ENGLISH PROSE AND POETRY

1660–1800

EDITED BY

ODELL SHEPARD

Formerly James J. Goodwin Professor of English Literature
Trinity College

AND

PAUL SPENCER WOOD

Ames Professor of English Language and Rhetoric
in Grinnell College

HOUGHTON MIFFLIN COMPANY

The Riverside Press Cambridge

The Riverside Press
CAMBRIDGE · MASSACHUSETTS
PRINTED IN THE U.S.A.

IN MEMORIAM
IRVING BABBITT
MAGISTRI BENE MERENTIS
QUI UT PRÆSENTIA DITARET
PRÆTERITA SCRUTABATUR
HUNC LIBRUM
DISCIPULI GRATO AC PIO ANIMO
DEDICAVERUNT

PREFACE

The editors of this book have held steadily in mind, as their chief criterion in every problem of selection and of interpretation, the probable needs of a student making his first long excursion into English neo-classical literature. Several peculiarities of the book are thus explained. In the first place, it has seemed clear that the prose and verse of this period, even more than of most others, ought to be read together, without such artificial separation as the editorial work hitherto done upon them has enforced. The present book brings ample selections from the whole field of neo-classical prose and poetry between two covers for the first time. Its extensive and numerous introductions, moreover, constitute a sufficient historical account of the period, besides providing adequate critical comment upon each author represented and upon each of the more important selections. It may therefore be used independently — that is, without any other textbook or "collateral reading" — in college and university courses dealing with the period as a whole or with one of its major subdivisions, such as the Eighteenth Century or the Restoration. The paths leading to further study are sufficiently indicated, however, by the bibliographical notes.

Although frequently interpretative and, in a few instances, controversial, the notes upon the text are chiefly intended to give timely information. As they are obviously not addressed to the advanced scholar, no apology need be made for their number and fullness. In spite of a persistent faith to the contrary, the average American college student is not much given to ransacking books of reference, nor should he be when engaged in reading literature. The editors have not felt justified in assuming that such a student would have at his command bits of miscellaneous information which they themselves did not at first possess, or in hoping that he would instantly understand passages which remained obscure to them after repeated readings. One of their departures from custom, therefore, has been a certain neglect of the privilege of editorial silence. Several important pieces of literature — such, for example, as Smart's exceedingly difficult *Song to David* — are here set forth for the first time with at least an attempt, restricted by exigencies of space, at adequate annotation.

A governing consideration in the choice and handling of texts has been the fact that this book has not been designed for the use of textual scholars or for the entertainment of bookish antiquarians, who can be served, after all, only by original editions or by copies of them in *fácsimile.* Neo-classical writers disliked few things more than a "Gothic" oddity, and it was their sound opinion that a main task of scholarship in every generation is to make the past live in the present. Partly in justice to them, but also for weightier reasons, the editors have consistently chosen such texts, whatever their dates or provenience, as would present least difficulty to a modern student in his effort to grasp the thought and the original effect of this literature. The greater number of the texts thus chosen derive from the writers' own time, but others are the product of more recent editorial work. Such freedom of choice has involved a minor inconsistency in the representation of unstressed and elided syllables, which early printers usually marked with an apostrophe and many modern editors spell out; but it is believed that this inconsistency will not be troublesome — or, at any rate, not more so than that of the original texts themselves. In other respects, spelling has been modernized throughout. Punctuation has also been modernized to a considerable extent, though complete logical uniformity has not been imposed upon all the texts. Dates in square brackets at the ends of the selections indicate first publication. Where a second date appears after a dash, it indicates the later limit of the first edition; otherwise it indicates later publication in revised or augmented form.

Except in the few instances where the contrary is stated, all the selections are complete units, unexpurgated and continuous. Without exception, they are intelligible standing alone. Space has been saved by the reluctant omission of fiction and drama, of several minor authors who wrote in the Scottish dialect, and of certain poets — Marvell, Cotton, Milton, and Vaughan in the early years, and Bowles and Rogers in the later — whose more important writing was either not done within the period or else did not conform to its ethos. Even with these omissions, the book remains an ample introduction to the thought, the feeling, the society, the literary art, and the chief persons of a long and very complex period.

The editors are grateful for the co-operative enterprise of their publishers, which has enabled them to bring so large a harvest into one barn. To Thomas Wright, Esquire, Curator of the Cowper Museum at Olney they are indebted for permission to include lines 144 to 166 from William Cowper's *Yardley Oak* and an additional stanza of *To Mary* (ll. 41–44), first published in 1900 from manuscripts now in the Cowper Museum. To the Cambridge University Press, they are indebted for permission to include Matthew Prior's *Jinny the Just*, from the Longleat Manuscripts first published by A. R. Waller in his edition of Prior's *Dialogues of the Dead*, 1907. By permission of Harcourt, Brace and Company, Inc., they are enabled to use a selection from the text of *The Diary of Samuel Pepys*, in the edition of Henry B. Wheatley, 1893–99. They wish also to thank Professor Robert Morss Lovett, once their teacher, for expert counsel and personal co-operation in his capacity as general editor of the series in which this book appears. They are grateful for much valuable assistance to Professor Thurman Losson Hood, Professor Le Roy Carr Barret, Professor Frank Cole Babbitt, and President Remsen Brinckerhoff Ogilby of Trinity College, to Professor John Merrill Bridgham, Professor Edward Buckham Taylor Spencer, and Professor Evelyn M. Boyd of Grinnell College and to Professor Evelyn May Albright of the University of Chicago. To Mary and Margaret Wood and to Mary Farwell Shepard, who have greatly lightened the task of preparing the manuscript, their gratitude need not be expressed in print.

O. S.
P. S. W.

CONTENTS

GENERAL INTRODUCTION

I

The named and dated "periods" into which we divide human history are of course almost as artificial as the lines that separate one country from its neighbours on a map. We isolate them merely for convenience of thought and discourse, and we should use them only so long as they remain really helpful.

One of the more significant of the periods into which English literature may be divided is that extending from 1660 to 1800, or from the accession of Charles II to the death of William Cowper. Even those who see most clearly that "nothing begins, and nothing ever ends" will agree that within these fourteen decades occurred the rise and culmination and decline of English neo-classicism. We may therefore call this stretch of time *the neo-classical period*, although we should remember that the adjective is somewhat more appropriate to the middle of the epoch than to its beginning or to its end. The four decades between the Restoration and the death of Dryden correspond, roughly, to the rise of neo-classicism; the years from 1700 to the death of Pope in 1744 are those of its culmination; and during the remainder of the eighteenth century it was in gradual decline. The adjective "neo-classical," furthermore, is applicable not by any means to all of the literature produced in England during this period but only to that which had at the time the greater vogue and which has been accepted by later criticism as determining the literary tone of the time. Throughout the entire epoch, neo-classical modes of thought, feeling, and expression were opposed by others, less fashionable but more native. Strong and entrenched when the period opened, this native opposition was rapidly overpowered; during the dominance of Pope it almost disappeared from sight, though certainly not from life; its triumph, clearly foreshadowed long before the eighteenth century closed, we know as the romantic movement.

A period so intricate and various cannot be characterized as a unit without some difficulty and some danger. Each of its major characteristics is countered by another, found within the epoch itself. Thus, although we may say with assurance that neo-classicism rests upon the authority of the past, the powerful influence of scientific study was brought to bear against "authority" and in favour of "experience" before the period was well begun. We may call it an age of intense political and social activity, in which the individual tended to express himself chiefly as the member of a group, but the praise of solitude sounds without a pause from the time of Cowley to that of Cowper. We must certainly call it a time of decorum and moderation, yet it ranged all the way from brutal debauchery to "Sentimentalism," and the Wesleyan movement gave it the most violent emotional upheaval that modern England has ever known.

In spite of these dangers and difficulties, however, there are two clear advantages to be gained by surveying this long, complex, and self-contradictory period as a unit. In the first place — although of course there was neo-classicism in England before 1660, as, for example, in Ben Jonson, and also after 1800, in the writing of such men as Byron and Landor — it provides the student of English literature with his best opportunity to follow a single literary movement through something like its total sweep. Secondly, this division seems to be more in keeping with the facts than that which is ordinarily made. Critics and historians of literature have worked for the last hundred years upon the assumption that the ideas and emotions governing the English romantic movement were new discoveries toward which the writers of the earlier period had groped their way as though out of darkness into light, and it was recently an accepted way of praising certain minor poets of the eighteenth century, to say that they "anticipated" or "heralded" romanticism. But the truth is that the romantic temper is easily discernible in every decade between 1660 and 1800. Such a phrase, therefore, as "the beginnings of romanticism," is inapplicable to any portion of the eighteenth century in England, and the segregation of fifty or sixty years of that century as the period of such "beginnings" leads to a serious misconception. A first step in the correction of this error is taken when we give one name to the whole period during which neo-classicism was either a growing, a dominant, or a dying force in English life and letters.

Historians of literature who sacrifice accuracy to clean-cut statement often suggest that neo-classicism first came into England with the returning court of Charles II, and as a direct importation from the court of France. The actual contact with the French court established by the English royal party during its exile was slighter than this view implies, and neo-classicism was a much older and more pervasive thing than it suggests — an aspect, indeed, of the Renaissance, which had been alternately attracting and repelling England since the days of Chaucer. What the Restoration did was to provide highly favourable conditions for a tendency long latent. Among other things, it brought England back into the tradition of Continental culture after a period of exaggerated insularity. After an exhausting riot of individualism, it established a central power. It imposed order, moderation, and reason upon a country just recovering from a terrible experience of emotional debauch, anarchy, and misrule.

Neo-classicism was in several ways the literary and intellectual counterpart of that stabilizing political and social influence which the English people of 1660 hoped that the throne might exert. It returned to England, having also been in exile, almost as welcome, because almost as much needed, as the King. It came with every advantage to be gained from the favour of a court which was to control the taste and critical opinions of the upper classes as well as literary patronage. It came with its main doctrines already elaborated into a set of critical theories and rules more precise than English critics could have made them; it already had a superb body of French literature to its credit, in comparison with which the literature of England seemed bungling and crude; furthermore, it was closely congenial with just the form of government which the dominant party wished to establish. That preoccupation with political ideas which marks the whole history of neo-classicism in England is a constant reminder that its main theses were given final statement in a country which has seldom held politics and literature apart. In England, to be sure, the monarch and his court had not the power enjoyed by those of France, and from the first it was clear that English individualism and traditions of liberty would enforce many modifications in the doctrine and the practice of neo-classicism. The possible influence of the sovereign upon all activities of the realm, moreover, was soon to be greatly reduced, and the ignorance of later British monarchs concerning all literary matters was equalled only by their indifference. Neo-classical writers, however, retained so strong a feeling of social obligation and so close a contact with their times that some knowledge of the epoch is necessary to a comprehension of their work.

II

The restoration of the Stuart dynasty brought about some of the most far-reaching changes that had occurred in England since the Norman Conquest — changes working inward to the country's heart and mind. Outwardly, it meant a return to constitutional monarchy; it was a triumph of the upper over the lower social classes, and of the Established Church over Presbyterianism and Independency; it brought into power and influence a set of persons more or less connected with the court and in various ways indoctrinated with French ideas. King Charles gave England, so far as he was able, the absolute régime to be expected from a Stuart, and beneficial effects followed throughout the national life. Everywhere — in the reform of English verse and dramatic construction as well as in government and church and society — chaos gradually gave way to order; the individual was slowly subordinated to the social whole; reason and discipline gained the upper hand.

During the twenty-five years of this reign, political, religious and economic controversies gave rise to the Whig and Tory parties, the former resting upon Parliament and the latter siding usually with the throne. James II, the Roman Catholic brother of Charles, was driven from the country in 1688, and the crown was accepted by William of Orange and his wife Mary, daughter of James. The radical reforms carried through at this time, greatly restricting royal prerogative and increasing the power of Parliament, amounted to a peaceful revolution and made England the freest country on earth. They also gave a long ascendancy to the Whigs — that is, to certain great land-owners, merchants, and prosperous tradesmen, as against the country clergy and smaller country squires, who stood together in the Tory opposition. The Toleration Act of 1689 guaranteed liberty of religious belief and worship, although dissenters were still excluded from the universities and from public office. Six years later the freedom of the press for which Milton had contended was finally won. The necessities of King William in his war with Louis XIV obliged him to inaugurate the cabinet system of government. At the end of his reign he formed a Grand Alliance with the Netherlands and the Holy Roman Empire against France, and this was carried on to triumph during the reign of Queen Anne (1702–1714) by the military genius of Marlborough.

Through no merit of the dull, pious, and unfortunate Queen herself, the Age of Queen Anne was one of exceptional brilliancy, in political and social life as well as in its intellectual attainment. London became the recognized capital not of England alone but of the British Isles, drawing many of its most notable minds from Scotland and Ireland. As the recollection of the Civil War died out, the social classes drew more closely together and began once more to interpenetrate, with advantage to them all. Peace was made with France in 1713, and in the following year Anne was succeeded by the Elector of Hanover as George I, who never learned to speak English and regarded England chiefly as a source of income.

In the reigns of the first two Georges (1714–1727 and 1727–1760), both rather stupid men who were easily led by their ministers and mistresses, England as a whole settled into spiritual lethargy. As in America after the Great War, the heart of the nation grew fat with wealth and ease, and even the bursting of the "South Sea Bubble" in 1721, although it destroyed many of the greatest fortunes and reputations, had only a passing effect. England's chief military foe had been almost crushed; her trade and the treasures of India were bringing her great riches; her Whig minister, Sir Robert Walpole, gave her a corrupt but highly successful "business man's administration" lasting for twenty years. In the midst of such prosperity the brutal cynicism creeping upon almost all classes, the miseries of the poor, the prevalence of drunkenness and violent crime, the atrocities of the penal system and of press-gangs, went almost unnoticed. The universities and the Church had never been more timidly acquiescent or more inert, and political life had never been more corrupt; but those who held power were satisfied.

But England is never unprovided with an "opposition" to whatever party or social tendency may be in power. The conditions just described roused the indignation of many a satirist. The very worldliness and indifference of the Church led up to and necessitated the religious revival nicknamed "Methodism." As though in answer to the hard and cynical temper of the times a movement now known as "Sentimentalism" developed, attracting many of the best spirits of the age and beginning many urgently needed reforms. The intellect of the country had been quickened by the incessant controversies of the preceding hundred years. Science and exploration were swiftly extending the knowledge of nature; hostile philosophies and theologies were locked in combat; the audience for literature was rapidly growing with the spread of education and the rise of the middle classes; thinkers, scholars, and men of letters were given a prominence — even, at times, an influence — in society and government such as they had not enjoyed in England for many years and have seldom since known. Social life, if it was not so brilliant as that of Paris, was at any rate absorbing. Society learned to talk, and seemed to exist for talking. Little by little it absorbed newcomers from the ranks of the bourgeoisie whose grandparents had been Puritans, teaching them the urbanity and elegance which they were eager to learn, and gaining from them for itself a greater respect for conventional morality and a deepening seriousness of mood. It may well be that such social satires as *The Rape of the Lock* have given us an exaggerated notion of the triviality of the time. Against the view that the period in which neo-classicism flourished was effeminate and superficial, given over to gossip at card-parties and graceful chatter in coffee-houses, it is perhaps enough to point out that this age produced and nurtured and gave honour to a series of unquestionably great individuals such as few other epochs of English history can claim.

Except for the years of Walpole's administration, England was very frequently at war during this period, but as all her battles were fought on foreign soil and with armies of impressed or mercenary soldiers, these wars had little immediate effect upon daily life. During the eighteenth century she established her naval supremacy, carried on the great tradition of her earlier navigators and explorers, extended her trade to the ends of the earth, conquered India and Canada, began the colonization of Australia, and in spite of the loss of her American colonies, founded the world's greatest empire.

When George III came to the throne in 1760 the population of England and Wales was about seven millions, scarcely more than that of London today. When he died, in 1820, it had risen to twelve millions in spite of almost constant war and the ravages of diseases that have since been checked. The population of the metropolis grew from about four hundred thousand at the beginning of our period to one million at the end of it, at which time London was already the largest and the wealthiest city in the western world. This growth was of course related to the increase in wealth, and it was not unconnected with the "industrial revolution" which began in the early years of the reign of George III, taking several basic industries out of the homes of the people and concentrating them in great mills where improved or newly invented machinery was employed. These changes, in which England led the world toward labour organizations and amalgamations of capital, over-production and under-employment, drained the villages and the countryside into slums of appalling squalor, destroyed craftsmanship, and turned the yeoman into a hired hand. In order to feed the displaced millions in the cities, corresponding changes had to be made in agriculture, and they were made by the great landed gentry, who held almost unlimited power, without primary regard to the welfare of the people. During the entire period, and with steady acceleration toward its close, there went on the reclamation of waste lands which had belonged since Saxon times to the peasantry. Moreover, the "open fields" about the villages, usually owned and farmed in common by the villagers, were gradually "enclosed" and taken into private hands. This process, bitterly deplored by Goldsmith, was economically advantageous but, taken with the results of the industrial revolution, it destroyed "Merry England" forever.

III

By establishing, early in his reign, The Royal Society of London for Improving Natural Knowledge, Charles II made scientific study a reputable employment for the gentleman and the man of letters. The close relationship between literature and science with which the period opens was not maintained to its close, and there were always writers such as Butler, Swift, and Addison to whom scientific investigation seemed merely ridiculous — an idle and eccentric curiosity, proper to a "virtuoso" rather than to a sensible man, whose study should be always Man. Yet there can be no doubt that the growing hope of "mastery" over nature contributed to the optimism of the time, that the steady advance in scientific knowledge gave support to the rather recent faith in "progress," and that the dazzling achievements of such thinkers as Sir Isaac Newton strengthened the tendency to exalt the reason above other faculties of the mind. Using Bacon's now well-established "experimental method," the sciences of physics, astronomy, and chemistry took on during this period something of their modern aspect. Medicine made great advances, and political economy was born. England's knowledge of the globe and of primitive peoples was greatly extended by the amazing voyages of Dampier, Shelvock, Anson, and Cook, the accounts of which made some of the most popular reading of the time. As reflected in literature these voyages contributed to a growing interest in the remote and exotic, besides suggesting many unfavourable comparisons of European with Oriental civilizations. Although these advances and discoveries awoke less enthusiasm than the Elizabethans had shown, the men of this period lived with a sense of widening horizons, of deepening insight into nature, and of increasing control over their environment.

The philosophical and ethical thinking of the neo-classical period found its point of departure in the system of Thomas Hobbes (1588–1679), cynical in its estimate of human nature and entirely materialistic. Hobbes taught that the sole motive governing conduct is self-interest, that society and government are devices whereby each man gains a certain immunity from the self-seeking of others by restricting his aggression upon them, that morality is created by law and can be maintained only by force, that religion is wholly an affair of state, demanding no more than outward conformity, and that the best government is that of an unlimited monarch. Useful as it was to the party brought into power at the Restoration, this system was repugnant alike to the adherents of monarchy by divine right and to the supporters of civil liberty. Hobbes is significant because he used reason to buttress authority; but even while he wrote, tendencies of thought were gathering force that would arraign at the bar of reason all authority, whether human or divine. The effort of rationalism — usually traced to Descartes, but strongly seconded in England by the influence of natural science — was to use the abstract reason as much as possible in segregation from the other "faculties" and more particularly from the emotions. Intuition, mystic insight, tradition and the historic sense, all aspiration and enthusiasm, all the glamour of imagination and fancy, all the coloured lights of mood, it strove to shut away so as to secure a cold clear light for the quest of what it called "Truth" — a sufficiently empty and meaningless thing. In this extreme and early form, based as it obviously was upon a false psychology, rationalism could not long endure. Men of the world such as the Earl of Rochester ridiculed it from the standpoint of common sense, and John Locke demonstrated, before the end of the seventeenth century, that the supposed "innate ideas" upon which it depended have no real existence. What we find in the central years of the period is not a bigoted or even a confident assertion of the sufficiency of reason, but rather a strong tendency to fall back upon common sense. During the second half of the eighteenth century Locke's empiricism, basing all knowledge upon sense experience, resulted in the scepticism of David Hume. In the meantime such thinkers as Butler, Berkeley, Shaftesbury, and Hutcheson, all regarding Thomas Hobbes as their ideal antagonist, had strongly affirmed the benevolence of human nature, the presence of God in his creation, and the validity of emotional experience.

Two teachers, rather more literary than philosophical, played a large part in shaping ideals of conduct. The moral discourses and epistles of Seneca, widely known in French and English translations as well as in the Latin original, disseminated not only the ethics of ancient Stoicism but also its fundamental doctrine of self-reliance, modified by a deep realization of social duty and of the brotherhood of man. Even more influential was the Epicureanism of the poet Horace, familiar from schoolboy days to every educated gentleman, which gave powerful support to the contemporary ideals of moderation and decorum, good sense, and enlightened worldliness. Preached from many an orthodox pulpit during the long decline of the English Church, advocated in thousands of poems and essays, exemplified in the lives and minds of many prominent men, the teachings of these two ancient writers were at least as influential as those more peculiar to Christianity, and we must attribute partly to them that faint reminiscence of ancient Roman times which pervades the whole period and which has given to its middle decades the name, Age of the Augustans.

A period distrustful of mysticism, disgusted by "enthusiasm," and inclining to believe only the evidence of the senses, can scarcely be called deeply religious, and yet it would be absurd to regard as essentially irreligious an age that produced the poems of Traherne, the hymns of Watts and Wesley and Cowper, such a devotional book as Law's *Serious Call*, the Prayers of Dr. Johnson, and the greatest spiritual revival of modern times. The Deistic movement itself, in its essence an effort to harmonize theology with reason, was by no means the expression of indifference to religion which its popular antagonists made it appear, but rather of an intense, though an almost purely intellectual, interest. In this aspect of its life, as in many others, the period was far more complex and self-contradictory than is generally supposed. An inevitable recoil from earlier excesses gave a tone of impiety and even licentiousness to the fashionable life and literature of its first decades; and the effect of this was not erased in the Age of Pope by that concentration upon human things, as opposed to divine, which was enforced by neo-classical doctrine. It should be said, however, that the religious and spiritual life of the time has been judged, hitherto, by unsympathetic observers, and also that the evidence for a final estimate is not yet entirely before us. In thousands of obscure books, forgotten magazines, and private letters which scarcely any one has glanced at during the last hundred and fifty years, the simple piety of men and women who lived in this epoch speaks as clearly as it does out of any other Christian time. In such neo-classical religious utterances as Dryden's *Religio Laici*, Pope's *Universal Prayer*, Addison's *Hymn*, and Thomson's *Hymn on the Seasons*, we are likely to miss that same element of passion which is equally deficient in the secular poetry; but there is no such lack in the sacred verse of Cowper, in the sermons of George Whitefield, or in Smart's exultant *Song to David*.

In several of the arts England failed to recover, during these hundred and forty years, the ground lost during the decades of Puritan domination. Most obvious and most deplorable was the almost total loss of native English music. During the eighteenth century London had musical audiences perhaps as appreciative and well-informed as any in Europe, but what they heard was Italian opera and the works of Handel and Gluck. The theatre recovered only in part. What may be called the arts of the people — folk dances, festival games, mummings, popular ballads — survived sporadically but lost ground year by year. In the arts of space the record is far better. Water-colour painting was revived and carried forward as far as it has ever gone, by Englishmen who were born during the eighteenth century. In portrait painting the country set forth for herself, having learned what she could from Van Dyck, Kneller, and Lely, and produced such masters as Gainsborough, Reynolds, and Romney. Landscape painting, although its original debt to Poussin, Claude Lorraine, and Salvator Rosa was profound, attained a European importance in the work of the Cromes, Wilson, Gainsborough, Constable, and Turner. In the sister-art of landscape-gardening England began by imitating Continental models and ended by imposing her own. At least one architect of genius, Sir Christopher Wren, lived and worked in this period, erecting many monuments of neo-classical taste which endure today. In the rebuilding of London after the fire of 1666, Wren gave it the severe and uniform dignity still to be seen in many of the older squares, but England's rapidly increasing wealth was exhibited in the many new country houses of the time, built with a magnificence never before seen. The taste of the period was shown at its best in the furniture of Chippendale and Sheraton, in the interiors of the Adam brothers, and in the pottery of Josiah Wedgwood.

Nothing like the elementary public school system of America was known in England until the nineteeth century. The so-called Free Grammar Schools, restored by Edward VI and Elizabeth in a few towns after the destruction of a much larger number during the Reformation, maintained a languishing and continually less important existence throughout the neo-classical period. Strong efforts made by Parliament in the first years of Charles II not only to discourage all new foundations but to bring all the old ones under the control of Church of England men, reduced the established schools, by the end of the century, to a disgraceful condition. The dissenters met this attack, however, by founding a considerable number of private institutions, such as the one at Newington in which Defoe was admirably educated, free at once from ecclesiastical control and from the dead hand of the classical curriculum. At the same time the first schools for girls and young women were instituted. In the absence of all assistance or even encouragement from the State, local philanthropists began, about 1700, to establish "Charity" and "Blue Coat" Schools in many of the larger towns, and the vestries of rural parishes undertook the maintenance of schools in many villages; but in most of these only such instruction was given as it was considered safe for the poor to absorb, and they left the lower classes practically illiterate. During the eighteenth century the sons of gentlemen, formerly educated at home or in the old Free Grammar Schools, flocked more and more to Winchester, Eton, Harrow, and — by far the most important — Westminster. In these great schools the curriculum, throughout the neo-classical period and for long after it, included nothing whatever except the classical languages and literatures, with great emphasis laid upon the composition of Latin and Greek prose and of Latin verse. The effect of this training upon the most influential minds of the time can scarcely be exaggerated, and there can be no doubt that many traits of neo-classical literature, and especially of its poetry, are attributable directly to it. Docile subjection to "rules" and willing imitation of "models" came naturally to men who had first learned to write in a dead language under the eye of a schoolmaster, and mere "correctness" never ceased to seem a high virtue to those who had been praised in boyhood chiefly for the avoidance of error. Imagination, originality, creative power, and self-expression were qualities of which they might be vaguely aware in ancient authors but which they were not encouraged to emulate. The sharp distinction maintained between the work of these schools, on the one hand, and those in which dissenters and the middle classes were taught the vernacular and something of the natural sciences, gave a recognized social value to such classical training, and maintained the exhibition of it in literature long after it might otherwise have disappeared. Even more unfortunately, this distinction suggested that one of the marks of the gentleman is a certain ostentatious uselessness and contempt for exact scholarship. Nothing was done in the universities, which were in an even worse condition than the schools during most of the period, to correct these shortcomings. Scholars of the highest eminence, such as Barrow, Bentley, and Porson, resided at Oxford and Cambridge, and men of letters such as Gray and Thomas Warton were supported by college fellowships, but the intellectual life of the universities was sluggish and dull.

In an attempt to estimate the culture of the neo-classical period the student soon becomes aware that its really classical element — that is, its participation in the spirit of the ancient Greek civilization — was extremely slight, a matter of learning rather than of living, and more concerned with an anxious and negative kind of taste than with free creative activity. The neo-classic movement, although connected with the Renaissance, was less a rebirth of the ancient world than a recollection, distant and unimpassioned. The minds and characters it helped to shape had little of the ancient Greek's joy in life, of his delight in the flesh and the senses, of his feeling of kinship with earth on the one hand and the gods on the other. The undefeated Puritan temper permeated society, gradually abandoning theological dogma but not its hatred of the arts. Those who escaped it, like Lord Chesterfield, were often left hollow and cold-blooded, and the culture of those who did not escape was likely to be too literary and moralistic. We see the second result in one of the greatest men of the time, whom we still consider an excellent example of neo-classicism. Dr. Johnson was indifferent to sculpture and painting, ignorant of dancing, superficially interested in the theatre, not only deaf to music but contemptuous of it, blind to the beauty of landscape, gross in appearance, and graceless in manners. Out of the wealth of experience and expression which the classic mind embraced and the earlier Renaissance strove to recapture, he chose one item, the literary. Even here, he did his best work in criticism, and in this his judgments were ultimately moralistic.

IV

It has been already pointed out that the Restoration brought into power and influence a set of persons who were, at any rate in the earlier years of the period, more or less closely connected with the court and in various ways affected by French customs, standards, and ideas. These persons served as the nucleus of a society not unlike that of the Parisian *salons* — a society without organization or fixed personnel, never including more than a few hundred individuals, which came to be called "the Town." Contemporary allusions may exaggerate the Town's unanimity, but its mandates, issued from the drawing-rooms and coffee-houses of London, were likely to be obeyed. For many years it controlled the theatre, and it could make or mar a literary fame almost as easily as a social reputation. On the other hand, this society was unrepresentative, aristocratic, and cosmopolitan rather than English in sympathy. Its tenure of influence was therefore insecure, and its sway, absolute in the vicinity of Whitehall, did not at any time include all of London and never penetrated the countryside, which is England's stronghold. Neo-classical taste and manners might indeed be discovered in a few great country houses and in such fashionable resorts as Bath and Tunbridge Wells; they were, in fact, very influential in changing the outward aspect of the country, transforming both the more splendid rural mansions and the landscape about them in accord with Continental taste; but the proper *milieu* of neo-classicism was "the Town" in "the Season." It left the market-town, village, and farm untouched.

Much depended, therefore, upon a writer's place of residence. Living in London, he wrote for a known audience; he was at once strongly supported and severely restricted by the pressure of social criticism, oral and written; he belonged to a community of minds coherent and powerful enough to reward obedience and punish recalcitrancy. Strong men were strengthened by the Town, clever men learned to take advantage of it, weaklings were intimidated, but almost all conformed. This restraint, with all its manifest advantages for a literature which had seldom been curbed before, caused a certain stagnation in imaginative writing. Poets found it hard to avoid the debilitating conclusion of strictly interpreted neo-classical doctrine, that all the great themes had been exhausted, and all the great verses written, by the ancients. For their portion there seemed to remain only the imitation of those ancients, or else the elegant trifling of the mock-heroic style.

The Town's chief weapon was ridicule or social laughter, represented in literature by satire. Levelled at first against hypocrisy and dullness, it soon proceeded to attack eccentricity, usually dear to the English people, and at last, growing bolder, it began to deride as mere "enthusiasm" all strong emotion and unrestrained zeal. Nearly every one who was in any way dependent upon the Town lived in a fear of this ridicule which, though often wholesome, was often merely intimidating. Addison remarked that his generation surpassed the ancients in "Doggerel, Humour, Burlesque, and all the trivial arts of Ridicule," but there were certain other forms of literature and particularly those expressing intense personal passion, which could not continue to live at all in such an atmosphere. Poetry suffered far more than prose, and the lyric most of all, because the lyric impulse is most sensitive to social laughter. Such emotional intensity as there was in the poets of the time was likely to disguise itself in the garb of wit, as though anticipating ridicule and wishing to laugh first. In this way the talents of men such as Prior, Gay, and Shenstone may have been somewhat deflected from their natural channels. Passion, at any rate, is one quality of high art for which we look almost vainly in this literature. It was a period distrustful of the *furor poeticus* and incapable of soaring. From end to end, if we may except its many admirable hymns and the writings of Burns and Blake, it produced few strains of pure spontaneous song

This tension of the Town upon literature, however, may almost be said to have decreased as the square of the distance from London. Thomas Warton, living at Oxford, acknowledged neo-classical authority in perhaps half his work, though his essentially romantic heart was not with it. His brother Joseph, at Winchester, defied it, as his father had done at Basingstoke. John Dyer, in far-off Wales, knew it in his earlier years only as a distant rumour, with no compulsion upon his work. So long as she remained a member of the court circle, Lady Winchilsea wrote the conventional witty satire of her day; it was in her exile from the court and from London that she composed the highly "enthusiastic" and personal poems for which she is now remembered. James Thomson, on the other hand, arrived in London with a poem of strongly romantic tendency in manuscript, which his associations with the Town caused him to revise extensively, in later years, according to the orthodox mode.

These instances, together with the many more that might be cited to the same effect, and also the difficulty of finding any considerable author of the earlier period who steadily maintained a romantic tone of writing in London or a neo-classic tone outside of its influence, suggest that what we now call romanticism was as closely related to the country as neo-classicism was to the Town. A review of the evidence strengthens this surmise. One of the recurring themes of the period is the comparison of rural with metropolitan life. This theme had, indeed, been worn threadbare by ancient poets and rhetoricians, and it had been bandied back and forth during the entire Renaissance, but Englishmen returned to it during the neo-classical period with a fresh interest not to be entirely explained by their preference for customary topics. An early outcry from the one camp is the remark addressed to a town gentleman in Etherege's *The Man of Mode* (1676): "I know all beyond Hyde Park's a desert to you." Somewhat more than a hundred years later Cowper wrote his quietly assured line: "God made the Country and man made the Town." The champions of the Town are sometimes contemptuous of things peculiarly English, and the defenders of the Country, on the other hand, speak more proudly of the English past and are not a little resentful of the invasion of their land by European models of conduct and expression. This rigidity and local pride in the face of foreign influence is a perennial English attitude. We see it in Roger Ascham and also in Tennyson, three hundred years later. Unquestionably, it endured throughout the neo-classical period, surviving strongly in the country though it had to abandon the capital, so that it stood ready, after neo-classicism had run its course, to set English literature once more upon its natural and national road.

Similar conclusions would be reached by close study of all that the writers of this period had to say about solitude — which is as clearly romanticism's central word as "society" is the focal term of classicism. The interest displayed in this theme also is keener than even its great prominence in the literature of the ancient world, the Middle Ages, and the Renaissance, would lead one to expect. From the first decade of the neo-classic régime — when Cowley's essays on solitude, Sir George Mackenzie's *Solitude Preferred to Public Employment*, and John Evelyn's answer to Mackenzie all appeared within a few months — to the last years of the period, when Cowper praised it in two long didactic poems, the solitary life commanded an almost fascinated attention. This becomes significant when one realizes that "solitude" was a word of rich connotations, suggesting the contemplation both of nature and of God, pensive melancholy, self-reliant individualism, simplicity, and "sensibility." It was, in short, the antithesis of those characteristics — worldliness, pride, conventionality, ambition trivial gayety, and the like — which country-dwellers, rightly or wrongly, attributed to the Town. That solitude was also a central theme of the great romantic poets when their time arrived is common knowledge, and every one is aware that they had only brief and accidental connections with London.

We may picture England's neo-classicism, therefore, as an invasion vaguely like the Roman occupation of Britain, which, although it bore the external marks of absolute power and maintained itself for a long time, was never completed. Neo-classicism took the capital as Rome had done, and established camps elsewhere, but this did not mean the subjugation of England's innermost heart and mind. Its law was more widely recognized than obeyed. England learned from it many a necessary lesson in moderation, decorum, and self-restraint, as the people of Britain had learned from Rome — and then, when its time had passed, she returned to her own resources.

V

Certain literary forms were lost during the neo-classical period, others were revived and perfected, and one or two were invented. After the waning of the Cavalier impulse, the lyric, except in hymnology, dwindled in importance. The heroic drama, written in close imitation of French models, did not long retain the hold upon the stage which it gained in the early years of Charles II, and the comedy of manners, after a brilliant career of some four decades, gave way to a comedy, now called "sentimental," which was less witty and more sympathetic. Much of the best work done in the first and second sub-divisions of the period was in the form of satire, but this also declined as sentimentalism increased. Perhaps because of its immunity from ridicule, the mock-heroic method of satire was much employed, both in prose and verse. A favourite form of the period was the long didactic poem, sometimes primarily instructive and based upon Virgil's *Georgics*, sometimes intended for edification, as in Young's *Night Thoughts*. A large body of wholly delightful work, never excelled in its kind, was done in the personal letter and the informal essay. Clarendon, Gibbon, and Hume produced supreme examples of history writing, and James Boswell an unsurpassed biography. Perhaps the most remarkable literary achievement of the time, however, is the swift development of the novel out of bare and not very promising origins into the finished work of Richardson, Fielding, Smollett, and Sterne.

During these hundred and forty years the conditions of authorship were radically changed. At the time of the Restoration, and for long thereafter, a writer was usually obliged to seek support, social as well as financial, from a patron, to whom he returned thanks in fulsome dedications. But Daniel Defoe, by dint of exceptional gifts and enormous industry, was just able to live without this support, and the comfortable fortune amassed by Pope suggested to his contemporaries that they might make the public their patron. They could hope to do this, of course, only by adjusting their work to a larger public than English authors had yet learned to write for, and they made the adjustment by acquiring a new lightness of touch and some of the arts of the journalist. The reading public of England was still very small, however, and few writers of the period made a livelihood exclusively by serving it. The important thing is that the effort was made and that the old subserviency to individual patrons was thrown off.

The development of prose style in this period was what might be expected in a highly social and political, that is to say a talking and oratorical, age. The leaning of literary prose toward the standards of good speech was made evident very early, for we are told by Thomas Sprat, writing in 1667, that the Royal Society "exacted from all their members a close, naked, natural way of speaking; positive expressions, clear senses, a native easiness, bringing all things as near the mathematical plainness as they can; and preferring the language of artisans, countrymen, and merchants, before that of wits and scholars." It would have been well if the last clause in this admirable set of directions had been followed as closely as the others. That it was not so followed may be attributed in part to the fact that later neo-classical writers were not so assured of their own gentility as the first members of the Royal Society had been, and that they were therefore more anxious to distinguish themselves from merchants, artisans, and countrymen, and to ally themselves, rather, with scholars and wits. There was little evidence of this anxiety, to be sure, in the writing of John Dryden, generally regarded as the "father of modern English prose," and certainly one of its greatest masters. Addison refined and polished the prose of Dryden, with some loss of its vigour and a decided inclination toward the language of the wit and away from that of the artisan. He was accepted, in his turn, as the model of all excellence by most prose men of the next half-century. Dr. Johnson characterized the style of Addison, in a famous passage which illustrates sufficiently his own departure from it, as "the model of the middle type: on grave subjects not formal, on light occasions not grovelling; pure without scrupulosity and exact without apparent elaboration; always equable and always easy, without glowing words or pointed sentences." Clearly, its virtues were largely of the negative kind. It was, in fact, a somewhat timorous style, seldom risking a fall because it seldom soared. Its restraint, quietness, and urbane simplicity or "elegance" have been sufficiently praised, but we have forgotten at what a sacrifice of rhythmical richness these qualities were attained. The prose of Addison, thoroughly admirable in itself and quite necessary to the tasks that awaited English literature, opened the road downward from the noble cadences of Hooker, Taylor, and Browne toward the proletarian prose of our own day; and this road was quickly followed. First written by those who still heard the echoes of great imaginative and emotional writing, it was addressed to men who did not hear them, and after the generation of its chief masters — Addison himself, and Swift, and Bolingbroke — it was written by such men, who were unable to conceal its tendency toward inert dullness. Once more, however, and for almost the last time, ancient literature gave the impetus and the examples for a new advance — not, to be sure, toward the language of the artisan or countryman, but toward that of the scholar. Johnson, Gibbon, and Burke saved the best qualities in earlier neo-classical prose and enriched them by the addition of rhythms which seem to have been suggested by those of Latin and Greek. The defect of this later style was certainly not dullness, but rather a monotonous pomp in the sound and a rigidity in the parallelism of their phrases which sometimes has a similar effect.

Yet the accomplishment of the neo-classical period in the field of prose style was one of its chief glories. It found English prose a splendid chaos and left it an ordered realm. Out of many superb prose styles, possible only to the men of genius who devised them, it developed two, known by the names of Johnson and Addison, which any intelligent person may learn to write who will take the pains.

The history of verse style in this period is not dissimilar. It is a history, we may say without much exaggeration, of a single form, the heroic couplet, which, although known to Chaucer and much used during the earlier seventeenth century, was intensively, and at times, almost exclusively cultivated, during the Age of Pope. Here too the cardinal name is that of John Dryden, whose influence was like that which he exerted in prose, bringing the art under rules of law and order without impairing its vigour. Dryden's verse was perfected by Pope somewhat as his prose style was polished by Addison, and with results even more enduring and more questionable. Pope was himself a stylist of consummate gifts and attainments, with an extremely subtle ear for niceties of expression and verbal music; but Pope bestrode his narrow world like a Colossus — and he was not, after all, a large man. In consideration of his huge influence, it is somewhat unfortunate that he spent his powers almost entirely upon the heroic couplet. The form, to be sure, was exactly suited to his mind and temperament, being a perfect vehicle for the witty epigram pointed by malice, and also it was closely adjusted to the cautious temper of an age which delighted in the opportunity it offered to express tempered judgments with precision and balance. Too often, however, the heroic couplet was written with a mechanical and monotonous regularity, which the age did not need as a counterpoise for any excess of emotional fervour. Like the prose of the time, it contained no secrets which any one might not learn, and gave few chances to "snatch a grace beyond the reach of art."

The same leaning toward conformity seen in the prose and verse of this period is observable in the effort to regulate English grammar, pronunciation, and spelling. Believing, of course mistakenly, that the Greek and Latin languages had undergone no change during the great stretches of time represented by classic literature, it deduced the notion, by no means unfamiliar today, that the laws governing linguistic change all make for "corruption" and that they may and should be withstood. Dryden and Swift both favoured the founding of an English Academy to exert a stabilizing influence on the language, and Dr. Johnson said in the original Plan for his Dictionary that a primary purpose of the undertaking was "to fix the language." He succeeded in doing this only in one secondary and rather unfortunate particular — that of orthography, which has changed hardly at all since his Dictionary appeared in 1755. Upon the values of vowel sounds, which Johnson did not even indicate, this great work had little effect. The reader of neo-classic verse, in which the rhyming was far more exact than it has since become, is constantly reminded of vocalic changes that have taken place since the time of Dryden and Pope. Thus, Dryden rhymes *heat* with *great,* and Pope hears no difference between the vowel in *tea,* and that in *obey.* Dryden and Pope and Johnson all rhyme *toil* with *smile* and *join* with *divine.*

In these and several other respects neo-classical writers were following not the usages of "standard English," which had not yet been fully established, but rather the special dialect of fashionable London society. Even in the most dignified verse — as, for example, in the last line of Pope's *Eloisa to Abelard,* "He best can paint 'em who can feel 'em most" — they imitated the Town's habit of using elisions which to modern taste are the opposite of "genteel." The most obvious and most irritating of these class mannerisms is the suppression of unstressed syllables in such words as *vigorous, bravery, general,* and *interest,* which resulted not only in sprinkling every page of verse with apostrophes but withdrew from the poetic language many trisyllabic words which might have helped to lighten the heavily iambic and often flat-footed verse. A further use of the apostrophe, to mark the elision of *e* in final syllables where it was not to be pronounced, indicated little about the state of the language but was primarily a printer's device, inconsistently employed.

Neo-classical writers discriminated more and more as time went on against "the language of artisans, countrymen, and merchants," narrowing and enfeebling their vocabulary by casting out, as "low" and "vulgar," an increasing number of the native expressions commonly used by the lower classes. They diluted their language with tasteless circumlocutions and overloaded it with a cumbrous Latinity. For all this they were able, to be sure, to find a plausible excuse in terms of criticism. Addison, for example, remarks that "since it often happens that the most obvious phrases, and those which are used in ordinary conversations, become too familiar to the ear, and contract a kind of meanness by passing through the mouths of the vulgar, a poet should take particular care to guard himself against idiomatic ways of speaking." Dr. Johnson is equally positive that "the most heroic sentiments will lose their efficacy, and the most splendid ideas drop their magnificence, if they are conveyed by words used commonly upon low and trivial occasions, debased by vulgar mouths and contaminated by inelegant applications." One is often led to suspect, however, that this besetting fear of vulgarity in language had a foundation in the desire for social gentility, about which the writers of the period were sometimes amusingly anxious.

And yet it was for the good of the language and of literature that these men, not all of them to the manner born, strove to write like gentlemen. This meant that, with all their imitation of ancient and modern models, they never ceased to listen to cultivated conversation, learning to write at least in part by ear. Therefore the idiomatic tang and freedom of good English was not wholly lost. The language of artisans and of countrymen was not to return to literature until the time of Wordsworth, but in the meanwhile men could write wittily without false display and could give the flavour and aroma of scholarship to their pages without parade of erudition.

VI

One of the difficulties met by a modern reader in the neo-classical period is that of accustoming himself to a pace and rhythm very different from his own. At the opening of the period we find a society still rigidly stratified, a Church and State strongly conservative, domestic manufactures, traditional handicrafts, and an agriculture carried on with simple tools by methods of ancient use and wont. Although threatened more and more, these conditions remained to the end of the age as at least a vivid memory, making always for a deeper quiet than the twentieth century has known, or desires. The writers of such a time could count upon a far greater leisure in their audience than those of our day dare assume. They felt more sure of their audiences, and wrote less in fear of boring them. Not confined, as we are, to the comparatively crude effort to instruct, to excite, or to edify, they could play with ideas and pause upon the nuances of thought and feeling. What this would mean in the shaping of such works as those of Gibbon, Sterne, Cowper, and Boswell, is clear enough, and one can see that it might affect the cadences of paragraphs and even the length and intricacy of the single sentence. A considerable part of Pope's monumental translation of Homer was written in a mediæval tower standing among rich meadows far up the Thames. In New York, or even in London, today, it could scarcely be written at all.

Following a prolonged spell of national fever, the temperature of this age was steadily declining. Men were learning moderation and restraint, learning to limit their range, to direct their energies, and to think soberly "like people of this world." What the time aspired to, perhaps most of all, was simple good sense. A reader of our time, as feverish in its different way as that against which the neo-classical period was reacting, is likely to attribute the low pulse of the eighteenth century to deficient vitality, and indeed there was some suggestion of the elderly valetudinarian about it, in spite of the presence of such full-blooded men as Fielding, Wilkes, Smollett, Churchill, Johnson, and Burke. There is characterization not of the writer alone but of many men of his age as well in what Shenstone says of himself: "I begin too soon in life to slight the world more than is consistent with making a figure in it. The *non est tanti* of Ovid grows upon me so fast that in a few years I shall have no passions." The moderation and poise of neoclassicism were not always won by a bold mingling of all the elements of normal experience but, too frequently, by the mere excision of those regarded as dangerous. In particular, that eternal conflict between "passion and reason, self-division's cause," which had tormented but also deepened the poetry of the greater Elizabethans, and in which the intellectual world of today is again engaged, scarcely ruffled the surface of their literature. The teachings of Newton and Locke pointed toward a new earth if not a new heaven, but Englishmen of the neo-classical period, with their gaze fixed upon an immutable past, were in no haste to explore the emotional implications of doctrines which they accepted intellectually. In their poetry even more than in their prose, it is evident that many of them achieved their cool temperance not so much by the strong control as by the slow atrophy of the emotions.

Another impediment to our understanding of this literature is found in what may be called its impersonality. The age strove to restrain all peculiarities, whether of the individual or of the race or of the epoch, in favour of a representative and normal humanity, regarded as essentially the same for all times and lands and individuals. The typical writer of the period was less concerned with "self-expression" than with the communication of ideas considered binding upon all rational creatures, according to the laws of reason. He thought of himself less as an artist than as a teacher. Thus, at the opening of the period, the poet Waller said that he would gladly blot from his pages every line which did not conduce to some sort of improvement in his readers, and at the end of it William Cowper repeatedly expressed the same feeling. In such circumstances the main effort of poetry was not the suggestion of atmosphere, emotion, and mood, and certainly not the advertisement of the poet's idiosyncrasy, but the clear communication of moral ideas.

The tone of homily spreading from these convictions is hard to forgive in a generation like our own, firmly convinced of the "folly of preaching." Like all good homiletics, moreover, the literature of this age is chiefly concerned with commonplaces, undisguised by the glitter of paradox or the deliberate clowning practised by preachers of our time. Customary themes and conventionalized expressions were definitely preferred because they had the approval of "universal consent," and writers suspected themselves of eccentricity whenever they said, by accident, what had apparently never been said before. The civilizations of the classic past were less the objects of archæological study than they are with us, but they were much more a shaping influence upon thought and feeling, opinion and conduct. Hard as the fact may be for us to realize, many basic notions about the public career were derived from Plutarch, and, as we have seen, many ideals of private life were shaped by the poetry and example of Horace. And yet these men were far less antiquarian than we are. They escaped what might have been a merely slavish imitation of the past by means of the neo-classic conviction, well exemplified in Pope's *Homer* and Dr. Johnson's *London*, that a main function of scholarship is to bring the great past down to date, to lift its sunken treasure and turn it into current coin.

On the other hand, the feeling that all the basic themes had been exhausted and all the primary verses written long ago deprived the age of the sense of fresh adventure and contributed to its occasional tone of weariness. It seemed to reduce the writers of the time to the rôle of rhetoricians — phrase-finders rather than way-breakers in new countries of the mind. The neo-classic period was, in fact, the last great age of rhetoric, that highly questionable tradition handed on by the dying ancients to the modern world. Like bladders filled with air, it has sustained many a name that should have sunk and, in every century, has impeded a few minds that should have trusted to themselves. Wherever we study its influence — in Seneca, in Petrarch, or in Pope — we find it obtruding ready-made phrases, critical theories, notions of "decorum" and of "elegance," and other such secondary matters, between the writer and the precise thing he thinks or feels. The literature written in this tradition, often powerful and persuasive, has seldom the thrilling effect of immediacy which can be given only by a writer who is possessed by his theme. Perhaps it is the most severe criticism to be brought against the more typical writers of the neo-classical movement to say that they themselves were less moved than desirous of moving others by the approved traditional methods, and that they were less impressed than impressive. Preferring always to stand at several safe removes from vulgar actuality, they seldom realized life at first hand or helped their readers to do so. Joseph Addison, who had never seen a battle and could not vividly imagine one, represented them fairly enough as he sat in his bath-gown up two pairs of stairs balancing the chilly phrases of *The Campaign* and fabricating a picture of the Battle of Blenheim as stately as it was cold, as false to actual experience as it was nicely calculated to perpetuate the literary lie about warfare. Their occasional efforts to represent emotional experience were likely to be stiff and statuesque. Thus, William Collins's *Ode on the Passions* does not suggest that the poet either feels or remembers the emotions of fear, anger, love, and joy, but only that he has observed them — as represented in other works of art. They come before him as so many allegorical statues, with frozen features, each bearing its appropriate label. His effort is not to deepen the realization of life but to produce a work of art, cool, self-contained, harmonious with itself, like a sonata by Haydn or a vase by Wedgwood.

One of the clearest proofs that the inspiration of these men was literary and that their artistic effort was rhetorical is seen in their habitual use and abuse of personification — a device exactly suited to timid men who wish to hold life at arm's length and to observe without sharing it. Closely connected with their addiction to this figure of speech was their effort to sink the concrete and specific — "all singular forms, local customs, particularities, and details of every kind" — in seas of abstraction. This was supposed to produce that "grandeur of generality" which was praised by Johnson and Reynolds. It certainly kept art cool from the emotions, which always cling to the concrete, and it was perfectly consonant with that genteel spectatorial attitude which Addison praised and exemplified; but the first great artist, careless of gentility, who looked squarely at the doctrine brushed it contemptuously aside. "To generalize is to be an idiot," said William Blake. "To particularize is the great distinction of merit." Somewhat later he added, more temperately: "Grandeur of ideas is founded on precision of ideas."

The mere mention of Blake will remind the student once more that it is impossible to frame any formula which will include all the writers who happened to live within the neo-classical period. Throughout the second half of the eighteenth century there was a steady return, corresponding in part to the gradual decline of Pope's influence, toward direct simplicity of diction and open utterance of personal feeling. We watch this tendency grow in the work of Shenstone, Crabbe, Cowper, and Blake. Long before the century was out, Laurence Sterne represented emotion with startling actuality. Before the death of Cowper it was clear that the poets of the next period, already represented by the *Lyrical Ballads* of 1798, would make a clean break with the entire "genteel tradition," declaring war on rhetoric and negative taste and immersing themselves in the currents of common life. It is chiefly to the Age of Pope, when neo-classicism was at its height, that the generalizations made above are intended to apply. Of that age we may say, although with many reservations, that it simplified the problem of living, and so of literature, too drastically, by its repression of emotional experience. Several events that might be cited as exceptions to this statement are really proofs of it. The swift and wide-spread "enthusiasm" that swept through England during the Methodist Revival, the shallower and cultivated emotionality of "sentimentalism," and the excitement caused by such crude and literary stimulants as the Ossianic poems and the Gothic Romances, indicate a foregoing effort not to train and develop the emotions but to repress and stifle them. Instead of moderation and temperance, which should mean a balance of powers held high, the age secured what it loved to call "mediocrity," a very different thing. Our own time, disinclined to omit any essential phase of experience, cannot admire unreservedly the smug contentment of Pomfret's *The Choice* or the facile optimism of Pope's *Essay on Man*, or the soft effeminate comfort of Cowper's *Retirement.* In each of these typical poems we discern a tendency to run for the shore, whereas it is our growing determination to ride out the storm. Our conception of life's heights and depths, and also of its mystery, has been considerably extended since John Gilbert Cooper, echoing Pope, wrote these shallow but not unrepresentative lines:

> the sweet offspring of Content
> Flows from the mind's calm government.
> Thus, man, thy state is free from woe
> If thou wouldst choose to make it so.
> Murmur not, then at Heaven's decree;
> The gods have given thee liberty,
> And placed within thy conscious breast
> Reason, as an unerring test;
> And shouldst thou fix on misery,
> The fault is not in them, but thee.

VII

In all of this, to be sure, no allowance has been made for the seductive charm which an age so excited and noisy as ours may feel in a time like that of the Restoration or that of Queen Anne. Partly because of the distance at which they lie, those decades have fallen cool and quiet. The neo-classical period is one of the most delightful of all temporary refuges from modernity, but it is more important because of its bearing upon our own time. It spoke a language sufficiently like our own and was filled with people whom we can comprehend although they were not much like us. In spite of many hesitations, it managed to record itself with remarkable fullness and accuracy. It left an indelible memory, exact and minute to the finest detail, of perhaps a dozen great persons who are permanent members of the society of time. Though it may seem simple and even superficial to the first view, one who lives in it for even a little while discovers that it was extremely complex, various, and self-contradictory. Almost every problem with which the twentieth century is now confronted either had its origin within this period or else was inherited by it from an earlier epoch, and the result is that no one can hope to understand the modern world who has not spent some time in this fertile seed-plot of ideas.

An English critic of the neo-classical period, were he here to counsel us, might well say, now that the ancient classics have become mere learnings and are all but lost as living influences, that the best source still open to us for the poise, good sense, normality and cosmopolitanism of which we stand so dangerously in need is the period represented by the poetry and prose in this book. He would be right. Both for humility and guidance we need the example of a civilization other than our own. If "civilization" means order, if it implies the union of many minds under the sway of a generally accepted oligarchy of ideas, if it suggests that skill in social and political and economic arrangements which enables human beings to live successfully together, if it is based upon the sense of common traits and rights in all humanity, if it gives due regard to tradition without thwarting growth, if it includes the good sense that puts first things first and holds them there, then the men and women of England's neo-classical period were as civilized as we are, and in ways interestingly and instructively different. They produced a more coherent society of minds than any that has since appeared, at any rate in England or America. They produced great individuals, as we no longer do. It was the natural consequence of these achievements that they also produced a large and various body of great literature.

GENERAL BIBLIOGRAPHY

THE following selected list of books and articles is intended as a general introduction to the literature of the period 1660–1800; for special studies it must be supplemented by the bibliographies listed under the various authors. Names of technical journals to which most frequent reference is made are abbreviated as follows: *AJP*, *American Journal of Philology; JEGP*, *Journal of English and Germanic Philology; MLN*, *Modern Language Notes; MP*, *Modern Philology; PMLA*, *Publications of the Modern Language Association of America; PQ*, *Philological Quarterly; RES*, *Review of English Studies; RLC*, *Revue de la Littérature Comparée; SP*, *Studies in Philology*.

I. BIBLIOGRAPHICAL STUDIES

1. *Annual Bibliography of English Language and Literature*, Edited for the Modern Humanities Research Association, 1921–.
2. Crane, R. S., "English Literature of the Restoration and Eighteenth Century: A Current Bibliography," *PQ*, 1926–32; continued 1933– by Louis I. Bredvold.
3. Draper, J. W., *Eighteenth Century English Æsthetics: A Bibliography*. (*Anglistische Forschungen*, 71), 1931.
4. Northup, Clark S., *A Register of Bibliographies of the English Language and Literature*, 1925.
5. *The Year's Work in English Studies*, Edited for the English Association, 1922–.
6. Williams, I. A., *Seven XVIIIth Century Bibliographies*, 1924.

II. STUDIES IN THE HISTORICAL BACKGROUND

1. Ashton, John, *Social Life in the Reign of Queen Anne*, 1883.
2. Besant, Sir Walter, *London in the Eighteenth Century*, 1902.
3. Botsford, Jay B., *English Society in the Eighteenth Century*, 1924.
4. Bury, J. B., *The Idea of Progress: An Inquiry into its Origin and Growth*, 1920.
5. Chancellor, E. B., *The Eighteenth Century in London*, 1920.
6. Clark, Henry W., *A History of English Non-Conformity*, 2 vols. Vol. II. *From the Restoration to the Close of the Nineteenth Century*, 1913.
7. Dunning, William A., *A History of Political Ideas from Rousseau to Spencer*, 1920.
8. George, M. D., *London Life in the Eighteenth Century*, 1923.
9. Gooch, G. P., *English Democratic Ideas in the Seventeenth Century*, 2d ed., with notes by H. J. Laski, 1927.
10. Hunt, John, *Religious Thought in England to the End of the Eighteenth Century*, 3 vols., 1870–73.
11. Hunt, William, *The History of England from the Accession of George III to the Close of Pitt's First Administration* (*1760–1801*). (Vol. X in Hunt and Poole's *Political History of England*.) 1905.
12. Hutton, William H., *The English Church from the Accession of Charles I to the Death of Anne*, 1903.
13. Klingberg, F. J., *The Anti-Slavery Movement in England: A Study in English Humanitarianism*, 1926.
14. Laski, H. J., *Political Thought in England from Locke to Bentham*. (Home Univ. Lib.) 1920.
15. Leadam, I. S., *The History of England from the Accession of Anne to the Death of George II* (*1702–1760*). (Vol. IX in Hunt and Poole's *Political History of England*.) 1909.
16. Lecky, William E. H., *A History of England in the Eighteenth Century*, 8 vols., 1877–90.
17. Macaulay, Thomas B., *History of England from the Accession of James II*, 5 vols., 1849–61. Ed. Sir Charles H. Firth. 6 vols., 1913–15.
18. McCarthy, J. H., *The Reign of Queen Anne*, 2 vols., 1902.

19. Mantoux, Paul, *The Industrial Revolution in the Eighteenth Century.* Rev. ed., translated by Marjorie Vernon, 1928.
20. Manwaring, Elizabeth W., *Italian Landscape in Eighteenth Century England*, 1925.
21. Nicolson, Marjorie, "The Early Stage of Cartesianism in England," *SP*, XXVI (1929), 356–74.
22. Overton, J. H., *The English Church from the Accession of George I to the End of the Eighteenth Century (1714–1800)*, 1906.
23. Perdeck, A. A., *Theology in Augustan Literature*, 1928.
24. Quennell, M. and C. H. B., *A History of Everyday Things in England;* Part II, 1500–1799, 1922.
25. Randall, J. H., Jr., *The Making of the Modern Mind: A Survey of the Intellectual Background of the Present Age*, 1926.
26. Robertson, Sir Charles Grant, *England under the Hanoverians*, 1911. Rev. ed., 1930.
27. Toynbee, A., *The Industrial Revolution in the Eighteenth Century in England*, 1919.
28. Trevelyan, G. M., *England under the Stuarts* (Vol. V of *A History of England*, ed. by Charles Oman), 1904.
29. Trevelyan, G. M., *England under Queen Anne: Blenheim*, 1930; *Ramillies and the Union with Scotland*, 1932.
30. Traill, H. D., and Mann, J. A., *Social England*, 6 vols., 1896–97. (Vols. IV and V.)
31. Turberville, A. S., *English Men and Manners in the Eighteenth Century*, 1926.
32. Stephen, Sir Leslie, *History of English Thought in the Eighteenth Century*, 2 vols., 1876.
33. Sydney, W. C., *England and the English in the Eighteenth Century*, 2 vols., 1892.
34. Symonds, E. M., *Social Caricature in the Eighteenth Century*, 1905.
35. Warner, W. J., *The Wesleyan Movement in the Industrial Revolution*, 1930.

III. Studies in Foreign Influences on English Literature

1. Babbitt, Irving, *Rousseau and Romanticism*, 1919.
2. Bray, René, *La formation de la doctrine classique en France*, 1927.
3. Charlanne, Louis, *L'influence française en Angleterre au XVIIe siècle*, 1906.
4. Clark, A. F. B., *Boileau and the French Classical Critics in England (1660–1830)*, 1925.
5. Draper, J. W., "Aristotelian 'Mimesis' in Eighteenth Century England," *PMLA*, XXXVI (1921), 372–400.
6. Engel, Claire-Eliane, *La littérature alpestre en France et en Angleterre au XVIIIe et au XIXe siècle*, 1930.
7. Farley, F. E., *Scandinavian Influences in the English Romantic Movement*, 1903.
8. Goad, Caroline M., *Horace in English Literature of the Eighteenth Century*, 1918.
9. Herrick, M. T., *The Poetics of Aristotle in England*, 1930.
10. Hustvedt, Sigurd B., *Ballad Criticism in Scandinavia and Great Britain during the Eighteenth Century*, 1916.
11. Lilly, Marie L., *The Georgic: A Contribution to the Study of the Vergilian Type of Didactic Poetry*, 1919.
12. Lockitt, C. H., *The Relations of French and English Society, 1763–93*, 1920.
13. Lovejoy, A. O., "The Supposed Primitivism of Rousseau's *Discourse on Inequality*," *MP*, XXI (1923), 165–86.
14. Mantz, H. E., "Non-Dramatic Pastoral in Europe in the Eighteenth Century," *PMLA*, XXXI (1916), 421–47.
15. Mornet, Daniel, *French Thought in the Eighteenth Century.* Translated by L. M. Levin, 1929.
16. Mustard, W. P., "Virgil's *Georgics* and the British Poets," *AJP*, XXIX (1908), 1–32.
17. Nitchie, Elizabeth, *Virgil and the English Poets*, 1919.
18. Snyder, E. D., *The Celtic Revival in English Literature, 1760–1800*, 1923.
19. Texte, Joseph, *Rousseau et les origines du cosmopolitisme littéraire*, 1895; Eng. translation, 1899.
20. Torrey, Norman L., *Voltaire and the English Deists*, 1930.

21. Van Tieghem, Paul, *Le Préromantisme: études d'histoire littéraire européenne*, 1924.
22. Van Tieghem, Paul, "La sensibilité et la passion dans le roman européen au dix-huitième siècle," *RLC*, VI (1926), 424–35.
23. Van Tieghem, Paul, "L'automne dans la poésie ouest-européenne de Brockes à Lamartine (1720–1820)," *Mélanges Baldensperger*, II, 327–43, 1930.
24. West, A. H., *L'influence française dans la poésie burlesque en Angleterre entre 1660 et 1700*, 1931.
25. Whitford, R. C., "Juvenal in England, 1750–1802," *PQ*, VII (1928), 9–16.
26. Wollstein, Rose H., *English Opinions of French Poetry, 1660–1750*, 1923.

IV. Studies in English Literature and Criticism

1. Babbitt, Irving, *The New Laocoön; an Essay on the Confusion of the Arts*, 1910.
2. Babcock, R. W., *The Genesis of Shakespeare Idolatry, 1766–1799*, 1931.
3. Baldwin, Edward C., "The Relation of the Seventeenth Century Character to the Periodical Essay," *PMLA*, XIX (1904), 75–114.
4. Beers, H. A., *A History of English Romanticism in the Eighteenth Century*, 1899; second ed., 1910.
5. Beljame, A., *Le public et les hommes de lettres en Angleterre au dix-huitième siècle, 1660–1744*, 1881.
6. Bernbaum, Ernest, *Guide through the Romantic Movement*, 1930.
7. Bissell, Benjamin, *The American Indian in English Literature of the Eighteenth Century*, 1925.
8. Bosker, A., *Literary Criticism in the Age of Johnson*, 1930.
9. Bredvold, L. I., "The Element of Art in Eighteenth Century Poetry," Introduction to *Selected Poems of Alexander Pope*, 1926.
10. Brie, Friedrich, *Englische Rokoko-Epik (1710–1730)*, 1927.
11. Broadus, E. K., *The Laureateship, A Study of the Office of Poet Laureate in England*, 1921.
12. Burd, H. A., "The Golden Age Idea in Eighteenth Century Poetry," *Sewanee Review*, XXIII (1915), 172–85.
13. Cazamian, Louis, *L'évolution psychologique et la littérature en Angleterre, 1660–1914*, 1920.
14. Clark, Kenneth, *The Gothic Revival, an Essay in the History of Taste*, 1928.
15. Collins, A. S., "The Growth of the Reading Public during the Eighteenth Century," *RES*, II (1926), 284–93; 428–38.
16. Collins, A. S., *Authorship in the Days of Johnson, being a Study of the Relation between Author, Patron, Publisher, and Public, 1726–80*, 1927.
17. Collins, A. S., "The Growth of the Reading Public: 1780–1800," *Nineteenth Century, CI*, (1927), 749–58.
18. Conant, Martha P., *The Oriental Tale in England in the Eighteenth Century*, 1908.
19. Cory, H. E., "Spenser, Thomson, and Romanticism," *PMLA*, XXVI (1911), 51–91.
20. Courthope, W. J., *A History of English Poetry*, 6 vols., 1895–1910. Vols. III, V, VI, deal with this period.
21. Cowl, R. P., *The Theory of Poetry in England*, 1914.
22. Crane, R. S., "Imitation of Spenser and Milton in the Early Eighteenth Century: A New Document," *SP*, XV (1918), 195–206.
23. Crofts, J. E. V., "Enthusiasm," *Eighteenth Century Literature: An Oxford Miscellany*, 1909.
24. Crum, R. B., *Scientific Thought in Poetry*, 1931.
25. Das, P. K., *Evidences of a Growing Taste for Nature in the Age of Pope*, 1928.
26. De Maar, Harko G., *A History of Modern English Romanticism*, vol. I, *Elizabethan and Modern Romanticism in the Eighteenth Century*, 1924.
27. Dennis, John, *The Age of Pope*, 1894.
28. Dobson, Austin, *Eighteenth Century Vignettes*, first series, 1892; second series, 1894; third series, 1896.
29. Dodds, Mrs. A. E. Powell, *The Romantic Theory of Poetry*, 1926.
30. Doughty, Oswald, *English Lyric in the Age of Reason*, 1922.

31. Draper, John W., *The Funeral Elegy and the Rise of English Romanticism*, 1929.
32. Duncan, C. S., *The New Science and English Literature in the Classical Period*, 1913.
33. Eastlake, C. L., *A History of the Gothic Revival*, 1872.
34. Elton, Oliver, *The Augustan Ages*, 1899.
35. Elton, Oliver, *A Survey of English Literature, 1780–1830*, 2 vols., 1912.
36. Elton, Oliver, *A Survey of English Literature, 1730–1780*, 2 vols., 1928.
37. Elton, Oliver, "Reason and Enthusiasm in the Eighteenth Century," in *Essays and Studies by Members of the English Association*, vol. X, 1924.
38. Fairchild, Hoxie N., *The Noble Savage: A Study in Romantic Naturalism*, 1928.
39. Fairchild, Hoxie N., *The Romantic Quest*, 1931.
40. Garnett, Richard, *The Age of Dryden*, 1895.
41. Gertsch, Alfred, *Der steigende Ruhm Miltons*, 1927.
42. Gosse, Edmund, *From Shakespeare to Pope: An Inquiry into the Causes and Phenomena of the Rise of Classical Poetry in England*, 1885.
43. Gosse, Edmund, *History of Eighteenth Century Literature*, 1896.
44. Graham, W. J., *The Beginnings of English Literary Periodicals: A Study of Periodical Literature, 1665–1715*, 1926.
45. Grierson, H. J. C., *Classical and Romantic*, 1923. (Reprinted in *The Background of English Literature*, 1925.)
46. Grierson, H. J. C., *Cross Currents in English Literature of the XVIIth Century*, 1929.
47. Griffith, R. H., "The Progress Pieces of the Eighteenth Century," *Texas Review*, V (1920), 218–33.
48. Haas, C. E. de, *Nature and the Country in English Poetry of the First Half of the Eighteenth Century*, 1928.
49. Haferkorn, Reinhard, *Gothik und Ruine in der englischen Dichtung des Achtzehnten Jahrhunderts*, 1924.
50. Hamelius, Paul, *Die Kritik in der englischen Literatur des 17. und 18. Jahrhunderts*, 1897.
51. Havens, R. D., "Literature of Melancholy," *MLN*, XXIV (1909), 226–27.
52. Havens, R. D., "Romantic Aspects of the Age of Pope," *PMLA*, XXVII (1912), 297–324.
53. Havens, R. D., "The Poetic Diction of the English Classicists," in *Anniversary Papers by Colleagues and Pupils of George Lyman Kittredge*, 1913.
54. Havens, R. D., "Nature in the Early Eighteenth Century," *Nation*, March 26, 1914, p. 329.
55. Havens, R. D., *The Influence of Milton on English Poetry*, 1922.
56. Havens, R. D., "Changing Taste in the Eighteenth Century: A Study of Dryden's and Dodsley's Miscellanies," *PMLA*, XLIV (1929), 501–36.
57. Havens, R. D., "More Eighteenth Century Sonnets," *MLN*, XLV (1930), 77–84.
58. Hazlitt, William, *Lectures on the English Comic Writers*, 1819.
59. Howard, W. G., "Ut Pictura Poesis," *PMLA*, XXIV (1909), 40–123.
60. Howard, W. G., "Good Taste and Conscience," *PMLA*, XXV (1910), 486–97.
61. Hussey, Christopher, *The Picturesque: Studies in a Point of View*, 1927.
62. Jones, R. F., "The Background of the 'Battle of the Books,'" in *Washington University Studies*, vol. VII, Humanistic Series, 2, 1920.
63. Jones, R. F., "Eclogue Types in English Poetry of the Eighteenth Century," *JEGP*, XXIV (1925), 33–60.
64. Kalkühler, F., *Die Natur des Spleens bei dem englischen Schriftstellern in der ersten Hälfte des 18. Jahrhunderts*, 1920.
65. Kaufman, Paul, "Defining Romanticism," *MLN*, XL (1925), 193–204.
66. Kaufman, Paul, "Heralds of Original Genius," in *Essays in Memory of Barrett Wendell*, 1926.
67. Ker, W. P., "On the Value of the Terms 'Classical' and 'Romantic' as Applied to Literature," in *Collected Essays*, 2 vols., 1925.
68. Kitchin, George, *A Survey of Burlesque and Parody in English*, 1931.
69. Legouis, E., and Cazamian, L., *A History of English Literature*, translated from the French, new ed., 1929.

70. Longaker, Mark, *English Biography in the Eighteenth Century*, 1931.
71. Longueil, Alfred E., "The Word 'Gothic' in Eighteenth Century Criticism," *MLN*, XXXVIII (1923), 453–60.
72. Lovejoy, A. O., "'Pride' in Eighteenth Century Thought," *MLN*, XXXVI (1921), 31–37.
73. Lovejoy, A. O., "On the Discrimination of Romanticisms," *PMLA*, XXXIX (1924), 229–53.
74. Lovejoy, A. O., "Nature as Æsthetic Norm," *MLN*, XLII (1927), 444–50.
75. Lovejoy, A. O., "Optimism and Romanticism," *PMLA*, XLII (1927), 921–45.
76. Lovejoy, A. O., "The Parallel of Deism and Classicism," *MP*, XXIX (1932), 281–99.
77. McKillop, A. D., "Some Details of the Sonnet Revival," *MLN*, XXXIX (1924), 438–40.
78. Mainzer, P., *Die schöne Literatur Englands und die literarische Kritik in einigen der kleineren englischen Zeitschriften des 18. Jahrhunderts*, 1911.
79. Marr, G. S., *The Periodical Essayists of the Eighteenth Century*, 1924.
80. Martin, A. C., "The Love of Solitude in Eighteenth Century Poetry," *South Atlantic Quarterly*, XXIX (1930), 48–59.
81. Masterman, J. H. B., *The Age of Milton*, 1897.
82. Millar, J. H., *The Mid-Eighteenth Century*, 1902.
83. Miller, G. M., *The Historical Point of View in English Literary Criticism from 1570–1770* (*Anglistische Forschungen*, 35), 1913.
84. Minto, William, *The Literature of the Georgian Era*, 1894.
85. Moore, C. A., "The Return to Nature in the English Poetry of the Eighteenth Century," *SP*, XIV (1917), 243–91.
86. Moore, C. A., "Whig Panegyric Verse, 1700–1760: A Phase of Sentimentalism," *PMLA*, XLI (1926), 362–401.
87. More, P. E., *With the Wits; Shelburne Essays, Tenth Series*, 1919.
88. Morton, E. P., "The Spenserian Stanza before 1700," *MP*, IV (1907), 630–54.
89. Morton, E. P., "The Spenserian Stanza in the Eighteenth Century," *MP*, X (1913), 365–91.
90. Nethercot, A. H., "The Term 'Metaphysical Poets' before Johnson," *MLN*, XXXVIII (1922), 11–17.
91. Nethercot, A. H., "The Reputation of the 'Metaphysical Poets' during the Seventeenth Century," *JEGP*, XXIII (1924), 173–98.
92. Nethercot, A. H., "The Reputation of the 'Metaphysical Poets' during the Age of Pope," *PQ*, IV (1925), 161–79.
93. Nethercot, A. H., "The Reputation of the 'Metaphysical Poets' during the Age of Johnson and the 'Romantic Revival,'" *SP*, XXII (1925), 81–132.
94. Nichols, John, *Literary Anecdotes of the Eighteenth Century*, 9 vols., 1812–16.
95. Nichols, John, *Illustrations of the Literary History of the Eighteenth Century*, 8 vols., 1817–58.
96. Omond, T. S., *English Metrists in the Eighteenth and Nineteenth Centuries*, 1907.
97. Partridge, Eric, *Eighteenth Century English Romantic Poetry*, 1924.
98. Patton, Julia, *The English Village: A Literary Study, 1750–1850*, 1919.
99. Perry, T. S., *History of English Literature in the Eighteenth Century*, 1883.
100. Phelps, W. L., *The Beginnings of the English Romantic Movement*, 1893.
101. Plessow, Max, *Geschichte der Fabeldichtung in England bis zu John Gay (1726)*, 1906.
102. Previté-Orton, C. W., *Political Satire in English Poetry*, 1910.
103. Quayle, Thomas, *Poetic Diction: A Study of Eighteenth Century Verse*, 1924.
104. Quiller-Couch, Sir A., "On the Terms 'Classic' and 'Romantic,'" in *Studies in Literature*, 2 vols., 1922.
105. Railo, Eino, *The Haunted Castle: A Study of the Elements of English Romanticism*, translated from the Finnish, 1927.
106. Read, Herbert, *Reason and Romanticism*, 1926.
107. Reed, Amy L., *The Background of Gray's Elegy: A Study in the Taste for Melancholy Poetry, 1700–1751*, 1924.

108. Reynolds, Myra, *The Treatment of Nature in English Poetry between Pope and Wordsworth*, 1909.
109. Reynolds, Myra, *The Learned Lady in England, 1650–1760*, 1920.
110. Robertson, J. G., *Studies in the Genesis of Romantic Theory in the Eighteenth Century*, 1923.
111. Robertson, J. G., *The Reconciliation of Classic and Romantic*, 1925.
112. Robinson, H. S., *English Shakespearian Criticism in the Eighteenth Century*, 1931.
113. Saintsbury, George, *A History of Criticism and Literary Taste in Europe*, 3 vols., 1900–1904. The English chapters of this work have been reprinted as *A History of English Criticism*, 1911.
114. Saintsbury, George, *The Peace of the Augustans*, 1916.
115. Schelling, F. E., "Ben Jonson and the Classical School," *PMLA*, VI (1928), 221–49.
116. Schöffler, H., *Protestantismus und Literatur: neue Wege zur englischen Literatur des 18. Jahrhunderts*, 1922.
117. Seccombe, Thomas, *The Age of Johnson*, 1900.
118. Sherburn, George, "The Early Popularity of Milton's Minor Poems," *MP*, XVII (1919–1920), 259–78, 515–40.
119. Smith, David Nichol, *Shakespeare in the Eighteenth Century*, 1928.
120. Smith, L. P., "Four Romantic Words" [*Romantic, Originality, Creative, Genius*], in *Words and Idioms*, 1925.
121. Stephen, Sir Leslie, *English Literature and Society in the Eighteenth Century*, 1904.
122. Tatlock, J. S. P., "Origin of the Closed Couplet in English," *Nation*, April 9, 1914, p. 390.
123. Thackeray, William M., *English Humorists in the Eighteenth Century*, 1853.
124. Thüme, Hans, *Beiträge zur Geschichte des Geniebegriffs in England*, 1927.
125. Tinker, Chauncey B., *The Salon and English Letters*, 1915.
126. Tinker, Chauncey B., *Nature's Simple Plan*, 1922.
127. Vaughan, C. E., *The Romantic Revolt* (*Periods of European Literature*) 1900.
128. Vines, Sherard, *The Course of English Classicism from the Tudor to the Victorian Age*, 1930.
129. Walker, Hugh, *English Satire and Satirists*, 1925.
130. Ward, A. W., and Waller, A. R., editors, *The Cambridge History of English Literature*, 14 vols., 1907–18. Vols. VIII–XI deal with this period. *The Cambridge Bibliography of English Literature*, which is announced for early publication, will bring the bibliographies of this work down to date.
131. Wendell, Barrett, *The Temper of the Seventeenth Century in English Literature*, 1904.
132. Whibley, Charles, "The Court Poets," in *Literary Studies*, 1919.
133. Whitford, R. C., "Satire's View of Sentimentalism in the Days of George the Third," *JEGP*, XVIII (1919), 155–61.
134. Whitney, Lois, "English Primitivistic Theories of Epic Origins," *MP*, XXI (1924), 337–78.
135. Williams, George G., "The Beginnings of Nature Poetry in the Eighteenth Century," *SP*, XXVII (1930), 583–608.
136. Wood, Paul S., "Native Elements in English Neo-Classicism," *MP*, XXIV (1926), 201–08.
137. Wood, Paul S., "The Opposition to Neo-Classicism in England between 1660 and 1700," *PMLA*, XLIII (1928), 182–97.
138. Wyld, H. C., *Studies in English Rhymes from Surrey to Pope*, 1923.

SAMUEL BUTLER

There are few English writers of comparable importance of whom we know so little as we do about the author of *Hudibras*. Although his great poem was received with a prompt applause which has never quite subsided, the details of his life, the canon of his works, even the precise nature of his mind and character, are still uncertain. We know that he was born in 1612 near Worcester, that he attended the Cathedral School there under a good master, and that he was probably prevented by the poverty of his father, a small farmer, from attending the university. Until fifty years of age, at which time he married a woman whose considerable fortune was soon afterwards lost, Butler lived as clerk or secretary in various great country houses, notably that of the famous Puritan, Sir Samuel Luke, who is generally regarded as the original of Hudibras. In these situations, not unlike that occupied by Swift in the house of Sir William Temple, he accumulated ire and erudition and notes for many years until, early in 1663, the first part of *Hudibras* burst upon the world like an explosion. The second part met with equal success in the following year, but when the third part appeared in 1678 it made little stir in an England which had forgotten not only the poet but the animosities out of which he spoke. Butler died in 1680, poor and obscure, leaving much prose and verse which was not published for ninety years. A contemporary description brings the man before us: "of a leonine-coloured hair, sanguine, choleric, middle-sized, strong."

To most readers of our day *Hudibras* is a loose group of grotesque scenes and situations carelessly invented for a set of characters that never "come alive," yet rendered memorable, or at any rate unforgettable, by a rapid fire of epigram, a blaze of wit, and an audacity of language not to be found elsewhere in English. To Butler's first readers the poem was a shout of triumph over a defeated foe, and the violence that wearies us was the merely adequate expression of a mood which had long been violently repressed. To Butler himself, it is at least plausible to surmise, the poem was a reply to many personal indignities, edged by hatred of actual individuals and certain definite traits of English Puritanism. But *Hudibras* is a greater poem than these estimates indicate. It begins, indeed, as a satire against the Puritans, and in so far it may seem nothing more than exultation over a corpse, but it soon turns out to be a satire against humanity. As in the similar instance of Rabelais, Butler's superabundant wit and humour, taken with the power and profusion of his utterance, have impeded the realization of his essential greatness and have made it easy to ignore the extreme subtlety, not to say the cruelty, of his probing into the darker secrets of human egoism, hypocrisy, and self-deception. A fit companion for the deepest minds of his century, he had wandered for many years in the intellectual wilderness of Puritanism, and he was finally lost in the solitudes of the spirit, without hope either for himself or for mankind. As a complete sceptic, he could not write his satire from any settled point of view. If it was moderation that he set up as an ideal opposed to the intemperance of Puritanism, he did not attain or exemplify it; and if we are to suppose that the charity of complete understanding was his mark, again he fell far short. When one has read through Butler's verse and his at least equally brilliant prose, one can only say that he was a sincere lover of truth — and that he found it nowhere.

At the very beginning of the neo-classical period *Hudibras* strikes the note of ridicule — that is, of social laughter levelled at all aberrations from an ideal norm of character and conduct — which was to make itself increasingly feared. Unlike later English satire, however, the poem does not rest upon French precepts or examples, and Butler's voice is by no means that of the Court or of the Town. Instead of being urbane, genteel, cautious to keep the laugh on its side, striving chiefly for decorum and correctness, it is a burly, raucous, and always scornful English voice, delighting in its own harshness and in the pain it gives. The tone of derision is heard in the rugged cacophonous verse itself, which can be described only by the adjective "Hudibrastic." That crude native vigour in which many poets of the succeeding century were deficient, is here in excess, but of song, of rapture, and of the delicate simplicity which had been the greatness of the Elizabethan lyrists, there is not a hint from end to end.

HUDIBRAS

PART I, CANTO I

When civil dudgeon first grew high
And men fell out, they knew not why;
When hard words, jealousies, and fears
Set folks together by the ears,
And made them fight like mad or drunk
For Dame Religion as for *punk,
Whose honesty they all durst swear for
Tho' not a man of them knew wherefore;
When *gospel-trumpeter, surrounded
With long-ear'd rout, to battle sounded,
And pulpit, drum ecclesiastic,
Was beat with fist instead of a stick;
Then did Sir Knight abandon dwelling,
And out he rode a-colonelling.
  A wight he was whose very sight would
Entitle him Mirror of Knighthood,
That never bow'd his stubborn knee
To anything but chivalry,
Nor put up *blow but that which laid
Right Worshipful on shoulder-blade;
Chief of domestic knights and *errant,
Either for *chartel or for warrant,
Great on the bench, great in the saddle,
That could as well *bind o'er as *swaddle.
Mighty he was at both of these,
And styled of war as well as peace.
(So some rats of amphibious nature
Are either for the land or water.)
But here our authors make a doubt
Whether he were more wise or stout.
Some hold the one and some the other,
But, howsoe'er they make a pother,
The diff'rence was so small, his brain
Outweigh'd his rage but half a grain;
Which made some take him for a tool
That knaves do work with, call'd a fool.
For 't has been held by many that,
As Montaigne, playing with his cat,
Complains she thought him but an ass,
Much more she would Sir *Hudibras —
For that's the name our valiant knight
To all his challenges did write.
But they're mistaken very much;
'Tis plain enough he was no such.
We grant, altho' he had much wit,
H' was very shy of using it,
As being loath to wear it out,
And therefore bore it not about,
Unless on holidays or so,
As men their best apparel do.
Besides, 'tis known he could speak Greek
As naturally as pigs squeak,
That Latin was no more difficile
Than to a blackbird 'tis to whistle.
Being rich in both, he never scanted
His bounty unto such as wanted,
But much of either would afford
To many that had not one word.
For Hebrew roots, altho' they're found
To flourish most in barren ground,
He had such plenty as suffic'd
To make some think him circumcised:
And, truly, so he was, perhaps,
Not as a pros'lyte but for claps.
  He was in logic a great critic,
Profoundly skill'd in analytic;
He could distinguish and divide
A hair 'twixt south and south-west side,
On either which he would dispute,
Confute, change hands, and still confute.
He'd undertake to prove by force
Of argument, a man's no horse;
He'd prove a buzzard is no fowl,
And that a Lord may be an owl,
A calf an Alderman, a goose a Justice,
And rooks committee-men and trustees.
He'd run in debt by disputation
And pay with ratiocination.
All this by syllogism true
In mood and figure he would do.
For rhetoric, he could not ope
His mouth but out there flew a trope,
And when he happen'd to break off
I' th' middle of his speech, or cough,
H' had hard words ready to show why,
And tell what rules he did it by,
Else, when with greatest art he spoke,
You'd think he talk'd like other folk.
For all a rhetorician's rules
Teach nothing but to name his tools.
But when he pleas'd to show 't, his speech
In loftiness of sound was rich —
A Babylonish dialect
Which learnèd pedants much affect:
It was a party-colour'd dress
Of patch'd and piebald languages;
'Twas English cut on Greek and Latin
Like *fustian heretofore on satin.
It had an odd promiscuous tone
As if h' had talk'd three parts in one,
Which made some think, when he did gabble,
Th' had heard three labourers of Babel,

* Notes on Samuel Butler will be found in the Appendix, p. 937.

Or Cerberus himself pronounce
A *leash of languages at once.
This he as volubly would vent
As if his stock would ne'er be spent;
And truly, to support that *charge,
He had supplies as vast and large,
For he could coin or counterfeit
New words with little or no wit —
Words so debas'd and hard, no stone
Was hard enough *to touch them on.
And when with hasty noise he spoke 'em,
The ignorant for current took 'em,
That, had the *orator who once
Did fill his mouth with pebble stones
When he harangued, but known his phrase,
He would have us'd no other ways.
In mathematics he was greater
Than *Tycho Brahe or *Erra Pater,
For he by geometric scale
Could take the size of pots of ale,
Resolve by sines and tangents straight
If bread or butter wanted weight,
And wisely tell what hour o' th' day
The clock does strike, by algebra.
Besides, he was a shrewd philosopher,
And had read ev'ry text and gloss over;
Whate'er the crabbed'st author hath
He understood b' implicit faith;
Whatever sceptic could enquire for,
For every *why* he had a *wherefore;*
Knew more than forty of them do,
As far as words and terms could go.
All which he understood by rote,
And, as occasion serv'd, would quote,
No matter whether right or wrong.
They might be either said or sung.
His notions fitted things so well
That which was which he could not tell,
But oftentimes mistook the one
For th' other, as great clerks have done.
He could reduce all things to acts
And knew their nature by abstracts —
Where entity and *quiddity,
The ghosts of defunct bodies, fly,
Where Truth in person does appear,
Like words congeal'd in *northern air.
He knew what's what, and that's as high
As metaphysic wit can fly.
In *school-divinity as able
As he that hight *Irrefragable,
A second *Thomas — or, at once
To name them all, another *Duns.
Profound in all the *nominal
And real ways, beyond them all,
For he a rope of sand could twist
As tough as learned *Sorbonist,
And weave fine cobwebs fit for skull
That's empty when the moon is full,
Such as take lodgings in a head
That's to be let, unfurnishèd.
He could raise scruples dark and nice,
And, after, solve them in a trice,
As if Divinity had catch'd
The itch on purpose to be scratch'd,
Or, like a mountebank, did wound
And stab herself with doubts profound
Only to show with how small pain
The sores of faith are cur'd again —
Altho' by woful proof we find
They always leave a scar behind.
He knew the seat of Paradise,
Could tell in what degree it lies,
And, as he was dispos'd, could prove it
Below the moon or else above it;
What Adam dreamt of when his bride
Came from her closet in his side;
Whether the devil tempted her
By a High-Dutch interpreter;
If either of them had a navel;
Who first made music malleable;
Whether the serpent, at the Fall,
Had cloven feet or none at all.
All this, without a gloss or comment,
He could unriddle in a moment
In proper terms, such as men smatter
When they throw out and miss the matter.
For his religion, it was fit
To match his learning and his wit:
'Twas Presbyterian true blue,
For he was of that stubborn crew
Of errant saints whom all men grant
To be the true Church Militant,
Such as do build their faith upon
The holy text of pike and gun,
Decide all controversies by
Infallible artillery,
And prove their doctrine orthodox
By apostolic blows and knocks,
Call fire and sword and desolation
A godly, thorough reformation
Which always must be carried on
And still be doing, never done —
As if religion were intended
For nothing else but to be mended;
A sect whose chief devotion lies
In odd perverse antipathies,
In falling out with that or this
And finding somewhat still amiss;
More peevish, cross, and splenetic
Than dog distract or monkey sick;

That with more care keep holy-day
The wrong, than others the right way;
Compound for sins they are inclined to
By damning those they have no mind to;
Still so perverse and opposite
As if they worshipped God for spite.
The self-same thing they will abhor
One way, and long another for.
Free-will they one way disavow,
Another, nothing else allow.
All piety consists therein
In them, in other men all sin.
Rather than fail, they will defy
That which they love most tenderly,
Quarrel with minc'd pies and disparage
Their best and dearest friend, plum-porridge;
Fat pig and goose itself oppose,
And blaspheme custard thro' the nose.
Th' apostles of this fierce religion,
Like Mahomet's, were ass and *widgeon.
To whom our knight, by fast instinct
Of wit and temper, was so linked
As if hypocrisy and nonsense
Had got th' *advowson of his conscience.
  Thus was he gifted and accouter'd —
We mean on th' inside, not the outward.
That next of all we shall discuss;
Then listen, sirs, it follows thus:
His tawny beard was th' equal grace
Both of his wisdom and his face,
In cut and dye so like a tile
As sudden view it would beguile;
The upper part whereof was whey,
The nether orange mix'd with gray.
This hairy meteor did denounce
The fall of sceptres and of crowns,
With grisly *type did represent
Declining age of government,
And tell with hieroglyphic spade
Its own grave and the State's were made.
Like Samson's *heart-breakers, it grew
In time to make a nation rue,
Tho' it contributed its own fall
To wait upon the public downfall.
It was monastic, and did grow
In holy orders by strict vow
Of rule as sullen and severe
As that of rigid *Cordelier.
'Twas bound to suffer persecution
And martyrdom with resolution,
T' oppose itself against the hate
And vengeance of th' incensèd State
In whose defiance it was worn,
Still ready to be pull'd and torn,
With red-hot irons to be tortur'd,
Revil'd and spit upon and martyr'd.
*Maugre all which, 'twas to stand fast
As long as monarchy should last;
But when the State should hap to reel,
'Twas to submit to fatal steel
And fall, as it was consecrate,
A sacrifice to fall of State,
Whose thread of life the Fatal Sisters
Did twist together with its whiskers,
And twine so close that Time should never
In life or death their fortunes sever,
But with his rusty sickle mow
Both down together at a blow.
So learnèd *Taliacotius from
The brawny part of porter's bum
Cut supplemental noses which
Would last as long as parent breech,
But when the date of *Nock was out,
Off dropp'd the sympathetic snout.
His back, or rather burden, showed
As if it stoop'd with its own load,
For as Æneas bore his sire
Upon his shoulders thro' the fire,
Our knight did bear no less a pack
Of his own buttocks on his back,
Which now had almost got the upper
Hand of his head for want of crupper.
To poise this equally he bore
A paunch of the same bulk before,
Which still he had a special care
To keep well cramm'd with thrifty fare,
As white-pot, buttermilk, and curds
Such as a country house affords,
With other victual which anon
We farther shall dilate upon
When of his hose we come to treat —
The cupboard where he kept his meat.
  His doublet was of sturdy buff,
And tho' not sword, yet cudgel-proof,
Whereby 'twas fitter for his use
Who fear'd no blows but such as *bruise.
  His breeches were of rugged woollen,
And had been at the Siege of *Bullen.
To old King Harry so well known,
Some writers held they were his own.
Thro' they were lin'd with many a piece
Of *ammunition bread and cheese
And fat *black-puddings — proper food
For warriors that delight in blood;
For, as we said, he always chose
To carry victual in his hose,
That often tempted rats and mice
The ammunition to surprise,
And when he put a hand but in
The one or th' other magazine,

They stoutly in defence on't stood
And from the wounded foe drew blood;
And, till th' were storm'd and beaten out,
Ne'er left the fortified redoubt.
And tho' knights-errant, as some think,
Of old did neither eat nor drink,
Because when *thorough deserts vast
And regions desolate they passed,
Where belly-timber, above ground
Or under, was not to be found,
Unless they grazed, there's not a word
Of their provision on record,
Which made some confidently write
They had no stomachs, but to fight —
'Tis false, for Arthur *wore in hall
Round table like a *farthingale,
On which, with shirt pull'd out behind
And eke before, his good knights din'd —
Though 'twas no table, some suppose,
But a huge pair of round trunk-hose,
In which he carried as much meat
As he and all the knights could eat
When, laying by their swords and truncheons,
They took their breakfasts or their nuncheons.
But let that pass at present, lest
We should forget where we digressed
As learnèd authors use, to whom
We leave 't, and to the purpose come.
His puissant sword unto his side,
Near his undaunted heart, was tied,
With basket-hilt that would hold broth
And serve for fight and dinner both.
In it he melted lead for bullets
To shoot at foes — and, sometimes, pullets,
To whom he bore so fell a grutch
He ne'er gave quarter t' any such.
The trenchant blade, Toledo trusty,
For want of fighting was grown rusty,
And ate into itself for lack
Of somebody to hew and hack.
The peaceful scabbard where it dwelt
The rancour of its edge had felt,
For of the lower end two handful
It had devoured, 'twas so manful,
And so much scorn'd to lurk in ease
As if it durst not show its face.
In many desperate attempts
Of warrants, exigents, *contempts,
It had appear'd with courage bolder
Than Sergeant Bum invading *shoulder.
Oft had it ta'en possession,
And pris'ners too, or made them run.
This sword a dagger had, his page,
That was but little for his age,
And therefore waited on him so
As dwarfs upon knights-errant do.
It was a serviceable *dudgeon
Either for fighting or for drudging.
When it had stabb'd or broke a head,
It would scrape trenchers or chip bread,
Toast cheese or bacon; tho' it were
To bait a mouse trap, 'twould not care.
'Twould make clean shoes, and in the earth
Set leeks and onions and so forth.
It had been 'prentice to a brewer
Where this and more it did endure,
But left the trade as many more
Have lately done on the same *score.
In th' holsters at his saddle-bow
Two aged pistols he did stow
Among the surplus of such meat
As in his hose he could not get.
These would inveigle rats with th' scent
To forage when the cocks were *bent,
And sometimes catch 'em with a snap
As cleverly as th' ablest trap.
They were upon hard duty still,
And every night stood sentinel
To guard the magazine i' th' hose
From two-legg'd and from four-legg'd foes.
Thus clad and fortified, Sir Knight
From peaceful home set forth to fight,
But first with nimble active force
He got on th' outside of his horse;
For having but one stirrup tied
T' his saddle on the further side,
It was so short h' had much ado
To reach it with his desp'rate toe;
But, after many strains and heaves,
He got up to the saddle-eaves,
From whence he vaulted into th' seat
With so much vigour, strength, and heat
That he had almost tumbled over
With his own weight, but did recover
By laying hold on tail and mane,
Which oft he us'd instead of rein.
But now we talk of mounting steed,
Before we further do proceed,
It doth behove us to say something
Of that which bore our valiant bumkin.
The beast was sturdy, large, and tall,
With mouth of meal and eyes of wall —
I would say eye, for h' had but one,
As most agree, tho' some say none.
He was well *stay'd and in his gate
Preserv'd a grave majestic state.
At spur or switch no more he skipped
Or mended pace than Spaniard whipped,
And yet so fiery he would bound
As if he grieved to touch the ground;

That Cæsar's horse, who, as fame goes
Had corns upon his feet and toes,
Was not by half so tender-hoofed,
Nor trod upon the ground so *soft.
And as that beast would kneel and stoop,
Some write, to take his rider up,
So Hudibras *his, 'tis well known,
Would often do to set him down.
We shall not need to say what lack
Of leather was upon his back,
For that was hidden under pad,
And breech of knight gall'd full as bad.
His strutting ribs on both sides show'd
Like furrows he himself had plow'd;
For underneath the skirt of *panel,
'Twixt ev'ry two there was a channel.
His draggling tail hung in the dirt,
Which on his rider he would flirt
Still as his tender side he prick'd
With arm'd heel, or with unarm'd kick'd;
For Hudibras wore but one spur,
As wisely knowing, could he stir
To active trot one side of 's horse,
The other would not hang an arse. . . .

[1663]

THOMAS HOBBES

THOMAS HOBBES lived through two ages: born in the Armada year, 1588, he was personally acquainted with Bacon and Ben Jonson; though seventy-two years of age at the Restoration, he survived it more than nineteen years and became a literary contemporary of Dryden. He was a voluminous writer in Latin and English until the very end of his long life. The work by which he is most frequently remembered is *Leviathan; or the Matter, Form, and Power of a Commonwealth, Ecclesiastical and Civil,* first published in 1651, an elaborate argument in favour of the royal authority. Hobbes bases this authority on a social contract, which is, however, completely different from that of his successors in political theory. He describes the primitive state of nature as one of complete barbarism in which every man's hand is against all his neighbours. In exchange for the most elementary conditions of personal protection and as a first step toward civilization, he believes, men handed over absolute authority to kings. This authority, once established, was irrevocable. "He interprets," says Sir Leslie Stephen, "the doctrine of the social compact (which had been recently expounded by Hooker and Grotius) not as a compact between the sovereign and his subjects, but as between the subjects to obey the sovereign." This royal absolutism applies equally to religious and secular matters; in all respects the king is supreme.

These conclusions really pleased no one: they offended Parliamentarians by their high stand for royal authority, and they offended Cavaliers by their denial of divine right; they offended churchmen of all kinds, either because of intolerance, or because of flat Erastianism. In consequence Hobbes was assailed from all sides; Roman Catholics, High Churchmen, Low Churchmen, dissenters, even rationalists attacked him. He was accused of atheism, materialism, selfishness, bigotry, false reasoning. Hobbism was viewed with alarm as the school of debauchery and the enemy of Church and State. Its refutation was undertaken by clergymen, philosophers, and political theorists. At the same time Hobbes was recognized by his contemporaries and immediate successors as one of the leading philosophers of his time. On the Continent his influence was even more important, as shown in the work of Spinoza, Leibnitz, Diderot, and Rousseau.

In spite of the fact that it comes too early to be affected by the new prose, his English style is eminently readable. It is vigorous, direct, incisive, marked by native wit and shrewdness. Though a scholar of no mean acquisitions Hobbes is original both in thought and in expression. According to his contemporary, Aubrey, "He was wont to say that if he had read as much as other men, he should have continued still as ignorant as other men." At his best he writes clearly and with a homely tang all his own. Thus in the conclusion of *Leviathan*, when he is explaining why he does not follow the customary practice of ornamenting his writing by quotations from "ancient poets, orators, and philosophers," he includes the following among his reasons:

> "Fourthly, such opinions as are taken only upon credit of antiquity are not intrinsically the judgment of those that cite them, but words that pass (like gaping) from mouth to mouth. Fifthly, it is many times with a fraudulent design that men stick their corrupt doctrine with the cloves of other men's wit. Sixthly, I find not that the ancients they cite took it for an ornament to do the like with those that wrote before them. Seventhly, it is an argument of indigestion, when Greek and Latin sentences unchewed come up again, as they used to do, unchanged."

The last sentence of the book is not only a shrewd observation but a brilliant apothegm:

> "For such truth as opposeth no man's profit nor pleasure is to all men welcome."

Personally Hobbes was a timid man, but intellectually he was bold. He made a profound impression upon his contemporaries; and he has, through his direct influence and even more through the opposition that he stirred up, left a lasting impression upon the course of philosophical and political speculation.

LEVIATHAN

PART II

Chapter XVII

Of the Causes, Generation, and Definition of a Commonwealth

The final cause, end, or design of men, who naturally love liberty and dominion over others, in the introduction of that restraint upon themselves, in which we see them live in commonwealths, is the foresight of their own preservation, and of a more contented life thereby; that is to say, of getting themselves out from that miserable condition of war, which is necessarily consequent (as hath been shown) to the natural passions of men, when there is no visible power to keep them in awe, and tie them by fear of punishment to the performance of their covenants, and observation of those laws of nature set down in the fourteenth and fifteenth chapters.

For the laws of nature (as justice, equity, modesty, mercy, and, in sum, doing to others as we would be done to) of themselves, without the terror of some power to cause them to be observed, are contrary to our natural passions, that carry us to partiality, pride, revenge, and the like. And covenants, without the sword, are but words, and of no strength to secure a man at all. Therefore, notwithstanding the laws of nature (which every one hath then kept, when he has the will to keep them, when he can do it safely), if there be no power erected, or not great enough for our security, every man will and may lawfully rely on his own strength and art for caution against all other men. And in all places where men have lived by small families, to rob and spoil one another has been a trade, and so far from being reputed against the law of nature that the greater spoils they gained, the greater was their honour; and men observed no other laws therein but the laws of honour; that is, to abstain from cruelty, leaving to men their lives and instruments of husbandry. And as small families did then, so now do cities and kingdoms, which are but greater families for their own security, enlarge their dominions upon all pretences of danger and fear of invasion, or assistance that may be given to invaders; endeavour as much as they can to subdue or weaken their neighbours by open force and secret arts, for want of other caution, justly; and are remembered for it in after ages with honour.

Nor is it the joining together of a small number of men that gives them this security; because in small numbers, small additions on the one side or the other make the advantage of strength so great as is sufficient to carry the victory; and therefore gives encouragement to an invasion. The multitude sufficient to confide in for our security is not determined by any certain number, but by comparison with the enemy we fear; and is then sufficient, when the odds of the enemy is not of so visible and conspicuous moment, to determine the event of war, as to move him to attempt.

And be there never so great a multitude, yet if their actions be directed according to their particular judgments and particular appetites, they can expect thereby no defence, nor protection, neither against a common enemy nor against the injuries of one another. For being distracted in opinions concerning the best use and application of their strength, they do not help, but hinder one another; and reduce their strength by mutual opposition to nothing: whereby they are easily, not only subdued by a very few that agree together, but also when there is no common enemy, they make war upon each other for their particular interests. For if we could suppose a great multitude of men to consent in the observation of justice and other laws of nature without a common power to keep them all in awe, we might as well suppose all mankind to do the same; and then there neither would be, nor need to be, any civil government or commonwealth at all, because there would be peace without subjection.

Nor is it enough for the security, which men desire should last all the time of their life, that they be governed and directed by one judgment for a limited time, as in one battle or one war. For though they obtain a victory by their unanimous endeavour against a foreign enemy; yet afterwards, when either they have no common enemy, or he that by one part is held for an enemy is by another part held for a friend, they must needs by the difference of their interests dissolve, and fall again into a war amongst themselves.

It is true that certain living creatures, as bees and ants, live sociably one with another (which are therefore by Aristotle numbered amongst political creatures) and yet have no other direction than their particular judgments and appetites; nor speech, whereby one of them can signify to another what he thinks expedient for the common benefit: and therefore some man may perhaps desire to know why mankind cannot do the same. To which I answer:

First, that men are continually in competition for honour and dignity, which these creatures are not; and consequently amongst men there ariseth on that ground envy and hatred and finally war; but amongst these not so.

Secondly, that amongst these creatures the common good differeth not from the private; and being by nature inclined to their private, they procure thereby the common benefit. But man, whose joy consisteth in comparing himself with other men, can relish nothing but what is eminent.

Thirdly, that these creatures, having not, as man, the use of reason, do not see, nor think they see, any fault in the administration of their common business: whereas amongst men there are very many that think themselves wiser and abler to govern the public, better than the rest; and these strive to reform and innovate, one this way, another that way; and thereby bring it into distraction and civil war.

Fourthly, that these creatures, though they have some use of voice in making known to one another their desires and other affections; yet they want that art of words, by which some men can represent to others that which is good in the likeness of evil; and evil in the likeness of good; and augment or diminish the apparent greatness of good and evil; discontenting men, and troubling their peace at their pleasure.

Fifthly, irrational creatures cannot distinguish between injury and damage; and therefore as long as they be at ease, they are not offended with their fellows; whereas man is then most troublesome when he is most at ease; for then it is that he loves to show his wisdom, and control the actions of them that govern the commonwealth.

Lastly, the agreement of these creatures is natural; that of men is by covenant only, which is artificial: and therefore it is no wonder if there be somewhat else required, besides covenant, to make their agreement constant and lasting; which is a common power to keep them in awe, and to direct their actions to the common benefit.

The only way to erect such a common power as may be able to defend them from the invasion of foreigners and the injuries of one another, and thereby to secure them in such sort as that by their own industry and by the fruits of the earth they may nourish themselves and live contentedly, is to confer all their power and strength upon one man or upon one assembly of men that may reduce all their wills by plurality of voices unto one will; which is as much as to say, to appoint one man, or assembly of men, to bear their person; and every one to own and acknowledge himself to be author of whatsoever he that so beareth their person, shall act, or cause to be acted, in those things which concern the common peace and safety; and therein to submit their wills, every one to his will, and their judgments to his judgment. This is more than consent or concord; it is a real unity of them all in one and the same person, made by covenant of every man with every man in such manner, as if every man should say to every man, "I authorize and give up my right of governing myself to this man, or to this assembly of men, on this condition,— that thou give up thy right to him, and authorize all his actions in like manner." This done, the multitude so united in one person is called a *commonwealth*, in Latin, *civitas*. This is the generation of that great *Leviathan*, or rather, to speak more reverently, of that mortal god to which we owe under the immortal God our peace and defence. For by this authority, given him by every particular man in the commonwealth, he hath the use of so much power and strength conferred on him, that by terror thereof he is enabled to form the wills of them all, to peace at home and mutual aid against their enemies abroad. And in him consisteth the essence of the commonwealth; which, to define it, is one person, of whose acts a great multitude by mutual covenants one with another have made themselves every one the author, to the end he may use the strength and means of them all, as he shall think expedient for their peace and common defence.

And he that carrieth this person is called sovereign and said to have sovereign power; and every one besides, his subject.

The attaining to this sovereign power is by two ways. One, by natural force, as when a man maketh his children to submit themselves and their children to his government, as being able to destroy them if they refuse; or by war subdueth his enemies to his will, giving them their lives on that condition. The other is when men agree amongst themselves to submit to some man, or assembly of men, voluntarily, on confidence to be protected by him against all others. This latter may be called a political commonwealth, or commonwealth by institution; and the former a commonwealth by acquisition. And first, I shall speak of a commonwealth by institution.

Chapter XVIII

Of the Rights of Sovereigns by Institution

A commonwealth is said to be instituted when a multitude of men do agree and covenant, every one with every one, that to whatsoever man, or assembly of men shall be given by the major part the right to present the person of them all (that is to say, to be their representative); every one, as well he that voted for it as he that voted against it, shall authorize all the actions and judgments of that man, or assembly of men, in the same manner as if they were his own, to the end to live peaceably amongst themselves and be protected against other men.

From this institution of a commonwealth are derived all the rights and faculties of him, or them, on whom the sovereign power is conferred by the consent of the people assembled.

First, because they covenant, it is to be understood they are not obliged by former covenant to anything repugnant hereunto. And consequently they that have already instituted a commonwealth, being thereby bound by covenant to own the actions and judgments of one, cannot lawfully make a new covenant amongst themselves to be obedient to any other, in anything whatsoever without his permission. And therefore, they that are subjects to a monarch cannot without his leave cast off monarchy, and return to the confusion of a disunited multitude; nor transfer their person from him that beareth it to another man, or other assembly of men: for they are bound, every man to every man, to own and be reputed author of all that he that already is their sovereign shall do and judge fit to be done; so that any one man dissenting, all the rest should break their covenant made to that man, which is injustice; and they have also every man given the sovereignty to him that beareth their person; and therefore if they depose him, they take from him that which is his own, and so again it is injustice. Besides, if he that attempteth to depose his sovereign be killed or punished by him for such attempt, he is author of his own punishment, as being by the institution author of all his sovereign shall do; and because it is injustice for a man to do anything for which he may be punished by his own authority, he is also upon that title, unjust. And whereas some men have pretended for their disobedience to their sovereign * a new covenant made, not with men, but with God; this also is unjust: for there is no covenant with God but by mediation of somebody that representeth God's person; which none doth but God's lieutenant, who hath the sovereignty under God. But this pretence of covenant with God is so evident a lie, even in the pretenders' own consciences, that it is not only an act of an unjust, but also of a vile and unmanly disposition.

Secondly, because the right of bearing the person of them all is given to him they make sovereign, by covenant only of one to another, and not of him to any of them; there can happen no breach of covenant on the part of the sovereign; and consequently none of his subjects by any pretence of forfeiture can be freed from his subjection. That he which is made sovereign maketh no covenant with his subjects beforehand is manifest, because either he must make it with the whole multitude, as one party to the covenant, or he must make a several covenant with every man. With the whole as one party, it is impossible, because as yet they are not one person; and if he make so many several covenants as there be men, those covenants after he hath the sovereignty are void, because what act soever can be pretended by any one of them for breach thereof is the act both of himself and of all the rest, because done in the person and by the right of every one of them in particular. Besides, if any one, or more of them, pretend a breach of the covenant made by the sovereign at his in-

* Notes on Thomas Hobbes will be found in the Appendix, p. 928

stitution; and others, or one other of his subjects or himself alone, pretend there was no such breach, there is in this case no judge to decide the controversy: it returns therefore to the sword again; and every man recovereth the right of protecting himself by his own strength, contrary to the design they had in the institution. It is therefore in vain to grant sovereignty by way of precedent covenant. The opinion that any monarch receiveth his power by covenant, that is to say on condition, proceedeth from want of understanding this easy truth, that covenants being but words and breath, have no force to oblige, contain, constrain, or protect any man, but what it has from the public sword; that is, from the untied hands of that man, or assembly of men, that hath the sovereignty, and whose actions are avouched by them all, and performed by the strength of them all, in him united. But when an assembly of men is made sovereign; then no man imagineth any such covenant to have passed in the institution; for no man is so dull as to say, for example, the people of Rome made a covenant with the Romans to hold the sovereignty on such or such conditions; which not performed, the Romans might lawfully depose the Roman people. That men see not the reason to be alike in a monarchy and in a popular government, proceedeth from the ambition of some that are kinder to the government of an assembly, whereof they may hope to participate, than of monarchy, which they despair to enjoy.

Thirdly, because the major part hath by consenting voices declared a sovereign, he that dissented must now consent with the rest; that is, be contented to avow all the actions he shall do, or else justly be destroyed by the rest. For if he voluntarily entered into the congregation of them that were assembled, he sufficiently declared thereby his will, and therefore tacitly covenanted to stand to what the major part should ordain; and therefore if he refuse to stand thereto, or make protestation against any of their decrees, he does contrary to his covenant, and therefore unjustly. And whether he be of the congregation or not, and whether his consent be asked or not, he must either submit to their decrees, or be left in the condition of war he was in before; wherein he might without injustice be destroyed by any man whatsoever.

Fourthly, because every subject is by this institution author of all the actions and judgments of the sovereign instituted, it follows that whatsoever he doth, it can be no injury to any of his subjects, nor ought he to be by any of them accused of injustice. For he that doth anything by authority from another, doth therein no injury to him by whose authority he acteth; but by this institution of a commonwealth every particular man is author of all the sovereign doth; and consequently he that complaineth of injury from his sovereign, complaineth of that whereof he himself is author; and therefore ought not to accuse any man but himself, no nor himself of injury, because to do injury to oneself is impossible. It is true that they that have sovereign power may commit iniquity, but not injustice or injury in the proper signification.

Fifthly, and consequently to that which was said last, *no man that hath sovereign power can justly be put to death, or otherwise in any manner by his subjects punished. For seeing every subject is author of the actions of his sovereign, he punisheth another for the actions committed by himself.

And because the end of this institution is the peace and defence of them all, and whosoever has right to the end has right to the means, it belongeth of right to whatsoever man or assembly that hath the sovereignty, to be judge both of the means of peace and defence; and also of the hindrances and disturbances of the same; and to do whatsoever he shall think necessary to be done, both beforehand for the preserving of peace and security, by prevention of discord at home, and hostility from abroad; and, when peace and security are lost, for the recovery of the same. And therefore,

Sixthly, it is annexed to the sovereignty to be judge of what opinions and doctrines are averse and what conducing to peace; and consequently on what occasions, how far, and what men are to be trusted withal, in speaking to multitudes of people; and who shall examine the doctrines of all books before they be published. For the actions of men proceed from their opinions, and in the well-governing of opinions consisteth the well-governing of men's actions, in order to their peace and concord. And though in matter of doctrine nothing ought to be regarded but the truth, yet this is not repugnant to regulating of the same by peace. For doctrine repugnant to peace can no more be true than peace and concord can be against the law of nature. It is true that in a commonwealth, where by the negligence or unskillfulness of governors and teachers, false doctrines are by time generally received, the contrary truths may be generally offensive; yet the most sudden and rough bustling in of a new truth that can be, does never break the peace, but only sometimes awake the war. For those men that are so remissly governed that they dare take up arms to defend or introduce an opinion are still in war, and their condition not peace, but only a cessation of arms for fear of one another; and they live, as it were, in the procincts of battle continually. It belongeth therefore to him that hath the sovereign power to be judge, or constitute all judges of opinions and doctrines as a thing necessary to peace; thereby to prevent discord and civil war.

Seventhly, is annexed to the sovereignty the whole power of prescribing the rules whereby every man may know what goods he may enjoy and what actions he may do without being molested by any of his fellow subjects; and this is it men call propriety. For before constitution of sovereign power, as hath already been shown, all men had right to all things; which necessarily causeth war; and therefore this propriety, being necessary to peace, and depending on sovereign power, is the act of that power, in order to the public peace. These rules of propriety (or *meum* and *tuum*), and of good, evil, lawful, and unlawful in the actions of subjects, are the civil laws; that is to say, the laws of each commonwealth in particular; though the name of civil law be now restrained to the ancient civil laws of the city of Rome, which, being the head of a great part of the world, her laws at that time were in these parts the civil law.

Eighthly, is annexed to the sovereignty the right of judicature; that is to say, of hearing and deciding all controversies which may arise concerning law, either civil or natural, or concerning fact. For without the decision of controversies, there is no protection of one subject against the injuries of another; the laws concerning *meum* and *tuum* are vain; and to every man remaineth from the natural and necessary appetite of his own conservation the right of protecting himself by his private strength, which is the condition of war, and contrary to the end for which every commonwealth is instituted.

Ninthly, is annexed to the sovereignty the right of making war and peace with other nations and commonwealths; that is to say, of judging when it is for the public good, and how great forces are to be assembled, armed, and paid for that end; and to levy money upon the subjects to defray the expenses thereof. For the power by which the people are to be defended consisteth in their armies; and the strength of an army, in the union of their strength under one command; which command the sovereign instituted, therefore hath; because the command of the militia, without other institution, maketh him that hath it sovereign. And therefore whosoever is made general of an army, he that hath the sovereign power is always generalissimo.

Tenthly, is annexed to the sovereignty the choosing of all counsellors, ministers, magistrates, and officers, both in peace and war. For seeing the sovereign is charged with the end, which is the common peace and defence, he is understood to have power to use such means as he shall think most fit for his discharge.

Eleventhly, to the sovereign is committed the power of rewarding with riches or honour, and of punishing with corporal or pecuniary punishment, or with ignominy, every subject according to the law he hath formerly made; or if there be no law made, according as he shall judge most to conduce to the encouraging of men to serve the commonwealth, or deterring of them from doing disservice to the same.

Lastly, considering what values men are naturally apt to set upon themselves, what respect they look for from others, and how little they value other men; from whence continually arise amongst them emulation, quarrels, factions, and at last war, to the destroying of one another, and diminution of their strength against a common enemy; it is necessary that there be laws of honour, and a public rate of the worth of such men as have deserved, or are able to deserve, well of the commonwealth; and that there be force in the hands of some or other to put those laws in execution. But it hath already been shown that not only the whole militia, or forces of the commonwealth, but also the judicature of all controversies is annexed to the sovereignty. To the sovereign, therefore, it belongeth also to give titles of honour, and to appoint what order of place and dignity each man shall hold, and what signs of respect, in public or private meetings, they shall give to one another.

These are the rights which make the essence of sovereignty, and which are the marks whereby a man may discern in what man, or assembly of men, the sovereign power is placed and resideth. For these are incommunicable and inseparable. The power to coin money, to dispose of the estate and persons of infant heirs, to have pre-emption in markets, and all other statute prerogatives, may be transferred by the sovereign, and yet the power to protect his subjects be retained. But if he transfer the militia, he retains the judicature in vain, for want of execution of the laws; or if he grant away the power of raising money, the militia is in vain; or if he give away the government of doctrines, men will be frighted into rebellion with the fear of spirits. And so, if we consider any one of the said rights, we shall presently see that the holding of all the rest will produce no effect in the conservation of peace and justice, the end for which all commonwealths are instituted. And this division is it, whereof it is said, a kingdom divided in itself cannot stand; for unless this division precede, division into opposite armies can never happen. If there had not first been an opinion received of the greatest part of England, that these powers were divided between the King and the Lords and the House of Commons, the people had never been divided, and fallen into this civil war; first, between those that disagreed in politics; and after, between the dissenters about the liberty of religion, which have so instructed men in this point of sovereign right that there be few now in England that do not see that these rights are inseparable, and will be so generally acknowledged at the next return of peace; and so continue till their miseries are forgotten; and no longer, except the vulgar be better taught than they have hitherto been.

And because they are essential and inseparable rights, it follows necessarily that in whatsoever words any of them seem to be granted away, yet if the sovereign power itself be not in direct terms renounced, and the name of sovereign no more given by the grantees to him that grants them, the grant is void; for when he has granted all he can, if we grant back the sovereignty, all is restored, as inseparably annexed thereunto.

This great authority being indivisible and inseparably annexed to the sovereignty, there is little ground for the opinion of them that say of sovereign kings, though they be *singulis majores*, of greater power than every one of their subjects, yet they be *universis minores*, of less power than them all together. For if by all together they mean not the collective body as one person, then all together and every one signify the same; and the speech is absurd. But if by all together they understand them as one person, which person the sovereign bears, then the power of all together is the same with the sovereign's power; and so again the speech is absurd; which absurdity they see well enough when the sovereignty is in an assembly of the people; but in a monarch they see it not, and yet the power of sovereignty is the same in whomsoever it be placed.

And as the power, so also the honour of the sovereign ought to be greater than that of any or all the subjects. For in the sovereignty is the fountain of honour. The dignities of lord, earl, duke, and prince are his creatures. As in the presence of the master, the servants are equal and without any honour at all, so are the subjects in the presence of the sovereign. And though they shine some more, some less, when they are out of his sight, yet in his presence they shine no more than the stars in presence of the sun.

But a man may here object that the condition of subjects is very miserable, as being obnoxious to the lusts and other irregular passions of him or them that have so unlimited a power in their hands. And commonly they that live under a monarch think it the fault of monarchy, and they that live under the government of democracy or other sovereign assembly attribute all the inconvenience to that form of commonwealth; whereas the power in all forms, if they be perfect enough to protect them, is the same; not considering that the estate of man can never be without some incommodity or other, and that the greatest that in any form of government can possibly happen to the people in general is scarce sensible in respect of the miseries and horrible calamities that accompany a civil war, or that dissolute condition of masterless men, without subjection to laws and a coercive power to tie their hands from rapine and revenge: nor considering that the greatest pressure of sovereign governors proceedeth not from any delight or profit they can expect in the damage or weakening of their subjects, in whose vigour consisteth their own strength and glory; but in the restiveness of themselves that unwillingly contributing to their own defence, make it necessary for their governors to draw from them what they can in time of peace, that they may have means on any emergent occasion, or sudden need, to resist or take advantage on their enemies. For all men are by nature provided of notable multiplying glasses (that is, their passions and self-love), through which every little payment appeareth a great grievance, but are destitute of those *prospective-glasses (namely moral and civil science) to see afar off the miseries that hang over them, and cannot without such payments be avoided.

[1651]

ABRAHAM COWLEY

THE fame of Abraham Cowley began in 1633 when, at the age of fourteen, he published his first collection of poems. At the time of his death in 1667 he was the most admired poet in England; but later generations, admitting the brilliance of his wit and his skill as a rhetorician in verse, have concluded that he was scarcely a poet at all. In recent decades his prose has been rediscovered and given the high rating it deserves. He may be remembered longest as the man who brought the informal essay from France to England, where it has flourished ever since far more than in its native land.

Cowley himself attributed his remarkable precocity in verse-making to the influence of Spenser's *Faerie Queene*, which he read in childhood. His father, a wealthy London merchant, sent him to Westminster School and then to Cambridge University, but, as he says, he "was soon torn from thence by that violent public storm which would suffer nothing to stand where it did." He joined the Royalists on the outbreak of the Civil War and was consequently ejected from his college fellowship in 1643. Soon after, he went with the queen to Paris, serving as her secretary for the next twelve years and often risking his life on perilous political journeys. In 1656 he returned to London, was for a time imprisoned, and published his collected poems, including the *Pindaric Odes*, the *Davideis* — an unfinished epic in heroic couplets on the life of David which Cowley had begun in Latin while in Cambridge — *The Mistress*, and *Miscellanies*. He evidently regarded the *Davideis* as his masterpiece, the answer to his own question:

What shall I do to be forever known
And make the coming age my own?

but it made no great impression, and to modern taste, in spite of many vivid lines, it is intolerably dull. Cowley's contemporaries preferred the exceedingly clever amatory poems of *The Mistress*, probably the most popular book of verse of the time. Scholars have had most to say about the *Pindaric Odes*, not solely because they set a bad fashion for the eighteenth century and made way for the great irregular odes of the nineteenth, but primarily because they give them an opportunity to show that Cowley did not understand the versification of Pindar. The volume contained at least one beautiful and noble poem, the elegy on the poet Crashaw. This also helped to establish a fashion, that of the elegy of personal mourning, which the succeeding age did not soon forget.

At the time of the Restoration Cowley had well-founded hopes of political advancement, but when these were disappointed he went to live in the village of Chertsey on the Thames. Here he spent the last six years of his life in a celebrated literary seclusion, overseeing his small farm, working at a book on botany, producing a pamphlet on *The Advancement of Experimental Philosophy* which hastened the founding of the Royal Society, writing his eleven *Essays in Verse and Prose* as an apologia for his retirement from public life, and, finally, at the suggestion of his friend and correspondent, John Evelyn, composing his sound and thoughtful *Ode to the Royal Society*. Cowley died in Chertsey at the age of forty-nine and was buried with great pomp in Westminster Abbey.

Concerning Cowley's verse we can scarcely say more than that it is obviously the product of an exceedingly brilliant and well-stored mind driven by the Renaissance passion for fame. We read the half of his verse that can be read at all, with amazement at the flash of his tireless wit and ingenuity, but with a growing conviction that he never quite discovered what poetry is, and never had any deep need of it. Superficially, *The Mistress* suggests John Donne, but Cowley could imitate only the mannerisms of that great and sombre mind. He is graceful where Donne was grotesquely awkward; he is a better versifier than Donne tried to be; but also he is utterly cold, which Donne never was, so that his artifice is merely artificial to the end.

Cowley's prose may seem at first to be far more simple and "sincere," far less dependent than his verse upon the rhetorical tradition of the Renaissance. As compared with almost any of the more important prose written at about the same time — with that of Sir Thomas Browne, of Taylor or Barrow or Milton, even of Fuller — it is indeed remarkably direct and straight-grained, and there can be no doubt that it helped to prepare the way for the reforms of Dryden and the triumphs of Addison. Yet even here Cowley is a rhetorician of the Renaissance. He is almost as much an imitator and an echoer in his essays, where he asserts his independence, as in his verse. All the essays have one central theme — solitude, which had been a commonplace of rhetorical display for two thousand years. Cowley has the vast literature of this theme at his quill's tip, and he does little more than recapitulate its more famous passages. We need not entirely ignore the possibility, of which contemporaries made much, that his condemnation of public life was a crying of sour grapes; but we know that the strain of the Civil Wars taught many a man to sigh for country contentments, and Cowley had begun to long for them even as a child in London.

Somewhat more than a century after Cowley's death, Dr. Johnson treated him, in the first of his *Lives of the Poets*, with decided respect, calling him the last of the metaphysical poets and undoubtedly the best. In other respects Johnson evidently thought Cowley the earliest English poet of his own kind. This opinion was not entirely wrong. Although there was much of the earlier Renaissance in him, there was also something of the cool and moderate eighteenth century.

TO THE ROYAL SOCIETY

*Philosophy, the great and only heir
Of all that human knowledge which has been
Unforfeited by man's rebellious *sin,
Though full of years he do appear,
(Philosophy, I say, and call it, he,
For whatsoe'er the painter's fancy be,
It a male-virtue seems to me)
Has still been kept in nonage till of late,
Nor manag'd or enjoy'd his vast estate:
Three or four thousand years, one would have thought,
To ripeness and perfection might have brought
A science so well bred and nurs'd,
And of such hopeful parts, too, at the first;
But, oh, the guardians and the tutors then,
(Some negligent, and some ambitious men)
Would ne'er consent to set him free,
Or his own natural powers to let him see,
Lest that should put an end to their authority.

2

That his own business he might quite forget,
They amus'd him with the sports of wanton wit,
With the desserts of poetry they fed him,
Instead of solid meats t' increase his force;
Instead of vigorous exercise they led him
Into the pleasant labyrinths of ever-fresh discourse.
Instead of carrying him to see
The riches which do hoarded for him lie
In nature's endless treasury,
They chose his eye to entertain
(His *curious but not covetous eye)
With painted scenes, and pageants of the brain.
Some few exalted *spirits this latter age has shown,
That labour'd to assert the liberty
(From guardians, who were now usurpers grown)
Of this old minor still, captiv'd Philosophy;
But 'twas rebellion call'd, to fight
For such a long-oppressèd right.
Bacon at last, a mighty man, arose,
Whom a wise king, and Nature, chose
Lord Chancellor of both their *laws,
And boldly undertook the injur'd pupil's cause.

3

Authority, which did a body boast,
Though 'twas but air condens'd, and stalk'd about
Like some old giant's more gigantic ghost,
To terrify the learned *rout
With the plain magic of true reason's light,
He chas'd out of our sight,
Nor suffer'd living men to be misled
By the vain shadows of the dead:
To graves, from whence it rose, the conquer'd phantom fled;
He broke that monstrous *god which stood
In midst of th' orchard, and the whole did claim,
Which with a useless scythe of wood,
And something else not worth a name,
(Both vast for show, yet neither fit
Or to defend or to beget;
Ridiculous and senseless terrors!) made
Children and superstitious men afraid.
The orchard's open now, and free;
Bacon has broke that scarecrow deity.
Come, enter, all that will,
Behold the rip'ned fruit; come gather now your fill.
Yet still, methinks, we fain would be
Catching at the forbidden *tree,
We would be like the deity,
When truth and falsehood, good and evil, we
Without the sense's aid within ourselves would see;
For 'tis God only who can find
All nature in his mind.

4

From words, which are but pictures of the thought,
(Though we our thoughts from them perversely drew)

*Notes on Abraham Cowley will be found in the Appendix, pp. 938 ff.

To things, the mind's right object, he it brought.
Like foolish birds to painted grapes we *flew;
He sought and gather'd for our use the true;
And when on heaps the chosen bunches lay,
He press'd them wisely the *mechanic way,
Till all their juice did in one vessel join,
Ferment into a nourishment divine,
The thirsty soul's refreshing wine.
Who to the life an exact piece would make,
Must not from other's work a copy take —
No, not from Rubens or Vandyke;
Much less content himself to make it like
Th' ideas and the images which lie
In his own fancy, or his memory.
No, he before his sight must place
The natural and the living face;
The real object must command
Each judgment of his eye, and motion of his hand.

5

From these and all long *errors of the way
In which our wandering predecessors went,
And like th' old Hebrews many years did stray
In deserts but of small extent,
Bacon, like Moses, led us forth at last;
The barren wilderness he pass'd
Did on the very border stand
Of the blest promis'd land,
And from the mountain's top of his exalted wit,
Saw it himself, and show'd us it.
But life did never to one man allow
Time to discover worlds, and conquer too;
Nor can so short a line sufficient be
To fathom the vast depths of nature's sea.
The work he did we ought t' admire,
And were unjust if we should more require
From his few years, divided 'twixt excess
Of low affliction, and high happiness.
For who on things remote can fix his sight
That's always in a triumph, or a fight?

6

From *you, great champions, we expect to *get
These spacious countries but discover'd yet —
Countries where yet, instead of nature, we
Her images and idols worshipp'd see.
These large and wealthy regions to subdue,
Though Learning has whole armies at command
Quarter'd about in every land,
A better troop she ne'er together drew.
Methinks, like Gideon's little *band,
God with design has pick'd out you
To do these noble wonders by a few.
When the whole host he saw, "They are," said he,
"Too many to o'ercome for me."
And now he chooses out his men
Much in the way that he did then —
Not those many whom he found
Idly extended on the ground,
To drink with their dejected head
The stream just so as by their mouths it fled;
No, but those few who took the waters up
And made of their laborious hands the cup.

7

Thus you prepar'd, and in the glorious fight
Their wondrous pattern too you take:
Their old and empty pitchers first they brake,
And with their hands then lifted up the light.
*Io! Sound too the trumpets here!
Already your victorious lights appear;
New scenes of heaven already we espy,
And crowds of golden worlds on high;
Which from the spacious plains of earth and sea
Could never yet discover'd be
By sailors' or Chaldeans' watchful eye.
Nature's great works no distance can obscure,
No smallness her near objects can secure.
Y' have taught the curious sight to press
Into the privatest recess
Of her imperceptible littleness.
Y' have learn'd to read her smallest *hand,
And well begun her deepest sense to understand.

8

Mischief and true dishonour fall on *those
Who would to laughter or to scorn expose
So virtuous and so noble a design,
So human for its use, for knowledge so divine.
The things which these proud men despise, and call
Impertinent, and vain, and small,
Those smallest things of nature let me know
Rather than all their greatest actions do.
Whoever would deposèd truth advance
Into the throne usurped from it,
Must feel at first the blows of ignorance,
And the sharp points of envious wit.
So when, by various turns of the celestial dance,
In many thousand years
A star, so long unknown, appears,

Though heaven itself more beauteous by it grow,
It troubles and alarms the world below,
Does to the wise a star, to fools a meteor *show.

9

With courage and success you the bold work begin;
Your cradle has not idle been.
None e'er but Hercules and you could be
At five years age worthy a *history.
And ne'er did fortune better yet
Th' historian to the story fit
As you from all old errors free
And purge the body of philosophy,
So from all modern follies *he
Has vindicated eloquence and wit.
His candid style like a clean stream does slide,
And his bright fancy all the way
Does like the sunshine in it play;
It does like Thames, the best of rivers, glide,
Where the *god does not rudely overturn,
But gently pour the crystal urn,
And with judicious hand does the whole current guide.
'T has all the beauties nature can impart,
And all the comely dress without the paint of art.

[1667]

OF SOLITUDE

**Nunquam minus solus, quam cum solus*, is now become a very vulgar saying. Every man and almost every boy for these seventeen hundred years has had it in his mouth. But it was at first spoken by the excellent *Scipio, who was without question a most eloquent and witty person, as well as the most wise, most worthy, most happy, and the greatest of all mankind. His meaning no doubt was this, that he found more satisfaction to his mind, and more improvement of it by solitude than by company; and to show that he spoke not this loosely or out of vanity, after he had made Rome mistress of almost the whole world, he retired himself from it by voluntary exile, and at a private house in the middle of a wood near *Linternum, passed the remainder of his glorious life no less gloriously. This house Seneca went to see so long after with great *veneration, and among other things describes his baths to have been of so mean a structure, that now, says he, the basest of the people would despise them, and cry out, "Poor Scipio understood not how to live." What an authority is here for the credit of retreat? and how happy had it been for Hannibal, if adversity could have taught him as much wisdom as was learned by Scipio from the highest prosperities! This would be no wonder if it were as truly as it is *colourably and wittily said by Monsieur de *Montaigne that "Ambition itself might teach us to love solitude; there's nothing does so much hate to have companions." 'Tis true, it loves to have its elbows free; it detests to have company on either side; but it delights above all things in a train behind — aye, and ushers too before it. But the greatest part of men are so far from the opinion of that noble Roman, that if they chance at any time to be without company, they're like a becalmed ship, they never move but by the wind of other men's breath, and have no oars of their own to steer withal. It is very fantastical and contradictory in human nature, that men should love themselves above all the rest of the world, and yet never endure to be with themselves. When they are in love with a mistress, all other persons are importunate and burdensome to them. **Tecum vivere amem, tecum obeam lubens*, they would live and die with her alone.

> **Sic ego secretis possum bene vivere silvis*
> *Qua nulla humano sit via trita pede,*
> *Tu mihi curarum requies, tu nocte vel atra*
> *Lumen, et in solis tu mihi turba locis.*

> With thee forever I in woods could rest,
> Where never human foot the ground has press'd,
> Thou from all shades the darkness canst exclude,
> And from a desert banish solitude.

And yet our dear self is so wearisome to us that we can scarcely support its conversation for an hour together. This is such an odd temper of mind as Catullus expresses towards one of his mistresses, whom we may suppose to have been of a very unsociable humour.

> **Odi et amo: quare id faciam fortasse requiris.*
> *Nescio; sed fieri sentio, et excrucior.*

> I hate, and yet I love thee too;
> How can that be? I know not how;
> Only that so it is I know,
> And feel with torment that 'tis so.

It is a deplorable condition, this, and drives a man sometimes to pitiful shifts in seeking how to avoid himself.

The truth of the matter is that neither he who is a fop in the world is a fit man to be alone; nor he who has set his heart much upon the world, though he have never so much understanding; so that solitude can be well fitted and set right, but upon a very few persons. They must have enough knowledge of the world to see the vanity of it, and enough virtue to despise all vanity; if the mind be possessed with any lust or passions, a man had better be in a fair, than in a wood alone. They may, like petty thieves, cheat us perhaps, and pick our pockets in the midst of company, but like robbers they use to strip and bind, or murder us when they catch us alone. This is but to retreat from men, and fall into the hands of devils. 'Tis like the punishment of parricides among the Romans, to be sewed into a bag with an ape, a dog, and a serpent. The first work therefore that a man must do to make himself capable of the good of solitude, is the very eradication of all lusts, for how is it possible for a man to enjoy himself while his affections are tied to things without himself? In the second place, he must learn the art and get the habit of thinking; for this too, no less than well speaking, depends upon much practice, and cogitation is the thing which distinguishes the solitude of a god from a wild *beast. Now because the soul of man is not by its own nature or observation furnished with sufficient materials to work upon, it is necessary for it to have continual recourse to learning and books for fresh supplies, so that the solitary life will grow indigent, and be ready to starve without them; but if once we be thoroughly engaged in the love of letters, instead of being wearied with the length of any day, we shall only complain of the shortness of our whole life.

O vita, stulto longa, sapienti brevis!

O life, long to the fool, short to the wise!

The first Minister of State has not so much business in public as a wise man has in private. If the one have little leisure to be alone, the other has less leisure to be in company; the one has but part of the affairs of one nation, the other all the works of God and nature under his consideration. There is no saying shocks me so much as that which I hear very often, that a man does not know how to pass his time. 'Twould have been ill spoken by Methusalem in the nine hundred sixty-ninth year of his life, so far it is from us, who have not time enough to attain to the utmost perfection of any part of any science, to have cause to complain that we are forced to be idle for want of work. But this you'll say is work only for the learned; others are not capable either of the employments or divertisements that arrive from letters. I know they are not; and therefore cannot much recommend solitude to a man totally illiterate. But if any man be so unlearned as to want entertainment of the little intervals of accidental solitude, which frequently occur in almost all conditions (except the very meanest of the people, who have business enough in the necessary provisions for life), it is truly a great shame both to his parents and himself, for a very small portion of any ingenious art will stop up all those gaps of our time. Either music, or painting, or chemistry, or history, or gardening, or twenty other things will do it usefully and pleasantly; and if he happen to set his affections upon poetry (which I do not advise him too immoderately). that will overdo it. No wood will be thick enough to hide him from the importunities of company or business, which would abstract him from his beloved.

*— *O quis me gelidis sub montibus Æmi*
Sistat, et ingenti ramorum protegat umbra?

I

Hail, old patrician trees, so great and good!
Hail ye plebeian underwood,
Where the poetic birds rejoice,
And for their quiet nests and plenteous food,
Pay with their grateful voice!

II

Hail, the poor Muses' richest manor seat,
Ye country houses and retreat,
Which all the happy gods so love,
That for you oft they quit their bright and great
Metropolis above!

III

Here Nature does a house for me erect —
Nature, the wisest architect,
Who those fond artists does despise
That can the fair and living trees neglect,
Yet the dead timber prize.

IV

Here let me, careless and unthoughtful lying,
Hear the soft winds above me flying,
With all their wanton boughs dispute,
And the more tuneful birds to both replying,
Nor be myself too mute.

V

A silver stream shall roll his waters near,
Gilt with the sunbeams here and there
On whose enamell'd bank I'll walk
And see how prettily they smile, and hear
How prettily they talk.

VI

Ah wretched, and too solitary he
Who loves not his own company!
He'll feel the weight of 't many a day
Unless he call in sin and vanity
To help to bear 't away.

VII

Oh Solitude, first state of humankind!
Which blest remain'd till man did find
Even his own helper's company.
As soon as two (alas!) together join'd,
The serpent made up three.

VIII

Though God himself, through countless ages, thee
His sole companion chose to be —
Thee, sacred Solitude, alone,
Before the branchy head of number's tree
Sprang from the trunk of one.

IX

Thou (though men think thine an unactive part)
Dost break and tame th' unruly heart,
Which else would know no settled pace,
Making it move, well manag'd by thy art,
With swiftness and with grace.

X

Thou the faint beams of reason's scatter'd light
Dost like a burning-glass unite,
Dost multiply the feeble heat,
And fortify the strength, till thou dost bright
And noble fires beget.

XI

Whilst this hard truth I teach, methinks, I see
The monster London laugh at me.
I should at thee too, foolish city,
If it were fit to laugh at misery;
But thy estate I pity.

XII

Let but thy wicked men from out thee go,
And all the fools that crowd thee so,
Even thou, who dost thy millions boast,
A village less than Islington wilt grow —
A solitude, almost.

[1668]

EDMUND WALLER

THE long life of Edmund Waller, extending from 1606 to 1687, and the fact that his literary career covered six decades, leaves one in doubt whether to call him a Jacobean or a Caroline poet, a writer of the Protectorate or of the Restoration. His biography falls into no definite divisions and so gives little help. He entered Parliament at sixteen and was still a member when he died; closely related both to Hampden and to Cromwell, yet Royalist in sympathy, he was a turncoat and a time-server in politics, playing fast and loose with both parties; he wrote as well at eighty as he had at twenty years of age, though not better and not very differently. For present purposes, however, it is decisive that poets and critics of the following age found much to admire and emulate in his verse and regarded him as their kind of man. In his cool precision, his close attention to polish and to form, and his lack of passion, he is in fact strangely like them, although he was born before John Milton and ten years before the death of Shakespeare. For these reasons he is represented here by selections from the verse he wrote after the Restoration.

The tangled story of Waller's political life — of his disgraceful and cowardly conduct in "Waller's Plot" against Parliament, of his exile in Paris, and of his speeches for and against the Crown — need not be told here. His governing motive seems to have been vanity. Waller the poet and Waller the universally admired man of society is summed up in what Bishop Burnet says of him as a parliamentary speaker: "He was only concerned to say that which should make him applauded; he never laid the business of the House to heart, being a vain and empty, though a witty, man." These quietly damning words sketch the portrait of a man dominated by the rhetorical tradition. Like Petrarch at the opening of the Renaissance, Waller, at the end of it, was willing to say anything that could be said wittily, would adopt any opinion which gave him a chance for eloquence and "point" or enabled him to round off a period with an apt classical quotation. He composed many graceful but cold and shallow lyrics in paying court to Lady Dorothy Spencer, his "Sacharissa," maintaining all the while the self-composure of a fine gentleman going through the stately paces of the sarabande, and then, when she married another man, sent her one of the wittiest letters ever penned. Even more truly than John Keats he "looked upon fine phrases like a lover." They were, in fact, all that he could love.

Waller exhibits with exceptional clearness several of the weaker aspects of the late Renaissance — a doctrine of "imitation" debased and misunderstood, deficiency in inventive power, frigid fancy in the place of creative imagination, docile obedience to the rhetoricians ancient and modern. In his life and work alike we see mere phraseology eating into character, or taking its place. Correctness and smoothness of utterance are more important to him than the opinions or feelings he expresses.

The importance of these characteristics is by no means confined to their influence upon Waller's own work, now largely forgotten. They had their effect upon many English poets of the next hundred years, chilling and intimidating their imaginations and making them strive above all to be smooth and correct. How a man of such slight abilities as his could have wielded this influence is not immediately apparent, but, on the other hand, is not difficult to explain. Waller's prestige among the middle-class poets who followed him may have been assisted by the fact that he moved always in the highest society and was a man of considerable wealth — able, for example, to buy his life with a fine amounting to half a million dollars when his two chief fellow conspirators in "Waller's Plot" were hanged at their street doors. Further, he was one of the last English poets of importance who wrote not as members of the literary profession, for money or fame, but as gentlemen amusing themselves with a graceful accomplishment. The triviality of his themes and of his usual manner, which so disgusted Dr. Johnson, may be explained in part by his anxiety that no one should take him seriously or suppose that he worked hard at his verse. It is said that he once spent an entire summer polishing and revising ten lines of verse to be inscribed in a great lady's copy of Tasso, in order that when he finally wrote them down for her they might seem the inspiration of the moment. Mere accidents of fortune made him seem a model of that elegance which the less fortunate poets of later generations were to desire and emulate.

In justice to Waller and to his imitators it must be admitted that his elegance was not due solely to these accidents. Though trifling and superficial, it was not a mere garb to be donned and doffed; it was at least skin-deep. He had a stately gallantry inherited from the finer traditions of the past; considering his epoch it is worth while to mention the perfect cleanliness of all his writing — possibly due to his long residence in France; the fact that he drank nothing but water and yet was always the gayest man in any Bacchanalian assembly would have been almost enough, in that age, to make him famous. His chief strength lay in the *bon mot*; the two or three lyrics of his that are now remembered, such as *Go Lovely Rose* and *On a Girdle*, are really epigrams polished with incessant care. His longer productions — such as *The Triple Combat*, in which he anticipates the brittle grace of Pope's mock-heroic — tend to be mere successions of epigrams with little effect of flow, and in the charming artificialities of his *St. James's Park* we have a series of brilliant apothegms rather than a unified poem.

The gift for such things is cultivated in the polite conversation of a strongly centralized society such as the Paris that Waller knew and in which he "kept a table" for several years. It is far more French than English and is the product, at least in origin, of a leisured class. Obviously, therefore, it could not satisfy the deeper poetical feelings of an English literary public which was to be more and more composed of the middle classes, and though it might for a time maintain itself in fashion — having the Court and Town steadily in its favour, with some help from the universities — it could never draw into its channel the main stream of English verse. For Waller's epigram the closed couplet — long mistakenly supposed to have been his invention — was the most perfect vehicle of expression that could have been found; the two were handed down together to his successors.

Few writers have exerted so wide and deep an influence as Waller did while working with so slight a gift. He was made for, as well as by, his exact niche of time. Without passion or deep thought or even any real convictions, he taught English poets what they most needed to know and were at last ready to learn: precision of form and phrase, avoidance of the odd and the obscure and of all that seems deep only because it is dark. Perhaps it is his chief title to praise that he turned English verse permanently away from the vicious conceits of the "metaphysical school" toward clear and normal thinking — that is to say, away from "false wit" and toward "true wit." Remembering this really great and indispensable service, we can partly comprehend the hearty praise of Waller in which the young Addison expressed the view of his time:

> But now, my Muse, a softer strain rehearse;
> Turn every line with art and smooth thy verse!
> The courtly Waller next commands thy lays;
> Muse, tune thy verse with art to Waller's praise.
> While tender airs and lovely dames inspire
> Soft melting thoughts and propagate desire,
> So long shall Waller's strains our passion move,
> And Sacharissa's beauties kindle love.

ON ST. JAMES'S PARK

AS LATELY IMPROVED BY HIS MAJESTY

Of the first Paradise there's nothing found;
Plants set by Heaven are vanished, and the ground;
Yet the description *lasts. Who knows the fate
Of lines that shall this paradise relate?
Instead of rivers rolling by the side
Of Eden's garden, here flows in the *tide;
The sea, which always served his empire, now
Pays tribute to our prince's pleasure too.
Of famous cities we the founders know;
But rivers, old as seas to which they go,
Are nature's bounty; 'tis of more renown
To make a river than to build a town.
For future shade, young trees upon the banks
Of the new stream appear in even ranks;
The voice of Orpheus, or Amphion's *hand,
In better order could not make them stand;
May they increase as fast, and spread their boughs,
As the high fame of their great owner grows!
May he live long enough to see them all
Dark shadows cast, and as his palace tall!
Methinks I see the love that shall be made,
The lovers walking in that amorous shade;
The gallants dancing by the river's side;
They bathe in summer, and in winter slide.
Methinks I hear the music in the boats
And the loud echo which returns the notes,
While overhead a flock of new-sprung fowl
Hangs in the air, and does the sun control,
Darkening the sky; they hover o'er and shroud
The wanton sailors with a feathered cloud.
Beneath, a shoal of silver fishes glides
And plays about the gilded barges' sides;
The ladies, angling in the crystal lake,
Feast on the waters with the prey they take;
At once victorious with their lines and eyes,
They make the fishes and the men their prize.
A thousand Cupids on the billows ride,
And sea-nymphs enter with the swelling tide,
From *Thetis sent as spies, to make report,
And tell the wonders of her sovereign's *court.
All that can, living, feed the greedy eye,
Or dead, the palate, here you may descry;

*** Notes on Edmund Waller will be found in the Appendix, pp. 939 ff.**

The choicest things that furnished Noah's ark,
Or Peter's *sheet, inhabiting this park;
All with a border of rich fruit-trees crowned,
Whose loaded branches hide the lofty *mound.
Such various ways the spacious alleys lead,
My doubtful Muse knows not what path to tread.
Yonder, the harvest of cold months laid up,
Gives a fresh coolness to the royal cup;
There ice, like crystal firm, and never lost,
Tempers hot July with December's frost;
Winter's dark prison, whence he cannot fly
Though the warm spring, his enemy, draws nigh.
Strange, that extremes should thus preserve the snow,
High on the Alps or in deep caves below.
Here, a well-polished *Mall gives us the joy
To see our prince his matchless force employ;
His manly posture, and his graceful mien,
Vigour and youth, in all his motions seen,
His shape so lovely, and his limbs so strong,
Confirm our hopes we shall obey him long.
No sooner has he touched the flying ball,
But 'tis already more than half the Mall;
And such a fury from his arm has got,
As from a smoking culverin 'twere shot.
Near this my Muse, what most delights her, sees
A living gallery of aged trees;
Bold sons of earth, that thrust their arms so high,
As if once more they would invade the *sky.
In such green palaces the first kings reigned,
Slept in their shades, and angels *entertained;
With such old counsellors they did advise,
And, by frequenting sacred groves, grew wise.
Free from the impediments of light and noise,
Man, thus retired, his nobler thoughts employs.
Here Charles contrives the ordering of his states,
Here he resolves his neighbouring princes' fates:
What nation shall have peace, where war be made,
Determined is in this oraculous *shade;
The world, from India to the frozen north,
Concerned in what this solitude brings forth.
His fancy objects from his view receives;
The prospect thought and contemplation gives.
That seat of empire here salutes his eye
To which three kingdoms do themselves apply;
The structure by a *prelate raised, Whitehall,
Built with the fortune of Rome's capitol;
Both, disproportioned to the present state
Of their proud founders, were approved by Fate.
From hence he does that antique *pile behold
Where royal heads receive the sacred gold;
It gives them crowns and does their ashes keep;
There made like gods, like mortals there they sleep;
Making the circle of their reign complete,
Those suns of empire! where they rise, they set.
When others fell, this, standing, did presage
The crown should triumph over popular rage;
Hard by that *house, where all our ills were shaped,
The auspicious temple stood, and yet escaped.
So snow on Ætna does unmelted lie,
Whence rolling flames and scattered cinders fly;
The distant country in the ruin shares;
What falls from heaven the burning mountain spares.
Next, that capacious *hall he sees, the room
Where the whole nation does for justice come;
Under whose large roof flourishes the gown,
And judges grave, on high tribunals, frown.
Here, like the people's pastor he does go,
His flock subjected to his view below;
On which reflecting in his mighty mind,
No private passion does indulgence find;
*The pleasures of his youth suspended are,
And made a sacrifice to public care.
Here, free from court compliances, he walks,
And with himself, his best adviser, talks;
How peaceful olive may his temples shade
For mending laws and for restoring trade;
Or, how his brows may be with laurel charged,
For nations conquered, and our bounds enlarged.
Of ancient prudence here he ruminates,
Of rising kingdoms, and of falling states;
What ruling arts gave great Augustus fame,
And how *Alcides purchased such a name.
His eyes, upon his native *palace bent,
Close by, suggest a greater argument.
His thoughts rise higher when he does reflect
On what the world may from that *star expect
Which at his birth appeared, to let us see
Day, for his sake, could with the night agree;
A prince, on whom such different lights did smile,
Born the divided *world to reconcile!
Whatever Heaven, or high extracted blood
Could promise or foretell, he will make good;
Reform these nations, and improve them more,
Than this fair park, from what it was before.

[1661]

THE NIGHT-PIECE

OR, A PICTURE DRAWN IN THE DARK

Darkness, which fairest nymphs disarms,
Defends us ill from Mira's charms;
Mira can lay her beauty by,
Take no advantage of the eye,
Quit all that *Lely's art can take
And yet a thousand captives make.
Her speech is graced with sweeter sound
Than in another's song is found;
And all her well-placed words are darts,
Which need no light to reach our hearts.
As the bright stars and Milky Way,
Showed by the night, are hid by day;
So we, in that accomplished mind,
Helped by the night, new graces find,
Which, by the splendour of her *view
Dazzled before, we never knew.
While we converse with her, we mark
No want of day, nor think it dark;
Her shining image is a light
Fixed in our hearts, and conquers night.
Like jewels to advantage set,
Her beauty by the shade does *get;
There blushes, frowns, and cold disdain,
All that our passion might restrain,
Is hid, and our indulgent mind
Presents the fair idea kind.
Yet, friended by the night, we dare
Only in whispers tell our care;
He that on her his bold hand lays,
With Cupid's pointed arrows plays;
They with a touch (they are so keen!)
Wound us unshot, and she unseen.
All near approaches threaten death;
We may be shipwrecked by her breath;
Love, favoured once with that sweet gale,
Doubles his haste and fills his sail,
Till he arrive where she must prove
The haven, or the rock, of love.
So we the Arabian coast do know
At distance, when the spices blow;
By the rich odour taught to steer,
Though neither day nor stars appear.

[1668]

THE TRIPLE COMBAT

When through the world fair *Mazarin had run,
Bright as her fellow-traveller, the sun,
Hither at length the Roman eagle flies,
As the last triumph of her conquering eyes.
As heir to Julius, she may pretend
A second time to make this nation bend;
But *Portsmouth, springing from the ancient race
Of Britons, which the Saxon here did chase,
As they great Cæsar did oppose, makes head,
And does against this new invader lead.
That goodly nymph, the taller of the two,
Careless and fearless to the field does go.
Becoming blushes on the other wait,
And her young look excuses want of height.
Beauty gives courage; for she knows the day
Must not be won the Amazonian way.
Nor does her grace the better title want;
Our law's indulgent to the occupant.
Legions of beauties to the battle come,
For Little Britain these, and those for Rome.
Dressed to advantage, this illustrious pair 21
Arrived, for combat in the list appear.
What may the Fates design? For never yet
From distant regions two such beauties met.
Venus had been an equal friend to both,
And victory to declare herself seems loath;
Over the camp, with doubtful wings, she flies,
Till *Chloris shining in the field she spies.
The lovely Chloris well-attended came,
A thousand Graces waited on the dame;
Her matchless form made all the English glad,
And foreign beauties less assurance had;
Yet, like the *three on Ida's top, they all
Pretend alike, contesting for the ball;
Which to determine, Love himself declined,
Lest the neglected should become less kind.
Such killing looks, so thick the arrows fly,
That 'tis unsafe to be a stander-by.
Poets, approaching to describe the fight, 39
Are by their wounds instructed how to write.
They with less hazard might look on, and draw
The ruder combats in *Alsatia;
And, with that foil of violence and rage,
Set off the spendour of our golden age;
Where Love gives law, Beauty the sceptre sways,
And, uncompelled, the happy world obeys.

[1675]

OF THE LAST VERSES IN THE BOOK

When we for age could neither read nor write,
The subject made us able to indite;
The soul, with nobler resolutions decked,
The body stooping, does herself erect.

No mortal parts are requisite to raise
Her that, unbodied, can her Maker praise.
The seas are quiet when the winds give o'er;
So, calm are we when passions are no more!
For then we know how vain it was to boast
Of fleeting things, so certain to be lost.
Clouds of affection from our younger eyes
Conceal that emptiness which age descries.
The soul's dark cottage, battered and decayed,
Lets in new light through chinks that time has made;
Stronger by weakness, wiser men become,
As they draw near to their eternal home.
Leaving the old, both worlds at once they view,
That stand upon the threshold of the new.

[1686]

JOHN WILMOT, EARL OF ROCHESTER

No later generation of English readers, unless it be our own, has had the secret of Rochester's abandoned and despairing gaiety; and it is only in recent years that we have begun to do justice to the subtle intensity and charm of his mind. The all but universal admiration which he won in his own day was already crossed by envy, by fear, and by that moral obloquy which has been the chief revenge that mediocrity takes against superior persons. Even before his early death Rochester had become, like Lord Byron, the hero of a legend in which all the depravity attributed to the wits of the court by those who had neither wit nor social standing was ascribed to him as its type and symbol. Such a variety of vicious acts as he had scarcely time to commit, and also a number of poems which cannot possibly be his for the reason that, besides being indecent, they are also dull, have been confidently laid at his door, so that even so recent a writer as Sir Edmund Gosse could call him "a veritable devil." As though fascinated by the splendid wickedness of the portrait they have helped to paint, Rochester's critics have seldom seen that, whatever his morals may have been, his poems were good, his thought was powerful, and his genius was unquestionable.

Born in 1647, son of a famous Cavalier, Rochester took his master's degree at Oxford at the age of fourteen, and three years later, after a long residence abroad, took his place at court. His physical beauty, his engaging manners, and the surprising range of his knowledge, won him an immediate success which even his mordant wit did little to abate. Charles banished him frequently from the court, and even imprisoned him for his abduction of a wealthy and beautiful woman whom he married for her fortune, but though often technically in disgrace he was seldom out of favour as the king's boon companion. Much of his time was spent, apparently, in cynical and dissolute pleasure-seeking, and some of his exploits, such as the hiring of bullies to beat John Dryden, were disgraceful. On the other hand, his letters reveal a mind capable of tenderness and serious purpose. He died, worn out, at the age of thirty-three, after a death-bed repentance of which Bishop Burnet made all that the facts would warrant.

The code of the gentleman forbade Rochester either to polish or to publish his verses, but the poetry he dashed down between amours and drinking-bouts shows that in natural gifts he was inferior to no poet of the age. In the words of one of his friends, "His poetry has everywhere a tincture of that unaccountable charm in his fashion and conversation, that peculiar becomingness in all he said and did, that drew the eyes and won the hearts of all who came near him." Many of his love songs have the strange intensity that we associate with John Donne, and a hoarse passion of utterance that vibrates with metaphysical implications. He often suggests Donne's anger of a strong spirit caught in the trap of the flesh, and it is possible to surmise, considering that he died repentant at about the age at which Donne's conversion occurred, that if he had been given more time he might have rounded out his intellectual and spiritual life in a way not wholly unlike that of the great dean. As it is, Rochester's worthiest performance is *A Satire Against Mankind* — a perfectly original poem in spite of its indebtedness to Boileau, powerfully effective in spite of its contemptuous haste.

A SATIRE AGAINST MANKIND

Were I, who, to my cost, already am,
One of those strange, prodigious creatures, man,
A spirit free to choose for my own share
What sort of flesh and blood I pleased to wear,
I'd be a dog, a monkey, or a bear,
Or anything, but that vain animal,
Who is so proud of being rational.
The senses are too gross, and he'll contrive
A sixth to contradict the other five;
And before certain instinct will prefer
Reason, which fifty times for one does err —
Reason, an *ignis fatuus* of the mind,
Which leaves the light of nature, sense, behind.
Pathless and dangerous wand'ring ways it takes
Through error's fenny bogs and thorny brakes,
Whilst the misguided follower climbs with pain
Mountains of whimsies, heap'd in his own brain,
Stumbling from thought to thought, falls headlong down
Into doubt's boundless sea, where, like to drown,

Books bear him up a while and make him try
To swim with bladders of philosophy,
In hopes still to o'ertake the skipping light.
The vapour dances in his dazzled sight
Till, spent, it leaves him to eternal night.
Then old age and experience, hand in hand,
Lead him to death and make him understand
After a search so painful and so long,
That all his life he has been in the wrong.
Huddled in dirt, [the] reas'ning engine lies
Who was so proud, so witty, and so wise.
Pride drew him in, as cheats their *bubbles catch,
And made him venture to be made a wretch.
His wisdom did his happiness destroy,
Aiming to know the world he should enjoy;
And wit was his vain frivolous pretence
Of pleasing others at his own expense.
For wits are treated just like common whores;
First they're enjoy'd, and then kick'd out of doors.
The pleasure past, a threat'ning doubt remains,
That frights th' enjoyer with succeeding pains.
Women and men of wit are dang'rous tools,
And ever fatal to admiring fools.
Pleasure allures, and when the *fops escape,
'Tis not that they're belov'd, but fortunate,
And therefore what they fear, at heart they hate.
But now methinks some formal *band and beard
Takes me to task: "Come on, sir, I'm prepar'd."
"Then, by your favour, anything that's writ
Against this gibing, jingling knack, call'd wit,
Likes me abundantly; but you'll take care
Upon this point, not to be too severe.
Perhaps my *Muse were fitter for this part,
For I profess, I can be very smart
On wit, which I abhor with all my heart.
I long to lash it in some sharp essay,
But your grand indiscretion bids me stay,
And turns my tide of ink another way.
What rage ferments in your degen'rate mind
To make you rail at reason and mankind? —
Blest glorious man, to whom alone kind Heav'n
An everlasting soul hath freely giv'n;
Whom his great Maker took such care to make
That from himself he did the image take,
And this fair frame in shining reason dressed,
To dignify his nature above beast —
Reason, by whose aspiring influence
We take a flight beyond material sense,
Dive into mysteries, then soaring pierce
The flaming limits of the *universe,
Search heav'n and hell, find out what's acted there,
And give the world true grounds of hope and fear?"

"Hold, mighty man," I cry. "All this we know
From the pathetic pen of *Ingelo,
From Patrick's *Pilgrim, Sibb's *Soliloquies;
And 'tis this very reason I despise,
This supernat'ral gift, that makes a mite
Think he's the image of the infinite;
Comparing his short life, void of all rest,
To the eternal and the ever blest;
This busy puzzling stirrer up of doubt,
That frames deep mysteries, then finds 'em out,
Filling with frantic crowds of thinking fools
The reverend *bedlams, colleges and schools;
Borne on whose wings, each heavy sot can pierce
The limits of the boundless universe.
So *charming ointments make an old witch fly,
And bear a crippled carcase through the sky.
'Tis this exalted pow'r whose business lies
In nonsense and impossibilities;
This made a whimsical *philosopher,
Before the spacious world his tub prefer;
And we have many modern coxcombs who
Retire to think, 'cause they have nought to do.
But thoughts were giv'n for action's government;
Where action ceases, thought's impertinent.
Our sphere of action is life's happiness,
And he that thinks beyond thinks like an ass.
Thus whilst against false reas'ning I inveigh,
I own right reason, which I would obey —
That reason which distinguishes by *sense,
And gives us rules of good and ill from thence;
That bounds desires with a reforming will
To keep them more in vigour, not to kill.
Your reason hinders, mine helps to enjoy,
Renewing appetites, yours would destroy.
My reason is my friend, yours is a cheat:
Hunger calls out, my reason bids me eat;
Perversely yours, your appetite does mock;
This asks for food; that answers, 'What's o'clock?'

"This plain distinction, sir, your doubt secures;

*Notes on the Earl of Rochester will be found in the Appendix, pp. 940 ff.

'Tis not true reason I despise, but yours.
Thus I think reason righted; but for man,
I'll ne'er recant, defend him if you can.
For all his pride and his philosophy,
'Tis evident beasts are, in their degree,
As wise at least, and better far than he.
Those creatures are the wisest who attain
By surest means the ends at which they aim.
If therefore * Jowler finds and kills his hare
Better than * Meres supplies committee chair,
Though one's a statesman, th' other but a hound,
Jowler in justice will be wiser found.
You see how far man's wisdom here extends;
Look next if human nature makes amends,
Whose principles are most generous and just,
And to whose morals, you would sooner trust.
Be judge yourself, I'll bring it to the test,
Which is the basest creature, man or beast:
Birds feed on birds, beasts on each other prey;
But savage man alone does man betray.
Press'd by necessity, they kill for food;
Man undoes man to do himself no good.
With teeth, and claws, by nature arm'd they hunt
Nature's allowance, to supply their want;
But man with smiles, embraces, friendships, praise,
Inhumanly his fellow's life betrays,
With voluntary pains works his distress,
Not through necessity, but wantonness.
For hunger or for love they bite or tear,
Whilst wretched man is still in arms for fear:
For fear he arms, and is of arms afraid;
From fear to fear successively betray'd.
Base fear, the source whence his best passions came,
His boasted honour, and his dear-bought fame,
The lust of pow'r, to which he's such a slave,
And for the which alone he dares be brave;
To which his various projects are design'd,
Which makes him gen'rous, affable, and kind;
For which he takes such pains to be thought wise,
And screws his actions in a forc'd disguise;
Leads a most tedious life in misery,
Under laborious, mean hypocrisy.
Look to the bottom of his vast design,
Wherein man's wisdom, pow'r, and glory join —
The good he acts, the ill he does endure,
'Tis all from fear, to make himself secure.
Merely for safety, after fame they thirst,
For all men would be cowards if they durst;
And honesty's against all common sense —
Men must be knaves; 'tis in their own defence.
Mankind's dishonest; if they think it fair,
Amongst known cheats, to play upon the square,
You'll be undone —
Nor can weak truth, your reputation save;
The knaves will all agree to call you knave.
Wrong'd shall he live, insulted o'er, oppress'd,
Who dares be less a villain than the rest.
Thus here you see what human nature craves,
Most men are cowards, all men should be knaves.
The difference lies, as far as I can see,
Not in the thing itself, but the degree;
And all the subject-matter of debate,
Is only, who's a knave of the first rate."

[1675]

THOMAS TRAHERNE

ALTHOUGH the son of a shoemaker, Thomas Traherne was able to take his degree at Oxford in 1656, when he was some twenty years of age. For the remaining two decades of his life he served as a domestic chaplain near his native town of Hereford. Little of his work was published during his lifetime. In the last years of the nineteenth century the manuscript of his poems was discovered on a London bookstall and was at first attributed to Henry Vaughan, whom he imitated. Some ten years later the scholarly bookseller, Bertram Dobell, published the manuscript, with sufficient proof of Traherne's authorship.

Certainly a lesser poet, Traherne is not inferior to Vaughan in the steadiness or the depth of his mystic insight. The accent of his verse is usually prosaic, though his mood and matter are seldom so. His chief defect is a tendency toward the verbose, which, however, is not out of keeping with his prevailing tone of naïve wonder and childlike simplicity.

SHADOWS IN THE WATER

In unexperienced infancy
Many a sweet mistake doth lie, —
Mistake, tho' false, intending true;
A seeming somewhat more than view
  That doth instruct the mind
  In things that lie behind,
And many secrets to us show
Which afterwards we come to know.

Thus did I by the water's brink
Another world beneath me think;
And while the lofty spacious skies
Reversèd there abused mine eyes,
  I fancied other feet
  Came mine to touch or meet;
As by some puddle I did play
Another world within it lay.

Beneath the water people drowned,
Yet with another heaven crowned,
In spacious regions seemed to go
As freely moving to and fro;
  In bright and open space
  I saw their very face;
Eyes, hands, and feet they had like mine;
Another sun did with them shine.

'Twas strange that people there should walk
And yet I could not hear them talk,
That through a little wat'ry chink,
Which one dry ox or horse might drink,
  We other worlds should see,
  Yet not admitted be;
And other confines there behold
Of light and darkness, heat and cold.

I called them oft, but called in vain;
No speeches we could entertain:
Yet did I there expect to find
Some other world, to please my mind.
  I plainly saw by these
  A new Antipodes,
Whom, though they were so plainly seen,
A film kept off that stood between.

By walking men's reversèd feet
I chanced another world to meet;
Though it did not to view exceed
A phantasm, 'tis a world indeed,
  Where skies beneath us shine,
  And earth, by art divine,
Another face presents below,
Where people's feet against ours go.

Within the regions of the air,
Compassed about with heavens fair,
Great tracts of land there may be found
Enriched with fields and fertile ground;
  Where many num'rous hosts,
  In those far distant coasts,
For other great and glorious ends
Inhabit, my yet unknown friends.

O ye that stand upon the brink,
Whom I so near me, through the chink,
With wonder see; what faces there,
Whose feet, whose bodies, do ye wear?
  I my companions see
  In you, another me.
They seemèd others, but are we;
Our second selves those shadows be.

Look how far off those lower skies
Extend themselves! Scarce with mine eyes
I can them reach. O ye, my friends,
What secret borders on those ends?
Are lofty heavens hurled
'Bout your inferior world?
Are ye the representatives
Of other peoples' distant lives?
Of all the playmates which I knew
That here I do the image view
In other selves, what can it mean,
But that below the purling stream
Some unknown joys there be
Laid up in store for me,
To which I shall, when that thin skin
Is broken, be admitted in?

[1906]

JOHN DRYDEN

John Dryden was not only the greatest English man of letters during the last generation of the seventeenth century, but to a degree scarcely paralleled in the history of literature he embodied and gave expression to the spirit of his age. With the exception of the epic, he wrote all the higher forms of prose and verse that were attempted in his time, and he excelled in almost everything that he attempted. In most of these he was the leader of his age; he broke the ground for his contemporaries; and, what is even more important, he pointed the way for the next age. Saintsbury says, "The eighteen volumes of his works contain a faithful representation of the whole literary movement in England for the best part of half a century, and what is more, they contain the germs and indicate the direction of almost the whole literary movement for nearly a century more." He was a literary dictator during the first age of English neo-classicism, stating its principles, enforcing its discipline, and giving models for its imitation. The late seventeenth century in English literature is chiefly the figure of John Dryden, and the early eighteenth century is the prolongation of his shadow.

Dryden won his first reputation as a dramatist. Though his genius was not primarily dramatic, he continued during most of his career the composition of plays, chiefly because it was the form of writing most in demand in his day and the one by which a working man of letters might most easily support himself. Much of his energy was thus deflected into a type of composition in which he was not at his best, in the same way that the energy of some men of letters in our day has been attracted through the demand for prose fiction into the employment of an uncongenial mode of literary expression. Though he never attained the highest excellence as a dramatic poet, he wrote workmanlike comedy, and tragedy that falls short only of the greatest: *All for Love* is among the dramatic masterpieces of our language, and though Dryden freely yielded the pre-eminence, is worthy of comparison with Shakespeare's *Antony and Cleopatra*. As a verse satirist, Dryden takes one of the highest places in our literature in positive achievement, and the first place in priority; he was the first English poet to write satire of a strength and flexibility and finish comparable to that of his Latin models. In lyric verse he attained distinction; in didactic verse he did work of no mean order; and in translated verse he set new standards of excellence. In what he himself described as "the other harmony of prose" his fame is secure; he was not the first man to write the new prose, but he was a leader in the production of that clear, idiomatic, well-ordered prose that from his time to our own has been the ideal of normal English writing. As a literary critic he stands in the very front rank. It is hard to find another English man of letters who combines such versatility with such a uniformly high level of achievement.

The personal character of Dryden has suffered from the imputation of vacillation and time-serving. It has often been pointed out that he began life as a supporter of Cromwell, and later became a high Tory; that he was successively a Puritan, an Anglican, and a Roman Catholic. To make the matter worse, these changes came at times when they were open to the charges of personal advantage and political expediency. Without entering into the details of these charges, it is immediately evident that all the changes in Dryden's political and religious affiliations were consistently in one direction: from radicalism to conservatism, without variation from the extreme Left to the extreme Right. That they coincided with shifts of popular opinion or the changing fashions of the court does not necessarily prove him a hypocrite. What is most significant is that in spite of later temptations to change back, Dryden never recanted either his political or his religious opinions; after the Revolution he remained a supporter of the divine right of kings, and in the face of anti-Papal prejudices and legal disabilities he died a Roman Catholic. If he veered with the winds of royal favour in times both of sunshine and tempest, it was in only one direction. Such consistency is not common with time-servers.

ABSALOM AND ACHITOPHEL

A POEM

**Si propius stes*
Te capiet magis.
HOR. *Ars Poet., 361.*

In pious times, ere priestcraft did begin,
Before polygamy was made a sin;
When man on many multiplied his kind,
Ere one to one was cursedly confin'd;
When nature prompted, and no law denied
Promiscuous use of concubine and bride;
Then Israel's monarch after Heaven's own heart,
His vigorous warmth did variously impart
To wives and slaves; and, wide as his command,
Scatter'd his Maker's image thro' the land.
Michal, of royal blood, the crown did wear,
A soil ungrateful to the tiller's care:
Not so the rest; for several mothers bore
To godlike David several sons before.
But since like slaves his bed they did ascend,
No true succession could their seed attend.
Of all this numerous progeny was none
So beautiful, so brave, as Absalon:
Whether, inspir'd by some diviner lust,
His father got him with a greater gust;
Or that his conscious destiny made way,
By manly beauty, to imperial sway.
Early in foreign fields he won renown,
With kings and states allied to Israel's crown:
In peace the thoughts of war he could remove,
And seem'd as he were only born for love.
Whate'er he did, was done with so much ease,
In him alone 'twas natural to please:
His motions all accompanied with grace;
And paradise was open'd in his face.
With secret joy indulgent David view'd
His youthful image in his son renew'd:
To all his wishes nothing he denied;
And made the charming Annabel his bride.
What faults he had, (for who from faults is free?)
His father could not, or he would not see.
Some warm excesses which the law forbore,
Were construed youth that purg'd by boiling o'er,
And Amnon's murder, by a specious name,
Was call'd a just revenge for injur'd fame.
Thus prais'd and lov'd the noble youth remain'd,
While David, undisturb'd, in Sion reign'd.
But life can never be sincerely blest;
Heav'n punishes the bad, and proves the best.
The Jews, a headstrong, moody, murm'ring race,
As ever tried th' extent and stretch of grace;
God's pamper'd people, whom, debauch'd with ease,
No king could govern, nor no God could please;
(Gods they had tried of every shape and size,
That god-smiths could produce, or priests devise:)
These Adam-wits, too fortunately free,
Began to dream they wanted liberty;
And when no rule, no precedent was found,
Of men by laws less circumscrib'd and bound;
They led their wild desires to woods and caves,
And thought that all but savages were slaves.
They who, when Saul was dead, without a blow,
Made foolish Ishbosheth the crown forego;
Who banish'd David did from Hebron bring,
And with a general shout proclaim'd him king:
Those very Jews, who, at their very best,
Their * humour more than loyalty express'd,
Now wonder'd why so long they had obey'd
An idol monarch, which their hands had made;
Thought they might ruin him they could create,
Or melt him to that golden calf, a State.
But these were random bolts; no form'd design,
Nor interest made the factious crowd to join:
The sober part of Israel, free from stain,
Well knew the value of a peaceful reign;
And, looking backward with a wise affright,
Saw seams of wounds, dishonest to the sight:
In contemplation of whose ugly scars
They curs'd the memory of civil wars.
The moderate sort of men, thus qualified,

* Notes on John Dryden will be found in the Appendix, pp. 941 ff.

Inclin'd the balance to the better side;
And David's mildness manag'd it so well,
The bad found no occasion to rebel.
But when to sin our bias'd nature leans,
The careful Devil is still at hand with means;
And providently pimps for ill desires.
The * Good Old Cause reviv'd, a plot requires:
Plots, true or false, are necessary things,
To raise up commonwealths, and ruin kings.
  Th' inhabitants of old Jerusalem
Were Jebusites; the town so call'd from them;
And theirs the native right ——
But when the chosen people grew more strong,
The rightful cause at length became the wrong;
And every loss the men of Jebus bore,
They still were thought God's enemies the more.
Thus worn and weaken'd, well or ill content,
Submit they must to David's government:
Impoverish'd and depriv'd of all command,
Their taxes doubled as they lost their land;
And, what was harder yet to flesh and blood,
Their gods disgrac'd, and burnt like common wood.
This set the heathen priesthood in a flame;
For priests of all religions are the same:
Of whatsoe'er descent their godhead be,
Stock, stone, or other homely pedigree,
In his defence his servants are as bold,
As if he had been born of beaten gold.
The Jewish rabbins, tho' their enemies,
In this conclude them honest men and wise:
For 'twas their duty, all the learned think,
T' espouse his cause, by whom they eat and drink.
From hence began that * Plot, the nation's curse,
Bad in itself, but represented worse;
Rais'd in extremes, and in extremes decried;
With oaths affirm'd, with dying vows denied;
Not weigh'd or winnow'd by the multitude;
But swallow'd in the mass, unchew'd and crude.
Some truth there was, but dash'd and brew'd with lies,
To please the fools, and puzzle all the wise.
Succeeding times did equal folly call,
Believing nothing, or believing all.
Th' Egyptian rites the Jebusites embrac'd;
* Where gods were recommended by their taste.
Such sav'ry deities must needs be good,
As serv'd at once for worship and for food.
By force they could not introduce these gods,
For ten to one in former days was odds;
So fraud was us'd (the sacrificer's trade):
Fools are more hard to conquer than persuade.
Their busy teachers mingled with the Jews,
And rak'd for converts even the court and stews:
Which Hebrew priests the more unkindly took,
Because the fleece accompanies the flock.
Some thought they God's anointed meant to slay
By guns, invented since full many a day:
Our author swears it not; but who can know
How far the Devil and Jebusites may go?
This Plot, which fail'd for want of common sense,
Had yet a deep and dangerous consequence:
For, as when raging fevers boil the blood,
The standing lake soon floats into a flood,
And ev'ry hostile humour, which before
Slept quiet in its channels, bubbles o'er;
So several factions from this first ferment
Work up to foam, and threat the government.
Some by their friends, more by themselves thought wise,
Oppos'd the pow'r to which they could not rise.
Some had in courts been great, and thrown from thence,
Like fiends were harden'd in impenitence.
Some, by their monarch's fatal mercy, grown
From pardon'd rebels kinsmen to the throne,
Were rais'd in pow'r and public office high;
Strong bands, if bands ungrateful men could tie.
  Of these the false Achitophel was first;
A name to all succeeding ages curst:
For close designs and crooked counsels fit;
Sagacious, bold, and turbulent of wit;
Restless, unfix'd in principles and place;
In pow'r unpleas'd, impatient of disgrace:
A fiery soul, which, working out its way,
Fretted the pigmy body to decay,
And o'er-inform'd the tenement of clay.
A daring pilot in extremity;
Pleas'd with the danger, when the waves went high,
He sought the storms; but, for a calm unfit,
Would steer too nigh the sands, to boast his wit.
Great wits are sure to madness near allied,
And thin partitions do their bounds divide;
Else why should he, with wealth and honour blest,

Refuse his age the needful hours of rest?
Punish a body which he could not please;
Bankrupt of life, yet prodigal of ease?
And all to leave what with his toil he won,
To that *unfeather'd two-legg'd thing, a son;
Got, while his soul did huddled notions try;
And born a shapeless lump, like anarchy.
In friendship false, implacable in hate;
Resolv'd to ruin or to rule the State.
To compass this the *triple bond he broke;
The pillars of the public safety shook;
And fitted Israel for a foreign yoke:
Then seiz'd with fear, yet still affecting fame,
Usurp'd a patriot's all-atoning name.
So easy still it proves in factious times,
With public zeal to cancel private crimes.
How safe is treason, and how sacred ill,
Where none can sin against the people's will!
Where crowds can wink, and no offence be known,
Since in another's guilt they find their own!
Yet fame deserv'd no enemy can grudge;
The statesman we abhor, but praise the judge.
In Israel's courts ne'er sat an Abbethdin
With more discerning eyes, or hands more clean;
Unbrib'd, unsought, the wretched to redress;
Swift of dispatch, and easy of access.
Oh, had he been content to serve the crown,
With virtues only proper to the gown;
Or had the rankness of the soil been freed
From cockle, that oppress'd the noble seed;
David for him his tuneful harp had strung,
And Heav'n had wanted one *immortal song.
But wild Ambition loves to slide, not stand,
And fortune's ice prefers to virtue's land.
Achitophel, grown weary to possess
A lawful fame, and lazy happiness,
Disdain'd the golden fruit to gather free,
And lent the crowd his arm to shake the tree.
Now, manifest of crimes contriv'd long since,
He stood at bold defiance with his prince;
Held up the buckler of the people's cause
Against the crown, and skulk'd behind the laws.
The wish'd occasion of the Plot he takes;
Some circumstances finds, but more he makes.
By buzzing emissaries fills the ears
Of list'ning crowds with jealousies and fears
Of arbitrary counsels brought to light,
And proves the king himself a Jebusite.
Weak arguments! which yet he knew full well
Were strong with people easy to rebel.
For, govern'd by the moon, the giddy Jews
Tread the same track when she the prime renews;
And once in twenty years, their scribes record,
By natural instinct they change their lord.
Achitophel still wants a chief, and none
Was found so fit as warlike Absalon:
Not that he wish'd his greatness to create,
(For politicians neither love nor hate,)
But, for he knew his title not allow'd,
Would keep him still depending on the crowd:
That kingly pow'r, thus ebbing out, might be
Drawn to the *dregs of a democracy.
Him he attempts with studied arts to please,
And sheds his venom in such words as these:
"Auspicious prince, at whose nativity
Some royal planet rul'd the southern sky;
Thy longing country's darling and desire;
Their cloudy pillar and their guardian fire:
Their second Moses, whose extended wand
Divides the seas, and shows the promis'd land;
Whose dawning day in every distant age
Has exercis'd the sacred prophets' rage:
The people's pray'r, the glad diviners' theme,
The young men's vision, and the old men's dream!
Thee, saviour, thee, the nation's vows confess,
And, never satisfied with seeing, bless:
Swift unbespoken pomps thy steps proclaim,
And stammering babes are taught to lisp thy name.
How long wilt thou the general joy detain,
Starve and defraud the people of thy reign?
Content ingloriously to pass thy days
Like one of virtue's fools that feeds on praise;
Till thy fresh glories, which now shine so bright,
Grow stale and tarnish with our daily sight.
Believe me, royal youth, thy fruit must be
Or gather'd ripe, or rot upon the tree.
Heav'n has to all allotted, soon or late,
Some lucky revolution of their fate;
Whose motions if we watch and guide with skill,
(For human good depends on human will,)
Our fortune rolls as from a smooth descent,
And from the first impression takes the bent:
But, if unseiz'd, she glides away like wind,
And leaves repenting folly far behind.
Now, now she meets you with a glorious prize,
And spreads her locks before her as she flies.

Had thus old David, from whose loins you spring,
Not dar'd, when Fortune call'd him, to be king,
At Gath an exile he might still remain,
And Heaven's anointing oil had been in vain.
Let his successful youth your hopes engage;
But shun th' example of declining age:
Behold him setting in his western skies,
The shadows lengthening as the vapours rise.
He is not now, as when on Jordan's sand
The joyful people throng'd to see him land,
Cov'ring the beach, and black'ning all the strand;
But, like the Prince of Angels, from his height
Comes tumbling downward with diminish'd light;
Betray'd by one poor Plot to public scorn,
(Our only blessing since his curst return;)
Those heaps of people which one sheaf did bind,
Blown off and scatter'd by a puff of wind.
What strength can he to your designs oppose,
Naked of friends, and round beset with foes?
If Pharaoh's doubtful succour he should use,
A foreign aid would more incense the Jews:
Proud Egypt would dissembled friendship bring;
Foment the war, but not support the king:
Nor would the royal party e'er unite
With Pharaoh's arms t' assist the Jebusite;
Or if they should, their interest soon would break,
And with such odious aid make David weak.
All sorts of men by my successful arts,
Abhorring kings, estrange their alter'd hearts
From David's rule: and 'tis the general cry,
'Religion, commonwealth, and liberty.'
If you, as champion of the public good,
Add to their arms a chief of royal blood,
What may not Israel hope, and what applause
Might such a general gain by such a cause?
Not barren praise alone, that gaudy flow'r
Fair only to the sight, but solid pow'r;
And nobler is a limited command,
Giv'n by the love of all your native land,
Than a successive title, long and dark,
Drawn from the mouldy rolls of Noah's ark."
What cannot praise effect in mighty minds,
When flattery soothes, and when ambition blinds!
Desire of pow'r, on earth a vicious weed,
Yet, sprung from high, is of celestial seed:
In God 'tis glory; and when men aspire,
'Tis but a spark too much of heavenly fire.
Th' ambitious youth, too covetous of fame,
Too full of angels' metal in his frame,
Unwarily was led from virtue's ways,
Made drunk with honour, and debauch'd with praise.
Half loath, and half consenting to the ill,
(For loyal blood within him struggled still,)
He thus replied: "And what pretence have I
To take up arms for public liberty?
My father governs with unquestion'd right;
The faith's defender, and mankind's delight;
Good, gracious, just, observant of the laws:
And Heav'n by wonders has espous'd his cause.
Whom has he wrong'd in all his peaceful reign?
Who sues for justice to his throne in vain?
What millions has he pardon'd of his foes,
Whom just revenge did to his wrath expose?
Mild, easy, humble, studious of our good;
Inclin'd to mercy, and averse from blood;
If mildness ill with stubborn Israel suit,
His crime is God's beloved attribute.
What could he gain, his people to betray,
Or change his right for arbitrary sway?
Let haughty Pharaoh curse with such a reign
His fruitful Nile, and yoke a servile train.
If David's rule Jerusalem displease,
The Dog Star heats their brains to this disease.
Why then should I, encouraging the bad,
Turn rebel and run popularly mad?
Were he a tyrant, who, by lawless might
Oppress'd the Jews, and rais'd the Jebusite,
Well might I mourn; but nature's holy bands
Would curb my spirits and restrain my hands:
The people might assert their liberty;
But what was right in them were crime in me.
His favour leaves me nothing to require,
Prevents my wishes, and outruns desire.
What more can I expect while David lives?
All but his kingly diadem he gives:
And that" — But there he paus'd; then sighing, said —
"Is justly destin'd for a worthier head.
For, when my father from his toils shall rest,
And late augment the number of the blest,
His lawful issue shall the throne ascend,
Or the collat'ral line, where that shall end.
His brother, tho' oppress'd with vulgar spite,
Yet dauntless, and secure of native right,
Of every royal virtue stands possess'd;

Still dear to all the bravest and the best.
His courage foes, his friends his truth proclaim;
His loyalty the king, the world his fame.
His mercy ev'n th' offending crowd will find;
For sure he comes of a forgiving kind.
Why should I then repine at Heaven's decree,
Which gives me no pretence to royalty?
Yet oh that fate, propitiously inclin'd,
Had rais'd my birth, or had debas'd my mind;
To my large soul not all her treasure lent,
And then betray'd it to a mean descent!
I find, I find my mounting spirits bold,
And David's part disdains my mother's mould.
Why am I scanted by a niggard birth?
My soul disclaims the kindred of her earth;
And, made for empire, whispers me within,
'Desire of greatness is a godlike sin.'"

Him staggering so when hell's dire agent found,
While fainting Virtue scarce maintain'd her ground,
He pours fresh forces in, and thus replies:
"Th' eternal God, supremely good and wise,
Imparts not these prodigious gifts in vain:
What wonders are reserv'd to bless your reign!
Against your will, your arguments have shown,
Such virtue's only giv'n to guide a throne.
Not that your father's mildness I contemn;
But manly force becomes the diadem.
'Tis true he grants the people all they crave;
And more, perhaps, than subjects ought to have:
For lavish grants suppose a monarch tame,
And more his goodness than his wit proclaim.
But when should people strive their bonds to break,
If not when kings are negligent or weak?
Let him give on till he can give no more,
The thrifty Sanhedrin shall keep him poor;
And every shekel which he can receive,
Shall cost a limb of his prerogative.
To ply him with new plots shall be my care;
Or plunge him deep in some expensive war;
Which when his treasure can no more supply,
He must, with the remains of kingship, buy.
His faithful friends, our jealousies and fears
Call Jebusites, and Pharaoh's pensioners;
Whom when our fury from his aid has torn,
He shall be naked left to public scorn.
The next successor, whom I fear and hate,
My arts have made obnoxious to the state;
Turn'd all his virtues to his overthrow,
And gain'd our elders to pronounce a foe.
His right, for sums of necessary gold,
Shall first be pawn'd, and afterwards be sold;
Till time shall ever-wanting David draw,
To pass your doubtful title into law:
If not, the people have a right supreme
To make their kings; for kings are made for them.
All empire is no more than pow'r in trust,
Which, when resum'd, can be no longer just.
Succession, for the general good design'd,
In its own wrong a nation cannot bind;
If altering that the people can relieve,
Better one suffer than a nation grieve.
The Jews well know their pow'r: ere Saul they chose,
God was their king, and God they durst depose.
Urge now your piety, your filial name,
A father's right, and fear of future fame;
The public good, that universal call,
To which even Heav'n submitted, answers all
Nor let his love enchant your generous mind;
'Tis Nature's trick to propagate her kind.
Our fond begetters, who would never die,
Love but themselves in their posterity.
Or let his kindness by th' effects be tried,
Or let him lay his vain pretence aside.
God said he lov'd your father; could he bring
A better proof than to anoint him king?
It surely show'd he lov'd the shepherd well,
Who gave so fair a flock as Israel.
Would David have you thought his darling son?
What means he then, to alienate the crown?
The name of godly he may blush to bear:
'Tis after God's own heart to cheat his heir.
He to his brother gives supreme command,
To you a legacy of barren land:
Perhaps th' old harp, on which he thrums his lays,
Or some dull Hebrew ballad in your praise.
Then the next heir, a prince severe and wise,
Already looks on you with jealous eyes;
Sees thro' the thin disguises of your arts,
And marks your progress in the people's hearts.
Tho' now his mighty soul its grief contains,
He meditates revenge who least complains;
And, like a lion, slumb'ring in the way,

Or sleep dissembling, while he waits his prey,
His fearless foes within his distance draws,
Constrains his roaring, and contracts his paws;
Till at the last, his time for fury found,
He shoots with sudden vengeance from the ground;
The prostrate vulgar passes o'er and spares,
But with a lordly rage his hunters tears.
Your case no tame expedients will afford:
Resolve on death, or conquest by the sword,
Which for no less a stake than life you draw;
And self-defence is nature's eldest law.
Leave the warm people no considering time;
For then rebellion may be thought a crime.
Prevail yourself of what occasion gives,
But try your title while your father lives;
And that your arms may have a fair pretence,
Proclaim you take them in the king's defence;
Whose sacred life each minute would expose
To plots, from seeming friends, and secret foes.
And who can sound the depth of David's soul?
Perhaps his fear his kindness may control.
He fears his brother, tho' he loves his son,
For plighted vows too late to be undone.
If so, by force he wishes to be gain'd;
Like women's lechery, to seem constrain'd.
Doubt not; but, when he most affects the frown,
Commit a pleasing rape upon the crown.
Secure his person to secure your cause:
They who possess the prince, possess the laws."

He said, and this advice above the rest,
With Absalom's mild nature suited best:
Unblam'd of life, (ambition set aside,)
Not stain'd with cruelty, nor puff'd with pride;
How happy had he been, if destiny
Had higher plac'd his birth, or not so high!
His kingly virtues might have claim'd a throne,
And bless'd all other countries but his own.
But charming greatness since so few refuse,
'Tis juster to lament him than accuse.
Strong were his hopes a rival to remove,
With blandishments to gain the public love;
To head the faction while their zeal was hot,
And popularly prosecute the Plot.
To further this, Achitophel unites
The malcontents of all the Israelites;
Whose differing parties he could wisely join,
For several ends, to serve the same design:
The best, (and of the princes some were such,)
Who thought the pow'r of monarchy too much;
Mistaken men, and patriots in their hearts;
Not wicked, but seduc'd by impious arts.
By these the springs of property were bent,
And wound so high, they crack'd the government.
The next for interest sought t' embroil the state,
To sell their duty at a dearer rate;
And make their Jewish markets of the throne,
Pretending public good, to serve their own.
Others thought kings an useless heavy load,
Who cost too much, and did too little good.
These were for laying honest David by,
On principles of pure good husbandry.
With them join'd all th' haranguers of the throng,
That thought to get preferment by the tongue.
Who follow next, a double danger bring,
Not only hating David, but the king:
The Solymæan rout, well-vers'd of old
In godly faction, and in treason bold;
Cow'ring and quaking at a conqu'ror's sword;
But lofty to a lawful prince restor'd;
Saw with disdain an Ethnic plot begun,
And scorn'd by Jebusites to be outdone.
Hot Levites headed these; who, pull'd before
From th' ark, which in the Judges' days they bore,
Resum'd their cant, and with a zealous cry
Pursued their old belov'd Theocracy,
Where Sanhedrin and priest enslav'd the nation,
And justified their spoils by inspiration:
For who so fit for reign as Aaron's race,
If once dominion they could found in grace?
These led the pack; tho' not of surest scent,
Yet deepest mouth'd against the government.
A numerous host of dreaming * saints succeed,
Of the true old * enthusiastic breed:
'Gainst form and order they their pow'r employ,
Nothing to build, and all things to destroy.
But far more numerous was the herd of such,
Who think too little, and who talk too much.
These, out of mere instinct, they knew not why,
Ador'd their fathers' God and property;
And, by the same blind benefit of fate,
The Devil and the Jebusite did hate:
* Born to be sav'd, even in their own despite,
Because they could not help believing right.
Such were the tools; but a whole Hydra more

Remains, of sprouting heads too long to score.
Some of their chiefs were princes of the land:
In the first rank of these did Zimri stand;
A man so various that he seem'd to be
Not one, but all mankind's epitome:
Stiff in opinions, always in the wrong;
Was everything by starts, and nothing long;
But, in the course of one revolving moon,
Was chemist, fiddler, statesman, and buffoon:
Then all for women, painting, rhyming, drinking,
Besides ten thousand freaks that died in thinking.
Blest madman, who could every hour employ,
With something new to wish, or to enjoy!
Railing and praising were his usual themes;
And both (to show his judgment) in extremes:
So over-violent, or over-civil,
That every man, with him, was God or Devil.
In squand'ring wealth was his peculiar art:
Nothing went unrewarded but desert.
Beggar'd by fools, whom still he found too late,
He had his jest, and they had his estate.
He laugh'd himself from court; then sought relief
By forming parties, but could ne'er be chief;
For, spite of him, the weight of business fell
On Absalom and wise Achitophel:
Thus, wicked but in will, of means bereft,
He left not faction, but of that was left.
Titles and names 'twere tedious to rehearse
Of lords, below the dignity of verse.
Wits, warriors, Commonwealth's-men, were the best;
Kind husbands, and mere nobles, all the rest.
And therefore, in the name of dullness, be
The well-hung Balaam and cold Caleb, free;
And canting Nadab let oblivion damn,
Who made new porridge for the paschal lamb.
Let friendship's holy band some names assure;
Some their own worth, and some let scorn secure.
Nor shall the rascal rabble here have place,
Whom kings no titles gave, and God no grace:
Not bull-fac'd Jonas, who could statutes draw
To mean rebellion, and make treason law.
But he, tho' bad, is follow'd by a worse,
The wretch who Heav'n's anointed dar'd to curse:
Shimei, whose youth did early promise bring
Of zeal to God and hatred to his king,
Did wisely from expensive sins refrain,
And never broke the Sabbath, but for gain;
Nor ever was he known an oath to vent,
Or curse, unless against the government.
Thus heaping wealth, by the most ready way
Among the Jews, which was to cheat and pray,
The city, to reward his pious hate
Against his master, chose him magistrate.
His hand a *vare of justice did uphold;
His neck was loaded with a chain of gold.
During his office, treason was no crime;
The sons of Belial had a glorious time;
For Shimei, tho' not prodigal of pelf,
Yet lov'd his wicked neighbour as himself.
When two or three were gather'd to declaim
Against the monarch of Jerusalem,
Shimei was always in the midst of them;
And if they curs'd the king when he was by,
Would rather curse than break good company.
If any durst his factious friends accuse,
He pack'd a jury of dissenting Jews;
Whose fellow-feeling in the godly cause
Would free the suff'ring saint from human laws.
For laws are only made to punish those
Who serve the king, and to protect his foes.
If any leisure time he had from pow'r,
(Because 'tis sin to misemploy an hour,)
His bus'ness was, by writing, to persuade
That kings were useless, and a clog to trade;
And, that his noble style he might refine,
No Rechabite more shunn'd the fumes of wine.
Chaste were his cellars, and his shrieval board
The grossness of a city feast abhorr'd:
His cooks, with long disuse, their trade forgot;
Cool was his kitchen, tho' his brains were hot.
Such frugal virtue malice may accuse,
But sure 'twas necessary to the Jews;
For towns once burnt such magistrates require
As dare not tempt God's providence by fire.
With spiritual food he fed his servants well,
But free from flesh that made the Jews rebel;
And Moses' laws he held in more account,
For forty days of fasting in the mount.
To speak the rest, who better are forgot,
Would tire a well-breath'd witness of the Plot.
Yet, Corah, thou shalt from oblivion pass:
Erect thyself, thou monumental brass,
High as the serpent of thy metal made,
While nations stand secure beneath thy shade.
What tho' his birth were base, yet comets rise

From earthy vapours, ere they shine in skies.
Prodigious actions may as well be done
By weaver's issue, as by prince's son.
This arch-attestor for the public good
By that one deed ennobles all his blood.
Who ever ask'd the witnesses' high race,
Whose oath with martyrdom did Stephen grace?
Ours was a Levite, and as times went then,
His tribe were God Almighty's gentlemen.
Sunk were his eyes, his voice was harsh and loud,
Sure signs he neither choleric was nor proud:
His long chin prov'd his wit; his saintlike grace,
A church vermilion, and a Moses' face.
His memory, miraculously great,
Could plots, exceeding man's belief, repeat;
Which therefore cannot be accounted lies,
For human wit could never such devise.
Some future truths are mingled in his book;
But where the witness fail'd, the prophet spoke:
Some things like visionary flights appear;
The spirit caught him up, the Lord knows where;
And gave him his rabbinical degree,
Unknown to foreign university.
His judgment yet his mem'ry did excel;
Which piec'd his wondrous evidence so well,
And suited to the temper of the times,
Then groaning under Jebusitic crimes.
Let Israel's foes suspect his heav'nly call,
And rashly judge his writ apocryphal;
Our laws for such affronts have forfeits made:
He takes his life, who takes away his trade.
Were I myself in witness Corah's place,
The wretch who did me such a dire disgrace
Should whet my memory, tho' once forgot,
To make him an appendix of my plot.
His zeal to Heav'n made him his prince despise,
And load his person with indignities;
But zeal peculiar privilege affords,
Indulging latitude to deeds and words;
And Corah might for *Agag's murder call,
In terms as coarse as Samuel us'd to Saul.
What others in his evidence did join,
(The best that could be had for love or coin,)
In Corah's own predicament will fall;
For *witness* is a common name to all.
Surrounded thus with friends of every sort,
Deluded Absalom forsakes the court;
Impatient of high hopes, urg'd with renown,
And fir'd with near possession of a crown.
Th' admiring crowd are dazzled with surprise,
And on his goodly person feed their eyes.
His joy conceal'd, he sets himself to show,
On each side bowing popularly low;
His looks, his gestures, and his words he frames,
And with familiar ease repeats their names.
Thus form'd by nature, furnish'd out with arts,
He glides unfelt into their secret hearts.
Then, with a kind compassionating look,
And sighs, bespeaking pity ere he spoke,
Few words he said; but easy those and fit,
More slow than Hybla-drops, and far more sweet.
"I mourn, my countrymen, your lost estate;
Tho' far unable to prevent your fate:
Behold a banish'd man, for your dear cause
Expos'd a prey to arbitrary laws!
Yet oh! that I alone could be undone,
Cut off from empire, and no more a son!
Now all your liberties a spoil are made;
Egypt and Tyrus intercept your trade,
And Jebusites your sacred rites invade.
My father, whom with reverence yet I name,
Charm'd into ease, is careless of his fame;
And, brib'd with petty sums of foreign gold,
Is grown in Bathsheba's embraces old;
Exalts his enemies, his friends destroys;
And all his pow'r against himself employs.
He gives, and let him give, my right away;
But why should he his own and yours betray?
He, only he, can make the nation bleed,
And he alone from my revenge is freed.
Take then my tears," (with that he wip'd his eyes,)
"'Tis all the aid my present pow'r supplies:
No court-informer can these arms accuse;
These arms may sons against their fathers use:
And 'tis my wish, the next successor's reign
May make no other Israelite complain."
Youth, beauty, graceful action seldom fail;
But common interest always will prevail;
And pity never ceases to be shown
To him who makes the people's wrongs his own.
The crowd, that still believe their kings oppress,
With lifted hands their young Messiah bless:
Who now begins his progress to ordain
With chariots, horsemen, and a num'rous train;
From east to west his glories he displays,
And, like the sun, the promis'd land surveys.

Fame runs before him as the morning star,
And shouts of joy salute him from afar:
Each house receives him as a guardian god,
And consecrates the place of his abode.
But hospitable treats did most commend
Wise Issachar, his wealthy western friend.
This moving court, that caught the people's eyes,
And seem'd but pomp, did other ends disguise:
Achitophel had form'd it, with intent
To sound the depths, and fathom, where it went,
The people's hearts; distinguish friends from foes,
And try their strength, before they came to blows.
Yet all was colour'd with a smooth pretence
Of specious love, and duty to their prince.
Religion, and redress of grievances,
Two names that always cheat and always please,
Are often urg'd; and good King David's life
Endanger'd by a brother and a wife.
Thus in a pageant show a plot is made,
And peace itself is war in masquerade.
* Oh foolish Israel! never warn'd by ill!
Still the same bait, and circumvented still!
Did ever men forsake their present ease,
In midst of health imagine a disease;
Take pains contingent mischiefs to foresee,
Make heirs for monarchs, and for God decree?
What shall we think? Can people give away,
Both for themselves and sons, their native sway?
Then they are left defenceless to the sword
Of each unbounded, arbitrary lord:
And laws are vain, by which we right enjoy,
If kings unquestion'd can those laws destroy.
Yet if the crowd be judge of fit and just,
And kings are only officers in trust,
Then this resuming cov'nant was declar'd
When kings were made, or is for ever barr'd.
If those who gave the sceptre could not tie
By their own deed their own posterity,
How then could Adam bind his future race?
How could his forfeit on mankind take place?
Or how could heavenly justice damn us all,
Who ne'er consented to our father's fall?
Then kings are slaves to those whom they command,
And tenants to their people's pleasure stand.
Add, that the pow'r for property allow'd
Is mischievously seated in the crowd;
For who can be secure of private right,
If sovereign sway may be dissolv'd by might?
Nor is the people's judgment always true:
The most may err as grossly as the few;
And faultless kings run down, by common cry,
For vice, oppression, and for tyranny.
What standard is there in a fickle rout,
Which, flowing to the mark, runs faster out?
Nor only crowds, but Sanhedrins may be
Infected with this public lunacy,
And share the madness of rebellious times,
To murder monarchs for imagin'd crimes.
If they may give and take whene'er they please,
Not kings alone, (the Godhead's images,)
But government itself at length must fall
To nature's state, where all have right to all.
Yet, grant our lords the people kings can make,
What prudent men a settled throne would shake?
For whatsoe'er their sufferings were before,
That change they covet makes them suffer more.
All other errors but disturb a state,
But innovation is the blow of fate.
If ancient fabrics nod, and threat to fall,
To patch the flaws, and buttress up the wall,
Thus far 'tis duty: but here fix the mark;
For all beyond it is to touch our ark.
To change foundations, cast the frame anew,
Is work for rebels, who base ends pursue,
At once divine and human laws control,
And mend the parts by ruin of the whole.
The tamp'ring world is subject to this curse,
To physic their disease into a worse.
  Now what relief can righteous David bring?
How fatal 'tis to be too good a king!
Friends he has few, so high the madness grows:
Who dare be such, must be the people's foes.
Yet some there were, ev'n in the worst of days;
Some let me name, and naming is to praise.
  In this short file Barzillai first appears;
Barzillai, crown'd with honour and with years.
Long since, the rising rebels he withstood
In regions waste, beyond the Jordan's flood:
Unfortunately brave to buoy the state;
But sinking underneath his master's fate:
In exile with his godlike prince he mourn'd;
For him he suffer'd, and with him return'd.
The court he practis'd, not the courtier's art:

Large was his wealth, but larger was his heart,
Which well the noblest objects knew to choose,
The fighting warrior, and recording Muse.
His bed could once a fruitful issue boast;
Now more than half a father's name is lost.
His eldest hope, with every grace adorn'd,
By me (so Heav'n will have it) always mourn'd,
And always honour'd, snatch'd in manhood's prime
B' unequal fates, and Providence's crime;
Yet not before the goal of honour won,
All parts fulfill'd of subject and of son:
Swift was the race, but short the time to run.
Oh narrow circle, but of pow'r divine,
Scanted in space, but perfect in thy line!
By sea, by land, thy matchless worth was known,
Arms thy delight, and war was all thy own:
Thy force, infus'd, the fainting Tyrians propp'd;
And haughty Pharaoh found his fortune stopp'd.
Oh ancient honour! Oh unconquer'd hand,
Whom foes unpunish'd never could withstand!
But Israel was unworthy of thy name;
Short is the date of all immoderate fame.
It looks as Heav'n our ruin had design'd,
And durst not trust thy fortune and thy mind.
Now, free from earth, thy disencumber'd soul
Mounts up, and leaves behind the clouds and starry pole:
From thence thy kindred legions mayst thou bring,
To aid the guardian angel of thy king.
Here stop, my Muse, here cease thy painful flight;
No pinions can pursue immortal height:
Tell good Barzillai thou canst sing no more,
And tell thy soul she should have fled before.
Or fled she with his life, and left this verse
To hang on her departed patron's hearse?
Now take thy steepy flight from heav'n, and see
If thou canst find on earth another *he:*
Another *he* would be too hard to find;
See then whom thou canst see not far behind.
Zadoc the priest, whom, shunning pow'r and place,
His lowly mind advanc'd to David's grace.
With him the Sagan of Jerusalem,
Of hospitable soul, and noble stem;
Him of the western dome, whose weighty sense
Flows in fit words and heavenly eloquence.
The prophets' sons, by such example led,
To learning and to loyalty were bred:
For colleges on bounteous kings depend,
And never rebel was to arts a friend.
To these succeed the pillars of the laws;
Who best could plead, and best can judge a cause.
Next them a train of loyal peers ascend;
Sharp-judging Adriel, the Muses' friend;
Himself a Muse — in Sanhedrin's debate
True to his prince, but not a slave of state:
Whom David's love with honours did adorn,
That from his disobedient son were torn.
Jotham of piercing wit, and pregnant thought;
Endued by nature, and by learning taught
To move assemblies, who but only tried
The worse a while, then chose the better side:
Nor chose alone, but turn'd the balance too;
So much the weight of one brave man can do.
Hushai, the friend of David in distress;
In public storms, of manly steadfastness:
By foreign treaties he inform'd his youth,
And join'd experience to his native truth.
His frugal care supplied the wanting throne;
Frugal for that, but bounteous of his own:
'Tis easy conduct when exchequers flow,
But hard the task to manage well the low;
For sovereign power is too depress'd or high,
When kings are forc'd to sell, or crowds to buy.
Indulge one labour more, my weary Muse,
For Amiel: who can Amiel's praise refuse?
Of ancient race by birth, but nobler yet
In his own worth, and without title great:
The Sanhedrin long time as chief he rul'd,
Their reason guided, and their passion cool'd:
So dext'rous was he in the crown's defence,
So form'd to speak a loyal nation's sense,
That, as their band was Israel's tribes in small,
So fit was he to represent them all.
Now rasher charioteers the seat ascend,
Whose loose careers his steady skill commend:
They, like th' unequal ruler of the day,
Misguide the seasons, and mistake the way;
While he withdrawn at their mad labour smiles,
And safe enjoys the sabbath of his toils.
These were the chief, a small but faithful band
Of worthies, in the breach who dar'd to stand

And tempt th' united fury of the land.
With grief they view'd such powerful engines bent,
To batter down the lawful government:
A numerous faction, with pretended frights,
In Sanhedrins to plume the regal rights;
The true successor from the court remov'd;
The Plot, by hireling witnesses, improv'd.
These ills they saw, and, as their duty bound,
They show'd the king the danger of the wound;
That no concessions from the throne would please,
But lenitives fomented the disease;
That Absalom, ambitious of the crown,
Was made the lure to draw the people down;
That false Achitophel's pernicious hate
Had turn'd the Plot to ruin Church and State;
The council violent, the rabble worse;
That Shimei taught Jersualem to curse.
With all these loads of injuries oppress'd,
And long revolving in his careful breast
Th' event of things, at last, his patience tir'd,
Thus from his *royal throne, by Heav'n inspir'd,
The godlike David spoke: with awful fear
His train their Maker in their master hear.
"Thus long have I, by native mercy sway'd,
My wrongs dissembled, my revenge delay'd:
So willing to forgive th' offending age;
So much the father did the king assuage.
But now so far my clemency they slight,
Th' offenders question my forgiving right.
That one was made for many, they contend;
But 'tis to rule; for that's a monarch's end.
They call my tenderness of blood, my fear;
Tho' manly tempers can the longest bear.
Yet, since they will divert my native course,
'Tis time to show I am not good by force.
Those heap'd affronts that haughty subjects bring,
Are burdens for a camel, not a king.
Kings are the public pillars of the State,
Born to sustain and prop the nation's weight;
If my young Samson will pretend a call
To shake the column, let him share the fall:
But oh, that yet he would repent and live!
How easy 'tis for parents to forgive!
With how few tears a pardon might be won
From nature, pleading for a darling son!
Poor pitied youth, by my paternal care
Rais'd up to all the height his frame could bear!
Had God ordain'd his fate for empire born,
He would have giv'n his soul another turn:
Gull'd with a patriot's name, whose modern sense
Is one that would by law supplant his prince;
The people's brave, the politician's tool;
Never was patriot yet, but was a fool.
Whence comes it that religion and the laws
Should more be Absalom's than David's cause?
His old instructor, ere he lost his place,
Was never thought indued with so much grace.
Good heav'ns, how faction can a patriot paint!
My rebel ever proves my people's saint.
Would *they* impose an heir upon the throne?
Let Sanhedrins be taught to give their own.
A king's at least a part of government,
And mine as requisite as their consent;
Without my leave a future king to choose,
Infers a right the present to depose.
True, they petition me t' approve their choice;
But Esau's hands suit ill with Jacob's voice.
My pious subjects for my safety pray;
Which to secure, they take my pow'r away.
From plots and treasons Heav'n preserve my years,
But save me most from my petitioners!
Unsatiate as the barren womb or grave;
God cannot grant so much as they can crave.
What then is left, but with a jealous eye
To guard the small remains of royalty?
The law shall still direct my peaceful sway,
And the same law teach rebels to obey:
Votes shall no more establish'd pow'r control—
Such votes as make a part exceed the whole:
No groundless clamours shall my friends remove,
Nor crowds have pow'r to punish ere they prove;
For gods and godlike kings their care express,
Still to defend their servants in distress.
Oh that my pow'r to saving were confin'd!
Why am I forc'd, like Heav'n, against my mind,
To make examples of another kind?
Must I at length the sword of justice draw?
Oh curst effects of necessary law!
How ill my fear they by my mercy scan!
Beware the fury of a patient man.
Law they require, let Law then show her face;

They could not be content to look on Grace,
Her hinder parts, but with a daring eye
To tempt the terror of her front and die.
By their own arts, 'tis righteously decreed,
Those dire artificers of death shall bleed.
Against themselves their witnesses will swear,
Till viper-like their mother Plot they tear;
And suck for nutriment that bloody gore,
Which was their principle of life before.
Their Belial with their Belzebub will fight;
Thus on my foes, my foes shall do me right.
Nor doubt th' event; for factious crowds engage,
In their first onset, all their brutal rage.
Then let 'em take an unresisted course;
Retire, and traverse, and delude their force;
But, when they stand all breathless, urge the fight,
And rise upon 'em with redoubled might;
For lawful pow'r is still superior found;
When long driv'n back, at length it stands the ground."
He said. Th' Almighty, nodding, gave consent;
And peals of thunder shook the firmament.
Henceforth a series of new time began,
The mighty years in long procession ran:
Once more the godlike David was restor'd,
And willing nations knew their lawful lord.

[1681]

MAC FLECKNOE

OR, A SATIRE UPON THE TRUE-BLUE-PROTESTANT POET

T. S.

BY THE AUTHOR OF ABSALOM AND ACHITOPHEL

Mac Flecknoe is Dryden's most brilliant piece of literary satire, at once an attack upon Thomas Shadwell and a major engagement in the warfare between Wit and Dullness. In form it is a mock-heroic — not to be confused with travesty, which is an altogether different literary type. Mock-heroic or mock-epic poetry handles a trivial theme in a grand manner; travesty or burlesque poetry treats a grand theme in a trivial manner. The former was in the neo-classic tradition, but the latter was opposed to it. Thus Boileau wrote the mock-heroic, *Le Lutrin*, but in *L'Art Poétique*, (I: 81, 82) he also wrote the words that were Englished in the Soame-Dryden version:

> The dull burlesque appeared with impudence,
> And pleased by novelty, in spite of sense.

Pope later described *The Rape of the Lock* as "An Heroi-Comical Poem," and he not only followed the general form of *Mac Flecknoe*, but also adopted its special machinery in *The Dunciad*.

Dryden's authorship of *Mac Flecknoe* has during recent years been called in question; efforts have been made to prove that it was written by Oldham. In so doing, emphasis has been put upon the peculiar circumstances of publication, upon Shadwell's statement that Dryden had denied the authorship with execrations, and upon the inference to be drawn from the inclusion of a version of the poem in a late seventeenth-century manuscript volume in the Bodleian Library (Rawlinson Poetry 123) which contains a transcription of most of Oldham's works. All the evidence thus far published is easily susceptible of explanation without impugning Dryden's authorship, but the most important reason for the traditional attribution is the quality of the verse. Oldham never wrote anything else comparable in brilliancy to *Mac Flecknoe*; it is not likely that he would have published vastly inferior work under his own name and then have failed to claim this masterpiece. In fact it is better than anything else of the same kind that Dryden wrote. But there is no late seventeenth-century poet except Dryden whose known work can for a moment be set beside this. The internal evidence points unmistakably to Dryden and to Dryden alone. For a brief summary of the argument see the appendix to Mark Van Doren's *The Poetry of John Dryden*.

* All human things are subject to decay,
And when Fate summons, monarchs must obey.
This * Flecknoe found, who, like Augustus, young
Was call'd to empire, and had govern'd long;
In prose and verse, was own'd, without dispute,
Through all the realms of Nonsense, absolute.
This aged prince, now flourishing in peace,
And blest with issue of a large increase;
Worn out with business, did at length debate

To settle the succession of the State;
And, pond'ring which of all his sons was fit
To reign, and wage immortal war with wit,
Cried, "'Tis resolv'd; for nature pleads, that he
Should only rule, who most resembles me:
* Sh—— alone my perfect image bears,
Mature in dullness from his tender years;
Sh—— alone, of all my sons, is he
Who stands confirm'd in full stupidity.
The rest to some faint meaning make pretence,
But Sh—— never deviates into sense.
Some beams of wit on other souls may fall,
Strike through, and make a lucid interval;
But Sh——'s genuine night admits no ray,
His rising fogs prevail upon the day:
Besides, his goodly fabric fills the eye,
And seems design'd for thoughtless majesty:
Thoughtless as monarch oaks that shade the plain,
And, spread in solemn state, supinely reign.
* Heywood and Shirley were but types of thee,
Thou last great prophet of tautology:
Even I, a dunce of more renown than they,
Was sent before but to prepare thy way;
And, coarsely clad in * Norwich drugget, came
To teach the nations in thy greater name.
My warbling lute, the lute I whilom strung,
When to * King John of Portugal I sung,
Was but the prelude to that glorious day,
When thou on silver Thames didst cut thy way,
With well-tim'd oars before the royal barge,
Swell'd with the pride of thy celestial charge;
And big with hymn, commander of an host,
The like was ne'er in * Epsom blankets toss'd.
Methinks I see * the new Arion sail,
The lute still trembling underneath thy nail.
At thy well-sharpen'd thumb from shore to shore
The treble squeaks for fear, the basses roar;
Echoes from Pissing Alley Sh—— call,
And Sh—— they resound from Aston Hall.
About thy boat the little fishes throng,
As at the morning toast that floats along.
Sometimes, as prince of thy harmonious band,
Thou wield'st thy papers in thy threshing hand.
* St. André's feet ne'er kept more equal time,
Not ev'n the feet of thy own *Psyche's* rhyme,
Though they in number as in sense excel;
So just, so like tautology, they fell,
That, pale with envy, Singleton forswore
The lute and sword, which he in triumph bore,
And vow'd he ne'er would act Villerius more."
Here stopp'd the good old sire, and wept for joy
In silent raptures of the hopeful boy.
All arguments, but most his plays, persuade,
That for anointed dullness he was made.
Close to the walls which fair Augusta bind,
(The * fair Augusta much to fears inclin'd,)
An ancient fabric rais'd t' inform the sight,
There stood of yore, and Barbican it hight:
A watchtower once; but now, so fate ordains,
Of all the pile an empty name remains.
From its old ruins brothel-houses rise,
Scenes of lewd loves, and of polluted joys,
Where their vast courts the mother-strumpets keep,
And, undisturb'd by watch, in silence sleep.
Near these * a nursery erects its head,
Where queens are form'd, and future heroes bred;
Where unfledg'd actors learn to laugh and cry,
Where infant punks their tender voices try,
And * little Maximins the gods defy.
Great Fletcher never treads in buskins here,
Nor greater Jonson dares in socks appear;
But * gentle Simkin just reception finds
Amidst this monument of vanish'd minds:
Pure * clinches the suburban Muse affords,
And Panton waging harmless war with words.
Here Flecknoe, as a place to fame well known,
Ambitiously design'd his Sh——'s throne.
For ancient Dekker prophesied long since,
That in this pile should reign a mighty prince,
Born for a scourge of wit, and flail of sense;
To whom true dullness should some *Psyches* owe,
But worlds of **Misers* from his pen should flow;
Humorists and hypocrites it should produce,
Whole * Raymond families, and tribes of Bruce.
Now Empress Fame had publish'd the renown
Of Sh——'s coronation through the town.
Rous'd by report of Fame, the nations meet,
From near Bunhill, and distant Watling Street.
No Persian carpets spread th' imperial way,
But scatter'd limbs of mangled poets lay;
From dusty shops neglected authors come,
Martyrs of pies, and relics of the bum.
Much Heywood, Shirley, * Ogleby there lay,
But loads of Sh—— almost chok'd the way.
Bilk'd stationers for yeomen stood prepar'd,
And * Herringman was captain of the guard.
The hoary prince in majesty appear'd,
* High on a throne of his own labours rear'd.
At his right hand * our young Ascanius sate,
Rome's other hope, and pillar of the State.

His brows thick fogs, instead of glories, grace,
And lambent dullness play'd around his face.
As Hannibal did to the altars come,
Sworn by his sire, a mortal foe to Rome;
So Sh—— swore, nor should his vow be vain,
That he till death true dullness would maintain;
And, in his father's right, and realm's defence,
Ne'er to have peace with wit, nor truce with sense.
The king himself the sacred unction made,
As king by office, and as priest by trade.
In his sinister hand, instead of ball,
He plac'd a mighty mug of potent ale;
**Love's Kingdom* to his right he did convey,
At once his sceptre and his rule of sway;
Whose righteous lore the prince had practis'd young,
And from whose loins recorded *Psyche* sprung.
His temples, last, with poppies were o'er-spread,
That nodding seem'd to consecrate his head.
Just at that point of time, if fame not lie,
On his left hand twelve reverend owls did fly.
So Romulus, 'tis sung, by Tiber's brook,
Presage of sway from twice six vultures took.
Th' admiring throng loud acclamations make,
And omens of his future empire take.
The sire then shook the honours of his head,
And from his brows damps of oblivion shed
Full on the filial dullness: long he stood,
Repelling from his breast the raging god;
At length burst out in this prophetic mood:
"Heavens bless my son, from Ireland let him reign
To far Barbadoes on the western main;
Of his dominion may no end be known,
And greater than his father's be his throne;
Beyond *Love's Kingdom* let him stretch his pen!"
He paus'd, and all the people cried, "Amen."
Then thus continued he: "My son, advance
Still in new impudence, new ignorance.
Success let others teach, learn thou from me
Pangs without birth, and fruitless industry.
Let *Virtuosos* in five years be writ;
Yet not one thought accuse thy toil of wit.
Let *gentle George in triumph tread the stage,
Make Dorimant betray, and Loveit rage;
Let Cully, Cockwood, Fopling, charm the pit,
And in their folly show the writer's wit.
Yet still thy fools shall stand in thy defence,
And justify their author's want of sense.
Let 'em be all by thy own model made
Of dullness, and desire no foreign aid;
That they to future ages may be known,
Not copies drawn, but issue of thy own.
Nay, let thy men of wit too be the same,
All full of thee, and differing but in name.
But let no alien *S—dl—y interpose,
To lard with wit thy hungry *Epsom* prose.
And when false flowers of rhetoric thou wouldst cull,
Trust nature, do not labour to be dull;
But write thy best, and top; and, in each line,
*Sir Formal's oratory will be thine:
Sir Formal, though unsought, attends thy quill,
And does thy northern dedications fill.
Nor let false friends seduce thy mind to fame,
By arrogating Jonson's hostile name.
Let father Flecknoe fire thy mind with praise,
And uncle Ogleby thy envy raise.
Thou art my blood, where Jonson has no part:
What share have we in nature, or in art?
Where did his wit on learning fix a brand,
And rail at arts he did not understand?
Where made he love in *Prince Nicander's vein,
Or swept the dust in *Psyche's* humble strain?
Where *sold he bargains, 'whip-stitch, kiss my arse,'
Promis'd a play and dwindled to a farce?
When did his Muse from Fletcher scenes purloin,
As thou whole Eth'rege dost transfuse to thine?
But so transfus'd as oils on waters flow,
His always floats above, thine sinks below.
This is thy province, this thy wondrous way,
New humours to invent for each new play:
*This is that boasted bias of thy mind,
By which one way, to dullness, 'tis inclin'd;
Which makes thy writings lean on one side still,
And, in all changes, that way bends thy will.
Nor let thy mountain belly make pretence
Of likeness; thine's a tympany of sense.
A tun of man in thy large bulk is writ,
But sure thou'rt but a kilderkin of wit.
Like mine, thy gentle numbers feebly creep;
Thy tragic Muse gives smiles, thy comic sleep.
With whate'er gall thou sett'st thyself to write,
Thy inoffensive satires never bite.
In thy felonious heart though venom lies,
It does but touch thy Irish pen, and dies.
*Thy genius calls thee not to purchase fame
In keen iambics, but mild anagram.
Leave writing plays, and choose for thy command
Some peaceful province in Acrostic Land.

There thou may'st wings display and altars raise,
And torture one poor word ten thousand ways.
Or, if thou wouldst thy diff'rent talents suit,
Set thy own songs, and sing them to thy lute."
He said: but his last words were scarcely heard;
For *Bruce and Longvil had a trap prepar'd,
And down they sent the yet declaiming bard.
*Sinking he left his drugget robe behind,
Borne upwards by a subterranean wind.
The mantle fell to the young prophet's part,
With double portion of his father's art.

[1682]

THE HIND AND THE PANTHER

THE FIRST PART

Between November, 1681, and October, 1682, Dryden had published a group of satires such as had not previously appeared in the English language: *Absalom and Achitophel*, *The Medal*, and *Mac Flecknoe*. A month later, in November, 1682, he published *Religio Laici*, a serious verse argument in support of the doctrine and ecclesiastical organization of the English Church. As Saintsbury points out (E. M. L. *Dryden*, p. 91), such a production from the pen of a fifty-year-old man of letters chiefly famous for his loose plays "would nowadays be something more than a nine days' wonder. In Dryden's time it was somewhat less surprising." In the seventeenth century politics and religion were inextricably intertwined; furthermore, scarcely anybody wanted to separate them. Temporal and spiritual power were two aspects of the same thing; the King was the head of the English Church as well as of the English State; lords spiritual and lords temporal sat side by side in the upper house of that Parliament which had given legal assent to the Book of Common Prayer and had established a sacramental test for public service. Certain alliances in politics and religion were inevitable; it was natural for a high Tory to be a High Churchman and for a Whig to be a Low Churchman, while a generation before, the Commonwealth men had been equally zealous against the King and the bishops. Most questions of contemporary concern had direct religious connection: witness the "Popish Plot," for instance, or the attempt to exclude the Duke of York from succession to the throne. Monmouth's ambitions would have been unimportant or nonexistent apart from religious prejudice; it had seemed natural for Dryden to treat these by means of an allegory taken from Old Testament history. The publication of *Religio Laici*, with its defence of the Anglican Church against the Protestant dissenters on the one side and the Roman Catholics on the other, occasioned no special surprise. What did occasion surprise and recrimination was the publication less than five years later of *The Hind and the Panther*.

King Charles II died February 6, 1685, and was succeeded by his brother, the Duke of York, who reigned as James II. The new king was a zealous Roman Catholic, who desired so far as possible to make his religion prevail in England. It was not long before there were conversions in court circles; before the year was out, Dryden had seen the light and had renounced his former Anglican allegiance. Of course he was denounced as a time-serving hypocrite, though perhaps with less assurance by his contemporaries than by later historians. What led Dryden to take this step we cannot tell with certainty. Probably his motives were mingled; most men's are likely to be at any great crisis. But it is apparent that his conversion brought him no new appointments from the court, and it is not evident that it saved the positions he already held, those of poet laureate and historiographer royal. There can be no doubt that it entailed the active distrust and opposition of the great body of his countrymen. The most convincing argument for his sincerity is his conduct four years later when he refused to take the oaths of allegiance to William and Mary that would have been necessary to save his court appointments. Had he been the time-server that some have thought him, he might easily have recanted his Romanism and been restored to his Anglican allegiance by the same public profession of repentance that some of the other recent converts submitted to. Instead he gave up his appointments and his small pension and, what was more important, his influence in the court, and began resolutely the task of supporting his expensive family by the unaided labours of his pen. What must have been even more galling, he saw his old enemy, Thomas Shadwell, succeed him as poet laureate and historiographer royal.

The "Popish Plot" and the Exclusion Bill before the death of Charles II stirred up a perfect flood of religious controversy that was increased by the agitation over James the Second's use of the dispensing power and his appointments in the Church and the universities. In the pulpit and in the tavern and in public print the respective merits of the Roman and Anglican position were being argued as they seldom had been before. Books and pamphlets on both sides of the question were put out in great numbers. Every educated man in England was in the midst of the controversy; Dryden could not have escaped it if he would. That he was interested in it is sufficiently proved by *Religio Laici* even if other evidence were entirely lacking. It is likely that Dryden's conversion resulted from the investigation of the question as it was thus forced upon him. Already in the earlier poem he had shown that his sympathies were far from the extreme Protestant position; he was by temperament a conservative; he believed in authority. His turn to Rome was not out of character.

Early in 1687 he published *The Hind and the Panther,* where under the guise of a beast-fable he defended the Roman Catholic Church and satirized its enemies. To the Anglican Church he was more favourable than to the dissenting sects because it had less of heresy; it was "the fairest creature of the spotted kind"; but it was none the less the communion with which he had chief controversy. The poem was written during the earlier part of James's reign when the royal policy was to placate the High Church Anglicans, who believed that the King ruled by divine right and consequently that active resistance to him was wicked. Later, however, James found them continuing stubborn in their passive opposition to his exercise of the dispensing power; consequently he turned to the dissenters whom he tried to win over by his Declaration of Indulgence and by his suspension of the Test Act and of penal laws directed alike against Roman Catholic and Protestant Dissenter. This change in policy is noted in the prose address *To the Reader* which precedes the poem and praises toleration. But the poem itself is written in the spirit of the earlier policy in which the dissenting sects are severely arraigned, and there is still hope of reconciliation between the Hind and the Panther.

* A milk-white Hind, immortal and unchang'd,
Fed on the lawns and in the forest rang'd;
Without unspotted, innocent within,
She fear'd no danger, for she knew no sin.
Yet had she oft been chas'd with horns and hounds
And Scythian shafts; and many winged wounds
Aim'd at her heart; was often forc'd to fly,
And doom'd to death, though fated not to die.
Not so her young; for their unequal line
Was hero's make, half human, half divine.
Their earthly mould obnoxious was to fate,
Th' immortal part assum'd immortal state.
Of these a slaughter'd army lay in blood,
Extended o'er the * Caledonian wood,
Their native walk; whose vocal blood arose,
And cried for pardon on their perjur'd foes.
Their fate was fruitful, and the sanguine seed,
Indued with souls, increas'd the sacred breed.
So captive Israel multiplied in chains,
A numerous exile, and enjoy'd her pains.
With grief and gladness mix'd, their mother view'd
Her martyr'd offspring, and their race renew'd;
Their corpse to perish, but their kind to last,
So much the deathless plant the dying fruit surpass'd.
Panting and pensive now she rang'd alone,
And wander'd in the kingdoms, once her own.
The common hunt, though from their rage restrain'd
By sov'reign pow'r, her company disdain'd;
Grinn'd as they pass'd, and with a glaring eye
Gave gloomy signs of secret enmity.
'Tis true, she bounded by, and tripp'd so light,
They had not time to take a steady sight;
For Truth has such a face and such a mien,
As to be lov'd needs only to be seen.
The * bloody Bear, an *Independent* beast,
Unlick'd to form, in groans her hate express'd.
Among the timorous kind the * *Quaking* Hare
Profess'd neutrality, but would not swear.
Next her the **buffoon* Ape, as atheists use,
Mimick'd all sects, and had his own to choose;
Still when the * Lion look'd, his knees he bent,
And paid at church a courtier's compliment.
The bristled * *Baptist* Boar, impure as he,
(But whiten'd with the foam of sanctity,)
With fat pollutions fill'd the sacred place,
And mountains level'd in his furious race:
So first rebellion founded was in grace.
But since the mighty ravage which he made
In German forests had his guilt betray'd,
With broken tusks, and with a borrow'd name,
He shunn'd the vengeance, and conceal'd the shame;
So lurk'd in sects unseen. With greater guile
* False Reynard fed on consecrated spoil:
The graceless beast by Athanasius first
Was chas'd from Nice; then, by Socinus nurs'd,
His impious race their blasphemy renew'd,
And nature's King through nature's optics view'd.
Revers'd, they view'd him lessen'd to their eye,
Nor in an infant could a God descry:
New swarming sects to this obliquely tend,
Hence they began, and here they all will end.
What weight of ancient witness can prevail,
If private reason hold the public scale?
But, gracious God, how well dost thou provide
For erring judgments an unerring guide!
Thy throne is darkness in th' abyss of light,

A blaze of glory that forbids the sight.
Oh, teach me to believe thee thus conceal'd,
And search no farther than thyself reveal'd;
But her alone for my director take,
Whom thou hast promis'd never to forsake!
My thoughtless youth was wing'd with vain desires;
My manhood, long misled by wand'ring fires,
Follow'd false lights; and, when their glimpse was gone,
My pride struck out new sparkles of her own.
Such was I, such by nature still I am;
Be thine the glory, and be mine the shame.
Good life be now my task: my doubts are done:
(What more could * fright my faith than three in one?)
Can I believe eternal God could lie
Disguis'd in mortal mould and infancy?
That the great Maker of the world could die?
And after that trust my imperfect sense,
Which calls in question his omnipotence?
Can I my reason to my faith compel,
And shall my sight, and touch, and taste rebel?
Superior faculties are set aside;
Shall their subservient organs be my guide?
Then let the moon usurp the rule of day,
And winking tapers show the sun his way;
For what my senses can themselves perceive,
I need no revelation to believe.
* Can they who say the Host should be descried
By sense, define a body glorified?
Impassable, and penetrating parts?
Let them declare by what mysterious arts
He shot that body through th' opposing might
Of bolts and bars impervious to the light,
And stood before his train confess'd in open sight.

For since thus wondrously he pass'd, 'tis plain,
One single place two bodies did contain.
And sure the same Omnipotence as well
Can make one body in more places dwell.
Let Reason then at her own quarry fly,
But how can finite grasp infinity?

'Tis urg'd again that faith did first commence
By miracles, which are appeals to sense,
And thence concluded that our sense must be
The motive still of credibility.
For latter ages must on former wait,
And what began belief, must propagate.

But winnow well this thought, and you shall find
'Tis light as chaff that flies before the wind.
Were all those wonders wrought by pow'r divine
As means or ends of some more deep design?
Most sure as means, whose end was this alone,
To prove the Godhead of th' eternal Son.
God thus asserted: man is to believe
Beyond what sense and reason can conceive,
And for mysterious things of faith rely
On the proponent, Heav'n's authority.
If then our faith we for our guide admit,
Vain is the farther search of human wit;
As, when the building gains a surer stay,
We take th' unuseful scaffolding away.
Reason by sense no more can understand;
The game is play'd into another hand.
Why choose we then like * bilanders to creep
Along the coast, and land in view to keep,
When safely we may launch into the deep?
In the same vessel which our Saviour bore,
Himself the pilot, let us leave the shore,
And with a better guide a better world explore.
Could he his Godhead veil with flesh and blood,
And not veil these again to be our food?
His grace in both is equal in extent;
The first affords us life, the second nourishment.
And if he can, why all this frantic pain
To construe what his clearest words contain,
And make a riddle what he made so plain?
To take up half on trust, and half to try,
Name it not faith, but bungling bigotry.
Both knave and fool the merchant we may call,
To pay great sums, and to compound the small:
For who would break with Heav'n, and would not break for all?
Rest then, my soul, from endless anguish freed:
Nor sciences thy guide, nor sense thy creed.
Faith is the best ensurer of thy bliss;
The bank above must fail before the venture miss.
But Heav'n and Heav'n-born faith are far from thee,
Thou first apostate to divinity.
Unkennel'd range in thy * Polonian plains;
A fiercer foe the insatiate * Wolf remains.

Too boastful Britain, please thyself no more,
That beasts of prey are banish'd from thy shore:
The Bear, the Boar, and every savage name,
Wild in effect, though in appearance tame,
Lay waste thy woods, destroy thy blissful bow'r,
And, muzzled though they seem, the mutes devour.

More haughty than the rest, the *wolfish* race
Appear with belly gaunt, and famish'd face:
Never was so deform'd a beast of grace.
His *ragged tail betwixt his legs he wears,
Close clapp'd for shame; but his rough crest he rears,
And pricks up his *predestinating ears.
His wild disorder'd walk, his haggard eyes,
Did all the bestial citizens surprise.
Though fear'd and hated, yet he *rul'd a while
As captain or companion of the spoil.
Full *many a year his hateful head had been
For tribute paid, nor since in Cambria seen:
The *last of all the litter 'scap'd by chance,
And from Geneva first infested France.
Some authors thus his pedigree will trace,
But others write him of an upstart race;
Because of Wycliffe's brood no mark he brings,
But his innate antipathy to kings.
These last deduce him from th' *Helvetian kind,
Who near the Leman lake his consort lin'd:
That fi'ry Zuinglius first th' affection bred,
And meagre Calvin bless'd the nuptial bed.
In Israel some believe him *whelp'd long since,
When the proud Sanhedrim oppress'd the prince,
Or, since he will be Jew, derive him high'r,
When Corah with his brethren did conspire
From Moses' hand the sov'reign sway to wrest,
And Aaron of his ephod to divest:
Till opening earth made way for all to pass,
And could not bear the burden of a *class.
The Fox and he came shuffl'd in the dark,
If ever they were stow'd in Noah's ark:
Perhaps not made; for all their barking train
The Dog (a common species) will contain.
And some wild curs, who from their masters ran,
Abhorring the supremacy of man,
In woods and caves the rebel-race began.
  O happy pair, how well have you increas'd!
What ills in Church and State have you redress'd!
With teeth untried, and rudiments of claws,
Your first essay was on your native laws:
Those having torn with ease, and trampled down,
Your fangs you fasten'd on the *mitred crown,
And freed from God and monarchy your town.
What though your native kennel still be small,
Bounded betwixt a puddle and a wall;
Yet your victorious colonies are sent
Where the north ocean girds the continent.
Quicken'd with fire below, your monsters breed
In fenny Holland, and in *fruitful Tweed:
And, like the first, the last effects to be
*Drawn to the dregs of a democracy.
As, where in fields the fairy rounds are seen,
A rank, sour herbage rises on the green;
So, springing where these midnight elves advance,
Rebellion prints the footsteps of the dance.
Such are their doctrines, such contempt they show
To Heav'n above, and to their prince below,
As none but traitors and blasphemers know.
God, like the tyrant of the skies, is plac'd,
And kings, like slaves, beneath the crowd debas'd.
So fulsome is their food that flocks refuse
To bite, and only dogs for physic use.
As, where the lightning runs along the ground,
No husbandry can heal the blasting wound;
Nor bladed grass, nor bearded corn succeeds,
But scales of scurf and putrefaction breeds:
Such wars, such waste, such fiery tracks of dearth
Their zeal has left, and such a teemless earth.
But, as the poisons of the deadliest kind
Are to their own unhappy coasts confin'd;
As only Indian shades of sight deprive,
And magic plants will but in Colchos thrive;
So Presbyt'ry and pestilential zeal
Can only flourish in a *commonweal.
  From *Celtic woods is chas'd the *wolfish* crew;
But ah! some pity e'en to brutes is due:
Their native walks, methinks, they might enjoy,
Curb'd of their native malice to destroy.
Of all the tyrannies on humankind,
The worst is that which persecutes the mind.
Let us but weigh at what offence we strike;
'Tis but because we cannot think alike.
In punishing of this, we overthrow
The laws of nations and of nature too.
Beasts are the subjects of tyrannic sway,
Where still the stronger on the weaker prey;
Man only of a softer mould is made,
Not for his fellows' ruin, but their aid:
Created kind, beneficent, and free,
The noble image of the Deity.
  One portion of informing fire was giv'n
To brutes, th' inferior family of heav'n:
The Smith divine, as with a careless beat,
Struck out the mute creation at a heat;
But, when arriv'd at last to human race,

The Godhead took a deep consid'ring space;
And, to distinguish man from all the rest,
Unlock'd the sacred treasures of his breast;
And mercy mix'd with reason did impart,
One to his head, the other to his heart:
Reason to rule, but mercy to forgive;
The first is law, the last prerogative.
And like his mind his outward form appear'd,
When, issuing naked to the wond'ring herd,
He charm'd their eyes; and, for they lov'd, they fear'd:
Not arm'd with horns of arbitrary might,
Or claws to seize their furry spoils in fight,
Or with increase of feet t' o'ertake 'em in their flight;
Of easy shape, and pliant ev'ry way;
Confessing still the softness of his clay,
And kind as kings upon their coronation day,
With open hands, and with extended space
Of arms, to satisfy a large embrace.
Thus kneaded up with milk, the new-made man
His kingdom o'er his kindred world began;
Till knowledge misapplied, misunderstood,
And pride of empire sour'd his balmy blood.
Then, first rebelling, his own stamp he coins;
The murd'rer Cain was latent in his loins;
And blood began its first and loudest cry
For diff'ring worship of the Deity.
Thus persecution rose, and farther space
Produc'd the mighty hunter of his race.
Not so the *blessed Pan his flock increas'd,
Content to fold 'em from the famish'd beast:
Mild were his laws; the Sheep and harmless Hind
Were never of the persecuting kind.
Such pity now the pious Pastor shows,
Such mercy from the British Lion flows,
That both provide protection for their foes.
O happy regions, Italy and Spain,
Which never did those monsters entertain!
The Wolf, the Bear, the Boar, can there advance
No native claim of just inheritance.
And self-preserving laws, severe in show,
May guard their fences from th' invading foe.
Where birth has plac'd 'em, let 'em safely share
The common benefit of vital air.
Themselves unharmful, let them live unharm'd;
Their jaws disabl'd, and their claws disarm'd:
Here, only in nocturnal howlings bold,
They dare not seize the Hind, nor leap the fold.
More pow'rful, and as vigilant as they,
The Lion awfully forbids the prey.
Their rage repress'd, though pinch'd with famine sore,
They stand aloof, and tremble at his roar;
Much is their hunger, but their fear is more.
These are the chief; to number o'er the rest,
And stand, like Adam, naming ev'ry beast,
Were weary work: nor will the Muse describe
A slimy-born and sun-begotten tribe;
Who, far from steeples and their sacred sound,
In fields their sullen *conventicles found:
These gross, half-animated lumps I leave;
Nor can I think what thoughts they can conceive.
But if they think at all 'tis sure no high'r
Than matter, put in motion, may aspire:
Souls that can scarce ferment their mass of clay:
So drossy, so divisible are they,
As would but serve pure bodies for allay:
Such souls as shards produce, such beetle things
As only buzz to heav'n with ev'ning wings;
Strike in the dark, offending but by chance,
Such are the blindfold blows of ignorance.
They know not beings, and but hate a name;
To them the Hind and Panther are the same.
*The Panther, sure the noblest, next the Hind,
And fairest creature of the spotted kind;
Oh, could her inborn stains be wash'd away,
She were too good to be a beast of prey!
How can I praise, or blame, and not offend,
Or how divide the frailty from the friend!
Her faults and virtues lie so mix'd that she
Nor wholly stands condemn'd, nor wholly free.
Then, like her injur'd Lion, let me speak;
He cannot bend her, and he would not break.
Unkind already, and estrang'd in part,
The Wolf begins to share her wand'ring heart.
Though unpolluted yet with actual ill,
She half commits, who sins but in her will.
If, as our dreaming Platonists report,
There could be spirits of a middle sort,
Too black for heav'n, and yet too white for hell,
Who just dropp'd halfway down, nor lower fell;
So pois'd, so gently she descends from high,
It seems a soft dismission from the sky.
*Her house not ancient, whatsoe'er pretence
Her clergy heralds make in her defence;
A second century not halfway run,
Since the new honours of her blood begun.
*A Lion, old, obscene, and furious made
By lust, compress'd her mother in a shade;

Then, by a left-hand marriage, weds the dame,
Cov'ring adult'ry with a specious name:
So Schism begot; and Sacrilege and she,
A well-match'd pair, got graceless Heresy.
God's and kings' rebels have the same good cause,
To trample down divine and human laws;
Both would be call'd reformers, and their hate
Alike destructive both to Church and State:
The *fruit proclaims the plant; a lawless prince
By luxury reform'd incontinence;
By ruins, charity; by riots, abstinence.
Confessions, fasts, and penance set aside;
Oh, with what ease we follow such a guide,
Where souls are starv'd, and senses gratified;
Where marriage pleasures midnight pray'r supply,
And matin bells (a melancholy cry)
Are tun'd to merrier notes, increase and multiply!
Religion shows a rosy-colour'd face;
Not *hatter'd out with drudging works of grace;
A downhill reformation rolls apace.
What flesh and blood would crowd the narrow gate,
Or, till they waste their pamper'd paunches, wait?
All would be happy at the cheapest rate.

Though our lean faith these rigid laws has giv'n,
The full-fed Mussulman goes fat to heav'n;
For his Arabian prophet with delights
Of sense allur'd his Eastern proselytes.
The jolly Luther, reading him, began
T' interpret Scriptures by his Alcoran;
To grub the thorns beneath our tender feet,
And make the paths of paradise more sweet:
Bethought him of a wife ere halfway gone,
(For 'twas uneasy travelling alone;)
And, in this masquerade of mirth and love,
Mistook the bliss of heav'n for Bacchanals above.
Sure he presum'd of praise, who came to stock
Th' ethereal pastures with so fair a flock,
Burnish'd, and batt'ning on their food, to show
The diligence of careful herds below.

Our Panther, though like these she chang'd her head,
Yet, as the *mistress of a monarch's bed,
Her front erect with majesty she bore,
The crosier wielded, and the mitre wore.
Her upper part of decent discipline
Show'd affectation of an ancient line;
And Fathers, Councils, Church, and Church's Head,
Were on her reverend *phylacteries read.
But what disgrac'd and disavow'd the rest,
Was Calvin's brand, that stigmatiz'd the beast.
Thus, like *a creature of a double kind,
In her own labyrinth she lives confin'd;
To foreign lands no sound of her is come,
Humbly content to be despis'd at home.
Such is her faith; where good cannot be had,
At least she leaves the refuse of the bad:
Nice in her choice of ill, though not of best,
And least deform'd, because reform'd the least.
In doubtful points betwixt her diff'ring friends,
Where one for substance, one for sign contends,
Their contradicting terms she strives to join;
Sign shall be substance, substance shall be sign.
A Real Presence all her sons allow,
And yet 'tis flat idolatry to bow,
Because the Godhead's there they know not how.
*Her novices are taught that bread and wine
Are but the visible and outward sign,
Receiv'd by those who in communion join;
But th' inward grace, or the thing signified,
His Blood and Body, who to save us died:
The faithful this thing signified receive.
What is 't those faithful then partake or leave?
For what is signified and understood,
Is, by her own confession, Flesh and Blood.
Then, by the same acknowledgment, we know
They take the sign, and take the substance too
The lit'ral sense is hard to flesh and blood,
But nonsense never can be understood.

Her wild belief on ev'ry wave is toss'd;
But sure no church can better morals boast:
True to her king her principles are found;
Oh, that her practice were but half so sound!
Steadfast in various turns of state she stood,
And seal'd her vow'd affection with her blood:
Nor will I meanly tax her constancy,
That int'rest or obligement made the tie
(Bound to the fate of murder'd monarchy:)
Before the sounding ax so falls the vine,
Whose tender branches round the poplar twine.
She chose her ruin, and resign'd her life,
In death undaunted as an Indian wife:
A rare example! but some souls we see
Grow hard, and stiffen with adversity;
Yet these by fortune's favours are undone;
Resolv'd, into a baser form they run,
And bore the wind, but cannot bear the sun.

Let this be nature's frailty, or her fate,
Or *Isgrim's counsel, her new-chosen mate;
Still she's the fairest of the fallen crew,
No mother more indulgent, but the true.
  Fierce to her foes, yet fears her force to try,
Because she wants innate authority;
For how can she constrain them to obey,
Who has herself cast off the lawful sway?
Rebellion equals all, and those who toil
In common theft will share the common spoil.
Let her produce the title and the right
Against her old superiors first to fight;
If she reform by text, ev'n that's as plain
For her own rebels to reform again.
As long as words a diff'rent sense will bear,
And each may be his own interpreter,
Our airy faith will no foundation find;
The word's a weathercock for ev'ry wind:
The Bear, the Fox, the Wolf, by turns prevail;
The most in pow'r supplies the present gale.
The wretched Panther cries aloud for aid
To Church and Councils, whom she first betray'd;
No help from Fathers or tradition's train:
Those ancient guides she taught us to disdain,
And by that Scripture which she once abus'd
To reformation stands herself accus'd.
What bills for breach of laws can she prefer,
Expounding which she owns herself may err?
And, after all her winding ways are tried,
If doubts arise, she slips herself aside,
And leaves the private conscience for the guide.
If then that conscience set th' offender free,
It bars her claim to Church authority.
How can she censure, or what crime pretend,
But Scripture may be construed to defend?
Ev'n those whom for rebellion she transmits
To civil pow'r, her doctrine first acquits;
Because no disobedience can ensue
Where no submission to a judge is due;
Each judging for himself, by her consent,
Whom thus absolv'd she sends to punishment.
Suppose the magistrate revenge her cause,
'Tis only for transgressing human laws.
How answ'ring to its end a church is made,
Whose pow'r is but to counsel and persuade?
O solid rock, on which secure she stands!
Eternal house, not built with mortal hands!
O sure defence against th' infernal gate,
A patent during pleasure of the state!
  Thus is the Panther neither lov'd nor fear'd,
A mere mock queen of a divided herd,
Whom soon by lawful pow'r she might control,
Herself a part submitted to the whole.
Then, as the moon who first receives the light
By which she makes our nether regions bright,
So might she shine, reflecting from afar
The rays she borrow'd from a better star;
Big with the beams which from her mother flow,
And reigning o'er the rising tides below:
Now, mixing with a savage crowd, she goes,
And meanly flatters her invet'rate foes;
Rul'd while she rules, and losing ev'ry hour
Her wretched remnants of precarious pow'r.
  One evening, while the cooler shade she sought,
Revolving many a melancholy thought,
Alone she walk'd, and look'd around in vain,
With rueful visage, for her vanish'd train:
None of her sylvan subjects made their court;
*Levées and couchées pass'd without resort.
So hardly can usurpers manage well
Those whom they first instructed to rebel:
More liberty begets desire of more;
The hunger still increases with the store.
Without respect they brush'd along the wood,
Each in his clan, and, fill'd with loathsome food,
Ask'd no permission to the neighb'ring flood.
The Panther, full of inward discontent,
Since they would go, before 'em wisely went;
Supplying want of pow'r by drinking first,
As if she gave 'em leave to quench their thirst.
Among the rest, the Hind, with fearful face,
Beheld from far the common wat'ring place,
Nor durst approach; till with an awful roar
The sovereign Lion bade her fear no more.
Encourag'd thus she brought her younglings nigh,
Watching the motions of her patron's eye,
And drank a sober draught; the rest amaz'd
Stood mutely still, and on the stranger gaz'd;
Survey'd her part by part, and sought to find
*The ten-horn'd monster in the harmless Hind,
Such as the Wolf and Panther had design'd.
They thought at first they dream'd; for 'twas offence
With them to question certitude of sense,
Their guide in faith; but nearer when they drew,
And had the faultless object full in view,
Lord, how they all admir'd her heav'nly hue!
Some, who before her fellowship disdain'd,
Scarce, and but scarce, from inborn rage restrain'd,
Now frisk'd about her, and old kindred feign'd.

Whether for love or int'rest, ev'ry sect
Of all the savage nation show'd respect:
The viceroy Panther could not awe the herd;
The more the company, the less they fear'd.
The surly Wolf with secret envy burst, 551
Yet could not howl; *the Hind had seen him first:
But what he durst not speak, the Panther durst.
  For when the herd, suffic'd, did late repair
To ferny heaths, and to their forest lair,
She made a mannerly excuse to stay,
Proff'ring the Hind to wait her half the way;
That, since the sky was clear, an hour of talk
Might help her to beguile the tedious walk.
With much good will the motion was embrac'd,
To chat a while on their adventures pass'd;
Nor had the grateful Hind so soon forgot 562
Her friend and fellow-suff'rer in the Plot.
Yet wond'ring how of late she grew estrang'd,
Her forehead cloudy, and her count'nance chang'd,
She thought this hour th' occasion would present
To learn her secret cause of discontent,
Which well she hop'd might be with ease redress'd,
Consid'ring her a well-bred civil beast,
And more a gentlewoman than the rest. 570
After some common talk what rumours ran,
The lady of the spotted muff began.

[1687]

A SONG FOR ST. CECILIA'S DAY

1687

This poem and *Alexander's Feast* were written, in 1687 and in 1697 respectively, for celebrations of the Feast of Saint Cecilia, November 22. They were set to music and performed at the annual concerts of a London society, held on this day in honour of the patron saint of music. They have been justly prized as the greatest of Dryden's lyrics. Though the first is called a song and the second, in the sub-title, is called an ode, both are really in the same poetic tradition, that of the irregular Pindaric ode, which was to dominate the formal lyric of the eighteenth century to its hurt, and was eventually to produce the great odes of the nineteenth century.

I

From harmony, from heav'nly harmony,
  This universal frame began:
  When Nature underneath a heap
    Of jarring atoms lay,
  And could not heave her head,
The tuneful voice was heard from high:
    "Arise, ye more than dead."
Then * cold, and hot, and moist, and dry,
In order to their stations leap,
    And Music's pow'r obey.
From harmony, from heav'nly harmony,
  This universal frame began:
  From harmony to harmony
Through all the compass of the notes it ran,
The diapason closing full in Man.

II

What passion cannot Music raise and quell!
    When * Jubal struck the corded shell,
  His list'ning brethren stood around,
  And, wond'ring, on their faces fell
  To worship that celestial sound.
Less than a god they thought there could not dwell
    Within the hollow of that shell
    That spoke so sweetly and so well.
What passion cannot Music raise and quell!

III

  The * Trumpet's loud clangour
    Excites us to arms,
  With shrill notes of anger,
    And mortal alarms.
  The double double double beat
    Of the thund'ring Drum
Cries: "Hark! the foes come;
Charge, charge, 'tis too late to retreat."

IV

  The soft complaining Flute
  In dying notes discovers
  The woes of hopeless lovers,
Whose dirge is whisper'd by the warbling Lute.

V

  Sharp Violins proclaim
Their jealous pangs, and desperation,
Fury, frantic indignation,
Depth of pains, and height of passion,
  For the fair, disdainful dame.

VI

  But oh! what art can teach,
  What human voice can reach,
The sacred Organ's praise?
  Notes inspiring holy love,
Notes that wing their heav'nly ways
  To mend the choirs above.

VII

*Orpheus could lead the savage race;
And trees unrooted left their place,
Sequacious of the lyre;
But bright * Cecilia rais'd the wonder high'r:
When to her Organ vocal breath was giv'n,
An angel heard, and straight appear'd,
Mistaking earth for heav'n.

GRAND CHORUS

As from the pow'r of sacred lays
The spheres began to move,
And sung the great Creator's praise
To all the blest above;
So, when the last and dreadful hour
This crumbling pageant shall devour,
The Trumpet shall be heard on high.
The dead shall live, the living die,
And * Music shall untune the sky.

[1687]

ALEXANDER'S FEAST

OR, THE POWER OF MUSIC
AN ODE IN HONOUR OF ST. CECILIA'S DAY

I

'Twas at the royal feast, for Persia won
By Philip's warlike son:
Aloft in awful state
The godlike hero sate
On his imperial throne:
His valiant peers were plac'd around;
Their brows with roses and with myrtles bound:
(So should desert in arms be crown'd.)
The lovely Thais, by his side,
Sate like a blooming Eastern bride
In flow'r of youth and beauty's pride.
Happy, happy, happy pair!
None but the brave,
None but the brave,
*None but the brave deserves the fair.

CHORUS

Happy, happy, happy pair!
None but the brave,
None but the brave,
None but the brave deserves the fair.

II

Timotheus, plac'd on high
Amid the tuneful choir,
With flying fingers touch'd the lyre:
The trembling notes ascend the sky,
And heav'nly joys inspire.
*The song began from Jove,
Who left his blissful seats above,
(Such is the pow'r of mighty love.)
A dragon's fiery form belied the god:
Sublime on radiant spires he rode,
When he to fair Olympia press'd;
And while he sought her snowy breast:
Then round her slender waist he curl'd,
And stamp'd an image of himself, a sov'reign of the world.
The list'ning crowd admire the lofty sound;
"A present deity," they shout around;
"A present deity," the vaulted roofs rebound:
With ravish'd ears
The monarch hears,
Assumes the god,
Affects to nod,
And seems to shake the spheres.

CHORUS

With ravish'd ears
The monarch hears,
Assumes the god,
Affects to nod,
And seems to shake the spheres.

III

The praise of Bacchus then the sweet musician sung,
Of Bacchus ever fair and ever young:
The jolly god in triumph comes;
Sound the trumpets; beat the drums;
Flush'd with a purple grace
He shows his honest face:
Now give the hautboys breath; he comes, he comes.
Bacchus, ever fair and young,
Drinking joys did first ordain;
Bacchus' blessings are a treasure,
Drinking is the soldier's pleasure:
Rich the treasure,
Sweet the pleasure,
Sweet is pleasure after pain.

CHORUS

Bacchus' blessings are a treasure,
Drinking is the soldier's pleasure:
Rich the treasure,
Sweet the pleasure,
Sweet is pleasure after pain.

IV

Sooth'd with the sound, the king grew vain;
Fought all his battles o'er again;
And thrice he routed all his foes; and thrice he slew the slain.
The master saw the madness rise;
His glowing cheeks, his ardent eyes;
And, while he heav'n and earth defied,
Chang'd his hand, and check'd his pride.
He chose a mournful Muse,
Soft pity to infuse:
He sung Darius great and good,
By too severe a fate,
Fallen, fallen, fallen, fallen,
Fallen from his high estate,
And welt'ring in his blood;
Deserted, at his utmost need,
By those his former bounty fed;
On the bare earth expos'd he lies,
With not a friend to close his eyes.
With downcast looks the joyless victor sate,
Revolving in his alter'd soul
The various turns of chance below;
And, now and then, a sigh he stole;
And tears began to flow.

CHORUS

Revolving in his alter'd soul
The various turns of chance below;
And, now and then, a sigh he stole;
And tears began to flow.

V

The mighty master smil'd, to see
That love was in the next degree:
'Twas but a kindred sound to move,
For pity melts the mind to love.
Softly sweet, in Lydian measures,
Soon he sooth'd his soul to pleasures.
"War," he sung, "is toil and trouble;
Honour, but an empty bubble;
Never ending, still beginning,
Fighting still, and still destroying:
If the world be worth thy winning,
Think, oh, think it worth enjoying;
Lovely Thais sits beside thee,
Take the good the gods provide thee."
The many rend the skies with loud applause;
So Love was crown'd, but Music won the cause.
The prince, unable to conceal his pain,
Gaz'd on the fair
Who caus'd his care,
And sigh'd and look'd, sigh'd and look'd,
Sigh'd and look'd, and sigh'd again:
At length, with love and wine at once oppress'd,
The vanquish'd victor sunk upon her breast.

CHORUS

The prince, unable to conceal his pain,
Gaz'd on the fair
Who caus'd his care,
And sigh'd and look'd, sigh'd and look'd,
Sigh'd and look'd, and sigh'd again:
At length, with love and wine at once oppress'd,
The vanquish'd victor sunk upon her breast.

VI

Now strike the golden lyre again:
A louder yet, and yet a louder strain.
Break his bands of sleep asunder,
And rouse him, like a rattling peal of thunder.
Hark, hark, the horrid sound
Has rais'd up his head:
As awak'd from the dead,
And amaz'd, he stares around.
"Revenge, revenge!" Timotheus cries,
"See the Furies arise!
See the snakes that they rear,
How they hiss in their hair,
And the sparkles that flash from their eyes!
Behold a ghastly band,
Each a torch in his hand!
Those are Grecian ghosts, that in battle were slain,
And unburied remain
Inglorious on the plain:
Give the vengeance due
To the valiant crew.
Behold how they toss their torches on high,
How they point to the Persian abodes,
And glitt'ring temples of their hostile gods!"
The princes applaud, with a furious joy;
And the king seiz'd a flambeau with zeal to destroy;
Thais led the way,
To light him to his prey,
And, like another Helen, fir'd another Troy.

CHORUS

And the king seiz'd a flambeau with zeal to destroy;
Thais led the way,
To light him to his prey,
And, like another Helen, fir'd another Troy.

VII

Thus, long ago,
Ere heaving bellows learn'd to blow,
While organs yet were mute;
Timotheus, to his breathing flute,
And sounding lyre,
Could swell the soul to rage, or kindle soft desire.
At last, divine Cecilia came,
Inventress of the vocal frame;
*The sweet enthusiast, from her sacred store,
Enlarg'd the former narrow bounds,
And added length to solemn sounds,
With nature's mother wit, and arts unknown before.
Let old Timotheus yield the prize,
Or both divide the crown;
He rais'd a mortal to the skies;
She drew an angel down.

GRAND CHORUS

At last, divine Cecilia came,
Inventress of the vocal frame;
The sweet enthusiast, from her sacred store,
Enlarg'd the former narrow bounds,
And added length to solemn sounds,
With nature's mother wit, and arts unknown before.
Let old Timotheus yield the prize,
Or both divide the crown;
He rais'd a mortal to the skies;
She drew an angel down.

[1697]

TO THE PIOUS MEMORY OF THE ACCOMPLISHED YOUNG LADY, MRS. ANNE KILLIGREW

EXCELLENT IN THE TWO SISTER-ARTS OF POESY AND PAINTING

AN ODE

This poem, like the two preceding, is an irregular Pindaric ode. It was first published in the volume of Anne Killigrew's poems that appeared in 1686, the year after her death. It celebrates the virtues and talents of the gifted daughter of the Reverend Henry Killigrew (himself a dramatist), the niece of the dramatists, Thomas and Henry Killigrew. Written at the height of Dryden's powers, it is a graceful tribute in flowing verse; especially in the fourth stanza it reveals strong personal feeling. As elegy, however, it falls far short of the best. Lyrical gifts were a part of Dryden's many-sided genius, but his diffusion of energy and the spirit of the age were alike unfavourable to their full development.

I

Thou youngest virgin daughter of the skies,
Made in the last promotion of the blest;
Whose palms, new pluck'd from paradise,
In spreading branches more sublimely rise,
Rich with immortal green above the rest:
Whether, adopted to some neighbouring star,
Thou roll'st above us, in thy wand'ring race,
Or, in procession fix'd and regular,
Mov'd with the heavens' majestic pace;
Or, call'd to more superior bliss,
Thou tread'st, with seraphims, the vast abyss—
Whatever happy region is thy place,
Cease thy celestial song a little space;
(Thou wilt have time enough for hymns divine,
Since heav'n's eternal year is thine.)
Hear then a mortal Muse thy praise rehearse,
In no ignoble verse;
But such as thy own voice did practise here,
When thy first fruits of poesy were giv'n,
To make thyself a welcome inmate there;
While yet a young probationer,
And candidate of heav'n.

II

If by traduction came thy mind,
Our wonder is the less to find
A soul so charming from a stock so good;
Thy father was transfus'd into thy blood:
So wert thou born into the tuneful strain,
(An early, rich, and inexhausted vein.)
But if thy pre-existing soul
Was form'd, at first, with myriads more,
It did through all the mighty poets roll,
Who Greek or Latin laurels wore,
And was that Sappho last, which once it was before.
If so, then cease thy flight, O heav'n-born mind!
Thou hast no dross to purge from thy rich ore;
Nor can thy soul a fairer mansion find,
Than was the beauteous frame she left behind:
Return, to fill or mend the choir of thy celestial kind.

III

May we presume to say, that at thy birth
New joy was sprung in heav'n, as well as here on earth?
For sure the milder planets did combine
On thy auspicious horoscope to shine,
And ev'n the most malicious were *in trine.
Thy brother angels at thy birth
Strung each his lyre, and tun'd it high,
That all the people of the sky
Might know a poetess was born on earth.
And then, if ever, mortal ears
Had heard the music of the spheres!
And if no clust'ring *swarm of bees
On thy sweet mouth distill'd their golden dew,
'Twas that such vulgar miracles
Heav'n had not leisure to renew;
For all the blest fraternity of love
Solemniz'd there thy birth, and kept thy holiday above.

IV

O gracious God! how far have we
*Profan'd thy heav'nly gift of poesy!
Made prostitute and profligate the Muse,
Debas'd to each obscene and impious use,
Whose harmony was first ordain'd above
For tongues of angels, and for hymns of love!
O wretched we! why were we hurried down
This lubric and adult'rate age,
(Nay, added fat pollutions of our own,)
T' increase the steaming ordures of the stage?
What can we say t' excuse our second fall?
Let this thy vestal, Heav'n, atone for all:
Her Arethusian stream remains unsoil'd,
Unmix'd with foreign filth, and undefil'd;
Her wit was more than man, her innocence a child!

V

*Art she had none, yet wanted none;
For nature did that want supply:
So rich in treasures of her own,
She might our boasted stores defy:
Such noble vigour did her verse adorn
That it seem'd borrow'd, where 'twas only born.
Her morals too were in her bosom bred,
By great examples daily fed,
What in the best of books, her father's life, she read.
And to be read herself she need not fear;
Each test, and ev'ry light, her Muse will bear,
Though *Epictetus with his lamp were there.
Ev'n love (for love sometimes her Muse express'd)
Was but a lambent flame which play'd about her breast,
Light as the vapours of a morning dream:
So cold herself, whilst she such warmth express'd,
'Twas Cupid bathing in Diana's stream.

VI

Born to the spacious empire of the Nine,
One would have thought she should have been content
To manage well that mighty government;
But what can young ambitious souls confine?
To the next realm she stretch'd her sway,
For Painture near adjoining lay,
A plenteous province, and alluring prey.
A chamber of dependences was fram'd,
(As conquerors will never want pretence,
When arm'd, to justify th' offence,)
And the whole fief in right of poetry she claim'd.
The country open lay without defence;
For poets frequent inroads there had made,
And perfectly could represent
The shape, the face, with ev'ry lineament;
And all the large domains which the Dumb Sister sway'd,
All bow'd beneath her government;
Receiv'd in triumph wheresoe'er she went.
Her pencil drew whate'er her soul design'd,
And oft the happy draught surpass'd the image in her mind.
The sylvan scenes of herds and flocks,
And fruitful plains and barren rocks,
Of shallow brooks that flow'd so clear
The bottom did the top appear;
Of deeper too and ampler floods,
Which, as in mirrors, show'd the woods;
Of lofty trees, with sacred shades,
And *perspectives of pleasant glades,
Where nymphs of brightest form appear,
And shaggy satyrs standing near,
Which them at once admire and fear:
The ruins too of some majestic piece,
Boasting the pow'r of ancient Rome, or Greece,
Whose statues, friezes, columns broken lie,
And, though defac'd, the wonder of the eye:
What nature, art, bold fiction, e'er durst frame,

Her forming hand gave feature to the name.
So strange a concourse ne'er was seen before,
But when the peopled ark the whole creation bore.

VII

The scene then chang'd: with bold erected look
Our martial king the sight with reverence strook;
For, not content t' express his outward part,
Her hand call'd out the image of his heart:
His warlike mind, his soul devoid of fear,
His high-designing thoughts were figur'd there,
As when, by magic, ghosts are made appear.
Our Phœnix queen was portray'd too so bright,
Beauty alone could beauty take so right:
Her dress, her shape, her matchless grace,
Were all observ'd, as well as heav'nly face.
With such a peerless majesty she stands,
As in that day she took the crown from sacred hands;
Before a train of heroines was seen,
In beauty foremost, as in rank the queen.
Thus nothing to her genius was denied,
But like a ball of fire the farther thrown,
Still with a greater blaze she shone,
And her bright soul broke out on ev'ry side.
What next she had design'd, Heaven only knows;
*To such immod'rate growth her conquest rose
That fate alone its progress could oppose.

VIII

Now all those charms, that blooming grace,
The well proportion'd shape, and beauteous face,
Shall never more be seen by mortal eyes:
In earth the much-lamented virgin lies!
Not wit, nor piety could fate prevent;
Nor was the cruel destiny content
To finish all the murder at a blow,
To sweep at once her life and beauty too;
But, like a harden'd felon, took a pride
To work more mischievously slow,
And plunder'd first, and then destroy'd.
Oh double sacrilege on things divine,
To rob the relic, and deface the shrine!
*But thus Orinda died:
Heav'n, by the same disease, did both translate;
As equal were their souls, so equal was their fate.

IX

Meantime her warlike brother on the seas
His waving streamers to the winds displays,
And vows for his return, with vain devotion, pays.
Ah, generous youth, that wish forbear,
The winds too soon will waft thee here!
Slack all thy sails, and fear to come,
Alas, thou know'st not thou art wreck'd at home!
No more shalt thou behold thy sister's face;
Thou hast already had her last embrace.
But look aloft, and if thou kenn'st from far
Among the Pleiads a new-kindled star;
If any sparkles than the rest more bright,
'Tis she that shines in that propitious light.

X

When in mid air the golden trump shall sound,
To raise the nations under ground;
When in *the Valley of Jehosaphat
The judging God shall close the book of fate,
And there the last assizes keep
For those who wake and those who sleep;
When rattling bones together fly
From the four corners of the sky;
When sinews o'er the skeletons are spread,
Those cloth'd with flesh, and life inspires the dead;
The sacred poets first shall hear the sound,
And foremost from the tomb shall bound,
For they are cover'd with the lightest ground;
And straight, with inborn vigour, on the wing,
Like mounting larks, to the new morning sing.
There thou, sweet saint, before the choir shalt go,
As harbinger of heav'n, the way to show,
The way which thou so well hast learn'd below.

[1686]

EPISTLES

As their subject matter and form indicate, these epistles are not personal letters in verse but rather complimentary epistles, usually prefixed to the work of the authors to whom they are addressed. They are at once personal appreciations, and serious treatments of important subjects; they are therefore appropriately written in the heroic couplet. The two examples here given illustrate respectively the work of the first and the last decades of Dryden's literary career.

TO MY HONOURED FRIEND, DR. CHARLETON,

ON HIS LEARNED AND USEFUL WORKS; AND MORE PARTICULARLY THIS OF STONEHENGE, BY HIM RESTORED TO THE TRUE FOUNDERS

To my Honoured Friend, Dr. Charleton was published in 1663 with the latter's *Chorea Gigantum,* an archæological study which attempts to prove that Stonehenge was built by the Danes. Dryden's epistle is a striking illustration of his interest and that of his age in the new science.

*The longest tyranny that ever sway'd
Was that wherein our ancestors betray'd
Their free-born reason to the Stagirite,
And made his torch their universal light.
So truth, while only one supplied the state,
Grew scarce, and dear, and yet sophisticate;
Until 'twas bought, like emp'ric wares or charms,
Hard words seal'd up with Aristotle's arms.
Columbus was the first that shook his throne,
And found a temp'rate in a torrid zone:
The fev'rish air fann'd by a cooling breeze,
The fruitful vales set round with shady trees;
And guiltless men, who danc'd away their time,
Fresh as their groves, and happy as their clime.
Had we still paid that homage to a name
Which only God and nature justly claim,
The western seas had been our utmost bound,
Where poets still might dream the sun was drown'd:
And all the stars that shine in southern skies
Had been admir'd by none but savage eyes.
Among th' asserters of free reason's claim,
Th' English are not the least in worth or fame.
The world to *Bacon does not only owe
Its present knowledge, but its future too.
*Gilbert shall live, till loadstones cease to draw,
Or British fleets the boundless ocean awe;
And noble *Boyle, not less in nature seen,
Than his great brother read in states and men.
The circling streams, once thought but pools of blood
(Whether life's fuel, or the body's food)
From dark oblivion *Harvey's name shall save;
While *Ent keeps all the honour that he gave.
Nor are you, learned friend, the least renown'd;
Whose fame, not circumscrib'd with English ground,
Flies like the nimble journeys of the light;
And is, like that, unspent too in its flight.
Whatever truths have been, by art or chance,
Redeem'd from error, or from ignorance,
Thin in their authors, like rich veins of ore,
Your works unite, and still discover more.
Such is the healing virtue of your pen,
To perfect cures on books, as well as men.
Nor is this work the least: you well may give
To men new vigour, who make stones to live.
Through you, the Danes, their short dominion lost,
A longer conquest than the Saxons boast.
*Stonehenge, once thought a temple, you have found
A throne, where kings, our earthly gods, were crown'd;
Where by their wond'ring subjects they were seen,
Joy'd with their stature, and their princely mien.
Our sovereign here above the rest might stand,
And here be chose again to rule the land.
These ruins shelter'd once his sacred head,
Then when from *Wor'ster's fatal field he fled;
Watch'd by the genius of this royal place,
And mighty visions of the Danish race.
His refuge then was for a temple shown;
But, he restor'd, 'tis now become a throne.

[1663]

TO MY DEAR FRIEND, MR. CONGREVE, ON HIS COMEDY CALLED "THE DOUBLE-DEALER"

This epistle was prefixed to the first edition of William Congreve's comedy, *The Double-Dealer,* in 1694. Its importance lies in the statement of Dryden's mature views on the relations between the drama of his age and that of the Elizabethans, his critical insight in perceiving Congreve's genius before the latter had written his most important plays, and his generous appreciation of a young aspirant for literary fame. Seldom in the history of literature has there been such a generous reception of a young rival by an acknowledged dean of poets.

Well then, the promis'd hour is come at last;
The present age of wit obscures the past:
Strong were our sires, and as they fought they writ,
Conqu'ring with force of arms, and dint of wit:
Theirs was the giant race, before the flood;
And thus, when Charles return'd, our empire stood.
Like *Janus he the stubborn soil manur'd,
With rules of husbandry the rankness cur'd;
Tam'd us to manners, when the stage was rude;
And boist'rous English wit with art indued.
Our age was cultivated thus at length,
But what we gain'd in skill we lost in strength.
Our builders were with want of genius curs'd;
*The second temple was not like the first:
Till you, the best *Vitruvius, come at length;
Our beauties equal, but excel our strength.
Firm Doric pillars found your solid base;
The fair Corinthian crowns the higher space:
Thus all below is strength, and all above is grace.
In easy dialogue is Fletcher's praise;
He mov'd the mind, but had no power to raise.
Great Jonson did by strength of judgment please;
Yet, doubling Fletcher's force, he wants his ease.
In differing talents both adorn'd their age;
One for the study, t'other for the stage:
But both to Congreve justly shall submit,
One match'd in judgment, both o'ermatch'd in wit.
In him all beauties of this age we see,
*Etherege his courtship, Southerne's purity,
The satire, wit, and strength of manly Wycherley.
All this in blooming youth you have achiev'd,
Nor are your foil'd contemporaries griev'd.
So much the sweetness of your manners move,
We cannot envy you, because we love.
*Fabius might joy in Scipio, when he saw
A beardless consul made against the law;
And join his suffrage to the votes of Rome,
Though he with Hannibal was overcome.
Thus *old Romano bow'd to Raphael's fame,
And scholar to the youth he taught became.
Oh, that *your brows my laurel had sustain'd;
Well had I been depos'd, if you had reign'd!
The father had descended for the son;
For only you are lineal to the throne.
Thus, when the state one Edward did depose,
A *greater Edward in his room arose.
But now, not I, but poetry is curs'd;
For Tom the Second reigns like Tom the First.
But let 'em not mistake *my patron's part,
Nor call his charity their own desert.
Yet this I prophesy: thou shalt be seen
(Though with some short parenthesis between)
High on the throne of wit; and, seated there,
Not mine — that's little — but thy laurel wear.
Thy first attempt an early promise made;
That early promise this has more than paid.
So bold, yet so judiciously you dare,
That your least praise is to be regular.
Time, place, and action may with pains be wrought;
But *genius must be born, and never can be taught.
This is your portion; this your native store;
Heav'n, that but once was prodigal before,
To Shakespeare gave as much; she could not give him more.
Maintain your post: that's all the fame you need;
For 'tis impossible you should proceed.
Already I am worn with cares and age,
And just abandoning th' ungrateful stage;
Unprofitably kept at Heav'n's expense,
I live a rent-charge on his providence:
But you, whom ev'ry Muse and Grace adorn,
Whom I foresee to better fortune born,
*Be kind to my remains; and oh, defend,
Against your judgment, your departed friend!
Let not th' insulting foe my fame pursue,
But shade those laurels which descend to you;
And take for tribute what these lines express:
You merit more; nor could my love do less.

[1694]

PROLOGUES AND EPILOGUES

No part of Dryden's work shows more wit than these prologues and epilogues that the poet wrote for his own and some of his friends' plays, and no part shows nicer adaptation of means to ends. Intended as they were to catch the attention at the beginning of a play and to send the audience home amused, if not satisfied, they were perforce direct and forthright. While the essays, dedications, and prefaces that make up Dryden's prose criticism contain subtler thoughts and more learned appeals to the judicious readers, these prologues and epilogues are none the less significant in the critical history of the time and are indispensable to an understanding of Dryden's critical theory and practice. In reading them we come closer than in any other documents to the gossip of the greenroom and the talk of the coffee-houses, where public opinion was formulated and plays were approved or damned. Only a few of the prologues and epilogues that speak of poetic technique and critical judgment are here given.

EPILOGUE TO "THE WILD GALLANT," *REVIVED

Of all dramatic writing, comic wit,
As 'tis the best, so 'tis most hard to hit,
For it lies all in level to the eye,
Where all may judge, and each defect may spy.
*Humour is that which every day we meet,
And therefore known as every public street;
In which, if e'er the poet go astray,
You all can point, 'twas there he lost his way.
But, what's so common, to make pleasant too,
Is more than any wit can always do.
For 'tis like Turks, with hen and rice to treat;
To make regalios out of common meat.
But, in your diet, you grow savages:
Nothing but human flesh your taste can please;
And, as their feasts with slaughter'd slaves began,
So you, at each new play, must have a man.
Hither you come, as to see *prizes fought;
If no blood's drawn, you cry the prize is naught.
But fools grow wary now; and, when they see
A poet eyeing round the company,
Straight each man for himself begins to doubt;
They shrink like seamen when a press comes out.
Few of 'em will be found for public use,
Except you charge an oaf upon each house,
Like the trainbands, and every man engage
For a sufficient fool, to serve the stage.
And when, with much ado, you get him there,
Where he in all his glory should appear,
Your poets make him such rare things to say,
That he's more wit than any man i' th' play;
But of so ill a mingle with the rest,
As when a parrot's taught to break a jest.
Thus, aiming to be fine, they make a show,
As tawdry squires in country churches do.
Things well consider'd, 'tis so hard to make
A comedy which should the knowing take,
That our dull poet, in despair to please,
Does humbly beg, by me, his *writ of ease.
'Tis a land tax, which he's too poor to pay;
You therefore must some other impost lay.
Would you but change, for serious plot and verse
This motley garniture of fool and farce,
Nor scorn a mode, because 'tis taught at home,
Which does, like *vests, our gravity become,
Our poet yields you should this play refuse:
As tradesmen, by the change of fashions, lose,
With some content, their fripperies of France,
In hope it may their staple trade advance.

[1667]

PROLOGUE TO "THE TEMPEST

OR, THE ENCHANTED ISLAND"

An adaptation of Shakespeare's *The Tempest* by Dryden and Sir William Davenant was produced in 1667. This prologue is important because of its appreciation of Shakespeare. Compare the remarks in *An Essay of Dramatic Poesy*, published the following year.

As, when a tree's cut down, the secret root
Lives under ground, and thence new branches shoot;
So from old Shakespeare's honour'd dust, this day
Springs up and buds a new reviving play:
Shakespeare, who (taught by none) did first impart
To Fletcher wit, to labouring Jonson art.
He, monarch-like, gave those, his subjects, law;
And is that nature which they paint and draw;
Fletcher reach'd that which on his heights did grow,
Whilst Jonson crept, and gather'd all below.
This did his love, and this his mirth digest:
One imitates him most, the other best.

If they have since outwrit all other men,
'Tis with the drops which fell from Shakespeare's pen.
The storm which vanish'd on the neighb'ring shore,
Was taught by Shakespeare's *Tempest* first to roar.
That innocence and beauty which did smile
In Fletcher, grew on this *Enchanted Isle.*
But Shakespeare's magic could not copied be;
Within that circle none durst walk but he.
I must confess 'twas bold, nor would you now
That liberty to vulgar wits allow,
Which works by magic supernatural things;
But Shakespeare's pow'r is sacred as a king's.
Those legends from old priesthood were receiv'd,
And he then writ, as people then believ'd.
But if for Shakespeare we your grace implore,
We for our theatre shall want it more,
Who by our dearth of youths are forc'd t' employ
One of our women to present a boy;
And that's a transformation, you will say,
Exceeding all the magic in the play.
Let none expect in the last act to find
Her sex transform'd from man to womankind.
Whate'er she was before the play began,
All you shall see of her is perfect man.
Or if your fancy will be farther led
To find her woman, it must be abed.

[1670]

EPILOGUE

TO "THE CONQUEST OF GRANADA BY THE SPANIARDS," THE SECOND PART

This play was first acted in 1670 or 1671. The tone of the epilogue is in striking contrast to that of the prologue to *The Tempest.* While Dryden was not always entirely consistent in his criticism of the Elizabethans (see introductory note to *An Essay of Dramatic Poesy*), it must be remembered that he is here speaking of one particular thing, the improvement in the "wit" of discourse in his own age. There can be no doubt that the language had been refined and developed during the last generation and that the stage had reflected the changes. Dryden sincerely admired the Elizabethans, but he did not worship them. Even Shakespeare he regarded as a fellow-craftsman who had faults to be avoided as well as merits that often defied imitation. In 1672 Dryden published his *Defence of the Epilogue; or an Essay on the Dramatic Poetry of the Last Age,* in which he made this point of view perfectly clear. Here he said: "For we live in an age so sceptical, that as it determines little, so it takes nothing from antiquity on trust; and I profess to have no other ambition in this *Essay*, than that poetry may not go backward, when all other arts and sciences are advancing."

He sums up his argument thus: "To conclude all, let us render to our predecessors what is their due, without confining ourselves to a servile imitation of all they writ; and, without assuming to ourselves the title of better poets, let us ascribe to the gallantry and civility of our age the advantage which we have above them, and to our knowledge of the customs and manner of it the happiness we have to please beyond them."

They who have best succeeded on the stage
Have still conform'd their genius to their age.
Thus Jonson did mechanic humour show,
When men were dull, and conversation low.
Then comedy was faultless, but 'twas coarse:
*Cobb's tankard was a jest, and Otter's horse.
And, as their comedy, their love was mean;
Except, by chance, in some one labour'd scene
Which must atone for an ill written play.
They rose, but at their height could seldom stay.
Fame then was cheap, and the first comer sped;
And they have kept it since, by being dead.
But, were they now to write, when critics weigh
Each line, and ev'ry word, throughout a play,
None of 'em, no, not Jonson in his height,
Could pass, without allowing grains for weight.
Think it not envy that these truths are told;
Our poet's not malicious, though he's bold.
'Tis not to brand 'em that their faults are shown,
But, by their errors, to excuse his own.
If love and honour now are higher rais'd,
'Tis not the poet, but the age is prais'd.
Wit's now arriv'd to a more high degree;
Our native language more refin'd and free.
Our ladies and our men now speak more wit
In conversation, than those poets writ.
Then, one of these is, consequently, true:
That what this poet writes comes short of you,
And imitates you ill, (which most he fears,)
Or else his writing is not worse than theirs.
Yet, though you judge (as sure the critics will)
That some before him writ with greater skill,
In this one praise he has their fame surpass'd,
To please an age more gallant than the last.

[1672]

PROLOGUE TO "AURENG-ZEBE"

In this prologue to the last of his heroic plays, which was produced in 1675, Dryden announced his change of opinion on the use of rhyme in serious drama. About three years later he put into practice the opinions here stated when *All for Love* was produced.

Our author, by experience, finds it true,
'Tis much more hard to please himself than you;
And out of no feign'd modesty, this day
Damns his laborious trifle of a play:
Not that it's worse than what before he writ,
But he has now another taste of wit;
And, to confess a truth, (though out of time,)
Grows weary of his long-lov'd mistress, Rhyme.
Passion's too fierce to be in fetters bound,
And nature flies him like enchanted ground.
What verse can do, he has perform'd in this,
Which he presumes the most correct of his;
But spite of all his pride, a secret shame
Invades his breast at Shakespeare's sacred name:
Aw'd when he hears his godlike Romans rage,
He, in a just despair, would quit the stage;
And to an age less polish'd, more unskill'd,
Does, with disdain, the foremost honours yield.
As with the greater dead he dares not strive,
He would not match his verse with those who live:
Let him retire, betwixt two ages cast,
The first of this, and hindmost of the last.
A losing gamester, let him sneak away;
He bears no ready money from the play.
The fate which governs poets thought it fit
He should not raise his fortunes by his wit.
The clergy thrive, and the litigious bar;
Dull heroes fatten with the spoils of war:
All southern vices, Heav'n be prais'd, are here;
But wit's a luxury you think too dear.
When you to cultivate the plant are loath,
'Tis a shrewd sign 'twas never of your growth;
And wit in northern climates will not blow,
Except, like orange trees, 'tis hous'd from snow.
There needs no care to * put a playhouse down,
'Tis the most desert place of all the town:
We and our neighbours, to speak proudly, are
Like monarchs, ruin'd with expensive war;
While, like wise English, unconcern'd you sit,
And see us play the tragedy of wit.

[1676]

From AN ESSAY OF DRAMATIC POESY

An Essay of Dramatic Poesy was first published in 1668 and was republished in 1684 and 1693. Thus it was written during the early part of its author's literary career and was republished in his middle and later years. In the original dedication to Charles, Lord Buckhurst (later, Earl of Dorset), Dryden wrote:

"I confess I find many things in this discourse which I do not now approve; my judgment being a little altered since the writing of it; but whether for the better or the worse, I know not: neither is it much material, in an essay where all I have said is problematical."

In the edition of 1684 he changed the wording to read "my judgment being not a little altered," but he made only minor alterations in the text. (The present text follows the later edition.) It is avowedly an *essay*, which in the seventeenth century meant something even less complete and final than it does today. It differed from most of Dryden's critical works in being a separate publication rather than a dedication or preface to a volume of poetry; consequently its treatment was unaffected by the immediate need of explaining or defending its author's practice in an accompanying work.

In form, *An Essay of Dramatic Poesy* is a dialogue after the Platonic manner, attempting to get at truth by presenting various conflicting points of view. The introduction is highly artistic: it presents the scene vividly and introduces the critical discussion naturally. The brief conclusion returns to the method of the introduction and rounds out the whole. The *Essay* represents the conversation of gentlemen and not the controversies of pedantic scholars, a truly classical ideal and one which was in some measure embodied in the life of an age when poetry and criticism were the concerns of *un honnête homme.*

In 1692, Dryden, who was then drawing near the close of his life, wrote *A Discourse Concerning the Original and Progress of Satire* in which he recalled this *Essay*:

"When I was myself in the rudiments of my poetry,... when I was drawing the outlines of an art without any living master to instruct me in it; an art that had been better praised than studied here in England, wherein Shakespeare, who created the stage among us, had rather written happily, than knowingly and justly, and Jonson, who, by studying Horace, had been acquainted with the rules, yet seemed to envy to posterity that knowledge, and, like an inventor of some useful art, to make a monopoly of his learning; when thus, as I may say, before the use of the loadstone, or knowledge of the compass, I was sailing in a vast ocean, without other help than the pole-star of the ancients, and the rules of the French stage among the moderns, which are extremely different from ours, by reason of their opposite taste; yet even then, I had the presumption to dedicate to your Lordship, a very unfinished piece, I must confess, and which only can be excused by the little experience of the author, and the modesty of the title *An Essay*."

In these words Dryden presents his critical problem as it appeared not only at the beginning of his career but, in some measure, throughout his life. Literary criticism in France at this time was simple: into a medieval chaos had come the fiat of Aristotle, and straightway there emerged the poetry of the great age. But in England, where a splendid outburst of creative activity had preceded the general knowledge of the classical rules, the situation was much more complex: on the one hand stood the work of Shakespeare and the other Elizabethans, undoubtedly great; on the other hand stood the rules of classical criticism and the models of classical poetry. How could the two be reconciled? To appreciate Elizabethan literature and at the same time to hold a theory of poetry at variance with it was not easy. Recognition of this fact serves to explain a good deal of the apparent inconsistency of Dryden and also helps us to estimate at its true worth his critical achievement. In the attempt to hold to opposite poles of poetic truth Dryden developed a balanced and a tempered judgment, as far from mere dogmatism as it was from colourless neutrality, which made him the first great English critic.

TO THE READER

The drift of the ensuing discourse was chiefly to vindicate the honour of our English writers from the censure of those who unjustly prefer the French before them. This I intimate, lest any should think me so exceedingly vain as to teach others an art which they understand much better than myself. But if this incorrect essay, written in the country without the help of books or advice of friends, shall find any acceptance in the world, I promise to myself a better success of the *second part, wherein I shall more fully treat of the virtues and faults of the English poets who have written either in this, the epic, or the lyric way.

AN ESSAY OF DRAMATIC POESY

It was that *memorable day, in the first summer of the late war, when our navy engaged the Dutch; a day wherein the two most mighty and best appointed fleets which any age had ever seen, disputed the command of the greater half of the globe, the commerce of nations, and the riches of the universe. While these vast floating bodies, on either side, moved against each other in parallel lines, and our countrymen, under the happy conduct of his Royal Highness, went breaking, by little and little, into the line of the enemies; the noise of the cannon from both navies reached our ears about the city, so that all men being alarmed with it, and in a dreadful suspense of the event, which they knew was then deciding, every one went following the sound as his fancy led him; and leaving the town almost empty, some took towards the park, some cross the river, others down it; all seeking the noise in the depth of silence.

Among the rest, it was the fortune of *Eugenius, Crites, Lisideius, and Neander to be in company together; three of them persons whom their wit and quality have made known to all the town; and whom I have chose to hide under these borrowed names, that they may not suffer by so ill a relation as I am going to make of their discourse.

2. Taking then a barge, which a servant of Lisideius had provided for them, they made haste to *shoot the bridge, and left behind them that great fall of waters which hindered them from hearing what they desired: after which, having disengaged themselves from many vessels which rode at anchor in the Thames, and almost blocked up the passage towards Greenwich, they ordered the watermen to let fall their oars more gently; and then, every one favouring his own curiosity with a strict silence, it was not long ere they perceived the air to break about them like the noise of distant thunder, or of swallows in a chimney: those little undulations of sound, though almost vanishing before they reached them, yet still seeming to retain somewhat of their first horror, which they had betwixt the fleets.

After they had attentively listened till such time as the sound by little and little went from them, Eugenius, lifting up his head, and taking notice of it, was the first who congratulated to the rest that happy omen of our nation's victory: adding, that we had but this to desire in confirmation of it, that we might hear no more of that noise, which was now leaving the English coast. When the rest had concurred in the same opinion, Crites, a person of a sharp judgment, and somewhat too delicate a taste in wit, which the world have mistaken in him for ill-nature, said, smiling to us, that if the concernment of this battle had not been so exceeding great, he could scarce have wished the victory at the price he knew he must pay for it, in being subject to the reading and hearing of so many ill verses as he was sure would be made on that subject. Adding, that no argument could scape some of those eternal rhymers, who watch a battle with more diligence than the ravens and birds of prey; and the worst of them surest to be first in upon the quarry: while the better able, either out of modesty writ not at all, or set that due value upon their poems, as to let them be often desired and long expected. "There are some of those impertinent people of whom you speak," answered Lisideius, "who to my knowledge are already so provided, either way, that they can produce not only a panegyric upon the victory, but, if need be, a funeral elegy on the duke; wherein, after they have crowned his valour with many laurels, they will at last deplore the odds under which he fell, concluding that his courage deserved a better destiny." All the company smiled at the conceit of Lisideius; but Crites, more eager than before, began to make particular exceptions against some writers, and said the public magistrate ought to send betimes to forbid them; and that it concerned the peace and quiet of all honest people that ill poets should be as well silenced as seditious preachers. "In my opinion," replied Eugenius, "you pursue your point too far; for as to my own particular, I am so great a lover of poesy that I could wish them all rewarded who attempt but to do well; at least, I would not have them worse used than one of their brethren was by Sylla the Dictator: — **Quem in concione vidimus* (says Tully), *cum ei libellum malus poeta de populo subjecisset, quod epigramma in eum fecisset tantummodo alternis versibus longiusculis, statim ex iis rebus quas tunc vendebat jubere ei præmium tribui, sub ea conditione ne quid postea scriberet.*" "I could wish with all my heart," replied Crites, "that many whom we know were as bountifully thanked upon the same condition, — that they would never trouble us again. For amongst others, I have a mortal apprehension of * two poets, whom this victory, with the help of both her wings, will never be able to escape." "'Tis easy to guess whom you intend," said Lisideius; "and without naming them, I ask you, if one of them does not perpetually pay us with * clenches upon words, and a certain clownish kind of raillery? if now and then he does not offer at a * catachresis or Clevelandism, wresting and torturing a word into another meaning: in fine, if he be not one of those whom the French would call * *un mauvais buffon*; one who is so much a well-willer to the satire that he intends at least to spare no man; and though he cannot strike a blow to hurt any, yet he ought to be punished for the malice of the action, as our witches are justly hanged, because they think themselves to be such; and suffer deservedly for believing they did mischief, because they meant it." "You have described him," said Crites, "so exactly that I am afraid to come after you with my other extremity of poetry. He is one of those who, having had some advantage of education and converse, knows better than the other what a poet should be, but puts it into practice more unluckily than any man; his style and matter are everywhere alike: he is the most calm, peaceable writer you ever read: he never disquiets your passions with the least concernment, but still leaves you in as even a temper as he found you; he is * a very Leveller in poetry: he creeps along with ten little words in every line, and helps out his numbers with *for to*, and *unto*, and all the pretty expletives he can find, till he drags them to the end of another line; while the sense is left tired halfway behind it: he doubly starves all his verses, first for want of thought, and then of expression; his poetry neither has wit in it, nor seems to have it; like him in Martial:

> **Pauper videri Cinna vult, et est pauper.*

"He affects plainness, to cover his want of imagination: when he writes the serious way, the highest flight of his fancy is some miserable antithesis, or seeming contradiction; and in the comic he is still reaching at some thin conceit, the ghost of a jest, and that too flies before him, never to be caught; these swallows which we see before us on the Thames are the just resemblance of his wit: you may observe how near the water they stoop, how many proffers they make to dip, and yet how seldom they touch it; and when they do, 'tis but the surface: they skim over it but to catch a gnat, and then mount into the air and leave it."

3. "Well, gentlemen," said Eugenius, "you may speak your pleasure of these authors; but though I and some few more about the town may give you a peaceable hearing, yet assure yourselves, there are multitudes who would think you malicious and them injured: especially him whom you first described; he is *the very Withers of the City: they have bought more editions of his works than would serve to lay under all their pies at the lord mayor's Christmas. When his famous poem first came out in the year 1660, I have seen them reading it in the midst of 'Change time; nay so vehement they were at it, that they lost their bargain by the candles' ends; but what will you say if he has been received amongst great persons? I can assure you he is, this day, the envy of one who is lord in the art of quibbling, and who does not take it well that any man should intrude so far into his province." "All I would wish," replied Crites, "is, that they who love his writings, may still admire him, and his fellow poet: **Qui Bavium non odit*, etc., is curse sufficient." "And farther," added Lisideius, "I believe there is no man who writes well, but would think he had hard measure if their admirers should praise anything of his: **Nam quos contemnimus, eorum quoque laudes contemnimus*." "There are so few who write well in this age," says Crites, "that methinks any praises should be welcome; they neither rise to the dignity of the last age, nor to any of the ancients: and we may cry out of the writers of this time, with more reason than Petronius of his, *Pace vestra liceat dixisse, primi omnium eloquentiam perdidistis:* you have debauched the true old poetry so far, that nature, which is the soul of it, is not in any of your writings."

4. "If your quarrel," said Eugenius, "to those who now write, be grounded only on your reverence to antiquity, there is no man more ready to adore those great Greeks and Romans than I am: but on the other side, I cannot think so contemptibly of the age in which I live, or so dishonourably of my own country, as not to judge we equal the ancients in most kinds of poesy, and in some surpass them; neither know I any reason why I may not be as zealous for the reputation of our age as we find the ancients themselves were in reference to those who lived before them. For you hear your Horace saying:

> **Indignor quidquam reprehendi, non quia crasse*
> *Compositum, illepidеve putetur, sed quia nuper.*

And after,

> **Si meliora dies, ut vina, poemata reddit,*
> *Scire velim, pretium chartis quotus arroget annus?*

"But I see I am engaging in a wide dispute, where the arguments are not like to reach close on either side; for poesy is of so large an extent, and so many both of the ancients and moderns have done well in all kinds of it, that in citing one against the other, we shall take up more time this evening than each man's occasions will allow him: therefore I would ask Crites to what part of poesy he would confine his arguments, and whether he would defend the general cause of the ancients against the moderns, or oppose any age of the moderns against this of ours?"

5. Crites, a little while considering upon this demand, told Eugenius, that if he pleased, he would limit their dispute to dramatic poesy; in which he thought it not difficult to prove, either that the ancients were superior to the moderns, or the last age to this of ours.

Eugenius was somewhat surprised when he heard Crites make choice of that subject. "For aught I see," said he, "I have undertaken a harder province than I imagined; for though I never judged the plays of the Greek or Roman poets comparable to ours, yet, on the other side, those we now see acted come short of many which were written in the last age: but my comfort is, if we are o'ercome, it will be only by our own countrymen: and if we yield to them in this one part of poesy, we more surpass them in all the other: for in the epic or lyric way, it will be hard for them to show us one such amongst them, as we have many now living, or who lately were: they can produce nothing so courtly writ, or which expresses so much the conversation of a gentleman, as Sir John Suckling; nothing so even, sweet, and flowing as Mr. Waller; nothing so majestic, so correct, as Sir John Denham; nothing so elevated, so copious, and full of spirit as Mr. Cowley; as for the Italian, French, and Spanish plays, I can make it evident that those who now write surpass them; and that the drama is wholly ours."

* All of them were thus far of Eugenius his opinion that the sweetness of English verse was never understood or practised by our fathers; even Crites himself did not much oppose it: and every one was willing to acknowledge how much our poesy is improved by the happiness of some writers yet living; who first taught us to mould our thoughts into easy and significant words, to retrench the superfluities of expression, and to make our rhyme so properly a part of the verse that it should never mislead the sense, but itself be led and governed by it.

6. Eugenius was going to continue this discourse, when Lisideius told him that it was necessary, before they proceeded further, to take a standing measure of their controversy; for how was it possible to be decided who writ the best plays, before we know what a play should be? But, this once agreed on by both parties, each might have recourse to it, either to prove his own advantages, or to discover the failings of his adversary.

He had no sooner said this, but all desired the favour of him to give the definition of a play; and they were the more importunate, because neither Aristotle, nor Horace, nor any other who had writ of that subject had ever done it.

Lisideius, after some modest denials, at last confessed he had a rude notion of it; indeed, rather a description than a definition; but which served to guide him in his private thoughts, when he was to make a judgment of what others writ: that he conceived a play ought to be, *a just and lively image of human nature, representing its passions and humours, and the changes of fortune to which it is subject, for the delight and instruction of mankind.*

This definition, though Crites raised a logical objection against it: that it was only * *a genere et fine*, and so not altogether perfect, was yet well received by the rest: and after they had given order to the watermen to turn their barge, and row softly, that they might take the cool of the evening in their return, Crites, being desired by the company to begin, spoke on behalf of the ancients, in this manner:

"If confidence presage a victory, Eugenius, in his own opinion, has already triumphed over the ancients: nothing seems more easy to him than to overcome those whom it is our greatest praise to have imitated well; for we do not only build upon their foundations, but by their models. Dramatic poesy had time enough, reckoning from Thespis (who first invented it) to Aristophanes, to be born, to grow up, and to flourish in maturity. It has been observed of arts and sciences, that in one and the same century they have arrived to great perfection; and no wonder, since every age has a kind of universal genius, which inclines those that live in it to some particular studies: the work then, being pushed on by many hands, must of necessity go forward.

"Is it not evident, in these last hundred years, when the study of philosophy has been the business of all the virtuosi in Christendom, that almost a new nature has been revealed to us? That more errors of the school have been detected, more useful experiments in philosophy have been made, more noble secrets in optics, medicine, anatomy, astronomy, discovered, than in all * those credulous and doting ages from Aristotle to us? — so true it is, that nothing spreads more fast than science, when rightly and generally cultivated.

"Add to this, the more than common emulation that was in those times of writing well; which though it be found in all ages and all persons that pretend to the same reputation, yet poesy, being then in more esteem than now it is, had greater honours decreed to the professors of it, and consequently the rivalship was more high between them; they had judges ordained to decide their merit, and prizes to reward it; and historians have been diligent to record of Æschylus, Euripides, Sophocles, Lycophron, and the rest of them, both who they were that vanquished in these wars of the theatre, and how often they were crowned: while the Asian kings and Grecian commonwealths scarce afforded them a nobler subject than the unmanly luxuries of a debauched court, or giddy intrigues of a factious city. *Alit æmulatio ingenia* (says Paterculus), *et nunc invidia, nunc admiratio incitationem accendit:* emulation is the spur of wit; and sometimes envy, sometimes admiration, quickens our endeavours.

"But now, since the rewards of honour are taken away, that virtuous emulation is turned into direct malice; yet so slothful that it contents itself to condemn and cry down others, without attempting to do better: 'tis a reputation too unprofitable, to take the necessary pains for it; yet, wishing they had it, that desire is incitement enough to hinder others from it. And this, in short, Eugenius, is the reason why you have now so few good poets, and so many severe judges. Certainly, to imitate the ancients well, much labour and long study is required; which pains, I have already shown, our poets would want encouragement to take, if yet they had ability to go through the work. Those ancients have been faithful imitators and wise observers of that nature which is so torn and ill represented in our plays; they have handed down to us a perfect resemblance of her; which we, like ill copiers, neglecting to look on, have rendered monstrous, and disfigured. But, that you may know how much you are indebted to those your masters, and be ashamed to have so ill requited them, I must remember you that all the rules by which we practise the drama at this day (either such as relate to the justness and symmetry of the plot, or the episodical ornaments, such as descriptions, narrations, and other beauties, which are not essential to the play), were delivered to us from the observations which Aristotle made, of those poets who either lived before him or were his contemporaries: we have added nothing of our own, except we have the confidence to say our wit is better; of which, none boast in this our age, but such as understand not theirs. Of that book which Aristotle has left us, *περὶ τῆς Ποιητικῆς, Horace his *Art of Poetry* is an excellent comment, and, I believe, restores to us that Second Book of his concerning *Comedy*, which is wanting in him.

"Out of these two have been extracted the famous Rules, which the French call *Des Trois Unités*, or, the Three Unities, which ought to be observed in every regular play; namely, of Time, Place, and Action.

"The Unity of Time they comprehend in twenty-four hours, the compass of a natural day, or as near as it can be contrived; and the reason of it is obvious to every one, — that the time of the feigned action, or fable of the play, should be proportioned as near as can be to the duration of that time in which it is represented: since, therefore, all plays are acted on the theatre in a space of time much within the compass of twenty-four hours, that play is to be thought the nearest imitation of nature, whose plot or action is confined within that time; and, by the same rule which concludes this general proportion of time, it follows that all the parts of it are (as near as may be) to be equally subdivided; namely, that one act take not up the supposed time of half a day, which is out of proportion to the rest; since the other four are then to be straitened within the compass of the remaining half: for it is unnatural that one act, which being spoke or written is not longer than the rest, should be supposed longer by the audience; 'tis therefore the poet's duty, to take care that no act should be imagined to exceed the time in which it is represented on the stage; and that the intervals and inequalities of time be supposed to fall out between the acts.

"This rule of time, how well it has been observed by the ancients, most of their plays will witness; you see them in their tragedies (wherein to follow this rule is certainly most difficult), from the very beginning of their plays, falling close into that part of the story which they intend for the action or principal object of it, leaving the former part to be delivered by narration: so that they set the audience, as it were, at the post where the race is to be concluded; and, saving them the tedious expectation of seeing the poet set out and ride the beginning of the course, they suffer you not to behold him, till he is in sight of the goal, and just upon you.

"For the Second Unity, which is that of Place, the ancients meant by it, that the scene ought to be continued through the play, in the same place where it was laid in the beginning: for, the stage on which it is represented being but one and the same place, it is unnatural to conceive it many, — and those far distant from one another. I will not deny but, by the variation of painted scenes, the fancy, which in these cases will contribute to its own deceit, may sometimes imagine it several places, with some appearance of probability; yet it still carries the greater likelihood of truth if those places be supposed so near each other as in the same town or city; which may all be comprehended under the larger denomination of one place; for a greater distance will bear no proportion to the shortness of time which is allotted in the acting, to pass from one of them to another; for the observation of this, next to the ancients, the French are to be most commended. They tie themselves so strictly to the Unity of Place that you never see in any of their plays a scene changed in the middle of an act: if the act begins in a garden, a street, or chamber, 'tis ended in the same place; and that you may know it to be the same, the stage is so supplied with persons that it is never empty all the time: he who enters second, has business with him who was on before; and before the second quits the stage, a third appears who has business with him. This Corneille calls *la liaison des scènes*, the continuity or joining of the scenes; and 'tis a good mark of a well-contrived play, when all the persons are known to each other, and every one of them has some affairs with all the rest.

"As for the Third Unity, which is that of Action, the ancients meant no other by it than what the logicians do by their *finis*, the end or scope of any action; that which is the first in intention, and last in execution: now the poet is to aim at one great and complete action, to the carrying on of which all things in his play, even the very obstacles, are to be subservient; and the reason of this is as evident as any of the former.

For two actions, equally laboured and driven on by the writer, would destroy the unity of the poem; it would be no longer one play, but two: not but that there may be many actions in a play, as Ben Jonson has observed in his *Discoveries*; but they must be all subservient to the great one, which our language happily expresses in the name of *under-plots*: such as in Terence's *Eunuch* is the difference and reconcilement of Thais and Phædria, which is not the chief business of the play, but promotes the marriage of Chærea and Chremes's sister, principally intended by the poet. There ought to be but one action, says Corneille, that is, one complete action, which leaves the mind of the audience in a full repose; but this cannot be brought to pass but by many other imperfect actions, which conduce to it, and hold the audience in a delightful suspense of what will be.

"If by these rules (to omit many other drawn from the precepts and practice of the ancients) we should judge our modern plays, 'tis probable that few of them would endure the trial: that which should be the business of a day, takes up in some of them an age; instead of one action, they are the epitomes of a man's life; and for one spot of ground, which the stage should represent, we are sometimes in more countries than the map can show us.

"But if we will allow the ancients to have contrived well, we must acknowledge them to have written better. Questionless we are deprived of a great stock of wit in the loss of Menander among the Greek poets, and of Cæcilius, Afranius, and Varius, among the Romans; we may guess at Menander's excellency by the plays of Terence, who translated some of them; and yet wanted so much of him that he was called by C. Cæsar the half-Menander; and may judge of Varius, by the testimonies of Horace, Martial, and Velleius Paterculus. 'Tis probable that these, could they be recovered, would decide the controversy; but so long as Aristophanes and Plautus are extant, while the tragedies of Euripides, Sophocles, and Seneca, are in our hands, I can never see one of those plays which are now written but it increases my admiration of the ancients. And yet I must acknowledge farther, that to admire them as we ought, we should understand them better than we do. Doubtless many things appear flat to us, the wit of which depended on some custom or story which never came to our knowledge; or perhaps on some criticism in their language, which being so long dead, and only remaining in their books, 'tis not possible they should make us understand perfectly. To read Macrobius, explaining the propriety and elegancy of many words in Virgil, which I had before passed over without consideration as common things, is enough to assure me that I ought to think the same of Terence; and that in the purity of his style (which Tully so much valued that he ever carried his works about him) there is yet left in him great room for admiration, if I knew but where to place it. In the mean time I must desire you to take notice that the greatest man of the last age, Ben Jonson, was willing to give place to them in all things: he was not only a professed imitator of Horace, but a learned plagiary of all the others; you track him everywhere in their snow: if Horace, Lucan, Petronius Arbiter, Seneca, and Juvenal, had their own from him, there are few serious thoughts which are new in him: you will pardon me, therefore, if I presume he loved their fashion, when he wore their clothes. But since I have otherwise a great veneration for him, and you, Eugenius, prefer him above all other poets, I will use no farther argument to you than his example: I will produce before you Father Ben, dressed in all the ornaments and colours of the ancients; you will need no other guide to our party, if you follow him; and whether you consider the bad plays of our age, or regard the good plays of the last, both the best and worst of the modern poets will equally instruct you to admire the ancients."

Crites had no sooner left speaking, but Eugenius, who had waited with some impatience for it, thus began:

"I have observed in your speech, that the former part of it is convincing as to what the moderns have profited by the rules of the ancients; but in the latter you are careful to conceal how much they have excelled them; we own all the helps we have from them, and want neither veneration nor gratitude, while we acknowledge that, to overcome them, we must make use of the advantages we have received from them: but to these assistances we have joined our own industry; for, had we sat down with a dull imitation of them, we might then have lost somewhat of the old perfection, but never acquired any that was new. We draw not therefore after their lines, but those of nature; and having the life before us, besides the experience of all they knew, it is no wonder if we hit some airs and features which they have missed. I deny not what you urge of arts and sciences, that they have flourished in some ages more than others; but your instance in philosophy makes for me: for if natural causes be more known now than in the time of Aristotle, because more studied, it follows that poesy and other arts may, with the same pains, arrive still nearer to perfection; and, that granted, it will rest for you to prove that they wrought more perfect images of human life than we; which seeing in your discourse you have avoided to make good, it shall now be my task to show you some part of their defects, and some few excellencies of the moderns. And I think there is none among us can imagine I do it enviously, or with purpose to detract from them; for what interest of fame or profit can the living lose by the reputation of the dead? On the other side, it is a great truth which Velleius Paterculus affirms: **Audita visis libentius laudamus; et præsentia, invidia, præterita admiratione prosequimur; et his nos obrui, illis instrui credimus:* that praise or censure is certainly the most sincere, which unbribed posterity shall give us.

"Be pleased then in the first place to take notice that the Greek poesy, which Crites has affirmed to have arrived to perfection in the reign of the Old Comedy, was so far from it that the distinction of it into acts was not known to them; or if it were, it is yet so darkly delivered to us that we cannot make it out.

"All we know of it is from the singing of their Chorus; and that too is so uncertain, that in some of their plays we have reason to conjecture they sung more than five times. Aristotle indeed divides the integral parts of a play into four. First, the *Protasis*, or entrance, which gives light only to the characters of the persons, and proceeds very little into any part of the action. Secondly, the *Epitasis*, or working up of the plot; where the play grows warmer, the design or action of it is drawing on, and you see something promising that it will come to pass. Thirdly, the *Catastasis*, called by the Romans, *Status*, the height and full growth of the play: we may call it properly the counter-turn, which destroys that expectation, imbroils the action in new difficulties, and leaves you far distant from that hope in which it found you; as you may have observed in a violent stream resisted by a narrow passage, — it runs round to an eddy, and carries back the waters with more swiftness than it brought them on. Lastly, the *Catastrophe*, which the Grecians called λύσις, the French *le dênouement*, and we the discovery, or unravelling of the plot: there you see all things settling again upon their first foundations; and, the obstacles which hindered the design or action of the play once removed, it ends with that resemblance of truth and nature, that the audience are satisfied with the conduct of it. Thus this great man delivered to us the image of a play; and I must confess it is so lively that from thence much light has been derived to the forming it more perfectly into acts and scenes: but what poet first limited to five the number of the acts, I know not; only we see it so firmly established in the time of Horace, that he gives it for a rule in comedy, **Neu brevior quinto, neu sit productior actu.* So that you see the Grecians cannot be said to have consummated this art; writing rather by entrances than by acts, and having rather a general indigested notion of a play, than knowing how and where to bestow the particular graces of it.

"But since the Spaniards at this day allow but three acts, which they call *Jornadas*, to a play, and the Italians in many of theirs follow them, when I condemn the ancients, I declare it is not altogether because they have not five acts to every play, but because they have not confined themselves to one certain number: it is building an house without a model; and when they succeeded in such undertakings, they ought to have sacrificed to Fortune, not to the Muses.

"Next, for the plot, which Aristotle called ὁ μῦθος, and often τῶν πραγμάτων σύνθεσις, and from him the Romans *Fabula*; it has already been judiciously observed by a late writer that in their tragedies it was only some tale derived from Thebes or Troy, or at least something that happened in those two ages; which was worn so threadbare by the pens of all the epic poets, and even by tradition itself of the talkative Greeklings (as Ben Jonson calls them), that before it came upon the stage, it was already known to all the audience: and the people, so soon as ever they heard the name of Œdipus, knew as well as the poet, that he had killed his father by a mistake, and committed incest with his mother, before the play; that they were now to hear of a great plague, an oracle, and the ghost of Laius: so that they sat with a yawning kind of expectation, till he was to come with his eyes pulled out, and speak a hundred or more verses in a tragic tone, in complaint of his misfortunes. But one Œdipus, Hercules, or Medea had been tolerable: poor people, they 'scaped not so good cheap; they had still the **chapon bouillé* set before them till their appetites were cloyed with the same dish, and, the novelty being gone, the pleasure vanished; so that one main end of dramatic poesy in its definition, which was to cause delight, was of consequence destroyed.

"In their comedies the Romans generally borrowed their plots from the Greek poets; and theirs was commonly a little girl stolen or wandered from her parents, brought back unknown to the city, there got with child by some lewd young fellow, who, by the help of his servant, cheats his father; and when her time comes, to cry, **Juno Lucina, fer opem*, one or other sees a little box or cabinet which was carried away with her, and so discovers her to her friends, if some god do not prevent it, by coming down in a machine, and taking the thanks of it to himself.

"By the plot you may guess much of the characters of the persons. An old father, who would willingly, before he dies, see his son well married; his debauched son, kind in his nature to his mistress, but miserably in want of money; a servant or slave, who has so much wit to strike in with him, and help to dupe his father; a braggadocio captain, a parasite, and a lady of pleasure.

"As for the poor honest maid, on whom the story is built, and who ought to be one of the principal actors in the play, she is commonly a mute in it: she has the breeding of the old Elizabeth way, which was for maids to be seen and not to be heard; and it is enough you know she is willing to be married, when the fifth act requires it.

"These are plots built after the Italian mode of houses; you see through them all at once: the characters are indeed the imitations of nature, but so narrow, as if they had imitated only an eye or an hand, and did not dare to venture on the lines of a face, or the proportion of a body.

"But in how strait a compass soever they have bounded their plots and characters, we will pass it by, if they have regularly pursued them, and perfectly observed those three Unities of Time, Place, and Action, the knowledge of which you say is derived to us from them. But in the first place give me leave to tell you that the Unity of Place, however it might be practised by them, was never any of their rules: we neither find it in Aristotle, Horace, or any who have written of it, till in our age the French poets first made it a precept of the stage. The Unity of Time, even Terence himself, who was the best and most regular of them, has neglected: his *Heautontimorumenos*, or Self-Punisher, takes up visibly two days, says Scaliger; the two first acts concluding the first day, the three last the day ensuing; and Euripides, in tying himself to one day, has committed an absurdity never to be forgiven him; for in one of his tragedies he has made Theseus go from Athens to Thebes, which was about forty English miles, under the walls of it to give battle, and appear victorious in the next act; and yet, from the time of his departure to the return of the *Nuntius*, who gives the relation of his victory, Æthra and the Chorus have but thirty-six verses; which is not for every mile a verse.

"The like error is as evident in Terence his *Eunuch*, when Laches, the old man, enters by mistake into the house of Thais; where, betwixt his exit and the entrance of Pythias, who comes to give ample relation of the disorders he has raised within, Parmeno, who was left upon the stage, has not above five lines to speak. **C'est bien employer un temps* *si court*, says the French poet, who furnished me with one of the observations: and almost all their tragedies will afford us examples of the like nature.

"'Tis true, they have kept the continuity, or, as you called it, *liaison des scènes*, somewhat better: two do not perpetually come in together, talk, and go out together; and other two succeed them, and do the same throughout the act, which the English call by the name of single scenes; but the reason is, because they have seldom above two or three scenes, properly so called, in every act; for it is to be accounted a new scene, not only every time the stage is empty; but every person who enters, though to others, makes it so, because he introduces a new business. Now the plots of their plays being narrow, and the persons few, one of their acts was written in a less compass than one of our well-wrought scenes; and yet they are often deficient even in this. To go no further than Terence; you find in the *Eunuch*, Antipho entering single in the midst of the third act, after Chremes and Pythias were gone off; in the same play you have likewise Dorias beginning the fourth act alone; and after she had made a relation of what was done at the Soldiers' entertainment (which by the way was very *inartificial, because she was presumed to speak directly to the audience, and to acquaint them with what was necessary to be known, but yet should have been so contrived by the poet as to have been told by persons of the drama to one another, and so by them to have come to the knowledge of the people), she quits the stage, and Phædria enters next, alone likewise: he also gives you an account of himself, and of his returning from the country, in monologue; to which unnatural way of narration Terence is subject in all his plays. In his *Adelphi*, or Brothers, Syrus and Demea enter after the scene was broken by the departure of Sostrata, Geta, and Canthara; and indeed you can scarce look into any of his comedies, where you will not presently discover the same interruption.

"But as they have failed both in laying of their plots, and in the management, swerving from the rules of their own art by misrepresenting nature to us, in which they have ill satisfied one intention of a play, which was delight; so in the instructive part they have erred worse: instead of punishing vice and rewarding virtue, they have often shown a prosperous wickedness, and an unhappy piety: they have set before us a bloody image of revenge in Medea, and given her dragons to convey her safe from punishment; a Priam and Astyanax murdered, and Cassandra ravished, and the lust and murder ending in the victory of him who acted them: in short, there is no indecorum in any of our modern plays which, if I would excuse, I could not shadow with some authority from the ancients.

"And one farther note of them let me leave you: tragedies and comedies were not writ then as they are now, promiscuously, by the same person; but he who found his genius bending to the one, never attempted the other way. This is so plain that I need not instance to you that Aristophanes, Plautus, Terence, never any of them writ a tragedy; Æschylus, Euripides, Sophocles, and Seneca, never meddled with comedy: the sock and buskin were not worn by the same poet. Having then so much care to excel in one kind, very little is to be pardoned them, if they miscarried in it; and this would lead me to the consideration of their wit, had not Crites given me sufficient warning not to be too bold in my judgment of it; because, the languages being dead, and many of the customs and little accidents on which it depended lost to us, we are not competent judges of it. But though I grant that here and there we may miss the application of a proverb or a custom, yet a thing well said will be wit in all languages; and though it may lose something in the translation, yet to him who reads it in the original, 'tis still the same: he has an idea of its excellency, though it cannot pass from his mind into any other expression or words than those in which he finds it. When Phædria, in the *Eunuch*, had a command from his mistress to be absent two days, and, encouraging himself to go through with it, said, **Tandem ego non illa caream, si sit opus, vel totum triduum?* — Parmeno, to mock the softness of his master, lifting up his hands and eyes, cries out, as it were in admiration, **Hui! universum triduum!* the elegancy of which *universum*, though it cannot be rendered in our language, yet leaves an impression on our souls: but this happens seldom in him; in Plautus oftener, who is infinitely too bold in his metaphors and coining words, out of which many times his wit is nothing; which questionless was one reason why Horace falls upon him so severely in those verses:

**Sed proavi nostri Plautinos et numeros et*
Laudavere sales, nimium patienter utrumque,
Ne dicam stolide.

For Horace himself was cautious to obtrude a new word on his readers, and makes custom and common use the best measure of receiving it into our writings:

**Multa renascentur quæ nunc cecidere, cadentque*
Quæ nunc sunt in honore vocabula, si volet usus,
Quem penes arbitrium est, et jus, et norma loquendi.

"The not observing this rule is that which the world has blamed in our satirist, Cleveland: to express a thing hard and unnaturally, is his new way of elocution. 'Tis true, no poet but may sometimes use a catachresis: Virgil does it —

**Mistaque ridenti colocasia fundet acantho —*

in his eclogue of Pollio; and in his seventh Æneid:

**. . . mirantur et undæ,*
Miratur nemus insuetum fulgentia longe
Scuta virum fluvio pictasque innare carinas.

And Ovid once so modestly, that he asks leave to do it:

**. . . quem, si verbo audacia detur,*
Haud metuam summi dixisse Palatia cœli:

calling the court of Jupiter by the name of Augustus his palace; though in another place he is more bold, where he says, — **et longas visent Capitolia pompas*. But to do this always, and never be able to write a line without it, though it may be admired by some few pedants, will not pass upon those who know that wit is best conveyed to us in the most easy language; and is most to be admired when a great thought comes dressed in words so commonly received that it is understood by the meanest apprehensions, as the best meat is the most easily digested: but we cannot read a verse of Cleveland's without making a face at it, as if every word were a pill to swallow: he gives us many times a hard nut to break our teeth, without a kernel for our pains. So that there is this difference betwixt his satires and Doctor Donne's; that the one gives us deep thoughts in common language, though rough cadence; the other gives us common thoughts in abstruse words: 'tis true, in some places his wit is independent of his words, as in that of the *Rebel Scot*:

Had Cain been Scot, God would have chang'd his doom;
Not forc'd him wander, but confin'd him home.

*"*Si sic omnia dixisset!* This is wit in all languages: 'tis like mercury, never to be lost or killed: — and so that other —

For beauty, like white powder, makes no noise,
And yet the silent hypocrite destroys.

You see the last line is highly metaphorical, but it is so soft and gentle that it does not shock us as we read it.

"But, to return from whence I have digressed, to the consideration of the ancients' writing, and their wit, of which by this time you will grant us in some measure to be fit judges. Though I see many excellent thoughts in Seneca, yet he of them who had a genius most proper for the stage was Ovid; he had a way of writing so fit to stir up a pleasing admiration and concernment, which are the objects of a tragedy, and to show the various movements of a soul combating betwixt two different passions, that, had he lived in our age, or in his own could have writ with our advantages, no man but must have yielded to him; and therefore I am confident the *Medea* is none of his: for, though I esteem it for the gravity and sententiousness of it, which he himself concludes to be suitable to a tragedy, — **Omne genus scripti gravitate tragœdia vincit*, — yet it moves not my soul enough to judge that he, who in the epic way wrote things so near the drama as the story of Myrrha, of Caunus and Biblis, and the rest, should stir up no more concernment where he most endeavoured it. The masterpiece of Seneca I hold to be that scene in the *Troades*, where Ulysses is seeking for Astyanax to kill him: there you see the tenderness of a mother so represented in Andromache that it raises compassion to a high degree in the reader, and bears the nearest resemblance of anything in the tragedies of the ancients to the excellent scenes of passion in Shakespeare, or in Fletcher: for love-scenes, you will find few among them; their tragic poets dealt not with that soft passion, but with lust, cruelty, revenge, ambition, and those bloody actions they produced; which were more capable of raising horror than compassion in an audience: leaving love untouched, whose gentleness would have tempered them; which is the most frequent of all the passions, and which, being the private concernment of every person, is soothed by viewing its own image in a public entertainment.

"Among their comedies, we find a scene or

two of tenderness, and that where you would least expect it, in Plautus; but to speak generally, their lovers say little, when they see each other, but *_anima mea, vita mea_; Ζωὴ καὶ ψυχῆ, as the women in Juvenal's time used to cry out in the fury of their kindness. Any sudden gust of passion (as an ecstasy of love in an unexpected meeting) cannot better be expressed than in a word and a sigh, breaking one another. Nature is dumb on such occasions; and to make her speak would be to represent her unlike herself. But there are a thousand other concernments of lovers, as jealousies, complaints, contrivances, and the like, where not to open their minds at large to each other, were to be wanting to their own love, and to the expectation of the audience; who watch the movements of their minds, as much as the changes of their fortunes. For the imaging of the first is properly the work of a poet; the latter he borrows from the historian."

Eugenius was proceeding in that part of his discourse, when Crites interrupted him. "I see," said he, "Eugenius and I are never like to have this question decided betwixt us; for he maintains the moderns have acquired a new perfection in writing; I can only grant they have altered the mode of it. Homer described his heroes men of great appetites, lovers of beef broiled upon the coals, and good fellows; contrary to the practice of the French romances, whose heroes neither eat, nor drink, nor sleep, for love. Virgil makes Æneas a bold avower of his own virtues:

*_Sum pius Æneas, fama super æthera notus;_

which, in the civility of our poets is the character of a fanfaron or Hector: for with us the knight takes occasion to walk out, or sleep, to avoid the vanity of telling his own story, which the trusty squire is ever to perform for him. So in their love-scenes, of which Eugenius spoke last, the ancients were more hearty, we more talkative: they writ love as it was then the mode to make it; and I will grant thus much to Eugenius, that perhaps one of their poets had he lived in our age, _si foret hoc nostrum fato delapsus in ævum_ (as Horace says of Lucilius), he had altered many things; not that they were not natural before, but that he might accommodate himself to the age in which he lived. Yet in the mean time, we are not to conclude anything rashly against those great men, but preserve to them the dignity of masters, and give that honour to their memories, *_quos Libitina sacravit_, part of which we expect may be paid to us in future times."

This moderation of Crites, as it was pleasing to all the company, so it put an end to that dispute; which Eugenius, who seemed to have the better of the argument, would urge no farther: but Lisideius, after he had acknowledged himself of Eugenius his opinion concerning the ancients, yet told him he had forborne, till his discourse were ended, to ask him why he preferred the English plays above those of other nations, and whether we ought not to submit our stage to the exactness of our next neighbours.

"Though," said Eugenius, "I am at all times ready to defend the honour of my country against the French, and to maintain, we are as well able to vanquish them with our pens, as our ancestors have been with their swords; yet, if you please," added he, looking upon Neander, "I will commit this cause to my friend's management; his opinion of our plays is the same with mine: and besides, there is no reason, that Crites and I, who have now left the stage, should re-enter so suddenly upon it, which is against the laws of comedy."

"If the question had been stated," replied Lisideius, "who had writ best, the French or English, forty years ago, I should have been of your opinion, and adjudged the honour to our own nation; but since that time" (said he, turning towards Neander), *"we have been so long together bad Englishmen that we had not leisure to be good poets. Beaumont, Fletcher, and Jonson (who were only capable of bringing us to that degree of perfection which we have) were just then leaving the world; as if in an age of so much horror, wit and those milder studies of humanity had no farther business among us. But the Muses, who ever follow peace, went to plant in another country: it was then that the great Cardinal Richelieu began to take them into his protection; and that, by his encouragement, Corneille, and some other Frenchmen, reformed their theatre, which before was as much below ours, as it now surpasses it and the rest of Europe. But because Crites in his discourse for the ancients has prevented me, by observing many rules of the stage which the moderns have borrowed from them, I shall only, in short, demand of you, whether you are not convinced that of all nations the French have best observed them. In the Unity of Time you find them so scrupulous that it yet remains a dispute among their poets, whether the artificial day of twelve hours, more or less, be not meant by Aristotle, rather than the natural one of twenty-four; and consequently, whether all plays ought not to be reduced into that compass. This I can testify, that in all their dramas writ within these last twenty years and upwards, I have not observed any that have extended the time to thirty hours: in the Unity of Place they are full as scrupulous; for many of their critics limit it to that very spot of ground where the play is supposed to begin; none of them exceed the compass of the same town or city. The Unity of Action in all plays is yet more conspicuous; for they do not burden them with under-plots, as the English do: which is the reason why many scenes of our tragi-comedies carry on a design that is nothing of kin to the main plot; and that we see two distinct webs in a play, like those in ill-wrought stuffs; and two actions, that is, two plays, carried on together, to the confounding of the audience; who, before they are warm in their concernments for one part, are diverted to another; and by that means espouse the interest of neither. From hence likewise it arises that the one half of our actors are not known to the other. They keep their distances, as if they were *Montagues and Capulets, and seldom begin an acquaintance till the last scene of the fifth act, when they are all to meet upon the stage. There is no theatre in the world has anything so absurd as the English tragi-comedy; 'tis a drama of our own invention, and the fashion of it is enough to proclaim it so; here a course of mirth, there another of sadness and passion, and a third of honour and a duel: thus, in two hours and a half, we run through all the fits of Bedlam. The French affords you as much variety on the same day, but they do it not so unseasonably, or *mal à propos*, as we: our poets present you the play and the farce together; and our stages still retain somewhat of the original civility of the Red Bull:

**Atque ursum et pugiles media inter carmina poscunt.*

The end of tragedies or serious plays, says Aristotle, is to beget admiration, compassion, or concernment; but are not mirth and compassion things incompatible? and is it not evident that the poet must of necessity destroy the former by intermingling of the latter? that is, he must ruin the sole end and object of his tragedy, to introduce somewhat that is forced into it, and is not of the body of it. Would you not think that physician mad, who, having prescribed a purge, should immediately order you to take restringents?

"But to leave our plays and return to theirs. I have noted one great advantage they have had in the plotting of their tragedies; that is, they are always grounded upon some known history: according to that of Horace, **Ex noto fictum carmen sequar;* and in that they have so imitated the ancients that they have surpassed them. For the ancients, as was observed before, took for the foundation of their plays some poetical fiction, such as under that consideration could move but little concernment in the audience, because they already knew the event of it. But the French goes farther:

**Atque ita mentitur, sic veris falsa remiscet,*
Primo ne medium, medio ne discrepet imum.

He so interweaves truth with probable fiction that he puts a pleasing fallacy upon us; mends the intrigues of fate, and dispenses with the severity of history, to reward that virtue which has been rendered to us there unfortunate. Sometimes the story has left the success so doubtful that the writer is free, by the privilege of a poet, to take that which of two or more relations will best suit with his design: as for example, in the death of Cyrus, whom Justin and some others report to have perished in the Scythian war, but Xenophon affirms to have died in his bed of extreme old age. Nay more, when the event is past dispute, even then we are willing to be deceived, and the poet, if he contrives it with appearance of truth, has all the audience of his party; at least during the time his play is acting: so naturally we are kind to virtue, when our own interest is not in question, that we take it up as the general concernment of mankind. On the other side, if you consider the historical plays of Shakespeare, they are rather so many chronicles of kings, or the business many times of thirty or forty years, cramped into a representation of two hours and an half; which is not to imitate or paint nature, but rather to draw her in miniature, to take her in little; to look upon her through the wrong end of a *perspective, and receive her images not only much less, but infinitely more imperfect than the life: this, instead of making a play delightful, renders it ridiculous:

> **Quodcunque ostendis mihi sic, incredulus odi.*

For the spirit of man cannot be satisfied but with truth, or at least verisimility; and a poem is to contain, if not τὰ ἔτυμα, yet ἐτύμοισιν ὁμοῖα, as one of the Greek poets has expressed it.

"Another thing in which the French differ from us and from the Spaniards, is that they do not embarrass, or cumber themselves with too much plot; they only represent so much of a story as will constitute one whole and great action sufficient for a play; we, who undertake more, do but multiply adventures; which, not being produced from one another, as effects from causes, but rarely following, constitute many actions in the drama, and consequently make it many plays.

"But by pursuing closely one argument, which is not cloyed with many turns, the French have gained more liberty for verse, in which they write; they have leisure to dwell on a subject which deserves it; and to represent the passions (which we have acknowledged to be the poet's work), without being hurried from one thing to another, as we are in the plays of Calderon, which we have seen lately upon our theatres under the name of Spanish plots. I have taken notice but of one tragedy of ours whose plot has that uniformity and unity of design in it which I have commended in the French; and that is *Rollo*, or rather, under the name of Rollo, the story of Bassianus and Geta in Herodian: there indeed the plot is neither large nor intricate, but just enough to fill the minds of the audience, not to cloy them. Besides, you see it founded upon the truth of history, — only the time of the action is not reducible to the strictness of the rules; and you see in some places a little farce mingled, which is below the dignity of the other parts; and in this all our poets are extremely peccant: even Ben Jonson himself in *Sejanus* and *Catiline*, has given us this oleo of a play, this unnatural mixture of comedy and tragedy; which to me sounds just as ridiculously as the history of David with the merry humours of Golias. In *Sejanus* you may take notice of the scene betwixt Livia and the physician which is a pleasant satire upon the artificial helps of beauty: in *Catiline* you may see the parliament of women; the little envies of them to one another; and all that passes betwixt Curio and Fulvia: scenes admirable in their kind, but of an ill mingle with the rest.

"But I return again to the French writers, who, as I have said, do not burden themselves too much with plot, which has been reproached to them by an ingenious person of our nation as a fault; for, he says, they commonly make but one person considerable in a play; they dwell on him, and his concernments, while the rest of the persons are only subservient to set him off. If he intends this by it, that there is one person in the play who is of greater dignity than the rest, he must tax, not only theirs, but those of the ancients, and which he would be loath to do, the best of ours; for it is impossible but that one person must be more conspicuous in it than any other, and consequently the greatest share in the action must devolve on him. We see it so in the management of all affairs; even in the most equal aristocracy, the balance cannot be so justly poised but some one will be superior to the rest, either in parts, fortune, interest, or the consideration of some glorious exploit; which will reduce the greatest part of business into his hands.

"But, if he would have us to imagine that in exalting one character the rest of them are neglected, and that all of them have not some share or other in the action of the play, I desire him to produce any of Corneille's tragedies, wherein every person, like so many servants in a well-governed family, has not some employment, and who is not necessary to the carrying on of the plot, or at least to your understanding it.

"There are indeed some *protatic persons in the ancients, whom they make use of in their plays, either to hear or give the relation: but the French avoid this with great address, making their narrations only to, or by such, who are some way interested in the main design. And now I am speaking of relations, I cannot take a fitter opportunity to add this in favour of the French, that they often use them with better judgment and more *à propos* than the English do. Not that I commend narrations in general, — but there are two sorts of them. One, of those things which are antecedent to the play, and are related to make the conduct of it more clear to us. But 'tis a fault to choose such subjects for the stage as will force us on that rock, because we see they are seldom listened to by the audience and that is many times the ruin of the play; for, being once let pass without attention, the audience can never recover themselves to understand the plot: and indeed it is somewhat unreasonable that they should be put to so much trouble, as that, to comprehend what passes in their sight, they must have recourse to what was done, perhaps, ten or twenty years ago.

"But there is another sort of relations, that is, of things happening in the action of the play, and supposed to be done behind the scenes; and this is many times both convenient and beautiful; for by it the French avoid the tumult to which we are subject in England, by representing duels, battles, and the like; which renders our stage too like the theatres where they fight prizes. For what is more ridiculous than to represent an army with a drum and five men behind it; all which the hero of the other side is to drive in before him; or to see a duel fought, and one slain with two or three thrusts of the foils, which we know are so blunted that we might give a man an hour to kill another in good earnest with them.

"I have observed that in all our tragedies, the audience cannot forbear laughing when the actors are to die; it is the most comic part of the whole play. All *passions* may be lively represented on the stage, if to the well-writing of them the actor supplies a good commanded voice, and limbs that move easily, and without stiffness; but there are many *actions* which can never be imitated to a just height: dying especially is a thing which none but a Roman gladiator could naturally perform on the stage, when he did not imitate or represent, but do it; and therefore it is better to omit the representation of it.

"The words of a good writer, which describe it lively, will make a deeper impression of belief in us than all the actor can insinuate into us, when he seems to fall dead before us; as a poet in the description of a beautiful garden, or a meadow, will please our imagination more than the place itself can please our sight. When we see death represented, we are convinced it is but fiction; but when we hear it related, our eyes, the strongest witnesses, are wanting, which might have undeceived us; and we are all willing to favour the sleight, when the poet does not too grossly impose on us. They therefore who imagine these relations would make no concernment in the audience, are deceived, by confounding them with the other, which are of things antecedent to the play: those are made often in cold blood, as I may say, to the audience; but these are warmed with our concernments, which were before awakened in the play. What the philosophers say of motion, that, when it is once begun, it continues of itself, and will do so to eternity, without some stop put to it, is clearly true on this occasion: the soul being already moved with the characters and fortunes of those imaginary persons, continues going of its own accord; and we are no more weary to hear what becomes of them when they are not on the stage, than we are to listen to the news of an absent mistress. But it is objected, that if one part of the play may be related, then why not all? I answer, some parts of the action are more fit to be represented, some to be related. Corneille says judiciously that the poet is not obliged to expose to view all particular actions which conduce to the principal: he ought to select such of them to be seen, which will appear with the greatest beauty, either by the magnificence of the show, or the vehemence of passions which they produce, or some other charm which they have in them; and let the rest arrive to the audience by narration. 'Tis a great mistake in us to believe the French present no part of the action on the stage; every alteration or crossing of a design, every new-sprung passion, and turn of it, is a part of the action, and much the noblest, except we conceive nothing to be action till the players come to blows; as if the painting of the hero's mind were not more properly the poet's work than the strength of his body. Nor does this anything contradict the opinion of Horace, where he tells us,

> **Segnius irritant animos demissa per aurem,*
> *Quam quæ sunt oculis subjecta fidelibus.*

For he says immediately after,

> *Non tamem intus*
> *Digna geri promes in scenam; multaque tolles*
> *Ex oculis, quæ mox narret facundia præsens.*

Among which many he recounts some:

> *Nec pueros coram populo Medea trucidet,*
> *Aut in avem Progne mutetur, Cadmus in anguem,* etc.

That is, those actions which by reason of their cruelty will cause aversion in us, or by reason of their impossibility, unbelief, ought either wholly to be avoided by a poet, or only delivered by narration. To which we may have leave to add, such as, to avoid tumult (as was before hinted), or to reduce the plot into a more reasonable compass of time, or for defect of beauty in them, are rather to be related than presented to the eye. Examples of all these kinds are frequent, not only among all the ancients, but in the best received of our English poets. We find Ben Jonson using them in his *Magnetic Lady*, where one comes out from dinner, and relates the quarrels and disorders of it, to save the undecent appearance of them on the stage, and to abbreviate the story; and this in express imitation of Terence, who had done the same before him in his *Eunuch*, where Pythias makes the like relation of what had happened within at the Soldier's entertainment. The relations likewise of Sejanus's death, and the prodigies before it, are remarkable; the one of which was hid from sight, to avoid the horror and tumult of the representation; the other, to shun the introducing of things impossible to be believed. In that excellent play, *The King and no King*, Fletcher goes yet farther; for the whole unravelling of the plot is done by narration in the fifth act, after the manner of the ancients; and it moves great concernment in the audience, though it be only a relation of what was done many years before the play. I could multiply other instances, but these are sufficient to prove that there is no error in choosing a subject which requires this sort of narrations; in the ill management of them, there may.

"But I find I have been too long in this discourse, since the French have many other excellencies not common to us; as that you never see any of their plays end with a conversion, or simple change of will, which is the ordinary way which our poets use to end theirs. It shows little art in the conclusion of a dramatic poem, when they who have hindered the felicity during the four acts, desist from it in the fifth, without some powerful cause to take them off their design; and though I deny not but such reasons may be found, yet it is a path that is cautiously to be trod, and the poet is to be sure he convinces the audience that the motive is strong enough. As for example, the conversion of the usurer in *The Scornful Lady* seems to me a little forced; for, being an usurer, which implies a lover of money to the highest degree of covetousness (and such the poet has represented him), the account he gives for the sudden change is that he has been duped by the wild young fellow; which in reason might render him more wary another time, and make him punish himself with harder fare and coarser clothes, to get up again what he had lost: but that he should look on it as a judgment, and so repent, we may expect to hear in a sermon, but I should never endure it in a play.

"I pass by this; neither will I insist on the care they take that no person after his first entrance shall ever appear, but the business which brings him upon the stage shall be evident; which rule, if observed, must needs render all the events in the play more natural; for there you see the probability of every accident, in the cause that produced it; and that which appears chance in the play, will seem so reasonable to you, that you will there find it almost necessary: so that in the exit of the actor you have a clear account of his purpose and design in the next entrance (though, if the scene be well wrought, the event will commonly deceive you); for there is nothing so absurd, says Corneille, as for an actor to leave the stage only because he has no more to say.

"I should now speak of the beauty of their rhyme, and the just reason I have to prefer that way of writing in tragedies before ours in blank verse; but because it is partly received by us, and therefore not altogether peculiar to them, I will say no more of it in relation to their plays. For our own, I doubt not but it will exceedingly beautify them; and I can see but one reason why it should not generally obtain, that is, because our poets write so ill in it. This indeed may prove a more prevailing argument than all others which are used to destroy it, and therefore I am only troubled when great and judicious poets, and those who are acknowledged such, have writ or spoke against it: as for others, they are to be answered by that one sentence of an ancient author: — * *Sed ut primo ad consequendos eos quos priores ducimus, accendimur, ita ubi aut præteriri, aut æquari eos posse desperavimus, studium cum spe senescit: quod, scilicet, assequi non potest, sequi desinit, . . . præteritoque eo in quo eminere non possumus, aliquid in quo nitamur, conquirimus.*"

Lisideius concluded in this manner; and

Neander, after a little pause, thus answered him:

"I shall grant Lisideius, without much dispute, a great part of what he has urged against us; for I acknowledge that the French contrive their plots more regularly, and observe the laws of comedy, and decorum of the stage (to speak generally), with more exactness than the English. Farther, I deny not but he has taxed us justly in some irregularities of ours, which he has mentioned; yet, after all, I am of opinion that neither our faults nor their virtues are considerable enough to place them above us.

"For the lively imitation of nature being in the definition of a play, those which best fulfil that law ought to be esteemed superior to the others. 'Tis true, those beauties of the French poesy are such as will raise perfection higher where it is, but are not sufficient to give it where it is not: they are indeed the beauties of a statue, but not of a man, because not animated with the soul of poesy, which is imitation of humour and passions: and this Lisideius himself, or any other, however biassed to their party, cannot but acknowledge, if he will either compare the humours of our comedies, or the characters of our serious plays, with theirs. He who will look upon theirs which have been written till these last ten years, or thereabouts, will find it an hard matter to pick out two or three passable humours amongst them. Corneille himself, their arch-poet, what has he produced except *The Liar*, and you know how it was cried up in France; but when it came upon the English stage, though well translated, and that part of Dorant acted to so much advantage as I am confident it never received in its own country, the most favourable to it would not put it in competition with many of Fletcher's or Ben Jonson's. In the rest of Corneille's comedies you have little humour; he tells you himself, his way is first to show two lovers in good intelligence with each other; in the working up of the play to embroil them by some mistake, and in the latter end to clear it, and reconcile them.

"But of late years Molière, the younger Corneille, Quinault, and some others, have been imitating afar off the quick turns and graces of the English stage. They have mixed their serious plays with mirth, like our tragi-comedies, since the death of Cardinal Richelieu; which Lisideius and many others not observing, have commended that in them for a virtue which they themselves no longer practise. Most of their new plays are, like some of ours, derived from the Spanish novels. There is scarce one of them without a veil, and a trusty Diego, who drolls much after the rate of *The Adventures*. But their humours, if I may grace them with that name, are so thin-sown that never above one of them comes up in any play. I dare take upon me to find more variety of them in some one play of Ben Jonson's than in all theirs together; as he who has seen *The Alchemist*, *The Silent Woman*, or *Bartholomew Fair*, cannot but acknowledge with me.

"I grant the French have performed what was possible on the groundwork of the Spanish plays; what was pleasant before, they have made regular: but there is not above one good play to be writ on all those plots; they are too much alike to please often; which we need not the experience of our own stage to justify. As for their new way of mingling mirth with serious plot, I do not, with Lisideius, condemn the thing, though I cannot approve their manner of doing it. He tells us we cannot so speedily recollect ourselves after a scene of great passion and concernment, as to pass to another of mirth and humour, and to enjoy it with any relish: but why should he imagine the soul of man more heavy than his senses? Does not the eye pass from an unpleasant object to a pleasant in a much shorter time than is required to this? and does not the unpleasantness of the first commend the beauty of the latter? The old rule of logic might have convinced him that contraries, when placed near, set off each other. A continued gravity keeps the spirit too much bent; we must refresh it sometimes, as we bait in a journey that we may go on with greater ease. A scene of mirth, mixed with tragedy, has the same effect upon us which our music has betwixt the acts; which we find a relief to us from the best plots and language of the stage, if the discourses have been long. I must therefore have stronger arguments, ere I am convinced that compassion and mirth in the same subject destroy each other; and in the meantime cannot but conclude, to the honour of our nation, that we have invented, increased, and perfected a more pleasant way of writing for the stage, than was ever known to the ancients or moderns of any nation, which is tragi-comedy.

"And this leads me to wonder why Lisideius and many others should cry up the barrenness of the French plots above the variety and copiousness of the English. Their plots are single; they carry on one design, which is pushed forward by all the actors, every scene in the play contributing and moving towards it. Our plays, besides the main design, have under-plots or by-concernments, of less considerable persons and intrigues, which are carried on with the motion of the main plot: as they say the orb of the fixed stars, and those of the planets, though they have motions of their own, are whirled about by the motion of the * *primum mobile*, in which they are contained. That similitude expresses much of the English stage; for if contrary motions may be found in nature to agree; if a planet can go east and west at the same time, one way by virtue of his own motion, the other by the force of the first mover, it will not be difficult to imagine how the under-plot, which is only different, not contrary to the great design, may naturally be conducted along with it.

"Eugenius has already shown us, from the confession of the French poets, that the Unity of Action is sufficiently preserved, if all the imperfect actions of the play are conducing to the main design; but when those petty intrigues of a play are so ill ordered that they have no coherence with the other, I must grant that Lisideius has reason to tax that want of due connection; for * co-ordination in a play is as dangerous and unnatural as in a state. In the meantime he must acknowledge, our variety, if well ordered, will afford a greater pleasure to the audience.

"As for his other argument, that by pursuing one single theme they gain an advantage to express and work up the passions, I wish any example he could bring from them would make it good; for I confess their verses are to me the coldest I have ever read. Neither, indeed, is it possible for them, in the way they take, so to express passion, as that the effects of it should appear in the concernment of an audience, their speeches being so many declamations, which tire us with the length; so that instead of persuading us to grieve for their imaginary heroes, we are concerned for our own trouble, as we are in tedious visits of bad company; we are in pain till they are gone. When the French stage came to be reformed by Cardinal Richelieu, those long harangues were introduced to comply with the gravity of a churchman. Look upon the *Cinna* and the *Pompey;* they are not so properly to be called plays, as long discourses of reason of state; and *Polieucte* in matters of religion is as solemn as the long stops upon our organs. Since that time it is grown into a custom, and their actors speak by the hour-glass, like our parsons; nay, they account it the grace of their parts, and think themselves disparaged by the poet, if they may not twice or thrice in a play entertain the audience with a speech of an hundred lines. I deny not but this may suit well enough with the French; for as we, who are a more sullen people, come to be diverted at our plays, so they, who are of an airy and gay temper, come thither to make themselves more serious: and this I conceive to be one reason why comedies are more pleasing to us, and tragedies to them. But to speak generally, it cannot be denied that short speeches and replies are more apt to move the passions and beget concernment in us, than the other; for it is unnatural for any one in a gust of passion to speak long together, or for another in the same condition to suffer him, without interruption. Grief and passion are like floods raised in little brooks by a sudden rain; they are quickly up; and if the concernment be poured unexpectedly in upon us, it overflows us: but a long sober shower gives them leisure to run out as they came in, without troubling the ordinary current. As for comedy, repartee is one of its chiefest graces; the greatest pleasure of the audience is a chase of wit, kept up on both sides, and swiftly managed. And this our forefathers, if not we, have had in Fletcher's plays, to a much higher degree of perfection than the French poets can reasonably hope to reach.

"There is another part of Lisideius his discourse, in which he has rather excused our neighbours than commended them; that is, for aiming only to make one person considerable in their plays. 'Tis very true what he has urged, that one character in all plays, even without the poet's care, will have advantage of all the others; and that the design of the whole drama will chiefly depend on it. But this hinders not that there may be more shining characters in the play: many persons of a second magnitude, nay, some so very near, so almost equal to the first, that greatness may be opposed to greatness, and all the persons be made considerable, not only by their quality, but their action. 'Tis evident that the more the persons are, the greater will be the variety of the plot. If then the parts are managed so regularly that the beauty of the whole be kept entire, and that the variety become not a perplexed and confused mass of accidents, you will find it infinitely pleasing to be led in a labyrinth of design, where you see some of your way before you, yet discern not the end till you arrive at it. And that all this is practicable, I can produce for examples many of our English plays: as *The Maid's Tragedy*, *The Alchemist*, *The Silent Woman;* I was going to have named *The Fox*, but that the unity of design seems not exactly observed in it; for there appear two actions in the play; the first naturally ending with the fourth act; the second forced from it in the fifth; which yet is the less to be condemned in him, because the disguise of Volpone, though it suited not with his character as a crafty or covetous person, agreed well enough with that of a voluptuary; and by it the poet gained the end at which he aimed, the punishment of vice, and the reward of virtue, both which that disguise produced. So that to judge equally of it, it was an excellent fifth act, but not so naturally proceeding from the former.

"But to leave this, and pass to the latter part of Lisideius his discourse, which concerns relations: I must acknowledge with him that the French have reason to hide that part of the action which would occasion too much tumult on the stage, and to choose rather to have it made known by narration to the audience. Farther, I think it very convenient, for the reasons he has given, that all incredible actions were removed; but whether custom has so insinuated itself into our countrymen, or nature has so formed them to fierceness, I know not; but they will scarcely suffer combats and other objects of horror to be taken from them. And indeed, the indecency of tumults is all which can be objected against fighting: for why may not our imagination as well suffer itself to be deluded with the probability of it, as with any other thing in the play? For my part, I can with as great ease persuade myself that the blows are given in good earnest, as I can that they who strike them are kings or princes, or those persons which they represent. For objects of incredibility, I would be satisfied from Lisideius, whether we have any so removed from all appearance of truth, as are those of Corneille's *Andromède*: a play which has been frequented the most of any he has writ. If the Perseus, or the son of a heathen god, the Pegasus, and the Monster, were not capable to choke a strong belief, let him blame any representation of ours hereafter. Those indeed were objects of delight; yet the reason is the same as to the probability: for he makes it not a ballet or masque, but a play, which is to resemble truth. But for death, that it ought not to be represented, I have, besides the arguments alleged by Lisideius, the authority of Ben Jonson, who has forborne it in his tragedies; for both the death of Sejanus and Catiline are related: though in the latter I cannot but observe one irregularity of that great poet; he has removed the scene in the same act from Rome to Catiline's army, and from thence again to Rome; and besides, has allowed a very inconsiderable time, after Catiline's speech, for the striking of the battle, and the return of Petreius, who is to relate the event of it to the senate: which I should not animadvert on him, who was otherwise a painful observer of τὸ πρέπον, or the *decorum* of the stage, if he had not used extreme severity in his judgment on the incomparable Shakespeare for the same fault. — To conclude on this subject of relations; if we are to be blamed for showing too much of the action, the French are as faulty for discovering too little of it: a mean betwixt both should be observed by every judicious writer, so as the audience may neither be left unsatisfied by not seeing what is beautiful, or shocked by beholding what is either incredible or undecent.

"I hope I have already proved in this discourse, that though we are not altogether so punctual as the French in observing the laws of comedy, yet our errors are so few, and little, and those things wherein we excel them so considerable, that we ought of right to be preferred before them. But what will Lisideius say, if they themselves acknowledge they are too strictly bounded by those laws, for breaking which he has blamed the English? I will allege Corneille's words, as I find them in the end of his Discourse of the Three Unities: *Il est facile aux spéculatifs d'être sévères, etc.* "'Tis easy for speculative persons to judge severely; but if they would produce to public view ten or twelve pieces of this nature, they would perhaps give more latitude to the rules than I have done, when by experience they had known how much we are limited and constrained by them, and how many beauties of the stage they banished from it.' To illustrate a little what he has said: by their servile observations of the Unities of Time and Place, and integrity of scenes, they have brought on themselves that dearth of plot and narrowness of imagination, which may be observed in all their plays. How many beautiful accidents might naturally happen in two or three days, which cannot arrive with any probability in the compass of twenty-four hours? There is time to be allowed also for maturity of design, which, amongst great and prudent persons, such as are often represented in tragedy, cannot, with any likelihood of truth, be brought to pass at so short a warning. Farther, by tying themselves strictly to the Unity of Place, and unbroken scenes, they are forced many times to omit some beauties which cannot be shown where the act began; but might, if the scene were interrupted, and the stage cleared for the persons to enter in another place; and therefore the French poets are often forced upon absurdities; for if the act begins in a chamber, all the persons in the play must have some business or other to come thither, or else they are not to be shown that act; and sometimes their characters are very unfitting to appear there: as, suppose it were the king's bed-chamber; yet the meanest man in the tragedy must come and dispatch his business there, rather than in the lobby or courtyard (which is fitter for him), for fear the stage should be cleared, and the scenes broken. Many times they fall by it in a greater inconvenience; for they keep their scenes unbroken, and yet change the place; as in one of their newest plays, where the act begins in the street. There a gentleman is to meet his friend; he sees him with his man, coming out from his father's house; they talk together, and the first goes out: the second, who is a lover, has made an appointment with his mistress; she appears at the window, and then we are to imagine the scene lies under it. This gentleman is called away, and leaves his servant with his mistress; presently her father is heard from within; the young lady is afraid the serving-man should be discovered, and thrusts him into a place of safety, which is supposed to be her closet. After this, the father enters to the daughter, and now the scene is in a house; for he is seeking from one room to another for this poor Philipin, or French Diego, who is heard from within, drolling and breaking many a miserable conceit on the subject of his sad condition. In this ridiculous manner the play goes forward, the stage being never empty all the while: so that the street, the window, the houses, and the closet are made to walk about, and the persons to stand still. Now what, I beseech you, is more easy than to write a regular French play, or more difficult than to write an irregular English one, like those of Fletcher, or of Shakespeare?

"If they content themselves, as Corneille did, with some flat design, which, like an ill riddle, is found out ere it be half proposed, such plots we can make every way regular, as easily as they; but whene'er they endeavour to rise to any quick turns and counterturns of plot, as some of them have attempted since Corneille's plays have been less in vogue, you see they write as irregularly as we, though they cover it more speciously. Hence the reason is perspicuous why no French plays, when translated, have, or ever can succeed on the English stage. For, if you consider the plots, our own are fuller of variety; if the writing, ours are more quick and fuller of spirit; and therefore 'tis a strange mistake in those who decry the way of writing plays in verse, as if the English therein imitated the French. We have borrowed nothing from them; our plots are weaved in English looms: we endeavour therein to follow the variety and greatness of characters which are derived to us from Shakespeare and Fletcher; the copiousness and well-knitting of the intrigues we have from Jonson; and for the verse itself we have English precedents of elder date than any of Corneille's plays. Not to name our old comedies before Shakespeare, which were all writ in verse of six feet, or Alexandrines, such as the French now use, I can show in Shakespeare many scenes of rhyme together, and the like in Ben Jonson's tragedies: in *Catiline* and *Sejanus* sometimes thirty or forty lines, I mean besides the Chorus, or the monologues; which, by the way, showed Ben no enemy to this way of writing, especially if you read his *Sad Shepherd*, which goes sometimes on rhyme, sometimes on blank verse, like an horse who eases himself on trot and amble. You find him likewise commending Fletcher's pastoral of *The Faithful Shepherdess*, which is for the most part rhyme, though not refined to that purity to which it hath since been brought. And these examples are enough to clear us from a servile imitation of the French.

"But to return whence I have digressed, I dare boldly affirm these two things of the English drama: first, that we have many plays of ours as regular as any of theirs, and which, besides, have more variety of plot and characters; and secondly, that in most of the irregular plays of Shakespeare or Fletcher (for Ben Jonson's are for the most part regular) there is a more masculine fancy and greater spirit in the writing than there is in any of the French. I could produce, even in Shakespeare's and Fletcher's works, some plays which are almost exactly formed; as *The Merry Wives of Windsor*, and *The Scornful Lady:* but because (generally speaking) Shakespeare, who writ first, did not perfectly observe the laws of comedy, and Fletcher, who came nearer to perfection, yet through carelessness made many faults; I will take the pattern of a perfect play from Ben Jonson, who was a careful and learned observer of the dramatic laws, and from all his comedies, I shall select *The Silent Woman,* of which I will make a short examen, according to those rules which the French observe."

As Neander was beginning to examine *The Silent Woman,* Eugenius, earnestly regarding him; "I beseech you, Neander," said he, "gratify the company, and me in particular, so far, as before you speak of the play, to give us a character of the author; and tell us frankly your opinion, whether you do not think all writers, both French and English, ought to give place to him."

"I fear," replied Neander, "that in obeying your commands I shall draw some *envy on myself. Besides, in performing them, it will be first necessary to speak somewhat of Shakespeare and Fletcher, his rivals in poesy; and one of them, in my opinion, at least his equal, perhaps his superior.

"To begin, then, with Shakespeare. He was the man who of all modern, and perhaps ancient poets, had the largest and most comprehensive soul. All the images of nature were still present to him, and he drew them, not laboriously, but luckily; when he describes anything, you more than see it, you feel it too. Those who accuse him to have wanted learning, give him the greater commendation: he was naturally learned; he needed not the spectacles of books to read nature; he looked inwards, and found her there. I cannot say he is everywhere alike; were he so, I should do him injury to compare him with the greatest of mankind. He is many times flat, insipid; his comic wit degenerating into clenches, his serious swelling into bombast. But he is always great when some great occasion is presented to him; no man can say he ever had a fit subject for his wit, and did not then raise himself as high above the rest of poets,

**Quantum lenta solent inter viburna cupressi.*

The consideration of this made Mr. Hales of Eton say that there was no subject of which any poet ever writ, but he would produce it much better done in Shakespeare; and however others are now generally preferred before him, yet the age wherein he lived, which had contemporaries with him Fletcher and Jonson, never equalled them to him in their esteem: and in the last king's court, when Ben's reputation was at highest, Sir John Suckling, and with him the greater part of the courtiers, set our Shakespeare far above him.

"Beaumont and Fletcher, of whom I am next to speak, had, with the advantage of Shakespeare's wit, which was their precedent, great natural gifts, improved by study: Beaumont especially being so accurate a judge of plays that Ben Jonson, while he lived, submitted all his writings to his censure, and, 'tis thought, used his judgment in correcting, if not contriving, all his plots. What value he had for him appears by the verses he writ to him; and therefore I need speak no farther of it. The first play that brought Fletcher and him in esteem was their *Philaster*: for before that, they had written two or three very unsuccessfully, as the like is reported of Ben Jonson, before he writ *Every Man in his Humour*. Their plots were generally more regular than Shakespeare's, especially those which were made before Beaumont's death; and they understood and imitated the conversation of gentlemen much better; whose wild debaucheries, and quickness of wit in repartees, no poet before them could paint as they have done. Humour, which Ben Jonson derived from particular persons, they made it not their business to describe: they represented all the passions very lively, but above all, love. I am apt to believe the English language in them arrived to its highest perfection: what words have since been taken in, are rather superfluous than ornamental. Their plays are now the most pleasant and frequent entertainments of the stage; two of theirs being acted through the year for one of Shakespeare's or Jonson's: the reason is, because there is a certain gaiety in their comedies, and pathos in their more serious plays, which suits generally with all men's humours. Shakespeare's language is likewise a little obsolete, and Ben Jonson's wit comes short of theirs.

"As for Jonson, to whose character I am now arrived, if we look upon him while he was himself (for his last plays were but his dotages), I think him the most learned and judicious writer which any theatre ever had. He was a most severe judge of himself, as well as others. One cannot say he wanted wit, but rather that he was frugal of it. In his works you find little to retrench or alter. Wit, and language, and humour also in some measure, we had before him; but something of art was wanting to the drama till he came. He managed his strength to more advantage than any who preceded him. You seldom find him making love in any of his scenes, or endeavouring to move the passions; his genius was too sullen and saturnine to do it gracefully, especially when he knew he came after those who had performed both to such an height. Humour was his proper sphere; and in that he delighted most to represent mechanic people. He was deeply conversant in the ancients, both Greek and Latin, and he borrowed boldly from them: there is scarce a poet or historian among the Roman authors of those times whom he has not translated in *Sejanus* and *Catiline*. But he has done his robberies so openly that one may see he fears not to be taxed by any law. He invades authors like a monarch; and what would be theft in other poets is only victory in him. With the spoils of these writers he so represents old Rome to us, in its rites, ceremonies, and customs, that if one of their poets had written either of his tragedies, we had seen less of it than in him. If there was any fault in his language, 'twas that he weaved it too closely and laboriously, in his comedies especially: perhaps, too, he did a little too much Romanise our tongue, leaving the words which he translated almost as much Latin as he found them: wherein, though he learnedly followed their language, he did not enough comply with the idiom of ours. If I would compare him with Shakespeare, I must acknowledge him the more correct poet, but Shakespeare the greater wit. Shakespeare was the Homer, or father of our dramatic poets; Jonson was the Virgil, the pattern of elaborate writing; I admire him, but I love Shakespeare. To conclude of him; as he has given us the most correct plays, so in the precepts which he has laid down in his *Discoveries*, we have as many and profitable rules for perfecting the stage, as any wherewith the French can furnish us.

"Having thus spoken of the author, I proceed to the examination of his comedy, *The Silent Woman.*

EXAMEN OF "THE SILENT WOMAN"

"To begin first with the length of the action; it is so far from exceeding the compass of a natural day that it takes not up an artificial one. 'Tis all included in the limits of three hours and an half, which is no more than is required for the presentment on the stage: a beauty perhaps not much observed; if it had, we should not have looked on the Spanish translation of *Five Hours* with so much wonder. The scene of it is laid in London; the latitude of place is almost as little as you can imagine; for it lies all within the compass of two houses, and after the first act, in one. The continuity of scenes is observed more than in any of our plays, except his own *Fox* and *Alchemist.* They are not broken above twice or thrice at most in the whole comedy; and in the two best of Corneille's plays, the *Cid* and *Cinna*, they are interrupted once. The action of the play is entirely one; the end or aim of which is the settling Morose's estate on Dauphine. The intrigue of it is the greatest and most noble of any pure unmixed comedy in any language; you see in it many persons of various characters and humours, and all delightful: as first, Morose, or an old man to whom all noise but his own talking is offensive. Some who would be thought critics, say this humour of his is forced: but to remove that objection, we may consider him first to be naturally of a delicate hearing, as many are, to whom all sharp sounds are unpleasant; and secondly, we may attribute much of it to the peevishness of his age, or the wayward authority of an old man in his own house, where he may make himself obeyed; and to this the poet seems to allude in his name, Morose. Besides this, I am assured from divers persons that Ben Jonson was actually acquainted with such a man, one altogether as ridiculous as he is here represented. Others say it is not enough to find one man of such an humour; it must be common to more, and the more common the more natural. To prove this, they instance in the best of comical characters, Falstaff: there are many men resembling him; old, fat, merry, cowardly, drunken, amorous, vain, and lying. But to convince these people, I need but tell them that humour is the ridiculous extravagance of conversation, wherein one man differs from all others. If then it be common, or communicated to many, how differs it from other men's? or what indeed causes it to be ridiculous so much as the singularity of it? As for Falstaff, he is not properly one humour, but a miscellany of humours or images, drawn from so many several men that wherein he is singular is his wit, or those things he says *præter expectatum*, unexpected by the audience; his quick evasions, when you imagine him surprised, which, as they are extremely diverting of themselves, so receive a great addition from his person; for the very sight of such an unwieldy, old, debauched fellow is a comedy alone. And here having a place so proper for it, I cannot but enlarge somewhat upon this subject of humour into which I am fallen. The ancients had little of it in their comedies; for the *τὸ γελοῖον of the Old Comedy, of which Aristophanes was chief, was not so much to imitate a man, as to make the people laugh at some odd conceit, which had commonly somewhat of unnatural or obscene in it. Thus, when you see Socrates brought upon the stage, you are not to imagine him made ridiculous by the imitation of his actions, but rather by making him perform something very unlike himself; something so childish and absurd as, by comparing it with the gravity of the true Socrates, makes a ridiculous object for the spectators. In their New Comedy, which succeeded, the poets sought indeed to express the *ἦθος, as in their tragedies the *πάθος of mankind. But this ἦθος contained only the general characters of men and manners; as old men, lovers, serving-men, courtesans, parasites, and such other persons as we see in their comedies; all which they made alike: that is, one old man or father, one lover, one courtesan, so like another, as if the first of them had begot the rest of every sort: **Ex homine hunc natum dicas*. The same custom they observed likewise in their tragedies. As for the French, though they have the word *humeur* among them, yet they have small use of it in their comedies or farces; they being but ill imitations of the *ridiculum*, or that which stirred up laughter in the Old Comedy. But among the English 'tis otherwise: where by humour is meant some extravagant habit, passion, or affection, particular (as I said before) to some one person, by the oddness of which, he is immediately distinguished from the rest of men; which being lively and naturally represented, most frequently begets that malicious pleasure in the audience which is testified by laughter; as all things which are deviations from customs are ever the aptest to produce it: though by the way this laughter is only accidental, as the person represented is fantastic or bizarre; but pleasure is essential to it, as the imitation of what is natural. The description of these humours, drawn from the knowledge and observation of particular persons, was the peculiar genius and talent of Ben Jonson, to whose play I now return.

"Besides Morose, there are at least nine or ten different characters and humours in *The Silent Woman,* all which persons have several concernments of their own, yet are all used by the poet to the conducting of the main design to perfection. I shall not waste time in commending the writing of this play; but I will give you my opinion that there is more wit and acuteness of fancy in it than in any of Ben Jonson's. Besides, that he has here described the conversation of gentlemen in the persons of True-Wit, and his friends, with more gaiety, air, and freedom, than in the rest of his comedies. For the contrivance of the plot, 'tis extreme, elaborate, and yet withal easy; for the λύσις, or untying of it, 'tis so admirable that when it is done, no one of the audience would think the poet could have missed it; and yet it was concealed so much before the last scene that any other way would sooner have entered your thoughts. But I dare not take upon me to commend the fabric of it, because it is altogether so full of art that I must unravel every scene in it to commend it as I ought. And this excellent contrivance is still the more to be admired, because 'tis comedy, where the persons are only of common rank, and their business private, not elevated by passions or high concernments, as in serious plays. Here every one is a proper judge of all he sees; nothing is represented but that with which he daily converses: so that by consequence all faults lie open to discovery, and few are pardonable. 'Tis this which Horace has judiciously observed:

**Creditur, ex medio quia res arcessit, habere*
Sudoris minimum; sed habet comedia tanto
Plus oneris, quanto veniæ minus.

"But our poet, who was not ignorant of these difficulties, has made use of all advantages; as he who designs a large leap takes his rise from the highest ground. One of these advantages is that which Corneille has laid down as the greatest which can arrive to any poem, and which he himself could never compass above thrice in all his plays; viz., the making choice of some signal and long-expected day, whereon the action of the play is to depend. This day was that designed by Dauphine for the settling of his uncle's estate upon him; which to compass, he contrives to marry him. That the marriage had been plotted by him long beforehand, is made evident by what he tells True-Wit in the second act, that in one moment he had destroyed what he had been raising many months.

"There is another artifice of the poet, which I cannot here omit, because by the frequent practice of it in his comedies he has left it to us almost as a rule; that is, when he has any character or humour wherein he would show a *coup de maître*, or his highest skill, he recommends it to your observation by a pleasant description of it before the person first appears. Thus, in *Bartholomew Fair* he gives you the pictures of Numps and Cokes, and in this those of Daw, Lafoole, Morose, and the Collegiate Ladies; all which you hear described before you see them. So that before they come upon the stage, you have a longing expectation of them, which prepares you to receive them favourably; and when they are there, even from their first appearance you are so far acquainted with them that nothing of their humour is lost to you.

"I will observe yet one thing further of this admirable plot; the business of it rises in every act. The second is greater than the first; the third than the second; and so forward to the fifth. There too you see, till the very last scene, new difficulties arising to obstruct the action of the play; and when the audience is brought into despair that the business can naturally be effected, then, and not before, the discovery is made. But that the poet might entertain you with more variety all this while, he reserves some new characters to show you, which he opens not till the second and third act; in the second, Morose, Daw, the Barber, and Otter; in the third, the Collegiate Ladies: all which he moves afterwards in by-walks, or under-plots, as diversions to the main design, lest it should grow tedious, though they are still naturally joined with it, and somewhere or other subservient to it. Thus, like a skillful chess-player, by little and little he draws out his men, and makes his pawns of use to his greater persons.

"If this comedy and some others of his were translated into French prose (which would now be no wonder to them, since Molière has lately given them plays out of verse, which have not displeased them), I believe the controversy would soon be decided betwixt the two nations, even making them the judges. But we need not call our heroes to our aid; be it spoken to the honour of the English, our nation can never want in any age such who are able to dispute the empire of wit with any people in the universe. And though the fury of a civil war, and power for twenty years together abandoned to a barbarous race of men, enemies of all good learning, had buried the Muses under the ruins of monarchy; yet, with the restoration of our happiness, we see revived poesy lifting up its head, and already shaking off the rubbish which lay so heavy on it. We have seen since his Majesty's return, many dramatic poems which yield not to those of any foreign nation, and which deserve all laurels but the English. I will set aside flattery and envy: it cannot be denied but we have had some little blemish either in the plot or writing of all those plays which have been made within these seven years (and perhaps there is no nation in the world so quick to discern them, or so difficult to pardon them, as ours); yet if we can persuade ourselves to use the candour of that poet, who, though the most severe of critics, has left us this caution by which to moderate our censures —

> * . . . *ubi plura nitent in carmine, non ego paucis*
> *Offendar maculis;* —

if, in consideration of their many and great beauties, we can wink at some slight and little imperfections, if we, I say, can be thus equal to ourselves, I ask no favour from the French. And if I do not venture upon any particular judgment of our late plays, 'tis out of the consideration which an ancient writer gives me: *vivorum, ut magna admiratio, ita censura difficilis:* betwixt the extremes of admiration and malice, 'tis hard to judge uprightly of the living. Only I think it may be permitted me to say, that as it is no lessening to us to yield to some plays, and those not many, of our own nation in the last age, so can it be no addition to pronounce of our present poets, that they have far surpassed all the ancients, and the modern writers of other countries."

This was the substance of what was then spoke on that occasion; and Lisideius, I think, was going to reply, when he was prevented thus by Crites: "I am confident," said he, "that the most material things that can be said have been already urged on either side; if they have not, I must beg of Lisideius that he will defer his answer till another time: for I confess I have a joint quarrel to you both, because you have concluded, without any reason given for it, that rhyme is proper for the stage. . . ."

Neander was pursuing this discourse so eagerly that Eugenius had called to him twice or thrice, ere he took notice that the barge stood still, and that they were at the foot of Somerset Stairs, where they had appointed it to land. The company were all sorry to separate so soon, though a great part of the evening was already spent; and stood a while looking back on the water, upon which the moonbeams played, and made it appear like floating quicksilver: at last they went up through a crowd of French people, who were merrily dancing in the open air, and nothing concerned for the noise of guns which had alarmed the town that afternoon. Walking thence together to the Piazza, they parted there; Eugenius and Lisideius to some pleasant appointment they had made, and Crites and Neander to their several lodgings.

[1668 and 1684]

PREFACE TO "FABLES ANCIENT AND MODERN"

Published in March, 1700, less than three months before his death, the *Fables . . . from Homer, Ovid, Boccace, and Chaucer* represent the last important work of Dryden. Even better known today than the poems of this volume is the admirable preface, the ripest and most interesting of his critical works. "The *Preface to the Fables* is more full of life than anything else in Dryden's prose; not inferior even to the *Essay of Dramatic Poesy*; while nothing, either in prose or verse, brings out more admirably or to better advantage the qualities of Dryden as the great English man of letters. For this is what he was, rather than essentially a poet; his genius is one that commands both vehicles of expression, it is not one that is specially inclined to verse; and the free movement of his mind and speech is scarcely less wonderful in a prose tract like this Preface than in the verse of *Absalom and Achitophel.*" W. P. Ker, Introduction to *Essays of John Dryden.*

This mature critical preface is a contrast to the tentative conclusions of *An Essay of Dramatic Poesy* and is also a development of the same habit of mind. The one is the production of a young man who had yet to win his spurs in criticism; the other is the final pronouncement of the acknowledged dean of English letters: both are the works of a seeker after truth, who is ready to state his opinions but who is always willing to consider both sides of a question. Particularly interesting in this preface are Dryden's references to Jeremy Collier and the controversy that had been precipitated by the latter's *Short View of the Immorality and Profaneness of the English Stage,* published two years before. The old poet's acknowledgement of his errors and his refusal to defend certain parts of his dramatic work that his conscience told him were indefensible are not less characteristic than his castigation of Collier's arrogance and extravagance in pressing the charges. Dryden is humble in confessing his faults, but he is far from humble toward the man who has occasioned the confession. Even Christian humility had its limits.

PREFACE TO "FABLES ANCIENT AND MODERN, TRANSLATED INTO VERSE FROM HOMER, OVID, BOCCACE, AND CHAUCER"

'Tis with a poet, as with a man who designs to build, and is very exact, as he supposes, in casting up the cost beforehand; but, generally speaking, he is mistaken in his account, and reckons short of the expense he first intended. He alters his mind as the work proceeds, and will have this or that convenience more, of which he had not thought when he began. So has it happened to me; I have built a house where I intended but a lodge; yet with better success than a certain nobleman, who, beginning with a dog-kennel, never lived to finish the palace he had contrived.

From translating the first of Homer's *Iliads* (which I intended as an essay to the whole work), I proceeded to the translation of the Twelfth Book of Ovid's *Metamorphoses*, because it contains, among other things, the causes, the beginning, and ending, of the Trojan War. Here I ought in reason to have stopped; but the speeches of Ajax and Ulysses lying next in my way, I could not *balk 'em. When I had compassed them, I was so taken with the former part of the Fifteenth Book (which is the masterpiece of the whole *Metamorphoses*), that I enjoined myself the pleasing task of rendering it into English. And now I found, by the number of my verses, that they began to swell into a little volume, which gave me an occasion of looking backward on some beauties of my author in his former books: there occurred to me the *Hunting of the Boar*, *Cinyras and Myrrha*, the good-natured story of *Baucis and Philemon*, with the rest, which I hope I have translated closely enough, and given them the same turn of verse which they had in the original; and this, I may say, without vanity, is not the talent of every poet. He who has arrived the nearest to it is the ingenious and learned Sandys, the best versifier of the former age; if I may properly call it by that name, which was the former part of this concluding century. For Spenser and Fairfax both flourished in the reign of Queen Elizabeth; great masters in our language, and who saw much further into the beauties of our numbers than those who immediately followed them. Milton was the poetical son of Spenser, and Mr. Waller of Fairfax; for we have our lineal descents and clans as well as other families. Spenser more than once insinuates that the soul of Chaucer was transfused into his body, and that he was begotten by him two hundred years after his decease. Milton has acknowledged to me that Spenser was his original; and many besides myself have heard our famous Waller own that he derived the harmony of his numbers from *Godfrey of Bulloign*, which was turned into English by Mr. Fairfax.

But to return: having done with Ovid for this time, it came into my mind that our old English poet, Chaucer, in many things resembled him, and that with no disadvantage on the side of the modern author, as I shall endeavour to prove when I compare them; and as I am, and always have been, studious to promote the honour of my native country, so I soon resolved to put their merits to the trial, by turning some of the *Canterbury Tales* into our language, as it is now refined; for by this means, both the poets being set in the same light, and dressed in the same English habit, story to be compared with story, a certain judgment may be made betwixt them by the reader, without obtruding my opinion on him. Or, if I seem partial to my countryman and *predecessor in the laurel, the friends of antiquity are not few; and, besides many of the learned, Ovid has almost all the beaux, and the whole fair sex, his declared patrons. Perhaps I have assumed somewhat more to myself than they allow me, because I have adventured to sum up the evidence; but the readers are the jury, and their privilege remains entire, to decide according to the merits of the cause; or, if they please, to bring it to another hearing before some other court. In the mean time, to follow the thread of my discourse (as thoughts, according to Mr. Hobbes, have always some connection), so from Chaucer I was led to think on Boccace, who was not only his contemporary, but also pursued the same studies; wrote novels in prose, and many works in verse; particularly is said to have invented the octave rhyme, or stanza of eight lines, which ever since has been maintained by the practice of all Italian writers who are, or at least assume the title of heroic poets.

He and Chaucer, among other things, had this in common, that they refined their mother-tongues; but with this difference, that Dante had begun to file their language, at least in verse, before the time of Boccace, who likewise received no little help from his master Petrarch; but the reformation of their prose was wholly owing to Boccace himself, who is yet the standard of purity in the Italian tongue, though many of his phrases are become obsolete, as in process of time it must needs happen. Chaucer (as you have formerly been told by our learned Mr. Rymer) first adorned and amplified our barren tongue from the *Provençal, which was then the most polished of all the modern languages; but this subject has been copiously treated by that great critic, who deserves no little commendation from us his countrymen. For these reasons of time, and resemblance of genius, in Chaucer and Boccace, I resolved to join them in my present work; to which I have added some original papers of my own, which whether they are equal or inferior to my other poems, an author is the most improper judge; and therefore I leave them wholly to the mercy of the reader. I will hope the best, that they will not be condemned; but if they should, I have the excuse of an old gentleman, who, mounting on horseback before some ladies, when I was present, got up somewhat heavily, but desired of the fair spectators that they would count fourscore and eight before they judged him. By the mercy of God, I am already come within twenty years of his number; a cripple in my limbs, but what decays are in my mind, the reader must determine. I think myself as vigorous as ever in the faculties of my soul, excepting only my memory, which is not impaired to any great degree; and if I lose not more of it, I have no great reason to complain. What judgment I had increases rather than diminishes; and thoughts, such as they are, come crowding in so fast upon me that my only difficulty is to choose or to reject, to run them into verse, or to give them the other harmony of prose: I have so long studied and practised both that they are grown into a habit, and become familiar to me. In short, though I may lawfully plead some part of the old gentleman's excuse, yet I will reserve it till I think I have greater need, and ask no grains of allowance for the faults of this my present work but those which are given of course to human frailty. I will not trouble my reader with the shortness of time in which I writ it, or the several intervals of sickness. They who think too well of their own performances are apt to boast in their prefaces how little time their works have cost them, and what other business of more importance interfered; but the reader will be as apt to ask the question, why they allowed not a longer time to make their works more perfect, and why they had so despicable an opinion of their judges as to thrust their indigested stuff upon them, as if they deserved no better.

With this account of my present undertaking, I conclude the first part of this discourse; in the second part, as at a second sitting, though I alter not the draught, I must touch the same features over again, and change the dead-colouring of the whole. In general I will only say that I have written nothing which savours of *immorality or profaneness; at least, I am not conscious to myself of any such intention. If there happen to be found an irreverent expression, or a thought too wanton, they are crept into my verses through my inadvertency; if the searchers find any in the cargo, let them be staved or forfeited, like counterbanded goods; at least let their authors be answerable for them, as being but imported merchandise, and not of my own manufacture. On the other side, I have endeavoured to choose such fables, both ancient and modern, as contain in each of them some instructive moral; which I could prove by induction, but the way is tedious, and they leap foremost into sight, without the reader's trouble of looking after them. I wish I could affirm, with a safe conscience, that I had taken the same care in all my former writings; for it must be owned that, supposing verses are never so beautiful or pleasing, yet, if they contain anything which shocks religion or good manners, they are at best what Horace says of good numbers without good sense, **Versus inopes rerum, nugæque canoræ*. Thus far, I hope, I am right in court, without renouncing to my other right of self-defence, where I have been wrongfully accused, and my sense wire-drawn into blasphemy or bawdry, as it has often been by a religious lawyer, in a late pleading against the stage; in which he mixes truth with falsehood, and has not forgotten the old rule of calumniating strongly, that something may remain.

I resume the thread of my discourse with the first of my translations, which was the first *Iliad* of Homer. If it shall please God to give me longer life, and moderate health, my intentions are to translate the whole *Ilias*; provided still that I meet with those encouragements from the public which may enable me to proceed in my undertaking with some cheerfulness. And this I dare assure the world beforehand that I have found by trial, Homer a more pleasing task than Virgil, though I say not the translation will be less laborious; for the Grecian is more according to my genius than the Latin poet. In the works of the two authors we may read their manners, and natural inclinations, which are wholly different. Virgil was of a quiet, sedate temper; Homer was violent, impetuous, and full of fire. The chief talent of Virgil was propriety of thoughts, and ornament of words: Homer was rapid in his thoughts, and took all the liberties, both of numbers and of expressions, which his language, and the age in which he lived, allowed him. Homer's invention was more copious, Virgil's more confined; so that if Homer had not led the way, it was not in Virgil to have begun heroic poetry; for nothing can be more evident than that the Roman poem is but the second part of the *Ilias*; a continuation of the same story, and the persons already formed. The manners of Æneas are those of Hector, superadded to those which Homer gave him. The adventures of Ulysses in the *Odysseis* are imitated in the first six books of Virgil's *Æneis*; and though the accidents are not the same (which would have argued him of a servile copying, and total barrenness of invention), yet the seas were the same in which both the heroes wandered; and Dido cannot be denied to be the poetical daughter of Calypso. The six latter books of Virgil's poem are the four-and-twenty *Iliads* contracted: a quarrel occasioned by a lady, a single combat, battles fought, and a town besieged. I say not this in derogation to Virgil, neither do I contradict anything which I have formerly said in his just praise; for his episodes are almost wholly of his own invention, and the form which he has given to the telling makes the tale his own, even though the original story had been the same. But this proves, however, that Homer taught Virgil to design; and if invention be the first virtue of an epic poet, then the Latin poem can only be allowed the second place. Mr. Hobbes, in the preface to his own bald translation of the *Ilias* (studying poetry as he did mathematics, when it was too late), Mr. Hobbes, I say, begins the praise of Homer where he should have ended it. He tells us that the first beauty of an epic poem consists in diction; that is, in the choice of words, and harmony of numbers. Now the words are the colouring of the work, which, in the order of nature, is last to be considered. The design, the disposition, the manners, and the thoughts are all before it: where any of those are wanting or imperfect, so much wants or is imperfect in the imitation of human life, which is in the very definition of a poem. Words, indeed, like glaring colours, are the first beauties that arise and strike the sight; but, if the draught be false or lame, the figures ill disposed, the manners obscure or inconsistent, or the thoughts unnatural, then the finest colours are but daubing, and the piece is a beautiful monster at the best. Neither Virgil nor Homer were deficient in any of the former beauties; but in this last, which is expression, the Roman poet is at least equal to the Grecian, as I have said elsewhere: supplying the poverty of his language by his musical ear, and by his diligence.

But to return: our two great poets being so different in their tempers, one choleric and sanguine, the other phlegmatic and melancholic; that which makes them excel in their several ways is that each of them has followed his own natural inclination, as well in forming the design as in the execution of it. The very heroes show their authors: Achilles is hot, impatient, revengeful —

**Impiger, iracundus, inexorabilis, acer*, etc.,

Æneas patient, considerate, careful of his people, and merciful to his enemies; ever submissive to the will of heaven —

*... *quo fata trahunt retrahuntque, sequamur.*

I could please myself with enlarging on this subject, but am forced to defer it to a fitter time. From all I have said, I will only draw this inference, that the action of Homer, being more full of vigour than that of Virgil, according to the temper of the writer, is of consequence more pleasing to the reader. One warms you by degrees; the other sets you on fire all at once, and never intermits his heat. 'Tis the same difference which Longinus makes betwixt the effects of eloquence in Demosthenes and Tully; one persuades, the other commands. You never cool while you read Homer, even not in the second book (a graceful flattery to his countrymen); but he hastens from the ships, and concludes not that book till he has made you an amends by the violent playing of a new machine. From thence he hurries on his action with variety of events, and ends it in less compass than two months. This vehemence of his, I confess, is more suitable to my temper; and, therefore, I have translated his first book with greater pleasure than any part of Virgil; but it was not a pleasure without pains. The continual agitations of the spirits must needs be a weakening of any constitution, especially in age; and many pauses are required for refreshment betwixt the heats; the *Iliad* of itself being a third part longer than all Virgil's works together.

This is what I thought needful in this place to say of Homer. I proceed to Ovid and Chaucer; considering the former only in relation to the latter. With Ovid ended the Golden Age of the Roman tongue; from Chaucer the purity of the English tongue began. The manners of the poets were not unlike. Both of them were well-bred, well-natured, amorous, and libertine, at least in their writings; it may be also in their lives. Their studies were the same, philosophy and *philology. Both of them were knowing in astronomy; of which Ovid's books of the *Roman Feasts*, and Chaucer's *Treatise of the Astrolabe*, are sufficient witnesses. But Chaucer was likewise an astrologer, as were Virgil, Horace, Persius, and Manilius. Both writ with wonderful facility and clearness; neither were great inventors: for Ovid only copied the Grecian fables, and most of Chaucer's stories were taken from his Italian contemporaries, or their predecessors. *Boccace his *Decameron* was first published, and from thence our Englishman has borrowed many of his *Canterbury Tales*: yet that of *Palamon and Arcite* was written, in all probability, by some Italian wit, in a former age, as I shall prove hereafter. *The tale of *Grizild* was the invention of Petrarch; by him sent to Boccace, from whom it came to Chaucer. *Troilus and Cressida* was also written by a Lombard author, but much amplified by our English translator, as well as beautified; the genius of our countrymen, in general, being rather to improve an invention than to invent themselves, as is evident not only in our poetry, but in many of our manufactures. I find I have anticipated already, and taken up from Boccace before I come to him: but there is so much less behind; and I am of the temper of most kings, who love to be in debt, are all for present money, no matter how they pay it afterwards: besides, the nature of a preface is rambling, never wholly out of the way, nor in it. This I have learned from the practice of honest Montaigne, and return at my pleasure to Ovid and Chaucer, of whom I have little more to say.

Both of them built on the inventions of other men; yet since Chaucer had something of his own, as **The Wife of Bath's Tale, The Cock and the Fox*, which I have translated, and some others, I may justly give our countryman the precedence in that part; since I can remember nothing of Ovid which was wholly his. Both of them understood the manners; under which name I comprehend the passions, and in a larger sense, the descriptions of persons, and their very habits. For an example, I see Baucis and Philemon as perfectly before me as if some ancient painter had drawn them; and all the Pilgrims in the *Canterbury Tales*, their humours, their features, and the very dress, as distinctly as if I had supped with them at the Tabard in Southwark. Yet even there, too, the figures of Chaucer are much more lively, and set in a better light; which though I have not time to prove, yet I appeal to the reader, and am sure he will clear me from partiality. The thoughts and words remain to be considered, in the comparison of the two poets, and I have saved myself one-half of the labour by owning that Ovid lived when the Roman tongue was in its meridian, Chaucer in the dawning of our language; therefore, that part of the comparison stands not on an equal foot, any more than the diction of Ennius and Ovid, or of Chaucer and our present English. The words are given up, as a post not to be defended in our poet, because he wanted the modern art of fortifying. The thoughts remain to be considered; and they are to be measured only by their propriety; that is, as they flow more or less naturally from the persons described, on such and such occasions. The vulgar judges, which are nine parts in ten of all nations, who call conceits and jingles wit, who see Ovid full of them, and Chaucer altogether without them, will think me little less than mad for preferring the Englishman to the Roman. Yet, with their leave, I must presume to say that the things they admire are only glittering trifles, and so far from being witty, that in a serious poem they are nauseous, because they are unnatural. Would any man, who is ready to die for love, describe his passion like Narcissus? Would he think of **inopem me copia fecit*, and a dozen more of such expressions, poured on the neck of one another, and signifying all the same thing? If this were wit, was this a time to be witty, when the poor wretch was in the agony of death? This is just *John Littlewit, in *Bartholomew Fair*, who had a conceit (as he tells you) left him in his misery, a miserable conceit. On these occasions the poet should endeavour to raise pity; but, instead of this, Ovid is tickling you to laugh. Virgil never made use of such machines when he was moving you to commiserate the death of Dido: he would not destroy what he was building. Chaucer makes Arcite violent in his love, and unjust in the pursuit of it; yet, when he came to die, he made him think more reasonably: he repents not of his love, for that had altered his character; but acknowledges the injustice of his proceedings, and resigns Emilia to Palamon. What would Ovid have done on this occasion? He would certainly have made Arcite witty on his deathbed; he had complained he was further off from possession, by being so near, and a thousand such boyisms, which Chaucer rejected as below the dignity of the subject. They who think otherwise would, by the same reason, prefer Lucan and Ovid to Homer and Virgil, and Martial to all four of them. As for the turn of words, in which Ovid particularly excels all poets, they are sometimes a fault, and sometimes a beauty, as they are used properly or improperly; but in strong passions always to be shunned, because passions are serious, and will admit no playing. The French have a high value for them; and, I confess, they are often what they call delicate, when they are introduced with judgment; but Chaucer writ with more simplicity, and followed nature more closely than to use them. I have thus far, to the best of my knowledge, been an upright judge betwixt the parties in competition, not meddling with the design nor the disposition of it; because the design was not their own; and in the disposing of it they were equal. It remains that I say somewhat of Chaucer in particular.

In the first place, as he is the father of English poetry, so I hold him in the same degree of veneration as the Grecians held Homer, or the Romans Virgil. He is a perpetual fountain of good sense; learned in all sciences; and, therefore, speaks properly on all subjects. As he knew what to say, so he knows also when to leave off; a continence which is practised by few writers, and scarcely by any of the ancients, excepting Virgil and Horace. *One of our late great poets is sunk in his reputation because he could never forgive any conceit which came in his way; but swept like a drag-net, great and small. There was plenty enough, but the dishes were ill sorted; whole pyramids of sweetmeats for boys and women but little of solid meat for men. All this proceeded not from any want of knowledge, but of judgment. Neither did he want that in discerning the beauties and faults of other poets, but only indulged himself in the luxury of writing; and perhaps knew it was a fault, but hoped the reader would not find it. For this reason, though he must always be thought a great poet, he is no longer esteemed a good writer; and for ten impressions, which his works have had in so many successive years, yet at present a hundred books are scarcely purchased once a twelvemonth; for, as my last Lord Rochester said, though somewhat profanely, "not being of God, he could not stand."

Chaucer followed Nature everywhere, but was never so bold to go beyond her; and there is a great difference of being **poeta* and *nimis poeta*, if we may believe Catullus, as much as betwixt a modest behaviour and affectation. The verse of Chaucer, I confess, is not harmonious to us; but 'tis like the eloquence of one whom Tacitus commends, it was **auribus istius temporis accommodata:* they who lived with him, and some time after him, thought it musical; and it continues so, even in our judgment, if compared with the numbers of Lydgate and Gower, his contemporaries; there is the rude sweetness of a Scotch tune in it, which is natural and pleasing, though not perfect. 'Tis true, I cannot go so far as *he who published the last edition of him; for he would make us believe the fault is in our ears, and that there were really ten syllables in a verse where we find but nine: but this opinion is not worth confuting; 'tis so gross and obvious an error that common sense (which is a rule in everything but matters of faith and revelation) must convince the reader that equality of numbers, in every verse which we call *heroic*, was either not known, or not always practised, in Chaucer's age. It were an easy matter to produce some thousands of his verses which are lame for want of half a foot, and sometimes a whole one, and which no pronunciation can make otherwise. We can only say that he lived in the infancy of our poetry, and that nothing is brought to perfection at the first. We must be children before we grow men. There was an Ennius and in process of time a Lucilius and a Lucretius, before Virgil and Horace; even after Chaucer there was a Spenser, a Harrington, a Fairfax, before Waller and Denham were in being; and our numbers were in their nonage till these last appeared. I need say little of his *parentage, life, and fortunes; they are to be found at large in all the editions of his works. He was employed abroad, and favoured, by Edward the Third, Richard the Second, and Henry the Fourth, and was poet, as I suppose, to all three of them. In Richard's time, I doubt, he was a little dipped in the rebellion of the Commons; and being brother-in-law to John of Gaunt, it was no wonder if he followed the fortunes of that family; and was well with Henry the Fourth when he had deposed his predecessor. Neither is it to be admired that Henry, who was a wise as well as a valiant prince, who claimed by succession, and was sensible that his title was not sound, but was rightfully in Mortimer, who had married the heir of York; it was not to be admired, I say, if that great politician should be pleased to have the greatest wit of those times in his interests, and to be the trumpet of his praises. Augustus had given him the example, by the advice of Mæcenas, who recommended Virgil and Horace to him; whose praises helped to make him popular while he was alive, and after his death have made him precious to posterity. As for the religion of our poet, he seems to have some little bias towards the opinions of Wiclif, after John of Gaunt, his patron; somewhat of which appears in * the tale of *Piers Plowman*; yet I cannot blame him for inveighing so sharply against the vices of the clergy in his age: their pride, their ambition, their pomp, their avarice, their worldly interest deserved the lashes which he gave them, both in that, and in most of his *Canterbury Tales*. Neither has his contemporary Boccace spared them: yet both those poets lived in much esteem with good and holy men in orders; for the scandal which is given by particular priests reflects not on the sacred function. Chaucer's Monk, his Canon, and his Friar took not from the character of his Good Parson. A satirical poet is the check of the laymen on bad priests. We are only to take care that we involve not the innocent with the guilty in the same condemnation. The good cannot be too much honoured, nor the bad too coarsely used, for the corruption of the best becomes the worst. When a clergyman is whipped, his gown is first taken off, by which the dignity of his order is secured. If he be wrongfully accused, he has his action of slander; and 'tis at the poet's peril if he transgress the law. But they will tell us that all kind of satire, though never so well deserved by particular priests, yet brings the whole order into contempt. Is then the peerage of England anything dishonoured when a peer suffers for his treason? If he be libelled, or any way defamed, he has his **scandalum magnatum* to punish the offender. They who use this kind of argument seem to be conscious to themselves of somewhat which has deserved the poet's lash, and are less concerned for their public capacity than for their private; at least there is pride at the bottom of their reasoning. If the faults of men in orders are only to be judged among themselves, they are all in some sort parties; for, since they say the honour of their order is concerned in every member of it, how can we be sure that they will be impartial judges? How far I may be allowed to speak my opinion in this case, I know not; but I am sure a dispute of this nature caused mischief in abundance betwixt * a King of England and an Archbishop of Canterbury; one standing up for the laws of his land, and the other for the honour (as he called it) of God's Church; which ended in the murder of the prelate, and in the whipping of his Majesty from post to pillar for his penance. The *learned and ingenious Dr. Drake has saved me the labour of inquiring into the esteem and reverence which the priests have had of old; and I would rather extend than diminish any part of it; yet I must needs say that when a priest provokes me without any occasion given him, I have no reason, unless it be the charity of a Christian, to forgive him: **prior læsit* is justification sufficient in the civil law. If I answer him in his own language, self-defence, I am sure, must be allowed me; and if I carry it further, even to a sharp recrimination, somewhat may be indulged to human frailty. Yet my resentment has not wrought so far but that I have followed Chaucer in his character of a holy man, and have enlarged on that subject with some pleasure; reserving to myself the right, if I shall think fit hereafter, to describe another sort of priests, such as are more easily to be found than the Good Parson; such as have given the last blow to Christianity in this age, by a practice so contrary to their doctrine. But this will keep cold till another time. In the meanwhile, I take up Chaucer where I left him.

He must have been a man of a most wonderful comprehensive nature, because, as it has been truly observed of him, he has taken into the compass of his *Canterbury Tales* the various manners and humours (as we now call them) of the whole English nation in his age. Not a single character has escaped him. All his pilgrims are severally distinguished from each other; and not only in their inclinations, but in their very physiognomies and persons. *Baptista Porta could not have described their natures better, than by the marks which the poet gives them. The matter and manner of their tales, and of their telling, are so suited to their different educations, humours, and callings that each of them would be improper in any other mouth. Even the grave and serious characters are distinguished by their several sorts of gravity: their discourses are such as belong to their age, their calling, and their breeding; such as are becoming of them, and of them only. Some of his persons are vicious, and some virtuous; some are unlearned, or (as Chaucer calls them) lewd, and some are learned. Even the ribaldry of the low characters is different: the Reeve, the Miller, and the Cook are several men, and distinguished from each other as much as the mincing Lady Prioress and the broad-speaking, gap-toothed Wife of Bath. But enough of this; there is such a variety of game springing up before me that I am distracted in my choice, and know not which to follow. 'Tis sufficient to say, according to the proverb, that "here is God's plenty." We have our forefathers and great-grand-dames all before us, as they were in Chaucer's days: their general characters are still remaining in mankind, and even in England, though they are called by other names than those of Monks, and Friars, and Canons, and Lady Abbesses, and Nuns; for mankind is ever the same, and nothing lost out of nature, though everything is altered. May I have leave to do myself the justice (since my enemies will do me none, and are so far from granting me to be a good poet that they will not allow me so much as to be a Christian, or a moral man), may I have leave, I say, to inform my reader that I have confined my choice to such tales of Chaucer as savour nothing of immodesty. If I had desired more to please than to instruct, the Reeve, the Miller, the Shipman, the Merchant, the Summoner, and, above all, the Wife of Bath, in the Prologue to her Tale, would have procured me as many friends and readers as there are beaux and ladies of pleasure in the town. But I will no more offend against good manners: I am sensible as I ought to be of the scandal I have given by my loose writings; and make what reparation I am able, by this public acknowledgment. If anything of this nature, or of profaneness be crept into these poems, I am so far from defending it that I disown it. **Totum hoc indictum volo.* Chaucer makes another manner of apology for his broad speaking, and Boccace makes the like; but I will follow neither of them. Our countryman, in the end of his Characters, before the *Canterbury Tales*, thus excuses the ribaldry, which is very gross in many of his novels—

But firste, I pray you, of your courtesy,
That ye ne arrete it nought my villany,
Though that I plainly speak in this mattere,
To tellen you her words, and eke her chere:
Ne though I speak her words properly,
For this ye knowen as well as I,
Who shall tellen a tale after a man,
He mote rehearse as nye as ever he can:
Everich word of it ben in his charge,
All speke he, never so rudely, ne large:
Or else he mote tellen his tale untrue,
Or feine things, or find words new:
He may not spare, altho he were his brother,
He mote as wel say o word as another.
Crist spake himself ful broad in holy Writ,
And well I wote no villany is it.
Eke Plato saith, who so can him rede,
The words mote been cousin to the dede.

Yet if a man should have enquired of Boccace or of Chaucer what need they had of introducing such characters, where obscene words were proper in their mouths, but very undecent to be heard; I know not what answer they could have made; for that reason, such tales shall be left untold by me. You have here a specimen of Chaucer's language, which is so obsolete that his sense is scarce to be understood; and you have likewise more than one example of his unequal numbers, which were mentioned before. Yet many of his verses consist of ten syllables, and the words not much behind our present English: as for example, these two lines, in the description of the Carpenter's young wife —

> Wincing she was, as is a jolly colt,
> Long as a mast, and upright as a bolt.

I have almost done with Chaucer, when I have answered some objections relating to my present work. I find some people are offended that I have turned these tales into modern English, because they think them unworthy of my pains, and look on Chaucer as a dry, old-fashioned wit, not worth reviving. I have often heard the late Earl of Leicester say that Mr. Cowley himself was of that opinion; who, having read him over at my Lord's request, declared he had no taste of him. I dare not advance my opinion against the judgment of so great an author; but I think it fair, however, to leave the decision to the public. Mr. Cowley was too modest to set up for a dictator; and being shocked perhaps with his old style, never examined into the depth of his good sense. Chaucer, I confess, is a rough diamond, and must first be polished ere he shines. I deny not likewise that, living in our early days of poetry, he writes not always of a piece; but sometimes mingles trivial things with those of greater moment. Sometimes also, though not often, he runs riot, like Ovid, and knows not when he has said enough. But there are more great wits besides Chaucer, whose fault is their excess of conceits, and those ill sorted. An author is not to write all he can, but only all he ought. Having observed this redundancy in Chaucer (as it is an easy matter for a man of ordinary parts to find a fault in one of greater), I have not tied myself to a literal translation; but have often omitted what I judged unnecessary, or not of dignity enough to appear in the company of better thoughts. I have presumed farther, in some places, and added somewhat of my own where I thought my author was deficient, and had not given his thoughts their true lustre, for want of words in the beginning of our language. And to this I was the more emboldened, because (if I may be permitted to say it of myself) I found I had a soul congenial to his, and that I had been conversant in the same studies. Another poet, in another age, may take the same liberty with my writings; if at least they live long enough to deserve correction. It was also necessary sometimes to restore the sense of Chaucer, which was lost or mangled in the errors of the press. Let this example suffice at present: in the story of *Palamon and Arcite*, where the temple of Diana is described, you find these verses in all the editions of our author: —

> There saw I Danè turned unto a tree,
> I mean not the goddess Diane,
> But Venus daughter, which that hight Danè.

Which, after a little consideration, I knew was to be reformed into this sense, that Daphne, the daughter of Peneus, was turned into a tree. I durst not make thus bold with Ovid, lest *some future Milbourne should arise and say I varied from my author because I understood him not.

But there are other judges who think I ought not to have translated Chaucer into English, out of a quite contrary notion: they suppose there is a certain veneration due to his old language, and that it is little less than profanation and sacrilege to alter it. They are farther of opinion that somewhat of his good sense will suffer in this transfusion, and much of the beauty of his thoughts will infallibly be lost, which appear with more grace in their old habit. Of this opinion was that excellent person, whom I mentioned, the late Earl of Leicester, who valued Chaucer as much as Mr. Cowley despised him. My Lord dissuaded me from this attempt (for I was thinking of it some years before his death) and his authority prevailed so far with me, as to defer my undertaking while he lived, in deference to him: yet my reason was not convinced with what he urged against it. If the first end of a writer be to be understood, then, as his language grows obsolete, his thoughts must grow obscure —

> **Multa renascentur, quæ nunc cecidere; cadentque*
> *Quæ nunc sunt in honore vocabula, si volet usus,*
> *Quem penes arbitrium est et jus et norma loquendi.*

When an ancient word, for its sound and significancy, deserves to be revived, I have that reasonable veneration for antiquity to restore it. All beyond this is superstition. Words are not like landmarks, so sacred as never to be removed; customs are changed, and even statutes are silently repealed, when the reason ceases for which they were enacted. As for the other part of the argument, that his thoughts will lose of their original beauty by the innovation of words; in the first place, not only their beauty, but their being is lost, where they are no longer understood, which is the present case. I grant that something must be lost in all transfusion, that is, in all translations; but the sense will remain, which would otherwise be lost, or at least be maimed, when it is scarce intelligible, and that but to a few. How few are there who can read Chaucer so as to understand him perfectly? And if imperfectly, then with less profit, and no pleasure. It is not for the use of some old Saxon friends that I have taken these pains with him: let them neglect my version, because they have no need of it. I made it for their sakes, who understand sense and poetry as well as they, when that poetry and sense is put into words which they understand. I will go farther, and dare to add, that what beauties I lose in some places, I give to others which had them not originally: but in this I may be partial to myself; let the reader judge, and I submit to his decision. Yet I think I have just occasion to complain of them, who because they understand Chaucer, would deprive the greater part of their countrymen of the same advantage, and hoard him up, as misers do their grandam gold, only to look on it themselves, and hinder others from making use of it. In sum, I seriously protest that no man ever had, or can have, a greater veneration for Chaucer than myself. I have translated some part of his works, only that I might perpetuate his memory, or at least refresh it, amongst my countrymen. If I have altered him anywhere for the better, I must at the same time acknowledge that I could have done nothing without him. * *Facile est inventis addere* is no great commendation; and I am not so vain to think I have deserved a greater. I will conclude what I have to say of him singly, with this one remark: a lady of my acquaintance, who keeps a kind of correspondence with some authors of the fair sex in France, has been informed by them that * Mademoiselle de Scudéry, who is as old as Sibyl, and inspired like her by the same god of poetry, is at this time translating Chaucer into modern French. From which I gather that he has been formerly translated into the old Provençal; for how she should come to understand old English, I know not. But the matter of fact being true, it makes me think that there is something in it like fatality; that, after certain periods of time, the fame and memory of great wits should be renewed, as Chaucer is both in France and England. If this be wholly chance, 'tis extraordinary; and I dare not call it more, for fear of being taxed with superstition.

Boccace comes last to be considered, who, living in the same age with Chaucer, had the same genius, and followed the same studies. Both writ novels, and each of them cultivated his mother tongue. But the greatest resemblance of our two modern authors being in their familiar style and pleasing way of relating comical adventures, I may pass it over, because I have translated nothing from Boccace of that nature. In the serious part of poetry, the advantage is wholly on Chaucer's side, for though the Englishman has borrowed many tales from the Italian, yet it appears that those of Boccace were not generally of his own making, but taken from authors of former ages, and by him only modelled; so that what there was of invention, in either of them, may be judged equal. But Chaucer has refined on Boccace, and has mended the stories which he has borrowed, in his way of telling; though prose allows more liberty of thought, and the expression is more easy when unconfined by numbers. Our countryman carries weight, and yet wins the race at disadvantage. I desire not the reader should take my word; and, therefore, I will set two of their discourses, on the same subject, in the same light, for every man to judge betwixt them. I translated Chaucer first, and, amongst the rest, pitched on *The Wife of Bath's Tale;* not daring, as I have said, to adventure on her Prologue, because 'tis too licentious. There Chaucer introduces an old woman, of mean parentage, whom a youthful knight, of noble blood, was forced to marry, and consequently loathed her. The crone being in bed with him on the wedding-night, and finding his aversion, endeavours to win his affection by reason, and speaks a good word for herself (as who could blame her?) in hope to mollify the sullen bridegroom. She takes her topics from the benefits of poverty, the advantages of old age and ugliness, the vanity of youth, and the silly pride of ancestry and titles, without inherent virtue, which is the true nobility. When I had closed Chaucer, I returned to Ovid, and translated some more of his fables; and, by this time, had so far forgotten *The Wife of Bath's Tale*, that, when I took up Boccace, unawares I fell on the same argument, of preferring virtue to nobility of blood and titles, in the story of *Sigismonda;* which I had certainly avoided, for the resemblance of the two discourses, if my memory had not failed me. Let the reader weigh them both; and, if he thinks me partial to Chaucer, 'tis in him to right Boccace.

I prefer, in our countryman, far above all his other stories, the noble poem of *Palamon and Arcite*, which is of the epic kind, and perhaps not much inferior to the *Ilias*, or the *Æneis*. The story is more pleasing than either of them, the manners as perfect, the diction as poetical, the learning as deep and various, and the disposition full as artful: only it includes a greater length of time, as taking up seven years at least; but Aristotle has left undecided the duration of the action; which yet is easily reduced into the compass of a year, by a narration of what preceded the return of Palamon to Athens. I had thought, for the honour of our narration, and more particularly for his, whose laurel, though unworthy, I have worn after him, that this story was of English growth, and Chaucer's own: but I was undeceived by Boccace; for, casually looking on the end of his seventh *Giornata*, I found Dioneo (under which name he shadows himself), and Fiametta (who represents his mistress, the natural daughter of Robert, King of Naples), of whom these words are spoken: **Dioneo e Fiametta gran pezza cantarono insieme d'Arcita, e di Palemone;* by which it appears that this story was written before the time of Boccace; but the name of its author being wholly lost, Chaucer is now become an original; and I question not but the poem has received many beauties, by passing through his noble hands. Besides this tale, there is another of his own invention, after the manner of the Provençals, called * *The Flower and the Leaf*, with which I was so particularly pleased, both for the invention and the moral, that I cannot hinder myself from recommending it to the reader.

As a corollary to this preface, in which I have done justice to others, I owe somewhat to myself; not that I think it worth my time to enter the lists with one M——, and one * B——, but barely to take notice that such men there are, who have written scurrilously against me, without any provocation. M——, who is in orders, pretends, amongst the rest, this quarrel to me, that I have fallen foul on priesthood: if I have, I am only to ask pardon of good priests, and am afraid his part of the reparation will come to little. Let him be satisfied that he shall not be able to force himself upon me for an adversary. I contemn him too much to enter into competition with him. His own translations of Virgil have answered his criticisms on mine. If (as they say, he has declared in print) he prefers the version of * Ogilby to mine, the world has made him the same compliment, for 'tis agreed, on all hands, that he writes even below Ogilby. That, you will say, is not easily to be done; but what cannot M—— bring about? I am satisfied, however, that, while he and I live together, I shall not be thought the worst poet of the age. It looks as if I had desired him underhand to write so ill against me; but upon my honest word I have not bribed him to do me this service, and am wholly guiltless of his pamphlet. 'Tis true, I should be glad if I could persuade him to continue his good offices, and write such another critique on anything of mine; for I find, by experience, he has a great stroke with the reader, when he condemns any of my poems, to make the world have a better opinion of them. He has taken some pains with my poetry; but nobody will be persuaded to take the same with his. If I had taken to the Church, as he affirms, but which was never in my thoughts, I should have had more sense, if not more grace, than to have turned myself out of my benefice, by writing libels on my parishioners. But his account of my manners and my principles are of a piece with his cavils and his poetry; and so I have done with him for ever.

As for the City Bard, or Knight Physician, I hear his quarrel to me is that I was the author of *Absalom and Achitophel*, which, he thinks, is a little hard on his fanatic patrons in London.

But I will deal the more civilly with his two poems, because nothing ill is to be spoken of the dead; and therefore peace be to the *manes* of his *Arthurs*. I will only say that it was not for this noble knight that I drew the plan of an epic poem on King Arthur, in my preface to the translation of Juvenal. The Guardian Angels of kingdoms were machines too ponderous for him to manage; and therefore he rejected them, as Dares did * the whirl-bats of Eryx when they were thrown before him by Entellus: yet from that preface, he plainly took his hint; for he began immediately upon the story, though he had the baseness not to acknowledge his benefactor, but instead of it, to traduce me in a libel.

I shall say the less of * Mr. Collier, because in many things he has taxed me justly; and I have pleaded guilty to all thoughts and expressions of mine which can be truly argued of obscenity, profaneness, or immorality, and retract them. If he be my enemy, let him triumph; if he be my friend, as I have given him no personal occasion to be otherwise, he will be glad of my repentance. It becomes me not to draw my pen in the defence of a bad cause, when I have so often drawn it for a good one. Yet it were not difficult to prove that in many places he has perverted my meaning by his glosses, and interpreted my words into blasphemy and bawdry, of which they were not guilty. Besides that, he is too much given to horseplay in his raillery, and comes to battle like a dictator from the plough. I will not say, "The zeal of God's house has eaten him up"; but I am sure it has devoured some part of his good manners and civility. It might also be doubted whether it were altogether zeal which prompted him to this rough manner of proceeding; perhaps it became not one of his function to rake into the rubbish of ancient and modern plays: a divine might have employed his pains to better purpose than in the nastiness of Plautus and Aristophanes, whose examples, as they excuse not me, so it might be possibly supposed that he read them not without some pleasure. They who have written commentaries on those poets, or on Horace, Juvenal, and Martial, have explained some vices, which, without their interpretation, had been unknown to modern times. Neither has he judged impartially betwixt the former age and us. There is more bawdry in one play of Fletcher's, called *The Custom of the Country*, than in all ours together. Yet this has been often acted on the stage, in my remembrance. Are the times so much more reformed now than they were five-and-twenty years ago? If they are, I congratulate the amendment of our morals. But I am not to prejudice the cause of my fellow poets, though I abandon my own defence: they have some of them answered for themselves; and neither they nor I can think Mr. Collier so formidable an enemy that we should shun him. He has lost ground, at the latter end of the day, by pursuing his point too far, like the Prince of Condé, at the battle of Senneph: from immoral plays to no plays, **ab abusu ad usum, non valet consequentia.* But, being a party, I am not to erect myself into a judge. As for the rest of those who have written against me, they are such scoundrels that they deserve not the least notice to be taken of them. B—— and M—— are only distinguished from the crowd by being remembered to their infamy:

> *. . . *Demetri, teque, Tigelli,*
> *Discipulorum inter jubeo plorare cathedras.*

[1700]

SAMUEL PEPYS

Under the date, May 26, 1703, John Evelyn, then in his eighty-second year, wrote in his diary: "This day died Mr. Samuel Pepys, a very worthy, industrious, and curious person, none in England exceeding him in knowledge of the navy, in which he had passed through all the most considerable offices, Clerk of the Acts and Secretary of the Admiralty, all of which he performed with great integrity. When King James II went out of England, he laid down his office, and would serve no more; but withdrawing himself from all public affairs, he lived at Clapham with his partner, Mr. Hewer, formerly his clerk, in a very noble house and sweet place, where he enjoyed the fruit of his labours in great prosperity. He was universally beloved, hospitable, generous, learned in many things, skilled in music, a very great cherisher of learned men of whom he had the conversation. His library and collection of other curiosities were the most considerable, the models of ships especially. Besides what he published of an account of the navy, as he found and left it, he had for divers years under his hand the History of the Navy, or *Navalia*, as he called it; but how far advanced, and what will follow of his, is left, I suppose, to his sister's son, Mr. Jackson, a young gentleman whom Mr. Pepys had educated in all sorts of useful learning, sending him to travel abroad, from whence he returned with extraordinary accomplishments, and worthy to be heir. Mr. Pepys had been for near forty years so much my particular friend that Mr. Jackson sent me complete mourning, desiring me to be one to hold up the pall at his magnificent obsequies; but my indisposition hindered me from doing him this last office."

Such was the man as he appeared to his contemporaries. If, today, we know him more intimately than was possible to his particular friend of near forty years' standing, we owe our insight to the pages of a work which Evelyn did not mention, one which was read by no one except its author until more than a century after his magnificent obsequies. This was the diary that he kept in a shorthand cipher between January 1, 1660, and May 31, 1669, when he discontinued it because of his failing eyesight. This diary was bound in six volumes and included among the books which he left by will to Magdalene College, Cambridge, where it is preserved in the Pepsian Library. Here it was deciphered by the Reverend John Smith, and a complete transcript made, but only an incomplete edition was first published. This edition was several times reprinted with some additions of the deleted matter. Later, the Reverend Mynors Bright made a second transcription and printed a new and somewhat more complete edition in six volumes (1875–79). Still later H. B. Wheatley published the whole diary, with the exception of a few words here and there which are replaced by dots.

Nowhere else in the world's literature have we so complete and intimate a picture of the life of a distant period of history as we have in Pepys's *Diary*, together with such a complete revelation of the inner life of a human being. For Samuel Pepys was not only in a position to know most of what was going on in the world about him, but he was a close observer with an insatiable curiosity and a keen delight in experiences of every sort, and he had both the desire and the power to show himself as he really was. Many men and some women have written confessions designed to show that they were better or worse than the world supposed. Pepys is never confessional; he never poses and never pretends. Simply, directly, and vividly he presents his thoughts and words and deeds and hopes and fears and most secret emotions. Not even James Joyce in *Ulysses* has portrayed the secret soul of an imaginary character more unsparingly than Pepys has laid bare his own. And because he has told the truth, there is no reader who cannot find the best and the worst, and more than these, the most trivial and withal the most characteristic aspects of his own life here reflected. What most of us are unwilling to admit even to ourselves he has here set down.

It is often asked why Pepys wrote his *Diary* in a secret code and then included it among the books that he bequeathed to a college library. In the first place he used a shorthand system that was quick and economical of space. It was not a secret writing as the term is usually understood; probably any one of half a dozen clerks in the Navy Office could have decoded it, but it could not be read either by his wife or by any casual visitor who picked it up. Some have supposed that it was included by accident among the books of the Pepsian Collection. Such a supposition is hardly tenable when we recall that the books in question were not the whole of his library but the best of them carefully selected, beautifully bound, and arranged in cases made to fit them. The volumes of the *Diary* were preserved by design. Their author certainly had some conception of their value to posterity.

In accordance with the design of this volume to present wholes rather than selections, one complete month, January, 1661, has been included rather than the selections that are usually reprinted. Though at first reading, entries chosen at intervals appear more interesting, they do not give the acquaintance with the author that is provided by the complete *Diary*, even for a single month.

From the DIARY

*1660–61. At the end of the last and the beginning of this year, I do live in one of the houses belonging to the Navy Office, as *one of the principal officers, and have done now about half a year. After much trouble with workmen I am now almost settled; my family being myself, my wife, Jane, Will Hewer, and Wayneman, my girl's brother. Myself in constant good health, and in a most handsome and thriving condition. Blessed be Almighty God for it. I am now taking my sister to come and live with me. As to things of state.—The King settled, and loved of all. The Duke of York matched to my Lord Chancellor's daughter, which do not please many. The Queen upon her return to France with the Princess Henrietta. The *Princess of Orange lately dead, and we into new mourning for her. We have been lately frighted with *a great plot, and many taken up on it, and the fright not quite over. The Parliament, which had done all this great good to the King, beginning to grow factious, the King did dissolve it December 29th last, and another likely to be chosen speedily. I take myself now to be worth £300 clear in money, and all my goods and all manner of debts paid, which are none at all.

1660–61. January 1st. Called up this morning by Mr. Moore, who brought me my last things for me to sign for the last month, and to my great comfort tells me that my fees will come to £80 clear to myself, and about £25 for him, which he hath got out of the pardons, though there be no fee due to me at all out of them. Then comes in my brother Thomas, and after him my father, Dr. Thomas Pepys, my Uncle Fenner and his two sons (Anthony's only child dying this morning, yet he was so civil to come, and was pretty merry) to breakfast; and I had for them a barrel of oysters, a dish of neat's tongues, and a dish of anchovies, wine of all sorts, and Northdown ale. We were very merry till about eleven o'clock, and then they went away. At noon I carried my wife by coach to my cousin, Thomas Pepys, where we, with my father, Dr. Thomas, Cousin Stradwick, Scott, and their wives, dined. Here I first saw his second wife, which is a very respectful woman, but his dinner a sorry, poor dinner for a man of his estate, there being nothing but ordinary meat in it. Today the King dined at a lord's, two doors from us. After dinner I took my wife to Whitehall, I sent her to Mrs. Pierce's (where we should have dined today), and I to the *Privy Seal, where Mr. Moore took out all his money, and he and I went to Mr. Pierce's; in our way seeing the Duke of York bring his lady this day to wait upon the Queen, the first time that ever she did since that great business; and the Queen is said to receive her now with much respect and love; and there he cast up the fees, and I told the money; by the same token one £100 bag, after I had told it, fell all about the room, and I fear I have lost some of it. That done I left my friends and went to *my Lord's, but he being not come in I lodged the money with Mr. Shepley, and bade good night to Mr. Moore, and so returned to Mr. Pierce's, and there supped with them, and Mr. Pierce, the purser, and his wife and mine, where we had a calf's head carboned, but it was raw, we could not eat it, and a good hen. But she is such a slut that I do not love her victuals. After supper I sent them home by coach, and I went to my Lord's and there played until 12 at night at cards at *Best with J. Goods and N. Osgood, and then to bed with Mr. Shepley.

2d. Up early, and being called up to my Lord he did give me many commands in his business. As about taking care to write to my uncle that Mr. Barnewell's papers should be locked up, in case he should die, he being suspected to be very ill. Also about consulting with Mr. W. Montagu for the settling of the £4000 a year that the King had promised my Lord. As also about getting of Mr. George Montagu to be chosen at Huntingdon this next Parliament, &c. That done he to Whitehall stairs with much company, and I with him; where we took water for Lambeth, and there coach for Portsmouth. The Queen's things were all in Whitehall Court ready to be sent away, and her Majesty ready to be gone an hour after to Hampton Court tonight, and so to be at Portsmouth on Saturday next.

* Notes on Samual Pepys will be found in the Appendix, pp. 955 ff.

I by water to my office, and there all the morning, and so home to dinner, where I found *Pall (my sister) was come; but I do not let her sit down at table with me, which I do at first that she may not expect it hereafter from me. After dinner I to Westminster by water, and there found *my brother Spicer at the Leg with all the rest of the Exchequer men (most of whom I now do not know) at dinner. Here I stayed and drank with them, and then to Mr. George Montagu about the business of election, and he did give me a piece in gold; so to my Lord's and got the chest of plate brought to the Exchequer, and my brother Spicer put it into his treasury. So to *Will's with them to a pot of ale, and so parted. I took a turn in the hall, and bought the King and Chancellor's speeches at the dissolving the Parliament last Saturday. So to my Lord's, and took my money I brought thither last night and the silver candlesticks, and by coach left the latter at Alderman Backwell's, I having no use for them, and the former home. There stood a man at our door, when I carried it in, and saw me, which made me a little afeared. Up to my chamber and wrote letters to Huntingdon and did other business. This day I lent *Sir W. Batten and Captn. Rider my chine of beef for to serve dinner tomorrow at Trinity House, the Duke of Albemarle to be there and all the rest of the brethren, it being a great day for the reading over of their new charter, which the King hath newly given them.

3d. Early in the morning to the Exchequer, where I told over what money I had of my Lord's and my own there, which I found to be £970. Thence to Will's, where Spicer and I eat our dinner of a roasted leg of pork which Will did give us, and after that to the Theatre, where was acted *_Beggar's Bush_, it being very well done; and here the first time that ever I saw women come upon the stage. From thence to my father's, where I found my mother gone by Bird, the carrier, to Brampton, upon my uncle's great desire, my aunt being now in despair of life. So home.

4th. Office all the morning, my wife and Pall being gone to my father's to dress dinner for Mr. Honiwood, my mother being gone out of town. Dined at home, and Mr. Moore with me, with whom I had been early this morning at Whitehall, at the Jewel Office, to choose a piece of gilt plate for my Lord, in return of his offering to the King (which it seems is usual at this time of year, and an earl gives twenty pieces in gold in a purse to the King). I chose a gilt tankard, weighing 31 ounces and a half, and he is allowed 30; so I paid 12_s._ for the ounce and half over what he is to have; but strange it was to me to see what a company of small fees I was called upon by a great many to pay there, which I perceive is the manner that courtiers do get their estates. After dinner Mr. Moore and I to the Theatre, where was *_The Scornful Lady_, acted very well, it being the first play that ever he saw. Thence with him to drink a cup of ale at Hercules Pillars, and so parted. I called to see my father, who told me by the way how Will and Mary Joyce do live a strange life together, nothing but fighting, &c., so that sometimes her father has a mind to have them divorced. Thence home.

5th. Home all the morning. Several people came to me about business, among others *the great Tom Fuller, who came to desire a kindness for a friend of his, who hath a mind to go to Jamaica with these two ships that are going, which I promised to do. So to Whitehall to my Lady, whom I found at dinner and dined with her, and stayed with her talking all the afternoon, and thence walked to Westminster Hall. So to Will's, and drank with Spicer, and thence by coach home, staying a little in Paul's Churchyard to bespeak Ogilby's Æsop's _Fables_ and Tully's _Offices_ to be bound for me. So home and to bed.

6th (Lord's day). My wife and I to church this morning, and so home to dinner to a boiled leg of mutton all alone. To church again, where, before sermon, a long Psalm was set that lasted an hour, while the sexton gathered his year's contribution through the whole church. After sermon home, and there I went to my chamber and wrote a letter to send to *Mr. Coventry, with a piece of plate along with it, which I do preserve among my other letters. So to supper, and thence after prayers to bed.

7th. This morning, news was brought to me to my bedside that there had been a great stir in the City this night by the Fanatics, who had been up and killed six or seven men, but all are fled. My Lord Mayor and the whole City had been in arms, above 40,000. To the office, and after that to dinner, where my brother Tom came and dined with me, and after dinner (leaving 12_d._ with the servants to buy a cake with at night, this day being kept as Twelfth Day) Tom and I and my wife to the Theatre, and there saw **The Silent Woman.* The first time that ever I did see it, and it is an excellent play. Among other things here, Kinaston, the boy, had the good turn to appear in three shapes: first, as a poor woman in ordinary clothes, to please Morose; then in fine clothes, as a gallant, and in them was clearly the prettiest woman in the whole house, and lastly, as a man; and then likewise did appear the handsomest man in the house. From thence by link to my Cousin Stradwick's, where my father and we and Dr. Pepys, Scott, and his wife, and one Mr. Ward and his; and after a good supper, we had an excellent cake, where *the mark for the queen was cut, and so there was two queens, my wife and Mrs. Ward; and the king being lost, they chose the doctor to be king; so we made him send for some wine, and then home, and in our way home we were in many places strictly examined, more than in the worst of times, there being great fears of these Fanatics rising again: for the present I do not hear that any of them are taken. Home, it being a clear moonshine and after 12 o'clock at night. Being come home we found that my people had been very merry, and my wife tells me afterwards that she had heard that they had got young Davis and some other neighbours with them to be merry, but no harm.

8th. My wife and I lay very long in bed today talking and pleasing one another in discourse. Being up, Mr. Warren came, and he and I agreed for the deals that my Lord is to have. Then Will and I to Westminster, where I dined with *my Lady. After dinner I took my Lord Hinchinbroke and Mr. Sidney to the Theatre, and showed them **The Widow,* an indifferent good play, but wronged by the women being to seek in their parts. That being done, my Lord's coach waited for us, and so back to my Lady's, where she made me drink of some Florence wine, and did give me two bottles for my wife. From thence walked to my Cousin Stradwick's, and there chose a small banquet and some other things against our entertainment on Thursday next. Thence to Tom Pepys and bought a dozen of trenchers, and so home. Some talk today of a head of Fanatics that do appear about Barnett, but I do not believe it. However, my Lord Mayor, Sir Richd. Browne, hath carried himself very honourably, and hath caused one of their meeting-houses in London to be pulled down.

9th. Waked in the morning about six o'clock, by people running up and down in Mr. Davis's house, talking that the Fanatics were up in arms in the City. And so I rose and went forth; where in the street I found everybody in arms at the doors. So I returned (though with no good courage at all, but that I might not seem to be afeared), and got my sword and pistol, which, however, I had no powder to charge; and went to the door, where I found Sir R. Ford, and with him I walked up and down as far as the Exchange, and there I left him. In our way, the streets full of Train-band, and great stories, what mischief these rogues have done; and I think near a dozen have been killed this morning on both sides. Seeing the City in this condition, the shops shut, and all things in trouble, I went home and sat, it being office day, till noon. So home, and dined at home, my father with me, and after dinner he would needs have me go to my Uncle Wight's (where I have been so long absent that I am ashamed to go). I found him at home and his wife, and I can see they have taken my absence ill, but all things are past and we good friends, and here I sat with my aunt, till it was late, my uncle going forth about business. My aunt being very fearful to be alone. So home to my lute till late, and then to bed, there being strict guards all night in the City, though most of the enemies, they say, are killed or taken. This morning my wife and Pall went forth early, and I stayed within.

10th. There comes Mr. Hawley to me and brings me my money for the quarter of a year's salary of my place under Downing that I was at sea. So I did give him half, whereof he did in his nobleness give the odd 5*s.* to my Jane. So we both went forth (calling first to see how *Sir W. Penn do, whom I found very ill), and at the Hoop by the bridge we drank two pints of wormwood and sack. Talking of his wooing afresh of Mrs. Lane, and of his going to serve the Bishop of London. Thence by water to Whitehall, and found my wife at Mrs. Hunt's. Leaving her to dine there, I went and dined with my Lady, and stayed to talk a while with her. After dinner Will comes to tell me that he had presented my piece of plate to Mr. Coventry, who takes it very kindly, and sends me a very kind letter, and the plate back again; of which my heart is very glad. So to Mrs. Hunt, where I found a Frenchman, a lodger of hers, at dinner, and just as I came in was kissing my wife, which I did not like, though there could not be any hurt in it. Thence by coach to my Uncle Wight's with my wife, but they being out of doors we went home, where after I had put some papers in order and entered some letters in my book which I have a mind to keep, I went with my wife to see Sir W. Penn, who we found ill still, but he do make very much of it. Here we sat a great while; at last comes in Mr. Davis and his lady (who takes it very ill that my wife never did go to see her), and so we fell to talk. Among other things Mr. Davis told us the particular examinations of these Fanatics that are taken: and in short it is this, of all these Fanatics that have done all this, viz., routed all the Train-bands that they met with, put the King's lifeguards to the run, killed about twenty men, broke through the City gates twice; and all this in the daytime, when all the City was in arms; — are not in all above 31. Whereas we did believe them (because they were seen up and down in every place almost in the City, and had been about Highgate two or three days, and in several other places) to be at least 500. A thing that was never heard of, that so few men should dare and do so much mischief. Their word was, "The King Jesus, and *the heads upon the gates." Few of them would receive any quarter, but such as were taken by force and kept alive; expecting Jesus to come here and reign in the world presently, and will not believe yet but their work will be carried on though they do die. The King this day came to town.

11th. Office day. This day comes news, by letters from Portsmouth, that the Princess Henrietta is fallen sick of the measles on board the *London*, after the Queen and she was under sail. And so was forced to come back again into Portsmouth Harbour; and in their way, by negligence of the pilot, run upon the Horse Sand. The Queen and she continue aboard, and do not intend to come on shore till she sees what will become of the young Princess. This news do make people think something indeed, that three of the Royal Family should fall sick of the same disease, one after another. This morning likewise, we had order to see guards set in all the King's yards; and so we do appoint who and who should go to them. Sir Wm. Batten to Chatham, *Colonel Slingsby and I to Deptford and Woolwich. Portsmouth, being a garrison, needs none. Dined at home, discontented that my wife do not go neater now she has two maids. After dinner comes in Kate Sterpin (whom we had not seen a great while) and her husband to see us, with whom I stayed a while, and then to the office, and left them with my wife. At night walked to Paul's Churchyard, and bespoke some books against next week, and from thence to the Coffee-house, where I met Captain Morrice, the upholsterer, who would fain have lent me a horse tonight to have rid with him upon the City-guards, with the Lord Mayor, there being some new expectations of these rogues; but I refused by reason of my going out of town tomorrow. So home to bed.

12th. With Colonel Slingsby and a friend of his, Major Waters (a deaf and most amorous melancholy gentleman, who is under a despair in love, as the colonel told me, which makes him bad company, though a most good-natured man), by water to Redriffe, and so on foot to Deptford (our servants by water), where we fell to choosing four captains to command the guards, and choosing the places where to keep them, and other things in order thereunto. We dined at the Globe, having our messenger with us to take care for us. Never till now did I see the great authority of my place, all the captains of the fleet coming cap in hand to us. Having stayed very late there talking with the colonel, I went home with Mr. Davis, storekeeper (whose wife is ill and so I could not see her) and was there most prince-like lodged, with so great respect and honour that I was at a loss how to behave myself.

13th. In the morning we all went to church, and sat in the pew belonging to us, where a cold sermon of a young man that never had preached before. Here commissioner came with his wife and daughters, the eldest being his wife's daughter is a very comely *black woman. So to the Globe to dinner, and then with Commissioner Pett to his lodgings there (which he hath for the present while he is building the King's yacht, which will be a pretty thing, and much beyond the Dutchman's), and from thence with him and his wife and daughter-in-law by coach to Greenwich Church, where a good sermon, a fine church, and a great company of handsome women. After sermon to Deptford again; where, at the commissioner's and the Globe, we stayed long. And so I to Mr. Davis's to bed again. But no sooner in bed, than we had an alarm, and so we rose; and the Comptroller comes into the yard to us; and seamen of all the ships present repair to us, and there we armed with every one a handspike, with which they were as fierce as could be. At last we hear that it was only five or six men that did ride through the guard in the town, without stopping to the guard that was there; and, some say, shot at them. But all being quiet there, we caused the seamen to go on board again. And so we all to bed (after I had sat awhile with Mr. Davis in his study, which is filled with good books and some very good song books); I likewise to bed.

14th. The arms being come this morning from the Tower, we caused them to be distributed. I spent much time walking with Lieutenant Lambert, walking up and down the yards, who did give me much light into things there, and so went along with me and dined with us. After dinner, Mrs. Pett, her husband being gone this morning with Sir W. Batten to Chatham, lent us her coach, and carried us to Woolwich, where we did also dispose of the arms there and settle the guards. So to Mr. Pett's, the shipwright, and there supped, where he did treat us very handsomely (and strange it is to see what neat houses all the officers of the King's yards have), his wife a proper woman, and has been handsome, and yet has a very pretty hand. Thence I with Mr. Ackworth to his house, where he has a very pretty house, and a very proper lovely woman to his wife, who both sat with me in my chamber, and they being gone, I went to bed, which was also most neat and fine.

15th. Up and down the yard all the morning and seeing the seamen exercise, which they do already very handsomely. Then to dinner at Mr. Ackworth's, where there also dined with us one Captain Bethell, a friend of the comptroller's. A good dinner and very handsome. After that and taking our leaves of the officers of the yard, walked to the waterside and in our way walked into the rope-yard, where I do look into the tar-houses and other places, and took great notice of all the several works belonging to the making of a cable. So after a cup of burnt wine at the tavern there, we took barge and went to Blackwall and viewed the dock and the new wet dock, which is newly made there, and a brave new merchantman which is to be launched shortly, and they say to be called the *Royal Oak*. Hence we walked to Dick-Shore, and thence to the Tower and so home. Where I found my wife and Pall abroad, so I went to see Sir W. Penn, and there found Mr. Coventry come to see him, and now had an opportunity to thank him, and he did express much kindness to me. I sat a great while with Sir Wm. after he was gone and had much talk with him. I perceive none of our officers care much for one another, but I do keep in with them all as much as I can. Sir W. Penn is still very ill as when I went. Home, where my wife not yet come home; so I went up to put my papers in order, and then was much troubled my wife was not come, it being 10 o'clock just now striking as I write this last line. This day I hear the Princess is recovered again. The King hath been this afternoon at Deptford, to see the yacht that Commissioner Pett is building, which will be very pretty; as also that that his brother at Woolwich is in making. By and by comes in my boy and tells me that his mistress do lie this night at Mrs. Hunt's, who is very ill, with which being something satisfied, I went to bed.

16th. This morning I went early to the comptroller's and so with him by coach to Whitehall, to wait upon Mr. Coventry to give him an account of what we have done, which having done, I went away to wait upon my Lady; but coming to her lodgings I find that she is gone this morning to Chatham by coach, thinking to meet me there, which did trouble me exceedingly, and I did not know what to do, being loath to follow her, and yet could not imagine what she would do when she found me not there. In this trouble, I went to take a walk in Westminster Hall and by chance met with Mr. Child, who went forth with my Lady today, but his horse being bad, he come back again, which then did trouble me more, so that I did resolve to go to her; and so by boat home and put on my boots, and so over to Southwark to the posthouse, and there took horse and guide to Dartford and thence to Rochester (I having good horses and good way, come thither about half an hour after daylight, which was before 6 o'clock and I set forth after two), where I found my Lady and her daughter Jem., and Mrs. Browne and five servants, all at a great loss, not finding me here, but at my coming she was overjoyed. The sport was how she had intended to have kept herself unknown, and how the captain (whom she had sent for) of the *Charles* had *forsoothed her, though he knew her well and she him. In fine we supped merry and so to bed, there coming several of the *Charles's* men to see me before I got to bed. The page lay with me.

17th. Up, and breakfast with my Lady. Then come Captains Cuttance and Blake to carry her in the barge on board, and so we went through Ham Creek to the *Sovereign* (a goodly sight all the way to see the brave ships that lie here) first, which is a most noble ship. I never saw her before. My Lady Sandwich, My Lady Jemimah, Mrs. Browne, Mrs. Grace, and Mary and the page, my Lady's servants and myself, all went into *the lantern together. From thence to the *Charles*, where my Lady took great pleasure to see all the rooms, and to hear me tell her how things are when my Lord is there. After we had seen all, then the officers of the ship had prepared a handsome breakfast for her, and while she was pledging my Lord's health they give her five guns. That done, we went off, and then they give us thirteen guns more. I confess it was a great pleasure to myself to see the ship that I began my good fortune in. From thence on board the *Newcastle*, to show my Lady the difference between a great and a small ship. Among these ships I did give away £7. So back again and went on shore at Chatham, where I had ordered the coach to wait for us. Here I heard that Sir William Batten and his lady (who I knew were here, and did endeavour to avoid) were now gone this morning to London. So we took coach, and I went into the coach, and went through the town, without making stop at our inn, but left J. Goods to pay the reckoning. So I rode with my Lady in the coach, and the page on the horse that I should have rid on — he desiring it. It begun to be dark before we could come to Dartford, and to rain hard, and the horses to fail, which was our great care to prevent, for fear of my Lord's displeasure; so here we set up for tonight, as also Captains Cuttance and Blake, who came along with us. We sat and talked till supper, and at supper my Lady and I entered into a great dispute concerning what were best for a man to do with his estate — whether to make his elder son heir, which my Lady is for, and I against, but rather to make all equal. This discourse took us much time, till it was time to go to bed; but we being merry, we bade my Lady good-night and intended to have gone to the post-house to drink, and hear a pretty girl play of the cittern (and indeed we should have lain there, but by a mistake we did not), but it was late, and we could not hear her, and the guard came to examine what we were; so we returned to our inn and to bed, the page and I in one bed, and the two captains in another, all in one chamber, where we had very good mirth with our most abominable lodging.

18th. The captains went with me to the posthouse about 9 o'clock, and after a morning draft I took horse and guide for London; and through some rain, and a great wind in my face, I got to London at eleven o'clock. At home found all well, but the monkey loose, which did anger me, and so I did strike her till she was almost dead, that they might make her fast again, which did still trouble me more. In the afternoon we met at the office and sat till night, and then I to see my father who I found well, and took him to Standing's to drink a cup of ale. He told me my aunt at Brampton is yet alive and my mother well there. In comes Will Joyce to us drunk, and in a talking, vapouring humour of his state, and I know not what, which did vex me cruelly. After him Mr. Hollier had learned at my father's that I was here (where I had appointed to meet him) and so he did give me some things to take for prevention. Will Joyce not letting us talk as I would, I left my father and him and took Mr. Hollier to the Greyhound, where he did advise me above all things, both as to the stone and the decay of my memory (of which I now complain to him), to avoid drinking often, which I am resolved, if I can, to leave off. Hence home, and took home with me from the bookseller's Ogilby's Æsop, which he had bound for me, and indeed I am very much pleased with the book. Home and to bed.

19th. To the comptroller's, and with him by coach to Whitehall; in our way meeting Venner and Pritchard upon a sledge, who with two more Fifth Monarchy men were hanged today, and the two first drawn and quartered. Where we walked up and down, and at last found *Sir G. Carteret, whom I had not seen a great while, and did discourse with him about our assisting the commissioners in paying off the fleet, which we think to decline. Here the treasurer did tell me that he did suspect *Thos. Hater to be an informer of them in this work, which we do take to be a diminution of us, which do trouble me, and I do intend to find out the truth. Hence to my Lady, who told me how Mr. Hetley is dead of the smallpox going to Portsmouth with my Lord. My Lady went forth to dinner to her father's, and so I went to the Leg in King Street and had a rabbit for myself and my Will, and after dinner I sent him home and myself went to the Theatre, where I saw **The Lost Lady*, which do not please me much. Here I was troubled to be seen by four of our office clerks, which sat in the half-crown box and I in the 1*s.* 6*d.* From thence by link, and bought two mouse traps of Thomas Pepys, the turner, and so went and drank a cup of ale with him, and so home and wrote by post to Portsmouth to my Lord, and so to bed.

20th (Lord's day). To church in the morning. Dined at home. My wife and I to church in the afternoon, and that being done we went to see my Uncle and Aunt Wight. There I left my wife and came back, and sat with Sir W. Penn, who is not yet well again. Thence back again to my wife and supped there, and were very merry, and so home, and after prayers to write down my journal for the last five days, and so to bed.

21st. This morning Sir W. Batten, the comptroller and I to Westminster, to the commissioners for paying off the army and navy, where the Duke of Albemarle was; and we sat with our hats on, and did discourse about paying off the ships and do find that they do intend to undertake it without our help; and we are glad of it, for it is a work that will much displease the poor seamen, and so we are glad to have no hand in it. From thence to the Exchequer, and took £200 and carried it home, and so to the office till night, and then to see Sir W. Penn, whither came my Lady Batten and her daughter, and then I sent for my wife, and so we sat talking till it was late. So home to supper and then to bed, having eat no dinner today. It is strange what weather we have had all this winter, no cold at all; but the ways are dusty, and the flies fly up and down, and the rosebushes are full of leaves, such a time of the year as was never known in this world before here. This day many more of the Fifth Monarchy men were hanged.

22nd. To the comptroller's house, where I read over his proposals to the Lord Admiral for the regulating of the officers of the navy, in which he hath taken much pains, only he do seem to have too good opinion of them himself. From thence in his coach to Mercer's Chapel, and so up to the great hall, where we met with the King's Council for Trade, upon some proposals of theirs settling convoys for the whole English trade, and that by having 33 ships (four fourth-rates, nineteen fifths, ten sixths) settled by the King for that purpose, which indeed was argued very finely by many persons of honour and merchants that were there. It pleased me much now to come in this condition to this place, where I was once a petitioner for *my exhibition in Paul's School; and also where Sir G. Downing (my late master) was chairman, and so but equally concerned with me. From thence home, and after a little dinner my wife and I by coach into London, and bought some glasses, and then to Whitehall to see Mrs. Fox, but she not within, my wife to my mother Bowyer, and I met with Dr. Thomas Fuller, and took him to the Dog, where he tells me of his last and great book that is coming out: that is, his history of all the families in England; and could tell me more of my own than I knew myself. And also to what perfection he hath now brought the art of memory; that he did lately to four eminently great scholars dictate together in Latin, upon different subjects of their proposing, faster than they were able to write, till they were tired; and by the way in discourse tells me that the best way of beginning a sentence, if a man should be out and forget his last sentence (which he never was), that then his last refuge is to begin with an **utcunque*. From thence I to Mr. Bowyer's and there sat a while, and so to Mr. Fox's, and sat with them a very little while, and then by coach home, and so to see Sir Wm. Penn, where we found Mrs. Martha Batten and two handsome ladies more, and so we stayed supper and were very merry, and so home to bed.

23rd. To the office all the morning. My wife and people at home busy to get things ready for tomorrow's dinner. At noon, without dinner, went into the City, and there meeting with Greatorex, we went and drank a pot of ale. He told me that he was upon a design to go to Teneriffe to try experiments there. With him to *Gresham College (where I never was before), and saw the manner of the house, and found great company of persons of honour there; thence to my bookseller's, and for books, and to Stevens, the silversmith, to make clean some plate against tomorrow, and so home, by the way paying many little debts for wine and pictures, &c., which is my great pleasure. Home and found all things in a hurry of business, Slater, our messenger, being here as my cook till very late. I in our chamber all the evening looking over my Osborn's works and new Emanuel Thesaurus *Patriarchæ*. So late to bed, having ate nothing today but a piece of bread and cheese at the alehouse with Greatorex, and some bread and butter at home.

24th. At home all day. There dined with me Sir William Batten and his lady and daughter, Sir W. Penn, Mr. Fox (his lady being ill could not come), and Captain Cuttance; the first dinner I have made since I came hither. This cost me above £5, and merry we were — only my chimney smokes. In the afternoon Mr. Hater bringing me my last quarter's salary, which I received of him, and so I have now Mr. Barlow's money in my hands. The company all go away, and by and by Sir Wms. both and my Lady Batten and his daughter come again and supped with me and talked till late, and so to bed, being glad that the trouble is over.

25th. At the office all the morning. Dined at home and Mr. Hater with me, and so I did make even with him for the last quarter. After dinner he and I to look upon the instructions of my Lord Northumberland's, but we were interrupted by Mr. Salisbury's coming in, who came to see me and to show me my Lord's picture in little, of his doing. And truly it is strange to what a perfection he is come in a year's time. From thence to Paul's Churchyard about books, and so back again home. This night comes two cages, which I bought this evening for my canary birds, which Captain Rooth this day sent me. So to bed.

26th. Within all the morning. About noon comes one that had formerly known me and I him, but I know not his name, to borrow £5 of me, but I had the wit to deny him. There dined with me this day both the Pierces and their wives, and Captain Cuttance, and Lieutenant Lambert, with whom we made ourselves very merry by *taking away his ribbons and garters, having made him to confess that he is lately married. The company being gone I went to my lute till night, and so to bed.

27th (Lord's day). Before I rose, letters come to me from Portsmouth, telling me that the Princess is now well, and my Lord Sandwich set sail with the Queen and her yesterday from thence for France. To church, leaving my wife sick . . . at home, a poor dull sermon of a stranger. Home, and at dinner was very angry at my people's eating a fine pudding (made me by Slater, the cook, last Thursday) without my wife's leave. To church again, a good sermon of Mr. Mills, and after sermon Sir W. Penn and I an hour in the garden talking, and he did answer me to many things; I asked Mr. Coventry's opinion of me, and Sir W. Batten's of my Lord Sandwich, which do both please me. Then to Sir W. Batten's, where very merry, and here I met the comptroller and his lady and daughter (the first time I ever saw them) and Mrs. Turner, who and her husband supped with us here (I having fetched my wife thither), and after supper we fell to oysters, and then Mr. Turner went and fetched some strong waters, and so being very merry we parted, and home to bed. This day the parson read a proclamation at church, for the keeping of Wednesday next, the 30th of January, a fast for the murder of the late King.

28th. At the office all the morning; dine at home, and after dinner to Fleet Street, with my sword to Mr. Brigden (lately made Captain of the Auxiliaries) to be refreshed, and with him to an alehouse, where I met Mr. Davenport, and after some talk of Cromwell, Ireton, and Bradshaw's bodies being taken out of their graves today, I went to Mr. Crew's and thence to the Theatre, where I saw again *The Lost Lady*, which do now please me better than before; and here I sitting behind in a dark place, a lady spit backward upon me by mistake, not seeing me, but after seeing her to be a very pretty lady, I was not troubled at it at all. Thence to Mr. Crew's, and there met Mr. Moore, who came lately to me, and went with me to my father's, and with him to Standing's, whither came to us Dr. Fairbrother, who I took and my father to the Bear and gave a pint of sack and a pint of claret. He do still continue his expressions of respect and love to me, and tells me my brother John will make a good scholar. Thence to see the doctor at his lodging at Mr. Holden's, where I bought a hat, cost me 35*s*. So home by moonshine, and by the way was overtaken by the comptroller's coach, and so home to his house with him. So home and to bed. This noon I had my press set up in my chamber for papers to be put in.

29th. Mr. Moore making up accounts with me all this morning till Lieut. Lambert came, and so with them over the water to Southwark, and so over the fields to Lambeth, and there drank, it being a most glorious and warm day, even to amazement for this time of the year. Thence to my Lord's, where we found my Lady gone with some company to see Hampton Court; so we three went to Blackfriars (the first time I ever was there since plays begun), and there after great patience and little expectation, from so poor beginning, I saw three acts of **The Maid in the Mill* acted to my great content. But it being late, I left the play and them, and by water through bridge home, and so to Mr. Turner's house, where the comptroller, Sir William Batten, and Mr. Davis and their ladies; and here we had a most neat little but costly and genteel supper, and after that a great deal of impertinent mirth by Mr. Davis, and some catches, and so broke up, and going away, Mr. Davis's eldest son took up my old Lady Slingsby in his arms, and carried her to the coach, and is said to be able to carry three of the biggest men that were in the company, which I wonder at. So home and to bed.

30th (Fast day). The first time that this day hath been yet observed; and Mr. Mills made a most excellent sermon, upon "Lord forgive us our former iniquities," speaking excellently of the justice of God in punishing men for the sins of their ancestors. Home, and John Goods comes, and after dinner I did pay him £30 for my Lady, and after that Sir W. Penn and I into Moorfields and had a brave talk, it being a most pleasant day, and besides much discourse did please ourselves to see young Davis and Whitton, two of our clerks, going by us in the field, who we observe to take much pleasure together, and I did most often see them at play together. Back to the Old James in Bishopsgate Street, where Sir W. Batten and Sir Wm. Rider met him about business of the Trinity House. So I went home, and there understand that my mother is come home well from Brampton, and had a letter from my brother John, a very ingenious one, and he therein begs to have leave to come to town at the Coronation. Then to my Lady Batten's, where my wife and she are lately come back again from being abroad, and seeing of Cromwell, Ireton, and Bradshaw hanged and buried at Tyburn. Then I home.

31st. This morning with Mr. Coventry at Whitehall about getting a ship to carry my Lord's deals to Lynne, and we have chosen the *Gift*. Thence at noon to my Lord's, where my Lady not well; so I eat a mouthful of dinner there, and thence to the Theatre, and there sat in the pit among the company of fine ladies, &c.; and the house was exceeding full to see **Argalus and Parthenia*, the first time that it hath been acted: and indeed it is good, though wronged by my over great expectations, as all things else are. Thence to my father's to see my mother, who is pretty well after her journey from Brampton. She tells me my aunt is pretty well, yet cannot live long. My uncle pretty well too, and she believes would marry again were my aunt dead, which God forbid. So home.

[1825, 1893]

JOHN EVELYN

BETWEEN 1641, when he was twenty-one years of age, and 1706, shortly before his death at the age of eighty-six, John Evelyn kept a diary, which has been preserved in the library of his family seat at Wotton, Surrey. In this diary are mirrored the man and the stirring times in which he lived. If there has been in the public mind of this generation a reaction against the traditional opinion that the Cavaliers were all drunken roisterers, devoid of moral earnestness and spiritual virility, it has been brought about in large measure by J. H. Shorthouse's historical novel, *John Inglesant*, a work which owes not a little to the character of John Evelyn as portrayed in this diary. He was a Cavalier who disliked both asceticism and debauchery, a royalist who hated arbitrary government alike in Parliament and King, a devoted churchman who, without bigotry, set himself against superstition and fanaticism, and a patriotic Englishman who knew the Continent and served his native land without narrowness or insularity.

Throughout the latter part of the reign of Charles I, the Commonwealth, and the reigns of Charles II, James II, William III, and the first part of the reign of Anne, he was a close observer of public affairs; under two kings he took a prominent part in public affairs. He has thus left a historical document of the first importance as well as a contribution to literature. More austere and far less intimate than the revelations of his friend, Pepys, Evelyn's *Diary* shows a high-spirited gentleman whom we neither despise nor love. The one shows its author in dressing gown and slippers; the other maintains the dignity of the drawing room and the library.

Though he wrote numerous other books and pamphlets, John Evelyn's reputation today is based chiefly on his correspondence and on the *Diary*. The extract here reprinted covers all the published entries for the months of September and October, 1666.

From the DIARY

2nd September, [1666.] This fatal night, about ten, began the deplorable fire, near Fish Street, in London.

3rd. I had public prayers at home. The fire continuing, after dinner I took coach with my wife and son, and went to the Bankside in Southwark, where we beheld that dismal spectacle, the whole city in dreadful flames near the waterside; all the houses from the Bridge, all Thames Street, and upwards towards Cheapside, down to the Three Cranes were now consumed; and so returned, exceeding astonished what would become of the rest.

The fire having continued all this night (if I may call that night which was light as day for ten miles round about, after a dreadful manner), when conspiring with a fierce eastern wind in a very dry season, I went on foot to the same place; and saw the whole south part of the City burning from Cheapside to the Thames, and all along Cornhill (for it likewise kindled back against the wind as well as forward), Tower Street, Fenchurch Street, Gracious Street, and so along to Baynard's Castle, and was now taking hold of St. Paul's Church, to which the scaffolds contributed exceedingly. The conflagration was so universal, and the people so astonished, that, from the beginning, I know not by what despondency or fate, they hardly stirred to quench it; so that there was nothing heard or seen but crying out and lamentation, running about like distracted creatures, without at all attempting to save even their goods; such a strange consternation there was upon them, so as it burned both in breadth and length the churches, public halls, Exchange, hospitals, monuments, and ornaments, leaping after a prodigious manner from house to house, and street to street, at great distances one from the other. For the heat, with a long set of fair and warm weather, had even ignited the air, and prepared the materials to conceive the fire, which devoured, after an incredible manner, houses, furniture, and everything. Here we saw the Thames covered with goods floating, all the barges and boats laden with what some had time and courage to save, as on the other side carts, &c., carrying out to the fields, which for many miles were strewed with movables of all sorts, and tents erecting to shelter both people and what goods they could get away. Oh, the miserable and calamitous spectacle, such as haply the world had not seen since the foundation of it, nor can be outdone till the universal conflagration thereof! All the sky was of a fiery aspect, like the top of a burning oven, and the light seen above forty miles round about for many nights. God grant mine eyes may never behold the like, who now saw above 10,000 houses all in one flame! The noise and cracking and thunder of the impetuous flames, the shrieking of women and children, the hurry of people, the fall of towers, houses, and churches, was like a hideous storm; and the air all about so hot and inflamed that at the last one was not able to approach it, so that they were forced to stand still and let the flames burn on, which they did, for near two miles in length and one in breadth. The clouds also of smoke were dismal, and reached, upon computation, near fifty miles in length. Thus, I left it this afternoon burning, a resemblance of Sodom or the last day. It forcibly called to my mind that passage — * *non enim hic habemus stabilem civitatem*, the ruins resembling the picture of Troy. London was, but is no more! Thus, I returned.

4th September. The burning still rages, and it is now gotten as far as the Inner Temple. All Fleet Street, the Old Bailey, Ludgate Hill, Warwick Lane, Newgate, Paul's Chain, Watling Street, now flaming, and most of it reduced to ashes; the stones of Paul's flew like grenados, the melting lead running down the streets in a stream, and the very pavements glowing with fiery redness, so as no horse, nor man, was able to tread on them, and the demolition had stopped all the passages so that no help could be applied. The eastern wind still more impetuously driving the flames forward. Nothing but the almighty power of God was able to stop them; for vain was the help of man.

5th September. It crossed towards Whitehall; but oh, the confusion there was then at that court! It pleased his Majesty to command me, among the rest, to look after the quenching of Fetter Lane end, to preserve (if possible) that part of Holborn, whilst the rest of the gentlemen took their several posts, some at one part, and some at another (for now they began to bestir themselves, and not till now, who hitherto had stood as men intoxicated, with their hands across), and began to consider that nothing was likely to put a stop but the blowing up of so many houses as might make a wider gap than any had yet been made by the ordinary method of pulling them down with engines. This some stout seamen proposed early enough to have saved near the whole city, but this some tenacious and avaricious men, aldermen, &c., would not permit, because their houses must have been of the first. It was, therefore, now commended to be practised; and my concern being particularly for the hospital of St. Bartholomew, near Smithfield, * where I had many wounded and sick men, made me the more diligent to promote it; nor was my care for the Savoy less. It now pleased God, by abating the wind, and by the industry of the people, when almost all was lost infusing a new spirit into them, that the fury of it began sensibly to abate about noon, so as it came no farther than the Temple westward, nor than the entrance of Smithfield, north; but continued all this day and night so impetuous towards Cripplegate and the Tower, as made us all despair. It also brake out again in the Temple; but the courage of the multitude persisting, and many houses being blown up, such gaps and desolations were soon made, as, with the former three days' consumption, the back fire did not so vehemently urge upon the rest as formerly. There was yet no standing near the burning and glowing ruins by near a furlong's space.

The coal and wood-wharfs, and magazines of oil, rosin, &c., did infinite mischief, so as the invective which a little before I had dedicated to his Majesty and published, giving warning what probably might be the issue of suffering those shops to be in the City was looked upon as a prophecy.

The poor inhabitants were dispersed about St. George's Fields, and Moorfields, as far as Highgate, and several miles in circle, some under tents, some under miserable huts and hovels, many without a rag, or any necessary utensils, bed or board, who from delicateness, riches, and easy accommodations in stately and well furnished houses, were now reduced to extremest misery and poverty.

In this calamitous condition, I returned with a sad heart to my house, blessing and adoring the distinguishing mercy of God to me and mine, who, in the midst of all this ruin, was like Lot, in my little Zoar, safe and sound.

6th September. Thursday. I represented to his Majesty the case of the French prisoners at war in my custody and besought him that there might be still the same care of watching at all places contiguous to unseized houses. It is not indeed imaginable how extraordinary the vigilance and activity of the King and the Duke was, even labouring in person, and being present to command, order, reward, or

* Notes on John Evelyn will be found in the Appendix, p. 957.

encourage workmen, by which he showed his affection to his people, and gained theirs. Having, then, disposed of some under cure at the Savoy, I returned to Whitehall, where I dined at Mr. Offley's, the groom-porter, who was my relation.

7th. I went this morning on foot from Whitehall as far as London Bridge, through the late Fleet Street, Ludgate Hill by St. Paul's, Cheapside, Exchange, Bishopsgate, Aldersgate, and out to Moorfields, thence through Cornhill, &c., with extraordinary difficulty, clambering over heaps of yet smoking rubbish, and frequently mistaking where I was, the ground under my feet so hot that it even burnt the soles of my shoes. In the meantime, his Majesty got to the Tower by water to demolish the houses about *the graff, which, being built entirely about it, had they taken fire and attacked the White Tower, where the magazine of powder lay, would undoubtedly not only have beaten down and destroyed all the bridge, but sunk and torn the vessels in the river, and rendered the demolition beyond all expression for several miles about the country.

At my return, I was infinitely concerned to find that goodly church, St. Paul's, now a sad ruin, and that beautiful portico (for structure comparable to any in Europe, as not long before repaired by the late King) now rent in pieces, flakes of large stones split asunder, and nothing remaining entire but the inscription in the architrave, showing by whom it was built, which had not one letter of it defaced! It was astonishing to see what immense stones the heat had in a manner calcined, so that all the ornaments, columns, friezes, capitals, and projectures of massy Portland stone flew off, even to the very roof, where a sheet of lead covering a great space (no less than six acres by measure) was totally melted. The ruins of the vaulted roof falling, broke into St. Faith's, which being filled with the magazines of books belonging to the stationers, and carried thither for safety, they were all consumed, burning for a week following. It is also observable that the lead over the altar at the east end was untouched, and among the divers monuments the body of one bishop remained entire. Thus lay in ashes that most venerable church, one of the most ancient pieces of early piety in the Christian world, besides near one hundred more. The lead, iron-work, bells, plate, &c., melted, the exquisitely wrought Mercers' Chapel, the sumptuous Exchange, the august fabric of Christ Church, all the rest of the Companies' Halls, splendid buildings, arches, entries, all in dust; the fountains dried up and ruined, whilst the very waters remained boiling; the *voragos of subterranean cellars, wells, and dungeons, formerly warehouses, still burning in stench and dark clouds of smoke; so that in five or six miles traversing about I did not see one load of timber unconsumed, nor many stones but what were calcined white as snow.

The people, who now walked about the ruins, appeared like men in some dismal desert, or rather, in some great city laid waste by a cruel enemy, to which was added the stench that came from some poor creatures' bodies, beds, and other combustible goods. Sir Thomas Gresham's statue, though fallen from its niche in the Royal Exchange, remained entire, when all those of the Kings since the Conquest were broken to pieces. Also the standard in Cornhill, and Queen Elizabeth's effigies, with some arms on Ludgate, continued with but little detriment, whilst the vast iron chains of the City streets, hinges, bars, and gates of prisons, were many of them melted and reduced to cinders by the vehement heat. Nor was I yet able to pass through any of the narrow streets, but kept the widest; the ground and air, smoke and fiery vapour, continued so intense that my hair was almost singed and my feet unsufferably *surbated. The bye-lanes and narrow streets were quite filled up with rubbish; nor could one have possibly known where he was, but by the ruins of some church or hall that had some remarkable tower or pinnacle remaining.

I then went towards Islington and Highgate, where one might have seen 200,000 people of all ranks and degrees dispersed, and lying along by their heaps of what they could save from the fire, deploring their loss, and, though ready to perish for hunger and destitution, yet not asking one penny for relief, which to me appeared a stranger sight than any I had yet beheld. His Majesty and Council indeed took all imaginable care for their relief, by proclamation for the country to come in and refresh them with provisions.

In the midst of all this calamity and confusion there was, I know not how, an alarm begun that the French and Dutch, with whom we were now in hostility, were not only landed but even entering the City. There was, in truth, some days before, great suspicion of those two nations joining, and now that they had been the occasion of firing the town. This report did so terrify that on a sudden there was such an uproar and tumult that they run from their goods, and, taking what weapons they could come at, they could not be stopped from falling on some of those nations whom they casually met, without sense or reason. The clamour and peril grew so excessive that it made the whole Court amazed, and they did with infinite pains and great difficulty reduce and appease the people, sending troops of soldiers and guards to cause them to retire into the fields again, where they were watched all this night. I left them pretty quiet and came home sufficiently weary and broken. Their spirits thus a little calmed, and the affright abated, they now began to repair into the suburbs about the City, where such as had friends or opportunity, got shelter for the present, to which his Majesty's proclamation also invited them.

Still, the plague continuing in our parish, I could not without danger adventure to our church.

10th September. I went again to the ruins, for it was now no longer a city.

13th September. I presented his Majesty with a survey of the ruins, and a plot for a new City, with a discourse on it; whereupon, after dinner, his Majesty sent for me into the Queen's bedchamber, her Majesty and the Duke only being present. They examined each particular, and discoursed on them for near an hour, seeming to be extremely pleased with what I had so early thought on. The Queen was now in her cavalier riding-habit, hat and feather, and horseman's coat, going to take the air.

16th. I went to Greenwich Church, where Mr. Plume preached very well from this text: "Seeing, then, all these things shall be dissolved," &c., taking occasion from the late unparalleled conflagration to mind us how we ought to walk more holy in all manner of conversation.

27th. Dined at Sir William D'Oyly's with that worthy gentleman, Sir John Holland, of Suffolk.

10th October. This day was ordered a general fast through the nation, to humble us on the late dreadful conflagration, added to the plague and war, the most dismal judgments that could be inflicted; but which indeed we highly deserved for our prodigious ingratitude, burning lusts, dissolute court, profane and abominable lives, under such dispensations of God's continued favour in restoring Church, Prince, and People from our late intestine calamities, of which we were altogether unmindful, even to astonishment. This made me resolve to go to our parish assembly, where our doctor preached on Luke xix:41, piously applying it to the occasion. After which was a collection for the distressed losers in the late fire.

18th October. To Court. It being the first time his Majesty put himself solemnly into *the Eastern fashion of vest, changing doublet, stiff collar, bands and cloak, into a comely dress, after the Persian mode, with girdles or straps, and shoe-strings and garters into buckles, of which some were set with precious stones, resolving never to alter it, and to leave the French mode, which had hitherto obtained to our great expense and reproach. Upon which divers courtiers and gentlemen gave his Majesty gold by way of wager that he would not persist in this resolution. I had sometime before presented an invective against that unconstancy, and our so much affecting the French fashion, to his Majesty; in which I took occasion to describe the comeliness and usefulness of the Persian clothing, in the very same manner his Majesty now clad himself. This pamphlet I entitled *Tyrannus, or the Mode*, and gave it to the King to read. I do not impute to this discourse the change which soon happened, but it was an identity that I could not but take notice of.

This night was acted my Lord Broghill's tragedy, called **Mustapha*, before their Majesties at Court, at which I was present; very seldom going to the public theatres for many reasons now, as they were abused to an atheistical liberty; foul and undecent women now (and never till now) permitted to appear and act, who inflaming several young noblemen and gallants, became their misses, and to some, their wives. Witness the Earl of Oxford, Sir R. Howard, Prince Rupert, the Earl of Dorset, and *another greater person than any of them, who fell into their snares, to the reproach of their noble families, and ruin of both body and soul. I was invited by my Lord Chamberlain to see this tragedy, exceedingly well written, though in my mind I did not approve of any such pastime in a time of such judgments and calamities.

21st October. This season, after so long and extraordinary a drought in August and September, as if preparatory for the dreadful fire, was so very wet and rainy as many feared an ensuing famine.

28th. The pestilence, through God's mercy, began now to abate considerably in our town.

30th. To London to our office, and now had I on the vest and surcoat, or tunic, as it was called, after his Majesty had brought the whole court to it. It was a comely and manly habit, too good to hold, it being impossible for us in good earnest to leave the Monsieurs' vanities long.

31st. I heard the signal cause of my Lord Cleveland pleaded before the House of Lords; and was this day forty-six years of age, wonderfully protected by the mercies of God, for which I render him immortal thanks.

[1818]

EDWARD HYDE, EARL OF CLARENDON

Edward Hyde was a trusted counsellor of Charles I during the Civil War, and afterwards of Charles II during his "travels." In 1660 he came into power as chief minister of the restored monarchy; the following year he was created first Earl of Clarendon. The last seven years of his life were spent in exile in France, where he had leisure for the cultivation of letters, in which he had always been interested. Here, besides essays and less important historical works, he finished *The History of the Rebellion and Civil Wars in England,* which he had begun in 1646. It was not published until 1702–04, more than a quarter-century after his death. The manuscripts were left to the University of Oxford, and the profits were spent upon various university projects, chiefly a building for the press which bears his name.

The History is a royalist apology by one of the chief actors in the drama that it presents. As such, it is rather a historical document than a finished and rounded history, but by reason of its literary qualities it has exerted much influence upon historical writing in England. Composed at different times, and embodying considerable portions of a *Life* by himself, it combines the characteristics of memoir and history. Its most striking feature is the series of portraits of the chief participants in the Civil War. These sketches owe something of their form to the seventeenth-century character writers, though Clarendon's chief models in this, as in most respects, are the ancients. The two extracts here reprinted give the character of Charles I, from Book XI, and that of Cromwell, from Book XV. The first illustrates the cult of St. Charles the Martyr, yet it discriminates between the virtues of the man and the weakness of the king. In the second there is recognition of the personal force and the executive vigour of Cromwell, especially as manifested in the foreign relations of England under the Protectorate, qualities that the old statesman admired even in the slayer of the Lord's anointed.

THE HISTORY OF THE REBELLION AND CIVIL WARS IN ENGLAND

From Book XI

CHARLES I

The several unheard of insolences which this excellent prince was forced to submit to, at the other times he was brought before that odious judicatory, his majestic behaviour under so much insolence, and resolute insisting upon his own dignity, and defending it by manifest authorities in the law, as well as by the clearest deductions from reason, the pronouncing that horrible sentence upon the most innocent person in the world, the execution of that sentence by the most execrable murder that was ever committed since that of our blessed Saviour, and the circumstances thereof; the application and interposition that was used by some noble persons to prevent that woful murder, and the hypocrisy with which that interposition was eluded, the saintlike behaviour of that blessed martyr, and his Christian courage and patience at his death, are all particulars so well known, and have been so much enlarged upon in a treatise peculiarly writ to that purpose, that the farther mentioning it in this place would but afflict and grieve the reader, and make the relation itself odious as well as needless; and therefore no more shall be said here of that lamentable tragedy, so much to the dishonour of the nation, and the religion professed by it.

But it will not be unnecessary to add a short character of his person, that posterity may know the inestimable loss which the nation then underwent, in being deprived of a prince whose example would have had a greater influence upon the manners and piety of the nation than the most strict laws can have. To speak first of his private qualifications as a man, before the mention of his princely and royal virtues; he was, if ever any, the most worthy of the title of an honest man, so great a lover of justice that no temptation could dispose him to a wrongful action, except it was so disguised to him that he believed it to be just. He had a tenderness and compassion of nature, which restrained him from ever doing a hardhearted thing; and therefore he was so apt to grant pardon to malefactors that the judges of the land represented to him the damage and insecurity to the public that flowed from such his indulgence. And then he restrained himself from pardoning either murders or highway robberies, and quickly discerned the fruits of his severity by a wonderful reformation of those enormities. He was very punctual and regular in his devotions; he was never known to enter upon his recreations or sports, though never so early in the morning, before he had been at public prayers; so that on hunting days his chaplains were bound to a very early attendance. He was likewise very strict in observing the hours of his private cabinet devotions, and was so severe an exactor of gravity and reverence in all mention of religion that he could never endure any light or profane word, with what sharpness of wit soever it was covered; and though he was well pleased and delighted with reading verses made upon any occasion, no man durst bring before him anything that was profane or unclean. That kind of wit had never any countenance then. He was so great an example of conjugal affection that they who did not imitate him in that particular did not brag of their liberty; and he did not only permit, but direct his bishops to prosecute those scandalous vices in the ecclesiastical courts against persons of eminence and near relation to his service.

His kingly virtues had some mixture and allay, that hindered them from shining in full lustre and from producing those fruits they should have been attended with. He was not in his nature very bountiful, though he gave very much. This appeared more after the *Duke of Buckingham's death, after which those showers fell very rarely; and he paused too long in giving, which made those to whom he gave less sensible of the benefit. He kept state to the full, which made his court very orderly, no man presuming to be seen in a place where he had no pretence to be. He saw and observed men long before he received them about his person, and did not love strangers nor very confident men. He was a patient hearer of causes, which he frequently accustomed himself to at the council board, and judged very well, and was dexterous in the mediating part, so that he often put an end to causes by persuasion, which the stubbornness of men's humours made dilatory in courts of justice.

He was very fearless in his person, but not very enterprising. He had an excellent understanding, but was not confident enough of it, which made him oftentimes change his own opinion for a worse, and follow the advice of men that did not judge so well as himself. This made him more irresolute than the conjuncture of his affairs would admit; if he had been of a rougher and more imperious nature, he would have found more respect and duty. And his not applying some severe cures to approaching evils proceeded from the lenity of his nature and the tenderness of his conscience, which, in all cases of blood, made him choose the softer way, and not hearken to severe counsels, how reasonably soever urged. This only restrained him from pursuing his advantage in the first Scottish expedition, when, humanly speaking, he might have reduced that nation to the most slavish obedience that could have been wished. But no man can say he had then many who advised him to it, but the contrary, by a wonderful indisposition all his council had to fighting, or any other fatigue. He was always an immoderate lover of the Scottish nation, having not only been born there, but educated by that people, and besieged by them always, having few English about him till he was king, and the major number of his servants being still of that nation, who he thought could never fail him. And among these, no man had such an ascendant over him, by the humblest insinuations, as Duke Hamilton had.

As he excelled in all other virtues, so in temperance he was so strict that he abhorred all debauchery to that degree, that, at a great festival solemnity where he once was, when very many of the nobility of the English and Scots were entertained, being told by one who withdrew from thence what vast draughts of wine they drank, and "that there was one earl, who had drank most of the rest down, and was not himself moved or altered," the king said that he deserved to be hanged; and that earl coming shortly after into the room where his majesty was, in some gayety, to show how unhurt he was from that battle, the king sent one to bid him withdraw from his majesty's presence; nor did he in some days after appear before him.

So many miraculous circumstances contributed to his ruin that men might well think that heaven and earth conspired it and that the stars designed it. Though he was, from the first declension of his power, so much betrayed by his own servants that there were very few who remained faithful to him, yet

* Notes on Clarendon will be found in the Appendix, pp. 957 ff.

that treachery proceeded not from any treasonable purpose to do him any harm, but from particular and personal animosities against other men. And, afterwards, the terror all men were under of the Parliament, and the guilt they were conscious of themselves, made them watch all opportunities to make themselves gracious to those who could do them good; and so they became spies upon their master, and from one piece of knavery were hardened and confirmed to undertake another, till at last they had no hope of preservation but by the destruction of their master. And after all this, when a man might reasonably believe that less than a universal defection of three nations could not have reduced a great king to so ugly a fate, it is most certain that, in that very hour when he was thus wickedly murdered in the sight of the sun, he had as great a share in the hearts and affections of his subjects in general, was as much beloved, esteemed, and longed for by the people in general of the three nations, as any of his predecessors had ever been. To conclude, he was the worthiest gentleman, the best master, the best friend, the best husband, the best father, and the best Christian that the age in which he lived produced. And if he were not the best king, if he were without some parts and qualities which have made some kings great and happy, no other prince was ever unhappy who was possessed of half his virtues and endowments, and so much without any kind of vice.

This unparalleled murder and parricide was committed upon the thirtieth of January, in *the year, according to the account used in England, 1648, in the forty and ninth year of his age, and when he had such excellent health and so great vigour of body that when his murderers caused him to be opened, (which they did, and were some of them present at it with great curiosity) they confessed and declared "that no man had ever all his vital parts so perfect and unhurt; and that he seemed to be of so admirable a composition and constitution that he would probably have lived as long as nature could subsist." His body was immediately carried into a room at Whitehall, where he was exposed for many days to the public view, that all men might know that he was not alive. And he was then embalmed, and put into a coffin, and so carried to St. James's, where he likewise remained several days. They who were qualified to look after that province declared, "that he should be buried at Windsor in a decent manner, provided that the whole expense should not exceed five hundred pounds." The Duke of Richmond, the Marquis of Hertford, the Earls of Southampton and Lindsey, who had been of his bedchamber and always very faithful to him, desired those who governed, that they might have leave to perform the last duty to their dead master, and to wait upon him to his grave; which, after some pauses, they were permitted to do, with this, that they should not attend the corpse out of the town; since they resolved it should be privately carried to Windsor without pomp or noise, and then they should have timely notice, that, if they pleased they might be at his interment. And accordingly it was committed to four of those servants who had been by them appointed to wait upon him during his imprisonment that they should convey the body to Windsor, which they did. And it was, that night, placed in that chamber which had usually been his bedchamber; the next morning, it was carried into the great hall, where it remained till the lords came; who arrived there in the afternoon, and immediately went to Colonel Whitchcot, the governor of the castle, and showed the order they had from the Parliament to be present at the burial, which he admitted: but when they desired that his majesty might be buried according to the form of the Common Prayer Book, the Bishop of London being present with them to officiate, he expressly, positively, and roughly refused to consent to it; and said it was not lawful; that the Common Prayer Book was put down, and he would not suffer it to be used in that garrison where he commanded; nor could all the reasons, persuasions, and entreaties prevail with him to suffer it. Then they went into the church to make choice of a place for burial. But when they entered into it, which they had been so well acquainted with, they found it so altered and transformed, all tombs, inscriptions, and those landmarks pulled down, by which all men knew every particular place in that church, and such a dismal mutation over the whole, that they knew not where they were; nor was there one old officer that had belonged to it, or knew where our princes had used to be interred. At last there was a fellow of the town who undertook to tell them the place, where, he said, "there was a vault, in which King Harry the Eighth and Queen Jane Seymour were interred." As near that place as could conveniently be, they caused the grave to be made. There the king's body was laid without any words, or other ceremonies than the tears and sighs of the few beholders. Upon the coffin was a plate of silver fixed with these words only, *King Charles, 1648*. When the coffin was put in, the black velvet pall that had covered it was thrown over it, and then the earth thrown in, which the governor stayed to see perfectly done, and then took the keys of the church, which was seldom put to any use.

From Book XV

OLIVER CROMWELL

He seemed to be much afflicted at the death of his friend, the Earl of Warwick, with whom he had a fast friendship, though neither their humours nor their natures were like. And the heir of that house, who had married his youngest daughter, died about the same time, so that all his relation to, or confidence in, that family was at an end, the other branches of it abhorring his alliance. His domestic delights were lessened every day; he plainly discovered that *his son Falconbridge's heart was set upon an interest destructive to his, and grew to hate him perfectly. But that which chiefly broke his peace was the death of his daughter Claypole, who had been always his greatest joy, and who, in her sickness, which was of a nature the physicians knew not how to deal with, had several conferences with him, which exceedingly perplexed him. Though nobody was near enough to hear the particulars, yet her often mentioning, in the pains she endured, the blood her father had spilt, made people conclude that she had presented his worst actions to his consideration. And though he never made the least show of remorse for any of those actions, it is very certain that either what she said or her death affected him wonderfully.

Whatever it was, about the middle of August, he was seized on by a common tertian ague, from which, he believed, a little ease and divertisement at Hampton Court would have freed him. But the fits grew stronger, and his spirits much abated: so that he returned again to Whitehall, when his physicians began to think him in danger, though the preachers, who prayed always about him, and told God Almighty what great things he had done for him, and how much more need he had still of his service, declared as from God, that he should recover; and he himself did not think he should die, till even the time that his spirits failed him. Then he declared to them that he did appoint his son to succeed him, his eldest son, Richard, and so expired upon the third day of September, 1658, a day he thought always very propitious to him, and on which he had twice triumphed for several victories, a day very memorable for the greatest storm of wind that had been ever known, for some hours before and after his death, which overthrew trees, houses, and made great wrecks at sea; and was so universal that the effects of it were terrible both in France and Flanders, where all people trembled at it, for, besides the wrecks all along the sea-coast, many boats were cast away in the very rivers; and within few days after, the circumstance of his death, that accompanied that storm, was known.

He was one of those men, **quos vituperare ne inimici quidem possunt, nisi ut simul laudent*, for he could never have done half that mischief without great parts of courage, industry, and judgment. He must have had a wonderful understanding in the natures and humours of men, and as great a dexterity in applying them; who, from a private and obscure birth, (though of a good family,) without interest or estate, alliance, or friendship, could raise himself to such a height, and compound and knead such opposite and contradictory tempers, humours, and interests into a consistence that contributed to his designs and to their own destruction, whilst himself grew insensibly powerful enough to cut off those by whom he had climbed, in the instant that they projected to demolish their own building. What Velleius Paterculus said of Cinna may very justly be said of him, **Ausum eum, quæ nemo auderet bonus; perfecisse, quæ a nullo, nisi fortissimo, perfici possent*. Without doubt, no man with more wickedness ever attempted anything, or brought to pass what he desired more wickedly, more in the face and contempt of religion and moral honesty; yet wickedness as great as his could never have accomplished those trophies, without the assistance of a great spirit, and admirable circumspection and sagacity, and a most magnanimous resolution.

When he appeared first in the Parliament, he seemed to have a person in no degree gracious, no ornament of discourse, none of those talents which use to reconcile the affections of the stander-by; yet as he grew into place and authority, his parts seemed to be raised, as if he had had concealed faculties, till he had occasion to use them; and when he was to act the part of a great man, he did it without any indecency, notwithstanding the want of custom.

After he was confirmed and invested Protector by the humble Petition and Advice, he consulted with very few upon any action of importance, nor communicated any enterprise he resolved upon, with more than those who were to have principal parts in the execution of it; nor with them sooner than was absolutely necessary. What he once resolved, in which he was not rash, he would not be dissuaded from, nor endure any contradiction of his power and authority, but extorted obedience from them who were not willing to yield it.

When he had laid some very extraordinary tax upon the City, one Cony, an eminent fanatic, and one who had heretofore served him very notably, positively refused to pay his part, and loudly dissuaded others from submitting to it, "as an imposition notoriously against the law, and the property of the subject, which all honest men were bound to defend." Cromwell sent for him, and cajoled him with the memory of the old kindness and friendship that had been between them; and that of all men he did not expect this opposition from him, in a matter that was so necessary for the good of the commonwealth. But it was always his fortune to meet with the most rude and obstinate behaviour from those who had formerly been absolutely governed by him; and they commonly put him in mind of some expressions and sayings of his own, in cases of the like nature: so this man remembered him, how great an enemy he had expressed himself to such grievances and had declared, "that all who submitted to them, and paid illegal taxes, were more to blame, and greater enemies to their country, than they who had imposed them; and that the tyranny of princes could never be grievous, but by the tameness and stupidity of the people." When Cromwell saw that he could not convert him, he told him that he had a will as stubborn as his, and he would try which of them two should be master. Thereupon, with some terms of reproach and contempt, he committed the man to prison, whose courage was nothing abated by it; but as soon as the term came, he brought his habeas corpus in the King's Bench, which they then called the Upper Bench. Maynard, who was of council with the prisoner, demanded his liberty with great confidence, both upon the illegality of the commitment, and the illegality of the imposition, as being laid without any lawful authority. The judges could not maintain or defend either, and enough declared what their sentence would be; and therefore the Protector's attorney required a farther day, to answer what had been urged. Before that day, Maynard was committed to the Tower for presuming to question or make doubt of his authority; and the judges were sent for, and severely reprehended for suffering that licence; when they, with all humility, mentioned the law and Magna Charta, Cromwell told them, their magna f—— should not control his actions, which he knew were for the safety of the commonwealth. He asked them, who made them judges; whether they had any authority to sit there, but what he gave them; and if his authority were at an end, they knew well enough what would become of themselves; and therefore advised them to be more tender of that which could only preserve them; and so dismissed them with caution that they should not suffer the lawyers to prate what it would not become them to hear.

Thus he subdued a spirit that had been often troublesome to the most sovereign power, and made Westminster Hall as obedient, and subservient to his commands, as any of the rest of his quarters. In all other matters which did not concern the life of his jurisdiction he seemed to have great reverence for the law, rarely interposing between party and party. As he proceeded with this kind of indignation and haughtiness with those who were refractory, and dared to contend with his greatness, so towards all who complied with his good pleasure, and courted his protection, he used a wonderful civility, generosity, and bounty.

To reduce three nations, which perfectly hated him, to an entire obedience to all his dictates, to awe and govern those nations by an army that was indevoted to him, and wished his ruin, was an instance of a very prodigious address. But his greatness at home was but a shadow of the glory he had abroad. It was hard to discover which feared him most, France, Spain, or the Low Countries, where his friendship was current at the value he put upon it. As they did all sacrifice their honour and their interest to his pleasure, so there is nothing he could have demanded that either of them would have denied him. To manifest which, there needs only two instances. The first is, when those of the valley of Lucerne had unwarily rebelled against the Duke of Savoy, which gave occasion to the Pope, and the neighbour princes of Italy, to call and solicit for their extirpation, and their prince positively resolved upon it, Cromwell sent his agent to the Duke of Savoy, a prince with whom he had no correspondence, or commerce, and so engaged the cardinal, and even terrified the Pope himself, without so much as doing any grace to the English Roman Catholics, (nothing being more usual than his saying that his ships in the Mediterranean should visit Civita Vecchia; and that the sound of his cannon should be heard in Rome), that the Duke of Savoy thought it necessary to restore all that he had taken from them, and did renew all those privileges they had formerly enjoyed, and newly forfeited.

The other instance of his authority was yet greater, and more incredible. In the city of Nismes, which is one of the fairest in the province of Languedoc and where * those of the religion do most abound, there was a great faction at that season when the consuls (who are the chief magistrates) were to be chosen. Those of the reformed religion had the confidence to set up one of themselves for that magistracy, which they of the Roman religion resolved to oppose with all their power. The dissension between them made so much noise that the intendant of the province, who is the supreme minister in all civil affairs throughout the whole province, went thither to prevent any disorder that might happen. When the day of election came, those of the religion possessed themselves with many armed men of the town-house, where the election was to be made. The magistrates sent to know what their meaning was; to which they answered, they were there to give their voices for the choice of the new consuls, and to be sure that the election should be fairly made. The bishop of the city, the intendant of the province, with all the officers of the church, and the present magistrates of the town, went together in their robes to be present at the election, without any suspicion that there would be any force used. When they came near the gate of the town-house, which was shut, and they supposed would be opened when they came, they within poured out a volley of musket-shot upon them, by which the dean of the church and two or three of the magistrates of the town were killed upon the place, and very many others wounded, whereof some died shortly after. In this confusion, the magistrates put themselves into as good a posture to defend themselves as they could, without any purpose of offending the other, till they should be better provided; in order to which they sent an express to the court with a plain relation of the whole matter of fact, "and that there appeared to be no manner of combination with those of the religion in other places of the province; but that it was an insolence in those of the place, upon the presumption of their great numbers, which were little inferior to those of the Catholics." The court was glad of the occasion, and resolved that this provocation, in which other places were not involved, and which nobody could excuse, should warrant all kind of severity in that city, even to the pulling down their temples and expelling many of them forever out of the city; which, with the execution and forfeiture of many of the principal persons, would be a general mortification to all of the religion in France, with whom they were heartily offended; and a part of the army was forthwith ordered to march towards Nismes, to see this executed with the utmost rigour.

Those of the religion in the town were quickly sensible into what condition they had brought themselves, and sent, with all possible submission, to the magistrates to excuse themselves, and to impute what had been done to the rashness of particular men, who had no order for what they did. The magistrates answered that they were glad they were sensible of their miscarriage; but they could say nothing upon the subject till the king's pleasure should be known, to whom they had sent a full relation of all that had passed. The others very well knew what the king's pleasure would be, and forthwith sent an express, one Moulins, a Scotchman who had lived many years in that place and in Montpellier, to Cromwell, to desire his protection and interposition. The express made so much haste and found so good a reception the first hour he came, that Cromwell, after he had received the whole account, bade him refresh himself after so long a journey, and he would take such care of his business that by the time he came to Paris he should find it despatched; and, that night, sent away another messenger to his ambassador Lockhart, who, by the time Moulins came thither, had so far prevailed with the cardinal that orders were sent to stop the troops, which were upon their march towards Nismes; and, within few days after, Moulins returned with a full pardon and amnesty from the king, under the great seal of France, so fully confirmed with all circumstances that there was never farther mention made of it, but all things passed as if there had never been any such thing. So that nobody can wonder that his memory remains still in those parts, and with those people, in great veneration.

He would never suffer himself to be denied anything he ever asked of the cardinal, alleging "that the people would not be otherwise satisfied"; which the cardinal bore very heavily, and complained of to those with whom he would be free. One day he visited Madam Turenne; and when he took his leave of her, she, according to her custom, besought him to continue gracious to the churches. Whereupon the cardinal told her that he knew not how to behave himself; if he advised the king to punish and suppress their insolence, Cromwell threatened him to join with the Spaniard; and if he showed any favour to them, at Rome they accounted him an heretic.

He was not a man of blood, and totally declined Machiavel's method, which prescribes, upon any alteration of government, as a thing absolutely necessary, to cut off all the heads of those, and extirpate their families, who are friends to the old one. It was confidently reported that, in the council of officers, it was more than once proposed "that there might be a general massacre of all the royal party, as the only expedient to secure the government," but that Cromwell would never consent to it; it may be, out of too much contempt of his enemies. In a word, as he had all the wickednesses against which damnation is denounced, and for which hellfire is prepared, so he had some virtues which have caused the memory of some men in all ages to be celebrated; and he will be looked upon by posterity as a brave bad man.

[1702–04]

JOHN BUNYAN

Bunyan was out of the main current of English literature in his time; in background, themes, and forms of expression he had little in common with the age of Dryden. Indeed, he probably did not consider himself a man of letters at all, and he would have been surprised could he have foreseen his inclusion among the company of major English authors. He was an unlettered tinker who became a Baptist minister and who consecrated his life to gospel preaching. Had he not been imprisoned after the Restoration because of his refusal to submit to the laws against religious dissent, it is unlikely that he would have turned to the pen as a means of carrying on this one activity to which he was passionately devoted. Of formal education he had nothing; except for the Bible his reading was limited to a few books of evangelical piety. The English Bible, however, was for him school and university and literary model; its subject-matter was his subject-matter, and its cadences formed his style.

Seventeenth-century Puritanism had a profound influence on English literature, but it found direct, positive, typical expression only in Bunyan among the important writers of the time. Milton had a large infusion of Puritanism, which affected particularly his writings on religion and government (though even here he was far from being a typical Puritan); but in his major literary productions he was a Renaissance humanist whose critical principles were formed in the neoclassical mould. Marvell, in spite of his political associations with the Commonwealth government, wrote poetry which typical Puritans neither understood nor approved. Indeed, it was inevitable that Puritanism, which despised art and opposed it as one of the lures of Satan, should not have produced it or found its expression congenial. Bunyan wrote to awaken conscience, to strengthen faith, to win souls, just as hundreds of other dissenters did; but to him alone was it given to produce books of abiding literary merit and to elevate tracts into prose masterpieces.

The man to whom Bunyan is most frequently compared is Defoe. In some respects the comparison holds: each was a representative of the lower middle classes among whom Puritanism found most of its adherents; each wrote a simple colloquial prose, careless of structure yet singularly effective for its purpose; each is remembered for a single masterpiece that is known the world over. In fundamentals, however, the two men were antithetical: Defoe was a professional writer who was willing to serve any cause that paid; Bunyan used his talents only as a divine stewardship; Defoe appears at times to have indited moral treatises with his tongue in his cheek because his audience demanded them; Bunyan wrote at all times with genuine zeal and integrity of purpose.

While Bunyan's works all have the same purpose, they differ considerably in outward form. *Pilgrim's Progress* is an allegory of human life and universal religious experience; *The Holy War* represents the same things under a different allegory, the siege of the city of Mansoul by Diabolus and his hosts; *The Life and Death of Mr. Badman* forsakes allegory and presents through the medium of a dialogue between Mr. Wiseman and Mr. Attentive a realistic account of a bourgeois rascal, such a man as must have been familiar to the author and his readers. *Grace Abounding to the Chief of Sinners*, the first part of which is here reprinted, stands high among the most famous spiritual autobiographies. It is one of his earliest works, published in 1666. Though it contains less homely downrightness than *Pilgrim's Progress*, its style is not without a tang of picturesque colloquial English which diversifies Bunyan's prevailingly Scriptural phraseology. It tells the story of a richly emotional nature, gifted with unusual powers of imagination, to which the terrors of the last judgment and the tortures of hell were more vivid than the experiences of daily life. Yet Bunyan was no earth-scorning fanatic, unaware of the material world about him; *Grace Abounding* is a narrative of spiritual adventure, the scene of which is laid in a real English village. Though dates and names are omitted as of relative unimportance, Bunyan shows the game of cat with its interested spectators, the bell-ringers at the church, the poor women sitting before a door in the sun, the puddles in the road when the temptation was hot upon him to stake salvation on a single cast. The book shows too the experiences of the dreamer when the people of Bedford appeared as "in a kind of vision" on the sunny side of a high mountain while he shivered in storm and cold, shut out by an encompassing wall. Of such mingled realism and fantasy the *Pilgrim's Progress* was later to be compounded.

Bunyan's spiritual experiences were, of course, conditioned by his sect and his time; they centred about his individual use and interpretation of Scripture. Not for him was the concept of the Holy Church throughout all the world or the mystical following of the inner light. The Bible alone provided all the weapons of his warfare with Apollyon. His use of Scriptural verses, and even phrases, detached from their context, and often interpreted with the most grotesque disregard of their literal meaning, appears fantastic to the modern reader. His desperate heart-searching, his passionate yearning for signs of the divine grace within himself, his alternate despair and ineffable joy are experiences not easy for us to share with him even in imagination. Yet beneath the vesture of seventeenth-century Calvinism we can see the common humanity of the man, making him brother to poets and prophets and seers of all ages who have striven to know God and do his will, and in his will have found their peace. Though his religious experience took a form that was not theirs, it had much in common with that of St. Paul and St. Augustine and George Fox and John Wesley and George Herbert. It is a document in the spiritual history of mankind.

From GRACE ABOUNDING TO THE CHIEF OF SINNERS

In this my relation of the merciful working of God upon my soul, it will not be amiss, if, in the first place, I do, in a few words, give you a hint of my pedigree and manner of bringing up, that thereby the goodness and bounty of God towards me may be the more advanced and magnified before the sons of men.

For my descent then, it was, as is well known by many, of a low and inconsiderable generation; my father's house being of that rank that is meanest and most despised of all the families in the land. Wherefore I have not here, as others, to boast of noble blood, or of a high-born state, according to the flesh; though, all things considered, I magnify the heavenly Majesty, for that by this door he brought me into this world, to partake of the grace and life that is in Christ by the Gospel.

But yet, notwithstanding the meanness and inconsiderableness of my parents, it pleased God to put it into their hearts to put me to school, to learn both to read and write; the which I also attained, according to the rate of other poor men's children; though, to my shame I confess, I did soon lose that little I learnt, even almost utterly, and that long before the Lord did work his gracious work of conversion upon my soul.

As for my own natural life, for the time that I was without God in the world, it was indeed "according to the course of this world, and the spirit that now worketh in the children of disobedience" (Eph. 2:2, 3). It was my delight to be "taken captive by the devil at his will" (II Tim. 2:26), being filled with all unrighteousness; the which did also so strongly work and put forth itself, both in my heart and life, and that from a child, that I had but few equals (especially considering my years, which were tender, being few), both for cursing, swearing, lying, and blaspheming the holy name of God.

Yea, so settled and rooted was I in these things that they became as a second nature to me; the which, as I also have with soberness considered since, did so offend the Lord that even in my childhood he did scare and affright me with fearful dreams, and did terrify me with dreadful visions; for often, after I had spent this and the other day in sin, I have in my bed been greatly afflicted, while asleep, with the apprehensions of devils and wicked spirits, who still, as I then thought, laboured to draw me away with them, of which I could never be rid.

Also I should at these years be greatly afflicted and troubled with the thoughts of the day of judgment, and that both night and day, and should at the thoughts of the fearful torments of hell-fire; still fearing that it would be my lot to be found at last among those devils and hellish fiends, who are there bound down with the chains and bonds of darkness, "unto the judgment of the great day."

These things, I say, when I was but a child about nine or ten years old, did so distress my soul that when in the midst of my many sports and childish vanities, amidst my vain companions, I was often much cast down and afflicted in my mind therewith, yet could I not let go my sins. Yea, I was also then so overcome with despair of life and heaven that I should often wish either that there had been no hell, or that I had been a devil — supposing they were only tormentors; that if it must needs be that I indeed went thither, I might be rather a tormentor, than be tormented myself.

A while after, these terrible dreams did leave me, which also I soon forgot; for my pleasures did quickly cut off the remembrance of them, as if they had never been: wherefore, with more greediness, according to the strength of nature, I did still let loose the reins to my lust, and delighted in all transgression against the law of God: so that, until I came to the state of marriage, I was the very ringleader of all the youth that kept me company, in all manner of vice and ungodliness.

Yea, such prevalency had the lusts and fruits of the flesh in this poor soul of mine, that had not a miracle of precious grace prevented, I had not only perished by the stroke of eternal justice, but had also laid myself open, even to the stroke of those laws which bring some to disgrace and open shame before the face of the world.

In these days the thoughts of religion were very grievous to me. I could neither endure it myself, nor that any other should; so that, when I have seen some read in those books that concerned Christian piety, it would be as it were a prison to me. Then I said unto God, "Depart from me, for I desire not the knowledge of thy ways" (Job 21:14). I was now void of all good consideration, heaven and hell were both out of sight and mind; and as for saving and damning, they were least in my thoughts. "O Lord, thou knowest my life, and my ways were not hid from thee."

But this I well remember, that though I could myself sin with the greatest delight and ease, and also take pleasure in the vileness of my companions; yet, even then, if I have at any time seen wicked things, by those who professed goodness, it would make my spirit tremble. As once, above all the rest, when I was in my height of vanity, yet hearing one to swear that was reckoned for a religious man, it had so great a stroke upon my spirit that it made my heart ache.

But God did not utterly leave me, but followed me still, not now with convictions, but judgments; yet such as were mixed with mercy. For once I fell into a creek of the sea, and hardly escaped drowning. Another time I fell out of a boat into Bedford river, but mercy yet preserved me alive. Besides, another time, being in the field with one of my companions, it chanced that an adder passed over the highway; so I, having a stick in my hand, struck her over the back; and having stunned her, I forced open her mouth with my stick, and plucked her sting out with my fingers; by which act, had not God been merciful to me, I might, by my desperateness, have brought myself to mine end.

This also have I taken notice of with thanksgiving; *when I was a soldier, I, with others, were drawn out to go to such a place to besiege it; but when I was just ready to go, one of the company desired to go in my room; to which, when I had consented, he took my place; and coming to the siege, as he stood sentinel, he was shot into the head with a musket bullet, and died.

Here, as I said, were judgments and mercy, but neither of them did awaken my soul to righteousness; wherefore I sinned still, and grew more and more rebellious against God, and careless of mine own salvation.

Presently after this, I changed my condition into a married state, and my mercy was to light upon a wife whose father was counted godly. This woman and I, though we came together as poor as poor might be, not having so much household stuff as a dish or spoon betwixt us both, yet this she had for her part, *The Plain Man's Pathway to Heaven*, and *The Practice of Piety*, which her father had left her when he died. In these two books I should sometimes read with her, wherein I also found some things that were somewhat pleasing to me; but all this while I met with no conviction. She also would be often telling of me what a godly man her father was, and how he would reprove and correct vice, both in his house, and amongst his neighbours; what a strict and holy life he lived in his day, both in word and deed.

Wherefore these books with this relation, though they did not reach my heart, to awaken it about my sad and sinful state, yet they did beget within me some desires to religion; so that, because I knew no better, I fell in very eagerly with the religion of the times, to wit, to go to church twice a day, and that too with the foremost; and there should very devoutly, both say and sing as others did, yet retaining my wicked life; but withal, I was so overrun with a spirit of superstition that I adored, and that with great devotion, even all things, both the high place, priest, clerk, vestments, service, and what else belonging to the church; counting all things holy that were therein contained, and especially the priest and clerk most happy, and without doubt, greatly blessed because they were the servants, as I then thought, of God, and were principal in the holy temple, to do his work therein.

This conceit grew so strong in little time upon my spirit that had I but seen a priest, though never so sordid and debauched in his life, I should find my spirit fall under him, reverence him, and knit unto him; yea, I thought for the love I did bear unto them, supposing they were the ministers of God, I could have lain down at their feet, and have been trampled upon by them; their name, their garb, and work did so intoxicate and bewitch me.

After I had been thus for some considerable time, another thought came in my mind; and that was, whether we were of the Israelites, or

* Notes on John Bunyan will be found in the Appendix, pp. 958 ff.

no. For finding in the Scriptures that they were once the peculiar people of God, thought I, if I were one of this race, my soul must needs be happy. Now again, I found within me a great longing to be resolved about this question, but could not tell how I should. At last I asked my father of it, who told me, no, we were not. Wherefore then I fell in my spirit as to the hopes of that, and so remained.

But all this while I was not sensible of the danger and evil of sin; I was kept from considering that sin would damn me, what religion soever I followed, unless I was found in Christ. Nay, I never thought of him, nor whether there was such an one, or no. Thus man, while blind, doth wander, but wearieth himself with vanity, for he knoweth not the way to the city of God (Eccles. 10:15).

But one day, amongst all the sermons our parson made, his subject was to treat of the Sabbath day and of the evil of breaking that, either with labour, sports, or otherwise. Now I was, notwithstanding my religion, one that took much delight in all manner of vice, and especially that was the day that I did solace myself therewith, wherefore I fell in my conscience under his sermon, thinking and believing that he made that sermon on purpose to show me my evil doing; and at that time I felt what guilt was, though never before that I can remember; but then I was, for the present, greatly loaden therewith, and so went home when the sermon was ended, with a great burden upon my spirit.

This, for that instant, did benumb the sinews of my best delights, and did imbitter my former pleasures to me; but, behold, it lasted not, for before I had well dined the trouble began to go off my mind, and my heart returned to its old course: but oh! how glad was I, that this trouble was gone from me, and that the fire was put out, that I might sin again without control! Wherefore, when I had satisfied nature with my food, I shook the sermon out of my mind, and to my old custom of sports and gaming I returned with great delight.

But the same day, as I was in the midst of a *game at cat, and having struck it one blow from the hole, just as I was about to strike it the second time, a voice did suddenly dart from heaven into my soul, which said, "Wilt thou leave thy sins and go to heaven, or have thy sins and go to hell?" At this I was put to an exceeding maze; wherefore, leaving my cat upon the ground, I looked up to heaven, and was as if I had, with the eyes of my understanding, seen the Lord Jesus looking down upon me, as being very hotly displeased with me, and as if he did severely threaten me with some grievous punishment for these and other my ungodly practices.

I had no sooner thus conceived in my mind, but suddenly this conclusion was fastened on my spirit, for the former hint did set my sins again before my face, that I had been a great and grievous sinner, and that it was now too late for me to look after heaven; for Christ would not forgive me, nor pardon my transgressions. Then I fell to musing upon this also; and while I was thinking on it, and fearing lest it should be so, I felt my heart sink in despair, concluding it was too late; and therefore I resolved in my mind I would go on in sin: for, thought I, if the case be thus, my state is surely miserable, miserable if I leave my sins, and but miserable if I follow them; I can but be damned, and if I must be so, I had as good be damned for many sins as to be damned for few.

Thus I stood in the midst of my play, before all that then were present, but yet I told them nothing: but I say, I having made this conclusion, I returned desperately to my sport again; and I well remember that presently this kind of despair did so possess my soul that I was persuaded I could never attain to other comfort than what I should get in sin; for heaven was gone already, so that on that I must not think; wherefore I found within me a great desire to take my fill of sin, still studying what sin was yet to be committed, that I might taste the sweetness of it; and I made as much haste as I could to fill my belly with its delicates, lest I should die before I had my desire; for that I feared greatly. In these things, I protest before God, I lie not, neither do I feign this sort of speech; these were really, strongly, and with all my heart, my desires; the good Lord, whose mercy is unsearchable, forgive me my transgressions!

And I am very confident that this temptation of the devil is more usual amongst poor creatures than many are aware of, even to overrun their spirits with a scurvy and seared frame of heart, and benumbing of conscience; which frame, he stilly and slily supplieth with such despair that though not much guilt attendeth souls, yet they continually have a secret conclusion within them that there is no hopes for them; for they have loved sins,

"Therefore after them they will go" (Jer. 2:25; and 18:12).

Now therefore I went on in sin with great greediness of mind, still grudging that I could not be so satisfied with it as I would. This did continue with me about a month, or more; but one day, as I was standing at a neighbour's shop-window, and there cursing and swearing, and playing the madman, after my wonted manner, there sat within the woman of the house, and heard me, who, though she was a very loose and ungodly wretch, yet protested that I swore and cursed at that most fearful rate that she was made to tremble to hear me; and told me further, that I was the ungodliest fellow for swearing that ever she heard in all her life; and that I, by thus doing, was able to spoil all the youth in the whole town, if they came but in my company.

After this reproof I was silenced, and put to secret shame, and that too, as I thought, before the God of heaven; wherefore, while I stood there, and hanging down my head, I wished with all my heart that I might be a little child again, that my father might learn me to speak without this wicked way of swearing; for, thought I, I am so accustomed to it that it is in vain for me to think of a reformation, for I thought it could never be.

But how it came to pass I know not; I did from this time forward so leave my swearing that it was a great wonder to myself to observe it; and whereas before, I knew not how to speak unless I put an oath before, and another behind, to make my words have authority; now, I could, without it, speak better and with more pleasantness than ever I could before. All this while I knew not Jesus Christ, neither did I leave my sports and play.

But quickly after this I fell in company with one poor man that made profession of religion, who, as I then thought, did talk pleasantly of the Scriptures and of the matters of religion; wherefore, falling into some love and liking to what he said, I betook me to my Bible, and began to take great pleasure in reading, but especially with the historical part thereof; for, as for Paul's epistles and scriptures, I could not away with them, being as yet ignorant, either of the corruptions of my nature, or of the want and worth of Jesus Christ to save me.

Wherefore I fell to some outward reformation, both in my words and life, and did set the commandments before me for my way to heaven; which commandments I also did strive to keep, and, as I thought, did keep them pretty well sometimes, and then I should have comfort, yet now and then should break one, and so afflict my conscience; but then I should repent, and say I was sorry for it, and promise God to do better next time, and there get help again, for then I thought I pleased God as well as any man in England.

Thus I continued about a year; all which time our neighbours did take me to be a very godly man, a new and religious man, and did marvel much to see such a great and famous alteration in my life and manners; and, indeed, so it was, though yet I knew not Christ, nor grace, nor faith, nor hope; and, truly, as I have well seen since, had I then died, my state had been most fearful.

But, I say, my neighbours were amazed at this my great conversion from prodigious profaneness to something like a moral life; and, truly, so they well might; for this my conversion was as great as for *Tom of Bedlam to become a sober man. Now, therefore, they began to praise, to commend, and to speak well of me, both to my face and behind my back. Now I was, as they said, become godly; now I was become a right honest man. But, oh! when I understood that these were their words and opinions of me, it pleased me mighty well. For though as yet I was nothing but a poor painted hypocrite, yet I loved to be talked of as one that was truly godly; I was proud of my godliness, and, indeed, I did all I did, either to be seen of, or to be well spoken of, by men. And thus I continued for about a twelvemonth or more.

Now, you must know, that before this I had taken much delight in ringing, but my conscience beginning to be tender, I thought such practice was but vain, and therefore forced myself to leave it, yet my mind hankered; wherefore I should go to the steeple house, and look on it, though I durst not ring. But I thought this did not become religion neither, yet I forced myself, and would look on still; but quickly after, I began to think, "How, if one of the bells should fall?" Then I chose to stand under a main beam that lay overthwart the steeple from side to side thinking there I might stand sure, but then I should think again, "Should the bell fall with a swing, it might first hit the wall, and then rebounding upon me, might kill me for all this beam." This made me stand in the steeple door; and,

"Now," thought I, "I am safe enough; for, if a bell should then fall, I can slip out behind these thick walls, and so be preserved notwithstanding."

So, after this, I would yet go to see them ring, but would not go further than the steeple door; but then it came into my head, "How, if the steeple itself should fall?" And this thought, it may fall for aught I know, when I stood and looked on, did continually so shake my mind that I durst not stand at the steeple door any longer, but was forced to flee, for fear the steeple should fall upon my head.

Another thing was my dancing; I was a full year before I could quite leave that; but all this while, when I thought I kept this or that commandment, or did, by word or deed, anything that I thought was good, I had great peace in my conscience; and should think with myself, God cannot choose but be now pleased with me; yea, to relate it in mine own way, I thought no man in England could please God better than I.

But poor wretch as I was, I was all this while ignorant of Jesus Christ and going about to establish my own righteousness; and had perished therein, had not God, in mercy, showed me more of my state by nature.

But upon a day, the good providence of God did cast me to Bedford, to work on my calling; and in one of the streets of that town, I came where there were three or four poor women sitting at a door in the sun, and talking about the things of God; and being now willing to hear them discourse, I drew near to hear what they said, for I was now a brisk talker also myself in the matters of religion, but I may say, I heard, but I understood not; for they were far above, out of my reach; for their talk was about a new birth, the work of God on their hearts, also how they were convinced of their miserable state by nature; they talked how God had visited their souls with his love in the Lord Jesus, and with what words and promises they had been refreshed, comforted, and supported against the temptations of the devil. Moreover, they reasoned of the suggestions and temptations of Satan in particular; and told to each other by which they had been afflicted, and how they were borne up under his assaults. They also discoursed of their own wretchedness of heart, of their unbelief; and did contemn, slight, and abhor their own righteousness, as filthy and insufficient to do them any good.

And methought they spake as if joy did make them speak; they spake with such pleasantness of Scripture language, and with such appearance of grace in all they said, that they were to me as if they had found a new world, as if they were "People that dwelt alone, and were not to be reckoned amongst their neighbours" (Num. 23:9).

At this I felt my own heart began to shake, as mistrusting my condition to be naught; for I saw that in all my thoughts about religion and salvation, the new birth did never enter into my mind; neither knew I the comfort of the Word and promise, nor the deceitfulness and treachery of my own wicked heart. As for secret thoughts, I took no notice of them; neither did I understand what Satan's temptations were, nor how they were to be withstood and resisted, etc.

Thus, therefore, when I had heard and considered what they said, I left them, and went about my employment again, but their talk and discourse went with me; also my heart would tarry with them, for I was greatly affected with their words, both because by them I was convinced that I wanted the true tokens of a truly godly man, and also because by them I was convinced of the happy and blessed condition of him that was such an one.

Therefore I should often make it my business to be going again and again into the company of these poor people, for I could not stay away; and the more I went amongst them, the more I did question my condition; and as I still do remember, presently I found two things within me, at which I did sometimes marvel, especially considering what a blind, ignorant, sordid, and ungodly wretch but just before I was; the one was a very great softness and tenderness of heart, which caused me to fall under the conviction of what by Scripture they asserted; and the other was a great bending in my mind to a continual meditating on them, and on all other good things which at any time I heard or read of.

By these things my mind was now so turned that it lay like a horse-leech at the vein, still crying out, "Give, give," (Prov. 30:15); yea, it was so fixed on eternity and on the things about the kingdom of heaven (that is, so far as I knew, though as yet, God knows, I knew but little), that neither pleasures nor profits, nor persuasions, nor threats could loosen it, or make it let go its hold; and though I may speak it with shame, yet it is in very deed a certain truth, it would then have been as difficult for me to have taken my mind from heaven to earth, as I have found it often since to get it again from earth to heaven.

One thing I may not omit: there was a young man in our town, to whom my heart before was knit more than to any other, but he being a most wicked creature for cursing and swearing and whoring, I now shook him off, and forsook his company; but about a quarter of a year after I had left him, I met him in a certain lane, and asked him how he did; he, after his old swearing and mad way, answered, he was well. "But, Harry," said I, "why do you swear and curse thus? What will become of you if you die in this condition?" He answered me in a great chafe, "What would the devil do for company, if it were not for such as I am?"

About this time I met with some *Ranters' books, that were put forth by some of our countrymen, which books were also highly in esteem by several old *professors; some of these I read, but was not able to make a judgment about them; wherefore as I read in them, and thought upon them, feeling myself unable to judge, I should betake myself to hearty prayer in this manner: "O Lord, I am a fool, and not able to know the truth from error: Lord, leave me not to my own blindness, either to approve of, or condemn this doctrine; if it be of God, let me not despise it; if it be of the devil, let me not embrace it. Lord, I lay my soul, in this matter, only at thy foot; let me not be deceived, I humbly beseech thee." I had one religious intimate companion all this while, and that was the poor man that I spoke of before; but about this time he also turned a most devilish Ranter, and gave himself up to all manner of filthiness, especially uncleanness; he would also deny that there was a God, angel, or spirit; and would laugh at all exhortations to sobriety. When I laboured to rebuke his wickedness, he would laugh the more, and pretend that he had gone through all religions, and could never light on the right till now. He told me also that in a little time I should see all professors turn to the ways of the Ranters. Wherefore, abominating those cursed principles, I left his company forthwith, and became to him as great a stranger as I had been before a familiar.

Neither was this man only a temptation to me; but my calling lying in the country, I happened to light into several people's company, who, though strict in religion formerly, yet were also swept away by these Ranters. These would also talk with me of their ways, and condemn me as legal and dark; pretending that they only had attained to perfection that could do what they would, and not sin. Oh! these temptations were suitable to my flesh, I being but a young man, and my nature in its prime; but God, who had, as I hope, designed me for better things, kept me in the fear of his name, and did not suffer me to accept of such cursed principles. And blessed be God, who put it into my heart to cry to him to be kept and directed, still distrusting mine own wisdom; for I have since seen even the effect of that prayer, in his preserving me not only from ranting errors, but from those also that have sprung up since. The Bible was precious to me in those days.

And now, methought, I began to look into the Bible with new eyes, and read as I never did before; and especially the epistles of the apostle St. Paul were sweet and pleasant to me; and, indeed, I was then never out of the Bible, either by reading or meditation; still crying out to God that I might know the truth, and way to heaven and glory.

And, as I went on and read, I lighted on that passage, "To one is given by the Spirit the word of wisdom; to another the word of knowledge by the same Spirit; and to another faith," etc. (*I Cor. 12:8, 9). And though, as I have since seen, that by this Scripture the Holy Ghost intends, in special, things extraordinary, yet on me it did then fasten with conviction that I did want things ordinary, even that understanding and wisdom that other Christians had. On this word I mused, and could not tell what to do; especially this word [faith] put me to it, for I could not help it, but sometimes must question whether I had any faith or no; but I was loath to conclude I have no faith; for if I do so, thought I, then I shall count myself a very castaway indeed.

"No," said I with myself, "though I am convinced that I am an ignorant sot, and that I want those blessed gifts of knowledge and understanding that other good people have; yet, at a venture, I will conclude I am not altogether faithless, though I know not what faith is." For it was showed me, and that too, as I have seen since, by Satan, that those who conclude themselves in a faithless state, have neither rest nor quiet in their souls; and I was loath to fall quite into despair.

Wherefore, by this suggestion, I was for a while made afraid to see my want of faith; but God would not suffer me thus to undo and destroy my soul, but did continually, against this my blind and sad conclusion, create still within me such suppositions, insomuch that I could not rest content until I did now come to some certain knowledge, whether I had faith or no; this always running in my mind. But how if you want faith indeed? But how can you tell you have faith? And, besides, I saw for certain, if I had it not, I was sure to perish forever.

So that though I endeavoured at the first to look over the business of faith, yet in a little time, I, better considering the matter, was willing to put myself upon the trial, whether I had faith or no. But, alas, poor wretch, so ignorant and brutish was I that I knew to this day no more how to do it than I know how to begin and accomplish that rare and curious piece of art which I never yet saw or considered.

Wherefore, while I was thus considering, and being put to my plunge about it (for you must know that as yet I had in this matter broken my mind to no man, only did hear and consider), the tempter came in with his delusion: that there was no way for me to know I had faith, but by trying to work some miracle; urging those Scriptures that seem to look that way, for the enforcing and strengthening his temptation. Nay, one day as I was betwixt Elstow and Bedford, the temptation was hot upon me to try if I had faith by doing some miracle: which miracle at that time was this, I must say to the puddles that were in the horse-pads, "Be dry"; and to the dry places, "Be you the puddles." And, truly, one time I was going to say so indeed; but just as I was about to speak, this thought came into my mind, but go under yonder hedge and pray first, that God would make you able. But when I had concluded to pray, this came hot upon me, that if I prayed, and came again and tried to do it, and yet did nothing notwithstanding, then be sure I had no faith, but was a castaway and lost. "Nay," thought I, "if it be so, I will never try yet, but will stay a little longer."

So I continued at a great loss; for I thought, if they only had faith, which could do so wonderful things, then I concluded that, for the present, I neither had it, nor yet, for time to come, were ever like to have it. Thus I was tossed betwixt the devil and my own ignorance, and so perplexed, especially at some times, that I could not tell what to do.

About this time, the state and happiness of these poor people at Bedford was thus, in a kind of vision, presented to me. I saw, as if they were set on the sunny side of some high mountain, there refreshing themselves with the pleasant beams of the sun, while I was shivering and shrinking in the cold, afflicted with frost, snow, and dark clouds. Methought, also, betwixt me and them, I saw a wall that did compass about this mountain; now, through this wall my soul did greatly desire to pass; concluding, that if I could, I would go even into the very midst of them, and there also comfort myself with the heat of their sun.

About this wall I thought myself to go again and again, still prying as I went, to see if I could find some way or passage by which I might enter therein; but none could I find for some time. At the last, I saw, as it were, a narrow gap, like a little doorway in the wall, through which I attempted to pass; but the passage being very strait and narrow, I made many efforts to get in, but all in vain, even until I was well-nigh quite beat out, by striving to get in; at last, with great striving, methought I at first did get in my head, and after that, by a sideling striving, my shoulders, and my whole body; then was I exceedingly glad, and went and sat down in the midst of them, and so was comforted with the light and heat of their sun.

Now, this mountain and wall, etc., was thus made out to me — the mountain signified the church of the living God; the sun that shone thereon, the comfortable shining of his merciful face on them that were therein; the wall, I thought, was the Word, that did make separation between the Christians and the world; and the gap which was in this wall, I thought, was Jesus Christ, who is the way to God the Father (John 14:6; Matt. 7:14). But forasmuch as the passage was wonderful narrow, even so narrow that I could not, but with great difficulty, enter in thereat, it showed me that none could enter into life but those that were in downright earnest, and unless also they left this wicked world behind them; for here was only room for body and soul, but not for body and soul and sin.

This resemblance abode upon my spirit

many days; all which time I saw myself in a forlorn and sad condition, but yet was provoked to a vehement hunger and desire to be one of that number that did sit in the sunshine. Now also I should pray wherever I was, whether at home or abroad, in house or field, and should also often, with lifting up of heart, sing that of the 51st Psalm, "O Lord, consider my distress"; for as yet I knew not where I was.

Neither as yet could I attain to any considerable persuasion that I had faith in Christ; but instead of having satisfaction, here I began to find my soul to be assaulted with fresh doubts about my future happiness, especially with such as these: Whether I was elected? But how if the day of grace should now be past and gone?

By these two temptations I was very much afflicted and disquieted; sometimes by one, and sometimes by the other of them. And first, to speak of that about my questioning my election, I found at this time that though I was in a flame to find the way to heaven and glory, and though nothing could beat me off from this, yet this question did so offend and discourage me that I was, especially at some times, as if the very strength of my body also had been taken away by the force and power thereof. This Scripture did also seem to me to trample upon all my desires, "It is neither in him that willeth, nor in him that runneth, but in God that showeth mercy." (Rom. 9:16.)

With this Scripture I could not tell what to do; for I evidently saw, unless that the great God, of his infinite grace and bounty, had voluntarily chosen me to be a vessel of mercy, though I should desire, and long and labour until my heart did break, no good could come of it. Therefore, this would still stick with me. How can you tell you are elected? And what if you should not? How then?

"O Lord," thought I, "what if I should not, indeed?" "It may be you are not," said the tempter. "It may be so, indeed," thought I. "Why, then," said Satan, "you had as good leave off, and strive no further; for if, indeed, you should not be elected and chosen of God, there is no talk of your being saved; 'For it is neither in him that willeth, nor in him that runneth, but in God that showeth mercy.' "

By these things I was driven to my wits' end, not knowing what to say, or how to answer these temptations. Indeed, I little thought that Satan had thus assaulted me, but that rather it was my own prudence, thus to start the question; for, that the elect only attained eternal life, that I, without scruple, did heartily close withal; but that myself was one of them, there lay the question.

Thus, therefore, for several days, I was greatly assaulted and perplexed, and was often, when I have been walking, ready to sink where I went, with faintness in my mind; but one day, after I had been so many weeks oppressed and cast down therewith, as I was now quite giving up the ghost of all my hopes of ever attaining life, that sentence fell with weight upon my spirit, "Look at the generations of old and see; did ever any trust in God and were confounded?"

At which I was greatly lightened and encouraged in my soul; for thus, at that very instant, it was expounded to me, "Begin at the beginning of Genesis, and read to the end of the Revelations, and see if you can find that there was ever any that trusted in the Lord, and was confounded." So, coming home, I presently went to my Bible to see if I could find that saying, not doubting but to find it presently; for it was so fresh, and with such strength and comfort on my spirit, that. I was as if it talked with me.

Well, I looked, but I found it not; only it abode upon me; then I did ask first this good man and then another if they knew where it was, but they knew no such place. At this I wondered that such a sentence should so suddenly, and with such comfort and strength, seize and abide upon my heart, and yet that none could find it, for I doubted not but it was in holy Scripture.

Thus I continued above a year, and could not find the place; but at last, casting my eye into the Apocrypha books, I found it in Ecclesiasticus 2:10. This, at the first, did somewhat daunt me; but because, by this time, I had got more experience of the love and kindness of God, it troubled me the less; especially when I considered that though it was not in those texts that we call holy and canonical, yet forasmuch as this sentence was the sum and substance of many of the promises, it was my duty to take the comfort of it; and I bless God for that word, for it was of God to me: that word doth still, at times, shine before my face.

After this, that other doubt did come with strength upon me, but how if the day of grace should be past and gone? How if you have overstood the time of mercy? Now, I remember that one day, as I was walking into the country, I was much in the thoughts of this: but how if the day of grace be past? And to aggravate my trouble, the tempter presented to my mind those good people of Bedford, and suggested thus unto me: that these being converted already, they were all that God would save in those parts; and that I came too late, for these had got the blessing before I came.

Now was I in great distress, thinking in very deed that this might well be so; wherefore I went up and down bemoaning my sad condition, counting myself far worse than a thousand fools, for standing off thus long, and spending so many years in sin as I have done; still crying out, "Oh, that I had turned sooner! Oh, that I had turned seven years ago!" It made me also angry with myself, to think that I should have no more wit but to trifle away my time till my soul and heaven were lost.

But when I had been long vexed with this fear, and was scarce able to take one step more, just about the same place where I received my other encouragement, these words broke in upon my mind, "Compel them to come in, that my house may be filled"; "and yet there is room." (Luke 14:22, 23.) These words, but especially them, "and yet there is room," were sweet words to me; for, truly, I thought that by them I saw there was place enough in heaven for me; and, moreover, that when the Lord Jesus did speak these words, he then did think of me; and that he, knowing the time would come that I should be afflicted with fear that there was no place left for me in his bosom, did before speak this word, and leave it upon record, that I might find help thereby against this vile temptation. This I then verily believed.

In the light and encouragement of this word, I went a pretty while; and the comfort was the more when I thought that the Lord Jesus should think on me so long ago, and that he should speak them [*sic*] words on purpose for my sake; for I did then think, verily, that he did on purpose speak them, to encourage me withal.

But I was not without my temptations to go back again; temptations, I say, both from Satan, mine own heart, and carnal acquaintance; but I thank God these were outweighed by that sound sense of death and of the day of judgment, which abode, as it were, continually in my view; I should often also think on Nebuchadnezzar, of whom it is said, he had given him all the kingdoms of the earth (Dan. 5:18, 19). "Yet," thought I, "if this great man had all his portion in this world, one hour in hell fire would make him forget all." Which consideration was a great help to me.

I was almost made, about this time, to see something concerning the beasts that Moses counted clean and unclean. I thought those beasts were types of men; the clean, types of them that were the people of God; but the unclean, types of such as were the children of the wicked one. Now, I read that the clean beasts chewed the cud; that is, thought I, they show us we must feed upon the Word of God. They also parted the hoof; I thought that signified we must part, if we would be saved, with the ways of ungodly men. And also, in further reading about them I found that though we did chew the cud as the hare, yet if we walked with claws like a dog, or if we did part the hoof like the swine, yet if we did not chew the cud as the sheep, we were still, for all that, but unclean; for I thought the hare to be a type of those that talk of the Word, yet walk in the ways of sin; and that the swine was like him that parted with his outward pollutions, but still wanteth the Word of faith, without which there could be no way of salvation, let a man be never so devout (Deut. 14:8). After this I found, by reading the Word, that those that must be glorified with Christ in another world must be called by him here; called to the partaking of a share in his Word and righteousness, and to the comforts and first fruits of his Spirit, and to a peculiar interest in all those heavenly things which do indeed fore-fit the soul for that rest and house of glory which is in heaven above.

Here, again, I was at a very great stand, not knowing what to do, fearing I was not called; for, thought I, "If I be not called, what then can do me good?" None but those who are effectually called inherit the kingdom of heaven. But oh! how I now loved those words that spake of a Christian's calling! as when the Lord said to one, "Follow me," and to another, "Come after me." "And oh!" thought I, "that he would say so to me too, how gladly would I run after him!"

I cannot now express with what longings and breakings in my soul I cried to Christ to call me. Thus I continued for a time, all on a flame to be converted to Jesus Christ; and did also see at that day, such glory in a converted state that I could not be contented without a share therein. Gold! could it have been gotten for gold, what could I have given for it! Had I had a whole world, it had all gone ten thousand times over for this, that my soul might have been in a converted state....

[1666]

DANIEL DEFOE

DEFOE is remembered today chiefly as the author of *Robinson Crusoe*, yet he was the very opposite of a one-book writer, for he left more than 250 known publications. In spite of the activity of his pen he was primarily a man of action, whose busy life and checkered fortunes would have been a fit subject for one of his own romances had he dared to reveal its intimate details. While we are not even yet fully acquainted with all these details, the studies of the past two generations have cast so much light upon them that we can see the man more clearly than could any of his contemporaries.

The date of his birth has been commonly given as 1661, though there is some reason to put it a year or two earlier. His father was a London butcher named Foe; Daniel did not assume the more impressive form, Defoe, until he reached middle life. He was educated for the dissenting ministry, took part in Monmouth's rebellion in 1685, became a wholesale merchant, went into bankruptcy, played more than one important part in public affairs, was imprisoned, was employed for many years in the secret service (changing his politics whenever it became necessary, and sometimes taking pay from both sides at the same time), and died poor and discredited, in 1731. First and foremost, however, Defoe was a journalist, a great sensational journalist at a time when English journalism was in its formative period. He edited newspapers, contributed to newspapers, and wrote a large number of occasional pamphlets. Indeed, from one point of view practically all his writing was journalistic, since it was addressed to the general public and dealt with matters of immediate popular concern such as news, political propaganda, and "human interest."

Defoe was not in the main current of English literature in his time; he had few associations with the better known men of letters. As a dissenter, a bourgeois, and a secret political agent whose shady dealings were suspected even when they were not fully known, he had few direct dealings with his more aristocratic and reputable contemporaries. He was too prolific, too hasty in writing and publishing, too much of a journalist to give literary form to the bulk of his writing. Swift could write rapidly and produce masterpieces of thought and style; Addison could dash off a *Spectator* article while the press was waiting, and give it the qualities of enduring perfection. Defoe's works, on the other hand, are often deficient in form and usually careless in style. He seldom took pains to do his best.

The selections here reprinted illustrate two aspects of his work. *An Essay upon Projects* (1697) is a relatively early piece of writing, apparently done with more than usual care. It is interesting today chiefly because it gives expression to many ideas that were in the air at the time; few of his projects were original with Defoe though all bear the impress of his mind. Among them are reforms in banking, in taxation, and in the care of idiots, improvement of highways, and establishment of an insurance system and various academies. While some of his ideas seem prophetic of the future, few of them have actually been put into practice in the forms that he suggested. As William Minto points out, they are a "strange mixture of steady sense with incontinent flightiness." These characteristics are amply illustrated in the treatment of the project for "An Academy for Women," which is here quoted in full.

In March, 1722, Defoe published *A Journal of the Plague Year: Being Observations or Memorials of the Most Remarkable Occurrences, as Well Public as Private which Happened in London during the Last Great Visitation in 1665. Written by a Citizen who Continued all the While in London. Never Made Public Before.* Like practically all his other writings this had a journalistic purpose, for the plague had been raging at Marseilles during the two preceding years, and there was grave apprehension that it would again visit England. In such circumstances a detailed account of the last great visitation in London, combined with remarks upon methods for its prevention and cure as well as edifying moral observations, was well calculated to the popular interest.

Such verisimilitude does the *Journal* possess that it has frequently been accepted as the genuine narrative of a London tradesman who personally experienced the events which he records. Chronology, however, immediately proves it to be fiction of a type comparable to *Robinson Crusoe* or *Mcll Flanders* or *Captain Singleton.* Even if the birthdate of 1659 is accepted, Defoe was only six years of age in the plague year and could have remembered few of the details. However, he grew up among the surroundings that he describes, many of which must have remained with little change in spite of the Great Fire; furthermore, he would certainly have heard stories about the plague during the most impressionable years of his boyhood. With this background of personal experience and with the assistance of numerous books and pamphlets about the plague, he was much better supplied with authentic information than he was for most of his other fictions. The man who could bring before us Crusoe's island and the interior of Africa had no difficulty in presenting with extraordinary vividness dramatic scenes in the London of his early boyhood.

The ostensible writer of the *Journal* is a hard-headed, unimaginative tradesman, whose unimpassioned account of what he professes to have seen and heard carries conviction. Such a man, especially when he appears to discriminate between matters of fact and those of hearsay, is a most convincing narrator of strange and surprising events. The heroes of Defoe's first-person narratives are commonly such men, whom he knew intimately and who were typical of the class for which he wrote. Even Swift, though addressing a higher audience, makes Lemuel Gulliver just such a man.

A Journal of the Plague Year is as good as anything that Defoe ever wrote. The vivid, circumstantial detail and the low-toned realism produce an extraordinary effect of verisimilitude which enhances the effect of the terrible scenes presented. The selection here reprinted is a single passage taken without omission from the second quarter of the book.

From AN ESSAY UPON PROJECTS

* Under this head of Academies I might bring in a project for —

AN ACADEMY FOR WOMEN

I have often thought of it as one of the most barbarous customs in the world, considering us as a civilized and a Christian country, that we deny the advantages of learning to women. We reproach the sex every day with folly and impertinence, while I am confident, had they the advantages of education equal to us, they would be guilty of less than ourselves.

One would wonder, indeed, how it should happen that women are conversible at all, since they are only beholden to natural parts for all their knowledge. Their youth is spent to teach them to stitch and sew or make baubies. They are taught to read, indeed, and perhaps to write their names or so, and that is the height of a woman's education. And I would but ask any who slight the sex for their understanding, what is a man (a gentleman, I mean) good for that is taught no more?

I need not give instances, or examine the character of a gentleman with a good estate, and of a good family, and with tolerable parts, and examine what figure he makes for want of education.

The soul is placed in the body like a rough diamond, and must be polished, or the lustre of it will never appear: and 'tis manifest that as the rational soul distinguishes us from brutes, so education carries on the distinction and makes some less brutish than others. This is too evident to need any demonstration. But why then should women be denied the benefit of instruction? If knowledge and understanding had been useless additions to the sex, God Almighty would never have given them capacities, for he made nothing needless. Besides, I would ask such what they can see in ignorance that they should think it a necessary ornament to a woman? or how much worse is a wise woman than a fool? or what has the woman done to forfeit the privilege of being taught? Does she plague us with her pride and impertinence? Why did we not let her learn, that she might have had more wit? Shall we upbraid women with folly, when 'tis only the error of this inhuman custom that hindered them being made wiser?

The capacities of women are supposed to be greater and their senses quicker than those of the men; and what they might be capable of being bred to is plain from some instances of female wit, which this age is not without; which upbraids us with injustice, and looks as if we denied women the advantages of education for fear they should vie with the men in their improvements.

To remove this objection, and that women might have at least a needful opportunity of education in all sorts of useful learning, I propose the draught of an Academy for that purpose.

I know 'tis dangerous to make public appearances of the sex. They are not either to be confined or exposed; the first will disagree with their inclinations, and the last with their reputations, and therefore it is somewhat difficult; and I doubt a method proposed by an ingenious lady in a little book called **Advice to the Ladies* would be found impracticable, for, saving my respect to the sex, the levity, which perhaps is a little peculiar to them, at least in

* Notes on Daniel Defoe will be found in the Appendix, pp. 959 ff.

their youth, will not bear the restraint; and I am satisfied nothing but the height of bigotry can keep up a nunnery. Women are extravagantly desirous of going to heaven, and will punish their pretty bodies to get thither; but nothing else will do it, and even in that case sometimes it falls out that nature will prevail.

When I talk, therefore, of an academy for women, I mean both the model, the teaching, and the government different from what is proposed by that ingenious lady, for whose proposal I have a very great esteem, and also a great opinion of her wit; different, too, from all sorts of religious confinement, and, above all, from vows of celibacy.

Wherefore the academy I propose should differ but little from public schools, wherein such ladies as were willing to study should have all the advantages of learning suitable to their genius.

But since some severities of discipline more than ordinary would be absolutely necessary to preserve the reputation of the house, that persons of quality and fortune might not be afraid to venture their children thither, I shall venture to make a small scheme by way of essay.

The house I would have built in a form by itself, as well as in a place by itself. The building should be of three plain fronts, without any jettings or bearing-work, that the eye might at a glance see from one coin to the other; the gardens walled in the same triangular figure, with a large moat, and but one entrance.

When thus every part of the situation was contrived as well as might be for discovery, and to render intriguing dangerous, I would have no guards, no eyes, no spies set over the ladies, but shall expect them to be tried by the principles of honour and strict virtue.

And if I am asked why, I must ask pardon of my own sex for giving this reason for it:

I am so much in charity with women and so well acquainted with men that it is my opinion there needs no other care to prevent intriguing than to keep the men effectually away; for though inclination, which we prettily call love, does sometimes move a little too visibly in the sex, and frailty often follows, yet I think, verily, custom, which we miscall modesty, has so far the ascendant over the sex that solicitation always goes before it.

Custom with women 'stead of virtue rules;
It leads the wisest and commands the fools;
For this alone, when inclinations reign,
Though virtue's fled, will acts of vice restrain.
Only by custom 'tis that virtue lives,
And love requires to be asked before it gives;
For that which we call modesty is pride;
They scorn to ask, and hate to be denied.
'Tis custom thus prevails upon their want;
They'll never beg what asked they easily grant;
And when the needless ceremony is over,
Themselves the weakness of the sex discover.
If then desires are strong and nature free,
Keep from her men and opportunity;
Else 'twill be vain to curb her by restraint,
But keep the question off, you keep the saint.

In short, let a woman have never such a coming principle, she will let you ask before she complies, at least if she be a woman of any honour.

Upon this ground I am persuaded such measures might be taken that the ladies might have all the freedom in the world within their own walls, and yet no intriguing, no indecencies, nor scandalous affairs happen; and in order to this the following customs and laws should be observed in the colleges, of which I propose one at least in every county in England, and about ten for the City of London.

After the regulation of the form of the building as before:

(1) All the ladies who enter into the house should set their hands to the orders of the house, to signify their consent to submit to them.

(2) As no woman should be received but who declared herself willing, and that it was the act of her choice to enter herself, so no person should be confined to continue there a moment longer than the same voluntary choice inclined her.

(3) The charges of the house being to be paid by the ladies, every one that entered should have only this encumbrance, that she should pay for the whole year, though her mind should change as to her continuance.

(4) An Act of Parliament should make it a *felony without clergy for any man to enter by force or fraud into the house, or to solicit any woman, though it were to marry, while she was in the house. And this law would by no means be severe, because any woman who was willing to receive the addresses of a man might discharge herself of the house when she pleased; and, on the contrary, any woman who had occasion, might discharge herself of

the impertinent addresses of any person she had an aversion to by entering into the house.

In this house, the persons who enter should be taught all sorts of breeding suitable to both their genius and their quality, and in particular music and dancing, which it would be cruelty to bar the sex of, because they are their darlings; but besides this, they should be taught languages, as particularly French and Italian; and I would venture the injury of giving a woman more tongues than one.

They should, as a particular study, be taught all the graces of speech and all the necessary air of conversation, which our common education is so defective in that I need not expose it. They should be brought to read books, and especially history, and so to read as to make them understand the world, and be able to know and judge of things when they hear of them.

To such whose genius would lead them to it I would deny no sort of learning; but the chief thing in general is to cultivate the understandings of the sex, that they may be capable of all sorts of conversation; that, their parts and judgments being improved, they may be as profitable in their conversation as they are pleasant.

Women, in my observation, have little or no difference in them, but as they are or are not distinguished by education. Tempers indeed may in some degree influence them, but the main distinguishing part is their breeding.

The whole sex are generally quick and sharp. I believe I may be allowed to say generally so, for you rarely see them lumpish and heavy when they are children, as boys will often be. If a woman be well-bred, and taught the proper management of her natural wit, she proves generally very sensible and retentive; and without partiality, a woman of sense and manners is the finest and most delicate part of God's creation, the glory of her Maker, and the great instance of his singular regard to man, his darling creature, to whom he gave the best gift either God could bestow or man receive. And 'tis the sordidest piece of folly and ingratitude in the world to withhold from the sex the due lustre which the advantages of education gives to the natural beauty of their minds.

A woman well bred and well taught, furnished with the additional accomplishments of knowledge and behaviour, is a creature without comparison; her society is the emblem of sublimer enjoyments; her person is angelic and her conversation heavenly; she is all softness and sweetness, peace, love, wit, and delight. She is every way suitable to the sublimest wish, and the man that has such a one to his portion has nothing to do but to rejoice in her and be thankful.

On the other hand, suppose her to be the very same woman, and rob her of the benefit of education, and it follows thus:

If her temper be good, want of education makes her soft and easy. Her wit, for want of teaching, makes her impertinent and talkative. Her knowledge, for want of judgment and experience, makes her fanciful and whimsical. If her temper be bad, want of breeding makes her worse, and she grows haughty, insolent, and loud. If she be passionate, want of manners makes her termagant and a scold, which is much at one with lunatic. If she be proud, want of discretion (which still is breeding) makes her conceited, fantastic, and ridiculous. And from these she degenerates to be turbulent, clamorous, noisy, nasty, and the devil.

Methinks mankind for their own sakes — since, say what we will of the women, we all think fit at one time or other to be concerned with them — should take some care to breed them up to be suitable and serviceable, if they expected no such thing as delight from them. Bless us! what care do we take to breed up a good horse and to break him well, and what a value do we put upon him when it is done, and all because he should be fit for our use; and why not a woman? Since all her ornaments and beauty without suitable behaviour is a cheat in nature, like the false tradesman, who puts the best of his goods uppermost, that the buyer may think the rest are of the same goodness.

Beauty of the body, which is the woman's glory, seems to be now unequally bestowed, and Nature, or rather Providence, to lie under some scandal about it, as if 'twas given a woman for a snare to men, and so make a kind of a she-devil of her; because, they say, exquisite beauty is rarely given with wit, more rarely with goodness of temper, and never at all with modesty. And some, pretending to justify the equity of such a distribution, will tell us 'tis the effect of the justice of Providence in dividing particular excellencies among all his creatures, share and share alike, as it were, that all might for something or other be acceptable to one another, else some would be despised.

I think both these notions false, and yet the last, which has the show of respect to Providence, is the worst, for it supposes Providence to be indigent and empty, as if it had not wherewith to furnish all the creatures it had made, but was fain to be parsimonious in its gifts, and distribute them by piecemeal for fear of being exhausted.

If I might venture my opinion against an almost universal notion, I would say most men mistake the proceedings of Providence in this case, and all the world at this day are mistaken in their practice about it. And because the assertion is very bold, I desire to explain myself.

That Almighty First Cause which made us all is certainly the fountain of excellence, as it is of being, and by an invisible influence could have diffused equal qualities and perfections to all the creatures it has made, as the sun does its light, without the least ebb or diminution to himself, and has given indeed to every individual sufficient to the figure his providence had designed him in the world.

I believe it might be defended if I should say that I do suppose God has given to all mankind equal gifts and capacities in that he has given them all souls equally capable, and that the whole difference in mankind proceeds either from accidental difference in the make of their bodies or from the foolish difference of education.

1. *From Accidental Difference in Bodies.* I would avoid discoursing here of the philosophical position of the soul in the body. But if it be true, as philosophers do affirm, that the understanding and memory is dilated or contracted according to the accidental dimensions of the organ through which 'tis conveyed, then, though God has given a soul as capable to me as another, yet if I have any natural defect in those parts of the body by which the soul should act, I may have the same soul infused as another man, and yet he be a wise man and I a very fool. For example, if a child naturally have a defect in the organ of hearing, so that he could never distinguish any sound, that child shall never be able to speak or read, though it have a soul capable of all the accomplishments in the world. The brain is the centre of the soul's actings, where all the distinguishing faculties of it reside; and 'tis observable a man who has a narrow contracted head, in which there is not room for the due and necessary operations of nature by the brain, is never a man of very great judgment; and that proverb, "A great head and little wit," is not meant by nature, but is a reproof upon sloth, as if one should, by way of wonder, say, "Fie, fie! you that have a great head have but little wit; that's strange! that must certainly be your own fault." From this notion I do believe there is a great matter in the breed of men and women — not that wise men shall always get wise children, but I believe strong and healthy bodies have the wisest children, and sickly, weakly bodies affect the wits as well as the bodies of their children. We are easily persuaded to believe this in the breeds of horses, cocks, dogs, and other creatures, and I believe 'tis as visible in men.

But to come closer to the business, the great distinguishing difference which is seen in the world between men and women is in their education, and this is manifested by comparing it with the difference between one man or woman and another.

And herein it is that I take upon me to make such a bold assertion that all the world are mistaken in their practice about women; for I cannot think that God Almighty ever made them so delicate, so glorious creatures, and furnished them with such charms, so agreeable and so delightful to mankind, with souls capable of the same accomplishments with men, and all to be only stewards of our houses, cooks, and slaves.

Not that I am for exalting the female government in the least; but, in short, I would have men take women for companions, and educate them to be fit for it. A woman of sense and breeding will scorn as much to encroach upon the prerogative of the man as a man of sense will scorn to oppress the weakness of the woman. But if the women's souls were refined and improved by teaching, that word would be lost; to say, the *weakness of the sex* as to judgment, would be nonsense, for ignorance and folly would be no more to be found among women than men. I remember a passage which I heard from a very fine woman; she had wit and capacity enough, an extraordinary shape and face, and a great fortune, but had been cloistered up all her time, and, for fear of being stolen, had not had the liberty of being taught the common necessary knowledge of women's affairs; and when she came to converse in the world, her natural wit made her so sensible of the want of education that she gave this short reflection on herself: "I am ashamed to talk with my very maids," says she, "for I don't know when they do right or wrong. I had more need go to school than be married."

I need not enlarge on the loss the defect of education is to the sex, nor argue the benefit of the contrary practice; 'tis a thing will be more easily granted than remedied. This chapter is but an essay at the thing, and I refer the practice to those happy days, if ever they shall be, when men shall be wise enough to mend it.

[1697]

From A JOURNAL OF THE PLAGUE YEAR

.. It was now the beginning of August, and the plague grew very violent and terrible in *the place where I lived; and *Dr. Heath coming to visit me, and finding that I ventured so often out in the streets, earnestly persuaded me to lock myself up, and my family, and not to suffer any of us to go out of doors; to keep all our windows fast, shutters and curtains close, and never to open them, but first to make a very strong smoke in the room, where the window or door was to be opened, with rosin and pitch, brimstone and gunpowder, and the like; and we did this for some time. But as I had not laid in a store of provision for such a retreat, it was impossible that we could keep within doors entirely. However, I attempted, though it was so very late, to do something towards it; and first, as I had convenience both for brewing and baking, I went and bought two sacks of meal, and for several weeks, having an oven, we baked all our own bread; also I bought malt and brewed as much beer as all the casks I had would hold, and which seemed enough to serve my house for five or six weeks; also I laid in a quantity of salt butter and Cheshire cheese; but I had no flesh-meat, and the plague raged so violently among the butchers and the slaughter-houses on the other side of our street, where they are known to dwell in great numbers, that it was not advisable so much as to go over the street among them.

And here I must observe again that this necessity of going out of our houses to buy provisions was in a great measure the ruin of the whole city; for the people catched the distemper, on these occasions, one of another; and even the provisions themselves were often tainted, at least I have great reason to believe so; and, therefore, I cannot say with satisfaction, what I know is repeated with great assurance, that the market-people and such as brought provisions to town were never infected. I am certain the butchers of Whitechapel, where the greatest part of the flesh-meat was killed, were dreadfully visited, and that at last to such a degree that few of their shops were kept open; and those that remained of them killed their meat at Mile-End, and that way, and brought it to market upon horses.

However, the poor people could not lay up provisions, and there was a necessity that they must go to market to buy, and others to send servants or their children; and, as this was a necessity which renewed itself daily, it brought abundance of unsound people to the markets; and a great many that went thither sound brought death home with them.

It is true, people used all possible precaution. *When any one bought a joint of meat in the market, they would not take it out of the butcher's hand, but took it off the hooks themselves. On the other hand, the butcher would not touch the money, but have it put into a pot full of vinegar which he kept for that purpose. The buyers carried always small money to make up any odd sum, that they might take no change. They carried bottles for scents and perfumes in their hands, and all the means that could be used were used; but then the poor could not do even these things, and they went at all hazards.

Innumerable dismal stories we heard every day on this very account. Sometimes a man or woman dropped down dead in the very markets; for many people that had the plague upon them knew nothing of it till the inward gangrene had affected their vitals, and they died in a few moments. This caused that many died frequently in that manner in the street suddenly, without any warning; others, perhaps, had time to go to the next bulk or stall, or to any door or porch, and just sit down and die, as I have said before.

These objects were so frequent in the streets that when the plague came to be very raging on one side, there was scarce any passing by the streets but that several dead bodies would be lying here and there upon the ground. On the other hand, it is observable that, though at first the people would stop as they went along, and call to the neighbours to come out on such an occasion, yet afterward no notice was taken of them; but that, if at any time we found a corpse lying, go across the way and not come near it; or, if in a narrow lane or passage, go back again, and seek some other way to go on the business we were upon; and in those cases the corpse was always left till the officers had notice to come and take them away, or till night, when the bearers attending the dead-cart would take them up and carry them away. Nor did those undaunted creatures who performed these offices fail to search their pockets, and sometimes strip off their clothes, if they were well dressed, as sometimes they were, and carry off what they could get.

But to return to the markets. The butchers took that care, that, if any person died in the market, they had the officers always at hand to take them up upon handbarrows, and carry them to the next churchyard; and this was so frequent that such were not entered in *the weekly bill, "found dead in the streets or fields," as is the case now, but they went into the general articles of the great distemper.

But now the fury of the distemper increased to such a degree that even the markets were but very thinly furnished with provisions, or frequented with buyers, compared to what they were before; and the Lord Mayor caused the country people who brought provisions to be stopped in the streets leading into the town, and to sit down there with their goods, where they sold what they brought, and went immediately away. And this encouraged the country people greatly to do so, for they sold their provisions at the very entrances into the town, and even in the fields, as particularly in the fields beyond Whitechapel, in Spittlefields. Note, those streets now called Spittlefields were then indeed open fields: also in St. George's Fields in Southwark, in Bunhill Fields, and in a great field called Wood's Close, near Islington. Thither the Lord Mayor, aldermen, and magistrates sent their officers and servants to buy for their families, themselves keeping within doors as much as possible; and the like did many other people; and after this method was taken, the country people came with great cheerfulness, and brought provisions of all sorts, and very seldom got any harm, which, I suppose, added also to that report of their being miraculously preserved.

As for my little family, having thus, as I have said, laid in a store of bread, butter, cheese, and beer, I took my friend and physician's advice, and locked myself up, and my family, and resolved to suffer the hardship of living a few months without flesh-meat rather than to purchase it at the hazard of our lives.

But though I confined my family, I could not prevail upon my unsatisfied curiosity to stay within entirely myself, and, though I generally came frighted and terrified home, yet I could not restrain, only that, indeed, I did not do it so frequently as at first.

I had some little obligations, indeed, upon me to go to my brother's house, which was in Coleman Street Parish, and which he had left to my care; and I went at first every day, but afterwards only once or twice a week.

In these walks I had many dismal scenes before my eyes, as, particularly, of persons falling dead in the streets, terrible shrieks and screechings of women, who in their agonies would throw open their chamber windows, and cry out in a dismal, surprising manner. It is impossible to describe the variety of postures in which the passions of the poor people would express themselves.

Passing through Token-House Yard in Lothbury, of a sudden a casement violently opened just over my head, and a woman gave three frightful screeches, and then cried, "Oh! death, death, death!" in a most inimitable tone, and which struck me with horror, and a chillness in my very blood. There was nobody to be seen in the whole street, neither did any other window open, for people had no curiosity now in any case, nor could anybody help one another; so I went on to pass into Bell Alley.

Just in Bell Alley, on the right hand of the passage, there was a more terrible cry than that, though it was not so directed out at the window. But the whole family was in a terrible fright, and I could hear women and children run screaming about the rooms like distracted, when a garret window opened, and somebody from a window on the other side the alley called and asked, "What is the matter?" Upon which from the first window it was answered, "O Lord, my old master has hanged himself!" The other asked again, "Is he quite dead?" and the first answered, "Ay, ay, quite dead; quite dead and cold!" This person was a merchant and a deputy alderman, and very rich. I care not to mention his name, though I knew his name too; but that would be an hardship to the family, which is now flourishing again.

But this is but one. It is scarce credible what dreadful cases happened in particular families every day, — people, in the rage of the distemper, or in the torment of their swellings, which was indeed intolerable, running out of their own government, raving and distracted, and oftentimes laying violent hands upon themselves, throwing themselves out at their windows, shooting themselves, etc.; mothers murdering their own children in their lunacy; some dying of mere grief as a passion, some of mere fright and surprise without any infection at all; others frighted into idiotism and foolish distractions, some into despair and lunacy, others into melancholy madness.

The pain of the swelling was in particular very violent, and to some intolerable. The physicians and surgeons may be said to have tortured many poor creatures even to death. The swellings in some grew hard, and they applied violent drawing plasters, or poultices, to break them; and, if these did not do, they cut and scarified them in a terrible manner. In some, those swellings were made hard, partly by the force of the distemper, and partly by their being too violently drawn, and were so hard that no instrument could cut them; and then they burned them with caustics, so that many died raving mad with the torment, and some in the very operation. In these distresses, some, for want of help to hold them down in their beds or to look to them, laid hands upon themselves as above; some broke out into the streets, perhaps naked, and would run directly down to the river, if they were not stopped by the watchmen or other officers, and plunge themselves into the water wherever they found it.

It often pierced my very soul to hear the groans and cries of those who were thus tormented. But of the two, this was counted the most promising particular in the whole infection: for if these swellings could be brought to a head, and to break and run, or, as the surgeons call it, to "digest," the patient generally recovered; whereas those who, like the gentlewoman's daughter, were struck with death at the beginning, and had the tokens come out upon them, often went about indifferently easy till a little before they died, and some till the moment they dropped down, as in apoplexies and epilepsies is often the case. Such would be taken suddenly very sick, and would run to a bench or bulk, or any convenient place that offered itself, or to their own houses, if possible, as I mentioned before, and there sit down, grow faint, and die. This kind of dying was much the same as it was with those who die of common mortifications, who die swooning, and, as it were, go away in a dream. Such as died thus had very little notice of their being infected at all till the gangrene was spread through their whole body; nor could physicians themselves know certainly how it was with them till they opened their breasts, or other parts of their body, and saw the tokens.

We had at this time a great many frightful stories told us of nurses and watchmen who looked after the dying people, that is to say, hired nurses, who attended infected people, using them barbarously, starving them, smothering them, or by other wicked means hastening their end, that is to say, murdering of them: and watchmen being set to guard houses that were shut up, when there has been but one person left, and perhaps that one lying sick, that they have broke in and murdered that body, and immediately thrown them out into the dead-cart; and so they have gone scarce cold to the grave.

I cannot say but that some such murders were committed, and I think two were sent to prison for it, but died before they could be tried; and I have heard that three others, at several times, were executed for murders of that kind. But I must say I believe nothing of its being so common a crime as some have since been pleased to say; nor did it seem to be so rational, where the people were brought so low as not to be able to help themselves; for such seldom recovered, and there was no temptation to commit a murder, at least not equal to the fact, where they were sure persons would die in so short a time, and could not live.

That there were a great many robberies and wicked practices committed even in this dreadful time, I do not deny. The power of avarice was so strong in some that they would run any hazard to steal and to plunder; and, particularly in houses where all the families or inhabitants have been dead and carried out, they would break in at all hazards, and, without regard to the danger of infection, take even the clothes off the dead bodies, and the bedclothes from others where they lay dead.

This, I suppose, must be the case of a family in Houndsditch, where a man and his daughter, the rest of the family being, as I suppose, carried away before by the dead-cart, were found stark naked, one in one chamber and one in another, lying dead on the floor, and the clothes of the beds, from whence 'tis supposed they were rolled off by thieves, stolen, and carried quite away.

It is indeed to be observed that the women were, in all this calamity, the most rash, fearless, and desperate creatures; and, as there were vast numbers that went about as nurses to tend those that were sick, they committed a great many petty thieveries in the houses where they were employed; and some of them were publicly whipped for it, when perhaps they ought rather to have been hanged for examples, for numbers of houses were robbed on these occasions; till at length the parish officers were sent to recommend nurses to the sick, and always took an account who it was they sent, so as that they might call them to account if the house had been abused where they were placed.

But these robberies extended chiefly to wearing-clothes, linen, and what rings or money they could come at, when the person died who was under their care, but not to a general plunder of the houses; and I could give you an account of one of these nurses, who several years after, being on her deathbed, confessed with the utmost horror the robberies she had committed at the time of her being a nurse, and by which she had enriched herself to a great degree. But as for murders, I do not find that there was ever any proofs of the fact in the manner as it has been reported, except as above.

They did tell me, indeed, of a nurse in one place that laid a wet cloth upon the face of a dying patient whom she tended, and so put an end to his life, who was just expiring before; and another that smothered a young woman she was looking to, when she was in a fainting fit, and would have come to herself; some that killed them by giving them one thing, some another, and some starved them by giving them nothing at all. But these stories had two marks of suspicion that always attended them, which caused me always to slight them, and to look on them as mere stories that people continually frighted one another with. First — that wherever it was that we heard it, they always placed the scene at the farther end of the town, opposite or most remote from where you were to hear it. If you heard it in Whitechapel, it had happened at St. Giles's, or at Westminster, or Holborn, or that end of the town; if you heard of it at that end of the town, then it was done in Whitechapel, or the Minories, or about Cripplegate Parish; if you heard of it in the city, why, then, it happened in Southwark; and, if you heard of it in Southwark, then it was done in the city, and the like.

In the next place, of what part soever you heard the story, the particulars were always the same, especially that of laying a wet double clout on a dying man's face, and that of smothering a young gentlewoman: so that it was apparent, at least to my judgment, that there was more of tale than of truth in those things.

However, I cannot say, but it had some effect upon the people; and particularly, that, as I said before, they grew more cautious who they took into their houses, and whom they trusted their lives with, and had them always recommended, if they could; and where they could not find such, for they were not very plenty, they applied to the parish officers.

But here again, the misery of that time lay upon the poor, who, being infected, had neither food nor physic: neither physician nor apothecary to assist them, nor nurse to attend them. Many of those died calling for help, and even for sustenance, out at their windows, in a most miserable and deplorable manner; but it must be added that whenever the cases of such persons or families were represented to my Lord Mayor, they always were relieved.

It is true that in some houses where the people were not very poor, yet, where they had sent perhaps their wives and children away, and if they had any servants, they had been dismissed; I say, it is true, that to save the expenses, many such as these shut themselves in, and, not having help, died alone.

A neighbour and acquaintance of mine, having some money owing to him from a shopkeeper in Whitecross Street or thereabouts, sent his apprentice, a youth about eighteen years of age, to endeavour to get the money. He came to the door, and finding it shut, knocked pretty hard, and, as he thought, heard somebody answer within, but was not sure; so he waited, and after some stay knocked again, and then a third time, when he heard somebody coming downstairs.

At length the man of the house came to the door; he had on his breeches, or drawers, and a yellow flannel waistcoat, no stockings, a pair of slipped-shoes, a white cap on his head, and, as the young man said, "death in his face."

When he opened the door, says he, "What do you disturb me thus for?" The boy, though a little surprised, replied, "I come from such a one; and my master sent me for the money, which he says you know of." "Very well, child," returns the living ghost; "call, as you go by, at Cripplegate Church, and bid them ring the bell"; and with these words shut the door again, and went up again, and died the same day, nay, perhaps the same hour. This the young man told me himself, and I have reason to believe it. This was while the plague was not come to a height. I think it was in June, towards the latter end of the month. It must be before the dead-carts came about, and while they used the ceremony of ringing the bell for the dead, which was over for certain, in that parish at least, before the month of July; for by the 25th of July there died five hundred and fifty and upwards in a week, and then they could no more bury in form rich or poor.

I have mentioned above, that notwithstanding this dreadful calamity, yet numbers of thieves were abroad upon all occasions where they had found any prey, and that these were generally women. It was one morning about eleven o'clock, I had walked out to my brother's house in Coleman Street Parish, as I often did, to see that all was safe.

My brother's house had a little court before it, and a brick wall and a gate in it, and, within that, several warehouses, where his goods of several sorts lay. It happened that in one of these warehouses were several packs of women's high-crowned hats, which came out of the country, and were, as I suppose, for exportation, whither I know not.

I was surprised that when I came near my brother's door, which was in a place they called Swan Alley, I met three or four women with high-crowned hats on their heads; and, as I remembered afterwards, one, if not more, had some hats likewise in their hands: but as I did not see them come out at my brother's door, and not knowing that my brother had any such goods in his warehouse, I did not offer to say anything to them, but went across the way to shun meeting them, as was usual to do at that time, for fear of the plague. But when I came nearer to the gate, I met another woman, with more hats, come out of the gate. "What business, mistress," said I, "have you had there?" "There are more people there," said she; "I have had no more business there than they." I was hasty to get to the gate then, and said no more to her; by which means she got away. But just as I came to the gate, I saw two more coming across the yard, to come out, with hats also on their heads and under their arms; at which I threw the gate to behind me, which, having a spring-lock, fastened itself; and turning to the women, "Forsooth," said I, "what are you doing here?" and seized upon the hats, and took them from them. One of them, who, I confess, did not look like a thief, — "Indeed," says she, "we are wrong; but we were told they were goods that had no owner: be pleased to take them again; and look yonder, there are more such customers as we." She cried, and looked pitifully; so I took the hats from her, and opened the gate, and bade them be gone, for I pitied the women indeed; but when I looked towards the warehouse, as she directed, there were six or seven more, all women, fitting themselves with hats, as unconcerned and quiet as if they had been at a hatter's shop buying for their money.

I was surprised, not at the sight of so many thieves only, but at the circumstances I was in; being now to thrust myself in among so many people, who for some weeks had been so shy of myself that if I met anybody in the street, I would cross the way from them.

They were equally surprised, though on another account. They all told me they were neighbours, that they had heard any one might take them, that they were nobody's goods, and the like. I talked big to them at first; went back to the gate and took out the key, so that they were all my prisoners; threatened to lock them all into the warehouse, and go and fetch my Lord Mayor's officers for them.

They begged heartily, protested they found the gate open, and the warehouse door open, and that it had no doubt been broken open by some who expected to find goods of greater value, which indeed was reasonable to believe, because the lock was broke, and a padlock that hung to the door on the outside also loose, and not abundance of the hats carried away.

At length I considered that this was not a time to be cruel and rigorous; and besides that, it would necessarily oblige me to go much about, to have several people come to me, and I go to several, whose circumstances of health I knew nothing of: and that, even at this time, the plague was so high as that there died four thousand a week; so that, in showing my resentment, or even in seeking justice for my brother's goods, I might lose my own life. So I contented myself with taking the names and places where some of them lived, who were really inhabitants in the neighbourhood, and threatening that my brother should call them to an account for it when he returned to his habitation.

Then I talked a little upon another footing with them, and asked them how they could do such things as these in a time of such general calamity, and, as it were, in the face of God's most dreadful judgments, when the plague was at their very doors, and, it may be, in their very houses, and they did not know but that the dead-cart might stop at their doors in a few hours, to carry them to their graves.

I could not perceive that my discourse made much impression upon them all that while, till it happened that there came two men of the neighbourhood, hearing of the disturbance, and knowing my brother, for they had been both dependents upon his family, and they came to my assistance. These being, as I said, neighbours, presently knew three of the women, and told me who they were, and where they lived; and it seems they had given me a true account of themselves before.

This brings these two men to a further remembrance. The name of one was John Hayward, who was at that time under-sexton of the parish of St. Stephen, Coleman Street: by under-sexton was understood at that time gravedigger and bearer of the dead. This man carried, or assisted to carry, all the dead to their graves, which were buried in that large parish, and who were carried in form, and, after that form of burying was stopped, went with the dead-cart and the bell to fetch the dead bodies from the houses where they lay, and fetched many of them out of the chambers and houses; for the parish was, and is still, remarkable, particularly above all the parishes in London, for a great number of alleys and thoroughfares, very long, into which no carts could come, and where they were obliged to go and fetch the bodies a very long way, which alleys now remain to witness it; such as White's Alley, Cross Key Court, Swan Alley, Bell Alley, White Horse Alley, and many more. Here they went with a kind of handbarrow, and laid the dead bodies on it, and carried them out to the carts; which work he performed, and never had the distemper at all, but lived about twenty years after it, and was sexton of the parish to the time of his death. His wife at the same time was a nurse to infected people, and tended many that died in the parish, being for her honesty recommended by the parish officers; yet she never was infected, neither.

He never used any preservative against the infection other than holding garlic and rue in his mouth, and smoking tobacco. This I also had from his own mouth. And his wife's remedy was washing her head in vinegar, and sprinkling her head-clothes so with vinegar as to keep them always moist; and, if the smell of any of those she waited on was more than ordinarily offensive, she snuffed vinegar up her nose, and sprinkled vinegar upon her head-clothes, and held a handkerchief wetted with vinegar to her mouth.

It must be confessed that though the plague was chiefly among the poor, yet were the poor the most venturous and fearless of it, and went about their employment with a sort of brutal courage; I must call it so, for it was founded neither on religion or prudence. Scarce did they use any caution, but ran into any business which they could get employment in, though it was the most hazardous; such was that of tending the sick, watching houses shut up, carrying infected persons to the pest-house, and, which was still worse, carrying the dead away to their graves.

It was under this John Hayward's care, and within his bounds, that the story of the piper, with which people have made themselves so merry, happened; and he assured me that it was true. It is said that it was a blind piper; but, as John told me, the fellow was not blind, but an ignorant, weak, poor man, and usually went his rounds about ten o'clock at night, and went piping along from door to door. And the people usually took him in at public houses where they knew him, and would give him drink and victuals, and sometimes farthings; and he in return would pipe and sing, and talk simply, which diverted the people; and thus he lived. It was but a very bad time for this diversion while things were as I have told; yet the poor fellow went about as usual, but was almost starved: and when anybody asked how he did, he would answer, the dead-cart had not taken him yet, but that they had promised to call for him next week.

It happened one night that this poor fellow, whether somebody had given him too much drink or no — John Hayward said he had not drink in his house, but that they had given him a little more victuals than ordinary at a public house in Coleman Street — and the poor fellow having not usually had a bellyful, or perhaps not a good while, was laid all along upon the top of a bulk or stall, and fast asleep at a door in the street near London Wall, towards Cripplegate; and that, upon the same bulk or stall, the people of some house in the alley of which the house was a corner, hearing a bell, which they always rung before the cart came, had laid a body really dead of the plague just by him, thinking too that this poor fellow had been a dead body as the other was, and laid there by some of the neighbours.

Accordingly, when John Hayward with his bell and the cart came along, finding two dead bodies lie upon the stall, they took them up with the instrument they used, and threw them into the cart; and all this while the piper slept soundly.

From hence they passed along, and took in other dead bodies, till, as honest John Hayward told me, they almost buried him alive in the cart; yet all this while he slept soundly. At length the cart came to the place where the bodies were to be thrown into the ground, which, as I do remember, was at Mountmill; and, as the cart usually stopped some time before they were ready to shoot out the melancholy load they had in it, as soon as the cart stopped, the fellow awaked, and struggled a little to get his head out from among the dead bodies; when, raising himself up in the cart, he called out, "Hey, where am I?" This frighted the fellow that attended about the work; but, after some pause, John Hayward, recovering himself, said, "Lord bless us! There's somebody in the cart not quite dead!" So another called to him, and said, "Who are you?" The fellow answered, "I am the poor piper. Where am I?" "Where are you?" says Hayward. "Why, you are in the dead-cart, and we are going to bury you." "But I an't dead, though, am I?" says the piper, which made them laugh a little, though, as John said, they were heartily frighted at first. So they helped the poor fellow down, and he went about his business.

I know the story goes, he set up his pipes in the cart, and frighted the bearers and others, so that they ran away; but John Hayward did not tell the story so, nor say anything of his piping at all: but that he was a poor piper, and that he was carried away as above, I am fully satisfied of the truth of.

It is to be noted here that the dead-carts in the city were not confined to particular parishes; but one cart went through several parishes, according as the number of dead presented; nor were they tied to carry the dead to their respective parishes; but many of the dead taken up in the city were carried to the burying-ground in the out-parts for want of room.

I have already mentioned the surprise that this judgment was, at first, the occasion of among the people. I must be allowed to give some of my observations on the more serious and religious part. Surely never city, at least of this bulk and magnitude, was taken in a condition so perfectly unprepared for such a dreadful visitation, whether I am to speak of the civil preparations, or religious; they were, indeed, as if they had had no warning, no expectation, no apprehensions, and consequently, the least provision imaginable was made for it in a public way; for example:

The Lord Mayor and sheriffs had made no provision, as magistrates, for the regulations which were to be observed; they had gone into no measures for the relief of the poor.

The citizens had no public magazines, or store-houses for corn, or meal, for the subsistence of the poor; which, if they had provided themselves with, as in such cases is done abroad, many miserable families, who were now reduced to the utmost distress, would have been relieved, and that in a better manner than now could be done.

The stock of the city's money I can say but little to; the Chamber of London was said to be exceeding rich; and it may be concluded that they were so, by the vast sums of money issued from thence, in the rebuilding the public edifices after the Fire of London, and in building new works, such as, for the first part, the Guildhall, Blackwell Hall, part of Leadenhall, half the Exchange, the Session House, the Compter, the prisons of Ludgate, Newgate, &c.; several of the wharfs, and stairs, and landing-places on the river; all which were either burnt down or damaged by the great Fire of London, the next year after the plague; and of the second sort, the Monument, Fleetditch, with its bridges, and the Hospital of Bethlem, or Bedlam, &c. But possibly the managers of the city's credit at that time made more conscience of breaking in upon the orphans' money, to show charity to the distressed citizens, than the managers in the following years did, to beautify the city, and re-edify the buildings, though in the first case, the losers would have thought their fortunes better bestowed, and the public faith of the city have been less subjected to scandal and reproach.

It must be acknowledged that the absent citizens, who, though they were fled for safety into the country, were yet greatly interested in the welfare of those whom they left behind, forgot not to contribute liberally to the relief of the poor, and large sums were also collected among trading towns in the remotest parts of England; and as I have heard also, the nobility and the gentry, in all parts of England, took the deplorable condition of the city into their consideration, and sent up large sums of money in charity, to the Lord Mayor and magistrates, for the relief of the poor. The King also, as I was told, ordered a thousand pounds a week to be distributed in four parts: one quarter to the city and liberties of Westminster; one quarter, or part, among the inhabitants of the Southwark-side of the water; one quarter to the liberties and parts without, of the city, exclusive of the city within the walls; and one fourth part to the suburbs in the county of Middlesex, and the east and north parts of the city; but this latter I only speak of as a report.

Certain it is, the greatest part of the poor, or families who formerly lived by their labour, or by retail trade, lived now on charity; and had there not been prodigious sums of money given by charitable, well-minded Christians, for the support of such, the city could never have subsisted. There were, no question, accounts kept of their charity, and of the just distribution of it by the magistrates: but as such multitudes of those very officers died, through whose hands it was distributed; and also that, as I have been told, most of the accounts of those things were lost in the great Fire which happened in the very next year, and which burnt even the chamberlain's office, and many of their papers; so I could never come at the particular account, which I used great endeavours to have seen.

It may, however, be a direction *in case of the approach of a like visitation, which God keep the city from! — I say, it may be of use to observe that by the care of the Lord Mayor and aldermen, at that time, in distributing weekly great sums of money for relief of the poor, a multitude of people, who would otherwise have perished, were relieved, and their lives preserved. And here let me enter into a brief state of the case of the poor at that time, and what was apprehended from them, from whence may be judged hereafter what may be expected, if the like distress should come upon the city.

At the beginning of the plague, when there was now no more hope but that the whole city would be visited; when, as I have said, all that had friends or estates in the country retired with their families; and when, indeed, one would have thought the very city itself was running out of the gates, and that there would be nobody left behind — you may be sure from that hour all trade, except such as related to immediate subsistence, was, as it were, at a full stop.

This is so lively a case, and contains in it so much of the real condition of the people, that I think I cannot be too particular in it, and therefore I descend to the several arrangements or classes of people who fell into immediate distress upon this occasion. For example:

1. All master workmen in manufactures, especially such as belonged to ornament and the less necessary parts of the people's dress, clothes, and furniture for houses; such as ribbon-weavers and other weavers, gold and silver lacemakers, and gold and silver wire drawers, sempstresses, milliners, shoemakers, hatmakers, and glovemakers, also upholsterers, joiners, cabinet-makers, looking-glass-makers, and innumerable trades which depend upon such as these — I say, the master workmen in such stopped their work, dismissed their journeymen and workmen and all their dependents.

2. As merchandising was at a full stop,

or very few ships ventured to come up the river, and none at all went out, so all the extraordinary officers of the customs, likewise the watermen, carmen, porters, and all the poor whose labour depended upon the merchants, were at once dismissed, and put out of business.

3. All the tradesmen usually employed in building or repairing of houses were at a full stop, for the people were far from wanting to build houses when so many thousand houses were at once stripped of their inhabitants; so that this one article turned all the ordinary workmen of that kind out of business, such as bricklayers, masons, carpenters, joiners, plasterers, painters, glaziers, smiths, plumbers, and all the labourers depending on such.

4. As navigation was at a stop, our ships neither coming in or going out as before, so the seamen were all out of employment, and many of them in the last and lowest degree of distress; and with the seamen were all the several tradesmen and workmen belonging to and depending upon the building and fitting out of ships; such as ship-carpenters, calkers, ropemakers, dry coopers, sailmakers, anchor-smiths, and other smiths, blockmakers, carvers, gunsmiths, ship-chandlers, ship-carvers, and the like. The masters of those, perhaps, might live upon their substance; but the traders were universally at a stop, and consequently all their workmen discharged. Add to these that the river was in a manner without boats, and all or most part of the watermen, lightermen, boat-builders, and lighter-builders in like manner idle and laid by.

5. All families retrenched their living as much as possible, as well those that fled as those that stayed, so that an innumerable multitude of footmen, serving men, shopkeepers, journeymen, merchants' bookkeepers, and such sort of people, and especially poor maidservants, were turned off, and left friendless and helpless, without employment and without habitation; and this was really a dismal article.

I might be more particular as to this part; but it may suffice to mention, in general, all trades being stopped, employment ceased, the labour, and by that the bread of the poor, were cut off; and at first, indeed, the cries of the poor were most lamentable to hear, though, by the distribution of charity, their misery that way was greatly abated. Many, indeed, fled into the country; but, thousands of them having stayed in London till nothing but desperation sent them away, death overtook them on the road, and they served for no better than the messengers of death; indeed, others carrying the infection along with them, spread it very unhappily into the remotest parts of the kingdom.

Many of these were the miserable objects of despair, which I have mentioned before, and were removed by the destruction which followed. These might be said to perish, not by the infection itself, but by the consequence of it: — namely, by hunger and distress, and the want of all things; being without lodging, without money, without friends, without means to get their bread, and without any one to give it them, for many of them were without what we call legal settlements, and so could not claim of the parishes; and all the support they had was by application to the magistrates for relief, which relief was (to give the magistrates their due) carefully and cheerfully administered, as they found it necessary; and those that stayed behind never felt the want and distress of that kind, which they felt who went away in the manner above noted.

Let any one who is acquainted with what multitudes of people get their daily bread in this city by their labour, whether artificers or mere workmen; — I say, let any man consider what must be the miserable condition of this town, if, on a sudden, they should be all turned out of employment, that labour should cease, and wages for work be no more.

This was the case with us at that time; and had not the sums of money, contributed in charity by well-disposed people of every kind, as well abroad as at home, been prodigiously great, it had not been in the power of the Lord Mayor and sheriffs to have kept the public peace: nor were they without apprehensions as it was, that desperation should push the people upon tumults, and cause them to rifle the houses of rich men, and plunder the markets of provisions: in which case, the country people, who brought provisions very freely and boldly to town, would have been terrified from coming any more, and the town would have sunk under an unavoidable famine.

But the prudence of my Lord Mayor, and the court of aldermen within the city, and of the justices of peace in the out-parts was such, and they were supported with money from all parts so well, that the poor people were kept quiet, and their wants everywhere relieved, as far as was possible to be done.

Two things, besides this, contributed to prevent *the mob doing any mischief: one was that really the rich themselves had not laid up stores of provisions in their houses, as, indeed, they ought to have done, and which, if they had been wise enough to have done, and locked themselves entirely up, as some few did, they had perhaps escaped the disease better; but as it appeared they had not, so the mob had no notion of finding stores of provisions there, if they had broken in, as it is plain they were sometimes very near doing, and which, if they had, they had finished the ruin of the whole city, for there were no regular troops to have withstood them; nor could the trained bands have been brought together to defend the city, no men being to be found to bear arms.

But the vigilance of the Lord Mayor, and such magistrates as could be had, for some, even of the aldermen, were dead, and some absent, prevented this; and they did it by the most kind and gentle methods they could think of, as particularly by relieving the most desperate with money, and putting others into business, and particularly that employment of watching houses that were infected and shut up; and as the number of these was very great, for, it was said, there was at one time ten thousand houses shut up; and every house had two watchmen to guard it, viz., one by night, and the other by day; this gave opportunity to employ a very great number of poor men at a time.

The women and servants that were turned off from their places were likewise employed as nurses to tend the sick in all places, and this took off a very great number of them

And which, though a melancholy article in itself, yet was a deliverance in its kind, namely, the plague, which raged in a dreadful manner from the middle of August to the middle of October, carried off in that time thirty or forty thousand of these very people, which, had they been left, would certainly have been an insufferable burden by their poverty; that is to say, the whole city could not have supported the expense of them, or have provided food for them, and they would in time have been even driven to the necessity of plundering either the city itself, or the country adjacent, to have subsisted themselves, which would, first or last, have put the whole nation, as well as the city, into the utmost terror and confusion.

It was observable, then, that this calamity of the people made them very humble; for now, for about nine weeks together, there died near a thousand a day, one day with another, even by the account of the weekly bills, which yet, I have reason to be assured, never gave a full account by many thousands; the confusion being such, and the carts working in the dark when they carried the dead, that in some places no account at all was kept, but they worked on; the clerks and sextons not attending for weeks together, and not knowing what number they carried. This account is verified by the following bills of mortality:

	Of All Diseases.	Of the Plague.
Aug. 8 to Aug. 15......	5,319	3,880
Aug. 15 to Aug. 22......	5,668	4,237
Aug. 22 to Aug. 29......	7,496	6,102
Aug. 29 to Sept. 5......	8,252	6,988
Sept. 5 to Sept. 12......	7,690	6,544
Sept. 12 to Sept. 19......	8,297	7,165
Sept. 19 to Sept. 26......	6,460	5,533
Sept. 26 to Oct. 3......	5,720	4,929
Oct. 3 to Oct. 10......	5,068	4,327
	59,870	49,705

So that the gross of the people were carried off in these two months; for, as the whole number which was brought in to die of the plague was but 68,590, here is 50,000 of them, within a trifle, in two months: I say 50,000, because as there wants 295 in the number above, so *there wants two days of two months in the account of time.

Now, when I say that the parish officers did not give in a full account, or were not to be depended upon for their account, let any one but consider how men could be exact in such a time of dreadful distress, and when many of them were taken sick themselves, and perhaps died in the very time when their accounts were to be given in, I mean the parish clerks, besides inferior officers: for though these poor men ventured at all hazards, yet they were far from being exempt from the common calamity, especially if it be true that the parish of Stepney had within the year one hundred and sixteen sextons, gravediggers, and their assistants; that is to say, bearers, bellmen, and drivers of carts for carrying off the dead bodies.

Indeed, the work was not of a nature to allow them leisure to take an exact tale of the dead bodies, which were all huddled together in the dark into a pit: which pit, or trench, no man could come nigh but at the utmost peril. I have observed often that in the parishes of Aldgate and Cripplegate, Whitechapel, and Stepney, there were five, six, seven, and eight hundred in a week in the bills; whereas, if we may believe the opinion of those that lived in the city all the time, as well as I, there died sometimes two thousand a week in those parishes. And I saw it under the hand of one that made as strict an examination as he could, that there really died an hundred thousand people of the plague in it that one year; whereas, in the bills, the articles of the plague formed but 68,590.

If I may be allowed to give my opinion, by what I saw with my eyes, and heard from other people that were eyewitnesses, I do verily believe the same, viz., that there died at least one hundred thousand of the plague only, besides other distempers, and besides those which died in the fields and highways and secret places, out of the compass of the communication, as it was called, and who were not put down in the bills, though they really belonged to the body of the inhabitants. It was known to us all that abundance of poor despairing creatures who had the distemper upon them, and were grown stupid or melancholy by their misery, as many were, wandered away into the fields and woods, and into secret uncouth places, almost anywhere, to creep into a bush or hedge, and die.

The inhabitants of the villages adjacent would in pity carry them food, and set it at a distance, that they might fetch it if they were able; and sometimes they were not able; and the next time they went they should find the poor wretches lie dead, and the food untouched. The number of these miserable objects were many; and I know so many that perished thus, and so exactly where, that I believe I could go to the very place, and dig their bones up still; for the country people would go and dig a hole at a distance from them, and then, with long poles and hooks at the end of them, drag the bodies into these pits, and then throw the earth in, from as far as they could cast it, to cover them, taking notice how the wind blew, and so coming on that side which the seamen call to windward, that the scent of the bodies might blow from them. And thus great numbers went out of the world who were never known, or any account of them taken, as well within the bills of mortality as without.

This, indeed, I had, in the main, only from the relation of others; for I seldom walked into the fields, except towards Bethnal Green and Hackney, or as hereafter. But when I did walk, I always saw a great many poor wanderers at a distance, but I could know little of their cases; for, whether it were in the street or in the fields, if we had seen anybody coming, it was a general method to walk away. Yet I believe the account is exactly true.

As this puts me upon mentioning my walking the streets and fields, I cannot omit taking notice what a desolate place the city was at that time. The great street I lived in, which is known to be one of the broadest of all the streets of London, I mean of the suburbs as well as the liberties, all the side where the butchers lived, especially *without the bars, was more like a green field than a paved street; and the people generally went in the middle with the horses and carts. It is true that the farthest end, towards Whitechapel Church, was not all paved, but even the part that was paved was full of grass also. But this need not seem strange, since the great streets within the city, such as Leadenhall Street, Bishopsgate Street, Cornhill, and even the Exchange itself, had grass growing in them in several places. Neither cart nor coach was seen in the streets from morning to evening, except some country carts to bring roots and beans, or peas, hay, and straw, to the market, and those but very few compared to what was usual. As for coaches, they were scarce used, but to carry sick people to the pesthouse and to other hospitals, and some few to carry physicians to such places as they thought fit to venture to visit; for really coaches were dangerous things, and people did not care to venture into them, because they did not know who might have been carried in them last; and sick infected people were, as I have said, ordinarily carried in them to the pesthouses; and sometimes people expired in them as they went along.

It is true, when the infection came to such a height as I have now mentioned, there were very few physicians which cared to stir abroad to sick houses, and very many of the most eminent of the faculty were dead, as well as the surgeons also; for now it was indeed a dismal time, and for about a month together, not taking any notice of the bills of mortality, I believe there did not die less than fifteen or seventeen hundred a day, one day with another.

One of the worst days we had in the whole time, as I thought, was in the beginning of September, when, indeed, good people began to think that God was resolved to make a full end of the people in this miserable city. This was at that time when the plague was fully come into the eastern parishes. The parish of Aldgate, if I may give my opinion, buried above one thousand a week for two weeks, though the bills did not say so many; but it surrounded me at so dismal a rate that there was not a house in twenty uninfected. In the Minories, in Houndsditch, and in those parts of Aldgate Parish about the Butcher Row, and the alleys over against me — I say, in those places death reigned in every corner. Whitechapel Parish was in the same condition, and though much less than the parish I lived in, yet buried near six hundred a week, by the bills, and in my opinion near twice as many. Whole families, and indeed whole streets of families, were swept away together, insomuch that it was frequent for neighbours to call to the bellman to go to such and such houses and fetch out the people, for that they were all dead.

And, indeed, the work of removing the dead bodies by carts was now grown so very odious and dangerous that it was complained of that the bearers did not take care to clear such houses where all the inhabitants were dead, but that sometimes the bodies lay several days unburied till the neighbouring families were offended by the stench, and consequently infected. And this neglect of the officers was such that the churchwardens and constables were summoned to look after it; and even the justices of the hamlets were obliged to venture their lives among them to quicken and encourage them; for innumerable of the bearers died of the distemper, infected by the bodies they were obliged to come so near. And had it not been that the number of poor people who wanted employment, and wanted bread, as I have said before, was so great that necessity drove them to undertake anything, and venture anything, they would never have found people to be employed; and then the bodies of the dead would have lain above ground, and have perished and rotted in a dreadful manner.

But the magistrates cannot be enough commended in this, that they kept such good order for the burying of the dead, that as fast as any of those they employed to carry off and bury the dead fell sick or died, as was many times the case, they immediately supplied the places with others; which, by reason of the great number of poor that was left out of business, as above, was not hard to do. This occasioned, that, notwithstanding the infinite number of people which died and were sick, almost all together, yet they were always cleared away, and carried off every night; so that it was never to be said of London that the living were not able to bury the dead.

As the desolation was greater during those terrible times, so the amazement of the people increased; and a thousand unaccountable things they would do in the violence of their fright, as others did the same in the agonies of their distemper: and this part was very affecting. Some went roaring, and crying and wringing their hands, along the street; some would go praying, and lifting up their hands to heaven, calling upon God for mercy. I cannot say, indeed, whether this was not in their distraction; but, be it so, it was still an indication of a more serious mind when they had the use of their senses, and was much better, even as it was, than the frightful yellings and cryings that every day, and especially in the evenings, were heard in some streets. I suppose the world has heard of the famous Solomon Eagle, an enthusiast. He, though not infected at all, but in his head, went about denouncing of judgment upon the city in a frightful manner, sometimes quite naked, and with a pan of burning charcoal on his head. What he said or pretended, indeed, I could not learn.

I will not say whether that clergyman was distracted or not, or whether he did it in pure zeal for the poor people, who went every evening through the streets of Whitechapel, and, with his hands lifted up, repeated that part of the liturgy of the church continually, "Spare us, good Lord; spare thy people whom thou hast redeemed with thy most precious blood." I say I cannot speak positively of these things, because these were only the dismal objects which represented themselves to me as I looked through my chamber windows; for I seldom opened the casements while I confined myself within doors during that most violent raging of the pestilence, when, indeed, as I have said, many began to think, and even to say, that there would none escape. And indeed I began to think so too, and therefore kept within doors for about a fortnight, and never stirred out. But I could not hold it. Besides, there were some people, who, notwithstanding the danger, did not omit publicly to attend the worship of God, even in the most dangerous times. And though it is true that a great many clergymen did shut up their churches and fled, as other people did, for the safety of their lives, yet all did not do so. Some ventured to officiate, and to keep up the assemblies of the people by constant prayers, and sometimes sermons, or brief exhortations to repentance and reformation, and this as long as they would hear them. And dissenters did the like also, and even in the very churches where the parish ministers were either dead or fled; nor was there any room for making a difference at such a time as this was.

It was indeed a lamentable thing to hear the miserable lamentations of poor dying creatures, calling out for ministers to comfort them and pray with them, to counsel them, and to direct them; calling out to God for pardon and mercy, and confessing aloud their past sins. It would make the stoutest heart bleed to hear how many warnings were then given by dying penitents to others, not to put off and delay their repentance to the day of distress; that such a time of calamity as this was no time for repentance, was no time to call upon God. I wish I could repeat the very sound of those groans, and of those exclamations that I heard from some poor dying creatures when in the height of their agonies and distress; and that I could make him that reads this, hear, as I imagine I now hear them, for the sound seems still to ring in my ears.

If I could but tell this part in such moving accents as should alarm the very soul of the reader, I should rejoice that I recorded these things, however short and imperfect. . . .

[1722]

JOHN LOCKE

John Locke, though best known as a philosopher, had a many-sided activity; he was a university lecturer on Greek and rhetoric, a member of the Royal Society, a physician, and the holder of several government appointments at home and abroad. He was the friend and follower of the first Earl of Shaftesbury (Dryden's "Achitophel"), and he supervised the education of the latter's son, the second earl, and afterwards of his grandson, the third earl, the famous author of *Characteristics*. Locke wrote on many subjects, and made for himself a prominent place in the history of English thought. Philosophy, morals, religion, education, and government were among the subjects to which he made important contributions.

Such varied activity can not be here illustrated within a few pages; nor is complete representation desirable, since many of Locke's writings diverge far from literature in subject-matter, and none are distinguished in style. Accordingly he is represented only by an extract from *Two Treatises of Government*, his most important work on political theory. This is not only valuable for the light it throws on the Revolution of 1688, but it falls into place naturally among the works of other political philosophers of the period, from Hobbes to Burke and Godwin.

Locke wrote his *Two Treatises of Government* (1690) as a defence of the Revolution of 1688 and in support of the Whig settlement of the throne upon William and Mary. He opposes the doctrine of the divine right of kings and argues that government is based upon a social contract which is revocable if its terms are not adhered to. In the first treatise he attacks the theories of Sir Robert Filmer, whose *Patriarcha*, published posthumously in 1680, had argued for the absolute authority of kings. Filmer agrees with Hobbes in this respect but differs from him in explaining the source of the royal authority. As the title, *Patriarcha*, indicates, he bases it upon the patriarchal system which derives ultimately from Adam. The power of the father over his children in primitive times is thus claimed as the original basis of Stuart absolutism. Locke completely demolishes this theory and shows its historical inadequacy.

In the second treatise, he goes more deeply into fundamental principles and provides the orthodox Whig answer to *Leviathan*. He does not, however, deal directly with Hobbes as he does with Filmer. Hobbes, in spite of his defence of the royal prerogative, was in bad odour with the Church because of his Erastian views and his reputation for impiety. Consequently, Locke, who was trying to justify the Revolution against High Church and Tory criticism, did not feel it necessary to refute him directly. But no one writing on government in the latter part of the seventeenth century could ignore the *Leviathan*. Locke, like Hobbes, predicates a social compact made originally in a state of nature: but his state of nature, far from being a state of anarchy and of constant war, was governed by the law of nature; his social compact was made between the people and their governors for the common good, and was revocable when it ceased so to function. The right to revolution thus remains inalienable, and the bad government of James II justified the title of William and Mary "in the consent of the people."

TWO TREATISES OF GOVERNMENT

Book II

Chapter VII

Of Political or Civil Society

...87. Man being born, as has been proved, with a title to perfect freedom and uncontrolled enjoyment of all the rights and privileges of the law of nature, equally with any other man, or number of men in the world, hath by nature a power not only to preserve his property — that is, his life, liberty, and estate — against the injuries and attempts of other men, but to judge of and punish the breaches of that law in others, as he is persuaded the offence deserves, even with death itself, in crimes where the heinousness of the fact, in his opinion, requires it. But because no political society can be, nor subsist, without having in itself the power to preserve the property, and in order thereunto punish the offences of all those of that society, there, and there only, is political society where every one of the members hath quitted his natural power, resigned it up into the hands of the community in all cases that exclude him not from appealing for protection to the law established by it. And thus all private judgment of every particular member being excluded, the community comes to be umpire, by settled, standing rules, indifferent, and the same to all parties; and by men having authority from the community for the execution of those rules, decides all the differences that may happen between any members of that society concerning any matter of right, and punishes those offences which any member hath committed against the society with such penalties as the law has established; whereby it is easy to discern who are, and who are not, in political society together. Those who are united into one body, and have a common established law and judicature to appeal to, with authority to decide controversies between them and punish offenders, are in civil society one with another; but those who have no such common appeal, I mean on earth, are still in the state of nature, each being where there is no other, judge for himself and executioner; which is, as I have before showed it, the perfect state of nature.

88. And thus the commonwealth comes by a power to set down what punishment shall belong to the several transgressions which they think worthy of it, committed amongst the members of that society (which is the power of making laws), as well as it has the power to punish any injury done unto any of its members by any one that is not of it (which is the power of war and peace); and all this for the preservation of the property of all the members of that society, as far as is possible. But though every man who has entered into civil society and is become a member of any commonwealth, has thereby quitted his power to punish offences against the law of nature in prosecution of his own private judgment, yet with the judgment of offences which he has given up to the legislative, in all cases where he can appeal to the magistrate, he has given a right to the commonwealth to employ his force for the execution of the judgments of the commonwealth whenever he shall be called to it, which, indeed, are his own judgments, they being made by himself or his representative. And herein we have the original of the legislative and executive power of civil society, which is to judge by standing laws how far offences are to be punished when committed within the commonwealth; and also to determine by occasional judgments founded on the present circumstances of the fact, how far injuries from without are to be vindicated, and in both these to employ all the force of all the members when there shall be need.

89. Wherever, therefore, any number of men are so united into one society as to quit every one his executive power of the law of nature, and to resign it to the public, there, and there only, is a political or civil society. And this is done wherever any number of men in the state of nature enter into society to make one people one body-politic under one supreme government; or else when any one joins himself to, and incorporates with, any government already made: for hereby he authorizes the society, or which is all one, the legislative thereof, to make laws for him as the public good of the society shall require, to the execution whereof his own assistance (as to his own degrees) is due. And this puts men out of a state of nature into that of a commonwealth, by setting up a judge on earth with authority to determine all the controversies and redress the injuries that may happen to any member of the commonwealth, which judge is the legislative or magistrate appointed by it. And wherever there are any number of men, however associated, that have no such decisive power to appeal to, there they are still in the state of nature.

90. Hence it is evident that absolute monarchy, which by some men is counted the only government in the world, is indeed inconsistent with civil society, and so can be no form of civil government at all: for the end of civil society being to avoid and remedy these inconveniencies of the state of nature which necessarily follow from every man being judge in his own case by setting up a known authority to which every one of that society may appeal upon any injury received, or controversy that may arise, and which every one of the society ought to obey; wherever any persons are, who have not such an authority to appeal to for the decision of any difference between them, there those persons are still in the state of nature; and so is every absolute prince, in respect of those who are under his dominion.

91. For he being supposed to have all, both legislative and executive, power in himself alone, there is no judge to be found; no appeal lies open to any one, who may fairly and indifferently and with authority decide, and from whose decision relief and

redress may be expected of any injury or inconveniency that may be suffered from the prince or by his order: so that such a man, however entitled, czar, or grand seignior, or how you please, is as much in the state of nature, with all under his dominion, as he is with the rest of mankind: for wherever any two men are, who have no standing rule and common judge to appeal to on earth, for the determination of controversies of right betwixt them, there they are still in the state of nature, and under all the inconveniencies of it, with only this woeful difference to the subject, or rather slave of an absolute prince; that whereas, in the ordinary state of nature, he has a liberty to judge of his right, and according to the best of his power to maintain it; now whenever his property is invaded by the will and order of his monarch, he has not only no appeal, as those in society ought to have, but, as if he were degraded from the common state of rational creatures, is denied a liberty to judge of or to defend his right; and so is exposed to all the misery and inconveniencies that a man can fear from one, who being in the unrestrained state of nature, is yet corrupted with flattery and armed with power.

92. For he that thinks absolute power purifies men's blood, and corrects the baseness of human nature, need read but the history of this, or any other age, to be convinced of the contrary. He that would have been so insolent and injurious in the woods of America would not probably be much better in a throne, where perhaps learning and religion shall be found out to justify all that he shall do to his subjects, and the sword presently silence all those that dare question it: for what the protection of absolute monarchy is, what kind of fathers of their countries it makes princes to be, and to what a degree of happiness and security it carries civil society, where this sort of government is grown to perfection, he that will look into *the late relation of Ceylon may easily see.

93. In absolute monarchies, indeed, as well as other governments of the world, the subjects have an appeal to the law, and judges to decide any controversies, and restrain any violence that may happen betwixt the subjects themselves, one amongst another. This every one thinks necessary, and believes he deserves to be thought a declared enemy to society and mankind who should go about to take it away. But whether this be from a true love of mankind and society, and such a charity as we all owe one to another, there is reason to doubt: for this is no more than what every man who loves his own power, profit, or greatness may, and naturally must do, keep those animals from hurting or destroying one another, who labour and drudge only for his pleasure and advantage; and so are taken care of, not out of any love the master has for them, but love of himself, and the profit they bring him: for if it be asked what security, what fence, is there in such a state against the violence and oppression of this absolute ruler, the very question can scarce be borne. They are ready to tell you that it deserves death only to ask after safety. Betwixt subject and subject, they will grant, there must be measures, laws, and judges for their mutual peace and security: but as for the ruler, he ought to be absolute, and is above all such circumstances; because he has power to do more hurt and wrong, it is right when he does it. To ask how you may be guarded from harm or injury on that side where the strongest hand is to do it, is presently the voice of faction and rebellion: as if when men, quitting the state of nature, entered into society, they agreed that all of them but one should be under the restraint of laws: but that he should still retain all the liberty of the state of nature, increased with power, and made licentious by impunity. This is to think that men are so foolish that they take care to avoid what mischiefs may be done them by polecats or foxes; but are content, nay, think it safety, to be devoured by lions.

94. But, whatever flatterers may talk to amuse people's understandings, it hinders not men from feeling; and when they perceive that any man, in what station soever, is out of the bounds of the civil society which they are of, and that they have no appeal on earth against any harm they may receive from him, they are apt to think themselves in the state of nature, in respect of him whom they find to be so; and to take care, as soon as they can, to have that safety and security in civil society, for which it was instituted, and for which only they entered into it. And therefore, though perhaps at first (as shall be showed more at large hereafter in the following part of this discourse) some one good and excellent man having got a pre-eminency

*** Notes on John Locke will be found in the Appendix, pp. 960 ff.**

amongst the rest, had this deference paid to his goodness and virtue, as to a kind of natural authority, that the chief rule, with arbitration of their differences, by a tacit consent devolved into his hands, without any other caution but the assurance they had of his uprightness and wisdom; yet when time, giving authority, and (as some men would persuade us) sacredness to customs, which the negligent and unforeseeing innocence of the first ages began, had brought in successors of another stamp; the people finding their properties not secure under the government as then it was (whereas government has no other end but the preservation of property), could never be safe nor at rest, nor think themselves in civil society, till the legislature was placed in collective bodies of men, call them senate, parliament, or what you please. By which means every single person became subject, equally with other the meanest men, to those laws, which he himself, as part of the legislative, had established; nor could any one, by his own authority, avoid the force of the law, when once made; nor by any pretence of superiority plead exemption, thereby to licence his own, or the miscarriages of any of his dependents. *"No man in civil society can be exempted from the laws of it": for if any man may do what he thinks fit and there be no appeal on earth for redress or security against any harm he shall do, I ask whether he be not perfectly still in the state of nature, and so can be no part or member of that civil society, unless any one will say the state of nature and civil socicty are one and the same thing, which I have never yet found any one so great a patron of anarchy as to affirm.

CHAPTER VIII

Of the Beginning of Political Societies

95. Men being, as has been said, by nature all free, equal, and independent, no one can be put out of this estate and subjected to the political power of another without his own consent. The only way whereby any one divests himself of his natural liberty and puts on the bonds of civil society is by agreeing with other men to join and unite into a community for their comfortable, safe, and peaceable living one amongst another, in a secure enjoyment of their properties, and a greater security against any that are not of it. This any number of men may do, because it injures not the freedom of the rest; they are left, as they were, in the liberty of the state of nature. When any number of men have so consented to make one community or government, they are thereby presently incorporated, and make one body-politic, wherein the majority have a right to act and conclude the rest.

96. For when any number of men have, by the consent of every individual, made a community, they have thereby made that community one body, with a power to act as one body, which is only by the will and determination of the majority: for that which acts any community, being only the consent of the individuals of it, and it being necessary to that which is one body to move one way, it is necessary the body should move that way whither the greater force carries it, which is the consent of the majority: or else it is impossible it should act or continue one body, one community, which the consent of every individual that united into it agreed that it should; and so every one is bound by that consent to be concluded by the majority. And therefore we see that in assemblies empowered to act by positive laws, where no number is set by that positive law which empowers them, the act of the majority passes for the act of the whole, and of course determines; as having, by the law of nature and reason, the power of the whole.

97. And thus every man, by consenting with others to make one body-politic under one government, puts himself under an obligation to every one of that society to submit to the determination of the majority, and to be concluded by it; or else this original compact, whereby he with others incorporate into one society, would signify nothing, and be no compact if he be left free, and under no other ties than he was in before in the state of nature. For what appearance would there be of any compact? What new engagement if he were no farther tied by any decrees of the society than he himself thought fit and did actually consent to? This would be still as great a liberty as he himself had before his compact, or any one else in the state of nature hath, who may submit himself and consent to any acts of it if he thinks fit.

98. For if the consent of the majority shall not in reason be received as the act of the

whole, and conclude every individual, nothing but the consent of every individual can make anything to be the act of the whole; but such a consent is next to impossible ever to be had, if we consider the infirmities of health and avocations of business, which in a number, though much less than that of a commonwealth, will necessarily keep many away from the public assembly. To which if we add the variety of opinions and contrariety of interest which unavoidably happen in all collections of men, the coming into society upon such terms would be only like Cato's coming into the theatre, only to go out again. Such a constitution as this would make * the mighty Leviathan of a shorter duration than the feeblest creatures, and not let it outlast the day it was born in, which cannot be supposed till we can think that rational creatures should desire and constitute societies only to be dissolved. For where the majority cannot conclude the rest, there they cannot act as one body, and consequently will be immediately dissolved again.

99. Whosoever, therefore, out of a state of nature unite into a community, must be understood to give up all the power necessary to the ends for which they unite into society, to the majority of the community, unless they expressly agreed in any number greater than the majority. And this is done by barely agreeing to unite into one political society, which is all the compact that is, or needs be, between the individuals that enter into or make up a commonwealth. And thus, that which begins and actually constitutes any political society is nothing but the consent of any number of freemen capable of a majority, to unite and incorporate into such a society. And this is that, and that only, which did or could give beginning to any lawful government in the world.

100. To this I find two objections made. First, "That there are no instances to be found in story of a company of men, independent and equal one amongst another, that met together, and in this way began and set up a government." Secondly, "It is impossible of right that men should do so, because all men being born under government, they are to submit to that, and are not at liberty to begin a new one."

101. To the first there is this to answer, that it is not at all to be wondered that history gives us but a very little account of men that lived together in the state of nature. The inconveniencies of that condition, and the love and want of society, no sooner brought any number of them together, but they presently united and incorporated if they designed to continue together. And if we may not suppose men ever to have been in the state of nature because we hear not much of them in such a state, we may as well suppose the armies of Salmanasser or Xerxes were never children, because we hear little of them till they were men and embodied in armies. Government is everywhere antecedent to records, and letters seldom come in amongst a people till a long continuation of civil society has, by other more necessary arts, provided for their safety, ease, and plenty: and then they begin to look after the history of their founders, and search into their original, when they have outlived the memory of it; for it is with commonwealths as with particular persons, they are commonly ignorant of their own births and infancies; and if they know anything of their original, they are beholden for it to the accidental records that others have kept of it. And those that we have of the beginning of any polities in the world, excepting that of the Jews, where God himself immediately interposed, and which favours not at all paternal dominion, are all either plain instances of such a beginning as I have mentioned, or at least have manifest footsteps of it.

102. He must show a strange inclination to deny evident matter of fact, when it agrees not with his hypothesis, who will not allow that the beginnings of Rome and Venice were by the uniting together of several men, free and independent one of another, amongst whom there was no natural superiority or subjection. And if * Josephus Acosta's word may be taken, he tells us that in many parts of America there was no government at all. "There are great and apparent conjectures," says he, "that these men [speaking of those of Peru] for a long time had neither kings nor commonwealths, but lived in troops, as they do this day in Florida, the Cheriquanas, those of Brazil, and many other nations, which have no certain kings, but, as occasion is offered in peace or war, they choose their captains as they please," lib. 1, cap. 25. If it be said that every man there was born subject to his father, or the head of his family, that the subjection due from a child to a father

took not away his freedom of uniting into what political society he thought fit, has been already proved. But be that as it will, these men, it is evident, were actually free; and whatever superiority some politicians now would place in any of them, they themselves claimed it not, but by consent were all equal, till by the same consent they set rulers over themselves. So that their politic societies all began from a voluntary union, and the mutual agreement of men freely acting in the choice of their governors and forms of government.

103. And I hope *those who went away from Sparta, with Palantus, mentioned by Justin, lib. III, cap. 4, will be allowed to have been freemen independent one of another, and to have set up a government over themselves by their own consent. Thus I have given several examples out of history, of people, free and in the state of nature, that, being met together, incorporated and began a commonwealth. And if the want of such instances be an argument to prove that governments were not, nor could not be so begun, I suppose the contenders for paternal empire were better let it alone than urge it against natural liberty: for if they can give so many instances out of history, of governments begun upon paternal right, I think (though at best an argument from what has been, to what should of right be, has no great force) one might, without any great danger, yield them the cause. But if I might advise them in the case, they would do well not to search too much into the original of governments as they have begun *de facto*, lest they should find at the foundation of most of them something very little favourable to the design they promote, and such a power as they contend for.

104. But, to conclude, reason being plain on our side that men are naturally free, and the examples of history showing that the governments of the world that were begun in peace had their beginning laid on that foundation, and were made by the consent of the people; there can be little room for doubt, either where the right is, or what has been the opinion or practice of mankind about the first erecting of governments.

105. I will not deny that if we look back as far as history will direct us, towards the original of commonwealths, we shall generally find them under the government and administration of one man. And I am also apt to believe that where a family was numerous enough to subsist by itself, and continued entire together, without mixing with others, as it often happens where there is much land and few people, the government commonly began in the father: for the father having, by the law of nature, the same power with every man else to punish, as he thought fit, any offences against that law, might thereby punish his transgressing children, even when they were men, and out of their pupilage; and they were very likely to submit to his punishment, and all join with him against the offender in their turns, giving him thereby power to execute his sentence against any transgression, and so, in effect, make him the law-maker and governor over all that remained in conjunction with his family. He was fittest to be trusted; paternal affection secured their property and interest under his care; and the custom of obeying him in their childhood made it easier to submit to him rather than any other. If, therefore, they must have one to rule them, as government is hardly to be avoided amongst men that live together; who so likely to be the man as he that was their common father, unless negligence, cruelty, or any other defect of mind or body, made him unfit for it? But when either the father died, and left his next heir, for want of age, wisdom, courage, or any other qualities, less fit for rule; or where several families met and consented to continue together; there, it is not to be doubted, but they used their natural freedom to set up him whom they judged the ablest and most likely to rule well over them. Conformable hereunto we find the people of America, who (living out of the reach of the conquering swords and spreading domination of the two great empires of Peru and Mexico) enjoyed their own natural freedom, though, *cæteris paribus*, they commonly prefer the heir of their deceased king; yet, if they find him any way weak or incapable, they pass him by, and set up the stoutest and bravest man for their ruler.

106. Thus, though looking back as far as records give us any account of peopling the world, and the history of nations, we commonly find the government to be in one hand; yet it destroys not that which I affirm, viz., that the beginning of politic society depends upon the consent of the individuals to join into and make one society; who, when they are thus

incorporated, might set up what form of government they thought fit. But this having given occasion to men to mistake and think that, by nature, government was monarchical, and belonged to the father; it may not be amiss here to consider why people in the beginning generally pitched upon this form; which, though perhaps the father's pre-eminency might in the first institution of some commonwealth, give rise to and place in the beginning the power in one hand; yet it is plain that the reason that continued the form of government in a single person was not any regard or respect to paternal authority; since all petty monarchies, that is, almost all monarchies, near their original, have been commonly, at least upon occasion, elective.

107. First, then, in the beginning of things, the father's government of the childhood of those sprung from him having accustomed them to the rule of one man, and taught them that where it was exercised with care and skill, with affection and love to those under it, it was sufficient to procure and preserve to men all the political happiness they sought for in society. It was no wonder that they should pitch upon and naturally run into that form of government which, from their infancy, they had been all accustomed to; and which, by experience, they had found both easy and safe. To which, if we add that monarchy being simple and most obvious to men, whom neither experience had instructed in forms of government, nor the ambition or insolence of empire had taught to beware of the encroachments of prerogative or the inconveniencies of absolute power, which monarchy in succession was apt to lay claim to, and bring upon them; it was not at all strange that they should not much trouble themselves to think of methods of restraining any exorbitances of those to whom they had given the authority over them, and of balancing the power of government by placing several parts of it in different hands. They had neither felt the oppression of tyrannical dominion, nor did the fashion of the age, nor their possessions or way of living (which afforded little matter for covetousness or ambition) give them any reason to apprehend or provide against it; and, therefore, it is no wonder they put themselves into such a frame of government as was not only, as I said, most obvious and simple, but also best suited to their present state and condition; which stood more in need of defence against foreign invasions and injuries, than of multiplicity of laws. The equality of a simple, poor way of living, confining their desires within the narrow bounds of each man's small property, made few controversies, and so no need of many laws to decide them, or variety of officers to superintend the process, or look after the execution of justice, where there were but few trespasses and few offenders. Since then those, who liked one another so well as to join into society, cannot but be supposed to have some acquaintance and friendship together, and some trust one in another; they could not but have greater apprehensions of others, than of one another: and therefore their first care and thought cannot but be supposed to be how to secure themselves against foreign force. It was natural for them to put themselves under a frame of government which might best serve to that end, and choose the wisest and bravest man to conduct them in their wars, and lead them out against their enemies, and in this chiefly be their ruler.

108. Thus we see that the kings of the Indians in America, which is still a pattern of the first ages in Asia and Europe, whilst the inhabitants were too few for the country, and want of people and money gave men no temptation to enlarge their possessions of land, or contest for wider extent of ground, are little more than generals of their armies; and though they command absolutely in war, yet at home, and in time of peace, they exercise very little dominion, and have but a very moderate sovereignty, the resolutions of peace and war being ordinarily either in the people or in a council. Though the war itself, which admits not of pluralities of governors, naturally devolves the command into the king's sole authority.

109. And thus, in Israel itself, the chief business of their judges and first kings seems to have been to be captains in war and leaders of their armies; which (besides what is signified by "going out and in before the people," which was to march forth to war and home again at the heads of their forces) appears plainly in the story of Jephtha. The Ammonites making war upon Israel, the Gileadites, in fear, send to Jephtha, a bastard of their family, whom they had cast off, and article with him, if he will assist them against the

Ammonites, to make him their ruler; which they do in these words, "And the people made him head and captain over them," Judg. 11:11, which was, as it seems, all one as to be judge. "And he judged Israel," Judg. 12:7, that is, was their captain-general, "six years." So when Jotham upbraids the Shechemites with the obligation they had to Gideon, who had been their judge and ruler, he tells them, "He fought for you, and adventured his life far, and delivered you out of the hands of Midian," Judg. 9:17. Nothing is mentioned of him but what he did as a general; and, indeed, that is all is found in his history, or in any of the rest of the judges. And Abimelech particularly is called king, though at most he was but their general. And when, being weary of the ill-conduct of Samuel's sons, the children of Israel desired a king, "like all the nations, to judge them, and to go out before them, and to fight their battles," 1 Sam. 8:20, God, granting their desire, says to Samuel, "I will send thee a man, and thou shalt anoint him to be captain over my people Israel, that he may save my people out of the hands of the Philistines," 9:16. As if the only business of a king had been to lead out their armies and fight in their defence; and, accordingly, Samuel at his inauguration, pouring a vial of oil upon him, declares to Saul that "the Lord had anointed him to be captain over his inheritance," 10:1. And therefore those who, after Saul's being solemnly chosen and saluted king by the tribes at Mizpeh, were unwilling to have him their king, made no other objection but this, "How shall this man save us?" 5:27, as if they should have said, "This man is unfit to be our king, not having skill and conduct enough in war to be able to defend us." And when God resolved to transfer the government to David, it is in these words, "But now thy kingdom shall not continue: the Lord hath sought him a man after his own heart, and the Lord hath commanded him to be captain over his people," 13:14. As if the whole kingly authority were nothing else but to be their general; and therefore the tribes who had stuck to Saul's family, and opposed David's reign, when they came to Hebron with terms of submission to him, they tell him, amongst other arguments, they had to submit to him as to their king, that he was, in effect, their king in Saul's time, and therefore they had no reason but to receive him as their king now. "Also," say they, "in time past, when Saul was king over us, thou wast he that leddest out, and broughtest in Israel, and the Lord said unto thee, Thou shalt feed my people Israel, and thou shalt be a captain over Israel."

110. Thus, whether a family by degrees grew up into a commonwealth, and the fatherly authority being continued on to the elder son, every one in his turn growing up under it, tacitly submitted to it; and the easiness and equality of it not offending any one, every one acquiesced, till time seemed to have confirmed it, and settled a right of succession by prescription: or whether several families, or the descendants of several families, whom chance, neighbourhood, or business brought together, uniting into society: the need of a general, whose conduct might defend them against their enemies in war, and the great confidence the innocence and sincerity of that poor but virtuous age (such are almost all those which begin governments, that ever come to last in the world) gave men to one another, made the first beginners of commonwealths generally put the rule into one man's hand, without any other express limitation or restraint, but what the nature of the thing and the end of government required: whichever of those it was that at first put the rule into the hands of a single person, certain it is that nobody was intrusted with it but for the public good and safety, and to those ends, in the infancies of commonwealths, those who had it, commonly used it. And unless they had done so, young societies could not have subsisted; without such nursing fathers, tender and careful of the public weal, all governments would have sunk under the weakness and infirmities of their infancy, and the prince and the people had soon perished together.

111. But though the golden age (before vain ambition, and *"*amor sceleratus habendi*," evil concupiscence, had corrupted men's minds into a mistake of true power and honour) had more virtue, and consequently better governors, as well as less vicious subjects; and there was then no stretching prerogative on the one side, to oppress the people; nor consequently on the other, any dispute about privilege, to lessen or restrain the power of the magistrate; and so no contest betwixt rulers and people about governors or government: yet when ambition and luxury in future ages would retain and increase the

power, without doing the business for which it was given; and, aided by flattery, taught princes to have distinct and separate interests from their people; men found it necessary to examine more carefully the original and rights of government, and to find out ways to restrain the exorbitancies and prevent the abuses of that power, which they having entrusted in another's hands, only for their own good, they found was made use of to hurt them.

112. Thus we may see how probable it is that people that were naturally free, and, by their own consent, either submitted to the government of their father, or united together, out of different families, to make a government, should generally put the rule into one man's hands, and choose to be under the conduct of a single person, without so much as by express conditions limiting or regulating his power, which they thought safe enough in his honesty and prudence; though they never dreamed of monarchy being [*] *jure divino*, which we never heard of among mankind till it was revealed to us by the divinity of this last age, nor ever allowed paternal power to have a right to dominion or to be the foundation of all government. And thus much may suffice to show that, as far as we have any light from history, we have reason to conclude that all peaceful beginnings of government have been laid in the consent of the people. I say peaceful, because I shall have occasion in another place to speak of conquest, which some esteem a way of beginning of governments.

The other objection I find urged against the beginning of polities, in the way I have mentioned, is this, viz.

113. "That all men being born under government, some or other, it is impossible any of them should ever be free and at liberty to unite together and begin a new one, or ever be able to erect a lawful government."

If this argument be good, I ask, how came so many lawful monarchies into the world? For if anybody, upon this supposition, can show me any one man in any age of the world free to begin a lawful monarchy, I will be bound to show him ten other free men at liberty at the same time to unite and begin a new government under a regal or any other form; it being demonstration that if any one born under the dominion of another may be so free as to have a right to command others in a new and distinct empire, every one that is born under the dominion of another may be so free too, and may become a ruler or subject of a distinct separate government. And so, by this their own principle, either all men, however born, are free, or else there is but one lawful prince, one lawful government in the world. And then they have nothing to do but barely to show us which that is, which when they have done, I doubt not but all mankind will easily agree to pay obedience to him.

114. Though it be a sufficient answer to their objection to show that it involves them in the same difficulties that it doth those they use it against, yet I shall endeavour to discover the weakness of this argument a little farther.

"All men," say they, "are born under government, and therefore they cannot be at liberty to begin a new one. Every one is born a subject to his father or his prince, and is therefore under the perpetual tie of subjection and allegiance." It is plain mankind never owned nor considered any such natural subjection that they were born in, to one or to the other, that tied them, without their own consents, to a subjection to them and their heirs.

115. For there are no examples so frequent in history, both sacred and profane, as those of men withdrawing themselves and their obedience from the jurisdiction they were born under, and the family or community they were bred up in, and setting up new governments in other places, from whence sprang all that number of petty commonwealths in the beginning of ages, and which always multiplied as long as there was room enough, till the stronger or more fortunate swallowed the weaker; and those great ones, again breaking to pieces, dissolved into lesser dominions. All which are so many testimonies against paternal sovereignty, and plainly prove that it was not the natural right of the father descending to his heirs that made governments in the beginning, since it was impossible, upon that ground, there should have been so many little kingdoms; all must have been but only one universal monarchy, if men had not been at liberty to separate themselves from their families and their government, be it what it will that was set up in it, and go and make distinct commonwealths and other governments as they thought fit.

116. This has been the practice of the world from its first beginning to this day; nor

is it now any more hindrance to the freedom of mankind, that they are born under constituted and ancient polities that have established laws and set forms of government, than if they were born in the woods amongst the unconfined inhabitants that run loose in them: for those who would persuade us that "by being born under any government we are naturally subjects to it," and have no more any title or pretence to the freedom of the state of nature; have no other reason (bating that of paternal power, which we have already answered) to produce for it, but only because our fathers or progenitors passed away their natural liberty, and thereby bound up themselves and their posterity to a perpetual subjection to the government which they themselves submitted to. It is true that whatever engagement or promises any one has made for himself, he is under the obligation of them, but cannot by any compact whatsoever bind his children or posterity: for his son, when a man, being altogether as free as the father, any "act of the father can no more give away the liberty of the son" than it can of anybody else: he may, indeed, annex such conditions to the land he enjoyed, as a subject of any commonwealth, as may oblige his son to be of that community, if he will enjoy those possessions which were his father's, because that estate being his father's property, he may dispose or settle it as he pleases.

117. And this has generally given the occasion to mistake in this matter; because commonwealths not permitting any part of their dominions to be dismembered, nor to be enjoyed by any but those of their community, the son cannot ordinarily enjoy the possessions of his father, but under the same terms his father did, by becoming a member of the society; whereby he puts himself presently under the government he finds there established, as much as any other subject of that commonwealth. And thus "the consent of freemen, born under government, which only makes them members of it," being given separately in their turns, as each comes to be of age, and not in a multitude together; people take no notice of it, and thinking it not done at all, or not necessary, conclude they are naturally subjects as they are men.

118. But, it is plain, governments themselves understand it otherwise; they claim "no power over the son, because of that they had over the father": nor look on children as being their subjects, by their fathers being so. If a subject of England have a child by an Englishwoman in France, whose subject is he? Not the King of England's; for he must have leave to be admitted to the privileges of it: nor the King of France's: for how then has his father a liberty to bring him away, and breed him as he pleases? and who ever was judged as a traitor or deserter, if he left, or warred against a country, for being barely born in it of parents that were aliens there? It is plain, then, by the practice of governments themselves, as well as by the law of right reason, that "a child is born a subject of no country or government." He is under his father's tuition and authority till he comes to age of discretion; and then he is a freeman, at liberty what government he will put himself under, what body-politic he will unite himself to: for if an Englishman's son born in France be at liberty, and may do so, it is evident there is no tie upon him by his father's being a subject of this kingdom; nor is he bound up by any compact of his ancestors. And why then hath not his son, by the same reason, the same liberty, though he be born anywhere else? Since the power that a father hath naturally over his children is the same wherever they be born, and the ties of natural obligations are not bounded by the positive limits of kingdoms and commonwealths.

119. Every man being, as has been showed, naturally free, and nothing being able to put him into subjection to any earthly power, but only his own consent; it is to be considered what shall be understood to be a sufficient declaration of a man's consent to make him subject to the laws of any government. There is a common distinction of an express and a tacit consent, which will concern our present case. Nobody doubts but an express consent of any man, entering into any society, makes him a perfect member of that society, a subject of that government. The difficulty is, what ought to be looked upon as a tacit consent, and how far it binds, i.e., how far any one shall be looked upon to have consented, and thereby submitted to any government, where he has made no expressions of it at all. And to this I say that every man that hath any possessions or enjoyment of any part of the dominions of any government doth thereby give his tacit consent, and is as far forth obliged to obedience to the laws of that

government, during such enjoyment, as any one under it; whether this his possession be of land to him and his heirs forever, or a lodging only for a week; or whether it be barely travelling freely on the highway; and, in effect, it reaches as far as the very being of any one within the territories of that government.

120. To understand this the better, it is fit to consider that every man when he at first incorporates himself into any commonwealth, he, by his uniting himself thereunto, annexes also, and submits to the community those possessions which he has, or shall acquire, that do not already belong to any other government; for it would be a direct contradiction for any one to enter into society with others for the securing and regulating of property, and yet to suppose his land, whose property is to be regulated by the laws of the society, should be exempt from the jurisdiction of that government to which he himself, the proprietor of the land, is a subject. By the same act, therefore, whereby any one unites his person, which was before free, to any commonwealth; by the same he unites his possessions, which were before free, to it also: and they become, both of them, person and possession, subject to the government and dominion of that commonwealth as long as it hath a being. Whoever, therefore, from thenceforth, by inheritance, purchase, permission, or otherwise, enjoys any part of the land so annexed to, and under the government of that commonwealth, must take it with the condition it is under; that is, of submitting to the government of the commonwealth under whose jurisdiction it is, as far forth as any subject of it.

121. But since the government has a direct jurisdiction only over the land and reaches the possessor of it (before he has actually incorporated himself in the society) only as he dwells upon and enjoys that; the obligation any one is under, by virtue of such enjoyment, to "submit to the government, begins and ends with the enjoyment": so that whenever the owner, who has given nothing but such a tacit consent to the government, will, by donation, sale, or otherwise, quit the said possession, he is at liberty to go and incorporate himself into any other commonwealth; or to agree with others to begin a new one **in vacuis locis*, in any part of the world they can find free and unpossessed: whereas he that has once, by actual agreement and any express declaration, given his consent to be of any commonwealth, is perpetually and indispensably obliged to be, and remain unalterably a subject to it, and can never be again in the liberty of the state of nature; unless by any calamity the government he was under comes to be dissolved, or else by some public act cuts him off from being any longer a member of it.

122. But submitting to the laws of any country, living quietly, and enjoying privileges and protection under them, makes not a man a member of that society: that is only a local protection and homage due to and from all those who, not being in a state of war, come within the territories belonging to any government, to all parts whereof the force of its laws extends. But this no more makes a man a member of that society, a perpetual subject of that commonwealth, than it would make a man a subject to another in whose family he found it convenient to abide for some time, though, whilst he continued in it, he were obliged to comply with the laws, and submit to the government he found there. And thus we see that foreigners, by living all their lives under another government, and enjoying the privileges and protection of it, though they are bound, even in conscience, to submit to its administration as far forth as any denizen, yet do not thereby come to be subjects or members of that commonwealth. Nothing can make any man so, but his actually entering into it by positive engagement and express promise and compact. This is that which I think, concerning the beginning of political societies, and that consent which makes any one a member of any commonwealth.

[1690]

SIR GEORGE SAVILE, MARQUIS OF HALIFAX

George Savile, Marquis of Halifax, the eloquent, brilliant minister of Charles II, of James II, and of William and Mary, was one of the chief English statesmen during the latter part of the seventeenth century. Though his connection with literature was that of the noble amateur or the anonymous pamphleteer, and though the quantity of his work is small, he succeeded in establishing through his keen intellect and sparkling wit a place as one of the foremost prose writers of his time.

Halifax's works include *The Character of King Charles the Second*, a shrewd and not unappreciative portrait, written soon after the king's death but not published until 1750; *A Letter to a Dissenter upon Occasion of His Majesty's Late Gracious Declaration of Indulgence*, 1687, and *The Anatomy of an Equivalent*, 1689, vigorous discussions of religious questions which were indissolubly connected with politics at that time; and *A Lady's Gift, or Advice to a Daughter*, 1688, a penetrating and witty letter of advice to his own daughter. He is most frequently remembered for *The Character of a Trimmer*, which was written in 1685, circulated in manuscript, and published in 1688. Though the title-page bears the name of his kinsman, Sir William Coventry, both internal and external evidence warrant its ascription to Halifax. Because he exemplified in public life the political philosophy which this pamphlet advocates, he has often been referred to as the Trimmer. In those days when party spirit ran high, this term had been applied in derision to any one who took the middle ground between the Whigs and Tories. Halifax accepted the designation and interpreted it favourably. In his Introduction he said, "This innocent word, Trimmer, signifieth no more than this: that if men are together in a boat, and one part of the company would weigh it down on one side, another would make it lean as much to the contrary; it happeneth there is a third opinion of those who conceive it would do as well if the boat went even, without endangering the passengers; now it is hard to imagine by what figure in language or by what rule in sense this cometh to be a fault, and it is much more a wonder it should be thought a heresy."

The Character of a Trimmer discusses the English government, the Protestant religion, the "Papists," and "Things Abroad." In most respects the Trimmer advocates moderation, tolerance, and common sense. In the State he is equally opposed to anarchy and absolutism; in the Church he dislikes both fanaticism and bigotry. His is the typical English middle way of intelligent conservatism, which prefers to mend the old rather than to experiment with things untried. While he regards the Roman Catholic Church as superstitious and dangerous, he does not wish to see its members persecuted; while he declares that "he would rather die than see a spire of English grass trampled down by a foreign trespasser," he does not wish to see English national policy dictated by hatred of any foreign nation. The English King and Church and People he loves because they are English and because they mediate between extremes.

"Our Trimmer, therefore, inspired by this divine virtue thinketh fit to conclude with these assertions: that our climate is a Trimmer between that part of the world where men are roasted, and the other where they are frozen; that our Church is a Trimmer between the frenzy of Platonic visions and the lethargic ignorance of Popish dreams; that our laws are Trimmers between the excess of unbounded power and the extravagance of liberty not enough restrained; that true virtue hath ever been thought a Trimmer, and to have its dwelling in the middle between the two extremes; that even God Almighty himself is divided between his two great attributes, his mercy and his justice.

"In such company, our Trimmer is not ashamed of his name, and willingly leaveth to the bold champions of either extreme the honour of contending with no less adversaries than nature, religion, liberty, prudence, humanity, and common sense."

Such a philosophy of life Halifax practised consistently. By nature tolerant and sceptical, he constantly opposed the extremes of partisanship. He threw his influence by turns on the side of royal authority when it was endangered by radicalism, and on the side of popular rights when they were imperilled by the extension of the royal prerogative. Though he was accused of religious indifference and political apostasy, he was no time-server, for he usually took the side that was unpopular at the moment. In so doing he exerted a beneficial influence at a time when partisan rancour was the greatest peril in Church and State. It was not by chance that he played an important part in the compromise of 1689.

The Character of a Trimmer, by title, and to some extent by form, shows the influence of the seventeenth-century character writers. It is at the same time in the tradition of La Bruyère and of Montaigne. Terse, epigrammatic, urbane, it is no less notable for its style than for its vigorous thought and its sturdy common sense. The selection here reprinted is from the first section, "The Trimmer's Opinion of the Laws and Government."

From THE CHARACTER OF A TRIMMER

...Our Trimmer thinketh that the king and kingdom ought to be one creature, not to be separated in their political capacity; and when either of them undertake to act apart, it is like the crawling of worms after they are cut in pieces, which cannot be a lasting motion, the whole creature not stirring at a time. If the body have a dead palsy, the head cannot make it move; and God hath not yet delegated such a healing power to princes as that they can in a moment say to a languishing people oppressed and in despair, "Take up your bed and walk."

The figure of a king is so comprehensive and exalted a thing that it is a kind of degrading him to lodge that power separately in his own natural person, which can never be safely or naturally great but where the people are so united to him as to be flesh of his flesh and bone of his bone. For when he is reduced to the single definition of a man, he sinketh into so low a character that it is a temptation upon men's allegiance, and an impairing that veneration which is necessary to preserve their duty to him; whereas a prince who is so joined to his people that they seem to be his limbs, rather than his subjects; clothed with mercy and justice rightly applied in their several places; his throne supported by love as well as by power; and the warm wishes of his devoted subjects, like never-failing incense, still ascending towards him, looketh so like the best image we can frame to ourselves of God Almighty that men would have much ado not to fall down and worship him, and would be much more tempted to the sin of idolatry than to that of disobedience.

Our Trimmer is of opinion that there must be so much dignity inseparably annexed to the royal function as may be sufficient to secure it from insolence and contempt; and there must be condescensions from the throne, like kind showers from Heaven, that the prince may look so much the more like God Almighty's deputy upon earth. For power without love hath a terrifying aspect, and the worship which is paid to it is like that which the Indians give out of fear to wild beasts and devils. He that feareth God only because there is an hell, must wish there were no God; and he who feareth the king only because he can punish, must wish there were no king. So that, without a principle of love, there can be no true allegiance; and there must remain perpetual seeds of resistance against a power that is built upon such an unnatural foundation as that of fear and terror. All force is a kind of foul play, and whosoever aimeth at it himself doth by implication allow it to those he playeth with, so that there will be ever matter prepared in the minds of people when they are provoked; and the prince, to secure himself, must live in the midst of his own subjects as if he were in a conquered country, raise arms as if he were immediately to meet or resist an invasion, and all this while sleep as unquietly from the fear of the remedies, as he did before from that of the disease; it being hard for him to forget that more princes have been destroyed by the guards than by their people; and that even at the time when the rule was **Quod principi placuit lex esto*, the armies and Prætorian Bands which were the instruments of that unruly power were frequently the means made use of to destroy them who had it. There will ever be this difference between God and his vicegerents, that God is still above the instruments he useth, and out of the danger of receiving hurt from them. But princes can never lodge power in any hands which may not at some time turn it back upon them; for though it is possible enough for a king to have power to satisfy his ambition, yet no kingdom hath money enough to satisfy the avarice of under-workmen, who learn from that prince who will exact more than belongeth to him to expect from him much more than they deserve, and, growing angry upon the first disappointment, they are the devils which grow terrible to the conjurers themselves who brought them up, and can't send them down again. And besides that there can be no lasting radical security but where the governed are satisfied with the governors, it must be a dominion very unpleasant to a prince of an elevated mind to impose an abject and sordid servility instead of receiving the willing sacrifice of duty and obedience. The bravest princes in all times, who were incapable of any other kind of fear, have feared to grieve their own people; such a fear is a glory, and in this sense 'tis an infamy not to be a coward. So that the mistaken heroes who are void of this generous kind of fear need no other aggravation to complete their ill characters.

When a despotic prince hath bruised all his

* Notes on Halifax will be found in the Appendix, p. 961.

subjects with a slavish obedience, all the force he can use cannot subdue his own fears, enemies of his own creation, to which he can never be reconciled, it being impossible to do injustice and not to fear revenge. There is no cure for this fear but the not deserving to be hurt; and therefore a prince who doth not allow his thoughts to stray beyond the rules of justice hath always the blessing of an inward quiet and assurance as a natural effect of his good meaning to his people; and though he will not neglect due precautions to secure himself in all events, yet he is incapable of entertaining vain and remote suspicions of those of whom he resolveth never to deserve ill.

It is very hard for a prince to fear rebellion, who neither doth, nor intendeth to do, anything to provoke it; therefore too great a diligence in the governors to raise and improve dangers and fears from the people is no very good symptom, and naturally begetteth an inference that they have thoughts of putting their subjects' allegiance to a trial; and therefore, not without some reason, fear beforehand that the irregularities they intend may raise men to a resistance.

Our Trimmer thinketh it no advantage to a government to endeavour the suppressing all kinds of right which may remain in the body of the people, or to employ small authors in it whose officiousness or want of money may encourage them to write, though it is not very easy to have abilities equal to such a subject. They forget that in their too high-strained arguments for the rights of princes, they very often plead against human nature, which will always give a bias to those reasons which seem of her side. It is the people that readeth those books and it is the people that must judge of them; and therefore no maxims should be laid down for the right of government to which there can be any reasonable objection; for the world hath an interest, and for that reason is more than ordinary discerning to find out the weak sides of such arguments as are intended to do them hurt; and it is a diminution to a government to promote or countenance such well-affected mistakes, which are turned upon it with disadvantage whenever they are detected and exposed. And naturally the too earnest endeavours to take from men the right they have, tempt them, by the example, to claim that which they have not.

In power, as in most things, the way for princes to keep it is not to grasp more than their arms can well hold; the nice and unnecessary inquiring into these things, or the licencing some books and suppressing some others without sufficient reason to justify the doing either, is so far from being an advantage to a government that it exposeth it to the censure of being partial, and to the suspicion of having some hidden designs to be carried on by these unusual methods.

When all is said, there is a natural reason of state, an undefinable thing grounded upon the common good of mankind, which is immortal, and in all changes and revolutions still preserveth its original right of saving a nation, when the letter of the law perhaps would destroy it; and by whatsoever means it moveth, carrieth a power with it that admitteth of no opposition, being supported by nature, which inspireth an immediate consent at some critical times into every individual member to that which visibly tendeth to preservation of the whole; and this being so, a wise prince, instead of controverting the right of this reason of state, will by all means endeavour it may be of his side, and then he will be secure.

Our Trimmer cannot conceive that the power of any prince can be lasting, but where 'tis built upon the foundation of his own unborrowed virtue; he must not only be the first mover and the fountain from whence the great acts of state originally flow, but he must be thought so to his people, that they may preserve their veneration for him; he must be jealous of his power, and not impart so much of it to any about him as that he may suffer an eclipse by it.

He cannot take too much care to keep himself up, for when a prince is thought to be led by those with whom he should only advise, and that the commands he giveth are transmitted through him, and are not of his own growth, the world will look upon him as a bird adorned with feathers that are not his own, or consider him rather as an engine than a living creature; besides, 'twould be a contradiction for a prince to fear a commonwealth and at the same time create one himself, by delegating such a power to any number of men near him as is inconsistent with the figure of a monarch; it is the worst kind of co-ordination the Crown can submit to; for it is the exercise of power that draweth the respect along with it, and when that is parted with, the bare character of a king is not sufficient to keep it up. But though it is a diminution to a prince to parcel out so liberally his power amongst his favourites, it is worse to divide it with any other man, and to bring himself in competition with a single rival; a partner in government is so unnatural a thing that it is a squint-eyed allegiance that must be paid to such a double-bottomed monarchy. The *two Czars of Muscovy are an example that the most civilized part of the world will not be prone to follow. Whatsoever gloss may be put upon this method by those to whom it may be of some use, the prince will do well to remember and reflect upon the story of certain men who had set up a statue in honour of the sun, yet in a very little time they turned their backs to the sun and their faces to the statue.

These mystical unions are better placed in the other world than they are in this, and we shall have much ado to find that in a monarchy God's vicegerency is delegated to more heads than that which is anointed.

Princes may lend some of their light to make another shine, but they must still preserve the superiority of being the brighter planet, and when it happeneth that the reversion is in men's eyes, there is more care necessary to keep up the dignity of possession that men may not forget who is king, either out of their hopes or fears who shall be. If the sun should part with all his light to any other stars, the Indians would not know where to find their god, after he had so deposed himself, and would make the light (wherever it went) the object of their worship.

All usurpation is alike upon sovereignty; it is no matter from what hand it cometh, and crowned heads are to be the more circumspect in respect men's thoughts are naturally apt to ramble beyond what is present; they love to work at a distance, and in their greedy expectations which their minds may be filled with of a new master, the old one may be left to look a little out of countenance.

Our Trimmer owneth a passion for liberty, yet so restrained that it doth not in the least impair or taint his allegiance; he thinketh it hard for a soul that doth not love liberty ever to raise itself to another world; he taketh it to be the foundation of all virtue, and the only seasoning that giveth a relish to life; and though the laziness of a slavish subjection hath its charms for the more gross and earthly part of mankind, yet to men made of a better sort of clay all that the world can give without liberty hath no taste. It is true nothing is sold so cheap by unthinking men; but that doth no more lessen the real value of it than a country fellow's ignorance doth that of a diamond in selling it for a pot of ale. Liberty is the mistress of mankind; she hath powerful charms which do so dazzle us that we find beauties in her which perhaps are not there, as we do in other mistresses. Yet if she was not a beauty, the world would not run mad for her; therefore, since the reasonable desire of it ought not to be restrained, and that even the unreasonable desire of it cannot be entirely suppressed, those who would take it away from a people possessed of it are likely to fail in the attempting, or be very unquiet in the keeping of it.

Our Trimmer admireth our blessed constitution, in which dominion and liberty are so well reconciled; it giveth to the prince the glorious power of commanding freemen, and to the subjects the satisfaction of seeing the power so lodged as that their liberties are secure. It doth not allow the Crown such a ruining power as that no grass can grow where'er it treadeth, but a cherishing and protecting power; such a one as hath a grim aspect only to the offending subjects, but is the joy and the pride of all the good ones; their own interest being so bound up in it as to engage them to defend and support it. And though in some instances the king is restrained, yet nothing in the government can move without him; our laws make a distinction between vassalage and obedience; between a devouring prerogative and a licentious ungovernable freedom; and as of all the orders of building the composite is the best, so ours by a happy mixture and a wise choice of what is best in others, is brought into a form that is our felicity who live under it, and the envy of our neighbours that cannot imitate it.

The Crown hath power sufficient to protect our liberties. The people have so much liberty as is necessary to make them useful to the Crown.

Our government is in a just proportion, no tympany, no unnatural swelling either of power or liberty; and whereas in all overgrown monarchies, reason, learning, and inquiry are hanged in effigy for mutineers, here they are encouraged and cherished as the surest friends to a government established upon the foundation of law and justice. When all is done, those who look for perfection in this world may look as the Jews have for their Messiah; and therefore our Trimmer is not so unreasonably partial as to free our government from all objections. No doubt there have been fatal instances of its sickness, and more than that, of its mortality for some time; though by a miracle it hath been revived again; but till we have another race of mankind, in all constitutions that are bounded there will ever be some matter of strife and contention, and, rather than want pretensions, men's passions and interests will raise them from the most inconsiderable causes.

Our government is like our climate. There are winds which are sometimes loud and unquiet; and yet, with all the trouble they give us, we owe part of our health unto them; they clear the air, which else would be like a standing pool, and instead of refreshment would be a disease unto us.

There may be fresh gales of asserting liberty without turning into such storms of hurricane as that the state should run any hazard of being cast away by them. These strugglings, which are natural to all mixed governments, while they are kept from growing into convulsions do by a mutual agitation from the several parts rather support and strengthen than weaken or maim the constitution; and the whole frame, instead of being torn or disjointed, cometh to be the better and closer knit by being thus exercised. But whatever faults our government may have, or a discerning critic may find in it, when he looketh upon it alone, let any other be set against it, and then it showeth its comparative beauty; let us look upon the most glittering outside of unbounded authority, and upon a nearer inquiry we shall find nothing but poor and miserable deformity within. Let us imagine a prince living in his kingdom, as if in a great galley, his subjects tugging at the oar, laden with chains, and reduced to real rags, that they may gain him imaginary laurels; let us represent him gazing among his flatterers, and receiving their false worship, like a child never contradicted, and therefore always cozened, or like a lady complimented only to be abused; condemned never to hear truth and consequently never to do justice; wallowing in the soft bed of wanton and unbridled greatness, not less odious to the instruments themselves than to the objects of his tyranny; blown up into an ambitious dropsy, never to be satisfied by the conquest of other people or by the oppression of his own. By aiming to be more than a man, he falleth lower than the meanest of them, a mistaken creature, swelled with panegyrics, and flattered out of his senses, and not only an incumbrance, but a nuisance to mankind, a hardened and unrelenting soul; and, like some creatures that grow fat with poisons, he groweth great by other men's miseries; an ambitious ape of the Divine greatness, an unruly giant that would storm even heaven itself, but that his scaling-ladders are not long enough; in short, a wild and devouring creature in rich trappings, and with all his pride, no more than a whip in God Almighty's hand, to be thrown into the fire when the world hath been sufficiently scourged with it. This picture laid in right colours would not incite men to wish for such a government, but rather to acknowledge the happiness of our own, under which we enjoy all the privilege reasonable men can desire, and avoid all the miseries many others are subject to; so that our Trimmer would keep it with all its faults, and doth as little forgive those who give the occasion of breaking it, as he doth those that take it.

Our Trimmer is a friend to parliaments, notwithstanding all their faults and excesses, which of late have given such matter of objection to them; he thinketh that though they may at some times be troublesome to authority, yet they add the greatest strength to it under a wise administration; he believeth no government is perfect except a kind of omnipotence reside in it to exercise upon great occasions. Now this cannot be obtained by force alone upon people, let it be never so great; there must be their consent, too, or else a nation moveth only by being driven, a sluggish and constrained motion, void of that life and vigour which is necessary to produce great things, whereas the virtual consent of the whole being included in their representatives, and the king giving the sanction to the united sense of the people, every act done by such an authority seemeth to be an effect of their choice as well as a part of their duty; and they do, with an eagerness of which men are uncapable whilst under a force, execute whatsoever is so enjoined as their own wills, better explained by parliament, rather than from the terror of incurring the penalty of the law for omitting it. And by means of this political omnipotence, whatever sap or juice there is in a nation may be to the last drop produced, whilst it riseth naturally from the root; whereas all power exercised without consent is like the giving wounds and gashes and tapping a tree at unseasonable times for the present occasion, which in a very little time must needs destroy it.

Our Trimmer believeth that by the advantage of our situation, there can hardly any such sudden disease come upon us, but that the king may have time enough left to consult with his physicians in parliament. Pretences indeed may be made, but a real necessity so pressing that no delay is to be admitted is hardly to be imagined, and it will be neither easy to give an instance of any such thing for the time past, or reasonable to presume it will ever happen for the time to come. But if that strange thing should fall out, our Trimmer is not so strait-laced as to let a nation die or to be stifled rather than it should be helped by any but the proper officers. The cases themselves will bring the remedies along with them; and he is not afraid to allow that, in order to its preservation, there is a hidden power in government, which would be lost if it was defined, a certain mystery, by virtue of which a nation may at some critical times be secured from ruin; but then it must be kept as a mystery; it is rendered useless when touched by unskillful hands; and no government ever had, or deserved to have, that power which was so unwary as to anticipate their claim to it. Our Trimmer cannot help thinking it had been better if *the Triennial Act had been observed; because 'tis the law, and he would not have the Crown by such an example teach the nation to break it; all irregularity is catching, it hath a contagion in it, especially in an age so much more inclined to follow ill patterns than good ones.

He would have had a parliament, because 'tis an essential part of the constitution, even without the law, it being the only provision in extraordinary cases in which there would be otherwise no remedy, and there can be no greater solecism in government than a failure of justice.

He would have had one because nothing else can unite and heal us; all other means are mere shifts and projects, houses of cards, to be blown down with the least breath, and cannot resist the difficulties which are ever presumed in things of this kind. And he would have had one because it might have done the king good, and could not possibly have done him hurt without his consent, which in that case is not to be supposed; and therefore for him to fear it is so strange and so little to be comprehended that the reasons can never be presumed to grow in our soil, or to thrive in it when transplanted from any other country. And no doubt there are such irresistible arguments for calling a parliament, that though it might be denied to the unmannerly mutinous petitions of men that are malicious and disaffected, it will be granted to the soft obsequious murmurs of his Majesty's best subjects, and there will be such rhetoric in their silent grief that it will at last prevail against the artifices of those who, either out of guilt or interest, are afraid to throw themselves upon their country, knowing how scurvily they have used it. That day of judgment will come, though we know neither the day nor the hour. And our Trimmer will live so as to be prepared for it, with full assurance in the meantime that the lamenting voice of a nation cannot long be resisted, and that a prince who could so easily forgive his people when they had been in the wrong, cannot fail to hear them when they are in the right....

[1688]

SIR WILLIAM TEMPLE

In 1689 Sir William Temple was known throughout Europe for his services in negotiating the Triple Alliance between England, Holland, and Sweden (1668), and in connection with the Peace of Nimeguen between Holland and France (1678). He had served for a time as one of the leading ministers of Charles II, had been responsible for the famous but short-lived plan for strengthening and giving additional power to the Privy Council, and had also played an important part in arranging the marriage of William of Orange and Princess Mary, by whose joint accession to the English throne he might have been expected to rise to any position in the gift of the crown. In addition to his fame as a statesman he was also well known as a man of letters. Yet by a curious twist of fate, he is remembered today less frequently for these things than for the fact that about this time he took into his service as secretary a distant relative of his wife's, an unknown young student from Ireland, Jonathan Swift.

In spite of his great reputation and unquestioned ability Temple did not re-enter public life after the Revolution, but remained at his estate of Moor Park, near Farnham, Surrey, where he wrote memoirs and essays. His most important works are *Observations upon the United Provinces of the Netherlands*, *Memoirs*, letters, and essays on various subjects. Among the more formal of these are *An Essay upon the Original and Nature of Government*, in which he argues against the idea of a primitive social contract, and *Upon Ancient and Modern Learning*, in which he espouses the side of the ancients in the ancient-modern controversy then waging in France. This last would scarcely be remembered if it had not been the occasion of Bentley's masterly *Dissertation on the Epistles of Phalaris*, and of Swift's more famous *The Battle of the Books*. Among Temple's less formal essays, which show the influence of Montaigne, are *Upon the Gardens of Epicurus*, *Of Heroic Virtue*, *Of Health and Long Life*. These are more graceful treatments of subjects upon which he was well qualified to discourse.

Dr. Johnson said, "Sir William Temple was the first writer who gave cadence to English prose. Before his time they were careless of arrangement, and did not mind whether a sentence ended with an important word or an insignificant word, or with what part of speech it was concluded." Neither here nor in the well-known passage in which Boswell reports Johnson to have said that his own style had been formed in part upon that of Temple are we to take the words quite literally: Taylor and Browne and Milton had written cadenced prose; and Johnson's own style is very different from Temple's. It is true, however, that among writers of the new, sinewy prose, which soon after the Restoration superseded the gorgeous but invertebrate periods of the earlier seventeenth century, Temple merits a high place, and it is probable that Johnson learned something of cadence from him. Saintsbury, who in spite of his own perverse practice had a feeling for style, wrote of Temple: "He holds with Tillotson, Halifax, and Dryden, the most distinguished place among those authors of the late seventeenth century who definitely expressed the tendencies of the present, and even of the future, among their contemporaries in matter of English prose style."

The extract which here represents Temple is the last third of the essay *Of Poetry*. In many respects this essay represents the commonplace viewpoint of a liberal-minded gentleman, significant rather because it shows the accepted critical judgments of the last decades of the seventeenth century than for any special shrewdness of judgment or originality of expression. The most striking part is that which discusses the humours. These are understood to be a special product of the English climate, and their representation is claimed as the peculiar merit of the English stage. Apparently it is not alone the satiric treatment of the humours to which Temple here refers, but their appreciative or at least tolerant portrayal. In so speaking he takes issue with the usual neo-classical judgment, and seems to give expression to an English point of view which seldom found utterance at this time, though its silent persistence offered a major obstacle to that social discipline which was one of the most important aspects of the neo-classical movement. The last sentence of this essay has frequently been singled out for praise; in diction, cadence, and tone it represents Temple's style at its happiest, and suggests the later development of the informal essay.

MISCELLANEA, The Second Part

From OF POETRY

. . .* In such poor wretched weeds as these was poetry clothed during those shades of ignorance that overspread all Europe for so many ages after the sunset of the Roman learning and empire together, which were succeeded by so many new dominions or plantations of the Gothic swarms, and by a new face of customs, habit, language, and almost of na-

* Notes on Sir William Temple will be found in the Appendix, pp. 961 ff.

ture; but upon the dawn of a new day, and the resurrection of other sciences, with the two learned languages among us, this of poetry began to appear very early, though very unlike itself, and in shapes as well as clothes, in humour and in spirit very different from the ancient. It was now all in rhyme, after the Gothic fashion; for indeed none of the several dialects of that language or alloy would bear the composure of such feet and measures as were in use among the Greeks and Latins; and some that attempted it soon left it off, despairing of success. Yet in this new dress, poetry was not without some charms, especially those of grace and sweetness, and the ore begun to shine in the hands and works of the first refiners. Petrarch, Ronsard, Spenser met with much applause upon the subjects of love, praise, grief, reproach. Ariosto and Tasso entered boldly upon the scene of heroic poems, but, having not wings for so high flights, began to learn of the old ones, fell upon their imitations, and chiefly of Virgil, as far as the force of their genius or disadvantages of new languages and customs would allow. The religion of the Gentiles had been woven into the contexture of all the ancient poetry with a very agreeable mixture, which made the moderns affect to give that of Christianity a place also in their poems. But *the true religion was not found to become fiction so well as a false had done, and all their attempts of this kind seemed rather to debase religion than to heighten poetry. Spenser endeavoured to supply this with morality, and to make instruction instead of story the subject of an epic poem. His execution was excellent, and his flights of fancy very noble and high, but his design was poor, and his moral lay so bare that it lost the effect; 'tis true, the pill was gilded, but so thin that the colour and the taste were too easily discovered.

*After these three, I know none of the moderns that have made any achievements in heroic poetry worth recording. The wits of the age soon left off such bold adventures and turned to other veins, as if, not worthy to sit down at the feast, they contented themselves with the scraps, with songs and sonnets, with odes and elegies, with satires and panegyrics, and what we call copies of verses upon any subjects or occasions; wanting either genius or application for nobler or more laborious productions, as painters that cannot succeed in great pieces turn to miniature.

But the modern poets, to value this small coin and make it pass, though of so much a baser metal than the old, gave it a new mixture from two veins which were little known or little esteemed among the ancients. There were indeed certain fairies in the old regions of poetry called epigrams, which seldom reached above the stature of two or four or six lines, and which, being so short, were all turned upon conceit, or some sharp hits of fancy or wit. The only ancient of this kind among the Latins were the Priapeïa, which were little voluntaries or extemporaries written upon the ridiculous wooden statues of Priapus among the gardens of Rome. In the decays of the Roman learning and wit as well as language, Martial, Ausonius, and others fell into this vein, and applied it indifferently to all subjects, which was before restrained to one, and dressed it something more cleanly than it was born. This vein of conceit seemed proper for such scraps or splinters into which poetry was broken, and was so eagerly followed, as almost to overrun all that was composed in our several modern languages. The Italian, the French, the Spanish, as well as English, were for a great while full of nothing else but conceit: it was an ingredient that gave taste to compositions which had little of themselves; 'twas a sauce that gave point to meat that was flat, and some life to colours that were fading; and, in short, those who could not furnish spirit supplied it with this salt, which may preserve things or bodies that are dead, but is, for ought I know, of little use to the living, or necessary to meats that have much or pleasing tastes of their own. However it were, this vein first overflowed our modern poetry, and with so little distinction or judgment that we would have conceit as well as rhyme in every two lines, and run through all our long scribbles as well as the short, and the whole body of the poem, whatever it is: this was just as if a building should be nothing but ornament, or clothes nothing but trimming; as if a face should be covered over with black patches, or a gown with spangles; which is all I shall say of it.

Another vein which has entered and helped to corrupt our modern poesy is that of ridicule, as if nothing pleased but what made one laugh, which yet come from two very different affections of the mind; for as men have no disposition to laugh at things they are most pleased with, so they are very little pleased with many things they laugh at.

But this mistake is very general, and such modern poets as found no better way of pleasing, thought they could not fail of it by ridiculing. This was encouraged by finding conversation run so much into the same vein, and the wits in vogue to take up with that part of it which was formerly left to those that were called fools, and were used in great families only to make the company laugh. What opinion the Romans had of this character appears in those lines of Horace:

**Absentum qui rodit amicum,*
Qui non defendit alio culpante, solutos
Qui captat risus hominum famamque dicasis,
Fingere qui non visa potest, commissa tacere
Qui nequit, hic niger est, hunc tu, Romane, caveto;

And 'tis a pity the character of a wit in one age should be so like that of a black in another.

Rabelais seems to have been father of the ridicule, a man of excellent and universal learning as well as wit; and though he had too much game given him for satire in that age, by the customs of courts and of convents, of processes and of wars, of schools and of camps, of romances and legends; yet he must be confessed to have kept up his vein of ridicule by saying many things so malicious, so smutty, and so profane, that either a prudent, a modest, or a pious man could not have afforded, though he had never so much of that coin about him: and it were to be wished that the wits who have followed his vein had not put too much value upon a dress that better understandings would not wear, at least in public, and upon a compass they gave themselves which other men would not take. The matchless writer of *Don Quixote* is much more to be admired for having made up so excellent a composition of satire or ridicule without those ingredients, and seems to be the best and highest strain that ever was, or will be reached by that vein.

It began first in verse with an Italian poem, called **La Secchia Rapita,* was pursued by *Scarron in French with his Virgil travesty, and in English by Sir John Mince, *Hudibras,* and Cotton, and with greater height of burlesque in the English than, I think, in any other language. But let the execution be what it will, the design, the custom, and example are very pernicious to poetry, and indeed to all virtue and good qualities among men, which must be disheartened by finding how unjustly and undistinguished they fall under the lash of raillery, and this vein of ridiculing the good as well as the ill, the guilty and the innocent together. 'Tis a very poor, though common, pretence to merit, to make it appear by the faults of other men. A mean wit or beauty may pass in a room, where the rest of the company are allowed to have none; 'tis something to sparkle among diamonds, but to shine among pebbles is neither credit nor value worth the pretending.

Besides these two veins brought in to supply the defects of the modern poetry, much application has been made to the smoothness of language or style, which has at the best but the beauty of colouring in a picture, and can never make a good one without spirit and strength. The academy set up by Cardinal Richelieu to amuse the wits of that age and country, and divert them from raking into his politics and ministry, brought this in vogue; and the French wits have for this last age been, in a manner, wholly turned to the refinement of their language, and indeed with such success that it can hardly be excelled, and runs equally through their verse and their prose. The same vein has been likewise much cultivated in our modern English poetry; and by such poor recruits have the broken forces of this empire been of late made up; with what success, I leave to be judged by such as consider it in the former heights and the present declines both of power and of honour; but this will not discourage, however it may affect, the true lovers of this mistress, who must ever think her a beauty in rags as well as in robes.

Among these many decays, there is yet one sort of poetry that seems to have succeeded much better with our moderns than any of the rest, which is dramatic, or that of the stage; in this, the Italian, the Spanish, and the French have all had their different merit, and received their just applauses. Yet I am deceived if our English has not in some kind excelled both the modern and the ancient, which has been by force of a vein natural perhaps to our country, and which with us is called *humour, a word peculiar to our language too, and hard to be expressed in any other; nor is it, that I know of, found in any foreign writers, unless it be Molière, and yet his itself has too much of the farce to pass for the same with ours. Shakespeare was the first that opened this vein upon our stage, which has run so freely and so pleasantly ever since that I have often wondered to find it appear so little upon any others, being a subject so proper for them, since humour is but a picture of particular life, as comedy is of general; and though it represents dispositions and customs less common, yet they are not less natural than those that are more frequent among men; for if humour itself be forced, it loses all the grace, which has been indeed the fault of some of our poets most celebrated in this kind.

It may seem a defect in the ancient stage that the characters introduced were so few, and those so common, as a covetous old man, an amorous young, a witty wench, a crafty slave, a bragging soldier; the spectators met nothing upon the stage, but what they met in the streets and at every turn.

All the variety is drawn only from different and uncommon events; whereas if the characters are so too, the diversity and the pleasure must needs be the more. But as of most general customs in a country there is usually some ground from the nature of the people or climate, so there may be amongst us for this vein of our stage, and a greater variety of humour in the picture, because there is a greater variety in the life. This may proceed from the native plenty of our soil, the unequalness of our climate, as well as the ease of our government, and the liberty of professing opinions and factions, which perhaps our neighbours may have about them, but are forced to disguise, and thereby they may come in time to be extinguished. Plenty begets wantonness and pride; wantonness is apt to invent, and pride scorns to imitate. Liberty begets stomach or heart, and stomach will not be constrained. Thus we come to have more originals, and more that appear what they are; we have more humour, because every man follows his own, and takes a pleasure, perhaps a pride, to show it.

On the contrary, where the people are generally poor and forced to hard labour, their actions and lives are all of a piece; where they serve hard masters, they must follow his examples as well as commands, and are forced upon imitation in small matters, as well as obedience in great; so that some nations look as if they were cast all by one mould, or cut out all by one pattern, — at least the common people in one, and the gentlemen in another; they seem all of a sort in their habits, their customs, and even their talk and conversation, as well as in the application and pursuit of their actions and their lives.

Besides all this, there is another sort of variety amongst us, which arises from our climate, and the dispositions it naturally produces. We are not only more unlike one another than any nation I know, but we are more unlike ourselves, too, at several times, and owe to our very air some ill qualities as well as many good. We may allow some distempers incident to our climate, since so much health, vigour, and length of life have been generally ascribed to it; for among the Greek and Roman authors themselves, we shall find the Britons observed to live the longest, and the Egyptians the shortest, of any nations that were known in those ages. Besides, I think none will dispute the native courage of our men and beauty of our women, which may be elsewhere as great in particulars, but nowhere so in general; they may be (what is said of diseases) as acute in other places, but with us they are epidemical. For my own part, who have conversed much with men of other nations, and such as have been both in great employments and esteem, I can say very impartially that I have not observed among any, so much true genius as among the English; nowhere more sharpness of wit, more pleasantness of humour, more range of fancy, more penetration of thought or depth of reflection among the better sort; nowhere more goodness of nature and of meaning, nor more plainness of sense and of life than among the common sort of country people, nor more blunt courage and honesty than among our seamen.

But, with all this, our country must be confessed to be what a great foreign physician called it, the region of spleen, which may arise a good deal from the great uncertainty and many sudden changes of our weather in all seasons of the year. And how much these affect the heads and hearts, especially of the finest tempers, is hard to be believed by men whose thoughts are not turned to such speculations. This makes us unequal in our humours, inconstant in our passions, uncertain in our ends, and even in our desires. Besides, our different opinions in religion, and the factions they have raised or animated for fifty years past, have had an ill effect upon our manners and customs, inducing more avarice, ambition, disguise, with the usual consequences of them, than were before in our constitution. From all this it may happen that there is nowhere more true zeal in the many different forms of devotion, and yet nowhere more knavery under the shows and pretences. There are nowhere so many disputers upon religion, so many reasoners upon government, so many refiners in politics, so many curious inquisitives, so many pretenders to business and state employments, greater porers upon books, nor plodders after wealth; and yet nowhere more abandoned libertines, more refined luxurists, extravagant debauchees, conceited gallants, more dabblers in poetry as well as politics, in philosophy, and in chemistry. I have had several servants far gone in divinity, others in poetry; have known, in the families of some friends, a keeper deep in the *Rosicrucian principles, and a laundress firm in those of Epicurus. What effect soever such a composition or medley of humours among us may have upon our lives or our government, it must needs have a good one upon our stage, and has given admirable play to our comical wits; so that in my opinion there is no vein of that sort, either ancient or modern, which excels or equals the humour of our plays. And for the rest, I cannot but observe, to the honour of our country, that the good qualities amongst us seem to be natural, and the ill ones more accidental, and such as would be easily changed by the examples of princes, and by the precepts of laws; such, I mean, as should be designed to form manners, to restrain excesses, to encourage industry, to prevent men's expenses beyond their fortunes, to countenance virtue, and raise that true esteem due to plain sense and common honesty.

But to spin off this thread which is already grown too long: what honour and request the ancient poetry has lived in, may not only be observed from the universal reception and use in all nations from China to Peru, from Scythia to Arabia, but from the esteem of the best and the greatest men as well as the vulgar. Among the Hebrews, David and Solomon, the wisest kings, Job and Jeremiah, the holiest men, were the best poets of their nation and language. Among the Greeks, the two most renowned sages and lawgivers were Lycurgus and Solon, whereof the last is known to have excelled in poetry, and the first was so great a lover of it that to his care and industry we are said by some authors to owe the collection and preservation of the loose and scattered pieces of Homer in the order wherein they have since appeared. Alexander is reported neither to have travelled nor slept without those admirable poems always in his company. *Phalaris, that was inexorable to all other enemies, relented at the charms of Stesichorus his muse. Among the Romans, the last and great Scipio passed the soft hours of his life in the conversation of Terence, and was thought to have a part in the composition of his comedies. Cæsar was an excellent poet as well as orator, and composed a poem in his voyage from Rome to Spain, relieving the tedious difficulties of his march with the entertainments of his muse. Augustus was not only a patron, but a friend and companion of Virgil and Horace, and was himself both an admirer of poetry and a pretender too, as far as his genius would reach or his busy scene allow. 'Tis true, since his age we have few such examples of great princes' favouring or affecting poetry, and as few perhaps of great poets deserving it. Whether it be that the fierceness of the Gothic humours, or noise of their perpetual wars, frighted it away, or that the unequal mixture of the modern languages would not bear it; certain it is that the great heights and excellency both of poetry and music fell with the Roman learning and empire, and have never since recovered the admiration and applauses that before attended them. Yet such as they are amongst us, they must be confessed to be the softest and sweetest, the most general and most innocent amusements of common time and life. They still find room in the courts of princes and the cottages of shepherds. They serve to revive and animate the dead calm of poor or idle lives, and to allay or divert the violent passions and perturbations of the greatest and the busiest men. And both these effects are of equal use to human life; for the mind of man is like the sea, which is neither agreeable to the beholder nor the voyager in a calm or in a storm, but is so to both when a little agitated by gentle gales; and so the mind, when moved by soft and easy passions and affections. I know very well that many who pretend to be wise by the forms of being grave are apt to despise both poetry and music as toys and trifles too light for the use or entertainment of serious men. But whoever find themselves wholly insensible to these charms would, I think, do well to keep their own counsel, for fear of reproaching their own temper, and bringing the goodness of their natures, if not of their understandings, into question; it may be thought at least an ill sign, if not an ill constitution, since some of the fathers went so far as to esteem the love of music a sign of predestination, as a thing divine, and reserved for the felicities of heaven itself. While this world lasts, I doubt not but the pleasure and request of these two entertainments will do so too; and happy those that content themselves with these or any other so easy and so innocent, and do not trouble the world or other men, because they cannot be quiet themselves, though nobody hurts them.

When all is done, human life is, at the greatest and the best, but like a froward child that must be played with and humoured a little to keep it quiet till it falls asleep, and then the care is over.

[1690]

ISAAC BARROW

Were apology necessary for inclusion of sermons in a volume of the prose and poetry of the classical period in English literature, it might be found in the words of Dr. Johnson to John Wilkes, "Why, sir, you are to consider that sermons make a considerable branch of English literature, so that a library must be very imperfect if it has not a numerous collection of sermons."

The seventeenth century was the golden age of the English pulpit, and its last forty years were in some respects the most important. That view of the Restoration period which shows it as a worldly reaction against the religious fervour of the saints, which emphasizes chiefly a corrupt court and a licentious theatre, is one-sided and misleading; at no period in English history has there been a more passionate interest in religion or a closer interpenetration of politics and literature. As Professor Arber has pointed out in the Preface to his reprint of *The Term Catalogues*, and as even the most cursory inspection of its pages reveals, a large part of the published writing of the time was on religious subjects. Especially important was preaching: practically every one went to church, and surprisingly large numbers of people were interested in sermons. Samuel Pepys was no zealot, yet he went to church even more regularly than he attended the theatre, and for substantially the same reason: because he enjoyed doing so. That his taste was not exceptional is abundantly proved by contemporary records. Sermons were published in every form, from cheap pamphlets to expensive folios; they were sold in immense numbers; and they found eager readers and intelligent critics.

While this interest survived to a considerable extent throughout the eighteenth century, it is particularly in the early part of our period that the sermon must be taken into account as literature. Not only is its content necessary for the right understanding of the social and the political history of the time, but its style is at once a formative influence and a reflection of English prose style. W. H. Hutton does not exaggerate when he says, "During the forty years which followed the return of Charles II, English divines, in their treatment of serious themes, laid the foundations on which Addison based his mastery over the language of his day."

Isaac Barrow had one of the most vigorous minds of his generation as well as great scholarship in several different subjects. He held, successively, professorships of Greek and of mathematics at Cambridge, in the latter of which he was succeeded by his pupil, Isaac Newton. His publications include important works on geometry and optics. But his chief interest was in preaching and in theology, to which he made important contributions. His last years were devoted to the Mastership of Trinity College, Cambridge, where he had a large part in founding the college library. He died at the age of forty-seven.

Barrow's sermons are marked by intellectual force putting to use the resources of vast learning, and by strong earnestness and directness. The great length for which his sermons were famous was copiousness rather than verbosity; he preached at length, sometimes at a length that exhausted even his hardiest listeners, because he had much to say. Addressing, as he commonly did, cultured, educated congregations at the court or the university, he discussed serious questions with convincing logic and rounded thoroughness. His style in most respects is modern, avoiding the extravagance and the forced conceits of pre-Restoration prose. Even when his sentences are longest, they are so coherent and so well organized that their meaning is immediately clear. His diction is choice and expressive, though, like all seventeenth-century writing, it occasionally misleads the present-day reader who is not watchful to detect archaic uses of familiar words. Barrow has neither the eloquence of Jeremy Taylor nor the finished perfection of Addision; he stands between the earlier and the later schools of prose; but he writes precisely, without pedantry, and clearly, with a sense of style supplied by his classical studies.

The selection here reprinted is the last part of a sermon preached May 29, 1676, the anniversary of the Restoration of King Charles II. Its subject is the duty of prayer and thanksgiving for kings. In developing his theme, Barrow gives a clear presentation of the High Church doctrines of the divine right of kings and of the duty of nonresistance to their authority. These doctrines, which were frequently promulgated from Anglican pulpits, especially between 1660 and 1689, are difficult for modern students to comprehend, because they are diametrically opposed to our customary theories of government. Yet, fantastic as they may seem to us, they were held by clear thinkers and conscientious men, who abundantly proved their devotion to principle.

From SERMON X. PRAYER FOR KINGS

I Tim., 2:1, 2. *"I exhort therefore, that, first of all, supplications, prayers, intercessions, and giving of thanks, be made for all men; for kings, and for all that are in authority."

... 9. Whereas God hath declared that he hath special regard to princes, and a more than ordinary care over them, because they have a peculiar relation to him, as his representatives, the ministers of his kingdom, the main instruments of his providence, whereby he conveyeth his favours, and dispenseth his justice to men; because also the good of mankind, which he especially tendereth, is mainly concerned in their welfare; whereas I say, "It is he that giveth salvation unto kings"; that "giveth great deliverance to his king, and showeth mercy to his anointed"; that hath the king's heart and his breath, and all his ways in his hand: even upon this account our prayers for them are the more required. For it is a method of God, and an established rule of divine providence, not to dispense special blessings without particular conditions, and the concurrence of our duty in observance of what he prescribeth in respect to them. Seeing then he hath enjoined that in order to our obtaining those great benefits which issue from his special care over princes, we should pray for it and seek it from his hands, the omission of this duty will intercept it, or bereave us of its advantages; nor in that case may we expect any blessings of that kind. As without praying for ourselves we must not expect private favours from heaven, so without praying for our prince we cannot well hope for public blessings. For, as a profane person, who in effect disavoweth God by not regarding to seek his favour and aid, is not qualified to receive any good from him; so a profane nation, which disclaimeth God's government of the world by not invoking his benediction on those who moderate it under him, is not well capable of common benefits. It is upon all accounts true which Ezra said, "The hand of our God is upon all them for good that seek him; but his power and his wrath is against all them that forsake him." If, therefore, we desire that our prince should not lose God's special regard, if we would not forfeit the benefits thereof to ourselves, we must conspire in hearty prayers for him.

10. To engage and encourage us in which practice, we may farther consider that such prayers, offered duly, with frequency and constancy, with sincerity and zeal, do always turn to good account and never want good effect: the which if it be not always easily discernible, yet it is certainly real; if it be not perfect as we may desire, yet it is competent, as expediency requireth, or as the condition of things will bear.

There may be impediments to a full success of the best prayers; they may not ever prevail to render princes completely good or extremely prosperous: for some concurrence of their own will is requisite to produce their virtue, God rarely working with irresistible power or fatal efficacy; and the state of things or the capacities of persons are not always fitly suited for prosperity. Yet are not such prayers ever wholly vain or fruitless: for God never prescribeth means unavailable to the end; he never would have commanded us particularly to pray for kings, if he did not mean to bestow a good issue to that practice.

And, surely, he that hath promised to hear all requests with faith and sincerity and incessant earnestness presented to him, cannot fail to hear those which are of such consequence, which are so agreeable to his will, which do include so much honesty and charity. In this case, surely, we may have some confidence, according to that of St. John, "This is the confidence we have in him, that if we ask anything according to his will, he heareth us."

*As the good bishop, observing St. Austin's mother, with what constancy and passionateness she did pray for her son, being then engaged in ways of error and vanity, did encourage her, saying, "It is impossible that a son of those devotions should perish": so may we hopefully presume and encourage ourselves that a prince will not miscarry, for whose welfare many good people do earnestly solicit: **Fieri non potest, ut princeps istarum lacrymarum pereat.*

You know in general the mighty efficacy of prayer, what pregnant assurances there are, and how wonderful instances thereof occur in Holy Scripture, both in relation to public and private blessings: how it is often promised that, *"All things, whatsoever we shall ask in prayer, believing, we shall receive"; and that, "Whoever asketh receiveth; and he that seeketh findeth; and to him that knocketh it shall be opened": how the prayer of Abraham did heal Abimelech and his family of barrenness;

* Notes on Isaac Barrow will be found in the Appendix, pp. 962 ff.

how the prayers of Moses did quench the fire, and cure the bitings of the fiery serpents; how the prayer of Joshua did arrest the sun; *how the prayer of Hannah did procure Samuel to her, as his name doth import; how *Elias his prayers did open and shut the heavens; how the same holy prophet's prayer did *reduce a departed soul, and that of Elisha did effect the same, and that of another prophet did restore Jeroboam's withered hand; how the prayers of God's people frequently did raise them up saviours, and, "When they cried unto the Lord in their trouble, he delivered them out of their distresses"; how the prayers of Asa discomfited a million of Arabians, and those of Jehoshaphat destroyed a numerous army of his enemies by their own hands, and those of Hezekiah brought down an angel from heaven to cut off the Assyrians, and those of Manasses restored him to his kingdom, and those of Esther saved her people from the brink of ruin, and those of Nehemiah inclined a pagan king's heart to favour his pious design for *re-edifying Jerusalem, and those of Daniel obtained strange visions and discoveries; how Noah, Job, Daniel, Moses, and Samuel are represented as powerful intercessors with God; and consequently it is intimated that the great things achieved by them were chiefly done by the force of their prayers.

And seeing prayers in so many cases are so effectual and work such miracles; what may we hope from them in this, wherein God so expressly and particularly directeth us to use them? If our prayers can so much avail to our personal and private advantage, if they may be very helpful to our friends, how much shall the devotions of many good men, all levelled at one mark, and aiming at a public most considerable good, be prevalent with the divine goodness? However, if God be not moved by prayers to convert a prince from all sin, to make him do all the good he might, to bless him in all matters; yet he may thence be induced to restrain him from much evil, to keep him from being worse, or from doing worse than otherwise would be; he may dispose him to do many things well, or better than of himself he would do; he may preserve him from many disasters otherwise incident to him, which will be considerable effects of prayer.

11. I shall add but one general consideration more, which is this, that prayer is the only allowable way of redressing our case, if we do suffer by, or for princes.

Are they bad, or do they misdemean themselves in their administration of government and justice? we may not by any violent or rough way attempt to reclaim them; for they are not accountable to us, or liable to our correction. "Where the word of a king is, there is power: and who shall say to him, What doest thou?" was *the Preacher's doctrine.

Do they oppress us, or abuse us? do they treat us harshly, or cruelly persecute us? we must not kick against them, or strive to right ourselves by resistance. For, "Against a king," saith the wise man, "there is no rising up": and, "Who," said David, "can stretch out his hand against the Lord's anointed, and be guiltless?" and, "They," saith St. Paul, "that resist shall receive to themselves damnation."

We must not so much as ease our *stomach, or discharge our passion, by railing or inveighing against them. For, "Thou shalt not speak evil of the ruler of thy people," is a divine law; and to blaspheme or revile dignities is by St. Peter and St. Jude reprehended as a notable crime.

We must not be bold or free in taxing their actions. For, "Is it fit," saith Elihu, "to say to a king, Thou art wicked? and to princes, Ye are ungodly?" and, to "reproach the footsteps of God's anointed," is implied to be an impious practice.

We must forbear even complaining and murmuring against them. For, murmurers are condemned as no mean sort of offenders; and the Jews in the wilderness were sorely punished for such behaviour.

We must not (according to the Preacher's advice) so much as "curse them in our thought"; or not entertain ill conceits and ill wishes in our minds toward them.

To do these things is not only high presumption in regard to them (inconsistent with the dutiful affection and respect which we owe to them), but it is flat impiety toward God, and an invasion of his authority; who alone is King of Kings, and hath reserved to himself the prerogative of judging, of rebuking, of punishing kings, when he findeth cause.

*These were the misdemeanours of those in the late times, who, instead of praying for their sovereign, did clamour and rail at him, did asperse him with foul imputations, did accuse his proceedings, did raise tumults, and levy war against him, pretending by rude force to reduce him unto his duty; so usurping on their prince, or rather on God himself, assuming his right, and taking his work out of his hands; discovering also therein great profaneness of mind, and distrust of God's providence; as if God, being implored by prayer, could not, or would not, had it been needful, without such irregular courses have redressed those evils in Church or State, which they pretended to feel or fear.

Nothing, therefore, in such cases is left to us for our remedy or ease, but having recourse to God himself, and seeking relief from his hand, in his good time, by converting our prince or directing him into a good course; however comforting ourselves in the conscience of submitting to God's will.

*This is the only method St. Paul did prescribe, even when Nero, a most vile, flagitious man, a sorry and naughty governor as could be, a monstrous tyrant, and most bloody persecutor (the very inventor of persecution), did sway the empire. He did not advise Christians to stand upon their guard, to contrive plots, to provide arms, to raise mutinies and insurrections against him; but to offer supplications, prayers, and intercessions for him, as the best means of their security and comfort. And this was the course of the primitive Christians, during their hard condition under the domination of heathen princes, impugners of their religion: prayers and tears were then the only arms of the Church; whereby they long defended it from ruin, and at last advanced it to most glorious prosperity.

Indeed, if, not assuming the liberty to find fault with princes, we would practise the duty of seeking God for his blessing on their proceedings; if, forbearing to scan and censure acts of state, we would earnestly implore God's direction of them; if, leaving to conceive disgusts, and vent complaints about the state of things, we would assiduously petition God for the settlement of them in good order; if, instead of being shrewd politicians or smart judges in such matters, we would be devout *orators and humble solicitors at the throne of grace; our endeavours surely would find much better effect toward public advantage: we certainly might do more good in our closets by a few hearty wishes uttered there than by all our tattling or jangling politics in corners.

There are great contrivances to settle things; every one hath his model of state or method of policy to communicate for ordering the state; each is zealous for his own conceit, and apt to be displeased with those who dissent from him: but it is, as the fairest and justest, so the surest and likeliest way of reducing things to a firm composure, (without more ado, letting the world alone to move on its own hinges, and not impertinently troubling ourselves or others with the conduct of it) simply to request of Almighty God, the Sovereign Governor and sole Disposer of things, that he would lead his own vicegerents in the management of the charge by himself committed to them. "Be careful for nothing; but in everything by prayer and supplication with thanksgiving let your requests be made known to God," is a rule very applicable to this case.

As God's providence is the only sure ground of our confidence, or hope for the preservation of Church and State, or for the restitution of things into a stable quiet; so it is only our hearty prayers, joined with a conscientious observance of God's laws, whereby we can incline Providence to favour us. By them alone we may hope to save things from sinking into disorder; we may assuage the factions; we may defeat the machinations against the public welfare.

12. Seeing then we have so many good arguments and motives inducing to pray for kings, it is no wonder that to back them we may also allege the practice of the Church, continually in all times performing this duty in its most sacred offices, especially in the celebration of the Holy Communion.

St. Paul indeed, when he saith, "I exhort first of all that prayers be made," doth chiefly impose this duty on Timothy, or supposeth it incumbent on the pastors of the Church, to take special care that prayers be made for this purpose, and offered up in the Church jointly by all Christians; and accordingly the ancient Christians, as Tertullian doth assure us, did, "always pray for all the emperors, that God would grant them a long life, a secure reign, a safe family, valiant armies, a faithful senate, a loyal people, a quiet world, and whatever they as men or as emperors could wish." Thus, addeth he, even for their persecutors, and in the very pangs of their sufferings, they did not fail to practice. Likewise of the Church in his time, St. Chrysostom telleth us that, "All communicants did know how every day both at even and morning they did make supplication for all the world and for the emperor and for all that are in authority."

And in the Greek liturgies (the composure whereof is fathered on St. Chrysostom) there are divers prayers interspersed for the emperors, couched in terms very pregnant and respectful.

If the officers of the Roman Church, and of the Churches truckling under it, in latter times, shall seem more defective or sparing in this point of service, the reason may be for that a superlative regard to the solar or pontifical authority (as Pope Innocent III distinguished) did obscure their devotion for the lunar or regal majesty. But our Church hath been abundantly careful that we should in most ample manner discharge this duty, having in each of her holy offices directed us to pray for our King in expressions most full, hearty, and lively.

She hath indeed been charged as somewhat lavish or over-liberal of her devotions in this case. But it is a good fault, and we little need fear overdoing in observance of a precept so very reasonable and so important; supposing that we have a due care to join our heart with the Church's words, and to the frequency of prayer for our prince do confer a suitable fervency. If we be not dead, or merely formal, we can hardly be too copious in this kind of devotion; reiteration of words can do no harm, being accompanied with renovation of our desires. Our text itself will bear us out in such a practice; the apostle therein by variety of expression appearing solicitous that abundance of prayers for kings should be offered in the Church, and no sort of them omitted.

There are so many general inducements to this duty at all times; and there are beside divers particular reasons enforcing it now in the present state and posture of things.

Times of trouble, of danger, of fear, of darkness and perplexity, of distraction and distress, of guilt and deserved wrath, are most seasonable for recourse to the divine help and mercy in prayer.

And are not ours such? are they not much like to those of which the Psalmist saith, "They know not, neither will they understand; they walk on in darkness: all the foundations of the earth are out of course"? or like those of which our Lord spake when there was "upon the earth distress of nations, with perplexity;... Men's hearts failing them for fear, and for looking after those things which were coming on the earth"?

Are not the days gloomy, so that no human providence can see far, no wisdom can descry the issue of things?

Is it not a very unsettled world, wherein all the public frames are shaken almost off the hinges, and the minds of men extremely discomposed with various passions; with fear, suspicion, anger, discontent, and impatience? How from dissensions in opinion do violent factions and feuds rage; the hearts of men boiling with fierce animosities and being exasperated against one another beyond any hopes or visible means of reconcilement?

Are not the fences of discipline cast down? is there any conscience made of violating laws? is not the dread of authority exceedingly abated, and all government overborne by unbridled licentiousness?

How many adversaries are there bearing ill will to our Sion? how many turbulent, malicious, crafty spirits, eagerly bent, and watching for occasion to subvert the Church, to disturb the State, to introduce confusion in all things? how many Edomites who say of Jerusalem (both ecclesiastical and civil), "Down with it, down with it even to the ground"?

Have we not great reason to be fearful of God's just displeasure, and that heavy judgments will be poured on us for our manifold heinous provocations and crying sins; for the prodigious growth of atheism, infidelity, and profaneness; for the rife practice of all impieties, iniquities, and impurities, with most impudent boldness, or rather with outrageous insolence; for the extreme dissoluteness in manners, the gross neglect or contempt of all duties, the great stupidity and coldness of people generally as to all concerns of religion; for the want of religious awe toward God, of charity toward our neighbour, of respect to our superiors, of sobriety in our conversation; for our ingratitude for many great mercies, and incorrigibleness under many sore chastisements, our insensibleness of many plain warnings, loudly calling us to repentance?

Is not all the world about us in combustion, cruel wars raging everywhere, and Christendom weltering in blood? and although at present, by God's mercy, we are free, who knows but that soon, by God's justice, the neighbouring flames may catch our houses?

In fine, is not our case palpably such, that

for any good composure or reinstatement of things in good order, for upholding truth and sound doctrine, for reducing charity and peace, for reviving the spirit of piety, and bringing virtue again into request, for preserving State and Church from ruin, we can have no confidence or reasonable hope but in the good providence and merciful succour of Almighty God; "beside whom there is no saviour"; who alone is "the hope of Israel, and saviour thereof in time of trouble"? we now having great cause to pray with our Lord's disciples in the storm, "Lord, save us; we perish."

Upon such considerations, and others whereof I suppose you are sufficiently apprehensive, we now especially are obliged earnestly to pray for our king, that God in mercy would preserve his royal person, and inspire his mind with light, and endue his heart with grace, and in all things bless him to us, to be "a repairer of our breaches, and a restorer of paths to dwell in"; so that under him we may lead a quiet life in all godliness and honesty.

I have done with the first duty, *prayer for kings,* upon which I have the rather so largely insisted, because it is very seasonable to our present condition.

II. The other, *thanksgiving,* I shall but touch, and need not perhaps to do more. For,

1. As to general inducements, they are the same, or very like to those which are for prayer; it being plain that whatever we are concerned to pray for, when we want it, that we are bound to thank God for, when he vouchsafeth to bestow it. And if common charity should dispose us to resent the good of princes with complacence; if their welfare be a public benefit; if ourselves are interested in it, and partake great advantages thereby; if in equity and ingenuity we are bound to seek it; then, surely, we are much engaged to thank God, the bountiful donor of it, for his goodness in conferring it.

2. As for particular motives, suiting the present occasion, I need not by information or impression of them farther to stretch your patience; seeing you cannot be ignorant or insensible of the grand benefits by the divine goodness bestowed on our king, and on ourselves, which this day we are bound with all grateful acknowledgment to commemorate. Wherefore, instead of reciting trite stories, and urging obvious reasons, which a small recollection will suggest to you, I shall only request you to join with me in the practice of the duty, and in acclamation of praise to God. Even so:

Blessed be God, who hath given to us so gracious and benign a prince, the * experiments of whose clemency and goodness no history can parallel, to sit on * the throne of his Blessed Father and renowned ancestors.

Blessed be God, who hath protected him in so many encounters, hath saved him from so many dangers and snares, hath delivered him from so great troubles.

Blessed be God, who in so wonderful a manner, by such miraculous trains of providence, did reduce him to his country, and reinstate him in the possession of his rights; thereby vindicating his own just providence, "declaring his salvation, and openly showing his righteousness in the sight of all people."

Blessed be God, who in him and with him did restore to us our ancient good constitution of government, our laws and liberties, our peace and quiet; rescuing us from lawless usurpations and tyrannical yokes, from the insultings of error and iniquity, from horrible distractions and confusions.

Ever blessed be God, who hath "turned the captivity of Sion"; hath raised our Church from the dust, and re-established the sound doctrine, the decent order, the wholesome discipline thereof; hath restored true religion with its supports, advantages, and encouragements.

Blessed be the Lord, who hath granted us to continue these sixteen years in the peaceable fruition of those blessings.

"Praised be God, who hath not cast out our prayer, nor turned his mercy from us."

Praised be God, who "hath turned our heaviness into joy, hath put off our sackcloth, and girded us with gladness."

"Let our mouth speak the praise of the Lord; and let all flesh bless his holy name for ever and ever."

"The Lord liveth; and blessed be our rock; and let the God of our salvation be exalted."

"Blessed be the Lord God of Israel, who only doeth wondrous things. And blessed be his glorious name for ever; and let the whole earth be filled with his glory; Amen, and Amen."

"Blessed be the Lord God of Israel from everlasting to everlasting: and let all the people say Amen. Praise ye the Lord."

[1678]

ROBERT SOUTH

ROBERT SOUTH was a slashing controversialist and a vigorous preacher, whose writing is marked by masculine forthrightness and ready wit. Throughout the course of his long and active life he was a constant supporter of High Church principles. Despite his indignation at James the Second's high-handed interference with the University of Oxford, South refused to countenance rebellion against the king. After the Revolution he, like other believers in divine right and nonresistance, felt conscientious scruples against swearing allegiance to William and Mary while King James still lived. Eventually, however, he took the ground that by fleeing the country James had really abdicated the crown; consequently South did not become a Nonjuror. He refused, however, to profit at the expense of those bishops who had decided otherwise, and declined episcopal preferment. Though South's character was far from amiable, and though he had little Christian charity for those who disagreed with him, he must be admired for his courage, his integrity, and his disinterested love of the Church.

Among the great English preachers South is probably the most interesting for the average reader today. He is learned but not pedantic, logical but not heavy, earnest but not dull. Though his style is not quite so modern as Tillotson's, it is clear and direct, with little of the old lumber of erudite quotation and unnecessary allusion; it completely eschews forced conceits and other ornaments of what Addison later denominated false wit. In his sermon, "The Scribe Instructed," which he preached before the University of Oxford, July 29, 1660, at the very beginning of the Restoration period, he said, "All vain, luxuriant allegories, rhyming cadences of similary words are such pitiful embellishments of speech, as serve for nothing but to embase divinity," and he ridiculed those whose "prayers shall be set out in such a dress as if they did not supplicate but compliment Almighty God; and their sermons so garnished with quibbles and trifles as if they played with truth and immortality.... Wit in divinity is nothing else but sacred truths suitably expressed. It is not shreds of Latin or Greek, nor a *Deus dixit*, and a *Deus benedixit*, nor those little quirks, or divisions into the ὅτι, the διότι, and the καθότι or the *egress*, *regress*, and *progress*, and other such stuff (much like the style of a lease) that can properly be called wit. For that is not wit which consists not with wisdom."

South has to an extraordinary degree the power of forceful, incisive speech. His writing is picturesque and frequently epigrammatic. With reference to the conjugal fidelity of Charles I, he says, "David was chiefly eminent for repenting in this matter, Charles for not needing repentance." The prosperous sinner "like a sot in a tavern, first drinks himself drunk and then forgets that there is a reckoning." "He that receives an injury may pardon it, but he that first does an injury is irreconcilable." "It is infinitely vain for a man to talk of heaven while he trades for hell, or to look upwards while he lives downwards." Concluding a sermon on "The wages of sin is death," he says, "He who likes the wages, let him go about the work." This power of lively and picturesque phrasing in the service of strong partisan feelings leads him occasionally to unseemly vigour of expression. Though he is never flat, he is often intemperate.

Much of his preaching is polemic. The Roman Catholics he berates in round terms, but it is against the Puritan dissenters that he is especially voluble. Both by denunciation and ridicule he attacks these constantly as enemies of King and Church. The extract which here represents South is the latter part of the first of two sermons in which he defends the liturgy of the Church of England. It is not only characteristic of its author, but it is important as a discussion of a question frequently debated between Anglicans and Nonconformists.

From SERMON XV. A DISCOURSE AGAINST LONG EXTEMPORARY PRAYERS

Text: Ecclesiastes V:2. — "Be not rash with thy mouth, and let not thine heart be hasty to utter any thing before God: for God is in heaven, and thou upon earth: therefore let thy words be few."

*... In fine, to state the whole matter of our prayers in one word; nothing can be fit for us to pray for, but what is fit and honourable for our great mediator and master of requests, Jesus Christ himself, to intercede for. This is to be the unchangeable rule and measure of all our petitions. And then, if Christ is to convey these our petitions to his Father, can any one dare to make him, who was holiness and purity itself, an advocate and solicitor for his lusts? Him who was nothing but meekness, lowliness, and humility, his proveditor for such things as can only feed his pride and

* Notes on Robert South will be found in the Appendix, p. 963.

flush his ambition? No, certainly; when we come as suppliants to the throne of grace, where Christ sits as intercessor at God's right hand, nothing can be fit to proceed out of our mouth but what is fit to pass through his.

The third and last thing that calls for a previous meditation to our prayers is the order and disposition of them; for though God does not command us to set off our prayers with dress and artifice, to flourish it in trope and metaphor, to beg our daily bread in blank verse, or to show anything of the poet in our devotions but indigence and want: I say, though God is far from requiring such things of us in our prayers, yet he requires that we should manage them with sense and reason. Fineness is not expected, but decency is; and though we cannot declaim as orators, yet he will have us speak like men, and tender him the results of that understanding and judgment that essentially constitute a rational nature.

But I shall briefly cast what I have to say upon this particular into these following assertions:

1st, That nothing can express our reverence to God in prayer, that would pass for irreverence towards a great man. Let any subject tender his prince a petition fraught with nonsense and incoherence, confusion and impertinence, and can he expect that majesty should answer it with anything but a deaf ear, a frowning eye, or (at best,) vouchsafe it any other reward but, by a gracious oblivion, to forgive the person, and forget the petition?

2dly, Nothing absurd and irrational, and such as a wise man would despise, can be acceptable to God in prayer. Solomon expressly tells us in Ecclesiastes v:4, that "God has no pleasure in fools"; nor is it possible that an infinite wisdom should. The Scripture all along expresses sin and wickedness by the name of folly; and therefore certainly folly is too near of kin to it to find any approbation from God in so great a duty: it is the simplicity of the heart, and not of the head, that is the best inditer of our petitions. That which proceeds from the latter is undoubtedly the sacrifice of fools; and God is never more weary of sacrifice than when a fool is the priest, and folly the oblation.

3dly, and lastly, Nothing rude, slight, and careless, or indeed less than the very best that a man can offer, can be acceptable or pleasing to God in prayer. "If ye offer the blind for sacrifice, is it not evil? If ye offer the lame and the sick, is it not evil? Offer it now to thy governor, and see whether he will be pleased with thee, or accept thy person, saith the Lord of hosts." (Malachi 1:8.) God rigidly expects a return of his own gifts; and where he has given ability, will be served by acts proportionable to it. And he who has parts to raise and propagate his own honour by, but none to employ in the worship of him that gave them, does (as I may so express it) refuse to wear God's livery in his own service, adds sacrilege to profaneness, strips and starves his devotions, and, in a word, falls directly under the dint of that curse denounced in the last verse of the first of Malachi, "Cursed be the deceiver, that hath in his flock a male, and voweth, and sacrificeth to the Lord a corrupt thing." The same is here, both the deceiver and the deceived too; for God very well knows what he gives men, and why; and where he has bestowed judgment, learning, and utterance, will not endure that men should be inaccurate in their discourse, and loose in their devotions; or think that the great "author of every good and perfect gift" will be put off with ramble and confused talk, babble, and tautology.

And thus much for the order and disposition of our prayers, which certainly requires precedent thought and meditation. God has declared himself the God of order in all things, and will have it observed in what he commands others, as well as in what he does himself. Order is the great rule or art by which God made the world, and by which he still governs it: nay, the world itself is nothing else; and all this glorious system of things is but the chaos put into order: and how then can God, who has so eminently owned himself concerned for this excellent thing, brook such absurdity and confusion as the slovenly and profane negligence of some treats him with, in their most solemn addresses to him? All which is the natural, unavoidable consequent of unpreparedness and want of premeditation; without which, whosoever presumes to pray cannot be so properly said to approach to, as to break in upon God. And surely he who is so hardy as to do so, has no reason in the earth to expect that the success which follows his prayers should be greater than the preparation that goes before them.

Now from what has been hitherto discoursed

of, this first and grand qualification of a pious and devout prayer, to wit, premeditation of thought, what can be so naturally and so usefully inferred, as the high expediency, or rather the absolute necessity of a set form of prayer to guide our devotions by? We have lived in an age that has despised, contradicted, and counteracted all the principles and practices of the primitive Christians, in taking the measures of their duty both to God and man, and of their behaviour both in matters civil and religious; but in nothing more scandalously than in their vile abuse of the great duty of prayer; concerning which, though it may with the clearest truth be affirmed that there has been no church yet of any account in the Christian world, but what has governed its public worship of God by a liturgy or set form of prayer; yet these enthusiastic innovators, the bold and blind reformers of all antiquity, and wiser than the whole catholic church besides, introduced into the room of it a saucy, senseless, extemporary way of speaking to God; affirming that this was a praying by the Spirit; and that the use of all set forms was stinting of the Spirit. A pretence, I confess, popular and plausible enough with such idiots as take the sound of words for the sense of them. But for the full confutation of it (which, I hope, shall be done both easily and briefly too) I shall advance this one assertion in direct contradiction to that; namely,

That the praying by a set form is not a stinting of the Spirit, and the praying extempore truly and properly is so.

For the proving and making out of which, we will first consider what it is to pray by the Spirit: a thing much talked of, but not so convenient for the talkers of it, and pretenders to it, to have it rightly stated and understood. In short, it includes in it these two things:

1st, A praying with the heart, which is sometimes called the spirit, or inward man; and so it is properly opposed to hypocritical lip-devotions, in which the heart or spirit does not go along with a man's words.

2dly, It includes in it also a praying according to the rules prescribed by God's holy Spirit, and held forth to us in his revealed word, which word was both dictated and confirmed by this Spirit; and so it is opposed to the praying unlawfully, or unwarrantably, and that either in respect of the matter or manner of our prayers. As, when we desire of God such things, or in such a way, as the Spirit of God, speaking in his holy word, does by no means warrant or approve of. So that to pray by the Spirit, signifies neither more nor less but to pray knowingly, heartily, and affectionately for such things, and in such a manner, as the Holy Ghost in Scripture either commands or allows of. As for any other kind of praying by the Spirit, upon the best inquiry that I can make into these matters, I can find none. And if some say (as I know they both impudently and blasphemously do) that, to pray by the Spirit is to have the Spirit immediately inspiring them, and by such inspiration speaking within them, and so dictating their prayers to them, let them either produce plain Scripture, or do a miracle to prove this by. But till then, he who shall consider what kind of prayers these pretenders to the Spirit have been notable for, will find that they have as little cause to father their prayers, as their practices, upon the Spirit of God.

These two things are certain, and I do particularly recommend them to your observation. One, that this way of praying by the Spirit, as they call it, was begun and first brought into use here in England in Queen Elizabeth's days, by *a Popish priest and Dominican friar, one Faithful Commin by name; who, counterfeiting himself a Protestant, and a zealot of the highest form, set up this new spiritual way of praying, with a design to bring the people first to a contempt, and from thence to an utter hatred and disuse of our Common Prayer; which he still reviled as only a translation of the Mass, thereby to distract men's minds, and to divide our Church. And this he did with such success that we have lived to see the effects of his labours in the utter subversion of Church and State. Which hellish negotiation, when this malicious hypocrite came to Rome to give the Pope an account of, he received of him (as so notable a service well deserved), besides a thousand thanks, two thousand ducats for his pains. So that now you see here the original of this extempore way of praying by the Spirit. The other thing that I would observe to you is that in the neighbour nation of Scotland *one of the greatest monsters of men that, I believe, ever lived, and actually in league with the devil, was yet, by the confession of all that heard him, the most excellent at this extempore way of praying by the

Spirit of any man in his time; none was able to come near him, or to compare with him. But surely now, he who shall venture to ascribe the prayers of such a wretch, made up of adulteries, incest, witchcraft, and other villainies not to be named, to the Spirit of God, may as well strike in with the Pharisees, and ascribe the miracles of Christ to the devil. And thus having shown both what ought to be meant by praying by the Spirit, and what ought not, cannot be meant by it, let us now see whether a set form, or this extemporary way, be the greater hinderer and stinter of it: in order to which, I shall lay down these three assertions:

1st, That the soul or mind of man is but of a limited nature in all its workings, and consequently cannot supply two distinct faculties at the same time, to the same height of operation.

2dly, That the finding words and expressions for prayer is the proper business of the brain and the invention; and that the finding devotion and affection to accompany and go along with those expressions is properly the work and business of the heart.

3dly, That this devotion and affection is indispensably required in prayer, as the principal and most essential part of it, and that in which the spirituality of it does most properly consist.

Now from these three things put together, this must naturally and necessarily follow: that as spiritual prayer, or praying by the Spirit, taken in the right sense of the word, consists properly in that affection and devotion that the heart exercises and employs in the work of prayer, so, whatsoever gives the soul scope and liberty to exercise and employ this affection and devotion, that does most effectually help and enlarge the spirit of prayer; and whatsoever diverts the soul from employing such affection and devotion, that does most directly stint and hinder it. Accordingly, let this now be our rule whereby to judge of the efficacy of a set form, and of the extemporary way in the present business. As for a set form, in which the words are ready prepared to our hands, the soul has nothing to do but to attend to the work of raising the affections and devotions, to go along with those words, so that all the powers of the soul are took up in applying the heart to this great duty; and it is the exercise of the heart (as has been already shown) that is truly and properly a praying by the Spirit. On the contrary, in all extempore prayer the powers and faculties of the soul are called off from dealing with the heart and the affections; and that both in the speaker and in the hearer; both in him who makes, and in him who is to join in such prayers.

And first, for the minister who makes and utters such extempore prayers. He is wholly employing his invention, both to conceive matter, and to find words and expressions to clothe it in: this is certainly the work which takes up his mind in this exercise; and since the nature of man's mind is such that it can not with the same vigour, at the same time, attend the work of invention and that of raising the affections also, nor measure out the same supply of spirits and intention for the carrying on the operations of the head and those of the heart too, it is certain that, while the head is so much employed, the heart must be idle and very little employed, and perhaps not at all; and consequently, if to pray by the Spirit be to pray with the heart and the affections, it is also as certain that while a man prays extempore, he does not pray by the Spirit; nay, the very truth of it is that while he is so doing he is not praying at all, but he is studying; he is beating his brain, while he should be drawing out his affections.

And then for the people that are to hear and join with him in such prayers; it is manifest that they, not knowing beforehand what the minister will say, must, as soon as they do hear him, presently busy and bestir their minds both to apprehend and understand the meaning of what they hear; and withal, to judge whether it be of such a nature as to be fit for them to join and concur with him in. So that the people also are, by this course, put to study, and to employ their apprehending and judging faculties, while they should be exerting their affections and devotions; and consequently, by this means, the spirit of prayer is stinted, as well in the congregation that follows, as in the minister who first conceives a prayer after their extempore way: which is a truth so clear, and indeed self-evident that it is impossible that it should need any further arguments to demonstrate or make it out.

The sum of all this is that, since a set form of prayer leaves the soul wholly free to employ its affections and devotions, in which the spirit of prayer does most properly consist, it follows that the spirit of prayer is thereby, in a singular manner, helped, promoted, and enlarged; and since, on the other hand, the extempore way withdraws and takes off the soul from employing its affections, and engages it chiefly, if not wholly, about the use of its invention, it as plainly follows that the spirit of prayer is by this means unavoidably cramped and hindered, and (to use their own word) stinted: which was the proposition that I undertook to prove. But there are two things, I confess, that are extremely hindered and stinted by a set form of prayer, and equally furthered and enlarged by the extempore way; which, without all doubt, is the true cause why the former is so much decried and the latter so much extolled by the men whom we are now pleading with. The first of which is pride and ostentation; the other, faction and sedition.

1, And first for pride. I do not in the least question but the chief design of such as use the extempore way is to amuse the unthinking rabble with an admiration of their gifts, their whole devotion proceeding from no other principle but only love to hear themselves talk. And I believe it would put Lucifer himself hard to it, to outvie the pride of one of those fellows pouring out his extempore stuff amongst his ignorant, whining, factious followers, listening to, and applauding his copious flow and cant with the ridiculous accents of their impertinent groans. And, the truth is, extempore prayer, even when best and most dexterously performed, is nothing else but a business of invention and wit (such as it is), and requires no more to it but a teeming imagination, a bold front, and a ready expression; and deserves much the same commendation (were it not in a matter too serious to be sudden upon) which is due to extempore verses: only with this difference that there is necessary to these latter a competent measure of wit and learning, whereas the former may be done with very little wit, and no learning at all.

And now, can any sober person think it reasonable that the public devotions of a whole congregation should be under the conduct and at the mercy of a pert, empty, conceited holderforth, whose chief (if not sole) intent is to vaunt his spiritual clack, and (as I may so speak) to pray prizes; whereas prayer is a duty that recommends itself to the acceptance of Almighty God by no other qualification so much as by the profoundest humility and the lowest esteem that a man can possibly have of himself?

Certainly the extemporizing faculty is never more out of its element than in the pulpit; though even here it is much more excusable in a sermon than in a prayer; forasmuch as in that, a man addresses himself but to men — men like himself, whom he may therefore make bold with; as no doubt for so doing they will also make bold with him. Besides the peculiar advantage attending all such sudden conceptions, that, as they are quickly born, so they quickly die: it being seldom known, where the speaker has so very fluent an invention, but the hearer also has the gift of as fluent a memory.

2dly, The other thing that has been hitherto so little befriended by a set form of prayer, and so very much by the extempore way, is faction and sedition. It has been always found an excellent way of girding at the government in Scripture phrase. And we all know the common dialect in which the great masters of this art used to pray for the king, and which may justly pass for only a cleanlier and more refined kind of libelling him in the Lord. As, "that God would turn his heart, and open his eyes": as if he were a pagan yet to be converted to Christianity; with many other sly, virulent, and malicious insinuations, which we may every day hear of from (those mints of treason and rebellion) their conventicles; and for which, and a great deal less, some princes and governments would make them not only eat their words, but the tongue that spoke them too. In fine, let all their extempore harangues be considered and duly weighed, and you shall find a spirit of pride, faction, and sedition predominant in them all, the only spirit which those impostors do really and indeed pray by.

I have been so much the longer and the earnester against this intoxicating, bewitching cheat of extempore prayer, being fully satisfied in my conscience that it has been all along the devil's masterpiece and prime engine to overthrow our Church by. For I look upon this as a most unanswerable truth, that whatsoever renders the public worship of God contemptible amongst us must, in the same degree, weaken and discredit our whole religion. And I hope I have also proved it to be a truth altogether as clear that this extempore way naturally brings all the contempt upon the worship of God, that both the folly and faction of men can possibly expose it to: and therefore, as a thing neither subservient to the true purposes of religion, nor grounded upon principles of reason, nor, lastly, suitable to the practice of antiquity, ought by all means to be exploded and cast out of every sober and well-ordered Church; or that will be sure to throw the Church itself out of doors.

And thus I have at length finished what I had to say of the first ingredient of a pious and reverential prayer, which was premeditation of thought, prescribed in these words, "Let not thy mouth be rash, nor thy heart be hasty to utter anything before God." Which excellent words and most wise advice of Solomon, whosoever can reconcile to the expediency, decency, or usefulness of extempore prayer, I shall acknowledge him a man of greater ability and parts of mind than Solomon himself.

The other ingredient of a reverential and duly qualified prayer is a pertinent brevity of expression, mentioned and recommended in that part of the text, "Therefore let thy words be few." *But this I cannot dispatch now, and therefore shall not enter upon at this time.

"Now to God the Father, God the Son, and God the Holy Ghost, three Persons and one God, be rendered and ascribed, as is most due, all praise, might, majesty, and dominion, both now and for evermore." Amen.

[1717]

JOHN TILLOTSON

John Tillotson was the most popular English preacher during the generation after the Restoration. He was born in 1630, one year before Dryden, and died in 1694, six years before him. Like Dryden he came of Puritan stock, was educated at Cambridge, and came into prominence soon after 1660. Tillotson, though he abandoned his Presbyterian allegiance after the Savoy Conference and submitted to the Act of Uniformity, did not, like Dryden, move completely away from his earlier political and religious position. In theology he was a Low Church latitudinarian; favouring comprehension of the Nonconformists, he was more vigorous in his attacks upon "Popery" than upon Dissent. In 1664 he became preacher at Lincoln's Inn, where his pulpit eloquence soon made him famous. In spite of his Whig politics he was made Dean of Canterbury by Charles II; after the Revolution he was in high favour with William III, who made him Dean of St. Paul's. When Archbishop Sancroft refused to take the oaths of allegiance to William and Mary, Tillotson was offered the Archbishopric of Canterbury. Though he is said to have been reluctant to accept this position during the lifetime of the venerable incumbent, he yielded to solicitation and accepted the Primacy. For so doing he was violently assailed by the Nonjurors and was blamed by many of the more moderate Churchmen. Yet even his enemies have admitted that he was remarkably free from worldly ambition and self-assertiveness. He survived his new honours only about three years.

His sermons were effective in oral delivery but had a much greater influence in their printed form. At a time when sermons were one of the most important forms of polite literature, Tillotson's were regarded as models. Shortly after his death the copyright of two volumes of his pulpit discourses was sold for the enormous sum of 2500 guineas. Though this popularity has long since faded — even by Johnson's time it had become dim — it has given Tillotson's name a place of importance among English prose writers. Congreve's statement in the Dedication of Dryden's *Dramatic Works* has been often quoted and is remembered in our day by multitudes who have never turned the yellowed pages of the folios in which Tillotson's sermons are preserved. "I have heard him [Dryden] frequently own with pleasure that if he had any talent for English prose, it was owing to his having often read the writings of the great Archbishop Tillotson." Whether or not Dryden's generous appreciation led him to overestimate the extent of this influence, there can be no doubt that Tillotson was one of the first writers of his day to make use of the new English prose, that simpler and more direct expression, with choice but familiar words arranged in workmanlike sentences, which had succeeded the fantastic language and magnificent but involved periods of the earlier part of the seventeenth century. Saintsbury, though disposed to minimize the claim that Tillotson was Dryden's teacher, ranks him with Dryden, Halifax, and Temple among the chief introducers of this new prose, "and as perhaps the most influential (in virtue of the potency of his special form on the literary habits of the nation) of the four. But he will, I think, rank as the least of them in original literary quality and in literary accomplishment within his own limits."

Tillotson's works will never again be popular. Few forms of literature age so fast as sermons; though religion may not change, it has to be interpreted afresh to every generation. But as historical documents his sermons are of immense value in understanding the spirit of the generation for which they were written and by which they were admired. The selection here given is the latter part of *A Thanksgiving Sermon for the Late Victory at Sea*, preached before the king and queen at Whitehall, October 27, 1692.

From SERMON XLI. A THANKSGIVING SERMON FOR THE LATE VICTORY AT SEA

Jer. IX:23, 24. *Thus saith the Lord, Let not the wise man glory in his wisdom, neither let the mighty man glory in his might, let not the rich man glory in his riches: But let him that glorieth, glory in this, that he understandeth and knoweth me, that I am the Lord which exercise lovingkindness, judgment, and righteousness in the earth: for in these things I delight, saith the Lord.

... The other inference is this, that the nature of God is the true idea and pattern of perfection and happiness; and therefore nothing but our own conformity to it can make us happy, and for this reason: to understand and know God is our great excellency and glory, because it is necessary to our imitation of him who is the best and happiest being. And so far as we are from resembling God, so far are we distant from happiness, and the true temper of the blessed. For goodness

* Notes on John Tillotson will be found in the Appendix, p. 964.

is an essential ingredient of happiness; and as without goodness there can be no true majesty and greatness, so neither any true felicity and blessedness.

Now goodness is a generous disposition of mind to diffuse and communicate itself by making others to partake of our happiness in such degrees as they are capable, for no being is so happy as it might be, that hath not the power and the pleasure to make others happy; this surely is the highest pleasure, I had almost said pride, of a great mind.

In vain, therefore, do we dream of happiness in anything without us. Happiness must be within us; the foundation of it must be laid in the inward frame and disposition of our spirits; and the very same causes and ingredients which make up the happiness of God must be found in us, though in a much inferior degree, or we cannot be happy. They understand not the nature of happiness, who hope for it upon any other terms: he who is the author and fountain of happiness cannot convey it to us by any other way than by planting in us such dispositions of mind as are in truth a kind of participation of the divine nature, and by enduing us with such qualities as are the necessary materials of happiness; and a man may as soon be well without health as happy without goodness.

If a wicked man were taken up into heaven, yet if he still continue the same bad man that he was before, * *cœlum non animum mutavit*, he may have changed the climate, and be gone into a far country; but because he carries himself still along with him, he will still be miserable from himself, because the man's mind is not changed all the while, which would signify a thousand times more to his happiness than change of place, or of any outward circumstances whatsoever, for a bad man hath a fiend in his own breast, and the fuel of hell in his guilty conscience.

There is a certain kind of temper and disposition which is necessary and essential to happiness, and that is holiness and goodness, which is the very nature of God; and so far as any man departs from this temper, so far he removes himself and runs away from happiness. And here the foundation of hell is laid, in the evil disposition of a man's own mind, which is naturally a torment to itself; and till this be cured, it is as impossible for him to be happy, as for a limb that is out of joint to be at ease, because the man's spirit is out of order, and off the hinges, and as it were tossed from its centre; and till that be set right and restored to its proper and natural state, the man will be perpetually unquiet, and can have no rest and peace within himself. "The wicked," saith the prophet, "is like the troubled sea, when it cannot rest: 'There is no peace,' saith my God, 'to the wicked,'" no peace with God, no peace with his own mind; for a bad man is at perpetual discord and wars within himself, and hence, as St. James tells us, "come wars and fightings without us, even from our own lusts, which war in our members."

And now that I have mentioned "wars and fightings without us," this cannot but bring to mind *the great and glorious occasion of this day, which gives us manifold cause of praise and thanksgiving to Almighty God, for several wonderful mercies and deliverances, and more particularly, for a most glorious victory at sea, vouchsafed to their majesties' fleet in this last summer's expedition.

For several great mercies and deliverances: for a wonderful deliverance indeed, from a sudden invasion designed upon us by the inveterate and implacable enemies of our peace and religion; which by the merciful providence of God was happily and strangely prevented, when it was just upon the point of execution.

Next for the preservation of our gracious sovereign, from *that horrid and most barbarous attempt designed upon his sacred person; and from those great and manifold dangers to which he was exposed in his late tedious expedition; and for his safe and most welcome return to us.

And lastly, for a most glorious victory at sea, the greatest and the cheapest that ever the sun saw, from his first setting out to run his course. The opportunity indeed of this victory was through the rashness and confidence of our enemies, by the wise providence of God, put into our hands; but the improvement of this opportunity into so great and happy a victory, we owe under God, to the matchless conduct and courage of the brave admiral, and to the invincible resolution and valour of the captains and seamen.

This great deliverance from the designed invasion, and this glorious victory God vouchsafed to us at home, whilst his sacred majesty was so freely hazarding his royal person abroad, in the public cause of the rights and liberties of almost all Europe.

And now what may God justly expect from us, as a meet return for his goodness to us? What, but that we should glorify him, first by offering praise and thanksgiving; and then, by ordering our conversation aright that he may still delight to show us his salvation?

God might have stood aloof from us in the day of our distress, and have said to us as he once did to the people of Israel, "So often have I delivered you from the hands of your enemies, but ye have still provoked me more and more; wherefore I will deliver you no more": he might have said of us, as he did of the same people, "I will hide my face from them; I will see what their end shall be; for they are a very froward generation, children in whom is no faith." Our resolutions and promises of better obedience are not to be trusted; all our repentance and righteousness are but "as the morning-cloud, and like the early dew that passeth away": nay, methinks God seems now to say to us, as he did of old to Jerusalem, "Be instructed, O Jerusalem, lest my soul depart from thee, and I make thee desolate, a land not inhabited."

We are here met together this day to pay our solemn acknowledgments to "the God of our salvation, who hath showed strength with his arm, and hath scattered the proud in the imagination of their heart": even to "him that exerciseth loving-kindness, and judgment, and righteousness in the earth": in him will we glory as our sure refuge and defence, as our mighty deliverer, and the rock of our salvation.

And now I have only to entreat your patience a little longer, whilst I apply what hath been discoursed upon this text a little more closely to the occasion of this day. I may be tedious, but I will not be long.

And blessed be God for this happy occasion: the greatest England ever had, and, in the true consequences of it, perhaps the greatest that Europe ever had of praise and thanksgiving.

You have heard two sorts of persons described in the text, by very different characters: the one, that glory in their wisdom, and might and riches; the other, that "glory in this, that" they "understand and know God to be the Lord, which exerciseth loving-kindness, and judgment, and righteousness in the earth."

And we have seen * these two characters exemplified, or rather drawn to the life, in this present age. We who live in this western part of Christendom have seen a mighty prince, by the just permission of God raised up to be a terror and scourge to all his neighbours: a prince who had in perfection all the advantages mentioned in the former part of the text; and who, in the opinion of many who had been long dazzled with his splendour and greatness, hath passed for many years for the most politic and powerful and richest monarch that hath appeared in these parts of the world for many ages.

Who hath governed his affairs by the deepest and steadiest counsels, and the most refined wisdom of this world: a prince mighty and powerful in his preparations for war; formidable for his vast and well disciplined armies, and for his great naval force; and who had brought the art of war almost to that perfection, as to be able to conquer and do his business without fighting, a mystery hardly known to former ages and generations: and all this skill and strength united under one absolute will, not hampered or bound up by any restraints of law or conscience.

A prince that commands the estates of all his subjects, and of all his conquests, which hath furnished him with an almost inexhaustible treasure and revenue; and one who, if the world doth not greatly mistake him, hath sufficiently gloried in all these advantages, and even beyond the rate of a mortal man.

But not "knowing God to be the Lord, which exercises loving-kindness and judgment and righteousness in the earth"; how hath the pride of all his glory been stained by tyranny and oppression, by injustice and cruelty; by enlarging his dominions without right, and by making war upon his neighbours without reason, or even colour of provocation? And this in a more barbarous manner than the most barbarous nations ever did; carrying fire and desolation wheresoever he went, and laying waste many and great cities without necessity and without pity.

And now behold what a terrible rebuke the providence of God hath given to this mighty monarch, in the full career of his fortune and fury. The consideration whereof brings to my thoughts those passages in the prophet concerning old Babylon, that standing and perpetual type of the great oppressors and persecutors of God's true church and religion: "How is the oppressor ceased? the exacter of gold ceased? he who smote the people in wrath with a continual stroke, he who ruled the nations in anger is himself persecuted, and none hindereth. The whole earth is at rest and is quiet, and breaks forth into singing: the grave beneath is moved for thee, to meet thee at thy coming; it stirreth up the dead for thee, even all the captains of the earth; it hath raised up from their thrones all the kings of the nations; all they shall speak and say unto thee, 'Art thou also become weak as we are? art thou also become like unto us? how art thou fallen from heaven, O Lucifer, son of the morning? how art thou cut down to the ground that didst weaken the nations? For thou hast said in thy heart, "I will ascend into heaven, I will exalt my throne above the stars of God: I will sit also upon the mount of the congregation in the sides of the north"'"—that is, upon Mount Zion; for just so the Psalmist describes it: "Beautiful for situation, the joy of the whole earth is Mount Zion, on the sides of the north." Here the king of Babylon threatens to take Jerusalem, and to demolish the temple where the congregation of Israel met for the worship of the true God: "I will also sit upon the mount of the congregation in the sides of the north." Much in the same style with the threatenings of modern Babylon, "I will destroy the reformation, I will extirpate the northern heresy."

And then he goes on, "'I will ascend above the height of the clouds, I will be like the most High': yet thou shalt be brought down to the grave, to the sides of the pit; they that see thee shall narrowly look upon thee, and consider thee, saying, 'Is this the man that made the earth to tremble, that did shake kingdoms; that made the world as a wilderness and destroyed the cities thereof, and opened not the house of his prisoners?'"

God seems already to have begun this work in the late glorious victory at sea; and I hope he will "cut it short in righteousness." I have sometimes heretofore wondered why at the destruction of modern and mystical Babylon the Scripture should make so express mention of great wailing and lamentation for the loss of her ships and seamen; little imagining, thirty years ago, that any of the kingdoms who had "given their power to the beast," would ever have arrived to that mighty naval force, but the "Scripture saith nothing in vain."

Whether, and how far, success is an argument of a good cause, I shall not now debate; but thus much, I think, may safely be affirmed that the providence of God doth sometimes, without plain and downright miracles, so visibly show itself that we cannot without great stupidity and obstinacy refuse to acknowledge it.

I grant, the cause must first be manifestly just before success can be made an argument of God's favour to it and approbation of it: and if the cause of true religion, and the necessary defence of it against a false and idolatrous worship, be a good cause, ours is so, and I do not here beg the question; we have abundantly proved it to the confusion of our adversaries: if the vindication of the common liberties of mankind against tyranny and oppression be a good cause, then ours is so; and this needs not to be proved: it is so glaringly evident to all the world. And as our cause is not like theirs; so neither hath "their rock" been "like our rock, our enemies themselves being judges."

And yet as bad an argument as success is of a good cause, I am sorry to say it, but I am afraid it is true, it is like in the conclusion to prove the best argument of all other to convince * those who have so long pretended conscience against submission to the present government.

Mere success is certainly one of the worst arguments in the world of a good cause, and the most improper to satisfy conscience; and yet we find by experience that in the issue it is the most successful of all other arguments; and does in a very odd, but effectual way, satisfy the consciences of a great many men by showing them their interest.

God has of late visibly made bare his arm on our behalf; though some are still so blind and obstinate that they will not see it, like those of whom the prophet complains, "Lord, when thy hand is lifted up they will not see, but they shall see, and be ashamed for their envy at thy people."

Thus have I represented unto you a mighty monarch who, like a fiery comet, hath hung over Europe for many years, and by his malignant influence hath made such terrible havoc and devastations in this part of the world.

Let us now turn our view to the other part of the text, and behold a greater than he is here: a prince of a quite different character, who does "understand and know God to be the Lord which doth exercise loving-kindness and judgment and righteousness in the earth"; and who hath made it the great study and endeavour of his life to imitate these divine perfections, as far as the imperfection of human nature in this mortal state will admit: I say a greater than he is here who never said or did an insolent thing, but instead of despising his enemies, has upon all occasions encountered them with an undaunted spirit and resolution.

This is the man whom God hath honoured to give a check to this mighty man of the earth, and to put a hook into the nostrils of this great Leviathan, who has so long had his pastime in the seas

But we will not insult, as he once did in a most unprincely manner over a man much better than himself when he *believed him to have been slain at the Boyne: and indeed death came then as near to him as was possible without killing him; but the merciful providence of God was pleased to step in for his preservation, almost by a miracle: for I do not believe that from the first use of great guns to that day, any mortal man ever had his shoulder so kindly kissed by a cannon bullet.

But I will not trespass any further upon that which is the great ornament of all his other virtues; though I have said nothing of him but what all the world does see and must acknowledge: *he is as much above being flattered as it is beneath an honest and generous mind to flatter.

Let us then glory in the Lord, and rejoice in the God of our salvation: let us now in the presence of all his people pay our most thankful acknowledgments to him "who is worthy to be praised," even to "the Lord God of Israel, who alone doth wondrous things," who "giveth victory unto kings," and hath "preserved" our "David his servant from the hurtful sword."

And let us humbly beseech Almighty God that he would long preserve to us the valuable blessing of our two excellent princes, whom the providence of God hath sent amongst us, like two good angels; not to rescue two or three persons, but almost a whole nation out of Sodom; by saving us, I hope, at last from our vices, as well as at first from that vengeance which was just ready to have been poured down upon us.

*Two sovereign princes reigning together, and in the same throne, and yet so entirely one as perhaps no nation, no age, can furnish us with a parallel: two princes perfectly united in the same design of promoting the true religion and the public welfare, by reforming our manners, and, as far as is possible, by repairing the breaches, and healing the divisions of a miserably distracted church and nation: in a word, two princes who are contented to sacrifice themselves and their whole time to the care of the public, and for the sake of that to deny themselves almost all sorts of ease and pleasure: to deny themselves, did I say? No, they have wisely and judiciously chosen the truest and highest pleasure that this world knows, the pleasure of doing good and being benefactors to mankind. May they have a long and happy reign over us, to make us happy, and to lay up in store for themselves a happiness without measure and without end, in God's glorious and everlasting kingdom: for his mercy's sake in Jesus Christ, to whom, with thee, O Father, and the Holy Ghost, be all honour and glory, thanksgiving and praise, both now and forever. Amen.

[1717]

THOMAS RYMER

ENGLISH literary criticism, like the English Constitution and the English Church, has generally taken the middle way between extremes; it has reconciled opposites and mediated between conflicting claims of opposing theories and between scarcely less hostile demands of theory and practice. Its characteristic virtues have been discrimination, balanced judgment, tempered opinion. This middle way in criticism has been taken not only because opposing parties and schools of thought have checked each other's extremes, but also because the best minds have usually been comprehensive, if not tolerant. Thomas Rymer is an exception to this tendency: with uncompromising logic he pursued an undeviating course no matter whither it led him. He was assertive, dogmatic, truculent, and so consistent that his conclusions have offended even when they were not manifestly wrong.

Educated at Cambridge University, he became a barrister at Gray's Inn, but was more interested in literature and criticism than in law. He read widely, and early familiarized himself with the work of the chief continental critics, from whom he imbibed the principles of Aristotelian formalism. In 1674 he published a translation of Père Rapin's *Reflections on Aristotle's Treatise of Poesie*, with a critical preface which gave him a high reputation. Four years later he published *The Tragedies of the Last Age Considered and Examined by the Practice of the Ancients and by the Common Sense of all Ages*. Here he criticizes some of the plays of Beaumont and Fletcher most severely, subjecting them to a careful analysis such as had rarely been applied before this time to any English poetry. As the title indicates, his criteria are "the practice of the ancients" and "the common sense of all ages." Of these he gives major emphasis to the second. He values ancient authority and neo-classical rule chiefly because they embody the common or general sense. His first demand is that the poet follow nature, by which he means the rational order characteristic of a well-governed world.

In 1693 he published *A Short View of Tragedy; Its Original, Excellency, and Corruption, with some Reflections on Shakespeare and Other Practitioners for the Stage*. This is the work that has most frequently been remembered to Rymer's discredit because of his vigorous and whole-hearted condemnation of Shakespeare. When neo-classical critical principles came to be generally accepted after the Restoration, the estimate of the Elizabethans, and especially of Shakespeare, involved particular difficulty, since it was obvious that most of their works had either ignored or run counter to the rules. The problem for Dryden and other discriminating critics was to reconcile the undoubted beauties of Shakespeare with the rules, or at least with the neo-classical system of which the rules were the most positive form of expression. Difficult as was this problem of historical judgment, it was intensified by the use to which the precedent of Shakespeare was being put by the more careless contemporary writers, who were citing it to justify almost any lapse from unity or propriety. To Rymer compromise was hateful. Any work which did not conform to right reason and the general sense must be condemned; even Shakespeare must be measured by these standards. So viewed, Rymer's attacks are evidence of the high regard in which Shakespeare was held at this time.

Rymer's method was direct and vigorous. He examined particular plays in accordance with the Aristotelian principles as interpreted by the Italian and French commentators, laying special emphasis on decorum and poetic justice. He had learning, dogmatic assurance, a homely, picturesque style, and rough, slashing methods of attack. Though his principal contemporaries, such as Dryden, Gildon, Dennis, disagreed with many of his conclusions, especially about Shakespeare, they respected him as a critic. Pope condemned his severity but described him as "on the whole, one of the best critics we ever had." Johnson's comparison of Dryden and Rymer as critics is included in the extract from *The Lives of the Poets*. With the ascendancy of the romantic movement, Rymer has been held up to ridicule, and there has been common assent to Macaulay's dictum that this contemner of Shakespeare was "the worst critic that ever lived." To the discriminating student who reads with historical perspective, Rymer's criticism is interesting as an extreme application of the principles of Aristotelian formalism, rare in England.

His estimate of Shakespeare throws light upon the appreciation characteristic of English criticism from Dryden to Johnson. Even apart from this historical importance, Rymer has some value for the student today; for in spite of his intemperance, his distortion, and his evident blindness to the most important aspects of Shakespeare's greatness, he does point out some real flaws. As a corrective to the equally extravagant panegyrics of the Shakespeare worshippers of the last generation, he has his place. The extract here reprinted includes the first and the last parts of Chapter VII of *A Short View of Tragedy*.

A SHORT VIEW OF TRAGEDY

Chapter VII

From all the tragedies acted on our English stage, *Othello* is said to bear the bell away. The subject is more of a piece, and there is indeed something like, there is, as it were, some phantom of a fable. The fable is always accounted the soul of tragedy. And it is the fable which is properly the poet's part. Because the other three parts of tragedy, to wit, the characters are taken from the moral philosopher; the thoughts, or sense, from them that teach rhetoric; and the last part, which is expression, we learn from the grammarians.

This fable is drawn from a novel composed in Italian by Giraldi Cinthio, who also was a writer of tragedies, and to that use employed such of his tales as he judged proper for the stage. But with this of the Moor he meddled no farther.

Shakespeare alters it from the original in several particulars, but always, unfortunately, for the worse. He bestows a name on his Moor, and styles him the Moor of Venice — a note of pre-eminence which neither history nor heraldry can allow him. Cinthio, who knew him best, and whose creature he was, calls him simply a Moor. We say the Piper of Strasbourg, the Jew of Florence, and, if you please, the Pindar of Wakefield, all upon record, and memorable in their places. But we see no such cause for the Moor's preferment to that dignity. And it is an affront to all chroniclers and antiquaries to top upon 'em a Moor, with that mark of renown, who yet had never fallen within the sphere of their cognizance.

Then is the Moor's wife, from a simple citizen in Cinthio, dressed up with her top knots, and raised to be Desdemona, a senator's daughter. All this is very strange, and therefore pleases such as reflect not on the improbability. This match might well be without the parent's consent. Old Horace long ago forbade the banns:

> * *Sed non ut placidis cœant immitia, non ut*
> *Serpentes avibus geminentur, tigribus agni.*

The Fable

Othello, a blackamoor captain, by talking of his prowess and feats of war, makes Desdemona, a senator's daughter, to be in love with him, and to be married to him without her parent's knowledge; and having preferred Cassio to be his lieutenant, a place which his ensign, Iago, sued for, Iago in revenge works the Moor into a jealousy that Cassio cuckolds him, which he effects by stealing and conveying a certain handkerchief which had at the wedding been by the Moor presented to his bride. Hereupon Othello and Iago plot the deaths of Desdemona and Cassio. Othello murders her, and soon after is convinced of her innocence. And as he is about to be carried to prison in order to be punished for the murder, he kills himself.

Whatever rubs or difficulty may stick on the bark, the moral, sure, of this fable is very instructive.

First, this may be a caution to all maidens of quality how, without their parents' consent, they run away with blackamoors.

> * *Di non si accompagnare con huomo cui la natura e il cielo e il modo della vita disgiunge da noi.* — Cinthio.

Secondly, this may be a warning to all good wives that they look well to their linen.

Thirdly, this may be a lesson to husbands that before their jealousy be tragical the proofs may be mathematical.

Cinthio affirms that she was not overcome by a womanish appetite, but by the virtue of the Moor. It must be a good-natured reader that takes Cinthio's word in this case, though in a novel. Shakespeare, who is accountable both to the eyes and to the ears, and to convince the very heart of an audience, shows that Desdemona was won by hearing Othello talk.

> *Othello.* I spake of most disastrous chances,
> Of moving accidents by flood and field,
> Of hair-breadth scapes i' th' imminent deadly breach,
> Of being taken by the insolent foe,
> And sold to slavery, of my redemption thence,
> And portents in my travel's history;
> Wherein of antres vast and deserts idle,
> Rough quarries, rocks, and hills whose heads touch heaven,
> It was my hint to speak, — such was my process—
> *And of the cannibals that each others eat,
> The Anthropophagi, and men whose heads
> Do grow beneath their shoulders.

This was the charm, this was the philtre, the love-powder, that took the daughter of this noble Venetian. This was sufficient to make the blackamoor white, and reconcile all, though there had been a cloven-foot into the bargain.

A meaner woman might be as soon taken by *Aqua Tetrachymagogon.

* Notes on Thomas Rymer will be found in the Appendix, pp. 964 ff.

Nodes, cataracts, tumours, chilblains, carnosity, shankers, or any cant in the bill of an High German doctor is as good fustian circumstance, and as likely to charm a senator's daughter. But, it seems, the noble Venetians have another sense of things. The Doge himself tells us:

Doge. I think this tale would win my daughter too.

Horace tells us:

**Intererit multum —*
Colchus an Assyrius, Thebis nutritus an Argis.

Shakespeare in this play calls them the supersubtle Venetians. Yet examine throughout the tragedy, there is nothing in the noble Desdemona that is not below any country chambermaid with us.

And the account he gives of their noblemen and senate can only be calculated for the *latitude of Gotham.

The character of that state is to employ strangers in their wars; but shall a poet thence fancy that they will set a negro to be their general, or trust a Moor to defend them against the Turk? With us a blackamoor might rise to be a trumpeter; but Shakespeare would not have him less than a lieutenant-general. With us a Moor might marry some little drab or small-coal wench; Shakespeare would provide him the daughter and heir of some great lord or privy-councillor: and all the town should reckon it a very suitable match. Yet the English are not bred up with that hatred and aversion to the Moors as are the Venetians, who suffer by a perpetual hostility from them,

**Littora littoribus contraria.*

Nothing is more odious in nature than an improbable lie; and certainly never was any play fraught like this of *Othello* with improbabilities.

The characters or manners, which are the second part in a tragedy, are not less unnatural and improper than the fable was improbable and absurd.

Othello is made a Venetian general. We see nothing done by him nor related concerning him that comports with the condition of a general, or indeed of a man, unless the killing himself to avoid a death the law was about to inflict upon him. When his jealousy had wrought him up to a resolution of his taking revenge for the supposed injury, he sets Iago to the fighting part to kill Cassio, and chooses himself to murder the silly woman, his wife, that was like to make no resistance.

His love and his jealousy are no part of a soldier's character, unless for comedy.

But what is most intolerable is Iago. He is no blackamoor soldier; so we may be sure he should be like other soldiers of our acquaintance; yet never in tragedy, nor in comedy, nor in nature, was a soldier with his character; take it in the author's own words:

Em. —— some eternal villain,
Some busy and insinuating rogue.
Some cogging, cozening slave, to get some office.

Horace describes a soldier otherwise:

**Impiger, iracundus, inexorabilis, acer.*

Shakespeare knew his character of Iago was inconsistent. In this very play he pronounces:

If thou dost deliver more or less than truth,
Thou art no soldier.

This he knew; but to entertain the audience with something new and surprising, against common sense and nature, he would pass upon us a close, dissembling, false, insinuating rascal instead of an open-hearted, frank, plain-dealing soldier, a character constantly worn by them for some thousands of years in the world.

Tiberius Cæsar had a poet arraigned for his life, because Agamemnon was brought upon the stage by him with a character unbecoming a soldier.

Our ensigns and subalterns, when disgusted by the captain, throw up their commissions, bluster, and are barefaced. Iago, I hope, is not brought on the stage in a red coat. I know not what livery the Venetians wear, but am sure they hold not these conditions to be * *alla soldatesca.*

**Non sia egli per far la vendetta con insidie, ma con la spada in mano.* — Cinthio.

Nor is our poet more discreet in his Desdemona. He had chosen a soldier for his knave, and a Venetian lady is to be the fool.

This senator's daughter runs away to a carrier's inn, the Sagittary, with a blackamoor; is no sooner wedded to him, but the very night she beds him is importuning and teasing him for a young smock-faced lieutenant, Cassio. And though she perceives the Moor jealous of Cassio, yet will she not forbear, but still rings "Cassio, Cassio," in both his ears.

Roderigo is the cully of Iago, brought in to be murdered by Iago, that Iago's hands might be the more in blood, and be yet the more abominable villain, who without that was too wicked on all conscience, and had more to answer for than any tragedy or furies could inflict upon him. So there can be nothing in the characters either for the profit or to delight an audience.

The third thing to be considered is the thoughts. But from such characters we need not expect many that are either true or fine or noble.

And without these, that is, without sense or meaning, the fourth part of tragedy, which is the expression, can hardly deserve to be treated on distinctly. The verse rumbling in our ears are of good use to help off the action.

In the neighing of an horse, or in the growling of a mastiff, there is a meaning, there is as lively expression; and, may I say, more humanity, than many times in the tragical flights of Shakespeare?

* Step then amongst the scenes to observe the conduct in this tragedy....

Then, after a little spurt of villainy and murder, we are brought to the most lamentable that ever appeared on any stage. A noble Venetian lady is to be murdered by our poet, in sober sadness, purely for being a fool. No pagan poet but would have found * some machine for her deliverance. Pegasus would have strained hard to have brought old Perseus on his back, time enough to rescue this Andromeda from so foul a monster. Has our Christian poetry no generosity, nor bowels? Ha, Sir Lancelot! ha, St. George! will no ghost leave the shades for us in extremity to save a distressed damosel?

But for our comfort, however felonious is the heart, hear with what soft language he does approach her, with a candle in his hand:

Oth. Put out the light, and then put out the light:
If I quench thee, thou flaming minister,
I can again thy former light restore.

Who would call him barbarian, monster, savage? Is this a blackamoor?

* *Soles occidere et redire possunt* —

* The very soul and quintessence of Sir George Etherege!

One might think the general should not glory much in this action, but make an hasty work on't, and have turned his eyes away from so unsoldierly an execution; yet is he all pause and deliberation, handles her as calmly and is as careful of her soul's health as it had been her father confessor. "Have you prayed tonight, Desdemona?" But the suspense is necessary that he might have a convenient while so to roll his eyes, and so to gnaw his nether lip to the spectators. Besides the greater cruelty, * *sub tam lentis maxillis*.

But, hark, a most tragical thing laid to her charge!

Oth. That handkerchief, that I so loved and gave thee,
Thou gav'st to Cassio.
Des. No, by my life and soul!
Send for the man, and ask him.
Oth. By heaven, I saw my handkerchief in his hand.
——— I saw the handkerchief.

So much ado, so much stress, so much passion and repetition about an handkerchief! Why was not this called the *Tragedy of the Handkerchief*? What can be more absurd than (as Quintilian expresses it) * *in parvis litibus has tragœdias movere*? We have heard of *Fortunatus his Purse* and of the invisible cloak, long ago worn threadbare and stowed up in the wardrobe of obsolete romances; one might think that were a fitter place for this handkerchief than that it, at this time of day be worn on the stage, to raise everywhere all this clutter and turmoil. Had it been Desdemona's garter, the sagacious Moor might have smelt a rat; but the handkerchief is so remote a trifle, no booby on this side Mauretania could make any consequence from it.

We may learn here that a woman never loses her tongue, even though after she is stifled:

Desd. Oh, falsely, falsely murdered!
Em. Sweet Desdemona, oh, sweet mistress speak!
Desd. A guiltless death I die.
Em. Oh, who has done the deed?
Desd. Nobody; I myself; farewell:
Commend me to my kind lord; oh, farewell!

This Desdemona is a black swan, or an old blackamoor is a bewitching bedfellow. If this be nature, it is a * *lâcheté* below what the English language can express.

For * Lardella to make love like an humblebee was, in *The Rehearsal*, thought a fancy odd enough.

But hark what follows:

Oth. ——— Oh, heavy hour!
Methinks it should be now a huge eclipse
Of sun and moon, and that the affrighted globe
Should yawn at alteration.

This is wonderful! Here is poetry to elevate and amuse. Here is sound all sufficient. It would be uncivil to ask * Flamsteed if the sun and moon can both together be so hugely eclipsed in any heavy hour whatsoever. Nor must the spectators consult * Gresham College whether a body is naturally frighted till he yawn again. The fortune of Greece is not concerned with these matters. These are physical circumstances a poet may be ignorant in, without any harm to the public. These slips have no influence on our manners and good life, which are the poet's province.

Rather may we ask here what unnatural crime Desdemona or her parents had committed, to bring this judgment down upon her: to wed a blackamoor, and, innocent, to be thus cruelly murdered by him? What instruction can we make out of this catastrophe? Or whither must our reflection lead us? Is not this to envenom and sour our spirits, to make us repine and grumble at Providence and the government of the world? If this be our end, what boots it to be virtuous?

Desdemona dropped the handkerchief, and missed it that very day after her marriage; it might have been rumpled up with her wedding sheets; and this night that she lay in her wedding sheets, the fairy napkin (whilst Othello was stifling her) might have started up to disarm his fury and stop his ungracious mouth. Then might she, in a trance for fear, have lain as dead. Then might he, believing her dead, touched with remorse, have honestly cut his own throat, by the good leave and with the applause of all the spectators, who might thereupon have gone home with a quiet mind, admiring the beauty of Providence, fairly and truly represented on the theatre.

Oth. ——— Why, how should she be murdered?
Em. Alas, who knows?
Oth. You heard her say herself, it was not I.
Em. She did so; I must needs report a truth.
Oth. She's, like a liar, gone to burn in hell.
'Twas I that did it.
Em. Oh, the more angel she,
And you the blacker devil!
Oth. She turned to folly, and she was an whore.
Em. Thou dost belie her, and thou art a devil.
Oth. She was false as water.
Em. Thou art rash as fire,
To say that she was false: oh, she was heavenly true.

In this kind of dialogue they continue for forty lines farther, before she bethinks herself to cry murder.

Em. ——— Help, help, oh, help!
The Moor has killed my mistress! Murder, murder!

But from this scene to the end of the play we meet with nothing but blood and butchery, described much-what to the style of the last speeches and confessions of the persons executed at Tyburn, with this difference, that there we have the fact and the due course of justice; whereas our poet, against all justice and reason, against all law, humanity, and nature, in a barbarous, arbitrary way, executes and makes havoc of his subjects, habnab, as they come to hand. Desdemona dropped her handkerchief; therefore she must be stifled. Othello, by law to be broken on the wheel, by the poet's cunning escapes with cutting his own throat. Cassio, for I know not what, comes off with a broken shin. Iago murders his benefactor, Roderigo, as this were poetical gratitude. Iago is not yet killed, because there yet never was such a villain alive. The devil, if once he brings a man to be dipped in a deadly sin, lets him alone to take his course; and now when the foul fiend has done with him, our wise authors take the sinner into their poetical service, there to accomplish him and do the devil's drudgery.

Philosophy tells us it is a principle in the nature of man to be grateful.

History may tell us that * John an Oaks, John a Stiles, or Iago were ungrateful. Poetry is to follow nature; philosophy must be his guide: history and fact in particular cases of John an Oaks or John a Stiles are no warrant or direction for a poet. Therefore Aristotle is always telling us that poetry is * *σπουδαιότερον και φιλοσοφώτερον*, is more general and abstracted, is led more by the philosophy, the reason and nature of things than history, which only records things higgledy-piggledy, right or wrong, as they happen. History might without any preamble or difficulty say that Iago was ungrateful. Philosophy then calls him unnatural. But the poet is, not without huge labour and preparation, to expose the monster, and after show the divine vengeance executed upon him. The poet is not to add wilful murder to his ingratitude; he has not antidote enough for the poison; his hell and furies are not punishment sufficient for one single crime of that bulk and aggravation.

Em. O thou dull Moor, that handkerchief thou speakest on
I found by fortune and did give my husband;
For often with a solemn earnestness,
More than indeed belong'd to such a trifle,
He begg'd of me to steal it.

Here we see the meanest woman in the play takes this handkerchief for a trifle below her husband to trouble his head about it. Yet we find it entered into our poet's head to make a tragedy of this trifle.

Then, for the unravelling of the plot, as they call it, never was old deputy recorder in a country town, with his spectacles, in summoning up the evidence, at such a puzzle, so blundered and bedoltefied as is our poet to have a good riddance and get the catastrophe off his hands.

What can remain with the audience to carry home with them from this sort of poetry for their use and edification? How can it work, unless (instead of settling the mind and purging our passions) to delude our senses, disorder our thoughts, addle our brain, pervert our affections, *hare our imaginations, corrupt our appetite, and fill our head with vanity, confusion, *tintamarre, and jingle-jangle beyond what all the parish clerks of London with their Old Testament farces and interludes, in Richard the Second's time could ever pretend to? Our only hopes for the good of their souls can be that these people go to the playhouse as they do to church, to sit still, look on one another, make no reflection, nor mind the play more than they would a sermon.

There is in this play some burlesque, some humour and ramble of comical wit, some show and some mimicry to divert the spectators; but the tragical part is plainly none other than a bloody farce without salt or savour.

[1693]

JEREMY COLLIER

It has often been assumed that Jeremy Collier in *A Short View of the Immorality and Profaneness of the English Stage* merely continued with greater success earlier Puritan attacks upon the stage. Such a conception is wide of the mark. The effectiveness of his crusade was due to the fact that Collier was the opposite of a Puritan. He was a High Church clergyman and a nonjuror; that is, he was one of a numerous party among the more conservative English clergy, who after the Revolution refused to take the oaths of allegiance to William and Mary because they adhered to the doctrines of the divine right of kings and nonresistance to royal authority, and because they could not conscientiously swear allegiance to the new sovereigns while James II lived and maintained his right to the throne. About two years before the publication of *A Short View* Collier had attended to the gallows at Tyburn two prisoners condemned for participation in a Jacobite plot against King William's life, and there had publicly absolved them, though they had given no public expression of repentance. For this action, which seemed to indicate that he regarded William as a usurper and that consequently it was not a mortal sin to conspire against his life, Collier had been indicted; and, upon his failure to give himself up, had been outlawed. Such a man obviously was no disciple of William Prynne.

At least in the beginning of his attack, Collier had taken the position of a defender of the stage against bad plays and dramatic abuses, though as he warmed up to the work he more and more laid himself open to the charge of hostility against the theatre itself. He was well acquainted with the drama, ancient and modern, and with the critical literature concerning it. In criticism his point of view was that of the Aristotelian formalists; he was evidently influenced both in subject-matter and in style by Thomas Rymer. Thus when he argued that the purpose of the drama is to teach, and that the duty of the poet is to observe poetic justice and to preserve strict decorum, he was enunciating principles which his opponents recognized and held in respect. He employed the orthodox vocabulary of critical discussion, appealed to the usual authorities, and judged plays, in part at least, according to the rules. None of the Puritan enemies of the stage had done these things.

Collier did not initiate the movement to reform the Restoration stage. Dr. Johnson in his *Lives of the Poets* remarked of Sir Richard Blackmore, "In his preface to *Prince Arthur* [1695] he had said of the dramatic writers almost all that was alleged afterwards by Collier; but Blackmore's censure was cold and general, Collier's was personal and ardent; Blackmore taught his reader to dislike what Collier incited him to abhor." Here as usual Johnson hits the nail on the head; more recent study has added to the list of those who between 1660 and 1698 called attention to the abuses of the English stage, but it has nowhere expressed more accurately the real importance of Collier's assault. *A Short View* was influential because it gave expression in vigorous and picturesque language to ideas that were in many men's minds. There has been much argument over the effect of Collier's attack. It produced an immediate sensation and was followed by a violent controversy. Dryden, who was now growing old, frankly admitted his faults (see Preface to *Fables*), though his reply showed that he could still strike back effectively when he was disposed to do so; Congreve and Vanbrugh took up the cudgels in earnest; Collier returned to the attack with pamphlet after pamphlet; and lesser men entered the arena from both sides. J. W. Krutch, in a "Bibliography of the Collier Controversy," published with his *Comedy and Conscience after the Restoration*, lists fifty-eight works on both sides which appeared between 1698 and 1730. Cibber in his *Apology* (1740), gives the impression that this controversy had a considerable effect in reforming the stage. There can be no doubt that during the first part of the eighteenth century the new sentimental comedy, which usually had a more moral tone, grew rapidly in popularity; and Richard Steele, its most prominent exponent, was a follower of Collier. On the other hand it has been pointed out that this sentimental comedy was largely the result of changed social conditions produced by the increased importance of the *bourgeoisie* after the Revolution of 1688, and that it had begun to show itself unmistakably before Collier wrote. It is also true that the old type of comedy of manners continued to be written for a long time and that the most objectionable of the Restoration plays were revived year after year with continuing popularity. The reformation of the stage was neither so sudden nor so complete as has often been supposed, yet there was some reformation. Of course Collier, like every one else in history, was a result as well as a cause; but through his vigorous and well-timed attack, and to some extent through his very intemperance and exaggeration, he left his stamp on the literary and social history of his time.

As the title, *A Short View of the Immorality and Profaneness of the English Stage*, indicates, Collier follows two main lines of attack. He shows not only that the language used in Restoration comedy is often immodest and sometimes obscene, but that the whole tendency is to ridicule virtue and exalt vice. In so doing he discusses drama from ancient to contemporary times, and draws the conclusion that, though many earlier dramatists had been justly censurable on moral grounds, recent ones were worse. Though he sometimes strains a point and condemns passages that seem to us comparatively harmless, on the whole he makes his case easily. His charge of profaneness is not so well substantiated: not only does he object to profane swearing on the stage, but he is unduly sensitive about the dignity of the clergy. Had he limited himself to condemnation of those plays in which religion is obviously scorned and the clergy are flagrantly abused, his case would have been stronger; but his excessive zeal weakens his cause. The passage here quoted is the first half of Chapter IV, in which he presses home one of his principal charges and shows clearly the critical principles upon which his denunciation is based.

A SHORT VIEW OF THE IMMORALITY AND PROFANENESS OF THE ENGLISH STAGE

Chapter IV

The Stage Poets Make their Principal Persons Vicious, and Reward them at the End of the Play.

The lines of virtue and vice are struck out by nature in very legible distinctions. They tend to a different point, and in the greater instances the space between them is easily perceived. Nothing can be more unlike than the original forms of these qualities: the first has all the sweetness, charms, and graces imaginable; the other has the air of a post ill carved into a monster, and looks both foolish and frightful together. These are the native appearances of good and evil; and they that endeavour to blot the distinctions, to rub out the colours, or change the marks, are extremely to blame. 'Tis confessed, as long as the mind is awake, and conscience goes true, there's no fear of being imposed on. But when vice is varnished over with pleasure and comes in the shape of convenience, the case grows somewhat dangerous; for then the fancy may be gained, and the guards corrupted, and reason suborned against itself. And thus a disguise often passes when the person would otherwise be stopped. To put lewdness into a thriving condition, to give it an equipage of quality, and to treat it with ceremony and respect, is the way to confound the understanding, to fortify the charm, and to make the mischief invincible. Innocence is often owing to fear, and appetite is kept under by shame; but when these restraints are once taken off, when profit and liberty lie on the same side, and a man can debauch himself into credit, what can be expected in such a case but that pleasure should grow absolute and madness carry all before it? The stage seems eager to bring matters to this issue; they have made a considerable progress and are still pushing their point with all the vigour imaginable. If this be not their aim, why is lewdness so much considered in character and success? Why are their favourites atheistical and their fine gentleman debauched? To what purpose is vice thus preferred, thus ornamented and caressed, unless for imitation? That matter of fact stands thus, I shall make good by several instances. To begin then with their men of breeding and figure. *Wildblood sets up for debauchery, ridicules marriage, and swears by Mahomet. *Bellamy makes sport with the devil, and *Lorenzo is vicious, and calls his father "bawdy magistrate." *Horner is horridly smutty, and *Harcourt false to his friend who used him kindly. In **The Plain Dealer* Freeman talks coarsely, cheats the widow, debauches her son and makes him undutiful. Bellmour is lewd and profane, and *Mellefont puts *Careless in the best way he can to debauch *Lady Plyant. These sparks generally marry the top ladies, and those that do not, are brought to no penance, but go off with the character of fine gentlemen. In **Don Sebastian*, Antonio, an atheistical bully, is rewarded with the Lady Morayma and half the Mufti's estate. Valentine, in **Love for Love*, is (if I may so call him) the hero of the play; this spark the poet would pass for a person of virtue, but he speaks too late. 'Tis true, he was hearty in his affection to Angelica. Now, without question, to be in love with a fine lady of £30,000 is a great virtue! But then, abating this single commendation, Valentine is altogether compounded of vice. He is a prodigal debauchee, unnatural, and profane, obscene, saucy, and undutiful; and yet this libertine is crowned for the man of merit, has his wishes thrown into his lap, and

* Notes on Jeremy Collier will be found in the Appendix, pp. 965 ff.

makes the happy exit. I perceive we should have a rare set of virtues if these poets had the making of them! How they hug a vicious character, and how profuse are they in their liberalities to lewdness! In * *The Provoked Wife* Constant swears at length, solicits Lady Brute, confesses himself lewd, and prefers debauchery to marriage. He handles the last subject very notably and worth the hearing. "There is," says he, "a poor, sordid slavery in marriage, that turns the flowing tide of honour, and sinks it to the lowest ebb of infamy. 'Tis a corrupted soil; ill nature, avarice, sloth, cowardice, and dirt are all its product." But then, "Constancy (alias whoring) is a brave, free, haughty, generous agent." This is admirable stuff both for the rhetoric and the reason! The character of young Fashion, in * *The Relapse*, is of the same staunchness, but this the reader may have in another place.

To sum up the evidence. A fine gentleman is a fine whoring, swearing, smutty, atheistical man. These qualifications, it seems, complete the idea of honour. They are the top improvements of fortune, and the distinguishing glories of birth and breeding! This is the stage test for quality, and those that can't stand it ought to be disclaimed. The restraints of conscience and the pedantry of virtue are unbecoming a cavalier: future securities and reaching beyond life are vulgar provisions; if he falls a-thinking at this rate, he forfeits his honour, for his head was only made to run against a post! Here you have a man of breeding and figure that burlesques the Bible, swears, and talks smut to ladies, speaks ill of his friend behind his back, and betrays his interest. A fine gentleman that has neither honesty nor honour, conscience nor manners, good-nature nor civil hypocrisy — fine only in the insignificancy of life, the abuse of religion, and the scandals of conversation. These worshipful things are the poets' favourites; they appear at the head of the fashion, and shine in character and equipage. If there is any sense stirring, they must have it, though the rest of the stage suffer never so much by the partiality. And what can be the meaning of this wretched distribution of honour? Is it not to give credit and countenance to vice, and to shame young people out of all pretence to conscience and regularity? They seem forced to turn lewd in their own defence; they can't otherwise justify themselves to the fashion, nor keep up the character of gentlemen: thus people not well furnished with thought and experience are debauched both in practice and in principle. And thus religion grows uncreditable, and passes for ill education. The stage seldom gives quarter to anything that's serviceable or significant, but persecutes worth and goodness under every appearance. He that would be safe from their satire must take care to disguise himself in vice, and hang out the colours of debauchery. How often is learning, industry, and frugality ridiculed in comedy? The rich citizens are often misers and cuckolds, and the universities schools of pedantry upon this score. In short, libertinism and profaneness, dressing, idleness, and gallantry are the only valuable qualities. As if people were not apt enough of themselves to be lazy, lewd, and extravagant, unless they were pricked forward, and provoked by glory and reputation. Thus the marks of honour and infamy are misapplied, and the ideas of virtue and vice confounded. Thus monstrousness goes for proportion, and the blemishes of human nature make up the beauties of it.

The fine ladies are of the same cut with the gentlemen. * Morayma is scandalously rude to her father, helps him to a beating, and runs away with Antonio. * Angelica talks saucily to her uncle, and * Belinda confesses her inclination for a gallant. And as I have observed already, the topping ladies in *The Mock Astrologer*, *Spanish Friar*, *Country Wife*, *Old Bachelor*, * *Orphan*, * *Double-Dealer*, and * *Love Triumphant*, are smutty, and sometimes profane.

And was licentiousness and irreligion always a mark of honour? No, I don't perceive but that the old poets had another notion of accomplishment, and bred their people of condition a different way. *Philolaches, in Plautus, laments his being debauched, and dilates upon the advantages of virtue and regularity. *Lysiteles, another young gentleman, disputes handsomely by himself against lewdness. And the discourse between him and Philto is moral and well managed. And afterwards he lashes luxury and debauching with a great deal of warmth and satire. *Chremes, in Terence, is a modest young gentleman; he is afraid of being surprised by Thais, and seems careful not to sully his reputation. And Pamphilus, in **Hecyra*, resolves rather to be governed by duty than inclination.

*Plautus's Pinacium tells her friend, Panegyris, that they ought to acquit themselves fairly to their husbands, though these should fail in their regards toward them. For all good people will do justice, though they don't receive it. Lady Brute, in *The Provoked Wife*, is governed by different maxims. She is debauched with ill usage, says, *"Virtue is an ass, and a gallant's worth forty on't." Pinacium goes on to another head of duty, and declares that a daughter can never respect her father too much, and that disobedience has a great deal of scandal and lewdness in't. The lady Jacintha, as I remember, does not treat her father at this rate of decency. Let us hear a little of her behaviour. *The Mock Astrologer* makes the men draw, and frights the ladies with the apprehension of a quarrel. Upon this, Theodosia cries, *"What will become of us!" Jacintha answers, "We'll die for company; nothing vexes me but that I am not a man, to have one thrust at that malicious old father of mine before I go." Afterwards the old gentleman, Alonzo, threatens his daughters with a nunnery. Jacintha spars again, and says, "I would have thee to know, thou graceless old man, that I defy a nunnery; name a nunnery once more, and I disown thee for my father." I could carry on the comparison between the old and modern poets somewhat farther. But this may suffice.

Thus we see what a fine time lewd people have on the English stage. No censure, no mark of infamy, no mortification must touch them. They keep their honour untarnished, and carry off the advantage of their character. They are set up for the standard of behaviour, and the masters of ceremony and sense. And at last, that the example may work the better, they generally make them rich and happy, and reward them with their own desires.

Mr. Dryden, in the preface to his *Mock Astrologer*, confesses himself blamed for this practice — for making debauched persons his protagonists, or chief persons of the drama, and for making them happy in the conclusion of the play, against the law of comedy, which is to reward virtue and punish vice. To this objection he makes a lame defence, and answers,

1st. That he knows no such law constantly observed in comedy by the ancient or modern poets. What then? Poets are not always exactly in rule. It may be a good law, though 'tis not constantly observed; some laws are constantly broken, and yet ne'er the worse for all that. He goes on, and pleads the authorities of Plautus and Terence. I grant there are instances of favour to vicious young people in those authors; but to this I reply,

1st. That those poets had a greater compass of liberty in their religion. Debauchery did not lie under those discouragements of scandal and penalty with them as it does with us. Unless, therefore, he can prove heathenism and Christianity the same, his precedents will do him little service.

2ly. *Horace, who was as good a judge of the stage as either of those comedians, seems to be of another opinion. He condemns the obscenities of Plautus, and tells you men of fortune and quality in his time would not endure immodest satire. He continues that poets were formerly admired for the great services they did: for teaching matters relating to religion and government; for refining the manners, tempering the passions, and improving the understandings of mankind; for making them more useful in domestic relations and the public capacities of life. This is a demonstration that vice was not the inclination of the Muses in those days, and that Horace believed the chief business of a poem was to instruct the audience. He adds farther that the chorus ought to turn upon the argument of the drama, and support the design of the acts, that they ought to speak in defence of virtue and frugality, and show a regard to religion. Now, from the rule of the chorus, we may conclude his judgment for the play. For, as he observes, there must be a uniformity between the chorus and the acts; they must have the same view, and be all of a piece. From hence 'tis plain that Horace would have no immoral characters have either countenance or good fortune upon the stage. If 'tis said the very mention of the chorus shows the directions were intended for tragedy, to this

I answer that the consequence is not good. For the use of a chorus is not inconsistent with comedy. The ancient comedians had it; Aristophanes is an instance. I know 'tis said the chorus was left out in that they call the New Comedy. But I can't see the conclusiveness of this assertion, for Aristophanes his *Plutus* is New Comedy with a chorus in't. And Aristotle, who lived after this revolution of the stage, mentions nothing of the omission of the chorus. He rather supposes its continuance by saying the * chorus was added by the government long after the invention of comedy. 'Tis true Plautus and Terence have none, but those before them probably might. * Molière has now revived them; and Horace might be of his opinion, for ought we know to the contrary.

Lastly, Horace, having expressly mentioned the beginning and progress of comedy, discovers himself more fully: he advises a poet to form his work upon the precepts of Socrates and Plato, and the models of moral philosophy. This was the way to preserve decency, and to assign a proper fate and behaviour to every character. Now, if Horace would have his poet governed by the maxims of morality, he must oblige him to sobriety of conduct, and a just distribution of rewards and punishments.

* Mr. Dryden makes homewards, and endeavours to fortify himself in modern authority. He lets us know that Ben Jonson, after whom he may be proud to err, gives him more than one example of this conduct; that in *The Alchemist* is notorious, where neither Face nor his master are corrected according to their demerits. But how proud soever Mr. Dryden may be of an error, he has not so much of Ben Jonson's company as he pretends. His instance of Face, etc., in *The Alchemist* is rather notorious against his purpose than for it.

For Face did not counsel his master, Lovewit, to debauch the widow; neither is it clear that the matter went thus far. He might gain her consent upon terms of honour, for ought appears to the contrary. 'Tis true, Face, who was one of the principal cheats, is pardoned and considered; but then his master confesses himself kind to a fault. He owns this indulgence was a breach of justice, and unbecoming the gravity of an old man, and then desires the audience to excuse him upon the score of the temptation. But Face continued in the cozenage till the last without repentance. Under favour I conceive this is a mistake. For does not Face make an apology before he leaves the stage? Does he not set himself at the bar, arraign his own practice, and cast the cause upon the clemency of the company? And are not all these signs of the dislike of what he had done? Thus careful the poet is to prevent the ill impressions of his play! He brings both man and master to confession. He dismisses them like malefactors, and moves for their pardon before he gives them their discharge. But *The Mock Astrologer* has a gentler hand; Wildblood and Jacintha are more generously used; there is no acknowledgment exacted, no hardship put upon them; they are permitted to talk on in their libertine way to the last, and take leave without the least appearance of reformation. *The Mock Astrologer* urges Ben Jonson's *Silent Woman* as another precedent to his purpose. For there Dauphine confesses himself in love with all the collegiate ladies. And yet this naughty Dauphine is crowned in the end with the possession of his uncle's estate, and with the hopes of all his mistresses. This charge, as I take it, is somewhat too severe. I grant Dauphine professes himself in love with the collegiate ladies at first. But when they invited him to a private visit, he makes them no promise, but rather appears tired and willing to disengage. Dauphine, therefore, is not altogether so naughty as this author represents him.

* Ben Jonson's *Fox* is clearly against Mr. Dryden. And here I have his own confession for proof. *He declares the poet's end in this play was the punishment of vice and the reward of virtue. Ben was forced to strain for this piece of justice, and break through the unity of design. This Mr. Dryden remarks upon him; however, he is pleased to commend the performance, and calls it an excellent fifth act.

Ben Jonson shall speak for himself afterwards in the character of a critic; in the mean time I shall take a testimony or two from Shakespeare. And here we may observe the admired * Falstaff goes off in disappointment. He is thrown out of favour as being a rake, and dies like a rat behind the hangings. The pleasure he had given would not excuse him. The poet was not so partial as to let his humour compound for his lewdness. If 'tis objected that this remark is wide of the point, because Falstaff is represented in tragedy, where the laws of justice are more strictly observed, to this I answer that you may call *Henry the Fourth* and *Fifth* tragedies if you please. But for all that, Falstaff wears no buskins; his character is perfectly comical from end to end.

The next instance shall be in * Flowerdale, the prodigal. This spark, notwithstanding his extravagance, makes a lucky hand on't at last, and marries up a rich lady. But then the poet qualifies him for his good fortune, and mends his manners with his circumstances. He makes him repent and leave off his intemperance, swearing, etc. And when his father warned him against a relapse, he answers very soberly,

> * Heaven helping me, I'll hate the course of hell.

I could give some instances of this kind out of Beaumont and Fletcher; but there's no need of any farther quotation, for Mr. Dryden is not satisfied with his apology from authority: he does as good as own that this may be construed no better than defending one ill practice by another. To prevent this very reasonable objection he endeavours to vindicate his precedents from the reason of the thing. To this purpose *he makes a wide difference between the rules of tragedy and comedy, that vice must be impartially prosecuted in the first, because the persons are great, etc.

It seems, then, executions are only for greatness and quality. Justice is not to strike much lower than a prince. Private people may do what they please. They are too few for mischief, and too little for punishment! This would be admirable doctrine for Newgate, and give us a general jail delivery without more ado. But in tragedy, says *The Mock Astrologer*, the crimes are likewise horrid, so that there is a necessity for severity and example. And how stands the matter in comedy? Quite otherwise. There the faults are but the sallies of youth and the frailties of human nature. For instance, there is nothing but a little whoring, pimping, gaming, profaneness, etc. And who could be so hard hearted to give a man any trouble for this? Such rigours would be strangely inhumane! A poet is a better-natured thing, I can assure you. These little miscarriages move pity and commiseration, and are not such as must of necessity be punished. This is comfortable casuistry! But to be serious, is dissolution of manners such a peccadillo? Does a profligate conscience deserve nothing but commiseration? And are people damned only for human frailties? I perceive the laws of religion and those of the stage differ extremely. The strength of his defence lies in this choice maxim, that the chief end of comedy is delight. He questions whether instruction has anything to do in comedy. If it has, he is sure 'tis no more than its secondary end, for the business of the poet is to make you laugh. Granting the truth of this principle, I somewhat question the serviceableness of it. For is there no diversion to be had unless vice appears prosperous and rides at the head of success? One would think such a preposterous distribution of rewards should rather shock the reason and raise the indignation of the audience. To laugh without reason is the pleasure of fools; and against it, of something worse. The exposing of knavery, and making lewdness ridiculous, is a much better occasion for laughter. And this, with submission, I take to be the end of comedy. And, therefore, it does not differ from tragedy in the end, but in the means. Instruction is the principal design of both. The one works by terror, the other by infamy. 'Tis true, they don't move in the same line, but they meet in the same point at last. For this opinion I have good authority, besides what has been cited already.

1st. * Monsieur Rapin affirms "that delight is the end that poetry aims at, but not the principal one. For poetry, being an art, ought to be profitable by the quality of its own nature, and by the essential subordination that all arts should have to polity, whose end in general is the public good. This is the judgment of Aristotle and of Horace, his chief interpreter." Ben Jonson, in his dedicatory epistle of his *Fox*, has somewhat considerable upon this argument; and declaims with a great deal of zeal, spirit, and good sense against the licentiousness of the stage. He lays it down for a principle, "that 'tis impossible to be a good poet without being a good man. That he (a good poet) is said to be able to inform young men to all good discipline, and inflame grown men to all great virtues, etc. — That the general complaint was that the writers of those days had nothing remaining in them of the dignity of a poet but the abused name. That now, especially in stage poetry, nothing but ribaldry, profanation, blasphemy, all licence of offence to God and man, is practised." He confesses a great part of this charge is over-true, and is sorry he dares not deny it. But then he hopes all are not embarked in this bold adventure for hell. "For my part," says he, "I can, and from a most clear conscience, affirm that I have ever trembled to think towards the least profaneness, and loathed the use of such foul and unwashed bawdry as is now made the food of the scene; — the increase of which lust in liberty what learned or liberal soul does not abhor? In whole interludes nothing but the filth of the time is uttered — with brothelry able to violate the ear of a pagan, and blasphemy to turn the blood of a Christian to water." He continues that the insolence of these men had brought the Muses into disgrace, and made poetry the lowest scorn of the age. He appeals to his patrons, the universities, that his labour has been heretofore, and mostly in this his latest work, to reduce not only the ancient forms, but manners of the scene, the innocence and the doctrine, which is the principal end of poesy, to inform men in the best reason of living. Lastly he adds, that he has imitated the conduct of the ancients in this play, the goings out (or conclusions) of whose comedies were not always joyful, but ofttimes the bawds, the slaves, the rivals, yea and the masters are mulcted, and fitly, it being the office of a comic poet (mark that!) to imitate justice and instruct to life, etc. Say you so! Why, then, if Ben Jonson knew anything of the matter, divertisement and laughing is not, as Mr. Dryden affirms, the chief end of comedy. This testimony is so very full and clear that it needs no explaining, nor any enforcement from reasoning and consequence....

[1698]

JOHN POMFRET

JOHN POMFRET'S chief hold upon fame is the remark of Dr. Johnson concerning his poem *The Choice*, that "no composition in our language has ever been oftener perused"; and this remark, hazardous when it was made, is certainly true no longer. Pomfret paid in full for the reputation the poem brought him. Two years after it was published, in 1700, he went up from his small parish in Bedfordshire to be instituted by the Bishop of London in a valuable church living, to which he had already been "presented." The bishop was reminded, however, of those lines in *The Choice* which declare the poet's intention to "have no wife" and to solace his Horatian retirement in the company of "witty nymphs." As a matter of fact the poet had married shortly after his poem was published, but while he was waiting in London for an opportunity to explain this discrepancy between his poetical and his actual conduct, he caught the smallpox, and died, at the age of thirty-six.

The Choice is interesting rather for its representative than for its intrinsic merit. English poems of the same purport and often of the same title, all resting upon Horace's doctrine of the Golden Mean, were written all the way from the beginning of the seventeenth century to the opening of the nineteenth, and there are at least as many more in French; but there is a peculiar timeliness and applicability in Pomfret's contribution. He speaks for many educated and refined Englishmen who had been tossed and worn in almost sixty years of civil turmoil, whose chief desire was for quiet, to whom mere safety seemed all they dared to ask. They erected "mediocrity" into an ideal; and their lives, as compared with those of their grandfathers, were orgies of moderation. Men of feeble pulse, genteel, anæmic, eager above all else to avoid eagerness, they entertained only the most probable wishes and hedged their "choice" about with anxious caution and distrust. We may catch the tones of this caution in some uses of the heroic couplet where every second line erases a part of what has been said in the preceding. It is fitting that Pomfret's clear expression of this mood which was to prevail, although of course not exclusively, until the death of Cowper in 1800, should have appeared in the century's opening year.

THE CHOICE

If Heaven the grateful liberty would give
That I might choose my method how to live,
And all those hours propitious fate should lend
In blissful ease and satisfaction *spend:

I. THE GENTLEMAN'S RETIREMENT

Near some fair town I'd have a private seat,
Built uniform, not little nor too great;
Better if on a rising ground it stood,
Fields on this side, on that a neighbouring wood.
It should, within, no other things contain
But what are useful, necessary, plain.
Methinks 'tis nauseous, and I'd ne'er endure
The needless pomp of gaudy furniture.
A little garden, grateful to the eye,
And a cool rivulet run murmuring by,
On whose delicious banks a stately row
Of shady limes or sycamores should grow;
At th' end of which a silent study placed
Should with the noblest authors there be graced:
Horace and Virgil, in whose mighty lines
Immortal wit and solid learning shines;
Sharp Juvenal and amorous Ovid too,
Who all the turns of love's soft passion knew.
He that with judgment reads the charming lines,
In which strong art with stronger nature joins,
Must grant his fancy does the best excel;
His thoughts so tender, and expressed so well;
With all those moderns, men of steady sense,
Esteemed for learning and for eloquence.
In some of these, as fancy should advise,
I'd always take my morning exercise;
For sure no moments bring us more content
Than those in pleasing, useful study spent.

II. HIS FORTUNE AND CHARITY

I'd have a clear and competent estate,
That I might live genteelly, but not great;
As much as I could moderately spend;
A little more sometimes t' oblige a friend.
Nor should the sons of poverty repine
At fortune's frown, for they should taste of mine;
And all that objects of true pity were
Should be relieved with what my wants could spare.
For what our Maker has too largely given
Should be returned in gratitude to Heaven.

* Notes on John Pomfret will be found in the Appendix, pp. 966 ff.

A frugal plenty should my table spread
With healthy, not luxurious, dishes fed;
Enough to satisfy, and something more
To feed the stranger and the neighb'ring poor.
Strong meat indulges vice, and pampering food
Creates diseases and inflames the blood;
But what's sufficient to make nature strong
And the bright lamp of life continue long
I'd freely take, and, as I did possess,
The bounteous Author of my plenty bless.

III. His Hospitality and Temperance

I'd have a little cellar cool and neat,
With humming ale and virgin wine replete.
Wine whets the wit, improves its native force,
And gives a pleasant flavour to discourse;
By making all our spirits debonair,
Throws off the lees and sediment of care.
But as the greatest blessing Heaven lends
May be debauched and serve ignoble ends,
So but too oft the grape's refreshing juice
Does many mischievous effects produce.
My house should no such rude disorders know
As from high drinking consequently flow,
Nor would I use what was so kindly given
To the dishonour of indulgent Heaven.
If any neighbour came, he should be free,
Used with respect and not uneasy be
In my retreat or to himself or me.
What freedom, prudence, and right reason give
All men may with impunity receive;
But the least swerving from their rule's too much,
And what's forbidden us 'tis death to touch.

IV. His Company

That life may be more comfortable yet,
And all my joys refined, sincere, and great,
I'd choose two friends whose company would be
A great advance to my felicity:
Well-born, of humours suited to my own,
Discreet, that men as well as books have known,
Brave, generous, witty, and exactly free
From loose behaviour or formality;
Airy and prudent, merry but not light,
Quick in discerning and in judging right.
They should be secret, faithful to their trust,
In reasoning cool, strong, temperate, and just;
Obliging, open, without *huffing brave;
Brisk in gay talking, and in sober, grave;
Close in dispute but not tenacious, tried
By solemn reason, and let that decide;
Not prone to lust, revenge, or envious hate,
Nor busy meddlers with intrigues of state;
Strangers to slander and sworn foes to spite,
Not quarrelsome, but stout enough to fight;
Loyal and pious, friends to *Cæsar, true
As dying martyrs to their Maker too.
In their society I could not miss
A permanent, sincere, substantial bliss.

V. His Lady and Converse

Would bounteous Heaven once more indulge, I'd choose
(For who would so much satisfaction lose
As witty nymphs in conversation give?)
Near some obliging modest fair to live;
For there's that sweetness in a female mind
Which in a man's we cannot hope to find,
That by a secret but a powerful art
Winds up the spring of life, and does impart
Fresh, vital heat to the transported heart.
I'd have her reason all her passions sway;
Easy in company, in private gay;
*Coy to a fop, to the deserving free;
Still constant to herself and just to me.
A soul she should have for great actions fit;
Prudence and wisdom to direct her wit;
Courage to look bold danger in the face,
No fear but only to be proud or base;
Quick to advise by an emergence pressed,
To give good counsel or to take the best.
I'd have th' expressions of her thoughts be such
She might not seem reserved, nor talk too much;
That shows a want of judgment and of sense;
More than enough is but impertinence.
Her conduct regular, her mirth refined,
Civil to strangers, to her neighbours kind,
Averse to vanity, revenge, and pride,
In all the methods of deceit untried;
So faithful to her friend and good to all,
No censure might upon her actions fall.
Then would e'en envy be compelled to say,
She goes the least of womankind astray.
To this fair creature I'd sometimes retire;
Her conversations would new joys inspire,
Give life an edge so keen, no surly care
Would venture to assault my soul or dare
Near my retreat to hide one secret snare.
But so divine, so noble a repast
I'd seldom and with moderation taste;

For highest cordials all their virtue lose
By a too frequent and too bold an use;
And what would cheer the spirits in distress
Ruins our health when taken to excess.

VI. His Peaceable Life

I'd be concerned in no litigious jar;
Beloved by all, not vainly popular.
Whate'er assistance I had power to bring
T' oblige my company or to serve my king,
Whene'er they called, I'd readily afford —
My tongue, my pen, my counsel, or my sword.
Lawsuits I'd shun with as much studious care
As I would dens where hungry lions are,
And rather put up injuries than be
A plague to him who'd be a plague to me.
I value quiet at a price too great
To give for my revenge so dear a *rate;
For what do we by all our bustle gain
But counterfeit delight for real pain?

VII. His Happy Death

If Heaven a date of many years would give,
Thus I'd in pleasure, ease, and plenty live;
And as I near approach'd the verge of life,
Some kind relation (for I'd have no wife)
Should take upon him all my worldly care
While I did for a better state prepare.
Then I'd not be with any trouble vexed,
Nor have the evening of my days perplexed;
But by a silent and a peaceful death,
Without a sigh, resign my aged breath;
And when committed to the dust I'd have
Few tears, but friendly, dropped into my grave;
Then would my exit so propitious be,
All men would wish to live and die like me.

[1700]

BERNARD MANDEVILLE

In 1705 there was published an anonymous sixpenny pamphlet containing a doggerel poem entitled *The Grumbling Hive: or Knaves Turned Honest.* The author was Bernard de Mandeville, a Dutch physician resident in London, who married an English wife and dropped the "de" from his name. Nine years later he republished these verses together with a considerable verse-commentary under the title, *The Fable of the Bees: or, Private Vices, Public Benefits.* Nine more years elapsed without the work attracting much attention; then in 1723 it was republished with the commentary still further enlarged and was followed by a second part in 1728. By 1723 it had begun to excite popular apprehension because of its bold attack on commonly received ethical principles. The book was presented as a public nuisance by the Grand Jury of Middlesex, and a controversy broke out that was to occupy much of the author's attention during the rest of his lifetime and was to rage long after his death.

Mandeville tried to show through his original verse fable that the welfare and prosperity of any community are dependent upon luxury, pride, avarice, and lust, which are nevertheless vices in the individual. The hive prospered while its members indulged their passions but fell upon evil days when they put into practice the ordinary rules of ethics. In the series of prose essays added to the revised volume, this thesis was elaborated and explained most ingeniously. F. B. Kaye in a full and illuminating introduction to his edition of *The Fable of the Bees* has traced the sources of Mandeville's thought and has shown that his reasoning is based upon two entirely different concepts of virtue common in the eighteenth century: one ascetic and the other rationalistic. By accepting at the same time both these conflicting definitions, Mandeville was able to demonstrate the social impracticability of the usual ideals of conduct and to present a most disturbing paradox.

He rejected Shaftesbury's teaching that human nature is essentially good, and argued that the underlying motive for human conduct is selfishness, either in the satisfaction of natural impulses or in the subjection of them through the desire of winning praise or avoiding censure. Against Shaftesbury's altruistic faith he emphasized egoism as the basis of human conduct; against Shaftesbury's sentimentalism he urged cynicism.

Mandeville's prose has liveliness and colloquial vigour that make it an admirable vehicle for his fresh and striking ideas. Even today *The Fable of the Bees* is interesting; to his early readers it was fascinating, irritating, and alarming. It went through numerous editions and was translated into French and German. Every one discussed it; numerous writers, including William Law, Francis Hutcheson, and Bishop Berkeley, replied to it. Mandeville took the place formerly occupied by Hobbes as the apostle of irreligion, repeatedly denounced from the pulpit and spoken of by the public in awed whispers. At the same time serious thinkers recognized, in spite of the author's obvious desire to be shocking, the real importance of the work. Even so conservative a critic as Dr. Johnson admitted that it had opened his views into real life very much. Professor Kaye has shown that its influence was greatest upon ethical and upon economic theory, the latter especially through Adam Smith and Voltaire.

The extracts in this volume include the original verse fable complete (but without Mandeville's extended *Remarks* on particular passages) and the first prose essay from Part I, as revised in the edition of 1732.

From THE FABLE OF THE BEES: OR, PRIVATE VICES, PUBLIC BENEFITS

The Grumbling Hive: or Knaves Turned Honest

A spacious hive well stock'd with bees,
That liv'd in luxury and ease;
And yet as fam'd for laws and arms,
As yielding large and early swarms;
Was counted the great nursery
Of sciences and industry.
*No bees had better government,
More fickleness, or less content:
They were not slaves to tyranny,
Nor rul'd by wild democracy;
But kings, that could not wrong, because
Their power was circumscrib'd by laws.

These insects liv'd like men, and all
Our actions they perform'd in small:
They did whatever's done in town,
And what belongs to sword or gown;
Tho' th' artful works, by nimble sleight
Of minute limbs, 'scap'd human sight;
Yet we've no engines, labourers,

* Notes on Bernard Mandeville will be found in the Appendix, p. 967.

Ships, castles, arms, artificers,
Craft, science, shop, or instrument,
But they had an equivalent;
Which, since their language is unknown,
Must be call'd as we do our own.
As grant, that among other things,
They wanted dice, yet they had kings;
And those had guards; from whence we may
Justly conclude, they had some play;
Unless a regiment be shown
Of soldiers that make use of none.

Vast numbers throng'd the fruitful hive;
Yet those vast numbers made 'em thrive;
Millions endeavouring to supply
Each other's lust and vanity;
While other millions were employ'd,
To see their handiworks destroy'd;
They furnish'd half the universe;
Yet had more work than labourers.
Some with vast stocks, and little pains,
Jump'd into business of great gains;
And some were damn'd to scythes and spades,
And all those hard laborious trades;
Where willing wretches daily sweat,
And wear out strength and limbs to eat:
While others follow'd mysteries,
To which few folks bind 'prentices;
That want no stock, but that of brass,
And may set up *without a cross;
As sharpers, parasites, pimps, players,
Pickpockets, coiners, quacks, soothsayers,
And all those that in enmity,
With downright working, cunningly
Convert to their own use the labour
Of their good-natur'd heedless neighbour.
These were call'd knaves, but, bar the name,
The grave industrious were the same;
All trades and places knew some cheat,
No calling was without deceit.

The lawyers, of whose art the basis
Was raising feuds and splitting cases,
Oppos'd all registers, that cheats
Might make more work with dipp'd estates;
As were 't unlawful that one's own,
Without a lawsuit, should be known.
They kept off hearings willfully,
To finger the refreshing fee;
And to defend a wicked cause,
Examin'd and survey'd the laws,
As burglars shops and houses do,
To find out where they'd best break through.

Physicians valu'd fame and wealth
Above the drooping patient's health,
Or their own skill; the greatest part
Studied, instead of rules of art,
Grave pensive looks and dull behaviour,
To gain th' apothecary's favour;
The praise of midwives, priests, and all
That serv'd at birth or funeral.
To bear with th' ever-talking tribe,
And hear my lady's aunt prescribe;
With formal smile, and kind how d'ye,
To fawn on all the family;
And, which of all the greatest curse is,
T' endure th' impertinence of nurses.

Among the many priests of Jove,
Hir'd to draw blessings from above,
Some few were learn'd and eloquent,
But thousands hot and ignorant;
Yet all pass'd muster that could hide
Their sloth, lust, avarice, and pride;
For which they were as fam'd as tailors
For *cabbage, or for brandy sailors:
Some meagre-look'd and meanly clad,
Would mystically pray for bread,
Meaning by that an ample store,
Yet lit'rally received no more;
And, while these holy drudges starv'd,
The lazy ones, for which they serv'd,
Indulg'd their ease, with all the graces
Of health and plenty in their faces.

The soldiers, that were forc'd to fight,
If they surviv'd, got honour by 't;
Tho' some, that shunn'd the bloody fray,
Had limbs shot off, that ran away:
Some valiant gen'rals fought the foe;
Others took bribes to let them go:
Some ventur'd always where 'twas warm,
Lost now a leg, and then an arm;
Till quite disabled, and put by,
They liv'd on half their salary;
While others never came in play,
And stayed at home for double pay.

Their kings were serv'd, but knavishly,
Cheated by their own ministry;
Many, that for their welfare slaved,
Robbing the very crown they saved;
Pensions were small, and they liv'd high,
Yet boasted of their honesty.
Calling, whene'er they strain'd their right,
The slipp'ry trick a perquisite;
And when folks understood their cant,
They chang'd that for emolument;

Unwilling to be short or plain
In anything concerning gain;
For there was not a bee but would
Get more, I won't say, than he should;
But than he dar'd to let them know,
That pay'd for 't; as your gamesters do,
That, tho' at fair play, ne'er will own
Before the losers what they've won.

But who can all their frauds repeat?
The very stuff, which in the street
They sold for dirt t' enrich the ground,
Was often by the buyers found
Sophisticated with a quarter
Of good-for-nothing stones and mortar;
Tho' Flail had little cause to mutter,
Who sold the other salt for butter.

Justice herself, fam'd for fair dealing,
By blindness had not lost her feeling;
Her left hand, which the scales should hold,
Had often dropt 'em, brib'd with gold;
And, tho' she seem'd impartial,
Where punishment was corporal,
Pretended to a reg'lar course,
In murder, and all crimes of force;
Tho' some, first pilloried for cheating,
Were hang'd in hemp of their own beating;
Yet, it was thought, the sword she bore
Check'd but the desp'rate and the poor;
That, urg'd by mere necessity,
Were tied up to the wretched tree
For crimes which not deserv'd that fate,
But to secure the rich and great.

Thus every part was full of vice,
Yet the whole mass a paradise;
Flatter'd in peace, and fear'd in wars,
They were th' esteem of foreigners,
And lavish of their wealth and lives,
The balance of all other hives.
Such were the blessings of that state;
Their crimes conspir'd to make them great;
And virtue, who from politics
Had learn'd a thousand cunning tricks,
Was by their happy influence
Made friends with vice: and ever since,
The worst of all the multitude
Did something for the common good.

This was the state's craft, that maintain'd
The whole of which each part complain'd:
This, as in music harmony,
Made jarrings in the main agree;
Parties directly opposite,
Assist each other, as 'twere for spite;
And temp'rance with sobriety,
Serve drunkenness and gluttony.

The root of evil, avarice,
That damn'd ill-natur'd baneful vice,
Was slave to prodigality,
That noble sin; whilst luxury
Employ'd a million of the poor,
And odious pride a million more:
Envy itself, and vanity,
Were ministers of industry;
Their darling folly, fickleness,
In diet, furniture, and dress,
That strange ridic'lous vice, was made
The very wheel that turn'd the trade.
Their laws and clothes were equally
Objects of mutability;
For, what was well done for a time,
In half a year became a crime;
Yet while they alter'd thus their laws,
Still finding and correcting flaws,
They mended by inconstancy
Faults, which no prudence could foresee.

Thus vice nurs'd ingenuity,
Which, join'd with time and industry,
Had carried life's conveniencies,
Its real pleasures, comforts, ease,
To such a height, the very poor
Liv'd better than the rich before,
And nothing could be added more.

How vain is mortal happiness!
Had they but known the bounds of bliss;
And that perfection here below
Is more than gods can well bestow;
The grumbling brutes had been content
With ministers and government.
But they, at every ill success,
Like creatures lost without redress,
Curs'd politicians, armies, fleets;
While every one cried, "Damn the cheats,"
And would, tho' conscious of his own,
In others barb'rously bear none.

One that had got a princely store,
By cheating master, king, and poor,
Dar'd cry aloud, "The land must sink
For all its fraud"; and whom d'ye think
The sermonizing rascal chid?
A glover that sold lamb for kid.

The least thing was not done amiss
Or cross'd the public business;

But all the rogues cried brazenly,
"Good gods, had we but honesty!"
Merc'ry smil'd at th' impudence,
And others call'd it want of sense,
Always to rail at what they lov'd:
But Jove, with indignation mov'd,
At last in anger swore he'd rid
The bawling hive of fraud; and did.
The very moment it departs,
And honesty fills all their hearts;
There shows 'em, like th' instructive tree,
Those crimes which they're asham'd to see;
Which now in silence they confess,
By blushing at their ugliness:
Like children that would hide their faults,
And by their colour own their thoughts:
Imag'ning, when they're look'd upon,
That others see what they have done.

But, oh, ye gods! What consternation,
How vast and sudden was th' alteration!
In half an hour, the nation round,
Meat fell a penny in the pound.
The mask hypocrisy's flung down,
From the great statesman to the clown:
And some in borrow'd looks well known,
Appear'd like strangers in their own.
The bar was silent from that day;
For now the willing debtors pay,
Ev'n what's by creditors forgot,
Who quitted them that had it not.
Those that were in the wrong stood mute,
And dropp'd the patch'd vexatious suit:
On which since nothing less can thrive
Than lawyers in an honest hive,
All, except those that got enough,
With inkhorns by their sides troop'd off.

Justice hang'd some, set others free;
And after jail delivery,
Her presence being no more requir'd,
With all her train and pomp retir'd.
First march'd some smiths with locks and grates,
Fetters, and doors with iron plates:
Next jailers, turnkeys, and assistants:
Before the goddess, at some distance,
Her chief and faithful minister,
*Squire Catch, the law's great finisher,
Bore not th' imaginary sword,
But his own tools, an ax and cord:
Then on a cloud the hoodwink'd fair,
Justice herself, was push'd by air:
About her chariot, and behind,
Were sergeants, *bums of every kind,
Tip-staffs, and all those officers,
That squeeze a living out of tears.

Tho' physic liv'd, while folks were ill,
None would prescribe, but bees of skill,
Which through the hive dispers'd so wide,
That none of them had need to ride;
Wav'd vain disputes, and strove to free
The patients of their misery;
Left drugs in cheating countries grown,
And us'd the product of their own;
Knowing the gods sent no disease
To nations without remedies.

Their clergy rous'd from laziness,
Laid not their charge on *journey-bees;
But serv'd themselves, exempt from vice,
The gods with pray'r and sacrifice;
All those that were unfit, or knew
Their service might be spar'd, withdrew:
Nor was there business for so many,
(If th' honest stand in need of any,)
Few only with the high priest stay'd,
To whom the rest obedience paid:
Himself employ'd in holy cares,
Resign'd to others state affairs.
He chas'd no starv'ling from his door,
Nor pinch'd the wages of the poor;
But at his house the hungry's fed,
The hireling finds unmeasur'd bread,
The needy trav'ler board and bed.

Among the king's great ministers,
And all th' inferior officers
The change was great; for frugally
They now liv'd on their salary:
That a poor bee should ten times come
To ask his due, a trifling sum,
And by some well-hir'd clerk be made
To give a crown, or ne'er be paid,
Would now be call'd a downright cheat,
Tho' formerly a perquisite.
All places manag'd first by three,
Who watch'd each other's knavery,
And often for a fellow feeling,
Promoted one another's stealing,
Are happily supplied by one,
By which some thousands more are gone.

No honour now could be content,
To live and owe for what was spent;
Liv'ries in brokers' shops are hung,
They part with coaches for a song;
Sell stately horses by whole sets,
And country houses, to pay debts.

Vain cost is shunn'd as much as fraud;
They have no forces kept abroad;
Laugh at th' esteem of foreigners,
And empty glory got by wars;
They fight, but for their country's sake,
When right or liberty's at stake.

Now mind the glorious hive, and see
How honesty and trade agree.
The show is gone; it thins apace
And looks with quite another face.
For 'twas not only that they went,
By whom vast sums were yearly spent;
But multitudes that liv'd on them,
Were daily forc'd to do the same.
In vain to other trades they'd fly;
All were o'erstock'd accordingly.

The price of land and houses falls;
Mirac'lous palaces, whose walls,
Like those of Thebes, were rais'd by play,
Are to be let; while the once gay,
Well seated household gods would be
More pleas'd to expire in flames, than see
The mean inscription on the door
Smile at the lofty ones they bore.
The building trade is quite destroy'd,
Artificers are not employ'd;
No limner for his art is fam'd,
Stonecutters, carvers are not nam'd.

Those that remain'd, grown temp'rate, strive,
Not how to spend, but how to live,
And, when they paid their tavern score,
Resolv'd to enter it no more:
No vintner's jilt in all the hive
Could wear now cloth of gold, and thrive;
Nor Torcol such vast sums advance,
For Burgundy and ortolans;
The courtier's gone, that with his miss
Supp'd at his house on Christmas peas,
Spending as much in two hours' stay,
As keeps a troop of horse a day.

The haughty Chloe, to live great,
Had made her husband rob the state:
But now she sells her furniture,
Which th' Indies had been ransack'd for;
Contracts th' expensive bill of fare,
And wears her strong suit a whole year:
The slight and fickle age is past;
And clothes, as well as fashions, last.
Weavers, that join'd rich silk with plate,
And all the trades subordinate,
Are gone. Still peace and plenty reign,
And everything is cheap, tho' plain:
Kind nature, free from gard'ners' force,
Allows all fruits in her own course;
But rarities cannot be had,
Where pains to get them are not paid.

As pride and luxury decrease,
So by degrees they leave the seas.
Not merchants now, but companies,
Remove whole manufactories.
All arts and crafts neglected lie;
Content, the bane of industry,
Makes 'em admire their homely store,
And neither seek nor covet more.

So few in the vast hive remain,
The hundredth part they can't maintain
Against th' insults of numerous foes;
Whom yet they valiantly oppose:
Till some well fenc'd retreat is found,
And here they die or stand their ground.
No hireling in their army's known;
But bravely fighting for their own,
Their courage and integrity
At last were crown'd with victory.
They triumph'd not without their cost,
For many thousand bees were lost.
Hard'ned with toils and exercise,
They counted ease itself a vice;
Which so improv'd their temperance;
That, to avoid extravagance,
They flew into a hollow tree,
Blest with content and honesty.

The Moral

Then leave complaints: fools only strive
To make a great, an honest hive.
T' enjoy the world's conveniencies,
Be fam'd in war, yet live in ease,
Without great vices, is a vain
Utopia seated in the brain.
Fraud, luxury, and pride must live,
While we the benefits receive:
Hunger's a dreadful plague, no doubt,
Yet who digests or thrives without?
Do we not owe the growth of wine
To the dry, shabby, crooked vine?
Which, while its shoots neglected stood,
Chok'd other plants, and ran to wood;
But blest us with its noble fruit,
As soon as it was tied and cut:
So vice is beneficial found,
When it's by justice lopp'd and bound;

Nay, where the people would be great,
As necessary to the state,
As hunger is to make 'em eat.
Bare virtue can't make nations live
In splendour; they that would revive
A golden age must be as free
For acorns as for honesty.

[1705]

From THE FABLE OF THE BEES: OR, PRIVATE VICES, PUBLIC BENEFITS

AN ENQUIRY INTO THE ORIGIN OF MORAL VIRTUE

All untaught animals are only solicitous of pleasing themselves, and naturally follow the bent of their own inclinations, without considering the good or harm that from their being pleased will accrue to others. This is the reason that in the wild state of nature those creatures are fittest to live peaceably together in great numbers that discover the least of understanding and have the fewest appetites to gratify; and consequently no species of animals is, without the curb of government, less capable of agreeing long together in multitudes than that of man; yet such are his qualities, whether good or bad, I shall not determine, that no creature besides himself can ever be made sociable: but being an extraordinary selfish and headstrong, as well as cunning, animal, however he may be subdued by superior strength, it is impossible by force alone to make him tractable, and receive the improvements he is capable of.

The chief thing, therefore, which lawgivers and other wise men that have laboured for the establishment of society have endeavoured, has been to make the people they were to govern believe that it was more beneficial for everybody to conquer than indulge his appetites, and much better to mind the public than what seemed his private interest. As this has always been a very difficult task, so no wit or eloquence has been left untried to compass it; and the moralists and philosophers of all ages employed their utmost skill to prove the truth of so useful an assertion. But whether mankind would have ever believed it or not, it is not likely that anybody could have persuaded them to disapprove of their natural inclinations, or prefer the good of others to their own, if at the same time he had not showed them an equivalent to be enjoyed as a reward for the violence, which by so doing they of necessity must commit upon themselves. Those that have undertaken to civilize mankind were not ignorant of this; but being unable to give so many real rewards as would satisfy all persons for every individual action, they were forced to contrive an imaginary one, that as a general equivalent for the trouble of self-denial should serve on all occasions, and without costing anything either to themselves or others, be yet a most acceptable recompense to the receivers.

They thoroughly examined all the strength and frailties of our nature, and observing that none were either so savage as not to be charmed with praise, or so despicable as patiently to bear contempt, justly concluded that flattery must be the most powerful argument that could be used to human creatures. Making use of this bewitching engine, they extolled the excellency of our nature above other animals, and setting forth with unbounded praises the wonders of our sagacity and vastness of understanding, bestowed a thousand encomiums on the rationality of our souls, by the help of which we were capable of performing the most noble achievements. Having by this artful way of flattery insinuated themselves into the hearts of men, they began to instruct them in the notions of honour and shame; representing the one as the worst of all evils, and the other as the highest good to which mortals could aspire: which being done, they laid before them how unbecoming it was the dignity of such sublime creatures to be solicitous about gratifying those appetites which they had in common with brutes, and at the same time unmindful of those higher qualities that gave them the pre-eminence over all visible beings. They indeed confessed that those impulses of nature were very pressing, that it was troublesome to resist and very difficult wholly to subdue them. But this they only used as an argument to demonstrate how glorious the conquest of them was on the one hand and how scandalous on the other not to attempt it.

To introduce, moreover, an emulation amongst men, they divided the whole species into two classes, vastly differing from one another; the one consisted of abject, low-minded people that, always hunting after immediate enjoyment, were wholly incapable of self-denial, and without regard to the good of others, had no higher aim than their private advantage; such as, being enslaved by voluptuousness, yielded without resistance to every gross desire, and made no use of their rational faculties but to heighten their sensual pleasures. These vile, grovelling wretches, they said, were the dross of their kind, and having only the shape of men, differed from brutes in nothing but their outward figure. But the other class was made up of lofty high-spirited creatures that, free from sordid selfishness, esteemed the improvements of the mind to be their fairest possessions; and setting a true value upon themselves, took no delight but in embellishing that part in which their excellency consisted; such as, despising whatever they had in common with irrational creatures, opposed by the help of reason their most violent inclinations, and making a continual war with themselves to promote the peace of others, aimed at no less than the public welfare and the conquest of their own passions.

**Fortior est qui se quam qui fortissima vincit Mœnia.*

These they called the true representatives of their sublime species, exceeding in worth the first class by more degrees than that itself was superior to the beasts of the field.

As in all animals that are not too imperfect to discover pride, we find that the finest and such as are the most beautiful and valuable of their kind, have generally the greatest share of it; so in man, the most perfect of animals, it is so inseparable from his very essence (how cunningly soever some may learn to hide or disguise it) that without it the compound he is made of would want one of the chiefest ingredients; which, if we consider, it is hardly to be doubted but lessons and remonstrances, so skillfully adapted to the good opinion man has of himself, as those I have mentioned, must, if scattered amongst a multitude, not only gain the assent of most of them, as to the speculative part, but likewise induce several, especially the fiercest, most resolute, and best among them, to endure a thousand inconveniences and undergo as many hardships, that they may have the pleasure of counting themselves men of the second class, and consequently appropriating to themselves all the excellences they have heard of it.

From what has been said, we ought to expect in the first place that the heroes who took such extraordinary pains to master some of their natural appetites, and preferred the good of others to any visible interest of their own, would not recede an inch from the fine notions they had received concerning the dignity of rational creatures, and having ever the authority of the government on their side, with all imaginable vigour assert the esteem that was due to those of the second class, as well as their superiority over the rest of their kind. In the second, that those who wanted a sufficient stock of either pride or resolution to buoy them up in mortifying of what was dearest to them, followed the sensual dictates of nature, would yet be ashamed of confessing themselves to be those despicable wretches that belonged to the inferior class, and were generally reckoned to be so little removed from brutes; and that therefore in their own defence they would say, as others did, and hiding their own imperfections as well as they could, cry up self-denial and public-spiritedness as much as any; for it is highly probable that some of them, convinced by the real proofs of fortitude and self-conquest they had seen, would admire in others what they found wanting in themselves; others be afraid of the resolution and prowess of those of the second class, and that all of them were kept in awe by the power of their rulers; wherefore it is reasonable to think that none of them (whatever they thought in themselves) would dare openly contradict what by everybody else was thought criminal to doubt of.

This was (or at least might have been) the manner after which savage man was broke; from whence it is evident that the first rudiments of morality, broached by skillful politicians, to render men useful to each other as well as tractable, were chiefly contrived that the ambitious might reap the more benefit from and govern vast numbers of them with the greater ease and security. This foundation of politics being once laid, it is impossible that man should long remain uncivilized; for even those who only strove to gratify their appetites, being continually crossed by others of the same stamp, could not but observe that whenever they checked their inclinations or but followed them with more circumspection, they avoided a world of troubles and often escaped many of the calamities that generally attended the too eager pursuit after pleasure.

First, they received, as well as others, the benefit of those actions that were done for the good of the whole society, and consequently could not forbear wishing well to those of the superior class that performed them. Secondly, the more intent they were in seeking their own advantage, without regard to others, the more they were hourly convinced that none were so obnoxious to them as those that were most like themselves.

It being the interest then of the very worst of them, more than any, to preach up public-spiritedness that they might reap the fruits of the labour and self-denial of others, and at the same time indulge their own appetites with less disturbance, they agreed with the rest to call everything which, without regard to the public, man should commit to gratify any of his appetites, VICE; if in that action there could be observed the least prospect that it might either be injurious to any of the society, or ever render himself less serviceable to others: and to give the name of VIRTUE to every performance by which man, contrary to the impulse of nature, should endeavour the benefit of others, or the conquest of his own passions out of a rational ambition of being good.

It shall be objected that no society was ever any ways civilized before the major part had agreed upon some worship or other of an overruling power, and consequently that the notions of good and evil and the distinction between virtue and vice were never the contrivance of politicians, but the pure effect of religion. Before I answer this objection, I must repeat what I have said already, that in this *Enquiry into the Origin of Moral Virtue* I speak neither of Jews or Christians, but man in his state of nature and ignorance of the true Deity; and then I affirm that the idolatrous superstitions of all other nations, and the pitiful notions they had of the Supreme Being, were incapable of exciting man to virtue, and good for nothing but to awe and amuse a rude and unthinking multitude. It is evident from history that in all considerable societies, how stupid or ridiculous soever people's received notions have been, as to the deities they worshipped, human nature has ever exerted itself in all its branches, and that there is no earthly wisdom or moral virtue but at one time or other men have excelled in it in all monarchies and commonwealths that for riches and power have been any ways remarkable.

The Egyptians, not satisfied with having deified all the ugly monsters they could think on, were so silly as to adore the onions of their own sowing; yet at the same time their country was the most famous nursery of arts and sciences in the world, and themselves more eminently skilled in the deepest mysteries of nature than any nation has been since.

No states or kingdoms under heaven have yielded more or greater patterns in all sorts of moral virtues than the Greek and Roman empires, more especially the latter, and yet how loose, absurd, and ridiculous were their sentiments as to sacred matters? For without reflecting on the extravagant number of their deities, if we only consider the infamous stories they fathered upon them, it is not to be denied but that their religion, far from teaching men the conquest of their passions and the way to virtue, seemed rather contrived to justify their appetites and encourage their vices. But if we would know what made them excel in fortitude, courage, and magnanimity, we must cast our eyes on the pomp of their triumphs, the magnificence of their monuments and arches; their trophies, statues and inscriptions; the variety of their military crowns, their honours decreed to the dead, public encomiums on the living, and other imaginary rewards they bestowed on men of merit; and we shall find that what carried so many of them to the utmost pitch of self-denial was nothing but their policy in making use of the most effectual means that human pride could be flattered with.

It is visible, then, that it was not any heathen religion or other idolatrous superstition that first put man upon crossing his appetites and subduing his dearest inclinations, but the skillful management of wary politicians; and the nearer we search into human nature, the more we shall be convinced that the moral virtues are the political offspring which flattery begot upon pride.

There is no man of what capacity or penetration soever, that is wholly proof against the witchcraft of flattery, if artfully performed and suited to his abilities. Children and fools will swallow personal praise, but those that are more cunning must be managed with greater circumspection; and the more general the flattery is, the less it is suspected by those it is levelled at. What you say in commendation of a whole town is received with pleasure by all the inhabitants; speak in commendation of letters in general, and every man of learning will think himself in particular obliged to you. You may safely praise the employment a man is of, or the country he was born in, because you give him an opportunity of screening the joy he feels upon his own account, under the esteem which he pretends to have for others.

It is common among cunning men that understand the power which flattery has upon pride, when they are afraid they shall be imposed upon, to enlarge, though much against their conscience, upon the honour, fair dealing, and integrity of the family, country, or sometimes the profession of him they suspect, because they know that men often will change their resolution and act against their inclination that they may have the pleasure of continuing to appear in the opinion of some what they are conscious not to be in reality. Thus sagacious moralists draw men like angels, in hopes that the pride at least of some will put them upon copying after the beautiful originals which they are represented to be.

When * the incomparable Mr. Steele, in the usual elegance of his easy style, dwells on the praises of his sublime species, and, with all the embellishments of rhetoric sets forth the excellency of human nature, it is impossible not to be charmed with his happy turns of thought, and the politeness of his expressions. But though I have been often moved by the force of his eloquence and ready to swallow the ingenious sophistry with pleasure, yet I could never be so serious, but, reflecting on his artful encomiums, I thought on the tricks made use of by the women that would teach children to be mannerly. When an awkward girl, before she can either speak or go, begins after many entreaties to make the first rude essays of curtsying, the nurse falls in an ecstasy of praise: "There's a delicate curtsy! O fine miss! There's a pretty lady! Mama! Miss can make a better curtsy than her sister Molly!" The same is echoed over by the maids, whilst mama almost hugs the child to pieces; only Miss Molly, who, being four years older, knows how to make a very handsome curtsy, wonders at the perverseness of their judgment, and swelling with indignation, is ready to cry at the injustice that is done her; till, being whispered in the ear that it is only to please the baby, and that she is a woman, she grows proud at being let into the secret, and rejoicing at the superiority of her understanding, repeats what has been said with large additions, and insults over the weakness of her sister, whom all this while she fancies to be the only bubble among them. These extravagant praises would by any one above the capacity of an infant, be called fulsome flatteries and, if you will, abominable lies, yet experience teaches us that by the help of such gross encomiums, young misses will be brought to make pretty curtsies and behave themselves womanly much sooner and with less trouble than they would without them. 'Tis the same with boys, whom they'll strive to persuade that all fine gentlemen do as they are bid and that none but beggar boys are rude, or dirty their clothes; nay, as soon as the wild brat with his untaught fist begins to fumble for his hat, the mother, to make him pull it off, tells him before he is two years old that he is a man, and if he repeats that action when she desires him, he's presently a captain, a lord mayor, a king, or something higher if she can think of it; till egged on by the force of praise, the little urchin endeavours to imitate man as well as he can and strains all his faculties to appear what his shallow noddle imagines he is believed to be.

The meanest wretch puts an inestimable value upon himself, and the highest wish of the ambitious man is to have all the world as to that particular of his opinion: so that the most insatiable thirst after fame that ever hero was inspired with, was never more than an ungovernable greediness to engross the esteem and admiration of others in future ages as well as his own; and (what mortification soever this truth might be to the second thoughts of an Alexander or a Cæsar) the great recompense in view, for which the most exalted minds have with so much alacrity sacrificed their quiet, health, sensual pleasures, and every inch of themselves, has never been anything else but the breath of man, the aërial coin of praise. Who can forbear laughing when he thinks on all the great men that have been so serious on the subject of that Macedonian madman, his capacious soul, that mighty heart, in one corner of which, according to * Lorenzo Gratian, the world was so commodiously lodged that in the whole there was room for six more? Who can forbear laughing, I say, when he compares the fine things that have been said of Alexander, with the end he proposed to himself from his vast exploits, to be proved from his own mouth; when the vast pains he took to pass the Hydaspes forced him to cry out, "O ye Athenians, could you believe what dangers I expose myself to, to be praised by you!" For, to define the reward of glory in the amplest manner, the most that can be said of it is that it consists in a superlative felicity which a man, who is conscious of having performed a noble action, enjoys in self-love, whilst he is thinking on the applause he expects of others.

But here I shall be told that besides the noisy exploits of war and public bustle of the ambitious, there are noble and generous actions that are performed in silence; that virtue being its own reward, those who are really good have a satisfaction in their consciousness of being so, which is all the recompense they expect from the most worthy performances; that among the heathens there have been men who, when they did good to others, were so far from coveting thanks and applause that they took all imaginable care to be forever concealed from those on whom they bestowed their benefits; and consequently that pride has no hand in spurring man on to the highest pitch of self-denial.

In answer to this I say that it is impossible to judge of a man's performance unless we are thoroughly acquainted with the principle and motive from which he acts. Pity, though it is the most gentle and the least mischievous of all our passions, is yet as much a frailty of our nature as anger, pride, or fear. The weakest minds have generally the greatest share of it, for which reason none are more compassionate than women and children. It must be owned that of all our weaknesses it is the most amiable and bears the greatest resemblance to virtue; nay, without a considerable mixture of it the society could hardly subsist: but as it is an impulse of nature that consults neither the public interest nor our own reason, it may produce evil as well as good. It has helped to destroy the honour of virgins and corrupted the integrity of judges; and whoever acts from it as a principle, what good soever he may bring to the society, has nothing to boast of but that he has indulged a passion that has happened to be beneficial to the public. There is no merit in saving an innocent babe ready to drop into the fire: the action is neither good nor bad, and what benefit soever the infant received, we only obliged ourselves; for to have seen it fall and not strove to hinder it, would have caused a pain, which self-preservation compelled us to prevent: nor has a rich prodigal that happens to be of a commiserating temper and loves to gratify his passions, greater virtue to boast of when he relieves an object of compassion with what to himself is a trifle.

But such men, as without complying with any weakness of their own, can part from what they value themselves, and, from no other motive but their love to goodness, perform a worthy action in silence, such men, I confess, have acquired more refined notions of virtue than those I have hitherto spoke of; yet even in these (with which the world has yet never swarmed) we may discover no small symptoms of pride, and the humblest man alive must confess that the reward of a virtuous action, which is the satisfaction that ensues upon it, consists in a certain pleasure he procures to himself by contemplating on his own worth: which pleasure, together with the occasion of it, are as certain signs of pride as looking pale and trembling at any imminent danger are the symptoms of fear.

If the too scrupulous reader should at first view condemn these notions concerning the origin of moral virtue, and think them perhaps offensive to Christianity, I hope he'll forbear his censures when he shall consider that nothing can render the unsearchable depth of the Divine Wisdom more conspicuous than that man, whom Providence had designed for society, should not only by his own frailties and imperfections be led into the road to temporal happiness, but likewise receive, from a seeming necessity of natural causes, a tincture of that knowledge in which he was afterwards to be made perfect by the true religion, to his eternal welfare.

[1714]

ANTHONY ASHLEY COOPER, EARL OF SHAFTESBURY

Anthony Ashley Cooper, third Earl of Shaftesbury, was the grandson of the first earl, whom Dryden had satirized as "Achitophel." Except for a short period at Winchester School, he was privately educated under the supervision of John Locke, and spent much time abroad. By inheritance and training he held strong Whig prejudices, opposing High Church sacerdotalism even more vigorously than dissenting enthusiasm. Though he always rendered nominal allegiance to the Church of England by law established, he had so little sympathy with its doctrines that he is usually reckoned among the Deists. In most respects he was tolerant to the verge of indifference, cosmopolitan in his culture, refined, with the tastes of a gentleman and the spirit of a virtuoso.

In philosophy he was an optimist, opposing both Hobbes's concept of the state of nature and the Christian doctrine of the fall of man. He believed in the harmony of nature presided over by an all-pervading God of supreme benevolence, who is to be discerned in nature and worshipped rationally. Evil, he conceived not as an interruption to this harmony but merely as an appearance resulting from our ignorance. "What is beautiful is harmonious and proportionable; what is harmonious and proportionable is true; and what is at once both beautiful and true is, of consequence, agreeable and good." Conversely he believed that ridicule is the most effective weapon against things inharmonious and disproportioned. "For nothing is ridiculous except what is deformed; nor is anything proof against raillery except what is handsome and just." So, too, he laid great emphasis upon taste, which, he taught, is not capricious but is based upon the fundamental harmony of nature, and consequently, when properly developed, provides a sure guide in religion, morals, and art.

Shaftesbury's concept of the divinity of nature and his advice to follow nature suggest at first sight the romantic point of view, but they are in reality very different. For him nature is universal harmony, ideal and unchanging, an expression of the divine perfection. When he speaks of following nature, he advises not obedience to animal impulses but self-discipline in accordance with the best. He was not a relativist but a believer in definite standards of judgment for art and for morals. He recognized the significance of universal values, and condemned the craze for mere novelty; he perceived the importance of criticism as an aid alike to the appreciation and the creation of literature. In one respect, however, he was at variance with the Christian and the classical tradition: his belief in the essential goodness of human nature. He did not perceive, and in his day no one could perceive, the consequences to which this idea would lead in Rousseau and his followers.

The influence of Shaftesbury was great, both directly and indirectly. Pope drew from him many of the ideas to which he gave brilliant expression in *An Essay on Man*; Swift reacted violently against his facile optimism; Mandeville attacked Shaftesbury's system; Hutcheson defended it; Berkeley criticized it. In France and in Germany his writings were influential.

The extracts here reprinted are from *Soliloquy, or Advice to an Author*, first published in 1710 included in *Characteristics*, and from *Miscellaneous Reflections*, published posthumously in 1714, included in later editions of *Characteristics*. However, since the later work is in large measure a commentary on the earlier, and since both extracts treat the same subjects, they form a coherent whole.

From CHARACTERISTICS OF MEN, MANNERS, OPINIONS, TIMES

Soliloquy, or Advice to an Author

Part III, Section III

We are now arrived to that part of our performance where it becomes us to cast our eye back on what has already passed. The observers of method generally make this the place of recapitulation. Other artists have substituted the practice of apology, or extenuation. For the anticipating manner of prefatory discourse is too well known to work any surprising effect in the author's behalf, preface being become only another word to signify excuse. Besides that the author is generally the most straitened in that preliminary part, which on other accounts is too apt to grow voluminous. He therefore takes the advantage of his corollary or winding up, and ends pathetically by endeavouring, in the softest manner, to reconcile his reader to those faults which he chooses rather to excuse than to amend.

General practice has made this a necessary part of elegance, hardly to be passed over by any writer. 'Tis the chief stratagem by which he engages in personal conference with his reader, and can talk immoderately of himself, with all the seeming modesty of one who is the furthest from any selfish views, or conceited thoughts of his own merit. There appears such a peculiar grace and ingenuity in the method of confessing laziness, precipitancy, carelessness, or whatever other vices have been the occasion of the author's deficiency, that it would seem a pity had the work itself been brought to such perfection as to have left no room for the penitent party to enlarge on his own demerits. For from the multiplicity of these, he finds subject to ingratiate himself with his reader, who doubtless is not a little raised by this submission of a confessing author and is ready on these terms to give him absolution and receive him into his good grace and favour.

In the gallant world, indeed, we easily find how far a humility of this kind prevails. They who hope to rise by merit are likeliest to be disappointed in their pretensions. The confessing lover, who ascribes all to the bounty of the fair one, meets his reward the sooner, for having studied less how to deserve it. For merit is generally thought presumptuous, and supposed to carry with it a certain assurance and ease with which a mistress is not so well contented. The claim of well deserving seems to derogate from the pure grace and favour of the benefactress, who then appears to herself most sovereign in power and likeliest to be obeyed without reserve when she bestows her bounty where there is least title or pretension.

Thus a certain adoration of the sex, which passes in our age without the least charge of profaneness or idolatry, may, according to vulgar imagination, serve to justify these gallant votaries in the imitation of the real religious and devout. The method of self-abasement may perhaps be thought the properest to make approaches to the sacred shrines; and the entire resignation of merit in each case may be esteemed the only ground of well deserving. But what we allow to heaven or to the fair should not, methinks, be made a precedent in favour of the world. Whatever deference is due to that body of men whom we call readers, we may be supposed to treat them with sufficient honour, if with thorough diligence and pains we endeavour to render our works perfect, and leave them to judge of the performance as they are able.

However difficult or desperate it may appear in any artist to endeavour to bring perfection into his work, if he has not at least the idea of perfection to give him aim, he will be found very defective and mean in his performance. Though his intention be to please the world, he must nevertheless be, in a manner, above it, and fix his eye upon that consummate grace, that beauty of nature, and that perfection of numbers, which the rest of mankind, feeling only by the effect whilst ignorant of the cause, term the **je ne sais quoi*, the unintelligible, or the "I know not what," and suppose to be a kind of charm or enchantment, of which the artist himself can give no account.

But here I find I am tempted to do what I have myself condemned. Hardly can I forbear making some apology for my frequent recourse to the rules of common artists, to the masters of exercise, to the academies of painters, statuaries, and to the rest of the virtuoso tribe. But in this I am so fully satisfied I have reason on my side, that, let custom be ever so strong against me, I had rather repair to these inferior schools to search for truth and nature, than to some other places where higher arts and sciences are professed.

I am persuaded that to be a *virtuoso (so far as befits a gentleman) is a higher step towards the becoming a man of virtue and good sense, than the being what in this age we call a scholar. For even rude nature itself, in its primitive simplicity, is a better guide to judgment than improved sophistry and pedantic learning. The **faciuntne intellegendo, ut nihil intellegant?* will ever be applied by men of discernment and free thought to such logic, such principles, such forms and rudiments of knowledge, as are established in certain schools of literature and science. The case is sufficiently understood even by those who are unwilling to confess the truth of it. Effects betray their causes. And the known turn and figure of those understandings which sprout from nurseries of this kind, give a plain idea

* Notes on Shaftesbury will be found in the Appendix, pp. 967 ff.

of what is judged on this occasion. 'Tis no wonder if, after so wrong a ground of education, there appears to be such need of redress and amendment from that excellent school which we call the world. The mere amusements of gentlemen are found more improving than the profound researches of pedants. And in the management of our youth we are forced to have recourse to the former, as an antidote against the genius peculiar to the latter. If the formalists of this sort were erected into patentees with a sole commission of authorship, we should undoubtedly see such writing in our days as would either wholly wean us from all books in general, or at least from all such as were the product of our own nation under such a subordinate and conforming government.

However this may prove, there can be no kind of writing which relates to men and manners where it is not necessary for the author to understand poetical and moral truth, the beauty of sentiments, the sublime of characters, and carry in his eye the model or exemplar of that natural grace which gives to every action its attractive charm. If he has naturally no eye or ear for these interior numbers, 'tis not likely he should be able to judge better of that exterior proportion and symmetry of composition which constitutes a legitimate piece.

Could we once convince ourselves of what is in itself so evident, that in the very nature of things there must of necessity be the foundation of a right and wrong taste, as well in respect of inward characters and features as of outward person, behaviour, and action, we should be far more ashamed of ignorance and wrong judgment in the former than in the latter of these subjects. Even in the arts, which are mere imitations of that outward grace and beauty, we not only confess a taste, but make it a part of refined breeding to discover amidst the many false manners and ill styles the true and natural one, which represents the real beauty and Venus of the kind. 'Tis the like moral grace and Venus which, discovering itself in the turns of character and the variety of human affection, is copied by the writing artist. If he knows not this Venus, these graces, nor was ever struck with the beauty, the decorum of this inward kind, he can neither paint advantageously after the life nor in a feigned subject where he has full scope. For never can he, on these terms, represent merit and virtue, or mark deformity and blemish. Never can he with justice and true proportion assign the boundaries of either part, or separate the distant characters. The schemes must be defective, and the draughts confused, where the standard is weakly established and the measure out of use. Such a designer, who has so little feeling of these proportions, so little consciousness of this excellence or these perfections, will never be found able to describe a perfect character; or, what is more according to art, express the effect and force of this perfection from the result of various and mixed characters of life. And thus the sense of inward numbers, the knowledge and practice of the social virtues, and the familiarity and favour of the moral graces, are essential to the character of a deserving artist and just favourite of the Muses. Thus are the arts and virtues mutually friends; and thus the science of virtuosos and that of virtue itself become, in a manner, one and the same.

One who aspires to the character of a man of breeding and politeness is careful to form his judgment of arts and sciences upon right models of perfection. If he travels to Rome, he inquires which are the truest pieces of architecture, the best remains of statues, the best paintings of a Raphael or a Carracci. However antiquated, rough, or dismal they may appear to him at first sight, he resolves to view them over and over, till he has brought himself to relish them, and finds their hidden graces and perfections. He takes particular care to turn his eye from everything which is gaudy, luscious, and of a false taste. Nor is he less careful to turn his ear from every sort of music besides that which is of the best manner and truest harmony.

'Twere to be wished we had the same regard to a right taste in life and manners. What mortal being, once convinced of a difference in inward character, and of a preference due to one kind above another, would not be concerned to make his own the best? If civility and humanity be a taste; if brutality, insolence, riot, be in the same manner a taste, who, if he could reflect, would not choose to form himself on the amiable and agreeable rather than the odious and perverse model? Who would not endeavour to force nature as well in this respect as in what relates to a taste or judgment in other arts and sciences? For in each place the force on nature is used only for its redress. If a natural good taste be not already formed in us, why should not we endeavour to form it, and cultivate it till it become natural?

"I like! I fancy! I admire! How? By accident, or as I please? No. But I learn to fancy, to admire, to please, as the subjects themselves are deserving, and can bear me out. Otherwise I like at this hour but dislike the next. I shall be weary of my pursuit, and, upon experience, find little pleasure in the main, if my choice and judgment in it be from no other rule than that single one, because I please. Grotesque and monstrous figures often please. Cruel spectacles and barbarities are also found to please, and, in some tempers, to please beyond all other subjects. But is this pleasure right? And shall I follow it if it presents? Not strive with it, or endeavour to prevent its growth or prevalency in my temper? How stands the case in a more soft and flattering kind of pleasure? Effeminacy pleases me. The Indian figures, the Japan work, the enamel strikes my eye. The luscious colours and glossy paint gain upon my fancy. A French or Flemish style is highly liked by me at first sight, and I pursue my liking. But what ensues? Do I not forever forfeit my good relish? How is it possible I should thus come to taste the beauties of an Italian master, or of a hand happily formed on nature and the ancients? 'Tis not by wantonness and humour that I shall attain my end and arrive at the enjoyment I propose. The art itself is severe, the rules rigid. And if I expect the knowledge should come to me by accident, or in play, I shall be grossly deluded, and prove myself, at best, a mock-virtuoso or mere pedant of the kind."

Here therefore we have once again exhibited our moral science in * the same method and manner of soliloquy as above. To this correction of humour and formation of a taste, our reading, if it be of the right sort, must principally contribute. Whatever company we keep, or however polite and agreeable their characters may be with whom we converse or correspond, if the authors we read are of another kind, we shall find our palate strangely turned their way. We are the unhappier in this respect for being scholars, if our studies be ill chosen. Nor can I, for this reason, think it proper to call a man well-read who reads many authors, since he must of necessity have more ill models than good, and be more stuffed with bombast, ill fancy, and wry thought, than filled with solid sense and just imagination.

But notwithstanding this hazard of our taste from a multiplicity of reading, we are not, it seems, the least scrupulous in our choice of subject. We read whatever comes next us. What was first put into our hand when we were young, serves us afterwards for serious study and wise research when we are old. We are many of us, indeed, so grave as to continue this exercise of youth through our remaining life. The exercising authors of this kind have been above described in the beginning of this treatise. The manner of exercise is called meditation and is of a sort so solemn and profound that we dare not so much as thoroughly examine the subject on which we are bid to meditate. This is a sort of task-reading in which a taste is not permitted. How little soever we take of this diet, it is sufficient to give full exercise to our grave humour and allay the appetite towards further research and solid contemplation. The rest is holiday, diversion, play, and fancy. We reject all rule, as thinking it an injury to our diversions to have regard to truth or nature, without which, however, nothing can be truly agreeable or entertaining, much less instructive or improving. Through a certain surfeit taken in a wrong kind of serious reading, we apply ourselves with full content to the most ridiculous. The more remote our pattern is from anything moral or profitable, the more freedom and satisfaction we find in it. We care not how Gothic or barbarous our models are, what ill-designed or monstrous figures we view, or what false proportions we trace or see described in history, romance, or fiction. And thus our eye and ear is lost. Our relish or taste must of necessity grow barbarous whilst barbarian customs, savage manners, Indian wars, and wonders of the *terra incognita*, employ our leisure hours and are the chief materials to furnish out a library.

These are in our present days, what books of chivalry were in those of our forefathers. I know not what faith our valiant ancestors may have had in the stories of their giants, their dragons, and St. Georges. But for our faith, indeed, as well as our taste, in this other way of reading, I must confess I can't consider it without astonishment.

It must certainly be something else than incredulity which fashions the taste and judgment of many gentlemen whom we hear censured as atheists for attempting to philosophize after a newer manner than any known of late. For my own part, I have ever thought this sort of men to be in general more credulous, though after another manner than the mere vulgar. Besides what I have observed in conversation with the men of this character, I can produce many anathematized authors, who if they want a true Israelitish faith, can make amends by a Chinese or Indian one. If they are short in Syria or the Palestine, they have their full measure in America or Japan. Histories of Incas or Iroquois written by friars and missionaries, pirates and renegades, sea captains and trusty travellers, pass for authentic records and are canonical with the virtuosos of this sort. Though Christian miracles may not so well satisfy them, they dwell with the highest contentment on the prodigies of Moorish and pagan countries. They have far more pleasure in hearing the monstrous accounts of monstrous men and manners than the politest and best narrations of the affairs, the governments, and lives of the wisest and most polished people.

'Tis the same taste which makes us prefer a Turkish history to a Grecian or a Roman, an Ariosto to a Virgil, and a romance or novel to an *Iliad*. We have no regard to the character or genius of our author, nor are so far curious as to observe how able he is in the judgment of facts, or how ingenious in the texture of his lies. For facts unably related, though with the greatest sincerity and good faith, may prove the worst sort of deceit; and mere lies, judiciously composed, can teach us the truth of things beyond any other manner. But to amuse ourselves with such authors as neither know how to lie nor tell truth discovers a taste which methinks one should not be apt to envy. Yet so enchanted we are with the travelling memoirs of any casual adventurer, that be his character or genius what it will, we have no sooner turned over a page or two than we begin to interest ourselves highly in his affairs. No sooner has he taken shipping at the mouth of the Thames, or sent his baggage before him to Gravesend, or buoy in * the Nore, than straight our attention is earnestly taken up. If in order to his more distant travels, he takes some part of Europe in his way, we can with patience hear of inns and ordinaries, passage boats and ferries, foul and fair weather; with all the particulars of the author's diet, habit of body, his personal dangers and mischances on land and sea. And thus, full of desire and hope, we accompany him till he enters on his great scene of action and begins by the description of some enormous fish or beast. From monstrous brutes he proceeds to yet more monstrous men. For in this race of authors he is ever completest and of the first rank who is able to speak of things the most unnatural and monstrous.

This humour our old tragic poet seems to have discovered. He hit our taste in giving us a Moorish hero full fraught with prodigy, a wondrous story teller! But for the attentive part, the poet chose to give it to womankind. What passionate reader of travels or student in the prodigious sciences can refuse to pity that fair lady who fell in love with the miraculous Moor? especially considering with what suitable grace such a lover could relate the most monstrous adventures and satisfy the wondering appetite with the most wondrous tales, wherein (says the hero traveller)

> * Of antres vast and deserts idle,
> It was my hint to speak, —
> And of the cannibals that each other eat!
> The Anthropophagi! and men whose heads
> Do grow beneath their shoulders. These to hear
> Would Desdemona seriously incline.

Seriously, 'twas a woeful tale! unfit, one would think, to win a tender fair one. It's true the poet sufficiently condemns her fancy, and makes her (poor lady!) pay dearly for it in the end. But why, amongst his Greek names, he should have chosen one which denoted the lady superstitious, I can't imagine; unless, as poets are sometimes prophets too, he should figuratively under this dark type have represented to us that about a hundred years after his time, the fair sex of this island should, by other monstrous tales, be so seduced as to turn their favour chiefly on the persons of the tale tellers, and change their natural inclination for fair, candid, and courteous knights into a passion for a mysterious race of black enchanters, such as of old were said to creep into houses and lead captive silly women.

'Tis certain there is a very great affinity between the passion of superstition and that of tales. The love of strange narrations and the ardent appetite towards unnatural objects has a near alliance with the like appetite towards the supernatural kind, such as are called prodigious and of dire omen. For so the mind forebodes on every such unusual sight or hearing. Fate, destiny, or the anger of heaven seems denoted, and as it were delineated, by the monstrous birth, the horrid fact, or dire event. For this reason the very persons of such relators or tale tellers with a small help of dismal habit, suitable countenance and tone, become sacred and tremendous in the eyes of mortals who are thus addicted from their youth. The tender virgins, losing their natural softness, assume this tragic passion, of which they are highly susceptible, especially when a suitable kind of eloquence and action attends the character of the narrator. A thousand Desdemonas are then ready to present themselves, and would frankly resign fathers, relations, countrymen, and country itself to follow the fortunes of a hero of the black tribe.

But whatever monstrous zeal or superstitious passion the poet might foretell, either in the gentlemen, ladies, or common people of an after age, 'tis certain that as to books, the same Moorish fancy in its plain and literal sense prevails strongly at this present time. Monsters and monster lands were never more in request; and we may often see a philosopher or a wit run a tale-gathering in those idle deserts, as familiarly as the silliest woman or merest boy.

One would imagine that our philosophical writers, who pretend to treat of morals, should far outdo mere poets in recommending virtue, and representing what was fair and amiable in human actions. One would imagine that, if they turned their eye towards remote countries (of which they affect so much to speak), they should search for that simplicity of manners and innocence of behaviour which has been often known among mere savages, ere they were corrupted by our commerce, and, by sad example, instructed in all kinds of treachery and inhumanity. 'Twould be of advantage to us to hear the causes of this strange corruption in ourselves, and be made consider of our deviation from nature, and from that just purity of manners which might be expected, especially from a people so assisted and enlightened by religion. For who would not naturally expect more justice, fidelity, temperance, and honesty from Christians than from Mahometans or mere pagans? But so far are our modern moralists from condemning any unnatural vices or corrupt manners, whether in our own or foreign climates, that they would have vice itself appear as natural as virtue, and from the worst examples would represent to us that all actions are naturally indifferent; that they have no note or character of good or ill in themselves, but are distinguished by mere fashion, law, or arbitrary decree. Wonderful philosophy! raised from the dregs of an illiterate, mean kind, which was ever despised among the great ancients, and rejected by all men of action or sound erudition, but in these ages imperfectly copied from the original, and, with much disadvantage, imitated and assumed in common both by devout and indevout attempters in the moral kind.

Should a writer upon music, addressing himself to the students and lovers of the art, declare to them that the measure or rule of harmony was caprice or will, humour or fashion, 'tis not very likely he should be heard with great attention or treated with real gravity. For harmony is harmony by nature, let men judge ever so ridiculously of music. So is symmetry and proportion founded still in nature, let men's fancy prove ever so barbarous, or their fashions ever so Gothic, in their architecture, sculpture, or whatever other designing art. 'Tis the same case where life and manners are concerned. Virtue has the same fixed standard. The same numbers, harmony, and proportion will have place in morals, and are discoverable in the characters and affections of mankind; in which are laid the just foundations of an art and science superior to every other of human practice and comprehension.

This I suppose, therefore, is highly necessary, that a writer should comprehend. For things are stubborn, and will not be as we fancy them, or as the fashion varies, but as they stand in nature. Now whether the writer be poet, philosopher, or of whatever kind, he is in truth no other than a copyist after nature. His style may be differently suited to the different times he lives in, or to the different humour of his age or nation; his manner, his dress, his colouring may vary. But if his drawing be uncorrect, or his design contrary to nature, his piece will be found ridiculous when it comes thoroughly to be examined. For nature will not be mocked.

The prepossession against her can never be very lasting. Her decrees and instincts are powerful, and her sentiments inbred. She has a strong party abroad, and as strong a one within ourselves; and when any slight is put upon her, she can soon turn the reproach and make large reprisals on the taste and judgment of her antagonist.

Whatever philosopher, critic, or author is convinced of this prerogative of nature, will easily be persuaded to apply himself to the great work of reforming his taste, which he will have reason to suspect, if he be not such a one as has deliberately endeavoured to frame it by the just standard of nature. Whether this be his case he will easily discover by appealing to his memory. For custom and fashion are powerful seducers; and he must, of necessity, have fought hard against these to have attained that justness of taste which is required in one who pretends to follow nature. But if no such conflict can be called to mind, 'tis a certain token that the party has his taste very little different from the vulgar. And on this account he should instantly betake himself to the wholesome practice recommended in this treatise. He should set afoot the powerfulest faculties of his mind and assemble the best forces of his wit and judgment, in order to make a formal descent on the territories of the heart, resolving to decline no combat nor hearken to any terms till he had pierced into its inmost provinces and reached the seat of empire. No treaties should amuse him, no advantages lead him aside. All other speculations should be suspended, all other mysteries resigned, till this necessary campaign was made and these inward conflicts learnt, by which he would be able to gain at least some tolerable insight into himself, and knowledge of his own natural principles....

[1710]

From CHARACTERISTICS OF MEN, MANNERS, OPINIONS, TIMES

Miscellaneous Reflections

Miscellany III, Chapter I

...It may be proper for us to remark *in favour of our author, that the sort of ridicule or raillery which is apt to fall upon philosophers is of the same kind with that which falls commonly on the virtuosos or refined wits of the age. In this latter general denomination we include the real, fine gentlemen, the lovers of art and ingenuity: such as have seen the world and informed themselves of the manners and customs of the several nations of Europe; searched into their antiquities and records; considered their police, laws, and constitutions; observed the situation, strength, and ornaments of their cities, their principal arts, studies, and amusements, their architecture, sculpture, painting, music, and their taste in poetry, learning, language, and conversation.

Hitherto there can lie no ridicule, nor the least scope for satiric wit or raillery. But when we push this virtuoso character a little further and lead our polished gentleman into more nice researches; when from the view of mankind and their affairs, our speculative genius and minute examiner of nature's works proceeds with equal or perhaps superior zeal in the contemplation of the insect life, the conveniencies, habitations, and economy of a race of shellfish; when he has erected a cabinet in due form and made it the real pattern of his mind, replete with the same trash and trumpery of correspondent empty notions and chimerical conceits, — he then indeed becomes the subject of sufficient raillery and is made the jest of common conversations.

A worse thing than this happens commonly to *these inferior virtuosos. In seeking so earnestly for rarities, they fall in love with rarity for rareness' sake. Now the greatest rarities in the world are monsters. So that the study and relish of these gentlemen, thus assiduously employed, becomes at last in reality monstrous; and their whole delight is found to consist in selecting and contemplating whatever is most monstrous, disagreeing, out of the way, and to the least purpose of anything in nature.

In philosophy, matters answer exactly to this virtuoso scheme. Let us suppose a man, who having this resolution merely, how to employ his understanding to the best purpose, considers who or what he is, whence he arose, or had his being, to what end he was designed, and to what course of action he is by his natural frame and constitution destined: should he descend on this account into himself and examine his inward powers and faculties, or should he ascend beyond his own immediate species, city, or community, to discover and recognize his higher polity or community (that common and universal one, of which he is born a member); nothing, surely, of this kind could reasonably draw upon him the least contempt or mockery. On the contrary, the finest gentleman must after all be considered but as an idiot who, talking much of the knowledge of the world and mankind, has never so much as thought of the study or knowledge of himself, or of the nature and government of that real public and world from whence he holds his being.

* *Quid sumus, et quidnam victuri gignimur?* ——

"Where are we? Under what roof? Or on board what vessel? Whither bound? On what business? Under whose pilotship, government, or protection?" are questions which every sensible man would naturally ask, if he were on a sudden transported into a new scene of life. 'Tis admirable, indeed, to consider that a man should have been long come into a world, carried his reason and sense about with him, and yet have never seriously asked himself this single question, "Where am I? or what?" but; on the contrary, should proceed regularly to every other study and inquiry, postponing this alone, as the least considerable, or leaving the examination of it to others commissioned, as he supposes, to understand and think for him, upon this head. To be bubbled or put upon by any sham advices in this affair, is, it seems, of no consequence! We take care to examine accurately by our own judgment, the affairs of other people and the concerns of the world which least belong to us; but what relates more immediately to ourselves, and is our chief self-interest, we charitably leave to others to examine for us, and readily take up with the first comers, on whose honesty and good faith 'tis presumed we may safely rely.

Here, methinks, the ridicule turns more against the philosophy haters than the virtuosos or philosophers. Whilst philosophy is taken (as in its prime sense it ought) for mastership in life and manners, 'tis like to make no ill figure in the world whatever impertinencies may reign, or however extravagant the times may prove. But let us view philosophy, like mere virtuosoship, in its usual career; and we shall find the ridicule rising full as strongly against the professors of the higher as the lower kind. Cockleshell abounds with each. Many things exterior and without ourselves, of no relation to our real interests or to those of society and mankind, are diligently investigated; nature's remotest operations, deepest mysteries and most difficult phenomena discussed and whimsically explained; hypotheses and fantastic systems erected; a universe anatomized; and by some notable scheme so solved and reduced as to appear an easy knack or secret to those who have the clew. Creation itself can upon occasion be exhibited; transmutations, projections, and other philosophical arcana, such as in the corporeal world can accomplish all things; whilst in the intellectual, a set frame of metaphysical phrases and distinctions can serve to solve whatever difficulties may be propounded either in logics, ethics, or any real science of whatever kind.

It appears from hence that the defects of philosophy and those of virtuosoship are of the same nature. Nothing can be more dangerous than a wrong choice or misapplication in these affairs. But as ridiculous as these studies are rendered by their senseless managers, it appears, however, that each of them are, in their nature, essential to the character of a fine gentleman and man of sense.

To philosophize in a just signification is but to carry good breeding a step higher. For the accomplishment of breeding is to learn whatever is decent in company or beautiful in arts; and the sum of philosophy is to learn what is just in society and beautiful in nature, and the order of the world.

'Tis not wit merely, but a temper which must form the well-bred man. In the same manner, 'tis not a head merely, but a heart and resolution which must complete the real philosopher. Both characters aim at what is excellent, aspire to a just taste, and carry in view the model of what is beautiful and becoming. Accordingly the respective conduct and distinct manners of each party are regulated, the one according to the perfectest ease and good entertainment of company, the other according to the strictest interest of mankind and society; the one according to a man's rank and quality in his private nation, the other according to his rank and dignity in nature.

Whether each of these officers or social parts are in themselves as convenient as becoming, is the great question which must someway be decided. The well-bred man has already decided this, in his own case, and declared on the side of what is handsome; for whatever he practises in this kind, he accounts no more than what he owes purely to himself, without regard to any further advantage. The pretender to philosophy, who either knows not how to determine this affair, or if he has determined, knows not how to pursue his point with constancy and firmness, remains in respect of philosophy what a clown or coxcomb is in respect of breeding and behaviour. Thus, according to our author, the taste of beauty and the relish of what is decent, just, and amiable, perfects the character of the gentleman and the philosopher. And the study of such a taste or relish will, as we suppose, be ever the great employment and concern of him who covets as well to be wise and good as agreeable and polite.

* *Quid verum atque decens, curo, et rogo, et omnis in hoc sum.*

Chapter II

By this time, surely, I must have proved myself sufficiently engaged in the project and design of our self-discoursing author whose defence I have undertaken. His pretension, as plainly appears in this third treatise, is to recommend morals on the same foot with what in a lower sense is called manners; and to advance philosophy (as harsh a subject as it may appear) on the very foundation of what is called agreeable and polite. And 'tis in this method and management that, as his interpreter or paraphrast, I have proposed to imitate and accompany him as far as my miscellaneous character will permit.

Our joint endeavour, therefore, must appear this: to show that nothing which is found charming or delightful in the polite world, nothing which is adopted as pleasure or entertainment of whatever kind, can any way be accounted for, supported, or established without the pre-establishment or supposition of a certain taste. Now a taste or judgment, 'tis supposed, can hardly come ready formed with us into the world. Whatever principles or materials of this kind we may possibly bring with us, whatever good faculties, senses, or anticipating sensations and imaginations, may be of nature's growth and arise properly, of themselves, without our art, promotion, or assistance; the general idea which is formed of all this management, and the clear notion we attain of what is preferable and principal in all these subjects of choice and estimation, will not, as I imagine, by any person, be taken for innate. Use, practice, and culture must precede the understanding and wit of such an advanced size and growth as this. A legitimate and just taste can neither be begotten, made, conceived, or produced without the antecedent labour and pains of criticism.

For this reason we presume not only to defend the cause of critics, but to declare open war against those indolent, supine authors, performers, readers, auditors, actors, or spectators, who making their humour alone the rule of what is beautiful and agreeable, and having no account to give of such their humour or odd fancy, reject the criticizing or examining art, by which alone they are able to discover the true beauty and worth of every object.

According to that affected ridicule which these insipid remarkers pretend to throw upon just critics, the enjoyment of all real arts or natural beauties would be entirely lost; even in behaviour and manners we should at this rate become in time as barbarous as in our pleasures and diversions. I would presume it, however, of these critic-haters, that they are not yet so uncivilized or void of all social sense as to maintain that the most barbarous life or brutish pleasure is as desirable as the most polished or refined.

For my own part, when I have heard sometimes men of reputed ability join in with that effeminate, plaintive tone of invective against critics, I have really thought they had it in their fancy to keep down the growing geniuses of the youth, their rivals, by turning them aside from that examination and search on which all good performance, as well as good judgment, depends. I have seen many a time a well-bred man who had himself a real, good taste, give way, with a malicious complaisance, to the humour of a company where, in favour chiefly of the tender sex, this soft, languishing contempt of critics and their labours has been the subject set afoot. "Wretched creatures!" says one, "impertinent things, these critics, as ye call them! — As if one couldn't know what was agreeable or pretty without their help. — 'Tis fine indeed that one shouldn't be allowed to fancy for oneself. — Now should a thousand critics tell me that Mr. A —— 's new play wa'n't the wittiest in the world, I wouldn't mind them one bit."

This our real man of wit hears patiently, and adds, perhaps of his own, that he thinks it, truly, somewhat hard, in what relates to people's diversion and entertainment, that they should be obliged to choose what pleased others and not themselves. Soon after this he goes himself to the play, finds one of his effeminate companions commending or admiring at a wrong place. He turns to the next person who sits by him and asks privately what he thinks of his companion's relish?

Such is the malice of the world! They who by pains and industry have acquired a real taste in arts, rejoice in their advantage over others, who have either none at all or such as renders them ridiculous. At an auction of books or pictures, you shall hear these gentlemen persuading every one to bid for what he fancies. But, at the same time, they would be soundly mortified themselves, if by such as they esteemed good judges they should be found to have purchased by a wrong fancy or ill taste. The same gentleman who commends his neighbour for ordering his garden or apartment as his humour leads him, takes care his own should be so ordered as the best judgments would advise. Being once a judge himself or but tolerably knowing in these affairs, his aim is not to change the being of things and bring truth and nature to his humour, but, leaving nature and truth just as he found them, to accommodate his humour and fancy to their standard. Would he do this in a yet higher case, he might in reality become as wise and great a man as he is already a refined and polished gentleman. By one of these tastes he understands how to lay out his garden, model his house, fancy his equipage, appoint his table; by the other he learns of what value these amusements are in life, and of what importance to a man's freedom, happiness, and self-enjoyment. For if he would try effectually to acquire the real science or taste of life, he would certainly discover that a right mind and generous affection had more beauty and charm than all other symmetries in the world besides. And that a grain of honesty and native worth was of more value than all the adventitious ornaments, estates, or preferments, for the sake of which some of the better sort so oft turn knaves, forsaking their principles and quitting their honour and freedom for a mean, timorous, shifting state of gaudy servitude....

[1714]

ANNE, COUNTESS OF WINCHILSEA

ANNE FINCH, in later life Countess of Winchilsea, was born near Southampton in 1661, of a titled family. She was left an orphan at the age of three, and nothing is known of her youth and education. In 1683 she was one of the maids of honour — together with Dryden's Mistress Anne Killigrew — in the household of the Duchess of York, and in the next year occurred her happy marriage to Colonel Heneage Finch, who was in the Duke's service. During the brief reign of James II the couple were members of the court circle, but after the Revolution of 1688 they shared, in some measure, their royal master's exile, Colonel Finch refusing to take the oath of allegiance to William and Mary. In 1690 they were established at the country seat of Colonel Finch's nephew in Kent, where the more important poems of Anne Finch were probably written. This nephew, the fourth Earl of Winchilsea, died in 1712 and Colonel Finch succeeded to the title. The Countess of Winchilsea died in London in 1720, leaving no children.

Unwilling to brave the ridicule levelled against women who were known to write, the Countess of Winchilsea allowed few of her poems to be published during her lifetime, and these few seemed to relate her either to the school of Cowley, a foremost name in English poetry during her youth, or else to Prior and Pope, with both of whom she maintained pleasant relations. She imitated these two assiduously, and also the court poets of the Restoration, but her wit and good sense, though indubitable, were not such as to raise her high in such company, and her name was almost entirely forgotten until Wordsworth called attention to her in his Preface to *Lyrical Ballads*. A brief article by Sir Edmund Gosse in Ward's *English Poets* brought to light in 1884 a considerable number of her unpublished poems and won for her the praise of Matthew Arnold. Some twenty years later a complete edition of her work, together with an adequate apparatus, was published in America, and since then the Countess of Winchilsea has quietly taken her place as one of the most delightful and significant minor poets of the eighteenth century.

The quality of Lady Anne's verse pointed out by Wordsworth was its direct and original rendering of nature, most apparent in her *Nocturnal Reverie*. Her mind lay open to minute and apparently trivial observations, such as that of the straying horse and the "torn up forage," and in an age prone to vague generalization she knew the æsthetic value of sharply incised detail. Had she been less orthodox in religious belief, her feeling for nature would probably have shown a pantheistic tendency, and in the *Petition for an Absolute Retreat* there is more than a hint of the mysticism of Henry Vaughan. The very title of this poem suggests, however, one of the basic moods of Lady Anne's mind, more fundamental and pervasive than her delight in nature: a strong, steady leaning toward seclusion which had, as its obverse, an equally strong distaste for the publicity of the Town. Her best poetry is written in praise of solitude and its country contentments, so that she is one of the several writers of her time who never quite abandoned the natural English preference for privacy. This portion of her work, or such of it as she saw fit to publish during her lifetime, was forgotten until the triumphant romantic movement — in part a reassertion of the right to privacy and a celebration of solitude in its many aspects — prepared for it a favourable hearing.

THE TREE

Fair tree, for thy delightful shade
'Tis just that some return be made;
Sure some return is due from me
To thy cool shadows and to thee.
When thou to birds dost shelter give
Thou music dost from them receive;
If travellers beneath thee stay
Till storms have worn themselves away,
That time in praising thee they spend,
And thy protecting power commend;
The shepherd here, from scorching freed,
Tunes to thy dancing leaves his reed,
Whilst his loved nymph in thanks bestows
Her flowery * chaplets on thy boughs.
Shall I then only silent be,
And no return be made by me?
No! let this wish upon thee wait,
And still to flourish be thy fate;
To future ages mayst thou stand
Untouched by the rash workman's hand,
Till that large stock of sap is spent
Which gives thy summer's ornament;
Till the fierce winds, that vainly strive
To shock thy greatness whilst alive,
Shall on thy lifeless hour attend,
* Prevent the axe, and grace thy end,
Their scattered strength together call
And to the clouds proclaim thy fall:

* Notes on Anne, Countess of Winchilsea, will be found in the Appendix, pp. 968 ff.

Who then their evening dews may spare,
When thou no longer art their care,
But shalt, like ancient heroes, burn,
And some bright hearth be made thy urn.

[1713]

TO THE NIGHTINGALE

Exert thy voice, sweet harbinger of spring!
This moment is thy time to sing;
This moment I attend to praise,
And set my numbers to thy lays.
Free as thine shall be my song;
As thy music, short or long.
Poets wild as thee were born,
Pleasing best when *unconfined,
When to please is least designed,
Soothing but their cares to rest.
Cares do still their thoughts molest,
And still th' unhappy poet's breast,
Like thine, when best he sings, is placed against a *thorn.

She begins, let all be still!
Muse, thy promise now fulfil!
Sweet, oh, sweet! still sweeter yet!
Can *thy words such accents fit?
Canst thou syllables *refine,
Melt a sense that shall retain
Still some spirit of the brain,
Till with sounds like these it join?
'Twill not be! then change thy note;
Let *division shake thy throat.
Hark! division now she tries,
Yet as far the Muse outflies.

Cease then, prithee, cease thy tune!
Trifler, wilt thou sing till June?
Till thy business all lies waste,
And the time of building's past?
Thus we poets that have speech
Unlike what thy forests teach,
If a *fluent vein be shown
That's transcendent to our own,
Criticize, reform, or preach,
Or censure what we cannot reach.

[1713]

A NOCTURNAL REVERIE

*In such a night, when every louder wind
Is to its distant cavern safe confined,
And only gentle Zephyr fans his wings,
And lonely Philomel, still waking, sings,
Or from some tree, famed for the owl's delight,
She, *hollowing clear, directs the wanderer right;
In such a night, when passing clouds give place,
Or thinly veil the heavens' mysterious face;
When in some river, overhung with green,
The waning moon and trembling leaves are seen;
When freshened grass now bears itself upright
And makes cool banks to pleasing rest invite;
When spring the woodbine and the bramble-rose,
And where the sleepy cowslip sheltered grows;
Whilst now a paler hue the foxglove takes,
Yet checkers still with red the dusky brakes;
When scattered glow-worms, but in twilight fine,
Show trivial beauties watch their hour to shine,
Whilst *Salisbury stands the test of every light
In perfect charms and perfect virtue bright;
When odours which decline repelling day
Through temperate air uninterrupted stray;
When darkened groves their softest shadows wear,
And falling waters we distinctly hear;
When through the gloom more venerable shows
Some ancient fabric, awful in repose;
While sunburnt hills their swarthy looks conceal,
And swelling haycocks thicken up the vale;
When the loosed horse now, as his pasture leads,
Comes slowly grazing through th' adjoining meads,
Whose stealing pace and lengthened shade we fear,
Till torn up forage in his teeth we hear;
When nibbling sheep at large pursue their food,
And unmolested kine re-chew the cud;
When curlews cry beneath the village walls,
And to her straggling brood the partridge calls;
Their short-lived jubilee the creatures keep,
Which but endures whilst tyrant-man does sleep;
When a sedate content the spirit feels,
And no fierce light disturbs whilst it reveals,
But silent musings urge the mind to seek
Something too high for syllables to speak,
Till the free soul, to a compos'dness charmed,
Finding the elements of rage disarmed,
O'er all below a solemn quiet grown,

Joys in th' inferior world and thinks it like
*her own:
In such a night let me abroad remain,
Till morning breaks and all's confused again,
Our cares, our toils, our clamours, are renewed,
Or pleasures, seldom reached, again pursued.

[1713]

From THE PETITION FOR AN ABSOLUTE RETREAT

Give me, O indulgent Fate!
Give me yet, before I die,
A sweet but absolute *retreat
'Mongst paths so lost and trees so high
That the world may ne'er invade,
Through such windings and such shade,
My unshaken liberty.

No intruders thither come
Who visit but to be from home!
None who their vain moments pass
Only studious of their glass.
News, that charm to listening ears,
That false alarm to hopes and fears,
That common theme for every fop
From the statesman to the shop,
In those coverts ne'er be spread
Of who's deceased or who's to wed!
Be no tidings thither brought,
But silent as a midnight thought
Where the world may ne'er invade
Be those windings and that shade!

Courteous Fate! afford me there
A table spread without my care
With what the neighbouring fields impart,
Whose cleanliness be all its art.
When, of old, the calf was dressed
(Though to make an angel's feast)
In the plain unstudied sauce
Nor *truffle nor *morillia was;
Nor could the mighty patriarch's board
One far-fetched *ortolan afford.
Courteous Fate, then give me there
Only plain and wholesome fare.
Fruits indeed (would Heaven bestow)
All that did in Eden grow,
All but the forbidden tree,
Would be coveted by me:
Grapes, with juice so crowded up
As breaking through the native *cup;
Figs, yet growing, candied o'er
By the sun's attractive power;
Cherries, with the downy peach,
All within my easy reach;
Whilst, creeping near the humble ground,
Should the strawberry be found
Springing wheresoe'er I strayed
Through those windings and that shade.

For my garments, let them be
What may with the time agree:
Warm when Phœbus does retire
And is ill-supplied by fire;
But when he renews the year
And verdant all the fields appear,
Beauty everything resumes,
Birds have dropped their winter plumes,
When the lily full-displayed
Stands in purer white arrayed
Than that vest which heretofore
The luxurious *monarch wore
When from Salem's gate he drove
To the soft retreat of love,
Lebanon's all burnished house
And the dear Egyptian spouse,—
Clothe me, Fate, though not so gay,
Clothe me light and fresh as May!
In the fountains let me view
All my habit cheap and new,
Such as, when sweet zephyrs fly,
With their motions may comply,
Gently waving to express
Unaffected carelessness....
Let me, when I must be fine,
In such natural colours shine,
Wove and painted by the sun;
Whose resplendent rays to shun
When they do too fiercely beat,
Let me find some close retreat
Where they have no passage made
Through those windings and that shade.

Give me there — since Heaven has shown
It was not good to be alone —
A partner suited to my mind,
Solitary, pleased, and kind,
Who, *partially, may something see
Preferred to all the world in me,
Slighting by my humble side
Fame and splendour, wealth and pride.
When but two the earth possessed,
'Twas their happiest days and best.
They by business nor by wars,
They by no domestic cares
From each other e'er were drawn,
But in some grove or flowery lawn
Spent the swiftly flying time,
Spent their own and nature's prime,

In love — that only passion given
To perfect man whilst friends with Heaven.
Rage and jealousy and hate,
Transports of his fallen state
When by Satan's wiles betrayed,
Fly those windings and that shade!...

Let me then, indulgent Fate,
Let me still in my retreat
From all roving thoughts be freed,
Or aims that may contention breed;
Nor be my endeavours led
By goods that perish with the dead.
Fitly might the life of man
Be indeed esteemed a span
If the present moment were
Of delight his only share,
If no other joys he knew
Than what round about him grew;
But as those who stars would trace
From a *subterranean place
Through some *engine lift their eyes
To the outward glorious skies,
So the immortal spirit may,
When descended to our clay,
From a rightly governed *frame
View the height from whence she came,
To her paradise be caught
And things unutterable taught.
Give me, then, in that retreat,
Give me, O indulgent Fate,
For all pleasures left behind,
Contemplations of the mind.
Let the fair, the gay, the vain,
Courtship and applause obtain;
Let the ambitious rule the earth;
Let the giddy fool have mirth;
Give the epicure his dish,
Every one their several wish;
Whilst my transports I employ
On that more extensive joy
When all Heaven shall be surveyed
From those windings and that shade.

[1713]

FRAGMENT

So here confined, and but to female clay,
*Ardelia's soul mistook the rightful way;
Whilst the soft breeze of pleasure's tempting air
Made her believe felicity was there,
And, basking in the warmth of early time,
To vain amusements *dedicate her prime;
Ambition next allured her towering eye,
For Paradise, she heard, was placed on high,
Then thought the court, with all its glorious show,
Was sure above the rest, and Paradise below.
There *placed, too soon the flaming sword appeared,
Removed those powers whom justly she revered,
Adhered to in their wreck and in their ruin shared.
Now, by the *wheel's inevitable round,
With them thrown prostrate to the humble ground,
No more she takes — instructed by that fall —
For fixed, or worth her thought, this rolling ball;
Towards a more certain station she aspires,
Unshaken by revolts, and owns no less desires.
But all *in vain are prayers, ecstatic thoughts,
Recovered moments, and retracted faults,
Retirement, which the world moroseness calls,
Abandoned pleasures in *monastic walls.
These, but at distance, towards that purpose tend,
The lowly means to an exalted end
Which He must perfect who allots her stay,
And, that accomplished, will direct the way,
Pity her restless cares and weary strife,
And point some issue to escaping life.
Which, so dismissed, no pen nor human speech
Th' *ineffable recess can ever teach —
Th' expanse, the light, the harmony, the throng,
The bride's attendance and the bridal song,
The numerous mansions and the immortal tree
No eye unpurged by death must ever see,
Or waves which through that wondrous city roll.
Rest then content, my too impatient soul!
Observe but here the easy precepts given,
Then wait with cheerful hope till Heaven be known in Heaven.

[1713]

JOHN DYER

Born in Wales about the year 1700, John Dyer attended Westminster School and spent his earlier manhood as a professional painter of portraits and landscape, a minor figure among the many British artists who were at just this time developing a new public taste for the romantically picturesque. A natural product of his wanderings in Wales and of his skill as a painter was the poem, *Grongar Hill*, first published by Richard Savage in 1726 in the form of an "Irregular Ode," but recast in the following year into octosyllabic couplets. A long residence abroad, spent in the study of art, produced in 1740 *The Ruins of Rome*, a poem of considerable length and dullness in blank verse. In 1741 he married, took orders, and settled down as a country clergyman. Dyer's last contribution to literature was *The Fleece*, a blank verse poem in four books dealing with the growth, manufacture, and sale of wool. In 1758, one year after *The Fleece* appeared, he died.

Critical estimates of Dyer's poetry have been diverse. Dr. Johnson, who could like no poetry not written in rhyme and who had little patience with any versified description of landscape, treated it with slightly qualified contempt. Thomas Gray, on the other hand, asserted in a letter to Walpole, that "Mr. Dyer has more of poetry in his imagination than almost any of our number," and Akenside — a close friend of the poet, to be sure — remarked concerning *The Fleece* that "if that were ill received he should not think it any longer reasonable to expect fame from excellence." A more familiar tribute is that in the sonnet by Wordsworth, who found a man after his own heart in the sauntering, view-hunting, mildly didactic clergyman:

> Yet pure and powerful minds, hearts meek and still,
> A grateful few, shall love thy modest lay
> Long as the shepherd's bleating flock shall stray
> O'er naked Snowdon's wide aerial waste,
> Long as the thrush shall pipe on Grongar Hill.

It is no great loss to literature that *Grongar Hill* alone, out of Dyer's slight literary production, has survived in public memory — although its companion-piece published in the same year, *The Country Walk*, may well go with it still. His *Epistle to a Friend in Town*, ultimately Horatian in origin, is one of the most graceful yet most compact of the many poems of its kind. There are good things in *The Ruins of Rome*, as even Dr. Johnson was forced to admit, and it is an interesting early example of the romantic treatment of a classic theme, but it is so stiff and cold with ossified poetic diction, suggesting the manner of Akenside at his worst, as to be in our time almost unreadable. *The Fleece* is full of poetic ideas rather than of poetry. Its audacious vindication of trade and manufacture as entirely fit for poetic treatment, its defence of the Inclosure Acts, and its clear prophecy of the Panama Canal are not sufficient to raise it near the level of Dyer's one true poem, written carelessly and with many defects but from the heart, before he had a reputation to sustain.

In the year 1726, when *Grongar Hill* appeared, Alexander Pope, feeling very secure upon his throne, was writing *The Dunciad*, perhaps the most vigorous English utterance ever pronounced from the Town's point of view — an utterance of the dominant common sense and of centralized intellectual authority. Dyer's poem had not then, and of course has not today, anything resembling the importance of the other, but it was on the side of what was growing, whereas Pope's great poem was the culmination of a movement bound thenceforth to decline. Little would have been accomplished by Dyer's graceful sketch in water-colour alone. It was, however, a clear, fresh, sufficiently vigorous expression of a mood which had never quite died out in England during the storms of the Civil Wars and the succeeding rule of neo-classical taste. Moreover, it was corroborated almost at once by many reinforcements, in painting as well as in poetry, and by a gradual change in landscape gardening. It was in this same year that James Thomson brought down from Scotland and published the first version of *Winter*.

Grongar Hill is merely the most famous and successful of the hundreds of poems written in more or less deliberate imitation of the verse, the moods, the themes, and the rambling structure, of Milton's *L'Allegro* and *Il Penseroso*. Like them, it is a poem of unchecked reverie rather than of directed thought, a loose gathering of scenes that chime with the antecedent mood, a drifting and a dreamy poem that grows without effort or apparent plan, like a summer cloud. Above all, it is a poem of solitude, as its two models also are, written by one who has for the time being forgotten all "the noise of busy man," who ignores politics, wit, the Town, the duty of poets to "instruct" as well as to "please," and indeed nearly everything that an eighteenth-century poet is supposed to attend to. Born and educated far from London, Dyer has no fears whatever of that social ridicule which the city poet of his time strove at any cost to avoid. He probably does not know that he is an "enthusiast." It would be difficult to imagine a sharper contrast, therefore, than that between *Grongar Hill* and the fierce, piercing, merciless poem, intensely social, on which Pope was working at Twickenham. There is one respect in which Dyer has a strong advantage over John Denham, whose somewhat too famous *Cooper's Hill* he had certainly to some extent in mind, and even over Milton: he sees the landscape with the eye of a painter, and strives to make words do as much as possible of the work of pigments. It is a time in which painting and poetry work together, for the most part unconsciously, in the gradual modification of the public taste, and the writing of John Dyer is one of the best examples of their partnership.

GRONGAR HILL

*Silent nymph with curious eye
Who, *the purple ev'ning, lie
On the mountain's lonely *van
Beyond the noise of busy man,
Painting fair the form of things
While the yellow linnet sings,
Or the tuneful nightingale
Charms the forest with her tale,
Come with all thy various hues,
Come and aid thy sister *Muse
Now while Phœbus riding high
Gives lustre to the land and sky!
*Grongar Hill invites my song,
Draw the landscape bright and strong;
Grongar, in whose mossy cells
Sweetly musing Quiet dwells;
Grongar, in whose silent shade,
For the modest Muses made,
So oft I have, the evening still,
At the fountain of a rill,
Sate upon a flow'ry bed
With my hand beneath my head,
While strayed my eyes o'er *Towy's flood,
Over mead and over wood,
From house to house, from hill to hill,
Till Contemplation had her fill.
  Above his chequered sides I wind
And leave his brooks and meads behind,
And groves and grottoes where I lay,
And vistas shooting beams of day.
Wide and wider spreads the vale,
As circles on a smooth canal;
The mountains round, — unhappy fate,
Sooner or later, of all height, —
Withdraw their summits from the skies
And lessen as the others rise:
Still the prospect wider spreads,
Adds a thousand woods and meads;
Still it widens, widens still,
And sinks the newly-risen hill.
  Now I gain the mountain's brow
What a landscape lies below!
No clouds, no vapours intervene,
But the gay, the open scene
Does the face of Nature show
In all the hues of heaven's bow,
And, swelling to embrace the light,
Spreads around beneath the sight.
  Old castles on the cliffs arise,
Proudly tow'ring in the skies;
Rushing from the woods, the spires
Seem from hence ascending fires!
Half his beams Apollo sheds
On the yellow mountain-heads,
Gilds the fleeces of the flocks,
And glitters on the broken rocks.
  Below me trees unnumbered rise,
Beautiful in various dyes:
The gloomy pine, the poplar blue,
The yellow beech, the sable yew,
The slender fir that taper grows,
The sturdy oak with broad-spread boughs.
And beyond the purple grove,
Haunt of Phyllis, queen of love,
Gaudy as the op'ning dawn
Lies a long and level *lawn
On which a dark hill, steep and high,
Holds and charms the wand'ring eye.
Deep are his feet in Towy's flood;
His sides are clothed with waving wood;
And ancient towers crown his brow
That cast an awful look below,
Whose ragged walls the ivy *creeps
And with her arms from falling keeps —
So both a safety from the wind
On mutual dependence find.
'Tis now the raven's bleak abode;
'Tis now th' apartment of the toad;
And there the fox securely feeds;
And there the pois'nous adder breeds,
Concealed in ruins, moss, and weeds;
While, ever and anon, there falls
Huge heaps of hoary mouldered walls.
Yet Time has seen, that lifts the low,
And level lays the lofty brow,
Has seen this broken pile complete,
Big with the vanity of state.
But transient is the smile of Fate!

* Notes on John Dyer will be found in the Appendix, p. 969.

A little rule, a little sway,
A sunbeam in a winter's day,
Is all the proud and mighty have
Between the cradle and the grave.

And see the rivers, how they run
Through woods and meads, in shade and sun;
Sometimes swift, sometimes slow,
Wave succeeding wave, they go
A various journey to the deep,
Like human life to endless sleep.
Thus is Nature's vesture wrought
To instruct our wand'ring thought;
Thus she dresses green and gay
To disperse our cares away.

Ever charming, ever new,
When will the landscape tire the view!
The fountain's fall, the river's flow,
The woody valleys, warm and low,
The windy summit, wild and high,
Roughly rushing on the sky,
The pleasant seat, the ruined tower,
The naked rock, the shady bower,
The town and village, dome and farm,
Each give each a double charm,
As *pearls upon an Æthiop's arm.

See on the mountain's southern side,
Where the prospect opens wide,
Where the evening gilds the tide,
How close and small the hedges lie,
What *streaks of meadows cross the eye!
A step methinks may pass the stream.
So little distant dangers seem;
So we mistake the future's face,
Eyed through hope's deluding glass;
As yon summits soft and fair,
Clad in colours of the air,
Which to those who journey near,
Barren, brown, and rough appear:
Still we tread the same coarse way;
The present's still a cloudy day.

Oh, may I with myself agree,
And never covet what I see;
Content me with an humble shade,
My passions tamed, my wishes *laid:
For while our wishes wildly roll,
We banish quiet from the soul:
'Tis thus the busy beat the air,
And misers gather wealth and care.

Now, even now, my joys run high,
As on the mountain turf I lie;
While the wanton Zephyr sings
And in the vale perfumes his wings;
While the waters murmur deep,
While the shepherd charms his sheep,
While the birds unbounded fly
And with music fill the sky;
Now, even now, my joys run high.

Be full, ye courts; be great who will;
Search for Peace with all your skill;
Open wide the lofty door,
Seek her on the marble floor;
In vain you search, she is not there;
In vain ye search the domes of care!
Grass and flowers Quiet treads,
On the meads and mountain-heads,
Along with Pleasure, close allied,
Ever by each other's side.
And often, by the murm'ring rill,
Hears the thrush, while all is still,
Within the groves of Grongar Hill.

[1726]

THE COUNTRY WALK

The morning's fair; the lusty sun
With ruddy cheek begins to run;
And early birds, that wing the skies,
Sweetly sing to see him rise.

I am resolved, this charming day,
In the open field to stray,
And have no roof above my head
But that whereon the gods do tread.
Before the yellow barn I see
A beautiful variety
Of strutting cocks advancing stout
And flirting empty chaff about,
Hens, ducks, and geese, and all their brood,
And turkeys gobbling for their food;
While rustics thrash the wealthy floor,
And tempt them all to crowd the door.

What a fair face does nature show!
*Augusta, wipe thy dusty brow!
A landscape wide salutes my sight,
Of shady vales and mountains bright,
And azure heavens I behold,
And clouds of silver and of gold.
And now into the fields I go
Where thousand flaming flowers glow,
And every neighbouring hedge I greet
With honeysuckles smelling sweet.
Now o'er the daisy meads I stray,
And meet with, as I pace my way,
Sweetly shining on the eye,
A rivulet, gliding smoothly by,
Which shows with what an easy tide
The moments of the happy glide.
Here, finding pleasure after pain,
Sleeping, I see a wearied swain,
While his full scrip lies open by,
That does his healthy food supply.

Happy swain, sure happier far
Than lofty kings and princes are!
Enjoy sweet sleep, which shuns the crown,
With all its easy beds of down.
The sun now shows his noontide blaze,
And sheds around me burning rays.
A little onward, and I go
Into the shade that groves bestow,
And on green moss I lay me down
That o'er the root of oak has grown,
Where all is silent, but some flood
That sweetly murmurs in the wood,
But birds that warble in the sprays,
And charm e'en silence with their lays.
O powerful silence, how you reign
In the poet's busy brain!
His numerous thoughts obey the calls
Of the tuneful waterfalls;
Like moles, whene'er the coast is clear,
They rise before thee without fear,
And range in parties here and there.
Some wildly to Parnassus wing
And view the fair Castalian spring,
Where they behold a lonely well
Where now no tuneful Muses dwell,
But now and then a slavish hind
Paddling the troubled pool they find.
Some trace the pleasing paths of joy;
Others the blissful scene destroy —
In thorny tracks of sorrow stray,
And pine for Clio far away.
But stay — methinks her lays I hear,
So smooth! so sweet! so deep! so clear!
No, 'tis not her voice, I find,
'Tis but the echo stays behind.
Some meditate ambition's brow,
And the black gulf that gapes below;
Some peep in courts, and there they see
The sneaking tribe of flattery.
But, striking to the ear and eye,
A nimble deer comes bounding by;
When rushing from yon rustling spray,
It made them vanish all away.
I rouse me up, and on I rove;
'Tis more than time to leave the grove.
The sun declines, the evening breeze
Begins to whisper through the trees:
And, as I leave the sylvan gloom,
As to the glare of day I come,
An old man's smoky nest I see,
Leaning on an aged tree:
Whose willow walls, and furzy brow,
A little garden sway below.
Through spreading beds of blooming green,
Matted with herbage sweet and clean,
A vein of water limps along,
And makes them ever green and young.
Here he puffs upon his spade,
And digs up cabbage in the shade:
His tatter'd rags are sable brown;
His beard and hair are hoary grown:
The dying sap descends apace,
And leaves a withered hand and face.
Up Grongar Hill I labour now,
And reach at last his bushy brow.
Oh, how fresh, how pure the air!
Let me breath a little here.
Where am I, nature? I descry
Thy magazine before me lie!
Temples! — and towns! — and towers! — and woods!
And hills! — and vales! — and fields! — and floods!
Crowding before me, edged around
With naked wilds, and barren ground.
See, below, the pleasant dome,
The poet's pride, the poet's home,
Which the sunbeams shine upon
To the even, from the dawn.
See her woods, where Echo talks,
Her gardens trim, her terrace walks,
Her * wildernesses, fragrant brakes,
Her gloomy bowers, and shining lakes.
Keep, ye gods, this humble seat,
For ever pleasant, private, neat.
See yonder hill, uprising steep
Above the river slow and deep:
It looks from hence a pyramid,
Beneath a verdant forest hid,
On whose high top there rises great,
The mighty remnant of a seat,
An old green tower, whose batter'd brow
Frowns upon the vale below.
Look upon that flowery plain,
How the sheep surround their swain,
How they crowd to hear his strain!
All careless with his legs across,
Leaning on a bank of moss,
He spends his empty hours at play,
Which fly as light as down away.
And there behold a bloomy mead,
A silver stream, a willow shade,
Beneath the shade a fisher stand,
Who, with the angle in his hand,
Swings the nibbling fry to land.
In blushes the descending sun
Kisses the streams, while slow they run;
And yonder hill remoter grows,
Or dusky clouds do interpose.
The fields are left, the labouring hind

His weary oxen does unbind;
And vocal mountains, as they low,
Re-echo to the vales below;
The jocund shepherds piping come,
And drive the herd before them home;
And now begin to light their fires,
Which send up smoke in curling spires;
While with light heart all homeward tend,
To Abergasney I descend.
  But, oh! how bless'd would be the day,
Did I with Clio pace my way,
And not alone and solitary stray!

[1726]

AN EPISTLE TO A FRIEND IN TOWN

Have my friends in the town, in the gay busy town,
  Forgot such a man as John Dyer?
Or heedless despise they, or pity the clown
  Whose bosom no pageantries fire?
No matter, no matter, content in the shades,
  (Contented? Why, everything charms me.)
Fall in tunes all adown the green steep, ye cascades,
  Till hence rigid *Virtue alarms me.

Till Outrage arises, or Misery needs
  The swift, the intrepid avenger;
Till sacred Religion or Liberty bleeds.
  Then mine be the deed and the danger!

Alas! what a folly, that wealth and domain
  We heap up in sin and in sorrow!
Immense is the toil, yet the labour how vain!
  Is not life to be over tomorrow?

Then glide on my moments, the few that I have,
  Smooth-shaded and quiet and even,
While gently the body descends to the grave,
  And the spirit arises to Heaven.

[1770]

THE TATLER

THOUGH the publication of the *Tatler* marks a major event in the history of British journalism, the paper had numerous predecessors. Most of these had been newspapers or journals of political controversy, but some, like John Dunton's *Athenian Mercury*, had been more general in their scope. As first conceived by Richard Steele the *Tatler* included news both foreign and domestic (see the prospectus in No. 1), but largely through the influence of Joseph Addison this feature became of decreasing importance as time passed. From the beginning Steele had been interested in the reform of morals and the amelioration of social conditions. The author of *The Christian Hero* (1701) and of such sentimental comedies as *The Tender Husband* (1705) had shown his characteristic bent long before he began the publication of the *Tatler*.

The new periodical would never have attained to importance had it been entirely didactic in purpose and method; it reflected the interests and activities of the town when London was still small enough to be reflected in a single mirror. Not only did the *Tatler* profess to present the gossip of the coffee-houses, but in large measure it did actually represent the lively curiosity in public affairs, fashions, scandals, as well as in letters, the theatre, and learning in its more popular aspects. It was better talk than the talk of the coffee-houses, more varied, more stimulating, better presented. Therefore, it was eagerly read in the coffee-houses; it helped to define and formulate average middle-class opinion as well as to reflect it.

Steele's sensitiveness to the public mind, even in its undefined tendencies and unconscious aspirations, his initiative, his warmth of heart, and his quixotic enthusiasm would not have been enough by themselves to carry his project through successfully; but he was fortunate in finding able assistants, especially his old schoolfellow, Joseph Addison. The latter brought to the journal a cultured and well-stocked mind, a rounded personality, a power of delicate, urbane satire, and a gift of literary expression that could give classical finish to an article while the printer's boy waited for the copy. Steele created a magazine; through Addison's influence that magazine became literature.

The *Tatler* was published three times a week from April 12, 1709, until January 2, 1711. The price was at first a penny but was afterwards doubled. Though the original form was rough, "tobacco paper and scurvy letter," the essays were at once collected and published in royal octavo volumes that sold by subscription at the high price of a guinea a volume.

From No. 1, Tuesday, April 12, 1709

* *Quicquid agunt homines . . . nostri farrago libelli.*
Juv., *Sat.* I, 85, 86.

[Whate'er men do, or say, or think, or dream,
Our motley paper seizes for its theme.
Pope.]

Though the other papers which are published for the use of the good people of England have certainly very wholesome effects, and are laudable in their particular kinds, yet they do not seem to come up to the main design of such narrations, which, I humbly presume, should be principally intended for the use of politic persons, who are so public-spirited as to neglect their own affairs to look into transactions of state. Now these gentlemen, for the most part, being men of strong zeal and weak intellects, it is both a charitable and a necessary work to offer something whereby such worthy and well-affected members of the commonwealth may be instructed, after their reading, what to think; which shall be the end and purpose of this my paper; wherein I shall from time to time report and consider all matters of what kind soever that shall occur to me, and publish such my advices and reflections every Tuesday, Thursday, and Saturday in the week, for the convenience of the post. I have also resolved to have something which may be of entertainment to the fair sex, in honour of whom I have taken the title of this paper. I therefore earnestly desire all persons, without distinction, to take it in for the present gratis, and hereafter at the price of one penny, forbidding all hawkers to take more for it at their peril. And I desire my readers to consider that I am at a very great charge for proper materials for this work, as well as that, before I resolved upon it, I had settled a correspondence in all parts of the known and knowing world. And forasmuch as this globe is not trodden upon by mere drudges of business only, but that men of spirit and genius are justly to be esteemed as considerable agents in it, we shall not, upon a dearth of news, present you

* Notes on the *Tatler* will be found in the Appendix, pp. 970 ff.

with musty foreign edicts, or dull proclamations, but shall divide our relation of the passages which occur in action or discourse throughout this town, as well as elsewhere, under such dates of places as may prepare you for the matter you are to expect, in the following manner:

All accounts of gallantry, pleasure, and entertainment shall be under the article of *White's Chocolate-house; poetry, under that of *Will's Coffee-house; learning, under the title of *Grecian; foreign and domestic news you will have from *St. James's Coffee-house; and what else I shall on any other subject offer, shall be dated from my own apartment.

I once more desire my readers to consider that, as I cannot keep an ingenious man to go daily to Will's under twopence each day merely for his charges, to White's under sixpence, nor to the Grecian without allowing him some plain Spanish, to be as able as others at the learned table, and that a good observe cannot speak with even *Kidney at St. James's without clean linen, — I say, these considerations will, I hope, make all persons willing to comply with my humble request (when my gratis stock is exhausted) of a penny apiece; especially since they are sure of some proper amusement, and that it is impossible for me to want means to entertain them, — having, besides the helps of my own parts, *the power of divination, and that I can, by casting a figure, tell you all that will happen before it comes to pass. But this last faculty I shall use very sparingly, and not speak of anything until it is passed, for fear of divulging matters which may offend our superiors.

White's Chocolate-house, April 11

The deplorable condition of a very pretty gentleman, who walks here at the hours when men of quality first appear, is what is very much lamented. His history is, that on the ninth of September, 1705, being in his one-and-twentieth year, he was washing his teeth at a tavern window in Pall Mall, when a fine equipage passed by, and in it a young lady who looked up at him; away goes the coach, and the young gentleman pulled off his night-cap, and instead of rubbing his gums, as he ought to do, out of the window till about four o'clock, he sits him down and spoke not a word till twelve at night; after which he began to inquire if anybody knew the lady. The company asked, "What lady?" But he said no more until they broke up at six in the morning. All the ensuing winter he went from church to church every Sunday, and from play-house to play-house all the week; but could never find the original of the picture which dwelt in his bosom. In a word, his attention to anything but his passion was utterly gone. He has lost all the money he ever played for, and been confuted in every argument he has entered upon, since the moment he first saw her. He is of a noble family, has naturally a very good air, and is of a frank, honest temper; but this passion has so extremely mauled him that his features are set and uninformed, and his whole visage is deadened by a long absence of thought. He never appears in any alacrity, but when raised by wine; at which time he is sure to come hither, and throw away a great deal of wit on fellows who have no sense further than just to observe that our poor lover has most understanding when he is drunk, and is least in his senses when he is sober.

Will's Coffee-house, April 8

On Thursday last was presented, for the benefit of Mr. Betterton, the celebrated comedy called **Love for Love*. Those excellent players, Mrs. Barry, Mrs. Bracegirdle, and Mr. Doggett, though not at present concerned in the house, acted on that occasion. There has not been known so great a concourse of persons of distinction as at that time; the stage itself was covered with gentlemen and ladies, and when the curtain was drawn, it discovered even there a very splendid audience. This unusual encouragement, which was given to a play for the advantage of so great an actor, gives an undeniable instance that the true relish for manly entertainments and rational pleasures is not wholly lost. All the parts were acted to perfection; the actors were careful of their carriage, and no one was guilty of the affectation to insert witticisms of his own; but a due respect was had to the audience, for encouraging this accomplished player. It is not now doubted but plays will revive, and take their usual place in the opinion of persons of wit and merit, notwithstanding their late apostacy in favour of dress and sound. This place is very much altered since Mr. Dryden frequented it; where you used to see songs, epigrams, and satires, in the hands of every man you met, you have now only a pack of cards; and instead of the cavils about the turn of the expression, the elegance of the style, and the like, the learned now dispute only about the truth of the game. But, however the company is altered, all have shown a great respect for Mr. Betterton; and the very gaming part of this house have been so much touched with a sense of the uncertainty of human affairs (which alter with themselves every moment) that in this gentleman they pitied Mark Antony of Rome, Hamlet of Denmark, Mithridates of Pontus, Theodosius of Greece, and Henry the Eighth of England. It is well known he has been in the condition of each of those illustrious personages for several hours together, and behaved himself in those high stations, in all the changes of the scene, with suitable dignity. For these reasons, we intend to repeat this favour to him on a proper occasion, lest he, who can instruct us so well in personating feigned sorrows, should be lost to us by suffering under real ones. The town is at present in very great expectation of seeing a comedy now in rehearsal, which is the twenty-fifth production of my honoured friend, *Mr. Thomas D'Urfey; who, besides his great abilities in the dramatic, has a peculiar talent in the lyric way of writing, and that with a manner wholly new and unknown to the ancient Greeks and Romans, wherein he is but faintly imitated in the translations of the modern Italian operas.

**From My Own Apartment*

I am sorry I am obliged to trouble the public with so much discourse upon a matter which I at the very first mentioned as a trifle, viz., the death of *Mr. Partridge, under whose name there is an almanac come out for the year 1709, in one page of which it is asserted by the said John Partridge that he is still living, and that not only so, but that he was also living some time before, and even at the instant when I writ of his death. I have in another place, and in a paper by itself, sufficiently convinced this man that he is dead; and if he has any shame, I don't doubt but that by this time he owns it to all his acquaintance; for though the legs and arms and whole body of that man may still appear and perform their animal functions, yet since, as I have elsewhere observed, his art is gone, the man is gone. I am, as I said, concerned that this little matter should make so much noise; but since I am engaged, I take myself obliged in honour to go on in my lucubrations, and by the help of these arts of which I am master, as well as my skill in astrological speculations, I shall, as I see occasion, proceed to confute other dead men, who pretend to be in being, that they are actually deceased. I therefore give all men fair warning to mend their manners, for I shall from time to time print bills of mortality; and I beg the pardon of all such who shall be named therein, if they who are good for nothing shall find themselves in the number of the deceased.

[Steele]

From NO. 25, JUNE 6, 1709

Quicquid agunt homines . . . nostri farrago libelli.
JUV. *Sat.* I, 85, 86.

[Whate'er men do, or say, or think, or dream,
Our motley paper seizes for its theme.
POPE.]

White's Chocolate-house, June 6

A letter from a young lady, written in the most passionate terms, wherein she laments the misfortune of a gentleman, her lover, who was lately wounded in a duel, has turned my thoughts to that subject, and inclined me to examine into the causes which precipitate men into so fatal a folly. And as it has been proposed to treat of subjects of gallantry in the article from hence, and no one point of nature is more proper to be considered by the company who frequent this place, than that of duels, it is worth our consideration to examine into this chimerical groundless humour, and to lay every other thought aside till we have stripped it of all its false pretences to credit and reputation amongst men. But I must confess, when I consider what I am going about, and run over in my imagination all the endless crowd of men of honour who will be offended at such a discourse, I am undertaking, methinks, a work worthy an invulnerable hero in romance, rather than a private gentleman with a single rapier. But as I am pretty well acquainted by great opportunities with the nature of man, and know of a truth that all men fight against their will, the danger vanishes, and resolution rises upon this subject. For this reason I shall talk very freely on a custom which all men wish exploded, though no man has courage enough to resist it. But there is one unintelligible word which I fear will extremely perplex my dissertation, and I confess to you I find very hard to explain, which is the term "satisfaction." An honest country gentleman had the misfortune to fall into company with two or three modern men of honour, where he happened to be very ill-treated; and one of the company, being conscious of his offence, sends a note to him in the morning, and tells him he was ready to give him satisfaction. "This is fine doing," says the plain fellow; "last night he sent me away cursedly out of humour, and this morning he fancies it would be a satisfaction to be run through the body." As the matter at present stands, it is not to do handsome actions denominates a man of honour; it is enough if he dares to defend ill ones. Thus you often see a common sharper in competition with a gentleman of the first rank, though all mankind is convinced that a fighting gamester is only a pickpocket with the courage of a highwayman. One cannot with any patience reflect on the unaccountable jumble of persons and things in this town and nation, which occasions very frequently that a brave man falls by a hand below that of the common hangman, and yet his executioner escapes the clutches of the hangman for doing it. I shall therefore hereafter consider how the bravest men in other ages and nations have behaved themselves upon such incidents as we decide by combat, and show, from their practice, that this resentment neither has its foundation from true reason nor solid fame, but is an imposture, made up of cowardice, falsehood, and want of understanding. For this work, a good history of quarrels would be very edifying to the public, and I apply myself to the town for particulars and circumstances within their knowledge, which may serve to embellish the dissertation with proper cuts. Most of the quarrels I have ever known have proceeded from some valiant coxcomb's persisting in the wrong, to defend some prevailing folly, and preserve himself from the ingenuity of owning a mistake.

By this means it is called "giving a man satisfaction" to urge your offence against him with your sword; which puts me in mind of Peter's order to the keeper, in the *Tale of a Tub:* "If you neglect to do all this, damn you and your generation for ever; and so we bid you heartily farewell." If the contradiction in the very terms of one of our challenges were as well explained, and turned into plain English, would it not run after this manner?

"Sir: Your extraordinary behaviour last night, and the liberty you were pleased to take with me, makes me this morning give you this, to tell you, because you are an ill-bred puppy, I will meet you in Hyde Park an hour hence; and because you want both breeding and humanity, I desire you would come with a pistol in your hand, on horseback, and endeavour to shoot me through the head, to teach you more manners. If you fail of doing me this pleasure, I shall say you are a rascal on every post in town. And so, sir, if you will not injure me more, I shall never forgive what you have done already. Pray, sir, do not fail of getting everything ready, and you will infinitely oblige,

Sir,

Your most obedient,

humble servant, &c."

From My Own Apartment, June 6

Among the many employments I am necessarily put upon by my friends, that of giving advice is the most unwelcome to me; and, indeed, I am forced to use a little art in the matter; for some people will ask counsel of you when they have already acted what they tell you is still under deliberation. I had almost lost a very good friend the other day, who came to know how I liked his design to marry such a lady. I answered, "By no means; and I must be positive against it, for very solid reasons, which are not proper to communicate." "Not proper to communicate!" said he, with a grave air; "I will know the bottom of this." I saw him moved, and knew from thence he was already determined; therefore evaded it by saying, "To tell you the truth, dear Frank, of all women living, I would have her myself." "Isaac," said he, "thou art too late, for we have been both one these two months." I learned this caution by a gentleman's consulting me formerly about his son. He railed at his damned extravagance, and told me, in a very little time he would beggar him by the exorbitant bills which came from Oxford every quarter. "Make the rogue bite upon the bridle," said I; "pay none of his bills; it will but encourage him to further trespasses." He looked plaguy sour at me. His son soon after sent up a paper of verses, forsooth, in print, on the last public occasion; upon which, he is convinced the boy has parts, and a lad of spirit is not to be too much cramped in his maintenance, lest he take ill courses. Neither father nor son can ever since endure the sight of me. These sort of people ask opinions only out of the fullness of their heart on the subject of their perplexity, and not from a desire of information. There is nothing so easy as to find out which opinion the person in doubt has a mind to; therefore the sure way is to tell him that is certainly to be chosen. Then you are to be very clear and positive; leave no handle for scruple. "Bless me! sir, there is no room for a question." This rivets you into his heart, for you at once applaud his wisdom and gratify his inclination. However, I had too much bowels to be insincere to a man who came yesterday to know of me, with which of two eminent men in the city he should place his son. Their names are Paulo and Avaro. This gave me much debate with myself, because not only the fortune of the youth but his virtue also depended upon this choice. The men are equally wealthy; but they differ in the use and application of their riches, which you immediately see upon entering their doors.

The habitation of Paulo has at once the air of a nobleman and a merchant. You see the servants act with affection to their master and satisfaction in themselves; the master meets you with an open countenance, full of benevolence and integrity; your business is dispatched with that confidence and welcome which always accompanies honest minds. His table is the image of plenty and generosity, supported by justice and frugality. After we had dined here, our affair was to visit Avaro. Out comes an awkward fellow, with a careful countenance: "Sir, would you speak with my master? May I crave your name?" After the first preambles, he leads us into a noble solitude, a great house that seemed uninhabited; but from the end of the spacious hall moves towards us Avaro, with a suspicious aspect, as if he believed us thieves; and, as for my part, I approached him as if I knew him a cut-purse. We fell into discourse of his noble dwelling, and the great estate all the world knew he had to enjoy in it; and I, to plague him, fell a-commending Paulo's way of living. "Paulo," answered Avaro, "is a very good man; but we, who have smaller estates, must cut our coat according to our cloth." "Nay," says I, "every man knows his own circumstances best; you are in the right, if you haven't wherewithal." He looked very sour; for it is, you must know, the utmost vanity of a mean-spirited rich man to be contradicted when he calls himself poor. But I was resolved to vex him, by consenting to all he said, the main design of which was that he would have us find out he was one of the wealthiest men in London, and lived like a beggar. We left him, and took a turn on the Change. My friend was ravished with Avaro. "This," said he, "is certainly a sure man." I contradicted him with much warmth, and summed up their different characters as well as I could. "This Paulo," said I, "grows wealthy by being a common good; Avaro, by being a general evil; Paulo has the art, Avaro, the craft of trade. When Paulo gains, all men he deals with are the better; whenever Avaro profits, another certainly loses. In a word, Paulo is a citizen, and Avaro a cit." I convinced my friend and carried the young gentleman the next day to Paulo, where he will learn the way both to gain and enjoy a good fortune. And though I cannot say I have, by keeping him from Avaro, saved him from the gallows, I have prevented his deserving it every day he lives; for with Paulo he will be an honest man, without being so for fear of the law; as with Avaro he would have been a villain within the protection of it.

[Steele]

No. 106, December 13, 1709

Invenies dissecti membra poetæ. Hor. *Sat.*, I, iv, 62.

[You will find the limbs of a dismembered poet.]

Will's Coffee-house, December 12

I was this evening sitting at the side-table, and reading one of my own papers with great satisfaction, not knowing that I was observed by any in the room. I had not long enjoyed this secret pleasure of an author, when a gentleman, some of whose works I have been highly entertained with, accosted me after the following manner: "Mr. Bickerstaff, you know I have for some years devoted myself wholly to the Muses, and, perhaps, you will be surprised when I tell you I am resolved to take up, and apply myself to business. I shall, therefore, beg you will stand my friend, and recommend a customer to me for several goods that I have now upon my hands." I desired him to *let me have a particular, and I would do my utmost to serve him. "I have, first of all," says he, "the progress of an amour digested into *sonnets, beginning with a poem to the unknown fair, and ending with an epithalamium. I have celebrated in it her cruelty, her pity, her face, her shape, her wit, her good humour, her dancing, her singing ——" I could not forbear interrupting him: "This is a most accomplished lady," said I; "but has she really, with all these perfections, a fine voice?" "Pugh," says he, "you do not believe there is such a person in nature. This was only my employment *in solitude last summer, when I had neither friends nor books to divert me." "I was going," says I, "to ask her name, but I find it is only an imaginary mistress." "That's true," replied my friend; "but her name is Flavia." "I have," continued he, "in the second place, a collection of lampoons, calculated either for the Bath, Tunbridge, or any place where they drink waters, with blank spaces for the names of such person or persons as may be inserted in them on occasion. Thus much I have told only of what I have by me, proceeding from love and malice. I have also at this time the sketch of an heroic poem upon the next peace: several, indeed, of the verses are either too long or too short, it being a rough draft of my thoughts upon that subject." I thereupon told him that, as it was, *it might probably pass for a very good Pindaric, and I believed I knew one who would be willing to deal with him for it upon that foot. "I must tell you also, I have made a dedication to it, which is about four sides close written, that may serve any one that is tall, and understands Latin. I have further, about fifty similes that were never yet applied, besides three-and-twenty descriptions of the sun rising, that might be of great use to an epic poet. These are my more bulky commodities: besides which, I have several small wares that I would part with at easy rates; as, observations upon life, and moral sentences, reduced into several couplets, very proper to close up acts of plays, and may be easily introduced by two or three lines of prose, either in tragedy or comedy. If I could find a purchaser curious in Latin poetry, I could accommodate him with two dozen of epigrams, which, by reason of a few false quantities, should come for little or nothing."

I heard the gentleman with much attention, and asked him whether he would break bulk and sell his goods by retail, or designed they should all go in a lump. He told me that he should be very loath to part them unless it was to oblige a man of quality, or any person for whom I had a particular friendship. "My reason for asking," said I, "is, only because I know a young gentleman who intends to appear next spring in a new jingling chariot, with the figures of the nine Muses on each side of it; and, I believe would be glad to come into the world in verse." We could not go on in our treaty, by reason of two or three critics that joined us. They had been talking, it seems, of the two letters which were found in the coffin, and mentioned in *one of my late lucubrations, and came with a request to me that I would communicate any others of them that were legible. One of the gentlemen was pleased to say that it was a very proper instance of a widow's constancy, and said he wished I had subjoined, as a foil to it, the following passage in *Hamlet*. The young prince was not yet acquainted with all the guilt of his mother, but turns his thoughts on her sudden forgetfulness of his father, and the indecency of her hasty marriage.

That it should come to this!
But two months dead! Nay, not so much, not two!
So excellent a king! that was to this,
Hyperion to a satyr! So loving to my mother,
That he permitted not the winds of heaven
To visit her face too roughly! Heaven and earth!
Must I remember? Why, she would hang on him,
As if increase of appetite had grown
By what it fed on. And yet, within a month!
Let me not think on't — Frailty, thy name is woman!
A little month! or ere those shoes were old,
With which she followed my poor father's body,
Like Niobe, all tears; why she, even she —
O Heaven! a brute, that wants discourse of reason,
Would have mourned longer! — married with mine uncle,
My father's brother! But no more like my father
Than I to Hercules! Within a month!
Ere yet the salt of most unrighteous tears
Had left the flushing of her gallèd eyes,
She married — O most wicked speed! to post
With such dexterity to incestuous sheets!
It is not, nor it cannot come to good!
But break, my heart; for I must hold my tongue!

The several emotions of mind, and breaks of passion, in this speech, are admirable. He has touched every circumstance that aggravated the fact, and seemed capable of hurrying the thoughts of a son into distraction.

His father's tenderness for his mother, expressed in so delicate a particular; his mother's fondness for his father, no less exquisitely described; the great and amiable figure of his dead parent drawn by a true filial piety; his disdain of so unworthy a successor to his bed; but above all, the shortness of the time between his father's death and his mother's second marriage, brought together with so much disorder, make up as noble a part as any in that celebrated tragedy. The circumstance of time I never could enough admire. The widowhood had lasted two months. This is his first reflection: but, as his indignation rises, he sinks to scarce two months: afterwards into a month; and at last, into a little month: but all this so naturally that the reader accompanies him in the violence of his passion, and finds the time lessen insensibly, according to the different workings of his disdain. I have not mentioned the incest of her marriage, which is so obvious a provocation; but cannot forbear taking notice that when his fury is at its height, he cries, "Frailty, thy name is woman!" as railing at the sex in general, rather than giving himself leave to think his mother worse than others.—*Desiderantur multa.*

Whereas Mr. Jeffery Groggram has surrendered himself, by his letter bearing date December 7, and has sent an acknowledgment that he is dead, praying an order to the * Company of Upholders for interment at such a reasonable rate as may not impoverish his heirs: the said Groggram having been dead ever since he was born, and added nothing to his small patrimony, Mr. Bickerstaff has taken the premises into consideration; and being sensible of the ingenuous and singular behaviour of this petitioner, pronounces the said Jeffery Groggram a live man, and will not suffer that he should bury himself out of modesty; but requires him to remain among the living, as an example to those obstinate dead men, who will neither labour for life, nor go to their grave.

N.B. Mr. Groggram is the first person that has come in upon * Mr. Bickerstaff's dead warrant.

Florinda demands, by her letter of this day, to be allowed to pass for a living woman, having danced the Derbyshire hornpipe in the presence of several friends on Saturday last.

Granted: provided she can bring proof that she can make a pudding on the 24th instant.

[Steele]

No. 163, April 25, 1710

Idem inficeto est inficetior rure,
Simul poemata attigit; neque idem unquam
Æque est beatus, ac poema cum scribit:
Tam gaudet in se, tamque se ipse miratur.
Nimirum idem omnes fallimur; neque est quisquam
Quem non in aliqua re videre Suffenum
Possis.

Catullus, XXII, 14.

[Suffenus has no more wit than a mere clown, when he attempts to write verses; and yet he is never happier than when he is scribbling; so much does he admire himself and his compositions. And, indeed, this is the foible of every one of us; for there is no man living who is not a Suffenus in one thing or other.]

Will's Coffee-house, April 24

I yesterday came hither about two hours before the company generally make their appearance, with a design to read over all the newspapers; but upon my sitting down, I was accosted by Ned Softly, who saw me from a corner in the other end of the room, where I found he had been writing something. "Mr. Bickerstaff," says he, "I observe by a late paper of yours that you and I are just of a humour; for you must know, of all impertinences, there is nothing which I so much hate as news. I never read a Gazette in my life, and never trouble my head about our armies, whether they win or lose, or in what part of the world they lie encamped." Without giving me time to reply, he drew a paper of verses out of his pocket, telling me that he had something which would entertain me more agreeably, and that he would desire my judgment upon every line, for that we had time enough before us till the company came in.

Ned Softly is a very pretty poet, and a great admirer of easy lines. Waller is his favourite; and as that admirable writer has the best and worst verses of any among our great English poets, Ned Softly has got all the bad ones without book, which he repeats upon occasion, to show his reading and garnish his conversation. Ned is indeed a true English reader, incapable of relishing the great and masterly strokes of this art, but wonderfully pleased with the *little Gothic ornaments of epigrammatical conceits, turns, points, and quibbles, which are so frequent in the most admired of our English poets, and practised by those who want genius and strength to represent, after the manner of the ancients, simplicity in its natural beauty and perfection.

Finding myself unavoidably engaged in such a conversation, I was resolved to turn my pain into a pleasure, and to divert myself as well as I could with so very odd a fellow. "You must understand," says Ned, "that the *sonnet I am going to read to you was written upon a lady who showed me some verses of her own making, and is perhaps the best poet of our age. But you shall hear it." Upon which he began to read as follows:

TO MIRA ON HER INCOMPARABLE POEMS

I

When dressed in laurel wreaths you shine,
And tune your soft melodious notes,
You seem a sister of the Nine,
Or Phœbus' self in petticoats.

II

I fancy, when your song you sing
(Your song you sing with so much art),
Your pen was plucked from Cupid's wing;
For ah! it wounds me like his dart.

"Why," says I, "this is a little nosegay of conceits, a very lump of salt: every verse has something in it that piques; and then the dart in the last line is certainly as pretty a sting in the tail of an epigram (for so I think your critics call it) as ever entered into the thought of a poet." "Dear Mr. Bickerstaff," says he, shaking me by the hand, "everybody knows you to be a judge of these things; and to tell you truly, I read over Roscommon's translation of Horace's 'Art of Poetry' three several times before I sat down to write the sonnet which I have shown you. But you shall hear it again, and pray observe every line of it, for not one of them shall pass without your approbation.

When dressed in laurel wreaths you shine.

"That is," says he, "when you have your garland on, when you are writing verses." To which I replied, "I know your meaning, a metaphor!" "The same," said he, and went on:

And tune your soft melodious notes.

"Pray observe the gliding of that verse; there is scarce a consonant in it: I took care to make it run upon liquids. Give me your opinion of it." "Truly," said I, "I think it as good as the former." "I am very glad to hear you say so," says he; "but mind the next:

You seem a sister of the Nine.

"That is," says he, "you seem a sister of the Muses; for if you look into ancient authors, you will find it was their opinion that there were nine of them." "I remember it very well," said I; "but pray proceed."

"Or Phœbus' self in petticoats.

"Phœbus," says he, "was the God of Poetry. These little instances, Mr. Bickerstaff, show a gentleman's reading. Then to take off from the air of learning, which Phœbus and the Muses have given to this first stanza, you may observe how it falls all of a sudden into the familiar, 'in petticoats!'

Or Phœbus' self in petticoats."

"Let us now," says I, "enter upon the second stanza. I find the first line is still a continuation of the metaphor:

I fancy, when your song you sing."

"It is very right," says he; "but pray observe the turn of words in those two lines. I was a whole hour in adjusting of them, and have still a doubt upon me, whether in the second line it should be, 'Your song you sing'; or, 'You sing your song'? You shall hear them both:

I fancy when your song you sing
(Your song you sing with so much art).

Or,

"I fancy, when your song you sing
(You sing your song with so much art.)"

"Truly," said I, "the turn is so natural either way that you have made me almost giddy with it." "Dear sir," said he, grasping me by the hand, "you have a great deal of patience; but pray what do you think of the next verse:

Your pen was plucked from Cupid's wing?"

"Think!" says I; "I think you have made Cupid look like a little goose." "That was my meaning," says he; "I think the ridicule is well enough hit off. But we now come to the last, which sums up the whole matter:

For ah! it wounds me like his dart.

"Pray, how do you like that 'Ah!' Does it not make a pretty figure in that place?

'Ah!' It looks as if I felt the dart, and cried out at being pricked with it:

For ah! it wounds me like his dart.

"My friend, Dick Easy," continued he, "assured me he would rather have written that 'Ah!' than to have been the author of the *Æneid*. He indeed objected that I made Mira's pen like a quill in one of the lines, and like a dart in the other. But as to that——" "Oh! as to that," says I, "it is but supposing Cupid to be like a porcupine, and his quills and darts will be the same thing." He was going to embrace me for the hint; but half a dozen critics coming into the room, whose faces he did not like, he conveyed the sonnet into his pocket, and whispered me in the ear, he would show it me again as soon as his man had written it over fair.

[Addison]

No. 165, April 29, 1710

From My Own Apartment, April 28

It has always been my endeavour to distinguish between realities and appearances, and to separate true merit from the pretence to it. As it shall ever be my study to make discoveries of this nature in human life, and to settle the proper distinctions between the virtues and perfections of mankind, and those false colours and resemblances of them that shine alike in the eyes of the vulgar; so I shall be more particularly careful to search into the various merits and pretences of the learned world. This is the more necessary, because there seems to be a general combination among the pedants to extol one another's labours and cry up one another's parts; while men of sense, either through that modesty which is natural to them, or the scorn they have for such trifling commendations, enjoy their stock of knowledge like a hidden treasure, with satisfaction and silence. Pedantry, indeed, in learning is like hypocrisy in religion, a form of knowledge without the power of it, that attracts the eyes of the common people, breaks out in noise and show, and finds its reward not from any inward pleasure that attends it, but from the praises and approbations which it receives from men.

Of this shallow species there is not a more importunate, empty, and conceited animal than *that which is generally known by the name of a critic. This, in the common acceptation of the word, is one that without entering into the sense and soul of an author has a few general rules which, like mechanical instruments, he applies to the works of every writer, and as they quadrate with them pronounces the author perfect or defective. He is master of a certain set of words, as "unity, style, fire, phlegm, easy, natural, turn, sentiment," and the like; which he varies, compounds, divides, and throws together in every part of his discourse without any thought or meaning. The marks you may know him by are an elevated eye, and dogmatical brow, a positive voice, and a contempt for everything that comes out, whether he has read it or not. He dwells altogether in generals. He praises or dispraises in the lump. He shakes his head very frequently at the pedantry of universities, and bursts into laughter when you mention an author that is not known at Will's. He has formed his judgment upon Homer, Horace, and Virgil, not from their own works, but from those of *Rapin and Bossu. He knows his own strength so well that he never dares praise anything in which he has not a French author for his voucher.

With these extraordinary talents and accomplishments, Sir Timothy Tittle puts men in vogue, or condemns them to obscurity, and sits as judge of life and death upon every author that appears in public. It is impossible to represent the pangs, agonies, and convulsions which Sir Timothy expresses in every feature of his face, and muscle of his body, upon the reading of a bad poet.

About a week ago I was engaged at a friend's of mine in an agreeable conversation with his wife and daughters, when in the height of our mirth, Sir Timothy, who makes love to my friend's eldest daughter, came in amongst us puffing and blowing as if he had been very much out of breath. He immediately called for a chair, and desired leave to sit down, without any further ceremony. I asked him where he had been, whether he was out of order. He only replied that he was quite spent, and fell a-cursing in soliloquy. I could hear him cry, "A wicked rogue!" "An execrable wretch!" "Was there ever such a monster?"

The young ladies upon this began to be affrighted, and asked whether any one had hurt him. He answered nothing, but still talked to himself. "To lay the first scene," says he, "in St. James's Park, and the last in Northamptonshire." "Is that all?" says I. "Then I suppose you have been at the rehearsal of a play this morning?" "Been!" says he; "I have been at Northampton, in the Park, in a lady's bedchamber, in a dining-room, everywhere; the rogue has led me such a dance." Though I could scarce forbear laughing at his discourse, I told him I was glad it was no worse, and that he was only metaphorically weary. "In short, sir," says he, "the author has not observed a single unity in his whole play; the scene shifts in every dialogue; the villain has hurried me up and down at such a rate that I am tired off my legs." I could not but observe with some pleasure that the young lady whom he made love to conceived a very just aversion to him, upon seeing him so very passionate in trifles. And as she had *that natural sense which makes her a better judge than a thousand critics, she began to rally him upon this foolish humour. "For my part," says she, "I never knew a play take that was written up to your rules, as you call them." "How, madam!" says he; "is that your opinion? I am sure you have a better taste." "It is a pretty kind of magic," says she, "the poets have, to transport an audience from place to place without the help of a coach and horses. I could travel round the world at such a rate. 'Tis such an entertainment as an enchantress finds when she fancies herself in a wood, or upon a mountain, at a feast, or a solemnity; though at the same time she has never stirred out of her cottage." "Your simile, madam," says Sir Timothy, "is by no means just." "Pray," says she, "let my similes pass without a criticism. I must confess," continued she, for I found she was resolved to exasperate him, "I laughed very heartily at the last new comedy which you found so much fault with." "But, madam," says he, "you ought not to have laughed, and I defy any one to show me a single rule that you could laugh by." "Ought not to laugh!" says she. "Pray, who should hinder me?" "Madam," says he, "there are such people in the world as Rapin, *Dacier, and several others, that ought to have spoiled your mirth." "I have heard," says the young lady, "that your great critics are always very bad poets: I fancy there is as much difference between the works of one and the other as there is between the carriage of a dancing-master and a gentleman. I must confess," continued she, "I would not be troubled with so fine a judgment as yours is; for I find you feel more vexation in a bad comedy than I do in a deep tragedy." "Madam," says Sir Timothy, "that is not my fault. They should learn the art of writing." "For my part," says the young lady, "I should think the greatest art in your writers of comedies is to please." "To please!" says Sir Timothy; and immediately fell a-laughing. "Truly," says she, "that is my opinion." Upon this, he composed his countenance, looked upon his watch, and took his leave.

I hear that Sir Timothy has not been at my friend's house since this notable conference, to the great satisfaction of the young lady, who by this means has got rid of a very impertinent fop.

I must confess I could not but observe, with a great deal of surprise, how this gentleman, by his ill nature, folly, and affectation, has made himself capable of suffering so many imaginary pains, and looking with such a senseless severity upon the common diversions of life.

[Addison]

No. 181, June 6, 1710

— Dies, ni fallor, adest, quem semper acerbum,
Semper honoratum (sic di voluistis) habebo.
Virg., *Æn.* V, 49.]

[And now the rising day renews the year:
A day for ever sad, for ever dear.
Dryden.]

From My Own Apartment, June 5

There are those among mankind who can enjoy no relish of their being, except the world is made acquainted with all that relates to them, and think everything lost that passes unobserved; but others find a solid delight in stealing by the crowd and modelling their life after such a manner, as is as much above the approbation as the practice of the vulgar. Life being too short to give instances great enough of true friendship or goodwill, some sages have thought it pious to preserve a certain reverence for the manes of their deceased friends, and have withdrawn themselves from the rest of the world at certain seasons to commemorate in their own thoughts such of their acquaintance who have gone before them out of this life; and, indeed, when we are advanced in years, there is not a more pleasing entertainment than to recollect in a gloomy moment the many we have parted with that have been dear and agreeable to us, and to cast a melancholy thought or two after those with whom, perhaps, we have indulged ourselves in whole nights of mirth and jollity. With such inclinations in my heart I went to my closet yesterday in the evening, and *resolved to be sorrowful; upon which occasion I could not but look with disdain upon myself, that though all the reasons which I had to lament the loss of many of my friends are now as forcible as at the moment of their departure, yet did not my heart swell with the same sorrow which I felt at that time; but I could, without tears, reflect upon many pleasing adventures I have had with some who have long been blended with common earth. Though it is by the benefit of nature that length of time thus blots out the violence of afflictions; yet with tempers too much given to pleasure, it is almost necessary to revive the old places of grief in our memory, and ponder step by step on past life, to lead the mind into that sobriety of thought which poises the heart and makes it beat with due time, without being quickened with desire or retarded with despair, from its proper and equal motion. When we wind up a clock that is out of order, to make it go well for the future, we do not immediately set the hand to the present instant, but we make it strike the round of all its hours, before it can recover the regularity of its time. "Such," thought I, "shall be my method this evening; and since it is that day of the year which I dedicate to the memory of such in another life as I much delighted in when living, an hour or two shall be sacred to sorrow and their memory, while I run over all the melancholy circumstances of this kind which have occurred to me in my whole life."

The first sense of sorrow I ever knew was upon the death of my father, at which time I was not quite five years of age, but was rather amazed at what all the house meant, than possessed with a real understanding why nobody was willing to play with me. I remember I went into the room where his body lay, and my mother sat weeping alone by it. I had my battledore in my hand, and fell a-beating the coffin, and calling "Papa"; for, I know not how, I had some slight idea that he was locked up there. My mother catched me in her arms, and, transported beyond all patience of the silent grief she was before in, she almost smothered me in her embrace, and told me, in a flood of tears, papa could not hear me, and would play with me no more, for they were going to put him under ground, whence he could never come to us again. She was a very beautiful woman, of a noble spirit, and there was a dignity in her grief amidst all the wildness of her transport, which, methought, struck me with an instinct of sorrow which, before I was sensible of what it was to grieve, seized my very soul, and has made pity the weakness of my heart ever since. The mind in infancy is, methinks, like the body in embryo, and receives impressions so forcible that they are as hard to be removed by reason as any mark with which a child is born is to be taken away by any future application. Hence it is that good nature in me is no merit, but, having been so frequently overwhelmed with her tears before I knew the cause of any affliction, or could draw defences from my own judgment, I imbibed commiseration, remorse, and an unmanly gentleness of mind, which has since ensnared me into ten thousand calamities, and from whence I can reap no advantage, except it be that in such a humour as I am now in, I can the better indulge myself in the softnesses of humanity, and enjoy that sweet anxiety which arises from the memory of past afflictions.

We that are very old are better able to remember things which befell us in our distant youth, than the passages of later days. For this reason it is that the companions of my strong and vigorous years present themselves more immediately to me in this office of sorrow. Untimely or unhappy deaths are what we are most apt to lament, so little are we able to make it indifferent when a thing happens, though we know it must happen. Thus we groan under life, and bewail those who are relieved from it. Every object that returns to our imagination raises different passions according to the circumstance of their departure. Who can have lived in an army, and in a serious hour reflect upon the many gay and agreeable men that might long have flourished in the arts of peace, and not join with the imprecations of the fatherless and widow on the tyrant to whose ambition they fell sacrifices? But gallant men who are cut off by the sword move rather our veneration than our pity, and we gather relief enough from their own contempt of death, to make it no evil, which was approached with so much cheerfulness and attended with so much honour. But when we turn our thoughts from the great parts of life on such occasions, and, instead of lamenting those who stood ready to give death to those from whom they had the fortune to receive it, — I say, when we let our thoughts wander from such noble objects, and consider the havoc which is made among the tender and the innocent, pity enters with an unmixed softness, and possesses all our souls at once.

Here, were there words to express such sentiments with proper tenderness, I should record the beauty, innocence, and untimely death of the first object my eyes ever beheld with love. The beauteous virgin! How ignorantly did she charm, how carelessly excel! O Death! thou hast right to the bold, to the ambitious, to the high, and to the haughty; but why this cruelty to the humble, to the meek, to the undiscerning, to the thoughtless? Nor age, nor business, nor distress can erase the dear image from my imagination. In the same week I saw her dressed for a ball, and in a shroud. How ill did the habit of Death become the pretty trifler! I still behold the smiling earth —

A large train of disasters were coming on to my memory, when my servant knocked at my closet door, and interrupted me with a letter, attended with *a hamper of wine, of the same sort with that which is to be put to sale on Thursday next at Garraway's Coffee-house. Upon the receipt of it, I sent for three of my friends. We are so intimate that we can be company in whatever state of mind we meet, and can entertain each other without expecting always to rejoice. The wine we found to be generous and warming, but with such a heat as moved us rather to be cheerful than frolicsome. It revived the spirits without firing the blood. We commended it till two of the clock this morning, and, having today met a little before dinner, we found that, though we drank two bottles a man, we had much more reason to recollect than forget what had passed the night before.

[Steele]

No. 196, July 11, 1710

Dulcis inexperto cultura potentis amici:
Expertus metuit —

Hor., I *Ep.* XVIII, 86.

[Untried, how sweet a court attendance!
When tried, how dreadful the dependence!
Francis.]

From My Own Apartment, July 10

The intended course of my studies was altered this evening by a visit from an old acquaintance, who complained to me, mentioning one upon whom he had long depended, that he found his labour and perseverance in his *patron's service and interests wholly ineffectual; and he thought now, after his best years were spent in a professed adherence to him and his fortunes, he should in the end be forced to break with him, and give over all further expectations from him. He sighed, and ended his discourse by saying, "You, Mr. Censor, some time ago, gave us your thoughts of the behaviour of great men to their creditors. This sort of demand upon them, for what they invite men to expect, is a debt of honour, which, according to custom, they ought to be most careful of paying, and would be a very worthy subject for a lucubration.

Of all men living, I think, I am the most proper to treat of this matter, because in the character and employment of censor, I have had encouragement so infinitely above my desert that what I say cannot possibly be supposed to arise from peevishness or any disappointment in that kind which I myself have met with. When we consider patrons and their clients, those who receive addresses, and those who are addressed to, it must not be understood that the dependants as such are worthless in their natures, abandoned to any vice or dishonour, or such as without a call thrust themselves upon men in power; nor when we say patrons, do we mean such as have it not in their power, or have no obligation, to assist their friends; but we speak of such leagues where there are power and obligation on the one part, and merit and expectation on the other. Were we to be very particular on this subject, I take it that the division of patron and client may include a third part of our nation. The want of merit and real worth will strike out about ninety-nine in the hundred of these, and want of ability in the patron will dispose of as many of that order. He who out of mere vanity to be applied to, will take up another's time and fortune in his service, where he has no prospect of returning it, is as much more unjust as those who took up my friend * the upholder's goods without paying him for them. I say, he is as much more unjust as our life and time is more valuable than our goods and movables. Among many whom you see about the great, there is a contented, well-pleased set, who seem to like the attendance for its own sake, and are early at the abodes of the powerful out of mere fashion. This sort of vanity is as well grounded as if a man should lay aside his own plain suit, and dress himself up in a gay livery of another's.

There are many of this species who exclude others of just expectation, and make those proper dependants appear impatient, because they are not so cheerful as those who expect nothing. I have made use of the penny post for the instruction of these voluntary slaves, and informed them that they will never be provided for; but they double their diligence upon admonition. Will Afterday has told his friends that he was to have the next thing these ten years, and Harry Linger has been fourteen within a month of a considerable office. However the fantastic complaisance which is paid to them may blind the great from seeing themselves in a just light, they must needs (if they in the least reflect) at some times have a sense of the injustice they do in raising in others a false expectation. But this is so common a practice in all the stages of power that there are not more cripples come out of the wars than from the attendance of patrons. You see in one a settled melancholy, in another a bridled rage, a third has lost his memory, and a fourth his whole constitution and humour. In a word, when you see a particular cast of mind or body, which looks a little upon the distracted, you may be sure the poor gentleman has formerly had great friends. For this reason, I have thought it a prudent thing to take a nephew of mine out of a lady's service, where he was a page, and have bound him to a shoemaker.

But what of all the humours under the sun is the most pleasant to consider is that you see some men lay, as it were, a set of acquaintance by them, to converse with when they are out of employment, who had no effect of their power when they were in. Here patrons and clients both make the most fantastical figure imaginable. Friendship indeed is most manifested in adversity; but I do not know how to behave myself to a man who thinks me his friend at no other time but that. Dick Reptile of our club had this in his head the other night, when he said, "I am afraid of ill news when I am visited by any of my old friends." These patrons are a little like some fine gentlemen, who spend all their hours of gaiety with their wenches, but when they fall sick, will let no one come near them but their wives. It seems truth and honour are companions too sober for prosperity. It is certainly the most black ingratitude to accept of a man's best endeavours to be pleasing to you, and return it with indifference.

I am so much of this mind that Dick Estcourt, the comedian, for coming one night to our club, though he laughed at us all the time he was there, shall have our company at his play on Thursday. A man of talents is to be favoured, or never admitted. Let the ordinary world truck for money and wares, but men of spirit and conversation should in every kind do others as much pleasure as they receive from them. But men are so taken up with outward forms that they do not consider their actions. Else how should it be that a man shall deny that to the entreaties and almost tears of an old friend, which he shall solicit a new one to accept of? I remember, when I first came out of Staffordshire, I had an intimacy with a man of quality, in whose gift there fell a very good employment. All the town cried, "There's a thing for Mr. Bickerstaff!" when, to my great astonishment, I found my patron had been forced upon twenty artifices to surprise a man with it who never thought of it. But sure it is a degree of murder to amuse men with vain hopes. If a man takes away another's life, where is the difference, whether he does it by taking away the minutes of his time, or the drops of his blood? But indeed, such as have hearts barren of kindness are served accordingly by those whom they employ, and pass their lives away with an empty show of civility for love, and an insipid intercourse of a commerce in which their affections are no way concerned. But on the other side, how beautiful is the life of a patron who performs his duty to his inferiors? a worthy merchant who employs a crowd of artificers? a great lord who is generous and merciful to the several necessities of his tenants? a courtier who uses his credit and power for the welfare of his friends? These have in their several stations a quick relish of the exquisite pleasure of doing good. In a word, good patrons are like the guardian angels of Plato, who are ever busy, though unseen, in the care of their wards; but ill patrons are like the deities of Epicurus, supine, indolent, and unconcerned, though they see mortals in storms and tempests even while they are offering incense to their power.

[Steele]

No. 216, August 26, 1710

- *Nugis addere pondus.* Hor., I *Ep.* XIX, 42.

[Weight and importance some to trifles give.
R. Wynne.]

From My Own Apartment, Aug. 25

Nature is full of wonders; every atom is a standing miracle, and endowed with such qualities as could not be impressed on it by a power and wisdom less than infinite. For this reason I would not discourage any searches that are made into the most minute and trivial parts of the creation. However, since the world abounds in the noblest fields of speculation, it is, methinks, the mark of a little genius to be wholly conversant among insects, reptiles, animalcules, and those trifling rarities that furnish out the apartment of *a virtuoso.

There are some men whose heads are so oddly turned this way, that though they are utter strangers to the common occurrences of life, they are able to discover the sex of a cockle, or describe the generation of a mite, in all its circumstances. They are so little versed in the world that they scarce know a horse from an ox; but at the same time will tell you, with a great deal of gravity, that a flea is a rhinoceros, and a snail an hermaphrodite. I have known one of these whimsical philosophers who has set a greater value upon a collection of spiders than he would upon a flock of sheep, and has sold his coat off his back to purchase a tarantula.

I would not have a scholar wholly unacquainted with these secrets and curiosities of nature; but certainly the mind of man, that is capable of so much higher contemplations, should not be altogether fixed upon such mean and disproportioned objects. Observations of this kind are apt to alienate us too much from the knowledge of the world, and to make us serious upon trifles, by which means they expose philosophy to the ridicule of the witty, and contempt of the ignorant. In short, studies of this nature should be the diversions, relaxations, and amusements; not the care, business, and concern of life.

It is indeed wonderful to consider that there should be a sort of learned men who are wholly employed in gathering together the refuse of nature, if I may call it so, and hoarding up in their chests and cabinets such creatures as others industriously avoid the sight of. One does not know how to mention some of the most precious parts of their treasure without a kind of an apology for it. I have been shown a beetle valued at twenty crowns, and a toad at a hundred; but we must take this for a general rule, that whatever appears trivial or obscene in the common notions of the world, looks grave and philosophical in the eye of a virtuoso.

To show this humour in its perfection I shall present my reader with the legacy of a certain virtuoso, who laid out a considerable estate in natural rarities and curiosities, which upon his deathbed he bequeathed to his relations and friends in the following words:

The Will of a Virtuoso

I, Nicholas Gimcrack, being in sound health of mind, but in great weakness of body, do by this my last will and testament bestow my worldly goods and chattels in manner following:

Imprimis, to my dear wife,
One box of butterflies,
One drawer of shells,
A female skeleton,
A dried cockatrice.

Item, to my daughter Elizabeth,
My receipt for preserving dead caterpillars.
As also my preparations of winter Maydew, and embryo pickle.

Item, to my little daughter Fanny,
Three crocodile's eggs.
And upon the birth of her first child, if she marries with her mother's consent
The nest of a humming bird.

Item, to my eldest brother, as an acknowledgment for the lands he has vested in my son Charles, I bequeath
My last year's collection of grasshoppers.

Item, to his daughter Susanna, being his only child, I bequeath my
English weeds pasted on royal paper.
With my large folio of Indian cabbage.

Item, to my learned and worthy friend Dr. Johannes Elscrikius, Professor in Anatomy, and my associate in the studies of nature, as an eternal monument of my affection and friendship for him, I bequeath
My rat's testicles, and
Whale's pizzle,
to him and his issue male; and in default of such issue in the said Dr. Elscrikius, then to return to my executor and his heirs for ever.

Having fully provided for my nephew Isaac, by making over to him some years since
A horned scarabæus,
The skin of a rattlesnake, and
The mummy of an Egyptian king,
I make no further provision for him in this my will.

My eldest son John having spoken disrespectfully of his little sister, whom I keep by me in spirits of wine, and in many other instances behaved himself undutifully towards me, I do disinherit, and wholly cut off from any part of this my personal estate, by giving him a single cockleshell.

To my second son Charles, I give and bequeath all my flowers, plants, minerals, mosses, shells, pebbles, fossils, beetles, butterflies, caterpillars, grasshoppers, and vermin, not above specified: as also all my monsters, both wet and dry, making the said Charles whole and sole executor of this my last will and testament; he paying, or causing to be paid, the aforesaid legacies within the space of six months after my decease. And I do hereby revoke all other wills whatsoever by me formerly made.

ADVERTISEMENT

Whereas an ignorant upstart in astrology has publicly endeavoured to persuade the world that he is the late John Partridge, who died the 28th of March, 1708, these are to certify all whom it may concern that the true John Partridge was not only dead at that time, but continues so to this present day.

Beware of counterfeits, for such are abroad.

[Addison]

No. 263, December 14, 1710

—*Minima contentos nocte Britannos.* Juv., *Sat.* II, 161.

[Britons contented with the shortest night.]

From My Own Apartment, Dec. 13

An old friend of mine being lately come to town, I went to see him on Tuesday last about eight o'clock in the evening, with a design to sit with him an hour or two and talk over old stories; but upon inquiring after him, his servant told me he was just gone to bed. The next morning as soon as I was up and dressed, and had despatched a little business, I came again to my friend's house about eleven o'clock, with a design to renew my visit; but upon asking for him, his servant told me he was just sat down to dinner. In short, I found that my old-fashioned friend religiously adhered to the example of his forefathers, and observed the same hours that had been kept in the family ever since the Conquest.

It is very plain that the night was much longer formerly in this island than it is at present. By the night I mean that portion of time which nature has thrown into darkness, and which the wisdom of mankind had formerly dedicated to rest and silence. This used to begin at eight o'clock in the evening and conclude at six in the morning. The curfew, or eight o'clock bell, was the signal throughout the nation for putting out their candles and going to bed.

Our grandmothers, though they were wont to sit up the last in the family, were all of them fast asleep at the same hours that their daughters are busy at *crimp and basset. Modern statesmen are concerting schemes, and engaged in the depth of politics, at the time when their forefathers were laid down quietly to rest, and had nothing in their heads but dreams. As we have thus thrown business and pleasure into the hours of rest, and by that means made the natural night but half as long as it should be, we are forced to piece it out with a great part of the morning, so that near two-thirds of the nation lie fast asleep for several hours in broad daylight. This irregularity is grown so very fashionable at present that there is scarce a lady of quality in Great Britain that ever saw the sun rise. And if the humour increases in proportion to what it has done of late years, it is not impossible but our children may hear the bellman going about the streets at nine o'clock in the morning, and the watch making their rounds till eleven. This unaccountable disposition in mankind to continue awake in the night, and sleep in sunshine, has made me inquire whether the same change of inclination has happened to any other animals. For this reason I desired a friend of mine in the country to let me know whether the lark rises as early as he did formerly, and whether the cock begins to crow at his usual hour. My friend has answered me that his poultry are as regular as ever, and that all the birds and the beasts of his neighbourhood keep the same hours that they have observed in the memory of man, and the same which, in all probability, they have kept for these five thousand years.

If you would see the innovations that have been made among us in this particular, you may only look into the hours of colleges, where they still dine at eleven and sup at six, which were doubtless the hours of the whole nation at the time when those places were founded. But at present the courts of justice are scarce opened in Westminster Hall at the time when William Rufus used to go to dinner in it. All business is driven forward: the landmarks of our fathers (if I may so call them) are removed, and planted further up into the day, insomuch that I am afraid our clergy will be obliged (if they expect full congregations) not to look any more upon ten o'clock in the morning as a canonical hour. In my own memory the dinner has crept by degrees from twelve o'clock to three, and where it will fix nobody knows.

I have sometimes thought to draw up a memorial in the behalf of supper against dinner, setting forth that the said dinner has made several encroachments upon the said supper and entered very far upon his frontiers; that he has banished him out of several families, and in all has driven him from his headquarters, and forced him to make his retreat into the hours of midnight; and in short, that he is now in danger of being entirely confounded and lost in a breakfast. Those who have read Lucian, and seen the complaints of the letter "t" against "s" upon account of many injuries and usurpations of the same nature, will not, I believe, think such a memorial forced and unnatural. If dinner has been thus postponed, or (if you please) kept back from time to time, you may be sure that it has been in compliance with the other business of the day, and that supper has still observed a proportionable distance. There is a venerable proverb, which we have all of us heard in our infancy, of "putting the children to bed, and laying the goose to the fire." This was one of the jocular sayings of our forefathers, but may be properly used in the literal sense at present. Who would not wonder at this perverted relish of those who are reckoned the most polite part of mankind, that prefer sea-coals and candles to the sun, and exchange so many cheerful morning hours for the pleasures of midnight revels and debauches? If a man was only to consult his health, he would choose to live his whole time (if possible) in daylight, and to retire out of the world into silence and sleep, while the raw damps and unwholesome vapours fly abroad without a sun to disperse, moderate, or control them. For my own part, I value an hour in the morning as much as common libertines do an hour at midnight. When I find myself awakened into being, and perceive my life renewed within me, and at the same time see the whole face of nature recovered out of the dark, uncomfortable state in which it lay for several hours, my heart overflows with such secret sentiments of joy and gratitude as are a kind of implicit praise to the great Author of Nature. The mind in these early seasons of the day is so refreshed in all its faculties, and borne up with such new supplies of animal spirits, that she finds herself in a state of youth, especially when she is entertained with the breath of flowers, the melody of birds, the dews that hang upon the plants, and all those other sweets of nature that are peculiar to the morning.

It is impossible for a man to have this relish of being, this exquisite taste of life, who does not come into the world before it is in all its noise and hurry; who loses the rising of the sun, the still hours of the day, and immediately upon his first getting up plunges himself into the ordinary cares or follies of the world.

I shall conclude this paper with Milton's inimitable description of Adam's awakening his Eve in Paradise, which indeed would have been a place as little delightful as a barren heath or desert to those who slept in it. The fondness of the posture in which Adam is represented, and the softness of his whisper, are passages in this divine poem that are above all commendation, and rather to be admired than praised.

Now morn, her rosy steps in th' eastern clime
Advancing, sowed the earth with orient pearl,
When Adam waked, so customed; for his sleep
Was airy-light from pure digestion bred,
And temperate vapours bland, which th' only sound
Of leaves and fuming rills, Aurora's fan,
Lightly dispersed, and the shrill matin song
Of birds on every bough; so much the more
His wonder was to find unwakened Eve,
With tresses discomposed, and glowing cheek,
As through unquiet rest: he on his side
Leaning half-raised, with looks of cordial love
Hung over her enamoured, and beheld
Beauty, which whether waking or asleep,
Shot forth peculiar graces. Then with voice
Mild, as when Zephyrus on Flora breathes,
Her hand soft touching, whispered thus: "Awake,
My fairest, my espoused, my latest found,
Heaven's last best gift, my ever new delight;
Awake, the morning shines, and the fresh field
Calls us; we lose the prime, to mark how spring
Our tended plants, how blows the citron grove,
What drops the myrrh, and what the balmy reed,
How Nature paints her colours, how the bee
Sits on the bloom extracting liquid sweet."
Such whispering waked her, but with startled eye
On Adam, whom embracing, thus she spake:
"O soul! in whom my thoughts find all repose,
My glory, my perfection, glad I see
Thy face, and morn returned."

[Steele]

No. 271, January 2, 1710–11

The printer having informed me that there are as many of these papers printed as will make four volumes, I am now come to the end of my ambition in this matter, and have nothing further to say to the world under the character of Isaac Bickerstaff. This work has indeed for some time been disagreeable to me, and *the purpose of it wholly lost by my being so long understood as the author. I never designed in it to give any man any secret wound by my concealment, but spoke in the character of an old man, a philosopher, a humorist, an astrologer, and a censor, to allure my reader with the variety of my subjects, and insinuate, if I could, the weight of reason with the agreeableness of wit. The general purpose of the whole has been to recommend truth, innocence, honour, and virtue, as the chief ornaments of life; but I considered that severity of manners was absolutely necessary to him who would censure others, and for that reason, and that only, chose to talk in a mask. I shall not carry my humility so far as to call myself a vicious man; but at the same time must confess, my life is at best but pardonable. And with no greater character than this, a man would make but an indifferent progress in attacking prevailing and fashionable vices, which Mr. Bickerstaff has done with a freedom of spirit that would have lost both its beauty and efficacy, had it been pretended to by Mr. Steele.

As to the work itself, the acceptance it has met with is the best proof of its value; but I should err against that candour which an honest man should always carry about him, if I did not own that the most approved pieces in it were written by others, and those which have been most excepted against by myself. *The hand that has assisted me in those noble discourses upon the immortality of the soul, the glorious prospects of another life, and the most sublime ideas of religion and virtue, is a person who is too fondly my friend ever to own them; but I should little deserve to be his, if I usurped the glory of them. I must acknowledge at the same time that I think the finest strokes of wit and humour in all Mr. Bickerstaff's lucubrations are those for which he is also beholden to him.

As for the satirical parts of these writings, those against the gentlemen who profess gaming are the most licentious; but the main of them I take to come from losing gamesters, as invectives against the fortunate; for in very many of them I was very little else but the transcriber. If any have been more particularly marked at, such persons may impute it to their own behaviour (before they were touched upon) in publicly speaking their resentment against the author, and professing they would support any man who should insult him. When I mention this subject, I hope *Major General Davenport, Brigadier Bisset, and my Lord Forbes will accept of my thanks for their frequent good offices in professing their readiness to partake any danger that should befall me in so just an undertaking, as the endeavour to banish fraud and cozenage from the presence and conversation of gentlemen.

But what I find is the least excusable part of all this work is that I have in some places touched upon matters which concern both the Church and State. All I shall say for this is that the points I alluded to are such as concerned every Christian and freeholder in England; and I could not be cold enough to conceal my opinion on subjects which related to either of those characters. But politics apart, I must confess, it has been a most exquisite pleasure to me to frame characters of domestic life, and put those parts of it which are least observed into an agreeable view; to inquire into the seeds of vanity and affectation, to lay before my readers the emptiness of ambition: in a word, to trace human life through all its mazes and recesses, and show much shorter methods than men ordinarily practise, to be happy, agreeable, and great.

But to inquire into men's faults and weaknesses has something in it so unwelcome that I have often seen people in pain to act before me, whose modesty only makes them think themselves liable to censure. This and a thousand other nameless things have made it an irksome task to me to personate Mr. Bickerstaff any longer; and I believe it does not often happen that the reader is delighted where the author is displeased.

All I can now do for the further gratification of the town is to give them a faithful index and explication of passages and allusions, and sometimes of persons intended in the several scattered parts of the work. At the same time, the succeeding volumes shall discover which of the whole have been written by me, and which by others, and by whom, as far as I am able, or permitted.

Thus I have voluntarily done what I think all authors should do when called upon. I have published my name to my writings and given myself up to the mercy of the town (as Shakespeare expresses it) with all my imperfections on my head. The indulgent reader's

Most obliged,

Most obedient,

Humble Servant,

Richard Steele

THE SPECTATOR

THE last number of the *Tatler* appeared January 2, 1711. On March 1 of the same year Addison and Steele began the publication of a new paper, the *Spectator*, which appeared six times a week and ran until December 6, 1712. It was afterwards issued three times a week from June 18, 1714, to December 20, 1714, but this later issue, in spite of Dr. Johnson's opinion to the contrary, has generally been considered of less importance than the 555 numbers of the original publication. As first issued, the *Spectator* was printed in double columns on both sides of a single sheet of foolscap folio. These sheets were afterwards republished in monthly parts, and later in octavo volumes. The daily circulation of the *Spectator* has been the subject of considerable controversy. In Number 10 Addison said that three thousand copies were already being distributed each day. But beginning August 1, 1712, a stamp duty was required, which of course increased the price. Steele wrote in Number 555, "The tax on each half-sheet has brought into the stamp-office, one week with another, above £20 a week arising from this single paper, notwithstanding it at first reduced it to less than half the number that was usually printed before this tax was laid." But large as was the daily circulation, the sale of the collected volumes was much greater. In the last number of Volume VII, just quoted, Steele wrote that above nine thousand copies of each of the first four volumes had already been sold. Since that time the *Spectator* has been republished in a long series of editions.

The *Tatler* had been to a considerable degree tentative and experimental, developing under the hands of Steele and his associates as the newspaper features were eliminated and the short reports from the various coffee-houses gave way to longer essays more frequently headed, "From my own Apartment." The *Spectator* seems to have been more definitely planned. While it is improbable that either Steele or Addison realized anything like the full possibilities of the club, they had a well-formulated procedure in mind, and they undertook the new daily publication with confidence in their resources. Though Addison's well-known statement in the tenth number must not be taken too seriously, it represents, with due allowance for the bantering tone, the purpose of the new publication:

"Since I have raised to myself so great an audience, I shall spare no pains to make their instruction agreeable, and their diversion useful. For which reasons I shall endeavour to enliven morality with wit, and to temper wit with morality, that my readers may, if possible, both ways find their account in the speculation of the day.... It was said of Socrates that he brought philosophy down from heaven, to inhabit among men; and I shall be ambitious to have it said of me that I have brought philosophy out of closets and libraries, schools and colleges, to dwell in clubs and assemblies, at tea-tables and in coffee-houses."

The members of the Spectator Club correspond in some measure to the coffee-houses from which the earlier numbers of the *Tatler* ostensibly issued. The "accounts of gallantry, pleasure, and entertainment," which had formerly been dated from White's Chocolate-house, were now to be associated with the name of Will Honeycomb; poetry, which had been connected with Will's Coffee-house, was the special province of the Templar; learning, which was to have been treated at the Grecian, now had no single representative but was considered by the Spectator himself, assisted by the Templar and the Clergyman; foreign and domestic news, which had been picked up at St. James's Coffee-house, had little place in the new publication, but it would have been appropriate to Sir Andrew Freeport and Captain Sentry. Finally, Isaac Bickerstaff gave place to the Spectator. An entirely new feature was the presence of Sir Roger de Coverley, the country gentleman who was soon to overshadow the other members of the club.

These were well chosen, not only to cover the different subjects thus allotted, but also to represent the different classes of contemporary society and so to furnish a canvas for its satiric delineation. Though politics was deliberately excluded from consideration and the excesses of party rivalry were made the object of ridicule, so typical a Tory as Sir Roger and so typical a Whig as Sir Andrew were certainly not introduced accidentally. In spite of the fact that they are represented as friends and fellow club-members, thereby indicating that political enemies could lie down together, their opinions would none the less be perpetually clashing. And though Addison and Steele were for the moment out of politics, both were Whigs. *A priori* one would have expected Sir Roger to come off rather badly at their hands. It is remarkable that the exact opposite came to pass: Sir Roger's character was the object of loving and appreciative development, while

Sir Andrew's was neglected. It is not easy to find in literature a more striking example of the triumph of literary creation over personal prejudice.

In still another respect is the delineation of Sir Roger de Coverley surprising, for the worthy gentleman was from the beginning the outstanding example among the club-members of a character of "humour." To the classicist humours are objects of reprehension. The humourist is a social nonconformist; he sets up his personal idiosyncrasy against the received standards of the best. In so doing he becomes the legitimate object of satire that he may be corrected or that, if he is beyond cure, other men may be warned by his example. Such was the Jonsonian concept of humour, and such, after the Restoration, had been the practically unanimous treatment of humour by English men of letters. In spite of the prevalence of this point of view for two generations, the native English tolerance and admiration of individualism, even of idiosyncratic and perverse individualism, had resisted the pressure of the classical discipline. In the generally accepted theory humours were defects in character; in literature they were commonly so represented for satirical purposes; but in actual life this theory was imperfectly realized. The character of Sir Roger as it developed under the hand of Addison was one of the first important literary creations after 1660 to revert to the pre-Restoration treatment of a humour as something to be admired or loved with slight admixture of reprehension. The Town smiled a little at this representative of the Country, but none the less received him with tolerance and growing affection.

The Spectator himself, separated as he is from participation in the ordinary concerns of life, looks on the world from a position of artificial detachment where he can observe to advantage its incongruities and its shortcomings and vain pretensions and also its confused strugglings toward dimly perceived goals. To expose the bad by gentle satire and to assist the good by encouragement and timely advice is his conscious design. The two purposes are scarcely separable; satire and didactic writing are obverse and reverse of the same medal.

The papers are on all manner of subjects: ladies' fashions, the cries of London, applause at the theatre, the absurdities of Italian opera, eccentric clubs, the improvement of the language, the discrimination of false and true wit, the popular ballads, the pleasures of the imagination. Some are light and amusing; others are distinctly serious. There are walks about the city, suggestions for lovers, humorous journals, stories, moral allegories, discussions of religion, and a long series of criticisms of Milton's *Paradise Lost*. The use of letters from the public, which had been employed to advantage in the *Tatler*, was continued and developed. Some of these letters are mere literary devices, but others are genuine. There was give-and-take between Mr. Spectator and his readers: answers to correspondents, comments on recent essays, echoes, and suggestions. The Town was amused, piqued, instructed, but seldom bored, for Mr. Spectator was evidently a man of the world, even though he stood apart from the world. His papers had wit in every sense of that protean word.

The influence of the *Spectator* has been twofold: on journalism and on literature. It set the tone for a long series of imitators throughout the eighteenth century and into the nineteenth. Even more important was its influence on the familiar essay and, indirectly, on the novel. It is both an introduction to the familiar life and the characteristic ideas of Queen Anne's time, and a link between Bacon and Hazlitt; it illuminates the pages of Pope and Swift and of Richardson and Fielding and Goldsmith. Whoever would know the eighteenth century in its social aspects and its literary relations may profitably give his days and his nights to the volumes of the *Spectator*.

No. 2, Friday, March 2, 1711

—— *Hæc alii sex*
Vel plures uno conclamant ore.
Juv., *Sat.* VII, 167.

[Six more at least join their consenting voice.]

The first of our society is a gentleman of Worcestershire, of ancient descent, a baronet, his name Sir Roger de Coverley. His great-grandfather was inventor of that famous country-dance which is called after him. All who know that shire are very well acquainted with the parts and merits of Sir Roger. He is a gentleman that is very singular in his behaviour, but his singularities proceed from his good sense, and are contradictions to the manners of the world only as he thinks the world is in the wrong. However, this humour creates him no enemies, for he does nothing with sourness or obstinacy; and his being unconfined to modes and forms makes him but the readier and more capable to please and oblige all who know him. When he is in town, he lives in * Soho Square. It is said he keeps himself a bachelor by reason he was crossed in love by a perverse, beautiful widow of the next county to him. Before this disappointment, Sir Roger was what you call a fine gentleman, had often supped with my Lord Rochester and Sir George Etherege, fought a duel upon his first coming to town, and kicked Bully Dawson in a public coffee-house for

* Notes on the *Spectator* will be found in the Appendix, pp. 972 ff.

calling him "youngster." But being ill used by the above mentioned widow, he was very serious for a year and a half; and though, his temper being naturally jovial, he at last got over it, he grew careless of himself, and never dressed afterwards. He continues to wear a coat and doublet of the same cut that were in fashion at the time of his repulse, which, in his merry humours, he tells us has been in and out twelve times since he first wore it. 'Tis said Sir Roger grew humble in his desires after he had forgot this cruel beauty, insomuch that it is reported he has frequently offended in point of chastity with beggars and gypsies; but this is looked upon by his friends rather as matter of raillery than truth. He is now in his fifty-sixth year, cheerful, gay, and hearty; keeps a good house in both town and country; a great lover of mankind; but there is such a mirthful cast in his behaviour that he is rather beloved than esteemed. His tenants grow rich, his servants look satisfied, all the young women profess love to him, and the young men are glad of his company; when he comes into a house, he calls the servants by their names, and talks all the way upstairs to a visit. I must not omit that Sir Roger is a justice of the quorum; that he fills the chair at a quarter-session with great abilities; and, three months ago, gained universal applause by explaining a passage in the Game Act.

The gentleman next in esteem and authority among us is another bachelor, who is a member of the Inner Temple; a man of great probity, wit, and understanding; but he has chosen his place of residence rather to obey the direction of an old, humoursome father, than in pursuit of his own inclinations. He was placed there to study the laws of the land, and is the most learned of any of the house in those of the stage. Aristotle and *Longinus are much better understood by him than Littleton or Coke. The father sends up every post questions relating to marriage-articles, leases, and tenures, in the neighbourhood; all which questions he agrees with an attorney to answer and take care of in the lump. He is studying the passions themselves, when he should be inquiring into the debates among men which arise from them. He knows the argument of each of the orations of Demosthenes and Tully, but not one case in the reports of our own courts. No one ever took him for a fool, but none, except his intimate friends, know he has a great deal of wit. This turn makes him at once both disinterested and agreeable: as few of his thoughts are drawn from business, they are most of them fit for conversation. His taste of books is a little too just for the age he lives in; he has read all, but approves of very few. His familiarity with the customs, manners, actions, and writings of the ancients makes him a very delicate observer of what occurs to him in the present world. He is an excellent critic, and the time of the play is his hour of business; *exactly at five he passes through New Inn, crosses through Russell Court, and takes a turn at Will's till the play begins; he has his shoes rubbed and his periwig powdered at the barber's as you go into the Rose. It is for the good of the audience when he is at a play, for the actors have an ambition to please him.

The person of next consideration is Sir Andrew Freeport, a merchant of great eminence in the city of London, a person of indefatigable industry, strong reason, and great experience. His notions of trade are noble and generous, and (as every rich man has usually some sly way of jesting, which would make no great figure were he not a rich man) he calls the sea the British Common. He is acquainted with commerce in all its parts, and will tell you that it is a stupid and barbarous way to extend dominion by arms; for true power is to be got by arts and industry. He will often argue that if this part of our trade were well cultivated, we should gain from one nation; and if another, from another. I have heard him prove that diligence makes more lasting acquisitions than valour, and that sloth has ruined more nations than the sword. He abounds in several frugal maxims, among which the greatest favourite is, "A penny saved is a penny got." A general trader of good sense is pleasanter company than a general scholar; and Sir Andrew having a natural, unaffected eloquence, the perspicuity of his discourse gives the same pleasure that wit would in another man. He has made his fortunes himself, and says that England may be richer than other kingdoms by as plain methods as he himself is richer than other men; though at the same time I can say this of him, that there is not a point in the compass but blows home a ship in which he is an owner.

Next to Sir Andrew in the club-room sits

Captain Sentry, a gentleman of great courage, good understanding, but invincible modesty. He is one of those that deserve very well, but are very awkward at putting their talents within the observation of such as should take notice of them. He was some years a captain, and behaved himself with great gallantry in several engagements and at several sieges; but having a small estate of his own, and being next heir to Sir Roger, he has quitted a way of life in which no man can rise suitably to his merit who is not something of a courtier as well as a soldier. I have heard him often lament that in a profession where merit is placed in so conspicuous a view, impudence should get the better of modesty. When he has talked to this purpose I never heard him make a sour expression, but frankly confess that he left the world because he was not fit for it. A strict honesty and an even, regular behaviour are in themselves obstacles to him that must press through crowds, who endeavour at the same end with himself, — the favour of a commander. He will, however, in this way of talk excuse generals for not disposing according to men's desert, or inquiring into it: "For," says he, "that great man who has a mind to help me, has as many to break through to come at me, as I have to come at him"; therefore he will conclude that the man who would make a figure, especially in a military way, must get over all false modesty, and assist his patron against the importunity of other pretenders by a proper assurance in his own vindication. He says it is a civil cowardice to be backward in asserting what you ought to expect, as it is a military fear to be slow in attacking when it is your duty. With this candour does the gentleman speak of himself and others. The same frankness runs through all his conversation. The military part of his life has furnished him with many adventures, in the relation of which he is very agreeable to the company; for he is never overbearing, though accustomed to command men in the utmost degree below him, nor ever too obsequious from a habit of obeying men highly above him.

But that our society may not appear a set of humorists unacquainted with the gallantries and pleasures of the age, we have among us the gallant Will Honeycomb, a gentleman who according to his years should be in the decline of his life, but having ever been very careful of his person, and always had a very easy fortune, time has made but very little impression either by wrinkles on his forehead, or traces in his brain. His person is well turned, of a good height. He is very ready at that sort of discourse with which men usually entertain women. He has all his life dressed very well, and remembers habits as others do men. He can smile when one speaks to him, and laughs easily. He knows the history of every mode, and can inform you from which of the French king's wenches our wives and daughters had this manner of curling their hair, that way of placing their hoods; whose frailty was covered by such a sort of petticoat, and whose vanity to show her foot made that part of the dress so short in such a year; in a word, all his conversation and knowledge has been in the female world. As other men of his age will take notice to you what such a minister said upon such and such an occasion, he will tell you when the Duke of Monmouth danced at court such a woman was then smitten, another was taken with him at the head of his troop in the Park. In all these important relations, he has ever about the same time received a kind glance or a blow of a fan from some celebrated beauty, mother of the present Lord Such-a-one. If you speak of a young commoner that said a lively thing in the House, he starts up: "He has good blood in his veins; Tom Mirabel begot him; the rogue cheated me in that affair: that young fellow's mother used me more like a dog than any woman I ever made advances to." This way of talking of his very much enlivens the conversation among us of a more sedate turn; and I find there is not one of the company, but myself, who rarely speak at all, but speaks of him as of that sort of man who is usually called a well-bred, fine gentleman. To conclude his character, where women are not concerned, he is an honest, worthy man.

I cannot tell whether I am to account him whom I am next to speak of as one of our company, for he visits us but seldom; but when he does, it adds to every man else a new enjoyment of himself. He is a clergyman, a very philosophic man, of general learning, great sanctity of life, and the most exact good breeding. He has the misfortune to be of a very weak constitution, and consequently cannot accept of such cares and business as preferments in his function would oblige him to; he is therefore among divines what a chamber-counsellor is among lawyers. The probity of his mind and the integrity of his life create him followers, as being eloquent or loud advances others. He seldom introduces the subject he speaks upon; but we are so far gone in years that he observes, when he is among us, an earnestness to have him fall on some divine topic, which he always treats with much authority, as one who has no interests in this world, as one who is hastening to the object of all his wishes, and conceives hope from his decays and infirmities. These are my ordinary companions.

[Steele]

No. 35, Tuesday, April 10, 1711

*— *Risu inepto res ineptior nulla est.*
Catullus, XXXIX, 16.

[Nothing so foolish as the laughter of fools.]

Among all kinds of writing, there is none in which authors are more apt to miscarry than in works of humour, as there is none in which they are more ambitious to excel. It is not an imagination that teems with monsters, an head that is filled with extravagant conceptions, which is capable of furnishing the world with diversions of this nature; and yet, if we look into the productions of several writers, who set up for men of humour, what wild, irregular fancies, what unnatural distortions of thought do we meet with? If they speak nonsense, they believe they are talking humour; and when they have drawn together a scheme of absurd, inconsistent ideas, they are not able to read it over to themselves without laughing. These poor gentlemen endeavour to gain themselves the reputation of wits and humourists, by such monstrous conceits as almost qualify them for Bedlam; not considering that humour should always lie under the check of reason, and that it requires the direction of the nicest judgment, by so much the more as it indulges itself in the most boundless freedoms. There is a kind of nature that is to be observed in this sort of compositions, as well as in all other; and a certain regularity of thought which must discover the writer to be a man of sense, at the same time that he appears altogether given up to caprice. For my part, when I read the delirious mirth of an unskillful author, I cannot be so barbarous as to divert myself with it, but am rather apt to pity the man, than to laugh at anything he writes.

*The deceased Mr. Shadwell, who had himself a great deal of the talent which I am treating of, represents an empty rake, in one of his plays, as very much surprised to hear one say that breaking of windows was not humour; and I question not but several English readers will be as much startled to hear me affirm that many of those raving, incoherent pieces, which are often spread among us, under odd chimerical titles, are rather the offsprings of a distempered brain than works of humour.

It is, indeed, much easier to describe what is not humour than what is; and very difficult to define it otherwise than *as Cowley has done wit, by negatives. Were I to give my own notions of it, I would deliver them after Plato's manner, in a kind of allegory, and, by supposing Humour to be a person, deduce to him all his qualifications, according to the following genealogy. Truth was the founder of the family, and the father of Good Sense. Good Sense was the father of Wit, who married a lady of a collateral line called Mirth, by whom he had issue Humour. Humour therefore being the youngest of this illustrious family, and descended from parents of such different dispositions, is very various and unequal in his temper; sometimes you see him putting on grave looks and a solemn habit, sometimes airy in his behaviour and fantastic in his dress; insomuch that at different times he appears as serious as a judge, and as jocular as a merry-andrew. But, as he has a great deal of the mother in his constitution, whatever mood he is in, he never fails to make his company laugh.

But since there is an impostor abroad, who takes upon him the name of this young gentleman, and would willingly pass for him in the world; to the end that well-meaning persons may not be imposed upon by cheats, I would desire my readers, when they meet with this pretender, to look into his parentage, and to examine him strictly, whether or no he be remotely allied to Truth, and lineally descended from Good Sense; if not, they may conclude him a counterfeit. They may likewise distinguish him by a loud and excessive laughter, in which he seldom gets his company to join with him. For as True Humour generally looks serious while everybody laughs about him, False Humour is always laughing whilst everybody about him looks serious. I shall only add, if he has not in him a mixture of both parents — that is, if he would pass for the offspring of Wit without Mirth, or Mirth without Wit, you may conclude him to be altogether spurious and a cheat.

The impostor of whom I am speaking descends originally from Falsehood, who was the mother of Nonsense, who was brought to bed of a son called Frenzy, who married one of the daughters of Folly, commonly known by the name of Laughter, on whom he begot that monstrous infant of which I have been here speaking. I shall set down at length the genealogical table of False Humour, and, at the same time, place under it the genealogy of True Humour, that the reader may at one view behold their different pedigrees and relations:

Falsehood.
Nonsense.
Frenzy,—— Laughter.
False Humour.

Truth.
Good Sense.
Wit,—— Mirth.
Humour.

I might extend the allegory, by mentioning several of the children of False Humour, who are more in number than the sands of the sea, and might in particular enumerate the many sons and daughters which he has begot in this island. But as this would be a very invidious task, I shall only observe in general that False Humour differs from the True as a monkey does from a man.

First of all, he is exceedingly given to little apish tricks and buffooneries.

Secondly, he so much delights in mimicry that it is all one to him whether he exposes by it vice and folly, luxury and avarice; or, on the contrary, virtue and wisdom, pain and poverty.

Thirdly, he is wonderfully unlucky, insomuch that he will bite the hand that feeds him, and endeavour to ridicule both friends and foes indifferently. For, having but small talents, he must be merry where he can, not where he should.

Fourthly, being entirely void of reason, he pursues no point either of morality or instruction, but is ludicrous only for the sake of being so.

Fifthly, being incapable of having anything but mock representations, his ridicule is always personal, and aimed at the vicious man, or the writer; not at the vice, or at the writing.

I have here only pointed at the whole species of false humorists; but, as one of my principal designs in this paper is to beat down that malignant spirit which discovers itself in the writings of the present age, I shall not scruple, for the future, to single out any of the small wits that infest the world with such compositions as are ill-natured, immoral, and absurd. This is the only exception which I shall make to the general rule I have prescribed myself, of attacking multitudes; since every honest man ought to look upon himself as in a natural state of war with the libeller and lampooner, and to annoy them wherever they fall in his way. This is but retaliating upon them, and treating them as they treat others. [Addison]

No. 41, Tuesday, April 17, 1711

Tu non inventa reperta es.
Ovid, *Met.* I, 654.

[So found, is worse than lost.
Addison.]

Compassion for the gentleman who writes the following letter should not prevail upon me to fall upon the fair sex, if it were not that I find they are frequently fairer than they ought to be. Such impostures are not to be tolerated in civil society, and I think his misfortune ought to be made public, as a warning for other men always to examine into what they admire:

"Sir,

Supposing you to be a person of general knowledge, I make my application to you on a very particular occasion. I have a great mind to be rid of my wife, and hope, when you consider my case, you will be of opinion I have very just pretensions to a divorce. I am a mere man of the town and have very little improvement but what I have got from plays. I remember in * *The Silent Woman*, the learned Dr. Cutberd — or Dr. Otter, I forget which — makes one of the causes of separation to be *error personæ* (when a man marries a woman, and finds her not to be the same woman whom he intended to marry, but another). If that be law, it is, I presume, exactly my case. For you are to know, Mr. Spectator, that there are women who do not let their husbands see their faces till they are married.

"Not to keep you in suspense, I mean plainly that part of the sex who paint. They are some of them so exquisitely skillful this way that, give them but a tolerable pair of eyes to set up with, and they will make bosom, lips, cheeks, and eyebrows, by their own industry. As for my dear, never man was so enamoured as I was of her fair forehead, neck, and arms, as well as the bright jet of her hair; but, to my great astonishment, I find they were all the effect of art. Her skin is so tarnished with this practice that, when she first wakes in a morning, she scarce seems young enough to be the mother of her whom I carried to bed the night before. I shall take the liberty to part with her by the first opportunity, unless her father will make her portion suitable to her real, not her assumed, countenance. This I thought fit to let him and her know by your means.

I am, sir,

Your most obedient humble servant."

I cannot tell what the law or the parents of the lady will do for this injured gentleman, but must allow he has very much justice on his side. I have indeed very long observed this evil, and distinguished those of our women who wear their own from those in borrowed complexions by the Picts and the British. There does not need any great discernment to judge which are which. The British have a lively, animated aspect; the Picts, though never so beautiful, have dead, uninformed countenances. The muscles of a real face sometimes swell with soft passion, sudden surprise, and are flushed with agreeable confusions, according as the objects before them, or the ideas presented to them, affect their imagination. But the Picts behold all things with the same air, whether they are joyful or sad; the same fixed insensibility appears upon all occasions. A Pict, though she takes all pains to invite the approach of lovers, is obliged to keep them at a certain distance; a sigh in a languishing lover, if fetched too near her, would dissolve a feature; and a kiss snatched by a forward one, might transfer the complexion of the mistress to the admirer. It is hard to speak of these fair false ones without saying something uncomplaisant; but I would only recommend to them to consider how they like coming into a room new painted: they may assure themselves the near approach of a lady who uses this practice is much more offensive.

Will Honeycomb told us one day an adventure he once had with a Pict. The lady had wit, as well as beauty, at will; and made it her business to gain hearts for no other reason but to rally the torments of her lovers. She would make great advances to ensnare men, but without any manner of scruple break off when there was no provocation. Her ill-nature and vanity made my friend very easily proof against the charms of her wit and conversation; but her beauteous form, instead of being blemished by her falsehood and inconstancy, every day increased upon him, and she had new attractions every time he saw her. When she observed Will irrevocably her slave, she began to use him as such, and after many steps towards such a cruelty, she at last utterly banished him. The unhappy lover strove in vain, by servile epistles, to revoke his doom; till at length he was forced to the last refuge, a round sum of money to her maid. This corrupt attendant placed him early in the morning behind the hangings in her mistress's dressing-room. He stood very conveniently to observe, without being seen. The Pict begins the face she designed to wear that day, and I have heard him protest she had worked a full half-hour before he knew her to be the same woman. As soon as he saw the dawn of that complexion for which he had so long languished, he thought fit to break from his concealment, repeating that [verse] of Cowley:

"Th' adorning thee with so much art
 Is but a barbarous skill;
'Tis like the pois'ning of a dart,
 Too apt before to kill."

The Pict stood before him in the utmost confusion, with the prettiest smirk imaginable on the finished side of her face, pale as ashes on the other. Honeycomb seized all her gallipots and washes, and carried off his handkerchief full of brushes, scraps of Spanish wools, and phials of unguents. The lady went into the country; the lover was cured.

It is certain no faith ought to be kept with cheats, and an oath made to a Pict is of itself void. I would therefore exhort all the British ladies to single them out, nor do I know any but Lindamira who should be exempt from discovery; for her own complexion is so delicate that she ought to be allowed the covering it with paint, as a punishment for choosing to be the worst piece of art extant, instead of the masterpiece of nature. As for my part, who have no expectations from women, and consider them only as they are part of the species, I do not half so much fear offending a beauty as a woman of sense; I shall therefore produce several faces which have been in public this many years, and never appeared. It will be a very pretty entertainment in the playhouse, when I have abolished this custom, to see so many ladies, when they first lay it down, *incog.* in their own faces.

In the mean time, as a pattern for improving their charms, let the sex study the agreeable Statira. Her features are enlivened with the cheerfulness of her mind, and good-humour gives an alacrity to her eyes. She is graceful without affecting an air, and unconcerned without appearing careless. Her having no manner of art in her mind makes her want none in her person.

How like is this lady, and how unlike is a Pict, to that description Dr. Donne gives of his mistress!

> Her pure and eloquent blood
> Spoke in her cheeks, and so distinctly wrought
> That one would almost say her body thought.

ADVERTISEMENT

A young gentlewoman of about nineteen years of age, bred in the family of a person of quality lately deceased, who paints the finest flesh-colour, wants a place, and is to be heard of at the house of Mynheer Grotesque, a Dutch painter, in Barbican.

N.B. — She is also well skilled in the drapery part and puts on hoods and mixes ribbons so as to suit the colours of the face with great art and success.

[Steele]

No. 50, Friday, April 27, 1711

Nunquam aliud natura, aliud sapientia dicit.
Juv., *Sat.* XIV, 321.

[Good taste and nature always speak the same.]

When *the four Indian kings were in this country about a twelvemonth ago, I often mixed with the rabble, and followed them a whole day together, being wonderfully struck with the sight of everything that is new or uncommon. I have, since their departure, employed a friend to make many inquiries of their landlord, the upholsterer, relating to their manners and conversation, as also concerning the remarks which they made in this country; for, next to the forming a right notion of such strangers, I should be desirous of learning what ideas they have conceived of us.

The upholsterer, finding my friend very inquisitive about these his lodgers, brought him some time since a little bundle of papers, which he assured him were written by King Sa Ga Yean Qua Rash Tow, and, as he supposes, left behind by some mistake. These papers are now translated, and contain abundance of very odd observations, which I find this little fraternity of kings made during their stay in the isle of Great Britain. I shall present my reader with a short specimen of them in this paper, and may perhaps communicate more to him hereafter. In the article of London are the following words, which without doubt are meant of the church of St. Paul.

"On the most rising part of the town there stands a huge house, big enough to contain the whole nation of which I am king. Our good brother E Tow O Koam, King of the Rivers, is of opinion it was made by the hands of that great God to whom it is consecrated. The Kings of Granajah and of the Six Nations believe that it was created with the earth, and produced on the same day with the sun and moon. But for my own part, by the best information that I could get of this matter, I am apt to think that this prodigious pile was fashioned into the shape it now bears by several tools and instruments, of which they have a wonderful variety in this country. It was probably at first an huge misshapen rock that grew upon the top of he hill, which the natives of the country (after having cut it into a kind of regular figure) bored and hollowed with incredible pains and industry, till they had wrought in it all those beautiful vaults and caverns into which it is divided at this day. As soon as this rock was thus curiously scooped to their liking, a prodigious number of hands must have been employed in chipping the outside of it, which is now as smooth as the surface of a pebble, and is in several places hewn out into pillars, that stand like the trunks of so many trees bound about the top with garlands of leaves. It is probable that when this great work was begun, which must have been many hundred years ago, there was some religion among this people; for they give it the name of a temple, and have a tradition that it was designed for men to pay their devotions in. And indeed there are several reasons which make us think that the natives of this country had formerly among them some sort of worship, for they set apart every seventh day as sacred; but upon my going into one of these holy houses on that day, I could not observe any circumstance of devotion in their behaviour. There was indeed a man in black who was mounted above the rest, and seemed to utter something with a great deal of vehemence; but as for those underneath him, instead of paying their worship to the deity of the place, they were most of them bowing and curtsying to one another, and a considerable number of them fast asleep.

"The queen of the country appointed two men to attend us, that had enough of our language to make themselves understood in some few particulars. But we soon perceived these two were great enemies to one another, and did not always agree in the same story. We could make a shift to gather out of one of them that this island was very much infested with a monstrous kind of animals, in the shape of men, called Whigs; and he often told us that he hoped we should meet with none of them in our way, for that if we did, they would be apt to knock us down for being kings.

"Our other interpreter used to talk very much of a kind of animal called a Tory, that was as great a monster as the Whig, and would treat us as ill for being foreigners. These two creatures, it seems, are born with a secret antipathy to one another, and engage when they meet as naturally as the elephant and the rhinoceros. But as we saw none of either of these species, we are apt to think that our guides deceived us with misrepresentations and fictions, and amused us with an account of such monsters as are not really in their country.

"These particulars we made a shift to pick out from the discourse of our interpreters, which we put together as well as we could, being able to understand but here and there a word of what they said, and afterwards making up the meaning of it among ourselves. The men of the country are very cunning and ingenious in handicraft works, but withal so very idle that we often saw young lusty rawboned fellows carried up and down the streets in little covered rooms by a couple of porters, who are hired for that service. Their dress is likewise very barbarous, for they almost strangle themselves about the neck, and bind their bodies with many ligatures, that we are apt to think are the occasion of several distempers among them, which our country is entirely free from. Instead of those beautiful feathers with which we adorn our heads, they often buy up a monstrous bush of hair, which covers their heads and falls down in a large fleece below the middle of their backs; with which they walk up and down the streets, and are as proud of it as if it was of their own growth.

"We were invited to one of their public diversions, where we hoped to have seen the great men of their country running down a stag or pitching a bar, that we might have discovered who were the persons of the greatest abilities among them; but instead of that, they conveyed us into a huge room lighted up with abundance of candles, where this lazy people sat still above three hours to see several feats of ingenuity performed by others, who it seems were paid for it.

"As for the women of the country, not being able to talk with them, we could only make our remarks upon them at a distance. They let the hair of their heads grow to a great length; but as the men make a great show with heads of hair that are none of their own, the women, who they say have very fine heads of hair, tie it up in a knot, and cover it from being seen. The women look like angels, and would be more beautiful than the sun, were it not for *little black spots that are apt to break out in their faces, and sometimes rise in very odd figures. I have observed that those little blemishes wear off very soon; but when they disappear in one part of the face, they are very apt to break out in another, insomuch that I have seen a spot upon the forehead in the afternoon, which was upon the chin in the morning."

The author then proceeds to show the absurdity of breeches and petticoats, with many other curious observations, which I shall reserve for another occasion. I cannot, however, conclude this paper without taking notice that, amidst these wild remarks, there now and then appears something very reasonable. I cannot likewise forbear observing that we are all guilty in some measure of the same narrow way of thinking which we meet with in this abstract of the Indian journal, when we fancy the customs, dresses, and manners of other countries are ridiculous and extravagant, if they do not resemble those of our own.

[Addison]

No. 58, Monday, May 7, 1711

* *Ut pictura poesis erit* —
Hor., *Ars Poet.* 361.

[Poems like pictures are.]

Nothing is so much admired, and so little understood, as wit. No author that I know of has written professedly upon it. As for those who make any mention of it, they only treat on the subject as it has accidentally fallen in their way, and that too in little short reflections, or in general declamatory flourishes, without entering into the bottom of the matter. I hope, therefore, I shall perform an acceptable work to my countrymen if I treat at large upon this subject; which I shall endeavour to do in a manner suitable to it, that I may not incur * the censure which a famous critic bestows upon one who had written a treatise upon "the sublime," in a low, grovelling style. I intend to lay aside a whole week for this undertaking, that the scheme of my thoughts may not be broken and interrupted; and I dare promise myself, if my readers will give me a week's attention, that this great city will be very much changed for the better by next Saturday night. I shall endeavour to make what I say intelligible to ordinary capacities; but if my readers meet with any paper that in some parts of it may be a little out of their reach, I would not have them discouraged, for they may assure themselves the next shall be much clearer.

As the great and only end of these my speculations is to banish vice and ignorance out of the territories of Great Britain, I shall endeavour, as much as possible, to establish among us a taste of polite writing. It is with this view that I have endeavoured to set my readers right in several points relating to operas and tragedies, and shall, from time to time, impart my notions of comedy, as I think they may tend to its refinement and perfection. I find by my bookseller that these papers of criticism, with that upon humour, have met with a more kind reception than indeed I could have hoped for from such subjects; for which reason I shall enter upon my present undertaking with greater cheerfulness.

In this, and one or two following papers, I shall trace out the history of false wit, and distinguish the several kinds of it as they have prevailed in different ages of the world. This I think the more necessary at present, because I observed there were attempts on foot last winter to revive some of those antiquated modes of wit that have been long exploded out of the commonwealth of letters. There were several satires and panegyrics handed about in an acrostic, by which means some of the most arrant, undisputed blockheads about the town began to entertain ambitious thoughts, and to set up for polite authors. I shall therefore describe at length those many arts of false wit, in which a writer does not show himself a man of a beautiful genius, but of great industry.

The first species of false wit which I have met with is very venerable for its antiquity, and has produced several pieces which have lived very near as long as the *Iliad* itself: I mean, those short poems printed among the minor Greek poets which resemble the figure of an egg, a pair of wings, an axe, a shepherd's pipe, and an altar.

As for the first, it is a little oval poem, and may not improperly be called a scholar's egg. I would endeavour to hatch it, or, in more intelligible language, to translate it into English, did not I find the interpretation of it very difficult; for the author seems to have been more intent upon the figure of his poem than upon the sense of it.

The pair of wings consists of twelve verses, or rather feathers, every verse decreasing gradually in its measure according to its situation in the wing. The subject of it, as in the rest of the poems which follow, bears some remote affinity with the figure, for it describes a god of love, who is always painted with wings.

The axe, methinks, would have been a good figure for a lampoon, had the edge of it consisted of the most satirical parts of the work; but as it is in the original, I take it to have been nothing else but the posy of an axe which was consecrated to Minerva, and was thought to have been the same that Epeus made use of in the building of the Trojan horse; which is a hint I shall leave to the consideration of the critics. I am apt to think that the posy was written originally upon the axe, like those which our modern cutlers inscribe upon their knives; and that, therefore, the posy still remains in its ancient shape, though the axe itself is lost.

The shepherd's pipe may be said to be full of music, for it is composed of nine different kinds of verses, which by their several lengths resemble the nine stops of the old musical instrument that is likewise the subject of the poem.

The altar is inscribed with the epitaph of Troilus the son of Hecuba; which, by the way, makes me believe that these false pieces of wit are much more ancient than the authors to whom they are generally ascribed; at least, I will never be persuaded that so fine a writer as Theocritus could have been the author of any such simple works.

It was impossible for a man to succeed in these performances who was not a kind of painter, or at least a designer. He was first of all to draw the outline of the subject which he intended to write upon, and afterwards conform the description to the figure of his subject. The poetry was to contract or dilate itself according to the mould in which it was cast. In a word, the verses were to be cramped or extended to the dimensions of the frame that was prepared for them; and to undergo the fate of those persons whom the tyrant Procrustes used to lodge in his iron bed: if they were too short, he stretched them on a rack; and if they were too long, chopped off a part of their legs, till they fitted the couch which he had prepared for them.

Mr. Dryden hints at this obsolete kind of wit in one of the following verses in his *Mac Flecknoe*, which an English reader cannot understand who does not know that there are those little poems above mentioned in the shape of wings and altars:

> — Choose for thy command
> Some peaceful province in Acrostic Land;
> There may'st thou wings display, and altars raise,
> And torture one poor word a thousand ways.

This fashion of false wit was revived by several poets of the last age, and in particular may be met with among *Mr. Herbert's poems; and, if I am not mistaken, in the translation of *Du Bartas. I do not remember any other kind of work among the moderns which more resembles the performances I have mentioned than that famous picture of King Charles the First, which has the whole Book of Psalms written in the lines of the face, and the hair of the head. When I was last at Oxford, I perused one of the whiskers, and was reading the other, but could not go so far in it as I would have done, by reason of the impatience of my friends and fellow-travellers, who all of them pressed to see such a piece of curiosity. I have since heard that there is now an eminent writing master in town, who has transcribed all the Old Testament in a full-bottomed periwig; and if the fashion should introduce the thick kind of wigs which were in vogue some few years ago, he promises to add two or three supernumerary locks that shall contain all the Apocrypha. He designed this wig originally for King William, having disposed of the two Books of Kings in the two forks of the foretop; but that glorious monarch dying before the wig was finished, there is a space left in it for the face of any one that has a mind to purchase it.

But to return to our ancient poems in picture. I would humbly propose, for the benefit of our modern smatterers in poetry, that they would imitate their brethren among the ancients in those ingenious devices. I have communicated this thought to a young poetical lover of my acquaintance, who intends to present his mistress with a copy of verses made in the shape of her fan; and, if he tells me true, has already finished the three first sticks of it. He has likewise promised me to get the measure of his mistress's marriage finger with a design to make a posy in the fashion of a ring, which shall exactly fit it. It is so very easy to enlarge upon a good hint that I do not question but my ingenious readers will apply what I have said to many other particulars; and that we shall see the town filled in a very little time with poetical tippets, handkerchiefs, snuff-boxes, and the like female ornaments. I shall therefore conclude with a word of advice to those admirable English authors who call themselves *Pindaric writers, that they would apply themselves to this kind of wit without loss of time, as being provided better than any other poets with verses of all sizes and dimensions.

[Addison]

* No. 61, Thursday, May 10, 1711

Non equidem hoc studeo, bullatis ut mihi nugis
Pagina turgescat, dare pondus idonea fumo.
Pers., *Sat.* V, 19.

['Tis not indeed my talent to engage
In lofty trifles, or to swell my page
With wind and noise. Dryden.]

There is no kind of false wit which has been so recommended by the practice of all ages as that which consists in a jingle of words, and is comprehended under the general name of punning. It is indeed impossible to kill a weed which the soil has a natural disposition to produce. The seeds of punning are in the minds of all men, and though they may be subdued by reason, reflection, and good sense, they will be very apt to shoot up in the greatest genius that is not broken and cultivated by the rules of art. Imitation is natural to us, and when it does not raise the mind to poetry, painting, music, or other more noble arts, it often breaks out in puns and quibbles.

Aristotle, in the eleventh chapter of his book of rhetoric, describes two or three kinds of puns, which he calls paragrams, among the beauties of good writing, and produces instances of them out of some of the greatest authors in the Greek tongue. Cicero has sprinkled several of his works with puns, and, in his book where he lays down the rules of oratory, quotes abundance of sayings as pieces of wit, which also, upon examination, prove arrant puns. But the age in which the pun chiefly flourished was the reign of King James the First. That learned monarch was himself a tolerable punster, and made very few bishops or Privy Councillors that had not some time or other signalized themselves by a clinch, or a conundrum. It was, therefore, in this age that the pun appeared with pomp and dignity. It had before been admitted into merry speeches and ludicrous compositions, but was now delivered with great gravity from the pulpit, or pronounced in the most solemn manner at the council-table. The greatest authors, in their most serious works, made frequent use of puns. The sermons of Bishop Andrewes, and the tragedies of Shakespeare, are full of them. The sinner was punned into repentance by the former; as in the latter, nothing is more usual than to see a hero weeping and quibbling for a dozen lines together.

I must add to these great authorities, which seem to have given a kind of sanction to this piece of false wit, that all the writers of rhetoric have treated of punning with very great respect, and divided the several kinds of it into hard names, that are reckoned among the figures of speech, and recommended as ornaments in discourse. I remember a country schoolmaster of my acquaintance told me once, that he had been in company with a gentleman whom he looked upon to be the greatest paragrammatist among the moderns. Upon inquiry, I found my learned friend had dined that day with Mr. Swan, the famous punster; and desiring him to give me some account of Mr. Swan's conversation, he told me that he generally talked in the *Paranomasia*, that he sometimes gave in to the *Plocé*, but that in his humble opinion he shined most in the *Antanaclasis*.

I must not here omit that *a famous university of this land was formerly very much infested with puns; but whether or no this might not arise from the fens and marshes in which it was situated, and which are now drained, I must leave to the determination of more skillful naturalists.

After this short history of punning, one would wonder how it should be so entirely banished out of the learned world as it is at present, especially since it had found a place in the writings of the most ancient polite authors. To account for this we must consider that the first race of authors, who were the great heroes in writing, were destitute of all rules and arts of criticism; and for that reason, though they excel later writers in greatness of genius, they fall short of them in accuracy and correctness. The moderns cannot reach their beauties, but can avoid their imperfections. When the world was furnished with these authors of the first eminence, there grew up another set of writers, who gained themselves a reputation by the remarks which they made on the works of those who preceded them. It was one of the employments of these secondary authors to distinguish the several kinds of wit by terms of art, and to consider them as more or less perfect, according as they were founded in truth. It is no wonder, therefore, that even such authors as Isocrates, Plato, and Cicero, should have such little blemishes as are not to be met with in authors of a much inferior character who have written since those several blemishes were discovered. I do not find that there was a proper separation made between puns and true wit by any of the ancient authors, except Quintilian and Longinus. But when this distinction was once settled, it was very natural for all men of sense to agree in it. As for the revival of this false wit, it happened about the time of the revival of letters; but as soon as it was once detected, it immediately vanished and disappeared. At the same time there is no question but, as it has sunk in one age and rose in another, it will again *recover itself in some distant period of time, as pedantry and ignorance shall prevail upon wit and sense. And, to speak the truth, I do very much apprehend, by some of the last winter's productions, which had their sets of admirers, that our posterity will in a few years degenerate into a race of punsters: at least, a man may be very excusable for any apprehensions of this kind, that has seen acrostics handed about the town with great secrecy and applause; to which I must also add a little epigram called the "Witches' Prayer," that fell into verse when it was read either backward or forward, excepting only that it cursed one way, and blessed the other. When one sees there are actually such pains-takers among our British wits, who can tell what it may end in? If we must lash one another, let it be with the manly strokes of wit and satire; for I am of the old philosopher's opinion, that, if I must suffer from one or the other, I would rather it should be from the paw of a lion than the hoof of an ass. I do not speak this out of any spirit of party. There is a most crying dullness on both sides. I have seen Tory acrostics and Whig anagrams, and do not quarrel with either of them because they are Whigs or Tories, but because they are anagrams and acrostics.

But to return to punning. Having pursued the history of a pun, from its original to its downfall, I shall here define it to be a conceit arising from the use of two words that agree in the sound, but differ in the sense. The only way, therefore, to try a piece of wit is to translate it into a different language. If it bears the test, you may pronounce it true; but if it vanishes in the experiment, you may conclude it to have been a pun. In short, one may say of a pun, as the countryman described his nightingale, that it is *vox et prœterea nihil* — "a sound, and nothing but a sound." On the contrary, one may represent true wit by the description which Aristænetus makes of a fine woman: — "When she is dressed she is beautiful: when she is undressed she is beautiful"; or, as Mercerus has translated it more emphatically, *_Induitur, formosa est: exuitur, ipsa forma est._

[Addison]

NO. 62, FRIDAY, MAY 11, 1711

Scribendi recte sapere est et principium, et fons.
HOR., *Ars Poet.* 309.

[Sound judgment is the ground of writing well.
— ROSCOMMON.]

Mr. Locke has an admirable reflection upon the difference of wit and judgment, whereby he endeavours to show the reason why they are not always the talents of the same person. His words are as follow: "And hence, perhaps, may be given some reason of that common observation, that men who have a great deal of wit, and prompt memories, have not always the clearest judgment or deepest reason. For wit lying most in the assemblage of ideas, and putting those together with quickness and variety wherein can be found any resemblance or congruity, thereby to make up pleasant pictures, and agreeable visions in the fancy; judgment, on the contrary, lies quite on the other side, in separating carefully one from another, ideas wherein can be found the least difference, thereby to avoid being misled by similitude, and by affinity to take one thing for another. This is a way of proceeding quite contrary to metaphor and allusion, wherein, for the most part, lies that entertainment and pleasantry of wit, which strikes so lively on the fancy, and is therefore so acceptable to all people."

This is, I think, the best and most philosophical account that I have ever met with of wit, which generally, though not always, consists in such a resemblance and congruity of ideas as this author mentions. I shall only add to it, by way of explanation, that every resemblance of ideas is not that which we call wit, unless it be such an one that gives delight and surprise to the reader. These two properties seem essential to wit, more particularly the last of them. In order, therefore, that the resemblance in the ideas be wit, it is necessary that the ideas should not lie too near one another in the nature of things; for where the likeness is obvious, it gives no surprise. To compare one man's singing to that of another, or to represent the whiteness of any object by that of milk and snow, or the variety of its colours by those of the rainbow, cannot be called wit, unless, besides this obvious resemblance, there be some further congruity discovered in the two ideas, that is capable of giving the reader some surprise. Thus when a poet tells us the bosom of his mistress is as white as snow, there is no wit in the comparison; but when he adds, with a sigh, that it is as cold too, it then grows into wit. Every reader's memory may supply him with innumerable instances of the same nature. For this reason the similitudes in heroic poets, who endeavour rather to fill the mind with great conceptions than to divert it with such as are new and surprising, have seldom anything in them that can be called wit. Mr. Locke's account of wit, with this short explanation, comprehends most of the species of wit, — as metaphors, similitudes, allegories, enigmas, mottoes, parables, fables, dreams, visions, dramatic writings, burlesque, and all the methods of allusion: as there are many other pieces of wit, how remote soever they may appear at first sight from the foregoing description, which upon examination will be found to agree with it.

As true wit generally consists in this resemblance and congruity of ideas, false wit chiefly consists in the resemblance and congruity, sometimes of single letters, as in anagrams, chronograms, lipograms, and acrostics; sometimes of syllables, as in echoes and doggerel rhymes; sometimes of words, as in puns and quibbles; sometimes of whole sentences or poems cast into the figures of eggs, axes, or altars. Nay, some carry the notion of wit so far as to ascribe it even to external mimicry, and to look upon a man as an ingenious person that can resemble the tone, posture, or face of another.

As true wit consists in the resemblance of ideas, and false wit in the resemblance of words, according to the foregoing instances, there is another kind of wit which consists partly in the resemblance of ideas, and partly in the resemblance of words, which for distinction sake I shall call mixed wit. This kind of wit is that which abounds in Cowley, more than in any author that ever wrote. Mr. Waller has likewise a great deal of it. Mr. Dryden is very sparing in it. Milton had a genius much above it. Spenser is in the same class with Milton. The Italians, even in their epic poetry, are full of it. Monsieur Boileau, who formed himself upon the ancient poets, has everywhere rejected it with scorn. If we look after mixed wit among the Greek writers, we shall find it nowhere but in the epigrammatists. There are indeed some strokes of it in the little poem ascribed to Musæus, which by that as well as many other marks betrays itself to be a modern composition. If we look into the Latin writers, we find none of this mixed wit in Virgil, Lucretius, or Catullus; very little in Horace, but a great deal of it in Ovid, and scarce anything else in Martial.

Out of the innumerable branches of mixed wit, I shall choose one instance which may be met with in all the writers of this class. The passion of love in its nature has been thought to resemble fire, for which reason the words *fire* and *flame* are made use of to signify love. The witty poets therefore have taken an advantage from the doubtful meaning of the word *fire*, to make an infinite number of witticisms. Cowley, observing the cold regard of his mistress's eyes, and at the same time their power of producing love in him, considers them as burning-glasses made of ice; and, finding himself able to live in the greatest extremities of love, concludes the torrid zone to be habitable. When his mistress has read his letter written in juice of lemon, by holding it to the fire, he desires her to read it over a second time by love's flames. When she weeps, he wishes it were inward heat that distilled those drops from the limbeck. When she is absent, he is beyond eighty, — that is, thirty degrees nearer the pole than when she is with him. His ambitious love is a fire that naturally mounts upwards; his happy love is the beams of heaven, and his unhappy love flames of hell. When it does not let him sleep, it is a flame that sends up no smoke; when it is opposed by counsel and advice, it is a fire that rages the more by the winds blowing upon it. Upon the dying of a tree in which he had cut his loves, he observes that his written flames had burnt up and withered the tree. When he resolves to give over his passion, he tells us that one burnt like him forever dreads the fire. His heart is an Ætna, that, instead of Vulcan's shop, encloses Cupid's forge in it. His endeavouring to drown his love in wine is throwing oil upon the fire. He would insinuate to his mistress that the fire of love, like that of the sun (which produces so many living creatures), should not only warm, but beget. Love, in another place, cooks pleasure at his fire. Sometimes the poet's heart is frozen in every breast, and sometimes scorched in every eye. Sometimes he is drowned in tears and burnt in love, like a ship set on fire in the middle of the sea.

The reader may observe in every one of these instances that the poet mixes the qualities of fire with those of love; and, in the same sentence speaking of it both as a passion and as real fire, surprises the reader with those seeming resemblances or contradictions that make up all the wit in this kind of writing. Mixed wit, therefore, is a composition of pun and true wit, and is more or less perfect as the resemblance lies in the ideas or in the words. Its foundations are laid partly in falsehood and partly in truth; reason puts in her claim for one half of it, and extravagance for the other. The only province, therefore, for this kind of wit is epigram, or those little occasional poems that in their own nature are nothing else but a tissue of epigrams. I cannot conclude this head of mixed wit without owning that the admirable poet out of whom I have taken the examples of it, had as much true wit as any author that ever writ, and indeed all other talents of an extraordinary genius.

It may be expected, since I am upon this subject, that I should take notice of *Mr. Dryden's definition of wit; which, with all the deference that is due to the judgment of so great a man, is not so properly a definition of wit as of good writing in general. Wit, as he defines it, is "a propriety of words and thoughts adapted to the subject." If this be a true definition of wit, I am apt to think that Euclid was the greatest wit that ever set pen to paper. It is certain there never was a greater propriety of words and thoughts adapted to the subject than what that author has made use of in his *Elements*. I shall only appeal to my reader if this definition agrees with any notion he has of wit. If it be a true one, I am sure Mr. Dryden was not only a better poet, but a greater wit, than Mr. Cowley, and Virgil a much more facetious man than either Ovid or Martial.

*Bouhours, whom I look upon to be the most penetrating of all the French critics, has taken pains to show that it is impossible for any thought to be beautiful which is not just, and has not its foundation in the nature of things; that the basis of all wit is truth; and that no thought can be valuable of which good sense is not the groundwork. Boileau has endeavoured to inculcate the same notion in several parts of his writings, both in prose and verse. This is that natural way of writing, that beautiful simplicity, which we so much admire in the compositions of the ancients, and which nobody deviates from but those who want strength of genius to make a thought shine in its own natural beauties. Poets who want this strength of genius to give that majestic simplicity to nature which we so much admire in the works of the ancients, are forced to hunt after foreign ornaments, and not to let any piece of wit of what kind soever escape them. I look upon these writers as Goths in poetry, who, like those in architecture, not being able to come up to the beautiful simplicity of the old Greeks and Romans, have endeavoured to supply its place with all the extravagancies of an irregular fancy. Mr. Dryden makes a very handsome observation on Ovid's writing a letter from Dido to Æneas, in the following words: "Ovid," says he, speaking of Virgil's fiction of Dido and Æneas, "takes it up after him, even in the same age, and makes an ancient heroine of Virgil's new-created Dido; dictates a letter for her just before her death to the ungrateful fugitive, and, very unluckily for himself, is for measuring a sword with a man so much superior in force to him on the same subject. I think I may be judge of this, because I have translated both. The famous author of *The Art of Love* has nothing of his own; he borrows all from a greater master in his own profession, and, which is worse, improves nothing which he finds. Nature fails him; and, being forced to his old shift, he has recourse to witticism. This passes indeed with his soft admirers, and gives him the preference to Virgil in their esteem."

Were not I supported by so great an authority as that of Mr. Dryden, I should not venture to observe that the taste of most of our English poets, as well as readers, is extremely *Gothic. *He quotes Monsieur Segrais for a threefold distinction of the readers of poetry; in the first of which he comprehends the rabble of readers, whom he does not treat as such with regard to their quality, but to their numbers and the coarseness of their taste. His words are as follow: "Segrais has distinguished the readers of poetry, according to their capacity of judging, into three classes." (He might have said the same of writers too if he had pleased.) "In the lowest form he places those whom he calls *Les Petits Esprits*, such things as our upper-gallery audience in a playhouse, who like nothing but the husk and rind of wit, prefer a quibble, a conceit, an epigram, before solid sense and elegant expression. These are *mob readers. If Virgil and Martial stood for Parliament-men, we know already who would carry it. But though they make the greatest appearance in the field, and cry the loudest, the best on't is they are but a sort of French Huguenots, or Dutch boors, brought over in herds, but not naturalized, who have not lands of two pounds per annum in Parnassus, and therefore are not privileged to poll. Their authors are of the same level, fit to represent them on a mountebank's stage, or to be masters of the ceremonies in a bear-garden; yet these are they who have the most admirers. But it often happens, to their mortification, that as their readers improve their stock of sense, as they may by reading better books, and by conversation with men of judgment, they soon forsake them."

I must not dismiss this subject without observing that, as Mr. Locke, in the passage above mentioned, has discovered the most fruitful source of wit, so there is another of a quite contrary nature to it, which does likewise branch itself out into several kinds. For not only the resemblance, but the opposition of ideas does very often produce wit, as I could show in several little points, turns, and antitheses that I may possibly enlarge upon in some future speculation.

[Addison]

No. 63, Saturday, May 12, 1711

Humano capiti cervicem pictor equinam
Jungere si velit, et varias inducere plumas,
Undique collatis membris, ut turpiter atrum
Desinat in piscem mulier formosa superne;
Spectatum admissi risum teneatis, amici?
Credite, Pisones, isti tabulæ fore librum
Persimilem, cujus, velut ægri somnia, vanæ
Fingentur species.

Hor., *Ars Poet.* 1–8.

[If in a picture, Piso, you should see
A handsome woman with a fish's tail,
Or a man's head upon a horse's neck,
Or limbs of beasts, of the most different kinds,
Cover'd with feathers of all sorts of birds,
Would you not laugh, and think the painter mad?
Trust me, that book is as ridiculous
Whose incoherent style, like sick men's dreams,
Varies all shapes, and mixes all extremes.

Roscommon.]

It is very hard for the mind to disengage itself from a subject in which it has been long employed. The thoughts will be rising of themselves from time to time, though we give them no encouragement: as the tossings and fluctuations of the sea continue several hours after the winds are laid.

It is to this that I impute my last night's dream or vision, which formed into one continued allegory the several schemes of wit, whether false, mixed, or true, that have been the subject of my late papers.

Methought I was transported into a country that was filled with prodigies and enchantments, governed by the goddess of Falsehood, and entitled the Region of False Wit. There was nothing in the fields, the woods, and the rivers that appeared natural. Several of the trees blossomed in leaf-gold, some of them produced bone-lace, and some of them precious stones. The fountains bubbled in an opera tune, and were filled with stags, wild boars, and mermaids, that lived among the waters; at the same time that dolphins and several kinds of fish played upon the banks, or took their pastime in the meadows. The birds had many of them golden beaks, and human voices. The flowers perfumed the air with smells of incense, ambergris, and *pulvillios; and were so interwoven with one another that they grew up in pieces of embroidery. The winds were filled with sighs and messages of distant lovers. As I was walking to and fro in this enchanted wilderness, I could not forbear breaking out into soliloquies upon the several wonders which lay before me, when, to my great surprise, I found there were artificial echoes in every walk, that, by repetitions of certain words which I spoke, agreed with me or contradicted me in everything I said. In the midst of my conversation with these invisible companions, I discovered in the centre of a very dark grove a monstrous fabric built after the Gothic manner, and covered with innumerable devices in that barbarous kind of sculpture. I immediately went up to it, and found it to be a kind of heathen temple consecrated to the god of Dullness. Upon my entrance I saw the deity of the place, dressed in the habit of a monk, with a book in one hand and a rattle in the other. Upon his right hand was Industry, with a lamp burning before her; and on his left, Caprice, with a monkey sitting on her shoulder. Before his feet there stood an altar of a very odd make, which, as I afterwards found, was shaped in that manner to comply with the inscription that surrounded it. Upon the altar there lay several offerings of axes, wings, and eggs, cut in paper, and inscribed with verses. The temple was filled with votaries, who applied themselves to different diversions, as their fancies directed them. In one part of it I saw a regiment of anagrams, who were continually in motion, turning to the right or to the left, facing about, doubling their ranks, shifting their stations, and throwing themselves into all the figures and countermarches of the most changeable and perplexed exercises.

Not far from these was the body of acrostics, made up of very disproportioned persons. It was disposed into three columns, the officers planting themselves in a line on the left hand of each column. The officers were all of them at least six foot high, and made three rows of very proper men; but the common soldiers, who filled up the spaces between the officers, were such dwarfs, cripples, and scarecrows, that one could hardly look upon them without laughing. There were behind the acrostics two or three files of chronograms, which differed only from the former as their officers were equipped, like the figure of Time, with an hourglass in one hand, and a scythe in the other, and took their posts promiscuously among the private men whom they commanded.

In the body of the temple, and before the very face of the deity, methought I saw the phantom of Tryphiodorus, the lipogrammatist, engaged in a ball with four-and-twenty persons, who pursued him by turns through all the intricacies and labyrinths of a country dance, without being able to overtake him.

Observing several to be very busy at the western end of the temple, I inquired into what they were doing, and found there was in that quarter the great magazine of rebuses. These were several things of the most different natures tied up in bundles, and thrown upon one another in heaps like fagots. You might behold an anchor, a night-rail, and a hobbyhorse bound up together. One of the workmen, seeing me very much surprised, told me there was an infinite deal of wit in several of those bundles, and that he would explain them to me if I pleased; I thanked him for his civility, but told him I was in very great haste at that time. As I was going out of the temple, I observed in one corner of it a cluster of men and women laughing very heartily, and diverting themselves at a game of crambo. I heard several double rhymes as I passed by them, which raised a great deal of mirth.

Not far from these was another set of merry people engaged at a diversion, in which the whole jest was to mistake one person for another. To give occasion for these ludicrous mistakes, they were divided into pairs, every pair being covered from head to foot with the same kind of dress, though perhaps there was not the least resemblance in their faces. By this means an old man was sometimes mistaken for a boy, a woman for a man, and a blackamoor for an European, which very often produced great peals of laughter. These I guessed to be a party of puns. But being very desirous to get out of this world of magic, which had almost turned my brain, I left the temple and crossed over the fields that lay about it with all the speed I could make. I was not gone far before I heard the sound of trumpets and alarms, which seemed to proclaim the march of an enemy; and, as I afterwards found, was in reality what I apprehended it. There appeared at a great distance a very shining light, and in the midst of it a person of a most beautiful aspect; her name was Truth. On her right hand there marched a male deity, who bore several quivers on his shoulders, and grasped several arrows in his hand; his name was Wit. The approach of these two enemies filled all the territories of False Wit with an unspeakable consternation, insomuch that the goddess of those regions appeared in person upon her frontiers, with the several inferior deities and the different bodies of forces which I had before seen in the temple, who were now drawn up in array, and prepared to give their foes a warm reception. As the march of the enemy was very slow, it gave time to the several inhabitants who bordered upon the regions of Falsehood to draw their forces into a body, with a design to stand upon their guard as neuters, and attend the issue of the combat.

I must here inform my reader that the frontiers of the enchanted region, which I have before described, were inhabited by the species of Mixed Wit, who made a very odd appearance when they were mustered together in an army. There were men whose bodies were stuck full of darts, and women whose eyes were burning-glasses; men that had hearts of fire, and women that had breasts of snow. It would be endless to describe several monsters of the like nature that composed this great army, which immediately fell asunder, and divided itself into two parts, the one half throwing themselves behind the banners of Truth, and the others behind those of Falsehood.

The goddess of Falsehood was of a gigantic stature, and advanced some paces before the front of her army; but as the dazzling light which flowed from Truth began to shine upon her, she faded insensibly; insomuch that in a little space she looked rather like an huge phantom than a real substance. At length, as the goddess of Truth approached still nearer to her, she fell away entirely, and vanished amidst the brightness of her presence; so that there did not remain the least trace or impression of her figure in the place where she had been seen.

As at the rising of the sun the constellations grow thin, and the stars go out one after another, till the whole hemisphere is extinguished; such was the vanishing of the goddess, and not only of the goddess herself, but of the whole army that attended her, which sympathized with their leader, and shrunk into nothing, in proportion as the goddess disappeared. At the same time the whole temple sunk, the fish betook themselves to the streams, and the wild beasts to the woods, the fountains recovered their murmurs, the birds their voices, the trees their leaves, the flowers their scents, and the whole face of nature its true and genuine appearance. Though I still continued asleep, I fancied myself, as it were, awakened out of a dream, when I saw this region of prodigies restored to woods and rivers, fields, and meadows.

Upon the removal of that wild scene of wonders, which had very much disturbed my imagination, I took a full survey of the persons of Wit and Truth; for indeed it was impossible to look upon the first without seeing the other at the same time. There was behind them a strong and compact body of figures. The genius of Heroic Poetry appeared with a sword in her hand, and a laurel on her head. Tragedy was crowned with a cypress, and covered with robes dipped in blood. Satire had smiles in her look, and a dagger under her garment. Rhetoric was known by her thunderbolt, and Comedy by her mask. After several other figures, Epigram marched up in the rear, who had been posted there at the beginning of the expedition, that he might not revolt to the enemy, whom he was suspected to favour in his heart. I was very much awed and delighted with the appearance of the god of Wit; there was something so amiable, and yet so piercing, in his looks, as inspired me at once with love and terror. As I was gazing on him, to my unspeakable joy, he took a quiver of arrows from his shoulder, in order to make me a present of it; but as I was reaching out my hand to receive it of him, I knocked it against a chair, and by that means awaked.

[Addison]

No. 70, Monday, May 21, 1711

Interdum vulgus rectum videt.

Hor., *Ep.* II, i, 63.

[Sometimes the vulgar see and judge aright.]

When I travelled, I took a particular delight in hearing the songs and fables that are come from father to son, and are most in vogue among the common people of the countries through which I passed; for it is impossible that anything should be universally tasted and approved by a multitude, though they are only the rabble of a nation, which hath not in it some peculiar aptness to please and gratify the mind of man. Human nature is the same in all reasonable creatures; and whatever falls in with it will meet with admirers amongst readers of all qualities and conditions. Molière, as we are told by Monsieur Boileau, used to read all his comedies to an old woman who was his housekeeper as she sat with him at her work by the chimney-corner, and could foretell the success of his play in the theatre from the reception it met at his fireside; for he tells us the audience always followed the old woman, and never failed to laugh in the same place.

I know nothing which more shows the essential and inherent perfection of simplicity of thought, above that which I call the Gothic manner in writing, than this, that the first pleases all kinds of palates, and the latter only such as have formed to themselves a wrong, artificial taste upon little fanciful authors and writers of epigram. Homer, Virgil, or Milton, so far as the language of their poems is understood, will please a reader of plain common sense, who would neither relish nor comprehend an epigram of Martial, or a poem of Cowley; so, on the contrary, an ordinary song or ballad that is the delight of the common people cannot fail to please all such readers as are not unqualified for the entertainment by their affectation or ignorance; and the reason is plain, because the same paintings of nature which recommend it to the most ordinary reader will appear beautiful to the most refined.

The old song of "Chevy Chase" is the favourite ballad of the common people of England, and Ben Jonson used to say he had rather have been the author of it than of all his works. *Sir Philip Sidney, in his discourse of poetry, speaks of it in the following words: "I never heard the old song of Percy and Douglas that I found not my heart more moved than with a trumpet; and yet it is sung by some blind crowder with no rougher voice than rude style, which, being so evil apparelled in the dust and cobweb of that uncivil age, what would it work trimmed in the gorgeous eloquence of Pindar?" For my own part, I am so professed an admirer of this antiquated song that I shall give my reader a critique upon it without any further apology for so doing.

The greatest modern critics have laid it down as a rule that an heroic poem should be founded upon some important precept of morality adapted to the constitution of the country in which the poet writes. Homer and Virgil have formed their plans in this view. As Greece was a collection of many governments, who suffered very much among themselves, and gave the Persian emperor, who was their common enemy, many advantages over them by their mutual jealousies and animosities, Homer, in order to establish among them an union which was so necessary for their safety, grounds his poem upon the discords of the several Grecian princes who were engaged in a confederacy against an Asiatic prince, and the several advantages which the enemy gained by such their discords. At the *time the poem we are now treating of was written, the dissensions of the barons, who were then so many petty princes, ran very high, whether they quarrelled among themselves or with their neighbours, and produced unspeakable calamities to the country. The poet, to deter men from such unnatural contentions, describes a bloody battle and dreadful scene of death, occasioned by the mutual feuds which reigned in the families of an English and Scotch nobleman. That he designed this for the instruction of his poem we may learn from his four last lines, in which, after the example of the modern tragedians, he draws from it a precept for the benefit of his readers:

God save the king, and bless the land
  In plenty, joy, and peace;
And grant henceforth that foul debate
  'Twixt noblemen may cease.

The next point observed by the greatest heroic poets hath been to celebrate persons and actions which do honour to their country: thus Virgil's hero was the founder of Rome; Homer's a prince of Greece; and for this reason Valerius Flaccus and Statius, who were both Romans, might be justly derided for having chosen the expedition of the Golden Fleece and the Wars of Thebes for the subjects of their epic writings.

The poet before us has not only found out a hero in his own country, but raises the reputation of it by several beautiful incidents. The English are the first who take the field and the last who quit it. The English bring only fifteen hundred to the battle, the Scotch two thousand. The English keep the field with fifty-three; the Scotch retire with fifty-five, all the rest on each side being slain in battle. But the most remarkable circumstance of this kind is the different manner in which the Scotch and English kings receive the news of this fight, and of the great men's deaths who commanded in it:

This news was brought to Edinburgh,
  Where Scotland's king did reign,
That brave Earl Douglas suddenly
  Was with an arrow slain.

"O heavy news!" King James did say,
  "Scotland can witness be,
I have not any captain more
  Of such account as he."

Like tidings to King Henry came,
  Within as short a space,
That Percy of Northumberland
  Was slain in Chevy Chase.

"Now God be with him," said our king,
  "Sith 'twill no better be,
I trust I have within my realm
  Five hundred as good as he.

"Yet shall not Scot nor Scotland say
But I will vengeance take,
And be revenged on them all
For brave Lord Percy's sake."

This vow full well the king performed
After on Humble-down,
In one day fifty knights were slain,
With lords of great renown.

And of the rest of small account
Did many thousands die, &c.

At the same time that our poet shows a laudible partiality to his countrymen, he represents the Scots after a manner not unbecoming so bold and brave a people:

Earl Douglas on a milk-white steed,
Most like a baron bold,
Rode foremost of the company,
Whose armour shone like gold.

His sentiments and actions are every way suitable to an hero. "One of us two," says he, "must die: I am an earl as well as yourself, so that you can have no pretence for refusing the combat; however," says he, "'tis pity, and indeed would be a sin, that so many innocent men should perish for our sakes: rather let you and I end our quarrel in single fight":

"Ere thus I will out-braved be,
One of us two shall die;
I know thee well, an earl thou art;
Lord Percy, so am I.

"But trust me, Percy, pity it were
And great offence to kill
Any of these our harmless men,
For they have done no ill.

"Let thou and I the battle try,
And set our men aside."
"Accurst be he," Lord Percy said,
"By whom this is deny'd."

When these brave men had distinguished themselves in the battle and in single combat with each other, in the midst of a generous parley, full of heroic sentiments, the Scotch earl falls, and with his dying words encourages his men to revenge his death, representing to them, as the most bitter circumstance of it, that his rival saw him fall:

With that there came an arrow keen
Out of an English bow,
Which struck Earl Douglas to the heart
A deep and deadly blow.

Who never spoke more words than these,
"Fight on, my merry men all,
For why, my life is at an end,
Lord Percy sees my fall."

Merry men, in the language of those times, is no more than a cheerful word for companions and fellow-soldiers. A passage in the eleventh book of Virgil's *Æneid* is very much to be admired, where Camilla, in her last agonies, instead of weeping over the wound she had received, as one might have expected from a warrior of her sex, considers only, like the hero of whom we are now speaking, how the battle should be continued after her death:

Tum sic exspirans, &c.
VIRG., *Æn.* XI, 820.

A gathering mist o'erclouds her cheerful eyes;
And from her cheeks the rosy colour flies,
Then turns to her, whom of her female train
She trusted most, and thus she speaks with pain:
"Acca, 'tis past! he swims before my sight,
Inexorable Death, and claims his right.
Bear my last words to Turnus; fly with speed
And bid him timely to my charge succeed:
Repel the Trojans, and the town relieve;
Farewell." DRYDEN.

Turnus did not die in so heroic a manner, though our poet seems to have had his eye upon Turnus's speech in the last verse:

Lord Percy sees my fall.

— *Vicisti, et victum tendere palmas*
Ausonnii videre.
VIRG., *Æn.* XII, 936.

The Latian chiefs have seen me beg my life.
DRYDEN.

Earl Percy's lamentation over his enemy is generous, beautiful, and passionate. I must only caution the reader not to let the simplicity of the style, which one may well pardon in so old a poet, prejudice him against the greatness of the thought:

Then leaving life, Earl Percy took
The dead man by the hand,
And said, "Earl Douglas, for thy life
Would I had lost my land.

"O Christ! my very heart doth bleed
With sorrow for thy sake;
For sure a more renowned knight
Mischance did never take."

That beautiful line, "Taking the dead man by the hand," will put the reader in mind of Æneas's behaviour towards Lausus, whom he himself had slain as he came to the rescue of his aged father:

At vero ut vultum vidit morientis, et ora,
Ora modis Anchisiades pallentia miris;
Ingemuit, miserans graviter, dextramque tetendit.
VIRG., *Æn.* X, 821.

The pious prince beheld young Lausus dead;
He griev'd, he wept; then grasp'd his hand and said,
"Poor hapless youth! what praises can be paid
To worth so great?"

[DRYDEN.]

I shall take *another opportunity to consider the other parts of this old song.

[Addison]

* No. 102, Wednesday, June 27, 1711

—— *Lusus animo debent aliquando dari*
Ad cogitandum melior ut redeat sibi.
Phæd., *Fab.* III, xiv, 12, 13.

[The mind ought sometimes to be diverted, that it may return the better to thinking.]

I do not know whether to call the following letter a satire upon coquettes, or a representation of their several fantastical accomplishments, or what other title to give it; but as it is I shall communicate it to the public. It will sufficiently explain its own intentions so that I shall give it my reader at length without either preface or postscript.

"*Mr. Spectator,*

Women are armed with fans as men with swords, and sometimes do more execution with them: to the end, therefore, that ladies may be entire mistresses of the weapon which they bear, I have erected an academy for the training up of young women in the exercise of the fan, according to the most fashionable airs and motions that are now practised at court. The ladies who carry fans under me are drawn up twice a day in my great hall, where they are instructed in the use of their arms, and exercised by the following words of command:

Handle your fans,
Unfurl your fans,
Discharge your fans,
Ground your fans,
Recover your fans,
Flutter your fans.

"By the right observation of these few plain words of command a woman of a tolerable genius, who will apply herself diligently to her exercise for the space of but one half year shall be able to give her fan all the graces that can possibly enter into that little modish machine.

"But to the end that my readers may form to themselves a right notion of this exercise, I beg leave to explain it to them in all its parts. When my female regiment is drawn up in array, with every one her weapon in her hand, upon my giving the word to handle their fans, each of them shakes her fan at me with a smile, then gives her right-hand woman a tap upon the shoulder, then presses her lips with the extremity of her fan, then lets her arms fall in an easy motion, and stands in a readiness to receive the next word of command. All this is done with a close fan and is generally learned in the first week.

"The next motion is that of unfurling the fan, in which are comprehended several little flirts and vibrations, as also gradual and deliberate openings, with many voluntary fallings asunder in the fan itself, that are seldom learned under a month's practice. This part of the exercise pleases the spectators more than any other, as it discovers on a sudden an infinite number of Cupids, garlands, altars, birds, beasts, rainbows, and the like agreeable figures that display themselves to view whilst every one in the regiment holds a picture in her hand. Upon my giving the word to discharge their fans, they give a general crack that may be heard at a considerable distance when the wind sits fair. This is one of the most difficult parts of the exercise; but I have several ladies with me, who at their first entrance could not give a pop loud enough to be heard at the further end of a room, who can now discharge a fan in such a manner that it shall make a report like a pocket pistol. I have likewise taken care (in order to hinder young women from letting off their fans in wrong places or unsuitable occasions) to show upon what subject the crack of a fan may come in properly; I have likewise invented a fan with which a girl of sixteen, by the help of a little wind which is enclosed about one of the largest sticks, can make as loud a crack as a woman of fifty with an ordinary fan.

"When the fans are thus discharged, the word of command in course is to ground their fans. This teaches a lady to quit her fan gracefully when she throws it aside in order to take up a pack of cards, adjust a curl of hair, replace a falling pin, or apply herself to any other matter of importance. This part of the exercise, as it only consists in tossing a fan with an air upon a long table (which stands by for that purpose) may be learned in two days' time as well as in a twelvemonth.

"When my female regiment is thus disarmed, I generally let them walk about the room for some time; when on a sudden (like ladies that look upon their watches after a long visit) they all of them hasten to their arms, catch them up in a hurry, and place themselves in their proper stations upon my calling out, "Recover your fans." This part of the exercise is not difficult, provided a woman applies her thoughts to it.

"The fluttering of the fan is the last, and indeed the masterpiece of the whole exercise; but if a lady does not misspend her time, she may make herself mistress of it in three months. I generally lay aside the dog days and the hot time of the summer for the teaching this part of the exercise; for as soon as ever I pronounce, "Flutter your fans," the place is filled with so many zephyrs and gentle breezes as are very refreshing in that season of the year, though they might be dangerous to ladies of a tender constitution in any other.

"There is an infinite variety of motions to be made use of in the flutter of a fan: there is the angry flutter, the modest flutter, the timorous flutter, the confused flutter, the merry flutter, and the amorous flutter. Not to be tedious, there is scarce any emotion in the mind which does not produce a suitable agitation in the fan; insomuch, that if I only see the fan of a disciplined lady, I know very well whether she laughs, frowns, or blushes. I have seen a fan so very angry that it would have been dangerous for the absent lover who provoked it to have come within the wind of it; and at other times so very languishing that I have been glad for the lady's sake the lover was at a sufficient distance from it. I need not add that a fan is either a prude or coquette, according to the nature of the person who bears it. To conclude my letter, I must acquaint you that I have from my own observations compiled a little treatise for the use of my scholars, entitled the "Passions of the Fan," which I will communicate to you, if you think it may be of use to the public. I shall have a general review on Thursday next, to which you shall be very welcome if you will honour it with your presence.

I am, &c.

"P.S. *I teach young gentlemen the whole art of gallanting a fan.

"N.B. I have several little plain fans made for this use, to avoid expense."

[Addison]

No. 119, Tuesday, July 17, 1711

Urbem quam dicunt Romam, Melibœe, putavi
Stultus ego huic nostræ similem.

VIRGIL, *Bucolica* I, 20.

[Fool that I was, I thought imperial Rome
Like Mantua. DRYDEN.]

The first and most obvious reflections which arise in a man who changes the city for the country are upon the different manners of the people whom he meets with in those two different scenes of life. By manners I do not mean morals, but behaviour and good-breeding as they show themselves in the town and in the country.

And here, in the first place, I must observe a very great revolution that has happened in this article of good-breeding. Several obliging deferences, condescensions, and submissions, with many outward forms and ceremonies that accompany them, were first of all brought up among the politer part of mankind, who lived in courts and cities, and distinguished themselves from the rustic part of the species (who on all occasions acted bluntly and naturally) by such a mutual complaisance and intercourse of civilities. These forms of conversation by degrees multiplied and grew troublesome; the modish world found too great a constraint in them, and have therefore thrown most of them aside. Conversation, like the Romish religion, was so encumbered with show and ceremony that it stood in need of a reformation to retrench its superfluities, and restore it to its natural good sense and beauty. At present, therefore, an unconstrained carriage and a certain openness of behaviour are the height of good-breeding. The fashionable world is grown free and easy; our manners sit more loose upon us. Nothing is so modish as an agreeable negligence. In a word, good-breeding shows itself most, where to an ordinary eye it appears the least.

If after this we look on the people of mode in the country, we find in them the manners of the last age. They have no sooner fetched themselves up to the fashion of the polite world, but the town has dropped them, and are nearer to the first state of nature than to those refinements which formerly reigned in the court, and still prevail in the country. One may now know a man that never conversed in the world by his excess of good-breeding. A polite country squire shall make you as many bows in half an hour as would serve a courtier for a week. There is infinitely more to-do about place and precedency in a meeting of justices' wives than in an assembly of duchesses.

This rural politeness is very troublesome to a man of my temper, who generally take the chair that is next me, and walk first or last, in the front or in the rear, as chance directs. I have known my friend Sir Roger's dinner almost cold before the company could adjust the ceremonial, and be prevailed upon to sit down; and have heartily pitied my old friend, when I have seen him forced to pick and cull his guests, as they sat at the several parts of his table, that he might drink their healths according to their respective ranks and qualities. Honest Will Wimble, who I should have thought had been altogether uninfected with ceremony, gives me abundance of trouble in this particular. Though he has been fishing all the morning, he will not help himself at dinner till I am served. When we are going out of the hall, he runs behind me; and last night, as we were walking in the fields, stopped short at a stile till I came up to it, and upon my making signs to him to get over, told me, with a serious smile, that sure I believed they had no manners in the country.

There has happened another revolution in the point of good-breeding, which relates to the *conversation among men of mode, and which I cannot but look upon as very extraordinary. It was certainly one of the first distinctions of a well-bred man to express everything that had the most remote appearance of being obscene in modest terms and distant phrases; whilst the clown, who had no such delicacy of conception and expression, clothed his ideas in those plain, homely terms that are the most obvious and natural. This kind of good manners was perhaps carried to an excess, so as to make conversation too stiff, formal, and precise: for which reason (as hypocrisy in one age is generally succeeded by atheism in another) conversation is in a great measure relapsed into the first extreme; so that at present several of our men of the town, and particularly those who have been polished in France, make use of the most coarse, uncivilized words in our language, and utter themselves often in such a manner as a clown would blush to hear.

This infamous piece of good-breeding, which reigns among the coxcombs of the town, has not yet made its way into the country; and as it is impossible for such an irrational way of conversation to last long among a people that make any profession of religion, or show of modesty, if the country gentlemen get into it, they will certainly be left in the lurch. Their good-breeding will come too late to them, and they will be thought a parcel of lewd clowns, while they fancy themselves talking together like men of wit and pleasure.

As the two points of good-breeding which I have hitherto insisted upon regard behaviour and conversation, there is a third, which turns upon dress. In this, too, the country are very much behindhand. The rural beaus are not yet got out of the fashion that took place at the time of the Revolution, but ride about the country in red coats and laced hats, while the women in many parts are still trying to outvie one another in the height of their head-dresses.

But a friend of mine who is now upon the western circuit, having promised to give me an account of the several modes and fashions that prevail in the different parts of the nation through which he passes, I shall defer the enlarging upon this last topic till I have received a letter from him, which I expect every post.

[Addison]

No. 135, Saturday, August 4, 1711

Est brevitate opus, ut currat sententia.
Hor., *Sat.* I, x, 9.

[Express your sentiments with brevity.]

I have somewhere read of an eminent person who used in his private offices of devotion to give thanks to Heaven that he was born a Frenchman: for my own part I look upon it as a peculiar blessing that I was born an Englishman. Among many other reasons, I think myself very happy in my country, as the language of it is wonderfully adapted to a man who is sparing of his words, and an enemy to loquacity.

As I have frequently reflected on my good fortune in this particular, I shall communicate to the public my speculations upon the English tongue, not doubting but they will be acceptable to all my curious readers.

The English delight in silence more than any other European nation, if the remarks which are made on us by foreigners are true. Our discourse is not kept up in conversation, but falls into more pauses and intervals than in our neighbouring countries; as it is observed that the matter of our writings is thrown much closer together, and lies in a narrower compass, than is usual in the works of foreign authors; for, to favour our natural taciturnity, when we are obliged to utter our thoughts, we do it in the shortest way we are able, and give as quick a birth to our conceptions as possible.

This humour shows itself in several remarks that we may make upon the English language. As, first of all, by its abounding in monosyllables, which gives us an opportunity of delivering our thoughts in few sounds. This indeed takes off from the elegance of our tongue, but at the same time expresses our ideas in the readiest manner, and consequently answers the first design of speech better than the multitude of syllables which make the words of other languages more tuneable and sonorous. The sounds of our English words are commonly like those of string music, short and transient, which rise and perish upon a single touch; those of other languages are like the notes of wind instruments, sweet and swelling, and lengthened out into variety of modulation.

In the next place we may observe that, where the words are not monosyllables, we often make them so, as much as lies in our power, by our rapidity of pronunciation; as it generally happens in most of our long words which are derived from the Latin, where we contract the length of the syllables, that gives them a grave and solemn air in their own language, to make them more proper for despatch, and more conformable to the genius of our tongue. This we may find in a multitude of words, as "liberty," "conspiracy," "theatre," "orator," &c.

The same natural aversion to loquacity has of late years made a very considerable alteration in our language, by closing in one syllable the termination of our preterperfect tense, as in these words "drown'd," "walk'd," "arriv'd," for "drowned," "walked," "arrived," which has very much disfigured the tongue, and turned a tenth part of our smoothest words into so many clusters of consonants. This is the more remarkable because the want of vowels in our language has been the general complaint of our politest authors, who nevertheless are the men that have made these retrenchments, and consequently very much increased our former scarcity.

This reflection on the words that end in "ed" I have heard in conversation from *one of the greatest geniuses this age has produced. I think we may add to the foregoing observation, the change which has happened in our language by the abbreviation of several words that are terminated in "eth," by substituting an "s" in the room of the last syllable, as in "drowns," "walks," "arrives," and innumerable other words, which in the pronunciation of our forefathers were "drowneth," "walketh," "arriveth." This has wonderfully multiplied a letter which was before too frequent in the English tongue, and added to that hissing in our language which is taken so much notice of by foreigners but, at the same time humours our taciturnity, and eases us of many superfluous syllables.

I might here observe that the same *single letter on many occasions does the office of a whole word, and represents the "his" and "her" of our forefathers. There is no doubt but the ear of a foreigner, which is the best judge in this case, would very much disapprove of such innovations, which indeed we do ourselves in some measure, by retaining the old termination in writing, and in all the solemn offices of our religion.

As, in the instances I have given, we have epitomised many of our particular words to the detriment of our tongue, so on other occasions we have drawn two words into one, which has likewise very much untuned our language, and clogged it with consonants, as "mayn't," "can't," "shan't," "won't," and the like, for "may not," "can not," "shall not," "will not," &c.

It is perhaps this humour of speaking no more than we needs must which has so miserably curtailed some of our words, that in familiar writings and conversations they often lose all but their first syllables, as in "mob.," "rep.," "pos.," "incog.," and the like; and as all ridiculous words make their first entry into a language by familiar phrases, I dare not answer for these that they will not in time be looked upon as a part of our tongue. We see some of our poets have been so indiscreet as to imitate Hudibras's doggrel expressions in their serious compositions, by throwing out the signs of our substantives which are essential to the English language. Nay, this humour of shortening our language had once run so far that some of our celebrated authors, among whom we may reckon *Sir Roger L'Estrange in particular, began to prune their words of all superfluous letters, as they termed them, in order to adjust the spelling to the pronunciation; which would have confounded all our etymologies, and have quite destroyed our tongue.

We may here likewise observe that our proper names, when familiarised in English, generally dwindle to monosyllables, whereas in other modern languages they receive a softer turn on this occasion, by the addition of a new syllable. Nick, in Italian, is Nicolini; Jack, in French, Janot; and so of the rest.

There is another particular in our language which is a great instance of our frugality of words, and that is the suppressing of several particles which must be produced in other tongues to make a sentence intelligible. This often perplexes the best writers, when they find the relatives "whom," "which," or "they," at their mercy, whether they may have admission or not; and will never be decided till we have something like an *academy, that by the best authorities, and rules drawn from the analogy of languages, shall settle all controversies between grammar and idiom.

I have only considered our language as it shows the genius and natural temper of the English, which is modest, thoughtful, and sincere, and which, perhaps, may recommend the people, though it has spoiled the tongue. We might, perhaps, carry the same thought into other languages, and deduce a great part of what is peculiar to them from the genius of the people who speak them. It is certain the light, talkative humour of the French has not a little infected their tongue, which might be shown by many instances; as the genius of the Italians, which is so much addicted to music and ceremony, has moulded all their words and phrases to those particular uses. The stateliness and gravity of the Spaniards shows itself to perfection in the solemnity of their language; and the blunt, honest humour of the Germans sounds better in the roughness of the High Dutch than it would in a politer tongue.

[Addison]

No. 157, Thursday, August 30, 1711

Genius, natale comes qui temperat astrum,
Naturæ deus humanæ, mortalis in unum
Quodque caput.

Hor., *Epist.* II, ii, 187–89.

[That directing pow'r
Who forms the genius in the natal hour;
That God of nature who, within us still,
Inclines our action, not constrains our will.

Pope.]

I am very much at a loss to express by any word that occurs to me in our language that which is understood by **indoles* in Latin. The natural disposition to any particular art, science, profession, or trade is very much to be consulted in the care of youth, and studied by men for their own conduct when they form to themselves any scheme of life. It is wonderfully hard indeed for a man to judge of his own capacity impartially. That may look great to me which may appear little to another, and I may be carried by fondness towards myself so far as to attempt things too high for my talents and accomplishments. But it is not, methinks, so very difficult a matter to make a judgment of the abilities of others, especially of those who are in their infancy. My commonplace book directs me on this occasion to mention the dawning of greatness in Alexander, who, being asked in his youth to contend for a prize in the Olympic games, answered he would if he had kings to run against him. Cassius, who was one of the conspirators against Cæsar, gave as great a proof of his temper when in his childhood he struck a playfellow, the son of Sulla, for saying his father was master of the Roman people. Scipio is reported to have answered, when some flatterers at supper were asking him what the Romans should do for a general after his death, "Take Marius." Marius was then a very boy, and had given no instances of his valour; but it was visible to Scipio, from the manners of the youth, that he had a soul formed for the attempt and execution of great undertakings. I must confess I have very often with much sorrow bewailed the *misfortune of the children of Great Britain, when I consider the ignorance and undiscerning of the generality of schoolmasters. The boasted liberty we talk of is but a mean reward for the long servitude, the many heartaches and terrors to which our childhood is exposed in going through a grammar school. Many of these stupid tyrants exercise their cruelty without any manner of distinction of the capacities of children, or the intention of parents in their behalf. There are many excellent tempers which are worthy to be nourished and cultivated with all possible diligence and care, that were never designed to be acquainted with Aristotle, Tully, or Virgil; and there are as many who have capacities for understanding every word those great persons have writ, and yet were not born to have any relish of their writings. For want of this common and obvious discerning in those who have the care of youth, we have so many hundred unaccountable creatures every age whipped up into great scholars that are for ever near a right understanding, and will never arrive at it. These are the scandal of letters, and these are generally the men who are to teach others. The sense of shame and honour is enough to keep the world itself in order without corporal punishment, much more to train the minds of uncorrupted and innocent children. It happens, I doubt not, more than once in a year that a lad is chastised for a blockhead, when it is good apprehension that makes him incapable of knowing what his teacher means. A brisk imagination very often may suggest an error which a lad could not have fallen into if he had been as heavy in conjecturing as his master in explaining. But there is no mercy even towards a wrong interpretation of his meaning; the sufferings of the scholar's body are to rectify the mistakes of his mind.

I am confident that no boy who will not be allured to letters without blows will ever be brought to anything with them. A great or good mind must necessarily be the worse for such indignities, and it is a sad change to lose of its virtue for the improvement of its knowledge. No one who has gone through what they call a great school but must remember to have seen children of excellent and ingenuous natures, as has afterwards appeared in their manhood — I say no man has passed through this way of education but must have seen an ingenuous creature expiring with shame, with pale looks, beseeching sorrow, and silent tears, throw up its honest eyes and kneel on its tender knees to an inexorable blockhead to be forgiven the false quantity of a word in making a Latin verse. The child is punished, and the next day he commits a like crime, and so a third with the same consequence. I would fain ask any reasonable man whether this lad, in the simplicity of his native innocence, full of shame, and capable of any impression from that grace of soul, was not fitter for any purpose in this life than after that spark of virtue is extinguished in him, though he is able to write twenty verses in an evening?

Seneca says, after his exalted way of talking, "As the immortal gods never learned any virtue, though they are endued with all that is good, so there are some men who have so natural a propensity to what they should follow that they learn it almost as soon as they hear it." Plants and vegetables are cultivated into the production of finer fruit than they would yield without that care; and yet we cannot entertain hopes of producing a tender, conscious spirit into acts of virtue without the same methods as are used to cut timber, or give new shape to a piece of stone.

It is wholly to this dreadful practice that we may attribute a certain hardness and ferocity which some men, though liberally educated, carry about them in all their behaviour. To be bred like a gentleman, and punished like a malefactor, must, as we see it does, produce that illiberal sauciness which we see sometimes in men of letters.

The Spartan boy who suffered the fox which he had stolen and hid under his coat to eat into his bowels, I dare say, had not half the wit or petulance which we learn at great schools among us; but the glorious sense of honour, or rather fear of shame, which he demonstrated in that action, was worth all the learning in the world without it.

It is, methinks, a very melancholy consideration that a little negligence can spoil us, but great industry is necessary to improve us; the most excellent natures are soon depreciated, but evil tempers are long before they are exalted into good habits. To help this by punishments is the same thing as killing a man to cure him of a distemper; when he comes to suffer punishment in that one circumstance, he is brought below the existence of a rational creature, and is in the state of a brute that moves only by the admonition of stripes. But since this custom of educating by the lash is suffered by the gentry of Great Britain, I would prevail only that honest, heavy lads may be dismissed from slavery sooner than they are at present, and not whipped on to their fourteenth or fifteenth year, whether they expect any progress from them or not. Let the child's capacity be forthwith examined, and he sent to some mechanic way of life, without respect to his birth, if nature designed him for nothing higher; let him go before he has innocently suffered, and is debased into a dereliction of mind for being what it is no guilt to be, a plain man. I would not here be supposed to have said that our learned men *of either robe who have been whipped at school are not still men of noble and liberal minds; but I am sure they had been much more so than they are had they never suffered that infamy.

But though there is so little care, as I have observed, taken, or observation made of the natural strain of men, it is no small comfort to me, as a Spectator, that there is any right value set upon the *bona indoles* of other animals, as appears by the following advertisement handed about the county of Lincoln, and subscribed by Enos Thomas, a person whom I have not the honour to know, but suppose to be profoundly learned in horseflesh:

"A chestnut horse called Cæsar, bred by James Darcy, Esq., at Sedbury, near Richmond, in the county of York; his granddam was his old royal mare, and got by Blunderbuss, which was got by Hemsly-Turk, and he got by Mr. Corant's Arabian, which got Mr. Minshul's Jew's-trump. *Mr. Cæsar sold him to a nobleman (coming five years old, when he had but one sweat) for three hundred guineas. A guinea a leap and trial, and a shilling the man.

ENOS THOMAS."

[Steele]

No. 160, Monday, September 3, 1711

— Cui mens divinior, atque os
Magna sonaturum, des nominis hujus honorem.
HOR., *Sat.* I, iv, 43.

[On him confer the poet's sacred name,
Whose lofty voice declares the heavenly flame.]

There is no character more frequently given to a writer than that of being a genius. I have heard many a little sonneteer called a fine genius. There is not a heroic scribbler in the nation that has not his admirers who think him a great genius; and as for your smatterers in tragedy, there is scarce a man among them who is not cried up by one or other for a prodigious genius.

My design in this paper is to consider what is properly a great genius, and to throw some thoughts together on so uncommon a subject.

Among great geniuses those few draw the admiration of all the world upon them, and stand up as the prodigies of mankind, who, by the mere strength of natural parts, and without any assistance of art or learning, have produced works that were the delight of their own times and the wonder of posterity. There appears something nobly wild and extravagant in these great *natural geniuses, that is infinitely more beautiful than all the turn and polishing of what the French call a *bel esprit*, by which they would express a genius refined by conversation, reflection, and the reading of the most polite authors. The greatest genius which runs through the arts and sciences takes a kind of tincture from them and falls unavoidably into imitation.

Many of these great natural geniuses, that were never disciplined and broken by rules of art, are to be found among the ancients, and in particular among those of the more eastern parts of the world. Homer has innumerable flights that Virgil was not able to reach, and in the Old Testament we find several passages more elevated and sublime than any in Homer. At the same time that we allow a greater and more daring genius to the ancients, we must own that the greatest of them very much failed in, or, if you will, that they were much above the nicety and correctness of the moderns. In their similitudes and allusions, provided there was a likeness, they did not much trouble themselves about the decency of the comparison: thus Solomon resembles the nose of his beloved to the tower of Lebanon which looketh toward Damascus, as the coming of a thief in the night is a similitude of the same kind in the New Testament. It would be endless to make collections of this nature. Homer illustrates one of his heroes encompassed with the enemy, by an ass in a field of corn that has his sides belaboured by all the boys of the village without stirring a foot for it; and another of them tossing to and fro in his bed, and burning with resentment, to a piece of flesh broiled on the coals. This particular failure in the ancients opens *a large field of raillery to the little wits, who can laugh at an indecency, but not relish the sublime in these sorts of writings. The present Emperor of Persia, conformable to this eastern way of thinking, amidst a great many pompous titles, denominates himself "the sun of glory" and "the nutmeg of delight." In short, to cut off all cavilling against the ancients, and particularly those of the warmer climates, who had most heat and life in their imaginations, we are to consider that the rule of observing what the French call the **bienséance* in an allusion has been found out of latter years, and in the colder regions of the world, where we would make some amends for our want of force and spirit by a scrupulous nicety and exactness in our compositions. Our countryman, Shakespeare, was a remarkable instance of this first kind of great geniuses.

I cannot quit this head without observing that Pindar was a great genius of the first class, who was hurried on by a natural fire and impetuosity to vast conceptions of things and noble sallies of imagination. At the same time can anything be more ridiculous than for men of a sober and moderate fancy to imitate this poet's way of writing in those monstrous compositions which go among us under the name of *Pindarics? When I see people copying works which, as Horace has represented them, are singular in their kind, and inimitable; when I see men following irregularities by rule, and by the little tricks of art straining after the most unbounded flights of nature, I cannot but apply to them that passage in Terence:

> *— *Incerta hæc si tu postules*
> *Ratione certa facere, nihilo plus agas,*
> *Quam si des operam, ut cum ratione insanias.*

In short, a modern Pindaric writer compared with Pindar is like a sister among the *Camisars compared with Virgil's Sibyl; there is the distortion, grimace, and outward figure, but nothing of that divine impulse which raises the mind above itself, and makes the sounds more than human.

There is another kind of great geniuses which I shall place in a second class, not as I think them inferior to the first, but only for distinction's sake, as they are of a different kind. This second class of great geniuses are those that have formed themselves by rules, and submitted the greatness of their natural talents to the corrections and restraints of art. Such among the Greeks were Plato and Aristotle; among the Romans, Virgil and Tully; among the English, Milton and Sir Francis Bacon.

The genius in both these classes of authors may be equally great, but shows itself after a different manner. In the first it is like a rich soil in a happy climate, that produces a whole wilderness of noble plants rising in a thousand beautiful landscapes without any certain order or regularity; in the other it is the same rich soil, under the same happy climate, that has been laid out in walks and parterres, and cut into shape and beauty by the skill of the gardener.

The great danger in these latter kind of geniuses is lest they cramp their own abilities too much by imitation, and form themselves altogether upon models, without giving the full play to their own natural parts. An imitation of the best authors is not to compare with a good original; and I believe we may observe that very few writers make an extraordinary figure in the world who have not something in their way of thinking or expressing themselves that is peculiar to them, and entirely their own.

It is odd to consider what great geniuses are sometimes thrown away upon trifles.

"I once saw a shepherd," says a famous Italian author, "who used to divert himself in his solitudes with tossing up eggs and catching them again without breaking them; in which he had arrived to so great a degree of perfection that he would keep up four at a time for several minutes together playing in the air, and falling into his hand by turns. I think," says the author, "I never saw a greater severity than in this man's face, for by his wonderful perseverance and application he had contracted the seriousness and gravity of a privy councillor, and I could not but reflect with myself that the same assiduity and attention, had they been rightly applied, might have made him a greater mathematician than Archimedes."

[Addison]

No. 262, Monday, December 31, 1711

> *Nulla venenato littera mista joco est.*
> Ovid, *Tristia* II, 566.

> [My paper flows from no satiric vein,
> Contains no poison, and conveys no pain.]

I think myself highly obliged to the public for their kind acceptance of a paper which visits them every morning, and has in it none of those seasonings that recommend so many of the writings which are in vogue among us.

As, on the one side, my paper has not in it a single word of news, a reflection in politics, nor a stroke of party; so, on the other, there are no fashionable touches of infidelity, no obscene ideas, no satires upon priesthood, marriage, and the like popular topics of ridicule; no private scandal, nor anything that may tend to the defamation of particular persons, families, or societies.

There is not one of these above mentioned subjects that would not sell a very indifferent paper, could I think of gratifying the public by such mean and base methods. But notwithstanding I have rejected everything that savours of party, everything that is loose and immoral, and everything that might create uneasiness in the minds of particular persons, I find that the demand for my papers has increased every month since their appearance in the world. This does not perhaps reflect so much honour upon myself as on my readers, who give a much greater attention to discourses of virtue and morality than ever I expected or indeed could hope.

When I broke loose from that great body of writers who have employed their wit and parts in propagating vice and irreligion, I did not question but I should be treated as an odd kind of fellow that had a mind to appear singular in my way of writing. But the general reception I have found convinces me that the world is not so corrupt as we are apt to imagine, and that if those men of parts who have been employed in vitiating the age had endeavoured to rectify and amend it, they needed not have sacrificed their good sense and virtue to their fame and reputation. No man is so sunk in vice and ignorance but there are still some hidden seeds of goodness and knowledge in him, which give him a relish of such reflections and speculations as have an aptness to improve the mind and to make the heart better.

I have shown in a former paper, with how much care I have avoided all such thoughts as are loose, obscene, or immoral; and I believe my reader would still think the better of me, if he knew the pains I am at in qualifying what I write after such a manner that nothing may be interpreted as aimed at private persons. For this reason when I draw any faulty character, I consider all those persons to whom the malice of the world may possibly apply it, and take care to dash it with such particular circumstances as may prevent all such ill-natured applications. If I write anything on a black man, I run over in my mind all the eminent persons in the nation who are of that complexion. When I place an imaginary name at the head of a character, I examine every syllable and letter of it, that it may not bear any resemblance to one that is real. I know very well the value which every man sets upon his reputation, and how painful it is to be exposed to the mirth and derision of the public, and should therefore scorn to divert my reader at the expense of any private man.

As I have been thus tender of every particular person's reputation, so I have taken more than ordinary care not to give offence to those who appear in the higher figures of life. I would not make myself merry even with a piece of pasteboard that is invested with a public character; for which reason I have never glanced upon *the late designed procession of his Holiness and his attendants notwithstanding it might have afforded matter to many ludicrous speculations. Among those advantages which the public may reap from this paper, it is not the least that it draws men's minds off from the bitterness of party and furnishes them with subjects of discourse that may be treated without warmth or passion. This is said to have been the first design of those gentlemen who set on foot the Royal Society, and had then a very good effect, as it turned many of the greatest geniuses of that age to the disquisitions of natural knowledge, who, if they had engaged in politics with the same parts and application, might have set their country in a flame. The air-pump, the barometer, the quadrant, and the like inventions were thrown out to those busy spirits *as tubs and barrels are to a whale, that he may let the ship sail on without disturbance while he diverts himself with those innocent amusements.

I have been so very scrupulous in this particular of not hurting any man's reputation that I have forborne mentioning even such authors as I could not name with honour. This I must confess to have been a piece of very great self-denial; for as the public relishes nothing better than the ridicule which turns upon a writer of any eminence, so there is nothing which a man that has but a very ordinary talent in ridicule may execute with greater ease. One might raise laughter for a quarter of a year together upon the works of a person who has published but a very few volumes. For which reasons I am astonished that those who have appeared against this paper have made so very little of it. The criticisms which I have hitherto published have been made with an intention rather to discover beauties and excellencies in the writers of my own time than to publish any of their faults and imperfections. In the mean while I should take it for a very great favour from some of my underhand detractors if they would break all measures with me so far as to give me a pretence for examining their performances with an impartial eye; nor shall I look upon it as any breach of charity to criticise the author, so long as I keep clear of the person.

In the mean while, till I am provoked to such hostilities, I shall from time to time endeavour to do justice to those who have distinguished themselves in the politer parts of learning, and to point out such beauties in their works as may have escaped the observation of others.

As the first place among our English poets is due to Milton, and as I have drawn more quotations out of him than from any other, I shall enter into a regular criticism upon his *Paradise Lost*, which I shall publish every Saturday till I have given my thoughts upon that poem. I shall not, however, presume to impose upon others my own particular judgment on this author, but only deliver it as my private opinion. Criticism is of a very large extent, and every particular master in this art has his favourite passages in an author, which do not equally strike the best judges. It will be sufficient for me if I discover many beauties or imperfections which others have not attended to, and I should be very glad to see any of our eminent writers publish their discoveries on the same subject. In short, I would always be understood to write my papers of criticism in the spirit which Horace has expressed in those two famous lines:

— Si quid novisti rectius istis,
Candidus imperti; si non, his utere mecum.
[*Ep.* I, vi, 67, 68]

If you have made any better remarks of your own, communicate them with candour; if not, make use of these I present you with.

[Addison]

No. 409, Thursday, June 19, 1712

Musæo contingens cuncta lepore.
Lucr. I, 933.

[Gracing each subject with enlivening wit.]

Gratian very often recommends the fine taste as the utmost perfection of an accomplished man. As this word arises very often in conversation, I shall endeavour to give some account of it, and to lay down rules how we may know whether we are possessed of it, and how we may acquire that fine taste of writing which is so much talked of among the polite world.

Most languages make use of this metaphor to express that faculty of the mind which distinguishes all the most concealed faults and nicest perfections in writing. We may be sure this metaphor would not have been so general in all tongues, had there not been a very great conformity between that mental taste, which is the subject of this paper, and that sensitive taste which gives us a relish of every different flavour that affects the palate. Accordingly we find there are as many degrees of refinement in the intellectual faculty as in the sense which is marked out by this common denomination.

I knew a person who possessed the one in so great a perfection, that, after having tasted ten different kinds of tea, he would distinguish, without seeing the colour of it, the particular sort which was offered him; and not only so, but any two sorts of them that were mixed together in an equal proportion. Nay, he has carried the experiment so far as, upon tasting the composition of three different sorts, to name the parcels from whence the three several ingredients were taken. A man of a fine taste in writing will discern, after the same manner, not only the general beauties and imperfections of an author, but discover the several ways of thinking and expressing himself which diversify him from all other authors, with the several foreign infusions of thought and language, and the particular authors from whom they were borrowed.

After having thus far explained what is generally meant by a fine taste in writing, and shown the propriety of the metaphor which is used on this occasion, I think I may define it to be "that faculty of the soul which discerns the beauties of an author with pleasure, and the imperfections with dislike." If a man would know whether he is possessed of this faculty, I would have him read over the celebrated works of antiquity, which have stood the test of so many different ages and countries, or those works among the moderns which have the sanction of the politer part of our contemporaries. If, upon the perusal of such writings, he does not find himself delighted in an extraordinary manner, or if, upon reading the admired passages in such authors, he finds a coldness and indifference in his thoughts, he ought to conclude, not — as is too usual among tasteless readers — that the author wants those perfections which have been admired in him, but that he himself wants the faculty of discovering them.

He should, in the second place, be very careful to observe whether he tastes the distinguishing perfections, or — if I may be allowed to call them so — the specific qualities of the author whom he peruses; whether he is particularly pleased with Livy for his manner of telling a story, with Sallust for his entering into those internal principles of action which arise from the characters and manners of the persons he describes, or with Tacitus for his displaying those outward motives of safety and interest which gave birth to the whole series of transactions which he relates.

He may likewise consider how differently he is affected by the same thought which presents itself in a great writer, from what he is when he finds it delivered by a person of an ordinary genius; for there is as much difference in apprehending a thought clothed in Cicero's language, and that of a common author, as in seeing an object by the light of a taper or by the light of the sun.

It is very difficult to lay down rules for the acquirement of such a taste as that I am here speaking of. The faculty must in some degree be born with us; and it very often happens that those who have other qualities in perfection are wholly void of this. One of the most eminent mathematicians of the age has assured me that the greatest pleasure he took in reading Virgil was in examining Æneas his voyage by the map; as I question not but many a modern compiler of history would be delighted with little more in that divine author than the bare matters of fact.

But, notwithstanding this faculty must in some measure be born with us, there are several methods for cultivating and improving it, and without which it will be very uncertain and of little use to the person that possesses it. The most natural method for this purpose is to be conversant among the writings of the most polite authors. A man who has any relish for fine writing either discovers new beauties, or receives stronger impressions, from the masterly strokes of a great author, every time he peruses him; besides that he naturally wears himself into the same manner of speaking and thinking.

Conversation with men of a polite genius is another method for improving our natural taste. It is impossible for a man of the greatest parts to consider anything in its whole extent and in all its variety of lights. Every man, besides those general observations which are to be made upon an author, forms several reflections that are peculiar to his own manner of thinking; so that conversation will naturally furnish us with hints which we did not attend to, and make us enjoy other men's parts and reflections, as well as our own. This is the best reason I can give for the observation which several have made, that men of great genius in the same way of writing seldom rise up singly, but at certain periods of time appear together, and in a body; as they did at Rome in the reign of Augustus, and in Greece about the age of Socrates. I cannot think that Corneille, Racine, Molière, Boileau, La Fontaine, Bruyère, Bossu, or the Daciers, would have written so well as they have done, had they not been friends and contemporaries.

It is likewise necessary for a man who would form to himself a finished taste of good writing, to be well versed in the works of the best critics, both ancient and modern. I must confess that I could wish there were authors of this kind, who, besides the mechanical rules, which a man of very little taste may discourse upon, would enter into the very spirit and soul of fine writing, and show us the several sources of that pleasure which rises in the mind upon the perusal of a noble work. Thus, although in poetry it be absolutely necessary that the unities of time, place, and action, with other points of the same nature, should be thoroughly explained and understood, there is still something more essential to the art, something that elevates and astonishes the fancy, and gives a greatness of mind to the reader, which few of the critics besides Longinus have considered.

Our general taste in England is for epigram, turns of wit, and forced conceits, which have no manner of influence either for the bettering or enlarging the mind of him who reads them, and have been carefully avoided by the greatest writers, both among the ancients and moderns. I have endeavoured in several of my speculations to banish this Gothic taste which has taken possession among us. *I entertained the town for a week together with an essay upon wit, in which I endeavoured to detect several of those false kinds which have been admired in the different ages of the world, and at the same time to show wherein the nature of true wit consists. *I afterwards gave an instance of the great force which lies in a natural simplicity of thought to affect the mind of the reader, from such vulgar pieces as have little else besides this single qualification to recommend them. *I have likewise examined the works of the greatest poet which our nation, or perhaps any other, has produced, and particularized most of those rational and manly beauties which give a value to that divine work. I shall next Saturday enter upon an essay on *The Pleasures of the Imagination*, which, though it shall consider that subject at large, will perhaps suggest to the reader what it is that gives a beauty to many passages of the finest writers both in prose and verse. As an undertaking of this nature is entirely new, I question not but it will be received with candour.

[Addison]

No. 419, Tuesday, July 1, 1712

— Mentis gratissimus error.

Hor., *Epist.* II, ii, 140.

[A most pleasing delusion of the mind.]

There is a kind of writing wherein the poet quite loses sight of nature, and entertains his reader's imagination with the characters and actions of such persons as have, many of them, no existence but what he bestows on them. Such are fairies, witches, magicians, demons, and departed spirits. This Mr. Dryden calls "the *fairy way of writing," which is indeed more difficult than any other that depends on the poet's fancy, because he has no pattern to follow in it, and must work altogether out of his own invention.

There is a very odd turn of thought required for this sort of writing, and it is impossible for a poet to succeed in it who has not a particular cast of fancy, and an imagination naturally fruitful and superstitious. Besides this, he ought to be very well versed in legends and fables, antiquated romances, and the traditions of nurses and old women, that he may fall in with our natural prejudices, and humour those notions which we have imbibed in our infancy. For otherwise he will be apt to make his fairies talk like people of his own species, and not like other sets of beings, who converse with different objects and think in a different manner from that of mankind.

**Sylvis deducti caveant, me judice, Fauni*
Ne velut innati triviis ac pene forenses,
Aut nimium teneris juvenentur versibus —

Horace.

I do not say, with *Mr. Bayes in *The Rehearsal*, that spirits must not be confined to speak sense, but it is certain their sense ought to be a little discoloured, that it may seem particular, and proper to the person and condition of the speaker.

These descriptions raise a pleasing kind of horror in the mind of the reader, and amuse his imagination with the strangeness and novelty of the persons who are represented in them. They bring up into our memory the stories we have heard in our childhood, and favour those secret terrors and apprehensions to which the mind of man is naturally subject. We are pleased with surveying the different habits and behaviours of foreign countries; how much more must we be delighted and surprised when we are led, as it were, into a new creation, and see the persons and manners of another species! Men of cold fancies and philosophical dispositions object to this kind of poetry that it has not probability enough to affect the imagination. But to this it may be answered that we are sure, in general, there are many intellectual beings in the world besides ourselves, and several species of spirits, who are subject to different laws and economies from those of mankind. When we see, therefore, any of these represented naturally, we cannot look upon the representation as altogether impossible; nay, many are prepossessed with such false opinions as dispose them to believe these particular delusions; at least we have all heard so many pleasing relations in favour of them that we do not care for seeing through the falsehood, and willingly give ourselves up to so agreeable an imposture.

The ancients have not much of this poetry among them; for, indeed, almost the whole substance of it owes its original to the darkness and superstition of later ages, when pious frauds were made use of to amuse mankind, and frighten them into a sense of their duty. Our forefathers looked upon nature with more reverence and horror, before the world was enlightened by learning and philosophy, and loved to astonish themselves with the apprehensions of witchcraft, prodigies, charms, and enchantments. There was not a village in England that had not a ghost in it; the churchyards were all haunted; every large common had a circle of fairies belonging to it; and there was scarce a shepherd to be met with who had not seen a spirit.

Among all the poets of this kind our English are much the best, by what I have yet seen; whether it be that we abound with more stories of this nature, or that the genius of our country is fitter for this sort of poetry. For the English are naturally fanciful, and very often disposed, by that gloominess and melancholy of temper which is so frequent in our nation, to many wild notions and visions to which others are not so liable. Among the English, Shakespeare has incomparably excelled all others. That noble extravagance of fancy which he had in so great perfection thoroughly qualified him to touch this weak superstitious part of his reader's imagination, and made him capable of succeeding where he had nothing to support him besides the strength of his own genius. There is something so wild, and yet so solemn, in the speeches of his ghosts, fairies, witches, and the like imaginary persons that we cannot forbear thinking them natural, though we have no rule by which to judge of them, and must confess, if there are such beings in the world, it looks highly probable they should talk and act as he has represented them.

There is another sort of imaginary beings that we sometimes meet with among the poets, when the author represents any passion, appetite, virtue, or vice under a visible shape, and makes it a person or an actor in his poem. Of this nature are the descriptions of Hunger and Envy in Ovid, of Fame in Virgil, and of Sin and Death in Milton. We find a whole creation of the like shadowy persons in Spenser, who had an admirable talent in representations of this kind. I have discoursed of these emblematical persons in former papers, and shall therefore only mention them in this place. Thus we see how many ways poetry addresses itself to the imagination, as it has not only the whole circle of nature for its province, but makes new worlds of its own, shows us persons who are not to be found in being, and represents even the faculties of the soul, with her several virtues and vices, in a sensible shape and character. I shall in my two following papers consider in general how other kinds of writing are qualified to please the imagination; with which I intend to conclude this essay.

[Addison]

THOMAS TICKELL

THE relationship between Tickell and Addison was somewhat like that between Boswell and Dr. Johnson. Each rested upon a profound admiration of the lesser for the greater man, and each disciple left a tribute to his master finer than anything his master produced in that kind. Boswell has other claims to attention, but Tickell has been remembered almost entirely as a satellite. His association with Addison began in 1707, when he was twenty-one and still a student at Oxford, with a complimentary poem which he addressed to the essayist, then not widely known. He was the innocent cause of quarrels between Addison and Pope and Steele. Addison corrected Tickell's verses, praised his translation from Homer, secured for him a government post, and made him his literary executor. For his posthumous edition of Addison's works, which appeared in 1721, Tickell wrote his noble *Elegy*, the only poem of his that is now remembered. It is a poem that takes rather high literary rank by virtue chiefly of the moral and emotional rather than the intellectual qualities of its author.

Tickell's other poems do not reflect much credit upon Addison as a preceptor. He contributed a few papers to the *Spectator* and the *Guardian*. After Addison's death he spent many years in Ireland, dying in 1740.

TO THE EARL OF WARWICK ON THE DEATH OF MR. ADDISON

If dumb too long the drooping Muse hath stay'd
And left her debt to Addison unpaid,
Blame not her silence, *Warwick, but bemoan,
And judge, oh judge my bosom by your own!
What mourner ever felt poetic fires?
Slow comes the verse that real woe inspires;
Grief unaffected suits but ill with art,
Or flowing numbers with a bleeding heart.
Can I forget the dismal night that gave
My soul's best part forever to the grave?
How silent did his old companions tread,
By midnight lamps, the mansions of the *dead —
Through breathing statues, then unheeded things,
Through rows of warriors and through walks of kings!
What awe did the slow, solemn knell inspire,
The pealing organ and the pausing choir,
The duties by the lawn-robed prelate paid,
And the last words that dust to dust convey'd!
While speechless o'er thy closing grave we bend,
Accept these tears, thou dear departed friend.
Oh, gone forever, take this long adieu,
And sleep in peace next thy lov'd *Montagu.
To strew fresh laurels let the task be mine,
A frequent pilgrim at thy sacred shrine;
Mine with true sighs thy absence to bemoan
And grave with faithful epitaphs thy stone.
If e'er from me thy lov'd *memorial part,
May shame afflict this alienated heart;
Of thee forgetful, if I form a song,
My lyre be broken and untun'd my tongue;
My griefs be doubled, from thy image free,
And mirth a torment unchastised by thee.
Oft let me range the gloomy aisles *alone
(Sad luxury, to vulgar minds unknown)
Along the walls where speaking marbles show
What worthies form the hallow'd mould below —
Proud names who once the reins of empire held,
In arms who triumph'd or in arts excell'd;
Chiefs grac'd with scars and prodigal of blood,
Stern patriots who for sacred freedom stood,
Just men by whom impartial laws were given,
And saints who taught and led the way to heaven.
Ne'er to these chambers where the mighty rest,
Since their foundation, came a nobler guest,
Nor e'er was to the bowers of bliss convey'd
A fairer spirit or more welcome shade.
In what new region, to the just assign'd,
What new employments please th' unbody'd mind?
A winged Virtue thro' th' ethereal sky
From world to world unweary'd does he fly,
Or curious trace the long laborious maze
Of heaven's decrees where wondering angels gaze?
Does he delight to hear bold Seraphs tell
How Michael battled and the Dragon fell,
Or, mix'd with milder Cherubim, to glow

* Notes on Thomas Tickell will be found in the Appendix, p. 976.

In *hymns of love not ill essay'd below?
Or dost thou warn poor mortals left behind —
A task well suited to thy gentle mind?
Oh, if sometimes thy spotless form descend,
To me thy aid, thou guardian Genius, lend!
When rage misguides me or when fear alarms,
When pain distresses or when pleasure charms,
In silent whisperings purer thoughts impart,
And turn from ill a frail and feeble heart.
Lead through the paths thy virtue trod before,
Till bliss shall join, nor death can part us more.

That awful form which, so ye heavens decree,
Must still be lov'd and still deplor'd by me,
In nightly visions seldom fails to rise,
Or, rous'd by fancy, meets my waking eyes.
If business calls or crowded courts invite,
Th' unblemish'd statesman seems to strike my sight;
If in the stage I seek to soothe my care,
I meet his soul which breathes in *Cato there;
If, pensive, to the rural shades I rove,
His shape o'ertakes me in the lonely *grove.
'Twas there of just and good he reason'd strong,
Clear'd some great truth or rais'd some serious song;
There patient show'd us the wise course to steer,
A candid censor and a friend severe;
There taught us how to live and (oh, too high
The price for knowledge!) taught us how to *die.

Thou *hill whose brow the antique structures grace,
Rear'd by bold chiefs of Warwick's noble race,
Why, once so lov'd, whene'er thy bower appears
O'er my dim eyeballs glance the sudden tears?
How sweet were once thy prospects fresh and fair,
Thy sloping walks and unpolluted air!
How sweet the glooms beneath thy aged trees,
Thy noontide shadow and thy evening breeze!
His image thy forsaken bowers restore;
Thy walks and airy prospects charm no more;
No more the summer in thy glooms allay'd,
Thy ev'ning breezes and thy noonday shade.

From other ills, however fortune frown'd,
Some refuge in the Muse's art I found.
Reluctant now I touch the trembling string,
Bereft of him who taught me how to sing,
And these sad accents murmur'd o'er his urn
Betray that absence they attempt to mourn.
Oh, must I then (now fresh my bosom bleeds,
And *Craggs in death to Addison succeeds)
The verse begun to one lost friend prolong,
And weep a second in th' unfinish'd song?

These works divine which, on his deathbed laid,
To thee, O Craggs, th' expiring sage *convey'd,
Great but ill-omen'd monument of fame,
Nor he surviv'd to give, nor thou to claim.
Swift after him thy social spirit flies,
And close to his, how soon! thy coffin *lies.
Blest pair, whose union future bards shall tell
In future tongues, each other's boast! Farewell!
Farewell, whom join'd in fame, in friendship tried,
No chance could sever nor the grave divide.

[1721]

ISAAC WATTS

One of the earlier indications that Court and Town did not comprise the sole literary audience in England was given by the appearance, in 1706, of Watts' *Horæ Lyricæ*, and, in the following year, of his *Hymns*. In the preface to the former collection Watts inveighs against the "profanation and debasement" of Restoration verse which he says "has tempted many weak Christians to imagine that poetry and vice are naturally akin," contending strongly for the sensible view that religious experience provides ample poetic material and opportunity. His own verse is almost exclusively religious, although he also wrote a *Logic* and a treatise *On the Improvement of the Mind* which are not yet quite forgotten. During the Wesleyan revival, Watts' hymns had great vogue, and this popularity has never since subsided. Indeed, when we consider that scores of his hymns are still in general use, it seems probable that he has now a larger audience than any other poet of his century. It is fortunate, therefore, that Watts was a man of taste and of considerable intellectual attainment. He wrote Latin verse as readily as he did English and shows in his best hymns the influence of classic models. He is often somewhat absurd in his Cowleyan "Pindarics," and in the condescending tone of his poems for children his almost incessant moralizing seldom rises above the level of bourgeois respectability; and yet in those hymns in which he tried to phrase the basic Christian beliefs and emotions there is a strong simplicity and unerring rightness that deserve high praise. Without their violence and queerness, Watts kept some of the intensity of the greater religious poets — Donne, Herbert, Crashaw, Traherne, and Vaughan — who went before him. Like most of them, he was an innovator in versification, and he seems to have striven deliberately to find a distinguishing form for his religious lyrics. The movement of his better hymns is so orderly and English that it has stood the test of two centuries.

THE DAY OF JUDGMENT

(*An Ode Attempted in English Sapphic*)

When the fierce north wind with his airy forces
Rears up the Baltic to a foaming fury,
And the red lightning with a storm of hail comes
Rushing amain down,

How the poor sailors stand amazed and tremble,
While the hoarse thunder, like a bloody trumpet,
Roars a loud onset to the gaping waters
Quick to devour them!

Such shall the noise be, and the wild disorder,
If things eternal may be like those earthly,
Such the dire terror, when the great Archangel
Shakes the creation,

Tears the strong pillars of the vault of heaven,
Breaks up old marble, the repose of princes.
See the graves open, and the bones arising,
Flames all around 'em!

Hark the shrill outcries of the guilty wretches!
Lively bright horror and amazing anguish
Stare through their eyelids, while the living worm lies
Gnawing within them.

Thoughts like old vultures prey upon their heartstrings,
And the smart twinges, when their eye beholds the
Lofty Judge frowning, and a flood of vengeance
Rolling afore him.

Hopeless immortals! How they scream and shiver
While devils push them to the pit wide yawning,
Hideous and gloomy, to receive them headlong
Down to the centre.

Stop here, my fancy. All away, ye horrid,
Doleful ideas. Come, arise to Jesus.
How he sits Godlike! and the saints around him
Thron'd, yet adoring!

Oh, may I sit there when he comes triumphant,
*Dooming the nations; then ascend to glory,
While our hosannas all along the passage
Shout the Redeemer!

[1706]

* Notes on Isaac Watts will be found in the Appendix, p. 976.

A PROSPECT OF HEAVEN MAKES DEATH EASY

There is a land of pure delight
  Where saints immortal reign;
Infinite day excludes the night,
  And pleasures banish pain.

There everlasting spring abides,
  And never-withering flowers;
Death, like a narrow sea, divides
  This heavenly land from ours.

Sweet fields beyond the swelling flood
  Stand dressed in living green;
So to the Jews old Canaan stood
  While Jordan rolled between.

But timorous mortals start and shrink
  To cross this narrow sea,
And linger shivering on the brink
  And fear to launch away.

Oh, could we make our doubts remove,
  These gloomy doubts that rise,
And see the Canaan that we love
  With unbeclouded eyes,

Could we but climb where Moses stood
  And view the landscape o'er,
Not Jordan's stream nor death's cold flood
  Should fright us from the shore.

[1706]

CRUCIFIXION TO THE WORLD BY THE CROSS OF CHRIST

When I survey the wondrous cross
  On which the Prince of Glory died,
My richest gain I count but loss
  And pour contempt on all my pride.

Forbid it, Lord, that I should boast
  Save in the death of Christ, my God;
All the vain things that charm me most,
  I sacrifice them to his blood.

See from his head, his hands, his feet,
  Sorrow and love flow mingled down!
Did e'er such love and sorrow meet;
  Or thorns compose so rich a crown?

His dying crimson like a robe
  Spread o'er his body on the tree;
Then am I dead to all the globe,
  And all the globe is dead to me.

Were the whole realm of nature mine,
  That were a present far too small;
Love so amazing, so divine,
  Demands my soul, my life, my all.

[1707]

MAN FRAIL, AND GOD ETERNAL

Our God, our help in ages past,
  Our hope for years to come,
Our shelter from the stormy blast,
  And our eternal home.

Under the shadow of thy throne
  Thy saints have dwelt secure;
Sufficient is thine arm alone,
  And our defence is sure.

Before the hills in order stood,
  Or earth received her *frame,
From everlasting thou art God,
  To endless years the same.

Thy word commands our flesh to dust:
  "Return, ye sons of men."
All nations rose from earth at first
  And turn to earth again.

A thousand ages in thy sight
  Are like an evening gone,
Short as the watch that ends the night
  Before the rising sun.

The busy tribes of flesh and blood,
  With all their lives and cares,
Are carried downwards by thy flood
  And lost in following years.

Time, like an ever-rolling stream,
  Bears all its sons away;
They fly forgotten, as a dream
  Dies at the opening day.

Like flowery fields the nations stand
  Pleased with the morning light;
The flowers beneath the mower's hand
  Lie withering ere 'tis night.

Our God, our help in ages past,
  Our hope for years to come,
Be thou our guard while troubles last,
  And our eternal home.

[1719]

WILLIAM LAW

William Law was a High Churchman who sowed the seed of Methodism, a slashing theological controversialist who gave his life to deeds of simple charity, and a mystic who wrote one of the most influential books of practical divinity in the English language. As a man and as a thinker he won the respect of critics as diverse as Gibbon, Johnson, and John Wesley, though all three disagreed with him in essentials. No important English writer of the eighteenth century presents more paradoxes or more striking divergencies from the spirit of his age.

Law belongs to the second generation of Nonjurors. On the accession of George I he forfeited his fellowship at Emmanuel College, Cambridge, and gave up all hope of preferment in the Church rather than take the required oaths. For a number of years he lived in the family of Edward Gibbon as tutor to his son, the father of the historian, and afterwards as spiritual director to the family. His later years were spent at his native village of King's Cliffe, Northamptonshire, where in company with two wealthy disciples, Miss Hester Gibbon and Mrs. Hutcheson, he lived a life of primitive Christian devotion and good works. He wrote much on a variety of subjects: in support of High Church principles against Benjamin Hoadly, King's Chaplain and latitudinarian Bishop of Bangor; in opposition to stage plays (a belated echo of the Collier controversy); in answer to Mandeville's *The Fable of the Bees;* in support of orthodox Christianity against the Deists; and in defence of the mystical writers, especially of Jacob Boehme, the famous seventeenth-century German, who influenced Law in increasing degree during the latter part of his life.

Of wider popular appeal than any of his other works, however, were the practical books of Christian devotion which he published in middle life: *A Practical Treatise upon Christian Perfection,* 1726, and *A Serious Call to a Devout and Holy Life,* 1728. The latter exerted the wider influence and is generally accounted Law's masterpiece. It is vibrant with the power of simple Christianity, which transfigures the heart of the believer and expresses itself in a life of single-hearted devotion to the literal precepts of the Gospel. At the same time it has high literary excellence, is written in a chaste and vigorous style admirably adapted to its purpose, and is marked by wit, satiric keenness, and incisive logic. Sir Leslie Stephen, the agnostic historian of English thought in the eighteenth century, says that *A Serious Call* "may be read with pleasure by the purely literary critic," but adds, "Perhaps there is a touch of profanity in reading in cold blood a book which throughout palpitates with the deepest emotions of its author, and which has thrilled so many sympathetic spirits. The power can only be felt by readers who can study it on their knees." Dr. Johnson told Boswell that it had been instrumental in overcoming his own early indifference to religion. "When at Oxford, I took up Law's 'Serious Call to a Holy Life,' expecting to find it a dull book (as such books generally are,) and perhaps to laugh at it. But I found Law quite an overmatch for me."

The extract here given is the first chapter of *A Serious Call.* Though a few pages can not adequately illustrate the logical continuity of Law's thought or the sustained intensity of his emotion, they can illustrate the purity and raciness of his style, and the earnestness of his purpose.

A SERIOUS CALL TO A DEVOUT AND HOLY LIFE

Chapter I

Concerning the Nature and Extent of Christian Devotion

Devotion is neither private nor public prayer; but prayers, whether private or public, are particular parts or instances of devotion. Devotion signifies a life given, or devoted, to God.

He, therefore, is the devout man who lives no longer to his own will, or the way and spirit of the world, but to the sole will of God; who considers God in everything, who serves God in everything, who makes all the parts of his common life parts of piety, by doing everything in the name of God, and under such rules as are conformable to his glory.

We readily acknowledge that God alone is to be the rule and measure of our prayers; that in them we are to look wholly unto him, and act wholly for him; that we are only to pray in such a manner, for such things, and such ends, as are suitable to his glory.

Now, let any one but find out the reason why he is to be thus strictly pious in his prayers, and he will find the same as strong a reason to be as strictly pious in all the other parts of his life. For there is not the least shadow of a reason why we should make God the rule and measure of our prayers, why we should then look wholly unto him, and pray according to his will, but what equally proves it necessary for us to look wholly unto God, and make him the rule and measure of all the other actions of our life. For any ways of life, any employment of our talents, whether of our parts, our time, or money, that is not strictly according to the will of God, that is not for such ends as are suitable to his glory, are as great absurdities and failings as prayers that are not according to the will of God. For there is no other reason why our prayers should be according to the will of God, why they should have nothing in them but what is wise and holy and heavenly; there is no other reason for this but that our lives may be of the same nature, full of the same wisdom, holiness, and heavenly tempers, that we may live unto God in the same spirit that we pray unto him. Were it not our strict duty to live by reason, to devote all the actions of our lives to God, were it not absolutely necessary to walk before him in wisdom and holiness and all heavenly conversation, doing everything in his name and for his glory, there would be no excellency or wisdom in the most heavenly prayers. Nay, such prayers would be absurdities; they would be like prayers for wings when it was no part of our duty to fly.

As sure, therefore, as there is any wisdom in praying for the Spirit of God, so sure is it that we are to make that Spirit the rule of all our actions; as sure as it is our duty to look wholly unto God in our prayers, so sure is it that it is our duty to live wholly unto God in our lives. But we can no more be said to live unto God, unless we live unto him in all the ordinary actions of our life, unless he be the rule and measure of all our ways, than we can be said to pray unto God, unless our prayers look wholly unto him. So that unreasonable and absurd ways of life, whether in labour or diversion, whether they consume our time or our money, are like unreasonable and absurd prayers, and are as truly an offence unto God.

It is for want of knowing, or at least considering this, that we see such a mixture of ridicule in the lives of many people. You see them strict as to some times and places of devotion, but when the service of the church is over, they are but like those that seldom or never come there. In their way of life, their manner of spending their time and money, in their cares and fears, in their pleasures and indulgences, in their labour and diversions, they are like the rest of the world. This makes the loose part of the world generally make a jest of those that are devout, because they see their devotion goes no farther than their prayers, and that when they are over, they live no more unto God, till the time of prayer returns again; but live by the same humour and fancy, and in as full an enjoyment of all the follies of life as other people. This is the reason why they are the jest and scorn of careless and worldly people; not because they are really devoted to God, but because they appear to have no other devotion but that of occasional prayers.

*Julius is very fearful of missing prayers; all the parish supposes Julius to be sick if he is not at church. But if you were to ask him why he spends the rest of his time by humour or chance, why he is a companion of the silliest people in their most silly pleasures, why he is ready for every impertinent entertainment and diversion; if you were to ask him why there is no amusement too trifling to please him, why he is busy at all balls and assemblies, why he gives himself up to an idle, gossiping conversation, why he lives in foolish friendships and fondness for particular persons that neither want nor deserve any particular kindness, why he allows himself in foolish hatreds and resentments against particular persons without considering that he is to love everybody as himself; if you ask him why he never puts his conversation, his time, and fortune, under the rules of religion, Julius has no more to say for himself than the most disorderly person. For the whole tenor of Scripture lies as directly against such a life, as against debauchery and intemperance: he that lives in such a course of idleness and folly, lives no more according to the religion of Jesus Christ than he that lives in gluttony and intemperance.

If a man were to tell Julius that there was no occasion for so much constancy at prayers, and that he might, without any harm to himself, neglect the service of the church, as the generality of people do, Julius would think such a one to be no Christian, and that he ought to avoid his company. But if a person only tells him that he may live as the generality of the world does, that he may enjoy himself as others do, that he may spend his time and money as people of fashion do, that he may

* Notes on William Law will be found in the Appendix, pp. 976 ff.

conform to the follies and frailties of the generality, and gratify his tempers and passions as most people do, Julius never suspects that man to want a Christian spirit, or that he is doing the devil's work.

And if Julius were to read all the New Testament from the beginning to the end, he would find his course of life condemned in every page of it.

And indeed there cannot anything be imagined more absurd in itself, than wise and sublime and heavenly prayers added to a life of vanity and folly, where neither labour nor diversions, neither time nor money, are under the direction of the wisdom and heavenly tempers of our prayers. If we were to see a man pretending to act wholly with regard to God in everything that he did, that would neither spend time nor money, or take any labour or diversion, but so far as he could act according to strict principles of reason and piety, and yet at the same time neglect all prayer, whether public or private, should we not be amazed at such a man, and wonder how he could have so much folly along with so much religion?

Yet this is as reasonable as for any person to pretend to strictness in devotion, to be careful of observing times and places of prayer, and yet letting the rest of his life, his time and labour, his talents and money, be disposed of without any regard to strict rules of piety and devotion. For it is as great an absurdity to suppose holy prayers and divine petitions, without an holiness of life suitable to them, as to suppose an holy and divine life without prayers.

Let any one therefore think how easily he could confute a man that pretended to great strictness of life without prayer, and the same arguments will as plainly confute another that pretends to strictness of prayer, without carrying the same strictness into every other part of life. For to be weak and foolish in spending our time and fortune is no greater a mistake than to be weak and foolish in relation to our prayers. And to allow ourselves in any ways of life that neither are nor can be offered to God, is the same irreligion as to neglect our prayers, or use them in such a manner as makes them an offering unworthy of God.

The short of the matter is this: either reason and religion prescribe rules and ends to all the ordinary actions of our life, or they do not; if they do, then it is as necessary to govern all our actions by those rules, as it is necessary to worship God. For if religion teaches us anything concerning eating and drinking, or spending our time and money; if it teaches us how we are to use and contemn the world; if it tells us what tempers we are to have in common life, how we are to be disposed towards all people, how we are to behave towards the sick, the poor, the old and destitute; if it tells us whom we are to treat with a particular love, whom we are to regard with a particular esteem; if it tells us how we are to treat our enemies, and how we are to mortify and deny ourselves; he must be very weak that can think these parts of religion are not to be observed with as much exactness as any doctrines that relate to prayers.

It is very observable that there is not one command in all the Gospel for public worship; and perhaps it is a duty that is least insisted upon in Scripture of any other. The frequent attendance at it is never so much as mentioned in all the New Testament. Whereas that religion or devotion which is to govern the ordinary actions of our life is to be found in almost every verse of Scripture. Our blessed Saviour and his apostles are wholly taken up in doctrines that relate to common life. They call us to renounce the world, and differ in every temper and way of life from the spirit and way of the world; to renounce all its goods, to fear none of its evils, to reject its joys, and have no value for its happiness; to be as new-born babes that are born into a new state of things; to live as pilgrims in spiritual watching, in holy fear, and heavenly aspiring after another life; to take up our daily cross, to deny ourselves, to profess the blessedness of mourning, to seek the blessedness of poverty of spirit; to forsake the pride and vanity of riches, to take no thought for the morrow, to live in the profoundest state of humility, to rejoice in worldly sufferings; to reject the lust of the flesh, the lust of the eyes, and the pride of life; to bear injuries, to forgive and bless our enemies, and to love mankind as God loveth them; to give up our whole hearts and affections to God, and strive to enter through the strait gate into a life of eternal glory.

This is the common devotion which our blessed Saviour taught, in order to make it the common life of all Christians. Is it not therefore exceeding strange that people should place so much piety in the attendance upon public worship, concerning which there is not one precept of our Lord's to be found, and yet neglect these common duties of our ordinary life, which are commanded in every page of the Gospel? I call these duties the devotion of our common life, because if they are to be practised, they must be made parts of our common life; they can have no place anywhere else.

If contempt of the world and heavenly affection is a necessary temper of Christians, it is necessary that this temper appear in the whole course of their lives, in their manner of using the world, because it can have no place anywhere else. If self-denial be a condition of salvation, all that would be saved must make it a part of their ordinary life. If humility be a Christian duty, then the common life of a Christian is to be a constant course of humility in all its kinds. If poverty of spirit be necessary, it must be the spirit and temper of every day of our lives. If we are to relieve the naked, the sick, and the prisoner, it must be the common charity of our lives, as far as we can render ourselves able to perform it. If we are to love our enemies, we must make our common life a visible exercise and demonstration of that love. If content and thankfulness, if the patient bearing of evil, be duties to God, they are the duties of every day, and in every circumstance of our life. If we are to be wise and holy as the new-born sons of God, we can no otherwise be so, but by renouncing everything that is foolish and vain in every part of our common life. If we are to be in Christ new creatures, we must show that we are so, by having new ways of living in the world. If we are to follow Christ, it must be in our common way of spending every day.

Thus it is in all the virtues and holy tempers of Christianity; they are not ours unless they be the virtues and tempers of our ordinary life. So that Christianity is so far from leaving us to live in the common ways of life, conforming to the folly of customs, and gratifying the passions and tempers which the spirit of the world delights in; it is so far from indulging us in any of these things that all its virtues which it makes necessary to salvation are only so many ways of living above and contrary to the world, in all the common actions of our life. If our common life is not a common course of humility, self-denial, renunciation of the world, poverty of spirit, and heavenly affection, we do not live the lives of Christians.

But yet though it is thus plain that this, and this alone, is Christianity, an uniform, open, and visible practice of all these virtues, yet it is as plain that there is little or nothing of this to be found, even amongst the better sort of people. You see them often at church, and pleased with fine preachers; but look into their lives, and you see them just the same sort of people as others are that make no pretences to devotion. The difference that you find betwixt them is only the difference of their natural tempers. They have the same taste of the world, the same worldly cares and fears and joys; they have the same turn of mind, equally vain in their desires. You see the same fondness for state and equipage, the same pride and vanity of dress, the same self-love and indulgence, the same foolish friendships and groundless hatreds, the same levity of mind and trifling spirit, the same fondness for diversions, the same idle dispositions and vain ways of spending their time in visiting and conversation, as the rest of the world that make no pretences to devotion.

I do not mean this comparison betwixt people seemingly good and professed rakes, but betwixt people of sober lives. Let us take an instance in two modest women: let it be supposed that one of them is careful of times of devotion, and observes them through a sense of duty, and that the other has no hearty concern about it, but is at church seldom or often, just as it happens. Now it is a very easy thing to see this difference betwixt these persons. But when you have seen this, can you find any further difference betwixt them? Can you find that their common life is of a different kind? Are not the tempers and customs and manners of the one, of the same kind as of the other? Do they live as if they belonged to different worlds, had different views in their heads, and different rules and measures of all their actions? Have they not the same goods and evils? Are they not pleased and displeased in the same manner, and for the same things? Do they not live in the same course of life? Does one seem to be of this world, looking at the things that are temporal, and the other to be of another world, looking wholly at the things that are eternal? Does the one live in pleasure, delighting herself in show or dress, and the other live in self-denial and mortification, renouncing everything that looks like vanity, either of person, dress, or carriage? Does the one follow public diversions, and trifle away her time in idle visits, and corrupt conversation; and does the other study all the arts of improving her time, living in prayer and watching, and such good works as may make all her time turn to her advantage, and be placed to her account at the last day? Is the one careless of expense, and glad to be able to adorn herself with every costly ornament of dress; and does the other consider her fortune as a talent given her by God, which is to be improved religiously, and no more to be spent in vain and needless ornaments than it is to be buried in the earth? Where must you look, to find one person of religion differing in this manner from another that has none? And yet if they do not differ in these things which are here related, can it with any sense be said the one is a good Christian, and the other not?

Take another instance amongst the men. Leo has a great deal of good nature, has kept what they call good company, hates everything that is false and base, is very generous and brave to his friends, but has concerned himself so little with religion that he hardly knows the difference betwixt a Jew and a Christian.

Eusebius, on the other hand, has had early impressions of religion, and buys books of devotion. He can talk of all the feasts and fasts of the Church, and knows the names of most men that have been eminent for piety. You never hear him swear or make a loose jest; and when he talks of religion, he talks of it as of a matter of the last concern.

Here you see that one person has religion enough, according to the way of the world, to be reckoned a pious Christian, and the other is so far from all appearance of religion that he may fairly be reckoned a heathen; and yet if you look into their common life, if you examine their chief and ruling tempers in the greatest articles of life, or the greatest doctrines of Christianity, you will find the least difference imaginable.

Consider them with regard to the use of the world, because that is what everybody can see.

Now to have right notions and tempers with relation to this world is as essential to religion as to have right notions of God. And it is as possible for a man to worship a crocodile, and yet be a pious man, as to have his affections set upon this world, and yet be a good Christian.

But now if you consider Leo and Eusebius in this respect, you will find them exactly alike, seeking, using, and enjoying all that can be got in this world in the same manner, and for the same ends. You will find that riches, prosperity, pleasures, indulgences, state, equipage, and honour, are just as much the happiness of Eusebius as they are of Leo. And yet if Christianity has not changed a man's mind and temper with relation to these things, what can we say that it has done for him? For if the doctrines of Christianity were practised, they would make a man as different from other people, as to all worldly tempers, sensual pleasures, and the pride of life, as a wise man is different from * a natural; it would be as easy a thing to know a Christian by his outward course of life as it is now difficult to find anybody that lives it. For it is notorious that Christians are now not only like other men in their frailties and infirmities; this might be in some degree excusable, but the complaint is they are like heathens in all the main and chief articles of their lives. They enjoy the world and live every day in the same tempers and the same designs and the same indulgences, as they do who know not God, nor of any happiness in another life. Everybody that is capable of any reflection must have observed that this is generally the state even of devout people, whether men or women. You may see them different from other people, so far as to times and places of prayer, but generally like the rest of the world in all the other parts of their lives. That is adding Christian devotion to a heathen life. I have the authority of our blessed Saviour for this remark, where he says, "Take no thought, saying, What shall we eat? or, What shall we drink? or, Wherewithal shall we be clothed? For after all these things do the Gentiles seek." But if to be thus affected even with the necessary things of this life shows that we are not yet of a Christian spirit, but are like the heathens, surely to enjoy the vanity and folly of the world as they did, to be like them in the main chief tempers of our lives, in self-love, and indulgence, in sensual pleasures and diversions, in the vanity of dress, the love of show and greatness, or any other gaudy distinctions of fortune, is a much greater sign of a heathen temper. And, consequently, they who add devotion to such a life, must be said to pray as Christians, but live as heathens.

[1728]

COLLEY CIBBER

Colley Cibber was the son of a Danish sculptor resident in England, who married an English woman named Colley. The son became an actor, achieved success in eccentric rôles, wrote numerous comedies of the sentimental type popular in the early eighteenth century, became a theatrical manager, and upon the death of Eusden in 1730 was appointed poet-laureate. His obvious unfitness for this last position, except for his strong Whig sympathies; the badness of his official odes, even at a time when the laureateship had sunk very low; and the attacks of Pope and the other wits, have obscured the value of his services to the stage and have injured his reputation. Dr. Johnson's well-known epigram was doubtless intended chiefly as an attack on George II, but it cuts with a double edge.

> Augustus still survives in Maro's strain,
> And Spenser's verse prolongs Eliza's reign;
> Great George's acts let tuneful Cibber sing;
> For nature form'd the poet for the king.

Yet Johnson, in spite of his political prejudice and his low estimate of the actor's profession, on a later occasion did Cibber more justice when he told Boswell, "Colley Cibber, sir, was by no means a blockhead, but by arrogating to himself too much he was in danger of losing that degree of estimation to which he was entitled. His friends gave out that he *intended* his birthday odes should be bad, but that was not the case, sir... Cibber's familiar style, however, was better than that which Whitehead has assumed. *Grand* nonsense is insupportable."

Some misunderstanding has arisen because Pope in later editions of *The Dunciad* dethroned Theobald as monarch of Dullness and elevated Cibber to his place. In the modern sense of the word Cibber was not dull; indeed his faults of pertness and coxcombry denote the opposite quality. It must be remembered, however, that as Pope used the word, dullness was the opposite of wit; it embraced all the faults of bad taste in literature and life; what was disproportioned, incongruous, ridiculous was a form of false wit or dullness; sauciness and impertinence as well as pedantry and stupidity were qualities of the dunce.

Though Cibber's plays have been forgotten, and his verses fell from the press stillborn, one of his writings has preserved its vitality to our own day. *An Apology for the Life of Mr. Colley Cibber, Comedian, and Late Patentee of the Theatre-Royal*, 1740, as he designated his memoirs, is one of the most interesting books of its period. Here Cibber presents himself, with a vanity that will not conceal itself, as a comedian off the stage as well as upon it, and at the same time gives us, as the title-page asserts, "An Historical View of the Stage during his own Time." Here we have the greenroom gossip of the closing years of the seventeenth and the first third of the eighteenth century; here we have admirable portraits of the leading actors: Booth, Wilks, Betterton, Nokes, Leigh, Doggett, Mrs. Barry, Mrs. Bracegirdle, Mrs. Oldfield — to mention but a few. It is a vivid portrayal of the stage in one of its greatest periods. When Boswell asked Johnson whether he had read the *Apology*, the doctor replied, "Yes, it is very entertaining. But as for Cibber himself, taking from his conversation all that he ought not to have said, he was a poor creature." Whether or not we subscribe to the "poor creature," we may be thankful that Cibber did not take from his book "all that he ought not to have said."

The selection here given is the first half of Chapter VIII, which deals with the Collier controversy and records some of the actors' experiences with stage censorship.

APOLOGY

Chapter VIII

Though *the master of our theatre had no conception himself of theatrical merit, either in authors or actors, yet his judgment was governed by a saving rule in both: he looked into his receipts for the value of a play, and from common fame he judged of his actors. But by whatever rule he was governed, while he had prudently reserved to himself a power of not paying them more than their merit could get, he could not be much deceived by their being over, or undervalued. In a word, he had with great skill inverted the constitution of the stage, and quite changed the channel of profits arising from it; formerly, (when there was but one company) the proprietors punctually paid the actors their appointed salaries, and took to themselves only the clear profits; but our wiser proprietor, took first out of every day's receipts

* Notes on Colley Cibber will be found in the Appendix p. 977.

two shillings in the pound to himself, and left their salaries to be paid only as the less or greater deficiencies of acting (according to his own accounts) would permit. What seemed most extraordinary in these measures, was that at the same time he had persuaded us to be contented with our condition, upon his assuring us that as fast as money would come in, we should all be paid our arrears; and that we might not have it always in our power to say he had never intended to keep his word, I remember in a few years after this time he once paid us nine days in one week: this happened when * *The Funeral, or Grief à la Mode* was first acted, with more than expected success. Whether this well timed bounty was only allowed us to save appearances, I will not say, but if that was his real motive for it, it was too costly a frolic to be repeated, and was, at least, the only grimace of its kind he vouchsafed us, we never having received one day more of those arrears in above fifteen years' service.

While the actors were in this condition, I think I may very well be excused in my presuming to write plays, which I was forced to do for the support of my increasing family, my precarious income as an actor being then too scanty to supply it with even the necessaries of life.

It may be observable too that my Muse and my spouse were equally prolific, that the one was seldom the mother of a child but in the same year the other made me the father of a play; I think we had a dozen of each sort between us; of both which kinds some died in their infancy and near an equal number of each were alive when I quitted the theatre —— but it is no wonder, when a Muse is only called upon by family duty, she should not always rejoice in the fruit of her labour. To this necessity of writing, then, I attribute the defects of my second play, which, coming out too hastily the year after my first, turned to very little account. But having got as much by my first as I ought to have expected from the success of them both, I had no great reason to complain; not but, I confess, so bad was my second that I do not choose to tell you the name of it, and that it might be peaceably forgotten, I have not given it a place in the two volumes of those I published in quarto in the year 1721. And whenever I took upon me to make some dormant play of an old author to the best of my judgment fitter for the stage, it was, honestly, not to be idle that set me to work, as a good housewife will mend old linen when she has not better employment; but when I was more warmly engaged by a subject entirely new, I only thought it a good subject when it seemed worthy of an abler pen than my own, and might prove as useful to the hearer as profitable to myself: therefore, whatever any of my productions might want of skill, learning, wit, or humour, or however unqualified I might be to instruct others, who so ill governed myself, yet such plays (entirely my own) were not wanting, at least, in what our most admired writers seemed to neglect, and without which I cannot allow the most taking play to be intrinsically good, or to be a work upon which a man of sense and probity should value himself, — I mean when they do not, as well *prodesse* as *delectare*, give profit with delight! The * *utile dulci* was, of old, equally the point, and has always been my aim, however wide of the mark I may have shot my arrow. It has often given me amazement that our best authors of that time could think the wit and spirit of their scenes could be an excuse for making the looseness of them public. The many instances of their talents so abused are too glaring to need a closer comment and are sometimes too gross to be recited. If then to have avoided this imputation, or rather to have had the interest and honour of virtue always in view, can give merit to a play, I am contented that my readers should think such merit the all that mine have to boast of. Libertines of mere wit and pleasure may laugh at these grave laws that would limit a lively genius, but every sensible, honest man, conscious of their truth and use, will give these ralliers smile for smile and show a due contempt for their merriment.

But while our authors took these extraordinary liberties with their wit, I remember the ladies were then observed to be decently afraid of venturing barefaced to a new comedy till they had been assured they might do it without the risk of an insult to their modesty; or if their curiosity were too strong for their patience, they took care at least to save appearances, and rarely came upon the first days of acting but in masks (then daily worn and admitted in the pit, the side-boxes, and gallery), which custom, however, had so many ill consequences attending it that it has been abolished these many years.

These immoralities of the stage had by an

avowed indulgence been creeping into it ever since King Charles' time: nothing that was loose could then be too low for it; the *London Cuckolds*, the most rank play that ever succeeded, was then in the highest court favour. In this almost general corruption, Dryden, whose plays were more famed for their wit than their chastity, led the way, which he fairly confesses and endeavours to excuse in his epilogue to * *The Pilgrim*, revived in 1700 for his benefit in his declining age and fortune. The following lines of it will make good my observation:

Perhaps the parson stretch'd a point too far,
When with our theatres he wag'd a war.
He tells you that this very moral age
Receiv'd the first infection from the stage.
But sure, a banish'd court, with lewdness fraught,
The seeds of open vice, returning, brought.
Thus lodg'd (as vice by great example thrives,)
It first debauch'd the daughters and the wives.
London, a fruitful soil, yet never bore
So plentiful a crop of horns before.
The poets, who must live by courts, or starve,
Were proud so good a government to serve;
And, mixing with buffoons and pimps profane,
Tainted the stage, for some small snip of gain.
For they, like harlots, under bawds profess'd,
Took all th' ungodly pains, and got the least.
Thus did the thriving malady prevail,
The court its head, the poets but the tail.
The sin was of our native growth, 'tis true;
The scandal of the sin was wholly new.
Misses there were, but modestly conceal'd;
Whitehall the naked Venus first reveal'd,
Who standing, as at Cyprus, in her shrine,
The strumpet was ador'd with rites divine.

This epilogue and the prologue to the same play, written by Dryden, I spoke myself, which not being usually done by the same person, I have a mind, while I think of it, to let you know on what occasion they both fell to my share, and how other actors were affected by it.

Sir John Vanbrugh, who had given some light touches of his pen to *The Pilgrim* to assist the benefit day of Dryden, had the disposal of the parts, and I being then, as an actor, in some favour with him, he read the play first with me alone, and was pleased to offer me my choice of what I might like best for myself in it. But as the chief characters were not (according to my taste) the most shining, it was no great self-denial in me that I desired he would first take care of those who were more difficult to be pleased; I therefore only chose for myself two short incidental parts, that of the stuttering cook and the mad Englishman. In which homely characters I saw more matter for delight than those that might have a better pretence to the amiable, and when the play came to be acted, I was not deceived in my choice. Sir John, upon my being contented with so little a share in the entertainment, gave me the epilogue to make up my mess, which being written so much above the strain of common authors, I confess I was not a little pleased with. And Dryden, upon his hearing me repeat it to him, made me a farther compliment of trusting me with the prologue. This so particular distinction was looked upon by the actors as something too extraordinary. But no one was so impatiently ruffled at it as Wilks, who seldom chose soft words when he spoke of anything he did not like. The most gentle thing he said of it was that he did not understand such treatment, that for his part he looked upon it as an affront to all the rest of the company, that there should be but one out of the whole judged fit to speak either a prologue or an epilogue! To quiet him, I offered to decline either in his favour, or both, if it were equally easy to the author; but he was too much concerned to accept of an offer that had been made to another in preference to himself, and which he seemed to think his best way of resenting was to contemn. But from that time, however, he was resolved to the best of his power never to let the first offer of a prologue escape him, which little ambition sometimes made him pay too dear for his success: the flatness of the many miserable prologues that by this means fell to his lot seemed woefully unequal to the few good ones he might have reason to triumph in.

I have given you this fact only as a sample of those frequent rubs and impediments I met with when any step was made to my being distinguished as an actor; and from this incident too, you may partly see what occasioned so many prologues, after the death of Betterton, to fall into the hands of one speaker, but it is not every successor to a vacant post that brings into it the talents equal to those of a predecessor. To speak a good prologue well is, in my opinion, one of the hardest parts and strongest proofs of sound elocution, of which, I confess, I never thought that any of the several who attempted it showed themselves by far equal masters to Betterton. Betterton, in the delivery of a good prologue, had a natural gravity that gave strength to a good sense, a tempered spirit that gave life to wit, and a dry reserve in his smile that threw ridicule into its brightest colours. Of these qualities, in the speaking of a prologue, Booth only had the first, but attained not to the other two; Wilks had spirit, but gave too loose a rein to it, and it was seldom he could speak a grave and weighty verse harmoniously. His accents were frequently too sharp and violent, which sometimes occasioned his eagerly cutting off half the sound of syllables that ought to have been gently melted into the melody of metre; in the verses of humour, too, he would sometimes carry the mimicry farther than the hint would bear, even to a trifling light, as if himself were pleased to see it so glittering. In the truth of this criticism, I have been confirmed by those whose judgment I dare more confidently rely on than my own. Wilks had many excellencies, but if we leave prologue speaking out of the number, he will still have enough to have made him a valuable actor. And I only make this exception from them to caution others from imitating what in his time they might have too implicitly admired. But I have a word or two more to say concerning the immoralities of the stage.

Our theatrical writers were not only accused of immorality, but profaneness; many flagrant instances of which were collected and published by a nonjuring clergyman, Jeremy Collier, in his **View of the Stage, etc.*, about the year, 1697. However just his charge against the authors that then wrote for it might be, I cannot but think his sentence against the stage itself is unequal; reformation he thinks too mild a treatment for it, and is therefore for laying his axe to the root of it. If this were to be a rule of judgment for offences of the same nature, what might become of the pulpit, where many a seditious and corrupted teacher has been known to cover the most pernicious doctrine with the mask of religion? This puts me in mind of what the noted Jo. Hains, the comedian, a fellow of a wicked wit, said upon this occasion; who being asked what could transport Mr. Collier into so blind a zeal for a general suppression of the stage, when only some particular authors had abused it, whereas the stage, he could not but know, was generally allowed, when rightly conducted, to be a delightful method of mending our morals: "For that reason," replied Hains, "Collier is by profession a moral-mender himself, and two of trade, you know, can never agree."

*The authors of *The Old Bachelor* and of *The Relapse* were those whom Collier most laboured to convict of immorality, to which they severally published their reply; the first seemed too much hurt to be able to defend himself, and the other felt him so little that his wit only laughed at his lashes.

My first play of *The Fool in Fashion*, too, being then in a course of success, perhaps for that reason only this severe author thought himself obliged to attack it, in which, I hope, he has shown more zeal than justice: his greatest charge against it is that it sometimes uses the word, *Faith*! as an oath, in the dialogue; but if *faith* may as well signify our given word, or credit, as our religious belief, why might not his charity have taken it in the less criminal sense? Nevertheless, Mr. Collier's book was upon the whole thought so laudable a work that King William, soon after it was published, granted him a **nolo prosequi*, when he stood answerable to the law for his having absolved two criminals, just before they were executed for high treason. And it must be farther granted that his calling our dramatic writers to this strict account had a very wholesome effect upon those who writ after this time. They were now a great deal more upon their guard; indecencies were no longer writ; and by degrees the fair sex came again to fill the boxes on the first day of a new comedy, without fear or censure. But the Master of the Revels, who then licensed all plays for the stage, assisted this reformation with a more zealous severity than ever. He would strike out whole scenes of a vicious or immoral character, though it were visibly shown to be reformed or punished. A severe instance of this kind falling upon myself may be an excuse for my relating it. When *Richard the Third* (as I altered it from Shakespeare) came from his hands to the stage, he expunged the whole first act, without sparing a line of it. This extraordinary stroke of a **sic volo* occasioned my applying to him for the small indulgence of a speech or two, that the other four acts might limp on with a little less absurdity. No! he had not leisure to consider what might be separately inoffensive. He had an objection to the whole act, and the reason he gave for it was that the distresses of *King Henry the Sixth, who is killed by Richard in the first act, would put weak people too much in mind of King James, then living in France, — a notable proof of his zeal for the government! Those who have read either the play or the history, I dare say, will think he strained hard for the parallel. In a word, we were forced for some few years to let the play take its fate, with only four acts, divided into five. By the loss of so considerable a limb may one not modestly suppose it was robbed of at least a fifth part of that favour it afterwards met with? For though his first act was at last recovered, and made the play whole again, yet the relief came too late to repay me for the pains I had taken in it. Nor did I ever hear that this zealous severity of the Master of the Revels was afterwards thought justifiable. But my good fortune in process of time gave me an opportunity to talk with my oppressor in my turn.

*The patent granted by His Majesty, King George the First, to Sir Richard Steele and his assigns, of which I was one, made us sole judges of what plays might be proper for the stage without submitting them to the approbation or licence of any other particular person. Notwithstanding which the Master of the Revels demanded his fee of forty shillings upon our acting a new one, though we had spared him the trouble of perusing it. This occasioned my being deputed to him to enquire into the right of his demand, and to make an amicable end of our dispute. I confess I did not dislike the office, and told him, according to my instructions, that I came not to defend even our own right, in prejudice to his, that if our patent had inadvertently superseded the grant of any former power or warrant whereon he might ground his pretensions, we would not insist upon our broad seal, but would readily answer his demands upon sight of such his warrant, anything in our patent to the contrary notwithstanding. This I had reason to think he could not do; and when I found he made no direct reply to my question, I repeated it with greater civilities and offers of compliance till I was forced in the end to conclude with telling him that as his pretensions were not backed with any visible instrument of right, and as his strongest plea was custom, we could not so far extend our complaisance as to continue his fees upon so slender a claim to them: and from that time, neither our plays or his fees gave either of us any farther trouble. In this negotiation I am the bolder to think justice was on our side, because the law lately passed, by which the power of licencing plays etc. is given to a proper person, is a strong presumption that no law had ever given that power to any such person before....

[1740]

LADY MARY WORTLEY MONTAGU

Lady Mary Wortley Montagu is remembered today for three things: her place as a learned lady, her controversy with Pope, and her letters.

Although facilities for the education of women were almost entirely lacking in England during the first half of the eighteenth century, educated women were more numerous than is often supposed. Mrs. Eliza Haywood, Mrs. Mary Manley, Mrs. Susanna Centlivre, Mary Astell, Hester Van Homrigh (Swift's Vanessa), Lady Winchilsea, are but a few of those who won contemporary fame. Prominent in this group was the beautiful and accomplished daughter of Evelyn Pierrepont (later Duke of Kingston), who married Edward Wortley Montagu and travelled with him to Constantinople, where he was British ambassador to the Porte in 1717 and 1718. Here she learned the method of inoculating against the smallpox, then a scourge of all classes in western Europe, and after her return to England, she did much to encourage its practice. Since she belonged to the Whig aristocracy, and since she was witty and talented, she occupied a prominent place in society. Lady Mary was at once a learned lady and a brilliant hostess who, in happier conditions, might have become the centre of an influential literary group.

While English women of letters thus had some importance in her generation, they left much less impress upon the age than did contemporary French women. In France, from the time of Louis XIV to the Revolution, feminine influence found expression in the *salon*, where great ladies brought together the social and literary worlds, imparting cultivation to the one and grace to the other. It was not until the latter part of the eighteenth century that the *salon* became important in England. During the early part of the century, England was distinctly masculine: the coffee-house remained its characteristic meeting-place and set the tone of its conversation and its writing.

In the rough give-and-take of early Georgian literary controversy Lady Mary held her place among the men. Without hesitation she could pen a coarse ballad or indulge in personal lampoon. It was her misfortune, however, to be pitted against the most dangerous personal and literary opponent of the century; as a consequence she is remembered by the "Sappho" passages in Pope's satires, the author of which has frequently been condemned for what have been taken for unprovoked attacks upon a helpless woman. The two were at first friends and admirers, and Pope paid her personal addresses that she seems not to have discouraged. After a time, however, they quarrelled, whether, as gossip reported, because she laughed in his face at a declaration from so puny a man, or because of other and more obscure reasons, it is now impossible to say. Whatever the origin of the quarrel, it is evident that Pope used with incomparably greater effectiveness the weapons that the lady was equally willing to use against him.

The only part of Lady Mary's writings that is now read is her letters. These have a shrewdness and a sparkle that distinguish them in an age which produced some of the best letters in English literary history. Though they are seldom so malicious as Horace Walpole's, like his they view the contemporary scene through disillusioned and slightly cynical eyes. They deal brilliantly with the materials of conversation; their ideas are stimulating but seldom profound; their matter ranges from vivid description to frothy gossip. Like all good letter writers she is always herself even while she adapts subject and form to suit her correspondents. Her letters extend over a period of more than fifty years, from 1709, when she was but nineteen, through her travels in the East, her residence in England, and her long self-imposed exile in Italy apart from her husband, until shortly before her death in 1762.

LETTERS

To Mr. Pope

Adrianople, April 1, O.S. [1717.]

I dare say you expect at least something very new in this letter, after I have gone *a journey not undertaken by any Christian for some hundred years. The most remarkable accident that happened to me was my being very near overturned into the Hebrus; and, if I had much regard for the glories that one's name enjoys after death, I should certainly be sorry for having missed the romantic conclusion of swimming down the same river in which the musical head of Orpheus repeated verses so many ages since:

**Caput a cervice revulsum,*
Gurgite cum medio portans Œagrius Hebrus
Volveret, Eurydicen vox ipsa, et frigida lingua,
Ah! miserum Eurydicen! anima fugiente vocabat,
Eurydicen toto referebant flumine ripæ.
[Virg., *Georg.* IV, 523–27.]

* Notes on Lady Mary Wortley Montagu will be found in the Appendix, pp. 977 ff.

Who knows but some of your bright wits might have found it a subject affording many poetical turns, and have told the world, in an heroic elegy, that,

*As equal were our souls, so equal were our fates?

I despair of ever having so many fine things said of me as so extraordinary a death would have given occasion for.

I am at this present writing in a house situated on the banks of the Hebrus, which runs under my chamber window. My garden is full of tall cypress trees, upon the branches of which several couple of true turtles are saying soft things to one another from morning till night. How naturally do boughs and vows come into my head at this minute! And must not you confess, to my praise, that 'tis more than ordinary discretion that can resist the wicked suggestions of poetry, in a place where truth, for once, furnishes all the ideas of pastoral? The summer is already far advanced in this part of the world; and, for some miles round Adrianople, the whole ground is laid out in gardens, and the banks of the river set with rows of fruit trees, under which all the most considerable Turks divert themselves every evening — not with walking, that is not one of their pleasures; but a set party of them choose out a green spot where the shade is very thick, and there they spread a carpet, on which they sit drinking their coffee, and generally attended by some slave with a fine voice, or that plays on some instrument. Every twenty paces you may see one of these little companies listening to the dashing of the river; and this taste is so universal that the very gardeners are not without it. I have often seen them and their children sitting on the banks, and playing on a rural instrument, perfectly answering the description of the ancient *fistula*, being composed of unequal reeds, with a simple but agreeable softness in the sound.

Mr. Addison might here make the experiment he speaks of in his travels, there not being one instrument of music among the Greek or Roman statues that is not to be found in the hands of the people of this country. The young lads generally divert themselves with making garlands for their favourite lambs, which I have often seen painted and adorned with flowers, lying at their feet while they sung or played. It is not that they ever read romances, but these are the ancient amusements here, and as natural to them as cudgel-playing and football to our British swains; the softness and warmth of the climate forbidding all rough exercises, which were never so much as heard of amongst them, and naturally inspiring a laziness and aversion to labour, which the great plenty indulges. These gardeners are the only happy race of country people in Turkey. They furnish all the city with fruit and herbs, and seem to live very easily. They are most of them Greeks, and have little houses in the midst of their gardens, where their wives and daughters take a liberty not permitted in the town, I mean, to go unveiled. These wenches are very neat and handsome, and pass their time at their looms under the shade of their trees.

I no longer look upon Theocritus as a romantic writer; he has only given a plain image of the way of life amongst the peasants of his country, who, before oppression had reduced them to want, were, I suppose, all employed as the better sort of them are now. I don't doubt, had he been born a Briton, his *Idylliums* had been filled with descriptions of threshing and churning, both which are unknown here, the corn being all trod out by oxen, and butter (I speak it with sorrow) unheard of.

*I read over your Homer here with an infinite pleasure, and find several little passages explained, that I did not before entirely comprehend the beauty of, many of the customs, and much of the dress then in fashion, being yet retained; and I don't wonder to find more remains here of an age so distant than is to be found in any other country, the Turks not taking that pains to introduce their own manners as has been generally practised by other nations that imagine themselves more polite. It would be too tedious to you to point out all the passages that relate to present customs. But I can assure you that the princesses and great ladies pass their time at their looms, embroidering veils and robes, surrounded by their maids, which are always very numerous, in the same manner as we find Andromache and Helen described. The description of the belt of Menelaus exactly resembles those that are now worn by the great men, fastened before with broad golden clasps, and embroidered round with rich work. The snowy veil that Helen throws over her face is still fashionable; and I never see (as I do very often) half a dozen of old pashas with their reverend beards, sitting basking in the sun, but I recollect good King Priam and his counsellors. Their manner of dancing is certainly the same that Diana is sung to have danced on the banks of the Eurotas. The great lady still leads the dance, and is followed by a troop of young girls, who imitate her steps, and, if she sings, make up the chorus. The tunes are extremely gay and lively, yet with something in them wonderfully soft. The steps are varied according to the pleasure of her that leads the dance, but always in exact time, and infinitely more agreeable than any of our dances, at least in my opinion. I sometimes make one in the train, but am not skillful enough to lead; these are Grecian dances, the Turkish being very different.

I should have told you, in the first place, that the Eastern manners give a great light into many Scripture passages that appear odd to us, their phrases being commonly what we should call Scripture language. The vulgar Turk is very different from what is spoken at court, or amongst the people of figure, who always mix so much Arabic or Persian in their discourse that it may very well be called another language. And 'tis as ridiculous to make use of the expressions commonly used, in speaking to a great man or a lady, as it would be to talk broad Yorkshire or Somersetshire in the drawing-room. Besides this distinction, they have what they call the *sublime*, that is, a style proper for poetry, and which is the exact Scripture style. I believe you would be pleased to see a genuine example of this; and I am very glad I have it in my power to satisfy your curiosity, by sending you a faithful copy of the verses that Ibrahim Pasha, the reigning favourite, has made for the young princess, his contracted wife, whom he is not yet permitted to visit without witnesses, though she is gone home to his house. He is a man of wit and learning; and whether or no he is capable of writing good verse himself, you may be sure, that, on such an occasion, he would not want the assistance of the best poets in the empire. Thus the verses may be looked upon as a sample of their finest poetry; and I don't doubt you'll be of my mind, that it is most wonderfully resembling *The Song of Solomon*, which was also addressed to a royal bride.

TURKISH VERSES *addressed to the* SULTANA, *eldest daughter of Sultan* ACHMET III.

STANZA I.

1. The nightingale now wanders in the vines;
 Her passion is to seek roses.

2. I went down to admire the beauty of the vines;
 The sweetness of your charms has ravish'd my soul.

3. Your eyes are black and lovely,
 But wild and disdainful as those of a stag.

STANZA II.

1. The wish'd possession is delay'd from day to day;
 The cruel Sultan Achmet will not permit me
 To see those cheeks more vermilion than roses.

2. I dare not snatch one of your kisses;
 The sweetness of your charms has ravish'd my soul.

3. Your eyes are black and lovely,
 But wild and disdainful as those of a stag.

STANZA III.

1. The wretched Pasha Ibrahim sighs in these verses;
 One dart from your eyes has pierc'd thro' my heart.

2. Ah! when will the hour of possession arrive?
 Must I yet wait a long time?
 The sweetness of your charms has ravish'd my soul.

3. Ah! Sultana! stag-ey'd — an angel amongst angels!
 I desire, — and my desire remains unsatisfied.
 Can you take delight to prey upon my heart?

STANZA IV.

1. My cries pierce the heavens!
 My eyes are without sleep!
 Turn to me, Sultana — let me gaze on thy beauty.

2. Adieu! I go down to the grave.
 If you call me, I return.
 My heart is hot as sulphur; sigh, and it will flame.

3. Crown of my life! fair light of my eyes!
 My Sultana! my princess!
 I rub my face against the earth; — I am drown'd in scalding tears — I rave!
 Have you no compassion? Will you not turn to look upon me?

I have taken abundance of pains to get these verses in a literal translation; and if you were acquainted with my interpreters, I might spare myself the trouble of assuring you that they have received no poetical touches from their hands. In my opinion (allowing for the inevitable faults of a prose translation into a language so very different) there is a good deal of beauty in them. The epithet of *stag-ey'd* (though the sound is not very agreeable in English) pleases me extremely; and is, I think, a very lively image of the fire and indifference in his mistress's eyes. Monsieur Boileau has very justly observed, we are never to judge of the elevation of an expression in an ancient author by the sound it carries with us; which may be extremely fine with them, at the same time it looks low or uncouth to us. You are so well acquainted with Homer, you cannot but have observed the same thing, and you must have the same indulgence for all Oriental poetry.

The repetitions at the end of the two first stanzas are meant for a sort of chorus, and agreeable to the ancient manner of writing; the music of the verses apparently changes in the third stanza, where the burden is altered; and I think he very artfully seems more passionate at the conclusion, as 'tis natural for people to warm themselves by their own discourse, especially on a subject where the heart is concerned, and is far more touching than our modern custom of concluding a song of passion with a turn which is inconsistent with it. The first verse is a description of the season of the year; all the country being now full of nightingales, whose amours with roses is an Arabian fable, as well known here as any part of Ovid amongst us, and is much the same thing as if an English poem should begin by saying — "Now Philomela sings." Or what if I turned the whole into the style of English poetry, to see how it would look?

STANZA I.

Now Philomel renews her tender strain,
Indulging all the night her pleasing pain;

I sought the groves to hear the wanton sing,
There saw a face more beauteous than the spring.

Your large stag-eyes, where thousand glories play,
As bright, as lively, but as wild as they.

STANZA II.

In vain I'm promised such a heav'nly prize;
Ah! cruel Sultan! who delays my joys!

While piercing charms transfix my am'rous heart,
I dare not snatch one kiss to ease the smart,

Those eyes! like, etc.

STANZA III.

Your wretched lover in these lines complains;
From those dear beauties rise his killing pains.

When will the hour of wish'd-for bliss arrive?
Must I wait longer? Can I wait and live?

Ah! bright Sultana! maid divinely fair!
Can you, unpitying, see the pain I bear?

STANZA IV.

The heavens, relenting, hear my piercing cries,
I loathe the light, and sleep forsakes my eyes;
Turn thee, Sultana, ere thy lover dies:

Sinking to earth I sigh the last adieu;
Call me, my goddess, and my life renew.

My queen! my angel! my fond heart's desire!
I rave — my bosom burns with heav'nly fire!
Pity that passion which thy charms inspire.

I have taken the liberty, in the second verse, of following what I suppose is the true sense of the author, though not literally expressed. By his saying he went down to admire the beauty of the vines, and her charms ravished his soul, I understand by this a poetical fiction, of having first seen her in a garden, where he was admiring the beauty of the spring. But I could not forbear retaining the comparison of her eyes to those of a stag, though, perhaps, the novelty of it may give it a burlesque sound in our language. I cannot determine upon the whole how well I have succeeded in the translation, neither do I think our English proper to express such violence of passion, which is very seldom felt amongst us, and we want those compound words which are very frequent and strong in the Turkish language.

You see I am pretty far gone in Oriental learning; and, to say truth, I study very hard. I wish my studies may give me an occasion of entertaining your curiosity, which will be the utmost advantage hoped for from it by, etc.

*To *the Countess of Mar*

PERA OF CONSTANTINOPLE,
March 10, O.S. [1718.]

I have not written to you, dear sister, these many months: — a great piece of self-denial. But I know not where to direct, or what part of the world you were in. I have received no letter from you since that short note of April last, in which you tell me that you are on the point of leaving England, and promise me a direction for the place you stay in; but I have in vain expected it till now: and now I only learn from the gazette that you are returned, which induces me to venture this letter to your house at London. I had rather ten of my letters should be lost than you imagine I don't write; and I think it is hard fortune if one in ten don't reach you. However, I am resolved to keep the copies, as testimonies of my inclination to give you, to the utmost of my power, all the diverting part of my travels, while you are exempt from all the fatigues and inconveniences.

In the first place, I wish you joy of your niece; for I was brought to bed of a daughter five weeks ago. I don't mention this as one of my diverting adventures; though I must own that it is not half so mortifying here as in England, there being as much difference as there is between a little cold in the head, which sometimes happens here, and the consumptive coughs, so common in London. Nobody keeps their house a month for lying in; and I am not so fond of any of our customs to retain them when they are not necessary. I returned my visits at three weeks' end; and about four days ago crossed the sea, which divides this place from Constantinople, to make a new one, where I had the good fortune to pick up many curiosities.

I went to see the Sultana Hafitên, favourite of the late Emperor Mustapha, who, you know (or perhaps you don't know) was deposed by his brother, the reigning Sultan Achmet, and died a few weeks after, being poisoned, as it was generally believed. This lady was, immediately after his death, saluted with an absolute order to leave the seraglio, and choose herself a husband from the great men at the Porte. I suppose you may imagine her overjoyed at this proposal. Quite contrary: these women, who are called, and esteem themselves, queens, look upon this liberty as the greatest disgrace and affront that can happen to them. She threw herself at the Sultan's feet, and begged him to poignard her, rather than use his brother's widow with that contempt. She represented to him, in agonies of sorrow, that she was privileged from this misfortune, by having brought five princes into the Ottoman family, but all the boys being dead, and only one girl surviving, this excuse was not received, and she [was] compelled to make her choice. She chose Bekir Effendi, then secretary of state, and above fourscore years old, to convince the world that she firmly intended to keep the vow she had made, of never suffering a second husband to approach her bed; and since she must honour some subject so far as to be called his wife, she would choose him as a mark of her gratitude, since it was he that had presented her at the age of ten years old, to her last lord. But she has never permitted him to pay her one visit; though it is now fifteen years she has been in his house, where she passes her time in uninterrupted mourning, with a constancy very little known in Christendom, especially in a widow of twenty-one, for she is now but thirty-six. She has no black eunuchs for her guard, her husband being obliged to respect her as a queen, and not inquire at all into what is done in her apartment, where I was led into a large room, with a sofa the whole length of it, adorned with white marble pillars like a **ruelle*, covered with pale blue figured velvet on a silver ground, with cushions of the same, where I was desired to repose till the Sultana appeared, who had contrived this manner of reception to avoid rising up at my entrance, though she made me an inclination of her head, when I rose up to her. I was very glad to observe a lady that had been distinguished by the favour of an emperor, to whom beauties were every day presented from all parts of the world. But she did not seem to me to have ever been half so beautiful as the fair Fatima I saw at Adrianople; though she had the remains of a fine face, more decayed by sorrow than time. But her dress was something so surprisingly rich, I cannot forbear describing it to you. She wore a vest called *donalma*, and which differs from a *caftán* by longer sleeves, and folding over at the bottom. It was of purple cloth, straight to her shape, and thick set, on each side, down to her feet, and round the sleeves, with pearls of the best water, of the same size as their buttons commonly are. You must not suppose I mean as large as those of my Lord ——, but about the bigness of a pea; and to these buttons large loops of diamonds, in the form of those gold loops so common upon birthday coats. This habit was tied, at the waist, with two large tassels of smaller pearl, and round the arms embroidered with large diamonds: her shift fastened at the bottom with a great diamond, shaped like a lozenge; her girdle as broad as the broadest English ribbon, entirely covered with diamonds. Round her neck she wore three chains, which reached to her knees: one of large pearl, at the bottom of which hung a fine coloured emerald, as big as a turkey-egg; another, consisting of two hundred emeralds, close joined together, of the most lively green, perfectly matched, every one as large as a half-crown piece, and as thick as three crown pieces; and another of small emeralds, perfectly round. But her earrings eclipsed all the rest. They were two diamonds, shaped exactly like pears, as large as a big hazel nut. Round her *talpoche* she had four strings of pearl, the whitest and most perfect in the world, at least enough to make four necklaces, every one as large as the Duchess of Marlborough's, and of the same size, fastened with two roses, consisting of a large ruby for the middle stone, and round them twenty drops of clean diamonds to each. Besides this, hei headdress was covered with bodkins of emeralds and diamonds. She wore large diamond bracelets, and had five rings on her fingers, all single diamonds, (except Mr. Pitt's) the largest I ever saw in my life. It is for jewellers to compute the value of these things; but, according to the common estimation of jewels in our part of the world, her whole dress must be worth above a hundred thousand pounds sterling. This I am very sure of, that no European queen has half the quantity; and the empress's jewels, though very fine, would look very mean near hers.

She gave me a dinner of fifty dishes of meat, which (after their fashion) were placed on the table but one at a time, and was extremely tedious. But the magnificence of her table answered very well to that of her dress. The knives were of gold, the hafts set with diamonds. But the piece of luxury that grieved my eyes was the tablecloth and napkins, which were all tiffany, embroidered with silks and gold, in the finest manner, in natural flowers. It was with the utmost regret that I made use of these costly napkins, as finely wrought as the finest handkerchiefs that ever came out of this country. You may be sure that they were entirely spoiled before dinner was over. The sherbet (which is the liquor they drink at meals) was served in china bowls; but the covers and salvers massy gold. After dinner, water was brought in a gold basin, and towels of the same kind of the napkins, which I very unwillingly wiped my hands upon; and coffee was served in china, with gold *_soucoupes_.

The Sultana seemed in very good humour, and talked to me with the utmost civility. I did not omit this opportunity of learning all that I possibly could of the seraglio, which is so entirely unknown among us. She assured me that the story of the Sultan's throwing a handkerchief is altogether fabulous; and the manner upon that occasion, no other but that he sends the *kyslár agá*, to signify to the lady the honour he intends her. She is immediately complimented upon it by the others, and led to the bath, where she is perfumed and dressed in the most magnificent and becoming manner. The Emperor precedes his visit by a royal present, and then comes into her apartment; neither is there any such thing as her creeping in at the bed's foot. She said that the first he made choice of was always after the first in rank, and not the mother of the eldest son, as other writers would make us believe. Sometimes the Sultan diverts himself in the company of all his ladies, who stand in a circle round him. And she confessed that they were ready to die with jealousy and envy of the happy she that he distinguished by any appearance of preference. But this seemed to me neither better nor worse than the circles in most courts, where the glance of the monarch is watched, and every smile waited for with impatience, and envied by those who cannot obtain it.

She never mentioned the Sultan without tears in her eyes, yet she seemed very fond of the discourse. "My past happiness," said she, "appears a dream to me. Yet I cannot forget that I was beloved by the greatest and most lovely of mankind. I was chosen from all the rest, to make all his campaigns with him; I would not survive him if I was not passionately fond of the princess my daughter. Yet all my tenderness for her was hardly enough to make me preserve my life. When I lost him, I passed a whole twelvemonth without seeing the light. Time has softened my despair; yet I now pass some days every week in tears, devoted to the memory of my Sultan."

There was no affectation in these words. It was easy to see she was in a deep melancholy, though her good humour made her willing to divert me.

She asked me to walk in her garden, and one of her slaves immediately brought her a *pellice* of rich brocade lined with sables. I waited on her into the garden, which had nothing in it remarkable but the fountains; and from thence she showed me all her apartments. In her bedchamber her toilet was displayed, consisting of two looking-glasses, the frames covered with pearls, and her night *talpoche* set with bodkins of jewels, and near it three vests of fine sables, every one of which is, at least, worth a thousand dollars (two hundred pounds English money). I don't doubt these rich habits were purposely placed in sight, but they seemed negligently thrown on the sofa. When I took my leave of her, I was complimented with perfumes, as at the grand vizier's, and presented with a very fine embroidered handkerchief. Her slaves were to the number of thirty, besides ten little ones, the eldest not above seven years old. These were the most beautiful girls I ever saw, all richly dressed; and I observed that the Sultana took a great deal of pleasure in these lovely children, which is a vast expense; for there is not a handsome girl of that age to be bought under a hundred pounds sterling. They wore little garlands of flowers, and their own hair, braided, which was all their head-dress; but their habits all of gold stuffs. These served her coffee, kneeling; brought water when she washed, etc. It is a great part of the business of the older slaves to take care of these girls, to learn them to embroider, and serve them as carefully as if they were children of the family.

Now, do I fancy that you imagine I have entertained you, all this while, with a relation that has, at least, received many embellishments from my hand? This is but too like (say you) the Arabian Tales: these embroidered napkins! and a jewel as large as a turkey's egg! — You forget, dear sister, those very tales were written by an author of this country, and (excepting the enchantments) are a real representation of the manners here. We travellers are in very hard circumstances: If we say nothing but what has been said before us, we are dull, and we have observed nothing. If we tell anything new, we are laughed at as fabulous and romantic, not allowing for the difference of ranks, which afford difference of company, more curiosity, or the change of customs, that happen every twenty years in every country. But people judge of travellers exactly with the same candour, good nature, and impartiality they judge of their neighbours upon all occasions. For my part, if I live to return amongst you, I am so well acquainted with the morals of all my dear friends and acquaintance that I am resolved to tell them nothing at all, to avoid the imputation (which their charity would certainly incline them to) of my telling too much. But I depend upon your knowing me enough to believe whatever I seriously assert for truth, though I give you leave to be surprised at an account so new to you.

But what would you say if I told you that I have been in a harem where the winter apartment was wainscoted with inlaid work of mother-of-pearl, ivory of different colours, and olive wood, exactly like the little boxes you have seen brought out of this country; and those rooms designed for summer, the walls all crusted with japan china, the roofs gilt, and the floors spread with the finest Persian carpets? Yet there is nothing more true; such is the palace of my lovely friend, the fair Fatima, whom I was acquainted with at Adrianople. I went to visit her yesterday; and, if possible, she appeared to me handsomer than before. She met me at the door of her chamber, and, giving me her hand with the best grace in the world, — "You Christian ladies," said she, with a smile that made her as handsome as an angel, "have the reputation of inconstancy, and I did not expect, whatever goodness you expressed for me at Adrianople, that I should ever see you again. But I am now convinced that I have really the happiness of pleasing you; and if you knew how I speak of you amongst our ladies, you would be assured that you do me justice if you think me your friend." She placed me in the corner of the sofa, and I spent the afternoon in her conversation, with the greatest pleasure in the world.

The Sultana Hafitén is, what one would naturally expect to find a Turkish lady, willing to oblige, but not knowing how to go about it; and it is easy to see in her manner that she has lived secluded from the world. But Fatima has all the politeness and good breeding of a court, with an air that inspires at once respect and tenderness; and now I understand her language, I find her wit as engaging as her beauty. She is very curious after the manners of other countries, and has not that partiality for her own, so common to little minds. A Greek that I carried with me, who had never seen her before, (nor could have been admitted now, if she had not been in my train,) showed that surprise at her beauty and manner which is unavoidable at the first sight, and said to me in Italian, "This is no Turkish lady, she is certainly some Christian." Fatima guessed she spoke of her, and asked what she said. I would not have told, thinking she would have been no better pleased with the compliment than one of our court beauties to be told she had the air of a Turk; but the Greek lady told it her; and she smiled, saying, "It is not the first time I have heard so: my mother was a * Poloneze, taken at the siege of Caminiec; and my father used to rally me, saying he believed his Christian wife had found some Christian gallant; for I had not the air of a Turkish girl." I assured her that, if all the Turkish ladies were like her, it was absolutely necessary to confine them from public view, for the repose of mankind; and proceeded to tell her what a noise such a face as hers would make in London or Paris. "I can't believe you," replied she, agreeably. "If beauty was so much valued in your country as you say, they would never have suffered you to leave it." Perhaps, dear sister, you laugh at my vanity in repeating this compliment; but I only do it as I think it very well turned, and give it you as an instance of the spirit of her conversation.

Her house was magnificently furnished, and very well fancied; her winter rooms being furnished with figured velvet on gold grounds, and those for summer with fine Indian quilting embroidered with gold. The houses of the great Turkish ladies are kept clean with as much nicety as those in Holland. This was situated in a high part of the town; and from the windows of her summer apartment we had the prospect of the sea, the islands, and the Asian mountains.

My letter is insensibly grown so long, I am ashamed of it. This is a very bad symptom. 'Tis well if I don't degenerate into a downright story-teller. It may be our proverb, that knowledge is no burden, may be true as to one's self, but knowing too much is very apt to make us troublesome to other people.

*To * the Countess of Pomfret*

1738 O.S. [*March,* 1739]

I am so well acquainted with the lady you mention that I am not surprised at any proof of her want of judgment; she is one of those who has passed upon the world vivacity in the place of understanding; for me, who think with Boileau,

> * *Rien n'est beau que le vrai, le vrai seul est aimable,*

I have always thought those geniuses much inferior to the plain sense of a cookmaid, who can make a good pudding and keep the kitchen in good order.

Here is no news to be sent you from this place, which has been for this fortnight and still continues overwhelmed with politics, and which are of so mysterious a nature, one ought to have some of * the gifts of Lilly or Partridge to be able to write about them; and I leave all those dissertations to those distinguished mortals who are endowed with the talent of divination; though I am at present the only one of my sex who seems to be of that opinion, the ladies having shown their zeal and appetite for knowledge in a most glorious manner. At the last warm debate in the House of Lords, it was unanimously resolved there should be no crowd of unnecessary auditors; consequently the fair sex were excluded, and the gallery destined to the sole use of the House of Commons. Notwithstanding which determination, a tribe of dames resolved to show on this occasion that neither men nor laws could resist them. These heroines were Lady Huntingdon, the Duchess of Queensberry, the Duchess of Ancaster, Lady Westmoreland, Lady Cobham, Lady Charlotte Edwin, Lady Archibald Hamilton and her daughter, Mrs. Scott, and Mrs. Pendarves, and Lady Frances Saunderson. I am thus particular in their names, since I look upon them to be the boldest assertors, and most resigned sufferers for liberty, I ever read of. They presented themselves at the door at nine o'clock in the morning, where Sir William Saunderson respectfully informed them the chancellor had made an order against their admittance. The Duchess of Queensberry, as head of the squadron, pished at the ill-breeding of a mere lawyer, and desired him to let them upstairs privately. After some modest refusals, he swore by G— he would not let them in. Her Grace, with a noble warmth, answered, by G— they would come in, in spite of the chancellor and the whole House. This being reported, the Peers resolved to starve them out; an order was made that the doors should not be opened till they had raised their siege. These Amazons now showed themselves qualified for the duty even of foot soldiers; they stood there till five in the afternoon, without either sustenance or evacuation, every now and then playing volleys of thumps, kicks, and raps against the door, with so much violence that the speakers in the House were scarce heard. When the

Lords were not to be conquered by this, the two duchesses (very well apprised of the use of stratagems in war) commanded a dead silence of half an hour; and the chancellor, who thought this a certain proof of their absence (the Commons also being very impatient to enter), gave order for the opening of the door; upon which they all rushed in, pushed aside their competitors, and placed themselves in the front rows of the gallery. They stayed there till after eleven, when the House rose; and during the debate gave applause, and showed marks of dislike, not only by smiles and winks (which have always been allowed in these cases), but by noisy laughs and apparent contempts, which is supposed the true reason why poor Lord Hervey spoke miserably. I beg your pardon, dear madam, for this long relation; but 'tis impossible to be short on so copious a subject; and you must own this action very well worthy of record, and I think not to be paralleled in history, ancient or modern. I look so little in my own eyes (who was at that time ingloriously sitting over a tea-table) I hardly dare subscribe myself even,

Yours.

*To *the Countess of Bute*

Jan. 28, N.S. [1753]

DEAR CHILD,

You have given me a great deal of satisfaction by your account of your eldest daughter. I am particularly pleased to hear she is a good arithmetician; it is the best proof of understanding; the knowledge of numbers is one of the chief distinctions between us and the brutes. If there is anything in blood, you may reasonably expect your children should be endowed with an uncommon share of good sense. Mr. Wortley's family and mine have both produced some of the greatest men that have been born in England: I mean Admiral Sandwich, and my grandfather, who was distinguished by the name of Wise William. I have heard Lord Bute's father mentioned as an extraordinary genius, though he had not many opportunities of showing it; and his uncle, the present Duke of Argyll, has one of the best heads I ever knew. I will therefore speak to you as supposing Lady Mary not only capable, but desirous of learning: in that case by all means let her be indulged in it. You will tell me I did not make it a part of your education: your prospect was very different from hers. As you had no defect either in mind or person to hinder, and much in your circumstances to attract, the highest offers, it seemed your business to learn how to live in the world, as it is hers to know how to be easy out of it. It is the common error of builders and parents to follow some plan they think beautiful (and perhaps is so), without considering that nothing is beautiful that is displaced. Hence we see so many edifices raised that the raisers can never inhabit, being too large for their fortunes. Vistas are laid open over barren heaths, and apartments contrived for a coolness very agreeable in Italy, but killing in the north of Britain: thus every woman endeavours to breed her daughter a fine lady, qualifying her for a station in which she will never appear, and at the same time incapacitating her for that retirement to which she is destined. Learning, if she has a real taste for it, will not only make her contented, but happy in it. No entertainment is so cheap as reading, nor any pleasure so lasting. She will not want new fashions, nor regret the loss of expensive diversions, or variety of company, if she can be amused with an author in her closet. To render this amusement extensive, she should be permitted to learn the languages. I have heard it lamented that boys lose so many years in mere learning of words; this is no objection to a girl, whose time is not so precious: she cannot advance herself in any profession, and has therefore more hours to spare; and as you say her memory is good, she will be very agreeably employed this way. There are two cautions to be given on this subject: first, not to think herself learned when she can read Latin, or even Greek. Languages are more properly to be called vehicles of learning than learning itself, as may be observed in many schoolmasters, who, though perhaps critics in grammar, are the most ignorant fellows upon earth. True knowledge consists in knowing things, not words. I would wish her no further a linguist than to enable her to read books in their originals, that are often corrupted, and always injured, by translations. Two hours' application every morning will bring this about much sooner than you can imagine, and she will have leisure enough besides to run over the English poetry, which is a more important part of a woman's education than it is generally supposed. Many a young damsel has been ruined by a fine copy of verses, which she would have laughed at if she had known it had been stolen from Mr. Waller. I remember, when I was a girl, I saved one of my companions from destruction, who communicated to me an epistle she was quite charmed with. As she had a natural good taste, she observed the lines were not so smooth as Prior's or Pope's, but had more thought and spirit than any of theirs. She was wonderfully delighted with such a demonstration of her lover's sense and passion, and not a little pleased with her own charms, that had force enough to inspire such elegancies. In the midst of this triumph I showed her that they were taken from *Randolph's poems, and the unfortunate transcriber was dismissed with the scorn he deserved. To say truth, the poor plagiary was very unlucky to fall into my hands; that author, being no longer in fashion, would have escaped any one of less universal reading than myself. You should encourage your daughter to talk over with you what she reads; and, as you are very capable of distinguishing, take care she does not mistake pert folly for wit and humour, or rhyme for poetry, which are the common errors of young people, and have a train of ill consequences. The second caution to be given her (and which is most absolutely necessary) is to conceal whatever learning she attains, with as much solicitude as she would hide crookedness or lameness; the parade of it can only serve to draw on her the envy, and consequently the most inveterate hatred, of all he and she fools, which will certainly be at least three parts in four of all her acquaintance. The use of knowledge in our sex, besides the amusement of solitude, is to moderate the passions, and learn to be contented with a small expense, which are the certain effects of a studious life; and it may be preferable even to that fame which men have engrossed to themselves, and will not suffer us to share. You will tell me I have not observed this rule myself; but you are mistaken: it is only inevitable accident that has given me any reputation that way. I have always carefully avoided it, and ever thought it a misfortune. The explanation of this paragraph would occasion a long digression, which I will not trouble you with, it being my present design only to say what I think useful for the instruction of my granddaughter, which I have much at heart. If she has the same inclination (I should say passion) for learning that I was born with, history, geography, and philosophy will furnish her with materials to pass away cheerfully a longer life than is allotted to mortals. I believe there are few heads capable of making Sir I. Newton's calculations, but the result of them is not difficult to be understood by a moderate capacity. Do not fear this should make her affect the character of *Lady ——, or Lady ——, or Mrs. ——: those women are ridiculous, not because they have learning, but because they have it not. One thinks herself a complete historian, after reading Echard's *Roman History*; another a profound philosopher, having got by heart some of *Pope's unintelligible essays; and a third an able divine, on the strength of Whitefield's sermons: thus you hear them screaming politics and controversy.

It is a saying of Thucydides, ignorance is bold, and knowledge reserved. Indeed, it is impossible to be far advanced in it without being more humbled by a conviction of human ignorance, than elated by learning. At the same time I recommend books, I neither exclude work nor drawing. I think it as scandalous for a woman not to know how to use a needle, as for a man not to know how to use a sword. I was once extreme fond of my pencil, and it was a great mortification to me when my father turned off my master, having made a considerable progress for a short time I learnt. My over-eagerness in the pursuit of it had brought a weakness on my eyes, that made it necessary to leave it off; and all the advantage I got was the improvement of my hand. I see, by hers, that practice will make her a ready writer: she may attain it by serving you for a secretary, when your health or affairs make it troublesome to you to write yourself; and custom will make it an agreeable amusement to her. She cannot have too many for that station of life which will probably be her fate. The ultimate end of your education was to make you a good wife (and I have the comfort to hear that you are one): hers ought to be, to make her happy in a virgin state. I will not say it is happier; but it is undoubtedly safer than any marriage. In a lottery, where there are (at the lowest computation) ten thousand blanks to a prize, it is the most prudent choice not to venture. I have always been so thoroughly persuaded of this truth, that, notwithstanding the flattering views I had for you (as I never intended you a sacrifice to my vanity),

I thought I owed you the justice to lay before you all the hazards attending matrimony; you may recollect I did so in the strongest manner. Perhaps you may have more success in the instructing your daughter: she has so much company at home, she will not need seeking it abroad, and will more readily take the notions you think fit to give her. As you were alone in my family, it would have been thought a great cruelty to suffer you no companions of your own age, especially having so many near relations, and I do not wonder their opinions influenced yours. I was not sorry to see you not determined on a single life, knowing it was not your father's intention, and contented myself with endeavouring to make your home so easy that you might not be in haste to leave it.

I am afraid you will think this a very long and insignificant letter. I hope the kindness of the design will excuse it, being willing to give you every proof in my power that I am

Your most affectionate mother.

[1763 and 1837]

MATTHEW PRIOR

THE son of a Nonconformist carpenter of Dorsetshire, Matthew Prior was born in London in 1664. After his father's early death he was taken from school and worked for a time in his uncle's wine-shop. There, when the boy was ten years of age, the Earl of Dorset one day found him reading Horace, and was so much taken by his skill at impromptu and verse translation that he became his patron and sent him back to school. At Westminster School Prior formed a lasting friendship with Charles Montagu, later to become Earl of Halifax and a powerful politician. With him he went to Cambridge University, where he finally won a fellowship which he retained throughout his life. In 1687 appeared the travesty upon Dryden's *The Hind and the Panther* called *The City Mouse and the Country Mouse*, a joint production of Prior and Montagu in which the former seems to have furnished most of the wit and for which the second appears to have taken, at first, most of the credit. The Whigs rewarded Prior for his attack upon Dryden by making him Secretary to the Embassy at the Hague. He seems to have won the friendship of King William and to have acted to some extent as his secretary. During the reign of Anne he was often engaged in diplomatic services, particularly in France, and his influence in shaping the Peace of Utrecht was such that it was popularly known as "Matt's Peace." When the Whigs, whom he had deserted early in his public career, regained power after the death of Anne, he was imprisoned for two years, writing his long humorous poem *Alma, or the Progress of the Mind*, while in custody. This poem, published in 1718 together with his very serious and ambitious *Solomon*, brought him four thousand pounds and a present of an equal sum from Harley. Thus enabled to live in comfort without further activity, he retired to his newly purchased estate, Down Hall, in Essex. Two years later, in 1721, he died and was buried under a monument of his own provision in Westminster Abbey.

Prior's successful combination of the literary life with business, politics, and diplomacy reminds one of Geoffrey Chaucer; and many of his traits, such as his equanimity, his smiling but underisive comprehension of human frailties, his laughter of the mind, and an inward serenity which was based upon moderate expectations, still more vividly recall the Father of English verse. An even stronger likeness, however, is soon discovered between him and the poet he was reading when the Earl of Dorset found him at his uncle's shop. The spirit and mood of Horace, diffused throughout the first half of the eighteenth century, was personified in this worldly place-hunter who knew so exactly the little worth of the preferments he sought. Loose in conduct and occasionally obscene in verse, epicurean both for good and ill, self-centred and self-serving, yet universally liked — capable without effort, as one of his many hostesses, the Duchess of Portland, said, of making himself "beloved by every living thing in the house" — never profound in thought or deeply sincere in feeling, yet seldom quite trivial, Prior is the English Horace.

Before Pope was born, Prior had set for himself the French and Horatian ideal of "correctness," in pursuit of which he was to be as successful, though in different fields, as Pope himself. Even Dr. Johnson, who does not like him, admits that "his diligence has justly placed him amongst the most correct of English poets; and he was one of the first that resolutely endeavoured at correctness." This is a quality that makes for success in the versified epigram, in which Prior has few English rivals. His thought is often shallow and his verse shows more glitter than depth, but this does not prevent him from excelling in *vers de société*. There is a certain literary effect, narrowly restricted and perhaps hardly poetical at all, in which Prior's gayety, his play of mind, and his wit devoid of malice, give him an easy supremacy. The fact that he is utterly unsentimental need not hide the charming tenderness of his famous lines, *To a Child of Quality*, or of his letter to "little Peggy." What he lacked was intensity, passion, a sense of life's mystery, and the power of rising occasionally above himself; but this was the general lack of his time and the very "defect of its qualities." Once only did he attain even for a moment the effect of magic which is now regarded as pre-eminently poetical — in the few stanzas quoted below from his long jesting poem, *Down Hall*.

TO A LADY

SHE REFUSING TO CONTINUE A DISPUTE WITH ME, AND LEAVING ME IN THE ARGUMENT

Spare, generous victor, spare the slave,
  Who did unequal war pursue,
That more than triumph he might have,
  In being overcome by you.

In the dispute whate'er I said,
  My heart was by my tongue belied;
And in my looks you might have read
  How much I argued on your side.

You, far from danger as from fear,
  Might have sustained an open fight;
For seldom your opinions err;
  Your eyes are always in the right.

Why, fair one, would you not rely
  On reason's force with beauty's joined?
Could I their prevalence deny,
  I must at once be deaf and blind.

Alas! not hoping to subdue,
  I only to the fight aspired;
To keep the beauteous foe in view
  Was all the glory I desired.

But she, howe'er of victory sure,
  Contemns the wreath too long delayed;
And, armed with more immediate power,
  Calls cruel silence to her aid.

Deeper to wound, she shuns the fight;
  She drops her arms, to gain the field;
Secures her conquest by her flight;
  And triumphs when she seems to yield.

So when the Parthian turned his steed
  And from the hostile camp withdrew,
With cruel skill the backward *reed
  He sent, and as he fled he slew.

[1704]

TO A CHILD OF QUALITY

FIVE YEARS OLD, MDCCIV, THE AUTHOR THEN FORTY

Lords, knights, and squires, the numerous band
  That wear the fair Miss Mary's fetters,
Were summoned by her high command,
  To show their passions by their letters.

My pen among the rest I took,
  Lest those bright eyes that cannot read
Should dart their kindling fires, and look
  The power they have to be obeyed.

Nor quality nor reputation
  Forbid me yet my flame to tell;
Dear five years old befriends my passion,
  And I may write till she can spell.

For while she makes her silkworms beds
  With all the tender things I swear,
Whilst all the house my passion reads
  In papers round her baby hair,

She may receive and own my flame,
  For, though the strictest prudes should know it,
She'll pass for a most virtuous dame,
  And I for an unhappy poet.

Then too, alas! when she shall tear
  The lines some younger rival sends,
She'll give me leave to write, I fear,
  And we shall still continue friends.

For, as our different ages move,
  'Tis so ordained, (would Fate but mend it!)
That I shall be past making love,
  When she begins to comprehend it.

[1704]

A BETTER ANSWER

(TO CLOE JEALOUS)

Dear Cloe, how blubbered is that pretty face,
  Thy cheek all on fire, and thy hair all uncurled!
Prithee quit this caprice; and (as old Falstaff says)
  Let us e'en talk a little like folks of this world.

How canst thou presume thou hast leave to destroy
  The beauties which Venus but lent to thy keeping?
Those looks were designed to inspire love and joy;
  More ord'nary eyes may serve people for weeping.

To be vexed at a trifle or two that I writ,
  Your judgment, at once, and my passion you wrong;
You take that for fact which will scarce be found wit.
  Od's life! must one swear to the truth of a song?

What I speak, my fair Cloe, and what I write shows
  The difference there is betwixt nature and art;
I court others in verse, but I love thee in prose;
  And they have my whimsies, but thou hast my heart!

The god of us verse-men (you know, child), the sun,
  How after his journeys he sets up his rest;
If at morning o'er earth 'tis his fancy to run,
  At night he reclines on his *Thetis's breast.

* Notes on Matthew Prior will be found in the Appendix, pp. 978 ff.

So when I am wearied with wand'ring all day,
To thee, my delight, in the evening I come;
No matter what beauties I saw in my way,
They were but my visits, but thou art my home.

Then finish, dear Cloe, this pastoral war,
And let us like Horace and Lydia agree;
For thou art a girl as much brighter than her,
As he was a poet sublimer than me.

[1718]

AN EPITAPH

Interred beneath this marble stone
Lie sauntering Jack and idle Joan.
While rolling threescore years and one
Did round this globe their courses run,
If human things went ill or well,
If changing empires rose or fell,
The morning past, the evening came,
And found this couple still the same.
They walked and eat, good folks, what then?
Why then they walked and eat again!
They soundly slept the night away;
They just did nothing all the day;
And having buried children four,
Would not take pains to try for more;
Nor sister either had, nor brother;
They seemed just tallied for each other.
Their moral and economy
Most perfectly they made agree;
Each virtue kept its proper bound,
Nor trespassed on the other's ground:
Nor fame nor censure they regarded;
They neither punished nor rewarded.
He cared not what the footmen did;
Her maids she neither praised nor chid;
So every servant took his course,
And, bad at first, they all grew worse.
Slothful disorder filled his stable
And sluttish plenty decked her table.
Their beer was strong, their wine was port,
Their meal was large, their grace was short.
They gave the poor the remnant meat
Just when it grew not fit to eat.
They paid the church and parish rate,
And took, but read not, the receipt,
For which they claimed their Sunday's due
Of slumbering in an upper pew.
No man's defects sought they to know,
So never made themselves a foe;
No man's good deeds did they commend,
So never raised themselves a friend;
Nor cherished they relations poor
That might decrease their present store;
Nor barn nor house did they repair
That might oblige their future heir.
They neither added nor confounded;
They neither wanted nor abounded.
Each Christmas they accounts did clear,
And wound their *bottom round the year.
Nor tear nor smile did they employ
At news of public grief, or joy.
When bells were rung, and bonfires made,
If asked, they ne'er denied their aid;
Their jug was to the *ringers carried,
Whoever either died or married;
Their billet at the fire was found,
Whoever was deposed, or crowned.
Nor good, nor bad, nor fools, nor wise,
They would not learn, nor could advise;
Without love, hatred, joy, or fear,
They led — a kind of — as it were;
Nor wished, nor cared, nor laughed, nor cried;
And so they lived, and so they died.

[1718]

A LETTER

TO THE HONOURABLE LADY MISS MARGARET CAVENDISH HOLLES HARLEY, WHEN A CHILD

My noble, lovely little Peggy,
Let this, my first epistle, beg ye,
At dawn of morn and close of even,
To lift your heart and hands to heaven.
In double duty say your prayer —
Our Father first, then *Notre Père*.
And, dearest child, along the day,
In everything you do and say,
Obey and please my lord and lady,
So God shall love and angels aid ye.

If to these precepts you attend,
No second letter need I send.
And so I rest your constant friend.

[1740]

JINNY THE JUST

Releas'd from the noise of the butcher and baker
Who, my old friends be thanked, did seldom forsake her,
And from the soft duns of my landlord the Quaker,

From chiding the footmen and watching the lasses,
From Nell that burn'd milk, and Tom that broke glasses
(Sad mischiefs through which a good housekeeper passes!)

From some real care but more fancied vexation,
From a life parti-coloured, half reason, half passion,
Here lies, after all, the best wench in the nation.

From the Rhine to the Po, from the Thames to the Rhone,
Joanna or Janneton, Jinny or Joan,
'Twas all one to her by what name she was known.

For the idiom of words very little she heeded,
Provided the matter she drove at succeeded,
She took and gave languages just as she needed.

So for kitchen and market, for bargain and sale,
She paid English or Dutch or French down on the nail,
But in telling a story she sometimes did fail;

Then begging excuse as she happen'd to stammer,
With respect to her betters but none to her grammar,
Her blush help'd her out and her jargon became her.

Her habit and mien she endeavour'd to frame
To the different *gout* of the place where she came;
Her outside still chang'd, but her inside the same:

At the Hague in her slippers and hair as the mode is,
At Paris all falbalow'd fine as a goddess,
And at censuring London in smock sleeves and bodice.

She order'd affairs that few people could tell
In what part about her that mixture did dwell
Of Vrough, or Mistress, or Mademoiselle.

For her surname and race let the heralds e'en answer;
Her own proper worth was enough to advance her,
And he who lik'd her, little valu'd her grandsire.

But from what house so ever her lineage may come
I wish my own Jinny but out of her tomb,
Though all her relations were there in her room.

Of such terrible beauty she never could boast
As with absolute sway o'er all hearts rules the roast
When J— bawls out to the chair for a toast,

But of good household features her person was made,
Nor by faction cry'd up nor of censure afraid,
And her beauty was rather for use than parade.

Her blood so well mix'd and flesh so well pasted
That though her youth faded her comeliness lasted;
The blue was wore off, but the plum was well tasted.

Less smooth than her skin and less white than her breast
Was this polish'd stone beneath which she lies press'd:
Stop, reader, and sigh while thou think'st on the rest.

With a just trim of virtue her soul was endu'd,
Not affectedly pious nor secretly lewd,
She cut even between the coquette and the prude.

Her will with her duty so equally stood
That, seldom oppos'd, she was commonly good,
And did pretty well, doing just what she would.

Declining all power, she found means to persuade,
Was then most regarded when most she obey'd,
The mistress in truth when she seem'd but the maid.

Such care of her own proper actions she took
That on other folks' lives she had no time to look,
So censure and praise were struck out of her book.

Her thought still confin'd to her own little sphere,
She minded not who did excel or did err
But just as the matter related to her.

Then too when her private tribunal was rear'd,
Her mercy so mix'd with her judgment appear'd
That her foes were condemn'd and her friends always clear'd.

Her religion so well with her learning did suit
That, in practice sincere and in controverse mute,
She show'd she knew better to live than dispute.

Some parts of the Bible by heart she recited,
And much in historical chapters delighted,
But in points about faith she was something shortsighted;

So notions and modes she referr'd to the schools,
And in matters of conscience adher'd to the rules:
To advise with no bigots, and jest with no fools.

And scrupling but little, enough she believ'd,
By charity ample small sins she retriev'd,
And when she had new clothes, she always receiv'd.

Thus still whilst her morning unseen fled away
In ord'ring the linen and making the tea
That she scarce could have time for the Psalm of the Day;

And while after dinner the night came so soon
That half she propos'd very seldom was done;
With twenty "God bless me's how this day is gone!"

While she read and accounted and paid and abated,
Eat and drank, play'd and work'd, laugh'd and cry'd, lov'd and hated,
As answer'd the end of her being created;

In the midst of her age came a cruel disease
Which neither her juleps nor receipts could appease;
So down dropp'd her clay. May her soul be at peace!

Retire from this sepulchre all the profane;
You that love for debauch, or that marry for gain.
Retire least ye trouble the *manes* of J—

But thou that know'st love above interest or lust,
Strew the myrtle and rose on this once belov'd dust,
And shed one pious tear upon Jinny the Just.

Tread soft on her grave, and do right to her honour;
Let neither rude hand nor ill tongue light upon her;
Do all the small favours that now can be done her.

And when what thou lik'st shall return to her clay,
(For so I'm persuaded she must do one day
What ever fantastic J— Asgil may say,)

When as I have done now, thou shalt set up a stone
For something however distinguish'd or known,
May some pious friend the misfortune bemoan,
And make thy concern by reflection his own.

[1907]

From DOWN HALL

"Come here, my sweet landlady. Pray, how d' ye do?
Where is Cicely so cleanly, and Prudence, and Sue?
And where is the widow that dwelt here below,
And the ostler that sung about eight years ago?

"And where is your sister, so mild and so dear,
Whose voice to her maids like a trumpet was clear?"
"By my troth!" she replies, "you grow younger, I think.
And pray, sir, what wine does the gentleman drink?

"Why now, let me die, sir, or live upon trust,
If I know to which question to answer you first.
Why, things, since I saw you, most strangely have varied.
The ostler is hanged and the widow is married.

"And Prue left a child for the parish to nurse,
And Cicely went off with a gentleman's purse,
And as to my sister so mild and so dear,
She has lain in the churchyard full many a year."

[1723]

FOR MY OWN MONUMENT

As doctors give physic by way of prevention,
Mat, alive, and in health, of his tombstone took care;
For delays are unsafe, and his pious intention
May haply be never fulfilled by his heir.

Then take Mat's word for it, the sculptor is paid;
That the figure is fine, pray believe your own eye;
Yet credit but lightly what more may be said,
For we flatter ourselves, and teach marble to lie.

Yet, counting as far as to fifty his years,
His virtues and vices were as other men's are;
High hopes he conceived, and he smothered great fears,
In life parti-coloured, half pleasure, half care.
Nor to business a drudge, nor to faction a slave,
He strove to make interest and freedom agree;
In public employments industrious and grave,
And alone with his friends, lord, how merry was he!
Now in equipage stately, now humbly on foot,
Both fortunes he tried but to neither would trust;
And whirled in the round, as the wheel turned about,
He found riches had wings and knew man was but dust.

This verse little polished, though mighty sincere,
Sets neither his titles nor merit to view;
It says that his relics collected lie here,
And no mortal yet knows too if this may be true.

Fierce robbers there are that infest the highway,
So Mat may be killed and his bones never found;
False witness at court and fierce tempests at sea,
So Mat may yet chance to be hanged, or be drowned.

If his bones lie on earth, roll in sea, fly in air,
To fate we must yield, and the thing is the same;
And if passing thou giv'st him a smile or a tear,
He cares not — yet prithee be kind to his fame.

[1740]

THOMAS PARNELL

Thomas Parnell, born in Dublin in 1679, came of an English family long established in Cheshire which emigrated to Ireland after the Restoration, and in the nineteenth century produced the Irish patriot, Charles Stewart Parnell. He entered Trinity College, Dublin, at the age of thirteen, and gained sufficient classical scholarship so that he was able in later years to give Pope material assistance in the translation of Homer. After taking his master's degree in 1700 he entered the church, married, and began the uneasy life, made familiar by his friend and protector, Dean Swift, of the witty and ambitious Anglican clergyman whose work lay in Ireland but whose heart was in London. His considerable private fortune seems merely to have confirmed his indolence and discontent. At first a strong Whig, he became intimate with the circle of Addison and Steele, but when the Tories came into power in 1710 he transferred allegiance and was much courted by the new party leaders and their literary henchmen. Swift, Pope, Gay, and Bolingbroke did all they could, though vainly, to get him the fashionable London pulpit he longed for. Parnell's life was made unhappy and his work was disintegrated by his contempt for the country in which his duty lay. After the death of his wife and his two sons he did not much care to live, and he died at the age of thirty-eight, indifferent and a good deal given to drink, while on the way from London back to Ireland.

Parnell's work, both in prose and verse, shows an easy competence in all the miscellaneous forms and themes he undertook, but memorable excellence almost nowhere. As Dr. Johnson says, "In his verses there is more happiness than pains," and "It is impossible to say whether they are the productions of nature so excellent as not to want the help of art, or of art so refined as to resemble nature." The tradition of the gentleman, who is supposed to do all things easily but nothing with the finished perfection of an expert, is obvious in his whole career. More clearly than any of his associates, unless perhaps the versatile Bolingbroke, he exemplifies "*l'honnête homme qui ne se pique de rien.*" Parnell lacked the power of concentration and never made up his mind. He wrote songs, elegies, verse-epistles, allegories, social satire, eclogues, humorous verse and epigrams, a translation of the *Pervigilium Veneris*, even a fairy tale in what he considered "the ancient English style." His *Night Piece on Death* is clearly one of the almost innumerable sources of Gray's *Elegy*, and his *Hymn to Contentment*, half clerical and half Horatian, is a sensible contribution to the controversy about retirement that went on endlessly throughout the century. His chief contemporary success, due to a shallow and highly dubious moralizing with which no one of his time found fault, was made with *The Hermit*, the story of which came down to him through James Howell's *Familiar Letters* from the *Gesta Romanorum* and a dim Oriental source. One of the most memorable of Parnell's performances is a poem which has not been at all remembered, his letter *To Mr. Pope*. Here, for all the suffocating incense, it is not difficult to see complete sincerity, with something of the master's own precision of epithet and brilliance of metaphor. The possibility is not to be ignored, however, that this is one of the several poems by Parnell that Pope retouched.

TO MR. POPE

To praise, yet still with due respect to praise,
A bard triumphant in immortal bays,
The learn'd to show, the sensible to commend,
Yet still preserve the province of the friend —
What life, what vigour, must the lines require,
What music tune them, what affection fire!
  Oh! might thy genius in my bosom shine,
Thou shouldst not fail of numbers worthy thine;
The brightest ancients might at once agree
To sing within my lays, and sing of thee.
  Horace himself would own thou dost excel
In candid arts, to play the critic well.
  Ovid himself might wish to sing the dame
Whom Windsor Forest sees a gliding stream;
On silver feet, with annual osier crown'd,
She runs forever through poetic ground.
  How flame the glories of Belinda's hair,
Made by thy Muse the envy of the fair!
Less shone the tresses * Egypt's princess wore,
Which sweet Callimachus so sung before;
Here courtly trifles set the world at odds,
Belles war with beaux, and whims descend * for gods;
The * new machines in names of ridicule,
Mock the grave frenzy of the * chymic fool.
But know, ye fair, a point conceal'd with art,
The sylphs and gnomes are but a woman's heart;

* Notes on Thomas Parnell will be found in the Appendix, pp. 979 ff.

The Graces stand in sight; a * satyr train
Peep o'er their heads, and laugh behind the scene.
In Fame's fair temple, o'er the boldest wits
Enshrined on high, the sacred Virgil sits,
And sits in measures, such as Virgil's Muse
To place thee near him might be fond to choose.
How might he tune th' alternate reed with thee,
Perhaps a Strephon thou, a Daphnis he,
While some old Damon, o'er the vulgar wise,
Thinks he deserves, and thou deserv'st the prize!
Rapt with the thought, my fancy seeks the plains,
And turns me shepherd while I hear the strains.
Indulgent nurse of every tender gale,
Parent of flowerets, old Arcadia, hail!
Here in the cool my limbs at ease I spread,
Here let thy poplars whisper o'er my head,
Still slide thy waters soft among the trees,
Thy aspens quiver in a breathing breeze,
Smile all thy valleys in eternal spring,
Be hush'd, ye winds! while Pope and Virgil sing.
In English lays, and all sublimely great,
Thy Homer warms with all his ancient heat;
He shines in council, thunders in the fight,
And flames with every sense of great delight.
Long has that poet reign'd, and long unknown,
Like monarchs sparkling on a distant throne,
In all the majesty of Greek retired,
Himself unknown, his mighty name admired;
His language, failing, wrapp'd him round with night;
Thine, raised by thee, recalls the work to light.
So wealthy mines, that ages long before
Fed the large realms around with golden ore,
When choked by sinking banks, no more appear,
And shepherds only say, "The mines were here":
Should some rich youth (if nature warm his heart,
And all his projects stand inform'd with art)
Here clear the caves, there ope the leading vein;
The mines, detected, flame with gold again.
How vast, how copious are thy new designs!
How every music varies in thy lines!
Still as I read, I feel my bosom beat,
And rise in raptures by another's heat.
Thus in the wood, when summer dress'd the days,
When Windsor lent us tuneful hours of ease,
Our ears the lark, the thrush, the turtle bless'd,
And Philomela sweetest o'er the rest:
The shades resound with song — oh, softly tread!
While a whole season warbles round my head
This to my friend — and when a friend inspires,
My silent harp its master's hand requires,
Shakes off the dust, and makes these rocks resound;
For fortune placed me in * unfertile ground,
Far from the joys that with my soul agree,
From wit, from learning — far, oh far from thee!
Here moss-grown trees expand the smallest leaf,
Here half an acre's corn is half a sheaf;
Here hills with naked heads the tempest meet,
Rocks at their side, and torrents at their feet,
Or lazy lakes, unconscious of a flood,
Whose dull brown naiads ever sleep in mud.
Yet here content can dwell, and learned ease,
A friend delight me, and an author please;
Even here I sing, while Pope supplies the theme, —
Show my own love, though not increase his fame.

[1721]

A HYMN TO CONTENTMENT

"Lovely, lasting peace of mind,
Sweet delight of humankind,
Heavenly born and bred on high,
To crown the favourites of the sky
With more of happiness below
Than victors in a triumph know,
Whither, oh whither art thou fled,
To lay thy meek, contented head?
What happy region dost thou please
To make the seat of calms and ease?
"Ambition searches all its sphere
Of pomp and state, to meet thee there.
Increasing avarice would find
Thy presence in its gold enshrined.
The bold advent'rer ploughs his way
Through rocks amidst the foaming sea,
To gain thy love, and then perceives

Thou wert not in the rocks and waves.
The silent heart which grief assails
Treads soft and lonesome o'er the vales,
Sees daisies open, rivers run,
And seeks, as I have vainly done,
Amusing thought, but learns to know
That solitude's the nurse of woe.
No real happiness is found
In *trailing purple o'er the ground;
Or in a soul exalted high
To range the circuit of the sky,
Converse with stars above, and know
All nature in its forms below;
The rest it seeks, in seeking dies,
And doubts at last, for knowledge, rise.
"Lovely, lasting peace, appear!
This world itself, if thou art here,
Is once again with Eden blest,
And man contains it in his breast."
'Twas thus, as under shade I stood,
I sung my wishes to the wood,
And, lost in thought, no more perceived
The branches whisper as they waved;
It seemed as all the quiet place
Confessed the presence of the *Grace;
When thus she spoke: "Go rule thy will;
Bid thy wild passions all be still;
Know God, and bring thy heart to know
The joys which from religion flow:
Then every Grace shall prove its guest,
And I'll be there to crown the rest."
Oh, by yonder mossy seat,
In my hours of sweet retreat,
Might I thus my soul employ
With sense of gratitude and joy,
Raised, as ancient prophets were,
In heavenly vision, praise, and prayer,
Pleasing all men, hurting none,
Pleased and bless'd with God alone!
Then, while the gardens take my sight
With all the colours of delight,
While silver waters glide along
To please my ear and court my song,
I'll lift my voice, and tune my string,
And thee, great Source of Nature, sing.
The sun, that walks his airy way
To light the world and give the day;
The moon, that shines with borrowed light;
The stars, that gild the gloomy night;
The seas, that roll unnumbered waves;
The wood, that spreads its shady leaves;
The field, whose ears conceal the grain,
The yellow treasure of the plain;
All of these, and all I see,
Should be sung, and sung by me.
They *speak their Maker as they can,
But want and ask the tongue of man.
Go search among your idle dreams,
Your busy or your vain extremes,
And find a life of equal bliss,
Or own the next begun in this.

[1714]

A NIGHT-PIECE ON DEATH

By the blue taper's trembling light,
No more I waste the wakeful night,
Intent with endless view to pore
The schoolmen and the sages o'er.
Their books from wisdom widely stray,
Or point at best the longest way;
I'll seek a readier path, and go
Where wisdom's surely taught below.
How deep yon azure dyes the sky,
Where orbs of gold unnumbered lie,
While through their ranks in silver pride
The nether crescent seems to glide!
The slumb'ring breeze forgets to breathe;
The lake is smooth and clear beneath,
Where once again the spangled show
Descends to meet our eyes below.
The grounds which on the right aspire
In dimness from the view retire;
The left presents a place of graves,
Whose wall the silent water laves;
That steeple guides thy doubtful sight
Among the livid gleams of night.
There pass, with melancholy state,
By all the solemn heaps of fate,
And think, as softly-sad you tread
Above the venerable dead,
"Time was, like thee they life possessed,
And time shall be that thou shalt rest."
Those graves, with bending *osier bound,
That nameless heave the crumbled ground,
Quick to the glancing thought disclose
Where Toil and Poverty repose.
The flat, smooth stones that bear a name,
The chisel's slender help to fame
(Which ere our set of friends decay
Their frequent steps may wear away),
A middle race of mortals own,
Men half ambitious, all unknown.
The marble tombs that rise on high,
Whose dead in vaulted arches lie,
Whose pillars swell with sculptured stones —
Arms, angels, epitaphs, and bones, —
These, all the poor remains of state,
Adorn the rich or praise the great,
Who, while on earth in fame they live,

Are senseless of the fame they give.
Ha! while I gaze, pale Cynthia fades;
The bursting earth unveils the shades!
All slow, and wan, and wrapped with shrouds,
They rise in *visionary crowds,
And all with sober accent cry,
"Think, mortal, what it is to die!"
Now from yon black and funeral yew,
That bathes the charnel house with dew,
Methinks I hear a voice begin
(Ye ravens, cease your croaking din!
Ye tolling clocks, no time resound
O'er the long lake and midnight ground!);
It sends a peal of hollow groans,
Thus speaking from among the bones:
"When men my scythe and darts supply,
How great a King of Fears am I!
They view me like the last of things;
They make, and then they dread, my stings.
Fools! if you less provoked your fears,
No more my spectre-form appears.
Death's but a path that must be trod,
If man would ever pass to God;
A port of calms, a state of ease
From the rough rage of swelling seas."
Why, then, thy flowing sable *stoles,
Deep pendant *cypress, *mourning poles,
Loose scarfs to fall athwart thy *weeds,
Long palls, drawn hearses, covered steeds,
And plumes of black, that, as they tread,
Nod o'er the *'scutcheons of the dead?
Nor can the parted body know,
Nor wants the soul, these forms of woe.
As men who long in prison dwell,
With lamps that glimmer round the cell,
Whene'er their suffering years are run,
Spring forth to greet the glittering sun,
Such joy, though far transcending sense,
Have pious souls at parting hence;
On earth, and in the body placed,
A few and evil years they waste,
But, when their chains are cast aside,
See the glad scene unfolding wide,
Clap the glad wing, and tow'r away,
And mingle with the blaze of day.

[1721]

THE HERMIT

Far in a wild, unknown to public view,
From youth to age a reverend hermit grew;
The moss his bed, the cave his humble cell,
His food the fruits, his drink the crystal well.
Remote from man, with God he passed the days,
Prayer all his business, all his pleasure praise.
A life so sacred, such serene repose,
Seemed heaven itself till one suggestion rose:
That vice should triumph, virtue vice obey.
This *sprung some doubt of Providence's sway;
His hopes no more a certain prospect boast,
And all the tenour of his soul is lost.
So when a smooth expanse receives imprest
Calm nature's image on its watery breast,
Down bend the banks, the trees depending grow,
And skies beneath with answering colours glow;
But if a stone the gentle scene divide,
Swift ruffling circles curl on every side,
And glimmering fragments of a broken sun,
Banks, trees, and skies, in thick disorder run.
To clear this doubt, to know the world by sight,
To find if books or swains report it right
(For yet by swains alone the world he knew,
Whose feet came wandering o'er the nightly dew),
He quits his cell: the pilgrim-staff he bore,
And fixed the *scallop in his hat before;
Then, with the sun arising, journey went,
Sedate to think and watching each event.
The morn was wasted in the pathless grass,
And long and lonesome was the wild to pass;
But when the southern sun had warmed the day,
A youth came posting o'er a crossing way —
His raiment decent, his complexion fair,
And soft in graceful ringlets waved his hair.
Then, near approaching, "Father, hail!" he cried;
"And hail, my son!" the reverend sire replied.
Words followed words, from question answer flowed,
And talk of various kind *deceived the road;
Till, each with other pleased and loath to part,
While in their age they differ, join in heart:
Thus stands an aged elm, in ivy bound;
Thus youthful ivy clasps an elm around.
Now sunk the sun; the closing hour of day
Came onward, mantled o'er with sober gray;
Nature in silence bid the world repose;
When near the road a stately palace rose.
There by the moon through ranks of trees they pass,
Whose verdure crowned their sloping sides of grass.
It chanced the noble master of the dome

Still made his house the wandering stranger's home;
Yet still the kindness, from a thirst of praise,
Proved the vain *flourish of expensive ease.
The pair arrive; the liveried servants wait;
Their lord receives them at the pompous gate;
The table groans with costly piles of food,
And all is more than hospitably good;
Then, led to rest, the day's long toil they drown,
Deep sunk in sleep and silk and heaps of down.
At length 'tis morn, and at the dawn of day
Along the wide canals the zephyrs play;
Fresh o'er the gay parterres the breezes creep,
And shake the neighbouring wood to banish sleep.
Up rise the guests, obedient to the call;
An early banquet decked the splendid hall;
Rich luscious wine a golden goblet graced,
Which the kind master forced the guests to taste;
Then, pleased and thankful, from the porch they go,
And but the landlord none had cause of woe—
His cup was vanished, for in secret guise
The younger guest purloined the glittering prize.
As one who spies a serpent in his way,
Glistening and basking in the summer ray,
Disordered stops to shun the danger near,
Then walks with faintness on and looks with fear;
So seemed the sire, when, far upon the road,
The shining spoil his wily partner showed.
He stopped with silence, walked with trembling heart,
And much he wished, but durst not ask, to part;
Murmuring he lifts his eyes, and thinks it hard
That generous actions meet a base reward.
While thus they pass, the sun his glory shrouds;
The changing skies hang out their sable clouds;
A sound in air presaged approaching rain,
And beasts to covert scud across the plain.
Warned by the signs, the wandering pair retreat
To seek for shelter at a neighbouring seat.
'Twas built with turrets, on a rising ground,
And strong, and large, and unimproved around;
Its owner's temper, timorous and severe,
Unkind and griping, caused a desert there.
As near the miser's heavy doors they drew,
Fierce rising gusts with sudden fury blew;
The nimble lightning, mixed with showers, began,
And o'er their heads loud-rolling thunders ran.
Here long they knock, but knock or call in vain,
Driven by the wind and battered by the rain.
At length some pity warmed the master's breast
('Twas then his threshold first received a guest);
Slow creaking, turns the door with jealous care,
And half he welcomes in the shivering pair.
One frugal faggot lights the naked walls, 101
And nature's fervour through their limbs recalls;
Bread of the coarsest sort, with *eager wine,
Each hardly granted, served them both to dine;
And when the tempest first appeared to cease,
A ready warning bid them part in peace.
With still remark the pondering hermit viewed
In one so rich a life so poor and rude;
"And why should such," within himself he cried,
"Lock the lost wealth a thousand want beside?"
But what new marks of wonder soon took place
In every settling feature of his face,
When from his vest the young companion bore
That cup the generous landlord owned before,
And paid profusely, with the precious bowl,
The stinted kindness of this churlish soul!
But now the clouds in airy tumult fly;
The sun, emerging, opes an azure sky;
A fresher green the smelling leaves display,
And, glittering as they tremble, cheer the day.
The weather courts them from the poor retreat,
And the glad master bolts the wary gate.
While hence they walk, the pilgrim's bosom wrought
With all the travail of uncertain thought:
His partner's acts without their cause appear;
'Twas there a vice, and seemed a madness here;
Detesting that, and pitying this, he goes,

Lost and confounded with the various shows.
  Now night's dim shades again involve the sky;
Again the wanderers want a place to lie;
Again they search, and find a lodging nigh:
The soil improved around, the mansion neat,
And neither poorly low nor idly great;
It seemed to speak its master's turn of mind —
Content, and not for praise, but virtue, kind.
  Hither the walkers turn with weary feet,
Then bless the mansion and the master greet.
Their greeting, fair bestowed, with modest guise
The courteous master hears, and thus replies:
  "Without a vain, without a grudging heart,
To him who gives us all I yield a part;
From him you come, for him accept it here,
A frank and sober more than costly cheer."
He spoke, and bid the welcome table spread,
Then talked of virtue till the time of bed,
When the grave household round his hall repair,
Warned by a bell, and close the hours with prayer.
  At length the world, renewed by calm repose,
Was strong for toil; the dappled morn arose.
Before the pilgrims part, the younger crept
Near the closed cradle where an infant slept,
And *writhed his neck; the landlord's little pride
(Oh, strange return!) grew black and gasped and died!
Horror of horrors! what! his only son!
How looked our hermit when the fact was done?
Not hell, though hell's black jaws in sunder part
And breathe blue fire, could more assault his heart.
  Confused, and struck with silence at the deed,
He flies, but, trembling, fails to fly with speed;
His steps the youth pursues. The country lay
*Perplexed with roads; a servant showed the way.
A river crossed the path; the passage o'er
Was *nice to find; the servant trod before;
Long arms of oaks an open bridge supplied,
And deep the waves beneath the bending glide.
The youth, who seemed to watch a time to sin,
Approached the careless guide, and thrust him in;
Plunging he falls, and, rising, lifts his head,
Then flashing turns and sinks among the dead.
  Wild, sparkling rage inflames the father's eyes;
He bursts the bands of fear, and madly cries,
"Detested wretch!" — but scarce his speech began,
When the strange partner seemed no longer man:
His youthful face grew more serenely sweet;
His robe turned white, and flowed upon his feet;
Fair rounds of radiant points invest his hair;
Celestial odours breathe through purpled air;
And wings, whose colours glittered on the day,
Wide at his back their *gradual plumes display.
The form ethereal bursts upon his sight,
And moves in all the majesty of light.
  Though loud at first the pilgrim's passion grew,
Sudden he gazed, and *wist not what to do:
Surprise in secret chains his words suspends,
And in a calm his settling temper ends.
But silence here the beauteous angel broke;
The voice of music ravished as he spoke:
  "Thy prayer, thy praise, thy life to vice unknown,
In sweet memorial rise before the throne.
These charms success in our bright region find,
And force an angel down to calm thy mind;
For this commissioned, I forsook the sky —
Nay, cease to kneel! thy fellow-servant I.
  "Then know the truth of government divine,
And let these scruples be no longer thine.
  "The Maker justly claims that world he made;
In this the right of Providence is laid;
Its sacred majesty through all depends
On using *second means to work his ends.
'Tis thus, withdrawn in state from human eye,
The Power exerts his attributes on high,
Your actions uses, not controls your will,
And bids the doubting sons of men be still.
  "What strange events can strike with more surprise
Than those which lately struck thy wondering eyes?
Yet, taught by these, confess th' Almighty just,
And where you can't unriddle, learn to trust!

"The great, vain man, who fared on costly food,
Whose life was too luxurious to be good,
Who made his ivory stands with goblets shine,
And forced his guests to morning draughts of wine,
Has, with the cup, the graceless custom lost,
And still he welcomes but with less of cost.
"The mean, suspicious wretch, whose bolted door
Ne'er moved in duty to the wandering poor,
With him I left the cup, to teach his mind
That Heaven can bless if mortals will be kind.
Conscious of wanting worth, he views the bowl,
And feels compassion touch his grateful soul.
Thus *artists melt the sullen ore of lead
With heaping *coals of fire upon its head;
In the kind warmth the metal learns to glow,
And, loose from dross, the silver runs below.
"Long had our pious friend in virtue trod,
But now the child half weaned his heart from God;
Child of his age, for him he lived in pain,
And measured back his steps to earth again.
To what excesses had his dotage run!
But God, to save the father, took the son.
To all but thee in fits he seemed to *go,
And 'twas my ministry to deal the blow.
The poor, fond parent, humbled in the dust,
Now owns in tears the punishment was just.
"But how had all his fortune felt a wrack
Had that false servant sped in safety back!
This night his treasured heaps he meant to steal,
And what a fund of charity would fail!
"Thus Heav'n instructs thy mind; this trial o'er,
Depart in peace, resign, and sin no more!"
On sounding pinions here the youth withdrew;
The sage stood wondering as the seraph flew:
Thus looked Elisha, when, to mount on high,
His master took the chariot of the sky;
The fiery pomp, ascending, left the view;
The prophet gazed, and wished to follow too.
The bending hermit here a prayer begun:
"Lord, as in heaven, on earth thy will be done!"
Then, gladly turning, sought his ancient place,
And passed a life of piety and peace.

[1721]

JOHN GAY

Born in the west of England in 1685, John Gay arrived in London, after a good grammar school education in his native town, as apprentice to a silk mercer. His talent for making influential friends was brought early into play. In 1713 he attracted the attention and regard of Pope by dedicating to him a poem, in two cantos of workmanlike couplets, called *Rural Sports*. Pope was at this time smarting under the praise recently won by the pastoral poems of Ambrose Philips, a praise that seemed to threaten his own pre-eminence as "the English Theocritus," and he suggested that Gay might use his knowledge of English country life to ridicule the work of Philips and destroy its vogue. The six pastorals called *The Shepherd's Week*, which appeared in 1714, were the result. Two years later he published *Trivia, or the Art of Walking the Streets of London*, in which he owed something to hints from Dean Swift. The publication of his collected poems in 1720 brought him a thousand pounds, all of which he lost at once in the South Sea Bubble. For several years he lived upon sinecures in the gift of the government and at the homes of his wealthy patrons. His *Fifty-One Fables in Verse* was composed in 1727 for Prince William, then five years old. In the following year appeared *The Beggar's Opera*, Gay's chief success, enthusiastically received in London and in the country and echoing even through the court. This play of criminal life, really a satire upon society and politics, made Gay for a time one of the most famous men in England. Sir Robert Walpole, who was caricatured in it, forbade the performance of its sequel, *Polly*, which sold so well in book form, however, that Gay was in easy circumstances during the last few years of his life. He died in 1732 and was buried in Westminster Abbey under the famous epitaph from his own pen:

Life is a jest, and all things show it;
I thought so once, and now I know it.

There is far more revelation of Gay's essential nature in this distich than in the elaborate epitaph Pope wrote for his friend:

Of manners gentle, of affections mild,
In wit a man, simplicity a child;
With native humour temp'ring virtuous rage,
Form'd to delight at once and lash the age;
Above temptation in a low estate,
And uncorrupted ev'n among the great;
A safe companion and an easy friend,
Unblamed through life, lamented in thy end....

This is rather Pope's notion of what a poet should be than an accurate picture of what his flattering and always useful friend actually was. The fact is that Gay was a good deal corrupted, or at least weakened and demoralized, by the patronage upon which he felt obliged to depend, that he was quite incapable of "rage" of any sort, and that he could not swing the "lash" even when he was egged on to do so, instructed, and assisted by his sterner associates. "Cheerfulness was always breaking through" and dissipating his best satiric intentions. In each of his four chief productions he tried to reach and maintain the fashionable tone of ridicule, but was defeated by his natural zest and his delight in the outward shows of things.

Both as man and writer Gay won the affection of all who knew him, but not always their respect. His helplessness in practical affairs coupled with charming good humour made many eager to help him, and upon these he soon learned to depend. Even *The Beggar's Opera*, suggested by Swift, was overseen during the composition by Arbuthnot and Pope. Gay wrote with a fluent and versatile pen almost anything he was told to write, and whatever he thought might gain him a pension or a patron, but he wrote nothing under the purely artistic compulsion, so that perhaps it is not unfair to regard him as a hackwriter peculiarly favoured and highly gifted.

In *The Shepherd's Week* Gay is so hampered by Pope's difficult commission, and so concerned to avoid polite ridicule by an assumed contempt for his rustics, that his knowledge of rural England and his sincere love for it do not get fair play, yet these poems contain passages of affecting simplicity by no means common at the time. Although *Trivia* is marred by discursiveness and a bungling use of the mock-heroic style, it is filled with the stir of life, it is crammed with facts keenly observed and accurately set down, and it holds its place as the most vivid description of London written during the first half of the century. Gay's most satisfactory performance, however, is his *Fables*, upon which he spent real labour. In this interesting form he had many predecessors, and in particular he had the recent example of La Fontaine, but his work was none the less original. Widely read in eight or ten different languages for more than two hundred years, these poems are kept alive even today by their amiable wit, lively verse, and the sort of shrewd but not ignoble worldly wisdom which their author seldom practised.

THE SHEPHERD'S WEEK

For the group of pastorals called *The Shepherd's Week*, Gay wrote an interesting Proem to the Courteous Reader, using an affectedly archaic language not unlike that of the poems themselves, in which he made clear his general purpose. He begins with the assertion that no English poet "hath hit on the right, simple eclogue, after the true ancient guise of Theocritus, before this mine attempt." With special reference to Ambrose Philips, he speaks of the "rout and rabblement of critical gallimawfry which hath been made of late days by certain young men of insipid delicacy, concerning I know not what Golden Age, and other outrageous conceits to which they would confine pastoral." For his own part he is convinced that "it behoveth a pastoral to be such as nature in the country affordeth, and the manners also meetly copied from the rustical folk therein.... It is my purpose, gentle reader, to set before thee as it were a picture, or rather, lively landscape, of thy own country just as thou mightest see it didst thou take a walk into the fields at the proper season; even as Master Milton hath elegantly set forth the same. Thou wilt not find my shepherdesses idly piping on oaten reeds, but milking the kine, tying up the sheaves, or, if the hogs are astray, driving them to their styes." He takes for his model *The Shepherd's Calendar* of Spenser, whom he acknowledges "a bard of sweetest memorial," although he admits that in that poem the shepherd's boy "hath at some times raised his rustic reed to rhymes more rumbling than rural," and that "diverse grave points also hath he handled of churchly matter and doubts in religion daily arising, to great clerks only appertaining." This fault he promises to avoid by making his rustics speak and sing only of matters within their knowledge.

Gay's preface is most interesting in its apology for the language he has used, "which is, soothly to say, such as is neither spoken by the country maiden or the courtly dame; nay, not only such as in the present times is not uttered, but was never uttered in times past... it having too much of the country to be fit for the court, too much of the court to be fit for the country, too much of the language of old times to be fit for the present, too much of the present to have been fit for the old, and too much of both to be fit for any time to come." In other words, he admits the truth of Ben Jonson's remark that Spenser, in imitating the ancients, "writ no language," so that he has no excuse to make for his archaisms. "For this point," says he, "no reason can I allege, only deep learned ensamples having led me thereunto." It is significant in this connection that Gay wrote glossarial footnotes explaining many of the obsolete or West-Country words of his text that would be unknown to the polite London reader. This he seems to have done at the suggestion of Lord Bolingbroke, to whom the series was dedicated, for in his versified prologue, speaking of Bolingbroke, Gay writes:

> Thus he told me on a day:
> "Trim are thy sonnets, gentle Gay,
> And certes, mirth it were to see
> Thy joyous madrigals twice three,
> With preface meet and notes profound,
> Imprinted fair and well y-bound."
> All suddenly then home I sped
> And did even as my lord had said.

Gay's claim that he is representing the actualities of rural life is of course no more tenable than a similar claim would be for the eclogues of Theocritus himself; yet it is remarkable enough that even the assertion should have been made. The mental background of these poems is not unlike that revealed by the reworkings of Thomson's *Seasons* and of Shenstone's *Schoolmistress*: real knowledge of country things and deep affection for them stand somewhat shamefaced before the dominant taste of the Town, finding expression for themselves only by indirection and trying to escape ridicule by laughing first.

THE SHEPHERD'S WEEK

From TUESDAY, OR THE DITTY

Ah, Colin! canst thou leave thy sweetheart true?
What I have done for thee, will Cic'ly do?
Will she thy linen wash or hosen darn,
And knit thee gloves made of her own spun yarn?
Will she with housewife's hand provide thy meat,
And every Sunday morn thy neckcloth plait,
Which, o'er thy kersey doublet spreading wide,

In service-time drew Cic'ly's eyes aside?...
If in the soil you guide the crooked share,
Your early breakfast is my constant care;
And when with even hand you strow the grain,
I fright the thievish rooks from off the plain.
In *misling days when I my thresher heard,
With *nappy beer I to the barn repaired;
Lost in the music of the whirling flail,
To gaze on thee I left the smoking pail.
In harvest when the sun was mounted high,
My leathern bottle did thy drought supply;
Whene'er you mowed I followed with the rake,
And have full oft been sunburnt for thy sake;
When in the welkin gathering showers were seen,
I lagged the last with Colin on the green;
And when, at eve returning with thy car,
Awaiting, heard the jingling bells from far,
Straight on the fire the sooty pot I placed;
To warm thy broth I burnt my hands for haste.
When hungry thou stood'st staring like an oaf,
I sliced the luncheon from the barley loaf;
With crumbled bread I thickened well thy mess —
Ah, love me more, or love thy pottage less!

FRIDAY; OR THE DIRGE

Bumkinet, Grubbinol

Bumkinet. Why, Grubbinol, dost thou so wistful seem?
There's sorrow in thy look, if right I deem.
'Tis true, yon oaks with yellow tops appear,
And chilly blasts begin to nip the year;
From the tall elm a shower of leaves is borne,
And their lost beauty riven beeches mourn.
Yet even this season pleasance blithe affords,
Now the squeez'd press foams with our apple hoards.
Come, let us hie, and quaff a cheery bowl;
Let cider now wash sorrow from the soul.

Grubbinol. Ah Bumkinet! since thou from hence wert gone.
From these sad plains all merriment is flown;
Should I reveal my grief, 'twould spoil thy cheer,
And make thine eye o'erflow with many a tear.

Bumkinet. Hang sorrow! Let's to yonder hut repair,
And with trim *sonnets cast away our care.
Gillian of Croydon well thy pipe can play,
Thou sing'st most sweet, "O'er hills and far away."
Of *Patient Grissel I *devise to sing,
And catches quaint shall make the valleys ring.
Come, Grubbinol, beneath this shelter come;
From hence we view our flocks securely roam.

Grubbinol. Yes, blithesome lad, a tale I mean to sing,
But with my woe shall distant valleys ring;
The tale shall make our kidlings droop their head,
For woe is me! — our Blouzelind is dead.

Bumkinet. Is Blouzelinda dead? farewell my glee!
No happiness is now reserv'd for me.
As the wood-pigeon coos without his mate,
So shall my doleful dirge bewail her fate.
Of Blouzelinda fair I mean to tell,
The peerless maid that did all maids excel.

Henceforth the morn shall dewy sorrow shed,
And ev'ning tears upon the grass be spread;
The rolling streams with watery grief shall flow,
And winds shall moan aloud when loud they blow.
Henceforth, as oft as autumn shall return,
The dropping trees, whene'er it rains, shall mourn;
This season quite shall strip the country's pride,
For 'twas in autumn Blouzelinda died.

Where'er I gad, I Blouzelind shall view.
Woods, dairy, barn, and mows our passion knew.
When I direct my eyes to yonder wood,
Fresh rising sorrow curdles in my blood.
Thither I've often been the damsel's guide,
When rotten sticks our fuel have supplied;
There I remember how her faggots large
Were frequently these happy shoulders' charge.
Sometimes this crook drew hazel boughs adown
And stuff'd her apron wide with nuts so brown;
Or when her feeding hogs had miss'd their way,
Or wallowing 'mid a feast of acorns lay,

***Notes on John Gay will be found in the Appendix, pp. 980 ff.**

Th' untoward creatures to the sty I drove
And whistled all the way — or told my love.

If by the dairy's *hatch I chance to hie,
I shall her goodly countenance espy,
For there her goodly countenance I've seen,
Set off with kerchief starch'd and *pinners clean.
Sometimes, like wax, she rolls the butter round,
Or with the wooden *lily prints the pound.
Whilom I've seen her skim the clotted cream,
And press from spongy curds the milky stream.
But now, alas! these ears shall hear no more
The whining swine surround the dairy door;
No more her care shall fill the hollow tray,
To fat the guzzling hogs with floods of whey.
Lament, ye swine; in grunting spend your grief;
For you, like me, have lost your sole relief.

When in the barn the sounding flail I ply,
Where from her sieve the chaff was wont to fly,
The poultry there will seem around to stand,
Waiting upon her charitable hand.
No succour meet the poultry now can find,
For they, like me, have lost their Blouzelind.

Whenever by yon barley mow I pass,
Before my eyes will trip the tidy lass.
I pitch'd the sheaves (oh, could I do so now!)
Which she in rows pil'd on the growing mow.
There *every deal my heart by love was gain'd,
There the sweet kiss my courtship has explain'd.
Ah Blouzelind! that mow I ne'er shall see,
But thy memorial will revive in me.

Lament, ye fields, and rueful symptoms show!
Henceforth let not the smelling primrose grow;
Let weeds instead of *butter-flowers appear,
And meads, instead of daisies, *hemlock bear;
For cowslips sweet let dandelions spread,
For Blouzelinda, blithesome maid, is dead!
Lament, ye swains, and o'er her grave bemoan,
And spell ye right this verse upon her stone:
"Here Blouzelinda lies — Alas, alas!
Weep shepherds — and remember flesh is grass."

Grubbinol. Albeit thy songs are sweeter to mine ear
Than to the thirsty cattle rivers clear,
Or winter porridge to th' lab'ring youth,
Or buns and sugar to the damsel's tooth,
Yet Blouzelinda's name shall tune my lay,
Of her I'll sing for ever and for aye.

When Blouzelind expir'd, the *wether's bell
Before the drooping flock toll'd forth her knell;
The solemn deathwatch click'd the hour she died,
And shrilling crickets in the chimney cried;
The boding raven on her cottage sate,
And with hoarse croaking warn'd us of her fate;
The lambkin which her wonted tendance bred
Dropp'd on the plains that fatal instant dead;
Swarm'd on a rotten stick the bees I spied,
Which erst I saw when Goody Dobson died.

How shall I, void of tears, her death relate!
While on her darling's bed her mother sate,
These words the dying Blouzelinda spoke,
And of the dead let none the will revoke:

"Mother," quoth she, "let not the poultry need,
And give the goose wherewith to raise her breed;
Be these my sister's care — and ev'ry morn
Amid the ducklings let her scatter corn;
The sickly calf that's hous'd, be sure to tend,
Feed him with milk, and from bleak colds defend;
Yet ere I die — see, mother, yonder shelf,
There secretly I've hid my worldly pelf.
Twenty good shillings in a rag I laid.
Be ten the parson's, for my sermon paid;
The rest is yours. My spinning wheel and rake,
Let Susan keep for her dear sister's sake;
My new straw hat that's trimly lin'd with green,
Let Peggy wear, for she's a damsel clean.
My leathern bottle, long in harvests tried,
Be Grubbinol's — this silver ring beside;
Three silver pennies, and a ninepence bent,
A token kind to Bumkinet is sent."
Thus spoke the maiden, while her mother cried,
And peaceful, like the harmless lamb, she died.

To show their love, the neighbours far and near
Follow'd with wistful look the damsel's bier.
*Sprigg'd rosemary the lads and lasses bore,
While dismally the parson walk'd before.
Upon her grave the rosemary they threw,
The daisy, butter-flow'r, and endive blue.

After the good man warn'd us from his text
That none could tell whose turn would be the next,
He said that heaven would take her soul, no doubt,
And spoke the hourglass, in her praise, quite out.

To her sweet mem'ry, flow'ry garlands strung,
O'er her now empty seat aloft were hung.
With wicker rods we fenc'd her tomb around,
To ward from man and beast the hallow'd ground,
Lest her new grave the parson's cattle raze,
For both his horse and cow the churchyard graze.

Now we trudg'd homeward to her mother's farm,
To drink new cider mull'd, with ginger warm.
For *Gaffer Treadwell told us, by the bye,
Excessive sorrow is exceeding dry.

While bulls bear horns upon their curled brow,
Or lasses with soft strokings milk the cow;
While paddling ducks the *standing lake desire,
Or batt'ning hogs roll in the sinking mire;
While moles the crumbled earth in hillocks raise,
So long shall swains tell Blouzelinda's praise.

Thus wail'd the louts in melancholy strain,
Till bonny Susan sped across the plain;
They seiz'd the lass in apron clean array'd,
And to the ale-house forc'd the willing maid.
In ale and kisses they forgot their cares,
And Susan, Blouzelinda's loss repairs.

[1714]

TRIVIA OR THE ART OF WALKING THE STREETS OF LONDON

Gay's first intention in writing *Trivia* — this word is the plural form of the Latin *trivium*, a cross-road or public square — may have been primarily to ridicule the numerous didactic poems of his time on the "Art" of this and that by the presentation of a trifling subject-matter in grandiose language. Had he succeeded in this, he would have produced a mock-heroic poem congenial to an age which tried to ensure itself against enthusiasm by raillery, and which had recently put forth, as one of its most characteristic works, *The Rape of the Lock*. He did not succeed, partly because his wit was insufficient for the task, but chiefly because London was not ridiculous to him but an absorbing spectacle. His use of classical analogues, such as the likening of mud thrown up by dray-horses on Ludgate Hill to Parthian shafts, is often absurd in a way he did not intend, and even his frequent ridicule of classic diction is seldom witty enough to have the effect of literary criticism. The poem's failure in this way is atoned for, however, by its brilliant success as a record of the actual look and feeling of London in one of its most fascinating epochs. Intended as a *jeu d'esprit*, it takes its place among the many celebrations of the great city extending from Langland and Lydgate down to Wordsworth and Richard Jefferies and Edward Thomas — countrymen all.

From BOOK II

OF WALKING THE STREETS BY DAY

...For ease and for dispatch, the morning's best;
No tides of passengers the streets molest.
You'll see a draggled damsel here and there
From *Billingsgate her filthy traffic bear;
On doors the sallow milkmaid chalks her gains —
Ah! how unlike the milkmaid of the plains!
Before proud gates attending *asses bray,
Or arrogate with solemn pace the way;
These grave physicians with their milky cheer
The love-sick maid and dwindling beau repair;
Here rows of *drummers stand in martial file,
And with their vellum thunder shake the pile
To greet the new-made bride. Are sounds like these
The proper prelude to a *state of peace?
Now industry awakes her busy sons;
Full charg'd with news the breathless *hawker runs;
Shops open, coaches roll, carts shake the ground,
And all the streets with passing cries resound.

If cloth'd in black, you tread the busy town,
Or if distinguish'd by the reverend gown,
Three trades avoid: oft in the mingling press,
The barber's apron soils the sable dress;
Shun the perfumer's touch with cautious eye;
Nor let the baker's step advance too nigh.
Ye walkers too that youthful colours wear,
Three sullying trades avoid with equal care:
The little chimney-sweeper skulks along
And marks with sooty stains the heedless throng;
When *small-coal murmurs in the hoarser throat,
From smutty dangers guard thy threaten'd coat;
The dustman's cart offends thy clothes and eyes,
When through the street a cloud of ashes flies.
But whether black or lighter dyes are worn,
The chandler's basket, on his shoulder borne,
With tallow spots thy coat; resign the way,
To shun the surly butcher's greasy tray —
Butchers, whose hands are dy'd with blood's foul stain,
And always foremost in the hangman's train.

Let due civilities be strictly paid.
*The wall surrender to the hooded maid,
Nor let thy sturdy elbow's hasty rage
Jostle the feeble steps of trembling age;
And when the porter bends beneath his load
And pants for breath, clear thou the crowded road;
But, above all, the groping blind direct,
And from the pressing throng the lame protect.
You'll sometimes meet a fop, of nicest tread,
Whose *mantling peruke veils his empty head,
At ev'ry step he dreads the wall to lose,
And risks, to save a coach, his red-heel'd shoes.
Him, like the miller, pass with caution by,
Lest from his shoulder clouds of powder fly.
But when the bully, with assuming pace,
Cocks his broad hat, edg'd round with tarnish'd lace,
Yield not the way; defy his strutting pride,
And thrust him to the muddy *kennel's side;
He never turns again, nor dares oppose,
But mutters coward curses as he goes.

If drawn by business to a street unknown,
Let the sworn porter point thee through the town;
Be sure observe the *signs, for signs remain,
Like faithful landmarks to the walking train.
Seek not from 'prentices to learn the way;
Those fabling boys will turn thy steps astray:
Ask the grave tradesman to direct thee right,
He ne'er deceives, but when he profits by 't.

Where fam'd *St. Giles's ancient limits spread,
An inrail'd column rears its lofty head,
Here to sev'n streets *sev'n dials count the day,
And from each other catch the circling ray.
Here oft the peasant, with enquiring face,
Bewildered, trudges on from place to place;
He dwells on every sign with stupid gaze,
Enters the narrow alley's doubtful maze,
Tries every winding court and street in vain,
And doubles o'er his weary steps again.
Thus hardy Theseus with intrepid feet,
Traversed the dangerous labyrinth of Crete;
But still the wandering passes forced his stay
Till Ariadne's clue unwinds the way.
But do not thou, like that bold chief, confide
Thy venturous footsteps to a female guide;
She'll lead thee with delusive smiles along,
Dive in thy *fob, and drop thee in the throng.

When waggish boys the *stunted besom ply
To *rid the *slabby pavement, pass not by
Ere thou hast held their hands; some heedless flirt
Will overspread thy calves with sputt'ring dirt.
Where porters' hogsheads roll from carts aslope,
Or brewers down steep cellars stretch the rope,
Where counted *billets are by carmen toss'd,
Stay thy rash step, and walk without the *post....

Where elevated o'er the gaping crowd,
Clasp'd in the *board the perjur'd head is bow'd,
Betimes retreat; here, thick as hailstones pour,
Turnips, and half-hatch'd eggs, (a mingled show'r)
Among the rabble rain. Some random throw
May with the trickling yolk thy cheek o'erflow.

Though expedition bids, yet never stray
Where no rang'd posts defend the rugged way.
Here laden carts with thund'ring wagons meet,

Wheels clash with wheels, and bar the narrow street;
The lashing whip resounds, and horses strain,
And blood in anguish bursts the swelling vein.
O barb'rous men, your cruel breasts assuage!
Why vent ye on the gen'rous steed your rage?
Does not his service earn your daily bread?
Your wives, your children, by his labours fed!
If, as the * Samian taught, the soul revives,
And, shifting seats, in other bodies lives;
Severe shall be the brutal coachman's change,
Doom'd in a hackney horse the town to range:
Carmen, transform'd, the groaning load shall draw,
Whom other tyrants with the lash shall awe.

Who would of * Watling Street the dangers share,
When the broad pavement of Cheapside is near?
Or who that * rugged street would traverse o'er,
That stretches, O * Fleet-ditch, from thy black shore
To the Tow'r's moated walls? Here steams ascend
That, in mix'd fumes, the wrinkled nose offend.
Where chandlers cauldrons boil; where fishy prey
Hide the wet stall, long absent from the sea;
And where the cleaver chops the heifer's spoil,
And where huge hogsheads sweat with * trainy oil,
Thy breathing nostril hold. But how shall I
Pass, where in piles * Cornavian cheeses lie —
Cheese, that the table's closing rites denies,
And bids me with th' unwilling * chaplain rise?

Oh, bear me to the paths of fair *Pell Mell!
Safe are thy pavements, grateful is thy smell,
At distance rolls along the gilded coach,
Nor sturdy carmen on thy walks encroach.
No * lets would bar thy ways were chairs deny'd —
The soft supports of laziness and pride;
Shops breathe perfumes, thro' sashes ribbons glow,
The mutual arms of ladies, and the beau.
Yet still even here, when rains the passage hide,
Oft the loose stone spirts up a muddy tide
Beneath thy careless foot; and from on high,
Where masons mount the ladder, fragments fly;
Mortar, and crumbled lime in show'rs descend,
And o'er thy head destructive tiles impend.

But sometimes let me leave the noisy roads,
And silent wander in the close abodes
Where wheels ne'er shake the ground; there pensive stray,
In studious thought, the long uncrowded way.
Here I remark each walker's diff'rent face,
And in their look their various bus'ness trace.
The broker here his spacious * beaver wears,
Upon his brow sit jealousies and cares;
Bent on some mortgage (to avoid reproach)
He seeks by-streets, and saves th' expensive coach.
Soft, at low doors, old letchers tap their cane,
For fair recluse that travels Drury Lane.
Here roams uncomb'd the lavish rake, to shun
His Fleet Street * draper's everlasting dun.

Careful observers, studious of the town,
Shun the misfortunes that disgrace the clown.
Untempted, they contemn the juggler's feats,
Pass by the * Meuse, nor try the * thimble's cheats.
When drays bound high, they never cross behind,
Where bubbling yeast is blown by gusts of wind;
And when up Ludgate Hill huge carts move slow,
Far from the straining steeds securely go,
Whose dashing hoofs behind them fling the mire,
And mark with muddy blots the gazing squire.
The Parthian thus his jav'lin backward throws,
And as he flies infests pursuing foes. . . .

[1716]

SWEET WILLIAM'S FAREWELL TO BLACK-EYED SUSAN

A BALLAD

All in the Downs the fleet was moored,
The streamers waving in the wind,
When black-eyed Susan came aboard,
"Oh! where shall I my true love find?
Tell me, ye jovial sailors, tell me true,
If my sweet William sails among the crew?"

William, who high upon the yard
Rocked with the billow to and fro,
Soon as her well-known voice he heard,
He sighed, and cast his eyes below;
The cord slides swiftly through his glowing hands,
And, quick as lightning, on the deck he stands.

So the sweet lark, high poised in air,
Shuts close his pinions to his breast —
If chance his mate's shrill call he hear —
And drops at once into her nest.
The noblest captain in the British fleet
Might envy William's lips those kisses sweet.

"O Susan, Susan, lovely dear,
My vows shall ever true remain;
Let me kiss off that falling tear;
We only part to meet again.
Change as ye list, ye winds! my heart shall be
The faithful compass that still points to thee.

"Believe not what the landsmen say,
Who tempt with doubts thy constant mind;
They'll tell thee, sailors, when away,
In every port a mistress find;
Yes, yes, believe them when they tell thee so,
For thou art present wheresoe'er I go.

"If to fair India's coast we sail,
Thy eyes are seen in diamonds bright,
Thy breath is Afric's spicy gale,
Thy skin is ivory so white.
Thus every beauteous object that I view,
Wakes in my soul some charm of lovely Sue.

"Though battle call me from thy arms,
Let not my pretty Susan mourn;
Though cannons roar, yet safe from harms,
William shall to his dear return.
Love turns aside the balls that round me fly,
Lest precious tears should drop from Susan's eye."

The boatswain gave the dreadful word;
The sails their swelling bosom spread;
No longer must she stay aboard;
They kissed — she sighed — he hung his head.
Her lessening boat unwilling rows to land,
"Adieu!" she cries, and waved her lily hand.

[1720]

From FABLES

THE TWO OWLS AND THE SPARROW

Two formal owls together sat,
Conferring thus in solemn chat:
"How is the modern taste decayed!
Where's the respect to wisdom paid?
Our worth the Grecian sages knew;
They gave our sires the honour due;
They weighed the dignity of fowls,
And pried into the depth of owls.
Athens, the seat of learned fame,
With general voice revered our name;
On merit, title was conferred,
And all adored th' Athenian bird."
"Brother, you reason well," replies
The solemn mate, with half-shut eyes;
"Right. Athens was the seat of learning,
And truly wisdom is discerning.
Besides, on Pallas' helm we sit,
The type and ornament of wit:
But now, alas! we're quite neglected,
And a pert sparrow's more respected."
A sparrow, who was lodged beside,
O'erhears them soothe each other's pride,
And thus he nimbly vents his heat:
"Who meets a fool must find conceit.
I grant, you were at Athens graced,
And on Minerva's helm were placed;
But every bird that wings the sky,
Except an owl, can tell you why.
From hence they taught their schools to know
How false we judge by outward show;
That we should never looks esteem,
Since fools as wise as you might seem.
Would ye contempt and scorn avoid,
Let your vainglory be destroyed;
Humble your arrogance of thought,
Pursue the ways by nature taught;
So shall you find delicious fare,
And grateful farmers praise your care;
So shall sleek mice your chase reward,
And no keen cat find more regard."

THE TWO MONKEYS

The learned, full of inward pride,
The fops of outward show deride;
The fop, with learning at defiance,
Scoffs at the pedant, and the science;
The *Don, a formal, solemn strutter,
Despises *Monsieur's airs and flutter;
While Monsieur mocks the formal fool,
Who looks, and speaks, and walks by rule.
Britain, a medley of the twain,

As pert as France, as grave as Spain,
In fancy wiser than the rest,
Laughs at them both, of both the jest.
Is not the poet's chiming close
Censured by all the sons of prose,
While bards of quick imagination
Despise the sleepy prose narration?
Men laugh at apes, they men contemn;
For what are we, but apes to them?
Two monkeys went to Southwark Fair;
No critics had a sourer air.
They forced their way through draggled folks
Who gaped to catch jack-pudding's jokes;
Then took their tickets for the show
And got by chance the foremost row.
To see their grave, observing face,
Provoked a laugh throughout the place.
"Brother," says Pug, and turned his head,
"The rabble's monstrously ill-bred."
Now through the booth loud hisses ran;
Nor ended till the show began.
The tumbler whirls the flip-flap round,
With somersets he shakes the ground;
The cord beneath the dancer springs;
Aloft in air the vaulter swings;
Distorted now, now prone depends,
Now through his twisted arms ascends;
The crowd, in wonder and delight,
With clapping hands applaud the sight.
With smiles quoth Pug, "If pranks like these
The giant apes of reason please,
How would they wonder at our arts!
They must adore us for our parts.
High on the twig I've seen you cling;
Play, twist, and turn in airy ring.
How can those clumsy things, like me,
Fly with a bound from tree to tree?
But yet, by this applause, we find
These emulators of our kind
Discern our worth, our parts regard,
Who our mean mimics thus reward."
"Brother," the grinning mate replies,
"In this I grant that man is wise.
While good example they pursue,
We must allow some praise is due;
But when they strain beyond their guide,
I laugh to scorn the mimic pride,
For how fantastic is the sight,
To meet men always bolt upright,
Because we sometimes walk on two!
I hate the imitating crew."

THE HARE AND MANY FRIENDS

Friendship, like love, is but a name,
Unless to one you * stint the flame.
The child whom many fathers share
Hath seldom known a father's care.
'Tis thus in friendships; who depend
On many, rarely find a friend.
A hare, who in a civil way,
Complied with everything, like Gay,
Was known by all the bestial train
Who haunt the wood, or graze the plain.
Her care was never to offend,
And every creature was her friend.
As forth she went at early dawn,
To taste the dew-besprinkled lawn,
Behind she hears the hunter's cries,
And from the deep-mouthed thunder flies.
She starts, she stops, she pants for breath;
She hears the near advance of death;
She doubles to mislead the hound,
And measures back her mazy round;
Till fainting in the public way,
Half-dead with fear, she gasping lay.
What transport in her bosom grew,
When first the horse appeared in view!
"Let me," says she, "your back ascend,
And owe my safety to a friend.
You know my feet betray my flight;
To friendship every burden's light."
The horse replied: "Poor honest puss,
It grieves my heart to see thee thus;
Be comforted, relief is near;
For all your friends are in the rear."
She next the stately bull implored;
And thus replied the mighty lord:
"Since every beast alive can tell
That I sincerely wish you well,
I may, without offence, pretend
To take the freedom of a friend.
Love calls me hence; a favourite cow
Expects me near yon barley mow;
And when a lady's in the case,
You know all other things give place.
To leave you thus might seem unkind;
But see, the goat is just behind."
The goat remarked her pulse was high,
Her languid head, her heavy eye;
"My back," says he, "may do you harm;
The sheep's at hand, and wool is warm."
The sheep was feeble, and complained
His sides a load of wool sustained;
Said he was slow, confessed his fears;
For hounds eat sheep, as well as hares.

She now the trotting calf addressed,
To save from death a friend distressed.
"Shall I," says he, "of tender age,
In this important care engage?
Older and abler passed you by;
How strong are those! how weak am I!
Should I presume to bear you hence,
Those friends of mine may take offence.
Excuse me then. You know my heart,
But dearest friends, alas! must part.
How shall we all lament! Adieu!
For see, the hounds are just in view!"

[1727]

MATTHEW GREEN

CONCERNING the life of Matthew Green little is known, except that he was born in 1696 of a Quaker family, that he was employed in the Custom House, and that he died a bachelor at the age of forty-one. Not a member of either university and unconnected with any literary group, Green wrote little, and he is remembered only for *The Spleen*, which appeared in 1737, shortly after his death. This is a poem of the second order of merit, kept alive by its brisk versification, good spirits, and bubbling wit. In the Introductory Epistle the author promises to show how he has cured himself of "spleen" — a half-fanciful disease vaguely related to the "melancholy" of Elizabethan and Jacobean days and also to the "vapours" and "hypochondria" of later times. His method of cure is related to the cardinal virtue of his epoch, which was variously called moderation, contentment, good sense, and sometimes "mediocrity." It consisted in steady avoidance of all extremes, particularly those of emotion, in a distaste for "enthusiasms" of conduct and belief, in a disposition to make the best of the world as it is, and to regard the human show with good-humoured toleration. This, of course, is exactly the mood and philosophy of the poet Horace, and indeed Green's picture of his ideal rural retreat can scarcely be independent of the sixth satire of Horace's second book. Unlike most of his poetic contemporaries, however, Green was not a Latin scholar, and his description of the *via media* may have derived from one or more of the many eighteenth century poems, such as Pomfret's *The Choice*, in which the same Horatian ideal is depicted. Although it contains little that is original and nothing that is at all profound, *The Spleen* has high representative value; and moreover it shines throughout with a witty common sense less brilliant than Pope's but hardly less wise, not so merry as that of Gay and Prior but quite as charming. The passage here chosen is near the end of the poem, which extends to somewhat more than eight hundred lines.

From THE SPLEEN

...Contentment, parent of delight,
So much a stranger to our sight,
Say, goddess, in what happy place
Mortals behold thy blooming face.
Thy gracious auspices impart
And for thy temple choose my heart.
They whom thou deignest to inspire
Thy science learn, to bound desire;
By happy alchemy of mind
They turn to pleasure all they find;
They both disdain in outward mien
The grave and solemn garb of spleen
And meretricious arts of dress,
To feign a joy, and hide distress;
Unmoved when the rude tempest blows,
Without an opiate they repose,
And covered by your shield, defy
The whizzing shafts that round them fly;
Nor, meddling with the gods' affairs,
Concern themselves with distant cares,
But place their bliss in mental rest
And feed upon the good possess'd.
  Forced by soft violence of prayer,
The blithesome goddess soothes my care.
I feel the deity inspire,
And thus she models my desire:
Two hundred pounds half-yearly paid,
Annuity securely made,
A farm some twenty miles from town,
Small, tight, salubrious, and my own;
Two maids that never saw the town,
A serving-man not quite a clown,
A boy to help to tread the mow,
And drive, while t'other holds the plough;
A *chief, of temper formed to please,
Fit to converse and keep the keys,
And, better to preserve the peace,
Commissioned by the name of niece;
With understandings of a size
To think their master very wise.
May heaven (it's all I wish for) send
One genial room to treat a friend,
Where decent cupboard, little *plate,
Display benevolence, not state.
And may my humble dwelling stand
Upon some chosen spot of land,
A pond before full to the brim
Where cows may cool and geese may swim,
Behind, a green like velvet neat,
Soft to the eye and to the feet,
Where odorous plants in evening fair
Breathe all around ambrosial air;
From *Eurus, foe to kitchen ground,
Fenced by a slope with bushes crowned,
Fit dwelling for the feathered throng
Who pay their *quit-rents with a song,
With opening views of hill and dale
Which sense and fancy too regale.

* Notes on Matthew Green will be found in the Appendix, pp. 981 ff.

Where the half-cirque which vision bounds
Like amphitheatre surrounds,
And woods impervious to the breeze,
Thick phalanx of *embodied trees,
From hills through plains in dusk array
Extended far, repel the day.
Here stillness, height, and solemn shade
Invite, and contemplation aid;
Here nymphs from hollow oaks relate
The *dark decrees and will of fate,
And dreams beneath the spreading beech
Inspire, and docile fancy teach,
While, soft as breezy breath of wind,
Impulses rustle through the mind;
Here Dryads, scorning Phœbus' ray,
While Pan melodious pipes away,
In measured motions frisk about
Till old Silenus puts them out.
There see the clover, pea, and bean
Vie in variety of green;
Fresh pastures speckled o'er with sheep,
Brown fields their fallow sabbaths keep,
Plump Ceres' golden tresses wear,
And poppy top-knots deck her hair,
And silver streams through meadows stray,
And Naiads on the margin play,
And lesser nymphs on side of hills
From plaything urns pour down the rills.
Thus sheltered, free from care and strife,
May I enjoy a calm through life,
See faction, safe in low degree,
As men at land see storms at sea,
And laugh at miserable elves
Not kind so much as to themselves,
Cursed with such souls of base alloy
As can possess but not enjoy;
Debarred the pleasure to impart
By avarice, *sphincter of the heart,
Who wealth, hard earned by guilty cares,
Bequeath untouched to thankless heirs.
May I, with look ungloom'd by guile,
And wearing virtue's *livery-smile,
Prone the distressèd to relieve
And little trespasses forgive,
With income not in fortune's power
And skill to make a busy hour,
With trips to town, life to amuse,
To purchase books and hear the news,
To see old friends, brush off the clown,
And quicken taste at *coming down,
Unhurt by sickness' blasting rage,
And slowly mellowing in age,
When fate extends its gathering gripe,
Fall off like fruit grown fully ripe,
Quit a worn being without pain,
Perhaps to blossom soon again....

[1737]

ALEXANDER POPE

Pope has suffered alike at the hands of his enemies and his friends. His character has been the subject of endless debate in which it has been attacked and apologized for, but seldom understood. One thing, however, has been generally admitted, though its full implications have not always been realized: he lived above all else for his art. Few of his literary contemporaries were primarily men of letters: Addison was a statesman, Prior was a diplomat, Steele was a journalist, Swift was a clergyman, Arbuthnot was a physician; Pope alone lived for poetry, unplaced, unpensioned, unpatronized. This single-hearted devotion to letters came about in the first place because he was excluded from other professions: as an invalid and almost a cripple he could take no part in the more active business of the world; as a Roman Catholic he was barred from the universities and from public service. Poetry was his natural refuge, but it would have been his choice had he been free to choose without restriction. Environment and innate tendency coincided most happily.

The art to which Pope was thus devoted became his professional support; it was never merely his trade. His little patrimony enabled him to go through his time of preparation without the necessity of hack work; his translation of Homer brought in funds, which, wisely invested, made him financially independent. He was never a poor-devil author; he never drudged in a garret. From the beginning he associated with gentlemen; in the height of his reputation he was the intimate of bishops and peers. Poetry gave to the son of a retired London merchant, not the patronage but the friendship of the great. Grub Street he saw from afar and despised.

In a very special sense, then, he lived for and by his art; it was his chief concern in life. And he naturally became the champion of what the age called *wit*. A classical period is always distinguished by the public recognition of certain standards of the best; it holds to universal judgments of reason and taste that are approved by the "general sense." The man of letters who most completely embodies these standards and who most conspicuously takes upon himself their public defence becomes a literary dictator. What Malherbe and Boileau had been in France, what Dryden had been in England during the preceding age, and what Johnson was most completely to become during the next age, Pope became during the first generation of the eighteenth century. These men were strong because they had behind them the force of enlightened public opinion, because their judgments were based upon generally accepted standards of the best. In some respects, however, Pope realized this ideal of the champion of wit less completely than did the other literary dictators of the neo-classical period. He lacked the necessary personal force and the physical virility; he was too much a recluse and too little the representative of all classes of contemporary letters to be generally acknowledged. Hence his campaigns against dullness were, sometimes in his own day, and almost always later, considered as partisan or personal warfare. A waspish little man who satirized his enemies and waged a private war with Grub Street, — this is the usual estimate of Pope as a critic.

There is thus much of truth in the accusation: he was a good hater and an implacable foe. But if the personal enemies of Pope were the same as the enemies of wit, if his private and his professional animosities coincided, was he therefore the less fitted to champion wit? For the most part, his friendships were as strong and as representative as his hatreds. With the notable exception of Addison, he numbered the most distinguished men of letters in the generation among his friends, and kept them to the end. He was not a man with whom it was easy to get along; he was naturally suspicious, vindictive, disingenuous, nor were these qualities lessened by pain and ill-health; yet his friendships were more notable than his hatreds. Both were connected with his ruling passion.

In spite of his lifelong devotion to poetry and the high estimate of his time, a succeeding age was to question, first, whether Pope was a poet of the highest rank and, finally, whether he was a poet at all. That the supreme representative of the Augustan Age should be regarded with diminished favour in a romantic generation is not surprising — he naturally became the focal point of controversy; satire had so completely gone out of favour that it was not understood; and Nature in the Wordsworthian sense had become the chief subject-matter of a poetry surcharged with complex emotion. More recently there has been a return of appreciation for Pope, though too often it has been a romantic idealization of a picturesque figure from a long-past age, as in Austin Dobson's *Dialogue to the Memory of Mr. Alexander Pope.* Only within the past two decades has there begun to take shape a truer understanding based on a juster comprehension of his real merit. We are learning to attune our ears to the delicate harmonies of the Popean verse and to recognize that its beauties are different from the richness of Keats or the complex orchestration of Swinburne — different but no less genuine. Pope's clarity, his incisiveness, his sure sense of the right word, are as evident as his mellifluousness. He had wit and wisdom and taste; he gave to universal subjects final poetic expression. Johnson asked, "If Pope be not a poet, where is poetry to be found?" English poetry has been enriched since the eighteenth century by new themes and varied harmonies; but now as then, any definition of poetry which excludes *The Rape of the Lock* and the *Epistle to Dr. Arbuthnot* and the conclusion of *The Dunciad* is sadly incomplete. The world has not yet outgrown the art to which Pope gave his life.

AN ESSAY ON CRITICISM

An Essay on Criticism was published in 1711; it seems to have been mostly written about 1709, when Pope was not yet twenty-one. Obviously, it is a precocious work even though its author's claims of still earlier composition are not accepted.

At bottom it is not original, nor was it intended to be; not presentation of new critical theories but judicious application of old principles was the purpose in writing. Pope accepted the classical theory of poetry as presented by Aristotle, Horace, Longinus; adapted to modern conditions by Vida, Boileau, Le Bossu, Rapin, and Bouhours; and applied to English letters by Dryden and his followers. His poem differs from Roscommon's *Essay on Translated Verse* and the Earl of Mulgrave's *Essay on Poetry* by reason of its point of view — it deals with the art of criticism instead of the art of poetry — and by the happiness with which it illustrates the accepted principles.

> True wit is nature to advantage dress'd,
> What oft was thought, but ne'er so well express'd.

While *An Essay on Criticism* thus accepted the orthodox classical doctrines, it was distinctly liberal in their interpretation. Pope was not an Aristotelian formalist, who laid major emphasis on the rules as infallible guides. Instead, he followed Boileau, who had tried to refound the rules in nature and reason, who believed that they are useful guides only to the poet with genius and the inner fire; and he was especially interested in the new "school of taste," which emphasized the *je ne sais quoi*, something beyond the rules and transcending them. He was thus in line with Dryden and Addison in his critical theory, orthodox but not reactionary, conservative in the best sense of the word. The logical thoroughness and the critical severity of Rymer he respected but did not follow.

Pope modestly called his poem not an art of criticism but an essay, thus indicating that its treatment was informal and without the thoroughgoing completeness of a treatise. In so planning his work he maintained an aristocratic tradition that went back to Horace, and he justly estimated his own powers, for his strength lay rather in elaboration and adaptation than in methodical regularity or systematic planning. The prose argument before each of the parts indicates the general order of the topics, which are roughly: 1, the basis of criticism; 2, hindrances to just judgment; 3, the qualities necessary in a good critic and their exemplification in some of the most eminent critics of the past.

PART I

INTRODUCTION. That it is as great a fault to judge ill as to write ill, and a more dangerous one to the public. That a true taste is as rare to be found as a true genius. That most men are born with some taste, but spoiled by false education. The multitude of critics, and causes of them. That we are to study our own taste, and know the limits of it. Nature the best guide of judgment. Improved by art and rules, which are but methodized nature. Rules derived from the practice of the ancient poets. That therefore the ancients are necessary to be studied by a critic, particularly Homer and Virgil. Of licenses, and the use of them by the ancients. Reverence due to the ancients, and praise of them.

'Tis hard to say if greater want of skill
Appear in writing or in judging ill;
But of the two less dang'rous is th' offence
To tire our patience than mislead our sense.
Some few in that, but numbers err in this;
Ten censure wrong for one who writes amiss;
A fool might once himself alone expose;
Now one in verse makes many more in prose.
'Tis with our judgments as our watches: none
Go just alike, yet each believes his own.
In poets as true genius is but rare,
True taste as seldom is the critic's share;
Both must alike from Heav'n derive their light,
These born to judge, as well as those to write.
Let such teach others who themselves excel,
And censure freely who have written well.
Authors are partial to their wit, 'tis true,
But are not critics to their judgment too?

Yet if we look more closely, we shall find
Most have the seeds of judgment in their mind:
Nature affords at least a glimm'ring light;
The lines, tho' touch'd but faintly, are drawn right.
But as the slightest sketch, if justly trac'd,
Is by ill-colouring but the more disgrac'd,

So by false learning is good sense defac'd:
Some are bewilder'd in the maze of schools,
And some made coxcombs nature meant but fools.
In search of wit these lose their common sense,
And then turn critics in their own defence:
Each burns alike, who can or cannot write,
Or with a rival's or an eunuch's spite.
All fools have still an itching to deride,
And fain would be upon the laughing side.
If *Mævius scribble in Apollo's spite,
There are who judge still worse than he can write.

Some have at first for wits, then poets pass'd;
Turn'd critics next, and prov'd plain fools at last.
Some neither can for wits nor critics pass,
As heavy mules are neither horse nor ass.
Those half-learn'd witlings, num'rous in our isle
As half-form'd insects on the banks of Nile;
Unfinish'd things, one knows not what to call,
Their generation's so equivocal;
To tell 'em would a hundred tongues require,
Or one vain wit's, that might a hundred tire.

But you who seek to give and merit fame,
And justly bear a critic's noble name,
Be sure yourself and your own reach to know,
How far your genius, taste, and learning go;
Launch not beyond your depth, but be discreet,
And mark that point where sense and dullness meet.

Nature to all things fix'd the limits fit,
And wisely curb'd proud man's pretending wit.
As on the land while here the ocean gains,
In other parts it leaves wide sandy plains;
Thus in the soul while memory prevails,
The solid pow'r of understanding fails;
Where beams of warm imagination play,
The memory's soft figures melt away.
One science only will one genius fit;
So vast is art, so narrow human wit—
Not only bounded to peculiar arts,
But oft in those confin'd to single parts.
Like kings, we lose the conquests gain'd before
By vain ambition still to make them more;
Each might his sev'ral province well command,
Would all but stoop to what they understand.

*First follow Nature, and your judgment frame
By her just standard, which is still the same:
Unerring Nature, still divinely bright,
One clear, unchang'd, and universal light,
Life, force, and beauty must to all impart,
At once the source, and end, and test of art.
Art from that fund each just supply provides,
Works without show, and without pomp presides:
In some fair body thus th' informing soul
With spirits feeds, with vigour fills the whole,
Each motion guides and every nerve sustains;
Itself unseen, but in th' effects remains.
Some, to whom Heav'n in wit has been profuse,
Want as much more to turn it to its use;
For wit and judgment often are at strife,
Tho' meant each other's aid, like man and wife.
'Tis more to guide than spur the Muse's steed,
Restrain his fury than provoke his speed;
The winged courser, like a gen'rous horse,
Shows most true mettle when you check his course.

*Those rules of old, discover'd, not devis'd,
Are Nature still, but Nature methodiz'd;
Nature, like liberty, is but restrain'd
By the same laws which first herself ordain'd.

Hear how learn'd Greece her useful rules indites,
When to repress and when indulge our flights:
High on Parnassus' top her sons she show'd,
And pointed out those arduous paths they trod;
Held from afar, aloft, th' immortal prize,
And urg'd the rest by equal steps to rise.
Just precepts thus from great examples giv'n,
She drew from them what they deriv'd from Heav'n.
The gen'rous critic fann'd the poet's fire,
And taught the world with reason to admire.
Then Criticism the Muse's handmaid prov'd,
To dress her charms, and make her more belov'd:
But following wits from that intention stray'd:
Who could not win the mistress woo'd the maid;
Against the poets their own arms they turn'd,
Sure to hate most the men from whom they learn'd.
So modern 'pothecaries, taught the art
By doctor's bills to play the doctor's part,
Bold in the practice of mistaken rules,
Prescribe, apply, and call their masters fools.
*Some on the leaves of ancient authors prey;
Nor time nor moths e'er spoil'd so much as they;
Some drily plain, without invention's aid,
Write *dull receipts how poems may be made;
These leave the sense their learning to display,

*** Notes on Alexander Pope will be found in the Appendix, pp. 982 ff.**

And those explain the meaning quite away.

You then whose judgment the right course would steer,
Know well each ancient's proper character;
His fable, subject, scope in every page;
Religion, country, genius of his age:
Without all these at once before your eyes,
Cavil you may, but never criticise.
Be Homer's works your study and delight,
Read them by day, and meditate by night;
Thence form your judgment, thence your maxims bring,
And trace the Muses upward to their spring.
Still with itself compared, his text peruse;
And let your comment be the * Mantuan Muse.

When first young Maro in his boundless mind
A work t' outlast immortal Rome design'd,
Perhaps he seem'd above the critic's law,
And but from nature's fountains scorn'd to draw;
But when t' examine ev'ry part he came,
Nature and Homer were, he found, the same.
Convinc'd, amaz'd, he checks the bold design,
And rules as strict his labour'd work confine
As if *the Stagirite o'erlook'd each line.
Learn hence for ancient rules a just esteem;
To copy nature is to copy them.

Some beauties yet no precepts can declare,
For there's a happiness as well as care.
Music resembles poetry; in each
Are nameless graces which no methods teach,
And which a master-hand alone can reach.
If, where the rules not far enough extend,
(Since rules were made but to promote their end)
Some lucky license answer to the full
Th' intent proposed, that license is a rule.
Thus Pegasus, a nearer way to take,
May boldly deviate from the common track.
Great wits sometimes may gloriously offend,
And rise to faults true critics dare not mend;
From vulgar bounds with brave disorder part,
And snatch a grace beyond the reach of art,
Which, without passing thro' the judgment, gains
The heart, and all its end at once attains.
In prospects thus some objects please our eyes,
Which out of nature's common order rise,
The shapeless rock, or hanging precipice.
But tho' the ancients thus their rules invade,
(As kings dispense with laws themselves have made)
Moderns, beware! or if you must offend
Against the precept, ne'er transgress its end;
Let it be seldom, and compell'd by need;
And have at least their precedent to plead.
The critic else proceeds without remorse,
Seizes your fame, and puts his laws in force.

I know there are to whose presumptuous thoughts
Those freer beauties, ev'n in them, seem faults.
Some figures monstrous and misshap'd appear,
Consider'd singly, or beheld too near,
Which, but proportion'd to their light or place,
Due distance reconciles to form and grace.
A prudent chief not always must display
His pow'rs in equal ranks and fair array,
But with th' occasion and the place comply,
Conceal his force, nay, seem sometimes to fly.
Those oft are stratagems which errors seem,
Nor is it Homer nods, but we that dream.

Still green with bays each ancient altar stands
Above the reach of sacrilegious hands,
Secure from flames, from envy's fiercer rage,
Destructive war, and all-involving age.
See from each clime the learn'd their incense bring!
Hear in all tongues consenting pæans ring!
In praise so just let ev'ry voice be join'd,
And fill the gen'ral chorus of mankind.
Hail, bards triumphant! born in happier days,
Immortal heirs of universal praise!
Whose honours with increase of ages grow,
As streams roll down, enlarging as they flow;
Nations unborn your mighty names shall sound,
And worlds applaud that must not yet be found!
Oh, may some spark of your celestial fire
The last, the meanest of your sons inspire,
(That on weak wings, from far, pursues your flights,
Glows while he reads, but trembles as he writes)
To teach vain wits a science little known,
T' admire superior sense, and doubt their own.

PART II

Causes hindering a true judgment. 1. Pride. 2. Imperfect learning. 3. Judging by parts, and not by the whole. Critics in wit, language, versification only. 4. Being too hard to please, or too apt to admire. 5. Partiality— too much love to a sect— to the ancients or moderns. 6. Prejudice or prevention. 7. Singularity. 8. Inconstancy. 9. Party spirit. 10. Envy. Against envy, and in praise of good-nature. When severity is chiefly to be used by critics.

Of all the causes which conspire to blind
Man's erring judgment, and misguide the mind,
What the weak head with strongest bias rules,
Is pride, the never-failing vice of fools.

Whatever nature has in worth denied,
She gives in large recruits of needful pride:
For as in bodies, thus in souls, we find
What wants in blood and spirits swell'd with wind;
Pride, where wit fails, steps in to our defence,
And fills up all the mighty void of sense.
If once right reason drives that cloud away,
Truth breaks upon us with resistless day.
Trust not yourself; but, your defects to know,
Make use of ev'ry friend — and ev'ry foe.
A little learning is a dang'rous thing:
Drink deep, or taste not * the Pierian spring;
There shallow draughts intoxicate the brain,
And drinking largely sobers us again.
Fired at first sight with what the Muse imparts,
In fearless youth we tempt the heights of arts,
While from the bounded level of our mind
Short views we take, nor see the lengths behind;
But more advanc'd, behold with strange surprise
New distant scenes of endless science rise!
So pleas'd at first the tow'ring Alps we try,
Mount o'er the vales, and seem to tread the sky;
Th' eternal snows appear already past,
And the first clouds and mountains seem the last:
But those attain'd, we tremble to survey
The growing labours of the lengthen'd way;
Th' increasing prospect tires our wand'ring eyes,
Hills peep o'er hills, and Alps on Alps arise!
A perfect judge will read each work of wit
With the same spirit that its author writ:
Survey the whole, nor seek slight faults to find
Where nature moves, and rapture warms the mind;
Nor lose, for that malignant dull delight,
The gen'rous pleasure to be charm'd with wit.
But in such lays as neither ebb nor flow,
Correctly cold, and regularly low,
That shunning faults one quiet tenor keep,
We cannot blame indeed — but we may sleep.
In wit, as nature, what affects our hearts
Is not th' exactness of peculiar parts;
'Tis not a lip or eye we beauty call,
But the joint force and full result of all.
Thus when we view some well proportion'd dome,
(The world's just wonder, and ev'n thine, O Rome!)
No single parts unequally surprise,
All comes united to th' admiring eyes;
No monstrous height, or breadth, or length, appear;
The whole at once is bold and regular.
Whoever thinks a faultless piece to see,
Thinks what ne'er was, nor is, nor e'er shall be.
In every work regard the writer's end,
Since none can compass more than they intend;
And if the means be just, the conduct true,
Applause, in spite of trivial faults, is due.
As men of breeding, sometimes men of wit,
T' avoid great errors must the less commit,
Neglect the rules each verbal critic lays,
For not to know some trifles is a praise.
Most critics, fond of some subservient art,
Still make the whole depend upon a part;
They talk of principles, but notions prize,
And all to one lov'd folly sacrifice.
Once on a time * La Mancha's knight, they say,
A certain bard encount'ring on the way,
Discours'd in terms as just, with looks as sage,
As e'er could Dennis, of the Grecian stage;
Concluding all were desperate sots and fools
Who durst depart from Aristotle's rules.
Our author, happy in a judge so nice,
Produced his play, and begg'd the knight's advice;
Made him observe the subject and the plot,
The manners, passions, unities — what not?
All which exact to rule were brought about,
Were but a combat in the lists left out.
"What! leave the combat out?" exclaims the knight;
"Yes, or we must renounce the Stagirite."
"Not so, by Heaven!" he answers in a rage,
"Knights, squires, and steeds must enter on the stage."
"So vast a throng the stage can ne'er contain."
"Then build a new, or act it in a plain."
Thus critics of less judgment than caprice,
Curious, not knowing, not exact, but nice,
Form short ideas, and offend in arts
(As most in manners) by a love to parts.
Some to conceit alone their taste confine,
And glitt'ring thoughts struck out at ev'ry line;
Pleas'd with a work where nothing's just or fit,
One glaring chaos and wild heap of wit.
Poets, like painters, thus unskill'd to trace
The naked nature and the living grace,
With gold and jewels cover ev'ry part,

And hide with ornaments their want of art.
True wit is nature to advantage dress'd,
What oft was thought, but ne'er so well express'd;
Something whose truth convinc'd at sight we find,
That gives us back the image of our mind.
As shades more sweetly recommend the light,
So modest plainness sets off sprightly wit;
For works may have more wit than does 'em good,
As bodies perish thro' excess of blood.
Others for language all their care express,
And value books, as women men, for dress:
Their praise is still, — the style is excellent;
The sense they humbly take upon content.
Words are like leaves; and where they most abound,
Much fruit of sense beneath is rarely found:
False eloquence, like the prismatic glass,
Its gaudy colours spreads on ev'ry place;
The face of nature we no more survey;
All glares alike, without distinction gay:
But true expression, like th' unchanging sun,
Clears and improves whate'er it shines upon;
It gilds all objects, but it alters none.
Expression is the dress of thought, and still
Appears more decent as more suitable;
A vile conceit in pompous words express'd
Is like a clown in regal purple dress'd.
For diff'rent styles with diff'rent subjects sort,
As sev'ral garbs with country, town, and court.
Some by old words to fame have made pretence,
Ancients in phrase, mere moderns in their sense;
Such labour'd nothings, in so strange a style,
Amaze th' unlearn'd, and make the learned smile;
Unlucky as *Fungoso in the play,
These sparks with awkward vanity display
What the fine gentleman wore yesterday;
And but so mimic ancient wits at best,
As apes our grandsires in their doublets dress'd.
In words as fashions the same rule will hold,
Alike fantastic if too new or old:
Be not the first by whom the new are tried,
Nor yet the last to lay the old aside.
But most by numbers judge a poet's song,
And smooth or rough with them is right or wrong.
In the bright Muse tho' thousand charms conspire,
Her voice is all these tuneful fools admire;
Who haunt Parnassus but to please their ear,
Not mend their minds; as some to church repair,
Not for the doctrine, but the music there.
*These equal syllables alone require,
Tho' oft the ear the open vowels tire;
While expletives their feeble aid do join,
And ten low words oft creep in one dull line:
While they ring round the same unvaried chimes,
With sure returns of still expected rhymes;
Where'er you find "the cooling western breeze,"
In the next line, it "whispers thro' the trees";
If crystal streams "with pleasing murmurs creep,"
The reader's threaten'd (not in vain) with "sleep":
Then, at the last and only couplet fraught
With some unmeaning thing they call a thought,
A needless Alexandrine ends the song,
That, like a wounded snake, drags its slow length along.
Leave such to tune their own dull rhymes, and know
What's roundly smooth, or languishly slow;
And praise the easy vigour of a line
Where Denham's strength and Waller's sweetness join.
True ease in writing comes from art, not chance,
As those move easiest who have learn'd to dance.
'Tis not enough no harshness gives offence;
The sound must seem an echo to the sense.
Soft is the strain when zephyr gently blows,
And the smooth stream in smoother numbers flows;
But when loud surges lash the sounding shore,
The hoarse, rough verse should like the torrent roar:
When Ajax strives some rock's vast weight to throw,
The line, too, labours, and the words move slow:
*Not so when swift Camilla scours the plain,
Flies o'er th' unbending corn, and skims along the main.
Hear how *Timotheus' varied lays surprise,
And bid alternate passions fall and rise!
While at each change the son of Libyan Jove
Now burns with glory, and then melts with love;
Now his fierce eyes with sparkling fury glow,
Now sighs steal out, and tears begin to flow:

Persians and Greeks like turns of nature found,
And the world's victor stood subdued by sound!
The pow'r of music all our hearts allow,
And what Timotheus was, is Dryden now.
  Avoid extremes, and shun the fault of such
Who still are pleas'd too little or too much.
At ev'ry trifle scorn to take offence;
That always shows great pride or little sense:
Those heads, as stomachs, are not sure the best
Which nauseate all, and nothing can digest.
Yet let not each gay turn thy rapture move;
*For fools admire, but men of sense approve:
As things seem large which we thro' mists descry,
Dullness is ever apt to magnify.
  Some foreign writers, some our own despise;
The ancients only, or the moderns prize.
Thus wit, like faith, by each man is applied
To one small sect, and all are damn'd beside.
Meanly they seek the blessing to confine,
And force that sun but on a part to shine,
Which not alone the southern wit sublimes,
But ripens spirits in cold northern climes;
Which from the first has shone on ages past,
Enlights the present, and shall warm the last;
Tho' each may feel increases and decays,
And see now clearer and now darker days.
Regard not then if wit be old or new,
But blame the false and value still the true.
  Some ne'er advance a judgment of their own,
But catch the spreading notion of the town;
They reason and conclude by precedent,
And own stale nonsense which they ne'er invent.
Some judge of authors' names, not works, and then
Nor praise nor blame the writings, but the men.
Of all this servile herd, the worst is he
That in proud dullness joins with quality,
A constant critic at the great man's board,
To fetch and carry nonsense for my lord.
What woful stuff this madrigal would be
In some starv'd hackney sonneteer or me!
But let a lord once own the happy lines,
How the wit brightens! how the style refines!
Before his sacred name flies ev'ry fault,
And each exalted stanza teems with thought!
  The vulgar thus thro' imitation err,
As oft the learn'd by being singular;
So much they scorn the crowd, that if the throng
By chance go right, they purposely go wrong;
So schismatics the plain believers quit,
And are but damn'd for having too much wit.
Some praise at morning what they blame at night,
But always think the last opinion right.
A Muse by these is like a mistress used,
This hour she's idolized, the next abused;
While their weak heads, like towns unfortified,
'Twixt sense and nonsense daily change their side.
Ask them the cause — they're wiser still, they say;
And still tomorrow's wiser than today.
We think our fathers fools, so wise we grow;
Our wiser sons no doubt will think us so.
Once school-divines this zealous isle o'erspread;
Who knew most sentences was deepest read.
Faith, gospel, all seem'd made to be disputed,
And none had sense enough to be confuted.
*Scotists and Thomists now in peace remain
Amidst their kindred cobwebs in *Duck Lane
If faith itself has diff'rent dresses worn,
What wonder modes in wit should take their turn?
Oft, leaving what is natural and fit,
The current folly proves the ready wit;
And authors think their reputation safe,
Which lives as long as fools are pleas'd to laugh.
  Some, valuing those of their own side or mind,
Still make themselves the measure of mankind:
Fondly we think we honour merit then,
When we but praise ourselves in other men.
Parties in wit attend on those of state,
And public faction doubles private hate.
Pride, Malice, Folly, against Dryden rose,
In various shapes of *parsons, critics, beaux;
But sense surviv'd when merry jests were past;
For rising merit will buoy up at last.
Might he return and bless once more our eyes,
New *Blackmores and new Milbournes must arise.
Nay, should great Homer lift his awful head,
*Zoilus again would start up from the dead.
Envy will merit as its shade pursue,
But like a shadow proves the substance true;
For envied wit, like Sol eclips'd, makes known
Th' opposing body's grossness, not its own.
When first that sun too pow'rful beams displays,
It draws up vapours which obscure its rays;

But ev'n those clouds at last adorn its way,
Reflect new glories, and augment the day.
Be thou the first true merit to befriend;
His praise is lost who stays till all commend.
Short is the date, alas! of modern rhymes,
And 'tis but just to let them live betimes.
No longer now that Golden Age appears,
When patriarch wits survived a thousand years;
Now length of fame, our second life, is lost,
And bare threescore is all ev'n that can boast:
Our sons their fathers' failing language see,
And such as Chaucer is shall Dryden be.
So when the faithful pencil has design'd
Some bright idea of the master's mind,
Where a new world leaps out at his command,
And ready nature waits upon his hand;
When the ripe colours soften and unite,
And sweetly melt into just shade and light;
When mellowing years their full perfection give,
And each bold figure just begins to live,
The treach'rous colours the fair art betray,
And all the bright creation fades away!
Unhappy wit, like most mistaken things,
Atones not for that envy which it brings.
In youth alone its empty praise we boast,
But soon the short-lived vanity is lost;
Like some fair flower the early spring supplies,
That gaily blooms, but ev'n in blooming dies.
What is this wit, which must our cares employ?
The owner's wife that other men enjoy;
Then most our trouble still when most admir'd,
And still the more we give, the more requir'd;
Whose fame with pains we guard, but lose with ease,
Sure some to vex, but never all to please;
'Tis what the vicious fear, the virtuous shun;
By fools 'tis hated, and by knaves undone!
If wit so much from ign'rance undergo,
Ah, let not learning too commence its foe!
Of old those met rewards who could excel,
And such were prais'd who but endeavour'd well;
Tho' triumphs were to gen'rals only due,
Crowns were reserv'd to grace the soldiers too.
Now they who reach Parnassus' lofty crown
Employ their pains to spurn some others down;
And while self-love each jealous writer rules,
Contending wits become the sport of fools:
But still the worst with most regret commend,
For each ill author is as bad a friend.
To what base ends, and by what abject ways,
Are mortals urged thro' sacred lust of praise!
Ah, ne'er so dire a thirst of glory boast,
Nor in the critic let the man be lost.
Good nature and good sense must ever join;
To err is human; to forgive, divine.
But if in noble minds some dregs remain,
Not yet purged off, of spleen and sour disdain,
Discharge that rage on more provoking crimes,
Nor fear a dearth in these flagitious times.
No pardon vile obscenity should find,
Tho' wit and art conspire to move your mind;
But dullness with obscenity must prove
As shameful sure as impotence in love.
In the fat age of pleasure, wealth, and ease
Sprung the rank weed, and thrived with large increase:
When love was all an easy monarch's care,
Seldom at council, never in a war;
Jilts ruled the state, and statesmen farces writ;
Nay wits had pensions, and young lords had wit;
The fair sat panting at a courtier's play,
And not a mask went unimprov'd away;
The modest fan was lifted up no more,
And virgins smil'd at what they blush'd before.
The following license of a foreign reign
Did all * the dregs of bold Socinus drain;
Then unbelieving priests reform'd the nation,
And taught more pleasant methods of salvation;
Where Heav'n's free subjects might their rights dispute,
Lest God himself should seem too absolute;
Pulpits their sacred satire learn'd to spare,
And vice admir'd to find a flatt'rer there!
Encourag'd thus, wit's Titans braved the skies,
And the press groan'd with licens'd blasphemies.
These monsters, critics! with your darts engage,
Here point your thunder, and exhaust your rage!
Yet shun their fault, who, scandalously nice,
Will needs mistake an author into vice:
All seems infected that th' infected spy,
As all looks yellow to the jaundic'd eye.

PART III

Rules for the conduct and manners in a critic. 1. Candour. Modesty. Good breeding. Sincerity and freedom of advice. 2. When one's counsel is to be restrained. Character of an incorrigible poet. And of an impertinent critic. Character of a good critic. The history of criticism, and characters of the best critics. Aristotle, Horace, Dionysius, Petronius, Quintilian, Longinus. Of the decay of criticism, and its revival. Erasmus. Vida. Boileau. Lord Roscommon, &c. Conclusion.

Learn then what morals critics ought to show,
For 'tis but half a judge's task to know.
'Tis not enough taste, judgment, learning join;
In all you speak let truth and candour shine,
That not alone what to your sense is due
All may allow, but seek your friendship too.
  Be silent always when you doubt your sense,
And speak, tho' sure, with seeming diffidence:
Some positive persisting fops we know,
Who if once wrong will needs be always so;
But you with pleasure own your errors past,
And make each day a critic on the last.
  'Tis not enough your counsel still be true;
Blunt truths more mischief than nice falsehoods do;
Men must be taught as if you taught them not,
And things unknown propos'd as things forgot.
Without good breeding truth is disapprov'd;
That only makes superior sense belov'd.
  Be niggards of advice on no pretence,
For the worst avarice is that of sense.
With mean complacence ne'er betray your trust,
Nor be so civil as to prove unjust.
Fear not the anger of the wise to raise;
Those best can bear reproof who merit praise.
  'Twere well might critics still this freedom take,
*But Appius reddens at each word you speak,
And stares tremendous, with a threat'ning eye,
Like some fierce tyrant in old tapestry.
Fear most to tax an Honourable fool,
Whose right it is, uncensur'd to be dull;
Such, without wit, are poets when they please,
As without learning they can take degrees.
Leave dang'rous truths to unsuccessful satires,
And flattery to fulsome dedicators,
Whom, when they praise, the world believes no more
Than when they promise to give scribbling o'er.
'Tis best sometimes your censure to restrain,
And charitably let the dull be vain;
Your silence there is better than your spite,
For who can rail so long as they can write?
Still humming on their drowsy course they keep,
And lash'd so long, like tops, are lash'd asleep.
False steps but help them to renew the race,
As, after stumbling, jades will mend their pace.
What crowds of these, impenitently bold,
In sounds and jingling syllables grown old,
Still run on poets, in a raging vein,
Ev'n to the dregs and squeezings of the brain,
Strain out the last dull droppings of their sense,
And rhyme with all the rage of impotence.
  Such shameless bards we have; and yet 'tis true
There are as mad abandon'd critics too.
The bookful blockhead ignorantly read,
With loads of learned lumber in his head,
With his own tongue still edifies his ears,
And always list'ning to himself appears.
All books he reads, and all he reads assails,
From Dryden's *Fables* down to *Durfey's *Tales*.
With him most authors steal their works, or buy;
*Garth did not write his own *Dispensary*.
Name a new play, and he's the poet's friend;
Nay, show'd his faults — but when would poets mend?
No place so sacred from such fops is barr'd,
Nor is Paul's church more safe than *Paul's churchyard:
Nay, fly to altars; there they'll talk you dead;
For fools rush in where angels fear to tread.
Distrustful sense with modest caution speaks,
It still looks home, and short excursions makes;
But rattling nonsense in full volleys breaks,
And never shock'd, and never turn'd aside,
Bursts out, resistless, with a thund'ring tide.
  But where's the man who counsel can bestow,
Still pleas'd to teach, and yet not proud to know?
Unbiass'd or by favour or by spite;
Not dully prepossess'd nor blindly right;
Tho' learn'd, well-bred, and tho' well-bred sincere;
Modestly bold, and humanly severe;
Who to a friend his faults can freely show,
And gladly praise the merit of a foe?
Bless'd with a taste exact, yet unconfin'd;
A knowledge both of books and humankind;
Gen'rous converse; a soul exempt from pride:

And love to praise, with reason on his side?
Such once were critics; such the happy few
Athens and Rome in better ages knew.
The mighty Stagirite first left the shore,
Spread all his sails, and durst the deeps explore;
He steer'd securely, and discover'd far,
Led by the light of * the Mæonian star.
Poets, a race long unconfin'd and free,
Still fond and proud of savage liberty,
Receiv'd his laws, and stood convinc'd 'twas fit
Who conquer'd nature should preside o'er wit.
Horace still charms with graceful negligence,
And without method talks us into sense;
Will, like a friend, familiarly convey
The truest notions in the easiest way.
He who, supreme in judgment as in wit,
Might boldly censure as he boldly writ,
Yet judg'd with coolness, though he sung with fire;
His precepts teach but what his works inspire.
Our critics take a contrary extreme:
They judge with fury, but they write with phlegm;
Nor suffers Horace more in wrong translations
By wits, than critics in as wrong quotations.
See * Dionysius Homer's thoughts refine,
And call new beauties forth from ev'ry line!
Fancy and art in * gay Petronius please,
The scholar's learning with the courtier's ease.
In * grave Quintilian's copious work we find
The justest rules and clearest method join'd:
Thus useful arms in magazines we place,
All rang'd in order, and dispos'd with grace,
But less to please the eye than arm the hand,
Still fit for use, and ready at command.
Thee, bold Longinus! all the Nine inspire,
And bless their critic with a poet's fire:
An ardent judge, who, zealous in his trust,
With warmth gives sentence, yet is always just;
Whose own example strengthens all his laws,
And is himself that great sublime he draws.
Thus long succeeding critics justly reign'd,
Licence repress'd, and useful laws ordain'd.
Learning and Rome alike in empire grew,
And arts still follow'd where her eagles flew;
From the same foes at last both felt their doom,
And the same age saw learning fall and Rome.
With tyranny then superstition join'd,
As that the body, this enslav'd the mind;
Much was believ'd, but little understood,
And to be dull was constru'd to be good;
A second deluge learning thus o'errun,
And the monks finish'd what the Goths begun.
At length Erasmus, that great injur'd name,
(The glory of the priesthood and the shame!)
Stemm'd the wild torrent of a barb'rous age,
And drove those holy Vandals off the stage.
But see! each muse in * Leo's golden days
Starts from her trance, and trims her wither'd bays.
Rome's ancient genius, o'er its ruins spread,
Shakes off the dust, and rears his rev'rend head.
Then sculpture and her sister arts revive;
Stones leap'd to form, and rocks began to live;
With sweeter notes each rising temple rung;
A Raphael painted and a Vida sung:
Immortal Vida! on whose honour'd brow
The poet's bays and critic's ivy grow;
* Cremona now shall ever boast thy name,
As next in place to Mantua, next in fame!
But soon by impious arms from Latium chas'd,
Their ancient bounds the banish'd Muses pass'd;
Thence arts o'er all the northern world advance,
But critic learning flourish'd most in France;
The rules a nation born to serve obeys,
And Boileau still in right of Horace sways.
But we, brave Britons, foreign laws despised,
And kept unconquer'd and unciviliz'd;
Fierce for the liberties of wit, and bold,
We still defied the Romans, as of old.
Yet some there were, among the sounder few
Of those who less presumed and better knew.
Who durst assert the juster ancient cause,
And here restor'd wit's fundamental laws.
Such was the Muse whose rules and practice tell
"Nature's chief masterpiece is writing well."
Such was Roscommon, not more learn'd than good,
With manners gen'rous as his noble blood;
To him the wit of Greece and Rome was known,
And ev'ry author's merit but his own.
Such late was * Walsh — the Muse's judge and friend,
Who justly knew to blame or to commend;
To failings mild but zealous for desert,
The clearest head, and the sincerest heart.
This humble praise, lamented shade! receive:

This praise at least a grateful Muse may give:
The Muse whose early voice you taught to sing,
Prescribed her heights, and pruned her tender wing,
(Her guide now lost) no more attempts to rise,
But in low numbers short excursions tries;
Content if hence th' unlearn'd their wants may view,
The learn'd reflect on what before they knew:
Careless of censure, nor too fond of fame;
Still pleas'd to praise, yet not afraid to blame;
Averse alike to flatter or offend;
Not free from faults, nor yet too vain to mend.

[1711]

THE RAPE OF THE LOCK

The Rape of the Lock was published in its original form, in two cantos, in 1712. The story of how Pope tried to end a family quarrel that had grown out of Lord Petre's theft of a lock of hair from Miss Arabella Fermor is too well known to need repetition. The success of the poem in its first form induced Pope to expand it into five cantos by adding considerable new material, including the machinery of the sylphs and gnomes. In the hands of most poets such a studied attempt to improve a happy trifle would have been foredoomed to failure; but it suited the genius of Pope. The poem in its complete form was published early in 1714 and was so popular that 3000 copies sold within four days.

This popularity has continued. *The Rape of the Lock* has been a favourite with all classes of readers, even those who care little for Pope's other work; it is a famous example of what the French call *vers de société*, the delicate treatment of a topic suggested by contemporary society in which satire and seriousness, whimsicality and sentiment are blended in exactly the right proportion.

Pope described *The Rape of the Lock* as an Heroi-Comical Poem, by which he meant what we commonly call a mock-epic, a literary form which must not be confused with burlesque or travesty. Vida's *The Game of Chess* and Boileau's *Le Lutrin* were two of Pope's best known models. Not only are the conventions of the classical epic here delightfully adapted, — as in the heroic opening, the supernatural machinery, the Homeric combat, the descent into the lower world (represented as the Cave of Spleen); but many well known quotations are cleverly suggested or reset. The poem may be enjoyed by any one, but it can be appreciated to the full only by a reader who is well acquainted with Homer and Virgil and Milton.

This setting of a society theme in the mock-epic form is Pope's happiest and most graceful, though not his greatest poem. In it he has given the very spirit of English society in one of its splendid periods; here are reflected the light humours of the *Tatler* and the sparkling wit of *The Way of the World*; feminine foibles are perceived without condemnation, and court life is shown at once petty and delightful. The wax candles of Hampton Court shine on brocade and lawn, snuff-box and fan, with a mellow glow that illuminates youth and beauty and wit, gay pretence and hollow masquerade.

THE RAPE OF THE LOCK

AN HEROI-COMICAL POEM

Nolueram, Belinda, tuos violare capillos;
Sed juvat, hoc precibus me tribuisse tuis.
Mart., [*Epig.* XII, 84, 5.]

CANTO I

*What dire offence from am'rous causes springs,
What mighty contests rise from trivial things,
I sing — This verse to **Caryll*, Muse! is due:
This, ev'n Belinda may vouchsafe to view:
Slight is the subject, but not so the praise,
If she inspire, and he approve my lays.
Say what strange motive, goddess! could compel
A well-bred lord t' assault a gentle belle!
O say what stranger cause, yet unexplor'd,
Could make a gentle belle reject a lord!
In tasks so bold can little men engage,
And in soft bosoms dwells such mighty rage?
Sol thro' white curtains shot a tim'rous ray,
And oped those eyes that must eclipse the day:
Now lap dogs give themselves the rousing shake,
And sleepless lovers just at twelve awake:
Thrice rung the bell, the slipper knock'd the ground,
And the press'd watch return'd a silver sound.
Belinda still her downy pillow press'd;
Her guardian sylph prolong'd the balmy rest:
'Twas he had summon'd to her silent bed
The morning-dream that hover'd o'er her head,
A youth more glitt'ring than a birthnight beau

(That ev'n in slumber caus'd her cheek to glow)
Seem'd to her ear his winning lips to lay,
And thus in whispers said, or seem'd to say:
"Fairest of mortals, thou distinguish'd care
Of thousand bright inhabitants of air!
If e'er one vision touch'd thy infant thought,
Of all the nurse and all the priest have taught:
Of airy elves by moonlight shadows seen,
The silver token, and the circled green,
Or virgins visited by angel-pow'rs,
With golden crowns and wreaths of heav'nly flow'rs;
Hear and believe! thy own importance know,
Nor bound thy narrow views to things below.
Some secret truths, from learned pride conceal'd,
To maids alone and children are reveal'd:
What tho' no credit doubting wits may give?
The fair and innocent shall still believe.
Know, then, unnumber'd spirits round thee fly,
The light militia of the lower sky:
These, tho' unseen, are ever on the wing,
Hang o'er * the box, and hover round the ring.
Think what an equipage thou hast in air,
And view with scorn two pages and a chair.
As now your own, our beings were of old,
And once inclosed in woman's beauteous mould;
Thence, by a soft transition, we repair
From earthly vehicles to these of air.
Think not, when woman's transient breath is fled,
That all her vanities at once are dead;
Succeeding vanities she still regards,
And, tho' she plays no more, o'erlooks the cards.
Her joy in gilded chariots, when alive,
And love of ombre, after death survive.
For when the fair in all their pride expire,
To their first elements their souls retire:
The sprites of fiery termagants in flame
Mount up, and take a salamander's name.
Soft yielding minds to water glide away,
And sip, with nymphs, their elemental tea.
The graver prude sinks downward to a gnome
In search of mischief still on earth to roam.
The light coquettes in sylphs aloft repair,
And sport and flutter in the fields of air.
"Know further yet: whoever fair and chaste
Rejects mankind, is by some sylph embraced;
For spirits, freed from mortal laws, with ease.
Assume what sexes and what shapes they please.
What guards the purity of melting maids,
In courtly balls, and midnight masquerades,
Safe from the treach'rous friend, the daring spark,
The glance by day, the whisper in the dark;
When kind occasion prompts their warm desires,
When music softens, and when dancing fires?
'Tis but their sylph, the wise celestials know,
Tho' honour is the word with men below.
"Some nymphs there are, too conscious of their face,
For life predestin'd to the gnome's embrace.
These swell their prospects and exalt their pride,
When offers are disdain'd, and love denied:
Then gay ideas crowd the vacant brain,
While peers, and dukes, and all their sweeping train,
And garters, stars, and coronets appear,
And in soft sounds, 'Your Grace' salutes their ear.
'Tis these that early taint the female soul,
Instruct the eyes of young coquettes to roll,
Teach infant cheeks a bidden blush to know,
And little hearts to flutter at a beau.
"Oft, when the world imagine women stray,
The sylphs thro' mystic mazes guide their way;
Thro' all the giddy circle they pursue,
And old impertinence expel by new.
What tender maid but must a victim fall
To one man's treat, but for another's ball?
When Florio speaks, what virgin could withstand,
If gentle Damon did not squeeze her hand?
With varying vanities, from ev'ry part,
They shift the moving toyshop of their heart;
Where wigs with wigs, with sword-knots sword-knots strive,
Beaux banish beaux, and coaches coaches drive.
This erring mortals levity may call;
Oh blind to truth! the sylphs contrive it all.
"Of these am I, who thy protection claim,
A watchful sprite, and Ariel is my name.
Late, as I ranged the crystal wilds of air,
In the clear mirror of thy ruling star
I saw, alas! some dread event impend,
Ere to the main this morning sun descend,

But Heav'n reveals not what, or how or where:
Warn'd by the sylph, O pious maid, beware!
This to disclose is all thy guardian can:
Beware of all, but most beware of man!"
He said; when Shock, who thought she slept too long,
Leap'd up, and waked his mistress with his tongue.
'Twas then, Belinda, if report say true,
Thy eyes first open'd on a billet-doux;
Wounds, charms, and ardours were no sooner read,
But all the vision vanish'd from thy head.
And now, unveil'd, the toilet stands display'd,
Each silver vase in mystic order laid.
First, rob'd in white, the nymph intent adores,
With head uncover'd, the cosmetic pow'rs.
A heav'nly image in the glass appears;
To that she bends, to that her eyes she rears.
Th' inferior priestess, at her altar's side,
Trembling begins the sacred rites of Pride.
Unnumber'd treasures ope at once, and here
The various off'rings of the world appear;
From each she nicely culls with curious toil,
And decks the goddess with the glitt'ring spoil.
This casket India's glowing gems unlocks,
And all Arabia breathes from yonder box.
The tortoise here and elephant unite,
Transform'd to combs, the speckled, and the white.
Here files of pins extend their shining rows,
Puffs, powders, patches, bibles, billets-doux.
Now awful beauty puts on all its arms;
The fair each moment rises in her charms,
Repairs her smiles, awakens ev'ry grace,
And calls forth all the wonders of her face;
Sees by degrees a purer blush arise,
And keener lightnings quicken in her eyes.
The busy sylphs surround their darling care,
These set the head, and those divide the hair,
Some fold the sleeve, whilst other plait the gown;
And Betty's prais'd for labours not her own.

CANTO II

Not with more glories, in th' ethereal plain,
The sun first rises o'er the purpled main,
Than, issuing forth, the rival of his beams
Launch'd on the bosom of the silver Thames.
Fair nymphs, and well-dress'd youths around her shone,
But ev'ry eye was fix'd on her alone.
On her white breast a sparkling cross she wore,
Which Jews might kiss, and infidels adore.
Her lively looks a sprightly mind disclose,
Quick as her eyes, and as unfix'd as those:
Favours to none, to all she smiles extends;
Oft she rejects, but never once offends.
Bright as the sun, her eyes the gazers strike,
And, like the sun, they shine on all alike.
Yet graceful ease, and sweetness void of pride,
Might hide her faults, if belles had faults to hide;
If to her share some female errors fall,
Look on her face, and you'll forget 'em all.
This nymph, to the destruction of mankind,
Nourish'd two locks, which graceful hung behind
In equal curls, and well conspired to deck
With shining ringlets the smooth iv'ry neck.
Love in these labyrinths his slaves detains,
And mighty hearts are held in slender chains.
With hairy springes we the birds betray,
Slight lines of hair surprise the finny prey,
Fair tresses man's imperial race ensnare,
And beauty draws us with a single hair.
Th' advent'rous baron the bright locks admir'd;
He saw, he wish'd, and to the prize aspired.
Resolv'd to win, he meditates the way,
By force to ravish, or by fraud betray;
For when success a lover's toil attends,
Few ask if fraud or force attain'd his ends.
For this, ere Phœbus rose, he had implor'd
Propitious Heav'n, and ev'ry pow'r ador'd,
But chiefly Love — to Love an altar built
Of twelve vast French romances, neatly gilt.
There lay three garters, half a pair of gloves,
And all the trophies of his former loves;
With tender billets-doux he lights the pyre,
And breathes three am'rous sighs to raise the fire.
Then prostrate falls, and begs with ardent eyes
Soon to obtain, and long possess the prize:
The pow'rs gave ear, and granted half his prayer,
The rest the winds dispers'd in empty air.
But now secure the painted vessel glides,
The sunbeams trembling on the floating tides:
While melting music steals upon the sky,
And soften'd sounds along the waters die;
Smooth flow the waves, the zephyrs gently play,

Belinda smil'd, and all the world was gay.
All but the sylph — with careful thoughts oppress'd
Th' impending woe sat heavy on his breast.
He summons straight his denizens of air;
The lucid squadrons round the sails repair:
Soft o'er the shrouds aërial whispers breathe
That seem'd but zephyrs to the train beneath.
Some to the sun their insect-wings unfold,
Waft on the breeze, or sink in clouds of gold;
Transparent forms too fine for mortal sight,
Their fluid bodies half dissolv'd in light,
Loose to the wind their airy garments flew,
Thin glitt'ring textures of the filmy dew,
Dipt in the richest tincture of the skies,
Where light disports in ever-mingling dyes,
While ev'ry beam new transient colours flings,
Colours that change whene'er they wave their wings.
Amid the circle, on the gilded mast,
Superior by the head was Ariel plac'd;
His purple pinions opening to the sun,
He raised his azure wand, and thus begun:
"Ye sylphs and sylphids, to your chief give ear!
Fays, fairies, genii, elves, and dæmons, hear!
Ye know the spheres and various tasks assign'd
By laws eternal to th' aërial kind.
Some in the fields of purest ether play,
And bask and whiten in the blaze of day:
Some guide the course of wand'ring orbs on high,
Or roll the planets thro' the boundless sky.
Some, less refin'd, beneath the moon's pale light
Pursue the stars that shoot athwart the night,
Or suck the mists in grosser air below,
Or dip their pinions in the painted bow,
Or brew fierce tempests on the wintry main,
Or o'er the glebe distil the kindly rain.
Others, on earth, o'er human race preside,
Watch all their ways, and all their actions guide:
Of these the chief the care of nations own,
And guard with arms divine the British throne.
"Our humbler province is to tend the fair,
Not a less pleasing, tho' less glorious care;
To save the powder from too rude a gale;
Nor let th' imprison'd essences exhale;
To draw fresh colours from the vernal flow'rs;
To steal from rainbows, ere they drop in show'rs,
A brighter wash; to curl their waving hairs,
Assist their blushes and inspire their airs;
Nay oft, in dreams invention we bestow,
To change a flounce, or add a furbelow.
"This day black omens threat the brightest fair,
That e'er deserv'd a watchful spirit's care;
Some dire disaster, or by force or slight;
But what, or where, the Fates have wrapt in night.
Whether the nymph shall break Diana's law,
Or some frail china jar receive a flaw;
Or stain her honour, or her new brocade,
Forget her pray'rs, or miss a masquerade;
Or lose her heart, or necklace, at a ball;
Or whether Heav'n has doom'd that Shock must fall.
Haste, then, ye spirits! to your charge repair:
The flutt'ring fan be Zephyretta's care;
The drops to thee, Brillante, we consign;
And, Momentilla, let the watch be thine;
Do thou, Crispissa, tend her fav'rite lock;
Ariel himself shall be the guard of Shock.
"To fifty chosen sylphs, of special note,
We trust th' important charge, the petticoat;
Oft have we known that sev'n-fold fence to fail,
Tho' stiff with hoops, and arm'd with ribs of whale;
Form a strong line about the silver bound,
And guard the wide circumference around.
"Whatever spirit, careless of his charge,
His post neglects, or leaves the fair at large,
Shall feel sharp vengeance soon o'ertake his sins,
Be stopp'd in vials, or transfix'd with pins;
Or plung'd in lakes of bitter washes lie,
Or wedg'd whole ages in a bodkin's eye:
Gums and pomatums shall his flight restrain,
While clogg'd he beats his silken wings in vain;
Or alum styptics with contracting pow'r
Shrink his thin essence like a *rivell'd flow'r:
Or, as Ixion fix'd, the wretch shall feel
The giddy motion of the whirling mill,
In fumes of burning chocolate shall glow,
And tremble at the sea that froths below!"
He spoke; the spirits from the sails descend:
Some, orb in orb, around the nymph extend;
Some thread the mazy ringlets of her hair;

Some hang upon the pendants of her ear;
With beating hearts the dire event they wait,
Anxious, and trembling for the birth of Fate.

CANTO III

Close by those meads, forever crown'd with flow'rs,
Where Thames with pride surveys his rising tow'rs,
There stands *a structure of majestic frame,
Which from the neighb'ring Hampton takes its name.
Here Britain's statesmen oft the fall foredoom
Of foreign tyrants, and of nymphs at home;
Here thou, great Anna! whom three realms obey,
Dost sometimes counsel take — and sometimes tea.
  Hither the heroes and the nymphs resort,
To taste awhile the pleasures of a court;
In various talk th' instructive hours they pass'd,
Who gave the ball, or paid the visit last;
One speaks the glory of the British Queen,
And one describes a charming Indian screen;
A third interprets motions, looks, and eyes;
At ev'ry word a reputation dies.
Snuff, or the fan, supply each pause of chat,
With singing, laughing, ogling, *and all that.*
  Meanwhile, declining from the noon of day,
The sun obliquely shoots his burning ray;
The hungry judges soon the sentence sign,
And wretches hang that jurymen may dine;
The merchant from th' Exchange returns in peace,
And the long labours of the toilet cease.
Belinda now, whom thirst of fame invites,
Burns to encounter two advent'rous knights,
At *ombre singly to decide their doom;
And swells her breast with conquests yet to come.
Straight the three bands prepare in arms to join,
Each band the number of the sacred Nine.
Soon as she spreads her hand, th' aërial guard
Descend, and sit on each important card:
First Ariel perch'd upon a Matadore,
Then each according to the rank they bore;
For sylphs, yet mindful of their ancient race,
Are, as when women, wondrous fond of place.
  Behold four kings in majesty rever'd,
With hoary whiskers and a forky beard;
And four fair queens, whose hands sustain a flow'r,
Th' expressive emblem of their softer pow'r;
Four knaves, in garbs succinct, a trusty band,
Caps on their heads, and halberts in their hand;
And parti-colour'd troops, a shining train,
Draw forth to combat on the velvet plain.
  The skillful nymph reviews her force with care:
"Let spades be trumps!" she said, and trumps they were.
  Now move to war her sable Matadores,
In show like leaders of the swarthy Moors.
Spadillio first, unconquerable lord!
Led off two captive trumps, and swept the board.
As many more Manillio forced to yield,
And march'd a victor from the verdant field.
Him Basto follow'd, but his fate more hard
Gain'd but one trump and one plebeian card.
With his broad sabre next, a chief in years,
The hoary majesty of spades appears,
Puts forth one manly leg, to sight reveal'd;
The rest his many-colour'd robe conceal'd.
The rebel knave, who dares his prince engage,
Proves the just victim of his royal rage.
Ev'n mighty Pam, that kings and queens o'erthrew,
And mow'd down armies in the fights of loo,
Sad chance of war! now destitute of aid,
Falls undistinguish'd by the victor spade!
  Thus far both armies to Belinda yield;
Now to the baron Fate inclines the field.
His warlike amazon her host invades,
Th' imperial consort of the crown of spades.
The club's black tyrant first her victim died,
Spite of his haughty mien and barb'rous pride:
What boots the regal circle on his head,
His giant limbs, in state unwieldy spread;
That long behind he trails his pompous robe,
And of all monarchs only grasps the globe?
  The baron now his diamonds pours apace;
Th' embroider'd king who shows but half his face,
And his refulgent queen, with pow'rs combin'd,
Of broken troops an easy conquest find.
Clubs, diamonds, hearts, in wild disorder seen,
With throngs promiscuous strew the level green.
Thus when dispers'd, a routed army runs,

Of Asia's troops, and Afric's sable sons,
With like confusion diff'rent nations fly,
Of various habit, and of various dye;
The pierced battalions disunited fall
In heaps on heaps; one fate o'erwhelms them all.
The knave of diamonds tries his wily arts,
And wins (oh shameful chance!) the queen of hearts.
At this, the blood the virgin's cheek forsook,
A livid paleness spreads o'er all her look;
She sees, and trembles at th' approaching ill,
Just in the jaws of ruin, and Codille.
And now (as oft in some distemper'd state)
On one nice trick depends the gen'ral fate.
An ace of hearts steps forth: the king unseen
Lurk'd in her hand, and mourn'd his captive queen:
He springs to vengeance with an eager pace,
And falls like thunder on the prostrate ace.
The nymph, exulting, fills with shouts the sky;
The walls, the woods, and long canals reply.
Oh thoughtless mortals! ever blind to fate,
Too soon dejected, and too soon elate.
Sudden these honours shall be snatch'd away,
And curs'd forever this victorious day.
For lo! the board with cups and spoons is crown'd,
The berries crackle, and the mill turns round;
On *shining altars of japan they raise
The silver lamp; the fiery spirits blaze:
From silver spouts the grateful liquors glide,
While China's earth receives the smoking tide:
At once they gratify their scent and taste,
And frequent cups prolong the rich repast.
Straight hover round the fair her airy band;
Some, as she sipp'd, the fuming liquor fann'd,
Some o'er her lap their careful plumes display'd,
Trembling, and conscious of the rich brocade.
Coffee (which makes the politician wise,
And see thro' all things with his half-shut eyes)
Sent up in vapours to the baron's brain
New stratagems, the radiant lock to gain.
Ah, cease, rash youth! desist ere 'tis too late,
Fear the just gods, and think of Scylla's fate!
*Changed to a bird, and sent to flit in air,
She dearly pays for Nisus' injured hair!
But when to mischief mortals bend their will,
How soon they find fit instruments of ill!
Just then, Clarissa drew with tempting grace
A two-edg'd weapon from her shining case:
So ladies in romance assist their knight,
Present the spear, and arm him for the fight.
He takes the gift with rev'rence, and extends
The little engine on his fingers' ends;
This just behind Belinda's neck he spread,
As o'er the fragrant steams she bends her head.
Swift to the lock a thousand sprites repair;
A thousand wings, by turns, blow back the hair;
And thrice they twitch'd the diamond in her ear;
Thrice she look'd back, and thrice the foe drew near.
Just in that instant, anxious Ariel sought
The close recesses of the virgin's thought:
As on the nosegay in her breast reclin'd,
He watch'd th' ideas rising in her mind,
Sudden he view'd, in spite of all her art,
An earthly lover lurking at her heart.
Amaz'd, confus'd, he found his pow'r expir'd,
Resign'd to fate, and with a sigh retir'd.
The peer now spreads the glitt'ring *forfex wide,
T' inclose the lock; now joins it, to divide.
Ev'n then, before the fatal engine closed,
A wretched sylph too fondly interpos'd;
Fate urged the shears, and cut the sylph in twain
(But airy substance soon unites again).
The meeting points the sacred hair dissever
From the fair head, forever, and forever!
Then flash'd the living lightning from her eyes,
And screams of horror rend th' affrighted skies.
Not louder shrieks to pitying Heav'n are cast,
When husbands, or when lap dogs breathe their last;
Or when rich china vessels, fall'n from high,
In glitt'ring dust and painted fragments lie!
"Let wreaths of triumph now my temples twine,"
The victor cried; "the glorious prize is mine!
While fish in streams, or birds delight in air,
Or in a coach and six the British fair,
As long as *Atalantis* shall be read,
Or the small pillow grace a lady's bed,
While visits shall be paid on solemn days,
When num'rous wax-lights in bright order blaze,
While nymphs take treats, or assignations give,

So long my honour, name, and praise shall live!
What time would spare, from steel receives its date,
And monuments, like men, submit to fate!
Steel could the labour of the gods destroy,
And strike to dust th' imperial tow'rs of Troy;
Steel could the works of mortal pride confound
And hew triumphal arches to the ground.
What wonder, then, fair nymph! thy hairs should feel
The conquering force of unresisted steel?"

CANTO IV

But anxious cares the pensive nymph oppress'd,
And secret passions labour'd in her breast.
Not youthful kings in battle seiz'd alive,
Not scornful virgins who their charms survive,
Not ardent lovers robb'd of all their bliss,
Not ancient ladies when refused a kiss,
Not tyrants fierce that unrepenting die,
Not Cynthia when her manteau's pinn'd awry,
E'er felt such rage, resentment, and despair,
As thou, sad virgin! for thy ravish'd hair.
For, that sad moment, when the sylphs withdrew,
And Ariel weeping from Belinda flew,
Umbriel, a dusky, melancholy sprite
As ever sullied the fair face of light,
Down to the central earth, his proper scene,
Repair'd to search the gloomy * Cave of Spleen.
Swift on his sooty pinions flits the gnome,
And in a vapour reach'd the dismal dome.
No cheerful breeze this sullen region knows;
The dreaded east is all the wind that blows.
Here in a grotto shelter'd close from air,
And screen'd in shades from day's detested glare,
She sighs for ever on her pensive bed,
Pain at her side, and * Megrim at her head.
Two handmaids wait the throne, alike in place,
But diff'ring far in figure and in face.
Here stood Ill-nature, like an ancient maid,
Her wrinkled form in black and white array'd;
With store of pray'rs for mornings, nights, and noons,
Her hand is fill'd; her bosom with lampoons.
There Affectation, with a sickly mien,
Shows in her cheek the roses of eighteen,
Practis'd to lisp, and hang the head aside,
Faints into airs, and languishes with pride;
On the rich quilt sinks with becoming woe,
Wrapp'd in a gown for sickness and for show.
The fair ones feel such maladies as these,
When each new nightdress gives a new disease.
A constant vapour o'er the palace flies;
Strange phantoms rising as the mists arise;
Dreadful as hermits' dreams in haunted shades,
Or bright as visions of expiring maids.
Now glaring fiends, and snakes on rolling spires,
Pale spectres, gaping tombs, and purple fires;
Now lakes of liquid gold, Elysian scenes,
And crystal domes, and angels in machines.
Unnumber'd throngs on ev'ry side are seen,
Of bodies changed to various forms by Spleen.
Here living teapots stand, one arm held out,
One bent; the handle this, and that the spout:
A pipkin there, like Homer's tripod walks;
Here sighs a jar, and there a goose-pie talks;
Men prove with child, as pow'rful fancy works,
And maids turn'd bottles call aloud for corks.
Safe pass'd the gnome thro' this fantastic band,
* A branch of healing spleenwort in his hand.
Then thus address'd the pow'r: "Hail, wayward queen!
Who rule the sex to fifty from fifteen:
Parent of vapours and of female wit,
Who give th' hysteric or poetic fit,
On various tempers act by various ways,
Make some take physic, others scribble plays;
Who cause the proud their visits to delay,
And send the godly in a pet to pray.
A nymph there is that all thy pow'r disdains,
And thousands more in equal mirth maintains.
But oh! if e'er thy gnome could spoil a grace,
Or raise a pimple on a beauteous face,
* Like citron-waters matrons' cheeks inflame,
Or change complexions at a losing game;
If e'er with airy horns I planted heads,
Or rumpled petticoats, or tumbled beds,
Or caused suspicion when no soul was rude,
Or discomposed the head-dress of a prude,
Or e'er to costive lap dog gave disease,
Which not the tears of brightest eyes could ease,
Hear me, and touch Belinda with chagrin;
That single act gives half the world the spleen."
The goddess, with a discontented air,
Seems to reject him tho' she grants his pray'r.
A wondrous bag with both her hands she binds,
Like that where once Ulysses held the winds

There she collects the force of female lungs,
Sighs, sobs, and passions, and the war of tongues.
A vial next she fills with fainting fears,
Soft sorrows, melting griefs, and flowing tears.
The gnome rejoicing bears her gifts away,
Spreads his black wings, and slowly mounts to day.
Sunk in Thalestris' arms the nymph he found,
Her eyes dejected, and her hair unbound.
Full o'er their heads the swelling bag he rent,
And all the Furies issued at the vent.
Belinda burns with more than mortal ire,
And fierce Thalestris fans the rising fire.
"O wretched maid!" she spread her hands, and cried
(While Hampton's echoes, "Wretched maid!" replied),
"Was it for this you took such constant care
The bodkin, comb, and essence to prepare?
For this your locks in paper durance bound?
For this with tort'ring irons wreath'd around?
For this with fillets strain'd your tender head,
And bravely bore the double loads of lead?
Gods! shall the ravisher display your hair,
While the fops envy, and the ladies stare!
Honour forbid! at whose unrivall'd shrine
Ease, pleasure, virtue, all, our sex resign.
Methinks already I your tears survey,
Already hear the horrid things they say,
Already see you a degraded toast,
And all your honour in a whisper lost!
How shall I, then, your helpless fame defend?
'Twill then be infamy to seem your friend!
And shall this prize, th' inestimable prize,
Exposed thro' crystal to the gazing eyes,
And heighten'd by the diamond's circling rays,
On that rapacious hand forever blaze?
Sooner shall grass in Hyde Park Circus grow,
And * wits take lodgings in the sound of Bow;
Sooner let earth, air, sea, to chaos fall,
Men, monkeys, lap dogs, parrots, perish all!"
She said; then raging to * Sir Plume repairs,
And bids her beau demand the precious hairs:
(Sir Plume, of amber snuffbox justly vain,
And the nice conduct of a clouded cane)
With earnest eyes, and round, unthinking face,
He first the snuffbox open'd, then the case,
And thus broke out, "My lord, why, what the devil!
Z—ds! damn the lock! 'fore Gad, you must be civil!
Plague on't! 'tis past a jest — nay, prithee, pox!
Give her the hair." — He spoke, and rapp'd his box.
"It grieves me much," replied the peer again,
"Who speaks so well should ever speak in vain:
But by this lock, this sacred lock, I swear,
(Which never more shall join its parted hair:
Which never more its honours shall renew,
Clipp'd from the lovely head where late it grew)
That, while my nostrils draw the vital air,
This hand, which won it, shall forever wear."
He spoke, and speaking, in proud triumph spread
The long-contended honours of her head.
But Umbriel, hateful gnome, forbears not so;
He breaks the vial whence the sorrows flow.
Then see! the nymph in beauteous grief appears,
Her eyes half languishing, half drown'd in tears;
On her heav'd bosom hung her drooping head,
Which with a sigh she rais'd, and thus she said:
"Forever curs'd be this detested day,
Which snatch'd my best, my fav'rite curl away!
Happy! ah, ten times happy had I been,
If Hampton Court these eyes had never seen!
Yet am not I the first mistaken maid,
By love of courts to numerous ills betray'd.
Oh, had I rather unadmired remain'd
In some lone isle, or distant northern land;
Where the gilt chariot never marks the way,
Where none learn ombre, none e'er taste bohea!
There kept my charms conceal'd from mortal eye,
Like roses, that in deserts bloom and die.
What mov'd my mind with youthful lords to roam?
Oh, had I stay'd, and said my pray'rs at home;
'Twas this the morning omens seem'd to tell:
Thrice from my trembling hand the patchbox fell;
The tott'ring china shook without a wind;
Nay, Poll sat mute, and Shock was most unkind!
A sylph, too, warn'd me of the threats of fate,
In mystic visions, now believ'd too late!
See the poor remnants of these slighted hairs!

My hands shall rend what ev'n thy rapine spares:
These, in two sable ringlets taught to break,
Once gave new beauties to the snowy neck;
The sister-lock now sits uncouth alone,
And in its fellow's fate foresees its own;
Uncurl'd it hangs, the fatal shears demands,
And tempts once more thy sacrilegious hands.
Oh, hadst thou, cruel! been content to seize
Hairs less in sight, or any hairs but these!"

CANTO V

She said: the pitying audience melt in tears;
But Fate and Jove had stopp'd the baron's ears.
In vain Thalestris with reproach assails,
For who can move when fair Belinda fails?
*Not half so fix'd the Trojan could remain,
While Anna begg'd and Dido raged in vain.
Then grave Clarissa graceful waved her fan;
Silence ensued, and thus the nymph began:
"Say, why are beauties prais'd and honour'd most,
The wise man's passion, and the vain man's toast?
Why deck'd with all that land and sea afford,
Why angels call'd, and angel-like ador'd?
Why round our coaches crowd the white-glov'd beaux?
Why bows the side-box from its inmost rows?
How vain are all these glories, all our pains,
Unless good sense preserve what beauty gains;
That men may say when we the front-box grace,
'Behold the first in virtue as in face!'
Oh! if to dance all night, and dress all day,
Charm'd the smallpox, or chased old age away;
Who would not scorn what housewife's cares produce,
Or who would learn one earthly thing of use?
To patch, nay ogle, might become a saint,
Nor could it sure be such a sin to paint.
But since, alas! frail beauty must decay,
Curl'd or uncurl'd, since locks will turn to gray;
Since painted, or not painted, all shall fade,
And she who scorns a man must die a maid;
What then remains, but well our power to use,
And keep good humour still whate'er we lose?
And trust me, dear, good humour can prevail,
When airs, and flights, and screams, and scolding fail.
Beauties in vain their pretty eyes may roll;
Charms strike the sight, but merit wins the soul."
So spoke the dame, but no applause ensued;
Belinda frown'd, Thalestris call'd her prude.
"To arms, to arms!" the fierce virago cries,
And swift as lightning to the combat flies.
All side in parties, and begin th' attack;
Fans clap, silks rustle, and tough whalebones crack;
Heroes' and heroines' shouts confusedly rise,
And bass and treble voices strike the skies.
No common weapons in their hands are found:
Like gods they fight nor dread a mortal wound
So when bold Homer makes the gods engage,
And heav'nly breasts with human passions rage;
'Gainst Pallas, Mars; Latona, Hermes arms;
And all Olympus rings with loud alarms;
Jove's thunder roars, Heav'n trembles all around,
Blue Neptune storms, the bell'wing deeps resound:
Earth shakes her nodding tow'rs, the ground gives way,
And the pale ghosts start at the flash of day!
*Triumphant Umbriel, on a sconce's height,
Clapp'd his glad wings, and sate to view the fight:
Propp'd on their bodkin-spears, the sprites survey
The growing combat, or assist the fray.
While thro' the press enraged Thalestris flies,
And scatters death around from both her eyes,
A beau and witling perish'd in the throng,
One died in metaphor, and one in song:
"O cruel nymph! a living death I bear,"
Cried Dapperwit, and sunk beside his chair.
A mournful glance Sir Fopling upwards cast,
"Those eyes are made so killing" — was his last.
Thus on Mæander's flow'ry margin lies
Th' expiring swan, and as he sings he dies.
When bold Sir Plume had drawn Clarissa down,
Chloe stepp'd in, and kill'd him with a frown;
She smiled to see the doughty hero slain,
But, at her smile, the beau revived again.
Now Jove suspends his golden scales in air,
Weighs the men's wits against the lady's hair;
The doubtful beam long nods from side to side;
At length the wits mount up, the hairs subside.
See fierce Belinda on the baron flies,
With more than usual lightning in her eyes;
Nor fear'd the chief th' unequal fight to try,
Who sought no more than on his foe to die.

But this bold lord, with manly strength endued,
She with one finger and a thumb subdued:
Just where the breadth of life his nostrils drew,
A charge of snuff the wily virgin threw;
The gnomes direct, to ev'ry atom just,
The pungent grains of titillating dust.
Sudden, with starting tears each eye o'erflows,
And the high dome re-echoes to his nose.
"Now meet thy fate," incens'd Belinda cried,
And drew a deadly bodkin from her side.
(The same, his ancient personage to deck,
Her great-great-grandsire wore about his neck,
In three seal-rings; which after, melted down,
Form'd a vast buckle for his widow's gown:
Her infant grandame's whistle next it grew,
The bells she jingled, and the whistle blew;
Then in a bodkin graced her mother's hairs,
Which long she wore and now Belinda wears.)
"Boast not my fall," he cried, "insulting foe!
Thou by some other shalt be laid as low:
Nor think to die dejects my lofty mind;
All that I dread is leaving you behind!
Rather than so, ah, let me still survive,
And burn in Cupid's flames — but burn alive."
"Restore the lock!" she cries; and all around
"Restore the lock!" the vaulted roofs rebound.
Not fierce Othello in so loud a strain
Roar'd for the handkerchief that caus'd his pain.
But see how oft ambitious aims are cross'd,
And chiefs contend till all the prize is lost!
The lock, obtain'd with guilt, and kept with pain,
In ev'ry place is sought, but sought in vain:
With such a prize no mortal must be blest;
So Heav'n decrees! with Heav'n who can contest?
Some thought it mounted to the lunar sphere,
Since all things lost on earth are treasured there.
There heroes' wits are kept in pond'rous vases,
And beaux' in snuffboxes and tweezer-cases.
There broken vows, and deathbed alms are found,
And lovers' hearts with ends of ribbon bound,
The courtier's promises, and sick man's prayers,
The smiles of harlots, and the tears of heirs,
Cages for gnats, and chains to yoke a flea,
Dried butterflies, and tomes of casuistry.
But trust the Muse — she saw it upward rise,
Tho' mark'd by none but quick poetic eyes
(*So Rome's great founder to the heav'ns withdrew,
To Proculus alone confess'd in view):
A sudden star, it shot thro' liquid air,
And drew behind a radiant trail of hair.
Not *Berenice's locks first rose so bright,
The heav'ns bespangling with dishevell'd light.
The sylphs behold it kindling as it flies,
And pleas'd pursue its progress thro' the skies.
This the beau monde shall from *the Mall survey,
And hail with music its propitious ray;
This the blest lover shall for Venus take,
And send up vows from *Rosamonda's lake;
This *Partridge soon shall view in cloudless skies,
When next he looks thro' Galileo's eyes;
And hence th' egregious wizard shall foredoom
The fate of Louis, and the fall of Rome.
Then cease, bright nymph! to mourn thy ravish'd hair,
Which adds new glory to the shining sphere!
Not all the tresses that fair head can boast,
Shall draw such envy as the lock you lost.
For after all the murders of your eye,
When, after millions slain, yourself shall die;
When those fair suns shall set, as set they must,
And all those tresses shall be laid in dust,
This lock the Muse shall consecrate to fame,
And 'midst the stars inscribe Belinda's name.

[1714]

AN ESSAY ON MAN

IN FOUR EPISTLES TO LORD BOLINGBROKE

Pope was not a great original thinker; he worked best when elaborating rather than constructing for himself. Thus *An Essay on Criticism* deals with the usual concepts of neo-classical literary judgment; his Homer is a translation; the best of the *Satires* are reworked from Horace; *The Dunciad* was, in part at least, suggested by the Scriblerus Club and inspired by Swift. *An Essay on Man* was written under the influence of Bolingbroke. That brilliant man of the world, politician, philosopher, and amateur of letters, after his return from banishment in 1723 lived for a time at Dawley, where he was a neighbour of Pope's. The two saw much of each other and conversed on philosophical topics. The poet's attention was thus turned to a type of deistic speculation with which he had been previously little acquainted. It is too much to say that he merely versified Bolingbroke's ideas, but he certainly drew upon them to no small degree.

An Essay on Man is, as the opening lines assert, an attempt to "vindicate the ways of God to man." In so doing, Pope makes no direct mention of the Christian hope but limits himself to abstract questions of philosophy. Bolingbroke was a free-thinker, but Pope seems to have accepted the central dogmas of the Roman Catholic Church, even though he was willing to dabble in heretical ideas. When the *Essay* was attacked as deistic, he was much disturbed and was grateful for Warburton's defence.

The philosophical ideas of the poem now concern us much less than the brilliant, epigrammatic phrasing which has passed into our stock of current aphorism. Book I, which is here reprinted, contains the fundamental ideas of the whole and sufficiently illustrates its quality.

EPISTLE I

OF THE NATURE AND STATE OF MAN, WITH RESPECT TO THE UNIVERSE

ARGUMENT

Of man in the abstract. I. That we can judge only with regard to our own system, being ignorant of the relations of systems and things, verse 17, etc. II. That man is not to be deemed imperfect, but a being suited to his place and rank in the creation, agreeable to the general order of things, and conformable to ends and relations to him unknown, verse 35, etc. III. That it is partly upon his ignorance of future events, and partly upon the hope of a future state, that all his happiness in the present depends, verse 77, etc. IV. The pride of aiming at more knowledge, and pretending to more perfection, the cause of man's error and misery. The impiety of putting himself in the place of God, and judging of the fitness or unfitness, perfection or imperfection, justice or injustice, of his dispensations, verse 113, etc. V. The absurdity of conceiting himself the final cause of the creation, or expecting that perfection in the moral world which is not in the natural, verse 131, etc. VI. The unreasonableness of his complaints against Providence, while, on the one hand, he demands the perfections of the angels, and, on the other, the bodily qualifications of the brutes; though to possess any of the sensitive faculties in a higher degree would render him miserable, verse 173, etc. VII. That throughout the whole visible world an universal order and gradation in the sensual and mental faculties is observed, which causes a subordination of creature to creature, and of all creatures to man. The gradations of sense, instinct, thought, reflection, reason; that reason alone countervails all the other faculties, verse 207, etc. VIII. How much further this order and subordination of living creatures may extend above and below us; were any part of which broken, not that part only, but the whole connected creation must be destroyed, verse 233, etc. IX. The extravagance, madness and pride of such a desire, verse 259, etc. X. The consequence of all, the absolute submission due to Providence, both as to our present and future state, verse 281, etc., to the end.

Awake, my *St. John! leave all meaner things
To low ambition and the pride of kings.
Let us, since life can little more supply
Than just to look about us and to die,
Expatiate free o'er all this scene of man;
A mighty maze! but not without a plan;
A wild, where weeds and flow'rs promiscuous
  shoot;
Or garden, tempting with forbidden fruit.
Together let us beat this ample field,
Try what the open, what the covert yield;
The latent tracts, the giddy heights, explore
Of all who blindly creep or sightless soar;
Eye nature's walks, shoot folly as it flies,
And catch the manners living as they rise;
Laugh where we must, be *candid where we
  can,
But vindicate the ways of God to man.
  I. Say first, of God above or man below,
What can we reason but from what we know?
Of man what see we but his station here,
From which to reason, or to which refer?
Thro' worlds unnumber'd tho' the God be
  known,
'Tis ours to trace him only in our own.
He who thro' vast immensity can pierce,
See worlds on worlds compose one universe,
Observe how system into system runs,
What other planets circle other suns,
What varied being peoples ev'ry star,
May tell why Heav'n has made us as we are.
But of this frame, the bearings and the ties,
The strong connections, nice dependencies,
Gradations just, has thy pervading soul
Look'd thro'? or can a part contain the whole?
  Is the great chain that draws all to agree,
And drawn supports, upheld by God or thee?
  II. Presumptuous man! the reason wouldst
  thou find,
Why form'd so weak, so little, and so blind?
First, if thou canst, the harder reason guess
Why form'd no weaker, blinder, and no less!
Ask of thy mother earth why oaks are made
Taller or stronger than the weeds they shade!
Or ask of yonder argent fields above
Why Jove's *satellites are less than Jove!
  Of systems possible, if 'tis confess'd
That wisdom infinite must form the best,
Where all must fall or not coherent be,
And all that rises, rise in due degree;
Then in the scale of reas'ning life 'tis plain
There must be, somewhere, such a rank as man:
And all the question (wrangle e'er so long)
Is only this — if God has placed him wrong.

Respecting man, whatever wrong we call,
May, must be right, as relative to all.
In human works, tho' labour'd on with pain,
A thousand movements scarce one purpose gain;
In God's, one single can its end produce,
Yet serves to second too some other use.
So man, who here seems principal alone,
Perhaps acts second to some sphere unknown,
Touches some wheel, or verges to some goal;
'Tis but a part we see, and not a whole.

When the proud steed shall know why man restrains
His fiery course, or drives him o'er the plains;
When the dull ox, why now he breaks the clod,
Is now a victim, and now Egypt's god;
Then shall man's pride and dullness comprehend
His actions', passions', being's, use and end;
Why doing, suff'ring, check'd, impell'd; and why
This hour a slave, the next a deity.

Then say not man's imperfect, Heav'n in fault;
Say rather man's as perfect as he ought;
His knowledge measured to his state and place,
His time a moment, and a point his space.
If to be perfect in a certain sphere,
What matter soon or late, or here or there?
The blest today is as completely so
As who began a thousand years ago.

III. Heav'n from all creatures hides the book of fate,
All but the page prescribed, their present state;
From brutes what men, from men what spirits know;
Or who could suffer being here below?
The lamb thy riot dooms to bleed today,
Had he thy reason, would he skip and play?
Pleas'd to the last, he crops the flow'ry food,
And licks the hand just rais'd to shed his blood.
Oh blindness to the future! kindly giv'n,
That each may fill the circle mark'd by Heav'n;
Who sees with equal eye, as God of all,
A hero perish or a sparrow fall,
Atoms or systems into ruin hurl'd,
And now a bubble burst, and now a world.

Hope humbly then; with trembling pinions soar;
Wait the great teacher, Death, and God adore.
What future bliss he gives not thee to know,
But gives that hope to be thy blessing now.
Hope springs eternal in the human breast;
Man never is, but always to be, bless'd.
The soul, uneasy and confin'd from home,
Rests and expatiates in a life to come.

Lo, the poor Indian! whose untutor'd mind
Sees God in clouds, or hears him in the wind;
His soul proud science never taught to stray
Far as the solar walk or milky way;
Yet simple nature to his hope has giv'n,
Behind the cloud-topt hill, an humbler heav'n,
Some safer world in depth of woods embrac'd,
Some happier island in the wat'ry waste,
Where slaves once more their native land behold,
No fiends torment, no Christians thirst for gold.
To be, contents his natural desire;
He asks no angel's wing, no seraph's fire;
But thinks, admitted to that equal sky,
His faithful dog shall bear him company.

IV. Go, wiser thou! and in thy scale of sense
Weigh thy opinion against Providence;
Call imperfection what thou fanciest such;
Say, here he gives too little, there too much;
Destroy all creatures for thy sport or gust,
Yet cry, if man's unhappy, God's unjust;
If man alone engross not Heav'n's high care,
Alone made perfect here, immortal there:
Snatch from his hand the balance and the rod,
Rejudge his justice, be the god of God.
In pride, in reas'ning pride, our error lies;
All quit their sphere, and rush into the skies!
Pride still is aiming at the bless'd abodes,
Men would be angels, angels would be gods.
Aspiring to be gods if angels fell,
Aspiring to be angels men rebel:
And who but wishes to invert the laws
Of order, sins against th' Eternal Cause.

V. Ask for what end the heav'nly bodies shine,
Earth for whose use — Pride answers, "'Tis for mine!
For me kind nature wakes her genial pow'r,
Suckles each herb, and spreads out ev'ry flower;
Annual for me the grape, the rose renew
The juice nectareous and the balmy dew;
For me the mine a thousand treasures brings;
For me health gushes from a thousand springs;
Seas roll to waft me, suns to light me rise;
My footstool earth, my canopy the skies."

But errs not nature from this gracious end,
From burning suns when livid deaths descend,
When earthquakes swallow, or when tempests sweep
Towns to one grave, whole nations to the deep?
"No," 'tis replied, "the first Almighty Cause

Acts not by partial but by gen'ral laws:
Th' exceptions few; some change since all began;
And what created perfect?" — Why then man?
If the great end be human happiness,
Then nature deviates; and can man do less?
As much that end a constant course requires
Of show'rs and sunshine, as of man's desires;
As much eternal springs and cloudless skies,
As men forever temp'rate, calm and wise.
If plagues or earthquakes break not Heav'n's design,
Why then *a Borgia or a Catiline?
Who knows but He, whose hand the lightning forms,
Who heaves old ocean, and who wings the storms;
Pours fierce ambition in a Cæsar's mind,
Or turns *young Ammon loose to scourge mankind?
From pride, from pride, our very reas'ning springs;
Account for moral as for natural things:
Why charge we Heav'n in those, in these acquit?
In both, to reason right is to submit.
 Better for us, perhaps, it might appear,
Were there all harmony, all virtue here;
That never air or ocean felt the wind;
That never passion discomposed the mind.
But all subsists by elemental strife;
And passions are the elements of life.
The gen'ral order, since the whole began,
Is kept in nature, and is kept in man.
 VI. What would this man? Now upward will he soar,
And little less than angel, would be more;
Now looking downwards, just as griev'd appears
To want the strength of bulls, the fur of bears.
Made for his use all creatures if he call,
Say what their use, had he the powers of all?
Nature to these without profusion kind,
The proper organs, proper pow'rs assign'd;
Each seeming want compensated of course,
Here with degrees of swiftness, there of force;
All in exact proportion to the state;
Nothing to add, and nothing to abate.
Each beast, each insect, happy in its own:
Is Heav'n unkind to man, and man alone?
Shall he alone, whom rational we call,
Be pleas'd with nothing if not bless'd with all?
 The bliss of man (could pride that blessing find)
Is not to act or think beyond mankind;
No pow'rs of body or of soul to share,
But what his nature and his state can bear.
Why has not man a microscopic eye?
For this plain reason, man is not a fly.
Say, what the use, were finer optics giv'n,
T' inspect a mite, not comprehend the Heav'n?
Or touch, if tremblingly alive all o'er,
To smart and agonize at every pore?
Or quick effluvia darting thro' the brain,
Die of a rose in aromatic pain?
If nature thunder'd in his op'ning ears,
And stunn'd him with the music of the spheres,
How would he wish that Heav'n had left him still
The whisp'ring zephyr and the purling rill?
Who finds not Providence all good and wise,
Alike in what it gives and what denies?
 VII. Far as creation's ample range extends,
The scale of sensual, mental pow'rs ascends:
Mark how it mounts to man's imperial race
From the green myriads in the peopled grass;
What modes of sight betwixt each wide extreme,
The mole's dim curtain and the lynx's beam:
Of smell, the headlong lioness between,
And hound sagacious on the tainted green:
Of hearing, from the life that fills the flood
To that which warbles thro' the vernal wood:
The spider's touch, how exquisitely fine!
Feels at each thread, and lives along the line:
In the nice bee what sense so subtly true,
From pois'nous herbs extracts the healing dew?
How instinct varies in the grov'lling swine,
Compared, half-reas'ning elephant, with thine!
'Twixt that and reason what a nice barrier!
Forever sep'rate, yet forever near!
Remembrance and reflection how allied;
What thin partitions sense from thought divide:
And middle natures how they long to join,
Yet never pass th' insuperable line!
Without this just gradation could they be
Subjected, these to those, or all to thee?
The pow'rs of all subdu'd by thee alone,
Is not thy reason all these pow'rs in one?
 VIII. See, thro' this air, this ocean, and this earth,
All matter quick, and bursting into birth.
Above, how high progressive life may go!
Around, how wide! how deep extend below!
Vast chain of being! which from God began,
Natures ethereal, human, angel, man,
Beast, bird, fish, insect, what no eye can see,
No glass can reach; from infinite to thee,

From thee to nothing. On superior pow'rs
Were we to press, inferior might on ours:
Or in the full creation leave a void,
Where, one step broken, the great scale's destroy'd:
From nature's chain whatever link you strike,
Tenth, or ten thousandth, breaks the chain alike.
  And if each system in gradation roll,
Alike essential to th' amazing whole,
The least confusion but in one, not all
That system only, but the whole must fall.
Let earth unbalanced from her orbit fly,
Planets and suns run lawless thro' the sky;
Let ruling angels from their spheres be hurl'd,
Being on being wreck'd, and world on world;
Heav'n's whole foundations to their centre nod,
And nature tremble to the throne of God!
All this dread order break — for whom? for thee?
Vile worm! — oh, madness! pride! impiety!
  IX. What if the foot, ordain'd the dust to tread,
Or hand to toil, aspir'd to be the head?
What if the head, the eye, or ear repin'd
To serve mere engines to the ruling mind?
Just as absurd for any part to claim
To be another in this gen'ral frame;
Just as absurd to mourn the tasks or pains
The great directing Mind of All ordains.
  All are but parts of one stupendous whole,
Whose body nature is, and God the soul;
That chang'd thro' all, and yet in all the same,
Great in the earth as in th' ethereal frame,
Warms in the sun, refreshes in the breeze,
Glows in the stars, and blossoms in the trees;
Lives thro' all life, extends thro' all extent,
Spreads undivided, operates unspent;
Breathes in our soul, informs our mortal part,
As full, as perfect, in a hair as heart;
As full, as perfect, in vile man that mourns,
As the rapt seraph that adores and burns.
To him no high, no low, no great, no small;
He fills, he bounds, connects, and equals all.
  X. Cease, then, nor order imperfection name:
Our proper bliss depends on what we blame.
Know thy own point: this kind, this due degree
Of blindness, weakness, Heav'n bestows on thee.
Submit: in this or any other sphere,
Secure to be as bless'd as thou canst bear;
Safe in the hand of one disposing Pow'r,
Or in the natal or the mortal hour.
All nature is but art, unknown to thee;
All chance, direction which thou canst not see;
All discord, harmony not understood;
All partial evil, universal good:
And spite of pride, in erring reason's spite,
One truth is clear, WHATEVER IS, IS RIGHT.

[1733]

SATIRES, EPISTLES, THE DUNCIAD

In his satires Pope reached the high point of his poetry and gave the world the unique product of his genius. Pastoral, elegy, criticism, mock-heroic, translation, didactic poetry he wrote excellently; but satire was his peculiar talent. Here he took up the mantle of Dryden with a double portion of his master's power. For the past century satire has so far been out of vogue that to many readers it seems mere scolding. In an age when standards of judgment are personal, and one man's opinion is thought as good as another's, satire loses its power, it is no longer the means of enforcing the "general sense." Pope expresses the classical attitude when he says:

Yes, I am proud; I must be proud to see
Men, not afraid of God, afraid of me;
Safe from the bar, the pulpit, and the throne,
Yet touch'd and shamed by ridicule alone.
  O sacred weapon! left for Truth's defence,
Sole dread of Folly, Vice, and Insolence,
To all but Heav'n-directed hands denied,
The Muse may give thee, but the gods must guide!
Rev'rent I touch thee! but with honest zeal,
To rouse the watchmen of the public weal,
To Virtue's work provoke the tardy hall,
And goad the prelate, slumb'ring in his stall.

(Epilogue to *The Satires*, Dialogue II, ll. 208–219.)

It would be extravagant to assert that Pope always lived up to this high ideal, but he cannot be understood if it is unrecognized. The gods did not always guide him aright; imperfect vision, personal and partisan considerations too often warped his judgment and misdirected his shafts. In the main, however, after all allowance has been made for frailty and imperfection, he was true to his trust: in criticism, literary, social, and ethical, he was usually on the right side. That his satire was cutting is no valid objection; satire must be keenly edged if it is to accomplish its purpose. Pope used no two-handed sword but a thin blade of right Damascus steel.

The *Satires* proper were published between 1733 and 1738, after the first version of *The Dunciad* and before the final version, which included the fourth book. They consist of six imitations of Horace, reworkings of two of John Donne's satires (apparently made some time before their publication), a Prologue and an Epilogue. The *Imitations of Horace* are not translations but adaptations; they follow the outlines of the original satires and epistles rather closely, but they introduce English references in place of Latin and Greek. They are thus attempts to write in the spirit of Horace, as he might have done had he lived in eighteenth-century England. The Prologue, in the form of an epistle, and the Epilogue in that of two satiric dialogues, do not imitate individual poems of Horace, but are none the less in his style and to some extent in his mood.

The Dunciad, which is here represented only by the first book, is Pope's most important long satire. In form it is a mock-epic, and follows the same plan as Dryden's *Mac Flecknoe*. In the original edition it placed on the throne of Dullness, Lewis Theobald, the rival editor of Shakespeare, who had in 1726 published *Shakespeare Restored*, an attack upon Pope's editorial work. The poem seems to have grown out of the Scriblerus Club's satire upon dullness in poets and pedantry in scholars. When *The Dunciad* was finally revised in 1742–43, Theobald was dethroned and Colley Cibber, the Poet Laureate was elevated as Monarch of Dullness. The criticism that Cibber, whatever his faults, was a sprightly person rather than a dullard is based upon the modern understanding of the word. In Pope's time *dullness* was conceived as the antithesis of wit; hence a poet might be described as dull because his work was in bad taste, because it did not conform to the generally accepted standards of good poetry.

Another common criticism of *The Dunciad* is that it attacked nobodies, mere poetasters who would be forgotten today had they not been here given the immortality of ridicule. In one respect this is merely to affirm that Pope knew a dunce when he saw one, but it ignores the fact that some of these men had considerable reputation in their own day until it was laughed away by his satire. That Pope's judgments have been for the most part confirmed by time is a recognition of his ability as a critic.

Though many nineteenth-century readers were repelled by the venom of the poem and by its Swiftian coarseness, the present generation is learning better to understand the forthrightness of the eighteenth century and to prefer it to Victorian fastidiousness. More important for its true understanding is a recognition that *The Dunciad* embodies its author's hatred, not only of particular dunces but of incarnate dullness. As such it becomes the final expression of Pope's ruling passion, and at the same time it transcends the local and too often petty concerns in which it originated.

EPISTLE TO DR. ARBUTHNOT

BEING THE PROLOGUE TO THE SATIRES

P. "Shut, shut the door, *good John!" fatigued, I said;
"Tie up the knocker; say I'm sick, I'm dead."
The Dog Star rages! nay, 'tis past a doubt
All Bedlam or Parnassus is let out:
Fire in each eye, and papers in each hand,
They rave, recite, and madden round the land.
What walls can guard me, or what shades can hide?
They pierce my thickets, *thro' my grot they glide,
By land, by water, they renew the charge,
They stop the chariot, and they board the barge.
No place is sacred; not the church is free;
Ev'n Sunday shines no Sabbath-day to me:
Then from *the Mint walks forth the man of rhyme,
Happy to catch me just at dinner time.
Is there a parson much bemused in beer,
A maudlin poetess, a rhyming peer,
A clerk, foredoom'd his father's soul to cross,
Who pens a stanza when he should engross?
Is there who, lock'd from ink and paper, scrawls
With desp'rate charcoal round his darken'd walls?
All fly to *Twit'nam, and in humble strain
Apply to me to keep them mad or vain.
*Arthur, whose giddy son neglects the laws,
Imputes to me and my damn'd works the cause:
Poor Cornus sees his frantic wife elope
And curses wit and poetry, and Pope.
Friend to my life (which did not you prolong,
The world had wanted many an idle song),
What drop or nostrum can this plague remove?
Or which must end me, a fool's wrath or love?
A dire dilemma! either way I'm sped;

If foes, they write, if friends, they read me dead.
Seiz'd and tied down to judge, how wretched I!
Who can't be silent, and who will not lie.
To laugh were want of goodness and of grace,
And to be grave exceeds all power of face.
I sit with sad civility, I read
With honest anguish and an aching head;
And drop at last, but in unwilling ears,
This saving counsel, * "Keep your piece nine years."
"Nine years!" cries he, who, high in Drury Lane,
Lull'd by soft zephyrs thro' the broken pane,
Rhymes ere he wakes, and prints before Term ends,
* Obliged by hunger, and request of friends:
"The piece, you think, is incorrect? why, take it;
I'm all submission; what you'd have it, make it."
Three things another's modest wishes bound,
My friendship, and a prologue, and ten pound.
* Pitholeon sends to me: "You know his Grace;
I want a patron; ask him for a place."
Pitholeon libell'd me — "But here's a letter
Informs you, sir, 'twas when he knew no better.
Dare you refuse him? * Curll invites to dine;
He'll write a Journal, or he'll turn divine."
Bless me! a packet. "'Tis a stranger sues,
A virgin tragedy, an orphan Muse."
If I dislike it, "Furies, death, and rage!"
If I approve, "Commend it to the stage."
There (thank my stars) my whole commission ends;
The play'rs and I are, luckily, no friends.
Fired that the house reject him, "'Sdeath, I'll print it,
And shame the fools — your int'rest, sir, with * Lintot."
Lintot, dull rogue, will think your price too much:
"Not, sir, if you revise it, and retouch."
All my demurs but double his attacks;
At last he whispers, "Do, and we go snacks."
Glad of a quarrel, straight I clap the door:
"Sir, let me see your works and you no more."
'Tis sung, when Midas' ears began to spring,
(Midas, a sacred person and a king)
His very minister who spied them first,
(Some say his queen) was forc'd to speak or burst.
And is not mine, my friend, a sorer case,
When ev'ry coxcomb perks them in my face?
A. Good friend, forbear! you deal in dang'rous things;
I'd never name queens, ministers, or kings;
Keep close to ears, and those let asses prick,
'Tis nothing — *P.* Nothing? if they bite and kick?
Out with it, *Dunciad!* let the secret pass,
That secret to each fool, that he's an ass:
The truth once told (and wherefore should we lie?)
The queen of Midas slept, and so may I.
You think this cruel? take it for a rule,
No creature smarts so little as a fool.
Let peals of laughter, * Codrus! round thee break,
Thou unconcern'd canst hear the mighty crack:
Pit, box, and gall'ry in convulsions hurl'd,
Thou stand'st unshook amidst a bursting world.
Who shames a scribbler? break one cobweb thro',
He spins the slight self-pleasing thread anew:
Destroy his fib, or sophistry — in vain!
The creature's at his dirty work again,
Thron'd in the centre of his thin designs,
Proud of a vast extent of flimsy lines!
Whom have I hurt? has poet yet, or peer
Lost the arch'd eyebrow or Parnassian sneer?
And has not Colley still his lord and whore?
* His butchers, Henley? his freemasons, Moore?
Does not one table * Bavius still admit?
* Still to one bishop, Philips seem a wit?
Still * Sappho — *A.* Hold! for God's sake! — you'll offend:
No names — be calm — learn prudence of a friend.
I too could write, and I am twice as tall;
But foes like these — *P.* One flatt'rer's worse than all.
Of all mad creatures, if the learn'd are right,
It is the slaver kills, and not the bite.
A fool quite angry is quite innocent:
Alas! 'tis ten times worse when they repent.
One dedicates in high heroic prose,
And ridicules beyond a hundred foes:
One from all Grub Street will my fame defend,
And, more abusive, calls himself my friend.
This prints my letters, that expects a bribe,
And others roar aloud, "Subscribe, subscribe!"
There are who to my person pay their court:

I cough like Horace; and tho' lean, am short;
Ammon's great son one shoulder had too high,
Such Ovid's nose, and, "Sir! you have an eye."
Go on, obliging creatures, make me see
All that disgrac'd my betters met in me.
Say, for my comfort, languishing in bed,
"Just so immortal Maro held his head":
And when I die, be sure you let me know
Great Homer died three thousand years ago.
Why did I write? what sin to me unknown
Dipp'd me in ink, my parents', or my own?
As yet a child, nor yet a fool to fame,
I lisp'd in numbers, for the numbers came.
I left no calling for this idle trade,
No duty broke, no father disobey'd:
The Muse but serv'd to ease some friend, not wife,
To help me thro' this long disease, my life;
To second, Arbuthnot! thy art and care,
And teach the being you preserv'd, to bear.
A. But why then publish? *P*. * Granville the polite,
And knowing Walsh, would tell me I could write;
Well-natured Garth inflam'd with early praise,
And Congreve lov'd, and Swift endur'd my lays;
The courtly * Talbot, Somers, Sheffield, read;
Ev'n * mitred Rochester would nod the head,
And St. John's self (great Dryden's friends before)
With open arms receiv'd one poet more.
Happy my studies, when by these approv'd!
Happier their author, when by these belov'd!
From these the world will judge of men and books,
Not from the * Burnets, Oldmixons, and Cookes.
Soft were my numbers; who could take offence
While * pure description held the place of sense?
* Like gentle Fanny's was my flowery theme,
A painted mistress, or a purling stream.
Yet then did * Gildon draw his venal quill;
I wish'd the man a dinner, and sat still.
Yet then did * Dennis rave in furious fret;
I never answer'd, — I was not in debt.
If want provok'd, or madness made them print,
I wag'd no war with Bedlam or the Mint.
Did some more sober critic come abroad;
If wrong, I smiled; if right, I kiss'd the rod.
Pains, reading, study, are their just pretence,
And all they want is spirit, taste, and sense.
Commas and points they set exactly right,
And 'twere a sin to rob them of their mite.
Yet ne'er one sprig of laurel graced these ribalds,
From * slashing Bentley down to piddling Tibbalds.
Each wight who reads not, and but scans and spells,
Each word-catcher that lives on syllables,
Ev'n such small critics some regard may claim,
Preserv'd in Milton's or in Shakespeare's name.
Pretty! in amber to observe the forms
Of hairs, or straws, or dirt, or grubs, or worms!
The things, we know, are neither rich nor rare,
But wonder how the devil they got there.
Were others angry, I excuse them too;
Well might they rage, I gave them but their due.
A man's true merit 'tis not hard to find;
But each man's secret standard in his mind,
That casting-weight pride adds to emptiness,
This, who can gratify? for who can guess?
* The bard whom pilfer'd pastorals renown,
Who turns a Persian tale for half a crown,
Just writes to make his barrenness appear,
And strains from hard-bound brains eight lines a year;
He who still wanting, tho' he lives on theft,
Steals much, spends little, yet has nothing left;
And he who now to sense, now nonsense leaning,
Means not, but blunders round about a meaning;
And he whose fustian's so sublimely bad,
It is not poetry, but prose run mad:
All these my modest satire bade translate,
And own'd that * nine such poets made a Tate.
How did they fume, and stamp, and roar, and chafe!
And swear not Addison himself was safe.
* Peace to all such! but were there one whose fires
True genius kindles, and fair fame inspires;
Bless'd with each talent and each art to please,
And born to write, converse, and live with ease:
Should such a man, too fond to rule alone,
Bear, like the Turk, no brother near the throne;
View him with scornful, yet with jealous eyes,
And hate for arts that caus'd himself to rise;
Damn with faint praise, assent with civil leer,

And, without sneering, teach the rest to sneer;
Willing to wound, and yet afraid to strike,
Just hint a fault, and hesitate dislike;
Alike reserv'd to blame or to commend,
A tim'rous foe, and a suspicious friend;
Dreading ev'n fools, by flatterers besieged,
And so obliging that he ne'er obliged;
Like Cato, give his little senate laws,
And sit attentive to his own applause:
While wits and Templars ev'ry sentence raise,
And wonder with a foolish face of praise —
Who but must laugh if such a man there be?
Who would not weep, if Atticus were he?
  What tho' my name stood rubric on the walls,
Or plaster'd posts, with claps, in capitals?
Or smoking forth, a hundred hawkers' load,
On wings of winds came flying all abroad?
I sought no homage from the race that write;
I kept, like Asian Monarchs, from their sight:
Poems I heeded (now be-rhymed so long)
No more than thou, great George! a birthday song.
I ne'er with wits or witlings pass'd my days
To spread about the itch of verse and praise;
Nor like a puppy daggled thro' the town
To fetch and carry sing-song up and down;
Nor at rehearsals sweat, and mouth'd and cried,
With handkerchief and orange at my side;
But sick of fops, and poetry, and prate,
To *Bufo left the whole Castalian state.
  Proud as Apollo on his forked hill
Sat full-blown Bufo, puff'd by ev'ry quill;
Fed with soft dedication all day long,
Horace and he went hand in hand in song.
His library (where busts of poets dead,
And a true Pindar stood without a head)
Receiv'd of wits an undistinguish'd race,
Who first his judgment ask'd, and then a place:
Much they extoll'd his pictures, much his seat,
And flatter'd ev'ry day, and some days eat:
'Till grown more frugal in his riper days,
He paid some bards with port, and some with praise;
To some a dry rehearsal was assign'd,
And others (harder still) he paid in kind.
Dryden alone (what wonder?) came not nigh;
Dryden alone escaped this judging eye:
But still the great have kindness in reserve;
He help'd to bury whom he help'd to starve.
  May some choice patron bless each gray goose quill!
May every Bavius have his Bufo still!
So when a statesman wants a day's defence,
Or envy holds a whole week's war with sense,
Or simple pride for flatt'ry makes demands,
May dunce by dunce be whistled off my hands!
Bless'd be the great! for those they take away,
And those they left me — for they left me Gay;
Left me to see neglected genius bloom,
Neglected die, and tell it on his tomb:
Of all thy blameless life the sole return
My verse, and *Queensb'ry weeping o'er thy urn!
  Oh let me live my own, and die so too,
(To live and die is all I have to do)
Maintain a poet's dignity and ease,
And see what friends, and read what books I please:
Above a patron, tho' I condescend
Sometimes to call a minister my friend.
I was not born for courts or great affairs:
I pay my debts, believe, and say my prayers;
Can sleep without a poem in my head,
Nor know if Dennis be alive or dead.
  Why am I ask'd what next shall see the light?
Heav'ns! was I born for nothing but to write?
Has life no joys for me? or (to be grave)
Have I no friend to serve, no soul to save?
"I found him close with Swift" — "Indeed? no doubt,"
Cries prating Balbus, "something will come out."
'Tis all in vain, deny it as I will.
"No, such a genius never can lie still";
And then for mine obligingly mistakes
The first lampoon *Sir Will or Bubo makes.
Poor guiltless I! and can I choose but smile,
When ev'ry coxcomb knows me by my style?
  Curs'd be the verse, how well soe'er it flow,
That tends to make one worthy man my foe,
Give virtue scandal, innocence a fear,
Or from the soft-eyed virgin steal a tear!
But he who hurts a harmless neighbour's peace,
Insults fall'n worth, or beauty in distress,
Who loves a lie, lame slander helps about,
Who writes a libel, or who copies out;
That fop whose pride affects a patron's name,
Yet absent, wounds an author's honest fame;
Who can your merit selfishly approve,
And show the sense of it without the love;
Who has the vanity to call you friend,
Yet wants the honour, injur'd, to defend;
Who tells whate'er you think, whate'er you say,
And, if he lie not, must at least betray;
*Who to the *dean* and *silver bell* can swear,

And sees at Canons what was never there;
Who reads but with a lust to misapply,
Make satire a lampoon, and fiction lie:
A lash like mine no honest man shall dread,
But all such babbling blockheads in his stead.
Let * Sporus tremble — *A.* What? that thing of silk,
Sporus, that mere white curd of ass's milk?
Satire or sense, alas! can Sporus feel?
Who breaks a butterfly upon a wheel?
P. Yet let me flap this bug with gilded wings,
This painted child of dirt, that stinks and stings;
Whose buzz the witty and the fair annoys,
Yet wit ne'er tastes, and beauty ne'er enjoys:
So well-bred spaniels civilly delight
In mumbling of the game they dare not bite.
Eternal smiles his emptiness betray,
As shallow streams run dimpling all the way,
Whether in florid impotence he speaks,
And, as the prompter breathes, the puppet squeaks;
Or * at the ear of Eve, familiar toad,
Half froth, half venom, spits himself abroad,
In puns, or politics, or tales, or lies,
Or spite, or smut, or rhymes, or blasphemies.
His wit all see-saw between that and this,
Now high, now low, now master up, now miss,
And he himself one vile antithesis.
Amphibious thing! that acting either part,
The trifling head, or the corrupted heart;
Fop at the toilet, flatt'rer at the board,
Now trips a lady, and now struts a lord.
Eve's tempter thus the Rabbins have express'd,
A cherub's face, a reptile all the rest;
Beauty that shocks you, parts that none will trust,
Wit that can creep, and pride that licks the dust.
Not fortune's worshipper, nor fashion's fool,
Not lucre's madman, nor ambition's tool,
Not proud nor servile; — be one poet's praise,
That if he pleas'd, he pleas'd by manly ways:
That flatt'ry, ev'n to kings, he held a shame,
And thought a lie in verse or prose the same;
That not in fancy's maze he wander'd long,
But stoop'd to truth, and moraliz'd his song:
That not for fame, but virtue's better end,
He stood the furious foe, the timid friend,
The damning critic, half-approving wit,
The coxcomb hit, or fearing to be hit;
Laugh'd at the loss of friends he never had,
The dull, the proud, the wicked, and the mad;
The distant threats of vengeance on his head,
The blow unfelt, the tear he never shed;
The tale reviv'd, the lie so oft o'erthrown,
Th' imputed trash and dullness not his own;
The morals blacken'd when the writings 'scape,
The libell'd person, and the pictur'd shape;
Abuse on all he lov'd, or lov'd him, spread,
A friend in exile, or a father dead;
The whisper that, to greatness still too near,
Perhaps yet vibrate on his sov'reign's ear, —
Welcome for thee, fair Virtue! all the past:
For thee, fair Virtue! welcome ev'n the last!
A. But why insult the poor? affront the great?
P. A knave's a knave to me in ev'ry state;
Alike my scorn, if he succeed or fail,
Sporus at court, or * Japhet in a jail;
A hireling scribbler, or a hireling peer,
* Knight of the post corrupt, or of the shire;
If on a pillory, or near a throne,
He gain his prince's ear, or lose his own.
Yet soft by nature, more a dupe than wit,
Sappho can tell you how this man was bit:
This dreaded satirist * Dennis will confess
Foe to his pride, but friend to his distress:
So humble, he has knock'd at Tibbald's door,
Has drunk with Cibber, nay, has rhymed for Moore.
Full ten years slander'd, did he once reply?
Three thousand suns went down on Welsted's lie.
To please a mistress one aspers'd his life;
He lash'd him not, but let her be his wife:
* Let Budgell charge low Grub Street on his quill,
And write whate'er he pleas'd, except his will;
Let * the two Curlls of town and court abuse
His father, mother, body, soul, and Muse.
Yet why? that father held it for a rule,
It was a sin to call our neighbour fool:
That harmless mother thought no wife a whore:
Hear this, and spare his family, James Moore!
Unspotted names, and memorable long,
If there be force in virtue, or in song.
Of gentle blood (part shed in honour's cause,
While yet in Britain honour had applause)
Each parent sprung — *A.* What fortune, pray? —
P. Their own;
* And better got than Bestia's from the throne.
Born to no pride, inheriting no strife,

Nor marrying discord in a noble wife,
Stranger to civil and religious rage,
The good man walk'd innoxious thro' his age.
No courts he saw, no suits would ever try,
*Nor dar'd an oath, nor hazarded a lie.
Unlearn'd, he knew no schoolman's subtle art,
No language but the language of the heart.
By nature honest, by experience wise,
Healthy by temp'rance and by exercise;
His life, tho' long, to sickness pass'd unknown,
His death was instant and without a groan.
Oh grant me thus to live, and thus to die!
Who sprung from kings shall know less joy than I.

O friend! may each domestic bliss be thine!
Be no unpleasing melancholy mine:
Me, let the tender office long engage
To rock the cradle of reposing age,
With lenient arts extend a mother's breath,
Make languor smile, and smooth the bed of death;
Explore the thought, explain the asking eye,
And keep awhile one parent from the sky!
On cares like these if length of days attend,
May Heav'n, to bless those days, preserve my friend,
Preserve him social, cheerful, and serene,
And just as rich as when he serv'd a queen.
A. Whether that blessing be denied or giv'n,
Thus far was right; — the rest belongs to Heav'n.

[1735]

SATIRES, EPISTLES, AND ODES OF HORACE IMITATED

THE FIRST SATIRE OF THE SECOND BOOK OF HORACE

TO * MR. FORTESCUE

P. There are (I scarce can think it, but am told),
There are to whom my satire seems too bold:
Scarce to *wise Peter complaisant enough,
And something said of *Chartres much too rough.
The lines are weak, another's pleas'd to say;
Lord Fanny spins a thousand such a day.
Tim'rous by nature, of the rich in awe,
I come to counsel learned in the law:
You'll give me, like a friend both sage and free,
Advice; and (as you use) without a fee.

F. I'd write no more.
P. Not write? but then I think,
And for my soul I cannot sleep a wink.
I nod in company, I wake at night;
Fools rush into my head, and so I write.
F. You could not do a worse thing for your life.
Why, if the nights seem tedious — take a wife:
Or rather, truly, if your point be rest,
Lettuce and cowslip wine; **probatum est.*
But talk with *Celsus, Celsus will advise
Hartshorn, or something that shall close your eyes.
Or if you needs must write, write Cæsar's praise;
You'll gain at least a knighthood or the bays.
P. What? like *Sir Richard, rumbling, rough, and fierce,
With arms, and George, and Brunswick, crowd the verse;
Rend with tremendous sound your ears asunder,
With gun, drum, trumpet, blunderbuss, and thunder?
Or nobly wild, with Budgell's fire and force,
Paint angels trembling round his falling horse?
F. Then all your Muse's softer art display,
Let *Carolina smooth the tuneful lay;
Lull with *Amelia's liquid name the Nine,
And sweetly flow thro' all the royal line.
P. Alas! few verses touch their nicer ear;
They scarce can bear their Laureate twice a year;
And justly Cæsar scorns the poet's lays;
It is to history he trusts for praise.
F. Better be Cibber, I'll maintain it still,
Than ridicule all taste, blaspheme quadrille,
Abuse the city's best good men in metre,
And laugh at peers that put their trust in Peter.
Ev'n those you touch not, hate you.
P. What should ail 'em?
F. A hundred smart in *Timon and in Balaam:
The fewer still you name, you wound the more;
*Bond is but one, but Harpax is a score.
P. Each mortal has his pleasure: none deny
*Scarsdale his bottle, Darty his ham-pie;
*Ridotta sips and dances till she see
The doubling lustres dance as fast as she;
*F— loves the senate, Hockley Hole his brother,
Like in all else, as one egg to another.
I love to pour out all myself as plain
As *downright Shippen, or as old Montaigne:

In them, as certain to be lov'd as seen,
The soul stood forth, nor kept a thought within;
In me what spots (for spots I have) appear,
Will prove at least the medium must be clear.
In this impartial glass my Muse intends
Fair to expose myself, my foes, my friends;
Publish the present age; but where my text
Is vice too high, reserve it for the next:
My foes shall wish my life a longer date,
And ev'ry friend the less lament my fate.
My head and heart thus flowing thro' my quill,
Verse-man or prose-man, term me which you will,
* Papist or Protestant, or both between,
Like good Erasmus, in an honest mean,
In moderation placing all my glory,
While Tories call me Whig, and Whigs a Tory.
Satire's my weapon, but I'm too discreet
To run amuck, and tilt at all I meet;
I only wear it in a land of Hectors,
Thieves, supercargoes, sharpers, and directors.
Save but our army! and let Jove incrust
Swords, pikes, and guns, with everlasting rust!
* Peace is my dear delight — not Fleury's more:
But touch me, and no minister so sore.
Whoe'er offends, at some unlucky time
Slides into verse, and hitches in a rhyme,
Sacred to ridicule his whole life long,
And the sad burden of some merry song.
Slander or * poison dread from Delia's rage;
Hard words or hanging, if your judge be * Page.
From * furious Sappho scarce a milder fate,
P–x'd by her love, or libell'd by her hate.
Its proper pow'r to hurt each creature feels;
Bulls aim their horns, and asses lift their heels;
'Tis a bear's talent not to kick, but hug;
And no man wonders he's not stung by pug.
So drink with Walters, or with Chartres eat,
They'll never poison you; they'll only cheat.
Then, learned sir! (to cut the matter short)
Whate'er my fate, or well or ill at court,
Whether old age, with faint but cheerful ray,
Attends to gild the ev'ning of my day,
Or death's black wing already be display'd,
To wrap me in the universal shade;
Whether the darken'd room to muse invite,
Or whiten'd wall provoke the skewer to write;
In durance, exile, Bedlam, or the Mint,
Like * Lee or Budgell I will rhyme and print.
F. Alas, young man! your days can ne'er be long;
In flow'r of age you perish for a song!
Plums and directors, * Shylock and his wife,
Will club their * testers now to take your life.
P. What? arm'd for virtue when I point the pen,
Brand the bold front of shameless guilty men,
Dash the proud gamester in his gilded car,
Bare the mean heart that lurks beneath a star;
Can there be wanting, to defend her cause,
Lights of the Church, or guardians of the laws?
Could pension'd Boileau lash in honest strain
Flatt'rers and bigots ev'n in Louis' reign?
Could Laureate Dryden pimp and friar engage,
Yet neither Charles nor James be in a rage?
And I not strip the gilding off a knave,
Unplac'd, unpension'd, no man's heir or slave?
I will, or perish in the gen'rous cause.
Hear this, and tremble! you who 'scape the laws:
Yes, while I live, no rich or noble knave
Shall walk the world in credit to his grave.
To Virtue only and her friends a friend,
The world beside may murmur or commend.
Know, all the distant din that world can keep,
Rolls o'er my grotto and but soothes my sleep.
There my retreat the best companions grace,
Chiefs out of war, and statesmen out of place:
There St. John mingles with my friendly bowl
The feast of reason and the flow of soul:
And * he, whose lightning pierced th' Iberian lines,
Now forms my quincunx, and now ranks my vines,
Or tames the genius of the stubborn plain,
Almost as quickly as he conquer'd Spain.
Envy must own I live among the great,
No pimp of pleasure, and no spy of state,
With eyes that pry not, tongue that ne'er repeats,
Fond to spread friendships, but to cover heats;
To help who want, to forward who excel;
This, all who know me, know; who love me, tell:
And who unknown defame me, let them be
Scribblers or peers, alike are mob to me.
This is my plea, on this I rest my cause —
What saith my counsel, learned in the laws?
F. Your plea is good; but still I say, beware!
Laws are explain'd by men — so have a care.
It stands on record, that in Richard's times
A man was hang'd for very honest rhymes.
Consult the statute: * *quart.* I think it is,
Edwardi sext. or *prim. et quint. Eliz.*
See Libels, Satires,— here you have it — read.
P. * Libels and satires! lawless things indeed!
But grave epistles, bringing vice to light,
Such as a king might read, a bishop write;
Such as Sir Robert would approve —

F. Indeed!
The case is alter'd — you may then proceed;
In such a cause the plaintiff will be hiss'd,
My lords the judges laugh, and you're dismiss'd.

[1733]

THE FIRST EPISTLE OF THE SECOND BOOK OF HORACE

ADVERTISEMENT

The reflections of Horace, and the judgments passed in his Epistle to Augustus, seemed so seasonable to the present times that I could not help applying them to the use of my own country. The author thought them considerable enough to address them to his prince, whom he paints with all the great and good qualities of a monarch upon whom the Romans depended for the increase of an absolute empire; but to make the poem entirely English, I was willing to add one or two of those which contribute to the happiness of a free people, and are more consistent with the welfare of our neighbours.

This epistle will show the learned world to have fallen into two mistakes: one, that Augustus was a patron of poets in general; whereas he not only prohibited all but the best writers to name him, but recommended that care even to the civil magistrate: *Admonebat prætores, ne paterentur nomen suum obsolefieri*, &c. The other, that this piece was only a general discourse of poetry; whereas it was an apology for the poets, in order to render Augustus more their patron. Horace here pleads the cause of his contemporaries; first, against the taste of the town, whose humour it was to magnify the authors of the preceding age; secondly, against the court and nobility, who encouraged only the writers for the theatre; and, lastly, against the Emperor himself, who had conceived them of little use to the government. He shows (by a view of the progress of learning, and the change of taste among the Romans) that the introduction of the polite arts of Greece had given the writers of his time great advantages over their predecessors; that their morals were much improved, and the licence of those ancient poets restrained; that satire and comedy were become more just and useful; that whatever extravagancies were left on the stage were owing to the ill taste of the nobility; that poets, under due regulations, were in many respects useful to the state; and concludes, that it was upon them the Emperor himself must depend for his fame with posterity.

We may further learn from this epistle, that Horace made his court to this great prince by writing with a decent freedom toward him, with a just contempt of his low flatterers, and with a manly regard to his own character.

POPE

* TO AUGUSTUS

* While you, great patron of mankind! sustain
The balanced world, and open all the main;
Your country, chief, in arms abroad defend,
At home with morals, arts, and laws amend;
How shall the Muse, from such a monarch, steal
An hour, and not defraud the public weal?
Edward and Henry, now the boast of fame,
And virtuous Alfred, a more sacred name,
After a life of gen'rous toils endur'd,
The Gaul subdu'd, or property secur'd,
Ambition humbled, mighty cities storm'd,
Or laws establish'd, and the world reform'd;
Clos'd their long glories with a sigh, to find
Th' unwilling gratitude of base mankind!
All human virtue, to its latest breath,
Finds envy never conquer'd but by death.
The great Alcides, ev'ry labour past,
Had still this monster to subdue at last.
Sure fate of all, beneath whose rising ray
Each star of meaner merit fades away!
Oppress'd we feel the beam directly beat;
Those suns of glory please not till they set.
To thee the world its present homage pays,
The harvest early, but mature the praise:
Great friend of liberty! in kings a name
Above all Greek, above all Roman fame;
Whose word is truth, as sacred and rever'd
As Heav'n's own oracles from altars heard.
Wonder of kings! like whom to mortal eyes
None e'er has risen, and none e'er shall rise.
Just in one instance, be it yet confess'd
Your people, sir, are partial in the rest;
Foes to all living worth except your own,
And advocates for folly dead and gone.
Authors, like coins, grow dear as they grow old;
It is the rust we value, not the gold.
Chaucer's worst ribaldry is learn'd by rote,
And * beastly Skelton heads of houses quote;
One likes no language but *The Fairy Queen*;
A Scot will fight for * *Christ's Kirk o' the Green*;
And each true Briton is to * Ben so civil,
He swears the Muses met him at the Devil.
Tho' justly Greece her eldest sons admires,
Why should not we be wiser than our sires?
In every public virtue we excel,
We build, we paint, we sing, we dance, as well;
And learned Athens to our art must stoop,
Could she behold us tumbling thro' a hoop.
If time improve our wit as well as wine,
Say at what age a poet grows divine?
Shall we, or shall we not, account him so
Who died, perhaps an hundred years ago?
End all dispute; and fix the year precise
When British bards begin t' immortalize?
"Who lasts a century can have no flaw;
I hold that wit a classic, good in law."
Suppose he wants a year, will you compound?
And shall we deem him ancient, right, and sound,
Or damn to all eternity at once
At ninety-nine a modern and a dunce?
"We shall not quarrel for a year or two;
By courtesy of England he may do."
Then by the rule that made the horsetail bare,
I pluck out year by year, as hair by hair,
And melt down ancients like a heap of snow,
While you, to measure merits, look in * Stowe,
And estimating authors by the year,
Bestow a garland only on a bier.

Shakespeare (whom you and every play-house-bill
Style the divine! the matchless! what you will)
For gain, not glory, wing'd his roving flight,
And grew immortal in his own despite.
Ben, old and poor, as little seem'd to heed
The life to come in every poet's creed.
Who now reads Cowley? if he pleases yet,
His moral pleases, not his pointed wit;
Forgot his epic, nay, Pindaric art,
But still I love the language of his heart.
"Yet surely, surely these were famous men!
What boy but hears the sayings of old Ben?
In all debates where critics bear a part
Not one but nods, and talks of Jonson's art,
Of Shakespeare's nature, and of Cowley's wit;
How Beaumont's judgment check'd what Fletcher writ;
How Shadwell hasty, Wycherley was slow;
But for the passions, Southern sure, and Rowe.
These, only these, support the crowded stage,
From * eldest Heywood down to Cibber's age."
All this may be; the people's voice is odd;
It is, and it is not, the voice of God.
To * *Gammer Gurton* if it give the bays,
And yet deny * *The Careless Husband* praise,
Or say our fathers never broke a rule;
Why then, I say, the public is a fool.
But let them own that greater faults than we
They had, and greater virtues, I'll agree.
Spenser himself affects the obsolete,
And * Sidney's verse halts ill on Roman feet;
Milton's strong pinion now not Heav'n can bound,
Now, serpent-like, in prose he sweeps the ground.
In quibbles angel and archangel join,
And God the Father turns a school-divine.
Not that I'd lop the beauties from his book,
Like slashing Bentley with his desp'rate hook;
Or damn all Shakespeare, like th' affected fool
At court, who hates whate'er he read at school.
But for the wits of either Charles's days,
The mob of gentlemen who wrote with ease;
Sprat, Carew, Sedley, and a hundred more
(Like twinkling stars the Miscellanies o'er),
One simile that solitary shines
In the dry desert of a thousand lines,
Or lengthen'd thought that gleams through many a page,
Has sanctified whole poems for an age.
I lose my patience, and I own it too,
When works are censur'd not as bad, but new;
While, if our elders break all reason's laws,
These fools demand not pardon, but applause.
On Avon's bank, where flow'rs eternal blow,
If I but ask if any weed can grow,
One tragic sentence if I dare deride,
Which * Betterton's grave action dignified,
Or well-mouth'd Booth with emphasis proclaims,
(Tho' but perhaps a muster-roll of names),
How will our fathers rise up in a rage,
And swear all shame is lost in George's age!
You'd think no fools disgrac'd the former reign,
Did not some grave examples yet remain,
Who scorn a lad should teach his father skill,
And having once been wrong, will be so still.
He who, to seem more deep than you or I,
Extols old bards, or * Merlin's prophecy—
Mistake him not; he envies, not admires,
And to debase the sons exalts the sires.
Had ancient times conspir'd to disallow
What then was new, what had been ancient now?
Or what remain'd, so worthy to be read
By learned critics of the mighty dead?
In days of ease, when now the weary sword
Was sheath'd, and luxury with Charles restor'd,
In ev'ry taste of foreign courts improv'd,
"All by the king's example liv'd and lov'd,"
Then peers grew proud in horsemanship t' excel;
* Newmarket's glory rose, as Britain's fell;
The soldier breath'd the gallantries of France,
And ev'ry flow'ry courtier writ romance.
Then marble, soften'd into life, grew warm,
And yielding metal flow'd to human form;
* Lely on animated canvas stole
The sleepy eye that spoke the melting soul.
No wonder then, when all was love and sport,
The willing Muses were debauch'd at court:
* On each enervate string they taught the note
To pant, or tremble thro' a eunuch's throat.
But Britain, changeful as a child at play,
Now calls in princes, and now turns away.
Now Whig, now Tory, what we lov'd we hate;
Now all for pleasure, now for Church and State;
Now for prerogative, and now for laws;
Effects unhappy, from a noble cause.
Time was, a sober Englishman would knock
His servants up, and rise by five o'clock;
Instruct his family in ev'ry rule,
And send his wife to church, his son to school
To worship like his fathers was his care;
To teach their frugal virtues to his heir;
To prove that luxury could never hold,
And place on good security his gold.

Now times are chang'd, and one poetic itch
Has seized the court and city, poor and rich:
Sons, sires, and grandsires, all will wear the bays;
Our wives read Milton, and our daughters plays;
To theatres and to rehearsals throng,
And all our grace at table is a song.
I, who so oft renounce the Muses, lie:
Not —'s self e'er tells more fibs than I;
When sick of Muse, our follies we deplore,
And promise our best friends to rhyme no more;
We wake next morning in a raging fit,
And call for pen and ink to show our wit.
  He serv'd a 'prenticeship who sets up shop;
* Ward tried on puppies and the poor his drop;
Ev'n * Radcliffe's doctors travel first to France,
Nor dare to practise till they've learn'd to dance.
Who builds a bridge that never drove a pile?
(* Should Ripley venture, all the world would smile),
But those who cannot write, and those who can,
All rhyme, and scrawl, and scribble, to a man.
  Yet, sir, reflect; the mischief is not great;
These madmen never hurt the Church or State:
Sometimes the folly benefits mankind;
And rarely av'rice taints the tuneful mind.
Allow him but his plaything of a pen,
He ne'er rebels, or plots, like other men:
Flight of cashiers, or mobs, he'll never mind,
And knows no losses while the Muse is kind.
To cheat a friend or ward, he leaves to Peter;
The good man heaps up nothing but mere metre,
Enjoys his garden and his book in quiet;
And then — a perfect hermit in his diet.
  Of little use the man you may suppose
Who says in verse what others say in prose;
Yet let me show a poet's of some weight,
And (tho' no soldier) useful to the state.
What will a child learn sooner than a song?
What better teach a foreigner the tongue?
What's long or short, each accent where to place,
And speak in public with some sort of grace?
I scarce can think him such a worthless thing,
Unless he praise some monster of a king;
Or virtue or religion turn to sport,
To please a lewd or unbelieving court.
Unhappy Dryden! — In all Charles's days
Roscommon only boasts unspotted bays;
And in our own (excuse some courtly stains)
No whiter page than Addison remains.
He from the taste obscene reclaims our youth,
And sets the passions on the side of truth,
Forms the soft bosom with the gentlest art,
And pours each human virtue in the heart.
Let Ireland tell how wit upheld her cause,
Her trade supported, and supplied her laws;
And leave on Swift this grateful verse engraved,
"The rights a court attack'd, a poet sav'd."
Behold the hand that wrought a nation's cure,
Stretch'd to relieve the idiot and the poor;
Proud vice to brand, or injur'd worth adorn,
And stretch the ray to ages yet unborn.
Not but there are, who merit other palms;
* Hopkins and Sternhold glad the heart with psalms:
The boys and girls whom charity maintains
Implore your help in these pathetic strains:
How could devotion touch the country pews
Unless the gods bestow'd a proper Muse?
Verse cheers their leisure, verse assists their work,
Verse prays for peace, or sings down pope and Turk.
The silenc'd preacher yields to potent strain,
And feels that grace his pray'r besought in vain;
The blessing thrills thro' all the lab'ring throng,
And Heav'n is won by violence of song.
  Our rural ancestors, with little blest,
Patient of labour when the end was rest,
Indulg'd the day that hous'd their annual grain
With feasts, and off'rings, and a thankful strain:
The joy their wives, their sons, and servants share,
Ease of their toil, and partners of their care:
The laugh, the jest, attendants on the bowl,
Smooth'd ev'ry brow, and open'd ev'ry soul:
With growing years the pleasing license grew,
And taunts alternate innocently flew.
But times corrupt, and nature, ill-inclin'd,
Produc'd the point that left a sting behind;
Till friend with friend, and families at strife,
Triumphant malice rag'd thro' private life.
Who felt the wrong, or fear'd it, took th' alarm,
Appeal'd to law, and Justice lent her arm.
At length by wholesome dread of statutes bound,
The poets learn'd to please, and not to wound:

Most warp'd to flatt'ry's side; but some, more nice,
Preserv'd the freedom, and forbore the vice.
Hence satire rose, that just the medium hit,
And heals with morals what it hurts with wit.
  We conquer'd France, but felt our captive's charms,
Her arts victorious triumph'd o'er our arms;
Britain to soft refinements less a foe,
Wit grew polite, and numbers learn'd to flow.
Waller was smooth; but Dryden taught to join
The varying verse, the full resounding line,
The long majestic march, and energy divine;
Tho' still some traces of our rustic vein
And splay-foot verse remain'd, and will remain.
Late, very late, correctness grew our care,
When the tir'd nation breath'd from civil war
Exact Racine and Corneille's noble fire
Show'd us that France had something to admire.
Not but the tragic spirit was our own,
And full in Shakespeare, fair in Otway, shone;
But Otway fail'd to polish or refine,
And fluent Shakespeare scarce effac'd a line.
Ev'n copious Dryden wanted, or forgot,
The last and greatest art — the art to blot.
Some doubt if equal pains or equal fire
The humbler Muse of comedy require.
But in known images of life I guess
The labour greater, as th' indulgence less.
Observe how seldom ev'n the best succeed:
Tell me if Congreve's fools are fools indeed?
What pert, low dialogue has Farquhar writ!
How * Van wants grace, who never wanted wit!
The stage how loosely does * Astræa tread,
Who fairly puts all characters to bed!
And idle Cibber, how he breaks the laws,
To make * poor Pinkey eat with vast applause!
But fill their purse, our poet's work is done,
Alike to them by pathos or by pun.
  O you! whom vanity's light bark conveys
On fame's mad voyage by the wind of praise,
With what a shifting gale your course you ply,
For ever sunk too low, or borne too high!
Who pants for glory finds but short repose;
A breath revives him, or a breath o'erthrows.
Farewell the stage! if just as thrives the play
The silly bard grows fat or falls away.
  There still remains, to mortify a wit,
The many-headed monster of the pit:
A senseless, worthless, and unhonour'd crowd,
Who, to disturb their betters, mighty proud
Clatt'ring their sticks before ten lines are spoke,
Call for the farce, the bear, or the * black-joke.
What dear delight to Britons farce affords!
Ever the taste of mobs, but now of lords;
(Taste, that eternal wanderer, which flies
From heads to ears, and now from ears to eyes.)
The play stands still; damn action and discourse,
Back fly the scenes, and enter foot and horse;
Pageants on pageants, in long order drawn,
Peers, heralds, bishops, ermine, gold, and lawn;
* The Champion too! and, to complete the jest,
Old Edward's armour beams on Cibber's breast.
With laughter sure * Democritus had died,
Had he beheld an audience gape so wide.
Let bear or elephant be e'er so white,
The people sure, the people are the sight!
Ah, luckless poet! stretch thy lungs and roar,
That bear or elephant shall heed thee more;
While all its throats the gallery extends,
And all the thunder of the pit ascends!
Loud as the wolves on * Orcas' stormy steep
Howl to the roarings of the northern deep,
Such is the shout, the long applauding note,
At * Quin's high plume, or Oldfield's petticoat;
Or when from court a birthday suit bestow'd,
Sinks the lost actor in the tawdry load.
Booth enters — hark! the universal peal!
"But has he spoken?" Not a syllable.
What shook the stage, and made the people stare?
* Cato's long wig, flow'r'd gown, and lacquer'd chair.
  Yet lest you think I rally more than teach,
Or praise malignly arts I cannot reach,
Let me for once presume t' instruct the times,
To know the poet from the man of rhymes:
'Tis he who gives my breast a thousand pains,
Can make me feel each passion that he feigns;
Enrage, compose, with more than magic art,
With pity and with terror tear my heart;
And snatch me o'er the earth, or thro' the air,
To Thebes, to Athens, when he will, and where.
  But not this part of the poetic state
Alone deserves the favour of the great;
Think of those authors, sir, who would rely
More on a reader's sense than gazer's eye.
Or who shall wander where the Muses sing?
Who climb their mountain, or who taste their spring?
* How shall we fill a library with wit,

When Merlin's Cave is half unfurnish'd yet?
My liege! why writers little claim your thought,
I guess; and, with their leave, will tell the fault.
We poets are (upon a poet's word)
Of all mankind the creatures most absurd:
The season when to come, and when to go,
To sing, or cease to sing, we never know;
And if we will recite nine hours in ten,
You lose your patience just like other men.
Then, too, we hurt ourselves when, to defend
A single verse, we quarrel with a friend;
Repeat, unask'd; lament, the wit's too fine
For vulgar eyes, and point out ev'ry line.
But most, when straining with too weak a wing
We needs will write epistles to the king;
And from the moment we oblige the town,
Expect a place or pension from the crown;
Or dubb'd historians by express command,
T' enroll your triumphs o'er the seas and land,
Be call'd to court to plan some work divine,
As once for Louis, Boileau and Racine.
Yet think, great sir! (so many virtues shown)
Ah think, what poet best may make them known?
Or choose at least some minister of grace,
Fit to bestow the Laureate's weighty place.
*Charles, to late times to be transmitted fair,
Assign'd his figure to Bernini's care;
*And great Nassau to Kneller's hand decreed
To fix him graceful on the bounding steed;
So well in paint and stone they judg'd of merit:
But kings in wit may want discerning spirit.
The hero William, and the martyr Charles,
One knighted *Blackmore, and one pension'd Quarles,
Which made old Ben and surly Dennis swear
"No Lord's anointed, but a Russian bear."
Not with such majesty, such bold relief,
The forms august of king, or conqu'ring chief,
E'er swell'd on marble, as in verse have shin'd
(In polish'd verse) the manners and the mind.
Oh! could I mount on the Mæonian wing,
Your arms, your actions, *your repose, to sing!
What seas you travers'd, and what fields you fought!
Your country's peace how oft, how dearly bought!
How barb'rous rage subsided at your word,
And nations wonder'd while they dropp'd the sword!
How, when you nodded, o'er the land and deep,
Peace stole her wing, and wrapp'd the world in sleep;
Till earth's extremes your mediation own,
And Asia's tyrants tremble at your throne —
But verse, alas! your Majesty disdains;
*And I'm not us'd to panegyric strains.
The zeal of fools offends at any time,
But most of all the zeal of fools in rhyme.
Besides, a fate attends on all I write,
That when I aim at praise, they say I bite.
A vile encomium doubly ridicules:
There's nothing blackens like the ink of fools.
If true, a woful likeness; and, if lies,
"Praise undeserv'd is scandal in disguise":
Well may he blush who gives it, or receives;
And when I flatter, let my dirty leaves
(Like journals, odes, and such forgotten things,
As *Eusden, Philips, Settle, writ of kings)
Clothe spice, line trunk, or, flutt'ring in a row,
Befringe the rails of *Bedlam and Soho.

[1737]

EPILOGUE TO THE SATIRES

IN TWO DIALOGUES. WRITTEN IN MDCCXXXVIII

DIALOGUE I

**Fr.* Not twice a twelvemonth you appear in print,
And when it comes, the court see nothing in 't:
You grow correct, that once with rapture writ,
And are, besides, too moral for a wit.
Decay of parts, alas! we all must feel —
Why now, this moment, don't I see you steal?
'Tis all from Horace; Horace long before ye
Said *"Tories call'd him Whig, and Whigs a Tory";
And taught his Romans, in much better metre,
"To laugh at fools who put their trust in Peter."
But Horace, sir, was delicate, was nice;
*Bubo observes, he lash'd no sort of vice:
Horace would say, Sir Billy served the crown,
Blunt could do business, *H–ggins knew the town;
In Sappho touch the failings of the sex,
In rev'rend bishops note some small neglects,
*And own the Spaniard did a waggish thing,
Who cropt our ears, and sent them to the king.
His sly, polite, insinuating style

Could please at court, and make Augustus smile:
An artful manager, that crept between
His friend and shame, and was a kind of screen.
But, 'faith, your very friends will soon be sore;
*Patriots there are who wish you'd jest no more —
And where's the glory? 'twill be only thought
The great man never offer'd you a groat.
Go see Sir Robert —
P. See Sir Robert! — hum —
And never laugh — for all my life to come!
Seen him I have; but in his happier hour
Of social pleasure, ill-exchanged for power;
Seen him, uncumber'd with the venal tribe,
Smile without art, and win without a bribe.
Would he oblige me? let me only find
He does not think me *what he thinks mankind.
Come, come, at all I laugh he laughs, no doubt;
The only diff'rence is — I dare laugh out.
F. Why, yes: with Scripture still you may be free;
A horse-laugh, if you please, at honesty;
*A joke on Jekyl, or some odd old Whig,
Who never chang'd his principle or wig:
A patriot is a fool in ev'ry age,
Whom all Lord Chamberlains allow the stage:
These nothing hurts; they keep their fashion still,
And wear their strange old virtue as they will.
If any ask you, "Who's the man so near
His prince, that writes in verse, and has his ear?"
Why, answer, *Lyttleton! and I'll engage
The worthy youth shall ne'er be in a rage;
But were his verses vile, his whisper base,
You'd quickly find him in Lord Fanny's case.
*Sejanus, Wolsey, hurt not honest Fleury,
But well may put some statesmen in a fury.
Laugh then at any but at fools or foes;
These you but anger, and you mend not those.
Laugh at your friends, and if your friends are sore,
So much the better, you may laugh the more.
To vice and folly to confine the jest
Sets half the world, God knows, against the rest,
Did not the sneer of more impartial men
At sense and virtue, balance all again.
Judicious wits spread wide the ridicule,
And charitably comfort knave and fool.
P. Dear sir, forgive the prejudice of youth:
Adieu distinction, satire, warmth, and truth!
Come, harmless characters that no one hit;
Come, Henley's oratory, *Osborne's wit!
The honey dropping from Favonio's tongue,
The flowers of Bubo, and the flow of *Y–ng!
The gracious dew of pulpit eloquence,
And all the well-whipt cream of courtly sense
That first was *H— vy's, F—'s next, and then
The S— te's, and then H— vy's once again.
Oh, come, that easy Ciceronian style,
So Latin, yet so English all the while,
As, tho' the pride of *Middleton and Bland,
All boys may read, and girls may understand!
Then might I sing without the least offence,
And all I sung should be the nation's sense;
Or teach the melancholy Muse to mourn,
Hang the sad verse on Carolina's urn,
And hail her passage to the realms of rest,
*All parts perform'd, and all her children blest!
So — satire is no more — I feel it die —
No gazetteer more innocent than I —
And let, a' God's name! ev'ry fool and knave
Be grac'd thro' life, and flatter'd in his grave.
F. Why so? if satire knows its time and place,
You still may lash the greatest — in disgrace:
For merit will by turns forsake them all;
Would you know when? exactly when they fall.
But let all satire in all changes spare
*Immortal S—k, and grave De— re.
Silent and soft, as saints remove to heav'n,
All ties dissolv'd, and ev'ry sin forgiv'n,
These may some gentle ministerial wing
Receive, and place for ever near a king!
There where no passion, pride, or shame transport,
Lull'd with the sweet nepenthe of a court:
There where no father's, brother's, friend's disgrace
Once break their rest, or stir them from their place:
But past the sense of human miseries,
All tears are wip'd for ever from all eyes;
No cheek is known to blush, no heart to throb,
Save when they lose a question, or a job.
P. Good Heav'n forbid that I should blast their glory,
Who know how like Whig ministers to Tory,
And when three sov'reigns died could scarce be vext,
Consid'ring what a gracious prince was next.
Have I, in silent wonder, seen such things
As pride in slaves, and avarice in kings?

And at a peer or peeress shall I fret,
*Who starves a sister or forswears a debt?
Virtue, I grant you, is an empty boast;
But shall the dignity of vice be lost?
Ye gods! shall Cibber's son, without rebuke,
Swear like a lord; or Rich outwhore a duke?
A fav'rite's porter with his master vie,
Be brib'd as often, and as often lie?
Shall *Ward draw contracts with a statesman's skill?
Or *Japhet pocket, like his Grace, a will?
Is it for Bond or Peter (paltry things)
To pay their debts, or keep their faith, like kings?
*If Blount dispatch'd himself, he play'd the man,
And so may'st thou, illustrious Passeran!
But shall a printer, weary of his life,
Learn from their books to hang himself and wife?
This, this, my friend, I cannot, must not bear;
Vice thus abus'd demands a nation's care;
This calls the Church to deprecate our sin,
And *hurls the thunder of the laws on gin.
*Let modest Foster, if he will, excel
Ten metropolitans in preaching well;
A simple Quaker, or a Quaker's wife,
Outdo *Llandaff in doctrine — yea, in life;
*Let humble Allen, with an awkward shame,
Do good by stealth, and blush to find it fame.
Virtue may choose the high or low degree,
'Tis just alike to virtue and to me;
Dwell in a monk, or light upon a king,
She's still the same belov'd, contented thing.
Vice is undone, if she forgets her birth,
And stoops from angels to the dregs of earth:
But 'tis the fall degrades her to a whore;
Let greatness own her, and she's mean no more:
Her birth, her beauty, crowds and courts confess;
Chaste matrons praise her, and grave bishops bless;
In golden chains the willing world she draws,
And hers the gospel is, and hers the laws;
Mounts the tribunal, lifts her scarlet head,
And sees *pale Virtue carted in her stead.
Lo! at the wheels of her triumphal car,
Old England's genius, rough with many a scar,
Dragg'd in the dust! his arms hang idly round,
His flag inverted trails along the ground!
Our youth, all liv'ried o'er with foreign gold,
Before her dance: behind her crawl the old!
See thronging millions to the pagod run,
And offer country, parent, wife, or son!
Hear her black trumpet thro' the land proclaim,
That not to be corrupted is the shame.
In soldier, churchman, patriot, man in power,
'Tis av'rice all, ambition is no more!
See all our nobles begging to be slaves!
See all our fools aspiring to be knaves!
The wit of cheats, the courage of a whore,
Are what ten thousand envy and adore:
All, all look up with reverential awe,
At crimes that 'scape, or triumph o'er the law:
While truth, worth, wisdom, daily they decry —
"Nothing is sacred now but villainy."
Yet may this verse (if such a verse remain)
Show there was one who held it in disdain.

[1738]

THE DUNCIAD

TO DR. JONATHAN SWIFT

BOOK I

ARGUMENT

The Proposition, the Invocation, and the Inscription. Then the original of the great empire of Dullness, and cause of the continuance thereof. The college of the goddess in the city, with her private academy for poets in particular; the governors of it, and the four cardinal virtues. Then the poem hastes into the midst of things, presenting her, on the evening of a Lord Mayor's Day, revolving the long succession of her sons, and the glories past and to come. She fixes her eye on Bayes, to be the instrument of that great event which is the subject of the poem. He is described pensive among his books, giving up the cause, and apprehending the period of her empire: after debating whether to betake himself to the Church, or to gaming, or to party-writing, he raises an altar of proper books, and (making first his solemn prayer and declaration) purposes thereon to sacrifice all his unsuccessful writings. As the pile is kindled, the goddess, beholding the flame from her seat, flies and puts it out, by casting upon it the poem of Thule. She forthwith reveals herself to him, transports him to her temple, unfolds her arts, and initiates him into her mysteries; then announcing the death of Eusden, the Poet Laureate, anoints him, carries him to court, and proclaims him successor.

The mighty mother, and her son who brings
*The Smithfield Muses to the ear of kings,
I sing. Say you, her instruments the great!
Call'd to this work by Dullness, Jove, and Fate:
You by whose care, in vain decried and curst,
*Still Dunce the second reigns like Dunce the first;
Say how the goddess bade Britannia sleep,
And pour'd her spirit, o'er the land and deep.
In eldest time, ere mortals writ or read,
Ere Pallas issu'd from the Thund'rer's head,
Dullness o'er all possess'd her ancient right,
Daughter of Chaos and eternal Night:
Fate in their dotage this fair idiot gave,
Gross as her sire, and as her mother grave;
Laborious, heavy, busy, bold, and blind,

She rul'd, in native anarchy, the mind.
  Still her old empire to restore she tries,
For, born a goddess, Dullness never dies.
  *O thou! whatever title please thine ear,
Dean, Drapier, Bickerstaff, or Gulliver!
Whether thou choose Cervantes' serious air,
Or laugh and shake in Rabelais' easy chair,
Or praise the court, or magnify mankind,
Or thy griev'd country's copper chains unbind;
From thy Bœotia tho' her power retires,
Mourn not, my Swift, at aught our realm acquires.
Here, pleas'd, behold her mighty wings outspread
To hatch a new Saturnian Age of Lead.
  Close to those walls where Folly holds her throne,
And laughs to think *Monroe would take her down,
*Where o'er the gates, by his famed father's hand,
Great Cibber's brazen, brainless brothers stand;
One cell there is, conceal'd from vulgar eye,
The cave of poverty and poetry.
Keen, hollow winds howl thro' the bleak recess,
Emblem of music caus'd by emptiness.
Hence bards, like Proteus long in vain tied down,
Escape in monsters, and amaze the town.
Hence miscellanies spring, the weekly boast
Of *Curll's chaste press, and Lintot's rubric post:
Hence hymning *Tyburn's elegiac lines;
Hence journals, medleys, merc'ries, magazines;
Sepulchral lies, our holy walls to grace,
And new-year odes, and all the Grub Street race.
  In clouded majesty here Dullness shone;
Four guardian Virtues, round, support her throne:
Fierce champion Fortitude, that knows no fears
Of hisses, blows, or want, or loss of ears:
Calm Temperance, whose blessings those partake,
Who hunger and who thirst for scribbling sake:
Prudence, whose glass presents th' approaching jail:
Poetic Justice, with her lifted scale,
Where, in nice balance, truth with gold she weighs,
And solid pudding against empty praise.
  Here she beholds the chaos dark and deep,
Where nameless somethings in their causes sleep,
*Till genial Jacob, or a warm third day,
Call forth each mass, a poem or a play:
How hints, like spawn, scarce quick in embryo lie,
How new-born nonsense first is taught to cry,
Maggots, half-form'd, in rhyme exactly meet,
And learn to crawl upon poetic feet.
Here one poor word an hundred *clenches makes,
And ductile Dullness new meanders takes;
There motley images her fancy strike,
Figures ill pair'd, and similes unlike.
She sees a mob of metaphors advance,
Pleas'd with the madness of the mazy dance;
How Tragedy and Comedy embrace;
How Farce and Epic get a jumbled race;
How Time himself stands still at her command,
Realms shift their place, and ocean turns to land.
Here gay description Egypt glads with showers,
Or gives to Zembla fruits, to Barca flowers;
Glitt'ring with ice here hoary hills are seen,
There painted valleys of eternal green;
In cold December fragrant chaplets blow,
And heavy harvests nod beneath the snow.
  All these, and more, the cloud-compelling queen
Beholds thro' fogs that magnify the scene.
She, tinsel'd o'er in robes of varying hues,
With self-applause her wild creation views;
Sees momentary monsters rise and fall,
And with her own fools-colours gilds them all.
  *'Twas on the day when **, rich and grave,
Like Cimon, triumph'd both on land and wave:
(Pomps without guilt, of bloodless swords and maces,
Glad chains, warm furs, broad banners, and broad faces)
Now night descending, the proud scene was o'er,
But liv'd in *Settle's numbers one day more.
Now may'rs and shrieves all hush'd and satiate lay,
Yet ate, in dreams, the custard of the day;
While pensive poets painful vigils keep,
Sleepless themselves to give their readers sleep.
Much to the mindful queen the feast recalls
What city swans once sung within the walls;

Much she revolves their arts, their ancient praise,
And sure succession down from *Heywood's days.
She saw with joy the line immortal run,
Each sire imprest and glaring in his son:
So watchful bruin forms, with plastic care,
Each growing lump, and brings it to a bear.
She saw *old Prynne in restless Daniel shine,
And Eusden eke out Blackmore's endless line;
She saw slow Philips creep like Tate's poor page,
And all the mighty mad in Dennis rage.
In each she marks her image full exprest,
But chief in *Bayes's monster-breeding breast:
Bayes, form'd by nature stage and town to bless,
And act, and be, a coxcomb with success.
Dullness with transport eyes the lively dunce,
Rememb'ring she herself was Pertness once.
Now (shame to Fortune!) an ill run at play
Blank'd his bold visage, and a thin third day:
Swearing and supperless the hero sate,
Blasphem'd his gods, the dice, and damn'd his fate;
Then gnaw'd his pen, then dash'd it on the ground,
Sinking from thought to thought, a vast profound!
Plung'd for his sense, but found no bottom there,
Yet wrote and flounder'd on in mere despair.
Round him much embryo, much abortion lay,
Much future ode, and abdicated play;
Nonsense precipitate, like running lead,
That slipp'd thro' cracks and zigzags of the head;
All that on Folly Frenzy could beget,
Fruits of dull heat, and *sooterkins of wit.
Next o'er his books his eyes began to roll,
In pleasing memory of all he stole;
How here he sipp'd, how there he plunder'd snug,
And suck'd all o'er like an industrious bug.
Here lay *poor Fletcher's half-eat scenes, and here
The frippery of crucified Molière;
There *hapless Shakespeare, yet of Tibbald sore,
*Wish'd he had blotted for himself before.
The rest on outside merit but presume,
Or serve (like other fools) to fill a room;
Such with their shelves as due proportion hold,
Or their fond parents drest in red and gold;
Or where the pictures for the page atone,
And Quarles is saved by beauties not his own.
Here swells the shelf with *Ogilby the great;
There, stamp'd with arms, *Newcastle shines complete:
Here all his suff'ring brotherhood retire,
And 'scape the martyrdom of jakes and fire:
A Gothic library! of Greece and Rome
Well purged, and worthy Settle, *Banks, and Broome.
But, high above, more solid learning shone,
The classics of an age that heard of none;
There *Caxton slept, with Wynkyn at his side,
One clasp'd in wood, and one in strong cow-hide;
There, sav'd by spice, like mummies, many a year,
Dry bodies of divinity appear:
*De Lyra there a dreadful front extends,
And here the groaning shelves *Philemon bends.
Of these, twelve volumes, twelve of amplest size,
Redeem'd from tapers and defrauded pies,
Inspir'd he seizes: these an altar raise;
A hecatomb of pure unsullied lays
That altar crowns; a folio Commonplace
Founds the whole pile, of all his works the base;
Quartos, octavos, shape the less'ning pyre,
A twisted birthday ode completes the spire.
Then he: "Great tamer of all human art!
First in my care, and ever at my heart;
Dullness! whose good old cause I yet defend,
With whom my Muse began, with whom shall end,
*E'er since Sir Fopling's periwig was praise,
To the last honours of the butt and bays:
O thou! of bus'ness the directing soul!
To this our head, like bias to the bowl,
Which, as more pond'rous, made its aim more true,
Obliquely waddling to the mark in view:
Oh! ever gracious to perplex'd mankind,
Still spread a healing mist before the mind;
And, lest we err by wit's wild dancing light,
Secure us kindly in our native night.
Or, if to wit a coxcomb make pretence,
Guard the sure barrier between that and sense;
Or quite unravel all the reas'ning thread,
And hang some curious cobweb in its stead!
As, forc'd from wind-guns, lead itself can fly,
And pond'rous slugs cut swiftly thro' the sky;
As clocks to weight their nimble motion owe,
The wheels above urg'd by the load below;
Me Emptiness and Dullness could inspire,
And were my elasticity and fire.

Some Demon stole my pen (forgive th' offence),
And once betray'd me into common sense:
Else all my prose and verse were much the same;
This prose on stilts, that poetry fall'n lame.
Did on the stage my fops appear confin'd?
My life gave ampler lessons to mankind.
Did the dead letter unsuccessful prove?
The brisk example never fail'd to move.
Yet sure, had Heav'n decreed to save the state,
Heav'n had decreed these works a longer date.
Could Troy be sav'd by any single hand,
This gray-goose weapon must have made her stand.
What can I now? my Fletcher cast aside,
Take up * the Bible, once my better guide?
Or tread the path by vent'rous heroes trod,
This box my thunder, this right hand my god?
Or chair'd * at White's amidst the doctors sit,
Teach oaths to gamesters, and to nobles wit?
Or bidd'st thou rather party to embrace?
(A friend to party thou, and all her race;
'Tis the same rope at diff'rent ends they twist;
To Dullness * Ridpath is as dear as Mist.)
Shall I, like Curtius, desp'rate in my zeal,
O'er head and ears plunge for the commonweal?
Or rob Rome's ancient geese of all their glories,
And cackling save the monarchy of Tories?
Hold — to the minister I more incline;
To serve his cause, O queen! is serving thine.
And see! thy very gazetteers give o'er,
Ev'n * Ralph repents, and Henley writes no more.
What then remains? Ourself. Still, still remain
Cibberian forehead, and Cibberian brain.
This brazen brightness to the 'squire so dear;
This polish'd hardness that reflects the peer;
This arch absurd, that wit and fool delights;
* This mess, toss'd up of Hockley Hole and White's;
Where dukes and butchers join to wreathe my crown,
At once the bear and fiddle of the town.
*"Oh, born in sin, and forth in folly brought!
Works damn'd or to be damn'd (your father's fault)!
Go, purified by flames, ascend the sky,
My better and more Christian progeny!
Unstain'd, untouch'd, and yet in maiden sheets,
While all your smutty sisters walk the streets.
*Ye shall not beg, like gratis-given Bland,
Sent with a pass and vagrant thro' the land;
Not * sail with Ward to ape-and-monkey climes,
Where vile * mundungus trucks for viler rhymes:
Not sulphur-tipt, emblaze an alehouse fire;
Not wrap up oranges to pelt your sire!
Oh! pass more innocent, in infant state,
To the mild limbo of our father * Tate:
Or peaceably forgot, at once be blest
In Shadwell's bosom with eternal rest!
Soon to that mass of nonsense to return,
Where things destroy'd are swept to things unborn."

With that, a tear (portentous sign of grace!)
Stole from the master of the sev'nfold face;
And thrice he lifted high the birthday brand,
And thrice he dropp'd it from his quiv'ring hand;
Then lights the structure with averted eyes:
The rolling smoke involves the sacrifice.
The op'ning clouds disclose each work by turns,
Now flames *_The Cid_, and now _Perolla_ burns;
Great _Cæsar_ roars and hisses in the fires;
King John in silence modestly expires;
No merit now the dear _Nonjuror_ claims,
Molière's old stubble in a moment flames.
Tears gush'd again, as from pale Priam's eyes,
When the last blaze sent Ilion to the skies.

Rous'd by the light, old Dullness heav'd the head,
Then snatch'd a sheet of * _Thule_ from her bed;
Sudden she flies, and whelms it o'er the pyre:
Down sink the flames, and with a hiss expire.

Her ample presence fills up all the place;
A veil of fogs dilates her awful face:
Great in her charms! as when on shrieves and mayors
She looks, and breathes herself into their airs.
She bids him wait her to her sacred dome:
Well pleas'd he enter'd, and confess'd his home.
So spirits ending their terrestrial race
Ascend, and recognize their native place.
This the great mother dearer held than all
The clubs of *quidnuncs, or her own Guildhall:
Here stood her opium, here she nurs'd her owls,
And here she plann'd th' imperial seat of fools.

Here to her chosen all her works she shows,
Prose swell'd to verse, verse loit'ring into prose:
How random thoughts now meaning chance to find,
Now leave all memory of sense behind;
How prologues into prefaces decay,
And these to notes are fritter'd quite away:

How index-learning turns no student pale,
Yet holds the eel of science by the tail:
How, with *less reading than makes felons scape,
Less human genius than God gives an ape,
Small thanks to France, and none to Rome or Greece,
A vast, vamp'd future, old, reviv'd, new piece,
'Twixt Plautus, Fletcher, Shakespeare, and Corneille,
Can make a Cibber, Tibbald, or *Ozell.
The goddess then o'er his anointed head,
With mystic words, the sacred opium shed.
And lo! her bird (a monster of a fowl,
Something betwixt *a heideggre and owl)
Perch'd on his crown. "All hail! and hail again,
My son, the promis'd land expects thy reign.
Know *Eusden thirsts no more for sack or praise;
He sleeps among the dull of ancient days;
Safe where no critics damn, no duns molest,
Where wretched *Withers, Ward, and Gildon rest,
And *high-born Howard, more majestic sire,
With fool of quality completes the quire.
Thou, Cibber! thou his laurel shalt support;
Folly, my son, has still a friend at court.
Lift up your gates, ye princes, see him come!
Sound, sound ye viols, be the cat-call dumb!
Bring, bring the madding bay, the drunken vine,
The creeping, dirty, courtly ivy join.
*And thou! his aid-de-camp, lead on my sons,
Light-arm'd with points, antitheses, and puns.
Let bawdry, Billingsgate, my daughters dear,
Support his front, and oaths bring up the rear:
And under his, and under Archer's wing,
Gaming and Grub Street skulk behind the king.
"Oh! when shall rise a monarch all our own,
And I, a nursing mother, rock the throne;
'Twixt prince and people close the curtain draw,
Shade him from light, and cover him from law;
Fatten the courtier, starve the learned band,
And suckle armies, and dry-nurse the land:
Till senates nod to lullabies divine,
And all be sleep, as at an ode of thine."
She ceas'd. Then swells the Chapel Royal throat:
"God save King Cibber!" mounts in every note.
Familiar White's, "God save King Colley!" cries,
"God save King Colley!" Drury Lane replies.
To Needham's quick the voice triumphal rode,
But *pious Needham dropp'd the name of God;
*Back to the Devil the last echoes roll,
And "Coll!" each butcher roars at Hockley Hole.
*So when Jove's block descended from on high
(As sings thy great forefather Ogilby),
Loud thunder to its bottom shook the bog,
And the hoarse nation croak'd, "God save King Log!"

[1728, 1743]

THE PROSE OF POPE

THOUGH his poetry overshadows it, Pope's prose bulks large in his collected work and is important for its own sake as well as for the light that it throws on his personality and literary methods. Roughly, it falls into the following divisions: essays published in the *Guardian* and other periodicals, personal and literary controversy, prefaces to his translations from Homer and to his edition of Shakespeare, and letters.

Among his essays, the *Guardian* No. 173 is most famous. This is a plea for naturalness in gardening and is a witty presentation of the absurdities of the formal style then in vogue. In the revolt against the French and Dutch styles of gardening Pope took a prominent part not only by his writing but also by his practice in his own garden at Twickenham.

A Receipt to Make an Epic Poem first appeared in the *Guardian* No. 78 and was afterwards published as chapter XV of Περὶ Βαθοῦς, or *The Art of Sinking in Poetry*, which comprises Book II of *Memoirs of the Extraordinary Life, Works, and Discoveries of Martinus Scriblerus*. This satire grew out of the meetings of the Scriblerus Club, which numbered among its members Pope, Swift, Arbuthnot, Congreve, Atterbury, and other wits. Here was conceived the project of a satire on the abuses of learning through "the character of a man of capacity enough, that had dipped into every art and science, but injudiciously in each." The project was abandoned when the members of the club were scattered in 1714, but it bore fruit in *Gulliver's Travels* and to some extent in *The Dunciad*. *The Art of Sinking in Poetry* was published in vol. III of *Miscellanies* by Pope, Swift, Arbuthnot, and

Gay in 1728. The title parodies the Περὶ Ὕψους of Longinus, and the work gives directions how to attain, not the *Sublime* but the *Low* in poetry. The chapter here reprinted is a satire on the formalistic critics who emphasize rules at the expense of genius and taste.

The facts about the publication of Pope's letters are involved in obscurity and have been the subject of much controversy. There is no doubt that Pope used devious and underhand methods both in altering the text of his letters and in giving it to the world. For these things he has been furiously attacked, and his motives have been given the worst possible interpretation. It should not be forgotten, however, that letters were looked upon as literary exercises in the eighteenth century, though their publication involved delicate questions of personal and literary ethics. Pope can not be blamed for wishing before publication to delete matters of merely private concern, even if he can not be excused for the freedom with which he not only altered but added matter, changed dates, and even substituted the names of his correspondents. It has not been proved, however, that he had any more sinister motive than the publication of witty literary exercises that would advance his reputation and prove interesting to the purchasers.

Pope's prose style has not the charm of Dryden's or the forthrightness of Swift's; but it is at once dignified, terse, and at times epigrammatic. It illustrates once more the fact that good prose is often a by-product of the art and craft of poetry.

THE GUARDIAN

No. 173, September 29, 1713

Nec sera comantem
Narcissum, aut flexi tacuissem vimen acanthi,
Pallentesque hederas, et amantes littora myrtos.
—Virg., [*Georgics*, IV, 122–24.]

[Nor should I have failed to speak of the late-flowering narcissus, or of the bending stem of the acanthus, or of the pale ivy, or of the myrtle that loves the coast.]

I lately took a particular friend of mine to my house in the country, not without some apprehension that it could afford little entertainment to a man of his polite taste particularly in architecture and gardening, who had so long been conversant with all that is beautiful and great in either. But it was a pleasant surprise to me to hear him often declare he had found in my little retirement that beauty which he always thought wanting in the most celebrated seats (or, if you will, villas) of the nation. This he described to me in those verses with which Martial begins one of his epigrams:

**Baiana nostri villa, Basse, Faustini,*
Non otiosis ordinata myrtetis,
Viduaque platano, tonsilique buxeto,
Ingrata lati spatia detinet campi;
Sed rure vero, barbaroque lætatur.

There is certainly something in the amiable simplicity of unadorned nature that spreads over the mind a more noble sort of tranquillity and a loftier sensation of pleasure than can be raised from the nicer scenes of art.

This was the taste of the ancients in their gardens, as we may discover from the descriptions extant of them. The two most celebrated wits of the world have each of them left us a particular picture of a garden, wherein those great masters being wholly unconfined and painting at pleasure, may be thought to have given a full idea of what they esteemed most excellent in this way. These (one may observe) consist entirely of the useful part of horticulture, fruit trees, herbs, water, etc. The pieces I am speaking of are *Virgil's account of the garden of the old Corycian and *Homer's of that of Alcinous in the seventh Odyssey, to which I refer the reader.

*Sir William Temple has remarked that this garden of Homer contains all the justest rules and provisions which can go toward composing the best gardens. Its extent was four acres, which, in those times of simplicity, was looked upon as a large one, even for a prince. It was inclosed all round for defence, and for conveniency joined close to the gates of the palace.

He mentions next *the trees, which were standards, and suffered to grow to their full height. The fine description of the fruits that never failed and the eternal zephyrs is only a more noble and poetical way of expressing the continual succession of one fruit after another throughout the year.

The vineyard seems to have been a plantation distinct from the garden; as also the beds of greens mentioned afterwards at the extremity of the inclosure, in the usual place of our kitchen gardens.

The two fountains are disposed very remarkably. They rose within the inclosure, and were brought in by conduits or ducts; one of them to water all parts of the gardens, and the other underneath the palace into the town, for the service of the public.

How contrary to this simplicity is the modern practice of gardening! We seem to make it our study to recede from nature, not only in the various tonsure of greens into the most regular and formal shapes, but even in monstrous attempts beyond the reach of the art itself; we run into sculpture, and are yet better pleased to have our trees in the most awkward figures of men and animals, than in the most regular of their own.

**Hinc et nexilibus videas e frondibus hortos,*
Implexos late muros, et mœnia circum
Porrigere, et latas e ramis surgere turres;
Deflexam et myrtum in puppes, atque ærea rostra:
In buxisque undare fretum, atque e rore rudentes.
Parte alia frondere suis tentoria castris:
Scutaque, spiculaque, et jaculantia citra vallos.

I believe it is no wrong observation that persons of genius and those who are most capable of art are always most fond of nature, as such are chiefly sensible that all art consists in the imitation and study of nature. On the contrary, people of the common level of understanding are principally delighted with the little niceties and fantastical operations of art, and constantly think that finest which is least natural. A citizen is no sooner proprietor of a couple of yews but he entertains thoughts of erecting them into *giants, like those of Guildhall. I know an eminent cook, who beautified his country seat with a coronation dinner in greens, where you see * the Champion flourishing on horseback at one end of the table, and the queen in perpetual youth at the other.

For the benefit of all my loving countrymen of this curious taste, I shall here publish a catalogue of greens to be disposed of by an eminent town gardener who has lately applied to me upon this head. He represents that for the advancement of a politer sort of ornament in the villas and gardens adjacent to this great city, and in order to distinguish those places from the mere barbarous countries of gross nature, the world stands much in need of a virtuoso gardener who has a turn to sculpture, and is thereby capable of improving upon the ancients, in the imagery of evergreens. I proceed to his catalogue:

Adam and Eve in yew; Adam a little shattered by the fall of the Tree of Knowledge in the great storm; Eve and the serpent very flourishing.

Noah's ark in holly, the ribs a little damaged for want of water.

The Tower of Babel, not yet finished.

St. George in box; his arm scarce long enough, but will be in a condition to stick the dragon by next April.

A green dragon of the same, with a tail of ground ivy for the present.

N.B. These two not to be sold separately.

Edward the Black Prince in cypress.

A laurustine bear in blossom, with a juniper hunter in berries.

A pair of giants, stunted, to be sold cheap.

A Queen Elizabeth in phyllirea, a little inclining to the green sickness, but of full growth.

Another Queen Elizabeth in myrtle, which was very forward, but miscarried by being too near a savine.

An old maid of honour in wormwood.

A topping Ben Jonson in laurel.

Divers eminent modern poets in bays, somewhat blighted, to be disposed of a pennyworth.

A quick-set hog shot up into a porcupine, by being forgot a week in rainy weather.

A lavender pig, with sage growing in his belly.

A pair of maidenheads in fir, in great forwardness.

He also cutteth family pieces of men, women, and children, so that any gentleman may have his lady's effigies in myrtle, or his own in hornbeam.

*"Thy wife shall be as the fruitful vine, and thy children as olive branches round thy table."

MARTINUS SCRIBLERUS, Περὶ βαθοῦς: OR THE ART OF SINKING IN POETRY

A RECEIPT TO MAKE AN EPIC POEM

An epic poem, the critics agree, is the greatest work human nature is capable of. They have already laid down many mechanical rules for compositions of this sort; but at the same time they cut off almost all undertakers from the possibility of ever performing them, for the first qualification they unanimously require in a poet is a genius. I shall here endeavour (for the benefit of my countrymen) to make it manifest that epic poems may be made without a genius, nay without learning or much reading. This must necessarily be of great use to all those who confess they never read, and of whom the world is convinced they never learn. Molière observes of making a dinner that any man can do it with money, and if a professed cook can not do it without, he has his art for nothing: the same may be said of making a poem; 'tis easily brought about by him that has a genius, but the skill lies in doing it without one. In pursuance of this end, I shall present the reader with a plain and certain recipe, by which any author in the Bathos may be qualified for this grand performance.

*For the *fable.* Take out of any old poem, history book, romance, or legend (for instance, *Geoffrey of Monmouth or *Don Belianis of*

Greece) those parts of story which afford most scope for long descriptions; put these pieces together, and throw all the adventures you fancy into one tale. Then take a hero, whom you may choose for the sound of his name, and put him into the midst of these adventures: there let him work for twelve books; at the end of which you may take him out, ready prepared to conquer or to marry, it being necessary that the conclusion of an epic poem be fortunate.

To make an episode. Take any remaining adventure of your former collection, in which you could no way involve your hero; or any unfortunate accident that was too good to be thrown away; and it will be of use, applied to any other person who may be lost and evaporate in the course of the work, without the least damage to the composition.

*For * the moral and allegory.* These you may extract out of the fable afterwards, at your leisure: be sure you strain them sufficiently.

For the manners. For those of the hero, take all the best qualities you can find in the most celebrated heroes of antiquity; if they will not be reduced to a consistency, lay them all on a heap upon him. But be sure they are qualities which your patron would be thought to have; and to prevent any mistake which the world may be subject to, select from the alphabet those capital letters that compose his name, and set them at the head of a dedication before your poem. However, do not absolutely observe the exact quantity of these virtues, it not being determined whether or no it be necessary for the hero of a poem to be an honest man. For the under characters, gather them from Homer and Virgil, and change the names as occasion serves.

For the machines. Take of deities, male and female, as many as you can use: separate them into two equal parts, and keep Jupiter in the middle; let Juno put him in a ferment, and Venus mollify him. Remember on all occasions to make use of volatile Mercury. If you have need of devils, draw them out of Milton's *Paradise*, and extract your spirits from Tasso. The use of these machines is evident; since no epic poem can possibly subsist without them, the wisest way is to reserve them for your greatest necessities: when you cannot extricate your hero by any human means, or yourself by your own wit, seek relief from heaven, and the gods will do your business very readily. This is according to the direct prescription of Horace in his *Art of Poetry*,

> * *Nec deus intersit, nisi dignus vindice nodus*
> *Inciderit* —

That is to say, a poet should never call upon the gods for their assistance, but when he is in great perplexity.

For the descriptions. For a tempest. Take Eurus, Zephyr, Auster, and Boreas, and cast them together in one verse: add to these of rain, lightning and thunder (the loudest you can) * *quantum sufficit:* mix your clouds and billows well together till they foam, and thicken your description here and there with a quicksand. Brew your tempest well in your head, before you set it a-blowing.

For a battle. Pick a large quantity of images and descriptions from Homer's *Iliads*, with a spice or two of Virgil, and if there remain any overplus, you may lay them by for a skirmish. Season it well with similes, and it will make an excellent battle.

For a burning town. If such a description be necessary (because it is certain there is one in Virgil), old Troy is ready burnt to your hands. But if you fear that would be thought borrowed, a chapter or two of * the Theory of the Conflagration, well circumstanced and done into verse, will be a good * *succedaneum*.

As for similes and metaphors, they may be found all over the creation; the most ignorant may gather them, but the difficulty is in applying them. For this, advise with your bookseller.

ALEXANDER POPE TO *THE BISHOP OF ROCHESTER

November 20, 1717

My Lord, — I am truly obliged by your kind condolence on my father's death, and the desire you express that I should improve this incident to my advantage. I know your lordship's friendship to me is so extensive that you include in that wish both my spiritual and my temporal advantage; and it is what I owe to that friendship, to open my mind unreservedly to you on this head. It is true I have lost a parent for whom no gains I could make would be any equivalent. But that was not my only tie; I thank God another still remains (and long may it remain) of the same tender nature. *_Genetrix est mihi_, and excuse me if I say with Euryalus,

> *_Nequeam lacrymas perferre parentis._

A rigid divine may call it a carnal tie, but sure it is a virtuous one. At least I am more certain that it is a duty of nature to preserve a good parent's life and happiness, than I am of any speculative point whatever.

> *_Ignaram hujus quodcunque pericli_
> _Hanc ego, nunc, linquam?_

For she, my lord, would think this separation more grievous than any other; and I, for my part, know as little as poor Euryalus did, of the success of such an adventure; for an adventure it is, and no small one, in spite of the most positive divinity. Whether the change would be to my spiritual advantage, God only knows; this I know that I mean as well in the religion I now profess, as I can possibly ever do in another. Can a man who thinks so justify a change, even if he thought both equally good? To such an one the part of joining with any one body of Christians might perhaps be easy, but I think it would not be so to renounce the other.

Your lordship has formerly advised me to read the best controversies between the churches. Shall I tell you a secret? I did so at fourteen years old, for I loved reading, and my father had no other books; there was a collection of *all that had been written on both sides in the reign of King James the Second. I warmed my head with them, and the consequence was that I found myself a Papist and a Protestant by turns, according to the last book I read. I am afraid most seekers are in the same case, and when they stop, they are not so properly converted as outwitted. You see how little glory you would gain by my conversion. And after all, I verily believe your lordship and I are both of the same religion, if we were thoroughly understood by one another; and that all honest and reasonable Christians would be so, if they did but talk enough together every day, and had nothing to do together but to serve God and live in peace with their neighbour.

As to the temporal side of the question, I can have no dispute with you; it is certain all the beneficial circumstances of life and all the shining ones lie on the part you would invite me to. But, if I could bring myself to fancy what I think you do but fancy, that I have any talents for active life, I want health for it; and besides it is a real truth I have less inclination (if possible) than ability. Contemplative life is not only my scene, but it is my habit too. I begun my life where most people end theirs, with a disrelish of all that the world call ambition. I do not know why it is called so, for to me it always seemed to be rather stooping than climbing. I will tell you my politic and religious sentiments in a few words. In my politics, I think no further than how to preserve the peace of my life in any government under which I live; nor in my religion, than to preserve the peace of my conscience in any church with which I communicate. I hope all churches and all governments are so far of God, as they are rightly understood and rightly administered; and where they are or may be wrong, I leave it to God alone to mend or reform them; which whenever he does, it must be by greater instruments than I am. *I am not a Papist, for I renounce the temporal invasions of the papal power, and detest their arrogated authority over princes and states. I am a Catholic in the strictest sense of the word. If I was born under an absolute prince, I would be a quiet subject; but I thank God I was not. I have a due sense of the excellence of the British constitution. In a word, the things I have always wished to see are not a Roman Catholic or a French Catholic or a Spanish Catholic, but a true Catholic: not a King of Whigs or a King of Tories, but a King of England; which God of his mercy grant his present Majesty may be, and all future Majesties. You see, my lord, I end like a preacher: that is *_sermo ad clerum_ not _ad populum._ Believe me, with infinite obligation and sincere thanks, ever your, etc.

JOHN GAY AND ALEXANDER POPE TO SWIFT

November 17, 1726

About ten days ago a book was published here of *the Travels of one Gulliver, which has been the conversation of the whole town ever since: the whole impression sold in a week; and nothing is more diverting than to hear the different opinions people give of it, though all agree in liking it extremely. It is generally said that you are the author; but I am told the bookseller declares he knows not from what hand it came. From the highest to the lowest it is universally read, from the cabinet-council to the nursery. The politicians to a man agree that it is free from particular reflections, but that the satire on general societies of men is too severe. Not but we now and then meet with people of greater perspicuity, who are in search for particular applications in every leaf; and it is highly probable we shall have keys published to give light into Gulliver's design. Lord [Bolingbroke] is the person who least approves it, blaming it as a design of evil consequence to depreciate human nature, at which it can not be wondered that he takes most offence, being himself the most accomplished of his species, and so losing more than any other of that praise which is due both to the dignity and virtue of a man. *Your friend, my Lord Harcourt, commends it very much, though he thinks in some places the matter too far carried. *The Duchess Dowager of Marlborough is in raptures at it; she says she can dream of nothing else since she read it. She declares that she has now found out that her whole life has been lost in caressing the worst part of mankind, and treating the best as her foes; and that if she knew Gulliver, though he had been the worst enemy she ever had, she should give up her present acquaintance for his friendship. You may see by this that you are not much injured by being supposed the author of this piece. If you are, you have disobliged us, and two or three of your best friends, in not giving us the least hint of it while you were with us; and in particular Dr. Arbuthnot, who says it is ten thousand pities he had not known it, he could have added such abundance of things upon every subject. Among the lady critics, some have found out that Mr. Gulliver had a particular malice to maids of honour. Those of them who frequent the church say his design is impious, and that it is an insult on Providence, depreciating the works of the Creator. Notwithstanding, I am told the princess has read it with great pleasure. As to other critics, they think the flying island is the least entertaining; and so great an opinion the town have of the impossibility of Gulliver's writing at all below himself, it is agreed that part was not writ by the same hand, though this has its defenders too. It has passed Lords and Commons, **nemine contradicente*; and the whole town, men, women, and children are quite full of it. Perhaps I may all this time be talking to you of a book you have never seen, and which has not yet reached Ireland. If it has not, I believe what we have said will be sufficient to recommend it to your reading, and that you will order me to send it to you. But it will be much better to come over yourself, and read it here, where you will have the pleasure of variety of commentators to explain the difficult passages to you.

We all rejoice that you have fixed the precise time of your coming to be **cum hirundine prima*, which we modern naturalists pronounce ought to be reckoned, contrary to Pliny, in this northern latitude of fifty-two degrees, from the end of February, *style Gregorian, at farthest. But to us, your friends, the coming of such a black swallow as you, will make a summer in the worst of seasons. We are no less glad at your mention of Twickenham and Dawley; and in town you know you have a lodging at court.

The princess is clothed in Irish silk; pray give our service to the weavers. We are strangely surprised to hear that the bells in Ireland ring without your money. I hope you do not write *"the thing that is not." We are afraid that B—— has been guilty of that crime, that you, like a Houyhnhnm, have treated him as a Yahoo, and discarded him your service. I fear you do not understand these modish terms, which every creature now understands but yourself.

You tell us your wine is bad, and that the clergy do not frequent your house, which we look upon to be tautology. The best advice we can give you is to make them a present of your wine, and come away to better. You fancy we envy you, but you are mistaken; we envy those you are with, for we cannot envy the man we love. Adieu.

ALEXANDER POPE TO *MRS. MARTHA BLOUNT

December, 1732

Your letter dated at nine o'clock on Tuesday (night as I suppose) has sunk me quite. Yesterday I hoped; and yesterday I sent you a line or two for our poor friend Gay, inclosed in a few words to you; about twelve or one o'clock you should have had it. I am troubled about that, though the present cause of our trouble be so much greater. Indeed I want a friend to help me to bear it better. We want each other. I bear a hearty share with *Mrs. Howard, who has lost a man of a most honest heart, so honest an one that I wish her master had none less honest about him. The world after all is a little, pitiful thing; not performing any one promise it makes us for the future, and every day taking away and annulling the joys of the past. Let us comfort one another, and, if possible, study to add as much more friendship to each other as death has deprived us of in him: I promise you more and more of mine, which will be the way to deserve more and more of yours.

I purposely avoid saying more. The subject is beyond writing upon, beyond cure or ease by reason or reflection, beyond all but one thought, that it is the will of God.

So will the death of my mother be, which now I tremble at, now resign to, now bring close to me, now set farther off: every day alters, turns me about, and confuses my whole frame of mind. Her dangerous distemper is again returned, her fever coming onward again, though less in pain; for which last, however, I thank God.

I am unfeignedly tired of the world, and receive nothing to be called a pleasure in it, equivalent to countervail either the death of one I have so long lived with, or of one I have so long lived for. I have nothing left but to turn my thoughts to one comfort; the last we usually think of, though the only one we should in wisdom depend upon, in such a disappointing place as this. I sit in her room, and she is always present before me, but when I sleep. I wonder I am so well; I have shed many tears, but now I weep at nothing. I would above all things see you, and think it would comfort you to see me so equal-tempered and so quiet. But pray dine here; you may, and she know nothing of it, for she dozes much, and we tell her of no earthly thing lest it run in her mind, which often trifles have done. If *Mr. Bethel had time, I wish he were your companion hither. Be as much as you can with each other: be assured I love you both, and be farther assured that friendship will increase as I live on.

[1737]

HENRY ST. JOHN, VISCOUNT BOLINGBROKE

Henry St. John, Viscount Bolingbroke, fills a large place in English political and literary history. Between 1710 and 1714 he was the principal associate of Robert Harley, Earl of Oxford, in the Tory ministry that negotiated the Peace of Utrecht. At this time, as a patron and friend of Swift, he figures largely in the *Journal to Stella*. After the death of Queen Anne he was impeached by the Whigs in connection with a plot to bring back the "Pretender" and defeat the Hanoverian succession. He fled to France, where for a short time he acted as Secretary of State in the Jacobite court at Saint Germain. In 1716 he was dismissed from this position, where both his religious skepticism and his political principles were uncongenial, after which he devoted his enforced leisure to literary and philosophical studies. Seven years later he was permitted to return to England, and in 1725 his forfeited estates were returned to him, though he was still excluded from the House of Lords. For some time he was a neighbour of Alexander Pope, with whom he became intimate and whom he influenced in the composition of *An Essay on Man*. Though unable to take a direct part in politics, he was active in the opposition to Walpole and was an important contributor to *The Craftsman*, a political journal through which for nearly a decade after 1726 the opposition wits attacked the government. His works include historical studies, some pieces of memoir, philosophical essays, and political discussions. Among these last is *The Idea of a Patriot King*, which endeavours to show how a king, by rising above the animosities of partisan rivalry can not only reign but govern to the advantage of the nation. Such a king was eagerly expected in Frederick, Prince of Wales, and formed the early ideal of George III, who was educated upon the precepts of this work.

It has long been customary to describe Bolingbroke as brilliant and versatile but shallow and insincere. Certainly his more pretentious writings have not stood the test of time: his philosophic system is deistic optimism, shallow and often inconsistent; his history is special pleading; and his political system is founded on party prejudice even when it declaims most loudly of liberty and patriotism. Yet, admitting that Bolingbroke was not a great thinker and that his writings have suffered the tarnish of time from which none but the greatest are exempt, we are not justified in dismissing him as a mere glittering mediocrity. He was generally considered the best orator of his day in a brilliant era of political oratory; he was an able statesman when in office, and, even when debarred from public life, a power in the opposition; and he was esteemed among the most celebrated wits of the age of Queen Anne. Charges of double dealing and untruthfulness must be balanced against those qualities of personal character that kept unbroken the close friendship of the irritable Pope, and the admiration and love of the outspoken Swift. That he was a great nobleman is not sufficient to account for the praise of these men who quarrelled with lords and satirized ministers in office and out.

Judgments of his prose style have varied greatly, yet so exacting a critic as Arnold says, "Power of style, properly so-called, as manifested in masters of style like Dante and Milton in poetry, Cicero, Bossuet or Bolingbroke in prose... has for its characteristic effect this: to add dignity and distinction." Whether or not one accepts this high estimate of Bolingbroke's style, one may readily admit its clarity, beauty, and adaptation to varied purposes. Bolingbroke is here represented by a letter, "Of the True Use of Retirement and Study," not his best piece of work but a complete whole, short enough for inclusion, in which some of his characteristic ideas are expressed with classical vigour and distinction.

OF THE TRUE USE OF RETIREMENT AND STUDY: TO *THE RIGHT HONOURABLE LORD BATHURST

Since my last to your lordship, this is the first favourable opportunity I have had of keeping the promise I made you. I will avoid prolixity, as much as I can, in a first draught of my thoughts; but I must give you them as they rise in my mind, without staying to marshal them in close order.

As proud as we are of human reason, nothing can be more absurd than the general system of human life and human knowledge. This faculty of distinguishing true from false, right from wrong, and what is agreeable from what is repugnant to nature, either by one act or by a longer process of intuition, has not been given with so sparing an hand as many

* Notes on Bolingbroke will be found in the Appendix, pp. 992 ff.

appearances would make us apt to believe. If it was cultivated, therefore, as early and as carefully as it might be, and if the exercise of it was left generally as free as it ought to be, our common notions and opinions would be more consonant to truth than they are; and, truth being but one, they would be more uniform likewise.

But this rightful mistress of human life and knowledge, whose proper office it is to preside over both, and to direct us in the conduct of one and the pursuit of the other, becomes degraded in the intellectual economy. She is reduced to a mean and servile state, to the vile drudgery of conniving at principles, defending opinions, and confirming habits that are none of hers. They who do her most honour, who consult her oftenest, and obey her too, very often are still guilty of limiting her authority according to maxims and rules and schemes that chance or ignorance or interest first devised and that custom sanctifies; custom, that result of the passions and prejudices of many, and of the designs of a few; that ape of reason, who usurps her seat, exercises her power, and is obeyed by mankind in her stead. Men find it easy, and government makes it profitable to concur in established systems of speculation and practice, and the whole turn of education prepares them to live upon credit all their lives. Much pains are taken and time bestowed to teach us what to think, but little or none of either to instruct us how to think. The magazine of the memory is stored and stuffed betimes; but the conduct of the understanding is all along neglected, and the free exercise of it is, in effect, forbid in all places, and in terms in some.

There is a strange distrust of human reason in every human institution: this distrust is so apparent that an habitual submission to some authority or other is forming in us from our cradles; that principles of reasoning and matters of fact are inculcated in our tender minds before we are able to exercise that reason; and that, when we are able to exercise it, we are either forbid or frightened from doing so, even on things that are themselves the proper objects of reason, or that are delivered to us upon an authority whose sufficiency or insufficiency is so most evidently.

On many subjects, such as the general laws of natural religion and the general rules of society and good policy, men of all countries and languages who cultivate their reason judge alike. The same premises have led them to the same conclusions, and so, following the same guide, they have trod in the same path: at least the differences are small, easily reconciled, and such as could not of themselves contradistinguish nation from nation, religion from religion, and sect from sect. How comes it, then, that there are other points on which the most opposite opinions are entertained, and some of these with so much heat and fury that the men on one side of the hedge will die for the affirmative, and the men on the other for the negative? *"*Toute opinion est assez forte pour se fair épouser au prix de la vie*," says Montaigne, whom I often quote, as I do Seneca, rather for the smartness of expression than the weight or newness of matter. Look narrowly into it, and you will find that the points agreed on and the points disputed are not proportionable to the common sense and general reason of mankind. Nature and truth are the same everywhere, and reason shows them everywhere alike. But the accidental and other causes which give rise and growth to opinions, both in speculation and practice, are of infinite variety; and wherever these opinions are once confirmed by custom and propagated by education, various, inconsistent, contradictory as they are, they all pretend (and all their pretences are backed by pride, by passion, and by interest) to have reason, or revelation, or both, on their side; though neither reason nor revelation can be possibly on the side of more than one and may be possibly on the side of none.

Thus it happens that the people of Thibet are Tartars and idolaters, that they are Turks and Mahometans at Constantinople, Italians and Papists at Rome; and how much soever education may be less confined, and the means of knowledge more attainable, in France and our own country, yet thus it happens in great measure that Frenchmen and Roman Catholics are bred at Paris, and Englishmen and Protestants at London. For men, indeed, properly speaking, are bred nowhere; every one thinks the system, as he speaks the language, of his country. At least there are few that think, and none that act, in any country, according to the dictates of pure unbiased reason; unless they may be said to do so when reason directs them to speak and act according to the system of their country or sect, at the same time as she leads them to think according to that of nature and truth.

Thus the far greatest part of mankind appears reduced to a lower state than other animals, in that very respect on account of which we claim so great superiority over them; because instinct, that has its due effect, is preferable to reason that has not. I suppose in this place, with philosophers and the vulgar, that which I am in no wise ready to affirm, that other animals have no share of human reason; for, let me say by the way, it is much more likely other animals should share the human, which is denied, than that man should share the divine reason, which is affirmed. But, supposing our monopoly of reason, would not your lordship choose to walk upon four legs, to wear a long tail, and to be called a beast, with the advantage of being determined by irresistible and unerring instinct to those truths that are necessary to your well-being, rather than to walk on two legs, to wear no tail, and to be honoured with the title of man, at the expense of deviating from them perpetually? Instinct acts spontaneously whenever its action is necessary, and directs the animal according to the purpose for which it was implanted in him. Reason is a nobler and more extensive faculty, for it extends to the unnecessary as well as necessary, and to satisfy our curiosity as well as our wants: but reason must be excited, or she will remain inactive; she must be left free, or she will conduct us wrong, and carry us farther astray from her own precincts than we should go without her help: in the first case we have no sufficient guide; and in the second, the more we employ our reason the more unreasonable we are.

Now if all this be so, if reason has so little, and ignorance, passion, interest, and custom so much to do, in forming our opinions and our habits, and in directing the whole conduct of human life; is it not a thing desirable by every thinking man, to have the opportunity, indulged to so few by the course of accidents, the opportunity *secum esse, et secum vivere*, of living some years, at least, to ourselves and for ourselves, in a state of freedom, under the laws of reason, instead of passing our whole time in a state of vassalage under those of authority and custom? Is it not worth our while to contemplate ourselves and others and all the things of this world, once before we leave them, through the medium of pure, and, if I may say so, of undefiled reason? Is it not worth our while to approve or condemn, on our own authority, what we receive in the beginning of life on the authority of other men, who were not then better able to judge for us than we are now to judge for ourselves?

That this may be done, and has been done to some degree, by men who remained much more mingled than I design to be for the future, in the company and business of the world, I shall not deny; but still it is better done in retreat and with greater ease and pleasure. Whilst we remain in the world, we are all fettered down, more or less, to one common level, and have neither all the leisure, nor all the means and advantages to soar above it, which we may procure to ourselves by breaking these fetters in retreat. To talk of abstracting ourselves from matter, laying aside body, and being resolved, as it were, into pure intellect, is proud, metaphysical, unmeaning jargon: but to abstract ourselves from the prejudices and habits and pleasures and business of the world is no more than many are, though all are not capable of doing. They who can do this may elevate their souls in retreat to an higher station, and may take from thence such a view of the world * as the second Scipio took in his dream, from the seats of the blessed, when the whole earth appeared so little to him that he could scarce discern that speck of dirt, the Roman Empire. Such a view as this will increase our knowledge by showing us our ignorance; will distinguish every degree of probability from the lowest to the highest, and mark the distance between that and certainty; will dispel the intoxicating fumes of philosophical presumption, and teach us to establish our peace of mind, where alone it can rest securely in resignation: in short, such a view will render life more agreeable and death less terrible. Is not this business, my lord? Is not this pleasure too, the highest pleasure? The world can afford us none such; we must retire from the world to taste it with a full gust; but we shall taste it the better for having been in the world. The share of sensual pleasures that a man of my age can promise himself is hardly worth attention: he should be sated, he will be soon disabled; and very little reflection surely will suffice to make his habits of this kind lose their power over him, in proportion at least as his power of indulging them diminishes. Besides, your lordship knows that my scheme of retirement excludes none of these pleasures that can be taken with decency and conveniency; and to say the truth, I believe that I allow myself more in speculation than I shall find I want in practice. As to the habits of business, they can have no hold on one who has been so long tired with it. You may object that though a man has discarded these habits, and has not even the embers of ambition about him to revive them, yet he can not renounce all public business as absolutely as I seem to do; because a better principle, a principle of duty, may summon him to the service of his country. I will answer you with great sincerity. No man has higher notions of this duty than I have. I think that scarce any age or circumstances can discharge us entirely from it; no, not my own. But as we are apt to take the impulse of our own passions for a call to the performance of this duty; so when these passions impel us no longer, the call that puts us upon action must be real and loud too.

Add to this that there are different methods proportioned to different circumstances and situations, of performing the same duty. In the midst of retreat, wherever it may be fixed, I may contribute to defend and preserve the British constitution of government: and you, my lord, may depend upon me, that whenever I can, I will. Should any one ask you, in this case, from whom I expect my reward: answer him by declaring to whom I pay this service, **Deo immortale, qui me non accipere modo hæc a majoribus voluit, sed etiam posteris prodere.*

But, to lead the life I propose with satisfaction and profit, renouncing the pleasures and business of the world, and breaking the habits of both, is not sufficient: the supine creature whose understanding is superficially employed through life, about a few general notions, and is never bent to a close and steady pursuit of truth, may renounce the pleasures and business of the world, for even in the business of the world we see such creatures often employed, and may break the habits; nay, he may retire and drone away life in solitude, like a monk, or like him over the door of whose house, as if his house had been his tomb, somebody writ, "Here lies such an one." But no such man will be able to make the true use of retirement. The employment of his mind, that would have been agreeable and easy if he had accustomed himself to it early, will be unpleasant and impracticable late: such men lose their intellectual powers for want of exerting them, and, having trifled away youth, are reduced to the necessity of trifling away age. It fares with the mind just as it does with the body. He who was born with a texture of brain as strong as that of Newton, may become unable to perform the common rules of arithmetic: just as he who has the same elasticity in his muscles, the same suppleness in his joints, and *all his nerves and sinews as well braced as Jacob Hall, may become a fat, unwieldy sluggard. Yet farther, the implicit creature, who has thought it all his life needless or unlawful to examine the principles or facts that he took originally on trust, will be as little able as the other to improve his solitude to any good purpose; unless we call it a good purpose, for that sometimes happens, to confirm and exalt his prejudices so that he may live and die in one continued delirium. The confirmed prejudices of a thoughtful life are as hard to change as the confirmed habits of an indolent life: and as some must trifle away age because they have trifled away youth, others must labour on in a maze of error, because they have wandered there too long to find their way out.

There is a prejudice in China in favour of little feet, and therefore the feet of girls are swathed and bound up from the cradle so that the women of that country are unable to walk without tottering and stumbling all their lives. Among the savages of America there are some who hold flat heads and long ears in great esteem, and therefore press the one, and draw down the others so hard from their infancy that they destroy irrecoverably the true proportions of nature, and continue all their lives ridiculous to every sight but their own. Just so, the first of these characters can not make any progress, and the second will not attempt to make any, in an impartial search after real knowledge.

To set about acquiring the habits of meditation and study late in life, is like getting into a go-cart with a grey beard, and learning to walk when we have lost the use of our legs. In general, the foundations of an happy old age must be laid in youth; and in particular, he who has not cultivated his reason young, will be utterly unable to improve it old. **Manent ingenia senibus, modo permaneant studium et industria.*

Not only a love of study, and a desire of knowledge, must have grown up with us, but such an industrious application likewise, as requires the whole vigour of the mind to be exerted in the pursuit of truth, through long trains of ideas, and all those dark recesses wherein man, not God, has hid it.

This love and this desire I have felt all my life, and I am not quite a stranger to this industry and application. There has been something always ready to whisper in my ear, whilst I ran the course of pleasure and of business,

**Solve senescentem mature sanus equum.*

But my genius, unlike *the demon of Socrates, whispered so softly that very often I heard him not, in the hurry of those passions by which I was transported. Some calmer hours there were; in them I hearkened to him. Reflection had often its turn, and the love of study and the desire of knowledge have never quite abandoned me. I am not therefore entirely unprepared for the life I will lead, and it is not without reason that I promise myself more satisfaction in the latter part of it than I ever knew in the former.

Your lordship may think this perhaps a little too sanguine for one who has lost so much time already; you may put me in mind that human life had no second spring, no second summer; you may ask me what I mean by sowing in autumn, and whether I hope to reap in winter. My answer will be that I think very differently from most men of the time we have to pass and the business we have to do in this world. I think we have more of one, and less of the other, than is commonly supposed. Our want of time and the shortness of human life are some of the principal commonplace complaints which we prefer against the established order of things; they are the grumblings of the vulgar, and the pathetic lamentations of the philosopher; but they are impertinent and impious in both. The man of business despises the man of pleasure for squandering his time away; the man of pleasure pities or laughs at the man of business for the same thing: and yet both concur superciliously and absurdly to find fault with the Supreme Being for having given them so little time. The philosopher, who misspends it very often as much as the others, joins in the same cry, and authorizes this impiety. Theophrastus thought it extremely hard to die at ninety, and to go out of the world when he had just learned how to live in it. His master, Aristotle, found fault with nature for treating man in this respect worse than several other animals: both very unphilosophically! and I love Seneca the better for his quarrel with the *Stagirite on this head. We see, in so many instances, a just proportion of things, according to their several relations to one another, that philosophy should lead us to conclude this proportion preserved, even where we cannot discern it; instead of leading us to conclude that it is not preserved where we do not discern it, or where we think that we see the contrary. To conclude otherwise is shocking presumption. It is to presume that the system of the universe would have been more wisely contrived if creatures of our low rank among intellectual natures had been called to the councils of the Most High, or that the Creator ought to mend his work by the advice of the creature. That life which seems to our self-love so short, when we compare it with the ideas we frame of eternity, or even with the duration of some other beings, will appear sufficient, upon a less partial view, to all the ends of our creation, and of a just proportion in the successive course of generations. The term itself is long: we render it short; and the want we complain of flows from our profusion, not from our poverty. We are all arrant spendthrifts; some of us dissipate our estates on the trifles, some on the superfluities, and then we all complain that we want the necessaries of life. The much greatest part never reclaim, but die bankrupts to God and man. Others reclaim late, and they are apt to imagine, when they make up their accounts and see how their fund is diminished, that they have not enough remaining to live upon, because they have not the whole. But they deceive themselves: they were richer than they thought, and they are not yet poor. If they husband well the remainder, it will be found sufficient for all the necessaries, and for some of the superfluities, and trifles too perhaps, of life: but then the former order of expense must be inverted; and the necessaries of life must be provided, before they put themselves to any cost for the trifles or superfluities.

Let us leave the men of pleasure and of business, who are often candid enough to own that they throw away their time, and thereby to confess that they complain of the Supreme Being for no other reason than this, that he has not proportioned his bounty to their extravagance: let us consider the scholar and the philosopher; who, far from owning that he throws any time away, reproves others for doing it: that solemn mortal, who abstains from the pleasures, and declines the business of the world, that he may dedicate his whole time to the search of truth, and the improvement of knowledge. When such an one complains of the shortness of human life in general, or of his remaining share in particular; might not a man, more reasonable though less solemn, expostulate thus with him?

"Your complaint is indeed consistent with your practice; but you would not, possibly, renew your complaint if you reviewed your practice. Though reading makes a scholar, yet every scholar is not a philosopher, nor every philosopher a wise man. It cost you twenty years to devour all the volumes on one side of your library: you came out a great critic in Latin and Greek, in the oriental tongues, in history and chronology; but you was not satisfied: you confessed that these were the *'*literæ nihil sanantes*'; and you wanted more time to acquire other knowledge. You have had this time: you have passed twenty years more on the other side of your library, among philosophers, rabbies, commentators, schoolmen, and whole legions of modern doctors. You are extremely well versed in all that has been written concerning the nature of God, and of the soul of man; about matter and form, body and spirit; and space, and eternal essences, and incorporeal substances; and the rest of those profound speculations. You are a master of the controversies that have arisen about nature and grace, about predestination and free will, and all the other abstruse questions that have made so much noise in the schools, and done so much hurt in the world. You are going on, as fast as the infirmities you have contracted will permit, in the same course of study; but you begin to foresee that you shall want time, and you make grievous complaints of the shortness of human life. Give me leave now to ask you how many thousand years God must prolong your life in order to reconcile you to his wisdom and goodness. It is plain, at least highly probable, that a life as long as that of the most aged of the patriarchs would be too short to answer your purposes; since the researches and disputes in which you are engaged, have been already for a much longer time the objects of learned enquiries, and remain still as imperfect and undetermined as they were at first. But let me ask you again, and deceive neither yourself nor me; have you, in the course of these forty years, once examined the first principles, and the fundamental facts, on which all those questions depend, with an absolute indifference of judgment, and with a scrupulous exactness? with the same that you have employed in examining the various consequences drawn from them, and the heterodox opinions about them? Have you not taken them for granted in the whole course of your studies? Or, if you have looked now and then on the state of the proofs brought to maintain them, have you not done it as a mathematician looks over a demonstration formerly made, to refresh his memory, not to satisfy any doubt? If you have thus examined, it may appear marvellous to some that you have spent so much time in many parts of those studies which have reduced you to this hectic condition of so much heat and weakness. But if you have not thus examined, it must be evident to all, nay to yourself on the least cool reflection, that you are still, notwithstanding all your learning, in a state of ignorance. For knowledge can alone produce knowledge; and without such an examination of axioms and facts, you can have none about inferences."

In this manner one might expostulate very reasonably with many a great scholar, many a profound philosopher, many a dogmatical casuist. And it serves to set the complaints about want of time, and the shortness of human life, in a very ridiculous but a true light. All men are taught their opinions, at least on the most important subjects, by rote, and are bred to defend them with obstinacy. They may be taught true opinions; but whether true or false, the same zeal for them, and the same attachment to them, is everywhere inspired alike. *The Tartar believes as heartily that the soul of Foe inhabits in his Dairo, as the Christian believes *the hypostatic union, or any article in the Athanasian Creed. Now this may answer the ends of society in some respects, and do well enough for the vulgar of all ranks; but it is not enough for the man who cultivates his reason, who is able to think, and who ought to think, for himself. To such a man, every opinion that he has not himself either framed, or examined strictly, and then adopted, will pass for nothing more than what it really is, the opinion of other men, which may be true or false for aught he knows. And this is a state of uncertainty in which no such man can remain, with any peace of mind, concerning those things that are of greatest importance to us here, and may be so hereafter. He will make them, therefore, the objects of his first and greatest attention. If he has lost time, he will lose no more; and when he has acquired all the knowledge he is capable of acquiring on these subjects, he will be the less concerned whether he has time to acquire any farther. Should he have passed his life in the pleasures or business of the world, whenever he sets about this work, he will soon have the advantage over the learned philosopher. For he will soon have secured what is necessary to his happiness, and may sit down in the peaceful enjoyment of that knowledge, or proceed with greater advantage and satisfaction to the acquisition of new knowledge; whilst the other continues his search after things that are in their nature, to say the best of them, hypothetical, precarious, and superfluous.

But this is not the only rule, by observing of which we may redeem our time, and have the advantage over those who imagine they have so much in point of knowledge over your lordship or me, for instance, and who despise our ignorance. The rule I mean is this: to be on our guard against the common arts of delusion, spoken of already; which, every one is ready to confess, have been employed to mislead those who differ from him. Let us be diffident of ourselves, but let us be diffident of others too; our own passions may lead us to reason wrong, but the passions and interest of others may have the same effect. It is in every man's power, who sets about it in good earnest, to prevent the first; and when he has done so, he will have a conscious certainty of it. To prevent the last there is one, and but one, sure method; and that is, to remount, in the survey of our opinions, to the first and even remotest principles on which they are founded. No respect, no habit, no seeming certainty whatever, must divert us from this; any affectation of diverting us from it ought to increase our suspicion: and the more important our examination is, the more important this method of conducting it becomes. Let us not be frighted from it, either by the supposed difficulty or length of such an enquiry; for, on the contrary, this is the easiest and the shortest, as well as the only sure way of arriving at real knowledge; and of being able to place the opinions we examine in the different classes of true, probable, or false, according to the truth, probability, or falsehood of the principles from whence they are deduced. If we find these principles false, and that will be the case in many instances, we stop our enquiries on these heads at once; and save an immense deal of time that we should otherwise misspend. The Mussulman who enters on the examination of all * the disputes that have arisen between the followers of Omar and Ali and other doctors of his law, must acquire a thorough knowledge of the whole Mahometan system; and will have as good a right to complain of want of time, and the shortness of human life, as any pagan or Christian divine or philosopher: but without all this time and learning, he might have discovered that Mahomet was an impostor, and that the Koran is an heap of absurdities.

In short, my lord, he who retires from the world with a resolution of employing his leisure in the first place to re-examine and settle his opinions, is inexcusable if he does not begin with those that are most important to him, and if he does not deal honestly by himself. To deal honestly by himself, he must observe the rule I have insisted upon, and not suffer the delusions of the world to follow him into his retreat. Every man's reason is every man's oracle; this oracle is best consulted in the silence of retirement; and when we have so consulted, whatever the decision be, whether in favour of our prejudices or against them, we must rest satisfied; since nothing can be more certain than this, that he who follows that guide in the search of truth, as that was given him to lead him to it, will have a much better plea to make, whenever or wherever he may be called to account, than he who has resigned himself, either deliberately or inadvertently, to any authority upon earth.

When we have done this, concerning God, ourselves, and other men; concerning the relations in which we stand to him and to them, the duties that result from these relations; and the positive will of the Supreme Being, whether revealed to us in a supernatural, or discovered by the right use of our reason in a natural way — we have done the great business of our lives. Our lives are so sufficient for this, that they afford us time for more, even when we begin late; especially if we proceed in every other enquiry by the same rule. To discover error in axioms, or in first principles grounded on facts, is like the breaking of a charm. The enchanted castle, the steepy rock, the burning lake disappear; and the paths that lead to truth, which we imagined to be so long, so embarrassed, and so difficult, show as they are, short, open, and easy. When we have secured the necessaries, there may be time to amuse ourselves with the superfluities, and even with the trifles of life. *"*Dulce est desipere*," said Horace: *"*Vive la bagatelle!*" says Swift. I oppose neither; not the Epicurean, much less the Christian philosopher, but I insist that a principal part of these amusements be the amusements of study and reflection, of reading and conversation. You know what conversation I mean; for we lose the true advantage of our nature and constitution, if we suffer the mind to come, as it were, to a stand. When the body, instead of acquiring new vigour, and tasting new pleasures, begins to decline, and is sated with pleasures, or grown incapable of taking them, the mind may continue still to improve and indulge itself in new enjoyments. Every advance in knowledge opens a new scene of delight; and the joy that we feel in the actual possession of one, will be heightened by that which we expect to find in another, so that before we can exhaust this fund of successive pleasures, death will come to end our pleasures and our pains at once. **In his studiis laboribusque viventi, non intelligitur quando obrepit senectus: ita sensim sine sensu ætas senescit, nec subito frangitur, sed diuturnitate extinguitur.*

This, my lord, is the wisest, and the most agreeable manner in which a man of sense can wind up the thread of life. Happy is he whose situation and circumstances give him the opportunity and means of doing it! Though he should not have made any great advances in knowledge, and should set about it late, yet the task will not be found difficult, unless he has gone too far out of his way; and unless he continues too long to halt between the dissipations of the world and the leisure of a retired life:

*— *Vivendi recte qui prorogat horam,*
Rusticus expectat dum defluat amnis, —

You know the rest. I am sensible, more sensible than any enemy I have, of my natural infirmities, and acquired disadvantages: but I have begun, and I will persist; for he who jogs forward on a battered horse, in the right way, may get to the end of his journey; which he cannot do, who gallops * the fleetest courser of Newmarket, out of it.

Adieu, my dear lord. Though I have much more to say on this subject, yet I perceive, and I doubt you have long perceived, that I have said too much, at least for a letter, already. The rest shall be reserved for conversation whenever we meet; and then I hope to confirm, under your lordship's eye, my speculations by my practice. In the meantime let me refer you to our friend Pope. He says I made a philosopher of him; I am sure he has contributed very much, and I thank him for it, to the making an hermit of me.

(1752)

JONATHAN SWIFT

Jonathan Swift is not only one of the greatest writers in English literature but a figure of major importance in world literature. In vigour of mind, originality of concept, and sheer literary craftsmanship he has few rivals anywhere. Summing up, as he does, many of the salient characteristics of the neo-classical period, he has expressed them through the medium of a strong personality which was enriched by classical imitation but was never submerged by it.

This personality is at first sight unattractive: pride, ferocity, misanthropy are its most evident characteristics. Beneath the surface, however, to one who knows the whole man, love, tenderness, playfulness, and friendship appear none the less distinctly. Swift was a mass of contradictions. If he hated and detested that animal called man, as he himself said, he heartily loved individual men, John, Peter, Thomas, and the rest; if he scorned society, he constantly laboured to improve it; if he despised Ireland, the land of his birth and his long residence, he made himself the most popular Englishman who ever lived in Dublin. He broke the heart of Vanessa, and he gave to Stella a life of devoted but frustrate love. Always beating fiercely at the bars of life, he lived in savage indignation the life of a cruelly embittered man, and, before passing under the cloud of madness, left his little fortune "to build a house for fools and mad."

The key to Swift's life — and incidentally to his literary production — is to be found in his practicality. What would have remained for most men unembodied fancies were by him translated into actualities. The story about his reading Matins when no one but his clerk was present in the church may be apocryphal, but it is typical of the man. Instead of beginning, "Dearly beloved brethren," he is said to have opened the service: "Dearly beloved Roger, the Scripture moveth us in sundry places to acknowledge and confess our manifold sins and wickedness." Any one might have thought of so doing; Swift was not satisfied until he put his thoughts into practice. Other men smiled at the predictions of such almanac makers as Partridge; Swift exposed them by issuing Bickerstaff's *Predictions*. Other men were furious at the jobbery of Wood's halfpence; he wrote *The Drapier's Letters* and frustrated it. So too he translated his scorn of ordinary social converse into *A Complete Collection of Genteel and Ingenious Conversation*, and his irritation at the knaveries of servants into the ironical *Directions to Servants*. *A Modest Proposal* is merely an elaboration of the remark, which must have occurred to fifty persons, that the English people, having eaten everything else in Ireland, might as well eat the children too. Dr. Johnson's remark about *Gulliver's Travels*, "When once you have thought of big men and little men, it is very easy to do all the rest," is an unconscious tribute to Swift. Given the concepts of little people, big people, virtuosi untouched by the ordinary limitations of a practical world, or aging immortals, all the rest follows inevitably. The fourth voyage is merely an expansion of the idea that men are often more brutish than beasts. Always there is the intense desire to put into practice, in life or in literature, what to others were mere fancies.

Swift is one of the foremost satirists of all time. His chief standard of comparison is common sense: what is unconformable to right reason he ridicules mercilessly. Wit, in the eighteenth century sense of the word, is a lambent flame about every subject that he touches.

His prose style is unexcelled. Plain, direct, exquisitely adapted to the task in hand, it has the art that effectively conceals art. In his hands the new prose reaches its highest point of excellence. Simpler than Dryden's, more finished than Steele's, more colloquial than Addison's, more direct than Johnson's, it has been the delight and the despair of imitators.

The coarseness of Swift's language has appeared to many discriminating critics as its worst fault, though it offends this generation less than it did the last. In part it is a reflection of a time of plain speaking when the conversation of gentlemen was not over nice. But it goes beyond the ordinary practice of the early eighteenth century; it shocked his contemporaries. In the *Character of Mrs. Johnson*, Swift commended Stella's dislike of vulgarity; in his own familiar speech he does not seem to have been wantonly nasty. But in his satires he availed himself of verbal coarseness as a weapon to attack the things he despised; he threw dirt at things hateful; he attached disgusting ideas to things disgusting. When, however, he rose to his greatest heights, he abandoned this method; in such passages as the eulogy of England and the King of Brobdingnag's observations upon it, or the description of the Struldbrugs, for example, there is scarcely a word to offend modesty. Evil at its worst is most effectively shown in its natural meanness: it needs nothing but stark revelation.

JOURNAL TO STELLA

THE relations of Swift and Esther Johnson are mysterious; because of their mystery, scarcely less than their romance, they have bulked larger in biographical and literary discussions than their actual importance warrants. Whether Stella was married to Swift is not of great significance, since it is apparent that the marriage, even if its existence could be proved, must have been merely nominal. Neither do the reasons that interfered with their marriage make a great deal of difference to us: whether physical, emotional, or economic, their effect on the man and his work was much the same. What does concern us is the close companionship and the sincere regard which began when Swift, as Sir William Temple's secretary, supervised the girl's education, which found expression in numerous writings, and which continued as a dominant factor in both their lives. To her Swift addressed some of his most graceful poems; for her he wrote some of his most sincere prayers; after her he left important literary memorials and the relic that he marked, "Only a woman's hair."

Most important of all is the series of letters which Swift addressed to her between 1710 and 1713, while he was in England and she was in Ireland. These letters, now commonly known as the *Journal to Stella*, are an intimate day by day record of Swift's life during its most busy and interesting years. He had been sent to England by the Irish bishops in 1707 to negotiate for important Church legislation before Parliament. The appointment was doubtless made because Swift, through his position with Temple, was better acquainted than any other Irish clergyman with the Whig leaders. The negotiations were protracted until 1710, when the Tories came into power. Swift had been until then nominally a Whig, because of his connection with Temple. But his interests were primarily with the Church; the welfare of the Church was his main concern, personally and professionally, all through his life. As it became apparent that the Tories were better friends of the Established Church, he was drawn more and more to them.

In September, 1710, he was again in England negotiating with the new ministry, of which Harley and St. John were the leaders. Then began the great years of Swift's life, the time in which he occupied that position of importance for which he was fitted but which, during the greater part of his life, was denied him by perverse fate. The Tory leaders recognized the power of his pen and immediately cultivated him. The long-continued negotiations were speedily concluded, but he remained to support the ministry and to have an important, though unofficial, part in public affairs. His letters to Esther Johnson and her companion, Rebecca Dingley, give an intimate record of his daily doings and his association with the leaders of the government. They are at once an historical chronicle of great importance and a personal document in which the man is revealed in a light in which none of his other writings show him. Here for once irony is dropped and the satiric mask is withdrawn, showing the man as he really was, with his most intimate friends. Without this piece of self portrayal — as intimate in its way as Pepys' *Diary*, though not at all like it in purpose or tone — the author of *A Modest Proposal* and *Gulliver's Travels* would be unintelligible. The Swift of these letters is proud, sensitive, domineering but tender also and playful and sincerely natural.

Most striking of the peculiarities in the *Journal* is the "little language," evidently a recollection of Esther's childish speech, the same sort of thing which most families preserve in some measure as an intimate special vocabulary, full of significance to their own members, but scarcely intelligible to outsiders. This "little language" has been much modified in most of the published letters (the originals of forty of the sixty-five have been lost); but from those manuscripts which remain we can reconstruct it and interpret what the editors have left of it.

The last letter of the series was written on June 6, shortly before Swift returned to Dublin to assume his new duties as Dean of St Patrick's Cathedral. The great years were over, but the once obscure parson was going back to one of the best positions in the Irish Church. Probably it was not the one that he would have chosen, but it was none the less a valued promotion, and it was taking him to Stella.

Each letter was written in a small hand on a folio sheet, and is usually in the form of a journal for two weeks. As internal evidence shows, the individual entries were commonly made in the morning before Swift left his lodgings, or at night after his return. The specimen here printed is one complete letter, No. XIX. While it would have been possible to give brief extracts that contain more famous passages, the complete record of a fortnight is obviously a better representation of the *Journal*.

JOURNAL TO STELLA

LETTER XIX

LONDON, *March* 24, 1710–11

It was a little cross in *Presto not to send today to the coffee-house to see whether there was a letter from *MD before I sent away mine; but faith I did it on purpose, because I would scorn to answer two letters of yours successively. This way of journal is the worst in the world for writing of news, unless one does it the last day; and so I will observe henceforward, if there be any politics or stuff worth sending. *My shin mends in spite of the scratching last night. I dined today at *Ned Southwell's with the Bishop of Ossory and a parcel of Irish gentlemen. Have you yet seen any of the Spectators? Just three weeks today since I had your last, N. 11. I am afraid I have lost one by the packet that was taken; that will vex me, considering the pains MD take to write, especially poor pretty *Stella, and her weak eyes: God bless them and the owner, and send them well, and little me together, I hope ere long. *This illness of Mr. Harley puts everything backwards, and he is still down and like to be so by that extravasated blood which comes from his breast to the wound; it was by the second blow Guiscard gave him after the penknife was broken. I am shocked at that villainy whenever I think of it. *Biddy Floyd is past danger but will lose all her beauty: she had them mighty thick, especially about her nose.

25. Morning. I wish you *a merry new year: this is the first day of the year, you know, with us, and 'tis Lady Day. I must rise and go to *my Lord-Keeper; it is not shaving day today, so I shall be early. I am to dine with *Mr. Secretary St. John. Good morrow, my mistresses both, good morrow. Stella will be peeping out of her room at *Mrs. de Caudres' down upon the folks as they come from church; and there comes Mrs. Proby, and that's my Lady Southwell, and there's Lady Betty Rochfort. I long to hear how you are settled in your new lodgings. I wish I were rid of my old ones, and that Mrs. Brent could contrive to put up my books in boxes and lodge them in some safe place, and you keep my papers of importance. But I must rise, I tell you.—At night. So I visited and dined as I told you, and what of that? We have let Guiscard be buried at last, after showing him pickled in a trough this fortnight for twopence apiece; and the fellow that showed would point to his body, and, "See, gentlemen, this is the wound that was given him by his Grace the Duke of Ormond; and this is the wound," &c.; and then the show was over, and another set of rabble came in. 'Tis hard that our laws would not suffer us to hang his body in chains because he was not tried; and in the eye of our law every man is innocent till then.—Mr. Harley is still very weak and never out of bed.

26. This was a most delicious day; and my shin being past danger, I walked like lightning above two hours in the Park. We have generally one fair day, and then a great deal of rain for three or four days together. All things are at a stop in Parliament for want of Mr. Harley; they cannot stir an inch without him in their most material affairs: and we fear by *the caprice of Radcliffe, who will admit none but his own surgeon, he has not been well looked after. I dined at an alehouse with Mr. Lewis but had his wine. Don't you begin to see the flowers and blossoms of the field? How busy should I now be at *Laracor? No news of your box? I hope you have it and are this minute drinking the chocolate and that the smell of the Brazil tobacco has not affected it. I would be glad to know whether you like it, because I would send you more by people that are now every day thinking of going to Ireland; therefore pray tell me, and tell me soon, and I will have the strong box.

27. A rainy, wretched, scurvy day from morning till night: and *my neighbour Vanhomrigh invited me to dine with them; and this evening I passed at Mr. Prior's with *Dr. Freind; and 'tis now past twelve; so I must go sleep.

28. Morning. Oh, faith, you're an impudent saucy couple of sluttekins for presuming to write so soon, said I to myself this morning; who knows but there may be a letter from MD at the coffee-house? Well, you must know, and so I just now sent *Patrick, and he brought me three letters, but not one from MD; no indeed, for I read all the superscriptions, and not one from MD. One I opened; it was from the Archbishop; t'other I opened, it was from Staunton; the third I took and looked at the hand. Whose hand is this? says I; yes, says I, whose hand is this? then there was wax between the folds; then I began to suspect; then I peeped; faith, it was *Walls's hand after all;

* Notes on Jonathan Swift will be found in the Appendix, pp. 993 ff.

then I opened it in a rage, and then it was little MD's hand, dear, little, pretty, charming, MD's sweet hand again. O lord, en't here a clutter and a stir, and a bustle, never saw the like! Faith, I believe yours lay some days at the post office, and that it came before my eighteenth went, but that I did not expect it, and I hardly ever go there. Well, and so you think I'll answer this letter now? no, faith, and so I won't. I'll make you wait, young women; but I'll enquire immediately about poor Dingley's *exchequer trangum. What, is that Vedel again a soldier? Was he broke? I'll put it in *Ben Tooke's hand. I hope Vedel could not sell it. — At night. Vedel, Vedel, poh, pox, I think it is *Vedeau, ay, Vedeau, now I have it; let me see, do you name him in yours? Yes, Mr. John Vedeau is the brother; but where does this brother live? I'll enquire. This was a fast-day for the public; so I dined late with Sir Matthew Dudley, whom I have not been with a great while. He is one of those that must lose his employment whenever the great shake comes: and I can't contribute to keep him in, though I have dropped words in his favour to the ministry; but he has been too violent a Whig, and friend to *the Lord Treasurer to stay in. 'Tis odd to think how long they let those people keep their places; but the reason is they have not enough to satisfy all expecters, and so they keep them all in hopes that they may be good boys in the mean time; and thus the old ones hold in still. The comptroller told me that there are eight people expect his staff. I walked after dinner today round the Park. — What, do I write politics to little young women? Hold your tongue, and go to *your dean's.

29. Morning. If this be a fine day, I will walk into the city and see *Charles Barnard's library. What care I for your letter, your saucy N. 12? I will say nothing to it yet; faith, I believe this will be full before its time, and then go it must. I will always write once a fortnight; and if it goes sooner by filling sooner, why then there is so much clear gain. Morrow, morrow, rogues and lasses both; I can't lie scribbling here in bed for your play: I must rise, and so morrow again.— At night. Your friend Montgomery and his sister are here, as I am told by Patrick; I have seen him often but take no notice of him; he is grown very ugly and pimpled. They tell me he is a gamester and wins money. How could I help it, pray? Patrick snuffed the candle too short, and *the grease ran down upon the paper. It en't my fault; 'tis Patrick's fault; pray now don't blame Presto. I walked today in the city and dined at a private house and went to see the auction of poor Charles Barnard's books; they were in the middle of the physic books; so I bought none; and they are so dear I believe I shall buy none, and there's an end; and go to Stoyte's, and I'll go sleep.

30. Morning. This is Good Friday, you must know, and I must rise and go to Mr. Secretary about some business, and Mrs. Vanhomrigh desires me to breakfast with her because she is to intercede for Patrick who is so often drunk and quarrelsome in the house that I was resolved to send him over; but he knows all the places where I send and is so used to my ways that it would be inconvenient to me; but when I come to Ireland, I will discharge him. *Sir Thomas Mansel, one of the Lords of the Treasury, setting me down at my door today, saw Patrick and swore he was a *Teaguelander. I am so used to his face I never observed it, but thought him a pretty fellow. Sir Andrew Fountaine and I supped this fast-day with Mrs. Vanhomrigh. We were afraid Mr. Harley's wound would turn to a fistula; but we think the danger is now past. He rises every day and walks about his room, and we hope he will be out in a fortnight. Prior showed me a handsome paper of verses he has writ on Mr. Harley's accident: they are not out; I will send them to you if he will give me a copy.

31. Morning. What shall we do to make April fools this year, now it happens on Sunday? Patrick brings word that Mr. Harley still mends and is up every day. I design to see him in a few days; and he brings me word too that he has found out Vedeau's brother's shop; I shall call there in a day or two. It seems the wife lodges next door to the brother. I doubt the scoundrel was broke, and got a commission, or perhaps is a volunteer gentleman, and expects to get one by his valour. Morrow, sirrahs, let me rise.— At night. I dined today with Sir Thomas Mansel. We were walking in the Park, and Mr. Lewis came to us. Mansel asked where we dined. We said, together. He said we should dine with him, only his wife desired him to bring nobody because she had only a leg of mutton. I said I would dine with him to choose; but he would send a servant to

order a plate or two; yet this man has ten thousand pounds a year in land, and is a lord of the treasury, and is not covetous neither, but runs out merely by slattering and negligence. The worst dinner I ever saw at the dean's was better, but so it is with abundance of people here. I called at night at Mr. Harley's, who begins to walk in his room with a stick, but is mighty weak. See how much I have lost with *that ugly grease. 'Tis your fault, pray; and I'll go to bed.

April 1. The Duke of Buckingham's house fell down last night with an earthquake and is half swallowed up; — Won't you go and see it? — An April fool, an April fool, Oh, ho, young women. — Well, don't be angry; I'll make you an April fool no more till the next time: we had no sport here because it is Sunday, and Easter Sunday. I dined with the secretary, who seemed terribly down and melancholy, which Mr. Prior and Lewis observed as well as I: perhaps something is gone wrong; perhaps there is nothing in it. God bless my own dearest MD, and all is well.

2. We have such windy weather, 'tis troublesome walking, yet all the rabble have got into our Park these Easter holidays. I am plagued with one Richardson, an Irish parson, and his project of printing Irish Bibles, &c. to make you Christians in that country; I befriend him what I can on account of the Archbishop and Bishop of Clogher. But what business have I to meddle? &c. Don't you remember that, sirrah Stella? What was that about, when you thought I was meddling with something that was not my business? Oh, faith, you are an impudent slut; I remember your doings, I'll never forget you as long as I live. Lewis and I dined together at his lodgings. But where's the answer to this letter of MD's? Oh, faith, Presto, you must think of that. Time enough, says saucy Presto.

3. I was this morning to see *Mrs. Barton; I love her better than anybody here, and see her seldomer. Why, really now, so it often happens in the world, that where one loves a body best — pshah, pshah, you are so silly with your moral observations. — Well, but she told me a very good story. An old gentlewoman died here two months ago, and left in her will to have eight men and eight maids bearers, who should have two guineas apiece, ten guineas to the parson for a sermon, and two guineas to the clerk. But bearers, parson, and clerk must be all true virgins, and not to be admitted till they took their oaths of virginity; so the poor woman lies still unburied, and so must do till the general resurrection. I called at Mr. Secretary's to see what the D—— ailed him on Sunday; I made him a very proper speech, told him I observed he was much out of temper, that I did not expect he would tell me the cause, but would be glad to see he was in better; and one thing I warned him of, never to appear cold to me, for I would not be treated like a schoolboy; that I had felt too much of that in my life already (meaning from Sir William Temple), that I expected every great minister who honoured me with his acquaintance, if he heard or saw anything to my disadvantage, would let me know in plain words, and not put me in pain to guess by the change or coldness of his countenance or behaviour; for it was what I would hardly bear from a crowned head, and I thought no subject's favour was worth it; and that I designed to let my Lord Keeper and Mr. Harley know the same thing that they might use me accordingly. He took all right; said I had reason; vowed nothing ailed him but sitting up whole nights at business, and one night at drinking; would have had me dine with him and *Mrs. Masham's brother to make up matters; but I would not. I don't know, but I would not. But indeed I was engaged with *my old friend, Rollinson; you never heard of him before.

4. I sometimes look a line or two back and see plaguy mistakes of the pen; how do you get over them? You are puzzled sometimes. Why, I think what I said to Mr. Secretary was right. Don't you remember how I used to be in pain when Sir William Temple would look cold and out of humour for three or four days, and I used to suspect a hundred reasons? I have plucked up my spirit since then, faith; he spoiled a fine gentleman. I dined with my neighbour Vanhomrigh, and MD, poor MD, at home on a loin of mutton and half a pint of wine, and the mutton was raw; poor Stella could not eat, poor dear rogue, and Dingley was so vexed; but we'll dine at Stoyte's tomorrow. Mr. Harley promised to see me in a day or two; so I called this evening: but his son and others were abroad, and he asleep; so I came away and found out Mrs. Vedeau. She drew out a letter from Dingley, and said she would get a friend to receive the money. I told her I would employ Mr. Tooke in it

henceforward. Her husband bought a lieutenancy of foot and is gone to Portugal. He sold his share of the shop to his brother, and put out the money to maintain her, all but what bought the commission. She lodges within two doors of her brother. She told me it made her very melancholy to change her manner of life thus, but trade was dead, &c. She says she will write to you soon. I design to engage Ben Tooke, and then receive the parchment from her. I gave *Mr. Dopping a copy of Prior's verses on Mr. Harley; he sent them yesterday to Ireland; so go look for them, for I won't be at the trouble to transcribe them here. — They will be printed in a day or two. Give my hearty service to *Stoyte and Catherine; upon my word I love them dearly, and desire you will tell them so: pray desire Goody Stoyte not to let Mrs. Walls and Mrs. Johnson cheat her of her money at ombre, but assure her from me that she is a bungler. Dine with her today, and tell her so, and drink my health, and good voyage, and speedy return, and so you're a rogue.

5. Morning. Now let us proceed to examine a saucy letter from one Madame MD. God Almighty bless poor dear Stella, and send her a great many birthdays, all happy and healthy and wealthy, and with me ever together, and never asunder again, unless by chance. When I find you are happy or merry there, it makes me so here, and I can hardly imagine you absent when I am reading your letter or writing to you. No, faith, you are just here upon this little paper, and therefore I see and talk with you every evening constantly, and sometimes in the morning, but not always in the morning because that is not so modest to young ladies. What, you would fain palm a letter upon me more than you sent; and I, like a fool, must look over all yours to see whether this was really N. 12, or more. Patrick has this moment brought me letters from the Bishop of Clogher, and *Parvisol; my heart was at my mouth for fear of one from MD; what a disgrace would it be to have two of yours to answer together? But faith, this shall go tonight, for fear, and then come when it will, I defy it. No, you are not naughty at all; write when you are disposed. And so the dean told you the story of Mr. Harley, from the archbishop; I warrant it never spoiled your supper, or broke off your game. Nor yet, have not you the box? I wish *Mrs. Edgworth had the ——. But you have it now, I suppose; and is the chocolate good, or has the tobacco spoiled it? *Leigh stays till Sterne has done his business, no longer; and when that will be, God knows: I befriend him as much as I can, but Mr. Harley's accident stops that as well as all things else. You guess, Madam Dingley, that I shall stay a round twelvemonth; as hope saved, I would come over, if I could, this minute; but we will talk of that by and by. Your affair of Vedeau I have told you of already; now to the next, turn over the leaf. Mrs. Dobbins lies; I have no more provision here or in Ireland than I had. I am pleased that Stella the conjurer approves *what I did with Mr. Harley; but your generosity makes me mad; I know you repine inwardly at Presto's absence; you think he has broken his word of coming in three months, and that this is always his trick; and now Stella says she does not see possibly how I can come away in haste, and that MD is satisfied, &c. An't you a rogue to overpower me thus? I did not expect to find such friends as I have done. They may indeed deceive me too. But there are important reasons (pox on this grease, this candle tallow!) why they should not. I have been used barbarously by the late ministry; I am a little piqued in honour to let people see I am not to be despised. The assurances they give me, without any scruple or provocation, are such as are usually believed in the world; they may come to nothing, but the first opportunity that offers, and is neglected, I shall depend no more, but come away. I could say a thousand things on this head if I were with you. I am thinking why Stella should not go to the Bath, if she be told it will do her good; I will make Parvisol get up fifty pounds and pay it you; and you may be good housewives, and live cheap there some months, and return in autumn, or visit London, as you please: pray think of it. I writ to Bernage, directed to Curry's; I wish he had the letter. I will send the bohea tea if I can. The Bishop of Kilmore — I don't keep such company; an old dying fool, whom I was never with in my life. So I am no godfather; all the better. Pray, Stella, explain those two words of yours to me, what you mean by *Villain* and *Dainger*, and you, Madam Dingley, what is *Christianing*? — Lay your letters **this way, this way*, and the devil a bit of difference between this way and t'other way. No; I'll show you, lay them *this*

way, this way, and not that way, that way.— You shall have your aprons; and I'll put all your commissions as they come in a paper together, and don't think I'll forget MD's orders, because they are friends; I'll be as careful as if they were strangers. I know not what to do about * this Clements. Walls will not let me say anything, as if Mr. Pratt was against him; and now the Bishop of Clogher has written to me in his behalf. This thing does not rightly fall in my way, and that people never consider: I always give my good offices where they are proper, and that I am judge of; however, I will do what I can. But if he has the name of a Whig, it will be hard, considering my Lord Anglesea and Hyde are very much otherwise, and you know they have the employment of deputy treasurer. If the frolic should take you of going to the Bath, I here send you a note on Parvisol; if not, you may tear it, and there's an end. Farewell.

If you have an imagination that the Bath will do you good, I say again, I would have you go; if not, or it be inconvenient, burn this note. Or, if you would go, and not take so much money, take thirty pounds, and I will return you twenty from hence. Do as you please, sirrahs. I suppose it will not be too late for the first season; if it be, I would have you resolve, however, to go the second season, if the doctors say it will do you good, and you fancy so.

[1768]

GULLIVER'S TRAVELS

In form *Gulliver's Travels* belongs among the imaginary journeys common in the eighteenth century, and best known to the general reader today by Defoe's *Robinson Crusoe.* Because of its simple directness of presentation and its realistic detail, as well as its imaginative fertility, it remains one of the world's chief books of adventure, the perennial delight of boys and girls, who read it in expurgated form without thought of any deeper purpose.

In spirit it is satire, the greatest prose satire in our language and one of the greatest in all literature. So much will be admitted even by those who dislike the book, belonging as it does to a form of literature little cultivated and comparatively unappreciated during the past century. Many who feel the power of *Gulliver's Travels* are repelled by it and protest indignantly against the low estimate of humanity therein presented. The Fourth Voyage in particular has been denounced and has been described as the product of a disordered mind, by some who admit that the earlier voyages contain large elements of universal truth.

From one point of view Gulliver's voyage to the land of the Houyhnhnms describes an ideal commonwealth, comparable to Sir Thomas More's *Utopia* or Bacon's *New Atlantis.* It is a country which is ruled and guided by reason, where the highest possibilities of the rational soul have been developed and given full expression in a life of pastoral simplicity; a country without pretense or deceit, without ambition except emulation in well-doing, without passion or luxury or vice or the accompanying disorders of mind and body; a country of sanity and moderation and virtue. What often prevents this ideal country from being recognized as such is the attribution of these qualities, not to men but to horses. At the same time is presented the picture of complete degradation and bestiality in the Yahoos, a race of beings who realize all the lowest possibilities of the human animal. It is not enough to perceive that the Yahoos are shown as men lower than beasts; one must recognize also that in Swift's belief the possession of reason and the living of a life according to its dictates would raise even animals above the present level of men, while the neglect of reason and the unrestrained following of the lower impulses may debase men below the animals.

Of course this view of the Fourth Voyage is far from complete; Swift's purpose was primarily denunciation. Satire and Utopianism have much in common, but they are not identical. The ideal of what man might become is here used to intensify the contrast with what he actually is; though he has the capacity for reason, he is not a rational creature. Swift was terribly angered as he looked about him at the deceit and cruelty and stupidity of mankind, and probably even more as he looked at the ugliness of human nature within himself. Gulliver first protests that he is not a Yahoo, but as he learns through association with the wise Houyhnhnms, who represent the perfection of nature, he perceives that he too is one of the loathsome creatures whom he abhors. All mankind are Yahoos; civilization has merely given scope and opportunity to native vileness; and his own image in the lake he looks upon with horror and detestation.

So Swift lashes the whole human race. Why did he write such satire? He declared to Pope that his chief purpose was to vex the world rather than to divert it. In his own apology he avowed his desire,

To cure the vices of mankind,

and he asserted that,

> His satire points at no defect,
> But what all mortals may correct.

To vex the world may be the first step toward its amendment, but Swift certainly had little hope of thoroughgoing reformation. He wrote less for the world than for a few friends; but chiefly he wrote for himself, because he could not remain silent, because he found savage joy in expression. He scorned the world and struck it viciously.

Gulliver's Travels is many-sided, at once simple and bafflingly complex. Its author recognized the potentialities of human nature and sounded the depths of its baseness. He went to the edge of human life and looked over. What he saw there is not the whole truth, but it contains so much truth that it makes the thoughtful man shudder. In proportion as we recognize our own lineaments in the picture, we are repelled and fascinated.

GULLIVER'S TRAVELS

PART IV

A VOYAGE TO THE COUNTRY OF THE HOUYHNHNMS

CHAPTER I

The author sets out as captain of a ship. His men conspire against him, confine him a long time to his cabin, set him on shore in an unknown land. He travels up into the country. The Yahoos, *a strange sort of animal, described. The Author meets two* Houyhnhnms.

I continued at home with my wife and children about five months in a very happy condition, if I could have learned the lesson of knowing when I was well. I left my poor wife big with child, and accepted an advantageous offer made me to be captain of the *Adventure*, a stout merchantman of 350 tons: for I understood navigation well, and being grown weary of a surgeon's employment at sea, which however I could exercise upon occasion, I took a skillful young man of that calling, one Robert Purefoy, into my ship. We set sail from Portsmouth upon the seventh day of September, 1710; on the fourteenth we met with Captain Pocock of Bristol, at Teneriffe, who was going to the bay of Campechy, to cut logwood. On the sixteenth, he was parted from us by a storm; I heard since my return that his ship foundered, and none escaped but one cabin boy. He was an honest man, and a good sailor, but a little too positive in his own opinions, which was the cause of his destruction, as it hath been of several others. For if he had followed my advice, he might have been safe at home with his family at this time, as well as myself.

I had several men died in my ship of calentures, so that I was forced to get recruits out of Barbadoes, and the Leeward Islands, where I touched by the direction of the merchants who employed me, which I had soon too much cause to repent; for I found afterwards that most of them had been buccaneers. I had fifty hands on board, and my orders were that I should trade with the Indians in the South Sea, and make what discoveries I could. These rogues whom I had picked up debauched my other men, and they all formed a conspiracy to seize the ship and secure me; which they did one morning, rushing into my cabin, and binding me hand and foot, threatening to throw me overboard, if I offered to stir. I told them I was their prisoner, and would submit. This they made me swear to do, and then they unbound me, only fastening one of my legs with a chain near my bed, and placed a sentry at my door with his piece charged, who was commanded to shoot me dead, if I attempted my liberty. They sent me down victuals and drink, and took the government of the ship to themselves. Their design was to turn pirates, and plunder the Spaniards, which they could not do till they got more men. But first they resolved to sell the goods in the ship, and then go to Madagascar for recruits, several among them having died since my confinement. They sailed many weeks, and traded with the Indians, but I knew not what course they took, being kept a close prisoner in my cabin, and expecting nothing less than to be murdered, as they often threatened me.

Upon the ninth day of May, 1711, one James Welch came down to my cabin; and said he had orders from the captain to set me ashore. I expostulated with him, but in vain; neither would he so much as tell me who their new captain was. They forced me into the long-boat, letting me put on my best suit of clothes, which were as good as new, and a small bundle of linen, but no arms except my hanger; and they were so civil as not to search my pockets, into which I conveyed what money I had, with some other little necessaries. They rowed about a league, and then set me down on a strand. I desired them to tell me * what country it was. They all swore they knew no more than myself, but said that the captain (as they called him) was resolved, after they had sold the lading, to get rid of me in the first place where they could discover land. They pushed off immediately, advising me to make haste, for fear of being overtaken by the tide, and so bade me farewell.

In this desolate condition I advanced forward, and soon got upon firm ground, where I sat down on a bank to rest myself, and consider what I had best to do. When I was a little refreshed, I went up into the country, resolving to deliver myself to the first savages I should meet, and purchase my life from them by some bracelets, glass rings, and other toys which sailors usually provide themselves with in those voyages, and whereof I had some about me. The land was divided by long rows of trees, not regularly planted, but naturally growing; there was great plenty of grass, and several fields of oats. I walked very circumspectly for fear of being surprised, or suddenly shot with an arrow from behind or on either side. I fell into a beaten road, where I saw many tracks of human feet, and some of cows, but most of horses. At last I beheld several animals in a field, and one or two of the same kind sitting in trees. Their shape was very singular, and deformed, which a little discomposed me, so that I lay down behind a thicket to observe them better. Some of them coming forward near the place where I lay, gave me an opportunity of distinctly marking their form. Their heads and breasts were covered with a thick hair, some frizzled and others lank; they had beards like goats, and a long ridge of hair down their backs and the fore parts of their legs and feet, but the rest of their bodies were bare, so that I might see their skins, which were of a brown buff colour. They had no tails, nor any hair at all on their buttocks, except about the anus; which, I presume, nature had placed there to defend them as they sat on the ground; for this posture they used, as well as lying down, and often stood on their hind feet. They climbed high trees, as nimbly as a squirrel, for they had strong extended claws before and behind, terminating in sharp points, and hooked. They would often spring, and bound, and leap with prodigious agility. The females were not so large as the males; they had long lank hair on their heads, but none on their faces, nor anything more than a sort of down on the rest of their bodies, except about the anus, and pudenda. Their dugs hung between their fore-feet, and often reached almost to the ground as they walked. The hair of both sexes was of several colours, brown, red, black, and yellow. Upon the whole, I never beheld in all my travels so disagreeable an animal, nor one against which I naturally conceived so strong an antipathy. So that thinking I had seen enough, full of contempt and aversion, I got up and pursued the beaten road, hoping it might direct me to the cabin of some Indian. I had not got far when I met one of these creatures full in my way, and coming up directly to me. The ugly monster, when he saw me, distorted several ways every feature of his visage, and stared as at an object he had never seen before; then approaching nearer, lifted up his fore-paw, whether out of curiosity or mischief, I could not tell. But I drew my hanger, and gave him a good blow with the flat side of it, for I durst not strike with the edge, fearing the inhabitants might be provoked against me, if they should come to know, that I had killed or maimed any of their cattle. When the beast felt the smart, he drew back, and roared so loud that a herd of at least forty came flocking about me from the next field, howling and making odious faces; but I ran to the body of a tree, and leaning my back against it, kept them off by waving my hanger. Several of this cursed brood getting hold of the branches behind, leapt up into the tree, from whence they began to discharge their excrements on my head; however, I escaped pretty well, by sticking close to the stem of the tree, but was almost stifled with the filth, which fell about me on every side.

In the midst of this distress, I observed them all to run away on a sudden as fast as they could, at which I ventured to leave the tree, and pursue the road, wondering what it was that could put them into this fright. But looking on my left hand, I saw a horse walking softly in the field; which my persecutors having sooner discovered, was the cause of their flight. The horse started a little when he came near me, but soon recovering himself, looked full in my face with manifest tokens of wonder; he viewed my hands and feet, walking round me several times. I would have pursued my journey, but he placed himself directly in the way, yet looking with a very mild aspect, never offering the least violence. We stood gazing at each other for some time; at last I took the boldness to reach my hands towards his neck, with a design to stroke it, using the common style and whistle of jockeys when they are going to handle a strange horse. But this animal seeming to receive my civilities with disdain, shook his head, and bent his brows, softly raising up his right fore-foot to remove my hand. Then he neighed three or four times, but in so different a cadence, that I almost began to think he was speaking to himself in some language of his own.

While he and I were thus employed, another horse came up; who applying himself to the first in a very formal manner, they gently struck each other's right hoof before, neighing several times by turns, and varying the sound, which seemed to be almost articulate. They went some paces off, as if it were to confer together, walking side by side, backward and forward, like persons deliberating upon some affair of weight, but often turning their eyes towards me, as it were to watch that I might not escape. I was amazed to see such actions and behaviour in brute beasts, and concluded with myself that if the inhabitants of this country were endued with a proportionable degree of reason, they must needs be the wisest people upon earth. This thought gave me so much comfort that I resolved to go forward until I could discover some house or village, or meet with any of the natives, leaving the two horses to discourse together as they pleased. But the first, who was a dapple gray, observing me to steal off, neighed after me in so expressive a tone that I fancied myself to understand what he meant; whereupon I turned back, and came near him, to expect his farther commands: but concealing my fear as much as I could, for I began to be in some pain, how this adventure might terminate; and the reader will easily believe I did not much like my present situation.

The two horses came up close to me, looking with great earnestness upon my face and hands. The gray steed rubbed my hat all round with his right fore-hoof, and discomposed it so much that I was forced to adjust it better, by taking it off, and settling it again; whereat both he and his companion (who was a brown bay) appeared to be much surprised: the latter felt the lappet of my coat, and finding it to hang loose about me, they both looked with new signs of wonder. He stroked my right hand, seeming to admire the softness and colour; but he squeezed it so hard between his hoof and his pastern, that I was forced to roar; after which they both touched me with all possible tenderness. They were under great perplexity about my shoes and stockings, which they felt very often, neighing to each other, and using various gestures, not unlike those of a philosopher, when he would attempt to solve some new and difficult phenomenon.

Upon the whole, the behaviour of these animals was so orderly and rational, so acute and judicious, that I at last concluded they must needs be magicians, who had thus metamorphosed themselves upon some design, and seeing a stranger in the way, were resolved to divert themselves with him; or perhaps were really amazed at the sight of a man so very different in habit, feature, and complexion from those who might probably live in so remote a climate. Upon the strength of this reasoning, I ventured to address them in the following manner: "Gentlemen, if you be conjurers, as I have good cause to believe, you can understand any language; therefore I make bold to let your worships know that I am a poor distressed Englishman, driven by his misfortunes upon your coast, and I entreat one of you, to let me ride upon his back, as if he were a real horse, to some house or village, where I can be relieved. In return of which favour, I will make you a present of this knife and bracelet," (taking them out of my pocket). The two creatures stood silent while I spoke, seeming to listen with great attention; and when I had ended, they neighed frequently towards each other, as if they were engaged in serious conversation. I plainly observed that their language expressed the passions very well, and the words might with little pains be resolved into an alphabet more easily than the Chinese.

I could frequently distinguish the word *Yahoo*, which was repeated by each of them several times; and although it was impossible for me to conjecture what it meant, yet while the two horses were busy in conversation, I endeavoured to practise this word upon my tongue; and as soon as they were silent, I boldly pronounced *Yahoo* in a loud voice, imitating, at the same time, as near as I could, the neighing of a horse; at which they were both visibly surprised, and the gray repeated the same word twice, as if he meant to teach me the right accent, wherein I spoke after him as well as I could, and found myself perceivably to improve every time, though very far from any degree of perfection. Then the bay tried me with a second word, much harder to be pronounced; but reducing it to the English orthography, may be spelt thus, **Houyhnhnm*. I did not succeed in this so well as the former, but after two or three farther trials, I had better fortune; and they both appeared amazed at my capacity.

After some further discourse, which I then conjectured might relate to me, the two friends took their leaves, with the same compliment of striking each other's hoof; and the gray made me signs that I should walk before him, wherein I thought it prudent to comply, till I could find a better director. When I offered to slacken my pace, he would cry *Hhuun, hhuun*; I guessed his meaning, and gave him to understand, as well as I could, that I was weary, and not able to walk faster; upon which, he would stand a while to let me rest.

CHAPTER II

The author conducted by a Houyhnhnm *to his house. The house described. The author's reception. The food of the* Houyhnhnms. *The author in distress for want of meat, is at last relieved. His manner of feeding in this country.*

Having travelled about three miles, we came to a long kind of building, made of timber, stuck in the ground, and wattled across; the roof was low, and covered with straw. I now began to be a little comforted, and took out some toys, which travellers usually carry for presents to the savage Indians of America and other parts, in hopes the people of the house would be thereby encouraged to receive me kindly. The horse made me a sign to go in first; it was a large room with a smooth clay floor, and a rack and manger extending the whole length on one side. There were three nags and two mares, not eating, but some of them sitting down upon their hams, which I very much wondered at; but wondered more to see the rest employed in domestic business. These seemed but ordinary cattle; however, this confirmed my first opinion that a people who could so far civilise brute animals, must needs excel in wisdom all the nations of the world. The gray came in just after, and thereby prevented any ill treatment which the others might have given me. He neighed to them several times in a style of authority, and received answers.

Beyond this room there were three others, reaching the length of the house, to which you passed through three doors, opposite to each other, in the manner of a vista; we went through the second room towards the third; here the gray walked in first, beckoning me to attend; I waited in the second room, and got ready my presents for the master and mistress of the house: they were two knives, three bracelets of false pearl, a small looking-glass, and a bead necklace. The horse neighed three or four times, and I waited to hear some answers in a human voice, but I heard no other returns than in the same dialect, only one or two a little shriller than his. I began to think that this house must belong to some person of great note among them, because there appeared so much ceremony before I could gain admittance. But, that a man of quality should be served all by horses, was beyond my comprehension. I feared my brain was disturbed by my sufferings and misfortunes: I roused myself, and looked about me in the room where I was left alone; this was furnished like the first, only after a more elegant manner. I rubbed my eyes often, but the same objects still occurred. I pinched my arms and sides, to awake myself, hoping I might be in a dream. I then absolutely concluded that all these appearances could be nothing else but necromancy and magic. But I had no time to pursue these reflections; for the gray horse came to the door, and made me a sign to follow him into the third room, where I saw a very comely mare, together with a colt and foal, sitting on their haunches, upon mats of straw, not unartfully made, and perfectly neat and clean.

The mare soon after my entrance rose from her mat, and coming up close, after having nicely observed my hands and face, gave me a most contemptuous look; then turning to the horse, I heard the word *Yahoo* often repeated betwixt them; the meaning of which word I could not then comprehend, although it were the first I had learned to pronounce; but I was soon better informed, to my everlasting mortification: for the horse beckoning to me with his head, and repeating the word *Hhuun, hhuun*, as he did upon the road, which I understood was to attend him, led me out into a kind of court, where was another building at some distance from the house. Here we entered, and I saw three of those detestable creatures, whom I first met after my landing, feeding upon roots, and the flesh of some animals, which I afterwards found to be that of asses and dogs, and now and then a cow dead by accident or disease. They were all tied by the neck with strong withes, fastened to a beam; they held their food between the claws of their fore-feet, and tore it with their teeth.

The master horse ordered a sorrel nag, one of his servants, to untie the largest of these animals, and take him into the yard. The beast and I were brought close together, and our countenances diligently compared, both by master and servant, who thereupon repeated several times the word *Yahoo*. My horror and astonishment are not to be described, when I observed, in this abominable animal, a perfect human figure: the face of it indeed was flat and broad, the nose depressed, the lips large, and the mouth wide. But these differences are common to all savage nations, where the lineaments of the countenance are distorted by the natives suffering their infants to lie grovelling on the earth, or by carrying them on their backs, nuzzling with their face against the mother's shoulders. The fore-feet of the *Yahoo* differed from my hands in nothing else but the length of the nails, the coarseness and brownness of the palms, and the hairiness on the backs. There was the same resemblance between our feet, with the same differences, which I knew very well, though the horses did not, because of my shoes and stockings; the same in every part of our bodies, except as to hairiness and colour, which I have already described.

The great difficulty that seemed to stick with the two horses was to see the rest of my body so very different from that of a *Yahoo*, for which I was obliged to my clothes, whereof they had no conception. The sorrel nag offered me a root, which he held (after their manner, as we shall describe in its proper place) between his hoof and pastern; I took it in my hand, and having smelt it, returned it to him again as civilly as I could. He brought out of the *Yahoo's* kennel a piece of ass's flesh, but it smelt so offensively that I turned from it with loathing; he then threw it to the *Yahoo*, by whom it was greedily devoured. He afterwards showed me a wisp of hay, and * a fetlock full of oats; but I shook my head, to signify, that neither of these were food for me. And indeed, I now apprehended that I must absolutely starve, if I did not get to some of my own species; for as to those filthy *Yahoos*, although there were few greater lovers of mankind, at that time, than myself, yet I confess I never saw * any sensitive being so detestable on all accounts; and the more I came near them, the more hateful they grew, while I stayed in that country. This the master horse observed by my behaviour, and therefore sent the *Yahoo* back to his kennel. He then put his fore-hoof to his mouth, at which I was much surprised, although he did it with ease, and with a motion that appeared perfectly natural, and made other signs to know what I would eat; but I could not return him such an answer as he was able to apprehend; and if he had understood me, I did not see how it was possible to contrive any way for finding myself nourishment. While we were thus engaged, I observed a cow passing by, whereupon I pointed to her, and expressed a desire to let me go and milk her. This had its effect; for he led me back into the house, and ordered a mare-servant to open a room, where a good store of milk lay in earthen and wooden vessels, after a very orderly and cleanly manner. She gave me a large bowl full, of which I drank very heartily, and found myself well refreshed.

About noon I saw coming towards the house a kind of vehicle, drawn like a sledge by four *Yahoos*. There was in it an old steed, who seemed to be of quality; he alighted with his hind-feet forward, having by accident got a hurt on his left fore-foot. He came to dine with our horse, who received him with great civility. They dined in the best room, and had oats boiled in milk for the second course, which the old horse eat warm, but the rest cold. Their mangers were placed circular in the middle of the room, and divided into several partitions, round which they sat on their haunches upon bosses of straw. In the middle was a large rack with angles answering to every partition of the manger, so that each horse and mare eat their own hay, and their own mash of oats and milk, with much decency and regularity. The behaviour of the young colt and foal appeared very modest, and that of the master and mistress extremely cheerful and complaisant to their guest. The gray ordered me to stand by him, and much discourse passed between him and his friend concerning me, as I found by the stranger's often looking on me, and the frequent repetition of the word *Yahoo*.

I happened to wear my gloves, which the master gray observing, seemed perplexed, discovering signs of wonder what I had done to my fore-feet; he put his hoof three or four times to them, as if he would signify that I should reduce them to their former shape, which I presently did, pulling off both my gloves, and putting them into my pocket. This occasioned farther talk, and I saw the company was pleased with my behaviour, whereof I soon found the good effects. I was ordered to speak the few words I understood, and while they were at dinner, the master taught me the names for oats, milk, fire, water, and some others; which I could readily pronounce after him, having from my youth a great facility in learning languages.

When dinner was done, the master horse took me aside, and by signs and words made me understand the concern that he was in, that I had nothing to eat. Oats in their tongue are called *hlunnh*. This word I pronounced two or three times; for although I had refused them at first, yet upon second thoughts, I considered that I could contrive to make of them a kind of bread, which might be sufficient with milk to keep me alive till I could make my escape to some other country, and to creatures of my own species. The horse immediately ordered a white mare-servant of his family to bring me a good quantity of oats in a sort of wooden tray. These I heated before the fire as well as I could, and rubbed them till the husks came off, which I made a shift to winnow from the grain; I ground and beat them between two stones, then took water and made them into a paste or cake, which I toasted at the fire, and ate warm with milk. It was at first a very insipid diet, though common enough in many parts of Europe, but grew tolerable by time; and having been often reduced to hard fare in my life, this was not the first experiment I had made how easily nature is satisfied. And I cannot but observe that I never had one hour's sickness while I stayed in this island. 'Tis true, I sometimes made a shift to catch a rabbit, or bird, by springes made of *Yahoo's* hairs, and I often gathered wholesome herbs, which I boiled, and eat as salads with my bread, and now and then, for a rarity, I made a little butter, and drank the whey. I was at first * at a great loss for salt; but custom soon reconciled the want of it; and I am confident that the frequent use of salt among us is an effect of luxury, and was first introduced only as a provocative to drink; except where it is necessary for preserving of flesh in long voyages, or in places remote from great markets. For we observe no animal to be fond of it but man; and as to myself, when I left this country, it was a great while before I could endure the taste of it in anything that I eat.

This is enough to say upon the subject of my diet, wherewith other travellers fill their books, as if the readers were personally concerned whether we fared well or ill. However, it was necessary to mention this matter, lest the world should think it impossible that I could find sustenance for three years in such a country, and among such inhabitants.

When it grew towards evening, the master horse ordered a place for me to lodge in; it was but six yards from the house, and separated from the stable of the *Yahoos*. Here I got some straw, and covering myself with my own clothes, slept very sound. But I was in a short time better accommodated, as the reader shall know hereafter, when I come to treat more particularly about my way of living.

CHAPTER III

The author studious to learn the language, the Houyhnhnm *his master assists in teaching him. The language described. Several* Houyhnhnms *of quality come out of curiosity to see the author. He gives his master a short account of his voyage.*

My principal endeavour was to learn the language, which my master (for so I shall henceforth call him), and his children, and every servant of his house, were desirous to teach me. For they looked upon it as a prodigy that a brute animal should discover such marks of a rational creature. I pointed to every thing, and enquired the name of it, which I wrote down in my journal-book when I was alone, and corrected my bad accent by desiring those of the family to pronounce it often. In this employment a sorrel nag, one of the under servants, was very ready to assist me.

In speaking, they pronounce through the nose and throat, and their language approaches nearest to the High-Dutch, or German, of any I know in Europe; but is much more graceful and significant. The Emperor Charles V made almost the same observation, when he said that if he were to speak to his horse, it should be in High-Dutch.

The curiosity and impatience of my master

were so great that he spent many hours of his leisure to instruct me. He was convinced (as he afterwards told me) that I must be a *Yahoo*, but my teachableness, civility, and cleanliness, astonished him; which were qualities altogether so opposite to those animals. He was most perplexed about my clothes, reasoning sometimes with himself, whether they were a part of my body: for I never pulled them off till the family were asleep, and got them on before they waked in the morning. My master was eager to learn from whence I came, how I acquired those appearances of reason which I discovered in all my actions, and to know my story from my own mouth, which he hoped he should soon do by the great proficiency I made in learning and pronouncing their words and sentences. To help my memory, I formed all I learned into the English alphabet, and writ the words down with the translations. This last, after some time, I ventured to do in my master's presence. It cost me much trouble to explain to him what I was doing; for the inhabitants have not the least idea of books or literature.

In about ten weeks' time I was able to understand most of his questions, and in three months could give him some tolerable answers. He was extremely curious to know from what part of the country I came, and how I was taught to imitate a rational creature, because the *Yahoos* (whom he saw I exactly resembled in my head, hands, and face, that were only visible), with some appearance of cunning, and the strongest disposition to mischief, were observed to be the most unteachable of all brutes. I answered that I came over the sea from a far place, with many others of my own kind, in a great hollow vessel made of the bodies of trees. That my companions forced me to land on this coast, and then left me to shift for myself. It was with some difficulty, and by the help of many signs, that I brought him to understand me. He replied, that I must needs be mistaken, or that I *said the thing which was not*. (For they have no word in their language to express lying or falsehood.) He knew it was impossible that there could be a country beyond the sea, or that a parcel of brutes could move a wooden vessel whither they pleased upon water. He was sure no *Houyhnhnm* alive could make such a vessel, nor would trust *Yahoos* to manage it.

The word *Houyhnhnm*, in their tongue, signifies a *horse*, and in its etymology, *the perfection of nature*. I told my master that I was at a loss for expression, but would improve as fast as I could; and hoped in a short time I should be able to tell him wonders: he was pleased to direct his own mare, his colt and foal, and the servants of the family, to take all opportunities of instructing me, and every day for two or three hours, he was at the same pains himself. Several horses and mares of quality in the neighbourhood came often to our house upon the report spread of a wonderful *Yahoo* that could speak like a *Houyhnhnm*, and seemed in his words and actions to discover some glimmerings of reason. These delighted to converse with me; they put many questions, and received such answers as I was able to return. By all these advantages, I made so great a progress that in five months from my arrival, I understood whatever was spoke, and could express myself tolerably well.

The *Houyhnhnms* who came to visit my master, out of a design of seeing and talking with me, could hardly believe me to be a right *Yahoo*, because my body had a different covering from others of my kind. They were astonished to observe me without the usual hair or skin, except on my head, face, and hands; but I discovered that secret to my master, upon an accident, which happened about a fortnight before.

I have already told the reader that every night when the family were gone to bed, it was my custom to strip and cover myself with my clothes: it happened one morning early, that my master sent for me, by the sorrel nag, who was his valet; when he came, I was fast asleep, my clothes fallen off on one side, and my shirt above my waist. I awakened at the noise he made, and observed him to deliver his message in some disorder; after which he went to my master, and in a great fright gave him a very confused account of what he had seen. This I presently discovered; for going as soon as I was dressed to pay my attendance upon his Honour, he asked me the meaning of what his servant had reported, that I was not the same thing when I slept as I appeared to be at other times; that his valet assured him, some part of me was white, some yellow, at least not so white, and some brown.

I had hitherto concealed the secret of my dress, in order to distinguish myself, as much as possible, from that cursed race of *Yahoos*; but now I found it in vain to do so any longer. Besides, I considered that my clothes and shoes would soon wear out, which already were in a declining condition, and must be supplied by some contrivance from the hides of *Yahoos* or other brutes; whereby the whole secret would be known. I therefore told my master that in the country from whence I came, those of my kind always covered their bodies with the hairs of certain animals prepared by art, as well for decency, as to avoid the inclemencies of air, both hot and cold; of which, as to my own person, I would give him immediate conviction, if he pleased to command me: only desiring his excuse, if I did not expose those parts that nature taught us to conceal. He said my discourse was all very strange, but especially the last part; for he could not understand why nature should teach us to conceal what nature had given. That neither himself nor family were ashamed of any parts of their bodies; but however I might do as I pleased. Whereupon, I first unbuttoned my coat, and pulled it off. I did the same with my waistcoat; I drew off my shoes, stockings, and breeches. I let my shirt down to my waist, and drew up the bottom, fastening it like a girdle about my middle to hide my nakedness.

My master observed the whole performance with great signs of curiosity and admiration. He took up all my clothes in his pastern, one piece after another, and examined them diligently; he then stroked my body very gently, and looked round me several times, after which he said it was plain I must be a perfect *Yahoo*; but that I differed very much from the rest of my species, in the softness, and whiteness, and smoothness of my skin, my want of hair in several parts of my body, the shape and shortness of my claws behind and before, and my affectation of walking continually on my two hinder feet. He desired to see no more, and gave me leave to put on my clothes again, for I was shuddering with cold.

I expressed my uneasiness at his giving me so often the appellation of *Yahoo*, an odious animal for which I had so utter a hatred and contempt. I begged he would forbear applying that word to me, and take the same order in his family, and among his friends whom he suffered to see me. I requested, likewise, that the secret of my having a false covering to my body might be known to none but himself, at least as long as my present clothing should last; for as to what the sorrel nag, his valet, had observed, his Honour might command him to conceal it.

All this my master very graciously consented to, and thus the secret was kept till my clothes began to wear out, which I was forced to supply by several contrivances that shall hereafter be mentioned. In the meantime, he desired I would go on with my utmost diligence to learn their language, because he was more astonished at my capacity for speech and reason, than at the figure of my body, whether it were covered or no; adding, that he waited with some impatience to hear the wonders which I promised to tell him.

From thenceforward he doubled the pains he had been at to instruct me; he brought me into all company, and made them treat me with civility, because, as he told them privately, this would put me into good humour, and make me more diverting.

Every day when I waited on him, beside the trouble he was at in teaching, he would ask me several questions concerning myself, which I answered as well as I could; and by these means he had already received some general ideas, though very imperfect. It would be tedious to relate the several steps by which I advanced to a more regular conversation; but the first account I gave of myself in any order and length, was to this purpose:

That I came from a very far country, as I already had attempted to tell him, with about fifty more of my own species; that we travelled upon the seas in a great hollow vessel made of wood, and larger than his Honour's house. I described the ship to him in the best terms I could, and explained by the help of my handkerchief displayed, how it was driven forward by the wind. That upon a quarrel among us, I was set on shore on this coast, where I walked forward without knowing whither, till he delivered me from the persecution of those execrable *Yahoos*. He asked me who made the ship, and how it was possible that the *Houyhnhnms* of my country would leave it to the management of brutes. My answer was that I durst proceed no further in my relation, unless he would give me his word and honour that he would not be offended, and then I would tell him the wonders I had so often promised. He agreed; and I went on by assuring him that the ship was made by creatures like myself, who in all the countries I had travelled, as well as in my own, were the only governing, rational animals; and that upon my arrival hither, I was as much astonished to see the *Houyhnhnms* act like rational beings, as he or his friends could be in finding some marks of reason in a creature he was pleased to call a *Yahoo*, to which I owned my resemblance in every part, but could not account for their degenerate and brutal nature. I said farther, that if good fortune ever restored me to my native country, to relate my travels hither, as I resolved to do, every body would believe that I *said the thing which was not*; that I invented the story out of my own head; and with all possible respect to himself, his family and friends, and under his promise of not being offended, our countrymen would hardly think it probable that a *Houyhnhnm* should be the presiding creature of a nation, and a *Yahoo* the brute.

CHAPTER IV

The Houyhnhnm's *notion of truth and falsehood. The author's discourse disapproved by his master. The author gives a more particular account of himself, and the accidents of his voyage.*

My master heard me with great appearances of uneasiness in his countenance, because *doubting*, or *not believing*, are so little known in this country that the inhabitants cannot tell how to behave themselves under such circumstances. And I remember in frequent discourses with my master concerning the nature of manhood, in other parts of the world, having occasion to talk of *lying* and *false representation*, it was with much difficulty that he comprehended what I meant, although he had otherwise a most acute judgment. For he argued thus: that the use of speech was to make us understand one another, and to receive information of facts; now if any one *said the thing which was not*, these ends were defeated; because I cannot properly be said to understand him; and I am so far from receiving information that he leaves me worse than in ignorance, for I am led to believe a thing black when it is white, and short when it is long. And these were all the notions he had concerning that faculty of *lying*, so perfectly well understood, and so universally practised, among human creatures.

To return from this digression; when I asserted that the *Yahoos* were the only governing animals in my country, which my master said was altogether past his conception, he desired to know whether we had *Houyhnhnms* among us, and what was their employment: I told him we had great numbers, that in summer they grazed in the fields, and in winter were kept in houses, with hay and oats, where *Yahoo* servants were employed to rub their skins smooth, comb their manes, pick their feet, serve them with food, and make their beds. "I understand you well"; said my master, "it is now very plain, from all you have spoken, that whatever share of reason the *Yahoos* pretend to, the *Houyhnhnms* are your masters; I heartily wish our *Yahoos* would be so tractable." I begged his Honour would please to excuse me from proceeding any farther, because I was very certain that the account he expected from me would be highly displeasing. But he insisted in commanding me to let him know the best and the worst: I told him he should be obeyed. I owned that the *Houyhnhnms* among us, whom we called horses, were the most generous and comely animals we had, that they excelled in strength and swiftness; and when they belonged to persons of quality, employed in travelling, racing, or drawing chariots, they were treated with much kindness and care, till they fell into diseases, or became foundered in the feet; and then they were sold, and used to all kind of drudgery till they died; after which their skins were stripped and sold for what they were worth, and their bodies left to be devoured by dogs and birds of prey. But the common race of horses had not so good fortune, being kept by farmers and carriers, and other mean people, who put them to greater labour, and fed them worse. I described, as well as I could, our way of riding, the shape and use of a bridle, a saddle, a spur, and a whip, of harness and wheels. I added that we fastened plates of a certain hard substance called iron at the bottom of their feet, to preserve their hoofs from being broken by the stony ways on which we often travelled.

My master, after some expressions of great indignation, wondered how we dared to venture upon a *Houyhnhnm's* back, for he was sure that the weakest servant in his house would be able to shake off the strongest *Yahoo*, or by lying down, and rolling on his back, squeeze the brute to death. I answered that our horses were trained up from three or four years old to the several uses we intended them for; that if any of them proved intolerably vicious, they were employed for carriages; that they were severely beaten while they were young, for any mischievous tricks; that the males, designed for common use of riding or draught, were generally castrated about two years after their birth, to take down their spirits, and make them more tame and gentle; that they were indeed sensible of rewards and punishments; but his Honour would please to consider that they had not the least tincture of reason any more than the *Yahoos* in this country.

It put me to the pains of many circumlocutions to give my master a right idea of what I spoke; for their language doth not abound in variety of words, because their wants and passions are fewer than among us. But it is impossible to express his noble resentment at our savage treatment of the *Houyhnhnm* race, particularly after I had explained the manner and use of castrating horses among us, to hinder them from propagating their kind, and to render them more servile. He said, if it were possible there could be any country where *Yahoos* alone were endued with reason, they certainly must be the governing animal, because reason will in time always prevail against brutal strength. But, considering the frame of our bodies, and especially of mine, he thought no creature of equal bulk was so ill-contrived for employing that reason in the common offices of life; whereupon he desired to know whether those among whom I lived resembled me or the *Yahoos* of his country. I assured him, that I was as well shaped as most of my age; but the younger and the females were much more soft and tender, and the skins of the latter generally as white as milk. He said I differed indeed from other *Yahoos*, being much more cleanly, and not altogether so deformed, but, in point of real advantage, he thought I differed for the worse. That my nails were of no use either to my fore or hinder-feet; as to my fore-feet, he could not properly call them by that name, for he never observed me to walk upon them; that they were too soft to bear the ground; that I generally went with them uncovered, neither was the covering I sometimes wore on them of the same shape, or so strong as that on my feet behind. That I could not walk with any security, for if either of my hinder-feet slipped, I must inevitably fall. He then began to find fault with other parts of my body, the flatness of my face, the prominence of my nose, my eyes placed directly in front, so that I could not look on either side without turning my head: that I was not able to feed myself, without lifting one of my fore-feet to my mouth: and therefore nature had placed those joints to answer that necessity. He knew not what could be the use of those several clefts and divisions in my feet behind; that these were too soft to bear the hardness and sharpness of stones without a covering made from the skin of some other brute; that my whole body wanted a fence against heat and cold, which I was forced to put on and off every day with tediousness and trouble. And lastly, that he observed every animal in this country naturally to abhor the *Yahoos*, whom the weaker avoided, and the stronger drove from them. So that supposing us to have the gift of reason, he could not see how it were possible to cure that natural antipathy which every creature discovered against us; nor consequently, how we could tame and render them serviceable. However, he would, (as he said,) debate the matter no farther, because he was more desirous to know my own story, the country where I was born, and the several actions and events of my life before I came hither.

I assured him how extremely desirous I was that he should be satisfied on every point; but I doubted much, whether it would be possible for me to explain myself on several subjects whereof his Honour could have no conception, because I saw nothing in his country to which I could resemble them. That, however, I would do my best, and strive to express myself by similitudes, humbly desiring his assistance when I wanted proper words; which he was pleased to promise me.

I said my birth was of honest parents in an island called England, which was remote from this country, as many days' journey as the strongest of his Honour's servants could travel in the annual course of the sun. That I was bred a surgeon, whose trade it is to cure wounds and hurts in the body, got by accident or violence; that my country was governed by a female man, whom we called a queen. That I left it to get riches, whereby I might maintain myself and family when I should return. That, in my last voyage, I was commander of the ship, and had about fifty *Yahoos* under me, many of which died at sea, and I was forced to supply them by others picked out from several nations. That our ship was twice in danger of being sunk; the first time by a great storm, and the second, by striking against a rock. Here my master interposed, by asking me how I could persuade strangers out of different countries to venture with me, after the losses I had sustained, and the hazards I had run. I said they were fellows of desperate fortunes, forced to fly from the places of their birth, on account of their poverty or their crimes. Some were undone by lawsuits; others spent all they had in drinking, whoring, and gaming; others fled for treason; many for murder, theft, poisoning, robbery, perjury, forgery, coining false money, for committing rapes or sodomy, for flying from their colours, or deserting to the enemy, and most of them had broken prison; none of these durst return to their native countries for fear of being hanged, or of starving in a jail; and therefore were under the necessity of seeking a livelihood in other places.

During this discourse, my master was pleased to interrupt me several times; I had made use of many circumlocutions in describing to him the nature of the several crimes, for which most of our crew had been forced to fly their country. This labour took up several days' conversation, before he was able to comprehend me. He was wholly at a loss to know what could be the use or necessity of practising those vices. To clear up which I endeavoured to give some ideas of the desire of power and riches, of the terrible effects of lust, intemperance, malice, and envy. All this I was forced to define and describe by putting of cases, and making of suppositions. After which, like one whose imagination was struck with something never seen or heard of before, he would lift up his eyes with amazement and indignation. Power, government, war, law, punishment, and a thousand other things had no terms wherein that language could express them, which made the difficulty almost insuperable to give my master any conception of what I meant. But being of an excellent understanding, much improved by contemplation and converse, he at last arrived at a competent knowledge of what human nature in our parts of the world is capable to perform, and desired I would give him some particular account of that land which we call Europe, but especially of my own country.

CHAPTER V

The author, at his master's commands, informs him of the state of England. *The causes of war among the princes of* Europe. *The author begins to explain the* English *constitution.*

The reader may please to observe that the following extract of many conversations I had with my master contains a summary of the most material points, which were discoursed at several times for above two years; his Honour often desiring fuller satisfaction as I farther improved in the *Houyhnhnm* tongue. I laid before him, as well as I could, the whole state of Europe; I discoursed of trade and manufactures, of arts and sciences; and the answers I gave to all the questions he made, as they arose upon several subjects, were a fund of conversation not to be exhausted. But I shall here only set down the substance of what passed between us concerning my own country, reducing it into order as well as I can, without any regard to time or other circumstances, while I strictly adhere to truth. My only concern is that I shall hardly be able to do justice to my master's arguments and expressions, which must needs suffer by my want of capacity, as well as by a translation into our barbarous English.

In obedience, therefore, to his Honour's commands, I related to him the Revolution under the Prince of Orange; the long war with France entered into by the said prince, and renewed by his successor, the present queen, wherein the greatest powers of Christendom were engaged, and which still continued: I computed, at his request, that about a million of *Yahoos* might have been killed in the whole progress of it; and perhaps a hundred or more cities taken, and thrice as many ships burnt or sunk.

He asked me what were the usual causes or motives that made one country go to war with another. I answered they were innumerable, but I should only mention a few of the chief. Sometimes the ambition of princes, who never think they have land or people enough to govern; sometimes the corruption of ministers, who engage their master in a war in order to stifle or divert the clamour of the subjects against their evil administration. Difference in opinions hath cost many millions of lives: for instance, * whether flesh be bread, or bread be flesh; whether the juice of a certain berry be blood or wine; * whether whistling be a vice or a virtue; whether it be better * to kiss a post, or throw it into the fire; * what is the best colour for a coat, whether black, white, red, or gray: and whether it should be long or short, narrow or wide, dirty or clean; with many more. Neither are any wars so furious and bloody, or of so long continuance, as those occasioned by difference in opinion, especially if it be in things indifferent.

Sometimes the quarrel between two princes is to decide which of them shall dispossess a third of his dominions, where neither of them pretend to any right. Sometimes one prince quarrelleth with another, for fear the other should quarrel with him. Sometimes a war is entered upon because the enemy is too strong, and sometimes because he is too weak. Sometimes our neighbours want the things which we have, or have the things which we want; and we both fight till they take ours or give us theirs. It is a very justifiable cause of a war to invade a country after the people have been wasted by famine, destroyed by pestilence, or embroiled by factions among themselves. It is justifiable to enter into war against our nearest ally, when one of his towns lies convenient for us, or a territory of land that would render our dominions round and complete. If a prince sends forces into a nation, where the people are poor and ignorant, he may lawfully put half of them to death, and make slaves of the rest, in order to civilize and reduce them from their barbarous way of living. It is a very kingly, honourable, and frequent practice, when one prince desires the assistance of another to secure him against an invasion, that the assistant, when he hath driven out the invader, should seize on the dominions himself, and kill, imprison, or banish the prince he came to relieve. Alliance by blood or marriage is a frequent cause of war between princes; and the nearer the kindred is, the greater is their disposition to quarrel: poor nations are hungry, and rich nations are proud; and pride and hunger will ever be at variance. For these reasons, the trade of a soldier is held the most honourable of all others; because a soldier is a *Yahoo* hired to kill in cold blood as many of his own species, who have never offended him, as possibly he can.

There is likewise a kind of beggarly princes in Europe, not able to make war by themselves, who hire out their troops to richer nations, for so much a day to each man; of which they keep three fourths to themselves, and it is the best part of their maintenance; such are those in Germany and other northern parts of Europe.

"What you have told me," said my master, "upon the subject of war, does indeed discover most admirably the effects of that reason you pretend to: however, it is happy that the shame is greater than the danger; and that nature hath left you utterly uncapable of doing much mischief.

"For your mouths lying flat with your faces, you can hardly bite each other to any purpose, unless by consent. Then as to the claws upon your feet before and behind, they are so short and tender that one of our *Yahoos* would drive a dozen of yours before him. And therefore in recounting the numbers of those who have been killed in battle, I cannot but think that you have said the thing which is not."

I could not forbear shaking my head, and smiling a little at his ignorance. And being no stranger to the art of war, I gave him a description of cannons, culverins, muskets, carabines, pistols, bullets, powder, swords, bayonets, battles, sieges, retreats, attacks, undermines, countermines, bombardments, sea fights; ships sunk with a thousand men, twenty thousand killed on each side; dying groans, limbs flying in the air, smoke, noise, confusion, trampling to death under horses' feet; flight, pursuit, victory; fields strewed with carcases left for food to dogs, and wolves, and birds of prey; plundering, stripping, ravishing, burning, and destroying. And to set forth the valour of my own dear countrymen, I assured him, that I had seen them blow up a hundred enemies at once in a siege, and as many in a ship, and beheld the dead bodies come down in pieces from the clouds, to the great diversion of the spectators.

I was going on to more particulars, when my master commanded me silence. He said whoever understood the nature of *Yahoos* might easily believe it possible for so vile an animal to be capable of every action I had named, if their strength and cunning equalled their malice. But as my discourse had increased his abhorrence of the whole species, so he found it gave him a disturbance in his mind, to which he was wholly a stranger before. He thought his ears being used to such abominable words, might by degrees admit them with less detestation. That although he hated the *Yahoos* of this country, yet he no more blamed them for their odious qualities, than he did a *gnnayh* (a bird of prey) for its cruelty, or a sharp stone for cutting his hoof. But when a creature pretending to reason could be capable of such enormities, he dreaded lest the corruption of that faculty might be worse than brutality itself. He seemed therefore confident that, instead of reason, we were only possessed of some quality fitted to increase our natural vices; as the reflection from a troubled stream returns the image of an ill-shapen body, not only larger, but more distorted.

He added that he had heard too much upon the subject of war, both in this, and some former discourses. There was another point which a little perplexed him at present. I had informed him that some of our crew left their country on account of being ruined by law, that I had already explained the meaning of the word; but he was at a loss how it should come to pass that the law which was intended for every man's preservation, should be any man's ruin. Therefore he desired to be farther satisfied what I meant by law, and the dispensers thereof, according to the present practice in my own country; because he thought nature and reason were sufficient guides for a reasonable animal, as we pretended to be, in showing us what we ought to do, and what to avoid.

I assured his Honour that law was a science wherein I had not much conversed, further than by employing advocates, in vain, upon some injustices that had been done me; however, I would give him all the satisfaction I was able.

I said there was a society of men among us, bred up from their youth in the art of proving by words multiplied for the purpose, that white is black, and black is white, according as they are paid. To this society all the rest of the people are slaves. For example, if my neighbour hath a mind to my cow, he hires a lawyer to prove that he ought to have my cow from me. I must then hire another to defend my right, it being against all rules of law that any man should be allowed to speak for himself. Now in this case, I, who am the right owner, lie under two great disadvantages. First, my lawyer, being practised almost from his cradle in defending falsehood, is quite out of his element when he would be an advocate for justice, which as an office unnatural, he always attempts with great awkwardness, if not with ill-will. The second disadvantage is that my lawyer must proceed with great caution, or else he will be reprimanded by the judges, and abhorred by his brethren, as one that would lessen the practice of the law. And therefore I have but two methods to preserve my cow. The first is to gain over my adversary's lawyer with a double fee; who will then betray his client, by insinuating that he hath justice on his side. The second way is for my lawyer to make my cause appear as unjust as he can, by allowing the cow to belong to my adversary; and this, if it be skillfully done, will certainly bespeak the favour of the bench.

Now, your Honour is to know, that these judges are persons appointed to decide all controversies of property, as well as for the trial of criminals, and picked out from the most dexterous lawyers, who are grown old or lazy, and having been biassed all their lives against truth and equity, are under such a fatal necessity of favouring fraud, perjury, and oppression that I have known several of them refuse a large bribe from the side where justice lay, rather than injure the faculty by doing anything unbecoming their nature or their office.

It is a maxim among these lawyers that whatever hath been done before may legally be done again; and therefore they take special care to record all the decisions formerly made against common justice, and the general reason of mankind. These, under the name of *precedents*, they produce as authorities, to justify the most iniquitous opinions; and the judges never fail of directing accordingly.

In pleading, they studiously avoid entering into the merits of the cause; but are loud, violent, and tedious in dwelling upon all circumstances which are not to the purpose. For instance, in the case already mentioned: they never desire to know what claim or title my adversary hath to my cow; but whether the said cow were red or black; her horns long or short; whether the field I graze her in be round or square; whether she was milked at home or abroad; what diseases she is subject to, and the like; after which they consult precedents, adjourn the cause from time to time, and in ten, twenty, or thirty years come to an issue.

It is likewise to be observed that this society hath a peculiar cant and jargon of their own that no other mortal can understand, and wherein all their laws are written, which they take special care to multiply;

whereby they have wholly confounded the very essence of truth and falsehood, of right and wrong; so that it will take thirty years to decide whether the field left me by my ancestors for six generations belongs to me, or to a stranger three hundred miles off.

In the trial of persons accused for crimes against the state, the method is much more short and commendable: the judge first sends to sound the disposition of those in power, after which he can easily hang or save the criminal, strictly preserving all due forms of law.

Here my master, interposing, said it was a pity that creatures endowed with such prodigious abilities of mind as these lawyers, by the description I gave of them, must certainly be, were not rather encouraged to be instructors of others in wisdom and knowledge. In answer to which, I assured his Honour that in all points out of their own trade, they were usually the most ignorant and stupid generation among us, the most despicable in common conversation, avowed enemies to all knowledge and learning, and equally disposed to pervert the general reason of mankind in every other subject of discourse, as in that of their own profession.

CHAPTER VI

A continuation of the state of England *under Queen* Anne. *The character of a first minister of state in the courts of* Europe.

My master was yet wholly at a loss to understand what motives could incite this race of lawyers to perplex, disquiet, and weary themselves, and engage in a confederacy of injustice, merely for the sake of injuring their fellow-animals; neither could he comprehend what I meant in saying they did it for hire. Whereupon I was at much pains to describe to him the use of money, the materials it was made of, and the value of the metals; that when a *Yahoo* had got a great store of this precious substance, he was able to purchase whatever he had a mind to: the finest clothing, the noblest houses, great tracts of land, the most costly meats and drinks, and have his choice of the most beautiful females. Therefore since money alone was able to perform all these feats, our *Yahoos* thought they could never have enough of it to spend or to save, as they found themselves inclined from their natural bent either to profusion or avarice. That the rich man enjoyed the fruit of the poor man's labour, and the latter were a thousand to one in proportion to the former. That the bulk of our people were forced to live miserably, by labouring every day for small wages to make a few live plentifully. I enlarged myself much on these and many other particulars to the same purpose; but his Honour was still to seek; for he went upon a supposition that all animals had a title to their share in the productions of the earth, and especially those who presided over the rest. Therefore he desired I would let him know what these costly meats were, and how any of us happened to want them. Whereupon I enumerated as many sorts as came into my head, with the various methods of dressing them, which could not be done without sending vessels by sea to every part of the world, as well for liquors to drink, as for sauces, and innumerable other conveniences. I assured him that this whole globe of earth must be at least three times gone round, before one of our better female *Yahoos* could get her breakfast, or a cup to put it in. He said that must needs be a miserable country which cannot furnish food for its own inhabitants. But what he chiefly wondered at was how such vast tracts of ground as I described should be wholly without fresh water, and the people put to the necessity of sending over the sea for drink. I replied, that England (the dear place of my nativity) was computed to produce three times the quantity of food, more than its inhabitants are able to consume, as well as liquors extracted from grain, or pressed out of the fruit of certain trees, which made excellent drink, and the same proportion in every other convenience of life. But, in order to feed the luxury and intemperance of the males, and the vanity of the females, we sent away the greatest part of our necessary things to other countries, from whence in return we brought the materials of diseases, folly, and vice to spend among ourselves. Hence it follows, of necessity, that vast numbers of our people are compelled to seek their livelihood by begging, robbing, stealing, cheating, pimping, forswearing, flattering, suborning, forging, gaming, lying, fawning, hectoring, voting, scribbling, star-gazing, poisoning, whoring, canting, libelling, freethinking, and the like occupations: every one of which terms, I was at much pains to make him understand.

That wine was not imported among us from foreign countries to supply the want of water or other drinks, but because it was a sort of liquid which made us merry, by putting us out of our senses; diverted all melancholy thoughts, begat wild extravagant imaginations in the brain, raised our hopes, and banished our fears, suspended every office of reason for a time, and deprived us of the use of our limbs, till we fell into a profound sleep; although it must be confessed that we always awaked sick and dispirited, and that the use of this liquor filled us with diseases, which made our lives uncomfortable and short.

But beside all this, the bulk of our people supported themselves by furnishing the necessities or conveniences of life to the rich, and to each other. For instance, when I am at home and dressed as I ought to be, I carry on my body the workmanship of an hundred tradesmen; the building and furniture of my house employ as many more, and five times the number to adorn my wife.

I was going on to tell him of another sort of people, who get their livelihood by attending the sick, having upon some occasions informed his Honour that many of my crew had died of diseases. But here it was with the utmost difficulty that I brought him to apprehend what I meant. He could easily conceive, that a *Houyhnhnm* grew weak and heavy a few days before his death, or by some accident might hurt a limb. But that nature, who works all things to perfection, should suffer any pains to breed in our bodies, he thought impossible, and desired to know the reason of so unaccountable an evil. I told him we fed on a thousand things which operated contrary to each other; that we eat when we were not hungry, and drank without the provocation of thirst; that we sat whole nights drinking strong liquors without eating a bit, which disposed us to sloth, inflamed our bodies, and precipitated or prevented digestion. That prostitute female *Yahoos* acquired a certain malady which bred rottenness in the bones of those who fell into their embraces; that this and many other diseases were propagated from father to son, so that great numbers come into the world with complicated maladies upon them; that it would be endless to give him a catalogue of all diseases incident to human bodies; for they would not be fewer than five or six hundred, spread over every limb and joint; in short, every part, external and intestine, having diseases appropriated to each. To remedy which, there was a sort of people bred up among us, in the profession or pretence of curing the sick. And because I had some skill in the faculty, I would in gratitude to his Honour, let him know the whole mystery and method by which they proceed.

Their fundamental is that all diseases arise from repletion, from whence they conclude that a great evacuation of the body is necessary, either through the natural passage, or upwards at the mouth. Their next business is, from herbs, minerals, gums, oils, shells, salts, juices, seaweed, excrements, barks of trees, serpents, toads, frogs, spiders, dead men's flesh and bones, birds, beasts, and fishes, to form a composition for smell and taste the most abominable, nauseous, and detestable they can possibly contrive, which the stomach immediately rejects with loathing; and this they call a vomit; or else from the same store-house, with some other poisonous additions, they command us to take in at the orifice above or below (just as the physician then happens to be disposed) a medicine equally annoying and disgustful to the bowels; which relaxing the belly, drives down all before it, and this they call a purge, or a clyster. For nature (as the physicians allege) having intended the superior anterior orifice only for the intromission of solids and liquids, and the inferior posterior for ejection, these artists ingeniously considering that in all diseases nature is forced out of her seat, therefore to replace her in it, the body must be treated in a manner directly contrary, by interchanging the use of each orifice; forcing solids and liquids in at the anus, and making evacuations at the mouth.

But, besides real diseases, we are subject to many that are only imaginary, for which the physicians have invented imaginary cures; these have their several names, and so have the drugs that are proper for them, and with these our female *Yahoos* are always infested.

One great excellency in this tribe is their skill at prognostics, wherein they seldom fail; their predictions in real diseases, when they rise to any degree of malignity, generally portending death, which is always in their power, when recovery is not: and therefore, upon any unexpected signs of amendment, after they have pronounced their sentence, rather than be accused as false prophets, they know how to approve their sagacity to the world by a seasonable dose.

They are likewise of special use to husbands

and wives who are grown weary of their mates; to eldest sons, to great ministers of state, and often to princes.

I had formerly upon occasion discoursed with my master upon the nature of government in general, and particularly of our own excellent constitution, deservedly the wonder and envy of the whole world. But having here accidentally mentioned a minister of state, he commanded me some time after to inform him what species of *Yahoo* I particularly meant by that appellation.

I told him that a first or chief minister of state, who was the person I intended to describe, was a creature wholly exempt from joy and grief, love and hatred, pity and anger; at least made use of no other passions but a violent desire of wealth, power, and titles; that he applies his words to all uses, except to the indication of his mind; that he never tells a truth, but with an intent that you should take it for a lie; nor a lie, but with a design that you should take it for a truth; that those he speaks worst of behind their backs are in the surest way of preferment; and whenever he begins to praise you to others or to yourself, you are from that day forlorn. The worst mark you can receive is a promise, especially when it is confirmed with an oath; after which every wise man retires, and gives over all hopes.

There are three methods by which a man may rise to be chief minister: the first is by knowing how with prudence to dispose of a wife, a daughter, or a sister: the second, by betraying or undermining his predecessor: and the third is by a furious zeal in public assemblies against the corruptions of the court. But a wise prince would rather choose to employ those who practise the last of these methods because such zealots prove always the most obsequious and subservient to the will and passions of their master. That these ministers having all employments at their disposal, preserve themselves in power by bribing the majority of a senate or great council; and at last, by an expedient called an Act of Indemnity (whereof I described the nature to him) they secure themselves from after-reckonings, and retire from the public, laden with the spoils of the nation.

The palace of a chief minister is a seminary to breed up others in his own trade: the pages, lackeys, and porters, by imitating their master, become ministers of state in their several districts, and learn to excel in the three principal ingredients of insolence, lying, and bribery. Accordingly, they have a subaltern court paid to them by persons of the best rank, and sometimes by the force of dexterity and impudence, arrive through several gradations to be successors to their lord.

He is usually governed by a decayed wench, or favourite footman, who are the tunnels through which all graces are conveyed, and may properly be called, in the last resort, the governors of the kingdom.

One day in discourse my master, having heard me mention the nobility of my country, was pleased to make me a compliment which I could not pretend to deserve: that he was sure I must have been born of some noble family, because I far exceeded in shape, colour, and cleanliness all the *Yahoos* of his nation, although I seemed to fail in strength and agility, which must be imputed to my different way of living from those other brutes; and besides, I was not only endowed with the faculty of speech, but likewise with some rudiments of reason, to a degree that with all his acquaintance I passed for a prodigy.

He made me observe that among the *Houyhnhnms*, the white, the sorrel, and the iron-gray, were not so exactly shaped as the bay, the dapple-gray, and the black; nor born with equal talents of the mind, or a capacity to improve them; and therefore continued always in the condition of servants, without ever aspiring to match out of their own race, which in that country would be reckoned monstrous and unnatural.

I made his Honour my most humble acknowledgements for the good opinion he was pleased to conceive of me; but assured him at the same time that my birth was of the lower sort, having been born of plain, honest parents, who were just able to give me a tolerable education; that nobility among us was altogether a different thing from the idea he had of it; that our young noblemen are bred from their childhood in idleness and luxury; that as soon as years will permit, they consume their vigour, and contract odious diseases among lewd females; and when their fortunes are almost ruined, they marry some woman of mean birth, disagreeable person, and unsound constitution, merely for the sake of money, whom they hate and despise. That the productions of such marriages are generally scrofulous, rickety, or deformed children; by which means the family seldom continues above three generations, unless the wife takes care to provide a healthy father among her neighbours or domestics, in order to improve and continue the breed. That a weak, diseased body, a meagre countenance, and sallow complexion, are the true marks of noble blood; and a healthy, robust appearance is so disgraceful in a man of quality, that the world concludes his real father to have been a groom or a coachman. The imperfections of his mind run parallel with those of his body, being a composition of spleen, dullness, ignorance, caprice, sensuality, and pride.

Without the consent of this illustrious body no law can be enacted, repealed, or altered; and these have the decision of all our possessions without appeal.

CHAPTER VII

The author's great love of his native country. His master's observations upon the constitution and administration of England, *as described by the author, with parallel cases and comparisons. His master's observations upon human nature.*

The reader may be disposed to wonder how I could prevail on myself to give so free a representation of my own species, among a race of mortals who are already too apt to conceive the vilest opinion of human kind, from that entire congruity betwixt me and their *Yahoos*. But I must freely confess that the many virtues of those excellent quadrupeds placed in opposite view to human corruptions, had so far opened my eyes and enlarged my understanding that I began to view the actions and passions of man in a very different light, and to think the honour of my own kind not worth managing; which, besides, it was impossible for me to do before a person of so acute a judgment as my master, who daily convinced me of a thousand faults in myself, whereof I had not the least perception before, and which with us would never be numbered even among human infirmities. I had likewise learned from his example an utter detestation of all falsehood or disguise; and truth appeared so amiable to me that I determined upon sacrificing everything to it.

Let me deal so candidly with the reader as to confess that there was yet a much stronger motive for the freedom I took in my representation of things. I had not been a year in this country before I contracted such a love and veneration for the inhabitants that I entered on a firm resolution never to return to human kind, but to pass the rest of my life among these admirable *Houyhnhnms* in the contemplation and practice of every virtue, where I could have no example or incitement to vice. But it was decreed by fortune, my perpetual enemy, that so great a felicity should not fall to my share. However, it is now some comfort to reflect that in what I said of my countrymen, I extenuated their faults as much as I durst before so strict an examiner, and upon every article gave as favourable a turn as the matter would bear. For, indeed, who is there alive that will not be swayed by his bias and partiality to the place of his birth?

I have related the substance of several conversations I had with my master, during the greatest part of the time I had the honour to be in his service, but have indeed for brevity sake omitted much more than is here set down.

When I had answered all his questions, and his curiosity seemed to be fully satisfied, he sent for me one morning early, and commanding me to sit down at some distance, (an honour which he had never before conferred upon me) he said he had been very seriously considering my whole story, as far as it related both to myself and my country; that he looked upon us as a sort of animals to whose share, by what accident he could not conjecture, some small pittance of reason had fallen, whereof we made no other use than by its assistance to aggravate our natural corruptions, and to acquire new ones, which nature had not given us. That we disarmed ourselves of the few abilities she had bestowed, had been very successful in multiplying our original wants, and seemed to spend our whole lives in vain endeavours to supply them by our own inventions. That as to myself, it was manifest I had neither the strength or agility of a common *Yahoo*; that I walked infirmly on my hinder feet; had found out a contrivance to make my claws of no use or defence, and to remove the hair from my chin, which was intended as a shelter from the sun and the weather. Lastly, that I could neither run with speed, nor climb trees like my brethren (as he called them) the *Yahoos* in this country.

That our institutions of government and law were plainly owing to our gross defects in reason and, by consequence, in virtue; because reason alone is sufficient to govern a rational creature; which was therefore a character we had no pretence to challenge, even from the account I had given of my own people; although he manifestly perceived that in order to favour them, I had concealed many particulars, and often *said the thing which was not.*

He was the more confirmed in this opinion because he observed that as I agreed in every feature of my body with other *Yahoos*, except where it was to my real disadvantage in point of strength, speed and activity, the shortness of my claws, and some other particulars where nature had no part; so from the representation I had given him of our lives, our manners, and our actions, he found as near a resemblance in the disposition of our minds. He said the *Yahoos* were known to hate one another more than they did any different species of animals; and the reason usually assigned was the odiousness of their own shapes, which all could see in the rest, but not in themselves. He had therefore begun to think it not unwise in us to cover our bodies, and by that invention conceal many of our own deformities from each other, which would else be hardly supportable. But he now found he had been mistaken, and that the dissensions of those brutes in his country were owing to the same cause with ours, as I had described them. For if (said he) you throw among five *Yahoos* as much food as would be sufficient for fifty, they will, instead of eating peaceably, fall together by the ears, each single one impatient to have all to itself; and therefore a servant was usually employed to stand by while they were feeding abroad, and those kept at home were tied at a distance from each other: that if a cow died of age or accident, before a *Houyhnhnm* could secure it for his own *Yahoos*, those in the neighbourhood would come in herds to seize it, and then would ensue such a battle as I had described, with terrible wounds made by their claws on both sides, although they seldom were able to kill one another, for want of such convenient instruments of death as we had invented. At other times the like battles have been fought between the *Yahoos* of several neighbourhoods without any visible cause; those of one district watching all opportunities to surprise the next before they are prepared. But if they find their project hath miscarried, they return home, and, for want of enemies, engage in what I call a civil war among themselves.

That in some fields of his country, there are certain shining stones of several colours, whereof the *Yahoos* are violently fond, and when part of these stones is fixed in the earth, as it sometimes happeneth, they will dig with their claws for whole days to get them out, then carry them away, and hide them by heaps in their kennels; but still looking round with great caution, for fear their comrades should find out their treasure. My master said he could never discover the reason of this unnatural appetite, or how these stones could be of any use to a *Yahoo*; but now he believed it might proceed from the same principle of avarice which I had ascribed to mankind: that he had once, by way of experiment, privately removed a heap of these stones from the place where one of his *Yahoos* had buried it: whereupon, the sordid animal missing his treasure, by his loud lamenting brought the whole herd to the place, there miserably howled, then fell to biting and tearing the rest, began to pine away, would neither eat, nor sleep, nor work, till he ordered a servant privately to convey the stones into the same hole, and hide them as before; which when his *Yahoo* had found, he presently recovered his spirits and good humour, but took good care to remove them to a better hiding place, and hath ever since been a very serviceable brute.

My master farther assured me, which I also observed myself, that in the fields where the shining stones abound, the fiercest and most frequent battles are fought, occasioned by perpetual inroads of the neighbouring *Yahoos*.

He said it was common when two *Yahoos* discovered such a stone in a field, and were contending which of them should be the proprietor, a third would take the advantage, and carry it away from them both; which my master would needs contend to have some kind of resemblance with our suits at law; wherein I thought it for our credit not to undeceive him; since the decision he mentioned was much more equitable than many decrees among us; because the plaintiff and defendant there lost nothing beside the stone they contended for, whereas our courts of equity would never have dismissed the cause while either of them had anything left.

My master, continuing his discourse, said there was nothing that rendered the *Yahoos* more odious than their undistinguishing appetite to devour everything that came in their way, whether herbs, roots, berries, the corrupted flesh of animals, or all mingled together; and it was peculiar in their temper that they were fonder of what they could get by rapine or stealth at a greater distance, than much better food provided for them at home. If their prey held out, they would eat till they were ready to burst, after which nature had pointed out to them a certain root that gave them a general evacuation.

There was also another kind of root very juicy, but somewhat rare and difficult to be found, which the *Yahoos* sought for with much eagerness, and would suck it with great delight; and it produced in them the same effects that wine hath upon us. It would make them sometimes hug, and sometimes tear one another; they would howl, and grin, and chatter, and reel, and tumble, and then fall asleep in the mud.

I did indeed observe that the *Yahoos* were the only animals in this country subject to any diseases; which, however, were much fewer than horses have among us, and contracted not by any ill-treatment they meet with, but by the nastiness and greediness of that sordid brute. Neither has their language any more than a general appellation for those maladies, which is borrowed from the name of the beast, and called *Hnea-Yahoo*, or *Yahoos's evil*, and the cure prescribed is a mixture of their own dung and urine forcibly put down the *Yahoo's* throat. This I have since often known to have been taken with success, and do freely recommend it to my countrymen, for the public good, as an admirable specific against all diseases produced by repletion.

As to learning, government, arts, manufactures, and the like, my master confessed he could find little or no resemblance between the *Yahoos* of that country and those in ours. For he only meant to observe what parity there was in our natures. He had heard, indeed, some curious *Houyhnhnms* observe that in most herds there was a sort of ruling *Yahoo* (as among us there is generally some leading or principal stag in a park), who was always more deformed in body, and mischievous in disposition, than any of the rest. That this leader had usually a favourite as like himself as he could get, whose employment was to lick his master's feet and posteriors, and drive the female *Yahoos* to his kennel; for which he was now and then rewarded with a piece of ass's flesh. This favourite is hated by the whole herd, and therefore to protect himself, keeps always near the person of his leader. He usually continues in office till a worse can be found; but the very moment he is discarded, his successor, at the head of all the *Yahoos* in that district, young and old, male and female, come in a body, and discharge their excrements upon him from head to foot. But how far this might be applicable to our courts and favourites and ministers of state, my master said I could best determine.

I durst make no return to this malicious insinuation, which debased human understanding below the sagacity of a common hound, who has judgment enough to distinguish and follow the cry of the ablest dog in the pack, without being ever mistaken.

My master told me there were some qualities remarkable in the *Yahoos*, which he had not observed me to mention, or at least very slightly, in the accounts I had given him of human kind. He said those animals, like other brutes, had their females in common; but in this they differed, that the she-*Yahoo* would admit the male while she was pregnant; and that the he's would quarrel and fight with the females as fiercely as with each other. Both which practices were such degrees of infamous brutality that no other sensitive creature ever arrived at.

Another thing he wondered at in the *Yahoos* was their strange disposition to nastiness and dirt, whereas there appears to be a natural love of cleanliness in all other animals. As to the two former accusations, I was glad to let them pass without any reply, because I had not a word to offer upon them in defence of my species, which otherwise I certainly had done from my own inclinations. But I could have easily vindicated human kind from the imputation of singularity upon the last article, if there had been any swine in that country (as unluckily for me there were not), which although it may be a sweeter quadruped than a *Yahoo*, cannot I humbly conceive in justice pretend to more cleanliness; and so his Honour himself must have owned, if he had seen their filthy way of feeding, and their custom of wallowing and sleeping in the mud.

My master likewise mentioned another quality which his servants had discovered in several *Yahoos*, and to him was wholly unaccountable. He said a fancy would sometimes take a *Yahoo* to retire into a corner, to lie down and howl, and groan, and spurn away all that came near him, although he were young and fat, wanted neither food nor water; nor did the servants imagine what could possibly ail him. And the only remedy they found was to set him to hard work, after which he would infallibly come to himself. To this I was silent out of partiality to my own kind; yet here I could plainly discover the true seeds of spleen, which only seizeth on the lazy, the luxurious, and the rich; who, if they were forced to undergo the same regimen, I would undertake for the cure.

His Honour had further observed that a female *Yahoo* would often stand behind a bank or a bush, to gaze on the young males passing by, and then appear, and hide, using many antic gestures and grimaces, at which time it was observed that she had a most offensive smell; and when any of the males advanced, would slowly retire, looking often back, and with a counterfeit show of fear, run off into some convenient place where she knew the male would follow her.

At other times if a female stranger came among them, three or four of her own sex would get about her, and stare, and chatter, and grin, and smell her all over; and then turn off with gestures that seemed to express contempt and disdain.

Perhaps my master might refine a little in these speculations, which he had drawn from what he observed himself, or had been told him by others; however, I could not reflect without some amazement, and much sorrow, that the rudiments of lewdness, coquetry, censure, and scandal should have place by instinct in womankind.

I expected every moment that my master would accuse the *Yahoos* of those unnatural appetites in both sexes, so common among us. But nature, it seems, hath not been so expert a school-mistress; and these politer pleasures are entirely the productions of art and reason, on our side of the globe.

CHAPTER VIII

The author relates several particulars of the Yahoos. *The great virtues of the* Houyhnhnms. *The education and exercise of their youth. Their general assembly.*

As I ought to have understood human nature much better than I supposed it possible for my master to do, so it was easy to apply the character he gave of the *Yahoos* to myself and my countrymen; and I believed I could yet make farther discoveries from my own observation. I therefore often begged his favour to let me go among the herds of *Yahoos* in the neighbourhood, to which he always very graciously consented, being perfectly convinced that the hatred I bore those brutes would never suffer me to be corrupted by them; and his Honour ordered one of his servants, a strong sorrel nag, very honest and good-natured, to be my guard, without whose protection I durst not undertake such adventures. For I have already told the reader how much I was pestered by those odious animals upon my first arrival. And I afterwards failed very narrowly three or four times of falling into their clutches, when I happened to stray at any distance without my hanger. And I have reason to believe they had some imagination that I was of their own species, which I often assisted myself, by stripping up my sleeves, and showing my naked arms and breast in their sight, when my protector was with me. At which times they would approach as near as they durst, and imitate my actions after the manner of monkeys, but ever with great signs of hatred; as a tame jackdaw with cap and stockings, is always persecuted by the wild ones, when he happens to be got among them.

They are prodigiously nimble from their infancy; however, I once caught a young male of three years old, and endeavoured by all marks of tenderness to make it quiet; but the little imp fell a-squalling, and scratching, and biting with such violence that I was forced to let it go; and it was high time, for a whole troop of old ones came about us at the noise, but finding the cub was safe (for away it ran), and my sorrel nag being by, they durst not venture near us. I observed the young animal's flesh to smell very rank, and the stink was somewhat between a weasel and a fox, but much more disagreeable. I forgot another circumstance (and perhaps I might have the reader's pardon if it were wholly omitted), that while I held the odious vermin in my hands, it voided its filthy excrements of a yellow liquid substance, all over my clothes; but by good fortune there was a small brook hard by, where I washed myself as clean as I could; although I durst not come into my master's presence, until I were sufficiently aired.

By what I could discover, the *Yahoos* appear to be the most unteachable of all animals, their capacities never reaching higher than to draw or carry burdens. Yet I am of opinion, this defect ariseth chiefly from a perverse, restive disposition. For they are cunning, malicious, treacherous, and revengeful. They are strong and hardy, but of a cowardly spirit, and by consequence, insolent, abject, and cruel. It is observed that the red-haired of both sexes are more libidinous and mischievous than the rest, whom yet they much exceed in strength and activity.

The *Houyhnhnms* keep the *Yahoos* for present use in huts not far from the house; but the rest are sent abroad to certain fields, where they dig up roots, eat several kinds of herbs, and search about for carrion, or sometimes catch weasels and *luhimuhs* (a sort of wild rat), which they greedily devour. Nature hath taught them to dig deep holes with their nails on the side of a rising ground, wherein they lie by themselves; only the kennels of the females are larger, sufficient to hold two or three cubs.

They swim from their infancy like frogs, and are able to continue long under water, where they often take fish, which the females carry home to their young. And upon this occasion, I hope the reader will pardon my relating an odd adventure.

Being one day abroad with my protector, the sorrel nag, and the weather exceeding hot, I entreated him to let me bathe in a river that was near. He consented, and I immediately stripped myself stark naked, and went down softly into the stream. It happened that a young female *Yahoo*, standing behind a bank, saw the whole proceeding, and inflamed by desire, as the nag and I conjectured, came running with all speed, and leaped into the water, within five yards of the place where I bathed. I was never in my life so terribly frighted; the nag was grazing at some distance, not suspecting any harm. She embraced me after a most fulsome manner; I roared as loud as I could, and the nag came galloping towards me, whereupon she quitted her grasp with the utmost reluctancy, and leaped upon the opposite bank, where she stood gazing and howling all the time I was putting on my clothes.

This was matter of diversion to my master and his family, as well as of mortification to myself. For now I could no longer deny that I was a real *Yahoo* in every limb and feature, since the females had a natural propensity to me, as one of their own species. Neither was the hair of this brute of a red colour (which might have been some excuse for an appetite a little irregular), but black as a sloe, and her countenance did not make an appearance altogether so hideous as the rest of the kind, for I think she could not be above eleven years old.

Having lived three years in this country, the reader I suppose will expect that I should, like other travellers, give him some account of the manners and customs of its inhabitants, which it was indeed my principal study to learn.

As these noble *Houyhnhnms* are endowed by nature with a general disposition to all virtues, and have no conceptions or ideas of what is evil in a rational creature, so their grand maxim is to cultivate reason, and to be wholly governed by it. Neither is reason among them a point problematical as with us, where men can argue with plausibility on both sides of the question; but strikes you with immediate conviction; as it must needs do where it is not mingled, obscured, or discoloured by passion and interest. I remember it was with extreme difficulty that I could bring my master to understand the meaning of the word *opinion*, or how a point could be disputable; because reason taught us to affirm or deny only where we are certain; and beyond our knowledge we cannot do either. So that controversies, wranglings, disputes, and positiveness in false or dubious propositions are evils unknown among the *Houyhnhnms*. In the like manner when I used to explain to him our several systems of natural philosophy, he would laugh that a creature pretending to reason should value itself upon the knowledge of other people's conjectures, and in things where that knowledge, if it were certain, could be of no use. Wherein he agreed entirely with the sentiments of Socrates, as Plato delivers them; which I mention as the highest honour I can do that prince of philosophers. I have often since reflected what destruction such a doctrine would make in the libraries of Europe; and how many paths to fame would be then shut up in the learned world.

Friendship and benevolence are the two principal virtues among the *Houyhnhnms*; and these not confined to particular objects, but universal to the whole race. For a stranger from the remotest part is equally treated with the nearest neighbour, and wherever he goes, looks upon himself as at home. They preserve decency and civility in the highest degrees, but are altogether ignorant of ceremony. They have no fondness for their colts or foals, but the care they take in educating them proceeds entirely from the dictates of reason. And I observed my master to show the same affection to his neighbour's issue that he had for his own. They will have it that nature teaches them to love the whole species, and it is reason only that maketh a distinction of persons, where there is a superior degree of virtue.

When the matron *Houyhnhnms* have produced one of each sex, they no longer accompany with their consorts, except they lose one of their issue by some casualty, which very seldom happens; but in such a case they meet again, or when the like accident befalls a person whose wife is past bearing, some other couple bestow him one of their own colts, and then go together again till the mother is pregnant. This caution is necessary to prevent the country from being overburdened with numbers. But the race of inferior *Houyhnhnms* bred up to be servants is not so strictly limited upon this article; these are allowed to produce three of each sex, to be domestics in the noble families.

In their marriages they are exactly careful to choose such colours as will not make any disagreeable mixture in the breed. Strength is chiefly valued in the male, and comeliness in the female; not upon the account of love, but to preserve the race from degenerating; for where a female happens to excel in strength, a consort is chosen with regard to comeliness. Courtship, love, presents, jointures, settlements have no place in their thoughts; or terms whereby to express them in their language. The young couple meet and are joined merely because it is the determination of their parents and friends: it is what they see done every day, and they look upon it as one of the necessary actions of a reasonable being. But the violation of marriage, or any other unchastity, was never heard of: and the married pair pass their lives with the same friendship and mutual benevolence that they bear to all others of the same species who come in their way, without jealousy, fondness, quarrelling, or discontent.

In educating the youth of both sexes, their method is admirable, and highly deserves our imitation. These are not suffered to taste a grain of oats, except upon certain days, till eighteen years old; nor milk, but very rarely; and in summer they graze two hours in the morning, and as many in the evening, which their parents likewise observe; but the servants are not allowed above half that time, and a great part of their grass is brought home, which they eat at the most convenient hours, when they can be best spared from work.

Temperance, industry, exercise, and cleanliness are the lessons equally enjoined to the young ones of both sexes; and my master thought it monstrous in us to give the females a different kind of education from the males, except in some articles of domestic management; whereby, as he truly observed, one half of our natives were good for nothing but bringing children into the world: and to trust the care of our children to such useless animals, he said, was yet a greater instance of brutality.

But the *Houyhnhnms* train up their youth to strength, speed, and hardiness by exercising them in running races up and down steep hills and over hard, stony grounds; and when they are all in a sweat, they are ordered to leap over head and ears into a pond or a river. Four times a year the youth of a certain district meet to show their proficiency in running and leaping, and other feats of strength and agility, where the victor is rewarded with a song made in his or her praise. On this festival the servants drive a herd of *Yahoos* into the field, laden with hay and oats and milk, for a repast to the *Houyhnhnms*; after which these brutes are immediately driven back again, for fear of being noisome to the assembly.

Every fourth year, at the vernal equinox, there is a representative council of the whole nation, which meets in a plain about twenty miles from our house, and continues about five or six days. Here they enquire into the state and condition of the several districts; whether they abound or be deficient in hay or oats, or cows or *Yahoos*. And wherever there is any want (which is but seldom) it is immediately supplied by unanimous consent and contribution. Here likewise the regulation of children is settled: as for instance, if a *Houyhnhnm* hath two males, he changeth one of them with another that hath two females; and when a child hath been lost by any casualty, where the mother is past breeding, it is determined what family in the district shall breed another to supply the loss.

CHAPTER IX

A grand debate at the general assembly of the Houyhnhnms, *and how it was determined. The learning of the* Houyhnhnms. *Their buildings. Their manner of burials. The defectiveness of their language.*

One of these grand assemblies was held in my time, about three months before my departure, whither my master went as the representative of our district. In this council was resumed their old debate, and indeed, the only debate which ever happened in that country; whereof my master after his return gave me a very particular account.

The question to be debated was whether the *Yahoos* should be exterminated from the face of the earth. One of the members for the affirmative offered several arguments of great strength and weight, alleging, that as the *Yahoos* were the most filthy, noisome, and deformed animal which nature ever produced, so they were the most restive and * indocible, mischievous and malicious: they would privately suck the teats of the *Houyhnhnms*' cows, kill and devour their cats, trample down their oats and grass, if they were not continually watched, and commit a thousand other extravagancies. He took notice of a general tradition that *Yahoos* had not been always in that country; but, that many ages ago, two of these brutes appeared together upon a mountain; whether produced by the heat of the sun upon corrupted mud and slime, or from the ooze and froth of the sea, was never known. That these *Yahoos* engendered, and their brood in a short time grew so numerous as to overrun and infest the whole nation. That the *Houyhnhnms* to get rid of this evil, made a general hunting, and at last enclosed the whole herd; and destroying the elder, every *Houyhnhnm* kept two young ones in a kennel, and brought them to such a degree of tameness as an animal so savage by nature can be capable of acquiring; using them for draught and carriage. That there seemed to be much truth in this tradition, and that those creatures could not be *Ylnhniamshy* (or *aborigines* of the land), because of the violent hatred the *Houyhnhnms*, as well as all other animals, bore them; which although their evil disposition sufficiently deserved, could never have arrived at so high a degree, if they had been aborigines, or else they would have long since been rooted out. That the inhabitants taking a fancy to use the service of the *Yahoos*, had very imprudently neglected to cultivate the breed of asses, which were a comely animal, easily kept, more tame and orderly, without any offensive smell, strong enough for labour, although they yield to the other in agility of body; and if their braying be no agreeable sound, it is far preferable to the horrible howlings of the *Yahoos*.

Several others declared their sentiments to the same purpose, when my master proposed an expedient to the assembly, whereof he had indeed borrowed the hint from me. He approved of the tradition mentioned by the honourable member who spoke before, and affirmed that the two *Yahoos* said to be first seen among them, had been driven thither over the sea; that coming to land, and being forsaken by their companions, they retired to the mountains, and degenerating by degrees, became in process of time much more savage than those of their own species in the country from whence these two originals came. The reason of this assertion was that he had now in his possession a certain wonderful *Yahoo*, (meaning myself) which most of them had heard of, and many of them had seen. He then related to them how he first found me; that my body was all covered with an artificial composure of the skins and hairs of other animals; that I spoke in a language of my own, and had thoroughly learned theirs; that I had related to him the accidents which brought me thither: that when he saw me without my covering, I was an exact *Yahoo* in every part, only of a whiter colour, less hairy, and with shorter claws. He added how I had endeavoured to persuade him that in my own and other countries the *Yahoos* acted as the governing, rational animal, and held the *Houyhnhnms* in servitude; that he observed in me all the qualities of a *Yahoo*, only a little more civilized by some tincture of reason, which however was in a degree as far inferior to the *Houyhnhnm* race, as the *Yahoos* of their country were to me: that, among other things, I mentioned a custom we had of castrating *Houyhnhnms* when they were young, in order to render them tame; that the operation was easy and safe; that it was no shame to learn wisdom from brutes, as industry is taught by the ant, and building by the swallow. (For so I translate the word *lyhannh*, although it be a much larger fowl.) That this invention might be practiced upon the younger *Yahoos* here, which, besides rendering them tractable and fitter for use, would in an age put an end to the whole species without destroying life. That in the mean time the *Houyhnhnms* should be exhorted to cultivate the breed of asses, which, as they are in all respects more valuable brutes, so they have this advantage, to be fit for service at five years old, which the others are not till twelve.

This was all my master thought fit to tell me at that time, of what passed in the grand council. But he was pleased to conceal one particular which related personally to myself, whereof I soon felt the unhappy effect, as the reader will know in its proper place, and from whence I date all the succeeding misfortunes of my life.

The *Houyhnhnms* have no letters, and consequently their knowledge is all traditional. But there happening few events of any moment among a people so well united, naturally disposed to every virtue, wholly governed by reason, and cut off from all commerce with other nations, the historical part is easily preserved without burdening their memories. I have already observed that they are subject to no diseases, and therefore can have no need of physicians. However, they have excellent medicines composed of herbs, to cure accidental bruises and cuts in the pastern or frog of the foot by sharp stones, as well as other maims and hurts in the several parts of the body.

They calculate the year by the revolution of the sun and moon, but use no subdivisions into weeks. They are well enough acquainted with the motions of those two luminaries, and understand the nature of eclipses; and this is the utmost progress of their astronomy.

In poetry they must be allowed to excel all other mortals; wherein the justness of their similes, and the minuteness, as well as exactness of their descriptions, are indeed inimitable. Their verses abound very much in both of these, and usually contain either some exalted notions of friendship and benevolence, or the praises of those who were victors in races, and other bodily exercises. Their buildings, although very rude and simple, are not inconvenient, but well contrived to defend them from all injuries of cold and heat. They have a kind of tree, which at forty years old loosens in the root, and falls with the first storm; it grows very straight, and being pointed like stakes with a sharp stone (for the *Houyhnhnms* know not the use of iron), they stick them erect in the ground about ten inches asunder, and then weave in oat-straw, or sometimes wattles betwixt them. The roof is made after the same manner, and so are the doors.

The *Houyhnhnms* use the hollow part between the pastern and the hoof of their fore-feet, as we do our hands, and this with greater dexterity than I could at first imagine. I have seen a white mare of our family thread a needle (which I lent her on purpose) with that joint. They milk their cows, reap their oats, and do all the work which requires hands, in the same manner. They have a kind of hard flints, which by grinding against other stones, they form into instruments that serve instead of wedges, axes, and hammers. With tools made of these flints, they likewise cut their hay, and reap their oats, which there groweth naturally in several fields; the *Yahoos* draw home the sheaves in carriages, and the servants tread them in certain covered huts, to get out the grain, which is kept in stores. They make a rude kind of earthen and wooden vessels, and bake the former in the sun.

If they can avoid casualties, they die only of old age, and are buried in the obscurest places that can be found, their friends and relations expressing neither joy nor grief at their departure; nor does the dying person discover the least regret that he is leaving the world, any more than if he were upon returning home from a visit to one of his neighbours. I remember my master having once made an appointment with a friend and his family to come to his house upon some affair of importance, on the day fixed, the mistress and her two children came very late; she made two excuses, first for her husband, who, as she said, happened that very morning to *shnuwnh.* The word is strongly expressive in their language, but not easily rendered into English; it signifies *to retire to his first mother.* Her excuse for not coming sooner was that her husband dying late in the morning, she was a good while consulting her servants about a convenient place where his body should be laid; and I observed she behaved herself at our house as cheerfully as the rest. She died about three months after.

They live generally to seventy or seventy-five years, very seldom to fourscore; some weeks before their death they feel a gradual decay, but without pain. During this time they are much visited by their friends, because they cannot go abroad with their usual ease and satisfaction. However, about ten days before their death, which they seldom fail in computing, they return the visits that have been made them by those who are nearest in the neighbourhood, being carried in a convenient sledge drawn by *Yahoos,* which vehicle they use, not only upon this occasion, but when they grow old, upon long journeys, or when they are lamed by any accident. And therefore when the dying *Houyhnhnms* return those visits, they take a solemn leave of their friends, as if they were going to some remote part of the country, where they designed to pass the rest of their lives.

I know not whether it may be worth observing that the *Houyhnhnms* have no word in their language to express anything that is evil, except what they borrow from the deformities or ill qualities of the *Yahoos.* Thus they denote the folly of a servant, an omission of a child, a stone that cuts their feet, a continuance of foul or unseasonable weather, and the like, by adding to each the epithet of *Yahoo.* For instance, *Hhnm Yahoo, Whnaholm Yahoo, Ynlhmndwihlma Yahoo,* and an ill-contrived house *Ynholmhnmrohlnw Yahoo.*

I could with great pleasure enlarge further upon the manners and virtues of this excellent people; but intending in a short time to publish a volume by itself expressly upon that subject, I refer the reader thither. And in the mean time, proceed to relate my own sad catastrophe.

CHAPTER X

The author's economy, and happy life among the Houyhnhnms. *His great improvement in virtue, by conversing with them. Their conversations. The author has notice given him by his master that he must depart from the country. He falls into a swoon for grief, but submits. He contrives and finishes a canoe, by the help of a fellow-servant, and puts to sea at a venture.*

I had settled my little economy to my own heart's content. My master had ordered a room to be made for me after their manner, about six yards from the house; the sides and floors of which I plastered with clay, and covered with rush-mats of my own contriving; I had beaten hemp, which there grows wild, and made of it a sort of ticking: this I filled with the feathers of several birds I had taken with springes made of *Yahoos'* hairs, and were excellent food. I had worked two chairs with my knife, the sorrel nag helping me in the grosser and more laborious part. When my clothes were worn to rags, I made myself others with the skins of rabbits, and of a certain beautiful animal about the same size, called *nnuhnoh,* the skin of which is covered with a fine down. Of these I likewise made very tolerable stockings. I soled my shoes with wood which I cut from a tree, and fitted to the upper leather, and when this was worn out, I supplied it with the skins of *Yahoos* dried in the sun. I often got honey out of hollow trees, which I mingled with water, or eat with my bread. No man could more verify the truth of these two maxims, *That nature is very easily satisfied*; and *That necessity is the mother of invention.* I enjoyed perfect health of body, and tranquillity of mind; I did not feel the treachery or inconstancy of a friend, nor the injuries of a secret or open enemy. I had no occasion of bribing, flattering, or pimping, to procure the favour of any great man or of his minion. I wanted no fence against fraud or oppression; here was neither physician to destroy my body, nor lawyer to ruin my fortune; no informer to watch my words and actions, or forge accusations against me for hire: here were no gibers, censurers, backbiters, pickpockets, highwaymen, housebreakers, attorneys, bawds, buffoons, gamesters, politicians, wits, splenetics, tedious talkers, controvertists, ravishers, murderers, robbers, virtuosos; no leaders or followers of party and faction; no encouragers to vice, by seducement or examples; no dungeon, axes, gibbets, whipping-posts, or pillories; no cheating shopkeepers or mechanics; no pride, vanity, or affectation; no fops, bullies, drunkards, strolling whores, or poxes; no ranting, lewd, expensive wives; no stupid, proud pedants; no importunate, overbearing, quarrelsome, noisy, roaring, empty, conceited, swearing companions; no scoundrels raised from the dust for the sake of their vices, or nobility thrown into it on account of their virtues; no lords, fiddlers, judges, or dancing-masters.

I had the favour of being admitted to several *Houyhnhnms* who came to visit or dine with my master; where his Honour graciously suffered me to wait in the room, and listen to their discourse. Both he and his company would often descend to ask me questions, and receive my answers. I had also sometimes the honour of attending my master in his visits to others. I never presumed to speak, except in answer to a question; and then I did it with inward regret, because it was a loss of so much time for improving myself: but I was infinitely delighted with the station of an humble auditor in such conversations, where nothing passed but what was useful, expressed in the fewest and most significant words; where (as I have already said) the greatest decency was observed, without the least degree of ceremony; where no person spoke without being pleased himself, and pleasing his companions; where there was no interruption, tediousness, heat, or difference of sentiments. They have a notion that when people are met together, a short silence doth much improve conversation: this I found to be true; for during those little intermissions of talk, new ideas would arise in their thoughts, which very much enlivened the discourse. Their subjects are generally on friendship and benevolence, or order and economy; sometimes upon the visible operations of nature, or ancient traditions; upon the bounds and limits of virtue; upon the unerring rules of reason, or upon some determinations to be taken at the next great assembly; and often upon the various excellencies of poetry. I may add, without vanity, that my presence often gave them sufficient matter for discourse, because it afforded my master an occasion of letting his friends into the history of me and my country, upon which they were all pleased to descant in a manner not very advantageous to humankind; and for that reason I shall not repeat what they said: only I may be allowed to observe that his Honour, to my great admiration, appeared to understand the nature of *Yahoos* much better than myself. He went through all our vices and follies, and discovered many which I had never mentioned to him, by only supposing what qualities a *Yahoo* of their country, with a small proportion of reason, might be capable of exerting; and concluded, with too much probability, how vile as well as miserable such a creature must be.

I freely confess that all the little knowledge I have of any value was acquired by the lectures I received from my master, and from hearing the discourses of him and his friends; to which I should be prouder to listen than to dictate to the greatest and wisest assembly in Europe. I admired the strength, comeliness, and speed of the inhabitants; and such a constellation of virtues in such amiable persons produced in me the highest veneration. At first, indeed, I did not feel that natural awe which the *Yahoos* and all other animals bear towards them; but it grew upon me by degrees, much sooner than I imagined, and was mingled with a respectful love and gratitude that they would condescend to distinguish me from the rest of my species.

When I thought of my family, my friends, my countrymen, or human race in general, I considered them as they really were, *Yahoos* in shape and disposition, perhaps a little more civilized, and qualified with the gift of speech, but making no other use of reason than to improve and multiply those vices, whereof their brethren in this country had only the share that nature allotted them. When I happened to behold the reflection of my own form in a lake or fountain, I turned away my face in horror and detestation of myself, and could better endure the sight of a common *Yahoo* than of my own person. By conversing with the *Houyhnhnms*, and looking upon them with delight, I fell to imitate their gait and gesture, which is now grown into a habit, and my friends often tell me in a blunt way that I trot like a horse; which, however, I take for a great compliment. Neither shall I disown that in speaking I am apt to fall into the voice and manner of the *Houyhnhnms*, and hear myself ridiculed on that account without the least mortification.

In the midst of all this happiness, and when I looked upon myself to be fully settled for life, my master sent for me one morning a little earlier than his usual hour. I observed by his countenance that he was in some perplexity, and at a loss how to begin what he had to speak. After a short silence, he told me he did not know how I would take what he was going to say; that in the last general assembly, when the affair of the *Yahoos* was entered upon, the representatives had taken offence at his keeping a *Yahoo* (meaning myself) in his family more like a *Houhynhnm* than a brute animal. That he was known frequently to converse with me, as if he could receive some advantage or pleasure in my company; that such a practice was not agreeable to reason or nature, or a thing ever heard of before among them. The assembly did therefore exhort him, either to employ me like the rest of my species, or command me to swim back to the place from whence I came. That the first of these expedients was utterly rejected by all the *Houyhnhnms* who had ever seen me at his house or their own: for they alleged that because I had some rudiments of reason, added to the natural pravity of those animals, it was to be feared I might be able to seduce them into the woody and mountainous parts of the country, and bring them in troops by night to destroy the *Houyhnhnms'* cattle, as being naturally of the ravenous kind, and averse from labour.

My master added that he was daily pressed by the *Houyhnhnms* of the neighbourhood to have the assembly's exhortation executed, which he could not put off much longer. He doubted it would be impossible for me to swim to another country, and therefore wished I would contrive some sort of vehicle resembling those I had described to him, that might carry me on the sea; in which work I should have the assistance of his own servants, as well as those of his neighbours. He concluded that for his own part, he could have been content to keep me in his service as long as I lived; because he found I had cured myself of some bad habits and dispositions, by endeavouring, as far as my inferior nature was capable, to imitate the *Houyhnhnms.*

I should here observe to the reader that a decree of the general assembly in this country is expressed by the word *hnhloayn*, which signifies an exhortation, as near as I can render it; for they have no conception how a rational creature can be compelled, but only advised, or exhorted; because no person can disobey reason, without giving up his claim to be a rational creature.

I was struck with the utmost grief and despair at my master's discourse; and being unable to support the agonies I was under, I fell into a swoon at his feet; when I came to myself, he told me that he concluded I had been dead (for these people are subject to no such imbecilities of nature). I answered, in a faint voice, that death would have been too great an happiness; that although I could not blame the assembly's exhortation, or the urgency of his friends; yet, in my weak and corrupt judgment, I thought it might consist with reason to have been less rigorous. That I could not swim a league, and probably the nearest land to theirs might be distant above an hundred: that many materials, necessary for making a small vessel to carry me off, were wholly wanting in this country, which, however, I would attempt in obedience and gratitude to his Honour, although I concluded the thing to be impossible, and therefore looked on myself as already devoted to destruction. That the certain prospect of an unnatural death was the least of my evils: for, supposing I should escape with life by some strange adventure, how could I think with temper of passing my days among *Yahoos*, and relapsing into my old corruptions, for want of examples to lead and keep me within the paths of virtue. That I knew too well upon what solid reasons all the determinations of the wise *Houyhnhnms* were founded, not to be shaken by arguments of mine, a miserable *Yahoo*; and therefore, after presenting him with my humble thanks for the offer of his servants' assistance in making a vessel, and desiring a reasonable time for so difficult a work, I told him I would endeavour to preserve a wretched being; and, if ever I returned to England, was not without hopes of being useful to my own species, by celebrating the praises of the renowned *Houyhnhnms*, and proposing their virtues to the imitation of mankind.

My master in a few words made me a very gracious reply, allowed me the space of two months to finish my boat; and ordered the sorrel nag, my fellow-servant (for so at this distance I may presume to call him) to follow my instructions, because I told my master that his help would be sufficient, and I knew he had a tenderness for me.

In his company my first business was to go to that part of the coast where my rebellious crew had ordered me to be set on shore. I got upon a height, and looking on every side into the sea, fancied I saw a small island towards the northeast: I took out my pocket-glass, and could then clearly distinguish it about five leagues off, as I computed; but it appeared to the sorrel nag to be only a blue cloud: for, as he had no conception of any country beside his own, so he could not be as expert in distinguishing remote objects at sea, as we who so much converse in that element.

After I had discovered this island, I considered no farther; but resolved it should, if possible, be the first place of my banishment, leaving the consequence to fortune.

I returned home, and consulting with the sorrel nag, we went into a copse at some distance, where I with my knife, and he with a sharp flint fastened very artificially, after their manner, to a wooden handle, cut down several oak wattles about the thickness of a walking-staff, and some larger pieces. But I shall not trouble the reader with a particular description of my own mechanics; let it suffice to say that in six weeks' time, with the help of the sorrel nag, who performed the parts that required most labour, I finished a sort of Indian canoe, but much larger, covering it with the skins of *Yahoos* well stitched together with hempen threads of my own making. My sail was likewise composed of the skins of the same animal; but I made use of the youngest I could get, the older being too tough and thick; and I likewise provided myself with four paddles. I laid in a stock of boiled flesh, of rabbits and fowls, and took with me two vessels, one filled with milk, and the other with water.

I tried my canoe in a large pond near my master's house, and then corrected in it what was amiss; stopping all the chinks with *Yahoos'* tallow, till I found it staunch, and able to bear me, and my freight. And when it was as complete as I could possibly make it, I had it drawn on a carriage very gently by *Yahoos* to the seaside, under the conduct of the sorrel nag and another servant.

When all was ready, and the day came for my departure, I took leave of my master and lady, and the whole family, my eyes flowing with tears, and my heart quite sunk with grief. But his Honour, out of curiosity, and, perhaps (if I may speak it without vanity) partly out of kindness, was determined to see me in my canoe, and got several of his neighbouring friends to accompany him. I was forced to wait above an hour for the tide, and then observing the wind very fortunately bearing towards the island to which I intended to steer my course, I took a second leave of my master: but as I was going to prostrate myself to kiss his hoof, he did me the honour to raise it gently to my mouth. I am not ignorant how much I have been censured for mentioning this last particular. For my detractors are pleased to think it improbable that so illustrious a person should descend to give so great a mark of distinction to a creature so inferior as I. Neither have I forgot how apt some travellers are to boast of extraordinary favours they have received. But if these censurers were better acquainted with the noble and courteous disposition of the *Houyhnhnms*, they would soon change their opinion.

I paid my respects to the rest of the *Houyhnhnms* in his Honour's company; then getting into my canoe, I pushed off from shore.

CHAPTER XI

The author's dangerous voyage. He arrives at New Holland, *hoping to settle there. Is wounded with an arrow by one of the natives. Is seized and carried by force into a* Portuguese *ship. The great civilities of the captain. The author arrives at* England.

I began this desperate voyage on February 15, 1714-15, at 9 o'clock in the morning. The wind was very favourable; however, I made use at first only of my paddles; but considering I should soon be weary, and that the wind might chop about, I ventured to set up my little sail; and thus, with the help of the tide, I went at the rate of a league and a half an hour, as near as I could guess. My master and his friends continued on the shore till I was almost out of sight; and I often heard the sorrel nag (who always loved me) crying out "*Hnuy illa nyha majah Yahoo,*" take care of thyself, gentle *Yahoo.*

My design was, if possible, to discover some small island uninhabited, yet sufficient by my labour to furnish me with the necessaries of life, which I would have thought a greater happiness than to be first minister in the politest court of Europe; so horrible was the idea I conceived of returning to live in the society and under the government of *Yahoos.* For in such a solitude as I desired, I could at least enjoy my own thoughts, and reflect with delight on the virtues of those inimitable *Houyhnhnms*, without any opportunity of degenerating into the vices and corruptions of my own species.

The reader may remember what I related when my crew conspired against me, and confined me to my cabin. How I continued there several weeks, without knowing what course we took; and when I was put ashore in the longboat, how the sailors told me with oaths, whether true or false, that they knew not in what part of the world we were. However, I did then believe us to be about ten degrees southward of the Cape of Good Hope, or about 45 degrees southern latitude, as I gathered from some general words I overheard among them, being I supposed to the southeast in their intended voyage to

Madagascar. And although this were but little better than conjecture, yet I resolved to steer my course eastward, hoping to reach the southwest coast of New Holland, and perhaps some such island as I desired, lying westward of it. The wind was full west, and by six in the evening I computed I had gone eastward at least eighteen leagues, when I spied a very small island about half a league off, which I soon reached. It was nothing but a rock with one creek, naturally arched by the force of tempests. Here I put in my canoe, and climbing up a part of the rock, I could plainly discover land to the east, extending from south to north. I lay all night in my canoe; and repeating my voyage early in the morning, I arrived in seven hours to the southeast point of New Holland. This confirmed me in the opinion I have long entertained that the maps and charts place this country at least three degrees more to the east than it really is; which thought I communicated many years ago to my worthy friend, * Mr. Herman Moll, and gave him my reasons for it, although he hath rather chosen to follow other authors.

I saw no inhabitants in the place where I landed, and being unarmed, I was afraid of venturing far into the country. I found some shellfish on the shore, and eat them raw, not daring to kindle a fire, for fear of being discovered by the natives. I continued three days feeding on oysters and limpets, to save my own provisions; and I fortunately found a brook of excellent water, which gave me great relief.

On the fourth day, venturing out early a little too far, I saw twenty or thirty natives upon a height, not above five hundred yards from me. They were stark naked, men, women, and children round a fire, as I could discover by the smoke. One of them spied me, and gave notice to the rest; five of them advanced towards me, leaving the women and children at the fire. I made what haste I could to the shore, and getting into my canoe, shoved off: the savages observing me retreat, ran after me; and before I could get far enough into the sea, discharged an arrow, which wounded me deeply on the inside of my left knee (I shall carry the mark to my grave). I apprehended the arrow might be poisoned, and paddling out of the reach of their darts (being a calm day), I made a shift to suck the wound, and dress it as well as I could.

I was at a loss what to do, for I durst not return to the same landing-place, but stood to the north, and was forced to paddle; for the wind, though very gentle, was against me, blowing northwest. As I was looking about for a secure landing-place, I saw a sail to the north-northeast, which appearing every minute more visible, I was in some doubt whether I should wait for them or no; but at last my detestation of the *Yahoo* race prevailed, and turning my canoe, I sailed and paddled together to the south, and got into the same creek from whence I set out in the morning, choosing rather to trust myself among these barbarians, than live with European *Yahoos*. I drew up my canoe as close as I could to the shore, and hid myself behind a stone by the little brook, which, as I have already said, was excellent water.

The ship came within half a league of this creek, and sent her longboat with vessels to take in fresh water (for the place it seems was very well known), but I did not observe it till the boat was almost on shore, and it was too late to seek another hiding-place. The seamen at their landing observed my canoe, and rummaging it all over, easily conjectured that the owner could not be far off. Four of them well armed searched every cranny and lurking-hole, till at last they found me flat on my face behind the stone. They gazed awhile in *admiration at my strange, uncouth dress; my coat made of skins, my wooden-soled shoes, and my furred stockings; from whence, however, they concluded I was not a native of the place, who all go naked. One of the seamen in Portuguese bid me rise, and asked who I was. I understood that language very well, and getting upon my feet, said I was a poor *Yahoo*, banished from the *Houyhnhnms*, and desired they would please to let me depart. They admired to hear me answer them in their own tongue, and saw by my complexion I must be an European; but were at a loss to know what I meant by *Yahoos* and *Houyhnhnms*, and at the same time fell a-laughing at my strange tone in speaking, which resembled the neighing of a horse. I trembled all the while betwixt fear and hatred: I again desired leave to depart, and was gently moving to my canoe; but they laid hold of me, desiring to know what country I was of; whence I came; with many other questions. I told them I was born in England, from whence I came about five years ago, and then their country and ours were at peace. I therefore hoped they would not treat me as an enemy, since I meant them no harm, but was a poor *Yahoo*, seeking some desolate place where to pass the remainder of his unfortunate life.

When they began to talk, I thought I never heard or saw any thing so unnatural; for it appeared to me as monstrous as if a dog or a cow should speak in England, or a *Yahoo* in *Houyhnhnm-land*. The honest Portuguese were equally amazed at my strange dress, and the odd manner of delivering my words, which however they understood very well. They spoke to me with great humanity, and said they were sure their captain would carry me *gratis* to Lisbon, from whence I might return to my own country; that two of the seamen would go back to the ship, inform the captain of what they had seen, and receive his orders; in the mean time, unless I would give my solemn oath not to fly, they would secure me by force. I thought it best to comply with their proposal. They were very curious to know my story, but I gave them very little satisfaction; and they all conjectured that my misfortunes had impaired my reason. In two hours the boat, which went loaden with vessels of water, returned with the captain's command to fetch me on board. I fell on my knees to preserve my liberty; but all was in vain, and the men having tied me with cords, heaved me into the boat, from whence I was taken into the ship, and from thence into the captain's cabin.

His name was Pedro de Mendez; he was a very courteous and generous person; he entreated me to give some account of myself, and desired to know what I would eat or drink; said I should be used as well as himself, and spoke so many obliging things that I wondered to find such civilities from a *Yahoo*. However, I remained silent and sullen; I was ready to faint at the very smell of him and his men. At last I desired something to eat out of my own canoe; but he ordered me a chicken and some excellent wine, and then directed that I should be put to bed in a very clean cabin. I would not undress myself, but lay on the bed-clothes, and in half an hour stole out, when I thought the crew was at dinner, and getting to the side of the ship was going to leap into the sea, and swim for my life, rather than continue among *Yahoos*. But one of the seamen prevented me, and having informed the captain, I was chained to my cabin.

After dinner Don Pedro came to me, and desired to know my reason for so desperate an attempt; assured me he only meant to do me all the service he was able; and spoke so very movingly that at last I descended to treat him like an animal which had some little portion of reason. I gave him a very short relation of my voyage; of the conspiracy against me by my own men; of the country where they set me on shore, and of *my three years' residence there. All which he looked upon as if it were a dream or a vision; whereat I took great offence; for I had quite forgot the faculty of lying, so peculiar to *Yahoos* in all countries where they preside, and, consequently the disposition of suspecting truth in others of their own species. I asked him whether it were the custom in his country to say the thing that was not. I assured him I had almost forgot what he meant by falsehood, and if I had lived a thousand years in *Houyhnhnm-land*, I should never have heard a lie from the meanest servant; that I was altogether indifferent whether he believed me or no; but, however, in return for his favours, I would give so much allowance to the corruption of his nature as to answer any objection he would please to make, and then he might easily discover the truth.

The captain, a wise man, after many endeavours to catch me tripping in some part of my story, at last began to have a better opinion of my veracity. But he added that since I professed so inviolable an attachment to truth, I must give him my word of honour to bear him company in this voyage, without attempting anything against my life, or else he would continue me a prisoner till we arrived at Lisbon. I gave him the promise he required; but at the same time protested that I would suffer the greatest hardships rather than return to live among *Yahoos*.

Our voyage passed without any considerable accident. In gratitude to the captain I sometimes sat with him at his earnest request, and strove to conceal my antipathy to humankind, although it often broke out, which he suffered to pass without observation. But the greatest part of the day I confined myself to my cabin, to avoid seeing any of the crew. The captain had often entreated me to strip myself of my savage dress, and offered to lend me the best suit of clothes he had. This I would not be prevailed on to accept, abhorring to cover myself with anything that had been on the back of a *Yahoo.* I only desired he would lend me two clean shirts, which having been washed since he wore them, I believed would not so much defile me. These I changed every second day, and washed them myself.

We arrived at Lisbon, Nov. 5, 1715. At our landing the captain forced me to cover myself with his cloak to prevent the rabble from crowding about me. I was conveyed to his own house, and at my earnest request, he led me up to the highest room backwards. I conjured him to conceal from all persons what I had told him of the *Houyhnhnms*, because the least hint of such a story would not only draw numbers of people to see me, but probably put me in danger of being imprisoned, or burnt by the Inquisition. The captain persuaded me to accept a suit of clothes newly made; but I would not suffer the tailor to take my measure; however, Don Pedro being almost of my size, they fitted me well enough. He accoutred me with other necessaries all new, which I aired for twenty-four hours before I would use them.

The captain had no wife, nor above three servants, none of which were suffered to attend at meals, and his whole deportment was so obliging, added to very good *human* understanding, that I really began to tolerate his company. He gained so far upon me that I ventured to look out of the back window. By degrees I was brought into another room, from whence I peeped into the street, but drew my head back in a fright. In a week's time he seduced me down to the door. I found my terror gradually lessened, but my hatred and contempt seemed to increase. I was at last bold enough to walk the street in his company, but kept my nose well stopped with rue, or sometimes with tobacco.

In ten days Don Pedro, to whom I had given some account of my domestic affairs, put it upon me as a matter of honour and conscience that I ought to return to my native country, and live at home with my wife and children. He told me there was an English ship in the port just ready to sail, and he would furnish me with all things necessary. It would be tedious to repeat his arguments and my contradictions. He said it was altogether impossible to find such a solitary island as I desired to live in; but I might command in my own house, and pass my time in a manner as recluse as I pleased.

I complied at last, finding I could not do better. I left Lisbon the 24th day of November, in an English merchantman, but who was the master I never inquired. Don Pedro accompanied me to the ship, and lent me twenty pounds. He took kind leave of me, and embraced me at parting, which I bore as well as I could. During this last voyage I had no commerce with the master or any of his men; but pretending I was sick, kept close in my cabin. On the fifth of December, 1715, we cast anchor in the Downs about nine in the morning, and at three in the afternoon I got safe to my house at Rotherhithe.

My wife and family received me with great surprise and joy, because they concluded me certainly dead; but I must freely confess the sight of them filled me only with hatred, disgust, and contempt, and the more by reflecting on the near alliance I had to them. For, although since my unfortunate exile from the *Houyhnhnm* country, I had compelled myself to tolerate the sight of *Yahoos*, and to converse with Don Pedro de Mendez; yet my memory and imagination were perpetually filled with the virtues and ideas of those exalted *Houyhnhnms.* And when I began to consider that by copulating with one of the *Yahoo* species I had become a parent of more, it struck me with the utmost shame, confusion, and horror.

As soon as I entered the house, my wife took me in her arms, and kissed me; at which, having not been used to the touch of that odious animal for so many years, I fell in a swoon for almost an hour. At the time I am writing, it is five years since my last return to England: during the first year I could not endure my wife or children in my presence, the very smell of them was intolerable; much less could I suffer them to eat in the same room. To this hour they dare not presume to touch my bread, or drink out of the same cup; neither was I ever able to let one of them take me by the hand. The first money I laid out was to buy two young *stone-horses, which I keep in a good stable, and next to them the groom is my greatest favourite;

for I feel my spirits revived by the smell he contracts in the stable. My horses understand me tolerably well; I converse with them at least four hours every day. They are strangers to bridle or saddle; they live in great amity with me, and friendship to each *other....

[1726]

ON THE DEATH OF MRS. JOHNSON

The circumstances in which Swift wrote this character of Stella are sufficiently explained in the opening paragraphs. In its combination of suppressed emotion and of simple, matter of fact statement it is one of the most revealing documents that came from his hands. Churton Collins wrote of it, "Sorrow and despair have many voices, but seldom have they found expression so affecting as in those calm and simple words."

This day being Sunday, January 28, 1727–28, about eight o'clock at night, a servant brought me a note, with an account of the death of the truest, most virtuous, and valuable friend, that I, or perhaps any other person ever was blessed with. She expired about six in the evening of this day; and *as soon as I am left alone, which is about eleven at night, I resolve, for my own satisfaction, to say something of her life and character.

She was born at Richmond, in Surrey, on the thirteenth day of March, in the year 1681. Her father was a younger brother of a good family in Nottinghamshire, her mother of a lower degree; and indeed she had little to boast of her birth. I knew her from six years old, and had some share in her education, by directing what books she should read, and perpetually instructing her in the principles of honour and virtue; from which she never swerved in any one action or moment of her life. She was sickly from her childhood until about the age of fifteen; but then grew into perfect health, and was looked upon as one of the most beautiful, graceful, and agreeable young women in London, only a little too fat. Her hair was blacker than a raven, and every feature of her face in perfection. She lived generally in the country with a family, where she contracted an intimate friendship with *another lady of more advanced years. I was then (to my mortification) settled in Ireland; and about a year after, going to visit my friends in England, I found she was a little uneasy upon the death of *a person on whom she had some dependence. Her fortune, at that time, was in all not above fifteen hundred pounds, the interest of which was but a scanty maintenance, in so dear a country, for one of her spirit. Upon this consideration, and indeed very much for my own satisfaction, who had few friends or acquaintance in Ireland, I prevailed with her and her dear friend and companion, the other lady, to draw what money they had into Ireland, a great part of their fortune being in annuities upon funds. Money was then ten per cent in Ireland, besides the advantage of turning it, and all necessaries of life at half the price. They complied with my advice, and soon after came over; but, I happening to continue some time longer in England, they were much discouraged to live in Dublin, where they were wholly strangers. She was at that time about nineteen years old, and her person was soon distinguished. But the adventure looked so like a frolic, the censure held for some time, as if there were a secret history in such a removal; which, however, soon blew off by her excellent conduct. She came over with her friend on the *—— in the year 170–; and they both lived together until this day, when death removed her from us. For some years past she had been visited with continual ill health; and several times, within these two years, her life was despaired of. But, for this twelvemonth past, she never had a day's health; and, properly speaking, she hath been dying six months, but kept alive, almost against nature, by the generous kindness of two physicians, and the care of her friends. Thus far I writ the same night between eleven and twelve.

Never was any of her sex born with better gifts of the mind, or more improved them by reading and conversation. Yet her memory was not of the best, and was impaired in the latter years of her life. But I can not call to mind that I ever once heard her make a wrong judgment of persons, books, or affairs. Her advice was always the best, and with the greatest freedom, mixed with the greatest decency. She had a gracefulness, somewhat more than human, in every motion, word, and action. Never was so happy a conjunction of civility, freedom, easiness, and sincerity. There seemed to be a combination among all that knew her, to treat her with a dignity much beyond her rank; yet people of all sorts were never more easy than in her company. Mr. Addison, when he was in Ireland, being introduced to her, immediately found her out; and, if he had not soon after left the kingdom, assured me he would have used all endeavours to cultivate her friendship. A rude or conceited coxcomb passed his time very ill upon the least breach of respect; for in such a case she had no mercy, but was sure to expose him to the contempt of the standers-by, yet in such a manner as he was ashamed to complain, and durst not resent. All of us who had the happiness of her friendship, agreed unanimously that, in an afternoon or evening's conversation, she never failed, before we parted, of delivering the best thing that was said in the company. Some of us have written down *several of her sayings, or what the French call *bons mots*, wherein she excelled almost beyond belief. She never mistook the understanding of others; nor ever said a severe word, but where a much severer was deserved.

Her servants loved, and almost adored her at the same time. She would, upon occasions, treat them with freedom; yet her demeanour was so awful that they durst not fail in the least point of respect. She chid them seldom, but it was with severity, which had an effect upon them for a long time after.

January 29. My head aches, and I can write no more.

January 30. Tuesday. This is the night of the funeral, which my sickness will not suffer me to attend. It is now nine at night, and I am removed into another apartment, that I may not see the light in the church, which is just over against the window of my bedchamber.

With all the softness of temper that became a lady, she had the personal courage of a hero. She and her friend having removed their lodgings to a new house which stood solitary, a parcel of rogues, armed, attempted the house, where there was only one boy. She was then about four-and-twenty; and having been warned to apprehend some such attempt, she learned the management of a pistol; and the other women and servants being half dead with fear, she stole softly to her dining-room window, put on a black hood to prevent being seen, primed the pistol fresh, gently lifted up the sash, and having taken her aim with the utmost presence of mind, discharged the pistol, loaden with the bullets, into the body of one villain who stood the fairest mark. The fellow, mortally wounded, was carried off by the rest and died the following morning; but his companions could not be found. The Duke of Ormond hath often drank her health to me upon that account and had always an high esteem of her. She was indeed under some apprehensions of going in a boat, after some danger she had narrowly escaped by water, but she was reasoned thoroughly out of it. She was never known to cry out or discover any fear in a coach or on horseback; or any uneasiness by those sudden accidents with which most of her sex, either by weakness or affectation, appear so much disordered.

She never had the least absence of mind in conversation, nor [was] given to interruption, or appeared eager to put in her word, by waiting impatiently until another had done. She spoke in a most agreeable voice, in the plainest words, never hesitating, except out of modesty before new faces, where she was somewhat reserved; nor, among her nearest friends, ever spoke much at a time. She was but little versed in the common topics of female chat; scandal, censure, and detraction never came out of her mouth; yet, among a few friends, in private conversation, she made little ceremony in discovering her contempt of a coxcomb, and describing all his follies to the life; but the follies of her own sex she was rather inclined to extenuate or to pity.

When she was once convinced, by open facts, of any breach of truth or honour in a person of high station, especially in the Church, she could not conceal her indignation, nor hear them named without showing her displeasure in her countenance; particularly one or two of the latter sort, whom she had known and esteemed, but detested above all mankind, when it was manifest that they had sacrificed those two precious virtues to their ambition, and would much sooner have forgiven them the common immoralities of the laity.

Her frequent fits of sickness, in most parts of her life, had prevented her from making that progress in reading which she would otherwise have done. She was well versed in the Greek and Roman story, and was not unskilled in that of France and England.

She spoke French perfectly, but forgot much of it by neglect and sickness. She had read carefully all the best books of travels, which serve to open and enlarge the mind. She understood the Platonic and Epicurean philosophy, and judged very well of the defects of the latter. She made very judicious abstracts of the best books she had read. She understood the nature of government and could point out all the errors of Hobbes, both in that and religion. She had a good insight into physic and knew somewhat of anatomy; in both which she was instructed in her younger days by an eminent physician who had her long under his care, and bore the highest esteem for her person and understanding. She had a true taste of wit and good sense, both in poetry and prose, and was a perfect good critic of style; neither was it easy to find a more proper or impartial judge whose advice an author might better rely on if he intended to send a thing into the world, provided it was on a subject that came within the compass of her knowledge. Yet, perhaps, she was sometimes too severe, which is a safe and pardonable error. She preserved her wit, judgment, and vivacity to the last but often used to complain of her memory.

Her fortune, with some accession, could not, as I have heard say, amount to much more than two thousand pounds, whereof a great part fell with her life, having been placed upon annuities in England and one in Ireland.

In a person so extraordinary perhaps it may be pardonable to mention some particulars, although of little moment, further than to set forth her character. Some presents of gold pieces being often made to her while she was a girl by her mother and other friends, on promise to keep them, she grew into such a spirit of thrift that in about three years they amounted to above two hundred pounds. She used to show them with boasting; but her mother, apprehending she would be cheated of them, prevailed, in some months and by great importunities, to have them put out to interest; when the girl lost the pleasure of seeing and counting her gold, which she never failed of doing several times in a day, and despaired of heaping up such another treasure, her humour took the quite contrary turn; she grew careless and squandering of every new acquisition, and so continued until about two-and-twenty; when, by advice of some friends and the fright of paying large bills of tradesmen who enticed her into their debt, she began to reflect upon her own folly, and was never at rest until she had discharged all her shop bills and refunded herself a considerable sum she had run out. After which, by the addition of a few years and a superior understanding, she became, and continued all her life, a most prudent economist; yet still with a strong bent to the liberal side, wherein she gratified herself by avoiding all expense in clothes (which she ever despised) beyond what was merely decent. And, although her frequent returns of sickness were very chargeable, except fees to physicians, of which she met with several so generous that she could force nothing on them (and indeed she must otherwise have been undone), yet she never was without a considerable sum of ready money. Insomuch that, upon her death, when her nearest friends thought her very bare, her executors found in her strong box about a hundred and fifty pounds in gold. She lamented the narrowness of her fortune in nothing so much as that it did not enable her to entertain her friends so often, and in so hospitable a manner, as she desired. Yet they were always welcome; and, while she was in health to direct, were treated with neatness and elegance, so that the revenues of her and her companion passed for much more considerable than they really were. They lived always in lodgings; their domestics consisted of two maids and one man. She kept an account of all the family expenses, from her arrival in Ireland to some months before her death; and she would often repine, when looking back upon the annals of her household bills, that everything necessary for life was double the price, while interest for money was sunk almost to one half, so that the addition made to her fortune was indeed grown absolutely necessary.

(I since writ as I found time.)

But her charity to the poor was a duty not to be diminished, and therefore became a tax upon those tradesmen who furnish the fopperies of other ladies. She bought clothes as seldom as possible and those as plain and cheap as consisted with the situation she was in, and wore no lace for many years. Either her judgment or fortune was extraordinary in the choice of those on whom she bestowed her charity, for it went further in doing good than double the sum from any other hand. And I have heard her say she always met with gratitude from the poor, which must be owing to her skill in distinguishing proper objects, as well as her gracious manner in relieving them.

But she had another quality that much delighted her, although it may be thought a kind of check upon her bounty; however, it was a pleasure she could not resist: I mean that of making agreeable presents; wherein I never knew her equal, although it be an affair of as delicate a nature as most in the course of life. She used to define a present: that it was a gift to a friend of something he wanted, or was fond of, and which could not be easily gotten for money. I am confident, during my acquaintance with her, she hath, in these and some other kinds of liberality, disposed of to the value of several hundred pounds. As to presents made to herself, she received them with great unwillingness, but especially from those to whom she had ever given any, being on all occasions the most disinterested mortal I ever knew or heard of.

From her own disposition, at least as much as from the frequent want of health, she seldom made any visits; but her own lodgings, from before twenty years old, were frequented by many persons of the graver sort, who all respected her highly upon her good sense, good manners, and conversation. Among these were the late Primate Lindsay, Bishop Lloyd, Bishop Ashe, Bishop Brown, Bishop Stearne, Bishop Pulleyn, with some others of later date; and indeed the greatest number of her acquaintance was among the clergy. Honour, truth, liberality, good nature, and modesty were the virtues she chiefly possessed and most valued in her acquaintance: and where she found them would be ready to allow for some defects; nor valued them less, although they did not shine in learning or in wit: but would never give the least allowance for any failures in the former, even to those who made the greatest figure in either of the two latter. She had no use of any person's liberality, yet her detestation of covetous people made her uneasy if such a one was in her company, upon which occasion she would say many things very entertaining and humorous.

She never interrupted any person who spoke; she laughed at no mistakes they made, but helped them out with modesty; and if a good thing were spoken, but neglected, she would not let it fall, but set it in the best light to those who were present. She listened to all that was said and had never the least distraction or absence of thought.

It was not safe, nor prudent, in her presence * to offend in the least word against modesty; for she then gave full employment to her wit, her contempt, and resentment, under which even stupidity and brutality were forced to sink into confusion; and the guilty person, by her future avoiding him like a bear or a satyr, was never in a way to transgress a second time.

It happened one single coxcomb of the pert kind was in her company among several other ladies, and in his flippant way began to deliver some double meanings; the rest flapped their fans and used the other common expedients practised in such cases, of appearing not to mind or comprehend what was said. Her behaviour was very different, and perhaps may be censured. She said thus to the man: "Sir. all these ladies and I understand your meaning very well, having, in spite of our care, too often met with those of your sex who wanted manners and good sense. But, believe me, neither virtuous nor even vicious women love such kind of conversation. However, I will leave you and report your behaviour; and whatever visit I make, I shall first enquire at the door whether you are in the house that I may be sure to avoid you." I know not whether a majority of ladies would approve of such a proceeding; but I believe the practice of it would soon put an end to that corrupt conversation, the worst effect of dullness, ignorance, impudence, and vulgarity, and the highest affront to the modesty and understanding of the female sex.

By returning very few visits she had not much company of her own sex, except those whom she most loved for their easiness, or esteemed for their good sense: and those, not insisting on ceremony, came often to her. But she rather chose men for her companions, the usual topics of ladies' discourse being such as she had little knowledge of, and less relish. Yet no man was upon the rack to entertain her, for she easily descended to anything that was innocent and diverting. News, politics, censure, family management, or town-talk she always diverted to something else; but these indeed seldom happened, for she chose her company better: and therefore many who mistook her and themselves having solicited her acquaintance, and finding themselves disappointed, after a few visits dropped off; and she was never known to enquire into the reason or ask what was become of them.

She was never positive in arguing; and she usually treated those who were so in a manner which well enough gratified that unhappy disposition, yet in such a sort as made it very contemptible, and at the same time did some hurt to the owners. Whether this proceeded from her easiness in general, or from her indifference to persons, or from her despair of mending them, or from the same practice which she much liked in Mr. Addison, I cannot determine; but when she saw any of the company very warm in a wrong opinion, she was more inclined to confirm them in it than oppose them. The excuse she commonly gave, when her friends asked the reason, was that it prevented noise and saved time. Yet I have known her very angry with some whom she much esteemed for sometimes falling into that infirmity.

She loved Ireland much better than the generality of those who owe both their birth and riches to it; and having brought over all the fortune she had in money, left the reversion of the best part of it, one thousand pounds, to Dr. Stephens's Hospital. She detested the tyranny and injustice of England in their treatment of this kingdom. She had indeed reason to love a country where she had the esteem and friendship of all who knew her and the universal good report of all who ever heard of her, without one exception, if I am told the truth by those who keep general conversation. Which character is the more extraordinary in falling to a person of so much knowledge, wit, and vivacity, qualities that are used to create envy and consequently censure; and must be rather imputed to her great modesty, gentle behaviour, and inoffensiveness than to her superior virtues.

Although her knowledge from books and company was much more extensive than usually falls to the share of her sex, yet she was so far from making a parade of it that her female visitants, on their first acquaintance, who expected to discover it by what they call hard words and deep discourse, would be sometimes disappointed and say they found she was like other women. But wise men, through all her modesty, whatever they discoursed on, could easily observe that she understood them very well by the judgment shown in her observations as well as in her questions.

[1765]

ON THE DEATH OF DR. SWIFT

Though Swift is now remembered chiefly as a prose writer, his published poems are by no means inconsiderable in number or in bulk: they include verses serious and playful, personal and occasional, odes, elegies, narratives, satires, epigrams, riddles, classical imitations, and epistles. Most of his earlier poems were written in the more dignified forms, including Pindarics and heroic couplets, but the later and more characteristic work commonly employed the short couplet, the usual eighteenth-century form for light verse. Interesting as this poetry is, and important as it is for a rounded knowledge of Swift's literary production, it remains so much less important than the prose that in a limited selection such as the present it can receive but brief representation. The lines *On the Death of Dr. Swift* are here included because they are the best known verses of their author and also because they throw much light on his character and constitute his own apology for his life and literary work. They were written in 1731, when Swift was sixty-three years of age, about fourteen years before his death. He showed them in manuscript to a number of his friends but did not intend to publish them until after the event which they celebrate. In 1733, however, a pirated version was printed, after which he gave permission for the publication of a correct copy.

Occasioned by reading the following maxim in Rochefoucauld, *Dans l'adversité de nos meilleurs amis, nous trauvons toujours quelque chose qui ne nous déplaît pas.*

As Rochefoucauld his maxims drew
From nature, I believe 'em true:
They argue no corrupted mind
In him; the fault is in mankind.
This maxim more than all the rest
Is thought too base for human breast:
"In all distresses of our friends,
We first consult our private ends;
While nature, kindly bent to ease us,
Points out some circumstance to please us."
If this perhaps your patience move,
Let reason and experience prove.
We all behold with envious eyes
Our equal raised above our size.

Who would not at a crowded show
Stand high himself, keep others low?
I love my friend as well as you,
But why should he obstruct my view?
Then let me have the higher post;
Suppose it but an inch at most.
If in a battle you should find
One whom you love of all mankind,
Had some heroic action done,
A champion kill'd, or trophy won;
Rather than thus be overtopp'd,
Would you not wish his laurels cropp'd?
Dear honest Ned is in the gout,
Lies rack'd with pain, and you without:
How patiently you hear him groan!
How glad the case is not your own!
  What poet would not grieve to see
His brethren write as well as he?
But rather than they should excel
He'd wish his rivals all in hell.
  Her end when Emulation misses,
She turns to Envy, stings and hisses;
The strongest friendship yields to pride,
Unless the odds be on our side.
Vain human kind! fantastic race!
Thy various follies who can trace?
Self-love, ambition, envy, pride,
Their empire in our hearts divide.
Give others riches, power, and station,
'Tis all on me an usurpation.
I have no title to aspire;
Yet, when you sink, I seem the higher.
In Pope I cannot read a line,
But with a sigh I wish it mine;
When he can in one couplet fix
More sense than I can do in six,
It gives me such a jealous fit,
I cry, "Pox take him and his wit!"
I grieve to be outdone by Gay
In my own hum'rous biting way.
Arbuthnot is no more my friend,
Who dares to irony pretend,
Which I was born to introduce,
Refin'd it first, and show'd its use.
*St. John, as well as *Pultney, knows
That I had some repute for prose;
And, till they drove me out of date
Could maul a minister of state.
If they have mortified my pride,
And made me throw my pen aside;
If with such talents Heav'n has blest 'em,
Have I not reason to detest 'em?
  To all my foes, dear Fortune, send
Thy gifts, but never to my friend;
I tamely can endure the first;
But this with envy makes me burst.
  Thus much may serve by way of proem;
Proceed we therefore to our poem.
  The time is not remote, when I
Must by the course of nature die,
When, I foresee, my special friends
Will try to find their private ends;
Tho' it is hardly understood
Which way my death can do them good,
Yet thus, methinks, I hear 'em speak:
"See, how the Dean begins to break!
Poor gentleman, he droops apace!
You plainly find it in his face.
*That old vertigo in his head
Will never leave him till he's dead.
Besides, his memory decays:
He recollects not what he says;
He can not call his friends to mind;
Forgets the place where last he din'd;
Plies you with stories o'er and o'er;
He told them fifty times before.
How does he fancy we can sit
To hear his out-of-fashion'd wit?
But he takes up with younger folks,
Who for his wine will bear his jokes.
Faith! he must make his stories shorter,
Or change his comrades once a quarter;
In half the time he talks them round,
There must another set be found.
  "For poetry he's past his prime:
He takes an hour to find a rhyme;
His fire is out, his wit decay'd,
His fancy sunk, his Muse a jade.
I'd have him throw away his pen; —
But there's no talking to some men!"
  And then their tenderness appears,
By adding largely to my years;
"He's older than he would be reckon'd,
And *well remembers Charles the Second.
He hardly drinks a pint of wine;
And that, I doubt, is no good sign.
His stomach too begins to fail;
Last year we thought him strong and hale;
But now he's quite another thing:
I wish he may hold out till spring!"
Then hug themselves, and reason thus:
"It is not yet so bad with us!"
  In such a case, they talk in tropes,
And by their fears express their hopes;
Some great misfortune to portend,
No enemy can match a friend.
With all the kindness they profess,
The merit of a lucky guess
(When daily how d'ye's come of course,
And servants answer, "Worse and worse!")

Would please 'em better, than to tell,
That, "God be prais'd, the Dean is well."
Then he who prophesied the best,
Approves his foresight to the rest:
"You know I always fear'd the worst,
And often told you so at first."
He'd rather choose that I should die,
Than his prediction prove a lie.
Not one foretells I shall recover;
But all agree to give me over.

Yet, should some neighbour feel a pain
Just in the parts where I complain;
How many a message would he send!
What hearty prayers that I should mend!
Inquire what regimen I kept;
What gave me ease, and how I slept?
And more lament when I was dead,
Than all the sniv'llers round my bed.

My good companions, never fear;
For though you may mistake a year,
Though your prognostics run too fast,
They must be verified at last.

Behold the fatal day arrive!
"How is the Dean?"—"He's just alive."
Now the departing prayer is read;
"He hardly breathes."—"The Dean is dead."

Before the passing-bell begun,
The news thro' half the town has run.
"Oh! may we all for death prepare!
What has he left? and who's his heir?"
"I know no more than what the news is;
*'Tis all bequeath'd to public uses."
"To public use! a perfect whim!
What had the public done for him?
Mere envy, avarice, and pride;
He gave it all—but first he died.
And had the Dean, in all the nation,
*No worthy friend, no poor relation?
So ready to do strangers good,
Forgetting his own flesh and blood!"

Now, Grub Street wits are all employ'd;
With elegies the town is cloy'd:
Some paragraph in ev'ry paper
*To curse the Dean, or bless the Drapier.

The doctors, tender of their fame,
Wisely on me lay all the blame:
"We must confess, his case was nice;
But he would never take advice.
Had he been ruled, for aught appears,
He might have lived these twenty years;
For, when we open'd him, we found
That all his vital parts were sound."

From Dublin soon to London spread,
'Tis told at court, "The Dean is dead."
*Kind Lady Suffolk, in the spleen,
Runs laughing up to tell the queen.
The queen, so gracious, mild, and good,
Cries, "Is he gone! 'tis time he should.
He's dead, you say; why, let him rot:
I'm glad *the medals were forgot.
I promised him, I own; but when?
I only was a princess then;
But now, as consort of a king,
You know, 'tis quite a different thing."
Now *Chartres, at *Sir Robert's levee,
Tells with a sneer the tidings heavy:
"Why, is he dead without his shoes?"
Cries Bob, "I'm sorry for the news:
Oh, were the wretch but living still,
And in his place *my good friend Will!
Or had a mitre on his head,
Provided Bolingbroke were dead!"
Now *Curll his shop from rubbish drains;
Three genuine tomes of Swift's remains!
And then to make them pass the glibber,
Revised by *Tibbalds, Moore, and Cibber.
He'll treat me as he does my betters,
Publish my will, my life, my letters;
Revive the libels born to die,
Which Pope must bear, as well as I.

Here shift the scene, to represent
How those I love my death lament.
Poor Pope will grieve a month, and Gay
A week, and Arbuthnot a day.

St. John himself will scarce forbear
To bite his pen, and drop a tear.
The rest will give a shrug, and cry,
"I'm sorry—but we all must die!"

Indifference, clad in Wisdom's guise,
All fortitude of mind supplies:
For how can stony bowels melt
In those who never pity felt!
When *we* are lash'd, *they* kiss the rod,
Resigning to the will of God.

The fools, my juniors by a year,
Are tortur'd with suspense and fear;
Who wisely thought my age a screen,
When death approach'd, to stand between:
The screen removed, their hearts are trembling;
They mourn for me without dissembling.

My female friends, whose tender hearts
Have better learn'd to act their parts,
Receive the news in doleful dumps:
"The Dean is dead: (and what is trumps?)
Then, Lord have mercy on his soul!
(Ladies, *I'll venture for the vole.)
Six deans, they say, must bear the pall;
(I wish I knew what king to call.)

Madam, your husband will attend
The funeral of so good a friend."
"No, madam, 'tis a shocking sight,
And he's engaged to-morrow night;
My Lady Club would take it ill,
If he should fail her at quadrille.
He loved the Dean — (I lead a heart,)
But dearest friends, they say, must part.
His time was come: he ran his race;
We hope he's in a better place."

Why do we grieve that friends should die?
No loss more easy to supply.
One year is past; a different scene!
No further mention of the Dean;
Who now, alas! no more is miss'd
Than if he never did exist.
Where's now this fav'rite of Apollo!
Departed: — and his works must follow;
Must undergo the common fate;
His kind of wit is out of date.

Some country squire to *Lintot goes,
Inquires for "Swift in Verse and Prose."
Says Lintot, "I have heard the name;
He died a year ago." — "The same."
He searches all the shop in vain.
"Sir, you may find them in *Duck Lane.
I sent them with a load of books,
Last Monday to the pastry-cook's.
To fancy they could live a year!
I find you're but a stranger here.
The Dean was famous in his time,
And had a kind of knack at rhyme.
His way of writing now is past;
The town has got a better taste;
I keep no antiquated stuff,
But spick and span I have enough.
Pray do but give me leave to show 'em;
Here's Colley Cibber's birthday poem.
This ode you never yet have seen,
By *Stephen Duck, upon the queen.
Then here's a letter finely penned
Against the Craftsman and his friend;
It clearly shows that all reflection
On ministers is disaffection.
Next, here's Sir Robert's vindication,
And *Mr. Henley's last oration.
The hawkers have not got them yet.
Your honour please to buy a set?

"Here's *Woolston's tracts, the twelfth edition;
'Tis read by every politician:
The country members, when in town,
To all their boroughs send them down;
You never met a thing so smart;
The courtiers have them all by heart:
Those maids of honour (who can read),
Are taught to use them for their creed.
The rev'rend author's good intention
Has been rewarded with a pension.
He does an honour to his gown,
By bravely running priestcraft down:
He shows, as sure as God's in Gloucester,
That Moses was a grand impostor;
That all his miracles were cheats,
Perform'd as jugglers do their feats:
The church had never such a writer;
A shame he has not got a mitre!"

Suppose me dead; and then suppose
A club assembled at the Rose;
Where, from discourse of this and that,
I grow the subject of their chat.
And while they toss my name about,
With favour some, and some without,
One, quite indiff'rent in the cause,
My character impartial draws:

"The Dean, if we believe report,
Was never ill receiv'd at court.
As for his works in verse and prose
I own myself no judge of those;
Nor can I tell what critics thought 'em:
But this I know, all people bought 'em.
As with a moral view design'd
To cure the vices of mankind;
And, if he often miss'd his aim,
The world must own it, to their shame,
The praise is his, and theirs the blame."
"Sir, I have heard another story:
He was a most confounded Tory,
And grew, or he is much belied,
Extremely dull before he died."

"Can we the Drapier then forget?
Is not our nation in his debt?
'Twas he that writ the Drapier's letters!"
"He should have left them for his betters;
We had a hundred abler men,
Nor need depend upon his pen.
Say what you will about his reading,
You never can defend his breeding;
Who in his satires running riot,
Could never leave the world in quiet,
Attacking, when he took the whim,
Court, city, camp — all one to him.

"But why should he, except he slobber't,
Offend our patriot, great Sir Robert,
Whose counsels aid the sov'reign power
To save the nation every hour?
What scenes of evil he unravels
In satires, libels, lying travels!
Not sparing his own clergy-cloth,

But eats into it, like a moth!"
"His vein, ironically grave,
Exposed the fool, and lash'd the knave.
To steal a hint was never known,
But what he writ was all his own.
"He never thought an honour done him,
Because a duke was proud to own him,
Would rather slip aside and choose
To talk with wits in dirty shoes;
Despised the fools with stars and garters,
So often seen caressing Chartres.
He never courted men in station,
Nor persons held in admiration;
Of no man's greatness was afraid,
Because he sought for no man's aid.
Though trusted long in great affairs
He gave himself no haughty airs:
Without regarding private ends,
Spent all his credit for his friends;
And only chose the wise and good;
No flatterers; no allies in blood:
But succour'd virtue in distress,
And seldom fail'd of good success;
As numbers in their hearts must own,
Who, but for him had been unknown.
"With princes kept a due decorum,
But never stood in awe before 'em.
He follow'd David's lesson just;
In princes never put thy trust:
And would you make him truly sour,
Provoke him with a slave in power.
The Irish senate if you named,
With what impatience he declaim'd!
Fair Liberty was all his cry,
For her he stood prepared to die;
For her he boldly stood alone;
For her he oft exposed his own.
*Two kingdoms, just as faction led,
Had set a price upon his head;
But not a traitor could be found,
To sell him for six hundred pound.
"Had he but spared his tongue and pen
He might have rose like other men:
But power was never in his thought,
And wealth he valued not a groat;
Ingratitude he often found,
And pitied those who meant the wound,
But kept the tenor of his mind,
To merit well of human kind;
Nor made a sacrifice of those
Who still were true, to please his foes.
He labour'd many a fruitless hour,
To reconcile his friends in power;
Saw mischief by a faction brewing,
While they pursued each other's ruin.
But finding vain was all his care,
He left the court in mere despair.
"And, oh! how short are human schemes!
Here ended all our golden dreams.
What St. John's skill in state affairs,
What Ormond's valour, Oxford's cares,
To save their sinking country lent,
Was all destroy'd by one event.
*Too soon that precious life was ended,
On which alone our weal depended.
When up a dangerous faction starts,
With wrath and vengeance in their hearts;
By solemn League and Cov'nant bound,
To ruin, slaughter, and confound;
To turn religion to a fable,
And make the government a Babel;
Pervert the laws, disgrace the gown,
Corrupt the senate, rob the crown;
To sacrifice old England's glory,
And make her infamous in story:
When such a tempest shook the land,
How could unguarded Virtue stand!
With horror, grief, despair, the Dean
Beheld the dire destructive scene:
His friends in exile, or the tower,
Himself within the frown of power,
Pursued by base envenom'd pens,
Far to the land of slaves and fens;
A servile race in folly nursed,
Who truckle most, when treated worst.
"By innocence and resolution,
He bore continual persecution,
While numbers to preferment rose,
Whose merits were, to be his foes;
When ev'n his own familiar friends,
Intent upon their private ends,
Like renegadoes now he feels,
Against him lifting up their heels.
"The Dean did, by his pen, defeat
An infamous, destructive cheat;
Taught fools their int'rest how to know,
And gave them arms to ward the blow.
Envy has own'd it was his doing,
To save that hapless land from ruin;
While they who at the steerage stood,
And reap'd the profit, sought his blood.
"To save them from their evil fate,
In him was held a crime of state;
*A wicked monster on the bench,
Whose fury blood could never quench,
As vile and profligate a villain
As modern Scroggs, or old Tresilian,
Who long all justice had discarded,
Nor fear'd he God, nor man regarded,
Vow'd on the Dean his rage to vent,

And make him of his zeal repent:
But Heaven his innocence defends,
The grateful people stand his friends;
Not strains of law, nor judge's frown,
Nor topics brought to please the crown,
Nor witness hired, nor jury pick'd,
Prevail to bring him in convict.
"In exile, with a steady heart,
He spent his life's declining part;
Where folly, pride, and faction sway,
Remote from St. John, Pope, and Gay."
"Alas, poor Dean! his only scope
Was to be held a misanthrope.
This into gen'ral odium drew him,
Which if he liked, much good may't do him.
His zeal was not to lash our crimes,
But discontent against the times;
For had we made him timely offers
To raise his post, or fill his coffers,
Perhaps he might have truckled down,
Like other brethren of his gown.
For party he would scarce have bled;
I say no more — because he's dead.
What writings has he left behind?
I hear, they're of a different kind;
A few in verse; but most in prose —
Some high-flown pamphlets, I suppose; —
All scribbled in the worst of times,
To palliate his friend Oxford's crimes,
To praise Queen Anne, nay more, defend her,
As never fav'ring the Pretender;
Or libels yet conceal'd from sight,
Against the court to show his spite;
Perhaps his travels, part the third;
A lie at every second word —
Offensive to a loyal ear:
But not one sermon, you may swear."
"His friendships there, to few confined
Were always of the middling kind;
No fools of rank, a mongrel breed,
Who fain would pass for lords indeed:
Where titles give no right or power,
And peerage is a wither'd flower;
He would have held it a disgrace,
If such a wretch had known his face.
On rural squires, that kingdom's bane,
He vented oft his wrath in vain;
[*Biennial] squires to market brought;
Who sell their souls and [votes] for nought;
The [nation stripped,] go joyful back,
To *—— the church, their tenants rack,
Go snacks with [rogues and *rapparees,]
And keep the peace to pick up fees;
In every job to have a share,
A jail or barrack to repair;
And turn the tax for public roads,
Commodious to their own abodes.
"Perhaps I may allow the Dean,
Had too much satire in his vein;
And seem'd determined not to starve it,
Because no age could more deserve it.
Yet malice never was his aim;
He lash'd the vice, but spared the name;
No individual could resent,
Where thousands equally were meant;
His satire points at no defect,
But what all mortals may correct;
For he abhorr'd that senseless tribe
Who call it humour when they gibe:
He spared a hump, or crooked nose,
Whose owners set not up for beaux.
True genuine dullness moved his pity,
Unless it offer'd to be witty.
Those who their ignorance confess'd,
He ne'er offended with a jest;
But laughed to hear an idiot quote
A verse from Horace learn'd by rote.
"Vice, if it e'er can be abash'd,
Must be or ridiculed or lash'd.
If you resent it, who's to blame?
He neither knew you nor your name.
Should vice expect to 'scape rebuke,
Because its owner is a duke?
"He knew an hundred pleasant stories,
With all the turns of Whigs and Tories;
Was cheerful to his dying day;
And friends would let him have his way.
"He gave the little wealth he had
To build a house for fools and mad;
And show'd by one satiric touch
No nation wanted it so much.
That kingdom he hath left his debtor.
I wish it soon may have a better.
And, since you dread no farther lashes
*Methinks you may forgive his ashes."

[1739]

From A COMPLETE COLLECTION OF GENTEEL AND INGENIOUS CONVERSATION

ACCORDING TO THE MOST POLITE MODE AND METHOD NOW USED AT COURT, AND IN THE BEST COMPANIES OF ENGLAND. IN THREE DIALOGUES.

BY SIMON WAGSTAFF, ESQ.

Among Swift's numerous works dealing with language none is more interesting than these dialogues of *Polite Conversation.* In the Introduction (the greater part of which is here reprinted) he praises ironically the "flowers of wit and language" that adorn the conversation of "the polite persons of both sexes," and he congratulates the people of England upon having developed this noble art to the height of perfection. The dialogues that follow (space permits the quotation of only the beginning of the first dialogue) illustrate the pert remarks, the vapid commonplaces, the trite witticisms, the outworn proverbs, the hackneyed raillery, and the flat repartee which made up the stock in trade of Sir Plume and Lady Modish. Here are the worn discs of conversational coin, the *clichés* of familiar discourse, which provided a substitute for thinking and tricked out dullness in cast finery and threadbare wit. Yet this talk, which Swift thus satirized two hundred years ago, has more than an antiquarian curiosity; though Lord Sparkish and Colonel Atwit and Lady Smart and Miss Notable belong to an age that has long passed away, the very phrases of their polite conversation still do duty in the smart talk of their descendants. Few readers today can turn at random to the pages of these dialogues without lighting on some of their own favourite expressions and cherished witticisms, still being used as they were in the eighteenth century, when Swift pilloried them as stupid, pointless, and conventional.

A Complete Collection of Genteel and Ingenious Conversation was published in 1738, both in London and in Dublin. It seems likely that Swift had had the idea in mind for a long time, probably at least since 1709 or 1710 when he had written *Hints toward an Essay on Conversation,* which treats some of the same matters that are here developed more fully. However, there is no evidence from his correspondence that he did anything more with the idea until the summer of 1731, when he wrote to Gay that he was working upon these dialogues and also upon his *Directions to Servants.* It is pleasing to know that Swift gave the manuscript of *Polite Conversation* before publication to Mrs. Barber, the wife of a poor Dublin tailor, and that the profits from its publication were sufficient to relieve her family from their most pressing want. Mrs. Barber is said to have won Swift's regard through her poetical ability (she published a volume of poems in 1734) and through her heroic efforts to assist her husband and give an education to her children. That such a piece of satire should have been the means of benefiting a friend in distress is typical of its author's relations to society and to individuals.

AN INTRODUCTION TO THE FOLLOWING TREATISE

As my life hath been chiefly spent in consulting the honour and welfare of my country for more than forty years past, not without answerable success, if the world and my friends have not flattered me; so, there is no point wherein I have so much laboured as that of improving and polishing all parts of conversation between persons of quality, whether they meet by accident or invitation, at meals, tea, or visits, mornings, noons, or evenings.

I have passed perhaps more time than any other man of my age and country in visits and assemblies, where the polite persons of both sexes distinguish themselves, and could not without much grief observe how frequently both gentlemen and ladies are at a loss for questions, answers, replies, and rejoinders; however, my concern was much abated when I found that these defects were not occasioned by any want of materials, but because those materials were not in every hand: for instance, one lady can give an answer better than ask a question; one gentleman is happy at a reply; another excels in a rejoinder; one can revive a languishing conversation by a sudden surprising sentence; another is more dextrous in seconding; a third can fill the gap with laughing, or commending what hath been said. Thus fresh hints may be started, and the ball of discourse kept up.

But, alas! this is too seldom the case, even in the most select companies: how often do we see at court, at public visiting days, at great men's levees, and other places of general meeting, that the conversation falls and drops to nothing, like a fire without supply of fuel; this is what we ought to lament; and against this dangerous evil I take upon me to affirm that I have in the following papers provided an infallible remedy.

It was in the year 1695, and the sixth of his late majesty King William the Third, of ever glorious and immortal memory, who rescued three kingdoms from popery and slavery; when, being about the age of six-and-thirty, my judgment mature, of good reputation in the world, and well acquainted with the best families in town, I determined to spend five mornings, to dine four times, pass three afternoons and six evenings every week in the houses of the most polite families, of which I would confine myself to fifty; only changing as the masters or ladies died, or left the town, or grew out of vogue, or sunk in their fortunes, (which to me was of the highest moment) or became disaffected to the government; which practice I have followed ever since to this very day, except when I happened to be sick, or in the spleen upon cloudy weather; and except when I entertained four of each sex at my lodgings once a month, by way of retaliation.

I always kept a large table-book in my pocket; and as soon as I left the company, I immediately entered the choicest expressions that passed during the visit; which, returning home, I transcribed in a fair hand, but somewhat enlarged; and had made the greatest part of my collection in twelve years, but not digested into any method; for this I found was a work of infinite labour, and what required the nicest judgment, and consequently could not be brought to any degree of perfection in less than sixteen years more.

Herein I resolved to exceed the advice of Horace, a Roman poet, (which I have read in * Mr. Creech's admirable translation) that an author should keep his works nine years in his closet, before he ventured to publish them; and finding that I still received some additional flowers of wit and language, although in a very small number, I determined to defer the publication, to pursue my design, and exhaust, if possible, the whole subject, that I might present a complete system to the world: for, I am convinced by long experience that the critics will be as severe as their old envy against me can make them; I foretell they will object that I have inserted many answers and replies which are neither witty, humorous, polite, nor authentic, and have omitted others that would have been highly useful, as well as entertaining; but let them come to particulars, and I will boldly engage to confute their malice.

For these last six or seven years I have not been able to add above nine valuable sentences to enrich my collection; from whence I conclude that what remains will amount only to a trifle. However, if after the publication of this work any lady or gentleman, when they have read it, shall find the least thing of importance omitted, I desire they will please to supply my defects by communicating to me their discoveries; and their letters may be directed to * Simon Wagstaff, Esq. at his lodgings next door to the Gloucester-Head in St. James's Street, (they paying the postage). In return of which favour, I shall make honourable mention of their names in a short preface to the second edition.

In the meantime, I can not, but with some pride and much pleasure, congratulate with my dear country, which hath outdone all the nations of Europe in advancing the whole art of conversation to the greatest height it is capable of reaching; and, therefore, being entirely convinced that the collection I now offer to the public is full and complete, I may at the same time boldly affirm that the whole genius, humour, politeness, and eloquence of England are summed up in it: nor is the treasure small wherein are to be found at least a thousand shining questions, answers, repartees, replies, and rejoinders, fitted to adorn every kind of discourse that an assembly of English ladies and gentlemen, met together for their mutual entertainment, can possibly want, especially when the several flowers shall be set off and improved by the speakers, with every circumstance of preface and circumlocution, in proper terms, and attended with praise, laughter, or admiration.

There is a natural, involuntary distortion of the muscles which is the anatomical cause of laughter; but there is another cause of laughter which decency requires, and is the undoubted mark of a good taste, as well as of a polite, obliging behaviour; neither is this to be acquired without much observation, long practice, and a sound judgment: I did therefore once intend, for the ease of the learner, to set down in all parts of the following dialogues certain marks, asterisks, or *nota-bene's* (in English, mark-well's) after most questions, and every reply or answer, directing exactly the moment when one, two, or all the company are to laugh; but having duly considered that the expedient would too much enlarge the bulk of the volume, and consequently the price; and likewise that something ought to be left for ingenious readers to find out, I have determined to leave that whole affair, although of great importance, to their own discretion.

The readers must learn by all means to distinguish between * proverbs and those polite speeches which beautify conversation; for, as to the former, I utterly reject them out of all ingenious discourse. I acknowledge indeed that there may possibly be found in this treatise a few sayings, among so great a number of smart turns of wit and humour as I have produced, which have a proverbial air: however, I hope it will be considered that even these were not originally proverbs, but the genuine productions of superior wits, to embellish and support conversation; from whence, with great impropriety, as well as plagiarism (if you will forgive a hard word), they have most injuriously been transferred into proverbial maxims; and therefore in justice ought to be resumed out of vulgar hands, to adorn the drawing-rooms of princes, both male and female, the levees of great ministers, as well as the toilet and tea-table of the ladies.

I can faithfully assure the reader that there is not one single witty phrase in this whole collection which hath not received the stamp and approbation of at least one hundred years, and how much longer it is hard to determine; he may therefore be secure to find them all genuine, sterling, and authentic.

But before this elaborate treatise can become of universal use and ornament to my native country, two points, that will require time and much application, are absolutely necessary.

For, first, whatever person would aspire to be completely witty, smart, humorous, and polite, must by hard labour be able to retain in his memory every single sentence contained in this work, so as never to be once at a loss in applying the right answers, questions, repartees, and the like, immediately, and without study or hesitation.

And, secondly, after a lady or gentleman hath so well overcome this difficulty as to be never at a loss upon any emergency, the true management of every feature, and almost of every limb, is equally necessary; without which an infinite number of absurdities will inevitably ensue: for instance, there is hardly a polite sentence in the following dialogues which doth not absolutely require some peculiar graceful motion in the eyes or nose or mouth or forehead or chin, or suitable toss of the head, with certain offices assigned to each hand; and, in ladies, * the whole exercise of the fan, fitted to the energy of every word they deliver; by no means omitting the various turns and cadences of the voice, the twistings and movements and different postures of the body, the several kinds and gradations of laughter, which the ladies must daily practise by the looking-glass, and consult upon them with their waiting-maids.

My readers will soon observe what a great compass of real and useful knowledge this science includes; wherein, although nature, assisted by a genius, may be very instrumental, yet a strong memory and constant application, together with example and precept, will be highly necessary: for these reasons I have often wished that certain male and female instructors, perfectly versed in this science, would set up schools for the instruction of young ladies and gentlemen therein.

I remember about thirty years ago there was a Bohemian woman, of that species commonly known by the name of gipsies, who came over hither from France, and generally attended * Isaac the dancing-master when he was teaching his art to misses of quality; and while the young ladies were thus employed, the Bohemian, standing at some distance, but full in their sight, acted before them all proper airs and turnings of the head and motions of the hands and twistings of the body, whereof you may still observe the good effects in several of our elder ladies.

After the same manner, it were much to be desired that some expert gentlewomen gone to decay would set up public schools, wherein young girls of quality or great fortunes might first be taught to repeat this following system of conversation which I have been at so much pains to compile; and then to adapt every feature of their countenances, every turn of their hands, every screwing of their bodies, every exercise of their fans, to the humour of the sentences they hear or deliver in conversation. But above all to instruct them in every species and degree of laughing in the proper seasons at their own wit or that of the company. And, if the sons of the nobility and gentry, instead of being sent to common schools or put into the hands of tutors at home, to learn nothing but words, were consigned to able instructors in the same art, I cannot find what use there could be of books, except in the hands of those who are to make learning their trade, which is below the dignity of persons born to titles or estates.

It would be another infinite advantage that, by cultivating this science, we should wholly avoid the vexations and impertinence of pedants, who affect to talk in a language not to be understood; and whenever a polite person offers accidentally to use any of their jargon terms, have the presumption to laugh at us for pronouncing those words in a genteeler manner. Whereas, I do here affirm that whenever any fine gentleman or lady condescends to let a hard word pass out of their mouths, every syllable is smoothed and polished in the passage; and it is a true mark of politeness, both in writing and reading, to vary the orthography as well as the sound, because we are infinitely better judges of what will please a distinguishing ear than those who call themselves scholars can possibly be; who, consequently, ought to correct their books and manner of pronouncing by the authority of our example, from whose lips they proceed with infinitely more beauty and significancy.

But, in the meantime, until so great, so useful, and so necessary a design can be put in execution, (which, considering the good disposition of our country at present, I shall not despair of living to see) let me recommend the following treatise to be carried about as a pocket companion by all gentlemen and ladies, when they are going to visit or dine or drink tea, or where they happen to pass the evening without cards, (as I have sometimes known it to be the case upon disappointments or accidents unforeseen) desiring they would read their several parts in their chairs or coaches to prepare themselves for every kind of conversation that can possibly happen.

Although I have, in justice to my country, allowed the genius of our people to excel that of any other nation upon earth, and have confirmed this truth by an argument not to be controlled, I mean, by producing so great a number of witty sentences in the ensuing dialogues, all of undoubted authority, as well as of our own production; yet I must confess at the same time that we are wholly indebted for them to our ancestors; at least, for as long as my memory reacheth, I do not recollect one new phrase of importance to have been added, which defect in us moderns I take to have been occasioned by the introduction of *cant words in the reign of King Charles the Second. And those have so often varied that hardly one of them, of above a year's standing, is now intelligible, nor anywhere to be found, excepting a small number strewed here and there in the comedies and other fantastic writings of that age.

The Honourable *Colonel James Graham, my old friend and companion, did likewise, towards the end of the same reign, invent a set of words and phrases which continued almost to the time of his death. But, as those terms of art were adapted only to courts and politicians, and extended little further than among his particular acquaintance (of whom I had the honour to be one) they are now almost forgotten.

Nor did *the late D. of R—— and E. of E—— succeed much better, although they proceeded no further than single words, whereof, except *bite*, *bamboozle*, and one or two more, the whole vocabulary is antiquated.

The same fate hath already attended those other town-wits who furnish us with a great variety of new terms, which are annually changed, and those of the last season sunk in oblivion. Of these I was once favoured with a complete list by the Right Honourable the Lord and Lady ——, with which I made a considerable figure one summer in the country; but returning up to town in winter, and venturing to produce them again, I was partly hooted, and partly not understood.

The only invention of late years which hath any way contributed towards politeness in discourse is that of *abbreviating or reducing words of many syllables into one by lopping off the rest. This refinement, having begun about the time of the Revolution, I had some share in the honour of promoting it, and I observe, to my great satisfaction, that it makes daily advancements, and I hope in time will raise our language to the utmost perfection; although, I must confess, to avoid obscurity I have been very sparing of this ornament in the following dialogues.

But, as for phrases invented to cultivate conversation, I defy all the clubs of coffeehouses in this town to invent a new one equal in wit, humour, smartness, or politeness to the very worst of my set; which clearly shows, either that we are much degenerated or that the whole stock of materials hath been already employed. I would willingly hope, as I do confidently believe, the latter, because, having myself for several months racked my invention (if possible) to enrich this treasury with some additions of my own (which, however, should have been printed in a different character, that I might not be charged with imposing upon the public) and having shown them to some judicious friends, they dealt very sincerely with me; all unanimously agreeing that mine were infinitely below the true old helps to discourse, drawn up in my present collection, and confirmed their opinion with reasons by which I was perfectly convinced, as well as ashamed, of my great presumption.

But I lately met a much stronger argument to confirm me in the same sentiments; for, as the * great Bishop Burnet of Salisbury informs us in the preface to his admirable *History of his Own Times* that he intended to employ himself in polishing it every day of his life, (and indeed in its kind it is almost equally polished with this work of mine): so, it hath been my constant business for some years past to examine, with the utmost strictness, whether I could possibly find the smallest lapse in style or propriety through my whole collection, that, in emulation with the bishop, I might send it abroad as the most finished piece of the age.

It happened one day as I was dining in good company of both sexes and watching, according to my custom, for new materials wherewith to fill my pocket-book, I succeeded well enough till after dinner, when the ladies retired to their tea and left us over a bottle of wine. But I found we were not able to furnish any more materials that were worth the pains of transcribing; for the discourse of the company was all degenerated into smart sayings of their own invention, and not of the true old standard, so that in absolute despair I withdrew and went to attend the ladies at their tea. From whence I did then conclude, and still continue to believe, either that wine doth not inspire politeness or that our sex is not able to support it without the company of women, who never fail to lead us into the right way, and there to keep us.

It much increaseth the value of these apophthegms that unto them we owe the continuance of our language for at least an hundred years; neither is this to be wondered at, because indeed, besides the smartness of the wit and fineness of the raillery, such is the propriety and energy of expression in them all that they never can be changed but to disadvantage, except in the circumstance of using abbreviations; which, however, I do not despair in due time to see introduced, having already met them at some of the choice companies in town.

Although this work be calculated for all persons of quality and fortune of both sexes, yet the reader may perceive that my particular view was to the officers of the army, the gentlemen of the inns of court, and of both the universities, to all courtiers, male and female, but principally to the maids of honour, of whom I have been personally acquainted with two-and-twenty sets, all excelling in this noble endowment; till for some years past, I know not how, they came to degenerate into * selling of bargains, and * free-thinking; not that I am against either of these entertainments at proper seasons, in compliance with company who may want a taste for more exalted discourse, whose memories may be short, who are too young to be perfect in their lessons, or (although it be hard to conceive) who have no inclination to read and learn my instructions. And, besides, there is a strong temptation for court-ladies to fall into the two amusements above mentioned that they may avoid the censure of affecting singularity, against the general current and fashion of all about them. But, however, no man will pretend to affirm that either bargains or blasphemy, which are the principal ornaments of free-thinking, are so good a fund of polite discourse as what is to be met with in my collection. For, as to bargains, few of them seem to be excellent in their kind and have not much variety, because they all terminate in one single point; and to multiply them would require more invention than people have to spare. And, as to blasphemy or free-thinking, I have known some scrupulous persons of both sexes who, by a prejudiced education, are afraid of sprights. I must, however, except maids of honour, who have been fully convinced by an infamous court-chaplain that there is no such place as hell.

I cannot, indeed, controvert the lawfulness of free-thinking because it hath been universally allowed that thought is free. But however, although it may afford a large field of matter; yet in my poor opinion it seems to contain very little of wit or humour because it hath not been ancient enough among us to furnish established authentic expressions, I mean, such as must receive a sanction from the polite world before their authority can be allowed; neithei was the art of blasphemy or free-thinking invented by the court or by persons of great quality, who, properly speaking, were patrons rather than inventors of it, but first brought in by the fanatic faction, towards the end of their power, and, after the Restoration, carried to Whitehall by * the converted rumpers, with very good reasons; because they knew that King Charles the Second, from a wrong education occasioned by the troubles of his father, had time enough to observe that fanatic enthusiasm directly led to atheism, which agreed with the dissolute inclinations of his youth; and, perhaps, these principles were further cultivated in him by the French Huguenots, who have been often charged with spreading them among us. however, I cannot see where the necessity lies of introducing new and foreign topics for conversation while we have so plentiful a stock of our own growth.

I have likewise, for some reasons of equal weight, been very sparing in *doubles entendres* because they often put ladies upon affected constraints and affected ignorance. In short, they break, or very much entangle, the thread of discourse; neither am I master of any rules to settle the disconcerted countenances of the females in such a juncture; I can, therefore, only allow innuendoes of this kind to be delivered in whispers and only to young ladies under twenty, who, being in honour obliged to blush, it may produce a new subject for discourse.

Perhaps the critics may accuse me of a defect in my following system of Polite Conversation, that there is one great ornament of discourse whereof I have not produced a single example, which, indeed, I purposely omitted for some reasons that I shall immediately offer; and, if those reasons will not satisfy the male part of my gentle readers, the defect may be *applied in some manner by an appendix to the second edition, which appendix shall be printed by itself and sold for sixpence, stitched, and with a marble cover, that my readers may have no occasion to complain of being defrauded.

The defect I mean is my not having inserted into the body of my book all the oaths now most in fashion for embellishing discourse, especially since it could give no offence to * the clergy, who are seldom or never admitted to these polite assemblies. And it must be allowed that oaths, well chosen, are not only very useful expletives to matter but great ornaments of style.

What I shall here offer in my own defence upon this important article will, I hope, be some extenuation of my fault.

First, I reasoned with myself that a just collection of oaths, repeated as often as the fashion requires, must have enlarged this volume at least to double the bulk, whereby it would not only double the charge but likewise make the volume less commodious for pocket carriage.

Secondly, I have been assured by some judicious friends that themselves have known certain ladies to take offence (whether seriously or no) at too great a profusion of cursing and swearing, even when that kind of ornament was not improperly introduced, which, I confess, did startle me not a little, having never observed the like in the compass of my own several acquaintance, at least for twenty years past. However, I was forced to submit to wiser judgments than my own.

Thirdly, as this most useful treatise is calculated for all future times, I considered, in this maturity of my age, how great a variety of oaths I have heard since I began to study the world and to know men and manners. And here I found it to be true what I have read in * an ancient poet.

> For, nowadays, men change their oaths,
> As often as they change their clothes.

In short, oaths are the children of fashion; they are in some sense almost annuals, like what I observed before of cant words; and I myself can remember about forty different sets. The old stock oaths, I am confident, do not mount to above forty-five or fifty at most; but the way of mingling and compounding them is almost as various as that of the alphabet.

Sir John Perrot was the first man of quality whom I find upon record to have sworn by *God's wounds*. He lived in the reign of Q. Elizabeth and was supposed to have been a natural son of Henry the Eighth, who might also have probably been his instructor. This oath indeed still continues and is a stock oath to this day; so do several others that have kept their natural simplicity; but infinitely the greater number hath been so frequently changed and dislocated that if the inventors were now alive, they could hardly understand them.

Upon these considerations I began to apprehend that if I should insert all the oaths that are now current, my book would be out of vogue with the first change of fashion and grow as useless as an old dictionary; whereas the case is quite otherways with my collection of polite discourse, which, as I before observed, hath descended by tradition for at least an hundred years, without any change in the phraseology. I, therefore, determined with myself to leave out the whole system of swearing, because, both the male and female oaths are all perfectly well known and distinguished; new ones are easily learnt, and with a moderate share of discretion may be properly applied on every fit occasion. However, I must here, upon this article of swearing, most earnestly recommend to my male readers that they would please a little to study variety. For it is the opinion of our most refined swearers that the same oath or curse cannot consistent with true politeness be repeated above nine times in the same company, by the same person, and at one sitting.

I am far from desiring or expecting that all the polite and ingenious speeches contained in this work should, in the general conversation between ladies and gentlemen, come in so quick and so close as I have here delivered them. By no means; on the contrary, they ought to be husbanded better and spread much thinner. Nor do I make the least question but that by a discreet thrifty management they may serve for the entertainment of a whole year to any person who does not make too long or too frequent visits in the same family. The flowers of wit, fancy, wisdom, humour, and politeness scattered in this volume amount to one thousand, seventy and four. Allowing then to every gentleman and lady thirty visiting families, (not insisting upon fractions) there will want but a little of an hundred polite questions, answers, replies, rejoinders, repartees, and remarks, to be daily delivered fresh in every company for twelve solar months; and even this is a higher pitch of delicacy than the world insists on, or hath reason to expect. But I am altogether for exalting this science to its utmost perfection.

It may be objected that the publication of my book may, in a long course of time, prostitute this noble art to mean and vulgar people; but I answer that it is not so easy an acquirement as a few ignorant pretenders may imagine. A footman may swear, but he cannot swear like a lord. He can swear as often; but, can he swear with equal delicacy, propriety, and judgment? No, certainly, unless he be a lad of superior parts, of good memory, a diligent observer, one who hath a skillful ear, some knowledge of music, and an exact taste, which hardly fall to the share of one in a thousand among that fraternity, in as high favour as they now stand with their ladies; neither hath one footman in six so fine a genius as to relish and apply those exalted sentences comprised in this volume which I offer to the world. It is true, I cannot see that the same ill consequences would follow from the waiting-woman, who, if she hath been bred to read romances, may have some small subaltern, or second-hand politeness; and if she constantly attends the tea, and be a good listener, may, in some years, make a tolerable figure which will serve, perhaps, to draw in the young chaplain or the old steward. But, alas! after all, how can she acquire those hundreds of graces and motions and airs, the whole military management of the fan, the contortions of every muscular motion in the face, the risings and fallings, the quickness and slowness of the voice, with the several turns and cadences; the proper juncture of smiling and frowning, how often and how loud to laugh, when to jibe and when to flout, with all the other branches of doctrine and discipline above recited?

I am, therefore, not under the least apprehension that this art will ever be in danger of falling into common hands, which requires so much time, study, practice, and genius before it arrives to perfection; and, therefore, I must repeat my proposal for erecting public schools, provided with the best and ablest masters and mistresses, at the charge of the nation.

I have drawn this work into the form of a dialogue after the patterns of other famous writers in history, law, politics, and most other arts and sciences; and I hope it will have the same success: for, who can contest it to be of greater consequence to the happiness of these kingdoms than all human knowledge put together? Dialogue is held the best method of inculcating any part of knowledge; and as I am confident that public schools will soon be founded for teaching wit and politeness, after my scheme, to young people of quality and fortune, I have determined next sessions to deliver a petition to the House of Lords for an Act of Parliament to establish my book as the standard grammar in all the principal cities of the kingdom where this art is to be taught by able masters, who are to be approved and recommended by me, which is no more than * Lilly obtained only for teaching words in a language wholly useless: neither shall I be so far wanting to myself as not to desire a patent granted of course to all useful projectors; I mean, that I may have the sole profit of giving a licence to every school to read my grammar for fourteen years.

The reader cannot but observe what pains I have been at in polishing the style of my book to the greatest exactness; nor, have I been less diligent in refining the orthography, by spelling the words in the very same manner that they are pronounced by the chief patterns of politeness at court, at levees, at assemblies, at playhouses, at the prime visiting-places, by young templars, and by gentleman-commoners of both universities who have lived at least a twelvemonth in town and kept the best company. Of these spellings the public will meet with many examples in the following book. For instance, *can't*, *han't*, *shan't*, *didn't*, *couldn't*, *wouldn't*, *isn't*, * *e'n't*, with many more; besides several words which scholars pretend are derived from Greek and Latin, but not pared into a polite sound by ladies, officers of the army, courtiers, and templars, such as *jommetry* for *geometry*, *verdi* for *verdict*, *lierd* for *lord*, *larnen* for *learning*, together with some abbreviations exquisitely refined; as *pozz* for *positive*, *mobb* for *mobile*; *phizz* for *physiognomy*; *rep* for *reputation*; *plenipo* for *plenipotentiary*; *incog* for *incognito*; *hypps* or *hippo*, for *hypochondriacs*, *bam* for *bamboozle*; and *bamboozle* for *God knows what*; whereby much time is saved and the high road to conversation cut short by many a mile.

I have, as it will be apparent, laboured very much, and, I hope, with felicity enough, to make every character in the dialogue agreeable with itself, to a degree, that, whenever any judicious person shall read my book aloud, for the entertainment and instruction of a select company, he need not so much as * name the particular speakers, because all the persons, throughout the several subjects of conversation, strictly observe a different manner, peculiar to their characters, which are of different kinds; but this I leave entirely to the prudent and impartial reader's discernment.

Perhaps the very manner of introducing the several points of wit and humour may not be less entertaining and instructing than the matter itself. In the latter I can pretend to little merit, because it entirely depends upon memory and the happiness of having kept polite company. But the art of contriving that those speeches should be introduced naturally, as the most proper sentiments to be delivered upon so great variety of subjects, I take to be a talent somewhat uncommon and a labour that few people could hope to succeed in, unless they had a genius particularly turned that way, added to a sincere, disinterested love of the public.

Although every curious question, smart answer, and witty reply be little known to many people, yet there is not one single sentence in the whole collection for which I cannot bring most authentic vouchers whenever I shall be called; and, even for some expressions, which to a few nice ears may perhaps appear somewhat gross, I can produce the stamp of authority from courts, chocolate-houses, theatres, assemblies, drawing-rooms, levees, card-meetings, balls, and masquerades, from persons of both sexes, and of the highest titles next to royal. However, to say the truth, I have been very sparing in my quotations of such sentiments that seem to be over free, because, when I began my collection, such kind of converse was almost in its infancy, till it was taken into the protection of my honoured patronesses at court, by whose countenance and sanction it hath become a choice flower in the nosegay of wit and politeness.

Some will perhaps object that when I bring my company to dinner I mention too great a variety of dishes, not always consistent with the art of cookery or proper for the season of the year, and part of the first course mingled with the second, besides a failure in politeness by introducing a black pudden to a lord's table and at a great entertainment; but, if I had omitted the black pudden, I desire to know what would have become of that exquisite reason given by Miss Notable for not eating it; the world perhaps might have lost it for ever, and I should have been justly answerable for having left it out of my collection. I therefore cannot but hope that such hypercritical readers will please to consider my business was to make so full and complete a body of refined sayings as compact as I could; only taking care to produce them in the most natural and probable manner, in order to allure my readers into the very substance and marrow of this most admirable and necessary art.

I am heartily sorry, and was much disappointed, to find that so universal and polite an entertainment as cards hath hitherto contributed very little to the enlargement of my work. I have sat by many hundred times with the utmost vigilance, and my table-book ready, without being able in eight hours to gather matter for one single phrase in my book. But this, I think, may be easily accounted for by the turbulence and justling of passions upon the various and surprising turns, incidents, revolutions, and events of good and evil fortune that arrive in the course of a long evening at play, the mind being wholly taken up, and the consequence of non-attention so fatal.

Play is supported upon the two great pillars of deliberation and action. The terms of art are few, prescribed by law and custom, no time allowed for digressions or trials of wit. Quadrille in particular bears some resemblance to a state of nature, which, we are told, is a state of war, wherein every woman is against every woman: the unions short, inconstant, and soon broke, the league made this minute without knowing the ally, and dissolved in the next. Thus, at the game of quadrille, female brains are always employed in stratagem, or their hands in action. Neither can I find that our art hath gained much by the happy revival of masquerading among us, the whole dialogue in those meetings being summed up in one (sprightly I confess, but) single question, and as sprightly an answer. "Do you know me?" "Yes, I do." And, "Do you know me?" "Yes, I do." For this reason I did not think it proper to give my readers the trouble of introducing a masquerade merely for the sake of a single question and a single answer. Especially, when to perform this in a proper manner I must have brought in a hundred persons together, of both sexes, dressed in fantastic habits for one minute, and dismiss them the next.

Neither is it reasonable to conceive that our science can be much improved by masquerades, where the wit of both sexes is altogether taken up in continuing singular and humoursome disguises, and their thoughts entirely employed in bringing intrigues and assignations of gallantry to a happy conclusion.

The judicious reader will readily discover that I make Miss Notable my heroine and Mr. Thomas Neverout my hero. I have laboured both their characters with my utmost ability. It is into their mouths that I have put the liveliest questions, answers, repartees, and rejoinders, because my design was to propose them both as patterns for all young bachelors and single ladies to copy after. By which I hope very soon to see polite conversation flourish between both sexes in a more consummate degree of perfection than these kingdoms have yet ever known....

I shall conclude this long but necessary introduction with a request, or indeed rather, a just and reasonable demand from all lords, ladies, and gentlemen that while they are entertaining and improving each other with those polite questions, answers, repartees, replies, and rejoinders, which I have with infinite labour and close application, during the space of thirty-six years, been collecting for their service and improvement, they shall, as an instance of gratitude, on every proper occasion, quote my name, after this or the like manner. "Madam, as our Master Wagstaff says." "My lord, as our friend Wagstaff has it." I do likewise expect that all my pupils shall drink my health every day at dinner and supper during my life; and that they, or their posterity, shall continue the same ceremony to my not inglorious memory, after my decease, forever.

From THE FIRST DIALOGUE

DRAMATIS PERSONÆ

The Men	*The Ladies*
Lord Sparkish	Lady Smart
Lord Smart	Miss Notable
Sir John Linger	Lady Answerall
Mr. Neverout	
Colonel Atwit	

St. James's Park

Lord Sparkish *meeting* Col. Atwit.

Colonel. Well met, my lord.

Ld. Sparkish. Thank ye, colonel. A parson would have said, I hope we shall meet in heaven. When did you see Tom Neverout?

Col. He's just coming towards us. Talk of the devil —

NEVEROUT *comes up.*

Col. How do you do, Tom?

Neverout. Never the better for you.

Col. I hope you're never the worse. But where's your manners? Don't you see my Lord Sparkish?

Neverout. My Lord, I beg your lordship's pardon.

Ld. Sparkish. Tom, how is it that you can't see the wood for trees? What wind blew you hither?

Neverout. Why, my lord, it is an ill wind blows nobody good, for it gives me the honour of seeing your lordship.

Col. Tom, you must go with us to Lady Smart's to breakfast.

Neverout. Must? Why, colonel, must's for the king.

[COL. *offering in jest to draw his sword.*]

Col. Have you spoke with all your friends?

Neverout. Colonel, as you're stout, be merciful.

Ld. Sparkish. Come, agree, agree; the law's costly.

[COL. *taking his hand from the hilt.*]

Col. Well, Tom, you are never the worse man to be afraid of me. Come along.

Neverout. What, do you think I was born in a wood, to be afraid of an owl? I'll wait on you. I hope Miss Notable will be there; 'egad she's very handsome and has wit at will.

Col. Why every one as they like, as the good woman said when she kiss'd her cow.

LORD SMART'S *house; they knock at the door; the* porter *comes out.*

Ld. Sparkish. Pray, are you the porter?

Porter. Yes, for want of a better.

Ld. Sparkish. Is your lady at home?

Porter. She was at home just now; but she's not gone out yet.

Neverout. I warrant this rogue's tongue is well hung.

LADY SMART'S *antechamber.*

LADY SMART *and* LADY ANSWERALL *at the tea-table.*

Lady Smart. My lord, your lordship's most humble servant.

Ld. Sparkish. Madam, you spoke too late; I was your ladyship's before.

Lady Smart. Oh! colonel, are you here?

Col. As sure as you're there, madam.

Lady Smart. Oh, Mr. Neverout! what, such a man alive!

Neverout. Ay, madam; alive, and alive like to be, at your ladyship's service.

Lady Smart. Well, I'll get a knife and nick it down that Mr. Neverout came to our house. And pray, what news, Mr. Neverout?

Neverout. Why, madam, Queen Elizabeth's dead.

Lady Smart. Well, Mr. Neverout, I see you are no changeling.

MISS NOTABLE *comes in.*

Neverout. Miss, your slave; I hope your early rising will do you no harm. I hear you are but just come out of the cloth-market.

Miss. I always rise at eleven, whether it be day or no.

Col. Miss, I hope you are up for all day.

Miss. Yes, if I don't get a fall before night.

Col. Miss, I heard you were out of order; pray, how are you now?

Miss. Pretty well, colonel, I thank you.

Col. Pretty and well, miss! that's two very good things.

Miss. I mean I am better than I was.

Neverout. Why then, 'tis well you were sick.

Miss. What, Mr. Neverout, you take me up before I'm down.

Lady Smart. Come, let us leave off children's play and come to *push-pin.

Miss. [*To* LADY SMART.] Pray, madam, give me some more sugar to my tea.

Col. Oh! miss, you must needs be very good humour'd, you love sweet things so well.

Neverout. Stir it up with the spoon, miss; for the deeper the sweeter.

Lady Smart. I assure you, miss, the colonel has made you a great compliment.

Miss. I am sorry for it; for I have heard say that complimenting is lying.

Lady Smart. [*To* LD. SPARKISH.] My lord, methinks the sight of you is good for sore eyes; if we had known of your coming, we would have strewn rushes for you. How has your lordship done this long time?

Col. Faith, madam, he's better in health than in good conditions.

Ld. Sparkish. Well, I see there's no worse friend than one brings from home with one;

and I am not the first man has carried a rod to whip himself.

Neverout. Here's miss, has not a word to throw at a dog. Come; a penny for your thoughts.

Miss. It is not worth a farthing, for I was thinking of you. [COLONEL *rising up.*]

Lady Smart. Colonel, where are you going so soon? I hope you did not come to fetch fire.

Col. Madam, I must needs go home for half an hour.

Miss. Why, colonel, they say the devil's at home.

Lady Answ. Well, but sit down while you stay; 'tis as cheap sitting as standing.

Col. No, madam; while I'm standing I'm going.

Miss. Nay, let him go; I promise him we won't tear his clothes to hold him.

Lady Smart. I suppose, colonel, we keep you from better company; I mean only as to myself.

Col. Madam, I am all obedience.

[COLONEL *sits down.*]

Lady Smart. Lord, miss, how can you drink your tea so hot? Sure your mouth's pav'd. How do you like this tea, colonel?

Col. Well enough, madam; but methinks it is a little more-ish.

Lady Smart. Oh! colonel, I understand you. Betty, bring the canister. I have but very little of this tea left; but I don't love to make two wants of one: want when I have it, and want when I have it not. He, he, he, he!

[*Laughs.*]

Lady Answ. [*To the maid.*] Why, sure, Betty, you are bewitched; the cream is burnt too.

Betty. Why, madam, *the bishop has set his foot in it.

Lady Smart. Go, run, girl, and warm some fresh cream.

Betty. Indeed, madam, there's none left, for the cat has eaten it all.

Lady Smart. I doubt, it was a cat with two legs.

Miss. Colonel, don't you love bread and butter with your tea?

Col. Yes, in a morning, miss; for they say butter is gold in a morning, silver at noon, but it is lead at night.

Neverout. Miss, the weather is so hot that my butter melts on my bread.

Lady Answ. Why, butter, I've heard 'em say, is mad twice a year.

Ld. Sparkish. [*To the maid.*] Mrs. Betty, how does your body politic?

Col. Fie, my lord, you'll make Mrs. Betty blush.

Lady Smart. Blush! ay, blush like a blue dog.

Neverout. Pray, Mrs. Betty, are you not Tom Johnson's daughter?

Betty. So my mother tells me, sir.

Ld. Sparkish. But, Mrs. Betty, I hear you are in love.

Betty. My lord, I thank God, I hate nobody; I am in charity with all the world.

Lady Smart. Why, wench, I think thy tongue runs upon wheels this morning. How came you by that scratch upon your nose? Have you been fighting with the cats?

Col. [*To* MISS.] Miss, when will you be married?

Miss. One of these odd-come-shortly's, colonel.

Neverout. Yes, they say the match is half made; the spark is willing, but miss is not.

Miss. I suppose the gentleman has got his own consent for it.

Lady Answ. Pray, my lord, did you walk through the Park in the rain?

Ld. Sparkish. Yes, madam, we were neither sugar nor salt; we were not afraid the rain would melt us. He, he, he! [*Laugh.*]

Col. It rained, and the sun shone at the same time.

Neverout. Why, then, *the devil was beating his wife behind the door with a shoulder of mutton. [*Laugh.*]

Col. A blind man would be glad to see that.

Lady Smart. Mr. Neverout, methinks you stand in your own light.

Neverout. Ah! madam, I have done so all my life.

Ld. Sparkish. I'm sure he sits in mine. Pr'ythee, Tom, sit a little farther; I believe your father was no glazier.

Lady Smart. Miss, dear girl, fill me out a dish of tea, for I'm very lazy.

[MISS *fills a dish of tea, sweetens it, and then tastes it.*]

Lady Smart. What, miss, will you be my taster?

Miss. No, madam; but they say 'tis an ill cook that can't lick her own fingers.

Neverout. Pray, miss, fill me another.

Miss. Will you have it now, or stay till you get it?

Lady Answ. But, colonel, they say you went to court last night very drunk; nay, I'm told for certain you had been among the Philistines: no wonder the cat wink'd when both her eyes were out.

Col. Indeed, madam, that's a lie.

Lady Answ. 'Tis better I should lie than you should lose your good manners: besides, I don't lie; I sit.

Neverout. Oh! faith, colonel, you must own you had a drop in your eye; when I left you, you were half seas over.

Ld. Sparkish. Well, I fear Lady Answerall can't live long; she has so much wit.

Neverout. No, she can't live, that's certain; but she may linger thirty or forty years.

Miss. Live long! ay, longer than a cat or a dog or a better thing.

Lady Answ. Oh! miss, you must give your vardi too!

Ld. Sparkish. Miss, shall I fill you another dish of tea?

Miss. Indeed, my lord, I have drank enough.

Ld. Sparkish. Come, it will do you more good than a month's fasting; here, take it.

Miss. No, I thank your lordship; enough's as good as a feast.

Ld. Sparkish. Well; but if you always say no, you'll never be married.

Lady Answ. Do, my lord, give her a dish; for they say maids will say no, and take it.

Ld. Sparkish. Well; and I dare say miss is a maid in thought, word, and deed.

Neverout. I would not take my oath of that.

Miss. Pray, sir, speak for yourself.

Lady Smart. Fie, miss; they say maids should be seen and not heard.

Lady Answ. Good miss, stir the fire, that the teakettle may boil. — You have done it very well; now it burns purely. Well, miss, you'll have a cheerful husband.

Miss. Indeed, your ladyship could have stirred it much better.

Lady Answ. I know that very well, hussy; but I won't keep a dog and bark myself.

Neverout. What! you are sick, miss.

Miss. Not at all; for her ladyship meant you.

Neverout. Oh! faith, miss, you are in *Lob's pound; get out as you can.

Miss. I won't quarrel with my bread and butter for all that; I know when I'm well.

Lady Answ. Well; but, miss ——

Neverout. Ah! dear madam, let the matter fall; take pity on poor miss; don't throw water on a drowned rat.

Miss. Indeed, Mr. Neverout, you should be cut for the simples this morning; say a word more, and you had as good eat your nails.

Ld. Sparkish. Pray, miss, will you be so good as to favour us with a song?

Miss. Indeed, my lord, I can't, for I have a great cold.

Col. Oh! miss, they say all good singers have colds.

Ld. Sparkish. Pray, madam, does not miss sing very well?

Lady Answ. She sings, as one may say, my lord.

Miss. I hear Mr. Neverout has a very good voice.

Col. Yes, Tom sings well, but his luck's nought.

Neverout. Faith, colonel, you hit yourself a devilish box on the ear.

Col. Miss, will you take a pinch of snuff?

Miss. No, colonel, you must know that *I never take snuff, but when I'm angry.

Lady Answ. Yes, yes, she can take snuff, but she has never a box to put it in.

Miss. Pray, colonel, let me see that box.

Col. Madam, there's never a C upon it.

Miss. Maybe there is, colonel.

Col. Ay, but May bees don't fly now, miss.

Neverout. Colonel, why so hard upon poor miss? Don't set your wit against a child. Miss, give me a blow, and I'll beat him.

Miss. So she prayed me to tell you.

Ld. Sparkish. Pray, my Lady Smart, what kin are you to Lord Pozz?

Lady Smart. Why, his grandmother and mine had four elbows.

Lady Answ. Well, methinks here's a silent meeting. Come, miss, hold up your head, girl; there's money bid for you.

[MISS *starts.*]

Miss. Lord, madam, you frighten me out of my seven senses!

Ld. Sparkish. Well, I must be going.

Lady Answ. I have seen hastier people than you stay all night.

Col. [*To* LADY SMART.] Tom Neverout and I are to leap tomorrow for a guinea.

Miss. I believe, colonel, Mr. Neverout can leap at a crust better than you.

Neverout. Miss, your tongue runs before your wit; nothing can tame you but a husband.

Miss. Peace! I think I hear the church-clock.

Neverout. Why, you know, as the fool thinks ——

Lady Smart. Mr. Neverout, your handkerchief's fallen.

Miss. Let him set his foot on it, that it mayn't fly in his face.

Neverout. Well, miss ——

Miss. Ay, ay; many a one says well that thinks ill.

Neverout. Well, miss, I'll think of this.

Miss. That's rhyme, if you take it in time.

Neverout. What! I see you are a poet.

Miss. Yes, if I had but the wit to show it.

Neverout. Miss, will you be so kind as to fill me a dish of tea?

Miss. Pray, let your betters be served before you; I'm just going to fill one for myself; and, you know, the parson always christens his own child first.

Neverout. But I saw you fill one just now for the colonel; well, I find kissing goes by favour.

Miss. But pray, Mr. Neverout, what lady was that you were talking with in the side-box last Tuesday?

Neverout. Miss, can you keep a secret?

Miss. Yes, I can.

Neverout. Well, miss, and so can I.

Col. Odd-so! I have cut my thumb with this cursed knife!

Lady Answ. Ay; that was your mother's fault, because she only warned you not to cut your fingers.

Lady Smart. No, no; 'tis only fools cut their fingers, but wise folks cut their thumbs.

Miss. I'm sorry for it, but I can't cry.

Col. Don't you think miss is grown?

Lady Answ. Ay, ill weeds grow apace....

[1738]

JOHN ARBUTHNOT

ON MARCH 19, 1711, Swift wrote in the *Journal to Stella*, "The Duke of Argyle is gone; and whether he has my memorial I know not, till I see Dr. Arbuthnot, to whom I gave it. That hard name belongs to a Scotch doctor, an acquaintance of the duke's and me; Stella cannot pronounce it." Whether Stella succeeded in pronouncing the name is uncertain, but Swift himself seems never to have been quite certain whether to accent it on the second syllable, as pronounced in Scotland, or to Anglicize it with the accent on the first syllable.

Dr. John Arbuthnot, when Swift made his acquaintance, shortly before the date of this entry, was Physician in Ordinary to Queen Anne, a Fellow of the Royal Society, and a Fellow of the College of Physicians. His position at court, his staunch Tory politics, and his reputation as a wit made him an important member of the Brothers' Club, to which Swift, as well as other leading Tory statesmen and writers also belonged. Somewhat later was organized the more famous Scriblerus Club, which included Swift, Pope, Arbuthnot, Gay, Parnell, Congreve, and Bishop Atterbury. This brilliant assemblage of wits found a congenial occupation in planning satires upon pedantry and other forms of dullness. The most direct result of their collaboration was the *Memoirs of the Extraordinary Life, Works, and Discoveries of Martinus Scriblerus*, the first and only part of which waited for publication until 1741. Arbuthnot probably wrote most of it, though other members of the club, especially Pope, seem to have had a hand in the composition. *The Art of Sinking in Poetry*, which is closely connected with the *Memoirs*, appears to have been chiefly composed by Pope. The death of Queen Anne in August, 1714, and the downfall of the Tory ministry scattered the members of the Scriblerus Club and suspended its activities, but the projects there discussed found later expression in parts of *The Dunciad* as well as in *Gulliver's Travels*, which seems to have been projected as the travels of Martin.

In addition to medical and other scientific treatises and his part in the comedy, *Three Hours after Marriage*, in which he collaborated with Pope and Gay, Arbuthnot is the reputed author of a number of satirical pamphlets, which were published anonymously, and in some cases have been attributed to others. By far the most important of these, *The History of John Bull*, has frequently been assigned to Swift. Dr. Teerink has recently examined the evidence in detail, and come to the conclusion that Swift worked out an idea that Arbuthnot had originated. He has, therefore, ascribed the authorship, though not the actual writing, to the latter. In vigour and directness of execution the work is worthy of Swift, though the satire is less scathing and the wit less mordant than might be expected from him.

The work originally appeared in five parts between February and July, 1712: *Law is a Bottomless-Pit, John Bull in his Senses, John Bull still in his Senses, An Appendix to John Bull still in his Senses, Lewis Baboon turned Honest and John Bull Politician*. Its purpose was political, to present the Tory opposition to the War of the Spanish Succession and to create sentiment in favour of those proposals for peace which were incorporated the next year into the Treaty of Utrecht. It was Arbuthnot's fortune so to impress upon his readers the name and character of John Bull that this stout, ruddy-faced, choleric, obstinate, simple-minded fellow has ever since been accepted as representative of the English nation. In so doing he contributed not only to the cause for which he wrote immediately, but he exerted an enduring influence upon the future. The figure of John Bull has not only maintained its hold upon the popular mind, but has helped to affect the English national character at home, and to determine the attitude toward it abroad.

THE HISTORY OF JOHN BULL

From PART I

CHAPTER I

The Occasion of the Law Suit.

I need not tell you of the great quarrels that happened in our neighbourhood since the death of * the late Lord Strutt; how * the parson and a cunning attorney got him to settle his estate upon * his cousin, Philip Baboon, to the great disappointment of * his cousin Esquire South. Some stick not to say that the parson and the attorney forged a will, for which they were well paid by the family of the Baboons; let that be as it will, it is matter of fact that the honour and estate have continued ever since in the person of Philip Baboon.

You know that the Lord Strutts have for many years been possessed of a very great landed estate, well conditioned, wooded, watered, with coal, salt, tin, copper, iron, &c., all within themselves; that it has been the misfortune of that family to be the property of their stewards, tradesmen, and inferior servants, which has brought great incumbrances upon them; at the same time, their not abating of their expensive way of

* Notes on John Arbuthnot will be found in the Appendix, pp. 998 ff.

living has forced them to mortgage their best manors. It is credibly reported that the butcher's and baker's bill of a Lord Strutt that lived two hundred years ago are not yet paid.

When Philip Baboon came first to the possession of the Lord Strutt's estate, his tradesmen, as is usual upon such occasions, waited upon him to wish him joy and bespeak his custom. The two chief were * John Bull, the clothier, and *Nic. Frog, the linen-draper: they told him that the Bulls and Frogs had served the Lord Strutts with draperyware for many years; that they were honest and fair dealers; that their bills had never been questioned; that the Lord Strutts lived generously, and never used to dirty their fingers with pen, ink, and counters; that his lordship might depend upon their honesty; that they would use him as kindly as they had done his predecessors. The young lord seemed to take all in good part, and dismissed them with a deal of seeming content, assuring them he did not intend to change any of the honourable maxims of his predecessors.

CHAPTER II

How Bull and Frog grew jealous that the Lord Strutt intended to give all his custom to his grandfather, *Lewis Baboon.

It happened, unfortunately for the peace of our neighbourhood, that this young lord had an old cunning rogue, or (as the Scots call it) a false loon of a grandfather, that one might justly call a Jack-of-all-Trades; sometimes you would see him behind his counter selling broadcloth, sometimes measuring linen; next day he would be dealing in merceryware; high-heads, ribbons, gloves, fans, and lace he understood to a nicety. * Charles Mather could not bubble a young beau better with a toy; nay, he would descend even to the selling of tape, garters, and shoe-buckles; when shop was shut up, he would go about the neighbourhood and earn half a crown by teaching the young men and maids to dance. By these methods he had acquired immense riches, which he used to squander away at back-sword, quarter-staff, and cudgel-play, in which he took great pleasure, and challenged all the country. You will say it is no wonder if Bull and Frog should be jealous of this fellow. "It is not impossible," says Frog to Bull, "but this old rogue will take the management of the young lord's business into his hands; besides, the rascal has good ware, and will serve him as cheap as anybody. In that case I leave you to judge what must become of us and our families; we must starve, or turn journeyman to old Lewis Baboon. Therefore, neighbour, I hold it advisable that we write to young Lord Strutt to know the bottom of this matter."

CHAPTER III

A Copy of Bull and Frog's Letter to Lord Strutt.

My Lord, — I suppose your lordship knows that the Bulls and the Frogs have served the Lord Strutts with all sorts of draperyware time out of mind. And whereas we are jealous, not without reason, that your lordship intends henceforth to buy of your grandsire, old Lewis Baboon, this is to inform your lordship that this proceeding does not suit with the circumstances of our families, who have lived and made a good figure in the world by the generosity of the Lord Strutts. Therefore we think fit to acquaint your lordship that you must find sufficient security to us, our heirs and assigns, that you will not employ Lewis Baboon; or else we will take our remedy at law, clap an action upon you of £20,000 for old debts, seize and distrain your goods and chattels, which, considering your lordship's circumstances, will plunge you into difficulties, from which it will not be easy to extricate yourself; therefore we hope, when your lordship has better considered on it, you will comply with the desire of

Your loving friends,

John Bull,
Nic. Frog.

Some of Bull's friends advised him to take gentler methods with the young lord, but John naturally loved rough play. It is impossible to express the surprise of the Lord Strutt upon the receipt of this letter. He was not flush in ready, either to go to law or clear old debts; neither could he find good bail: he offered to bring matters to a friendly accommodation; and promised, upon his word of honour, that he would not change his drapers; but all to no purpose, for Bull and Frog saw clearly that old Lewis would have the cheating of him.

CHAPTER IV

How Bull and Frog went to Law with Lord Strutt about the Premises, and were Joined by the Rest of the Tradesmen.

All endeavours of accommodation between Lord Strutt and his drapers proved vain;

jealousies increased, and, indeed, it was rumoured abroad that Lord Strutt had bespoke his new liveries of old Lewis Baboon. This *coming to Mrs. Bull's ears, when John Bull came home, he found all his family in an uproar. Mrs. Bull, you must know, was very apt to be choleric. "You sot," says she, "you loiter about alehouses and taverns, spend your time at billiards, ninepins, or puppet-shows, or flaunt about the streets in your new gilt chariot, never minding me nor your numerous family. Don't you hear how Lord Strutt has bespoke his liveries at Lewis Baboon's shop? Don't you see how that old fox steals away your customers, and turns you out of your business every day, and you sit like an idle drone, with your hands in your pockets? Fie upon it! Up man, rouse thyself; I'll sell to my shift before I'll be so used by that knave." You must think Mrs. Bull had been pretty well tuned up by Frog, who chimed in with her learned harangue. No further delay now, but to counsel learned in the law they go, who unanimously assured them both of the justice and infallible success of *their lawsuit.

I told you before that old Lewis Baboon was a sort of a Jack-of-all-trades, which made the rest of the tradesmen jealous, as well as Bull and Frog; they, hearing of the quarrel, were glad of an opportunity of joining against old Lewis Baboon, provided that Bull and Frog would bear the charges of the suit. Even *lying Ned, the chimney-sweeper of Savoy, and *Tom, the Portugal dustman, put in their claims, and the cause was put into the hands of *Humphry Hocus, the attorney.

A declaration was drawn up to show "that Bull and Frog had undoubted right by prescription to be drapers to the Lord Strutts; that there were several old contracts to that purpose; that Lewis Baboon had taken up the trade of clothier and draper without serving his time or purchasing his freedom; that he sold goods that were not marketable, without the stamp; that he himself was more fit for a bully than a tradesman, and went about through all the country fairs challenging people to fight prizes, wrestling and cudgel play"; and abundance more to this purpose.

CHAPTER V

The True Character of John Bull, Nic. Frog, and Hocus.

For the better understanding the following history the reader ought to know that Bull, in the main, was an honest, plain-dealing fellow, choleric, bold, and of a very unconstant temper; he dreaded not old Lewis either at back-sword, single falchion, or cudgel-play; but then he was very apt to quarrel with his best friends, especially if they pretended to govern him: if you flattered him, you might lead him like a child. John's temper depended very much upon the air; his spirits rose and fell with the weather-glass. John was quick and understood his business very well; but no man alive was more careless in looking into his accounts, or more cheated by partners, apprentices, and servants. This was occasioned by his being a boon companion, loving his bottle and his diversion; for, to say truth, no man kept a better house than John, nor spent his money more generously. By plain and fair dealing John had acquired some plums, and might have kept them, had it not been for his unhappy lawsuit.

Nic. Frog was a cunning, sly whoreson, quite the reverse of John in many particulars; covetous, frugal; minded domestic affairs; would pinch his belly to save his pocket; never lost a farthing by careless servants or bad debtors. He did not care much for any sort of diversions, except tricks of High German artists and legerdemain: no man exceeded Nic. in these; yet it must be owned that Nic. was a fair dealer, and in that way acquired immense riches.

Hocus was an old, cunning attorney; and, though this was the first considerable suit that ever he was engaged in, he showed himself superior in address to most of his profession. He kept always good clerks, he loved money, was smooth-tongued, gave good words, and seldom lost his temper. He was not worse than an infidel, for he provided plentifully for his family; but he loved himself better than them all. The neighbours reported that he was henpecked, which was impossible by such a mild-spirited woman as his wife was.

CHAPTER VI

Of the Various Success of the Lawsuit.

Law is a bottomless pit; it is a cormorant, a harpy that devours everything. John Bull was flattered by the lawyers that his suit would not last above a year or two at most, that before that time he would be in quiet possession of his business; yet ten long years did Hocus steer his cause through all the meanders of the law and all the courts. No skill, no address was wanting; and, to say truth, John did not starve his cause; there wanted not yellowboys to fee counsel, hire witnesses, and bribe juries: Lord Strutt was generally cast, never had one verdict in his favour; and John was promised that the next, and the next, would be the final determination; but, alas! that final determination and happy conclusion was like an enchanted island; the nearer John came to it, the further it went from him: new trials upon new points still arose; new doubts, new matters to be cleared; in short, lawyers seldom part with so good a cause till they have got the oyster, and their clients the shell. John's ready money, book-debts, bonds, mortgages, all went into the lawyers' pockets; then John began to borrow money upon bank stock and East India bonds; now and then a farm went to pot; at last it was thought a good expedient to set up Esquire South's title, to prove the will forged, and dispossess Philip Lord Strutt at once. Here again was a new field for the lawyers, and the cause grew more intricate than ever. John grew madder and madder; wherever he met any of Lord Strutt's servants, he tore off their clothes; now and then you would see them come home naked, without shoes, stockings, and linen. As for old Lewis Baboon, he was reduced to his last shirt, though he had as many as any other; his children were reduced from rich silks to *Doily stuffs, his servants in rags, and barefooted; instead of good victuals they now lived upon neck beef and bullock's liver; in short, nobody got much by the matter but the men of law.

CHAPTER VII

How John Bull was so Mightily Pleased with his Success that he was going to Leave off his Trade and turn Lawyer.

It is wisely observed by a great philosopher that habit is a second nature; this was verified in the case of John Bull, who, from an honest and plain tradesman, had got such a haunt about the courts of justice, and such a jargon of law words that he concluded himself as able a lawyer as any that pleaded at the bar, or sat on the bench. He was overheard one day talking to himself after this manner: "How capriciously does fate or chance dispose of mankind? How seldom is that business allotted to a man for which he is fitted by nature? It is plain I was intended for a man of law; how did my guardians mistake my genius in placing me, like a mean slave, behind a counter? Bless me, what immense estates these fellows raise by the law! Besides, it is the profession of a gentleman. What a pleasure is it to be victorious in a cause, to swagger at the bar! What a fool am I to drudge any more in this woollen trade! For a lawyer I was born, and a lawyer I will be; one is never too old to learn." All this while John had conned over such a catalogue of hard words as were enough to conjure up the devil; these he used to babble indifferently in all companies, especially at coffee-houses, so that his neighbour tradesmen began to shun his company as a man that was cracked. Instead of the affairs at *Blackwell Hall and price of broadcloth, wool, and baizes, he talks of nothing but actions upon the case, returns, capias, alias capias, demurrers, *venire facias*, replevins, *supersedeases*, certioraris, writs of error, actions of trover and conversion, trespasses, *precipes*, and *dedimus*. This was matter of jest to the learned in law; however, Hocus and the rest of the tribe encouraged John in his fancy, assuring him that he had a great genius for law; that they questioned not but in time he might raise money enough by it to reimburse him all his charges; that, if he studied, he would undoubtedly arrive to the dignity of a Lord Chief Justice: as for the advice of honest friends and neighbours, John despised it; he looked upon them as fellows of a low genius, poor grovelling mechanics; John reckoned it more honour to have got one favourable verdict than to have sold a bale of broadcloth. As for Nic. Frog, to say the truth, he was more prudent; for, though he followed his lawsuit closely, he neglected not his ordinary business, but was both in court and in his shop at the proper hours.

CHAPTER VIII

How John Discovered that Hocus had an Intrigue with his Wife; and what Followed thereupon.

John had not run on a-madding so long, had it not been for an extravagant bitch of a wife, whom Hocus perceiving John to be fond of, was resolved to win over to his side. It is a true saying that the last man of the parish that knows of his cuckoldom is himself. It was observed by all the neighbourhood that *Hocus had dealings with John's wife that were not so much for his honour; but this was perceived by John a little too late. She was a luxurious jade, loved splendid equipages, plays, treats, and balls, differing very much from the sober manners of her ancestors, and by no means fit for a tradesman's wife. Hocus fed her extravagancy (what was still more shameful) with John's own money. Everybody said that Hocus had a month's mind to her body; be that as it will, it is matter of fact that upon all occasions she ran out extravagantly on the praise of Hocus. When John used to be finding fault with his bills, she used to reproach him as ungrateful to his greatest benefactor, one that had taken so much pains in his lawsuit, and retrieved his family from the oppression of old Lewis Baboon. A good swingeing sum of John's readiest cash went towards building of *Hocus's country-house. This affair between Hocus and Mrs. Bull was now so open that all the world were scandalised at it; John was not so clodpated, but at last he took the hint. *The parson of the parish preaching one day with more zeal than sense against adultery, Mrs. Bull told her husband that he was a very uncivil fellow to use such coarse language before people of condition; that Hocus was of the same mind, and that they would join to have him turned out of his living for using personal reflections. "How do you mean," says John, "by personal reflections? I hope in God, wife, he did not reflect upon you?" "No, thank God, my reputation is too well established in the world to receive any hurt from such a foul-mouthed scoundrel as he; his doctrine tends only to make husbands tyrants, and wives slaves; must we be shut up, and husbands left to their liberty? Very pretty indeed! a wife must never go abroad with a Platonic to see a play or a ball; she must never stir without her husband; nor walk in Spring Garden with a cousin. I do say, husband, and I will stand by it, that without the innocent freedoms of life, matrimony would be a most intolerable state; and that a wife's virtue ought to be the result of her own reason, and not of her husband's government: for my part, I would scorn a husband that would be jealous, if he saw a fellow abed with me." All this while John's blood boiled in his veins: he was now confirmed in all his suspicions; jade, bitch, and whore, were the best words that John gave her. Things went from better to worse, till Mrs. Bull aimed a knife at John, though John threw a bottle at her head very brutally indeed; and after this there was nothing but confusion; bottles, glasses, spoons, plates, knives, forks, and dishes flew about like dust; the result of which was that Mrs. Bull received a bruise in her right side of which she died half a year after. The bruise imposthumated, and afterwards turned to a stinking ulcer, which made everybody shy to come near her; yet she wanted not the help of many able physicians, who attended very diligently, and did what men of skill could do; but all to no purpose, for her condition was now quite desperate, all regular physicians and her nearest relations having given her over.

CHAPTER IX

How some Quacks Undertook to Cure Mrs. Bull of her Ulcer.

There is nothing so impossible in nature, but mountebanks will undertake; nothing so incredible, but they will affirm: Mrs. Bull's condition was looked upon as desperate by all the men of art; but there were those that bragged they had an infallible ointment and plaster, which, being applied to the sore, would cure it in a few days; at the same time they would give her a pill that would purge off all her bad humours, sweeten her blood, and rectify her disturbed imagination. In spite of all applications, the patient grew worse every day; she stunk so, nobody durst come within a stone's throw of her, except those quacks who attended her close, and apprehended no danger. If one asked them how Mrs. Bull did, "Better and better," said they; "the parts heal, and her constitution mends; if she submits to our government, she will be abroad in a little time." Nay, it is reported that they wrote to her friends in the country that she would dance a jig next October in Westminster Hall, and that her illness had been chiefly owing to bad physicians. At last, one of them was sent for in great haste; his patient grew worse and worse: when he came, he affirmed that it was a gross mistake, and that she was never in a fairer way, "Bring hither the salve," says he, "and give a plentiful draught of my cordial." As he was applying his ointments and administering the cordial, the patient gave up the ghost, to the great confusion of the quack, and the great joy of Bull and his friends. The quack flung away out of the house in great disorder, and swore there was foul play, for he was sure his medicines were infallible. Mrs. Bull having died without any signs of repentance or devotion, the clergy would hardly allow her a Christian burial. The relations had once resolved to sue John for the murder, but considering better of it, and that such a trial would rip up old sores, and discover things not so much to the reputation of the deceased, they dropped their design. She left no will, only there was found in her strong box the following words wrote on a scrip of paper, "My curse on John Bull and all my posterity, if ever they come to any composition with the Lord Strutt."

She left him three daughters, whose names were * Polemia, Discordia, and Usuria.

CHAPTER X

Of *John Bull's Second Wife, and the good Advice that she Gave Him.

John quickly got the better of his grief, and, seeing that neither his constitution nor the affairs of his family could permit him to live in an unmarried state, he resolved to get him another wife; a cousin of his last wife's was proposed, but John would have no more of the breed: in short, he wedded a sober country gentlewoman, of a good family and a plentiful fortune, the reverse of the other in her temper; not but that she loved money, for she was saving, and applied her fortune to pay John's clamorous debts, that the unfrugal methods of his last wife, and this ruinous lawsuit had brought him into. One day, as she had got her husband in a good humour, she talked to him after the following manner: "My dear, since I have been your wife, I have observed great abuses and disorders in your family; your servants are mutinous and quarrelsome, and cheat you most abominably; your cookmaid is in a combination with your butcher, poulterer, and fishmonger; your butler purloins your liquor, and the brewer sells you hogwash; your baker cheats both in weight and in tale; even your milkwoman and your nursery-maid have a fellow feeling; your tailor, instead of shreds, cabbages whole yards of cloth; besides, leaving such long scores, and not going to market with ready money forces us to take bad ware of the tradesmen at their own price. You have not posted your books these ten years; how is it possible for a man of business to keep his affairs even in the world at this rate? Pray God this Hocus be honest; would to God you would look over his bills, and see how matters stand between Frog and you; prodigious sums are spent in this lawsuit, and more must be borrowed of scriveners and usurers at heavy interest. Besides, my dear, let me beg of you to lay aside that wild project of leaving your business to turn lawyer, for which, let me tell you, nature never designed you. Believe me, these rogues do but flatter, that they may pick your pocket; observe what a parcel of hungry, ragged fellows live by your cause; to be sure they will never make an end on it. I foresee this haunt you have got about the courts will one day or other bring your family to beggary. Consider, my dear, how indecent it is to abandon your shop and follow pettifoggers; the habit is so strong upon you that there is hardly a plea between two country esquires, about a barren acre upon a common, but you draw yourself in as bail, surety, or solicitor." John heard her all this while with patience, till she pricked his maggot, and touched him in the tender point. Then he broke out into a violent passion: "What, I not fit for a lawyer? let me tell you, my clodpated relations spoiled the greatest genius in the world when they bred me a mechanic. Lord Strutt and his old rogue of a grandsire have found to their cost that I can manage a lawsuit as well as another." "I don't deny what you say," says Mrs. Bull; "nor do I call in question your parts; but I say it does not suit with your circumstances: you and your predecessors have lived in good reputation among your neighbours by this same clothing-trade, and it were madness to leave it off. Besides, there are few that know all the tricks and cheats of these lawyers; does not your own experience teach you how they have drawn you on from one term to another, and how you have danced the round of all the courts, still flattering you with a final issue; and, for aught I can see, your cause is not a bit clearer than it was seven years ago?" "I will be damned," says John, "if I accept of any composition from Strutt or his grandfather; I'll rather wheel about the streets an engine to grind knives and scissors; however, I'll take your advice, and look over my accounts."

CHAPTER XI

How John Looked over his Attorney's Bill.

When John first brought out the bills, the surprise of all the family was inexpressible at the prodigious dimensions of them; they would have measured with the best bale of cloth in John's shop. Fees to judges, puisnijudges, clerks, prothonotaries, filacers, chirographers, under-clerks, proclamators, counsel, witnesses, jurymen, marshals, tipstaffs, criers, porters; for enrollings, exemplifications, bails, vouchers, returns, caveats, examinations, filings of writs, entries, declarations, replications, recordats, *nolle prosequis*, *certioraris*, mittimuses, demurrers, special verdicts, informations, *scire facias*, *supersedeas*, *habeas corpus*, coach-hire, treating of witnesses, &c. "Verily," says John, "there are a prodigious number of learned words in this law; what a pretty science it is!" "Ay but, husband, you have paid for every syllable and letter of these fine words; bless me, what immense sums are at the bottom of the account!" John spent several weeks in looking over his bills, and, by comparing and stating his accounts, he discovered that, besides the extravagance of every article, he had been egregiously cheated; that he had paid for counsel that were never feed, for writs that were never drawn, for dinners that were never dressed, and journeys that were never made: in short, that the tradesmen, lawyers, and Frog had agreed to throw the burden of the lawsuit upon his shoulders.

CHAPTER XII

How John Grew Angry, and Resolved to Accept a Composition; and what Methods were Practised by the Lawyers for Keeping Him from it.

Well might the learned * Daniel Burgess say that a lawsuit is a suit for life. He that sows his grain upon marble will have many a hungry belly before harvest. This John felt by woeful experience. John's cause was a good milch cow, and many a man subsisted his family out of it. However, John began to think it high time to look about him. He had a cousin in the country, one * Sir Roger Bold, whose predecessors had been bred up to the law, and knew as much of it as anybody; but, having left off the profession for some time, they took great pleasure in compounding lawsuits among their neighbours, for which they were the aversion of the gentlemen of the long robe, and at perpetual war with all the country attorneys. John put his cause in Sir Roger's hands, desiring him to make the best of it; the news had no sooner reached the ears of the lawyers, but they were all in an uproar. They brought all the rest of the tradesmen upon John: Squire South swore he was betrayed, that he would starve before he compounded; Frog said he was highly wronged; even lying Ned, the chimney-sweeper, and Tom, the dustman, complained that their interest was sacrificed. The lawyers, solicitors, Hocus and his clerks, were all up in arms at the news of the composition; they abused him and his wife most shamefully. "You silly, awkward, ill-bred country sow," quoth one, "have you no more manners than to rail at Hocus, that has saved that clodpated, numskulled ninnyhammer of yours from ruin, and all his family? It is well known how he has rose early and sat up late to make him easy, when he was sotting at every alehouse in town. I knew his last wife; she was a woman of breeding, good humour, and complaisance — knew how to live in the world: as for you, you look like a puppet moved by clockwork; your clothes hang upon you as they were upon tenterhooks; and you come into a room as if you were going to steal away a piss-pot: get you gone into the country to look after your mother's poultry, to milk the cows, churn the butter, and dress up nosegays for a holiday, and not meddle with matters which you know no more of than the sign-post before your door. It is well known that Hocus had an established reputation; he never swore an oath, nor told a lie in all his life; he is grateful to his benefactors, faithful to his friends, liberal to his dependents, and dutiful to his superiors; he values not your money more than the dust under his feet, but he hates to be abused. Once for all, Mrs. Minx, leave off talking of Hocus, or I will pull out those saucer-eyes of yours, and make that redstreak country face look as raw as an ox-cheek upon a butcher's stall; remember, I say, that there are pillories and ducking-stools." With this away they flung, leaving Mrs. Bull no time to reply. No stone was left unturned to fright John from his composition: sometimes they spread reports at coffee-houses that John and his wife were run mad; that they intended to give up house, and make over all their estate to Lewis Baboon; that John had been often heard talking to himself, and seen in the streets without shoes or stockings; that he did nothing from morning till night but beat his servants, after having been the best master alive; as for his wife, she was a mere natural. Sometimes John's house was beset with a whole regiment of attorneys' clerks, bailiffs, and bailiffs' followers, and other small retainers of the law, who threw stones at his windows, and dirt at himself as he went along the street. When John complained of want of ready money to carry on his suit, they advised him to pawn his plate and jewels, and that * Mrs. Bull should sell her linen and wearing-clothes....

[1712, 1727]

JAMES THOMSON

James Thomson was born in Scotland in 1700, the son of a minister, and was educated at Edinburgh. When twenty-five he went to London with the manuscript of *Winter*, intending to enter the Church, but introductions to the circle of Pope turned him toward literature. For some years he served as tutor to the sons of noblemen, publishing *Winter* in 1726, *Summer* in 1727, *Spring* in 1728, and the completed *Seasons*, including *Autumn*, in 1730. Throughout his active life he also wrote, with moderate success, for the stage. Assiduous cultivation of patrons brought him certain small sinecures, but he was usually poor and in debt. *Liberty*, a laborious blank-verse poem in which the preacher almost silenced the poet, appeared in 1736. From that year to the end of his life he lived at Richmond, near Pope and Horace Walpole, in a rather sleepy retirement. At about the same time he began *The Castle of Indolence*, which was not finished until 1748, the year of his death.

Thomson was a man of easy-going nature who quarrelled with no one and tried to adopt every man's opinions. Inclusive and sympathetic rather than critical, his thought never attained self-consistency, yet for that reason it was the more open to the ideas, hopes, and modes of feeling current at the time. Even in his style and verse he tried to ride two horses. His natural gift lay in a delicate realism like that of his famous passage about the redbreast, but this the southern poets and critics taught him to overlay and obscure with the generality which almost ruins *Liberty* and enfeebles later versions of *The Seasons*. In his blank verse his attempt to mingle the artificial diction and balanced epithets of Pope with the sonorous periods of Milton often results in mere pomposity. Yet even his blank verse has many passages — ornate and studied, to be sure, like Handel's oratorios — of true nobility and grandeur, and the man who wrote *The Castle of Indolence* was clearly one of the few adept versifiers of his century.

Some patience is required to discern, beneath the banal conventionality of Thomson's usual style, that directness of vision and thrilling delight in nature which he never wholly lost; but it is matter of history that these qualities of his were discerned by several generations of readers, European as well as English, and that they produced important results. Without intending it, Thomson gave the most emphatic answer to Pope's too restricting assertion, "the proper study of mankind is man," by showing that there is "no subject more elevating, more amusing, more ready to awake the poetical enthusiasm, the philosophical reflection, and the moral sentiment, than the works of nature." These words, taken from the Preface to the second edition of *Winter*, might have been written by Wordsworth, by Herder, or by Lamartine, but there was only one man who could have written them in 1726. At wide intervals in the poetry of Thomson, moreover, we come upon sudden gleams of pure magic — it may be a glamorous stanza of *The Castle* in which sound and sense are perfectly united or such a mere phrase of blank verse as that in which the whales of the Arctic are said to "tempest the loosened brine," or, more probably, in *A Hymn*, which Keats himself could not have bettered:

> "ye harvests, wave to him —
> Breathe your still song into the reaper's heart
> As home he goes beneath the joyous moon."

Such things as these show clearly enough that just when the supreme work of Pope, unsurpassable in its kind, was closing one epoch of English poetry, another epoch was opening. Yet there was nothing revolutionary or even innovating in Thomson's work. He only brought the poetry of England back somewhat closer to its main and natural channel.

WINTER

With the first edition of *Winter*, published when he was twenty-six, Thomson made his reputation. During the twenty years that followed he altered the poem in many ways, as he did also the other three "Seasons," enlarging it from 787 to 1069 lines by several digressions and amplifications which are not always improvements. The text here given is that of 1746, modernized in spelling.

See, Winter comes to rule the varied year,
Sullen and sad, with all his rising train —
Vapours, and clouds, and storms. Be these my theme;
These, that exalt the soul to solemn thought
And heavenly musing. Welcome, kindred glooms!
Congenial*horrors, hail! With frequent foot.

* Notes on James Thomson will be found in the Appendix, pp. 999 ff.

Pleased have I, in my cheerful morn of life,
When nursed by careless solitude I lived
And sung of nature with unceasing joy,
Pleased have I wandered through your rough domain;
Trod the pure virgin-snows, myself as pure;
Heard the winds roar, and the big torrent burst;
Or seen the deep-fermenting tempest brewed
In the grim evening-sky. Thus passed the time,
Till through the lucid chambers of the south
Looked out the joyous Spring — looked out and smiled.

To thee, the patron of this first *essay,
The Muse, O Wilmington! renews her song.
Since has she rounded the revolving year;
Skimm'd the gay spring; on eagle-pinions borne,
Attempted through the summer blaze to rise;
Then swept o'er autumn with the shadowy gale.
And now among the wintry clouds again,
Rolled in the doubling storm, she tries to soar,
To swell her note with all the rushing winds,
To suit her sounding cadence to the floods —
As is her theme, her numbers wildly great.
Thrice happy, could she fill thy judging ear
With bold description and with manly thought!
Nor art thou skilled in awful schemes alone,
And how to make a mighty people thrive;
But equal goodness, sound integrity,
A firm, unshaken, uncorrupted soul
Amid a sliding age, and burning strong,
Not vainly blazing, for thy country's weal,
A steady spirit, regularly free —
These, each exalting each, the statesman light
Into the patriot; these the public hope
And eye to thee converting, bid the Muse
Record what envy dares not flattery call.

Now when the cheerless empire of the sky
To Capricorn the Centaur-Archer yields,
And fierce Aquarius stains the inverted *year —
Hung o'er the farthest verge of heaven, the sun
Scarce spreads o'er ether the dejected day.
Faint are his gleams, and ineffectual shoot
His struggling rays in horizontal lines
Through the thick air, as, clothed in cloudy storm,
Weak, wan, and broad, he skirts the southern sky,
And, soon descending, to the long dark night,
Wide-shading all, the prostrate world resigns.
Nor is the night unwished, while vital heat,
Light, life, and joy the dubious day forsake.
Meantime, in sable cincture, shadows vast,
Deep-tinged and damp, and congregated clouds,
And all the vapoury turbulence of heaven
Involve the face of things. Thus winter falls,
A heavy gloom oppressive o'er the world,
Through nature shedding influence malign,
And rouses up the seeds of dark disease.
The soul of man dies in him, loathing life,
And black with more than melancholy views.
The cattle droop; and o'er the furrowed land,
Fresh from the plough, the dun discoloured flocks,
Untended spreading, crop the wholesome *root.
Along the woods, along the moorish fens,
Sighs the sad genius of the coming storm;
And up among the loose disjointed cliffs
And fractured mountains wild, the brawling brook
And cave, presageful, send a hollow moan,
Resounding long in listening fancy's ear.

Then comes the father of the tempest forth,
Wrapped in black glooms. First, joyless rains obscure
Drive through the mingling skies with vapour foul,
Dash on the mountain's brow, and shake the woods
That grumbling wave below. The unsightly plain
Lies a brown deluge, as the low-bent clouds
Pour flood on flood, yet unexhausted still
Combine, and, deepening into night, shut up
The day's fair face. The wanderers of heaven,
Each to his home, retire, save those that love
To take their pastime in the troubled air,
Or skimming flutter round the dimply pool.
The cattle from the untasted fields return
And ask, with meaning low, their wonted stalls,
Or ruminate in the contiguous shade.
Thither the household feathery people crowd —
The crested cock with all his female train,
Pensive and dripping; while the cottage-hind
Hangs o'er the enlivening blaze, and taleful there
Recounts his simple frolic. Much he talks,
And much he laughs, nor recks the storm that blows
Without, and rattles on his humble roof.

Wide o'er the brim, with many a torrent swelled
And the mixed ruin of its banks o'erspread,
At last, the roused-up river pours along.
Resistless, roaring, dreadful, down it comes,
From the rude mountain and the mossy wild
Tumbling through rocks abrupt, and sounding far;
Then o'er the sanded valley floating spreads,
Calm, sluggish, silent; till again, constrained
Between two meeting hills, it bursts a way
Where rocks and woods o'erhang the turbid stream;
There, gathering triple force, rapid and deep,
It boils, and wheels, and foams, and thunders through.

Nature! great parent! whose unceasing hand
Rolls round the seasons of the changeful year,
How mighty, how majestic are thy works!
With what a pleasing dread they swell the soul,
That sees astonished, and astonished sings!
Ye too, ye winds! that now begin to blow
With boisterous sweep, I raise my voice to you.
Where are your stores, ye powerful beings! say,
Where your aërial magazines reserved
To swell the brooding terrors of the storm?
In what far-distant region of the sky,
Hushed in deep silence, sleep you when 'tis calm?

When from the pallid sky the sun descends,
With many a spot that o'er his glaring orb
Uncertain wanders, stained, red fiery streaks
Begin to flush around. The reeling clouds
Stagger with dizzy poise, as doubting yet
Which master to obey; while, rising slow,
Blank in the leaden-coloured east, the moon
Wears a wan circle round her blunted horns.
Seen through the turbid, fluctuating air,
The stars obtuse emit a shivering ray;
Or frequent seem to shoot athwart the gloom,
And long behind them trail the whitening blaze.
Snatched in short eddies, plays the withered leaf,
And on the flood the dancing feather floats.
With broadened nostrils to the sky upturned,
The conscious heifer snuffs the stormy gale,
Even as the matron, at her nightly task,
With pensive labour draws the flaxen thread,
The wasted taper and the crackling flame
Foretell the blast. But chief the plumy race,
The tenants of the sky, its changes speak.
Retiring from the * downs where all day long
They picked their scanty fare, a blackening train
Of clamorous rooks thick-urge their weary flight,
And seek the closing shelter of the grove.
Assiduous, in his bower, the wailing owl
Plies his sad song. The * cormorant on high
Wheels from the deep, and screams along the land.
Loud shrieks the soaring * hern; and with wild wing
The circling sea-fowl cleave the flaky clouds.
Ocean, unequal pressed, with broken tide
And blind commotion heaves; while from the shore,
* Eat into caverns by the restless wave,
And forest-rustling mountain comes a voice
That, solemn-sounding, bids the world prepare.
Then issues forth the storm with sudden burst,
And hurls the whole precipitated air
Down in a torrent. On the passive main
Descends the ethereal force, and with strong gust
Turns from its bottom the discoloured deep.
Through the black night that sits immense around,
Lashed into foam, the fierce-conflicting brine
Seems o'er a thousand raging waves to burn.
Meantime the mountain-billows, to the clouds
In dreadful tumult swelled, surge above surge,
Burst into chaos with tremendous roar,
And anchored navies from their stations drive
Wild as the winds, across the howling waste
Of mighty waters: now the inflated wave
Straining they scale, and now impetuous shoot
Into the secret chambers of the deep,
The wintry Baltic thundering o'er their head.
Emerging thence again, before the breath
Of full-exerted heaven they wing their course.
And dart on distant coasts — if some sharp rock
Or shoal insidious break not their career,
And in loose fragments fling them floating * round.

Nor less at land the loosened tempest reigns
The mountain thunders, and its sturdy sons
Stoop to the bottom of the rocks they shade
Lone on the midnight steep, and all aghast,
The dark wayfaring stranger breathless toils,
And, often falling, climbs against the blast.
Low waves the rooted forest, vexed, and sheds
What of its tarnished honours yet remain —

Dashed down and scattered, by the tearing wind's
Assiduous fury, its gigantic limbs.
Thus, struggling through the dissipated grove,
The whirling tempest raves along the plain,
And, on the cottage thatched or lordly roof
Keen-fastening, shakes them to the solid base.
Sleep, frighted, flies; and round the rocking *dome,
For entrance eager, howls the savage blast.
Then too, they say, through all the burdened air
Long groans are heard, shrill sounds, and distant sighs,
That, uttered by the demon of the night,
Warn the *devoted wretch of woe and death.
 Huge uproar lords it wide. The clouds, commixed
With stars swift-gliding, sweep along the sky.
All nature reels: till nature's King, who oft
Amid tempestuous darkness dwells alone,
And on the wings of the careering wind
Walks dreadfully serene, commands a calm;
Then straight air, sea, and earth are hushed at once.
 As yet 'tis midnight deep. The weary clouds,
Slow-meeting, mingle into solid gloom.
Now, while the drowsy world lies lost in sleep,
Let me associate with the serious Night
And Contemplation, her sedate compeer;
Let me shake off the intrusive cares of day,
And lay the meddling senses all *aside.
 Where now, ye lying vanities of life!
Ye ever-tempting, ever-cheating train!
Where are you now? and what is your amount?
Vexation, disappointment, and remorse.
Sad, sickening thought! and yet deluded man,
A scene of crude disjointed visions past,
And broken slumbers, rises still resolved,
With new-flushed hopes, to run the giddy round.
 Father of light and life! thou Good Supreme!
O teach me what is good! teach me thyself!
Save me from folly, vanity, and vice,
From every low pursuit; and feed my soul
With knowledge, conscious peace, and virtue pure —
Sacred, substantial, never-fading bliss!
 The keener tempests come: and, fuming dun
From all the livid east or piercing north,
Thick clouds ascend, in whose capacious womb
A vapoury deluge lies, to snow congealed.
Heavy they roll their fleecy world along,
And the sky saddens with the gathered storm.
Through the hushed air the whitening shower descends,
At first thin-wavering; till at last the flakes
Fall broad and wide and fast, dimming the day
With a continual flow. The cherished fields
Put on their winter robe of purest white.
'Tis brightness all, save where the new snow melts
Along the mazy current. Low the woods
Bow their hoar head; and, ere the languid sun
Faint from the west emits his evening ray,
Earth's universal face, deep-hid and chill,
Is one wild, dazzling waste that buries wide
The works of man. Drooping, the labourer-ox
Stands covered o'er with snow, and then demands
The fruit of all his toil. The fowls of heaven,
Tamed by the cruel season, crowd around
The winnowing * store, and claim the little boon
Which Providence assigns them. One alone,
The redbreast, sacred to the household gods,
Wisely regardful of the embroiling sky,
In joyless fields and thorny thickets leaves
His shivering mates, and pays to trusted man
His annual visit. Half afraid, he first
Against the window beats; then brisk alights
On the warm hearth, then, hopping o'er the floor,
Eyes all the smiling family askance,
And pecks, and starts, and wonders where he is —
Till, more familiar grown, the table-crumbs
Attract his slender feet. The foodless wilds
Pour forth their brown inhabitants. The hare,
Though timorous of heart, and hard beset
By death in various forms — dark snares, and dogs,
And more unpitying men — the garden seeks,
Urged on by fearless want. The bleating kind
Eye the bleak heaven and next the glistening earth
With looks of dumb despair; then, sad-dispersed,
Dig for the withered herb through heaps of snow.
 Now, shepherds, to your helpless charge be kind:
Baffle the raging year, and fill their pens
With food *at will; lodge them below the storm,
And watch them strict, for, from the bellowing east

In this dire season, oft the whirlwind's wing
Sweeps up the burden of whole wintry plains
In one wide waft, and o'er the hapless flocks,
Hid in the hollow of two neighbouring hills,
The billowy tempest whelms, till, upward urged,
The valley to a shining mountain swells,
Tipt with a wreath high-curling in the sky.

As thus the snows arise, and, foul and fierce,
All winter drives along the darkened air;
In his own loose-revolving fields the swain
Disastered stands; sees other hills ascend,
Of unknown joyless brow, and other scenes,
Of horrid prospect, shag the trackless plain;
Nor finds the river nor the forest, hid
Beneath the formless wild, but wanders on
From hill to dale, still more and more astray —
Impatient flouncing through the drifted heaps,
Stung with the thoughts of home. The thoughts of home
Rush on his nerves and call their vigour forth
In many a vain attempt. How sinks his soul!
What black despair, what horror fills his heart,
When, for the dusky spot which fancy feigned
His tufted cottage rising through the snow,
He meets the roughness of the middle waste,
Far from the track and blest abode of man;
While round him night resistless closes fast,
And every tempest, howling o'er his head,
Renders the savage wilderness more wild.
Then throng the busy shapes into his mind
Of covered pits, unfathomably deep,
A dire descent! beyond the power of frost;
Of faithless bogs; of precipices huge,
Smoothed up with snow; and (what is land unknown,
What water) of the still unfrozen spring,
In the loose marsh or solitary lake,
Where the fresh fountain from the bottom boils.
These check his fearful steps; and down he sinks
Beneath the shelter of the shapeless drift,
Thinking o'er all the bitterness of death,
Mixed with the tender anguish nature shoots
Through the wrung bosom of the dying man —
His wife, his children, and his friends unseen.
In *vain for him the officious wife prepares
The fire fair-blazing and the vestment warm;
In vain his little children, peeping out
Into the mingling storm, demand their sire
With tears of artless innocence. Alas!
Nor wife nor children more shall he behold,
Nor friends, nor sacred home. On every nerve
The deadly winter seizes, shuts up sense,
And, o'er his inmost vitals creeping cold,
Lays him along the snows a stiffened corse,
Stretched out, and bleaching in the northern blast.

Ah! little think the gay licentious *proud,
Whom pleasure, power, and affluence surround —
They, who their thoughtless hours in giddy mirth,
And wanton, often cruel, riot waste —
Ah! little think they, while they dance along,
How many feel, this very moment, death
And all the sad variety of pain;
How many sink in the devouring flood,
Or more devouring flame; how many bleed,
By shameful variance betwixt man and man;
How many pine in want, and dungeon-glooms,
Shut from the common air and common use
Of their own limbs; how many drink the cup
Of baleful grief, or eat the bitter bread
Of misery; sore pierced by wintry winds,
How many shrink into the sordid hut
Of cheerless poverty; how many shake
With all the fiercer tortures of the mind,
Unbounded passion, madness, guilt, remorse —
Whence, tumbled headlong from the height of life,
They furnish matter for the tragic muse;
Even in the vale, where wisdom loves to dwell,
With friendship, peace, and contemplation joined,
How many, racked with honest passions, droop
In deep retired distress; how many stand
Around the death-bed of their dearest friends,
And point the parting anguish! Thought fond man
Of these, and all the thousand nameless ills
That one incessant struggle render life,
One scene of toil, of suffering, and of fate,
Vice in his high career would stand appalled,
And heedless rambling impulse learn to think;
The conscious heart of charity would warm,
And her wide wish benevolence dilate;
The social tear would rise, the social sigh;
And, into clear perfection, gradual bliss,
Refining still, the social passions *work.

And here can I forget the generous *band
Who, touched with human woe, redressive searched
Into the horrors of the gloomy jail?

Unpitied and unheard where misery moans,
Where sickness pines, where thirst and hunger burn,
And poor misfortune feels the lash of vice;
While in the land of liberty — the land
Whose every street and public meeting glow
With open freedom — little tyrants raged:
Snatched the lean morsel from the starving mouth,
Tore from cold wintry limbs the tattered weed,
Even robbed them of the last of comforts, sleep;
The free-born Briton to the dungeon chained
Or, as the lust of cruelty prevailed,
At pleasure marked him with inglorious stripes,
And crushed out lives, by secret barbarous ways,
That for their country would have toiled or bled.
Oh, great design! if executed well,
With patient care and wisdom-tempered zeal.
Ye sons of mercy! yet resume the search;
Drag forth the legal monsters into light,
Wrench from their hands Oppression's iron rod,
And bid the cruel feel the pains they give.
Much still untouched remains; in this rank age,
Much is the patriot's weeding hand required.
The toils of law — what dark insidious men
Have cumbrous added to perplex the truth
And lengthen simple justice into trade —
How glorious were the day that saw these broke,
And every man within the reach of right!

By wintry famine roused, from all the tract
Of *horrid mountains which the shining Alps
And wavy Apennines and Pyrenees
Branch out stupendous into distant lands,
Cruel as death, and hungry as the grave,
Burning for blood, bony, and gaunt, and grim,
Assembling wolves in raging troops descend;
And, pouring o'er the country, bear along
Keen as the north wind sweeps the glossy snow.
All is their prize. They fasten on the steed,
Press him to earth, and pierce his mighty heart.
Nor can the bull his awful front defend,
Or shake the murdering savages away.
Rapacious, at the mother's throat they fly,
And tear the screaming infant from her breast.
The godlike face of man avails him naught.
Even Beauty, force divine! at whose bright glance
The generous lion *stands in softened gaze,
Here bleeds, a hapless undistinguished prey.
But if, apprised of the severe attack,
The country be shut up, lured by the scent,
On churchyards drear (inhuman to relate!)
The disappointed prowlers fall, and dig
The shrouded body from the grave; o'er which,
Mixed with foul shades and frighted ghosts, they howl.

Among those hilly regions, where, embraced
In peaceful vales, the happy *Grisons dwell,
Oft, rushing sudden from the loaded cliffs,
Mountains of snow their gathering terrors roll.
From steep to steep, loud thundering, down they come,
A wintry waste in dire commotion all;
And herds, and flocks, and travellers, and swains,
And sometimes whole brigades of marching troops,
Or hamlets sleeping in the dead of night,
Are deep beneath the smothering ruin whelmed.

*Now, all amid the rigours of the year,
In the wild depth of winter, while without
The ceaseless winds blow ice, be my retreat,
Between the groaning forest and the shore,
Beat by the boundless multitude of waves,
A rural, sheltered, solitary scene;
Where ruddy fire and beaming tapers join
To cheer the gloom. There, studious, let me sit,
And hold high converse with the mighty dead —
Sages of ancient time, as gods revered,
As gods beneficent, who blessed mankind
With arts and arms, and humanized a world.
Roused at the inspiring thought, I throw aside
The long-lived *volume, and, deep-musing, hail
The sacred shades that slowly rising pass
Before my wondering eyes. First Socrates,
Who, firmly good in a corrupted state,
Against the rage of tyrants single stood
Invincible! calm reason's holy law,
That voice of God within the attentive mind,
Obeying, fearless or in life or death:
Great moral teacher! wisest of mankind!
*Solon the next, who built his commonweal
On equity's wide base; by tender laws
A lively people curbing, yet undamped
Preserving still that quick peculiar fire,

Whence in the laurelled field of finer arts,
And of bold freedom, they unequalled shone,
The pride of smiling Greece and humankind.
*Lycurgus then, who bowed beneath the force
Of strictest discipline, severely wise,
All human passions. Following him I see,
As at Thermopylæ he glorious fell,
The firm devoted *chief, who proved by deeds
The hardest lesson which the other taught.
Then *Aristides lifts his honest front;
Spotless of heart, to whom the unflattering voice
Of freedom gave the noblest name of Just;
In pure majestic poverty revered;
Who, even his glory to his country's weal
Submitting, swelled a haughty rival's *fame.
Reared by his care, of softer ray appears
*Cimon, sweet-souled; whose genius, rising strong,
Shook off the load of young debauch; abroad
The scourge of Persian pride, at home the friend
Of every worth and every splendid art;
Modest and simple in the pomp of wealth.
Then the last worthies of declining Greece,
Late-called to glory, in unequal times,
Pensive appear. The fair Corinthian boast,
*Timoleon, tempered happy, mild, and firm,
Who wept the brother while the tyrant bled;
And, equal to the best, the Theban *pair,
Whose virtues, in heroic concord joined,
Their country raised to freedom, empire, fame.
He, too, with whom Athenian honour sunk,
And left a mass of sordid lees behind, —
*Phocion the Good; in public life severe,
To virtue still inexorably firm;
But when, beneath his low illustrious roof,
Sweet peace and happy wisdom smoothed his brow,
Not friendship softer was, nor love more kind.
And he, the last of old Lycurgus' sons,
The generous victim to that vain attempt
To save a rotten state — *Agis, who saw
Even Sparta's self to servile avarice sunk.
The two Achaian heroes close the train —
*Aratus, who a while relumed the soul
Of fondly lingering liberty in Greece;
And he, her darling, as her latest hope,
The gallant *Philopœmen, who to arms
Turned the luxurious pomp he could not cure,
Or toiling in his farm, a simple swain,
Or bold and skillful thundering in the field.
  Of rougher front, a mighty people come,
A race of heroes! in those virtuous times
Which knew no stain, save that with partial flame
Their dearest country they too fondly loved.
Her better founder first, the light of Rome,
*Numa, who softened her rapacious sons;
*Servius, the king who laid the solid base
On which o'er earth the vast republic spread.
Then the great consuls venerable rise:
The public *father who the private quelled,
As on the dread tribunal, sternly sad;
He, whom his thankless country could not lose,
*Camillus, only vengeful to her foes;
*Fabricius, scorner of all-conquering gold,
And *Cincinnatus, awful from the plough;
Thy willing *victim, Carthage! bursting loose
From all that pleading nature could oppose,
From a whole city's tears, by rigid faith
Imperious called, and honour's dire command;
*Scipio, the gentle chief, humanely brave,
Who soon the race of spotless glory ran,
And, warm in youth, to the poetic shade
With friendship and philosophy retired;
*Tully, whose powerful eloquence a while
Restrained the rapid fate of rushing Rome;
Unconquered *Cato, virtuous in extreme;
And thou, unhappy *Brutus, kind of heart,
Whose steady arm, by awful virtue urged,
Lifted the Roman steel against thy friend.
Thousands besides the tribute of a verse
Demand; but who can count the stars of heaven?
Who sing their influence on this lower world?
  Behold, who yonder comes! in sober state,
Fair, mild, and strong as is a vernal sun:
'Tis Phœbus' self, or else the *Mantuan swain!
Great Homer too appears, of daring wing,
Parent of song! and equal by his side,
The British Muse; join'd hand in hand they walk,
Darkling, full up the middle steep to fame.
Nor absent are those shades, whose skillful touch
Pathetic drew the impassioned heart, and charmed
Transported Athens with the moral scene;
Nor those who, tuneful, waked the enchanting lyre.
  First of your kind! society divine!
Still visit thus my nights, for you reserved,
And mount my soaring soul to thoughts like yours.
Silence, thou lonely power! the door be thine;
See on the hallowed hour that none intrude,
Save a few chosen friends, who sometimes deign

To bless my humble roof, with sense refined,
Learning digested well, exalted faith,
Unstudied wit, and humour ever gay.
Or from the Muses' hill will Pope descend,
To raise the sacred hour, to bid it smile,
And with the social spirit warm the heart;
For, though not sweeter his own Homer sings,
Yet is his life the more endearing song.
 Where art thou, *Hammond? thou the darling pride,
The friend and lover of the tuneful throng!
Ah! why dear youth, in all the blooming prime
Of vernal genius, where, disclosing fast,
Each active worth, each manly virtue lay,
Why wert thou ravished from our hope so soon?
What now avails that noble thirst of fame,
Which stung thy fervent breast? that treasured store
Of knowledge, early gained? that eager zeal
To serve thy country, glowing in the band
Of youthful patriots who sustain her name?
What now, alas! that life-diffusing charm
Of sprightly wit? that rapture for the Muse,
That heart of friendship, and that soul of joy,
Which bade with softest light thy virtues smile?
Ah! only showed to check our fond pursuits,
And teach our humbled hopes that life is vain.
 Thus in some deep retirement would I pass
The winter-glooms with friends of pliant soul,
Or blithe or solemn, as the theme inspired:
With them would search if nature's boundless frame
Was called, late-rising, from the void of night,
Or sprung eternal from the Eternal Mind;
Its life, its laws, its progress, and its end.
Hence larger prospects of the beauteous whole
Would gradual open on our opening minds;
And each diffusive harmony unite
In full perfection to the astonished eye.
Then would we try to scan the moral world,
Which, though to us it seems embroiled, moves on
In higher order, fitted and impelled
By wisdom's finest hand, and issuing all
In general *good. The sage historic Muse
Should next conduct us through the deeps of time,
Show us how empire grew, declined, and fell
In scattered states; what makes the nations smile,
Improves their soil, and gives them double suns;
And why they pine beneath the brightest skies
In nature's richest lap. As thus we talked,
Our hearts would burn within us, would inhale
That portion of divinity, that ray
Of purest heaven which lights the public soul
Of patriots and of heroes. But, if doomed
In powerless humble fortune to repress
These ardent risings of the kindling soul,
Then, even superior to ambition, we
Would learn the private virtues—how to glide
Through shades and plains along the smoothest stream
Of rural *life; or, snatched away by hope
Through the dim spaces of futurity,
With earnest eye anticipate those scenes
Of happiness and wonder where the mind,
In endless growth and infinite ascent,
Rises from state to state, and world to world.
But, when with these the serious thought is foiled,
We, shifting for relief, would play the shapes
Of frolic Fancy; and incessant form
Those rapid pictures, that assembled train
Of fleet ideas, never joined before,
Whence lively Wit excites to gay surprise,
Or folly-painting Humour, grave himself,
Calls laughter forth, deep-shaking every nerve.

*Meantime the village rouses up the fire;
While, well attested, and as well believed,
Heard solemn, goes the goblin-story round,
Till superstitious horror creeps o'er all.
Or frequent in the sounding hall they wake
The rural gambol. Rustic mirth goes round—
The simple joke that takes the shepherd's heart,
Easily pleased, the long loud laugh sincere;
The kiss, snatched hasty from the sidelong maid
On purpose guardless, or pretending sleep;
The leap, the slap, the haul; and, shook to notes
Of native music, the respondent dance.
Thus jocund fleets with them the winter night.
 The *city swarms intense. The public haunt,
Full of each theme and warm with mixed discourse,
Hums indistinct. The sons of riot flow
Down the loose stream of false enchanted joy
To swift destruction. On the rankled soul
The gaming fury falls; and in one gulf
Of total ruin, honour, virtue, peace,
Friends, families, and fortune headlong sink.
Up springs the dance along the lighted dome,

Mixed and evolved a thousand sprightly ways.
The glittering court effuses every pomp;
The circle deepens; beamed from gaudy robes,
Tapers, and sparkling gems, and radiant eyes,
A soft effulgence o'er the palace waves —
While, a gay insect in his summer shine,
The fop, light-fluttering, spreads his mealy wings.
Dread o'er the scene the ghost of Hamlet stalks;
Othello rages; poor *Monimia mourns;
And *Belvidera pours her soul in love.
Terror alarms the breast; the comely tear
Steals o'er the cheek; or else the comic Muse
Holds to the world a picture of itself,
And raises sly the fair impartial laugh.
Sometimes she lifts her *strain, and paints the scenes
Of beauteous life — whate'er can deck mankind,
Or charm the heart, in generous *Bevil showed.

O thou, whose wisdom, solid yet refined,
Whose patriot virtues, and consummate skill
To touch the finer springs that move the world,
Joined to whate'er the graces can bestow,
And all Apollo's animating fire,
Give thee with pleasing dignity to shine
At once the guardian, ornament, and joy
Of polished life — permit the rural Muse,
O *Chesterfield, to grace with thee her song.
Ere to the shades again she humbly flies,
Indulge her fond ambition, in thy train
(For every Muse has in thy train a place)
To mark thy various full-accomplished mind —
To mark that spirit which with British scorn
Rejects the allurements of corrupted power;
That elegant politeness which excels,
Even in the judgment of presumptuous France,
The boasted manners of her shining court;
That wit, the vivid energy of sense,
The truth of nature, which with Attic point,
And kind well-tempered satire, smoothly keen,
Steals through the soul and without pain corrects.
Or, rising thence with yet a brighter flame,
Oh, let me hail thee on some glorious day,
When to the listening senate, ardent, crowd
Britannia's sons to hear her pleaded cause!
Then, dressed by thee more amiably fair,
Truth the soft robe of mild persuasion wears;
Thou to assenting reason giv'st again
Her own enlightened thoughts; called from the heart,
The obedient passions on thy voice attend;
And even reluctant party feels a while
Thy gracious power, as through the varied maze
Of eloquence, now smooth, now quick, now strong,
Profound and clear, you roll the copious flood.

To thy loved haunt return, my happy Muse;
For now, behold! the joyous winter days,
Frosty, succeed; and through the blue serene,
For sight too fine, the ethereal nitre flies,
Killing infectious damps, and the spent air
Storing afresh with elemental life.
Close crowds the shining atmosphere, and binds
Our strengthened bodies in its cold embrace,
Constringent; feeds, and animates our blood;
Refines our spirits, through the new-strung nerves
In swifter sallies darting to the brain
Where sits the soul, intense, collected, cool,
Bright as the skies, and as the season keen.
All nature feels the renovating force
Of winter; only to the thoughtless eye
In ruin seen. The frost-concocted glebe
Draws in abundant vegetable soul,
And gathers vigour for the coming year;
A stronger glow sits on the lively cheek,
Of ruddy fire; and *luculent along
The purer rivers flow; their sullen deeps,
Transparent, open to the shepherd's gaze,
And murmur hoarser at the fixing frost.
What art thou, frost? and whence are thy keen *stores
Derived, thou secret all-invading power,
Whom even the illusive fluid cannot fly?
Is not thy potent energy, unseen,
Myriads of little salts, or hooked, or shaped
Like double wedges, and diffused immense
Through water, earth, and ether? Hence at eve,
Steamed eager from the red horizon round,
With the fierce rage of winter deep suffused,
An icy gale, oft shifting, o'er the pool
Breathes a blue film, and in its mid-career
Arrests the bickering stream. The loosened ice,
Let down the flood and half dissolved by day,
Rustles no more, but to the sedgy bank
Fast grows, or gathers round the pointed stone,
A crystal pavement, by the breath of heaven
Cemented firm; till, seized from shore to shore,

The whole imprisoned river growls below.
Loud rings the frozen earth, and hard reflects
A double noise; while, at his evening watch,
The village dog deters the nightly thief;
The heifer lows; the distant waterfall
Swells in the breeze; and with the hasty tread
Of traveller the hollow-sounding plain
Shakes from afar. The full ethereal round,
Infinite worlds disclosing to the view,
Shines out intensely keen, and, all one *cope
Of starry glitter, glows from pole to pole.
From pole to pole the rigid influence falls
Through the still night incessant, heavy, strong,
And seizes nature fast. It freezes on,
Till morn, late-rising o'er the drooping world,
Lifts her pale eye unjoyous. Then appears
The various labour of the silent night:
Prone from the dripping eave and dumb cascade,
Whose idle torrents only seem to roar,
The pendent icicle; the frost-work fair,
Where transient hues and fancied figures rise;
Wide-spouted o'er the hill the frozen brook,
A livid tract, cold-gleaming on the morn;
The forest bent beneath the plumy wave;
And by the frost refined the whiter snow
Incrusted hard, and sounding to the tread
Of early shepherd, as he pensive seeks
His pining flock, or from the mountain top,
Pleased with the slippery surface, swift descends.

On blithesome frolics bent, the youthful swains,
While every work of man is laid at rest,
Fond o'er the river crowd, in various sport
And revelry dissolved; where, mixing glad,
Happiest of all the train, the raptured boy
Lashes the whirling top. Or, where the Rhine
Branched out in many a long canal extends,
From every province swarming, void of care,
*Batavia rushes forth; and, as they sweep
On sounding skates a thousand different ways
In circling poise swift as the winds along,
The then gay land is maddened all to joy.
Nor less the northern courts, wide o'er the snow,
Pour a new pomp. Eager, on rapid sleds,
Their vigorous youth in bold contention wheel
The long-resounding course. Meantime, to raise
The manly strife, with highly blooming charms
Flushed by the season, Scandinavia's dames
Or Russia's buxom daughters glow around.

Pure, quick, and sportful is the wholesome day,
But soon elapsed. The horizontal sun
Broad o'er the south hangs at his utmost noon;
And ineffectual strikes the *gelid cliff.
His azure gloss the mountain still maintains,
Nor feels the feeble touch. Perhaps the vale
Relents a while to the reflected ray;
Or from the forest falls the clustered snow,
Myriads of gems, that in the waving gleam
Gay-twinkle as they scatter. Thick around
Thunders the sport of those who with the gun,
And dog impatient bounding at the shot,
Worse than the season desolate the fields,
And, adding to the ruins of the year,
Distress the footed or the feathered game.

But what is this? Our infant Winter sinks
Divested of his grandeur should our eye
Astonished shoot into the frigid zone,
Where for relentless months continual night
Holds o'er the glittering waste her starry reign.
There, through the prison of unbounded wilds,
Barred by the hand of nature from escape,
Wide roams the Russian exile. Naught around
Strikes his sad eye but deserts lost in snow,
And heavy-loaded groves, and solid floods
That stretch athwart the solitary *vast
Their icy horrors to the frozen main,
And cheerless towns far distant — never blessed,
Save when its annual course the caravan
Bends to the golden coast of rich Cathay,
With news of humankind. Yet there life glows;
Yet, cherished there, beneath the shining waste
The furry nations harbour — tipped with jet,
Fair ermines spotless as the snows they press;
*Sables of glossy black; and, dark-embrowned,
Or beauteous *freaked with many a mingled hue,
Thousands besides, the costly pride of courts.
There, warm together pressed, the trooping deer
Sleep on the new-fallen snows; and, scarce his head
Raised o'er the heapy wreath, the branching elk
Lies slumbering sullen in the white abyss.
The ruthless hunter wants nor dogs nor *toils,
Nor with the dread of sounding bows he drives
The fearful flying race; with ponderous clubs,
As weak against the mountain-heaps they push
Their beating breast in vain, and piteous *bray,
He lays them quivering on the ensanguined snows,

And with loud shouts rejoicing bears them home.
There, through the piny forest * half-absorbed,
Rough tenant of these shades, the shapeless bear,
With dangling ice all horrid, stalks forlorn;
Slow-paced, and sourer as the storms increase,
He makes his bed beneath the inclement drift,
And, with stern patience, scorning weak complaint,
Hardens his heart against assailing want.
  Wide o'er the spacious regions of the north,
That see * Boötes urge his tardy wain,
A boisterous race, by frosty * Caurus pierced,
Who little pleasure know and fear no pain,
Prolific swarm. They once relumed the flame
Of lost mankind in polished slavery sunk;
Drove martial horde on horde, with dreadful sweep
Resistless rushing o'er the enfeebled south,
And gave the vanquished world another form.
Not such the sons of Lapland: wisely they
Despise the insensate barbarous trade of war;
They ask no more than simple nature * gives;
They love their mountains and enjoy their storms.
No false desires, no pride-created wants,
Disturb the peaceful current of their time,
And through the restless ever tortured maze
Of pleasure or ambition bid it rage.
Their reindeer form their riches. These their tents,
Their robes, their beds, and all their homely wealth
Supply, their wholesome fare, and cheerful cups.
Obsequious at their call, the docile tribe
Yield to the sled their necks, and whirl them swift
O'er hill and dale, heaped into one expanse
Of marbled snow, or, far as eye can sweep,
With a blue crust of ice unbounded glazed.
By dancing meteors then, that ceaseless shake
A waving blaze refracted o'er the heavens,
And vivid moons, and stars that keener play
With doubled lustre from the radiant waste,
Even in the depth of polar night they find
A wondrous day — enough to light the chase
Or guide their daring steps to Finland fairs.
Wished spring returns; and from the hazy south,
While dim Aurora slowly moves before,
The welcome sun, just verging up at first,
By small degrees extends the swelling curve;
Till, seen at last for gay rejoicing months,
Still round and round his spiral course he winds,
And, as he nearly dips his flaming orb,
Wheels up again and re-ascends the sky.
In that glad season, from the lakes and floods,
Where pure * Niëmi's fairy mountains rise,
And, fringed with roses, Tenglio rolls his stream,
They draw the copious fry. With these at eve
They, cheerful-loaded, to their tents repair,
Where, all day long in useful cares employed,
Their kind unblemished wives the fire prepare.
Thrice happy race! by poverty secured
From legal plunder and rapacious power,
In whom fell interest never yet has sown
The seeds of vice, whose spotless swains ne'er knew
Injurious deed, nor, blasted by the breath
Of faithless love, their blooming daughters * woe.
  Still pressing on, beyond * Tornea's lake,
And * Hecla flaming through a waste of snow,
And farthest Greenland, to the pole itself,
Where, failing gradual, life at length goes out,
The Muse expands her solitary flight;
And, hovering o'er the wild stupendous scene,
Beholds new seas beneath another * sky.
Throned in his palace of cerulean ice,
Here Winter holds his unrejoicing court;
And through his airy hall the loud misrule
Of driving tempest is forever heard:
Here the grim tyrant meditates his wrath;
Here arms his winds with all subduing frost;
Moulds his fierce hail, and treasures up his snows,
With which he now oppresses half the * globe.
  Thence winding *eastward to the Tartar's coast,
She sweeps the howling margin of the main;
Where, undissolving from the first of time,
Snows swell on snows amazing to the sky;
And icy mountains high on mountains piled
Seem to the shivering sailor from afar,
Shapeless and white, an atmosphere of clouds.
Projected huge and horrid o'er the surge,
Alps frown on Alps, or, rushing hideous down,
As if old Chaos was again returned,
Wide-rend the deep and shake the solid * pole.
Ocean itself no longer can resist
The binding fury; but, in all its rage
Of tempest, taken by the boundless frost,
Is many a fathom to the bottom chained,

And bid to roar no more — a bleak expanse
Shagged o'er with wavy rocks, cheerless and void
Of every life, that from the dreary months
Flies conscious southward. Miserable they
Who, here entangled in the gathering ice,
Take their last look of the descending sun;
While, full of death and fierce with tenfold frost,
The long, long night, incumbent o'er their heads,
Falls horrible! Such was the * Briton's fate,
As with first prow (what have not Britons dared?)
He for the passage sought, attempted since
So much in vain, and seeming to be shut
By jealous nature with eternal bars.
In these fell regions, in * Arzina caught,
And to the stony deep his idle ship
Immediate sealed, he with his hapless crew,
Each full exerted at his several task,
Froze into statues — to the cordage glued
The sailor, and the pilot to the helm.
  Hard by these shores, where scarce his freezing stream
Rolls the wild * Oby, live the last of men;
And, half enlivened by the distant sun,
That rears and ripens man as well as plants,
Here human nature wears its rudest form.
Deep from the piercing season sunk in caves,
Here by dull fires and with unjoyous cheer
They waste the tedious gloom: immersed in furs
Doze the gross race — nor sprightly jest, nor song,
Nor tenderness they know, nor aught of life
Beyond the kindred bears that stalk without —
Till Morn at length, her roses drooping all,
Sheds a long twilight brightening o'er their fields
And calls the quivered savage to the chase.
  What cannot active government perform,
New-moulding man? Wide-stretching from these shores,
A people savage from remotest time,
A huge neglected empire, one vast mind
By heaven inspired from Gothic darkness called.
Immortal * Peter! first of monarchs! He
His stubborn country tamed, — her rocks, her fens,
Her floods, her seas, her ill-submitting sons;
And, while the fierce barbarian he subdued,
To more exalted soul he raised the man.
Ye shades of ancient heroes, ye who toiled
Through long successive ages to build up
A labouring plan of state, behold at once
The wonder done! behold the matchless prince!
Who left his native throne, where reigned till then
A mighty shadow of unreal power;
Who greatly spurned the slothful pomp of courts;
And, roaming every land, in every port
His sceptre laid aside, with glorious hand
Unwearied plying the mechanic tool,
Gathered the seeds of trade, of useful arts,
Of civil wisdom, and of martial * skill.
Charged with the stores of Europe home he goes!
Then cities rise amid the illumined waste;
O'er joyless deserts smiles the rural reign;
Far-distant flood to flood is social joined;
The astonished Euxine hears the Baltic * roar;
Proud navies ride on seas that never foamed
With daring keel before; and armies stretch
Each way their dazzling files, repressing here
The frantic * Alexander of the north,
And awing there stern Othman's shrinking * sons.
Sloth flies the land, and ignorance and vice,
Of old dishonour proud: it glows around,
Taught by the royal hand that roused the whole,
One scene of arts, of arms, of rising trade —
For, what his wisdom planned and power enforced,
More potent still his great example showed.

  Muttering, the winds at eve with blunted point
Blow hollow-blustering from the south. Subdued,
The frost resolves into a trickling thaw.
Spotted the mountains shine: loose sleet descends,
And floods the country round. The rivers swell,
Of bonds impatient. Sudden from the hills,
O'er rocks and woods, in broad brown cataracts,
A thousand snow-fed torrents shoot at once;
And, where they rush, the wide-resounding plain
Is left one slimy waste. Those sullen seas
That washed the ungenial pole, will rest no more
Beneath the shackles of the mighty north,
But, rousing all their waves, resistless heave

And, hark! the lengthening roar continuous runs
Athwart the rifted deep: at once it bursts,
And piles a thousand mountains to the clouds.
Ill fares the bark, with trembling wretches charged,
That, tossed amid the floating fragments, moors
Beneath the shelter of an icy isle,
While night o'erwhelms the * sea, and horror looks
More horrible. Can human force endure
The assembled mischiefs that besiege them round?—
Heart-gnawing hunger, fainting weariness,
The roar of winds and waves, the crush of ice,
Now ceasing, now renewed with louder rage,
And in dire echoes bellowing round the main.
More to embroil the deep, Leviathan
And his unwieldy train in dreadful sport
Tempest the loosened brine; while through the gloom
Far from the bleak inhospitable shore,
Loading the winds, is heard the hungry howl
Of famished monsters, there awaiting wrecks.
Yet Providence, that ever-waking Eye,
Looks down with pity on the feeble toil
Of mortals lost to hope, and lights them safe
Through all this dreary labyrinth of fate.

'Tis done! Dread Winter spreads his latest glooms,
And reigns tremendous o'er the conquered year.
How dead the vegetable kingdom lies!
How dumb the tuneful! Horror wide extends
His desolate domain. Behold, fond man!
See here thy pictured life; pass some few years,
Thy flowering spring, thy summer's ardent strength,
Thy sober autumn fading into age,
And pale concluding winter comes at last
And shuts the scene. Ah! whither now are fled
Those dreams of greatness, those unsolid hopes
Of happiness, those longings after fame,
Those restless cares, those busy bustling days,
Those gay-spent festive nights, those veering thoughts,
Lost between good and ill, that shared thy life?
All now are vanished! Virtue sole survives —
Immortal, never-failing friend of man,
His guide to happiness on high. And see,
'Tis come, the glorious morn, the second birth
Of heaven and earth! Awakening nature hears
The new-creating word, and starts to life
In every heightened form, from pain and death
Forever free. The great eternal scheme,
Involving all, and in a perfect whole
Uniting, as the prospect wider spreads,
To reason's eye refined, clears up apace.
Ye vainly wise! ye blind presumptuous! now,
Confounded in the dust, adore that Power
And Wisdom — oft arraigned. See now the cause
Why unassuming worth in secret lived
And died neglected; why the good man's share
In life was gall and bitterness of soul;
Why the lone widow and her orphans pined
In starving solitude, while luxury
In palaces lay straining her low thought
To form unreal wants; why heaven-born truth
And moderation fair wore the red marks
Of superstition's scourge; why licensed pain,
That cruel spoiler, that embosomed foe,
Embittered all our bliss. Ye good distressed,
Ye noble few, who here unbending stand
Beneath life's pressure, yet bear up a while,
And what your bounded view, which only saw
A little part, deemed evil is no more.
The storms of wintry time will quickly pass,
And one unbounded spring encircle all.

[1726, 1746]

A HYMN

It was one of the central ideas of the English Deists that God had made a sufficient revelation, not only of himself but also of moral truth, in the natural world. From this position it followed that by the study of nature we may know God, and that in the contemplation of nature we worship him. In the writings of John Toland (1670–1722) these doctrines were given a pantheistic tendency, which, though Thomson was not a Deist, coloured his *Hymn* on the Seasons. An interesting comparison may be made between this poem and Coleridge's *Hymn Before Sunrise, in the Vale of Chamouni.*

*These, as they change, Almighty Father! these
Are but the varied God. The rolling year
Is full of thee. Forth in the pleasing spring
Thy beauty walks, thy tenderness and love.
Wide flush the fields; the softening air is balm;
Echo the mountains round; the forest smiles;
And every sense, and every heart, is joy.
Then comes thy glory in the summer months,
With light and heat refulgent. Then thy sun
Shoots full perfection through the swelling year;
And oft thy voice in dreadful thunder speaks,
And oft, at dawn, deep noon, or falling eve,
By brooks and groves, in hollow-whispering gales.
Thy bounty shines in autumn unconfined,
And spreads a common feast for all that lives.
In winter, awful, thou! With clouds and storms
Around thee thrown, tempest o'er tempest rolled,
Majestic darkness, on the whirlwind's wing
Riding sublime, thou bidst the world adore,
And humblest nature with thy northern blast.

Mysterious *round! what skill, what force divine,
Deep-felt in these appear! a simple *train,
Yet so delightful mixed, with such kind art,
Such beauty and beneficence combined,
Shade unperceived so softening into shade,
And all so forming an harmonious whole
That, as they still succeed, they ravish still.
But, wandering oft with brute unconscious gaze,
Man marks not thee, marks not the mighty hand
That, ever busy, wheels the silent spheres,
Works in the secret deep, shoots steaming thence
The fair profusion that o'erspreads the spring,
Flings from the sun direct the flaming day,
Feeds every creature, hurls the tempest forth,
And, as on earth this grateful change revolves,
With transport touches all the springs of life.

Nature, attend! join, every living soul
Beneath the spacious temple of the sky,
In adoration join; and ardent raise
One general song! To him, ye vocal gales,
Breathe soft, whose spirit in your freshness breathes;
Oh, talk of him in solitary glooms,
Where, o'er the rock, the scarcely-waving pine
Fills the brown shade with a religious awe.
And ye, whose bolder note is heard afar,
Who shake the astonished world, lift high to Heaven
The impetuous song, and say from whom you rage.
His praise, ye brooks, attune, ye trembling rills;
And let me catch it as I muse along.
Ye headlong torrents, rapid and profound;
Ye softer floods, that lead the humid maze
Along the vale; and thou, majestic main,
A secret world of wonders in thyself,
Sound his stupendous praise, whose greater voice
Or bids you roar or bids your roarings fall.
Soft roll your incense, herbs, and fruits, and flowers,
In mingled clouds to him, whose sun exalts,
Whose breath perfumes you, and whose pencil paints.
Ye forests, bend; ye harvests, wave to him —
Breathe your still song into the reaper's heart
As home he goes beneath the joyous moon.
Ye that keep watch in heaven, as earth asleep
Unconscious lies, effuse your mildest beams,
Ye constellations! while your angels strike
Amid the spangled sky the silver lyre.
Great source of day! best image here below
Of thy Creator, ever pouring wide
From world to world the vital ocean round!
On nature write with every beam his praise.
The thunder rolls: be hushed the prostrate world,
While cloud to cloud returns the solemn hymn.
Bleat out afresh, ye hills; ye mossy rocks,
Retain the sound; the broad responsive low,
Ye valleys, raise; for the Great Shepherd reigns,
And his unsuffering kingdom yet will come.
Ye woodlands all, awake: a boundless song
Burst from the groves; and, when the restless day,
Expiring, lays the warbling world asleep,
Sweetest of birds, sweet Philomela! charm
The listening shades, and teach the night his praise!
Ye, chief, for whom the whole creation smiles,
At once the head, the heart, the tongue of all,
Crown the great hymn! In swarming cities vast,

Assembled men, to the deep organ join
The long-resounding voice, oft breaking clear
At solemn pauses through the swelling bass;
And, as each mingling flame increases each,
In one united ardour rise to heaven.
Or, if you rather choose the rural shade,
And find a fane in every sacred grove,
There let the shepherd's flute, the virgin's lay,
The prompting seraph, and the poet's lyre
Still sing the God of Seasons as they roll.
For me, when I forget the darling theme,
Whether the blossom blows, the summer-ray
Russets the plain, inspiring autumn gleams,
Or winter rises in the blackening east,
Be my tongue mute, may fancy paint no more,
And, dead to joy, forget my heart to beat!

Should fate command me to the farthest verge
Of the green earth, to distant barbarous climes,
Rivers unknown to song, where first the sun
Gilds Indian mountains, or his setting beam
Flames on the Atlantic isles, 'tis naught to me;
Since God is ever present, ever felt,
In the void waste as in the city full,
And where he vital spreads there must be joy.
When even at last the solemn hour shall come,
And wing my mystic flight to future worlds,
I cheerful will obey; there, with new powers,
Will rising wonders sing. I cannot go
Where universal love not smiles around,
Sustaining all yon orbs and all their sons,
From seeming evil still educing good,
And better thence again, and better still,
In infinite progression. But I lose
Myself in him, in Light Ineffable!
Come then, expressive Silence, muse his praise.

[1730, 1746]

TO THE MEMORY OF SIR ISAAC *NEWTON

Although Sir Isaac Newton wrote little in English, his indirect importance in English literature is considerable because of the support given by his achievements to certain main doctrines of Rationalism, and, in spite of his own religious orthodoxy, to the Deists. His discoveries, destined in their later results to multiply the problems of philosophy, seemed at first to indicate an ordered, harmonious, simple, and easily intelligible universe, for the early and complete comprehension of which human reason would be quite sufficient. They gave an impetus, also, to the still novel idea of progress, and prepared the way for the doctrine of perfectibility.

Thomson's elegy on Newton, though little read, is, intellectually considered, his most interesting performance. At a time when a thinker of even Dean Swift's intelligence could still deride scientific investigation as lunacy, he understands and celebrates the essential beauty of science and proclaims its high imaginative value. In sharp contrast with almost all the later poets of the romantic school, he asserts that the scientific imagination, both for its energy and for the dignity of its objects, must be placed at least on a level with that of the poet himself.

Shall the great soul of Newton quit this earth
To mingle with *his stars, and every *Muse,
Astonished into silence, shun the weight
Of honours due to his illustrious name?
But what can man? Even now the sons of *light,
In strains high warbled to seraphic lyre,
Hail his arrival on the coast of bliss.
Yet am not I deterred, though high the theme,
And sung to harps of angels, for with you,
Ethereal flames! ambitious, I aspire
In nature's general symphony to join.

And what new wonders can ye show your guest,
Who, while on this dim spot where mortals toil
Clouded in dust, from motion's simple laws
Could trace the secret hand of Providence,
Wide-working through this universal frame?

Have ye not listened while he *bound the suns
And planets to their spheres, the *unequal task
Of humankind till then? Oft had they rolled
O'er erring man the year, and oft disgraced
The pride of schools, before their course was known
Full in its causes and effects to him,
All-piercing sage! who sat not down and dreamed
Romantic schemes, defended by the din
Of specious words, and tyranny of *names;
But, bidding his amazing mind attend,
And with heroic patience years on years
Deep-searching, saw at last the system dawn,
And shine, of all his race, on him alone.

What were his raptures then! how pure! how strong!
And what the triumphs of old Greece and Rome,
By his diminished, but the pride of boys
In some small fray victorious! when instead
Of shattered parcels of this earth usurped
By violence unmanly, and sore deeds
Of cruelty and blood, Nature herself
Stood all subdued by him, and open laid
Her every latent glory to his view.
All intellectual eye, our solar round
First gazing through, he, by the blended power
Of gravitation and projection, saw
The whole in silent harmony revolve.
From unassisted vision hid, the moons
To cheer remoter planets numerous formed,
By him in all their mingled *tracts were seen.
He also fixed our wandering Queen of Night,
Whether she wanes into a scanty orb,
Or, waxing broad, with her pale shadowy light
In a soft deluge overflows the sky.
Her every motion clear-discerning, he
Adjusted to the mutual *main, and taught
Why now the mighty mass of waters swells
Resistless, heaving on the broken rocks,
And the full river turning — till again
The tide revertive, unattracted, leaves
A yellow waste of idle sands behind.
Then, breaking hence, he took his ardent flight
Through the blue infinite; and every star
Which the clear concave of a winter's night
Pours on the eye, or astronomic tube,
Far stretching, snatches from the dark abyss,
Or such as further in successive skies
To fancy shine alone, at his approach
Blazed into suns, the living centre each
Of an harmonious system — all combined,
And ruled unerring by that single power
Which draws the stone projected to the ground.
Oh, unprofuse magnificence divine!
Oh, wisdom truly perfect! thus to call
From a few causes such a scheme of things,
Effects so various, beautiful and great,
An universe complete! And O beloved
Of Heaven! whose well-purged penetrating eye
The mystic veil transpiercing, inly scanned
The rising, moving, wide-established frame.
He, first of men, with awful wing pursued
The comet through the long elliptic curve,
As round innumerous worlds he wound his way,
Till, to the forehead of our evening sky
Returned, the blazing wonder glares anew,
And o'er the trembling nations shakes dismay.
The heavens are all his own, from the wide rule
Of whirling vortices and circling spheres
To their first great simplicity restored.
The schools astonished stood; but found it vain
To combat still with demonstration strong,
And, unawakened, dream beneath the blaze
Of truth. At once their *pleasing visions fled,
With the gay shadows of the morning mixed,
When Newton rose, our philosophic sun!
The aërial flow of sound was known to him,
From whence it first in wavy circles breaks
Till the touched organ takes the message in.
Nor could the darting beam, of speed immense,
Escape his swift pursuit and measuring eye.
Even light itself, which everything displays,
Shone undiscovered till his brighter mind
Untwisted all the shining robe of day;
And, from the whitening undistinguished blaze
Collecting every ray into *his kind,
To the charmed eye educed the gorgeous train
Of parent colours. First the flaming red
Sprung vivid forth; the tawny orange next;
And next delicious yellow; by whose side
Fell the kind beams of all-refreshing green.
Then the pure blue, that swells autumnal skies,
Ethereal played; and then, of sadder hue,
Emerged the deepened indigo, as when
The heavy-skirted evening droops with frost;
While the last gleamings of refracted light
Died in the fainting violet away.
These, when the clouds distil the rosy shower,
Shine out distinct adown the watery bow;
While o'er our heads the dewy vision bends
Delightful, melting on the fields beneath.
Myriads of mingling dyes from these result,
And myriads still remain — infinite source
Of beauty, ever flushing, ever *new.
Did ever poet image aught so fair,
Dreaming in whispering groves by the hoarse brook?
Or prophet, to whose rapture Heaven descends?
Even now the setting sun and shifting clouds,
Seen, Greenwich, from thy lovely heights, declare
How just, how beauteous the refractive law.
The noiseless tide of time, all bearing down
To vast eternity's unbounded sea

Where the green islands of the happy shine,
He stemmed alone; and, to the source (involved
Deep in primeval gloom) ascending, raised
His lights at equal distances, to guide
Historian wildered on his darksome * way.

But who can number up his labours? who
His high discoveries sing? When but a few
Of the deep-studying race can stretch their minds
To what he knew — in fancy's lighter thought
How shall the Muse then grasp the mighty theme?

What wonder thence that his devotion swelled
Responsive to his knowledge? For could he,
Whose piercing mental eye diffusive saw
The finished university of things
In all its order, magnitude, and parts,
Forbear incessant to adore that Power
Who fills, sustains, and actuates the * whole?

Say, ye who best can tell, ye happy few,
Who saw him in the softest lights of life,
All unwithheld, indulging to his friends
The vast unborrowed treasures of his mind —
Oh, speak the wondrous man! how mild, how calm,
How greatly humble, how divinely good,
How firmly stablished on eternal truth;
Fervent in doing well, with every nerve
Still pressing on, forgetful of the past,
And panting for perfection; far above
Those little cares and visionary joys
That so perplex the fond impassioned heart
Of ever cheated, ever trusting man.
This, * Conduitt, from thy rural hours we hope,
As through the pleasing shade where nature pours
Her every sweet in studious ease you walk,
The social passions smiling at thy heart
That glows with all the recollected sage.

And you, ye hopeless gloomy-minded tribe,
You who, unconscious of those nobler flights
That reach impatient at immortal life,
Against the prime endearing * privilege
Of being dare contend, — say, can a soul
Of such extensive, deep, tremendous powers,
Enlarging still, be but a finer breath
Of spirits dancing through their tubes awhile,
And then forever lost in vacant air?

But hark! methinks I hear a warning voice,
Solemn as when some awful change is come,
Sound through the world — "'Tis done! — the measure's full;
And I resign my charge." — Ye mouldering stones
That build the towering pyramid, the proud
Triumphal arch, the monument effaced
By ruthless ruin, and whate'er supports
The worshipped name of hoar antiquity —
Down to the dust! What grandeur can ye boast
While Newton lifts his column to the skies,
Beyond the waste of time. Let no weak drop
Be shed for him. The virgin in her bloom
Cut off, the joyous youth, and darling child —
These are the tombs that claim the tender tear
And elegiac song. But Newton calls
For other notes of gratulation high,
That now he wanders through those endless worlds
He here so well descried, and wondering talks
And hymns their Author with his glad compeers.

Oh, Britain's boast! whether with angels thou
Sittest in dread discourse, or fellow-blessed,
Who joy to see the honour of their kind;
Or whether, mounted on cherubic wing,
Thy swift career is with the whirling orbs,
Comparing things with things, in rapture lost,
And grateful adoration for that light
So plenteous rayed into thy mind below
From Light himself; oh, look with pity down
On humankind, a frail erroneous race!
Exalt the spirit of a downward world!
O'er thy dejected country chief preside,
And be her Genius called! her studies raise,
Correct her manners, and inspire her youth;
For, though depraved and sunk, she brought thee forth,
And glories in thy name! she points thee out
To all her sons, and bids them eye thy star:
While, in expectance of the second life
When time shall be no more, thy sacred dust
Sleeps with her * kings, and dignifies the scene.

[1727]

THE CASTLE OF INDOLENCE

Although not published until 1748, Thomson's imitation of Spenser was begun at about the same time as that by William Shenstone, *The Schoolmistress*, which first appeared in 1737. As in that poem and also in John Gay's *The Shepherd's Week*, Spenser's archaistic language is used spasmodically, not quite seriously, and without exact knowledge. *The Castle of Indolence* shows the skill in painting vignettes of landscape which readers of *The Seasons* would expect and which Spenser also had, but the beauty of its versification is greater by far than any of the poet's earlier work had shown. Thomson comes closest to his original, indeed, in the varied, ample, always somewhat indolent music of his Spenserian stanzas. The charm of the verse, the theme, and the poet's prevailing mood combine to produce one of the minor masterpieces of the century and one of the most delightful of English poems. In the first canto, where Thomson is content merely to "please," he succeeds because he writes from his real convictions; in the second canto he attempts to "instruct," and descends from poetry to didacticism.

CANTO I

*The Castle * hight of* Indolence,
And its false luxury;
Where for a little time, alas!
We lived right jollily.

O mortal man, who livest here by toil,
Do not complain of this thy hard estate;
That like an * emmet thou must ever * moil
Is a sad * sentence of an ancient date:
And, certes, there is for it reason great;
For, though sometimes it makes thee weep and wail,
And curse thy stars, and early drudge and late,
Withouten that would come an heavier * bale,
Loose life, unruly passions, and diseases pale.

In lowly * dale, fast by a river's side,
With woody hill o'er hill encompassed round,
A most enchanting wizard did abide,
Than whom a fiend more fell is nowhere found.
It was, I ween, a lovely spot of ground;
And there a season atween June and May,
Half prankt with spring, with summer half imbrowned,
A listless climate made, where, sooth to say,
No living * wight could work, * ne carèd even play.

Was nought around but images of rest:
Sleep-soothing groves, and quiet lawns between;
And flowery beds that slumbrous influence * kest,
From poppies breathed; and beds of pleasant green,
Where never yet was creeping creature seen.
Meantime unnumbered glittering streamlets played,
And hurlèd everywhere their waters * sheen;
That, as they bickered through the sunny glade,
Though restless * still themselves, a lulling murmur made.

Joined to the prattle of the purling rills
Were heard the lowing herds along the vale,
And flocks loud-bleating from the distant hills,
And * vacant shepherds piping in the dale:
And now and then sweet Philomel would wail,
Or stock-doves plain amid the forest deep
That drowsy rustled to the sighing gale;
And still a * coil the grasshopper did * keep:
Yet all these sounds * yblent inclinèd all to sleep.

Full in the passage of the vale, above,
A sable, silent, solemn forest stood;
Where nought but shadowy forms were seen to move,
As * Idless fancied in her dreaming mood.
And up the hills, on either side, a wood
Of blackening pines, aye waving to and fro,
Sent forth a sleepy horror through the blood;
And where this valley winded out, below,
The murmuring main was heard, and scarcely heard, to flow.

A pleasing land of * drowsyhed it was:
Of dreams that wave before the half-shut eye;
And of gay castles in the clouds that pass,
Forever flushing round a summer sky:
There eke the soft delights, that witchingly
Instil a wanton sweetness through the breast,
And the calm pleasures, always hovered nigh:

But whate'er smacked of noyance, or unrest,
Was far, far off expelled from this delicious nest.

The *landskip such, inspiring perfect ease;
Where Indolence (for so the wizard hight)
Close hid his castle mid embowering trees,
That half shut out the beams of Phœbus bright,
And made a kind of checkered day and night.
Meanwhile, unceasing, at the massy gate,
Beneath a spacious palm, the wicked wight
Was placed; and, to his lute, of cruel fate
And labour harsh complained, lamenting man's estate.

Thither continual pilgrims crowded still
From all the roads of earth that pass thereby:
For, as they chaunced to *breathe on neighbouring hill,
The freshness of this valley smote their eye
And drew them ever and anon more nigh,
Till clustering round the enchanter false they hung,
*Ymolten with his siren melody;
While o'er th' enfeebling lute his hand he flung,
And to the trembling chord these tempting verses sung:

"Behold! ye pilgrims of this earth, behold!
See all but man with unearned pleasure gay.
See her bright robes the butterfly unfold,
Broke from her wintry tomb in prime of May.
What youthful bride can equal her array?
Who can with her for easy pleasure vie?
From mead to mead with gentle wing to stray,
From flower to flower on balmy gales to fly,
Is all she has to do beneath the radiant sky.

"Behold the merry minstrels of the morn,
The swarming songsters of the careless grove,
Ten thousand throats that, from the flowering thorn,
Hymn their good God, and carol sweet of love,
Such grateful kindly raptures them *emove!
They neither plough nor sow; ne, fit for flail,
E'er to the barn the nodding sheaves they drove;
Yet theirs each harvest dancing in the gale,
Whatever crowns the hill, or smiles along the vale.

"Outcast of nature, man! the wretched thrall
Of bitter-dropping sweat, of sweltry pain,
Of cares that eat away thy heart with gall,
And of the vices, an inhuman train,
That all proceed from savage thirst of gain:
For when hard-hearted *Interest first began
To poison earth, *Astræa left the plain;
Guile, Violence, and Murder seized on man,
And, for soft milky streams, with blood the rivers ran.

"Come, ye, who still the cumbrous load of life
Push hard up hill; but, as the farthest steep
You trust to gain, and put an end to strife,
Down thunders back the stone with mighty *sweep,
And hurls your labours to the valley deep,
Forever vain: come, and withouten fee
I in oblivion will your sorrows steep,
Your cares, your toils; will steep you in a sea
Of full delight: O come, ye weary wights, to me!

"With me, you need not rise at early dawn,
To pass the joyless day in various *stounds;
Or, *louting low, on upstart fortune fawn,
And sell fair honour for some paltry pounds;
Or through the city take your dirty rounds
To cheat, and dun, and lie, and visit pay,
Now flattering base, now giving secret wounds;
Or prowl in courts of law for human prey,
In venal senate thieve, or rob on broad highway.

"No cocks, with me, to rustic labour call,
From village on to village sounding clear;
To tardy swain no shrill-voiced matrons squall;
No dogs, no babes, no wives to stun your ear;
No hammers thump; no horrid blacksmith sear,
Ne noisy tradesman your sweet slumbers start
With sounds that are a misery to hear:

But all is calm as would delight the heart
Of * Sybarite of old — all nature, and all art.

"Here nought but candour reigns, indulgent ease,
Good-natured lounging, sauntering up and down;
They who are pleased themselves must always please;
On others' ways they never squint a frown,
Nor heed what haps in hamlet or in town.
Thus, from the source of tender Indolence,
With milky blood the heart is overflown,
Is soothed and sweetened by the social sense;
For interest, envy, pride, and strife are banished hence.

"What, what is virtue but repose of mind?
A pure ethereal calm that knows no storm,
Above the reach of wild ambition's wind,
Above those passions that this world deform,
And torture man, a proud malignant worm!
But here, instead, soft gales of passion play,
And gently stir the heart, thereby to form
A quicker sense of joy; as breezes stray
Across the enlivened skies, and make them still more gay.

"The best of men have ever loved repose;
They hate to mingle in the filthy fray,
Where the soul sours, and gradual rancour grows,
Imbittered more from peevish day to day.
Even those whom fame has lent her fairest ray,
The most renowned of worthy wights of yore,
From a base world at last have stolen away:
So * Scipio, to the soft * Cumæan shore
Retiring, tasted joy he never knew before.

"But if a little exercise you choose,
Some zest for ease, 'tis not forbidden here.
Amid the groves you may indulge the Muse,
Or tend the blooms, and deck the vernal year;
Or softly stealing with your watery gear
Along the brooks, the crimson-spotted * fry
You may delude; the whilst, amused, you hear
Now the hoarse stream, and now the zephyr's sigh,
Attunèd to the birds, and woodland melody.

"Oh, grievous folly! to heap up estate,
Losing the days you see beneath the sun;
When, sudden, comes blind unrelenting fate,
And gives the untasted portion you have won
With ruthless toil, and many a wretch undone,
To those who mock you, gone to Pluto's reign,
There with sad ghosts to pine, and shadows dun:
But sure it is of vanities most vain,
To toil for what you here untoiling may obtain."

He ceased. But still their * trembling ears retained
The deep vibrations of his witching song;
That, by a kind of magic power, constrained
To enter in, pell-mell, the listening throng.
Heaps poured on heaps, and yet they slipt along
In silent ease: as when, beneath the beam
Of summer moons, the distant woods among,
Or by some flood all silvered with the gleam,
The soft-embodied fays through airy portal * stream.

By the * smooth demon so it ordered was,
And here his baneful bounty first began:
Though some there were who would not further pass,
And his alluring baits suspected * han.
The wise distrust the too fair-spoken man.
Yet through the gate they cast a wishful eye
Not to move on, * perdie, is all they can;
For, do their very best, they cannot fly,
But often each way look, and often sorely sigh.

When this the watchful wicked wizard saw,
With sudden spring he leaped upon them strait;
And, soon as touched by his unhallowed paw,
They found themselves within the cursèd gate,
Full hard to be repassed, like that of fate.
Not stronger were of old the * giant-crew,
Who sought to pull high Jove from regal state,

Though feeble wretch he seemed, of sallow hue:
Certes, who bides his grasp, will that encounter rue.

For whomsoe'er the villain takes in hand,
Their joints unknit, their sinews melt apace;
As lithe they grow as any willow wand,
And of their vanished force remains no trace:
So when a maiden fair, of modest grace,
In all her buxom blooming May of charms,
Is seizèd in some *losel's hot embrace,
She waxeth very weakly as she warms,
Then sighing yields her up to love's delicious harms.

Waked by the crowd, slow from his bench arose
A comely full-spread porter, swoln with sleep;
His calm, broad, thoughtless aspect breathed repose,
And in sweet torpor he was plungèd deep,
Ne could himself from ceaseless yawning keep;
While o'er his eyes the drowsy liquor ran,
Through which his half-waked soul would faintly peep.
Then, taking his black staff, he called his man,
And roused himself as much as rouse himself he can.

The lad leaped lightly at his master's call.
He was, *to weet, a little roguish page,
Save sleep and play who minded nought at all,
Like most the untaught striplings of his age.
This boy he kept each band to disengage,
Garters and buckles, task for him unfit,
But ill becoming his grave personage,
And which his portly paunch would not permit.
So this same limber page to all performèd it.

Meantime the master-porter wide displayed
Great store of caps, of slippers, and of gowns,
Wherewith he those who entered in arrayed,
Loose as the breeze that plays along the downs,
And waves the summer woods when evening frowns.
Oh, fair undress, best dress! it checks no vein,
But every flowing limb in pleasure drowns,
And heightens ease with grace. This done right *fain
Sir Porter sat him down, and turned to sleep again.

Thus easy robed, they to the fountain sped,
That in the middle of the court up-threw
A stream, high-spouting from its liquid bed,
And falling back again in drizzly dew;
There each deep draughts, as deep he thirsted, drew.
It was a fountain of *nepenthe rare:
Whence, as *Dan Homer *sings, huge pleasaunce grew,
And sweet oblivion of vile earthly care,
Fair gladsome waking thoughts, and joyous dreams more fair.

This rite performed, all inly pleased and still,
Withouten *trump was proclamation made:
"Ye sons of Indolence, do what you *will;
And wander where you list, through hall or glade:
Be no man's pleasure for another's stayed:
Let each as likes him best his hours employ,
And curst be he who minds his neighbour's trade!
Here dwells kind ease, and unreproving joy;
He little merits bliss who others can annoy."

Straight of these endless numbers, swarming round
As thick as idle motes in sunny ray,
Not one *eftsoons in view was to be found,
But every man strolled off his own glad way.
Wide o'er this ample court's blank area,
With all the lodges that thereto pertained,
No living creature could be seen to stray;
While solitude and perfect silence reigned:
So that to think you dreamt you almost *was constrained.

As when a shepherd of the Hebrid Isles
Placed far amid the melancholy main,
(Whether it be lone fancy him beguiles,
Or that aërial beings sometimes deign
To stand embodied to our senses plain)
Sees on the naked hill, or valley low,
The whilst in ocean Phœbus dips his *wain,
A vast assembly moving to and fro;
Then all at once in air dissolves the wondrous show.

Ye gods of quiet, and of sleep profound,
Whose soft dominion o'er this castle sways,
And all the widely-silent places round,
Forgive me, if my trembling pen displays
What never yet was sung in mortal lays.
But how shall I attempt such arduous string?
I who have spent my nights and nightly days
In this soul-deadening *place, loose loitering —
Ah! how shall I for this uprear my moulted wing?

Come on, my Muse, nor stoop to low despair,
Thou *imp of Jove, touched by celestial fire!
Thou yet shalt sing of war and actions fair
Which the bold sons of Britain will inspire;
Of ancient bards thou yet shalt sweep the lyre;
Thou yet shalt tread in tragic pall the stage,
Paint love's enchanting woes, the hero's ire,
The sage's calm, the patriot's noble rage,
Dashing corruption down through every worthless *age.

The doors, that knew no shrill alarming bell,
Ne cursèd knocker plied by villain's hand,
Self-opened into halls where, who can tell
What elegance and grandeur wide expand
The pride of Turkey and of Persia land?
Soft quilts on quilts, on carpets carpets spread,
And couches stretched around in seemly band;
And endless pillows rise to prop the head;
So that each spacious room was one full-swelling bed.

And everywhere huge covered tables stood,
With wines high-flavoured and rich viands crowned;
Whatever sprightly juice or tasteful food
On the green bosom of this earth are found,
And all old ocean genders in his round —
Some hand unseen these silently displayed,
Even undemanded by a sign or sound;
You need but wish, and, instantly obeyed,
Fair-ranged the dishes rose, and thick the glasses *played.

Here freedom reigned without the least alloy;
Nor gossip's tale, nor ancient maiden's gall,
Nor saintly spleen durst murmur at our joy,
And with envenomed tongue our pleasures pall.
For why? there was but one great rule for all;
To wit, that each should work his own *desire,
And eat, drink, study, sleep, as it may fall,
Or melt the time in love, or wake the lyre,
And carol what, unbid, the Muses might inspire.

The rooms with costly tapestry were hung,
Where was inwoven many a gentle tale,
Such as of old the rural poets sung
Or of Arcadian or Sicilian vale:
Reclining lovers in the lonely dale
Poured forth at large the sweetly tortured heart;
Or, looking tender passion, swelled the gale,
And taught charmed echo to resound their smart;
While flocks, woods, streams around, repose and peace impart.

Those pleased the most, where, by a cunning hand,
*Depeinten was the patriarchal age;
What time Dan Abraham left the Chaldee *land,
And pastured on from verdant stage to stage,
Where fields and fountains fresh could best engage.
Toil was not then. Of nothing took they heed,
But with wild beasts the silvan war to wage
And o'er vast plains their herds and flocks to feed.
Blest sons of nature they! true golden age indeed!

Sometimes the *pencil, in cool airy halls,
Bade the gay bloom of vernal landskips rise,
Or autumn's varied shades imbrown the walls.
Now the black tempest strikes the astonished eyes;
Now down the steep the flashing torrent flies;
The trembling sun now plays o'er ocean blue.

And now rude mountains frown amid the skies;
Whate'er *Lorrain light-touched with softening hue,
Or savage *Rosa dashed, or learnèd *Poussin drew.

Each sound too here to languishment inclined,
Lulled the weak bosom, and inducèd ease.
Aërial music in the warbling wind,
At distance rising oft, by small degrees,
Nearer and nearer came, till o'er the trees
It hung, and breathed such soul-dissolving airs
As did, alas! with soft perdition please.
Entangled deep in its enchanting snares,
The listening heart forgot all duties and all cares.

A certain music, never known *before,
Here soothed the pensive melancholy mind;
Full easily obtained. Behoves no more,
But sidelong to the gently-waving wind
To lay the well-tuned instrument reclined;
From which, with airy flying fingers light,
Beyond each mortal touch the most refined,
The god of winds drew sounds of deep delight:
Whence, with just cause, the harp of Æolus it hight.

Ah me! what hand can touch the strings so fine?
Who up the lofty diapason roll
Such sweet, such sad, such solemn airs divine,
Then let them down again into the soul?
Now rising love they fanned; now pleasing dole
They breathed, in tender musings, through the heart;
And now a graver sacred strain they stole,
As when seraphic hands an hymn impart:
Wild warbling nature all, above the reach of art!

Such the gay splendour, the luxurious state,
Of Caliphs old, who on the Tigris' shore,
In mighty Bagdad, populous and great,
Held their bright court, where was of ladies store;
And verse, love, music still the garland wore:
When sleep was coy, the bard in waiting there
Cheered the lone midnight with the Muse's lore;
Composing music, bade his dreams be fair,
And music lent new gladness to the morning air.

Near the pavilions where we slept, still ran
Soft-tinkling streams, and dashing waters fell,
And sobbing breezes sighed, and oft began
(So worked the wizard) wintry storms to swell,
As heaven and earth they would together *mell.
At doors and windows, threatening, seemed to call
The demons of the tempest, growling fell;
Yet the least entrance found they none at all;
Whence sweeter grew our sleep, secure in massy hall.

And hither Morpheus sent his kindest dreams,
Raising a world of gayer tinct and grace;
O'er which were shadowy cast Elysian gleams,
That played in waving lights from place to place,
And shed a roseate smile on nature's face.
Not *Titian's pencil e'er could so array,
So fleece with clouds the pure ethereal space;
Ne could it e'er such melting forms display,
As loose on flowery beds all languishingly lay.

No, fair illusions! artful phantoms, no!
My Muse will not attempt your fairyland.
She has no colours that like you can glow;
To catch your vivid scenes too gross her hand.
But sure it is, was ne'er a subtler band
Than these same guileful angel-seeming sprights,
Who thus in dreams voluptuous, soft, and bland,
Poured all the Arabian *heaven upon our nights,
And blessed them oft besides with more refined delights.

They were in sooth a most enchanting train,
Even feigning virtue; skillful to unite
With evil good, and strew with pleasure pain.

But, *for those *fiends whom blood and broils delight,
Who hurl the wretch as if to hell outright
Down, down black gulfs where sullen waters sleep,
Or hold him clambering all the fearful night
On beetling cliffs, or pent in ruins deep:
They, till due time should serve, were bid far hence to keep.

Ye guardian spirits to whom man is dear,
From these foul demons shield the midnight gloom!
Angels of fancy and of love, be near,
And o'er the wilds of sleep diffuse a bloom;
Evoke the sacred shades of Greece and Rome,
And let them virtue with a look impart!
But chief, a while, oh, lend us from the tomb
Those long-lost friends for whom in love we smart,
And fill with pious awe and joy-mixt woe the heart!

Or are you sportive? Bid the morn of youth
Rise to new light, and beam afresh the days
Of innocence, simplicity, and truth;
To cares estranged, and manhood's thorny ways.
What transport to retrace our boyish plays,
Our easy bliss, when each thing joy supplied:
The woods, the mountains, and the warbling maze
Of the wild brooks! But, fondly wandering wide,
My Muse, resume the task that yet doth thee *abide.

One great amusement of our household was
In a huge crystal magic globe to spy,
Still as you turned it, all things that do pass
Upon this ant-hill earth; where constantly
Of idly-busy men the restless fry
Run bustling to and fro with foolish haste
In search of pleasures vain, that from them fly,
Or which, obtained, the caitiffs dare not taste:
When nothing is enjoyed, can there be greater waste?

Of Vanity the Mirror this was called.
Here you a muckworm of the town might see
At his dull desk, amid his ledgers stalled,
Eat up with carking care and penury,
Most like to carcase parched on gallow-tree.
"A penny savèd is a penny got":
Firm to this scoundrel maxim keepeth he,
Ne of its rigour will he bate a jot,
Till it has quenched his fire, and banishèd his *pot.

Straight from the filth of this low grub, behold!
Comes fluttering forth a gaudy spendthrift heir,
All glossy gay, enamelled all with gold,
The silly tenant of the summer air.
In folly lost, of nothing takes he care;
Pimps, lawyers, stewards, harlots, flatterers vile,
And thieving tradesmen him among them share:
His father's ghost from Limbo-lake the while
Sees this, which more damnation doth upon him pile.

This globe portrayed the race of learned men,
Still at their books and turning o'er the page
Backwards and forwards; oft they snatch the pen
As if inspired and in a *Thespian rage,
Then write, and blot, as would your ruth engage.
Why, authors, all this scrawl and scribbling sore?
To lose the present, gain the future age,
Praisèd to be when you can hear no more,
And much enriched with fame when useless worldly store!

Then would a splendid city rise to view,
With carts, and cars, and coaches roaring all.
Wide-poured abroad, behold the prowling crew;
See how they dash along from wall to wall!
At every door, hark how they thundering call!
Good Lord! what can this giddy *rout excite?
Why? each on each to prey, by guile or gall;

With flattery these, with slander those to blight,
And make new tiresome parties for the coming night.

The puzzling sons of party next appeared,
In dark *cabals and nightly *juntos met;
And now they whispered close, now shrugging reared
The important shoulder; then, as if to get
New light, their twinkling eyes were inward set.
No sooner *Lucifer recalls affairs,
Than forth they various rush in mighty fret;
When lo! pushed up to power, and crowned their cares,
In comes another set, and kicketh them downstairs.

But what most showed the vanity of life
Was to behold the nations all on fire,
In cruel broils engaged, and deadly strife;
Most Christian kings, inflamed by black desire,
With honourable ruffians in their hire,
Cause war to rage, and blood around to pour.
Of this sad work when each begins to tire,
They sit them down just where they were before,
Till for new scenes of woe peace shall their force restore.

To number up the thousands dwelling here,
An useless were, and eke an endless task:
From kings, and those who at the helm appear,
To gipsies brown in summer-glades who bask.
Yea, many a man, perdie, I could unmask,
Whose desk and table make a solemn show
With tape-tied trash, and suits of fools that ask
For place or pension, laid in decent row;
But these I passen by, with nameless numbers *moe.

Of all the gentle tenants of the place,
There was a *man of special grave remark:
A certain tender gloom o'erspread his face,
Pensive, not sad; in thought involved, not dark:
As *soote this man could sing as morning-lark,
And teach the noblest morals of the heart;
But these his talents were yburied *stark;
Of the fine stores he nothing would impart,
Which or *boon nature gave or nature-painting art.

To noontide shades *incontinent he ran
Where purls the brook with sleep-inviting sound;
Or, when Dan Sol to slope his wheels began,
Amid the *broom he basked him on the ground
Where the wild thyme and camomile are found.
There would he linger till the latest ray
Of light sat quivering on the welkin's bound;
Then homeward through the twilight shadows stray,
Sauntering and slow. So had he passèd many a day.

Yet not in thoughtless slumber were they passed;
For oft the heavenly fire that lay concealed
Emongst the sleeping embers mounted fast,
And all its native light anew revealed.
Oft as he traversed the cerulean field,
And marked the clouds that drove before the wind,
Ten thousand glorious systems would he build,
Ten thousand great ideas filled his mind;
But with the clouds they fled, and left no trace behind.

With him was sometimes joined in silent walk
(Profoundly silent, for they never spoke)
*One shyer still, who quite detested talk:
Oft, stung by spleen, at once away he broke
To groves of pine and broad o'ershadowing oak;
There, inly thrilled, he wandered all alone,
And on himself his pensive fury *wroke,
Ne ever uttered word, save when first shone
The glittering star of eve — "Thank heaven! the day is done."

Here lurked a *wretch who had not crept abroad
For forty years, ne face of mortal seen;
In chamber brooding like a loathly toad;
And sure his linen was not very clean.

Through secret loophole, that had practised been
Near to his bed, his dinner vile he took;
Unkempt, and rough, of squalid face and mien,
Our castle's shame! whence, from his filthy nook,
We drove the villain out for fitter lair to look.

One day there chanced into these halls to rove
A joyous * youth, who took you at first sight.
Him the wild wave of pleasure hither drove,
Before the sprightly tempest tossing light.
Certes, he was a most engaging wight,
Of social glee, and wit humane though keen,
Turning the night to day and day to night:
For him the merry bells had rung, I ween,
If, in this nook of quiet, bells had ever been.

But not even pleasure to excess is good:
What most elates then sinks the soul as low;
When springtide joy pours in with copious flood,
The higher still the exulting billows flow,
The farther back again they flagging go,
And leave us grovelling on the dreary shore.
Taught by this son of joy, we found it so;
Who, whilst he staid, kept in a gay uproar
Our maddened castle all, the abode of sleep no more.

As when in prime of June a burnished fly,
Sprung from the meads o'er which he sweeps along,
Cheered by the breathing bloom and vital sky,
Tunes up amid these airy halls his song,
Soothing at first the gay reposing throng;
And oft he sips their bowl, or, nearly drowned,
He, thence recovering, drives their beds among,
And scares their tender sleep with trump profound;
Then out again he flies, to wing his mazy round.

Another * guest there was, of sense refined,
Who felt each worth, — for every worth he had;
Serene yet warm, humane yet firm his mind,
As little touched as any man's with bad:
Him through their inmost walks the Muses * lad,
To him the sacred love of nature lent;
And sometimes would he make our valley glad.
Whenas we found he would not here be pent,
To him the better sort this friendly message sent:

"Come dwell with us! true son of virtue, come!
But if, alas! we cannot thee persuade
To lie content beneath our peaceful dome,
Ne ever more to quit our quiet glade;
Yet, when at last thy toils, but ill apaid,
Shall dead thy fire and damp its heavenly spark,
Thou wilt be glad to seek the rural shade,
There to indulge the Muse, and nature mark:
We then a lodge for thee will rear in * Hagley Park."

Here * whilom ligged * the Esopus of the age;
But, called by fame, in soul yprickèd deep,
A noble pride restored him to the stage,
And roused him like a giant from his sleep.
Even from his slumbers we advantage reap:
With double force the astonished scene he wakes,
Yet quits not nature's bounds. He knows to keep
Each due decorum: now the heart he shakes,
And now with well-urged sense the enlightened judgment takes.

A bard here * dwelt, more fat then bard beseems,
Who, void of envy, guile, and lust of gain,
On virtue still, and nature's pleasing themes,
Poured forth his unpremeditated strain,
The world forsaking with a calm disdain;
Here laughed he careless in his easy seat,
Here quaffed, encircled with the joyous train,
Oft moralizing sage; his ditty sweet
He loathèd much to write, ne carèd to repeat.

Full oft by holy feet our ground was trod;
Of clerks good plenty here you * mote espy.
A little, round, fat, * oily man of God
Was one I chiefly marked among the fry:
He had a roguish twinkle in his eye,
And shone all glittering with ungodly dew,
If a * tight damsel chanced to trippen by;
Which when observed, he shrunk into his * mew,
And straight would recollect his piety anew.

Nor be forgot a tribe who minded nought
(Old inmates of the place) but state affairs:
They looked, perdie, as if they deeply thought;
And on their brow sat every nation's cares.
The world by them is parcelled out in shares,
When in the Hall of Smoke they congress hold,
And the sage berry sun-burnt Mocha bears
Has cleared their inward eye: then, smoke-enrolled,
Their oracles break forth, mysterious as of old.

Here languid Beauty kept her pale-faced court:
Bevies of dainty dames of high degree
From every quarter hither made resort;
Where, from gross mortal care and business free,
They lay poured out in ease and luxury.
Or, should they a vain show of work assume,
Alas! and well-a-day! what can it be?
To *knot, to twist, to range the vernal bloom;
But far is cast the distaff, spinning-wheel, and loom.

Their only labour was to kill the time;
And labour dire it is, and weary woe.
They sit, they loll, turn o'er some idle rhyme;
Then, rising sudden, to the glass they go,
Or saunter forth with tottering step and slow.
This soon too rude an exercise they find;
Strait on the couch their limbs again they throw,
Where, hours on hours, they sighing lie reclined,
And court the *vapoury god soft-breathing in the wind.

Now must I mark the villany we found,
But ah! too late, as shall eftsoons be shown.
A place here was, deep, dreary, under ground;
Where still our inmates, when unpleasing grown,
Diseased, and loathsome, privily were thrown.
Far from the light of heaven they languished there,
Unpitied, uttering many a bitter groan;
For of these wretches taken was no care:
Fierce fiends and hags of hell their only nurses were.

Alas the *change! from scenes of joy and rest
To this dark den, where sickness tossed alway.
Here Lethargy, with deadly sleep oppressed,
Stretched on his back, a mighty lubbard lay,
Heaving his sides, and snorèd night and day;
To stir him from his traunce it was not *eath,
And his half-opened eyne he shut straitway;
He led, I wot, the softest way to death,
And taught withouten pain and strife to yield the breath.

Of limbs enormous, but withal unsound,
Soft-swoln, and pale, here lay the Hydropsy:
Unwieldy man! with belly monstrous round,
Forever fed with watery supply;
For still he drank, and yet he still was dry.
And moping here did Hypochondria sit,
Mother of Spleen, in robes of various dye,
Who vexèd was full oft with ugly fit;
And some her *frantic deemed, and some her deemed a wit.

A lady proud she was, of ancient blood,
Yet oft her fear her pride made crouchen low:
She felt, or fancied in her fluttering mood,
All the diseases which the *spittles know,
And sought all physic which the shops bestow,
And still new leeches and new drugs would try,
Her humour ever wavering to and fro;
For sometimes she would laugh, and sometimes cry,
Then sudden waxèd wroth; and all she knew not why.

Fast by her side a listless maiden pined,
With aching head and squeamish heart-burnings;
Pale, bloated, cold, she seemed to hate mankind,
Yet loved in secret all forbidden things.
And here the *Tertian shakes his chilling wings;
The sleepless Gout here counts the crowing cocks —
A wolf now gnaws him, now a serpent stings;
Whilst Apoplexy crammed Intemperance knocks
Down to the ground at once, as butcher felleth ox.

[1748]

MARK AKENSIDE

Born the son of a butcher in 1721, the poet Akenside rose at the end of his life to be physician to Queen Charlotte. This success was due in part to the fame he won at the age of twenty-three by the publication of his chief poem, *The Pleasures of Imagination*, partly to his well-earned eminence as a physician, but perhaps chiefly to the fact that on the accession of George III he became a Tory after having been for half a lifetime a violent Whig. What Dr. Johnson says of his politics, that he showed "an impetuous eagerness to subvert and confound, with very little care what should be established," is applicable, within limits, to his literary theory. In his almost forgotten *Remonstrance of Shakespeare* the natural alliance between the doctrines which we now regard as foreshadowings of the romantic movement, on the one hand, and British patriotism, insularity, and dislike of France on the other, is made exceptionally clear. Akenside shows his romantic leanings by preferring "native wood-notes wild" to the most correct but imported song. In him as in Charles Churchill, this preference is related to Whig principles, and it has a nationalistic as well as a literary motive.

And yet, so even did the balance hang at the middle of the century, classical elements are as readily discerned as the romantic in Akenside's verse. His unusually deep study of the ancient languages not only trained his ear to a finer sense of verbal harmonies than most poets of his time possessed, but they shaped his imagination, as may be seen in his chaste and cool *Inscription for a Grotto*. He rises too seldom, however, above the pompous ostentation of learning and the chilly rhetoric that ruin for modern taste what might otherwise have been his best poem, the *Hymn to the Naiads*.

Akenside's chief model of style in *The Pleasures of Imagination* is of course John Milton, whom he follows closely enough to write at any rate the most musical blank verse of the century. The thought of this poem, badly arranged and often obscurely phrased, is borrowed from Shaftesbury's *Characteristics* and from certain of Addison's papers in the *Spectator*. The theme, which we should now classify as belonging to æsthetics and psychology, is ill-suited to poetical treatment. Nevertheless, turgid and pretentious as it often is, this poem contains some passages of cloudy splendour highly creditable to the poet who composed them, apparently, before he reached the age of twenty, without the advantages of higher education.

In the last months of his life, which ended in 1770, Akenside rewrote *The Pleasures of Imagination* without improving it. The present selection is taken from the opening lines of the first of the three books into which the earlier version was divided.

THE PLEASURES OF IMAGINATION

From Book I

With what attractive charms this goodly frame
Of nature touches the consenting hearts
Of mortal men; and what the pleasing stores
Which beauteous imitation thence derives
To deck the poet's or the painter's toil,
My verse unfolds. Attend, ye gentle powers
Of musical delight! and while I sing
Your gifts, your honours, dance around my strain.
Thou, smiling queen of every tuneful breast,
Indulgent Fancy! from the fruitful banks
Of Avon, whence thy rosy fingers cull
Fresh flowers and dews to sprinkle on the turf
Where Shakespeare lies, be present: and with thee
Let Fiction come, upon her vagrant wings
Wafting ten thousand colours through the air,
Which, by the glances of her magic eye,
She blends and shifts at will, through countless forms,
Her wild creation. Goddess of the lyre,
Which rules the accents of the moving sphere,
Wilt thou, eternal Harmony, descend
And join this festive train? for with thee comes
The guide, the guardian of their lovely sports,
Majestic Truth; and where Truth deigns to come,
Her sister Liberty will not be far.
Be present all ye Genii who conduct
The wandering footsteps of the youthful bard,
New to your springs and shades, who touch his ear
With finer sounds, who heighten to his eye
The bloom of nature, and before him turn
The gayest, happiest attitude of things.
Oft have the laws of each poetic strain

The critic-verse employ'd; yet still unsung
Lay this prime subject, though importing most
A poet's name: for fruitless is the attempt,
By dull obedience and by creeping toil
Obscure to conquer the severe ascent
Of high Parnassus. Nature's kindling breath
Must fire the chosen genius; Nature's hand
Must string his nerves, and imp his eagle-wings,
Impatient of the painful steep, to soar
High as the summit; there to breathe at large
Ethereal air, with bards and sages old,
Immortal sons of praise. These flattering scenes,
To this neglected labour court my song;
Yet not unconscious what a doubtful task
To paint the finest features of the mind,
And to most subtile and mysterious things
Give colour, strength, and motion. But the love
Of nature and the Muses bids explore,
Through secret paths erewhile untrod by man,
The fair poetic region, to detect
Untasted springs, to drink inspiring draughts,
And shade my temples with unfading flowers
Cull'd from the laureate vale's profound recess,
Where never poet gain'd a wreath before.

From Heaven my strains begin; from Heaven descends
The flame of genius to the human breast,
And love and beauty, and poetic joy
And inspiration. Ere the radiant sun
Sprang from the east, or 'mid the vault of night
The moon suspended her serener lamp;
Ere mountains, woods, or streams adorn'd the globe,
Or Wisdom taught the sons of men her lore;
Then liv'd the Almighty One: then, deep re-tir'd
In his unfathom'd essence, view'd the forms,
The *forms eternal of created things;
The radiant sun, the moon's nocturnal lamp,
The mountains, woods, and streams, the roll-ing globe,
And Wisdom's mien celestial. From the first
Of days, on them his love divine he fix'd,
His admiration; till in time complete
What he admir'd and lov'd, his vital smile
Unfolded into being. Hence the breath
Of life informing each organic frame;
Hence the green earth, and wild resounding waves;
Hence light and shade alternate, warmth and cold,
And clear autumnal skies and vernal showers,
And all the fair variety of things.

But not alike to every mortal eye
Is this great scene unveil'd. For, since the claims
Of social life to different labours urge
The active powers of man, with wise intent
The hand of Nature on peculiar minds
Imprints a different bias, and to each
Decrees its province in the common toil.
To some she taught the fabric of the sphere,
The changeful moon, the circuit of the stars,
The golden zones of heaven; to some she gave
To weigh the moment of eternal things,
Of time, and space, and fate's unbroken chain,
And will's quick impulse; others by the hand
She led o'er vales and mountains, to explore
What healing virtue swells the tender veins
Of herbs and flowers; or what the beams of morn
Draw forth, distilling from the clifted rind
In balmy tears. But some, to higher hopes
Were destin'd; some within a finer mould
She wrought and temper'd with a purer flame.
To these the Sire Omnipotent unfolds
The world's harmonious volume, there to read
The transcript of himself. On every part
They trace the bright impressions of his hand:
In earth or air, the meadow's purple stores,
The moon's mild radiance, or the virgin's form
Blooming with rosy smiles, they see portray'd
That uncreated beauty which delights
The Mind Supreme. They also feel her charms,
Enamour'd: they partake the eternal joy.

For as old Memnon's image, long renown'd
By fabling Nilus, to the quivering touch
Of Titan's ray, with each repulsive string
Consenting, sounded through the warbling air
Unbidden strains, even so did Nature's hand
To certain species of external things,
Attune the finer organs of the mind;
So the glad impulse of congenial powers,
Or of sweet sound, or fair proportion'd form,
The grace of motion, or the bloom of light,
Thrills through Imagination's tender frame,
From nerve to nerve; all naked and alive
They catch the spreading rays; till now the soul
At length discloses every tuneful spring,
To that harmonious movement from without
Responsive. Then the inexpressive strain
Diffuses its enchantment: Fancy dreams

*Notes on Mark Akenside will be found in the Appendix, p. 1004.

Of sacred fountains and Elysian groves,
And vales of bliss; the intellectual power
Bends from his awful throne a wondering ear,
And smiles; the passions, gently soothed away,
Sink to divine repose, and love and joy
Alone are waking; love and joy, serene
As airs that fan the summer. Oh! attend,
Whoe'er thou art, whom these delights can touch,
Whose candid bosom the refining love
Of Nature warms, oh! listen to my song;
And I will guide thee to her favourite walks,
And teach thy solitude her voice to hear,
And point her loveliest features to thy view.

Know then, whate'er of Nature's pregnant stores,
Whate'er of mimic Art's reflected forms
With love and admiration thus inflame
The powers of Fancy, her delighted sons
To three illustrious orders have referr'd;
Three sister Graces, whom the painter's hand,
The poet's tongue confesses: the Sublime,
The Wonderful, the Fair. I see them dawn!
I see the radiant visions, where they rise,
More lovely than when Lucifer displays
His beaming forehead through the gates of morn,
To lead the train of Phœbus and the spring.

Say, why was man so eminently rais'd
Amid the vast creation; why ordain'd
Through life and death to dart his piercing eye,
With thoughts beyond the limit of his frame;
But that the Omnipotent might send him forth
In sight of mortal and immortal powers,
As on a boundless theatre, to run
The great career of justice; to exalt
His generous aim to all diviner deeds;
To chase each partial purpose from his breast;
And through the mists of passion and of sense,
And through the tossing tide of chance and pain,
To hold his course unfaltering, while the voice
Of truth and virtue, up the steep ascent
Of nature, calls him to his high reward,
The applauding smile of Heaven? Else wherefore burns
In mortal bosoms this unquenched hope,
That breathes from day to day sublimer things,
And mocks possession? Wherefore darts the mind,
With such resistless ardour to embrace
Majestic forms; impatient to be free,
Spurning the gross control of willful might;
Proud of the strong contention of her toils;
Proud to be daring? Who but rather turns
To heaven's broad fire his unconstrained view,
Than to the glimmering of a waxen flame?
Who that, from Alpine heights, his labouring eye
Shoots round the wide horizon, to survey
Nilus or Ganges rolling his bright wave
Through mountains, plains, through empires black with shade,
And continents of sand, will turn his gaze
To mark the windings of a scanty rill
That murmurs at his feet? The high-born soul
Disdains to rest her heaven-aspiring wing
Beneath its native quarry. Tir'd of earth
And this diurnal scene, she springs aloft
Through fields of air; pursues the flying storm;
Rides on the volley'd lightning through the heavens;
Or, yok'd with whirlwinds and the northern blast,
Sweeps the long tract of day. Then high she soars
The blue profound, and, hovering round the sun,
Beholds him pouring the redundant stream
Of light; beholds his unrelenting sway
Bend the reluctant planets to absolve
The fated rounds of Time. Thence far effus'd
She darts her swiftness up the long career
Of devious comets; through its burning signs
Exulting measures the perennial wheel
Of Nature, and looks back on all the stars,
Whose blended light, as with a milky zone,
Invests the orient. Now amaz'd she views
The empyreal waste, where happy spirits hold,
Beyond this concave heaven, their calm abode;
And fields of radiance, whose unfading light
Has travell'd the profound six thousand years,
Nor yet arrives in sight of mortal things.
Even on the barriers of the world untir'd
She meditates the eternal depth below;
Till, half recoiling, down the headlong steep
She plunges; soon o'erwhelm'd and swallow'd up
In that immense of being. There her hopes
Rest at the fated goal. For from the birth
Of mortal man, the Sovereign Maker said,
That not in humble nor in brief delight,
Not in the fading echoes of renown,

Power's purple robes, nor Pleasure's flowery lap,
The soul should find enjoyment: but from these
Turning disdainful to an equal good,
Through all the ascent of things enlarge her view,
Till every bound at length should disappear,
And infinite perfection close the scene....

[1744]

THE REMONSTRANCE OF SHAKESPEARE

SUPPOSED TO HAVE BEEN SPOKEN AT THE THEATRE-ROYAL, WHILE THE FRENCH COMEDIANS WERE ACTING BY SUBSCRIPTION. 1749.

If, yet regardful of your native land,
Old Shakespeare's tongue you deign to understand,
Lo, from the blissful bowers where heaven rewards
Instructive sages and unblemish'd bards,
I come, the ancient founder of the stage,
Intent to learn, in this discerning age,
What form of wit your fancies have embrac'd,
And whither tends your elegance of taste,
That thus at length our homely toils you spurn,
That thus to foreign scenes you proudly turn,
That from my brow the laurel wreath you claim
To crown the rivals of your country's fame.
What though the footsteps of my devious Muse
The measured walks of Grecian art refuse?
Or though the frankness of my hardy style
Mock the nice touches of the critic's file?
Yet, what my age and climate held to view,
Impartial I survey'd and fearless drew.
And say, ye skillful in the human heart,
Who know to prize a poet's noblest part,
What age, what clime, could e'er an ampler field
For lofty thought, for daring fancy, yield?
I saw this England break the *shameful bands
Forged for the souls of men by sacred hands:
I saw each groaning realm her aid implore;
Her sons the heroes of each warlike shore:
Her naval standard (the dire Spaniard's bane)
Obey'd through all the circuit of the main.
Then, too, great Commerce, for a late-found world,
Around your coast her eager sails unfurl'd!
New hopes, new passions, thence the bosom fir'd;
New plans, new arts, the genius thence inspir'd;
Thence every scene, which private fortune knows,
In stronger life, with bolder spirit, rose.
Disgrac'd I this full prospect which I drew,
My colours languid, or my strokes untrue?
Have not your sages, warriors, swains, and kings,
Confess'd the living draught of men and things?
What other bard in any clime appears
Alike the master of your smiles and tears?
Yet have I deign'd your audience to entice
With wretched bribes to luxury and vice?
Or have my various scenes a purpose known
Which freedom, virtue, glory, might not own?
Such from the first was my dramatic plan;
It should be yours to crown what I began:
And now that England spurns her Gothic chain,
And equal laws and social science reign,
I thought, now surely shall my zealous eyes
View nobler bards and juster critics rise,
Intent with learned labour to refine
The copious ore of Albion's native mine,
Our stately Muse more graceful airs to teach,
And form her tongue to more attractive speech,
Till rival nations listen at her feet,
And own her polish'd as they own her great.
But do you thus my favourite hopes fulfill?
Is France at last the standard of your skill?
Alas for you! that so betray a mind
Of art unconscious and to beauty blind.
Say, does her language your ambition raise,
Her barren, trivial, unharmonious phrase,
Which fetters eloquence to scantiest bounds,
And maims the cadence of poetic sounds?
Say, does your humble admiration choose
The gentle prattle of her Comic Muse,
While wits, plain-dealers, fops, and fools appear,
Charged to say naught but what the king may hear?
Or rather melt your sympathizing hearts
Won by her tragic scene's romantic arts,
Where old and young declaim on soft desire,
And heroes never, but for love, expire?
No. Though the charms of novelty a while,
Perhaps too fondly, win your thoughtless smile,
Yet not for you design'd indulgent fate
The modes or manners of the Bourbon state.

And ill your minds my partial judgment reads,
And many an augury my hope misleads,
If the fair maids of yonder blooming train
To their light courtship would an audience deign,
Or those chaste matrons a Parisian wife
Choose for the model of domestic life;
Or if one youth of all that generous band,
The strength and splendour of their native land,
Would yield his portion of his country's fame,
And quit old freedom's patrimonial claim,
With lying smiles oppression's pomp to see,
And judge of glory by a king's decree.
Oh! bless'd at home with justly envied laws,
Oh! long the chiefs of Europe's general cause,
Whom heaven hath chosen at each dangerous hour
To check the inroads of barbaric power,
The rights of trampled nations to reclaim,
And guard the social world from bonds and shame;
Oh! let not luxury's fantastic charms
Thus give the lie to your heroic arms:
Nor for the ornaments of life embrace
Dishonest lessons from that *vaunting race,
Whom fate's dread laws (for, in eternal fate
Despotic rule was heir to freedom's hate),
Whom in each warlike, each commercial part,
In civic council, and in pleasing art,
The judge of earth predestined for your foes,
And made it fame and virtue to oppose.

[1772]

INSCRIPTION FOR A GROTTO

To me, whom in their lays the shepherds call
Actæa, daughter of the neighbouring stream,
This cave belongs. The fig tree and the vine,
Which o'er the rocky entrance downward shoot,
Were placed by Glycon. He with cowslips pale,
Primrose, and purple lychnis, deck'd the green
Before my threshold, and my shelving walls
With honeysuckle cover'd. Here at noon,
Lull'd by the murmur of my rising fount,
I slumber; here my clustering fruits I tend;
Or from the humid flowers, at break of day,
Fresh garlands weave, and chase from all my bounds
Each thing impure or noxious. Enter in,
O stranger, undismay'd. Nor bat, nor toad
Here lurks; and if thy breast of blameless thoughts
Approve thee, not unwelcome shalt thou tread
My quiet mansion; chiefly, if thy name
Wise Pallas and the immortal Muses own.

[1758]

EDWARD YOUNG

THOUGH his period of literary composition spanned a half-century, Edward Young wrote those works upon which his present reputation is chiefly based very late in life. His earlier work comprised odes, elegies, satires, essays, tragedies. After seeking in vain for secular preferment he took holy orders in 1727 and three years later was given the living of Welwyn in Hertfordshire, which he occupied until his death in 1765.

The Complaint, or Night Thoughts on Life, Death, and Immortality (1742–44), attained immediate popularity, was reprinted almost forty times within a generation after its publication, and has maintained its position as an English classic. Abroad, its popularity was no less great; it had a phenomenal influence in Germany, and it was translated into practically all the European languages, including Portuguese and Magyar. Like most of the other poems important in the early history of the romantic movement, this poem is a curious blend of the old and the new. In form it is a serious argument in support of orthodox Christianity, a philosophical work such as an eighteenth-century clergyman might have been expected to write on a subject comparable to that of Pope's *Essay on Man.* At the same time it is full of romantic notes: love of gloom and a not unpleasing melancholy, the *Il Penseroso* tradition which blossomed in the "Graveyard" poetry of Blair and Gray and their imitators; emotional self-expression and the new sensibility; dissatisfaction with the world, and the effort to escape through romantic solitude and through religious aspiration. It has many points of contact with James Hervey's *Meditations among the Tombs* (1746–47), which enjoyed a comparable popularity in England, though it is practically forgotten today. Such works, which gave expression to vague romantic concepts and emotions and at the same time associated them with sound orthodoxy, made a powerful appeal in the latter half of the eighteenth century.

Much has been made of the blank verse of *Night Thoughts* as marking a break with the heroic couplet, following the influence of Thomson and, more remotely, of Milton. That Young's rejection of rhyme for serious poetry was duly considered is proved by his remarks on the subject in his *Conjectures*; that it had a considerable influence on his followers is not to be doubted. Verse form, however, has received undue emphasis in some discussions of the beginnings of the romantic movement, probably because it is easy to see and to point out, in contrast to subtler and more important ideas and attitudes of mind. Dr. Johnson, whose lifelong advocacy of rhyme makes his testimony the more significant, said in the notes that he appended to Henry Croft's letter (which comprises the bulk of the treatment of Young in *The Lives of the English Poets*), "This is one of the few poems in which blank verse could not be changed for rhyme but with disadvantage." The structure of the blank verse, however, is very different from Milton's, or even Thomson's: it has few wide-wheeling periods; it is often broken; at times it suggests couplets without rhyme. Partly for this last reason and partly because of Young's rhetorical power, the poem contains an unusually large number of familiar quotations.

In 1759, when he was seventy-six years of age, Young published anonymously *Conjectures on Original Composition in a Letter to the Author of Sir Charles Grandison*, a pamphlet which has received much attention among recent students of the romantic movement. It has been said to mark a definite epoch in English criticism even more clearly than *Night Thoughts* marks an epoch in English poetry. At the same time one must realize that neither publication was original in a startling sense; both merely gave concrete expression to what was floating in the intellectual air. Young was mistaken in his assertion that nothing had previously been written on this theme, for it is really a phase of the ancient-modern controversy, in the course of which many writers had expressed similar sentiments. What makes the publication of the *Conjectures* notable is the clear-cut and, at times, exaggerated praise of originality in contrast to imitation. On the other hand there is no evidence to prove that the *Conjectures*, like *Night Thoughts*, exerted a very wide influence on contemporaries and successors. It is, however, a convenient statement of what was to develop into one of the central ideas of romanticism.

The classical point of view demands that the individual discipline himself in accordance with universally received standards of the best: in literature he follows the models; in life he develops his truest individuality by restraining his tendencies toward eccentricity. The chief precept is "Follow nature," which means almost exactly the opposite of the Rousseauistic counsel to follow one's natural impulses. This idealized and universalized nature is found expressed in the great classical models, such as Homer or Virgil; hence to imitate them is to follow nature. It forms the basis for the rules of the critics, which teach us to judge aright. Finally, since the world is a planned and consistent whole, nature, wherever encountered and however expressed, will be in accord with reason; and whatever purports to be natural must be reasonable. On this fourfold foundation of nature, models, rules, and reason stood the whole edifice of neo-classical criticism. For a century after the Restoration this foundation was unshaken; those who were disposed to protest had no considered body of critical doctrine to which they might appeal against it.

In the latter part of the eighteenth century was developed the theory of original genius. According to this theory the genius does not need models, but is actually hampered by them; he needs only to look within himself to find his true inspiration and his guide to the highest truth. The emphasis shifted from the universal to the particular, from nature to the individual. Those eccentricities which had been ridiculed as "humours," were now regarded as signs of genius, unavoidable and usually desirable; to be an "original," was no longer a reproach.

Toward the concept of original genius, there had been many previous approaches. Shakespearean criticism during the latter part of the seventeenth and the first part of the eighteenth century had tried to reconcile Shakespeare's violations of the rules and his unquestionable primacy in English literature by representing him as an untaught genius. In the *Spectator* No. 160 as well as in the series on "The Pleasures of the Imagination," Addison had dealt further with this idea and had unconsciously forecast its later development, which was eventually to destroy the foundations of neo-classical criticism. About the same time Shaftesbury, in *Characteristics* (1711), had discussed the same idea. Thus we can account for Dr. Johnson's comment, which Boswell records in *Journal of a Tour to the Hebrides*, that "he was surprised to find Young receive as novelties what he thought very common maxims." That Johnson, who had extraordinary sensitiveness to everything opposed to received neo-classical doctrine, should have failed to perceive the danger latent here, shows the slow and as yet unsuspected development of the original genius concept. Only in the light of later events could its implications become evident.

The passages here reprinted include the first book of *Night Thoughts* (the complete poem is in nine *Nights*) and the greater part of the *Conjectures*. The conclusion of this pamphlet presents an appreciation of Addison's work, which Young contrasts most favourably with that of Pope and Swift, and then concludes with what he asserts to be his "chief inducement for writing at all," an edifying account of Addison's death.

THE COMPLAINT, OR, NIGHT THOUGHTS ON LIFE, DEATH, AND IMMORTALITY

NIGHT THE FIRST

Tired Nature's sweet restorer, balmy Sleep!
He, like the world, his ready visit pays
Where Fortune smiles; the wretched he forsakes;
Swift on his downy pinion flies from woe,
And lights on lids unsullied with a tear.
  From short (as usual) and disturb'd repose,
I wake: how happy they who wake no more!
Yet that were vain, if dreams infest the grave.
I wake, emerging from a sea of dreams
Tumultuous; where my wreck'd desponding thought
From wave to wave of fancied misery
At random drove, her helm of reason lost.
Though now restored, 'tis only change of pain,
(A bitter change!) severer for severe.
*The day too short for my distress; and night,
Even in the zenith of her dark domain,
Is sunshine to the colour of my fate.
  Night, sable goddess! from her ebon throne,
In rayless majesty, now stretches forth
Her leaden sceptre o'er a slumbering world.
Silence, how dead! and darkness, how profound!
Nor eye, nor list'ning ear, an object finds;
Creation sleeps. 'Tis as the general pulse
Of life stood still, and nature made a pause;
An awful pause! prophetic of her end.
And let her prophecy be soon fulfill'd;
Fate! drop the curtain; I can lose no more.
  Silence and Darkness! solemn sisters! twins
From ancient Night, who nurse the tender thought
To reason, and on reason build resolve,
(That column of true majesty in man)
Assist me: I will thank you in the grave;
The grave, your kingdom; there this frame shall fall
A victim sacred to your dreary shrine.
But what are ye?—
                Thou, who didst put to flight
Primeval Silence, when the morning stars,
Exulting, shouted o'er the rising ball;
O thou, whose word from solid darkness struck
That spark, the sun; strike wisdom from my soul;

* Notes on Edward Young will be found in the Appendix, pp. 1004 ff.

My soul, which flies to thee, her trust, her treasure,
As misers to their gold, while others rest.
Through this opaque of nature, and of soul,
This double night, transmit one pitying ray,
To lighten, and to cheer. Oh, lead my mind,
(A mind that fain would wander from its woe)
Lead it through various scenes of life and death;
And from each scene the noblest truths inspire.
Nor less inspire my conduct, than my song;
Teach my best reason, reason; my best will
Teach rectitude; and fix my firm resolve
Wisdom to wed, and pay her long arrear:
Nor let the phial of thy vengeance, pour'd
On this devoted head, be pour'd in vain.
The bell strikes one. We take no note of time
But from its loss. To give it then a tongue
Is wise in man. As if an angel spoke,
I feel the solemn sound. If heard aright,
It is the knell of my departed hours:
Where are they? With the years beyond the flood.
It is the signal that demands despatch:
How much is to be done? My hopes and fears
Start up alarm'd, and o'er life's narrow verge
Look down — on what? a fathomless abyss;
A dread eternity! how surely mine!
And can eternity belong to me,
Poor pensioner on the bounties of an hour?
How poor, how rich, how abject, how august,
How complicate, how wonderful is man!
How passing wonder he who made him such!
Who centred in our make such strange extremes!
From diff'rent natures marvellously mix'd,
Connection exquisite of distant worlds!
Distinguish'd link in being's endless chain!
Midway from nothing to the Deity!
A beam ethereal, sullied and absorb'd!
Though sullied and dishonour'd, still divine!
Dim miniature of greatness absolute!
An heir of glory! a frail child of dust!
Helpless immortal! insect infinite!
A worm! a god! — I tremble at myself,
And in myself am lost! At home a stranger,
Thought wanders up and down, surprised, aghast,
And wond'ring at her own: how reason reels!
Oh, what a miracle to man is man,
Triumphantly distress'd! what joy, what dread!
Alternately transported and alarm'd!
What can preserve my life! or what destroy?
An angel's arm can't snatch me from the grave;
Legions of angels can't confine me there.
'Tis past conjecture; all things rise in proof:
While o'er my limbs Sleep's soft dominion spread,
What though my soul fantastic measures trod
O'er fairy fields; or mourn'd along the gloom
Of pathless woods; or down the craggy steep
Hurl'd headlong, swam with pain the mantled pool;
Or scaled the cliff; or danced on hollow winds,
With antic shapes, wild natives of the brain?
Her ceaseless flight, though devious, speaks her nature
Of subtler essence than the trodden clod;
Active, aërial, towering, unconfined,
Unfetter'd with her gross companion's fall.
Ev'n silent night proclaims my soul immortal:
Ev'n silent night proclaims eternal day.
For human weal, Heaven husbands all events;
Dull sleep instructs, nor sport vain dreams in vain.
Why then their loss deplore that are not lost?
Why wanders wretched thought their tombs around,
In infidel distress? Are angels there?
Slumbers, raked up in dust, ethereal fire?
They live! they greatly live a life on earth
Unkindled, unconceived; and from an eye
Of tenderness let heavenly pity fall
On me, more justly number'd with the dead.
This is the desert, this the solitude:
How populous, how vital, is the grave!
This is creation's melancholy vault,
The vale funereal, the sad cypress gloom;
The land of apparitions, empty shades!
All, all on earth is shadow, all beyond
Is substance; the reverse is Folly's creed:
How solid all, where change shall be no more!
This is the bud of being, the dim dawn,
The twilight of our day, the vestibule.
Life's theatre as yet is shut, and Death,
Strong Death, alone can heave the massy bar,
This gross impediment of clay remove,
And make us embryos of existence free.
From real life, but little more remote
Is he, not yet a candidate for light,
The future embryo, slumbering in his sire.
Embryos we must be, till we burst the shell,
Yon ambient azure shell, and spring to life,
The life of gods, oh transport! and of man.

Yet man, fool man! here buries all his thoughts;
Inters celestial hopes without one sigh.
Prisoner of earth, and pent beneath the moon,
Here pinions all his wishes; wing'd by Heaven
To fly at infinite; and reach it there,
Where seraphs gather immortality,
On life's fair tree, fast by the throne of God.
What golden joys ambrosial clustering glow
In his full beam, and ripen for the just,
Where momentary ages are no more!
Where time, and pain, and chance, and death expire!
And is it in the flight of threescore years
To push eternity from human thought,
And smother souls immortal in the dust?
A soul immortal, spending all her fires,
Wasting her strength in strenuous idleness,
Thrown into tumult, raptured, or alarm'd,
At aught this scene can threaten or indulge,
Resembles ocean into tempest wrought,
To waft a feather, or to drown a fly.

Where falls this censure? It o'erwhelms myself;
How was my heart incrusted by the world!
Oh, how self-fetter'd was my grov'lling soul!
How, like a worm, was I wrapt round and round
In silken thought, which reptile Fancy spun,
Till darken'd reason lay quite clouded o'er
With soft conceit of endless comfort here,
Nor yet put forth her wings to reach the skies!

Night-visions may befriend (as sung above):
Our waking dreams are fatal. How I dreamt
Of things impossible! (Could sleep do more?)
Of joys perpetual in perpetual change!
Of stable pleasures on the tossing wave!
Eternal sunshine in the storms of life!
How richly were my noontide trances hung
With gorgeous tapestries of pictured joys!
Joy behind joy, in endless perspective!
Till at Death's toll, whose restless iron tongue
Calls daily for his millions at a meal,
Starting I woke, and found myself undone.
Where now my frenzy's pompous furniture?
The cobwebb'd cottage, with its ragged wall
Of mouldering mud, is royalty to me!
The spider's most attenuated thread
Is cord, is cable, to man's tender tie
On earthly bliss; it breaks at every breeze.

Oh, ye blest scenes of permanent delight!
Full above measure! lasting beyond bound!
A perpetuity of bliss is bliss.
Could you, so rich in rapture, fear an end,
That ghastly thought would drink up all your joy,
And quite unparadise the realms of light.
Safe are you lodged above these rolling spheres,
The baleful influence of whose giddy dance
Sheds sad vicissitude on all beneath.
Here teems with revolutions every hour;
And rarely for the better; or the best,
More mortal than the common births of Fate.
Each moment has its sickle, emulous
Of Time's enormous scythe, whose ample sweep
Strikes empires from the root; each moment plays
His little weapon in the narrower sphere
Of sweet domestic comfort, and cuts down
The fairest bloom of sublunary bliss.

Bliss! sublunary bliss! — proud words, and vain!
Implicit treason to divine decree!
A bold invasion of the rights of Heaven!
I clasp'd the phantoms, and I found them air.
Oh, had I weigh'd it ere my fond embrace!
What darts of agony had miss'd my heart!

Death! great proprietor of all! 'tis thine
To tread out empire, and to quench the stars.
The sun himself by thy permission shines;
And, one day, thou shalt pluck him from his sphere.
Amid such mighty plunder, why exhaust
Thy partial quiver on a mark so mean?
Why thy peculiar rancour wreak'd on me?
Insatiate archer! could not one suffice?
Thy shaft flew thrice; and thrice my peace was slain;
And thrice, ere thrice yon moon had fill'd her horn.
O Cynthia! why so pale? dost thou lament
Thy wretched neighbour? grieve to see thy wheel
Of ceaseless change outwhirl'd in human life?
How wanes my borrow'd bliss! from Fortune's smile,
Precarious courtesy! Not Virtue's sure,
Self-given, solar ray of sound delight.

In every varied posture, place, and hour,
How widow'd every thought of every joy!
Thought, busy thought! too busy for my peace!
Through the dark postern of time long elapsed,
Led softly, by the stillness of the night,
Led, like a murderer, (and such it proves!)
Strays (wretched rover!) o'er the pleasing past;
In quest of wretchedness perversely strays:

And finds all desert now; and meets the ghosts
Of my departed joys; a numerous train!
I rue the riches of my former fate;
Sweet comfort's blasted clusters I lament;
I tremble at the blessings once so dear;
And every pleasure pains me to the heart.
Yet why complain? or why complain for one?
Hangs out the sun his lustre but for me,
The single man? Are angels all beside?
I mourn for millions: 'tis the common lot;
In this shape, or in that, has fate entail'd
The mother's throes on all of woman born,
Not more the children, than sure heirs, of pain.
War, famine, pest, volcano, storm, and fire,
Intestine broils, oppression, with her heart
Wrapt up in triple brass, besiege mankind.
God's image disinherited of day,
Here, plunged in mines, forgets a sun was made.
There, beings deathless as their haughty lord,
Are hammer'd to the galling oar for life;
And plough the winter's wave, and reap despair.
Some, for hard masters, broken under arms,
In battle lopp'd away, with half their limbs,
Beg bitter bread through realms their valour saved,
If so the tyrant, or his minion, doom.
Want and incurable disease, (fell pair!)
On hopeless multitudes remorseless seize
At once; and make a refuge of the grave.
How groaning hospitals eject their dead!
What numbers groan for sad admission there!
What numbers, once in Fortune's lap high-fed,
Solicit the cold hand of Charity!
To shock us more, solicit it in vain!
Ye silken sons of Pleasure! since in pains
You rue more modish visits, visit here,
And breathe from your debauch: give, and reduce
Surfeit's dominion o'er you; but so great
Your impudence, you blush at what is right.
Happy, did sorrow seize on such alone!
Not prudence can defend, or virtue save;
Disease invades the chastest temperance;
And punishment the guiltless; and alarm,
Through thickest shades pursues the fond of peace.
Man's caution often into danger turns,
And, his guard falling, crushes him to death.
Not happiness itself makes good her name!
Our very wishes give us not our wish.
How distant oft the thing we doat on most,
From that for which we doat, felicity!
The smoothest course of nature has its pains;
And truest friends, through error, wound our rest.
Without misfortune, what calamities!
And what hostilities, without a foe!
Nor are foes wanting to the best on earth.
But endless is the list of human ills,
And sighs might sooner fail, than cause to sigh.
A part how small of the terraqueous globe
Is tenanted by man! the rest a waste,
Rocks, deserts, frozen seas, and burning sands.
Wild haunts of monsters, poisons, stings, and death.
Such is earth's melancholy map! But, far
More sad! this earth is a true map of man.
So bounded are its haughty lord's delights
To woe's wide empire; where deep troubles toss,
Loud sorrows howl, envenom'd passions bite,
Ravenous calamities our vitals seize,
And threatening Fate wide opens to devour.
What then am I, who sorrow for myself?
In age, in infancy, from others' aid
Is all our hope; to teach us to be kind.
That, Nature's first, last lesson to mankind;
The selfish heart deserves the pain it feels;
More generous sorrow, while it sinks, exalts;
And conscious virtue mitigates the pang.
Nor virtue, more than prudence, bids me give
Swoln thought a second channel; who divide,
They weaken, too, the torrent of their grief.
Take then, O world! thy much-indebted tear:
How sad a sight is human happiness,
To those whose thought can pierce beyond an hour!
O thou! whate'er thou art, whose heart exults!
Would'st thou I should congratulate thy fate?
I know thou would'st; thy pride demands it from me.
Let thy pride pardon, what thy nature needs,
The salutary censure of a friend.
Thou happy wretch! by blindness art thou blest;
By dotage dandled to perpetual smiles.
Know, smiler! at thy peril art thou pleased;
Thy pleasure is the promise of thy pain.
Misfortune, like a creditor severe,
But rises in demand for her delay;
She makes a scourge of past prosperity,
To sting thee more, and double thy distress.
*Lorenzo, Fortune makes her court to thee,
Thy fond heart dances, while the siren sings.
Dear is thy welfare; think me not unkind;
I would not damp, but to secure thy joys.

Think not that fear is sacred to the storm:
Stand on thy guard against the smiles of Fate.
Is Heaven tremendous in its frowns? Most sure;
And in its favours formidable too:
Its favours here are trials, not rewards;
A call to duty, not discharge from care;
And should alarm us, full as much as woes;
Awake us to their cause and consequence;
And make us tremble, weigh'd with our desert;
Awe Nature's tumult, and chastise her joys,
Lest, while we clasp, we kill them; nay, invert
To worse than simple misery, their charms.
Revolted joys, like foes in civil war,
Like bosom friendships to resentment sour'd,
With rage envenom'd rise against our peace.
Beware what earth calls happiness; beware
All joys, but joys that never can expire.
Who builds on less than an immortal base,
Fond as he seems, condemns his joys to death.
  Mine died with thee, *Philander! thy last sigh
Dissolved the charm; the disenchanted earth
Lost all her lustre. Where her glittering towers?
Her golden mountains, where? all darken'd down
To naked waste; a dreary vale of tears:
The great magician's dead! Thou poor, pale piece
Of outcast earth, in darkness! what a change
From yesterday! Thy darling hope so near
(Long-labour'd prize!) Oh, how Ambition flush'd
Thy glowing cheek! Ambition truly great,
Of virtuous praise. Death's subtle seed within
(Sly, treacherous miner!) working in the dark,
Smiled at thy well-concerted scheme, and beckon'd
The worm to riot on that rose so red,
Unfaded ere it fell, — one moment's prey!
  Man's foresight is conditionally wise;
Lorenzo! wisdom into folly turns
Oft, the first instant, its idea fair
To labouring thought is born. How dim our eye!
The present moment terminates our sight;
Clouds, thick as those on doomsday, drown the next;
We penetrate, we prophesy in vain.
Time is dealt out by particles; and each,
Ere mingled with the streaming sands of life,
By Fate's inviolable oath is sworn
Deep silence, "Where eternity begins."
  By Nature's law, what may be, may be now;
There's no prerogative in human hours.
In human hearts what bolder thought can rise,
Than man's presumption on tomorrow's dawn?
Where is tomorrow? In another world.
For numbers this is certain; the reverse
Is sure to none; and yet on this perhaps,
This peradventure, infamous for lies,
As on a rock of adamant, we build
Our mountain hopes; spin out eternal schemes,
As we the Fatal Sisters could out-spin,
And, big with life's futurities, expire.
  Not ev'n Philander had bespoke his shroud;
Nor had he cause; a warning was denied:
How many fall as sudden, not as safe!
As sudden, though for years admonish'd home.
Of human ills the last extreme beware,
Beware, Lorenzo! a slow sudden death.
How dreadful that deliberate surprise!
Be wise to-day; 'tis madness to defer;
Next day the fatal precedent will plead;
Thus on, till wisdom is push'd out of life.
Procrastination is the Thief of time;
Year after year it steals, till all are fled,
And to the mercies of a moment leaves
The vast concerns of an eternal scene.
If not so frequent, would not this be strange?
That 'tis so frequent, this is stranger still.
  Of man's miraculous mistakes, this bears
The palm, "That all men are about to live,"
Forever on the brink of being born.
All pay themselves the compliment to think
They one day shall not drivel: and their pride
On this reversion takes up ready praise;
At least, their own; their future selves applauds;
How excellent that life they ne'er will lead!
Time lodged in their own hands is Folly's *vails;
That lodged in Fate's, to wisdom they consign;
The thing they can't but purpose, they postpone;
'Tis not in Folly, not to scorn a fool;
And scarce in human wisdom to do more.
All promise is poor dilatory man,
And that through every stage: when young, indeed,
In full content we, sometimes, nobly rest,
Unanxious for ourselves; and only wish,
As duteous sons, our fathers were more wise.
At thirty, man suspects himself a fool;

Knows it at forty, and reforms his plan;
At fifty, chides his infamous delay,
Pushes his prudent purpose to resolve;
In all the magnanimity of thought
Resolves; and re-resolves; then dies the same.
And why? Because he thinks himself immortal.
All men think all men mortal, but themselves:
Themselves, when some alarming shock of Fate
Strikes through their wounded hearts the sudden dread;
But their hearts wounded, like the wounded air,
Soon close; where pass'd the shaft, no trace is found.
As from the wing no scar the sky retains;
The parted wave no furrow from the keel;
So dies in human hearts the thought of death.
Even with the tender tear which nature sheds
O'er those we love, we drop it in their grave.
Can I forget Philander? That were strange!
Oh, my full heart!—But should I give it vent,
The longest night, though longer far, would fail,
And the lark listen to my midnight song.
The sprightly lark's shrill matin wakes the morn;
Grief's sharpest thorn hard pressing on my breast,
I strive, with wakeful melody, to cheer
The sullen gloom, sweet Philomel! like thee,
And call the stars to listen: every star
Is deaf to mine, enamour'd of thy lay.
Yet be not vain; there are, who thine excel,
And charm through distant ages: wrapt in shade,
Prisoner of darkness! to the silent hours,
How often I repeat their rage divine,
To lull my griefs, and steal my heart from woe!
I roll their raptures, but not catch their flames.
Dark, though not blind, like thee, * Mæonides!
Or, Milton! thee; ah, could I reach your strain!
Or * his, who made Mæonides our own.
Man too he sung: immortal man I sing;
Oft bursts my song beyond the bounds of life;
What, now, but immortality, can please?
Oh, had he press'd his theme, pursued the track,
Which opens out of darkness into day!
Oh, had he, mounted on his wing of fire,
Soar'd where I sink, and sung immortal man!
How had it bless'd mankind, and rescued me!

[1742]

From CONJECTURES ON ORIGINAL COMPOSITION

IN A LETTER TO * THE AUTHOR OF SIR CHARLES GRANDISON

Dear Sir,—We confess the follies of youth without a blush; not so those of age. However, keep me a little in countenance, by considering that age wants amusements more, though it can justify them less, than the preceding periods of life. How you may relish the pastime here sent you, I know not. It is miscellaneous in its nature, somewhat licentious in its conduct; and, perhaps, not over important in its end. However, I have endeavoured to make some amends, by digressing into * subjects more important, and more suitable to my season of life. A serious thought, standing single among many of a lighter nature, will sometimes strike the careless wanderer after amusement only, with useful awe, as monumental marbles scattered in a wide pleasure garden (and such there are) will call to recollection those who would never have sought it in a churchyard walk of mournful yews.

To one such monument I may conduct you, in which is a hidden lustre, like the sepulchral lamps of old; but not like those will this be extinguished, but shine the brighter for being produced, after so long concealment, into open day.

You remember that your worthy patron, and our common friend, put some questions on the serious drama, at the same time when he desired our sentiments on original and on moral composition. Though I despair of breaking through the frozen obstructions of age, and care's incumbent cloud, into that flow of thought, and brightness of expression which subjects so polite require; yet will I hazard some conjectures on them.

I begin with * original composition; and the more willingly, as it seems an original subject to me, who have seen nothing hitherto written on it: but first, a few thoughts on composition in general. Some are of opinion that its growth, at present, is too luxuriant; and that the press is overcharged. Overcharged, I think, it could never be, if none were admitted, but such as brought their imprimatur from sound understanding and the public good. Wit, indeed, however brilliant, should not be permitted to gaze self-enamoured on its useless charms, in that fountain of fame (if so I may call the press), if beauty is all that it has to boast; but, like * the first Brutus, it should sacrifice its most darling offspring to the sacred interests of virtue, and real service of mankind.

This restriction allowed, the more composition the better. To men of letters, and leisure, it is not only a noble amusement, but a sweet refuge; it improves their parts, and promotes their peace: it opens a back-door out of the bustle of this busy and idle world into a delicious garden of moral and intellectual fruits and flowers, the key of which is denied to the rest of mankind. When stung with idle anxieties, or teased with fruitless impertinence, or yawning over insipid diversions, then we perceive the blessing of a lettered recess. With what a gust do we retire to our disinterested and immortal friends in our closet, and find our minds, when applied to some favourite theme, as naturally, and as easily quieted and refreshed, as a peevish child (and peevish children are we all till we fall asleep) when laid to the breast? Our happiness no longer lives on charity; nor bids fair for a fall, by leaning on that most precarious and thorny pillow, another's pleasure, for our repose. How independent of the world is he who can daily find new acquaintance that at once entertain and improve him, in the little world, the minute but fruitful creation, of his own mind?

These advantages composition affords us, whether we write ourselves, or in more humble amusement peruse the works of others. While we bustle through the thronged walks of public life, it gives us a respite, at least, from care; a pleasing pause of refreshing recollection. If the country is our choice, or fate, there it rescues us from sloth and sensuality, which, like obscene vermin, are apt gradually to creep unperceived into the delightful bowers of our retirement, and to poison all its sweets. Conscious guilt robs the rose of its scent, the lily of its lustre; and makes an Eden a deflowered and dismal scene.

Moreover, if we consider life's endless evils, what can be more prudent than to provide for consolation under them? A consolation under them the wisest of men have found in the pleasures of the pen. Witness, among many more, Thucydides, Xenophon, Tully, Ovid, Seneca, Pliny the Younger, who says, **In uxoris infirmitate, et amicorum periculo, aut morte turbatus, ad studia, unicum doloris levamentum, confugio.* And why not add to these their modern equals, Chaucer, Raleigh, Bacon, Milton, Clarendon, under the same shield, unwounded by misfortune, and nobly smiling in distress?

Composition was a cordial to these under the frowns of fortune; but evils there are which her smiles cannot prevent or cure. Among these are the languors of old age. If those are held honourable, who in a hand benumbed by time have grasped the just sword in defence of their country; shall they be less esteemed, whose unsteady pen vibrates to the last in the cause of religion, of virtue, of learning? Both these are happy in this, that by fixing their attention on objects most important, they escape numberless little anxieties, and that * *tædium vitæ* which often hangs so heavy on its evening hours. May not this insinuate some apology for my spilling ink, and spoiling paper, so late in life?

But there are who write with vigour, and success, to the world's delight and their own renown. These are the glorious fruits where genius prevails. The mind of a man of genius is a fertile and pleasant field, pleasant as Elysium, and fertile as Tempe; it enjoys a perpetual spring. Of that spring originals are the fairest flowers; * imitations are of quicker growth, but fainter bloom. Imitations are of two kinds: one of nature, one of authors; the first we call originals, and confine the term imitation to the second. I shall not enter into the curious inquiry of what is, or is not, strictly speaking, original, content with what all must allow, that some compositions are more so than others; and the more they are so, I say, the better. Originals are, and ought to be, great favourites, for they are great benefactors; they extend the republic of letters, and add a new province to its dominion: imitators only give us a sort of duplicates of what we had, possibly much better, before; increasing the mere drug of books, while all that makes them valuable, knowledge and genius, are at a stand. The pen of an original writer, like *Armida's wand, out of a barren waste calls a blooming spring; out of that blooming spring an imitator is a transplanter of laurels, which sometimes die on removal, always languish in a foreign soil.

But suppose an imitator to be most excellent (and such there are), yet still he but nobly builds on another's foundation; his debt is, at least, equal to his glory; which, therefore, on the balance, cannot be very great. On the contrary, an original, though but indifferent (its originality being set aside), yet has something to boast; it is something to say with him in Horace,

**Meo sum pauper in ære;*

and to share ambition with no less than Cæsar, who declared he had rather be the first in a village than the second at Rome.

Still farther, an imitator shares his crown, if he has one, with the chosen object of his imitation; an original enjoys an undivided applause. An original may be said to be of a vegetable nature; it rises spontaneously from the vital root of genius; it grows, it is not made. Imitations are often a sort of manufacture wrought up by those mechanics, art and labour, out of pre-existent materials not their own.

Again, we read imitation with somewhat of his languor who listens to a twice-told tale; our spirits rouse at an original; that is a perfect stranger, and all throng to learn what news from a foreign land: and though it comes, like an Indian prince, adorned with feathers only, having little of weight; yet of our attention it will rob the more solid, if not equally new: thus every telescope is lifted at a new-discovered star; it makes a hundred astronomers in a moment, and denies equal notice to the sun. But if an original, by being as excellent as new, adds admiration to surprise, then are we at the writer's mercy; on the strong wing of his imagination we are snatched from Britain to Italy, from climate to climate, from pleasure to pleasure; we have no home, no thought, of our own; till the magician drops his pen: and then falling down into ourselves, we awake to flat realities, lamenting the change, like the beggar who dreamt himself a prince.

It is with thoughts as it is with words; and with both as with men; they may grow old and die. Words tarnished, by passing through the mouths of the vulgar, are laid aside as inelegant and obsolete. So thoughts, when become too common, should lose their currency; and we should send new metal to the mint, that is, new meaning to the press. The division of tongues at Babel did not more effectually debar men from making themselves a name (as the Scripture speaks), than the too great concurrence, or union of tongues will do forever. We may as well grow good by another's virtue, or fat by another's food, as famous by another's thought. The world will pay its debt of praise but once; and, instead of applauding, explode a second demand, as a cheat.

If it is said that most of the Latin classics, and all the Greek, except, perhaps, Homer, Pindar, and Anacreon, are in the number of imitators, yet receive our highest applause; our answer is that they, though not real, are accidental originals; the works they imitated, few excepted, are lost; they, on their father's decease, enter as lawful heirs on their estates in fame: the fathers of our copyists are still in possession; and secured in it, in spite of Goths and flames, by the perpetuating power of the press. Very late must a modern imitator's fame arrive, if it waits for their decease.

An original enters early on reputation: Fame, fond of new glories, sounds her trumpet in triumph at its birth; and yet how few are awakened by it into the noble ambition of like attempts? Ambition is sometimes no vice in life; it is always a virtue in composition. High in the towering Alps is the fountain of the Po; high in fame and in antiquity is the fountain of an imitator's undertaking; but the river and the imitation, humbly creep along the vale. So few are our originals that, if all other books were to be burnt, the lettered world would resemble some metropolis in flames, where a few incombustible buildings, a fortress, temple, or tower, lift their heads, in melancholy grandeur, amid the mighty ruin. Compared with this conflagration, *old Omar lighted up but a small bonfire, when he heated the baths of the barbarians, for eight months together, with the famed Alexandrian library's inestimable spoils, that no profane book might obstruct the triumphant progress of his holy Alcoran round the globe.

But why are originals so few? not because the writer's harvest is over, the great reapers of antiquity having left nothing to be gleaned after them; nor because the human mind's teeming time is past, or because it is incapable of putting forth unprecedented births; but because illustrious examples engross, prejudice, and intimidate. They engross our attention, and so prevent a due inspection of ourselves; they prejudice our judgment in favour of their abilities, and so lessen the sense of our own; and they intimidate us with the splendour of their renown, and thus under diffidence bury our strength. Nature's impossibilities, and those of diffidence lie wide asunder.

Let it not be suspected that I would weakly insinuate anything in favour of the moderns, as compared with ancient authors; no, I am lamenting their great inferiority. But I think it is no necessary inferiority; that it is not from divine destination, but from some cause far beneath the moon: I think that human souls, through all periods, are equal; that due care and exertion would set us nearer our immortal predecessors than we are at present; and he who questions and confutes this, will show abilities not a little tending toward a proof of that equality which he denies.

After all, the first ancients had no merit in being originals; they could not be imitators. Modern writers have a choice to make, and therefore have a merit in their power. They may soar in the regions of liberty, or move in the soft fetters of easy imitation; and imitation has as many plausible reasons to urge, as pleasure had to offer to Hercules. Hercules made the choice of an hero, and so became immortal.

Yet let not assertors of classic excellence imagine that I deny the tribute it so well deserves. He that admires not ancient authors betrays a secret he would conceal, and tells the world that he does not understand them. Let us be as far from neglecting as from copying their admirable compositions; sacred be their rights, and inviolable their fame. Let our understanding feed on theirs; they afford the noblest nourishment; but let them nourish, not annihilate, our own. When we read, let our imagination kindle at their charms; when we write, let our judgment shut them out of our thoughts; treat even Homer himself as his royal admirer was treated by the cynic; bid him stand aside, nor shade our composition from the beams of our own genius; for nothing original can rise, nothing immortal can ripen, in any other sun.

Must we then, you say, not imitate ancient authors? Imitate them by all means; but imitate aright. He that imitates the divine *Iliad* does not imitate Homer; but he who takes the same method which Homer took for arriving at a capacity of accomplishing a work so great. Tread in his steps to the sole fountain of immortality; drink where he drank, at the true Helicon, that is, at the breast of Nature: imitate; but imitate not the composition but the man. For may not this paradox pass into a maxim? viz. "The less we copy the renowned ancients, we shall resemble them the more."

But possibly you may reply that * you must either imitate Homer or depart from nature. Not so: for suppose you was to change place, in time, with Homer; then, if you write naturally, you might as well charge Homer with an imitation of you. Can you be said to imitate Homer for writing so as you would have written, if Homer had never been? As far as a regard to nature, and sound sense, will permit a departure from your great predecessors; so far, ambitiously, depart from them; the farther from them in similitude, the nearer are you to them in excellence; you rise by it into an original, become a noble collateral, not an humble descendant from them. Let us build our compositions with the spirit, and in the taste, of the ancients, but not with their materials: thus will they resemble the structures of Pericles at Athens, which Plutarch commends for having had an air of antiquity as soon as they were built. All eminence, and distinction, lies out of the beaten road; excursion and deviation are necessary to find it; and the more remote your path from the highway, the more reputable, if, like poor Gulliver (of whom anon), you fall not into a ditch in your way to glory.

What glory to come near, what glory to reach, what glory (presumptuous thought!) to surpass our predecessors! And is that then in nature absolutely impossible? Or is it not, rather, contrary to nature to fail in it? Nature herself sets the ladder; all wanting is our ambition to climb. For by the bounty of nature we are as strong as our predecessors; and by the favour of time (which is but another round in nature's scale) we stand on higher ground. As to the first, were they more than men? Or are we less? Are not our minds cast in the same mould with those before the flood? The flood affected matter; mind escaped. As to the second: though we are moderns, the world is an ancient; more ancient far than when they whom we most admire filled it with their fame. Have we not their beauties, as stars, to guide; their defects, as rocks, to be shunned; the judgment of ages on both, as a chart to conduct, and a sure helm to steer us in our passage to greater perfection than theirs? And shall we be stopped in our rival pretensions to fame by this just reproof?

> **Stat contra, dicitque tibi tua pagina, fur es.*
> MARTIAL.

It is by a sort of noble contagion, from a general familiarity with their writings, and not by any particular sordid theft, that we can be the better for those who went before us. Hope we, from plagiarism, any dominion in literature; as that of Rome arose from a nest of thieves?

Rome was a powerful ally to many states; ancient authors are our powerful allies; but we must take heed that they do not succour till they enslave, after the manner of Rome. Too formidable an idea of their superiority, like a spectre, would fright us out of a proper use of our wits, and dwarf our understanding, by making a giant of theirs. Too great awe for them lays genius under restraint, and denies it that free scope, that full elbow-room, which is requisite for striking its most masterly strokes. Genius is a master-workman; learning is but an instrument, and an instrument, though most valuable, yet not always indispensable. Heaven will not admit of a partner in the accomplishment of some favourite spirits; but, rejecting all human means, assumes the whole glory to itself. Have not some, though not famed for erudition, so written as almost to persuade us that they shone brighter, and soared higher, for escaping the boasted aid of that proud ally?

Nor is it strange; for what, for the most part, mean we by genius, but the power of accomplishing great things without the means generally reputed necessary to that end? A genius differs from a good understanding as a magician from a good architect: that raises his structure by means invisible; this by the skillful use of common tools. Hence genius has ever been supposed to partake of something divine. **Nemo unquam vir magnus fuit, sine aliquo afflatu divino.*

Learning, destitute of this superior aid, is fond and proud of what has cost it much pains; is a great lover of rules, and boaster of famed examples: as beauties less perfect, who owe half their charms to cautious art, learning inveighs against natural unstudied graces, and small harmless inaccuracies, and sets rigid bounds to that liberty to which genius often owes its supreme glory; but the no-genius its frequent ruin. For unprescribed beauties, and unexampled excellence, which are characteristics of genius, lie without the pale of learning's authorities, and laws; which pale, genius must leap to come at them: but by that leap, if genius is wanting, we break our necks; we lose that little credit which possibly we might have enjoyed before. For rules, like crutches, are a needful aid to the lame, though an impediment to the strong. A Homer casts them away; and, like his Achilles,

> **Jura negat sibi nata, nihil non arrogat,*

by native force of mind. There is something in poetry beyond prose-reason; there are mysteries in it not to be explained, but admired; which render mere prose-men infidels to their divinity. And here pardon a second paradox; viz. "Genius often then deserves most to be praised when it is most sure to be condemned; that is, when its excellence, from mounting high, to weak eyes is quite out of sight."

If I might speak farther of learning, and genius, I would compare genius to virtue, and learning to riches. As riches are most wanted where there is least virtue; so learning where there is least genius. As virtue without much riches can give happiness, so genius without much learning can give renown. As it is said in Terence, **Pecuniam negligere interdum maximum est lucrum*; so to neglect of learning, genius sometimes owes its greater glory. Genius, therefore, leaves but the second place among men of letters to the learned. It is their merit, and ambition, to fling light on the works of genius, and point out its charms. We most justly reverence their informing radius for that favour; but we must much more admire the radiant stars pointed out by them.

A star of the first magnitude among the moderns was Shakespeare; among the ancients, Pindar, who (as *Vossius tells us) boasted of his no-learning, calling himself the eagle, for his flight above it. And such genii as these may, indeed, have much reliance on their own native powers. For genius may be compared to the natural strength of the body: learning to the super-induced accoutrements of arms: if the first is equal to the proposed exploit, the latter rather encumbers than assists; rather retards than promotes the victory. **Sacer nobis inest Deus*, says Seneca. With regard to the moral world, conscience, with regard to the intellectual, genius is that god within. Genius can set us right in composition without the rules of the learned; as conscience sets us right in life without the laws of the land: this, singly, can make us good, as men: that, singly, as writers, can sometimes make us great.

I say, sometimes, because there is a genius which stands in need of learning to make it shine. Of genius there are two species, an earlier and a later; or call them infantine and adult. An adult genius comes out of nature's hand, as Pallas out of Jove's head, at full growth and mature: Shakespeare's genius was of this kind; on the contrary, Swift stumbled at the threshold, and set out for distinction on feeble knees: his was an infantine genius; a genius, which, like other infants, must be nursed, and educated, or it will come to naught: learning is its nurse and tutor; but this nurse may overlay with an indigested load, which smothers common sense; and this tutor may mislead, with pedantic prejudice, which vitiates the best understanding: as too great admirers of the fathers of the Church have sometimes set up their authority against the true sense of Scripture; so too great admirers of the classical fathers have sometimes set up their authority, or example, against reason.

> **Neve minor, neu sit quinto productior actu*
> *Fabula.*

So says Horace; so says ancient example. But reason has not subscribed. I know but one book that can justify our implicit acquiescence in it: and (by the way) on that book a noble disdain of undue deference to prior opinion has lately cast, and is still casting, a new and inestimable light.

But, superstition for our predecessors set aside, the classics are forever our rightful and revered masters in composition; and our understandings bow before them: but when? When a master is wanted; which, sometimes, as I have shown, is not the case. Some are pupils of nature only, nor go farther to school: from such we reap often a double advantage; they not only rival the reputation of the great ancient authors, but also reduce the number of mean ones among the moderns. For when they enter on subjects which have been in former hands, such is their superiority that, like a tenth wave, they overwhelm and bury in oblivion all that went before: and thus not only enrich and adorn, but remove a load, and lessen the labour, of the lettered world.

"But," you say, "since originals can arise from genius only, and since genius is so very rare, it is scarce worth while to labour a point so much, from which we can reasonably expect so little." To show that genius is not so very rare as you imagine, I shall point out strong instances of it in a far distant quarter from that mentioned above. The minds of the schoolmen were almost as much cloistered as their bodies; they had but little learning, and few books; yet may the most learned be struck with some astonishment at their so singular natural sagacity, and most exquisite edge of thought. Who would expect to find Pindar and Scotus, Shakespeare and Aquinas, of the same party? Both equally show an original, unindebted energy; the **vigor igneus*, and *cœlestis origo*, burns in both; and leaves us in doubt whether genius is more evident in the sublime flights and beauteous flowers of poetry, or in the profound penetrations, and marvellously keen and minute distinctions, called the thorns of the schools. There might have been more able consuls called from the plough than ever arrived at that honour; many a genius probably there has been which could neither write nor read. So that genius, that supreme lustre of literature, is less rare than you conceive.

By the praise of genius we detract not from learning; we detract not from the value of gold by saying that diamond has greater still. He who disregards learning shows that he wants its aid; and he that overvalues it shows that its aid has done him harm. Overvalued indeed it cannot be, if genius, as to composition, is valued more. Learning we thank, genius we revere; that gives us pleasure, this gives us rapture; that informs, this inspires, and is itself inspired; for genius is from heaven, learning from man: this sets us above the low and illiterate; that, above the learned and polite. Learning is borrowed knowledge; genius is knowledge innate, and quite our own. Therefore, as Bacon observes, it may take a nobler name, and be called wisdom; in which sense of wisdom some are born wise

But here a caution is necessary against the most fatal of errors in those automaths, those self-taught philosophers of our age who set up genius, and often mere fancied genius, not only above human learning, but divine truth. I have called genius wisdom; but let it be remembered that in the most renowned ages of the most refined heathen wisdom (and theirs is not Christian) "the world by wisdom knew not God, and it pleased God by the foolishness of preaching to save those that believed." In the fairyland of fancy, genius may wander wild; there it has a creative power, and may reign arbitrarily over its own empire of chimeras. The wide field of nature also lies open before it, where it may range unconfined, make what discoveries it can, and sport with its infinite objects uncontrolled, as far as visible nature extends, painting them as wantonly as it will. But what painter of the most unbounded and exalted genius can give us the true portrait of a seraph? He can give us only what, by his own or others' eyes, has been seen; though that indeed infinitely compounded, raised, burlesqued, dishonoured, or adorned: in like manner, who can give us divine truth unrevealed? Much less should any presume to set aside divine truth when revealed, as incongruous to their own sagacities. Is this too serious for my subject? I shall be more so before I close.

Having put in a caveat against the most fatal of errors, from the too great indulgence of genius, return we now to that too great suppression of it, which is detrimental to composition; and endeavour to rescue the writer, as well as the man. I have said that some are born wise; but they, like those that are born rich, by neglecting the cultivation and produce of their own possessions, and by running in debt, may be beggared at last; and lose their reputations, as younger brothers estates, not by being born with less abilities than the rich heir, but at too late an hour.

Many a great man has been lost to himself, and the public, purely because great ones were born before him. Hermias, in his collections on Homer's blindness, says that Homer, requesting the gods to grant him a sight of Achilles, that hero rose, but in armour so bright, that it struck Homer blind with the blaze. Let not the blaze of even Homer's Muse darken us to the discernment of our own powers; which may possibly set us above the rank of imitators; who, though most excellent and even immortal (as some of them are) yet are still but **dii minorum gentium*, nor can expect the largest share of incense, the greatest profusion of praise, on their secondary altars.

But farther still: a spirit of imitation hath many ill effects; I shall confine myself to three. First, it deprives the liberal and politer arts of an advantage which the mechanic enjoy: in these, men are ever endeavouring to go beyond their predecessors; in the former, to follow them. And since copies surpass not their originals, as streams rise not higher than their spring, rarely so high; hence, while arts mechanic are in perpetual progress and increase, the liberal are in retrogradation and decay. These resemble pyramids, are broad at bottom, but lessen exceedingly as they rise; those resemble rivers which, from a small fountain-head, are spreading ever wider and wider as they run. Hence it is evident that different portions of understanding are not (as some imagine) allotted to different periods of time; for we see, in the same period, understanding rising in one set of artists and declining in another. Therefore nature stands absolved and our inferiority in composition must be charged on ourselves.

Nay, so far are we from complying with a necessity, which nature lays us under, that, secondly, by a spirit of imitation we counteract nature, and thwart her design. She brings us into the world all originals: no two faces, no two minds, are just alike; but all bear nature's evident mark of separation on them. Born originals, how comes it to pass that we die copies? That meddling ape, Imitation, as soon as we come to years of indiscretion (so let me speak), snatches the pen and blots out nature's mark of separation, cancels her kind intention, destroys all mental individuality; the lettered world no longer consists of singulars, it is a medley, a mass; and a hundred books, at bottom, are but one. Why are monkeys such masters of mimicry? Why receive they such a talent at imitation? Is it not as the Spartan slaves received a licence for ebriety, that their betters might be ashamed of it?

The third fault to be found with a spirit of imitation is that with great incongruity it makes us poor and proud: makes us think little, and write much; gives us huge folios, which are little better than more reputable cushions to promote our repose. Have not some sevenfold volumes put us in mind of Ovid's sevenfold channels of the Nile at the conflagration?

*Ostia septem
Pulverulenta vacant septem sine flumine valles.

Such leaden labours are like Lycurgus's iron money, which was so much less in value than in bulk that it required barns for strong-boxes, and a yoke of oxen to draw five hundred pounds.

But notwithstanding these disadvantages of imitation, imitation must be the lot (and often an honourable lot it is) of most writers. If there is a famine of invention in the land, like *Joseph's brethren we must travel far for food; we must visit the remote and rich ancients; but an inventive genius may safely stay at home; that, like *the widow's cruse, is divinely replenished from within; and affords us a miraculous delight. Whether our own genius be such or not, we diligently should inquire; that we may not go a-begging with gold in our purse. For there is a mine in man, which must be deeply dug ere we can conjecture its contents. Another often sees that in us which we see not ourselves; and may there not be that in us which is unseen by both? That there may, chance often discovers, either by a luckily chosen theme, or a mighty premium, or an absolute necessity of exertion, or a noble stroke of emulation from another's glory; as that on Thucydides from hearing Herodotus repeat part of his history at the Olympic games: had there been no Herodotus, there might have been no Thucydides, and the world's admiration might have begun at Livy for excellence in that province of the pen. Demosthenes had the same stimulation on hearing Callistratus; or Tully might have been the first of consummate renown at the bar.

Quite clear of the dispute concerning ancient and modern learning, we speak not of performance but powers. The modern powers are equal to those before them; modern performance in general is deplorably short. How great are the names just mentioned! Yet who will dare affirm that as great may not rise up in some future, or even in the present age? Reasons there are why talents may not appear, none why they may not exist as much in one period as another. An evocation of vegetable fruits depends on rain, air, and sun; an evocation of the fruits of genius no less depends on externals. What a marvellous crop bore it in Greece and Rome! And what a marvellous sunshine did it there enjoy! What encouragement from the nature of their governments, and the spirit of their people! Virgil and Horace owed their divine talents to Heaven; their immortal works to men; thank Mæcenas and Augustus for them. Had it not been for these, the genius of those poets had lain buried in their ashes. Athens expended on her theatre, painting, sculpture, and architecture a tax levied for the support of a war. Cæsar dropped his papers when Tully spoke; and Philip trembled at the voice of Demosthenes: and has there arisen but one Tully, one Demosthenes, in so long a course of years? The powerful eloquence of them both in one stream, should never bear me down into the melancholy persuasion that several have not been born, though they have not emerged. The sun as much exists in a cloudy day, as in a clear; it is outward, accidental circumstances that with regard to genius either in nation or age

Collectas fugat nubes, solemque reducit.
VIRGIL.

As great, perhaps greater than those mentioned (presumptuous as it may sound) may possibly arise; for who hath fathomed the mind of man? Its bounds are as unknown as those of the creation; since the birth of which, perhaps, not one has so far exerted, as not to leave his possibilities beyond his attainments, his powers beyond his exploits. Forming our judgments altogether by what *has* been done, without knowing, or at all inquiring, what possibly *might* have been done, we naturally enough fall into too mean an opinion of the human mind. If a sketch of the divine *Iliad* before Homer wrote, had been given to mankind by some superior being, or otherwise, its execution would, probably, have appeared beyond the power of man. Now, to surpass it, we think impossible. As the first of these opinions would evidently have been a mistake, why may not the second be so too? Both are founded on the same bottom, on our ignorance of the possible dimensions of the mind of man.

Nor are we only ignorant of the dimensions of the human mind in general, but even of our own. That a man may be scarce less ignorant of his own powers than an oyster of its pearl, or a rock of its diamond; that he may possess dormant, unsuspected abilities, till awakened by loud calls, or stung up by striking emergencies, is evident from the sudden eruption of some men, out of perfect obscurity, into public admiration, on the strong impulse of some animating occasion; not more to the world's great surprise than their own. Few authors of distinction but have experienced something of this nature, at the first beamings of their yet unsuspected genius on their hitherto dark composition: the writer starts at it, as at a lucid meteor in the night; is much surprised; can scarce believe it true. During his happy confusion it may be said to him, as to Eve at the lake,

What there thou seest, fair creature, is thyself.
MILTON.

Genius, in this view, is like a dear friend in our company under disguise; who, while we are lamenting his absence, drops his mask, striking us, at once, with equal surprise and joy. This sensation, which I speak of in a writer, might favour, and so promote, the fable of poetic inspiration: a poet of a strong imagination, and stronger vanity, on feeling it, might naturally enough realize the world's mere compliment, and think himself truly inspired. Which is not improbable; for enthusiasts of all kinds do no less.

Since it is plain that men may be strangers to their own abilities; and by thinking meanly of them without just cause, may possibly lose a name, perhaps a name immortal; I would find some means to prevent these evils. Whatever promotes virtue, promotes something more, and carries its good influence beyond the moral man; to prevent these evils, I borrow two golden rules from ethics, which are no less golden in composition than in life. 1. *Know thyself;* 2dly, *Reverence thyself:* I design to repay ethics in a future letter, by two rules from rhetoric for its service.

1st. *Know thyself.* Of ourselves it may be said, as Martial says of a bad neighbour,

**Nil tam prope, proculque nobis.*

Therefore dive deep into thy bosom; learn the depth, extent, bias, and full fort of thy mind; contract full intimacy with the stranger within thee; excite and cherish every spark of intellectual light and heat, however smothered under former negligence, or scattered through the dull, dark mass of common thoughts; and collecting them into a body, let thy genius rise (if a genius thou hast) as the sun from chaos; and if I should then say, like an Indian "Worship it," (though too bold) yet should I say little more than my second rule enjoins, (viz.) "Reverence thyself."

That is, let not great examples, or authorities, browbeat thy reason into too great a diffidence of thyself: thyself so reverence as to prefer the native growth of thy own mind to the richest import from abroad; such borrowed riches make us poor. The man who thus reverences himself will soon find the world's reverence to follow his own. His works will stand distinguished; his the sole property of them; which property alone can confer the noble title of an author; that is, of one who (to speak accurately) thinks and composes; while other invaders of the press, how voluminous and learned soever, (with due respect be it spoken) only read and write.

This is the difference between those two luminaries in literature, the well-accomplished scholar, and the divinely-inspired enthusiast; the first is as the bright morning star; the second, as the rising sun. The writer who neglects those two rules above will never stand alone; he makes one of a group, and thinks in wretched unanimity with the throng: incumbered with the notions of others, and impoverished by their abundance, he conceives not the least embryo of new thought; opens not the least vista through the gloom of ordinary writers, into the bright walks of rare imagination, and singular design; while the true genius is crossing all public roads into fresh untrodden ground; he, up to the knees in antiquity, is treading the sacred footsteps of great examples, with the blind veneration of a bigot saluting the papal toe; comfortably hoping full absolution for the sins of his own understanding, from the powerful charm of touching his idol's infallibility.

Such meanness of mind, such prostration of our own powers, proceeds from too great admiration of others. Admiration has, generally, a degree of two very bad ingredients in it: of ignorance, and of fear; and does mischief in composition, and in life. Proud as the world is, there is more superiority in it given than assumed; and its grandees of all kinds owe more of their elevation to the littleness of others' minds than to the greatness of their own. Were not prostrate spirits their voluntary pedestals, the figure they make among mankind would not stand so high. Imitators and translators are somewhat of the pedestal-kind, and sometimes rather raise their original's reputation by showing him to be by them inimitable, than their own. Homer has been translated into most languages; Ælian tells us that the Indians (hopeful tutors!) have taught him to speak their tongue. What expect we from them? Not Homer's Achilles, but something which, like Patroclus, assumes his name, and at its peril appears in his stead; nor expect we Homer's Ulysses, gloriously bursting out of his cloud into royal grandeur, but an Ulysses under disguise, and a beggar to the last. Such is that inimitable father of poetry, and oracle of all the wise, whom Lycurgus transcribed; and for an annual public recital of whose works Solon enacted a law; that it is much to be feared that his so numerous translations are but as the published testimonials of so many nations and ages, that this author so divine is untranslated still.

But here,

> **Cynthius aurem*
> *Vellit*, —
>
> VIRGIL.

and demands justice for his favourite, and ours. Great things he has done; but he might have done greater. What a fall is it from Homer's numbers, free as air, lofty and harmonious as the spheres, into childish shackles, and tinkling sounds! But, in his fall, he is still great:

> Nor appears
> Less than archangel ruin'd, and the excess
> Of glory obscur'd. —
>
> MILTON.

Had Milton never wrote, Pope had been less to blame: but when in Milton's genius, Homer, as it were, personally rose to forbid Britons doing him that ignoble wrong, it is less pardonable, by that effeminate decoration, to put Achilles in petticoats a second time: how much nobler had it been, if his numbers had rolled on in full flow, through the various modulations of masculine melody, into those grandeurs of solemn sound which are indispensably demanded by the native dignity of heroic song! How much nobler, if he had resisted the temptation of that Gothic demon, which, modern poesy tasting, became mortal! Oh, how unlike the deathless, divine harmony of three great names (how justly joined!), of Milton, Greece, and Rome! His verse, but for this little speck of mortality in its extreme parts, as his hero had in his heel, like him, had been invulnerable and immortal. But, unfortunately, that was undipped in Helicon, as this, in Styx. Harmony as well as eloquence is essential to poesy; and a murder of his music is putting half Homer to death. Blank is a term of diminution; what we mean by blank verse is verse unfallen, uncursed; verse reclaimed, reinthroned in the true language of the gods, who never thundered nor suffered their Homer to thunder, in rhyme; and therefore, I beg you, my friend, to crown it with some nobler term; nor let the greatness of the thing lie under the defamation of such a name.

But supposing Pope's *Iliad* to have been perfect in its kind; yet it is a translation still; which differs as much from an original as the moon from the sun:

> *— *Phœben alieno jusserat igne*
> *Impleri, solemque suo.*
>
> CLAUDIAN.

But as nothing is more easy than to write originally wrong, originals are not here recommended, but under the strong guard of my first rule — *Know thyself*. Lucian, who was an original, neglected not this rule, if we may judge by his reply to one who took some freedom with him. He was, at first, an apprentice to a statuary; and when he was reflected on as such, by being called Prometheus, he replied, "I am indeed the inventor of new work, the model of which I owe to none; and, if I do not execute it well, I deserve to be torn by twelve vultures, instead of one."

If so, O Gulliver! dost thou not shudder at thy brother Lucian's vultures hovering o'er thee? Shudder on! they cannot shock thee more than decency has been shocked by thee. How have thy Houyhnhnms thrown thy judgment from its seat and laid thy imagination in the mire! In what ordure hast thou dipped thy pencil! What a monster hast thou made of the

> Human face divine!
>
> MILTON.

This writer has so satirized human nature as to give a demonstration in himself that it deserves to be satirized. But, say his wholesale admirers, few could so have written; true, and fewer would. If it required great abilities to commit the fault, greater still would have saved him from it. But whence arise such warm advocates for such a performance? From hence, viz. before a character is established, merit makes fame; afterwards fame makes merit. Swift is not commended for this piece, but this piece for Swift. He has given us some beauties which deserve all our praise; and our comfort is that his faults will not become common; for none can be guilty of them but who have wit as well as reputation to spare. His wit had been less wild, if his temper had not jostled his judgment. If his favourite Houyhnhnms could write, and Swift had been one of them, every horse with him would have been an ass, and he would have written a panegyric on mankind, saddling with much reproach the present heroes of his pen: on the contrary, being born amongst men, and, of consequence, piqued by many, and peevish at more, he has blasphemed a nature little lower than that of angels, and assumed by far higher than they: but surely the contempt of the world is not a greater virtue than the contempt of mankind is a vice. Therefore I wonder that, though forborne by others, the laughter-loving Swift was not reproved by the venerable dean, who could sometimes be very grave.

For I remember, as I and others were taking with him an evening's walk, about a mile out of Dublin, he stopped short; we passed on; but perceiving that he did not follow us, I went back; and found him fixed as a statue, and earnestly gazing upward at a noble elm, which in its uppermost branches was much withered and decayed. Pointing at it, he said, "I shall be like that tree; I shall die at top." As in this he seemed to prophesy like the sibyls; if, like one of them, he had burnt part of his works, especially this blasted branch of a noble genius, like her too, he might have risen in his demand for the rest.

Would not his friend Pope have succeeded better in an original attempt? Talents untried are talents unknown. All that I know is that, contrary to these sentiments, he was not only an avowed professor of imitation, but a zealous recommender of it also. Nor could he recommend anything better, except emulation, to those who write. One of these all writers must call to their aid; but aids they are of unequal repute. Imitation is inferiority confessed; emulation is superiority contested, or denied; imitation is servile, emulation generous; that fetters, this fires; that may give a name; this, a name immortal: this made Athens to succeeding ages the rule of taste, and the standard of perfection. Her men of genius struck fire against each other; and kindled, by conflict, into glories which no time shall extinguish. We thank Æschylus for Sophocles; and *Parrhasius for Zeuxis; emulation, for both. That bids us fly the general fault of imitators; bids us not be struck with the loud report of former fame, as with a knell which damps the spirits; but as with a trumpet, which inspires ardour to rival the renowned. Emulation exhorts us, instead of learning our discipline forever, like raw troops, under ancient leaders in composition, to put those laurelled veterans in some hazard of losing their superior posts in glory.

Such is Emulation's high-spirited advice, such her immortalizing call. Pope would not hear, pre-engaged with Imitation, which blessed him with all her charms. He chose rather, with his namesake of Greece, to triumph in the old world than to look out for a new. His taste partook the error of his religion; it denied not worship to saints and angels; that is, to writers, who, canonized for ages, have received their apotheosis from established and universal fame. True poesy, like true religion, abhors idolatry; and though it honours the memory of the exemplary, and takes them willingly (yet cautiously) as guides in the way to glory; real, though unexampled, excellence is its only aim; nor looks it for any inspiration less than divine.

Though Pope's noble Muse may boast her illustrious descent from Homer, Virgil, Horace, yet is an original author more nobly born. As Tacitus says of Curtius Rufus, an original author is born of himself, is his own progenitor, and will probably propagate a numerous offspring of imitators, to eternize his glory: while mule-like imitators die without issue. Therefore, though we stand much obliged for his giving us an Homer, yet had he doubled our obligation by giving us — a Pope. Had he a strong imagination, and the true sublime? That granted, we might have had two Homers instead of one, if longer had been his life; for I heard the dying swan talk over an epic plan a few weeks before his decease.

Bacon, under the shadow of whose great name I would shelter my present attempt in favour of originals, says, "Men seek not to know their own stock and abilities; but fancy their possessions to be greater, and their abilities less, than they really are." Which is, in effect, saying "that we ought to exert more than we do; and that, on exertion, our probability of success is greater than we conceive."

Nor have I Bacon's opinion only, but his

assistance too, on my side. His mighty mind travelled round the intellectual world; and, with a more than eagle's eye, saw, and has pointed out, blank spaces, or dark spots in it, on which the human mind never shone: some of these have been enlightened since; some are benighted still.

Moreover, so boundless are the bold excursions of the human mind that, in the vast void beyond real existence, it can call forth shadowy beings, and unknown worlds, as numerous, as bright, and, perhaps, as lasting, as the stars; such quite-original beauties we may call paradisaical.

* *Natos sine semine flores.*

OVID.

When such an ample area for renowned adventure in original attempts lies before us, shall we be as mere leaden pipes, conveying to the present age small streams of excellence from its grand reservoir in antiquity; and those too, perhaps, mudded in the pass? Originals shine like comets; have no peer in their path; are rivalled by none, and the gaze of all; all other compositions (if they shine at all) shine in clusters; like the stars in the galaxy, where, like bad neighbours, all suffer from all, each particular being diminished, and almost lost in the throng.

If thoughts of this nature prevailed; if ancients and moderns were no longer considered as masters and pupils, but as hard-matched rivals for renown; then moderns, by the longevity of their labours, might, one day, become ancients themselves: and old Time, that best weigher of merits, to keep his balance even, might have the golden weight of an Augustan age in both his scales; or rather our scale might descend; and that of antiquity (as a modern match for it strongly speaks) might kick the beam.

And why not? For consider, since an impartial Providence scatters talents indifferently, as through all orders of persons, so through all periods of time; since, a marvellous light, unenjoyed of old, is poured on us by revelation, with larger prospects extending our understanding, with brighter objects enriching our imagination, with an inestimable prize setting our passions on fire, thus strengthening every power that enables composition to shine; since there has been no fall in man on this side Adam, who left no works, and the works of all other ancients are our auxiliars against themselves, as being perpetual spurs to our ambition, and shining lamps in our path to fame; since this world is a school, as well for intellectual as moral advance; and the longer human nature is at school, the better scholar it should be; since, as the moral world expects its glorious millennium, the world intellectual may hope, by the rules of analogy, for some superior degrees of excellence to crown her later scenes; nor may it only hope, but must enjoy them too; for Tully, Quintilian, and all true critics allow, that virtue assists genius, and that the writer will be more able, when better is the man — all these particulars, I say, considered, why should it seem altogether impossible that Heaven's latest editions of the human mind may be the most correct, and fair; that the day may come when the moderns may proudly look back on the comparative darkness of former ages, on the children of antiquity; reputing Homer and Demosthenes as the dawn of divine genius, and Athens as the cradle of infant fame; what a glorious revolution would this make in the rolls of renown?

What a rant, say you, is here? — I partly grant it; yet, consider, my friend! knowledge physical, mathematical, moral, and divine, increases; all arts and sciences are making considerable advance; with them, all the accommodations, ornaments, delights, and glories of human life; and these are new food to the genius of a polite writer; these are as the root, and composition as the flower; and as the root spreads and thrives, shall the flower fail? As well may a flower flourish when the root is dead. It is prudence to read, genius to relish, glory to surpass ancient authors; and wisdom to try our strength, in an attempt in which it would be no great dishonour to fail.

* Why condemned Maro his admirable epic to the flames? Was it not because his discerning eye saw some length of perfection beyond it? And what he saw, may not others reach? And who bid fairer than our countrymen for that glory? Something new may be expected from Britons particularly; who seem not to be more severed from the rest of mankind by the surrounding sea, than by the current in their veins; and of whom little more appears to be required, in order to give us originals, than a consistency of character, and making their compositions of a piece with their lives. May our genius shine; and proclaim us in that nobler view!

*... *minima contentos nocte Britannos.*
VIRGIL.

And so it does; for in polite composition, in natural and mathematical knowledge, we have great originals already — Bacon, Boyle, Newton, Shakespeare, Milton have showed us that all the winds cannot blow the British flag farther than an original spirit can convey the British fame; their names go round the world; and what foreign genius strikes not as they pass? Why should not their posterity embark in the same bold bottom of new enterprise, and hope the same success? Hope it they may; or you must assert either that those originals which we already enjoy were written by angels, or deny that we are men. As Simonides said to Pausanias, reason should say to the writer, "Remember thou art a man." And for man not to grasp at all which is laudable within his reach, is a dishonour to human nature, and a disobedience to the divine; for as Heaven does nothing in vain, its gift of talents implies an injunction of their use.

*A friend of mine has obeyed that injunction; he has relied on himself, and with a genius, as well moral as original (to speak in bold terms), has cast out evil spirits; has made a convert to virtue of a species of composition, once most its foe. As the first Christian emperors expelled demons, and dedicated their temples to the living God.

But you, I know, are sparing in your praise of this author; therefore I will speak of one, which is sure of your applause. Shakespeare mingled no water with his wine, lowered his genius by no vapid imitation. Shakespeare gave us a Shakespeare, nor could the first in ancient fame have given us more! Shakespeare is not their son, but brother, their equal; and that, in spite of all his faults. Think you this too bold? Consider, in those ancients what is it the world admires! Not the fewness of their faults, but the number and brightness of their beauties; and if Shakespeare is their equal (as he doubtless is) in that which in them is admired, then is Shakespeare as great as they; and not impotence, but some other cause, must be charged with his defects. When we are setting these great men in competition, what but the comparative size of their genius is the subject of our inquiry? And a giant loses nothing of his size, though he should chance to trip in his race. But it is a compliment to those heroes of antiquity to suppose Shakespeare their equal only in dramatic powers; therefore, though his faults had been greater, the scale would still turn in his favour. There is at least as much genius on the British as on the Grecian stage, though the former is not swept so clean — so clean from violations not only of the dramatic, but moral rule; for an honest heathen, on reading some of our celebrated scenes, might be seriously concerned to see that our obligations to the religion of nature were cancelled by Christianity.

Jonson, in the serious drama, is as much an imitator as Shakespeare is an original. He was very learned, as Sampson was very strong, to his own hurt: blind to the nature of tragedy, he pulled down all antiquity on his head, and buried himself under it; we see nothing of Jonson, nor indeed of his admired (but also murdered) ancients; for what shone in the historian is a cloud on the poet; and *Catiline* might have been a good play if Sallust had never writ.

Who knows whether Shakespeare might not have thought less, if he had read more? Who knows if he might not have laboured under the load of Jonson's learning, as Enceladus under Etna? His mighty genius, indeed, through the most mountainous oppression would have breathed out some of his inextinguishable fire; yet, possibly, he might not have risen up into that giant, that much more than common man, at which we now gaze with amazement, and delight. Perhaps he was as learned as his dramatic province required; for whatever other learning he wanted, he was master of two books, unknown to many of the profoundly read, though books which the last conflagration alone can destroy; the book of nature, and that of man. These he had by heart, and has transcribed many admirable pages of them into his immortal works. These are the fountain-head, whence the Castalian streams of original composition flow; and these are often mudded by other waters, though waters in their distinct channel, most wholesome and pure: as two chemical liquors, separately clear as crystal, grow foul by mixture, and offend the sight. So that he had not only as much learning as his dramatic province required, but, perhaps, as it could safely bear. If Milton had spared some of his learning, his Muse would have gained more glory than he would have lost by it.

Dryden, destitute of Shakespeare's genius, had almost as much learning as Jonson, and, for the buskin, quite as little taste. He was a stranger to the pathos, and, by numbers, expression, sentiment, and every other dramatic cheat strove to make amends for it; as if a saint could make amends for the want of conscience; a soldier, for the want of valour; or a vestal, of modesty. The noble nature of tragedy disclaims an equivalent; like virtue, it demands the heart; and Dryden had none to give. Let epic poets think, the tragedian's point is rather to feel; such distant things are a tragedian and a poet that the latter indulged destroys the former. Look on Barnwell, and Essex, and see how as to these distant characters Dryden excels, and is excelled. But the strongest demonstration of his no-taste for the buskin are his tragedies fringed with rhyme; which, in epic poetry, is a sore disease, in the tragic, absolute death. To Dryden's enormity, Pope's was a light offence. As lacemen are foes to mourning, these two authors, rich in rhyme, were no great friends to those solemn ornaments which the noble nature of their works required.

Must rhyme then, say you, be banished? I wish the nature of our language could bear its entire expulsion; but our lesser poetry stands in need of a toleration for it; it raises that, but sinks the great; as spangles adorn children, but expose men. Prince Henry bespangled all over in his oylet-hole suit, with glittering pins; and an Achilles, or an Almanzor, in his Gothic array, are very much on a level as to the majesty of the poet, and the prince. Dryden had a great, but a general capacity; and as for a general genius, there is no such thing in nature: a genius implies the rays of the mind concentred, and determined to some particular point; when they are scattered widely, they act feebly, and strike not with sufficient force, to fire, or dissolve, the heart. As what comes from the writer's heart reaches ours; so what comes from his head sets our brains at work, and our hearts at ease. It makes a circle of thoughtful critics, not of distressed patients; and a passive audience is what tragedy requires. Applause is not to be given, but extorted; and the silent lapse of a single tear does the writer more honour than the rattling thunder of a thousand hands. Applauding hands and dry eyes (which during Dryden's theatrical reign often met) are a satire on the writer's talent, and the spectator's taste. When by such judges the laurel is blindly given, and by such a poet proudly received, they resemble an intoxicated host, and his tasteless guests, over some sparkling adulteration, commending their champagne.

But Dryden has his glory, though not on the stage. What an inimitable original is his ode! A small one, indeed, but of the first lustre, and without a flaw; and, amid the brightest boasts of antiquity, it may find a foil....

[1759]

ROBERT BLAIR

BORN in 1699 of an ancient Scottish family, Robert Blair was educated in the university of his native Edinburgh and in Holland. After some years of private study and occasional preaching, he was appointed in 1731 to a church living in East Lothian, where he remained until his death in 1746. Blair was a man of some private means, which enabled him to devote ample time to the study of botany and of the earlier English dramatists, and his whole life as a clergyman seems to have resembled that of George Crabbe in his later years. His only composition of any importance is *The Grave*, which apparently was begun during his young manhood, long before he could have read Young's *Night Thoughts* (1742–44). First published in 1743, this poem was immediately successful, and remained for at least a century one of the most popular poems in the language. William Blake's series of twelve illustrative designs, appearing in 1808, gave it a new lease of life and won for it a somewhat more discerning audience.

In spite of its hackneyed theme which constantly tempts the poet to the utterance of trite commonplaces, its frequent bathos, and its rude versification, *The Grave* must be regarded as the rough sketch, at least, of a powerful poem. Its faults, like those of Smart's *Song to David*, are exactly the opposite of those usually found in more typical eighteenth-century verse, for they are the blunders of a hand too heavy and violent rather than too languid. "Blair may be a homely and even a gloomy poet in the eye of fastidious criticism," as Thomas Campbell said, "but there is a masculine and pronounced character even in his gloom and homeliness that keeps it most distinctly apart from either dullness or vulgarity. His style pleases us like the powerful expression of a countenance without regular beauty." Mediæval in thought and feeling, often strangely like some of the darker Jacobean dramatists in accent, the poem is in total effect distinctly "Gothic," or, as the times were learning to say, "Romantic." Its lasting popularity may have been due in part to the universal fascination of the theme, and it certainly found out a class of readers — those who kept alive *Robinson Crusoe* and *Pilgrim's Progress* — to whom the more polished literature of the day meant little; yet, in admitting this, we need not ignore its bold graphic power and easy opulence of execution. A comparison of Bryant's *Thanatopsis*, which is merely the finished rendering of one or two hints from Blair, will show that the Scottish poet is as much superior in native vigour and audacity as the American is a better artist.

From THE GRAVE

While some affect the sun and some the shade,
Some flee the city, some the hermitage,
Their aims as various as the roads they take
In journeying through life, the task be mine
To paint the gloomy horrors of the tomb,
The appointed place of rendezvous where all
These travellers meet. Thy succours I implore,
Eternal king, whose potent arm sustains
The keys of hell and death. The Grave, dread thing!
Men shiver when thou'rt named; Nature, appall'd,
Shakes off her wonted firmness. Ah, how dark
Thy long-extended realms and rueful wastes,
Where nought but silence reigns, and night, dark night,
Dark as was chaos ere the infant sun
Was roll'd together, or had tried his beams
Athwart the gloom profound! The sickly taper,
By glimmering through thy low-browed misty vaults,
Furr'd round with mouldy damps and ropy slime,
Lets fall a supernumerary horror,
And only serves to make the night more irksome.
Well do I know thee by thy trusty yew,
Cheerless unsocial plant that loves to dwell
'Midst skulls and coffins, epitaphs and worms,
Where light-heel'd ghosts and visionary shades
Beneath the wan cold moon, as fame reports,
Embodied, thick, perform their mystic rounds!
No other merriment, dull tree, is thine.

See yonder hallow'd fane, the pious work
Of names once fam'd, now dubious or forgot,
And buried 'midst the wreck of things which were;

*There lie interr'd the more illustrious dead.
The wind is up. Hark, how it howls! Methinks
Till now I never heard a sound so dreary.
Doors creak and windows clap, and night's foul bird
*Rook'd in the spire, screams loud. The gloomy aisles,
Black-plaster'd and hung round with shreds of 'scutcheons
And tatter'd coats of arms, send back the sound
Laden with heavier airs, from the low vaults,
The mansions of the dead. Rous'd from their slumbers,
In grim array the grisly spectres rise,
Grin horrible, and, obstinately sullen,
Pass and repass, hush'd as the foot of night.
Again the screech-owl shrieks. Ungracious sound!
I'll hear no more. It makes one's blood run chill.
  Quite round the *pile a row of reverend elms,
Co-eval near with that, all ragged show,
Long lash'd by the rude winds, some *rift half down
Their branchless trunks, others so thin at top
That scarce two crows could lodge in the same tree.
Strange things, the neighbours say, have happen'd here:
Wild shrieks have issued from the hollow tombs;
Dead men have come again and walk'd about;
And the great bell has toll'd, unrung, untouch'd!
(Such tales their cheer at wake or *gossiping,
When it draws near to witching time of night.)
  Oft in the lone churchyard at night I've seen,
By glimpse of moonshine checkering through the trees,
The schoolboy with his satchel in his hand
Whistling aloud to bear his courage up,
And lightly tripping o'er the long flat stones,
With nettles skirted and with moss o'ergrown,
That tell in homely phrase who lie below.
Sudden he starts and hears, or thinks he hears,
The sound of something purring at his heels;
Full fast he flies and dares not look behind him,
Till out of breath he overtakes his fellows,
Who gather round and wonder at the tale
Of horrid apparition, tall and ghastly,
That walks at dead of night, or takes his stand
O'er some new-open'd grave, and, strange to tell,
Evanishes at crowing of the cock.
  The new-made widow too I've sometimes spied—
Sad sight! — slow moving o'er the prostrate dead.
Listless she crawls along in doleful black
Whilst bursts of sorrow gush from either eye,
Fast falling down her now untasted cheek.
Prone on the lowly grave of the dear man
She drops, whilst busy meddling memory
In barbarous succession musters up
The past endearments of their softer hours,
Tenacious of its theme. Still, still she thinks
She sees him, and, indulging the fond thought,
Clings yet more closely to the senseless turf,
Nor heeds the passenger who looks that way.
  *Invidious grave, how dost thou rend in sunder
Whom love has knit and sympathy made one! —
A tie more stubborn far than nature's band.
Friendship, mysterious cement of the soul,
Sweetener of life and solder of society,
I owe thee much; thou has deserved from me
Far, far beyond what I can ever pay.
Oft have I prov'd the labours of thy love
And the warm efforts of the gentle heart
Anxious to please. Oh, when my friend and I
In some thick wood have wander'd heedless on
Hid from the vulgar eye, and sat us down
Upon the sloping cowslip-cover'd bank
Where the pure limpid stream has slid along
In grateful *errors through the underwood,
Sweet murmuring, methought the shrill-tongued thrush
Mended his song of love, the sooty blackbird
Mellow'd his pipe, and soften'd every note;
The eglantine smelt sweeter, and the rose
Assum'd a dye more deep; whilst every flower
Vied with its fellow plant in luxury
Of dress. Oh, then the longest summer's day
Seem'd too, too much in haste. Still the full heart
Had not imparted half. 'Twas happiness
Too exquisite to last. Of joys departed
Not to return, how painful the remembrance!
  Dull Grave, thou spoil'st the dance of youthful blood,
Strik'st out the dimple from the cheek of mirth,
And every *smirking feature from the face,

*Notes on Robert Blair will be found in the Appendix, p. 1006.

Branding our laughter with the name of madness.
Where are the jesters now, the men of health
*Complexionally pleasant? Where the droll
Whose every look and jesture was a joke
To clapping theatres and shouting crowds,
And made even thick-lipp'd musing melancholy
To gather up her face into a smile
Before she was aware? Ah! sullen now
And dumb as the green turf that covers them.
Where are the mighty thunderbolts of war,
The Roman Cæsars and the Grecian chiefs,
The boast of story? Where the hot-brain'd *youth
Who the tiara at his pleasure tore
From kings of all the then discover'd globe,
And cried, forsooth, because his arm was hamper'd,
And had not room enough to do its work?
Alas, how slim, dishonourably slim,
And cramm'd into a place we blush to name!
Proud royalty, how alter'd in thy looks,
How blank thy features, and how wan thy hue!
Son of the morning, whither art thou gone?
Where hast thou hid thy many-spangled head
And the majestic menace of thine eyes,
Felt from afar? Pliant and powerless now
Like new-born infant wound up in his swathes,
Or victim tumbled flat upon its back
That throbs beneath the sacrificer's knife.
Mute must thou bear the strife of little tongues
And coward insults of the base-born crowd
That grudge a privilege thou never hadst,
But only hoped for in the peaceful grave,
Of being unmolested and alone.
Arabia's gums and odoriferous drugs
And honours by the heralds duly paid
In mode and form even to a very scruple —
Oh, cruel irony! these come too late
And only mock whom they were meant to honour.
Surely there's not a dungeon slave that's buried
In the highway, unshrouded and uncoffin'd,
But lies as soft and sleeps as sound as he.
Sorry pre-eminence of high descent
Above the vulgar born, to rot in state!...
Tell us, ye dead! Will none of you in pity
To those you left behind disclose the secret?
Oh, that some courteous ghost would blab it out,
What 'tis you are, and we must shortly be!
I've heard that souls departed have sometimes
Forewarn'd men of their death. 'Twas kindly done
To knock and give the alarum. But what means
This stinted charity? 'Tis but lame kindness
That does its work by halves. Why might you not
Tell us what 'tis to die? Do the strict laws
Of your society forbid your speaking
Upon a point so nice? — I'll ask no more.
Sullen, like lamps in sepulchres, your shine
Enlightens but yourselves. Well, 'tis no matter;
A very little time will clear up all,
And make us learn'd as you are, and as close.
Death's shafts fly thick! Here falls the village swain,
And there his pamper'd lord. The cup goes round,
And who so artful as to put it by?
*'Tis long since death had the majority;
Yet, strange! the living lay it not to heart.
See yonder maker of the dead man's bed,
The sexton, hoary-headed chronicle,
Of hard, unmeaning face, down which ne'er stole
A gentle tear; with mattock in his hand
Digs through whole rows of kindred and acquaintance
By far his juniors. Scarce a skull's cast up
But well he knew its owner, and can tell
Some passage of his life. Thus hand in hand
The sot has walk'd with death twice twenty years,
And yet ne'er younker on the green laughs louder,
Or *clubs a smuttier tale; when drunkards meet,
None sings a merrier catch or lends a hand
More willing to his cup. Poor wretch, he minds not
That soon some trusty brother of the trade
Shall do for him what he has done for thousands.
On this side and on that, men see their friends
Drop off like leaves in autumn, yet launch out
Into fantastic schemes which the long livers
In the world's hale and undegenerate days
Could scarce have leisure for. Fools that we are!
Never to think of death and of ourselves
At the same time, as if to learn to die
Were no concern of ours. Oh! more than sottish

For creatures of a day, in gamesome mood,
To frolic on eternity's dread brink
Unapprehensive, when, for aught we know,
The very first swoln surge shall sweep us in!
Think we, or think we not, time hurries on
With a resistless, unremitting stream,
Yet treads more soft than e'er did midnight thief
That slides his hand under the miser's pillow
And carries off his prize. What is this world?
What but a spacious burial field unwall'd,
Strew'd with death's spoils, the spoils of animals,
Savage and tame, and full of dead men's bones!
The very turf on which we tread once lived,
And we that live must lend our carcasses
To cover our own offspring. In their turns
They too must cover theirs. 'Tis here all meet:
The shivering Icelander and sun-burnt Moor,
Men of all climes that never met before,
And of all creeds, the Jew, the Turk, the Christian.
Here the proud prince, and favourite yet prouder,
His sov'reign's keeper and the people's scourge,
Are huddled out of sight. Here lie abash'd
The great negotiators of the earth,
And celebrated masters of the * balance
Deep read in stratagems and wiles of courts.
Now vain their treaty skill: Death scorns to treat.
Here the o'erloaded slave flings down his burden
From his gall'd shoulders, and when the cruel tyrant
With all his guards and tools of power about him,
Is meditating new unheard-of hardships,
Mocks his short arm, and, quick as thought, escapes
Where tyrants vex not, and the weary rest.
Here the warm lover, leaving the cool shade,
The tell-tale echo, and the babbling stream
(Time out of mind the favourite seats of love)
Fast by his gentle mistress lays him down
Unblasted by foul tongue. Here friends and foes
Lie close, unmindful of their former feuds.
The *lawn-robed prelate and plain presbyter
Erewhile that stood aloof as shy to meet,
Familiar mingle here, like sister streams
That some rude interposing rock had split.
Here is the large-limb'd peasant, here the child
Of a span long, that never saw the sun
Nor press'd the nipple, strangled in life's porch.
Here is the mother with her sons and daughters,
The barren wife, the long-demurring maid
Whose lonely unappropriated sweets
Smiled like yon knot of cowslips on the cliff,
Not to be come at by the willing hand.
Here are the prude severe and gay coquette,
The sober widow and the young green virgin,
Cropp'd like a rose before 'tis fully blown
Or half its worth disclosed. Strange medley here!
Here garrulous old age winds up his tale,
And jovial youth, of lightsome vacant heart,
Whose every day was made of melody,
Hears not the voice of mirth. The shrill-tongued shrew
Meek as the turtledove, forgets her chiding.
Here are the wise, the generous, and the brave,
The just, the good, the worthless, the profane,
The *downright clown and perfectly well-bred,
The fool, the churl, the scoundrel and the mean,
The supple statesman and the patriot stern,
The wrecks of nations and the spoils of time,
With all the lumber of six thousand years...

[1743]

THOMAS GRAY

THE quiet life of Thomas Gray began in London, where his father was a prosperous broker. He spent his boyhood at Eton College and then went to Cambridge, where most of his later life slipped by in the literary leisure made possible by a university fellowship. His erudition, particularly in the ancient classics, was deep, wide, and exact. Perhaps the chief event of his career was his tour of Europe as companion of Horace Walpole in 1739–41. The death in 1742 of his closest friend, Richard West, a poet of some promise, increased the natural melancholy of Gray's disposition and deepened the tone of his thought and writing. The *Elegy Written in a Country Churchyard*, published in 1751, made him famous. Six years later appeared his *Pindaric Odes*, including *The Progress of Poesy* and *The Bard*. In later life he travelled through Wales and the Lake District in search of the picturesque, keeping an interesting diary of his impressions. Shortly before his death in 1771 he was made Professor of Modern History at Cambridge, having already declined an offer of the laureateship.

Interest in Thomas Gray, which has increased with the years, has several sources or aspects: he composed one of the most popular and influential poems in modern literature; he wrote a large body of letters seldom excelled in charm and urbanity; he was a somewhat timid and hesitant pioneer in the discovery of "northern antiquities" and of the natural picturesque as we now feel it; his career as poet and scholar illustrated vividly the antagonism between the accumulative and the creative tendencies in the intellectual life; his mental history provides a clear example, fascinating to the present day, of a first-rate mind in a transitional epoch, striving to retain what was good in the old while reaching forward toward the new. As a poet Gray has been somewhat overrated, perhaps partly because his reputation has grown under the hands of men who were primarily scholars, like himself. A vote taken among poets, at almost any time since 1800, would probably have rated him somewhat below William Collins. Those literary critics, moreover, who have been engaged for more than half a century in readjusting the balance, so greatly disturbed by the romantic movement, between art and genius, taste and inspiration, have chosen Gray as a fair approximation to their ideal, forgetting that the composition of true poetry is always a creative act and that Gray's creative force was slight. He had an accumulating, sifting, and appraising mind, strong in the sense of form and of proportion, delicately precise and clear, finely disciplined by intimate acquaintance with great models of expression, patient, earnest, aspiring — and yet not the mind of a true "maker." He scarcely experienced passion, and he had a narrower range of emotion to bring under control than is necessary to the equipment of a poet. His intellectual curiosity led him some little distance into territories soon to be annexed by the romantic school, and it is customary to distinguish two, three, or even four "periods" in the small body of his verse, in the last of which periods he is said to have been definitely romantic; but his later poems show as clearly as the earliest his effort to subject all thought and emotion to the restraints of strict form, and in this important respect he remained on the neo-classical side.

In a letter to William Mason written January 13, 1758, Gray says: "Extreme conciseness of expression, yet pure, perspicuous, and musical, is one of the grand beauties of lyric poetry. This I have always aimed at, and never could attain. The necessity of rhyming is one great obstacle to it." Certainly he did attain it in several stanzas of the *Elegy*, but only by dint of the most patient care. Verse never became to him an easy and natural mode of expression, and he never quite outgrew the habits of composition acquired in the writing of Latin verse. In prose he was an abler writer, a more interesting man, one might almost say a better poet.

SONNET

ON THE DEATH OF RICHARD WEST

In vain to me the smiling mornings shine,
  And redd'ning Phœbus lifts his golden fire;
The birds in vain their amorous descant join,
  Or cheerful fields resume their green attire:
These ears, alas! for other notes repine;
  A different object do these eyes require.
My lonely anguish melts no heart but mine,
  And in my breast the imperfect joys expire.
Yet morning smiles the busy race to cheer,
  And new-born pleasure brings to happier men;
The fields to all their wonted tribute bear;
  To warm their little loves the birds complain:
I fruitless mourn to him that cannot hear,
  And weep the more because I weep in vain.

[1775]

ODE ON A DISTANT PROSPECT OF ETON COLLEGE

A distant prospect of the spires of Eton and of Windsor Castle might have been had, in Gray's time, from the mound near the churchyard at Stoke Poges, which is at least the traditional scene of his *Elegy*. It is known, at any rate, that he was living in that village during the fruitful summer of 1742, when the present poem was written. His recollection of the joys of his own school days was darkened by the thought of their transiency. Of the three close friends he had made at Eton, Richard West, the dearest, had just died, and from the other two, Horace Walpole and Thomas Ashton, he was temporarily estranged.

Ye distant spires, ye antique towers,
  That crown the wat'ry glade,
Where grateful *Science still adores
  Her *Henry's holy shade;
And ye, that from the stately brow
Of *Windsor's heights th' expanse below
  Of grove, of lawn, of mead survey,
Whose turf, whose shade, whose flowers among
Wanders the hoary Thames along
  His silver-winding way.

Ah, happy hills! ah, pleasing shade!
  Ah, fields belov'd in vain!
Where once my careless childhood stray'd,
  A stranger yet to pain!
I feel the gales that from ye blow
A momentary bliss bestow,
  As, waving fresh their gladsome wing,
My weary soul they seem to soothe,
And, redolent of joy and youth,
  To breathe a second spring.

Say, Father Thames, for thou hast seen
  Full many a sprightly race
Disporting on thy margent green
  The paths of pleasure trace;
Who foremost now delight to cleave
With pliant arm thy glassy wave?
  The captive linnet which enthral?
What idle progeny *succeed
To chase the rolling *circle's speed,
  Or urge the flying ball?

While some on earnest business bent
  Their murm'ring *labours ply
'Gainst graver *hours that bring constraint
  To *sweeten liberty,
Some bold adventurers disdain
The limits of their little *reign,
  And unknown regions dare descry;
Still as they run they look behind;
They hear a voice in every wind,
  And snatch a fearful joy.

Gay hope is theirs, by fancy fed,
  Less pleasing when possessed;
The tear forgot as soon as shed;
  The sunshine of the breast;
Theirs buxom health of rosy hue,
Wild wit, invention ever new,
  And lively cheer, of vigour born,
The thoughtless day, the easy night,
The spirits pure, the slumbers light
  That fly th' approach of morn.

Alas! regardless of their doom
  The little victims play;
No sense have they of ills to come,
  Nor care beyond today!
Yet see, how all around 'em wait
The ministers of human fate,
  And black Misfortune's baleful train!
Ah, show them where in ambush stand,
To seize their prey, the murd'rous band!
  Ah, tell them, they are men!

These shall the fury Passions tear,
  The vultures of the mind,
Disdainful Anger, pallid Fear,
  And Shame that skulks behind;
Or pining Love shall waste their youth,
Or Jealousy with rankling tooth
  That inly gnaws the secret heart,
And Envy wan, and faded Care,
Grim-visag'd comfortless Despair,
  And Sorrow's piercing dart.

Ambition this shall tempt to rise,
  Then whirl the wretch from high,
To bitter Scorn a sacrifice,
  And grinning Infamy.
The stings of Falsehood those shall try,
And hard Unkindness' alter'd eye
  That mocks the tear it forc'd to flow;
And keen Remorse with blood defil'd,
And moody Madness laughing wild
  Amid severest woe.

Lo! in the vale of years *beneath
  A grisly troop are seen —
The painful *family of Death,
  More hideous than their queen.

* Notes on Thomas Gray will be found in the Appendix, pp. 1007 ff.

This racks the joints, this fires the veins,
That every labouring sinew strains,
  Those in the deeper vitals rage;
Lo! Poverty, to fill the band,
That numbs the soul with icy *hand,
  And slow-consuming Age.

To each his suff'rings; all are men,
  Condemn'd alike to groan —
The tender for another's pain,
  Th' unfeeling for his own.
Yet, ah! why should they know their fate,
Since sorrow never comes too late,
  And happiness too swiftly flies?
Thought would destroy their paradise.
No more; — where ignorance is bliss,
  'Tis folly to be wise.

[1747]

ODE ON THE SPRING

Lo, where the rosy-bosom'd *Hours,
  Fair Venus' train, appear,
Disclose the *long-expecting flowers,
  And wake the *purple year.
The Attic *warbler pours her throat,
Responsive to the cuckoo's note,
  The untaught harmony of spring;
While, whisp'ring pleasure as they fly,
Cool zephyrs through the clear blue sky
  Their gather'd fragrance fling.

Where'er the oak's thick branches stretch
  A broader, browner shade,
Where'er the rude and moss-grown beech
  O'er-canopies the glade,
Beside some water's rushy brink
With me the Muse shall sit, and think
  (At ease reclin'd in rustic state)
How vain the ardour of the crowd,
How low, how little are the proud,
  How indigent the great!

Still is the toiling hand of Care;
  The panting herds repose;
Yet hark how through the peopled air
  The busy murmur glows!
The insect youth are on the wing,
Eager to taste the honied spring
  And float amid the liquid noon;
Some lightly o'er the current skim,
Some show their gaily-gilded trim
  Quick glancing to the sun.

To Contemplation's sober eye
  Such is the race of man;
And they that creep, and they that fly,
  Shall end where they began:
Alike the busy and the gay
But flutter through life's little day,
  In Fortune's varying colours dress'd;
Brush'd by the hand of rough Mischance,
Or chill'd by Age, their airy dance
  They leave, in dust to rest.

Methinks I hear, in accents low,
  The sportive kind reply:
"Poor moralist, and what art thou?
  A solitary fly!
Thy joys no glittering female meets,
No hive hast thou of hoarded sweets,
  No painted plumage to display;
On hasty wings thy youth is flown,
Thy sun is set, thy spring is gone —
  We frolic while 'tis May."

[1748]

ELEGY WRITTEN IN A COUNTRY CHURCHYARD

This most familiar of English poems was probably begun at Stoke Poges in 1742, was published in 1751, and went through many editions during Gray's lifetime. The scene of the poem may have been the churchyard at Stoke Poges itself, where Gray lies buried. To one of Gray's classical scholarship the word "elegy" — although it had acquired since the Renaissance a more modern sense, illustrated in line 82 — suggested not a song of lamentation, like *Lycidas*, but a poem of meditative calm written in a measure conducive to thoughtfulness. The *Love Elegies* of James Hammond, who died in 1742, had recently shown, indeed, that there was no necessary connection between elegiac poems and the theme of death, and Gray's choice of this theme may have been determined largely by the mood in which he began to write, shortly after the death of his friend Richard West. It has been asserted, by Sir Edmund Gosse, that the *Elegy* "belongs to a class apart, as it is not addressed to the memory of any particular person." This is true of the poem in what may be called its original form, extending through line 92 and the four rejected stanzas, given in the notes. To this impersonal and generalized elegy, however, it would appear that Gray later attached eight stanzas of different tendency and origin, dealing not with his imagined future self, as is commonly said, but with his dead friend, West. So read, the completed poem takes its place beside *Lycidas*, *Adonais*, *Thyrsis*, and *In Memoriam* as a poem of personal mourning. Gray's reason for not making clear the ascription to West — or rather, for elaborately though clumsily concealing it — is suggested in the note to line 93.

For the rest, the *Elegy* is a noble phrasing of commonplace thought, "a thing of shreds and patches" gathered from the literature of the world and subdued into a rich and sober unity. In the language of the poet's time, it is a triumph of patient art rather than of genius.

The curfew tolls the knell of parting day;
The lowing herd wind slowly o'er the lea;
The ploughman homeward plods his weary way,
And leaves the world to darkness and to me.

Now fades the glimmering landscape on the sight,
And all the air a solemn stillness holds,
Save where the beetle wheels his droning flight,
And drowsy tinklings lull the distant folds;

Save that from yonder ivy-mantled tow'r
The moping owl does to the moon complain
Of such as, wand'ring near her secret bow'r,
Molest her ancient solitary reign.

Beneath those rugged elms, that yew tree's shade,
Where heaves the turf in many a mould'ring heap,
Each in his narrow cell forever laid,
The *rude forefathers of the hamlet sleep.

The breezy call of incense-breathing morn,
The swallow twitt'ring from the straw-built shed,
The cock's shrill clarion, or the echoing horn,
No more shall rouse them from their lowly bed.

For them no more the blazing hearth shall burn,
Or busy housewife ply her evening care;
No children run to lisp their sire's return,
Or climb his knees the envied kiss to *share.

Oft did the harvest to their sickle yield;
Their furrow oft the stubborn glebe has broke;
How jocund did they drive their team afield!
How bow'd the woods beneath their sturdy stroke!

Let not Ambition mock their useful toil,
Their homely joys, and destiny obscure;
Nor Grandeur hear with a disdainful smile
The short and simple annals of the poor.

The boast of *heraldry, the pomp of pow'r,
And all that beauty, all that wealth e'er gave,
*Awaits alike th' inevitable hour:
The paths of glory lead but to the grave.

Nor you, ye proud, impute to these the fault,
If Mem'ry o'er their tomb no *trophies raise,
Where through the long-drawn aisle and *fretted vault
The pealing anthem swells the note of praise.

Can *storied urn or *animated bust
Back to its mansion call the fleeting breath?
Can Honour's voice *provoke the silent dust,
Or Flatt'ry soothe the dull, cold ear of Death?

Perhaps in this neglected spot is laid
Some heart once pregnant with celestial fire;
Hands that the rod of empire might have sway'd,
Or wak'd to ecstasy the living lyre.

But Knowledge to their eyes her ample page,
Rich with the spoils of time, did ne'er unroll;
Chill Penury repress'd their noble *rage,
And froze the *genial current of the soul.

*Full many a gem of purest ray serene
The dark unfathom'd caves of ocean bear:
Full many a flower is born to blush unseen,
And waste its sweetness on the desert air.

Some village *Hampden that with dauntless breast
The little tyrant of his fields withstood,
Some mute, inglorious Milton here may rest,—
Some Cromwell, guiltless of his country's *blood.

Th' applause of list'ning senates to command,
The threats of pain and ruin to despise,
To scatter plenty o'er a smiling land,
And read their hist'ry in a nation's eyes,

Their lot forbade; nor circumscrib'd alone
Their growing virtues, but their crimes confined;
Forbade to wade thro' slaughter to a throne,
And shut the gates of mercy on mankind,

The struggling pangs of conscious truth to hide,
To quench the blushes of ingenuous shame,
Or heap the shrine of Luxury and Pride
With *incense kindled at the Muse's flame.

Far from the madding crowd's ignoble strife
Their sober wishes never learn'd to stray;
Along the cool, sequester'd vale of life
They kept the noiseless tenor of their way.

Yet ev'n these bones from insult to protect,
Some frail memorial *still erected nigh,
With uncouth rhymes and shapeless sculpture deck'd,
Implores the passing tribute of a sigh.

Their name, their years, spelt by th' unletter'd Muse,
The place of fame and *elegy supply;
And many a holy text around she strews,
That teach the rustic moralist to die.

For who, to dumb Forgetfulness a prey,
This pleasing anxious being e'er resign'd,
Left the warm precincts of the cheerful day,
Nor cast one longing, ling'ring look behind?

On some fond breast the parting soul relies,
Some pious drops the closing eye requires;
E'en from the tomb the voice of Nature cries,
E'en in our ashes live their wonted fires.

For *thee who, mindful of th' unhonour'd dead,
Dost in these lines their artless tale relate,
If chance, by lonely Contemplation led,
Some kindred spirit shall inquire thy fate,

Haply some hoary-headed swain may say:
"Oft have we seen him at the peep of dawn
Brushing with hasty steps the dews away,
To meet the sun upon the upland lawn.

"There, at the foot of yonder nodding beech
That wreathes its old fantastic roots so high,
His listless length at noontide would he stretch,
And pore upon the brook that babbles by.

"Hard by yon wood, now smiling as in scorn,
Mutt'ring his wayward fancies, he would rove,
Now drooping, woeful-wan, like one forlorn,
Or craz'd with care, or cross'd in hopeless love.

"One morn I miss'd him on the custom'd hill,
Along the heath, and near his fav'rite tree;
Another came; nor yet beside the rill,
Nor up the lawn, nor at the wood was he;

"The next, with dirges due, in sad array,
Slow through the church-way path we saw him borne.
Approach and read (for thou canst read) the lay
Grav'd on the stone beneath yon aged *thorn."

THE EPITAPH

Here rests his head upon the lap of Earth
A youth to fortune and to fame unknown;
*Fair *Science frown'd not on his humble birth,*
And Melancholy mark'd him for her own.

Large was his bounty, and his soul sincere;
Heav'n did a recompense as largely send:
He gave to misery all he had, a tear,
He gain'd from Heaven ('twas all he wish'd) a friend.

No farther seek his merits to disclose,
Or draw his frailties from their dread abode,
(There they alike in trembling hope repose,)
The bosom of his Father and his God.

[1751]

HYMN TO ADVERSITY

This poem, based upon Horace's *Ode to Fortune*, is important partly because of the hints it supplied for Wordsworth's *Ode to Duty*. Written in 1742, shortly after the death of Richard West, it is another veiled expression of the mood of grief which, in the same summer, produced the *Ode on a Distant Prospect of Eton College* and gave the first impulse toward the composition of the *Elegy*.

Daughter of Jove, relentless power,
Thou Tamer of the human breast,
Whose iron scourge and tort'ring hour
The bad affright, afflict the best!
Bound in thy adamantine chain,
The proud are taught to taste of pain,
And *purple tyrants vainly groan
With *pangs unfelt before, unpitied and alone.

When first thy sire to send on earth
Virtue, his darling child, design'd,
To thee he gave the heav'nly birth,
And bade to form her infant mind.
Stern rugged nurse! thy rigid *lore
*With patience many a year she bore;
What sorrow was, thou bad'st her know,
And from her own she learn'd to melt at others' *woe.

Scar'd at thy frown terrific, fly
Self-pleasing Folly's idle brood,
Wild Laughter, Noise, and thoughtless Joy,
And leave us leisure to be *good.
*Light they disperse, and with them go
The summer friend, the flatt'ring foe;
By vain Prosperity receiv'd,
To her they vow their truth, and are again believ'd.

Wisdom, in sable garb array'd,
Immers'd in rapt'rous thought profound,
And Melancholy, silent maid,
With *leaden eye that loves the ground,
Still on thy solemn steps attend:
Warm Charity, the gen'ral friend,
With Justice, to herself severe,
And Pity, dropping soft the sadly-pleasing tear.

Oh! gently on thy suppliant's head,
Dread goddess, lay thy chast'ning hand!
Not in thy Gorgon terrors clad,
Not circled with the vengeful *band
(As by the *impious thou art seen)
With thund'ring voice, and threat'ning mien,
With screaming Horror's fun'ral cry,
Despair, and fell Disease, and ghastly Poverty.

Thy form benign, O goddess, wear;
Thy milder influence impart;
Thy philosophic train be there
To soften, not to wound, my heart.
The gen'rous spark extinct revive;
Teach me to love and to forgive,
*Exact my own defects to scan,
What others are, to feel, and know myself a man.

[1753]

THE PROGRESS OF POESY

A PINDARIC ODE

As a close student of Greek literature, Gray knew that the irregular "Pindaric Odes" made popular by the example of Cowley were quite unlike the odes of Pindar himself, whose lyrics are remarkable for their strict though intricate symmetry. This fact had been pointed out by Congreve as early as 1696, but his *Discourse on the Pindaric Ode* did little to diminish the spate of poems which he described as "bundles of rambling incoherent thoughts expressed in a like parcel of irregular stanzas." Fifty years later, and almost exactly one hundred years after the publication of Cowley's *Pindaric Odes*, Gray set himself to show — even more clearly than Collins had done ten years earlier in his *Ode on the Poetical Character* — how the true Pindaric should be written. *The Progress of Poesy* and *The Bard*, whatever may be their merits in other respects, are impressive structures of verse. The former is in three parts, each extending to forty-one lines, and each of these parts is subdivided into three stanzas which derive their names — signifying the turn, the counter-turn, and the stand — from the choric dances of the Greek theatre. Strophes and antistrophes are identical in length and rhyme scheme, and epode corresponds with epode. At least the major divisions of this structure, moreover, correspond with major movements of the thought. The style of this poem, and of *The Bard* as well, is bold, abrupt, and highly metaphorical, in imitation of Pindar's manner. Gray's contemporaries had great difficulty in understanding these odes, even with the author's voluminous notes, and later opinion about them has been widely divided. Lowell says of *The Progress of Poesy* that "in reach, variety, and loftiness of poise, it overflies all other English lyrics like an eagle." Dr. Johnson is far nearer the truth when he asserts in his *Life of Gray* that "these odes are marked by a glittering accumulation of ungraceful ornaments; they strike, rather than please; the images are magnified by affectation; the language is laboured into harshness.... He has a kind of strutting dignity, and is tall by walking on tiptoe."

I

STROPHE

Awake, Æolian *lyre, awake,
And give to rapture all thy trembling strings.
From *Helicon's harmonious springs
A thousand rills their mazy progress take;
The laughing flowers that round them blow
Drink life and fragrance as they flow.
Now the rich stream of music winds along
Deep, majestic, smooth, and strong,
Thro' verdant vales and Ceres' golden *reign;
Now rolling down the steep amain,
Headlong, impetuous, see it pour;
The rocks and nodding groves rebellow to the roar.

ANTISTROPHE

Oh! Sovereign of the willing soul,
Parent of sweet and solemn-breathing airs,

Enchanting *shell! the sullen Cares
And frantic Passions hear thy soft control.
On Thracia's hills the Lord of War
Has curb'd the fury of his car
And dropp'd his thirsty lance at thy command.
Perching on the sceptred hand
Of Jove, thy magic lulls the feather'd *king
With ruffled plumes, and flagging wing;
Quench'd in dark clouds of slumber lie
The terror of his beak, and lightnings of his eye.

EPODE

Thee the voice, the dance, obey,
Temper'd to thy warbled lay.
O'er *Idalia's velvet-green
The rosy-crownèd Loves are seen
On Cytherea's day,
With antic Sports and blue-eyed Pleasures
Frisking light in frolic measures;
Now pursuing, now retreating,
Now in circling troops they meet;
To brisk notes in cadence beating
Glance their many-twinkling feet.
Slow melting strains their queen's approach declare;
Where'er she turns, the Graces homage pay.
With arms *sublime that float upon the air,
In gliding state she wins her easy way; 39
O'er her warm cheek and rising bosom move
The bloom of young desire and purple light of love.

II

STROPHE

Man's feeble race what ills await!
Labour, and penury, the racks of pain,
Disease, and sorrow's weeping train,
And death, sad refuge from the storms of fate!
The *fond complaint, my song, disprove,
And justify the laws of *Jove.
Say, has he given in vain the heavenly Muse?
Night, and all her sickly dews,
Her spectres wan, and birds of boding cry
He gives to range the dreary sky,
Till down the eastern cliffs afar
*Hyperion's march they spy, and glittering shafts of war.

ANTISTROPHE

In climes *beyond the solar road
Where shaggy forms o'er ice-built mountains roam,
The Muse has broke the twilight gloom
To cheer the shiv'ring native's dull abode.
And oft, beneath the od'rous shade
Of Chili's boundless forests laid,
She deigns to hear the savage youth *repeat
In loose numbers wildly sweet
Their feather-cinctured chiefs and dusky loves.
Her track, where'er the goddess roves,
Glory *pursue, and gen'rous shame,
Th' unconquerable mind, and freedom's holy flame.

EPODE

Woods that wave o'er Delphi's *steep,
Isles that crown th' Ægean deep,
Fields that cool *Ilissus laves,
Or where *Mæander's amber waves
In lingering lab'rinths creep,
How do your tuneful echoes languish,
Mute, but to the voice of anguish!
Where each old poetic mountain
Inspiration breath'd around,
Every shade and hallow'd fountain
Murmur'd deep a solemn sound,
Till the sad Nine, in Greece's evil hour,
Left their Parnassus for the Latian plains.
Alike they scorn the pomp of tyrant Power
And coward Vice, that revels in her chains.
When Latium had her lofty spirit lost, 81
They sought, oh, Albion! next, thy sea-encircled coast.

III

STROPHE

Far from the sun and summer gale
In thy green lap was Nature's *darling laid,
What time, where lucid Avon stray'd,
To him the mighty mother did unveil
Her awful face. The dauntless child
Stretch'd forth his little arms, and smil'd.
"This pencil take," she said, "whose colours clear
Richly paint the vernal year.
Thine, too, these golden keys, immortal boy!
This can unlock the gates of joy;
Of horror that, and thrilling fears,
Or ope the sacred source of sympathetic tears."

ANTISTROPHE

Nor second *he, that rode sublime
Upon the *seraph wings of Ecstasy
The secrets of the abyss to spy.
He pass'd the *flaming bounds of place and time;

The living throne, the sapphire blaze,
Where angels tremble while they gaze,
He saw; but, blasted with excess of light,
Clos'd his eyes in endless night.
Behold where Dryden's less presumptuous car
Wide o'er the fields of glory bear
*Two coursers of ethereal race,
With necks in thunder cloth'd, and long-resounding *pace.

EPODE

Hark, his hands the lyre explore!
Bright-eyed Fancy, hov'ring o'er,
Scatters from her pictur'd urn
Thoughts that breathe, and words that burn.
But ah! 'tis heard no more —
Oh! lyre divine, what daring *spirit
Wakes thee now? Tho' he inherit
Nor the pride, nor ample pinion,
That the *Theban eagle bear,
Sailing with supreme dominion
Thro' the azure deep of air,
Yet oft before his infant eyes would run
Such forms as glitter in the Muse's ray
With orient hues, unborrow'd of the sun;
Yet shall he mount, and keep his distant way
Beyond the limits of a vulgar fate —
Beneath the good how far! but far above the *great.

[1757]

THE BARD

A PINDARIC ODE

"The following ode is founded on a tradition current in Wales, that Edward the First, when he completed the conquest of that country, ordered all the bards that fell into his hands to be put to *death."

I

STROPHE

"Ruin seize thee, ruthless King!
*Confusion on thy banners wait;
Tho' fann'd by Conquest's crimson wing,
They mock the air with idle state.
Helm, nor hauberk's twisted mail,
Nor even thy virtues, Tyrant, shall avail
To save thy secret soul from nightly fears,
From *Cambria's curse, from Cambria's tears!"
Such were the sounds that o'er the crested pride
Of the first Edward scatter'd wild dismay,
As down the steep of Snowdon's shaggy side
He wound with toilsome march his long array.
Stout *Glo'ster stood aghast in speechless trance;
"To arms!" cried Mortimer, and couch'd his quiv'ring lance.

ANTISTROPHE

On a rock whose haughty brow
Frowns o'er old *Conway's foaming flood,
Robed in the sable garb of woe,
With haggard eyes the poet stood;
(Loose his beard and hoary hair
Stream'd, like a meteor, to the troubled *air)
And with a master's hand, and prophet's fire,
Struck the deep sorrows of his lyre.
"Hark, how each giant oak, and desert cave,
Sighs to the torrent's awful voice beneath!
O'er thee, O King! their hundred arms they wave,
Revenge on thee in hoarser murmurs breathe;
Vocal no more, since Cambria's fatal day,
To high-born *Hoel's harp, or soft Llewellyn's *lay.

EPODE

"Cold is Cadwallo's tongue,
That hush'd the stormy main;
Brave Urien sleeps upon his craggy bed;
Mountains, ye mourn in vain
*Modred, whose magic song
Made huge *Plinlimmon bow his cloud-topped head.
On dreary Arvon's *shore they lie,
Smear'd with gore, and ghastly pale;
Far, far aloof th' affrighted ravens sail;
The famish'd eagle screams, and passes by.

Dear lost companions of my tuneful art,
Dear as the light that visits these sad eyes,
Dear as the ruddy drops that warm my heart,
Ye died amidst your dying country's cries —
No more I weep. They do not sleep.
On yonder cliffs, a grisly band,
I see them sit; they linger yet,
Avengers of their native land:
With me in dreadful harmony they join,
And weave with bloody hands the tissue of thy line.

II

STROPHE

"'Weave the warp, and weave the woof,
The winding-sheet of Edward's race.
Give ample room, and verge enough
The characters of hell to trace.
Mark the year, and mark the night,
When Severn shall re-echo with affright
The shrieks of death thro' Berkley's roofs that ring,
Shrieks of an agonizing *king!
*She-wolf of France, with unrelenting fangs,
That tear'st the bowels of thy mangled mate,
From thee be born, who o'er thy country hangs
The scourge of Heav'n. What terrors round *him wait!
Amazement in his van, with Flight combin'd,
And Sorrow's faded form, and Solitude behind.

ANTISTROPHE

"'Mighty victor, mighty lord!
Low on his funeral couch he lies!
No pitying heart, no eye, afford
A tear to grace his obsequies.
Is the sable *warrior fled?
Thy son is gone. He rests among the dead.
The swarm that in thy noontide beam were born?
Gone to salute the rising morn.
*Fair laughs the morn, and soft the zephyr blows,
While proudly riding o'er the azure realm
In gallant trim the gilded vessel goes;
Youth on the prow, and Pleasure at the helm;
Regardless of the sweeping whirlwind's sway,
That, hush'd in grim repose, expects his evening prey.

EPODE

"'Fill high the sparkling bowl,
The rich repast prepare;
Reft of a crown, he yet may share the feast.
Close by the regal chair
Fell Thirst and Famine scowl
A baleful smile upon their baffled *guest.
Heard ye the din of battle bray,
Lance to lance, and horse to horse?
Long years of *havoc urge their destined course,
And thro' the kindred squadrons mow their way.
Ye *towers of Julius, London's lasting shame,
With many a foul and midnight murder fed,
Revere his *consort's faith, his *father's fame,
And spare the meek *usurper's holy head.
Above, below, the rose of snow,
Twin'd with her blushing *foe, we spread:
The bristled *boar in infant-gore
Wallows beneath the thorny shade.
Now, brothers, bending o'er the accursed loom,
Stamp we our vengeance deep, and ratify his doom.

III

STROPHE

"'Edward, lo! to sudden fate
(Weave we the woof. The thread is spun.)
Half of thy *heart we consecrate.
(The web is wove. The work is done.)'—
Stay, oh *stay! nor thus forlorn
Leave me unbless'd, unpitied, here to mourn!
In yon bright track that fires the western skies,
They melt, they vanish from my eyes.
But oh! what solemn scenes on Snowdon's height
Descending slow their glitt'ring skirts unroll?
Visions of glory, spare my aching sight!
Ye unborn ages, crowd not on my soul!
No more our long-lost *Arthur we bewail.
All hail, ye genuine *kings, Britannia's issue, hail!

ANTISTROPHE

"Girt with many a baron bold
Sublime their starry fronts they rear;
And gorgeous dames, and statesmen old
In bearded majesty, appear.
In the midst a *form divine!
Her eye proclaims her of the Briton-line;
Her lion-port, her awe-commanding face,
Attemper'd sweet to virgin-grace.
What strings symphonious tremble in the air,
What *strains of vocal transport round her play!
Hear from the grave, great *Taliessin, hear;
They breathe a soul to animate thy clay.
Bright Rapture calls, and soaring, as she sings,
Waves in the eye of Heav'n her many-colour'd wings.

EPODE

"The verse adorn again
Fierce War, and faithful Love,
And Truth severe, by fairy Fiction *drest.

In buskin'd *measures move
Pale Grief, and pleasing Pain,
With Horror, tyrant of the throbbing breast.
A *voice, as of the cherub-choir,
Gales from blooming Eden bear;
And distant *warblings lessen on my ear,
That, lost in long futurity, expire.
Fond impious *man, think'st thou yon sanguine cloud,
Rais'd by thy breath, has quench'd the orb of day?
Tomorrow he repairs the golden flood,
And warms the nations with redoubled ray.
Enough for me; with joy I see
The different doom our fates assign.
Be thine Despair, and sceptred Care;
To triumph, and to die, are mine."
He spoke, and headlong from the mountain's height
Deep in the roaring tide he plunged to endless night.

[1757]

THE FATAL SISTERS

In a note written for the first edition of *The Fatal Sisters* Gray gives the impression that he has translated the poem directly "from the Norse tongue," but it is now agreed that he knew little Old Norse and that he depended chiefly, in this instance, upon a Latin version of the original. Most of the difficulties of the poem are cleared up by the following passage from the same prefatory note: "In the eleventh century, Sigurd, Earl of the Orkney Islands, went with a fleet of ships and a considerable body of troops into Ireland, to the assistance of Sictryg with the Silken Beard, who was then making war on his father-in-law, Brian, King of Dublin. The earl and all his forces were cut to pieces, and Sictryg was in danger of a total defeat; but the enemy had a greater loss by the death of Brian, their king, who fell in the action. On Christmas Day (the day of the battle) a native of Caithness in Scotland saw at a distance a number of persons on horseback riding full speed towards a hill, and seeming to enter into it. Curiosity led him to follow them, till, looking through an opening in the rocks, he saw twelve gigantic figures resembling women: they were all employed about a loom, and, as they wove, they sung the following dreadful song; which when they had finished, they tore the web into twelve pieces and, each taking her portion, galloped six to the north and as many to the south."

These Fatal Sisters, several of whose names appear in the poem, are of course the Valkyrs or choosers of the slain.

Now the storm begins to lour;
(Haste, the loom of hell prepare!)
Iron sleet of arrowy shower
Hurtles in the darken'd air.

Glitt'ring lances are the loom
Where the dusky warp we strain,
Weaving many a soldier's doom,
Orkney's woe and Randver's bane.

See the grisly texture grow!
'Tis of human entrails made;
And the weights that play below,
Each a gasping warrior's head.

Shafts for shuttles, dipp'd in gore,
Shoot the trembling cords along.
Sword, that once a monarch bore,
Keep the tissue close and strong.

Mista, black, terrific maid,
Sangrida, and Hilda, see,
Join the wayward work to aid:
'Tis the woof of victory.

Ere the ruddy sun be set,
Pikes must shiver, javelins sing,
Blade with clattering buckler meet,
Hauberk crash, and helmet ring.

(Weave the crimson web of war!)
Let us go, and let us fly
Where our friends the conflict share,
Where they triumph, where they die.

As the paths of fate we tread,
Wading through th' ensanguin'd field,
Gondula and Geira, spread
O'er the youthful *king your shield.

We the reins to slaughter give;
Ours to kill, and ours to spare:
Spite of danger he shall live.
(Weave the crimson web of war!)

*They whom once the desert beach
Pent within its bleak domain,
Soon their ample sway shall stretch
O'er the plenty of the *plain.

Low the dauntless *earl is laid,
  Gor'd with many a gaping wound:
Fate demands a nobler head;
  Soon a *king shall bite the ground.

Long his loss shall Eirin weep,
  Ne'er again his likeness see;
Long her strains in sorrow steep,
  Strains of immortality!

Horror covers all the heath,
  Clouds of carnage blot the sun.
Sisters, weave the web of death!
  Sisters, cease; the work is done.

Hail the task, and hail the hands!
  Songs of joy and triumph sing!
Joy to the victorious bands;
  Triumph to the younger *king.

Mortal, thou that hear'st the tale,
  Learn the tenor of our song.
Scotland, through each winding vale
  Far and wide the notes prolong.

Sisters, hence with spurs of speed;
  Each her thundering falchion wield;
Each bestride her sable steed.
  Hurry, hurry to the field!

[1768]

ODE ON THE PLEASURE ARISING FROM *VICISSITUDE

Now the golden Morn aloft
  Waves her dew-bespangled wing;
With *vermeil cheek and whisper soft
  She woos the tardy Spring,
Till April starts and calls around
The sleeping fragrance from the ground,
And lightly o'er the living scene
Scatters his freshest, tenderest green.

New-born flocks, in rustic dance,
  Frisking ply their feeble feet;
Forgetful of their wintry trance
  The birds his presence greet;
But chief, the skylark warbles high
His trembling thrilling ecstasy,
And, lessening from the dazzled sight,
Melts into air and liquid light.

Rise, my soul, on wings of fire!
  Rise the rapt'rous choir among!
Hark! 'tis Nature strikes the lyre
  And leads the general song.

* * * * * * *

Yesterday the sullen year
  Saw the snowy whirlwind fly;
Mute was the music of the air,
  The herd stood drooping by.
Their raptures now, that wildly flow,
No yesterday nor morrow know;
'Tis man alone that joy descries
With forward and reverted eyes.

Smiles on past Misfortune's brow
  Soft Reflection's hand can trace,
And o'er the cheek of Sorrow throw
  A melancholy grace;
While Hope prolongs our happier hour
Or deepest shades, that dimly lour
And blacken round our weary way,
Gilds with a gleam of distant day.

*Still, where rosy Pleasure leads,
  See a kindred Grief pursue;
Behind the steps that Misery treads,
  Approaching Comfort view.
The hues of Bliss more brightly glow
Chastis'd by sabler tints of woe,
And, blended, form with artful strife
The strength and harmony of life.

See the wretch that long has toss'd
  On the thorny bed of pain,
At length repair his vigour lost
  And breathe and walk again:
The meanest floweret of the vale,
The simplest note that swells the gale,
The common sun, the air, the skies,
To him are opening Paradise.

Humble Quiet builds her cell
  Near the source where pleasure flows;
She eyes the clear crystalline well
  And tastes it as it goes.

* * * * * * *

[1775]

LETTERS

To Richard West

*PETERHOUSE, *December*, 1736

You must know that I do not take degrees, and, after this term, shall have nothing more of college impertinences to undergo, which I trust will be some pleasure to you, as it is a great one to me. I have endured lectures daily and hourly since I *came last, supported by the hopes of being shortly at full liberty to give myself up to my friends and classical *companions, who, poor souls! though I see them fallen into great contempt with most people here, yet I cannot help sticking to them, and, out of a spirit of obstinacy, I think, love them the better for it. And, indeed, what can I do else? Must I plunge into metaphysics? Alas, I cannot see in the dark; nature has not furnished me with the optics of a cat. Must I pore upon mathematics? Alas, I cannot see in too much light; I am no eagle. It is very possible that two and two make four, but I would not give four farthings to demonstrate this ever so clearly; and if these be the profits of life, give me the amusements of it. The people I behold all around me, it seems, know all this and more, and yet I do not know one of them who inspires me with any ambition of being like him. Surely it was of this place, now Cambridge, but formerly known by the name of Babylon, that the prophet spoke when he said, "the wild beasts of the desert shall build there, and their houses shall be full of doleful creatures, and owls shall build there, and satyrs shall dance there; their forts and towers shall be a den for ever, a joy of wild asses; there shall the great owl make her nest, and lay and hatch and gather under her shadow; it shall be a court of dragons; the screech owl also shall rest there, and find for herself a place of *rest." You see here is a pretty collection of desolate animals, which is verified in this town to a tittle, and perhaps it may also allude to your *habitation, for you know all types may be taken by abundance of handles; however, I defy your owls to match mine.

If the default of your spirits and nerves be nothing but the effect of the *hyp, I have no more to say. We all must submit to that wayward queen; I too in no small degree own her sway,

I feel her influence while I speak her power.

But if it be a real distemper, pray take more care of your health, if not for your own at least for our sakes, and do not be so soon weary of this little world. I do not know what refined friendships you may have contracted in the other, but pray do not be in a hurry to see your acquaintance above; among your terrestrial familiars, however, though I say it that should not say it, there positively is not one that has a greater esteem for you than

Yours most sincerely, etc.

*To *Richard West*

As I know you are a lover of Curiosities, I send you the following, which is a true and faithful Narrative of what passed in my study on Saturday the 16th, instant. I was sitting there very tranquil in my chair, when I was suddenly alarmd with a great hubbub of Tongues. In the Street, you suppose? No! in my Study, Sir. In your Study say you? Yes & between my books, which is more. For why should not books talks as well as Crabs & Mice & *files & serpents do in Esop. But as I listend with great attention so as to remember what I heard pretty exactly, I shall set down the whole conversation as methodically as I can, with the names prefixed.

**Mad. de Sévigné.* Mon cher Aristote! do get a little further or you will quite suffocate me.

Aristotle. * Οὐ ἔποτε γυνή... I have as much right to this place as you, and I sha'nt remove a jot.

M. Sévigné. Oh! the brute! Here's my poor Sixth tome is squeezed to death: for God's sake, Bussy, come & rescue me.

**Bussy Rabutin.* Ma belle Cousine! I would fly to your assistance. Mais voici un diable de Strabon qui me tue, and I have no one worth conversing with here but Catullus.

**Bruyère.* Patience! You must consider we are but books, and so ca'nt help ourselves. for my part I wonder who we belong to. We are a strange mixture here. I have a *Malebranche on one side of me, and a *Gronovius on t'other.

Locke. Certainly our owner must have very confused ideas, to jumble us so strangely together. He has associated me with Ovid and * Ray the Naturalist.

Virgil. *'Me vero primum dulces ante omnia Musæ
Accipiant!'

H. More. Of all the Speculations that the Soul of Man can entertain herself withall there is none of greater moment than this of her immortality.

**Cheyne.* Every man after fourty is either a fool or a Physician.

Euclid. Punctum est cujus nulla est....

Boileau. Peste soit de cet homme avec son Punctum! I wonder any man of sense will have a Mathematician in his Study.

Swift. In short, let us get the Mathematics banishd first, the Metaphysicks and Nat: Philosophy may follow them.

Vade Mecum. Pshaw! I and the Bible are enough for any one Library.

This last ridiculous egotism made me laugh so heartily that I disturbd the poor books & they talk'd no more.

To Richard West

LONDON, *April, Thursday* [1742]

You are the first who ever made a Muse of a *cough; to me it seems a much more easy task to versify in one's sleep (that indeed you were of old famous for) than for want of it. Not the wakeful nightingale, when she had a cough, ever sung so sweetly. I give you thanks for your warble, and wish you could sing yourself to rest. These wicked remains of your illness will sure give way to warm weather and gentle exercise; which I hope you will not omit as the season advances. Whatever low spirits and indolence, the effect of them, may advise to the contrary, I pray you add five steps to your walk daily for my sake; by the help of which, in a month's time, I propose to set you on horseback.

I talked of the **Dunciad* as concluding you had seen it; if you have not, do you choose I should get and send it you? I have myself, upon your recommendation, been reading **Joseph Andrews.* The incidents are ill laid and without invention; but the characters have a great deal of nature, which always pleases even in her lowest shapes. Parson Adams is perfectly well; so is Mrs. Slipslop, and the story of Wilson; and throughout he shows himself well read in stage-coaches, country squires, inns, and inns of court. His reflections upon high people and low people, and misses and masters, are very good. However the exaltedness of some minds (or rather, as I shrewdly suspect, their insipidity and want of feeling or observation) may make them insensible to these light things (I mean such as characterize and paint nature), yet surely they are as weighty and much more useful than your grave discourses upon the mind, the passions, and what not. Now as the paradisaical pleasures of the Mahometans consist in playing upon the flute and lying with houris, be mine to read eternal new romances of *Marivaux and *Crébillon.

You are very good in giving yourself the trouble to read and find fault with my long *harangues. Your freedom (as you call it) has so little need of apologies that I should scarce excuse your treating me any otherwise; which, whatever compliment it might be to my vanity, would be making a very ill one to my understanding. As to matter of style, I have this to say: the language of the age is never the language of poetry, except among the French, whose verse, where the thought or image does not support it, differs in nothing from prose. Our poetry, on the contrary, has a language peculiar to itself; to which almost every one that has written has added something by enriching it with foreign idioms and derivatives — nay sometimes words of their own composition or invention. Shakespeare and Milton have been great creators this way; and no one more licentious than Pope or Dryden, who perpetually borrow expressions from the former. Let me give you some instances from Dryden, whom everybody reckons a great master of our poetical tongue. — Full of *museful mopings* — unlike the *trim of love* — a pleasant *beverage* — a *roundelay* of love — stood silent in his *mood* — with knots and *knares* deformed — his *ireful mood* — in proud *array* — his *boon* was granted — and *disarray* and shameful rout — *wayward* but wise — *furbished* for the field — the *foiled dodderd* oaks — *disherited* — *smouldering* flames — *retchless* of laws — *crones* old and ugly — the *beldam* at his side — the *grandam-hag* — *villanize* his father's fame. — But they are infinite; and our language not being a settled thing (like the French) has an undoubted right to words of an hundred years old, provided antiquity have not rendered them unintelligible. In truth, Shakespeare's language is one of his principal beauties; and he has no less advantage over your Addisons and *Rowes in this than in those other great excellences you mention. Every word in him is a picture. Pray put me the following lines into the tongue of our modern dramatics:

*But I, that am not shaped for sportive tricks,
Nor made to court an amorous looking-glass:
I, that am rudely stamp'd, and want love's majesty
To strut before a wanton ambling nymph;
I, that am curtail'd of this fair proportion,
Cheated of feature by dissembling nature,
Deform'd, unfinish'd, sent before my time
Into this breathing world, scarce half made up —

and what follows. To me they appear untranslatable; and if this be the case, our language is greatly degenerated. However, the affectation of imitating Shakespeare may doubtless be carried too far; and is no sort of excuse for sentiments ill-suited or speeches ill-timed, which I believe is a little the case with me. I guess the most faulty *expression may be these: *silken* son of dalliance — *drowsier* pretensions — wrinkled *beldams* — *arched* the hearer's brow and *riveted* his eyes in *fearful ecstasy*. These are easily altered or omitted; and, indeed, if the thoughts be wrong or superfluous, there is nothing easier than to leave out the whole. The first ten or twelve lines are, I believe, the best; and as for the rest, I was betrayed into a good deal of it by Tacitus. Only what he has said in five words, I imagine I have said in fifty lines. Such is the misfortune of imitating the inimitable. Now, if you are of my opinion, **una litura* may do the business better than a dozen; and you need not fear unravelling my web. I am a sort of spider; and have little else to do but spin it over again, or creep to some other place and spin there. Alas! for one who has nothing to do but amuse himself, I believe my amusements are as little amusing as most folks'. But no matter; it makes the hours pass; and is better than *ἐν ἀμαθίᾳ καὶ ἀμουσίᾳ καταβιῶναι. Adieu.

To Horace Walpole

CAMBRIDGE, *February* 11, 1751

As you have brought me into a little sort of distress, you must assist me, I believe, to get out of it as well as I can. Yesterday I had the misfortune of receiving a letter from certain gentlemen (as their bookseller expresses it), who have taken the *Magazine of Magazines* into their hands. They tell me that an *ingenious* poem, called "Reflections in a Country Churchyard," has been communicated to them, which they are printing forthwith; that they are informed that the *excellent* author of it is I by name, and that they beg not only his *indulgence*, but the *honour* of his correspondence, etc. As I am not at all disposed to be either so indulgent or so correspondent as they desire, I have but one bad way left to escape the honour they would inflict upon me; and therefore am obliged to desire you would make *Dodsley print it immediately (which may be done in less than a week's time) from your copy, but without my name, in what form is most convenient for him, but on his best paper and character. He must correct the press himself, and print it without any interval between the stanzas, because the sense is in some places continued beyond them; and the title must be, — "Elegy, written in a Country Churchyard." If he would add a line or two to say it came into his hands by accident, I should like it better. If you behold the *Magazine of Magazines* in the light that I do, you will not refuse to give yourself this trouble on my account, which you have taken of your own accord before now. If Dodsley do not do this immediately, he may as well *let it alone.

*To *Richard Hurd*

STOKE, *August* 25, 1757

I do not know why you should thank me for what you had a *right and title to, but attribute it to the excess of your politeness; and the more so because almost no one else has made me the same compliment. As your acquaintance in the university (you say) do me the honour to admire, it would be ungenerous in me not to give them notice that they are doing a very unfashionable thing; for all people of condition are agreed not to admire, nor even to understand. One very great man, writing to an acquaintance of his and mine, says that he had read them seven or eight times; and that now when he next sees him, he shall not have above thirty questions to ask. Another (a peer) believes that the last stanza of the second ode relates to King Charles the First and Oliver Cromwell. Even my friends tell me they do not succeed, and write me moving topics of consolation on that head. In short I have heard of nobody but an actor and a doctor of divinity that profess their esteem for them. Oh yes, a lady of quality (a friend of *Mason's), who is a great reader. She knew there was a compliment to

Dryden, but never suspected there was anything said about Shakespeare or Milton till it was explained to her; and wishes that there had been titles prefixed to tell what they were about.

From this mention of Mason's name you may think, perhaps, we are great correspondents. No such thing; I have not heard from him these two months. I will be sure to scold in my own name, as well as in yours. I rejoice to hear you are so ripe for the press, and so voluminous; not for my own sake only, whom you flatter with the hopes of seeing your labours both public and private, but for yours too; for to be employed is o be happy. This principle of mine (and I am convinced of its truth) has, as usual, no influence on my practice. I am alone, and *ennuyé* to the last degree, yet do nothing. Indeed I have one excuse; my health, which you so kindly enquire after, is not extraordinary, ever since I came hither. It is no great malady, but several little ones that seem brewing no good to me.

It will be a particular pleasure to me to hear whether Content dwells in Leicestershire, and how she entertains herself there; only do not be too happy, nor forget entirely the quiet ugliness of Cambridge. I am, dear sir,

Your friend and obliged humble servant,

To Mr. Stonehewer

Cambridge, *August* 18, 1758

I am as sorry as you seem to be, that our acquaintance harped so much on the subject of materialism when I saw him with you in town, because it was plain to which side of the long-debated question he inclined. That we are indeed mechanical and dependent beings, I need no other proof than my own feelings; and from the same feelings I learn, with equal conviction, that we are not merely such: that there is a power within that struggles against the force and bias of that mechanism, commands its motion, and, by frequent practice, reduces it to that ready obedience which we call habit; and all this in conformity to a preconceived opinion (no matter whether right or wrong), to that least material of all agents, a thought. I have known many in his case, who, while they thought they were conquering an old prejudice, did not perceive they were under the influence of one far more dangerous, — one that furnishes us with a ready apology for all our worst actions, and opens to us a full license for doing whatever we please; and yet these very people were not at all the more indulgent to other men, as they naturally should have been; their indignation to such as offended them, their desire of revenge on anybody that hurt them was nothing mitigated; in short, the truth is, they wished to be persuaded of that opinion for the sake of its convenience, but were not so in their heart; and they would have been glad (as they ought in common prudence) that nobody else should think the same, for fear of the mischief that might ensue to themselves. His French author I never saw, but have read fifty in the same strain, and shall read no more. I can be wretched enough without them. They put me in mind of the Greek sophist that got immortal honour by discoursing so feelingly on the miseries of our condition, that fifty of his audience went home and hanged themselves; yet he lived himself (I suppose) many years after in very good plight.

You say you cannot conceive how Lord Shaftesbury came to be a philosopher in vogue; I will tell you. First, he was a lord; 2dly, he was as vain as any of his readers; 3dly, men are very prone to believe what they do not understand; 4thly, they will believe anything at all, provided they are under no obligation to believe it; 5thly, they love to take a new road, even when that road leads nowhere; 6thly, he was reckoned a fine writer, and seemed always to mean more than he said. Would you have any more reasons? An interval of above forty years has pretty well destroyed the charm. A dead lord ranks but with commoners. Vanity is no longer interested in the matter, for the new road has become an old one. The mode of free-thinking is like that of ruffs and farthingales, and has given place to the mode of not thinking at all. Once it was reckoned graceful half to discover and half conceal the mind, but now we have been long accustomed to see it quite naked. Primness and affectation of style, like the good breeding of Queen Anne's court, has turned to hoydening and rude familiarity.

[1775, 1816]

WILLIAM COLLINS

All the verse by William Collins now known to exist was written before he was twenty-nine. He produced little, he published less, and he even tried to destroy a portion of what he had published. A considerable number of the fifteen hundred lines he left, including certainly the *Persian Eclogues* (1742) and the *Epistle to Hanmer* (1743), are crude and immature, and of the twelve *Odes on Several Descriptive and Allegoric Subjects* (1746) upon which his fame chiefly rests, the majority are strained and frigid rhetoric. Few English poets have been more extravagantly and absurdly praised. The first important critical judgment of his work, that of his friend, Dr. Johnson, is still one of the soundest: "His diction was often harsh, unskillfully laboured, and injudiciously selected. He affected the obsolete when it was not worthy of revival; and he puts his words out of the common order, seeming to think... that not to write prose is certainly to write poetry. His lines commonly are of slow motion, clogged and impeded with clusters of consonants. As men are often esteemed who cannot be loved, so the poetry of Collins may sometimes extort praise when it gives little pleasure."

This opinion seems too severe only because it is delivered upon Collins's average accomplishment, ignoring the exquisite but never quite flawless beauty of the four or five poems that we now choose to remember. By these four or five, however, the reputation of Collins as one of the best poets of his century is entirely justified. In the restraint and poise of his finest achievement, the *Ode to Evening*, there is something as characteristic of that century at its best as in the architecture of the Adam brothers or in the *adagios* of Mozart. Collins seldom lived up to the ideal expressed in his *Ode to Simplicity*, but he had a few serene moments, such as that which gave us "How sleep the brave," in which his verse moved and grew like effortless, unpremeditated song.

Critical opinion has been somewhat swayed by the pathos and brevity of Collins's life, wishing to give him credit — as we tend to do with Keats and Chatterton — for what he might have done with a better chance. He was born at Chichester on Christmas Day, 1721, the son of a prosperous merchant. At Winchester College he began to write verse in association with Joseph Warton. After taking his degree at Oxford in 1743 he wavered between the church and the army, finally drifting into the literary circles of London and making spasmodic efforts to earn a livelihood by writing. These were frustrated by a natural indolence which probably had a physical cause, by the rapid increase of a nervous disorder, and perhaps by intemperate habits. The failure of his *Persian Eclogues* and of his *Odes* to attract any attention made it easier for him to retire to Chichester when, in 1749, he inherited a small fortune. In that year he met the Scottish dramatist, John Home, whose account of the Highlands and Hebrides fired his imagination, and the *Ode* in which he surveyed these new poetic realms shows him reaching eagerly forward, like Keats, at the very end of his intellectual life. He had already begun, however, to feel the approaches of mental disease, which increased until his death, in 1759.

The influence of Greek and Latin literature upon the formally educated poets of the eighteenth century has been discussed in the General Introduction. It can scarcely be overestimated. Beginning in childhood and lasting throughout their lives, it was not an influence which they deliberately chose but one which they inevitably absorbed. Subjection to it, moreover, gave one the mark of the gentleman — not the less desired now that literature had fallen into the hands of the middle classes. All this might have been pure gain to them and to poetry, had not the enthusiastic scholarship of the early Renaissance — to which the discovery of ancient art had been a discovery of life — cooled and dwindled into a mere rhetoric, a study of "elegance." Deriving their first notions of their art from an ancient tongue laboriously acquired by rote, learning rules of Greek and Latin versification before they had any use for them, they could not fail to regard verse as a very special and stately mode of making dignified remarks, a heightened oratory, the prerogative of scholars. Thus their tendency was to write and to think in phrases worn thin by centuries of use, to interpret modern in terms of ancient life, and to see even English landscape in patterns stamped by classic mythology.

Still more difficult to allow for, and seldom mentioned at all, is the effect upon these poets of verse-composition in the ancient languages, before the feeling for the vernacular was firmly established. The use of such aids as the *Gradus ad Parnassum* not only filled their minds with stock epithets and conventional elegances of expression but suggested that all verse-making is a matter of fitting rigid phrases into a mosaic design. The results are almost everywhere apparent in the poetry of the time. They are obvious in the work of Gray, who was a Latin poet before he was an English. They are conspicuous by their absence in the poetry of Burns and Blake, the direct and vivid freshness of whose writings is partly attributable to the simple fact that they did not undergo the ordinary training in Latin and Greek. In the work of Collins, who was not given time to outgrow his undergraduate habits of mind, they are perhaps clearest of all, both for good and ill. Such violent inversions of normal English word-order and such huge parentheses as are to be found in all his more elaborate poems were possible only to one who had first learned to think and write in a synthetic language like Latin. His merely decorative if not ostentatious allusions to classic literature, his excessive personification, and a kind of pedantic stiffness in all but his few best poems, remind us constantly that the milk of his *alma mater* is still in him.

But Collins was one of the rare students of the classics who pass now and then beyond the letter to the spirit. Greek art taught him at least to aspire toward simplicity, although he seldom attained it. We owe to the example of Horace the unlaboured beauty of his *Ode to Evening*, in which the music is an emanation of mood and the form is that of the thought itself. We may attribute to ancient mythology the faint flushes of life that sometimes tinge his personified abstractions. Classical influences may account for the sculpturesque quality of his work, — for its coldness, for its constant search for the typical rather than the individual, for the absence in it of all motion and emotion other than what a sculptor might show.

ODE TO SIMPLICITY

O thou by Nature taught
To breathe her genuine thought,
In numbers warmly pure and sweetly strong;
Who first, on mountains wild,
In Fancy, loveliest child,
Thy babe or Pleasure's, nurs'd the pow'rs of song!

Thou who with hermit heart
Disdain'st the wealth of art,
And *gauds, and pageant weeds, and trailing *pall;
But com'st a *decent maid,
In Attic robe array'd,
O chaste, unboastful nymph, to thee I call!

By all the honey'd store
On *Hybla's thymy shore,
By all her blooms and mingl'd murmurs dear;
By *her whose lovelorn woe,
In ev'ning musings slow,
Soothed sweetly sad Electra's *poet's ear;

By old *Cephisus deep,
Who spread his wavy sweep,
In warbled wand'rings round thy green *retreat;
On whose enamell'd side
When holy Freedom died,
No equal haunt allur'd thy future feet;

O sister meek of Truth,
To my admiring youth
Thy sober aid and native charms infuse!
The flow'rs that sweetest breathe,
Though Beauty cull'd the wreath,
Still ask thy hand to range their order'd hues.

While Rome could none esteem
But Virtue's patriot *theme,
You lov'd her hills, and led her laureate *band;
But staid to sing alone
To one distinguish'd *throne,
And turn'd thy face and fled her alter'd land.

No more, in hall or *bow'r,
The passions own thy pow'r;
Love, only love, *her forceless numbers mean:
For thou hast left her shrine;
Nor olive more, nor vine,
Shall gain thy feet to bless the servile *scene.

Though taste, though genius bless
To some divine excess,
Faints the cold work till thou inspire the whole:
What each, what all supply,
May court, may charm our eye;
Thou, only thou, canst raise the meeting soul!

Of *these let others ask,
To aid some mighty task;
I only seek to find thy temp'rate vale,
Where oft my reed might sound
To maids and shepherds round,
And all thy sons, O Nature, learn my tale.

[1747]

ODE TO EVENING

*If aught of oaten stop or pastoral song
May hope, chaste Eve, to soothe thy modest ear
Like thy own solemn springs,
Thy springs and dying gales,

*Notes on William Collins will be found in the Appendix, pp. 1011 ff.

O nymph reserv'd, while now the bright-hair'd sun
Sits in yon western tent, whose cloudy skirts,
With *brede ethereal wove,
O'erhang his wavy bed

(*Now air is hush'd, save where the weak-ey'd bat,
With short shrill shriek, flits by on leathern wing,
Or where the beetle winds
His small but sullen horn,

As oft he rises 'midst the twilight path,
Against the pilgrim borne in heedless hum)
Now teach me, maid compos'd,
To breathe some soften'd strain

Whose numbers, stealing through thy dark'n-ing vale,
May not unseemly with its stillness suit,
As, musing slow, I hail
Thy genial lov'd return!

For when thy *folding-star, arising, shows
His paly circlet, at his warning lamp,
The fragrant Hours, and elves
Who slept in flow'rs the day,

And many a nymph who wreathes her brows with sedge
And sheds the fresh'ning dew, and, lovelier still,
The pensive Pleasures sweet,
Prepare thy shadowy *car.

Then lead, calm *vot'ress, where some sheety lake
Cheers the lone heath, or some time-hallow'd pile
Or upland fallows gray
Reflect its last cool *gleam.

But when chill blust'ring winds or driving rain
Forbid my willing feet, be mine the hut
That from the mountain's side
Views wilds, and swelling floods,

And hamlets brown, and dim-discover'd spires,
And hears their simple bell, and marks o'er all
Thy dewy fingers draw
The gradual dusky veil.

While Spring shall pour his show'rs, as oft he *wont,
And bathe thy breathing tresses, meekest Eve;
While Summer loves to sport
Beneath thy ling'ring light;

While sallow Autumn fills thy lap with leaves;
Or Winter, yelling through the troublous air,
Affrights thy shrinking train,
And rudely rends thy robes;

So long, sure-found beneath the sylvan shed,
Shall Fancy, Friendship, Science, rose-lipp'd Health,
Thy gentlest influence own,
And hymn thy fav'rite name!

[1747]

ODE TO FEAR

STROPHE

Thou to whom the world unknown,
With all its shadowy shapes, is shown;
Who see'st, appall'd, th' unreal scene,
While Fancy lifts the veil between;
Ah Fear, ah frantic Fear,
I see, I see thee near!
I know thy hurried step, thy haggard eye!
Like thee I start, like thee disorder'd fly,
For, lo, what monsters in thy train appear!
Danger, whose limbs of giant mould
What mortal eye can fix'd behold?
Who stalks his round, an hideous form,
Howling amidst the midnight storm,
Or throws him on the ridgy steep
Of some loose-hanging rock to sleep.
And with him thousand phantoms join'd,
Who prompt to deeds accurs'd the mind;
And those, the fiends, who, near *allied,
O'er Nature's wounds and wrecks preside,
Whilst Vengeance in the lurid air
Lifts her red arm, expos'd and bare;
On whom that rav'ning *brood of Fate,
Who lap the blood of Sorrow, wait.
Who, Fear, this ghastly train can see,
And look not madly wild, like thee?

EPODE

In earliest Greece to thee, with partial choice,
The grief-full Muse address'd her infant tongue;
The maids and matrons on her awful voice,
Silent and pale, in wild amazement hung.

Yet he, the *bard who first invok'd thy name,
Disdain'd in Marathon its pow'r to feel; 31

For not alone he nurs'd the poet's flame,
But *reach'd from Virtue's hand the patriot's steel.

But who is *he whom later garlands grace,
Who left awhile o'er *Hybla's dews to rove,
With trembling eyes thy dreary steps to trace,
Where thou and Furies shared the baleful *grove?

Wrapt in thy cloudy *veil, th' incestuous *queen
Sighed the sad call her son and husband heard,
When once alone it broke the silent scene,
And he, the wretch of Thebes, no more appear'd.

O Fear, I know thee by my throbbing heart;
Thy with'ring pow'r inspir'd each mournful *line;
Though gentle Pity claim her mingl'd part,
Yet all the thunders of the *scene are thine!

ANTISTROPHE

Thou who such weary lengths hast passed,
Where wilt thou rest, mad nymph, at last?
Say, wilt thou shroud in haunted cell,
Where gloomy Rape and Murder dwell?
Or in some hollow'd seat,
'Gainst which the big waves beat,
Hear drowning seamen's cries, in tempests brought?
Dark pow'r, with shudd'ring, meek, submitted thought
Be mine to read the visions old
Which thy awak'ning bards have told,
And, lest thou meet my blasted view,
Hold each strange tale devoutly true!
Ne'er be I found, by thee o'eraw'd,
In that thrice-hallowed *eve abroad
When ghosts, as cottage maids believe,
Their pebbled beds permitted leave,
And goblins haunt, from fire, or fen,
Or mine, or flood, the walks of men!
O thou whose spirit most possess'd
The sacred seat of Shakespeare's breast,
By all that from thy prophet broke,
In thy divine emotions spoke,
Hither again thy fury deal!
Teach me but once like him to feel,
His *cypress wreath my meed decree,
And I, O Fear, will dwell with *thee!

[1747]

ODE ON THE POETICAL CHARACTER

STROPHE

*As once, if not with light regard
I read aright that gifted *bard
(Him whose school above the rest
His loveliest Elfin *Queen has blest),
One, only one, unrivall'd fair
Might hope the magic girdle *wear,
At solemn tourney hung on high,
The wish of each love-darting eye;
(Lo! to each other nymph in turn applied,
As if, in air unseen, some hov'ring hand,
Some chaste and angel friend to virgin fame,
With whispered spell had burst the starting band,
It left unblest her loath'd, dishonour'd side;
Happier, hopeless fair, if never
Her baffled hand, with vain endeavour,
Had touched that fatal zone to her denied!)
Young Fancy thus, to me divinest name,
To whom, prepar'd and bath'd in heav'n,
The *cest of amplest pow'r is giv'n,
To few the godlike gift assigns
To gird their blest, prophetic loins,
And *gaze her visions wild, and feel unmix'd her flame!

EPODE

The band, as fairy legends say,
Was wove on that creating day
When he who called with thought to birth
Yon tented sky, this laughing earth,
And dress'd with springs and forests tall,
And pour'd the main engirting all,
Long by the lov'd *enthusiast *woo'd,
Himself in some diviner mood,
Retiring, sate with her alone,
And placed her on his sapphire throne,
The whiles, the vaulted shrine around,
Seraphic wires were heard to sound,
Now sublimest triumph swelling,
Now on love and mercy dwelling;
And she, from out the veiling cloud,
Breath'd her magic notes aloud,
And thou, thou rich-haired *youth of morn,
And all thy subject life, was born!
The dang'rous passions kept aloof,
Far from the sainted growing woof:
But near it sate ecstatic Wonder,
List'ning the deep applauding thunder;
And Truth, in sunny vest array'd,
By *whose the *tarsel's eyes were made.

All the shad'wy tribes of mind,
In braided dance, their murmurs join'd,
And all the bright uncounted pow'rs
Who feed on heav'n's ambrosial flow'rs.
Where is the bard whose soul can now
Its high presuming hopes avow?
Where he who thinks, with rapture blind,
This hallow'd *work for him design'd?

ANTISTROPHE

High on some *cliff, to heav'n up-pil'd,
Of rude access, of prospect wild,
Where, tangled round the *jealous steep,
Strange shades o'erbrow the valleys deep,
And holy genii guard the rock,
Its glooms embrown, its springs unlock,
While on its rich ambitious head
An Eden, like his own, lies spread.
I view that *oak, the fancied glades among,
By which as Milton lay, his ev'ning ear,
From many a cloud that dropp'd ethereal dew,
Nigh *spher'd in heav'n, its native strains could hear,
On which that ancient *trump he reached was hung.
Thither oft, his glory greeting,
From Waller's *myrtle shades retreating,
With many a vow from Hope's aspiring tongue,
My trembling feet his guiding steps pursue.
In vain — such bliss to one *alone
Of all the sons of soul was known,
And Heav'n and Fancy, kindred pow'rs,
Have now o'erturn'd th' inspiring bow'rs
Or curtain'd close such scene from ev'ry future view.

[1747]

THE *PASSIONS

AN ODE FOR MUSIC

When Music, heav'nly maid, was young,
While yet in early Greece she sung,
The Passions oft, to hear her *shell,
Thronged around her magic cell,
Exulting, trembling, raging, fainting,
Possess'd beyond the Muse's painting;
By turns they felt the glowing mind
Disturb'd, delighted, rais'd, refin'd.
Till once, 'tis said, when all were fir'd,
Fill'd with fury, rapt, inspir'd,
From the supporting *myrtles round
They snatch'd her instruments of sound;
And, as they oft had heard apart
Sweet lessons of her forceful art,
Each (for madness rul'd the hour)
Would prove his own expressive pow'r.

First Fear his hand, its skill to try,
Amid the chords bewilder'd laid,
And back recoil'd, he knew not why,
Ev'n at the sound himself had made.

Next Anger rush'd; his eyes on fire,
In lightnings own'd his secret stings;
In one rude clash he struck the lyre,
And swept with hurried hand the strings.

With woful measures wan Despair,
Low sullen *sounds, his grief beguil'd;
A solemn, strange, and mingled air —
'Twas sad by fits, by starts 'twas wild.

But thou, O Hope, with eyes so fair,
What was thy delightful measure?
Still it whisper'd promis'd pleasure,
And bade the lovely scenes at distance hail!
Still would her touch the strain prolong;
And from the rocks, the woods, the vale,
She called on Echo still, through all the song;
And where her sweetest *theme she chose,
A soft responsive voice was heard at ev'ry close,
And Hope, enchanted, smiled, and wav'd her golden hair.

And longer had she sung; but with a frown
Revenge impatient rose:
He threw his blood-stain'd sword in thunder down,
And with a with'ring look
The war-*denouncing trumpet took,
And blew a blast so loud and dread,
Were ne'er prophetic sounds so full of woe.
And ever and anon he beat
The doubling drum with furious heat;
And though sometimes, each dreary pause between,
Dejected Pity, at his side,
Her soul-subduing voice applied,
Yet still he kept his wild unalter'd mien,
While each strain'd ball of sight seem'd bursting from his head.

Thy numbers, Jealousy, to naught were fix'd,
Sad proof of thy distressful state;

Of diff'ring themes the veering song was mix'd;
And now it courted Love, now raving call'd on Hate.
With eyes uprais'd, as one inspir'd,
Pale Melancholy sate retir'd,
And from her wild sequester'd seat,
In notes by distance made more sweet,
Pour'd through the mellow horn her pensive soul;
And, dashing soft from rocks around,
Bubbling runnels join'd the sound;
Through glades and glooms the mingled measure stole,
Or o'er some haunted stream, with fond delay,
Round an holy calm diffusing,
Love of peace and lonely musing,
In hollow murmurs died away.

But oh, how alter'd was its sprightlier tone
When Cheerfulness, a nymph of healthiest hue,
Her bow across her shoulder flung,
Her buskins gemm'd with morning dew,
Blew an inspiring air, that dale and thicket rung,
The hunter's call, to faun and dryad known!
The oak-crowned *sisters, and their chaste-eyed *queen,
Satyrs, and sylvan boys were seen
Peeping from forth their alleys green;
Brown Exercise rejoic'd to hear;
And Sport leap'd up, and seiz'd his beechen spear.

Last came Joy's ecstatic trial:
He, with *viny crown advancing,
First to the lively pipe his hand address'd;
But soon he saw the brisk awak'ning viol,
Whose sweet entrancing voice he lov'd the best.
They would have thought, who heard the strain,
They saw in Tempe's *vale her native maids,
Amidst the festal-sounding shades,
To some unwearied minstrel dancing,
While, as his flying fingers kiss'd the strings,
Love fram'd with Mirth a gay fantastic round;
Loose were her tresses seen, her zone unbound,
And he, amidst his frolic play,
As if he would the charming air repay,
Shook thousand odours from his dewy wings.

O Music! sphere-descended maid!
Friend of Pleasure, Wisdom's aid!
Why, goddess, why, to us denied,
Lay'st thou thy ancient lyre aside?
As in that lov'd Athenian bow'r
You learn'd an all-commanding pow'r,
Thy mimic soul, O nymph endear'd,
Can well recall what then it heard.
Where is thy native simple heart,
Devote to Virtue, Fancy, Art?
Arise as in that elder time,
Warm, energic, chaste, sublime!
Thy wonders, in that godlike age,
Fill thy recording *sister's page.
'Tis said, and I believe the tale,
Thy humblest *reed could more prevail,
Had more of strength, diviner rage,
Than all which charms this laggard age,
Ev'n all at once together found,
Cecilia's mingled *world of sound.
Oh, bid our vain *endeavours cease;
Revive the just designs of Greece;
Return in all thy simple state;
Confirm the tales her sons *relate!

[1747]

ODE

WRITTEN IN THE BEGINNING OF THE YEAR *1746

How sleep the brave who sink to rest
By all their country's wishes bless'd!
When Spring, with dewy fingers cold,
Returns to deck their hallow'd mould,
She there shall dress a sweeter sod
Than Fancy's feet have ever trod.

By fairy hands their knell is rung;
By forms unseen their dirge is sung;
There Honour comes, a pilgrim gray,
To bless the turf that wraps their clay;
And Freedom shall awhile repair,
To dwell a weeping hermit there!

[1747]

A SONG FROM SHAKESPEARE'S "CYMBELINE"

SUNG BY *GUIDERUS AND ARVIRAGUS OVER FIDELE, SUPPOSED TO BE *DEAD

To fair Fidele's grassy tomb
Soft maids and village hinds shall bring
Each op'ning sweet of earliest bloom,
And rifle all the breathing spring.

No wailing ghost shall dare appear,
To vex with shrieks this quiet grove;
But shepherd lads assemble here,
And melting virgins own their love.

No wither'd witch shall here be seen,
No goblins lead their nightly crew;
The female fays shall haunt the green,
And dress thy grave with pearly dew.

The redbreast oft, at ev'ning hours,
Shall kindly lend his little aid,
With hoary moss and gathered flow'rs,
To deck the ground where thou art laid.

When howling winds and beating rain
In tempests shake the sylvan cell,
Or 'midst the chase, on ev'ry plain,
The tender thought on thee shall dwell.

Each lonely scene shall thee restore;
For thee the tear be duly shed;
Belov'd till life could charm no more,
And mourned till Pity's self be dead.

[1749]

AN ODE ON THE POPULAR SUPERSTITIONS OF THE HIGHLANDS OF SCOTLAND

CONSIDERED AS THE SUBJECT OF POETRY

This poem, probably written in 1749, was first published, lacking a stanza and a half, besides several half-lines, in 1788. Shortly after, there appeared another version in which these gaps were, for the most part, adequately filled. Although it is by no means certain that this second version is entirely from the pen of Collins, it does at any rate present a complete, though not a finally revised, poem. For this reason, it is the one here used, the passages omitted in the first version being enclosed in square brackets.

*H——, thou return'st from Thames, whose naiads long
Have seen thee ling'ring with a fond delay
'Mid those soft friends whose hearts, some future day,
Shall melt, perhaps, to hear thy tragic song.
Go, not unmindful of that cordial *youth
Whom, long endear'd, thou leav'st by Lavant's side;
Together let us wish him lasting truth
And joy untainted with his destined bride.
Go! nor regardless, while these numbers boast
My short-liv'd bliss, forget my social name;
But think, far off, how, on the southern coast,
I met thy friendship with an equal flame.
Fresh to that * soil thou turn'st whose ev'ry vale
Shall prompt the poet and his song demand.
To thee thy copious subjects ne'er shall fail;
Thou need'st but take the pencil to thy hand
And paint what all believe who own thy genial land.

There must thou wake perforce thy *Doric quill;
'Tis Fancy's land to which thou sett'st thy feet,
Where still, 'tis said, the fairy people meet
Beneath each * birken shade on mead or hill.
There each trim lass that skims the milky store
To the swart * tribes their creamy bowl allots;
By night they sip it round the cottage door,
While airy minstrels warble jocund notes.
There ev'ry * herd, by sad experience, knows
How, wing'd with fate, their elf-shot arrows fly,
When the sick ewe her summer food foregoes,
Or, stretch'd on earth, the heart-smit heifers lie.
Such airy beings awe th' untutor'd swain,
Nor thou, though learn'd, his homelier thoughts neglect;
Let thy sweet Muse the rural faith sustain:
These are the themes of simple, sure effect,
That add new conquests to her boundless reign,
And fill with double force her heart-commanding strain.

Ev'n yet preserv'd, how often may'st thou hear,
Where to the pole the boreal mountains * run,
Taught by the father to his list'ning son,
Strange lays whose pow'r had charm'd a Spenser's ear.
At ev'ry pause, before thy mind * possest,
Old Runic * bards shall seem to rise around,
With uncouth lyres, in many-colour'd * vest,
Their matted hair with boughs fantastic crown'd:
Whether thou bid'st the well-taught * hind repeat
The choral * dirge that mourns some chieftain brave,
When ev'ry shrieking maid her bosom beat

And strew'd with choicest herbs his scented grave,
Or whether, sitting in the shepherd's * shiel,
Thou hear'st some sounding tale of war's alarms,
When, at the bugle's call, with fire and steel
The sturdy clans pour'd forth their bony swarms
And hostile brothers met to * prove each other's arms.

'Tis thine to sing how, framing hideous spells,
In Skye's lone isle the gifted wizard seer
Lodg'd in the wintry cave with [Fate's fell spear]
Or in the depth of * Uist's dark forests dwells;
How they whose * sight such dreary dreams engross,
With their own visions oft astonish'd droop,
When o'er the wat'ry * strath or quaggy moss
They see the gliding ghosts unbodied troop;
Or if, in sports or on the festive green,
Their [destined] glance some fated youth descry
Who, now perhaps in lusty vigour seen
And rosy health, shall soon lamented die.
For them the viewless forms of air obey,
Their bidding heed, and at their beck repair.
They know what spirit brews the stormful day
And, * heartless, oft like moody madness stare
To see the phantom train their secret work prepare.

[To monarchs dear, some hundred miles astray,
Oft have they seen Fate give the fatal blow!
The seer in Skye shriek'd as the blood did flow
When headless * Charles warm on the scaffold lay.
As Boreas threw his young Aurora forth
In the first year of the first George's reign
And battles rag'd in welkin of the north,
They mourn'd in air fell, fell Rebellion * slain.
And as, of late, they joy'd in Preston's fight,
Saw at sad Falkirk all their hopes near crown'd,
They rav'd, divining thro' their second sight,
Pale red * Culloden, where these hopes were drown'd.
Illustrious William! Britain's guardian name!
One * William sav'd us from a tyrant's stroke;
He, for a sceptre, gain'd heroic fame,
But * thou, more glorious, Slavery's chain hast broke
To reign a private man and bow to Freedom's yoke.

These, too, thou'lt sing, for well thy magic Muse
Can to the topmost heav'n of grandeur soar
Or stoop to wail the swain that is no more.
Ah, homely swains, your homeward steps ne'er lose;
Let not dank * Will mislead you to the heath!
Dancing in mirky night o'er fen and lake
He glows to draw you downward to your death
In his bewitch'd, low, marshy willow brake!]
What tho' far off, from some dark dell espied,
His glimm'ring mazes cheer th' excursive sight,
Yet turn, ye wand'rers, turn your steps aside,
Nor trust the guidance of that faithless light;
For, watchful, lurking 'mid th' unrustling reed,
At those mirk hours the wily monster lies
And listens oft to hear the passing steed,
And frequent round him rolls his sullen eyes
If chance his savage wrath may some weak wretch surprise.

Ah, luckless swain, o'er all unblest, indeed,
Whom, late bewilder'd in the dank, dark fen,
Far from his flocks and smoking hamlet then,
To that sad spot [where hums the sedgy weed:]
On him, enrag'd, the fiend, in angry mood,
Shall never look with pity's kind concern,
But instant, furious, raise the whelming flood
O'er its drown'd bank, forbidding all return.
Or, if he meditate his wish'd escape
To some dim hill that seems uprising near,
To his faint eye the grim and grisly shape,
In all its terrors clad, shall wild appear.
Meantime the wat'ry surge shall round him rise,
Pour'd sudden forth from ev'ry swelling source.
What now remains but tears and hopeless sighs?
His fear-shook limbs have lost their youthly force,
And down the waves he floats, a pale and breathless corse.

For him, in vain, his anxious wife shall *wait,
Or wander forth to meet him on his way;
For him, in vain, at to-fall of the day,
His babes shall linger at th' unclosing gate.
Ah, ne'er shall he return! Alone, if night
*Her *travell'd limbs in broken slumbers steep,
With dropping willows drest, his mournful sprite
Shall visit sad, perchance, her silent sleep;
Then he, perhaps, with moist and wat'ry hand,
Shall fondly seem to press her shudd'ring cheek,
And with his blue-swoln face before her stand,
And, shiv'ring cold, these piteous accents speak:
"Pursue, dear wife, thy daily toils pursue
At dawn or dusk, industrious as before;
Nor e'er of me one hapless thought renew,
While I lie welt'ring on the *osier'd shore,
Drowned by the *kelpie's wrath, nor e'er shall aid thee *more!"

Unbounded is thy range; with varied style
Thy Muse may, like those feath'ry *tribes which spring
From their rude rocks, extend her skirting wing
Round the moist marge of each cold Hebrid isle,
To that hoar *pile which still its ruin shows,
In whose small vaults a pigmy-folk is found,
Whose bones the delver with his spade upthrows,
And culls them, wond'ring, from the hallow'd ground!
Or thither, where, beneath the show'ry west,
The mighty *kings of three fair realms are laid;
Once foes, perhaps, together now they rest.
No slaves revere them, and no wars invade:
Yet frequent now, at midnight's solemn hour,
The rifted mounds their yawning cells unfold,
And forth the monarchs stalk with sov'reign pow'r,
In pageant robes, and wreath'd with sheeny gold,
And on their twilight tombs aërial council hold.

But oh! o'er all, forget not Kilda's *race,
On whose bleak rocks, which brave the wasting tides,
Fair Nature's daughter, Virtue, yet abides.
Go, just as they, their blameless manners trace!
Then to my ear transmit some gentle song
Of those whose lives are yet sincere and plain,
Their bounded walks the rugged cliffs along,
And all their prospect *but the wintry main.
With sparing temp'rance, at the needful time,
They drain the *sainted spring, or, hunger-press'd,
Along th' Atlantic rock undreading climb,
And of its eggs despoil the *solan's nest.
Thus blest in primal innocence they live,
Suffic'd and happy with that frugal fare
Which *tasteful toil and hourly danger give.
Hard is their shallow soil, and bleak and bare;
Nor ever vernal bee was heard to murmur there!

Nor need'st thou blush that such *false themes engage
Thy *gentle mind, of fairer stores possest;
For not alone they touch the village breast,
But fill'd in elder time th' historic page.
There Shakespeare's self, with ev'ry garland crown'd —
[Flew to those fairy climes his fancy sheen!] —
In*musing hour, his wayward *sisters found,
And with their terrors dress'd the magic scene.
From them he sung when, 'mid his bold design,
Before the Scot afflicted and aghast,
The *shadowy kings of Banquo's fated line
Thro' the dark cave in gleamy pageant passed.
Proceed, nor quit the tales which, simply told,
Could once so well my answ'ring bosom pierce;
Proceed! in forceful sounds and colours bold,
The native legends of thy land rehearse;
To such adapt thy lyre and suit thy pow'rful verse.

In scenes like these, which, daring to depart
From sober truth, are still to nature true,
And call forth fresh delight to fancy's view,
Th' heroic muse employ'd her Tasso's art!
How have I trembled, when, at Tancred's stroke,
Its gushing blood the gaping cypress pour'd;

When each live plant with mortal accents spoke,
And the wild blast upheav'd the vanish'd sword!
How have I sat, when pip'd the pensive wind,
To hear his harp, by British *Fairfax strung—
Prevailing poet, whose undoubting mind
Believ'd the magic wonders which he sung!
Hence at each sound imagination glows;
[Hence, at each picture, vivid life starts here!]
Hence his warm lay with softest sweetness flows;
Melting it flows, pure, *num'rous, strong, and clear,
And fills th' impassion'd heart, and wins th' harmonious ear.

All hail, ye scenes that o'er my soul prevail!
Ye [splendid] *friths and lakes which, far away,
Are by smooth Annan fill'd, or past'ral Tay,
Or Don's romantic springs; at distance, hail!
The time shall come when I, perhaps, may tread
Your lowly glens, o'erhung with spreading broom,
Or o'er your stretching heaths by fancy led,
[Or o'er your mountains creep, in awful gloom.]
Then will I dress once more the faded bow'r
Where Jonson sat in Drummond's [classic] *shade,
Or crop from Tiviot's *dale each [lyric flower,]
*And mourn on Yarrow's banks [where Willy's laid!]
Meantime, ye Pow'rs that on the plains which bore
The cordial *youth, on Lothian's plains, attend,
Where'er he dwell, on hill or lowly muir,
To him I lose, your kind protection lend,
And, touch'd with love like mine, preserve my absent friend!

[1788]

THOMAS WARTON, THE ELDER

THE elder Thomas Warton, father of Joseph and Thomas, was born in the south of England about the year 1688 and was educated at Magdalen College, Oxford. In his most prominent position, as Professor of Poetry at Oxford, he seems not to have been entirely successful, perhaps on account of a natural indolence which was later shown by his younger son while he held the same office. After leaving Oxford he was made vicar of Basingstoke, a small market town in Hampshire, and also master of the excellent grammar school in that town, where the naturalist, Gilbert White, was one of his pupils. Most of his verse was written in his early years, but very little of it was published until three years after his death, when his son, Joseph, brought out his *Poems on Several Occasions*, 1748.

Until recent decades the verse of the elder Warton has been entirely neglected. This has meant a loss not so much to literature as to the understanding of literary history, for his significance lies far more in his influence upon others than in his personal accomplishment. It is true that he was one of the earlier experimenters with the Spenserian stanza and the Miltonic couplet; he had enough interest in northern antiquities to make two English versions, from the Latin translation published by Sir William Temple, of *The Death Song of Ragnar Lodbrok*; his choice of themes, and in particular, his liking for the theme of solitude, is often surprising, in consideration of his dates, to those who still believe that romanticism was a fresh discovery made in the eighteenth century. Belonging to the Country as against the Town, preferring nature to art and the old to the new, somewhat timidly antiquarian and sentimental, his tone of thought and feeling often suggests either the simplicities of Elizabethan lyric or else the more conscious naïveté of the Wordsworthian school. All this would matter little if only his own rather trifling verses were involved. His importance is understood only when it is realized that all the tentative and experimental tendencies found in his work were amplified and consciously defended in the work of his two sons, and were handed on by them to many still younger men, their pupils or imitators. There is, in fact, one unbroken literary tradition easily traceable from the elder Warton, Pope's contemporary, through his son, Joseph, who lived until 1800 and taught thousands of English boys, into the work of William Lisle Bowles, Joseph's pupil, and thence to Wordsworth and Coleridge, both of whom acknowledge their debt to Bowles. The elder Warton is therefore one of the better examples out of the many that may be cited to prove that what we now call romanticism never died out in England but was merely for a time submerged.

RETIREMENT

AN ODE

Although of slight literary value, these verses are an interesting indication of the deep influence exerted by Milton's minor poems, and particularly by *Il Penseroso*, upon the Wartons and the many to whom their influence extended. Not only does Warton imitate Milton's verse-form as closely as he is able, gathering the couplets to be sure into stanzas of equal length, but he adapts Milton's peculiar use of personification and of allegorical figures to the eighteenth-century taste for abstraction. What is most worthy of attention, however, is the strong emphasis he places upon solitude, in Milton's poem only the chief of several themes, asserting that it is safer, happier, more thoughtful and more virtuous than public life. This praise of retirement was already, of course, very old, but the poets of Warton's time found their warrant for it chiefly in *Il Penseroso*.

On beds of daisies idly laid,
The willow waving o'er my head,
Now morning on the bending stem,
Hangs the round and glittering gem,
Lull'd by the lapse of yonder spring,
Of nature's various charms I sing;
Ambition, Pride, and Pomp, adieu!
For what has Joy to do with you?

Joy, rose-lipped dryad, loves to dwell
In sunny field or mossy cell,
Delights on echoing hills to hear
The reaper's song or lowing steer;
Or view with tenfold plenty spread
The crowded cornfield, blooming mead;
While beauty, health, and innocence
Transport the eye, the soul, the sense.

Not fresco'd roofs, not beds of state,
Not guards that round a monarch wait,
Not crowds of flatterers can scare
From loftiest courts intruding Care;
Midst odours, splendours, banquets, wine,
While minstrels sound, while tapers shine,

In sable stole sad Care will come
And darken the gay drawing-room.

Nymphs of the groves, in green array'd,
Conduct me to your thickest shade,
Deep in the bosom of the vale,
Where haunts the lonesome nightingale;
Where Contemplation, maid divine,
Leans against some aged pine,
Wrapt in steadfast thought profound,
Her eyes fix'd steadfast on the ground.

O Virtue's nurse! retired queen,
By saints alone and hermits seen,
Beyond vain mortals' wishes wise,
Teach me *St. James's to despise;
For what are courts but schools
For fops, or hospitals for fools,
Where slaves and madmen, young and old,
Meet to adore some calf of gold?

[1748]

AN ODE

WRITTEN IN A GROTTO NEAR FARNHAM IN SURREY, CALLED MOTHER LUDLOW'S CAVE

Close in this deep *retreat
Oh, coolly let me sit,
Shelter'd from the sultry day!
*Sirius and Sol with burning beams
So strike the gasping fields below
That not an ox is heard to low,
Or little warbler from his throat
To pour the sweetly-winding note.

The nymphs that keep this *circling wood
And beauteous naiads of the neighb'ring *flood,
With their dew-dropping hair,
Oft to this cave repair,
To dance and trip it in a round
On the smooth and hallow'd ground;
And say that Dian's grot and Thetis' bow'rs
Must yield in coolness and in shade to ours.

'Twas here, as old traditions tell,
A wither'd *witch was wont to dwell;
The magic mutterings of whose voice could call
A thousand demons from their darksome hall,
Bid haste the wild winds from their northern caves,
Obscure the moon, and rouse the roaring waves.
Here *Lud, retiring from fierce battle, came,
And from his helmit quaff'd the cooling stream;
Leant on his spear, unrein'd his foaming steed,
To pasture on the green, refreshful mead.

Here what a solemn silence reigns,
Save the tinklings of a rill
That, gushing from the hollow hill,
Pensive as it runs, complains!
But hark! methinks a spirit speaks,
A voice from the remotest cavern breaks:
"From the vain world learn, mortal, to retire,
With true ambition to Heav'n aspire;
Grandeur and glory trifling hearts *trepan;
These toys disdain, for virtue makes the man."

Let me therefore ever dwell
In this twilight, solemn cell;
For musing Melancholy made,
Whose entrance venerable oaks o'ershade,
And whose roof that lowly bends,
With awful gloom my serious thoughts befriends.
Here let me dwell,
Till Death shall say, "Thy cavern leave,
Change it for a darker grave."

[1748]

AN INVOCATION TO A WATER-NYMPH

Fair pearl-crown'd nymph, whose gushing torrent laves
This marble rock with hollow-tinkling waves;
Who wont'st in secret solitude to dwell
On coral beds beneath thy sapphire cell;
Whose virgin-power can break the magic charm,
Whose look the black enchanter's hand disarm;
Whom swains in neighb'ring vales to sing delight,
Kind guardian of their flocks from *blasting sprite;
Permit me, goddess, from thy silver lake,
With cooling draught my glowing thirst to slake!
So, when thou bath'st, may no rude satyr's eye,
From some deep brake thy naked beauties spy:
May no chill blast the ivied oak invade,
That o'er thy cavern waves his solemn shade.

[1748]

* Notes on Thomas Warton, the Elder, will be found in the Appendix, p. 1014.

THOMAS WARTON, THE YOUNGER

Thomas Warton, younger son of Thomas Warton Senior, was born at Basingstoke, Hampshire, in 1728, and was educated by his father in the grammar school of that town. At seventeen he wrote *The Pleasures of Melancholy*, a companion-piece for his brother's *The Enthusiast* and an enlargement of many hints and sketches to be found in his father's verse. Proceeding to Trinity College, Oxford, he took his master's degree at twenty-three and was elected fellow. He remained at Oxford for the rest of his life, never marrying, paying no attention to his various church livings, spending his evenings at ale-houses with boon companions and his days among the mediæval records in the Bodleian Library, growing more careless of his personal appearance, more eccentric, and more learned every year. Before he was thirty years of age he was chosen for the important Professorship of Poetry which his father had held before him. In various ways, by poems serious or burlesque about his beloved city and by various monographs on the antiquities of the place, as well as by his apparent indolence and his really great industry, Warton made himself the very type of the Oxford don of his century. The greater part of his verse was written before he was twenty-three. His important *Observations on the Poetry of Spenser* appeared in 1754, and twenty years later he published the first volume of his chief work, *The History of English Poetry*, a masterpiece of scholarship which, for its range of erudition and bold way-breaking through new territory, deserves to stand beside Gibbon's *Decline and Fall*, its contemporary. This work, originally planned by Pope and later by Thomas Gray, Warton brought down in a third volume to the age of Elizabeth, but left it a fragment at that point. His most pleasing piece of work, an admirable edition of Milton's minor poems, appeared in 1785. In the same year he was made Camden Professor of History and Poet-Laureate of England. He died in 1790, of a paralytic stroke.

Thomas Warton's most satisfactory work in verse was done in the humorous and mock-heroic vein well exemplified by his *Panegyric Upon Oxford Ale*. In his serious verse, of which his sonnets are the best, he is haunted by the spirit of Milton's *Il Penseroso*, and dominated by the "passion for the past," the strongest emotion he knew in life.

THE PLEASURES OF *MELANCHOLY

Mother of musings, Contemplation sage,
Whose grotto stands upon the topmost rock
Of Teneriffe; 'mid the tempestuous night,
On which, in calmest meditation held,
Thou hear'st with howling winds the beating rain
And drifting hail descend; or if the skies
Unclouded shine, and through the blue serene
Pale Cynthia rolls her silver-axled car,
Whence gazing steadfast on the spangled vault
Raptured thou sitt'st, while murmurs indistinct
Of distant billows soothe thy pensive ear
With hoarse and hollow sounds; secure, self-blest,
There oft thou listen'st to the *wild uproar
Of fleets encountering, that in whispers low
Ascends the rocky summit, where thou dwell'st
Remote from man, conversing with the spheres!
O lead me, queen sublime, to solemn glooms
Congenial with my soul; to cheerless shades,
To ruin'd *seats, to twilight cells and bow'rs,
Where thoughtful Melancholy loves to muse,
Her favourite midnight haunts. The laughing scenes
Of purple spring, where all the wanton train
Of Smiles and Graces seem to lead the dance
In sportive round, while from their hands they show'r
Ambrosial blooms and flow'rs, no longer charm;
*Tempe, no more I court thy balmy breeze;
Adieu, green vales! Ye broider'd meads, adieu!

Beneath yon *ruin'd abbey's moss-grown piles
Oft let me sit, at twilight hour of eve,
Where through some western window the pale moon
Pours her long-levell'd rule of streaming *light;
While *sullen sacred silence reigns around,
Save the lone screech-owl's note, who builds his bow'r
Amid the mould'ring caverns dark and damp,
Or the calm breeze, that rustles in the leaves
Of flaunting ivy, that with mantle green
Invests some wasted tow'r. Or let me tread

* Notes on Thomas Warton, the Younger, will be found in the Appendix, pp. 1014 ff.

Its neighbouring walk of pines, where mused of old
The cloister'd brothers; through the gloomy void
That far extends beneath their ample arch
As on I pace, religious *horror wraps
My soul in dread repose. But when the world
Is clad in midnight's raven-colour'd robe,
'Mid hollow charnel let me watch the flame
Of taper dim, shedding a livid glare
O'er the wan heaps, while *airy voices talk
Along the glimmering walls, or ghostly shape
At distance seen, invites with beckoning hand
My lonesome steps, through the far-winding vaults.
Nor undelightful is the solemn noon
Of night, when, haply, wakeful from my couch
I start: lo, all is motionless around!
Roars not the rushing wind; the sons of men
And every beast in mute oblivion lie;
All nature's hush'd in silence and in sleep.
Oh, then how fearful is it to reflect
That through the still globe's awful solitude,
No being wakes but me! till stealing sleep
My drooping temples bathes in opiate dews.
Nor then let dreams, of wanton folly born,
My senses lead through flowery paths of joy;
But let the sacred Genius of the night
Such mystic visions send, as *Spenser saw,
When through bewildering Fancy's magic maze,
To the fell house of Busyrane he led
Th' unshaken Britomart; or *Milton knew,
When in abstracted thought he first conceived
All heav'n in tumult, and the Seraphim
Come towering, arm'd in adamant and gold.

Let others love soft Summer's evening smiles
As, listening to the distant waterfall,
They mark the blushes of the streaky west;
I choose the pale December's foggy glooms.
Then, when the sullen shades of evening close,
Where through the room a blindly-glimmering gleam
The dying embers scatter, far remote
From Mirth's mad shouts, that through th' illumin'd roof
Resound with festive echo, let me sit,
Blest with the lowly cricket's drowsy dirge.
Then let my thought contemplative explore
This fleeting state of things, the vain delights,
The fruitless toils that still our search elude,
As through the wilderness of life we rove.
This sober hour of silence will unmask
False Folly's smile, that like the dazzling spells
Of wily Comus cheat th' *unweeting eye
With *blear illusion, and persuade to drink
That *charmèd cup, which Reason's mintage fair
Unmoulds, and stamps the monster on the man.
Eager we taste, but in the luscious draught
Forget the poisonous dregs that lurk beneath.

Few know that *elegance of soul refined,
Whose soft sensation feels a *quicker joy
From Melancholy's scenes, than the dull pride
Of tasteless splendour and magnificence
Can e'er afford. Thus Eloïse, whose mind
Had languish'd to the pangs of melting love,
More genuine transport found, as on some tomb
Reclined, she watch'd the *tapers of the dead;
Or through the pillar'd aisles, amid pale shrines
Of imaged saints, and intermingled graves,
Mus'd a veil'd votaress; than Flavia feels
As through the mazes of the festive ball,
Proud of her conquering charms and beauty's blaze,
She floats amid the silken sons of dress
And shines the fairest of th' assembled fair.

When azure noontide cheers the *dædal globe,
And the blest regent of the golden day
Rejoices in his bright meridian tower,
How oft my wishes ask the night's return
That best befriends the melancholy mind!
Hail, sacred Night! thou too shalt share my song!
Sister of ebon-sceptred Hecate, hail!
Whether in congregated clouds thou wrap'st
Thy viewless chariot, or with silver crown
Thy beaming head encirclest, ever hail!
What tho' beneath thy gloom the sorceress-train,
Far in obscurèd haunt of Lapland moors,
With rhymes uncouth the bloody cauldron bless;
Though Murder wan beneath thy shrouding shade
Summons her slow-eyed votaries to *devise
Of secret slaughter, while by one blue lamp
In hideous conference sits the listening band,
And starts at each low wind, or wakeful sound;
What though thy stay the pilgrim curseth oft
As, all benighted in Arabian wastes,
He hears the wilderness around him howl
With roaming monsters, while on his hoar head

The black-descending tempest ceaseless beats;
Yet more delightful to my pensive mind
Is thy return than blooming morn's approach,
Ev'n then, in youthful pride of opening May,
When from the portals of the saffron east
She sheds fresh roses, and ambrosial dews.
Yet not ungrateful is the morn's approach,
When dropping wet she comes, and clad in clouds,
While through the damp air scowls the louring south,
Blackening the landscape's face, that grove and hill
In formless vapours undistinguish'd swim:
Th' afflicted songsters of the sadden'd groves
Hail not the sullen gloom; the waving elms
That, hoar thro' time and ranged in thick array,
Enclose with stately row some rural hall,
Are mute, nor echo with the clamours hoarse
Of rooks rejoicing on their airy boughs;
While to the shed the dripping poultry crowd,
A mournful train; secure the village hind
Hangs o'er the crackling blaze, nor tempts the storm;
Fix'd in th' unfinish'd furrow rests the plough:
Rings not the high wood with enliven'd shouts
Of early hunter: all is silence drear;
And deepest sadness wraps the face of things.

Thro' Pope's soft song tho' all the Graces breathe,
And happiest art adorn his *Attic page;
Yet does my mind with sweeter transport glow,
As at the root of mossy trunk reclined,
In magic Spenser's wildly-warbled song
I see deserted Una wander wide
Through *wasteful solitudes and *lurid heaths,
Weary, forlorn; than when the fated *fair
Upon the bosom bright of silver Thames
Launches in all the lustre of brocade,
Amid the splendours of the laughing sun.
The gay description palls upon the sense,
And coldly strikes the mind with feeble bliss.

Ye youths of Albion's beauty-blooming isle,
Whose brows have worn the wreath of luckless love,
Is there a pleasure like the pensive mood,
Whose magic wont to soothe your soften'd souls?
Oh, tell how rapturous the joy, to melt
To Melody's *assuasive voice; to bend
Th' uncertain step along the midnight mead,
And pour your sorrows to the pitying moon,
By many a slow trill from the bird of woe
Oft interrupted; in embowering woods
By darksome brook to muse, and there forget
The solemn dullness of the tedious world,
While fancy grasps the visionary fair;
And now no more th' abstracted ear attends
The water's murmuring lapse, th' entranc'd eye
Pierces no longer through th' extended rows
Of thick-ranged trees, till haply from the depth
The woodman's stroke, or distant tinkling team,
Or heifers rustling through the brake, alarms
Th' *illuded sense, and mars the golden dream.
These are delights that absence drear has made
Familiar to my soul, e'er since the form
Of young Sapphira, beauteous as the Spring,
When from her violet-woven couch awaked
By frolic Zephyr's hand, her tender cheek
Graceful she lifts, and blushing from her bow'r
Issues to clothe in gladsome-glistering green
The genial globe, first met my dazzled sight:
These are delights unknown to minds profane,
And which alone the pensive soul can *taste.

The *taper'd choir, at the late hour of prayer,
Oft let me tread, while to th' according voice
The many-sounding organ peals on high
The clear, slow-dittied chaunt, or varied hymn,
Till all my soul is bathed in ecstasies,
And lapp'd in Paradise. Or let me sit
Far in sequester'd aisles of the deep dome,
There lonesome listen to the sacred sounds,
Which, as they lengthen through the Gothic vaults,
In hollow murmurs reach my ravish'd ear.
Nor when the lamps expiring yield to night,
And solitude returns, would I forsake
The solemn mansion, but attentive mark
The due clock swinging slow with sweepy sway,
Measuring Time's flight with momentary sound.

Nor let me fail to cultivate my mind
With the soft thrillings of the tragic Muse,
Divine Melpomene, sweet Pity's nurse,
Queen of the stately step, and flowing pall.
Now let *Monimia mourn with streaming eyes
Her joys incestuous, and polluted love;
Now let soft Juliet in the gaping tomb

Print the last kiss on her true Romeo's lips,
His lips yet reeking from the deadly draught;
Or *Jaffier kneel for one forgiving look.
Nor seldom let the Moor on Desdemone
Pour the misguided threats of jealous rage.
By soft degrees the manly torrent steals
From my swoln eyes; and at a brother's woe
My big heart melts in sympathizing tears.

What are the splendours of the gaudy court,
Its tinsel trappings, and its pageant pomps?
To me far happier seems the banish'd lord,
Amid Siberia's unrejoicing wilds
Who pines all lonesome, in the chambers hoar
Of some high castle shut, whose windows dim
In distant *ken discover trackless plains,
Where Winter ever whirls his icy car;
While, still repeated objects of his view,
The gloomy battlements and ivied spires,
That crown the solitary dome, arise;
While from the topmost turret the slow clock,
Far heard along th' inhospitable wastes,
With sad-returning chime awakes new grief.
Even he far happier seems than is the proud,
The potent satrap, whom he left behind
'Mid Moscow's golden palaces, to drown
In ease and luxury the laughing hours.

Illustrious objects strike the gazer's mind
With feeble bliss, and but allure the sight,
Nor rouse with impulse quick th' unfeeling heart.
Thus, seen by shepherd from *Hymettus' brow,
What dædal landscapes smile! Here palmy groves
Resounding once with *Plato's voice, arise,
Amid whose umbrage green her silver head
Th' unfading olive lifts; here vine-clad hills
Lay forth their purple store, and sunny vales
In prospect vast their level laps expand,
Amid whose beauties glistering Athens towers.
Though through the blissful scenes Ilissus roll
His *sage-inspiring flood, whose winding marge
The thick-wove laurel shades; though roseate Morn
Pour all her splendours on th' empurpled scene,
Yet feels the hoary hermit truer joys,
As from the cliff that o'er his cavern hangs,
He views the piles of fall'n *Persepolis
In deep arrangement hide the darksome plain.
Unbounded waste! the mouldering obelisk
Here, like a blasted oak, ascends the clouds;
Here *Parian domes their vaulted halls disclose
*Horrid with thorn, where lurks th' unpitying thief,
Whence flits the twilight-loving bat at eve,
And the deaf adder wreathes her spotted train,
The dwellings once of elegance and art.
Here temples rise, amid whose hallow'd bounds
*Spires the black pine, while through the naked street,
Once haunt of tradeful merchants, springs the grass:
Here columns heap'd on prostrate columns, torn
From their firm base, increase the mouldering mass.
Far as the sight can pierce, appear the spoils
Of sunk magnificence! a blended scene
Of *moles, fanes, arches, domes, and palaces,
Where, with his brother Horror, Ruin sits.

O come then, Melancholy, queen of thought!
O come, with saintly look and steadfast step
From forth thy cave embower'd with mournful yew,
Where ever to the curfew's solemn sound
Listening thou sitt'st, and with thy cypress bind
Thy votary's hair, and seal him for thy son.
But never let *Euphrosyne beguile
With toys of wanton mirth my fixèd mind,
Nor in my path her primrose garland cast.
Though 'mid her train the dimpled Hebe bare
Her rosy bosom to th' enamour'd view;
Though Venus, mother of the Smiles and Loves,
And Bacchus, ivy-crown'd in citron bower
With her on nectar-streaming fruitage feast.
What though 'tis hers to calm the louring skies,
And at her presence mild th' embattled clouds
Disperse the air, and o'er the face of heaven
New day diffusive gleam at her approach,
Yet are these joys that Melancholy gives,
Than all her witless revels happier far —
These deep-felt joys, by Contemplation taught.

Then ever, beauteous Contemplation, hail!
From thee began, auspicious maid, my song,
With thee shall end; for thou art fairer far
Than are the nymphs of *Cirrha's mossy grot;
To loftier rapture thou canst wake the thought,
Than all the fabling poet's boasted powers.
Hail, queen divine! whom, as tradition tells.

Once in his evening walk a Druid found,
Far in a hollow glade of *Mona's woods;
And piteous bore with hospitable hand
To the close shelter of his oaken bower.
There soon the sage admiring mark'd the dawn
Of solemn musing in your pensive thought;
For, when a smiling babe, you loved to lie
Oft deeply list'ning to the rapid roar
Of wood-hung *Menai, stream of Druids old.

[1747]

ON THE APPROACH OF SUMMER

One of the clearest examples of the persisting influence of Milton's minor poems — in this case, of *L'Allegro* — and of their important bearing upon the romantic movement, is provided by Thomas Warton's *Lines on the Approach of Summer*. It is a strange but significant paradox that the preparation for this movement, which was to overthrow the classical doctrine of imitation in favour of "original genius," should have been helped forward by work so slavishly imitative.

Hence, iron-sceptred Winter, haste
To bleak Siberian waste!
Haste to thy polar solitude;
'Mid cataracts of ice,
Whose torrents dumb are stretch'd in fragments rude
From many an airy precipice,
Where, ever beat by sleety showers,
Thy gloomy Gothic castle towers;
Amid whose howling aisles and halls,
Where no gay sunbeam paints the walls,
On ebon throne thou lov'st to shroud
Thy brows in many a murky cloud.

E'en now, before the vernal heat
Sullen I see thy *train retreat:
Thy ruthless host stern *Eurus guides,
That on a ravenous tiger rides,
Dim-figur'd on whose robe are shown
Shipwrecks, and villages o'erthrown;
Grim *Auster, dropping all with dew,
In mantle clad of *watchet hue;
And Cold, like Zemblan savage seen,
Still threatening with his arrows keen;
And next, in furry coat emboss'd
With icicles, his brother Frost.

Winter farewell! thy forests hoar,
Thy frozen floods delight no more;
Farewell the fields, so bare and wild!
But come thou rose-cheek'd cherub mild,
Sweetest Summer! haste thee here,
Once more to crown the gladden'd year.
Thee April blithe, as long of yore
Bermuda's lawns he frolick'd o'er,
With musky nectar-trickling wing
(In the new world's first dawning spring)
To gather balm of choicest dews
And patterns fair of various hues
With which to paint, in changeful dye,
The youthful earth's embroidery,
To cull the essence of rich smells
In which to dip his new-born bells;
Thee, as he skimm'd with pinions fleet,
He found an infant, smiling sweet,
Where a tall citron's shade *embrown'd
The soft lap of the fragrant ground.
There, on an *amaranthine bed,
Thee with rare nectarine fruits he fed,
Till soon beneath his forming care
You bloom'd a goddess debonair;
And then he gave the blessed isle
Aye to be sway'd beneath thy smile;
There plac'd thy green and grassy shrine,
With myrtle bower'd and jessamine,
And to thy care the task assign'd
With quickening hand, and nurture kind,
His roseate infant-births to rear,
Till Autumn's mellowing reign appear.

Haste thee, nymph! and hand in hand,
With thee lead a buxom band;
Bring fantastic-footed Joy,
With Sport, that yellow-tressed boy:
Leisure, that through the balmy sky
Chases a crimson butterfly.
Bring Health, that loves in early dawn
To meet the milkmaid on the lawn;
Bring Pleasure, rural nymph, and Peace,
Meek, cottage-loving shepherdess!
And that sweet stripling, *Zephyr, bring,
Light, and forever on the wing.
Bring the dear Muse, that loves to lean
On river-margins, mossy green.
But who is she that bears thy train,
Pacing light the velvet plain?
The pale pink binds her auburn hair,
Her tresses flow with pastoral air;
'Tis May, the Grace — *confess'd she stands
By branch of hawthorn in her hands.
Lo! near her trip the lightsome Dews,
Their wings all ting'd in iris-hues;
With whom the powers of Flora play,
And paint with pansies all the way.

Oft when thy season, sweetest queen,
Has dress'd the groves in livery green;

When in each fair and fertile field
Beauty begins her bower to build;
While Evening, veil'd in shadows brown,
Puts her matron-mantle on,
And mists in spreading steams convey
More fresh the fumes of new-shorn hay;
Then, goddess, guide my pilgrim feet,
Contemplation hoar to meet,
As slow he winds in museful mood,
Near the rush'd marge of *Cherwell's flood:
Or o'er old Avon's magic edge,
Whence Shakespeare cull'd the spiky sedge,
All playful yet, in years unripe,
To frame a shrill and simple pipe.
There through the dusk but dimly seen,
Sweet ev'ning objects intervene:
His *wattled cotes the shepherd plants;
Beneath her elm the milkmaid chants;
The woodman, speeding home, awhile
Rests him at a shady stile.

Nor wants there fragrance to dispense
Refreshment o'er my soothed sense,
Nor tangled woodbine's balmy bloom,
Nor grass *besprent to breath perfume,
Nor lurking wild-thyme's spicy sweet
To bathe in dew my roving feet;
Nor wants there note of Philomel,
Nor sound of distant-tinkling bell,
Nor lowings faint of herds remote,
Nor mastiff's bark from *bosom'd cote;
Rustle the breezes lightly borne
O'er *deep-embattled *ears of corn:
Round ancient elm, with humming noise,
Full loud the *chaffer-swarms rejoice.
Meantime a thousand dyes invest
The ruby chambers of the west,
That all aslant the village tower
A mild reflected radiance pour,
While, with the level-streaming rays
Far seen its arched windows blaze:
And the tall grove's green top is *dight
In russet tints and gleams of light;
So that the gay scene by degrees
Bathes my blithe heart in ecstasies;
And Fancy to my ravish'd sight
Portrays her kindred visions bright.
At length the parting light subdues
My soften'd soul to calmer views,
And fainter shapes of pensive joy,
As twilight dawns, my mind employ,
Till from the path I fondly stray
In musings lapp'd, nor heed the way;
Wandering thro' the landscape still,
Till Melancholy has her fill;
And on each moss-wove border damp
The glow-worm hangs his fairy lamp.

But when the Sun, at noontide hour,
Sits throned in his highest tower,
Me, heart-rejoicing goddess, lead
*To the tann'd haycock in the mead,
To mix in rural mood among
The nymphs and swains, a busy throng;
Or, as the tepid odours breathe,
The russet piles to lean beneath:
There, as my listless limbs are thrown
On couch more soft than palace down,
I listen to the busy sound
Of mirth and toil that hums around,
And see the team *shrill-tinkling pass,
Alternate o'er the furrow'd grass.

But ever after summer shower,
When the bright Sun's returning power
With laughing beam has chased the storm
And cheer'd reviving Nature's form,
By sweetbrier hedges, bath'd in dew,
Let me my wholesome path pursue.
There issuing forth, the frequent snail
Wears the dank way with slimy trail,
While, as I walk, from pearled bush
The sunny-sparkling drop I brush;
And all the landscape fair I view
Clad in robe of fresher hue;
And so loud the blackbird sings,
That far and near the valley rings.
From shelter deep of shaggy rock
The shepherd drives his joyful flock;
From bowering beech the mower blithe
With new-born vigour grasps the scythe;
While o'er the smooth unbounded meads
His last faint gleam the rainbow spreads.

But ever against restless heat
Bear me to the rock-arch'd seat,
O'er whose dim mouth an ivied oak
Hangs nodding from the low-brow'd rock,
Haunted by that chaste nymph alone,
Whose waters cleave the smoothed stone;
Which, as they gush upon the ground,
Still scatter misty dews around:
A rustic, wild, grotesque alcove,
Its side with mantling woodbines wove,
Cool as the cave where *Clio dwells
Whence Helicon's fresh fountain wells,
Or noontide grot where *Sylvan sleeps
In hoar *Lycæum's piny steeps.

Me, goddess, in such cavern lay
While all without is scorch'd in day;

Sore sighs the weary swain beneath
His with'ring hawthorn on the heath;
The drooping *hedger wishes eve
In vain, of labour short reprieve!
Meantime, on Afric's glowing sands,
Smote with keen heat the trav'ller stands;
Low sinks his heart, while round his eye
Measures the scenes that boundless lie,
Ne'er yet by foot of mortal worn,
Where Thirst, wan pilgrim, walks forlorn.
How does he wish some cooling wave
To slake his lips, or limbs to lave!
And thinks in every whisper low
He hears a bursting fountain flow.

Or bear me to some antique wood,
Dim temple of sage Solitude!
There within a nook most dark,
Where none my musing mood may mark,
Let me in many a whisper'd rite
The *Genius old of Greece invite,
With that fair wreath my brows to bind,
Which for his chosen *imps he twined,
Well nurtur'd in *Pierian lore,
On clean, *Ilissus' laureate shore,
Till high on waving nest reclin'd,
The raven wakes my tranced mind!

Or to the forest-fringed vale,
Where widow'd turtles love to wail,
Where cowslips, clad in mantle meek,
Nod their tall heads to breezes weak.
In the midst, with sedges gray
Crown'd, a scant riv'let winds its way,
And, trembling through the weedy wreaths,
Around an oozy freshness breathes.
O'er the solitary green,
Nor cot nor loitering hind is seen;
Nor aught alarms the mute repose,
Save that by fits an heifer lows:
A *scene might tempt some peaceful sage
To rear him a lone hermitage.
Fit place his pensive eld might choose
On virtue's holy lore to muse.

Yet still the sultry noon t' appease,
Some more romantic scene might please:
Or fairy bank or magic lawn
By Spenser's lavish pencil drawn;
Or bower in Vallombrosa's shade,
By legendary pens portray'd.
Haste, let me shroud from painful light,
On that hoar hill's aërial height,
In solemn state, where waving wide,
Thick pines with darkening *umbrage hide
The rugged vaults and riven towers
Of that proud castle's painted bowers,
Whence *Hardyknute, a baron bold,
In Scotland's martial days of old,
Descended from the stately feast,
Begirt with many a warrior guest,
To quell the pride of Norway's king,
With quiv'ring lance and twanging string.
As through the caverns dim I wind,
Might I that holy legend find,
By fairies *spelt in magic rhymes,
To teach inquiring later times,
What open force, or secret guile,
Dash'd into dust the solemn pile.

But when mild Morn in saffron stole
First issues from her eastern goal,
*Let not my due feet fail to climb
Some breezy summit's brow sublime,
Whence Nature's universal face
Illumin'd smiles with new-born grace.
The misty streams that wind below
With silver-sparkling lustre glow;
The groves and castl'd cliffs appear
Invested all in radiance clear;
Oh, every village charm beneath!
The smoke that mounts in azure wreath!
Oh, beauteous, rural interchange!
The simple spire, and elmy *grange!
Content, indulging blissful hours,
Whistles o'er the fragrant flowers,
And cattle, rous'd to pasture new,
Shake jocund from their sides the dew.

'Tis thou alone, O Summer mild,
Canst bid me carol wood-notes wild:
Whene'er I view thy genial scenes,
Thy waving woods, embroider'd greens,
What fires within my bosom wake,
How glows my mind the *reed to take!
What charms like thine the Muse can call,
With whom 'tis youth and laughter all;
With whom each field's a paradise,
And all the globe a bower of bliss!
With thee conversing all the day,
I meditate my lightsome lay.
These *pedant cloisters let me leave,
To breathe my *votive song at eve,
In valleys where mild whispers *use
Of shade and stream, to court the Muse;
While wand'ring o'er the brook's dim verge,
I hear the stock-dove's dying dirge.

But when life's busier scene is o'er,
And Age shall give the tresses hoar,

I'd fly soft luxury's marble dome
And make an humble thatch my home,
Which sloping hills around enclose,
Where many a beech and brown oak grows,
Beneath whose dark and branching bowers
Its tides a far-famed river pours;
By Nature's beauties taught to please,
Sweet *Tusculane of rural ease!
Still grot of Peace! in lowly shed
Who loves to rest her gentle head.
For not the scenes of Attic art
Can comfort care, or soothe the heart;
Nor burning cheek, nor wakeful eye,
For gold and Tyrian purple fly.

Thither, kind Heaven, in pity lent,
Send me a little, and content:
The faithful friend, and cheerful night,
The social scene of dear delight;
The conscience pure, the temper gay,
The musing eve, the idle day.
Give me beneath cool shades to sit,
Rapt with the charms of classic wit;
To catch the bold heroic flame,
That built immortal Græcia's fame.
Nor let me fail, meantime, to raise
The solemn song to Britain's praise;
To spurn the shepherd's simple reeds,
And paint heroic ancient deeds;
To chant fam'd Arthur's magic tale,
And Edward, stern in sable mail;
Or wand'ring *Brutus' lawless doom.
Or brave *Bonduca, scourge of Rome.

Oh, ever to sweet Poesy
Let me live true votary!
She shall lead me by the hand,
Queen of sweet smiles, and solace bland!
She from her precious stores shall shed
Ambrosial flow'rets o'er my head:
She from my tender youthful cheek,
Can wipe, with lenient finger meek,
The secret, and unpitied tear,
Which still I drop in darkness drear.
She shall be my blooming bride;
With her, as years successive glide,
I'll hold divinest dalliance,
For ever held in holy trance.

[1753]

*TO THE RIVER LODON

Ah! what a weary race my feet have run
Since first I trod thy banks with alders crown'd,
And thought my way was all through fairy ground,
Beneath thy azure sky, and golden sun:
Where first my Muse to lisp her notes begun!
While pensive Memory traces back the round
Which fills the varied interval between;
Much pleasure, more of sorrow, marks the scene.
Sweet native stream! those skies and suns so pure
No more return, to cheer my evening road!
Yet still one joy remains, that not obscure,
Nor useless, all my vacant days have flow'd,
From youth's gay dawn to manhood's prime mature;
Nor with the Muse's laurel unbestow'd.

[1777]

VERSES

ON SIR JOSHUA REYNOLDS'S PAINTED WINDOW AT NEW COLLEGE, OXFORD

By showing how easily Warton was converted, at least for the time, from his preference for the "Gothic arts" of a "barbarous age," the following lines suggest that his alleged "romanticism" was never much more than quest for novelty, an emotional aberration unsanctioned by his better judgment. The fact seems to be that his reason was convinced by neo-classical doctrine, although his heart was not.

The older windows in the forechapel of New College, at Oxford, are good examples of fourteenth-century stained glass. About 1780 the old glass and the stone tracery of the great west window were removed — an act of vandalism to which it might have been expected that a man of Warton's taste would vigorously object. In their stead the painter Jervais executed, in monochrome laid on clear glass, seven pictures after designs by Reynolds, vaguely and coolly religious in suggestion. Admirable as these are, the placing of them in a Gothic chapel was an inexcusable blunder. The best thing to be said for the error is that it enforces active critical comparison, if not a choice, by bringing mediæval work into juxtaposition with its antithesis.

Ah, stay thy treacherous hand, forbear to trace
Those faultless forms of elegance and grace!
Ah, cease to spread the bright transparent mass,
With Titian's pencil, o'er the speaking glass!
Nor steal, by strokes of art with truth combin'd,
The fond illusions of my wayward mind!
For long enamour'd of a barbarous age,
A faithless truant to the classic page;
Long have I lov'd to catch the simple chime

Of minstrel-harps, and spell the fabling rhyme,
To view the festive rites, the knightly play,
That deck'd heroic Albion's elder day,
To mark the mouldering halls of barons bold,
And the rough castle, cast in giant mould,
With Gothic manners Gothic arts explore,
And muse on the magnificence of yore.

But chief, enraptur'd have I loved to roam,
A lingering votary, the vaulted dome,
Where the tall shafts, that mount in massy pride,
Their mingling branches shoot from side to side;
Where elfin sculptors, with fantastic clew
O'er the long roof their wild embroidery drew;
Where Superstition with capricious hand
In many a maze the wreath'd window plann'd,
With hues romantic ting'd the gorgeous pane,
To fill with holy light the wondrous fane,
To aid the builder's model, richly rude,
By no *Vitruvian symmetry subdued,
To suit the *genius of the mystic pile:
Whilst, as around the far-retiring aisle
And fretted shrines, with hoary trophies hung,
Her dark illumination wide she flung,
With new solemnity the nooks profound,
The caves of death, and the dim arches frown'd.

From bliss long felt unwillingly we part:
Ah, spare the weakness of a lover's heart!
Chase not the phantoms of my fairy dream,
Phantoms that shrink at Reason's painful gleam!
That softer touch, insidious artist, stay,
Nor to new joys my struggling breast betray!

Such was a pensive bard's mistaken strain.
But, oh, of ravish'd pleasures why complain?
No more the matchless skill I call unkind,
That strives to disenchant my cheated mind.
For when again I view thy chaste design,
The just proportion and the genuine line;
Those native portraitures of Attic art
That from the lucid surface seem to start;
Those tints that steal no glories from the day
Nor ask the sun to lend his streaming ray;
The doubtful radiance of contending dyes
That faintly mingle yet distinctly rise;
'Twixt light and shade the transitory strife,
The feature blooming with immortal life,
The *stole in casual foldings taught to flow,
Not with ambitious ornaments to glow,
The tread majestic and the beaming eye
That lifted speaks its commerce with the sky,
Heaven's golden emanation gleaming mild
O'er the mean cradle of the Virgin's child,
Sudden, the sombrous imagery is fled
Which late my visionary rapture fed:
Thy powerful hand has broke the Gothic chain,
And brought my bosom back to truth again —
To truth, by no peculiar taste confin'd,
Whose universal pattern strikes mankind;
To Truth, whose bold and unresisted aim
Checks frail Caprice and Fashion's fickle claim;
To Truth, whose charms Deception's magic quell,
And bind coy Fancy in a stronger spell.

Ye brawny prophets that, in robes so rich,
At distance due possess the crisped niche,
Ye rows of patriarchs that, sublimely rear'd,
Diffuse a proud primeval length of beard,
Ye saints who, clad in crimson's bright array,
More pride than humble poverty display,
Ye virgins meek, that wear the palmy crown
Of patient faith, and yet so fiercely frown,
Ye angels that from clouds of gold recline
But boast no semblance to a race divine,
Ye tragic tales of legendary lore
That draw devotion's ready tear no more,
Ye martyrdoms of unenlighten'd days,
Ye miracles that now no wonder raise,
Shapes that with one broad glare the gazer strike,
Kings, bishops, nuns, apostles, all alike!
Ye colours that th' unwary sight amaze
And only dazzle in the noontide blaze!
No more the sacred window's *round disgrace,
But yield to Grecian groups the shining space.
Lo, from the canvas Beauty shifts her throne!
Lo, *Picture's powers a new formation own!
Behold, she prints upon the *crystal plain,
With her own energy, th' expressive stain!
The mighty master spreads his mimic toil
More wide, nor only blends the breathing oil;
But calls the lineaments of life complete
From genial alchemy's creative heat;
Obedient forms to the bright fusion gives,
While in the warm enamel nature lives.

Reynolds, 'tis thine, from the broad window's height,
To add new lustre to religious light;
Not of its pomp to strip this ancient shrine,
But bid that pomp with purer radiance shine;
With arts unknown before to reconcile
The willing Graces to the Gothic pile.

[1782]

JOSEPH WARTON

Joseph Warton, eldest son of Thomas Warton Senior, was born in 1722. At Winchester School he formed a close friendship, deeply influential upon both poets, with William Collins, who went with him to Oxford. After serving as his father's curate at Basingstoke and then as rector of various rural parishes, he became in 1755 one of the masters at Winchester and, eleven years later, headmaster. His rule was by no means peaceful, and when seventy-one years of age he was forced to resign by the last of three mutinies among his boys. Joseph Warton was fond of society, far more polished in manners than his brother Thomas, and so frequent a visitor in London that he was elected a member of Johnson's Literary Club. He endured with courage and equanimity a good deal of ridicule of his critical opinions and died, in 1800, with a sound though not a great reputation as poet, critic, editor, translator, and scholar.

The literary work of this long life was begun early. Even while at school Warton contributed, with Collins, to the *Gentleman's Magazine*, attracting the favourable attention of Dr. Johnson. At eighteen he wrote *The Enthusiast, or the Lover of Nature*, a remarkably bold challenge of critical orthodoxy even though it is not what Sir Edmund Gosse calls it, "the earliest expression of complete revolt against the classical attitude." Warton's precocity is to be explained, in part, by the fact that he had both the precept and the example of his father to guide him, so that the critical dicta of *The Enthusiast* came to him ready made. He had, in any case, by no means an original mind, and nearly all his verse is highly imitative, particularly of the minor poems of Milton. *The Enthusiast* shows him already opposed to the School of Pope, and in the Preface to his *Odes on Several Occasions*, published when he was twenty-two, he gives one reason for this opposition in saying that "the fashion of moralizing in verse has been carried too far" and that he "looks upon invention and imagination to be the chief faculties of a poet." But unfortunately it was just these faculties in which Warton's learned and cultivated mind least excelled.

The most important of Warton's productions was an *Essay on the Genius and Writings of Pope*, 1757–1782, which ranks Pope below Milton, Shakespeare, and Spenser on the ground that although he was certainly more "correct" he had less "original genius." Warton also published an edition of Pope and prepared an edition of Dryden, besides editing Virgil with a creditable translation of the *Georgics* and *Eclogues* into English verse. His own verse is perhaps chiefly remarkable for the antiquarian tendency of thought it reveals — a nostalgia for the Middle Ages like that of his brother Thomas — and for his steady preference of "nature" to "art."

THE ENTHUSIAST
OR THE
LOVER OF NATURE

In spite of its blunderings and absurdities, *The Enthusiast* is a remarkable poem for a youth of seventeen to have written. It phrases clearly a surprising number of the more fundamental romantic moods and theories: preference of nature to art and of "original genius" to "correctness," preference of wild landscapes to the cultivated; the belief that man is corrupted by society and that in the wilderness he comes into direct contact with divine or supernatural sources of wisdom; yearning for the imagined simplicities and freedom of a Golden Age, placed both in the remote past and in America; above all, an essentially romantic yearning for solitude.

Ye green-rob'd dryads, oft at dusky eve
By wondering shepherds seen, — to forests brown,
To unfrequented meads and pathless wilds
Lead me, from gardens deck'd with art's vain pomps!
Can gilt alcoves, can marble-mimic gods,
*Parterres embroider'd, obelisks, and urns
Of high relief; can the long, spreading lake
Or vista lessening to the sight; can *Stowe
With all her Attic fanes, such raptures raise,
As the thrush-haunted copse, where lightly leaps
The fearful fawn the rustling leaves along,
And the brisk squirrel sports from bough to bough,
While from an hollow oak, whose naked roots
O'erhang a pensive rill, the busy bees
Hum drowsy lullabies? The bards of old,
Fair Nature's friends, sought such retreats, to charm
Sweet Echo with their songs; oft too they met
In summer evenings, near sequester'd bowers,

*Notes on Joseph Warton will be found in the Appendix, pp. 1016 ff.

Or mountain-nymph, or Muse, and eager learnt
The moral strains she taught to mend mankind.
As to a secret grot Ægeria stole
With patriot * Numa, and in silent night
Whisper'd him sacred laws, he listening sat,
Rapt with her virtuous voice, old Tiber lean'd
Attentive on his urn, and hushed his waves.
Rich in her weeping country's spoils, * Versailles
May boast a thousand fountains that can cast
The tortur'd waters to the distant heavens;
Yet let me choose some pine-topp'd precipice
Abrupt and shaggy, whence a foamy stream,
Like *Anio, tumbling roars; or some bleak heath,
Where straggling stands the mournful juniper
Or yew tree scath'd; while in clear prospect round,
From the grove's bosom spires emerge, and smoke
In bluish wreaths ascends, ripe harvests wave,
Low, lonely cottages, and ruin'd tops
Of Gothic battlements appear, and streams
Beneath the sunbeams twinkle. The shrill lark,
That wakes the woodman to his early task,
Or love-sick Philomel whose luscious lays
Soothe lone night-wanderers, the moaning dove
Pitied by list'ning milkmaid, far excel
The deep-mouthed viol, the soul-lulling lute,
And battle-breathing trumpet. Artful sounds!
That please not like the choristers of air,
When first they hail th' approach of laughing May.
Can * Kent design like Nature? Mark where Thames
Plenty and pleasure pours through Lincoln's meads!
Can the great artist, though with taste supreme
Endued, one beauty to this Eden add?
Though he, by rules unfetter'd, boldly scorns
Formality and method, round and square
Disdaining, plans irregularly great.
Creative Titian, can thy vivid strokes,
Or thine, O graceful Raphael, dare to vie
With the rich tints that paint the breathing mead?
The thousand-colour'd tulip, violet's bell
Snow-clad and meek, the vermeil-tinctur'd rose,
And golden crocus? Yet with these the maid,
Phillis or Phœbe at a feast or wake,
Her jetty locks enamels; fairer she,
In innocence and home-spun vestments dress'd,
Than if cerulean sapphires at her ears
Shone pendent, or a precious diamond cross
Heav'd gently on her panting bosom white.
Yon shepherd idly stretched on the rude rock,
Listening to dashing waves, and sea-mew's clang
High-hovering o'er his head, who views beneath
The dolphin dancing o'er the level brine,
Feels more true bliss than the proud admiral,
Amid his vessels bright with burnished gold
And silken streamers, though his lordly nod
Ten thousand war-worn mariners revere.
And great Æneas gaz'd with more delight
On the rough mountain shagg'd with * horrid shades,
(Where cloud-compelling Jove, as fancy dream'd,
Descending, shook his direful * ægis black)
Than if he enter'd the high Capitol
On golden columns rear'd, a conquer'd world
Exhausted, to enrich its stately head.
More pleas'd he slept in poor * Evander's cot
On shaggy skins, lull'd by sweet nightingales,
Than if a Nero, in an age refin'd,
Beneath a gorgeous canopy had plac'd
His royal guest, and bade his minstrels sound
Soft slumb'rous * Lydian airs, to soothe his rest.
* Happy the first of men, ere yet confin'd
To smoky cities; who in sheltering groves,
Warm caves, and deep-sunk valleys liv'd and lov'd,
By cares unwounded; what the sun and showers,
And genial earth untillag'd, could produce,
They gather'd grateful, or the acorn brown,
Or blushing berry; by the liquid lapse
Of murm'ring waters call'd to slake their thirst,
Or with fair nymphs their sun-brown limbs to bathe, —
With nymphs who fondly clasp'd their favourite youths,
Unaw'd by shame, beneath the beechen shade,
Nor wiles, nor artificial coyness knew.
Then doors and walls were not; the melting maid
Nor frown of parents fear'd, nor husband's threats;
Nor had curs'd gold their tender hearts allur'd:

Then beauty was not venal. Injur'd Love,
Oh! whither, god of raptures, art thou fled?
While Avarice waves his golden wand around,
Abhorr'd magician, and his costly cup
Prepares with baneful drugs, t' enchant the souls
Of each low-thoughted fair to wed for gain.
In earth's first infancy (as sung the *bard
Who strongly painted what he boldly thought),
Though the fierce north oft smote with iron whip
Their shiv'ring limbs, though oft the bristly boar
Or hungry lion woke them with their howls,
And scar'd them from their moss-grown caves, to rove
Houseless and cold in dark tempestuous nights;
Yet were not myriads in embattl'd fields
Swept off at once, nor had the raging seas
O'erwhelm'd the foundering bark and shrieking crew.
In vain the glassy ocean smil'd to tempt
The jolly sailor, unsuspecting harm,
For commerce ne'er had spread her swelling sails,
Nor had the wondering Nereids ever heard
The dashing oar; then famine, want, and *pine
Sunk to the grave their fainting limbs; but us,
Diseaseful dainties, riot, and excess,
And feverish luxury destroy. In brakes
Or marshes wild unknowingly they cropp'd
Herbs of malignant juice; to realms remote
While we for powerful poisons madly roam,
From every noxious herb collecting death.
What though unknown to those primeval sires
The well-arch'd dome, peopled with breathing forms
By fair Italia's skillful hand, unknown
The shapely column, and the crumbling busts
Of awful ancestors in long descent?
Yet why should man, mistaken, deem it nobler
To dwell in palaces, and high-roof'd halls,
Than in God's forests, architect supreme!
Say, is the Persian carpet, than the field's
Or meadow's mantle gay, more richly wov'n;
Or softer to the votaries of ease
Than bladed grass, perfum'd with dew-dropp'd flowers?
Oh, taste corrupt! that luxury and pomp,
In specious names of polish'd manners veil'd,
Should proudly banish Nature's simple charms!
All beauteous Nature! by thy boundless charms
Oppress'd, oh, where shall I begin thy praise,
Where turn th' ecstatic eye, how ease my breast
That pants with wild astonishment and love!
Dark forests, and the opening lawn, refresh'd
With ever-gushing brooks, hill, meadow, dale,
The balmy bean-field, the gay-clover'd *close,
So sweetly interchang'd, the lowing ox,
The playful lamb, the distant waterfall
Now faintly heard, now swelling with the breeze,
The sound of pastoral reed from hazel-bower,
The choral birds, the neighing steed that snuffs
His dappled mate, stung with intense desire,
The ripen'd orchard when the ruddy orbs
Betwixt the green leaves blush, the azure skies,
The cheerful sun that through earth's vitals pours
Delight and health and heat: all, all conspire,
To raise, to soothe, to harmonize the mind,
To lift on wings of praise, to the great Sire
Of being and of beauty, at whose nod
Creation started from the gloomy vault
Of dreary Chaos, while the grisly king
Murmur'd to feel his boisterous power confin'd.
What are the lays of artful Addison,
Coldly correct, to *Shakespeare's warblings wild?
Whom on the winding Avon's willow'd banks
Fair Fancy found, and bore the smiling babe
To a close cavern. Still the shepherds show
The sacred place, whence with religious awe
They hear, returning from the field at eve,
Strange whisperings of sweet music through the air.
Here, as with honey gather'd from the rock,
She fed the little prattler, and with songs
Oft sooth'd his wondering ears; with deep delight
On her soft lap he sat, and caught the sounds.
Oft near some crowded city would I *walk,
Listening the far-off noises, rattling cars,
Loud shouts of joy, sad shrieks of sorrow, knells
Full slowly tolling, instruments of trade,
Striking mine ears with one deep-swelling hum.
Or wandering near the sea, attend the sounds
Of hollow winds, and ever-beating waves.
Ev'n when wild tempests swallow up the plains,
And Boreas' blasts, big hail, and rains combine
To shake the groves and mountains, would I sit,

Pensively musing on th' outrageous crimes
That wake Heaven's vengeance. At such solemn hours,
Demons and goblins through the dark air shriek,
While Hecat, with her black-brow'd sisters nine,
Rides o'er the earth, and scatters woes and death.
Then too, they say, in drear Egyptian wilds
The lion and the tiger prowl for prey
With roarings loud! the listening traveller
Starts fear-struck, while the hollow-echoing vaults
Of pyramids increase the deathful sounds.
  But let me never fail in cloudless nights,
When silent Cynthia in her silver car
Through the blue concave slides, when shine the hills,
Twinkle the streams, and woods look tipp'd with gold,
To seek some level mead, and there invoke
Old Midnight's sister, Contemplation sage,
Queen of the rugged brow, and stern-fix'd eye,
To lift my soul above this little earth,
This folly-fetter'd world: to purge my ears,
That I may hear the rolling planet's song,
And tuneful turning spheres. If this be barr'd,
The little Fays that dance in neighbouring dales,
Sipping the night-dew, while they laugh and love,
Shall charm me with aërial notes. As thus
I wander musing, lo, what awful forms
Yonder appear! Sharp-ey'd Philosophy
Clad in dun robes, an eagle on his wrist,
First meets my eye; next virgin Solitude
Serene, who blushes at each gazer's sight;
Then Wisdom's hoary head, with crutch in hand,
Trembling, and bent with age; last, Virtue's self,
Smiling, in white array'd, who with her leads
Sweet Innocence, that prattles by her side,
A naked boy! — Harass'd with fear I stop,
I gaze, when Virtue thus: "Whoe'er thou art,
Mortal, by whom I deign to be beheld
In these my midnight walks, depart, and say
That henceforth I and my immortal train
Forsake Britannia's isle, who fondly stoops
To Vice, her favourite paramour.' *She spoke,
And as she turn'd, her round and rosy neck,
Her flowing train, and long ambrosial hair,
Breathing rich odours, I enamour'd view.
  Oh, who will bear me then to *western climes,
(Since Virtue leaves our wretched land) to fields
Yet unpolluted with *Iberian swords:
The isles of Innocence, from mortal view
Deeply retir'd, beneath a plantane's shade,
Where Happiness and Quiet sit enthron'd,
With simple Indian swains, that I may hunt
The boar and tiger through savannahs wild,
Through fragrant deserts, and through citron-groves?
There, fed on dates and herbs, would I despise
The far-fetch'd cates of luxury, and hoards
Of narrow-hearted avarice; nor heed
The distant din of the tumultuous world.
So when rude whirlwinds rouse the roaring main,
Beneath, fair *Thetis sits, in coral caves,
Serenely gay, nor sinking sailors' cries
Disturb her sportive nymphs, who round her form
The light fantastic dance, or for her hair
Weave rosy crowns, or with according lutes
Grace the soft warbles of her honied voice.

[1744]

ODE TO SOLITUDE

Thou, that at deep dead of night
Walk'st forth beneath the pale moon's light,
In robe of flowing black array'd,
While cypress-leaves thy brows o'ershade;
Listening to the crowing cock,
And the distant sounding clock;
Or, sitting in the cavern low,
Dost hear the bleak winds loudly blow,
Or the hoarse death-boding owl,
Or village mastiff's wakeful howl,
While through thy melancholy room
A dim lamp casts an awful gloom;
Thou, that on the meadow green
Or daisied upland art not seen,
But wandering by the dusky nooks,
And the pensive falling brooks,
Or near some rugged, herbless rock,
Where no shepherd keeps his flock!
Musing maid, to thee I come,
Hating the tradeful city's hum.
Oh, let me calmly dwell with thee,
From noisy mirth and business free,
With meditation seek the skies,
This folly-fetter'd world despise!

[1746]

ODE TO FANCY

O Parent of each lovely Muse,
Thy spirit o'er my soul diffuse,
O'er all my artless songs preside,
My footsteps to thy temple, guide,
To offer at thy turf-built shrine,
In golden cups no costly wine,
No murder'd fatling of the flock,
But flowers and honey from the rock.
O Nymph with loosely-flowing hair,
With buskin'd leg, and bosom bare,
Thy waist with myrtle-girdle bound,
Thy brows with Indian feathers crown'd,
Waving in thy snowy hand
An all-commanding magic wand,
Of power to bid fresh gardens blow,
'Mid cheerless Lapland's barren snow,
Whose rapid wings thy flight convey
Through air, and over earth and sea,
While the vast various landscape lies
Conspicuous to thy piercing eyes.
O lover of the desert, hail!
Say, in what deep and pathless vale,
Or on what hoary mountain's side,
'Mid fall of waters, you reside,
'Mid broken rocks, a rugged scene,
With green and grassy dales between,
'Mid forests dark of aged oak,
Ne'er echoing with the woodman's stroke,
Where never human art appear'd,
Nor ev'n one straw-roof'd cot was rear'd,
Where Nature seems to sit alone,
Majestic on a craggy throne.
Tell me the path, sweet wanderer, tell,
To thy unknown sequester'd cell,
Where woodbines cluster round the door,
Where shells and moss o'erlay the floor,
And on whose top an hawthorn blows,
Amid whose thickly-woven boughs
Some nightingale still builds her nest,
Each evening warbling thee to rest:
Then lay me by the haunted stream,
Rapt in some wild poetic dream,
In converse while methinks I rove
With Spenser through a fairy grove;
Till, suddenly awoke, I hear
Strange whisper'd music in my ear,
And my glad soul in bliss is drown'd
By the sweetly-soothing sound!
Me, goddess, by the right hand lead,
Sometimes through the yellow mead,
Where Joy and white-rob'd Peace resort,
And Venus keeps her festive court,
Where Mirth and Youth each evening meet,
And lightly trip with nimble feet,
Nodding their lily-crowned heads,
Where Laughter rose-lipp'd Hebe leads,
Where Echo walks steep hills among,
Listening to the shepherd's song:
Yet not those flowery fields of joy
Can long my pensive mind employ.
Haste, Fancy, from these scenes of folly,
To meet the matron Melancholy,
Goddess of the tearful eye,
That loves to fold her arms, and sigh!
Let us with silent footsteps go
To charnels and the house of woe,
To Gothic churches, vaults, and tombs,
Where each sad night some virgin comes,
With throbbing breast, and faded cheek,
Her promis'd bridegroom's urn to seek;
Or to some abbey's mouldering towers,
Where, to avoid cold wintry showers,
The naked beggar shivering lies,
While whistling tempests round her rise,
And trembles lest the tottering wall
Should on her sleeping infants fall.
Now let us louder strike the lyre,
For my heart glows with martial fire;
I feel, I feel, with sudden heat,
My big tumultuous bosom beat;
The trumpet's clangours pierce my ear;
A thousand widows' shrieks I hear;
"Give me another horse," I cry,
"Lo, the base Gallic squadrons fly!"
Whence is this rage? What spirit, say,
To battle hurries me away?
'Tis Fancy, in her fiery car,
Transports me to the thickest war,
There whirls me o'er the hills of slain,
Where Tumult and Destruction reign;
Where, mad with pain, the wounded steed
Tramples the dying and the dead;
Where giant Terror stalks around,
With sullen joy surveys the ground,
And, pointing to the ensanguin'd field,
Shakes his dreadful Gorgon-shield!
Oh, guide me from this horrid scene
To high-arch'd walks and alleys green,
Which lovely Laura seeks, to shun
The fervours of the midday sun;
The pangs of absence, oh, remove!
For thou canst place me near my love,
Canst fold in visionary bliss,
And let me think I steal a kiss,
While her ruby lips dispense
Luscious nectar's quintessence!
When young-eyed Spring profusely throws
From her green lap the pink and rose;

When the soft turtle of the dale
To Summer tells her tender tale;
When Autumn cooling caverns seeks,
And stains with wine his jolly cheeks;
When Winter, like poor pilgrim old,
Shakes his silver beard with cold;
At every season let my ear
Thy solemn whispers, Fancy, hear.
O warm, enthusiastic maid,
Without thy powerful, vital aid,
That breathes an energy divine,
That gives a soul to every line,
Ne'er may I strive with lips profane
To utter an unhallow'd strain,
Nor dare to touch the sacred string,
Save when with smiles thou bid'st me sing.
O hear our prayer, O hither come
From thy lamented Shakespeare's tomb,
On which thou lov'st to sit at eve,
Musing o'er thy darling's grave;
O queen of numbers, once again
Animate some chosen swain,
Who, fill'd with unexhausted fire,
May boldly smite the sounding lyre,
Who with some new, unequall'd song,
May rise above the rhyming throng,
O'er all our listening passions reign,
O'erwhelm our souls with joy and pain;
With terror shake, with pity move,
Rouse with revenge, or melt with love.
Oh, deign t' attend his evening walk,
With him in groves and grottoes talk;
Teach him to scorn with frigid art
Feebly to touch the unraptur'd heart;
Like lightning, let his mighty verse
The bosom's inmost foldings pierce;
With native beauties win applause,
Beyond cold critics' studied laws.
Oh, let each Muse's fame increase!
Oh, bid Britannia rival Greece!

[1746]

WILLIAM SHENSTONE

Born in 1714 in the west of England, William Shenstone attended school in his native village, at first under the tutelage of one Sarah Lloyd whom he celebrates in his most famous poem, and spent four years at Pembroke College, Oxford. Indolence and indecision prevented him from taking a degree or choosing a fixed occupation. When about thirty years of age he retired to the Leasowes, the small patrimonial estate where he was born, and there spent the remainder of his life, partly engaged in desultory writing and reading, often rather eagerly occupied with the cultivation of his grounds, but for the most part given over to gentlemanly idleness. The improvement of his estate, in which he tried to compromise between the older formal gardening and the new feeling for the wild, brought him both fame and debts. His love of the country was sincere, but he soon showed the lack of the intellectual stimulus and guidance which London or even Oxford might have given him, and his life of retirement was not happy. Shenstone had a rather wide circle of friends and correspondents, however, among whom were the poet Jago, Lord Lyttleton, and Richard Graves, author of *The Spiritual Quixote*, from whom we have, in addition to a lively biography of the poet, an amusing and not very sympathetic account of his life at the Leasowes, called *Columella, or the Distressed Anchoret*. In several unostentatious ways Shenstone exerted considerable influence in the shaping of the public taste. He assisted Robert Dodsley in the preparation of his *Poetical Miscellanies*, and it was chiefly by his advice and encouragement that Bishop Percy was brought to publish his *Reliques of Ancient Poetry*. Shenstone died at the Leasowes in his fiftieth year. Dr. Johnson's unsympathetic account of him in *The Lives of the Poets* (1779–81) did nothing at the time to increase a fame already declining, and it has tended ever since to lower the critical estimate of a graceful poet, an interesting and influential mind, and one of the masters of English aphoristic prose.

A main object of Shenstone's rather purposeless life seems to have been to avoid making himself ridiculous, but even in this he was not entirely successful. On an income of three hundred pounds he tried to emulate the glories of Hagley Park, owned by his very wealthy neighbour, Lord Lyttleton. His delight in nature escaped "enthusiasm" by a narrow margin, and he had some marks of the still despised "virtuoso." In all his activities, except perhaps in his gardening, he gives the impression of a cultivated trifler. But perhaps the most ludicrous thing about him, in the eyes of his contemporaries, was his attempt to live the life of a man of letters while residing two days' journey from the metropolis in which, down to his time, nearly all of England's literature had been produced. He was in fact one of the first revolters in the long process of decentralization which was to cause the greater poets of the romantic era to live by preference almost anywhere except in London. These very traits, however, which prevented Shenstone from winning the respect of his own time, are of a sort that make him highly interesting to ours. There are surprises in store for one who reads patiently through his neglected, frequently tedious, half-hearted, but always highly intelligent verse. No one who examines his *Essays on Men and Manners* can fail to discover in them a critic of fine gifts and one of the few English masters of *pensée* writing.

Shenstone's fear of ridicule, his effort to ride two horses at once, and the enfeebling of his creative powers by self-doubt, are illustrated in the history of his best poem, *The Schoolmistress*. The first version of this poem, extending to only twelve stanzas, was written at Oxford and was published there in a small edition of *Poems upon Various Occasions* which the young poet later tried to suppress. In 1742 there appeared a new version, in twenty-eight stanzas, with a "Ludicrous Index." Six years later, Dodsley reprinted this version, with slight changes, in his *Collection of Poems by Various Hands*. The second edition of Dodsley, 1748, gives the poem as we now read it, with many alterations, in thirty-five stanzas, and without the Index. These details imply not a little of Shenstone's character, and also of the intellectual history of his time. The first version is obviously a sincere expression of the poet's love for Spenser, for his native village, and for rural simplicities. But these things were not yet in fashion. When the poem was first printed, Thomson's *Castle of Indolence*, also in Spenserians, had been composed but not published. Never having the full courage of his convictions, Shenstone added the Ludicrous Index to his second version in order, as he said in a letter, "to show fools that I am in jest." Only fools could be shown any such thing. He really wrote the Index in fear of the charge of sentimentality; and only later, when his own reputation had increased and the public taste had changed somewhat, did he dare to dispense with it. There are few better examples of the way in which literary tendencies, at just this time, were shifting and wavering.

The Schoolmistress is important in the history of literature not merely for its "romantic" use of the Spenserian stanza and its bungling attempt at archaic diction. Greatly admired both by Goldsmith and Burns, it gave them hints for the general tone and atmosphere if not for the style of *The Deserted Village* and *The Cotter's Saturday Night*, as these poems in turn led on to Wordsworth's and Tennyson's idylls, to Goethe's *Hermann und Dorothea*, and to Longfellow's *Evangeline*. It lies near the source, therefore, of a considerable stream of literature, and, what is more important, of modern feeling. Yet its chief value, of course, consists in its delicate harmonies of effect and in its charming admixture of laughter and tenderness. The same thing may be said of Shenstone's other completely successful poem, *A Pastoral Ballad*, a triumph of delicate artificiality somewhat in the manner of Watteau, never quite sinking into the trivial or insincere.

Although the eighteenth-century gentleman, William Shenstone, tried to avoid singularity, he was in fact something of an innovator. In his criticism and his original writing alike he turned his back upon the influences which had dominated English letters for eighty years. He did this not abruptly, indeed, and perhaps not even consciously; still he did it. While remaining as "correct" as Pope, he abandoned the Popean couplet and all the external traits of style that went therewith. He too wished to "follow nature," but he interpreted that Protean word with a slight difference of emphasis which was to have considerable results. Ease, grace, and simplicity, the main traits of his verse when at its best, are the qualities he chose to emphasize in the "natural." Artificial in every good sense that abused word may contain, he strove against its bad senses. Yet his revolt against what was desiccated and moribund in the culture of his time was actuated by the ideal of *l'honnête homme*, of the gentleman who strives to regulate his life by good taste, moderation, and decorum. He took his manners with him to the country, and did not humble himself, in the fashion of later lovers of nature, before peasants and the beasts of the field. "Everything disgusts but mere simplicity," he wrote to Bishop Percy; but this was said from the point of view of "taste."

THE SCHOOLMISTRESS

IN IMITATION OF SPENSER

**Auditæ voces, vagitus et ingens,*
Infantumque animæ flentes in limine primo.

VIRGIL

ADVERTISEMENT

What particulars in Spenser were imagined most proper for the author's imitation on this occasion are his language, his simplicity, his manner of description, and a peculiar tenderness of sentiment remarkable throughout his works.

Ah me! full sorely is my heart forlorn,
To think how modest worth neglected lies,
While partial fame doth with her blasts adorn
Such deeds alone, as pride and pomp disguise;
Deeds of ill sort, and mischievous emprize:
Lend me thy clarion, goddess! let me try
To sound the praise of merit, ere it dies;
Such as I oft have chaunced to espy
Lost in the dreary shades of dull obscurity.

In every village mark'd with little spire,
Embow'r'd in trees, and hardly known to fame,
There dwells, in lowly shed and mean attire,
A matron old, whom we schoolmistress name,
Who boasts unruly brats with birch to tame;
They grieven sore, in piteous durance pent,
Aw'd by the power of this relentless dame,
And ofttimes, on vagaries idly bent,
For unkempt hair, or task unconn'd, are sorely *shent.

And all in sight doth rise a birchen tree,
Which Learning near her little *dome did stow,
*Whilom a twig of small regard to see,
Though now so wide its waving branches flow,
And work the simple vassals *mickle woe;
For not a wind might curl the leaves that blew,
But their limbs shudder'd, and their pulse beat low,
And as they look'd they found their horror grew,
And shap'd it into rods, and tingl'd at the view.

So have I seen (who has not may conceive)
A lifeless *phantom near a garden placed,
So doth it *wanton birds of peace bereave,
Of sport, of song, of pleasure, of repast;
They start, they stare, they wheel, they look aghast;
Sad servitude! such comfortless annoy
May no bold Briton's riper age e'er taste!
*Ne superstition clog his dance of joy,
Ne vision empty, vain, his native bliss destroy.

Near to this dome is found a patch so green,
On which the tribe their gambols do display.
And at the door imprisoning board is seen,
Lest weakly wights of smaller size should stray,

*Notes on William Shenstone will be found in the Appendix, pp. 1017 ff.

Eager, *perdie, to bask in sunny day!
The noises intermix'd, which thence resound,
Do learning's little tenement betray;
Where sits the dame, disguis'd in look profound,
And eyes her fairy throng, and turns her *wheel around.

Her cap, far whiter than the driven snow,
Emblem right meet of decency does yield;
Her apron, dyed in grain, as blue, I trow,
As is the harebell that adorns the field;
And in her hand, for sceptre, she does wield
Tway birchen sprays; with anxious fear entwined,
With dark distrust, and sad repentance fill'd,
And steadfast hate, and sharp affliction join'd,
And fury uncontroll'd, and chastisement unkind.

Few but have kenn'd, in semblance meet portrayed,
The childish *faces of old Æol's train,
Libs, Notus, Auster: these in frowns array'd,
How then would fare or earth, or sky, or main,
Were the stern god to give his slaves the rein?
And were not she rebellious breasts to quell,
And were not she her statutes to maintain,
The cot no more, I ween, were deemed the cell
Where comely peace of mind, and decent order dwell.

A russet stole was o'er her shoulders thrown,
A russet *kirtle fenc'd the nipping air;
'Twas simple russet, but it was her own;
'Twas her own country bred the flock so fair;
'Twas her own labour did the fleece prepare;
And, sooth to say, her pupils, ranged around,
Through pious awe, did term it passing rare;
For they in gaping wonderment abound,
And think, no doubt, she been the greatest *wight on ground.

Albeit *ne flattery did corrupt her truth,
Ne pompous title did debauch her ear;
*Goody, good-woman, *gossip, *n'aunt, forsooth,
Or dame, the sole *additions she did hear;
Yet these she challeng'd, these she held right dear;
Ne would esteem him act *as mought behove,
Who should not honour'd eld with these revere;
For never title yet so mean could prove,
But there was eke a mind which did that title love.

One ancient hen she took delight to feed,
The plodding pattern of the busy dame,
Which ever and anon, impell'd by need,
Into her school, begirt with chickens, came.
Such favour did her past deportment claim;
And, if neglect had lavish'd on the ground
Fragment of bread, she would collect the same;
For well she knew, and quaintly could expound,
What sin it were to waste the smallest crumb she found.

Herbs too, she knew, and well of each could speak,
That in her garden sipp'd the silvery dew,
Where no vain flower disclos'd a gaudy streak,
But herbs for use, and physick, not a few,
Of *gray renown, within those borders grew;
The tufted basil, pun-provoking thyme,
Fresh *baum, and marigold of cheerful hue,
The lowly gill, that never dares to climb,
And more I fain would sing, disdaining here to rhyme.

Yet euphrasy may not be left unsung,
That gives dim eyes to wander leagues around;
And pungent radish, biting infant's tongue;
And plantain ribb'd, that heals the reaper's wound;
And marjoram sweet, in shepherd's posie found;
And lavender, whose pikes of azure bloom
Shall be, erewhile, in arid bundles bound,
To lurk amidst the labours of her loom,
And crown her kerchiefs clean with mickle rare perfume.

And here trim rosemarine, that whilom crown'd
The daintiest garden of the proudest peer;
Ere, driven from its envied site, it found
A sacred shelter for its branches here;
Where edg'd with gold its glittering skirts appear.
Oh, *wassel days! Oh, customs meet and well!
Ere this was banish'd from its lofty sphere;
Simplicity then sought this humble cell,
Nor ever would she more with *thane and lordling dwell.

Here oft the dame, on Sabbath's decent eve,
Hymnèd such psalms as *Sternhold forth did *mete;
If winter 'twere, she to her hearth did cleave,
But in her garden found a summer seat:
Sweet melody! to hear her then repeat
How Israel's sons, beneath a foreign *king,
While taunting foemen did a song entreat,
All for the nonce untuning every string,
Uphung their useless lyres — small heart had they to sing.

For she was just, and friend to virtuous lore,
And pass'd much time in truly virtuous deed;
And, in those *elfins' ears, would oft deplore
The times when truth by popish rage did bleed,
And *tortious death was true devotion's meed;
And simple faith in iron chains did mourn,
That *nould on wooden image place her creed;
And *lawny saints in smouldering flames did burn:
Ah! dearest Lord! *forfend *thilk days should e'er return.

In elbow-chair, like that of Scottish *stem
By the sharp tooth of cankering eld defaced,
In which, when he receives his diadem,
Our sovereign prince and *liefest liege is placed,
The matron sate; and some with rank she graced,
(The source of children's and of courtiers' pride!)
Redress'd affronts, for vile affronts there pass'd,
And warn'd them not the fretful to deride,
But love each other dear, whatever them betide.

Right well she knew each temper to descry,
To thwart the proud, and the submiss to raise;
Some with vile copper prize exalt on high,
And some entice with pittance small of praise;
And other some with baleful sprig she 'frays:
Ev'n absent, she the reins of power doth hold,
While with quaint arts the giddy crowd she sways;
Forewarn'd, if little bird their pranks behold,
'Twill whisper in her ear, and all the scene unfold.

Lo! now with state she utters the command;
Eftsoons the urchins to their tasks repair;
Their books, of stature small, they take in hand,
Which with pellucid horn secured are,
To save from finger wet the letters fair;
The work so gay, that on their back is seen,
St. George's high achievements does declare,
On which thilk wight that has y-gazing been
Kens the forthcoming rod, unpleasing sight, I ween!

Ah! luckless he, and born beneath the beam
Of evil star! it irks me whilst I write!
As erst the *bard by Mulla's silver stream,
Oft as he told of deadly dolorous plight,
Sigh'd as he sung, and did in tears indite.
For brandishing the rod, she doth begin
To loose the *brogues, the stripling's late delight!
And down they drop! appears his dainty skin,
Fair as the furry coat of whitest *ermilin.

Oh, ruthful scene! when from a nook obscure
His little sister doth his peril see;
All playful as she sate she grows demure,
She finds full soon her wonted spirits flee;
She meditates a prayer to set him free;
Nor gentle pardon could this dame deny,
(If gentle pardon could with dames agree)
To her sad grief that swells in either eye,
And wrings her so that all for pity she could die.

Nor longer can she now her shrieks command,
And hardly she forbears, through awful fear,
To rushen forth, and, with presumptuous hand,
To stay harsh justice in its mid career.
On thee she calls, on thee, her parent dear!
(Ah! too remote to ward the shameful blow!)
She sees no kind domestic visage near,
And soon a flood of tears begins to flow,
And gives a loose at last to unavailing woe.

But, ah! what pen his piteous plight may trace?
Or what *device his loud laments explain?
The form uncouth of his disguised face?
The pallid hue that dyes his looks amain?
The plenteous shower that does his cheek distain?
When he, in abject wise, implores the dame,
Ne hopeth aught of sweet reprieve to gain;
Or when from high she levels well her aim,
And, through the thatch, his cries each falling stroke proclaim.

The other tribe, aghast, with sore dismay,
Attend, and con their tasks with mickle care;
By turns, astonied, every twig survey,
And from their fellow's hateful wounds beware,
Knowing, I wist, how each the same may share;
Till fear has taught them a performance meet,
And to the well known chest the dame repair,
Whence oft with sugar'd cates she doth them greet,
And gingerbread *y-rare; now, certes, doubly sweet!

See to their seats they hye with merry glee,
And in beseemly order sitten there;
All but the wight of bum y-gallèd, he
Abhorreth bench, and stool, and *fourm, and chair,
(This hand in mouth y-fixed, that rends his hair;)
And eke with *snubs profound, and heaving breast,
Convulsions intermitting! does declare
His grievous wrong, his dame's unjust behest,
And scorns her offered love, and shuns to be caressed.

His face besprent with liquid crystal shines,
His blooming face, that seems a purple flower,
Which low to earth its drooping head declines,
All smear'd and sullied by a vernal shower.
Oh, the hard bosoms of despotic power!
All, all, but she, the author of his shame,
All, all, but she, regret this mournful hour;
Yet hence the youth, and hence the flower shall claim,
If so I deem aright, transcending worth and fame.

Behind some door, in melancholy thought,
Mindless of food, he, dreary *caitiff! pines;
Ne for his fellows' joyaunce careth aught,
But to the wind all merriment resigns,
And deems it shame if he to peace inclines;
And many a sullen look askaunce is sent,
Which for his dame's annoyance he designs;
And still the more to pleasure him she's bent,
The more doth he, perverse, her 'haviour past resent.

Ah me! how much I fear lest pride it be!
But if that pride it be, which thus inspires,
Beware, ye dames! with nice discernment see
Ye quench not, too, the sparks of nobler fires:
Ah! better far than all the Muses' lyres,
All coward arts, is valour's generous heat;
The firm fixt breast which fit and right requires,
Like *Vernon's patriot soul! more justly great
Than craft that *pimps for ill, or flowery false deceit.

Yet nursed with skill! what dazzling fruits appear!
Ev'n now sagacious foresight points to show
A little bench of heedless bishops here,
And there a chancellour in embryo,
Or bard sublime, if bard may e'er be so,
As Milton, Shakespeare, names that ne'er shall die!
Though now he crawl along the ground so low,
Nor *weeting how the Muse should soar on high,
Wisheth, poor starveling elf! his paper kite may fly.

And this, perhaps, who, censuring the design,
Low lays the house which that of cards doth *build,
Shall *Dennis be! if rigid fates incline,
And many an epic to his rage shall yield,
And many a poet quit th' *Aonian field;
And, sour'd by age, profound he shall appear,
As he who now with 'sdainful fury thrill'd
Surveys mine work, and levels many a sneer,
And furls his wrinkly front, and cries, "What stuff is here!"

But now Dan Phœbus gains the middle sky,
And liberty unbars her prison door,
And like a rushing torrent out they fly,
And now the grassy cirque *han covered o'er
With boisterous revel rout and wild uproar;
A thousand ways in wanton rings they run,
Heaven shield their shortlived pastimes I implore!
For well may freedom, erst so dearly won,
Appear to British elf more gladsome than the sun.

Enjoy, poor imps! enjoy your sportive trade,
And chase gay flies, and cull the fairest flowers,
For when my bones in grass-green sods are laid;
For never may ye taste more careless hours
In knightly castles or in ladies' bowers.
Oh, vain to seek delight in earthly thing!
But most in courts, where proud ambition towers;
Deluded wight! who weens fair peace can spring
Beneath the pompous dome of *kesar or of king.

See in each sprite some various bent appear!
These rudely carol most incondite lay:
Those sauntering on the green, with jocund leer
Salute the stranger passing on his way;
Some builden fragile tenements of clay;
Some to the standing lake their courses bend,
With pebbles smooth at duck and drake to play;
Thilk to the huxter's savoury cottage tend,
In pastry kings and queens th' allotted mite to spend.

Here, as each season yields a different store.
Each season's stores in order rangèd been;
Apples with cabbage-net y-covered o'er,
Galling full sore the unmoneyed wight, are seen,
And gooseb'rie, clad in livery red or green;
And here of lovely dye the Catherine pear,
Fine pear! as lovely for thy juice I ween;
Oh, may no wight e'er pennyless come there,
Lest smit with ardent love he pine with hopeless care!

See! cherries here, ere cherries yet abound,
With thread so white in tempting *posies ty'd,
Scattering like blooming maid their glances round,
With pampered look draw little eyes aside,
And must be bought, though penury betide;
The plum all azure, and the nut all brown;
And here each season do those *cakes abide,
Whose honoured names th' inventive city own,
Rendering through Britain's isle Salopia's praises known.

Admired Salopia! that with venial pride
Eyes her bright form in Severn's ambient wave,
Famed for her loyal cares in perils try'd,
Her daughters lovely, and her striplings brave;
Ah! midst the rest, may flowers adorn his grave
Whose art did first these dulcet cates display!
A motive fair to learning's imps he gave,
Who cheerless o'er her darkling region stray!
Till reason's morn arise, and light them on their way.

[1737, 1748]

A PASTORAL BALLAD, PART II
HOPE

My banks they are furnish'd with bees
Whose murmur invites one to sleep;
My grottos are shaded with trees,
And my hills are white over with sheep.
I seldom have met with a loss,
Such health do my fountains bestow;
My fountains all border'd with moss,
Where the harebells and violets grow.

Not a pine in my grove is there seen
But with tendrils of woodbine is bound;
Not a beech's more beautiful green
But a sweetbriar entwines it around.
Not my fields in the prime of the year,
More charms than my cattle unfold;
Not a brook that is limpid and clear
But it glitters with fishes of gold.

One would think she might like to retire
To the bower I have labour'd to rear:
Not a shrub that I heard her admire,
But I hasted and planted it there.
Oh, how sudden the jessamine strove
With the lilac to render it gay!
Already it calls for my love
To prune the wild branches away.

From the plains, from the woodlands, and groves,
What strains of wild melody flow!
How the nightingales warble their loves
From thickets of roses that blow!
And when her bright form shall appear,
Each bird shall harmoniously join
In a concert so soft and so clear
As — she may not be *fond to resign.

I have found out a gift for my fair;
I have found where the wood-pigeons breed;
But let me that plunder forbear,
She will say 'twas a barbarous deed:
For he ne'er could be true, she averr'd,
Who could rob a poor bird of its young;
And I loved her the more when I heard
Such tenderness fall from her tongue.

I have heard her with sweetness unfold
How that pity was due to — a dove;
That it ever attended the bold,
And she call'd it the sister of Love.
But her words such a pleasure convey,
So much I her accents adore,
Let her speak, and whatever she say,
Methinks I should love her the more.

Can a bosom so gentle remain
Unmoved when her Corydon sighs?
Will a nymph that is fond of the plain,
These plains and this valley despise?
Dear regions of silence and shade:
Soft scenes of contentment and ease!
Where I could have pleasingly stray'd,
If aught in her absence could please.

But where does my Phyllida stray?
And where are her grots and her bowers?
Are the groves and the valleys as gay,
And the shepherds as gentle as ours?
The groves may perhaps be as fair,
And the face of the valleys as fine;
The swains may in manners compare,
But their love is not equal to mine.

[1755]

ODE TO MEMORY

O Memory! celestial maid!
  Who glean'st the flowerets cropp'd by time;
And, suffering not a leaf to fade,
  Preserv'st the blossoms of our prime;
Bring, bring those moments to my mind
When life was new and Lesbia kind.

And bring that garland to my sight,
  With which my favour'd crook she bound;
And bring that wreath of roses bright,
  Which then my festive temples crown'd;
And to my raptured ear convey
The gentle things she deign'd to say.

And sketch with care the Muse's bower,
  Where *Isis rolls her silver tide;
Nor yet omit one reed or flower
  That shines on *Cherwell's verdant side;
If so thou mayst those hours prolong,
When polish'd *Lycon join'd my song.

The song it 'vails not to recite;
  But, sure, to soothe our youthful dreams,
Those banks and streams appear'd more bright
  Than other banks, than other streams —
Or, by thy softening pencil shown,
Assume they beauties not their own?

And paint that sweetly-vacant scene,
  When, all beneath the poplar bough,
My spirits light, my soul serene,
  I breathed in verse one cordial vow,
That nothing should my soul inspire
But friendship warm and love entire.

Dull to the sense of new delight,
  On thee the drooping Muse attends;
As some fond lover, robb'd of sight,
  On thy expressive power depends,
Nor would exchange thy glowing lines,
To live the lord of all that shines.

But let me chase those vows away,
  Which at Ambition's shrine I made;
Nor ever let thy skill display

Those anxious moments, ill repaid:
Oh! from my breast that season rase,
And bring my childhood in its place.

Bring me the bells, the rattle bring,
And bring the hobby I bestrode,
When pleased in many a sportive ring,
Around the room I jovial rode;
Ev'n let me bid my lyre adieu,
And bring the whistle that I blew.

Then will I muse, and, pensive, say,
Why did not these enjoyments last?
How sweetly wasted I the day,
While innocence allow'd to waste!
Ambition's toils alike are vain,
But ah! for pleasure yield us pain.

[1764]

INSCRIPTION ON THE BACK OF A GOTHIC SEAT

Shepherd, wouldst thou here obtain
Pleasure unalloy'd with pain?
Joy that suits the rural sphere?
Gentle shepherd, lend an ear.

Learn to relish calm delight,
Verdant vales and fountains bright;
Trees that nod o'er sloping hills,
Caves that echo tinkling rills.

If thou canst no charm disclose
In the simplest bud that blows,
Go, forsake thy plain and fold;
Join the crowd, and toil for gold.

Tranquil pleasures never cloy;
Banish each tumultuous joy;
All but love — for love inspires
Fonder wishes, warmer fires.

Love and all its joys be thine —
Yet, ere thou the reins resign,
Hear what reason seems to say,
Hear attentive, and obey:

Crimson leaves the rose adorn,
But beneath them lurks a thorn;
Fair and flowery is the brake,
Yet it hides the vengeful snake.

"Think not she, whose empty pride
Dares the fleecy garb deride,
Think not she, who, light and vain,
Scorns the sheep, can love the swain.

"Artless deed and simple dress
Mark the chosen shepherdess;
Thoughts by decency controll'd,
Well conceived and freely told.

"Sense that shuns each conscious air,
Wit that falls ere well aware;
Generous pity, prone to sigh
If her kid or lambkin die.

"Let not lucre, let not pride,
Draw thee from such charms aside;
Have not those their proper sphere?
Gentler passions triumph here.

"See, to sweeten thy repose,
The blossom buds, the fountain flows;
Lo! to crown thy healthful board,
All that milk and fruits afford.

"Seek no more — the rest is vain;
Pleasure ending soon in pain:
Anguish lightly gilded o'er:
Close thy wish, and seek no more."

[1764]

WRITTEN AT AN INN AT HENLEY

To thee, fair Freedom, I retire
From flattery, cards, and dice, and din;
Nor art thou found in mansions higher
Than the low cot or humble inn.

'Tis here with boundless power I reign,
And every health which I begin
Converts dull port to bright champagne;
Such freedom crowns it, at an inn.

I fly from pomp, I fly from plate,
I fly from Falsehood's specious grin!
Freedom I love and form I hate,
And choose my lodgings at an inn.

Here, waiter, take my sordid ore,
Which lackeys else might hope to win;
It buys, what courts have not in store;
It buys me freedom, at an inn.

Whoe'er has travell'd life's dull round,
Where'er his stages may have been,
May sigh to think he still has found
The warmest welcome at an inn.

[1758]

SELECTIONS FROM "ESSAYS ON MEN AND MANNERS"

In his Introduction to the original edition of Shenstone's *Essays on Men and Manners*, Robert Dodsley wrote: "His character, as a man of clear judgment and deep penetration, will best appear from his prose works. It is there we must search for the acuteness of his understanding, and his profound knowledge of the human heart." This is true, and it may be added that Shenstone's prose brings before us a mind at once more alert and more serious than we find in his poems, yet this prose has been even more neglected and undervalued than his verse. One reason for this neglect may be the fact that Shenstone excelled chiefly in a form of prose-writing unfamiliar to English readers — the detached, brief, epigrammatic observation to which the French give the name *pensée*. His natural indolence and fear of ridicule, coupled with his wit, his sensibility, and his delight in polishing trifles, enabled him to challenge comparison, occasionally, in this delightful form, with Vauvenargues, Chamfort, and even Joubert. He was in fact almost the only important writer of *pensées* in the whole range of English literature, although in American writing we have admirable examples of the form in the Journals of Emerson and Thoreau and in Mr. Logan Pearsall Smith's *Trivia*.

As there is only a semblance of order in Shenstone's own arrangement of his prose jottings, it seems justifiable to represent them here by selections chosen at random. The essay entitled *An Humorist* — in which the author is apparently writing to some extent about himself — is, however, represented almost entire.

AN HUMORIST

... Not the entrance of a cathedral, not the sound of a passing bell, not the furs of a magistrate, nor the sables of a funeral, were fraught with half the solemnity of face!

Nay, so wonderfully serious was he observed to be on all occasions that it was found hardly possible to be otherwise in his company. He quashed the loudest tempest of laughter whenever he entered the room; and men's features, though ever so much roughened, were sure to grow smooth at his approach.

The man had nothing vicious or even ill-natured in his character, yet he was the dread of all jovial conversation. The young, the gay, found their spirits fly before him. Even the kitten and the puppy, as it were by instinct, would forego their frolics, and be still. The depression he occasioned was like that of a damp or vitiated air. Unconscious of any apparent cause, you found your spirits sink insensibly: and were any one to sit for the picture of ill-luck, it is not possible the painter could select a more proper person.

Yet he did not fail to boast of a superior share of reason, even for the want of that very faculty, risibility, with which it is supposed to be always joined.

Indeed he acquired the character of the most ingenious person of his county from this meditative temper. Not that he had ever made any great *discovery of his talents, but a few oracular declarations, joined with a common opinion that he was writing somewhat for posterity, completed his reputation.

Numbers would have willingly depreciated his character, had not his known sobriety and reputed sense deterred them.

He was one day overheard at his devotions, returning his most fervent thanks for some particularities in his situation which the generality of mankind would have but little regarded.

"Accept," said he, "the gratitude of thy most humble yet most happy creature, not for silver or gold, the tinsel of mankind, but for those amiable peculiarities which thou hast so graciously interwoven both with my fortune and my *complexion, — for those treasures so well adapted to that frame of mind thou hast assigned me.

"That the surname which has descended to me is liable to no pun.

"That it runs chiefly upon vowels and liquids.

"That I have a picturesque countenance, rather than one that is esteemed of regular features.

"That there is an intermediate hill intercepting my view of a nobleman's *seat, whose ill-obtained superiority I can not bear to recollect.

"That my estate is overrun with brambles, resounds with cataracts, and is beautifully varied with rocks and precipices, rather than an even cultivated spot, fertile of corn or wine or oil, or those kinds of productions in which the sons of men delight themselves.

"That as thou dividest thy bounties impartially, giving riches to one and the contempt of riches to another, so thou hast given me, in the midst of poverty, to despise the insolence of riches, and by declining all emulation that is founded upon wealth, to maintain the dignity and superiority of the Muses.

"That I have a disposition either so elevated or so *ingenuous that I can derive to myself amusement from the very expedients and contrivances with which rigorous necessity furnishes my invention.

"That I can laugh at my own follies, foibles, and infirmities, and that I do not *want infirmities to employ this disposition."

This poor gentleman caught cold one winter's night as he was *contemplating, by the side of a crystal stream, by moonshine. This afterwards terminated in a fever that was fatal to him. Since his death I have been favoured with the inspection of his poetry, of which I preserved a catalogue for the benefit of my readers.

OCCASIONAL POEMS

On his dog, that, growing corpulent, refused a crust when it was offered him.

To the memory of a pair of breeches that had done him excellent service.

Having lost his trusty walking-staff, he complaineth.

To his mistress, on her declaring that she loved parsnips better than potatoes.

On an *earwig that crept into a *nectarine that it might be swallowed by Cloe.

On cutting an artichoke in his garden the day that Queen Anne cut her little finger.

Epigram on a wooden peg.

Ode to the memory of the great modern — who first invented shoe-buckles.

DETACHED THOUGHTS

Art should never be allowed to set foot in the province of nature, otherwise than clandestinely and by night. Whenever she is allowed to appear here, and men begin to *compromise the difference — night, Gothicism, confusion, and absolute chaos are come again.

The works of a person that builds begin immediately to decay, while those of him who plants begin directly to improve. In this, planting promises a more lasting pleasure than building, which, were it to remain in equal perfection, would at best begin to moulder and want repairs in imagination.

It was the wise remark of some sagacious observer that familiarity is for the most part productive of contempt. Graceless offspring of so amiable a parent! Unfortunate beings that we are, whose enjoyments must be either checked or prove destructive of themselves! Our passions are permitted to sip a little pleasure, but are extinguished by indulgence like a lamp overwhelmed with oil. Hence we neglect the beauty with which we have been intimate, nor would any addition it could receive prove an equivalent for the advantage it derived from the first impression. Thus, negligent of graces that have the merit of reality, we too often prefer imaginary ones that have only the charm of novelty. And hence we may account, in general, for the preference of art to nature in our old-fashioned gardens.

Indolence is a kind of centripetal force.

If a person ought heartily to *stickle for any cause, it should be for that of moderation. Moderation should be his party.

Inanimates, toys, utensils, seem to merit a kind of affection from us when they have been our companions through various vicissitudes. I have often viewed my watch, *standish, snuff-box, with this kind of tender regard, allotting them a degree of friendship which there are some men who do not deserve. — *"Midst many faithless only faithful found!"

I begin too soon in life to slight the world more than is consistent with making a figure in it. The **non est tanti* of Ovid grows upon me so fast that in a few years I shall have no passion.

I cannot avoid comparing the ease and freedom I enjoy to the ease of an old shoe, where a certain degree of shabbiness is joined with the convenience.

The chief advantage that ancient writers can boast over modern ones seems owing to simplicity. Every noble truth and sentiment was expressed by the former in the natural manner — in word and phrase simple, perspicuous, and incapable of improvement. What then remained for later writers but affectation, witticism, and *conceit?

Everything disgusts but mere simplicity. The scriptural writers describe their heroes using only some such phrase as this: "Alas, my brother!" "O Absolom, my son! my son!" etc. The lamentation of Saul over Jonathan is more diffuse, but at the same time entirely simple.

A plain narrative of any remarkable fact, emphatically related, has a more striking effect than the author's comment.

I think nothing truly poetic, at least no poetry worth composing, that does not strongly affect one's passions, and this is but slenderly effected by fables, allegories, and lies.

I hate a style, as I do a garden, that is wholly flat and regular, that slides along like an eel, and never rises to what one can call an inequality.

The world may be divided into people that read, people that write, people that think, and fox-hunters.

Superficial writers, like the mole, often fancy themselves deep when they are exceeding near the surface.

Pope's talent lay remarkably in what one may naturally enough term the condensation of thoughts. I think no other English poet ever brought so much sense into the same number of lines with equal smoothness, ease, and poetical beauty. Let him who doubts of this peruse his *Essay on Man* with attention. Perhaps this was a talent from which he could not easily have swerved. Perhaps he could not have sufficiently rarefied his thoughts to produce that flimsiness which is required in a ballad or love-song.

I durst not have censured Mr. Pope's writings in his lifetime, you say. True. A writer surrounded with all his fame, engaging with another that is hardly known, is a man in armour attacking another in his * nightgown and slippers.

Poetry and consumptions are the most flattering diseases.

Every good poet includes a critic. The reverse will not hold.

Men of fine parts, they say, are often proud. I answer, dull people are seldom so, and both act upon appearance of reason.

There is nothing more universally commended than a fine day. The reason is that people can commend it without envy.

Virtue seems to be nothing more than a motion consonant to the system of things. Were a planet to fly from its orbit, it would represent a vicious man.

Virtue should be considered as a part of taste (and perhaps it is so more in this age than in any preceding one) and should as much avoid deceit or sinister meanings in discourse as they would puns, bad language, or false grammar.

The state of man is not unlike that of a fish hooked by an angler. Death allows us a little line. We flounce and sport and vary our situation; but when we would extend our schemes, we discover our confinement, checked and limited by a superior hand who drags us from our element whenever he pleases.

[1764]

WILLIAM WHITEHEAD

THE later life of William Whitehead (1715–1785) was an illustration of the poem he composed while an undergraduate at Cambridge, *On the Danger of Writing Verse.* Considering that he was all his life a butt of satire, and that he suffered particularly at the violent hands of Charles Churchill, there is unintended humour in his chief poetic effort, a versified *Essay on Ridicule* (1743), in which, following the lead of the sentimentalists, he deprecates all satire as likely to do more harm than good. He did not take the best way of avoiding ridicule when he accepted, in 1757, the office of poet-laureate, which had just been refused by Thomas Gray, and indeed he soon produced *A Pathetic Apology for all Laureates, Past, Present, and to Come.* Whitehead was not, however, at all contemptible, although there was little of the poet in him and nothing of the thinker. He had wit and humour; he wrote a large amount of creditable light verse; and his plays were moderately successful.

The Enthusiast deserves to be remembered as a sensible statement of orthodox opinion levelled at a heresy — the worship of nature and preference of the solitary to the social life — which had long been increasing and was soon to triumph. The word "enthusiast" meant at this time a wild emotional dreamer, the sort of person who prefers solitude because it leaves him free to "abound in his own sense" and to ignore the rational criticism of society — in short, a romantic and original "genius." Against this fugitive temperament reason brings to bear several arguments drawn from Christianity, from the Stoics, and from recent humanitarianism. The poem is an echo of a controversy which began in the ancient world, which raged throughout the Middle Ages, and in which the eighteenth century was always deeply interested.

THE ENTHUSIAST

AN ODE

Once — I remember well the day,
'Twas ere the blooming sweets of May
Had lost their freshest hues,
When every flower on every hill,
In every vale, had drank its fill
Of sunshine and of dews;

In short, 'twas that sweet season's prime
When Spring gives up the reins of time
To Summer's glowing hand,
And doubting mortals hardly know
By whose command the breezes blow
Which fan the smiling land —

'Twas then, beside a greenwood shade
Which cloth'd a lawn's aspiring head,
I urg'd my devious way
With loitering steps, regardless where,
So soft, so genial was the air,
So wond'rous bright the day.

And now my eyes with transport rove
O'er all the blue expanse above,
Unbroken by a cloud!
And now beneath delighted pass
Where, winding thro' the deep-green grass,
A full-brimm'd river flow'd.

I stop, I gaze; in accents rude
To thee, serenest Solitude,
Bursts forth th' unbidden lay;
"Begone vile world! The learn'd, the wise,
The great, the busy, I despise,
And pity e'en the gay.

"These, these are joys alone," I cry;
"'Tis here, divine Philosophy,
Thou deign'st to fix thy throne.
Here Contemplation points the road
Thro' nature's charms to nature's God.
These, these are joys alone.

"Adieu ye vain, low-thoughted cares,
Ye human hopes and human fears,
Ye pleasures and ye pains!"
While thus I spake, o'er all my soul
A philosophic calmness stole;
A Stoic stillness reigns.

The tyrant passions all subside;
Fear, anger, pity, shame, and pride
No more my bosom move;
Yet still I felt, or seem'd to feel,
A kind of visionary zeal
Of universal love.

When lo! a voice, a voice I hear!
'Twas Reason whisper'd in my ear

These monitory strains:
"What mean'st thou, man? Wouldst thou unbind
The ties which constitute thy kind,
The pleasures and the pains?

"The same Almighty Power unseen
Who spreads the gay or solemn scene
To Contemplation's eye
Fix'd every movement of the soul,
Taught every wish its destin'd goal,
And quicken'd every joy.

"He bids the tyrant passions rage,
He bids them war eternal wage,
And combat each his foe,
Till from dissensions concords rise,
And beauties from deformities,
And happiness from woe.

"Art thou not man, and dar'st thou find
A bliss which leans not to mankind?
Presumptuous thought and vain!
Each bliss unshar'd is unenjoy'd;
Each power is weak unless employ'd
Some social good to gain.

"Shall light and shade and warmth and air
With those exalted joys compare
Which active Virtue feels,
When on she drags as lawful prize
Contempt and Indolence and Vice
At her triumphant wheels?

"As rest to labour still succeeds,
To man, whilst Virtue's glorious deeds
Employ his toilsome day,
This fair variety of things
Are merely life's refreshing springs
To sooth him on his way.

"Enthusiast, go, unstring thy lyre;
In vain thou sing'st if none admire,
How sweet soe'er the strain.
And is not thy o'erflowing mind,
Unless thou mixest with thy kind,
Benevolent in vain?

"Enthusiast, go, try every sense,
If not thy bliss, thy excellence,
Thou yet hast learn'd to scan;
At least thy wants, thy weakness know,
And see them all uniting show
That man was made for man."

[1754]

CHARLES CHURCHILL

Although he once "blazed the comet of a season," as Byron said of him, Charles Churchill is less known today than almost any other English poet of his ability. One reason for this is that nearly all his work was done in the form of satire and that much of it deals with persons and themes never important and now forgotten; but it must be said, in addition, that Churchill wasted and misused his fine powers, partly through lack of early discipline and training, partly in a spirit of bravado and sheer recklessness. Even his admirers admit the truth of the words he is said to have uttered on his deathbed, "What a fool I have been!"

During the last four years of his life, which extended only from 1731 to 1764, Churchill poured forth a surprising quantity of hastily written verse, scorning the patient care by which Pope and his followers strove for perfection and preferring what he calls "the generous roughness of a nervous line." This he often attained, and one reason for his immediate success and fame is that he brought back into English verse a crude vigour which for some decades had seldom been heard there. His writing has a rush of thoughts and images, a speed, a virility, which relate him to poets of high rank such, for example, as Lord Byron. He believed that he had rejected Pope as a model in favour of Dryden, but he misunderstood the genius of the one poet as much as he underestimated that of the other, so that, although he is to be remembered as one of the last satiric poets of the Dryden-Pope tradition, he fell far short of both his great predecessors. Churchill's most serious defects — digressiveness, failure in unity and construction, frequent bathos and triviality — are precisely such as close study of Pope might have corrected. But he was restive against all restraint, whether of moral obligation, of law, or of art; and indeed it would be possible to draw a striking parallel between his conduct as a dissolute rake on the one hand — conduct which finally forced him to abandon the Church as a profession — and his theory and practice of poetry on the other. In this and several other respects he reminds us of the French *libertin*, Théophile de Viaud, whose lyric powers, however, he did not possess. The preoccupation of eighteenth-century verse with political and social questions is nowhere more clearly illustrated than in his work. As we should expect from a close friend of John Wilkes, his cry is always for "liberty," never very clearly conceived or defined, as against all authorities of Church and State. Equally opposed to the "musty rules" of literary criticism, he bases his claim to poetic honours upon the *furor poeticus*; yet a mere glance at his pages shows that he retained without question several of the most frigid and hackneyed devices of the old poetic diction.

Too much of Churchill's work was written in attempted justification of his own irregularities and excesses, or of his friends. His fame was made almost over night in 1761 by *The Rosciad*, a witty but gratuitous onslaught upon nearly the whole roster of contemporary London actors. This brought him many enemies, to each of whom he gave full measure of his gift for vituperation. Among the more important of his later poems are *The Prophecy of Famine*, an attack upon the Scotch people and Scottish influence at Court; an *Epistle to William Hogarth*, in which he defends John Wilkes; *The Ghost*, containing a vigorous lampoon upon Dr. Johnson; and *The Duellist.*

From THE AUTHOR

The Author was perhaps more generally admired by Churchill's contemporaries than any other of his works. It has been chosen here because it is less concerned with forgotten persons and events than his other poems, because it reveals his literary purposes even better than his *Apology*, but chiefly because it shows how much — and how little — of the great tradition of satire survived the attacks of sentimentalism and lived on into the second half of the century. The poem bears an obvious relation to Pope's *Epistle to Dr. Arbuthnot*, but is less personal, for once, in its attack and self-justification. Its assertion of "genius" against the "rules" and of the common man against entrenched authority points forward to Paine and Burns, even to Byron and Shelley. The basis of this assertion is an ideal "liberty" regarded as peculiarly English, which Churchill thought threatened by foreign influences emanating from Scotland and France.

Two passages dealing with Churchill's political foes have been omitted.

Accursed the man whom fate ordains, in spite,
And cruel parents teach, to read and write!
What need of letters? Wherefore should we spell?
Why write our names? A mark will do as well.

Much are the precious hours of youth misspent
In climbing learning's rugged steep ascent.
When to the top the bold adventurer's got,
He reigns, vain monarch, o'er a barren spot;
Whilst in the vale of ignorance below
Folly and vice to rank luxuriance grow,
Honours and wealth pour in on every side
And proud preferment rolls her golden tide.
O'er crabbed authors life's gay prime to waste,
To cramp wild genius in the chains of taste,
To bear the slavish drudgery of schools,
And tamely stoop to every pedant's rules;
For seven long years debarr'd of liberal ease,
To plod in college trammels to degrees;
Beneath the weight of solemn toys to groan,
*Sleep over books, and leave mankind unknown;
To praise each senior blockhead's threadbare tale,
And laugh till reason blush and spirits fail;
Manhood with vile submission to disgrace,
And cap the fool whose merit is his place,
Vice-chancellors whose knowledge is but small,
And chancellors who nothing know at all —
Ill brook'd the generous spirit in those days
When learning was the certain road to praise,
When nobles, with a love of science bless'd,
Approved in others what themselves possess'd.
But now, when Dullness rears aloft her throne,
When lordly vassals her wide empire own,
When Wit, seduced by Envy, starts aside
And basely leagues with Ignorance and Pride,
What now should tempt us, by false hopes misled,
Learning's unfashionable paths to tread,
To bear those labours which our fathers bore,
That crown withheld which they in triumph wore?
When with much pains this boasted learning's got,
'Tis an affront to those who have it not:
In some it causes hate, in others fear,
Instructs our foes to rail, our friends to sneer.
With prudent haste the worldly-minded fool
Forgets the little which he learn'd at school.
The elder brother, to vast fortunes born,
Looks on all science with an eye of scorn;
Dependent brethren the same features wear,
And younger sons are stupid as the heir.
In senates, at the bar, in church and state,
Genius is vile, and learning out of date.
Is this — oh, death to think! — is this the land
Where merit and reward went hand in hand?
Where heroes, parent-like, the poet view'd,
By whom they saw their glorious deeds renew'd?
Where poets, true to honour, tuned their lays,
And by their patrons sanctified their praise?
Is this the land where, on our Spenser's tongue,
Enamour'd of his voice, Description hung?
Where Jonson rigid Gravity beguiled,
Whilst Reason through her critic fences smiled?
Where Nature listening stood whilst Shakespear play'd,
And wonder'd at the work herself had made?
Is this the land where, mindful of her charge
And office high, fair Freedom walk'd at large?
Where, finding in our laws a sure defence,
She mock'd at all restraints but those of sense?
Where, Health and Honour trooping by her side,
She spread her sacred empire far and wide;
Pointed the way, Affliction to beguile,
And bade the face of Sorrow wear a smile;
Bade those who dare obey the generous call
Enjoy her blessings which God meant for all?
Is this the land where, in some tyrant's reign,
When a weak, wicked ministerial train,
The tools of power, the slaves of interest, plann'd
Their country's ruin and with bribes unmann'd
Those wretches who, ordain'd in Freedom's cause,
Gave up our liberties, and sold our laws;
When Power was taught by Meanness where to go,
Nor dared to love the virtue of a foe;
When, like a leprous plague, from the foul head
To the foul heart her sores Corruption spread;
Her iron arm when stern Oppression rear'd;
And Virtue, from her broad base shaken, fear'd
The scourge of Vice; when, impotent and vain,
Poor Freedom bow'd the neck to Slavery's chain —

*Notes on Charles Churchill will be found in the Appendix, p. 1019.

Is this the land where, in those worst of times,
The hardy poet raised his honest rhymes
To dread rebuke, and bade Controlment speak
In guilty blushes on the villain's cheek,
Bade Power turn pale, kept mighty rogues in awe,
And made them fear the Muse who fear'd not law?

How do I laugh when men of narrow souls
Whom Folly guides, and Prejudice controls;
Who, one dull drowsy track of business trod,
Worship their Mammon and neglect their God;
Who, breathing by one musty set of rules,
Dote from their birth and are by system fools;
Who, form'd to dullness from their very youth,
Lies of the day prefer to gospel truth;
Pick up their little knowledge from reviews,
And lay out all their stock of faith in news —
How do I laugh, when creatures form'd like these,
Whom Reason scorns, and I should blush to please,
Rail at all liberal arts, deem verse a crime,
And hold not truth as truth, if told in rhyme!...

How do I laugh when men, by fortune placed
Above their betters, and by rank disgraced,
Who found their pride on titles which they stain,
And, mean themselves, are of their fathers vain,
Who would a * bill of privilege prefer,
And treat a poet like a creditor,
The generous ardour of the Muse condemn,
And curse the storm they know must break on them!
"What! shall a reptile bard, a wretch unknown,
Without one badge of merit but his own,
Great nobles lash, and lords, like common men,
Smart from the vengeance of a scribbler's pen?"

What's in this name of lord, that I should fear
To bring their vices to the public ear?
Flows not the honest blood of humble swains
Quick as the tide which swells a monarch's veins?
Monarchs, who wealth and titles can bestow,
Can not make virtues in succession flow.
Wouldst thou, proud man, be safely placed above
The censure of the Muse? Deserve her love,
Act as thy birth demands, as nobles ought;
Look back, and by thy worthy father taught,
Who earn'd those honours thou wert born to wear,
Follow his steps and be his virtue's heir.
But if, regardless of the road to fame,
You start aside and tread the paths of shame;
If such thy life that, should thy sire arise,
The sight of such a son would blast his eyes,
Would make him curse the hour which gave thee birth,
Would drive him shuddering from the face of earth,
Once more, with shame and sorrow, 'mongst the dead
In endless night to hide his reverend head;
If such thy life, though kings had made thee more
Than ever king a scoundrel made before;
Nay, to allow thy pride a deeper spring,
Though God in vengeance had made thee a king,
Taking on Virtue's wing her daring flight,
The Muse should drag thee, trembling, to the light,
Probe thy foul wounds and lay thy bosom bare
To the keen question of the searching air.

Gods! with what pride I see the titled slave
Who smarts beneath the stroke which Satire gave,
Aiming at ease, and with dishonest art
Striving to hide the feelings of his heart!
How do I laugh when, with affected air,
(Scarce able through despite to keep his chair,
Whilst on his trembling lip pale anger speaks,
And the chafed blood flies mounting to his cheeks)
He talks of conscience, which good men secures
From all those evil moments guilt endures,
And seems to laugh at those who pay regard
To the wild ravings of a frantic bard.
"Satire, whilst envy and ill humour sway
The mind of man, must always make her way;
Nor to a bosom with discretion fraught
Is all her malice worth a single thought.
The wise have not the will, nor fools the power,
To stop her headstrong course; within the hour,
Left to herself, she dies; opposing strife
Gives her fresh vigour and prolongs her life.
All things her prey, and every man her aim,
I can no patent for exemption claim,
Nor would I wish to stop that harmless dart

Which plays around, but cannot wound, my heart.
Though pointed at myself, be Satire free;
To her 'tis pleasure, and no pain to me."
Dissembling wretch, hence to the Stoic school,
And there amongst thy brethren play the fool;
There, unrebuked, these wild vain doctrines preach.
Lives there a man whom Satire cannot reach?
Lives there a man who calmly can stand by
And see his conscience ripp'd with steady eye?
When Satire flies abroad on Falsehood's wing,
Short is her life and impotent her sting;
But when to Truth allied, the wound she gives
Sinks deep, and to remotest ages lives.
When in the tomb thy pamper'd flesh shall rot,
And e'en by friends thy memory be forgot,
Still shalt thou live, recorded for thy crimes,
Live in her page, and stink to aftertimes.
Hast thou no feeling yet? Come, throw off pride,
And own those passions which thou shalt not hide.
* Sandwich, who from the moment of his birth
Made human nature a reproach on earth,
Who never dared, nor wish'd, behind to stay
When Folly, Vice, and Meanness led the way,
Would blush, should he be told by Truth and Wit
Those actions which he blush'd not to commit.
Men the most infamous are fond of fame,
And those who fear not guilt yet start at shame.
But whither runs my zeal, whose rapid force,
Turning the brain, bears Reason from her course,
Carries me back to times when poets, bless'd
With courage, graced the science they profess'd;
When they, in honour rooted, firmly stood
The bad to punish and reward the good;
When, to a flame by public virtue wrought,
The foes of freedom they to justice brought,
And dared expose those slaves who dared support
A tyrant plan and call'd themselves a court?
Ah, what are poets now? As slavish those
Who deal in verse as those who deal in prose.
Is there an author, search the kingdom round,
In whom true worth and real spirit's found?
The slaves of booksellers or — doom'd by fate
To baser chains — vile pensioners of state;
Some, dead to shame, and of those shackles proud
Which Honour scorns, for slavery roar aloud;
Others, half-palsied only, mutes become,
And what makes * Smollett write makes Johnson dumb....

[1763]

CHRISTOPHER SMART

Born in Kent in 1722, Christopher Smart was educated at Durham School and at Pembroke College, Cambridge, where he won a fellowship and made the acquaintance of Thomas Gray. His improvident and intemperate habits did not prevent him from gaining considerable scholarship, and for five successive years he won the Seatonian prize for a poem on "One of the Attributes of the Supreme Being." At thirty, having married the stepdaughter of a London publisher, he forfeited his fellowship and had to set to work with his pen in Grub Street. His prose translation of Horace, finished in 1756, although highly popular for more than a century among the college students of England and America, brought him little money, and the weekly essays which he undertook to produce for the remainder of his life were even less successful. At about this time he began to show signs of a harmless religious mania, interpreting literally the Biblical injunctions concerning continual prayer, and for some two years he was confined in an asylum. His great poem, *A Song to David*, appeared in April, 1763, probably less than a year after his release, but there is no internal or external evidence for the legend that it was written during his confinement — as some say, indented with a key on the walls of his cell. To most readers of the eighteenth century, as of the twentieth, it seemed precisely the sort of poem that a madman would write, and it made little stir. During Smart's last years his affairs went from bad to worse; and he died, at the age of forty-nine, in a debtor's prison.

The later history of the *Song* has not been creditable either to editorship or to criticism. Although it is the only production of Smart's that rises above mediocrity, it was excluded from the collected edition of his work, made twenty years after his death, on the ground that it bore "melancholy proofs of the recent estrangement of his mind" — an assertion which indicates only that Smart's first editor, like most of his followers, did not read the poem intelligently. Most anthologists have either ignored the *Song* entirely or have misrepresented its closely reasoned structure by excerpts, and by none of them has it ever been adequately annotated. The critics have erred both in blame and praise. Thomas Campbell wrote in his *Specimens of the British Poets*, 1801: "If Smart had any talent above mediocrity, it was a slight turn for humour. In his serious attempts at poetry he reminds one of those

> Whom Phœbus, in his ire,
> Hath blasted with poetic fire."

Dante Gabriel Rossetti advertised the limitations of his knowledge and taste almost as absurdly by calling the *Song* "the only great accomplished poem of the last century," although there is nothing to retract from his further remark that it is "a masterpiece of rich imagery, exhaustive resources, and reverberant sound." Many commentators, however, have at least seen that the poem stands alone. "Its noble wildness," says Palgrave, "and its transitions from grandeur to tenderness, from earth to heaven, are unique in our poetry." Churton Collins considers it "the most extraordinary phenomenon, perhaps, in our literature; the one rapt strain in the poetry of the eighteenth century." But the most emphatic praise of *A Song to David*, and also the most discerning, is that found in the poem addressed to Smart in Robert Browning's *Parleyings with Certain People*. Browning calls it

> A song where flute-breath silvers trumpet-clang,
> And stations you for once on either hand
> With Milton and with Keats....
> Such success
> Befell Smart only out of throngs between
> Milton and Keats that donned the singing-dress —
> Smart, solely of such songmen, pierced the screen
> 'Twixt thing and word, lit language straight from soul, —
> Left no fine film-flake on the naked coal
> Live from the censer — shapely or uncouth,
> Fire-suffused through and through, one blaze of truth
> Undeadened by a lie, — (you have my mind).

The salient feat of Smart's poem is perfectly described in the assertion that he "pierced the screen 'twixt thing and word" — a screen more than usually opaque to the poets of his day. He wrenched himself free, for a time, from the clutch of the rhetorical tradition, according to which the decorous and accepted ways of saying things are always paramount to the things said. Closer to Keats than to Milton, he made words do a double and treble duty. While his mind was on fire with this poem, his imagination flashed from high to low, linked the far to the near and the august to the most humble, at a speed Keats himself never attained. He saw nature not in Keats's way, as a rich spectacle, but with the ecstatic innocence and freshness of vision which we associate with Traherne, Vaughan, and Blake. The mere naming of God's creatures, whether worm or star, was a religious delight to him, for he saw them bound together in one universal prayer. Either from Cabalistic and Rosicrucian literature or else, more probably, by direct intuition, he had won a fleeting realization of the world's unity beneath "the one Spirit's plastic stress" which reminds us far less of Keats than of Shelley in his greater moments.

There is no century of English literature in which *A Song to David* might not have appeared more appropriately than in the eighteenth. Precisely those qualities of intensity, spermatic vigour, and audacious speed in which the time was most deficient are its most obvious strength. It is a great lyric composed in a period in which the lyric languished and all but died — a mighty song chanted fearlessly in the church of the world in a time which had forgotten how to sing.

To modern readers Smart's title is not prepossessing. He may have wished to round out, in lyric mode, the theme Cowley had left unfinished in his *Davideis*. The *Song* is the most important document in the contemporary effort, by no means restricted to English literature, to find in the Bible a substitute for the overworked fields of classic myth and legend — an effort in which Robert Lowth's important *Prœlectiones de Sacra Poesi Hebrœorum*, 1753, led the way. But David is hardly more than Smart's ostensible theme, chosen partly, it may be, as a healer of madness, and partly for the great range of his experience and consequent understanding, but chiefly because he, like his singer, was in all his error and weakness always a "God-intoxicated man" and always "instant in prayer." In the final analysis *A Song to David* is an attempt to express and communicate the glory of the mystic vision. Like every other such attempt, it was foredoomed to be regarded as mere raving by those to whom this vision is nonsense, but it is destined also to be treasured by a few in every generation as poetry of the highest order.

A SONG TO DAVID

ARGUMENT. Invocation, I–III. The excellence and lustre of David's character (in twelve points of view), proved from the history of his life, IV–XVI. He consecrates his genius for consolation and edification: — the subjects he made choice of — the Supreme Being — angels, men of renown, the works of nature in all directions, either particularly or collectively considered, XVII–XXVI. He obtains power over infernal spirits, and the malignity of his enemies; wins the heart of Michal, XXVII–XXIX. Shows that the pillars of knowledge are the monuments of God's works in the first week, XXX–XXXVII.

An exercise upon the Decalogue, XL–XLIX. The transcendent virtue of praise and adoration, L–LI. An exercise upon the seasons and the right use of them, LII–LXIII. An exercise upon the senses, and how to subdue them, LXIV–LXXI. An amplification in five degrees, which is wrought up to this conclusion: — that the best poet who ever lived, was thought worthy of the highest honour which possibly can be conceived, as the Saviour of the world was ascribed to his house, and called his son in the body, LXXII. The end.

O thou, that sitt'st upon a throne,
With harp of high, majestic tone,
  To praise the King of kings,
And voice of heaven-ascending swell,
Which, while its deeper notes excel,
  Clear as a clarion rings,

To bless each valley, grove, and coast,
And charm the cherubs to the post
  Of gratitude in throngs;
To keep the days on Zion's mount,
And send the year to his account
  With dances and with songs;

O servant of God's holiest *charge,
The minister of praise at large,
  Which thou mayst now receive;
From thy blest mansion hail and hear,
From topmost eminence appear
  To this the wreath I weave.

Great, valiant, pious, good, and clean,
Sublime, contemplative, serene,
  Strong, constant, pleasant, wise!
Bright effluence of exceeding grace;
Best man! the swiftness and the race,
  The peril and the prize!

Great — from the lustre of his crown,
From Samuel's *horn and God's renown,
  Which is the people's voice;
For all the host, from rear to van,
Applauded and embraced the man —
  The man of God's own choice.

Valiant — the word, and up he rose:
The fight — he triumphed o'er the foes
  Whom God's just laws abhor;
And, armed in gallant faith, he took
Against the boaster, from the brook,
  The weapons of the *war.

Pious — magnificent and grand,
'Twas he the famous temple *plann'd,
  The seraph in his soul;
Foremost to give his Lord his dues,

* Notes on Christopher Smart will be found in the Appendix, pp. 1019 ff.

Foremost to bless the welcome news,
And foremost to condole.

Good — from Jehudah's genuine *vein,
From God's best nature, good in *grain,
His aspect and his heart,
To pity, to forgive, to save, —
Witness En-gedi's conscious *cave,
And Shimei's blunted *dart.

Clean — if perpetual prayer be pure,
And love, which could itself inure
To fasting and to fear —
Clean in his gestures, hands, and feet,
To smite the lyre, the dance complete,
To play the sword and spear.

Sublime — invention ever young,
Of vast conception, tow'ring tongue,
To God the eternal theme;
Notes from yon exaltations caught,
Unrivall'd royalty of thought,
O'er meaner strains supreme.

Contemplative — on God to fix
His musings, and above the six
The Sabbath-day he blessed;
'Twas then his thoughts self-conquest prun'd,
And heavenly melancholy tun'd,
To bless and bear the rest.

Serene — to sow the seeds of peace,
Remembering, when he watched the fleece,
How sweetly *Kidron purled —
To further knowledge, silence vice,
And plant perpetual paradise,
When God had calm'd the world.

Strong — in the Lord, who could defy
Satan, and all his powers that lie
In sempiternal night;
And hell, and horror, and despair
Were as the lion and the *bear
To his undaunted might.

Constant — in love to God, the truth,
Age, manhood, infancy, and youth:
To Jonathan his friend
Constant, beyond the verge of death;
And Ziba and Mephibosheth
His endless fame *attend.

Pleasant — and various as the year;
Man, soul, and angel without peer,
Priest, champion, sage, and boy;
In armour or in *ephod clad,
His pomp, his piety was glad;
Majestic was his joy.

Wise — in recovery from his *fall,
Whence rose his eminence o'er all,
Of all the most reviled;
The light of Israel in his ways,
Wise are his precepts, prayer, and praise,
And counsel to his *child.

His Muse, bright angel of his verse,
Gives balm for all the thorns that pierce,
For all the pangs that rage;
Blest light, still gaining on the gloom,
The more than *Michal of his bloom,
The *Abishag of his age.

He *sung of God — the mighty source
Of all things, the stupendous force
On which all strength depends,
From whose right arm, beneath whose eyes,
All period, power, and enterprise
Commences, reigns, and ends;

Angels — their ministry and meed,
Which to and fro with blessings speed,
Or with their *citterns wait;
Where Michael with his millions bows,
Where dwells the seraph and his spouse
The cherub and her mate;

Of man — the semblance and effect
Of God and love, the saint elect
For infinite applause,
To rule the land, and briny broad,
To be laborious in *his laud,
And heroes in his cause;

The world — the clustering spheres he made,
The glorious light, the soothing shade,
Dale, champaign, grove, and hill;
The multitudinous abyss,
Where Secrecy remains in bliss,
And Wisdom hides her skill;

Trees, plants, and flowers — of *virtuous root;
*Gem yielding blossom, yielding fruit,
Choice gums and precious balm;
Bless ye the nosegay in the vale,
And with the sweetness of the gale
Enrich the thankful psalm;

Of fowl — e'en every beak and wing
Which cheer the winter, hail the spring,

That live in peace or prey;
They that make music, or that mock,
The quail, the brave domestic cock,
The raven, swan, and jay;

Of fishes — every size and shape,
Which nature frames of light escape
Devouring man to shun;
The shells are in the wealthy deep,
The *shoals upon the surface leap,
And love the glancing sun;

Of beasts — the beaver plods his task,
While the sleek tigers roll and bask,
Nor yet the shades arouse;
Her cave the mining *coney scoops;
Where o'er the mead the mountain stoops,
The kids exult and browse;

Of gems — their virtue and their price,
Which, hid in earth from man's *device,
Their darts of lustre sheathe;
The jasper of the master's stamp,
The topaz blazing like a lamp,
Among the mines beneath.

Blest was the tenderness he felt,
When to his graceful harp he knelt,
And did for audience call;
When Satan with his hand he quell'd,
And in serene suspense he held
The frantic throes of *Saul.

His furious foes no more malign'd
As he such melody divin'd,
And sense and soul detain'd;
Now striking strong, now soothing soft,
He sent the godly sounds aloft,
Or in delight refrain'd.

When up to heaven his thoughts he pil'd
From fervent lips fair Michal smil'd,
As blush to blush she *stood,
And chose herself the queen, and gave
Her utmost from her heart — "so brave,
And plays his hymns so good."

The pillars of the Lord are *seven,
Which stand from earth to topmost heaven;
His wisdom drew the plan;
His Word accomplished the design,
From brightest gem to deepest mine,
From Christ enthroned to man.

Alpha, the cause of causes, first
In station, fountain, whence the burst
Of light and blaze of day;
Whence bold attempt, and brave advance,
Have motion, life, and ordinance,
And heaven itself its stay.

Gamma supports the glorious arch
On which angelic legions march,
And is with sapphires pav'd;
Thence the fleet clouds are sent adrift,
And thence the painted folds that lift
The crimson veil, are wav'd.

Eta with living sculpture breathes,
With verdant carvings, flowery wreaths,
Of never-wasting bloom;
In strong relief his goodly base
All instruments of labour grace,
The trowel, spade, and loom.

Next Theta stands to the *Supreme —
Who formed in number, *sign, and scheme,
The illustrious lights that are;
And *one addressed his saffron robe,
And one clad in a silver globe,
Held rule with every star.

Iota's tun'd to choral hymns
Of those that fly, while he that swims
In thankful safety lurks;
And foot and chapiter and niche
The various histories enrich
Of God's recorded works.

Sigma presents the social droves,
With him that solitary roves,
And man of all the chief;
Fair on whose face and stately frame
Did God impress his hallowed name,
For ocular belief.

Omega! greatest and the best,
Stands sacred to the day of rest,
For gratitude and thought;
Which blessed the world upon his pole,
And gave the universe his goal,
And closed the infernal *draught.

O David, scholar of the Lord!
Such is thy science, whence reward,
And infinite *degree;
O strength, O sweetness, lasting, ripe!
God's harp thy symbol, and thy type
The lion and the *bee!

There is but One who ne'er rebelled,
But One by passion unimpelled,
By pleasures unenticed;
He from himself his semblance sent,
Grand object of his own content,
And saw the God in Christ.

"Tell them, I am," Jehovah said
To Moses; while earth heard in dread,
And, smitten to the heart,
At once above, beneath, around,
All nature, without voice or sound,
Replied, "O Lord, Thou art."

Thou art — to give and to confirm,
For each his talent and his term;
All flesh thy bounties share:
Thou shalt not call thy brother *fool;
The porches of the Christian school
Are meekness, peace, and prayer.

Open and naked of offence,
Man's made of mercy, soul, and sense;
God armed the snail and *wilk;
Be good to him that pulls thy plough;
Due food and care, due rest allow
For her that yields thee milk.

Rise up before the hoary head,
And God's benign commandment dread,
Which says thou shalt not die;
"Not as I will, but as thou *wilt,"
Prayed he whose conscience knew no guilt;
With whose bless'd pattern vie.

Use all thy passions! Love is thine,
And joy, and jealousy divine;
Thine hope's eternal fort,
And care, thy leisure to disturb,
With fear, concupiscence to curb,
And rapture, to transport.

Act simply, as occasion asks;
Put mellow wine in season'd casks;
Till not with ass and *bull;
Remember thy baptismal bond;
Keep from commixtures foul and fond,
Nor work thy flax with *wool.

Distribute; pay the Lord his tithe,
And make the widow's heartstrings blithe;
Resort with those that weep:
As you from all and each expect,
For all and each thy love direct,
And render as you reap.

The slander and its bearer spurn,
And propagating praise sojourn
To make thy welcome last;
Turn from old Adam to the New;
By hope futurity pursue;
Look upwards to the past.

Control thine eye, salute success,
Honour the wiser, happier bless,
And for their neighbour feel;
*Grutch not of Mammon and his leaven
Work emulation up to heaven
By knowledge and by zeal.

O David, highest in the list
Of worthies, on God's ways insist,
The genuine word repeat!
Vain are the documents of men,
And vain the flourish of the pen
That keeps the fool's conceit.

Praise above all — for praise prevails;
Heap up the measure, load the scales,
And good to goodness add.
The generous soul her Saviour aids,
But peevish obloquy degrades;
The Lord is great and glad.

For adoration all the ranks
Of angels yield eternal thanks,
And David in the midst:
With God's good poor, which, last and least
In man's esteem, thou to thy feast,
O blessèd Bridegroom, bidst.

For adoration seasons change,
And order, truth, and beauty range,
Adjust, attract, and fill:
The grass the polyanthus *checks,
And polish'd porphyry reflects
By the descending rill.

Rich almonds colour to the *prime
For adoration; tendrils climb,
And fruit trees pledge their *gems;
And *Ivis, with her gorgeous vest,
Builds for her eggs her cunning nest,
And *bell-flowers bow their stems.

With vinous syrup cedars spout;
From rocks pure honey gushing out,
For adoration springs:
All scenes of painting crowd the map
Of *nature; to the mermaid's pap
The scalèd infant clings.

The spotted ounce and playsome cubs
Run rustling 'mongst the flowering shrubs,
And lizards *feed the moss;
For adoration beasts *embark,
While waves upholding halcyon's *ark
No longer roar and toss.

While Israel sits beneath his *fig,
With coral root and amber sprig
The wean'd adventurer sports;
Where to the palm the jasmine cleaves,
For adoration 'mongst the leaves
The gale his peace reports.

Increasing days their reign exalt,
Nor in the pink and mottled vault
Th' opposing *spirits tilt;
And by the *coasting reader spied,
The *silverlings and *crusions glide
For adoration gilt.

For adoration ripening canes,
And cocoa's purest milk detains
The western pilgrim's staff;
Where rain in clasping boughs enclosed,
And vines with oranges disposed
Embower the social laugh.

Now labour his reward receives,
For adoration counts his sheaves,
To peace, her bounteous prince;
The nectarine his strong tint imbibes,
And apples of ten thousand tribes,
And quick peculiar quince.

The wealthy crops of whitening rice
'Mongst *thyine woods and groves of spice,
For adoration grow;
And, marshall'd in the fencèd land,
The peaches and pomegranates stand,
Where wild carnations blow.

The laurels with the winter strive;
The crocus burnishes alive
Upon the snow-clad earth;
For adoration myrtles stay
To keep the garden from dismay,
And bless the sight from dearth.

The pheasant shows his pompous neck;
And ermine, jealous of a speck,
With fear eludes offence:
The sable, with his glossy pride,
For adoration is descried,
Where frosts the wave condense.

The cheerful holly, pensive yew,
The holy *thorn, their trim renew;
The squirrel hoards his nuts;
All creatures batten o'er their stores,
And careful nature all her doors
For adoration shuts.

For adoration, David's Psalms
Lift up the heart to deeds of alms;
And he, who kneels and chants,
Prevails his passions to control,
Finds meat and medicine to the soul,
Which for *translation pants.

For adoration, beyond match,
The scholar *bullfinch aims to catch
The soft flute's ivory touch;
And, careless, on the hazel spray
The daring redbreast keeps at bay
The damsel's greedy clutch.

For adoration, in the skies,
The Lord's *philosopher espies
The dog, the ram, and rose,
The planet's *ring, Orion's sword;
Nor is his greatness less adored
In the vile worm that glows.

For adoration, on the *strings
The western breezes work their wings,
The captive ear to soothe —
Hark! 'tis a *voice — how still, and small —
That makes the cataracts to fall,
Or bids the sea be smooth!

For adoration, incense comes
From *bezoar, and Arabian gums,
And on the civet's *fur;
But as for prayer, or e'er it faints,
Far better is the breath of saints
Than *galbanum and myrrh.

For adoration, from the down
Of damsons to th' anana's *crown,
God sends to tempt the taste;
And while the luscious zest invites
The sense, that in the scene delights,
Commands desire be chaste.

For adoration, all the paths
Of grace are open, all the baths
Of purity refresh;
And all the rays of glory beam
To deck the man of God's esteem,
Who triumphs o'er the flesh.

For adoration, in the dome
Of Christ, the sparrows find an home;
And on his olives perch:
The swallow also dwells with thee,
O man of God's humility,
Within his Saviour's *Church.

Sweet is the dew that falls betimes,
And drops upon the leafy limes;
Sweet, Hermon's fragrant air:
Sweet is the lily's silver bell,
And sweet the wakeful tapers smell
That watch for early prayer.

Sweet the young nurse, with love intense,
Which smiles o'er sleeping innocence;
Sweet when the lost arrive;
Sweet the musician's ardour beats,
While his vague mind's in quest of sweets,
The choicest flowers to hive.

Sweeter, in all the strains of love,
The language of thy turtledove,
Pair'd to thy swelling chord;
Sweeter, with every grace endued,
The glory of thy gratitude
Respir'd unto the Lord.

Strong is the horse upon his *speed;
Strong in pursuit the rapid *glede,
Which makes at once his game:
Strong the tall ostrich on the ground;
Strong through the turbulent profound
Shoots *xiphias to his aim.

Strong is the lion — like a coal
His eyeball — like a bastion's *mole
His chest against the foes:
Strong the *gier-eagle on his sail,
Strong against tide th' enormous whale
Emerges as he goes.

But stronger still in earth and air,
And in the sea, the man of prayer,
And far beneath the tide:
And in the seat to faith assigned,
Where ask is have, where seek is find,
Where knock is open *wide.

Beauteous the fleet before the gale;
Beauteous the multitudes in mail,
Ranked arms, and crested heads;
Beauteous the garden's umbrage mild,
Walk, water, *meditated wild,
And all the bloomy beds.

Beauteous the moon full on the lawn;
And beauteous, when the veil's withdrawn,
The virgin to her spouse:
Beauteous the temple, decked and filled,
When to the heaven of heavens they build
Their heart-directed vows.

Beauteous, yea beauteous more than these,
The Shepherd King upon his knees,
For his momentous trust;
With wish of infinite *conceit,
For man, beast, mute, the small and great,
And prostrate *dust to dust.

Precious the bounteous widow's *mite;
And precious, for extreme delight,
The largess from the *churl:
Precious the ruby's blushing blaze,
And *alba's blest imperial rays,
And pure cerulean pearl.

Precious the penitential tear;
And precious is the sigh sincere;
Acceptable to God:
And precious are the winning flowers,
In gladsome Israel's feast of bowers,
Bound on the hallowed *sod.

More precious that diviner part
Of David, even the Lord's own *heart,
Great, beautiful, and new;
In all things where it was intent,
In all extremes, in each event,
Proof — answering true to true.

Glorious the sun in mid career;
Glorious th' assembled fires appear;
Glorious the comet's train:
Glorious the trumpet and alarm;
Glorious th' Almighty's stretched-out arm;
Glorious th' enraptured main:

Glorious the northern lights a-stream;
Glorious the song, when God's the theme;
Glorious the thunder's roar:
Glorious Hosannah from the *den;
Glorious the catholic amen;
Glorious the martyr's gore:

Glorious, — more glorious, is the crown
Of him that brought salvation down,
By meekness called thy Son:
Thou that stupendous truth believed; —
And now the matchless deed's achieved,
Determined, dared, and done.

[1763]

DAVID HUME

David Hume holds a large place in the history of thought: he was a philosopher second to none in England and among the most important in Europe, one of the first modern English historians, and a political theorist of unusual abilities. He had a clear mind and a power of close, logical thought that was ruthless in its criticism of every system which it scrutinized. Ideas interested him not only abstractly but as embodied in literary expression. Indeed, he declared shortly before his death that a passion for literature had been the ruling passion of his whole life and the chief source of his enjoyments.

His sceptical philosophy was clearly set forth in *A Treatise of Human Nature*, which was written when he was in his early twenties and was published in 1739–40. This book made almost no impression at first, but the *Essays Moral and Political*, which followed it, won him a measure of popular recognition. In these and later essays he applied his fundamental ideas to a variety of subjects, stimulating his readers by his brilliant analysis and shocking many of them by his destructive criticism. Though he was cautious enough to leave his most scathing attacks upon orthodox religion for posthumous publication, he was frequently denounced during his lifetime as an enemy of Christianity. Frequently his most heretical conclusions are expressed in words of unmistakable import but double meaning, as in the famous concluding paragraphs of the essay, "Of Miracles."

The selection that here represents Hume is the short treatise, "Of the Standard of Taste," in which he brings to bear his usual close reasoning and his searching examination upon a basic problem of criticism. His conclusions, which may well be compared with those of Addison in the *Spectator*, No. 409, illustrate the eighteenth-century establishment of classical teaching on universal human qualities rather than authority or prescriptive rule. Hume's style, though Dr. Johnson criticised the French manner of its sentence structure and gibed at its Scotticisms, has generally been admired for its clearness and effectiveness. Without attaining to the highest literary art, it is a good example of vigorous thinking and perspicuous expression.

OF THE STANDARD OF TASTE

The great variety of taste, as well as of opinion, which prevails in the world, is too obvious not to have fallen under every one's observation. Men of the most confined knowledge are able to remark a difference of taste in the narrow circle of their acquaintance, even where the persons have been educated under the same government and have early imbibed the same prejudices. But those who can enlarge their view to contemplate distant nations and remote ages are still more surprised at the great inconsistence and contrariety. We are apt to call *barbarous* whatever departs widely from our own taste and apprehension, but soon find the epithet of reproach retorted on us. And the highest arrogance and self-conceit is at last startled, on observing an equal assurance on all sides, and scruples, amidst such a contest of sentiment, to pronounce positively in its own favour.

As this variety of taste is obvious to the most careless inquirer, so will it be found, on examination, to be still greater in reality than in appearance. The sentiments of men often differ with regard to beauty and deformity of all kinds, even while their general discourse is the same. There are certain terms in every language which import blame, and others praise; and all men who use the same tongue must agree in their application of them. Every voice is united in applauding elegance, propriety, simplicity, spirit in writing, and in blaming fustian, affectation, coldness, and a false brilliancy. But when critics come to particulars, this seeming unanimity vanishes; and it is found that they had affixed a very different meaning to their expressions. In all matters of opinion and science, the case is opposite; the difference among men is there oftener found to lie in generals than in particulars, and to be less in reality than in appearance. An explanation of the terms commonly ends the controversy, and the disputants are surprised to find that they had been quarrelling while at bottom they agreed in their judgment.

Those who found morality on sentiment, more than on reason, are inclined to comprehend ethics under the former observation, and to maintain, that, in all questions which regard conduct and manners, the difference among men is really greater than at first sight it appears. It is indeed obvious that writers of all nations and all ages concur in applauding justice, humanity, magnanimity, prudence, veracity, and in blaming the opposite qualities. Even poets and other authors, whose compositions are chiefly calculated to please the imagination, are yet found, from Homer down to * Fénelon, to inculcate the same moral precepts, and to bestow their applause and blame on the same virtues and vices. This great unanimity is usually ascribed to the influence of plain reason, which, in all these cases, maintains similar sentiments in all men, and prevents those controversies to which the abstract sciences are so much exposed. So far as the unanimity is real, this account may be admitted as satisfactory. But we must also allow that some part of the seeming harmony in morals may be accounted for from the very nature of language. The word *virtue*, with its equivalent in every tongue, implies praise, as that of *vice* does blame; and no one, without the most obvious and grossest impropriety, could affix reproach to a term, which in general acceptation is understood in a good sense, or bestow applause where the idiom requires disapprobation. Homer's general precepts, where he delivers any such, will never be controverted; but it is obvious that when he draws particular pictures of manners, and represents heroism in Achilles and prudence in Ulysses, he intermixes a much greater degree of ferocity in the former and of cunning and fraud in the latter than Fénelon would admit of. The sage Ulysses, in the Greek poet, seems to delight in lies and fictions, and often employs them without any necessity, or even advantage. But his more scrupulous son, in the French epic writer, exposes himself to the most imminent perils, rather than depart from the most exact line of truth and veracity.

The admirers and followers of the Alcoran insist on the excellent moral precepts interspersed throughout that wild and absurd performance. But it is to be supposed that the Arabic words which correspond to the English *equity*, *justice*, *temperance*, *meekness*, *charity* were such as, from the constant use of that tongue, must always be taken in a good sense; and it would have argued the greatest ignorance, not of morals, but of language, to have mentioned them with any epithets, besides those of applause and approbation. But would we know whether the pretended prophet had really attained a just sentiment of morals, let us attend to his narration, and we shall soon find that he bestows praise on such instances of treachery, inhumanity, cruelty, revenge, bigotry, as are utterly incompatible with civilized society. No steady rule of right seems there to be attended to; and every action is blamed or praised, so far only as it is beneficial or hurtful to the true believers.

The merit of delivering true general precepts in ethics is indeed very small. Whoever recommends any moral virtues, really does no more than is implied in the terms themselves. That people who invented the word *charity*, and used it in a good sense, inculcated more clearly, and much more efficaciously, the precept, "Be charitable," than any pretended legislator or prophet who should insert such a maxim in his writings. Of all expressions, those which, together with their other meaning, imply a degree either of blame or approbation, are the least liable to be perverted or mistaken.

It is natural for us to seek a *standard of taste*, a rule by which the various sentiments of men may be reconciled, at least a decision afforded, confirming one sentiment and condemning another.

There is a species of philosophy which cuts off all hopes of success in such an attempt, and represents the impossibility of ever attaining any standard of taste. The difference, it is said, is very wide between judgment and sentiment. All sentiment is right; because sentiment has a reference to nothing beyond itself, and is always real, wherever a man is conscious of it. But all determinations of the understanding are not right; because they have a reference to something beyond themselves, to wit, real matter of fact, and are not always conformable to that standard. Among a thousand different opinions which different men may entertain of the same subject, there is one, and but one, that is just and true; and the only difficulty is to fix and ascertain it. On the contrary, a thousand different sentiments, excited by the same object, are all right, because no sentiment represents what is really in the object. It only marks a certain conformity or relation between the object and the organs or faculties of the mind; and if that conformity did not really exist, the sentiment could never possibly have being. Beauty is no quality in things themselves: it exists merely in the mind which contemplates them:

* Notes on David Hume will be found in the Appendix, pp. 1021 ff.

and each mind perceives a different beauty. One person may even perceive deformity, where another is sensible of beauty; and every individual ought to acquiesce in his own sentiment, without pretending to regulate those of others. To seek the real beauty, or real deformity, is as fruitless an inquiry as to pretend to ascertain the real sweet or real bitter. According to the disposition of the organs, the same object may be both sweet and bitter, and the proverb has justly determined it to be fruitless to dispute concerning tastes. It is very natural, and even quite necessary, to extend this axiom to mental as well as bodily taste; and thus common sense, which is so often at variance with philosophy, especially with the skeptical kind, is found in one instance at least to agree in pronouncing the same decision.

But though this axiom, by passing into a proverb, seems to have attained the sanction of common sense, there is certainly a species of common sense which opposes it, at least serves to modify and restrain it. Whoever would assert an equality of genius and elegance between *Ogilby and Milton, or *Bunyan and Addison, would be thought to defend no less an extravagance than if he had maintained a molehill to be as high as Teneriffe, or a pond as extensive as the ocean. Though there may be found persons who give the preference to the former authors, no one pays attention to such a taste; and we pronounce without scruple the sentiment of these pretended critics to be absurd and ridiculous. The principle of the natural equality of tastes is then totally forgot, and while we admit it on some occasions, where the objects seem near an equality, it appears an extravagant paradox, or rather a palpable absurdity, where objects so disproportioned are compared together.

It is evident that none of the rules of composition are fixed by reasonings *a priori*, or can be esteemed abstract conclusions of the understanding, from comparing those habitudes and relations of ideas which are eternal and immutable. Their foundation is the same with that of all the practical sciences, experience; nor are they anything but general observations concerning what has been universally found to please in all countries and in all ages. Many of the beauties of poetry and even of eloquence are founded on falsehood and fiction, on hyperboles, metaphors, and an abuse or perversion of terms from their natural meaning. To check the sallies of the imagination, and to reduce every expression to geometrical truth and exactness, would be the most contrary to the laws of criticism, because it would produce a work which, by universal experience, has been found the most insipid and disagreeable. But though poetry can never submit to exact truth, it must be confined by rules of art, discovered to the author either by genius or observation. If some negligent or irregular writers have pleased, they have not pleased by their transgressions of rule or order, but in spite of these transgressions; they have possessed other beauties, which were conformable to just criticism, and the force of these beauties has been able to overpower censure, and give the mind a satisfaction superior to the disgust arising from the blemishes. Ariosto pleases, but not by his monstrous and improbable fictions, by his bizarre mixture of the serious and comic styles, by the want of coherence in his stories, or by the continual interruptions of his narration. He charms by the force and clearness of his expression, by the readiness and variety of his inventions, and by his natural pictures of the passions, especially those of the gay and amorous kind; and however his faults may diminish our satisfaction, they are not able entirely to destroy it. Did our pleasure really arise from those parts of his poem which we denominate faults, this would be no objection to criticism in general; it would only be an objection to those particular rules of criticism which would establish such circumstances to be faults, and would represent them as universally blamable. If they are found to please, they cannot be faults, let the pleasure which they produce be ever so unexpected and unaccountable.

But though all the general rules of art are founded only on experience, and on the observation of the common sentiments of human nature, we must not imagine that, on every occasion, the feelings of men will be conformable to these rules. Those finer emotions of the mind are of a very tender and delicate nature, and require the concurrence of many favourable circumstances to make them play with facility and exactness, according to their general and established principles. The least exterior hinderance to such small springs, or the least internal disorder, disturbs their motion, and confounds the operation of the whole machine. When we would make an experiment of this nature, and would try the force of any beauty or deformity, we must choose with care a proper time and place, and bring the fancy to a suitable situation and disposition. A perfect serenity of mind, a recollection of thought, a due attention to the object; if any of these circumstances be wanting, our experiment will be fallacious, and we shall be unable to judge of the catholic and universal beauty. The relation which nature has placed between the form and the sentiment will at least be more obscure, and it will require greater accuracy to trace and discern it. We shall be able to ascertain its influence, not so much from the operation of each particular beauty, as from the durable admiration which attends those works that have survived all the caprices of mode and fashion, all the mistakes of ignorance and envy.

The same Homer who pleased at Athens and Rome two thousand years ago, is still admired at Paris and at London. All the changes of climate, government, religion, and language have not been able to obscure his glory. Authority or prejudice may give a temporary vogue to a bad poet or orator, but his reputation will never be durable or general. When his compositions are examined by posterity or by foreigners, the enchantment is dissipated, and his faults appear in their true colours. On the contrary, a real genius, the longer his works endure, and the more wide they are spread, the more sincere is the admiration which he meets with. Envy and jealousy have too much place in a narrow circle, and even familiar acquaintance with his person may diminish the applause due to his performances: but when these obstructions are removed, the beauties, which are naturally fitted to excite agreeable sentiments, immediately display their energy; and, while the world endures, they maintain their authority over the minds of men.

It appears, then, that, amidst all the variety and caprice of taste, there are certain general principles of approbation or blame, whose influence a careful eye may trace in all operations of the mind. Some particular forms or qualities, from the original structure of the internal fabric, are calculated to please, and others to displease; and if they fail of their effect in any particular instance, it is from some apparent defect or imperfection in the organ. A man in a fever would not insist on his palate as able to decide concerning flavours, nor would one affected with the jaundice pretend to give a verdict with regard to colours. In each creature there is a sound and a defective state, and the former alone can be supposed to afford us a true standard of taste and sentiment. If, in the sound state of the organ, there be an entire or a considerable uniformity of sentiment among men, we may thence derive an idea of the perfect beauty; in like manner as the appearance of objects in daylight, to the eye of a man in health, is denominated their true and real colour, even while colour is allowed to be merely a phantasm of the senses.

Many and frequent are the defects in the internal organs, which prevent or weaken the influence of those general principles on which depends our sentiment of beauty or deformity. Though some objects, by the structure of the mind, be naturally calculated to give pleasure, it is not to be expected that in every individual the pleasure will be equally felt. Particular incidents and situations occur, which either throw a false light on the objects or hinder the true from conveying to the imagination the proper sentiment and perception.

One obvious cause why many feel not the proper sentiment of beauty is the want of that delicacy of imagination which is requisite to convey a sensibility of those finer emotions. This delicacy every one pretends to; every one talks of it, and would reduce every kind of taste or sentiment to its standard. But as our intention in this essay is to mingle some light of the understanding with the feelings of sentiment, it will be proper to give a more accurate definition of delicacy than has hitherto been attempted. And not to draw our philosophy from too profound a source, we shall have recourse to a noted story in *Don Quixote*.

"It is with good reason," says Sancho to the squire with the great nose, "that I pretend to have a judgment in wine; this is a quality hereditary in our family. Two of my kinsmen were once called to give their opinion of a hogshead which was supposed to be excellent, being old and of a good vintage. One of them tastes it, considers it, and, after mature reflection, pronounces the wine to be good, were it not for a small taste of leather which he perceived in it. The other, after using the same precautions, gives also his verdict in favour of the wine, but with the reserve of a taste of iron which he could easily distinguish. You cannot imagine how much they were both ridiculed for their judgment. But who laughed in the end? On emptying the hogshead, there was found at the bottom an old key with a leathern thong tied to it."

The great resemblance between mental and bodily taste will easily teach us to apply this story. Though it be certain that beauty and deformity, more than sweet and bitter, are not qualities in objects, but belong entirely to the sentiment, internal or external, it must be allowed that there are certain qualities in objects which are fitted by nature to produce those particular feelings. Now, as these qualities may be found in a small degree, or may be mixed and confounded with each other, it often happens that the taste is not affected with such minute qualities, or is not able to distinguish all the particular flavours, amidst the disorder in which they are presented. Where the organs are so fine as to allow nothing to escape them, and at the same time so exact as to perceive every ingredient in the composition, this we call delicacy of taste, whether we employ these terms in the literal or metaphorical sense. Here then the general rules of beauty are of use, being drawn from established models, and from the observation of what pleases or displeases, when presented singly and in a high degree; and if the same qualities, in a continued composition and in a smaller degree, affect not the organs with a sensible delight or uneasiness, we exclude the person from all pretensions to this delicacy. To produce these general rules or avowed patterns of composition is like finding the key with the leathern thong, which justified the verdict of Sancho's kinsmen, and confounded those pretended judges who had condemned them. Though the hogshead had never been emptied, the taste of the one was still equally delicate, and that of the other equally dull and languid; but it would have been more difficult to have proved the superiority of the former to the conviction of every bystander. In like manner, though the beauties of writing had never been methodized or reduced to general principles, though no excellent models had ever been acknowledged, the different degrees of taste would still have subsisted, and the judgment of one man been preferable to that of another; but it would not have been so easy to silence the bad critic, who might always insist upon his particular sentiment, and refuse to submit to his antagonist. But when we show him an avowed principle of art; when we illustrate this principle by examples whose operation, from his own particular taste, he acknowledges to be conformable to the principle; when we prove that the same principle may be applied to the present case, where he did not perceive or feel its influence, — he must conclude, upon the whole, that the fault lies in himself, and that he wants the delicacy which is requisite to make him sensible of every beauty and every blemish in any composition or discourse.

It is acknowledged to be the perfection of every sense or faculty, to perceive with exactness its most minute objects, and allow nothing to escape its notice and observation. The smaller the objects are which become sensible to the eye, the finer is that organ, and the more elaborate its make and composition. A good palate is not tried by strong flavours, but by a mixture of small ingredients, where we are still sensible of each part, notwithstanding its minuteness and its confusion with the rest. In like manner, a quick and acute perception of beauty and deformity must be the perfection ot our mental taste; nor can a man be satisfied with himself while he suspects that any excellence or blemish in a discourse has passed him unobserved. In this case the perfection of the man, and the perfection of the sense of feeling, are found to be united. A very delicate palate, on many occasions, may be a great inconvenience both to a man himself and to his friends. But a delicate taste of wit or beauty must always be a desirable quality, because it is the source of all the finest and most innocent enjoyments of which human nature is susceptible. In this decision the sentiments of all mankind are agreed. Wherever you can ascertain a delicacy of taste, it is sure to meet with approbation; and the best way of ascertaining it is to appeal to those models and principles which have been established by the uniform consent and experience of nations and ages.

But though there be naturally a wide difference, in point of delicacy, between one person and another, nothing tends further to increase and improve this talent than practice in a particular art, and the frequent survey or contemplation of a particular species of beauty. When objects of any kind are first presented to the eye or imagination the sentiment which attends them is obscure and confused; and the mind is, in a great measure, incapable of pronouncing concerning their merits or defects. The taste cannot perceive the several excellences of the performance, much less distinguish the particular character of each excellency, and ascertain its quality and degree. If it pronounce the whole in general to be beautiful or deformed, it is the utmost that can be expected; and even this judgment, a person so unpractised will be apt to deliver with great hesitation and reserve. But allow him to acquire experience in those objects, his feeling becomes more exact and nice; he not only perceives the beauties and defects of each part, but marks the distinguishing species of each quality, and assigns it suitable praise or blame. A clear and distinct sentiment attends him through the whole survey of the objects; and he discerns that very degree and kind of approbation or displeasure which each part is naturally fitted to produce. The mist dissipates which seemed formerly to hang over the object; the organ acquires greater perfection in its operations, and can pronounce, without danger of mistake, concerning the merits of every performance. In a word, the same address and dexterity which practice gives to the execution of any work, is also acquired by the same means in the judging of it.

So advantageous is practice to the discernment of beauty that, before we can give judgment on any work of importance, it will even be requisite that that very individual performance be more than once perused by us, and be surveyed in different lights with attention and deliberation. There is a flutter or hurry of thought which attends the first perusal of any piece, and which confounds the genuine sentiment of beauty. The relation of the parts is not discerned; the true characters of style are little distinguished. The several perfections and defects seem wrapped up in a species of confusion, and present themselves indistinctly to the imagination. Not to mention that there is a species of beauty, which, as it is florid and superficial, pleases at first; but being found incompatible with a just expression either of reason or passion, soon palls upon the taste, and is then rejected with disdain, at least rated at a much lower value.

It is impossible to continue in the practice of contemplating any order of beauty, without being frequently obliged to form comparisons between the several species and degrees of excellence, and estimating their proportion to each other. A man who has had no opportunity of comparing the different kinds of beauty is indeed totally unqualified to pronounce an opinion with regard to any object presented to him. By comparison alone we fix the epithets of praise or blame, and learn how to assign the due degree of each. The coarsest daubing contains a certain lustre of colours and exactness of imitation, which are so far beauties, and would affect the mind of a peasant or Indian with the highest admiration. *The most vulgar ballads are not entirely destitute of harmony or nature; and none but a person familiarized to superior beauties would pronounce their numbers harsh, or narration uninteresting. A great inferiority of beauty gives pain to a person conversant in the highest excellence of the kind, and is for that reason pronounced a deformity; as the most finished object with which we are acquainted is naturally supposed to have reached the pinnacle of perfection, and to be entitled to the highest applause. One accustomed to sec, and examine, and weigh the several performances, admired in different ages and nations, can alone rate the merits of a work exhibited to his view, and assign its proper rank among the productions of genius.

But to enable a critic the more fully to execute this undertaking, he must preserve his mind free from all prejudice, and allow nothing to enter into his consideration but the very object which is submitted to his examination. We may observe that every work of art, in order to produce its due effect on the mind, must be surveyed in a certain point of view, and cannot be fully relished by persons whose situation, real or imaginary, is not conformable to that which is required by the performance. An orator addresses himself to a particular audience, and must have a regard to their particular genius, interests, opinions, passions, and prejudices; otherwise he hopes in vain to govern their resolutions, and inflame their affections. Should they even have entertained some prepossessions against him, however unreasonable, he must not overlook this disadvantage; but, before he enters upon the subject, must endeavour to conciliate their affection, and acquire their good graces. A critic of a different age or nation, who should peruse this discourse, must have all these circumstances in his eye, and must place himself in the same situation as the audience, in order to form a true judgment of the oration. In like manner, when any work is addressed to the public, though I should have a friendship or enmity with the author, I must depart from this situation, and, considering myself as a man in general, forget, if possible, my individual being and my peculiar circumstances. A person influenced by prejudice complies not with this condition, but obstinately maintains his natural position, without placing himself in that point of view which the performance supposes. If the work be addressed to persons of a different age or nation, he makes no allowance for their peculiar views and prejudices; but, full of the manners of his own age and country, rashly condemns what seemed admirable in the eyes of those for whom alone the discourse was calculated. If the work be executed for the public, he never sufficiently enlarges his comprehension, or forgets his interest as a friend or enemy, as a rival or commentator. By this means his sentiments are perverted; nor have the same beauties and blemishes the same influence upon him, as if he had imposed a proper violence on his imagination, and had forgotten himself for a moment. So far his taste evidently departs from the true standard, and of consequence loses all credit and authority.

It is well known that, in all questions submitted to the understanding, prejudice is destructive of sound judgment, and perverts all operations of the intellectual faculties: it is no less contrary to good taste; nor has it less influence to corrupt our sentiment of beauty. It belongs to good sense to check its influence in both cases; and in this respect, as well as in many others, reason, if not an essential part of taste, is at least requisite to the operations of this latter faculty. In all the nobler productions of genius there is a mutual relation and correspondence of parts; nor can either the beauties or blemishes be perceived by him whose thought is not capacious enough to comprehend all those parts, and compare them with each other, in order to perceive the consistence and uniformity of the whole. Every work of art has also a certain end or purpose for which it is calculated; and is to be deemed more or less perfect, as it is more or less fitted to attain this end. The object of eloquence is to persuade, of history to instruct, of poetry to please, by means of the passions and the imagination. These ends we must carry constantly in our view when we peruse any performance; and we must be able to judge how far the means employed are adapted to their respective purposes. Besides, every kind of composition, even the most poetical, is nothing but a chain of propositions and reasonings; not always, indeed, the justest and most exact, but still plausible and specious, however disguised by the colouring of the imagination. The persons introduced in tragedy and epic poetry must be represented as reasoning and thinking and concluding and acting, suitably to their character and circumstances; and without judgment, as well as taste and invention, a poet can never hope to succeed in so delicate an undertaking. Not to mention that the same excellence of faculties which contributes to the improvement of reason, the same clearness of conception, the same exactness of distinction, the same vivacity of apprehension, are essential to the operations of true taste, and are its infallible concomitants. It seldom or never happens that a man of sense, who has experience in any art, cannot judge of its beauty; and it is no less rare to meet with a man who has a just taste without a sound understanding.

Thus, though the principles of taste be universal, and nearly, if not entirely, the same in all men, yet few are qualified to give judgment on any work of art, or establish their own sentiment as the standard of beauty. The organs of internal sensation are seldom so perfect as to allow the general principles their full play, and produce a feeling correspondent to those principles. They either labour under some defect, or are vitiated by some disorder; and by that means excite a sentiment which may be pronounced erroneous. When the critic has no delicacy, he judges without any distinction, and is only affected by the grosser and more palpable qualities of the object; the finer touches pass unnoticed and disregarded. Where he is not aided by practice, his verdict is attended with confusion and hesitation. Where no comparison has been employed, the most frivolous beauties, such as rather merit the name of defects, are the object of his admiration. Where he lies under the influence of prejudice, all his natural sentiments are perverted. Where good sense is wanting, he is not qualified to discern the beauties of design and reasoning, which are the highest and most excellent. Under some or other of these imperfections the generality of men labour, and hence a true judge in the finer arts is observed, even during the most polished ages, to be so rare a character. Strong sense, united to delicate sentiment, improved by practice, perfected by comparison, and cleared of all prejudice, can alone entitle critics to this valuable character; and the joint verdict of such, wherever they are to be found, is the true standard of taste and beauty.

But where are such critics to be found? By what marks are they to be known? How distinguish them from pretenders? These questions are embarrassing; and seem to throw us back into the same uncertainty from which, during the course of this essay, we have endeavoured to extricate ourselves.

But if we consider the matter aright, these are questions of fact, not of sentiment. Whether any particular person be endowed with good sense and a delicate imagination, free from prejudice, may often be the subject of dispute, and be liable to great discussion and inquiry; but that such a character is valuable and estimable will be agreed in by all mankind. Where these doubts occur, men can do no more than in other disputable questions which are submitted to the understanding: they must produce the best arguments that their invention suggests to them; they must acknowledge a true and decisive standard to exist somewhere, to wit, real existence and matter of fact; and they must have indulgence to such as differ from them in their appeals to this standard. It is sufficient for our present purpose if we have proved that the taste of all individuals is not upon an equal footing, and that some men in general, however difficult to be particularly pitched upon, will be acknowledged by universal sentiment to have a preference above others.

But, in reality, the difficulty of finding, even in particulars, the standard of taste, is not so great as it is represented. Though in speculation we may readily avow a certain criterion in science, and deny it in sentiment, the matter is found in practice to be much more hard to ascertain in the former case than in the latter. Theories of abstract philosophy, systems of profound theology, have prevailed during one age; in a successive period these have been universally exploded; their absurdity has been detected; other theories and systems have supplied their place, which again gave place to their successors: and nothing has been experienced more liable to the revolutions of chance and fashion than these pretended decisions of science. The case is not the same with the beauties of eloquence and poetry. Just expressions of passion and nature are sure, after a little time, to gain public applause, which they maintain forever. Aristotle and Plato and Epicurus and Descartes, may successively yield to each other; but Terence and Virgil maintain an universal, undisputed empire over the minds of men. The abstract philosophy of Cicero has lost its credit; the vehemence of his oratory is still the object of our admiration.

Though men of delicate taste be rare, they are easily to be distinguished in society by the soundness of their understanding, and the superiority of their faculties above the rest of mankind. The ascendant which they acquire gives a prevalence to that lively approbation with which they receive any productions of genius, and renders it generally predominant. Many men, when left to themselves, have but a faint and dubious perception of beauty, who yet are capable of relishing any fine stroke which is pointed out to them. Every convert to the admiration of the real poet or orator is the cause of some new conversion. And though prejudices may prevail for a time, they never unite in celebrating any rival to the true genius, but yield at last to the force of nature and just sentiment. Thus, though a civilized nation may easily be mistaken in the choice of their admired philosopher, they never have been found long to err in their affection for a favourite epic or tragic author.

But notwithstanding all our endeavours to fix a standard of taste, and reconcile the discordant apprehensions of men, there still remain two sources of variation, which are not sufficient indeed to confound all the boundaries of beauty and deformity, but will often serve to produce a difference in the degrees of our approbation or blame. The one is the different humours of particular men; the other, the particular manners and opinions of our age and country. The general principles of taste are uniform in human nature: where men vary in their judgments, some defect or perversion in the faculties may commonly be remarked, proceeding either from prejudice, from want of practice, or want of delicacy; and there is just reason for approving one taste and condemning another. But where there is such a diversity in the internal frame or external situation as is entirely blameless on both sides, and leaves no room to give one the preference above the other; in that case a certain degree of diversity in judgment is unavoidable, and we seek in vain for a standard by which we can reconcile the contrary sentiments.

A young man, whose passions are warm, will be more sensibly touched with amorous and tender images than a man more advanced in years, who takes pleasure in wise, philosophical reflections concerning the conduct of life and moderation of the passions. At twenty, Ovid may be the favourite author, Horace at forty, and perhaps Tacitus at fifty. Vainly would we, in such cases, endeavour to enter into the sentiments of others, and divest ourselves of those propensities which are natural to us. We choose our favourite author as we do our friend, from a conformity of humour and disposition. Mirth or passion, sentiment or reflection; whichever of these most predominates in our temper, it gives us a peculiar sympathy with the writer who resembles us.

One person is more pleased with the sublime, another with the tender, a third with raillery. One has a strong sensibility to blemishes, and is extremely studious of correctness; another has a more lively feeling of beauties, and pardons twenty absurdities and defects for one elevated or pathetic stroke. The ear of this man is entirely turned towards conciseness and energy; that man is delighted with a copious, rich, and harmonious expression. Simplicity is affected by one; ornament by another. Comedy, tragedy, satire, odes have each its partisans, who prefer that particular species of writing to all others. It is plainly an error in a critic to confine his approbation to one species or style of writing, and condemn all the rest. But it is almost impossible not to feel a predilection for that which suits our particular turn and disposition. Such preferences are innocent and unavoidable, and can never reasonably be the object of dispute, because there is no standard by which they can be decided.

For a like reason we are more pleased, in the course of our reading, with pictures and characters that resemble objects which are found in our own age or country than with those which describe a different set of customs. It is not without some effort that we reconcile ourselves to the simplicity of ancient manners, and behold princesses carrying water from the spring, and kings and heroes dressing their own victuals. We may allow in general that the representation of such manners is no fault in the author, nor deformity in the piece; but we are not so sensibly touched with them. For this reason, comedy is not easily transferred from one age or nation to another. A Frenchman or Englishman is not pleased with the *Andria* of Terence, or * *Clitia* of Machiavel; where the fine lady, upon whom all the play turns, never once appears to the spectators, but is always kept behind the scenes, suitably to the reserved humour of the ancient Greeks and modern Italians. A man of learning and reflection can make allowance for these peculiarities of manners; but a common audience can never divest themselves so far of their usual ideas and sentiments, as to relish pictures which nowise resemble them.

But here there occurs a reflection, which may, perhaps, be useful in examining the celebrated controversy concerning ancient and modern learning; where we often find the one side excusing any seeming absurdity in the ancients from the manners of the age, and the other refusing to admit this excuse, or at least admitting it only as an apology for the author, not for the performance. In my opinion, the proper boundaries in this subject have seldom been fixed between the contending parties. Where any innocent peculiarities of manners are represented, such as those above mentioned, they ought certainly to be admitted; and a man who is shocked with them gives an evident proof of false delicacy and refinement. The poet's "monument more durable than brass," must fall to the ground like common brick or clay, were men to make no allowance for the continual revolutions of manners and customs, and would admit of nothing but what was suitable to the prevailing fashion. Must we throw aside the pictures of our ancestors, because of their ruffs and farthingales? But where the ideas of morality and decency alter from one age to another, and where vicious manners are described, without being marked with the proper characters of blame and disapprobation, this must be allowed to disfigure the poem, and to be a real deformity. I cannot, nor is it proper I should, enter into such sentiments; and however I may excuse the poet on account of the manners of his age, I can never relish the composition. The want of humanity and of decency, so conspicuous in the characters drawn by several of the ancient poets, even sometimes by Homer and the

Greek tragedians, diminishes considerably the merit of their noble performances, and gives modern authors an advantage over them. We are not interested in the fortunes and sentiments of such rough heroes; we are displeased to find the limits of vice and virtue so much confounded; and whatever indulgence we may give to the writer on account of his prejudices, we can not prevail on ourselves to enter into his sentiments, or bear an affection to characters which we plainly discover to be blamable.

The case is not the same with moral principles as with speculative opinions of any kind. These are in continual flux and revolution. The son embraces a different system from the father. Nay, there scarcely is any man who can boast of great constancy and uniformity in this particular. Whatever speculative errors may be found in the polite writings of any age or country, they detract but little from the value of those compositions. There needs but a certain turn of thought or imagination to make us enter into all the opinions which then prevailed, and relish the sentiments or conclusions derived from them. But a very violent effort is requisite to change our judgment of manners, and excite sentiments of approbation or blame, love or hatred, different from those to which the mind, from long custom, has been familiarized. And where a man is confident of the rectitude of that moral standard by which he judges, he is justly jealous of it,—and will not pervert the sentiments of his heart for a moment, in complaisance to any writer whatsoever.

*Of all speculative errors, those which regard religion are the most excusable in compositions of genius; nor is it ever permitted to judge of the civility or wisdom of any people, or even of single persons, by the grossness or refinement of their theological principles. The same good sense that directs men in the ordinary occurrences of life, is not hearkened to in religious matters, which are supposed to be placed altogether above the cognizance of human reason. On this account all the absurdities of the Pagan system of theology must be overlooked by every critic who would pretend to form a just notion of ancient poetry; and our posterity, in their turn, must have the same indulgence to their forefathers. No religious principles can ever be imputed as a fault to any poet, while they remain merely principles, and take not such strong possession of his heart as to lay him under the imputation of bigotry or superstition. Where that happens, they confound the sentiments of morality, and alter the natural boundaries of vice and virtue. They are therefore eternal blemishes, according to the principle above mentioned; nor are the prejudices and false opinions of the age sufficient to justify them.

It is essential to the Roman Catholic religion to inspire a violent hatred of every other worship, and to represent all Pagans, Mahometans, and heretics as the objects of divine wrath and vengeance. Such sentiments, though they are in reality very blamable, are considered as virtues by the zealots of that communion, and are represented in their tragedies and epic poems as a kind of divine heroism. This bigotry has disfigured two very fine tragedies of the French theatre *Polyeucte* and *Athalie*; where an intemperate zeal for particular modes of worship is set off with all the pomp imaginable, and forms the predominant character of the heroes. "What is this?" says the sublime Joad to Josabet, finding her in discourse with Mathan the priest of Baal; "Does the daughter of David speak to this traitor? Are you not afraid lest the earth should open, and pour forth flames to devour you both! Or lest these holy walls should fall and crush you together? What is his purpose? Why comes that enemy of God hither to poison the air which we breathe with his horrid presence?" Such sentiments are received with great applause on the theatre of Paris; but at London the spectators would be full as much pleased to hear Achilles tell Agamemnon that he was a dog in his forehead, and a deer in his heart, or Jupiter threaten Juno with a sound drubbing, if she will not be quiet.

Religious principles are also a blemish in any polite composition, when they rise up to superstition, and intrude themselves into every sentiment, however remote from any connection with religion. It is no excuse for the poet that the customs of his country had burdened life with so many religious ceremonies and observances that no part of it was exempt from that yoke. It must forever be ridiculous in Petrarch to compare his mistress, Laura, to Jesus Christ. Nor is it less ridiculous in that agreeable libertine, Boccace, very seriously to give thanks to God Almighty and the ladies, for their assistance in defending him against his enemies.

[1757]

PHILIP DORMER STANHOPE, EARL OF CHESTERFIELD

Philip Dormer Stanhope, Lord Chesterfield, is still remembered as "the glass of fashion and the mould of form"; his example has enriched the language with the adjective "Chesterfieldian"; and in America, a century and a half after his death, his name is familiar to multitudes who are ignorant of his contemporaries. Curiously enough, he owes his fame quite as much to his detractors as to his admirers, for both have granted him pre-eminence in grace and elegance and worldly wisdom. Balancing these qualities and setting them off by contrast, insincerity, heartlessness, and immorality have been attributed to him by adverse critics. The public has accepted this grouping of complementary qualities as appropriate, thus giving just the spice of scandal required to add piquancy to the Chesterfield legend.

Though Lord Chesterfield was ambassador to Holland where he conducted important diplomatic negotiations with great skill, Lord Lieutenant of Ireland where he made an enviable reputation as an executive, and Secretary of State, his tenure of these important offices was shorter than his abilities appeared to warrant. In February, 1746, when he was fifty-three years of age, he retired from public office; thenceforth, except for attendance in the House of Lords, he took no official part in state affairs. While his speeches have not been preserved, we know that his associates regarded him as an orator of unusual ability. As a wit he was famous in a generation of wits. His literary taste and his social prestige were acknowledged. He was the great Lord Chesterfield, whose patronage Johnson sought for his *Dictionary*. Such a man was, of course, a literary amateur rather than a professional author.

Chesterfield had an illegitimate son, the result of an *amour* with Mlle. du Bouchet, while he was ambassador at the Hague before his marriage. Since he had no legitimate children, he took a keen interest in this son, bestowed upon him his own name, Philip Stanhope, and gave him the best possible education to fit him for the diplomatic service. The boy attended the Westminster School; and, when he was about fourteen, in 1746, he embarked upon the grand tour, in the course of which he visited Germany, Italy, and France, familiarizing himself with the language and society of each. His tutor, Walter Harte, was an Oxford graduate, the author of several books, a worthy but somewhat pedantic individual. His father secured the boy's admission to the best society in each of the places visited.

From the time that Philip was five years of age, the earl wrote to him frequently, giving him advice about his studies and especially, as the lad grew older, about those social graces which belong to the education of a gentleman. In spite of the care expended upon his education, the boy disappointed his father; he became a decent, hopelessly commonplace man, notably deficient in those qualities upon which the earl had laid constant emphasis. He held minor diplomatic posts and died abroad in 1768, when he was about thirty-six. Only then did the news transpire that he had been secretly married for some years to an undistinguished woman by whom he had two sons. Shortly after Chesterfield's death, in 1773, his son's widow added to her resources by selling for £1575 the letters which had been addressed by the earl to Philip Stanhope. They were an immediate success, three editions appearing in 1774, and eleven editions being published by 1800.

Chesterfield's *Letters to his Son* are a series of 431 letters written over a period of more than thirty years; they are for the most part in English, though a considerable number are in French and a few in Latin. Their principal subject is education, especially social education; they seldom speak of religion (that seems to have been left to the care of Mr. Harte), though they assume a fashionable acquiescence in the forms of the Anglican Church. Their ethics are not Christian morality but the artificial code of the gentleman. Dr. Johnson, who, in addition to being an uncompromising moralist, probably bore some malice concerning a little matter of the dedication to his *Dictionary*, has branded the *Letters* for all time with the epigram: "They teach the morals of a whore and the manners of a dancing-master." In reality they do neither; they teach the morals and the manners of a man of the world. About both Chesterfield wrote from a point of view that is more common in France than in England, with Gallic directness and Gallic abhorrence of pretence. That a father should counsel his son against crude debauchery, yet speak with tolerance and even approbation of intrigues with ladies of fashion, is shocking to English ears. Chesterfield, it must be remembered, was not writing for publication; he was advising a son whom he knew to be deficient in the graces. His primary concern was to warn that son against his besetting sins of crudeness and vulgarity. Consciously, and probably with a sense of the contradiction involved, the earl tried to avoid the usual tone of father-and-son correspondence by writing as one man of the world to another. He tried to teach manners, decorum, restraint, to counsel against the excesses of the clown, the pedant, the fop, to produce neither the trifler nor the professional, but the gentleman amateur, *l'honnête homme qui ne se pique de rien.* Rightly understood, there is more of the classical spirit in Chesterfield's *Letters* than in most English documents of the eighteenth century. The gentleman who is here held up to view as an ideal would have been at home in the court of Augustus, or of Louis XIV. Even Johnson bore testimony to the value of the work when he said, "Lord Chesterfield's *Letters to his Son*, I think might be made a very pretty book. Take out the immorality, and it should be put into the hands of every young gentleman." And again, apropos of the same subject, "Every man of any education would rather be called a rascal than accused of deficiency in the graces."

LETTERS TO HIS SON

LETTER CXLII

BATH, *February* 22, O.S. 1748

Dear Boy: Every excellency and every virtue has its kindred vice or weakness, and, if carried beyond certain bounds, sinks into one or the other. Generosity often runs into profusion, economy into avarice, courage into rashness, caution into timidity, and so on:—insomuch that, I believe, there is more judgment required for the proper conduct of our virtues, than for avoiding their opposite vices. Vice in its true light is so deformed that it shocks us at first sight, and would hardly ever seduce us, if it did not at first wear the mask of some virtue. But virtue is in itself so beautiful that it charms us at first sight; engages us more and more upon further acquaintance; and, as with other beauties, we think excess is impossible: it is here that judgment is necessary to moderate and direct the effects of an excellent cause. I shall apply this reasoning, at present, not to any particular virtue, but to an excellency, which for want of judgment is often the cause of ridiculous and blamable effects; I mean, great learning, which, if not accompanied with sound judgment, frequently carries us into error, pride, and pedantry. As I hope you will possess that excellency in its utmost extent, and yet without its too common failings, the hints which my experience can suggest may probably not be useless to you.

Some learned men, proud of their knowledge, only speak to decide, and give judgment without appeal; the consequence of which is that mankind, provoked by the insult and injured by the oppression, revolt; and, in order to shake off the tyranny, even call the lawful authority in question. The more you know, the modester you should be; and (by the by) that modesty is the surest way of gratifying your vanity. Even where you are sure, seem rather doubtful; represent, but do not pronounce; and, if you would convince others, seem open to conviction yourself.

Others, to show their learning, or often from the prejudices of a school education, where they hear of nothing else, are always talking of the ancients as something more than men, and of the moderns as something less. They are never without a classic or two in their pockets; they stick to the old good sense; they read none of the modern trash; and will show you plainly that no improvement has been made in any one art or science these last seventeen hundred years. I would by no means have you disown your acquaintance with the ancients, but still less would I have you brag of an exclusive intimacy with them. Speak of the moderns without contempt, and of the ancients without idolatry; judge them all by their merits, but not by their ages; and, if you happen to have *an Elzevir classic in your pocket, neither show it nor mention it.

Some general scholars, most absurdly, draw all their maxims, both for public and private life, from what they call parallel cases in the ancient authors; without considering that, in the first place, there never were, since the creation of the world, two cases exactly parallel; and, in the next place, that there never was a case stated, or even known, by any historian, with every one of its circumstances; which, however, ought to be known in order to be reasoned from. Reason upon the case itself and the several circumstances that attend it, and act accordingly, but not from the authority of ancient poets or historians. Take into your consideration, if you please, cases seemingly analogous; but take them as helps only, not as guides. We are really so prejudiced by our education that, as the ancients deified their heroes, we deify their mad-

* Notes on Philip Dormer Stanhope, Earl of Chesterfield, will be found in the Appendix, pp. 1022 ff.

men; of which, with all due regard for antiquity, I take *Leonidas and Curtius to have been two distinguished ones. And yet a solid pedant would, in a speech in Parliament relative to a tax of twopence in the pound upon some commodity or other, quote those two heroes as examples of what we ought to do and suffer for our country. I have known these absurdities carried so far by people of injudicious learning that I should not be surprised if some of them were to propose, while we are at war with the Gauls, that a number of geese should be kept in the Tower, upon account of the infinite advantage which Rome received, in a parallel case, from a certain number of *geese in the Capitol. This way of reasoning and this way of speaking will always form a poor politician and a puerile declaimer.

There is another species of learned men who, though less dogmatical and supercilious, are not less impertinent. These are the communicative and shining pedants, who adorn their conversation, even with women, by happy quotations of Greek and Latin, and who have contracted such a familiarity with the Greek and Roman authors that they call them by certain names or epithets denoting intimacy. As "old" Homer, that "sly rogue" Horace, "Maro" instead of Virgil, and "Naso" instead of Ovid. These are often imitated by coxcombs who have no learning at all, but who have got some names and some scraps of ancient authors by heart, which they improperly and impertinently retail in all companies, in hopes of passing for scholars. If, therefore, you would avoid the accusation of pedantry on one hand, or the suspicion of ignorance on the other, abstain from learned ostentation. Speak the language of the company that you are in; speak it purely, and unlarded with any other. Never seem wiser nor more learned than the people you are with. Wear your learning, like your watch, in a private pocket, and do not pull it out and strike it merely to show that you have one. If you are asked what o'clock it is, tell it; but do not proclaim it hourly and unasked, like the watchman.

Upon the whole, remember that learning (I mean Greek and Roman learning) is a most useful and necessary ornament, which it is shameful not to be master of; but, at the same time, most carefully avoid those errors and abuses which I have mentioned, and which too often attend it. Remember, too, that great modern knowledge is still more necessary than ancient, and that you had better know perfectly the present than the old state of Europe, though I would have you well acquainted with both.

I have this moment received your letter of the 17th N.S. Though, I confess, there is no great variety in your present manner of life, yet materials can never be wanting for a letter; you see, you hear, or you read something new every day, a short account of which, with your own reflections thereupon, will make out a letter very well. But, since you desire a subject, pray send me an account of the Lutheran establishment in Germany; their religious tenets, their church government, the maintenance, authority, and titles of their clergy.

* *Vittorio Siri*, complete, is a very scarce and very dear book here; but I do not want it. If your own library grows too voluminous, you will not know what to do with it when you leave Leipsig. Your best way will be, when you go away from thence, to send to England, by Hamburg, all the books that you do not absolutely want.

Yours.

Letter CLXI

London, *September* 5, O.S. 1748

Dear Boy: I have received yours, with the inclosed German letter to *Mr. Grevenkop, which he assures me is extremely well written, considering the little time that you have applied yourself to that language. As you have now got over the most difficult part, pray go on diligently, and make yourself absolutely master of the rest. Whoever does not entirely possess a language will never appear to advantage, or even equal to himself, either in speaking or writing it. His ideas are fettered, and seem imperfect or confused, if he is not master of all the words and phrases necessary to express them. I therefore desire that you will not fail writing a German letter once every fortnight to Mr. Grevenkop, which will make the writing of that language familiar to you; and moreover, when you shall have left Germany and be arrived at Turin, I shall require you to write even to me in German, that you may not forget with ease what you have with difficulty learned. I likewise desire that while you are in Germany you will take all opportunities of conversing in German, which is the only way of knowing that, or any other language, accurately. You will also desire your German master to teach you the proper titles and superscriptions to be used to people of all ranks; which is a point so material, in Germany, that I have known many a letter returned unopened, because one title in twenty has been omitted in the direction.

St. Thomas's day now draws near, when you are to leave Saxony and go to Berlin; and I take it for granted that if anything is yet wanting to complete your knowledge of the state of that electorate, you will not fail to procure it before you go away. I do not mean, as you will easily believe, the number of churches, parishes, or towns; but I mean the constitution, the revenues, the troops, and the trade of that electorate. A few questions, sensibly asked, of sensible people, will produce you the necessary informations, which I desire you will enter in your little book. Berlin will be entirely a new scene to you, and I look upon it, in a manner, as your first step into the great world; take care that step be not a false one, and that you do not stumble at the threshold. You will there be in more company than you have yet been; manners and attentions will therefore be more necessary. Pleasing in company is the only way of being pleased in it yourself. Sense and knowledge are the first and necessary foundations for pleasing in company; but they will by no means do alone, and they will never be perfectly welcome if they are not accompanied with manners and attentions. You will best acquire these by frequenting the companies of people of fashion; but then you must resolve to acquire them, in those companies, by proper care and observation; for I have known people, who, though they have frequented good company all their lifetime, have done it in so inattentive and unobserving a manner as to be never the better for it, and to remain as disagreeable, as awkward, and as vulgar, as if they had never seen any person of fashion. When you go into good company (by good company is meant the people of the first fashion of the place) observe carefully their turn, their manners, their address; and conform your own to them. But this is not all neither; go deeper still; observe their characters, and pry, as far as you can, into both their hearts and their heads. Seek for their particular merit, their predominant passion, or their prevailing weakness; and you will then know what to bait your hook with to catch them. Man is a composition of so many, and such various ingredients that it requires both time and care to analyze him: for though we have all the same ingredients in our general composition, as reason, will, passions, and appetites; yet the different proportions and combinations of them in each individual produce that infinite variety of characters, which, in some particular or other, distinguishes every individual from another. Reason ought to direct the whole, but seldom does. And he who addresses himself singly to another man's reason, without endeavouring to engage his heart in his interest also, is no more likely to succeed than a man who should apply only to a king's nominal minister, and neglect his favourite. I will recommend to your attentive perusal, now that you are going into the world, two books, which will let you as much into the characters of men, as books can do. I mean, *_Les Réflexions Morales de Monsieur de la Rochefoucauld_, and *_Les Caractères de la Bruyère_; but remember, at the same time, that I only recommend them to you as the best general maps to assist you in your journey, and not as marking out every particular turning and winding that you will meet with. There your own sagacity and observation must come to their aid. La Rochefoucauld, is, I know, blamed, but I think without reason, for deriving all our actions from the source of self-love. For my own part, I see a great deal of truth, and no harm at all, in that opinion. It is certain that we seek our own happiness in everything we do; and it is as certain that we can only find it in doing well, and in conforming all our actions to the rule of right reason, which is the great law of nature. It is only a mistaken self-love that is a blamable motive, when we take the immediate and indiscriminate gratification of a passion, or appetite, for real happiness. But am I blamable if I do a good action, upon account of the happiness which that honest consciousness will give me? Surely not. On the contrary, that pleasing consciousness is a proof of my virtue. The reflection which is the most censured in Monsieur de la Rochefoucauld's book as a very ill-natured one, is this, *_On trouve dans le malheur de son meilleur ami, quelque chose qui ne déplaît pas_. And why not? Why may I not feel a very tender and real concern for the misfortune of my friend, and yet at the same time feel a pleasing consciousness at having discharged my duty to him, by comforting and assisting him to the utmost of my power in that misfortune? Give me but virtuous actions, and I will not quibble and chicane about the motives. And I will give anybody their choice of these two truths, which amount to the same thing: He who loves himself best is the honestest man; or, The honestest man loves himself best.

The characters of La Bruyère are pictures from the life; most of them finely drawn, and highly coloured. Furnish your mind with them first, and when you meet with their likeness, as you will every day, they will strike you the more. You will compare every feature with the original; and both will reciprocally help you to discover the beauties and the blemishes.

As women are a considerable, or at least a pretty numerous part of company, and as their suffrages go a great way towards establishing a man's character in the fashionable part of the world (which is of great importance to the fortune and figure he proposes to make in it), it is necessary to please them. I will therefore, upon this subject, let you into certain *arcana*, that will be very useful for you to know, but which you must with the utmost care conceal, and never seem to know. Women, then, are only children of a larger growth; they have an entertaining tattle and sometimes wit, but for solid reasoning, good sense, I never knew in my life one that had it, or who reasoned or acted consequentially for four-and-twenty hours together. Some little passion or humour always breaks in upon their best resolutions. Their beauty neglected or controverted, their age increased, or their supposed understandings depreciated, instantly kindles their little passions, and overturns any system of consequential conduct that in their most reasonable moments they might have been capable of forming. A man of sense only trifles with them, plays with them, humours and flatters them, as he does with a sprightly, forward child; but he neither consults them about, nor trusts them with, serious matters, though he often makes them believe that he does both, which is the thing in the world that they are proud of; for they love mightily to be dabbling in business (which, by the way, they always spoil), and, being justly distrustful that men in general look upon them in a trifling light, they almost adore that man who talks more seriously to them, and who seems to consult and trust them; I say, who seems, — for weak men really do, but wise ones only seem to do it. No flattery is either too high or too low for them. They will greedily swallow the highest, and gratefully accept of the lowest; and you may safely flatter any woman, from her understanding down to the exquisite taste of her fan. Women who are either indisputably beautiful or indisputably ugly are best flattered upon the score of their understandings; but those who are in a state of mediocrity are best flattered upon their beauty, or at least their graces; for every woman who is not absolutely ugly thinks herself handsome, but, not hearing often that she is so, is the more grateful and the more obliged to the few who tell her so; whereas a decided and conscious beauty looks upon every tribute paid to her beauty only as her due, but wants to shine and to be considered on the side of her understanding; and a woman who is ugly enough to know that she is so, knows that she has nothing left for it but her understanding, which is consequently (and probably in more senses than one) her weak side. But these are secrets which you must keep inviolably, if you would not, like Orpheus, be torn to pieces by the whole sex; on the contrary, a man who thinks of living in the great world must be gallant, polite, and attentive to please the women. They have, from the weakness of men, more or less influence in all courts; they absolutely stamp every man's character in the *beau monde*, and make it either current, or cry it down and stop it in payments. It is, therefore, absolutely necessary to manage, please, and flatter them, and never to discover the least mark of contempt, which is what they never forgive; but in this they are not singular, for it is the same with men, who will much sooner forgive an injustice than an insult. Every man is not ambitious, or covetous, or passionate; but every man has pride enough in his composition to feel and resent the least slight and contempt. Remember, therefore, most carefully to conceal your contempt, however just, wherever you would not make an implacable enemy. Men are much more unwilling to have their weaknesses and their imperfections known than their crimes; and if you hint to a man that you think him silly, ignorant, or even ill bred or awkward, he will hate you more and longer than if you tell him plainly that you think him a rogue. Never yield to that temptation, which to most young men is very strong, of exposing other people's weakness and infirmities, for the sake either of diverting the company, or showing your own superiority. You may get the laugh on your side by it for the present; but you will make enemies by it forever; and even those who laugh with you then, will, upon reflection fear, and consequently hate you: besides that it is ill natured, and a good heart desires rather to conceal than expose other people's weaknesses or misfortunes. If you have wit, use it to please, and not to hurt: you may shine, like the sun in the temperate zones, without scorching. Here it is wished for; under *the line it is dreaded.

These are some of the hints which my long experience in the great world enables me to give you, and which, if you attend to them, may prove useful to you in your journey through it. I wish it may be a prosperous one; at least, I am sure that it must be your own fault if it is not.

Make my compliments to Mr. Harte, who, I am very sorry to hear, is not well. I hope by this time he is recovered. Adieu!

Letter CCXXIV

London, *May* 8, O.S. 1750

**My dear Friend:* At your age the love of pleasures is extremely natural, and the enjoyment of them not unbecoming; but the danger, at your age, is mistaking the object, and setting out wrong in the pursuit. The character of a man of pleasure dazzles young eyes; they do not see their way to it distinctly, and fall into vice and profligacy. I remember a strong instance of this a great many years ago. A young fellow, determined to shine as a man of pleasure, was at the play called the *Libertine Destroyed*, a translation of *Le Festin de Pierre* of Molière's. He was so struck with what he thought the fine character of the libertine that he swore he would be the "Libertine destroyed." Some friends asked him whether he had not better content himself with being only the libertine, but without being "destroyed." To which he answered with great warmth, "No, for that being destroyed was the perfection of the whole." This, extravagant as it seems in this light, is really the case of many an unfortunate young fellow, who, captivated by the name of pleasures, rushes indiscriminately, and without taste, into them all, and is finally destroyed. I am not stoically advising, not parsonically preaching to you to be a Stoic at your age; far from it: I am pointing out to you the paths to pleasures, and am endeavouring only to quicken and heighten them for you. Enjoy pleasures, but let them be your own, and then you will taste them; but adopt none; trust to nature for genuine ones. The pleasures that you would feel, you must earn; the man who gives himself up to all, feels none sensibly. *Sardanapalus, I am convinced, never felt any in his life. Those only who join serious occupations with pleasures, feel either as they should do. *Alcibiades, though addicted to the most shameful excesses, gave some time to philosophy, and some to business. Julius Cæsar joined business with pleasure so properly, that they mutually assisted each other; and though he was the husband of all the wives at Rome, he found time to be one of the best scholars, almost the best orator, and absolutely the best general there. An uninterrupted life of pleasures is as insipid as contemptible. Some hours given every day to serious business must whet both the mind and the senses to enjoy those of pleasure. A surfeited glutton, an emaciated sot, and an enervated, rotten whoremaster never enjoy the pleasures to which they devote themselves; but they are only so many human sacrifices to false gods. The pleasures of low life are all of this mistaken, merely sensual, and disgraceful nature; whereas those of high life, and in good company, (though possibly in themselves not more moral) are more delicate, more refined, less dangerous, and less disgraceful; and, in the common course of things, not reckoned disgraceful at all. In short, pleasure must not, nay cannot, be the business of a man of sense and character; but it may be, and is, his relief, his reward. It is particularly so with regard to the women, who have the utmost contempt for those men that, having no character nor consideration with their own sex, frivolously pass their whole time in **ruelles* and at *toilettes*. They look upon them as their lumber, and remove them whenever they can get better furniture. Women choose their favourites more by the ear than by any other of their senses, or even their understandings. The man whom they hear the most commended by the men, will always be the best received by them. Such a conquest flatters their vanity, and vanity is their universal, if not their strongest passion. A distinguished thining character is irresistible with them; shey crowd to, nay they even quarrel for the danger, in hopes of the triumph. Though, by the way (to use a vulgar expression), she who conquers only catches a Tartar, and becomes the slave of her captive. **Mais c'est là leur affaire.* Divide your time between useful occupations and elegant pleasures. The morning seems to belong to study, business, or serious conversations with men of learning and figure; not that I exclude an occasional hour at a *toilette.* From sitting down to dinner, the proper business of the day is pleasure, unless real business, which must never be postponed for pleasure, happens accidentally to interfere. In good company, the pleasures of the table are always carried to a certain point of delicacy and gratification, but never to excess and riot. Plays, operas, balls, suppers, gay conversations in polite and cheerful companies, properly conclude the evenings; not to mention the tender looks that you may direct, and the sighs that you may offer, upon these several occasions, to some propitious or unpropitious female deity, whose character and manners will neither disgrace nor corrupt yours. This is the life of a man of real sense and character; and by this distribution of your time, and choice of your pleasures, you will be equally qualified for the busy, or the *beau monde.* You see I am not rigid, and do not require that you and I should be of the same age. What I say to you, therefore, should have the more weight, as coming from a friend, not a father. But low company, and their low vices, their indecent riots and profligacy, I never will bear, nor forgive.

I have lately received two volumes of treaties, in German and Latin, from Hawkins, with your orders, under your own hand, to take care of them for you, which orders I shall most dutifully and punctually obey, and they wait for you in my library, together with your great collection of rare books, which your mamma sent me upon removing from her old house.

I hope you not only keep up, but *improve in your German, for it will be of great use to you when you come into business, and the more so, as you will be almost the only Englishman who either can speak or understand it. Pray speak it constantly to all Germans, wherever you meet them, and you will meet multitudes of them at Paris. Is Italian now become easy and familiar to you? Can you speak it with the same fluency that you can speak German? You cannot conceive what an advantage it will give you in negotiations, to possess Italian, German, and French perfectly, so as to understand all the force and *finesse* of those three languages. If two men of equal talents negotiate together, he who best understands the language in which the negotiation is carried on, will infallibly get the better of the other. The signification and force of one single word is often of great consequence in a treaty, and even in a letter.

Remember the *graces*, for without them **ogni fatica è vana.* Adieu.

[1774]

HORACE WALPOLE

THE life of Horace Walpole covered almost the whole of the eighteenth century. He was born in 1717, the youngest of the six children of the first Lady Walpole and the famous Prime Minister of George I and George II. In person, temperament, and tastes he was the antithesis of Sir Robert Walpole: he was slender, delicate, fastidious, and esthetic, a typical dilettante; while the old statesman was robust, coarse, hearty, and practical-minded, the very figure of John Bull. In view of these facts and the known estrangement of Sir Robert and his first wife during the later years of their life, it is not surprising that gossip should have noted the similarity between Horace and Carr, Lord Hervey, a friend of Lady Walpole's. A supposition which he would have been the first to entertain concerning the parentage of another seems to have been quite neglected or rejected by the son, whose devotion to his mother was equalled only by his filial pride in Sir Robert. In spite of physical weakness and martyrdom to the gout, Horace Walpole outlived his generation and attained his eightieth year. In 1791 he succeeded his nephew as Earl of Orford, being the fourth and last holder of this title, which had been bestowed upon Sir Robert Walpole when he retired from the premiership.

Horace Walpole lives in English literature by reason of his connection with the Gothic revival, the development of English printing, his historical and biographical writing, and his voluminous correspondence. With strong antiquarian interests and a passion for collecting, and with a large income, chiefly from sinecure political appointments, he indulged his taste for Gothic architecture at Strawberry Hill, his country home at Twickenham, a short distance from Pope's villa near London. When he purchased this estate in 1748, it was occupied only by a cottage, but he rebuilt and altered and added for a generation until he had an elaborate structure in imitation of the Gothic style. Here he housed his collection of antiquarian and artistic rarities. As might be expected from such amateur attempts at a time when little was known about mediæval building and design, his castle was fantastic and abounded in historical anomalies and architectural monstrosities. In his own time it was ridiculed as an artificial and unsubstantial imitation of the barbaric past, and later, as an uninspired aping of the glories of the Middle Ages. There can be no doubt, however, that this early experiment attracted wide interest and had an important part in the Gothic revival, which was a significant aspect of nascent romanticism. His Gothic novel, *The Castle of Otranto*, 1764, an experiment of a similar kind in another *genre*, had no small part in the development of a taste for mediæval romance. *The Castle of Otranto* bore to the Waverley Novels the same relation that Strawberry Hill bore to Abbotsford.

In 1757 he set up a private press at the Strawberry Hill estate and published several of his own works as well as numerous other volumes of prose and verse (including poems by his friend, Thomas Gray) which are now much sought after by book collectors. Walpole's publications include *A Catalogue of the Royal and Noble Authors of England*, 1758; *Anecdotes of Painting in England*, 1762–71; a tragedy, *The Mysterious Mother*, 1768; numerous political pamphlets and contributions to periodicals, as well as reminiscences, memoirs, and journals.

It is, however, as a letter writer that Horace Walpole is chiefly remembered today. Whatever disagreement there may be concerning his personal character or literary merits, there is general agreement that he is one of the most important English letter writers. Nor is the reason far to seek. He lived in the centre of political and social activity; he knew every one; he took his correspondence seriously, and he had leisure to practice it as an art and an avocation. From the letters of Gray and especially from those of Madame de Sévigné he learned much; of the latter he was a conscious student, striving to produce in English something of the same effects that she had attained in French. He had the qualities necessary for a brilliant correspondent: he was gay, whimsical, slightly malicious; he was interested in everything but not too serious about anything. To the faculty of keen observation he added the practice of constantly noting down bits of news, *bons mots*, anything that he could turn to account in his correspondence. In his hands gossip was transformed into literature. With the heights and the depths of human experience his letters have little concern; they deal brilliantly with the surface of life. A valuable reflection of upper-class English society in the eighteenth century, an engaging revelation of a fascinating, if not always admirable personality, they are among the best examples of a *genre* in which English literature has not had many masters.

LETTERS

To *the Hon. Henry Seymour Conway

Twickenham, *June* 8, 1747

You perceive by my date that I am got into a new camp, and have left my tub at Windsor. It is a little plaything-house that I got out of *Mrs. Chenevix's shop, and is the prettiest bauble you ever saw. It is set in enameled meadows, with filigree hedges:

> *A small Euphrates through the piece is roll'd,
> And little finches wave their wings in gold.

Two delightful roads, that you would call dusty, supply me continually with coaches and chaises; barges as solemn as Barons of the Exchequer move under my window; Richmond Hill and Ham Walks bound my prospect; but thank God! the Thames is between me and the Duchess of Queensberry. Dowagers as plenty as flounders inhabit all around, and Pope's ghost is just now skimming under my window by a most poetical moonlight. I have about land enough to keep such a farm as Noah's, when he set up in the ark with a pair of each kind; but my cottage is rather cleaner than I believe his was after they had been cooped up together forty days. The Chenevixes had tricked it out for themselves; up two pair of stairs is what they call Mr. Chenevix's library, furnished with three maps, one shelf, a bust of Sir Isaac Newton, and a lame telescope without any glasses. Lord John Sackville *predecessed* me here, and instituted certain games called *cricketalia*, which have been celebrated this very evening in honour of him in a neighbouring meadow.

You will think I have removed my philosophy from Windsor with my tea-things hither; for I am writing to you in all this tranquillity while a Parliament is bursting about my ears. You know it is going to be dissolved: I am told you are taken care of, though I don't know where, nor whether anybody that chooses you will quarrel with me because he does choose you, as that little bug, *the Marquis of Rockingham did — one of the calamities of my life which I have bore as abominably well as I do most about which I don't care. They say the prince has taken up two hundred thousand pounds to carry elections which he won't carry; he had much better have saved it to buy the Parliament after it is chosen. A new set of peers are in embryo, to add more dignity to the silence of the House of Lords.

I make no remarks on *your campaign because, as you say, you do nothing at all, which, though very proper nutriment for a thinking head, does not do quite so well to write upon. If any one of you can but contrive to be shot upon your post, it is all we desire, shall look upon it as a great curiosity, and will take care to set up a monument to the person so slain; as we are doing by vote to Captain Cornewall, who was killed at the beginning of the action in the Mediterranean four years ago. In the present dearth of glory, he is canonized; though, poor man! he had been tried twice the year before for cowardice.

I could tell you much election news, none else; though not being thoroughly attentive to so important a subject as, to be sure, one ought to be, I might now and then mistake, and give you a candidate for Durham in place of one for Southampton, or name the returning officer instead of the candidate. In general, I believe, it is much as usual — those sold in detail that afterwards will be sold in the representation — the ministers bribing Jacobites to choose friends of their own — the name of well-wishers to the present establishment, and patriots outbidding ministers that they may make the better market of their own patriotism: in short, all England, under some name or other, is just now to be bought and sold; though, whenever we become posterity and forefathers, we shall be in high repute for wisdom and virtue. My great-great-grandchildren will figure me with a white beard down to my girdle, and Mr. Pitt's will believe him unspotted enough to have walked over nine hundred hot ploughshares without hurting the sole of his foot. How merry my ghost will be, and shake its ears to hear itself quoted as a person of consummate prudence!

Adieu, dear Harry!

Yours ever,

Hor. Walpole

To *George Montagu

Strawberry Hill, *Aug.* 12, 1760

In what part of the island you are just now, I don't know — flying about somewhere or other, I suppose — well, it is charming to be

* Notes on Horace Walpole will be found in the Appendix, pp. 1023 ff.

so young! Here am I, lying upon a couch, wrapped up in flannels, with the gout in both feet — oh, yes! gout in all the forms. Six years ago I had it, and nobody would believe me; now they may have proof. My legs are as big as your cousin Guilford's, and they don't use to be quite so large. I was seized yesterday se'nnight, have had little pain in the day, but most uncomfortable nights; however, I move about again a little with a stick. If either my father or mother had had it, I should not dislike it so much. I am herald enough to approve it if descended genealogically; but it is an absolute upstart in me; and what is more provoking, I had trusted to my great abstinence for keeping me from it: but thus it is; if I had any gentleman-like virtue, as patriotism or loyalty, I might have got something by them; I had nothing but that beggarly virtue, temperance, and she had not interest enough to keep me from a fit of the gout. Another plague is that everybody that ever knew anybody that had it are so good as to come with advice and direct me how to manage it — that is, how to contrive to have it for a great many years. I am very refractory; I say to the gout, as great personages do to the executioners, "Friend, do your work as quick as you can." They tell me of wine to keep it out of my stomach; but I will starve temperance itself, — I will be virtuous indeed; that is, I will stick to virtue, though I find it is not its own reward.

This confinement has kept me from Yorkshire: I hope, however, to be at Ragley by the 20th, from whence I shall still go to Lord Strafford's; and by this delay you may possibly be at Greatworth by my return, which will be about the beginning of September. Write me a line as soon as you receive this; direct it to Arlington Street; it will be sent after me. Adieu.

Yours ever,

H. W.

P.S. My tower erects its battlements bravely; my *Anecdotes of Painting* thrive exceedingly, thanks to the gout that has pinned me to my chair. Think of Ariel the sprite in a slit shoe!

To George Montagu, Esq.

Arlington Street, *Nov.* 13, 1760

Even *the honeymoon of a new reign don't produce events every day. There is nothing but the common toying of addresses and kissing hands. The chief difficulty is settled: Lord Gower yields the Mastership of the Horse to Lord Huntingdon, and removes to the Great Wardrobe, from whence Sir Thomas Robinson was to have gone into Ellis's place, but he is saved and Sir Thomas remains as lumber not yet disposed of. The City, however, have a mind to be out of humour; a paper has been fixed on the Royal Exchange, with these words, *"No petticoat government, no Scotch minister, no Lord George Sackville," — two hints totally unfounded, and the other scarce true. No petticoat ever governed less, it is left at Leicester House; Lord George's breeches are as little concerned; and except *Lady Susan Stuart and *Sir Harry Erskine, nothing has yet been done for any Scots. For the King himself, he seems all good-nature, and wishing to satisfy everybody; all his speeches are obliging. I saw him again yesterday, and was surprised to find the levee-room had lost so entirely the air of the lion's den. This young man don't stand in one spot with his eyes fixed royally on the ground, and dropping bits of German news; he walks about, and speaks to everybody. I saw him afterwards on the throne, where he is graceful and genteel, sits with dignity, and reads his answers to addresses well. It was the Cambridge address carried by *the Duke of Newcastle in his doctor's gown, and looking like the **Médecin malgré lui*. He had been vehemently solicitous for attendance for fear *my Lord Westmoreland, who vouchsafes himself to bring the address from Oxford, should outnumber him. Lord Lichfield and several other Jacobites have kissed hands; George Selwyn says, "They go to St. James's because now there are so many *Stuarts* there."

Do you know, I had the curiosity to go to *the burying t'other night; I had never seen a royal funeral. Nay, I walked as a rag of quality, which I found would be — and so it was — the easiest way of seeing it. It is absolutely a noble sight. The prince's chamber, hung with purple and a quantity of silver lamps, the coffin under a canopy of purple velvet, and six vast chandeliers of silver on high stands, had a very good effect. The Ambassador from Tripoli and his son were carried to see that chamber. The procession, through a line of footguards, every seventh man bearing a torch, the horseguards lining the outside, their officers with drawn sabres and crape sashes on horseback, the drums muffled, the fifes, bells tolling, and minute guns — all this was very solemn. But the charm was the entrance of the Abbey, where we were received by the dean and chapter in rich copes, the choir and almsmen all bearing torches; the whole Abbey so illuminated that one saw it to greater advantage than by day; the tombs, long aisles, and fretted roof, all appearing distinctly, and with the happiest *chiaroscuro*. There wanted nothing but incense, and little chapels here and there, with priests saying Mass for the repose of the defunct; yet one could not complain of its not being Catholic enough. * I had been in dread of being coupled with some boy of ten years old; but the heralds were not very accurate, and I walked with George Grenville, taller and older enough, to keep me in countenance. When we came to the chapel of Henry the Seventh, all solemnity and decorum ceased: no order was observed, people set or stood where they could or would; the yeomen of the guard were crying out for help, oppressed by the immense weight of the coffin; the bishop read sadly, and blundered in the prayers; the fine chapter, "Man that is born of a woman," was chanted, not read; and the anthem, besides being unmeasurably tedious, would have served as well for a nuptial. The real serious part was the figure of the Duke of Cumberland, heightened by a thousand melancholy circumstances. He had * a dark brown adonis, and a cloak of black cloth, with a train of five yards. Attending the funeral of a father, how little reason soever he had to love him, could not be pleasant; his leg extremely bad, yet forced to stand upon it near two hours; his face bloated and distorted with his late paralytic stroke, which has affected, too, one of his eyes; and, placed over the mouth of the vault, into which, in all probability, he must himself so soon descend — think how unpleasant a situation! He bore it all with a firm and unaffected countenance. This grave scene was fully contrasted by the burlesque Duke of Newcastle. He fell into a fit of crying the moment he came into the chapel, and flung himself back in a stall, the archbishop hovering over him with a smelling-bottle; but in two minutes his curiosity got the better of his hypocrisy, and he ran about the chapel with his glass to spy who was or was not there, spying with one hand, and mopping his eyes with t'other. Then returned the fear of catching cold; and the Duke of Cumberland, who was sinking with heat, felt himself weighed down, and, turning round, found it was the Duke of Newcastle standing upon his train, to avoid the chill of the marble. It was very theatric to look down into the vault, where the coffin lay, attended by mourners with lights. Clavering, the groom of the bedchamber, refused to sit up with the body, and was dismissed by the king's order.

I have nothing more to tell you but a trifle, a very trifle: * the King of Prussia has totally defeated Marshal Daun. This, which would have been prodigious news a month ago, is nothing today; it only takes its turn among the questions, "Who is to be groom of the bedchamber?" "What is Sir T. Robinson to have?" I have been to * Leicester Fields today; the crowd was immoderate; I don't believe it will continue so. Good night. Yours ever.

H. W.

To * John Chute

Bath, *Oct.* 10, 1766

I am impatient to hear that your charity to me has not ended in the gout to yourself; all my comfort is, if you have it, that you have good Lady Brown to nurse you.

My health advances faster than my amusement. However, I have been at one opera, Mr. Wesley's. They have boys and girls with charming voices that sing hymns, in parts, to Scotch ballad tunes; but indeed so long that one would think they were already in eternity, and knew how much time they had before them. The chapel is very neat, with true Gothic windows (yet I am not converted); but I was glad to see that luxury is creeping in upon them before persecution: they have very neat mahogany stands for branches, and brackets of the same in taste. At the upper end is a broad * *haut-pas* of four steps, advancing in the middle; at each end of the broadest part are * two of *my* eagles with red cushions for the parson and clerk. Behind them rise three more steps, in the midst of which is a third eagle for pulpit. Scarlet armed-chairs to all three. On either hand, a balcony for elect ladies. The rest of the congregation sit on forms. Behind the pit, in a dark niche, is a plain table within rails; so you see the throne is for the apostle. Wesley is a lean, elderly man, fresh-coloured, his hair smoothly combed, but with * a *soupçon* of curl at the ends. Wondrous clean, but as evidently an actor as Garrick. He spoke his sermon, but so fast, and with so little accent, that I am sure he has often uttered it, for it was like a lesson. There were parts and eloquence in it; but towards the end he exalted his voice, and acted very ugly enthusiasm; decried learning, and told stories, like Latimer, of the fool of his college, who said, "I *thanks* God for everything." Except a few from curiosity and some *honourable women*, the congregation was very mean. There was a Scotch Countess of Buchan, who is carrying a pure rosy, vulgar face to heaven, and who asked Miss Rich if that was the *author of the poets*. I believe she meant me and the *Noble Authors*.

The Bedfords came last night. Lord Chatham was with me yesterday two hours; looks and walks well, and is in excellent political spirits.

Yours ever,

Hor. Walpole

To * the Rev. William Mason

Arlington Street, *April* 3, 1775

Well! your book is walking the town in midday. How it is liked I do not yet know. Were I to judge from my own feelings, I should say there never was so entertaining or interesting a work, that it is the most perfect model of biography, and must make Tacitus, and Agricola too, detest you. But as the world and simple I are not often of the same opinion, it will perhaps be thought very dull. If it is, all we can do is to appeal to that undutiful urchin, Posterity, who commonly treats the judgment of its parents with contempt, though it has so profound a veneration for its most distant ancestors. As you have neither imitated the teeth-breaking diction of Johnson, nor coined slanders against the most virtuous names in story, like modern historians, you cannot hope to please the *reigning* taste. Few persons have had time, from their politics, diversions, and gaming, to have read much of so large a volume, which they will keep for the summer, when they have full as much of nothing to do. Such as love poetry, or think themselves poets, will have hurried to the verses and been disappointed at not finding half a dozen more Elegies in a Churchyard. A few fine gentlemen will have read one or two of the shortest letters, which, not being exactly such as they write themselves, they will dislike or copy next post; they who wish or intend to find fault with Gray, you, or even me, have, to be sure, skimmed over the whole, except the Latin, for even spite, * *non est tanti*—. The reviewers, no doubt, are already writing against you — not because they have read the whole, but because one's own name is always the first thing that strikes one in a book. The Scotch will be more deliberate, but not less angry; and if not less angry, not more merciful. Every Hume, however spelled, will I don't know what do; I should be sorry to be able to guess what. I have already been asked why I did not prevent publication of * the censure on David. The truth is (as you know) I never saw the whole together till now, and not that part; and if I had, why ought I to have prevented it? Voltaire will cast * an *imbelle* javelin *sine ictu* at Gray, for he loves to depreciate a *dead* great author, even when unprovoked, — even when he has commended him alive, or before he was so vain and so envious as he is now. The Rousseaurians will imagine that I interpolated the condemnation of his *Eloïse*. In short, we shall have many sins laid to our charge, of which we are innocent; but what can the malicious say against the innocent but what is not true?

I am here in brunt to the storm; you sit serenely aloof and smile at its sputtering. So should I too, were I out of sight, but I hate to be stared at, and the object of whispers before my face. The Maccaronis will laugh out, for you say I am still in the fashionable world. "What!" they will cry, as they read while their hair is curling, — "that old soul"; for old and old-fashioned are synonymous in the vocabulary of mode, alas! Nobody is so sorry as I to be in the world's fashionable purlieus; still, in truth, all this is a joke and touches me little. I seem to myself * a Strulbrug, who have lived past my time, and see almost my own life written before my face while I am yet upon earth, and as it were the only one of my contemporaries with whom I began the world. Well; in a month's time there will be little question of Gray, and less of me. America and feathers and masquerades will drive us into libraries; and there I am well content to live as an humble companion to Gray and you — and, thank my stars, not on the same shelf with * the Macphersons and Dalrymples.

One omission I have found, at which I wonder: you do not mention Gray's study of physic, of which he had read much, and I doubt to his hurt. I had not seen till now that delightful encomium on Cambridge, when empty of its inhabitants. It is as good as anything in the book, and has that true humour which I think equal to any of his excellencies. So has the apostrophe to Nicholls, "Why, you monster, I shall never be dirty and amused as long as I live"; but I will not quote any more, though I shall be reading it and reading it for the rest of my life.

But come, here is a task you must perform, and forthwith; and if you will not write to me, you shall *transcribble* to me, or I will *combustle* you. Send me incontinently all the proper names that are omitted. You know how I love writing marginal notes in my books, and there is not a word in or out of the book of which I will be ignorant. To save you trouble, here is a list of who is's. Page 152, fill up the asterisks; *do.* p. 174; *do.* 206; *do.* 232; 249; Peer, who is it? 250; *do.* the Lady of Quality? 251; the leader, 275; who the asterisk, 282? the Dr. who, 283? *do.* 284; the B's and E's, 288, where, whose is Stratton? 290, Lord?

You see my queries are not very numerous. If you do not answer them, I will not tell you a syllable of what the *fashionable* say of your book, and I do not believe you have another correspondent amongst them. At present they are labouring through a very short work, more peculiarly addressed to them, at least to a respectable part of them, the Jockey Club, who, to the latter's extreme surprise, have been consulted on a point of honour by Mr. Fitzgerald, which, however, he has already decided himself with as little conscience as they could do in their most punctilious moments.

If you will satisfy me, I will tell you the following *bon mot* of *Foote; but be sure you don't read what follows till you have obeyed my commands. Foote was at Paris in October, when *Dr. Murray was, who *admiring* or *dreading* his wit (for commentators dispute on the true reading) often invited him to dinner with his nephew. The ambassador produced a very small bottle of Tokay, and dispensed it in very small glasses. The uncle, to prove how precious every drop, said it was of the most exquisite growth, and very old. Foote, taking up the diminutive glass, and examining it, replied, "It is very little of its age." Return me my story if you don't perform the conditions. I wish I could send you anybody's else life to write.

To *Sir Horace Mann

Strawberry Hill, *Dec.* 1, 1776

Though I wrote to you but the other day, and have nothing new to tell you, I must say a few words in answer to yours by Mr. Hull, and to that of Nov. 16th which I have just received.

As you are my first consideration, I could but state to you what reason and experience dictated for your personal security. I have, however, no doubt but you will find all honour and justice in your nephew, who I am sure has sense, and, as I told you before you saw him, appeared to me to have an excellent heart. It pleased me to see that he answered so thoroughly in your eyes to the character I had given you of him. As he is Gal's son, I must be glad too that you have made his mind at ease about his daughters. Still as I have so much friendship for your whole family, and think so well of Mr. and Mrs. Foote, I am not at all sorry that the step you have taken was transacted without my advice. I could never have brought myself to have decided on a point in which one part or other of your family would think itself wounded, as I doubt may be the case now; though I believe Mr. and Mrs. Foote are too good and reasonable to do more than think. You yourself have been originally ill used by both your brothers, James and Edward. The former was very weak; the other had not very good sense, with an abominable temper — but he is gone and I will say no more.

I did tell you I received the packet from Mr. Gyles, who, I suppose, is the person you mean by Mr. Price; you might easily forget the name of a man you knew so little.

I don't know who the Englishwoman is of whom you give so ridiculous a description, but it will suit thousands. I distrust my age continually, and impute to it half the contempt I feel for my countrymen and women. If I think the other half well founded, it is by considering what must be said hereafter of the present age. What is to impress a great idea of us on posterity? In truth, what do our contemporaries of all other countries think of us? They stare at and condemn our politics and follies; and if they retain any respect for us, I doubt it is for the sense we have had. I do know, indeed, one man who still worships us, but his adoration is testified so very absurdly as not to do us much credit. It is a Monsieur de Marchais, first *valet de chambre* to the King of France. He has the *anglomanie* so strong that he has not only read more English than French books, but if any valuable work appears in his own language, he waits to peruse it till it is translated into English; and, to be sure, our translations of French are admirable things!

To do the rest of the French justice — I mean such as like us — they adopt only our egregious follies, and in particular the flower of them, horseracing! "Le Roi Pepin," a racer, is the horse in fashion. I suppose the next shameful practice of ours they naturalize will be personal scurrilities in the newspapers, especially on young and handsome women, in which we certainly are originals! Voltaire, who first brought us into fashion in France, is stark mad at his own success. Out of envy to writers of his own nation he cried up Shakespeare; and now is distracted at the just encomiums bestowed on that first genius of the world in the new translation. He sent to the French Academy an invective that bears all the marks of passionate dotage. * Mrs. Montagu happened to be present when it was read. Suard, one of their writers, said to her, **Je crois, madame, que vous êtes un peu fâchée de ce que vous venez d'entendre.* She replied, **Moi, monsieur! point du tout! Je ne suis pas amie de Monsieur Voltaire.* I shall go to town the day after tomorrow, and will add a postscript, if I hear any news.

Dec. 3rd.

I am come late, have seen nobody, and must send away my letter.

[1798, 1859]

SAMUEL JOHNSON

Dr. Samuel Johnson bulks large in English literature by reason of his personality and his literary dictatorship as well as by reason of his writings. No one could enter his presence without realizing that he was a distinguished man. Some persons were repelled by his uncouth manners and his personal eccentricities, but most of his associates were undeterred by these externals. In any company he was the central figure. His club contained many of the most distinguished men of the day; statesmen, scholars, artists, half a dozen lords, as many bishops, and several of the most prominent authors; yet in the presence of Burke and Fox; Adam Smith, Gibbon, and Sir William Jones; Reynolds, Dr. Burney, and Garrick; Goldsmith, the Wartons, and Sheridan, Johnson shone the more brightly. To dominate such an assembly required a keen intellect, a ready wit, and a vigorous personality.

Johnson was the last of the literary dictators in England. He spoke with the voice of authority not only by reason of his personal qualities but far more because he was the mouthpiece of the "general sense" at a time when men still believed in literary and social standards and were able to reach valid and acceptable conclusions through their right application. He gave vigorous and happy expression to conclusions that embodied the best thought of his generation.

As a writer he achieved distinction in several fields. He is still remembered as a poet, an essayist, an editor, and a controversial writer. If he failed to win high place as a dramatist, he succeeded in writing a piece of prose fiction that has been many times reprinted and is still widely read. Though his *Dictionary* has long been superseded, its importance has always been realized. His chief title to literary fame, however, is in his criticism: he is among the half dozen most important English literary critics.

His prose style has been imitated and parodied and praised and ridiculed; it combines high excellence and outstanding defects. The diction is Latinate to an unusual degree, but it is liberally mixed with racy English idiom. The words are chosen with precision to express exact shades of meaning. The sentences march steadily forward uninterrupted by parenthesis or excessive subordination; they are frequently periodic and are carefully balanced internally and externally. Johnson's style, like everything else with which he had to do, is highly individual, yet it shows classical discipline and sense of proportion. In his earlier works it is often stiff, heavy, and mannered; but in his later works, especially in *The Lives of the English Poets,* written after he had been relieved from the pressure of poverty, it shows more of the qualities that made his conversation famous. Here the style most truly expresses the man.

THE VANITY OF HUMAN WISHES

THE TENTH SATIRE OF JUVENAL, IMITATED

Though the eighteenth century has been denominated "an age of prose," in no age has poetic composition been esteemed more essential for a well-rounded man of letters. Few important writers of this period limited themselves to prose. Johnson was no exception to the rule; indeed, his earlier literary reputation was based on his verse. Much of this has been forgotten in our day, but two of his poems are still read: *London* (1738) and *The Vanity of Human Wishes* (1749). Both are classical imitations of the same type as Pope's *Imitations of Horace,* modern poems that adapt rather than translate the ancient poems upon which they are based. While Pope went to the urbane satire of Horace, Johnson chose to imitate the fiercer invective of Juvenal. *London* is based on Juvenal's Third *Satire* and *The Vanity of Human Wishes* on his Tenth.

In the latter poem Johnson follows the outlines of his original and treats the same general topics in the same order, using for the most part modern and even contemporary illustrations; but at the same time he expresses his unique personality. Here is his characteristic melancholy as the result of clear-eyed perception of the vanities of the world; and here too is his Christian stoicism, which enabled him to face the dismal prospect undismayed. Neither shallow optimism nor distorting pessimism is here, neither sentimentalism nor cynicism: its subject is the vanity of human *wishes,* not the futility of human life. The subject is of frequent recurrence in Johnson; the point of view is characteristically his; the conclusion is typical of his thought.

Johnson was not a great poet; *The Vanity of Human Wishes* lacks many of the finest qualities of poetry. None the less it has merits indisputable: a sane and honest view of life presented with literary background and adequacy of expression. Though the verses lack grace, they attain sonority; though they lack the correctness of Pope's, the mellifluousness of Gray's, the sensuousness of Keats's, they have a marmoreal quality which suits their content. Johnson's poems are among the least of his claims to immortality, but if he had written nothing else they would give him a place in English literature.

Let observation, with extensive view,
Survey mankind from China to Peru;
Remark each anxious toil, each eager strife,
And watch the busy scenes of crowded life;
Then say how hope and fear, desire and hate,
O'erspread with snares the clouded maze of fate,
Where wav'ring man, betray'd by vent'rous pride
To tread the dreary paths without a guide,
As treach'rous phantoms in the mist delude,
Shuns fancied ills, or chases airy good;
How rarely reason guides the stubborn choice,
Rules the bold hand, or prompts the suppliant voice;
How nations sink, by darling schemes oppress'd,
When Vengeance listens to the fool's request.
Fate wings with ev'ry wish th' afflictive dart,
Each gift of nature, and each grace of art;
With fatal heat impetuous courage glows,
With fatal sweetness elocution flows;
Impeachment stops the speaker's pow'rful breath,
And restless fire precipitates on death.
  But, scarce observ'd, the knowing and the bold
Fall in the gen'ral massacre of gold;
Wide-wasting pest! that rages unconfin'd,
And crowds with crimes the records of mankind:
For gold his sword the hireling ruffian draws,
For gold the hireling judge distorts the laws;
Wealth heap'd on wealth, nor truth nor safety buys,
The dangers gather as the treasures rise.
  Let hist'ry tell, where rival kings command,
And dubious title shakes the madded land,
When statutes glean the refuse of the sword,
How much more safe the vassal than the lord;
Low skulks the hind beneath the rage of pow'r,
And leaves the wealthy traitor in the Tow'r;
Untouch'd his cottage, and his slumbers sound,
Though confiscation's vultures hover round.
  The needy traveller, serene and gay,
Walks the wild heath, and sings his toil away.
Does envy seize thee? Crush th' upbraiding joy,
Increase his riches, and his peace destroy;
New fears in dire vicissitude invade,
The rustling brake alarms, and quiv'ring shade;
Nor light nor darkness bring his pain relief,
One shows the plunder, and one hides the thief.
  Yet still one gen'ral cry the skies assails,
And gain and grandeur load the tainted gales;
Few know the toiling statesman's fear or care,
Th' insidious rival and the gaping heir.
  Once more, *Democritus, arise on earth,
With cheerful wisdom and instructive mirth,
See motley life in modern trappings dress'd,
And feed with varied fools th' eternal jest:
Thou who couldst laugh where want enchain'd caprice,
Toil crush'd conceit, and man was of a piece;
Where wealth unlov'd without a mourner died;
And scarce a sycophant was fed by pride;
Where ne'er was known the form of mock debate,
Or seen a new-made mayor's unwieldly state;
Where change of fav'rites made no change of laws,
And senates heard before they judg'd a cause;
How wouldst thou shake at Britain's modish tribe,
Dart the quick taunt, and edge the piercing gibe,
Attentive truth and nature to descry,
And pierce each scene with philosophic eye!
To thee were solemn toys, or empty show,
The robes of pleasure and the veils of woe;
All aid the farce, and all thy mirth maintain,
Whose joys are causeless, or whose griefs are vain.
  Such was the scorn that fill'd the sage's mind,
Renew'd at ev'ry glance on human kind;
How just that scorn ere yet thy voice declare,
Search ev'ry state, and canvass ev'ry pray'r.
  Unnumber'd suppliants crowd preferment's gate,
Athirst for wealth, and burning to be great;
Delusive fortune hears th' incessant call,
They mount, they shine, evaporate, and fall.
On ev'ry stage the foes of peace attend;
Hate dogs their flight, and insult mocks their end.

* Notes on Samuel Johnson will be found in the Appendix, pp. 1025 ff.

Love ends with hope; the sinking statesman's door
Pours in the morning worshipper no more;
For growing names the weekly scribbler lies,
To growing wealth the dedicator flies;
From ev'ry room descends the painted face,
That hung the bright palladium of the place;
And, smok'd in kitchens, or in auctions sold,
To better features yields the frame of gold;
For now no more we trace in ev'ry line
Heroic worth, benevolence divine:
The form distorted justifies the fall,
And detestation rids th' indignant wall.

But will not Britain hear the last appeal,
Sign her foes' doom, or guard her fav'rites' zeal?
Through Freedom's sons no more remonstrance rings,
Degrading nobles and controlling kings;
Our supple tribes repress their patriot throats,
And ask no questions but the price of votes;
With weekly libels and *septennial ale,
Their wish is full to riot and to rail.

In full-blown dignity see *Wolsey stand,
Law in his voice, and fortune in his hand:
To him the church, the realm, their pow'rs consign,
Through him the rays of regal bounty shine,
Turn'd by his nod the stream of honour flows,
His smile alone security bestows:
Still to new heights his restless wishes tow'r,
Claim leads to claim, and pow'r advances pow'r;
Till conquest unresisted ceas'd to please,
And rights submitted left him none to seize.
At length his sov'reign frowns — the train of state
Mark the keen glance, and watch the sign to hate.
Where'er he turns, he meets a stranger's eye,
His suppliants scorn him, and his followers fly:
Now drops at once the pride of awful state,
The golden canopy, the glitt'ring plate,
The regal palace, the luxurious board,
The liv'ried army, and the menial lord.
With age, with cares, with maladies oppress'd,
He seeks the refuge of monastic rest.
Grief aids disease, remember'd folly stings,
And his last sighs reproach the faith of kings.

Speak thou, whose thoughts at humble peace repine,
Shall Wolsey's wealth, with Wolsey's end, be thine?
Or liv'st thou now, with safer pride content,
The wisest justice on the banks of Trent?
For, why did Wolsey, near the steeps of fate,
On weak foundations raise th' enormous weight?
Why, but to sink beneath misfortune's blow,
With louder ruin to the gulfs below?

*What gave great Villiers to th' assassin's knife,
And fix'd disease on *Harley's closing life?
*What murder'd Wentworth, and what exil'd Hyde,
By kings protected, and to kings allied?
What but their wish indulg'd in courts to shine,
And pow'r too great to keep, or to resign?

When first the college rolls receive his name,
The young enthusiast quits his ease for fame;
Through all his veins the fever of renown
Spreads from the strong contagion of the gown;
O'er *Bodley's dome his future labours spread,
*And Bacon's mansion trembles o'er his head.
Are these thy views? Proceed, illustrious youth,
And Virtue guard thee to the throne of Truth!
Yet should thy soul indulge the gen'rous heat
Till captive Science yields her last retreat;
Should Reason guide thee with her brightest ray,
And pour on misty Doubt resistless day;
Should no false kindness lure to loose delight,
Nor praise relax, nor difficulty fright;
Should tempting Novelty thy cell refrain,
And Sloth diffuse her opiate fumes in vain;
Should Beauty blunt on fops her fatal dart,
Nor claim the triumph of a letter'd heart;
Should no disease thy torpid veins invade,
Nor melancholy's phantoms haunt thy shade;
Yet hope not life from grief or danger free,
Nor think the doom of man revers'd for thee:
Deign on the passing world to turn thine eyes,
And pause awhile from letters to be wise;
There mark what ills the scholar's life assail —
Toil, envy, want, *the patron, and the jail.
See nations, slowly wise and meanly just,
To buried merit raise the tardy bust.
If dreams yet flatter, once again attend,
*Here Lydiat's life, and Galileo's end.

Nor deem, when Learning her last prize bestows,
The glitt'ring eminence exempt from foes;
See, when the vulgar 'scape, despis'd or aw'd,
*Rebellion's vengeful talons seize on Laud!
From meaner minds, though smaller fines content,
The plunder'd palace, or sequester'd rent,

Mark'd out by dang'rous parts, he meets the shock,
And fatal Learning leads him to the block:
Around his tomb let Art and Genius weep,
But hear his death, ye blockheads, hear and sleep.

The festal blazes, the triumphal show,
The ravish'd standard, and the captive foe,
The senate's thanks, the gazette's pompous tale,
With force resistless o'er the brave prevail.
Such bribes *the rapid Greek o'er Asia whirl'd;
For such the steady Romans shook the world;
For such in distant lands the Britons shine,
And stain with blood *the Danube or the Rhine:
This pow'r has praise that virtue scarce can warm
Till fame supplies the universal charm.
Yet Reason frowns on war's unequal game,
Where wasted nations raise a single name,
And mortgag'd states their grandsires' wreaths regret,
From age to age in everlasting debt;
Wreaths which at last the dear-bought right convey
To rust on medals, or on stones decay.

On what foundation stands the warrior's pride,
How just his hopes, let *Swedish Charles decide:
A frame of adamant, a soul of fire,
No dangers fright him, and no labours tire;
O'er love, o'er fear, extends his wide domain,
Unconquer'd lord of pleasure and of pain;
No joys to him pacific sceptres yield,
War sounds the trump, he rushes to the field;
Behold surrounding kings their pow'rs combine,
And one capitulate, and one resign.
Peace courts his hand, but spreads her charms in vain;
"Think nothing gain'd," he cries, "till nought remain,
On Moscow's walls till Gothic standards fly,
And all be mine beneath the polar sky."
The march begins in military state,
And nations on his eye suspended wait;
Stern Famine guards the solitary coast,
And Winter barricades the realms of Frost;
He comes; nor want nor cold his course delay;—
Hide, blushing Glory, hide Pultowa's day:
The vanquish'd hero leaves his broken bands,
And shows his miseries in distant lands;
Condemn'd a needy supplicant to wait,
While ladies interpose, and slaves debate.
But did not Chance at length her error mend?
Did no subverted empire mark his end?
Did rival monarchs give the fatal wound?
Or hostile millions press him to the ground?
His fall was destin'd to a barren strand,
A petty fortress, and a dubious hand.
He left the name at which the world grew pale,
To point a moral, or adorn a tale.

All times their scenes of pompous woes afford,
From Persia's tyrant to Bavaria's lord.
In gay hostility and barb'rous pride,
With half mankind embattled at his side,
*Great Xerxes comes to seize the certain prey,
And starves exhausted regions in his way.
Attendant Flatt'ry counts his myriads o'er,
Till counted myriads soothe his pride no more;
Fresh praise is tried till madness fires his mind,
The waves he lashes, and enchains the wind;
New pow'rs are claim'd, new pow'rs are still bestow'd,
Till rude resistance lops the spreading god;
The daring Greeks deride the martial show,
And heap their valleys with the gaudy foe;
Th' insulted sea with humbler thought he gains,
A single skiff to speed his flight remains;
Th' encumber'd oar scarce leaves the dreaded coast
Through purple billows and a floating host.

*The bold Bavarian, in a luckless hour,
Tries the dread summits of Cæsarean pow'r,
With unexpected legions bursts away,
And sees defenseless realms receive his sway;
Short sway! fair Austria spreads her mournful charms,
The queen, the beauty, sets the world in arms;
From hill to hill the beacon's rousing blaze
Spreads wide the hope of plunder and of praise;
The fierce Croatian, and the wild Hussar,
With all the sons of ravage, crowd the war:
The baffl'd prince, in honour's flatt'ring bloom
Of hasty greatness, finds the fatal doom,
His foe's derision, and his subjects' blame,
And steals to death from anguish and from shame.

"Enlarge my life with multitude of days!"
In health, in sickness, thus the suppliant prays;
Hides from himself his state, and shuns to know,
That life protracted is protracted woe.
Time hovers o'er, impatient to destroy,

And shuts up all the passages of joy:
In vain their gifts the bounteous seasons pour,
The fruit autumnal, and the vernal flow'r;
With listless eyes the dotard views the store,
He views, and wonders that they please no more;
Now pall the tasteless meats, and joyless wines,
And Luxury with sighs her slave resigns.
Approach, ye minstrels, try the soothing strain,
Diffuse the tuneful lenitives of pain:
No sounds, alas! would touch th' impervious ear,
Though dancing mountains witness'd Orpheus near;
Not lute nor lyre his feeble pow'rs attend,
Nor sweeter music of a virtuous friend;
But everlasting dictates crowd his tongue,
Perversely grave, or positively wrong.
The still returning tale, and ling'ring jest
Perplex the fawning niece and pampered guest,
While growing hopes scarce awe the gath'ring sneer,
And scarce a legacy can bribe to hear;
The watchful guests still hint the last offence;
The daughter's petulance, the son's expense,
Improve his heady rage with treach'rous skill,
And mould his passions till they make his will.
Unnumber'd maladies his joints invade,
Lay siege to life, and press the dire blockade;
But unextinguish'd Av'rice still remains,
And dreaded losses aggravate his pains:
He turns, with anxious heart and crippled hands,
His bonds of debt, and mortgages of lands;
Or views his coffers with suspicious eyes,
Unlocks his gold, and counts it till he dies.
But grant, the virtues of a temp'rate prime
Bless with an age exempt from scorn or crime;
An age that melts with unperceiv'd decay,
And glides in modest innocence away;
Whose peaceful day Benevolence endears,
Whose night congratulating Conscience cheers;
The gen'ral fav'rite as the gen'ral friend:
Such age there is, and who shall wish its end?
Yet ev'n on this her load Misfortune flings,
To press the weary minutes' flagging wings;
New sorrow rises as the day returns,
A sister sickens, or a daughter mourns.
Now kindred merit fills the sable bier,
Now lacerated friendship claims a tear.
Year chases year, decay pursues decay,
Still drops some joy from with'ring life away;
New forms arise, and diff'rent views engage,
Superfluous lags the vet'ran on the stage,
Till pitying Nature signs the last release,
And bids afflicted worth retire to peace.
But few there are whom hours like these await,
Who set unclouded in the gulfs of fate.
From *Lydia's monarch should the search descend,
By Solon caution'd to regard his end,
In life's last scene what prodigies surprise —
Fears of the brave, and follies of the wise!
*From Marlb'rough's eyes the streams of dotage flow,
*And Swift expires a driv'ller and a show.
The teeming mother, anxious for her race,
Begs for each birth the fortune of a face;
*Yet Vane could tell what ills from beauty spring;
And *Sedley curs'd the form that pleas'd a king.
Ye nymphs of rosy lips and radiant eyes,
Whom Pleasure keeps too busy to be wise;
Whom joys with soft varieties invite,
By day the frolic, and the dance by night;
Who frown with vanity, who smile with art,
And ask the latest fashion of the heart;
What care, what rules your heedless charms shall save,
Each nymph your rival, and each youth your slave?
Against your fame with fondness hate combines,
The rival batters, and the lover mines.
With distant voice neglected Virtue calls,
Less heard and less, the faint remonstrance falls:
Tir'd with contempt, she quits the slipp'ry reign,
And Pride and Prudence take her seat in vain.
In crowd at once, where none the pass defend,
The harmless freedom and the private friend.
The guardians yield, by force superior plied:
To Int'rest, Prudence; and to Flatt'ry, Pride.
Here Beauty falls betray'd, despis'd, distress'd,
And hissing Infamy proclaims the rest.
Where then shall Hope and Fear their objects find?
Must dull Suspense corrupt the stagnant mind?
Must helpless man, in ignorance sedate,
Roll darkling down the torrent of his fate?
Must no dislike alarm, no wishes rise,
No cries invoke the mercies of the skies?
Enquirer, cease; petitions yet remain

Which Heav'n may hear, nor deem religion vain.
Still raise for good the supplicating voice,
But leave to Heav'n the measure and the choice.
Safe in his pow'r, whose eyes discern afar
The secret ambush of a specious pray'r;
Implore his aid, in his decisions rest,
Secure, whate'er he gives, he gives the best.
Yet, when the sense of sacred presence fires,
And strong devotion to the skies aspires,
Pour forth thy fervours for a healthful mind,
Obedient passions, and a will resign'd;
For love, which scarce collective man can fill;
For patience, sov'reign o'er transmuted ill;
For faith, that panting for a happier seat,
Counts death kind Nature's signal of retreat.
These goods for man the laws of Heav'n ordain;
These goods he grants, who grants the pow'r to gain;
With these celestial Wisdom calms the mind,
And makes the happiness she does not find.

[1749]

THE RAMBLER *and* THE IDLER

Among the many eighteenth-century periodicals in the *Spectator* tradition Johnson's *Rambler* and *Idler* hold an important place. Johnson had some of the requisites for successful essay writing: a keen mind, an active interest in all people and in most things, a facile pen, and a strong individuality. Lightness, however, and delicacy and grace were not his. He was a moralist more grave than Steele, a social censor more earnest than Addison, a literary critic more profound than Goldsmith. His style, especially at this period, was heavy and Latinate. In view of his personality and literary equipment it is surprising that he succeeded at all as a popular essayist.

The *Rambler* appeared twice a week between March 20, 1750, and March 14, 1752. Johnson wrote practically all the numbers, receiving assistance from his friends but rarely. The circulation was not large, but the essays in bound form reached a far wider audience. That these essays should have been written while Johnson was engaged on the *Dictionary* is an evidence of his power of continuous hard work in spite of a constitutional tendency toward indolence. During a second period of two years in 1758–60 he published another series of essays, weekly this time, which he called the *Idler*. Though these are somewhat less ponderous than the *Rambler*, they are seldom light reading.

The selections here reprinted are necessarily brief. *Rambler* 161 shows Johnson at his best as a popular philosopher; the fortunes of the garret here described are typical of human life. In the portrayal of the poet, he gives us a glimpse of Grub Street as he had known it himself. The character of Dick Minim, the critic, in the *Idler*, 60 and 61, satirizes the pretender to critical knowledge and taste at a time when it was fashionable for men-about-town to make such pretensions. Minim reflects the superficial conventionalities of eighteenth-century English literary criticism in much the same way that Sinclair Lewis's Lowell Schmalz reflects the superficial conventionalities of twentieth-century American Babbitry. The type of false critic here presented should be compared with that in Dryden, Addison, Pope, and Swift.

THE RAMBLER

No. 161. Tuesday, October 1, 1751

οἵη περ φύλλων γενεή, τοίη δὲ καὶ ἀνδρῶν.
— Homer, *Iliad*, vi, 146.

Frail as the leaves that quiver on the sprays,
Like them man flourishes, like them decays.

Mr. Rambler. Sir:

You have formerly observed that curiosity often terminates in barren knowledge, and that the mind is prompted to study and inquiry rather by the uneasiness of ignorance than the hope of profit. Nothing can be of less importance to any present interest than the fortune of those who have been long lost in the grave, and from whom nothing now can be hoped or feared. Yet, to rouse the zeal of a true antiquary, little more is necessary than to mention a name which mankind have conspired to forget; he will make his way to remote scenes of action through obscurity and contradiction, as *Tully sought amidst bushes and brambles the tomb of Archimedes.

It is not easy to discover how it concerns him that gathers the produce or receives the rent of an estate, to know through what families the land has passed, who is registered in the Conqueror's survey as its possessor, how often it has been forfeited by treason, or how often sold by prodigality. The power or wealth of the present inhabitants of a country can not be much increased by an inquiry after the names of those barbarians who destroyed one another, twenty centuries ago, in contests for the shelter of woods or convenience of pasturage. Yet we see that no man can be at rest in the enjoyment of a new purchase till he has learned the history of his grounds from the ancient inhabitants of the parish, and that no nation omits to record the actions of their ancestors, however bloody, savage, and rapacious.

The same disposition, as different opportunities call it forth, discovers itself in great or little things. I have always thought it unworthy of a wise man to slumber in total inactivity, only because he happens to have no employment equal to his ambition or genius. It is therefore my custom to apply my attention to the objects before me; and as I cannot think any place wholly unworthy of notice that affords a habitation to a man of letters, I have collected the history and antiquities of the several garrets in which I have resided.

Quantulacunque estis, vos ego magna voco.

How small to others, but how great to me!

Many of these narratives my industry has been able to extend to a considerable length; but the woman with whom I now lodge has lived only eighteen months in the house, and can give no account of its ancient revolutions: the plasterer having at her entrance obliterated, by his whitewash, all the smoky memorials which former tenants had left upon the ceiling, and perhaps drawn the veil of oblivion over politicians, philosophers, and poets.

When I first cheapened my lodgings, the landlady told me that she hoped I was not an author, for the lodgers on the first floor had stipulated that the upper rooms should not be occupied by a noisy trade. I very readily promised to give no disturbance to her family, and soon despatched a bargain on the usual terms.

I had not slept many nights in my new apartment before I began to inquire after my predecessors, and found my landlady, whose imagination is filled chiefly with her own affairs, very ready to give me information.

Curiosity, like all other desires, produces pain as well as pleasure. Before she began her narrative, I had heated my head with expectations of adventures and discoveries, of elegance in disguise, and learning in distress, and was somewhat mortified when I heard that the first tenant was a tailor, of whom nothing was remembered but that he complained of his room for want of light, and, after having lodged in it a month, and paid only a week's rent, pawned a piece of cloth which he was trusted to cut out, and was forced to make a precipitate retreat from this quarter of the town.

The next was a young woman newly arrived from the country, who lived for five weeks with great regularity, and became by frequent treats very much the favourite of the family, but at last received visits so frequently from a cousin in Cheapside that she brought the reputation of the house into danger, and was therefore dismissed with good advice.

The room then stood empty for a fortnight; my landlady began to think that she had judged hardly, and often wished for such another lodger. At last, an elderly man of a grave aspect read the bill, and bargained for the room at the very first price that was asked. He lived in close retirement, seldom went out till evening, and then returned early, sometimes cheerful and at other times dejected. It was remarkable that, whatever he purchased, he never had small money in his pocket; and, though cool and temperate on other occasions, was always vehement and stormy till he received his change. He paid his rent with great exactness, and seldom failed once a week to requite my landlady's civility with a supper. At last — such is the fate of human felicity — the house was alarmed at midnight by the constable, who demanded to search the garrets. My landlady, assuring him that he had mistaken the door, conducted him upstairs, where he found the tools of a coiner. But the tenant had crawled along the roof to an empty house, and escaped, much to the joy of my landlady, who declares him a very honest man, and wonders why anybody should be hanged for making money, when such numbers are in want of it. She, however, confesses that she shall, for the future, always question the character of those who take her garret without beating down the price.

The bill was then placed again in the window, and the poor woman was teased for seven weeks by innumerable passengers, who obliged her to climb with them every hour up five stories, and then disliked the prospect, hated the noise of a public street, thought the stairs narrow, objected to a low ceiling, required the walls to be hung with fresher paper, asked questions about the neighbourhood, could not think of living so far from their acquaintance wished the windows had looked to the south rather than the west, told how the door and chimney might have been better disposed, bid her half the price that she asked, or promised to give her earnest the next day, and came no more.

At last, a short, meagre man, in a tarnished waistcoat, desired to see the garret, and, when he had stipulated for two long shelves and a larger table, hired it at a low rate. When the affair was completed, he looked round him with great satisfaction, and repeated some words which the woman did not understand. In two days he brought a great box of books, took possession of his room, and lived very inoffensively, except that he frequently disturbed the inhabitants of the next floor by unseasonable noises. He was generally in bed at noon, but from evening to midnight he sometimes talked aloud with great vehemence, sometimes stamped as in rage, sometimes threw down his poker, then clattered his chairs, then sat down in deep thought, and again burst out into loud vociferations; sometimes he would sigh as oppressed with misery, and sometimes shake with convulsive laughter. When he encountered any of the family, he gave way or bowed, but rarely spoke, except that as he went up stairs he often repeated, —

ὅς ὑπέρτατα δώματα ναίει

This habitant th' aërial regions boast

— hard words, to which his neighbours listened so often that they learned them without understanding them. What was his employment she did not venture to ask him, but at last heard a printer's boy inquire for "the author." My landlady was very often advised to beware of this strange man, who, though he was quiet for the present, might perhaps become outrageous in the hot months; but, as she was punctually paid, she could not find any sufficient reason for dismissing him, till one night he convinced her, by setting fire to his curtains, that it was not safe to have an author for her inmate.

She had then for six weeks a succession of tenants, who left the house on Saturday, and, instead of paying their rent, stormed at their landlady. At last she took in two sisters, one of whom had spent her little fortune in procuring remedies for a lingering disease, and was now supported and attended by the other; she climbed with difficulty to the apartment, where she languished eight weeks without impatience or lamentation, except for the expense and fatigue which her sister suffered, and then calmly and contentedly expired. The sister followed her to the grave, paid the few debts which they had contracted, wiped away the tears of useless sorrow, and, returning to the business of common life, resigned to me the vacant habitation.

Such, Mr. Rambler, are the changes which have happened in the narrow space where my present fortune has fixed my residence. So true it is that amusement and instruction are always at hand for those who have skill and willingness to find them; and, so just is the observation of Juvenal that a single house will show whatever is done or suffered in the world.

I am, sir, &c.

THE IDLER

No. 60. Saturday, June 9, 1759

Criticism is a study by which men grow important and formidable at a very small expense. The power of invention has been conferred by nature upon few, and the labour of learning those sciences which may by mere labour be obtained is too great to be willingly endured; but every man can exert such judgment as he has upon the works of others; and he whom nature has made weak, and idleness keeps ignorant, may yet support his vanity by the name of a critic.

I hope it will give comfort to great numbers who are passing through the world in obscurity when I inform them how easily distinction may be obtained. All the other powers of literature are coy and haughty; they must be long courted, and at last are not always gained; but Criticism is a goddess easy of access and forward of advance, who will meet the slow and encourage the timorous; the want of meaning she supplies with words, and the want of spirit she recompenses with malignity.

This *profession has one recommendation peculiar to itself, that it gives vent to malignity without real mischief. No genius was ever blasted by the breath of critics. The poison which, if confined, would have burst the heart, fumes away in empty hisses, and malice is set at ease with very little danger to merit. The critic is the only man whose triumph is without another's pain, and whose greatness does not rise upon another's ruin.

To a study at once so easy and so reputable, so malicious and so harmless, it cannot be necessary to invite my readers by a long or laboured exhortation; it is sufficient, since all would be critics if they could, to show by one eminent example that all can be critics if they will.

Dick Minim, after the common course of puerile studies, in which he was no great proficient, was put an apprentice to a brewer, with whom he had lived two years when his uncle died in the city and left him a large fortune in the stocks. Dick had for six months before used the company of the lower players, of whom he had learned to scorn a trade, and, being now at liberty to follow his genius, he resolved to be a man of wit and humour. That he might be properly initiated in his new character, he frequented the coffee-houses near the theatres, where he listened very diligently day after day to those who talked of language and sentiments and unities and catastrophes, till by slow degrees he began to think that he understood something of the stage, and hoped in time to talk himself.

But he did not trust so much to natural sagacity as wholly to neglect the help of books. When the theatres were shut, he retired to Richmond with a few select writers, whose opinions he impressed upon his memory by unwearied diligence; and, when he returned with other wits to the town, was able to tell in very proper phrases that the chief business of art is to copy nature; that a perfect writer is not to be expected, because genius decays as judgment increases; that the great art is the art of blotting; and that, according to the rule of Horace, every piece should be kept nine years.

Of the great authors he now began to display the characters, laying down as an universal position that all had beauties and defects. His opinion was that Shakespeare, committing himself wholly to the impulse of nature, wanted that correctness which learning would have given him; and that Jonson, trusting to learning, did not sufficiently cast his eye on nature. He blamed the stanza of Spenser, and could not bear the hexameters of Sidney. Denham and Waller he held the first reformers of English numbers, and thought that if Waller could have obtained the strength of Denham, or Denham the sweetness of Waller, there had been nothing wanting to complete a poet. He often expressed his commiseration of Dryden's poverty, and his indignation at the age which suffered him to write for bread; he repeated with rapture the first lines of *All for Love*, but wondered at the corruption of taste which could bear anything so unnatural as rhyming tragedies. In *Otway he found uncommon powers of moving the passions, but was disgusted by his general negligence, and blamed him for making a conspirator his hero, and never concluded his disquisition without remarking how happily the sound of the clock is made to alarm the audience. *Southerne would have been his favourite but that he mixes comic with tragic scenes, intercepts the natural course of the passions, and fills the mind with a wild confusion of mirth and melancholy. The versification of Rowe he thought too melodious for the stage, and too little varied in different passions. He made it the great fault of Congreve that all his persons were wits and that he always wrote with more art than nature. He considered *Cato* rather as a poem than a play, and allowed Addison to be the complete master of allegory and grave humour, but paid no great deference to him as a critic. He thought the chief merit of Prior was in his easy tales and lighter poems, though he allowed that his *Solomon* had many noble sentiments elegantly expressed. In Swift he discovered an inimitable vein of irony and an easiness which all would hope and few would attain. Pope he was inclined to degrade from a poet to a versifier, and thought his numbers rather luscious than sweet. He often lamented the neglect of **Phædra and Hippolitus*, and wished to see the stage under better regulations.

These assertions passed commonly uncontradicted; and if now and then an opponent started up, he was quickly repressed by the suffrages of the company, and Minim went away from every dispute with elation of heart and increase of confidence.

He now grew conscious of his abilities and began to talk of the present state of dramatic poetry, wondered what was become of the comic genius which supplied our ancestors with wit and pleasantry, and why no writer could be found that durst now venture beyond a farce. He saw no reason for thinking that the vein of humour was exhausted, since we live in a country where liberty suffers every character to spread itself to its utmost bulk, and which therefore produces more originals than all the rest of the world together. Of tragedy he concluded business to be the soul, and yet often hinted that love predominates too much upon the modern stage.

He was now an acknowledged critic and had his own seat in a coffee-house and headed a party in the pit. Minim has more vanity than ill-nature and seldom desires to do much mischief; he will, perhaps, murmur a little in the ear of him that sits next him, but endeavours to influence the audience to favour by clapping when an actor exclaims, "Ye gods!" or laments the misery of his country.

By degrees he was admitted to rehearsals; and many of his friends are of opinion that our present poets are indebted to him for their happiest thoughts; by his contrivance *the bell was rung twice in *Barbarossa*, and by his persuasion *the author of *Cleone* concluded his play without a couplet; for what can be more absurd, said Minim, than that part of a play should be rhymed, and part written in blank verse? And by what acquisition of faculties is the speaker, who never could find rhymes before, enabled to rhyme at the conclusion of an act?

He is the great investigator of hidden beauties, and is particularly delighted when he finds *"the sound an echo to the sense." He has read all our poets with particular attention to this delicacy of versification, and wonders at the supineness with which their works have been hitherto perused, so that no man has found the sound of a drum in this distich:

> *And pulpit, drum ecclesiastic,
> Was beat with fist instead of a stick;

and that the wonderful lines upon honour and a bubble have hitherto passed without notice:

> *Honour is like the glassy bubble
> Which costs philosophers such trouble;
> Where, one part crack'd, the whole does fly,
> And wits are crack'd to find out why.

In these verses, says Minim, we have two striking accommodations of the sound to the sense. It is impossible to utter the two lines emphatically without an act like that which they describe: *bubble* and *trouble* causing a momentary inflation of the cheeks by the retention of the breath, which is afterwards forcibly emitted, as in the practice of *blowing bubbles.* But the greatest excellence is in the third line, which is *crack'd* in the middle to express a crack, and then shivers into monosyllables. Yet has this diamond lain neglected with common stones, and among the innumerable admirers of *Hudibras* the observation of this superlative passage has been reserved for the sagacity of Minim.

No. 61. Saturday, June 16, 1759

Mr. Minim had now advanced himself to the zenith of critical reputation; when he was in the pit, every eye in the boxes was fixed upon him; when he entered his coffee-house, he was surrounded by circles of candidates who passed their novitiate of literature under his tuition: his opinion was asked by all who had no opinion of their own, and yet loved to debate and decide; and no composition was supposed to pass in safety to posterity till it had been secured by Minim's approbation.

Minim professes great admiration of the wisdom and munificence by which the academies of the continent were raised, and often wishes for some standard of taste, for some tribunal, to which merit may appeal from caprice, prejudice, and malignity. He has formed a plan for *an academy of criticism, where every work of imagination may be read before it is printed, and which shall authoritatively direct the theatres what pieces to receive or reject, to exclude or to revive.

Such an institution would, in Dick's opinion, spread the fame of English literature over Europe and make London the metropolis of elegance and politeness, the place to which the learned and ingenious of all countries would repair for instruction and improvement, and where nothing would any longer be applauded or endured that was not conformed to the nicest rules and finished with the highest elegance.

Till some happy conjunction of the planets shall dispose our princes or ministers to make themselves immortal by such an academy, Minim contents himself to preside four nights in a week in a critical society selected by himself, where he is heard without contradiction, and whence his judgment is disseminated through *"the great vulgar and the small."

When he is placed in the chair of criticism, he declares loudly for the noble simplicity of our ancestors, in opposition to the petty refinements and ornamental luxuriance. Sometimes he is sunk in despair, and perceives false delicacy daily gaining ground, and sometimes brightens his countenance with a gleam of hope, and predicts the revival of the true sublime. He then fulminates his loudest censures against *the monkish barbarity of rhyme; wonders how beings that pretend to reason can be pleased with one line always ending like another; tells how unjustly and unnaturally sense is sacrificed to sound; how often the best thoughts are mangled by the necessity of confining or extending them to the dimensions of a couplet; and rejoices that genius has, in our days, shaken off the shackles which had encumbered it so long. Yet he allows that rhyme may sometimes be borne, if the lines be often broken, and the pauses judiciously diversified.

From blank verse he makes an easy transition to Milton, whom he produces as an example of the slow advance of lasting reputation. Milton is the only writer in whose books Minim can read forever without weariness. What cause it is that exempts this pleasure from satiety he has long and diligently inquired, and believes it to consist in the perpetual variation of the numbers, by which the ear is gratified and the attention awakened. The lines that are commonly thought rugged and unmusical, he conceives to have been written to temper the melodious luxury of the rest, or to express things by a proper cadence: for he scarcely finds a verse that has not this favourite beauty; he declares that he could shiver in a hot-house when he reads that

> *the ground
> Burns frore, and cold performs th' effect of fire;

and that, when Milton bewails his blindness, the verse,

> *So thick a drop serene hath quench'd their orbs,

has, he knows not how, something that strikes him with an obscure sensation like that which he fancies would be felt from the sound of darkness.

Minim is not so confident of his rules of judgment as not very eagerly to catch new light from the name of the author. He is commonly so prudent as to spare those whom he cannot resist, unless, as will sometimes happen, he finds the public combined against them. But a fresh pretender to fame he is strongly inclined to censure, till his own honour requires that he commend him. Till he knows the success of a composition, he entrenches himself in general terms: there are some new thoughts and beautiful passages, but there is likewise much which he would have advised the author to expunge. He has several favourite epithets of which he has never settled the meaning, but which are very commodiously applied to books which he has not read, or can not understand. One is *manly*, another is *dry*, another *stiff*, and another *flimsy*; sometimes he discovers *delicacy of style*, and sometimes meets with *strange expressions*.

He is never so great or so happy as when a youth of promising parts is brought to receive his directions for the prosecution of his studies. He then puts on a very serious air; he advises the pupil to read none but the best authors, and when he finds one congenial to his own mind, to study his beauties, but avoid his faults; and, when he sits down to write, to consider how his favourite author would think at the present time on the present occasion. He exhorts him to catch those moments when he finds his thoughts expanded and his genius exalted, but to take care lest imagination hurry him beyond the bounds of nature. He holds diligence the mother of success; yet enjoins him, with great earnestness, not to read more than he can digest, and not to confuse his mind by pursuing studies of contrary tendencies. He tells him that every man has his genius, and that Cicero could never be a poet. The boy retires illuminated, resolves to follow his genius, and to think how Milton would have thought: and Minim feasts upon his own beneficence till another day brings him another pupil.

From PREFACE TO SHAKESPEARE

In 1745 Johnson first issued his "Proposals for a New Edition of Shakespeare," but he encountered so many delays in the execution of the task that the completed work did not appear until some twenty years later. Though his edition of Shakespeare is an important piece of work, it is less frequently remembered in our day than is its Preface.

This Preface shows Johnson's characteristic sanity and sound judgment; it is a discriminating appreciation of Shakespeare by a great critic who was neither acrimonious in dislike nor servile in worship. Johnson judged the plays from a point of view strikingly different from Shakespeare's and quite as far from our own: he applied to his subject critical standards which Shakespeare neither knew nor recognized, and he lacked much knowledge which is the product of more modern research. Yet in spite of these differences, partly because of them, Johnson's conclusions have perennial interest: they enlighten both their author and their subject.

Most striking of the pronouncements is that on the dramatic unities. Most students learn with surprise that the most important mid-eighteenth-century protest against the universal application of the rule of the unities came from the acknowledged leader of neo-classical thought. Johnson respected the unities, but he valued them at their true worth, as instruments for attaining organic unity, not as unfailing marks of satisfactory dramatic structure. That one who valued authority so much as Johnson did, should have perceived the inadequacy of an opinion almost universally accepted by his predecessors and contemporaries is an example of that intellectual vigour which was one of his salient qualities.

The selection here reprinted includes the first half of the Preface. The omitted part deals with the work of the earlier Shakespearean editors and with Johnson's own treatment of the text.

That praises are without reason lavished on the dead, and that the honours due only to excellence are paid to antiquity is a complaint likely to be always continued by those, who, being able to add nothing to truth, hope for eminence from the heresies of paradox; or those, who, being forced by disappointment upon consolatory expedients, are willing to hope from posterity what the present age refuses, and flatter themselves that the regard which is yet denied by envy will be at last bestowed by time.

Antiquity, like every other quality that attracts the notice of mankind, has undoubtedly votaries that reverence it, not from reason but from prejudice. Some seem to admire indiscriminately whatever has been long preserved, without considering that time has sometimes co-operated with chance; all perhaps are more willing to honour past than present excellence; and the mind contemplates genius through the shades of age, as the eye surveys the sun through artificial opacity. The great contention of criticism is to find the faults of the moderns and the beauties of the ancients. While an author is yet living, we estimate his powers by his worst performance; and when he is dead, we rate them by his best.

To works, however, of which the excellence is not absolute and definite, but gradual and comparative; to works not raised upon principles demonstrative and scientific, but appealing wholly to observation and experience, no other test can be applied than length of duration and continuance of esteem. What mankind have long possessed, they have often examined and compared; and if they persist to value the possession, it is because frequent comparisons have confirmed opinion in its favour. As among the works of nature no man can properly call a river deep or a mountain high without the knowledge of many mountains and many rivers, so in the production of genius nothing can be styled excellent till it has been compared with other works of the same kind. Demonstration immediately displays its power, and has nothing to hope or fear from the flux of years; but works tentative and experimental must be estimated by their proportion to the general and collective ability of man as it is discovered in a long succession of endeavours. Of the first building that was raised, it might be with certainty determined that it was round or square; but whether it was spacious or lofty must have been referred to time. The *Pythagorean scale of numbers was at once discovered to be perfect; but the poems of Homer we yet know not to transcend the common limits of human intelligence, but by remarking that nation after nation, and century after century, has been able to do little more than transpose his incidents, new name his characters, and paraphrase his sentiments.

The reverence due to writings that have long subsisted arises therefore not from any credulous confidence in the superior wisdom of past ages, or gloomy persuasion of the degeneracy of mankind, but is the consequence of acknowledged and indubitable positions, that what has been longest known has been most considered, and what is most considered is best understood.

The poet of whose works I have undertaken the revision may now begin to assume the dignity of an ancient, and claim the privilege of established fame and prescriptive veneration. He has long outlived his century, the term commonly fixed as the test of literary merit. Whatever advantages he might once derive from personal allusions, local customs, or temporary opinions have for many years been lost; and every topic of merriment or motive of sorrow which the modes of artificial life afforded him now only obscure the scenes which they once illuminated. The effects of favour and competition are at an end; the tradition of his friendships and his enmities has perished; his works support no opinion with arguments, nor supply any faction with invectives; they can neither indulge vanity nor gratify malignity; but are read without any other reason than the desire of pleasure, and are therefore praised only as pleasure is obtained; yet, thus unassisted by interest or passion, they have passed through variations of taste and changes of manners, and, as they devolved from one generation to another, have received new honours at every transmission.

But because human judgment, though it be gradually gaining upon certainty, never becomes infallible, and approbation, though long continued, may yet be only the approbation of prejudice or fashion, it is proper to inquire by what peculiarities of excellence Shakespeare has gained and kept the favour of his countrymen.

Nothing can please many, and please long, but just representations of general nature. Particular manners can be known to few, and therefore few only can judge how nearly they are copied. The irregular combinations of fanciful invention may delight awhile, by that novelty of which the common satiety of life sends us all in quest; but the pleasures of sudden wonder are soon exhausted, and the mind can only repose on the stability of truth.

Shakespeare is, above all writers — at least above all modern writers — the poet of nature, the poet that holds up to his readers a faithful mirror of manners and of life. His characters are not modified by the customs of particular places, unpractised by the rest of the world; by the peculiarities of studies or professions, which can operate but upon small numbers; or by the accidents of transient fashions or temporary opinions: they are the genuine progeny of common humanity, such as the world will always supply, and observation will always find. His persons act and speak by the influence of those general passions and principles by which all minds are agitated, and the whole system of life is continued in motion. In the writings of other poets * a character is too often an individual; in those of Shakespeare it is commonly a species.

It is from this wide extension of design that so much instruction is derived. It is this which fills the plays of Shakespeare with practical axioms and domestic wisdom. It was said of Euripides that every verse was a precept; and it may be said of Shakespeare that from his works may be collected a system of civil and economical prudence. Yet his real power is not shown in the splendour of particular passages, but by the progress of his fable and the tenor of his dialogue; and he that tries to recommend him by select quotations will succeed like the pedant in Hierocles, who, when he offered his house to sale, carried a brick in his pocket as a specimen.

It will not easily be imagined how much Shakespeare excels in accommodating his sentiments to real life, but by comparing him with other authors. It was observed of the ancient schools of declamation that the more diligently they were frequented, the more was the student disqualified for the world, because he found nothing there which he should ever meet in any other place. The same remark may be applied to every stage but that of Shakespeare. The theatre, when it is under any other direction, is peopled by such characters as were never seen, conversing in a language which was never heard, upon topics which will never arise in the commerce of mankind. But the dialogue of this author is often so evidently determined by the incident which produces it, and is pursued with so much ease and simplicity, that it seems scarcely to claim the merit of fiction, but to have been gleaned by diligent selection out of common conversation and common occurrences.

Upon every other stage the universal agent is love, by whose power all good and evil is distributed, and every action quickened or retarded. To bring a lover, a lady, and a rival into the fable; to entangle them in contradictory obligations, perplex them with oppositions of interest, and harass them with violence of desires inconsistent with each other; to make them meet in rapture, and part in agony; to fill their mouths with hyperbolical joy and outrageous sorrow; to distress them as nothing human ever was distressed; to deliver them as nothing human ever was delivered, is the business of a modern dramatist. For this, probability is violated, life is misrepresented, and language is depraved. But love is only one of many passions; and as it has no great influence upon the sum of life, it has little operation in the dramas of a poet who caught his ideas from the living world, and exhibited only what he saw before him. He knew that any other passion, as it was regular or exorbitant, was a cause of happiness or calamity.

Characters thus ample and general were not easily discriminated and preserved, yet perhaps no poet ever kept his personages more distinct from each other. I will not say, with Pope, that every speech may be assigned to the proper speaker, because many speeches there are which have nothing characteristical; but, perhaps, though some may be equally adapted to every person, it will be difficult to find that any can be properly transferred from the present possessor to another claimant. The choice is right, when there is reason for choice.

Other dramatists can only gain attention by hyperbolical or aggravated characters, by fabulous and unexampled excellence or depravity, as the writers of barbarous romances invigorated the reader by a giant and a dwarf; and he that should form his expectations of human affairs from the play, or from the tale, would be equally deceived. Shakespeare has no heroes; his scenes are occupied only by men who act and speak as the reader thinks that he should himself have spoken or acted on the same occasion: even where the agency is supernatural, the dialogue is level with life. Other writers disguise the most natural passions and most frequent incidents, so that he who contemplates them in the book will not know them in the world. Shakespeare approximates the remote, and familiarizes the wonderful; the event which he represents will not happen, but, if it were possible, its effects would probably be such as he has assigned; and it may be said that he has not only shown human nature as it acts in real exigencies, but as it would be found in trials to which it cannot be exposed.

This, therefore, is the praise of Shakespeare, that his drama is the mirror of life; that he who has mazed his imagination in following the phantoms which other writers raise up before him, may here be cured of his delirious ecstasies, by reading human sentiments in human language; by scenes from which a hermit may estimate the transactions of the world, and a confessor predict the progress of the passions.

His adherence to general nature has exposed him to the censure of critics who form their judgments on narrower principles. *Dennis and Rymer think his Romans not sufficiently Roman, and *Voltaire censures his kings as not completely royal. Dennis is offended that Menenius, a senator of Rome, should play the buffoon; and Voltaire perhaps thinks decency violated when the Danish usurper is represented as a drunkard. But Shakespeare always makes nature predominate over accident; and, if he preserves the essential character, is not very careful of distinctions superinduced and adventitious. His story requires Romans or kings, but he thinks only on men. He knew that Rome, like every other city, had men of all dispositions; and wanting a buffoon, he went into the senate-house for that which the senate-house would certainly have afforded him. He was inclined to show an usurper and a murderer not only odious but despicable; he therefore added drunkenness to his other qualities, knowing that kings love wine like other men, and that wine exerts its natural power upon kings. These are the petty cavils of petty minds; a poet overlooks the casual distinction of country and condition, as a painter, satisfied with the figure, neglects the drapery.

The censure which he has incurred by mixing *comic and tragic scenes, as it extends to all his works, deserves more consideration. Let the fact be first stated, and then examined.

Shakespeare's plays are not, in the rigorous and critical sense, either tragedies or comedies, but compositions of a distinct kind, exhibiting the real state of sublunary nature, which partakes of good and evil, joy and sorrow, mingled with endless variety of proportion and innumerable modes of combination, and expressing the course of the world, in which the loss of one is the gain of another; in which, at the same time, the reveller is hasting to his wine, and the mourner burying his friend; in which the malignity of one is sometimes defeated by the frolic of another; and many mischiefs and many benefits are done and hindered without design.

Out of this chaos of mingled purposes and casualties the ancient poets, according to the laws which custom had prescribed, selected some the crimes of men, and some their absurdities; some the momentous vicissitudes of life, and some the lighter occurrences; some the terrors of distress, and some the gaieties of prosperity. Thus rose the two modes of imitation, known by the names of *tragedy* and *comedy*, compositions intended to promote different ends by contrary means, and considered as so little allied that I do not recollect among the Greeks or Romans a single writer who attempted both.

Shakespeare has united the powers of exciting laughter and sorrow not only in one mind, but in one composition. Almost all his plays are divided between serious and ludicrous characters, and, in the successive evolutions of the design, sometimes produce seriousness and sorrow, and sometimes levity and laughter.

That this is a practice contrary to the rules of criticism will be readily allowed; but there is always an appeal open from criticism to nature. The end of writing is to instruct; the end of poetry is to instruct by pleasing. That the mingled drama may convey all the instruction of tragedy or comedy cannot be denied, because it includes both in its alternations of exhibition, and approaches nearer than either to the appearance of life, by showing how great machinations and slender designs may promote or obviate one another, and the high and the low co-operate in the general system by unavoidable concatenation.

It is objected that by this change of scenes the passions are interrupted in their progression, and that the principal event, being not advanced by a due gradation of preparatory incidents, wants at last the power to move, which constitutes the perfection of dramatic poetry. This reasoning is so specious that it is received as true even by those who in daily experience feel it to be false. The interchanges of mingled scenes seldom fail to produce the intended vicissitudes of passion. Fiction cannot move so much but that the attention may be easily transferred; and though it must be allowed that pleasing melancholy be sometimes interrupted by unwelcome levity, yet let it be considered likewise that melancholy is often not pleasing, and that the disturbance of one man may be the relief of another; that different auditors have different habitudes; and that upon the whole all pleasure consists in variety.

*The players, who in their edition divided our author's works into comedies, histories, and tragedies, seem not to have distinguished the three kinds by any very exact or definite ideas. An action which ended happily to the principal persons, however serious or distressful through its intermediate incidents, in their opinion constituted a comedy. This idea of a comedy continued long amongst us; and plays were written which, by changing the catastrophe, were tragedies today and comedies tomorrow. Tragedy was not in those times a poem of more general dignity or elevation than comedy; it required only a calamitous conclusion, with which the common criticism of that age was satisfied, whatever lighter pleasure it afforded in its progress.

History was a series of actions with no other than chronological succession, independent on each other, and without any tendency to introduce or regulate the conclusion. It is not always very nicely distinguished from tragedy. There is not much nearer approach to unity of action in the tragedy of *Antony and Cleopatra* than in the history of *Richard the Second*. But a history might be continued through many plays; as it had no plan, it had no limits.

Through all these denominations of the drama, Shakespeare's mode of composition is the same: an interchange of seriousness and merriment, by which the mind is softened at one time, and exhilarated at another. But whatever be his purpose, whether to gladden or depress, or to conduct the story, without vehemence or emotion, through tracts of easy and familiar dialogue, he never fails to attain his purpose. As he commands us, we laugh or mourn, or sit silent with quiet expectation, in tranquillity without indifference.

When Shakespeare's plan is understood, most of the criticisms of Rymer and Voltaire vanish away. The play of *Hamlet* is opened, without impropriety, by two sentinels; Iago bellows at Brabantio's window without injury to the scheme of the play, though in terms which a modern audience would not easily endure; the character of Polonius is seasonable and useful, and the grave-diggers themselves may be heard with applause.

Shakespeare engaged in dramatic poetry with the world open before him; the rules of the ancients were yet known to few; the public judgment was unformed; he had no example of such fame as might force him upon imitation, nor critics of such authority as might restrain his extravagance: he therefore indulged his natural disposition; and his disposition, as Rymer has remarked, led him to comedy. In tragedy he often writes with great appearance of toil and study what is written at last with little felicity; but in his comic scenes he seems to produce, without labour, what no labour can improve. In tragedy he is always struggling after some occasion to be comic; but in comedy he seems to repose, or to luxuriate, as in a mode of thinking congenial to his nature. In his tragic scenes there is always something wanting, but his comedy often surpasses expectation or desire. His comedy pleases by the thoughts and the language, and his tragedy for the greater part by incident and action. His tragedy seems to be skill, his comedy to be instinct.

The force of his comic scenes has suffered little diminution from the changes made by a century and a half, in manners or in words. As his personages act upon principles arising from genuine passion, very little modified by particular forms, their pleasures and vexations are communicable to all times and to all places; they are natural, and therefore durable. The adventitious peculiarities of personal habits are only superficial dyes, bright and pleasing for a little while, yet soon fading to a dim tinct, without any remains of former lustre; but the discriminations of true passion are the colours of nature: they pervade the whole mass, and can only perish with the body that exhibits them. The accidental compositions of heterogeneous modes are dissolved by the chance which combined them, but the uniform simplicity of primitive qualities neither admits increase nor suffers decay. The sand heaped by one flood is scattered by another, but the rock always continues in its place. The stream of time, which is continually washing the dissoluble fabrics of other poets, passes without injury by the adamant of Shakespeare.

If there be, what I believe there is, in every nation, a style which never becomes obsolete — a certain mode of phraseology so consonant and congenial to the analogy and principles of its respective language, as to remain settled and unaltered — this style is probably to be sought in the common intercourse of life, among those who speak only to be understood, without ambition of elegance. The polite are always catching modish innovations, and the learned depart from established forms of speech in hope of finding or making better; those who wish for distinction forsake the vulgar, when the vulgar is right; but there is a conversation above grossness and below refinement, where propriety resides, and where this poet seems to have gathered his comic dialogue. He is therefore more agreeable to the ears of the present age than any other author equally remote, and, among his other excellencies, deserves to be studied as one of the original masters of our language.

These observations are to be considered not as unexceptionably constant, but as containing general and predominant truth. Shakespeare's familiar dialogue is affirmed to be smooth and clear, yet not wholly without ruggedness or difficulty, as a country may be eminently fruitful, though it has spots unfit for cultivation: his characters are praised as natural, though their sentiments are sometimes forced and their actions improbable, as the earth upon the whole is spherical, though its surface is varied with protuberances and cavities.

Shakespeare, with his excellencies, has likewise faults, and faults sufficient to obscure and overwhelm any other merit. I shall show them in the proportion in which they appear to me, without envious malignity or superstitious veneration. No question can be more innocently discussed than a dead poet's pretensions to renown, and little regard is due to that bigotry which sets *candour higher than truth.

His first defect is that to which may be imputed most of the evil in books or in men. He sacrifices virtue to convenience, and is so much more careful to please than to instruct that he seems to write without any moral purpose. From his writings, indeed, a system of social duty may be selected, for he that thinks reasonably must think morally; but his precepts and axioms drop casually from him; he makes no just distribution of good or evil, nor is always careful to show in the virtuous a disapprobation of the wicked. He carries his persons indifferently through right and wrong, and at the close dismisses them without further care, and leaves their examples to operate by chance. This fault the barbarity of his age cannot extenuate, for it is always a writer's duty to make the world better, and justice is a virtue independent on time or place.

The plots are often so loosely formed that a very slight consideration may improve them, and so carelessly pursued that he seems not always fully to comprehend his own design. He omits opportunities of instructing or delighting, which the train of his story seems to force upon him, and apparently rejects those exhibitions which would be more affecting, for the sake of those which are more easy.

It may be observed that in many of his plays the latter part is evidently neglected. When he found himself near the end of his work, and in view of his reward, he shortened the labour to snatch the profit. He therefore remits his efforts where he should most vigorously exert them, and his catastrophe is improbably produced or imperfectly represented.

He had no regard to distinction of time or place, but gives to one age or nation, without scruple, the customs, institutions, and opinions of another, at the expense not only of likelihood but of possibility. These faults Pope has endeavoured, with more zeal than judgment, to transfer to his imagined interpolators. We need not wonder to find *Hector quoting Aristotle, when we see *the loves of Theseus and Hippolyta combined with the Gothic mythology of fairies. Shakespeare, indeed, was not the only violator of chronology, for in the same age Sidney, who wanted not the advantages of learning, has, in his *Arcadia*, confounded the pastoral with the feudal times, the days of innocence, quiet, and security with those of turbulence, violence, and adventure.

In his comic scenes he is seldom very successful when he engages his characters in reciprocations of smartness and contests of sarcasm. Their jests are commonly gross, and their pleasantry licentious; neither his gentlemen nor his ladies have much delicacy, nor are sufficiently distinguished from his clowns by any appearance of refined manners. Whether he represented the real conversation of his time is not easy to determine; the reign of Elizabeth is commonly supposed to have been a time of stateliness, formality, and reserve, yet perhaps the relaxations of that severity were not very elegant. There must, however, have been always some modes of gaiety preferable to others, and a writer ought to choose the best.

In tragedy his performance seems constantly to be worse as his labour is more. The effusions of passion which exigence forces out are for the most part striking and energetic; but whenever he solicits his invention, or strains his faculties, the offspring of his throes is tumour, meanness, tediousness, and obscurity.

In narration he affects a disproportionate pomp of diction and a wearisome train of circumlocution, and tells the incident imperfectly in many words, which might have been more plainly delivered in few. Narration in dramatic poetry is naturally tedious, as it is unanimated and inactive, and obstructs the progress of the action; it should therefore always be rapid, and enlivened by frequent interruption. Shakespeare found it an encumbrance, and instead of lightening it by brevity, endeavoured to recommend it by dignity and splendour.

His declamations or set speeches are commonly cold and weak, for his power was the power of nature. When he endeavoured, like other tragic writers, to catch opportunities of amplification, and, instead of inquiring what the occasion demanded, to show how much his stores of knowledge could supply, he seldom escapes without the pity or resentment of his reader.

It is incident to him to be now and then entangled with an unwieldy sentiment, which he cannot well express, and will not reject. He struggles with it a while, and, if it continues stubborn, comprises it in words such as occur, and leaves it to be disentangled and evolved by those who have more leisure to bestow upon it.

Not that always where the language is intricate the thought is subtle, or the image always great where the line is bulky. The equality of words to things is very often neglected, and trivial sentiments and vulgar ideas disappoint the attention, to which they are recommended by sonorous epithets and swelling figures.

But the admirers of this great poet have most reason to complain when he approaches nearest to his highest excellence, and seems fully resolved to sink them in dejection, and mollify them with tender emotions, by the fall of greatness, the danger of innocence, or the crosses of love. What he does best, he soon ceases to do. He is not long soft and pathetic without some idle conceit or contemptible equivocation. He no sooner begins to move than he counteracts himself; and terror and pity, as they are rising in the mind, are checked and blasted by sudden frigidity.

A quibble is to Shakespeare what luminous vapours are to the traveller: he follows it at all adventures; it is sure to lead him out of his way, and sure to engulf him in the mire. It has some malignant power over his mind, and its fascinations are irresistible. Whatever be the dignity or profundity of his disquisition, whether he be enlarging knowledge or exalting affection, whether he be amusing attention with incidents, or enchaining it in suspense, let but a quibble spring up before him, and he leaves his work unfinished. A quibble is the golden apple for which he will always turn aside from his career, or stoop from his elevation. A quibble, poor and barren as it is, gave him such delight that he was content to purchase it by the sacrifice of reason, propriety, and truth. A quibble was to him the fatal Cleopatra for which he lost the world, and was content to lose it.

It will be thought strange that, in enumerating the defects of this writer, I have not yet mentioned his neglect of the unities: his violation of those laws which have been instituted and established by the joint authority of poets and critics.

For his other deviations from the art of writing I resign him to critical justice, without making any other demand in his favour than that which must be indulged to all human excellence — that his virtues be rated with his failings: but from the censure which this irregularity may bring upon him, I shall, with due reverence to that learning which I must oppose, adventure to try how I can defend him.

His histories, being neither tragedies nor comedies, are not subject to any of their laws. Nothing more is necessary to all the praise which they expect, than that the changes of action be so prepared as to be understood, that the incidents be various and affecting, and the characters consistent, natural, and distinct. No other unity is intended, and therefore none is to be sought.

In his other works he has well enough preserved the unity of action. He has not, indeed, an intrigue regularly perplexed and regularly unravelled; he does not endeavour to hide his design only to discover it, for this is seldom the order of real events, and Shakespeare is the poet of nature: but his plan has commonly what Aristotle requires, a beginning, a middle, and an end; one event is concatenated with another, and the conclusion follows by easy consequence. There are perhaps some incidents that might be spared, as in other poets there is much talk that only fills up time upon the stage; but the general system makes gradual advances, and the end of the play is the end of expectation.

To the unities of time and place he has shown no regard; and perhaps a nearer view of the principles on which they stand will diminish their value, and withdraw from them the veneration which, from the time of Corneille, they have very generally received, by discovering that they have given more trouble to the poet than pleasure to the auditor.

The necessity of observing the unities of time and place arises from the supposed necessity of making the drama credible. The critics hold it impossible that an action of months or years can be possibly believed to pass in three hours; or that the spectator can suppose himself to sit in the theatre while ambassadors go and return between distant kings, while armies are levied and towns besieged, while an exile wanders and returns, or till he whom they saw courting his mistress shall lament the untimely fall of his son. The mind revolts from evident falsehood, and fiction loses its force when it departs from the resemblance of reality.

From the narrow limitation of time necessarily arises the contraction of place. The spectator who knows that he saw the first act at Alexandria cannot suppose that he sees the next at Rome, at a distance to which not the dragons of Medea could, in so short a time, have transported him; he knows with certainty that he has not changed his place, and he knows that place cannot change itself: that what was a house cannot become a plain; that what was Thebes can never be Persepolis.

Such is the triumphant language with which a critic exults over the misery of an irregular poet, and exults commonly without resistance or reply. It is time, therefore, to tell him, by the authority of Shakespeare, that he assumes as an unquestionable principle a position which, while his breath is forming it into words, his understanding pronounces to be false. It is false that any representation is mistaken for reality; that any dramatic fable in its materiality was ever credible, or for a single moment was ever credited.

The objection arising from the impossibility of passing the first hour at Alexandria, and the next at Rome, supposes that when the play opens, the spectator really imagines himself at Alexandria, and believes that his walk to the theatre has been a voyage to Egypt, and that he lives in the days of Antony and Cleopatra. Surely he that imagines this may imagine more. He that can take the stage at one time for the palace of the Ptolemies, may take it in half an hour for the promontory of Actium. Delusion, if delusion be admitted, has no certain limitation; if the spectator can be once persuaded that his old acquaintance are Alexander and Cæsar, that a room illuminated with candles is the plain of Pharsalia, or the bank of Granicus, he is in a state of elevation above the reach of reason or of truth, and from the heights of empyrean poetry may despise the circumscriptions of terrestrial nature. There is no reason why a mind thus wandering in ecstasy should count the clock, or why an hour should not be a century in that calenture of the brain that can make the stage a field.

The truth is that the spectators are always in their senses and know, from the first act to the last, that the stage is only a stage and that the players are only players. They come to hear a certain number of lines recited with just gesture and elegant modulation. The lines relate to some action, and an action must be in some place; but the different actions that complete a story may be in places very remote from each other; and where is the absurdity of allowing that space to represent first Athens, and then Sicily, which was always known to be neither Sicily nor Athens, but a modern theatre?

By supposition, as place is introduced, time may be extended. The time required by the fable elapses for the most part between the acts; for, of so much of the action as is represented, the real and poetical duration is the same. If, in the first act, preparations for war against Mithridates are represented to be made in Rome, the event of the war may, without absurdity, be represented, in the catastrophe, as happening in Pontus; we know that there is neither war nor preparation for war; we know that we are neither in Rome nor Pontus; that neither Mithridates nor Lucullus are before us. The drama exhibits successive imitations of successive actions; and why may not the second imitation represent an action that happened years after the first, if it be so connected with it that nothing but time can be supposed to intervene? Time is, of all modes of existence, most obsequious to the imagination; a lapse of years is as easily conceived as a passage of hours. In contemplation we easily contract the time of real actions, and therefore willingly permit it to be contracted when we only see their imitation.

It will be asked how the drama moves, if it is not credited. It is credited with all the credit due to a drama. It is credited, whenever it moves, as a just picture of a real original; as representing to the auditor what he would himself feel if he were to do or suffer what is there feigned to be suffered or to be done. The reflection that strikes the heart is not that the evils before us are real evils, but that they are evils to which we ourselves may be exposed. If there be any fallacy, it is not that we fancy the players, but that we fancy ourselves unhappy for a moment; but we rather lament the possibility than suppose the presence of misery, as a mother weeps over her babe when she remembers that death may take it from her. The delight of tragedy proceeds from our consciousness of fiction; if we thought murders and treasons real, they would please no more.

Imitations produce pain or pleasure, not because they are mistaken for realities, but because they bring realities to mind. When the imagination is recreated by a painted landscape, the trees are not supposed capable to give us shade, or the fountains coolness; but we consider how we should be pleased with such fountains playing beside us, and such woods waving over us. We are agitated in reading the history of *Henry the Fifth*, yet no man takes his book for the field of Agincourt. A dramatic exhibition is a book recited with concomitants that increase or diminish its effect. Familiar comedy is often more powerful on the theatre than in the page; imperial tragedy is always less. *The humour of Petruchio may be heightened by grimace; but what voice or what gesture can hope to add dignity or force to *the soliloquy of Cato?

A play read affects the mind like a play acted. It is therefore evident that the action is not supposed to be real; and it follows that between the acts a longer or shorter time may be allowed to pass, and that no more account of space or duration is to be taken by the auditor of a drama than by the reader of a narrative, before whom may pass in an hour the life of a hero or the revolutions of an empire.

Whether Shakespeare knew the unities, and rejected them by design, or deviated from them by happy ignorance, it is, I think, impossible to decide and useless to inquire. We may reasonably suppose that, when he rose to notice, he did not want the counsels and admonitions of scholars and critics, and that he at last deliberately persisted in a practice which he might have begun by chance. As nothing is essential to the fable but unity of action, and as the unities of time and place arise evidently from false assumptions, and, by circumscribing the extent of the drama, lessen its variety, I cannot think it much to be lamented that they were not known by him, or not observed; nor, if such another poet could arise, should I very vehemently reproach him that his first act passed at Venice and his next in Cyprus. Such violations of rules merely positive become the comprehensive genius of Shakespeare, and such censures are suitable to the minute and slender criticism of Voltaire:

*Non usque adeo permiscuit imis
Longus summa dies, ut non, si voce Metelli
Serventur leges, malint a Cæsare tolli.

Yet when I speak thus slightly of dramatic rules, I cannot but recollect how much wit and learning may be produced against me; before such authorities I am afraid to stand, not that I think the present question one of those that are to be decided by mere authority, but because it is to be suspected that these precepts have not been so easily received, but for better reasons than I have yet been able to find. The result of my enquiries, in which it would be ludicrous to boast of impartiality, is that the unities of time and place are not essential to a just drama; that, though they may sometimes conduce to pleasure, they are always to be sacrificed to the nobler beauties of variety and instruction; and that a play written with nice observation of critical rules is to be contemplated as an elaborate curiosity, as the product of superfluous and ostentatious art, by which is shown rather what is possible than what is necessary.

He that, without diminution of any other excellence, shall preserve all the unities unbroken, deserves the like applause with the architect who shall display all the orders of architecture in a citadel, without any deduction from its strength; but the principal beauty of a citadel is to exclude the enemy, and the greatest graces of a play are to copy nature and instruct life.

Perhaps what I have here not dogmatically but deliberately written may recall the principles of the drama to a new examination. I am almost frighted at my own temerity; and, when I estimate the fame and the strength of those that maintain the contrary opinion, am ready to sink down in reverential silence, as *Æneas withdrew from the defence of Troy when he saw Neptune shaking the wall, and Juno heading the besiegers.

Those whom my arguments cannot persuade to give their approbation to the judgment of Shakespeare will easily, if they consider the condition of his life, make some allowance for his ignorance.

*Every man's performances, to be rightly estimated, must be compared with the state of the age in which he lived, and with his own particular opportunities; and though to a reader a book be not worse or better for the circumstances of the author, yet as there is always a silent reference of human works to human abilities, and as the enquiry, how far man may extend his designs, or how high he may rate his native force, is of far greater dignity than in what rank we shall place any particular performance, curiosity is always busy to discover the instruments, as well as to survey the workmanship, to know how much is to be ascribed to original powers, and how much to casual and adventitious help. The palaces of Peru or Mexico were certainly mean and incommodious habitations, if compared to the houses of European monarchs; yet who could forbear to view them with astonishment, who remembered that they were built without the use of iron?

The English nation in the time of Shakespeare was yet struggling to emerge from barbarity. *The philology of Italy had been transplanted hither in the reign of Henry the Eighth; and the learned languages had been successfully cultivated by Lilly, Linacre, and More; by Pole, Cheke, and Gardiner; and afterwards by Smith, Clerk, Haddon, and Ascham. Greek was now taught to boys in the principal schools; and those who united elegance with learning, read, with great diligence, the Italian and Spanish poets. But literature was yet confined to professed scholars or to men and women of high rank. The public was gross and dark; and to be able to read and write was an accomplishment still valued for its rarity.

Nations, like individuals, have their infancy. A people newly awakened to literary curiosity, being yet unacquainted with the true state of things, knows not how to judge of that which is proposed as its resemblance. Whatever is remote from common appearances is always welcome to vulgar, as to childish credulity;

and of a country unenlightened by learning, the whole people is the vulgar. The study of those who then aspired to plebeian learning was laid out upon adventures, giants, dragons, and enchantments. * *The Death of Arthur* was the favourite volume.

The mind which has feasted on the luxurious wonders of fiction has no taste of the insipidity of truth. A play which imitated only the common occurrences of the world would, upon the admirers of * *Palmerin* and *Guy of Warwick*, have made little impression; he that wrote for such an audience was under the necessity of looking round for strange events and fabulous transactions, and that incredibility by which maturer knowledge is offended was the chief recommendation of writings to unskillful curiosity.

Our author's plots are generally borrowed from novels; and it is reasonable to suppose that he chose the most popular, such as were read by many, and related by more; for his audience could not have followed him through the intricacies of the drama had they not held the thread of the story in their hands.

The stories which we now find only in remoter authors were in his time accessible and familiar. The fable of * *As You Like It*, which is supposed to be copied from Chaucer's *Gamelyn*, was a little pamphlet of those times; and old Mr. Cibber remembered * the tale of *Hamlet* in plain English prose, which the critics have now to seek in Saxo Grammaticus.

His English histories he took from English chronicles and English ballads; and as the ancient writers were made known to his countrymen by versions, they supplied him with new subjects; he dilated some of Plutarch's lives into plays, when they had been translated by North.

His plots, whether historical or fabulous, are always crowded with incidents, by which the attention of a rude people was more easily caught than by sentiment or argumentation; and such is the power of the marvellous, even over those who despise it, that every man finds his mind more strongly seized by the tragedies of Shakespeare than of any other writer; others please us by particular speeches, but he always makes us anxious for the event, and has perhaps excelled all but Homer in securing the first purpose of a writer, by exciting restless and unquenchable curiosity, and compelling him that reads his work to read it through.

The shows and bustle with which his plays abound have the same original. As knowledge advances, pleasure passes from the eye to the ear, but returns, as it declines, from the ear to the eye. Those to whom our author's labours were exhibited had more skill in pomps or processions than in poetical language, and perhaps wanted some visible and discriminated events, as comments on the dialogue. He knew how he should most please; and whether his practice is more agreeable to nature, or whether his example has prejudiced the nation, we still find that on our stage something must be done as well as said, and inactive declamation is very coldly heard, however musical or elegant, passionate or sublime.

Voltaire expresses his wonder that our author's extravagancies are endured by a nation which has seen the tragedy of *Cato*. Let him be answered that Addison speaks the language of poets, and Shakespeare of men. We find in *Cato* innumerable beauties which enamour us of its author, but we see nothing that acquaints us with human sentiments or human actions; we place it with the fairest and the noblest progeny which judgment propagates by conjunction with learning; but *Othello* is the vigorous and vivacious offspring of observation impregnated by genius. *Cato* affords a splendid exhibition of artificial and fictitious manners, and delivers just and noble sentiments, in diction easy, elevated, and harmonious, but its hopes and fears communicate no vibration to the heart; the composition refers us only to the writer; we pronounce the name of Cato, but we think on Addison.

The work of a correct and regular writer is a garden accurately formed and diligently planted, varied with shades and scented with flowers; the composition of Shakespeare is a forest, in which oaks extend their branches, and pines tower in the air, interspersed sometimes with weeds and brambles, and sometimes giving shelter to myrtles and to roses; filling the eye with awful pomp, and gratifying the mind with endless diversity. Other poets display cabinets of precious rarities, minutely finished, wrought into shape, and polished into brightness. Shakespeare opens a mine which contains gold and diamonds in unexhaustible plenty, though clouded by incrustations, debased by impurities, and mingled with a mass of meaner minerals.

It has been much disputed whether Shakespeare owed his excellence to his own native force, or whether he had the common helps of scholastic education, the precepts of critical science, and the examples of ancient authors.

There has always prevailed a tradition that Shakespeare wanted learning, that he had no regular education, nor much skill in the dead languages. Jonson, his friend, affirms that "he had small Latin, and less Greek"; who, besides that he had no imaginable temptation to falsehood, wrote at a time when the character and acquisitions of Shakespeare were known to multitudes. His evidence ought therefore to decide the controversy, unless some testimony of equal force could be opposed.

Some have imagined that they have discovered deep learning in many imitations of old writers; but the examples which I have known urged were drawn from books translated in his time, or were such easy coincidences of thought as will happen to all who consider the same subjects, or such remarks on life or axioms of morality as float in conversation, and are transmitted through the world in proverbial sentences.

I have found it remarked that in this important sentence, *"Go before, I'll follow," we read a translation of *I præ, sequar*. I have been told that when Caliban, after a pleasing dream, says, *"I cried to sleep again," the author imitates Anacreon, who had, like every other man, the same wish on the same occasion.

There are a few passages which may pass for imitations, but so few that the exception only confirms the rule; he obtained them from accidental quotations, or by oral communication, and as he used what he had, would have used more if he had obtained it.

The Comedy of Errors is confessedly taken from the *Menæchmi* of Plautus, from the only play of Plautus which was then in English. What can be more probable than that he who copied that, would have copied more, but that those which were not translated were inaccessible?

Whether he knew the modern languages is uncertain. That his plays have some French scenes proves but little; he might easily procure them to be written, and probably, even though he had known the language in the common degree, he could not have written it without assistance. In the story of *Romeo and Juliet* he is observed to have followed the English translation where it deviates from the Italian, but this on the other part proves nothing against his knowledge of the original. He was to copy, not what he knew himself, but what was known to his audience.

It is most likely that he had learned Latin sufficiently to make him acquainted with construction, but that he never advanced to an easy perusal of the Roman authors. Concerning his skill in modern languages I can find no sufficient ground of determination; but as no imitations of French or Italian authors have been discovered, though the Italian poetry was then in high esteem, I am inclined to believe that he read little more than English, and chose for his fables only such tales as he found translated.

That much knowledge is scattered over his works is very justly observed by Pope, but it is often such knowledge as books did not supply. He that will understand Shakespeare must not be content to study him in the closet; he must look for his meaning sometimes among the sports of the field, and sometimes among the manufactures of the shop.

There is, however, proof enough that he was a very diligent reader, nor was our language then so indigent of books but that he might very liberally indulge his curiosity without excursion into foreign literature. Many of the Roman authors were translated, and some of the Greek; the Reformation had filled the kingdom with theological learning; most of the topics of human disquisition had found English writers; and poetry had been cultivated, not only with diligence, but success. This was a stock of knowledge sufficient for a mind so capable of appropriating and improving it.

But the greater part of his excellence was the product of his own genius. He found the English stage in a state of the utmost rudeness; no essays either in tragedy or comedy had appeared, from which it could be discovered to what degree of delight either one or other might be carried. Neither character nor dialogue were yet understood. Shakespeare may be truly said to have introduced them both amongst us, and in some of his happier scenes to have carried them both to the utmost height.

By what gradations of improvement he proceeded, is not easily known, for the chronology of his works is yet unsettled. *Rowe is of opinion that "perhaps we are not to look for his beginning, like those of other writers, in his least perfect works; art had so little, and nature so large a share in what he did that, for aught I know," says he, "the performances of his youth, as they were the most vigorous, were the best." But the power of nature is only the power of using to any certain purpose the materials which diligence procures, or opportunity supplies. Nature gives no man knowledge, and when images are collected by study and experience, can only assist in combining or applying them. Shakespeare, however favoured by nature, could impart only what he had learned; and as he must increase his ideas, like other mortals, by gradual acquisition, he, like them, grew wiser as he grew older, could display life better, as he knew it more, and instruct with more efficacy, as he was himself more amply instructed.

There is a vigilance of observation and accuracy of distinction which books and precepts cannot confer; from this almost all original and native excellence proceeds. Shakespeare must have looked upon mankind with perspicacity, in the highest degree curious and attentive. Other writers borrow their characters from preceding writers, and diversify them only by the accidental appendages of present manners; the dress is a little varied, but the body is the same. Our author had both matter and form to provide; for, except the characters of Chaucer, to whom I think he is not much indebted, there were no writers in English, and perhaps not many in other modern languages, which showed life in its native colours.

The contest about the original benevolence or malignity of man had not yet commenced. Speculation had not yet attempted to analyze the mind, to trace the passions to their sources, to unfold the seminal principles of vice and virtue, or sound the depths of the heart for the motives of action. All those enquiries, which from that time that human nature became the fashionable study, have been made, sometimes with nice discernment, but often with idle subtilty, were yet unattempted. The tales with which the infancy of learning was satisfied, exhibited only the superficial appearances of action, related the events, but omitted the causes, and were formed for such as delighted in wonders rather than in truth. Mankind was not then to be studied in the closet; he that would know the world was under the necessity of gleaning his own remarks by mingling as he could in its business and amusements.

*Boyle congratulated himself upon his high birth, because it favoured his curiosity, by facilitating his access. Shakespeare had no such advantage; he came to London a needy adventurer, and lived for a time by very mean employments. Many works of genius and learning have been performed in states of life that appear very little favourable to thought or to enquiry; so many, that he who considers them is inclined to think that he sees enterprize and perseverance predominating over all external agency, and bidding help and hindrance vanish before them. The genius of Shakespeare was not to be depressed by the weight of poverty, nor limited by the narrow conversation to which men in want are inevitably condemned; the incumbrances of his fortune were shaken from his mind, *"as dewdrops from a lion's mane."

Though he had so many difficulties to encounter, and so little assistance to surmount them, he has been able to obtain an exact knowledge of many modes of life, and many casts of native dispositions; to vary them with great multiplicity; to mark them by nice distinctions; and to show them in full view by proper combinations. In this part of his performances he had none to imitate, but has himself been imitated by all succeeding writers; and it may be doubted whether from all his successors more maxims of theoretical knowledge or more rules of practical prudence can be collected, than he alone has given to his country.

Nor was his attention confined to the actions of men; he was an exact surveyor of the inanimate world; his descriptions have always some peculiarities, gathered by contemplating things as they really exist. It may be observed that the oldest poets of many nations preserve their reputation, and that the following generations of wit, after a short celebrity, sink into oblivion. The first, whoever they may be, must take their sentiments and descriptions immediately from knowledge; the resemblance is therefore just, their descriptions are verified by every eye, and their sentiments acknowledged by every breast. Those whom their fame invites to the same studies copy partly them, and partly nature, till the books of one age gain such authority as to stand in the place of nature to another, and imitation, always deviating a little, becomes at last capricious and casual. Shakespeare, whether life or nature be his subject, shows plainly that he has seen with his own eyes; he gives the image which he receives, not weakened or distorted by the intervention of any other mind; the ignorant feel his representations to be just, and the learned see that they are complete.

Perhaps it would not be easy to find any author, except Homer, who invented so much as Shakespeare, who so much advanced the studies which he cultivated, or effused so much novelty upon his age or country. The form, the characters, the language, and the shows of the English drama are his. *"He seems," says Dennis, "to have been the very original of our English tragical harmony, that is, the harmony of blank verse, diversified often by dissyllable and trisyllable terminations. For the diversity distinguishes it from heroic harmony, and by bringing it nearer to common use makes it more proper to gain attention and more fit for action and dialogue. Such verse we make when we are writing prose; we make such verse in common conversation."

I know not whether this praise is rigorously just. The dissyllable termination, which the critic rightly appropriates to the drama, is to be found, though, I think, not in *Gorboduc*, which is confessedly before our author, yet in **Hieronymo*, of which the date is not certain, but which there is reason to believe at least as old as his earliest plays. This however is certain, that he is the first who taught either tragedy or comedy to please, there being no theatrical piece of any older writer of which the name is known, except to antiquaries and collectors of books, which are sought because they are scarce, and would not have been scarce had they been much esteemed.

To him we must ascribe the praise, unless Spenser may divide it with him, of having first discovered to how much smoothness and harmony the English language could be softened. He has speeches, perhaps sometimes scenes, which have all the delicacy of Rowe, without his effeminacy. He endeavours, indeed, commonly to strike by the force and vigour of his dialogue, but he never executes his purpose better than when he tries to soothe by softness.

Yet it must be at last confessed that as we owe everything to him, he owes something to us; that, if much of his praise is paid by perception and judgment, much is likewise given by custom and veneration. We fix our eyes upon his graces, and turn them from his deformities, and endure in him what we should in another loathe or despise. If we endured without praising, respect for the father of our drama might excuse us; but I have seen in the *book of some modern critic a collection of anomalies which show that he has corrupted language by every mode of depravation, but which his admirer has accumulated as a monument of honour.

He has scenes of undoubted and perpetual excellence, but perhaps not one play which, if it were now exhibited as the work of a contemporary writer, would be heard to the conclusion. I am indeed far from thinking that his works were wrought to his own ideas of perfection; when they were such as would satisfy the audience, they satisfied the writer. It is seldom that authors, though more studious of fame than Shakespeare, rise much above the standard of their own age; to add a little to what is best will always be sufficient for present praise, and those who find themselves exalted into fame are willing to credit their encomiasts, and to spare the labour of contending with themselves.

It does not appear that Shakespeare thought his works worthy of posterity, that he levied any ideal tribute upon future times, or had any further prospect than of present popularity and present profit. When his plays had been acted, his hope was at an end; he solicited no addition of honour from the reader. He therefore made no scruple to repeat the same jests in many dialogues, or to entangle different plots by the same knot of perplexity, which may be at least forgiven him by those who recollect that of Congreve's four comedies two are concluded by a marriage in a mask, by a deception which perhaps never happened, and which, whether likely or not, he did not invent.

So careless was this great poet of future fame, that though he retired to ease and plenty, while he was yet little *"declined into the vale of years," before he could be disgusted with fatigue, or disabled by infirmity, he made no collection of his works, nor desired to rescue those that had been already published from the depravations that obscured them, or secure to the rest a better destiny, by giving them to the world in their genuine state....

[1765]

THE LIVES OF THE ENGLISH POETS

From DRYDEN

"The edition of the poets, now printing, will do honour to the English press; and a concise account of the life of each author, by Dr. Johnson, will be a very valuable addition, and stamp the reputation of this edition superior to anything that is gone before.... A select number of the most respectable booksellers met...; and, on consulting together, agreed that all the proprietors of copyright in the various poets [from Chaucer to the present time] should be summoned together; and when their opinions were given, to proceed immediately on the business. Accordingly a meeting was held, consisting of about forty of the most respectable booksellers of London, when it was agreed that an elegant and uniform edition of 'The English Poets' should be immediately printed, with a concise account of the life of each author by Dr. Samuel Johnson; and that three persons should be deputed to wait upon Dr. Johnson to solicit him to undertake the lives, viz. T. Davies, Strahan, and Cadell. The doctor very politely undertook it, and seemed exceedingly pleased with the proposal. As to the terms, it was left entirely to the doctor to name his own; he mentioned two hundred guineas; it was immediately agreed to; and a further compliment, I believe, will be made him. A committee was likewise appointed to engage the best engravers, viz. Bartolozzi, Sherwin, Hall, &c. Likewise another committee for giving directions about the paper, printing &c. so that the whole will be conducted with spirit, and in the best manner with respect to authorship, editorship, engravings, &c. &c."

So wrote Edward Dilly, the bookseller, to James Boswell under date of September 26, 1777. In 1781, after unforeseen delays, Johnson completed his task, and the work was published, though not quite as it had been planned, since the earlier poets were not included, and the edition began with Cowley. Johnson had expected to treat his subject briefly, giving to each poet only "a few dates and a general character," but the work grew under his hand to an extent that had not been anticipated. The booksellers added another hundred pounds to his fee, which was certainly most moderate: Malone estimated that "they have probably got five thousand guineas by this work in the course of twenty-five years."

The Lives of the English Poets is Johnson's maturest and most representative work, into which he poured the accumulated treasures of a lifetime devoted to literature. The biographies themselves did not involve, for the most part, elaborate study or research, but they included a large amount of personal anecdote and oral tradition that might otherwise have been lost. Some of the poets Johnson had known personally; others he had known through the medium of persons yet living in his youth who had known the previous generation. The biographical part of literature, he once declared, he loved most. Thus, both by opportunity and by personal taste, he was especially qualified for his task.

It is, however, his critical discussion of the poets' works which is the most important part of *The Lives of the English Poets*. Here we have the final judgment of the last recognized critic of the neoclassical period upon the literature of that period. Though Johnson represented his generation, he was much more than a mirror of its accepted critical conclusions. The standardized judgments of classical tradition submerge the individuality of the small critic, but they merely steady that of the great critic and create the conditions in which it can reach its fullest development. Johnson spoke with assurance because he was the recognized mouthpiece of the "general sense," but had he not spoken for himself the less Johnson he! Indeed he has been most frequently criticised, both in his own day and since, because of the prejudice he has shown against Milton and Gray. His tolerance was not universal; his judgment was not impeccable; his taste was not perfect: if they had been, he would have ranked, not as one of the half dozen chief English critics, but, as the critical paragon of all times. Though many things lay outside his vision, he saw the things that he saw at all with extraordinary clearness: his faults are chiefly those of omission, and his errors of judgment are usually those due to insufficient critical perspective.

Among the fullest and the best of *The Lives of the English Poets* is that of Dryden. The selection here reprinted is taken, with indicated omissions, from the latter part, and treats Dryden's contributions to criticism and to poetry; the life proper, the remarks upon his character, and the criticism of his translation are all omitted.

...Dryden may be properly considered as the father of English criticism, as the writer who first taught us to determine upon principles the merit of composition. Of our former poets the greatest dramatist wrote without rules, conducted through life and nature by a genius that rarely misled and rarely deserted him. Of the rest, those who knew the laws of propriety had neglected to teach them.

Two *Arts of English Poetry* were written in

the days of Elizabeth by Webbe and Puttenham, from which something might be learned, and a few hints had been given by Jonson and Cowley; but Dryden's *Essay on Dramatic Poetry* was the first regular and valuable treatise on the art of writing.

He who, having formed his opinions in the present age of English literature, turns back to peruse this dialogue, will not perhaps find much increase of knowledge or much novelty of instruction; but he is to remember that critical principles were then in the hands of a few, who had gathered them partly from the ancients and partly from the Italians and French. The structure of dramatic poems was then not generally understood. Audiences applauded by instinct, and poets perhaps often pleased by chance.

A writer who obtains his full purpose loses himself in his own lustre. Of an opinion which is no longer doubted, the evidence ceases to be examined. Of an art universally practised, the first teacher is forgotten. Learning once made popular is no longer learning; it has the appearance of something which we have bestowed upon ourselves, as the dew appears to rise from the field which it refreshes.

To judge rightly of an author, we must transport ourselves to his time, and examine what were the wants of his contemporaries, and what were his means of supplying them. That which is easy at one time was difficult at another. Dryden at least imported his science, and gave his country what it wanted before; or rather, he imported only the materials, and manufactured them by his own skill.

The dialogue on the drama was one of his first essays of criticism, written when he was yet a timorous candidate for reputation, and therefore laboured with that diligence which he might allow himself somewhat to remit, when his name gave sanction to his positions, and his awe of the public was abated, partly by custom, and partly by success. It will not be easy to find, in all the opulence of our language, a treatise so artfully variegated with successive representations of opposite probabilities, so enlivened with imagery, so brightened with illustrations. His portraits of the English dramatists are wrought with great spirit and diligence. The account of Shakespeare may stand as a perpetual model of encomiastic criticism: exact without minuteness, and lofty without exaggeration. * The praise lavished by Longinus on the attestation of the heroes of Marathon, by Demosthenes, fades away before it. In a few lines is exhibited a character, so extensive in its comprehension, and so curious in its limitations, that nothing can be added, diminished, or reformed; nor can the editors and admirers of Shakespeare, in all their emulation of reverence, boast of much more than of having diffused and paraphrased this epitome of excellence, of having changed Dryden's gold for baser metal, of lower value though of greater bulk.

In this, and in all his other essays on the same subject, the criticism of Dryden is the criticism of a poet; not a dull collection of theorems, nor a rude detection of faults, which perhaps the censor was not able to have committed; but a gay and vigorous dissertation, where delight is mingled with instruction, and where the author proves his right of judgment by his power of performance.

The different manner and effect with which critical knowledge may be conveyed was perhaps never more clearly exemplified than in the performances of Rymer and Dryden. It was said of a dispute between two mathematicians, *malim cum Scaligero errare, quam cum Clavio recte sapere;* that "it was more eligible to go wrong with one than right with the other." A tendency of the same kind every mind must feel at the perusal of Dryden's prefaces and Rymer's discourses. With Dryden we are wandering in quest of Truth; whom we find, if we find her at all, dressed in the graces of elegance, and if we miss her, the labour of the pursuit rewards itself; we are led only through fragrance and flowers. Rymer, without taking a nearer, takes a rougher way; every step is to be made through thorns and brambles; and Truth, if we meet her, appears repulsive by her mien, and ungraceful by her habit. Dryden's criticism has the majesty of a queen; Rymer's has the ferocity of a tyrant.

As he had studied with great diligence the art of poetry, and enlarged or rectified his notions by experience perpetually increasing, he had his mind stored with principles and observations; he poured out his knowledge with little labour; for of labour, notwithstanding the multiplicity of his productions, there is sufficient reason to suspect that he was not a lover. To write *con amore,* with fondness for the employment, with perpetual touches and retouches, with unwillingness to take leave of his own idea, and an unwearied pursuit of unattainable perfection was, I think, no part of his character.

His criticism may be considered as general or occasional. In his general precepts, which depend upon the nature of things and the structure of the human mind, he may doubtless be safely recommended to the confidence of the reader; but his occasional and particular positions were sometimes interested, sometimes negligent, and sometimes capricious. It is not without reason that *Trapp, speaking of the praises which he bestows on *Palamon and Arcite*, says, *"*Novimus judicium Drydeni de poemate quodam Chauceri, pulchro sane illo, et admodum laudando; nimirum quod non modo vere epicum sit, sed Iliada etiam atque Æneada æquet, imo superet. Sed novimus eodem tempore viri illius maximi non semper accuratissimas esse censuras, nec ad severissimam critices normam exactas: illo judice id plerumque optimum est, quod nunc præ manibus habet, et in quo nunc occupatur.*"

He is therefore by no means constant to himself. His defence and desertion of dramatic rhyme is generally known. *Spence, in his remarks on Pope's *Odyssey*, produces what he thinks an unconquerable quotation from Dryden's preface to the *Æneid*, in favour of translating an epic poem into blank verse; but he forgets that when his author attempted the *Iliad*, some years afterwards, he departed from his own decision, and translated into rhyme.

When he has any objection to obviate, or any licence to defend, he is not very scrupulous about what he asserts, nor very cautious, if the present purpose be served, not to entangle himself in his own sophistries. But when all arts are exhausted, like other hunted animals, he sometimes stands at bay; when he cannot disown the grossness of one of his plays, he declares that he knows not any law that prescribes morality to a comic poet.

His remarks on ancient or modern writers are not always to be trusted. His parallel of the versification of Ovid with that of Claudian has been very justly censured by *Sewel. His comparison of the first line of Virgil with the first of Statius is not happier. Virgil, he says, is soft and gentle, and would have thought Statius mad if he had heard him thundering out

**Quæ superimposito moles geminata colosso.*

Statius perhaps heats himself, as he proceeds, to exaggerations somewhat hyperbolical; but undoubtedly Virgil would have been too hasty if he had *condemned him to straw for one sounding line. Dryden wanted an instance, and the first that occurred was impressed into the service.

What he wishes to say, he says at hazard; he cited **Gorboduc*, which he had never seen; gives a false account of *Chapman's versification; and discovers, in the preface to his *Fables*, that he translated the first book of the *Iliad*, without knowing what was in the second.

It will be difficult to prove that Dryden ever made any great advances in literature. As, having distinguished himself at Westminster under *the tuition of Busby, who advanced his scholars to a height of knowledge very rarely attained in grammar schools, he resided afterwards at Cambridge, it is not to be supposed that his skill in the ancient languages was deficient, compared with that of common students; but his scholastic acquisitions seem not proportionate to his opportunities and abilities. He could not, like Milton or Cowley, have made his name illustrious merely by his learning. He mentions but few books, and those such as lie in the beaten track of regular study; from which if ever he departs, he is in danger of losing himself in unknown regions.

In his dialogue on the drama, he pronounces with great confidence that the Latin tragedy of *Medea* is not Ovid's, because it is not sufficiently interesting and pathetic. He might have determined the question upon surer evidence; for it is quoted by Quintilian as the work of Seneca; and the only line which remains of Ovid's play, for one line is left us, is not there to be found. There was, therefore, no need of the gravity of conjecture, or the discussion of plot or sentiment, to find what was already known upon higher authority than such discussions can ever reach.

His literature, though not always free from ostentation, will be commonly found either obvious, and made his own by the art of dressing it; or superficial, which, by what he gives, shows what he wanted; or erroneous, hastily collected, and negligently scattered.

Yet it cannot be said that his genius is ever unprovided of matter, or that his fancy languishes in penury of ideas. His works abound with knowledge and sparkle with illustrations. There is scarcely any science or faculty that does not supply him with occasional images and lucky similitudes; every page discovers a mind very widely acquainted both with art and nature, and in full possession of great stores of intellectual wealth. Of him that knows much, it is natural to suppose that he has read with diligence; yet I rather believe that the knowledge of Dryden was gleaned from accidental intelligence and various conversation, by a quick apprehension, a judicious selection, and a happy memory, a keen appetite of knowledge and a powerful digestion; by vigilance that permitted nothing to pass without notice, and a habit of reflection that suffered nothing useful to be lost. A mind like Dryden's, always curious, always active, to which every understanding was proud to be associated, and of which every one solicited the regard by an ambitious display of himself, had a more pleasant, perhaps a nearer, way to knowledge than by the silent progress of solitary reading. I do not suppose that he despised books, or intentionally neglected them; but that he was carried out, by the impetuosity of his genius, to more vivid and speedy instructors; and that his studies were rather desultory and fortuitous than constant and systematical.

It must be confessed that he scarcely ever appears to want book learning but when he mentions books; and to him may be transferred the praise which he gives his master, Charles:

> *His conversation, wit, and parts,
> His knowledge in the noblest useful arts,
> Were such, dead authors could not give,
> But habitudes of those that live;
> Who, lighting him, did greater lights receive:
> He drain'd from all, and all they knew,
> His apprehension quick, his judgment true:
> That the most learn'd with shame confess
> His knowledge more, his reading only less.

Of all this, however, if the proof be demanded, I will not undertake to give it; the atoms of probability, of which my opinion has been formed, lie scattered over all his works; and by him who thinks the question worth his notice, his works must be perused with very close attention.

Criticism, either didactic or defensive, occupies almost all his prose, except those pages which he has devoted to his patrons; but none of his prefaces were ever thought tedious. They have not the formality of a settled style, in which the first half of the sentence betrays the other. The clauses are never balanced, nor the periods modelled; every word seems to drop by chance, though it falls into its proper place. Nothing is cold or languid; the whole is airy, animated, and vigorous; what is little is gay; what is great is splendid. He may be thought to mention himself too frequently; but while he forces himself upon our esteem, we cannot refuse him to stand high in his own. Everything is excused by the play of images and the spriteliness of expression. Though all is easy, nothing is feeble; though all seems careless, there is nothing harsh; and though, since his earlier works, more than a century has passed, they have nothing yet uncouth or obsolete.

He who writes much will not easily escape a manner, such a recurrence of particular modes as may be easily noted. Dryden is always "another and the same"; he does not exhibit a second time the same elegances in the same form, nor appears to have any art other than that of expressing with clearness what he thinks with vigour. His style could not easily be imitated, either seriously or ludicrously; for, being always equable and always varied, it has no prominent or discriminative characters. The beauty who is totally free from disproportion of parts and features, cannot be ridiculed by an overcharged resemblance.

From his prose, however, Dryden derives only his accidental and secondary praise; the veneration with which his name is pronounced by every cultivator of English literature, is paid to him as he refined the language, improved the sentiments, and tuned the numbers of English poetry.

After about half a century of forced thoughts and rugged metre, some advances towards nature and harmony had been already made by Waller and Denham; they had shown that long discourses in rhyme grew more pleasing when they were broken into couplets, and that verse consisted not only in the number but the arrangement of syllables.

But though they did much, who can deny that they left much to do? Their works were not many, nor were their minds of very ample comprehension. More examples of more modes of composition were necessary for the establishment of regularity, and the introduction of propriety in word and thought.

Every language of a learned nation necessarily divides itself into diction scholastic and popular, grave and familiar, elegant and gross; and from a nice distinction of these different parts arises a great part of the beauty of style.

But if we except a few minds, the favourites of nature, to whom their own original rectitude was in the place of rules, this delicacy of selection was little known to our authors; our speech lay before them in a heap of confusion, and every man took for every purpose what chance might offer him.

There was therefore before the time of Dryden no poetical diction, no system of words at once refined from the grossness of domestic use, and free from the harshness of terms appropriated to particular arts. Words too familiar, or too remote, defeat the purpose of a poet. From those sounds which we hear on small or on coarse occasions, we do not easily receive strong impressions or delightful images; and words to which we are nearly strangers, whenever they occur, draw that attention on themselves which they should transmit to things.

Those happy combinations of words which distinguish poetry from prose, had been rarely attempted; we had few elegances or flowers of speech, the roses had not yet been plucked from the bramble, or different colours had not been joined to enliven one another.

It may be doubted whether Waller and Denham could have overborne the prejudices which had long prevailed, and which even then were sheltered by the protection of Cowley. The new versification, as it was called, may be considered as owing its establishment to Dryden, from whose time it is apparent that English poetry has had no tendency to relapse to its former savageness.

The affluence and comprehension of our language is very illustriously displayed in our poetical translations of ancient writers, a work which the French seem to relinquish in despair, and which we were long unable to perform with dexterity. Ben Jonson thought it necessary to copy Horace almost word by word; *Feltham, his contemporary and adversary, considers it as indispensably requisite in a translation to give line for line. It is said that *Sandys, whom Dryden calls the best versifier of the last age, has struggled hard to comprise every book of his English *Metamorphoses* in the same number of verses with the original. *Holyday had nothing in view but to show that he understood his author, with so little regard to the grandeur of his diction, or the volubility of his numbers, that his metres can hardly be called verses; they can not be read without reluctance, nor will the labour always be rewarded by understanding them. Cowley saw that such copiers were a "servile race"; he asserted his liberty, and spread his wings so boldly that he left his authors. It was reserved for Dryden to fix the limits of poetical liberty, and give us just rules and examples of translation.

When languages are formed upon different principles, it is impossible that the same modes of expression should always be elegant in both. While they run on together, the closest translation may be considered as the best; but when they divaricate, each must take its natural course. Where correspondence can not be obtained, it is necessary to be content with something equivalent. *"Translation therefore," says Dryden, "is not so loose as paraphrase, nor so close as metaphrase."

All polished languages have different styles; the concise, the diffuse, the lofty, and the humble. In the proper choice of style consists the resemblance which Dryden principally exacts from the translator. He is to exhibit his author's thoughts in such a dress of diction as the author would have given them, had his language been English: rugged magnificence is not to be softened: hyperbolical ostentation is not to be repressed, nor sententious affectation to have its points blunted. A translator is to be like his author: it is not his business to excel him.

The reasonableness of these rules seems sufficient for their vindication; and the effects produced by observing them were so happy that I know not whether they were ever opposed but by *Sir Edward Sherburne, a man whose learning was greater than his powers of poetry; and who, being better qualified to give the meaning than the spirit of Seneca, has introduced his version of three tragedies by a defence of close translation. The authority of Horace, which the new translators cited in defence of their practice, he has, by a judicious explanation, taken fairly from them; but reason wants not Horace to support it.

It seldom happens that all the necessary causes concur to any great effect: will is wanting to power, or power to will, or both are impeded by external obstructions. The exigences in which Dryden was condemned to pass his life are reasonably supposed to have blasted his genius, to have driven out his works in a state of immaturity, and to have intercepted the full-blown elegance which longer growth would have supplied.

Poverty, like other rigid powers, is sometimes too hastily accused. If the excellence of Dryden's works was lessened by his indigence, their number was increased; and I know not how it will be proved that if he had written less he would have written better; or that, indeed, he would have undergone the toil of an author, if he had not been solicited by something more pressing than the love of praise.

But as is said by his Sebastian,

*What had been, is unknown; what is, appears.

We know that Dryden's several productions were so many successive expedients for his support; his plays were therefore often borrowed, and his poems were almost all occasional.

In an occasional performance no height of excellence can be expected from any mind, however fertile in itself, and however stored with acquisitions. He whose work is general and arbitrary has the choice of his matter, and takes that which his inclination and his studies have best qualified him to display and decorate. He is at liberty to delay his publication till he has satisfied his friends and himself, till he has reformed his first thoughts by subsequent examination, and polished away those faults which the precipitance of ardent composition is likely to leave behind it. Virgil is related to have poured out a great number of lines in the morning, and to have passed the day in reducing them to fewer.

The occasional poet is circumscribed by the narrowness of his subject. Whatever can happen to man has happened so often that little remains for fancy or invention. We have been all born; we have most of us been married; and so many have died before us, that our deaths can supply but few materials for a poet. In the fate of princes the public has an interest; and what happens to them of good or evil, the poets have always considered as business for the Muse. But after so many inauguratory gratulations, nuptial hymns, and funeral dirges, he must be highly favoured by nature, or by fortune, who says anything not said before. Even war and conquest, however splendid, suggest no new images; the triumphal chariot of a victorious monarch can be decked only with those ornaments that have graced his predecessors.

Not only matter but time is wanting. The poem must not be delayed till the occasion is forgotten. The lucky moments of animated imagination cannot be attended; elegances and illustrations cannot be multiplied by gradual accumulation; the composition must be dispatched while conversation is yet busy, and admiration fresh; and haste is to be made, lest some other event should lay hold upon mankind.

Occasional compositions may, however, secure to a writer the praise both of learning and facility; for they cannot be the effect of long study, and must be furnished immediately from the treasures of the mind.

The death of Cromwell was the first public event which called forth Dryden's poetical powers. His heroic stanzas have beauties and defects; the thoughts are vigorous, and though not always proper, show a mind replete with ideas; the numbers are smooth, and the diction, if not altogether correct, is elegant and easy.

Davenant was perhaps at this time his favourite author, though *Gondibert* never appears to have been popular; and from Davenant he learned to please his ear with the stanza of four lines alternately rhymed.

Dryden very early formed his versification: there are in this early production no traces of Donne's or Jonson's ruggedness; but he did not so soon free his mind from the ambition of *forced conceits. In *his verses on the Restoration, he says of the king's exile:

He, toss'd by Fate,...
Could taste no sweets of youth's desired age,
But found his life too true a pilgrimage.

And afterwards, to show how virtue and wisdom are increased by adversity, he makes this remark:

Well might the ancient poets then confer
On Night the honour'd name of "counsellor,"
Since, struck with rays of prosperous fortune blind,
We light alone in dark afflictions find.

His praise of *Monk's dexterity comprises such a cluster of thoughts unallied to one another, as will not elsewhere be easily found:

'Twas Monk, whom Providence design'd to loose
Those real bonds false freedom did impose.
The blessed saints that watch'd this turning scene,
Did from their stars with joyful wonder lean
To see small clues draw vastest weights along,
Not in their bulk, but in their order strong.
Thus pencils can by one slight touch restore
Smiles to that changed face that wept before.
With ease such fond chimæras we pursue,
As fancy frames for fancy to subdue;
But, when ourselves to action we betake,
It shuns the mint like gold that chemists make:
How hard was then his task, at once to be

What in the body natural we see!
Man's Architect distinctly did ordain
The charge of muscles, nerves, and of the brain,
Through viewless conduits spirits to dispense
The springs of motion from the seat of sense.
'Twas not the hasty product of a day,
But the well-ripen'd fruit of wise delay.
He, like a patient angler, ere he strook,
Would let them play awhile upon the hook.
Our healthful food the stomach labours thus,
At first embracing what it straight doth crush.
Wise leeches will not vain receipts obtrude,
While growing pains pronounce the humours crude;
Deaf to complaints, they wait upon the ill,
Till some safe crisis authorize their skill.

He had not yet learned, indeed he never learned well, to forbear the improper use of mythology. After having rewarded the heathen deities for their care,

With alga who the sacred altar strows?
To all the sea-gods Charles an offering owes;
A bull to thee, Portunus, shall be slain;
A ram to you, ye Tempests of the Main:

he tells us, in the language of religion,

Prayer storm'd the skies, and ravish'd Charles from thence,
As heaven itself is took by violence.

And afterwards mentions one of the most awful passages of sacred history.

Other conceits there are, too curious to be quite omitted; as,

For by example most we sinn'd before,
And, glass-like, clearness mix'd with frailty bore.

How far he was yet from thinking it necessary to found his sentiments on nature, appears from the extravagance of his fictions and hyperboles:

The winds, that never moderation knew,
Afraid to blow too much, too faintly blew;
Or, out of breath with joy, could not enlarge
Their straiten'd lungs.

It is no longer motion cheats your view;
As you meet it, the land approacheth you;
The land returns, and in the white it wears
The marks of penitence and sorrow bears.

I know not whether this fancy, however little be its value, was not borrowed. A French poet read to Malherbe some verses, in which he represents France as moving out of its place to receive the king. "Though this," said Malherbe, "was in my time, I do not remember it." …

Absalom and Achitophel is a work so well known that particular criticism is superfluous. If it be considered as a poem political and controversial, it will be found to comprise all the excellences of which the subject is susceptible; acrimony of censure, elegance of praise, artful delineation of characters, variety and vigour of sentiment, happy turns of language, and pleasing harmony of numbers; and all these raised to such a height as can scarcely be found in any other English composition.

It is not, however, without faults; some lines are inelegant or improper, and too many are irreligiously licentious. The original structure of the poem was defective; allegories drawn to great length will always break; Charles could not run continually parallel with David.

The subject had likewise another inconvenience: it admitted little imagery or description, and a long poem of mere sentiments easily becomes tedious; though all the parts are forcible, and every line kindles new rapture, the reader, if not relieved by the interposition of something that soothes the fancy, grows weary of admiration, and defers the rest.

As an approach to historical truth was necessary, the action and catastrophe were not in the poet's power; there is therefore an unpleasing disproportion between the beginning and the end. We are alarmed by a faction formed out of many sects various in their principles, but agreeing in their purpose of mischief, formidable for their numbers, and strong by their supports, while the king's friends are few and weak. The chiefs on either part are set forth to view; but when expectation is at the height, the king makes a speech, and

Henceforth a series of new times began.

Who can forbear to think of an enchanted castle, with a wide moat and lofty battlements, walls of marble and gates of brass, which vanishes at once into air, when the destined knight blows his horn before it?

In the *second part, written by Tate, there is a long insertion, which, for poignancy of satire, exceeds any part of the former. Personal resentment, though no laudable motive to satire, can add great force to general principles. Self-love is a busy prompter.

The *Medal*, written upon the same principles with *Absalom and Achitophel*, but upon a narrower plan, gives less pleasure, though it discovers equal abilities in the writer. The superstructure cannot extend beyond the foundation; a single character or incident cannot furnish as many ideas as a series of events or multiplicity of agents. This poem, therefore, since time has left it to itself, is not much read, nor perhaps generally understood, yet it abounds with touches both of humorous and serious satire. The picture of a man whose propensions to mischief are such that his best actions are but inability of wickedness, is very skillfully delineated and strongly coloured:

Power was his aim: but, thrown from that pretence,
The wretch turn'd loyal in his own defence,
And malice reconcil'd him to his prince.
Him, in the anguish of his soul, he serv'd;
Rewarded faster still than he deserv'd:
Behold him now exalted into trust;
His counsels oft convenient, seldom just.
Ev'n in the most sincere advice he gave,
He had a grudging still to be a knave.
The frauds he learnt in his fanatic years,
Made him uneasy in his lawful gears:
At least as little honest as he could:
And, like white witches, mischievously good.
To his first bias, longingly, he leans;
And rather would be great by wicked means.

The *Threnodia*, which, by a term I am afraid neither authorized nor analogical, he calls *Augustalis*, is not among his happiest productions. Its first and obvious defect is the irregularity of its metre, to which the ears of that age, however, were accustomed. What is worse, it has neither tenderness nor dignity; it is neither magnificent nor pathetic. He seems to look round him for images which he cannot find, and what he has he distorts by endeavouring to enlarge them. "He is," he says, "petrified with grief"; but the marble sometimes relents, and trickles in a joke:

The sons of art all med'cines tried,
And every noble remedy applied:
With emulation each essay'd
His utmost skill; *nay, more, they pray'd:*
Never was losing game with better conduct play'd.

He had been a little inclined to merriment before upon the prayers of a nation for their dying sovereign, nor was he serious enough to keep heathen fables out of his religion.

With him th' innumerable crowd of armed prayers
Knock'd at the gates of heaven, and knock'd aloud;
The first well-meaning rude petitioners.
All for his life assail'd the throne,
All would have brib'd the skies by offering up their own.
So great a throng not Heaven itself could bar;
'Twas almost borne by force *as in the giants' war.*
The prayers, at least, for his reprieve were heard;
His death, like Hezekiah's, was deferr'd.

There is throughout the composition a desire of splendour without wealth. In the conclusion he seems too much pleased with the prospect of the new reign to have lamented his old master with much sincerity.

He did not miscarry in this attempt for want of skill either in lyric or elegiac poetry. His poem *On the Death of Mrs. Killigrew* is undoubtedly the noblest ode that our language ever has produced. The first part flows with a torrent of enthusiasm. *Fervet immensusque ruit.* All the stanzas, indeed, are not equal. An imperial crown cannot be one continued diamond; the gems must be held together by some less valuable matter.

In his first *Ode for Cecila's Day*, which is lost in the splendour of the second, there are passages which would have dignified any other poet. The first stanza is vigorous and elegant, though the word *diapason* is too technical, and the rhymes are too remote from one another.

From harmony, from heavenly harmony,
This universal frame began:
When Nature underneath a heap
Of jarring atoms lay,
And could not heave her head,
The tuneful voice was heard from high,
"Arise, ye more than dead."
Then cold and hot, and moist and dry,
In order to their stations leap,
And Music's power obey.
From harmony, from heavenly harmony,
This universal frame began:
From harmony to harmony
Through all the compass of the notes it ran,
The diapason closing full in man.

The conclusion is likewise striking, but it includes an image so awful in itself that it can owe little to poetry; and I could wish the antithesis of music untuning had found some other place.

As from the power of sacred lays
The spheres began to move,
And sung the great Creator's praise
To all the bless'd above:
So when the last and dreadful hour
This crumbling pageant shall devour,
The trumpet shall be heard on high,
The dead shall live, the living die,
And Music shall untune the sky.

Of his skill in elegy he has given a specimen in his *Eleonora*, of which the following lines discover their author:

Though all these rare endowments of the mind
Were in a narrow space of life confin'd,
The figure was with full perfection crown'd;
Though not so large an orb, as truly round.
As when in glory, through the public place,
The spoils of conquer'd nations were to pass,
And but one day for triumph was allow'd,
The consul was constrain'd his pomp to crowd;

And so the swift procession hurried on,
That all, though not distinctly, might be shown:
So in the straiten'd bounds of life confin'd,
She gave but glimpses of her glorious mind:
And multitudes of virtues pass'd along;
Each pressing foremost in the mighty throng,
Ambitious to be seen, and then make room
For greater multitudes that were to come.
Yet unemploy'd no minute slipp'd away;
Moments were precious in so short a stay.
The haste of heaven to have her was so great,
That some were single acts, though each complete;
And every act stood ready to repeat.

This piece, however, is not without its faults; there is so much likeness in the initial comparison that there is no illustration. As a king would be lamented, Eleonora was lamented.

As when some great and gracious monarch dies,
Soft whispers, first, and mournful murmurs rise
Among the sad attendants; then the sound
Soon gathers voice, and spreads the news around,
Through town and country, till the dreadful blast
Is blown to distant colonies at last;
Who, then, perhaps, were offering vows in vain,
For his long life, and for his happy reign:
So slowly by degrees, unwilling Fame
Did matchless Elecnora's fate proclaim,
Till public as the loss the news became.

This is little better than to say in praise of a shrub that it is as green as a tree, or of a brook, that it waters a garden as a river waters a country.

Dryden confesses that he did not know the lady whom he celebrates; the praise being therefore inevitably general, fixes no impression on the reader, nor excites any tendency to love, nor much desire of imitation. Knowledge of the subject is to the poet what durable materials are to the architect.

The *Religio Laici*, which borrows its title from *the *Religio Medici* of Browne, is almost the only work of Dryden which can be considered as a voluntary effusion; in this, therefore, it might be hoped that the full effulgence of his genius would be found. But unhappily the subject is rather argumentative than poetical: he intended only a specimen of metrical disputation:

And this unpolish'd rugged verse I chose,
As fittest for discourse, and nearest prose.

This, however, is a composition of great excellence in its kind, in which the familiar is very properly diversified with the solemn, and the grave with the humorous; in which metre has neither weakened the force, nor clouded the perspicuity of argument; nor will it be easy to find another example equally happy of this middle kind of writing, which, though prosaic in some parts, rises to high poetry in others, and neither towers to the skies, nor creeps along the ground.

Of the same kind, or not far distant from it, is *The Hind and Panther*, the longest of all Dryden's original poems; an allegory intended to comprise and to decide the controversy between the Romanists and Protestants. The scheme of the work is injudicious and incommodious; for what can be more absurd than that one beast should counsel another to rest her faith upon a pope and council? He seems well enough skilled in the usual topics of argument, endeavours to show the necessity of an infallible judge, and reproaches the Reformers with want of unity; but is weak enough to ask, why, since we see without knowing how, we may not have an infallible judge without knowing where.

The Hind at one time is afraid to drink at the common brook, because she may be worried; but walking home with the Panther, talks by the way of the *Nicene Fathers, and at last declares herself to be the Catholic Church.

This absurdity was very properly ridiculed in **The City Mouse and Country Mouse* of Montague and Prior; and in the detection and censure of the incongruity of the fiction chiefly consists the value of their performance, which, whatever reputation it might obtain by the help of temporary passions, seems to readers almost a century distant not very forcible or animated.

Pope, whose judgment was perhaps a little bribed by the subject, used to mention this poem as the most correct specimen of Dryden's versification. It was, indeed, written when he had completely formed his manner, and may be supposed to exhibit, negligence excepted, his deliberate and ultimate scheme of metre.

We may therefore reasonably infer that he did not approve the perpetual uniformity which confines the sense to couplets, since he has broken his lines in the initial paragraph:

A milk-white Hind, immortal and unchang'd,
Fed on the lawns, and in the forest rang'd;
Without unspotted, innocent within,
She fear'd no danger, for she knew no sin.
Yet had she oft been chas'd with horns and hounds
And Scythian shafts, and many winged wounds
Aim'd at her heart; was often forc'd to fly,
And doom'd to death, though fated not to die.

These lines are lofty, elegant, and musical, notwithstanding the interruption of the pause, of which the effect is rather increase of pleasure by variety than offence by ruggedness.

To the first part it was his intention, he says, "to give the majestic turn of heroic poesy"; and perhaps he might have executed his design not unsuccessfully, had not an opportunity of satire, which he cannot forbear, fallen sometimes in his way. The character of a Presbyterian, whose emblem is the Wolf, is not very heroically majestic:

> More haughty than the rest, the wolfish race
> Appear with belly gaunt and famish'd face:
> Never was so deform'd a beast of grace.
> His ragged tail betwixt his legs he wears,
> Close clapp'd for shame; but his rough crest he rears,
> And pricks up his predestinating ears.

His general character of the other sorts of beasts that never go to church, though spritely and keen, has, however, not much of heroic poesy:

> These are the chief; to number o'er the rest,
> And stand like Adam naming every beast,
> Were weary work; nor will the Muse describe
> A slimy-born and sun-begotten tribe;
> Who, far from steeples and their sacred sound,
> In fields their sullen conventicles found.
> These gross, half-animated, lumps I leave;
> Nor can I think what thoughts they can conceive;
> But if they think at all, 'tis sure no higher
> Than matter, put in motion, may aspire;
> Souls that can scarce ferment their mass of clay,
> So drossy, so divisible are they,
> As would but serve pure bodies for allay:
> Such souls as shards produce, such beetle things
> As only buzz to heaven with evening wings;
> Strike in the dark, offending but by chance;
> Such are the blindfold blows of ignorance.
> They know not beings, and but hate a name;
> To them the Hind and Panther are the same.

One more instance, and that taken from the narrative part, where style was more in his choice, will show how steadily he kept his resolution of heroic dignity:

> For when the herd, suffic'd, did late repair
> To ferny heaths, and to their forest lair,
> She made a mannerly excuse to stay,
> Proffering the Hind to wait her half the way;
> That, since the sky was clear, an hour of talk
> Might help her to beguile the tedious walk.
> With much good-will the motion was embrac'd,
> To chat awhile on their adventures past:
> Not had the grateful Hind so soon forgot
> Her friend and fellow-sufferer in the plot.
> Yet wondering how of late she grew estrang'd,
> Her forehead cloudy and her count'nance chang'd,
> She thought this hour th' occasion would present
> To learn her secret cause of discontent,
> Which well she hop'd, might be with ease redress'd,
> Considering her a well-bred civil beast,
> And more a gentlewoman than the rest.
> After some common talk what rumours ran,
> The lady of the spotted muff began.

The second and third parts he professes to have reduced to diction more familiar and more suitable to dispute and conversation; the difference is not, however, very easily perceived; the first has familiar, and the two others have sonorous, lines. The original incongruity runs through the whole; the king is now Cæsar, and now the Lion; and the name Pan is given to the Supreme Being.

But when this constitutional absurdity is forgiven, the poem must be confessed to be written with great smoothness of metre, a wise extent of knowledge, and an abundant multiplicity of images; the controversy is embellished with pointed sentences, diversified by illustrations, and enlivened by sallies of invective. Some of the facts to which allusions are made, are now become obscure, and perhaps there may be many satirical passages little understood.

As it was by its nature a work of defiance, a composition which would naturally be examined with the utmost acrimony of criticism, it was probably laboured with uncommon attention; and there are, indeed, few negligences in the subordinate parts. The original impropriety, and the subsequent unpopularity of the subject, added to the ridiculousness of its first elements, has sunk it into neglect; but it may be usefully studied as an example of poetical ratiocination, in which the argument suffers little from the metre.

In *the poem *On the Birth of the Prince of Wales*, nothing is very remarkable but the exorbitant adulation, and that insensibility of the precipice on which the king was then standing, which the Laureate apparently shared with the rest of the courtiers. A few months cured him of controversy, dismissed him from court, and made him again a playwright and translator....

Since the English ear has been accustomed to the mellifluence of Pope's numbers, and the diction of poetry has become more splendid, new attempts have been made to translate Virgil; and all his works have been attempted by men better qualified to contend with Dryden. I will not engage myself in an invidious comparison by opposing one passage to another; a work of which there would be no end, and which might be often offensive without use.

It is not by comparing line with line that the merit of great works is to be estimated, but by their general effects and ultimate result. It is easy to note a weak line, and write one more vigorous in its place; to find a happiness of expression in the original, and transplant it by force into the version: but what is given to the parts may be subducted from the whole, and the reader may be weary though the critic may commend. Works of imagination excel by their allurement and delight, by their power of attracting and detaining the attention. That book is good in vain which the reader throws away. He only is the master who keeps the mind in pleasing captivity; whose pages are perused with eagerness, and in hope of new pleasure are perused again; and whose conclusion is perceived with an eye of sorrow, such as the traveller casts upon departing day.

By his proportion of this predomination I will consent that Dryden should be tried; of this, which, in opposition to reason, makes Ariosto the darling and the pride of Italy; of this, which, in defiance of criticism, continues Shakespeare the sovereign of the drama.

His last work was his *Fables*, in which he gave us the first example of a mode of writing which the Italians call *rifacimento*, a renovation of ancient writers, by modernizing their language. Thus * the old poem of Boiardo has been new-dressed by Domenichi and Berni. The works of Chaucer, upon which this kind of rejuvenescence has been bestowed by Dryden, require little criticism. The tale of *The Cock* seems hardly worth revival; and the story of *Palamon and Arcite*, containing an action unsuitable to the times in which it is placed, can hardly be suffered to pass without censure of the hyperbolical commendation which Dryden has given it in the general Preface, and in a poetical Dedication, a piece where his original fondness of remote conceits seems to have revived.

Of the three pieces borrowed from Boccace, *Sigismunda* may be defended by the celebrity of the story. *Theodore and Honoria*, though it contains not much moral, yet afforded opportunities of striking description. And *Cymon* was formerly a tale of such reputation, that, at the revival of letters, it was translated into Latin by * one of the Beroalds.

Whatever subjects employed his pen, he was still improving our measures and embellishing our language.

In this volume are interspersed some short original poems, which with his prologues, epilogues, and songs, may be comprised in Congreve's remark, that even those, if he had written nothing else, would have entitled him to the praise of excellence in his kind.

One composition must, however, be distinguished. * The *Ode for Saint Cecilia's Day*, perhaps the last effort of his poetry, has been always considered as exhibiting the highest flight of fancy and the exactest nicety of art. This is allowed to stand without a rival. If, indeed, there is any excellence beyond it in some other of Dryden's works, that excellence must be found. Compared with the *Ode on Killigrew*, it may be pronounced perhaps superior in the whole; but without any single part equal to the first stanza of the other.

It is said to have cost Dryden a fortnight's labour; but it does not want its negligences: some of the lines are without correspondent rhymes; a defect, which I never detected but after an acquaintance of many years, and which the enthusiasm of the writer might hinder him from perceiving.

His last stanza has less emotion than the former; but is not less elegant in the diction. The conclusion is vicious; the music of Timotheus, which "raised a mortal to the skies," had only a metaphorical power; that of Cecilia, which "drew an angel down," had a real effect: the crown therefore could not reasonably be divided.

In a general survey of Dryden's labours, he appears to have had a mind very comprehensive by nature, and much enriched with acquired knowledge. His compositions are the effects of a vigorous genius operating upon large materials.

The power that predominated in his intellectual operations was rather strong reason than quick sensibility. Upon all occasions that were presented, he studied rather than felt, and produced sentiments not such as nature enforces, but meditation supplies. With the simple and elemental passions, as they spring separate in the mind, he seems not much acquainted; and seldom describes them but as they are complicated by the various relations of society, and confused in the tumults and agitations of life.

What he says of love may contribute to the explanation of his character:

*Love various minds does variously inspire;
It stirs in gentle bosoms gentle fire,
Like that of incense on the altar laid;
But raging flames tempestuous souls invade,
A fire which every windy passion blows;
With pride it mounts, or with revenge it glows.

Dryden's was not one of the "gentle bosoms." Love, as it subsists in itself, with no tendency but to the person loved, and wishing only for correspondent kindness, such love as shuts out all other interest, the love of the golden age, was too soft and subtle to put his faculties in motion. He hardly conceived it but in its turbulent effervescence with some other desires: when it was inflamed by rivalry or obstructed by difficulties; when it invigorated ambition, or exasperated revenge.

He is, therefore, with all his variety of excellence, not often pathetic; and had so little sensibility of the power of effusions purely natural that he did not esteem them in others. Simplicity gave him no pleasure; and for the first part of his life he looked on *Otway with contempt, though at last, indeed very late, he confessed that in his play "there was nature, which is the chief beauty."

We do not always know our own motives. I am not certain whether it was not rather the difficulty which he found in exhibiting the genuine operations of the heart, than a servile submission to an injudicious audience, that filled his plays with false magnificence. It was necessary to fix attention; and the mind can be captivated only by recollection, or by curiosity; by reviving natural sentiments, or impressing new appearances of things: sentences were readier at his call than images; he could more easily fill the ear with some splendid novelty, than awaken those ideas that slumber in the heart.

The favourite exercise of his mind was ratiocination; and, that argument might not be too soon at an end, he delighted to talk of liberty and necessity, destiny and contingence; these he discusses in the language of the school with so much profundity that the terms which he uses are not always understood. It is indeed learning, but learning out of place.

When once he had engaged himself in disputation, thoughts flowed in on either side: he was now no longer at a loss; he had always objections and solutions at command, *verbaque provisam rem* — give him matter for his verse, and he finds without difficulty verse for his matter.

In comedy, for which he professes himself not naturally qualified, the mirth which he excites will perhaps not be found so much to arise from any original humour, or peculiarity of character nicely distinguished and diligently pursued, as from incidents and circumstances, artifices and surprises; from jests of action rather than of sentiment. What he had of humorous or passionate, he seems to have had not from nature, but from other poets; if not always as a plagiary, at least as an imitator.

Next to argument, his delight was in wild and daring sallies of sentiment, in the irregular and eccentric violence of wit. He delighted to tread upon the brink of meaning, where light and darkness begin to mingle; to approach the precipice of absurdity, and hover over the abyss of unideal vacancy. This inclination sometimes produced nonsense, which he knew; as,

*Move swiftly, sun, and fly a lover's pace,
Leave weeks and months behind thee in thy race.

*Amariel flies...
To guard thee from the demons of the air;
My flaming sword above them to display,
All keen, and ground upon the edge of day.

And sometimes it issued in absurdities, of which, perhaps, he was not conscious:

*Then we upon our orb's last verge shall go,
And see the ocean leaning on the sky;
From thence our rolling neighbours we shall know,
And on the lunar world securely pry.

These lines have no meaning; but may we not say, in imitation of Cowley on another book,

*'Tis so like *sense* 'twill serve the turn as well?

This endeavour after the grand and the new produced many sentiments either great or bulky, and many images either just or splendid:

*I am as free as Nature first made man,
Ere the base laws of servitude began,
When wild in woods the noble savage ran.

*— 'Tis but because the living death ne'er knew,
They fear to prove it as a thing that's new:
Let me th' experiment before you try,
I'll show you first how easy 'tis to die.

*— There with a forest of their darts he strove,
And stood like Capaneus defying Jove,
With his broad sword the boldest beating down,
While Fate grew pale lest he should win the town,
And turn'd the iron leaves of his dark book
To make new dooms, or mend what it mistook.

*— I beg no pity for this mouldering clay;
For if you give it burial, there it takes
Possession of your earth;
If burnt, and scatter'd in the air, the winds
That strew my dust diffuse my royalty,
And spread me o'er your clime; for where one atom
Of mine shall light, know there Sebastian reigns.

Of these quotations the two first may be allowed to be great, the two latter only tumid.

Of such selection there is no end. I will add only a few more passages; of which the first, though it may perhaps not be quite clear in prose, is not too obscure for poetry, as the meaning that it has is noble:

*No, there is a necessity in fate,
Why still the brave bold man is fortunate;
He keeps his object ever full in sight,
And that assurance holds him firm and right,
True, 'tis a narrow way that leads to bliss,
But right before there is no precipice;
Fear makes men look aside, and so their footing miss.

Of the images which the two following citations afford, the first is elegant, the second magnificent; whether either be just, let the reader judge:

*What precious drops are these,
Which silently each other's track pursue,
Bright as young diamonds in their infant dew?

*—— Resign your castle ——
— Enter, brave sir; for when you speak the word,
The gates shall open of their own accord;
The genius of the place its lord shall meet,
And bow its towery forehead at your feet.

These bursts of extravagance Dryden calls the *"Delilahs of the theatre," and owns that many noisy lines of Maxamin and Almanzor call out for vengeance upon him; "but I knew," says he, "that they were bad enough to please, even when I wrote them." There is surely reason to suspect that he pleased himself as well as his audience; and that these, like the harlots of other men, had his love, though not his approbation.

He had sometimes faults of a less generous and splendid kind. He makes, like almost all other poets, very frequent use of mythology, and sometimes connects religion and fable too closely without distinction.

He descends to display his knowledge with pedantic ostentation; as when, in translating Virgil, he says *"tack to the larboard" — and "veer starboard"; and talks in another work of *"virtue spooming before the wind." His vanity now and then betrays his ignorance:

*They Nature's King through Nature's optics view'd;
Revers'd, they view'd him lessen'd to their eyes.

He had heard of reversing a telescope, and unluckily reverses the object.

He is sometimes unexpectedly mean. When he describes the Supreme Being as moved by prayer to stop the Fire of London, what is his expression?

*A hollow crystal pyramid he takes,
In firmamental waters dipp'd above,
Of this a broad *extinguisher* he makes,
And *hoods* the flames that to their quarry strove.

When he describes the Last Day, and the decisive tribunal, he intermingles this image:

*When rattling bones together fly,
From the four quarters of the sky.

It was, indeed, never in his power to resist the temptation of a jest. In his elegy on Cromwell:

No sooner was the Frenchman's cause embrac'd,
Than the *light Monsieur* the *grave Don* outweigh'd;
His fortune turn'd the scale.

He had a vanity, unworthy of his abilities, to show, as may be suspected, the rank of the company with whom he lived, by the use of French words, which had then crept into conversation; such as *fraîcheur* for coolness, *fougue* for turbulence, and a few more, none of which the language has incorporated or retained. They continue only where they stood first, perpetual warnings to future innovators.

These are his faults of affectation; his faults of negligence are beyond recital. Such is the unevenness of his compositions that ten lines are seldom found together without something of which the reader is ashamed. Dryden was no rigid judge of his own pages; he seldom struggled after supreme excellence, but snatched in haste what was within his reach; and when he could content others, was himself contented. He did not keep present to his mind an idea of pure perfection; nor compare his works, such as they were, with what they might be made. He knew to whom he should be opposed. He had more music than Waller, more vigour than Denham, and more nature than Cowley; and from his contemporaries he was in no danger. Standing, therefore, in the highest place, he had no care to rise by contending with himself; but while there was no name above his own, was willing to enjoy fame on the easiest terms.

He was no lover of labour. What he thought sufficient, he did not stop to make better; and allowed himself to leave many parts unfinished, in confidence that the good lines would overbalance the bad. What he had once written, he dismissed from his thoughts; and, I believe, there is no example to be found of any correction or improvement made by him after publication. The hastiness of his productions might be the effect of necessity; but his subsequent neglect could hardly have any other cause than impatience of study.

What can be said of his versification will be little more than a dilatation of the praise given it by Pope:

> *Waller was smooth; but Dryden taught to join
> The varying verse, the full-resounding line,
> The long majestic march, and energy divine.

Some improvements had been already made in English numbers; but the full force of our language was not yet felt; the verse that was smooth was commonly feeble. If Cowley had sometimes a finished line, he had it by chance. Dryden knew how to choose the flowing and the sonorous words; to vary the pauses, and adjust the accents; to diversify the cadence, and yet preserve the smoothness of his metre.

Of triplets and Alexandrines, though he did not introduce the use, he established it. The triplet has long subsisted among us. Dryden seems not to have traced it higher than to Chapman's *Homer*; but it is to be found in Phaer's *Virgil*, written in the reign of Mary, and in Hall's *Satires*, published five years before the death of Elizabeth.

The Alexandrine was, I believe, first used by Spenser, for the sake of closing his stanza with a fuller sound. We had a longer measure of fourteen syllables, into which the *Æneid* was translated by Phaer, and other works of the ancients, by other writers; of which Chapman's *Iliad* was, I believe, the last.

The two first lines of Phaer's third *Æneid* will exemplify this measure:

> When Asia's state was overthrown, and Priam's kingdom stout,
> All guiltless, by the power of gods above was rooted out.

As these lines had their break, or *cæsura*, always at the eighth syllable, it was thought, in time, commodious to divide them; and quatrains of lines alternately consisting of eight and six syllables, make the most soft and pleasing of our lyric measures; as,

> *Relentless Time, destroying power,
> Which stone and brass obey,
> Who giv'st to every flying hour
> To work some new decay.

In the Alexandrine, when its power was once felt, some poems, as *Drayton's *Polyolbion*, were wholly written; and sometimes the measures of twelve and fourteen syllables were interchanged with one another. Cowley was the first that inserted the Alexandrine at pleasure among the heroic lines of ten syllables, and from him Dryden professes to have adopted it.

*The triplet and Alexandrine are not universally approved. Swift always censured them, and wrote some lines to ridicule them. In examining their propriety, it is to be considered that the essence of verse is regularity, and its ornament is variety. To write verse is to dispose syllables and sounds harmonically by some known and settled rule; a rule, however, lax enough to substitute similitude for identity, to admit change without breach of order, and to relieve the ear without disappointing it. Thus a Latin hexameter is formed from dactyls and spondees differently combined; the English heroic admits of acute or grave syllables variously disposed. The Latin never deviates into seven feet, or exceeds the number of seventeen syllables; but the English Alexandrine breaks the lawful bounds, and surprises the reader with two syllables more than he expected.

The effect of the triplet is the same: the ear has been accustomed to expect a new rhyme in every couplet; but is on a sudden surprised with three rhymes together, to which the reader could not accommodate his voice, did he not obtain notice of the change from *the braces of the margins. Surely there is something unskillful in the necessity of such mechanical direction.

Considering the metrical art simply as a science, and consequently excluding all casualty, we must allow that triplets and Alexandrines, inserted by caprice, are interruptions of that constancy to which science aspires. And though the variety which they produce may very justly be desired, yet to make our poetry exact, there ought to be some stated mode of admitting them.

But till some such regulation can be formed, I wish them still to be retained in their present state. They are sometimes grateful to the reader, and sometimes convenient to the poet.

*Fenton was of opinion that Dryden was too liberal and Pope too sparing in their use.

The rhymes of Dryden are commonly just, and he valued himself for his readiness in finding them; but he is sometimes open to objection.

It is the common practice of our poets to end the second line with a weak or grave syllable:

> *Together o'er the Alps methinks we fly,
> Fill'd with ideas of fair *Italy*.

Dryden sometimes puts the weak rhyme in the first:

> *Laugh all the powers that favour *tyranny*,
> And all the standing army of the sky.

Sometimes he concludes a period or paragraph with the first line of a couplet, which, though the French seem to do it without irregularity, always displeases in English poetry.

The Alexandrine, though much his favourite, is not always very diligently fabricated by him. It invariably requires a break at the sixth syllable, a rule which the modern French poets never violate, but which Dryden sometimes neglected:

> *And with paternal thunder vindicates his throne.

Of Dryden's works it was said by Pope that he "could select from them better specimens of every mode of poetry than any other English writer could supply." Perhaps no nation ever produced a writer that enriched his language with such variety of models. To him we owe the improvement, perhaps the completion of our metre, the refinement of our language, and much of the correctness of our sentiments. By him we were taught *sapere et fari*, to think naturally and express forcibly. *Though Davies has reasoned in rhyme before him, it may be perhaps maintained that he was the first who joined argument with poetry. He showed us the true bounds of a translator's liberty. What was said of Rome, adorned by Augustus, may be applied by an easy metaphor to English poetry embellished by Dryden, **lateritiam invenit, marmoream reliquit:* he found it brick, and he left it marble....

[1779–81]

JAMES BOSWELL

It is now a century since Macaulay wrote that magnificent paradox about Boswell and his *Life of Johnson*: "Boswell is the first of biographers. He has no second.... Many of the greatest men that ever lived have written biography. Boswell was one of the smallest men that ever lived, and he has beaten them all." Then, after enumerating his faults, Macaulay continued: "That such a man should have written one of the best books in the world is strange enough. But this is not all. Many persons... have... attained literary eminence in spite of their weaknesses. Boswell attained it by reason of his weaknesses. If he had not been a great fool, he would never have been a great writer." Carlyle indignantly protested: "Falser hypothesis, we may venture to say, never rose in a human soul.... Boswell wrote a good Book because he had a heart and an eye to discern Wisdom and an utterance to render it forth; because of his free insight, his lively talent, above all, of his Love and childlike Open-mindedness." In spite of the evident truth of this protest, which many men have perceived and echoed, Macaulay's paradox, because of its brilliancy and the half truth that it embodies, has captivated the popular mind for a century.

Today, however, we are coming to know Boswell better than has ever been possible before. New evidence has been discovered; new documents are becoming available, which are transforming our ideas of the man and his work. We now know Boswell, not as a man of one book, but as a busy writer with much experience and many interests; we have his correspondence and his journals. The man has become at once more understandable and more complex; the old generalizations no longer suffice.

Yet with these changes our estimate of the place of *The Life of Johnson* remains unaltered. What was apparent to the clearer-sighted of his contemporaries, what even Macaulay and Carlyle agreed upon, what newer investigation has confirmed, is the importance of the book. It has been proclaimed by all as the best biography in English and probably the best in any language. The last decade has witnessed a renaissance of biographical writing, but it has produced nothing to dispute this pre-eminence.

Though Boswell had been preparing the materials almost from the time of his first acquaintance with Johnson, he was slow in completing *The Life*. In 1786, he published his *Journal of a Tour to the Hebrides*, in which he presented Johnson's character and recorded his words with extraordinary brilliancy for the short period of his visit to Scotland in 1773. This was a sort of trial balloon by which he not only tested his powers but from which he also profited by the criticism of friends and enemies. In 1791, almost seven years after Johnson's death, he published the *magnum opus*. There is no better comment on his biographical methods than the following paragraph from the Advertisement to the first edition:

> "The labour and anxious attention with which I have collected and arranged the materials of which these volumes are composed will hardly be conceived by those who read them with careless facility. The stretch of mind and prompt assiduity by which so many conversations were preserved, I myself, at some distance or time, contemplate with wonder; and I must be allowed to suggest that the nature of the work, in other respects, as it consists of innumerable detached particulars, all which, even the most minute, I have spared no pains to ascertain with a scrupulous authenticity, has occasioned a degree of trouble far beyond that of any other species of composition. Were I to detail the books which I have consulted, and the inquiries which I have found it necessary to make by various channels, I should probably be thought ridiculously ostentatious. Let me only observe, as a specimen of my trouble, that I have sometimes been obliged to run half over London, in order to fix a date correctly; which, when I had accomplished, I well knew would obtain me no praise, though a failure would have been to my discredit. And after all, perhaps, hard as it may be, I shall not be surprised if omissions or mistakes be pointed out with invidious severity. I have also been extremely careful as to the exactness of my quotations; holding that there is a respect due to the public which should oblige every author to attend to this, and never to presume to introduce them with, — 'I think I have read'; — or — 'If I remember right,' when the originals may be examined."

Accuracy and industry, however indispensable to such a task, were but a part of his equipment. Skill in arrangement, imagination, clear and forceful presentation were necessary to produce such a biography as this. Boswell loved Johnson and honoured his memory on this side idolatry as much as any, but he realized that the best service he could do his hero was to show him as he was, confident that the whole man in his weakness and his idiosyncrasy, as well as in his strength and his majesty, was great enough for unsparing revelation. Though the book was the object of immediate attack by many who had not this assurance, when the dust of controversy had cleared, it became apparent that Boswell was right. Despite the fact that he was one of the vainest of men, Boswell did not overestimate his achievement when he wrote in the opening pages of *The Life of Johnson*: "I will venture to say that he will be seen in this work more completely than any man who has ever yet lived."

Carlyle asserted that "all Johnson's own Writings, laborious and in their kind genuine above most, stand on a quite inferior level to it." While this statement is not true as it stands, it contains this element of truth: Johnson's work was of two kinds, oral and written; Boswell has preserved much of the talk which in its way is as valuable as anything that the doctor committed to paper. Besides this, it has preserved much of his correspondence. Without this supplementary material no student could know Johnson as he was.

The portions here reprinted are first, those that treat of Johnson's famous letter to the Earl of Chesterfield and, second, the narrative of the year 1763 from Boswell's first meeting with Johnson to their parting at Harwich when the former sailed for Holland. The first has been chosen because it illustrates Johnson's sturdy independence and also because it is a notable chapter in the history of literary patronage; the second and larger extract has been chosen because it records many of Johnson's most famous utterances. So far as they go, both are given without abridgment.

THE LIFE OF SAMUEL JOHNSON

From 1754, ÆTAT. 45

Lord Chesterfield, to whom Johnson had paid the high compliment of addressing to his Lordship * the "Plan" of his *Dictionary*, had behaved to him in such a manner as to excite his contempt and indignation. The world has been for many years amused with a story confidently told, and as confidently repeated with additional circumstances, that a sudden disgust was taken by Johnson upon occasion of his having been one day kept long in waiting in his Lordship's antechamber, for which the reason assigned was that he had company with him; and that at last, when the door opened, out walked * Colley Cibber; and that Johnson was so violently provoked when he found for whom he had been so long excluded that he went away in a passion and never would return. I remember having mentioned this story to * George Lord Lyttelton, who told me he was very intimate with Lord Chesterfield; and holding it as a well-known truth, defended Lord Chesterfield by saying, that "Cibber, who had been introduced familiarly by the backstairs, had probably not been there above ten minutes." It may seem strange even to entertain a doubt concerning a story so long and so widely current, and thus implicitly adopted, if not sanctioned, by the authority which I have mentioned; but Johnson himself assured me that there was not the least foundation for it. He told me that there never was any particular incident which produced a quarrel between Lord Chesterfield and him; but that his Lordship's continued neglect was the reason why he resolved to have no connection with him. When the *Dictionary* was upon the eve of publication, Lord Chesterfield, who, it is said, had flattered himself with expectations that Johnson would dedicate the work to him, attempted, in a courtly manner, to soothe and insinuate himself with the sage, conscious, as it should seem, of the cold indifference with which he had treated its learned author; and further attempted to conciliate him by writing two papers in * the *World*, in recommendation of the work; and it must be confessed that they contain some studied compliments, so finely turned that, if there had been no previous offence, it is probable that Johnson would have been highly delighted. Praise, in general, was pleasing to him; but by praise from a man of rank and elegant accomplishments he was peculiarly gratified.

His Lordship says, "I think the public in general, and the republic of letters in particular, are greatly obliged to Mr. Johnson for having undertaken and executed so great and desirable a work. Perfection is not to be expected from man: but if we are to judge by the various works of Mr. Johnson already published, we have good reason to believe that he will bring this as near to perfection as any man could do. The 'Plan' of it, which he published some years ago, seems to me to be a proof of it. Nothing can be more rationally imagined, or more accurately and elegantly expressed. I therefore recommend the previous perusal of it to all those who intend to

*** Notes on James Boswell will be found in the Appendix, pp. 1030 ff.**

buy the *Dictionary*, and who, I suppose, are all those who can afford it."

* * * * * * * *

"It must be owned that our language is at present in a state of anarchy, and hitherto, perhaps, it may not have been the worse for it. During our free and open trade, many words and expressions have been imported, adopted, and naturalized from other languages, which have greatly enriched our own. Let it still preserve what real strength and beauty it may have borrowed from others; but let it not, like the Tarpeian maid, be overwhelmed and crushed by unnecessary foreign ornaments. The time for discrimination seems to be now come. Toleration, adoption, and naturalization have run their lengths. Good order and authority are now necessary. But where shall we find them and, at the same time, the obedience due to them? We must have recourse to the old Roman expedient in times of confusion, and choose a dictator. Upon this principle, I give my vote for Mr. Johnson to fill that great and arduous post. And I hereby declare that I make a total surrender of all my rights and privileges in the English language, as a free-born British subject, to the said Mr. Johnson, during the term of his dictatorship. Nay more, I will not only obey him, like an old Roman, as my dictator, but, like a modern Roman, I will implicitly believe in him as my Pope, and hold him to be infallible while in the chair, but no longer. More than this he cannot well require; for, I presume that obedience can never be expected, when there is neither terror to enforce, nor interest to invite it."

* * * * * * * *

"But a grammar, a dictionary, and a history of our language, through its several stages, were still wanting at home, and importunately called for from abroad. Mr. Johnson's labours will now, and I dare say, very fully supply that want, and greatly contribute to the farther spreading of our language in other countries. Learners were discouraged by finding no standard to resort to; and, consequently, thought it incapable of any. They will now be undeceived and encouraged."

This courtly device failed of its effect. Johnson, who thought that "all was false and hollow," despised the honeyed words, and was even indignant that Lord Chesterfield should for a moment, imagine that he could be the dupe of such an artifice. His expression to me concerning Lord Chesterfield, upon this occasion, was, "Sir, after making great professions, he had, for many years, taken no notice of me; but when my *Dictionary* was coming out, he fell a-scribbling in the *World* about it. Upon which, I wrote him a letter expressed in civil terms, but such as might show him that I did not mind what he said or wrote, and that I had done with him."

This is that celebrated letter of which so much has been said, and about which curiosity has been so long excited, without being gratified. I for many years solicited Johnson to favour me with a copy of it, that so excellent a composition might not be lost to posterity. He delayed from time to time to give it me; till at last in 1781, when we were on a visit at *Mr. Dilly's, at Southill in Bedfordshire, he was pleased to dictate it to me from memory. He afterwards found among his papers a copy of it, which he had dictated to *Mr. Baretti, with its title and corrections in his own handwriting. This he gave to *Mr. Langton; adding that if it were to come into print, he wished it to be from that copy. By Mr. Langton's kindness, I am enabled to enrich my work with a perfect transcript of what the world has so eagerly desired to see.

"TO THE RIGHT HONOURABLE
THE EARL OF CHESTERFIELD.

February 7, 1755

"MY LORD,

"I have been lately informed, by the proprietor of the *World*, that two papers, in which my *Dictionary* is recommended to the public, were written by your Lordship. To be so distinguished is an honour, which, being very little accustomed to favours from the great, I know not well how to receive, or in what terms to acknowledge.

"When, upon some slight encouragement, I first visited your Lordship, I was overpowered, like the rest of mankind, by the enchantment of your address, and could not forbear to wish that I might boast myself **le vainqueur du vainqueur de la terre*, that I might obtain that regard for which I saw the world contending; but I found my attendance so little encouraged that neither pride nor modesty would suffer me to continue it. When I had once addressed your Lordship in public, I had exhausted all the art of pleasing which a retired and uncourtly scholar can possess. I had done all that I could; and no man is well pleased to have his all neglected, be it ever so little.

"Seven years, my Lord, have now passed since I waited in your outward rooms, or was repulsed from your door; during which time I have been pushing on my work through difficulties of which it is useless to complain, and have brought it, at last, to the verge of publication, without one act of assistance, one word of encouragement, or one smile of favour. Such treatment I did not expect, for I never had a patron before.

*"The shepherd in Virgil grew at last acquainted with Love, and found him a native of the rocks.

"Is not a patron, my Lord, one who looks with unconcern on a man struggling for life in the water, and, when he has reached ground, encumbers him with help? The notice which you have been pleased to take of my labours, had it been early, had been kind; but it has been delayed till I am indifferent, and cannot enjoy it; *till I am solitary, and cannot impart it; till I am known, and do not want it. I hope it is no very cynical asperity not to confess obligations where no benefit has been received, or to be unwilling that the public should consider me as owing that to a patron, which Providence has enabled me to do for myself.

"Having carried on my work thus far with so little obligation to any favourer of learning, I shall not be disappointed though I should conclude it, if less be possible, with less; for I have been long wakened from that dream of hope, in which I once boasted myself with so much exultation,

"My Lord,

"Your Lordship's most humble

"Most obedient servant,

"SAM. JOHNSON."

"While this was the talk of the town," says *Dr. Adams, in a letter to me, "I happened to visit *Dr. Warburton, who, finding that I was acquainted with Johnson, desired me earnestly to carry his compliments to him, and to tell him that he honoured him for his manly behaviour in rejecting these condescensions of Lord Chesterfield, and for resenting the treatment he had received from him, with a proper spirit. Johnson was visibly pleased with this compliment, for he had always a high opinion of Warburton. Indeed, the force of mind which appeared in this letter was congenial with that which Warburton himself amply possessed.

There is a curious minute circumstance which struck me, in comparing the various editions of Johnson's **Imitations of Juvenal.* In the tenth *Satire* one of the couplets upon the vanity of wishes even for literary distinction stood thus:

> Yet think what ills the scholar's life assail,
> Toil, envy, want, the *garret,* and the jail.

But after experiencing the uneasiness which Lord Chesterfield's fallacious patronage made him feel, he dismissed the word *garret* from the sad group, and in all the subsequent editions the line stands,

> Toil, envy, want, the *patron,* and the jail.

That Lord Chesterfield must have been mortified by the lofty contempt, and polite, yet keen, satire with which Johnson exhibited him to himself in this letter, it is impossible to doubt. He, however, with that glossy duplicity which was his constant study, affected to be quite unconcerned. Dr. Adams mentioned to *Mr. Robert Dodsley that he was sorry Johnson had written his letter to Lord Chesterfield. Dodsley, with the true feelings of trade, said he was very sorry too; for that he had a property in the *Dictionary,* to which his Lordship's patronage might have been of consequence. He then told Mr. Adams that Lord Chesterfield had shown him the letter. "I should have imagined," replied Dr. Adams, "that Lord Chesterfield would have concealed it." "Poh!" said Dodsley, "do you think a letter from Johnson could hurt Lord Chesterfield? Not at all, sir. It lay upon his table, where anybody might see it. He read it to me; said, 'This man has great powers,' pointed out the severest passages, and observed how well they were expressed." This air of indifference, which imposed upon the worthy Dodsley, was certainly nothing but a specimen of that dissimulation which Lord Chesterfield inculcated as one of the most essential lessons for the conduct of life. His Lordship endeavoured to justify himself to Dodsley from the charges brought against him by Johnson; but we may judge of the flimsiness of his defence, from his having excused his neglect of Johnson by saying that he had heard he had changed his lodgings, and did not know where he lived; as if there could have been the smallest difficulty to inform himself of that circumstance, by enquiring in the literary circle with which his Lordship was well acquainted, and was, indeed, himself, one of its ornaments.

Dr. Adams expostulated with Johnson, and suggested that his not being admitted when he called on him was probably not to be imputed to Lord Chesterfield; for his Lordship had declared to Dodsley that he would have turned off the best servant he ever had, if he had known that he denied him to a man who would have been always more than welcome; and in confirmation of this, he insisted on Lord Chesterfield's general affability and easiness of access, especially to literary men. "Sir," said Johnson, "that is not Lord Chesterfield; he is the proudest man this day existing." "No," said Dr. Adams, "there is one person, at least, as proud; I think, by your own account, you are the prouder man of the two." "But mine," replied Johnson instantly, "was *defensive* pride." This, as Dr. Adams well observed, was one of those happy turns for which he was so remarkably ready.

Johnson having now explicitly avowed his opinion of Lord Chesterfield, did not refrain from expressing himself concerning that nobleman with pointed freedom: "This man," said he, "I thought had been a lord among wits; but I find he is only a wit among lords!" And when his *Letters* to his natural son were published, he observed that "they teach the morals of a whore, and the manners of a dancing-master."

The character of "a respectable Hottentot," in Lord Chesterfield's letters, has been generally understood to be meant for Johnson, and I have no doubt that it was. But I remember when the literary property of those letters was contested in the Court of Session in Scotland, and Mr. Henry Dundas, one of the counsel for the proprietors, read this character as an exhibition of Johnson, Sir David Dalrymple, Lord Hailes, one of the judges, maintained, with some warmth, that it was not intended as a portrait of Johnson, but of a late noble lord, distinguished for abstruse science. I have heard Johnson himself talk of the character, and say that it was meant for George, Lord Lyttelton, in which I could by no means agree; for his Lordship had nothing of that violence which is a conspicuous feature in the composition. Finding that my illustrious friend could bear to have it supposed that it might be meant for him, I said, laughingly, that there was one trait which unquestionably did not belong to him; "He throws his meat anywhere but down his throat." "Sir," said he, "Lord Chesterfield never saw me eat in his life."...

From 1763, ÆTAT. 54

This is to me a memorable year; for in it I had the happiness to obtain the acquaintance of that extraordinary man whose memoirs I am now writing, an acquaintance which I shall ever esteem as one of the most fortunate circumstances in my life. Though then but two-and-twenty, I had for several years read his works with delight and instruction, and had the highest reverence for their author, which had grown up in my fancy into a kind of mysterious veneration, by figuring to myself a state of solemn elevated abstraction, in which I supposed him to live in the immense metropolis of London. Mr. Gentleman, a native of Ireland, who passed some years in Scotland as a player, and as an instructor in the English language, a man whose talents and worth were depressed by misfortunes, had given me a representation of the figure and manner of Dictionary Johnson! as he was then generally called; and during my first visit to London, which was for three months in 1760, *Mr. Derrick, the poet, who was Gentleman's friend and countryman, flattered me with hopes that he would introduce me to Johnson, an honour of which I was very ambitious. But he never found an opportunity, which made me doubt that he had promised to do what was not in his power; till Johnson some years afterwards told me, "Derrick, sir, might very well have introduced you. I had a kindness for Derrick, and am sorry he is dead."

In the summer of 1761 *Mr. Thomas Sheridan was at Edinburgh, and delivered lectures upon the English language and public speaking to large and respectable audiences. I was often in his company, and heard him frequently expatiate upon Johnson's extraordinary knowledge, talents, and virtues, repeat his pointed sayings, describe his particularities, and boast of his being his guest sometimes till two or three in the morning. At his house I hoped to have many opportunities of seeing the sage, as Mr. Sheridan obligingly assured me I should not be disappointed.

When I returned to London in the end of 1762, to my surprise and regret I found an irreconcilable difference had taken place between Johnson and Sheridan. A pension of two hundred pounds a year had been given to Sheridan. Johnson, who, as has been already mentioned, thought slightingly of Sheridan's art, upon hearing that he was also pensioned, exclaimed, "What! have they given *him* a pension? Then it is time for me to give up mine." Whether this proceeded from a momentary indignation, as if it were an affront to his exalted merit that a player should be rewarded in the same manner with him, or was the sudden effect of a fit of peevishness, it was unluckily said, and, indeed, cannot be justified. Mr. Sheridan's pension was granted to him not as a player, but as a sufferer in the cause of government, when he was manager of the Theatre Royal in Ireland, when parties ran high in 1753. And it must also be allowed that he was a man of literature, and had considerably improved the arts of reading and speaking with distinctness and propriety.

Besides, Johnson should have recollected that Mr. Sheridan taught pronunciation to *Mr. Alexander Wedderburne, whose sister was married to Sir Harry Erskine, an intimate friend of Lord Bute, who was the favourite of the king; and surely the most outrageous Whig will not maintain that, whatever ought to be the principle in the disposal of offices, a pension ought never to be granted from any bias of court connection. Mr. Macklin, indeed, shared with Mr. Sheridan the honour of instructing Mr. Wedderburne; and though it was too late in life for a Caledonian to acquire the genuine English cadence, yet so successful were Mr. Wedderburne's instructors, and his own unabating endeavours, that he got rid of the coarse part of his Scotch accent, retaining only as much of the "native woodnote wild," as to mark his country; which, if any Scotchman should affect to forget, I should heartily despise him. Notwithstanding the difficulties which are to be encountered by those who have not had the advantage of an English education, he by degrees formed a mode of speaking to which Englishmen do not deny the praise of elegance. Hence his distinguished oratory, which he exerted in his own country as an advocate in the Court of Session, and a ruling elder of the Kirk, has had its fame and ample reward in much higher spheres. When I look back on this noble person at Edinburgh, in situations so unworthy of his brilliant powers, and behold Lord Loughborough at London, the change seems almost like one of the metamorphoses in Ovid; and as his two preceptors, by refining his utterance, gave currency to his talents, we may say in the words of that poet, **Nam vos mutastis*.

I have dwelt the longer upon this remarkable instance of successful parts and assiduity, because it affords animating encouragement to other gentlemen of North Britain to try their fortunes in the southern part of the island, where they may hope to gratify their utmost ambition; and, now that we are one people by the Union, it would surely be illiberal to maintain that they have not an equal title with the natives of any other part of his Majesty's dominions.

Johnson complained that a man who disliked him repeated his sarcasm to Mr. Sheridan, without telling him what followed, which was that, after a pause, he added, "However, I am glad that Mr. Sheridan has a pension, for he is a very good man." Sheridan could never forgive this hasty contemptuous expression. It rankled in his mind; and though I informed him of all that Johnson said, and that he would be very glad to meet him amicably, he positively declined repeated offers which I made, and once went off abruptly from a house where he and I were engaged to dine, because he was told that Dr. Johnson was to be there. I have no sympathetic feeling with such persevering resentment. It is painful when there is a breach between those who have lived together socially and cordially; and I wonder that there is not, in all such cases, a mutual wish that it should be healed. I could perceive that Mr. Sheridan was by no means satisfied with Johnson's acknowledging him to be a good man. That could not soothe his injured vanity. I could not but smile, at the same time that I was offended, to observe Sheridan in the *Life of Swift*, which he afterwards published, attempting, in the writhings of his resentment, to depreciate Johnson by characterising him as "a writer of gigantic fame, in these days of little men"; that very Johnson whom he once so highly admired and venerated.

This rupture with Sheridan deprived Johnson of one of his most agreeable resources for amusement in his lonely evenings; for Sheridan's well-informed, animated, and bustling mind never suffered conversation to stagnate; and Mrs. Sheridan was a most agreeable companion to an intellectual man. She was sensible, ingenious, unassuming, yet communicative. I recollect with satisfaction many pleasing hours which I passed with her under the hospitable roof of her husband, who was to me a very kind friend. Her novel, entitled *Memoirs of Miss Sydney Biddulph,* contains an excellent moral, while it inculcates a future state of retribution; and what it teaches is impressed upon the mind by a series of as deep distress as can affect humanity, in the amiable and pious heroine who goes to her grave unrelieved, but resigned, and full of hope of "Heaven's mercy." Johnson paid her this high compliment upon it: "I know not, madam, that you have a right, upon moral principles, to make your readers suffer so much."

Mr. Thomas Davies, the actor, who then kept a bookseller's shop in Russell Street, Covent Garden, told me that Johnson was very much his friend, and came frequently to his house, where he more than once invited [illegible]e to meet him: but by some unlucky accident [illegible]ther he was prevented from coming to us. [illegible]Thomas Davies was a man of good [illegible]ding and talents, with the advantage [illegible] education. Though somewhat [illegible] an entertaining companion; [illegible] performances have no incon-[illegible]re of merit. He was a friendly and [illegible]ble man. Both he and his wife [illegible]en celebrated for her beauty), [illegible] stage for many years, main-[illegible]n decency of character; and [illegible]med them, and lived in as easy [illegible] with them as with any family [illegible] used to visit. Mr. Davies recol-[illegible] several of Johnson's remarkable say-[illegible]s, and was one of the best of the many imitators of his voice and manner, while relating them. He increased my impatience more and more to see the extraordinary man whose works I highly valued, and whose conversation was reported to be so peculiarly excellent.

At last, on Monday the 16th of May, when I was sitting in Mr. Davies's back-parlour, after having drunk tea with him and Mrs. Davies, Johnson unexpectedly came into the shop; and Mr. Davies having perceived him through the glass-door in the room in which we were sitting, advancing towards us — he announced his awful approach to me, somewhat in the manner of an actor in the part of Horatio, when he addresses Hamlet on the appearance of his father's ghost, "Look, my Lord, it comes." I found that I had a very perfect idea of Johnson's figure, from the portrait of him painted by Sir Joshua Reynolds soon after he had published his *Dictionary*, in the attitude of sitting in his easy chair in deep meditation; which was the first picture his friend did for him, which Sir Joshua very kindly presented to me, and from which an engraving has been made for this work. Mr. Davies mentioned my name, and respectfully introduced me to him. I was much agitated; and recollecting his prejudice against the Scotch, of which I had heard much, I said to Davies, "Don't tell where I come from." — "From Scotland," cried Davies, roguishly. "Mr. Johnson," said I, "I do indeed come from Scotland, but I cannot help it." I am willing to flatter myself that I meant this as light pleasantry to soothe and conciliate him, and not as an humiliating abasement at the expense of my country. But however that might be, this speech was somewhat unlucky; for with that quickness of wit for which he was so remarkable, he seized the expression "come from Scotland," which I used in the sense of being of that country; and, as if I had said that I had come away from it, or left it, retorted, "That, sir, I find, is what a very great many of your countrymen cannot help." This stroke stunned me a good deal; and when we had sat down, I felt myself not a little embarrassed, and apprehensive of what might come next. He then addressed himself to Davies: "What do you think of * Garrick? He has refused me an order for the play for *Miss Williams, because he knows the house will be full, and that an order would be worth three shillings." Eager to take any opening to get into conversation with him, I ventured to say, "Oh, sir, I cannot think Mr. Garrick would grudge such a trifle to you." "Sir," said he, with a stern look, "I have known David Garrick longer than you have done, and I know no right you have to talk to me on the subject." Perhaps I deserved this check; for it was rather presumptuous in me, an entire stranger, to express any doubt of the justice of his animadversion upon his old acquaintance and pupil. I now felt myself much mortified, and began to think that the hope which I had long indulged of obtaining his acquaintance was blasted. And, in truth, had not my ardour been uncommonly strong, and my resolution uncommonly persevering, so rough a reception might have deterred me forever from making any further attempts. Fortunately, however, I remained upon the field not wholly discomfited; and was soon rewarded by hearing some of his conversation, of which I preserved the following short minute, without marking the questions and observations by which it was produced.

"People," he remarked, "may be taken in once, who imagine that an author is greater in private life than other men. Uncommon parts require uncommon opportunities for their exertion."

"In barbarous society superiority of parts is of real consequence. Great strength or great wisdom is of much value to an individual. But in more polished times there are people to do everything for money; and then there are a number of other superiorities, such as those of birth and fortune and rank, that dissipate men's attention, and leave no extraordinary share of respect for personal and intellectual superiority. This is wisely ordered by Providence, to preserve some equality among mankind."

"Sir, this book," **The Elements of Criticism,* which he had taken up, "is a pretty essay, and deserves to be held in some estimation, though much of it is chimerical."

Speaking of one who with more than ordinary boldness attacked public measures and the royal family, he said, "I think he is safe from the law, but he is an abusive scoundrel; and instead of applying to my Lord Chief Justice to punish him, I would send half a dozen footmen and have him well ducked."

"The notion of liberty amuses the people of England, and helps to keep off the **tædium vitæ.* When a butcher tells you that his heart bleeds for his country, he has, in fact, no uneasy feeling."

"Sheridan will not succeed at Bath with his oratory. Ridicule has gone down before him, and I doubt, Derrick is his enemy."

"Derrick may do very well, as long as he can outrun his character; but the moment his character gets up with him, it is all over."

It is, however, but just to record that some years afterwards, when I reminded him of this sarcasm, he said, "Well, but Derrick has now got a character that he need not run away from."

I was highly pleased with the extraordinary vigour of his conversation, and regretted that I was drawn away from it by an engagement at another place. I had, for a part of the evening, been left alone with him, and had ventured to make an observation now and then, which he received very civilly; so that I was satisfied that, though there was a roughness in his manner, there was no ill-nature in his disposition. Davies followed me to the door, and when I complained to him a little of the hard blows which the great man had given me, he kindly took upon him to console me by saying, "Don't be uneasy. I can see he likes you very well."

A few days afterwards I called on Davies, and asked him if he thought I might take the liberty of waiting on Mr. Johnson at his chambers in the Temple. He said I certainly might, and that Mr. Johnson would take it as a compliment. So upon Tuesday, the 24th of May, after having been enlivened by the witty sallies of *Messieurs Thornton, Wilkes, Churchill, and Lloyd, with whom I had passed the morning, I boldly repaired to Johnson. His chambers were on the first floor of No. 1, Inner Temple Lane, and I entered them with an impression given me by the Reverend *Dr. [illegible] of Edinburgh, who had been introd[illegible] him not long before, and described [illegible] "found the giant in his den"; a[illegible] which, when I came to be[illegible] quainted with Johnson, I re[illegible] and he was diverted at this pic[illegible] count of himself. Dr. Blair ha[illegible] sented to him by Dr. James Ford[illegible] time the controversy conce[illegible] published by *Mr. James [illegible] translations of Ossian, was a[illegible] Johnson had all along denied th[illegible] ticity; and, what was still more prov[illegible] their admirers, maintained that they [illegible] merit. The subject having been introdu[illegible] by Dr. Fordyce, Dr. Blair, relying on the internal evidence of their antiquity, asked Dr. Johnson whether he thought any man of a modern age could have written such poems. Johnson replied, "Yes, sir, many men, many women, and many children." Johnson at this time did not know that Dr. Blair had just published a dissertation, not only defending their authenticity, but seriously ranking them with the poems of Homer and Virgil; and when he was afterwards informed of this circumstance, he expressed some displeasure at Dr. Fordyce's having suggested the topic, and said, "I am not sorry that they got thus much for their pains. Sir, it was like leading one to talk of a book when the author is concealed behind the door."

He received me very courteously; but, it must be confessed that his apartment and furniture and morning dress were sufficiently uncouth. His brown suit of clothes looked very rusty: he had on a little old shrivelled unpowdered wig, which was too small for his head; his shirt-neck and knees of his breeches were loose; his black worsted stockings ill drawn up; and he had a pair of unbuckled shoes by way of slippers. But all these slovenly particularities were forgotten the moment that he began to talk. Some gentlemen, whom I do not recollect, were sitting with him; and when they went away, I also rose; but he said to me, "Nay, don't go." — "Sir," said I, "I am afraid that I intrude upon you. It is benevolent to allow me to sit and hear you." He seemed pleased with this compliment, which I sincerely paid him, and answered, "Sir, I am obliged to any man who visits me." I have preserved the following short minute of what passed this day.

"Madness frequently discovers itself merely by unnecessary deviation from the usual modes of the world. *My poor friend Smart showed the disturbance of his mind, by falling upon his knees, and saying his prayers in the street, or in any other unusual place. Now although, rationally speaking, it is greater madness not to pray at all than to pray as Smart did, I am afraid there are so many who do not pray that their understanding is not called in question."

Concerning this unfortunate poet, Christopher Smart, who was confined in a madhouse, he had, at another time, the following conversation with Dr. Burney. — Burney. "How does poor Smart do, sir? is he likely to recover?" Johnson. "It seems as if his mind had ceased to struggle with the disease, for he grows fat upon it." Burney. "Perhaps, sir, that may be from want of exercise." Johnson. "No, sir; he has partly as much exercise as he used to have, for he digs in the garden. Indeed, before his confinement, he used for exercise to walk to the alehouse; but he was carried back again. I did not think he ought to be shut up. His infirmities were not noxious to society. He insisted on people praying with him; and I'd as lief pray with Kit Smart as any one else. Another charge was that he did not love clean linen; and I have no passion for it." Johnson continued. "Mankind have a great aversion to intellectual labour; but even supposing knowledge to be easily attainable, more people would be content to be ignorant than would take even a little trouble to acquire it."

"The morality of an action depends on the motive from which we act. If I fling half a crown to a beggar with intention to break his head, and he picks it up and buys victuals with it, the physical effect is good; but, with respect to me, the action is very wrong. So, religious exercises, if not performed with an intention to please God, avail us nothing. As our Saviour says of those who perform them from other motives, 'Verily they have their reward.'"

"The Christian religion has very strong evidences. It, indeed, appears in some degree strange to reason; but in history we have undoubted facts, against which, reasoning *à priori*, we have more arguments than we have for them; but then, testimony has great weight, and casts the balance. I would recommend to every man whose faith is yet unsettled, *Grotius, *Dr. Pearson, and *Dr. Clarke."

Talking of Garrick, he said, "He is the first man in the world for sprightly conversation."

When I rose a second time, he again pressed me to stay, which I did.

He told me that he generally went abroad at four in the afternoon, and seldom came home till two in the morning. I took the liberty to ask if he did not think it wrong to live thus, and not make more use of his great talents. He owned it was a bad habit. On reviewing, at the distance of many years, my journal of this period, I wonder how, at my first visit, I ventured to talk to him so freely, and that he bore it with so much indulgence.

Before we parted, he was so good as to promise to favour me with his company one evening at my lodgings; and, as I took my leave, shook me cordially by the hand. It is almost needless to add that I felt no little elation at having now so happily established an acquaintance of which I had been so long ambitious.

My readers will, I trust, excuse me for being thus minutely circumstantial, when it is considered that the acquaintance of Dr. Johnson was to me a most valuable acquisition, and laid the foundation of whatever instruction and entertainment they may receive from my collections concerning the great subject of the work which they are now perusing.

I did not visit him again till Monday, June 13, at which time I recollect no part of his conversation, except that when I told him I had been to see *Johnson ride upon three horses, he said, "Such a man, sir, should be encouraged; for his performances show the extent of the human powers in one instance, and thus tend to raise our opinion of the faculties of man. He shows what may be attained by persevering application, so that every man may hope that by giving as much application, although perhaps he may never ride three horses at a time or dance upon a wire, yet he may be equally expert in whatever profession he has chosen to pursue."

He again shook me by the hand at parting, and asked me why I did not come oftener to him. Trusting that I was now in his good graces, I answered that he had not given me much encouragement, and reminded him of the check I had received from him at our first interview. "Poh, poh!" said he, with a complacent smile, "never mind these things. Come to me as often as you can. I shall be glad to see you."

I had learned that his place of frequent resort was the Mitre Tavern in Fleet Street, where he loved to sit up late, and I begged I might be allowed to pass an evening with him there soon, which he promised I should. A few days afterwards I met him near Temple Bar, about one o'clock in the morning, and asked if he would then go to the Mitre. "Sir," said he, "it is too late; they won't let us in. But I'll go with you another night with all my heart."

A revolution of some importance in my plan of life had just taken place; for instead of procuring a commission in the foot-guards, which was my own inclination, I had, in compliance with my father's wishes, agreed to study the law, and was soon to set out for Utrecht, to hear the lectures of an excellent civilian in that university, and then to proceed on my travels. Though very desirous of obtaining Dr. Johnson's advice and instructions on the mode of pursuing my studies, I was at this time so occupied (shall I call it?) or so dissipated, by the amusements of London that our next meeting was not till Saturday, June 25, when happening to dine at Clifton's eating-house, in Butcher Row, I was surprised to perceive Johnson come in and take his seat at another table. The mode of dining, or rather being fed, at such houses in London, is well known to many to be particularly unsocial, as there is no ordinary, or united company, but each person has his own mess, and is under no obligation to hold any intercourse with any one. A liberal and full-minded man, however, who loves to talk, will break through this churlish and unsocial restraint. Johnson and an Irish gentleman got into a dispute concerning the cause of some part of mankind being black. "Why, sir," said Johnson, "it has been accounted for in three ways: either by supposing that they are the posterity of Ham, who was cursed; or that God at first created two kinds of men, one black and another white; or that by the heat of the sun the skin is scorched, and so acquires a sooty hue. This matter has been much canvassed among naturalists, but has never been brought to any certain issue." What the Irishman said is totally obliterated from my mind; but I remember that he became very warm and intemperate in his expressions; upon which Johnson rose, and quietly walked away. When he had retired, his antagonist took his revenge, as he thought, by saying, "He has a most ungainly figure, and an affectation of pomposity, unworthy of a man of genius."

Johnson had not observed that I was in the room. I followed him, however, and he agreed to meet me in the evening at the Mitre. I called on him, and we went thither at nine. We had a good supper, and port wine, of which he then sometimes drank a bottle. The orthodox high-church sound of the Mitre, the figure and manner of the celebrated Samuel Johnson, the extraordinary power and precision of his conversation, and the pride arising from finding myself admitted as his companion, produced a variety of sensations, and a pleasing elevation of mind beyond what I had ever before experienced. I find in my journal the following minute of our conversation, which, though it will give but a very faint notion of what passed, is, in some degree, a valuable record; and it will be curious in this view, as showing how habitual to his mind were some opinions which appear in his works.

"Colley Cibber, sir, was by no means a blockhead; but by arrogating to himself too much, he was in danger of losing that degree, of estimation to which he was entitled. His friends gave out that he intended his birthday odes should be bad: but that was not the case, sir; for he kept them many months by him, and a few years before he died he showed me one of them, with great solicitude to render it as perfect as might be, and I made some corrections, to which he was not very willing to submit. I remember the following couplet in allusion to the king and himself:

Perch'd on the eagle's soaring wing,
The lowly linnet loves to sing.

Sir, he had heard something of the fabulous tale of the wren sitting upon the eagle's wing, and he had applied it to a linnet. Cibber's familiar style, however, was better than that which *Whitehead has assumed. *Grand* nonsense is insupportable. Whitehead is but a little man to inscribe verses to players."

I did not presume to controvert this censure, which was tinctured with his prejudice against players, but I could not help thinking that a dramatic poet might with propriety pay a compliment to an eminent performer, as Whitehead has very happily done in his verses to Mr. Garrick.

"Sir, I do not think *Gray a first-rate poet. He has not a bold imagination, nor much command of words. The obscurity in which he has involved himself will not persuade us that he is sublime. His *Elegy in a Churchyard* has a happy selection of images, but I don't like what are called his great things. His ode which begins

Ruin seize thee, ruthless king,
Confusion on thy banners wait!

has been celebrated for its abruptness, and plunging into the subject all at once. But such arts as these have no merit, unless when they are original. We admire them only once; and this abruptness has nothing new in it. We have had it often before. Nay, we have it in the old song of *Johnny Armstrong*

Is there ever a man in all Scotland,
From the highest estate to the lowest degree, &c.

And then, sir,

Yes, there is a man in Westmoreland
And Johnny Armstrong they do him call.

There, now, you plunge at once into the subject. You have no previous narration to lead you to it. The two next lines in that ode are, I think, very good:

Though fann'd by Conquest's crimson wing,
They mock the air with idle state."

Here let it be observed that although his opinion of Gray's poetry was widely different from mine, and I believe from that of most men of taste, by whom it is with justice highly admired, there is certainly much absurdity in the clamour which has been raised, as if he had been culpably injurious to the merit of that bard, and had been actuated by envy. Alas! ye little short-sighted critics, could Johnson be envious of the talents of any of his contemporaries? That his opinion on this subject was what in private and in public he uniformly expressed, regardless of what others might think, we may wonder, and perhaps regret; but it is shallow and unjust to charge him with expressing what he did not think.

Finding him in a placid humour, and wishing to avail myself of the opportunity which I fortunately had of consulting a sage, to hear whose wisdom, I conceived, in the ardour of youthful imagination, that men filled with a noble enthusiasm for intellectual improvement would gladly have resorted from distant lands;—I opened my mind to him ingenuously, and gave him a little sketch of my life, to which he was pleased to listen with great attention.

I acknowledged that, though educated very strictly in the principles of religion, I had for some time been misled into a certain degree of infidelity; but that I was come now to a better way of thinking, and was fully satisfied of the truth of the Christian revelation, though I was not clear as to every point considered to be orthodox. Being at all times a curious examiner of the human mind, and pleased with an undisguised display of what had passed in it, he called to me with warmth, "Give me your hand; I have taken a liking to you." He then began to descant upon the force of testimony, and the little we could know of final causes; so that the objections of, why was it so? or why was it not so? ought not to disturb us: adding, that he himself had at one period been guilty of a temporary neglect of religion, but that it was not the result of argument, but mere absence of thought.

After having given credit to reports of his bigotry, I was agreeably surprised when he expressed the following very liberal sentiment, which has the additional value of obviating an objection to our holy religion, founded upon the discordant tenets of Christians themselves: "For my part, sir, I think all Christians, whether Papists or Protestants, agree in the essential articles, and that their differences are trivial, and rather political than religious."

We talked of belief in ghosts. He said, "Sir, I make a distinction between what a man may experience by the mere strength of his imagination, and what imagination cannot possibly produce. Thus, suppose I should think that I saw a form, and heard a voice cry, 'Johnson, you are a very wicked fellow, and unless you repent you will certainly be punished'; my own unworthiness is so deeply impressed upon my mind that I might imagine I thus saw and heard, and therefore I should not believe that an external communication had been made to me. But if a form should appear, and a voice should tell me that a particular man had died at a particular place, and a particular hour, a fact which I had no apprehension of, nor any means of knowing, and this fact, with all its circumstances, should afterwards be unquestionably proved, I should, in that case, be persuaded that I had supernatural intelligence imparted to me."

Here it is proper, once for all, to give a true and fair statement of Johnson's way of thinking upon the question, whether departed spirits are ever permitted to appear in this world, or in any way to operate upon human life. He has been ignorantly misrepresented as weakly credulous upon that subject; and, therefore, though I feel an inclination to disdain and treat with silent contempt so foolish a notion concerning my illustrious friend, yet as I find it has gained ground, it is necessary to refute it. The real fact then is that Johnson had a very philosophical mind, and such a rational respect for testimony as to make him submit his understanding to what was authentically proved, though he could not comprehend why it was so. Being thus disposed, he was willing to inquire into the truth of any relation of supernatural agency, a general belief of which has prevailed in all nations and ages. But so far was he from being the dupe of implicit faith that he examined the matter with a jealous attention, and no man was more ready to refute its falsehood when he had discovered it. Churchill in his poem entitled *The Ghost*, availed himself of the absurd credulity imputed to Johnson, and drew a caricature of him under the name of "Pomposo," representing him as one of the believers of the story of a ghost in Cock Lane, which, in the year 1762, had gained very general credit in London. Many of my readers, I am convinced, are to this hour under an impression that Johnson was thus foolishly deceived. It will therefore surprise them a good deal when they are informed upon undoubted authority that Johnson was one of those by whom the imposture was detected. The story had become so popular that he thought it should be investigated; and in this research he was assisted by the Reverend Dr. Douglas, now Bishop of Salisbury, the great detecter of impostures; who informs me, that after the gentlemen who went and examined into the evidence were satisfied of its falsity, Johnson wrote in their presence an account of it, which was published in the newspapers and *Gentleman's Magazine*, and undeceived the world.

Our conversation proceeded. "Sir," said he, "I am a friend to subordination, as most conducive to the happiness of society. There is a reciprocal pleasure in governing and being governed."

"Dr. Goldsmith is one of the first men we now have as an author, and he is a very worthy man too. He has been loose in his principles, but he is coming right."

I mentioned *Mallet's tragedy of *Elvira*, which had been acted the preceding winter at Drury Lane, and that the Honourable Andrew Erskine, Mr. Dempster, and myself, had joined in writing a pamphlet, entitled *Critical Strictures* against it. That the mildness of Dempster's disposition had, however, relented; and he had candidly said, "We have hardly a right to abuse this tragedy; for bad as it is, how vain should either of us be to write one not near so good." JOHNSON. "Why no, sir; this is not just reasoning. You *may* abuse a tragedy, though you cannot write one. You may scold a carpenter who has made you a bad table, though you cannot make a table. It is not your trade to make tables."

When I talked to him of the *paternal estate to which I was heir, he said, 'Sir, let me tell you that to be a Scotch landlord, where you have a number of families dependent upon you, and attached to you, is, perhaps, as high a situation as humanity can arrive at. A merchant upon the 'Change of London, with a hundred thousand pounds, is nothing; an English duke, with an immense fortune, is nothing: he has no tenants who consider themselves as under his patriarchal care, and who will follow him to the field upon an emergency."

His notion of the dignity of a Scotch landlord had been formed upon what he had heard of the Highland chiefs; for it is long since a Lowland landlord has been so curtailed in his feudal authority that he has little more influence over his tenants than an English landlord; and of late years most of the Highland chiefs have destroyed, by means too well known, the princely power which they once enjoyed.

He proceeded: "Your going abroad, sir, and breaking off idle habits, may be of great importance to you. I would go where there are courts and learned men. There is a good deal of Spain that has not been perambulated. I would have you go thither. A man of inferior talents to yours may furnish us with useful observations upon that country." His supposing me, at that period of life, capable of writing an account of my travels that would deserve to be read, elated me not a little.

I appeal to every impartial reader whether this faithful detail of his frankness, complacency, and kindness to a young man, a stranger and a Scotchman, does not refute the unjust opinion of the harshness of his general demeanour. His occasional reproofs of folly, impudence, or impiety, and even the sudden sallies of his constitutional irritability of temper, which have been preserved for the poignancy of their wit, have produced that opinion among those who have not considered that such instances, though collected by * Mrs. Piozzi into a small volume, and read over in a few hours, were, in fact, scattered through a long series of years: years, in which his time was chiefly spent in instructing and delighting mankind by his writings and conversation, in acts of piety to God, and good will to men.

I complained to him that I had not yet acquired much knowledge, and asked his advice as to my studies. He said, "Don't talk of study now. I will give you a plan, but it will require some time to consider of it."—"It is very good in you," I replied, "to allow me to be with you thus. Had it been foretold to me some years ago that I should pass an evening with the author of the *Rambler*, how should I have exulted!" What I then expressed was sincerely from the heart. He was satisfied that it was, and cordially answered, "Sir, I am glad we have met. I hope we shall pass many evenings and mornings too, together." We finished a couple of bottles of port, and sat till between one and two in the morning.

He wrote this year in the *Critical Review* the account of *Telemachus, a Mask*, by the Reverend George Graham, of Eton College. The subject of this beautiful poem was particularly interesting to Johnson, who had much experience of "the conflict of opposite principles," which he describes as "the contention between pleasure and virtue, a struggle which will always be continued while the present system of nature shall subsist; nor can history or poetry exhibit more than pleasure triumphing over virtue, and virtue subjugating pleasure."

As * Dr. Oliver Goldsmith will frequently appear in this narrative, I shall endeavour to make my readers in some degree acquainted with his singular character. He was a native of Ireland, and a contemporary with Mr. Burke, at Trinity College, Dublin, but did not then give much promise of future celebrity. He, however, observed to * Mr. Malone that "though he made no great figure in mathematics, which was a study in much repute there, he could turn an ode of Horace into English better than any of them." He afterwards studied physic at Edinburgh, and upon the Continent; and I have been informed, was enabled to pursue his travels on foot, partly by demanding at universities to enter the lists as a disputant, by which, according to the custom of many of them, he was entitled to the premium of a crown, when luckily for him his challenge was not accepted, so that, as I once observed to Dr. Johnson, he *disputed* his passage through Europe. He then came to England, and was employed successively in the capacities of an usher to an academy, a corrector of the press, a reviewer, and a writer for a newspaper. He had sagacity enough to cultivate assiduously the acquaintance of Johnson, and his faculties were gradually enlarged by the contemplation of such a model. To me and many others it appeared that he studiously copied the manner of Johnson, though, indeed, upon a smaller scale.

At this time I think he had published nothing with his name, though it was pretty generally known that one Dr. Goldsmith was the author of *An Enquiry into the Present State of Polite Learning in Europe*, and of *The Citizen of the World*, a series of letters supposed to be written from London by a Chinese. No man had the art of displaying with more advantage as a writer, whatever literary acquisitions he made. **Nihil quod tetigit non ornavit.* His mind resembled a fertile, but thin soil. There was a quick, but not a strong vegetation of whatever chanced to be thrown upon it. No deep root could be struck. The oak of the forest did not grow there, but the elegant shrubbery and the fragrant parterre appeared in gay succession. It has been generally circulated and believed that he was a mere fool in conversation; but, in truth, this has been greatly exaggerated. He had, no doubt, a more than common share of that hurry of ideas which we often find in his countrymen, and which sometimes produces a laughable confusion in expressing them. He was very much what the French call **un étourdi*, and from vanity and an eager desire of being conspicuous wherever he was, he frequently talked carelessly without knowledge of the subject, or even without thought. His person was short, his countenance coarse and vulgar, his deportment that of a scholar awkwardly affecting the easy gentleman. Those who were in any way distinguished excited envy in him to so ridiculous an excess that the instances of it are hardly credible. When accompanying two beautiful young ladies with their mother on a tour in France, he was seriously angry that more attention was paid to them than to him; and once at the exhibition of the **Fantoccini* in London, when those who sat next him observed with what dexterity a puppet was made to toss a pike, he could not bear that it should have such praise, and exclaimed with some warmth, "Pshaw! I can do it better myself."

He, I am afraid, had no settled system of any sort, so that his conduct must not be strictly scrutinized; but his affections were social and generous, and when he had money he gave it away very liberally. His desire of imaginary consequence predominated over his attention to truth. When he began to rise into notice, he said he had a brother who was *Dean of Durham, a fiction so easily detected that it is wonderful how he should have been so inconsiderate as to hazard it. He boasted to me at this time of the power of his pen in commanding money, which I believe was true in a certain degree, though in the instance he gave he was by no means correct. He told me that he had sold a novel for four hundred pounds. This was his *Vicar of Wakefield*. But Johnson informed me that he had made the bargain for Goldsmith, and the price was sixty pounds. "And, sir," said he, "a sufficient price too, when it was sold; for then the fame of Goldsmith had not been elevated, as it afterwards was, by his *Traveller*; and the bookseller had such faint hopes of profit by his bargain that he kept the manuscript by him a long time, and did not publish it till after the *Traveller* had appeared. Then, to be sure, it was accidentally worth more money."

Mrs. Piozzi and *Sir John Hawkins have strangely misstated the history of Goldsmith's situation and Johnson's friendly interference, when this novel was sold. I shall give it authentically from Johnson's own exact narration:

"I received one morning a message from poor Goldsmith that he was in great distress, and as it was not in his power to come to me, begging that I would come to him as soon as possible. I sent him a guinea and promised to come to him directly. I accordingly went as soon as I was dressed, and found that his landlady had arrested him for his rent, at which he was in a violent passion. I perceived that he had already changed my guinea, and had got a bottle of Madeira and glass before him. I put the cork into the bottle, desired he would be calm, and began to talk to him of the means by which he might be extricated. He then told me that he had a novel ready for the press, which he produced to me. I looked into it and saw its merit; told the landlady I should soon return, and having gone to a bookseller, sold it for sixty pounds. I brought Goldsmith the money, and he discharged his rent, not without rating his landlady in a high tone for having used him so ill."

My next meeting with Johnson was on Friday the 1st of July, when he and I and Dr. Goldsmith supped together at the Mitre. I was before this time pretty well acquainted with Goldsmith, who was one of the brightest ornaments of the Johnsonian school. Goldsmith's respectful attachment to Johnson was then at its height, for his own literary reputation had not yet distinguished him so much as to excite a vain desire of competition with his great master. He had increased my admiration of the goodness of Johnson's heart, by incidental remarks in the course of conversation, such as, when I mentioned *Mr. Levet, whom he entertained under his roof, "He is poor and honest, which is recommendation enough to Johnson"; and when I wondered that he was very kind to a man of whom I had heard a very bad character, "He is now become miserable, and that insures the protection of Johnson."

Goldsmith attempting this evening to maintain, I suppose from an affectation of paradox, "that knowledge was not desirable on its own account, for it often was a source of unhappiness." JOHNSON. "Why, sir, that knowledge may in some cases produce unhappiness, I allow. But, upon the whole, knowledge, *per se*, is certainly an object which every man would wish to attain, although, perhaps, he may not take the trouble necessary for attaining it."

Dr. John Campbell, the celebrated political and biographical writer, being mentioned, Johnson said, "Campbell is a man of much knowledge, and has a good share of imagination. His *Hermippus Redivivus* is very entertaining, as an account of the Hermetic philosophy, and as furnishing a curious history of the extravagancies of the human mind. If it were merely imaginary, it would be nothing at all. Campbell is not always rigidly careful of truth in his conversation; but I do not believe there is anything of this carelessness in his books. Campbell is a good man, a pious man. I am afraid he has not been in the inside of a church for many years; but he never passes a church without pulling off his hat. This shows that he has good principles. I used to go pretty often to Campbell's on a Sunday evening till I began to consider that the shoals of Scotchmen who flocked about him might probably say, when anything of mine was well done, 'Ay, ay, he has learned this of Cawmell!'"

He talked very contemptuously of Churchill's poetry, observing, that "it had a temporary currency, only from its audacity of abuse, and being filled with living names, and that it would sink into oblivion." I ventured to hint that he was not quite a fair judge, as Churchill had attacked him violently. JOHNSON. "Nay, sir, I am a very fair judge. He did not attack me violently till he found I did not like his poetry; and his attack on me shall not prevent me from continuing to say what I think of him, from an apprehension that it may be ascribed to resentment. No, sir, I called the fellow a blockhead at first, and I will call him a blockhead still. However, I will acknowledge that I have a better opinion of him now than I once had; for he has shown more fertility than I expected. To be sure, he is a tree that cannot produce good fruit: he only bears crabs. But, sir, a tree that produces a great many crabs is better than a tree which produces only a few."

In this depreciation of Churchill's poetry I could not agree with him. It is very true that the greatest part of it is upon the topics of the day, on which account, as it brought him great fame and profit at the time, it must proportionally slide out of the public attention as other occasional objects succeed. But Churchill had extraordinary vigour both of thought and expression. His portraits of the players will ever be valuable to the true lovers of the drama; and his strong caricatures of several eminent men of his age will not be forgotten by the curious. Let me add that there are in his works many passages which are of a general nature; and his *Prophecy of Famine* is a poem of no ordinary merit. It is, indeed, falsely injurious to Scotland, but therefore may be allowed a greater share of invention.

Bonnell Thornton had just published a burlesque *Ode on St. Cecilia's Day*, "adapted to the ancient British music, viz. the salt-box, the jew's-harp, the marrow-bones and cleaver, the hum-strum or hurdy-gurdy, &c." Johnson praised its humour, and seemed much diverted with it. He repeated the following passage:

In strains more exalted the salt-box shall join,
And clattering and battering and clapping combine;
With a rap and a tap while the hollow side sounds,
Up and down leaps the flap, and with rattling rebounds.

I mentioned the periodical paper called the **Connoisseur*. He said it wanted matter. No doubt it has not the deep thinking of Johnson's writings. But surely it has just views of the surface of life, and a very sprightly manner. His opinion of the *World* was not much higher than of the *Connoisseur*.

Let me here apologize for the imperfect manner in which I am obliged to exhibit Johnson's conversation at this period. In the early part of my acquaintance with him, I was so wrapt in admiration of his extraordinary colloquial talents, and so little accustomed to his peculiar mode of expression that I found it extremely difficult to recollect and record his conversation with its genuine vigour and vivacity. In progress of time, when my mind was, as it were, strongly impregnated with the Johnsonian æther, I could with much more facility and exactness carry in my memory and commit to paper the exuberant variety of his wisdom and wit.

At this time *Miss* Williams, as she was then called, though she did not reside with him in the Temple under his roof, but had lodgings in Bolt Court, Fleet Street, had so much of his attention that he every night drank tea with her before he went home, however late it might be, and she always sat up for him. This, it may be fairly conjectured, was not alone a proof of his regard for her, but of his own unwillingness to go into solitude, before that unseasonable hour at which he had habituated himself to expect the oblivion of repose. Dr. Goldsmith, being a privileged man, went with him this night, strutting away, and calling to me with an air of superiority, like that of an esoteric over an exoteric disciple of a sage of antiquity, "I go to Miss Williams." I confess I then envied him this mighty privilege, of which he seemed so proud; but it was not long before I obtained the same mark of distinction.

On Tuesday the 5th of July, I again visited Johnson. He told me he had looked into the poems of a pretty voluminous writer, Mr. (now Dr.) John Ogilvie, one of the Presbyterian ministers of Scotland, which had lately come out, but could find no thinking in them. BOSWELL. "Is there not imagination in them, sir?" JOHNSON. "Why, sir, there is in them what *was* imagination, but it is no more imagination in *him*, than sound is sound in the echo. And his diction too is not his own. We have long ago seen *white-robed innocence*, and *flower-bespangled meads*."

Talking of London, he observed, "Sir, if you wish to have a just notion of the magnitude of this city, you must not be satisfied with seeing its great streets and squares, but must survey the innumerable little lanes and courts. It is not in the showy evolutions of buildings, but in the multiplicity of human habitations which are crowded together, that the wonderful immensity of London consists." I have often amused myself with thinking how different a place London is to different people. They, whose narrow minds are contracted to the consideration of some one particular pursuit, view it only through that medium. A politician thinks of it merely as the seat of government in its different departments; a grazier, as a vast market for cattle; a mercantile man, as a place where a prodigious deal of business is done upon 'Change; a dramatic enthusiast, as the grand scene of theatrical entertainments; a man of pleasure, as an assemblage of taverns, and the great emporium for ladies of easy virtue. But the intellectual man is struck with it, as comprehending the whole of human life in all its variety, the contemplation of which is inexhaustible.

On Wednesday, July 6, he was engaged to sup with me at my lodgings in Downing Street, Westminster. But on the preceding night my landlord having behaved very rudely to me and some company who were with me, I had resolved not to remain another night in his house. I was exceedingly uneasy at the awkward appearance I supposed I should make to Johnson and the other gentleman whom I had invited, not being able to receive them at home, and being obliged to order supper at the Mitre. I went to Johnson in the morning, and talked of it as of a serious distress. He laughed, and said, "Consider, sir, how insignificant this will appear a twelvemonth hence." Were this consideration to be applied to most of the little vexatious incidents of life by which our quiet is too often disturbed, it would prevent many painful sensations. I have tried it frequently with good effect. "There is nothing," continued he, "in this mighty misfortune; nay, we shall be better at the Mitre." I told him that I had been at * Sir John Fielding's office, complaining of my landlord, and had been informed that, though I had taken my lodgings for a year, I might, upon proof of his bad behaviour, quit them when I pleased, without being under an obligation to pay rent for any longer time than while I possessed them. The fertility of Johnson's mind could show itself even upon so small a matter as this. "Why, sir," said he, "I suppose this must be the law, since you have been told so in Bow Street. But, if your landlord could hold you to your bargain, and the lodgings should be yours for a year, you may certainly use them as you think fit. So, sir, you may quarter two life-guardsmen upon him; or you may send the greatest scoundrel you can find into your apartments; or you may say that you want to make some experiments in natural philosophy, and may burn a large quantity of assafœtida in his house."

I had as my guests this evening at the Mitre Tavern, Dr. Johnson, Dr. Goldsmith, Mr. Thomas Davies, Mr. Eccles, an Irish gentleman, for whose agreeable company I was obliged to Mr. Davies, and the Reverend Mr. John Ogilvie, who was desirous of being in company with my illustrious friend, while I in my turn, was proud to have the honour of showing one of my countrymen upon what easy terms Johnson permitted me to live with him.

Goldsmith, as usual, endeavoured, with too much eagerness, to shine, and disputed very warmly with Johnson against the well known maxim of the British constitution, "The king can do no wrong"; affirming, that "what was morally false could not be politically true; and as the king might, in the exercise of his regal power, command and cause the doing of what was wrong, it certainly might be said, in sense and in reason, that he could do wrong." JOHNSON. "Sir, you are to consider that in our constitution, according to its true principles, the king is the head; he is supreme: he is above everything, and there is no power by which he can be tried. Therefore, it is, sir, that we hold the king can do no wrong; that whatever may happen to be wrong in government may not be above our reach, by being ascribed to majesty. Redress is always to be had against oppression, by punishing the immediate agents. The king, though he should command, cannot force a judge to condemn a man unjustly; therefore it is the judge whom we prosecute and punish. Political institutions are formed upon the consideration of what will most frequently tend to the good of the whole, although now and then exceptions may occur. Thus it is better in general that a nation should have a supreme legislative power, although it may at times be abused. And then, sir, there is this consideration, that *if the abuse be enormous, nature will rise up, and claiming her original rights, overturn a corrupt political system.*" I mark this animated sentence with peculiar pleasure, as a noble instance of that truly dignified spirit of freedom which ever glowed in his heart, though he was charged with slavish tenets by superficial observers; because he was at all times indignant against that false patriotism, that pretended love of freedom, that unruly restlessness which is inconsistent with the stable authority of any good government.

This generous sentiment, which he uttered with great fervour, struck me exceedingly, and stirred my blood to that pitch of fancied resistance, the possibility of which I am glad to keep in mind, but to which I trust I never shall be forced.

"Great abilities," said he, "are not requisite for an historian; for in historical composition, all the greatest powers of the human mind are quiescent. He has facts ready to his hand; so there is no exercise of invention. Imagination is not required in any high degree, only about as much as is used in the lower kinds of poetry. Some penetration, accuracy, and colouring, will fit a man for the task, if he can give the application which is necessary."

*"Bayle's *Dictionary* is a very useful work for those to consult who love the biographical part of literature, which is what I love most."

Talking of the eminent writers in Queen Anne's reign, he observed, "I think Dr. Arbuthnot the first man among them. He was the most universal genius, being an excellent physician, a man of deep learning, and a man of much humour. Mr. Addison was, to be sure, a great man; his learning was not profound; but his morality, his humour, and his elegance of writing, set him very high."

Mr. Ogilvie was unlucky enough to choose for the topic of his conversation the praises of his native country. He began with saying that there was very rich land round Edinburgh. Goldsmith, who had studied physic there, contradicted this, very untruly, with a sneering laugh. Disconcerted a little by this, Mr. Ogilvie then took new ground, where, I suppose, he thought himself perfectly safe; for he observed that Scotland had a great many noble wild prospects. JOHNSON. "I believe, sir, you have a great many. Norway, too, has noble wild prospects; and Lapland is remarkable for prodigious noble wild prospects. But, sir, let me tell you the noblest prospect which a Scotchman ever sees is the high road that leads him to England!" This unexpected and pointed sally produced a roar of applause. After all, however, those who admire the rude grandeur of nature, cannot deny it to Caledonia.

On Saturday, July 9, I found Johnson surrounded with a numerous levee, but have not preserved any part of his conversation. On the 14th we had another evening by ourselves at the Mitre. It happening to be a very rainy night, I made some commonplace observations on the relaxation of nerves and depression of spirits which such weather occasioned, adding, however, that it was good for the vegetable creation. Johnson, who, as we have already seen, denied that the temperature of the air had any influence on the human frame, answered, with a smile of ridicule, "Why, yes, sir, it is good for vegetables, and for the animals who eat those vegetables, and for the animals who eat those animals." This observation of his aptly enough introduced a good supper; and I soon forgot, in Johnson's company, the influence of a moist atmosphere.

Feeling myself now quite at ease as his companion, though I had all possible reverence for him, I expressed a regret that I could not be so easy with my father, though he was not much older than Johnson, and certainly, however respectable, had not more learning and greater abilities to depress me. I asked him the reason of this. JOHNSON. "Why, sir, I am a man of the world. I live in the world, and I take, in some degree, the colour of the world as it moves along. Your father is a judge in a remote part of the island, and all his notions are taken from the old world. Besides, sir, there must always be a struggle between a father and son, while one aims at power and the other at independence." I said I was afraid my father would force me to be a lawyer. JOHNSON. "Sir, you need not be afraid of his forcing you to be a laborious practising lawyer; that is not in his power. For as the proverb says, 'One man may lead a horse to the water, but twenty cannot make him drink.' He may be displeased that you are not what he wishes you to be, but that displeasure will not go far. If he insists only on your having as much law as is necessary for a man of property, and then endeavours to get you into Parliament, he is quite in the right."

He enlarged very convincingly upon the excellence of rhyme over blank verse in English poetry. I mentioned to him that *Dr. Adam Smith, in his lectures upon composition, when I studied under him in the College of Glasgow, had maintained the same opinion strenuously, and I repeated some of his arguments. JOHNSON. "Sir, I was once in company with Smith, and we did not take to each other; but had I known that he loved rhyme as much as you tell me he does, I should have hugged him."

Talking of those who denied the truth of Christianity, he said, "It is always easy to be on the negative side. If a man were now to deny that there is salt upon the table, you could not reduce him to an absurdity. Come, let us try this a little further. I deny that *Canada is taken, and I can support my denial by pretty good arguments. The French are a much more numerous people than we; and it is not likely that they would allow us to take it. 'But the ministry have assured us, in all the formality of the *Gazette*, that it is taken.' — Very true. But the ministry have put us to an enormous expense by the war in America, and it is their interest to persuade us that we have got something for our money. — 'But the fact is confirmed by thousands of men who were at the taking of it.' — Ay, but these men have still more interest in deceiving us. They don't want that you should think the French have beat them, but that they have beat the French. Now suppose you should go over and find that it is really taken, that would only satisfy yourself; for when you come home, we will not believe you. We will say you have been bribed. — Yet, sir, notwithstanding all these plausible objections, we have no doubt that Canada is really ours. Such is the weight of common testimony. How much stronger are the evidences of the Christian religion!"

"Idleness is a disease which must be combated; but I would not advise a rigid adherence to a particular plan of study. I myself have never persisted in any plan for two days together. A man ought to read just as inclination leads him, for what he reads as a task will do him little good. A young man should read five hours in a day, and so may acquire a great deal of knowledge."

To a man of vigorous intellect and ardent curiosity like his own, reading without a regular plan may be beneficial; though even such a man must submit to it, if he would attain a full understanding of any of the sciences.

To such a degree of unrestrained frankness had he now accustomed me, that in the course of this evening I talked of the numerous reflections which had been thrown out against him on account of his having accepted a pension from his present Majesty. "Why, sir," said he, with a hearty laugh, "it is a mighty foolish noise that they make. I have accepted of a pension as a reward which has been thought due to my literary merit; and now that I have this pension, I am the same man in every respect that I have ever been; I retain the same principles. It is true that I cannot now curse," smiling, "the House of Hanover; nor would it be decent for me to drink King James's health in the wine that King George gives me money to pay for. But, sir, I think that the pleasure of cursing the House of Hanover, and drinking *King James's health, are amply overbalanced by three hundred pounds a year."

There was here, most certainly, an affectation of more Jacobitism than he really had; and indeed an intention of admitting, for the moment, in a much greater extent than it really existed, the charge of disaffection imputed to him by the world, merely for the purpose of showing how dexterously he could repel an attack, even though he were placed in the most disadvantageous position; for I have heard him declare that if holding up his right hand would have secured victory at Culloden to Prince Charles's army, he was not sure he would have held it up; so little confidence had he in the right claimed by the house of Stuart, and so fearful was he of the consequences of another revolution on the throne of Great-Britain; and Mr. Topham Beauclerk assured me he had heard him say this before he had his pension. At another time he said to Mr. Langton, "Nothing has ever offered that has made it worth my while to consider the question fully." He, however, also said to the same gentleman, talking of King James the Second, "It was become impossible for him to reign any longer in this country." He no doubt had an early attachment to the House of Stuart; but his zeal had cooled as his reason strengthened. Indeed, I heard him once say "that after the death of a violent Whig, with whom he used to contend with great eagerness, he felt his Toryism much abated," I suppose he meant *Mr. Walmsley.

Yet there is no doubt that at earlier periods he was wont often to exercise both his pleasantry and ingenuity in talking Jacobitism. My much respected friend, Dr. Douglas, now Bishop of Salisbury, has favoured me with the following admirable instance from his lordship's own recollection. One day when dining at old Mr. Langton's, where Miss Roberts, his niece, was one of the company, Johnson, with his usual complacent attention to the fair sex, took her by the hand and said, "My dear, I hope you are a Jacobite." Old Mr. Langton, who, though a high and steady Tory, was attached to the present royal family, seemed offended, and asked Johnson, with great warmth, what he could mean by putting such a question to his niece. "Why, sir," said Johnson, "I meant no offence to your niece; I meant her a great compliment. A Jacobite, sir, believes in the divine right of kings. He that believes in the divine right of kings believes in a Divinity. A Jacobite believes in the divine right of bishops. He that believes in the divine right of bishops believes in the divine authority of the Christian religion. Therefore, sir, a Jacobite is neither an atheist not a Deist. That cannot be said of a Whig; for Whiggism is a negation of all principle."

He advised me when abroad to be as much as I could with the professors in the universities, and with the clergy; for from their conversation I might expect the best accounts of everything in whatever country I should be, with the additional advantage of keeping my learning alive.

It will be observed that, when giving me advice as to my travels, Dr. Johnson did not dwell upon cities, and palaces, and pictures, and shows, and Arcadian scenes. He was of Lord Essex's opinion, who advises his kinsman, Roger Earl of Rutland, "rather to go an hundred miles to speak with one wise man, than five miles to see a fair town."

I described to him an impudent fellow from Scotland, who affected to be a savage, and railed at all established systems. JOHNSON. "There is nothing surprising in this, sir. He wants to make himself conspicuous. He would tumble in a hogstye, as long as you looked at him and called to him to come out. But let him alone; never mind him, and he'll soon give it over."

I added that the same person maintained that there was no distinction between virtue and vice. JOHNSON. "Why, sir, if the fellow does not think as he speaks, he is lying; and I see not what honour he can propose to himself from having the character of a liar. But if he does really think that there is no distinction between virtue and vice, why, sir, when he leaves our houses let us count our spoons."

Sir David Dalrymple, now one of the judges of Scotland by the title of Lord Hailes, had contributed much to increase my high opinion of Johnson, on account of his writings, long before I attained to a personal acquaintance with him; I, in return, had informed Johnson of Sir David's eminent character for learning and religion; and Johnson was so much pleased that at one of our evening meetings he gave him for his toast. I at this time kept up a very frequent correspondence with Sir David; and I read to Dr. Johnson to-night the following passage from the letter which I had last received from him:

"It gives me pleasure to think that you have obtained the friendship of Mr. Samuel Johnson. He is one of the best moral writers which England has produced. At the same time, I envy you the free and undisguised converse with such a man. May I beg you to present my best respects to him, and to assure him of the veneration which I entertain for the author of the *Rambler* and of *Rasselas*? Let me recommend this last work to you; with the *Rambler* you certainly are acquainted. In *Rasselas* you will see a tender-hearted operator, who probes the wound only to heal it. Swift, on the contrary, mangles human nature. He cuts and slashes, as if he took pleasure in the operation, like the tyrant who said, *_Ita feri ut se sentiat emori_." Johnson seemed to be much gratified by this just and well turned compliment.

He recommended to me to keep a journal of my life, full and unreserved. He said it would be a very good exercise, and would yield me great satisfaction when the particulars were faded from my remembrance. I was uncommonly fortunate in having had a previous coincidence of opinion with him upon this subject, for I had kept such a journal for some time; and it was no small pleasure to me to have this to tell him, and to receive his approbation. He counselled me to keep it private, and said I might surely have a friend who would burn it in case of my death. From this habit I have been enabled to give the world so many anecdotes which would otherwise have been lost to posterity. I mentioned that I was afraid I put into my journal too many little incidents. JOHNSON. "There is nothing, sir, too little for so little a creature as man. It is by studying little things that we attain the great art of having as little misery and as much happiness as possible."

Next morning Mr. Dempster happened to call on me, and was so much struck even with the imperfect account which I gave him of Dr. Johnson's conversation, that to his honour be it recorded, when I complained that drinking port and sitting up late with him, affected my nerves for some time after, he said, "One had better be palsied at eighteen than not keep company with such a man."

On Tuesday, July 18, I found *tall Sir Thomas Robinson sitting with Johnson. Sir Thomas said that the King of Prussia valued himself upon three things: upon being a hero, a musician, and an author. JOHNSON. "Pretty well, sir, for one man. As to his being an author, I have not looked at his poetry; but his prose is poor stuff. He writes just as you might suppose Voltaire's footboy to do, who has been his amanuensis. He has such parts as the valet might have, and about as much of the colouring of the style as might be got by transcribing his works." When I was at Ferney, I repeated this to Voltaire, in order to reconcile him somewhat to Johnson, whom he, in affecting the English mode of expression, had previously characterised as "a superstitious dog"; but after hearing such a criticism on Frederick the Great, with whom he was then on bad terms, he exclaimed, "An honest fellow!"

But I think the criticism much too severe; For the *Memoirs of the House of Brandenburgh* are written as well as many works of that kind. His poetry, for the style of which he himself makes a frank apology, *"_jargonnant un François barbare_," though fraught with pernicious ravings of infidelity, has, in many places, great animation, and in some a pathetic tenderness.

Upon this contemptuous animadversion on the King of Prussia, I observed to Johnson, "It would seem then, sir, that much less parts are necessary to make a king, than to make an author: for the King of Prussia is confessedly the greatest king now in Europe, yet you think he makes a very poor figure as an author."

Mr. Levet this day showed me Dr. Johnson's library, which was contained in two garrets over his chambers, where Lintot, son of the celebrated bookseller of that name, had formerly his warehouse. I found a number of good books, but very dusty and in great confusion. The floor was strewed with manuscript leaves, in Johnson's own handwriting, which I beheld with a degree of veneration, supposing they perhaps might contain portions of the *Rambler*, or of *Rasselas*. I observed an apparatus for chemical experiments, of which Johnson was all his life very fond. The place seemed to be very favourable for retirement and meditation. Johnson told me that he went up thither without mentioning it to his servant when he wanted to study secure from interruption; for he would not allow his servant to say he was not at home when he really was. "A servant's strict regard for truth," said he, "must be weakened by such a practice. A philosopher may know that it is merely a form of denial; but few servants are such nice distinguishers. If I accustom a servant to tell a lie for *me*, have I not reason to apprehend that he will tell many lies for *himself*?" I am, however, satisfied that every servant, of any degree of intelligence, understands saying his master is not at home, not at all as the affirmation of a fact, but as customary words intimating that his master wishes not to be seen, so that there can be no bad effect from it.

Mr. Temple, now vicar of St. Gluvias, Cornwall, who had been my intimate friend for many years, had at this time chambers in Farrar's Buildings, at the bottom of Inner Temple Lane, which he kindly lent me upon my quitting my lodgings, he being to return to Trinity Hall, Cambridge. I found them particularly convenient for me, as they were so near Dr. Johnson's.

On Wednesday, July 20, Dr. Johnson, Mr. Dempster, and my uncle, Dr. Boswell, who happened to be now in London, supped with me at these chambers. JOHNSON. "Pity is not natural to man. Children are always cruel. Savages are always cruel. Pity is acquired and improved by the cultivation of reason. We may have uneasy sensations from seeing a creature in distress, without pity; for we have not pity unless we wish to relieve them. When I am on my way to dine with a friend, and finding it late, have bid the coachman make haste, if I happen to attend when he whips his horses, I may feel unpleasantly that the animals are put to pain, but I do not wish him to desist. No, sir, I wish him to drive on."

Mr. Alexander Donaldson, bookseller, of Edinburgh, had for some time opened a shop in London, and sold his cheap editions of the most popular English books, in defiance of the supposed common-law right of literary property. Johnson, though he concurred in the opinion which was afterwards sanctioned by a judgment of the House of Lords, that there was no such right, was at this time very angry that the booksellers of London, for whom he uniformly professed much regard, should suffer from an invasion of what they had ever considered to be secure; and he was loud and violent against Mr. Donaldson. "He is a fellow who takes advantage of the law to injure his brethren; for notwithstanding that the statute secures only fourteen years of exclusive right, it has always been understood by the trade, that he, who buys the copyright of a book from the author, obtains a perpetual property; and upon that belief, numberless bargains are made to transfer that property after the expiration of the statutory term. Now Donaldson, I say, takes advantage here, of people who have really an equitable title from usage; and if we consider how few of the books, of which they buy the property, succeed so well as to bring profit, we should be of opinion that the term of fourteen years is too short; it should be sixty years." DEMPSTER. "Donaldson, sir, is anxious for the encouragement of literature. He reduces the price of books so that poor students may buy them." JOHNSON, (laughing). "Well, sir, allowing that to be his motive, he is no better than Robin Hood, who robbed the rich in order to give to the poor."

It is remarkable that when the great question concerning literary property came to be ultimately tried before the supreme tribunal of this country in consequence of the very spirited exertions of Mr. Donaldson, Dr. Johnson was zealous against a perpetuity; but he thought that the term of the exclusive right of authors should be considerably enlarged. He was then for granting a hundred years.

The conversation now turned upon *Mr. David Hume's style. JOHNSON. "Why, sir, his style is not English; the structure of his sentences is French. Now the French structure and the English structure may, in the nature of things, be equally good. But if you allow that the English language is established, he is wrong. My name might originally have been Nicholson, as well as Johnson; but were you to call me Nicholson now, you would call me very absurdly."

*Rousseau's treatise on the inequality of mankind was at this time a fashionable topic. It gave rise to an observation by Mr. Dempster that the advantages of fortune and rank were nothing to a wise man, who ought to value only merit. JOHNSON. "If man were a savage, living in the woods by himself, this might be true; but in civilized society we all depend upon each other, and our happiness is very much owing to the good opinion of mankind. Now, sir, in civilized society, external advantages make us more respected. A man with a good coat upon his back meets with a better reception than he who has a bad one. Sir, you may analyse this, and say, 'What is there in it?' But that will avail you nothing, for it is a part of a general system. Pound St. Paul's Church into atoms, and consider any single atom; it is, to be sure, good for nothing: but, put all these atoms together, and you have St. Paul's Church. So it is with human felicity, which is made up of many ingredients, each of which may be shown to be very insignificant. In civilized society, personal merit will not serve you so much as money will. Sir, you may make the experiment. Go into the street, and give one man a lecture on morality, and another a shilling, and see which will respect you most. If you wish only to support nature, *Sir William Petty fixes your allowance at three pounds a year; but as times are much altered, let us call it six pounds. This sum will fill your belly, shelter you from the weather, and even get you a strong lasting coat, supposing it to be made of good bull's hide. Now, sir, all beyond this is artificial, and is desired in order to obtain a greater degree of respect from our fellow creatures. And, sir, if six hundred pounds a year procure a man more consequence, and, of course, more happiness than six pounds a year, the same proportion will hold as to six thousand, and so on, as far as opulence can be carried. Perhaps he who has a large fortune may not be so happy as he who has a small one; but that must proceed from other causes than from his having the large fortune: for, *_cæteris paribus_, he who is rich in a civilized society, must be happier than he who is poor; as riches, if properly used, (and it is a man's own fault if they are not) must be productive of the highest advantages. Money, to be sure, of itself is of no use; for its only use is to part with it. Rousseau and all those who deal in paradoxes are led away by a childish desire of novelty. When I was a boy, I used always to choose the wrong side of a debate, because most ingenious things, that is to say, most new things, could be said upon it. Sir, there is nothing for which you may not muster up more plausible arguments than those which are urged against wealth and other external advantages. Why, now, there is stealing; why should it be thought a crime? When we consider by what unjust methods property has been often acquired, and that what was unjustly got, it must be unjust to keep, where is the harm in one man's taking the property of another from him? Besides, sir, when we consider the bad use that many people make of their property, and how much better use the thief may make of it, it may be defended as a very allowable practice. Yet, sir, the experience of mankind has discovered stealing to be so very bad a thing, that they make no scruple to hang a man for it. When I was running about this town a very poor fellow, I was a great arguer for the advantages of poverty; but I was, at the same time, very sorry to be poor. Sir, all the arguments which are brought to represent poverty as no evil, show it to be evidently a great evil. You never find people labouring to convince you that you may live very happily upon a plentiful fortune. So you hear people talking how miserable a king must be; and yet they all wish to be in his place."

It was suggested that kings must be unhappy, because they are deprived of the greatest of all satisfactions, easy and unreserved society. JOHNSON. "That is an ill-founded notion. Being a king does not exclude a man from such society. Great kings have always been social. The King of Prussia, the only great king at present, is very social. Charles the Second, the last king of England who was a man of parts, was social; and our Henrys and Edwards were all social."

Mr. Dempster having endeavoured to maintain that intrinsic merit ought to make the only distinction amongst mankind: JOHNSON. "Why, sir, mankind have found that this cannot be. How shall we determine the proportion of intrinsic merit? Were that to be the only distinction amongst mankind, we should soon quarrel about the degrees of it. Were all distinctions abolished, the strongest would not long acquiesce, but would endeavour to obtain a superiority by their bodily strength. But, sir, as subordination is very necessary for society, and contentions for superiority very dangerous, mankind, that is to say, all civilized nations, have settled it upon a plain invariable principle. A man is born to hereditary rank; or his being appointed to certain offices, gives him a certain rank. Subordination tends greatly to human happiness. Were we all upon an equality, we should have no other enjoyment than mere animal pleasure."

I said, I considered distinction of rank to be of so much importance in civilized society that if I were asked on the same day to dine with the first duke in England, and with the first man in Britain for genius, I should hesitate which to prefer. JOHNSON. "To be sure, sir, if you were to dine only once, and it were never to be known where you dined, you would choose rather to dine with the first man for genius; but to gain most respect, you should dine with the first duke in England. For nine people in ten that you meet with, would have a higher opinion of you for having dined with a duke; and the great genius himself would receive you better, because you had been with the great duke."

He took care to guard himself against any possible suspicion that his settled principles of reverence for rank and respect for wealth were at all owing to mean or interested motives, for he asserted his own independence as a literary man. "No man," said he, "who ever lived by literature has lived more independently than I have done." He said he had taken longer time than he needed to have done in composing his *Dictionary*. He received our compliments upon that great work with complacency, and told us that the *Academy *della Crusca* could scarcely believe that it was done by one man.

Next morning I found him alone, and have preserved the following fragments of his conversation. Of a gentleman who was mentioned, he said, "I have not met with any man for a long time who has given me such general displeasure. He is totally unfixed in his principles, and wants to puzzle other people." I said his principles had been poisoned by a noted infidel writer, but that he was, nevertheless, a benevolent good man. Johnson. "We can have no dependence upon that instinctive, that constitutional goodness which is not founded upon principle. I grant you that such a man may be a very amiable member of society. I can conceive him placed in such a situation that he is not much tempted to deviate from what is right; and as every man prefers virtue, when there is not some strong incitement to transgress its precepts, I can conceive him doing nothing wrong. But if such a man stood in need of money, I should not like to trust him; and I should certainly not trust him with young ladies, for *there* there is always temptation. Hume, and other sceptical innovators, are vain men, and will gratify themselves at any expense. Truth will not afford sufficient food to their vanity; so they have betaken themselves to error. Truth, sir, is a cow which will yield such people no more milk, and so they are gone to milk the bull. If I could have allowed myself to gratify my vanity at the expense of truth, what fame might I have acquired! Everything which Hume has advanced against Christianity had passed through my mind long before he wrote. Always remember this, that after a system is well settled upon positive evidence, a few partial objections ought not to shake it. The human mind is so limited that it cannot take in all the parts of a subject, so that there may be objections raised against anything. There are objections against a **plenum*, and objections against a *vacuum*; yet one of them must certainly be true."

I mentioned Hume's argument against the belief of miracles, that it is more probable that the witnesses to the truth of them are mistaken, or speak falsely, than that the miracles should be true. Johnson. "Why, sir, the great difficulty of proving miracles should make us very cautious in believing them. But let us consider: although God has made nature to operate by certain fixed laws, yet it is not unreasonable to think that he may suspend those laws, in order to establish a system highly advantageous to mankind. Now the Christian religion is a most beneficial system, as it gives us light and certainty where we were before in darkness and doubt. The miracles which prove it are attested by men who had no interest in deceiving us; but who, on the contrary, were told that they should suffer persecution, and did actually lay down their lives in confirmation of the truth of the facts which they asserted. Indeed, for some centuries the heathens did not pretend to deny the miracles; but said they were performed by the aid of evil spirits. This is a circumstance of great weight. Then, sir, when we take the proofs derived from prophecies which have been so exactly fulfilled, we have most satisfactory evidence. Supposing a miracle possible, as to which, in my opinion, there can be no doubt, we have as strong evidence for the miracles in support of Christianity, as the nature of the thing admits."

At night, Mr. Johnson and I supped in a private room at the Turk's Head Coffeehouse, in the Strand. "I encourage this house," said he, "for the mistress of it is a good civil woman, and has not much business."

"Sir, I love the acquaintance of young people; because, in the first place, I don't like to think myself growing old. In the next place, young acquaintances must last longest, if they do last; and then, sir, young men have more virtue than old men; they have more generous sentiments in every respect. I love the young dogs of this age; they have more wit and humour and knowledge of life than we had; but then the dogs are not so good scholars. Sir, in my early years I read very hard. It is a sad reflection but a true one, that I knew almost as much at eighteen as I do now. My judgment, to be sure, was not so good; but, I had all the facts. I remember very well, when I was at Oxford, an old gentleman said to me, 'Young man, ply your book diligently now, and acquire a stock of knowledge; for when years come upon you, you will find that poring upon books will be but an irksome task.'"

This account of his reading, given by himself in plain words, sufficiently confirms what I have already advanced upon the disputed question as to his application. It reconciles any seeming inconsistency in his way of talking upon it at different times; and shows that idleness and reading hard were with him relative terms, the import of which, as used by him, must be gathered from a comparison with what scholars of different degrees of ardour and assiduity have been known to do. And let it be remembered that he was now talking spontaneously, and expressing his genuine sentiments; whereas at other times he might be induced, from his spirit of contradiction, or more properly from his love of argumentative contest, to speak lightly of his own application to study. It is pleasing to consider that the old gentleman's gloomy prophecy as to the irksomeness of books to men of an advanced age, which is too often fulfilled, was so far from being verified in Johnson that his ardour for literature never failed, and his last writings had more ease and vivacity than any of his earlier productions.

He mentioned to me now, for the first time, that he had been distressed by melancholy, and for that reason had been obliged to fly from study and meditation, to the dissipating variety of life. Against melancholy he recommended constant occupation of mind, a great deal of exercise, moderation in eating and drinking, and especially to shun drinking at night. He said melancholy people were apt to fly to intemperance for relief, but that it sunk them much deeper in misery. He observed that labouring men who work hard, and live sparingly, are seldom or never troubled with low spirits.

He again insisted on the duty of maintaining subordination of rank. "Sir, I would no more deprive a nobleman of his respect, than of his money. I consider myself as acting a part in the great system of society, and I do to others as I would have them to do to me. I would behave to a nobleman as I should expect he would behave to me, were I a nobleman and he Sam. Johnson. Sir, there is one Mrs. Macaulay in this town, a great republican. One day when I was at her house, I put on a very grave countenance, and said to her, 'Madam, I am now become a convert to your way of thinking. I am convinced that all mankind are upon an equal footing; and to give you an unquestionable proof, madam, that I am in earnest, here is a very sensible, civil, well behaved fellow-citizen, your footman; I desire that he may be allowed to sit down and dine with us.' I thus, sir, showed her the absurdity of the levelling doctrine. She has never liked me since. Sir, your levellers wish to level *down* as far as themselves; but they cannot bear levelling *up* to themselves. They would all have some people under them; why not then have some people above them?" I mentioned a certain author who disgusted me by his forwardness, and by showing no deference to noblemen into whose company he was admitted. JOHNSON. "Suppose a shoemaker should claim an equality with him, as he does with a lord: how he would stare! 'Why, sir, do you stare?' says the shoemaker, 'I do great service to society. 'Tis true, I am paid for doing it; but so are you, sir, and I am sorry to say it, paid better than I am, for doing something not so necessary. For mankind could do better without your books than without my shoes.' Thus, sir, there would be a perpetual struggle for precedence, were there no fixed invariable rules for the distinction of rank, which creates no jealousy, as it is allowed to be accidental."

He said *Dr. Joseph Warton was a very agreeable man, and his *Essay on the Genius and Writings of Pope*, a very pleasing book. I wondered that he delayed so long to give us the continuation of it. JOHNSON. "Why, sir, I suppose he finds himself a little disappointed, in not having been able to persuade the world to be of his opinion as to Pope."

We have now been favoured with the concluding volume, in which, to use a parliamentary expression, he has *explained*, so as not to appear quite so adverse to the opinion of the world, concerning Pope, as was at first thought; and we must all agree that his work is a most valuable accession to English literature.

A writer of deserved eminence being mentioned, Johnson said, "Why, sir, he is a man of good parts, but being originally poor, he has got a love of mean company and low jocularity, a very bad thing, sir. To laugh is good, and to talk is good. But you ought no more to think it enough if you laugh, than you are to think it enough if you talk. You may laugh in as many ways as you talk; and surely *every* way of talking that is practised cannot be esteemed."

I spoke of Sir James Macdonald as a young man of most distinguished merit, who united the highest reputation at Eton and Oxford, with the patriarchal spirit of a great Highland chieftain. I mentioned that Sir James had said to me that he had never seen Mr. Johnson, but he had a great respect for him, though at the same time it was mixed with some degree of terror. JOHNSON. "Sir, if he were to be acquainted with me, it might lessen both."

The mention of this gentleman led us to talk of the Western Islands of Scotland, to visit which he expressed a wish that then appeared to be a very romantic fancy, which I little thought would be afterwards realised. He told me that his father had put Martin's account of those islands into his hands when he was very young, and that he was highly pleased with it; that he was particularly struck with the St. Kilda man's notion that the high church of Glasgow had been hollowed out of a rock, a circumstance to which old Mr. Johnson had directed his attention. He said he would go to the Hebrides with me, when I returned from my travels, unless some very good companion should offer when I was absent, which he did not think probable, adding, "There are few people whom I take so much to, as you." And when I talked of my leaving England, he said with a very affectionate air, "My dear Boswell, I should be very unhappy at parting, did I think we were not to meet again." I cannot too often remind my readers that, although such instances of his kindness are doubtless very flattering to me, yet I hope my recording them will be ascribed to a better motive than to vanity; for they afford unquestionable evidence of his tenderness and complacency, which some, while they were forced to acknowledge his great powers, have been so strenuous to deny.

He maintained that a boy at school was the happiest of human beings. I supported a different opinion, from which I have never yet varied, that a man is happier; and I enlarged upon the anxiety and sufferings which are endured at school. JOHNSON. "Ah! sir, a boy's being flogged is not so severe as a man's having the hiss of the world against him. Men have a solicitude about fame; and the greater share they have of it, the more afraid they are of losing it." I silently asked myself, "Is it possible that the great Samuel Johnson really entertains any such apprehension, and is not confident that his exalted fame is established upon a foundation never to be shaken?"

He this evening drank a bumper to Sir David Dalrymple, "as a man of worth, a scholar, and a wit." "I have," said he, "never heard of him, except from you, but let him know my opinion of him: for as he does not show himself much in the world, he should have the praise of the few who hear of him."

On Tuesday, July 26, I found Mr. Johnson alone. It was a very wet day, and I again complained of the disagreeable effects of such weather. JOHNSON. "Sir, this is all imagination, which physicians encourage; for man lives in air, as a fish lives in water, so that if the atmosphere press heavy from above, there is an equal resistance from below. To be sure, bad weather is hard upon people who are obliged to be abroad; and men cannot labour so well in the open air in bad weather, as in good: but, sir, a smith or a tailor, whose work is within doors, will surely do as much in rainy weather, as in fair. Some very delicate frames, indeed, may be affected by wet weather; but not common constitutions."

We talked of the education of children; and I asked him what he thought was best to teach them first. JOHNSON. "Sir, it is no matter what you teach them first, any more than what leg you shall put into your breeches first. Sir, you may stand disputing which is best to put in first, but in the mean time your breech is bare. Sir, while you are considering which of two things you should teach your child first, another boy has learnt them both."

On Thursday, July 28, we again supped in private at the Turk's Head Coffee-house. JOHNSON. "Swift has a higher reputation than he deserves. His excellence is strong sense; for his humour, though very well, is not remarkably good. I doubt whether the *_Tale of a Tub_ be his; for he never owned it, and it is much above his usual manner."

"Thomson, I think, had as much of the poet about him as most writers. Everything appeared to him through the medium of his favourite pursuit. He could not have viewed those two candles burning but with a poetical eye."

"Has not —— a great deal of wit, sir?" JOHNSON. "I do not think so, sir. He is, indeed, continually attempting wit, but he fails. And I have no more pleasure in hearing a man attempting wit and failing, than in seeing a man trying to leap over a ditch and tumbling into it."

He laughed heartily when I mentioned to him a saying of his concerning Mr. Thomas Sheridan, which *Foote took a wicked pleasure to circulate. "'Why, sir, Sherry is dull, naturally dull; but it must have taken him a great deal of pains to become what we now see him. Such an excess of stupidity, sir, is not in nature.'" — "So," said he, "I allowed him all his own merit."

He now added, "Sheridan cannot bear me. I bring his declamation to a point. I ask him a plain question, 'What do you mean to teach?' Besides, sir, what influence can Mr. Sheridan have upon the language of this great country, by his narrow exertions? Sir, it is burning a farthing candle at Dover, to show light at Calais."

Talking of a young man who was uneasy from thinking that he was very deficient in learning and knowledge, he said, "A man has no reason to complain who holds a middle place, and has many below him; and perhaps he has not six of his years above him; — perhaps not one. Though he may not know any thing perfectly, the general mass of knowledge that he has acquired is considerable. Time will do for him all that is wanting."

The conversation then took a philosophical turn. JOHNSON. "Human experience, which is constantly contradicting theory, is the great test of truth. A system built upon the discoveries of a great many minds is always of more strength than what is produced by the mere workings of any one mind, which, of itself, can do little. There is not so poor a book in the world that would not be a prodigious effort were it wrought out entirely by a single mind, without the aid of prior investigators. The French writers are superficial, because they are not scholars, and so proceed upon the mere power of their own minds; and we see how very little power they have."

"As to the Christian religion, sir, besides the strong evidence which we have for it, there is a balance in its favour from the number of great men who have been convinced of its truth, after a serious consideration of the question. Grotius was an acute man, a lawyer, a man accustomed to examine evidence, and he was convinced. Grotius was not a recluse, but a man of the world, who certainly had no bias to the side of religion. *Sir Isaac Newton set out an infidel, and came to be a very firm believer."

He this evening again recommended me to perambulate Spain. I said it would amuse him to get a letter from me dated at Salamanca. JOHNSON. "I love the University of Salamanca; for when the Spaniards were in doubt as to the lawfulness of their conquering America, the University of Salamanca gave it as their opinion that it was not lawful." He spoke this with great emotion, and with that generous warmth which dictated the lines in his *London*, against Spanish encroachment.

"I expressed my opinion of my friend, Derrick, as but a poor writer. JOHNSON. "To be sure, sir, he is; but you are to consider that his being a literary man has got for him all that he has. It has made him King of Bath. Sir, he has nothing to say for himself but that he is a writer. Had he not been a writer, he must have been sweeping the crossings in the streets, and asking halfpence from everybody that passed."

In justice, however, to the memory of Mr. Derrick, who was my first tutor in the ways of London, and showed me the town in all its variety of departments, both literary and sportive, the particulars of which Dr. Johnson advised me to put in writing, it is proper to mention what Johnson, at a subsequent period, said of him both as a writer and an editor: "Sir, I have often said that if Derrick's letters had been written by one of a more established name, they would have been thought very pretty letters." And, "I sent Derrick to Dryden's relations to gather materials for his life; and I believe he got all that I myself should have got."

Poor Derrick! I remember him with kindness. Yet I cannot withhold from my readers a pleasant humorous sally which could not have hurt him had he been alive, and now is perfectly harmless. In his collection of poems, there is one upon entering the harbour of Dublin, his native city, after a long absence. It begins thus:

Eblana! much lov'd city, hail!
Where first I saw the light of day.

And after a solemn reflection on his being

"numbered with forgotten dead," there is the following stanza:

> Unless my lines protract my fame,
> And those, who chance to read them, cry,
> I knew him! Derrick was his name,
> In yonder tomb his ashes lie.

which was thus happily parodied by Mr. John Home, to whom we owe the beautiful and pathetic tragedy of *Douglas*:

> Unless my *deeds* protract my fame,
> *And he who passes sadly sings,*
> I knew him! Derrick was his name,
> *On yonder tree his carcase swings!*

I doubt much whether the amiable and ingenious author of these burlesque lines will recollect them; for they were produced extempore one evening while he and I were walking together in the dining room at Eglintoune Castle, in 1760, and I have never mentioned them to him since.

Johnson said once to me, "Sir, I honour Derrick for his presence of mind. One night, when Floyd, another poor author, was wandering about the streets in the night, he found Derrick fast asleep upon a bulk; upon being suddenly waked, Derrick started up, 'My dear Floyd, I am sorry to see you in this destitute state: will you go home with me to *my lodgings*?'"

I again begged his advice as to my method of study at Utrecht. "Come," said he, "let us make a day of it. Let us go down to Greenwich and dine, and talk of it there." The following Saturday was fixed for this excursion.

As we walked along the Strand tonight, arm in arm, a woman of the town accosted us, in the usual enticing manner. "No, no, my girl," said Johnson, "it won't do." He, however, did not treat her with harshness; and we talked of the wretched life of such women, and agreed that much more misery than happiness, upon the whole, is produced by illicit commerce between the sexes.

On Saturday, July 30, Dr. Johnson and I took a sculler at the Temple Stairs, and set out for Greenwich. I asked him if he really thought a knowledge of the Greek and Latin languages an essential requisite to a good education. Johnson. "Most certainly, sir; for those who know them have a very great advantage over those who do not. Nay, sir, it is wonderful what a difference learning makes upon people even in the common intercourse of life, which does not appear to be much connected with it." "And yet," said I, "people go through the world very well, and carry on the business of life to good advantage, without learning." Johnson. "Why, sir, that may be true in cases where learning cannot possibly be of any use; for instance, this boy rows us as well without learning, as if he could sing the song of Orpheus to the Argonauts, who were the first sailors." He then called to the boy, "What would you give, my lad, to know about the Argonauts?" "Sir," said the boy, "I would give what I have." Johnson was much pleased with his answer, and we gave him a double fare. Dr. Johnson then turning to me, "Sir," said he, "a desire of knowledge is the natural feeling of mankind; and every human being, whose mind is not debauched, will be willing to give all that he has, to get knowledge."

We landed at the Old Swan, and walked to Billingsgate, where we took oars and moved smoothly along the silver Thames. It was a very fine day. We were entertained with the immense number and variety of ships that were lying at anchor, and with the beautiful country on each side of the river.

I talked of preaching, and of the great success which those called Methodists have. Johnson. "Sir, it is owing to their expressing themselves in a plain and familiar manner, which is the only way to do good to the common people, and which clergymen of genius and learning ought to do from a principle of duty, when it is suited to their congregations, a practice, for which they will be praised by men of sense. To insist against drunkenness as a crime, because it debases reason, the noblest faculty of man, would be of no service to the common people; but to tell them that they may die in a fit of drunkenness, and show them how dreadful that would be, cannot fail to make a deep impression. Sir, when your Scotch clergy give up their homely manner, religion will soon decay in that country." Let this observation, as Johnson meant it, be ever remembered.

I was much pleased to find myself with Johnson at Greenwich, which he celebrates in his *London* as a favourite scene. I had the poem in my pocket, and read the lines aloud with enthusiasm:

> On Thames's banks in silent thought we stood,
> Where Greenwich smiles upon the silver flood:
> Pleas'd with the seat which gave Eliza birth,
> We kneel, and kiss the consecrated earth.

He remarked that the structure of Greenwich Hospital was too magnificent for a place of charity, and that its parts were too much detached to make one great whole.

*Buchanan, he said, was a very fine poet; and observed that he was the first who complimented a lady, by ascribing to her the different perfections of the heathen goddesses; but that *Johnston improved upon this by making his lady, at the same time, free from their defects.

He dwelt upon Buchanan's elegant verses to Mary Queen of Scots, *Nympha Caledoniæ*, &c. and spoke with enthusiasm of the beauty of Latin verse. "All the modern languages," said he, "cannot furnish so melodious a line as

**Formosam resonare doces Amarillida silvas.*"

Afterwards he entered upon the business of the day, which was to give me his advice as to a course of study. And here I am to mention with much regret that my record of what he said is miserably scanty. I recollect with admiration an animating blaze of eloquence, which roused every intellectual power in me to the highest pitch, but must have dazzled me so much that my memory could not preserve the substance of his discourse; for the note which I find of it is no more than this: "He ran over the grand scale of human knowledge; advised me to select some particular branch to excel in, but to acquire a little of every kind." The defect of my minutes will be fully supplied by a long letter upon the subject, which he favoured me with, after I had been some time at Utrecht, and which my readers will have the pleasure to peruse in its proper place.

We walked in the evening in Greenwich Park. He asked me, I suppose by way of trying my disposition, "Is not this very fine?" Having no exquisite relish of the beauties of nature, and being more delighted with "the busy hum of men," I answered, "Yes, sir; but not equal to Fleet Street." JOHNSON. "You are right, sir."

I am aware that many of my readers may censure my want of taste. Let me, however, shelter myself under the authority of a very fashionable baronet in the brilliant world, who, on his attention being called to the fragrance of a May evening in the country, observed, "This may be very well; but for my part, I prefer the smell of a flambeau at the playhouse."

We stayed so long at Greenwich that our sail up the river, in our return to London, was by no means so pleasant as in the morning; for the night air was so cold that it made me shiver. I was the more sensible of it from having sat up all the night before recollecting and writing in my journal what I thought worthy of preservation; an exertion, which, during the first part of my acquaintance with Johnson, I frequently made. I remember having sat up four nights in one week, without being much incommoded in the day time.

Johnson, whose robust frame was not in the least affected by the cold, scolded me, as if my shivering had been a paltry effeminacy, saying, "Why do you shiver?" Sir William Scott, of the Commons, told me, that when he complained of a headache in the post-chaise, as they were travelling together to Scotland, Johnson treated him in the same manner: "At your age, sir, I had no headache." It is not easy to make allowance for sensations in others which we ourselves have not at the time. We must all have experienced how very differently we are affected by the complaints of our neighbours, when we are well and when we are ill. In full health, we can scarcely believe that they suffer much, so faint is the image of pain upon our imagination; when softened by sickness, we readily sympathize with the sufferings of others.

We concluded the day at the Turk's Head Coffee-house very socially. He was pleased to listen to a particular account which I gave him of my family, and of its hereditary estate, as to the extent and population of which he asked questions, and made calculations; recommending, at the same time, a liberal kindness to the tenantry, as people over whom the proprietor was placed by Providence. He took delight in hearing my description of the romantic seat of my ancestors. "I must be there, sir," said he, "and we will live in the old castle; and if there is not a room in it remaining, we will build one." I was highly flattered, but could scarcely indulge a hope that Auchinleck would indeed be honoured by his presence, and celebrated by a description, as it afterwards was, in his *Journey to the Western Islands*.

After we had again talked of my setting out for Holland, he said, "I must see thee out of England; I will accompany you to Harwich." I could not find words to express what I felt upon this unexpected and very great mark of his affectionate regard.

Next day, Sunday, July 31, I told him I had been that morning at a meeting of the people called Quakers, where I had heard a woman preach. Johnson. "Sir, a woman's preaching is like a dog's walking on his hinder legs. It is not done well; but you are surprised to find it done at all."

On Tuesday, August 2, (the day of my departure from London having been fixed for the 5th) Dr. Johnson did me the honour to pass a part of the morning with me at my chambers. He said that "he always felt an inclination to do nothing." I observed that it was strange to think that the most indolent man in Britain had written the most laborious work, *The English Dictionary*.

I mentioned an imprudent publication, by a certain friend of his, at an early period of life, and asked him if he thought it would hurt him. Johnson. "No, sir; not much. It may, perhaps, be mentioned at an election."

I had now made good my title to be a privileged man, and was carried by him in the evening to drink tea with Miss Williams, whom, though under the misfortune of having lost her sight, I found to be agreeable in conversation; for she had a variety of literature, and expressed herself well; but her peculiar value was the intimacy in which she had long lived with Johnson, by which she was well acquainted with his habits, and knew how to lead him on to talk.

After tea he carried me to what he called his walk, which was a long narrow paved court in the neighbourhood, overshadowed by some trees. There we sauntered a considerable time; and I complained to him that my love of London and his company was such that I shrunk almost from the thought of going away even to travel, which is generally so much desired by young men. He roused me by manly and spirited conversation. He advised me, when settled in any place abroad, to study with an eagerness after knowledge, and to apply to Greek an hour every day; and when I was moving about, to read diligently the great book of mankind.

On Wednesday, August 3, we had our last social evening at the Turk's Head Coffeehouse, before my setting out for foreign parts. I had the misfortune, before we parted, to irritate him unintentionally. I mentioned to him how common it was in the world to tell absurd stories of him, and to ascribe to him very strange sayings. Johnson. "What do they make me say, sir?" Boswell. "Why, sir, as an instance very strange indeed," laughing heartily as I spoke, "David Hume told me you said that you would stand before a battery of cannon to *restore the Convocation to its full powers." Little did I apprehend that he had actually said this: but I was soon convinced of my error; for, with a determined look, he thundered out, "And would I not, sir? Shall the Presbyterian *Kirk* of Scotland have its General Assembly, and the Church of England be denied its Convocation?" He was walking up and down the room, while I told him the anecdote; but when he uttered this explosion of High Church zeal, he had come close to my chair, and his eyes flashed with indignation. I bowed to the storm, and diverted the force of it, by leading him to expatiate on the influence which religion derived from maintaining the church with great external respectability.

I must not omit to mention that he this year wrote *The Life of Ascham,* and the Dedication to the Earl of Shaftesbury, prefixed to the edition of that writer's English works, published by Mr. Bennet.

On Friday, August 5, we set out early in the morning in the Harwich stage-coach. A fat elderly gentlewoman and a young Dutchman seemed the most inclined among us to conversation. At the inn where we dined, the gentlewoman said that she had done her best to educate her children; and, particularly, that she had never suffered them to be a moment idle. Johnson. "I wish, madam, you would educate me too; for I have been an idle fellow all my life." "I am sure, sir," said she, "you have not been idle." Johnson. "Nay, madam, it is very true; and that gentleman there," pointing to me, "has been idle. He was idle at Edinburgh. His father sent him to Glasgow, where he continued to be idle. He then came to London, where he has been very idle; and now he is going to Utrecht, where he will be as idle as ever." I asked him privately how he could expose me so. Johnson. "Poh, poh!" said he, "they knew nothing about you, and will think of it no more." In the afternoon the gentlewoman talked violently against the Roman Catholics, and of the horrors of the Inquisition. To the utter astonishment of all the passengers but myself, who knew that he could talk upon any side of a question, he defended the Inquisition, and maintained that "false doctrine should be checked on its first appearance; that the civil power should unite with the church in punishing those who dare to attack the established religion, and that such only were punished by the Inquisition." He had in his pocket *Pomponius Mela *De Situ Orbis*, in which he read occasionally, and seemed very intent upon ancient geography. Though by no means niggardly, his attention to what was generally right was so minute that having observed at one of the stages that I ostentatiously gave a shilling to the coachman, when the custom was for each passenger to give only sixpence, he took me aside and scolded me, saying that what I had done would make the coachman dissatisfied with all the rest of the passengers who gave him no more than his due. This was a just reprimand; for in whatever way a man may indulge his generosity or his vanity in spending his money, for the sake of others he ought not to raise the price of any article for which there is a constant demand.

He talked of *Mr. Blacklock's poetry, so far as it was descriptive of visible objects; and observed, that "as its author had the misfortune to be blind, we may be absolutely sure that such passages are combinations of what he has remembered of the works of other writers who could see. *That foolish fellow, Spence, has laboured to explain philosophically how Blacklock may have done, by means of his own faculties, what it is impossible he should do. The solution, as I have given it, is plain. Suppose, I know a man to be so lame that he is absolutely incapable to move himself, and I find him in a different room from that in which I left him; shall I puzzle myself with idle conjectures, that, perhaps, his nerves have by some unknown change all at once become effective? No, sir, it is clear how he got into a different room: he was *carried*."

Having stopped a night at Colchester, Johnson talked of that town with veneration, for having stood a siege for Charles the First. The Dutchman alone now remained with us. He spoke English tolerably well; and thinking to recommend himself to us by expatiating on the superiority of the criminal jurisprudence of this country over that of Holland, he inveighed against the barbarity of putting an accused person to the torture, in order to force a confession. But Johnson was as ready for this, as for the Inquisition. "Why, sir, you do not, I find, understand the law of your own country. The torture of Holland is considered as a favour to an accused person; for no man is put to the torture there, unless there is as much evidence against him as would amount to conviction in England. An accused person among you, therefore, has one chance more to escape punishment than those who are tried among us."

At supper this night he talked of good eating with uncommon satisfaction. "Some people," said he, "have a foolish way of not minding, or pretending not to mind, what they eat. For my part, I mind my belly very studiously, and very carefully; for I look upon it that he who does not mind his belly will hardly mind any thing else." He now appeared to me **Jean Bull philosophe*, and he was, for the moment, not only serious but vehement. Yet I have heard him, upon other occasions, talk with great contempt of people who were anxious to gratify their palates; and the 206th number of his *Rambler* is a masterly essay against gulosity. His practice, indeed, I must acknowledge, may be considered as casting the balance of his different opinions upon this subject; for I never knew any man who relished good eating more than he did. When at table, he was totally absorbed in the business of the moment; his looks seemed rivetted to his plate; nor would he, unless when in very high company, say one word, or even pay the least attention to what was said by others, till he had satisfied his appetite, which was so fierce, and indulged with such intenseness, that while in the act of eating, the veins of his forehead swelled, and generally a strong perspiration was visible. To those whose sensations were delicate, this could not but be disgusting; and it was doubtless not very suitable to the character of a philosopher, who should be distinguished by self-command. But it must be owned that Johnson, though he could be rigidly abstemious, was not a temperate man either in eating or drinking. He could refrain, but he could not use moderately. He told me that he had fasted two days without inconvenience, and that he had never been hungry but once. They who beheld with wonder how much he eat upon all occasions, when his dinner was to his taste, could not easily conceive what he must have meant by hunger; and not only was he remarkable for the extraordinary quantity which he eat, but he was, or affected to be, a man of very nice discernment in the science of cookery. He used to descant critically on the dishes which had been at table where he had dined or supped, and to recollect very minutely what he had liked. I remember when he was in Scotland, his praising *"Gordon's palates," (a dish of palates at the Honourable Alexander Gordon's) with a warmth of expression which might have done honour to more important subjects. "As for Maclaurin's imitation of a *made dish*, it was a wretched attempt." He about the same time was so much displeased with the performances of a nobleman's French cook that he exclaimed with vehemence, "I'd throw such a rascal into the river"; and he then proceeded to alarm a lady at whose house he was to sup, by the following manifesto of his skill: "I, madam, who live at a variety of good tables, am a much better judge of cookery than any person who has a very tolerable cook but lives much at home; for his palate is gradually adapted to the taste of his cook: whereas, madam, in trying by a wider range, I can more exquisitely judge." When invited to dine, even with an intimate friend, he was not pleased if something better than a plain dinner was not prepared for him. I have heard him say on such an occasion, "This was a good dinner enough, to be sure, but it was not a dinner to *ask* a man to." On the other hand, he was wont to express, with great glee, his satisfaction when he had been entertained quite to his mind. One day when we had dined with his neighbour and landlord, in Bolt Court, Mr. Allen, the printer, whose old housekeeper had studied his taste, in everything, he pronounced this eulogy: "Sir, we could not have had a better dinner, had there been a *Synod of Cooks*."

While we were left by ourselves, after the Dutchman had gone to bed, Dr. Johnson talked of that studied behaviour which many have recommended and practised. He disapproved of it; and said, "I never considered whether I should be a grave man, or a merry man, but just let inclination, for the time, have its course."

He flattered me with some hopes that he would, in the course of the following summer, come over to Holland, and accompany me in a tour through the Netherlands.

I teased him with fanciful apprehensions of unhappiness. A moth having fluttered round the candle, and burnt itself, he laid hold of this little incident to admonish me; saying, with a sly look, and in a solemn but a quiet tone, "That creature was its own tormentor, and I believe its name was Boswell."

Next day we got to Harwich to dinner; and my passage in the packet boat to Helvoetsluys being secured, and my baggage put on board, we dined at our inn by ourselves. I happened to say it would be terrible if he should not find a speedy opportunity of returning to London, and be confined in so dull a place. JOHNSON. "Don't, sir, accustom yourself to use big words for little matters. It would *not* be *terrible*, though I *were* to be detained some time here." The practice of using words of disproportionate magnitude, is, no doubt, too frequent everywhere; but, I think, most remarkable among the French, of which, all who have travelled in France must have been struck with innumerable instances.

We went and looked at the church, and having gone into it, and walked up to the altar, Johnson, whose piety was constant and fervent, sent me to my knees, saying, "Now that you are going to leave your native country, recommend yourself to the protection of your Creator and Redeemer."

After we came out of the church, we stood talking for some time together of *Bishop Berkeley's ingenious sophistry to prove the non-existence of matter, and that everything in the universe is merely ideal. I observed that though we are satisfied his doctrine is not true, it is impossible to refute it. I never shall forget the alacrity with which Johnson answered, striking his foot with mighty force against a large stone, till he rebounded from it, — "I refute it *thus*." This was a stout exemplification of the *first truths* of *Père Bouffier, or the *original principles* of *Reid and of Beattie; without admitting which, we can no more argue in metaphysics than we can argue in mathematics without axioms. To me it is not conceivable how Berkeley can be answered by pure reasoning; but I know that the nice and difficult task was to have been undertaken by *one of the most luminous minds of the present age, had not politics "turned him from calm philosophy aside." What an admirable display of subtilty, united with brilliance, might his contending with Berkeley have afforded us! How must we, when we reflect on the loss of such an intellectual feast, regret that he should be characterised as the man,

Who, born for the universe, narrow'd his mind,
And to party gave up what was meant for mankind?

My revered friend walked down with me to the beach, where we embraced and parted with tenderness, and engaged to correspond by letters. I said, "I hope, sir, you will not forget me in my absence." JOHNSON. "Nay, sir, it is more likely you should forget me, than that I should forget you." As the vessel put out to sea, I kept my eyes upon him for a considerable time, while he remained rolling his majestic frame in his usual manner; and at last I perceived him walk back into the town, and he disappeared....

[1791]

FRANCES BURNEY (MADAME D'ARBLAY)

FRANCES BURNEY in middle life married a French *émigré*, General D'Arblay, and is in consequence officially listed as Madame D'Arblay, through the same zeal for accurate nomenclature that has been known to record the name of George Eliot as Mary Ann Cross. In literature, however, she is remembered by her maiden name, usually written Fanny Burney. She was the daughter of Dr. Charles Burney, an eminent musician and a member of Dr. Johnson's Club. Though without formal education, the girl began to write early; in 1778, when she was in her twenty-sixth year, she published anonymously her first novel, *Evelina, or a Young Lady's Entrance into the World.* At first no one but her brother and sisters knew the secret of her authorship, but as the novel had an unusual success the secret spread. She was invited by Mrs. Thrale to Streatham, where Dr. Johnson praised her highly, and so she made her own entrance into the world.

During practically her whole life Fanny Burney kept a diary. Here she set down the details of her daily life with the same keen observation and shrewd insight that distinguish her fiction. First as a girl at home, then as a rising young authoress in the literary world, afterwards as second keeper of the robes to Queen Charlotte, still later as wife and widow, she shows us widely varied scenes with vividness and charm. Written only for herself and her most intimate friends, this diary is, especially in its earlier parts, delightfully fresh and informal, while at the same time it shows a high degree of narrative skill. The character portrayal is especially good, and during the course of her eighty-seven years she had the chance to meet most of the people best worth portraying

Though the descriptions of the royal family and of Burke and Warren Hastings are famous, the most interesting part of the *Diary* is that between 1778 and 1784, in which Dr. Johnson frequently appears Seeing him chiefly at the Thrales' and in his less serious moments, she gives us a picture of the doctor scarcely less vivid than Boswell's, but different in tone. In a well-known passage of the *Diary* she records how Boswell tried in vain to get her help shortly before the publication of his *Life of Johnson.* The time was October, 1790; the place, Windsor, between Saint George's Chapel and the Queen's Lodge

"I asked him about Mr. Burke's book. 'Oh,' cried he, 'it will come out next week; 'tis the first book in the world, except my own, and that's coming out also very soon; only I want your help.'

"'My help?'

"'Yes, madam, you must give me some of your choice little notes of the doctor's; we have seen him long enough upon stilts; I want to show him in a new light. Grave Sam, and great Sam, and solemn Sam, and learned Sam — all these he has appeared over and over. Now I want to entwine a wreath of the graces across his brow; I want to show him as gay Sam, agreeable Sam, pleasant Sam; so you must help me with some of his beautiful billets to yourself.'

"I evaded this by declaring I had not any stores at hand. He proposed a thousand curious expedients to get at them, but I was invincible."

The passage here reprinted shows her at the moment when she is first tasting the sweets of literary success. It would be hard, in the whole range of literature, to find pages more full of simple joy and breathless apprehension than this account of Fanny's dinner with the great Dr. Johnson.

From the DIARY

August 3 [1778] — I have an immensity to write. *Susan has copied me a letter which *Mrs. Thrale had written to my father, upon the occasion of returning my mother two novels by Madame *Riccoboni. It is so honourable to me, and so sweet in her, that I must copy it for my faithful journal.

Wednesday, 22 [July], 1778
Streatham.

"Dear Sir — I forgot to give you the novels home in your carriage which I now send by Mr. Abingdon's. *Evelina* certainly excels them far enough, both in probability of story, elegance of sentiment, and general power over the mind, whether exerted in humour or pathos. Add to this, that Riccoboni is a veteran author, and all she ever can be; but I cannot tell what might not be expected from *Evelina*, was she to try her genius at comedy. So far had I written of my letter, when Mr. Johnson returned home, full of the praises of the book I had lent him, and protesting there were passages in it which might do honour to Richardson. We talk of it for-

* Notes on Frances Burney will be found in the Appendix, pp. 1034 ff.

ever, and he feels ardent after the *dénouement*; he could not get rid of the rogue, he said! I lent him the second volume, and he is now busy with the other two. You must be more a philosopher, and less a father than I wish you, not to be pleased with this letter; and the giving such pleasure yields to nothing but receiving it. Long, my dear sir, may you live to enjoy the just praises of your children! and long may they live to deserve and delight such a parent! These are things that you would say in verse; but poetry implies fiction, and all this is naked truth.

"Give my letter to my little friend, and a warm invitation to come and eat fruit while the season lasts. My compliments to Mrs. Burney, and kindest wishes to all your flock, etc."

How sweet, how amiable in this charming woman is her desire of making my dear father satisfied with his scribbler's attempt! I do, indeed, feel the most grateful love for her.

But Dr. Johnson's approbation! — it almost crazed me with agreeable surprise — it gave me such a flight of spirits that I danced a jig to *Mr. Crisp, without any preparation, music, or explanation — to his no small amazement and diversion. I left him, however, to make his own comments upon my friskiness, without affording him the smallest assistance.

Susan also writes me word that when my father went last to Streatham Dr. Johnson was not there, but Mrs. Thrale told him that when he gave her the first volume of *Evelina*, which she had lent him, he said, "Why, madam, why, what a charming book you lent me!" and eagerly inquired for the rest. He was particularly pleased with the Snow Hill scenes, and said that Mr. Smith's vulgar gentility was admirably portrayed; and when Sir Clement joins them, he said there was a shade of character prodigiously well marked. Well may it be said that the greatest minds are ever the most candid to the inferior set! I think I should love Dr. Johnson for such lenity to a poor mere worm in literature, even if I were not myself the identical grub he has obliged.

Susan has sent me a little note which has really been less pleasant to me, because it has alarmed me for my future concealment. It is from *Mrs. Williams, an exceeding pretty poetess, who has the misfortune to be blind, but who has, to make some amends, the honour of residing in the house of Dr. Johnson: for though he lives almost wholly at Streatham, he always keeps his apartments in town, and this lady acts as mistress of his house.

July 25

"Mrs. Williams sends compliments to Dr. Burney, and begs he will intercede with Miss Burney to do her the favour to lend her the reading of *Evelina*."

I was quite confounded at this request, which proves that Mrs. Thrale has told Dr. Johnson of my secret, and that he has told Mrs. Williams, and that she has told the person, whoever it be, whom she got to write the note.

I instantly scrawled a hasty letter to town to entreat my father would be so good as to write to her, to acquaint her with my earnest and unaffected desire to remain unknown.

And yet I am frightened at this affair, I am by no means insensible to the honour which I receive from the certainty that Dr. Johnson must have spoken very well of the book to have induced Mrs. Williams to send to our house for it. She has known my father indeed for some years, but not with any intimacy; and I never saw her, though the perusal of her poems has often made me wish to be acquainted with her.

I now come to last Saturday evening, when my beloved father came to Chessington, in full health, charming spirits, and all kindness, openness, and entertainment.

I inquired what he had done about Mrs. Williams. He told me he went to her himself at my desire, for if he had written she could not herself have read the note. She apologised very much for the liberty she had taken, and spoke highly of the book, though she had only heard the first volume, as she was dependent upon a lady's good nature and time for hearing any part of it; but she went so far as to say that his daughter was certainly the first writer, in that way, now living.

In his way hither he had stopped at Streatham, and he settled with Mrs. Thrale that he would call on her again in his way to town, and carry me with him! and Mrs. Thrale said, "We all long to know her."

I have been in a kind of twitter ever since, for there seems something very formidable in the idea of appearing as an authoress! I ever dreaded it, as it is a title which must raise more expectations than I have any chance of answering. Yet I am highly flattered by her invitation, and highly delighted in the prospect of being introduced to the Streatham society.

She sent me some very serious advice to write for the theatre, as, she says, I so naturally run into conversations that *Evelina* absolutely and plainly points out that path to me; and she hinted how much she should be pleased to be honoured with my confidence.

My dear father communicated this intelligence, and a great deal more, with a pleasure that almost surpassed that with which I heard it, and he seems quite eager for me to make another attempt. He desired to take upon himself the communication to my daddy Crisp, and as it is now in so many hands that it is possible accident might discover it to him, I readily consented.

Sunday evening, as I was going into my father's room I heard him say, "The variety of characters — the variety of scenes — and the language — why she has had very little education but what she has given herself, — less than any of the others!" and Mr. Crisp exclaimed, "Wonderful — it's wonderful!"

I now found what was going forward, and therefore deemed it most fitting to decamp.

About an hour after, as I was passing through the hall, I met my daddy [Crisp]. His face was all animation and archness; he doubled his fist at me, and would have stopped me, but I ran past him into the parlour.

Before supper, however, I again met him, and he would not suffer me to escape; he caught both my hands, and looked as if he would have looked me through, and then exclaimed, "Why, you little hussy, — you young devil! — an't you ashamed to look me in the face, you Evelina you! Why what a dance have you led me about it! Young friend indeed! Oh, you little hussy, what tricks have you served me!"

I was obliged to allow of his running on with these gentle appellations for I know not how long, ere he could sufficiently compose himself after his great surprise, to ask or hear any particulars; and then, he broke out every three instants with exclamations of astonishment at how I had found time to write so much unsuspected, and how and where I had picked up such various materials; and not a few times did he, with me, as he had with my father, exclaim, "Wonderful!"

He has, since, made me read him all my letters upon this subject. He said * Lowndes would have made an estate had he given me £1000 for it, and that he ought not to have given less! "You have nothing to do now," continued he, "but to take your pen in hand, for your fame and reputation are made, and any bookseller will snap at what you write."

I then told him that I could not but really and unaffectedly regret that the affair was spread to Mrs. Williams and her friends.

"Pho," said he, "if those who are proper judges think it right that it should be known, why should you trouble yourself about it? You have not spread it; there can be no imputation of vanity fall to your share; and it cannot come out more to your honour than through such a channel as Mrs. Thrale."

London, August. — I have now to write an account of the most consequential day I have spent since my birth: namely, my Streatham visit.

Our journey to Streatham was the least pleasant part of the day, for the roads were dreadfully dusty, and I was really in the fidgets from thinking what my reception might be, and from fearing they would expect a less awkward and backward kind of person than I was sure they would find.

Mr. Thrale's house is white, and very pleasantly situated, in a fine paddock. Mrs. Thrale was strolling about, and came to us as we got out of the chaise.

"Ah," cried she, "I hear Dr. Burney's voice! And you have brought your daughter? — well, now you are good!"

She then received me, taking both my hands, and with mixed politeness and cordiality welcoming me to Streatham. She led me into the house, and addressed herself almost wholly for a few minutes to my father, as if to give me an assurance she did not mean to regard me as a show, or to distress or frighten me by drawing me out. Afterwards she took me upstairs, and showed me the house, and said she had very much wished to see me at Streatham, and should always think herself much obliged to Dr. Burney for his goodness in bringing me, which she looked upon as a very great favour.

But though we were some time together, and though she was so very civil, she did not hint at my book, and I love her much more than ever for her delicacy in avoiding a subject which she could not but see would have greatly embarrassed me.

When we returned to the music-room, we

found Miss Thrale was with my father. Miss Thrale is a very fine girl, about fourteen years of age, but cold and reserved, though full of knowledge and intelligence.

Soon after, Mrs. Thrale took me to the library; she talked a little while upon common topics, and then, at last, she mentioned *Evelina*.

"Yesterday at supper," said she, "we talked it all over, and discussed all your characters; but Dr. Johnson's favourite is *Mr. Smith. He declares the fine gentleman *manqué* was never better drawn; and he acted him all the evening, saying he was 'all for the ladies!' He repeated whole scenes by heart. I declare I was astonished at him. Oh, you can't imagine how much he is pleased with the book; he 'could not get rid of the rogue,' he told me. But was it not droll," said she, "that I should recommend it to Dr. Burney? and tease him, so innocently, to read it?"

I now prevailed upon Mrs. Thrale to let me amuse myself, and she went to dress. I then prowled about to choose some book, and I saw, upon the reading-table, *Evelina*. I had just fixed upon a new translation of Cicero's *Lælius* when the library door was opened, and *Mr. Seward entered. I instantly put away my book, because I dreaded being thought studious and affected. He offered his service to find anything for me, and then in the same breath, ran on to speak of the book with which I had myself "favoured the world!"

The exact words he began with I cannot recollect, for I was actually confounded by the attack; and his abrupt manner of letting me know he was *au fait* equally astonished and provoked me. How different from the delicacy of Mr. and Mrs. Thrale!

When we were summoned to dinner, Mrs. Thrale made my father and me sit on each side of her. I said that I hoped I did not take Dr. Johnson's place, for he had not yet appeared.

"No," answered Mrs. Thrale, "he will sit by you, which I am sure will give him great pleasure."

Soon after we were seated, this great man entered. I have so true a veneration for him that the very sight of him inspires me with delight and reverence, notwithstanding the cruel infirmities to which he is subject; for he has almost perpetual convulsive movements, either of his hands, lips, feet, or knees, and sometimes of all together.

Mrs. Thrale introduced me to him, and he took his place. We had a noble dinner, and a most elegant dessert. Dr. Johnson, in the middle of dinner, asked Mrs. Thrale what was in some little pies that were near him.

"Mutton," answered she; "so I don't ask you to eat any, because I know you despise it."

"No, madam, no," cried he, "I despise nothing that is good of its sort; but I am too proud now to eat of it. Sitting by Miss Burney makes me very proud today!"

"Miss Burney," said Mrs. Thrale, laughing, "you must take great care of your heart if Dr. Johnson attacks it; for I assure you he is not often successless."

"What's that you say, madam?" cried he. "Are you making mischief between the young lady and me already?"

A little while after he drank Miss Thrale's health and mine, and then added: "'Tis a terrible thing that we cannot wish young ladies well without wishing them to become old women!"

"But some people," said Mr. Seward, "are old and young at the same time, for they wear so well that they never look old."

"No, sir, no," cried the doctor, laughing; "that never yet was; you might as well say they are at the same time tall and short. I remember an epitaph to that purpose, which is in —" (I have quite forgot what, and also the name it was made upon, but the rest I recollect exactly:)

"—— lies buried here;
So early wise, so lasting fair,
That none, unless her years you told,
Thought her a child, or thought her old."

Mr. Thrale then repeated some lines in French, and Dr. Johnson some more in Latin. An epilogue of Mr. Garrick's to **Bonduca* was then mentioned, and Dr. Johnson said it was a miserable performance, and everybody agreed it was the worst he had ever made.

"And yet," said Mr. Seward, "it has been very much admired; but it is in praise of English valour, and so I suppose the subject made it popular."

"I don't know, sir," said Dr. Johnson, "anything about the subject, for I could not read on till I came to it; I got through half a dozen lines, but I could observe no other subject than eternal dullness. I don't know what is the matter with David; I am afraid he is grown superannuated, for his prologues and epilogues used to be incomparable."

"Nothing is so fatiguing," said Mrs. Thrale, "as the life of a wit. He and *Wilkes are the two oldest men of their ages I know, for they have both worn themselves out by being eternally on the rack to give entertainment to others."

"David, madam," said the doctor, "looks much older than he is; for his face has had double the business of any other man's. It is never at rest; when he speaks one minute, he has quite a different countenance to what he assumes the next; I don't believe he ever kept the same look for half an hour together in the whole course of his life; and such an eternal, restless, fatiguing play of the muscles must certainly wear out a man's face before its real time."

"Oh, yes," cried Mrs. Thrale, "we must certainly make some allowance for such wear and tear of a man's face."

The next name that was started was that of *Sir John Hawkins, and Mrs. Thrale said, "Why, now, Dr. Johnson, he is another of those whom you suffer nobody to abuse but yourself; Garrick is one, too; for if any other person speaks against him, you browbeat him in a minute!"

"Why, madam," answered he, "they don't know when to abuse him, and when to praise him. I will allow no man to speak ill of David that he does not deserve; and as to Sir John, why, really I believe him to be an honest man at the bottom; but to be sure he is penurious, and he is mean, and it must be owned he has a degree of brutality and a tendency to savageness that cannot easily be defended."

We all laughed, as he meant we should, at this curious manner of speaking in his favour; and he then related an anecdote that he said he knew to be true in regard to his meanness. He said that Sir John and he once belonged to the same club, but that as he eat no supper after the first night of his admission, he desired to be excused paying his share.

"And was he excused?"

"Oh, yes, for no man is angry at another for being inferior to himself; we all scorned him, and admitted his plea. For my part, I was such a fool as to pay my share for wine, though I never tasted any. But Sir John was a most *unclubbable* man!"

How delighted was I to hear this master of languages so unaffectedly and sociably and good-naturedly make words, for the promotion of sport and good humour. *And this," continued he, "reminds me of a gentleman and lady with whom I traveled once; I suppose I must call them gentleman and lady, according to form, because they traveled in their own coach and four horses. But at the first inn where we stopped, the lady called for — a pint of ale! and when it came, quarreled with the waiter for not giving full measure. Now *Madame Duval could not have done a grosser thing!"

Oh, how everybody laughed! and to be sure I did not glow at all, nor munch fast, nor look on my plate, nor lose any part of my usual composure! But how grateful do I feel to this dear Dr. Johnson, for never naming me and the book as belonging one to the other, and yet making an allusion that showed his thoughts led to it, and, at the same time, that seemed to justify the character as being natural! But indeed, the delicacy I met with from him, and from all the Thrales, was yet more flattering to me than the praise with which I have heard they have honoured my book.

After dinner, when Mrs. Thrale and I left the gentlemen, we had a conversation that to me could not but be delightful, as she was all good-humour, spirits, sense and **agreeability*. Surely I may make words, when at a loss, if Dr. Johnson does.

However I shall not attempt to write any more particulars of this day — than which I have never known a happier, because the chief subject that was started and kept up was an invitation for me to Streatham, and a desire that I might accompany my father thither next week, and stay with them some time.

We left Streatham at about eight o'clock, and Mr. Seward, who handed me into the chaise, added his interest to the rest that my father would not fail to bring me again next week to stay with them some time. In short I was loaded with civilities from them all. And my ride home was equally happy with the rest of the day, for my kind and most beloved father was so happy in my happiness, and congratulated me so sweetly, that he could, like myself, think on no other subject; and he told me that, after passing through such a house as that, I could have nothing to fear — meaning for my book, my honoured book.

[1842–46]

SIR JOSHUA REYNOLDS

Sir Joshua Reynolds was not only the most famous English painter of his day, but he was closely associated with literature both through his friends and his writings. He was one of the original members of Johnson's Club and was an intimate friend of Johnson, Burke, and Goldsmith; he contributed three essays to the *Idler*, published *A Journey to Flanders and Holland* and an annotated translation of Du Fresnoy's *Art of Painting.* But his most important work is *Fifteen Discourses.* These were delivered before the Royal Academy, of which he was the first president, over an interval of more than twenty years, from its opening in 1769 until he took his leave in 1790.

Boswell says of Johnson, "Though he had no taste for painting, he admired much the manner in which Sir Joshua Reynolds treated of his art in his *Discourses to the Royal Academy.* He observed one day of a passage in them, 'I think I might as well have said this myself.'" Johnson, indeed, always considered Reynolds as one of his literary school. The principles of art that the latter expounds and applies are the principles of neo-classicism; they apply equally to poetry and to painting. Reynolds constantly recognizes the fact that certain fundamental principles are common to all the arts: in the Thirteenth Discourse he shows the relation of imagination to nature by illustrations drawn from poetry, painting, acting, gardening, and architecture. Because of their clarity and directness Reynolds's *Discourses* form one of the best statements ever formulated of neo-classical critical principles. No single contemporary work devoted primarily to literature accomplished this task so well.

The Sixth Discourse, which is here given in full, is an admirable presentation of the theory of imitation. The student should compare it carefully with Young's *Conjectures on Original Composition,* published fifteen years before Reynolds spoke these words. These two documents sum up very well the controversy over original genius in the third quarter of the eighteenth century.

FIFTEEN DISCOURSES DELIVERED IN THE ROYAL ACADEMY

DISCOURSE VI

DELIVERED TO THE STUDENTS OF THE ROYAL ACADEMY, ON THE DISTRIBUTION OF THE PRIZES, DECEMBER 10, 1774.

Gentlemen,

When I have taken the liberty of addressing you on the course and order of your studies, I never proposed to enter into a minute detail of the art. This I have always left to the several professors, who pursue the end of our institution with the highest honour to themselves, and with the greatest advantage to the students.

My purpose in the discourses I have held in the Academy has been to lay down certain general positions which seem to me proper for the formation of a sound taste, principles necessary to guard the pupils against those errors into which the sanguine temper common to their time of life has a tendency to lead them, and which have rendered abortive the hopes of so many successions of promising young men in all parts of Europe. I wished also to intercept and suppress those prejudices which particularly prevail when the mechanism of painting is come to its perfection, and which, when they do prevail, are certain utterly to destroy the higher and more valuable parts of this literate and liberal profession.

These two have been my principal purposes; they are still as much my concern as ever; and if I repeat my own notions on the subject, you who know how fast mistake and prejudice, when neglected, gain ground upon truth and reason, will easily excuse me. I only attempt to set the same thing in the greatest variety of lights.

The subject of this discourse will be imitation, as far as a painter is concerned in it. By imitation, I do not mean imitation in its largest sense, but simply the following of other masters and the advantage to be drawn from the study of their works.

Those who have undertaken to write on our art, and have represented it as a kind of *inspiration,* as a *gift* bestowed upon peculiar favourites at their birth, seem to insure a much more favourable disposition from their readers, and have a much more captivating and liberal air, than he who attempts to examine, coldly, whether there are any means by which this art may be acquired, how the mind may be strengthened and expanded, and what guides will show the way to eminence.

It is very natural for those who are unacquainted with the *cause* of anything extraordinary, to be astonished at the *effect*, and to consider it as a kind of magic. They, who have never observed the gradation by which art is acquired, who see only what is the full result of long labour and application of an infinite number and infinite variety of acts, are apt to conclude from their entire inability to do the same at once that it is not only inaccessible to themselves, but can be done by those only who have some gift of the nature of inspiration bestowed upon them.

The travellers into the East tell us that when the ignorant inhabitants of those countries are asked concerning the ruins of stately edifices yet remaining amongst them, the melancholy monuments of their former grandeur and long-lost science, they always answer that they were built by magicians. The untaught mind finds a vast gulf between its own powers and those works of complicated art which it is utterly unable to fathom, and it supposes that such a void can be passed only by supernatural powers.

And, as for artists themselves, it is by no means their interest to undeceive such judges, however conscious they may be of the very natural means by which their extraordinary powers were acquired; though our art, being intrinsically imitative, rejects this idea of inspiration, more perhaps than any other.

It is to avoid this plain confession of truth, as it should seem, that this imitation of masters, indeed almost all imitation, which implies a more regular and progressive method of attaining the ends of painting, has ever been particularly inveighed against with great keenness, both by ancient and modern writers.

To derive all from native power, to owe nothing to another, is the praise which men who do not much think on what they are saying bestow sometimes upon others, and sometimes on themselves; and their imaginary dignity is naturally heightened by a supercilious censure of the low, the barren, the grovelling, the servile imitator. It would be no wonder if a student, frightened by these terrific and disgraceful epithets with which the poor imitators are so often loaded should let fall his pencil in mere despair (conscious as he must be, how much he has been indebted to the labours of others, how little, how very little of his art was born with him), and consider it as hopeless, to set about acquiring by the imitation of any human master what he is taught to suppose is matter of inspiration from heaven.

Some allowance must be made for what is said in the gaiety of rhetoric. We cannot suppose that any one can really mean to exclude all imitation of others. A position so wild would scarce deserve a serious answer; for it is apparent if we were forbid to make use of the advantages which our predecessors afford us, the art would be always to begin, and consequently remain always in its infant state; and it is a common observation that no art was ever invented and carried to perfection at the same time.

But to bring us entirely to reason and sobriety, let it be observed that a painter must not only be of necessity an imitator of the works of nature, which alone is sufficient to dispel this phantom of inspiration, but he must be as necessarily an imitator of the works of other painters; this appears more humiliating, but is equally true, and no man can be an artist, whatever he may suppose, upon any other terms.

However, those who appear more moderate and reasonable allow that our study is to begin by imitation, but maintain that we should no longer use the thoughts of our predecessors when we are become able to think for ourselves. They hold that imitation is as hurtful to the more advanced student as it was advantageous to the beginner.

For my own part, I confess I am not only very much disposed to maintain the absolute necessity of imitation in the first stages of the art, but am of opinion that the study of other masters, which I here call imitation, may be extended throughout our whole lives without any danger of the inconveniences with which it is charged, of enfeebling the mind, or preventing us from giving that original air which every work undoubtedly ought always to have.

I am on the contrary persuaded that by imitation only variety, and even originality of invention, is produced. I will go further; even genius, at least what generally is so called, is the child of imitation. But as this appears to be contrary to the general opinion, I must explain my position before I enforce it.

Genius is supposed to be a power of producing excellences which are out of the reach of the rules of art, a power which no precepts can teach and which no industry can acquire.

This opinion of the impossibility of acquiring those beauties which stamp the work with the character of genius supposes that it is something more fixed than in reality it is, and that we always do, and ever did, agree in opinion with respect to what should be considered as the characteristic of genius. But the truth is that the *degree* of excellence which proclaims *genius* is different in different times and different places, and what shows it to be so is that mankind have often changed their opinion upon this matter.

When the arts were in their infancy, the power of merely drawing the likeness of any object was considered as one of its greatest efforts. The common people, ignorant of the principles of art, talk the same language even to this day. But when it was found that every man could be taught to do this, and a great deal more, merely by the observance of certain precepts, the name of genius then shifted its application, and was given only to him who added the peculiar character of the object he represented; to him who had invention, expression, grace, or dignity; in short, those qualities or excellences the power of producing which could not *then* be taught by any known and promulgated rules.

We are very sure that the beauty of form, the expression of the passions, the art of composition, even the power of giving a general air of grandeur to a work, is at present very much under the dominion of rules. These excellences were, heretofore, considered merely as the effects of genius, and justly, if genius is not taken for inspiration, but as the effect of close observation and experience.

He who first made any of these observations, and digested them so as to form an invariable principle for himself to work by, had that merit, but probably no one went very far at once; and generally the first who gave the hint did not know how to pursue it steadily and methodically, at least not in the beginning. He himself worked on it and improved it; others worked more and improved further, until the secret was discovered and the practice made as general as refined practice can be made. How many more principles may be fixed and ascertained we cannot tell; but, as criticism is likely to go hand in hand with the art which is its subject, we may venture to say that as that art shall advance, its powers will be still more and more fixed by rules.

But by whatever strides criticism may gain ground, we need be under no apprehension that invention will ever be annihilated or subdued, or intellectual energy be brought entirely within the restraint of written law. Genius will still have room enough to expatiate, and keep always at the same distance from narrow comprehension and mechanical performance.

What we now call genius begins, not where rules, abstractedly taken, end, but where known vulgar and trite rules have no longer any place. It must of necessity be that even works of genius, like every other effect, as they must have their cause, must likewise have their rules; it cannot be by chance that excellences are produced with any constancy or any certainty, for this is not the nature of chance; but the rules by which men of extraordinary parts, and such as are called men of genius, work are either such as they discover by their own peculiar observations, or of such a nice texture as not easily to admit being expressed in words, especially as artists are not very frequently skillful in that mode of communicating ideas. Unsubstantial, however, as these rules may seem, and difficult as it may be to convey them in writing, they are still seen and felt in the mind of the artist; and he works from them with as much certainty as if they were embodied, as I may say, upon paper. It is true, these refined principles cannot be always made palpable, like the more gross rules of art; yet it does not follow but that the mind may be put in such a train that it shall perceive, by a kind of scientific sense, that propriety which words, particularly words of unpractised writers, such as we are, can but very feebly suggest.

Invention is one of the great marks of genius; but if we consult experience, we shall find that it is by being conversant with the inventions of others that we learn to invent, as by reading the thoughts of others we learn to think.

Whoever has so far formed his taste as to be able to relish and feel the beauties of the great masters has gone a great way in his study; for, merely from a consciousness of this relish of the right, the mind swells with an inward pride, and is almost as powerfully affected as if it had itself produced what it admires. Our hearts, frequently warmed in this manner by the contact of those whom we wish to resemble, will undoubtedly catch something of their way of thinking, and we shall receive in our own bosoms some radiation at least of their fire and splendour. That disposition which is so strong in children still continues with us, of catching involuntarily the general air and manner of those with whom we are most conversant; with this difference only, that a young mind is naturally pliable and imitative, but in a more advanced state it grows rigid, and must be warmed and softened before it will receive a deep impression.

From these considerations, which a little of your own reflection will carry a great way further, it appears of what great consequence it is that our minds should be habituated to the contemplation of excellence, and that, far from being contented to make such habits the discipline of our youth only, we should, to the last moment of our lives, continue a settled intercourse with all the true examples of grandeur. Their inventions are not only the food of our infancy, but the substance which supplies the fullest maturity of our vigour.

The mind is but a barren soil, a soil which is soon exhausted and will produce no crop, or only one, unless it be continually fertilised and enriched with foreign matter.

When we have had continually before us the great works of art to impregnate our minds with kindred ideas, we are then, and not till then, fit to produce something of the same species. We behold all about us with the eyes of those penetrating observers whose works we contemplate; and our minds, accustomed to think the thoughts of the noblest and brightest intellects, are prepared for the discovery and selection of all that is great and noble in nature. The greatest natural genius cannot subsist on its own stock: he who resolves never to ransack any mind but his own will be soon reduced, from mere barrenness, to the poorest of all imitations; he will be obliged to imitate himself, and to repeat what he has before often repeated. When we know the subject designed by such men, it will never be difficult to guess what kind of work is to be produced.

It is vain for painters or poets to endeavour to invent without materials on which the mind may work, and from which invention must originate. Nothing can come of nothing.

Homer is supposed to be possessed of all the learning of his time, and we are certain that Michael Angelo and Raphael were equally possessed of all the knowledge in the art which had been discovered in the works of their predecessors.

A mind enriched by an assemblage of all the treasures of ancient and modern art will be more elevated and fruitful in resources, in proportion to the number of ideas which have been carefully collected and thoroughly digested. There can be no doubt but that he who has the most materials has the greatest means of invention; and if he has not the power of using them, it must proceed from a feebleness of intellect, or from the confused manner in which those collections have been laid up in his mind.

The addition of other men's judgment is so far from weakening our own, as is the opinion of many, that it will fashion and consolidate those ideas of excellence which lay in embryo, feeble, ill-shaped, and confused, but which are finished and put in order by the authority and practice of those, whose works may be said to have been consecrated by having stood the test of ages.

The mind, or genius, has been compared to a spark of fire, which is smothered by a heap of fuel, and prevented from blazing into a flame: this simile, which is made use of by the younger Pliny, may be easily mistaken for argument or proof. But there is no danger of the mind's being overburdened with knowledge, or the genius extinguished by any addition of images; on the contrary, these acquisitions may as well, perhaps better, be compared, if comparisons signified anything in reasoning, to the supply of living embers, which will contribute to strengthen the spark that without the association of more fuel would have died away. The truth is, he whose feebleness is such as to make other men's thoughts an incumbrance to him can have no very great strength of mind or genius of his own to be destroyed, so that not much harm will be done at worst.

We may oppose to Pliny the greater authority of Cicero, who is continually enforcing the necessity of this method of study. In his dialogue on Oratory, he makes Crassus say that one of the first and most important precepts is to choose a proper model for our imitation. *Hoc sit primum in præceptis meis, ut demonstremus quem imitemur.*

When I speak of the habitual imitation and continued study of masters, it is not to be understood that I advise any endeavour to copy the exact peculiar colour and complexion of another man's mind; the success of such an attempt must always be like his, who imitates exactly the air, manner, and gestures of him whom he admires. His model may be excellent, but the copy will be ridiculous; this ridicule does not arise from his having imitated, but from his not having chosen the right mode of imitation.

It is necessary and warrantable pride to disdain to walk servilely behind any individual, however elevated his rank. The true and liberal ground of imitation is an open field, where, though he who precedes has had the advantage of starting before you, you may always propose to overtake him: it is enough, however, to pursue his course; you need not tread in his footsteps; and you certainly have a right to outstrip him if you can.

Nor whilst I recommend studying the art from artists can I be supposed to mean that nature is to be neglected; I take this study in aid, and not in exclusion, of the other. Nature is, and must be the fountain which alone is inexhaustible, and from which all excellences must originally flow.

The great use of studying our predecessors is to open the mind, to shorten our labour, and to give us the result of the selection made by those great minds of what is grand or beautiful in nature: her rich stores are all spread out before us; but it is an art, and no easy art, to know how or what to choose, and how to attain and secure the object of our choice. Thus the highest beauty of form must be taken from nature; but it is an art of long deduction and great experience to know how to find it. We must not content ourselves with merely admiring and relishing; we must enter into the principles on which the work is wrought: these do not swim on the superficies, and consequently are not open to superficial observers.

Art in its perfection is not ostentatious; it lies hid, and works its effect, itself unseen. It is the proper study and labour of an artist to uncover and find out the latent cause of conspicuous beauties, and from thence form principles of his own conduct; such an examination is a continual exertion of the mind, as great, perhaps, as that of the artist whose works he is thus studying.

The sagacious imitator does not content himself with merely remarking what distinguishes the different manner or genius of each master; he enters into the contrivance in the composition how the masses of lights are disposed, the means by which the effect is produced, how artfully some parts are lost in the ground, others boldly relieved, and how all these are mutually altered and interchanged according to the reason and scheme of the work. He admires not the harmony of colouring alone, but examines by what artifice one colour is a foil to its neighbour. He looks close into the tints, examines of what colours they are composed, till he has formed clear and distinct ideas, and has learned to see in what, harmony and good colouring consists. What is learned in this manner from the works of others, becomes really our own, sinks deep, and is never forgotten; nay, it is by seizing on this clue that we proceed forward, and get further and further in enlarging the principles and improving the practice of our art.

There can be no doubt but the art is better learned from the works themselves than from the precepts which are formed upon those works; but if it is difficult to choose proper models for imitation; it requires no less circumspection to separate and distinguish what in those models we ought to imitate.

I cannot avoid mentioning here, though it is not my intention at present to enter into the art and method of study, an error which students are too apt to fall into. He that is forming himself must look with great caution and wariness on those peculiarities, or prominent parts, which at first force themselves upon view, and are the marks, or what is commonly called the manner, by which that individual artist is distinguished.

Peculiar marks I hold to be, generally, if not always, defects, however difficult it may be wholly to escape them.

Peculiarities in the works of art are like those in the human figure; it is by them that we are cognizable and distinguished one from another; but they are always so many blemishes, which, however, both in real life and in painting, cease to appear deformities to those who have them continually before their eyes. In the works of art even the most enlightened mind, when warmed by beauties of the highest kind, will by degrees find a repugnance within him to acknowledge any defects; nay, his enthusiasm will carry him so far as to transform them into beauties and objects of imitation.

It must be acknowledged that a peculiarity of style, either from its novelty or by seeming to proceed from a peculiar turn of mind, often escapes blame; on the contrary, it is sometimes striking and pleasing: but this it is a vain labour to endeavour to imitate, because novelty and peculiarity being its only merit, when it ceases to be new, it ceases to have value.

A manner, therefore, being a defect, and every painter, however excellent, having a manner, it seems to follow that all kinds of faults, as well as beauties, may be learned under the sanction of the greatest authorities. Even the great name of Michael Angelo may be used to keep in countenance a deficiency, or rather neglect, of colouring and every other ornamental part of the art. If the young student is dry and hard, Poussin is the same. If his work has a careless and unfinished air, he has most of the Venetian school to support him. If he makes no selection of objects, but takes individual nature just as he finds it, he is like Rembrandt. If he is incorrect in the proportions of his figures, Correggio was likewise incorrect. If his colours are not blended and united, Rubens was equally crude. In short, there is no defect that may not be excused if it is a sufficient excuse that it can be imputed to considerable artists; but it must be remembered that it was not by these defects they acquired their reputation: they have a right to our pardon, but not to our admiration.

However, to imitate peculiarities or mistake defects for beauties, that man will be most liable who confines his imitation to one favourite master; and even though he chooses the best, and is capable of distinguishing the real excellences of his model, it is not by such narrow practice that a genius or mastery in the art is acquired. A man is as little likely to form a true idea of the perfection of the art by studying a single artist, as he would be to produce a perfectly beautiful figure by an exact imitation of any individual living model. And as the painter, by bringing together in one piece those beauties which are dispersed among a great variety of individuals, produces a figure more beautiful than can be found in nature, so that artist who can unite in himself the excellences of the various great painters, will approach nearer to perfection than any one of his masters. He who confines himself to the imitation of an individual, as he never proposes to surpass, so he is not likely to equal, the object of his imitation. He professes only to follow, and he that follows must necessarily be behind.

We should imitate the conduct of the great artists in the course of their studies, as well as the works which they produced when they were perfectly formed. Raphael began by imitating implicitly the manner of Pietro Perugino, under whom he studied; hence his first works are scarce to be distinguished from his master's; but, soon forming higher and more extensive views, he imitated the grand outline of Michael Angelo; he learned the manner of using colours from the works of Leonardo da Vinci and Fratre Bartolomeo: to all this he added the contemplation of all the remains of antiquity that were within his reach, and employed others to draw for him what was in Greece and distant places. And it is from his having taken so many models that he became himself a model for all succeeding painters, always imitating, and always original.

If your ambition, therefore, be to equal Raphael, you must do as Raphael did, take many models, and not even *him* for your guide alone, to the exclusion of others. And yet the number is infinite of those who seem, if one may judge by their style, to have seen no other works but those of their master, or of some favourite, whose *manner* is their first wish and their last.

I will mention a few that occur to me of this narrow, confined, illiberal, unscientific, and servile kind of imitators. *Guido was thus meanly copied by Elisabetta Sirani, and Simone Cantarini; Poussin, by Verdier and Cheron; Parmeggiano, by Jeronimo Mazzuoli. Paolo Veronese and Iacomo Bassan had for their imitators their brothers and sons. Pietro da Cortona was followed by Ciro Ferri and Romanelli; Rubens, by Jacques Jordaens and Diepenbeke; Guercino, by his own family, the Gennari. Carlo Maratti was imitated by Giuseppe Chiari and Pietro da Pietri; and Rembrandt, by Bramer, Eeckhout, and Flink. All these, to whom may be added a much longer list of painters, whose works among

* Notes on Sir Joshua Reynolds will be found in the Appendix, p. 1035.

the ignorant pass for those of their masters, are justly to be censured for barrenness and servility.

To oppose to this list a few that have adopted a more liberal style of imitation: Pellegrino Tibaldi, Rosso, and Primaticcio did not coldly imitate, but caught something of the fire that animates the works of Michael Angelo. The Caraccis formed their style from Pellegrino Tibaldi, Correggio, and the Venetian school. Domenichino, Guido, Lanfranco, Albano, Guercino, Cavidone, Schidone, Tiarini, though it is sufficiently apparent that they came from the school of the Caraccis, have yet the appearance of men who extended their views beyond the model that lay before them, and have shown that they had opinions of their own, and thought for themselves, after they had made themselves masters of the general principles of their schools.

Le Suer's first manner resembles very much that of his master Voüet; but as he soon excelled him, so he differed from him in every part of the art. Carlo Maratti succeeded better than those I have first named, and I think owes his superiority to the extension of his views; beside his master Andrea Sacchi, he imitated Raphael, Guido, and the Caraccis. It is true there is nothing very captivating in Carlo Maratti; but this proceeded from a want which cannot be completely supplied, that is, want of strength of parts. In this certainly men are not equal, and a man can bring home wares only in proportion to the capital with which he goes to market. Carlo by diligence made the most of what he had; but there was undoubtedly a heaviness about him which extended itself, uniformly, to his invention, expression, his drawing, colouring, and the general effect of his pictures. The truth is he never equalled any of his patterns in any one thing, and he added little of his own.

But we must not rest contented even in this general study of the moderns; we must trace back the art to its fountainhead, to that source from whence they drew their principal excellences, the monuments of pure antiquity. All the inventions and thoughts of the ancients, whether conveyed to us in statues, bas-reliefs, intaglios, cameos, or coins, are to be sought after and carefully studied; the genius that hovers over these venerable relics may be called the father of modern art.

From the remains of the works of the ancients the modern arts were revived, and it is by their means that they must be restored a second time. However it may mortify our vanity, we must be forced to allow them our masters; and we may venture to prophesy that when they shall cease to be studied, arts will no longer flourish, and we shall again relapse into barbarism.

The fire of the artist's own genius operating upon these materials which have been thus diligently collected, will enable him to make new combinations, perhaps superior to what had ever before been in the possession of the art; as in the mixture of the variety of metals, which are said to have been melted and run together at the burning of Corinth, a new and till then unknown metal was produced, equal in value to any of those that had contributed to its composition. And though a curious refiner should come with his crucibles, analyse and separate its various component parts, yet Corinthian brass would still hold its rank amongst the most beautiful and valuable of metals.

We have hitherto considered the advantages of imitation as it tends to form the taste, and as a practice by which a spark of that genius may be caught, which illumines those noble works that ought always to be present to our thoughts.

We come now to speak of another kind of imitation, the borrowing a particular thought, an action, attitude, or figure, and transplanting it into your own work; this will either come under the charge of plagiarism, or be warrantable and deserve commendation, according to the address with which it is performed. There is some difference likewise, whether it is upon the ancients or moderns that these depredations are made. It is generally allowed that no man need be ashamed of copying the ancients; their works are considered as a magazine of common property, always open to the public, whence every man has a right to take what materials he pleases; and if he has the art of using them, they are supposed to become to all intents and purposes his own property. The collection of the thoughts of the ancients, which Raphael made with so much trouble, is a proof of his opinion on this subject. Such collections may be made with much more ease, by means of an art scarce known in his time; I mean that of engraving, by which, at an easy rate, every man may now avail himself of the inventions of antiquity.

It must be acknowledged that the works of the moderns are more the property of their authors. He who borrows an idea from an ancient, or even from a modern artist not his contemporary, and so accommodates it to his own work that it makes a part of it, with no seam or joining appearing, can hardly be charged with plagiarism; poets practise this kind of borrowing without reserve. But an artist should not be contented with this only; he should enter into a competition with his original, and endeavour to improve what he is appropriating to his own work. Such imitation is so far from having anything in it of the servility of plagiarism that it is a perpetual exercise of the mind, a continual invention. Borrowing or stealing with such art and caution will have a right to the same lenity as was used by the Lacedemonians, who did not punish theft, but the want of artifice to conceal it.

In order to encourage you to imitation to the utmost extent, let me add that very finished artists in the inferior branches of the art will contribute to furnish the mind and give hints, of which a skillful painter, who is sensible of what he wants and is in no danger of being infected by the contact of vicious models, will know how to avail himself. He will pick up from dunghills what by a nice chemistry, passing through his own mind, shall be converted into pure gold; and under the rudeness of * Gothic essays, he will find original, rational, and even sublime inventions.

The works of Albert Dürer, Lucas Van Leyden, the numerous inventions of Tobias Stimmer and Jost Ammon afford a rich mass of genuine materials, which wrought up and polished to elegance, will add copiousness to what, perhaps, without such aid, could have aspired only to justness and propriety.

In * the luxuriant style of Paul Veronese, in the capricious compositions of Tintoret, he will find something that will assist his invention, and give points from which his own imagination shall rise and take flight, when the subject which he treats will with propriety admit of splendid effects.

In every school, whether Venetian, French, or Dutch, he will find either ingenious compositions, extraordinary effects, some peculiar expressions, or some mechanical excellence, well worthy of his attention and, in some measure, of his imitation. Even in the lower class of the French painters great beauties are often found, united with great defects. Though Coypel wanted a simplicity of taste, and mistook a presumptuous and assuming air for what is grand and majestic, yet he frequently has good sense and judgment in his manner of telling his stories, great skill in his compositions, and is not without a considerable power of expressing the passions. The modern affectation of grace in his works, as well as in those of Bosch and Watteau, may be said to be separated by a very thin partition from the more simple and pure grace of Correggio and Parmegiano.

Among the Dutch painters the correct, firm, and determined pencil, which was employed by Bamboccio and Jean Miel on vulgar and mean subjects, might, without any change, be employed on the highest, to which, indeed, it seems more properly to belong. The greatest style, if that style is confined to small figures such as Poussin generally painted, would receive an additional grace by the elegance and precision of pencil so admirable in the works of Teniers; and though the school to which he belonged more particularly excelled in the mechanism of painting, yet it produced many who have shown great abilities in expressing what must be ranked above mechanical excellences. In the works of Frans Hals the portrait-painter may observe the composition of a face, the features well put together, as the painters express it, from whence proceeds that strong-marked character of individual nature which is so remarkable in his portraits, and is not found in an equal degree in any other painter. If he had joined to this most difficult part of the art a patience in finishing what he had so correctly planned, he might justly have claimed the place which Vandyck, all things considered, so justly holds as the first of portrait-painters.

Others of the same school have shown great power in expressing the character and passions of those vulgar people which were the subjects of their study and attention. Among those Jan Steen seems to be one of the most diligent and accurate observers of what passed in those scenes which he frequented, and which were to him an academy. I can easily imagine that if this extraordinary man had had the good fortune to have been born in Italy instead of Holland, had he lived in Rome instead of Leyden, and been blessed with Michael Angelo and Raphael for his masters instead of Brouwer and Van Goyen, the same sagacity and penetration which distinguished so accurately the different characters and expression in his vulgar figures, would, when exerted in the selection and imitation of what was great and elevated in nature, have been equally successful; and he now would have ranged with the great pillars and supporters of our art.

Men who, although thus bound down by the almost invincible powers of early habits, have still exerted extraordinary abilities within their narrow and confined circle, and have, from the natural vigour of their mind, given a very interesting expression and great force and energy to their works, though they cannot be recommended to be exactly imitated, may yet invite an artist to endeavour to transfer, by a kind of parody, their excellences to his own performances. Whoever has acquired the power of making this use of the Flemish, Venetian, and French schools is a real genius, and has sources of knowledge open to him which were wanting to the great artists who lived in the great age of painting.

To find excellences, however dispersed, to discover beauties, however concealed by the multitude of defects with which they are surrounded, can be the work only of him who, having a mind always alive to his art, has extended his views to all ages and to all schools, and has acquired from that comprehensive mass, which he has thus gathered to himself, a well-digested and perfect idea of his art, to which everything is referred. Like a sovereign judge and arbiter of art he is possessed of that presiding power which separates and attracts every excellence from every school, selects both from what is great, and what is little, brings home knowledge from the East and from the West, making the universe tributary towards furnishing his mind and enriching his works with originality and variety of inventions.

Thus I have ventured to give my opinion of what appears to me the true and only method by which an artist makes himself master of his profession, which I hold ought to be one continued course of imitation that is not to cease but with his life.

Those who, either from their own engagements and hurry of business or from indolence or from conceit and vanity, have neglected looking out of themselves, as far as my experience and observation reaches, have from that time not only ceased to advance and improve in their performances, but have gone backward. They may be compared to men who have lived upon their principal, till they are reduced to beggary and left without resources.

I can recommend nothing better, therefore, than that you endeavour to infuse into your works what you learn from the contemplation of the works of others. To recommend this has the appearance of needless and superfluous advice; but it has fallen within my own knowledge that artists, though they were not wanting in a sincere love for their art, though they had great pleasure in seeing good pictures, and were well skilled to distinguish what was excellent or defective in them, yet have gone on in their own manner without any endeavour to give a little of those beauties which they admired in others to their own works. It is difficult to conceive how the present Italian painters, who live in the midst of the treasures of art, should be contented with their own style. They proceed in their commonplace inventions, and never think it worth while to visit the works of those great artists with which they are surrounded.

I remember, several years ago, to have conversed at Rome with an artist of great fame throughout Europe; he was not without a considerable degree of abilities, but those abilities were by no means equal to his own opinion of them. From the reputation he had acquired, he too fondly concluded that he stood in the same rank, when compared with his predecessors, as he held with regard to his miserable contemporary rivals. In conversation about some particulars of the works of Raphael, he seemed to have, or to affect to have, a very obscure memory of them. He told me that he had not set his foot in the Vatican for fifteen years together, that he had been in treaty to copy a capital picture of Raphael, but that the business had gone off; however, if the agreement had held, his copy would have greatly exceeded the original. The merit of this artist, however great we may suppose it, I am sure would have been far greater, and his presumption would have been far less, if he had visited the Vatican, as in reason he ought to have done, at least once every month of his life.

I address myself, gentlemen, to you who have made some progress in the art, and are to be, for the future, under the guidance of your own judgment and discretion. I consider you as arrived at that period when you have a right to think for yourselves, and to presume that every man is fallible; to study the masters with a suspicion that great men are not always exempt from great faults; to criticise, compare, and rank their works in your own estimation, as they approach to, or recede from, that standard of perfection which you have formed in your own minds, but which those masters themselves, it must be remembered, have taught you to make; and which you will cease to make with correctness when you cease to study them. It is their excellences which have taught you their defects.

I would wish you to forget where you are, and who it is that speaks to you; I only direct you to higher models and better advisers. We can teach you here but very little; you are henceforth to be your own teachers. Do this justice, however, to the English Academy, to bear in mind that in this place you contracted no narrow habits, no false ideas, nothing that could lead you to the imitation of any living master who may be the fashionable darling of the day. As you have not been taught to flatter us, do not learn to flatter yourselves. We have endeavoured to lead you to the admiration of nothing but what is truly admirable. If you choose inferior patterns, or if you make your own *former* works your patterns for your *latter*, it is your own fault.

The purport of this discourse, and, indeed, of most of my other discourses, is to caution you against that false opinion, but too prevalent among artists, of the imaginary powers of native genius and its sufficiency in great works. This opinion, according to the temper of mind it meets with, almost always produces either a vain confidence or a sluggish despair, both equally fatal to all proficiency.

Study, therefore, the great works of the great masters, forever. Study, as nearly as you can, in the order, in the manner, and on the principles on which they studied. Study nature attentively, but always with those masters in your company; consider them as models which you are to imitate, and at the same time as rivals with whom you are to contend.

[1774, 1797]

OLIVER GOLDSMITH

Oliver Goldsmith achieved major excellence in four types of English literature: comedy, non-dramatic poetry, novel, and essay; and also wrote history, natural history, biography, criticism, and translation. As Dr. Johnson said of him in the famous epitaph in Westminster Abbey, there were few kinds of writing that he did not touch and none which he touched that he did not adorn. This astonishing versatility was partly the result of his genius, which enabled him to stamp his personality upon the most widely separated literary *genres*, and partly the result of the conditions of his work, which forced him to turn his facile pen to anything by which he could earn money. He achieved success in literature after having failed at almost everything else: he had prepared himself half-heartedly for holy orders and been rejected; he had set out for London to study law but had lost his funds to a sharper before reaching his destination; he had studied medicine at Edinburgh and continued his studies at Leyden and perhaps elsewhere on the continent, attaining a medical degree of questionable validity; he had wandered over Europe, and had returned to England where he had been successively an apothecary's assistant, an unsuccessful physician, a teacher, and perhaps a player. Inevitably he drifted into Grub Street, working first as a corrector for the press, afterwards as a magazine contributor, and as a writer-of-all-work for various booksellers. His superficial acquaintance with many aspects of life, his cosmopolitan experience, and his knowledge of literature had provided him with an exceptional preparation for the career upon which he had embarked almost in spite of himself.

From Grub Street he never emerged. Johnson, after his pension had provided for his material needs, came up out of Grub Street into the sunshine where literature is the delight of gentlemen and not the task of booksellers' drudges; yet even Johnson bore the marks of his earlier associations. Goldsmith was a bondservant for ever: no pension could have kept him out of debt or relieved him from the consequences of his impecuniosity. Yet the very lighthearted irresponsibility that prevented his emancipation shielded him from the worst results of his servitude. His genial Irish nature remained unspoiled to the end.

Goldsmith's personal peculiarities have been so much emphasized that the real importance of his literary contribution has at times been obscured. The epigram which declares that he "wrote like an angel but talked like poor Poll" presents something less than a half truth at best, but it has usually served to suggest the household pest rather than the superhuman penman. Goldsmith with his petty vanities and his social incapacity and his grotesque appearance has seduced many of his critics into Macaulay-like antitheses. To make the matter worse, Boswell, who obviously did not like him, has left a distorted picture in *The Life of Johnson*. Yet the man who by sheer force of personality and literary art won the recognition of his contemporaries and was honoured by charter membership in Johnson's Club, and has ever since been recognized as a major figure among English men of letters, could never have been the inspired idiot of popular tradition. Johnson recognized the danger of such misunderstanding and tried to guard others against it when he said, "Let not his frailties be remembered; he was a very great man."

ESSAYS

Goldsmith's essays were written chiefly during the earlier part of his literary career. *An Enquiry into the Present State of Polite Learning in Europe*, published in 1759, is properly speaking a treatise, though the chapter that is here excerpted may be read as an independent essay. In *The Bee*, a short-lived periodical published in the autumn of 1759 and reissued late in the same year, he successfully attempted the informal essay. The first *Bee* selection here printed shows him in the familiar rôle of an observant but by no means savage critic of contemporary manners. The second, a Lucianic *Reverie*, illustrates his shrewd though not unbiased estimate of recent literature.

His most important series of essays appeared in the *Public Ledger* between January 24, 1760, and August 14, 1761, under the title, *Chinese Letters*; in 1762 they were published separately in two volumes as *The Citizen of the World: or Letters from a Chinese Philosopher Residing in London to his Friends in the East*. This work was directly influenced by the fashionable Orientalism of the time. Montesquieu's *Lettres Persanes*, 1721, was the most famous exemplar of this type, though not the first, for fourteen years earlier Dufresny had adopted the expedient of showing Paris through the eyes of a visitor from Siam, and Marana in the *Turkish Spy* had employed a similar device as early as 1684. Among many other uses may be mentioned D'Argens' *Lettres Chinoises*, 1739–42, and

Horace Walpole's *Letter from Xo Ho, a Chinese Philosopher at London to his Friend Lien Chi at Peking*, 1757. Recent scholarship has shown that Goldsmith not only borrowed freely but that occasionally he introduced into his essays unacknowledged translations from the French.

However important these Oriental predecessors may have been, Goldsmith's work in *The Citizen of the World* was none the less a legitimate continuation of the *Tatler* and the *Spectator* tradition. Addison had written in *Spectator* No. 50 of the visit of the four Indian kings to London, but this idea had not been followed up. The important point is that Isaac Bickerstaff had been a detached figure, who viewed the humours of the Town somewhat apart from the current of life about him; Mr. Spectator continued this pose even more successfully; his very name indicated his detachment. What Steele and Addison had thus done somewhat artificially, Goldsmith was able to do more naturally under the guise of a philosopher learned in the lore of the East and acquainted with a highly developed but alien society. To such an observer, a true spectator of the pageant of English life, perception of inconsistencies and incongruities would be inevitable. A real citizen of the world would have the basis for an unusual estimate of values as he compared the manners of widely separated peoples. Of course Goldsmith's knowledge of the Orient was inadequate for full realization of the possibilities of his literary device, though he was to a greater degree than most of his countrymen prepared for the rôle of international observer by his Continental experience and especially by his "grand tour afoot."

The Citizen of the World is also important as a link between the collection of essays and the romance. Though the selections here given do not illustrate it, a thread of story runs through these letters, just as a rather large thread of essay runs through *The Vicar of Wakefield*.

In his prose style Goldsmith shows simplicity and colloquial ease. If at times it approaches the journalistic manner, it is saved by his innate taste and also by his acquaintance with French models. He had also learned enough of the Johnsonian balance to add vigour without ponderousness. His style is lucid, direct, and at the same time charming. Addison is more finished, Swift more concise, Burke more magnificent; but Goldsmith is unexcelled in the easy expression of a delightful personality.

*AN INQUIRY INTO THE PRESENT STATE OF POLITE LEARNING IN EUROPE

CHAPTER X

OF THE MARKS OF LITERARY DECAY IN FRANCE AND ENGLAND

The faults already mentioned are such as learning is often found to flourish under; but there is one of a much more dangerous nature, which has begun to fix itself among us: I mean criticism, which may properly be called the natural destroyer of polite learning. We have seen that critics, or those whose only business is to write books upon other books, are always more numerous as learning is more diffused; and experience has shown that, instead of promoting its interest, which they profess to do, they generally injure it. This decay which criticism produces may be deplored, but can scarcely be remedied; as the man who writes against the critics is obliged to add himself to the number. Other depravations in the republic of letters, such as affectation in some popular writer leading others into vicious imitation; political struggles in the state; a depravity of morals among the people; ill directed encouragement or no encouragement from the great, — these have been often found to co-operate in the decline of literature; and it has sometimes declined, as in modern Italy, without them; but an increase of criticism has always portended a decay. * Of all misfortunes, therefore, in the commonwealth of letters, this of judging from rule, and not from feeling, is the most severe. At such a tribunal no work of original merit can please. Sublimity, if carried to an exalted height, approaches burlesque, and humour sinks into vulgarity. The person who cannot feel may ridicule both as such, and bring rules to corroborate his assertion. There is, in short, no excellence in writing that such judges may not place among the neighbouring defects. Rules render the reader more difficult to be pleased, and abridge the author's power of pleasing.

If we turn to either country, we shall perceive evident symptoms of this natural decay beginning to appear. Upon a moderate calculation, there seem to be as many volumes of criticism published in those countries as of all other kinds of polite erudition united. Paris sends forth not less than four literary journals every month — the *Annêe Littêraire* and the *Feuille*, by Fréron; the *Journal Étranger*, by the Chevalier d'Arc, and *Le*

*** Notes on Oliver Goldsmith will be found in the Appendix, pp. 1036 ff.**

Mercure, by Marmontel. We have two literary reviews in London, with critical newspapers and magazines without number. The compilers of these resemble the commoners of Rome; they are all for levelling property, not by increasing their own, but by diminishing that of others. The man who has any good-nature in his disposition must, however, be somewhat displeased to see distinguished reputations often the sport of ignorance, to see by one false pleasantry the future peace of a worthy man's life disturbed, and this only because he has unsuccessfully attempted to instruct or amuse us. Though ill-nature is far from being wit, yet it is generally laughed at as such. The critic enjoys the triumph, and ascribes to his parts what is only due to his effrontery. I fire with indignation when I see persons wholly destitute of education and genius indent to the press, and thus turn book makers, adding to the sin of criticism the sin of ignorance also; whose trade is a bad one, and who are bad workmen in the trade.

When I consider those industrious men as indebted to the works of others for a precarious subsistence, when I see them coming down at stated intervals to rummage the bookseller's counter for materials to work upon, it raises a smile, though mixed with pity. It reminds me of an animal called by naturalists the soldier. "This little creature," says the historian, "is passionately fond of a shell; but not being supplied with one by nature, has recourse to the deserted shell of some other. I have seen these harmless reptiles," continues he, "come down once a year from the mountains, rank and file, cover the whole shore, and ply busily about, each in quest of a shell to please it. Nothing can be more amusing than their industry upon this occasion. One shell is too big, another too little: they enter and keep possession sometimes for a good while, until one is at last found entirely to please. When all are thus properly equipped, they march up again to the mountains, and live in their new acquisition till under a necessity of changing."

There is, indeed, scarcely an error of which our present writers are guilty, that does not arise from their opposing systems; there is scarcely an error that criticism cannot be brought to excuse. From this proceeds the affected security of our odes, the tuneless flow of our blank verse, the pompous epithet, laboured diction, and every other deviation from common sense which procures the poet the applause of the month: he is praised by all, read by a few, and soon forgotten.

There never was an unbeaten path trodden by the poet that the critic did not endeavour to reclaim him by calling his attempt innovation. This might be instanced in Dante, who first followed nature, and was persecuted by the critics as long as he lived. Thus novelty, one of the greatest beauties in poetry, must be avoided, or the connoisseur be displeased. It is one of the chief privileges, however, of genius, to fly from the herd of imitators by some happy singularity; for should he stand still, his heavy pursuers will at length certainly come up, and fairly dispute the victory.

*The ingenious Mr. Hogarth used to assert that every one except the connoisseur was a judge of painting. The same may be asserted of writing: the public in general set the whole piece in the proper point of view; the critic lays his eye close to all its minuteness, and condemns or approves in detail. And this may be the reason why so many writers at present are apt to appeal from the tribunal of criticism to that of the people.

From a desire in the critic of grafting the spirit of ancient languages upon the English have proceeded of late several disagreeable instances of pedantry. Among the number I think we may reckon blank verse. Nothing but the greatest sublimity of subject can render such a measure pleasing; however, we now see it used upon the most trivial occasions. It has particularly found its way into our didactic poetry, and is likely to bring that species of composition into disrepute, for which the English are deservedly famous.

Those who are acquainted with writing know that our language runs almost naturally into blank verse. The writers of our novels, romances, and all of this class who have no notion of style, naturally hobble into this unharmonious measure. If rhymes, therefore, be more difficult, for that very reason I would have our poets write in rhyme. Such a restriction upon the thought of a good poet often lifts and increases the vehemence of every sentiment; for fancy, like a fountain, plays highest by diminishing the aperture. But rhymes, it will be said, are a remnant of monkish stupidity, an innovation upon the poetry of the ancients. They are but indifferently acquainted with antiquity who make the assertion. Rhymes are probably of older date than either the Greek or Latin dactyl and spondee. *The Celtic, which is allowed to be the first language spoken in Europe, has ever preserved them, as we may find in the Edda of Iceland, and the Irish carols, still sung among the original inhabitants of that island. *Olaus Wormius gives us some of the Teutonic poetry in this way; and *Pontoppidan, Bishop of Bergen, some of the Norwegian. In short, this jingle of sounds is almost natural to mankind; at least it is so to our language, if we may judge from many unsuccessful attempts to throw it off.

I should not have employed so much time in opposing this erroneous innovation, if it were not apt to introduce another in its train, I mean a disgusting solemnity of manner, into our poetry; and, as the prose writer has been ever found to follow the poet, it must consequently banish in both all that agreeable trifling which, if I may so express it, often deceives us into instruction. The finest sentiment and the most weighty truth may put on a pleasant face, and it is even virtuous to jest when serious advice must be disgusting. But instead of this, the most trifling performance among us now assumes all the didactic stiffness of wisdom. The most diminutive son of fame or of famine has his *we* and *us*, his *firstlies* and *secondlies*, as methodical as if bound in cowhide and closed with clasps of brass. Were these monthly reviews and magazines frothy, pert, or absurd, they might find some pardon; but to be dull and dronish is an encroachment on the prerogative of a folio. These things should be considered as pills to purge melancholy; they should be made up in our splenetic climate to be taken as physic, and not so as to be used when we take it.

However, by the power of one single monosyllable, our critics have almost got the victory over humour among us. Does the poet paint the absurdities of the vulgar, then he is *low*; does he exaggerate the features of folly to render it more thoroughly ridiculous, he is then *very low*. In short, they have proscribed the comic or satirical muse from every walk but high life; which, though abounding in fools as well as the humblest station, is by no means so fruitful in absurdity. Among well-bred fools we may despise much, but have little to laugh at; nature seems to present us with a universal blank of silk, ribbons, smiles, and whispers. Absurdity is the poet's game, and good breeding is the nice concealment of absurdities. The truth is, the critic generally mistakes humour for wit, which is a very different excellence. Wit raises human nature above its level; *humour acts a contrary part, and equally depresses it. To expect exalted humour is a contradiction in terms; and the critic, by demanding an impossibility from the comic poet, has, in effect, banished new comedy from the stage. But to put the same thought in a different light, when an unexpected similitude in two objects strikes the imagination; in other words, when a thing is wittily expressed, all our pleasure turns into admiration of the artist who had fancy enough to draw the picture. When a thing is humorously described, our burst of laughter proceeds from a very different cause; we compare the absurdity of the character represented with our own, and triumph in our conscious superiority. No natural defect can be a cause of laughter, because it is a misfortune to which ourselves are liable. A defect of this kind changes the passion into pity or horror. We only laugh at those instances of moral absurdity to which we are conscious we ourselves are not liable. For instance, should I describe a man as wanting his nose, there is no humour in this, as it is an accident to which human nature is subject, and may be any man's case; but should I represent this man without his nose as extremely curious in the choice of his snuff-box, we here see him guilty of an absurdity of which we imagine it impossible for ourselves to be guilty, and therefore applaud our own good sense on the comparison. Thus, then, the pleasure we receive from wit turns on the admiration of another; that which we feel from humour centres in the admiration of ourselves. The poet, therefore, must place the object he would have the subject of humour in a state of inferiority; in other words, the subject of humour must be low.

The solemnity worn by many of our modern writers is, I fear, often the mask of dullness; for certain it is, it seems to fit every author who pleases to put it on. By the complexion of many of our late publications one might be apt to cry out with Cicero, **Civem, mehercule! non puto esse qui his temporibus ridere possit.* On my conscience, I believe we have all forgot to laugh in these days. Such writers probably make no distinction between what is praised and what is pleasing: between those commendations which the reader pays his own discernment, and those which are the genuine result of his sensations. It were to be wished, therefore, that we no longer found pleasure with the inflated style that has for some years been looked upon as fine writing, and which every young writer is now obliged to adopt, if he chooses to be read. We should now dispense with loaded epithet and dressing up trifles with dignity; for, to use an obvious instance, it is not those who make the greatest noise with their wares in the streets that have most to sell. Let us, instead of writing finely, try to write naturally; not hunt after lofty expressions to deliver mean ideas, nor be forever gaping, when we only mean to deliver a whisper.

[1759, 1774]

THE BEE

From *No. 2, *Saturday*, October 13, 1759

ON DRESS

Foreigners observe that there are no ladies in the world more beautiful or more ill-dressed than those of England. Our country-women have been compared to those pictures where the face is the work of a Raphael, but the draperies thrown out by some empty pretender, destitute of taste, and entirely unacquainted with design.

If I were a poet, I might observe on this occasion that so much beauty set off with all the advantages of dress, would be too powerful an antagonist for the opposite sex, and therefore it was wisely ordered that our ladies should want taste, lest their admirers should entirely want reason.

But, to confess a truth, I do not find they have a greater aversion to fine clothes than the women of any other country whatsoever. I cannot fancy that a shopkeeper's wife in Cheapside has a greater tenderness for the fortune of her husband than a citizen's wife in Paris; or that miss in a boarding-school is more an economist in dress than mademoiselle in a nunnery.

Although Paris may be accounted the soil in which almost every fashion takes its rise, its influence is never so general there as with us. They study there the happy method of uniting grace and fashion, and never excuse a woman for being awkwardly dressed by saying her clothes are made in the mode. A Frenchwoman is a perfect architect in dress; she never, with Gothic ignorance, mixes the orders; she never tricks out a squabby Doric shape with Corinthian finery; or, to speak without metaphor, she conforms to general fashion only when it happens not to be repugnant to private beauty.

Our ladies, on the contrary, seem to have no other standard for grace but the run of the town. If fashion gives the word, every distinction of beauty, complexion, or stature ceases. Sweeping trains, Prussian bonnets, and *trollopees, as like each other as if cut from the same piece, level all to one standard. The Mall, the gardens, and the playhouses are filled with ladies in uniform, and their whole appearance shows as little variety or taste as if their clothes were bespoke by the colonel of a marching regiment, or fancied by the same artist who dresses the three battalions of guards.

But not only ladies of every shape and complexion, but of every age, too, are possessed of this unaccountable passion of dressing in the same manner. A lady of no quality can be distinguished from a lady of some quality only by the redness of her hands; and a woman of sixty, masked, might easily pass for her granddaughter. I remember, a few days ago, to have walked behind a damsel tossed out in all the gayety of fifteen; her dress was loose, unstudied, and seemed the result of conscious beauty. I called up all my poetry on this occasion, and fancied twenty Cupids prepared for execution in every folding of her white negligee. I had prepared my imagination for an angel's face; but what was my mortification to find that the imaginary goddess was no other than my cousin Hannah, four years older than myself, and I shall be sixty-two the twelfth of next November.

After the transports of our first salute were over, I could not avoid running my eye over her whole appearance. Her gown was of cambric, cut short before, in order to discover a high-heeled shoe, which was buckled almost at the toe. Her cap — if cap it might be called that cap was none — consisted of a few bits of cambric and flowers of painted paper, stuck on one side of her head. Her bosom, that had felt no hand but the hand of time these twenty years, rose suing, but in vain, to be pressed. I could, indeed, have wished her more than an handkerchief of Paris net to shade her beauties; for, as Tasso says of the rosebud, **Quanto si mostra men, tanto è più bella*, I should think hers most pleasing when least discovered.

As my cousin had not put on all this finery for nothing, she was at that time sallying out to the Park when I had overtaken her. Perceiving, however, that I had on my best wig, she offered, if I would 'squire her there, to send home the footman. Though I trembled for our reception in public, yet I could not with any civility refuse; so, to be as gallant as possible, I took her hand in my arm, and thus we marched on together.

When we made our entry at the Park, two antiquated figures, so polite and so tender as we seemed to be, soon attracted the eyes of the company. As we made our way among crowds who were out to show their finery as well as we, wherever we came, I perceived we brought good-humour in our train. The polite could not forbear smiling, and the vulgar burst out into a hoarse laugh at our grotesque figures. Cousin Hannah, who was perfectly conscious of the rectitude of her own appearance, attributed all this mirth to the oddity of mine; while I as cordially placed the whole to her account. Thus, from being two of the best-natured creatures alive, before we got half-way up the Mall, we both began to grow peevish, and, like two mice on a string, endeavoured to revenge the impertinence of others upon ourselves. "I am amazed, Cousin Jeffrey," says miss, "that I can never get you to dress like a Christian. I knew we should have the eyes of the Park upon us, with your great wig, so frizzed, and yet so beggarly, and your monstrous muff. I hate *those odious muffs." I could have patiently borne a criticism on all the rest of my equipage; but, as I had always a peculiar veneration for my muff, I could not forbear being piqued a little; and, throwing my eyes with a spiteful air on her bosom, "I could heartily wish, madam," replied I, "that for your sake my muff was cut into a tippet."

As my cousin, by this time, was grown heartily ashamed of her gentleman usher, and as I was never very fond of any kind of exhibition myself, it was mutually agreed to retire for a while to one of the seats, and from that retreat remark on others as freely as they had remarked on us.

When seated, we continued silent for some time, employed in very different speculations. I regarded the whole company now passing in review before me as drawn out merely for my amusement. For my entertainment the beauty had all that morning been improving her charms, the beau had put on lace, and the young doctor a big wig, merely to please me. But quite different were the sentiments of Cousin Hannah; she regarded every well-dressed woman as a victorious rival, hated every face that seemed dressed in good-humour, or wore the appearance of greater happiness than her own. I perceived her uneasiness, and attempted to lessen it by observing that there was no company in the Park today. To this she readily assented; "And yet," says she, "it is full enough of scrubs of one kind or another." My smiling at this observation gave her spirits to pursue the bent of her inclination, and now she began to exhibit her skill in secret history, as she found me disposed to listen. "Observe," says she to me, "that old woman in tawdry silk, and dressed out even beyond the fashion. That is Miss Biddy Evergreen. Miss Biddy, it seems, has money; and as she considers that money was never so scarce as it is now, she seems resolved to keep what she has to herself. She is ugly enough, you see; yet, I assure you she has refused several offers, to my knowledge, within this twelvemonth. Let me see, three gentlemen from Ireland who study the law, two waiting captains, a doctor, and a Scotch preacher, who had like to have carried her off. All her time is passed between sickness and finery. Thus she spends the whole week in a close chamber, with no other company but her monkey, her apothecary, and cat; and comes dressed out to the Park every Sunday to show her airs, to get new lovers, to catch a new cold, and to make new work for the doctor.

"There goes Mrs. Roundabout; I mean the fat lady in the lutestring trollopee. Between you and I, she is but a cutler's wife. See how she's dressed, as fine as hands and pins can make her, while her two marriageable daughters, like bunters, in stuff gowns, are now taking sixpennyworth of tea at *the White Conduit House. Odious puss! how she waddles along, with her train two yards behind her! She puts me in mind of my Lord Bantam's Indian sheep, which are obliged to have their monstrous tails trundled along in a go-cart. For all her airs, it goes to her husband's heart to see four yards of good lutestring wearing against the ground like one of his knives on a grindstone. To speak my mind, Cousin Jeffrey, I never liked tails; for, suppose a young fellow should be rude, and the lady should offer to step back in a fright, instead of retiring, she treads upon her train, and falls fairly on her back; and then you know, cousin — her clothes may be spoiled.

"Ah, Miss Mazzard! I knew we should not miss her in the Park; she in the monstrous Prussian bonnet. Miss, though so very fine, was bred a milliner, and might have had some custom if she had minded her business; but the girl was fond of finery, and, instead of dressing her customers, laid out all her goods in adorning herself. Every new gown she put on impaired her credit; she still, however, went on improving her appearance and lessening her little fortune, and is now, you see, become a belle and a bankrupt."

My cousin was proceeding in her remarks, which were interrupted by the approach of the very lady she had been so freely describing. Miss had perceived her at a distance, and approached to salute her. I found, by the warmth of the two ladies' protestations, that they had been long intimate, esteemed friends and acquaintance. Both were so pleased at this happy rencounter that they were resolved not to part for the day. So we all crossed the Park together, and I saw them into a hackney-coach at the gate of St. James's. I could not, however, help observing "that they are generally most ridiculous themselves who are apt to see most ridicule in others."

THE BEE

From No. 5, *Saturday*, November 3, 1759

A REVERIE

Scarce a day passes in which we do not hear compliments paid to Dryden, Pope, and other writers of the last age, while not a month comes forward that is not loaded with invective against the writers of this. Strange that our critics should be fond of giving their favours to those who are insensible of the obligation, and their dislike to those who, of all mankind, are most apt to retaliate the injury.

Even though our present writers had not equal merit with their predecessors, it would be politic to use them with ceremony. Every compliment paid them would be more agreeable in proportion as they least deserved it. Tell a lady with a handsome face that she is pretty, she only thinks it her due; it is what she has heard a thousand times before from others, and disregards the compliment: but assure a lady the cut of whose visage is something more plain that she looks killing today, she instantly bridles up, and feels the force of the well-timed flattery the whole day after. Compliments which we think are deserved we accept only as debts with indifference; but those which conscience informs us we do not merit, we receive with the same gratitude that we do favours given away.

Our gentlemen, however, who preside at the distribution of literary fame seem resolved to part with praise neither from motives of justice nor generosity: one would think, when they take pen in hand, that it was only to blot reputations, and to put their seals to the packet which consigns every new-born effort to oblivion.

Yet, notwithstanding the republic of letters hangs at present so feebly together, though those friendships which once promoted literary fame seem now to be discontinued, though every writer who now draws the quill seems to aim at profit, as well as applause, many among them are probably laying in stores for immortality, and are provided with a sufficient stock of reputation to last the whole journey.

As I was indulging these reflections, in order to eke out the present page, I could not avoid pursuing the metaphor of going a journey in my imagination, and formed the following reverie, too wild for allegory, and too regular for a dream.

I fancied myself placed in the yard of a large inn, in which there were an infinite number of wagons and stage-coaches, attended by fellows who either invited the company to take their places, or were busied in packing their baggage. Each vehicle had its inscription, showing the place of its destination. On one I could read, The Pleasure Stage-Coach; on another, The Wagon of Industry; on a third, The Vanity Whim; and on a fourth, The Landau of Riches. I had some inclination to step into each of these, one after another; but, I know not by what means, I passed them by, and at last fixed my eye upon a small carriage, Berlin fashion, which seemed the most convenient vehicle at a distance in the world, and upon my nearer approach found it to be The Fame Machine.

I instantly made up to the coachman, whom I found to be an affable and seemingly good-natured fellow. He informed me that he had but a few days ago returned from the Temple of Fame, to which he had been carrying Addison, Swift, Pope, Steele, Congreve, and *Colley Cibber; that they made but indifferent company by the way, and that he once or twice was going to empty his berlin of the whole cargo; "However," says he, "I got them all safe home, with no other damage than a black eye which Colley gave Mr. Pope, and am now returned for another coachful." "If that be all, friend," said I, "and if you are in want of company, I'll make one with all my heart. Open the door; I hope the machine rides easy." "Oh, for that, sir, extremely easy." But, still keeping the door shut, and measuring me with his eye, "Pray, sir, have you no luggage? You seem to be a good-natured sort of a gentleman; but I don't find you have got any luggage, and I never permit any to travel with me but such as have something valuable to pay for coach-hire." Examining my pockets, I own I was not a little disconcerted at this unexpected rebuff; but, considering that I carried a number of the *Bee* under my arm, I was resolved to open it in his eyes and dazzle him with the splendour of the page. He read the title and contents, however, without any emotion, and assured me he had never heard of it before. "In short, friend," said he, now losing all his former respect, "you must not come in. I expect better passengers; but as you seem an harmless creature, perhaps, if there be room left, I may let you ride a while for charity." I now took my stand by the coachman at the door, and, since I could not command a seat, was resolved to be as useful as possible, and earn by my assiduity what I could not by my merit.

*The next that presented for a place was a most whimsical figure indeed. He was hung round with papers of his own composing, not unlike those who sing ballads in the streets, and came dancing up to the door with all the confidence of instant admittance. The volubility of his motion and address prevented my being able to read more of his cargo than the word, *Inspector*, which was written in great letters at the top of some of the papers. He opened the coach-door himself without any ceremony, and was just slipping in when the coachman, with as little ceremony, pulled him back. Our figure seemed perfectly angry at this repulse, and demanded gentleman's satisfaction. "Lord, sir!" replied the coachman, "instead of proper luggage, by your bulk you seem loaded for a West India voyage. You are big enough, with all your papers, to crack twenty stage-coaches. Excuse me, indeed, sir, for you must not enter." Our figure now began to expostulate: he assured the coachman that, though his baggage seemed so bulky, it was perfectly light, and that he would be contented with the smallest corner of room. But Jehu was inflexible, and the carrier of the *Inspectors* was sent to dance back again, with all his papers fluttering in the wind. We expected to have no more trouble from this quarter, when, in a few minutes, the same figure changed his appearance, like Harlequin upon the stage, and with the same confidence again made his approaches, dressed in lace, and carrying nothing but a nosegay. Upon coming near, he thrust the nosegay to the coachman's nose, grasped the brass, and seemed now resolved to enter by violence. I found the struggle soon begin to grow hot, and the coachman, who was a little old, unable to continue the contest; so, in order to ingratiate myself, I stepped in to his assistance, and our united efforts sent our literary Proteus, though worsted, unconquered still, clear off, dancing a rigadoon, and smelling to his own nosegay.

*The person who after him appeared as candidate for a place in the stage came up with an air not quite so confident, but somewhat, however, theatrical; and, instead of entering, made the coachman a very low bow, which the other returned, and desired to see his baggage; upon which he instantly produced some farces, a tragedy, and other miscellany productions. The coachman, casting his eye upon the cargo, assured him at present he could not possibly have a place, but hoped in time he might aspire to one, as he seemed to have read in the book of nature, without a careful perusal of which none ever found entrance at the Temple of Fame. "What!"

replied the disappointed poet, "shall my tragedy, in which I have vindicated the cause of liberty and virtue —" "Follow nature," returned the other, "and never expect to find lasting fame by topics which only please from their popularity. Had you been first in the cause of freedom, or praised in virtue more than an empty name, it is possible you might have gained admittance; but at present I beg, sir, you will stand aside for another gentleman whom I see approaching."

This was *a very grave personage, whom at some distance I took for one of the most reserved, and even disagreeable, figures I had seen; but as he approached, his appearance improved, and when I could distinguish him thoroughly, I perceived that, in spite of the severity of his brow, he had one of the most good-natured countenances that could be imagined. Upon coming to open the stage-door, he lifted a parcel of folios into the seat before him, but our inquisitorial coachman at once shoved them out again. "What! not take in my dictionary?" exclaimed the other, in a rage. "Be patient, sir," replied the coachman; "I have drove a coach, man and boy, these two thousand years; but I do not remember to have carried above one dictionary during the whole time. That little book which I perceive peeping from one of your pockets — may I presume to ask what it contains?" "A mere trifle," replied the author; "it is called the *Rambler*." "The *Rambler!*" says the coachman; "I beg, sir, you'll take your place. I have heard our ladies in the court of Apollo frequently mention it with rapture; and Clio, who happens to be a little grave, has been heard to prefer it to the *Spectator*; though others have observed that the reflections, by being refined, sometimes become minute."

This grave gentleman was scarcely seated when *another, whose appearance was something more modern, seemed willing to enter, yet afraid to ask. He carried in his hand a bundle of essays, of which the coachman was curious enough to inquire the contents. "These," replied the gentleman, "are rhapsodies against the religion of my country." "And how can you expect to come into my coach, after thus choosing the wrong side of the question?" "Ay, but I am right," replied the other; "and if you give me leave, I shall in a few minutes state the argument." "Right or wrong," said the coachman, "he who disturbs religion is a blockhead, and he shall never travel in a coach of mine." "If, then," said the gentleman, mustering up all his courage, "if I am not to have admittance as an essayist, I hope I shall not be repulsed as an historian; the last volume of my history met with applause." "Yes," replied the coachman, "but I have heard only the first approved at the Temple of Fame; and as I see you have it about you, enter, without further ceremony." My attention was now diverted to a crowd who were pushing forward *a person that seemed more inclined to the Stagecoach of Riches; but by their means he was driven forward to the same machine, which he nevertheless seemed heartily to despise. Impelled, however, by their solicitations, he steps up, flourishing a voluminous history, and demanding admittance. "Sir, I have formerly heard your name mentioned," says the coachman, "but never as an historian. Is there no other work upon which you may claim a place?" "None," replied the other, "except a romance. But this is a work of too trifling a nature to claim future attention." "You mistake," says the inquisitor; "a well-written romance is no such easy task as is generally imagined. I remember formerly to have carried Cervantes and *Segrais; and, if you think fit, you may enter."

Upon our three literary travellers coming into the same coach, I listened attentively to hear what might be the conversation that passed upon this extraordinary occasion; when, instead of agreeable or entertaining dialogue, *I found them grumbling at each other, and each seemed discontented with his companions. Strange, thought I to myself, that they who are thus born to enlighten the world should still preserve the narrow prejudices of childhood, and, by disagreeing, make even the highest merit ridiculous. Were the learned and the wise to unite against the dunces of society, instead of sometimes siding into opposite parties with them, they might throw a lustre upon each other's reputation, and teach every rank of subordinate merit, if not to admire, at least not to avow dislike.

In the midst of these reflections I perceived the coachman, unmindful of me, had now mounted the box. Several were approaching to be taken in, whose pretensions I was sensible were very just; I therefore desired him to stop and take in more passengers; but he replied, as he had now mounted the box, it would be improper to come down, but that he should take them all, one after the other, when he should return. So he drove away; and for myself, as I could not get in, I mounted behind, in order to hear the conversation on the way.

(*To be continued.)

THE CITIZEN OF THE WORLD

LETTER IV

From Lien Chi Altangi, to the Care of Fipsihi, Resident in Moscow; to be Forwarded by the Russian Caravan to Fum Hoam, First President of the Ceremonial Academy at Pekin, in China.

ENGLISH PRIDE. — LIBERTY. — AN INSTANCE OF BOTH. -- NEWSPAPERS. — POLITENESS.

The English seem as silent as the Japanese, yet vainer than the inhabitants of Siam. Upon my arrival I attributed that reserve to modesty, which I now find has its origin in pride. Condescend to address them first, and you are sure of their acquaintance; stoop to flattery, and you conciliate their friendship and esteem. They bear hunger, cold, fatigue, and all the miseries of life without shrinking; danger only calls forth their fortitude; they even exult in calamity; but contempt is what they cannot bear. An Englishman fears contempt more than death; he often flies to death as a refuge from its pressure, and dies when he fancies the world has ceased to esteem him.

Pride seems the source not only of their national vices, but of their national virtues also. An Englishman is taught to love his king as his friend, but to acknowledge no other master than the laws which himself has contributed to enact. He despises those nations who, that one may be free, are all content to be slaves; who first lift a tyrant into terror, and then shrink under his power as if delegated from heaven. Liberty is echoed in all their assemblies; and thousands might be found ready to offer up their lives for the sound, though perhaps not one of all the number understands its meaning. The lowest mechanic, however, looks upon it as his duty to be a watchful guardian of his country's freedom, and often uses a language that might seem haughty, even in the mouth of the great emperor who traces his ancestry to the moon.

A few days ago, passing by one of their prisons, I could not avoid stopping, in order to listen to a dialogue which I thought might afford me some entertainment. The conversation was carried on between a debtor through the grate of his prison, a porter who had stopped to rest his burden, and a soldier at the window. The subject was upon a threatened invasion from France, and each seemed extremely anxious to rescue his country from the impending danger. "For my part," cries the prisoner, "the greatest of my apprehensions is for our freedom; if the French should conquer, what would become of English liberty? My dear friends, liberty is the Englishman's prerogative; we must preserve that at the expense of our lives; of that the French shall never deprive us; it is not to be expected that men who are slaves themselves would preserve our freedom, should they happen to conquer." "Ay, slaves," cries the porter, "they are all slaves, fit only to carry burdens, every one of them. Before I would stoop to slavery, may this be my poison (and he held the goblet in his hand), may this be my poison — but I would sooner list for a soldier."

The soldier, taking the goblet from his friend, with much awe fervently cried out, "It is not so much our liberties as our religion that would suffer by such a change, ay, our religion, my lads. May the devil sink me into flames," such was the solemnity of his adjuration, "if the French should come over, but our religion would be utterly undone." So saying, instead of a libation, he applied the goblet to his lips, and confirmed his sentiments with a ceremony of the most persevering devotion.

In short, every man here pretends to be a politician; even the fair sex are sometimes found to mix the severity of national altercation with the blandishments of love, and often become conquerors by more weapons of destruction than their eyes.

This universal passion for politics is gratified by daily gazettes, as with us at China. But as in ours the emperor endeavours to instruct his people, in theirs the people endeavour to instruct the administration. You must not, however, imagine that they who compile these papers have any actual knowledge of the politics or the government of a state; they only collect their materials from the oracle of some coffee-house; which oracle has himself gathered them the night before from a beau at a gaming-table, who has pillaged his knowledge from a great man's porter, who has had his information from *the great man's gentleman who has invented the whole story for his own amusement the night preceding.

The English, in general, seem fonder of gaining the esteem than the love of those they converse with. This gives a formality to their amusements; their gayest conversations have something too wise for innocent relaxation; though in company you are seldom disgusted with the absurdity of a fool, you are seldom lifted into rapture by those strokes of vivacity which give instant, though not permanent, pleasure.

What they want, however, in gayety, they make up in politeness. You smile at hearing me praise the English for their politeness; you who have heard very different accounts from the missionaries at Pekin, who have seen such a different behaviour in their merchants and seamen at home. But I must still repeat it, the English seem more polite than any of their neighbours; their great art in this respect lies in endeavouring, while they oblige, to lessen the force of the favour. Other countries are fond of obliging a stranger, but seem desirous that he should be sensible of the obligation. The English confer their kindness with an appearance of indifference, and give away benefits with an air as if they despised them.

Walking a few days ago, between an English and a French man, into the suburbs of the city, we were overtaken by a heavy shower of rain. I was unprepared; but they had each large coats, which defended them from what seemed to me a perfect inundation. The Englishman, seeing me shrink from the weather, accosted me thus: "Pshaw, man, what dost shrink at? here, take this coat; I don't want it; I find it no way useful to me; I had as lief be without it." The Frenchman began to show his politeness in turn. "My dear friend," cries he, "why won't you oblige me by making use of my coat? You see how well it defends me from the rain; I should not choose to part with it to others, but to such a friend as you I could even part with my skin to do him service."

For such minute instances as these, most reverend Fum Hoam, I am sensible your sagacity will collect instruction. The volume of nature is the book of knowledge; and he becomes most wise who makes the most judicious selection. Farewell.

LETTER XXX

From the Same

THE PROCEEDINGS OF THE CLUB OF AUTHORS

By my last advices from Moscow I find the caravan has not yet departed for China: I still continue to write, expecting that you may receive a large number of letters at once. In them you will find rather a minute detail of English peculiarities than a general picture of their manners or disposition. Happy it were for mankind if all travellers would thus, instead of characterizing a people in general terms, lead us into a detail of those minute circumstances which first influenced their opinion. The genius of a country should be investigated with a kind of experimental inquiry: by this means we should have more precise and just notions of foreign nations, and detect travellers themselves when they happened to form wrong conclusions.

My friend and I *repeated our visit to the club of authors; where, upon our entrance, we found the members all assembled and engaged in a loud debate.

The poet, in shabby finery, holding a manuscript in his hand, was earnestly endeavouring to persuade the company to hear him read the first book of an heroic poem which he had composed the day before. But against this all the members very warmly objected. They knew no reason why any member of the club should be indulged with a particular hearing, when many of them had published whole volumes which had never been looked in. They insisted that the law should be observed, where reading in company was expressly noticed. It was in vain that the plaintiff pleaded the peculiar merit of his piece: he spoke to an assembly insensible to all his remonstrances; the book of laws was opened, and read by the secretary, where it was expressly enacted, "That whatsoever poet, speech-maker, critic, or historian should presume to engage the company by reading his own works, he was to lay down sixpence previous to opening the manuscript, and should be charged one shilling an hour while he continued reading: the said shilling to be equally distributed among the company as a recompense for their trouble."

Our poet seemed at first to shrink at the penalty, hesitating for some time whether he should deposit the fine, or shut up the poem, but looking round, and perceiving two strangers in the room, his love of fame outweighed his prudence, and laying down the sum by law established, he insisted on his prerogative.

A profound silence ensuing, he began by explaining his design. "Gentlemen," says he, "the present piece is not one of your common epic poems, which come from the press like paper kites in summer: there are none of your Turnuses or Didos in it; it is an heroical description of nature. I only beg you'll endeavour to make your souls unison with mine, and hear with the same enthusiasm with which I have written. The poem begins with the description of an author's bedchamber: the picture was sketched in my own apartment; for you must know, gentlemen, that I am myself the hero." Then putting himself into the attitude of an orator, with all the emphasis of voice and action, he proceeded:

Where the Red Lion flaring o'er the way
Invites each passing stranger that can pay;
Where Calvert's butt, and Parson's black champagne
Regale the drabs and bloods of Drury Lane;
There in a lonely room, from bailiffs snug,
The Muse found Scroggen stretch'd beneath a rug.
A window patch'd with paper lent a ray,
That dimly show'd the state in which he lay:
The sanded floor that grits beneath the tread;
The humid wall with paltry pictures spread;
*The royal game of goose was there in view,
And the twelve rules the royal martyr drew;
The seasons fram'd with *listing found a place,
And brave Prince William show'd his lamp-black face;
The morn was cold: he views with keen desire
The rusty grate, unconscious of a fire;
With beer and milk arrears the frieze was scor'd,
And five crack'd teacups dress'd the chimney board.
A nightcap deck'd his brows instead of bay,
A cap by night — a stocking all the day!

With this last line he seemed so much elated that he was unable to proceed. "There, gentlemen," cries he, "there is a description for you; Rabelais' bedchamber is but a fool to it.

A cap by night — a stocking all the day!

There is sound and sense, and truth and nature in the trifling compass of ten little syllables."

He was too much employed in self-admiration to observe the company, who, by nods, winks, shrugs, and stifled laughter, testified every mark of contempt. He turned severally to each for their opinion, and found all, however, ready to applaud. One swore it was inimitable; another said it was damned fine; and a third cried out in rapture, "Carissimo!" At last, addressing himself to the president, "And pray, Mr. Squint," says he, "let us have your opinion." "Mine!" answered the president, taking the manuscript out of the author's hand, "may this glass suffocate me, but I think it equal to anything I have seen; and I fancy," continued he, doubling up the poem, and forcing it into the author's pocket, "that you will get great honour when it comes out; so I shall beg leave to put it in. We will not intrude upon your good nature in desiring to hear more of it at present; **ex ungue Herculem*, we are satisfied, perfectly satisfied." The author made two or three attempts to pull it out a second time, and the president made as many to prevent him. Thus, though with reluctance, he was at last obliged to sit down, contented with the commendations for which he had paid.

When this tempest of poetry and praise was blown over, one of the company changed the subject by wondering how any man could be so dull as to write poetry at present, since prose itself would hardly pay. "Would you think it, gentlemen," continued he, "I have actually written last week sixteen prayers, twelve bawdy jests, and three sermons, all at the rate of sixpence apiece; and what is still more extraordinary, the bookseller has lost by the bargain? Such sermons would once have gained me a prebend's stall; but now, alas! we have neither piety, taste, nor humour among us. Positively, if this season does not turn out better than it has begun, unless the ministry commit some blunders to furnish us with a new topic of abuse, I shall resume my old business of working at the press, instead of finding it employment."

The whole club seemed to join in condemning the season as one of the worst that had come for some time; a gentleman particularly observed that the nobility were never known to subscribe worse than at present. "I know not how it happens," said he; "though I follow them up as close as possible, yet I can hardly get a single subscription in a week. The houses of the great are as inaccessible as a frontier garrison at midnight. I never see a nobleman's door half-opened that some surly porter or footman does not stand full in the breach. I was yesterday to wait with a subscription-proposal upon *my Lord Squash, the Creolian. I had posted myself at his door the whole morning, and just as he was getting into his coach, thrust my proposal snug into his hand, folded up in the form of a letter from myself. He just glanced at the superscription, and not knowing the hand, consigned it to his *valet-de-chambre,* this respectable personage treated it as his master, and put it into the hands of the porter; the porter grasped my proposal frowning; and measuring my figure from top to toe, put it back into my own hands unopened."

"To the devil I pitch all the nobility!" cries a little man, in a peculiar accent; "I am sure they have of late used me most scurvily. You must know, gentlemen, some time ago, upon the arrival of a certain noble duke from his travels, I set myself down, and vamped up a fine, flaunting poetical panegyric, which I had written in such a strain that I fancied it would have even wheedled milk from a mouse. In this I represented the whole kingdom welcoming his grace to his native soil, not forgetting the loss France and Italy would sustain in their arts by his departure. I expected to touch for a bank bill at least; so folding up my verses in gilt paper, I gave my last half-crown to a genteel servant to be the bearer. My letter was safely conveyed to his grace, and the servant, after four hours' absence, during which time I led the life of a fiend, returned with a letter four times as big as mine. Guess my ecstacy at the prospect of so fine a return. I eagerly took the packet into my hands, that trembled to receive it. I kept it some time unopened before me, brooding over the expected treasure it contained; when, opening it, as I hope to be saved, gentlemen, his grace had sent me in payment for my poem, no bank bills, but six copies of verse, each longer than mine, addressed to him upon the same occasion."

"A nobleman," cries a member who had hitherto been silent, "is created for the confusion of us authors as the catchpoll. I'll tell you a story, gentlemen, which is as true as that this pipe is made of clay. When I was delivered of my first book, I owed my tailor for a suit of clothes; but that is nothing new, you know, and may be any man's case as well as mine. Well, owing him for a suit of clothes, and hearing that my book took very well, he sent for his money, and insisted upon being paid immediately; though I was at that time rich in fame, for my book ran like wildfire, yet I was very short of money, and being unable to satisfy his demand, prudently resolved to keep my chamber, preferring a prison of my own choosing at home to one of my tailor's choosing abroad. In vain the bailiffs used all their arts to decoy me from my citadel; in vain they sent to let me know that a gentleman wanted to speak with me at the next tavern; in vain they came with an urgent message from my aunt in the country; in vain I was told that a particular friend was at the point of death, and desired to take his last farewell; I was deaf, insensible, rock, adamant; the bailiffs could make no impression on my hard heart, for I effectually kept my liberty by never stirring out of the room.

"This was very well for a fortnight; when one morning I received a most splendid message from the Earl of Doomsday, importing that he had read my book and was in raptures with every line of it; he impatiently longed to see the author and had some designs which might turn out greatly to my advantage. I paused upon the contents of this message, and found there could be no deceit, for the card was gilt at the edges, and the bearer, I was told, had quite the looks of a gentleman. Witness, ye powers, how my heart triumphed at my own importance! I saw a long perspective of felicity before me: I applauded the taste of the times, which never saw genius forsaken; I had prepared a set introductory speech for the occasion, five glaring compliments for his lordship, and two more modest for myself. The next morning, therefore, in order to be punctual to my appointment, I took coach, and ordered the fellow to drive to the street and house mentioned in his lordship's address. I had the precaution to pull up the window as I went along to keep off the busy part of mankind; and, big with expectation, fancied the coach never went fast enough. At length, however, the wished-for moment of its stopping arrived; this for some time I impatiently expected, and letting down the window in a transport in order to take a previous view of his lordship's magnificent palace and situation, I found — poison to my sight! — I found myself, not in an elegant street, but a paltry lane; not at a nobleman's door, but the * door of a sponging-house; I found the coachman had all this while been just driving me to jail, and I saw the bailiff, with a devil's face, coming out to secure me."

To a philosopher no circumstance, however trifling, is too minute; he finds instruction and entertainment in occurrences which are passed over by the rest of mankind as low, trite, and indifferent; it is from the number of these particulars, which to many appear insignificant, that he is at last enabled to form general conclusions: this, therefore, must be my excuse for sending so far as China accounts of manners and follies which, though minute in their own nature, serve more truly to characterize this people than histories of their public treaties, courts, ministers, negotiations, and ambassadors. Adieu.

LETTER LI

To the Same

A BOOKSELLER'S VISIT TO THE CHINESE

As I was yesterday seated at breakfast over a pensive dish of tea, my meditations were interrupted by * my old friend and companion, who introduced a stranger, dressed pretty much like himself. The gentleman made several apologies for his visit, begged of me to impute his intrusion to the sincerity of his respect and the warmth of his curiosity.

As I am very suspicious of my company when I find them very civil without any apparent reason, I answered the stranger's caresses at first with reserve; which my friend perceiving, instantly let me into my visitant's trade and character, asking Mr. Fudge whether he had lately published anything new. I now conjectured that my guest was no other than a bookseller, and his answer confirmed my suspicions.

"Excuse me, sir," says he, "it is not the season; books have their time as well as cucumbers. I would no more bring out a new work in summer than I would sell pork in the dog days. Nothing in my way goes off in summer, except very light goods indeed. A review, a magazine, or a sessions' paper may amuse a summer reader; but all our stock of value we reserve for a spring and winter trade." "I must confess, sir," says I, "a curiosity to know what you call a valuable stock, which can only bear a winter perusal." "Sir," replied the bookseller, "it is not my way to cry up my own goods; but, without exaggeration, I will venture to show with any of the trade: my books at least have the peculiar advantage of being always new; and it is my way to clear off my old to the trunk-makers every season. I have ten new title-pages now about me, which only want books to be added to make them the finest things in nature. Others may pretend to direct the vulgar, but that is not my way; I always let the vulgar direct me; wherever popular clamour arises, I always echo the million. For instance, should the people in general say that such a man is a rogue, I instantly give orders to set him down in print a villain; thus every man buys the book, not to learn new sentiments, but to have the pleasure of seeing his own reflected." "But, sir," interrupted I, "you speak as if you yourself wrote the books you publish; may I be so bold as to ask a sight of some of those intended publications which are shortly to surprise the world?" "As to that, sir," replied the talkative bookseller, "I only draw out the plans myself; and though I am very cautious of communicating them to any, yet, as in the end I have a favour to ask, you shall see a few of them. Here, sir, here they are, diamonds of the first water, I assure you. *Imprimis*, a translation of several medical precepts for the use of such physicians as do not understand Latin. *Item*, the young clergyman's art of placing patches regularly, with a dissertation on the different manners of smiling without distorting the face. *Item*, the whole art of love made perfectly easy, by a broker of 'Change Alley. *Item*, the proper manner of cutting black-lead pencils and making crayons, by the Right Hon. the Earl of —. *Item*, the muster-master-general, or the review of reviews." "Sir," cried I, interrupting him, "my curiosity with regard to title-pages is satisfied; I should be glad to see some longer manuscript, a history, or an epic poem." "Bless me!" cries the man of industry, "now you speak of an epic poem, you shall see an excellent farce. Here it is; dip into it where you will, it will be found replete with true modern humour. Strokes, sir; it is filled with strokes of wit and satire in every line." "Do you call these dashes of the pen strokes," replied I, "for I must confess I can see no other?" "And pray, sir," returned he, "what do you call them? Do you see anything good nowadays that is not filled with * strokes — and dashes? Sir, a well placed dash makes half the wit of our writers of modern humour. I bought a piece last season that had no other merit upon earth than nine hundred and ninety-five breaks, * seventy-two ha-ha's, three good things, and a garter. And yet it played off, and bounced, and cracked, and made more sport than a firework." "I fancy then, sir, you were a considerable gainer?" "It must be owned the piece did pay; but, upon the whole, I cannot much boast of last winter's success: I gained by two murders, but then I lost by an ill-timed charity sermon. I was a considerable sufferer by my 'Direct Road to an Estate,' but the 'Infernal Guide' brought me up again. Ah, sir, that was a piece touched off by the hand of a master, filled with good things from one end to the other. The author had nothing but the jest in view; no dull moral lurking beneath, nor ill-natured satire to sour the reader's good-humour; he wisely considered that moral and humour at the same time were quite overdoing the business." "To what purpose, was the book then published?" cried I. "Sir, the book was published in order to be sold; and no book sold better, except the criticisms upon it, which came out soon after: of all kinds of writing, that goes off best at present; and I generally fasten a criticism upon every selling book that is published.

"I once had an author who never left the least opening for the critics; close was the word, always very right, and very dull — ever on the safe side of an argument; yet, with all his qualifications, incapable of coming into favour. I soon perceived that his bent was for criticism; and, as he was good for nothing else, supplied him with pens and paper, and planted him at the beginning of every month as a censor on the works of others. In short, I found him a treasure; no merit could escape him: but what is most remarkable of all, he ever wrote best and bitterest when drunk." "But are there not some works," interrupted I, "that from the very manner of their composition must be exempt from criticism, particularly such as profess to disregard its laws?" "There is no work whatsoever but he can criticise," replied the bookseller; "even though you wrote in Chinese he would have a pluck at you. *Suppose you should take it into your head to publish a book, let it be a volume of Chinese Letters, for instance; write how you will, he shall show the world you could have written better. Should you, with the most local exactness, stick to the manners and customs of the country from whence you come — should you confine yourself to the narrow limits of Eastern knowledge, and be perfectly simple and perfectly natural — he has then the strongest reason to exclaim. He may, with a sneer, send you back to China for readers. He may observe that after the first or second letter the iteration of the same simplicity is insupportably tedious; but the worst of all is the public in such a case will anticipate his censures, and leave you with all your instructive simplicity to be mauled at discretion."

"Yes," cried I, "but in order to avoid his indignation and, what I should fear more, that of the public, I would in such a case write with all the knowledge I was master of. As I am not possessed of much learning, at least I would not suppress what little I had; nor would I appear more stupid than nature has made me." "Here, then," cries the bookseller, "we should have you entirely in our power: unnatural, uneastern, quite out of character, erroneously sensible would be the whole cry; sir, we should then hunt you down like a rat." "Head of my father!" said I, "sure there are but two ways: the door must either be shut or it must be open. I must either be natural or unnatural." "Be what you will, we shall criticise you," returned the bookseller, "and prove you a dunce in spite of your teeth. But, sir, it is time that I should come to business. I have just now in the press a history of China; and if you will but put your name to it as the author, I shall repay the obligation with gratitude." "What, sir," replied I, "put my name to a work which I have not written! Never, while I retain a proper respect for the public and myself." The bluntness of my reply quite abated the ardour of the bookseller's conversation; and, after about half an hour's disagreeable reserve, he, with some ceremony, took his leave and withdrew. Adieu.

*LETTER LIV

From the Same

THE CHARACTER OF AN IMPORTANT TRIFLER

Though naturally pensive, yet I am fond of gay company, and take every opportunity of thus dismissing the mind from duty. From this motive I am often found in the centre of a crowd; and wherever pleasure is to be sold am always a purchaser. In those places, without being remarked by any, I join in whatever goes forward, work my passions into a similitude of frivolous earnestness, shout as they shout, and condemn as they happen to disapprove. A mind thus sunk for a while below its natural standard is qualified for stronger flights, as those first retire who would spring forward with greater vigour.

Attracted by the serenity of the evening, my friend and I lately went to gaze upon the company in one of the public walks near the city. Here we sauntered together for some time, either praising the beauty of such as were handsome, or the dresses of such as had nothing else to recommend them. We had gone thus deliberately forward for some time, when, stopping on a sudden, my friend caught me by the elbow, and led me out of the public walk. I could perceive by the quickness of his pace, and by his frequently looking behind, that he was attempting to avoid somebody who followed: we now turned to the right, then to the left; as we went forward, he still went faster, but in vain; the person whom he attempted to escape hunted us through every doubling, and gained upon us each moment; so that at last we fairly stood still, resolving to face what we could not avoid.

Our pursuer soon came up, and joined us with all the familiarity of an old acquaintance. "My dear Drybone," cries he, shaking my friend's hand, "where have you been hiding this half a century? Positively I had fancied you were gone down to cultivate matrimony and your estate in the country."

During the reply I had an opportunity of surveying the appearance of our new companion: his hat was pinched up with peculiar smartness; his looks were pale, thin, and sharp; round his neck he wore a broad black ribbon, and in his bosom a buckle studded with glass; his coat was trimmed with tarnished twist; he wore by his side a sword with a black hilt; and his stockings of silk, though newly washed, were grown yellow by long service. I was so much engaged with the peculiarity of his dress that I attended only to the latter part of my friend's reply, in which he complimented Mr. Tibbs on the taste of his clothes and the bloom in his countenance.

"Pshaw, pshaw, Will," cried the figure, "no more of that, if you love me. You know I hate flattery, — on my soul I do; and yet, to be sure, an intimacy with the great will improve one's appearance, and a course of venison will fatten; and yet, faith, I despise the great as much as you do: but there are a great many damned honest fellows among them; and we must not quarrel with one half, because the other wants breeding. If they were all such as my Lord Mudler, one of the most good-natured creatures that ever squeezed a lemon, I should myself be among the number of their admirers. I was yesterday to dine at the Duchess of Piccadilly's. My lord was there. 'Ned,' says he to me, 'Ned,' says he, 'I'll hold gold to silver I can tell where you were poaching last night.' 'Poaching, my lord?' says I; 'faith, you have missed already; for I stayed at home, and let the girls poach for me. That's my way; I take a fine woman as some animals do their prey — stand still, and, swoop, they fall into my mouth.'"

"Ah, Tibbs, thou art a happy fellow," cried my companion, with looks of infinite pity; "I hope your fortune is as much improved as your understanding in such company?" "Improved," replied the other; "you shall know — but let it go no farther — a great secret — five hundred a year to begin with. My lord's word of honour for it — his lordship took me down in his own chariot yesterday, and we had a *tête-à-tête* dinner in the country, where we talked of nothing else." "I fancy you forget, sir," cried I; "you told us but this moment of your dining yesterday in town." "Did I say so?" replied he coolly; "to be sure, if I said so, it was so — dined in town: egad, now I do remember, I did dine in town; but I dined in the country too; for you must know, my boys, I eat two dinners. By the by, I am grown as nice as the devil in my eating. I'll tell you a pleasant affair about that: we were a select party of us to dine at Lady Grogram's, an affected piece, but let it go no farther — a secret; well, there happened to be no asafœtida in the sauce to a turkey, upon which, says I, 'I'll hold a thousand guineas, and say done first, that —' But, dear Drybone, you are an honest creature; lend me half-a-crown for a minute or two, or so, just till — but harkee, ask me for it the next time we meet, or it may be twenty to one but I forget to pay you."

When he left us, our conversation naturally turned upon so extraordinary a character. "His very dress," cries my friend, "is not less extraordinary than his conduct. If you meet him this day, you find him in rags, if the next, in embroidery. With those persons of distinction of whom he talks so familiarly, he has scarce a coffee-house acquaintance.

However, both for the interests of society, and perhaps for his own, Heaven has made him poor; and while all the world perceive his wants, he fancies them concealed from every eye. An agreeable companion, because he understands flattery; and all must be pleased with the first part of his conversation, though all are sure of its ending with a demand on their purse. While his youth countenances the levity of his conduct, he may thus earn a precarious subsistence; but when age comes on, the gravity of which is incompatible with buffoonery, then will he find himself forsaken by all; condemned in the decline of life to hang upon some rich family whom he once despised, there to undergo all the ingenuity of studied contempt, to be employed only as a spy upon the servants, or a bugbear to fright the children into obedience." Adieu.

*LETTER LV

To the Same

HIS CHARACTER CONTINUED; WITH THAT OF HIS WIFE, HIS HOUSE, AND FURNITURE

I am apt to fancy I have contracted a new acquaintance whom it will be no easy matter to shake off. My little beau yesterday overtook me again in one of the public walks, and, slapping me on the shoulder, saluted me with an air of the most perfect familiarity. His dress was the same as usual, except that he had more powder in his hair, wore a dirtier shirt, a pair of temple spectacles, and his hat under his arm.

As I knew him to be a harmless, amusing little thing, I could not return his smiles with any degree of severity; so we walked forward on terms of the utmost intimacy, and in a few minutes discussed all the usual topics preliminary to particular conversation.

The oddities that marked his character, however, soon began to appear; he bowed to several well-dressed persons, who, by their manner of returning the compliment, appeared perfect strangers. At intervals he drew out a pocket-book, seeming to take memorandums before all the company, with much importance and assiduity. In this manner he led me through the length of the whole walk, fretting at his absurdities, and fancying myself laughed at not less than him by every spectator.

When we were got to the end of our procession, "Blast me," cries he, with an air of vivacity, "I never saw the Park so thin in my life before! There's no company at all today; not a single face to be seen." "No company!" interrupted I peevishly; "no company, where there is such a crowd? Why, man, there's too much. What are the thousand that have been laughing at us but company?" "Lord, my dear," returned he, with the utmost good-humour, "you seem immensely chagrined; but, blast me, when the world laughs at me, I laugh at the world, and so we are even. My Lord Trip, Bill Squash the Creolian, and I sometimes make a party at being ridiculous; and so we say and do a thousand things for the joke's sake. But I see you are grave, and if you are for a fine grave sentimental companion, you shall dine with me and my wife today; I must insist on 't. I'll introduce you to Mrs. Tibbs, a lady of as elegant qualifications as any in nature; she was bred — but that's between ourselves — under the inspection of the Countess of All-night. A charming body of voice; but no more of that; she shall give us a song. You shall see my little girl too, Carolina Wilhelmina Amelia Tibbs, a sweet pretty creature! I design her for my Lord Drumstick's eldest son; but that's in friendship — let it go no farther: she's but six years old, and yet she walks a minuet, and plays on the guitar immensely already. I intend she shall be as perfect as possible in every accomplishment. In the first place, I'll make her a scholar; I'll teach her Greek myself, and learn that language purposely to instruct her; but let that be a secret."

Thus saying, without waiting for a reply, he took me by the arm and hauled me along. We passed through many dark alleys and winding ways; for, from some motives to me unknown, he seemed to have a particular aversion to every frequented street; at last, however, we got to the door of a dismal-looking house in the outlets of the town, where he informed me he chose to reside for the benefit of the air.

We entered the lower door, which ever seemed to lie most hospitably open, and I began to ascend an old and creaking staircase when, as he mounted to show me the way, he demanded whether I delighted in prospects; to which answering in the affirmative, "Then," says he, "I shall show you one of the most charming in the world, out of my windows; we shall see the ships sailing, and the whole country for twenty miles round, tip-top, quite high. My Lord Swamp would give ten thousand guineas for such a one; but, as I sometimes pleasantly tell him, I always love to keep my prospects at home, that my friends may come to see me the oftener."

By this time we were arrived as high as the stairs would permit us to ascend, till we came to what he was facetiously pleased to call the first floor down the chimney; and knocking at the door, a voice from within demanded, "Who's there?" My conductor answered that it was him. But this not satisfying the querist, the voice again repeated the demand; to which he answered louder than before; and now the door was opened by an old woman with cautious reluctance.

When we were got in, he welcomed me to his house with great ceremony, and, turning to the old woman, asked where was her lady. "Good troth," replied she, in a peculiar dialect, "she's washing your twa shirts at the next door, because they have taken an oath against lending out the tub any longer." "My two shirts!" cried he in a tone that faltered with confusion, "what does the idiot mean?" "I ken what I mean weel enough," replied the other; "she's washing your twa shirts at the next door, because——" "Fire and fury! no more of thy stupid explanations!" cried he; "go and inform her we have got company. Were that Scotch hag," continued he, turning to me, "to be forever in my family, she would never learn politeness, nor forget that absurd poisonous accent of hers, or testify the smallest specimen of breeding or high life; and yet it is very surprising too, as I had her from a parliament man, a friend of mine from the Highlands, one of the politest men in the world; but that's a secret."

We waited some time for Mrs. Tibbs's arrival, during which interval I had a full opportunity of surveying the chamber and all its furniture, which consisted of four chairs with old wrought bottoms, that he assured me were his wife's embroidery; a square table that had been once japanned; a cradle in one corner, a lumbering cabinet in the other; a broken shepherdess, and a mandarin without a head were stuck over the chimney; and round the walls several paltry unframed pictures, which, he observed, were all his own drawing. "What do you think, sir, of that head in the corner, done *in the manner of Grisoni? There's the true keeping in it; it's my own face, and though there happens to be no likeness, a countess offered me an hundred for its fellow: I refused her, for, hang it, that would be mechanical, you know."

The wife at last made her appearance, at once a slattern and a coquette; much emaciated, but still carrying the remains of beauty. She made twenty apologies for being seen in such odious dishabille, but hoped to be excused, as she had stayed out all night at the Gardens with the countess, who was excessively fond of the horns. "And indeed, my dear," added she, turning to her husband, "his lordship drank your health in a bumper." "Poor Jack!" cries he, "a dear good-natured creature; I know he loves me: but I hope, my dear, you have given orders for dinner; you need make no great preparations neither — there are but three of us; something elegant and little will do: a turbot, an ortolan, or a——" "Or what do you think, my dear," interrupts the wife, "of a nice pretty bit of ox-cheek, piping hot, and dressed with a little of my own sauce?" "The very thing!" replies he; "it will eat best with some smart bottled beer; but be sure to let us have the sauce his grace was so fond of. I hate your immense loads of meat; that is country all over; extreme disgusting to those who are in the least acquainted with high life."

By this time my curiosity began to abate, and my appetite to increase: the company of fools may at first make us smile, but at last never fails of rendering us melancholy; I therefore pretended to recollect a prior engagement, and, after having shown my respect to the house, according to the fashion of the English, by giving the old servant a piece of money at the door, I took my leave; Mrs. Tibbs assuring me that dinner, if I stayed, would be ready at least in less than two hours.

LETTER LXXXIX

To the Same

*THE FOLLY OF REMOTE OR USELESS DISQUISITIONS AMONG THE LEARNED

I am amused, my dear Fum, with the labours of some of the learned here. One shall write you a whole folio on the dissection of a caterpillar. Another shall swell his works with a description of the plumage on the wing of a butterfly; a third shall see a little world on a peach leaf, and publish a book to describe what his readers might see more clearly in two minutes, only by being furnished with eyes and a microscope.

I have frequently compared the understandings of such men to their own glasses. Their field of vision is too contracted to take in the whole of any but minute objects; they view all nature bit by bit: now the proboscis, now the antennæ, now the pinnæ of — a flea. Now the polypus comes to breakfast upon a worm; now it is kept up to see how long it will live without eating; now it is turned inside outward; and now it sickens and dies. Thus they proceed, laborious in trifles, constant in experiment, without one single abstraction, by which alone knowledge may be properly said to increase; till at last their ideas, ever employed upon minute things, contract to the size of the diminutive object, and a single mite shall fill the whole mind's capacity.

Yet, believe me, my friend, ridiculous as these men are to the world, they are set up as objects of esteem for each other. They have particular places appointed for their meetings in which one shows his cockle-shell and is praised by all the society; another produces his powder, makes some experiments that result in nothing, and comes off with admiration and applause; a third comes out with the important discovery of some new process in the skeleton of a mole, and is set down as the accurate and sensible; while one still more fortunate than the rest, by pickling, potting, and preserving monsters, rises into unbounded reputation.

The labours of such men, instead of being calculated to amuse the public, are laid out only in diverting each other. The world becomes very little the better or the wiser for knowing what is the peculiar food of an insect that is itself the food of another, which in its turn is eaten by a third; but there are men who have studied themselves into a habit of investigating and admiring such minutiæ. To these such subjects are pleasing, as there are some who contentedly spend whole days in endeavouring to solve enigmas, or disentangle the puzzling-sticks of children.

But of all the learned those who pretend to investigate remote antiquity have least to plead in their own defence, when they carry this passion to a faulty excess. They are generally found to supply by conjecture the want of record, and then by perseverance are wrought up into a confidence of the truth of opinions which even to themselves at first appeared founded only in imagination.

The Europeans have heard much of the kingdom of China; its politeness, arts, commerce, laws, and morals are, however, but very imperfectly known among them. They have even now in their Indian warehouses numberless utensils, plants, minerals, and machines of the use of which they are entirely ignorant; nor can any among them even make a probable guess for what they might have been designed. Yet, though this people be so ignorant of the present real state of China, the philosophers I am describing have entered into long, learned, laborious disputes about what China was two thousand years ago. China and European happiness are but little connected even at this day; but European happiness and China two thousand years ago have certainly no connection at all. However, the learned have written on and pursued the subject through all the labyrinths of antiquity; though the early dews and the tainted gale be passed away, though no footsteps remain to direct the doubtful chase, yet still they run forward, open upon the uncertain scent, and, though in fact they follow nothing, are earnest in the pursuit. In this chase, however, they all take different ways. One, for example, confidently assures us that China was peopled by a colony from Egypt. * Sesostris, he observes, led his army as far as the Ganges; therefore, if he went so far, he might still have gone as far as China, which is but about a thousand miles from thence; therefore he did go to China; therefore China was not peopled before he went there; therefore it was peopled by him. Besides, the Egyptians have pyramids; the Chinese have in like manner their porcelain tower: the Egyptians used to light up candles upon every rejoicing; the Chinese have lanterns upon the same occasion: the Egyptians had their great river; so have the Chinese. But what serves to put the matter past a doubt is that the ancient kings of China and those of Egypt were called by the same names. The Emperor Ki is certainly the same with King Atoes; for if we only change *K* into *A*, and *i* into *toes*, we shall have the name Atoes; and with equal ease Menes may be proved to be the same with the Emperor Yu; therefore the Chinese are a colony from Egypt.

But another of the learned is entirely different from the last; and he will have the Chinese to be a colony planted by Noah just after the deluge. First, from the vast similitude there is between the name of Fohi, the founder of the Chinese monarchy, and that of Noah, the preserver of the human race; Noah, Fohi — very like each other, truly; they have each but four letters, and only two of the four happen to differ. But, to strengthen the argument, Fohi, as the Chinese chronicle asserts, had no father. Noah, it is true, had a father, as the European Bible tells us; but then, as this father was probably drowned in the flood, it is just the same as if he had no father at all: therefore Noah and Fohi are the same. Just after the flood the earth was covered with mud; if it was covered with mud it must have been incrustated mud; if it was incrustated, it was clothed with verdure; this was a fine, unembarrassed road for Noah to fly from his wicked children: he therefore did fly from them, and took a journey of two thousand miles for his own amusement; therefore Noah and Fohi are the same.

Another sect of literati — for they all pass among the vulgar for very great scholars — assert that the Chinese came neither from the colony of Sesostris nor from Noah, but are descended from *Magog, Meshech, and Tubal, and therefore neither Sesostris nor Noah nor Fohi are the same.

It is thus, my friend, that indolence assumes the airs of wisdom, and, while it tosses the cup-and-ball with infantine folly, desires the world to look on, and calls the stupid pastime philosophy and learning. Adieu.

LETTER XC

To the Same

THE ENGLISH SUBJECT TO THE SPLEEN

When the men of this country are once turned of thirty, they regularly retire every year, at proper intervals, to lie in of *the spleen. The vulgar, unfurnished with the luxurious comforts of the soft cushion, down bed, and easy-chair, are obliged, when the fit is on them, to nurse it up by drinking, idleness, and ill-humour. In such dispositions unhappy is the foreigner who happens to cross them; his long chin, tarnished coat, or pinched hat are sure to receive no quarter. If they meet no foreigner, however, to fight with, they are in such cases generally content with beating each other.

The rich, as they have more sensibility, are operated upon with greater violence by this disorder. Different from the poor, instead of becoming more insolent, they grow totally unfit for opposition. A general here, who would have faced a culverin when well, if the fit be on him shall hardly find courage to snuff a candle. An admiral, who could have opposed a broadside without shrinking, shall sit whole days in his chamber, mobbed up in double nightcaps, shuddering at the intrusive breeze, and distinguishable from his wife only by his black beard and heavy eyebrows.

In the country this disorder mostly attacks the fair sex; in town it is most unfavourable to the men. A lady who has pined whole years amidst cooing doves and complaining nightingales, in rural retirement, shall resume all her vivacity in one night at a city gaming-table; her husband, who roared, hunted, and got drunk at home, shall grow splenetic in town, in proportion to his wife's good-humour. Upon their arrival in London they exchange their disorders. In consequence of her parties and excursions, he puts on the furred cap and scarlet stomacher, and perfectly resembles an Indian husband, who, when his wife is safely delivered, permits her to transact business abroad, while he undergoes all the formality of keeping his bed, and receiving all the condolence in her place.

But those who reside constantly in town owe this disorder mostly to the influence of the weather. It is impossible to describe what a variety of transmutations an east wind shall produce; it has been known to change a lady of fashion into a parlor couch, an alderman into a plate of custards, and a dispenser of justice into a rat-trap. Even philosophers themselves are not exempt from its influence; it has often converted a poet into a coral and bells, and a patriot senator into a dumb-waiter.

Some days ago I went to visit the man in black, and entered his house with that cheerfulness which the certainty of a favourable reception always inspires. Upon opening the door of his apartment, I found him, with the most rueful face imaginable, in a morning-gown and flannel nightcap, earnestly employed in learning to blow the German flute. Struck with the absurdity of a man in the decline of life thus blowing away all his constitution and spirits, even without the consolation of being musical, I ventured to ask what could induce him to attempt learning so difficult an instrument so late in life. To this he made no reply, but, groaning, and still holding the flute to his lips, continued to gaze at me for some moments very angrily, and then proceeded to practise his gamut as before. After having produced a variety of the most hideous tones in nature, at last, turning to me, he demanded whether I did not think he had made a surprising progress in two days. "You see," continues he, "I have got the **ambusheer* already, and as for fingering, my master tells me I shall have that in a few lessons more." I was so much astonished with this instance of inverted ambition that I knew not what to reply, but soon discerned the cause of all his absurdities; my friend was under a metamorphosis by the power of spleen, and flute-blowing was unluckily become his adventitious passion.

In order, therefore, to banish his anxiety imperceptibly by seeming to indulge it, I began to descant on those gloomy topics by which philosophers often get rid of their own spleen, by communicating it; the wretchedness of a man in this life; the happiness of some wrought out of the miseries of others; the necessity that wretches should expire under punishment that rogues might enjoy affluence in tranquillity: I led him on from the inhumanity of the rich to the ingratitude of the beggar; from the insincerity of refinement to the fierceness of rusticity; and at last had the good fortune to restore him to his usual serenity of temper by permitting him to expatiate upon all the modes of human misery.

"Some nights ago," says my friend, "sitting alone by my fire, I happened to look into an account of the detection of a set of men called the thief-takers. I read over the many hideous cruelties of those haters of mankind; of their pretended friendship to wretches they meant to betray; of their sending men out to rob, and then hanging them. I could not avoid sometimes interrupting the narrative by crying out, 'Yet these are men!' As I went on, I was informed that they had lived by this practice several years, and had been enriched by the price of blood; 'And yet,' cried I, 'I have been sent into this world, and am desired to call these men my brothers!' I read that the very man who led the condemned wretch to the gallows was he who falsely swore his life away; 'And yet,' continued I, 'that perjurer had just such a nose, such lips, such hands, and such eyes as Newton.' I at last came to the account of the wretch that was searched after robbing one of the thief-takers of half-a-crown. Those of the confederacy knew that he had got but that single half-crown in the world; after a long search, therefore, which they knew would be fruitless, and taking from him the half-crown, which they knew was all he had, one of the gang compassionately cried out, 'Alas! poor creature, let him keep all the rest he has got; it will do him service in Newgate, where we are sending him.' This was an instance of such complicated guilt and hypocrisy that I threw down the book in an agony of rage, and began to think with malice of all the human kind. I sat silent for some minutes; and soon perceiving the ticking of my watch beginning to grow noisy and troublesome, I quickly placed it out of hearing and strove to resume my serenity. But the watchman soon gave me a second alarm. I had scarcely recovered from this when my peace was assaulted by the wind at my window; and when that ceased to blow, I listened for *deathwatches in the wainscot. I now found my whole system discomposed. I strove to find a resource in philosophy and reason; but what could I oppose, or where direct my blow when I could see no enemy to combat? I saw no misery approaching, nor knew any I had to fear, yet still I was miserable. Morning came; I sought for tranquillity in dissipation, sauntered from one place of public resort to another, but found myself disagreeable to my acquaintance and ridiculous to others. I tried at different times dancing, fencing, and riding; I solved geometrical problems, shaped tobacco-stoppers, wrote verses, and cut paper. At last I placed my affections on music, and find that earnest employment, if it cannot cure, at least will palliate every anxiety." Adieu.

LETTER XCIII

To the Same

THE FONDNESS OF SOME TO ADMIRE THE WRITINGS OF LORDS, ETC.

It is surprising what an influence titles shall have upon the mind, even though these titles be of our own making. Like children, we dress up the puppets in finery, and then stand in astonishment at the plastic wonder. I have been told of a rat-catcher here who strolled for a long time about the villages near town without finding any employment; at last, however, he thought proper to take the title of his Majesty's Rat-Catcher in Ordinary, and thus succeeded beyond his expectations: when it was known that he caught rats at court, all were ready to give him countenance and employment.

But of all the people, they who make books seem most perfectly sensible of the advantages of titular dignity. *All seem convinced that a book written by vulgar hands can neither instruct nor improve; none but kings, chams, and mandarins can write with any probability of success. If the titles inform me right, not only kings and courtiers, but emperors themselves, in this country periodically supply the press.

A man here who should write, and honestly confess that he wrote for bread, might as well send his manuscript to fire the baker's oven; not one creature will read him: all must be court-bred poets, or pretend at least to be court-bred, who can expect to please. Should the caitiff fairly avow a design of emptying our pockets and filling his own, every reader would instantly forsake him; even those who write for bread themselves would combine to worry him, perfectly sensible that his attempts only served to take the bread out of their mouths.

And yet this silly prepossession the more amazes me, when I consider that almost all the excellent productions in wit that have appeared here were purely the offspring of necessity; their Drydens, Butlers, Otways, and Farquhars were all writers for bread. Believe me, my friend, hunger has a most amazing faculty of sharpening the genius; and he who with a full belly can think like a hero, after a course of fasting shall rise to the sublimity of a demigod.

But what will most amaze is that this very set of men, who are now so much depreciated by fools, are, however, the very best writers they have among them at present. For my own part, were I to buy a hat, I would not have it from a stocking-maker, but a hatter; were I to buy shoes, I should not go to the tailor's for that purpose. It is just so with regard to wit: did I, for my life, desire to be well served, I would apply only to those who made it their trade and lived by it. You smile at the oddity of my opinion; but be assured, my friend, that wit is in some measure mechanical, and that a man long habituated to catch at even its resemblance will at last be happy enough to possess the substance. By a long habit of writing he acquires a justness of thinking, and a mastery of manner, which holiday writers, even with ten times his genius, may vainly attempt to equal.

How, then, are they deceived who expect from title, dignity, and exterior circumstance an excellence which is in some measure acquired by habit and sharpened by necessity? You have seen, like me, many literary reputations promoted by the influence of fashion, which have scarce survived the possessor; you have seen the poor hardly earn the little reputation they acquired, and their merit only acknowledged when they were incapable of enjoying the pleasures of popularity: such, however, is the reputation worth possessing; that which is hardly earned is hardly lost. Adieu.

LETTER CXI

To the Same

ON THE DIFFERENT SECTS IN ENGLAND, PARTICULARLY *METHODISTS

Religious sects in England are far more numerous than in China. Every man who has interest enough *to hire a conventicle here may set up for himself, and sell off a new religion. The sellers of the newest pattern at present give extreme good bargains, and let their disciples have a great deal of confidence for very little money.

Their shops are much frequented, and their customers every day increasing; for people are naturally fond of going to Paradise at as small expense as possible.

Yet you must not conceive this modern sect as differing in opinion from those of the established religion. Difference of opinion, indeed, formerly divided their sectaries, and sometimes drew their armies to the field: *white gowns and black mantles, flapped hats and cross pocket-holes were once the obvious causes of quarrel; men then had some reason for fighting, they knew what they fought about; but at present they are arrived at such refinement in religion-making that they have actually formed a new sect without a new opinion; they quarrel for opinions they both equally defend; they hate each other, and that is all the difference between them.

But though their principles are the same, their practice is somewhat different. Those of the established religion laugh when they are pleased, and their groans are seldom extorted but by pain or danger. The new sect, on the contrary, weep for their amusement, and use little music except a chorus of sighs and groans, or tunes that are made to imitate groaning. Laughter is their aversion; lovers court each other from the Lamentations; the bridegroom approaches the nuptial couch in sorrowful solemnity, and the bride looks more dismal than an undertaker's shop. Dancing round the room is with them running in a direct line to the devil; and as for gaming, though but in jest, they would sooner play with a rattle-snake's tail than finger a dice-box.

By this time you perceive that I am describing a sect of enthusiasts, and you have already compared them with the Fakirs, Brahmins and Talapoins of the East. Among these, you know, are generations that have never been known to smile, and voluntary affliction makes up all the merit they can boast of. Enthusiasm in every country produces the same effects; stick the Fakir with pins, or confine the Brahmin to a vermin hospital; spread the Talapoin on the ground, or load the sectary's brow with contrition: those worshippers who discard the light of reason are ever gloomy; their fears increase in proportion to their ignorance, as men are continually under apprehensions who walk in darkness.

Yet there is still a stronger reason for the enthusiast's being an enemy to laughter; namely, his being himself so proper an object of ridicule. It is remarkable that the propagators of false doctrines have ever been averse to mirth, and always begin by recommending gravity when they intended to disseminate imposture. Fohi, the idol of China, is represented as having never laughed; *Zoroaster, the leader of the Brahmins, is said to have laughed but twice — upon his coming into the world, and upon his leaving it; and Mohammed himself, though a lover of pleasure, was a professed opposer of gayety. Upon a certain occasion, telling his followers that they would all appear naked at the resurrection, his favorite wife represented such an assembly as immodest and unbecoming. "Foolish woman!" cried the grave prophet, "though the whole assembly be naked, on that day they shall have forgotten to laugh." Men like him opposed ridicule, because they knew it to be a most formidable antagonist, and preached up gravity to conceal their own want of importance.

*Ridicule has ever been the most powerful enemy of enthusiasm, and properly the only antagonist that can be opposed to it with success. Persecution only serves to propagate new religions; they acquire fresh vigour beneath the executioner and the axe; and, like some vivacious insects, multiply by dissection. It is also impossible to combat enthusiasm with reason, for though it makes a show of resistance, it soon eludes the pressure; refers you to distinctions not to be understood, and feelings which it cannot explain. A man who would endeavour to fix an enthusiast by argument might as well attempt to spread quick-silver with his fingers. The only way to conquer a visionary is to despise him; the stake, the fagot, and the disputing doctor in some measure ennoble the opinions they are brought to oppose: they are harmless against innovating pride; contempt alone is truly dreadful. Hunters generally know the most vulnerable part of the beasts they pursue, by the care which every animal takes to defend the side which is weakest; on what side the enthusiast is most vulnerable may be known by the care which he takes in the beginning to work his disciples into gravity, and guard them against the power of ridicule.

When Philip the Second was King of Spain there was a contest in Salamanca between two orders of friars for superiority. The legend of one side contained more extraordinary miracles, but the legend of the other was reckoned most authentic. They reviled each other, as is usual in disputes of divinity; the people were divided into factions, and a civil war appeared unavoidable. In order to prevent such an imminent calamity, the combatants were prevailed upon to submit their legends to the fiery trial, and that which came forth untouched by the fire was to have the victory, and to be honoured with a double share of reverence. Whenever the people flock to see a miracle, it is a hundred to one but that they see a miracle; incredible, therefore, were the numbers that were gathered round upon this occasion. The friars on each side approached and confidently threw their respective legends into the flames, when lo! to the utter disappointment of all the assembly, instead of a miracle, both legends were consumed. Nothing but thus turning both parties into contempt could have prevented the effusion of blood. The people now laughed at their former folly, and wondered why they fell out. Adieu.

[1760, 61. 1762]

THE TRAVELLER AND THE DESERTED VILLAGE

Though Goldsmith's poetry is small in bulk, it has sufficed to place him among the most popular English poets. His two most important long poems won immediate success: *The Traveller*, published late in 1764, went through nine editions during its author's lifetime; *The Deserted Village*, published in 1770, went through five editions the first year. Since that time, despite fluctuations in taste that have endangered the literary reputation of most eighteenth-century poets, they have maintained their place in popular and critical favour; and *The Deserted Village* remains one of a small sheaf of English poems that almost every one has read, and that supply the current coin of familiar quotation.

In spite of its variety of literary forms Goldsmith's work is astonishingly of a piece: much of it has a well marked autobiographical colouring; the same ideas recur, at times with little variation in phrasing, and the same genial, whimsical personality permeates the whole. *The Traveller* is a series of reflections based on his wanderings through central Europe, many of which had already been presented in *The Citizen of the World*, while similar matter appears new-dressed in Chapter XX of *The Vicar of Wakefield*, "The History of a Philosophic Vagabond, Pursuing Novelty, but Losing Content." *The Deserted Village* draws largely upon Goldsmith's boyhood memories, and the innocent simplicity of the Primrose home in the opening chapters of *The Vicar* makes excellent use of the same material.

It has been the fashion recently to claim Goldsmith, especially in his poetry, among those precursors of romanticism, whose separate treatment in histories of English literature abridges the space devoted to classicism and apparently decreases its importance. Of course Goldsmith, like every other author of importance, had links with the future as well as with the past. His love of nature, his genial simplicity, his sentimentality, and his interest in lowly characters have all been emphasized as romantic tendencies. He appreciated nature, but not as the romanticists did for its own sake; for him it was rather a background to human nature. Simplicity is distinctly a classical quality. Geniality has no necessary opposition to the classical temper, for though it is a handicap to a satirist, not all classicists are satirists. Like his fellow countryman, Steele, he had a tender heart, gaiety, and high spirits. He had a strain of sensibility that sometimes crossed the line of sentimentality, but he always held it in check; and in theory and practice alike he steadily opposed sentimental comedy. He wrote of peasants and of rural life, rather because he was acquainted with them than from a belief that they are essentially better than the upper classes. His opinion of Rousseauism he expressed in *An Inquiry into the Present State of Polite Learning in Europe*, "Rousseau of Geneva, a professed man-hater, or more properly speaking, a philosopher enraged with one half of mankind because they unavoidably make the other half unhappy. Such sentiments are generally the result of much good nature and little experience." His glorification of the past was neither mediævalism nor primitivism. Goldsmith was a friend of Johnson's and an adherent of his literary principles; he wrote in the orthodox manner, rejecting blank verse, and clinging to descriptive and didactic poetry. In most important respects he was a man of his age.

THE TRAVELLER

or, A PROSPECT OF SOCIETY

Remote, unfriended, melancholy, slow,
Or by the lazy Scheldt or wandering Po;
Or onward, where the rude Carinthian boor
Against the houseless stranger shuts the door;
Or where Campania's plain forsaken lies,
A weary waste expanding to the skies:
Where'er I roam, whatever realms to see,
My heart untravell'd fondly turns to *thee;
Still to my brother turns, with ceaseless pain,
And drags at each remove a lengthening chain.

Eternal blessings crown my earliest friend,
And round his dwelling guardian saints attend:
Blest be that spot, where cheerful guests retire
To pause from toil, and trim their evening fire;
Blest that abode, where want and pain repair,
And every stranger finds a ready chair;
Blest be those feasts with simple plenty crown'd,
Where all the ruddy family around
Laugh at the jests or pranks that never fail,
Or sigh with pity at some mournful tale,
Or press the bashful stranger to his food,
And learn the luxury of doing good.

But me, not destin'd such delights to share,
My prime of life in wandering spent, and care;
Impell'd, with steps unceasing, to pursue
Some fleeting good, that mocks me with the view;
That, like the circle bounding earth and skies,
Allures from far, yet, as I follow, flies;
My fortune leads to traverse realms alone,
And find no spot of all the world my own.
Ev'n now, where Alpine solitudes ascend,
I sit me down a pensive hour to spend;
And, plac'd on high above the storm's career,
Look downward where an hundred realms appear:
Lakes, forests, cities, plains, extending wide,
The pomp of kings, the shepherd's humbler pride.

When thus creation's charms around combine,
Amidst the store, should thankless pride repine?
Say, should the philosophic mind disdain
That good which makes each humbler bosom vain?
Let school-taught pride dissemble all it can,
These little things are great to little man;
And wiser he, whose sympathetic mind
Exults in all the good of all mankind.
Ye glittering towns, with wealth and splendour crown'd;
Ye fields, where summer spreads profusion round;
Ye lakes, whose vessels catch the busy gale;
Ye bending swains, that dress the flowery vale;
For me your tributary stores combine:
Creation's heir, the world — the world is mine!

As some lone miser, visiting his store,
Bends at his treasure, counts, recounts it o'er;
Hoards after hoards his rising raptures fill,
Yet still he sighs, for hoards are wanting still:
Thus to my breast alternate passions rise,
Pleas'd with each good that Heaven to man supplies;
Yet oft a sigh prevails, and sorrows fall,
To see the hoard of human bliss so small;
And oft I wish, amidst the scene, to find
Some spot to real happiness consign'd,
Where my worn soul, each wandering hope at rest,
May gather bliss to see my fellows blest.

But where to find that happiest spot below,
Who can direct, when all pretend to know?
The shuddering tenant of the frigid zone
Boldly proclaims that happiest spot his own,
Extols the treasures of his stormy seas,
And his long nights of revelry and ease;
The naked negro, panting at *the line,
Boasts of his golden sands and palmy wine,
Basks in the glare, or stems the tepid wave,
And thanks his gods for all the good they gave.
Such is the patriot's boast, where'er we roam,
His first, best country ever is at home.
And yet, perhaps, if countries we compare,
And estimate the blessings which they share,
Though patriots flatter, still shall wisdom find
An equal portion dealt to all mankind;
As different good, by Art or Nature given,
To different nations makes their blessings even.

Nature, a mother kind alike to all,
Still grants her bliss at labour's earnest call;
With food as well the peasant is supplied
On Idra's cliffs as Arno's shelvy side;
And, though the rocky-crested summits frown,
These rocks by custom turn to beds of down.
From Art more various are the blessings sent:
Wealth, commerce, honour, liberty, content.
Yet these each other's power so strong contest,
That either seems destructive of the rest.
Where wealth and freedom reign, contentment fails,
And honour sinks where commerce long prevails.
Hence every state, to one lov'd blessing prone,
Conforms and models life to that alone.
Each to the favorite happiness attends,
And spurns the plan that aims at other ends;
Till, carried to excess in each domain,
This favorite good begets peculiar pain.

But let us try these truths with closer eyes,
And trace them through the prospect as it lies:
Here, for a while, my proper cares resign'd,
Here let me sit in sorrow for mankind;
Like yon neglected shrub at random cast,
That shades the steep, and sighs at every blast.

Far to the right, where Apennine ascends,
Bright as the summer, Italy extends;

Its uplands sloping deck the mountain's side,
Woods over woods in gay theatric pride;
While oft some temple's mouldering tops between
With venerable grandeur mark the scene.

Could Nature's bounty satisfy the breast,
The sons of Italy were surely blest.
Whatever fruits in different climes are found,
That proudly rise, or humbly court the ground;
Whatever blooms in torrid tracts appear,
Whose bright succession decks the varied year;
Whatever sweets salute the northern sky
With vernal lives, that blossom but to die;
These, here disporting, own the kindred soil,
Nor ask luxuriance from the planter's toil;
While sea-born gales their gelid wings expand
To winnow fragrance round the smiling land.

But small the bliss that sense alone bestows,
And sensual bliss is all the nation knows.
In florid beauty groves and fields appear,
Man seems the only growth that dwindles here.
Contrasted faults through all his manners reign:
Though poor, luxurious; though submissive, vain;
Though grave, yet trifling; zealous, yet untrue;
And ev'n in penance planning sins anew.
All evils here contaminate the mind,
That opulence departed leaves behind:
For wealth was theirs; not far remov'd the date,
When commerce proudly flourish'd through the state.
At her command the palace learnt to rise;
Again the long-fall'n column sought the skies;
The canvas glow'd beyond ev'n nature warm;
The pregnant quarry teem'd with human form;
Till, more unsteady than the southern gale,
Commerce on other shores display'd her sail;
While nought remain'd of all that riches gave,
But towns unmann'd, and lords without a slave:
And late the nation found, with fruitless skill,
Its former strength was but plethoric ill.

Yet still the loss of wealth is here supplied
By arts, the splendid wrecks of former pride;
From these the feeble heart and long-fall'n mind
An easy compensation seem to find.
Here may be seen, in bloodless pomp array'd,
The pasteboard triumph and the cavalcade;
Processions form'd for piety and love,
A mistress or a saint in every grove.
By sports like these are all their cares beguil'd,
The sports of children satisfy the child;
Each nobler aim, repress'd by long control,
Now sinks at last, or feebly mans the soul;
While low delights, succeeding fast behind,
In happier meanness occupy the mind:
As in those domes where Cæsars once bore sway,
Defac'd by time and tottering in decay,
There in the ruin, heedless of the dead,
The shelter-seeking peasant builds his shed;
And, wondering man could want the larger pile,
Exults, and owns his cottage with a smile.

My soul, turn from them; turn we to survey
Where rougher climes a nobler race display,
Where the bleak Swiss their stormy mansions tread,
And force a churlish soil for scanty bread:
No product here the barren hills afford,
But man and steel, the soldier and his sword;
No vernal blooms their torpid rocks array,
But winter lingering chills the lap of May;
No zephyr fondly sues the mountain's breast,
But meteors glare, and stormy glooms invest.

Yet still, even here, content can spread a charm,
Redress the clime, and all its rage disarm.
Though poor the peasant's hut, his feasts though small,
He sees his little lot the lot of all;
Sees no contiguous palace rear its head
To shame the meanness of his humble shed;
No costly lord the sumptuous banquet deal
To make him loathe his vegetable meal;
But calm, and bred in ignorance and toil,
Each wish contracting, fits him to the soil.
Cheerful, at morn, he wakes from short repose,
Breasts the keen air, and carols as he goes;
With patient angle trolls the finny deep,
Or drives his venturous ploughshare to the steep;

Or seeks the den where snow-tracks mark the way,
And drags *the struggling savage into day.
At night returning, every labour sped,
He sits him down, the monarch of a shed;
Smiles by his cheerful fire, and round surveys
His children's looks, that brighten at the blaze;
While his lov'd partner, boastful of her hoard,
Displays her cleanly platter on the board;
And haply too some pilgrim, thither led,
With many a tale repays the nightly bed.

Thus every good his native wilds impart,
Imprints the patriot passion on his heart;
And ev'n those ills that round his mansion rise,
Enhance the bliss his scanty fund supplies.
Dear is that shed to which his soul conforms,
And dear that hill which lifts him to the storms;
And as a child, when scaring sounds molest,
Clings close and closer to the mother's breast,
So the loud torrent and the whirlwind's roar
But bind him to his native mountains more.

Such are the charms to barren states assign'd;
Their wants but few, their wishes all confin'd.
Yet let them only share the praises due;
If few their wants, their pleasures are but few;
For every want that stimulates the breast
Becomes a source of pleasure when redrest.
Whence from such lands each pleasing science flies,
That first excites desire, and then supplies;
Unknown to them, when sensual pleasures cloy,
To fill the languid pause with finer joy;
Unknown those powers that raise the soul to flame,
Catch every nerve, and vibrate through the frame.
Their level life is but a smouldering fire,
Unquench'd by want, unfann'd by strong desire;
Unfit for raptures, or, if raptures cheer
On some high festival of once a year,
In wild excess the vulgar breast takes fire,
Till, buried in debauch, the bliss expire.

But not their joys alone thus coarsely flow;
Their morals, like their pleasures, are but low;
For, as refinement stops, from sire to son
Unalter'd, unimprov'd the manners run;
And love's and friendship's finely pointed dart
Fall blunted from each indurated heart.
Some sterner virtues o'er the mountain's breast
May sit, like falcons cowering on the nest;
But all the gentler morals, such as play
Through life's more cultur'd walks, and charm the way,
These, far dispers'd, on timorous pinions fly,
To sport and flutter in a kinder sky.

To kinder skies, where gentler manners reign,
I turn; and France displays her bright domain.
Gay, sprightly land of mirth and social ease,
Pleas'd with thyself, whom all the world can please,
How often have I led thy sportive choir,
With tuneless pipe, beside the murmuring Loire!
Where shading elms along the margin grew,
And freshen'd from the wave the zephyr flew;
And haply, though my harsh touch, faltering still,
But mock'd all tune, and marr'd the dancer's skill,
Yet would the village praise my wondrous power,
And dance, forgetful of the noontide hour.
Alike all ages: dames of ancient days
Have led their children through the mirthful maze;
And the gay grandsire, skill'd in *gestic lore,
Has frisk'd beneath the burden of threescore.

So blest a life these thoughtless realms display;
Thus idly busy rolls their world away.
Theirs are those arts that mind to mind endear,
For honour forms the social temper here.
Honour, that praise which real merit gains,
Or e'en imaginary worth obtains,
Here passes current; paid from hand to hand,
It shifts in splendid traffic round the land;
From courts to camps, to cottages it strays,
And all are taught an avarice of praise.
They please, are pleas'd; they give to get esteem,
Till, seeming blest, they grow to what they seem.

But while this softer art their bliss supplies
It gives their follies also room to rise;

For praise too dearly lov'd, or warmly sought,
Enfeebles all internal strength of thought:
And the weak soul, within itself unblest,
Leans for all pleasure on another's breast.
Hence ostentation here, with tawdry art,
Pants for the vulgar praise which fools impart;
Here vanity assumes her pert grimace,
And trims her robes of frieze with copper lace;
Here beggar pride defrauds her daily cheer,
To boast one splendid banquet once a year:
The mind still turns where shifting fashion draws,
Nor weighs the solid worth of self-applause.

To men of other minds my fancy flies,
Embosom'd in the deep where Holland lies.
Methinks her patient sons before me stand,
Where the broad ocean leans against the land,
And, sedulous to stop the coming tide,
Lift the tall *rampire's artificial pride.
Onward, methinks, and diligently slow,
The firm connected bulwark seems to grow,
Spreads its long arms amidst the watery roar,
Scoops out an empire, and usurps the shore.
While the pent ocean, rising o'er the pile,
Sees an amphibious world beneath him smile;
The slow canal, the yellow-blossom'd vale,
The willow-tufted bank, the gliding sail,
The crowded mart, the cultivated plain,
A new creation rescued from his reign.

Thus, while around the wave-subjected soil
Impels the native to repeated toil,
Industrious habits in each bosom reign,
And industry begets a love of gain.
Hence all the good from opulence that springs,
With all those ills superfluous treasure brings,
Are here display'd. Their much-lov'd wealth imparts
Convenience, plenty, elegance, and arts;
But, view them closer, craft and fraud appear;
Even liberty itself is barter'd here.
At gold's superior charms all freedom flies;
The needy sell it, and the rich man buys.
A land of tyrants, and a den of slaves,
Here wretches seek dishonourable graves,
And calmly bent, to servitude conform,
Dull as their lakes that slumber in the storm.

Heavens! how unlike their Belgic sires of old —
Rough, poor, content, ungovernably bold;
War in each breast, and freedom on each brow;
How much unlike the sons of Britain now!

Fir'd at the sound, my genius spreads her wing,
And flies where Britain courts the western spring;
Where lawns extend that scorn Arcadian pride,
And brighter streams than fam'd Hydaspes glide.
There all around the gentlest breezes stray,
There gentle music melts on every spray;
Creation's mildest charms are there combin'd:
Extremes are only in the master's mind!
Stern o'er each bosom reason holds her state,
With daring aims irregularly great;
Pride in their port, defiance in their eye,
I see the lords of human kind pass by;
Intent on high designs, a thoughtful band,
By forms unfashion'd, fresh from Nature's hand,
Fierce in their native hardiness of soul,
True to imagin'd right, above control;
While even the peasant boasts these rights to scan,
And learns to venerate himself as man.

Thine, Freedom, thine the blessings pictur'd here,
Thine are those charms that dazzle and endear;
Too blest, indeed, were such without alloy;
But, foster'd even by freedom, ills annoy:
That independence Britons prize too high
Keeps man from man, and breaks the social tie;
The self-dependent lordlings stand alone,
All claims that bind and sweeten life unknown.
Here, by the bonds of nature feebly held,
Minds combat minds, repelling and repell'd;
Ferments arise, imprison'd factions roar,
Repress'd ambition struggles round her shore;
Till, overwrought, the general system feels
Its motions stop, or frenzy fire the wheels.

Nor this the worst. As nature's ties decay,
As duty, love, and honour fail to sway,
Fictitious bonds, the bonds of wealth and law,
Still gather strength, and force unwilling awe.
Hence all obedience bows to these alone,
And talent sinks, and merit weeps unknown;
Till time may come, when, stripp'd of all her charms,
The land of scholars, and the nurse of arms,
Where noble stems transmit the patriot flame,
Where kings have toil'd and poets wrote for fame,

One sink of level avarice shall lie,
And scholars, soldiers, kings, unhonour'd die.

Yet think not, thus when Freedom's ills I state,
I mean to flatter kings, or court the great:
Ye powers of truth, that bid my soul aspire,
Far from my bosom drive the low desire!
And thou, fair Freedom, taught alike to feel
The rabble's rage, and tyrant's angry steel;
Thou transitory flower, alike undone
By proud contempt, or favour's fostering sun,
Still may thy blooms the changeful clime endure!
I only would repress them to secure:
For just experience tells, in every soil,
That those who think must govern those that toil;
And all that Freedom's highest aims can reach
Is but to lay proportion'd loads on each.
Hence, should one order disproportion'd grow,
Its double weight must ruin all below.

Oh, then how blind to all that truth requires,
Who think it freedom when a part aspires!
Calm is my soul, nor apt to rise in arms,
Except when fast approaching danger warms:
But when contending chiefs blockade the throne,
Contracting regal power to stretch their own;
When I behold a factious band agree
To call it freedom when themselves are free;
Each wanton judge new penal statutes draw,
Laws grind the poor, and rich men rule the law;
The wealth of climes, where savage nations roam,
Pillag'd from slaves to purchase slaves at home;
Fear, pity, justice, indignation, start,
Tear off reserve, and bare my swelling heart;
Till, half a patriot, half a coward grown,
I fly from petty tyrants to the throne.

Yes, brother, curse with me that baleful hour,
When first ambition struck at regal power;
And thus polluting honour in its source,
Gave wealth to sway the mind with double force.
Have we not seen, round Britain's peopled shore,
Her useful sons exchang'd for useless ore?
Seen all her triumphs but destruction haste,
Like flaring tapers brightening as they waste?
Seen opulence, her grandeur to maintain,
Lead stern depopulation in her train,
And over fields where scatter'd hamlets rose,
In barren, solitary pomp repose?
Have we not seen, at pleasure's lordly call,
The smiling, long frequented village fall?
Beheld the duteous son, the sire decay'd,
The modest matron, and the blushing maid,
Forc'd from their homes, a melancholy train,
To traverse climes beyond the western main;
Where wild Oswego spreads her swamps around,
And Niagàra stuns with thundering sound?

E'en now, perhaps, as there some pilgrim strays
Through tangled forests, and through dangerous ways,
Where beasts with man divided empire claim,
And the brown Indian marks with murderous aim;
There, while above the giddy tempest flies,
And all around distressful yells arise,
The pensive exile, bending with his woe,
*To stop too fearful, and too faint to go,
Casts a long look where England's glories shine,
And bids his bosom sympathize with mine.

Vain, very vain, my weary search to find
That bliss which only centres in the mind:
Why have I stray'd from pleasure and repose,
To seek a good each government bestows?
In every government, though terrors reign,
Though tyrant kings or tyrant laws restrain,
How small, of all that human hearts endure,
That part which laws or kings can cause or cure!
Still to ourselves in every place consign'd,
Our own felicity we make or find:
With secret course, which no loud storms annoy,
Glides the smooth current of domestic joy.
The lifted axe, the agonizing wheel,
*Luke's iron crown, and *Damiens' bed of steel,
To men remote from power but rarely known,
Leave reason, faith, and conscience, all our own.

[1764]

THE DESERTED VILLAGE

Sweet Auburn! loveliest village of the plain,
Where health and plenty cheer'd the labouring swain,
Where smiling spring its earliest visit paid,
And parting summer's lingering blooms delay'd;
Dear lovely bowers of innocence and ease,
Seats of my youth, when every sport could please,
How often have I loiter'd o'er thy green,
Where humble happiness endear'd each scene!
How often have I paus'd on every charm,
The shelter'd cot, the cultivated farm,
The never-failing brook, the busy mill,
The decent church that topp'd the neighbouring hill,
The hawthorn bush, with seats beneath the shade,
For talking age and whispering lovers made!
How often have I blest the coming day,
When toil remitting lent its turn to play,
And all the village train, from labour free,
Led up their sports beneath the spreading tree;
While many a pastime circled in the shade,
The young contending as the old survey'd;
And many a gambol frolick'd o'er the ground,
And sleights of art and feats of strength went round;
And still, as each repeated pleasure tir'd,
Succeeding sports the mirthful band inspir'd;
The dancing pair that simply sought renown,
By holding out to tire each other down;
The swain mistrustless of his smutted face,
While secret laughter titter'd round the place;
The bashful virgin's sidelong looks of love,
The matron's glance that would those looks reprove:
These were thy charms, sweet village! sports like these,
With sweet succession, taught e'en toil to please;
These round thy bowers their cheerful influence shed,
These were thy charms — but all these charms are fled.

Sweet smiling village, loveliest of the lawn!
Thy sports are fled, and all thy charms withdrawn:
Amidst thy bowers the tyrant's hand is seen,
And desolation saddens all thy green;
One only master grasps the whole domain,
And half a tillage stints thy smiling plain;
No more thy glassy brook reflects the day,
But, chok'd with sedges, works its weedy way;
Along thy glades, a solitary guest,
The hollow-sounding bittern guards its nest;
Amidst thy desert walks the lapwing flies,
And tires their echoes with unvaried cries.
Sunk are thy bowers in shapeless ruin all,
And the long grass o'ertops the mouldering wall;
And, trembling, shrinking from the spoiler's hand,
Far, far away thy children leave the land.

Ill fares the land, to hastening ills a prey,
Where wealth accumulates, and men decay:
Princes and lords may flourish, or may fade —
A breath can make them, as a breath has made;
But a bold peasantry, their country's pride,
When once destroy'd, can never be supplied.

A time there was, ere England's griefs began,
When every rood of ground maintain'd its man;
For him light labour spread her wholesome store,
Just gave what life requir'd, but gave no more;
His best companions, innocence and health;
And his best riches, ignorance of wealth.

But times are alter'd; trade's unfeeling train
Usurp the land, and dispossess the swain:
Along the lawn, where scatter'd hamlets rose,
Unwieldy wealth and cumbrous pomp repose;
And every want to opulence allied,
And every pang that folly pays to pride.
Those gentle hours that plenty bade to bloom,
Those calm desires that ask'd but little room,
Those healthful sports that grac'd the peaceful scene,
Liv'd in each look, and brighten'd all the green:
These, far departing, seek a kinder shore,
And rural mirth and manners are no more.

Sweet Auburn! parent of the blissful hour,
Thy glades forlorn confess the tyrant's power.
Here, as I take my solitary rounds,
Amidst thy tangling walks and ruin'd grounds,
And, many a year elaps'd, return to view
Where once the cottage stood, the hawthorn grew,
Remembrance wakes, with all her busy train,
Swells at my breast, and turns the past to pain.

In all my wanderings round this world of care,
In all my griefs — and God has given my share —
I still had hopes, my latest hours to crown,
Amidst these humble bowers to lay me down;
To husband out life's taper at the close,
And keep the flame from wasting by repose.
I still had hopes — for pride attends us still —
Amidst the swains to show my book-learn'd skill,
Around my fire an evening group to draw,
And tell of all I felt, and all I saw;
And, as a hare whom hounds and horns pursue,
Pants to the place from whence at first she flew,
I still had hopes, my long vexations past,
Here to return, — and die at home at last.

Oh, blest retirement! friend to life's decline,
Retreats from care, that never must be mine,
How happy he who crowns in shades like these
A youth of labour with an age of ease;
Who quits a world where strong temptations try,
And, since 'tis hard to combat, learns to fly!
For him no wretches, born to work and weep,
Explore the mine, or tempt the dangerous deep;
No surly porter stands in guilty state,
To spurn imploring famine from the gate:
But on he moves to meet his latter end,
Angels around befriending virtue's friend;
Bends to the grave with unperceiv'd decay,
While resignation gently slopes the way;
And, all his prospects brightening to the last,
His heaven commences ere the world be past.

Sweet was the sound, when oft at evening's close
Up yonder hill the village murmur rose;
There, as I pass'd with careless steps and slow,
The mingling notes came soften'd from below:
The swain responsive as the milkmaid sung,
The sober herd that low'd to meet their young;
The noisy geese that gabbled o'er the pool,
The playful children just let loose from school;
The watch-dog's voice that bay'd the whispering wind,
And the loud laugh that spoke the vacant mind —
These all in sweet confusion sought the shade,
And fill'd each pause the nightingale had made.
But now the sounds of population fail,
No cheerful murmurs fluctuate in the gale;
No busy steps the grass-grown footway tread,
For all the bloomy flush of life is fled.
All but yon widow'd, solitary thing
That feebly bends beside the plashy spring;
She, wretched matron, forc'd in age, for bread,
To strip the brook with mantling cresses spread,
To pick her wintry fagot from the thorn,
To seek her nightly shed, and weep till morn —
She only left of all the harmless train,
The sad historian of the pensive plain.

Near yonder copse, where once the garden smil'd,
And still where many a garden flower grows wild,
There, where a few torn shrubs the place disclose,
The village preacher's modest mansion rose.
A man he was to all the country dear,
And passing rich with forty pounds a year;
Remote from towns he ran his godly race,
Nor e'er had chang'd, nor wish'd to change, his place;
Unpractis'd he to fawn, or seek for power,
By doctrines fashion'd to the varying hour;
Far other aims his heart had learn'd to prize,
More skill'd to raise the wretched than to rise.
His house was known to all the vagrant train,
He chid their wanderings, but reliev'd their pain;
The long-remember'd beggar was his guest,
Whose beard descending swept his aged breast;
The ruin'd spendthrift, now no longer proud,
Claim'd kindred there, and had his claims allow'd;
The broken soldier, kindly bade to stay,
Sat by his fire, and talk'd the night away;
Wept o'er his wounds, or, tales of sorrow done,
Shoulder'd his crutch, and show'd how fields were won.
Pleas'd with his guests, the good man learn'd to glow,
And quite forgot their vices in their woe;
Careless their merits or their faults to scan,
His pity gave ere charity began.

Thus to relieve the wretched was his pride,
And e'en his failings lean'd to virtue's side;

But in his duty prompt at every call,
He watch'd and wept, he pray'd and felt for all;
And, as a bird each fond endearment tries
To tempt its new-fledg'd offspring to the skies,
He tried each art, reprov'd each dull delay,
Allur'd to brighter worlds, and led the way.

Beside the bed where parting life was laid,
And sorrow, guilt, and pain, by turns dismay'd,
The reverend champion stood. At his control,
Despair and anguish fled the struggling soul;
Comfort came down the trembling wretch to raise,
And his last faltering accents whisper'd praise.

At church, with meek and unaffected grace,
His looks adorn'd the venerable place;
Truth from his lips prevail'd with double sway,
And fools who came to scoff remain'd to pray.
The service past, around the pious man,
With steady zeal, each honest rustic ran;
E'en children follow'd, with endearing wile,
And pluck'd his gown, to share the good man's smile.
His ready smile a parent's warmth express'd,
Their welfare pleas'd him, and their cares distress'd;
To them his heart, his love, his griefs were given,
But all his serious thoughts had rest in heaven.
As some tall cliff that lifts its awful form,
Swells from the vale, and midway leaves the storm,
Though round its breast the rolling clouds are spread,
Eternal sunshine settles on its head.

Beside yon straggling fence that skirts the way,
With blossom'd furze unprofitably gay,
There, in his noisy mansion, skill'd to rule,
The village master taught his little school.
A man severe he was, and stern to view;
I knew him well, and every truant knew:
Well had the boding tremblers learn'd to trace
The day's disasters in his morning face;
Full well they laugh'd, with counterfeited glee,
At all his jokes, for many a joke had he;
Full well the busy whisper, circling round,
Convey'd the dismal tidings when he frown'd.
Yet he was kind, or, if severe in aught,
The love he bore to learning was in fault.
The village all declar'd how much he knew;
'Twas certain he could write, and cipher too;
Lands he could measure, terms and tides presage,
And e'en the story ran — that he could gauge:
In arguing, too, the parson own'd his skill,
For e'en though vanquish'd, he could argue still;
While words of learned length and thundering sound
Amaz'd the gazing rustics rang'd around;
And still they gaz'd, and still the wonder grew
That one small head could carry all he knew.

But past is all his fame. The very spot
Where many a time he triumph'd is forgot.
Near yonder thorn that lifts its head on high,
Where once the sign-post caught the passing eye,
Low lies that house where nut-brown draughts inspir'd,
Where graybeard mirth and smiling toil retir'd,
Where village statesmen talk'd with looks profound,
And news much older than their ale went round.
Imagination fondly stoops to trace
The parlour splendours of that festive place:
The whitewash'd wall, the nicely sanded floor,
The varnish'd clock that click'd behind the door;
The chest contriv'd a double debt to pay,
A bed by night, a chest of drawers by day;
The pictures plac'd for ornament and use,
*The twelve good rules, *the royal game of goose;
The hearth, except when winter chill'd the day,
With aspen boughs, and flowers, and fennel gay,
While broken teacups, wisely kept for show,
Rang'd o'er the chimney, glisten'd in a row.

Vain, transitory splendours! could not all
Reprieve the tottering mansion from its fall?
Obscure it sinks, nor shall it more impart
An hour's importance to the poor man's heart.
Thither no more the peasant shall repair
To sweet oblivion of his daily care;
No more the farmer's news, the barber's tale,
No more the woodman's ballad shall prevail;

No more the smith his dusky brow shall clear,
Relax his ponderous strength, and lean to hear;
The host himself no longer shall be found
Careful to see the mantling bliss go round;
Nor the coy maid, half willing to be press'd,
Shall kiss the cup to pass it to the rest.

Yes! let the rich deride, the proud disdain,
These simple blessings of the lowly train;
To me more dear, congenial to my heart,
One native charm, than all the gloss of art.
Spontaneous joys, where nature has its play,
The soul adopts, and owns their first-born sway;
Lightly they frolic o'er the vacant mind,
Unenvied, unmolested, unconfin'd.
But the long pomp, the midnight masquerade,
With all the freaks of wanton wealth array'd,—
In these, ere triflers half their wish obtain,
The toiling pleasure sickens into pain;
And e'en while fashion's brightest arts decoy,
The heart, distrusting, asks if this be joy.

Ye friends to truth, ye statesmen, who survey
The rich man's joys increase, the poor's decay,
'Tis yours to judge how wide the limits stand
Between a splendid and a happy land.
Proud swells the tide with loads of freighted ore,
And shouting Folly hails them from her shore;
Hoards e'en beyond the miser's wish abound,
And rich men flock from all the world around.
Yet count our gains: this wealth is but a name
That leaves our useful products still the same.
Not so the loss: the man of wealth and pride
Takes up a space that many poor supplied;
Space for his lake, his park's extended bounds,
Space for his horses, equipage, and hounds:
The robe that wraps his limbs in silken sloth
Has robb'd the neighbouring fields of half their growth;
His seat, where solitary sports are seen,
Indignant spurns the cottage from the green;
Around the world each needful product flies,
For all the luxuries the world supplies;
While thus the land, adorn'd for pleasure, all
In barren splendour feebly waits the fall.

As some fair female, unadorn'd and plain,
Secure to please while youth confirms her reign,
Slights every borrow'd charm that dress supplies,
Nor shares with art the triumph of her eyes;
But when those charms are past, for charms are frail,
When time advances, and when lovers fail,
She then shines forth, solicitous to bless,
In all the glaring impotence of dress:
Thus fares the land, by luxury betray'd;
In nature's simplest charms at first array'd;
But verging to decline, its splendours rise,
Its vistas strike, its palaces surprise;
While, scourged by famine from the smiling land,
The mournful peasant leads his humble band;
And while he sinks, without one arm to save,
The country blooms — a garden and a grave.

Where then, ah! where shall poverty reside,
To 'scape the pressure of contiguous pride?
If to some common's fenceless limits stray'd,
He drives his flock to pick the scanty blade,
Those fenceless fields the sons of wealth divide,
And e'en the bare-worn common is denied.

If to the city sped, what waits him there?
To see profusion that he must not share;
To see ten thousand baneful arts combin'd
To pamper luxury, and thin mankind;
To see those joys the sons of pleasure know
Extorted from his fellow-creature's woe.
Here, while the courtier glitters in brocade,
There the pale *artist plies the sickly trade;
Here, while the proud their long-drawn pomps display,
There the black gibbet glooms beside the way.
The dome where Pleasure holds her midnight reign,
Here, richly deck'd, admits the gorgeous train;
Tumultuous grandeur crowds the blazing square,
The rattling chariots clash, the torches glare.
Sure scenes like these no troubles e'er annoy!
Sure these denote one universal joy!
Are these thy serious thoughts? Ah! turn thine eyes
Where the poor houseless shivering female lies.
She once, perhaps, in village plenty blest,
Has wept at tales of innocence distrest;
Her modest looks the cottage might adorn,
Sweet as the primrose peeps beneath the thorn;

Now lost to all — her friends, her virtue fled —
Near her betrayer's door she lays her head,
And, pinch'd with cold, and shrinking from the shower,
With heavy heart deplores that luckless hour,
When idly first, ambitious of the town,
She left her wheel, and robes of country brown.

Do thine, sweet Auburn, thine, the loveliest train,
Do thy fair tribes participate her pain?
E'en now, perhaps, by cold and hunger led,
At proud men's doors they ask a little bread.

Ah, no! To distant climes, a dreary scene,
Where half the convex world intrudes between,
Through torrid tracts with fainting steps they go,
Where wild Altama murmurs to their woe.
Far different there from all that charm'd before,
The various terrors of that horrid shore;
Those blazing suns that dart a downward ray,
And fiercely shed intolerable day;
Those matted woods where birds forget to sing,
But silent bats in drowsy clusters cling;
Those pois'nous fields with rank luxuriance crown'd,
Where the dark scorpion gathers death around;
Where at each step the stranger fears to wake
The rattling terrors of the vengeful snake;
Where crouching tigers wait their hapless prey,
And savage men more murderous still than they;
While oft in whirls the mad tornado flies,
Mingling the ravag'd landscape with the skies.
Far different these from every former scene,
The cooling brook, the grassy-vested green,
The breezy covert of the warbling grove,
That only shelter'd thefts of harmless love.

Good Heaven! what sorrows gloom'd that parting day
That call'd them from their native walks away;
When the poor exiles, every pleasure past,
Hung round the bowers, and fondly look'd their last,
And took a long farewell, and wish'd in vain
For seats like these beyond the western main;
And, shuddering still to face the distant deep,
Return'd and wept, and still return'd to weep!
The good old sire the first prepar'd to go
To new-found worlds, and wept for others' woe;
But for himself, in conscious virtue brave,
He only wish'd for worlds beyond the grave.
His lovely daughter, lovelier in her tears,
The fond companion of his helpless years,
Silent went next, neglectful of her charms,
And left a lover's for a father's arms.
With louder plaints the mother spoke her woes,
And bless'd the cot where every pleasure rose;
And kiss'd her thoughtless babes with many a tear
And clasp'd them close, in sorrow doubly dear;
Whilst her fond husband strove to lend relief
In all the silent manliness of grief.

O Luxury! thou curst by Heaven's decree,
How ill exchang'd are things like these for thee!
How do thy potions, with insidious joy,
Diffuse their pleasures only to destroy!
Kingdoms by thee, to sickly greatness grown,
Boast of a florid vigour not their own:
At every draught more large and large they grow,
A bloated mass of rank, unwieldy woe;
Till sapp'd their strength, and every part unsound,
Down, down they sink, and spread a ruin round.

E'en now the devastation is begun,
And half the business of destruction done;
E'en now, methinks, as pondering here I stand,
I see the rural virtues leave the land.
Down where yon anchoring vessel spreads the sail
That idly waiting flaps with every gale,
Downward they move, a melancholy band,
Pass from the shore, and darken all the strand.
Contented toil, and hospitable care,
And kind connubial tenderness, are there;
And piety with wishes plac'd above,
And steady loyalty, and faithful love.
And thou, sweet Poetry, thou loveliest maid,
Still first to fly where sensual joys invade;
Unfit, in these degenerate times of shame,
To catch the heart, or strike for honest fame;
Dear charming nymph, neglected and decried,
My shame in crowds, my solitary pride;

Thou source of all my bliss and all my woe,
That found'st me poor at first, and keep'st me so;
Thou guide by which the nobler arts excel,
Thou nurse of every virtue, fare thee well!
Farewell! and oh! where'er thy voice be tried,
On Torno's cliffs, or Pambamarca's side,
Whether where equinoctial fervours glow,
Or winter wraps the polar world in snow,
Still let thy voice, prevailing over time,
Redress the rigours of the inclement clime;
Aid slighted truth with thy persuasive strain;
Teach erring man to spurn the rage of gain;
Teach him that states of native strength possest,
Though very poor, may still be very blest;
*That trade's proud empire hastes to swift decay,
As ocean sweeps the labour'd mole away;
While self-dependent power can time defy,
As rocks resist the billows and the sky.

[1770]

EDWARD GIBBON

GIBBON is representative of the eighteenth century; in his work neo-classicism found characteristic expression. Though his education was irregular, it gave him a thorough grounding in the Latin and Greek classics; without making him un-English it emancipated him from British insularity and brought him into contact with French as well as English culture. He was interested in ideas, and had a cultivated taste and sound scholarship. The best part of his life was given to one huge task, *The History of the Decline and Fall of the Roman Empire.* With painstaking thoroughness he made himself master of all the available source material; he planned a great historical structure and completed it with unswerving determination. Accuracy of detail has seldom been combined with greater imaginative sweep. To the task of the historian he brought the intellect of a philosopher and the lively fancy of a poet. He was clear-minded, sceptical, somewhat detached. If he sometimes failed to attain insight, he had sight of extraordinary keenness and strength. Later historians have had access to materials that were not known to Gibbon; they have supplemented his work, corrected it, retouched it here and there, but they have not superseded it. Yet Gibbon was not a professional historian; he was a gentleman amateur living for rather than by his work. Varied activities diversified his interests and enriched his experience: travel, society, scholarly correspondence, service in the Hampshire militia, a seat in Parliament. He was the better historian because he was more than a mere historian. He was the better representative of his age because he was a man of the world.

After completing *The Decline and Fall of the Roman Empire*, 1776–88, Gibbon began to write his *Memoirs.* "Truth," he asserted, "naked, unblushing truth, the first virtue of more serious history, must be the sole recommendation of this personal narrative.... My own amusement is my motive, and will be my reward." The work was never completed, but from the fragments that were left, his friend, Lord Sheffield, pieced together and published two years after the author's death the *Autobiography*, which has taken its place alongside the great history as a second and scarcely less valid claim to enduring reputation. In this little book he reveals himself with uncommon clarity. The picture is not altogether pleasing; it shows at the same time the devotion of the author and the vanity of the man. He was too egotistical to hide his own egotism and too faithful a historian to conceal his own foibles. The result is a piece of self-portraiture such as might result if the methods of the "new biography" were applied to autobiography. It is not without significance that the greatest literary life and one of the outstanding autobiographies in English should have been written at about the same time by two members of Dr. Johnson's Club.

Gibbon's prose style in *The Decline and Fall* has something of the Johnsonian sweep without the Johnsonian stiffness. It is clear, stately, antithetical, and to some extent oratorical. In the *Autobiography* it is simpler and more familiar without losing its essential characteristics.

The two extracts here reprinted show both aspects of his work. The first, from Chapter LII of *The Decline and Fall of the Roman Empire*, presents one of the crises in the mighty drama of Moslem conquest. The second is from the first part of the *Autobiography.* While the view of Oxford that it gives is undoubtedly biased, it sheds much light on English university life in the eighteenth century as well as on the character and personality of its author. It should be remembered, however, that Gibbon was not yet sixteen when he went up to Oxford and that he had just recovered from an illness which had threatened to leave him a permanent invalid. Had he entered the university under more normal conditions, his experiences might have been happier, though it is unlikely that under any circumstances he would have found much profit in the academic discipline which then prevailed.

THE HISTORY OF THE DECLINE AND FALL OF THE ROMAN EMPIRE

From CHAPTER LII

...*Constantinople and the Greek fire might exclude the Arabs from the eastern entrance of Europe; but in the west, on the side of the Pyrenees, the provinces of Gaul were threatened and invaded by the conquerors of Spain. The decline of the French monarchy invited the attack of these insatiate fanatics. The descendants of Clovis had lost the inheritance of his martial and ferocious spirit; and their misfortune or demerit has affixed the epithet of *lazy* to the last kings of the Merovingian race. They ascended the throne without

* Notes on Edward Gibbon will be found in the Appendix, pp. 1039 ff.

power, and sunk into the grave without a name. A country palace, in the neighbourhood of Compiègne, was allotted for their residence or prison; but each year, in the month of March or May, they were conducted in a wagon drawn by oxen to the assembly of the Franks, to give audience to foreign ambassadors, and to ratify the acts of the Mayor of the Palace. That domestic officer was become the minister of the nation, and the master of the prince. A public employment was converted into the patrimony of a private family; the elder Pepin left a king of mature years under the guardianship of his own widow and her child; and these feeble regents were forcibly dispossessed by the most active of his bastards. A government, half savage and half corrupt, was almost dissolved; and the tributary dukes, the provincial counts, and the territorial lords were tempted to despise the weakness of the monarch and to imitate the ambition of the mayor. Among these independent chiefs, one of the boldest and most successful was Eudes, Duke of Aquitaine, who, in the southern provinces of Gaul, usurped the authority and even the title of king. The Goths, the Gascons, and the Franks assembled under the standard of this Christian hero; he repelled the first invasion of the Saracens; and Zama, lieutenant of the caliph, lost his army and his life under the walls of Toulouse. The ambition of his successors was stimulated by revenge; they repassed the Pyrenees with the means and the resolution of conquest. The advantageous situation which had recommended Narbonne as the first Roman colony was again chosen by the Moslems: they claimed the province of Septimania, or Languedoc, as a just dependence of the Spanish monarchy: the vineyards of Gascony and the city of Bordeaux were possessed by the sovereign of Damascus and Samarcand; and the south of France, from the mouth of the Garonne to that of the Rhone, assumed the manners and religion of Arabia.

But these narrow limits were scorned by the spirit of Abdalrahman, or Abderame, who had been restored by the Caliph Hashem to the wishes of the soldiers and people of Spain. That veteran and daring commander adjudged to the obedience of the prophet whatever yet remained of France or of Europe; and prepared to execute the sentence, at the head of a formidable host, in the full confidence of surmounting all opposition, either of nature or of man. His first care was to suppress a domestic rebel, who commanded the most important passes of the Pyrenees: Munuza, a Moorish chief, had accepted the alliance of the Duke of Aquitaine; and Eudes, from a motive of private or public interest, devoted his beauteous daughter to the embraces of the African misbeliever. But the strongest fortresses of Cerdagne were invested by a superior force; the rebel was overtaken and slain in the mountains; and his widow was sent a captive to Damascus, to gratify the desires, or more probably the vanity, of the Commander of the Faithful. From the Pyrenees Abderame proceeded without delay to the passage of the Rhone and the siege of Arles. An army of Christians attempted the relief of the city; the tombs of their leaders were yet visible in the thirteenth century; and many thousands of their dead bodies were carried down the rapid stream into the Mediterranean Sea. The arms of Abderame were not less successful on the side of the ocean. He passed without opposition the Garonne and Dordogne, which unite their waters in the Gulf of Bordeaux; but he found, beyond those rivers, the camp of the intrepid Eudes, who had formed a second army, and sustained a second defeat, so fatal to the Christians that, according to their sad confession, God alone could reckon the number of the slain. The victorious Saracen overran the provinces of Aquitaine, whose Gallic names are disguised, rather than lost, in the modern appellations of Périgord, Saintonge, and Poitou: his standards were planted on the walls, or at least before the gates, of Tours and of Sens; and his detachments overspread the kingdom of Burgundy, as far as the well known cities of Lyons and Besançon. *The memory of these devastations, for Abderame did not spare the country or the people, was long preserved by tradition; and the invasion of France by the Moors or Mahometans affords the groundwork of those fables which have been so wildly disfigured in the romances of chivalry and so elegantly adorned by the Italian muse. In the decline of society and art, the deserted cities could supply a slender booty to the Saracens; their richest spoil was found in the churches and monasteries, which they stripped of their ornaments and delivered to the flames; and the tutelar saints, both Hilary of Poitiers and Martin of Tours, forgot their miraculous powers in the defence of their own sepulchres. A victorious line of march had been prolonged above a thousand miles from the rock of Gibraltar to the banks of the Loire; the repetition of an equal space would have carried the Saracens to the confines of Poland and the Highlands of Scotland; the Rhine is not more impassable than the Nile or Euphrates, and the Arabian fleet might have sailed without a naval combat into the mouth of the Thames. Perhaps the interpretation of the Koran would now be taught in the schools of Oxford, and her pulpits might demonstrate to a circumcised people the sanctity and truth of the revelation of Mahomet.

From such calamities was Christendom delivered by the genius and fortune of one man. Charles, the illegitimate son of the elder Pepin, was content with the titles of Mayor or Duke of the Franks, but he deserved to become the father of a line of kings. In a laborious administration of twenty-four years, he restored and supported the dignity of the throne; and the rebels of Germany and Gaul were successively crushed by the activity of a warrior, who, in the same campaign, could display his banner on the Elbe, the Rhone, and the shores of the ocean. In the public danger he was summoned by the voice of his country; and his rival, the Duke of Aquitaine, was reduced to appear among the fugitives and suppliants. "Alas!" exclaimed the Franks, "what a misfortune! what an indignity! We have long heard of the name and conquests of the Arabs: we were apprehensive of their attack from the east; they have now conquered Spain, and invade our country on the side of the west. Yet their numbers, and (since they have no buckler) their arms, are inferior to our own." "If you follow my advice," replied the prudent Mayor of the Palace, "you will not interrupt their march, nor precipitate your attack. They are like a torrent, which it is dangerous to stem in its career. The thirst of riches and the consciousness of success redouble their valour, and valour is of more avail than arms or numbers. Be patient till they have loaded themselves with the encumbrance of wealth. The possession of wealth will divide their counsels and assure your victory." This subtle policy is perhaps a refinement of the Arabian writers; and the situation of Charles will suggest a more narrow and selfish motive of procrastination: the secret desire of humbling the pride, and wasting the provinces, of the rebel Duke of Aquitaine. It is yet more probable that the delays of Charles were inevitable and reluctant. A standing army was unknown under the first and second race; more than half the kingdom was now in the hands of the Saracens; according to their respective situation, the Franks of *Neustria and Austrasia were too conscious or too careless of the impending danger; and the voluntary aids of the Gepidæ and Germans were separated by a long interval from the standard of the Christian general. No sooner had he collected his forces than he sought and found the enemy in the centre of France, between Tours and Poitiers. His well conducted march was covered by a range of hills, and Abderame appears to have been surprised by his unexpected presence. The nations of Asia, Africa, and Europe advanced with equal ardour to an encounter which would change the history of the whole world. In the six first days of desultory combat, the horsemen and archers of the East maintained their advantage; but in the closer onset of the seventh day the Orientals were oppressed by the strength and stature of the Germans, who, with stout hearts and iron hands, asserted the civil and religious freedom of their posterity. The epithet of *Martel*, the *Hammer*, which has been added to the name of Charles, is expressive of his weighty and irresistible strokes: the valour of Eudes was excited by resentment and emulation; and their companions, in the eye of history, are the true peers and paladins of French chivalry. After a bloody field, in which Abderame was slain, the Saracens, in the close of the evening, retired to their camp. In the disorder and despair of the night, the various tribes of Yemen and Damascus, of Africa and Spain, were provoked to turn their arms against each other; the remains of their host was suddenly dissolved, and each emir consulted his safety by an hasty and separate retreat. At the dawn of day, the stillness of an hostile camp was suspected by the victorious Christians: on the report of their spies, they ventured to explore the riches of the vacant tents; but, if we except some celebrated relics, a small portion of the spoil was restored to the innocent and lawful owners. The joyful tidings were soon diffused over the Catholic world, and the monks of Italy could affirm and believe that three hundred and fifty, or three hundred and seventy-five, thousand of the Mahometans had been crushed by the hammer of Charles; while no more than fifteen hundred Christians were slain in the field of Tours. But this incredible tale is sufficiently disproved by the caution of the French general, who apprehended the snares and accidents of a pursuit, and dismissed his German allies to their native forests. The inactivity of a conqueror betrays the loss of strength and blood, and the most cruel execution is inflicted, not in the ranks of battle, but on the backs of a flying enemy. Yet the victory of the Franks was complete and final; Aquitaine was recovered by the arms of Eudes; the Arabs never resumed the conquest of Gaul, and they were soon driven beyond the Pyrenees by Charles Martel and his valiant race. It might have been expected that the saviour of Christendom would have been canonized, or at least applauded, by the gratitude of the clergy, who are indebted to his sword for their present existence. But in the public distress the Mayor of the Palace had been compelled to apply the riches, or at least the revenues, of the bishops and abbots to the relief of the state and the reward of the soldiers. *His merits were forgotten; his sacrilege alone was remembered, and, in an epistle to a Carlovingian prince, a Gallic synod presumes to declare that his ancestor was damned; that on the opening of his tomb the spectators were affrighted by a smell of fire and the aspect of a horrid dragon; and that a saint of the times was indulged with a pleasant vision of the soul and body of Charles Martel burning, to all eternity, in the abyss of hell....

[1776–1788]

From THE MEMOIRS OF THE LIFE OF EDWARD GIBBON

...A traveller who visits Oxford or Cambridge is surprised and edified by the apparent order and tranquillity that prevail in the seats of the English Muses. In the most celebrated universities of Holland, Germany, and Italy the students, who swarm from different countries, are loosely dispersed in private lodgings at the houses of the burghers: they dress according to their fancy and fortune; and in the intemperate quarrels of youth and wine, their swords, though less frequently than of old, are sometimes stained with each other's blood. The use of arms is banished from our English universities; the uniform habit of the academics, the square cap and black gown, is adapted to the civil and even clerical profession; and from the doctor in divinity to the undergraduate, the degrees of learning and age are externally distinguished. Instead of being scattered in a town, the students of Oxford and Cambridge are united in colleges; their maintenance is provided at their own expense, or that of the founders; and the stated hours of the hall and chapel represent the discipline of a regular, and, as it were, a religious community. The eyes of the traveller are attracted by the size or beauty of the public edifices, and the principal colleges appear to be so many palaces which a liberal nation has erected and endowed for the habitation of science. My own introduction to the University of Oxford forms a new era in my life, and at the distance of forty years I still remember my first emotions of surprise and satisfaction. In my fifteenth year I felt myself suddenly raised from a boy to a man: the persons whom I respected as my superiors in age and academical rank entertained me with every mark of attention and civility; and my vanity was flattered by the velvet cap and silk gown which distinguish *a gentleman-commoner from a plebeian student. A decent allowance, more money than a schoolboy had ever seen, was at my own disposal; and I might command, among the tradesmen of Oxford, an indefinite and dangerous latitude of credit. A key was delivered into my hands, which gave me the free use of a numerous and learned library; my apartment consisted of three elegant and well-furnished rooms in the new building, a stately pile, of Magdalen College; and the adjacent walks, had they been frequented by Plato's disciples, might have been compared to the Attic shade on the banks of the Ilissus. Such was the fair prospect of my entrance (April 3, 1752) into the University of Oxford.

A venerable prelate, whose taste and erudition must reflect honour on the society in which they were formed, has drawn a very interesting picture of his academical life. "I was educated," says Bishop Lowth, "in the University of Oxford. I enjoyed all the advantages, both public and private, which that famous seat of learning so largely affords. I spent many years in that illustrious society, in a well-regulated course of useful discipline and studies, and in the agreeable and improving commerce of gentlemen and of scholars; in a society where emulation without envy, ambition without jealousy, contention without animosity, incited industry and awakened genius; where a liberal pursuit of knowledge, and a generous freedom of thought, was raised, encouraged, and pushed forward by example, by commendation, and by authority. I breathed the same atmosphere that *the Hookers, the Chillingworths, and the Lockes had breathed before; whose benevolence and humanity were as extensive as their vast genius and comprehensive knowledge; who always treated their adversaries with civility and respect; who made candour, moderation, and liberal judgment as much the rule and law as the subject of their discourse. And do you reproach me with my education in this place, and with my relation to this most respectable body, which I shall always esteem my greatest advantage and my highest honour?" I transcribe with pleasure this eloquent passage, without examining what benefits or what rewards were derived by Hooker, or Chillingworth, or Locke from their academical institution; without inquiring whether in this angry controversy the spirit of Lowth himself is purified from *the intolerant zeal which Warburton had ascribed to the genius of the place. The expression of gratitude is a virtue and a pleasure: a liberal mind will delight to cherish and celebrate the memory of its parents; and the teachers of science are the parents of the mind. I applaud the filial piety which it is impossible for me to imitate; since I must not confess an imaginary debt, to assume the merit of a just or generous retribution. To the University of Oxford I acknowledge no obligation, and she will as cheerfully renounce me for a son, as I am willing to disclaim her for a mother. I spent fourteen months at Magdalen College; they proved the fourteen months the most idle and unprofitable of my whole life: the reader will pronounce between the school and the scholar, but I cannot affect to believe that nature had disqualified me for all literary pursuits. The specious and ready excuse of my tender age, imperfect preparation, and hasty departure may doubtless be alleged; nor do I wish to defraud such excuses of their proper weight. Yet in my sixteenth year I was not devoid of capacity or application; even my childish reading had displayed an early though blind propensity for books; and the shallow flood might have been taught to flow in a deep channel and a clear stream. In the discipline of a well-constituted academy, under the guidance of skillful and vigilant professors, I should gradually have risen from translations to originals, from the Latin to the Greek classics, from dead languages to living science; my hours would have been occupied by useful and agreeable studies, the wanderings of fancy would have been restrained, and I should have escaped the temptations of idleness which finally precipitated my departure from Oxford.

Perhaps in a separate annotation I may coolly examine the fabulous and real antiquities of our sister universities, a question which has kindled such fierce and foolish disputes among their fanatic sons. In the meanwhile it will be acknowledged that these venerable bodies are sufficiently old to partake of all the prejudices and infirmities of age. The schools of Oxford and Cambridge were founded in a dark age of false and barbarous science, and they are still tainted with the vices of their origin. Their primitive discipline was adapted to the education of priests and monks; and the government still remains in the hands of the clergy, an order of men whose manners are remote from the present world, and whose eyes are dazzled by the light of philosophy. The legal incorporation of these societies by the charters of popes and kings had given them a monopoly of the public instruction; and the spirit of monopolists is narrow, lazy, and oppressive; their work is more costly and less productive than that of independent artists; and the new improvements so eagerly grasped by the competition of freedom are admitted with slow and sullen reluctance in those proud corporations, above the fear of a rival, and below the confession of an error. We may scarcely hope that any reformation will be a voluntary act; and so deeply are they rooted in law and prejudice that even the omnipotence of Parliament would shrink from an inquiry into the state and abuses of the two universities.

The use of academical degrees, as old as the thirteenth century, is visibly borrowed from the mechanic corporations, in which an apprentice, after serving his time, obtains a testimonial of his skill, and a licence to practise his trade and mystery. It is not my design to depreciate those honours which could never gratify or disappoint my ambition; and

I should applaud the institution, if the degrees of bachelor or licentiate were bestowed as the reward of manly and successful study, if the name and rank of doctor or master were strictly reserved for the professors of science who have approved their title to the public esteem.

The mysterious faculty of theology must not be scanned by a profane eye. The cloak of reason sits awkwardly on our fashionable divines, and in the ecclesiastical studies of the fathers and councils their modesty will yield to the Catholic universities. Our English civilians and canonists have never been famous. Their real business is confined to a small circle, and the double jurisprudence of Rome is overwhelmed by the enormous profession of common lawyers who, in the pursuit of honours and riches, disdain the mock majesty of our *budge doctors. We are justly proud of the skill and learning of our physicians. Their skill is acquired in the practice of the hospitals. They seek their learning in London, in Scotland, or on the continent, and few patients would trust their pulse to a medical student if he had passed the fourteen years of his novitiate at Oxford or Cambridge, whose degrees, however, are exclusively admitted in the Royal College. The arts are supposed to include the liberal knowledge of philosophy and literature, but I am informed that some tattered shreds of the old logic and metaphysics compose the exercises for a bachelor's and master's degree, and that modern improvements, instead of introducing a more rational trial, have only served to relax the forms which are now the object of general contempt.

In all the universities of Europe, except our own, the languages and sciences are distributed among a numerous list of effective professors; the students, according to their taste, their calling, and their diligence, apply themselves to the proper masters; and in the annual repetition of public and private lectures, these masters are assiduously employed. Our curiosity may inquire what number of professors has been instituted at Oxford (for I shall now confine myself to my own university); by whom are they appointed, and what may be the probable chances of merit or incapacity? How many are stationed to *the three faculties, and how many are left for the liberal arts? What is the form, and what the substance, of their lessons? But all these questions are silenced by one short and singular answer, "That in the University of Oxford the greater part of the public professors have for these many years given up altogether even the pretence of teaching." Incredible as the fact may appear, I must rest my belief on the positive and impartial evidence of a philosopher, who had himself resided at Oxford. *Dr. Adam Smith assigns as the cause of their indolence, that, instead of being paid by voluntary contributions, which would urge them to increase the number, and to deserve the gratitude of their pupils, the Oxford professors are secure in the enjoyment of a fixed stipend, without the necessity of labour or the apprehension of control. It has indeed been observed, nor is the observation absurd, that, except in experimental sciences, which demand a costly apparatus and a dexterous hand, the many valuable treatises that have been published on every subject of learning may now supersede the ancient mode of oral instruction. Were this principle true in its utmost latitude, I should only infer that the offices and salaries which are become useless ought without delay to be abolished. But there still remains a material difference between a book and a professor; the hour of the lecture enforces attendance; attention is fixed by the presence, the voice, and the occasional questions of the teacher; the most idle will carry something away; and the more diligent will compare the instructions which they have heard in the school with the volumes which they peruse in their chamber. The advice of a skillful professor will adapt a course of reading to every mind and every situation; his learning will remove difficulties and solve objections; his authority will discover, admonish, and at last chastise the negligence of his disciples; and his vigilant inquiries will ascertain the steps of their literary progress. Whatever science he professes he may illustrate in a series of discourses, composed in the leisure of his closet, pronounced on public occasions, and finally delivered to the press. I observe with pleasure that in the University of Oxford Dr. Lowth, with equal eloquence and erudition, has executed this task in his incomparable *Prælectiones* on the poetry of the Hebrews.

The college of St. Mary Magdalen (it is vulgarly pronounced Maudlin) was founded in the fifteenth century by the Bishop of Winchester, and now consists of a president, forty fellows, and a number of inferior students.

It is esteemed one of the largest and most wealthy of our academical corporations, which may be compared to the Benedictine abbeys of Catholic countries; and I have loosely heard that the estates belonging to Magdalen College, which are leased by those indulgent landlords at small quit-rents and occasional fines, might be raised in the hands of private avarice to an annual revenue of nearly thirty thousand pounds. Our colleges are supposed to be schools of science as well as of education; nor is it unreasonable to expect that a body of literary men, addicted to a life of celibacy, exempt from the care of their own subsistence, and amply provided with books, should devote their leisure to the prosecution of study, and that some effects of their studies should be manifested to the world. The shelves of their library groan under the weight of the Benedictine folios, of the editions of the Fathers, and the collections of the middle ages which have issued from the single abbey of St. Germain de Prés at Paris. A composition of genius must be the offspring of one mind; but such works of industry as may be divided among many hands, and must be continued during many years, are the peculiar province of a laborious community. If I inquire into the manufactures of *the monks of Magdalen, if I extend the inquiry to the other colleges of Oxford and Cambridge, a silent blush or a scornful frown will be the only reply. The fellows or monks of my time were decent, easy men, who supinely enjoyed the gifts of the founder: their days were filled by a series of uniform employments — the chapel and the hall, the coffee-house and *the common room — till they retired, weary and well satisfied, to a long slumber. From the toil of reading, or thinking, or writing they had absolved their conscience; and the first shoots of learning and ingenuity withered on the ground, without yielding any fruit to the owners or the public. The only student was a young fellow (a future bishop) who was deeply immersed in the follies of the Hutchinsonian system. The only author was an half-starved chaplain — Ballard was his name — who begged subscriptions for some *Memoirs* concerning the learned ladies of Great Britain. As a gentleman-commoner I was admitted to the society of the fellows, and fondly expected that some questions of literature would be the amusing and instructive topics of their discourse. Their conversation stagnated in a round of college business, Tory politics, personal stories, and private scandal; their dull and deep potations excused the brisk intemperance of youth; and their constitutional toasts were not expressive of the most lively loyalty for the house of Hanover. A general election was now approaching; the great Oxfordshire contest already blazed with all the malevolence of party zeal. Magdalen College was devoutly attached to the old interest, and the names of *Wenman and Dashwood were more frequently pronounced than those of Cicero and Chrysostom. The example of the senior fellows could not inspire the undergraduates with a liberal spirit or studious emulation; and I cannot describe, as I never knew, the discipline of the college. Some duties may possibly have been imposed on the poor scholars, whose ambition aspired to the peaceful honours of a fellowship (**ascribi quietis ordinibus... deorum*); but no independent members were admitted below the rank of a gentleman-commoner, and our velvet cap was the cap of liberty. A tradition prevailed that some of our predecessors had spoken Latin declamations in the hall, but of this ancient custom no vestige remained; the obvious methods of public exercises and examinations were totally unknown, and I have never heard that either the president or the society interfered in the private economy of the tutors and their pupils.

The silence of the Oxford professors, which deprives the youth of public instruction, is imperfectly supplied by the tutors, as they are styled, of the several colleges. Instead of confining themselves to a single science, which had satisfied the ambition of *Burmann or Bernoulli, they teach, or promise to teach, either history or mathematics or ancient literature or moral philosophy; and as it is possible that they may be defective in all, it is highly probable that of some they will be ignorant. They are paid, indeed, by private contributions, but their appointment depends on the head of the house; their diligence is voluntary and will consequently be languid, while the pupils themselves and their parents are not indulged in the liberty of choice or change. The first tutor into whose hands I was resigned appears to have been one of the best of the tribe; Dr. Waldegrave was a learned and pious man, of a mild disposition, strict morals, and abstemious life, who seldom mingled in the politics or the jollity of the college. But his knowledge of the world was confined to the university; his learning was of the last, rather than the present age; his temper was indolent; his faculties, which were not of the first rate, had been relaxed by the climate, and he was satisfied, like his fellows, with the slight and superficial discharge of an important trust. As soon as my tutor had sounded the insufficiency of his disciple in school-learning, he proposed that we should read every morning, from ten to eleven, the comedies of Terence. The sum of my improvement in the University of Oxford is confined to three or four Latin plays; and even the study of an elegant classic, which might have been illustrated by a comparison of ancient and modern theatres, was reduced to a dry and literal interpretation of the author's text. During the first weeks I constantly attended these lessons in my tutor's room; but as they appeared equally devoid of profit and pleasure, I was once tempted to try the experiment of a formal apology. The apology was accepted with a smile. I repeated the offence with less ceremony; the excuse was admitted with the same indulgence; the slightest motive of laziness or indisposition, the most trifling avocation at home or abroad, was allowed as a worthy impediment; nor did my tutor appear conscious of my absence or neglect. Had the hour of lecture been constantly filled, a single hour was a small portion of my academic leisure. No plan of study was recommended for my use; no exercises were prescribed for his inspection; and, at the most precious season of youth, whole days and weeks were suffered to elapse without labour or amusement, without advice or account. I should have listened to the voice of reason and of my tutor; his mild behaviour had gained my confidence. I preferred his society to that of the younger students, and in our evening walks to the top of Headington Hill we freely conversed on a variety of subjects. Since the days of * Pococke and Hyde, Oriental learning has always been the pride of Oxford, and I once expressed an inclination to study Arabic. His prudence discouraged this childish fancy, but he neglected the fair occasion of directing the ardour of a curious mind. During my absence in the summer vacation Dr. Waldegrave accepted a college living at Washington in Sussex, and on my return I no longer found him at Oxford. From that time I have lost sight of my first tutor; but at the end of thirty years (1781) he was still alive, and the practice of exercise and temperance had entitled him to an healthy old age....

[1796]

JAMES HERVEY

In 1746–47 the Reverend James Hervey, at this time curate to his father and afterwards his successor as rector of the two parishes of Collingtree and Weston Favell in Northamptonshire, published his *Meditations and Contemplations*, a work which so exactly suited the popular taste that it went through sixteen editions during the next twenty-one years and some twenty-five editions before the end of the century. To understand the reasons for its popularity is to penetrate a long way into the history of the romantic movement during the eighteenth century.

The two volumes of the original work are made up of the following independent pieces: *Meditations among the Tombs, Reflections on a Flower Garden, A Descant upon Creation, Contemplations on the Night, Contemplations on the Starry Heavens*, and *A Winter-Piece*. As the title of the first, *Meditations among the Tombs*, suggests, these productions are connected with the "Graveyard" school of poetry; they were published near the middle of the decade which produced Young's *Night Thoughts*, Blair's *The Grave*, and Gray's *Elegy*. In a florid style, artificially rhetorical and markedly rhythmic, they expatiate upon the wonders of creation and present unimpeachable moral lessons and religious observations; but chiefly they are concerned with a pleasing melancholy associated with the emblems of mortality. "Lonely walks," "sequestered bowers," "black-browed night," "the sable horrors of the skies," "gloomy vaults," "midnight phantoms," "the silent mansions of the dead," "the realms of horror and of death," — these are the subjects upon which Hervey waxes most eloquent and from which he extracts the most improving lessons.

> Divine instructor! lead through midnight glooms,
> To moralizing stars and preaching tombs:

so exclaims one of his admirers whose commendatory poems were published in successive editions of the *Meditations and Contemplations*. Sentimental melancholy united with religious teaching and expressed in language suitable to lower middle-class appreciation is the dominant characteristic of the work.

The emotionalism of the *Meditations and Contemplations* has a direct connection with the Methodist movement; Hervey had come under the influence of John Wesley at Oxford and was profoundly affected by evangelical teachings. At the same time, as Sir Leslie Stephen has pointed out, his work shows "that vaguer enthusiasm for nature represented soon afterwards by Ossian and Rousseau." At times this expansive appreciation of nature shows unmistakable signs of Deist phraseology.

> With thee the Muse should trace the pleasing road,
> That leads from nature up to nature's God;

wrote Peter Whalley of Northampton in his commendatory verses, echoing Pope's words. *Contemplations on the Starry Heavens* dallies with the idea of the multiplicity of worlds and some of the other wonders of astronomy, but overlays the whole so completely with evangelical theology that faith remains untroubled. Though the influence of Hervey has not been adequately studied, there is reason to believe that the wide popularity of his works was instrumental in preparing the ground for the nature worship of the early nineteenth-century poets.

No one in the present day can read Hervey's works with the serious admiration of his contemporaries and immediate followers. Like the once lauded rhapsodies of Ossian they have lost their power to charm. The modern reader finds in their sentimental pages a mildly ludicrous exaggeration, and the evidence of a popular taste that is a part of the complex century which it was once common to sum up in the misleading phrase, "The Age of Reason."

From CONTEMPLATIONS ON THE NIGHT

... Since sleep is so absolutely necessary, so inestimably valuable, observe what a fine apparatus Almighty Goodness has made, to accommodate us with the balmy blessing. With how kind a precaution he removes whatever might obstruct its access, or impede its influence! He draws around us the curtain of darkness, which inclines us to a drowsy indolence and conceals every object that might too strongly agitate the sense. He conveys peace into our apartments, and imposes silence on the whole creation. Every animal is bidden to tread softly, or rather to cease from its motion, when man is retiring to his repose. May we not discern, in this gracious disposition of things, the tender cares of a nursing mother, who hushes every noise and secludes every disturbance, when she has laid the child of her love to rest? So, by such soothing circumstances, and gently working opiates, "He giveth to his beloved sleep."

Another signal instance of a Providence intent upon our welfare is that we are preserved safe in the hours of slumber. How are we then lost to all apprehension of danger, even though the murderer be at our bed-side, or his naked sword at our breast! Destitute of all concern for ourselves, we are unable to think of, much more to provide for our own security. At these moments, therefore, we lie open to innumerable perils: perils from the resistless rage of flames; perils from the insidious artifices of thieves, or the outrageous violence of robbers; perils from the irregular workings of our own thoughts, and especially from the incursions of our spiritual enemy.

What dreadful mischief might that restless, that implacable adversary of mankind work was there not an invisible hand to control his rage, and protect poor mortals! What scenes of horror might he represent to our imaginations, and "scare us with dreams, or terrify us with visions!" But the Keeper of Israel, who never slumbers nor sleeps, interposes in our behalf, at once to cherish us under his wings, and to defend us as with a shield. It is said of Solomon, "that threescore valiant men were about his bed, all expert in war, every one with his sword upon his thigh, because of fear in the night." But one greater than Solomon, one mightier than myriads of armed hosts, even the great Jehovah, in whom is everlasting strength, he vouchsafes to encamp about our houses, to watch over our sleeping minutes, and to stop all the avenues of ill. Oh! the unwearied and condescending goodness of our Creator, who lulls us to our rest, by bringing on the silent shades; and plants his own ever-watchful eye as our sentinel, while we enjoy the needful repose.

Reason now resigns her sedate office, and fancy, extravagant fancy, leads the mind through a maze of vanity. The head is crowded with false images, and tantalized with the most ridiculous misapprehensions of things. Some are expatiating amidst fairy fields, and gathering garlands of visionary bliss, while their bodies are stretched on a wisp of straw, and sheltered by the cobwebs of a barn. Others, quite insensible of their rooms of state, are mourning in a doleful dungeon, or struggling with the raging billows. Perhaps, with hasty steps, they climb the craggy cliff, and with real anxiety fly from the imaginary danger. Or else, benumbed with sudden fear and finding themselves unable to escape, they give up at once their hopes and their efforts; and, though reclined on a couch of ivory, are sinking, all helpless and distressed, in the furious whirlpool. So unaccountable are the vagaries of the brain, while sleep maintains its dominion over the limbs!

But is this the only season when absurd and incoherent irregularities play their magic on our minds? Are there not those who dream, even in their waking moments? Some pride themselves in a notion of superior excellency because the royal favour has annexed a few splendid titles to their names, or because the dying silk-worm has bequeathed her finest threads to cover their nakedness. Others congratulate their own signal happiness because loads of golden lumber are amassed together in their coffers, or promise themselves a most superlative felicity indeed, when some thousands more are added to the useless heap. Nor are there wanting others, who gape after substantial satisfaction from airy applause, and flatter themselves with, I know not what, immortality in the momentary buzz of renown. Are any of these a whit more reasonable in their opinions than the poor ragged wretch in his reveries, who, while snoring under a hedge, exults in the possession of his stately palace and sumptuous furniture? If persons who are very vassals to their own domineering passions and led captive by numberless temptations, if these persons pique themselves with a conceit of their liberty, and fancy themselves the generous and gallant spirits of the age; where is the difference between theirs and the madman's frenzy; who, though chained to the floor, is throned in thought, and wielding an imaginary sceptre? In a word, as many as borrow their dignity from a plume of feathers, or the gaudy trappings of fortune; as many as send their souls to seek for bliss in the blandishments of sense, or in anything short of the divine favour, and a well-grounded hope of the incorruptible inheritance; what are they but dreamers with their eyes open; delirious, though in health?

Would you see their picture drawn to the very life, and the success of their schemes calculated with the utmost exactness, cast your eye upon that fine representation exhibited by the prophet: "It shall be even as when a hungry man dreameth, and behold, he eateth; but he awaketh, and his soul is empty: or, as when a thirsty man dreameth, and behold, he drinketh; but he awaketh, and behold, he is faint, and his soul hath appetite." Such is the race, and such the prize of all those candidates for honour and joy who run wide from the mark of the high calling of God in Christ Jesus. They live in vanity and die in woe. Awaken us, merciful Lord, from these noontide trances! Awaken us, while conviction may turn to our advantage, and not serve only to increase our torment. Oh! let our "eyes be enlightened to discern the things that are excellent"; and no longer be imposed upon by fantastic appearances, which, however pompous they may seem, will prove more empty than the visions of the night, more transient than the dream that is forgotten.

Having mentioned sleep and dreams, let me once again consider those remarkable incidents of our frame, so very remarkable that I may venture to call them a kind of experimental mystery, and little less than a standing miracle. Behold the most vigorous constitution, when stretched on the bed of ease, and totally resigned to the slumbers of the night. Its activity is oppressed with fetters of indolence; its strength is consigned over to a temporary annihilation; the nerves are like a bow unstrung, and the whole animal system is like a motionless log. Behold a person of the most delicate sensations and amiable dispositions. His eyes, though thrown wide open, admit not the visual ray, at least, distinguish not objects. His ears, with the organs unimpaired, and articulate accents beating upon the drum, perceive not the sound; at least, apprehend not the meaning. The senses and their exquisitely fine feelings, are overwhelmed with an unaccountable stupefaction. You call him a social creature; but where are his social affections? He knows not the father that begat him, and takes no notice of the friend that is as his own soul. The wife of his bosom may expire by his side, and he lie more unconcerned than a barbarian. The children of his body may be tortured with the severest pangs, and he, even in the same chamber, remain untouched with the least commiseration. Behold the most ingenious scholar, whose judgment is piercing, and able to trace the most intricate difficulties of science; his taste refined and quick to relish all the beauties of sentiment and composition. Yet at this juncture the thinking faculties are unhinged, and the intellectual economy quite disconcerted. Instead of close connected reasonings, nothing but a disjointed huddle of absurd ideas; instead of well digested principles, nothing but a disorderly jumble of crude conceptions. The most palpable delusions impose upon his imagination. The whole night passes, and he frequently mistakes it for a single minute; is not sensible of the transition, hardly sensible of any duration.

Yet no sooner does the morning dawn and daylight enter the room, but this strange enchantment vanishes. The man awakes and finds himself possessed of all the valuable endowments which for several hours were suspended or lost. His sinews are braced and fit for action; his senses are alert and keen. The romantic visionary brightens into the master of reason. The frozen or benumbed affections melt with tenderness, and glow with benevolence. And, what is beyond measure surprising, the intoxicated mind works itself sober, not by slow degrees, but in the twinkling of an eye recovers from its perturbation. Why does not the stupor which deadens all the nice operations of the animal powers, hold fast its possession? When the thoughts are once disadjusted, why are they not always in confusion? How is it that they are rallied in a moment, and from the wildest irregularity reduced to the most orderly array? From an inactivity resembling death, how is the body so suddenly restored to vigour and agility? From extravagancies bordering upon madness, how is the understanding instantaneously re-established in sedateness and harmony? Surely, "This is the Lord's doing, and it should be marvellous in our eyes"; should awaken our gratitude, and inspirit our praise.

This is the time in which ghosts are supposed to make their appearance. Now the timorous imagination teems with phantoms, and creates numberless terrors to itself. Now dreary forms in sullen state stalk along the gloom, or, swifter than lightning, glide across the shades. Now voices more than mortal are heard from the echoing vaults, and groans issue from the hollow tombs. Now melancholy spectres visit the ruins of ancient monasteries, and frequent the solitary dwellings of the dead. They pass and repass in unsubstantial images along the forsaken galleries, or take their determined stand over some lamented grave. *How often has the schoolboy fetched a long circuit and trudged many a needless step in order to avoid the haunted churchyard? Or, if necessity, sad necessity, has obliged him to cross the spot where human skulls are lodged below, and the baleful yews shed supernumerary horrors above, a thousand hideous stories rush into his memory. Fear adds wings to his feet; he scarce touches the ground, dares not once look behind him, and blesses his good fortune if no frightful sound purred at his heels, if no ghastly shape bolted upon his sight.

'Tis strange to observe the excessive timidity which possesses many people's minds on this fanciful occasion, while they are void of all concern on others of the most tremendous import. Those who are startled, in any dark and lonely walk, at the very apprehension of a single spectre are nevertheless unimpressed at the sure prospect of entering into a whole world of disembodied beings; nay, are without any emotions of awe, though they know themselves to be hastening into the presence of the great, infinite, and eternal Spirit. Should some pale messenger from the regions of the dead draw back our curtains at the hour of midnight, and, appointing some particular place, say as the horrid apparition to Brutus, *"I'll meet thee there;" I believe the boldest heart would feel something like a panic, would seriously think upon the adventure and be in pain for the event. But when a voice from heaven cries, in the awakening language of the prophet, "Prepare to meet thy God, O Israel;" how little is the warning regarded! How soon is it forgot! Preposterous stupidity! to be utterly unconcerned, where it is the truest wisdom to take the alarm; and to be all trepidation, where there is nothing really terrible! Do thou, my soul, remember thy Saviour's admonition: "I will forewarn you, whom you shall fear. Fear not these imaginary horrors of the night; but fear that awful Being, whose revelation of himself, though with expressions of peculiar mercy, made Moses, his favourite servant, tremble exceedingly; whose manifestation, when he appears with purposes of inexorable vengeance, will make mighty conquerors, who were familiar with dangers, and estranged to dismay, call upon the mountains to fall on them, and the rocks to cover them; the menace of whose majestic eye, when he comes attended with thousand thousands of his immortal hosts, will make the very heavens cleave asunder, and the earth flee away. Oh! dread his displeasure; secure his favour; and then thou mayest commit all thy other anxieties to the wind; thou mayest laugh at every other fear."

This brings to my mind a memorable and amazing occurrence, recorded in *the book of Job, which is, I think, no inconsiderable proof of the real existence of apparitions on some very extraordinary emergencies, while it discountenances those legions of idle tales which superstition has raised and credulity received. Since it teaches us that if, at any time, those visitants from the unknown world render themselves perceivable by mortals, it is not upon any errand of frivolous consequence; but to convey intelligences of the utmost moment, or to work impressions of the highest advantage.

'Twas in the dead of night. All nature lay shrouded in darkness. Every creature was buried in sleep. The most profound silence reigned through the universe. In these solemn moments, Eliphaz alone, all wakeful and solitary, was musing upon sublime and heavenly subjects. When lo! an awful being, from the invisible realms, burst into his apartment. A spirit passed before his face. Astonishment seized the beholder. His bones shivered within him; his flesh trembled all over him; and the hair of his head stood erect with horror. Sudden and unexpected was the appearance of the phantom; not such its departure. It stood still to present itself more fully to his view. It made a solemn pause to prepare his mind for some momentous message. After which a voice was heard, a voice, for the importance of its meaning, worthy to be had in everlasting remembrance; for the solemnity of its delivery, enough to alarm the heart of stone. *It spoke, and this was the purport of its words: "Shall man, frail man, be just before the mighty God? Shall even the most accomplished of mortals be pure in the sight of his Maker? Behold, and consider it attentively. He put no such trust in his most exalted servants, as should be-

* Notes on James Hervey will be found in the Appendix, pp. 1040 ff.

speak them incapable of defect. And his very angels he charged with folly, as sinking, even in the highest perfection of their holiness, infinitely beneath his transcendent glories; as falling, even in all the fidelity of their obedience, inexpressibly short of the homage due to his adorable Majesty. If angelic natures must not presume to justify either themselves or their services, before uncreated purity; how much more absurd is such a notion, how much more impious such an attempt in them that dwell in houses of clay; whose original is from the dust, and whose state is all imperfection!"

I would observe from hence the very singular necessity of that poverty of spirit which entirely renounces its own attainments, and most thankfully submits to the righteousness of the incarnate God. To inculcate this lesson the Son of the Blessed came down from heaven, and pressed no other principle with so repeated an importunity on his hearers. To instill the same doctrine the Holy Ghost touched the lips of the apostles with sacred eloquence, and made it an eminent part of their commission "to demolish every high imagination." That no expedient might be be wanting to give it a deep and lasting efficacy on the human mind, a phantom arises from the valley of the shadow of death, or a teacher descends from the habitation of spirits. Whatever then we neglect, let us not neglect to cultivate this grace, which has been so variously taught, so powerfully enforced.

Hark! a doleful voice. With sudden starts and hideous screams, it disturbs the silence of the peaceful night. 'Tis the screech-owl, sometimes in frantic, sometimes in disconsolate accents, uttering her woes. She flies the vocal grove and shuns the society of all the feathered choir. The blooming gardens and flowery meads have no charms for her. Obscene shades, ragged ruins, and walls overgrown with ivy are her favourite haunts. Above, the mouldering precipice nods, and threatens a fall; below, the toad crawls, or the poisonous adder hisses. The sprightly morning, which awakens other animals into joy, administers no pleasure to this gloomy recluse. Even the smiling face of day is her aversion, and all its lovely scenes create nothing but uneasiness.

So, just so, would it fare with the ungodly, were it possible to suppose their admission into the chaste and bright abodes of endless felicity. They would find nothing but disappointment and shame, even at the fountainhead of happiness and honour. For how could the tongue habituated to profaneness taste any delight in the harmonious adorations of heaven? How could the lips cankered with slander relish the raptures of everlasting praise? Where would be the satisfaction of the vain beauty or the supercilious grandee? Since, in the temple of the skies, no incense of flattery would be addressed to the former, nor any obsequious homage paid to the latter. The spotless and inconceivable purity of the blessed God would flash confusion on the lascivious eye. The envious mind must be on a rack of self-tormenting passions to observe millions of happy beings, shining in all the perfections of glory, and solacing themselves in the fullness of joy. In short, the unsanctified soul, amidst holy and triumphant spirits, even in the refined regions of bliss and immortality, would be, like this melancholy bird, dislodged from her darksome retirement, and imprisoned under the beams of day.

The voice of this creature screaming at our windows, or of the raven croaking over our houses, is, they say, a token of approaching death. There are persons who would regard such an incident with no small degree of solicitude. Trivial as it is, it would damp their spirits, perhaps break their rest. One cannot but wonder that people should suffer themselves to be affrighted at such fantastical, and yet be quite unaffected with real, presages of their dissolution. Real presages of this awful event address us from every quarter. What are these incumbent glooms which overwhelm the world, but a kind of pall provided for nature; and an image of that long night which will quickly cover the inhabitants of the whole earth! What an affinity has the sleep, which will very soon weigh down my drowsy eyelids, with that state of entire cessation in which all my senses must be laid aside! The silent chamber and the bed of slumber are a very significant representation of the land where all things are hushed, all things are forgotten. What meant that deep death-bell note which, the other evening, saddened the air? Laden with heaviest accents, it struck our ears, and seemed to knock at the door of our hearts. Surely, it brought a message to surviving mortals, and thus the tidings ran: "Mortals, the destroyer of your race is on his way. The last enemy has begun the pursuit, and is gaining ground upon you every moment. His paths are strewed with heaps of slain. Even now, his javelin has laid one of your neighbours in the dust; and will soon, very soon, aim the inevitable blow at each of your lives."

We need not go down to the charnel-house, nor carry our search into the repositories of the dead, in order to find memorials of our impending doom. A multitude of these remembrancers are planted in all our paths, and point the heedless passengers to their long home. I can hardly enter a considerable town, but I meet the funeral procession, or the mourners going about the streets. *The hatchment suspended on the wall, or the crape streaming in the air, are silent intimations that both rich and poor have been emptying their houses and replenishing their sepulchres. I can scarce join in any conversation, but mention is made of some that are given over by the physician, and hovering on the confines of eternity; of others that have just dropped their clay amidst weeping friends, and are gone to appear before the Judge of all the earth. There's not a newspaper comes to my hand, but, amidst all its entertaining narrations, reads several serious lectures of mortality. What else are the repeated accounts of age, worn out by slow-consuming sicknesses; of youth, dashed to pieces by some sudden stroke of casualty; of patriots, exchanging their seats in the senate for a lodging in the tomb; of misers, resigning their breath, and (O relentless destiny!) leaving their very riches for others? Even the vehicles of our amusement are registers of the deceased, and the voice of fame seldom sounds but in concert with a knell.

These monitors crowd every place; not so much as the scenes of our diversion excepted. What are the decorations of our public buildings and the most elegant furniture of our parlours, but the imagery of death and trophies of the tomb? That marble bust, and those gilded pictures; how solemnly they recognize the fate of others and speakingly remind us of our own! I see, I hear, and oh! I feel this great truth. It is interwoven with my constitution. The frequent decays of the structure foretell its final ruin. What are all the pains that have been darted through my limbs, what every disease that has assaulted my health, but the advanced guards of the foe? What are the languors and weariness that attend the labours of each revolving day, but the more secret practices of the adversary, slowly undermining the earthly tabernacle?

Amidst so many notices, shall we go on thoughtless and unconcerned? Can none of these prognostics, which are sure as oracles, awaken our attention and engage our circumspection? Noah, 'tis written, being warned of God, prepared an ark. Imitate, my soul, imitate this excellent example. Admonished by such a cloud of witnesses, be continually putting thyself in a readiness for the last change. Let not that day, of which thou hast so many infallible signs, come upon thee unawares. Get the ivy untwined, and thy affections disentangled from this enchanting world, that thou mayest be able to quit it without reluctance. Get the dreadful handwriting cancelled, and all thy sins blotted out, that thou mayest depart in peace, and have nothing to fear at the decisive tribunal. Get oh! get thyself interested in the Redeemer's merits, and transformed into his sacred image; then shalt thou be meet for the inheritance of saints in light, and mayest even desire to be dissolved, and to be with Christ.

[1746, 47]

JOHN WESLEY

John Wesley is important in English literature because of the Methodist movement and also because of the *Journal* in which he set down the external events of his long life and at the same time painted a memorable self-portrait.

The history of eighteenth-century England — literary, social, and even political — bears deep impress of that religious revival which eventuated in the separation of the Methodist communion and in the scarcely less important Evangelical movement within the Established Church. This revival has often been associated with the romantic movement and explained as one of its contributing causes or one of its manifestations. In its emotionalism and in its concern for the lowly and the under-privileged, it seems clearly to echo the romantic language of the heart as well as the humanitarian interest in the common folk. On the other hand, as has often been pointed out, the influence of the Wesleys was theologically conservative. To re-emphasize neglected aspects of orthodox Christian belief, and thereby to reanimate the love of many that had grown cold, was their purpose and method. They turned from intellectual subtleties and philosophical speculations, and appealed to personal experience of the Grace of God. They tolerated no polite scepticisms from the outer courts of the Deists, but read a fully inspired Bible written by the finger of God, encountered a personal and indefatigable Devil, and were miraculously helped by divine interpositions in the most material concerns of daily life. Any romantic illusions that John Wesley may have cherished about the simple children of nature were effectually dispelled by his experience with the Indians in Georgia. He taught uncompromisingly the doctrine of original sin, and, except as it was redeemed through divine Grace, he saw no good in natural humanity. John Wesley had no quarrel with the Anglican Church as an institution; he lived and died within its fold and laboured long to prevent the Methodist societies from becoming a dissenting sect. He was no revolutionist, but supported King and Church; he was no democrat in principle or in practice; he sought a moral rather than a political revolution. Methodism has a connection with the romantic movement, but its founder was no romantic.

Although during half a century of his ministry he traveled some 4500 miles each year and preached an average of twice daily — frequently to great throngs under the open sky, when he was denied the use of Anglican pulpits — John Wesley did an immense amount of writing. In 1771–74, nearly two decades before his death, his works were collected and published in thirty-two volumes. On horseback with the reins left slack, or bumping over the rough highways and rougher byways of the eighteenth century in stage-coach or carriage, he read constantly and wrote tirelessly. Of all these writings one book alone has made a place for itself in English literature, the *Journal* which he kept during the greater part of his life and published in a series of twenty-one separate parts. Here he recorded the story of his ministry, his trials and persecutions, his conduct of the affairs of the society, his journeyings, his controversies, his triumphs, and his reaping the fruit of his labours. In these pages can be read an authentic representation of eighteenth-century English life, and, better than that, a great spiritual revelation. The *Journal* has been called the work of "a pious Pepys"; it is perhaps better described as that of an educated Bunyan. It reflects the figure of a great preacher, an untiring worker, a popular but autocratic leader. It is shrewd, clear-sighted, with touches of occasional humour, yet constantly filled with the sense of a divine mission and consecration to the purposes of the Most High. Simply and directly, without literary pretensions yet in a style that bears the imprint of classical scholarship, Wesley sets down from day to day himself, and gives not only his own best life but one of the world's classics of religious autobiography.

The selection here printed covers all the entries during the period from June to December, 1768.

From the JOURNAL

Fri. [June] 3 [1768]. I rode to Richmond, intending to preach near the house of one of our friends; but some of the chief of the town sent to desire me to preach in the market-place. The Yorkshire militia were all there, just returned from their exercise; and a more rude rabble-rout I never saw, without sense, decency, or good manners.

In running down one of the mountains yesterday, I had got a sprain in my thigh. It was rather worse to-day; but as I rode to Barnard Castle, the sun shone so hot upon it that before I came to the town it was quite well. In the evening the commanding officer gave orders there should be no exercise, that all the Durham militia (what a contrast!) might be at liberty to attend the preaching. Accordingly, we had a little army of officers as well as soldiers, and all behaved well. A large number of them were present at five in the morning. I have not found so deep and lively a work in any other part of the kingdom as runs through the whole circuit, particularly in the vales that wind between * these horrid mountains. I returned to Newcastle in the evening.

Sun. 5. I preached in the morning at Plessey to some of the most lively colliers in England, and about two at Hartley to a still larger congregation, but to the largest of all in the Castlegarth at Newcastle.

Tues. 7. I went down by water to South Shields, and preached at noon to far more than could hear. We went, after dinner, to Tynemouth Castle, a magnificent heap of ruins. Within the walls are the remains of a very large church, which seems to have been of exquisite workmanship; and the stones are joined by so strong a cement that, but for Cromwell's cannon, they might have stood a thousand years.

Mon. 13. I left Newcastle, and in the residue of the month visited most of the societies in Yorkshire.

July 14, Thur. I crossed over into Lincolnshire, and after spending about ten days there, returned by Doncaster, Rotherham, and Sheffield, and thence crossed over to Madeley.

On Tuesday the 19th I wrote the following letter:

Swinfleet, July 19, 1768

Rev. and dear Sir,

One of Wintringham informed me yesterday that you said no sensible and well-meaning man could hear, and much less join the Methodists; because they all acted under a lie, professing themselves members of the Church of England, while they licenced themselves as Dissenters. You are a little misinformed. The greater part of the Methodist preachers are not licenced at all, and several that are, are not licenced as Dissenters. I instance particularly in Thomas Adams and Thomas Brisco. When Thomas Adams desired a licence, one of the justices said, "Mr. Adams, are not you of the Church of England? Why then do you desire a licence?" He answered, "Sir, I am of the Church of England; yet I desire a licence that I may legally defend myself from the illegal violence of oppressive men." T. Brisco being asked the same question in London, and the justice adding, "We will not grant you a licence," his lawyer replied, "Gentlemen, you cannot refuse it; the act is a mandatory act. You have no choice." One asked the chairman, "Is this true?" He shook his head and said, "He is in the right." The objection, therefore, does not lie at all against the greater part of the Methodist preachers, because they are either licenced in this form, or not licenced at all.

When others applied for a licence, the clerk or justice said, "I will not licence you but as Protestant Dissenters." They replied, "We are of the Church; we are not Dissenters; but if you will call us so, we cannot help it." They did call them so in their certificates, but this did not make them so. They still call themselves members of the Church of England, and they believe themselves so to be. Therefore neither do these act under a lie. They speak no more than they verily believe. Surely then, unless there are stronger objections than this, both well-meaning and sensible men may in perfect consistence with their sense and sincerity, not only hear, but join the Methodists.

We are in truth so far from being enemies to the Church that we are rather bigots to it. I dare not, like Mr. Venn, leave the parish church where I am, to go to an independent meeting. I dare not advise others to go thither rather than to church. I advise all, over whom I have any influence, steadily to keep to the Church. Meantime, I advise them to see that the kingdom of God is within them; that their hearts be full of love to God and man, and to look upon all, of whatever opinion, who are like-minded as their "brother and sister and mother." Oh, sir, what art of men or devils is this which makes you so studiously stand aloof from those who are thus minded? I cannot but say to you, as I did to Mr. Walker (and I say it the more freely because * *quid mea refert?* I am neither better nor worse whether you hear or forbear), "The Methodists do not want you, but you want them." You want the life, the spirit, the power which they have, not of themselves, but by the free grace of God: else how could it be (let me speak without reserve), that so good a man and so good a

*** Notes on John Wesley will be found in the Appendix, p. 1041.**

preacher should have so little fruit of his labour, his unwearied labour, for so many years? Have your parishioners the life of religion in their souls? Have they so much as the form of it? Are the people of Wintringham in general any better than those of Winterton, or Horton? Alas! sir, what is it that hinders your reaping the fruit of so much pains and so many prayers?

Is it not possible this may be the very thing, your setting yourself against those whom God owns, by the continual conviction and conversion of sinners?

I fear, as long as you in any wise oppose these, your rod will not blossom, neither will you see the desire of your soul, in the prosperity of the souls committed to your charge.

I pray God to give you a right judgment in all things, and am, dear sir,

Your affectionate brother,
John Wesley.

Sun. 31. I preached for Mr. Fletcher in the morning, and in the evening at Shrewsbury.

Aug. 1, Mon. I lodged at the abbey in Cardiganshire, and on Wednesday morning reached Haverfordwest. Here abundance of people flocked together, and willingly suffered the word of exhortation. Indeed a more quiet, humane, courteous people I have scarce ever seen. But I fear they were surfeited with preaching before we set foot in the town.

Sat. 6. I went to Pembroke. We were here several times before we had any place in Haverfordwest. But we have reason to fear lest the first become last.

Sun. 7. I took a good deal of pains to compose the little misunderstandings which have much obstructed the work of God. At ten, I read prayers, preached, and administered the Sacrament to a serious congregation at St. Daniel's; and the next morning left the people full of good desires, and in tolerable good humour with each other.

Mon. 8. I rode to Llanelly, and preached to a small, earnest company on "Ye are saved through faith." Thence we found a kind of a way to Oxwich, where I pressed the one thing needful on a plain, simple people, right willing to hear, with great enlargement of heart.

Tues. 9. I took a full view of the castle, situate on the top of a steep hill, and commanding a various and extensive prospect, both by sea and land. The building itself is far the loftiest which I have seen in Wales. What a taste had they who removed from hence to bury themselves in the hole at Margam!

When we came to Neath, I was a little surprised to hear I was to preach in the church, of which the churchwardens had the disposal, the minister being just dead. I began reading prayers at six, but was greatly disgusted at the manner of singing: (1) twelve or fourteen persons kept it to themselves, and quite shut out the congregation; (2) these repeated the same words, contrary to all sense and reason, six or eight or ten times over; (3) according to the shocking custom of modern music, different persons sung different words at one and the same moment, an intolerable insult on common sense, and utterly incompatible with any devotion.

Wed. 10. At five I had the pleasure of hearing the whole congregation at the room "sing with the spirit and with the understanding also"; and again, at one in the afternoon at Cowbridge, where I found uncommon liberty of speech, while I was explaining to many of the rich and gay, as well as to the poor, "The kingdom of God is within you."

I did not reach Cardiff till after seven; where, finding the congregation waiting, I began immediately in the town hall, strongly exhorting them not to "receive the grace of God in vain."

Fri. 12. I preached at that lovely place, Llanbradach; Saturday, 13th, about noon, at Chepstow. Thence I hastened to the passage, though every one told me I had time enough and to spare. I had so; for I waited six hours, the boat being just gone when we came. About nine we got over, and reached Bristol between eleven and twelve.

Sun. 14. Hearing my wife was dangerously ill, I took chaise immediately and reached * the Foundery before one in the morning. Finding the fever was turned, and the danger over, about two I set out again, and in the afternoon came (not at all tired) to Bristol.

Our Conference began on Tuesday, the 16th, and ended on Friday, the 19th. Oh, what can we do for more labourers? We can only cry to "the Lord of the harvest."

Sun. 21. Thousands of hearers, rich and poor, received the word near the new Square, with the deepest attention. This is the way to shake the trembling gates of hell. Still, I see nothing can do this so effectually as field-preaching.

Mon. 22. I rode through impetuous rain to Weston [Zoyland], a village near Bridgwater. A while ago the people here were lions, but now they are become lambs.

Tues. 23. I saw a serious congregation at Taunton. And shall we have fruit here also? In the evening I preached to the poor backsliders at Cullompton on, "Will the Lord be no more intreated?"

Wed. 24. I rode to Launceston, where both the seriousness and largeness of the congregation, evening and morning, gave us reason to hope that all our labour here will not be in vain.

Fri. 26. I came to Camelford, where the society is once more shrunk from seventy to fourteen. I preached in the market-place on "Oh, that thou hadst known, at least in this thy day, the things that make for thy peace!" Many were moved for the present, as they were the next day, while I was applying those awful words, "The harvest is past, the summer is ended, and we are not saved!"

Sat. 27. I went on to Port Isaac, now the liveliest place in the circuit. I preached from a balcony in the middle of the town, a circumstance I could not but observe. Before I came to Port Isaac the first time, one Richard Scantlebury invited me to lodge at his house; but when I came, seeing a large mob at my heels, he fairly shut the door upon me. Yet in this very house I now lodged, Richard Scantlebury being gone to his fathers, and the present proprietor, Richard Wood, counting it all joy to receive the servants of God. About this time I wrote to a friend as follows:

Dear Lawrence [Coughlan],

By a various train of providences you have been led to the very place where God intended you should be. And you have reason to praise him that he has not suffered your labour there to be in vain. In a short time, how little will it signify whether we had lived in the Summer Islands, or beneath

* The rage of Arctos and eternal frost!

How soon will this dream of life be at an end! And when we are once landed in eternity, it will be all one, whether we spent our time on earth in a palace, or had not where to lay our head.

You never learned either from my conversation, or preaching, or writings that "holiness consisted in a flow of joy." I constantly told you quite the contrary; I told you it was love: the love of God and our neighbour; the image of God stamped on the heart; the life of God in the soul of man; the mind that was in Christ, enabling us to walk as Christ also walked. If Mr. Maxfield or you took it to be anything else, it was your own fault, not mine. And whenever you waked out of that dream, you ought not to have laid the blame of it upon me. It is true that joy is one part of "the fruit of the Spirit," of the kingdom of God within us. But this is first "righteousness," then "peace," and "joy in the Holy Ghost." It is true, farther, that if you love God with "all your heart," you may "rejoice evermore." Nay, it is true still farther that many serious, humble, sober-minded believers, who do feel the love of God sometimes, and do then rejoice in God their Saviour, cannot be content with this, but pray continually that he would enable them to love and "rejoice in the Lord always." And no fact under heaven is more undeniable than that God does answer this prayer; that he does, for the sake of his Son, and through the power of his Spirit, enable one and another so to do. It is also a plain fact that this power does commonly overshadow them in an instant, and that from that time they enjoy that inward and outward holiness to which they were utter strangers before. Possibly you might be mistaken in this; perhaps you thought you had received what you had not. But pray do not measure all men by yourself; do not imagine you are the universal standard. If you deceived yourself (which yet I do not affirm), you should not infer that all others do. Many think they are justified, and are not; but we cannot infer that none are justified. So neither, if many think they are "perfected in love" and are not, will it follow that none are so? Blessed be God, though we set a hundred * enthusiasts aside, we are still "encompassed with a cloud of witnesses," who have testified and do testify in life and in death, that perfection which I have taught these forty years! This perfection cannot be a delusion, unless the Bible be a delusion too; I mean, "loving God with all our heart, and our neighbour as ourselves." I pin down all its opposers to this definition of it. No evasion! No shifting the question! Where is the delusion of this? Either you received this love, or you did not; if you did, dare you call it a delusion? You will not call it so for all the world. If you received anything else, it does not at all affect the question. Be it as much a delusion as you please, it is nothing to them who have received quite another thing, namely, that deep communion with the Father and the Son, whereby they are enabled to give him their whole heart, to love every man as their own soul, and to walk as Christ also walked.

O Lawrence, if Sister Coughlan and you ever did enjoy this, humble yourselves before God for casting it away; if you did not, God grant you may!

Mon. 29. I rode to St. Columb, intending to preach there; but finding no place that was tolerably convenient, I was going to take horse, when one offered me the use of his meadow close to the town. A large congregation quickly assembled, to whom I explained the nature and pleasantness of religion. I have seldom seen a people behave so well the first time I have preached to them.

Tues. 30. Calling at St. Agnes, I found a large congregation waiting; so I preached without delay. At Redruth likewise I found the people gathered from all parts, and God gave a loud call to the backsliders. Indeed there was need, for T. Rankin left between three and four hundred members in the society, and I found a hundred and ten!

In the evening I preached in the meadow at St. Ives to a very numerous and deeply serious congregation.

Wed. 31. I met the children, a work which will exercise the talents of the most able preachers in England.

Sept. 1, Thur. The grass being wet, we could not stand in the meadow, but we found an open space, where I called a listening multitude to return to him, who "hath not forgotten to be gracious."

Fri. 2. I preached at noon to an earnest company at Zennor, and in the evening to a far larger at St. Just. Here being informed that one of our sisters in the next parish, Morvah, who entertained the preachers formerly, was now decrepit, and had not heard a sermon for many years, I went on Saturday, the 3rd, at noon, to Alice Daniel's, and preached near the house on, "They who shall be accounted worthy to obtain that world, and the resurrection from the dead, are equal unto the angels, and are the children of God, being the children of the resurrection." I have always thought there is something venerable in persons worn out with age, especially when they retain their understanding and walk in the ways of God.

Sun. 4. I went to Sancreed church, where I heard an excellent sermon. Between one and two I confirmed it, by explaining that happy religion which our Lord describes in the eight beatitudes. About five in the evening I preached at Newlyn, about nine the next morning at Penzance. Surely God will have a people even in this place, where we have so long seemed only to beat the air. At noon I preached in St. Hilary, and at St. John's this and the next evening. I believe the most senseless then felt the word of God sharp as a two-edged sword.

Wed. 7. After the early preaching, the select society met, such a company of lively believers, full of faith and love, as I never found in this county before. This, and the three following days, I preached at as many places as I could, though I was at first in doubt whether I could preach eight days together, mostly in the open air, three or four times a day. But my strength was as my work; I hardly felt any weariness, first or last.

Sun. 11. About nine I preached at St. Agnes, and again between one and two. At five I took my old stand at Gwennap, in the natural amphitheatre. I suppose no human voice could have commanded such an audience on plain ground; but the ground rising all round gave me such an advantage that I believe all could hear distinctly.

Mon. 12. I preached about noon at Callestick, and in the evening at Keisilgey. It rained all the time, but that did not divert the attention of a large congregation. At noon, Tuesday the 13th, I preached in Truro, and in the evening at Mevagissey. It was a season of solemn joy; I have not often found the like. Surely God's thoughts are not as our thoughts! Can any good be done at Mevagissey?

Wed. 14. After preaching at St. Austell and Medrose, I rode over to Roche, and spent a comfortable evening with my old acquaintance, Mr. Furly.

Thur. 15. We had our Quarterly Meeting at Medrose, but it was not now as formerly, when the whole society was in a flame. "The love of many" is now "waxed cold."

Fri. 16. I rode through heavy rain to Polperro. Here the room over which we were to lodge, being filled with pilchards and conger eels, the perfume was too potent for me, so that I was not sorry when one of our friends invited me to lodge at her house. Soon after I began to preach, heavy rain began, yet none went away till the whole service was ended.

Sat. 17. When we came to Crimble Passage, we were at a full stop. The boatmen told us the storm was so high that it was not possible to pass; however, at length we persuaded them to venture out, and we did not ship one sea till we got over.

Sun. 18. Our room at the Dock contained the morning congregation tolerably well. Between one and two I began preaching on the quay at Plymouth. Notwithstanding the rain, abundance of people stood to hear. But one silly man talked without ceasing, till I desired the people to open to the right and left, and let me look him in the face. They did so. He pulled off his hat and quietly went away.

At five I preached in the square at the Dock, to an exceeding large congregation; and the rain, though it prevented some from coming, did not cause any to go away.

Mon. 19. In the evening I preached in what is vulgarly called Mr. Whitefield's room. Afterwards I met the society in our own, and exhorted them to "stand fast in one mind and one judgment." I set out early in the morning and in the evening preached at Tiverton.

Thur. 22. I rode to Axminster. The rain prevented my preaching abroad, though the room would ill contain the congregation. Observing many there who seemed quite unawakened, I opened and strongly applied Ezekiel's vision of the dry bones. Lord, "breathe upon these slain, that they may live."

Fri. 23. I rode across the country to Charlton, and found the congregation waiting. In the afternoon we went on to Lympsham, but not without some difficulty. The waters were out so that it was no easy matter either to ride or walk. My horse got into a ditch over his back in water; nor could I get to my lodgings the foot-way till an honest man took me on his shoulders, and so waded through.

Sat. 24. I returned to Bristol.

Tues. 27. I preached in Pensford at eight, in Shepton Mallet at one, and at Wincanton in the evening, with far greater freedom than I used to find among that dead people. About one, Wednesday the 28th, I preached at Stalbridge, to a large and serious attentive congregation. Hence I went on to cold, uncomfortable Shaftesbury, and spoke exceeding strong words. All seriously attended; some seemed to understand, and a few to feel what was spoken.

Thur. 29. I rode to Frome. The people here seem more alive than most I have seen in the circuit; and this is the more strange, because in this town only there is such a mixture of men of all opinions — Anabaptists, Quakers, Presbyterians, Arians, Antinomians, Moravians, and what not. If any hold to the truth in the midst of all these, surely the power must be of God.

Friday the 30th we observed as a day of fasting and prayer, and it was a good day for many, who no sooner called than God answered them in the joy of their heart.

Oct. 2. Sun. I preached at Kingswood, upon "Quench not the Spirit." Possibly this people may now have ears to hear, and may despise prophesyings no more. Hereby they have frequently quenched the Spirit, and destroyed his work in their hearts.

Wed. 5. I rode over to Maiden Bradley, and preached at a little distance from the town to as serious a congregation as I ever saw, many of whom were in tears. It is a wonder there should be room for the Gospel here, among so many lords and gentlemen! But indeed they neither meddle nor make, and this is all we desire of them.

Fri. 7. I spent an hour, much to my satisfaction, with the children at Kingswood. There is reason to hope that the grace of God is still working among them. Some are still alive to God, and all behave in such a manner that I have seen no other schoolboys like them.

Sun. 9. I began examining the society in Kingswood, much increased both in grace and number, chiefly by means of those meetings for prayer which God still blesses greatly. On Monday and Tuesday I examined the society at Bristol, and found cause to rejoice over these also; although there is still a heaviness of spirit upon many, indeed, on all who are not going on to perfection.

Wed. 12. In the evening I preached at Kingswood. I have not seen such a congregation there on a week day for above these twenty years. Nor have I seen such a congregation at Pill for many years, as was present on Thursday in the afternoon. It is possible, even on this barren soil, we may see a little fruit of much labour.

Fri. 14. I dined with Dr. Wrangel, one of the King of Sweden's chaplains, who has spent several years in Pennsylvania. His heart seemed to be greatly united to the American Christians, and he strongly pleaded for our sending some of our preachers to help them, multitudes of whom are as sheep without a shepherd.

Tues. 18. He preached at the new room, to a crowded audience, and gave general satisfaction by the simplicity and life which accompanied his sound doctrine.

Sat. 22. I was much surprised, in reading an **Essay on Music*, wrote by one who is a thorough master of the subject, to find that the music of the ancients was as simple as that of the Methodists; that their music wholly consisted of melody, or the arrangement of single notes; that what is now called harmony, singing in parts, the whole of counterpoint and fugues, is quite novel, being never known in the world till the popedom of Leo the Tenth. He farther observes that as the singing different words by different persons at the very same time necessarily prevents attention to the sense, so it frequently destroys melody for the sake of harmony; meantime it destroys the very end of music, which is to affect the passions.

Mon. 24. I left Bristol, and went by Bath and Bradford to Salisbury.

Wed. 26. At one, I preached in Romsey, to a very quiet, unaffected audience, and in the evening at Winchester, to a company of as poor people as I have seen for many years.

Thur. 27. The scene was changed; at Portsmouth rich and poor flocked together from all parts. Abundance of them came again at five in the morning. In the evening the house ill contained them, and never did I see any receive the word with greater earnestness. The next day I returned to London.

Mon. 31. I took horse at five, and just then found that my horse had scarce a shoe on his feet. However, I was obliged (not having a minute to spare) to ride on as far as Colney. There I procured one to shoe my horse all round, and lame him on both his fore-feet. However, he halted on to Hockliffe, where an honest and skillful smith so altered and removed the shoes that he did not halt any more. But by this means we had lost so much time that the sun set before we reached Whittlebury Forest. We had then wonderful road, some of the ridings (so called) being belly-deep. However, between six and seven we came safe to Whittlebury.

James Glassbrook was so wearied out that he could scarce stir hand or foot; so I desired him to go to rest. I was weary enough myself till I began to speak, but weariness then vanished away, and we all praised God with joyful lips.

Nov. 1, Tues. I preached at Weedon, and at five in the morning; about eleven at Towcester; and in the evening to many more than the house would hold at Northampton.

Fri. 4. James Glassbrook (who had a fit of an ague at Whittlebury) undertook to conduct me to Bedford, but he was taken ill on the road. I preached there at seven on "Awake, thou that sleepest." And never was more need, for a more sleepy audience I have not often seen.

Sat. 5. About noon I preached at Hertford, in the new room, to a large and serious congregation. The mayor's usage of Mr. Colley for preaching in the market-place, with Mr. Colley's firm and calm behaviour was the means of convincing Mr. Andrews, who built this room at his own expense.

Mon. 7. I set out for Oxfordshire, preached at Wycombe in the evening, and on Tuesday and Wednesday at Witney. On Thursday, in my return, I was desired to preach at Oxford. The room was thoroughly filled, and not with curious, but deeply serious hearers. Many of these desired that our travelling preachers would take them in their turn, with which I willingly complied.

In the evening I preached in the chapel at Henley, to a considerable number of serious people. One or two of the baser sort made some noise; but I reproved them, and, for once, they were ashamed.

Fri. 11. I returned to London. The next week I visited the classes, and at intervals read Mr. Boswell's *Account of Corsica*. But what a scene is opened therein! How little did we know of that brave people! How much less were we acquainted with the character of their general, Pascal Paoli, as great a lover of his country as Epaminondas, and as great a general as Hannibal!

Sat. 19. I read Dr. Nowell's answer to Mr. Hill, concerning *the expulsion of the students at Oxford. He has said all that could be said for that stretch of power, that instance of **summum jus*; and he says quite enough to clear the Church of England from the charge of predestination: a doctrine which he proves to be utterly inconsistent with the Common Prayer, the Communion Service, the Office of Baptism, the Articles, the Homilies, and the other writings of those that compiled them.

Mon. 28. In the evening I preached in the barracks at Chatham. I spoke louder than I have done for years, yet the skirts of the congregation could not hear. Few of those that did hear, heard in vain, for God was in the midst of them.

Tues. 29. At noon I preached at Sittingbourne to a deeply attentive audience, and in the evening at Canterbury in a house half filled — a sight I do not often see.

Wed. 30. I rode to Dover, and came in just before a violent storm began. It did not hinder the people. Many were obliged to go away after the house was filled. What a desire to hear runs through all the seaport towns wherever we come! Surely God is besieging this nation and attacking it at all the entrances!

Dec. 1, Thur. The storm was ready to bear away both man and beast. But it abated about noon so that, after preaching at Margate, I had a pleasant ride to Canterbury.

I made an odd observation here, which I recommend to all our preachers. The people of Canterbury have been so often reproved (and frequently without a cause) for being dead and cold, that it has utterly discouraged them, and made them cold as stones. How delicate a thing is it to reprove! To do it well requires more than human wisdom.

Fri. 2. Those who are called Mr. Whitefield's society, at Chatham, offered me the use of their preaching-house, which I suppose is nearly four times as large as that at the barracks. In the morning I walked on, ordering my servant to overtake me with my carriage; and he did so, but not till I had walked seven or eight miles.

Tues. 13. Having heard a heavy charge brought against W—— G——, a member of our society, I desired the parties concerned to meet me together. But this afternoon we could not get half through. At the second hearing I was convinced, (1) that he had spoken unkindly and unjustly; (2) that he had done wrong in leaving Mr. Dear at so short a warning; but I was equally convinced (3) that there had been no dishonesty on either side.

Wed. 14. I saw the Westminster scholars act the *Adelphi* of Terence, an entertainment not unworthy of a Christian. Oh, how do these heathens shame us! Their very comedies contain both excellent sense, the liveliest pictures of men and manners, and so fine strokes of genuine morality, as are seldom found in the writings of Christians.

Mon. 19. I spent an hour with B——a I——n. If the account she gives is true, what blessed creatures are both those gentlemen and their wives that would use the most scurrilous language, yea, strike and drive out of their house, and that in a rainy night, a young gentlewoman, a stranger, far from home, for joining with the Methodists! Do these call themselves Christians? Nay, and Protestants? Call them Turks. Papist is too good a name.

Tues. 20. I went to Shoreham. Here I read Mr. Archdeacon Blackburne's *Considerations on the Penal Laws against Papists*. In the appendix, p. 198, to my no small surprise, I read these words, said to be wrote by a gentleman at Paris: "The Popish party boast much of the increase of the Methodists, and talk of that sect with rapture. How far the Methodists and Papists stand connected in principles I know not, but I believe it is beyond a doubt that they are in constant correspondence with each other."

It seems this letter was published in the *St. James's Chronicle*, but I never saw or heard of it till these words were printed in the *Canterbury Journal* as Mr. Blackburne's own.

And he has nearly made them his own by his faint note upon them, "I would willingly hope some doubt may be made of this." Indeed he adds, "Mr. Whitefield took timely care to preclude all suspicions of his having any connections with Popery." Yea, and Mr. Wesley much more, even as early as Aug. 31, 1738. Again, in my *Journal*, Aug. 27, 1739, I published the only letter which I ever wrote to a Popish priest. And it is in proof of this proposition (an extraordinary proof of my connections with Popery!): "No Romanist, as such, can expect to be saved, according to the terms of the Christian covenant."

Many things to the same purpose occur in the *Journals*, and the *Appeals to Men of Reason and Religion*, over and above those whole treatises which I have published entirely upon the subject: *A Word to a Protestant*, a

Roman Catechism, and *The Advantages of the Members of the Church of England over the Members of the Church of Rome.*

What amazing ignorance, then, not to say impudence, does it imply, for any one at this time of day to tax me with having any connections with Popery!

In the latter end of the month I took some pains in reading over Dr. Young's *Night Thoughts*, leaving out the indifferent lines, correcting many of the rest, and explaining the hard words, in order to make that noble work more useful to all, and more intelligible to ordinary readers.

[1774]

CHARLES WESLEY

THE most important event occurring within the Church of England during the eighteenth century was the revival of religious fervour caused by Methodism. This movement, at first quite unconnected with Nonconformity, was a revulsion from the placid worldiness into which the Established Church had fallen since the Revolution, and a re-emphasis of truths and emotions once familiar to all devout Anglicans but now generally forgotten. Its chief distinguishing mark was a stronger earnestness, a deeper inwardness of religious feeling than the ordinary Churchmen of the time considered either desirable or decorous, and thus it came to be condemned by its enemies as an "enthusiasm."

Of this movement William Law was the herald and the deepest thinker, George Whitefield was the orator, James Hervey was the rather feeble popularizer, John Wesley was the organizer, and his brother Charles was the poet. Charles Wesley, eighteenth child of a country clergyman of good family who was himself a prolific versifier, was born in 1707. After receiving the best education afforded by the degenerate Oxford of his day, he worked for sixty years as the coadjutor of his brother John, than whom he was a less powerful but a more pleasing figure. The average excellence of his more than six thousand hymns is so high that he has been quite reasonably called "the greatest hymn-writer of the ages." The abundant humour and wit to be found in his secular verse, as also in that of his father and of his elder brother, Samuel, are not discernible in these hymns, but the manly vigour of them, the classic simplicity, and above all the pervading gentleness, are apparent to all readers who can give the religious lyric a fair hearing.

FOR CHRISTMAS DAY

Hark! how all the welkin rings
Glory to the King of Kings!
Peace on earth, and mercy mild,
God and sinners reconciled!
Joyful, all ye nations, rise,
Join the triumph of the skies;
Universal nature say,
Christ the Lord is born to-day!

Christ, by highest Heaven adored;
Christ, the Everlasting Lord;
Late in time behold Him come,
Offspring of a Virgin's womb:
Veiled in flesh the Godhead see;
Hail, th' Incarnate Deity,
Pleased as man with men to appear,
Jesus, our Immanuel here!

Hail! the heavenly Prince of Peace!
Hail! the Sun of Righteousness!
Light and life to all He brings,
Risen with healing in His wings.
Mild He lays His glory by,
Born that man no more may die,
Born to raise the sons of earth,
Born to give them second birth.

Come, Desire of nations, come,
Fix in us Thy humble home!
Rise, the Woman's conquering Seed,
Bruise in us the Serpent's head!
Now display Thy saving power,
Ruined nature now restore;
Now in mystic union join
Thine to ours, and ours to Thine!

Adam's likeness, Lord, efface;
Stamp Thy image in its place;
Second Adam from above,
Reinstate us in Thy love!
Let us Thee, though lost, regain,
Thee, the Life, the Inner Man:
Oh! to all Thyself impart,
Formed in each believing heart!

[1739]

WRESTLING JACOB

Come, O thou Traveller unknown,
  Whom still I hold, but cannot see;
My company before is gone,
  And I am left alone with Thee;
With Thee all night I mean to stay,
And wrestle till the break of day.

I need not tell Thee who I am,
  My misery or sin declare;
Thyself hast called me by my name;
  Look on Thy hands, and read it there!

But Who, I ask Thee, Who art Thou!
Tell me Thy Name, and tell me now.

In vain Thou strugglest to get free,
  I never will unloose my hold;
Art Thou the Man that died for me?
  The secret of Thy love unfold.
Wrestling, I will not let Thee go,
Till I Thy Name, Thy Nature know.

Wilt Thou not yet to me reveal
  Thy new, unutterable Name?
Tell me, I still beseech Thee, tell:
  To know it now, resolved I am:
Wrestling, I will not let Thee go,
Till I Thy Name, Thy Nature know.

'Tis all in vain to hold Thy tongue,
  Or touch the hollow of my thigh;
Though every sinew be unstrung,
  Out of my arms Thou shalt not fly:
Wrestling, I will not let Thee go,
Till I Thy Name, Thy Nature know.

What though my shrinking flesh complain,
  And murmur to contend so long?
I rise superior to my pain;
  When I am weak, then I am strong:
And when my all of strength shall fail,
I shall with the God-Man prevail.

My strength is gone; my nature dies;
  I sink beneath Thy weighty hand,
Faint to revive, and fall to rise;
  I fall, and yet by faith I stand:
I stand, and will not let Thee go,
Till I Thy Name, Thy Nature know.

Yield to me now, for I am weak,
  But confident in self-despair;
Speak to my heart, in blessings speak,
  Be conquer'd by my instant prayer!
Speak, or Thou never hence shalt move,
And tell me, if Thy Name is Love?

'Tis Love! 'tis Love! Thou diedst for me!
  I hear Thy whisper in my heart!
The morning breaks, the shadows flee;
  Pure universal Love Thou art!
To me, to all, Thy bowels move;
Thy Nature, and Thy Name is Love!

My prayer hath power with God; the grace
  Unspeakable I now receive;
Through faith I see Thee face to face,
  I see Thee face to face, and live:
In vain I have not wept and strove;
Thy Nature, and Thy Name is Love.

I know Thee, Saviour, Who Thou art;
  Jesus, the feeble sinner's Friend!
Nor wilt Thou with the night depart,
  But stay and love me to the end!
Thy mercies never shall remove,
Thy Nature, and Thy Name is Love!

The Sun of Righteousness on me
  Hath rose, with healing in his wings;
Withered my nature's strength, from Thee
  My soul its life and succour brings;
My help is all laid up above;
Thy Nature, and Thy Name is Love.

Contented now upon my thigh
  I halt, till life's short journey end;
All helplessness, all weakness, I
  On Thee alone for strength depend;
Nor have I power from Thee to move;
Thy Nature, and Thy Name is Love.

Lame as I am, I take the prey,
  Hell, earth, and sin, with ease o'ercome;
I leap for joy, pursue my way,
  And as a bounding hart fly home!
Through all eternity to prove,
Thy Nature, and Thy Name is Love!

[1742]

IN TEMPTATION

Jesu, lover of my soul,
  Let me to Thy bosom fly,
While the nearer waters roll,
  While the tempest still is high!
Hide me, O my Saviour, hide,
  Till the storm of life is past,
Safe into the haven guide;
  O receive my soul at last!

Other refuge have I none;
  Hangs my helpless soul on Thee;
Leave, ah! leave me not alone,
  Still support and comfort me!
All my trust on Thee is stay'd,
  All my help from Thee I bring:
Cover my defenceless head
  With the shadow of Thy wing!

Wilt Thou not regard my call?
Wilt Thou not accept my prayer?
Lo! I sink, I faint, I fall!
Lo! on Thee I cast my care!
Reach me out Thy gracious hand!
While I of Thy strength receive,
Hoping against hope I stand,
Dying, and behold I live!

Thou, O Christ, art all I want;
More than all in Thee I find:
Raise the fallen, cheer the faint,
Heal the sick, and lead the blind!
Just and holy is Thy Name;
I am all unrighteousness;
False and full of sin I am,
Thou art full of truth and grace.

Plenteous grace with Thee is found,
Grace to cover all my sin;
Let the healing streams abound;
Make and keep me pure within!
Thou of Life the Fountain art,
Freely let me take of Thee;
Spring Thou up within my heart,
Rise to all eternity!

[1749]

RICHARD HURD

"Of Dr. Hurd, Bishop of Worcester, Johnson said to a friend, 'Hurd, sir, is one of a set of men who account for everything systematically; for instance, it has been a fashion to wear scarlet breeches; these men would tell you that, according to causes and effects, no other wear could at that time have been chosen.' At another time, however, he said of him, 'Hurd, sir, is a man whose acquaintance is a valuable acquisition.'" These two remarks which Boswell reports are important for the understanding of Hurd's *Letters on Chivalry and Romance.* Not only was Hurd interested in the Middle Ages, but he wished systematically to account for the attraction that the chivalric romances had for "the greatest geniuses of our own and foreign countries, such as Ariosto and Tasso in Italy, and Spenser and Milton in England." Accordingly he set down in Letter I the following plan of investigation: "To form a judgment in the case, the rise, progress, and genius of Gothic chivalry must be explained. The circumstances in the Gothic fictions and manners which are proper to the ends of poetry (if any such there be) must be pointed out. Reasons for the decline and rejection of the Gothic taste in later times must be given." Because Hurd was "a man whose acquaintance is a valuable acquisition," both intellectually and socially, his book made the deeper impression upon the age.

Hurd was no innovator. Half a century before the publication of the *Letters on Chivalry and Romance* (1762), Addison had written on "The Fairy Way of Writing" in the *Spectator*, No. 419, and had discussed the poetic appeal of the ballads. Eight years before, in 1754, Thomas Warton had published *Observations on the Faerie Queene of Spenser;* six years before, in 1756, Joseph Warton had published the first part of his *Essay on the Genius and Writings of Pope.* Gray's *The Bard* had been published five years before, in 1757; *The Fatal Sisters* and *The Descent of Odin* had been written before 1762, but not yet published. Macpherson's *Fragments of Ancient Poetry Collected in the Highlands of Scotland* had appeared two years before, in 1760; *Fingal* was published the same year, 1762. Thus it is evident that interest in the Middle Ages and in the literature which had formerly been neglected because of its Gothic rudeness was becoming general when the Reverend Richard Hurd, not yet advanced to a high position in the Church, brought out his *Letters on Chivalry and Romance.* He was by no means a radical in literature or in life: he was intimate with Pope's editor and defender, Bishop Warburton, who had admired Hurd's commentary on Horace's *Ars Poetica;* his criticism seems to have been as orthodox as his theology. In politics he showed an early tendency to Whiggery, but later came to see his error, though Johnson suspected that he was after all "a Whig in his heart." At any rate he was made preceptor to the Prince of Wales and his brother, Prince Frederick. He was one of the last men in the country who might have been expected to be a precursor of romanticism.

Yet in spite of the fact that he was merely following a popular tendency of his time without thought of innovation, he reached conclusions in his *Letters on Chivalry and Romance* which were surprisingly favourable to the despised Gothic taste. He asserted that romance is not to be judged by the rules of the classical epic and that it has beauties unknown to the canons of Aristotle. Though he had no intention of advancing the claims of the mediæval romances (he refers to them as "barbarous volumes" in which he has done little reading), against the literature of his own day, he recognized the fact that the change in taste had involved loss as well as gain. He concludes:

> "What we have gotten by this revolution, you will say, is a world of good sense. What we have lost is a world of fine fabling, the illusion of which is so grateful to the charmed spirit that, in spite of philosophy and fashion, Fairy Spenser still ranks highest among the poets, — I mean with all those who are either come of that house or have any kindness for it. Earth-born critics, my friend, may blaspheme,
>
> But all the gods are ravish'd with delight
> Of his celestial song, and music's wondrous might."

Letters on Chivalry and Romance grew out of Hurd's *Moral and Political Dialogues,* 1759. The *Third Dialogue* represents Robert Digby, Dr. John Arbuthnot, and Joseph Addison as making a visit to the ruins of Kenilworth Castle in 1716 and while there discussing the "Golden Age of Queen Elizabeth." After viewing the remains of the hall and tilt-yard and recalling the magnificent entertainments provided for Queen Elizabeth on the occasion of her visit to the castle, they discuss the poetry of the Elizabethan period. Addison says, "Without doubt, the poetry of that time is of a better taste than could have been expected from its barbarism in other instances. But such prodigies as Shakespeare and Spenser could do great things in any age and under every disadvantage." Arbuthnot takes the ground that this poetry was especially favoured by the genius of the age. This point of view is further developed in the later work. The *Letters on Chivalry and Romance* is a small book containing twelve short letters, three of which, Numbers 6, 7, and 8, are here reprinted entire.

LETTERS ON CHIVALRY AND ROMANCE

LETTER VI

Let it be no surprise to you that, in the close of my last letter, I presumed to bring the **Gerusalemme Liberata* into competition with the *Iliad*.

So far as the *heroic and Gothic manners are the same, the pictures of each, if well taken, must be equally entertaining. But I go further, and maintain that the circumstances in which they differ are clearly to the advantage of the Gothic designers.

You see my purpose is to lead you from this forgotten chivalry to a more amusing subject, I mean the poetry we still read, and which was founded upon it.

Much has been said, and with great truth, of the felicity of Homer's age for poetical manners. But as Homer was a citizen of the world, when he had seen in Greece, on the one hand, the manners he has described, could he, on the other hand, have seen in the west the manners of the feudal ages, I make no doubt but he would certainly have preferred the latter. And the grounds of this preference would, I suppose, have been "the improved gallantry of the feudal times; and the superior solemnity of their superstitions."

If any great poet, like Homer, had lived amongst, and sung of, the Gothic knights (for after all Spenser and Tasso came too late, and it was impossible for them to paint truly and perfectly what was no longer seen or believed), this preference, I persuade myself, had been very sensible. But their fortune was not so happy.

*— *omnes illacrymabiles*
Urgentur, ignotique longa
Nocte, carent quia vate sacro.

As it is, we may take a guess of what the subject was capable of affording to real genius from the rude sketches we have of it in the old romancers. And it is but looking into any of them to be convinced that the gallantry, which inspirited the feudal times, was of a nature to furnish the poet with finer scenes and subjects of description in every view than the simple and uncontrolled barbarity of the Grecian.

The principal entertainment arising from the delineation of these consists in the exercise of the boisterous passions, which are provoked and kept alive from one end of the *Iliad* to the other, by every imaginable scene of rage, revenge, and slaughter. In the other, together with these, the gentler and more humane affections are awakened in us by the most interesting displays of love and friendship; of love, elevated to its noblest heights; and of friendship, operating on the purest motives. The mere variety of these paintings is a relief to the reader as well as writer. But their beauty, novelty, and pathos give them a vast advantage on the comparison.

Consider, withal, the surprises, accidents, adventures which probably and naturally attend on the life of wandering knights; the occasion there must be for describing the wonders of different countries, and of presenting to view the manners and policies of distant states: all which make so conspicuous a part of the materials of the greater poetry.

So that, on the whole, though the spirit, passions, rapine, and violence of the two sets of manners were equal, yet there was a dignity, a magnificence, a variety in the feudal, which the other wanted.

As to religious machinery, perhaps the popular system of each was equally remote from reason, yet the latter had something in it more amusing, as well as more awakening to the imagination.

The current popular tales of elves and fairies were even fitter to take the credulous mind, and charm it into a willing admiration of the specious miracles which wayward fancy delights in, than those of the old traditionary rabble of pagan divinities. And then, for the more solemn fancies of witchcraft and incantation, the horrors of the Gothic were above measure striking and terrible. The mummeries of the pagan priests were childish, but the Gothic enchanters shook and alarmed all nature.

We feel this difference very sensibly in reading the ancient and modern poets. You

* Notes on Richard Hurd will be found in the Appendix, p. 1042.

would not compare *the Canidia of Horace with the witches in *Macbeth*. And what are *Virgil's myrtles dropping blood, to Tasso's enchanted forest?

Ovid, indeed, who had a fancy turned to romance, makes Medea, in a rant, talk wildly. But was this the common language of their other writers? The enchantress in Virgil says coolly of the very chiefest prodigies of her charms and poisons,

**His ego sæpe lupum fieri, et se condere sylvis*
Mœrin; sæpe animas imis excire sepulchris,
Atque satas alio vidi traducere messes.

The admirable poet has given an air of the marvellous to his subject by the magic of his expression. Else, what do we find here, but the ordinary effects of melancholy, the vulgar superstition of evoking spirits, and the supposed influence of *fascination on the hopes of rural industry?

**Non isthic obliquo oculo mihi commoda quisquam*
Limat. . . .

says the poet of his country-seat, as if this security from a fascinating eye were a singular privilege, and the mark of a more than common good fortune.

Shakespeare, on the other hand, with a terrible sublime (which not so much the energy of his genius, as the nature of his subject drew from him) gives us another idea of the rough magic, as he calls it, of fairy enchantment:

*... I have bedimm'd
The noon-tide sun, call'd forth the mutinous winds,
And 'twixt the green sea and the azure vault
Set roaring war; to the dread rattling thunder
Have I giv'n fire, and rifted Jove's stout oak
With his own bolt; the strong-bas'd promontory
Have I made shake, and by the spurs pluck'd up
The pine and cedar: graves, at my command,
Have open'd, and let forth their sleepers. . . .

The last circumstance, you will say, is but the **animas imis excire sepulchris* of the Latin poet. But a very significant word marks the difference. The pagan necromancers had a hundred little tricks by which they pretended to call up the ghosts, or shadows of the dead: but these, in the ideas of paganism, were quite another thing from Shakespeare's sleepers.

This may serve for a cast of Shakespeare's magic; and I can't but think that when Milton wanted to paint the horrors of that night (one of the noblest parts in his *Paradise Regained*), which the devil himself is feigned to conjure up in the wilderness, the Gothic language and ideas helped him to work up his tempest with such terror. You will judge from these lines:

*... nor stay'd the terror there;
Infernal ghosts and hellish furies round
Environ'd thee; some howl'd, some yell'd,
some shriek'd,
Some bent at thee their fiery darts...

But above all from the following:

*Thus pass'd the night so foul, till morning fair
Came forth with pilgrim steps in amice gray,
Who with her *radiant finger* still'd the roar
Of thunder, chas'd the clouds, and laid the winds
And *grisly spectres*...

Where the radiant finger points at the potent wand of the Gothic magicians, which could reduce the calm of nature, upon occasion, as well as disturb it; and the grisly spectres laid by the approach of morn, were apparently of their raising, as a sagacious critic perceived when he took notice "how very injudicious it was to retail the popular superstition in this place."

After all, the conclusion is not to be drawn so much from particular passages, as from the general impression left on our minds in reading the ancient and modern poets. And this is so much in favour of the latter that Mr. Addison scruples not to say, *"The ancients have not much of this poetry among them; for, indeed," continues he, "almost the whole substance of it owes its original to the darkness and superstition of later ages. Our forefathers looked upon nature with more reverence and horror, before the world was enlightened by learning and philosophy, and loved to astonish themselves with the apprehensions of witchcraft, prodigies, charms, and enchantments. There was not a village in England that had not a ghost in it; the churchyards were all haunted; every large common had a circle of fairies belonging to it· and there was scarce a shepherd to be met with who had not seen a spirit."

We are upon enchanted ground, my friend; and you are to think yourself well used that I detain you no longer in this fearful circle. The glimpse you have had of it will help your imagination to conceive the rest. And without more words you will readily apprehend that the fancies of our modern bards are not only more gallant, but, on a change of the scene, more sublime, more terrible, more alarming than those of the classic fablers. In a word, you will find that the manners they paint, and the superstitions they adopt, are the more poetical for being Gothic.

LETTER VII

But nothing shows the difference of the two systems under consideration more plainly than the effect they really had on the two greatest of our poets; at least the two which an English reader is most fond to compare with Homer, I mean Spenser and Milton.

It is not to be doubted but that each of these bards had kindled his poetic fire from classic fables. So that, of course, their prejudices would lie that way. Yet they both appear, when most inflamed, to have been more particularly rapt with the Gothic fables of chivalry.

Spenser, though he had been long nourished with the spirit and substance of Homer and Virgil, chose the times of chivalry for his theme, and fairyland for the scene of his fictions. He could have planned, no doubt, an heroic design on the exact classic model; or, he might have trimmed between the Gothic and classic, as his contemporary Tasso did. But the charms of fairy prevailed. And if any think he was seduced by Ariosto into this choice, they should consider that it could be only for the sake of his subject; for the genius and character of these poets was widely different.

Under this idea, then, of a Gothic, not classical poem, the *Faerie Queene* is to be read and criticized. And on these principles, it would not be difficult to unfold its merit in another day than has been hitherto attempted.

Milton, it is true, preferred the classic model to the Gothic. But it was after long hesitation; and his favourite subject was Arthur and his knights of the round table. On this he had fixed for the greater part of his life. What led him to change his mind was, partly, as I suppose, *his growing fanaticism; partly, his ambition to take a different route from Spenser; but chiefly perhaps, the discredit into which the stories of chivalry had now fallen by * the immortal satire of Cervantes. Yet we see through all his poetry, where his enthusiasm flames out most, a certain predilection for the legends of chivalry before the fables of Greece.

This circumstance, you know, has given offence to the austerer and more mechanical critics. They are ready to censure his judgment, as juvenile and unformed, when they see him so delighted, on all occasions, with the Gothic romances. But do these censors imagine that Milton did not perceive the defects of these works, as well as they? No: it was not the composition of books of chivalry, but the manners described in them, that took his fancy; as appears from his *Allegro*:

> * Towered cities please us then
> And the busy hum of men,
> Where throngs of knights and barons bold
> In weeds of peace high triumphs hold,
> With store of ladies, whose bright eyes
> Rain influence, and judge the prize
> Of wit, or arms, while both contend
> To win her grace, whom all commend.

And when in the *Penseroso* he draws, by a fine contrivance, the same kind of image to soothe melancholy which he had before given to excite mirth, he indeed extols an author of one of these romances, as he had before, in general, extolled the subject of them; but it is an author worthy of his praise; not the writer of *Amadis* or *Sir Launcelot of the Lake*, but Chaucer himself, who has left an unfinished story on the Gothic or feudal model:

> * Or call up him that left half-told
> The story of Cambuscan bold,
> Of Camball and of Algarsife,
> And who had Canace to wife
> That own'd the virtuous ring and glass,
> And of the wondrous horse of brass,
> On which the Tartar king did ride;
> And if aught else great bards beside
> In sage and solemn tunes have sung
> Of tourneys and of trophies hung,
> Of forests and enchantments drear,
> Where more is meant than meets the ear.

The conduct, then, of these two poets may incline us to think with more respect than is commonly done of the Gothic manners, I mean as adapted to the uses of the greater poetry.

I say nothing of Shakespeare because the sublimity (the divinity, let it be, if nothing else will serve) of his genius kept no certain route, but rambled at hazard into all the regions of human life and manners. So that we can hardly say what he preferred or what he rejected on full deliberation. Yet one thing is clear, that even he is greater when he uses Gothic manners and machinery than when he employs classical: which brings us again to the same point, that the former have, by their nature and genius, the advantage of the latter in producing the sublime.

LETTER VIII

I spoke "of criticizing Spenser's poem under the idea not of a classical but Gothic composition."

It is certain much light might be thrown on that singular work, were an able critic to consider it in this view. For instance, he might go some way towards explaining, perhaps justifying, the general plan and conduct of the *Faerie Queene*, which to classical readers has appeared indefensible.

I have taken the fancy, with your leave, to try my hand on this curious subject.

When an architect examines a Gothic structure by Grecian rules, he finds nothing but deformity. But the Gothic architecture has its own rules, by which when it comes to be examined, it is seen to have its merit, as well as the Grecian. The question is not, which of the two is conducted in the simplest or truest taste, but whether there be not sense and design in both, when scrutinized by the laws on which each is projected.

The same observation holds of the two sorts of poetry. Judge of the *Faerie Queene* by the classic models, and you are shocked with its disorder; consider it with an eye to its Gothic original, and you find it regular. The unity and simplicity of the former are more complete; but the latter has that sort of unity and simplicity which results from its nature.

The *Faerie Queene* then, as a Gothic poem, derives its method, as well as the other characters of its composition, from the established modes and ideas of chivalry.

It was usual, in the days of knight-errantry, at the holding of any great feast, for knights to appear before the prince who presided at it, and claim the privilege of being sent on any adventure, to which the solemnity might give occasion. For it was supposed that, when such a throng of knights and barons bold as Milton speaks of, were got together, the distressed would flock in from all quarters, as to a place where they knew they might find and claim redress for all their grievances.

This was the real practice, in the days of pure and ancient chivalry. And an image of this practice was afterwards kept up in the castles of the great, on any extraordinary festival or solemnity: of which, if you want an instance, I refer you to the description of a feast made at Lisle in 1453 in the court of Philip the Good, Duke of Burgundy, for a crusade against the Turks, as you may find it given at large in the memoirs of Matthieu de Conci, Olivier de la Marche, and Monstrelet.

That feast was held for twelve days, and each day was distinguished by the claim and allowance of some adventure.

Now laying down this practice, as a foundation for the poet's design, you will see how properly the *Faerie Queene* is conducted.

"I devise," says the poet himself in his letter to Sir W. Raleigh, "that the Faery Queen kept her annual feaste xii days: upon which xii several days, the occasions of the xii several adventures happened; which being undertaken by xii several knights, are in these xii books severally handled."

Here you have the poet delivering his own method, and the reason of it. It arose out of the order of his subject. And would you desire a better reason for his choice?

Yes; you will say, a poet's method is not that of his subject. I grant you, as to the order of time, in which the recital is made; for here, as Spenser observes (and his own practice agrees to the rule) lies the main difference between the poet historical and the historiographer: the reason of which is drawn from the nature of epic composition itself, and holds equally, let the subject be what it will, and whatever the system of manners be on which it is conducted. Gothic or classic makes no difference in this respect.

But the case is not the same with regard to the general plan of a work, or what may be called the order of distribution, which is and must be governed by the subject-matter itself. It was as requisite for the *Faerie Queene* to consist of the adventures of twelve knights as for the *Odyssey* to be confined to the adventures of one hero: justice had otherwise not been done to his subject.

So that if you will say anything against the poet's method, you must say that he should not have chosen this subject. But this objection arises from your classic ideas of unity, which have no place here; and are in every view foreign to the purpose, if the poet has found means to give his work, though consisting of many parts, the advantage of unity. For in some reasonable sense or other it is agreed every work of art must be one, the very idea of a work requiring it.

If you ask, then, what is this unity of Spenser's poem, I say it consists in the relation of its several adventures to one common original, the appointment of the Faery Queen; and to one common end, the completion of the Faery Queen's injunctions. The knights issued forth on their adventures on the breaking up of this annual feast; and the next annual feast, we are to suppose, is to bring them together again from the achievement of their several charges.

This, it is true, is not the classic unity, which consists in the representation of one entire action, but it is an unity of another sort, an unity resulting from the respect which a number of related actions have to one common purpose. In other words, it is an unity of design and not of action.

This Gothic method of design in poetry may be, in some sort, illustrated by what is called the Gothic method of design in gardening. A wood or grove cut out into many separate avenues or glades was amongst the most favourite of the works of art which our fathers attempted in this species of cultivation. These walks were distinct from each other, had each their several destination, and terminated on their own proper objects. Yet the whole was brought together and considered under one view by the relation which these various openings had, not to each other, but to their common and concurrent centre. You and I are, perhaps, agreed that this sort of gardening is not of so true a taste as that which *Kent and Nature have brought us acquainted with, where the supreme art of the designer consists in disposing his ground and objects into an entire landscape, and grouping them, if I may use the term, in so easy a manner that the careless observer, though he be taken with the symmetry of the whole, discovers no art in the combination:

> **In lieto aspetto il bel giardin s'aperse,*
> *Acque stagnanti, mobili cristalli,*
> *Fior vari, e varie piante, herbe diverse,*
> *Apriche collinette, ombrose valli,*
> *Selve e spelunche in una vista offerse:*
> *E quel, che'l bello, e'l caro accresce à l'opre,*
> *L'arte, che tutto fà, nulla si scopre.*
>
> TASSO. C. xvi. S. ix.

This, I say, may be the truest taste in gardening because the simplest. Yet there is a manifest regard to unity in the other method; which has had its admirers, as it may have again, and is certainly not without its design and beauty.

But to return to our poet. Thus far he drew from Gothic ideas, and these ideas, I think, would lead him no farther. But, as Spenser knew what belonged to classic composition, he was tempted to tie his subject still closer together by one expedient of his own, and by another taken from his classic models.

His own was to interrupt the proper story of each book, by dispersing it into several; involving by this means, and as it were intertwisting the several actions together, in order to give something like the appearance of one action to his twelve adventures. And for this conduct, as absurd as it seems, he had some great examples in the Italian poets, though I believe they were led into it by different motives.

The other expedient which he borrowed from the classics, was by adopting one superior character which should be seen throughout. Prince Arthur, who had a separate adventure of his own, was to have his part in each of the others; and thus several actions were to be embodied by the interest which one principal hero had in them all. It is even observable that Spenser gives this adventure of Prince Arthur, in quest of Gloriana, as the proper subject of his poem. And upon this idea the late learned editor of the *Faerie Queene* has attempted, but I think without success, to defend the unity and simplicity of its fable. The truth was the violence of classic prejudices forced the poet to affect this appearance of unity, though in contradiction to his Gothic system. And as far as we can judge of the tenor of the whole work from the finished half of it, the adventure of Prince Arthur, whatever the author pretended, and his critic too easily believed, was but an afterthought; and at least with regard to the historical fable, which we are now considering, was only one of the expedients by which he would conceal the disorder of his Gothic plan.

And if this was his design, I will venture to say that both his expedients were injudicious. Their purpose was to ally two things, in nature incompatible, the Gothic, and the classic unity; the effect of which misalliance was to discover and expose the nakedness of the Gothic.

I am of opinion, then, considering the *Faerie Queene* as an epic or narrative poem constructed on Gothic ideas, that the poet had done well to affect no other unity than that of design, by which his subject was connected. But his poem is not simply narrative; it is throughout allegorical: he calls it "a perpetual allegory or dark conceit"; and this character, for reasons I may have occasion to observe hereafter, was even predominant in the

Faerie Queene. His narration is subservient to his moral, and but serves to colour it. This he tells us himself at setting out:

Fierce wars and faithful loves shall moralize my song,

that is, shall serve for a vehicle, or instrument to convey the moral.

Now under this idea the unity of the *Faerie Queene* is more apparent. His twelve knights are to exemplify as many virtues, out of which one illustrious character is to be composed. And in this view the part of Prince Arthur in each book becomes essential, and yet not principal; exactly as the poet has contrived it. They who rest in the literal story, that is, who criticize it on the footing of a narrative poem, have constantly objected to this management. They say it necessarily breaks the unity of design. Prince Arthur, they affirm, should either have had no part in the other adventures or he should have had the chief part. He should either have done nothing or more. And the objection is unanswerable; at least I know of nothing that can be said to remove it but what I have supposed above might be the purpose of the poet, and which I myself have rejected as insufficient.

But how faulty soever this conduct be in the literal story, it is perfectly right in the moral, and that for an obvious reason, though his critics seem not to have been aware of it. His chief hero was not to have the twelve virtues in the *degree* in which the knights had, each of them, their own; (such a character would be a monster) but he was to have so much of each as was requisite to form his superior character. Each virtue in its perfection is exemplified in its own knight; they are all, in a due degree, concentred in Prince Arthur.

This was the poet's moral: and what way of expressing this moral in the history but by making Prince Arthur appear in each adventure, and in a manner subordinate to its proper hero? Thus, though inferior to each in his own specific virtue, he is superior to all by uniting the whole circle of their virtues in himself; and thus he arrives, at length, at the possession of that bright form of glory, whose ravishing beauty, as seen in a dream or vision, had led him out into these miraculous adventures in the land of faery.

The conclusion is that, as an allegorical poem, the method of the *Faerie Queene* is governed by the justness of the moral; as a narrative poem it is conducted on the ideas and usages of chivalry. In either view, if taken by itself, the plan is defensible. But from the union of the two designs there arises a perplexity and confusion, which is the proper, and only considerable, defect of this extraordinary poem.

[1762]

JAMES MACPHERSON

One of the most startling and influential literary events of the eighteenth century was the appearance, in 1760, of a slight book entitled *Fragments of Ancient Poetry, Collected in the Highlands of Scotland.* The title-page bore the name of James Macpherson, at the time a schoolmaster twenty-four years of age, who asserted that he was only the translator of these "fragments." He had been encouraged to publish them by the dramatist, John Home, to whom William Collins had addressed his *Ode on the Superstitions of the Highlands* ten years before. There was something so fresh and strange in this heavily cadenced prose and the haunting images of wild nature, and they were so suited to the growing taste for the antique, the exotic, and the wild, that they made an immediate sensation. Thomas Gray wrote to a friend in the year they were published: "I am gone mad about them. They are said to be translations, literal and in prose, from the Erse tongue, done by one Macpherson, a young clergyman in the Highlands. He means to publish a collection he has of these specimens of antiquity — if it be antiquity; but what plagues me is, I cannot come to any certainty on that head." Dr. Johnson seems to have been perfectly certain at once, for reasons which have since been abundantly disproved, that they were spurious, and he could see in them no literary merit. In 1761 Macpherson brought out *Fingal, an Ancient Epic Poem, with Other Poems Composed by Ossian,* and two years later *Temora, an Epic Poem.* Here ended his connection with "Ossian," the third-century Gaelic bard, upon which his fame entirely rests. Although they were often demanded, he never produced any original manuscripts. He did, however, leave a Gaelic version of the poems which was probably retranslated from the English. In later life he served as secretary to the Governor of Florida, wrote history, translated the *Iliad,* bought an estate in the Highlands, and sat in Parliament from 1780 until his death in 1796.

Three lines of interest concerning the so-called Ossianic poems may be distinguished. There is, first, the question, not yet settled after a century and a half of debate, of just what Macpherson did in making them. That he had some original sources, oral or written, no one any longer doubts; but it seems equally certain that his treatment of these was not, for the most part, either translation or even paraphrase. The probability is that, with some knowledge of Gaelic and a rather extensive acquaintance among the actual singers of old Gaelic ballads attributed to Ossian, he expanded such fragments as he found into loosely connected narratives which he called epics. His rendering blurred the edges and softened the more violent tones of the original fragments, thus adjusting them to the taste of the time.

Secondly, the influence of the Ossianic poems, both at home and abroad, gives them an importance out of proportion to their merit. The echoes of their sonorous prose rolled through the literature of Europe and America for a hundred years. So great and original an artist as William Blake never outgrew the effect of them, and neither did Chateaubriand or Lamartine. The young Goethe said of them in *The Sorrows of Werther*: "Homer has been superseded in my heart by the divine Ossian." They had almost a determining influence upon the career of Herder. In the Italian translation they were Napoleon's favourite reading. Probably they did more than any other literary work, unless perhaps the *Reliques* of Bishop Percy, to hasten the triumph, in England and in Europe, of the romantic movement.

Finally, there is the question regarding the intrinsic literary worth of these writings. In recent years this has been rated very low, the ordinary critical view being that the style of Macpherson, once so admired, is pretentious, tawdry, and shallow. That it is monotonous and vague there can be no doubt, but to those few who do it the simple justice of reading it aloud, with an effort to visualize each simple picture, this very vagueness and monotony may still be impressive. Macpherson made good use, on the whole, of his two chief models, the Bible and Homer. There is a nobility of tone in these prose poems, a melancholy grandeur, which gives them place, whatever their origin, as a work of art. Matthew Arnold was certainly right when he said of them: "Choose any one of the better passages, and you can see at this day what an apparition of newness and of power such a strain must have been in the eighteenth century."

"OSSIAN"

Carthon

Argument

This poem is complete, and the subject of it, as of most of Ossian's compositions, tragical. In the time of Comhal, the son of Trathal, and father of the celebrated Fingal, Clessámmor, the son of Thaddu, and brother of Morna, Fingal's mother, was driven by a storm into the river Clyde, on the banks of which stood Balclutha, a town belonging to the Britons, between the walls. He was hospitably received by Reuthámir, the principal man in the place, who gave him Moina, his only daughter, in marriage. Reuda, the son of Cormo, a Briton, who was in love with Moina, came to Reuthámir's house, and behaved haughtily towards Clessámmor. A quarrel ensued, in which Reuda was killed; the Britons who attended him, pressed so hard on Clessámmor that he was obliged to throw himself into the Clyde and swim to his ship. He hoisted sail, and the wind, being favourable, bore him out to sea. He often endeavoured to return, and carry off his beloved Moina by night; but the wind continuing contrary, he was forced to desist.

Moina, who had been left with child by her husband, brought forth a son, and died soon after. Reuthámir named the child Carthon, i.e., "the murmur of waves," from the storm which carried off Clessámmor his father, who was supposed to have been cast away. When Carthon was three years old, Comhal, the father of Fingal, in one of his expeditions against the Britons, took and burnt Balclutha. Reuthámir was killed in the attack; and Carthon was carried safe away by his nurse, who fled farther into the country of the Britons. Carthon, coming to man's estate, was resolved to revenge the fall of Balclutha on Comhal's posterity. He set sail from the Clyde, and falling on the coast of Morven, defeated two of Fingal's heroes, who came to oppose his progress. He was, at last, unwittingly killed by his father, Clessámmor, in a single combat. This story is the foundation of the present poem, which opens on the night preceding the death of Carthon, so that what passed before is introduced by way of episode. The poem is addressed to Malvina, the daughter of * Toscar.

A tale of the times of old! The deeds of days of other years.

The murmur of thy streams, O Lora! brings back the memory of the past. The sound of thy woods, Garmaller, is lovely in mine ear. Dost thou not behold, Malvina, a rock with its head of heath? Three aged pines bend from its face; green is the narrow plain at its feet; there the flower of the mountain grows, and shakes its white head in the breeze. The thistle is there alone, shedding its aged beard. Two stones, half sunk in the ground, show their heads of moss. The deer of the mountain avoids the place, for he beholds a dim ghost standing there. The mighty lie, O Malvina! in the narrow plain of the rock.

A tale of the times of old! The deeds of days of other years!

Who comes from the land of strangers, with his thousands around him? The sunbeam pours its bright stream before him; his hair meets the wind of his hills. His face is settled from war. He is calm as the evening beam that looks from the cloud of the west, on Cona's silent vale. Who is it but Comhal's son, the king of mighty deeds! He beholds his hills with joy, he bids a thousand voices rise. "Ye have fled over your fields, ye sons of the distant land! The king of the world sits in his hall, and hears of his people's flight. He lifts his red eye of pride; he takes his father's sword. Ye have fled over your fields, sons of the distant land!"

Such were the words of the bards, when they came to Selma's halls. A thousand lights from the stranger's land rose in the midst of the people. The feast is spread around; the night passed away in joy. "Where is the noble Clessámmor?" said the fair-haired Fingal. "Where is the brother of Morna, in the hour of my joy? Sullen and dark, he passes his days in the vale of echoing Lora; but, behold, he comes from the hill, like a steed in his strength, who finds his companions in the breeze, and tosses his bright mane in the wind. Blest be the soul of Clessámmor. Why so long from Selma?"

"Returns the chief," said Clessámmor, "in the midst of his fame? Such was the renown of Comhal in the battles of his youth. Often did we pass over Carun to the land of the strangers; our swords returned, not unstained with blood; nor did the kings of the world rejoice. Why do I remember the times of our war? My hair is mixed with gray. My hand forgets to bend the bow; I lift a lighter spear. Oh, that my joy would return, as when I first beheld the maid; the white-bosomed daughter of strangers, Moina, with the dark blue eyes!"

"Tell," said the mighty Fingal, "the tale of thy youthful days. Sorrow, like a cloud on the sun, shades the soul of Clessámmor. Mournful are thy thoughts, alone, on the banks of the roaring Lora. Let us hear the sorrow of thy youth and the darkness of thy days!"

"It was in the days of peace," replied the great Clessámmor, "I came in my bounding ship to Balclutha's walls of towers. The winds had roared behind my sails, and Clutha's streams received my dark-bosomed ship. Three days I remained in Reuthámir's halls, and saw his daughter, that beam of light. The joy of the shell went round, and the aged hero gave the fair. Her breasts were like foam on the wave, and her eyes like stars of light; her hair was dark as the raven's wing; her soul was generous and mild. My love for Moina was great; my heart poured forth in joy.

"The son of a stranger came, a chief who loved the white-bosomed Moina. His words

* Notes on James Macpherson will be found in the Appendix, p. 1043.

were mighty in the hall; he often half-unsheathed his sword. 'Where,' said he, 'is the mighty Comhal, the restless wanderer of the heath? Comes he, with his host, to Balclutha, since Clessámmor is so bold?' 'My soul,' I replied, 'O warrior! burns in a light of its own. I stand without fear in the midst of thousands, though the valiant are distant far. Stranger! thy words are mighty, for Clessámmor is alone. But my sword trembles by my side, and longs to glitter in my hand. Speak no more of Comhal, son of the winding Clutha!'

"The strength of his pride arose. We fought: he fell beneath my sword. The banks of Clutha heard his fall; a thousand spears glittered around. I fought; the strangers prevailed; I plunged into the stream of Clutha. My white sails rose over the waves, and I bounded on the dark blue sea. Moina came to the shore, and rolled the red eye of her tears; her loose hair flew on the wind; and I heard her mournful, distant cries. Often did I turn my ship; but the winds of the east prevailed. Nor Clutha ever since have I seen, nor Moina of the dark brown hair. She fell in Balclutha, for I have seen her ghost. I knew her as she came through the dusky night, along the murmur of Lora; she was like the new moon, seen through the gathered mist, when the sky pours down its flaky snow, and the world is silent and dark."

"Raise, ye bards," said the mighty Fingal, "the praise of unhappy Moina. Call her ghost, with your songs, to our hills, that she may rest with the fair of Morven, the sunbeams of other days, the delight of heroes of old. I have seen the walls of Balclutha, but they were desolate. The fire had resounded in the halls; and the voice of the people is heard no more. The stream of Clutha was removed from its place by the fall of the walls. The thistle shook there its lonely head; the moss whistled to the wind. The fox looked out from the windows, the rank grass of the wall waved round its head. Desolate is the dwelling of Moina, silence is in the house of her fathers. Raise the song of mourning, O bards, over the land of strangers. They have but fallen before us; for one day we must fall. Why dost thou build the hall, son of the winged days? Thou lookest from thy towers today: yet a few years, and the blast of the desert comes; it howls in thy empty court, and whistles round thy half-worn shield. And let the blast of the desert come! We shall be renowned in our day! The mark of my arm shall be in battle; my name in the song of bards. Raise the song, send round the shell; let joy be heard in my hall. When thou, sun of heaven! shalt fail; if thou shalt fail, thou mighty light! if thy brightness is for a season, like Fingal, our fame shall survive thy beams."

Such was the song of Fingal in the day of his joy. His thousand bards leaned forward from their seats to hear the voice of the king. It was like the music of harps on the gale of the spring Lovely were thy thoughts, O Fingal! Why had not *Ossian the strength of thy soul? But thou standest alone, my father! Who can equal the king of Selma?

The night passed away in song; morning returned in joy. The mountains showed their gray heads; the blue face of ocean smiled. The white wave is seen tumbling round the distant rock; a mist rose slowly from the lake. It came, in the figure of an aged man, along the silent plain. Its large limbs did not move in steps, for a ghost supported it in mid air. It came towards Selma's hall, and dissolved in a shower of *blood.

The king alone beheld the sight; he foresaw the death of the people. He came in silence to his hall, and took his father's spear. The mail rattled on his breast. The heroes rose around. They looked in silence on each other, marking the eyes of Fingal. They saw battle in his face; the death of armies on his spear. A thousand shields at once are placed on their arms; they drew a thousand swords. The hall of Selma brightened around. The clang of arms ascends. The gray dogs howl in their place. No word is among the mighty chiefs. Each marked the eyes of the king and half assumed his spear.

"Sons of Morven," begun the king, "this is no time to fill the shell; the battle darkens near us; death hovers over the land. Some ghost, the friend of Fingal, has forewarned us of the foe. The sons of the stranger come from the darkly rolling sea; for from the water came the sign of Morven's gloomy danger. Let each assume his heavy spear, each gird on his father's sword. Let the dark helmet rise on every head; the mail pour its lightning from every side. The battle gathers like a storm; soon shall ye hear the roar of death."

The hero moved on before his host like a cloud before a ridge of green fire, when it pours on the sky of night, and mariners foresee a storm. On Cona's rising heath they stood: the white-bosomed maids beheld them above like a grove; they foresaw the death of the youth, and looked towards the sea with fear. The white wave deceived them for distant sails; the tear is on their cheek! The sun rose on the sea, and we beheld a distant fleet. Like the mist of ocean they came and poured their youth upon the coast. The chief was among them, like the stag in the midst of the herd. His shield is studded with gold; stately strode the king of spears. He moved towards Selma; his thousands moved behind.

"Go, with a song of peace," said Fingal; "go, Ullin, to the king of swords. Tell him that we are mighty in war, that the ghosts of our foes are many. But renowned are they who have feasted in my halls; they show the arms of my fathers in a foreign land; the sons of the strangers wonder, and bless the friends of Morven's race; for our names have been heard afar; the kings of the world shook in the midst of their host."

Ullin went with his song. Fingal rested on his spear; he saw the mighty foe in his armour; he blest the stranger's son. "How stately art thou, son of the sea!" said the king of woody Morven. "Thy sword is a beam of fire by thy side; thy spear is a pine that defies the storm. The varied face of the moon is not broader than thy shield. Ruddy is thy face of youth! soft the ringlets of thy hair! But this tree may fall, and his memory be forgot! The daughter of the stranger will be sad, looking to the rolling sea. The children will say, 'We see a ship; perhaps it is the king of Balclutha.' The tear starts from their mother's eye. Her thoughts are of him who sleeps in Morven!"

Such were the words of the king when Ullin came to the mighty Carthon. He threw down the spear before him; he raised the song of peace. "Come to the feast of Fingal, Carthon, from the rolling sea! Partake of the feast of the king, or lift the spear of war! The ghosts of our foes are many; but renowned are the friends of Morven! Behold that field, O Carthon! Many a green hill rises there, with mossy stones and rustling grass. These are the tombs of Fingal's foes, the sons of the rolling sea!"

"Dost thou speak to the weak in arms!" said Carthon, "bard of the woody Morven? Is my face pale for fear, son of the peaceful song? Why then dost thou think to darken my soul with the tales of those who fell? My arm has fought in battle; my renown is known afar. Go to the feeble in arms; bid them yield to Fingal. Have not I seen the fallen Balclutha? And shall I feast with Comhal's son — Comhal, who threw his fire in the midst of my father's hall? I was young, and knew not the cause why the virgins wept. The columns of smoke pleased mine eye, when they rose above my walls! I often looked back with gladness when my friends flew along the hill. But when the years of my youth came on, I beheld the moss of my fallen walls. My sigh arose with the morning, and my tears descended with night. 'Shall I not fight,' I said to my soul, 'against the children of my foes?' And I will fight, O bard! I feel the strength of my soul!"

His people gathered around the hero, and drew at once their shining swords. He stands in the midst, like a pillar of fire, the tear half-starting from his eye, for he thought of the fallen Balclutha. The crowded pride of his soul arose. Sidelong he looked up to the hill, where our heroes shone in arms; the spear trembled in his hand. Bending forward, he seemed to threaten the king.

"Shall I," said Fingal to his soul, "meet at once the youth? Shall I stop him in the midst of his course before his fame shall arise! But the bard hereafter may say, when he sees the tomb of Carthon, 'Fingal took his thousands to battle, before the noble Carthon fell.' No, bard of the times to come! thou shalt not lessen Fingal's fame! My heroes will fight the youth, and Fingal behold the war. If he overcomes, I rush in my strength, like the roaring stream of Cona. Who of my chiefs will meet the son of the rolling sea? Many are his warriors on the coast, and strong is his ashen spear!"

Cathul rose in his strength, the son of the mighty Lormar; three hundred youths attend the chief, the race of his native streams. Feeble was his arm against Carthon. He fell, and his heroes fled. Connal resumed the battle, but he broke his heavy spear; he lay bound on the field; Carthon pursued his people.

"Clessámmor," said the king of Morven, "where is the spear of thy strength? Wilt thou behold Connal bound — thy friend at the stream of Lora? Rise, in the light of thy steel, companion of valiant Comhal! Let the youth of Balclutha feel the strength of Morven's race." He rose in the strength of his steel, shaking his grisly locks. He fitted the steel to his side; he rushed in the pride of valour.

Carthon stood on a rock. He saw the hero rushing on. He loved the dreadful joy of his face — his strength in the locks of age! "Shall I lift that spear," he said, "that never strikes but once a foe? Or shall I, with the words of peace, preserve the warrior's life? Stately are his steps of age! Lovely the remnant of his years! Perhaps it is the husband of Moina, the father of car-borne Carthon. Often have I heard that he dwelt at the echoing stream of Lora."

Such were his words when Clessámmor came, and lifted high his spear. The youth received it on his shield, and spoke the words of peace. "Warrior of the aged locks! is there no youth to lift the spear? Hast thou no son to raise the shield before his father to meet the arm of youth? Is the spouse of thy love no more? Or weeps she over the tombs of thy sons? Art thou of the kings of men? What will be the fame of my sword, shouldst thou fall?"

"It will be great, thou son of pride!" began the tall Clessámmor. "I have been renowned in battle, but I never told my name to a *foe. Yield to me, son of the wave; then shalt thou know that the mark of my sword is in many a field."

"I never yielded, king of spears!" replied the noble pride of Carthon. "I have also fought in war; I behold my future fame. Despise me not, thou chief of men! My arm, my spear is strong. Retire among thy friends; let younger heroes fight."

"Why dost thou wound my soul?" replied Clessámmor, with a tear. "Age does not tremble on my hand. I still can lift the sword. Shall I fly in Fingal's sight — in the sight of him I love? Son of the sea, I never fled! Exalt thy pointed spear."

They fought like two contending winds that strive to roll the wave. Carthon bade his spear to err. He still thought that the foe was the spouse of Moina. He broke Clessámmor's beamy spear in twain; he seized his shining sword. But as Carthon was binding the chief, the chief drew the dagger of his fathers. He saw the foe's uncovered side, and opened there a wound.

Fingal saw Clessámmor low. He moved in the sound of his steel. The host stood silent in his presence; they turned their eyes to the king. He came like the sullen noise of a storm before the winds arise; the hunter hears it in the vale, and retires to the cave of the rock. Carthon stood in his place; the blood is rushing down his side; he saw the coming down of the king, his hopes of fame arose. But pale was his cheek; his hair flew loose; his helmet shook on high. The force of Carthon failed; but his soul was strong.

Fingal beheld the hero's blood; he stopped the uplifted spear. "Yield, king of swords!" said Comhal's son, "I behold thy blood; thou hast been mighty in battle, and thy fame shall never fade."

"Art thou the king so far renowned?" replied the car-borne Carthon. "Art thou that light of death that frightens the kings of the world? But why should Carthon ask? for he is like the stream of his hills, strong as a river in his course, swift as the eagle of heaven. Oh, that I had fought with the king, that my fame might be great in song! that the hunter, beholding my tomb, might say, 'He fought with the mighty Fingal.' But Carthon dies unknown; he has poured out his force on the weak."

"But thou shalt not die unknown," replied the king of woody Morven. "My bards are many, O Carthon! Their songs descend to future times. The children of years to come shall hear the fame of Carthon, when they sit round the burning oak, and the night is spent in songs of old. The hunter, sitting in the heath, shall hear the rustling blast, and, raising his eyes, behold the rock where Carthon fell. He shall turn to his son, and show the place where the mighty fought: 'There the king of Balclutha fought, like the strength of a thousand streams.'"

Joy rose in Carthon's face; he lifted his heavy eyes. He gave his sword to Fingal, to lie within his hall, that the memory of Balclutha's king might remain in Morven. The battle ceased along the field, the bard had sung the song of peace. The chiefs gathered round the falling Carthon; they heard his words with sighs. Silent they leaned on their spears, while Balclutha's hero spoke. His hair sighed in the wind, and his voice was sad and low.

"King of Morven," Carthon said, "I fall in the midst of my course. A foreign tomb receives, in youth, the last of Reuthámir's race. Darkness dwells in Balclutha; the shadows of grief in Crathmo. But raise my remembrance on the banks of Lora, where my fathers dwelt. Perhaps the husband of Moina will mourn over his fallen Carthon."

His words reached the heart of Clessámmor. He fell in silence on his son. The host stood darkened around. No voice is on the plain. Night came. The moon, from the east, looked on the mournful field; but still they stood, like a silent grove that lifts its head on Gormal, when the loud winds are laid, and dark autumn is on the plain.

Three days they mourned above Carthon; on the fourth his father died. In the narrow plain of the rock they lie; a dim ghost defends their tomb. There lovely Moina is often seen, when the sunbeam darts on the rock, and all around is dark. There she is seen, Malvina; but not like the daughters of the hill. Her robes are from the stranger's land, and she is still alone!

Fingal was sad for Carthon; he commanded his bards to mark the day when shadowy autumn returned; and often did they mark the day, and sing the hero's praise. "Who comes so dark from ocean's roar, like autumn's shadowy cloud? Death is trembling in his hand! His eyes are flames of fire! Who roars along dark Lora's heath? Who but Carthon, king of swords! The people fall! See how he strides like the sullen ghost of Morven! But there he lies, a goodly oak which sudden blasts overturned! When shalt thou rise, Balclutha's joy? When, Carthon, shalt thou arise? Who comes so dark from ocean's roar, like autumn's shadowy cloud?" Such were the words of the bards in the day of their mourning. Ossian often joined their voice, and added to their song. My soul has been mournful for Carthon; he fell in the days of his youth. And thou, O Clessámmor! where is thy dwelling in the wind? Has the youth forgot his wound? Flies he on clouds with thee?

I feel the sun, O Malvina! leave me to my rest. Perhaps they may come to my dreams; I think I hear a feeble voice! The beam of heaven delights to shine on the grave of Carthon; I feel it warm around.

O thou that rollest above, round as the shield of my fathers! Whence are thy beams, O sun! thy everlasting light? Thou comest forth in thy awful beauty; the stars hide themselves in the sky; the moon, cold and pale, sinks in the western wave; but thou thyself movest alone. Who can be a companion of thy course? The oaks of the mountains fall; the mountains themselves decay with years; the ocean shrinks and grows again; the moon herself is lost in heaven; but thou art forever the same, rejoicing in the brightness of thy course. When the world is dark with tempests, when thunder rolls and lightning flies, thou lookest in thy beauty from the clouds and laughest at the storm. But to Ossian thou lookest in vain, for he beholds thy beams no more: whether thy yellow hair flows on the eastern clouds, or thou tremblest at the gates of the west. But thou art, perhaps, like me, for a season; thy years will have an end. Thou shalt sleep in thy clouds, careless of the voice of the morning. Exult then, O sun, in the strength of thy youth! age is dark and unlovely; it is like the glimmering light of the moon, when it shines through broken clouds, and the mist is on the hills: the blast of the north is on the plain, the traveller shrinks in the midst of his journey.

[1760]

THOMAS CHATTERTON

On the twenty-fifth of August, 1770, there was found in the upper room of a poor London lodging house the dead body of a boy not yet eighteen years old, with a bottle of arsenic beside it surrounded by torn bits of manuscript. This was the final scene in one of the most pitiful stories of literary ambition. It was the end of a heroic struggle against almost every imaginable difficulty: galling poverty, total lack of guidance and suitable training, squalid environment, stupefying routine, dull associates, dishonest debtors, indifference in high places and ignorance in low, and Philistinism everywhere. A tyrannical pride and will, coupled with a fierce determination to escape by any means from his misery, had brought the lad thus far. It is useless to speculate whether he might have become a great artist, and Thomas Warton's assertion that if he had reached a maturer age he "would have proved the first of English poets" is pure gratuity, but he had in high degree that crude instinct of the "maker," that sheer fecundity, in which the most admired poets of his time were often deficient. Dropped into an age in which "art" was dying of inanition, he was a shining example of what that age had recently agreed to call a "genius."

Thomas Chatterton was born in Bristol, almost in the shadow of the fifteenth-century church of St. Mary Redcliffe, on November 20, 1752, four months after the death of his father. His home was poor, noisy, cramped, and squalid. In the great church where his ancestors had been sextons for two centuries his true education began and ended — as William Blake's was to do, some years later, in Westminster Abbey. There he found his only escape into beauty and peace from "Bristolia's dingy piles of brick." He learned in childhood to live in visions of the time when the church was new, rebuilt by the splendid Lord Mayor, William Canynge, according to the plans of an imaginary priest whom he called Thomas Rowley. Without any of that weariness of neo-classic conventionalities which at just this time was turning many other minds toward the "Gothic" ages, Chatterton succumbed in childhood to "the passion of the past," reacting not from Pope but from Bristol.

At the charity school which he attended for seven years Chatterton was taught only reading, writing, and arithmetic — for eight hours a day throughout the year. He consistently broke the rule requiring him to be in bed at eight o'clock by working in his garret through the dead of night, and in this way the writing that he did there took on from the first an air of secrecy. With the help of a few poor dictionaries of early English, he concocted a vocabulary which, in his utter ignorance of linguistics, he thought his priest of the fifteenth century might have used, and in this he began, when about fifteen, to compose verses. Such was the ignorance of Middle English, not to say of Anglo-Saxon, even among most educated persons of the time, that he had no difficulty in getting these verses accepted by his acquaintances as mediæval productions. Becoming bolder, he began to fabricate alleged manuscripts of the fifteenth century, and to dispose of them for small sums of money. In 1767 he entered an attorney's office, where he had more time for literary work, and was soon sending specimens of his "Rowley Poems" to the publisher Dodsley and to Horace Walpole — without immediate result. In April, 1770, having deliberately convinced his employer that he was insane, he went to London with high hopes. By writing at great speed in almost every form of literature then current, he managed to make about one pound a month. Publishers and editors broke their promises to him and were slow in paying what they owed. The great millionaire Beckford, Mayor of London, who had given him assurances of help, died during the summer. His best poem, *An Excelente Balade of Charitie*, was returned by all the magazines. He tried to get a berth as a surgeon's assistant on an African trader, and failed. Too proud either to accept charity or to go home, he drank poison to escape a slower death by starvation.

The Philistinism which had been one of Chatterton's chief enemies while he lived has never ceased to pursue him with charges of gross immorality. These are obviously absurd, considering the testimony of all who knew him and also the amazing amount of his work. Much more important was the controversy, closely parallel to that concerning the "Ossianic" fragments and even more amusing, about the authorship of the "Rowley Poems." Several learned champions of the priest appeared to argue with strict logic and at great length that the "Charity Boy" could not possibly have produced such works, but the sound sense of Dr. Johnson backed by the scholarship of Edmund Malone and Thomas Warton finally established the truth.

A literary scholar of our day would see at a glance that the "Rowley Poems" are written in what Ben Jonson called "no language." He would soon discover that they are the work of a brilliant unscholarly mind, almost utterly ignorant of formal grammar but with sure instinct for expressive speech, fabricating a vocabulary of its own with few and poor literary tools. Closer examination would show that Chatterton thought and composed in the language of his own time and then substituted as many artificial words and spellings as he thought would conduce to the desired effect. An example of this way of working may be found in Gay's *Shepherd's Week,* which he certainly read, or even in Thomson's *Castle of Indolence.* Chatterton's numerous borrowings from eighteenth-century poets, not to mention his many glaring anachronisms, should have been enough by themselves to show at once what he had done.

But there is one element in the "Rowley Poems" which we could not confidently expect a professional scholar of our time to discover, and that is their poetic power. To scholars he has been, too frequently, scarcely more than a detected forger, an ignoramus pretending to knowledge, while his fame has been advanced chiefly by such poets as Wordsworth and Keats, Rossetti and Swinburne and De Vigny, who have not failed to recognize the astonishing creative energy of his mind. When read aloud, with as little regard as may be to the vagaries of spelling, Chatterton's verse is as musical as any that his time produced, and it is also remarkably experimental and adventurous. It is fair to remember that he was cut short in the midst of that imitative period through which every artist must pass. He imitated a score of different styles, but under the familiar tones of Dryden, Gay, Collins, and the old ballads there is in his verse a timbre which we can attribute only to the "marvellous boy, the sleepless soul that perished in his pride" — to the erring, thwarted, but possibly great poet that England did not yet deserve. Even more important than Chatterton's verse, in later literature, has been the emblematic value of his career, generally accepted by his romantic successors as a clear example of what creative genius has to expect in a coarse and brutally bourgeois world.

BRISTOWE TRAGEDIE

OR, THE DETHE OF SYR CHARLES * BAWDIN

The feathered songster chaunticleer
 * Han wounde hys bugle horne,
And tolde the earlie villager
 The commynge of the morne.

Kynge Edwarde sawe the ruddie streakes
 Of lyghte eclypse the greie,
And herde the raven's crokyinge throte
 Proclayme the fated daie.

"Thou'rt righte," * quod hee, "for, by the Godde
 That syttes enthron'd on hyghe,
Charles Bawdin and hys fellowes twaine
 To-daie shall surelie die."

Thenne wythe a jugge of * nappy ale
 Hys knyghtes dydd onne hymm waite;
"Goe tell the traytour thatt to-daie
 Hee leaves thys mortall state."

Sir Canterlone thenne bendedd lowe
 With harte brymm-fulle of woe;
Hee journey'd to the castle-gate
 And to Syr Charles dydd goe.

Butt whenne hee came, hys children twaine,
 And eke hys lovynge wyfe,
Wythe brinie tears dydd wett the floore
 For goode Syr Charleses lyfe.

"O goode Syr Charles!" said Canterlone,
 "Badde tydyngs I doe brynge."
"Speke boldlie, manne," sayd brave Syr Charles,
 "Whatte says thie traytor kynge?"

"I greeve to telle; before yonne sonne
 Does fromme the welkinn flye,
Hee hath uponne hys honour sworne
 Thatt thou shalt surelie die."

"Wee all must die," quod brave Syr Charles;
 "Of thatte I'm not affearde.
Whatte bootes to lyve a little space?
 Thanke Jesu, I'm prepar'd;

"Butt telle thye kynge, for myne hee's not,
 I'de sooner die to-daie
Thanne lyve hys slave, as manie are,
 Though I should lyve for aie."

Thenne Canterlone hee dydd goe out
 To telle the maior straite
To gett all thynges ynne reddyness
 For goode Syr Charles's fate.

Thenne Maisterr * Canynge saughte the kynge
 And felle down onne hys knee;
"I'm come," quod hee, "unto your grace
 To move your clemencye."

Thenne quod the kynge, "Youre tale speke out.
 You have been much oure friende;

* Notes on Thomas Chatterton will be found in the Appendix, pp. 1043 ff.

Whatever youre request may bee,
  Wee wylle to ytte attende."

"My nobile leige, alle my request
  Ys for a nobile knyghte
Who, tho' may hap hee has donne wronge,
  Hee thoughte ytte stylle was ryghte:

"Hee has a spouse and children twaine;
  Alle * rewyn'd are for aie
Yff that you are resolv'd to lett
  Charles Bawdin die to-daie."

"Speke nott of such a traytour vile,"
  The kynge ynn furie sayde;
"Before the evening starre doth sheene
  Bawdin shall loose hys hedde;

"Justice does loudlie for hym calle,
  And hee shalle have hys * meede:
Speke, Maister Canynge! Whatte thynge else
  Att present doe you neede?"

"My nobile leige!" goode Canynge sayde,
  "Leave justice to our Godde,
And laye the yronne rule asyde;
  Be thyne the olyve rodde.

"Was Godde to serche our hertes and * reines,
  The best were synners grete;
* Christ's vycarr only knowes ne synne
  Ynne alle thys mortall state.

"Lett mercie rule thyne infante reigne;
  'Twylle * faste thye crowne fulle sure;
From race to race thy familie
  Alle sovereigns shall endure:

"But yff wythe bloode and slaughter thou
  Beginne thy infante reigne
Thy crowne uponne thy childrennes brows
  Wylle never long remayne."

"Canynge, awaie! thys traytour vile
  Has scorn'd my power and mee.
Howe canst thou thenne for such a manne
  Intreate my clemencye?"

"My nobile leige! the trulie brave
  Wylle valorous actions prize;
Respect a brave and nobile mynde,
  Altho' ynne enemies."

"Canynge, awaie! By Godde ynne Heaven
  That dydd mee beinge gyve,
I wylle nott taste a bitt of breade
  Whilst thys Syr Charles dothe lyve.

"By Marie and alle Seinctes ynne Heaven,
  Thys sunne shall be hys laste."
Thenne Canynge dropt a brinie teare
  And from the presence paste.

With herte brymm-fulle of gnawynge grief
  Hee to Syr Charles dydd goe,
And satt hymm downe uponne a stoole,
  And teares beganne to * flowe.

"Wee all must die," quod brave Syr Charles;
  "Whatte bootes ytte howe or whenne?
Dethe ys the sure, the certaine fate
  Of all wee mortall menne.

"Saye why, my friend, thie honest soul
  Runns overr att thyne eye.
Is ytte for my most welcome doome
  Thatt thou dost child-lyke crye?"

Quod godlie Canynge, "I doe weepe
  Thatt thou soe soone must dye
And leave thy sonnes and helpless wyfe;
  'Tys thys thatt wettes myne eye."

"Thenne drie the tears thatt out thyne eye
  From godlie fountaines sprynge;
Dethe I despise, and alle the power
  Of Edwarde, traytor kynge.

"Whan through the tyrant's welcom means
  I shall resigne my lyfe,
The Godde I serve wylle soone provyde
  For bothe mye sonnes and wyfe.

"Before I sawe the lyghtsome sunne
  Thys was appointed mee.
Shall mortal manne repyne or grudge
  What Godde ordeynes to bee?

"Howe oft ynne battaile have I stoode
  Whan thousands dy'd arounde,
Whan smokynge streemes of crimson bloode
  Imbrew'd the fattened grounde.

"Howe dydd I knowe thatt every darte
  That cutte the airie waie
Myghte nott fynde passage toe my harte,
  And close myne eyes for aie?

"And shall I nowe, forr feere of dethe,
Looke wanne and bee dysmayde?
Ne! fromm my herte flie childyshe feere.
Bee alle the manne displayed.

"Ah, goddelyke *Henrie, Godde *forfende
And guarde thee and thye sonne,
Yff 'tis hys wylle; but yff 'tis nott,
Why thenne hys wylle bee donne.

"My honest friende, my faulte has beene
To serve Godde and mye prynce,
And thatt I no tyme-server am
My dethe wylle soone convynce.

"Ynne Londonne citye was I borne
Of parents of grete note;
My fadre dydd a nobile armes
Emblazon onne hys cote:

"I make ne doubte butt hee ys gone
Where soone I hope to goe,
Where wee for ever shall bee blest,
From oute the reech of woe.

"Hee taughte mee justice and the laws
Wyth pitie to unite,
And eke hee taughte mee howe to knowe
The wronge cause fromm the ryghte:

"Hee taughte mee wyth a prudent hande
To feede the hungrie poore,
Ne lett mye sarvants dryve awaie
The hungrie fromme my doore;

"And none can saye butt alle mye lyfe
I have hys wordyes kept,
And summ'd the actyonns of the daie
Eche nyghte before I slept.

"I have a spouse; goe aske of her
Yff I defyl'd her bedde.
I have a kynge, and none can laie
Black treason onne my hedde.

"Ynne Lent, and onne the holie eve,
Fromm fleshe I dydd refrayne.
Whie should I thenne appeare dismay'd
To leave thys worlde of payne?

"Ne, hapless Henrie, I rejoyce!
I shall ne see thye dethe;
Moste willynglie ynne thye just cause
Doe I resign my brethe.

"Oh, fickle people! Rewyn'd londe!
Thou wylt kenne peace ne moe;
Whyle Richard's *sonnes exalt themselves,
Thye brookes wythe bloude wylle flowe.

"Saie, were ye tyr'd of godlie peace
And godlie Henrie's reigne,
Thatt you dydd *choppe your easie daies
For those of bloude and peyne?

"Whatte tho' I onne a sledde bee drawne
And mangled by a *hynde,
I doe defye the traytor's power,
Hee can ne harm my mynde;

"Whatte tho', uphoisted onne a pole,
Mye lymbes shall rotte ynne ayre,
And ne ryche monument of brasse
Charles Bawdin's name shall bear,

"Yett ynne the holie booke above
Whyche tyme can't eate awaie,
There wythe the sarvants of the Lorde
Mye name shall lyve for aie.

"Thenne welcome dethe! for lyfe eterne
I leave thys mortall lyfe;
Farewell, vayne worlde and alle that's deare,
Mye sonnes and lovynge wyfe!

"Nowe dethe as welcome to mee comes
As e'er the moneth of Maie,
Nor woulde I even wyshe to lyve,
Wyth my dere wyfe to staie."

Quod Canynge, "'Tys a goodlie thynge
To bee prepared to die;
And from thys world of peyne and grefe
To Godde ynne Heaven to flie."

And nowe the bell beganne to tolle,
And claryonnes to sounde;
Syr Charles hee herde the horses feete
A-prauncyng onne the grounde:

And just before the officers
His lovynge wyfe came ynne,
Weepynge unfeignèd teeres of woe,
Wythe loude and dysmalle dynne.

"Sweet Florence, nowe I praie forbere!
Ynne quiet lett mee die;
Praie Godde thatt ev'ry Christian soule
Maye looke onne dethe as I.

"Sweet Florence, why these brinie teeres?
  Theye washe my soule awaie,
And almost make mee wyshe for lyfe,
  Wyth thee, sweete dame, to staie.

"'Tys butt a journie I shalle goe
  Untoe the lande of blysse;
Nowe, as a proofe of husbande's love,
  Receive thys holie kysse."

Thenne Florence, fault'ring ynne her saie,
  Tremblynge these wordyes spoke:
"Ah, cruele Edwarde! bloudie kynge!
  My herte ys welle nyghe broke!

"Ah, sweete Syr Charles, why wylt thou goe
  Wythoute thye lovynge wyfe?
The cruelle axe thatt cuttes thye necke,
  Ytte eke shall ende mye lyfe."

And nowe the officers came ynne
  To brynge Syr Charles awaie,
Whoe turnèdd toe hys lovynge wyfe,
  And thus toe her dydd saie:

"I goe to lyfe, and nott to dethe;
  Truste thou ynne Godde above,
And teache thye sonnes to feare the Lorde,
  And ynne theyre hertes hym love:

"Teache them to runne the nobile race
  Thatt I theyre fader runne;
Florence, shou'd dethe thee take — adieu!
  Yee officers, leade onne."

Thenne Florence raved as anie madde,
  And dydd her tresses tere;
"Oh staie, mye husbande, lorde, and lyfe!"
  Syr Charles thenne dropt a teare.

'Tyll, tyrèdd oute wythe ravynge loud,
  Shee fellen onne the flore;
Syr Charles exerted alle hys myghte,
  And marched fromm oute the dore.

Uponne a sledde hee mounted thenne,
  Wythe lookes fulle brave and swete;
Lookes thatt *enshone ne moe concern
  Thanne anie ynne the strete.

Before hym went the council-menne,
  Ynne scarlett robes and golde,
And tassils spanglynge ynne the sunne,
  Muche glorious to beholde:

The *Freers of Seincte Augustyne next
  Appearèd to the syghte,
Alle cladd ynne homelie russett *weedes,
  Of godlie monkysh *plyghte;

Ynne diffraunt partes a godlie psaume
  Moste sweetlie theye dydd chaunt:
Behynde theyre backes syx mynstrelles came,
  Who tuned the strunge *bataunt.

Thenne fyve-and-twentye archers came;
  Echone the bowe dydd bende,
From rescue of kynge Henries friends
  Syr Charles forr to defend.

Bolde as a lyon came Syr Charles,
  Drawne, onne a clothe-layde sledde,
Bye two blacke stedes ynne trappynges white,
  Wyth plumes uponne theyre hedde;

Behynde hym fyve-and-twentye moe
  Of archers stronge and stoute,
Wyth bended bowe echone ynne hande,
  Marchèd ynne goodlie route.

Seincte Jameses Freers marchèd next;
  Echone hys parte dydd chaunt:
Behynde theyre backes syx mynstrelles came,
  Who tuned the strunge bataunt.

Thenne came the maior and eldermenne,
  Ynne clothe of scarlett deck't;
And theyre attendyng menne echone,
  Lyke easterne princes trickt:

And after them a multitude
  Of citizenns dydd thronge;
The wyndowes were alle fulle of heddes,
  As hee dydd passe alonge.

And whenne hee came to the hyghe crosse,
  Syr Charles dydd turne and saie,
"O thou thatt savest manne fromme synne,
  Washe mye soule clean thys daie!"

Att the grete mynsterr wyndowe sat
  The kynge ynne myckle state,
To see Charles Bawdin goe alonge
  To hys most welcom fate.

Soone as the sledde drewe nyghe enowe
  Thatt Edwarde hee myghte heare,
The brave Syr Charles hee dydd stande uppe,
  And thus hys wordes declare:

"Thou seest mee, Edwarde! traytour vile!
Exposed to infamie;
Butt bee assured, disloyall manne,
I'm greaterr nowe thanne thee!

"Bye foule proceedyngs, murdre, bloude,
Thou wearest nowe a crowne;
And hast appoynted mee to dye,
By power nott thyne owne.

"Thou thynkest I shall dye to-daie:
I have beene dede 'till nowe,
And soone shall lyve to weare a crowne
For aie uponne my browe;

"Whylst thou, perhapps, for som few yeares,
Shalt rule thys fickle lande,
To lett them knowe howe wyde the rule
'Twixt kynge and tyrant hande:

"Thye pow'r unjust, thou traytour slave,
Shall falle onne thye owne hedde" —
Fromm out of hearyng of the kynge
Departed thenne the sledde.

Kynge Edwarde's soule rushed to hys face;
Hee turned hys hedde awaie,
And to hys broder *Gloucester
Hee thus dydd speke and saie:

"To hym that soe-much-dreaded dethe
Ne ghastlie terrors brynge,
Beholde the manne! hee spake the truthe:
Hee's greater thanne a kynge!"

"Soe lett hym die!" Duke Richard sayde;
"And maye echone oure foes
Bende downe theyre neckes to bloudie axe
And feede the carryon crowes!"

And nowe the horses gentlie drewe
Syr Charles uppe the hyghe hylle;
The axe dydd glysterr ynne the sunne,
Hys pretious bloude to spylle.

Syrr Charles dydd uppe the scaffold goe
As uppe a gilded carre
Of victorye, bye val'rous chiefs
Gayned ynne the bloudie warre;

And to the people hee dydd saie,
"Beholde you see mee dye
For servynge loyally mye kynge,
Mye kynge most ryghtfullie.

"As longe as Edwarde rules thys land
Ne quiet you wylle knowe;
Youre sonnes and husbandes shalle bee slayne,
And brookes wythe bloude shalle flowe.

"You leave youre goode and lawfulle kynge
Whenne ynne adversitye;
Lyke mee, untoe the true cause stycke,
And for the true cause dye."

Thenne hee, wyth preestes, uponne hys knees
A pray'r to Godde dydd make,
Beseechynge hym unto hymselfe
Hys partynge soule to take.

Thenne, kneelynge downe, hee layd hys hedde
Most seemlie onne the blocke;
Whyche fromme hys bodie fayre at once
The able heddes-manne stroke:

And oute the bloude beganne to flowe,
And rounde the scaffolde twyne;
And teares, enow to washe 't awaie,
Dydd flowe fromme each mann's eyne.

The bloudie axe hys bodie fayre
Ynnto foure parties cutte;
And ev'rye parte, and eke hys hedde,
Uponne a pole was putte.

One parte dydd rotte onne Kynwulph-hylle,
One onne the mynster-tower,
And one from off the castle-gate
The crowen dydd devoure;

The other onne Seyncte Powle's goode gate,
A dreery spectacle;
Hys hedde was placed onne the hyghe crosse,
Ynne hyghe-streete most nobile.

Thus was the ende of Bawdin's fate
Godde prosper longe oure kynge,
And grante hee maye, wyth Bawdin's soule,
Ynne heav'n Godd's mercie synge!

[1772]

From ÆLLA, A TRAGYCAL ENTERLUDE

MYNSTRELLES SONGE

FYRSTE MYNSTRELLE

The *boddynge flourettes bloshes atte the lyghte;
The *mees be *sprenged wyth the yellowe hue;

Ynn daiseyd mantels ys the mountayne *dyghte;
The *nesh yonge coweslepe bendethe wyth the dewe;
The trees enlefèd, yntoe Heavenne *straughte,
Whenn gentle wyndes doe blowe to whestlyng dynne ys brought.

The evenynge commes, and brynges the dewe alonge;
*The roddie welkynne sheeneth to the eyne;
Arounde the *alestake mynstrells synge the songe;
Yonge ivie rounde the doore poste do entwyne;
I laie mee onn the grasse; yette, to mie wylle,
Albeytte alle ys fayre, there lackethe somethynge stylle.

SECONDE MYNSTRELLE

So Adam thoughtenne, whann, ynn Paradyse,
All heavenn and erthe dyd hommage to hys mynde;
Ynn womman alleyne mannès pleasaunce lyes;
As instrumentes of joie were made the *kynde.
Go, take a wyfe untoe thie armes, and see
Wynter and brownie hylles wyll have a charme for thee.

THYRDE MYNSTRELLE

Whanne autumpne *blake and sonne-brente doe appere,
With hys goulde honde *guylteynge the falleynge lefe,
Bryngeynge oppe wynterr to folfylle the yere,
Beerynge uponne hys backe the ripèd shefe;
Whan al the hyls wythe *woddie sede ys whyte;
Whanne *levynne-fyres and *lemes do mete from far the syghte;

Whann the fayre apple, rudde as *even skie,
Do bende the tree unto the *fructyle grounde;
When joicie peres, and berries of blacke die,
Doe daunce yn ayre, and call the eyne arounde;
Thann, bee the even foule or even fayre,
Meethynckes mie hartys joie ys *steyncèd wyth somme care.

SECONDE MYNSTRELLE

Angelles bee wroghte to bee of neidher *kynde;
Angelles alleyne fromme *chafe desyre bee free:
*Dheere ys a somwhatte evere yn the mynde,
*Yatte, wythout wommanne, cannot stylled bee;
Ne seyncte yn celles, *botte, havynge blodde and tere,
Do fynde the spryte to joie on syghte of wommanne fayre;

Wommen bee made, notte for hemselves, botte manne,
Bone of hys bone, and chyld of hys desire;
Fromme *an ynutyle membere fyrste beganne,
Ywroghte with moche of water, lyttele fyre;
Therefore theie seke the fyre of love, to hete
The milkyness of kynde, and make hemselfes complete.

Albeytte wythout wommen menne were *pheeres
To salvage kynde, and wulde botte lyve to slea,
Botte wommenne *efte the spryghte of peace so *cheres,
*Tochelod yn angel joie *heie angeles bee:
Go, take thee *swythyn to thie bedde a wyfe;
Bee *bante or blessed *hie yn proovynge marryage lyfe.

MYNSTRELLES SONGE

O, *synge untoe mie roundelaie!
O, droppe the brynie teare wythe mee!
Daunce ne moe atte *hallie daie;
Lycke a *reynynge ryver bee:
Mie love ys dedde,
Gon to hys death-bedde,
Al under the *wyllowe tree.

Blacke hys *cryne as the wyntere nyghte,
Whyte hys *rode as the sommer *snowe,
*Rodde hys face as the mornynge lyghte;
*Cale he lyes ynne the grave belowe:
Mie love ys dedde,
Gon to hys deathe-bedde,
Al under the wyllowe *tree.

*Swote hys tyngue as the throstles note,
Quycke ynn daunce as thoughte canne bee,
Defte hys *taboure, codgelle *stote;
O! hee lyes bie the wyllowe tree:
Mie love ys dedde,
Gonne to hys deathe-bedde,
Alle underre the wyllowe tree.

Harke! the ravenne flappes hys wynge,
In the briered delle belowe;
Harke! the dethe-owle loude dothe synge,
To the nyghte-mares as heie goe:
Mie love ys dedde,
Gonne to hys deathe-bedde,
Al under the wyllowe tree.

See! the whyte moone sheenes onne hie;
Whyterre ys mie true loves shroude,
Whyterre *yanne the mornynge skie,
Whyterre yanne the evenynge cloude:
Mie love ys dedde,
Gon to hys deathe-bedde,
Al under the wyllowe tree.

Heere, uponne mie true loves grave,
Schalle the baren fleurs be layde,
Nee one *hallie seyncte to save
Al the *celness of a mayde:
Mie love ys dedde,
Gonne to hys deathe-bedde,
Alle under the wyllowe tree.

Wythe mie hondes I'lle *dente the brieres
Rounde his hallie corse to *gre;
*Ouphante fairie, lyghte youre fyres,
Heere mie boddie stylle schalle bee:
Mie love ys dedde,
Gon to hys deathe-bedde,
Al under the wyllowe tree.

Comme, wythe acorne-coppe and thorne
Drayne mie hartys blodde awaie;
Lyfe and all yttes goode I scorne,
Daunce bie nete, or feaste by daie:
Mie love ys dedde,
Gon to hys death-bedde,
Al under the wyllowe tree.

Waterre wytches, crownede wythe *reytes,
Bere mee to yer *leathalle tyde.
I die! I comme! mie true love waytes.
*Thos the damselle spake and dyed.

[1777]

AN EXCELENTE BALADE OF *CHARITIE

AS WROTEN BIE THE GODE PRIESTE THOMAS ROWLEY, *1464

In *Virgynè the sweltrie sun *gan sheene,
And hotte upon the mees did caste his raie;
The apple rodded from its palie greene,
And the *mole peare did bende the leafy spraie;
*The peede chelandri sunge the livelong daie;
'Twas nowe the pride, the manhode, of the yeare,
And eke the grounde was dighte in its most defte *aumere.

The sun was glemeing in the middle of daie,
Deadde still the aire, and eke the welken blue,
When from the sea arist in drear arraie
A hepe of cloudes of sable sullen hue,
The which full fast unto the woodlande drewe,
*Hiltring attenes the sunnis fetive face,
And the blacke tempeste swolne and gatherd up apace.

Beneathe an *holme, faste by a pathwaie side
Which dide unto Seyncte Godwine's *covent lede,
A hapless pilgrim *moneynge dyd abide,
Pore in his viewe, *ungentle in his weede,
Longe *bretful of the miseries of neede.
Where from the hailstone coulde the *almer flie?
He had no housen theere, ne anie covent nie.

Look in his glommèd face, his sprighte there scanne:
Howe woe-be-gone, how withered, *forwynd, deade!
Haste to thie *church-glebe-house, asshrewed manne;
Haste to thie *kiste, thie onlie *dortoure bedde
Cale as the claie whiche will gre on thie hedde
Is charitie and love aminge highe elves;
Knightis and barons live for pleasure and themselves.

The gatherd storme is rype; the bigge drops falle;
The *forswat meadowes *smethe, and *drenche the raine;

The comyng *ghastness do the cattle pall,
And the full flockes are drivynge ore the plaine;
Dashde from the cloudes, the waters *flott againe;
The welkin opes, the yellow levynne flies,
And the hot fierie *smothe in the wide *lowings dies.

Liste! now the thunder's rattling *clymmynge sound
*Cheves slowie on, and then *embollen clangs,
Shakes the hie spyre, and, losst, dispended, drowned,
Still on the *gallard eare of terroure hanges;
The windes are up, the lofty elmen *swanges;
Again the levynne and the thunder poures,
And the full cloudes are braste attenes in stonen showers.

Spurreynge his palfrie oere the watrie plaine,
The Abbote of Seyncte Godwyne's convente came:
His *chapournette was *drented with the reine,
And his *pencte gyrdle met with mickle shame;
He aynewarde tolde his *bederoll at the same.
The storme encreasen, and he drew aside
With the *mist almes-craver neere to the holme to bide.

His *cope was all of Lyncolne clothe so fyne,
With a gold button fastened neere his chynne;
His *autremete was edged with golden twynne,
And *his shoone pyke a loverds mighte have binne
Full well it shewn he thoughten *coste no sinne;
The *trammels of the palfrye pleasde his sighte,
For the horse-millanare his head with roses dighte.

"An almes, sir prieste!" the droppynge pilgrim saide;
"O let me waite within your covente dore,
Till the sunne sheneth hie above our heade,
And the loude tempeste of the aire is oer.
Helpless and ould am I, alas! and poor;
No house, ne friend, ne moneie in my pouche;
All yatte I calle my owne is this my silver *crouche."

"Varlet," replyd the abbatte, "cease your dinne!
This is no season almes and prayers to give.
Mie porter never lets a *faitour in;
None touch mie *rynge who not in honour live."
And now the sonne with the blacke cloudes did stryve,
And *shettynge on he grounde his glairie raie:
The abbatte spurrde his steede, and eftsoones roadde awaie.

Once moe the skie was blacke, the thounder rolde:
Faste reyneynge oer the plaine a prieste was seen,
Ne dighte full proude, ne buttoned up in golde;
His cope and *jape were graie, and eke were clene;
*A limitoure he was of order seene.
And from the pathwaie side then turnèd hee,
Where the pore almer laie binethe the holmen tree.

"An almes, sir priest!" the droppynge pilgrim sayde,
"For sweete Seyncte Marie and your order sake!"
The limitoure then loosened his pouche threade,
And did thereoute a *groate of silver take:
The *mister pilgrim dyd for *halline shake.
"Here, take this silver; it maie *eathe thie care:
We are Goddes stewards all, *nete of oure owne we bare.

"But ah, *unhailie pilgrim, lerne of me
*Scathe anie give a *rentrolle to their Lorde.
Here, take my *semecope — thou arte bare, I see;
'Tis thyne; the seynctes will give me mie rewarde."
He left the pilgrim, and his waie *aborde.
Virgynne and hallie seyncte, who sitte yn *gloure,
Or give the *mittee *will or give the gode man power!

[1777]

JAMES BEATTIE

ALTHOUGH the son of a poor Scottish shopkeeper, James Beattie (1735–1803) managed to get so good an education that he was made professor of moral philosophy at Marischal College, Aberdeen, at the age of twenty-five. Ten years later he published his *Essay on the Nature and Immutability of Truth, in Opposition to Sophistry and Scepticism*, a work which had great vogue in religious circles not because of its philosophical or literary merit but because it was a violent attack upon David Hume — who never troubled to answer it except by saying that Beattie had not "used him like a gentleman." In the following year, 1771, appeared the first Book of *The Minstrel*. This also had immediate success, not so much on account of its intrinsic merits as because its sentimental humanitarianism, its exaltation of the poor and ignorant, its worship of nature, and, perhaps most of all, its preference of solitude to society and of the wild to the civilized, were in harmony with a mood by this time widely prevalent. In the year after Charles Churchill's death he wrote a scurrilous diatribe against the poet's memory, thereby demonstrating that his political orthodoxy was as staunch as his religious, so that when he visited London in 1773 George III received him cordially and gave him a pension of two hundred pounds a year. Whether for these or for better reasons, he was well liked by Dr. Johnson and his circle. Beattie's later years were darkened by personal sorrow. His wife lost her mind, and his two sons, one of them a poet of promise, died on the verge of manhood. From the loss of his second son in 1796, he never recovered.

All three of the poems by James Beattie that are now remembered — *Retirement*, *The Hermit*, and *The Minstrel* — are concerned with solitude, a theme to which more and more attention had been given by English poets since the time of George Dyer and Lady Winchilsea. Cowper was soon to consider it closely in his *Retirement*, and to make it the underlying *motif* of *The Task*. Round this theme, interpreted no more broadly than it was at the time, the whole history of the coming romantic movement might be written. In Beattie's *The Minstrel* the master-idea of solitude has already gathered a cluster of subsidiary notions, some of them social and political and others moral, religious, economic, educational, or psychological. Rousseau's basic contention, that man is good by nature and that only society makes him evil, is already strongly at work in it. The ancient belief, of which the Deists had recently made much, that nature is a teacher and provides a sufficient revelation of the Divine, had taken two courses: scientific investigation and emotional contemplation. The former laid some restraint upon the student and subjected him to some slight though shallow discipline, but there was neither discipline nor restraint for those whose study of nature amounted only to a vague admiration of the landscape. Indeed, it is precisely their revolt against restraint and discipline — or, in other words, against what had been known as civilization — that is most ominous of the future.

Quite as appropriately as Wordsworth's *Prelude*, Beattie's *The Minstrel* might have been given the sub-title: "The Growth of a Poet's Mind." In spite of its crudity, it is in fact a strangely close foreshadowing of Wordsworth's great poem. In the first book the young poet is educated almost entirely in solitude, by the shapes and sounds of the wilderness. The vague doctrines thus imbibed are corroborated in the second book by the piously anti-social counsels of an aged hermit whom the youth meets in the forest. The projected third book, in which presumably the powers and wisdom thus gained were to have been displayed, Beattie never wrote.

In purely literary merit *The Minstrel* does not stand high. A faint absurdity, seldom absent from Beattie's prose and verse, raises a smile at many a seriously intended line and stanza. The influence of Gray, who helped the author in the correction of his manuscript, is more apparent in occasional turns of phrase than in the management of thought and control of feeling. Beattie's Spenserian stanzas are greatly inferior to Thomson's in musical fluency, and indeed the effect of them is hardly Spenserian at all. Yet the poem has a considerable importance, partly for its pictures of northern landscape, but chiefly for the presentation of a set of ideas which were soon to transform literature.

THE MINSTREL
OR, THE PROGRESS OF GENIUS

BOOK I

Ah, who can tell how hard it is to climb
The steep where Fame's proud temple shines afar!
Ah, who can tell how many a soul sublime
Has felt the influence of malignant star
And waged with Fortune an eternal war —
Check'd by the scoff of Pride, by Envy's frown
And Poverty's unconquerable bar —
In life's low vale remote has pined alone
Then dropp'd into the grave unpitied and *unknown!

And yet the languor of inglorious days
Not equally oppressive is to all.
Him who ne'er listen'd to the voice of praise
The silence of neglect can ne'er appal.
There are, who, deaf to mad Ambition's call,
Would shrink to hear the *obstreperous trump of Fame,
Supremely blest if to their portion fall
Health, competence, and peace. Nor higher aim
Had he whose simple tale these artless lines proclaim.

The rolls of fame I will not now explore,
Nor need I here describe in learned lay
How forth the Minstrel fared in days of yore,
Right glad of heart though homely in array —
His waving locks and beard all hoary grey,
While from his bending shoulder decent hung
His harp, the sole companion of his way,
Which to the whistling wind responsive rung;
And ever as he went some merry lay he *sung.

Fret not thyself, thou glittering child of pride,
That a poor villager inspires my strain;
With thee let Pageantry and Power abide;
The gentle Muses haunt the sylvan reign
Where, through wild groves at eve, the lonely swain
Enraptured roams to gaze on Nature's charms:
They hate the sensual and scorn the vain;
The parasite their influence never warms,
Nor him whose sordid soul the love of gold alarms.

Though richest hues the peacock's plumes adorn,
Yet horror screams from his discordant throat.
Rise, sons of harmony, and hail the morn
While warbling larks on russet pinions float;
Or seek at noon the woodland scene remote,
Where the grey linnets carol from the hill.
Oh, let them ne'er, with artificial note,
To please a tyrant, strain the little bill,
But sing what Heaven inspires, and wander where they will!

Liberal, not lavish, is kind Nature's hand,
Nor was perfection made for man below;
Yet all her schemes with nicest art are plann'd,
Good counteracting ill, and gladness woe.
With gold and gems if Chilian mountains glow,
If bleak and barren Scotia's hills arise,
There plague and poison, lust and rapine grow;
Here, peaceful are the vales and pure the skies,
And Freedom fires the soul and sparkles in the eyes.

Then grieve not, thou to whom the indulgent Muse
Vouchsafes a portion of celestial fire,
Nor blame the partial Fates if they refuse
The imperial banquet and the rich attire.
Know thine own worth and reverence the lyre.
Wilt thou debase the heart which God refined?
No; let thy heaven-taught soul to Heaven aspire,
To fancy, freedom, harmony resign'd —
Ambition's grovelling crew forever left behind.

Canst thou forego the pure ethereal soul,
In each fine sense so exquisitely keen,
On the dull couch of Luxury to loll,
Stung with disease and stupefied with spleen;
Fain to implore the aid of Flattery's screen
Even from thyself thy loathsome heart to hide
(The mansion then no more of joy serene),
Where fear, distrust, malevolence abide,
And impotent desire, and disappointed pride?

* Notes on James Beattie will be found in the Appendix, p. 1046.

Oh, how canst thou renounce the boundless store
Of charms which Nature to her votary yields?
The warbling woodland, the resounding shore,
The pomp of groves and garniture of fields,
All that the genial ray of morning gilds
And all that echoes to the song of even,
All that the mountain's sheltering bosom shields,
And all the dread magnificence of heaven,
Oh, how canst thou renounce, and hope to be forgiven?

These charms shall work thy soul's eternal health,
And love and gentleness and joy impart.
But these thou must renounce if lust of wealth
E'er win its way to thy corrupted heart;
For ah! it poisons like a scorpion's dart,
Prompting the ungenerous wish, the selfish scheme,
The stern resolve unmoved by pity's smart,
The troublous day and long distressful dream.
Return, my roving Muse. Resume thy purposed theme.

There lived in * Gothic days, as legends tell,
A shepherd swain, a man of low degree,
Whose sires perchance in Fairyland might dwell,
Sicilian groves, or vales of Arcady;
But he, I ween, was of * the north countrie,—
A nation famed for song and beauty's charms,
Zealous yet modest, innocent though free,
Patient of toil, serene amidst alarms,
Inflexible in faith, invincible in arms.

The shepherd swain of whom I mention made
On Scotia's mountains fed his little flock;
The sickle, scythe, or plough he never sway'd;
An honest heart was almost all his stock;
His drink the living water from the rock;
The milky dams supplied his board and lent
Their kindly fleece to baffle winter's shock;
And he, though oft with dust and sweat besprent,
Did guide and guard their wanderings whereso'er they went.

From labour health, from health contentment springs;
Contentment opes the source of every joy.
He envied not, he never thought of kings,
Nor from those appetites sustain'd annoy
That chance may frustrate or indulgence cloy;
Nor Fate his calm and humble hopes beguiled;
He mourn'd no recreant friend nor mistress coy,
For on his vows the blameless Phœbe smiled,
And her alone he loved, and loved her from a child.

No jealousy their dawn of love o'ercast,
Nor blasted were their wedded days with strife;
Each season look'd delightful as it pass'd
To the fond husband and the faithful wife.
Beyond the lowly vale of shepherd life
They never * roam'd, secure beneath the storm
Which in Ambition's lofty hand is rife,
Where peace and love are canker'd by the worm
Of pride, each bud of joy industrious to deform.

The wight whose tale these artless lines unfold
Was all the offspring of this humble pair;
His birth no oracle or seer foretold;
No prodigy appear'd in earth or air,
Nor aught that might a strange event declare.
You guess each circumstance of Edwin's birth:
The parent's transport and the parent's care,
The gossip's prayer for wealth and wit and worth,
And one long summer day of indolence and mirth.

And yet poor Edwin was no * vulgar boy.
Deep thought oft seem'd to fix his infant eye;
Dainties he heeded not, nor * gaud, nor toy,
Save one short pipe of rudest minstrelsy.
Silent when glad, affectionate though shy;
And now his look was most demurely sad,
And now he laugh'd aloud, yet none knew why.

The neighbours stared and sigh'd, yet bless'd the lad;
Some deem'd him wondrous wise, and some believed him mad.

But why should I his childish feats display?
Concourse and noise and toil he ever fled,
Nor cared to mingle in the clamorous fray
Of squabbling imps, but to the forest sped
Or roamed at large the lonely mountain's head;
Or, where the maze of some bewilder'd stream
To deep untrodden groves his footsteps led,
There would he wander wild, till Phœbus' beam,
Shot from the western cliff, released the weary *team.

The exploit of strength, dexterity, or speed
To him nor vanity nor joy could bring.
His heart, from cruel sport estranged, would bleed
To work the woe of any living thing
By trap or net, by arrow or by sling;
These he detested, those he scorned to wield.
He wish'd to be the guardian, not the king,
Tyrant far less, or traitor of the field.
And sure the sylvan reign unbloody joy might yield.

Lo, where the stripling, wrapt in wonder, roves
Beneath the precipice o'erhung with pine,
And sees, on high, amidst the encircling groves,
From cliff to cliff the foaming torrents shine;
While waters, woods, and winds in concert join,
And Echo swells the chorus to the skies!
Would Edwin this majestic scene resign
For aught the huntsman's puny craft supplies?
Ah, no; he better knows great Nature's charms to prize.

And oft he traced the uplands to survey,
When o'er the sky advanced the kindling dawn,
The crimson cloud, blue main, and mountain gray,
And lake dim-gleaming on the *smoky lawn
Far to the west the long long vale withdrawn,
Where twilight loves to linger for a while;
And now he faintly kens the bounding fawn
And villager abroad at early toil.
But lo, the sun appears, and heaven, earth, ocean smile!

And oft the craggy cliff he loved to climb,
When all in mist the world below was lost.
What dreadful pleasure, there to stand *sublime,
Like shipwreck'd mariner on desert coast,
And view the enormous waste of vapour toss'd
In billows, lengthening to the horizon round,
Now scoop'd in gulfs, with mountains now emboss'd,
And hear the voice of mirth and song rebound,
Flocks, herds, and waterfalls, along the hoar profound!

In truth he was a strange and wayward wight,
Fond of each gentle and each dreadful scene.
In darkness and in storm he found delight,
Nor less than when on ocean-wave serene
The southern sun diffused his dazzling sheen.
Even sad vicissitude amused his *soul;
And if a sigh would sometimes intervene,
And down his cheek a tear of pity roll,
A sigh, a tear so sweet, he wish'd not to control.

"O ye wild groves, oh, where is now your bloom?"
(The Muse interprets thus his tender thought)
"Your flowers, your verdure, and your balmy gloom
Of late so grateful in the hour of drought?
Why do the birds that song and rapture brought
To all your bowers, their mansions now forsake?
Ah, why has fickle chance this ruin wrought?
For now the storm howls mournful through the brake
And the dead foliage flies in many a shapeless flake.

"Where now the rill, melodious, pure, and cool,
And meads with life and mirth and beauty crown'd?

Ah, see, the unsightly slime and sluggish pool
Have all the solitary vale imbrown'd!
Fled each fair form, and mute each melting sound;
The raven croaks forlorn on naked spray;
And hark! the river, bursting every mound,
Down the vale thunders, and with wasteful sway
Uproots the grove and rolls the shatter'd rocks away.

"Yet such the destiny of all on earth!
So flourishes and fades majestic man.
Fair is the bud his vernal morn brings forth,
And fostering gales awhile the nursling fan.
Oh smile, ye heavens serene! ye mildews wan,
Ye blighting whirlwinds, spare his balmy prime
Nor lessen of his life the little span!
Borne on the swift though silent wings of Time,
Old age comes on apace to ravage all the clime.

"And be it so. Let those deplore their doom
Whose hope still grovels in this dark sojourn;
But lofty souls who look beyond the tomb
Can smile at Fate, and wonder how they mourn.
Shall spring to these sad scenes no more return?
Is yonder wave the sun's eternal bed?
Soon shall the orient with new lustre burn,
And spring shall soon her vital influence shed,
Again attune the grove, again adorn the mead.

"Shall I be left forgotten in the dust
When Fate, relenting, lets the flower revive?
Shall Nature's voice, to man alone unjust,
Bid him, though doom'd to perish, hope to live?
Is it for this fair Virtue oft must strive
With disappointment, penury, and pain?
No! Heaven's immortal springs shall yet arrive,
And man's majestic beauty bloom again,
Bright through the eternal year of Love's triumphant reign."

This truth sublime his simple sire had taught.
In sooth, 'twas almost all the shepherd knew.
No subtle nor superfluous lore he sought,
Nor ever wish'd his Edwin to pursue.
"Let man's own sphere," said he, "confine his view;
Be man's peculiar work his sole delight."
And much and oft he warn'd him to eschew
Falsehood and guile, and aye maintain the right,
By pleasure unseduced, unawed by lawless might.

"And from the prayer of Want and plaint of Woe
Oh, never, never turn away thine ear!
Forlorn in this bleak wilderness below,
Ah, what were man should Heaven refuse to hear!
To others do (the law is not severe)
What to thyself thou wishest to be done.
Forgive thy foes, and love thy parents dear
And friends and native land; nor those alone:
All human weal and woe learn thou to make thine own."

See, in the rear of the warm sunny shower,
The visionary boy from shelter fly;
For now the storm of summer rain is o'er,
And cool and fresh and fragrant is the sky.
And lo, in the dark east expanded high,
The rainbow brightens to the setting sun!
Fond fool that deem'st the streaming glory nigh,
How vain the chase thine ardour has begun!
'Tis fled afar ere half thy purposed race be run.

Yet couldst thou learn that thus it fares with age
When pleasure, wealth, or power the bosom warm,
This baffled hope might tame thy manhood's rage,
And disappointment of her sting disarm.
But why should foresight thy fond heart alarm?
Perish the lore that deadens young desire!
Pursue, poor imp, the imaginary charm,
Indulge gay hope and fancy's pleasing fire;
Fancy and hope too soon shall of themselves expire.

When the long-sounding curfew from afar
Loaded with loud lament the lonely gale,
Young Edwin, lighted by the evening star,
Lingering and listening, wander'd down the vale.
There would he dream of graves and corses pale,
And ghosts that to the charnel-dungeon throng,
And drag a length of clanking chain, and wail,
Till silenced by the owl's terrific song,
Or blast that shrieks by fits the shuddering aisles along.

Or when the setting moon, in crimson dyed,
Hung o'er the dark and melancholy deep,
To haunted stream, remote from man, he hied,
Where fays of yore their revels wont to keep;
And there let Fancy rove at large, till sleep
A vision brought to his entrancèd sight.
And first, a wildly murmuring wind 'gan creep
Shrill to his ringing ear; then tapers bright,
With instantaneous gleam, illumed the vault of night.

Anon in view a portal's blazon'd arch
Arose; the trumpet bids the * valves unfold;
And forth an host of little warriors march,
Grasping the diamond lance and targe of gold.
Their look was gentle, their demeanour bold,
And green their helms and green their silk attire;
And here and there, right venerably old,
The long-robed minstrels wake the warbling wire,
And some with mellow breath the martial pipe inspire.

With merriment and song and timbrels clear,
A troop of dames from myrtle bowers advance;
The little warriors doff the targe and spear,
And loud enlivening strains provoke the dance.
They meet, they dart away, they wheel askance,
To right, to left, they thread the flying maze;
Now bound aloft with vigorous spring, then glance
Rapid along; with many-colour'd rays
Of tapers, gems, and gold the echoing forests blaze.

The dream is fled. Proud harbinger of day
Who scaredst the vision with thy clarion shrill,
Fell chanticleer, who oft hast reft away
My fancied good and brought substantial ill,
Oh, to thy cursèd scream, discordant still,
Let harmony aye shut her gentle ear!
Thy boastful mirth let jealous rivals * spill,
Insult thy crest, and glossy pinions tear,
And ever in thy dreams the ruthless fox appear!

Forbear, my Muse. Let love attune thy line.
Revoke the spell. Thine Edwin frets not so.
For how should he at wicked chance repine
Who feels from every change amusement flow?
Even now his eyes with smiles of rapture glow
As on he wanders through the scenes of morn,
Where the fresh flowers in living lustre blow,
Where thousand pearls the dewy lawns adorn,
A thousand notes of joy in every breeze are borne.

But who the melodies of morn can tell?
The wild brook babbling down the mountain side,
The lowing herd, the sheepfold's simple bell,
The pipe of early shepherd dim descried
In the lone valley, echoing far and wide
The clamorous horn along the cliffs above,
The hollow murmur of the ocean-tide,
The hum of bees, the linnet's lay of love,
And the full choir that wakes the universal grove.

The cottage curs at early pilgrim bark;
Crown'd with her pail the tripping milkmaid sings;
The whistling ploughman stalks afield; and hark!
Down the rough slope the ponderous wagon rings;
Through rustling corn the hare astonish'd springs;

Slow tolls the village clock the drowsy hour;
The partridge bursts away on whirring wings;
Deep mourns the turtle in sequester'd bower;
And shrill lark carols clear from her aërial tower.

O Nature, how in every charm supreme!
Whose votaries feast on raptures ever new.
Oh, for the voice and fire of seraphim
To sing thy glories with devotion due!
Blest be the day I 'scaped the wrangling crew,
From * Pyrrho's maze and * Epicurus' sty,
And held high converse with the godlike few
Who to the enraptured heart and ear and eye
Teach beauty, virtue, truth, and love, and melody.

Hence, ye who snare and stupify the mind,
Sophists! of beauty, virtue, joy, the bane!
Greedy and fell though impotent and blind,
Who spread your filthy nets in Truth's fair fane
And ever ply your venom'd fangs amain!
Hence to dark Error's den, whose rankling slime
First gave you form! Hence! lest the Muse should deign
(Though loth on theme so mean to waste a rhyme),
With vengeance to pursue your sacrilegious crime.

But hail ye mighty masters of the lay,
Nature's true sons, the friends of man and truth,
Whose song sublimely sweet, serenely gay,
Amused my childhood and inform'd my youth!
Oh, let your spirit still my bosom soothe,
Inspire my dreams and my wild wanderings guide!
Your voice each rugged path of life can smooth,
For well I know, wherever ye reside
There harmony and peace and innocence abide.

Ah me! neglected on the lonesome plain,
As yet poor Edwin never knew your lore,
Save when against the winter's drenching rain
And driving snow the cottage shut the door.
Then, as instructed by tradition hoar,
Her legend when the beldam 'gan impart,
Or chant the old heroic ditty o'er,
Wonder and joy ran thrilling to his heart;
Much he the tale admired, but more the tuneful art.

Various and strange was the long-winded tale,
And halls and knights and feats of arms display'd;
Or merry swains who quaff the nut-brown ale
And sing enamour'd of the nut-brown maid;
The moonlight revel of the fairy glade,
Or hags that suckle an infernal brood,
And ply in caves the unutterable * trade,
'Midst fiends and spectres quench the moon in blood,
Yell in the midnight storm, or ride the infuriate flood.

But when to horror his amazement rose,
A gentler strain the beldam would rehearse,
A tale of rural life, a tale of woes,
The orphan babes and guardian uncle fierce.
Oh, cruel! will no pang of pity pierce
That heart, by lust of lucre sear'd to stone?
For sure if aught of virtue last, or verse,
To latest times shall tender souls bemoan
Those hopeless orphan babes by thy fell arts undone.

Behold, with berries smear'd, with brambles torn,
The babes, now famish'd, lay them down to die!
Amidst the howl of darksome woods forlorn,
Folded in one another's arms they lie;
Nor friend nor stranger hears their dying cry:
"For from the town the man returns no more."
But thou who Heaven's just vengeance dar'st defy,
This deed with fruitless tears shalt soon deplore,
When death lays waste thy house and flames consume thy store.

A stifled smile of stern vindictive joy
Brighten'd one moment Edwin's starting tear,
"But why should gold man's feeble mind decoy,
And innocence thus die by doom severe?"
O Edwin! while thy heart is still sincere
The assaults of discontent and doubt repel;
Dark even at noontide is our mortal sphere;
But let us hope; to doubt is to rebel;
Let us exult in hope that all shall yet be well.

Nor be thy generous indignation check'd,
Nor check'd the tender tear to misery given;
From guilt's contagious power shall that protect,
This soften and refine the soul for Heaven.
But dreadful is their doom whom doubt has driven
To censure fate, and pious hope forego!
Like yonder blasted boughs by lightning riven,
Perfection, beauty, life, they never know,
But frown on all that pass, a monument of woe.

Shall he whose birth, maturity, and age
Scarce fill the circle of one summer day,
Shall the poor gnat, with discontent and rage,
Exclaim that Nature hastens to decay
If but a cloud obstruct the solar ray,
If but a momentary shower descend?
Or shall frail man Heaven's dread decree gainsay,
Which bade the series of events extend
Wide through unnumber'd worlds, and ages without end?

One part, one little part, we dimly scan
Through the dark medium of life's feverish dream;
Yet dare arraign the whole stupendous plan
If but that little part incongruous seem.
Nor is that part, perhaps, what mortals deem;
Oft from apparent ill our blessings rise.
Oh, then, renounce that impious self-esteem
That aims to trace the secrets of the skies;
For thou art but of dust; be humble, and be wise.

Thus Heaven enlarged his soul in riper years.
For Nature gave him strength and fire to soar
On Fancy's wing above this vale of tears,
Where dark cold-hearted sceptics, creeping, pore
Through microscope of metaphysic lore;
And much they grope for truth, but never hit.
For why? Their powers, inadequate before,
This idle art makes more and more unfit;
Yet deem they darkness light, and their vain blunders wit.

Nor was this ancient dame a foe to mirth.
Her ballad, jest, and riddle's quaint device
Oft cheer'd the shepherds round their social hearth,
Whom levity or spleen could ne'er entice
To purchase chat or laughter at the price
Of decency. Nor let it faith exceed
That Nature forms a rustic taste so * nice.
Ah, had they been of court or city breed
Such delicacy were right marvellous indeed!

Oft, when the winter storm had ceased to rave,
He roam'd the snowy waste at even, to view
The cloud stupendous, from the Atlantic wave
High-towering, sail along the horizon blue;
Where, 'midst the changeful scenery ever new,
Fancy a thousand wondrous forms des cries,
More wildly great than ever pencil drew;
Rocks, torrents, gulfs, and shapes of giant size,
And glittering cliffs on cliffs, and fiery ram-parts rise.

Thence musing onward to the sounding shore,
The lone enthusiast oft would take his way
Listening, with pleasing dread, to the deep roar
Of the wide-weltering waves. In black array,
When sulphurous clouds roll'd on the au-tumnal day,
Even then he hasten'd from the haunt of man
Along the trembling wilderness to stray,

What time the lightning's fierce career began,
And o'er heaven's rending arch the rattling thunder ran.

Responsive to the lively pipe, when all
In sprightly dance the village youth were join'd,
Edwin, of melody aye held in thrall,
From the rude gambol far remote reclined,
Soothed with the soft notes warbling in the wind.
Ah, then all jollity seem'd noise and folly
To the pure soul, by fancy's fire refined.
Ah, what is mirth but turbulence unholy
When with the charm compared of heavenly melancholy?

Is there a heart that music cannot melt?
Alas, how is that rugged heart forlorn!
Is there who ne'er those mystic transports felt
Of solitude and melancholy born?
He needs not woo the Muse; he is her scorn.
The sophist's rope of cobweb he shall twine;
Mope o'er the schoolman's peevish page, or mourn
And delve for life in Mammon's dirty mine;
Sneak with the scoundrel fox, or grunt with glutton swine.

For Edwin, Fate a nobler doom had plann'd;
Song was his favourite and first pursuit.
The wild harp rang to his adventurous hand,
And languish'd to his breath the plaintive flute.
His infant Muse, though artless, was not mute;
Of elegance as yet he took no care,
For this of time and culture is the fruit;
And Edwin gain'd at last this fruit so rare,
As in some future verse I purpose to declare.

Meanwhile, whate'er of beautiful or new,
Sublime or dreadful, in earth, sea, or sky,
By chance or search was offer'd to his view,
He scann'd with curious and romantic eye.
Whate'er of lore tradition could supply
From Gothic tale, or song, or fable old,
Roused him, still keen to listen and to pry.
At last, though long by penury controll'd
And solitude, his soul her graces 'gan unfold.

Thus on the chill *Lapponian's dreary land,
For many a long month lost in snow profound,
When Sol from Cancer sends the season bland,
And in their northern caves the storms are bound,
From silent mountains straight, with startling sound,
Torrents are hurl'd, green hills emerge; and lo!
The trees with foliage, cliffs with flowers are crown'd;
Pure rills through vales of verdure warbling go;
And wonder, love, and joy, the peasant's heart o'erflow.

Here pause, my Gothic lyre, a little while;
The leisure hour is all that thou canst claim.
But on this verse if *Montagu should smile,
New strains ere long shall animate thy frame.
And her applause to me is more than fame,
For still with truth accords her taste refined.
At lucre or renown let others aim;
I only wish to please the gentle mind,
Whom Nature's charms inspire and love of humankind.

[1771]

THOMAS RUSSELL

Born in a village of Dorsetshire in 1762, Thomas Russell attended Winchester School under the régime of Joseph Warton, graduated from New College, Oxford, and resided there for some years as a fellow. Shortly after taking orders in the Church, he died at the age of twenty-six, his life having been shortened apparently by sorrow and disappointment. Beyond these bare facts little is known about this poet, whose natural powers and attainments entitled him to something better than the oblivion in which his name has been sunk until very recent years. In several superficial respects he resembles William Lisle Bowles, who was born in the same year, attended the same school, responded to the literary influence of Joseph Warton in much the same way, and wrote on similar themes. Bowles's first publication appeared in the same year, 1789, as Russell's posthumous *Sonnets and Miscellaneous Poems*. Both poets are perhaps chiefly important as revivers of the sonnet and as links between the earlier poetic work of the Warton brothers and that of the major romantic poets. There was a thin vein of poetic originality in Russell, however, such as his contemporary did not possess. His sonnet on the Isle of Lemnos has an almost Miltonic sonority, and *The Maniac*, together with much dull and tasteless verbiage, contains several lines of direct and simple expression which relate it still more closely to the two poems it so much resembles in theme: Wordsworth's *Ruth* and Keats's *Meg Merrilies*.

THE MANIAC

Tho' grief had nipp'd her early bloom,
  Young Julia still was fair:
The rose indeed had left her cheek;
  The lily still was there.

Tho' of all other actions past
  Her memory bore no part,
The dear remembrance of her love
  Still linger'd in her heart.

Long in that heart had reign'd alone
  A swain of equal youth,
Of equal beauty too with hers,
  But not of equal truth.

Whole years her yielding breast he sooth'd
  With passion's tender tale,
Till avarice call'd him from her arms
  O'er the wide seas to sail.

With many a vow of quick return
  He cross'd the briny tide,
But when a foreign shore he reach'd,
  Soon found a wealthier bride.

Poor Julia sicken'd at the news,
  Yet never told her pain;
Long on her secret soul it prey'd,
  And turn'd at last her brain.

From brethren, parents, house, and home
  The mourning maniac fled;
The sky was all her roof by day,
  A bank by night her bed.

When thirst and hunger griev'd her most,
  If any food she took,
It was the berry from the thorn,
  The water from the brook.

Now hurrying o'er the heath she hied,
  Now wander'd thro' the wood,
Now o'er the precipice she peep'd,
  Now stood and eyed the flood.

From every hedge a flower she pluck'd,
  And moss from every stone,
To make a garland for her love —
  Yet left it still undone.

Still, as she rambled, was she wont
  To trill a plaintive song.
'Twas wild and full of fancies vain,
  Yet suited well her wrong.

All loose, yet lovely, to the wind
  Her golden tresses flew,
And now, alas! with heat were scorch'd,
  And now were drench'd with dew.

No friend was left the tears to wipe
  That dimm'd her radiant eyes,
Yet oft their beams like those would shine
  That gleam from wat'ry skies.

Oft too a smile, but not of joy,
  Play'd on her brow o'ercast;
It was the faint cold smile of spring
  Ere winter yet is past.

Those sorrows which her tongue conceal'd
  Her broken sighs confess'd;
Her cloak was too much torn to hide
  The throbbings of her breast.

From all who near her chanc'd to stray
  With wild affright she ran;
Each voice that reach'd her scar'd her breast,
  But most the voice of man.

To me alone, when oft we met,
  Her ear she would incline,
And with me weep, for well she knew
  Her woes resembled mine.

One morn I sought her; but too late—
  Her wound had bled so sore.
God rest thy spirit, gentle maid!
  Thou'rt gone forevermore!

[1789]

TO SILENCE

O Silence, maid of pensive mien,
That liv'st unknown, unheard, unseen,
  Within thy secret cell,
A pilgrim to thy shrine I come;
Oh, lead me to thy hallow'd home,
  That I with thee may dwell!

Say, dost thou love to drink the dew
That trickles from the churchyard yew
  At midnight's stillest hour;
Or, wrapt in melancholy fit,
In some drear charnel-house to sit,
  Or some dismantled tower?

Ah, no! the hoarse night-raven's song
Forbids thee there to linger long,
  When darkness shrouds the coast;
There too complains the wakeful owl,
With many a yelling demon foul,
  And many a shrieking ghost.

Or with thy sister Solitude
Dwell'st thou, mid Asia's deserts rude
  Beneath some craggy rock,
Where nor the roving robber hies
Nor Arab sees his tent arise,
  Nor shepherd folds his flock?

Yet even in that sequester'd sphere
The serpent's hiss assails thy ear,
  And fills thee with affright,
While lions, loud in angry mood,
And tigers roaming for their food
  Rage dreadful through the night.

Or dost thou, near the frozen pole
Where slumbering seas forget to roll,
  Brood o'er the stagnant deep,
Where nor is heard the dashing oar
Nor wave that murmurs on the shore
  To break thy charmed sleep?

Yet there each bird of harshest cry,
That bravely wings the wintry sky,
  Screams to the northern blast,
While on each ice-built mountain hoar
That parting falls with hideous roar,
  Grim monsters howl aghast.

Then where, ah, tell me! shall I find
Thy haunt untrodden by mankind,
  And undisturbed by noise,
Where, hush'd with thee in calm repose,
I may forget life's transient woes
  And yet more transient joys?

[1789]

SONNET

SUPPOSED TO BE WRITTEN AT LEMNOS

On this lone isle whose rugged rocks affright
  The cautious pilot, ten revolving years
  Great *Pæan's son, unwonted erst to tears,
Wept o'er his wound. Alike each rolling light
Of heaven he watch'd, and blam'd its lingering flight.
  By day the sea-mew screaming round his cave
  Drove slumber from his eyes; the chiding wave
And savage howlings chas'd his dreams by night.

Hope still was his. In each low breeze that sigh'd
  Thro' his rude grot he heard a coming oar;
In each white cloud a coming sail he spied;
  Nor seldom listened to the fancied roar
Of Œta's torrents, or the hoarser tide
  That parts fam'd Trachis from th' Euboic shore.

[1789]

* Notes on Thomas Russell will be found in the Appendix, p. 1046.

GILBERT WHITE

Gilbert White was a country vicar with the faculty of keen observation. Like Thoreau in Concord, he was interested in everything connected with his home surroundings; especially concerning the phenomena of nature was his curiosity insatiable. He noted the temperature and the rainfall in his parish of Selborne, the times when flowers blossomed and insects appeared, the habits of deer and hedgehogs and rabbits and otters, the growth of trees, the appearance of fossils, and the activities of earthworms. He speculated about the migrations of gypsies and the causes of leprosy; he noticed the peculiarities of echoes and the survival of village superstitions; he acquainted himself with the manufacture of rush-lights, and he was much concerned with the excavation of Roman remains. Most of all, however, he was interested in birds, of whose habits he was a tireless investigator. In his own day he had more than a local reputation as an ornithologist; in our day he is most frequently remembered for his contributions to bird lore. He was a born naturalist, and more than most men of his time he possessed the scientist's habit of mind.

White was educated with Joseph and Thomas Warton at their father's school at Basingstoke, and afterwards at Oriel College, Oxford; he entered the Church, and in 1755, when thirty-five, he was given the living of Selborne in Hampshire. Though only about fifty miles from London, Selborne village, because of the bad roads, was isolated. The parish was of considerable extent but numbered less than seven hundred inhabitants; it was heavily wooded and hilly. He lived here quietly for nearly fifty years, unmarried, occupied with his simple pastoral duties, and with abundant leisure for observing the wild life about him.

The Natural History and Antiquities of Selborne, the book that made Gilbert White famous, was published in 1789, four years before his death. It is in the form of letters which record simply and informally the results of his observation. *The Natural History*, which is the part of the work most frequently reprinted, is made up of letters to his friends, Thomas Pennant, the distinguished zoologist, and the Honourable Daines Barrington, a younger son of Viscount Barrington, a lawyer with interests similar to his own. The simple directness of these letters, accurate and scientific, yet unhampered by the technical language that has darkened much later scientific writing and made it a mystery not understanded of the people, is in large part responsible for the extraordinary popularity and the long life of this little book. It belongs in the same class with Isaac Walton's *Complete Angler* among a few books that please both the specialist and the general reader, forthright, wholesome, redolent of sunlight and rainwashed leaves, the work of men reared in the humanistic tradition, extraordinarily aware of the beauty of rural England and moved to share their experiences with others, unaffected by literary artifice and uncoloured by transcendental rapture and romantic yearning. The common assertion that the eighteenth century was incurious about nature and unappreciative of its wonders fails to take into account the Vicar of Selborne, who gave expression to the feelings of countless other Englishmen of his time, men whose days were spent in the open, whose lives were affected by their contact with nature, and who not only appreciated but, more than is commonly realized, helped to develop those natural beauties which have made rural England the delight of succeeding generations.

From THE NATURAL HISTORY AND ANTIQUITIES OF SELBORNE

To Thomas Pennant, Esq.

It has been my misfortune never to have had any neighbour whose studies have led him towards the pursuit of natural knowledge; so that, for want of a companion to quicken my industry and sharpen my attention, I have made but slender progress in a kind of information to which I have been attached from my childhood.

*As to swallows (*Hirundines rusticæ*) being found in a torpid state during the winter in the Isle of Wight, or any part of this country, I never heard any such account worth attending to. But a clergyman of an inquisitive turn assures me that, when he was a great boy, some workmen, in pulling down the battlements of a church tower early in the spring, found two or three swifts (*Hirundines apodes*) among the rubbish, which seemed, at their first appearance, dead; but, on being carried toward the fire, revived. He told me that, out of his great care to pre-

* Notes on Gilbert White will be found in the Appendix, pp. 1047 ff.

serve them, he put them in a paper bag, and hung them by the kitchen fire, where they were suffocated.

Another intelligent person has informed me that, while he was a schoolboy at *Brighthelmstone, in Sussex, a great fragment of the chalk cliff fell down one stormy winter on the beach, and that many people found swallows among the rubbish; but, on my questioning him whether he saw any of those birds himself, to my no small disappointment, he answered me in the negative, but that others assured him they did.

Young broods of swallows began to appear this year on July the eleventh, and young martins (*Hirundines urbicæ*) were then fledged in their nests. Both species will breed again once; for I see by my *fauna* of last year that young broods came forth so late as September the eighteenth. Are not these late hatchings more in favour of hiding than migration? Nay, some young martins remained in their nests last year so late as September the twenty-ninth; and yet they totally disappeared with us by the fifth of October. How strange it is that the swift, which seems to live exactly the same life with the swallow and house-martin, should leave us before the middle of August invariably! while the latter stay often till the middle of October; once I even saw numbers of house-martins on the seventh of November. The martins, redwings, and fieldfares were flying in sight together, an uncommon assemblage of summer and winter birds!

A little yellow bird (the *Motacilla trochilus*) still continues to make a sibilous shivering noise in the tops of tall woods. The *stoparola* of Ray is called, in *your *Zoölogy*, the flycatcher. There is one circumstance characteristic of this bird which seems to have escaped observation, and that is, it takes its stand on the top of some stake or post, from whence it springs forth on its prey, catching a fly in the air, and hardly ever touching the ground, but returning still to the same stand for many times together.

I perceive there are more than one species of the *Motacilla* which visits us. Mr. Derham supposes, in *Ray's *Philos. Letters*, that he has discovered three. In these there is again an instance of some very common birds that have as yet no English name.

*Mr. Stillingfleet makes a question whether the blackcap (*Motacilla atricapilla*) be a bird of passage or not; I think there is no doubt of it, for, in April, in the first fine weather, they come trooping, all at once, into these parts, but are never seen in the winter. They are delicate songsters.

Numbers of snipes breed every summer in some moory ground on the verge of this parish. It is very amusing to see the cock bird on wing at that time, and to hear his piping and humming notes.

I have had no opportunity yet of procuring any of those mice which I mentioned to you in town. The person that brought me the last says they are plentiful in harvest, at which time I will take care to get more; and will endeavour to put it out of doubt whether it be a nondescript species or not.

I suspect much there may be two species of water-rats. Ray says, and *Linnæus after him, that the water-rat is web-footed behind. Now I have discovered a rat on the banks of our little stream that is not web-footed, and yet is an excellent swimmer and diver; it answers exactly to the *Mus amphibius* of Linnæus, which, he says, swims and dives in ditches, "*natat in fossis et urinatur*." I should be glad to procure "one with the feet feathering out like a palm," "*plantis palmatis*." Linnæus seems to be in a puzzle about his *Mus amphibius*, and to doubt whether it differs from his *Mus terrestris*, which if it be, as he allows, the "*mus agrestis capite grandi brachyurus*," a field-mouse with "a large head and a short tail," is widely different from the water-rat, both in size, make, and manner of life.

As to the *falco*, which I mentioned in town, I shall take the liberty to send it down to you into Wales; presuming on your candour, that you will excuse me if it should appear as familiar to you as it is strange to me. "Though mutilated, such as you would say it had formerly been, seeing that the remains are what they are," "*qualem dices... antehac fuisse, tales cum sint reliquiæ!*"

It haunted a marshy piece of ground in quest of wild ducks and snipes, but, when it was shot, had just knocked down a rook, which it was tearing in pieces. I cannot make it answer to any of our English hawks; neither could I find any like it at the curious exhibition of stuffed birds in Spring Gardens. I found it nailed up at the end of a barn, which is the countryman's museum.

The parish I live in is a very abrupt, uneven country, full of hills and woods, and therefore full of birds.

August 4, 1767.

To the Honourable Daines Barrington.

It is the hardest thing in the world to shake off superstitious prejudices; they are sucked in, as it were, with our mother's milk; and, growing up with us at a time when they take the fastest hold and make the most lasting impressions, become so interwoven into our very constitutions that the strongest good sense is required to disengage ourselves from them. No wonder, therefore, that the lower people retain them their whole lives through, since their minds are not invigorated by a liberal education, and therefore not enabled to make any efforts adequate to the occasion.

Such a preamble seems to be necessary before we enter on the superstitions of this district, lest we should be suspected of exaggeration in a recital of practices too gross for this enlightened age.

But the people of Tring, in Hertfordshire, would do well to remember that no longer ago than the year 1751, and within twenty miles of the capital, they seized on two superannuated wretches, crazed with age and overwhelmed with infirmities, on a suspicion of witchcraft; and, by trying experiments, drowned them in a horse-pond.

In a farm-yard near the middle of this village stands, at this day, a row of pollard-ashes, which, by the seams and long cicatrices down their sides, manifestly show that, in former times, they have been cleft asunder. These trees, when young and flexible, were severed and held open by wedges, while ruptured children, stripped naked, were pushed through the apertures, under a persuasion that, by such a process, the poor babes would be cured of their infirmity. As soon as the operation was over, the tree, in the suffering part, was plastered with loam, and carefully swathed up. If the parts coalesced and soldered together, as usually fell out where the feat was performed with any adroitness at all, the party was cured; but where the cleft continued to gape, the operation, it was supposed, would prove ineffectual. Having occasion to enlarge my garden not long since, I cut down two or three such trees, one of which did not grow together.

We have several persons now living in the village, who, in their childhood, were supposed to be healed by this superstitious ceremony, derived down perhaps, from our Saxon ancestors, who practised it before their conversion to Christianity.

At the south corner of *the Plestor, or area, near the church, there stood, about twenty years ago, a very old grotesque hollow pollard-ash, which for ages had been looked on with no small veneration as a shrew-ash. Now a shrew-ash is an ash whose twigs or branches, when gently applied to the limbs of cattle, will immediately relieve the pains which a beast suffers from the running of a shrewmouse over the part affected; for it is supposed that a shrew-mouse is of so baneful and deleterious a nature, that wherever it creeps over a beast, be it a horse, cow, or sheep, the suffering animal is afflicted with cruel anguish, and threatened with the loss of the use of the limb. Against this accident, to which they are continually liable, our provident forefathers always kept a shrew-ash at hand, which, when once medicated, would maintain its virtue forever. A shrew-ash was made thus: into the body of the tree a deep hole was bored with an auger, and a poor devoted shrewmouse was thrust in alive, and plugged in, no doubt, with several quaint incantations long since forgotten. As the ceremonies necessary for such a consecration are no longer understood, all succession is at an end, and no such tree is known to subsist in the manor, or hundred.

As to that on the Plestor, for

*The late vicar stubb'd and burnt it,

when he was way-warden, regardless of the remonstrances of the bystanders, who interceded in vain for its preservation, urging its power and efficacy, and alleging that it had been "guarded through many years by the piety of our ancestors";

**Religione patrum multos servata per annos.*

Selborne, Jan. 8, 1776.

To the Honourable Daines Barrington.

**Forte puer, comitum seductus ab agmine fido,*
Dixerat, Ecquis adest? et, Adest, responderat Echo.
Hic stupet; utque aciem partes divisit in omnes;
Voce, Veni, clamat magna. Vocat illa vocantem.
(Ovid, *Met.* iii. 379.)

In a district so diversified as this, so full of hollow vales and hanging woods, it is no wonder that echoes should abound. Many we have discovered that return the cry of a pack of dogs, the notes of a hunting-horn, a tunable ring of bells, or the melody of birds very agreeably. But we were still at a loss for a polysyllabical articulate echo, till a young gentleman, who had parted from his company in a summer evening walk, and was calling after them, stumbled upon a very curious one in a spot where it might least be expected. At first he was much surprised, and could not be persuaded but that he was mocked by some boy; but repeating his trials in several languages, and finding his respondent to be a very adroit polyglot, he then discerned the deception.

This echo in an evening, before rural noises cease, would repeat ten syllables most articulately and distinctly, especially if quick dactyls were chosen. The last syllables of

** Tityre, tu patulæ recubans —*

were as audibly and intelligibly returned as the first; and there is no doubt, could trial have been made, but that at midnight, when the air is very elastic, and a dead stillness prevails, one or two syllables more might have been obtained; but the distance rendered so late an experiment very inconvenient.

Quick dactyls, we observed, succeeded best; for when we came to try its powers in slow, heavy, embarrassed spondees of the same number of syllables,

** Monstrum horrendum, informe, ingens —*

we could perceive a return but of four or five.

All echoes have some one place to which they are returned stronger and more distinct than to any other; and that is always the place that lies at right angles with the object of repercussion, and is not too near nor too far off. Buildings, or naked rocks, re-echo much more articulately than hanging wood or vales, because in the latter the voice is as it were entangled and embarrassed in the covert, and weakened in the rebound.

The true source of this echo, as we found by various experiments, is the stone-built, tiled hop-kiln in Gally Lane, which measures in front 40 feet, and from the ground to the eaves 12 feet. The true *centrum phonicum*, or just distance, is one particular spot in the King's Field, in the path to Nore Hill, on the very brink of the steep balk above the hollow cartway. In this case there is no choice of distance; but the path, by mere contingency, happens to be the lucky, the identical spot, because the ground rises or falls so immediately, if the speaker either retires or advances, that his mouth would at once be above or below the object.

We measured this polysyllabical echo with great exactness, and found the distance to fall very short of Dr. Plot's rule for distinct articulation: for the doctor, in his history of Oxfordshire, allows 120 feet for the return of each syllable distinctly; hence this echo, which gives ten distinct syllables, ought to measure 400 yards, or 120 feet to each syllable; whereas our distance is only 258 yards, or near 75 feet to each syllable. Thus our measure falls short of the doctor's, as five to eight; but then it must be acknowledged that this candid philosopher was convinced afterwards, that some latitude must be admitted of in the distance of echoes according to time and place.

When experiments of this sort are making, it should always be remembered that weather and the time of day have a vast influence on an echo; for a dull, heavy, moist air deadens and clogs the sound; and hot sunshine renders the air thin and weak, and deprives it of all its springiness; and a ruffling wind quite defeats the whole. In a still, clear, dewy evening the air is most elastic; and perhaps the later the hour the more so. Echo has always been so amusing to the imagination that the poets have personified her, and in their hands she has been the occasion of many a beautiful fiction. Nor need the gravest man be ashamed to appear taken with such a phenomenon, since it may become the subject of philosophical or mathematical inquiries.

One should have imagined that echoes, if not entertaining, must at least have been harmless and inoffensive; yet Virgil advances a strange notion that they are injurious to bees. After enumerating some probable and reasonable annoyances, such as prudent owners would wish far removed from their bee-gardens, he adds

**... aut ubi concava pulsu*
Saxa sonant, vocisque offensa resultat imago.

This wild and fanciful assertion will hardly be admitted by the philosophers of these days, especially as they all now seem agreed that insects are not furnished with any organs of hearing at all. But if it should be urged that though they cannot hear, yet perhaps they may feel the repercussion of sounds, I grant it is possible they may. Yet that these impressions are distasteful or hurtful, I deny, because bees, in good summers, thrive well in my outlet, where the echoes are very strong; for this village is another *Anathoth, a place of responses or echoes. Besides, it does not appear from experiment that bees are in any way capable of being affected by sounds; for I have often tried my own with a large speaking-trumpet held close to their hives, and with such an exertion of voice as would have hailed a ship at the distance of a mile, and still these insects pursued their various employments undisturbed, and without showing the least sensibility or resentment.

Some time since its discovery this echo is become totally silent, though the object, or hop-kiln, remains; nor is there any mystery in this defect, for the field between is planted as a hop-garden, and the voice of the speaker is totally absorbed and lost among the poles and entangled foliage of the hops. And when the poles are removed in autumn the disappointment is the same, because a tall quick-set hedge, nurtured up for the purpose of shelter to the hop-ground, interrupts the repercussion of the voice; so that till those obstructions are removed no more of its garrulity can be expected.

Should any gentleman of fortune think an echo in his park or outlet a pleasing incident, he might build one at little or no expense. For whenever he had occasion for a new barn, stable, dog kennel, or the like structure, it would be only needful to erect this building on the gentle declivity of a hill, with a like rising opposite to it, at a few hundred yards distance; and perhaps success might be the easier insured could some canal, lake, or stream, intervene. From a seat at the *centrum phonicum* he and his friends might amuse themselves sometimes of an evening with the prattle of this loquacious nymph; of whose complacency and decent reserve more may be said than can with truth of every individual of her sex; since she is "always ready with her vocal response, but never intrusive:"

** ... quæ nec reticere loquenti,*
Nec prior ipsa loqui didicit resonabilis Echo.

The classic reader will, I trust, pardon the following lovely quotation, so finely describing echoes, and so poetically accounting for their causes:

**Quæ bene quom videas, rationem reddere possis*
Tute tibi atque aliis, quo pacto per loca sola
Saxa pareis formas verborum ex ordine reddant,
Palanteis comites quom monteis inter opacos
Quærimus, et magna disperos voce ciemus.
Sex etiam, aut septem loca vidi reddere voces
Unam quom jaceres: ita colles collibus ipsis
Verba repulsantes iterabant dicta referre.
Hæc loca capripedes Satyros Nymphasque tenere
Finitimi fingunt, et Faunos esse loquuntur;
Quorum noctivago strepitu, ludoque jocanti
Adfirmant volgo taciturna silentia rumpi,
Chordarumque sonos fieri, dulceisque querelas,
Tibia quas fundit digitis pulsata canentum:
Et genus agricolum late sentiscere, quom Pan
Pinea semiferi capitis velamina quassans,
Unco sæpe labro calamos percurrit hianteis,
Fistula silvestrem ne cesset fundere musam.
(LUCRETIUS, lib. iv. l. 576.)

Selborne, Feb. 12, 1778.

To the Honourable Daines Barrington.

From the motion of birds, the transition is natural enough to their notes and language, of which I shall say something. Not that I would pretend to understand their language, like *the vizier of the *Spectator*, who, by the recital of a conversation which passed between two owls, reclaimed a sultan, before delighting in conquest and devastation; but I would be thought only to mean that many of the winged tribes have various sounds and voices adapted to express their various passions, wants, and feelings, such as anger, fear, love, hatred, hunger, and the like. All species are not equally eloquent; some are copious and fluent as it were in their utterance, while others are confined to a few important sounds: no bird, like the fish kind, is quite mute, though some are rather silent. The language of birds is very ancient, and, like other ancient modes of speech, very elliptical; little is said, but much is meant and understood.

The notes of the eagle-kind are shrill and piercing; and about the season of nidification much diversified, as I have been often assured by a curious observer of nature who long resided at Gibraltar, where eagles abound. The notes of our hawks much resemble those of the king of birds. Owls have very expressive notes; they hoot in a fine vocal sound, much resembling the **vox humana*, and reducible by a pitch-pipe to a musical key. This note seems to express complacency and rivalry among the males; they use also a quick call and a horrible scream, and can snore and hiss when they mean to menace. Ravens, besides their loud croak, can exert a deep and solemn note that makes the woods echo; the amorous sound of a crow is strange and ridiculous; rooks, in the breeding season, attempt sometimes in the gaiety of their hearts to sing, but with no great success; the parrot-kind may have many modulations of voice, as appears by their aptitude to learn human sounds; doves coo in an amorous and mournful manner, and are emblems of despairing lovers; the woodpecker sets up a sort of loud and hearty laugh; the fern-owl, or goatsucker, from the dusk till day-break, serenades his mate with the clattering of castanets. All the tuneful *passeres* express their complacency by sweet modulations and a variety of melody. The swallow, as has been observed in a former letter, by a shrill alarm bespeaks the attention of the other *hirundines*, and bids them be aware that the hawk is at hand. Aquatic and gregarious birds, especially the nocturnal, that shift their quarters in the dark, are very noisy and loquacious, as cranes, wild-geese, wild-ducks, and the like; their perpetual clamour prevents them from dispersing and losing their companions.

In so extensive a subject, sketches and outlines are as much as can be expected, for it would be endless to instance in all their infinite variety the notes of the feathered nation. I shall therefore confine the remainder of this letter to the few domestic fowls of our yards which are most known, and therefore best understood. And first the peacock, with his gorgeous train, demands our attention; but, like most of the gaudy birds, his notes are grating and shocking to the ear: the yelling of cats and the braying of an ass are not more disgustful. The voice of the goose is trumpet-like, and clanking, and once saved the Capitol at Rome, as grave historians assert; the hiss also of the gander is formidable and full of menace, and "protective of his young." Among ducks the sexual distinction of voice is remarkable; for, while the quack of the female is loud and sonorous, the voice of the drake is inward and harsh and feeble and scarce discernible. The cock turkey struts and gobbles to his mistress in a most uncouth manner; he hath also a pert and petulant note when he attacks his adversary. When a hen turkey leads forth her young brood, she keeps a watchful eye; and if a bird of prey appear, though ever so high in the air, the careful mother announces the enemy with a little inward moan, and watches him with a steady and attentive look; but, if he approach, her note becomes earnest and alarming, and her outcries are redoubled.

No inhabitants of the yard seem possessed of such a variety of expression, and so copious a language, as common poultry. Take a chicken of four or five days old, and hold it up to a window where there are flies, and it will immediately seize its prey with little twitterings of complacency; but if you tender it a wasp or a bee, at once its note becomes harsh, and expressive of disapprobation and a sense of danger. When a pullet is ready to lay, she intimates the event by a joyous, soft, and easy note. Of all the occurrences of their life that of laying seems to be the most important; for no sooner has a hen disburdened herself, than she rushes forth with a clamorous kind of joy, which the cock and the rest of his mistresses immediately adopt. The tumult is not confined to the family concerned, but catches from yard to yard, and spreads to every homestead within hearing, till at last the whole village is in an uproar. As soon as a hen becomes a mother, her new relation demands a new language; she then runs clucking and screaming about, and seems agitated as if possessed. The father of the flock has also a considerable vocabulary; if he finds food, he calls a favourite concubine to partake; and if a bird of prey passes over, with a warning voice he bids his family beware. The gallant chanticleer has, at command, his amorous phrases and his terms of defiance. But the sound by which he is best known is his crowing; by this he has been distinguished in all ages as the countryman's clock or larum, as the watchman that proclaims the divisions of the night. Thus the poet elegantly styles him

— * the crested cock, whose clarion sounds
The silent hours.

A neighbouring gentleman one summer had lost most of his chickens by a sparrow-hawk, that came gliding down between a faggot pile and the end of his house, to the place where the coops stood. The owner, inwardly vexed to see his flock thus diminishing, hung a setting net adroitly between the pile and the house, into which the caitiff dashed, and was entangled. Resentment suggested the law of retaliation; he therefore clipped the hawk's wings, cut off his talons, and, fixing a cork on his bill, threw him down among the brood.

hens. Imagination cannot paint the scene that ensued; the expressions that fear, rage, and revenge inspired were new, or at least such as had been unnoticed before; the exasperated matrons upbraided, they execrated, they insulted, they triumphed. In a word, they never desisted from buffeting their adversary till they had torn him in a hundred pieces.

Selborne, Sept. 9, 1778.

To the Honourable Daines Barrington.

*The old Sussex tortoise that I have mentioned to you so often is become my property. I dug it out of its winter dormitory in March last, when it was enough awakened to express its resentments by hissing; and, packing it in a box with earth, carried it eighty miles in post-chaises. The rattle and hurry of the journey so perfectly roused it that, when I turned it out on a border, it walked twice down to the bottom of my garden. However, in the evening, the weather being cold, it buried itself in the loose mould, and continues still concealed. As it will be under my eye, I shall now have an opportunity of enlarging my observations on its mode of life, and propensities; and perceive already that, towards the time of coming forth, it opens a breathing place in the ground near its head, requiring, I conclude, a freer respiration as it becomes more alive. This creature not only goes under the earth from the middle of November to the middle of April, but sleeps great part of the summer; for it goes to bed in the longest days at four in the afternoon, and often does not stir in the morning till late. Besides, it retires to rest for every shower, and does not move at all in wet days.

When one reflects on the state of this strange being, it is a matter of wonder to find that Providence should bestow such a profusion of days, such a seeming waste of longevity, on a reptile that appears to relish it so little as to squander more than two-thirds of its existence in a joyless stupor, and be lost to all sensation for months together in the profoundest of slumbers.

While I was writing this letter, a moist and warm afternoon, with the thermometer at fifty, brought forth troops of shell-snails; and at the same juncture the tortoise heaved up the mould and put out its head, and the next morning came forth, as it were, raised from the dead, and walked about till four in the afternoon. This was a curious coincidence! a very amusing occurrence! to see such a similarity of feelings between the two *φερέοικοι*, for so the Greeks call both the shell-snail and the tortoise.

Because we call "the old family tortoise" an abject reptile, we are too apt to undervalue his abilities and depreciate his powers of instinct. Yet he is, as Mr. Pope says of his lord,

> *Much too wise to walk into a well,

and has so much discernment as *not to fall down a haha, but to stop and withdraw from the brink with the readiest precaution. Though he loves warm weather, he avoids the hot sun, because his thick shell, when once heated, would, as the poet says of solid armour, "scald with safety." He therefore spends the more sultry hours under the umbrella of a large cabbage leaf, or amidst the waving forests of an asparagus bed. But, as he avoids heat in the summer, so, in the decline of the year, he improves the faint autumnal beams by getting within the reflection of a fruit-wall; and though he never has read that planes inclining to the horizon receive a greater share of warmth, he inclines his shell, by tilting it against the wall, to collect and admit every feeble ray.

Pitiable seems the condition of this poor embarrassed reptile: to be cased in a suit of ponderous armour, which he cannot lay aside; to be imprisoned, as it were, within his own shell, must preclude, we should suppose, all activity and disposition for enterprise. Yet there is a season of the year (usually the beginning of June) when his exertions are remarkable. He then walks on tiptoe, and is stirring by five in the morning; and, traversing the garden, examines every wicket and interstice in the fences, through which he will escape if possible; and often has eluded the care of the gardener, and wandered to some distant field. The motives that impel him to undertake these rambles seem to be of the amorous kind; his fancy then becomes intent on sexual attachments, which transport him beyond his usual gravity, and induce him to forget for a time his ordinary solemn deportment.

Summer birds are, this cold and backward spring, unusually late; I have seen but one swallow yet. This conformity with the weather convinces me more and more that they sleep in the winter.

Selborne, April 21, 1780.

To the Honourable Daines Barrington.

There were some circumstances attending the remarkable frost in January, 1776, so singular and striking that a short detail of them may not be unacceptable.

The most certain way to be exact will be to copy the passages from my journal, which were taken from time to time as things occurred. But it may be proper previously to remark that the first week in January was uncommonly wet, and drowned with vast rains from every quarter: from whence it may be inferred, as there is great reason to believe is the case, that intense frosts seldom take place till the earth is perfectly glutted and chilled with water; and hence dry autumns are seldom followed by rigorous winters.

January 7th. — Snow driving all the day, which was followed by frost, sleet, and some snow, till the 12th, when a prodigious mass overwhelmed all the works of men, drifting over the tops of the gates and filling the hollow lanes.

On the 14th the writer was obliged to be much abroad, and thinks he never, before or since, has encountered such rugged Siberian weather. Many of the narrow roads were now filled above the tops of the hedges, through which the snow was driven into most romantic and grotesque shapes, so striking to the imagination as not to be seen without wonder and pleasure. The poultry dared not stir out of their roosting-places, for cocks and hens are so dazzled and confounded by the glare of snow that they would soon perish without assistance. The hares also lay sullenly in their seats, and would not move till compelled by hunger, being conscious, poor animals, that the drifts and heaps treacherously betray their footsteps, and prove fatal to numbers of them.

From the 14th the snow continued to increase, and began to stop the road-wagons and coaches, which could no longer keep on their regular stages, more especially on the western roads, where the fall appears to have been deeper than in the south. The company at Bath that wanted to attend the Queen's birthday were strangely incommoded; the carriages of many persons who got on their way to town from Bath as far as Marlborough, after strange embarrassments, here met with a **ne plus ultra.* The ladies fretted, and offered large rewards to labourers if they would shovel them a track to London, but the relentless heaps of snow were too bulky to be removed; and so the 18th passed over, leaving the company in very uncomfortable circumstances at the Castle and other inns.

On the 20th the sun shone out for the first time since the frost began, a circumstance that has been remarked on before as much in favour of vegetation. All this time the cold was not very intense, for the thermometer stood at 29, 28, 25, and thereabout; but on the 21st it descended to 20. The birds now began to be in a very pitiable and starving condition. Tamed by the season, skylarks settled in the streets of towns because they saw the ground was bare; rooks frequented dunghills close to houses; and crows watched horses as they passed, and greedily devoured what dropped from them; hares now came into the gardens, and, scraping away the snow, devoured such plants as they could find.

On the 22nd the author had occasion to go to London through a sort of Laplandian scene, very wild and grotesque indeed. But the metropolis itself exhibited a still more singular appearance than the country; for, being bedded deep in snow, the pavement of the streets could not be touched by the wheels or the horses' feet, so that the carriages ran about without the least noise. Such an exemption from din and clatter was strange, but not pleasant; it seemed to convey an uncomfortable idea of desolation:

> . . . *ipsa silentia terrent.*
> By silence terrified.

On the 27th much snow fell all day, and in the evening the frost became very intense. At South Lambeth, for the four following nights, the thermometer fell to 11, 7, 6, 6; and at Selborne to 7, 6, 10; and on the 31st of January, just before sunrise, with rime on the trees and on the tube of the glass, the quicksilver sank exactly to zero, being 32 degrees below the freezing point: but by eleven in the morning, though in the shade, it sprang up to 16½ — a most unusual degree of cold this for the south of England! During these four nights the cold was so penetrating that it occasioned ice in warm chambers and under beds; and in the day the wind was so keen that persons of robust constitutions could scarcely endure to face it. The Thames was at once frozen over, both above and below bridge, so that crowds ran about on the ice. The streets were now strangely incumbered with snow, which crumbled and trod dusty, and soon turning grey, resembled bay-salt; what had fallen on the roofs was perfectly dry, that, from first to last, it lay twenty-six days on the houses in the city, a longer time than had been remembered by the oldest housekeepers living. According to all appearances we might now have expected the continuance of this rigorous weather for weeks to come, since every night increased in severity; but behold, without any apparent cause, on the 1st of February, a thaw took place, and some rain followed before night, making good the observation above, that frosts often go off as it were at once, without any gradual declension of cold. On the 2nd of February the thaw persisted; and on the 3rd swarms of little insects were frisking and sporting in a courtyard at South Lambeth, as if they had felt no frost. Why the juices in the small bodies, and smaller limbs, of such minute beings are not frozen is a matter of curious inquiry.

Severe frosts seem to be partial, or to run in currents; for, at the same juncture, as the author was informed by accurate correspondents, at Lyndon, in the county of Rutland, the thermometer stood at 19; at Blackburn, in Lancashire, at 19; and at Manchester at 21, 20, and 18. Thus does some unknown circumstance strangely overbalance latitude, and render the cold sometimes much greater in the southern than in the northern parts of this kingdom.

The consequences of this severity were that in Hampshire, at the melting of the snow, the wheat looked well, and the turnips came forth little injured. The laurels and laurustines were somewhat damaged, but only in hot aspects. No evergreens were quite destroyed; and not half the damage sustained that befell in January, 1768. Those laurels that were a little scorched on the south sides were perfectly untouched on their north sides. The care taken to shake the snow day by day from the branches seemed greatly to avail the author's evergreens. A neighbour's laurel hedge, in a high situation, and facing to the north, was perfectly green and vigorous; and the Portugal laurels remained unhurt.

As to the birds, the thrushes and blackbirds were mostly destroyed; and the partridges were so thinned by the weather and poachers that few remained to breed the following year

[1789]

JUNIUS

BETWEEN January, 1769, and January, 1772, there appeared in a London newspaper, the *Public Advertiser*, a series of letters bearing the signature "Junius," which caused an immediate storm of political and personal controversy and a scarcely less violent and a more enduring controversy about the identity of the author. These letters were brilliantly written by a bold, unscrupulous partisan who was intimately acquainted with the inner workings of public affairs, and who attacked some of the leading statesmen of the day with deadly effectiveness. In letter after letter of invective written in chaste and polished English he denounced the government and exposed its actions to ridicule. Employing by turns barbed innuendo and ringing philippic he struck at men prominent in public life, such as the Duke of Bedford, Lord Chief Justice Mansfield, and the Duke of Grafton. No such series of letters had ever been written in England, and seldom has public interest been more completely aroused. Speculation exhausted itself in fruitless efforts to discover the unknown writer, this "mighty boar of the forest," as Burke described him, who broke through the toils of the hunters and spread the fear of his tusks on every hand. Before long, "Junius" dared to go higher than the ministry and to turn upon the king himself. The publisher of the *Public Advertiser* was brought to trial for libel, but the prosecution failed because the jury returned a verdict of "Guilty of printing and publishing only." The circulation of the *Public Advertiser* grew rapidly; the letters were often copied, and were reprinted in numerous collected editions.

For more than a century the identification of "Junius" was hotly debated, and it has not been completely established even today. The question has taken its place with the identification of the Man in the Iron Mask as one of the insolvable problems of history. In hundreds of books and articles on the subject the names of more than two score persons have been proposed, including those of Bishop Butler, Lord Chatham, the Earl of Chesterfield, the Earl of Shelburne, Edmund Burke, Edward Hume, the Duke of Portland, General Lee, John Wilkes, John Horne Tooke, and Horace Walpole. Against most of these attributions the evidence is overwhelming; against several of them it is as near demonstration as negative evidence can be. Out of the confusion of charges and countercharges, claims and disclaimers, Sir Philip Francis eventually emerged as the most probable author. He was born in Dublin in 1740, the son of the Reverend Philip Francis; he held various political appointments, during the period of the "Junius" letters being the holder of a post in the War Office, and shortly afterwards being named a member of the Council of Bengal. While he was in India he quarrelled with Warren Hastings, and after his return to England he was active in the latter's impeachment. The evidence in support of Sir Philip Francis's identification consists of the similarity of his political views and those expressed in the letters, his known friendships and violent personal antipathies, his access to the sources of information used by "Junius," the correspondence between the dates of the letters and his own movements at the same times, the peculiarities of his handwriting, and the later testimony furnished by his widow. The only strong evidence against the "Franciscan theory" is that none of Sir Philip's acknowledged writings are equal to the "Junius" letters in political effectiveness or literary excellence. Though some of the other attributions have found supporters within recent years, the prevailing opinion today is that Sir Philip Francis had an important connection with the letters, and that he was probably their author.

While the mystery of the authorship has certainly had much to do with the fame of the letters, the controversy would not have continued through succeeding generations had they not possessed intrinsic value. Their style shows the full-dress dignity characteristic of eighteenth-century political papers, but it has also perfect lucidity and extraordinary vigour. The formal rhetoric of his rounded periods and elaborate antitheses does not obscure the precise beauty of his diction, the march of his rhythms, and the snap of his epigrams. He has pungent wit and telling sarcasm, feline grace of movement and dextrous use of lethal claws. The letters of "Junius" contain little that is notable in political theory or in such basic ideas of government as appear in the writings of Burke. Their controversies are chiefly personal; they exhibit partisan rancour rather than statesmanlike comprehension. Yet within their limitations they are unexcelled; "Junius" has a small compass of vision, but it is clear; his very hatred becomes magnificent; in his hands the political pamphlet attains the grand style. In the long struggle for the freedom of the press and in the development of governmental responsibility, not less than in the history of English prose, the *Letters of Junius* have an assured place.

THE LETTERS OF JUNIUS

TO *HIS GRACE THE DUKE OF BEDFORD

September 19, 1769.

MY LORD:

You are so little accustomed to receive any marks of respect or esteem from the public that if, in the following lines, a compliment or expression of applause should escape me, I fear you would consider it as a mockery of your established character, and perhaps an insult to your understanding. You have nice feelings, my lord, if we may judge from your resentments. Cautious, therefore, of giving offence where you have so little deserved it, I shall leave the illustration of your virtues to other hands. Your friends have a privilege to play upon the easiness of your temper, or possibly they are better acquainted with your good qualities than I am. You have done good by stealth. The rest is upon record. You have still left ample room for speculation, when panegyric is exhausted.

You are indeed a very considerable man. The highest rank, a splendid fortune, and a name, glorious till it was yours, were sufficient to have supported you with meaner abilities than I think you possess. From the first, you derived a constitutional claim to respect; from the second, a natural extensive authority; the last created a partial expectation of hereditary virtues. The use you have made of these uncommon advantages might have been more honourable to yourself, but could not be more instructive to mankind. We may trace it in the veneration of your country, the choice of your friends, and in the accomplishment of every sanguine hope which the public might have conceived from the illustrious name of Russell.

The eminence of your station gave you a commanding prospect of your duty. The road which led to honour was open to your view. You could not lose it by mistake, and you had no temptation to depart from it by design. Compare the natural dignity and importance of the richest peer of England, the noble independence which he might have maintained in Parliament, and the real interest and respect which he might have acquired, not only in Parliament, but through the whole kingdom, — compare these glorious distinctions with the ambition of holding a share in government, the emoluments of a place, the sale of a borough, or the purchase of a corporation; and, though you may not regret the virtues which create respect, you may see with anguish how much real importance and authority you have lost. Consider the character of an independent, virtuous Duke of Bedford; imagine what he might be in this country; then reflect one moment upon what you are. If it be possible for me to withdraw my attention from the fact, I will tell you in theory what such a man might be.

Conscious of his own weight and importance, his conduct in Parliament would be directed by nothing but the constitutional duty of a peer. He would consider himself as a guardian of the laws. Willing to support the just measures of government, but determined to observe the conduct of the minister with suspicion, he would oppose the violence of faction with as much firmness as the encroachments of prerogative. He would be as little capable of bargaining with the minister for places for himself or his dependents, as of descending to mix himself in the intrigues of opposition. Whenever an important question called for his opinion in Parliament, he would be heard by the most profligate minister with deference and respect. His authority would either sanctify or disgrace the measures of government. The people would look up to him as their protector, and a virtuous prince would have one honest man in his dominions, in whose integrity and judgment he might safely confide. If it should be the will of Providence to afflict him with *a domestic misfortune, he would submit to the stroke with feeling, but not without dignity. He would consider the people as his children, and receive a generous heartfelt consolation in the sympathizing tears and blessings of his country.

Your grace may probably discover something more intelligible in the negative part of this illustrious character. The man I have described would never prostitute his dignity in Parliament by an indecent violence, either in opposing or defending a minister. He would not at one moment rancorously persecute, at another basely cringe to, *the favourite of his sovereign. After outraging the royal dignity with peremptory conditions, little short of menace and hostility, he would never descend to the humility of soliciting an interview with the favourite, and of offer-

*** Notes on Junius will be found in the Appendix, pp. 1048 ff.**

ing to recover, at any price, the honour of his friendship. Though deceived, perhaps, in his youth, he would not, through the course of a long life, have invariably chosen his friends from among the most profligate of mankind. His own honour would have forbidden him from mixing his private pleasures of conversation with jockeys, gamesters, blasphemers, gladiators, or buffoons. He would then have never felt, much less would he have submitted to, the humiliating, dishonest necessity of engaging in the interest and intrigues of his dependents, of supplying their vices, or relieving their beggary, at the expense of his country. He would not have betrayed such ignorance or such contempt of the constitution as openly to avow, in a court of justice, *the purchase and sale of a borough. He would not have thought it consistent with his rank in the state, or even with his personal importance, to be the little tyrant of a little corporation. He would never have been insulted with virtues which he had laboured to extinguish, nor suffered the disgrace of a mortifying defeat which has made him ridiculous and contemptible even to the few by whom he was not detested. I reverence the afflictions of a good man — his sorrows are sacred. But how can we take part in the distresses of a man whom we can neither love nor esteem; or feel for a calamity of which he himself is insensible? Where was the father's heart when he could look for, or find an immediate consolation for the loss of an only son, in consultations and bargains for a place at court, and even in the misery of balloting at the India House!

Admitting, then, that you have mistaken or deserted those honourable principles which ought to have directed your conduct, admitting that you have as little claim to private affection as to public esteem, let us see with what abilities, with what degree of judgment, you have carried your own system into execution. A great man, in the success and even in the magnitude of his crimes, finds a rescue from contempt. Your grace is every way unfortunate. Yet I will not look back to those ridiculous scenes by which, in your earlier days, you thought it an honour to be distinguished — *the recorded stripes, the public infamy, your own sufferings, or Mr. Rigby's fortitude. These events undoubtedly left an impression, though not upon your mind. To *such* a mind it may, perhaps, be a pleasure to reflect that there is hardly a corner of *any of his Majesty's kingdoms, except France, in which, at one time or other, your valuable life has not been in danger. Amiable man! we see and acknowledge the protection of Providence, by which you have so often escaped the personal detestation of your fellow-subjects, and are still reserved for the public justice of your country.

Your history begins to be important at that auspicious period at which you were deputed to represent the Earl of Bute at the court of Versailles. It was an honourable office, and executed with the same spirit with which it was accepted. Your patrons wanted an ambassador who would submit to make concessions without daring to insist upon any honourable condition for his sovereign. Their business required a man who had as little feeling for his own dignity as for the welfare of his country; and they found him in the first rank of the nobility. *Belleisle, Goree, Guadaloupe, St. Louis, Martinique, the Fishery, and the Havanna, are glorious monuments of your grace's talents for negotiation My lord, we are too well acquainted with your pecuniary character to think it possible that so many public sacrifices should be made without some private compensations. Your conduct carries with it an internal evidence beyond all the legal proofs of a court of justice. Even the callous pride of Lord Egremont was alarmed. He saw and felt his own dishonour in corresponding with you; and there certainly was a moment at which he meant to have resisted, had not a fatal lethargy prevailed over his faculties, and carried all sense and memory away with it.

I will not pretend to specify the secret terms on which you were invited to support an administration which Lord Bute pretended to leave in full possession of their ministerial authority, and perfectly masters of themselves. He was not of a temper to relinquish power, though he retired from employment. Stipulations were certainly made between your grace and him, and certainly violated. After two years submission, you thought you had collected a strength sufficient to control his influence, and that it was your turn to be a tyrant, because you had been a slave. When you found yourself mistaken in your opinion of your gracious master's firmness, disappointment got the better of all your humble discretion, and carried you to an excess of outrage to his person, as distant from true spirit, as from all decency and respect. After robbing him of the rights of a king, *you would not permit him to preserve the honour of a gentleman. It was then Lord Weymouth was nominated to Ireland, and dispatched (we well remember with what indecent hurry) to plunder the treasury of the first fruits of an employment which you well knew he was never to execute.

This sudden declaration of war against the favourite might have given you a momentary merit with the public, if it had either been adopted upon principle, or maintained with resolution. Without looking back to all your former servility, we need only observe your subsequent conduct to see upon what motives you acted. Apparently united with Mr. Grenville, you waited until Lord Rockingham's feeble administration should dissolve in its own weakness. The moment their dismission was suspected, the moment you perceived that another system was adopted in the closet, you thought it no disgrace to return to your former dependence, and solicit once more the friendship of Lord Bute. You begged an interview, at which he had spirit enough to treat you with contempt.

It would now be of little use to point out by what a train of weak, injudicious measures, it became necessary, or was thought so, to call you back to a share in the administration. The friends whom you did not in the last instance desert were not of a character to add strength or credit to government, and at that time your alliance with the Duke of Grafton was, I presume, hardly foreseen. We must look for other stipulations to account for that sudden resolution of the closet, by which three of your dependants (whose characters, I think, cannot be less respected than they are) were advanced to offices through which you might again control the minister, and probably engross the whole direction of affairs.

The possession of absolute power is now once more within your reach. The measures you have taken to obtain and confirm it are too gross to escape the eyes of a discerning, judicious prince. His palace is besieged; the lines of circumvallation are drawing round him; and, unless he finds a resource in his own activity, or in the attachment of the real friends of his family, the best of princes must submit to the confinement of a state prisoner until your grace's death or some less fortunate event shall raise the siege. For the present, you may safely resume that style of insult and menace which even a private gentleman cannot submit to hear without being contemptible. *Mr. Mackenzie's history is not yet forgotten, and you may find precedents enough of the mode in which an imperious subject may signify his pleasure to his sovereign. Where will this gracious monarch look for assistance, when the wretched Grafton could forget his obligations to his master, and desert him for a hollow alliance with *such* a man as the Duke of Bedford!

Let us consider you, then, as arrived at the summit of worldly greatness; let us suppose that all your plans of avarice and ambition are accomplished, and your most sanguine wishes gratified in the fear as well as the hatred of the people. Can age itself forget that you are now in the last act of life? Can grey hairs make folly venerable? and is there no period to be reserved for meditation and retirement? For shame! my Lord: let it not be recorded of you that the latest moments of your life were dedicated to the same unworthy pursuits, the same busy agitations, in which your youth and manhood were exhausted. Consider that, although you cannot disgrace your former life, you are violating the character of age, and exposing the impotent imbecility, after you have lost the vigour, of the passions.

Your friends will ask, perhaps, whither shall this unhappy old man retire. Can he remain in the metropolis, where his life has been so often threatened, and his palace so often attacked? If he returns to *Woburn, scorn and mockery await him. He must create a solitude round his estate, if he would avoid the face of reproach and derision. At Plymouth, his destruction would be more than probable; at Exeter, inevitable. No honest Englishman will ever forget his attachment, nor any honest Scotchman forgive his treachery, to Lord Bute. At every town he enters he must change his liveries and his name. Whichever way he flies, the hue and cry of the country pursues him.

In another kingdom, indeed, the blessings of his administration have been more sensibly felt; his virtues better understood; or at worst, they will not, for him alone, forget their hospitality. *As well might Verres have returned to Sicily. You have twice escaped, my Lord; beware of a third experiment. The indignation of a whole people, plundered, insulted, and oppressed as they have been, will not always be disappointed.

It is in vain, therefore, to shift the scene. You can no more fly from your enemies than from yourself. Persecuted abroad, you look into your own heart for consolation, and find nothing but reproaches and despair. But, my Lord, you may quit the field of business, though not the field of danger; and though you cannot be safe, you may cease to be ridiculous. I fear you have listened too long to the advice of those pernicious friends with whose interests you have sordidly united your own, and for whom you have sacrificed everything that ought to be dear to a man of honour. They are still base enough to encourage the follies of your age, as they once did the vices of your youth. As little acquainted with the rules of decorum as with the laws of morality, they will not suffer you to profit by experience, nor even to consult the propriety of a bad character. Even now they tell you that life is no more than a dramatic scene, in which the hero should preserve his consistency to the last, and that, as you lived without virtue, you should die without repentance.

JUNIUS

*TO THE PRINTER OF THE "PUBLIC ADVERTISER"

December 19, 1769.

SIR:

When the complaints of a brave and powerful people are observed to increase in proportion to the wrongs they have suffered; when, instead of sinking into submission, they are roused to resistance, the time will soon arrive at which every inferior consideration must yield to the security of the sovereign and to the general safety of the state. There is a moment of difficulty and danger, at which flattery and falsehood can no longer deceive, and simplicity itself can no longer be misled. Let us suppose it arrived. Let us suppose a gracious, well-intentioned prince made sensible, at last, of the great duty he owes to his people, and of his own disgraceful situation; that he looks round him for assistance, and asks for no advice but how to gratify the wishes and secure the happiness of his subjects. In these circumstances, it may be matter of curious *speculation* to consider, if an honest man were permitted to approach a king, in what terms he would address himself to his sovereign. Let it be imagined, no matter how improbable, that the first prejudice against his character is removed, that the ceremonious difficulties of an audience are surmounted; that he feels himself animated by the purest and most honourable affections to his king and country; and that the great person whom he addresses has spirit enough to bid him speak freely, and understanding enough to listen to him with attention. Unacquainted with the vain impertinence of forms, he would deliver his sentiments with dignity and firmness, but not without respect.

Sir: It is the misfortune of your life, and originally the cause of every reproach and distress which has attended your government, that you should never have been acquainted with the language of truth until you heard it in the complaints of your people. It is not, however, too late to correct the error of your education. We are still inclined to make an indulgent allowance for *the pernicious lessons you received in your youth, and to form the most sanguine hopes from the natural benevolence of your disposition. We are far from thinking you capable of a direct, deliberate purpose to invade those original rights of your subjects on which all their civil and political liberties depend. Had it been possible for us to entertain a suspicion so dishonourable to your character, we should long since have adopted a style of remonstrance very distant from the humility of complaint. The doctrine inculcated by our laws, that "the king can do no wrong," is admitted without reluctance. We separate the amiable, good-natured prince from the folly and treachery of his servants, and the private virtues of the man from the vices of his government. Were it not for this just distinction, I know not whether your Majesty's condition or that of the English nation would deserve most to be lamented. I would prepare your mind for a favourable reception of truth by removing every painful, offensive idea of personal reproach. Your subjects, sir, wish for nothing but that, as *they* are reasonable and affectionate enough to separate your person from your government, so *you*, in your turn, should distinguish between the conduct which becomes the permanent dignity of a king and that which serves only to promote the temporary interest and miserable ambition of a minister.

You ascended the throne with a declared and, I doubt not, a sincere resolution of giving universal satisfaction to your subjects. You found them pleased with the novelty of a young prince whose countenance promised even more than his words, and loyal to you not only from principle but passion. It was not a cold profession of allegiance to the first magistrate, but a partial, animated attachment to a favourite prince, the native of their country. They did not wait to examine your conduct, nor to be determined by experience, but gave you a generous credit for the future blessings of your reign, and paid you in advance the dearest tribute of their affections. Such, sir, was once the disposition of a people who now surround your throne with reproaches and complaints. Do justice to yourself. Banish from your mind those unworthy opinions with which some interested persons have laboured to possess you. Distrust the men who tell you that the English are naturally light and inconstant — that they complain without a cause. Withdraw your confidence equally from all parties — from ministers, favourites, and relations; and let there be one moment in your life in which you have consulted your own understanding.

*When you affectedly renounced the name of Englishman, believe me, sir, you were persuaded to pay a very ill-judged compliment to one part of your subjects at the expense of another. While the natives of Scotland are not in actual rebellion, they are undoubtedly entitled to protection, nor do I mean to condemn the policy of giving some encouragement to the novelty of their affections for the house of Hanover. I am ready to hope for everything from their new-born zeal, and from the future steadiness of their allegiance. But hitherto they have no claim to your favour. To honour them with a determined predilection and confidence, in exclusion of your English subjects who placed your family, and in spite of treachery and rebellion have supported it, upon the throne, is a mistake too gross even for the unsuspecting generosity of youth. In this error we see a capital violation of the most obvious rules of policy and prudence. We trace it, however, to an original bias in your education, and are ready to allow for your inexperience.

To the same early influence we attribute it that you have descended to take a share not only in the narrow views and interests of particular persons, but in the fatal malignity of their passions. At your accession to the throne the whole system of government was altered, not from wisdom or deliberation, but because it had been adopted by your predecessor. A little personal motive of pique and resentment was sufficient to remove the ablest servants of the crown; but it is not in this country, sir, that such men can be dishonoured by the frowns of a king. They were dismissed, but could not be disgraced. Without entering into a minuter discussion of the merits of the peace, we may observe, in the imprudent hurry with which the first overtures from France were accepted, in the conduct of the negotiation, and terms of the treaty, the strongest marks of that precipitate spirit of concession with which a certain part of your subjects have been at all times ready to purchase a peace with the *natural enemies* of this country. On *your* part we are satisfied that everything was honourable and sincere, and if England was sold to France, we doubt not that your Majesty was equally betrayed. The conditions of the peace were matter of grief and surprise to your subjects, but not the immediate cause of their present discontent.

Hitherto, sir, you had been sacrificed to the prejudices and passions of others. With what firmness will you bear the mention of your own?

*A man, not very honourably distinguished in the world, commences a formal attack upon your favourite, considering nothing but how he might best expose his person and principles to detestation, and the national character of his countrymen to contempt. The natives of that country, sir, are as much distinguished by a peculiar character as by your Majesty's favour. Like another chosen people, they have been conducted into the land of plenty, where they find themselves effectually marked, and divided from mankind. There is hardly a period at which the most irregular character may not be redeemed. The mistakes of one sex find a retreat in patriotism; those of the other in devotion. Mr. Wilkes brought with him into politics the same liberal sentiments by which his private conduct had been directed, and seemed to think that as there are few excesses in which an English gentleman may not be permitted to indulge, the same latitude was allowed him in the choice of his political principles, and in the spirit of maintaining them. I mean to state, not entirely to defend, his conduct. In the earnestness of his zeal he suffered some unwarrantable insinuations to escape him. He said more than moderate men would justify, but not enough to entitle him to the honour of your Majesty's personal resentment. The rays of royal indignation collected upon him served only to illuminate, and could not consume. Animated by the favour of the people on one side, and heated by persecution on the other, his views and sentiments changed with his situation. Hardly serious at first, he is now an enthusiast. The coldest bodies warm with opposition, the hardest sparkle in collision. There is a holy mistaken zeal in politics as well as in religion. By persuading others, we convince ourselves. The passions are engaged, and create a maternal affection in the mind, which forces us to love the cause for which we suffer. Is this a contention worthy of a king? Are you not sensible how much the meanness of the cause gives an air of ridicule to the serious difficulties into which you have been betrayed? The destruction of one man has been now for many years the sole object of your government; and if there can be anything still more disgraceful, we have seen for such an object the utmost influence of the executive power and every ministerial artifice exerted, without success. Nor can you ever succeed, unless *he* should be imprudent enough to forfeit the protection of those laws to which you owe your crown, or unless your ministers should persuade you to make it a question of force alone, and try the whole strength of government in opposition to the people. The lessons *he* has received from experience, will probably guard him from such excess of folly, and in your Majesty's virtues we find an unquestionable assurance that no illegal violence will be attempted.

Far from suspecting you of so horrible a design, we would attribute the continued violation of the laws, and even this last enormous attack upon the vital principles of the constitution, to an ill-advised, unworthy personal resentment. From one false step you have been betrayed into another, and as the cause was unworthy of you, your ministers were determined that the prudence of the execution should correspond with the wisdom and dignity of the design. They have reduced you to the necessity of choosing out of a variety of difficulties — to a situation so unhappy that you can neither do wrong without ruin, nor right without affliction. These worthy servants have undoubtedly given you many singular proofs of their abilities. Not contented with making Mr. Wilkes a man of importance, they have judiciously transferred the question from the rights and interests of one man to the most important rights and interests of the people, and forced your subjects from wishing well to the cause of an individual, to unite with him in their own. Let them proceed as they have begun, and your Majesty need not doubt that the catastrophe will do no dishonour to the conduct of the piece.

The circumstances to which you are reduced will not admit of a compromise with the English nation. Undecisive, qualifying measures will disgrace your government still more than open violence, and without satisfying the people will excite their contempt. They have too much understanding and spirit to accept of an indirect satisfaction for a direct injury. Nothing less than a repeal, as formal as the resolution itself, can heal the wound which has been given to the constitution, nor will anything less be accepted. I can readily believe that there is an influence sufficient to recall that pernicious vote. The House of Commons undoubtedly consider their duty to the crown as paramount to all other obligations. To *us* they are only indebted for an accidental existence, and have justly transferred their gratitude from their parents to their benefactors — from those who gave them birth to the minister from whose benevolence they derive the comforts and pleasures of their political life, who has taken the tenderest care of their infancy, and relieves their necessities without offending their delicacy. But, if it were possible for their integrity to be degraded to a condition so vile and abject that, compared with it, the present estimation they stand in is a state of honour and respect, consider, sir, in what manner you will afterwards proceed. Can you conceive that the people of this country will long submit to be governed by so flexible a House of Commons? It is not in the nature of human society that any form of government, in such circumstances, can long be preserved. In ours, the general contempt of the people is as fatal as their detestation. Such, I am persuaded, would be the necessary effect of any base concession made by the present House of Commons, and, as a qualifying measure would not be accepted, it remains for you to decide whether you will, at any hazard, support a set of men who have reduced you to this unhappy dilemma, or whether you will gratify the united wishes of the whole people of England by dissolving the Parliament.

Taking it for granted, as I do very sincerely, that you have personally no design against the constitution, nor any views inconsistent with the good of your subjects, I think you cannot hesitate long upon the choice, which it equally concerns your interest and your honour to adopt. On one side you hazard the affections of all your English subjects — you relinquish every hope of repose to yourself, and you endanger the establishment of your family forever. All this you venture for no object whatsoever, or for such an object as it would be an affront to you to name. Men of sense will examine your conduct with suspicion, while those who are incapable of comprehending to what degree they are injured, afflict you with clamours equally insolent and unmeaning. Supposing it possible that no fatal struggle should ensue, you determine at once to be unhappy, without the hope of a compensation either from interest or ambition. If an English king be hated or despised, he *must* be unhappy; and this, perhaps, is the only political truth which he ought to be convinced of without experiment. But if the English people should no longer confine their resentment to a submissive representation of their wrongs; if, following the glorious example of their ancestors, they should no longer appeal to the creature of the constitution, but to that high Being who gave them the rights of humanity, whose gifts it were sacrilege to surrender — let me ask you, sir, upon what part of your subjects would you rely for assistance?

The people of Ireland have been uniformly plundered and oppressed. In return, they give you every day fresh marks of their resentment. They despise the miserable governor you have sent them, because he is the creature of Lord Bute; nor is it from any natural confusion in their ideas that they are so ready to confound the original of a king with the disgraceful representation of him.

The distance of the colonies would make it impossible for them to take an active concern in your affairs, if they were as well affected to your government as they once pretended to be to your person. They were ready enough to distinguish between *you* and your ministers. * They complained of an act of the legislature, but traced the origin of it no higher than to the servants of the crown; they pleased themselves with the hope that their sovereign, if not favourable to their cause, at least was impartial. The decisive personal part you took against them has effectually banished that first distinction from their minds. They consider you as united with your servants against America, and know how to distinguish the sovereign and a venal Parliament on one side, from the real sentiments of the English people on the other. Looking forward to independence, they might possibly receive you for their king; but if ever you retire to America, be assured they will give you such a Covenant to digest as the Presbytery of Scotland would have been ashamed to offer to Charles the Second. They left their native land in search of freedom, and found it in a desert. Divided as they are into a thousand forms of policy and religion, there is one point in which they all agree: they equally detest the pageantry of a king and the supercilious hypocrisy of a bishop.

It is not, then, from the alienated affections of Ireland or America that you can reasonably look for assistance; still less from the people of England, who are actually contending for their rights, and in this great question are parties against you. You are not, however, destitute of every appearance of support; you have all the Jacobites, Nonjurors, Roman Catholics, and Tories of this country, and all Scotland, without exception. Considering from what family you are descended, the choice of your friends has been singularly directed; and truly, sir, if you had not lost the Whig interest of England, I should admire your dexterity in turning the hearts of your enemies. Is it possible for you to place any confidence in men who, before they are faithful to you, must renounce every opinion and betray every principle, both in church and state, which they inherit from their ancestors, and are confirmed in by their education? whose numbers are so inconsiderable that they have long since been obliged to give up the principles and language which distinguish them as a party, and to fight under the banners of their enemies? Their zeal begins with hypocrisy, and must conclude in treachery. At first they deceive — at last they betray.

As to the Scotch, I must suppose your heart and understanding so biased, from your earliest infancy, in their favour, that nothing less than *your own* misfortunes can undeceive you. You will not accept of the uniform experience of your ancestors; and, when once a man is determined to believe, the very absurdity of the doctrine confirms him in his faith. A bigoted understanding can draw a proof of attachment to the house of Hanover from a notorious zeal for the house of Stuart, and find an earnest of future loyalty in former rebellions. Appearances are, however, in their favour — so strongly, indeed, that one would think they had forgotten that you are their lawful king, and had mistaken you for a pretender to the crown. Let it be admitted, then, that the Scotch are as sincere in their present professions as if you were in reality not an Englishman, but a Briton of the North. You would not be the first prince of their native country against whom they have rebelled, nor the first whom they have basely betrayed. Have you forgotten, sir, or has your favourite concealed from you * that part of our history when the unhappy Charles (and he too had private virtues) fled from the open, avowed indignation of his English subjects, and surrendered himself at discretion to the good faith of his own countrymen? Without looking for support in their affections as subjects, he applied only to their honour as gentlemen for protection. They received him as they would your Majesty, with bows, and smiles, and falsehood, and kept him until they had settled their bargain with the English Parliament; then basely sold their native king to the vengeance of his enemies. This, sir, was not the act of a few traitors, but the deliberate treachery of a Scotch Parliament representing the nation. A wise prince might draw from it two lessons of equal utility to himself. On one side he might learn to dread the undisguised resentment of a generous people, who dare openly assert their rights, and who, in a just cause, are ready to meet their sovereign in the field. On the other side, he would be taught to apprehend something far more formidable — a fawning treachery against which no prudence can guard, no courage can defend. The insidious smile upon the cheek would warn him of the canker in the heart.

From * the uses to which one part of the army has been too frequently applied, you have some reason to expect that there are no services they would refuse. Here, too, we trace the partiality of your understanding. You take the sense of the army from the conduct of the guards, with the same justice with which you collect the sense of the people from the representations of the ministry. Your marching regiments, sir, will not make the guards their example, either as soldiers or subjects. They feel, and resent — as they ought to do — that invariable, undistinguishing favour with which the guards are treated; while those gallant troops by whom every hazardous, every laborious service is performed, are left to perish in garrisons abroad, or pine in quarters at home, neglected and forgotten. If they had no sense of the great original duty they owe their country, their resentment would operate like patriotism, and leave your cause to be defended by those to whom you have lavished the rewards and honours of their profession. The Prætorian bands, enervated and debauched as they were, had still strength enough to awe the Roman populace; but when the distant legions took the alarm, they marched to Rome, and gave away the empire.

On this side, then, whichever way you turn your eyes, you see nothing but perplexity and distress. You may determine to support the very ministry who have reduced your affairs to this deplorable situation; you may shelter yourself under the forms of a Parliament, and set your people at defiance; but be assured, sir, that such a resolution would be as imprudent as it would be odious. If it did not immediately shake your establishment, it would rob you of your peace of mind forever.

On the other, how different is the prospect! How easy, how safe and honourable is the path before you! The English nation declare they are grossly injured by their representatives, and solicit your Majesty to exert your lawful prerogative, and give them an opportunity of recalling a trust which, they find, has been scandalously abused. You are not to be told that the power of the House of Commons is not original, but delegated to them for the welfare of the people from whom they received it. A question of right arises between the constituent and the representative body. By what authority shall it be decided? Will your Majesty interfere in a question in which you have properly no immediate concern? It would be a step equally odious and unnecessary. Shall the Lords be called upon to determine the rights and privileges of the Commons? They cannot do it without a flagrant breach of the constitution. Or will you refer it to the judges? They have often told your ancestors that the law of Parliament is above them. What party then remains but to leave it to the people to determine for themselves? They alone are injured; and, since there is no superior power to which the cause can be referred, they alone ought to determine.

I do not mean to perplex you with a tedious argument upon a subject already so discussed that inspiration could hardly throw a new light upon it. There are, however, two points of view in which it particularly imports your Majesty to consider the late proceedings of the House of Commons. By depriving a subject of his birthright, they have attributed to their own vote an authority equal to an act of the whole legislature; and, though perhaps not with the same motives, have strictly followed the example of * the Long Parliament, which first declared the regal office useless, and soon after, with as little ceremony, dissolved the House of Lords. The same pretended power which robs an English subject of his birthright may rob an English king of his crown. In another view, the resolution of the House of Commons, apparently not so dangerous to your Majesty, is still more alarming to your people. Not contented with divesting one man of his right, they have arbitrarily conveyed that right to another. They have set aside a return as illegal, without daring to censure those officers who were particularly apprized of Mr. Wilkes's incapacity, not only by the declaration of the House, but expressly by the writ directed to them, and who, nevertheless, returned him as duly elected. They have rejected the majority of votes, the only criterion by which our laws judge of the sense of the people; they have transferred the right of election from the collective to the representative body; and, by these acts, taken separately or together, they have essentially altered the original constitution of the House of Commons. Versed as your Majesty undoubtedly is in the English history, it cannot easily escape you how much it is your interest, as well as your duty, to prevent one of the three estates from encroaching upon the province of the other two, or assuming the authority of them all. When once they have departed from the great constitutional line by which all their proceedings should be directed, who will answer for their future moderation? Or what assurance will they give you that when they have trampled upon their equals they will submit to a superior? Your Majesty may learn hereafter how nearly the slave and tyrant are allied.

Some of your council, more candid than the rest, admit the abandoned profligacy of the present House of Commons, but oppose their dissolution upon an opinion, I confess not very unwarrantable, that their successors would be equally at the disposal of the treasury. I cannot persuade myself that the nation will have profited so little by experience. But if that opinion were well founded, you might then gratify our wishes at an easy rate, and appease the present clamour against your government, without offering any material injury to the favourite cause of corruption.

You still have an honourable part to act. The affections of your subjects may still be recovered. But before you subdue *their* hearts you must gain a noble victory over your own. Discard those little personal resentments which have too long directed your public conduct. Pardon this man the remainder of his punishment; and, if resentment still prevails, make it what it should have been long since — an act, not of mercy, but contempt. He will soon fall back into his natural station — a silent senator, and hardly supporting the weekly eloquence of a newspaper. The gentle breath of peace would leave him on the surface neglected and unremoved. It is only the tempest that lifts him from his place.

Without consulting your minister, call together your whole council. Let it appear to the public that you can determine and act for yourself. Come forward to your people. Lay aside the wretched formalities of a king, and speak to your subjects with the spirit of a man, and in the language of a gentleman. Tell them you have been fatally deceived. The acknowledgment will be no disgrace, but rather an honour to your understanding. Tell them you are determined to remove every cause of complaint against your government, that you will give your confidence to no man who does not possess the confidence of your subjects; and leave it to themselves to determine, by their conduct at a future election, whether or no it be in reality the general sense of the nation that their rights have been arbitrarily invaded by the present House of Commons, and the constitution betrayed. They will then do justice to their representatives and to themselves.

These sentiments, sir, and the style they are conveyed in, may be offensive, perhaps, because they are new to you. Accustomed to the language of courtiers, you measure their affections by the vehemence of their expressions; and when they only praise you indirectly, you admire their sincerity. But this is not a time to trifle with your fortune. They deceive you, sir, who tell you that you have many friends whose affections are founded upon a principle of personal attachment. The first foundation of friendship is not the power of conferring benefits, but the equality with which they are received and *may* be returned. The fortune which made you a king forbade you to have a friend. It is a law of nature, which cannot be violated with impunity. The mistaken prince who looks for friendship will find a favourite, and in that favourite the ruin of his affairs.

The people of England are loyal to the house of Hanover, not from a vain preference of one family to another, but from a conviction that the establishment of that family was necessary to the support of their civil and religious liberties. This, sir, is a principle of allegiance equally solid and rational, fit for Englishmen to adopt, and well worthy of your Majesty's encouragement. We cannot long be deluded by nominal distinctions. The name of Stuart, of itself, is only contemptible; armed with the sovereign authority, their principles are formidable. The prince who imitates their conduct should be warned by their example; and, while he plumes himself upon the security of his titie to the crown, should remember that, as it was acquired by one revolution, it may be lost by another.

JUNIUS

EDMUND BURKE

Among the strong men in Johnson's Club Edmund Burke was outstanding. Once, when Johnson was protesting against the attribution of extraordinary powers to any one, he said, "You do not see one man shoot a great deal higher than another." But when Boswell mentioned Burke, the doctor replied, "Yes, Burke *is* an extraordinary man. His stream of mind is perpetual." On another occasion, when Johnson was ill, he said of Burke, "That fellow calls forth all my powers. Were I to see Burke now it would kill me." In the course of a long life of public service Burke established in the wider field of statesmanship the same eminence that had been recognized long before by his associates in the club.

He was at the same time a statesman and a man of letters. "What makes Burke stand out so splendidly among politicians," said Matthew Arnold, "is that he treats politics with his thought and imagination." He treated political questions with the thought of a philosopher and the imagination of a poet. He raised political debate to the highest level of statesmanship, and he created literature while he was moulding public sentiment.

Burke's writings cover more than forty years and bulk large. *A Philosophical Inquiry into the Origin of our Ideas of the Sublime and the Beautiful*, 1756, is an important contribution to esthetics. The same year he published *A Vindication of Natural Society* in which he satirized the work of Bolingbroke. He did some historical writing and contributed to the *Annual Register* for many years, but with his active participation in politics he devoted more and more of his time and attention to speeches and pamphlets on public affairs.

The three questions in connection with which he is most frequently remembered are those concerned with American affairs in the seventies, Indian affairs, chiefly in the eighties, and the French Revolution in the nineties. His position on the first two was distinctly liberal: he favoured conciliation with the American colonies, and took a leading part in the prosecution of Warren Hastings for misconduct in India. In the first he was unsuccessful, for the American colonies were lost to Great Britain; in the second he failed of his immediate purpose, for Hastings was acquitted, but he did much to reform the administration of British government in India. In the third he was completely successful, for, though England would certainly have continued her traditional policy of opposition to France under the Revolutionary and Napoleonic régimes had Burke never lived, it was he who took the leading part in unifying popular sentiment during the crisis.

Many have contrasted the reactionary spirit of Burke during this last period of his life with the liberalism of the earlier periods and have attributed it to his advancing age. To the radical thinkers of his own time he appeared a lost leader. To the present-day reader, who surveys his work as a whole, however, it is evident that Burke was consistent. He was, in the true sense of the word, conservative throughout. He sought always to conserve the best in British traditions and in British institutions. Society was for him an organic whole which had slowly evolved in response to the most fundamental human needs; it was the product of the collective experience; it embodied the wisdom of the general sense. It was not perfect, but in its essentials it was right because it had the sanction of tradition and the prescription of custom. The wisdom of many generations was to be preferred to untried theories or to the vagaries of individual judgment.

In this insistence upon the general sense Burke was a classicist, for it can scarcely be too much emphasized that classicism is a way of life and not merely an attitude toward literature or even toward art in general. Burke applied to statesmanship the classical sense of moderation, the classical respect for antiquity, the classical standards based upon a conviction that those things are best which have been long tried and found satisfactory by the best qualified judges. The same principles that Johnson applied to literature and Reynolds to painting, Burke applied to government. To assert that he was romantic because of the imaginative power of his sympathy or because of his ability to invest with interest and colour the past experiences of the race is to assume that these powers of the poetic mind are the exclusive attributes of the romantic school. By such standards Virgil was a romantic.

A Letter to a Noble Lord, 1796, is at once Burke's *apologia* and an impassioned arraignment of those Englishmen who either from philosophical attachment to the "Rights of Man" or from opposition to the government, sympathized with the French Revolution. It is personal controversy elevated to the highest level of political thought and kindled by poetic imagination. This letter has been described as "the most splendid repartee in the English language."

Any consideration of Burke's prose style must take into account his many years of public speaking, just as any consideration of his oratory must take into account the fact that most of his speeches were more effective in the study than in the senate. If his oratory suffered because the thought was packed too close for ordinary hearers to follow, his writing certainly gained from the structural design and the passionate utterance that he had practised in oral delivery. His prose is direct, well articulated, economical; it is admirably adapted to his purpose, forthright, majestic, eloquent as occasion demands.

The selections here reprinted are from his last period. Both are in the form of the public letter, something between the rigidity of the treatise and the informality of private correspondence. It was a type popular in the eighteenth century and one suited to Burke's genius. The extract from *Reflections on the Revolution in France*, 1790, is from the first part and is complete so far as it goes; *A Letter to a Noble Lord* is quoted entire.

From * REFLECTIONS ON THE REVOLUTION IN FRANCE

... It is no wonder, therefore, that with these ideas of everything in their constitution and government at home, either in church or state, as illegitimate and usurped, or at best as a vain mockery, * they look abroad with an eager and passionate enthusiasm. Whilst they are possessed by these notions, it is vain to talk to them of the practice of their ancestors, the fundamental laws of their country, the fixed form of a constitution, whose merits are confirmed by the solid test of long experience, and an increasing public strength and national prosperity. They despise experience as the wisdom of unlettered men; and as for the rest, they have wrought underground a mine that will blow up, at one grand explosion, all examples of antiquity, all precedents, charters, and acts of Parliament. They have "the rights of men." Against these there can be no prescription; against these no agreement is binding: these admit no temperament and no compromise: anything withheld from their full demand is so much of fraud and injustice. Against these their rights of men let no government look for security in the length of its continuance, or in the justice and lenity of its administration. The objections of these speculatists, if its forms do not quadrate with their theories, are as valid against such an old and beneficent government, as against the most violent tyranny, or the greenest usurpation. They are always at issue with governments, not on a question of abuse, but a question of competency, and a question of title. I have nothing to say to the clumsy subtilty of their political metaphysics. Let them be their amusement in the schools. — * *Illa se jactet in aula — Æolus, et clauso ventorum carcere regnet.*— But let them not break prison to burst like * a *Levanter*, to sweep the earth with their hurricane, and to break up the fountains of the great deep to overwhelm us.

Far am I from denying in theory; full as far is my heart from withholding in practice (if I were of power to give or to withhold), the *real* rights of men. In denying their false claims of right, I do not mean to injure those which are real, and are such as their pretended rights would totally destroy. If civil society be made for the advantage of man, all the advantages for which it is made become his right. It is an institution of beneficence; and law itself is only beneficence acting by a rule. Men have a right to live by that rule; they have a right to do justice, as between their fellows, whether their fellows are in public function or in ordinary occupation. They have a right to the fruits of their industry, and to the means of making their industry fruitful. They have a right to the acquisitions of their parents, to the nourishment and improvement of their offspring, to instruction in life, and to consolation in death. Whatever each man can separately do, without trespassing upon others, he has a right to do for himself; and he has a right to a fair portion of all which society, with all its combinations of skill and force, can do in his favour. In this partnership all men have equal rights, but not to equal things. He that has but five shillings in the partnership, has as good a right to it, as he that has five hundred pounds has to his larger proportion. But he has not a right to an equal dividend in the product of the joint stock; and as to the share of power, authority, and direction which each individual ought to have in the management of the state, that I must deny to be amongst the direct original rights of man in civil society; for I have in my contemplation the civil social man, and no other. It is a thing to be settled by convention.

If civil society be the offspring of convention, that convention must be its law. That

* Notes on Edmund Burke will be found in the Appendix, pp. 1050 ff.

convention must limit and modify all the descriptions of constitution which are formed under it. Every sort of legislative, judicial, or executory power are its creatures. They can have no being in any other state of things; and how can any man claim, under the conventions of civil society, rights which do not so much as suppose its existence? rights which are absolutely repugnant to it? One of the first motives to civil society, and which becomes one of its fundamental rules, is *that no man should be judge in his own cause.* By this each person has at once divested himself of the first fundamental right of uncovenanted man, that is, to judge for himself, and to assert his own cause. He abdicates all right to be his own governor. He inclusively, in a great measure, abandons the right of self-defence, the first law of nature. Men cannot enjoy the rights of an uncivil and of a civil state together. That he may obtain justice, he gives up his right of determining what it is in points the most essential to him. That he may secure some liberty, he makes a surrender in trust of the whole of it.

Government is not made in virtue of natural rights, which may and do exist in total independence of it; and exist in much greater clearness, and in a much greater degree of abstract perfection: but their abstract perfection is their practical defect. By having a right to everything they want everything. Government is a contrivance of human wisdom to provide for human *wants.* Men have a right that these wants should be provided for by this wisdom. Among these wants is to be reckoned the want, out of civil society, of a sufficient restraint upon their passions. Society requires not only that the passions of individuals should be subjected, but that even in the mass and body, as well as in the individuals, the inclinations of men should frequently be thwarted, their will controlled, and their passions brought into subjection. This can only be done *by a power out of themselves*; and not, in the exercise of its function, subject to that will and to those passions which it is its office to bridle and subdue. In this sense the restraints on men, as well as their liberties, are to be reckoned among their rights. But as the liberties and the restrictions vary with times and circumstances, and admit of infinite modifications, they cannot be settled upon any abstract rule; and nothing is so foolish as to discuss them upon that principle.

The moment you abate anything from the full rights of men, each to govern himself, and suffer any artificial, positive limitation upon those rights, from that moment the whole organization of government becomes a consideration of convenience. This it is which makes the constitution of a state, and the due distribution of its powers, a matter of the most delicate and complicated skill. It requires a deep knowledge of human nature and human necessities, and of the things which facilitate or obstruct the various ends which are to be pursued by the mechanism of civil institutions. The state is to have recruits to its strength, and remedies to its distempers. What is the use of discussing a man's abstract right to food or medicine? The question is upon the method of procuring and administering them. In that deliberation I shall always advise to call in the aid of the farmer and the physician, rather than the professor of metaphysics.

The science of constructing a commonwealth, or renovating it, or reforming it, is, like every other experimental science, not to be taught *a priori.* Nor is it a short experience that can instruct us in that practical science, because the real effects of moral causes are not always immediate; but that which in the first instance is prejudicial may be excellent in its remoter operation; and its excellence may arise even from the ill effects it produces in the beginning. The reverse also happens; and very plausible schemes, with very pleasing commencements, have often shameful and lamentable conclusions. In states there are often some obscure and almost latent causes, things which appear at first view of little moment, on which a very great part of its prosperity or adversity may most essentially depend. The science of government being therefore so practical in itself, and intended for such practical purposes, a matter which requires experience, and even more experience than any person can gain in his whole life, however sagacious and observing he may be, it is with infinite caution that any man ought to venture upon pulling down an edifice, which has answered in any tolerable degree for ages the common purposes of society, or on building it up again, without having models and patterns of approved utility before his eyes.

These metaphysic rights entering into common life, like rays of light which pierce into a dense medium, are, by the laws of nature, refracted from their straight line. Indeed in the gross and complicated mass of human passions and concerns, the primitive rights of men undergo such a variety of refractions and reflections that it becomes absurd to talk of them as if they continued in the simplicity of their original direction. The nature of man is intricate; the objects of society are of the greatest possible complexity: and therefore no simple disposition or direction of power can be suitable either to man's nature, or to the quality of his affairs. When I hear the simplicity of contrivance aimed at and boasted of in any new political constitutions, I am at no loss to decide that the artificers are grossly ignorant of their trade, or totally negligent of their duty. The simple governments are fundamentally defective, to say no worse of them. If you were to contemplate society in but one point of view, all these simple modes of polity are infinitely captivating. In effect each would answer its single end much more perfectly than the more complex is able to attain all its complex purposes. But it is better that the whole should be imperfectly and anomalously answered, than that, while some parts are provided for with great exactness, others might be totally neglected, or perhaps materially injured, by the over-care of a favourite member.

The pretended rights of these theorists are all extremes; and in proportion as they are metaphysically true, they are morally and politically false. The rights of men are in a sort of *middle*, incapable of definition, but not impossible to be discerned. The rights of men in governments are their advantages; and these are often in balances between differences of good; in compromises sometimes between good and evil, and sometimes between evil and evil. Political reason is a computing principle; adding, subtracting, multiplying, and dividing, morally and not metaphysically, or mathematically, true moral denominations.

By these theorists the right of the people is almost always sophistically confounded with their power. The body of the community, whenever it can come to act, can meet with no effectual resistance; but till power and right are the same, the whole body of them has no right inconsistent with virtue, and the first of all virtues, prudence. Men have no right to what is not reasonable, and to what is not for their benefit; for though a pleasant writer said, * *Liceat perire poetis*, when one of them, in cold blood, is said to have leaped into the flames of a volcanic revolution, * *Ardentem frigidus Ætnam insiluit*, I consider such a frolic rather as an unjustifiable poetic licence than as one of the franchises of Parnassus; and whether he were poet, or divine, or politician that chose to exercise this kind of right, I think that more wise, because more charitable, thoughts would urge me rather to save the man, than to preserve his brazen slippers as the monuments of his folly.

The kind of anniversary sermons to which a great part of what I write refers, if men are not shamed out of their present course, in commemorating the fact will cheat many out of the principles, and deprive them of the benefits, of the revolution they commemorate. I confess to you, sir, I never liked this continual talk of resistance, and revolution, or the practice of making the extreme medicine of the constitution its daily bread. It renders the habit of society dangerously valetudinary: it is taking periodical doses of mercury sublimate, and swallowing down repeated provocatives of cantharides to our love of liberty.

This distemper of remedy, grown habitual, relaxes and wears out, by a vulgar and prostituted use, the spring of that spirit which is to be exerted on great occasions. It was in the most patient period of Roman servitude that themes of tyrannicide made the ordinary exercise of boys at school — * *cum perimit sævos classis numerosa tyrannos*. In the ordinary state of things, it produces in a country like ours the worst effects, even on the cause of that liberty which it abuses with the dissoluteness of an extravagant speculation. Almost all the high-bred republicans of my time have, after a short space, become the most decided, thorough-paced courtiers; they soon left the business of a tedious, moderate, but practical resistance, to those of us whom, in the pride and intoxication of their theories, they have slighted as not much better than Tories. Hypocrisy, of course, delights in the most sublime speculations; for, never intending to go beyond speculation, it costs nothing to have it magnificent. But even in cases where rather levity than fraud was to be suspected in these ranting speculations, the issue has been much the same. These professors, finding their extreme principles not applicable to cases which call only for a qualified, or, as I may say, civil and legal resistance, in such cases employ no resistance at all. It is with them a war or a revolution, or it is nothing. Finding their schemes of politics not adapted to the state of the world in which they live, they often come to think lightly of all public principle; and are ready, on their part, to abandon for a very trivial interest what they find of very trivial value. Some indeed are of more steady and persevering natures; but these are eager politicians out of Parliament, who have little to tempt them to abandon their favourite projects. They have some change in the church or state, or both, constantly in their view. When that is the case, they are always bad citizens, and perfectly unsure connections. For, considering their speculative designs as of infinite value, and the actual arrangement of the state as of no estimation, they are at best indifferent about it. They see no merit in the good, and no fault in the vicious, management of public affairs; they rather rejoice in the latter, as more propitious to revolution. They see no merit or demerit in any man, or any action, or any political principle, any further than as they may forward or retard their design of change: they therefore take up, one day, the most violent and stretched prerogative, and another time the wildest democratic ideas of freedom, and pass from the one to the other without any sort of regard to cause, to person, or to party.

In France you are now in the crisis of a revolution, and in the transit from one form of government to another — you cannot see that character of men exactly in the same situation in which we see it in this country. With us it is militant; with you it is triumphant; and you know how it can act when its power is commensurate to its will. I would not be supposed to confine those observations to any description of men, or to comprehend all men of any description within them. No! far from it. I am as incapable of that injustice, as I am of keeping terms with those who profess principles of extremities; and who, under the name of religion, teach little else than wild and dangerous politics. The worst of these politics of revolution is this: they temper and harden the breast, in order to prepare it for the desperate strokes which are sometimes used in extreme occasions. But as these occasions may never arrive, the mind receives a gratuitous taint; and the moral sentiments suffer not a little, when no political purpose is served by the deprivation. This sort of people are so taken up with their theories about the rights of man that they have totally forgotten his nature. Without opening one new avenue to the understanding, they have succeeded in stopping up those that lead to the heart. They have perverted in themselves, and in those that attend to them, all the well-placed sympathies of the human breast.

This famous sermon of *the Old Jewry breathes nothing but this spirit through all the political part. Plots, massacres, assassinations seem to some people a trivial price for obtaining a revolution. A cheap, bloodless reformation, a guiltless liberty, appear flat and vapid to their taste. There must be a great change of scene; there must be a magnificent stage effect; there must be a grand spectacle to rouse the imagination, grown torpid with the lazy enjoyment of sixty years' security, and the still unanimating repose of public prosperity. The preacher found them all in the French Revolution. This inspires a juvenile warmth through his whole frame. His enthusiasm kindles as he advances; and when he arrives at his peroration it is in a full blaze. Then viewing, from the Pisgah of his pulpit, the free, moral, happy, flourishing, and glorious state of France, as in a bird's-eye landscape of a promised land, he breaks out into the following rapture:

"What an eventful period is this! I am *thankful* that I have lived to it; I could almost say, *'Lord, now lettest thou thy servant depart in peace, for mine eyes have seen thy salvation.' I have lived to see a *diffusion* of knowledge, which has undermined superstition and error. I have lived to see *the rights of men* better understood than ever; and nations panting for liberty which seemed to have lost the idea of it. I have lived to see *thirty millions of people*, indignant and resolute, spurning at slavery, and demanding liberty with an irresistible voice. *Their king led in triumph, and an arbitrary monarch surrendering himself to his subjects.*"

Before I proceed further, I have to remark that Dr. Price seems rather to overvalue the great acquisitions of light which he has obtained and diffused in this age. The last century appears to me to have been quite as much enlightened. It had, though in a different place, a triumph as memorable as that of Dr. Price; and some of the great preachers of that period partook of it as eagerly as he has done in the triumph of France. On the trial of *the Rev. Hugh Peters for high treason, it was deposed that when King Charles was brought to London for his trial, the Apostle of Liberty in that day conducted the *triumph.* "I saw," says the witness, "his Majesty in the coach with six horses, and Peters riding before the king, *triumphing.*" Dr. Price, when he talks as if he had made a discovery, only follows a precedent; for, after the commencement of the king's trial, this precursor, the same Dr. Peters, concluding a long prayer at the Royal Chapel at Whitehall (he had very triumphantly chosen his place), said, "I have prayed and preached these twenty years; and now I may say with old Simeon, 'Lord, now lettest thou thy servant depart in peace, for mine eyes have seen thy salvation.'" Peters had not the fruits of his prayer; for he neither departed so soon as he wished, nor in peace. He became (what I heartily hope none of his followers may be in this country) himself a sacrifice to the triumph which he led as pontiff. They dealt at the Restoration, perhaps, too hardly with this poor good man. But we owe it to his memory and his sufferings that he had as much illumination and as much zeal, and had as effectually undermined all *the superstition and error* which might impede the great business he was engaged in, as any who follow and repeat after him, in this age, which would assume to itself an exclusive title to the knowledge of the rights of men, and all the glorious consequences of that knowledge.

After this sally of the preacher of the Old Jewry, which differs only in place and time, but agrees perfectly with the spirit and letter of the rapture of 1648, the Revolution Society, the fabricators of governments, the heroic band of *cashierers of monarchs*, electors of sovereigns, and leaders of kings in triumph, strutting with a proud consciousness of the diffusion of knowledge, of which every member had obtained so large a share in the donative, were in haste to make a generous diffusion of the knowledge they had thus gratuitously received. To make this bountiful communication, they adjourned from the church in the Old Jewry to the London Tavern; where the same Dr. Price, in whom the fumes of his oracular tripod were not entirely evaporated, moved and carried the resolution, or address of congratulation, transmitted by Lord Stanhope to the National Assembly of France.

I find a preacher of the gospel profaning the beautiful and prophetic ejaculation, commonly called *Nunc Dimittis*, made on the first presentation of our Savior in the temple, and applying it, with an inhuman and unnatural rapture, to the most horrid, atrocious, and afflicting spectacle that perhaps ever was exhibited to the pity and indignation of mankind. This "leading in triumph," a thing in its best form unmanly and irreligious, which fills our preacher with such unhallowed transports, must shock, I believe, the moral taste of every well-born mind. Several English were the stupified and indignant spectators of that triumph. It was (unless we have been strangely deceived) a spectacle more resembling a procession of American savages entering into Onondaga after some of their murders called victories, and leading into hovels hung round with scalps, their captives, overpowered with the scoffs and buffets of women as ferocious as themselves, much more than it resembled the triumphal pomp of a civilized, martial nation; — if a civilized nation, or any men who had a sense of generosity, were capable of a personal triumph over the fallen and afflicted.

This, my dear sir, was not the triumph of France. I must believe that, as a nation, it overwhelmed you with shame and horror. I must believe that the National Assembly find themselves in a state of the greatest humiliation in not being able to punish the authors of this triumph, or the actors in it; and that they are in a situation in which any inquiry they may make upon the subject must be destitute even of the appearance of liberty or impartiality. The apology of that assembly is found in their situation; but when we approve what they *must* bear, it is in us the degenerate choice of a vitiated mind.

With a compelled appearance of deliberation, they vote under the dominion of a stern necessity. They sit in the heart, as it were, of *a foreign republic; they have their residence in a city whose constitution has emanated neither from the charter of their king, nor from their legislative power. There they are surrounded by an army not raised either by the authority of their crown, or by their command; and which, if they should order to dissolve itself, would instantly dissolve them.

There they sit, after a gang of assassins had driven away some hundreds of the members; whilst those who held the same moderate principles, with more patience or better hope, continued every day exposed to outrageous insults and murderous threats. There a majority, sometimes real, sometimes pretended, captive itself, compels a captive king to issue as royal edicts, at third hand, the polluted nonsense of their most licentious and giddy coffee-houses. It is notorious that all their measures are decided before they are debated. It is beyond doubt that, under the terror of the bayonet, and the lamp-post, and the torch to their houses, they are obliged to adopt all the crude and desperate measures suggested by clubs composed of a monstrous medley of all conditions, tongues, and nations. Among these are found persons, in comparison of whom *Catiline would be thought scrupulous, and Cethegus a man of sobriety and moderation. Nor is it in these clubs alone that the public measures are deformed into monsters. They undergo a previous distortion in academies, intended as so many seminaries for these clubs, which are set up in all the places of public resort. In these meetings of all sorts, every counsel, in proportion as it is daring, and violent, and perfidious, is taken for the mark of superior genius. Humanity and compassion are ridiculed as the fruits of superstition and ignorance. Tenderness to individuals is considered as treason to the public. Liberty is always to be estimated perfect as property is rendered insecure. Amidst assassination, massacre, and confiscation, perpetrated or meditated, they are forming plans for the good order of future society. Embracing in their arms the carcasses of base criminals, and promoting their relations on the title of their offences, they drive hundreds of virtuous persons to the same end, by forcing them to subsist by beggary or by crime.

The assembly, their organ, acts before them the farce of deliberation with as little decency as liberty. They act like the comedians of a fair before a riotous audience; they act amidst the tumultuous cries of a mixed mob of ferocious men, and of women lost to shame, who, according to their insolent fancies, direct, control, applaud, *explode them; and sometimes mix and take their seats amongst them, domineering over them with a strange mixture of servile petulance and proud, presumptuous authority. As they have inverted order in all things, the gallery is in the place of the house. This assembly, which overthrows kings and kingdoms, has not even the physiognomy and aspect of a grave legislative body — **nec color imperii, nec frons ulla senatus*. They have a power given to them, like that of the evil principle, to subvert and destroy; but none to construct, except such machines as may be fitted for further subversion and further destruction.

Who is it that admires, and from the heart is attached to, national representative assemblies, but must turn with horror and disgust from such a profane burlesque, and abominable perversion of that sacred institute? Lovers of monarchy, lovers of republics must alike abhor it. The members of your assembly must themselves groan under the tyranny of which they have all the shame, none of the direction, and little of the profit. I am sure many of the members who compose even the majority of that body must feel as I do, notwithstanding the applauses of the Revolution Society. Miserable king! miserable assembly! How must that assembly be silently scandalized with those of their members who could call a day which seemed to blot the sun out of heaven, **un beau jour!* How must they be inwardly indignant at hearing others, who thought fit to declare to them, *"that the vessel of the state would fly forward in her course towards regeneration with more speed than ever," from the stiff gale of treason and murder, which preceded our preacher's triumph! What must they have felt, whilst, with outward patience, and inward indignation, they heard of the slaughter of innocent gentlemen in their houses, that "the blood spilled was not the most pure!" What must they have felt, when they were besieged by complaints of disorders which shook their country to its foundations, at being compelled coolly to tell the complainants that they were under the protection of the law, and that they would address the king (the captive king) to cause the laws to be enforced for their protection; when the enslaved ministers of that captive king had formally notified to them, that there were neither law, nor authority, nor power left to protect! What must they have felt at being obliged, as a felicitation on the present new year, to request their captive king to forget the stormy period of the last, on account of the great good which *he* was likely to produce to his people; to the complete attainment of which good they adjourned the practical demonstrations of their loyalty, assuring him of their obedience, when he should no longer possess any authority to command!

This address was made with much good nature and affection, to be sure. But among the revolutions in France must be reckoned a considerable revolution in their ideas of politeness. In England we are said to learn manners at second-hand from your side of the water, and that we dress our behaviour in the frippery of France. If so, we are still in the old cut; and have not so far conformed to the new Parisian mode of good breeding, as to think it quite in the most refined strain of delicate compliment (whether in condolence or congratulation) to say to the most humiliated creature that crawls upon the earth that great public benefits are derived from the murder of his servants, the attempted assassination of himself and of his wife, and the mortification, disgrace, and degradation that he has personally suffered. It is a topic of consolation which *our ordinary of Newgate would be too humane to use to a criminal at the foot of the gallows. I should have thought that the hangman of Paris, now that he is liberalized by the vote of the National Assembly, and is allowed his rank and arms in the herald's college of the rights of men, would be too generous, too gallant a man, too full of the sense of his new dignity, to employ that cutting consolation to any of the persons whom the **lèse nation* might bring under the administration of his executive power.

A man is fallen indeed, when he is thus flattered. The anodyne draught of oblivion, thus drugged, is well calculated to preserve a galling wakefulness, and to feed the living ulcer of a corroding memory. Thus to administer the opiate potion of amnesty, powdered with all the ingredients of scorn and contempt, is to hold to his lips, instead of *"the balm of hurt minds," the cup of human misery full to the brim, and to force him to drink it to the dregs.

Yielding to reasons at least as forcible as those which were so delicately urged in the compliment on the new year, the King of France will probably endeavour to forget these events and that compliment. But history, who keeps a durable record of all our acts, and exercises her awful censure over the proceedings of all sorts of sovereigns, will not forget either those events or the era of this liberal refinement in the intercourse of mankind. History will record that on the morning of the 6th of October, 1789, the King and Queen of France, after a day of confusion, alarm, dismay, and slaughter, lay down, under the pledged security of public faith, to indulge nature in a few hours of respite, and troubled, melancholy repose. From this sleep the queen was first startled by the voice of the sentinel at her door, who cried out to her to save herself by flight — that this was the last proof of fidelity he could give — that they were upon him, and he was dead. Instantly he was cut down. A band of cruel ruffians and assassins, reeking with his blood, rushed into the chamber of the queen, and pierced with a hundred strokes of bayonets and poniards the bed, from whence this persecuted woman had but just time to fly almost naked, and, through ways unknown to the murderers, had escaped to seek refuge at the feet of a king and husband, not secure of his own life for a moment.

This king, to say no more of him, and this queen, and their infant children (who once would have been the pride and hope of a great and generous people) were then forced to abandon the sanctuary of the most splendid palace in the world, which they left swimming in blood, polluted by massacre, and strewed with scattered limbs and mutilated carcasses. Thence they were conducted into the capital of their kingdom. Two had been selected from the unprovoked, unresisted, promiscuous slaughter, which was made of the gentlemen of birth and family who composed the king's body guard. These two gentlemen, with all the parade of an execution of justice, were cruelly and publicly dragged to the block, and beheaded in the great court of the palace. Their heads were stuck upon spears, and led the procession; whilst the royal captives who followed in the train were slowly moved along, amidst the horrid yells, and shrilling screams, and frantic dances, and infamous contumelies and all the unutterable abominations of the furies of hell, in the abused shape of the vilest of women. After they had been made to taste, drop by drop, more than the bitterness of death, in the slow torture of a journey of twelve miles, protracted to six hours, they were, under a guard, composed of those very soldiers who had thus conducted them through this famous triumph, lodged in one of the old palaces of Paris, now converted into a bastile for kings.

Is this a triumph to be consecrated at altars? to be commemorated with grateful thanksgiving? to be offered to the divine humanity with fervent prayer and enthusiastic ejaculation? — These Theban and Thracian orgies, acted in France, and applauded only in the Old Jewry, I assure you, kindle prophetic enthusiasm in the minds but of very few people in this kingdom; although a saint and apostle, who may have revelations of his own, and who has so completely vanquished all the mean superstitions of the heart, may incline to think it pious and decorous to compare it with the entrance into the world of the Prince of Peace, proclaimed in a holy temple by a venerable sage, and not long before not worse announced by the voice of angels to the quiet innocence of shepherds.

At first I was at a loss to account for this fit of unguarded transport. I knew, indeed, that the sufferings of monarchs make a delicious repast to some sort of palates. There were reflections which might serve to keep this appetite within some bounds of temperance. But when I took one circumstance into my consideration, I was obliged to confess that much allowance ought to be made for the society, and that the temptation was too strong for common discretion; I mean, the circumstance of the Io Pæan of the triumph, the animating cry which called "for all the bishops to be hanged on the lampposts," might well have brought forth a burst of enthusiasm on the foreseen consequences of this happy day. I allow to so much enthusiasm some little deviation from prudence. I allow this prophet to break forth into hymns of joy and thanksgiving on an event which appears like the precursor of the millennium, and *the projected fifth monarchy, in the destruction of all church establishments. There was, however, (as in all human affairs there is) in the midst of this joy, something to exercise the patience of these worthy gentlemen, and to try the long-suffering of their faith. The actual murder of the king and queen, and their child was wanting to the other auspicious circumstances of this "*beautiful day*." The actual murder of the bishops, though called for by so many holy ejaculations, was also wanting. A group of regicide and sacrilegious slaughter was indeed boldly sketched, but it was only sketched. It unhappily was left unfinished in this great history-piece of the massacre of innocents. What hardy pencil of a great master, from the school of the rights of men, will finish it, *is to be seen hereafter. The age has not yet the complete benefit of that diffusion of knowledge that has undermined superstition and error; and the King of France wants another object or two to consign to oblivion, in consideration of all the good which is to arise from his own sufferings, and the patriotic crimes of an enlightened age.

Although this work of our new light and knowledge did not go to the length that in all probability it was intended it should be carried, yet I must think that such treatment of any human creatures must be shocking to any but those who are made for accomplishing revolutions. But I cannot stop here. Influenced by the inborn feelings of my nature, and not being illuminated by a single ray of this new-sprung modern light, I confess to you, sir, that the exalted rank of the persons suffering, and particularly the sex, the beauty, and the amiable qualities of the descendant of so many kings and emperors, with the tender age of royal infants, insensible only through infancy and innocence of the cruel outrages to which their parents were exposed, instead of being a subject of exultation, adds not a little to my sensibility on that most melancholy occasion.

I hear that the august person who was the principal object of our preacher's triumph, though he supported himself, felt much on that shameful occasion. As a man, it became him to feel for his wife and his children and the faithful guards of his person that were massacred in cold blood about him; as a prince, it became him to feel for the strange and frightful transformation of his civilized subjects, and to be more grieved for them than solicitous for himself. It derogates little from his fortitude, while it adds infinitely to the honour of his humanity. I am very sorry to say it, very sorry indeed, that such personages are in a situation in which it is not becoming in us to praise the virtues of the great.

I hear, and I rejoice to hear, that the great lady, the other object of the triumph, has borne that day (one is interested that beings made for suffering should suffer well), and that she bears all the succeeding days, that she bears the imprisonment of her husband,

and her own captivity, and the exile of her friends, and the insulting adulation of addresses, and the whole weight of her accumulated wrongs with a serene patience, in a manner suited to her rank and race, and becoming the offspring of a sovereign distinguished for her piety and her courage: that, like her, she has lofty sentiments; that she feels with the dignity of a Roman matron; that in the last extremity she will save herself from the last disgrace; and that, if she must fall, she will fall by no ignoble hand.

It is now sixteen or seventeen years since I saw the Queen of France, then the Dauphiness, at Versailles; and surely never lighted on this orb, which she hardly seemed to touch, a more delightful vision. I saw her just above the horizon, decorating and cheering the elevated sphere she just began to move in — glittering like the morning-star, full of life and splendour and joy. Oh! what a revolution! and what a heart must I have to contemplate without emotion that elevation and that fall! Little did I dream when she added titles of veneration to those of enthusiastic, distant, respectful love, that she should ever be obliged to carry the sharp antidote against disgrace concealed in that bosom; little did I dream that I should have lived to see such disasters fallen upon her in a nation of gallant men, in a nation of men of honour, and of cavaliers. I thought ten thousand swords must have leaped from their scabbards to avenge even a look that threatened her with insult. But the age of chivalry is gone. That of sophisters, economists, and calculators has succeeded; and the glory of Europe is extinguished for ever. Never, never more shall we behold that generous loyalty to rank and sex, that proud submission, that dignified obedience, that subordination of the heart which kept alive, even in servitude itself, the spirit of an exalted freedom. The unbought grace of life, the cheap defence of nations, the nurse of manly sentiment and heroic enterprise is gone! It is gone, that sensibility of principle, that chastity of honour, which felt a stain like a wound, which inspired courage whilst it mitigated ferocity, which ennobled whatever it touched, and under which vice itself lost half its evil by losing all its grossness.

This mixed system of opinion and sentiment had its origin in the ancient chivalry; and the principle, though varied in its appearance by the varying state of human affairs, subsisted and influenced through a long succession of generations, even to the time we live in. If it should ever be totally extinguished, the loss I fear will be great. It is this which has given its character to modern Europe. It is this which has distinguished it under all its forms of government, and distinguished it to its advantage, from the states of Asia, and possibly from those states which flourished in the most brilliant periods of the antique world. It was this which, without confounding ranks, had produced a noble equality, and handed it down through all the gradations of social life. It was this opinion which mitigated kings into companions, and raised private men to be fellows with kings. Without force or opposition, it subdued the fierceness of pride and power; it obliged sovereigns to submit to the soft collar of social esteem, compelled stern authority to submit to elegance, and gave a dominating vanquisher of laws to be subdued by manners.

But now all is to be changed. All the pleasing illusions which made power gentle and obedience liberal, which harmonized the different shades of life, and which, by a bland assimilation, incorporated into politics the sentiments which beautify and soften private society, are to be dissolved by this new conquering empire of light and reason. All the decent drapery of life is to be rudely torn off. All the superadded ideas, furnished from the wardrobe of a moral imagination, which the heart owns, and the understanding ratifies, as necessary to cover the defects of our naked, shivering nature, and to raise it to dignity in our own estimation, are to be exploded as a ridiculous, absurd, and antiquated fashion.

On this scheme of things, a king is but a man, a queen is but a woman; a woman is but an animal, and an animal not of the highest order. All homage paid to the sex in general as such, and without distinct views, is to be regarded as romance and folly. Regicide and parricide and sacrilege are but fictions of superstition, corrupting jurisprudence by destroying its simplicity. The murder of a king, or a queen, or a bishop, or a father are only common homicide; and if the people are by any chance, or in any way, gainers by it, a sort of homicide much the most pardonable, and into which we ought not to make too severe a scrutiny.

On the scheme of this barbarous philosophy, which is the offspring of cold hearts and muddy understandings, and which is as void of solid wisdom as it is destitute of all taste and elegance, laws are to be supported only by their own terrors, and by the concern which each individual may find in them from his own private speculations, or can spare to them from his own private interests. In the groves of *their* academy, at the end of every vista, you see nothing but the gallows. Nothing is left which engages the affections on the part of the commonwealth. On the principles of this mechanic philosophy, our institutions can never be embodied, if I may use the expression, in persons, so as to create in us love, veneration, admiration, or attachment. But that sort of reason which banishes the affections is incapable of filling their place. These public affections, combined with manners, are required sometimes as supplements, sometimes as correctives, always as aids to law. The precept given by a wise man, as well as a great critic, for the construction of poems, is equally true as to states: — **Non satis est pulchra esse poemata, dulcia sunto.* There ought to be a system of manners in every nation, which a well-formed mind would be disposed to relish. To make us love our country, our country ought to be lovely.

But power, of some kind or other, will survive the shock in which manners and opinions perish; and it will find other and worse means for its support. The usurpation which, in order to subvert ancient institutions, has destroyed ancient principles, will hold power by arts similar to those by which it has acquired it. When the old feudal and chivalrous spirit of *fealty*, which, by freeing kings from fear, freed both kings and subjects from the precautions of tyranny, shall be extinct in the minds of men, plots and assassinations will be anticipated by preventive murder and preventive confiscation, and that long roll of grim and bloody maxims which form the political code of all power not standing on its own honour, and the honour of those who are to obey it. Kings will be tyrants from policy when subjects are rebels from principle.

When ancient opinions and rules of life are taken away, the loss cannot possibly be estimated. From that moment we have no compass to govern us, nor can we know distinctly to what port we steer. Europe, undoubtedly, taken in a mass, was in a flourishing condition the day on which your revolution was completed. How much of that prosperous state was owing to the spirit of our old manners and opinions is not easy to say; but as such causes cannot be indifferent in their operation, we must presume that, on the whole, their operation was beneficial.

We are but too apt to consider things in the state in which we find them, without sufficiently adverting to the causes by which they have been produced, and possibly may be upheld. Nothing is more certain than that our manners, our civilization, and all the good things which are connected with manners and with civilization, have, in this European world of ours, depended for ages upon two principles, and were indeed the result of both combined; I mean the spirit of a gentleman, and the spirit of religion. The nobility and the clergy, the one by profession, the other by patronage, kept learning in existence, even in the midst of arms and confusions, and whilst governments were rather in their causes, than formed. Learning paid back what it received to nobility and to priesthood, and paid it with usury, by enlarging their ideas, and by furnishing their minds. Happy if they had all continued to know their indissoluble union, and their proper place! Happy if learning, not debauched by ambition, had been satisfied to continue the instructor, and not aspired to be the master! Along with its natural protectors and guardians, learning will be *cast into the mire, and trodden down under the hoofs of a swinish multitude.

If, as I suspect, modern letters owe more than they are always willing to own to ancient manners, so do other interests which we value full as much as they are worth. Even commerce, and trade, and manufacture, the gods of our economical politicians, are themselves perhaps but creatures; are themselves but effects, which, as first causes, we choose to worship. They certainly grew under the same shade in which learning flourished. They too may decay with their natural protecting principles. With you, for the present at least, they all threaten to disappear together. Where trade and manufactures are wanting to a people, and the spirit of nobility and religion remains, sentiment supplies, and not always ill supplies, their place; but if commerce and the arts should be lost in an experiment to try how well a state may stand without these old fundamental principles, what sort of a thing must be a nation of gross, stupid, ferocious, and, at the same time, poor and sordid barbarians, destitute of religion, honour, or manly pride, possessing nothing at present, and hoping for nothing hereafter?

I wish you may not be going fast, and by the shortest cut, to that horrible and disgustful situation. Already there appears a poverty of conception, a coarseness and vulgarity, in all the proceedings of the Assembly and of all their instructors. Their liberty is not liberal. Their science is presumptuous ignorance. Their humanity is savage and brutal. . . .

[1790]

*A LETTER FROM THE RIGHT HON. EDMUND BURKE TO A NOBLE LORD

My Lord,

I could hardly flatter myself with the hope that so very early in the season I should have to acknowledge obligations to the Duke of Bedford and to the Earl of Lauderdale. These noble persons have lost no time in conferring upon me that sort of honour which it is alone within their competence, and which it is certainly most congenial to their nature, and their manners to bestow.

To be ill spoken of, in whatever language they speak, by the zealots of the new sect in philosophy and politics, of which these noble persons think so charitably, and of which others think so justly, to me, is no matter of uneasiness or surprise. To have incurred the displeasure of * the Duke of Orleans or the Duke of Bedford, to fall under the censure of *Citizen Brissot or of his friend, the Earl of Lauderdale, I ought to consider as proofs, not the least satisfactory, that I have produced some part of the effect I proposed by my endeavours. I have laboured hard to earn what the noble lords are generous enough to pay. Personal offence I have given them none. The part they take against me is from zeal to the cause. It is well! It is perfectly well! I have to do homage to their justice. I have to thank the Bedfords and the Lauderdales for having so faithfully and so fully acquitted towards me whatever arrear of debt was left undischarged by *the Priestleys and the Paines.

Some, perhaps, may think them executors in their own wrong; I at least have nothing to complain of. They have gone beyond the demands of justice. They have been (a little perhaps beyond their intention) favourable to me. They have been the means of bringing out, by their invectives, the handsome things which *Lord Grenville has had the goodness and condescension to say in my behalf. Retired as I am from the world, and from all its affairs and all its pleasures, I confess it does kindle, in my nearly extinguished feelings, a very vivid satisfaction to be so attacked and so commended. It is soothing to my wounded mind to be commended by an able, vigorous, and well-informed statesman, and at the very moment when he stands forth with a manliness and resolution, worthy of himself and of his cause, for the preservation of the person and government of our sovereign, and therein for the security of the laws, the liberties, the morals, and the lives of his people. To be in any fair way connected with such things is indeed a distinction. No philosophy can make me above it; no melancholy can depress me so low as to make me wholly insensible to such an honour.

Why will they not let me remain in obscurity and inaction? Are they apprehensive that, if an atom of me remains, the sect has something to fear? Must I be annihilated, lest, *like old John Zisca's, my skin might be made into a drum, to animate Europe to eternal battle against a tyranny that threatens to overwhelm all Europe, and all the human race?

My Lord, it is a subject of awful meditation. Before this of France, the annals of all time have not furnished an instance of a *complete* revolution. That revolution seems to have extended even to the constitution of the mind of man. It has this of wonderful in it, that it resembles what *Lord Verulam says of the operations of nature: it was perfect, not only in its elements and principles, but in all its members and its organs from the very beginning. The moral scheme of France furnishes the only pattern ever known, which they who admire will *instantly* resemble. It is indeed an inexhaustible repertory of one kind of examples. In my wretched condition, though hardly to be classed with the living, I am not safe from them. They have tigers to fall upon animated strength. They have hyenas to prey upon carcasses. The national menagerie is collected by the first physiologists of the time; and it is defective in no description of savage nature. They pursue even such as me into the obscurest retreats, and haul them before their revolutionary tribunals. Neither sex, nor age, nor the sanctuary of the tomb is sacred to them. They have so determined a hatred to all privileged orders that they deny even to the departed the sad immunities of the grave. They are not wholly without an object. Their turpitude purveys to their malice; and they *unplumb the dead for bullets to assassinate the living. If all revolutionists were not proof against all caution, I should recommend it to their consideration that no persons were ever known in history, either sacred or profane, to vex the sepulchre, and, by their sorceries, to call up the prophetic dead, with any other event than the prediction of their own disastrous fate. — "Leave me, oh leave me to repose!"

In one thing I can excuse the Duke of Bedford for his attack upon me and my mortuary pension. He cannot readily comprehend the transaction he condemns. What I have obtained was the fruit of no bargain; the production of no intrigue; the result of no compromise; the effect of no solicitation. The first suggestion of it never came from me, mediately or immediately, to his Majesty or any of his ministers. It was long known that the instant my engagements would permit it, and before *the heaviest of all calamities had forever condemned me to obscurity and sorrow, I had resolved on a total retreat. I had executed that design. I was entirely out of the way of serving or of hurting any statesman, or any party, when the ministers so generously and so nobly carried into effect the spontaneous bounty of the crown. Both descriptions have acted as became them. When I could no longer serve them, the ministers have considered my situation. When I could no longer hurt them, the revolutionists have trampled on my infirmity. My gratitude, I trust, is equal to the manner in which the benefit was conferred. It came to me, indeed, at a time of life, and in a state of mind and body, in which no circumstance of fortune could afford me any real pleasure. But this was no fault in the royal donor, or in his ministers, who were pleased, in acknowledging the merits of an invalid servant of the public, to assuage the sorrows of a desolate old man.

It would ill become me to boast of anything. It would as ill become me, thus called upon, to depreciate the value of a long life spent with unexampled toil in the service of my country. Since the total body of my services, on account of the industry which was shown in them, and the fairness of my intentions, have obtained the acceptance of my sovereign, it would be absurd in me to range myself on the side of the Duke of Bedford and the *Corresponding Society, or, as far as in me lies, to permit a dispute on the rate at which the authority appointed by *our* constitution to estimate such things has been pleased to set them.

Loose libels ought to be passed by in silence and contempt. By me they have been so always. I knew that as long as I remained in public I should live down the calumnies of malice and the judgments of ignorance. If I happened to be now and then in the wrong, (as who is not?) like all other men, I must bear the consequence of my faults and my mistakes. The libels of the present day are just of the same stuff as the libels of the past. But they derive an importance from the rank of the persons they come from, and the gravity of the place where they were uttered. In some way or other I ought to take some notice of them. To assert myself thus traduced is not vanity or arrogance. It is a demand of justice; it is a demonstration of gratitude. If I am unworthy, the ministers are worse than prodigal. On that hypothesis, I perfectly agree with the Duke of Bedford.

For whatever I have been (I am now no more) I put myself on my country. I ought to be allowed a reasonable freedom, because I stand upon my deliverance; and no culprit ought to plead in irons. Even in the utmost latitude of defensive liberty, I wish to preserve all possible decorum. Whatever it may be in the eyes of these noble persons themselves, to me their situation calls for the most profound respect. If I should happen to trespass a little, which I trust I shall not, let it always be supposed that a confusion of characters may produce mistakes; that, in the masquerades of the grand carnival of our age, whimsical adventures happen, odd things are said and pass off. If I should fail a single point in the high respect I owe to those illustrious persons, I cannot be supposed to mean the Duke of Bedford and the Earl of Lauderdale of the House of Peers, but the Duke of Bedford and the Earl of Lauderdale of Palace-Yard! — *The Dukes and Earls of Brentford. There they are on the pavement; there they seem to come nearer to my humble level, and, virtually at least, to have waived their high privilege.

Making this protestation, I refuse all revolutionary tribunals, where men have been put to death for no other reason than that they had obtained favours from the crown. I claim, not the letter, but the spirit, of the old English law, that is, to be tried by my peers. I decline his Grace's jurisdiction as a judge. I challenge the Duke of Bedford as a juror to pass upon the value of my services. Whatever his natural parts may be, I cannot recognize, in his few and idle years, the competence to judge of my long and laborious life. If I can help it, he shall not be on the inquest of my *_quantum meruit._ Poor rich man! He can hardly know anything of public industry in its exertions, or can estimate its compensations when its work is done. I have no doubt of his Grace's readiness in all the calculations of vulgar arithmetic; but I shrewdly suspect that he is little studied in the theory of moral proportions, and has never learned the rule of three in the arithmetic of policy and state.

His Grace thinks I have obtained too much. I answer that my exertions, whatever they have been, were such as no hopes of pecuniary reward could possibly excite; and no pecuniary compensation can possibly reward them. Between money and such services, if done by abler men than I am, there is no common principle of comparison; they are quantities incommensurable. Money is made for the comfort and convenience of animal life. It cannot be a reward for what mere animal life must indeed sustain, but never can inspire. With submission to his Grace, I have not had more than sufficient. As to any noble use, I trust I know how to employ, as well as he, a much greater fortune than he possesses. In a more confined application, I certainly stand in need of every kind of relief and easement much more than he does. When I say I have not received more than I deserve, is this the language I hold to majesty? No! Far, very far, from it! Before that presence I claim no merit at all. Everything towards me is favour and bounty. One style to a gracious benefactor; another to a proud and insulting foe.

His Grace is pleased to aggravate my guilt by charging my acceptance of his Majesty's grant as a departure from my ideas, and the spirit of my conduct with regard to economy. If it be, my ideas of economy were false and ill-founded. But they are the Duke of Bedford's ideas of economy I have contradicted, and not my own. If he means to allude to certain bills brought in by me on the message from the throne in 1782, I tell him that there is nothing in my conduct that can contradict either the letter or the spirit of those acts. Does he mean the pay-office act? I take it for granted he does not. The act to which he alludes, is, I suppose, the establishment act. I greatly doubt whether his Grace has ever read the one or the other. The first of these systems cost me, with every assistance which my then situation gave me, pains incredible. I found an opinion common through all the offices, and general in the public at large, that it would prove impossible to reform and methodize the office of paymaster-general. I undertook it, however; and I succeeded in my undertaking. Whether the military service, or whether the general economy of our finances, have profited by that act, I leave to those who are acquainted with the army, and with the treasury, to judge.

An opinion full as general prevailed also at the same time that nothing could be done for the regulation of the civil-list establishment. The very attempt to introduce method into it, and any limitations to its services, was held absurd. I had not seen the man, who so much as suggested one economical principle, or an economical expedient, upon that subject. Nothing but coarse amputation, or coarser taxation, were then talked of, both of them without design, combination, or the least shadow of principle. Blind and headlong zeal, or factious fury, were the whole contribution brought by the most noisy on that occasion, towards the satisfaction of the public, or the relief of the crown.

Let me tell my youthful censor that the necessities of that time required something very different from what others then suggested, or what his Grace now conceives. Let me inform him that it was one of the most critical periods in our annals. Astronomers have supposed that if a certain comet, whose path intersected the ecliptic, had met the earth in some (I forget what) sign, it would have whirled us along with it, in its eccentric course, into God knows what regions of heat and cold. Had the portentous comet of the rights of man, (which *"from its horrid hair shakes pestilence and war," and *"with fear of change perplexes monarchs,") had that comet crossed upon us in that internal state of England, nothing human could have prevented our being irresistibly hurried out of the highway of heaven, into all the vices, crimes, horrors, and miseries of the French Revolution.

Happily, France was not then Jacobinized. Her hostility was at a good distance. We had a limb cut off, but we preserved the body. We lost our colonies, but we kept our constitution. There was, indeed, much intestine heat; there was a dreadful fermentation. Wild and savage insurrection quitted the woods, and prowled about our streets in the name of reform. Such was the distemper of the public mind that there was no madman, in his maddest ideas and maddest projects, who might not count upon numbers to support his principles and execute his designs.

Many of the changes, by a great misnomer called parliamentary reforms, went, not in the intention of all the professors and supporters of them, undoubtedly, but went in their certain, and, in my opinion, not very remote effect, home to the utter destruction of the constitution of this kingdom. Had they taken place, not France, but England, would have had the honour of leading up the death-dance of a democratic revolution. Other projects, exactly coincident in time with those, struck at the very existence of the kingdom under any constitution. There are who remember the blind fury of some, and the lamentable helplessness of others; here, a torpid confusion, from a panic fear of the danger; there, the same inaction from a stupid insensibility to it; here, well-wishers to the mischief; there, indifferent lookers-on. At the same time, *a sort of national convention, dubious in its nature, and perilous in its example, nosed Parliament in the very seat of its authority, sat with a sort of superintendence over it, and little less than dictated to it, not only laws, but the very form and essence of legislature itself. In Ireland things ran in a still more eccentric course. Government was unnerved, confounded, and in a manner suspended. Its equipoise was totally gone. I do not mean to speak disrespectfully of *Lord North. He was a man of admirable parts, of general knowledge, of a versatile understanding fitted for every sort of business, of infinite wit and pleasantry, of a delightful temper, and with a mind most perfectly disinterested. But it would be only to degrade myself by a weak adulation, and not to honour the memory of a great man, to deny that he wanted something of the vigilance and spirit of command that the time required. Indeed, a darkness, next to the fog of this awful day, lowered over the whole region. For a little time the helm appeared abandoned —

**Ipse diem noctemque negat discernere cœlo,*
Nec meminisse viæ media Palinurus in unda.

At that time I was connected with men of high place in the community. They loved liberty as much as the Duke of Bedford can do, and they understood it at least as well. Perhaps their politics, as usual, took a tincture from their character, and they cultivated what they loved. The liberty they pursued was a liberty inseparable from order, from virtue, from morals, and from religion, and was neither hypocritically nor fanatically followed. They did not wish that liberty, in itself one of the first of blessings, should in its perversion become the greatest curse which could fall upon mankind. To preserve the constitution entire, and practically equal to all the great ends of its formation, not in one single part, but in all its parts, was to them the first object. Popularity and power they regarded alike. These were with them only different means of obtaining that object, and had no preference over each other in their minds, but as one or the other might afford a surer or a less certain prospect of arriving at that end. It is some consolation to me in the cheerless gloom which darkens the evening of my life, that with them I commenced my political career, and never for a moment, in reality nor in appearance, for any length of time, was separated from their good wishes and good opinion.

By what accident it matters not, nor upon what desert, but just then, and in the midst of that hunt of obloquy which ever has pursued me with a full cry through life, I had obtained a very considerable degree of public confidence. I know well enough how equivocal a test this kind of popular opinion forms of the merit that obtained it. I am no stranger to the insecurity of its tenure. I do not boast of it. It is mentioned to show, not how highly I prize the thing, but my right to value the use I made of it. I endeavoured to turn that short-lived advantage to myself into a permanent benefit to my country. Far am I from detracting from the merit of some gentlemen, out of office or in it, on that occasion. No! — It is not my way to refuse a full and heaped measure of justice to the aids that I receive. I have, through life, been willing to give everything to others, and to reserve nothing for myself but the inward conscience that I had omitted no pains to discover, to animate, to discipline, to direct the abilities of the country for its service, and to place them in the best light to improve their age, or to adorn it. This conscience I have. I have never suppressed any man, never checked him for a moment in his course, by any jealousy or by any policy. I was always ready, to the height of my means (and they were always infinitely below my desires), to forward those abilities which overpowered my own. He is an ill-furnished undertaker who has no machinery but his own hands to work with. Poor in my own faculties, I ever thought myself rich in theirs. In that period of difficulty and danger, more especially, I consulted and sincerely co-operated with men of all parties who seemed disposed to the same ends, or to any main part of them. Nothing to prevent disorder was omitted; when it appeared, nothing to subdue it was left uncounselled nor unexecuted, as far as I could prevail. At the time I speak of, and having a momentary lead, so aided and so encouraged, and as a feeble instrument in a mighty hand — I do not say I saved my country; I am sure I did my country important service. There were few, indeed, that did not at that time acknowledge it; and that time was thirteen years ago. It was but one voice that no man in the kingdom better deserved an honourable provision should be made for him.

So much for my general conduct through the whole of the portentous crisis from 1780 to 1782, and the general sense then entertained of that conduct by my country. But my character as a reformer, in the particular instances which the Duke of Bedford refers to, is so connected in principle with my opinions on the hideous changes which have since barbarized France, and, spreading thence, threatened the political and moral order of the whole world, that it seems to demand something of a more detailed discussion.

My economical reforms were not, as his Grace may think, the suppression of a paltry pension or employment, more or less. Economy in my plans was, as it ought to be, secondary, subordinate, instrumental. I acted on state principles. I found a great distemper in the commonwealth; and, according to the nature of the evil and of the object, I treated it. The malady was deep; it was complicated, in the causes and in the symptoms. Throughout it was full of contra-indicants. On one hand, government, daily growing more invidious from an apparent increase of the means of strength, was every day growing more contemptible by real weakness. Nor was this dissolution confined to government commonly so called. It extended to Parliament, which was losing not a little in its dignity and estimation, by an opinion of its not acting on worthy motives. On the other hand, the desires of the people (partly natural and partly infused into them by art) appeared in so wild and inconsiderate a manner, with regard to the economical object (for I set aside for a moment the dreadful tampering with the body of the constitution itself), that, if their petitions had literally been complied with, the state would have been convulsed, and a gate would have been opened through which all property might be sacked and ravaged. Nothing could have saved the public from the mischiefs of the false reform but its absurdity, which would soon have brought itself, and with it all real reform, into discredit. This would have left a rankling wound in the hearts of the people, who would know they had failed in the accomplishment of their wishes, but who, like the rest of mankind in all ages, would impute the blame to anything rather than to their own proceedings. But there were then persons in the world who nourished complaint, and would have been thoroughly disappointed if the people were ever satisfied. I was not of that humour. I wished that they *should* be satisfied. It was my aim to give to the people the substance of what I knew they desired, and what I thought was right, whether they desired it or not, before it had been modified for them into senseless petitions. I knew that there is a manifest, marked distinction, which ill men with ill designs, or weak men incapable of any design, will constantly be confounding — that is, a marked distinction between change and reformation. The former alters the substance of the objects themselves, and gets rid of all their essential good, as well as of all the accidental evil annexed to them. Change is novelty; and whether it is to operate any one of the effects of reformation at all, or whether it may not contradict the very principle upon which reformation is desired, cannot be certainly known beforehand. Reform is not a change in the substance, or in the primary modification, of the object, but a direct application of a remedy to the grievance complained of. So far as that is removed, all is sure. It stops there; and, if it fails, the substance which underwent the operation, at the very worst, is but where it was.

All this, in effect, I think, but am not sure, I have said elsewhere. It cannot at this time be too often repeated, line upon line, precept upon precept, until it comes into the currency of a proverb: *to innovate is not to reform.* The French revolutionists complained of everything; they refused to reform anything; and they left nothing, no, nothing at all unchanged. The consequences are before us, — not in remote history; not in future prognostication: they are about us; they are upon us. They shake the public security; they menace private enjoyment. They dwarf the growth of the young; they break the quiet of the old. If we travel, they stop our way. They infest us in town; they pursue us to the country. Our business is interrupted; our repose is troubled; our pleasures are saddened; our very studies are poisoned and perverted, and knowledge is rendered worse than ignorance, by the enormous evils of this dreadful innovation. The revolution harpies of France, sprung from night and hell, or from that chaotic anarchy which generates equivocally "all monstrous, all prodigious things," cuckoo-like, adulterously lay their eggs, and brood over, and hatch them in the nest of every neighbouring state. These obscene harpies, who deck themselves in I know not what divine attributes, but who in reality are foul and ravenous birds of prey (both mothers and daughters), flutter over our heads, and souse down upon our tables, and leave nothing unrent, unrifled, unravaged, or unpolluted with the slime of their filthy offal.

If his Grace can contemplate the result of this complete innovation, or, as some friends of his will call it, "reform," in the whole body of its solidity and compounded mass, at which, as *Hamlet says, the face of heaven glows with horror and indignation, and which, in truth, makes every reflecting mind and every feeling heart perfectly thought-sick without a thorough abhorrence of everything they say, and everything they do, I am amazed at the morbid strength or the natural infirmity of his mind.

It was then not my love, but my hatred, to innovation that produced my plan of reform. Without troubling myself with the exactness of the logical diagram, I considered them as things substantially opposite. It was to prevent that evil that I proposed the measures, which his Grace is pleased, and I am not sorry he is pleased, to recall to my recollection. I had (what I hope that noble duke will remember in all its operations) a state to preserve, as well as a state to reform. I had a people to gratify, but not to inflame or to mislead. I do not claim half the credit for what I did, as for what I prevented from being done. In that situation of the public mind, I did not undertake, as was then proposed, to new-model the House of Commons or the House of Lords; or to change the authority under which any officer of the crown acted, who was suffered at all to exist. Crown, Lords, Commons, judicial system, system of administration existed as they had existed before; and in the mode and manner in which they had always existed. My measures were, what I then truly stated them to the House to be, in their intent, healing and mediatorial. A complaint was made of too much influence in the House of Commons; I reduced it in both Houses; and I gave my reasons article by article for every reduction, and showed why I thought it safe for the service of the state. I heaved the lead every inch of way I made. A disposition to expense was complained of; to that I opposed not mere retrenchment but a system of economy which would make a random expense, without plan or foresight, in future not easily practicable. I proceeded upon principles of research to put me in possession of my matter; on principles of method to regulate it; and on principles in the human mind and in civil affairs to secure and perpetuate the operation. I conceived nothing arbitrarily; nor proposed anything to be done by the will and pleasure of others, or my own; but by reason, and by reason only. I have ever abhorred, since the first dawn of my understanding to this its obscure twilight, all the operations of opinion, fancy, inclination, and will in the affairs of government, where only a sovereign reason, paramount to all forms of legislation and administration, should dictate. Government is made for the very purpose of opposing that reason to will and caprice, in the reformers or in the reformed, in the governors or in the governed, in kings, in senates, or in people.

On a careful review, therefore, and analysis of all the component parts of the civil list, and on weighing them against each other, in order to make, as much as possible, all of them a subject of estimate (the foundation and corner-stone of all regular provident economy), it appeared to me evident that this was impracticable, whilst that part called the pension list was totally discretionary in its amount. For this reason, and for this only, I proposed to reduce it, both in its gross quantity, and in its larger individual proportions, to a certainty; lest, if it were left without a general limit, it might eat up the civil-list service; if suffered to be granted in portions too great for the fund, it might defeat its own end; and, by unlimited allowances to some, it might disable the crown in means of providing for others. The pension list was to be kept as a sacred fund; but it could not be kept as a constant, open fund, sufficient for growing demands, if some demands would wholly devour it. The tenour of the act will show that it regarded the civil list only, the reduction of which to some sort of estimate was my great object.

No other of the crown funds did I meddle with, because they had not the same relations. This of the four and a half per cents, does his Grace imagine had escaped me, or had escaped all the men of business who acted with me in those regulations? I knew that such a fund existed, and that pensions had been always granted on it, before his Grace was born. This fund was full in my eye. It was full in the eyes of those who worked with me. It was left on principle. On principle I did what was then done; and on principle what was left undone was omitted. I did not dare to rob the nation of all funds to reward merit. If I pressed this point too close, I acted contrary to the avowed principles on which I went. Gentlemen are very fond of quoting me; but if any one thinks it worth his while to know the rules that guided me in my plan of reform, he will read my printed speech on that subject; at least what is contained from page 230 to page 241 in the second volume of the collection which a friend has given himself the trouble to make of my publications. Be this as it may, these two bills (though achieved with the greatest labour, and management of every sort, both within and without the House) were only a part, and but a small part, of a very large system, comprehending all the objects I stated in opening my proposition, and, indeed, many more, which I just hinted at in my speech to the electors of Bristol, when I was put out of that representation. All these, in some state or other of forwardness, I have long had by me.

But do I justify his Majesty's grace on these grounds? I think them the least of my services! The time gave them an occasional value. What I have done in the way of political economy was far from confined to this body of measures. I did not come into Parliament to con my lesson. I had earned my pension before I set my foot in *St. Stephen's chapel. I was prepared and disciplined to this political warfare. The first session I sat in Parliament I found it necessary to analyze the whole commercial, financial, constitutional, and foreign interests of Great Britain and its empire. A great deal was then done; and more, far more, would have been done, if more had been permitted by events. Then, in the vigour of my manhood, my constitution sank under my labour. Had I then died (and I seemed to myself very near death), I had then earned for those who belonged to me more than the Duke of Bedford's ideas of service are of power to estimate. But, in truth, these services I am called to account for are not those on which I value myself the most. If I were to call for a reward (which I have never done), it should be for those in which for fourteen years, without intermission, I showed the most industry, and had the least success; I mean in the affairs of India. They are those on which I value myself the most; most for the importance; most for the labour; most for the judgment; most for constancy and perseverance in the pursuit. Others may value them most for the intention. In that, surely, they are not mistaken.

Does his Grace think that they who advised the crown to make my retreat easy, considered me only as an economist? That, well understood, however, is a good deal. If I had not deemed it of some value, I should not have made political economy an object of my humble studies, from my very early youth to near the end of my service in Parliament, even before (at least to any knowledge of mine) it had employed the thoughts of speculative men in other parts of Europe. At that time it was still in its infancy in England, where, in the last century, it had its origin. Great and learned men thought my studies were not wholly thrown away, and deigned to communicate with me now and then on some particulars of their immortal works. Something of these studies may appear incidentally in some of the earliest things I published.

The House has been witness to their effect, and has profited of them, more or less, for above eight-and-twenty years.

To their estimate I leave the matter. I was not, like his Grace of Bedford, swaddled and rocked and dandled into a legislator; **Nitor in adversum* is the motto for a man like me. I possessed not one of the qualities, nor cultivated one of the arts that recommend men to the favour and protection of the great. I was not made for a minion or a tool. As little did I follow the trade of winning the hearts by imposing on the understandings, of the people. At every step of my progress in life (for in every step was I traversed and opposed), and at every turnpike I met, I was obliged to show my passport, and again and again to prove my sole title to the honour of being useful to my country, by a proof that I was not wholly unacquainted with its laws and the whole system of its interests both abroad and at home. Otherwise no rank, no toleration even, for me. I had no arts but manly arts. On them I have stood, and, please God, in spite of the Duke of Bedford and the Earl of Lauderdale, to the last gasp will I stand.

Had his Grace condescended to inquire concerning the person whom he has not thought it below him to reproach, he might have found that, in the whole course of my life, I have never on any pretence of economy, or on any other pretence, so much as in a single instance, stood between any man and his reward of service, or his encouragement in useful talent and pursuit, from the highest of those services and pursuits to the lowest. On the contrary I have, on an hundred occasions, exerted myself with singular zeal to forward every man's even tolerable pretensions. I have more than once had good-natured reprehensions from my friends for carrying the matter to something bordering on abuse. This line of conduct, whatever its merits might be, was partly owing to natural disposition; but I think full as much to reason and principle. I looked on the consideration of public service, or public ornament, to be real and very justice; and I ever held a scanty and penurious justice to partake of the nature of a wrong. I held it to be, in its consequences, the worst economy in the world. In saving money, I soon can count up all the good I do; but when, by a cold penury, I blast the abilities of a nation, and stunt the growth of its active energies, the ill I may do is beyond all calculation. Whether it be too much or too little, whatever I have done has been general and systematic. I have never entered into those trifling vexations and oppressive details that have been falsely, and most ridiculously, laid to my charge.

Did I blame the pensions given to Mr. Barré and Mr. Dunning between the proposition and execution of my plan? No! Surely no! Those pensions were within my principles. I assert it, those gentlemen deserved their pensions, their titles, — all they had; and more had they had, I should have been but pleased the more. They were men of talents; they were men of service. I put the profession of the law out of the question in one of them. It is a service that rewards itself. But their public service, though, from their abilities unquestionably of more value than mine, in its quantity and its duration was not to be mentioned with it. But I never could drive a hard bargain in my life, concerning any matter whatever; and least of all do I know how to haggle and huckster with merit. Pension for myself I obtained none; nor did I solicit any. Yet I was loaded with hatred for everything that was withheld, and with obloquy for everything that was given. I was thus left to support the grants of a name ever dear to me, and ever venerable to the world, in favour of those, who were no friends of mine or of his, against the rude attacks of those who were at that time friends to the grantees, and their own zealous partisans. I have never heard the Earl of Lauderdale complain of these pensions. He finds nothing wrong till he comes to me. This is impartiality, in the true, modern, revolutionary style.

Whatever I did at that time, so far as it regarded order and economy, is stable and eternal, as all principles must be. A particular order of things may be altered; order itself cannot lose its value. As to other particulars, they are variable by time and by circumstances. Laws of regulation are not fundamental laws. The public exigencies are the masters of all such laws. They rule the laws, and are not to be ruled by them. They who exercise the legislative power at the time must judge.

It may be new to his Grace, but I beg leave to tell him, that mere parsimony is not economy. It is separable in theory from it; and in fact it may, or it may not, be a part of economy, according to circumstances. Expense, and great expense, may be an essential part in true economy. If parsimony were to be considered as one of the kinds of that virtue, there is however another and a higher economy. Economy is a distributive virtue, and consists not in saving, but in selection. Parsimony requires no providence, no sagacity, no powers of combination, no comparison, no judgment. Mere instinct, and that not an instinct of the noblest kind, may produce this false economy in perfection. The other economy has larger views. It demands a discriminating judgment and a firm, sagacious mind. It shuts one door to impudent importunity, only to open another, and a wider, to unpresuming merit. If none but meritorious service or real talent were to be rewarded, this nation has not wanted, and this nation will not want, the means of rewarding all the service it ever will receive, and encouraging all the merit it ever will produce. No state, since the foundation of society, has been impoverished by that species of profusion. Had the economy of selection and proportion been at all times observed, we should not now have had an overgrown Duke of Bedford, to oppress the industry of humble men, and to limit, by the standard of his own conceptions, the justice, the bounty, or, if he pleases, the charity of the crown.

His Grace may think as meanly as he will of my deserts in the far greater part of my conduct in life. It is free for him to do so. There will always be some difference of opinion in the value of political services. But there is one merit of mine which he, of all men living, ought to be the last to call in question. I have supported with very great zeal, and I am told with some degree of success, those opinions, or if his Grace likes another expression better, those old prejudices, which buoy up the ponderous mass of his nobility, wealth, and titles. I have omitted no exertion to prevent him and them from sinking to that level to which the meretricious French faction, his Grace at least coquets with, omit no exertion to reduce both. I have done all I could to discountenance their inquiries into the fortunes of those who hold large portions of wealth without any apparent merit of their own. I have strained every nerve to keep the Duke of Bedford in that situation which alone makes him my superior. Your Lordship has been a witness of the use he makes of that preeminence.

But be it that this is virtue! Be it that there is virtue in this well-selected rigour; yet all virtues are not equally becoming to all men and at all times. There are crimes, undoubtedly there are crimes, which in all seasons of our existence ought to put a generous antipathy in action; crimes that provoke an indignant justice, and call forth a warm and animated pursuit. But all things that concern what I may call the preventive police of morality, all things merely rigid, harsh, and censorial, the antiquated moralists, at whose feet I was brought up, would not have thought these the fittest matter to form the favourite virtues of young men of rank. What might have been well enough, and have been received with a veneration mixed with awe and terror, from an old, severe, crabbed Cato, would have wanted something of propriety in the young Scipios, the ornament of the Roman nobility, in the flower of their life. But the times, the morals, the masters, the scholars, have all undergone a thorough revolution. It is a vile illiberal school, this new French academy of the **sans-culottes*. There is nothing in it that is fit for a gentleman to learn.

Whatever its vogue may be, I still flatter myself that the parents of the growing generation will be satisfied with what is to be taught to their children in Westminster, in Eton, or in Winchester; I still indulge the hope that no grown gentleman or nobleman of our time will think of finishing at *Mr. Thelwall's lecture whatever may have been left incomplete at the old universities of his country. I would give to Lord Grenville and Mr. Pitt for a motto, what was said of a Roman censor or prætor (or what was he?) who, in virtue of a **Senatus consultum*, shut up certain academies,

> **Cludere ludum impudentiæ jussit.*

Every honest father of a family in the kingdom will rejoice at the breaking up for the holidays, and will pray that there may be a very long vacation in all such schools.

The awful state of the time, and not myself or my own justification, is my true object in what I now write, or in what I shall ever write or say. It little signifies to the world what becomes of such things as me, or even as the Duke of Bedford. What I say about either of us is nothing more than a vehicle, as you, my Lord, will easily perceive, to convey my sentiments on matters far more worthy of your attention. It is when I stick to my apparent first subject that I ought to apologize.

not when I depart from it. I therefore must beg your Lordship's pardon for again resuming it after this very short digression, assuring you that I shall never altogether lose sight of such matter as persons abler than I am may turn to some profit.

The Duke of Bedford conceives that he is obliged to call the attention of the House of Peers to his Majesty's grant to me, which he considers as excessive, and out of all bounds.

I know not how it has happened, but it really seems that, whilst his Grace was meditating his well-considered censure upon me, he fell into a sort of sleep. Homer nods, and the Duke of Bedford may dream; and as dreams (even his golden dreams) are apt to be ill-pieced and incongruously put together, his Grace preserved his idea of reproach to me, but took the subject-matter from the crown grants to his own family. This is *"the stuff of which his dreams are made." In that way of putting things together his Grace is perfectly in the right. The grants to the house of Russell were so enormous as, not only to outrage economy, but even to stagger credibility. The Duke of Bedford is the leviathan among all the creatures of the crown. He tumbles about his unwieldy bulk; he plays and frolics in the ocean of the royal bounty. Huge as he is, and whilst *"he lies floating many a rood," he is still a creature. His ribs, his fins, his whalebone, his blubber, the very spiracles through which he spouts a torrent of brine against his origin, and covers me all over with the spray, — everything of him and about him is from the throne. Is it for *him* to question the dispensation of the royal favour?

I really am at a loss to draw any sort of parallel between the public merits of his Grace, by which he justifies the grants he holds, and these services of mine, on the favourable construction of which I have obtained what his Grace so much disapproves. In private life I have not at all the honour of acquaintance with the noble duke. But I ought to presume, and it costs me nothing to do so, that he abundantly deserves the esteem and love of all who live with him. But as to public service, why, truly it would not be more ridiculous for me to compare myself in rank, in fortune, in splendid descent, in youth, strength, or figure, with the Duke of Bedford, than to make a parallel between his services and my attempts to be useful to my country. It would not be gross adulation, but uncivil irony, to say that he has any public merit of his own to keep alive the idea of the services by which his vast landed pensions were obtained. My merits, whatever they are, are original and personal; his are derivative. It is his ancestor, the original pensioner, that has laid up this inexhaustible fund of merit which makes his Grace so very delicate and exceptious about the merit of all other grantees of the crown. Had he permitted me to remain in quiet, I should have said, "'Tis his estate; that's enough. It is his by law; what have I to do with it or its history?" He would naturally have said on his side, "'Tis this man's fortune. He is as good now as my ancestor was two hundred and fifty years ago. I am a young man with very old pensions; he is an old man with very young pensions, — that's all."

Why will his Grace, by attacking me, force me reluctantly to compare my little merit with that which obtained from the crown those prodigies of profuse donation by which he tramples on the mediocrity of humble and laborious individuals? I would willingly leave him to the heralds' college, which the philosophy of the *sans-culottes* (prouder by far than all * the Garters, and Norroys, and Clarencieux, and Rouge Dragons that ever pranced in a procession of what his friends call aristocrats and despots) will abolish with contumely and scorn. These historians, recorders, and blazoners of virtues and arms differ wholly from that other description of historians who never assign any act of politicians to a good motive. These gentle historians, on the contrary, dip their pens in nothing but the milk of human kindness. They seek no further for merit than the preamble of a patent, or the inscription on a tomb. With them every man created a peer is first a hero ready-made. They judge of every man's capacity for office by the offices he has filled, and the more offices the more ability. Every general officer with them is a Marlborough; every statesman a Burleigh; every judge a Murray or a Yorke. They who, alive, were laughed at or pitied by all their acquaintance, make as good a figure as the best of them in the pages of * Guillim, Edmondson, and Collins.

To these recorders, so full of good-nature to to the great and prosperous, I would willingly leave the first Baron Russell and Earl of Bedford, and the merits of his grants. But the aulnager, the weigher, the meter of grants will not suffer us to acquiesce in the judgment of the prince reigning at the time when they were made. They are never good to those who earn them. Well, then, since the new grantees have war made on them by the old, and that the word of the sovereign is not to be taken, let us turn our eyes to history, in which great men have always a pleasure in contemplating the heroic origin of their house.

The first peer of the name, the first purchaser of the grants, was a Mr. Russell, a person of an ancient gentleman's family, raised by being a minion of Henry the Eighth. As there generally is some resemblance of character to create these relations, the favourite was in all likelihood much such another as his master. The first of those immoderate grants was not taken from the ancient demesne of the crown, but from the recent confiscation of the ancient nobility of the land. The lion, having sucked the blood of his prey, threw the offal carcass to the jackal in waiting. Having tasted once the food of confiscation, the favourites became fierce and ravenous. This worthy favourite's first grant was from the lay nobility. The second, infinitely improving on the enormity of the first, was from the plunder of the Church. In truth his Grace is somewhat excusable for his dislike to a grant like mine, not only in its quantity but in its kind so different from his own.

Mine was from a mild and benevolent sovereign; his from Henry the Eighth.

Mine had not its fund in the murder of any innocent person of illustrious rank, or in the pillage of any body of unoffending men. His grants were from the aggregate and consolidated funds of judgments iniquitously legal, and from possessions voluntarily surrendered by the lawful proprietors, with the gibbet at their door.

The merit of the grantee whom he derives from was that of being a prompt and greedy instrument of a levelling tyrant, who oppressed all descriptions of his people, but who fell with particular fury on everything that was great and noble. Mine has been, in endeavouring to screen every man, in every class, from oppression, and particularly in defending the high and eminent, who in the bad times of confiscating princes, confiscating chief governors, or confiscating demagogues, are the most exposed to jealousy, avarice, and envy.

The merit of the original grantee of his Grace's pensions was in giving his hand to the work and partaking the spoil, with a prince who plundered a part of the national Church of his time and country. Mine was in defending the whole of the national Church of my own time and my own country, and the whole of the national Churches of all countries, from the principles and the examples which lead to ecclesiastical pillage, thence to a contempt of all prescriptive titles, thence to the pillage of all property, and thence to universal desolation.

The merit of the origin of his Grace's fortune was in being a favourite and chief adviser to a prince who left no liberty to their native country. My endeavour was to obtain liberty for the municipal country in which I was born, and for all descriptions and denominations in it. Mine was to support with unrelaxing vigilance every right, every privilege, every franchise, in this my adopted, my dearer, and more comprehensive country; and not only to preserve those rights in this chief seat of empire, but in every nation, in every land, in every climate, language, and religion, in the vast domain that is still under the protection, and the larger that was once under the protection of the British crown.

His founder's merits were, by arts in which he served his master and made his fortune, to bring poverty, wretchedness, and depopulation on his country. Mine were, under a benevolent prince, in promoting the commerce, manufactures, and agriculture of his kingdom; in which his Majesty shows an eminent example, who even in his amusements is a patriot, and in hours of leisure an improver of his native soil.

His founder's merit was the merit of a gentleman raised by the arts of a court, and the protection of a Wolsey, to the eminence of a great and potent lord. His merit in that eminence was, by instigating a tyrant to injustice, to provoke a people to rebellion. My merit was to awaken the sober part of the country, that they might put themselves on their guard against any one potent lord, or any greater number of potent lords, or any combination of great leading men of any sort, if ever they should attempt to proceed in the same courses, but in the reverse order; that is, by instigating a corrupted populace to rebellion, and, through that rebellion, introducing a tyranny yet worse than the tyranny which his Grace's ancestor supported, and of which he profited in the manner we behold in the despotism of Henry the Eighth.

The political merit of the first pensioner of his Grace's house was that of being concerned as a counsellor of state in advising, and in his person executing, the conditions of a dishonourable peace with France, — the surrendering the fortress of Boulogne, then our outguard on the continent. By that surrender, Calais, the key of France, and the bridle in the mouth of that power, was, not many years afterwards, finally lost. My merit has been in resisting the power and pride of France, under any form of its rule, but in opposing it with the greatest zeal and earnestness when that rule appeared in the worst form it could assume, — the worst, indeed, which the prime cause and principle of all evil could possibly give it. It was my endeavour by every means to excite a spirit in the House where I had the honour of a seat, for carrying on, with early vigour and decision, the most clearly just and necessary war that this or any nation ever carried on, in order to save my country from the iron yoke of its power, and from the more dreadful contagion of its principles; to preserve, while they can be preserved, pure and untainted, the ancient, inbred integrity, piety, good-nature, and good humour of the people of England, from the dreadful pestilence which, beginning in France, threatens to lay waste the whole moral, and in a great degree the whole physical, world, having done both in the focus of its most intense malignity.

The labours of his Grace's founder merited the curses, not loud but deep, of the Commons of England, on whom he and his master had effected a complete parliamentary reform, by making them, in their slavery and humiliation, the true and adequate representatives of a debased, degraded, and undone people. My merits were in having had an active, though not always an ostentatious, share, in every one act, without exception, of undisputed constitutional utility in my time, and in having supported, on all occasions, the authority, the efficiency, and the privileges of the Commons of Great Britain. I ended my services by a recorded and fully reasoned assertion on their own journals of their constitutional rights, and a vindication of their constitutional conduct. I laboured in all things to merit their inward approbation, and (along with the assistance of the largest, the greatest, and best of my endeavours) I received their free, unbiased, public, and solemn thanks.

Thus stands the account of the comparative merits of the crown grants which compose the Duke of Bedford's fortune as balanced against mine. In the name of common sense, why should the Duke of Bedford think that none but of the house of Russell are entitled to the favour of the crown? Why should he imagine that no king of England has been capable of judging of merit but King Henry the Eighth? Indeed, he will pardon me; he is a little mistaken: all virtue did not end in the first Earl of Bedford; all discernment did not lose its vision when his creator closed his eyes. Let him remit his rigour on the disproportion between merit and reward in others, and they will make no inquiry into the origin of his fortune. They will regard with much more satisfaction, as he will contemplate with infinitely more advantage, whatever in his pedigree has been dulcified by an exposure to the influence of heaven in a long flow of generations, from the hard, acidulous, metallic tincture of the spring. It is little to be doubted that several of his forefathers in that long series have degenerated into honour and virtue. Let the Duke of Bedford (I am sure he will) reject with scorn and horror the counsels of the lecturers, those wicked panders to avarice and ambition, who would tempt him, in the troubles of his country, to seek another enormous fortune from the forfeitures of another nobility, and the plunder of another Church. Let him (and I trust that yet he will) employ all the energy of his youth, and all the resources of his wealth, to crush rebellious principles which have no foundation in morals, and rebellious movements that have no provocation in tyranny.

Then will be forgot the rebellions which, by a doubtful priority in crime, his ancestor had provoked and extinguished. On such a conduct in the noble duke, many of his countrymen might, and with some excuse might, give way to the enthusiasm of their gratitude, and, in the dashing style of some of the old declaimers, cry out that if the fates had found no other way in which they could give a Duke of Bedford and his opulence as props to a tottering world, then the butchery of the Duke of Buckingham might be tolerated; it might be regarded even with complacency, whilst in the heir of confiscation they saw the sympathizing comforter of the martyrs who suffer under the cruel confiscation of this day; whilst they behold with admiration his zealous protection of the virtuous and loyal nobility of France, and his manly support of his brethren, the yet standing nobility and gentry of his native land. Then his Grace's merit would be pure, and new, and sharp, as fresh from the mint of honour. As he pleased, he might reflect honour on his predecessors, or throw it forward on those who were to succeed him. He might be the propagator of the stock of honour, or the root of it, as he thought proper.

Had it pleased God to continue to me the hopes of succession, I should have been, according to my mediocrity, and the mediocrity of the age I live in, a sort of founder of a family; I should have left a son, who, in all the points in which personal merit can be viewed, in science, in erudition, in genius, in taste, in honour, in generosity, in humanity, in every liberal sentiment, and every liberal accomplishment, would not have shown himself inferior to the Duke of Bedford, or to any of those whom he traces in his line. His Grace very soon would have wanted all plausibility in his attack upon that provision which belonged more to mine than to me. He would soon have supplied every deficiency, and symmetrized every disproportion. It would not have been for that successor to resort to any stagnant, wasting reservoir of merit in me, or in any ancestry. He had in himself a salient, living spring of generous and manly action. Every day he lived, he would have repurchased the bounty of the crown, and ten times more, if ten times more he had received. He was made a public creature, and had no enjoyment whatever but in the performance of some duty. At this exigent moment, the loss of a finished man is not easily supplied.

But a Disposer whose power we are little able to resist, and whose wisdom it behooves us not at all to dispute, has ordained it in another manner, and (whatever my querulous weakness might suggest) a far better. The storm has gone over me; and I lie like one of those old oaks which the late hurricane has scattered about me. I am stripped of all my honours; I am torn up by the roots, and lie prostrate on the earth! There, and prostrate there, I most unfeignedly recognize the divine justice, and in some degree submit to it. But whilst I humble myself before God, I do not know that it is forbidden to repel the attacks of unjust and inconsiderate men. The patience of Job is proverbial. After some of the convulsive struggles of our irritable nature, he submitted himself, and repented in dust and ashes. But even so, I do not find him blamed for reprehending, and with a considerable degree of verbal asperity, those ill-natured neighbours of his, who visited his dunghill to read moral, political, and economical lectures on his misery. I am alone. I have none to meet my enemies in the gate. Indeed, my Lord, I greatly deceive myself if in this hard season I would give a peck of refuse wheat for all that is called fame and honour in the world. This is the appetite but of a few. It is a luxury, it is a privilege, it is an indulgence for those who are at their ease. But we are all of us made to shun disgrace, as we are made to shrink from pain and poverty and disease. It is an instinct; and under the direction of reason, instinct is always in the right. I live in an inverted order. They who ought to have succeeded me are gone before me. They who should have been to me as posterity are in the place of ancestors. I owe to the dearest relation (which ever must subsist in memory) that act of piety which he would have performed to me; I owe it to him to show that he was not descended, as the Duke of Bedford would have it, from an unworthy parent.

The crown has considered me after long service; the crown has paid the Duke of Bedford by advance. He has had a long credit for any service which he may perform hereafter. He is secure, and long may he be secure, in his advance, whether he performs any services or not. But let him take care how he endangers the safety of that constitution which secures his own utility or his own insignificance; or how he discourages those who take up even puny arms, to defend an order of things which, like the sun of heaven, shines alike on the useful and the worthless. His grants are ingrafted on the public law of Europe, covered with the awful hoar of innumerable ages. They are guarded by the sacred rules of prescription, found in that full treasury of jurisprudence from which the jejuneness and penury of our municipal law has, by degrees, been enriched and strengthened. This prescription I had my share (a very full share) in bringing to its perfection. The Duke of Bedford will stand as long as prescriptive law endures; as long as the great stable laws of property, common to us with all civilized nations, are kept in their integrity, and without the smallest intermixture of laws, maxims, principles, or precedents of the grand revolution. They are secure against all changes but one.

The whole revolutionary system — institutes, digest, code, novels, text, gloss, comment — are, not only not the same, but they are the very reverse, and the reverse fundamentally, of all the laws on which civil life has hitherto been upheld in all the governments of the world. The learned professors of the rights of man regard prescription, not as a title to bar all claim set up against all possession — but they look on prescription as itself a bar against the possessor and proprietor. They hold an immemorial possession to be no more than a long-continued, and therefore an aggravated, injustice.

Such are *their* ideas; such *their* religion, and such *their* law. But as to *our* country and *our* race, as long as the well-compacted structure of our Church and State, the sanctuary, the holy of holies of that ancient law, defended by reverence, defended by power, a fortress at once and a temple, shall stand inviolate on the brow of the British Sion — as long as the British monarchy, not more limited than fenced by the orders of the State, shall, like the proud Keep of Windsor, rising in the majesty of proportion, and girt with the double belt of its kindred and co-eval towers, as long as this awful structure shall oversee and guard the subjected land — so long the mounds and dikes of the low, fat Bedford level will have nothing to fear from all the pickaxes of all the levellers of France. As long as our sovereign lord the King, and his faithful subjects, the Lords and Commons of this realm, — the triple cord, which no man can break; the solemn, sworn, constitutional frank-pledge of this nation; the firm guarantees of each other's being and each other's rights; the joint and several securities, each in its place and order, for every kind and every quality of property and of dignity; — as long as these endure, so long the Duke of Bedford is safe: and we are all safe together, — the high from the blights of envy and the spoliations of rapacity; the low from the iron hand of oppression and the insolent spurn of contempt. Amen! and so be it: and so it will be,

**Dum domus Æneæ Capitoli immobile saxum*
Accolet; imperiumque pater Romanus habebit.

But if the rude inroad of Gallic tumult, with its sophistical rights of man to falsify the account, and its sword as a make-weight to throw into the scale, shall be introduced into our city by a misguided populace, set on by proud great men, themselves blinded and intoxicated by a frantic ambition, we shall all of us perish and be overwhelmed in a common ruin. If a great storm blow on our coast, it will cast the whales on the strand as well as the periwinkles. His Grace will not survive the poor grantee he despises, no, not for a twelvemonth. If the great look for safety in the services they render to this Gallic cause, it is to be foolish, even above the weight of privilege allowed to wealth. If his Grace be one of these whom they endeavour to proselytize, he ought to be aware of the character of the sect whose doctrines he is invited to embrace. With them insurrection is the most sacred of revolutionary duties to the State. Ingratitude to benefactors is the first of revolutionary virtues. Ingratitude is indeed their four cardinal virtues compacted and amalgamated into one; and he will find it in everything that has happened since the commencement of the philosophic revolution to this hour. If he pleads the merit of having performed the duty of insurrection against the order he lives (God forbid he ever should), the merit of others will be to perform the duty of insurrection against him. If he pleads (again God forbid he should, and I do not suspect he will) his ingratitude to the crown for its creation of his family, others will plead their right and duty to pay him in kind. They will laugh — indeed they will laugh — at his parchment and his wax. His deeds will be drawn out with the rest of the lumber of his evidence room, and burnt to the tune of **Ça ira* in the courts of Bedford (then Equality) House.

Am I to blame, if I attempt to pay his Grace's hostile reproaches to me with a friendly admonition to himself? Can I be blamed for pointing out to him in what manner he is likely to be affected, if the sect of the cannibal philosophers of France should proselytize any considerable part of this people, and, by their joint proselytizing arms, should conquer that government to which his Grace does not seem to me to give all the support his own security demands? Surely it is proper that he, and that others like him, should know the true genius of this sect: what their opinions are, what they have done, and to whom; and what (if a prognostic is to be formed from the dispositions and actions of men) it is certain they will do hereafter. He ought to know that they have sworn assistance, the only engagement they ever will keep to all in this country who bear a resemblance to themselves, and who think, as such, that "the whole duty of man" consists in destruction. They are a misallied and disparaged branch of the house of Nimrod. They are the Duke of Bedford's natural hunters; and he is their natural game. Because he is not very profoundly reflecting, he sleeps in profound security; they, on the contrary, are always vigilant, active, enterprising, and, though far removed from any knowledge which makes men estimable or useful, in all the instruments and resources of evil their leaders are not meanly instructed, or insufficiently furnished. In the French Revolution everything is new; and, from want of preparation to meet so unlooked-for an evil, everything is dangerous. Never before this time was a set of literary men converted into a gang of robbers and assassins. Never before did a den of bravoes and banditti assume the garb and tone of an academy of philosophers.

Let me tell his Grace that an union of such characters, monstrous as it seems, is not made for producing despicable enemies. But if they are formidable as foes, as friends they are dreadful indeed. The men of property in France, confiding in a force which seemed to be irresistible because it had never been tried, neglected to prepare for a conflict with their enemies at their own weapons. They were found in such a situation as the Mexicans were, when they were attacked by the dogs, the cavalry, the iron, and the gunpowder of a handful of bearded men whom they did not know to exist in nature. This is a comparison that some, I think, have made; and it is just. In France they had their enemies within their houses. They were even in the bosoms of many of them. But they had not sagacity to discern their savage character. They seemed tame and even caressing. They had nothing but **douce humanité* in their mouth. They could not bear the punishment of the mildest laws on the greatest criminals. The slightest severity of justice made their flesh creep. The very idea that war existed in the world disturbed their repose. Military glory was no more, with them, than a splendid infamy. Hardly would they hear of self-defence, which they reduced within such bounds as to leave it no defence at all. All this while they meditated the confiscations and massacres we have seen. Had any one told these unfortunate noblemen and gentlemen how, and by whom, the grand fabric of the French monarchy under which they flourished would be subverted, they would not have pitied him as a visionary, but would have turned from him as what they call a **mauvais plaisant*. Yet we have seen what has happened. The persons who have suffered from the cannibal philosophy of France are so like the Duke of Bedford that nothing but his Grace's probably not speaking quite so good French could enable us to find out any difference. A great many of them had as pompous titles as he, and were of full as illustrious a race; some few of them had fortunes as ample; several of them, without meaning the least disparagement to the Duke of Bedford, were as wise, and as virtuous, and as valiant, and as well educated, and as complete in all the lineaments of men of honour, as he is: and to all this they had added the powerful outguard of a military profession, which, in its nature, renders men somewhat more cautious than those who have nothing to attend to but the lazy enjoyment of undisturbed possessions. But security was their ruin. They are dashed to pieces in the storm, and our shores are covered with the wrecks. If they had been aware that such a thing might happen, such a thing never could have happened.

I assure his Grace that, if I state to him the designs of his enemies in a manner which may appear to him ludicrous and impossible, I tell him nothing that has not exactly happened, point by point, but twenty-four miles from our own shore. I assure him that the Frenchified faction, more encouraged than others are warned by what has happened in France, look at him and his landed possessions as an object at once of curiosity and rapacity. He is made for them in every part of their double character. As robbers, to them he is a noble booty; as speculatists, he is a glorious subject for their experimental philosophy. He affords matter for an extensive analysis in all the branches of their science, geometrical, physical, civil, and political. These philosophers are fanatics; independent of any interest, which if it operated alone would make them much more tractable, they are carried with such a headlong rage towards every desperate trial that they would sacrifice the whole human race to the slightest of their experiments. I am better able to enter into the character of this description of men than the noble duke can be. I have lived long and variously in the world. Without any considerable pretensions to literature in myself, I have aspired to the love of letters. I have lived for a great many years in habitudes with those who professed them. I can form a tolerable estimate of what is likely to happen from a character chiefly dependent for fame and fortune on knowledge and talent, as well in its morbid and perverted state as in that which is sound and natural. Naturally, men so formed and finished are the first gifts of Providence to the world. But when they have once thrown off the fear of God, which was in all ages too often the case, and the fear of man, which is now the case, and when in that state they come to understand one another, and to act in corps, a more dreadful calamity cannot arise out of hell to scourge mankind. Nothing can be conceived more hard than the heart of a thoroughbred metaphysician. It comes nearer to the cold malignity of a wicked spirit than to the frailty and passion of a man. It is like that of the principle of evil himself, incorporeal, pure, unmixed, dephlegmated, defecated evil. It is no easy operation to eradicate humanity from the human breast. What Shakespeare calls *"the compunctious visitings of nature" will sometimes knock at their hearts, and protest against their murderous speculations. But they have a means of compounding with their nature. Their humanity is not dissolved. They only give it a long prorogation. They are ready to declare that they do not think two thousand years too long a period for the good that they pursue. It is remarkable that they never see any way to their projected good but by the road of some evil. Their imagination is not fatigued with the contemplation of human suffering through the wild waste of centuries added to centuries of misery and desolation. Their humanity is at their horizon — and, like the horizon, it always flies before them. The geometricians and the chemists bring, the one from the dry bones of their diagrams, and the other from the soot of their furnaces, dispositions that make them worse than indifferent about those feelings and habitudes which are the supports of the moral world. Ambition is come upon them suddenly; they are intoxicated with it, and it has rendered them fearless of the danger which may from thence arise to others or to themselves. These philosophers consider men, in their experiments, no more than they do mice in an air-pump or in a recipient of mephitic gas. Whatever his Grace may think of himself, they look upon him, and everything that belongs to him, with no more regard than they do upon the whiskers of that little long-tailed animal that has been long the game of the grave, demure, insidious, spring-nailed, velvet-pawed, green-eyed philosophers, whether going upon two legs or upon four.

His Grace's landed possessions are irresistibly inviting to an agrarian experiment. They are a downright insult upon the rights of man. They are more extensive than the territory of many of the Grecian republics, and they are without comparison more fertile than most of them. There are now republics in Italy, in Germany, and in Switzerland, which do not possess anything like so fair and ample a domain. There is scope for seven philosophers to proceed in their analytical experiments upon *Harrington's seven different forms of republics, in the acres of this one duke. Hitherto they have been wholly unproductive to speculation, fitted for nothing but to fatten bullocks, and to produce grain for beer, still more to stupefy the dull English understanding. *Abbé Sieyès has whole nests of pigeonholes full of constitutions ready-made, ticketed, sorted, and numbered, suited to every season and every fancy: some with the top of the pattern at the bottom, and some with the bottom at the top; some plain, some flowered; some distinguished for their simplicity, others for their complexity; some of blood color, some of **boue de Paris*; some with directories, others without a direction; some with councils of elders, and councils of youngsters; some without any council at all; some where the electors choose the representatives; others, where the representatives choose the electors; some in long coats, and some in short cloaks; some with pantaloons; some without breeches; some with five-shilling qualifications; some totally unqualified. So that no constitution-fancier may go unsuited from his shop, provided he loves a pattern of pillage, oppression, arbitrary imprisonment, confiscation, exile, revolutionary judgment, and legalized premeditated murder, in any shapes into which they can be put. What a pity it is that the progress of experimental philosophy should be checked by his Grace's monopoly! Such are their sentiments, I assure him; such is their language, when they dare to speak; and such are their proceedings, when they have the means to act.

Their geographers and geometricians have been some time out of practice. It is some time since they have divided their own country into squares. That figure has lost the charms of its novelty. They want new lands for new trials. It is not only the geometricians of the republic that find him a good subject; the chemists have bespoken him, after the geometricians have done with him. As the first set have an eye on his Grace's lands, the chemists are not less taken with his buildings. They consider mortar as a very anti-revolutionary invention, in its present state, but, properly employed, an admirable material for overturning all establishments. They have found that the gunpowder of ruins is far the fittest for making other ruins, and so *ad infinitum*. They have calculated what quantity of matter convertible into nitre is to be found in Bedford House, in *Woburn Abbey, and in what his Grace and his trustees have still suffered to stand of that foolish royalist, Inigo Jones, in *Covent Garden. Churches, play-houses, coffee-houses, all alike are destined to be mingled and equalized and blended into one common rubbish; and, well sifted and lixiviated, to crystallize into true, democratic, explosive, insurrectionary nitre. Their academy *del Cimento* (**per antiphrasin*), with Morveau and Hassenfratz at its head, have computed that the brave *sans-culottes* may make war on all the aristocracy of Europe for a twelvemonth, out of the rubbish of the Duke of Bedford's buildings.

While the Morveaus and Priestleys are proceeding with these experiments upon the Duke of Bedford's houses, the Sieyès, and the rest of the analytical legislators and constitution-venders, are quite as busy in their trade of decomposing organization, in forming his Grace's vassals into primary assemblies, national guards, first, second, and third requisitioners, committees of research, conductors of the traveling guillotine, judges of revolutionary tribunals, legislative hangmen, supervisors of domiciliary visitation, exactors of forced loans, and assessors of the maximum.

The din of all this smithery may some time or other possibly wake this noble duke, and push him to an endeavour to save some little matter from their experimental philosophy. If he pleads his grants from the crown, he is ruined at the outset. If he pleads he has received them from the pillage of superstitious corporations, this indeed will stagger them a little, because they are enemies to all corporations, and to all religion. However, they will soon recover themselves, and will tell his Grace, or his learned counsel, that all such property belongs to the nation; and that it would be more wise for him, if he wishes to live the natural term of a citizen (that is, according to *Condorcet's calculation, six months on an average), not to pass for an usurper upon the national property. This is what the sergeants at law of the rights of man will say to the puny apprentices of the common law of England.

Is the genius of philosophy not yet known? You may as well think the garden of the Tuileries was well protected with the cords of ribbon insultingly stretched by the National Assembly to keep the sovereign *canaille* from intruding on the retirement of the poor King of the French, as that such flimsy cobwebs will stand between the savages of the revolution and their natural prey. Deep philosophers are no triflers; brave *sans-culottes* are no formalists. They will no more regard a *Marquis of Tavistock than an Abbot of Tavistock; the Lord of Woburn will not be more respectable in their eyes than the Prior of Woburn; they will make no difference between the superior of a Covent Garden of nuns, and of a Covent Garden of another description. They will not care a rush whether his coat is long or short, whether the colour be purple or blue-and-buff. They will not trouble their heads with what part of his head his hair is cut from; and they will look with equal respect on a tonsure and a crop. Their only question will be that of their *Legendre, or some other of their legislative butchers, — how he cuts up? how he tallows in the caul, or on the kidneys?

Is it not a singular phenomenon that, whilst the *sans-culotte* carcass-butchers and the philosophers of the shambles are pricking their dotted lines upon his hide, and, like the print of the poor ox that we see in the shop windows at Charing Cross, alive as he is, and thinking no harm in the world, he is divided into rumps, and sirloins, and briskets, and into all sorts of pieces for roasting, boiling, and stewing; that, all the while they are measuring him, his Grace is measuring me, is invidiously comparing the bounty of the crown with the deserts of the defender of his order, and in the same moment fawning on those who have the knife half out of the sheath? Poor innocent!

*Pleas'd to the last, he crops the flow'ry food,
And licks the hand just rais'd to shed his blood.

No man lives too long who lives to do with spirit, and suffer with resignation, what Providence pleases to command, or inflict; but indeed they are sharp incommodities which beset old age. It was but the other day that, on putting in order some things which had been brought here on my taking leave of London forever, I looked over a number of fine portraits, most of them of persons now dead, but whose society, in my better days, made this a proud and happy place. Amongst these was the picture of *Lord Keppel. It was painted by an artist worthy of the subject, the excellent friend of that excellent man from their earliest youth, and a common friend of us both, with whom we lived for many years without a moment of coldness, of peevishness, of jealousy, or of jar, to the day of our final separation.

I ever looked on Lord Keppel as one of the greatest and best men of his age; and I loved and cultivated him accordingly. He was much in my heart, and I believe I was in his to the very last beat. It was after his trial at Portsmouth that he gave me this picture. With what zeal and anxious affection I attended him through that his agony of glory, what part my son took in the early flush and enthusiasm of his virtue, and the pious passion with which he attached himself to all my connections, with what prodigality we both squandered ourselves in courting almost every sort of enmity for his sake, I believe he felt, just as I should have felt such friendship on such an occasion. I partook indeed of this honour, with several of the first, and best, and ablest in the kingdom, but I was behindhand with none of them; and I am sure that, if to the eternal disgrace of this nation, and to the total annihilation of every trace of honour and virtue in it, things had taken a different turn from what they did, I should have attended him to the quarter-deck with no less good will and more pride, though with far other feelings, than I partook of the general flow of national joy that attended the justice that was done to his virtue.

Pardon, my Lord, the feeble garrulity of age, which loves to diffuse itself in discourse of the departed great. At my years we live in retrospect alone; and, wholly unfitted for the society of vigorous life, we enjoy the best balm of all wounds, the consolation of friendship, in those only whom we have lost forever. Feeling the loss of Lord Keppel at all times, at no time did I feel it so much as on the first day when I was attacked in the House of Lords.

Had he lived, that reverend form would have risen in its place, and, with a mild, parental reprehension to his nephew, the Duke of Bedford, he would have told him that the favour of that gracious prince, who had honoured his virtues with the government of the navy of Great Britain, and with a seat in the hereditary great council of his kingdom, was not undeservedly shown to the friend of the best portion of his life, and his faithful companion and counsellor under his rudest trials. He would have told him, that to whomever else these reproaches might be becoming, they were not decorous in his near kindred. He would have told him that when men in that rank lose decorum they lose everything.

On that day I had a loss in Lord Keppel; but the public loss of him in this awful crisis —! I speak from much knowledge of the person; he never would have listened to any compromise with the rabble rout of this *sans-culotterie* of France. His goodness of heart, his reason, his taste, his public duty, his principles, his prejudices would have repelled him forever from all connection with that horrid medley of madness, vice, impiety, and crime.

Lord Keppel had two countries: one of descent, and one of birth. Their interest and their glory are the same; and his mind was capacious of both. His family was noble, and it was Dutch: that is, he was of the oldest and purest nobility that Europe can boast, among a people renowned above all others for love of their native land. Though it was never shown in insult to any human being, Lord Keppel was something high. It was a wild stock of pride, on which the tenderest of all hearts had grafted the milder virtues. He valued ancient nobility; and he was not disinclined to augment it with new honours. He valued the old nobility and the new, not as an excuse for inglorious sloth, but as an incitement to virtuous activity. He considered it as a sort of cure for selfishness and a narrow mind; conceiving that a man born in an elevated place in himself was nothing, but everything in what went before, and what was to come after him. Without much speculation, but by the sure instinct of ingenuous feelings, and by the dictates of plain, unsophisticated, natural understanding, he felt that no great commonwealth could by any possibility long subsist, without a body of some kind or other of nobility, decorated with honour, and fortified by privilege. This nobility forms the chain that connects the ages of a nation, which otherwise (with Mr. Paine) would soon be taught that no one generation can bind another. He felt that no political fabric could be well made without some such order of things as might, through a series of time, afford a rational hope of securing unity, coherence, consistency, and stability to the state. He felt that nothing else can protect it against the levity of courts, and the greater levity of the multitude. That to talk of hereditary monarchy, without anything else of hereditary reverence in the commonwealth, was a low-minded absurdity, fit only for those detestable "fools aspiring to be knaves," who began to forge in 1789 the false money of the French constitution — that it is one fatal objection to all new fancied and new fabricated republics (among a people, who, once possessing such an advantage, have wickedly and insolently rejected it) that the prejudice of an old nobility is a thing that cannot be made. It may be improved, it may be corrected, it may be replenished; men may be taken from it or aggregated to it, but the thing itself is matter of inveterate opinion, and therefore cannot be matter of mere positive institution. He felt that this nobility, in fact, does not exist in wrong of other orders of the state, but by them, and for them.

I knew the man I speak of: and, if we can divine the future out of what we collect from the past, no person living would look with more scorn and horror on the impious parricide committed on all their ancestry, and on the desperate attainder passed on all their posterity, by the Orleans, and the Rochefoucaulds, and the Fayettes, and the Vicomtes de Noailles, and the false Perigords, and the long *et cetera* of the perfidious *sans-culottes* of the court, who like demoniacs, possessed with a spirit of fallen pride, and inverted ambition, abdicated their dignities, disowned their families, betrayed the most sacred of all trusts, and, by breaking to pieces a great link of society and all the cramps and holdings of the state, brought eternal confusion and desolation on their country. For the fate of the miscreant parricides themselves he would have had no pity. Compassion for the myriads of men, of whom the world was not worthy, who by their means have perished in prisons, or on scaffolds, or are pining in beggary and exile, would leave no room in his, or in any well-formed mind, for any such sensation. We are not made at once to pity the oppressor and the oppressed.

Looking to his Batavian descent, how could he bear to behold his kindred, the descendants of the brave nobility of Holland, whose blood, prodigally poured out, had, more than all the canals, meres, and inundations of their country, protected their independence, to behold them bowed in the basest servitude to the basest and vilest of the human race; in servitude to those who in no respect were superior in dignity, or could aspire to a better place than that of hangmen to the tyrants, to whose sceptred pride they had opposed an elevation of soul that surmounted and overpowered the loftiness of Castile, the haughtiness of Austria, and the overbearing arrogance of France?

Could he with patience bear that the children of that nobility who would have deluged their country and given it to the sea rather than submit to Louis XIV, who was then in his meridian glory, when his arms were conducted by the Turennes, by the Luxembourgs, by the Boufflers; when his councils were directed by the Colberts, and the Louvois; when his tribunals were filled by the Lamoignons and the Daguessaus — that these should be given up to the cruel sport of the Pichegrus, the Jourdans, the Santerres, under the Rolands, the Brissots, and Gorfas, and Robespierres, the Reubels, the Carnots, and Talliens, and Dantons, and the whole tribe of regicides, robbers, and revolutionary judges that, from the rotten carcass of their own murdered country, have poured out innumerable swarms of the lowest, and at once the most destructive, of the classes of animated nature, which, like columns of locusts, have laid waste the fairest part of the world?

Would Keppel have borne to see the ruin of the virtuous patricians, that happy union of the noble and the burgher, who, with signal prudence and integrity, had long governed the cities of the confederate republic, the cherishing fathers of their country, who, denying commerce to themselves, made it flourish in a manner unexampled under their protection? Could Keppel have borne that a vile faction should totally destroy this harmonious construction, in favour of a robbing democracy, founded on the spurious rights of man?

He was no great clerk, but he was perfectly well versed in the interests of Europe, and he could not have heard with patience that the country of *Grotius, the cradle of the law of nations, and one of the richest repositories of all law, should be taught a new code by the ignorant flippancy of Thomas Paine, the presumptuous foppery of La Fayette, with his stolen rights of man in his hand, the wild, profligate intrigue, and turbulency, of Marat, and the impious sophistry of Condorcet, in his insolent addresses to the Batavian republic.

Could Keppel, who idolized *the house of Nassau, who was himself given to England along with the blessings of the British and Dutch revolutions; with revolutions of stability; with revolutions which consolidated and married the liberties and the interests of the two nations forever, could he see the fountain of British liberty itself in servitude to France? Could he see with patience a Prince of Orange expelled as a sort of diminutive despot, with every kind of contumely, from the country, which that family of deliverers had so often rescued from slavery, and obliged to live in exile in another country which owes its liberty to his house?

Would Keppel have heard with patience that the conduct to be held on such occasions was to become short by the knees to the faction of the homicides, to entreat them quietly to retire? or, if the fortune of war should drive them from their first wicked and unprovoked invasion, that no security should be taken, no arrangement made, no barrier formed, no alliance entered into for the security of that, which under a foreign name is the most precious part of England? What would he have said, if it was even proposed that the Austrian Netherlands (which ought to be a barrier to Holland, and the tie of an alliance, to protect her against any species of rule that might be erected, or even be restored in France) should be formed into a republic under her influence, and dependent upon her power?

But above all, what would he have said, if he had heard it made a matter of accusation against me, by his nephew the Duke of Bedford, that I was the author of the war? Had I a mind to keep that high distinction to myself, as from pride I might, but from justice I dare not, he would have snatched his share of it from my hand, and held it with the grasp of a dying convulsion to his end.

It would be a most arrogant presumption in me to assume to myself the glory of what belongs to his Majesty, and to his ministers, and to his Parliament, and to the far greater majority of his faithful people: but had I stood alone to counsel, and that all were determined to be guided by my advice, and to follow it implicitly, — then I should have been the sole author of a war. But it should have been a war on my ideas and my principles. However, let his Grace think as he may of my demerits with regard to the war with regicide, he will find my guilt confined to that alone. He never shall, with the smallest colour of reason, accuse me of being the author of a peace with regicide. But that is high matter; and ought not to be mixed with anything of so little moment as what may belong to me, or even to the Duke of Bedford.

I have the honour to be, &c.

EDMUND BURKE

[1796]

THOMAS PAINE

When in the autumn of 1774 Thomas Paine emigrated from England, he was thirty-seven years of age and had given little indication of unusual ability; twenty years later he was one of the most famous men in three different countries: he had taken a prominent part in the American Revolution; he had written an apology for the French Revolution, one of the most widely discussed books in Europe, which had led to his prosecution and outlawry in England for treason; and he had served in the French National Convention and had narrowly escaped the guillotine. When he died in America fifteen years later, he had become notorious because of *The Age of Reason.* Since then his memory has been reviled by many and passionately lauded by others, though he is still best known as "Tom" Paine, the enemy of Christianity.

Paine won his first reputation as a pamphleteer, and in spite of the bulk of some of his later works he continued a pamphleteer to the end. *Common Sense* was published in February, 1776, and immediately took the American colonies by storm, selling 120,000 copies within three months. No single cause contributed more than this little pamphlet to American independence. Late in the same year he began *The Crisis* papers, which were of great importance in strengthening the Continental army and its supporters. After the American Revolution was over, he returned to England, where in 1791–92 he published *The Rights of Man*, an answer to Burke's *Reflections on the French Revolution.* In a vigorous journalistic style that employed lucid explanation and telling argument, Paine here presented the claims of the French Revolution. Again he achieved a popular triumph, though the book was suppressed in England and all but the most radical of his supporters soon afterwards lost faith in the cause through the excesses of the Reign of Terror. In the three parts of *The Age of Reason* he continued his pamphleteering activities by an attack on organized religion, which he believed was no less inimical to human liberties than was monarchial government.

Paine was a Deist rather than an atheist; many of his objections to orthodox Christianity were the old Deist arguments against the inspiration of the Bible, and many of the conclusions have been accepted by Modernists in our day. It was chiefly the crude vigour of his attacks and the intemperate language in which they were expressed that made the book notorious. His political writing was popular rather than profound; it disseminated revolutionary ideas, but it contributed little to the theory of government. Today his doctrinaire teaching is old-fashioned when compared with Burke's concept of social evolution, yet many of Paine's radical conclusions have become orthodox. Beside the full-dress dignity of "Junius" or Burke, Paine's style appears less artistic than it really is: it has flexibility, concreteness, and directness; even its lapses from good taste probably contributed to its effectiveness with masses of people. To this style is due no small part of his success as a popularizer and controversialist.

From THE RIGHTS OF MAN

..."We have seen," says Mr. Burke, "the French rebel against a mild and lawful monarch with more fury, outrage, and insult than any people has been known to rise against the most illegal usurper, or the most sanguinary tyrant." This is one among a thousand other instances in which Mr. Burke shows that he is ignorant of the springs and principles of the French Revolution.

It was not against Louis XVI but against the despotic principles of the government that the nation revolted. These principles had not their origin in him, but in the original establishment, many centuries back; and they were become too deeply rooted to be removed, and the Augean stable of parasites and plunderers too abominably filthy to be cleansed by anything short of a complete and universal revolution. When it becomes necessary to do a thing, the whole heart and soul should go into the measure, or not attempt it. That crisis was then arrived, and there remained no choice but to act with determined vigour, or not to act at all. The king was known to be the friend of the nation, and this circumstance was favourable to the enterprise. Perhaps no man bred up in the style of an absolute king ever possessed a heart so little disposed to the exercise of that species of power as the present King of France. But the principles of the government itself still remained the same. The monarch and the monarchy were distinct and separate things; and it was against the established despotism of the latter, and not against the person or principles of the former, that the revolt commenced, and the revolution has been carried.

Mr. Burke does not attend to the distinction between men and principles, and, therefore, he does not see that a revolt may take place against the despotism of the latter, while there lies no charge of despotism against the former.

The natural moderation of Louis XVI contributed nothing to alter the hereditary despotism of the monarchy. All the tyrannies of former reigns, acted under that hereditary despotism, were still liable to be revived in the hands of a successor. It was not the respite of a reign that would satisfy France, enlightened as she then was become. A casual discontinuance of the *practice* of despotism, is not a discontinuance of its *principles*: the former depends on the virtue of the individual who is in immediate possession of the power; the latter, on the virtue and fortitude of the nation. In the case of Charles I and James II of England, the revolt was against the personal despotism of the men; whereas in France, it was against the hereditary despotism of the established government. But men who can consign over the rights of posterity forever on the authority of a mouldy parchment, like Mr. Burke, are not qualified to judge of this revolution. It takes in a field too vast for their views to explore, and proceeds with a mightiness of reason they cannot keep pace with.

But there are many points of view in which this revolution may be considered. When despotism has established itself for ages in a country, as in France, it is not in the person of the king only that it resides. It has the appearance of being so in show, and in nominal authority; but it is not so in practice and in fact. It has its standard everywhere. Every office and department has its despotism, founded upon custom and usage. Every place has its Bastille, and every Bastille its despot. The original hereditary despotism resident in the person of the king divides and subdivides itself into a thousand shapes and forms, till at last the whole of it is acted by deputation. This was the case in France; and against this species of despotism, proceeding on through an endless labyrinth of office till the source of it is scarcely perceptible, there is no mode of redress. It strengthens itself by assuming the appearance of duty, and tyrannizes under the pretence of obeying.

When a man reflects on the condition which France was in from the nature of her government, he will see other causes for revolt than those which immediately connect themselves with the person or character of Louis XVI. There were, if I may so express it, a thousand despotisms to be reformed in France, which had grown up under the hereditary despotism of the monarchy, and became so rooted as to be in a great measure independent of it. Between the Monarchy, the Parliament, and the Church there was a rivalship of despotism, besides the feudal despotism operating locally, and the ministerial despotism operating everywhere. But Mr. Burke, by considering the king as the only possible object of a revolt, speaks as if France was a village, in which everything that passed must be known to its commanding officer, and no oppression could be acted but what he could immediately control. Mr. Burke might have been in the Bastille his whole life, as well under Louis XVI as Louis XIV, and neither the one nor the other have known that such a man as Mr. Burke existed. The despotic principles of the government were the same in both reigns, though the dispositions of the men were as remote as tyranny and benevolence.

What Mr. Burke considers as a reproach to the French Revolution (that of bringing it forward under a reign more mild than the preceding ones) is one of its highest honours. The revolutions that have taken place in other European countries have been excited by personal hatred. The rage was against the man, and he became the victim. But, in the instance of France we see a revolution generated in the rational contemplation of the rights of man, and distinguishing from the beginning between persons and principles.

But Mr. Burke appears to have no idea of principles when he is contemplating governments. "Ten years ago," says he, "I could have felicitated France on her having a government, without inquiring what the nature of that government was or how it was administered." Is this the language of a rational man? Is it the language of a heart feeling as it ought to feel for the rights and happiness of the human race? On this ground, Mr. Burke must compliment all the governments in the world, while the victims who suffer under them, whether sold into slavery or tortured out of existence, are wholly forgotten. It is power, and not principles, that Mr. Burke venerates; and under this abominable depravity, he is disqualified to judge between them. Thus much for his opinion as to the occasions of the French Revolution. I now proceed to other considerations.

I know a place in America called Point-no-Point, because, as you proceed along the shore, gay and flowery as Mr. Burke's language, it continually recedes, and presents itself at a distance before you; but when you have got as far as you can go, there is no point at all. Just thus it is with Mr. Burke's three hundred and fifty-six pages. It is therefore difficult to reply to him. But as the points he wishes to establish may be inferred from what he abuses, it is in his paradoxes that we must look for his arguments.

As to the tragic paintings by which Mr. Burke has outraged his own imagination, and seeks to work upon that of his readers, they are very well calculated for theatrical representation, where facts are manufactured for the sake of show, and accommodated to produce, through the weakness of sympathy, a weeping effect. But Mr. Burke should recollect that he is writing history, and not plays, and that his readers will expect truth, and not the spouting rant of high-toned exclamation.

When we see a man dramatically lamenting, in a publication intended to be believed, that "the age of chivalry is gone!" that "the glory of Europe is extinguished forever!" that "the unbought grace of life [if any one knows what it is], the cheap defence of nations, the nurse of manly sentiment and heroic enterprise, is gone!" and all this because the Quixote age of chivalry nonsense is gone, what opinion can we form of his judgment, or what regard can we pay to his facts? In the rhapsody of his imagination he has discovered a world of windmills, and his sorrows are that there are no Quixotes to attack them. But if the age of aristocracy, like that of chivalry, should fall (and they had originally some connection), Mr. Burke, the trumpeter of the order, may continue his parody to the end, and finish with exclaiming, *"Othello's occupation's gone!"

Notwithstanding Mr. Burke's horrid paintings, when the French Revolution is compared with the revolutions of other countries, the astonishment will be that it is marked with so few sacrifices; but this astonishment will cease when we reflect that *principles*, and not *persons*, were the meditated objects of destruction. The mind of the nation was acted upon by a higher stimulus than what the consideration of persons could inspire, and sought a higher conquest than could be produced by the downfall of an enemy. *Among the few who fell, there do not appear to be any that were intentionally singled out. They all of them had their fate in the circumstances of the moment, and were not pursued with *that long, cold-blooded, unabated revenge which pursued the unfortunate Scotch in the affair of 1745.

Through the whole of Mr. Burke's book I do not observe that the Bastille is mentioned more than once, and that with a kind of implication as if he were sorry it was pulled down, and wished it were built up again. "We have rebuilt Newgate," says he, "and tenanted the mansion; and we have prisons almost as strong as the Bastille for those who dare to libel the queens of France." As for what *a madman, like the person called Lord G[eorge] G[ordon], might say, to whom Newgate is rather a bedlam than a prison, it is unworthy a rational consideration. It was a madman that libelled, and that is sufficient apology; and it afforded an opportunity for confining him, which was the thing that was wished for. But certain it is that Mr. Burke, who does not call himself a madman, whatever other people may do, has libelled, in the most unprovoked manner and in the grossest style of the most vulgar abuse, the whole representative authority of France; and yet Mr. Burke takes his seat in the British House of Commons! From his violence and his grief, his silence on some points and his excess on others, it is difficult not to believe that Mr. Burke is sorry, extremely sorry, that arbitrary power, the power of the Pope and the Bastille, are pulled down.

Not one glance of compassion, not one commiserating reflection, that I can find throughout his book, has he bestowed on those who lingered out the most wretched of lives, a life without hope in the most miserable of prisons. It is painful to behold a man employing his talents to corrupt himself. Nature has been kinder to Mr. Burke than he is to her. He is not affected by the reality of distress touching his heart, but by the showy resemblance of it striking his imagination. He

* Notes on Thomas Paine will be found in the Appendix, pp. 1053 ff.

pities the plumage, but forgets the dying bird. Accustomed to kiss the aristocratical hand that hath purloined him from himself, he degenerates into a composition of art, and the genuine soul of nature forsakes him. His hero or his heroine must be a tragedy-victim, expiring in show, and not the real prisoner of misery, sliding into death in the silence of a dungeon.

*As Mr. Burke has passed over the whole transaction of the Bastille (and his silence is nothing in his favour), and has entertained his readers with reflections on supposed facts distorted into real falsehoods, I will give, since he has not, some account of the circumstances which preceded that transaction. They will serve to show that less mischief could scarcely have accompanied such an event when considered with the treacherous and hostile aggravations of the enemies of the revolution....

I have now to follow Mr. Burke through a pathless wilderness of rhapsodies, and a sort of descant upon governments, in which he asserts whatever he pleases, on the presumption of its being believed, without offering either evidence or reasons for so doing.

Before anything can be reasoned upon to a conclusion, certain facts, principles, or data to reason from, must be established, admitted, or denied. Mr. Burke, with his usual outrage, abused the "Declaration of the Rights of Man," published by the National Assembly of France, as the basis on which the constitution of France is built. This he calls "paltry and blurred sheets of paper about the rights of man." Does Mr. Burke mean to deny that man has any rights? If he does, then he must mean that there are no such things as rights anywhere, and that he has none himself; for who is there in the world but man? But if Mr. Burke means to admit that man has rights, the question then will be: What are those rights, and how man came by them originally?

The error of those who reason by precedents drawn from antiquity, respecting the rights of man, is that they do not go far enough into antiquity. They do not go the whole way. They stop in some of the intermediate stages of an hundred or a thousand years, and produce what was then done, as a rule for the present day. This is no authority at all. If we travel still farther into antiquity, we shall find a direct contrary opinion and practice prevailing; and, if antiquity is to be authority, a thousand such authorities may be produced, successively contradicting each other; but if we proceed on, we shall at last come out right; we shall come to the time when man came from the hand of his Maker. What was he then? Man. Man was his high and only title, and a higher cannot be given him. But of titles I shall speak hereafter.

We are now got at the origin of man, and at the origin of his rights. As to the manner in which the world has been governed from that day to this, it is no farther any concern of ours than to make a proper use of the errors or the improvements which the history of it presents. Those who lived a hundred or a thousand years ago were then moderns, as we are now. They had *their* ancients, and those ancients had others, and we also shall be ancients in our turn. If the mere name of antiquity is to govern in the affairs of life, the people who are to live an hundred or a thousand years hence may as well take us for a precedent, as we make a precedent of those who lived an hundred or a thousand years ago. The fact is that portions of antiquity, by proving everything, establish nothing. It is authority against authority all the way, till we come to the divine origin of the rights of man, at the creation. Here our enquiries find a resting-place, and our reason finds a home. If a dispute about the rights of man had arisen at the distance of an hundred years from the creation, it is to this source of authority they must have referred, and it is to this same source of authority that we must now refer.

Though I mean not to touch upon any sectarian principle of religion, yet it may be worth observing that the genealogy of Christ is traced to Adam. Why, then, not trace the rights of man to the creation of man? I will answer the question. Because there have been upstart governments, thrusting themselves between, and presumptuously working to unmake man.

If any generation of men ever possessed the right of dictating the mode by which the world should be governed forever, it was the first generation that existed; and if that generation did it not, no succeeding generation can show any authority for doing it, nor can set any up. The illuminating and divine principle of the equal rights of man (for it has its origin from the Maker of man) relates not only to the living individuals, but to generations of men succeeding each other. Every generation is equal in rights to generations which preceded it, by the same rule that every individual is born equal in rights with his contemporary.

Every history of the creation, and every traditionary account, whether from the lettered or unlettered world, however they may vary in their opinion or belief of certain particulars, all agree in establishing one point, the unity of man; by which I mean that men are all of one degree, and consequently that all men are born equal, and with equal natural right, in the same manner as if posterity had been continued by creation instead of generation, the latter being the only mode by which the former is carried forward; and consequently, every child born into the world must be considered as deriving its existence from God. The world is as new to him as it was to the first man that existed, and his natural right in it is of the same kind.

The Mosaic account of the creation, whether taken as divine authority or merely historical, is full to this point, the unity or equality of man. The expression admits of no controversy. "And God said, let us make man in our own image. In the image of God created he him; male and female created he them." The distinction of sexes is pointed out, but no other distinction is even implied. If this be not divine authority, it is at least historical authority, and shows that the equality of man, so far from being a modern doctrine, is the oldest upon record.

It is also to be observed that all the religions known in the world are founded, so far as they relate to man, on the unity of man, as being all of one degree. Whether in heaven or in hell, or in whatever state man may be supposed to exist hereafter, the good and the bad are the only distinctions. Nay, even the laws of governments are obliged to slide into this principle, by making degrees to consist in crimes, and not in persons.

It is one of the greatest of all truths, and of the highest advantage to cultivate. By considering man in this light, and by instructing him to consider himself in this light, it places him in a close connection with all his duties, whether to his Creator, or to the creation of which he is a part; and it is only when he forgets his origin, or, to use a more fashionable phrase, his birth and family, that he becomes dissolute. It is not among the least of the evils of the present existing governments in all parts of Europe that man, considered as man, is thrown back to a vast distance from his Maker, and the artificial chasm filled up with a succession of barriers, or sort of turnpike gates, through which he has to pass. I will quote Mr. Burke's catalogue of barriers that he has set up between man and his Maker. Putting himself in the character of a herald, he says: "We fear God — we look with awe to kings — with affection to Parliaments — with duty to magistrates — with reverence to priests — and with respect to nobility." Mr. Burke has forgotten to put in "chivalry." He has also forgotten to put in Peter.

The duty of man is not a wilderness of turnpike gates, through which he is to pass by tickets from one to the other. It is plain and simple, and consists but of two points: his duty to God, which every man must feel, and, with respect to his neighbour, to do as he would be done by. If those to whom power is delegated do well, they will be respected: if not, they will be despised; and with regard to those to whom no power is delegated, but who assume it, the rational world can know nothing of them.

Hitherto we have spoken only (and that but in part) of the natural rights of man. We have now to consider the civil rights of man, and to show how the one originates from the other. Man did not enter into society to become *worse* than he was before, nor to have fewer rights than he had before, but to have those rights better secured. His natural rights are the foundation of all his civil rights. But in order to pursue this distinction with more precision, it will be necessary to mark the different qualities of natural and civil rights.

A few words will explain this. Natural rights are those which appertain to man in right of his existence. Of this kind are all the intellectual rights, or rights of the mind, and also all those rights of acting as an individual for his own comfort and happiness, which are not injurious to the natural rights of others. Civil rights are those which appertain to man in right of his being a member of society. Every civil right has for its foundation some natural right pre-existing in the individual, but to the enjoyment of which his individual power is not, in all cases, sufficiently competent. Of this kind are all those which relate to security and protection.

From this short review it will be easy to distinguish between that class of natural rights which man retains after entering into society and those which he throws into the common stock as a member of society.

The natural rights which he retains are all those in which the *power* to execute is as perfect in the individual as the right itself. Among this class, as is before mentioned, are all the intellectual rights, or rights of the mind; consequently religion is one of those rights. The natural rights which are not retained, are all those in which, though the right is perfect in the individual, the power to execute them is defective. They answer not his purpose. A man, by natural right, has a right to judge in his own cause; and so far as the right of the mind is concerned, he never surrenders it. But what availeth it him to judge, if he has not power to redress? He therefore deposits this right in the common stock of society, and takes the arm of society, of which he is a part, in preference and in addition to his own. Society grants him nothing. Every man is a proprietor in society, and draws on the capital as a matter of right.

From these premises two or three certain conclusions will follow:

First, That every civil right grows out of a natural right; or, in other words, is a natural right exchanged.

Secondly, That civil power properly considered as such is made up of the aggregate of that class of the natural rights of man, which becomes defective in the individual in point of power, and answers not his purpose, but when collected to a focus becomes competent to the purpose of every one.

Thirdly, That the power produced from the aggregate of natural rights, imperfect in power in the individual, cannot be applied to invade the natural rights which are retained in the individual, and in which the power to execute is as perfect as the right itself.

We have now, in a few words, traced man from a natural individual to a member of society, and shown, or endeavoured to show, the quality of the natural rights retained, and of those which are exchanged for civil rights. Let us now apply these principles to governments.

In casting our eyes over the world, it is extremely easy to distinguish the governments which have arisen out of society, or out of the social compact, from those which have not; but to place this in a clearer light than what a single glance may afford, it will be proper to take a review of the several sources from which governments have arisen and on which they have been founded.

They may be all comprehended under three heads. First, superstition. Secondly, power. Thirdly, the common interest of society and the common rights of man.

The first was a government of priestcraft, the second of conquerors, and the third of reason.

When a set of artful men pretended, through the medium of oracles, to hold intercourse with the Deity, as familiarly as they now march up the backstairs in European courts, the world was completely under the government of superstition. The oracles were consulted, and whatever they were made to say became the law; and this sort of government lasted as long as this sort of superstition lasted. After these a race of conquerors arose, whose government, like that of William the Conqueror, was founded in power, and the sword assumed the name of a sceptre. Governments thus established last as long as the power to support them lasts; but that they might avail themselves of every engine in their favour, they united fraud to force, and set up an idol which they called Divine Right, and which, in imitation of the Pope, who affects to be spiritual and temporal, and in contradiction to the Founder of the Christian religion, twisted itself afterwards into an idol of another shape, called Church and State. The key of St. Peter and the key of the treasury became quartered on one another, and the wondering cheated multitude worshipped the invention.

When I contemplate the natural dignity of man, when I feel (for nature has not been kind enough to me to blunt my feelings) for the honour and happiness of its character, I become irritated at the attempt to govern mankind by force and fraud, as if they were all knaves and fools, and can scarcely avoid disgust at those who are thus imposed upon.

We have now to review the governments which arise out of society, in contradistinction to those which arose out of superstition and conquest.

It has been thought a considerable advance towards establishing the principles of freedom to say that government is a compact between those who govern and those who are governed; but this cannot be true, because it is putting the effect before the cause; for as man must have existed before governments existed, there necessarily was a time when governments did not exist, and consequently there could originally exist no governors to form such a compact with.

The fact therefore must be that the individuals themselves, each in his own personal and sovereign right, entered into a compact with each other to produce a government; and this is the only mode in which governments have a right to arise, and the only principle on which they have a right to exist.

To possess ourselves of a clear idea of what government is, or ought to be, we must trace it to its origin. In doing this we shall easily discover that governments must have arisen either *out* of the people or *over* the people. Mr. Burke has made no distinction. He investigates nothing to its source, and therefore he confounds everything; but he has signified his intention of undertaking, at some future opportunity, a comparison between the constitution of England and France. As he thus renders it a subject of controversy by throwing the gauntlet, I take him upon his own ground. It is in high challenges that high truths have the right of appearing; and I accept it with the more readiness because it affords me, at the same time, an opportunity of pursuing the subject with respect to governments arising out of society.

But it will be first necessary to define what is meant by a constitution. It is not sufficient that we adopt the word; we must fix also a standard signification to it.

A constitution is not a thing in name only, but in fact. It has not an ideal, but a real existence; and wherever it cannot be produced in a visible form, there is none. A constitution is a thing antecedent to a government, and a government is only the creature of a constitution. The constitution of a country is not the act of its government, but of the people constituting its government. It is the body of elements to which you can refer, and quote article by article; and which contains the principles on which the government shall be established, the manner in which it shall be organized, the powers it shall have, the mode of elections, the duration of parliaments, or by what other name such bodies may be called; the powers which the executive part of the government shall have; and in fine, everything that relates to the complete organization of a civil government, and the principles on which it shall act, and by which it shall be bound. A constitution, therefore, is to a government what the laws made afterwards by that government are to a court of judicature. The court of judicature does not make the laws, neither can it alter them; it only acts in conformity to the laws made: and the government is in like manner governed by the constitution.

Can, then, Mr. Burke produce the English constitution? If he cannot, we may fairly conclude that though it has been so much talked about, no such thing as a constitution exists, or ever did exist, and consequently that the people have yet a constitution to form.

Mr. Burke will not, I presume, deny the position I have already advanced — namely, that governments arise either *out* of the people or *over* the people. The English government is one of those which arose out of a conquest, and not out of society, and consequently it arose over the people; and though it has been much modified from the opportunity of circumstances since the time of William the Conqueror, the country has never yet regenerated itself, and is therefore without a constitution.

I readily perceive the reason why Mr. Burke declined going into the comparison between the English and French constitutions, because he could not but perceive, when he sat down to the task, that no such a thing as a constitution existed on his side the question. His book is certainly bulky enough to have contained all he could say on this subject, and it would have been the best manner in which people could have judged of their separate merits. Why then has he declined the only thing that was worth while to write upon? It was the strongest ground he could take, if the advantages were on his side, but the weakest if they were not; and his declining to take it is either a sign that he could not possess it or could not maintain it.

Mr. Burke said, in a speech last winter in Parliament, "that when the National Assembly first met in three orders (the Tiers Etats, the Clergy, and the Noblesse), France had then a good constitution." This shows, among numerous other instances, that Mr. Burke does not understand what a constitution is. The persons so met were not a constitution, but a convention, to make a constitution.

The present National Assembly of France is, strictly speaking, the personal social compact. The members of it are the delegates of the nation in its original character; future assemblies will be the delegates of the nation in its organized character. The authority of the present assembly is different from what the authority of future assemblies will be. The authority of the present one is to form a constitution; the authority of future assemblies will be to legislate according to the principles and forms prescribed in that constitution; and if experience should hereafter show that alterations, amendments, or additions are necessary, the constitution will point out the mode by which such things shall be done, and not leave it to the discretionary power of the future government.

A government on the principles on which constitutional governments arising out of society are established, cannot have the right of altering itself. If it had, it would be arbitrary. It might make itself what it pleased; and wherever such a right is set up, it shows there is no constitution. The act by which the English Parliament empowered itself to sit seven years shows there is no constitution in England. It might, by the same self-authority, have sat any great number of years, or for life. The bill which the present Mr. Pitt brought into Parliament some years ago, to reform Parliament, was on the same erroneous principle. The right of reform is in the nation in its original character, and the constitutional method would be by a general convention elected for the purpose. There is. moreover, a paradox in the idea of vitiated bodies reforming themselves....

[1791]

WILLIAM GODWIN

William Godwin is most often remembered today as the impecunious father-in-law of Shelley and the author of a visionary system of political philosophy that provided the basis for the magnificent poetry of *Queen Mab* and *Prometheus Unbound*; but in the closing years of the eighteenth century he had a reputation second to none among the radical thinkers who welcomed the French Revolution as the herald of a new epoch for emancipated humanity. Even today, when his optimism has been discredited and his Utopian dreams have long since faded, his *Enquiry concerning Political Justice* remains an essential document for the understanding of those spacious times

> In which the meagre, stale, forbidding ways
> Of custom, law, and statute took at once
> The attraction of a country in romance!

Godwin's system is based on implicit belief in human perfectibility. Man, he thought, was fundamentally good, and all evil the result of tyranny and stupidity. Once freed from the perverting influences of false education and distorted social ideals, man would respond to the compelling force of right reason and would delight to do good. Since all government is evil and every constraint upon the individual is harmful, universal emancipation would result in universal benevolence. He conceived of a society with perfect freedom of speech and action, without king or priest or state-regulated education, where each man would do as he pleased and all would find their happiness in contributing to the general well-being. Illness would disappear; war would cease; and the earthly paradise would be restored in the reign of political justice. In this society of unhampered individuals there would be no coercion except the compulsion of reason; since the binding force of contracts and promises would be disavowed, there would be no marriage. Godwin's conception was the opposite of socialism: private property would remain but would be used for the general good; the co-operation of free individuals would be reduced to an absolute minimum. The ideal was philosophic anarchism.

An Enquiry concerning Political Justice was first published in 1793 and made an immediate sensation. In spite of its radical teachings it was not suppressed by the government, even in the days of extreme reaction, probably because it appeared in an expensive form calculated to appeal to philosophic speculation rather than to sway the passions of the mob. Nevertheless the common people clubbed together for its purchase and read it very widely. Three years later it was republished in a second edition in which Godwin modified some statements and explained certain matters that had been misunderstood. In 1799 there was a further revision, which toned down the work though it did not affect the main ideas. Among the rest of his voluminous writings little is of importance except his novels; the most notable of these is *Caleb Williams*, 1794, in which are embodied some of his characteristic teachings in the form of a detective story.

The elements of Godwin's philosophy are traceable to many sources, but the combination is original and the reasoning is cogent. His system, for all its extravagant impracticality, is that of a thinker; with characteristic revolutionary enthusiasm it devotes itself to an abstract idea of justice and ignores all human experience. He writes with classical lucidity in a somewhat Latinate diction, as far removed from the journalism of Paine as from the eloquence of Burke. His personal charm and his power of apt illustration relieve his work from philosophical aridity and make even his abstract reasoning interesting.

The selection here reprinted comprises the greater part of Book II of *An Enquiry concerning Political Justice*, which bears the title, "Principles of Society." It follows the text of the first edition.

AN ENQUIRY CONCERNING POLITICAL JUSTICE

Book II

PRINCIPLES OF SOCIETY

Chapter II

OF JUSTICE

From what has been said, it appears that the subject of the present enquiry is strictly speaking a department of the science of morals. Morality is the source from which its fundamental axioms must be drawn, and they will be made somewhat clearer in the present instance if we assume the term "justice" as a general appellation for all moral duty.

That this appellation is sufficiently expressive of the subject will appear if we consider for a moment mercy, gratitude, temperance, or any of those duties which in looser speaking are contradistinguished from justice. Why should I pardon this criminal, remunerate this favour, abstain from this indulgence? If it partake of the nature of morality, it must be either right oi wrong, just or unjust. It must tend to the benefit of the individual either without intrenching upon or with actual advantage to the mass of individuals. Either way it benefits the whole, because individuals are parts of the whole. Therefore to do it is just, and to forbear it is unjust. If justice have any meaning, it is just that I should contribute everything in my power to the benefit of the whole.

Considerable light will probably be thrown upon our investigation if, quitting for the present the political view, we examine justice merely as it exists among individuals. Justice is a rule of conduct originating in the connection of one percipient being with another. A comprehensive maxim which has been laid down upon the subject is "that we should love our neighbour as ourselves." But this maxim, though possessing considerable merit as a popular principle, is not modelled with the strictness of philosophical accuracy.

In a loose and general view I and my neighbour are both of us men, and of consequence entitled to equal attention. But in reality it is probable that one of us is a being of more worth and importance than the other. A man is of more worth than a beast, because, being possessed of higher faculties, he is capable of a more refined and genuine happiness. In the same manner *the illustrious Archbishop of Cambrai was of more worth than his chambermaid, and there are few of us that would hesitate to pronounce, if his palace were in flames and the life of only one of them could be preserved, which of the two ought to be preferred.

But there is another ground of preference beside the private consideration of one of them being farther removed from the state of a mere animal. We are not connected with one or two percipient beings, but with a society, a nation, and in some sense with the whole family of mankind. Of consequence that life ought to be preferred which will be most conducive to the general good. In saving the life of Fénelon, suppose at the moment when he was conceiving the project of his immortal *Telemachus*, I should be promoting the benefit of thousands who have been cured by the perusal of it of some error, vice, and consequent unhappiness. Nay, my benefit would extend farther than this, for every individual thus cured has become a better member of society and has contributed in his turn to the happiness, the information, and improvement of others.

Supposing I had been myself the chambermaid, I ought to have chosen to die rather than that Fénelon should have died. The life of Fénelon was really preferable to that of the chambermaid. But understanding is the faculty that perceives the truth of this and similar propositions; and justice is the principle that regulates my conduct accordingly. It would have been just in the chambermaid to have preferred the archbishop to herself. To have done otherwise would have been a breach of justice.

Supposing the chambermaid had been my wife, my mother, or my benefactor. This would not alter the truth of the proposition. The life of Fénelon would still be more valuable than that of the chambermaid; and justice — pure, unadulterated justice — would still have preferred that which was most valuable. Justice would have taught me to save the life of Fénelon at the expense of the other. What magic is there in the pronoun "my" to overturn the decisions of everlasting truth? My wife or my mother may be a fool or a prostitute, malicious, lying,

* Notes on William Godwin will be found in the Appendix, p. 1054.

or dishonest. If they be, of what consequence is it that they are mine?

"But my mother endured for me the pains of child bearing, and nourished me in the helplessness of infancy." When she first subjected herself to the necessity of these cares, she was probably influenced by no particular motives of benevolence to her future offspring. Every voluntary benefit however entitles the bestower to some kindness and retribution, But why so? Because a voluntary benefit is an evidence of benevolent intention; that is, of virtue. It is the disposition of the mind, not the external action, that entitles to respect. But the merit of this disposition is equal whether the benefit was conferred upon me or upon another. I and another man cannot both be right in preferring our own individual benefactor, for no man can be at the same time both better and worse than his neighbour. My benefactor ought to be esteemed, not because he bestowed a benefit upon me, but because he bestowed it upon a human being. His desert will be in exact proportion to the degree in which that human being was worthy of the distinction conferred. Thus every view of the subject brings us back to the consideration of my neighbour's moral worth and his importance to the general weal as the only standard to determine the treatment to which he is entitled. Gratitude, therefore, a principle which has so often been the theme of the moralist and the poet, is no part either of justice or virtue. By gratitude I understand a sentiment which would lead me to prefer one man to another from some other consideration than that of his superior usefulness or worth; that is, which would make something true to me (for example this preferableness) which cannot be true to another man and is not true in itself.

It may be objected "that my relation, my companion, or my benefactor will of course in many instances obtain an uncommon portion of my regard: for, not being universally capable of discriminating the comparative worth of different men, I shall inevitably judge most favourably of him of whose virtues I have received the most unquestionable proofs; and thus shall be compelled to prefer the man of moral worth whom I know, to another who may possess, unknown to me, an essential superiority."

This compulsion, however, is founded only in the present imperfection of human nature. It may serve as an apology for my error, but can never turn error into truth. It will always remain contrary to the strict and inflexible decisions of justice. The difficulty of conceiving this is owing merely to our confounding the disposition from which an action is chosen with the action itself. The disposition that would prefer virtue to vice and a greater degree of virtue to a less is undoubtedly a subject of approbation; the erroneous exercise of this disposition by which a wrong object is selected, if unavoidable, is to be deplored, but can by no colouring and under no denomination be converted into right.

It may in the second place be objected "that a mutual commerce of benefits tends to increase the mass of benevolent action, and that to increase the mass of benevolent action is to contribute to the general good." Indeed! Is the general good promoted by falsehood, by treating a man of one degree of worth as if he had ten times that worth? or as if he were in any degree different from what he really is? Would not the most beneficial consequences result from a different plan; from my constantly and carefully enquiring into the deserts of all those with whom I am connected, and from their being sure, after a certain allowance for the fallibility of human judgment, of being treated by me exactly as they deserved? Who can tell what would be the effects of such a plan of conduct universally adopted?

There seems to be more truth in the argument, derived chiefly from the unequal distribution of property, in favour of my providing in ordinary cases for my wife and children, my brothers and relations before I provide for strangers. As long as providing for individuals belongs to individuals, it seems as if there must be a certain distribution of the class needing superintendence and supply among the class affording it, that each man may have his claim and resource. But this argument, if admitted at all, is to be admitted with great caution. It belongs only to ordinary cases; and cases of a higher order or a more urgent necessity will perpetually occur, in competition with which these will be altogether impotent. We must be severely scrupulous in measuring out the quantity of supply, and with respect to money in particular, must remember how little is yet understood of the true mode of employing it for the public benefit.

Having considered the persons with whom justice is conversant, let us next enquire into the degree in which we are obliged to consult the good of others. And here I say that it is just that I should do all the good in my power. Does any person in distress apply to me for relief? It is my duty to grant it, and I commit a breach of duty in refusing. If this principle be not of universal application, it is because in conferring a benefit upon an individual I may in some instances inflict an injury of superior magnitude upon myself or society. Now the same justice that binds me to any individual of my fellow men binds me to the whole. If, while I confer a benefit upon one man, it appear, in striking an equitable balance, that I am injuring the whole, my action ceases to be right and becomes absolutely wrong. But how much am I bound to do for the general weal; that is, for the benefit of the individuals of whom the whole is composed? Everything in my power. What, to the neglect of the means of my own existence? No; for I am myself a part of the whole. Beside, it will rarely happen but that the project of doing for others everything in my power will demand for its execution the preservation of my own existence; or, in other words, it will rarely happen but that I can do more good in twenty years than in one. If the extraordinary case should occur in which I can promote the general good by my death more than by my life, justice requires that I should be content to die. In all other cases it is just that I should be careful to maintain my body and my mind in the utmost vigour and in the best condition for service.

I will suppose for example that it is right for one man to possess a greater portion of property than another, either as the fruit of his industry or the inheritance of his ancestors. Justice obliges him to regard this property as a trust and calls upon him maturely to consider in what manner it may best be employed for the increase of liberty, knowledge, and virtue. He has no right to dispose of a shilling of it at the will of his caprice. So far from being entitled to well-earned applause for having employed some scanty pittance in the service of philanthropy, he is in the eye of justice a delinquent if he withhold any portion from that service. Nothing can be more incontrovertible. Could that portion have been better or more worthily employed? That it could is implied in the very terms of the proposition. Then it was just it should have been so employed. In the same manner as my property I hold my person as a trust in behalf of mankind. I am bound to employ my talents, my understanding, my strength, and my time for the production of the greatest quantity of general good. Such are the declarations of justice; so great is the extent of my duty.

But justice is reciprocal. If it be just that I should confer a benefit, it is just that another man should receive it, and if I withhold from him that to which he is entitled, he may justly complain. My neighbour is in want of ten pounds that I can spare. There is no law of political institution that has been made to reach this case and to transfer this property from me to him. But in the eye of simple justice, unless it can be shown that the money can be more beneficently employed, his claim is as complete as if he had my bond in his possession or had supplied me with goods to the amount.

To this it has sometimes been answered that there is more than one person that stands in need of the money I have to spare, and of consequence I must be at liberty to bestow it as I please. I answer, if only one person offer himself to my knowledge or search, to me there is but one. Those others that I cannot find belong to other rich men to assist (rich men, I say, for every man is rich who has more money than his just occasions demand) and not to me. If more than one person offer, I am obliged to balance their fitness and conduct myself accordingly. It is scarcely possible to happen that two men shall be of exactly equal fitness or that I shall be equally certain of the fitness of the one as of the other.

It is therefore impossible for me to confer upon any man a favour; I can only do him a right. Whatever deviates from the law of justice, even I will suppose in the too much done in favour of some individual or some part of the general whole, is so much subtracted from the general stock — is so much of absolute injustice.

The inference most clearly afforded by the preceding reasonings is the competence of justice as a principle of deduction in all cases of moral enquiry. The reasonings themselves are rather of the nature of illustration and example, and any error that may be imputed to them in particulars will not invalidate the general conclusion, the propriety of applying moral justice as a criterion in the investigation of political truth.

Society is nothing more than an aggregation of individuals. Its claims and its duties must be the aggregate of their claims and duties, the one no more precarious and arbitrary than the other. What has the society a right to require from me? The question is already answered: everything that it is my duty to do. Anything more? Certainly not. Can they change eternal truth or subvert the nature of men and their actions? Can they make it my duty to commit intemperance, to maltreat or assassinate my neighbour? — Again. What is it that the society is bound to do for its members? Everything that can contribute to their welfare. But the nature of their welfare is defined by the nature of mind. That will most contribute to it which enlarges the understanding, supplies incitements to virtue, fills us with a generous consciousness of our independence, and carefully removes whatever can impede our exertions.

Should it be affirmed that it is not in the power of any political system to secure to us these advantages, the conclusion I am drawing will still be incontrovertible. It is bound to contribute everything it is able to these purposes, and no man was ever yet found hardy enough to affirm that it could do nothing. Suppose its influence in the utmost degree limited, there must be one method approaching nearer than any other to the desired object, and that method ought to be universally adopted. There is one thing that political institutions can assuredly do; they can avoid positively counteracting the true interests of their subjects. But all capricious rules and arbitrary distinctions do positively counteract them. There is scarcely any modification of society but has in it some degree of moral tendency. So far as it produces neither mischief nor benefit, it is good for nothing. So far as it tends to the improvement of the community, it ought to be universally adopted.

Chapter III

OF DUTY

There is a difficulty of considerable magnitude as to the subject of the preceding chapter, founded upon the difference which may exist between abstract justice and my apprehensions of justice. When I do an act wrong in itself, but which as to all the materials of judging extant to my understanding appears to be right, is my conduct virtuous or vicious?

Certain moralists have introduced a distinction upon this head between absolute and practical virtue. "There is one species of virtue," they say, "which rises out of the nature of things and is immutable, and another which rises out of the views extant to my understanding. Thus for example suppose I ought to worship Jesus Christ; but having been bred in the religion of Mahomet, I ought to adhere to that religion as long as its evidences shall appear to me conclusive. I am impanelled upon a jury to try a man arraigned for murder, and who is really innocent. Abstractedly considered, I ought to acquit him. But I am unacquainted with his innocence, and evidence is adduced such as to form the strongest presumption of his guilt. Demonstration in such cases is not to be attained; I am obliged in every concern of human life to act upon presumption; I ought therefore to convict him."

It may be doubted, however, whether any good purpose is likely to be answered by employing the terms of abstract science in this versatile and uncertain manner. Morality is, if anything can be, fixed and immutable; and there must surely be some strange deception that should induce us to give to an action eternally and unchangeably wrong the epithets of rectitude, duty, and virtue.

Nor have these moralists been thoroughly aware to what extent this admission would carry them. The human mind is incredibly subtle in inventing an apology for that to which its inclination leads. Nothing is so rare as pure and unmingled hypocrisy. There is no action of our lives which we were not ready at the time of adopting it to justify, unless so far as we were prevented by mere indolence and unconcern. There is scarcely any justification which we endeavour to pass upon others which we do not with tolerable success pass upon ourselves. The distinction, therefore, which is here set up would go near to prove that every action of every human being is entitled to the appellation of virtuous.

There is perhaps no man that cannot recollect the time when he secretly called in question the arbitrary division of property established in human society and felt inclined to appropriate to his use anything the possession of which appeared to him desirable. It is probably in some such way that men are usually influenced in the perpetration of robbery. They persuade themselves of the comparative inutility of the property to its present possessor and the inestimable advantage that would attend it in their hands. They believe that the transfer ought to be made. It is of no consequence that they are not consistent in these views, that the impressions of education speedily recur to their minds, and that in a season of adversity they readily confess the wickedness of their proceeding. It is not less true that they did what at the moment they thought to be right.

But there is another consideration that seems still more decisive of the subject before us. The worst actions, the most contrary to abstract justice and utility, have frequently been done from the most conscientious motives. *Clément, Ravaillac, Damiens, and Gerard had their minds deeply penetrated with anxiety for the eternal welfare of mankind. For these objects they sacrificed their ease, and cheerfully exposed themselves to tortures and death. It was benevolence probably that contributed to light *the fires of Smithfield and point *the daggers of Saint Bartholomew. The inventors of the *Gunpowder Treason were in general men remarkable for the sanctity of their lives and the severity of their manners. It is probable, indeed, that some ambitious views and some sentiments of hatred and abhorrence mixed with the benevolence and integrity of these persons. It is probable that no wrong action was ever committed from views entirely pure. But the deception they put upon themselves might nevertheless be complete. At all events their opinions upon the subject could not alter the real nature of the action.

The true solution of the question lies in observing that the disposition with which an action is adopted is one thing, and the action itself another. A right action may be done from a wrong disposition; in that case we approve the action but condemn the actor. A wrong action may be done from a right disposition; in that case we condemn the action but approve the actor. If the disposition by which a man is governed have a systematical tendency to the benefit of his species, he cannot fail to obtain our esteem, however mistaken he may be in his conduct.

But what shall we say to the duty of a man under these circumstances? Calvin, we will suppose, was clearly and conscientiously persuaded that he ought to burn *Servetus. Ought he to have burned him or not? If he burned him, he did an action detestable in its own nature; if he refrained, he acted in opposition to the best judgment of his own understanding as to a point of moral obligation. It is absurd, however, to say that it was in any sense his duty to burn him. The most that can be admitted is that his disposition was virtuous, and that in the circumstances in which he was placed, an action greatly to be deplored flowed from that disposition by invincible necessity.

Shall we say then that it was the duty of Calvin, who did not understand the principles of toleration, to act upon a truth of which he was ignorant? Suppose that a person is to be tried at York next week for murder and that my evidence would acquit him. Shall we say that it was my duty to go to York though I knew nothing of the matter? Upon the same principles we might affirm that it is my duty to go from London to York in half an hour, as the trial will come on within that time, the impossibility not being more real in one case than in the other. Upon the same principles we might affirm that it is my duty to be impeccable, omniscient, and almighty.

Duty is a term the use of which seems to be to describe the mode in which any being may best be employed for the general good. It is limited in its extent by the extent of the capacity of that being. Now capacity varies in its idea in proportion as we vary our view of the subject to which it belongs. What I am capable of, if you consider me merely as a man is one thing; what I am capable of as a man of a deformed figure, of weak understanding, of superstitious prejudices, or as the case may happen is another. So much cannot be expected of me under these disadvantages as if they were absent. But if this be the true definition of duty, it is absurd to suppose in any case that an action injurious to the general welfare can be classed in the rank of duties.

To apply these observations to the cases that have been stated. Ignorance, so far as it goes, completely annihilates capacity. As I was uninformed of the trial at York, I could not be influenced by any consideration respecting it. But it is absurd to say that it was my duty to neglect a motive with which I was unacquainted. If you allege that Calvin was ignorant of the principles of toleration and had no proper opportunity to learn them, it follows that in burning Servetus he did not violate his duty; but it does not follow that it was his duty to burn him. Upon the supposition here stated duty is silent. Calvin was unacquainted with the principles of justice, and therefore could not practise them. The duty of no man can exceed his capacity; but then neither can in any case an act of injustice be of the nature of duty.

There are certain inferences that flow from this view of the subject which it may be proper to mention. Nothing is more common than for individuals and societies of men to allege that they have acted to the best of their judgment, that they have done their duty, and therefore that their conduct, even should it prove to be mistaken, is nevertheless virtuous. This appears to be an error. An action, though done with the best intention in the world, may have nothing in it of the nature of virtue. In reality the most essential part of virtue consists in the incessantly seeking to inform ourselves more accurately upon the subject of utility and right. Whoever is greatly misinformed respecting them is indebted for his error to a defect in his philanthropy and zeal.

Secondly, since absolute virtue may be out of the power of a human being, it becomes us in the meantime to lay the greatest stress upon a virtuous disposition, which is not attended with the same ambiguity. A virtuous disposition is of the utmost consequence, since it will in the majority of instances be productive of virtuous actions; since it tends, in exact proportion to the quantity of virtue, to increase our discernment and improve our understanding; and since, if it were universally propagated, it would immediately lead to the great end of virtuous actions, the purest and most exquisite happiness of intelligent beings. But a virtuous disposition is principally generated by the uncontrolled exercise of private judgment and the rigid conformity of every man to the dictates of his conscience.

Chapter IV

OF THE EQUALITY OF MANKIND

The equality of mankind is either physical or moral. Their physical equality may be considered either as it relates to the strength of the body or the faculties of the mind.

This part of the subject has been exposed to cavil and objection. It has been said "that the reverse of this equality is the result of our experience. Among the individuals of our species we actually find that there are not two alike. One man is strong and another weak. One man is wise and another foolish. All that exists in the world of the inequality of conditions is to be traced to this as their source. The strong man possesses power to subdue, and the weak stands in need of an ally to protect. The consequence is inevitable: the equality of conditions is a chimerical assumption, neither possible to be reduced into practice nor desirable if it could be so reduced."

Upon this statement two observations are to be made. First, this inequality was in its origin infinitely less than it is at present. In the uncultivated state of man diseases, effeminacy, and luxury were little known; and of consequence the strength of every one much more nearly approached to the strength of his neighbour. In the uncultivated state of man the understandings of all were limited, their wants, their ideas, and their views nearly upon a level. It was to be expected that in their first departure from this state great irregularities would introduce themselves, and it is the object of subsequent wisdom and improvement to mitigate these irregularities.

Secondly, notwithstanding the encroachments that have been made upon the equality of mankind, a great and substantial equality remains. There is no such disparity among the human race as to enable one man to hold several other men in subjection, except so far as they are willing to be subject. All government is founded in opinion. Men at present live under any particular form because they conceive it their interest to do so. One part indeed of a community or empire may be held in subjection by force; but this cannot be the personal force of their despot; it must be the force of another part of the community who are of opinion that it is their interest to support his authority. Destroy this opinion, and the fabric which is built upon it falls to the ground. It follows, therefore, that all men are essentially independent. So much for the physical equality.

The moral equality is still less open to reasonable exception. By moral equality I understand the propriety of applying one unalterable rule of justice to every case that may arise. This cannot be questioned but upon arguments that would subvert the very nature of virtue. "Equality," it has been affirmed, "will always be an unintelligible fiction so long as the capacities of men shall be unequal and their pretended claims have neither guarantee nor sanction by which they can be enforced." But surely justice is sufficiently intelligible in its own nature, abstracted from the consideration whether it be or be not reduced into practice. Justice has relation to beings endowed with perception and capable of pleasure and pain. Now it immediately results from the nature of such beings, independently of any arbitrary constitution, that pleasure is agreeable and pain odious, pleasure to be desired and pain to be obviated. It is therefore just and reasonable that such beings should contribute, so far as it lies in their power, to the pleasure and benefit of each other. Among pleasures some are more exquisite, more unalloyed, and less precarious than others. It is just that these should be preferred.

From these simple principles we may deduce the moral equality of mankind. We are partakers of a common nature, and the same causes that contribute to the benefit of one contribute to the benefit of another. Our senses and faculties are of the same denomination. Our pleasures and pains will therefore be the same. We are all of us endowed with reason, able to compare, to judge and to infer. The improvement, therefore, which is to be desired for the one is to be desired for the other. We shall be provident for ourselves and useful to each other in proportion as we rise above the atmosphere of prejudice. The same independence, the same freedom from any such restraint as should prevent us from giving the reins to our own understanding or from uttering upon all occasions whatever we think to be true, will conduce to the improvement of all. There are certain opportunities and a certain situation most advantageous to every human being, and it is just that these should be communicated to all, as nearly at least as the general economy will permit.

There is indeed one species of moral inequality parallel to the physical inequality that has been already described. The treatment to which men are entitled is to be measured by their merits and their virtues. That country would not be the seat of wisdom and reason where the benefactor of his species was considered in the same point of view as their enemy. But in reality this distinction, so far from being adverse to equality in any tenable sense, is friendly to it and is accordingly known by the appellation of equity, a term derived from the same origin. Though in some sense an exception, it tends to the same purpose to which the principle itself is indebted for its value. It is calculated to infuse into every bosom an emulation of excellence. The thing really to be desired is the removing as much as possible arbitrary distinctions and leaving to talents and virtue the field of exertion unimpaired. We should endeavour to afford to all the same opportunities and the same encouragement, and to render justice the common interest and choice.

Chapter V

RIGHTS OF MAN

There is no subject that has been discussed with more eagerness and pertinacity than the rights of man. Has he any rights or has he none? Much may plausibly be alleged on both sides of this question, and in the conclusion those reasoners appear to express themselves with the greatest accuracy who embrace the negative. There is nothing that has been of greater disservice to the cause of truth than the hasty and unguarded manner in which its advocates have sometimes defended it; and it will be admitted to be peculiarly unfortunate if the advocates on one side of this question should be found to have the greatest quantity of truth while their adversaries have expressed themselves in a manner more consonant to reason and the nature of things. Where the question has been so extremely darkened by an ambiguous use of terms, it may at any rate be desirable to try whether by a patient and severe investigation of the first principles of political society it may be placed in a light considerably different from the views of both parties.

Political society, as has already been observed, is founded in the principles of morality and justice. It is impossible for intellectual beings to be brought into coalition and intercourse without a certain mode of conduct, adapted to their nature and connection, immediately becoming a duty incumbent on the parties concerned. Men would never have associated if they had not imagined that in consequence of that association they would mutually conduce to the advantage and happiness of each other. This is the real purpose, the genuine basis of their intercourse; and as far as this purpose is answered, so far does society answer the end of its institution.

There is only one postulate more that is necessary to bring us to a conclusive mode of reasoning upon this subject. Whatever is meant by the term "right" — for it will presently appear that the sense of the term itself has never been clearly understood — there can neither be opposite rights, nor rights and duties hostile to each other. The rights of one man cannot clash with or be destructive of the rights of another; for this, instead of rendering the subject an important branch of truth and morality, as the advocates of the rights of man certainly understand it to be, would be to reduce it to a heap of unintelligible jargon and inconsistency. If one man have a right to be free, another man cannot have a right to make him a slave; if one man have a right to inflict chastisement upon me, I cannot have a right to withdraw myself from chastisement; if my neighbour have a right to a sum of money in my possession, I cannot have a right to retain it in my pocket. It cannot be less incontrovertible that I have no right to omit what my duty prescribes.

From hence it inevitably follows that men have no rights. By right, as the word is employed in this subject, has always been understood discretion; that is, a full and complete power of either doing a thing or omitting it without the person's becoming liable to animadversion or censure from another; that is, in other words, without his incurring any degree of turpitude or guilt. Now in this sense I affirm that man has no rights, no discretionary power whatever.

It is commonly said that a man has a right to the disposal of his fortune, a right to the employment of his time, a right to the uncontrolled choice of his profession or pursuits. But this can never be consistently affirmed till it can be shown that he has no duties prescribing and limiting his mode of proceeding in all these respects. My neighbour has just as much right to put an end to my existence with dagger or poison as to deny me that pecuniary assistance without which I must starve, or as to deny me that assistance without which my intellectual attainments or my moral exertions will be materially injured. He has just as much right to amuse himself with burning my house or torturing my children upon the rack as to shut himself up in a cell careless about his fellow men and to hide his talent in a napkin.

If men have any rights, any discretionary powers, they must be in things of total indifference, as whether I sit on the right or on the left side of my fire, or dine on beef today or tomorrow. Even these rights are much fewer than we are apt to imagine, since before they can be completely established, it must be proved that my choice on one side or the other can in no possible way contribute to the benefit or injury of myself or of any other person in the world. Those must indeed be rights well worth the contending for, the very essence of which consists in their absolute nugatoriness and inutility.

In reality nothing can appear more wonderful to a careful enquirer than that two ideas so incompatible as man and rights should ever have been associated together. Certain it is that one of them must be utterly exclusive and annihilatory of the other. Before we ascribe rights to man, we must conceive of him as a being endowed with intellect and capable of discerning the differences and tendencies of things. But a being endowed with intellect and capable of discerning the differences and tendencies of things instantly becomes a moral being and has duties incumbent on him to discharge; and duties and rights, as has already been shown, are absolutely exclusive of each other.

It has been affirmed by the zealous advocates of liberty that princes and magistrates have no rights, and no position can be more incontrovertible. There is no situation of their lives that has not its correspondent duties. There is no power entrusted to them that they are not bound to exercise exclusively for the public good. It is strange that persons adopting this principle did not go a step farther and perceive that the same restrictions were applicable to subjects and citizens.

Nor is the fallacy of this language more conspicuous than its immoral tendency. To this inaccurate and unjust use of the term "right" we owe it that the miser, who accumulates to no end that which diffused would have conduced to the welfare of thousands, that the luxurious man, who wallows in indulgence and sees numerous families around him pining in beggary, never fail to tell us of their rights, and to silence animadversion and quiet the censure of their own mind by reminding us that they came fairly into possession of their wealth, that they owe no debts, and that of consequence no man has authority to enquire into their private manner of disposing of that which is their own. A great majority of mankind are conscious that they stand in need of this sort of defence, and are therefore very ready to combine against the insolent intruder who ventures to enquire into "things that do not concern him." They forget that the wise man and the honest man, the friend of his country and his kind, is concerned for everything by which they may be affected and carries about with him a diploma constituting him inquisitor general of the moral conduct of his neighbours, with a duty annexed to recall them to virtue by every lesson that truth can enable him to read and every punishment that plain speaking is competent to inflict.

It is scarcely necessary to add that if individuals have no rights, neither has society, which possesses nothing but what individuals have brought into a common stock. The absurdity of the common opinion, as applied to this subject, is still more glaring, if possible, than in the view in which we have already considered it. According to the usual sentiment every club assembling for any civil purpose, every congregation of religionists assembling for the worship of God, has a right to establish any provisions or ceremonies, no matter how ridiculous or detestable, provided they do not interfere with the freedom of others. Reason lies prostrate under their feet. They have a right to trample upon and insult her as they please. It is in the same spirit we have been told that every nation has a right to choose its form of government. A most acute, original, and inestimable author was probably misled by the vulgar phraseology on this subject when he asserted that *"at a time when neither the people of France nor the national assembly were troubling themselves about the affairs of England or the English Parliament, Mr. Burke's conduct was unpardonable in commencing an unprovoked attack upon them."

There are various objections that suggest themselves to the theory which subverts the rights of men; and if the theory be true, they will probably appear in the result to be so far from really hostile to it as to be found more fairly deducible from and consistent with its principles than with any of those with which they have inadvertently been connected.

In the first place it has sometimes been alleged, and seems to result from the reasonings already adduced under the head of justice, that men have a right to the assistance and co-operation of their fellows in every honest pursuit. But when we assert this proposition, we mean something by the word "right" exceedingly different from what is commonly understood by the term. We do not understand something discretionary, which, if not voluntarily fulfilled, cannot be considered as a matter of claim. On the contrary everything adduced upon that occasion was calculated to show that it was a matter of strict claim; and perhaps something would be gained with respect to perspicuity if we rather chose to distinguish it by that appellation than by a name so much abused and so ambiguous in its application as the term "right."

The true origin of this latter term is relative to the present state of political government, in which many of those actions which moral duty most strictly enjoins us are in no degree brought within the sphere of legislative sanction. Men uninfluenced by comprehensive principles of justice commit every species of intemperance, are selfish, hard-hearted, licentious and cruel, and maintain their right to all these caprices because the laws of their country are silent with regard to them. Philosophers and political enquirers have too frequently adopted the same principles with a certain degree of accommodation, though in fact men have no more right to these erroneous propensities in their most qualified sense than they had to them originally in all their extravagance. It is true that under the forms of society now existing in the world intemperance and the caprices of personal intercourse too frequently escape without animadversion. But in a more perfect form, though they may not fall under the cognisance of law, the offender will probably be so unequivocally reminded by the sincerity of his neighbours of the error he has committed as to be in no danger of running away with the opinion that he had a right to commit it.

A second and more important objection to the doctrine I am maintaining is derived from the rights, as they are called, of private judgment and the liberty of the press. But it may easily be shown that these, no more than

GEORGE CRABBE

Born in 1754, only three years after the publication of Gray's *Elegy*, George Crabbe lived and wrote until 1832, when the romantic movement had reached its height. Much of his best work was done in the nineteenth century, but he belonged in mind and spirit to the century preceding. Like most poets of his generation, he began, in fact, as an imitator of Pope, and throughout his career the closed couplet remained his favourite vehicle of expression. In other and more important respects he broke new ground, although it can scarcely be said that he grew a great profusion or variety of flowers upon it.

The strength and charm of Crabbe's writing consists in its simple honesty, which allows the facts to speak for themselves. He preferred to write about places and persons familiarly known to him, and these were for the most part connected with the region of his birthplace on the seacoast of Suffolk. Partly because his own youth and young manhood were spent in poverty among coarse and ignorant people, he resented what he considered the sentimental falsification of the lives of the rural poor which had come down into the eighteenth century on the stream of the pastoral tradition, and he resolved to report the facts as he had seen and felt them. Such is the purpose animating his most famous poem. *The Village*, published in 1783, was obviously written with special reference to Goldsmith's poem of similar title, then some thirteen years old, but it is probable that Crabbe had also in mind the still more favourable picture of rural felicity to be found in John Scott's *Amwell*, 1776. In a mood not wholly unlike that represented in Mr. Edgar Lee Masters' *Spoon River Anthology*, he set himself to destroy the roseate and ignorant dream of village life which had been built up by successive generations of poets dwelling in the city — feeling, perhaps, that the continuance of this dream could only postpone reform.

Critics of *The Village*, usually assuming that it is a rejoinder to *The Deserted Village* alone, have seldom expressed any doubt that Crabbe had the better of the argument — in which, to be sure, Goldsmith was given no opportunity for rebuttal — but the far greater popularity of Goldsmith's poem, even among good judges, may suggest that it is not enough for a poet merely to get his facts right. Goldsmith's facts were at least equally correct, as they had good reason to be, considering that his experience and observation of village life was wider than Crabbe's own; but he was able to add to them "the poet's vision and the dream," of which Crabbe had little notion. Whatever Crabbe saw he could render with exactitude, like one of the lesser Dutch painters, but he was intellectually short-sighted and emotionally restricted. While giving him full credit for his honesty, furthermore, we should not fail to see that his selection of detail is as much governed by personal predilection as that of any writer who has unquestioningly accepted the idyllic tradition of rural life. The fact that his picture of Aldeburgh in *The Village* is painted in darker colours and with deeper shadows than Goldsmith used in depicting Sweet Auburn does not prove that it is nearer "the truth." The region about Aldeburgh has, in reality, unusual charm.

George Crabbe is less known today, and he has been less read during the last hundred years, than his reputation in his own time seemed to promise. As a young man he won the praise and support of Burke, Reynolds, Johnson, and Fox. Thirty years later he was valued highly by such very different men as Wordsworth, Byron, Rogers, Jeffrey, Scott, and Lamb. In a still later generation, Tennyson and Edward Fitzgerald admired him, George Eliot imitated him, and Thomas Hardy acknowledged his influence. Even in our own time the American poet, Edwin Arlington Robinson, has expressed a deep admiration for Crabbe. Now it is evident that what these many critics and poets and novelists have meant to praise in Crabbe is chiefly his good sense and his fidelity to fact — admirable qualities both, but qualities which need not be at all confused with high poetic power. Many have seen, also, that Crabbe did indispensable service not to letters only but to society as well in his attack upon the false idyll of country life and in substituting the sober charm of actuality for it. Since his time, poets and novelists have not been content to dream irresponsibly about "nymphs" and "swains," but have been increasingly determined to know the country as it is. Here, then, he led the way, and in the right direction. A second characteristic of Crabbe, quite as prophetic of modern tendencies but less commonly recognized, is his unusual power of tracing thought and mood in the persons of his stories. In this he shows himself something of a psychological novelist in verse, and indeed his direct influence upon the novel — exerted in such a series of narratives as *The Parish Register*, 1810, and *The Borough*, 1812, or *Tales of the Hall*, 1817 — has not been inconsiderable. A third quality of Crabbe's work, which helped to prepare for the literature of the romantic movement, was due to his strong sense of what Wordsworth called the "influence of the articles already mentioned, are rights of discretion. If they were, they would prove that a man was strictly justifiable in publishing what he believed to be pernicious or false and that it was a matter of perfect moral indifference whether he conformed to the religious rites of Confucious, of Mahomet, or of Christ. The political freedom of conscience and of the press, so far from being as it is commonly supposed an extension, is a new case of the limitation of rights and discretion. Conscience and the press ought to be unrestrained, not because men have a right to deviate from the exact line that duty prescribes, but because society, the aggregate of individuals, has no right to assume the prerogative of an infallible judge and to undertake authoritatively to prescribe to its members in matters of pure speculation.

One obvious reason against this assumption on the part of the society is the impossibility by any compulsatory method of bringing men to uniformity of opinion. The judgment we form upon topics of general truth is or is imagined to be founded upon evidence; and however it may be soothed by gentle applications to the betraying its impartiality, it is apt to repel with no little pertinacity whatever comes under the form of compulsion. Persecution cannot persuade the understanding, even when it subdues our resolution. It may make us hypocrites, but cannot make us converts. The government, therefore, which is anxious above all things to imbue its subjects with integrity and virtue will be the farthest in the world from discouraging them in the explicit avowal of their sentiments.

But there is another reason of a higher order. Man is not, as has been already shown, a perfect being, but perfectible. No government that has yet existed or is likely presently to exist upon the face of the earth is faultless. No government ought, therefore, pertinaciously to resist the change of its own institutions; and still less ought it to set up a standard upon the various topics of human speculation, to restrain the excursions of an inventive mind. It is only by giving a free scope to these excursions that science, philosophy, and morals have arrived at their present degree of perfection or are capable of going on to that still greater perfection in comparison of which all that has been already done will perhaps appear childish. But a proceeding absolutely necessary for the purpose of exciting the mind to these salutary excursions, and still more necessary in order to give them their proper operation, consists in the unrestrained communication of men's thought and discoveries to each other. If every man have to begin again at the point from which his neighbour set out, the labour will be endless and the progress in an unvarying circle. There is nothing that more eminently contributes to intellectual energy than for every man to be habituated to follow without alarm the train of his speculations and to utter without fear the conclusions that have suggested themselves to him. But does all this imply that men have a right to act anything but virtue, and to utter anything but truth? Certainly not. It implies, indeed, that there are points with which society has no right to interfere, not that discretion and caprice are more free or duty less strict upon these points than upon any others with which human action is conversant.

[1793]

natural objects," both for good and ill, upon the mind of man. He understood as well as any writer of our own day the shaping effect of what we call environment; but he also understood, as he brilliantly shows in *The Lover's Journey*, that there is a reciprocal action by which the mind shapes and colours the external scene.

True in this respect to the critical dogma of his time, and also to the clerical profession which he finally adopted after a failure in medicine, Crabbe held before himself a definite didactic purpose in most of his versified fictions: to show how human happiness is wrecked by ungoverned passion. Many of these stories, like *Peter Grimes*, are for this reason painful in effect; yet they are almost always well told, with a strong sense of character, with some skill in management of plot, and often with not a little humour of a grim, unsmiling sort.

Beginning to write after he had reached manhood and without an adequate schooling, Crabbe never attained ease or even sure-footed correctness in the composition of verse. His couplets have neither the sparkle and speed of Pope nor the fluency that Leigh Hunt and Keats were soon to give the same measure. His rhymes are often hackneyed, monotonous, and dull. His verse is lifted so slightly above the level of prose that he is in constant danger of sinking below that level, and he often does so. Technical deficiencies of this sort, however, are not entirely out of keeping with his customary moods and themes. Now that we no longer regard these themes as "low" or these moods as "disgusting," and have learned from a long line of his successors stretching down to Mr. Robert Frost to trust the facts of life and to see their essential beauty, the time seems at hand for a revival of interest in George Crabbe.

THE VILLAGE

Book I

The village life, and every care that reigns
O'er youthful peasants and declining *swains;
What labour yields, and what, that labour past,
Age, in its hour of languor, finds at last;
What form the real picture of the poor,
Demand a song — the Muse can give no more.
Fled are those times when, in harmonious strains,
The rustic poet praised his native plains.
No shepherds now, in smooth alternate verse,
Their country's beauty or their nymphs' rehearse;
Yet still for these we frame the tender strain,
Still in our lays fond *Corydons complain,
And shepherds' boys their amorous pains reveal,
The only pains, alas! they never feel.
On *Mincio's banks, in Cæsar's bounteous reign,
If Tityrus found the Golden Age again,
Must sleepy bards the flattering dream prolong,
Mechanic echoes of the Mantuan song?
From Truth and Nature shall we widely stray,
Where Virgil, not where Fancy, leads the way?
Yes, thus the Muses sing of happy swains
Because the Muses never knew their pains.
They boast their peasants' pipes; but peasants now
Resign their pipes and plod behind the plough;
And few amid the rural tribe have time
To number syllables and play with rhyme.
Save *honest Duck, what son of verse could share
The poet's rapture and the peasant's care?
Or the great labours of the field degrade
With the new peril of a poorer trade?
From this chief cause these idle praises spring,
That themes so easy few forbear to sing,
For no deep thought the trifling subjects ask;
To sing of shepherds is an easy task.
The happy youth assumes the common strain,
A nymph his mistress and himself a swain;
With no sad scenes he clouds his tuneful prayer,
But all, to look like her, is painted fair.
I grant indeed that fields and flocks have charms
For him that grazes or for him that farms;
But when amid such pleasing scenes I trace
The poor laborious natives of the place,
And see the midday sun, with fervid ray,
On their bare heads and dewy temples play;
While some, with feebler heads and fainter hearts,
Deplore their fortune yet sustain their parts,
Then shall I dare these real ills to hide
In tinsel trappings of poetic pride?
No; cast by fortune on a *frowning coast
Which neither groves nor happy valleys boast,
Where other cares than those the Muse relates,
And other shepherds dwell with other mates:

* Notes on George Crabbe will be found in the Appendix, pp. 1054 ff.

By such examples taught, I paint the cot
As Truth will paint it, and as bards will not;
Nor you, ye poor, of letter'd scorn complain;
To you the smoothest song is smooth in vain.
O'ercome by labour and bow'd down by time,
Feel you the barren flattery of a rhyme?
Can poets soothe you when you pine for bread
By winding myrtles round your ruin'd shed?
Can their light tales your weighty griefs o'erpower,
Or glad with airy mirth the toilsome hour?

Lo! where the heath, with withering brake grown o'er,
Lends the light turf that warms the neighbouring poor;
From thence a length of burning sand appears,
Where the thin harvest waves its wither'd ears;
Rank weeds that every art and care defy
Reign o'er the land and rob the blighted rye:
There *thistles stretch their prickly arms afar
And to the ragged infant threaten war;
There poppies nodding mock the hope of toil;
There the blue bugloss paints the sterile soil;
Hardy and high above the slender sheaf
The slimy mallow waves her silky leaf;
O'er the young shoot the charlock throws a shade,
And clasping tares cling round the sickly blade;
With mingled tints the rocky coasts abound,
And a sad splendour vainly shines around.
So looks the nymph whom wretched arts adorn,
Betray'd by man, then left for man to scorn,
Whose cheek in vain assumes the mimic rose
While her sad eyes the troubled breast disclose;
Whose outward splendour is but folly's dress,
Exposing most when most it gilds distress.

Here joyless roam a wild amphibious race,
With sullen woe displayed in every face,
Who far from civil arts and social fly
And scowl at strangers with suspicious eye.

Here too the *lawless merchant of the main
Draws from his plough th' intoxicated swain;
Want only claim'd the labour of the day,
But vice now steals his nightly rest away.

Where are the swains, who, daily labour done,
With rural games play'd down the setting sun,
Who struck with matchless force the bounding ball
Or made the ponderous quoit obliquely fall;
While some huge Ajax, terrible and strong,
Engaged some artful stripling of the throng
And fell beneath him, foil'd, while far around
Hoarse triumph rose and rocks return'd the sound?
Where now are these? Beneath yon cliff they stand
To show the freighted pinnace where to land,
To load the ready steed with guilty haste,
To fly in terror o'er the pathless waste,
Or, when detected in their straggling course,
To foil their foes by cunning or by force,
Or, yielding part (which equal knaves demand),
To gain a lawless passport through the land.

Here, wandering long amid these frowning fields,
I sought the simple life that Nature yields.
Rapine and Wrong and Fear usurp'd her place,
And a bold, artful, surly, savage race
Who, only skill'd to take the finny tribe,
The yearly dinner or *septennial bribe,
Wait on the shore and, as the waves run high,
On the tossed vessel bend their eager eye
Which to their coast directs its venturous way —
Theirs, or the ocean's, miserable prey.

As on their neighbouring beach yon swallows stand
And wait for favouring winds to leave the land,
While still for flight the ready wing is spread,
So waited I the favouring hour, and *fled,
Fled from these shores where guilt and famine reign,
And cried "Ah! hapless they who still remain,
Who still remain to hear the ocean roar,
Whose greedy waves devour the lessening shore
Till some fierce tide, with more imperious sway,
Sweeps the low hut and all it holds away,
When the sad tenant weeps from door to door
And begs a poor protection from the poor."

But these are scenes where Nature's niggard hand
Gave a spare portion to the famish'd land;
Hers is the fault if here mankind complain
Of fruitless toil and labour spent in vain.
But yet in other scenes more fair in view,
Where Plenty smiles — alas! she smiles for few,
And those who taste not yet behold her store
Are as the slaves that dig the golden ore,
The wealth around them makes them doubly poor.

Or will you deem them amply paid in health,
Labour's fair child, that languishes with wealth?
Go then, and see them rising with the sun,
Through a long course of daily toil to run;
See them beneath the dog-star's raging heat,
When the knees tremble and the temples beat;
Behold them, leaning on their scythes, look o'er
The labour past, and toils to come explore;
See them alternate suns and showers engage,
And hoard up aches and anguish for their age;
Through fens and marshy moors their steps pursue
When their warm pores imbibe the evening dew;
Then own that labour may as fatal be
To these thy slaves as thine excess to thee.
Amid this tribe too oft a manly pride
Strives in strong toil the fainting heart to hide;
There may you see the youth of slender frame
Contend with weakness, weariness, and shame;
Yet, urged along, and proudly loath to yield,
He strives to join his fellows of the field,
Till long-contending nature droops at last,
Declining health rejects his poor repast,
His cheerless spouse the coming danger sees,
And mutual murmurs urge the slow disease.
Yet grant them health, 'tis not for us to tell,
Though the head droops not, that the heart is well;
Or will you praise that homely, healthy fare,
Plenteous and plain, that happy peasants share?
Oh! trifle not with wants you cannot feel,
Nor mock the misery of a stinted meal —
Homely, not wholesome, plain, not plenteous, such
As you who praise would never deign to touch.
Ye gentle souls who dream of rural ease,
Whom the smooth stream and smoother sonnet please,
Go, if the peaceful cot your praises share,
Go look within, and ask if peace be there:
If peace be his — that drooping weary sire,
Or theirs, that offspring round their feeble fire,
Or hers, that matron pale, whose trembling hand
Turns on the wretched hearth the expiring brand!
Nor yet can time itself obtain for these
Life's latest comforts, due respect and ease;
For yonder see that hoary swain whose age
Can with no cares except his own engage,
Who, propp'd on that rude staff, looks up to see
The bare arms broken from the withering tree
On which, a boy, he climb'd the loftiest bough,
Then his first joy, but his sad emblem now.
He once was chief in all the rustic trade;
His steady hand the straightest furrow made;
Full many a prize he won, and still is proud
To find the triumphs of his youth allowed.
A transient pleasure sparkles in his eyes,
He hears and smiles, then thinks again and sighs,
For now he journeys to his grave in pain;
The rich disdain him — nay, the poor disdain;
Alternate masters now their slave command,
Urge the weak efforts of his feeble hand,
And when his age attempts its task in vain,
With ruthless taunts of lazy poor complain.
Oft may you see him when he tends the sheep,
His winter-charge, beneath the hillock weep;
Oft hear him murmur to the winds that blow
O'er his white locks and bury them in snow,
When, roused by rage and muttering in the morn,
He mends the broken hedge with icy thorn:
"Why do I live, when I desire to be
At once from life and life's long labour free?
Like leaves in spring the young are blown away
Without the sorrows of a slow decay;
I, like yon wither'd leaf, remain behind
Nipp'd by the frost and shivering in the wind;
There it abides till younger buds come on,
As I, now all my fellow-swains are gone;
Then, from the rising generation thrust,
It falls, like me, unnoticed to the dust.
"These fruitful fields, these numerous flocks I see,
Are others' gain, but killing cares to me;
To me the children of my youth are lords,
Cool in their looks but hasty in their words;
Wants of their own demand their care: and who
Feels his own want and succours others too?
A lonely wretched man, in pain I go;
None need my help and none relieve my woe;
Then let my bones beneath the turf be laid,
And men forget the wretch they would not aid."
Thus groan the old till, by disease oppress'd,
They taste a final woe, and then they rest.
Theirs is yon house that holds the parish poor,
Whose walls of mud scarce bear the broken door;

There where the putrid vapours, flagging, play,
And the dull wheel hums doleful through the day —
There children dwell who know no parents' care,
Parents who know no children's love, dwell there!
Heart-broken matrons on their joyless bed,
Forsaken wives and mothers never wed,
Dejected widows with unheeded tears,
And crippled age with more than childhood fears,
The lame, the blind, and — far the happiest they! —
The moping idiot and the madman gay.
Here too the sick their final doom receive,
Here brought, amid the scenes of grief, to grieve,
Where the loud groans from some sad chamber flow,
Mix'd with the clamours of the crowd below;
Here, sorrowing, they each kindred sorrow scan,
And the cold charities of man to man,
Whose laws indeed for ruined age provide,
And strong compulsion plucks the scrap from pride;
But still that scrap is bought with many a sigh,
And pride embitters what it can't deny.
  Say ye, oppress'd by some fantastic woes,
Some jarring nerve that baffles your repose,
Who press the downy couch while slaves advance
With timid eye to read the distant glance,
Who with sad prayers the weary doctor tease
To name the nameless ever-new disease,
Who with mock patience dire complaints endure
Which real pain, and that alone, can cure;
How would ye bear in real pain to lie
Despised, neglected, left alone to die?
How would ye bear to draw your latest breath
Where all that's wretched paves the way for death?
  Such is that room which one rude beam divides,
And naked rafters form the sloping sides;
Where the vile bands that bind the thatch are seen,
And lath and mud are all that lie between,
Save one dull pane that, coarsely patch'd, gives way
To the rude tempest, yet excludes the day.
Here on a matted flock, with dust o'erspread,
The drooping wretch reclines his languid head;
For him no hand the cordial cup applies,
Or wipes the tear that stagnates in his eyes;
No friends with soft discourse his pain beguile,
Or promise hope till sickness wears a smile.
  But soon a loud and hasty summons calls,
Shakes the thin roof and echoes round the walls;
Anon a figure enters, quaintly neat,
All pride and business, bustle and conceit,
With looks unalter'd by these scenes of woe,
With speed that, entering, speaks his haste to go,
He bids the gazing throng around him fly
And carries fate and physic in his eye:
A *potent quack, long versed in human ills,
Who first insults the victim whom he kills,
Whose murderous hand a drowsy bench protect,
And whose most tender mercy is neglect.
  Paid by the parish for attendance here,
He wears contempt upon his sapient sneer;
In haste he seeks the bed where Misery lies,
Impatience mark'd in his averted eyes;
And, some habitual queries hurried o'er,
Without reply, he rushes on the door.
His drooping patient, long inured to pain,
And long unheeded, knows remonstrance vain;
He ceases now the feeble help to crave
Of man, and silent sinks into the grave.
  But ere his death some pious doubts arise,
Some simple fears which "bold bad" men despise;
Fain would he ask the parish priest to prove
His title certain to the joys above;
For this he sends the murmuring nurse, who calls
The holy stranger to these dismal walls.
And doth not he, the pious man, appear,
He, *"passing rich with forty pounds a year"?
Ah! no. A shepherd of a different stock,
And far unlike him, feeds this little flock:
A jovial youth who thinks his Sunday's task
As much as God or man can fairly ask;
The rest he gives to loves and labours light,
To fields the morning, and to feasts the night;
None better skill'd the noisy pack to guide,
To urge their chase, to cheer them or to chide;
A sportsman keen, he shoots through half the day,
And, skill'd at whist, devotes the night to play.

Then, while such honours bloom around his head,
Shall he sit sadly by the sick man's bed
To raise the hope he feels not, or with zeal
To combat fears that e'en the pious feel?

Now once again the gloomy scene explore,
Less gloomy now: the bitter hour is o'er;
The man of many sorrows sighs no more.
Up yonder hill, behold how sadly slow
The bier moves winding from the vale below;
There lie the happy dead, from trouble free,
And the glad parish pays the frugal fee.
No more, O Death, thy victim starts to hear
*Churchwarden stern or kingly overseer;
No more the *farmer claims his humble bow;
Thou art his lord, the best of tyrants thou!

Now to the church behold the mourners come,
Sedately torpid and devoutly dumb.
The village children now their games suspend
To see the bier that bears their ancient friend,
For he was one in all their idle sport
And like a monarch ruled their little court:
The pliant bow he form'd; the flying ball,
The bat, the wicket were his labours all;
Him now they follow to his grave, and stand
Silent and sad and gazing, hand in hand,
While, bending low, their eager eyes explore
The mingled relics of the parish poor.
The bell tolls late, the moping owl flies round,
Fear marks the flight and magnifies the sound;
The busy priest, detain'd by weightier care,
Defers his duty till the day of prayer,
And, waiting long, the crowd retired distressed
To think a poor man's bones should lie unblessed.

[1783]

THE BOROUGH

Letter XXII

PETER GRIMES

Old Peter Grimes made fishing his employ;
His wife he cabin'd with him and his boy,
And seem'd that life laborious to enjoy.
To town came quiet Peter with his fish,
And had of all a civil word and wish.
He left his trade upon the Sabbath day
And took young Peter in his hand to pray;
But soon the stubborn boy from care broke loose,
At first refused, then added his abuse;
His father's love he scorn'd, his power defied,
But, being drunk, wept sorely when he died.

Yes, then he wept, and to his mind there came
Much of his conduct, and he felt the shame:
How he had oft the good old man reviled
And never paid the duty of a child;
How when the father in his Bible read
He in contempt and anger left the shed.
"It is the Word of Life," the parent cried;
"This is the life itself," the boy replied,
And, while old Peter in amazement stood,
Gave the hot spirit to his boiling blood;
How he, with oath and furious speech, began
To prove his freedom and assert the man;
And when the parent check'd his impious rage
How he had cursed the tyranny of age —
Nay, once had dealt the sacrilegious blow
On his bare head, and laid his parent low.
The father groan'd: "If thou art old," said he,
"And hast a son, thou wilt remember me;
Thy mother left me in a happy time;
Thou kill'dst not her; Heaven spares the double crime."

On an inn-settle, in his maudlin grief,
This he revolved, and drank for his relief.

Now lived the youth in freedom, but debarr'd
From constant pleasure, and he thought it hard,
Hard that he could not every wish obey,
But must awhile relinquish ale and play;
Hard that he could not to his cards attend
But must acquire the money he would spend.

With greedy eye he look'd on all he saw;
He knew not justice and he laugh'd at law:
On all he marked he stretched his ready hand;
He fish'd by water and he filch'd by land.
Oft in the night has Peter dropp'd his oar,
Fled from his boat and sought for prey on shore;
Oft up the hedge-row glided, on his back
Bearing the orchard's produce in a sack,
Or farmyard load tugg'd fiercely from the stack;
And as these wrongs to greater numbers rose,
The more he look'd on all men as his foes.

He built a mud-walled hovel where he kept
His various wealth, and there he ofttimes slept:
But no success could please his cruel soul;
He wish'd for one to trouble and control;
He wanted some obedient boy to stand
And bear the blow of his outrageous hand,
And hoped to find in some propitious hour
A feeling creature subject to his power.

Peter had heard there were in London then —
Still have they being! — workhouse-clearing men
Who, undisturb'd by feelings just or kind,
Would parish-boys to needy tradesmen bind;
They in their want a trifling sum would take
And toiling slaves of piteous orphans make.

Such Peter sought, and, when a lad was found,
The sum was dealt him and the slave was bound.
Some few in town observed in Peter's trap
A boy, with jacket blue and woollen cap;
But none inquired how Peter used the rope,
Or what the bruise that made the stripling stoop;
None could the ridges on his back behold;
None sought him shivering in the winter's cold;
None put the question: "Peter, dost thou give
The boy his food? What, man! the lad must live:
Consider, Peter, let the child have bread;
He'll serve thee better if he's stroked and fed."
None reason'd thus, and some, on hearing cries,
Said calmly, "Grimes is at his exercise."

Pinn'd, beaten, cold, pinch'd, threaten'd, and abused,
His efforts punish'd and his food refused,
Awake tormented, soon aroused from sleep,
Struck if he wept and yet compell'd to weep,
The trembling boy dropp'd down and strove to pray,
Received a blow and trembling turn'd away,
Or sobb'd and hid his piteous face, while he,
The savage master, grinn'd in horrid glee;
He'd now the power he ever loved to show,
A feeling being subject to his blow.

Thus lived the lad in hunger, peril, pain,
His tears despised, his supplications vain.
Compell'd by fear to lie, by need to steal,
His bed uneasy and unbless'd his meal,
For three sad years the boy his tortures bore,
And then his pains and trials were no more.

"How died he, Peter?" when the people said,
He growl'd: "I found him lifeless in his bed";
Then tried for softer tone and sighed, "Poor Sam is dead."
Yet murmurs were there, and some questions asked,
How he was fed, how punish'd, and how task'd.
Much they suspected, but they little proved,
And Peter pass'd untroubled and unmoved.

Another boy with equal ease was found,
The money granted, and the victim bound.
And what his fate? One night it chanced he fell
From the boat's mast and perished in her well,
Where fish were living kept, and where the boy,
So reason'd men, could not himself destroy.

"Yes! so it was," said Peter, "in his play —
For he was idle both by night and day —
He climb'd the mainmast and then fell below";
Then show'd his corpse and pointed to the blow.
"What said the jury?" They were long in doubt,
But sturdy Peter faced the matter out;
So they dismiss'd him, saying at the time:
"Keep fast your *hatchway when you've boys who climb."
This hit the conscience, and he colour'd more
Than for the closest questions put before.

Thus all his fears the verdict set aside,
And at the slave-shop Peter still applied.

Then came a boy of manners soft and mild;
Our seamen's wives with grief beheld the child;
All thought — the poor themselves — that he was one
Of gentle blood, some noble sinner's son,
Who had, belike, deceived some humble maid,
Whom he had first seduced and then betray'd.
However this, he seem'd a gracious lad,
In grief submissive and with patience sad.

Passive he labour'd till his slender frame
Bent with his loads, and he at length was lame.
Strange that a frame so weak could bear so long
The grossest insult and the foulest wrong;
But there were causes: in the town they gave
Fire, food, and comfort to the gentle slave;
And though stern Peter, with a cruel hand
And knotted rope, enforced the rude command,
Yet he considered what he'd lately felt
And his vile blows with selfish pity dealt.

One day such draughts the cruel fisher made
He could not vend them in his borough-trade,
But sailed for London-mart; the boy was ill,
But ever humbled to his master's will,
And on the river, where they smoothly sail'd,
He strove with terror and a while prevail'd;

But new to danger on the angry sea,
He clung affrighten'd to his master's knee.
The boat grew leaky, and the wind was strong;
Rough was the passage, and the time was long;
His liquor fail'd, and Peter's wrath arose—
No more is known—the rest we must suppose,
Or learn of Peter: Peter says he "spied
The stripling's danger and for harbour tried;
Meantime the fish, and then the apprentice died."
The pitying women raised a clamour round,
And weeping said, "Thou hast thy 'prentice drown'd."
Now the stern man was summoned to the *hall
To tell his tale before the burghers all.
He gave th' account, profess'd the lad he loved,
And kept his brazen features all unmoved.
The mayor himself with tone severe replied:
"Henceforth with thee shall never boy abide;
Hire thee a freeman whom thou durst not beat,
But who, in thy despite, will sleep and eat.
Free thou art now. Again shouldst thou appear,
Thou'lt find thy sentence, like thy soul, severe."
Alas for Peter! Not a helping hand,
So was he hated, could he now command.
Alone he rowed his boat, alone he cast
His nets beside, or made his anchor fast;
To hold a rope or hear a curse was none—
He toil'd and rail'd, he groan'd and swore alone.
Thus by himself compell'd to live each day,
To wait for certain hours the tide's delay,
At the same times the same dull views to see:
The bounding marsh-bank and the blighted tree;
The water only, when the tides were high,
When low, the mud half-cover'd and half-dry;
The sunburnt tar that blisters on the planks,
And bank-side stakes in their uneven ranks;
Heaps of entangled weeds that slowly float
As the tide rolls by the impeded boat.
When tides were *neap and, in the sultry day,
Through the tall bounding mud-banks made their way,
Which on each side rose swelling, and below
The dark warm flood ran silently and slow;
There anchoring, Peter chose from man to hide,
There hang his head and view the lazy tide
In its hot slimy channel slowly glide;
Where the small eels that left the deeper way
For the warm shore within the shallows play;
Where gaping mussels, left upon the mud,
Slope their slow passage to the fallen flood:
Here dull and hopeless he'd lie down and trace
How sidelong crabs had scrawl'd their crooked race,
Or sadly listen to the tuneless cry
Of fishing gull or clanging golden-eye,
What time the sea-birds to the marsh would come,
And the loud bittern, from the bulrush home,
Gave from the salt-ditch side the bellowing boom.
He nursed the feelings these dull scenes produce,
And loved to stop beside the opening sluice,
Where the small stream, confined in narrow bound,
Ran with a dull, unvaried, saddening sound;
Where all presented to the eye or ear
Oppress'd the soul with misery, grief, and fear.
Besides these objects there were places three
Which Peter seemed with certain dread to see.
When he drew near them, he would turn from each
And loudly whistle till he pass'd the *reach.
A change of scene to him brought no relief;
In town, 'twas plain, men took him for a thief:
The sailors' wives would stop him in the street
And say, "Now, Peter, thou'st no boy to beat."
Infants at play, when they perceived him, ran,
Warning each other, "That's the wicked man."
He growl'd an oath, and in an angry tone
Cursed the whole place, and wish'd to be alone.
Alone he was, the same dull scenes in view,
And still more gloomy in his sight they grew.
Though man he hated, yet employ'd alone
At bootless labour, he would swear and groan,
Cursing the shoals that glided by the spot,
And gulls that caught them when his arts could not.
Cold nervous tremblings shook his sturdy frame,
And strange disease—he couldn't say the name;
Wild were his dreams, and oft he rose in fright
Waked by his view of horrors in the night,—
Horrors that would the sternest minds amaze,
Horrors that demons might be proud to raise;

And though he felt forsaken, grieved at heart
To think he lived from all mankind apart:
Yet, if a man approach'd, in terrors he would start.

A winter pass'd since Peter saw the town,
And summer lodgers were again come down;
These, idly curious, with their glasses spied
The ships in bay as anchor'd for the tide,
The river's craft, the bustle of the quay,
And seaport views which landmen love to see.

One, up the river, had a man and boat
Seen day by day, now anchor'd, now afloat;
Fisher he seem'd, yet used no net nor hook;
Of seafowl swimming by no heed he took,
But on the gliding waves still fix'd his lazy look;
At certain stations he would view the stream
As if he stood bewilder'd in a dream,
Or that some power had chain'd him for a time
To feel a curse or meditate on crime.

This known, some curious, some in pity went,
And others question'd, "Wretch, dost thou repent?"
He heard, he trembled, and in fear resign'd
His boat; new terror filled his restless mind;
Furious he grew, and up the country ran,
And there they seized him, a distemper'd man.
Him we received, and to a parish bed,
Follow'd and cursed, the groaning man was led.

Here when they saw him whom they used to shun,
A lost lone man, so harass'd and undone,
Our gentle females, ever prompt to feel,
Perceived compassion on their anger steal;
His crimes they could not from their memories blot,
But they were grieved, and trembled at his lot.

A priest too came, to whom his words are told,
And all the signs they shudder'd to behold.

"Look! look!" they cried; "his limbs with horror shake,
And as he grinds his teeth what noise they make!
How glare his angry eyes, and yet he's not awake.
See what cold drops upon his forehead stand,
And how he clenches that broad bony hand."

The priest attending found he spoke at times
As one alluding to his fears and crimes.
"It was the fall," he muttered. "I can show
The manner how — I never struck a blow."
And then aloud, "Unhand me, free my chain;
On oath, he fell. It struck him to the brain.
Why ask my father? That old man will swear
Against my life. Besides, he wasn't there.
What, all agreed? Am I to die today?
My Lord, in mercy, give me time to pray."

Then, as they watch'd him, calmer he became,
And grew so weak he couldn't move his frame,
But murmuring spake, while they could see and hear
The start of terror and the groan of fear,
See the large dew-beads on his forehead rise,
And the cold death-drop glaze his sunken eyes;
Nor yet he died, but with unwonted force
Seemed with some fancied being to discourse.
He knew not us, or with accustom'd art
He hid the knowledge yet exposed his heart;
'Twas part confession and the rest defence,
A madman's tale, with gleams of waking sense.

"I'll tell you all," he said; "the very day
When the old man first placed them in my way,
My father's spirit — he who always tried
To give me trouble, when he lived and died —
When he was gone, he could not be content
To see my days in painful labour spent,
But would appoint his meetings, and he made
Me watch at these and so neglect my trade.
'Twas one hot noon, all silent, still, serene,
No living being had I lately seen;
I paddled up and down and dipp'd my net
But (such his pleasure) I could nothing get —
A father's pleasure, when his toil was done,
To plague and torture thus an only son!
And so I sat and look'd upon the stream,
How it ran on, and felt as in a dream;
But dream it was not. No! I fixed my eyes
On the mid stream and saw the spirits rise;
I saw my father on the water stand
And hold a thin pale boy in either hand;
And there they glided ghastly on the top
Of the salt flood, and never touched a drop.
I would have struck them, but they knew the intent
And smiled upon the oar, and down they went.

"Now from that day, whenever I began
To dip my net, there stood the hard old man —
He and those boys. I humbled me and prayed
They would be gone; they heeded not, but stayed;

Nor could I turn, nor would the boat go by,
But, gazing on the spirits, there was I.
They bade me leap to death, but I was loth to die.
And every day, as sure as day arose,
Would these three spirits meet me ere the close.
To hear and mark them daily was my doom;
And 'Come,' they said, with weak sad voices, 'come.'
To row away with all my strength I tried,
But there were they, hard by me in the tide,
The three unbodied forms — and 'Come,' still 'come' they cried.

"Fathers should pity, but this old man shook
His hoary locks and froze me by a look.
Thrice, when I struck them, through the water came
A hollow groan that weakened all my frame.
'Father!' said I, 'have mercy!' He replied
I know not what — the angry spirit lied.
'Didst thou not draw thy knife?' said he; 'Twas true,
But I had pity and my arm withdrew.
He cried for mercy which I kindly gave,
But he has no compassion in his grave.

"There were three places where they ever rose.
The whole long river has not such as those —
Places accursed, where, if a man remain,
He'll see the things which strike him to the brain.
And there they made me on my paddle lean
And look at them for hours — accursed scene!
When they would glide to that smooth eddy-space,
Then bid me leap and join them in the place;
And at my groans each little villain sprite
Enjoy'd my pains and vanish'd in delight.

"In one fierce summer day, when my poor brain
Was burning hot, and cruel was my pain,
Then came this father-foe, and there he stood
With his two boys again upon the flood.
There was more mischief in their eyes, more glee
In their pale faces when they glared at me.
Still did they force me on the oar to rest,
And when they saw me fainting and oppress'd,
He, with his hand, the old man, scoop'd the flood,
And there came flame about him mix'd with blood.
He bade me stoop and look upon the place,
Then flung the hot-red liquor in my face;
Burning it blazed, and then I roar'd for pain,
I thought the demons would have turn'd my brain.

"Still there they stood, and forced me to behold
A place of horrors — they cannot be told —
Where the flood open'd, there I heard the shriek
Of tortured guilt no earthly tongue can speak.
'All days alike! forever!' did they say,
'And unremitted torments every day.'
Yes, so they said." — But here he ceased and gazed
On all around, affrighten'd and amazed;
And still he tried to speak, and looked in dread
Of frighten'd females gathering round his bed;
Then dropp'd exhausted and appear'd at rest,
Till the strong foe the vital powers possess'd;
Then with an inward broken voice he cried
"Again they come!" and mutter'd as he died.

[1810]

WILLIAM COWPER

The birth and death dates, 1731–1800, of William Cowper (pronounced "Cooper") were exactly one hundred years later than those of John Dryden. His mother was a descendant of John Donne and of Henry VII, and his father, a versifying but insensitive Rector of Great Berkhamstead, came of a family once eminent in the law. He attended Westminster School, where the poet Churchill and Warren Hastings were his classmates, and then studied law in company with Edward Thurlow, future Lord Chancellor. In 1754 he was called to the bar, and for some years thereafter he lived on small government sinecures, reading the classics, scribbling clever but trivial verses, and falling mildly in love with a cousin whose father forbade him to marry her. When about thirty he was required to pass a public examination before the House of Lords in order to secure a government post, and his apprehension of failure caused him to attempt suicide and then drove him mad. After a year in an asylum he retired to the village of Huntingdon, near Cambridge, and there met the family of Unwins with whom he went to live. With Mrs. Mary Unwin, after the death of her husband, he removed to the village of Olney, coming under the influence of John Newton, a coarse but powerful Evangelical curate who increased Cowper's religious morbidity. In 1773 his mind gave way again, so that his intended marriage to Mrs. Unwin was abandoned. At her suggestion he resumed the writing of verse, and in 1782 published a volume containing his *Table Talk*, *Conversation*, and *Retirement*. The moderate success of this collection encouraged him to proceed upon a hint made by his friend, Lady Austen, which culminated in his chief poetic effort, *The Task*. This long poem in blank verse, published in 1785, made Cowper famous, although he had previously gained some reputation by *John Gilpin*, 1782. In his remaining years he wrote an unsuccessful translation of Homer, struggled with an edition of Milton, cared for Mrs. Unwin during her protracted final illness, and after her death lived for three years more in agony and despair amounting to insanity.

Cowper's career was determined before he was eight years of age by the death of his mother and by the brutality of a bullying schoolmate. Naturally timid, deficient in vitality, and permanently disabled for normal living by the misery of his childhood, he spent his later years in a steady retreat from life. A substitute for the sheltering sympathy of his mother was found in a series of Platonic attachments to various women, and the place of the bully was taken by Jehovah, interpreted as a vengeful tyrant. Whether Cowper's logical mind ever quite accepted the doctrines of Calvin, it is certain that his emotional life, tragically disassociated from the intellectual, was tortured by them. A conviction that he was damned, fastening upon him in his early manhood, never permanently left him. In his least miserable hours he laboured not to avoid but only to forget the inevitable flames of hell by busying himself with his garden, his pets, his correspondence, or the writing of verse.

Unlike the world's great poetry, therefore, the verse of William Cowper was not produced in passionately joyous acts of creation unifying the poet with nature and God. He was incapable of passion; he seldom reached the higher levels of joy; nature, though he loved it as few have done, was never felt as his larger self but only as a spectacle of dying creatures that shared with him in the primal curse; from the terrible divinity whom he strove to worship as God he felt forever shut away by that God's hatred. Cowper did not begin to write the verse by which he is remembered until he was almost fifty, and even then he gave less time to it than to his gardening. It seldom engaged all his slight energy, but was written with the mere surface of his mind, for distraction.

The resulting defects of Cowper's verse, more observable in the longer than in the shorter poems, are these: failure in unity, loose connection of parts, diffuseness, pompous phrasing of commonplace ideas, and banality. He has little intellectual courage, slight powers of imaginative penetration, and none of that faith in the ultimate unity of the mind and the universe that great poets live by. He is everywhere able but almost nowhere brilliant in versification. His thought is clear, sensible, unexceptionable, rather than arresting, and in dealing with abstract ideas it is frequently vapid and dull. Perhaps the chief thing he has to say is that "God made the country and man made the town," but there is not one original idea in his voluminous praise of solitude, which he himself chose not for positive reasons but chiefly through fear of life.

On the other hand, Cowper is one of the most companionable of English poets, and one of the best beloved. His humour, his good taste, his intelligence that plays like a mild light of evening upon common objects and experience, even his gentle garrulity, have endeared him to millions in every generation since his death. A poet more utterly English has never lived. He came nearest to ecstasy, perhaps, in his praise of domestic comfort and safety — that shelter from the elemental and that postponement of the wrath of God which was his only approach to happiness. To compensate for his weakness in abstract thought, his fidelity in the rendering of concrete details, whether of the natural scene about him or of persons whom he knew, amounted almost to genius. His sympathy with suffering, his tenderness, his rejection of everything external and superfluous, and above all the charm of his innocence, indicate how profoundly the spirit of English poetry had changed since the days of Congreve, Rochester, and Sedley.

Cowper stands halfway between Pope and Wordsworth. We may think of him either as a neoclassic mind lacking in social courage and sense of community, or as a romantic lacking imaginative faith and full poetic passion.

RETIREMENT

The poem *Retirement*, although it has never been widely read, is one of Cowper's most representative productions. Dealing with the poet's own way of life and with a theme upon which he had meditated deeply, it is written *con amore*, with closer attention to logical development than his long poems usually show. Most of the ideas and attitudes it expresses were already commonplace, to be sure, for scores of poems in praise of solitude had been written during the eighteenth century — commonly regarded as a time which cared for nothing but "the Town" — and it rests rather heavily upon a poem of the same title, by the Reverend Robert Potter, which had been published eighteen years before. The identification of city life with moral evil and of retirement with virtue, which Cowper considers almost axiomatic, had been established ages before in the literature of Stoicism and in that of the early Christian Church. The special merit of the poem, considered in relation to the whole vast body of writing about solitude, lies in its clear discrimination of the various motives that lead to retirement, and this analysis had beneficial influence upon later treatments of the topic such as Zimmerman's highly important *Einsamkeit* and Wordsworth's *The Excursion*. During the second half of the century rural residence, at least for some part of the year, became increasingly fashionable. As a self-appointed "monitor" Cowper warns his countrymen that those who retire from active life merely to be in vogue, or for any other reason except the highest, are doomed to disappointment. His own real motive, obviously enough, is the desire to escape from a world he fears, but what he alleges as the highest motive is the desire for "divine communion."

* ... *studiis florens ignobilis oti.*
VIRGIL, *Georgics*, IV, 564.

*Hackney'd in business, wearied at that oar
Which thousands, once fast chain'd to, quit no more,
But which, when life at ebb runs weak and low,
All wish, or seem to wish, they could forego,
The statesman, lawyer, merchant, man of trade,
Pants for the refuge of some rural shade,
Where, all his long anxieties forgot
Amid the charms of a sequester'd spot,
Or recollected only to gild o'er
And add a smile to what was sweet before,
He may possess the joys he thinks he sees,
Lay his old age upon the lap of ease,
Improve the remnant of his wasted span,
And, having lived a trifler, die a man.
Thus conscience pleads her cause within the breast,
Though long rebell'd against, not yet suppress'd,
And calls a creature form'd for God alone,
For Heav'n's high purposes, and not his own,
Calls him away from selfish ends and aims,
From what debilitates and what inflames,
From cities humming with a restless crowd
Sordid as active, ignorant as loud,
Whose highest praise is that they live in vain,
The dupes of pleasure or the slaves of gain,
Where works of man are cluster'd close around
And works of God are hardly to be found,
To regions where, in spite of sin and woe,
Traces of Eden are still seen below,
Where mountain, river, forest, field, and grove
Remind him of his Maker's power and love.
'Tis well if, look'd for at so late a day,
In the last scene of such a senseless play,
True wisdom will attend his feeble call,
And grace his action ere the curtain fall.
Souls that have long despis'd their heavenly birth,
Their wishes all impregnated with earth,
For threescore years employ'd with ceaseless care
In catching smoke and feeding upon air,
Conversant only with the ways of men,
Rarely redeem the short remaining ten.

* Notes on William Cowper will be found in the Appendix, pp. 1055 ff.

Invet'rate habits choke th' unfruitful heart;
Their fibres penetrate its tenderest part,
And, draining its nutritious powers to feed
Their noxious growth, starve ev'ry better seed.

Happy, if full of days — but happier far,
If, ere we yet discern life's ev'ning star,
Sick of the service of a world that feeds
Its patient drudges with dry chaff and weeds,
We can escape from custom's idiot sway,
To serve the Sov'reign we were born t' obey.
Then sweet to muse upon his skill display'd
(Infinite skill) in all that he has made!
To trace, in nature's most minute design,
The signature and stamp of pow'r divine,
Contrivance intricate, expressed with ease,
Where unassisted sight no beauty sees,
The shapely limb and lubricated joint,
Within the small dimensions of a point,
Muscle and nerve miraculously spun,
His mighty work, who speaks and it is done,
Th' invisible in things scarce seen reveal'd,
To whom an atom is an ample field;
To wonder at a thousand insect forms,
These hatch'd, and those resuscitated worms,
New life ordain'd and brighter scenes to share,
Once prone on earth, now buoyant upon air,
Whose shape would make them, had they bulk and size,
More hideous foes than fancy can devise;
With helmet heads and dragon scales adorn'd,
The mighty myriads, now securely scorn'd,
Would mock the majesty of man's high birth,
Despise his bulwarks, and unpeople earth:
Then with a glance of fancy to survey,
Far as the faculty can stretch away,
Ten thousand rivers pour'd at his command
From urns that never fail through every land;
These like a deluge with impetuous force,
Those winding modestly a silent course;
The cloud-surmounting Alps, the fruitful vales;
Seas on which ev'ry nation spreads her sails;
The sun, a world whence other worlds drink light;
The crescent moon, the diadem of night;
Stars countless, each in his appointed place,
Fast-anchor'd in the deep abyss of space —
At such a sight to catch the poet's flame,
And with a rapture like his own exclaim:
"These are thy glorious works, thou source of good,
How dimly seen, how faintly understood!
Thine, and upheld by thy paternal care,
This universal frame, thus wondrous fair;
Thy pow'r divine, and bounty beyond thought,
Ador'd and prais'd in all that thou hast wrought.
Absorb'd in that immensity I see,
I shrink abas'd, and yet aspire to thee;
Instruct me, guide me, to that heav'nly day
Thy words more clearly than thy works display,
That, while thy truths my grosser thoughts refine,
I may resemble thee and call thee mine."

Oh blest proficiency! surpassing all
That men erroneously their glory call,
The recompense that arts or arms can yield.
The bar, the senate, or the tented field.
Compar'd with this sublimest life below,
Ye kings and rulers, what have courts to show?
Thus studied, us'd, and consecrated thus,
On earth what is, seems form'd indeed for us;
Not as the plaything of a froward child,
Fretful unless diverted and beguil'd,
Much less to feed and fan the fatal fires
Of pride, ambition, or impure desires,
But as a scale by which the soul ascends
From mighty means to more important ends,
Securely, though by steps but rarely trod,
Mounts from inferior beings up to God,
And sees, by no fallacious light or dim,
Earth made for man, and man himself for him.

Not that I mean t' approve, or would enforce,
A superstitious and monastic course:
Truth is not local; God alike pervades
And fills the world of traffic and the shades,
And may be fear'd amid the busiest scenes,
Or scorn'd where business never intervenes.
But 'tis not easy with a mind like ours
Conscious of weakness in its noblest pow'rs,
And in a world where, other ills apart,
The roving eye misleads the careless heart,
To limit thought, by nature prone to stray
Wherever freakish fancy points the way;
To bid the pleadings of self-love be still,
Resign our own and seek our Maker's will;
To spread the page of Scripture, and compare
Our conduct with the laws engraven there;
To measure all that passes in the breast,
Faithfully, fairly, by that sacred test;
To dive into the secret deeps within,
To spare no passion and no fav'rite sin,
And search the themes, important above all,
Ourselves, and our recov'ry from our fall.

But leisure, silence, and a mind releas'd
From anxious thoughts how wealth may be increas'd,
How to secure in some propitious hour
The point of int'rest or the post of pow'r,
A soul serene, and equally retir'd
From objects too much dreaded or desir'd,
Safe from the clamours of perverse dispute,
At least are friendly to the great pursuit.
  Op'ning the map of God's extensive plan,
We find a little isle, this life of man;
Eternity's unknown expanse appears
Circling around and limiting his years.
The busy race examine and explore
Each creek and cavern of the dang'rous shore,
With care collect what in their eyes excels,
Some shining pebbles, and some weeds and shells;
Thus laden, dream that they are rich and great,
And happiest he that groans beneath his weight:
The waves o'ertake them in their serious play,
And ev'ry hour sweeps multitudes away;
They shriek and sink, survivors start and weep,
Pursue their sport, and follow to the deep.
A few forsake the throng; with lifted eyes
Ask wealth of Heav'n, and gain a real prize —
Truth, wisdom, grace, and peace like that above,
Seal'd with his signet whom they serve and love;
Scorn'd by the rest, with patient hope they wait
A kind release from their imperfect state,
And, unregretted, are soon snatch'd away
From scenes of sorrow into glorious day.
  Nor these alone prefer a life recluse,
Who seek retirement for its proper use;
The love of change that lives in ev'ry breast,
Genius and temper, and desire of rest,
Discordant motives in one centre meet,
And each inclines its vot'ry to retreat.
Some minds by nature are averse to noise,
And hate the tumult half the world enjoys,
The lure of av'rice, or the pompous prize
That courts display before ambitious eyes;
The fruits that hang on pleasure's flow'ry stem,
Whate'er enchants them, are no snares to them.
To them the deep recess of dusky groves,
Or forest where the deer securely roves,
The fall of waters, and the song of birds,
And hills that echo to the distant herds
Are luxuries excelling all the glare
The world can boast, and her chief fav'rites share.
With eager step, and carelessly array'd,
For such a cause the poet seeks the shade;
From all he sees he catches new delight,
Pleas'd fancy claps her pinions at the sight,
The rising or the setting orb of day,
The clouds that flit or slowly float away,
Nature in all the various shapes she wears,
Frowning in storms, or breathing gentle airs,
The snowy robe her wintry state assumes,
Her summer heats, her fruits, and her perfumes —
All, all alike transport the glowing bard,
Success in rhyme his glory and reward.
Oh nature! whose Elysian scenes disclose
His bright perfections at whose word they rose,
Next to that Pow'r who form'd thee and sustains,
Be thou the great inspirer of my strains.
Still, as I touch the lyre, do thou expand
Thy genuine charms, and guide an artless hand,
That I may catch a fire but rarely known,
Give useful light though I should miss renown,
And, poring on thy page, whose ev'ry line
Bears proof of an intelligence divine,
May feel a heart enrich'd by what it pays,
That builds its glory on its Maker's praise.
Woe to the man whose wit disclaims its use,
Glitt'ring in vain, or only to seduce,
Who studies nature with a wanton eye,
Admires the work, but slips the lesson by;
His hours of leisure and recess employs
In drawing pictures of forbidden joys,
Retires to blazon his own worthless name,
Or shoot the careless with a surer aim.
  The lover too shuns business and alarms,
Tender idolater of absent charms.
Saints offer nothing in their warmest pray'rs
That he devotes not with a zeal like theirs;
'Tis consecration of his heart, soul, time,
And ev'ry thought that wanders is a crime.
In sighs he worships his supremely fair,
And weeps a sad libation in despair,
Adores a *creature, and, devout in vain,
Wins in return an answer of disdain.
As woodbine weds the plant within her reach,
Rough elm, or smooth-grain'd ash, or glossy beech,

In spiral rings ascends the trunk, and lays
Her golden tassels on the leafy sprays,
But does a mischief while she lends a grace,
*Strait'ning its growth by such a strict embrace, —
So love, that clings around the noblest minds,
Forbids th' advancement of the soul he binds;
The suitor's air indeed he soon improves,
And forms it to the taste of her he loves,
Teaches his eyes a language, and no less
Refines his speech, and fashions his address:
But farewell promises of happier fruits,
Manly designs, and learning's grave pursuits;
Girt with a chain he cannot wish to break,
His only bliss is sorrow for her sake;
Who will may pant for glory and excel,
Her smile his aim, all higher aims farewell!
Thyrsis, Alexis, or whatever name
May least offend against so pure a flame,
Though sage advice of friends the most sincere
Sounds harshly in so delicate an ear,
And lovers, of all creatures tame or wild,
Can least brook management, however mild,
Yet let a poet (poetry disarms
The fiercest animals with magic charms)
Risk an intrusion on thy pensive mood,
And woo and win thee to thy proper good.
Pastoral images and still retreats,
Umbrageous walks and solitary seats,
Sweet birds in concert with harmonious streams,
Soft airs, nocturnal vigils, and day-dreams
Are all enchantments in a case like thine,
Conspire against thy peace with one design,
Soothe thee to make thee but a surer prey,
And feed the fire that wastes thy pow'rs away.
Up! God has form'd thee with a wiser view,
Not to be led in chains, but to subdue;
Calls thee to cope with enemies, and first
Points out a conflict with thyself, the worst.
Woman, indeed, a gift he would bestow
When he design'd a paradise below,
The richest earthly boon his hands afford,
Deserves to be belov'd, but not ador'd.
Post away swiftly to more active scenes,
Collect the scatter'd truths that study gleans,
Mix with the world, but with its wiser part,
No longer give an image all thine heart;
Its empire is not hers, nor is it thine,
'Tis God's just claim, prerogative divine.
Virtuous and faithful *Heberden! whose skill
Attempts no task it cannot well fulfill,
Gives melancholy up to nature's care,
And sends the patient into purer air.
Look where he *comes — in this embower'd alcove
Stand close conceal'd, and see a statue move:
Lips busy, and eyes fix'd, foot falling slow,
Arms hanging idly down, hands clasp'd below,
Interpret to the marking eye distress
Such as its symptoms can alone express.
That tongue is silent now; that silent tongue
Could argue once, could jest or join the song,
Could give advice, could censure or commend,
Or charm the sorrows of a drooping friend.
Renounc'd alike its office and its sport,
Its brisker and its graver strains fall short;
Both fail beneath a fever's secret sway,
And, like a summer-brook, are past away.
This is a sight for Pity to peruse
Till she resemble faintly what she views,
Till Sympathy contract a kindred pain,
Pierc'd with the woes that she laments in vain.
This of all maladies that man infest,
Claims most compassion, and receives the least:
Job felt it when he groan'd beneath the rod
And the barb'd arrows of a frowning God;
And such emollients as his friends could spare,
Friends such as his for modern Jobs prepare.
Blest, rather curst, with hearts that never feel,
Kept snug in caskets of close-hammer'd steel,
With mouths made only to grin wide and eat,
And minds that deem derided pain a treat,
With limbs of British oak, and nerves of wire,
And wit that puppet-prompters might inspire,
Their sov'reign nostrum is a clumsy joke,
On pangs enforc'd with God's severest stroke.
But, with a soul that ever felt the sting
Of sorrow, sorrow is a sacred thing:
Not to molest, or irritate, or raise
A laugh at his expense, is slender praise;
He that has not usurp'd the name of man
Does all, and deems too little, all he can,
T'assuage the throbbings of the fester'd part,
And staunch the bleedings of a broken heart.
'Tis not, as heads that never ache suppose,
Forg'ry of fancy, and a dream of woes;
Man is a harp whose chords elude the sight,
Each yielding harmony dispos'd aright;
The screws revers'd (a task which if he please
God in a moment executes with ease),
Ten thousand thousand strings at once go loose,
Lost, till he tune them, all their pow'r and use.

Then neither heathy wilds, nor scenes as fair
As ever recompens'd the peasant's care,
Nor soft declivities with tufted hills,
Nor view of waters turning busy mills,
Parks in which Art preceptress Nature weds,
Nor gardens interspers'd with flow'ry beds,
Nor gales that catch the scent of blooming groves,
And waft it to the mourner as he roves,
Can call up life into his faded eye,
That passes all he sees unheeded by:
No wounds like those a wounded spirit feels;
No cure for such, till God who makes them, heals.
And thou, sad suff'rer under nameless ill,
That yields not to the touch of human skill,
Improve the kind occasion, understand
A Father's frown, and kiss his chast'ning hand:
To thee the day-spring, and the blaze of noon,
The purple ev'ning and resplendent moon,
The stars that, sprinkled o'er the vault of night,
Seem drops descending in a show'r of light,
Shine not, or undesir'd and hated shine,
Seen through the medium of a cloud like thine:
Yet seek him, in his favour life is found,
All bliss beside — a shadow or a sound:
Then heav'n, eclips'd so long, and this dull earth
Shall seem to start into a second birth;
Nature, assuming a more lovely face,
Borrowing a beauty from the works of grace,
Shall be despis'd and overlook'd no more,
Shall fill thee with delights unfelt before,
Impart to things inanimate a voice,
And bid her mountains and her hills rejoice;
The sound shall run along the winding vales,
And thou enjoy an Eden ere it fails.
"Ye groves," the statesman at his desk exclaims,
Sick of a thousand disappointed aims,
"My patrimonial treasure and my pride,
Beneath your shades your grey possessor hide;
Receive me languishing for that repose
The servant of the public never knows.
Ye saw me once (ah, those regretted days
When boyish innocence was all my praise!)
Hour after hour delightfully allot
To studies then familiar, since forgot,
And cultivate a taste for ancient song,
Catching its ardour as I mus'd along;
Nor seldom, as propitious Heav'n might send,
What once I valued and could boast, a friend,
Were witnesses how cordially I press'd
His undissembling virtue to my breast;
Receive me now, not uncorrupt as then,
Nor guiltless of corrupting other men,
But vers'd in arts that, while they seem to stay
A falling empire, hasten its decay.
To the fair haven of my native home,
The wreck of what I was, fatigu'd, I come;
For once I can approve the patriot's voice,
And make the course he recommends my choice;
We meet at last in one sincere desire,
His wish and mine both prompt me to retire."
'Tis done — he steps into the welcome chaise,
Lolls at his ease behind four handsome bays,
That whirl away from business and debate
The disencumber'd Atlas of the state.
Ask not the boy who, when the breeze of morn
First shakes the glitt'ring drops from every thorn
Unfolds his flock, then under bank or bush
Sits linking cherry stones, or platting rush,
How fair is freedom? — he was always free:
To carve his rustic name upon a tree,
To snare the mole, or with ill-fashion'd hook,
To draw th' incautious minnow from the brook,
Are life's prime pleasures in his simple view,
His flock the chief concern he ever knew;
She shines but little in his heedless eyes;
The good we never miss we rarely prize:
But ask the noble drudge in state affairs,
Escap'd from office and its constant cares,
What charms he sees in freedom's smile express'd,
In freedom lost so long, now repossess'd;
The tongue whose strains were cogent as commands,
Rever'd at home, and felt in foreign lands,
Shall own itself a stamm'rer in that cause,
Or plead its silence as its best applause.
He knows indeed that, whether dress'd or rude,
Wild without art, or artfully subdued,
Nature in ev'ry form inspires delight,
But never mark'd her with so just a sight.
Her hedge-row shrubs, a variegated store,
With woodbine and wild roses mantled o'er,
Green *balks and furrow'd lands, the stream that spreads
Its cooling vapour o'er the dewy meads,
Downs that almost escape th' inquiring eye,
That melt and fade into the distant sky,
Beauties he lately slighted as he pass'd,
Seem all created since he travell'd last.
Master of all th' enjoyments he design'd,
No rough annoyance rankling in his mind,

What early philosophic hours he keeps,
How regular his meals, how sound he sleeps!
No sounder he that on the mainmast head,
While morning kindles with a windy red,
Begins a long look-out for distant land,
Nor quits, till ev'ning watch, his giddy stand,
Then swift descending with a seaman's haste,
Slips to his hammock, and forgets the blast.
He chooses company, but not the squire's,
Whose wit is rudeness, whose good breeding tires;
Nor yet the parson's, who would gladly come,
Obsequious when abroad, though proud at home;
Nor can he much affect the neighb'ring peer,
Whose toe of emulation treads too near;
But wisely seeks a more convenient friend,
With whom, dismissing forms, he may unbend!
A man whom marks of condescending grace
Teach, while they flatter him, his proper place:
Who comes when call'd, and at a word withdraws,
Speaks with reserve, and listens with applause;
Some plain mechanic, who, without pretence
To birth or wit, nor gives nor takes offence;
On whom he rests well-pleas'd his weary pow'rs,
And talks and laughs away his vacant hours.
The tide of life, swift always in its course,
May run in cities with a brisker force,
But nowhere with a current so serene,
Or half so clear, as in the rural scene.
Yet how fallacious is all earthly bliss,
What obvious truths the wisest heads may miss!
Some pleasures live a month, and some a year,
But short the date of all we gather here;
No happiness is felt, except the true,
That does not charm the more for being new.
This observation, as it chanced, not made,
Or, if the thought occurr'd, not duly weigh'd,
He sighs — for, after all, by slow degrees,
The spot he lov'd has lost the pow'r to please.
To *cross his ambling pony day by day
Seems at the best but dreaming life away;
The prospect, such as might enchant despair,
He views it not, or sees no beauty there;
With aching heart and discontented looks
Returns at noon to billiards or to books,
But feels, while grasping at his faded joys,
A secret thirst of his renounced employs.
He chides the tardiness of ev'ry post,
Pants to be told of battles won or lost,
Blames his own indolence, observes, though late,
'Tis criminal to leave a sinking state,
Flies to the levee, and, receiv'd with grace,
Kneels, kisses hands, and shines again in place.
  Suburban villas, highway-side retreats,
That dread th' encroachment of our growing streets,
Tight boxes, neatly sash'd, and in a blaze
With all a July sun's collected rays,
Delight the citizen, who, gasping there,
Breathes clouds of dust, and calls it country air.
"Oh, sweet retirement, who would balk the thought,
That could afford retirement, or could not?
'Tis such an easy walk, so smooth and straight,
The second *milestone fronts the garden gate;
A step if fair, and, if a shower approach,
You find safe shelter in the next stagecoach."
There, prison'd in a parlour snug and small,
Like bottled wasps upon a southern wall,
The man of business and his friends compress'd,
Forget their labours, and yet find no rest;
But still 'tis rural — trees are to be seen
From ev'ry window, and the fields are green;
Ducks paddle in the pond before the door,
And what could a remoter scene show more?
A sense of elegance we rarely find
The portion of a mean or vulgar mind,
And ignorance of better things makes man,
Who cannot much, rejoice in what he can;
And he that deems his leisure well bestow'd
In contemplation of a turnpike road,
Is occupied as well, employs his hours
As wisely, and as much improves his pow'rs,
As he that slumbers in pavilions grac'd
With all the charms of an accomplish'd taste.
Yet hence, alas! insolvencies; and hence
The unpitied victim of ill-judg'd expense,
From all his wearisome engagements freed,
Shakes hands with business, and retires indeed.
  Your prudent grandmammas, ye modern belles,
Content with Bristol, Bath, and *Tunbridge Wells,
When health requir'd it would consent to roam,
Else more attach'd to pleasures found at home.
But now alike, gay widow, virgin, wife,
Ingenious to diversify dull life,

In coaches, chaises, *caravans, and *hoys,
Fly to the coast for daily, nightly joys,
And all, impatient of dry land, agree
With one consent, to rush into the sea.
Ocean exhibits, fathomless and broad,
Much of the power and majesty of God.
He swathes about the swelling of the deep,
That shines and rests, as infants smile and sleep;
Vast as it is, it answers as it flows
The breathings of the lightest air that blows;
Curling and whitening over all the waste,
The rising waves obey th' increasing blast,
Abrupt and horrid as the tempest roars,
Thunder and flash upon the steadfast shores,
Till he that rides the whirlwind checks the rein,
Then, all the world of waters sleeps again.
Nereids or Dryads, as the fashion leads,
Now in the floods, now panting in the meads,
Votaries of pleasure still, where'er she dwells,
Near barren rocks, in palaces, or cells,
Oh, grant a poet leave to recommend
(A poet fond of nature, and your friend)
Her slighted works to your admiring view;
Her works must needs excel, who fashion'd you.
Would ye, when rambling in your morning ride,
With some unmeaning coxcomb at your side,
Condemn the prattle for his idle pains,
To waste unheard the music of his strains,
And, deaf to all th' impertinence of tongue,
That, while it courts, affronts and does you wrong, —
Mark well the finish'd plan without a fault,
The seas globose and huge, th' o'erarching vault,
Earth's millions daily fed, a world employ'd
In gath'ring plenty yet to be enjoy'd,
Till gratitude grew vocal in the praise
Of God, beneficent in all his ways;
Grac'd with such wisdom, how would beauty shine!
Ye want but that to seem indeed divine.
  Anticipated *rents and bills unpaid
Force many a shining youth into the shade,
Not to redeem his time but his estate,
And play the fool, but at a cheaper rate;
There, hid in loath'd obscurity, remov'd
From pleasures left, but never more belov'd,
He just endures, and with a sickly spleen
Sighs o'er the beauties of the charming scene.
Nature indeed looks prettily in rhyme;
Streams tinkle sweetly in poetic chime:
The warblings of the blackbird, clear and strong,
Are musical enough in Thomson's song;
And *Cobham's groves, and Windsor's green retreats,
When Pope *describes them, have a thousand sweets;
He likes the country but, in truth, must own
Most likes it when he studies it in town.
  Poor Jack — no matter who, for when I blame
I pity, and must therefore sink the name —
Liv'd in his saddle, lov'd the chase, the course,
And always, ere he mounted, kiss'd his horse.
Th' estate his sires had own'd in ancient years
Was quickly distanced, match'd against a peer's.
Jack vanish'd, was regretted and forgot;
'Tis wild good-nature's never-failing lot.
At length, when all had long suppos'd him dead,
By cold submersion, razor, rope, or lead,
My lord, alighting at his usual place,
The Crown, took notice of an ostler's face.
Jack knew his friend, but hop'd in that disguise
He might escape the most observing eyes,
And whistling, as if unconcern'd and gay,
Curried his nag, and look'd another way.
Convinc'd at last, upon a nearer view,
'Twas he, the same, the very Jack he knew,
O'erwhelm'd at once with wonder, grief, and joy,
He press'd him much to quit his base employ;
His countenance, his purse, his heart, his hand,
Influence and power, were all at his command:
Peers are not always gen'rous as well-bred,
But *Granby was, meant truly what he said.
Jack bow'd, and was oblig'd, confess'd 'twas strange
That so retir'd he should not wish a change,
But knew no medium between guzzling beer,
And his old stint — three thousand pounds a year.
  Thus some retire to nourish hopeless woe;
Some seeking happiness not found below;
Some to comply with humour, and a mind
To social scenes by nature disinclin'd;
Some sway'd by fashion, some by deep disgust:
Some self-impoverish'd, and because they must;
But few that court retirement are aware
Of half the toils they must encounter there.

Lucrative offices are seldom lost
For want of pow'rs proportion'd to the post:
Give e'en a dunce th' employment he desires,
And he soon finds the talents it requires;
A business with an income at its heels
Furnishes always oil for its own wheels.
But in his arduous enterprise to close
His active years with indolent repose,
He finds the labours of that state exceed
His utmost faculties, severe indeed.
'Tis easy to resign a toilsome place,
But not to manage leisure with a grace,
Absence of occupation is not rest,
A mind quite vacant is a mind distress'd.
The veteran steed, excus'd his task at length
In kind compassion of his failing strength,
And turn'd into the park or mead to graze,
Exempt from future service all his days,
There feels a pleasure perfect in its kind,
Ranges at liberty, and snuffs the wind;
But when his lord would quit the busy road
To taste a joy like that he has bestow'd,
He proves, less happy than his favour'd brute,
A life of ease a difficult pursuit.
Thought, to the man that never thinks, may seem
As natural as, when asleep, to dream;
But reveries (for human minds will act)
Specious in show, impossible in fact,
Those flimsy webs that break as soon as wrought,
Attain not to the dignity of thought;
Nor yet the swarms that occupy the brain,
Where dreams of dress, intrigue, and pleasure reign;
Nor such as useless conversation breeds,
Or lust engenders, and indulgence feeds.
Whence, and what are we? to what end ordain'd?
What means the drama by the world sustain'd?
Business or vain amusement, care or mirth,
Divide the frail inhabitants of earth.
Is duty a mere sport, or an employ?
Life an intrusted talent, or a toy?
Is there, as reason, conscience, Scripture, say,
Cause to provide for a great future day,
When, earth's assign'd duration at an end,
Man shall be summon'd, and the dead attend?
The trumpet — will it sound? the curtain rise?
And show th' august tribunal of the skies,
Where no prevarication shall avail,
Where eloquence and artifice shall fail,
The pride of arrogant distinctions fall,
And conscience and our conduct judge us all?

Pardon me, ye that give the midnight oil
To learned cares or philosophic toil,
Though I revere your honourable names,
Your useful labours and important aims,
And hold the world indebted to your aid,
Enrich'd with the discoveries ye have made;
Yet let me stand excus'd, if I esteem
A mind employ'd on so sublime a theme,
Pushing her bold inquiry to the date
And outline of the present transient state,
And, after poising her adventurous wings,
Settling at last upon eternal things,
Far more intelligent, and better taught
The strenuous use of profitable thought,
Than ye, when happiest, and enlighten'd most,
And highest in renown, can justly boast.

A mind unnerv'd, or indispos'd to bear
The weight of subjects worthiest of her care,
Whatever hopes a change of scene inspires,
Must change her nature, or in vain retires.
An idler is a watch that wants both hands,
As useless if it goes as when it stands.
Books, therefore — not the scandal of the shelves,
In which lewd sensualists print out themselves;
Nor those in which the stage gives vice a blow,
With what success let modern manners show;
Nor *his who, for the bane of thousands born,
Built God a church, and laugh'd his word to scorn,
Skillful alike to seem devout and just,
And stab religion with a sly side-thrust;
Nor those of learn'd philologists, who chase
A panting syllable through time and space,
Start it at home, and hunt it in the dark
To Gaul, to Greece, and into Noah's ark —
But such as learning without false pretence,
The friend of truth, th' associate of sound sense,
And such as, in the zeal of good design,
Strong judgment lab'ring in the Scripture mine,
All such as manly and great souls produce,
Worthy to live, and of eternal use:
Behold in these what leisure hours demand,
Amusement and true knowledge hand in hand.
Luxury gives the mind a childish cast,
And, while she polishes, perverts the taste;
Habits of close attention, thinking heads,
Become more rare as dissipation spreads,
Till authors hear at length, one general cry,
"Tickle and entertain us, or we die."
The loud demand, from year to year the same,
Beggars invention and makes fancy lame,

Till farce itself, most mournfully jejune,
Calls for the kind assistance of a tune;
And novels (witness ev'ry month's review)
Belie their name, and offer nothing new.
The mind, relaxing into needful sport,
Should turn to writers of an abler sort,
Whose wit well manag'd, and whose classic style,
Give truth a lustre, and make wisdom smile.
Friends (for I cannot stint, as some have done,
Too rigid in my view, that name to one;
Though one, I grant it, in the generous breast,
Will stand advanc'd a step above the rest:
Flow'rs by that name promiscuously we call,
But one, the rose, the regent of them all),
Friends, not adopted with a school-boy's haste,
But chosen with a nice discerning taste,
Well-born, well-disciplin'd, who, plac'd apart
From vulgar minds, have honour much at heart,
And, though the world may think th' ingredients odd,
The love of virtue, and the fear of God!
Such friends prevent what else would soon succeed,
A temper rustic as the life we lead,
And keep the polish of the manners clean
As theirs who bustle in the busiest scene;
For solitude, however some may rave,
Seeming a sanctuary, proves a grave,
A sepulchre in which the living lie,
Where all good qualities grow sick and die.
I praise the *Frenchman, his remark was shrewd:
"How sweet, how passing sweet, is solitude!
But grant me still a friend in my retreat,
Whom I may whisper, 'Solitude is sweet.'"
Yet neither these delights, nor aught beside
That appetite can ask, or wealth provide,
Can save us always from a tedious day,
Or shine the dullness of still life away:
Divine communion, carefully enjoy'd,
Or sought with energy, must fill the void.
Oh, sacred art, to which alone life owes
Its happiest seasons, and a peaceful close,
Scorn'd in a world, indebted to that scorn
For evils daily felt and hardly borne, —
Not knowing thee, we reap, with bleeding hands,
Flowers of rank odour upon thorny lands,
And, while experience cautions us in vain,
Grasp seeming happiness, and find it pain.
Despondence, self-deserted in her grief,
Lost by abandoning her own relief,
Murmuring and ungrateful discontent
That scorns afflictions mercifully meant,
Those humours tart as wines upon the fret
Which idleness and weariness beget —
These, and a thousand plagues that haunt the breast,
Fond of the phantom of an earthly rest,
Divine communion chases, as the day
Drives to their dens th' obedient beasts of prey.
See Judah's promis'd *king, bereft of all,
Driv'n out an exile from the face of Saul.
To distant caves the lonely wand'rer flies
To seek that peace a tyrant's frown denies.
Hear the sweet accents of his tuneful voice,
Hear him, o'erwhelm'd with sorrow, yet rejoice;
No womanish or wailing grief has part,
No, not a moment, in his royal heart;
'Tis manly music, such as martyrs make,
Suff'ring with gladness for a Saviour's sake;
His soul exults, hope animates his lays,
The sense of mercy kindles into praise,
And wilds, familiar with the lion's roar,
Ring with ecstatic sounds unheard before:
'Tis love like his that can alone defeat
The foes of man, or make a desert sweet.
Religion does not censure or exclude
Unnumber'd pleasures harmlessly pursu'd:
To study culture, and with artful toil
To meliorate and tame the stubborn soil;
To give dissimilar yet fruitful lands
The grain, or herb, or plant that each demands;
To cherish virtue in an humble state,
And share the joys your bounty may create;
To mark the matchless workings of the pow'r
That shuts within its seed the future flow'r,
Bids these in elegance of form excel,
In colour these, and those delight the smell,
Sends Nature forth, the daughter of the skies,
To dance on earth, and charm all human eyes;
To teach the canvas innocent deceit,
Or lay the landscape on the snowy sheet —
These, these are arts pursu'd without a crime,
That leave no stain upon the wing of time.
Me poetry (or, rather, notes that aim
Feebly and vainly at poetic fame)
Employs, shut out from more important views,
Fast by the banks of the slow winding *Ouse;
Content if, thus sequester'd, I may raise
A monitor's, though not a poet's praise,
And while I teach an art too little known,
To close life wisely, may not waste my own.

[1782]

THE POPLAR FIELD

The Poplar Field, written in 1784 in mourning for a grove that had stood near Olney, is one of the most musical of eighteenth-century poems, remarkable for the skill with which a metre trivial in sound and association is compelled to produce a dignified effect. Cowper's own translation of the poem into Latin is given here partly because it is at least as successful as the original and partly to show his ability in this gentlemanly accomplishment.

The poplars are fell'd; farewell to the shade
And the whispering sound of the cool colonnade;
The winds play no longer and sing in the leaves,
Nor Ouse on his bosom their image receives.

Twelve years have elaps'd since I first took a view
Of my favourite field and the bank where they grew;
And now in the grass behold they are laid,
And the tree is my seat that once lent me a shade!

The blackbird has fled to another retreat
Where the hazels afford him a screen from the heat,
And the scene where his melody charm'd me before
Resounds with his sweet-flowing ditty no more.

My fugitive years are all hasting away,
And I must ere long lie as lowly as they,
With a turf on my breast and a stone at my head,
Ere another such grove shall arise in its stead.

'Tis a sight to engage me, if anything can,
To muse on the perishing pleasures of man;
Though his life be a dream, his enjoyments, I see,
Have a being less durable even than he.

[1785]

IDEM LATINE REDDITUM

Populeæ cecidit gratissima copia silvæ,
Conticuere susurri, omnisque evanuit umbra,
Nullæ jam levibus se miscent frondibus auræ
Et nulla in fluvio ramorum ludit imago.

Hei mihi! bis senos dum luctu torqueor annos,
His cogor silvis suetoque carere recessu,
Cum sero rediens stratasque in gramine cernens
Insedi arboribus sub queis errare solebam.

Ah ubi nunc merulæ cantus? Felicior illum
Silva tegit, duræ nondum permissa bipenni;
Scilicet exustos colles camposque patentes
Odit, et indignans et non rediturus abivit.

Sed qui succisas doleo succidar et ipse,
Et prius huic parilis quam creverit altera silva
Flebor, et, exequiis parvis donatus, habebo
Defixum lapidem tumulique cubantis acervum.

Tam subito periisse videns tam digna manere
Agnosco humanas sortes et tristia fata —
Sit licet ipse brevis, volucrique simillimus umbræ,
Est homini brevior citiusque obitura voluptas.

[1785]

YARDLEY OAK

Although written when the poet was sixty years of age and left unfinished, *Yardley Oak* is Cowper's highest imaginative utterance. Here he almost abandons his habitual method of detached objective description and comes nearest to a sympathetic penetration of his subject. In the literature of trees there is probably nothing that surpasses this poem unless in the two great elegies on an ancient oak by Victor de Laprade. The particular tree Cowper celebrates stood in the Yardley hunting ground near Olney. It was twenty-three feet in circumference, and local tradition asserted that it had been planted by the daughter of William the Conqueror.

Survivor sole, and hardly such, of all
That once liv'd here thy brethren! — at my birth
(Since which I number three-score winters past)
A shatter'd veteran, hollow-trunk'd perhaps
As now, and with *excoriate forks deform,
Relict of ages! Could a mind imbued
With truth from Heav'n created thing adore,
I might with rev'rence kneel and worship thee.

It seems idolatry with some excuse
When our forefather *Druids in their oaks

Imagin'd sanctity. The conscience yet
Unpurified by an authentic *act
Of amnesty, the meed of blood divine,
Lov'd not the light, but, gloomy into gloom
Of thickest shades, like Adam after taste
Of fruit proscrib'd, as to a refuge, fled.
Thou wast a bauble once; a cup and ball,
Which babes might play with; and the thievish jay
Seeking her food, with ease might have purloin'd
The auburn nut that held thee, swallowing down
Thy yet close-folded latitude of boughs
And all thine embryo vastness, at a gulp.
But fate thy growth decreed; autumnal rains
Beneath thy parent tree mellow'd the soil
Design'd thy cradle, and a skipping deer,
With pointed hoof dibbling the glebe, prepar'd
The soft receptacle in which secure
Thy rudiments should sleep the winter through.
So Fancy dreams. Disprove it, if ye can,
Ye reasoners broad awake, whose busy search
Of argument, employ'd too oft amiss, 31
Sifts half the pleasures of short life away!
Thou fell'st mature, and in the loamy clod
Swelling, with vegetative force *instinct,
Didst burst thine egg, as theirs the fabled *twins
Now stars; two lobes, protruding, pair'd exact;
A leaf succeeded, and another leaf,
And all the elements thy puny growth
Fost'ring propitious, thou becam'st a twig.
Who liv'd when thou wast such? Oh, couldst thou speak,
As in *Dodona once thy kindred trees
Oracular, I would not curious ask
The future, best unknown, but at thy mouth
Inquisitive, the less ambiguous past.
By thee I might correct, erroneous oft,
The clock of history, facts and events
Timing more punctual, unrecorded facts
Recov'ring, and misstated setting right —
Desp'rate attempt, till trees shall speak again!
Time made thee what thou wast — king of the woods;
And time hath made thee what thou art — a cave
For owls to roost in. Once thy spreading boughs
O'erhung the *champaign; and the numerous flock
That graz'd it stood beneath that ample cope
Uncrowded, yet safe-shelter'd from the storm.
No flock frequents thee now. Thou hast outliv'd
Thy popularity and art become
(Unless verse rescue thee awhile) a thing
Forgotten, as the foliage of thy youth.
While thus through all the stages thou hast push'd
Of treeship, first a seedling hid in grass,
Then twig, then sapling, and, as century roll'd
Slow after century, a giant bulk
Of girth enormous, with moss-cushion'd root
Upheav'd above the soil, and sides emboss'd
With prominent wens globose, till at the last
The rottenness, which time is charg'd t'inflict
On other mighty ones, found also thee.
What exhibitions various hath the world
Witness'd of mutability in all
That we account most durable below!
Change is the diet on which all subsist
Created changeable, and change at last
Destroys them. Skies uncertain now the heat
Transmitting cloudless, and the solar beam
Now quenching in a boundless sea of clouds, —
Calm and alternate storm, moisture and drought,
Invigorate by turns the springs of life
In all that live — plant, animal, and man —
And in conclusion mar them. Nature's threads,
Fine passing thought, ev'n in her coarsest works
Delight in agitation, yet sustain
The force that agitates, not unimpair'd;
But, worn by frequent impulse, to the cause
Of their best *tone their dissolution owe.
Thought cannot spend itself, comparing still
The great and little of thy lot, thy growth
From almost nullity into a state
Of matchless grandeur, and declension thence
Slow into such magnificent decay.
Time was, when settling on thy leaf, a fly
Could shake thee to the root — and time has been
When tempests could not. At thy firmest age
Thou hadst within thy bole solid contents
That might have ribb'd the sides and plank'd the deck
Of some flagg'd *admiral: and *tortuous arms,
The ship-wright's darling treasure, didst present
To the four-quarter'd winds, robust and bold,
Warp'd into tough knee-timber, many a load.

But the axe spar'd thee; in those thriftier days
Oaks fell not, hewn by thousands, to supply
The bottomless demands of contest wag'd
For senatorial *honours. Thus to Time
The task was left to whittle thee away
With his sly scythe, whose ever-nibbling edge
Noiseless, an atom and an atom more
Disjoining from the rest, has, unobserv'd,
Achiev'd a labour, which had, far and wide,
(By man perform'd) made all the forest ring.
*Embowell'd now, and of thy ancient self
Possessing nought but the scoop'd rind, that seems
A huge throat calling to the clouds for drink,
Which it would give in rivulets to thy root,
Thou temptest none, but rather much forbid'st
The feller's toil, which thou couldst ill requite.
Yet is thy root *sincere, sound as the rock,
A quarry of stout spurs and knotted fangs,
Which, crook'd into a thousand whimsies, clasp
The stubborn soil, and hold thee still erect.
So stands a kingdom, whose foundation yet
Fails not, in virtue and in wisdom laid,
Though all the superstructure, by the tooth
Pulveriz'd of venality, a shell
Stands now, and semblance only of itself.
Thine arms have left thee. Winds have rent them off
Long since, and rovers of the forest wild
With bow and shaft have burnt them. Some have left
A splinter'd stump bleach'd to a snowy white,
And some, memorial none where once they grew.
Yet life still lingers in thee, and puts forth
Proof not contemptible of what she can,
Even where death predominates. The spring
Thee finds not less alive to her sweet force
Than yonder upstarts of the neighbouring wood,
So much thy juniors, who their birth receiv'd
Half a millennium since the date of thine.
But since, although well qualified by age
To teach, no spirit dwells in thee, nor voice
May be expected from thee, seated here
On thy distorted root, with hearers none
Or prompter, save the scene, I will perform
Myself the oracle, and will discourse
In my own ear such matter as I may.
*Thou, like myself, hast stage by stage attain'd
Life's wintry *bourn; thou, after many years,
I after few; but few or many prove
A span in retrospect; for I can touch
With my least finger's end my own disease
And with extended thumb my natal hour,
And hadst thou also skill in measurement
As I, the past would seem as short to thee.
"Evil and few," said *Jacob — at an age
Thrice mine, and few and evil, I may think
The *prediluvian race, whose buxom youth
Endured two centuries, accounted *theirs.
"Shortliv'd as foliage is the race of man.
The wind shakes down the leaves, the budding grove
Soon teems with others, and in spring they grow.
So pass mankind. One generation meets
Its destin'd period, and a new succeeds."
Such was the tender but undue complaint
Of the *Mæonian in old time; for who
Would drawl out centuries in tedious strife
Severe with mental and corporeal ill,
And would not rather choose a shorter race
To glory, a few decades here below?
One man alone, the father of us all,
Drew not his life from woman; never gaz'd,
With mute unconsciousness of what he saw
On all around him; learn'd not by degrees,
Nor owed *articulation to his ear;
But, moulded by his Maker into man
At once, upstood intelligent, survey'd
All creatures, with precision understood
Their purport, uses, properties, assign'd
To each his name significant, and, fill'd
With love and wisdom, render'd back to heav'n
In praise harmonious the first air he drew.
He was excus'd the penalties of dull
Minority. No tutor charg'd his hand
With the thought-tracing quill, or task'd his mind
With problems; history, not wanted yet,
Lean'd on her elbow, watching time, whose course,
Eventful, should supply her with a theme:
* * * * * * * *

[1804]

THE TASK

The topics discussed by Cowper in his first volume of verse, published in 1782, were suggested to him chiefly by Mrs. Unwin. At least the title and the starting-point of his second effort, usually considered his masterpiece, were given him by his friend, Lady Austen, who, realizing that his only difficulty was in beginning, laughingly set him "the task" of writing about "this sofa." The blank-verse poem in six books which resulted is in fact a discursive treatment of a hundred different themes very loosely linked, although, as the poet himself asserted, "The whole has one tendency: to discountenance the modern enthusiasm after a London life, and to recommend rural ease and leisure, as friendly to the cause of piety and virtue." The main concern of *The Task* is identical, therefore, with that of *Retirement,* although it is superior to that poem in its greater wealth of concrete detail and in the weight and dignity as well as the ease of its versification. Thinking of the whole poem as Cowper's self-congratulation upon his escape from the storms of the outer world, we may find the very heart of it in the Fourth Book, where his sense of seclusion is deepest and his feeling of safety, for the brief time being, is strongest. The unobtrusive art with which he builds up the scene of domestic peace to make a picture intimate without sentimentality and vivid without violence, enhancing it by perfectly chosen contrasts, shows Cowper at his best.

Book IV

THE WINTER EVENING

Hark! 'tis the twanging horn! O'er yonder bridge
That with its wearisome but needful length
Bestrides the wintry flood, in which the moon
Sees her unwrinkled face reflected bright,
He comes, the herald of a noisy world,
With spatter'd boots, strapp'd waist, and frozen locks,
News from all nations lumb'ring at his back.
True to his charge, the close-pack'd load behind,
Yet careless what he brings, his one concern
Is to conduct it to the destin'd *inn,
And, having dropp'd the expected bag, pass on.
He whistles as he goes, light-hearted wretch,
Cold, and yet cheerful — messenger of grief
Perhaps to thousands, and of joy to some,
To him indiff'rent whether grief or joy.
Houses in ashes and the fall of stocks,
Births, deaths, and marriages, epistles wet
With tears that trickled down the writer's cheeks
Fast as the periods from his fluent quill,
Or charg'd with amorous sighs of absent swains
Or nymphs responsive, equally affect
His horse and him, unconscious of them all.
But oh, th' important budget! usher'd in
With such heart-shaking music, who can say
What are its tidings? Have our troops awak'd?
Or do they still, as if with opium drugg'd,
*Snore to the murmurs of th' Atlantic wave?
Is *India free, and does she wear her plum'd
And jewell'd turban with a smile of peace,
Or do we grind her still? The grand debate,
The popular harangue, the tart reply,
The logic and the wisdom and the wit
And the loud laugh — I long to know them all;
I burn to set th' imprison'd wranglers free
And give them voice and utterance once again.
  Now stir the fire, and close the shutters fast,
Let fall the curtains, wheel the sofa round,
And while the bubbling and loud-hissing urn
Throws up a steamy column, and the cups
That cheer but not inebriate, wait on each,
So let us welcome peaceful ev'ning in.
Not such his ev'ning, who with shining face
Sweats in the crowded theatre, and squeez'd
And bor'd with elbow-points through both his sides,
Outscolds the ranting actor on the stage;
Nor his who patient stands till his feet throb
And his head thumps to feed upon the breath
Of patriots bursting with heroic rage,
Or *placemen, all tranquillity and smiles.
This *folio of four pages, happy work,
Which not ev'n critics criticise, that holds
Inquisitive attention while I read,
Fast bound in chains of silence, which the fair,
Though eloquent themselves, yet fear to break —
What is it but a map of busy life,
Its fluctuations and its vast concerns?
Here runs the mountainous and craggy ridge
That tempts ambition. On the summit, see,
The seals of office glitter in his eyes;
He climbs, he pants, he grasps them! At his heels,
Close at his heels, a demagogue ascends

And with a dext'rous jerk soon twists him down,
And wins them, but to lose them in his turn.
Here rills of oily eloquence in soft
Meanders lubricate the course they take;
The modest speaker is asham'd and griev'd
T' engross a moment's notice, and yet begs,
Begs a propitious ear for his poor thoughts,
However trivial all that he conceives.
Sweet bashfulness! It claims, at least, this praise:
The dearth of information and good sense
That it foretells us always comes to pass.
Cat'racts of declamation thunder here;
There forests of no meaning spread the page
In which all comprehension wanders lost,
While fields of pleasantry amuse us there
With merry descants on a nation's woes.
The rest appears a *wilderness of strange
But gay confusion: roses for the cheeks
And lilies for the brows of faded age,
Teeth for the toothless, ringlets for the bald,
Heav'n, earth, and ocean plundered of their sweets,
Nectareous essences, Olympian dews,
Sermons and city feasts and favourite airs,
*Ethereal journeys, submarine exploits,
And *Katterfelto with his hair on end
At his own wonders, wond'ring for his bread.
'Tis pleasant through the loopholes of retreat
To peep at such a world; to see the stir
Of the great Babel and not feel the crowd;
To hear the roar she sends through all her gates
At a safe distance, where the dying sound
Falls, a soft murmur, on th' uninjur'd ear.
Thus sitting and surveying thus at ease
The globe and its concerns, I seem advanc'd
To some secure and more than mortal height
That liberates and exempts me from them all.
It turns submitted to my view, turns round
With all its generations. I behold
The tumult and am still. The sound of war
Has lost its terrors ere it reaches me,
Grieves, but alarms me not. I mourn the pride
And av'rice that make man a wolf to man,
Hear the faint echo of those brazen throats
By which he speaks the language of his heart,
And sigh, but never tremble at the sound.
He travels and *expatiates, as the bee
From flow'r to flow'r, so he from land to land;
The manners, customs, policy of all
Pay contribution to the store he gleans;
He sucks intelligence in ev'ry clime,
And spreads the honey of his deep research
At his return, a rich repast for me.
He travels, and I too. I tread his deck,
Ascend his topmast, through his peering eyes
Discover countries with a kindred heart,
Suffer his woes and share in his escapes,
While fancy, like the finger of a clock,
Runs the great circuit and is still at home.
O winter! ruler of the inverted year,
Thy scatter'd hair with sleet like ashes fill'd,
Thy breath congeal'd upon thy lips, thy cheeks
Fring'd with a beard made white with other snows
Than those of age, thy forehead wrapped in clouds,
A leafless branch thy sceptre, and thy throne
A sliding car indebted to no wheels,
But urg'd by storms along its slippery way,
I love thee, all unlovely as thou seem'st,
And dreaded as thou art. Thou hold'st the sun
A prisoner in the yet undawning east,
Short'ning his journey between morn and noon,
And hurrying him, impatient of his stay,
Down to the rosy west; but kindly still
Compensating his loss with added hours
Of social converse and instructive ease,
And gathering at short notice in one group
The family dispers'd, and fixing thought
Not less dispers'd by daylight and its cares.
I crown thee king of intimate delights,
Fireside enjoyments, homeborn happiness,
And all the comforts that the lowly roof
Of undisturb'd retirement and the hours
Of long uninterrupted evening know.
No rattling wheels stop short before these gates;
No powder'd pert proficient in the art
Of sounding an alarm assaults these doors
Till the street rings. No stationary steeds
Cough their own knell while, heedless of the sound,
The silent circle fan themselves and quake;
But here the needle plies its busy task;
The pattern grows, the well-depicted flow'r
Wrought patiently into the snowy lawn
Unfolds its bosom; buds, and leaves, and sprigs,
And curling tendrils, gracefully disposed,
Follow the nimble finger of the fair —
A wreath that cannot fade, of flow'rs that blow
With most success when all besides decay.

The poet's, or historian's page, by one
Made vocal for th' amusement of the rest,
The sprightly lyre whose treasure of sweet sounds
The touch from many a trembling chord shakes out,
And the clear voice symphonious, yet distinct,
And in the charming strife triumphant still,
Beguile the night and set a keener edge
On female industry; the threaded steel
Flies swiftly, and unfelt the task proceeds.
The volume clos'd, the customary rites
Of the last meal commence. A Roman meal
Such as the mistress of the world once found
Delicious when her patriots of high note,
Perhaps by moonlight, at their humble doors,
And under an old oak's domestic shade,
Enjoy'd, spare feast! a radish and an egg.
Discourse ensues, not trivial yet not dull,
Nor such as with a frown forbids the play
Of fancy, or proscribes the sound of mirth;
Nor do we madly, like an impious world,
Who deem religion frenzy, and the God
That made them an intruder on their joys,
Start at his awful name, or deem his praise
A jarring note — themes of a graver tone
Exciting oft our gratitude and love
While we retrace with mem'ry's pointing wand
That calls the past to our exact review
The dangers we have 'scap'd, the broken snare,
The disappointed foe, deliv'rance found
Unlook'd for, life preserv'd and peace restor'd,
Fruits of omnipotent eternal love.
"Oh ev'nings worthy of the gods!" exclaimed
The *Sabine bard. "Oh ev'nings," I reply,
"More to be prized and coveted than yours,
As more illumin'd and with nobler truths,
That I and mine and those we love, enjoy."
Is winter hideous in a garb like this?
Needs he the *tragic fur, the smoke of lamps,
The pent-up breath of an unsavoury throng,
To thaw him into feeling, or the smart
And snappish dialogue that flippant wits
Call comedy, to prompt him with a smile?
The self-complacent actor when he views,
Stealing a sidelong glance at a full house,
The slope of faces from the floor to th' roof,
As if one master-spring controlled them all,
Relax'd into an universal grin,
Sees not a countenance there that speaks a joy
Half so refin'd or so sincere as ours.
Cards were superfluous here, with all the tricks
That idleness has ever yet contriv'd
To fill the void of an unfurnish'd brain,
To palliate dullness and give time a shove.
Time, as he passes us, has a dove's wing,
Unsoil'd and swift and of a silken sound,
But the world's time is time in masquerade!
Theirs, should I paint him, has his pinions fledg'd
With motley plumes; and, where the peacock shows
His azure eyes, is tinctur'd black and red
With spots quadrangular of diamond form,
Ensanguin'd hearts, clubs typical of strife,
And spades, the emblem of untimely graves.
What should be and what was an hourglass once
Becomes a dice-box, and a billiard *mast
Well does the work of his destructive scythe.
Thus deck'd, he charms a world whom fashion blinds
To his true worth, most pleas'd when idle most,
Whose only happy are their wasted hours.
Ev'n misses, at whose age their mothers wore
The *back-string and the bib, assume the dress
Of womanhood, sit pupils in the school
Of card-devoted time, and, night by night,
Plac'd at some vacant corner of the board,
Learn every trick and soon play all the game.
But truce with censure. Roving as I rove
Where shall I find an end, or how proceed?
As he that travels far oft turns aside
To view some rugged rock or mould'ring tower
Which, seen, delights him not, then, coming home,
Describes and prints it, that the world may know
How far he went for what was nothing worth;
So I with brush in hand and pallet spread
With colours mix'd for a far different use,
Paint cards and dolls and ev'ry idle thing
That fancy finds in her excursive flights.
Come, Ev'ning, once again, season of peace,
Return, sweet Ev'ning, and continue long!
Methinks I see thee in the streaky west,
With matron step slow-moving, while the night
Treads on thy sweeping train — one hand employ'd
In letting fall the curtain of repose
On bird and beast, the other charg'd for man
With sweet oblivion of the cares of day;

Nor sumptuously adorn'd nor needing aid
Like homely-featur'd night, of clustering gems;
A star or two just twinkling on thy brow
Suffices thee, save that the moon is thine
No less than hers, not worn indeed on high
With ostentatious pageantry, but set
With modest grandeur in thy purple zone,
Resplendent less but of an ampler round.
Come, then, and thou shalt find thy vot'ry calm,
Or make me so. Composure is thy gift;
And whether I devote thy gentle hours
To books, to music, or the poet's toil,
To weaving nets for bird-alluring fruit,
Or twining silken threads round ivory reels
When they command whom man was born to please,
I slight thee not, but make thee welcome still.
Just when our drawing-rooms begin to blaze
With lights by clear reflection multiplied
From many a mirror, in which he of Gath,
Goliath, might have seen his giant bulk
Whole without stooping, tow'ring crest and all,
My pleasures too begin. But me perhaps
The glowing hearth may satisfy awhile
With faint illumination that uplifts
The shadow to the ceiling, there by fits
Dancing uncouthly to the quiv'ring flame.
Not undelightful is an hour to me
So spent in parlour twilight; such a gloom
Suits well the thoughtful or unthinking mind,
The mind contemplative, with some new theme
Pregnant, or indispos'd alike to all.
Laugh ye, who boast your more mercurial pow'rs
That never feel a stupor, know no pause,
Nor need one; I am conscious, and confess
Fearless, a soul that does not always think.
Me oft has fancy ludicrous and wild
Sooth'd with a waking dream of houses, tow'rs,
Trees, churches, and strange visages express'd
In the red cinders, while with poring eye
I gaz'd, myself creating what I saw.
Nor less amus'd have I quiescent watched
The sooty films that play upon the bars
Pendulous, and foreboding, in the view
Of superstition prophesying still
Though still deceiv'd, some stranger's near approach.
'Tis thus the understanding takes repose
In indolent vacuity of thought,
And sleeps and is refresh'd. Meanwhile the face
Conceals the mood lethargic with a mask
Of deep deliberation, as the man
Were task'd to his full strength, absorb'd and lost.
Thus oft reclined at ease I lose an hour
At evening, till at length the freezing blast
That sweeps the bolted shutter, summons home
The recollected powers, and snapping short
The glassy threads with which the fancy weaves
Her brittle toys, restores me to myself.
How calm is my recess, and how the frost
Raging abroad, and the rough wind endear
The silence and the warmth enjoyed within!
I saw the woods and fields at close of day
A variegated show: the meadows green
Though faded, and the *lands, where lately waved
The golden harvest, of a mellow brown,
Upturn'd so lately by the forceful share.
I saw far off the weedy fallows smile
With verdure not unprofitable, grazed
By flocks fast feeding, and selecting each
His fav'rite herb, while all the leafless groves
That skirt the horizon wore a sable hue,
Scarce notic'd in the kindred dusk of eve.
Tomorrow brings a change, a total change!
Which even now, though silently perform'd
And slowly, and by most unfelt, the face
Of universal nature undergoes.
Fast falls a fleecy show'r; the downy flakes
Descending and with never-ceasing lapse
Softly alighting upon all below,
Assimilate all objects. Earth receives
Gladly the thickening mantle, and the green
And tender blade that fear'd the chilling blast
Escapes unhurt beneath so warm a veil.
In such a world, so thorny, and where none
Finds happiness unblighted, or, if found,
Without some thistly sorrow at its side,
It seems the part of wisdom, and no sin
Against the law of love, to measure lots
With less distinguish'd than ourselves, that thus
We may with patience bear our moderate ills
And sympathize with others, suffering more.
Ill fares the trav'ller now, and he that stalks
In ponderous boots beside his reeking team.
The wain goes heavily, impeded sore
By congregated loads adhering close
To the clogg'd wheels, and in its sluggish pace
Noiseless appears a moving hill of snow.

The toiling steeds expand the nostril wide
While ev'ry breath by respiration strong
Forc'd downward, is consolidated soon
Upon their jutting chests. He, form'd to bear
The pelting brunt of the tempestuous night,
With half-shut eyes and pucker'd cheeks, and teeth
Presented bare against the storm, plods on.
One hand secures his hat, save when with both
He brandishes his pliant length of whip,
Resounding oft, and never heard in vain.
Oh happy; and, in my account, denied
That sensibility of pain with which
Refinement is endued, thrice happy thou!
The frame, robust and hardy, feels indeed
The piercing cold, but feels it unimpair'd.
The learned finger never need explore
Thy vig'rous pulse, and the unhealthful east
That breathes the spleen and searches every bone
Of the infirm, is wholesome air to thee.
Thy days roll on exempt from household care;
Thy wagon is thy wife, and the poor beasts
That drag the dull companion to and fro,
Thine helpless charge, dependent on thy care.
Ah, treat them kindly! Rude as thou appear'st,
Yet show that thou hast mercy, which the great,
With needless hurry whirl'd from place to place,
Humane as they would seem, not always show.
  Poor, yet industrious, modest, quiet, neat —
Such claim compassion in a night like this,
And have a friend in ev'ry feeling heart.
Warmed, while it lasts, by labour, all day long
They brave the season, and yet find at eve
Ill clad and fed but sparely, time to cool.
The frugal housewife trembles when she lights
Her scanty stock of brushwood, blazing clear
But dying soon, like all terrestrial joys.
The few small embers left she nurses well,
And while her infant race, with outspread hands
And crowded knees sit cow'ring o'er the sparks,
Retires, content to quake, so they be warm'd.
The man feels least, as more inur'd than she
To winter, and the current in his veins
More briskly mov'd by his severer toil;
Yet he too finds his own distress in theirs.
The taper soon extinguish'd, which I saw
Dangled along at the cold fingers' end
Just when the day declin'd, and the brown loaf
Lodg'd on the shelf, half eaten, without sauce
Of sav'ry cheese, or butter costlier still,
Sleep seems their only refuge; for, alas,
Where penury is felt the thought is chain'd,
And sweet colloquial pleasures are but few!
With all this thrift, they thrive not. All the care
Ingenious parsimony takes, but just
Saves the small inventory, bed and stool,
Skillet and old carved chest, from public sale.
They live, and live without extorted alms
From grudging hands, but other boast have none
To soothe their honest pride that scorns to beg,
Nor comfort else, but in their mutual love.
I praise you much, ye meek and patient pair,
For ye are worthy — choosing rather far
A dry but independent crust, hard-earn'd
And eaten with a sigh, than to endure
The rugged frowns and insolent rebuffs
Of knaves in office, partial in the work
Of distribution, lib'ral of their aid
To clam'rous importunity in rags,
But oft-times deaf to suppliants who would blush
To wear a tattered garb however coarse,
Whom famine cannot reconcile to filth:
These ask with painful shyness, and, refus'd,
Because deserving, silently retire.
But be ye of good courage. Time itself
Shall much befriend you. Time shall give increase,
And all your numerous progeny, well-train'd
But helpless, in few years shall find their hands,
And labour too. Meanwhile ye shall not want
What, conscious of your virtues, we can spare,
Nor what a wealthier than ourselves may send.
I mean the man who, when the distant poor
Need help, denies them nothing but his name.
  But poverty, with most who whimper forth
Their long complaints, is self-inflicted woe,
Th' effect of laziness or sottish waste.
Now goes the nightly thief prowling abroad
For plunder; much solicitous how best
He may compensate for a day of sloth
By works of darkness and nocturnal wrong.
Woe to the gardener's pale, the farmer's hedge
*Plash'd neatly, and secur'd with driven stakes
Deep in the loamy bank! Uptorn by strength,
Resistless in so bad a cause but lame
To better deeds, he bundles up the spoil —
An ass's burden — and, when laden most
And heaviest, light of foot steals fast away.

Nor does the boarded hovel better guard
The well-stack'd pile of riven logs and roots
From his pernicious force. Nor will he leave
Unwrench'd the door, however well secur'd,
Where chanticleer amidst his harem sleeps
In unsuspecting pomp. Twitch'd from the perch,
He gives the princely bird with all his wives
To his voracious bag, struggling in vain
And loudly wond'ring at the sudden change.
Nor this to feed his own. 'Twere some excuse
Did pity of their sufferings warp aside
His principle and tempt him into sin
For their support, so destitute. But they
Neglected pine at home, themselves, as more
Expos'd than others, with less scruple made
His victims, robb'd of their defenceless all.
Cruel is all he does. 'Tis quenchless thirst
Of ruinous *ebriety that prompts
His every action and imbrutes the man.
Oh, for a law to noose the villain's neck
Who starves his own! who persecutes the blood
He gave them in his children's veins, and hates
And wrongs the woman he has sworn to love!
 Pass where we may, through city or through town,
Village or hamlet, of this merry land,
Though lean and beggar'd, ev'ry twentieth pace
Conducts th' unguarded nose to such a whiff
Of stale debauch, forth-issuing from the styes
That law has licenc'd, as makes temperance reel.
There sit, involv'd and lost in curling clouds
Of *Indian fume, and guzzling deep, the boor,
The lackey, and the groom: the craftsman there
Takes a Lethean leave of all his toil;
Smith, cobbler, joiner, he that plies the shears,
And he that kneeds the dough; all loud alike,
All learned, and all drunk! The fiddle screams
Plaintive and piteous, as it wept and wailed
Its wasted tones and harmony unheard:
Fierce the dispute, whate'er the theme; while she,
Fell Discord, arbitress of such debate,
Perch'd on the signpost, holds with even hand
Her undecisive scales. In this she lays
A weight of ignorance; in that of pride;
And smiles, delighted with th' eternal poise.
Dire is the frequent curse, and its twin sound
The cheek-distending oath, not to be prais'd
As ornamental, musical, polite,
Like those which modern senators employ,
Whose oath is rhetoric, and who swear for fame!
Behold the schools in which plebeian minds,
Once simple, are initiated in arts
Which some may practise with politer grace,
But none with readier skill! 'Tis here they learn
The road that leads, from competence and peace,
To indigence and rapine; till at last
Society, grown weary of the load,
Shakes her encumber'd lap, and casts them out.
But censure profits little: vain the attempt
To advertise in verse a public pest,
That like the filth with which the peasant feeds
His hungry acres, stinks, and is of use.
The *excise is fatten'd with the rich result
Of all this riot; and ten thousand casks,
For ever dribbling out their base contents,
Touch'd by the Midas finger of the state,
Bleed gold for ministers to sport away.
Drink, and be mad, then; 'tis your country bids!
Gloriously drunk, obey th' important call!
Her cause demands th' assistance of your throats;
Ye all can swallow, and she asks no more.
 Would I had fall'n upon those happier days
That poets celebrate; those golden times
And those Arcadian scenes that Maro sings,
And Sidney, warbler of *poetic prose.
Nymphs were Dianas then, and swains had hearts
That felt their virtues: innocence, it seems,
From courts dismiss'd, found shelter in the groves;
The footsteps of Simplicity, impress'd
Upon the yielding herbage, (so they sing)
Then were not all effac'd: then speech profane,
And manners profligate, were rarely found;
Observ'd as prodigies, and soon reclaim'd.
Vain wish! those days were never: airy dreams
Sat for the picture; and the poet's hand,
Imparting substance to an empty shade,
Impos'd a gay delirium for a truth.
Grant it: I still must envy them an age
That favour'd such a dream, in days like these
Impossible, when Virtue is so scarce,
That to suppose a scene where she presides,

Is *tramontane, and stumbles all belief.
No: we are polish'd now! the rural lass,
Whom once her virgin modesty and grace,
Her artless manners, and her neat attire,
So dignified that she was hardly less
Than the fair shepherdess of old romance,
Is seen no more. The character is lost!
Her head adorn'd with *lappets pinn'd aloft,
And ribbons streaming gay, superbly rais'd,
And magnified beyond all human size,
Indebted to some smart wig-weaver's hand
For more than half the tresses it sustains;
Her elbows ruffled, and her tott'ring form
Ill propp'd upon French heels, she might be deem'd
(But that the basket dangling on her arm
Interprets her more truly) of a rank
Too proud for dairy work, or sale of eggs.
Expect her soon with foot-boy at her heels,
No longer blushing for her awkward load,
Her train and her umbrella all her care!
The town has ting'd the country; and the stain
Appears a spot upon a vestal's robe,
The worse for what it soils. The fashion runs
Down into scenes still rural; but, alas,
Scenes rarely grac'd with rural manners now!
Time was when, in the pastoral retreat,
Th' unguarded door was safe; men did not watch
T' invade another's right, or guard their own.
Then sleep was undisturb'd by fear, unscar'd
By drunken howlings; and the chilling tale
Of midnight murder was a wonder heard
With doubtful credit, told to frighten babes.
But farewell now to unsuspicious nights,
And slumbers unalarm'd! Now, ere you sleep,
See that your polish'd arms be prim'd with care,
And drop the night-bolt — ruffians are abroad;
And the first larum of the cock's shrill throat
May prove a trumpet summoning your ear
To horrid sounds of hostile feet within.
Ev'n daylight has its dangers; and the walk
Through pathless wastes and woods, unconscious once
Of other tenants than melodious birds,
Or harmless flocks, is hazardous and bold.
Lamented change! to which full many a cause
Inveterate, hopeless of a cure, conspires.
The course of human things from good to ill,
From ill to worse, is *fatal, never fails.
Increase of pow'r begets increase of wealth;
Wealth luxury, and luxury excess;
Excess, the scrofulous and itchy plague
That seizes first the opulent, descends
To the next rank contagious, and in time
Taints downward all the graduated scale
Of order, from the chariot to the plough.
The rich, and they that have an arm to check
The licence of the lowest in degree,
Desert their office; and themselves, intent
On pleasure, haunt the capital, and thus
To all the violence of lawless hands
Resign the scenes their presence might protect.
Authority herself not seldom sleeps,
Though resident, and witness of the wrong.
The plump convivial parson often bears
The *magisterial sword in vain, and lays
His rev'rence and his worship both to rest
On the same cushion of habitual sloth.
Perhaps timidity restrains his arm;
When he should strike he trembles, and sets free,
Himself enslav'd by terror of the band,
Th' audacious convict whom he dares not bind.
Perhaps, though, by profession *ghostly pure,
He too may have his vice, and sometimes prove
Less dainty than becomes his grave outside
In lucrative concerns. Examine well
His milk-white hand; the palm is hardly clean —
But here and there an ugly smutch appears.
Foh! 'twas a bribe that left it: he has touch'd
Corruption! Whoso seeks an audit here
Propitious, pays his tribute, game or fish,
Wild-fowl or ven'son, — and his errand speeds.
But faster far, and more than all the rest,
A noble cause, which none who bears a spark
Of public virtue ever wish'd remov'd,
Works the deplor'd and mischievous effect.
'Tis universal soldiership has stabb'd
The heart of merit in the meaner class
Arms, through the vanity and brainless rage
Of those that bear them, in whatever cause,
Seem most at variance with all moral good,
And incompatible with serious thought.
The clown, the child of nature, without guile,
Blest with an infant's ignorance of all
But his own simple pleasures — now and then
A wrestling-match, a foot-race, or a fair —
Is balloted, and trembles at the news;
Sheepish he doffs his hat, and, mumbling, swears
A Bible-oath to be whate'er they please,

To do he knows not what! The task perform'd,
That instant he becomes the sergeant's care,
His pupil, and his torment, and his jest.
His awkward gait, his introverted toes,
Bent knees, round shoulders, and dejected looks,
Procure him many a curse. By slow degrees,
Unapt to learn, and form'd of stubborn stuff,
He yet by slow degrees puts off himself,
Grows conscious of a change, and likes it well:
He stands erect; his slouch becomes a walk;
He steps right onward, martial in his air,
His form and movement; is as smart above
As meal and larded locks can make him; wears
His hat, or his plum'd helmet, with a grace;
And, his three years of heroship expir'd,
Returns indignant to the slighted plough.
He hates the field in which no fife or drum
Attends him; drives his cattle to a march;
And sighs for the smart comrades he has left.
'Twere well if his exterior change were all —
But with his clumsy port the wretch has lost
His ignorance and harmless manners too!
To swear, to game, to drink; to show at home
By lewdness, idleness, and Sabbath-breach,
The great proficiency he made abroad;
To astonish and to grieve his gazing friends,
To break some maiden's and his mother's heart;
To be a pest where he was useful once;
Are his sole aim, and all his glory now!
Man in society is like a flower
Blown in its native bed: 'tis there alone
His faculties, expanded in full bloom,
Shine out; there only reach their proper use.
But man associated and leagu'd with man
By regal warrant, or self-join'd by bond
For int'rest-sake, or swarming into clans
Beneath one head for purposes of war,
Like flowers selected from the rest and bound
And bundled close to fill some crowded vase,
Fades rapidly, and, by compression marr'd,
Contracts defilement not to be endur'd.
Hence charter'd boroughs are such public plagues,
And burghers, men immaculate, perhaps,
In all their private functions, once combin'd
Become a loathsome body, only fit
For dissolution, hurtful to the main.
Hence merchants, unimpeachable of sin
Against the charities of domestic life,
Incorporated, seem at once to lose
Their nature, and, disclaiming all regard
For mercy and the common rights of man,
Build *factories with blood, conducting trade
At the sword's point, and dyeing the white robe
Of innocent commercial justice red.
Hence, too, the field of glory, as the world
Misdeems it, dazzled by its bright array,
With all its majesty of thundering pomp,
Enchanting music, and immortal wreaths,
Is but a school where thoughtlessness is taught
On principle, where foppery atones
For folly, gallantry for ev'ry vice.
But, slighted as it is, and by the great
Abandon'd, and, which still I more regret,
Infected with the manners and the modes
It knew not once, the country wins me still.
I never fram'd a wish or form'd a plan
That flatter'd me with hopes of earthly bliss,
But there I laid the scene. There early stray'd
My fancy, ere yet liberty of choice
Had found me, or the hope of being free.
My very dreams were rural; rural, too,
The first-born efforts of my youthful Muse,
Sportive, and jingling her poetic bells
Ere yet her ear was mistress of their powers.
No bard could please me but whose lyre was tun'd
To nature's praises. Heroes and their feats
Fatigued me, never weary of the pipe
Of Tityrus, assembling, as he sang,
The rustic throng beneath his favourite beech.
Then Milton had indeed a poet's charms;
New to my taste, his Paradise surpass'd
The struggling efforts of my boyish tongue
To speak its excellence; I danced for joy.
I marvell'd much that, at so ripe an age
As twice sev'n years, his beauties had then first
Engag'd my wonder; and, admiring still,
And still admiring, with regret suppos'd
The joy half lost because not sooner found.
Thee too, enamour'd of the life I loved,
Pathetic in its praise, in its pursuit
Determin'd, and possessing it at last,
With transports such as favoured lovers feel,
I studied, priz'd, and wish'd that I had known,
Ingenious Cowley! and though now reclaim'd
By modern lights from an erroneous taste,
I cannot but lament thy splendid wit
Entangled in the cobwebs of the schools.
I still revere thee, courtly though retired;
Though stretch'd at ease in *Chertsey's silent bowers,
Not unemploy'd, and finding rich amends
For a lost world in solitude and verse.
'Tis born with all; the love of nature's works
Is an ingredient in the compound, man,

Infus'd at the creation of the kind.
And, though the Almighty Maker has throughout
Discriminated each from each, by strokes
And touches of his hand, with so much art
Diversified that two were never found
Twins at all points, yet this *obtains in all,
That all discern a beauty in his works,
And all can taste them, minds that have been form'd
And tutor'd, with a relish more exact,
But none without some relish, none unmov'd.
It is a flame that dies not even there
Where nothing feeds it. Neither business, crowds,
Nor habits of luxurious city-life,
Whatever else they smother of true worth
In human bosoms, quench it or abate.
The *villas with which London stands begirt
Like a swarth Indian with his belt of beads,
Prove it. A breath of unadulterate air,
The glimpse of a green pasture — how they cheer
The citizen, and brace his languid frame!
Even in the stifling bosom of the town,
A garden in which nothing thrives, has charms
That soothe the rich possessor, much consol'd
That here and there some sprigs of mournful mint,
Of nightshade or valerian grace the well
He cultivates. These serve him with a hint
That nature lives, that sight-refreshing green
Is still the livery she delights to wear,
Though sickly samples of the exuberant whole.
What are the casements lin'd with creeping herbs,
The prouder sashes fronted with a range
Of orange, myrtle, or the fragrant weed,
The *Frenchman's darling? Are they not all proofs
That man, immur'd in cities, still retains
His inborn inextinguishable thirst
Of rural scenes, compensating his loss
By supplemental shifts, the best he may?
The most, unfurnish'd with the means of life,
And they that never pass their brick-wall bounds
To range the fields and treat their lungs with air,
Yet feel the burning instinct, overhead
Suspend their crazy boxes, planted thick
And water'd duly. There the pitcher stands
A fragment, and the spoutless teapot there,
Sad witnesses how close-pent man regrets
The country, with what ardour he contrives
A peep at nature, when he can no more.
  Hail, therefore, patroness of health and ease
And contemplation, heart-consoling joys
And harmless pleasures, in the throng'd abode
Of multitudes unknown! Hail, rural life!
Address himself who will to the pursuit
Of honours or emolument or fame,
I shall not add myself to such a chase,
Thwart his attempts, or envy his success.
Some must be great. Great offices will have
Great talents; and God gives to every man
The virtue, temper, understanding, taste,
That lifts him into life, and lets him fall
Just in the niche he was ordained to fill.
To the deliverer of an injur'd land
He gives a tongue to enlarge upon, a heart
To feel, and courage to redress her wrongs;
To monarchs dignity; to judges sense;
To artists ingenuity and skill;
To me an unambitious mind, content
In the low vale of life, that early felt
A wish for ease and leisure, and ere long
Found here that leisure and that ease I wish'd.

[1785]

ON THE RECEIPT OF MY MOTHER'S PICTURE

OUT OF NORFOLK, THE GIFT OF MY COUSIN, ANN BODHAM

Writing to a friend on March 12, 1790, Cowper said: "I have lately received from a female cousin of mine in Norfolk... a picture of my mother. She died when I wanted two days of being six years old; yet I remember her perfectly, find the picture a strong likeness of her, and, because her memory has ever been precious to me, have written a poem on the receipt of it: a poem which, one excepted, I had more pleasure in writing than any that I ever wrote."

An interesting comparison may be made between this poem and *The Daguerreotype*, by William Vaughn Moody.

Oh, that those lips had language! Life has pass'd
With me but roughly since I heard thee last.
Those lips are thine — thy own sweet smile I see,
The same that oft in childhood solaced me;

Voice only fails, else how distinct they say,
"Grieve not, my child, chase all thy fears away!"
The meek intelligence of those dear eyes
(Blest be the art that can immortalize,
The art that baffles Time's tyrannic claim
To quench it!) here shines on me still the same.
Faithful remembrancer of one so dear,
Oh, welcome guest, though unexpected here!
Who bidd'st me honour with an artless song,
Affectionate, a mother lost so long,
I will obey, not willingly alone,
But gladly, as the precept were her own:
And, while that face renews my filial grief,
Fancy shall weave a charm for my relief,
Shall steep me in Elysian reverie,
A momentary dream that thou art she.
My mother! when I learn'd that thou wast dead,
Say, wast thou conscious of the tears I shed?
Hover'd thy spirit o'er thy sorrowing son,
Wretch even then, life's journey just begun?
Perhaps thou gav'st me, though unfelt, a kiss;
Perhaps a tear, if souls can weep in bliss —
Ah, that maternal smile! it answers — Yes.
I heard the bell toll'd on thy burial day,
I saw the hearse that bore thee slow away,
And, turning from my nursery window, drew
A long, long sigh, and wept a last adieu!
But was it such? — It was. — Where thou art gone
Adieus and farewells are a sound unknown.
May I but meet thee on that peaceful shore,
The parting word shall pass my lips no more!
Thy maidens, griev'd themselves at my concern,
Oft gave me promise of thy quick return.
What ardently I wish'd, I long believ'd,
And, disappointed still, was still deceiv'd;
By expectation every day beguil'd,
Dupe of tomorrow even from a child.
Thus many a sad tomorrow came and went,
Till, all my stock of infant sorrows spent,
I learn'd at last submission to my lot,
But, though I less deplor'd thee, ne'er forgot.
Where once we dwelt our name is heard no more;
Children not thine have trod my nursery floor,
And where the gardener, Robin, day by day;
Drew me to school along the public way,
Delighted with my bauble coach, and wrapped
In scarlet mantle warm, and velvet capped,
'Tis now become a history little known
That once we call'd the *pastoral house our own.
Shortliv'd possession! but the record fair,
That memory keeps of all thy kindness there,
Still outlives many a storm that has effac'd
A thousand other themes less deeply trac'd.
Thy nightly visits to my chamber made,
That thou might'st know me safe and warmly laid;
Thy morning bounties ere I left my home,
The biscuit, or confectionary plum;
The fragrant waters on my cheeks bestow'd
By thy own hand, till fresh they shone and glow'd:
All this, and more endearing still than all,
Thy constant flow of love, that knew no fall,
Ne'er roughen'd by those cataracts and breaks
That *humour interposed too often makes —
All this still legible in memory's page,
And still to be so to my latest age,
Adds joy to duty, makes me glad to pay
Such honours to thee as my numbers may;
Perhaps a frail memorial, but sincere,
Not scorn'd in heav'n, though little notic'd here.
Could Time, his flight revers'd, restore the hours,
When, playing with thy vesture's tissued flowers,
The violet, the pink, and jessamine,
I prick'd them into paper with a pin,
(And thou wast happier than myself the while,
Wouldst softly speak, and stroke my head and smile),
Could those few pleasant days again appear,
Might one wish bring them, would I wish them here?
I would not trust my heart — the dear delight
Seems so to be desir'd, perhaps I might.
But no — what here we call our life is such,
So little to be lov'd, and thou so much,
That I should ill requite thee to constrain
Thy unbound spirit into bonds again.
Thou, as a gallant bark from Albion's coast,
(The storms all weather'd and the ocean cross'd)
Shoots into port at some well-haven'd isle,
Where spices breathe, and brighter seasons smile,
There sits quiescent on the floods that show
Her beauteous form reflected clear below,
While airs impregnated with incense play
Around her, fanning light her streamers gay;

So thou, with sails how swift! hast reach'd the shore,
*"Where tempests never beat nor billows roar";
And thy loved consort on the dangerous tide
Of life long since has anchor'd by thy *side.
But me, scarce hoping to attain that rest,
Always from port withheld, always distress'd —
Me howling blasts drive devious, tempest-toss'd,
Sails ripp'd, seams opening wide, and compass lost,
And day by day some current's thwarting force
Sets me more distant from a prosperous course.
Yet oh, the thought that thou art safe, and he!
That thought is joy, arrive what may to me.
My boast is not that I deduce my *birth
From loins enthron'd, and rulers of the earth,
But higher far my proud pretensions rise, —
The son of parents pass'd into the skies.
And now, farewell! Time, unrevok'd, has run
His wonted course, yet what I wish'd is done.
By contemplation's help, not sought in vain,
I seem t' have liv'd my childhood o'er again;
To have renew'd the joys that once were mine,
Without the sin of violating thine;
And, while the wings of fancy still are free,
And I can view this mimic show of thee,
Time has but half succeeded in his theft, —
Thyself remov'd, thy power to soothe me left.

[1798]

TWO POEMS TO MRS. UNWIN

Cowper's two poems addressed to his closest friend, Mrs. Mary Unwin, were both written in 1793, after she had suffered two paralytic strokes and when she was rapidly declining. Mrs. Unwin was at this time seventy years of age, and she had been Cowper's constant companion for more than half his lifetime. The agonized care with which he watched over her probably hastened the mental ruin of his own final years. After her death in December, 1796, he looked once at her face, turned away with a cry, and never mentioned her name again.

TO MRS. UNWIN

Mary! I want a lyre with other strings,
Such aid from Heaven as some have feign'd they drew,
An eloquence scarce given to mortals, new,
And undebas'd by praise of meaner things,
That, ere through age or woe I shed my wings,
I may record thy worth with honour due
In verse as musical as thou art true, —
Verse that immortalizes whom it sings!

But thou hast little need. There is a book
By seraphs writ with beams of heav'nly light,
On which the eyes of God not rarely look;
A chronicle of actions just and bright.
There all thy deeds, my faithful Mary, shine;
And, since thou own'st that praise, I spare thee mine.

[1803]

TO MARY

The *twentieth year is well-nigh past
Since first our sky was overcast;
Ah, would that this might be the last,
My Mary!

Thy spirits have a fainter flow;
I see thee daily weaker grow;
'Twas my distress that brought thee low
My Mary!

Thy needles, once a shining store,
For my sake restless heretofore,
Now rust disus'd, and shine no more,
My Mary.

For though thou gladly wouldst fulfil
The same kind office for me still,
Thy sight now seconds not thy will,
My Mary.

But well thou play'd'st the housewife's part,
And all thy threads with magic art
Have wound themselves about this heart,
My Mary.

Thy *indistinct expressions seem
Like language utter'd in a dream,
Yet me they charm, whate'er the theme,
My Mary.

Thy silver locks, once auburn bright,
Are still more lovely in my sight
Than golden beams of orient light,
My Mary.

For, could I view nor them nor thee,
What sight worth seeing could I see?
The sun would rise in vain for me,
My Mary!

Partakers of thy sad decline,
Thy hands their little force resign,
Yet, gently pressed, press gently mine,
My Mary.

And then I feel that still I hold
A richer store ten thousandfold
Than misers fancy in their gold,
My Mary.

*Such feebleness of limbs thou prov'st
That now at every step thou mov'st
Upheld by two; yet still thou lov'st,
My Mary!

And still to love, though pressed with ill,
In wintry age to feel no chill,
With me is to be lovely still,
My Mary.

But ah, by constant heed I know
How oft the sadness that I show
Transforms thy smiles to looks of woe,
My Mary.

And should my future lot be cast
With much resemblance of the past,
Thy worn-out heart will break at last,
My Mary.

[1803]

THE CASTAWAY

Cowper frequently drew a parallel between his own mental and spiritual state and the situation of a shipwrecked or drowning mariner, but by far the most effective of these expressions of despair is *The Castaway*, written in 1799, one year before the poet's death. The incident at sea is taken from the *Voyage Round the World* of George Lord Anson, 1748, one of Cowper's favourite books.

Obscurest night involv'd the sky,
The Atlantic billows roar'd,
When such a *destin'd wretch as I,
Wash'd headlong from on board,
Of friends, of hope, of all bereft,
His floating home forever left.

No braver *chief could Albion boast
Than he with whom he went,
Nor ever ship left Albion's coast
With warmer wishes sent.
He lov'd them both, but both in vain,
Nor him beheld, nor her again.

Not long beneath the whelming brine,
Expert to swim, he lay;
Nor soon he felt his strength decline,
Or courage die away;
But wag'd with death a lasting strife,
Supported by despair of life.

He shouted: nor his friends had fail'd
To check the vessel's course,
But so the furious blast prevail'd,
That, pitiless perforce,
They left their outcast mate behind,
And scudded still before the wind.

Some succour yet they could afford,
And, such as storms allow,
The cask, the coop, the floated cord,
Delay'd not to bestow.
But he (they knew) nor ship nor shore,
Whate'er they gave, should visit more.

Nor, cruel as it seem'd, could he
Their haste himself condemn,
Aware that flight, in such a sea,
Alone could rescue them;
Yet bitter felt it still to die
Deserted, and his friends so nigh.

He long survives who lives an hour
In ocean, self-upheld;
And so long he, with unspent power,
His destiny repell'd;
And ever, as the minutes flew,
Entreated help, or cried, "Adieu!"

At length, his transient respite past,
His comrades, who before
Had heard his voice in every blast,
Could catch the sound no more;
For then, by toil subdued, he drank
The stifling wave, and then he sank

No poet wept him; but the page
Of narrative sincere
That tells his name, his worth, his age,
Is wet with Anson's tear:
And tears by bards or heroes shed
Alike immortalize the dead.

I therefore purpose not, or dream,
 Descanting on his fate,
To give the melancholy theme
 A more enduring date;
But misery still delights to trace
Its semblance in another's case.

No voice divine the storm allay'd,
 No light propitious shone,
When, snatch'd from all effectual aid,
 We perish'd, each alone:
But I beneath a rougher sea,
And whelm'd in deeper gulfs than he.

[1803]

LETTERS

Cowper's poetry revealed certain aspects of the man — his religious and moral interests, his love of nature, his classical scholarship, his devotion to his friends, even his despair, his sensibility, and to some extent his humour — but its disclosures are far from complete. Not until his personal letters were published, could the world know him as he appeared to a few intimates. In these letters he reveals the hidden charm of a winsome personality, where whimsicality and seriousness melt into each other and set each other off. Here are the delicacy and verve that lay concealed behind his usual diffidence. The letters are his talk, intimate, sprightly, allusive, reflecting his changing moods, — the talk that charmed Lady Austen and delighted Lady Hesketh, that won the love and respect of the ex-slaver, Newton, and floated about the summer-house in the garden with the pipe smoke of his eccentric friend, the Reverend William Bull.

The eighteenth century was the golden age of English letter-writing, and Cowper's letters are among the best written in the eighteenth century. They are as different, however, from the gay worldliness of Walpole as from the serious worldliness of Chesterfield, from the glitter of Lady Mary as from the planned effectiveness of Pope. They are as different as the shy recluse who wrote them was from his brilliant predecessors. They are nearer the delicate wit of Gray, but they are better letters, for they have more variety and more spontaneity. As one reads Cowper's correspondence, he realizes that it was composed with no discreet half-avowed suggestion of eventual publication, but that it was written *con amore*. Cowper's verse is sometimes artificial and not infrequently dull, but his letters are always natural and seldom uninteresting. Beneath his timidity, overlaid by his evangelical piety, often obscured by the irrational fears of ever-threatening madness, lay a delightful personality, which is best revealed in these familiar pages. Not only are Cowper's letters the best comment on his poetry, but they bid fair to outlive all but a slender sheaf of his poems and to be accepted as his most valid claim to enduring literary reputation.

To the Rev. *William Unwin

October 31, 1779

My dear Friend,

I wrote my last letter merely to inform you that I had nothing to say; in answer to which you have said nothing. I admire the propriety of your conduct, though I am a loser by it. I will endeavour to say something now, and shall hope for something in return.

I have been well entertained with Johnson's *biographies, for which I thank you; with one exception, and that a swingeing one, I think he has acquitted himself with his usual good sense and sufficiency. His treatment of Milton is unmerciful to the last degree. A pensioner is not likely to spare a republican; and the doctor, in order, I suppose, to convince his royal patron of the sincerity of his monarchical principles, has belaboured that great poet's character with the most industrious cruelty. As a man, he has hardly left him the shadow of one good quality. Churlishness in his private life, and a rancorous hatred of everything royal in his public, are the two colours with which he has smeared all the canvas. If he had any virtues, they are not to be found in the doctor's picture of him; and it is well for Milton that some sourness in his temper is the only vice with which his memory has been charged. It is evident enough that if his biographer could have discovered more, he would not have spared him. As a poet he has treated him with severity enough, and has plucked one or two of the most beautiful feathers out of his Muse's wing, and trampled them under his great foot. He has passed sentence of condemnation upon *Lycidas*, and has taken occasion, from that charming poem, to expose to ridicule (what is indeed ridiculous enough), the childish prattlement of pastoral compositions, as if *Lycidas* was the prototype and pattern of them all. The liveliness of the description, the sweetness of the numbers, the classical spirit of antiquity that prevails in it, go for nothing. I am convinced, by the way, that he has no ear for poetical numbers, or that it was stopped by prejudice against the harmony of Milton's. Was there ever anything so delightful as the music of the *Paradise Lost*? It is like that of a fine organ, has the fullest and the deepest tones of majesty, with all the softness and elegance of the Dorian flute. Variety without end and never equalled, unless perhaps by Virgil. Yet the doctor has little or nothing to say upon this copious theme, but talks something about the unfitness of the English language for blank verse, and how apt it is, in the mouth of some readers, to degenerate into declamation. Oh, I could thresh his old jacket, till I made his pension jingle in his pocket!

I could talk a good while longer, but I have no room. Our love attends yourself, Mrs. Unwin, and Miss Shuttleworth, not forgetting the two miniature pictures at your elbow.

Yours affectionately,

W. C.

To the Rev. William Unwin

October 10, 1784

My dear William,

I send you *four quires of verse, which having sent, I shall dismiss from my thoughts, and think no more of, till I see them in print. I have not after all found time or industry enough to give the last hand to the *points. I believe, however, they are not very erroneous, though in so long a work, and in a work that requires nicety in this particular, some inaccuracies will escape. Where you find any, you will oblige me by correcting them.

In some passages, especially in the second book, you will observe me very satirical. Writing on such subjects I could not be otherwise. I can write nothing without aiming at least at usefulness; it were beneath my years to do it, and still more dishonourable to my religion. I know that a reformation of such abuses as I have censured is not to be expected from the efforts of a poet; but to contemplate the world, its follies, its vices, its indifference to duty, and its strenuous attachment to what is evil, and not to reprehend, were to approve it. From this charge at least I shall be clear, for I have neither tacitly nor expressly flattered either its characters or its customs. I have paid one, and only one, *compliment, which was so justly due that I did not know how to withhold it, especially having so fair an occasion; — I forget myself, there is another in the first book to *Mr. Throckmorton, — but the compliment I mean is to *Mr. Smith. It is, however, so managed that nobody but himself can make the application and you, to whom I disclose the secret, — a delicacy on my part, which so much delicacy on his obliged me to the observance of.

What there is of a religious cast in the volume I have thrown towards the end of it, for two reasons: first, that I might not revolt the reader at his entrance, — and secondly, that my best impressions might be made last. Were I to write as many volumes as Lope de Vega or Voltaire, not one of them would be without this tincture. If the world like it not, so much the worse for them. I make all the concessions I can, that I may please them, but I will not please them at the expense of conscience.

My descriptions are all from nature — not one of them second-handed. My delineations of the heart are from my own experience — not one of them borrowed from books, or in the least degree conjectural. In my numbers, which I have varied as much as I could (for blank verse without variety of numbers is no better than bladder and string), I have imitated nobody, though sometimes perhaps there may be an apparent resemblance, because at the same time that I would not imitate, I have not affectedly differed.

If the work cannot boast a regular plan (in which respect however I do not think it altogether indefensible), it may yet boast that the reflections are naturally suggested always by the preceding passage, and that, except the fifth book, which is rather of a political aspect, the whole has one tendency: to discountenance the modern enthusiasm after a London life, and to recommend rural ease and leisure, as friendly to the cause of piety and virtue.

If it pleases you, I shall be happy, and collect from your pleasure in it an omen of its general acceptance.

Yours, my dear friend,

W. C.

Your mother's love. She wishes that you would buy her a second-hand cream-pot, small, either kit, jug, or ewer of silver.

I shall be glad of an immediate line to apprise me of its safe arrival.

To the Rev. *John Newton

December 13, 1784

My dear Friend,

Having imitated no man, I may reasonably hope that I shall not incur the disadvantage of a comparison with my betters. Milton's manner was peculiar. So is Thomson's. He that should write like either of them, would, in my judgment, deserve the name of copyist, but not of a poet. A judicious and sensible reader, therefore, like yourself, will not say that my manner is not good because it does not resemble theirs, but will rather consider what it is in itself. Blank verse is susceptible of a much greater diversification of manner than verse in rhyme; and why the modern writers of it have all thought proper to cast their numbers alike, I know not. Certainly it was not necessity that compelled them to do it. I flatter myself, however, that I have avoided that sameness with others which would entitle me to nothing but a share in one common oblivion with them all. It is possible that, as the reviewer of my former *volume found cause to say that he knew not to what class of writers to refer me, the reviewer of this, whosoever he shall be, may see occasion to remark the same singularity. At any rate, though as little apt to be sanguine as most men, and more prone to fear and despond than to overrate my own productions, I am persuaded that I shall not forfeit anything by this volume that I gained by the last.

As to the title, I take it to be the best that is to be had. It is not possible that a book, including such a variety of subjects, and in which no particular one is predominant, should find a title adapted to them all. In such a case, it seemed almost necessary to accommodate the name to the incident that gave birth to the poem; nor does it appear to me, that because I performed more than my task, therefore *The Task* is not a suitable title. A house would still be a house, though the builder of it should make it ten times as big as he at first intended. I might, indeed, following the example of the Sunday newsmonger, call it the *Olio. But I should do myself wrong; for though it have much variety, it has, I trust, no confusion.

For the same reason, none of the interior titles apply themselves to the contents at large of that book to which they belong. They are, every one of them, taken either from the leading (I should say the introductory) passage of that particular book, or from that which makes the most conspicuous figure in it. Had I set off with a design to write upon a gridiron, and had I actually written two hundred lines upon that utensil, as I have upon the Sofa, the Gridiron should have been my title. But the Sofa being, as I may say, the starting-post from which I addressed myself to the long race that I soon conceived a design to run, it acquired a just pre-eminence in my account, and was very worthily advanced to the titular honour it enjoys, its right being at least so far a good one that no word in the language could pretend a better.

*"The Time-piece" appears to me (though by some accident the import of that title has escaped you) to have a degree of propriety beyond the most of them. The book to which it belongs is intended to strike the hour that gives notice of approaching judgment, and, dealing pretty largely in the signs of the times, seems to be denominated, as it is, with a sufficient degree of accommodation to the subject....

We do not often see, or rather feel, so severe a frost before Christmas. Unexpected, at least by me, it had like to have been too much for my greenhouse, my myrtles having found themselves yesterday morning in an atmosphere so cold that the mercury was fallen eight degrees below the freezing point.

We are truly sorry for Mrs. Newton's indisposition, and shall be glad to hear of her recovery. We are most liable to colds at this season, and at this season a cold is most difficult of cure.

Be pleased to remember us to the young ladies, and to all under your roof and elsewhere, who are mindful of us. — And believe me,

Your affectionate

Wm. Cowper

Your letters are gone to their address. The oysters were very good.

To *Lady Hesketh

Olney, Nov. 9, 1785

My dearest Cousin,

Whose last most affectionate letter has run in my head ever since I received it, and which I now sit down to answer two days sooner than the post will serve me; I thank you for it, and with a warmth for which I am sure you will give me credit, though I do not spend many words in describing it. I do not seek new friends, not being altogether sure that I should find them, but have unspeakable pleasure in being still beloved by an old one. I hope that now our correspondence has suffered its last interruption, and that we shall go down together to the grave, chatting and chirping as merrily as such a scene of things as this will permit.

I am happy that my poems have pleased you. My volume has afforded me no such pleasure at any time, either while I was writing it, or since its publication, as I have derived from yours and my uncle's opinion of it. I make certain allowances for partiality, and for that peculiar quickness of taste with which you both relish what you like; and after all drawbacks upon those accounts duly made, find myself rich in the measure of your approbation that still remains. But above all I honour John Gilpin, since it was he who first encouraged you to write. I made him on purpose to laugh at, and he served his purpose well; but I am now in debt to him for a more valuable acquisition than all the laughter in the world amounts to, — the recovery of my intercourse with you, which is to me inestimable. My benevolent and generous cousin, when I was once asked if I wanted anything, and given delicately to understand that the inquirer was ready to supply all my occasions, I thankfully and civilly, but positively, declined the favour. I neither suffer, nor have suffered any such inconveniences as I had not much rather endure than come under obligations of that sort to a person comparatively with yourself a stranger to me. But to you I answer otherwise. I know you thoroughly, and the liberality of your disposition; and have that consummate confidence in the sincerity of your wish to serve me that delivers me from all awkward constraint, and from all fear of trespassing by acceptance. To you therefore I reply, yes. Whensoever, and whatsoever, and in what manner soever you please; and add moreover, that my affection for the giver is such as will increase to me tenfold the satisfaction that I shall have in receiving. It is necessary, however, that I should let you a little into the state of my finances, that you may not suppose them more narrowly circumscribed than they are. Since Mrs. Unwin and I have lived at Olney, we have had but one purse, although during the whole of that time, till lately, her income was nearly double mine. Her revenues, indeed, are now in some measure reduced, and do not much exceed my own. The worst consequence of this is that we are forced to deny ourselves some things which hitherto we have been better able to afford; but they are such things as neither life, nor the well-being of life depend upon. My own income has been better than it is, but when it was best, it would not have enabled me to live as my connections demanded that I should, had it not been combined with a better than itself — at least at this end of the kingdom. Of this I had full proof during three months that I spent in lodgings at Huntingdon, in which time, by the help of good management and a clear notion of economical matters, I contrived to spend the income of a twelvemonth. Now, my beloved cousin, you are in possession of the whole case as it stands. Strain no points to your own inconvenience or hurt, for there is no need of it, but indulge yourself in communicating (no matter what) that you can spare without missing it, since by so doing you will be sure to add to the comforts of my life one of the sweetest that I can enjoy — a token and proof of your affection.

In the affair of my next publication, toward which you also offer me so kindly your assistance, there will be no need that you should help me in the manner that you propose. It will be a large work, consisting, I should imagine, of six volumes at least. The twelfth of this month I shall have spent a year upon it, and it will cost me more than * another. I do not love the booksellers well enough to make them a present of such a labour, but intend to publish by subscription. Your vote and interest, my dear cousin, upon the occasion, if you please, but nothing more! I will trouble you with some papers of * proposals, when the time shall come, and I am sure that you will circulate as many for me as you can.

Now, my dear, I am going to tell you a secret. It is a great secret, that you must not whisper even to your cat. No creature is at this moment apprised of it but Mrs. Unwin and her son. I am making a new translation of Homer, and am on the point of finishing the twenty-first book of the *Iliad*. The reasons upon which I undertake this Herculean labour, and by which I justify an enterprise in which I seem so effectually anticipated by Pope, although in fact he has not anticipated me at all, I may possibly give you, if you wish for them, when I can find nothing more interesting to say — a period which I do not conceive to be very near!

I have not answered many things in your letter, nor can do it at present for want of room. I cannot believe but that I should know you, notwithstanding all that time may have done; there is not a feature of your face, could I meet it upon the road by itself, that I should not instantly recollect. I should say, "That is my cousin's nose," or "Those are her lips and her chin, and no woman upon earth can claim them but herself." As for me, I am a very smart youth of my years. I am not indeed grown gray so much as I am grown bald. No matter; there was more hair in the world than ever had the honour to belong to me. Accordingly having found just enough to curl a little at my ears, and to intermix with a little of my own that still hangs behind, I appear, if you see me in an afternoon, to have a very decent head-dress, not easily distinguished from my natural growth; which, being worn with a small bag and a black ribbon about my neck, continues to me the charms of my youth, even on the verge of age. Away with the fear of writing too often.

Yours, my dearest cousin,
W. C.

P.S. — That the view I give you of myself may be complete, I add the two following items: that I am in debt to nobody, and that I grow fat.

To Lady Hesketh

June 12, 1786

I am neither young nor superannuated, yet am I a child. When I had read your letter I grumbled: — not at you, my dearest cousin, for you are in no fault, but at the whole generation of coachmakers, as you may suppose, and at yours in particular. I foresaw and foreknew that he would fail in his promise, and yet was disappointed; was, in truth, no more prepared for what I expected with so much reason, than if I had not at all expected it. I grumbled till we went to dinner, and at intervals till we had dined; and when dinner was over, with very little encouragement, I could actually have cried. And if I had, I should in truth have thought them tears as well bestowed as most that I have shed for many years. At first I numbered months, then weeks, then days, and was just beginning to number hours, and now I am thrown back to days again. My first speech was, after folding up your letter (for I will honestly tell you all): "I am crazed with Mondays, Tuesdays, and Wednesdays, and St. Albans, and Totteridge, and Hadley. When is she to set out? When is she to be here? Do tell me, for perhaps you understand it better than I." "Why," says Mrs. Unwin (with much more composure in her air than properly belonged to her, for she also had her feelings on the occasion), "she sets out tomorrow se'nnight, and will be here on the Wednesday after." "And who knows that?" replied I. "Will the coachmaker be at all more punctual in repairing the old carriage, than in making the new one? For my part, I have no hope of seeing her this month; and if it be possible, I will not think of it, lest I should be again disappointed." And to say the truth, my dear, though hours have passed since thus I said, and I have had time for cooler consideration, the suspicion still sticks close to me that more delays may happen. A philosopher would prepare himself for such an event, but I am no philosopher, at least when the comfort of seeing you is in question. I believe in my heart that there have been just as many true philosophers upon earth as there have been men that have had little or no feeling, and not one more. Swift truly said:

> Indifference clad in reason's guise,
> All want of fortitude supplies.

When I wake in the night, I feel my spirits the lighter because you are coming. When I am not at * Troy, I am either occupied in the recollection of a thousand passages of my past life in which you were a partaker with me, or conversing about you with Mrs. Unwin. Thus my days and nights have been spent, principally, ever since you determined upon this journey, and especially, and almost without interruption from any other subject, since the time of your journey has seemed near at hand. While I despaired, as I did for many years that I should ever see you more, I thought of you, indeed, and often, but with less solicitude. I used to say to myself: "Providence has so ordered it, and it is my duty to submit. He has cast me at a distance from her, and from all whom I once knew. He did it, and not I; it is he who has chosen my situation for me. Have I not reason to be thankful that, since he designed me to pass a part of my life, and no inconsiderable one neither, in a state of the deepest melancholy, he appointed me a friend in Mrs. Unwin, who should share all my sorrows with me, and watch over me in my helpless condition, night and day? What, and where had I been without her?" Such considerations were sufficient to reconcile me at that time to perpetual separation even from you, because perpetual I supposed it must be, and without remedy. But now every hour of your absence seems long, for this very natural reason, because the same Providence has given me a hope that you will be present with me soon. A good that seems at an immeasurable distance, and that we cannot hope to reach, has therefore the less influence on our affections. But the same good brought nearer, made to appear practicable, promised to our hopes, and almost in possession, engages all our faculties and desires. All this is according to the natural and necessary course of things in the human heart; and the philosophy that would interfere with it is folly at least, if not frenzy. A throne has at present but little sensible attraction for me. And why? Perhaps only because I know that should I break my heart with wishes for a throne, I should never reach one. But did I know assuredly that I should put on a crown tomorrow, perhaps I too should feel ambition, and account the interposing night tedious. The sum of the whole matter, my dear, is this: that this villainous coachmaker has mortified me monstrously, and that I tremble lest he should do so again. From you I have no fears. I see in your letter, and all the way through it, what pains you take to assure me and give me comfort. I am and will be comforted for that very reason; and will wait still other ten days with all the patience that I can muster. You, I know, will be punctual if you can, and that at least is matter of real consolation.

I approve altogether, my cousin beloved, of your sending your goods to the wagon on Saturday, and cookee by the coach on Tuesday. She will be here perhaps by four in the afternoon, at the latest by five, and will have quite time enough to find out all the cupboards and shelves in her department before you arrive. But I declare and protest that cookee shall sleep that night at our house, and get her breakfast here next morning. You will break her heart, child, if you send her into a strange house where she will find nothing that has life but the curate, who has not much neither. Servant he keeps none. A woman makes his bed, and after a fashion as they say, dresses his dinner, and then leaves him to his lucubrations. I do therefore insist on it, and so does Mrs. Unwin, that cookee shall be our guest for that time; and from this we will not depart. I tell thee besides, that I shall be more glad to see her than ever I was in my life to see one whom I never saw before. Guess why, if you can.

You must number your miles fifty-six instead of * fifty-four. The fifty-sixth mile ends but a few yards beyond the vicarage. Soon after you shall have entered Olney, you will find an opening on your right hand. It is a lane that leads to your dwelling. There your coach may stop and set down Mrs. Eaton: when she has walked about forty yards, she will spy a green gate and rails on her left hand; and when she has opened the gate and reached the house-door, she will find herself at home. But we have another manœuvre to play off upon you, and in which we positively will not be opposed, or if we are, it shall be to no purpose. I have an honest fellow that works in my garden; his name is Kitchener, and we call him Kitch for brevity. He is sober, and as trusty as the day. He has a smart blue coat, that when I had worn it some years, I gave him, and he has now worn it some years himself. I shall set him on horseback, and order him to the Swan at * Newport, there to wait your arrival, and if you should not stop at that place, as perhaps you may not, immediately to throw himself into your suite, and to officiate as your guide. For though the way from Newport hither is short, there are turnings that might puzzle your coachman; and he will be of use, too, in conducting you to our house, which otherwise you might not easily find, partly through the stupidity of those of whom you might inquire, and partly from its out-of-the-way situation. My brother drove up and down Olney in quest of us, almost as often as you up and down Chancery Lane in quest of the Madans, with fifty boys and girls at his tail, before he could find us. The first man, therefore, you shall see in a blue coat with white buttons, in the famous town of Newport, cry "Kitch!" He will immediately answer, "My Lady!"

and from that moment you are sure not to be lost.

Your house shall be as clean as scrubbing and dry-rubbing can make it, and in all respects fit to receive you. My friend the Quaker, in all that I have seen of his doings has acquitted himself much to my satisfaction. Some little things, he says, will perhaps be missing at first, in such a multiplicity, but they shall be produced as soon as called for. Mrs. U. has bought you six ducks, and is fatting them for you. She has also rummaged up a coop that will hold six chickens, and designs to people it for you by the first opportunity; for these things are not to be got fit for the table at Olney. Thus, my dear, are all things in the best train possible, and nothing remains but that you come and show yourself. Oh, that moment! Shall we not both enjoy it? That we shall.

I have received an anonymous complimentary Pindaric Ode from a little poet who calls himself a schoolboy. I send you the first stanza by way of specimen. You shall see all soon.

TO WM. COWPER, OF THE INNER TEMPLE, ESQ.

ON HIS POEMS IN THE SECOND VOLUME

In what high strains, my Muse, wilt thou
Attempt great Cowper's worth to show?
Pindaric strains shall tune the lyre,
And 'twould require
A Pindar's fire
To sing great Cowper's worth,
The lofty bard, delightful Sage,
Ever the wonder of the age,
And blessing to the earth.

Adieu, my precious cousin, your lofty bard and delightful sage expects you with all possible affection.

Ever yours,
WM. COWPER.

I am truly sorry for your poor friend Burrows!

Our dinner hour is four o'clock. We will not surfeit you with delicacies; of that be assured. I know your palate, and am glad to know that it is easily pleased. Were it other than it is, it would stand but a poor chance to be gratified at Olney. I undertake for lettuce and cucumber, and Mrs. U. for all the rest. If she feeds you too well, you must humble her.

ROBERT BURNS

THE stormy life of Robert Burns began on the 25th of January, 1759, near the southwestern coast of Scotland in a cottage of two rooms which his father had built, of clay, and with his own hands. Here, during the pitifully brief childhood that could be allowed him, he had some three years of schooling. At fifteen he was already working beyond his strength as a day-labourer on his father's farm. He read "with avidity" every book that came his way; he learned French but not Latin; he gained wisdom and knowledge from association with his earnest-minded father; but by far the most important influence upon his youth was that of the folk-songs, legends, and local anecdotes of the countryside. He began early, as a local and almost parochial rhymester, what was to be his main task — the condensation into final form of this "oral literature." The first edition of his poems, printed in 1786 at the neighbouring town of Kilmarnock, was successful enough so that in the following year he went to Edinburgh, "on a borrowed nag," to superintend the publication of an enlarged edition.

The appearance of this peasant with the glowing eyes was the "sensation" of the year in the drawing-rooms of the Scottish capital. With "rustic manners but not clownish," with great powers of talk, and with a personal charm no one could withstand, Burns made at once a host of friends and admirers, most of whom remained true to the end. His fame filled Scotland and overflowed into England, where William Cowper was striving to understand the dialect of the Kilmarnock Edition and was making out enough of it to link the name of Burns with that of Shakespeare. In the meanwhile, the Edinburgh Edition was highly successful, bringing the poet by far the largest sum of money he ever possessed.

The strain of this prosperity was such as Burns's training and nature had not fitted him to bear. Although twenty-eight, he had never before been more than ten miles from his birthplace. He had long since learned, to be sure, "to mix without fear in a drunken squabble," and was already the father of more than one illegitimate child, but it was during this year among the rakish bachelors of the city that the hard and cynical tone, utterly out of keeping with his better self, was first clearly heard in his work. The best result for literature of this period was an agreement to furnish song-words for two publications called *The Musical Museum* and *Scottish Airs* — a task which he carried out with great enthusiasm in a spirit of patriotic devotion, refusing all financial reward.

Following his year in Edinburgh, his belated marriage to Jean Armour, and a last failure at farming, Burns moved to Dumfries and took up the hard work of an exciseman, which obliged him to ride two hundred miles every week and subjected him to constant temptation on his weakest side. His bold and tactless advocacy of the principles of the French Revolution may have prevented the advancement he expected. He lost the esteem of his neighbours, took to lower company, drank more and more, and lost hope in life and faith in himself. After he was thirty-five his health, never sound since the hard labour and exposure of his boyhood, declined rapidly, and he died, "burnt to a cinder," on July 21, 1797.

Burns has been judged chiefly by the *bourgeois* standards of morality which, as a peasant, he despised in theory and flouted in practice. His moral failure lay not so much, however, in his conformity to the standards of his class as in his imitation of the "buck" and rake, in whom the tradition of the gallant lost all charm by abandoning all its chivalry. He was, and knew himself to be, "a poor, damned, incautious, duped, unfortunate fool; the sport, the miserable victim of rebellious pride, hypochrondriac imaginations, agonizing sensibilities, and bedlam passions." All this should have tended, at least, to keep him spiritually alive, and might not have injured his poetry. The literature of Great Britain had been long enough in the hands of eminently respectable persons, and Burns's tang of earthy wildness, even with a strong savour of the goat-footed god, could do it no harm. But the sin of Burns, both as man and as poet, was that he learned to laugh at his own acknowledged wrong-doing, so as sometimes to give the impression that he thought all virtue a hypocrisy. To his unquestionable lewdness he added the fashionable leer, and thus became, in the words of W. E. Henley "a peasant of genius perverted from his peasanthood."

The numerous and almost equally lamentable blunders of Burns as a writer had a similar cause: unfaithfulness to his own class and its limitations. So long as he remained content with the language and scenes of his childhood he was a supreme singer. In his imitations of English poets and his efforts at what he took to be "the sublime" he was usually weak and often absurd.

Like Shakespeare, Burns was stronger in the imitation and perfecting of the work of others than in the invention of new ideas and forms. Besides the several English poets from whom he borrowed freely, he owed something to such known Scottish poets as Robert Fergusson and Allan Ramsay. For the most part, however, he drew upon the great wealth of song in the vernacular which had been built up in Scotland by hundreds of nameless singers. These unknown men made his triumph possible, and he in his turn gave their words — which could not have lived much longer without his help — an immortality. For most of his famous songs he had in mind some earlier version, a stanza or two, perhaps only a single line, or even a mere phrase. He could work, of course, in a totally different way, as he did in his masterpiece, *Tam O'Shanter*, but it was in this way that many of his best things were done.

One may say of Burns without any derogation from his genius that he was rather a maker of songs, like Béranger, than a poet in the sense that word has now acquired. There is no effect of magic in him, no glamour, no romance, little of the ecstatic vision of Shelley and Blake, little of Keats's devotion to pure beauty, and hardly a line that is memorable for independent poetic effect. His thought, moreover, when he is concerned with thought at all, is likely to be either borrowed or shallow. Even his emotion, in which he was strongest, is often sentimental and weak. This would seem a crushing indictment if he were not so clearly supreme in what is after all the poet's central and most precious gift, — the gift of music. Since the time of Chaucer, furthermore, there has been no humour in English verse more sunny and gay than his, and for tenderness also there is no one short of Chaucer with whom to compare him. What he lacks in glamour is atoned for by the vigorous adequacy and masculine force of expression which enables him nearly always to give in fewest words what is needed for his effect, and no more. In the depth and range of his sympathetic understanding and in the warmth of his humanity he has never been excelled.

THE COTTER'S SATURDAY NIGHT

INSCRIBED TO ROBERT AIKEN, ESQ.

Although it does not rank in the first or even the second flight of Burns's verse, *The Cotter's Saturday Night* has always been extremely popular, partly because of its exemplary moral tone, its flattery of the poor, and the fact that it falls well within the limits of the most elementary comprehension. It seems not unlikely that Burns wrote it with the deliberate intention of proving that he could compose, or at least concoct, a poem which the "unco guid" and all dull but respectable persons would approve; and he certainly forgot few of the necessary ingredients. He never wrote a second poem of the kind, although his literary advisers often implored him to do so.

The general idea and outline of the poem were suggested by Robert Fergusson's *The Farmer's Ingle*, which is decidedly superior to Burns's production as a realistic picture of Scottish peasant life. Burns imitated the Spenserian stanza not from Spenser himself but from Shenstone's *The Schoolmistress*, with some slight attention to Thomson and Beattie. Pope and Goldsmith are not ignored, and Gray's *Elegy*, from which Burns quoted a stanza to serve as motto, is a constant memory. All the few ideas and simple emotions the poem suggests might have been derived from the literature of sentimentalism, with which Burns was well acquainted.

And yet we need not suppose that these verses were insincerely written. They contain a faithful portrait of the poet's father, whom he had recently lost. Burns really held, and never outgrew, the naïve opinion — for which he could have quoted what he thought good literary authority — that the poor are superior to the rich in honesty, piety, and virtue. The poem is also a valuable indication, especially in the seventeenth stanza, of Burns's personal religion, which is not fully represented in such controversial and satiric pieces as *The Holy Fair* and *Holy Willie's Prayer*.

Let not Ambition mock their useful toil,
Their homely joys and destiny obscure;
Nor Grandeur hear with a disdainful smile
The short and simple annals of the poor.

My loved, my honoured, much respected *friend!
No mercenary bard his homage pays;
With honest pride, I scorn each selfish end,
My dearest meed a friend's esteem and praise:
To you I sing, in simple Scottish lays,
The lowly train in life's sequester'd scene;
The native feelings strong, the guileless ways;
What Aiken in a cottage would have been;
Ah, tho' his worth unknown, far happier there, I ween!

November chill blaws loud wi' angry *sugh;
The short'ning winter day is near a close
The miry beasts retreating frae the *pleugh;
The black'ning trains o' craws to their repose:
The toil-worn cotter frae his labour goes —
This night his weekly moil is at an end, —
Collects his spades, his mattocks, and his hoes,

* Notes on Robert Burns will be found in the Appendix, pp. 1058 ff.

Hoping the morn in ease and rest to spend,
And weary, o'er the moor, his course does hameward bend.

At length his lonely cot appears in view,
Beneath the shelter of an aged tree;
Th' expectant wee-things, toddlin' *stacher through
To meet their dad, wi' *flichterin noise and glee.
His wee bit *ingle, blinkin bonilie,
His clean hearth-stane, his thrifty wifie's smile,
The lisping infant, prattling on his knee,
Does a' his weary *kiaugh and care beguile,
And makes him quite forget his labour and his toil.

*Belyve the elder bairns come drapping in,
At service out, amang the farmers roun';
Some ca' the pleugh, some herd, some *tentie *rin
A cannie errand to a neebor town:
Their eldest hope, their Jenny, woman-grown,
In youthfu' bloom, love sparkling in her e'e,
Comes hame, perhaps to show a braw new gown,
Or *deposite her sair-worn penny-fee,
To help her parents dear if they in hardship be.

With joy unfeigned, brothers and sisters meet,
And each for other's weelfare kindly *spiers;
The social hours, swift-winged, unnoticed fleet;
Each tells the *uncos that he sees or hears.
The parents, partial, eye their hopeful years;
Anticipation forward points the view.
The mother, wi' her needle and her sheers,
Gars auld claes look amaist as weel's the new;
The father mixes a' wi' admonition due:

Their master's and their mistress's command
The younkers a' are warnèd to obey,
And mind their labours wi' an *eydent hand,
And ne'er, tho' out o' sight, to *jauk or play:
"And oh! be sure to fear the Lord alway,
And mind your duty duly, morn and night;
Lest in temptation's path ye gang astray,
Implore his counsel and assisting might:
They never sought in vain that sought the Lord aright."

But hark! a rap comes gently to the door;
Jenny, wha kens the meaning o' the same,
Tells how a neebor lad came o'er the moor,
To do some errands and convoy her hame.
The wily mother sees the conscious flame
Sparkle in Jenny's e'e, and flush her cheek;
With heart-struck anxious care enquires his name,
While Jenny *hafflins is afraid to speak;
Weel-pleased the mother hears it's nae wild, worthless rake.

With kindly welcome Jenny brings him *ben:
A strappin youth, he takes the mother's eye;
Blythe Jenny sees the visit's no ill-taen;
The father *cracks of horses, pleughs, and kye.
The youngster's artless heart o'erflows wi' joy,
But *blate and *laithfu', scarce can weel behave;
The mother, wi' a woman's wiles, can spy
What makes the youth sae bashfu' and sae grave,
Weel-pleased to think her bairn's respected like the *lave.

Oh, happy love, where love like this is found!
Oh, heart-felt raptures! bliss beyond compare!
I've pacèd much this weary, mortal round,
And sage experience bids me this declare:
"If Heaven a draught of heavenly pleasure spare,
One cordial in this melancholy vale,
'Tis when a youthful, loving, modest pair
In other's arms breathe out the tender tale,
Beneath the milk-white thorn that scents the evening gale."

Is there, in human form, that bears a heart,
A wretch! a villain! lost to love and truth!
That can, with studied, sly, ensnaring art,
Betray sweet Jenny's unsuspecting youth?
Curse on his perjured arts! dissembling, smooth!
Are honour, virtue, conscience, all exiled?
Is there no pity, no relenting ruth,

Points to the parents fondling o'er their child?
Then paints the ruined maid, and their distraction wild?

But now the supper crowns their simple board,
The healsome *parritch, chief o' Scotia's food:
The soupe their only *hawkie does afford,
That 'yont the *hallan snugly chows her cood;
The dame brings forth, in complimental mood,
To grace the lad, her *weel-hained kebbuck, *fell,
And aft he's prest and aft he ca's it guid;
The frugal wifie, garrulous, will tell
How 'twas a *towmond auld *sin' lint was i' the bell.

The cheerfu' supper done, wi' serious face
They round the ingle form a circle wide;
The sire turns o'er, wi' patriarchal grace,
The big ha'-Bible, ance his father's pride;
His bonnet rev'rently is laid aside,
His *lyart haffets wearing thin and bare;
Those strains that once did sweet in Zion glide,
He *wales a portion with judicious care,
And "Let us worship God!" he says, with solemn air.

They chant their artless notes in simple guise;
They tune their hearts, by far the noblest aim:
Perhaps "Dundee's" wild-warbling measures rise,
Or plaintive "Martyrs," worthy of the name;
Or noble "Elgin" *beets the heavenward flame,
The sweetest far of Scotia's holy lays.
Compared with these, Italian trills are tame;
The tickled ears no heart-felt raptures raise;
Nae unison hae they with our Creator's praise.

The priest-like father reads the sacred page:
How Abram was the friend of God on high;
Or Moses bade eternal warfare wage
With Amalek's ungracious progeny;
Or how the royal bard did groaning lie
Beneath the stroke of Heaven's avenging ire;
Or Job's pathetic plaint and wailing cry;
Or rapt Isaiah's wild, seraphic fire;
Or other holy seers that tune the sacred lyre.

Perhaps the Christian volume is the theme:
How guiltless blood for guilty man was shed;
How he who bore in Heaven the second name
Had not on earth whereon to lay his head;
How his first followers and servants sped;
The precepts sage they wrote to many a land;
How he, who lone in Patmos banishèd,
Saw in the sun a mighty angel stand,
And heard great Bab'lon's doom pronounced by Heaven's command.

Then kneeling down to heaven's Eternal King,
The saint, the father, and the husband prays;
Hope *"springs exulting on triumphant wing,"
That thus they all shall meet in future days,
There ever bask in uncreated rays,
No more to sigh or shed the bitter tear,
Together hymning their Creator's praise,
In such society, yet still more dear,
While circling time moves round in an eternal sphere.

Compared with this, how poor religion's pride,
In all the pomp of method and of art,
When men display to congregations wide
Devotion's ev'ry grace except the heart!
The Power, incensed, the pageant will desert,
The pompous strain, the sacerdotal stole;
But haply, in some cottage far apart,
May hear, well pleased, the language of the soul,
And in his Book of Life the inmates poor enroll.

Then homeward all take off their sev'ral way;
The youngling cottagers retire to rest;
The parent-pair their secret homage pay,
And proffer up to Heaven the warm request

That he who stills the raven's clam'rous nest,
And decks the lily fair in flow'ry pride,
Would, in the way his wisdom sees the best,
For them and for their little ones provide,
But chiefly in their hearts with grace divine preside.

From scenes like these old Scotia's grandeur springs,
That makes her loved at home, revered abroad:
Princes and lords are but the breath of kings,
*"An honest man's the noblest work of God."
And certes in fair virtue's heavenly road,
The cottage leaves the palace far behind:
What is a lordling's pomp? a cumbrous load,
Disguising oft the wretch of human kind,
Studied in arts of hell, in wickedness refined!

O Scotia! my dear, my native soil!
For whom my warmest wish to Heaven is sent!
Long may thy hardy sons of rustic toil
Be blest with health and peace and sweet content!
And oh, may Heaven their simple lives prevent
From luxury's contagion, weak and vile!
Then, howe'er crowns and coronets be rent,
A virtuous populace may rise the while,
And stand a wall of fire around their much-loved isle.

O thou, who poured the patriotic tide
That streamed thro' Wallace's undaunted heart,
Who dared to, nobly, stem tyrannic pride,
Or nobly die, the second glorious part!
(The patriot's God peculiarly thou art,
His friend, inspirer, guardian, and reward!)
Oh never, never Scotia's realm desert,
But still the patriot and the patriot-bard
In bright succession raise, her ornament and guard!

[1786]

THE HOLY FAIR

In the Presbyterian Church in Burns's time and district the Sacrament was observed only once a year, on the second Sunday in August. While the communion service was conducted inside the church, various ministers exhorted the crowd in a tent erected in the churchyard. The whole occasion, because of the numbers gathered from the countryside, was called a "holy fair." At Mauchline a tavern stood near the churchyard and almost in the shadow of the preaching-tent, a circumstance which gave Burns his opportunity for the strong satirical contrasts of his poem. In the bitter contemporary conflict that was being waged in the Scottish Presbyterian Church between the Old Lights and the New Lights — that is, between the stricter Calvinists and the Moderates — his sympathy was very strongly on the liberal side. He believed that orthodox theology is of little account beside the religion of the heart, and felt convinced also that strait-laced moralism is usually grounded in hypocrisy. In order to sympathize at all with the bitterness of his feeling on these matters and the savage force of his attack, one must know something about the powers that had been arrogated to themselves by the Puritanical ministers of the time as the censors of public morals.

The stanza, the refrain, and something of the general plan of *The Holy Fair* are borrowed from Robert Fergusson's *Leith Races*, yet it is obviously original in all important respects.

A robe of seeming truth and trust
Hid crafty observation;
And secret hung, with poison'd crust,
The dirk of defamation:
A mask that like the gorget show'd,
Dye-varying on the pigeon;
And for a mantle large and broad,
He wrapp'd him in religion.
Hypocrisy à-la-mode

Upon a simmer Sunday morn,
When Nature's face is fair,
I walkèd forth to view the corn,
An' snuff the *caller air.
The rising sun, owre Galston *Muirs,
Wi' glorious light was glintin;
The hares were *hirplin down the furs,
The lav'rocks they were chantin
Fu' sweet that day.

As lightsomely I glowered abroad,
To see a scene sae gay,

Three *hizzies, early at the road,
  Cam *skelpin up the way.
Twa had manteeles o' dolefu' black,
  But ane wi' *lyart lining;
The third, that gaed a wee a-back,
  Was in the fashion shining
      Fu' gay that day.

The twa appeared like sisters twin,
  In feature, form, an' claes;
Their visage withered, lang an' thin,
  An' sour as onie *slaes:
The third cam up, hap-step-an'-lowp,
  As light as onie lambie,
An' wi' a curchie low did stoop,
  As soon as e'er she saw me,
      Fu' kind that day.

Wi' bonnet aff, quoth I, "Sweet lass,
  I think ye seem to ken me;
I'm sure I've seen that bonie face,
  But yet I canna name ye."
Quo' she, an' laughin as she spak,
  An' taks me by the han's,
"Ye, for my sake, hae gi'en the *feck
  Of a' the Ten Comman's
      A *screed some day.

"My name is Fun — your cronie dear,
  The nearest friend ye hae;
An' this is Superstition here,
  An' that's Hypocrisy.
I'm gaun to Mauchline Holy Fair,
  To spend an hour in *daffin:
*Gin ye'll go there, yon *runkled pair,
  We will get famous laughin
      At them this day."

Quoth I, "Wi' a' my heart, I'll do 't:
  I'll get my Sunday's *sark on,
An' meet you on the holy spot;
  Faith, we'se hae fine remarkin!"
Then I gaed hame at *crowdie-time,
  An' soon I made me ready;
For roads were clad frae side to side
  Wi' monie a wearie body,
      In droves that day.

Here farmers *gash, in ridin *graith,
  Gaed *hoddin by their cotters;
There swankies young, in braw braid-claith,
  Are springin owre the gutters.
The lasses, skelpin barefit, *thrang,
  In silks an' scarlets glitter;
Wi' sweet-milk cheese in monie a *whang,
  An' *farls baked wi' butter,
      Fu' *crump that day.

When by the plate we set our nose,
  Weel heapèd up wi' ha'pence,
A greedy *glow'r *black bonnet throws,
  An' we maun draw our tippence.
Then in we go to see the show:
  On ev'ry side they're gath'rin,
Some carryin *dails, some chairs an' stools,
  An' some are busy *bleth'rin
      Right loud that day.

Here stands a shed to fend the show'rs,
  An' screen our countra gentry;
There Racer Jess, an' twa-three whores,
  Are blinkin at the entry.
Here sits a raw o' *tittlin jads,
  Wi' heavin breasts an' bare neck;
An' there a batch o' *wabster lads,
  Blackguardin frae Kilmarnock,
      For fun this day.

Here some are thinkin on their sins,
  An' some upo' their claes;
Ane curses feet that *fyl'd his shins,
  Anither sighs an' prays:
On this hand sits a chosen *swatch,
  Wi' screw'd-up, grace-proud faces;
On that a set o' chaps, at watch,
  Thrang winkin on the lasses
      To chairs that day.

Oh! happy is that man an' *blest
  (Nae wonder that it pride him!)
Wha's ain dear lass, that he likes best,
  Comes clinkin down beside him!
Wi' arm reposed on the chair-back,
  He sweetly does compose him;
Which, by degrees, slips round her neck,
  An's *loof upon her bosom,
      Unkend that day.

Now a' the congregation o'er
  Is silent expectation;
For *Moodie *speels the holy door
  Wi' tidings o' damnation.
Should *Hornie, as in ancient days,
  'Mang sons o' God present him,
The vera sight o' Moodie's face
  To's ain het hame had sent him
      Wi' fright that day

Hear how he clears the points o' faith
  Wi' rattlin an wi' thumpin!

Now meekly calm, now wild in wrath,
He's stampin an' he's jumpin!
His lengthened chin, his turned-up snout,
His eldritch squeel an' gestures,
Oh, how they fire the heart devout —
Like cantharidian plaisters,
On sic a day!

But hark! the tent has changed its voice;
There's peace an' rest nae langer;
For a' the real judges rise,
They canna sit for anger:
*Smith opens out his cauld harangues
On practice and on morals;
An' aff the godly pour in thrangs,
To gie the jars an' barrels
A lift that day.

What signifies his barren shine
Of moral pow'rs an' reason?
His English style an' gesture fine
Are a' clean out o' season.
Like Socrates or Antonine,
Or some auld pagan heathen,
The moral man he does define,
But ne'er a word o' faith in
That's right that day.

In guid time comes an antidote
Against sic poisoned nostrum;
For *Peebles, frae the *water-fit,
Ascends the holy rostrum:
See, up he's got the word o' God,
An' meek an' *mim has viewed it,
While Common Sense has taen the road,
An' aff, an' up the *Cowgate
Fast, fast that day.

Wee *Miller *niest the guard relieves,
An' orthodoxy *raibles,
Tho' in his heart he weel believes
An' thinks it auld wives' fables;
But faith! the *birkie wants a manse,
So cannilie he *hums them,
Altho' his carnal wit an' sense
Like *hafflins-wise o'ercomes him
At times that day.

Now *butt an' ben the *change-house fills
Wi' *yill-caup commentators;
Here's crying out for *bakes an' gills,
An' there the pint-stowp clatters;
While thick an' thrang, an' loud an' lang,
Wi' logic an' wi' Scripture,
They raise a din that in the end
Is like to breed a rupture
O' wrath that day.

*Leeze me on drink! it gies us mair
Than either school or college;
It kindles wit, it waukens *lear,
It *pangs us fou o' knowledge.
Be 't whisky-gill or *penny-wheep,
Or onie stronger potion,
It never fails, on drinkin deep,
To *kittle up our notion,
By night or day.

The lads an' lasses, blythely bent
To mind baith saul an' body,
Sit around the table weel content,
An' steer about the toddy.
On this ane's dress an' that ane's *leuk
They're makin observations;
While some are cozie i' the *neuk,
An' formin assignations
To meet some day.

But now the Lord's ain trumpet touts,
Till a' the hills are rairin,
And echoes back return the shouts;
Black *Russell is na spairin:
His piercin words, like Highlan' swords,
Divide the joints an' marrow;
His talk o' hell, where devils dwell,
Our verra "sauls does harrow"
Wi' fright that day.

A vast, unbottomed, boundless pit,
Filled fou o' *lowin brunstane,
Whase ragin flame an' scorchin heat
Wad melt the hardest *whun-stane!
The half-asleep start up wi' fear,
An' think they hear it roarin,
When presently it does appear
'Twas but some neebor snorin,
Asleep that day.

'Twad be owre lang a tale to tell
How monie stories passed,
An' how they crouded to the yill,
When they were a' dismissed;
How drink gaed round in *cogs an' caups,
Amang the furms an' benches,
An' cheese an' bread, frae women's laps,
Was dealt about in lunches
An' *dawds that day.

In comes a *gausie, *gash guidwife,
An' sits down by the fire,
Syne draws her *kebbuck an' her knife;
The lasses they are shyer;
The auld guidmen about the grace
Frae side to side they bother,
Till some ane by his bonnet lays
And gi'es them 't, like a tether,
Fu' lang that day.

*Waesucks for him that gets nae lass,
Or lasses that hae naething!
Sma' need has he to say a grace,
Or *melvie his braw claithing!
Oh, wives, be mindfu', ance yoursel
How bonie lads ye wanted,
An' dinna for a kebbuck-heel
Let lasses be affronted
On sic a day!

Now Clinkumbell, wi' rattlin *tow,
Begins to *jow an' croon;
Some swagger hame the best they *dow,
Some wait the afternoon.
At *slaps the billies halt a *blink,
Till lasses strip their shoon;
Wi' faith an' hope, an' love an' drink,
They're a' in famous tune
For *crack that day.

How monie hearts this day converts
O' sinners and o' lasses!
Their hearts o' stane, gin night, are gane
As saft as onie flesh is.
There's some are fou o' love divine,
There's some are fou o' brandy;
An' monie jobs that day begin,
May end in *houghmagandie
Some ither day.

[1786]

ADDRESS TO THE DEIL

Admiration of the rebellious angel, Satan, is a frequently recurring trait of the romantic temperament for which Milton himself had given more than the hint. In the time of Burns and after it, particularly in France, the feeling was strengthened by political considerations, and it has always been the natural result of a chivalrous sympathy with "the under-dog." When he wrote his *Address*, moreover, Burns had come to feel that if all the sombre Puritans about him were, as they said, on the side of Jehovah, then he was necessarily of the Devil's party. His poem differs from most productions of the "Satanic School" in its tone of jesting good-fellowship. He is genuinely sorry for Satan and holds nothing against him except his apparent hard-heartedness — always, to the sentimentalist, the one scarcely forgivable sin.

The swift and beautiful stanza used in this poem was invented by the Troubadours and had had a long history in Great Britain before Robert Fergusson made it the most familiar form of Scottish verse. Burns mastered it as no one had done before him. He thought and composed so habitually in terms of it that we might almost say it mastered him. Certain qualities of his style such as rapidity, compression, vigour, and wit, may reasonably be attributed to the opportunities and limitations the stanza offers.

> O prince! O chief of many throned pow'rs
> That led th' embattled seraphim to war.
> MILTON.

O thou! whatever title suit thee —
Auld Hornie, Satan, Nick, or Clootie —
Wha in yon cavern grim an' sootie,
Clos'd under hatches,
*Spairges about the brunstane cootie,
To scaud poor wretches!

Hear me, auld Hangie, for a wee,
An' let poor damnèd bodies be;
I'm sure sma' pleasure it can gie,
Ev'n to a deil,
To *skelp an' scaud poor dogs like me
An' hear us squeel.

Great is thy pow'r an' great thy fame;
Far kend an' noted is thy name;
An' tho' yon *lowin heugh's thy hame,
Thou travels far;
An' faith! thou's neither lag, nor lame,
Nor *blate, nor scaur.

Whyles, ranging like a roarin lion,
For prey, a' holes an' corners tryin;
Whyles, on the strong-wing'd tempest flyin,
*Tirlin the kirks;
Whyles, in the human bosom pryin,
Unseen thou lurks.

I've heard my rev'rend graunie say,
In lanely glens ye like to stray;
Or, where auld ruin'd castles grey
Nod to the moon,

Ye fright the nightly wand'rer's way
Wi' eldritch croon.

When twilight did my graunie summon,
To say her pray'rs, *douce, honest woman!
Aft *yont the dyke she's heard you bummin,
Wi' eerie drone;
Or, rustlin, thro' the *boortrees comin,
Wi' heavy groan.

Ae dreary, windy, winter night,
The stars shot down wi' sklentin light,
Wi' you mysel, I gat a fright:
Ayont the *lough,
Ye, like a *rash-buss, stood in sight,
Wi' waving *sugh.

The cudgel in my *nieve did shake;
Each bristl'd hair stood like a stake;
When wi' an eldritch, *stoor "quaick, quaick,"
Amang the springs,
Awa ye squatter'd like a drake,
On whistling wings.

Let warlocks grim, an' wither'd hags,
Tell how wi' you, on ragweed nags,
They skim the muirs an' dizzy crags,
Wi' wicked speed;
And in kirk-yards renew their leagues,
Owre *howkit dead.

Thence, countra wives, wi' toil an' pain,
May plunge an' plunge the *kirn in vain;
For oh! the yellow treasure's taen
By witching skill;
An' *dawtit, twal-pint hawkie's gaen
As yell's the bill.

Thence, mystic knots mak great abuse
On young guidmen, fond, keen, an' *croose;
When the best wark-lume i' the house,
By *cantraip wit,
Is instant made no worth a louse,
Just at the *bit.

When *thowes dissolve the snawy hoord,
An' float the jinglin icy boord,
Then, water-kelpies haunt the foord,
By your direction,
An' nighted trav'llers are allur'd
To their destruction.

And aft your moss-traversing *spunkies
Decoy the wight that late an' drunk is:
The bleezin, curst, mischievous monkies
Delude his eyes,
Till in some miry slough he sunk is,
Ne'er mair to rise.

When Masons' mystic word an' grip
In storms an' tempests raise you up,
Some cock or cat your rage maun stop,
Or, strange to tell!
The youngest brother ye wad whip
Aff straught to hell.

Lang syne in Eden's bonie yard,
When youthfu' lovers first were pair'd,
An' all the soul of love they shar'd,
The raptur'd hour,
Sweet on the fragrant flow'ry swaird,
In shady bow'r:

Then you, ye auld, *snick-drawing dog!
Ye cam to Paradise incog,
An' play'd on man a cursed *brogue
(Black be your fa'!),
An' gied the infant warld a *shog,
'Maist ruin'd a'.

D'ye mind that day when in a bizz
Wi' *reekit duds, an' reestit gizz,
Ye did present your smoutie phiz
'Mang better folk;
An' *sklented on the man of Uzz
Your spitefu' joke?

An' how ye gat him i' your thrall,
An' brak him out o' house an' hal',
While scabs an' botches did him gall,
Wi' bitter claw;
An' lows'd his ill-tongu'd wicked *scaul
Was warst *ava?

But a' your doings to rehearse,
Your wily snares an' *fechtin fierce,
Sin' that day Michael did you pierce
Down to this time,
Wad *ding a *Lallan tongue, or Erse,
In prose or rhyme.

An' now, auld Cloots, I ken ye're thinkin,
A certain bardie's rantin, drinkin,
Some luckless hour will send him *linkin,
To your black pit;
But, faith! he'll turn a corner *jinkin,
An' cheat you yet.

But fare-you-weel, auld Nickie-ben!
O, wad ye tak a thought an' men'!
Ye *aiblins might — I dinna ken —
Still hae a *stake;
I'm wae to think upo' yon den,
Ev'n for your sake!

[1786]

TO A MOUSE

ON TURNING HER UP IN HER NEST WITH THE PLOUGH, NOVEMBER, 1785

Wee, *sleekit, cowrin, tim'rous beastie,
Oh, what a panic's in thy breastie!
Thou need na start awa sae hasty,
Wi' *bickering brattle!
I wad be laith to rin an' chase thee,
Wi' murdering *pattle!

I'm truly sorry man's dominion
Has broken nature's social union,
An' justifies that ill opinion
Which makes thee startle
At me, thy poor, earth-born companion,
An' fellow-mortal!

I doubt na, *whyles, but thou may thieve;
What then? poor beastie, thou maun live!
*A daimen icker in a thrave
'S a sma' request;
I'll get a blessin wi' the *lave,
An' never miss't!

Thy wee bit housie, too, in ruin!
Its *silly wa's the win's are strewin!
An' naething now to *big a new ane,
O' *foggage green!
An' bleak December's win's ensuin,
Baith *snell an' keen!

Thou saw the fields laid bare an' waste,
An' weary winter comin fast,
An' cozie here, beneath the blast,
Thou thought to dwell —
Till, crash! the cruel coulter passed
Out thro' thy cell.

That wee bit heap o' leaves an' stibble
Has cost thee monie a weary nibble!
Now thou's turned out, for a' thy trouble,
*But house or *hald,
To *thole the winter's sleety dribble,
An' *cranreuch cauld!

But mousie, thou art *no thy lane
In proving foresight may be vain:
The best-laid schemes o' mice an' men
*Gang aft agley,
An' lea'e us naught but grief an' pain
For promised joy!

Still, thou art blest compared wi' me!
The present only toucheth thee;
But och! I backward cast my e'e,
On prospects drear!
An' forward, tho' I canna see,
I guess an' fear!

[1786]

TO A MOUNTAIN DAISY

ON TURNING ONE DOWN WITH THE PLOUGH IN APRIL, 1786

Wee, modest, crimson-tippèd flow'r,
Thou's met me in an evil hour,
For I maun crush amang the *stoure
Thy slender stem;
To spare thee now is past my pow'r,
Thou bonie *gem.

Alas! it's no thy neebor sweet,
The bonie lark, companion meet,
Bending thee 'mang the dewy weet,
Wi' spreckled breast,
When upward-springing, blythe, to greet
The purpling east.

Cauld blew the bitter-biting north
Upon thy early, humble birth;
Yet cheerfully thou glinted forth
Amid the storm,
Scarce reared above the parent-earth
Thy tender form.

The flaunting flow'rs our gardens yield,
High shelt'ring woods and wa's *maun shield;
But thou, beneath the random *bield
O' clod or stane,
Adorns the *histie stibble-field,
Unseen, alane.

There, in thy scanty mantle clad,
Thy snawie bosom sunward spread,
Thou lifts thy unassuming head
In humble guise;
But now the share uptears thy bed,
And low thou lies!

Such is the fate of artless maid,
Sweet flow'ret of the rural shade,
By love's simplicity betrayed,
And guileless trust,
Till she, like thee, all soiled is laid
Low i' the dust.

Such is the fate of simple bard,
On life's rough ocean luckless starred!

Unskillful he to note the *card
Of prudent lore,
Till billows rage, and gales blow hard,
And whelm him o'er!

Such fate to suffering worth is giv'n,
Who long with wants and woes has striv'n,
By human pride or cunning driv'n
To mis'ry's brink;
Till, wrenched of ev'ry stay but Heav'n,
He, ruined, sink!

Ev'n thou who mourn'st the daisy's fate,
That fate is thine — no distant date;
Stern Ruin's plough-share drives, elate,
Full on thy bloom,
Till crushed beneath the furrow's weight
Shall be thy doom!

[1786]

GREEN GROW THE RASHES, O

Chorus:
Green grow the *rashes, O;
Green grow the rashes, O;
The sweetest hours that e'er I spend
Are spent among the lasses, O!

I

There's naught but care on ev'ry han',
In every hour that passes, O;
What signifies the life o' man
An' 'twere na for the lasses, O?

II

The *war'ly race may riches chase,
An' riches still may fly them, O;
An' tho' at last they catch them fast,
Their hearts can ne'er enjoy them, O.

III

But gie me a *cannie hour at e'en,
My arms about my dearie, O,
An' war'ly cares an' war'ly men
May a' gae *tapsalteerie, O!

IV

For you sae *douce ye sneer at this,
Ye're naught but senseless asses, O:
The wisest man the warl' e'er saw,
He dearly loved the lasses, O.

V

Auld Nature swears the lovely dears
Her noblest work she classes, O;
Her prentice han' she tried on man,
An' then she made the lasses, O.

Chorus:
Green grow the rashes, O;
Green grow the rashes, O;
The sweetest hours that e'er I spend
Are spent among the lasses, O!

[1787]

THE RANTIN DOG, THE DADDIE O'T

O, wha my *babie-clouts will buy?
O, wha will *tent me when I cry?
Wha will kiss me where I lie? —
The *rantin dog, the daddie o't!

O, wha will own he did the *faut?
O, wha will buy the groanin *maut?
O, wha will tell me how to *ca't? —
The rantin dog, the daddie o't!

When I mount the *creepie-chair,
Wha will sit beside me there?
Gie me Rob, I'll seek nae mair —
The rantin dog, the daddie o't!

Wha will *crack to me *my lane?
Wha will mak me *fidgin fain?
Wha will kiss me o'er again? —
The rantin dog, the daddie o't!

[1788]

WHISTLE O'ER THE LAVE O'T

First when Maggie was my care,
Heav'n, I thought, was in her air;
Now we're married, *spier nae mair,
But — whistle o'er the *lave o't!
Meg was meek, and Meg was mild,
Sweet and harmless as a child:
Wiser men than me's beguiled —
Whistle o'er the lave o't!

How we live, my Meg and me,
How we love, and how we gree,
I care na by how few may see —
Whistle o'er the lave o't!
Wha I wish were maggots' meat,
Dish'd up in her winding-sheet,
I could write (but Meg wad see 't) —
Whistle o'er the lave o't!

[1790]

EPISTLE TO JAMES SMITH

Although less familiar than the *Epistle to J. Lapraik*, Burns's verse-letter to James Smith, his boon-companion of the Mauchline days, is an even more frank and delightful revelation of the young poet's thought about himself and his calling. It was written, probably, in 1786, just before he decided to have his poems published. Two years later his friend Smith — at this time a Mauchline shop-keeper some twenty years of age — left Scotland for Jamaica, as Burns himself was planning to do, and never returned. He seems to have been a youth of exceptional charm and of quite unexemplary morals.

Friendship! mysterious cement of the soul!
Sweet'ner of life and solder of society!
I owe thee much.

BLAIR.

Dear Smith, the slee'st, *pawkie thief,
That e'er attempted stealth or *rief!
Ye surely hae some *warlock-breef
Owre human hearts;
For ne'er a bosom yet was *prief
Against your arts.

For me, I swear by sun an' moon,
And ev'ry star that blinks aboon,
Ye've cost me twenty pair o' shoon,
Just gaun to see you;
And ev'ry ither pair that's done,
Mair taen I'm wi' you.

That auld, capricious carlin, Nature,
To mak amends for *scrimpit stature,
She's turn'd you off, a human creature
On her first plan;
And in her freaks, on ev'ry feature
She's wrote the man.

Just now I've taen the fit o' rhyme,
My *barmie noddle's working prime,
My fancy *yerkit up sublime,
Wi' hasty summon:
Hae ye a leisure-moment's time
To hear what's comin?

Some rhyme a neebor's name to lash;
Some rhyme (vain thought!) for needfu' cash;
Some rhyme to court the countra *clash,
An' raise a din;
For me, an aim I never *fash;
I rhyme for fun.

The star that rules my luckless lot,
Has fated me the russet coat,
An' damn'd my fortune to the groat;
But, in requit,
Has blest me with a random shot
O' countra wit.

This while *my notion's taen a sklent,
To try my fate in guid, black prent;
But still the mair I'm that way bent,
Something cries, *"Hoolie!
I *red you, honest man, tak *tent!
Ye'll shaw your folly:

"There's ither poets, much your betters,
Far seen in Greek, deep men o' letters,
Hae thought they had ensur'd their debtors,
A' future ages;
Now moths deform, in shapeless tatters,
Their unknown pages."

Then farewell hopes o' laurel-boughs
To garland my poetic brows!
Henceforth I'll rove where busy ploughs
Are whistling *thrang;
An' teach the lanely heights an' *howes
My rustic sang.

I'll wander on, wi' tentless heed
How never-halting moments speed,
Till fate shall snap the brittle thread;
Then, all unknown,
I'll lay me with th' inglorious dead,
Forgot and gone!

But why o' death begin a tale?
Just now we're living sound an' hale;
Then top and maintop crowd the sail,
Heave care o'er-side!
And large, before enjoyment's gale,
Let's tak the tide.

This life, sae far's I understand,
Is a' enchanted fairy-land,
Where pleasure is the magic-wand,
That, wielded right,
Maks hours like minutes, hand in hand,
Dance by fu' light.

The magic-wand then let us wield;
For, ance that five-an'-forty's *speel'd,
See, crazy, weary, joyless *Eild,
Wi' wrinkl'd face,

Comes *hostin, *hirplin owre the field,
Wi' creepin pace.

When ance life's day draws near the gloamin,
Then fareweel vacant, careless roamin;
An' fareweel chearfu' tankards foamin,
An' social noise:
An' fareweel dear, deluding woman,
The joy of joys!

O Life! how pleasant, in thy morning,
Young Fancy's rays the hills adorning!
Cold-pausing Caution's lesson scorning,
We frisk away,
Like schoolboys, at th' expected warning,
To joy an' play.

We wander there, we wander here,
We eye the rose upon the brier,
Unmindful that the thorn is near,
Among the leaves;
And tho' the puny wound appear,
Short while it grieves.

Some, lucky, find a flow'ry spot,
For which they never toil'd nor swat;
They drink the sweet and eat the fat,
*But care or pain;
And haply eye the barren hut
With high disdain.

With steady aim, some Fortune chase;
Keen Hope does ev'ry sinew brace;
Thro' fair, thro' foul, they urge the race,
And seize the prey:
Then cannie, in some cozie place,
They close the day.

And others, like your humble servan',
Poor wights! nae rules nor roads observin,
To right or left eternal swervin,
They zig-zag on;
Till, curst with age, obscure an' starvin,
They aften groan.

Alas! what bitter toil an' straining —
But truce with peevish, poor complaining!
Is Fortune's fickle *Luna* waning?
E'en let her gang!
Beneath what light she has remaining,
Let's sing our sang.

My pen I here fling to the door,
And kneel, ye Pow'rs! and warm implore,
"Tho' I should wander *Terra* o'er,
In all her climes,
Grant me but this, I ask no more,
Ay *rowth o' rhymes.

"Gie dreeping roasts to countra lairds,
Till icicles hing frae their beards;
Gie fine braw claes to fine life-guards
And maids of honour;
And *yill an' whisky gie to *cairds,
Until they *sconner.

"A title, Dempster merits it;
A garter gie to Willie Pitt;
Gie wealth to some be-ledger'd cit,
In cent. per cent.;
But give me real, sterling wit,
And I'm content.

"While ye are pleas'd to keep me hale,
I'll sit down o'er my scanty meal,
Be't *water-brose or *muslin-kail,
Wi' cheerfu' face,
As lang's the Muses dinna fail
To say the grace."

An anxious e'e I never throws
Behint my *lug, or by my nose;
I *jouk beneath misfortune's blows
As weel's I may;
Sworn foe to sorrow, care, and prose,
I rhyme away.

O ye *douce folk that live by rule,
Grave, tideless-blooded, calm an' cool,
Compar'd wi' you — O fool! fool! fool!
How much unlike!
Your hearts are just a standing pool,
Your lives a dyke!

Nae hair-brained, sentimental traces
In your unletter'd, nameless faces!
In *arioso* trills and graces
Ye never stray;
But *gravissimo*, solemn basses
Ye hum away.

Ye are sae grave, nae doubt ye're wise;
*Nae ferly tho' ye do despise
The harum-scarum, *ram-stam boys,
The rattling squad:
I see ye upward cast your eyes —
Ye ken the road!

Whilst I — but I shall haud me there,
Wi' you I'll scarce gang onie where —
Then, Jamie, I shall say nae mair,
But *quat my sang,
Content wi' you to mak a pair,
Whare'er I gang.

[1786]

WILLIE BREW'D A PECK O' MAUT

CHORUS

We are na *fou, we're nae that fou,
But just a *drappie in our e'e!
The cock may craw, the day may daw,
And ay we'll taste the *barley-bree!

I

O, Willie brew'd a peck o' maut,
And Rob and Allan cam to see.
Three blyther hearts that *lee-lang night
Ye wad na found in Christendie.

II

Here are we met, three merry boys,
Three merry boys I trow are we;
And monie a night we've merry been,
And monie *mae we hope to be!

III

It is the moon, I ken her horn,
That's blinkin in the *lift sae hie;
She shines sae bright to *wyle us hame,
But, by my sooth, she'll wait a wee!

IV

Wha first shall rise to gang awa,
A cuckold, coward *loun is he!
Wha first beside his chair shall fa',
He is the king amang us three!

CHORUS

We are na fou, we're nae that fou,
But just a drappie in our e'e!
The cock may craw, the day may daw,
And ay we'll taste the barley-bree!

[1790]

TAM O' SHANTER

A TALE

Burns's masterpiece is the most intensely local of all his larger productions. In *Tam O' Shanter* he is working entirely within the range of his own knowledge and homebred affections. The ruined Kirk of Alloway stood less than a mile from his birthplace; his father, who had repaired the wall of the churchyard, lay buried there; the legend and the character of the hero had been familiar to him from early childhood. Like all Burns's best work, the poem is addressed as it were to his neighbours, and is imagined less as a thing of print for all the world to read than as a tale in verse to be told in the tavern or at the fireside. It is, therefore, one of the chief glories of local patriotism, a triumph of parochial pride.

The tradition may be true which asserts that Burns composed *Tam O' Shanter* in a single day while walking by the river Nith on his farm at Ellisland, for the poem as we now read it has still the colloquial ease and the rushing speed of improvisation; yet it has also the "finishing polish" which Burns had to labour for like other men, and he himself admitted that he could never hope to excel it.

Of brownyis and of bogillis full is this buke.
GAWIN DOUGLAS.

When *chapman billies leave the street,
And *drouthy neebors neebors meet,
As market-days are wearing late,
An' folk begin to *tak the gate,
While we sit bousing at the *nappy,
An' getting fou and unco happy,
We think na on the lang *Scots miles,
The mosses, waters, *slaps, and stiles,
That lie between us and our hame,
Whare sits our sulky, sullen dame,
Gathering her brows like gathering storm,
Nursing her wrath to keep it warm.
This truth fand honest Tam o' Shanter,
As he frae Ayr ae night did canter
(Auld Ayr, wham ne'er a town surpasses
For honest men and bonie lasses).
O Tam, had'st thou but been sae wise
As taen thy ain wife Kate's advice!
She tauld thee weel thou was a *skellum,
A blethering, blustering, drunken *blellum,
That frae November till October
Ae market-day thou was nae sober;
That ilka *melder wi' the miller
Thou sat as lang as thou had siller;
That *ev'ry naig was ca'd a shoe on
The smith and thee gat roaring fou on;
That at the Lord's house, even on Sunday,
Thou drank wi' Kirkton Jean till Monday.
She prophesied that, late or soon,
Thou would be found deep drowned in Doon,
Or catched wi' *warlocks in the *mirk
By Alloway's auld, haunted kirk.
Ah, gentle dames, it *gars me greet
To think how monie counsels sweet,

How monie lengthened, sage advices,
The husband frae the wife despises!
But to our tale. Ae market-night
Tam had got planted unco right,
Fast by an ingle, bleezing finely,
Wi' *reaming swats, that drank divinely;
And at his elbow, *Souter Johnie,
His ancient, trusty, drouthy cronie:
Tam lo'ed him like a very brither;
They had been fou for weeks thegither.
The night drave on wi' sangs and clatter,
And ay the ale was growing better;
The landlady and Tam grew gracious,
Wi' secret favours, sweet and precious;
The souter tauld his queerest stories,
The landlord's laugh was ready chorus;
The storm without might rair and rustle,
Tam did na mind the storm a whistle.
Care, mad to see a man sae happy,
E'en drowned himsel amang the nappy;
As bees flee hame wi' lades o' treasure,
The minutes winged their way wi' pleasure:
Kings may be blest, but Tam was glorious,
O'er a' the ills o' life victorious!
But pleasures are like poppies spread —
You seize the flow'r, its bloom is shed;
Or like the snow falls in the river,
A moment white — then melts forever;
Or like the borealis race,
That flit ere you can point their place;
Or like the rainbow's lovely form,
Evanishing amid the storm.
Nae man can tether time or tide:
The hour approaches Tam maun ride;
That hour, o' night's black arch the key-stane,
That dreary hour Tam mounts his beast in,
And sic a night he taks the road in
As ne'er poor sinner was abroad in.
The wind blew as 'twad blawn its last;
The rattling showers rose on the blast;
The speedy gleams the darkness swallowed;
Loud, deep, and lang the thunder bellowed:
That night, a child might understand,
The Deil had business on his hand.
Weel-mounted on his gray mare Meg,
A better never lifted leg,
Tam *skelpit on thro' *dub and mire,
Despising wind and rain and fire;
*Whiles holding fast his guid blue bonnet,
Whiles crooning o'er some auld Scots *sonnet,
Whiles glow'ring round wi' prudent cares,
Lest *bogles catch him unawares:
Kirk-Alloway was drawing nigh,
Whare *ghaists and houlets nightly cry.
By this time he was cross the ford,
Whare in the snaw the chapman *smoored;
And past the *birks and *meikle stane,
Whare drunken Charlie brak's neck-bane;
And thro' the *whins and by the cairn,
Whare hunters fand the murdered bairn;
And near the thorn, aboon the well,
Whare Mungo's mither hanged hersel.
Before him Doon pours all his floods;
The doubling storm roars thro' the woods;
The lightnings flash from pole to pole;
Near and more near the thunders roll;
When, glimmering thro' the groaning trees,
Kirk-Alloway seemed in a bleeze:
Thro' ilka *bore the beams were glancing,
And loud resounded mirth and dancing.
Inspiring bold John Barleycorn,
What dangers thou canst make us scorn!
Wi' *tippenny, we fear nae evil;
Wi' *usquebae, we'll face the devil!
The swats sae reamed in Tammie's noddle,
Fair play, he cared na deils a *boddle.
But Maggie stood, right sair astonished,
Till, by the heel and hand admonished,
She ventured forward on the light;
And, vow! Tam saw an unco sight!
Warlocks and witches in a dance;
Nae cotillion, *brent new frae France,
But hornpipes, jigs, strathspeys, and reels
Put life and mettle in their heels.
A *winnock-bunker in the east,
There sat auld Nick, in shape o' beast;
A *towsie tyke, black, grim, and large,
To gie them music was his charge:
He screwed the pipes and *gart them skirl,
Till roof and rafters a' did *dirl.
Coffins stood round, like open presses,
That shawed the dead in their last dresses,
And, by some devilish *cantraip sleight,
Each in its cauld hand held a light:
By which heroic Tam was able
To note, upon the haly table,
A murderer's banes, in gibbet-airns;
Twa span-lang, wee, unchristened bairns;
A thief, new-cutted frae a rape,
Wi' his last gasp his gab did gape;
Five tomahawks, wi' bluid red-rusted;
Five scimitars, wi' murder crusted;
A garter which a babe had strangled;
A knife a father's throat had mangled,
Whom his ain son o' life bereft —
The grey-hairs yet stack to the heft;
Wi' mair of horrible and awfu',
Which even to name wad be unlawfu'.

As Tammie glowered, amazed and curious,
The mirth and fun grew fast and furious:
The piper loud and louder blew,
The dancers quick and quicker flew;
They reeled, they set, they crossed, they *cleekit,
*Till ilka carlin swat and reekit,
And *coost her duddies to the wark,
*And linket at it in her sark!
Now Tam, O Tam! had thae been *queans,
A' plump and strapping in their teens!
Their sarks, instead o' *creeshie flannen,
Been snaw-white *seventeen hunder linen!
*Thir breeks o' mine, my only pair,
That ance were plush, o' guid blue hair,
I wad hae gi'en them off my *hurdies,
For ae blink o' the bonie burdies!
But withered beldams, auld and droll,
*Rigwoodie hags wad spean a foal,
Louping and flinging on a *crummock,
I wonder didna turn thy stomach.
But Tam kend what was what fu' brawlie:
There was ae winsome wench and *wawlie,
That night enlisted in the *core,
(Lang after *kend on Carrick shore
For monie a beast to dead she shot,
An' perished monie a bonie boat,
And shook baith meikle corn and *bear,
And kept the country-side in fear);
Her *cutty sark, o' Paisley *harn
That while a lassie she had worn,
In longitude tho' sorely scanty,
It was her best, and she was *vauntie.
Ah, little kend thy reverend grannie
That sark she *coft for her wee Nannie,
Wi' twa *pund Scots ('twas a' her riches),
Wad ever graced a dance o' witches!
But here my Muse her wing maun cour;
Sic flights are far beyond her power:
To sing how Nannie lap and flang
(A souple jad she was and strang),
And how Tam stood like ane bewitched,
And thought his very een enriched;
Even Satan glowered and fidged fu' fain,
And *hotched and blew wi' might and main;
Till first ae caper, syne anither,
Tam *tint his reason a' thegither,
And roars out, "Weel done, Cutty-sark!"
And in an instant all was dark;
And scarcely had he Maggie rallied,
When out the hellish legion sallied.
As bees bizz out wi' angry *fyke,
When plundering *herds assail their *byke;
As open *pussie's mortal foes,
When, pop! she starts before their nose;
As eager runs the market-crowd,
When "Catch the thief!" resounds aloud;
So Maggie runs, the witches follow,
Wi' monie an eldritch skriech and hollo.
Ah, Tam! ah, Tam! thou'll get thy *fairin!
In hell they'll roast thee like a herrin!
In vain thy Kate awaits thy comin!
Kate soon will be a woefu' woman!
Now do thy speedy utmost, Meg,
And win the key-stane of the brig;
There at them thou thy tail may toss —
A running stream they dare na cross!
But ere the key-stane she could make,
The *fient a tail she had to shake!
For Nannie, far before the rest,
Hard upon noble Maggie prest,
And flew at Tam wi' furious *ettle;
But little wist she Maggie's mettle!
Ae spring brought off her master hale,
But left behind her ain grey tail:
The carlin *claught her by the rump,
And left poor Maggie scarce a stump.
Now, wha this tale o' truth shall read,
Ilk man and mother's son, take heed:
Whene'er to drink you are inclined,
Or cutty-sarks run in your mind,
Think ye may buy the joys o'er dear;
Remember Tam o' Shanter's mare.

[1791]

COMIN THRO' THE RYE

CHORUS

O, Jenny's a' weet, poor body,
Jenny's seldom dry;
She *draigl't a' her petticoatie,
Comin thro' the rye!

I

Comin thro' the rye, poor body,
Comin thro' the rye,
She draigl't a' her petticoatie,
Comin thro' the rye!

II

*Gin a body meet a body
Comin thro' the rye,
Gin a body kiss a body,
Need a body cry?

III

Gin a body meet a body
Comin thro' the glen,
Gin a body kiss a body,
Need the warld ken?

CHORUS

O, Jenny's a' weet, poor body,
Jenny's seldom dry:
She draigl't a' her petticoatie,
Comin thro' the rye!

[1788]

OF A' THE AIRTS

Of a' the *airts the wind can blaw,
I dearly like the west,
For there the bonie lassie lives,
The lassie I lo'e best:
There wild woods grow, and rivers *row,
And monie a hill between;
But day and night my fancy's flight
Is ever wi' my *Jean.

I see her in the dewy flowers,
I see her sweet and fair;
I hear her in the tunefu' birds,
I hear her charm the air:
There's not a bonie flower that springs
By fountain, *shaw, or green,
There's not a bonie bird that sings,
But minds me o' my Jean.

[1790]

I HAE A WIFE O' MY AIN

MADE A FEW DAYS AFTER HIS MARRIAGE

I hae a wife o' my ain,
I'll partake wi' naebody;
I'll take cuckold frae nane,
I'll gie cuckold to naebody.

I hae a penny to spend,
There — thanks to naebody!
I hae naething to lend,
I'll borrow frae naebody.

I am naebody's lord,
I'll be slave to naebody.
I hae a guid braid sword,
I'll tak *dunts frae naebody.

I'll be merry and free,
I'll be sad for naebody.
Naebody cares for me,
I care for naebody.

[1788]

JOHN ANDERSON, MY JO

John Anderson, my *jo, John,
When we were first acquent,
Your locks were like the raven,
Your bonie brow was *brent:
But now your brow is *beld, John,
Your locks are like the snaw;
But blessings on your frosty *pow,
John Anderson, my jo.

John Anderson, my jo, John,
We clamb the hill thegither;
And monie a *cantie day, John,
We've had wi' ane anither:
Now we maun totter down, John,
And hand in hand we'll go,
And sleep thegither at the foot,
John Anderson, my jo.

[1790]

SCOTS, WHA HAE

Scots, wha hae wi' Wallace bled,
Scots, wham Bruce has aften led,
Welcome to your gory bed,
Or to victorie!

Now's the day, and now's the hour!
See the front o' battle lour!
See approach proud Edward's power —
Chains and slaverie!

Wha will be a traitor knave?
Wha can fill a coward's grave?
Wha sae base as be a slave?
Let him turn and flee!

Wha for Scotland's king and law
Freedom's sword will strongly draw,
Freeman stand or freeman fa',
Let him follow me!

By oppression's woes and pains!
By your sons in servile chains!
We will drain our dearest veins,
But they shall be free!

Lay the proud usurpers low!
Tyrants fall in every foe!
Liberty's in every blow!
Let us do or die!

[1794]

FOR A' THAT AND A' THAT

Is there for honest poverty
  That hings his head, an' a' that?
The coward slave, we pass him by —
  We dare be poor for a' that!
For a' that, an' a' that,
  Our toils obscure, an' a' that,
The rank is but the guinea's stamp,
  The man's the * gowd for a' that.

What though on hamely fare we dine,
  Wear * hoddin grey, an' a' that?
Gie fools their silks, and knaves their wine —
  A man's a man for a' that.
For a' that, an' a' that,
  Their tinsel show, an' a' that,
The honest man, tho' e'er sae poor,
  Is king o' men for a' that.

Ye see yon * birkie ca'd "a lord,"
  Wha struts, an' stares, an' a' that?
Tho' hundreds worship at his word,
  He's but a * cuif for a' that.
For a' that, an' a' that,
  His ribbon, star, an' a' that,
The man o' independent mind,
  He looks an' laughs at a' that.

A prince can mak a belted knight,
  A marquis, duke, an' a' that!
But an honest man's aboon his might —
  Guid faith, he mauna * fa' that!
For a' that, an' a' that,
  Their dignities, an' a' that,
The pith o' sense an' pride o' worth
  Are higher rank than a' that.

Then let us pray that come it may
  (As come it will for a' that)
That Sense and Worth o'er a' the earth
  Shall bear the * gree an' a' that!
For a' that, an' a' that,
  It's comin yet for a' that,
That man to man the world o'er
  Shall brithers be for a' that.

[1795]

A RED, RED ROSE

O my luve is like a red, red rose,
  That's newly sprung in June;
O my luve is like the melodie
  That's sweetly played in tune.

As fair art thou, my bonie lass,
  So deep in luve am I;
And I will luve thee still my dear,
  Till a' the seas gang dry.

Till a' the seas gang dry, my dear,
  And the rocks melt wi' the sun;
And I will luve thee still, my dear,
  While the sands o' life shall run.

And fare thee weel, my only luve!
  And fare thee weel awhile!
And I will come again, my luve,
  Tho' it were ten thousand mile!

[1796]

*AULD LANG SYNE

CHORUS

For auld lang syne, my dear,
  For auld lang syne,
We'll tak a cup o' kindness yet,
  For auld lang syne.

I

Should auld acquaintance be forgot,
  And never brought to mind?
Should auld acquaintance be forgot,
  And auld lang syne?

II

And surely * ye'll be your pint-stowp,
  And surely I'll be mine;
And we'll tak a cup o' kindness yet
  For auld lang syne.

III

We twa hae run about the braes,
  And * pou'd the gowans fine;
But we've wandered monie a weary * fit
  Sin' auld lang syne.

IV

We twa hae * paidled in the burn,
  Frae morning sun till dine;
But seas between us * braid hae roared
  Sin' auld lang syne.

V

And there's a hand, my trusty * fiere,
  And gie's a hand o' thine;
And we'll tak a right * guid-willie * waught,
  For auld lang syne.

Chorus

For auld lang syne, my dear,
For auld lang syne,
We'll tak a cup o' kindness yet,
For auld lang syne.

[1796]

DUNCAN GRAY

Duncan Gray cam here to woo
(Ha, ha, the wooing o't!)
On blythe Yule Night when we were fou
(Ha, ha, the wooing o't!).
Maggie *coost her head fu' high,
Looked asklent and unco *skeigh,
*Gart poor Duncan stand *abeigh —
Ha, ha, the wooing o't!

Duncan *fleeched, and Duncan prayed
(Ha, ha, the wooing o't!);
Meg was deaf as *Ailsa craig
(Ha, ha, the wooing o't!).
Duncan sighed baith out and in,
*Grat his een baith bleer't an' blin',
Spak o' *lowpin o'er a linn —
Ha, ha, the wooing o't!

Time and chance are but a tide
(Ha, ha, the wooing o't!):
Slighted love is sair to *bide
(Ha, ha, the wooing o't!).
"Shall I, like a fool," quoth he,
"For a haughty hizzie die?
She may gae to — France for me!" —
Ha, ha, the wooing o't!

How it comes let doctors tell
(Ha, ha, the wooing o't!):
Meg grew sick as he grew hale
(Ha, ha, the wooing o't!);
Something in her bosom wrings,
For relief a sigh she brings;
And O her een, they spak sic things: —
Ha, ha, the wooing o't!

Duncan was a lad o' grace
(Ha, ha, the wooing o't!),
Maggie's was a piteous case
(Ha, ha, the wooing o't!):
Duncan could na be her death;
Swelling pity *smoored his wrath;
Now they're *crouse and canty baith —
Ha, ha, the wooing o't!

[1798]

HIGHLAND *MARY

Ye banks and *braes and streams around
The castle o' *Montgomery,
Green be your woods and fair your flowers,
Your waters never *drumlie!
There Summer first unfald her robes,
And there the langest tarry!
For there I took the last fareweel
O' my sweet Highland Mary.

How sweetly bloomed the gay green *birk,
How rich the hawthorn's blossom,
As, underneath their fragrant shade,
I clasped her to my bosom!
The golden hours, on angel wings,
Flew o'er me and my dearie;
For dear to me as light and life
Was my sweet Highland Mary.

Wi' monie a vow and locked embrace,
Our parting was fu' tender;
And, pledging aft to meet again,
We tore oursels asunder
But oh, fell death's untimely frost,
That nipt my flower sae early!
Now green's the sod and cauld's the clay
That wraps my Highland Mary!

Oh, pale, pale now those rosy lips
I aft hae kissed sae fondly!
And closed for ay the sparkling glance
That dwalt on me sae kindly!
And mouldering now in silent dust
That heart that lo'ed me dearly!
But still within my bosom's core
Shall live my Highland Mary!

[1799]

THE JOLLY BEGGARS

A CANTATA

Believing, as he wrote in his commonplace book, that "every man, even the worst, has something good about him," Burns often courted "the acquaintance of that part of mankind commonly known by the ordinary phrase of 'blackguards.'" *The Jolly Beggars*, if it does not reveal the lurking good in every man, does certainly exhibit the courage, the joy of life, and the remnants of self-respect which no circumstances can quite destroy. It is the expression of a robust faith that life is worth having even on the worst and lowest terms. Although the Cantata never received the poet's final revision and was left unpublished at his death, it is obviously a marvel of creative energy.

Recitativo

I

When *lyart leaves bestrow the *yird,
Or, wavering like the *bauckie-bird,
Bedim cauld Boreas' blast;
When hailstanes drive wi' bitter *skyte,
And infant frosts begin to bite,
In hoary *cranreuch drest;
Ae night at e'en a merry *core
O' *randie, gangrel bodies
In *Poosie-Nansie's held the *splore,
To *drink their orra duddies:
Wi' quaffing and laughing
They ranted an' they sang,
Wi' jumping an' thumping
The vera *girdle rang.

II

First, niest the fire, in auld red rags
Ane sat, weel brac'd wi' mealy bags
And knapsack a' in order;
His *doxy lay within his arm;
Wi' usquebae an' blankets warm,
She blinket on her sodger.
An' ay he gies the *tozie drab
The tither *skelpin kiss,
While she held up her greedy gab
Just like an *aumous dish:
Ilk smack still did crack still
Like onie *cadger's whup;
Then, swaggering an' staggering,
He roar'd this ditty up: —

Air

Tune: *Soldier's Joy*

I

I am a son of Mars, who have been in many wars,
And show my cuts and scars wherever I come:
This here was for a wench, and that other in a trench
When welcoming the French at the sound of the drum.
Lal de daudle, etc.

2

My prenticeship I past, where my leader breath'd his last,
When the bloody die was cast on the heights of *Abrám;
And I servèd out my trade when the gallant game was play'd,
And the *Moro low was laid at the sound of the drum.

3

I lastly was with Curtis among the floating *batt'ries,
And there I left for witness an arm and a limb;
Yet let my country need me, with *Eliott to head me
I'd clatter on my stumps at the sound of the drum.

4

And now, tho' I must beg with a wooden arm and leg
And many a tatter'd rag hanging over my bum,
I'm as happy with my wallet, my bottle, and my *callet
As when I us'd in scarlet to follow a drum.

5

What tho' with hoary locks I must stand the winter shocks,
Beneath the woods and rocks oftentimes for a home?

When the tother bag I sell, and the tother bottle tell,
I could meet a troop of hell at the sound of a drum.
Lal de daudle, etc.

RECITATIVO

He ended; and the *kebars sheuk
Aboon the chorus roar;
While frighted *rattons backward leuk,
An' seek the *benmost bore:
A fairy fiddler frae the *neuk,
He *skirl'd out Encore!
But up arose the martial *chuck,
An' laid the loud uproar:

AIR

TUNE: *Sodger Laddie*

1

I once was a maid, tho' I cannot tell when,
And still my delight is in proper young men.
Some one of a troop of dragoons was my daddie:
No wonder I'm fond of a sodger laddie!
Sing, lal de dal, etc.

2

The first of my loves was a swaggering blade:
To rattle the thundering drum was his trade;
His leg was so tight, and his cheek was so ruddy,
Transported I was with my sodger laddie.

3

But the godly old chaplain left him in the lurch;
The sword I forsook for the sake of the church;
He riskèd the soul, and I ventur'd the body:
'Twas then I prov'd false to my sodger laddie.

4

Full soon I grew sick of my sanctified sot;
The regiment at large for a husband I got;
From the gilded *spontoon to the fife I was ready:
I askèd no more but a sodger laddie.

5

But the peace it reduc'd me to beg in despair,
Till I met my old boy in a Cunningham Fair;
His rags regimental they flutter'd so gaudy:
My heart it rejoic'd at a sodger laddie.

6

And now I have liv'd — I know not how long!
But still I can join in a cup and a song;
And whilst with both hands I can hold the glass steady,
Here's to thee, my hero, my sodger laddie!
Sing, lal de dal, etc.

RECITATIVO

Poor *Merry-Andrew in the neuk
Sat guzzling wi' a *tinkler-hizzie;
They mind't na wha the chorus teuk,
Between themselves they were sae busy.
At length, wi' drink an' courting dizzy,
He *stoiter'd up an' made a face;
Then turn'd an' laid a smack on Grizzie,
Syne tun'd his pipes wi' grave grimace:

AIR

TUNE: *Auld Sir Symon*

1

Sir Wisdom's a fool when he's fou;
Sir Knave is a fool in a session:
He's there but a prentice I trow,
But I am a fool by profession.

2

My grannie she bought me a beuk,
An' I held awa to the school;
I fear I my talent misteuk,
But what will ye hae of a fool?

3

For drink I wad venture my neck;
A hizzie's the half of my craft:
But what could ye other expect
Of ane that's avowedly daft?

4

I ance was tyed up like a *stirk
For civilly swearing and quaffing;
I ance was abus'd i' the kirk
For towsing a lass i' my *daffin.

5

Poor Andrew that tumbles for sport
Let naebody name wi' a jeer;
There's even, I'm tauld, i' the court
A tumbler ca'd the *Premier.

6

Observ'd ye yon reverend lad
Mak faces to tickle the mob?

He rails at our mountebank squad —
  It's rivalship, just, i' the job!

7

And now my conclusion I'll tell,
  For faith! I'm confoundedly dry;
The *chiel that's a fool for himsel,
  Guid Lord! he's far dafter than I.

Recitativo

Then niest outspak a *raucle carlin,
Wha kent fu' weel to *cleek the sterlin,
For monie a pursie she had hookèd,
An' had in monie a well been *doukèd.
Her love had been a Highland laddie,
But *weary fa' the waefu' woodie!
Wi' sighs an' sobs she thus began
To wail her braw John Highlandman:

Air

Tune: *O An' Ye Were Dead, Guidman*

1

A Highland lad my love was born,
The *Lalland laws he held in scorn,
But he still was faithfu' to his clan,
My gallant, braw John Highlandman.

Chorus

Sing hey my braw John Highlandman!
Sing ho my braw John Highlandman!
There's not a lad in a' the lan'
Was match for my John Highlandman!

2

With his *philibeg, an' tartan plaid,
An' guid *claymore down by his side,
The ladies' hearts he did *trepan,
My gallant, braw John Highlandman.

3

We rangèd a' from Tweed to Spey,
An' liv'd like lords an' ladies gay,
For a Lalland face he fearèd none,
My gallant, braw John Highlandman.

4

They banish'd him beyond the sea,
But ere the bud was on the tree,
Adown my cheeks the pearls ran,
Embracing my John Highlandman.

5

But, och! they catch'd him at the last,
And bound him in a dungeon fast.
My curse upon them every one —
They've hang'd my braw John Highlandman!

6

And now a widow I must mourn
The pleasures that will ne'er return;
No comfort but a hearty *can
When I think on John Highlandman.

Chorus

Sing hey my braw John Highlandman!
Sing ho my braw John Highlandman!
There's not a lad in a' the lan'
Was match for my John Highlandman!

Recitativo

1

A pigmy scraper on a fiddle,
Wha us'd to *trystes an' fairs to *driddle,
Her strappin limb an' *gawsie middle
    (He reach'd nae higher)
Had *hol'd his heartie like a riddle,
    An' blawn 't on fire.

2

Wi' hand on hainch and upward e'e,
He croon'd his gamut, one, two, three;
Then in an *arioso* key
    The wee Apollo
Set off wi' *allegretto* glee
    His **giga* solo:

Air

Tune: *Whistle Owre the Lave O't*

1

Let me *ryke up to *dight that tear;
An' go wi' me an' be my dear,
An' then your every care an' fear
  May whistle owre the *lave o't.

Chorus

  I am a fiddler to my trade,
  An' a' the tunes that e'er I play'd,
  The sweetest still to wife or maid
    Was *Whistle Owre the Lave O't.*

2

At *kirns an' weddins we 'se be there,
An' O, sae nicely's we will fare!

We'll bowse about till Daddie Care
  Sing *Whistle Owre the Lave O't.*

3

Sae merrily the banes we'll * pyke,
An' sun oursels about the dyke;
An' at our leisure, when ye like,
  We'll — whistle owre the lave o't!

4

But bless me wi' your heav'n o' charms,
An' while I * kittle hair on thairms,
Hunger, cauld, an' a' sic harms
  May whistle owre the lave o't.

CHORUS

I am a fiddle to my trade,
  An' a' the tunes that e'er I play'd,
  The sweetest still to wife or maid
    Was *Whistle Owre the Lave O't.*

RECITATIVO

1

Her charms had struck a sturdy * caird
  As weel as poor gut-scraper;
He taks the fiddler by the beard,
  An' draws a roosty rapier;
He swore by a' was swearing worth
  To * speet him like a pliver,
Unless he would from that time forth
  Relinquish her forever.

2

Wi' ghastly e'e poor Tweedle-Dee
  Upon his * hunkers bended,
An' pray'd for grace wi' ruefu' face,
  An' sae the quarrel ended.
But tho' his little heart did grieve
  When round the tinkler prest her,
He feign'd to * snirtle in his sleeve
  When thus the caird address'd her:

AIR

TUNE: *Clout the Cauldron*

1

My bonie lass, I work in brass,
  A tinkler is my station;
I've travell'd round all Christian ground
  In this my occupation;
I've taen the gold, an' been enrolled
  In many a noble squadron;
But vain they search'd when off I march'd
  To go an' * clout the cauldron.

2

Despise that shrimp, that wither'd imp,
  With a' his noise an' cap'rin,
An' take a share wi' those that bear
  The * budget and the apron!
And by that * stowp, my faith an' houpe!
  And by that dear * Kilbaigie!
If e'er ye want, or meet wi' scant,
  May I ne'er weet my * craigie!

RECITATIVO

1

The caird prevail'd; th' unblushing fair
  In his embraces sunk,
Partly wi' love o'ercome sae sair,
  An' partly she was drunk.
Sir Violino, with an air
  That show'd a man o' spunk,
Wish'd unison between the pair,
  An' made the bottle clunk
    To their health that night.

2

But * hurchin Cupid shot a shaft,
  That play'd a dame a * shavie:
The fiddler rak'd her fore and aft
  Behint the chicken * cavie;
Her lord, a wight of * Homer's craft,
  Tho' limpin' wi' the * spavie,
He * hirpl'd up, an' * lap like daft,
  An' * shor'd them "Dainty Davie"
    O' * boot that night.

3

He was a care-defying blade
  As ever Bacchus listed!
Tho' Fortune sair upon him laid,
  His heart, she ever miss'd it.
He had no wish but — to be glad,
  Nor want but — when he thirsted;
He hated nought but — to be sad;
  An' thus the Muse suggested
    His sang that night.

AIR

TUNE: *For A' That, An' A' That*

1

I am a bard, of no regard
  Wi' gentle folks an' a' that,
But Homer-like the * glowrin byke,
  Frae town to town I draw that.

Chorus

For a' that, an' a' that,
An' twice as muckle 's a' that,
I've lost but ane, I've twa behin',
I've wife eneugh for a' that.

2

I never drank the Muses' * stank,
Castalia's * burn, an' a' that;
But * there it streams, an' richly reams —
My Helicon I ca' that.

3

Great love I bear to a' the fair,
Their humble slave an' a' that;
But lordly will, I hold it still
A mortal sin to * thraw that.

4

In raptures sweet this hour we meet
Wi' mutual love an' a' that;
But for how lang the flie may stang,
Let inclination * law that!

5

Their tricks an' craft hae put me daft,
They've taen me in, an' a' that;
But clear your decks, an' here's the sex!
I like the jads for a' that.

Chorus

For a' that, an' a' that,
An' twice as muckle 's a' that,
My dearest bluid, to do them guid,
They're welcome * till 't for a' that!

Recitativo

So sung the bard, and Nansie's wa's
Shook with a thunder of applause,
Re-echo'd from each mouth!
They * toom'd their pocks, they pawn'd their duds,
They scarcely left to * coor their fuds,
To quench their * lowin drouth.
Then owre again the jovial thrang
The poet did request
To lowse his pack, an' * wale a sang,
A ballad o' the best:
He rising, rejoicing
Between his twa Deborahs,
Looks round him, an' found them
Impatient for the chorus:

Air

Tune: *Jolly Mortals, Fill Your Glasses*

1

See the smoking bowl before us!
Mark our jovial, ragged ring!
Round and round take up the chorus,
And in raptures let us sing:

Chorus

A fig for those by law protected!
Liberty's a glorious feast,
Courts for cowards were erected,
Churches built to please the priest!

2

What is title, what is treasure,
What is reputation's care?
If we lead a life of pleasure,
'Tis no matter how or where!

3

With the ready trick and fable
Round we wander all the day;
And at night in barn or stable
Hug our doxies on the hay.

4

Does the train-attended carriage
Thro' the country lighter rove?
Does the sober bed of marriage
Witness brighter scenes of love?

5

Life is all a variorum,
We regard not how it goes;
Let them prate about decorum,
Who have character to lose.

6

Here's to budgets, bags, and wallets!
Here's to all the wandering train!
Here's our ragged brats and callets!
One and all, cry out, amen!

Chorus

A fig for those by law protected!
Liberty's a glorious feast,
Courts for cowards were erected,
Churches built to please the priest!

[1799]

MARY MORISON

O Mary, at thy window be!
It is the wish'd, the trysted hour.
Those smiles and glances let me see,
That make the miser's treasure poor.
How blythely wad I *bide the stoure,
A weary slave frae sun to sun,
Could I the rich reward secure —
The lovely Mary Morison!

Yestreen, when to the trembling string
The dance gaed thro' the lighted ha',
To thee my fancy took its wing,
I sat, but neither heard or saw:
Tho' this was fair, and that was *braw,
And yon the toast of a' the town,
I sigh'd and said amang them a':
"Ye are na Mary Morison!"

O Mary, canst thou wreck his peace
Wha for thy sake wad gladly die?
Or canst thou break that heart of his
Whase only faut is loving thee?
If love for love thou wilt na gie,
At least be pity to me shown;
A thought ungentle canna be
The thought o' Mary Morison.

[1800]

YE FLOWERY BANKS

Ye flowery banks o' bonie *Doon,
How can ye blume sae fair?
How can ye chant, ye little birds,
And I sae fu' o' care!

Thou'll break my heart, thou bonie bird
That sings upon the bough!
Thou minds me o' the happy days
When my fause luve was true.

Thou'll break my heart, thou bonie bird
That sings beside thy mate;
For sae I sat, and sae I sang,
And wist na o' my fate.

Aft hae I roved by bonie Doon,
To see the woodbine twine;
And ilka bird sang o' its luve,
And sae did I o' mine.

Wi' lightsome heart I pu'd a rose
Frae aff its thorny tree;
And my fause luver *staw my rose,
But left the thorn wi' me.

[1808]

WILLIAM BLAKE

On November 28, 1757, there was born to a London hosier a son who was to become, in the opinion of many modern critics, not only the greatest English poet but, even more certainly, the foremost English painter of his age. The influence of William Blake's childhood home, where he heard religious and theological questions discussed with utmost energy and freedom, was such as to encourage eccentricity and faith in private judgment as against orthodox belief. He absorbed the mysticism of Swedenborg almost before he knew the Apostles' Creed, and he began to have visions of God and angels and Hebrew prophets at the age of four. The only formal training he was ever to have was given him in a drawing school and during his apprenticeship to an engraver. He never learned Latin or Greek; he was subjected to no literary discipline whatever; the "rules" that were still supposed to govern poetical composition were unknown to him; even his grammar and his spelling were highly individual; and in short, it might be said that in the academic sense he never learned to write. Nevertheless, he began at the age of twelve to compose the marvellous lyrics which were later gathered into his *Poetical Sketches* (1783), in which the forgotten grace and charm of the Elizabethans is strangely united with the mystic's ecstasy. The most important of all educational influences playing upon him was that of Westminster Abbey, where he spent most of his time from the age of fifteen to twenty, copying the monuments in the Chapel of Edward the Confessor. At twenty-five he married a woman who could not then either read or write but who was his perfect friend and companion through all his remaining years.

In 1789 appeared *Songs of Innocence*, the first of many books which were not merely written but engraved, ornamented, printed, and coloured by Blake's own hand. Twenty-one copies of this very beautiful book are now known, each of them worth a fortune. During Blake's lifetime, when they were priced at four shillings, scarcely any were sold. The first of Blake's "Prophetic Books," *The Book of Thel*, was produced in the same manner in the same year. In 1794 he added *Songs of Experience*, with which his work as a lyrist was practically closed.

Literary students are likely to forget that poetry was never Blake's first concern, and that he worked steadily for fifty years, with ever-increasing power, as a designer and engraver. Neither his total genius nor his thought nor even his lyric verse can be fairly estimated without close study of his work as a plastic artist. It is certain that he intended his verse to be read only in the copies he made, where design and colour blend with sense and sound. He seems to have made no sharp distinction between painting and poetry. The distinction that should be made between his own productions in the two arts is that in his designs — sweeping up from the 537 illustrations of Young's *Night Thoughts* through the great series of twelve for Blair's *Grave* and those for Gray and for Dante to his masterpiece, the hundred for the Book of Job — there is a steady growth in power and clarity, while the development of his verse is in the opposite direction.

Except for a pastoral interlude of three years, spent on the coast of Sussex, Blake lived all his life in London. With far better claim to "inspiration" than most artists have had, he worked like any other craftsman except that he kept longer hours and was always at a white heat of intensity. No poet, not even Milton, has ever had a stronger sense of obligation to deliver a divine message. He drew and designed and wrote and fought with a growing conviction of spiritual presences. This suggested nothing but madness to most of his contemporaries, but it was in fact only the ordinary conviction of the mystic type of mind. Like all the mystics, Blake failed to find a language that could convey his intuitions to mankind, so that, as the years passed and the gulf widened between him and his generation, he was more and more content to be intelligible to himself. The later Prophetic Books, indeed, give the effect of a majestic soliloquy. The affection and deep respect of those who knew Blake was not won by such clouded glories as those of *Jerusalem*, *Milton*, and *Vala*, or the *Four Zoas*, but by the beauty of a blameless, happy, and utterly devoted life. Blake died on August 12, 1827, uttering cheerful songs to his Maker. He had been a poor man all his life; he had not won fame or influence; most of his contemporaries who knew of him at all regarded him as insane.

Interest in William Blake has grown and deepened with each decade since the appearance, in 1863, of Alexander Gilchrist's *Life and Selections*. By such editors and enthusiasts as Swinburne, Rossetti, Yeats, and Binyon, much has been done to atone for the neglect of Blake's contemporaries. His influence upon the verse of our own time is second only to that of John Donne. And yet critical opinion still ranges all the way from the absurd view that Blake was merely a madman to the view that he was the greatest creative genius England has ever produced. What we can be sure of is that he was a supreme master of the lyric, that his imagination was strangely penetrating and swift, that his thought was always vigorous, audacious, erratic, and original.

We should not go far wrong in saying that Blake was nearly everything that the eighteenth century was not. In an age of middle-class respectability when social caste was extremely important, he stood, as an artist and thinker, outside all classes; to the moderation of his time he opposed a "divine excess"; he confronted the religious orthodoxy of his age, which had dwindled too often into mere formalism, with the rebellion of a man who saw the spiritual world with his own eyes; wherever his contemporaries were cool and moderate he was hotly intemperate, and where they were eager — as in their quest for power and wealth — he was cold; in a period given to abstraction Blake spoke the clear word of the artist: "To generalize is to be an idiot. To particularize is the great distinction of merit." Such a poem as his *Marriage of Heaven and Hell*, if any one had been able to read it when it appeared, would have fallen into English society like a fire-ball into a tea-party. But English society, then solidifying itself against the French Revolution, bought twelve editions of *The Triumphs of Temper*, an utterly dull and pretentious poem by Blake's employer, William Hayley, and left Blake's masterpiece unread as the work of a madman. It is a significant fact that all three of the eighteenth-century poets — Smart, Chatterton, and Blake — in whom the pure poetic gift was strongest were considered insane by their contemporaries. Our modern attitude was expressed by Henry Crabb Robinson when he said of Blake: "There is something in the madness of this man which interests me more than the sanity of Byron or Walter Scott."

TO THE MUSES

Whether on Ida's shady brow,
Or in the chambers of the East,
The chambers of the sun that now
From ancient melody have ceased;

Whether in Heaven ye wander fair,
Or the green corners of the earth,
Or the blue regions of the air,
Where the melodious winds have birth;

Whether on crystal rocks ye rove
Beneath the bosom of the sea,
Wandering in many a coral grove;
Fair Nine, forsaking poetry:

How have you left the ancient love
That bards of old enjoyed in you!
The languid strings do scarcely move!
The sound is forced, the notes are few!

[1783]

TO SPRING

O thou with dewy locks, who lookest down
Through the clear windows of the morning, turn
Thine angel eyes upon our western isle,
Which in full choir hails thy approach, O Spring!

The hills tell each other, and the listening
Valleys hear; all our longing eyes are turned
Up to thy bright pavilions: issue forth,
And let thy holy feet visit our clime.

Come o'er the eastern hills, and let our winds
Kiss thy perfumèd garments; let us taste
Thy morn and evening breath; scatter thy pearls
Upon our love-sick land that mourns for thee.

Oh, deck her forth with thy fair fingers; pour
Thy soft kisses on her bosom; and put
Thy golden crown upon her languished head,
Whose modest tresses were bound up for thee.

[1783]

SONG

My silks and fine array,
My smiles and languished air,
By love are driven away;
And mournful lean Despair
Brings me yew to deck my grave:
Such end true lovers have.

His face is fair as heaven
When springing buds unfold;
Oh, why to him was't given
Whose heart is wintry cold?
His breast is love's all-worshipped tomb
Where all love's pilgrims come.

Bring me an axe and spade,
Bring me a winding sheet;
When I my grave have made,
Let winds and tempests beat;
Then down I'll lie as cold as clay.
True love doth pass away!

[1783]

SONG

Memory, hither come
And tune your merry notes;
And while upon the wind
Your music floats,
I'll pore upon the stream
Where sighing lovers dream.
And fish for fancies as they pass
Within the watery glass.

I'll drink of the clear stream,
And hear the linnet's song,
And there I'll lie and dream
The day along;
And when night comes I'll go
To places fit for woe,
Walking along the darkened valley,
With silent Melancholy.

[1783]

SONG

How sweet I roamed from field to field,
And tasted all the summer's pride;
Till I the Prince of Love beheld,
Who in the sunny beams did glide.

He showed me lilies for my hair,
And blushing roses for my brow;
He led me through his gardens fair,
Where all his golden pleasures grow.

With sweet May dews my wings were wet,
And Phœbus fired my vocal rage;
He caught me in his silken net,
And shut me in his golden cage.

He loves to sit and hear me sing,
Then, laughing, sports and plays with me,
Then stretches out my golden wing,
And mocks my loss of liberty.

[1783]

TO THE EVENING STAR

Thou fair-haired angel of the evening,
Now whilst the sun rests on the mountains, light
Thy bright torch of love; thy radiant crown
Put on and smile upon our evening bed!
Smile on our loves; and while thou drawest the
Blue curtains of the sky, scatter thy silver dew
On every flower that shuts its sweet eyes
In timely sleep. Let thy west wind sleep on
The lake; speak silence with thy glimmering eyes,
And wash the dusk with silver. Soon, full soon,
Dost thou withdraw: then the wolf rages wide,
And the lion glares through the dun forest
The fleeces of our flocks are covered with
Thy sacred dew; protect them with thine influence.

[1783]

INTRODUCTION
to the SONGS OF INNOCENCE

Piping down the valleys wild,
Piping songs of pleasant glee,
On a cloud I saw a child,
And he laughing said to me: —

"Pipe a song about a lamb!"
So I piped with merry cheer.
"Piper, pipe that song again:"
So I piped; he wept to hear.

"Drop thy pipe, thy happy pipe;
Sing thy songs of happy cheer:"
So I sang the same again,
While he wept with joy to hear.

"Piper, sit thee down and write
In a book that all may read."
So he vanished from my sight;
And I plucked a hollow reed,

And I made a rural pen,
And I stained the water clear,
And I wrote my happy songs,
Every child may joy to hear.

[1789]

LAUGHING SONG

When the green woods laugh with the voice of joy,
And the dimpling stream runs laughing by;
When the air does laugh with our merry wit,
And the green hill laughs with the noise of it;
When the meadows laugh with lively green,
And the grasshopper laughs in the merry scene;
When Mary and Susan and Emily
With their sweet round mouths sing "Ha ha he!"

When the painted birds laugh in the shade,
Where our table with cherries and nuts is spread,
Come live, and be merry, and join with me,
To sing the sweet chorus of "Ha ha he!"

[1789]

THE LITTLE BLACK BOY

My mother bore me in the southern wild,
And I am black, but oh, my soul is white!
White as an angel is the English child,
But I am black, as if bereaved of light.

My mother taught me underneath a tree,
And, sitting down before the heat of day,
She took me on her lap and kissèd me,
And, pointing to the east, began to say:

"Look on the rising sun; there God does live,
And gives his light, and gives his heat away,
And flowers and trees and beasts and men receive
Comfort in morning, joy in the noonday.

"And we are put on earth a little space
That we may learn to bear the beams of love;
And these black bodies and this sunburnt face
Are but a cloud, and like a shady grove.

"For, when our souls have learned the heat to bear,
The cloud will vanish; we shall hear his voice,
Saying: 'Come out from the grove, my love and care,
And round my golden tent like lambs rejoice.'"

Thus did my mother say, and kissèd me;
And thus I say to little English boy.
When I from black, and he from white cloud free,
And round the tent of God like lambs we joy,

I'll shade him from the heat till he can bear
To lean in joy upon our Father's knee;
And then I'll stand and stroke his silver hair,
And be like him, and he will then love me.
[1789]

THE LAMB

Little lamb, who made thee?
Dost thou know who made thee?
Gave thee life and bade thee feed
By the stream and o'er the mead;
Gave thee clothing of delight,
Softest clothing, woolly, bright;
Gave thee such a tender voice,
Making all the vales rejoice?
Little lamb who made thee?
Dost thou know who made thee?

Little lamb I'll tell thee;
Little lamb I'll tell thee:
He is callèd by thy name,
For he calls himself a Lamb.
He is meek and he is mild,
He became a little child.
I a child and thou a lamb,
We are callèd by his name.
Little lamb, God bless thee!
Little lamb, God bless thee!
[1789]

NIGHT

The sun descending in the west,
The evening star does shine;
The birds are silent in their nest,
And I must seek for mine.
The moon, like a flower
In heaven's high bower,
With silent delight
Sits and smiles on the night.

Farewell, green fields and happy grove,
Where flocks have ta'en delight;
Where lambs have nibbled, silent move
The feet of angels bright:
Unseen they pour blessing,
And joy without ceasing,
On each bud and blossom,
And each sleeping bosom.

They look in every thoughtless nest
Where birds are covered warm;
They visit caves of every beast,
To keep them all from harm.
If they see any weeping
That should have been sleeping,
They pour sleep on their head,
And sit down by their bed.

When wolves and tigers howl for prey
They pitying stand and weep,
Seeking to drive their thirst away,
And keep them from the sheep.
But if they rush dreadful
The angels, most heedful,
Receive each mild spirit
New worlds to inherit.

And there the lion's ruddy eyes
Shall flow with tears of gold:
And pitying the tender cries,
And walking round the fold,
Saying: "Wrath by his meekness,
And by his health sickness,
Are driven away
From our immortal day.

"And now beside thee, bleating lamb,
I can lie down and sleep,
Or think on him who bore thy name,
Graze after thee, and weep.
For, washed in life's river,
My bright mane forever
Shall shine like the gold
As I guard o'er the fold."

[1789]

THE MARRIAGE OF HEAVEN AND * HELL

THE ARGUMENT

* Rintrah roars and shakes his fires in the burden'd air;
Hungry clouds swag on the deep.

Once meek, and in a perilous path,
The just man kept his course along
The vale of death.
Roses are planted where thorns grow,
And on the barren heath
Sing the honey bees.

Then the perilous path was planted,
And a river and a spring
On every cliff and tomb,
And on the bleached bones
Red clay brought forth;

Till the villain left the paths of ease,
To walk in perilous paths, and drive
The just man into barren climes.

Now the sneaking serpent walks
In mild humility,
And the just man rages in the wilds
Where lions roam.

Rintrah roars and shakes his fires in the burden'd air;
Hungry clouds swag on the deep.

¶

As a new heaven is begun, and it is now thirty-three years since its * advent, the Eternal Hell revives. And lo! Swedenborg is the Angel sitting at the tomb: his writings are the linen clothes folded up. Now is the dominion of Edom, and the return of Adam into Paradise. See Isaiah XXXIV and XXXV Chap.

Without Contraries is no progression. Attraction and Repulsion, Reason and Energy, Love and Hate, are necessary to Human existence.

From these contraries spring what the religious call Good and Evil. Good is the passive that obeys Reason. Evil is the active springing from Energy.

Good is Heaven. Evil is Hell.

THE VOICE OF THE DEVIL

All Bibles or sacred codes have been the causes of the following Errors:

1. That Man has two real existing principles: Viz: a Body and a Soul.

2. That Energy, call'd Evil, is alone from the Body; and that Reason, call'd Good, is alone from the Soul.

3. That God will torment Man in Eternity for following his Energies.

But the following Contraries to these are True:

1. Man has no Body distinct from his Soul; for that call'd Body is a portion of Soul discern'd by the five Senses, the chief inlets of Soul in this age.

2. Energy is the only life, and is from the Body; and Reason is the bound or outward circumference of Energy.

3. Energy is Eternal Delight.

¶

Those who restrain desire, do so because theirs is weak enough to be restrained; and the restrainer, or reason, usurps its place and governs the unwilling.

And, being restrain'd, * it by degrees becomes passive, till it is only the shadow of desire.

The history of this is written in *Paradise Lost*, and the Governor, or Reason, is call'd Messiah.

And the original Archangel, or possessor of the command of the heavenly host, is call'd

* Notes on William Blake will be found in the Appendix, pp. 1066 ff.

the Devil or Satan, and his children are call'd Sin and Death.

But in the Book of Job, Milton's Messiah is call'd Satan.

For this history has been adopted by both parties.

It indeed appeared to Reason as if Desire was cast out; but the Devil's account is that the Messiah fell, and formed a heaven of what he stole from the Abyss.

This is shown in the Gospel, where he prays to the Father to send the comforter, or Desire, that Reason may have Ideas to build on; the Jehovah of the Bible being no other than he who dwells in flaming fire.

Know that after Christ's death, he became Jehovah.

But in Milton, the Father is Destiny, the Son a Ratio of the five senses, and the Holy Ghost Vacuum!

Note: the reason Milton wrote in fetters when he wrote of Angels and God, and at liberty when of Devils and Hell, is because he was a true Poet, and of the Devil's party without knowing it.

A MEMORABLE FANCY

As I was walking among the fires of hell, delighted with the enjoyments of Genius, which to Angels look like torment and insanity, I collected some of their Proverbs; thinking that as the sayings used in a nation mark its character, so the Proverbs of Hell show the nature of Infernal wisdom better than any description of buildings or garments.

When I came home: on the abyss of the five senses, where a flat sided steep frowns over the present world, I saw a mighty Devil folded in black clouds, hovering on the sides of the rock: with corroding fires he wrote the following sentence now perceived by the minds of men, and read by them on earth:

How do you know but ev'ry Bird that cuts the airy way,
Is an immense world of delight, clos'd by your senses five?

PROVERBS OF HELL

In seed time learn, in harvest teach, in winter enjoy.

Drive your cart and your plow over the bones of the dead.

The road of excess leads to the palace of wisdom.

Prudence is a rich, ugly old maid courted by Incapacity.

He who desires but acts not, breeds pestilence.

The cut worm forgives the plow.

Dip him in the river who loves water.

A fool sees not the same tree that a wise man sees.

He whose face gives no light shall never become a star.

Eternity is in love with the productions of time.

The busy bee has no time for sorrow.

The hours of folly are measur'd by the clock; but of wisdom, no clock can measure.

All wholesome food is caught without a net or a trap.

Bring out number, weight, and measure in a year of dearth.

No bird soars too high, if he soars with his own wings.

A dead body revenges not injuries.

The most sublime act is to set another before you.

If the fool would persist in his folly he would become wise.

Folly is the cloak of knavery.

Shame is Pride's cloak.

Prisons are built with stones of Law, Brothels with bricks of Religion.

The pride of the peacock is the glory of God.

The lust of the goat is the bounty of God.

The wrath of the lion is the wisdom of God.

The nakedness of woman is the work of God.

Excess of sorrow laughs. Excess of joy weeps.

The roaring of lions, the howling of wolves, the raging of the stormy sea, and the destructive sword are portions of eternity, too great for the eye of man.

The fox condemns the trap, not himself.

Joys impregnate. Sorrows bring forth.

Let man wear the fell of the lion, woman the fleece of the sheep.

The bird a nest, the spider a web, man friendship.

The selfish, smiling fool, and the sullen, frowning fool shall be both thought wise, that they may be a rod.

What is now proved was once only imagin'd.

The rat, the mouse, the fox, the rabbit watch the roots; the lion, the tiger, the horse, the elephant watch the fruits.

The cistern contains: the fountain overflows.

One thought fills immensity.

Always be ready to speak your mind, and a base man will avoid you.

Everything possible to be believ'd is an image of truth.

The eagle never lost so much time as when he submitted to learn of the crow.

The fox provides for himself, but God provides for the lion.

Think in the morning. Act in the noon. Eat in the evening. Sleep in the night.

He who has suffer'd you to impose on him, knows you.

As the plow follows words, so God rewards prayers.

The tigers of wrath are wiser than the horses of instruction.

Expect poison from the standing water.

You never know what is enough unless you know what is more than enough.

Listen to the fool's reproach! it is a kingly title!

The eyes of fire, the nostrils of air, the mouth of water, the beard of earth.

The weak in courage is strong in cunning.

The apple tree never asks the beech how he shall grow; nor the lion, the horse how he shall take his prey.

The thankful receiver bears a plentiful harvest.

If others had not been foolish, we should be so.

The soul of sweet delight can never be defil'd.

When thou seest an Eagle, thou seest a portion of Genius; lift up thy head!

As the caterpillar chooses the fairest leaves to lay her eggs on, so the priest lays his curse on the fairest joys.

To create a little flower is the labour of ages.

Damn braces. Bless relaxes.

The best wine is the oldest, the best water the newest.

Prayers plow not! Praises reap not!

Joys laugh not! Sorrows weep not!

The head Sublime, the heart Pathos, the genitals Beauty, the hands and feet Proportion.

As the air to a bird or the sea to a fish, so is contempt to the contemptible.

The crow wish'd everything was black, the owl that everything was white.

Exuberance is Beauty.

If the lion was advised by the fox, he would be cunning.

Improvement makes straight roads; but the crooked roads without Improvement are roads of Genius.

Sooner murder an infant in its cradle than nurse unacted desires.

Where man is not, nature is barren.

Truth can never be told so as to be understood, and not be believ'd.

Enough! or Too much.

¶

The ancient Poets animated all sensible objects with Gods or Geniuses, calling them by the names and adorning them with the properties of woods, rivers, mountains, lakes, cities, nations, and whatever their enlarged and numerous senses could perceive.

And particularly they studied the genius of each city and country, placing it under its mental deity;

Till a system was formed, which some took advantage of, and enslaved the vulgar by attempting to realize or abstract the mental deities from their objects: thus began Priesthood,

Choosing forms of worship from poetic tales.

And at length they pronounc'd that the Gods had order'd such things.

Thus men forgot that all deities reside in the human breast.

A MEMORABLE FANCY

The Prophets Isaiah and Ezekiel dined with me, and I asked them how they dared so roundly to assert that God spoke to them; and whether they did not think at the time that they would be misunderstood, and so be the cause of imposition.

Isaiah answer'd: "I saw no God, nor heard any, in a finite organical perception; but my senses discover'd the infinite in everything, and as I was then persuaded, and remain confirm'd that the voice of honest indignation is the voice of God; I cared not for consequences, but wrote."

Then I asked: "Does a firm persuasion that a thing is so, make it so?"

He replied: "All poets believe that it does, and in ages of imagination this firm persuasion removed mountains; but many are not capable of a firm persuasion of anything."

Then Ezekiel said: "The philosophy of the East taught the first principles of human perception; some nations held one principle for the origin, and some another: we of Israel taught that the Poetic Genius (as you now call it) was the first principle and all the others merely derivative, which was the cause of our despising the Priests and Philosophers of other countries, and prophesying that all Gods would at last be proved to originate in ours and to be the tributaries of the Poetic Genius; it was this that our great poet, King David, desired so fervently and invokes so pathetically saying by this he conquers enemies and governs kingdoms; and we so loved our God that we cursed in his name all the deities of surrounding nations, and asserted that they had rebelled: from these opinions the vulgar came to think that all nations would at last be subject to the Jews.

"This," said he, "like all firm persuasions, is come to pass; for all nations believe the Jews' code and worship the Jews' God, and what greater subjection can be?"

I heard this with some wonder, and must confess my own conviction. After dinner I ask'd Isaiah to favour the world with his lost works; he said none of equal value was lost. Ezekiel said the same of his.

I also asked Isaiah what made him go naked and barefoot three years. He answer'd: "The same that made our friend Diogenes, the Grecian."

I then asked Ezekiel why he ate dung, and lay so long on his right and left side. He answer'd, "The desire of raising other men into a perception of the infinite: this the North American tribes practised, and is he honest who resists his genius or conscience only for the sake of present ease or gratification?"

¶

The ancient tradition that the world will be consumed in fire at the end of six thousand years is true, as I have heard from Hell.

For the cherub with his flaming sword is hereby commanded to leave his guard at tree of life; and when he does, the whole creation will be consumed and appear infinite and holy, whereas it now appears finite and corrupt.

This will come to pass by an improvement of sensual enjoyment.

But first the notion that man has a body distinct from his soul is to be expunged; this I shall do by printing in the infernal method, by corrosives, which in Hell are salutary and medicinal, melting apparent surfaces away, and displaying the infinite which was hid.

If the doors of perception were cleansed, everything would appear to man as it is, infinite.

For man has closed himself up, till he sees all things thro' narrow chinks of his cavern.

A MEMORABLE FANCY

I was in a Printing house in Hell, and saw the method in which knowledge is transmitted from generation to generation.

In the first chamber was a Dragon-Man, clearing away the rubbish from a cave's mouth; within, a number of Dragons were hollowing the cave.

In the second chamber was a Viper folding round the rock and the cave, and others adorning it with gold, silver, and precious stones.

In the third chamber was an Eagle with wings and feathers of air: he caused the inside of the cave to be infinite; around were numbers of Eagle-like men who built palaces in the immense cliffs.

In the fourth chamber were Lions of flaming fire, raging around and melting the metals into living fluids.

In the fifth chamber were Unnam'd forms which cast the metals into the expanse.

There they were receiv'd by Men who occupied the sixth chamber, and took the forms of books and were arranged in libraries.

¶

The Giants who formed this world into its sensual existence, and now seem to live in it in chains, are in truth the causes of its life and the sources of all activity; but the chains are the cunning of weak and tame minds which have power to resist energy; according to the proverb, the weak in courage is strong in cunning.

Thus one portion of being is the Prolific, the other the Devouring: to the Devourer it seems as if the producer was in his chains; but it is not so; he only takes portions of existence and fancies that the whole.

But the Prolific would cease to be Prolific unless the Devourer, as a sea, received the excess of his delights.

Some will say: "Is not God alone the Prolific?" I answer: "God only Acts and Is, in existing beings or Men."

These two classes of men are always upon

earth, and they should be enemies: whoever tries to reconcile them seeks to destroy existence.

Religion is an endeavour to reconcile the two.

Note: Jesus Christ did not wish to unite, but to separate them, as in the Parable of sheep and goats! and he says: "I came not to send Peace, but a Sword."

Messiah or Satan or Tempter was formerly thought to be one of the Antediluvians who are our Energies.

A MEMORABLE FANCY

An Angel came to me and said: "O pitiable foolish young man! O horrible! O dreadful state! consider the hot burning dungeon thou art preparing for thyself to all eternity, to which thou art going in such career."

I said: "Perhaps you will be willing to show me my eternal lot, and we will contemplate together upon it, and see whether your lot or mine is most desirable."

So he took me thro' a stable and thro' a church and down into the church vault, at the end of which was a mill: thro' the mill we went, and came to a cave; down the winding cavern we groped our tedious way, till a void boundless as a nether sky appear'd beneath us, and we held by the roots of trees and hung over this immensity; but I said: "If you please, we will commit ourselves to this void, and see whether providence is here also; if you will not, I will"; but he answer'd: "Do not presume, O young man, but as we here remain, behold thy lot which will soon appear when the darkness passes away."

So I remain'd with him, sitting in the twisted root of an oak; he was suspended in a fungus, which hung with the head downward into the deep.

By degrees we beheld the infinite Abyss, fiery as the smoke of a burning city; beneath us, at an immense distance, was the sun, black but shining; round it were fiery tracks on which revolv'd vast spiders, crawling after their prey, which flew or rather swum, in the infinite deep, in the most terrific shapes of animals sprung from corruption; and the air was full of them, and seem'd composed of them: these are Devils, and are called Powers of the air. I now asked my companion which was my eternal lot. He said: "Between the black and white spiders."

But now, from between the black and white spiders, a cloud and fire burst and rolled thro' the deep, black'ning all beneath so that the nether deep grew black as a sea, and rolled with a terrible noise; beneath us was nothing now to be seen but a black tempest, till looking east between the clouds and the waves, we saw a cataract of blood mixed with fire, and not many stones' throw from us appear'd and sunk again the scaly fold of a monstrous serpent; at last to the east, distant about three degrees, appear'd a fiery crest above the waves; slowly it reared like a ridge of golden rocks, till we discover'd two globes of crimson fire, from which the sea fled away in clouds of smoke; and now we saw it was the head of Leviathan; his forehead was divided into streaks of green and purple like those on a tiger's forehead: soon we saw his mouth and red gills hang just above the raging foam, tinging the black deep with beams of blood, advancing toward us with all the fury of a spiritual existence.

My friend the Angel climb'd up from his station into the mill: I remain'd alone; and then this appearance was no more, but I found myself sitting on a pleasant bank beside a river by moonlight, hearing a harper, who sung to the harp; and his theme was: "The man who never alters his opinion is like standing water, and breeds reptiles of the mind."

But I arose and sought for the mill, and there I found my Angel, who, surprised, asked me how I escaped.

I answer'd: "All that we saw was owing to your metaphysics; for when you ran away, I found myself on a bank by moonlight hearing a harper. But now we have seen my eternal lot, shall I show you yours?" He laugh'd at my proposal; but I by force suddenly caught him in my arms, and flew westerly thro' the night, till we were elevated above the earth's shadow; then I flung myself with him directly into the body of the sun; here I clothed myself in white, and taking in my hand Swedenborg's volumes, sunk from the glorious clime, and passed all the planets till we came to Saturn: here I stay'd to rest, and then leap'd into the void between Saturn and the fixed stars.

"Here," said I, "is your lot, in this space — if space it may be call'd." Soon we saw the stable and the church, and I took him to the altar and open'd the Bible, and lo! it was a deep pit, into which I descended, driving the Angel before me; soon we saw seven houses of brick; one we enter'd; in it were a number of monkeys, baboons, and all of that species, chain'd by the middle, grinning and snatching at one another, but withheld by the shortness of their chains: however, I saw that they sometimes grew numerous, and then the weak were caught by the strong, and with a grinning aspect, first coupled with, and then devour'd, by plucking off first one limb and then another, till the body was left a helpless trunk; this, after grinning and kissing it with seeming fondness, they devour'd too; and here and there I saw one savourily picking the flesh off his own tail; as the stench terribly annoy'd us both, we went into the mill, and I in my hand brought the skeleton of a body, which in the mill was Aristotle's *Analytics*.

So the Angel said: "Thy phantasy has imposed upon me, and thou oughtest to be ashamed." I answer'd: "We impose on one another, and it is but lost time to converse with you whose works are only Analytics."

¶

Opposition is true Friendship.

¶

I have always found that Angels have the vanity to speak of themselves as the only wise; this they do with a confident insolence sprouting from systematic reasoning.

Thus Swedenborg boasts that what he writes is new; tho' it is only the Contents or Index of already publish'd books.

A man carried a monkey about for a show, and because he was a little wiser than the monkey, grew vain, and conceiv'd himself as much wiser than seven men. It is so with Swedenborg: he shows the folly of churches, and exposes hypocrites, till he imagines that all are religious, and himself the single one on earth that ever broke a net.

Now hear a plain fact: Swedenborg has not written one new truth. Now hear another: he has written all the old falsehoods.

And now hear the reason. He conversed with Angels who are all religious, and conversed not with Devils who all hate religion, for he was incapable thro' his conceited notions.

Thus Swedenborg's writings are a recapitulation of all superficial opinions, and an analysis of the more sublime — but no further.

Have now another plain fact. Any man of mechanical talents may, from the writings of Paracelsus or Jacob Behmen, produce ten thousand volumes of equal value with Swedenborg's, and from those of Dante or Shakespeare an infinite number.

But when he has done this, let him not say that he knows better than his master, for he only holds a candle in sunshine.

A MEMORABLE FANCY

Once I saw a Devil in a flame of fire, who arose before an Angel that sat on a cloud, and the Devil utter'd these words:

"The worship of God is honouring his gifts in other men, each according to his genius, and loving the greatest men best: those who envy or calumniate great men hate God, for there is no other God."

The Angel hearing this became almost blue; but mastering himself he grew yellow, and at last white, pink, and smiling, and then replied:

"Thou Idolater! is not God One? and is not he visible in Jesus Christ? and has not Jesus Christ given his sanction to the law of ten commandments? and are not all other men fools, sinners, and nothings?"

The Devil answer'd: "Bray a fool in a mortar with wheat, yet shall not his folly be beaten out of him! If Jesus Christ is the greatest man, you ought to love him in the greatest degree. Now hear how he has given his sanction to the law of ten commandments: did he not mock at the Sabbath, and so mock the Sabbath's God? murder those who were murder'd because of him? turn away the law from the woman taken in adultery? steal the labour of others to support him? bear false witness when he omitted making a defence before Pilate? covet when he pray'd for his disciples, and when he bid them shake off the dust of their feet against such as refused to lodge them? I tell you, no virtue can exist without breaking these ten commandments. Jesus was all virtue, and acted from impulse, not from rules."

When he had so spoken, I beheld the Angel, who stretched out his arms, embracing the flame of fire, and he was consumed and arose as Elijah.

Note: This Angel, who is now become a Devil, is my particular friend; we often read the Bible together in its infernal or diabolical sense, which the world shall have if they behave well.

I have also the Bible of Hell, which the world shall have whether they will or no.

¶

One Law for the Lion and Ox is Oppression.

A SONG OF *LIBERTY

1. The Eternal Female groan'd! it was heard over all the Earth.

2. Albion's coast is sick, silent; the American meadows faint!

3. Shadows of Prophecy shiver along by the lakes and the rivers, and mutter across the ocean: France, rend down thy dungeon!

4. Golden Spain, burst the barriers of old Rome!

5. Cast thy keys, O Rome, into the deep down falling, even to eternity down falling,

6. And weep.

7. In her trembling hands she took the new born terror, howling.

8. On these infinite mountains of light, now barr'd out by the Atlantic sea, the new born fire stood before the starry king!

9. Flag'd with grey brow'd snows and thunderous visages, the jealous wings wav'd over the deep.

10. The speary hand burned aloft, unbuckled was the shield; forth went the hand of jealousy among the flaming hair, and hurl'd the new born wonder thro' the starry night.

11. The fire, the fire is falling!

12. Look up! look up! O citizen of London, enlarge thy countenance! O Jew, leave counting gold! return to thy oil and wine. O African! black African! (go, winged thought, widen his forehead.)

13. The fiery limbs, the flaming hair, shot like the sinking sun into the western sea.

14. Wak'd from his eternal sleep, the hoary element roaring fled away.

15. Down rush'd, beating his wings in vain, the jealous king; his grey brow'd counsellors, thunderous warriors, curl'd veterans, among helms, and shields, and chariots, horses, elephants, banners, castles, slings, and * rocks.

16. Falling, rushing, ruining! buried in the ruins, on Urthona's dens;

17. All night beneath the ruins; then, their sullen flames faded, emerge round the gloomy king.

18. With thunder and fire, leading his starry hosts thro' the waste wilderness, he promulgates his ten * commands, glancing his beamy eyelids over the deep in dark dismay,

19. Where the son of fire in his eastern cloud, while the morning plumes her golden breast,

20. Spurning the clouds written with curses, stamps the stony law to dust, loosing the eternal horses from the dens of night, crying:

EMPIRE IS NO MORE! AND NOW THE LION AND WOLF SHALL CEASE,

CHORUS

Let the Priests of the Raven of dawn no longer, in deadly black, with hoarse note curse the sons of joy. Nor his accepted brethren — whom, tyrant, he calls free — lay the bound or build the roof. Nor pale religious lechery call that virginity that wishes but acts not!

For everything that lives is Holy.

[ca. 1793]

AH, SUNFLOWER

Ah, sunflower, weary of time,
Who countest the steps of the sun,
Seeking after that sweet golden clime
Where the traveller's journey is done —

Where the youth pined away with desire,
And the pale virgin, shrouded in snow,
Arise from their graves, and aspire
Where my sunflower wishes to go!

[1794]

THE TIGER

Tiger, tiger, burning bright
In the forests of the night,
What immortal hand or eye
Could frame thy fearful symmetry?

In what distant deeps or skies
Burnt the fire of thine eyes?
On what wings dare he aspire?
What the hand dare seize the fire?

And what shoulder, and what art,
Could twist the sinews of thy heart?
And when thy heart began to beat,
What dread hand? and what dread * feet?

What the hammer? what the chain?
In what furnace was thy brain?

What the anvil? What dread grasp
Dare its deadly terrors clasp?

When the stars threw down their spears,
And watered heaven with their tears,
Did he smile his work to see?
Did he who made the lamb, make thee?

Tiger, tiger, burning bright
In the forests of the night,
What immortal hand or eye
Dare frame thy fearful symmetry?

[1794]

THE CHIMNEY-SWEEPER

A little black thing among the snow,
Crying "weep! weep!" in notes of woe!
"Where are thy father and mother? Say!"
"They are both gone up to the church to pray.

"Because I was happy upon the heath,
And smiled among the winter's snow,
They clothed me in the clothes of death,
And taught me to sing the notes of woe.

"And because I am happy, and dance and sing,
They think they have done me no injury,
And are gone to praise God and his priest and king,
Who make up a heaven of our misery."

[1794]

From MILTON

And did those feet in ancient time
Walk upon England's mountains green?
And was the holy Lamb of God
On England's pleasant pastures seen?

And did the Countenance Divine
Shine forth upon our clouded hills?
And was Jerusalem builded here
Among these dark Satanic mills?

Bring me my bow of burning gold!
Bring me my arrows of desire!
Bring me my spear! O clouds, unfold!
Bring me my chariot of fire!

I will not cease from mental fight,
Nor shall my sword sleep in my hand,
Till we have built Jerusalem
In England's green and pleasant land.

[1804]

*AUGURIES OF INNOCENCE

To see a world in a grain of sand,
And a heaven in a wild flower;
Hold infinity in the palm of your hand,
And eternity in an hour.

A robin redbreast in a cage
Puts all heaven in a rage;
A dove-house filled with doves and pigeons
Shudders hell through all its regions.
A dog starved at his master's gate
Predicts the ruin of the state.
A game-cock clipped and armed for fight
Doth the rising sun affright;
A horse misused upon the road
Calls to heaven for human blood.
Every wolf's and lion's howl
Raises from hell a human soul;
Each outcry of the hunted hare
A fibre from the brain does tear;
A skylark wounded on the wing
Doth make a cherub cease to sing.

He who shall hurt the little wren
Shall never be beloved by men;
He who the ox to wrath has moved
Shall never be by woman loved;
He who shall train the horse to war
Shall never pass the polar bar.
The wanton boy that kills the fly
Shall feel the spider's enmity;
He who torments the chafer's sprite
Weaves a bower in endless night.
The caterpillar on the leaf
Repeats to thee thy mother's grief;
The wild deer wandering here and there
Keep the human soul from care;
The lamb misused breeds public strife,
And yet forgives the butcher's knife.
Kill not the moth nor butterfly,
For the last judgment draweth nigh;
The beggar's dog and widow's cat,
Feed them and thou shalt grow fat.
Every tear from every eye
Becomes a babe in eternity;
The bleat, the bark, bellow, and roar
Are waves that beat on heaven's shore.

The bat that flits at close of eve
Has left the brain that won't believe;
The owl that calls upon the night
Speaks the unbeliever's fright;
The gnat that sings his summer's song
Poison gets from Slander's tongue;

The poison of the snake and newt
Is the sweat of Envy's foot;
The poison of the honey-bee
Is the artist's jealousy;
The strongest poison ever known
Came from Cæsar's laurel crown.

Nought can deform the human race
Like to the armourer's iron brace;
The soldier armed with sword and gun
Palsied strikes the summer's sun.
When gold and gems adorn the plough,
To peaceful arts shall Envy bow.
The beggar's rags fluttering in air
Do to rags the heavens tear;
The prince's robes and beggar's rags
Are toadstools on the miser's bags.
One mite wrung from the labourer's hands
Shall buy and sell the miser's lands,
Or, if protected from on high,
Shall that whole nation sell and buy;
The poor man's farthing is worth more
Than all the gold on Afric's shore.
The whore and gambler, by the state
Licenced, build that nation's fate;
The harlot's cry from street to street
Shall weave Old England's winding sheet;
The winner's shout, the loser's curse,
Shall dance before dead England's hearse.

He who mocks the infant's faith
Shall be mocked in age and death;
He who shall teach the child to doubt
The rotting grave shall ne'er get out;
He who respects the infant's faith
Triumphs over hell and death.
The babe is more than swaddling-bands
Throughout all these human lands;
Tools were made, and born were hands,
Every farmer understands.
The questioner who sits so sly
Shall never know how to reply;
He who replies to words of doubt
Doth put the light of knowledge out;
A riddle, or the cricket's cry,
Is to doubt a fit reply.
The child's toys and the old man's reasons
Are the fruits of the two seasons.
The emmet's inch and eagle's mile
Make lame philosophy to smile.
A truth that's told with bad intent
Beats all the lies you can invent.
He who doubts from what he sees
Will ne'er believe, do what you please;
If the sun and moon should doubt
They'd immediately go out.

Every night and every morn
Some to misery are born;
Every morn and every night
Some are born to sweet delight;
Some are born to sweet delight,
Some are born to endless night.
Joy and woe are woven fine,
A clothing for the soul divine;
Under every grief and pine
Runs a joy with silken twine.
It is right it should be so;
Man was made for joy and woe;
And, when this we rightly know,
Safely through the world we go.

We are led to believe a lie
When we see *with* not *through* the eye,
Which was born in a night to perish in a night
When the soul slept in beams of light.
God appears, and God is light
To those poor souls who dwell in night,
But doth a human form display
To those who dwell in realms of day.

[1863]

APPENDIX

BIBLIOGRAPHIES AND NOTES

The figures in bold-face type in this Appendix indicate pages in the text to which the notes refer.

SAMUEL BUTLER

BIBLIOGRAPHY

Hudibras, ed. by A. R. Waller, 1905.
Characters and Passages from Notebooks, ed. by A. R. Waller, 1908.
Satires and Miscellaneous Poetry and Prose, ed. by René Lamar, 1928.
Edward Dowden, in *Puritan and Anglican: Studies in Literature*, 1900.
J. Veldkamp, *Samuel Butler, the Author of Hudibras*, 1924.
Dan Gibson, Jr., in *Seventeenth Century Studies by Members of the Graduate School, University of Cincinnati*, 1933.

NOTES

2, l. 6, *punk:* prostitute.
2, l. 9, *gospel-trumpeter:* a Presbyterian preacher advocating rebellion.
2, l. 19, *blow:* endured no blow except the king's accolade.
2, l. 21, *errant:* serving both at home — as Justice of the Peace — and in the field.
2, l. 22, *chartel:* a letter challenging to combat.
2, l. 24, *bind o'er:* "to keep the peace."
2, l. 24, *swaddle:* to beat with a cudgel.
2, l. 40, *Hudibras:* The name is taken from Spenser's *Faerie Queene*, II, 2, 17.
2, l. 98, *fustian:* a coarse cloth, often slashed or cut when used for sleeves to show a satin lining.
3, l. 104, *leash:* a sporting term meaning *three.* Cerberus, watch-dog of Hades, had three heads.
3, l. 107, *charge:* expense.
3, l. 112, *to touch them on:* the "touchstone" was used to test precious metals.
3, l. 115, *orator:* Demosthenes.
3, l. 120, *Tycho Brahe:* Danish astronomer, 1546–1601.
3, l. 120, *Erra Pater:* nickname of William Lilly, 1602–81, an astrologer lampooned by Butler as "Sidrophel."
3, l. 145, *quiddity:* real essence.
3, l. 148, *northern air:* The notion of "frozen words" that melt into audibility in a thaw is found in Lucian — and also in Mark Twain.
3, l. 151, *school-divinity:* scholastic theology.
3, l. 152, *Irrefragable:* nickname of the scholastic philosopher, Alexander of Hales, d. 1245.
3, l. 153, *Thomas:* Thomas Aquinas, 1227–1274, greatest of scholastic philosophers.
3, l. 154, *Duns:* Duns Scotus, a thirteenth-century philosopher, whose first name has given the word *dunce* because his followers opposed the New Learning.
3, l. 155, *nominal:* referring to the great philosophical struggle of the Middle Ages between the *Nominalists* and the *Realists.*
3, l. 158, *Sorbonist:* a doctor of the Sorbonne.
4, l. 232, *widgeon:* a pigeon that brought God's messages to the prophet. Mahomet rode into God's presence on an ass.
4, l. 236, *advowson:* legal obligation to defend an institution.
4, l. 249, *type:* symbol. He had sworn, as many did, not to shave until the king was dethroned.
4, l. 253, *heart-breakers:* long locks.
4, l. 260, *Cordelier:* a Franciscan.
4, l. 269, *Maugre:* in spite of.
4, l. 281, *Taliacotius:* an Italian surgeon to the Medici family.
4, l. 285, *Nock:* i.e., the porter. Nock was a vulgar nickname for Cromwell.
4, l. 308, *bruise:* because no gentleman would fight with him.
4, l. 310, *Bullen:* Boulogne, taken by siege in 1544 by Henry VIII.

4, l. 314, *ammunition:* distributed by a government to soldiers.
4, l. 315, *black-puddings:* sausages made of blood and suet.
5, l. 329, *thorough:* through
5, l. 337, *wore:* used.
5, l. 338, *farthingale:* a contrivance of whalebone to enlarge the circumference of skirts.
5, l. 370, *contempts:* legal terms of the country Justice's court.
5, l. 372, *shoulder:* a "bum-bailiff" making an arrest for debt by clapping his prisoner on the shoulder.
5, l. 379, *dudgeon:* a dagger with wooden hilt, carried by a civilian.
5, l. 390, *score:* Both Oliver Cromwell and Colonel Pride are said to have been brewers.
5, l. 396, *bent:* when the hammers were drawn back.
5, l. 427, *stay'd:* steady.
6, l. 436, *soft:* Cæsar's horse, according to Suetonius, had feet like a man's, with separate toes.
6, l. 439, *his:* old form of the possessive.
6, l. 447, *panel:* saddlecloth.

THOMAS HOBBES

BIBLIOGRAPHY

The standard edition and only complete reprint of Hobbes is that of Sir W. Molesworth, *Latin Works*, 5 vols., *English Works*, 11 vols., 1839–1845.

Modern editions of *Leviathan* include that ed. by A. R. Waller, 1904, and the Oxford reprint with an essay by W. G. Pogson Smith, 1909.

In the Modern Students' Library of Philosophy, F. J. E. Woodbridge has edited a useful volume, *Hobbes Selections*, 1929.

In addition to the standard histories of philosophy, the following biographies and critical discussions of Hobbes will be found useful.

G. C. Robertson, *Hobbes*, 1886.
G. Lyon, *La philosophie de Hobbes*, 1893.
F. Tönnies, *Hobbes, Leben und Lehre*, 1896.
G. Tarantino, *Saggio sulle idee morali e politiche di T. Hobbes*, 1900.
R. Mondolfo, *La morale di T. Hobbes*, 1903.
Sir Leslie Stephen, *Hobbes*, 1904.
A. E. Taylor, *Hobbes*, 1909.
R. Gadave, *Thomas Hobbes and his Theories of the Social Contract*, 1907.
G. Catbin, *Thomas Hobbes*, 1922.
Marjorie H. Nicolson, "Milton and Hobbes," *Studies in Phil.*, XXIII, 405–33, Oct., 1926.
Julius Lips, *Die Stellung des Thomas Hobbes zu den politischen Parteien der grossen englischen Revolution*, 1927, accompanying the first German translation of *Behemoth*.
V. Beonio-Brocchieri, *Studi sulla filosofia politica di Thomas Hobbes*, 1927.
Frithiof Brandt, *Thomas Hobbes' Mechanical Conception of Nature*, 1928.
L. I. Bredvold, "Dryden, Hobbes, and The Royal Society," *MP*, May, 1928.
Z. Lubiensky, *Die Grundlagen des ethisch-politischen Systems von Hobbes*, 1932.

NOTES

10, l. 20, *a new covenant made, not with men, but with God:* The reference is to the Solemn League and Covenant for the establishment of Presbyterianism and the putting down of the Episcopal Church, agreed to by the English and the Scottish Parliaments in 1643.

11, l. 20, *no man that hath sovereign power can justly be put to death:* In 1649, about two years before the publication of *Leviathan*, Charles I had been beheaded.

14, l. 3, *prospective-glasses:* perspective-glasses, or field-glasses.

ABRAHAM COWLEY

BIBLIOGRAPHY

The English Writings of Abraham Cowley, 2 vols., ed. by A. R. Waller, 1905.
Cowley's Essays, ed. by J. R. Lumby, revised by A. Tilley, 1923.
The Mistress, with Other Select Poems, ed. by J. Sparrow, 1926.

R. Shafer, *The English Ode to 1660*, 1918.
H. Ellis, in *The Philosophy of Conflict*, second series, 1919.
A. H. Nethercote, "The Reputation of Abraham Cowley," in *Publications of the Modern Language Association*, Sept., 1923.
H. W. Garrod, in *The Profession of Poetry*, 1929.

NOTES

TO THE ROYAL SOCIETY

16, l. 1, *Philosophy:* natural philosophy or science.
16, l. 3, *sin:* at the fall of man.
16, l. 29, *curious:* intelligently studious.
16, l. 31, *spirits:* a monosyllable.
16, l. 39, *laws:* of the realm and of nature.
16, l. 44, *rout:* crowd.
16, l. 50, *god:* Priapus, god of fertility, wooden images of whom were used as scarecrows.
16, l. 63, *tree:* cf. Genesis 2:9 and 3:3.
17, l. 72, *flew:* as in the story told of the picture of grapes by the Greek painter Zeuxis, fl. 420–390 B.C.
17, l. 75, *mechanic:* skillful.
17, l. 89, *errors:* wanderings.
17, l. 109, *you:* members of the Royal Society.
17, l. 109, *get:* conquer, acquire.
17, l. 117, *band: Cf.* Judges 7: 16–20. The ingenious working out of the parallel is in Cowley's most characteristic manner.
17, l. 134, *Io:* a Greek shout of triumph or joy.
17, l. 146, *hand:* handwriting.
17, l. 148, *those:* haters of the "virtuoso" such as Samuel Butler, who began to ridicule the Royal Society almost as soon as it was founded. See his *Elephant in the Moon.*
18, l. 165, *show:* seem.
18, l. 169, *history:* A *History of the Royal Society* written by Thomas Sprat, Cowley's friend and biographer, appeared in 1667. The present poem was written for that book.
18, l. 174, *he:* Thomas Sprat.
18, l. 180, *god:* Father Thames, the river-god.

OF SOLITUDE

18, l. 3, *Nunquam minus... solus:* "One is never less alone than when alone," a remark attributed to Scipio Africanus and quoted from him by Cicero in *De Officiis* III, 1, and *De Republica* I, 17.
18, l. 7, *Scipio:* surnamed "Africanus," conqueror of Hannibal.
18, l. 19, *Linternum:* a town in Campania.
18, l. 22, *veneration:* Seneca tells of his visit in *Epistles* XIII, 1.
18, l. 32, *colourably:* plausibly.
18, l. 33, *Montaigne: Essays* I, 38 — on *Solitude.*
18, l. 13, *Tecum vivere... lubens:* Horace, *Odes* III, ix, 24.
18, l. 16, *Sic ego... locis:* Tibullus IV, xiii, 9.
18, l. 31, *Odi et amo... excrucior:* Catullus LXXXV.
19, l. 30, *beast:* a reference to the remark of Aristotle that a man who loves solitude must be either a god or a beast.
19, l. 41, *O vita... brevis:* Publilius Syrus, *Sententiæ*, 202.
19, l. 27, *O quis... umbra:* "Oh, who will seat me under the cool mountains of Hæmus, and cover me with the spreading shade of boughs?" — inaccurately quoted from Virgil's *Georgics* II, 489.

EDMUND WALLER

BIBLIOGRAPHY

The Poems of Edmund Waller, ed. with Life by G. Thorn-Drury, 2 vols. (The Muses' Library), 1893.
Life in S. Johnson's *The Lives of the Poets.*
D. C. Tovey, in *Reviews and Essays in English Literature*, 1897.
Netty Roeckerath, *Der Nachruhm Herricks und Wallers*, 1931.

ON ST. JAMES'S PARK

22, l. 3, *lasts:* These lines were imitated by Pope in *Windsor Forest*, ll. 7, 8.

22, l. 6, *tide:* A small stream from the Thames, which is tidal at London, had been diverted into the Park.

22, l. 15, *hand:* Trees were supposed to obey the music of Orpheus, and Amphion was thought to have laid the stones of Thebes merely by playing his lyre.

22, l. 39, *Thetis:* goddess of the sea.

22, l. 40, *court:* playing upon the still rather novel idea that England is mistress of the sea.

23, l. 44, *sheet: Cf.* Acts 10: 11, 12.

23, l. 46, *mound:* an essential feature in the formal garden of the period.

23, l. 57, *Mall:* originally a shady walk along the northern border of the Park, where Charles II played the French game of pall mall.

23, l. 70, *sky:* like the Titans of Greek myth, also "sons of earth."

23, l. 72, *entertained: Cf.* Genesis 18: 2, 3.

23, l. 80, *shade:* referring to the Greek and Roman custom of interpreting the rustling of leaves as an oracle.

23, l. 87, *prelate:* Cardinal Wolsey, who did not build but merely beautified the mansion of Whitehall, using money gained from the dissolution of the monasteries.

23, l. 91, *pile:* Westminster Abbey.

23, l. 99, *house:* probably the Banqueting House at Whitehall where Charles I was executed.

23, l. 105, *hall:* Westminster Hall, for centuries a court of law.

23, l. 113, *The pleasures...:* Waller's adulation of Charles reaches the height of absurdity at this point, but it should be considered that the poem was written very early in the reign.

23, l. 124, *Alcides:* Hercules — referring to his choice between a life of pleasure and one of strenuous endeavour.

23, l. 125, *palace:* Charles II was born in St. James's Palace.

23, l. 128, *star:* seen at noon by Charles I while returning from St. Paul's where he had given thanks for the birth of his son.

23, l. 132, *world:* divided between the Roman Catholic and the Protestant faith.

THE NIGHT–PIECE

24, l. 5, *Lely's:* Sir Peter Lely, 1617–1680, was state-painter to Charles II.

24, l. 15, *view:* the sight of her.

24, l. 22, *get:* gain.

THE TRIPLE COMBAT

24, l. 1, *Mazarin:* the Duchess of Mazarin, one of the mistresses of Charles II, who was born in Rome and arrived in England in 1675.

24, l. 7, *Portsmouth:* the Duchess of Portsmouth, born in Lower Bretagne or "Little Britain," the chief mistress of the king at this time.

24, l. 28, *Chloris:* probably the Duchess of Cleveland, a third mistress of the king.

24, l. 33, *three:* referring to the contest of beauty between Juno, Venus, and Minerva, in which Paris was judge and a golden apple the prize.

24, l. 42, *Alsatia:* a quarter of London, inhabited by criminals. But the reference may be to the French campaign in Alsatia under Turenne in 1674.

JOHN WILMOT, EARL OF ROCHESTER

BIBLIOGRAPHY

Collected Works of John Wilmot, Earl of Rochester, ed. J. Hayward, 1926.
Thomas Longueville, *Rochester and Other Literary Rakes of the Court of Charles II*, 1902.
J. Prinz, *John Wilmot, Earl of Rochester, His Life and Writings*, 1927.

NOTES

27, l. 31, *bubbles:* gulls or victims.

27, l. 43, *fops:* i.e., the objects of witty ridicule.

27, l. 46, *band:* a neckcloth worn by certain Protestant clergymen.

27, l. 52, *Muse:* presumably one, unknown to Greek mythology, who presided over the writing of sermons.

27, l. 69, *universe:* a translation of Lucretius' famous words: *flammantia mœnia mundi, De Rerum Natura,* I, 73.

27, l. 73, *Ingelo:* Nathaniel Ingelo, 1621–1683, a scholar, musician, and dissenting clergyman, whose religious romance, *Bentivolio and Urania*, 1660, is here referred to.

27, l. 74, *Pilgrim: The Parable of the Pilgrim*, 1664, by Simon Patrick, Bishop of Ely.

27, l. 74, *Soliloquies:* probably the *Divine Meditations*, 1638, of Richard Sibbs, a Puritan divine, 1577-1635.

27, l. 83, *bedlams:* insane asylums.

27, l. 86, *charming:* thaumaturgic.

27, l. 90, *philosopher:* Diogenes.

27, l. 100, *sense:* common sense.

28, l. 119, *Jowler:* a common name for a dog.

28, l. 120, *Meres:* Sir Thomas Meres, 1635–1715, a Whig politician, stubborn opponent of Charles II and James II.

THOMAS TRAHERNE

BIBLIOGRAPHY

Poetical Works, ed. B. Dobell, 1906.
Centuries of Meditation, ed. B. Dobell, 1908.
Gladys E. Willett, *Traherne: An Essay*, 1919.
Frieda Löhrer, *Die Mystik und ihre Quellen in Thomas Traherne*, 1930.

JOHN DRYDEN

BIBLIOGRAPHY

The Works of John Dryden, ed. by Sir Walter Scott and revised by George Saintsbury, 18 vols., 1882–93. (The standard edition though out of date.)
The poems have been edited in several modern editions: by W. D. Christie, 1870, in the Globe Edition; by G. R. Noyes, 1909, in the Cambridge Edition; by John Sargeaunt, 1910, in the Oxford Edition.
Type-facsimile reprints of the first edition of *Mac Flecknoe*, 1924, and of *Annus Mirabilis*, 1927, have been published by the Oxford Univ. Press.
Songs of John Dryden, ed. by C. L. Day, 1932.
Essays of John Dryden, edited by W. P. Ker, 2 vols., 1900. (The best edition so far as it goes.)
Dramatic Essays, with an introduction by W. H. Hudson, Everyman's Library.
For the plays see George Saintsbury in the Mermaid Series, 2 vols., 1904.
G. R. Noyes, *Selected Dramas* (with *The Rehearsal*), 1915.
Montague Summers, *Dryden: The Dramatic Works*, 6 vols., 1931.
P. J. Dobell, *John Dryden: Bibliographical Memoranda*, 1922.
For biography and criticism, in addition to the memoirs in the various editions mentioned above and Dr. Johnson's "Dryden" in *The Lives of the English Poets* (part of which is reprinted in this volume) see the following:
George Saintsbury, *Dryden*, in the Eng. Men of Letters Series, 1881.
E. Dowden, *Puritan and Anglican: Studies in Literature*, 1900.
Mark Van Doren, *The Poetry of John Dryden*, 1920.
G. S. Collins, *Drydens Theorie und Praxis*, 1892.
M. Sherwood, *Dryden's Dramatic Theory and Practice*, 1899.
A. W. Verrall, *Lectures on Dryden*, 1914.
Allardyce Nicoll, *Dryden as an Adapter of Shakespeare*, 1922.
Allardyce Nicoll, *Dryden and his Poetry*, 1923.
B. J. Pendlebury, *Dryden's Heroic Plays: A Study of the Origins*, 1923.
T. S. Eliot, *Homage to John Dryden*, 1924.
John H. Smith, *Dryden's Critical Temper*, "Washington Univ. Studies." April, 1925, Humanistic Series, XII, 201–20.
G. Thorn-Drury, "Some Notes on Dryden," *RES*, Jan., 1925, I, 79–83; April, 1925, I, 187–97; July, 1925, I, 324–30.

G. L. Diffenbaugh, *The Rise and Development of the Mock Heroic Poem in England from 1660 to 1714: Dryden's "Mac Flecknoe."* 1926.

B. J. Wild, *Dryden und die römische Kirche*, 1928.

T. S. Eliot, *John Dryden, the Poet, the Dramatist, the Critic: Three Essays*, 1932.

Guido Fornelli, *La restaurazione inglese nell' opera di John Dryden*, 1932.

W. Jellie-Harvey, *Le théâtre classique en Angleterre dans l'âge de John Dryden*, 1932.

Wolfgang Jünemann, *Drydens Fabeln und ihre Quellen*, 1932.

Wolfgang Mann, *Drydens heroische Tragödien als Ausdruck höfischer Barockkultur in England*, 1932.

ABSALOM AND ACHITOPHEL

For the political situation in England in November, 1681, when this satire was published, see G. M. Trevelyan, *England under the Stuarts*. For the Biblical references to Absalom's rebellion, see II Samuel, chaps. 13 to 18. The parallel between certain events in the life of David and contemporary politics in the reign of Charles II had previously been observed; Dryden had referred to it casually in 1660 in *Astræa Redux*, lines 79–82. It had been developed in some detail in the anonymous pamphlet, *Absalom's Conspiracy, or The Tragedy of Treason*, reprinted in the Scott-Saintsbury ed., vol. IX, pp. 206–208.

The following table gives the interpretation of the Biblical proper names in *Absalom and Achitophel*, Part I:

Abbethdin: a rabbinical, not a Biblical, term for a high officer of justice among the Jews; Shaftesbury was Lord Chancellor.

Absalon or Absalom: James, Duke of Monmouth, an illegitimate son of Charles II.

Achitophel: (Ahithophel is the spelling in the Authorized Version.) Anthony Ashley Cooper, Earl of Shaftesbury.

Adriel: John Sheffield, Earl of Mulgrave, afterwards Duke of Buckingham, friend and patron of Dryden, and author of *Essay on Satire* and *Essay on Poetry*.

Agag: Sir Edmund Berry Godfrey, the magistrate before whom Titus Oates made his first charges of the Popish Plot; the finding of his dead body shortly afterwards added enormously to popular belief in Oates's charges.

Amiel: Edward Seymour, recently Speaker of the House of Commons.

Amnon: probably Sir John Coventry, who in 1671 had been attacked and brutally disfigured by some members of Monmouth's troop of the King's Horseguards. Since Coventry was not murdered, the parallel is not close.

Annabel: Anne Scott, Countess of Buccleuch, wife of Monmouth.

Balaam: Theophilus Hastings, Earl of Huntington.

Barzillai: James Butler, Duke of Ormond, a faithful old Cavalier of high repute.

Bathsheba: the Duchess of Portsmouth, at this time the favourite mistress of Charles II.

Caleb: Ford, Lord Grey; common scandal linked the name of his wife and that of Monmouth.

Corah: Titus Oates, the man whose testimony first alleged the existence of the "Popish Plot."

David: Charles II.

Egypt: France.

Gath: Brussels.

Hebron: Scotland. Charles II did not come directly from Scotland at the Restoration in 1660, but he had previously been crowned there just as David had been anointed in Hebron and had ruled there some seven years before he reigned in Jerusalem.

Hushai: Lawrence Hyde, Viscount Hyde and afterwards Earl of Rochester, a leading statesman and a patron of Dryden.

Ishbosheth: Richard Cromwell, son of the Protector; like the son of Saul, he proved too weak to rule the nation after his father's death.

Israel: England.

Issachar: Thomas Thynne of Longleat, who had recently entertained Monmouth at his magnificent home in Wiltshire.

Jebusites: Roman Catholics.

Jerusalem: London.

Jews: English.

Jonas: Sir William Jones, formerly the attorney-general who had conducted the prosecutions of the "Popish Plot," now an associate of Shaftesbury.

Jordan: the seas that surround England; in l. 270 "Jordan's sand" evidently means Dover, where Charles II landed at the Restoration, but in l. 820 the reference is to the Irish Channel.

Jotham: George Savile, Marquis of Halifax, known as the "Trimmer" because he was the leader of those who sought to mediate between the extremes of the rival parties. See p. 161.

Levites: Presbyterian ministers.
Michal: Catharine of Portugal, Queen of Charles II; like Michal she was childless.
Nadab: William, Lord Howard of Escrick, while in the Tower of London, accused of inciting a treasonable libel, had solemnly taken the Sacrament in proof of his innocence. Report, however, said that he had drunk "lamb's wool" (ale poured on roasted apples and sugar) instead of the sacramental wine.
Pharaoh: Louis XIV of France.
Sagan of Jerusalem: Henry Compton, Bishop of London.
Sanhedrin: Parliament.
Saul: Oliver Cromwell.
Shimei: one of the sheriffs of London in 1680, an old republican.
Sion: London.
Solymæan: pertaining to Jerusalem, from Solyma, Jerusalem.
Tyrus: Holland.
Zadoc: William Sancroft, Archbishop of Canterbury.
Zimri: George Villiers, Duke of Buckingham.

NOTES

32, Motto, *Si propius... magis:* "If you stand closer, it will affect you more."

32, l. 62, *humour:* For the development from the medieval meaning of *humour*, one of the four fluid elements of the human body, to the present meaning of a facetious turn of mind that perceives incongruities and moves to laughter, see *NED*. In the seventeenth and eighteenth centuries the word was undergoing a transformation in meaning which is important to the student of literature and society. Here it means capriciousness of disposition, eccentricity. In Dryden's time the word almost always had an unfavourable connotation.

33, l. 82, *Good Old Cause:* an ironic reference to the Commonwealth, frequent in the controversial writing of the period. Dryden is here trying to discredit the Whig politicians by associating them with the Cromwellian party.

33, l. 108, *Plot:* the "Popish Plot" which had excited England since the summer of 1678. It began with the charges of Titus Oates that the Jesuits were plotting to murder the king and restore the Roman Catholic religion. Recent investigation of the tangled mass of truth and falsehood in the charges has done much to vindicate Dryden's judgment in the following lines. It is remarkable that he could estimate the whole so accurately at a time when party spirit was running high and the available evidence was contradictory.

33, ll. 119–121, *Where gods were recommended by their taste:* With this attack on the doctrine of Transubstantiation compare Dryden's later references in *The Hind and the Panther*, Pt. I, ll. 72 ff., written after he had joined the Roman Catholic Church.

34, l. 170, *unfeather'd two-legg'd thing:* an application of the definition of a man, commonly attributed to Plato.

34, l. 175, *triple bond:* The Triple Alliance of 1668 between England, Sweden, and Holland against France. Shaftesbury had taken an influential part in breaking this alliance and in bringing on the war of 1672–74 against the Dutch.

34, l. 197, *immortal song:* On the assumption that these words refer to Dryden's *Absalom and Achitophel*, the author has been accused of arrogance. This interpretation is by no means necessary; the statement is that David would have made a song in honour of Achitophel instead of his lament for Absalom (II Sam. 13:33) or perhaps Psalm 3. The contemporary parallel is not complete, since Charles II was not a poet.

34, l. 227, *dregs of a democracy:* Few words have changed more in their connotations since the seventeenth century than "democracy"; in Dryden's time it meant about what we should describe as *mob rule.*

37, l. 529, *saints:* ironic use common at the time; compare note to l. 82.

37, l. 530, *enthusiastic:* Like "democracy" (*cf.* l. 227) this word has changed its ordinary significance since the seventeenth century; in Dryden's time it usually meant *fanatical.*

37, l. 539, *Born to be sav'd:* a contemptuous reference to the Calvinistic belief in predestination.

38, l. 595, *vare:* staff.

39, l. 676, *Agag's murder:* For the Biblical story of Samuel and Saul and Agag, see I Sam. 15.

40, ll. 753 ff., *Oh, foolish Israel:* It is significant that Dryden does not rest his case against rebellion on the High Tory doctrine of the divine right of kings. In the passage that follows, he shows himself equally against royal autocracy and popular anarchy: a typically English middle course is commended that respects ancient institutions and suspects innovation but applies the rule of reason and moderation to all things. The relation between this attitude of mind in political affairs and Dryden's literary criticism is interesting. See Paul Spencer Wood, "Native Elements in English Neo-Classicism," *Modern Philology*, vol. XXIV, No. 2, Nov., 1926.

42, ll. 936 ff., *royal throne:* David's speech, which follows, bears some resemblance to the speech of Charles II at the opening of the Parliament at Oxford, March 21, 1681.

MAC FLECKNOE

43, ll. 1, 2, *All human... obey:* The high-sounding platitude of these opening verses is, of course, intentional and in the mock-heroic vein.

43, l. 3, *Flecknoe:* Richard Flecknoe, said to have been an Irishman and a Roman Catholic priest, though he did not continue to officiate as such after the Restoration, had died in 1678. He seems to have had some contemporary notoriety as a bad poet, so that Dryden's placing him upon the throne of Dullness would have been understood in literary circles in much the same way that actors' "gags" at the expense of the neighbouring "joke town" delight our theatregoers. The title, *Mac Flecknoe*, the son of Flecknoe, derives part of its aptness from the Celtic reference.

44, l. 15, *Sh——:* Thomas Shadwell, 1642(?)–1692, was a minor poet and a comic dramatist. He avowed himself a disciple of Ben Jonson, whose use of *humours* he imitated. Though Shadwell is chiefly known at the present time because of Dryden's satiric attacks, he had no small contemporary reputation; his comedies are not without merit. He and Dryden had formerly been on good terms in spite of political differences. In 1682 Shadwell replied to the first part of *Absalom and Achitophel* and *The Medal*, in a scurrilous production entitled *The Medal of John Bayes: a Satire against Folly and Knavery*. Dryden struck back twice in rapid succession: in the present poem and, a month later, in his contributions to Nahum Tate's *Absalom and Achitophel*, Part II. In the latter he pilloried Elkanah Settle, "the City Poet" as Doeg, and Shadwell as Og. He describes them as

Two fools that crutch their feeble sense on verse,
Who, by my Muse, to all succeeding times
Shall live, in spite of their own dogg'rel rhymes.

The character of Og as here presented is one of the best things that Dryden ever did in the broader style of personal satire.

Now stop your noses, readers, all and some,
For here's a tun of midnight work to come,
Og, from a treason-tavern rolling home.
Round as a globe, and liquor'd ev'ry chink,
Goodly and great he sails behind his link.
With all this bulk there's nothing lost in Og,
For ev'ry inch that is not fool is rogue:
A monstrous mass of foul corrupted matter,
As all the devils had spew'd to make the batter.
When wine has given him courage to blaspheme,
He curses God, but God before curs'd him;
And if man could have reason, none has more,
That made his paunch so rich, and him so poor.
With wealth he was not trusted, for Heav'n knew
What 'twas of old to pamper up a Jew;
To what would he on quail and pheasant swell,
That ev'n on tripe and carrion could rebel?
But though Heav'n made him poor, (with rev'rence speaking,)
He never was a poet of God's making;
The midwife laid her hand on his thick skull,
With this prophetic blessing: *Be thou dull!*
Drink, swear, and roar, forbear no lewd delight
Fit for thy bulk, do anything but write.
Thou art of lasting make, like thoughtless men,
A strong nativity — but for the pen;
Eat opium, mingle arsenic in thy drink,
Still thou mayst live, avoiding pen and ink.
I see, I see, 'tis counsel given in vain,
For treason botch'd in rhyme will be thy bane;
Rhyme is the rock on which thou art to wreck,
'Tis fatal to thy fame and to thy neck:
Why should thy metre good King David blast?
A psalm of his will surely be thy last.
Dar'st thou presume in verse to meet thy foes,
Thou whom the penny pamphlet foil'd in prose?
Doeg, whom God for mankind's mirth has made,

O'ertops thy talent in thy very trade;
Doeg to thee, thy paintings are so coarse,
A poet is, though he's the poets' horse.
A double noose thou on thy neck dost pull,
For writing treason, and for writing dull;
To die for faction is a common evil,
But to be hang'd for nonsense is the devil.
Hadst thou the glories of thy king express'd,
Thy praises had been satire at the best;
But thou in clumsy verse, unlick'd, unpointed,
Hast shamefully defied the Lord's anointed:
I will not rake the dunghill of thy crimes,
For who would read thy life that reads thy rhymes?
But of King David's foes, be this the doom,
May all be like the young man Absalom;
And for my foes may this their blessing be,
To talk like Doeg, and to write like thee.

He lived to enjoy revenge, however, for when after the Revolution of 1688 Dryden lost the laureateship, Shadwell was presented as a Whig candidate and was given the position.

44, l. 29, *Heywood and Shirley:* Thomas Heywood (d. about 1650) and James Shirley (1596–1666) were two prolific dramatists of the earlier part of the century. Dryden probably had little acquaintance with their work, which has been much more highly appraised by nineteenth-century critics, but cited them merely as two old dramatic writers whose numerous works were not highly esteemed.

44, l. 33, *Norwich drugget:* a coarse cloth such as might be worn by impecunious poets.

44, l. 36, *King John of Portugal:* Flecknoe seems to have made much of the patronage of this monarch, by whom he was said to have been received when he visited Portugal.

44, l. 42, *Epsom blankets:* a double reference to Shadwell's comedy, *Epsom Wells* (1672) and to an episode in *The Virtuoso* (1676) in which one of the characters is tossed in a blanket.

44, l. 43, *the new Arion:* It has been surmised that Shadwell may have taken part in some pageant in which the classical story of Arion and the dolphins was either represented or called to mind. He refers to his own musical ability in the preface to his opera, *Psyche* (1675).

44, l. 53, *St. André's feet:* Scott identifies St. André as an eminent dancing master of the period.

44, l. 65, *fair Augusta:* a reference to the fears excited in London by the "Popish Plot."

44, l. 74, *a nursery:* A theatre for the training of boys and girls for the stage was so called.

44, l. 78, *little Maximins:* a reference to the hero of Dryden's own early heroic play, *Tyrannic Love*, whose ranting style he had now got away from.

44, l. 81, *gentle Simkin:* a well-known character in the farces and drolls which were performed for the amusement of the populace by strolling players.

44, l. 83, *clinches:* This word, sometimes written *clenches*, was the common seventeenth-century name for those puns or plays on words, which were objected to as false wit typical of the former age. Dryden in *Defence of the Epilogue to the Second Part of "The Conquest of Granada"* (1672) says that Ben Jonson "was not free from the lowest and most grovelling kind of wit, which we call clenches." *Cf. Spectator* No. 61.

44, l. 91, *Misers:* The reference is to Shadwell's comedy, *The Miser* (1672), adapted from Molière. In the following line there is a similar reference to *The Humorists* (1671).

44, l. 93, *Raymond... Bruce:* characters, respectively, in two of Shadwell's plays: *The Humorists* and *The Virtuoso* (1676).

44, l. 102, *Ogleby:* John Ogleby, or Ogilby (1600–1676), was a Scottish translator and epic poet, who was more than once referred to by Dryden as a horrible example.

44, l. 105, *Herringman:* a well-known London bookseller, who had formerly published for Dryden as well as for Shadwell. In 1678 or 1679 Dryden had broken with Herringman and had gone to Jacob Tonson, a young publisher, who was later to become famous in English literary history.

44, l. 107, *High on a throne:* evidently a parody of Milton's description of the throne of Satan from the opening of *Paradise Lost*, Bk. II.

44, l. 108, *our young Ascanius:* In the same way that Ascanius, the son of Æneas, is represented in the *Æneid* as the hope of his people, Shadwell is here referred to as the hope of the Empire of Dullness.

45, l. 122, *Love's Kingdom:* Flecknoe's only acted play, described as a "pastoral tragi-comedy."

45, ll. 151, 152, *gentle George:* Sir George Etherege (1635?–1691) was a contemporary wit and dramatist for whose comedies Dryden elsewhere expressed admiration. The names which follow are those of characters from Etherege's plays.

45, l. 163, *S—dl—y:* Sir Charles Sedley (1639?–1701). See note on *Lisideius*, page 64, lines 8, 9. The inference is that Sedley, who had written a prologue for Shadwell's comedy, *Epsom Wells*, had aided further in its composition.

45, l. 168, *Sir Formal's oratory:* Sir Formal Trifle in Shadwell's *The Virtuoso* is adequately described by his name.

45, l. 179, *Prince Nicander's vein:* The allusion is to a character in Shadwell's *Psyche.*

45, l. 181, *sold he bargains:* "To sell a bargain" is an expression now obsolete, meaning to entrap one into asking an innocent question to which a coarse or indelicate answer, such as is illustrated in the context, is unexpectedly given. Ben Jonson, whom Shadwell professed to follow, never condescended to the use of such farcical material.

45, ll. 189–192, *This is that boasted bias...:* These four lines are a direct parody of the following passage in the epilogue to Shadwell's *The Humorists:*

> A humour is the bias of the mind,
> By which with violence 'tis one way inclin'd:
> It makes our actions lean on one side still,
> And in all changes that way bends the will.

Shadwell had boasted in the Epistle Dedicatory to *The Virtuoso* of his success in embodying *humours* in his plays.

45, ll. 203–208, *Thy genius calls thee not...:* The meaning of this passage is that Shadwell is not suited by nature to produce classical satire but rather to follow the discredited ways of the "metaphysical" poets of the preceding generation. *Cf. An Essay of Dramatic Poesy* and Addison's contrast between true and false wit in the *Spectator,* No. 58. For illustration of the *wings* and *altars* of line 207, see George Herbert's two poems, *An Altar* and *Easter Wings,* in which the typographical appearance of long and short lines on the page actually imitates the shape of the objects mentioned. "Iambics" here means satire; Greek satire was often so denominated from its characteristic metrical form.

46, l. 212, *Bruce and Longvil:* two characters in Shadwell's *The Virtuoso* (*cf.* note to line 93) who play a similar trick upon Sir Formal Trifle.

46, ll. 214–217, *Sinking he left...:* The allusion is to the Biblical story of the translation of Elijah, II Kings 2:9–15. Here Elisha's possession of his predecessor's mantle is the visible symbol that a double portion of the older prophet's spirit has been transmitted to the younger.

THE HIND AND THE PANTHER

47, l. 1, *A milk-white Hind:* the Roman Catholic Church.

47, l. 14, *Caledonian wood:* Caledonian here seems to apply not only to Scotland but to all of Great Britain. The term, wood, is used in conformity with the beast allegory. The reference is to those Roman Catholics, especially those priests, who had suffered martyrdom for their faith since the Reformation, and perhaps with special thought of some of the recent victims of the "Popish Plot."

47, l. 35, *bloody Bear:* As the following word, *Independent,* indicates, the bear represents the Independents, or Congregationalists, who rejected all Episcopal or Presbyterian church government and made the individual congregation independent. The New England Puritans were mostly Independents.

47, l. 37, *Quaking Hare:* the Society of Friends, commonly called Quakers.

47, l. 39, *buffoon Ape:* the Freethinkers, who, having no scruples about conformity, were willing to acquiesce in the outward form of any denomination.

47, l. 41, *Lion:* James II, King of England. The allegory here, though not entirely consistent, is easily intelligible, since the lion is commonly known as the king of beasts and the lion is also familiar on the British royal arms.

47, l. 43, *Baptist Boar:* The Anabaptists, as they were originally called, were a sect whose early history in Germany had been associated with a peasant revolt which had led to excesses here referred to. They originally held the doctrine that the true believer becomes entirely sinless in this life. Lines 50–52 suggest that some of the English Independents were really Anabaptists.

47, l. 53, *False Reynard:* the Unitarians, who denied the divinity of Jesus. Dryden connects their teaching with the Arian heresy of the fourth century, which was condemned by the Council of Nicæa in 325 after being vigorously denounced by Bishop Athanasius. Lælius and Faustus Socinus, Italian reformers of the sixteenth century, founded the Socinian sect, which also denied the doctrine of the Trinity.

48, l. 79, *fright my faith...:* The following passage argues the point, much discussed between Anglican and Roman theologians, that the doctrine of the Trinity (taught by the Anglican Church) is fully as repugnant to human reason as the doctrine of Transubstantiation (rejected by the Anglican Church). The last-named doctrine teaches that the "accidents" of the elements remain unaltered after consecration at Mass but the substance is changed. Transubstantiation is the orthodox Roman Catholic explanation of the means by which the Bread and Wine become the Body and Blood of Christ. The English Church in rejecting this explanation does not necessarily reject the doctrine of the Real Presence; see ll. 417 ff.

48, l. 93, *Can they who say...:* See St. Luke 24:36–43 and St. John 20:19. The argument is that just as Christ's physical body could pass through the closed doors of the room, thus transcending the ordinary laws of matter, so it can in like manner transcend these laws by penetrating the consecrated Host, where the senses perceive only bread. Ll. 102, 103 reply to the statement of the rubric at the end of the Communion service in the English Book of Common Prayer: "... and the natural Body and Blood of our Saviour Christ are in Heaven, and not here; it being against the truth of Christ's natural Body to be at one time in more places than one."

48, l. 128, *bilanders:* small Dutch sailing vessels used chiefly for canal traffic; here, evidently referring to coasting vessels.

48, l. 152, *Polonian:* The Socinians had been especially active in Poland.

48, l. 153, *Wolf:* the Presbyterians.

49, l. 163, *ragged tail:* The Presbyterian clergy commonly wore the black Geneva gown.

49, l. 165, *predestinating ears:* The projecting ears of the "Roundheads" were a common subject of jest when fashionable gentlemen wore long hair or wigs. The ears of the Presbyterian clergy were made even more prominent by the contrast with their skull caps. "Predestinating," of course, refers to the Calvinistic doctrine of predestination. Dryden perhaps suggests that these were foreordained to be clipped on the scaffold.

49, l. 168, *rul'd a while:* During the Civil War Presbyterianism had for a time been set up as the national religion in England. Though later, under Cromwell, it was no longer "captain," it yet was a "companion of the spoil" of the Anglican Church, which was not restored until Charles II came to power in 1660.

49, l. 170, *many a year:* probably, as Christie pointed out, a reference to King Edgar's attempt in the tenth century to exterminate beasts of prey in his dominions by requiring a yearly tribute of three hundred wolves from his Welsh vassals. Dryden is here referring to actual wolves and not to the Presbyterians, who figure as wolves in his beast-fable; but he may well have had in mind the fact that it was in Scotland rather than in Wales (Cambria) that the Presbyterian Church was strong.

49, l. 172, *last of all the litter:* Dryden suggests that there may have been a connection between the Wycliffite heresy in England and the beginnings of the Calvinistic reformation in Switzerland, but points out that there was little in common between the two movements except that both showed "innate antipathy to kings," a common charge against all types of dissenters in England at this time.

49, l. 178, *Helvetian kind...:* British Presbyterianism had developed from the teaching of the Swiss reformers, Zuinglius (Ulric Zwingli, 1484–1531) and John Calvin (1509–1564).

49, l. 182, *whelp'd long since:* As Dryden's marginal note indicates, in ll. 182–189 he has followed suggestions from the preface to Peter Heylyn's *Aërius Redivivus; or, The History of the Presbyterians* (1670) which discusses the claim that the Jewish Sanhedrim, a body that set itself up even against princes, was the original of the presbyterial assembly. Heylin rejects such claims and suggests that the original Presbyterians were Korah, Dathan, and Abiram, who led a rebellion against Moses and Aaron and were punished by the Lord for so doing. See Numbers 16:1–35.

49, l. 189, *class:* An assembly of presbyters or elders was called a *classis* or *class.*

49, l. 202, *mitred crown:* Geneva before the Reformation had been ruled in temporal as well as in ecclesiastic matters by a bishop.

49, l. 209, *fruitful Tweed:* Scotland. The adjective seems to be used in a double sense; ironically as applied to the agricultural fertility of the country, and literally as applied to its productiveness of heresy and treason.

49, l. 211, *Drawn to the dregs of a democracy:* See note to *Absalom and Achitophel,* I, 227. While Dryden, here and elsewhere, makes capital of the unpopular political opinions of some dissenters and implies that opposition to Church and King go hand in hand, we must not forget that politics and religion were inextricably tangled in the seventeenth century and that few people thought of keeping them apart. Even in twentieth-century America, where the two are generally supposed to be separate, such a political campaign as that of 1928 shows that the separation is more theoretical than practical.

49, l. 234, *commonweal:* a commonwealth or democracy.

49, l. 235, *Celtic woods:* Ll. 235–290 decrying religious persecution may have been an interpolation shortly before the poem was published. As Scott pointed out, there is inconsistency between these lines which he applied to the revocation of the Edict of Nantes by Louis XIV in 1685, and the lines which immediately follow: "And just so our author, after blaming the persecution of the Huguenots, congratulates Italy and Spain upon possessing such just and excellent laws, as the rules of the inquisitorial church courts." Dryden attempts to draw a distinction between "self-preserving laws, severe in show," which "guard their fences from th' invading foe," and the treatment of dissenters who have a "native claim of just inheritance," but the two points of view have not been entirely reconciled. Dryden tells us in his prefatory address "To the Reader" that *The Hind and the Panther* "was written during the last winter and the beginning of this spring, tho' with long interruptions of ill health and other hindrances." The king's decree of limited toleration in Scotland appeared in February, 1687; the poem was licenced for publication on April 11, of the same year. This passage, appearing in connection with the character of the Wolf, may well have been inspired by this change in the royal policy. See the Introduction to *The*

Hind and the Panther for references to the Declaration of Indulgence in England, which appeared just one week before the poem was licenced.

50, l. 284, *blessed Pan:* The allegorical representation of Christ as Pan, the god of the shepherds, was not uncommon in English poetry, at least from the time of Spenser.

50, l. 313, *conventicles:* Dryden put the primary accent in this word sometimes on the first syllable and sometimes on the third. Conventicles were illegal religious meetings of dissenters, often held in the fields.

50, l. 327, *The Panther:* the Church of England.

50, l. 347, *Her house not ancient:* The Church of England claims apostolic foundation, asserting that the Reformation in no wise broke the continuity of its organization or the validity of its orders but that it merely swept away an accumulation of errors and abuses and restored primitive Catholic purity. The Roman Catholics deny these claims and assert that it was founded by Henry VIII.

50, l. 351, *A Lion, old:* Henry VIII. Saintsbury's note is too good to omit: "He was, at most, six-and-thirty, which may be old — for lions."

51, l. 361, *fruit proclaims the plant:* The following references are to the dissolution of the monasteries and the reforms in church discipline, including permission for the clergy to marry.

51, l. 371, *hatter'd out:* worn out.

51, l. 393, *mistress of a monarch's bed:* "The King being owned the head of the Church of England, contrary to the discipline of the other Reformed Churches." Scott.

51, l. 399, *phylacteries:* The word is here accented on the third syllable. Phylacteries are strips of parchment inscribed with words of Scripture and worn by the Jews attached to their foreheads and arms. The meaning is that the Church of England made formal avowal of respect for Catholic tradition (as Dryden had pointed out at length in *Religio Laici*) but had also been corrupted by Calvinistic doctrines.

51, l. 402, *a creature of a double kind:* "Referring to the Minotaur, half man and half bull, confined in the Cretan labyrinth." Noyes.

51, l. 417, *Her novices are taught:* See the *Catechism* of the Church of England, where "the outward part or sign of the Lord's Supper" is declared to be "Bread and Wine," and "the inward part, or thing signified" is "The Body and Blood of Christ."

52, l. 449, *Isgrim's:* In the mediæval beast-epic, *Reynard the Fox,* the wolf bears the name Isgrim. Here and elsewhere Dryden charges that the English Church is too friendly to the Presbyterian.

52, l. 516, *Levées* and *couchées:* morning and evening receptions for dependents and followers such as were held by great nobles. The allusion is to the growth of dissent in England, which Dryden obviously exaggerates.

52, l. 537, *The ten-horn'd monster*...: See Rev. 17. Protestants often used the symbolism of the Book of Revelations to describe the Roman Catholic Church.

53, l. 552, *the Hind had seen him first:* "There was a classical superstition, that, if a wolf saw a man before he saw the wolf, the person lost his voice.... Dryden has adopted, in the text, the converse of this superstitious belief." Scott.

A SONG FOR ST. CECILIA'S DAY

53, l. 8, *cold, and hot, and moist, and dry:* These are the four elements of mediæval physics, of which all things are compounded.

53, l. 17, *Jubal:* Gen. 4:21.

53, l. 25, *Trumpet's loud clangour:* It is scarcely necessary to call attention to the way in which the poet imitates the sounds of the various instruments that he treats.

54, l. 48, *Orpheus:* a legendary Thracian musician, inventor of the lyre. His skill in music is said to have been so great that not only animals but trees and rocks followed him as he played.

54, l. 51, *Cecilia:* St. Cecilia's invention of the organ is a late but popular addition to the legend of a Roman virgin, said to have been martyred in 176.

54, l. 63, *Music shall untune the sky:* When the trumpet of the last judgment shall sound and the whole world shall be destroyed, the music of the spheres will come to an end.

ALEXANDER'S FEAST

54, l. 15, *None but the brave deserves the fair:* Note that this line is usually misquoted.

54, l. 25, *The song began from Jove:* Alexander had been informed by an oracle that his father was not King Philip of Macedon but Jupiter himself. The name of Alexander's mother was Olympias, not Olympia, as Dryden writes it (l. 30).

56, l. 163, *The sweet enthusiast:* In the seventeenth century *enthusiast* is rarely used with a favourable connotation. See *NED.*

TO THE PIOUS MEMORY OF THE ACCOMPLISHED YOUNG LADY, MRS. ANNE KILLIGREW

57, l. 43, *in trine:* an astrological term denoting a special aspect of the stars interpreted as favourable. Though astrology was generally discredited in the latter part of the seventeenth century, its language still survived in poetry, as, indeed, it still does occasionally. Dryden is said to have had a belief in astrology, which was rare among educated men of his time.

57, l. 50, *swarm of bees:* Bees are said to have clustered about the lips of Plato when he was a small child.

57, l. 57, *Profan'd thy heav'nly gift of poesy:* Section IV of this poem has often been quoted as proof that Dryden in his secret heart was ashamed of the part that he took in the corruptions of the Restoration stage. Ashamed he undoubtedly was, as he freely confessed on more than one occasion. (See notes on the Preface to *Fables.*) But it is easy to make too much of this passage unless one considers its setting. He is here making a sharp contrast between the purity of the virgin poetess and the debasement of the "heav'nly gift of poesy." In similar circumstances an honest man might say the same about any age, including our own.

57, l. 71, *Art she had none:* This phrase, reminiscent of seventeenth- and eighteenth-century criticism of Shakespeare, is characteristic of an age that respected the rules but did not follow them servilely. For the relation of this idea to that of original genius see notes on the *Spectator*, No. 160, and on Young's *Conjectures on Original Composition.*

57, l. 82, *Epictetus:* As Noyes points out, Dryden has here apparently confused Epictetus with Diogenes, who searched with a lantern in daylight for an honest man.

57, l. 115, *perspectives:* This word is here accented on the first syllable.

58, l. 147, *To such immod'rate growth:* Noyes points out that ll. 147, 148 contain a reference to the words of Martial (VI, 29), *Immodicis brevis est ætas, et rara senectus* ("For extraordinary beings life is short and old age rare") quoted on the title-page of the edition of Anne Killigrew's *Poems* published in 1685. Dryden's poem was first published in this volume.

58, l. 162, *But thus Orinda died:* Katherine Phillips (1631–1684) was known as "Orinda"; like Anne Killigrew she died of the smallpox.

58, l. 180, *the Valley of Jehosaphat:* The name is taken from Joel 3:2 (where it is spelled Jehoshaphat), but the concept is that of the valley of dry bones, Ezekiel 37:1–17.

TO MY HONOURED FRIEND, DR. CHARLETON

59, l. 1, *The longest tyranny:* To one who thinks of the neo-classical as a period of blind devotion to authority these lines are incomprehensible except as another instance of Dryden's inconsistency. Yet if literature is regarded as an expression of the best thought of its age, the generation which witnessed the extraordinary outburst of interest in experimental science that found expression in the Royal Society (established 1660) must have been sceptical of authoritative pronouncements incapable of rational proof. At the moment when the leadership of Aristotle (the Stagirite) as a scientific teacher was being overthrown because it was clearly at variance with the proved facts of the physical world, the leadership of Aristotle as a literary critic was being established because it seemed in accord with the facts of literature and human experience.

59, l. 23, *Bacon:* Sir Francis Bacon (1561–1626), author of *Novum Organum* and leading exponent of the new experimental science.

59, l. 25, *Gilbert:* William Gilbert (1540–1603), author of a treatise on the magnet, important in the history of physics.

59, l. 27, *Boyle:* Robert Boyle (1627–1691), distinguished Irish chemist and physicist, one of the founders of the Royal Society, is most often remembered today as the promulgator of Boyle's law. "His great brother," Roger Boyle, Earl of Orrery (1621–1679), to whom about this time Dryden dedicated *The Rival Ladies*, was also interested in the new science.

59, l. 31, *Harvey's name:* William Harvey (1578–1657), discoverer of the circulation of the blood.

59, l. 32, *Ent:* Sir George Ent (1604–1689), physician, friend of Harvey, fellow of the Royal Society.

59, l. 47, *Stonehenge:* Dr. Charleton's conclusions have not been accepted by more recent archæologists.

59, l. 54, *Wor'ster's fatal field:* Charles II, after the defeat of his army at Worcester, Sept. 3, 1651, had a series of extraordinary adventures before he escaped from England.

TO MR. CONGREVE

60, l. 7, *Janus:* "The god Janus was fabled to have reigned in Italy, having his city near the hill Janiculum. Here he hospitably received Saturn who was fleeing from his son Jupiter, and from him he learned husbandry and other arts. Dryden here assigns to him a part that belongs rather to Saturn himself." Noyes.

60, l. 14, *The second temple was not like the first:* The temple built in Jerusalem after the return of the Jews from the Babylonian captivity was inferior to the temple of Solomon, which had been destroyed.

60, l. 15, *Vitruvius:* a famous Roman writer on architecture of the first century, B.C.

60, ll. 29, 30, *Etherege his courtship...:* Courtship here means courtliness. Sir George Etherege (1635?–1691), author of *The Man of Mode* and other well-known comedies, Thomas Southerne (1660–1746), author of *The Fatal Marriage* and other plays, and William Wycherley (1640?–1716), author of *The Plain Dealer* and three other comedies, were among the best known dramatists of the time. Wycherley was called "manly" because through Manly, the principal character in *The Plain Dealer*, the author was supposed to have expressed his own satirical views.

60, l. 35, *Fabius:* The allusion is to the jealousy of the old warrior, Fabius, toward Scipio, when the latter was elected consul, though not yet of legal age, and entrusted with the war against Hannibal. As Noyes points out, Dryden suggests that Fabius might have taken joy in the youthful leader had the latter shown the sweetness of Congreve's manners. The parallel between the old general and the young general, and the old poet and the young one is obvious.

60, l. 39, *old Romano bow'd to Raphael's fame:* Giulio Romano was some eleven years younger than Raphael and was his pupil.

60, l. 41, *your brows my laurel:* After the Revolution of 1688 Dryden refused to take the oaths of allegiance to William and Mary; consequently he lost his positions of Poet Laureate and Historiographer Royal. To the first was appointed Dryden's old enemy, Thomas Shadwell; after his death in 1692 he was succeeded in the laureateship by Nahum Tate who had collaborated with Dryden in the second part of *Absalom and Achitophel* and was longest remembered as one of the co-authors of Tate and Brady's metrical version of the Psalms, 1696. Scott understood by "Tom the Second" Thomas Rymer, the critic, who had been given Dryden's post as Historiographer Royal and to whom Dryden had referred in uncomplimentary terms in the dedication to *Examen Poeticum*. But the reference here is clearly to Dryden's successors in the Laureateship, and though Tate's first name was not Thomas, he may be referred to as a Tom or Tom-fool. Tate had been one of Dryden's assistants in the *Translations from Juvenal and Persius* in 1692, only two years before the publication of this epistle.

60, l. 46, *greater Edward:* Edward II was deposed by Parliament and succeeded by his son, Edward III, a greater king than his father.

60, l. 49, *my patron's part:* As Scott pointed out, the Earl of Dorset, who in his official capacity had been compelled to bestow Dryden's offices upon others, had none the less remained his friend. To Dorset the poet had the year before written *A Discourse concerning the Original and Progress of Satire*, in dedicating to him the volume of translations from Juvenal and Persius made by Dryden and a number of assistants.

60, l. 60, *genius must be born:* Not even the most extreme supporters of the school of rules asserted that good poetry could be made by the application of the rules alone, though they certainly minimized the importance of poetic aptitude. In France Boileau was emphasizing the importance of taste and the Longinian quality of inspiration. The opening lines of his *Art of Poetry* in the Dryden-Soame translation, or rather adaptation, 1683, lay stress upon this point as the first essential of the art:

> Rash author, 'tis a vain presumptuous crime
> To undertake the sacred art of rhyme,
> If at thy birth the stars that rul'd thy sense
> Shone not with a poetic influence;
> In thy strait genius thou wilt still be bound,
> Find Phœbus deaf, and Pegasus unsound.

60, l. 72, *Be kind to my remains:* Congreve edited an edition of Dryden's plays in 1717.

EPILOGUE TO "THE WILD GALLANT," REVIVED

61, Title, *Revived:* probably in 1667, four years after the original production.

61, l. 5, *Humour is that which every day we meet:* The following lines on the "humours" are important in their bearing upon the satiric element in Restoration comedy.

61, l. 17, *prizes:* contests, or as we now say, prize fights.

61, l. 38, *writ of ease:* certificate of discharge from employment.

61, l. 44, *vests:* About a year before this time King Charles II had attempted to introduce a new and "graver" style of dress for men. See note on Evelyn, *Diary*, Oct. 18, 1666.

EPILOGUE TO THE SECOND PART OF "THE CONQUEST OF GRANADA"

62, l. 6, *Cobb's tankard...: Otter's horse:* Cobb is a character in Jonson's *Every Man in his Humour*, and Otter is a character in the same author's *The Silent Woman*. Both are examples of somewhat farcical "humour."

PROLOGUE TO "AURENG-ZEBE"

63, l. 35, *put a playhouse down:* The comparison is between the two theatres engaged in expensive rivalry and Louis XIV at war with William of Orange and his allies. Just as the English nation was at this time neutral in the war, so the audience is represented as "unconcerned" at the warfare between the theatres.

AN ESSAY OF DRAMATIC POESY

64, ll. 13, 14, *second part:* The promised second part of this *Essay* was never written, though Dryden treated the subjects here indicated in many later works: see especially the *Dedication of the Æneis,* 1697, for a discussion of epic poetry.

64, l. 20, *memorable day:* June 3, 1665, when the English fleet under the command of the Duke of York, afterwards King James II, defeated the Dutch fleet near the English coast.

64, ll. 8, 9, *Eugenius, Crites, Lisideius, and Neander:* These characters represent not only four different points of view about the drama but four real people as well. Eugenius, as the name implies, was a nobleman, Charles Sackville, Lord Buckhurst, afterwards Earl of Middlesex and Dorset, Dryden's lifelong patron to whom this work was dedicated. He was actually at this time serving as a volunteer with the English fleet. Crites was Sir Robert Howard, Dryden's brother-in-law, a dramatist of some reputation. The preface to his *Four New Plays,* 1665, was the immediate occasion of the debate about rhyme in the latter part of the present work. Lisideius was Sir Charles Sedley (or Sidley, the Latin form of whose name, Sidleius, is made into an anagram), a courtier and an amateur man of letters, widely known at the time. Neander was Dryden himself.

64, l. 18, *shoot the bridge:* Old London bridge with its massive arches of stonework dammed the tidal waters of the Thames to such an extent that when the tide was receding, the river rushed through so furiously that "shooting the bridge" was difficult and dangerous.

65, l. 50, *Quem in concione... scriberet* (*Pro Archia,* X, 25): "When in the assembly we saw that a bad poet from the crowd presented him with a booklet, a complimentary poem in rough elegiacs, he immediately ordered that a reward from the goods he was now selling should be given to that one on condition that he should never afterwards write."

65, l. 6, *two poets:* The first of these bad poets has generally been identified as Robert Wild, the author of *Iter Boreale,* a poem in praise of General Monk; and the second has been conjectured to be Richard Flecknoe, the succession to whose throne of dullness is celebrated in *Mac Flecknoe.* They represent two aspects of bad poetry: the fantastic and the flat.

65, l. 12, *clenches upon words:* plays upon words, or puns. This species of false wit had flourished during the preceding generation but was now regarded as old-fashioned and "clownish." See *Spectator* Nos. 58–63.

65, l. 14, *catachresis or Clevelandism:* the strained use of a word, especially in a mixed metaphor. The most common type of Clevelandism was the far-fetched comparison to which Dr. Johnson later gave the name, metaphysical conceit. John Cleveland (1613–1658), in spite of the fact that he had been a Cavalier, was in bad repute as a poet because of the artificiality of his work.

65, l. 17, *un mauvais bouffon:* "A malicious buffoon." The following lines explain the meaning. *Cf. Mac Flecknoe,* ll. 200–203.

65, l. 37, *a very Leveller in poetry:* The Levellers were holders of communistic ideas during the period of the Civil War. Cromwell suppressed them.

65, l. 47, *Pauper videri Cinna...pauper* (Martial, *Epigr.* VIII, 19): "Cinna pretends to be poor, — and he is poor."

66, l. 15, *the very Withers of the City:* George Wither (Dryden miswrites the name), who died in 1667, the year preceding the publication of this *Essay,* was another poet of the old-fashioned type. The suggestion that he was, or had been, popular in the City, i.e., London, probably refers to the religious poetry that he wrote in his last years. Wither remained generally forgotten until he was rediscovered in the nineteenth century by Charles Lamb and others.

66, l. 31, *Qui Bavium non odit:* the beginning of a familiar quotation from Virgil's third *Eclogue,* l. 90. Dryden translates as follows:

> "Who hates not living Bavius, let him be,
> Dead Mævius, damn'd to love thy works and thee."

66, l. 36, *Nam quos contemnimus... contemnimus:* "For we also despise the praises of those persons whom we despise."

66, l. 7, *Indignor quidquam reprehendi... nuper* (*Epist.* II, 1, 76): "I resent anything's being condemned merely because it is new and not because it is judged to be crudely or coarsely written."

66, l. 10, *Si meliora dies... annus* (*Ib.* 34): "If time improves poems, as it does wines, I wish to know how many years give value to literature."

67, l. 1, *All of them... Eugenius his opinion:* To the student this unanimity of opinion will probably be surprising, for the common opinion today is that the sweetness of English verse had been better understood by the Elizabethans and that poetry had deteriorated since their time. Yet it may be that Dryden is more nearly right than at first appears. Notice carefully the respects in which verse is said to have been improved. Compare the Epilogue to the Second Part of *The Conquest of Granada.*

67, l. 41, *a genere et fine:* a term in logic meaning from genus and end. The objection, which Lisideius has already forestalled, is that his definition of a play is merely a description because it does not distinguish the species as well as the genus and end or purpose: it is applicable to a narrative poem, for example, as well as to a play.

67, l. 19, *those credulous and doting ages: Cf.* the notes to Dryden's *Epistle to Dr. Charleton.*

68, l. 28, *περὶ τῆς Ποιητικῆς:* The *Poetics.*

70, l. 44, *Audita visis libentius... credimus* (*Hist. Rom.* II, 92): "What is heard we praise more willingly than what is seen, and we follow the present with envy, the past with admiration; and we believe ourselves harmed by the former but edified by the latter."

70, l. 41, *Neu brevior quinto... actu* (*A. P.*, 189): "To five acts lengthened be the piece, not more." Howes.

71, l. 30, *chapon bouillé:* literally, "Boiled capon"; probably refers here to a piece of bread boiled in the soup.

71, l. 43, *Juno Lucina, fer opem:* a cry for help to Juno in her capacity as the goddess who assisted in childbirth.

71, l. 55, *C'est bien employer... court:* "This is using a short time to advantage."

72, l. 30, *inartificial:* without reference to the principles of art.

72, l. 42, *Tandem ego... triduum* (II, 1, 18): "Should I not then do without her, if need be, three whole days?"

72, l. 46, *Hui! universum triduum:* "Oh! three entire days." *Universum* as a noun means "the whole world, the universe"; thus the reply neatly suggests that three days may seem to be an eternity.

73, l. 1, *Sed proavi nostri... stolide* (*A. P.*, 270): Howes paraphrases as follows:

"Our forefathers, good-natured, easy folks,
Extolled the numbers and enjoyed the jokes
Of Plautus, prompt both these and those to hear
With tolerant — not to say with tasteless — ear;"

73, l. 8, *Multa renascentur... loquendi* (*Ib.* 70):

"Full many a word, now lost, again shall rise,
And many a word shall droop which now we prize,
As shifting fashion stamps the doom of each,
Sole umpire, arbitress, and guide of speech."

73, l. 17, *Mistaque ridenti... acantho* (*Ecl.* IV, 20): "[The earth] shall send forth colocasiums mingled with the smiling acanthus."

73, l. 22, *mirantur et undæ... carinas:* The quotation is from the eighth (not the seventh) book of the *Æneid*, ll. 91 ff., which Dryden renders thus:

"The woods and waters wonder at the gleam
Of shields, and painted ships that stem the stream."

73, l. 28, *quem, si verbo... cœli* (*Met.* I, 175): Dryden renders somewhat freely as follows:

"This place, as far as earth with heav'n may vie,
I dare to call the Louvre of the sky."

73, l. 32, *et longas visent Capitolia pompas* (*Ib.* 561): Dryden paraphrases this passage as follows:

"Thou shalt returning Cæsar's triumph grace,
When pomps shall in a long procession pass;"

73, l. 1, *Si sic omnia dixisset* (Juv. *Sat.* X, 123): "If he had always spoken thus!"

73, l. 28, *Omne genus scripti... vincit* (*Trist.* II, 381): "Tragedy surpasses in dignity every other kind of writing."

74, l. 4, *anima mea, vita mea* (Juv. *Sat.* VI, 195): "My soul, my life." The Greek repeats the same idea.

74, l. 36, *Sum pius Æneas... notus* (*Æneid*, I, 378, with the omission of some words): "I am pious Æneas famed above the skies."

74, l. 2, *quos Libitina sacravit* (Hor. *Epist.* II, 1, 49): "Whom death has sanctified."

74, l. 35, *we have been so long together bad Englishmen:* The reference is to the rebellion against the king in the recent Civil War.

75, l. 33, *Montagues and Capulets:* the two rival families in *Romeo and Juliet.*

75, l. 50, *Atque ursum... poscunt* (quoted inaccurately from Hor. *Epist.* II, 1, 185): "And they demand the bear and the boxers in the midst of the poems." The Red Bull had once been used for plays, but at this time was used for prize fights.

75, l. 14. *Ex noto fictum carmen sequar* (*A. P.*, 240): Howes translates:

"Some well-known legend should support my theme."

75, l. 23, *Atque ita mentitur... imum* (*Ib.* 151):

"And so adroitly mingles false with true,
So with his fair illusions cheats the view,
That all the parts — beginning, middle, end —
In one harmonious compound sweetly blend."

75, l. 55, *perspective:* a perspective-glass or telescope.

76, l 4, *Quodcunque ostendis mihi... odi* (Hor. *A. P.*, 188): "Whatever you thus show me I distrust and hate."

76, l. 40, *protatic persons:* characters appearing only in the introduction of a play, or the Protasis.

77, l. 43, *Segnius irritant animos... fidelibus:* This quotation and the two which follow it comprise, with brief omissions, ll. 180–187 of Horace, *Art of Poetry*. Howes's translation of the entire passage is as follows:

"Those which a tale shall through the ear impart
With fainter characters impress the heart
Than those which, subject to the eye's broad gaze,
The pleased spectator to himself conveys.
Yet drag not on the stage each horrid scene,
Nor shock the sight with what should pass within
This let description's milder medium show,
And leave to eloquence her tale of woe.
Let not the cruel Colchian mother slay
Her smiling infants in the face of day;
Nor Atreus crown the board with impious food,
And feast a brother with congenial blood:
Nor Procne's form the rising plumage take;
Nor Cadmus sink into a slimy snake."

78, l. 48, *Sed ut primo... conquirimus* (Velleius Paterculus I, 17): "But just as at first we burn to emulate those whom we account pre-eminent, so when we despair of being able either to surpass or to equal them, our zeal flags with our expectation: what it is not able to overtake, naturally it desists from following; and after we have abandoned what we are unable to excel in, we seek something else in which to exert ourselves."

80, l. 18, *primum mobile:* According to the Ptolemaic astronomy, this was the outermost of the revolving spheres of which the universe was supposed to be made up. While the Copernican astronomy had generally been substituted for the Ptolemaic by the latter part of the seventeenth century, the older concepts long survived, as in Milton's poetry, for literary purposes.

80, l. 36, *co-ordination:* i.e., the opposite of subordination.

83, l. 44, *envy:* odium, unpopularity.

83, l. 16, *Quantum lenta solent... cupressi* (Virg. *Ecl.* I, 25): "As cypress trees are wont to raise their heads above scraggly shrubs."

85, l. 38, *τὸ γελοῖον:* "The laughable"; *cf. ridiculum* below.

85, ll. 52, 53, *ἦθος* and *πάθος:* literally "character" and "suffering," but these words as used by Aristotle involve a great deal more than these literal meanings and go deep into the basic ideas of Greek literary criticism. As S. H. Butcher points out in *Aristotle's Theory of Poetry and Fine Art*, p. 116, *ἦθος* has to do with the permanent and universal qualities of the mind, while *πάθος* has to do with "more transient emotions, the passing moods of feeling." The student should consult the passage referred to.

85, l. 6, *Ex homine hunc natum dicas* (Terent. *Eun.* III, 2, 7): "One might call him the born image of the man." *Cf.* our expression, "A chip off the old block."

86, l. 14, *Creditur, ex medio... minus:* "Because it seeks its subject matter in middle class life, comedy is supposed to require very little toil; but comedy involves more labour to the extent that it receives less indulgence."

87, l. 3, ... *ubi plura nitent... maculis* (Hor. *A. P.*, 351): Howes translates

"If then a poem charm me in the main,
Slight faults I'll not too rigidly arraign."

87, l. 7, *rhyme... stage:* The omitted section deals with the use of rhyme in dramatic poetry.

PREFACE TO THE "FABLES"

88, l. 32, *balk:* omit.

88, l. 33, *predecessor in the laurel:* Dryden seems to have thought of Chaucer as Poet Laureate and thus his own predecessor in the position that he had lost in 1689. However, there is no evidence that Chaucer's pension was bestowed in recognition of literary services. Though several English poets had been described, more or less informally, as poets laureate, the history of the Laureateship as a regular institution dates only from the time of Ben Jonson.

89, l. 15, *Provençal:* The error here comes in the first place from Thomas Rymer, whom Dryden acknowledges as his authority. More recent scholarship sees little direct connection between Chaucer and the Provençal language and literature. As Ker points out, Dryden may have failed to distinguish between Old French and Provençal. Note the respectful treatment of Rymer, about whom Dryden had spoken in less complimentary terms a few years earlier.

89, l. 23, *immorality or profaneness:* The reference is of course to Jeremy Collier's work referred to in the introductory note. Collier is the "religious lawyer" mentioned a few lines later.

89, l. 48, *versus inopes rerum, nugæque canoræ* (Hor. *A. P.*, 322): "Verses without content and melodious trifles."

90, l. 41, *Impiger, iracundus inexorabilis, acer:* "Tireless, passionate, unyielding, fierce." The quotation is from Horace, *Art of Poetry*, l. 121, where the poet is advised to follow Homer in drawing his characters. In illustration of this precept the quoted words are applied to Achilles.

90, l. 45, ... *quo fata trahunt... sequamur* (Virg. *Æn.* V, 709): "Whither the fates draw us back and forth, let us follow."

91, l. 35, *philology:* literature in the broad sense, not merely linguistics.

91, l. 45, *Boccace his Decameron:* We have no evidence that Chaucer borrowed anything directly from the *Decameron* or, indeed, that he had ever read it, though he used other works of Boccaccio's, especially *Teseide* in *The Knight's Tale* (*Palamon and Arcite*) and *Il Filostrato* in *Troilus and Criseyde.*

91, l. 51, *The tale of Grizild:* The story of patient Griselda, used by Chaucer in *The Clerk's Tale*, was taken from Petrarch's Latin version which, in turn, came from Boccaccio's *Decameron.* Dryden's account is inaccurate.

91, ll. 19, 20, *The Wife of Bath's Tale, The Cock and the Fox:* While the immediate sources of these two tales of Chaucer's are not definitely established, the stories themselves long antedate his time. The latter is *The Nun's Priest's Tale.*

92, l. 11, *inopem me copia fecit* (*Metam.* III, 466): "Wealth has made me poor."

92, l. 16, *John Littlewit, in Bartholomew Fair:* The reference is an inexact one to a speech at the beginning of Ben Jonson's play in which John Littlewit speaks of his own ability to find pretty conceits.

92, l. 12, *One of our late great poets:* Abraham Cowley (1618–1667).

92, l. 36, *poeta and nimis poeta:* "A poet" and "too much a poet." As Ker points out, the quotation is taken from Martial (III, 44) and not from Catullus.

92, l. 41, *auribus istius temporis accommodata:* "Suited to the ears of that time," i.e., old-fashioned, adapted from *De Oratoribus*, 21.

92, l. 49, *he who published the last edition of him:* Thomas Speght, whose edition of Chaucer, originally published in 1598 and 1602, had been reprinted in 1687. Of course Dryden was completely wrong in this matter, though it was not until a much later date that by the patient labours of scholarship Chaucer's pronunciation came to be understood and Speght's judgment was vindicated. If the student will read with modern pronunciation the quotations from Chaucer given by Dryden, he will see how from a purely "common sense" point of view, unenlightened by linguistic research, Dryden's judgment seems inevitable.

93, l. 19, *parentage, life, and fortunes:* Knowledge of the facts of Chaucer's life was incomplete and inaccurate in the seventeenth century.

93, l. 48, *the tale of Piers Plowman:* not the poem that we now know as *The Vision of Piers the Plowman* but the pseudo-Chaucerian *Plowman's Tale*, in Dryden's time included as genuine in all editions of Chaucer.

93, l. 23, *scandalum magnatum:* a legal term (slander of magnates) to designate slander of a peer, a judge, or any other great officer of the realm.

93, l. 38, *a King of England and an Archbishop of Canterbury:* Henry II and St. Thomas à Becket.

93, l. 44, *learned and ingenious Dr. Drake:* The reference is to James Drake's *The Ancient and Modern Stages Survey'd*, published anonymously the year before in answer to Jeremy Collier.

93, l. 52, *prior læsit* (Terent. *Eun.* Prol. 4): "He struck first."

94, l. 25, *Baptista Porta:* an Italian physician of the sixteenth century who had written on human physiognomy.

94, l. 23, *Totum hoc indictum volo:* "I wish all this unsaid."

95, l. 15, *some future Milbourne should arise:* The Reverend Luke Milbourne (1649–1720), who had himself projected a translation of Virgil, had attacked Dryden's version two years before in *Notes on Dryden's Virgil.*

95, l. 41, *Multa renascentur... loquendi* (Hor. *A. P.*, 70): For translation see notes to Dryden's *Essay of Dramatic Poesy*, p. 73, l. 8.

96, l. 36, *Facile est inventis addere:* "It is easy to add to something already devised."

96, l. 43, *Mademoiselle de Scudéry:* one of the best known French writers of heroic romance. She was born in 1607 and lived until 1701. Dryden's informant seems to have been mistaken about the translation of Chaucer.

97, l. 28, *Dioneo e Fiametta... Palemone:* "Dioneo and Fiametta sang together for a good while of Arcite and of Palamon." For the real source of *The Knight's Tale*, see the note on *Boccace his Decameron*, above.

97, l. 37, *The Flower and the Leaf:* a pseudo-Chaucerian poem of the fifteenth century, included in early editions of Chaucer, and translated by Dryden under the mistaken impression that it was a genuine work of Chaucer's.

97, l. 45, *B——*: Sir Richard Blackmore (c. 1650–1729), "the City Bard or Knight Physician," as Dryden calls him in the next paragraph, was a physician who was the author of *Prince Arthur* (1695) and *King Arthur* (1697), two dull epics of unimpeachable morality. He had attacked Dryden, before Collier had done so, on the grounds of "irreligion and folly." *A Satire against Wit*, published about this time, had continued the attack.

97, l. 4, *Ogilby:* See note to *Mac Flecknoe*, l. 102.

97, l. 46, *the whirl-bats of Eryx:* cestus, or boxing gloves. See Virgil's *Æneid*, V, 400 ff.

97, l. 53, *Mr. Collier:* Here, after several references to the author of *A Short View*, Dryden acknowledges his faults and refuses to continue the controversy. Coming as they did from the acknowledged dean of English letters, these words of retraction are especially notable, since it is evident from what follows that Dryden's admissions are drawn from him by the consciousness of his offences and not through inability to meet Collier in controversy.

98, l. 20, *ab abusu... consequentia:* "No logical conclusion about the use of anything is to be drawn from its misuse."

98, l. 28, ... *Demetri, teque... cathedras* (Hor. 1 *Sat.* X, 90): "Demetrius and you, Tigellius, I bid weep among your scholars' chairs." Dr. Johnson in his *Life of Blackmore* (*Lives of the Poets*), says, "In some part of his [Blackmore's] life, it is not known when, his indigence compelled him to teach school, an humiliation with which, though it certainly lasted but a little while, his enemies did not forget to reproach him when he became conspicuous enough to excite malevolence; and let it be remembered for his honour, that to have been once a schoolmaster is the only reproach which all the perspicacity of malice, animated by wit, has ever fixed upon his private life."

SAMUEL PEPYS

BIBLIOGRAPHY

Memoirs of Samuel Pepys, Esq., Comprising his Diary from 1659 to 1669... and a Selection from his Private Correspondence, edited by Richard, Lord Braybrooke, 2 vols., 1825. Later editions, with additions, are usually in 4 vols.

Diary and Correspondence of Samuel Pepys, edited by Mynors Bright, 6 vols., 1875–1879.

The Diary of Samuel Pepys, edited by Henry B. Wheatley, 9 vols., 1893–1899.

Pepysiana or Additional Notes on the Particulars of Pepys' Life and on Some Passages in the Diary, 1899, is a supplement to the edition above.

Braybrooke's edition of the *Diary* was reprinted in Everyman's Library, 2 vols., 1906.

Diary with Introduction and Notes by G. G. Smith, Globe Edition, 1922.

Everybody's Pepys, edited and abridged by O. F. Morshead, 1926.

Private Correspondence and Miscellaneous Papers of Samuel Pepys, 1679–1703, in the Possession of J. Pepys Cockerell, edited by J. R. Tanner, 2 vols., 1926.

Further Correspondence of Samuel Pepys, 1662–1679, from the Family Papers in the Possession of J. Pepys Cockerell, 1929.

Walter H. Whitear, *More Pepysiana, being Notes on the Diary of Samuel Pepys and on the Genealogy of the Family*, 1927.

Letters and the Second Diary of Samuel Pepys, edited by R. G. Howarth, 1932. (The "Second Diary" deals with a trip in Tangier and Spain in 1683–84.)

Among the numerous works of biography and criticism the following are important:

H. B. Wheatley, *Samuel Pepys and the World he Lived in*, 1880.

Sir Frederick Bridge, *Samuel Pepys, Lover of Musique*, 1903.
Percy Lubbock, *Samuel Pepys*, in Literary Lives, 1909.
Mrs. Esther Hallam Meynell, *Samuel Pepys, Administrator, Observer, Gossip*, 1909.
Helen McAfee, *Pepys on the Restoration Stage*, 1916.
J. Lucas-Dubreton, *La petite vie de Samuel Pepys, Londonien*, 1923. English translation by H. J. Stenning under the title, *Samuel Pepys: A Portrait in Miniature*.
Gamaliel Bradford, *The Soul of Samuel Pepys*, 1924.
Joseph R. Tanner, *Mr. Pepys: An Introduction to the Diary together with a Sketch of his Later Life*, 1925.
Arthur Ponsonby, *Samuel Pepys*, in the Eng. Men of Letters Series, 1928.
John Drinkwater, *Pepys, his Life and Character*, 1930.

NOTES

100, l. 3, *1660–61:* According to the old style of reckoning the year began on March 25. Consequently the period between January 1 and March 25 for any year before 1752 belongs to the preceding year as it was then reckoned. By Pepys's time, however, January 1 was considered the actual, though not the legal, beginning of the year.

100, l. 5, *one of the principal officers:* Clerk of the Acts, an important position since it made him Secretary of the Navy Board and of equal rank with the other commissioners.

100, l. 19, *Princess of Orange:* Mary, Princess Royal, sister of the king and wife of William of Orange. She was the mother of William III.

100, l. 21, *a great plot:* that of the Fifth Monarchy men, whom Pepys refers to as the Fanatics, which came to a head during the following month.

100, l. 9, *Privy Seal:* In addition to his position of Clerk of the Acts Pepys was Lord Sandwich's deputy in a clerkship in the Privy Seal. This was a minor position which nevertheless brought him in some £3 a day for a time.

100, l. 20, *my Lord's:* Sir Edward Montagu, Earl of Sandwich, a distant relation of Pepys's, and his patron, is usually referred to in the *Diary* as my Lord. Pepys owed his position to this influential kinsman and had close relations with his family.

100, l. 31, *Best:* a card game, usually spelled and pronounced, *beast.*

101, l. 3, *Pall:* Paulina Pepys, Samuel's younger sister, who had arranged to come into his family as a servant. Later she married John Jackson. One of her sons was eventually made Pepys's heir. See the quotation from Evelyn's *Diary* in the Introduction.

101, l. 7, *my brother Spicer:* a brother clerk with Pepys at the Privy Seal.

101, l. 15, *Will's:* not the famous coffee-house to which Dryden was accustomed to resort, but a place of entertainment kept by William Joyce.

101, l. 28, *Sir W. Batten:* one of the Commissioners of the Navy and an associate of Pepys.

101, l. 41, *Beggar's Bush:* a comedy by Beaumont and Fletcher. Before the Restoration, women had not ordinarily appeared on the public stage.

101, l. 11, *The Scornful Lady:* another comedy by Beaumont and Fletcher.

101, l. 22, *the great Tom Fuller:* the Reverend Thomas Fuller (1608–1661), author of many works on theology, morals, history, and antiquities, among which *The Holy State and the Profane State* (1642) and *Worthies of England* (published posthumously in 1662) are famous in English literature. The latter book was being written at about this time; see Pepys's entry for January 22, 1660–61. Though Pepys had hopes that his family would be included, when he read the book, Feb. 10, 1661–62, he was much troubled to find that it had been entirely omitted.

101, l. 43, *Mr. Coventry:* afterwards Sir William Coventry, secretary to the Duke of York, and a warm friend of Pepys's.

102, l. 3, *The Silent Woman: Epicœne, or the Silent Woman,* a comedy by Ben Jonson.

102, l. 17, *the mark for the queen:* Among the traditional Twelfth Night customs was that of choosing a king and queen for the festival by the cutting of a cake in which were placed the "marks" to which Pepys refers. Since January 6 fell on a Sunday this year, the festival was kept on January 7. See R. Chambers, *The Book of Days.*

102, l. 38, *my Lady:* The Countess of Sandwich, the wife of Pepys's kinsman and patron.

102, l. 40, *The Widow:* a comedy by Jonson, Fletcher, and Middleton.

102, l. 43, *Sir W. Penn:* Sir William Penn, Admiral and Commissioner of the Navy (1621–70), an associate of Pepys. He was the father of William Penn, the Quaker, founder of Pennsylvania.

103, l. 31, *the heads upon the gates:* the heads of the Regicides, which had been set up on spikes.

103, l. 55, *Colonel Slingsby:* Colonel, afterwards Sir Robert, Slingsby, Comptroller of the Navy.

103, l. 44, *black woman:* the usual expression for a brunette.

105, l. 2, *forsoothed her:* addressed her in a very ceremonious manner.

105, l. 16, *the lantern: NED, Lantern,* sb. 3. c. is defined as "Some part of a ship," but only this passage is quoted to exemplify such use. Perhaps the worthy Clerk of the Acts confused his nautical terms.

105, l. 49, *Sir G. Carteret:* Sir George Carteret, Treasurer of the Navy.

105, l. 54, *Thos. Hater:* Pepys's clerk. In 1673 he succeeded Pepys as Clerk of the Acts, and later became Secretary of the Admiralty and Comptroller of the Navy.

106, l. 9, *The Lost Lady:* a tragi-comedy by Sir William Barclay. Like the other plays mentioned during the month this was an old play that had been revived. During the first years after the Restoration there was a dearth of new plays.

106, l. 13, *my exhibition in Paul's School:* An exhibition is a fixed sum of money given, usually from school funds, for the support of a student in an English university. In America we should call it a scholarship. St. Paul's is a well known public school in London, which Pepys had attended.

106, l. 36, *utcunque:* usually spelled *utcumque,* Lat., meaning *however.*

106, l. 51, *Gresham College:* the house of Sir Thomas Gresham, where early meetings of the Royal Society were held. Pepys became a Fellow of the Royal Society in 1664, was actively interested in its work, and was President for two years.

107, l. 50, *taking away his ribbons and garters:* At weddings it was customary to take away the groom's ribbons and garters, which were often cut up and divided among the guests.

108, l. 15, *The Maid in the Mill:* a comedy by Beaumont and Fletcher.

108, l. 28, *Argalus and Parthenia:* a tragi-comedy by Henry Glapthorne.

JOHN EVELYN

BIBLIOGRAPHY

Memoirs, Illustrative of the Life and Writings of John Evelyn, Esq., F.R.S., Comprising his Diary from the Year 1641 to 1705/06 and a Selection of his Familiar Letters, edited by William Bray, 2 vols., 1818. There have been numerous reprints of the *Diary and Letters,* usually in 4 vols. The *Diary* alone was reprinted in Everyman's Library, 2 vols., 1911, 1912.

The Diary of John Evelyn, with Introduction and Notes by Austin Dobson, 3 vols., 1906.

The Miscellaneous Writings, edited with notes by William Upcott, 1825; the second edition, 1834, bears the title, *Literary Remains.*

John Evelyn in Naples, 1645, edited by H. Maynard Smith, 1914.

The Early Life and Education of John Evelyn, 1620–41, with Commentary by H. Maynard Smith, 1920.

There is a brief *Life* by James Usher, and one by Henry Wheatley in the later editions of the *Memoirs.*

NOTES

110, ll. 18, 19, *non enim ... civitatem* (Heb. 13:14, Vulgate): "For here we have no continuing city."

110, l. 6, *where I had many wounded and sick men:* Evelyn was one of the Commissioners for the Care of the Sick and Wounded in the Dutch War.

111, l. 18, *the graff:* the ditch.

111, l. 7, *voragos:* abysses.

111, l. 34, *surbated:* bruised or made sore by walking.

112, l. 17, *the Eastern fashion of vest:* In 1661 Evelyn had published a pamphlet entitled *Tyrannus, or the Mode,* advocating a reform in men's dress. Under date of Oct. 17, 1666, Pepys wrote in his *Diary*: "The Court is all full of vests, only my Lord St. Albans not pinked but plain black; and they say the King says the pinking upon white makes them look too much like magpies, and therefore hath bespoke one of plain velvet." This protest against French fashions caused a stir at the time, but it was short-lived.

112, l. 41, *Mustapha: Mustapha, the Son of Solyman the Magnificent,* produced 1665, is a play by Roger Boyle, First Earl of Orrery (1621–1679).

112, l. 51, *another greater person:* an obvious reference to the king.

EDWARD HYDE, EARL OF CLARENDON

BIBLIOGRAPHY

There are numerous editions of *The History of the Rebellion and Civil Wars in England,* among them one published in 7 vols., including Bishop Warburton's notes, 1849.

An excellent volume of selections is G. D. Boyle's *Characters and Episodes of the Great Rebellion, Selected from the History and Autobiography of Edward Earl of Clarendon,* 1889.

C. H. Firth, *Edward Earl of Clarendon, as Statesman, Historian and Chancellor of the University*, 1909, is a brief discussion by one of the foremost recent British historians of the Civil War period. See also the same author's article in *DNB*.

Sir Henry Craik, *The Life of Edward, Earl of Clarendon*, 1911.

NOTES

115, l. 36, *Duke of Buckingham's death:* minister of Charles I, assassinated, 1628.

116, l. 37, *the year, according to the account used in England, 1648:* by the Old Style reckoning, 1649 by the New Style.

117, l. 30, *his son Falconbridge's heart:* One of Oliver Cromwell's daughters had married Viscount Falconbridge.

117, l. 25, *quos vituperare... laudent:* "Whom not even personal enemies can condemn without commending at the same time."

117, l. 45, *Ausum eum... possent* (*Historiæ Romanæ*, II, 24, 5): "He attempted those things which no good man durst have ventured on, and achieved those in which none but a valiant and great man could have succeeded."

119, l. 30, *those of the religion:* Protestants.

JOHN BUNYAN

BIBLIOGRAPHY

Works, edited by H. Stebbing, 4 vols., 1859.

Editions of *The Pilgrim's Progress* are very numerous; as is the case with the many books about Bunyan, their total was considerably augmented at the tercentenary celebration in 1928. A standard edition, which also includes *Grace Abounding to the Chief of Sinners*, is that edited by E. Venables, revised by Mabel Peacock, 1892. See also the editions ed. by Charles Whibley, 1926; J. B. Wharey, 1928; Noel Douglas, 1928, facsimile reprint of the first edition; G. B. Harrison, 1928, which also includes *The Life and Death of Mr. Badman*; Bonamy Dobrée in the World's Classics Series, 1928; G. A. Baker, 1928.

Bunyan's other works have not approached *The Pilgrim's Progress* in popularity; nevertheless some of them have been frequently reprinted.

The Holy War and *The Heavenly Footman*, ed. by Mabel Peacock, 1892.

The Life and Death of Mr. Badman, ed., with illustrations, by G. W. and L. Rhead, 1900; J. Brown, facsimile edition, 1905.

Grace Abounding to the Chief of Sinners and *The Life and Death of Mr. Badman* were published together in cheap form by Dent, 1928.

F. M. Harrison, *A Bibliography of the Works of John Bunyan*. Supplement to the *Bibliographical Society's Transactions*, No. 6, 1932.

Among works of biography and criticism are the following:

Robert Southey, *Life of John Bunyan*, 1830.
J. A. Froude, *Bunyan*, E. M. of L., 1880.
John Brown, *John Bunyan, His Life, Times, and Work*, 1887; revised by F. M. Harrison, 1928.
Edmund Venables, *Life of John Bunyan*, Great Writers Series, 1888.
W. Hale White, *John Bunyan*, in Literary Lives, 1904.
G. O. Griffith, *John Bunyan*, 1927.
F. M. Harrison, *John Bunyan: A Story of his Life*, 1928.
E. A. Knox, *John Bunyan in Relation to his Times*, 1928.
W. Y. Fullerton, *The Legacy of Bunyan*, 1928.
H. E. B. Speight, *The Life and Writings of John Bunyan*, 1928.
G. B. Harrison, *John Bunyan: A Study in Personality*, 1928.
W. H. Hutton, *John Bunyan*, 1928.
A. K. De Blois, *John Bunyan, the Man*, 1928.
A. R. Buckland, *John Bunyan: His Life and Times*, 1928.
W. H. Harding, *John Bunyan, Pilgrim and Dreamer*, 1928.

For study of Bunyan's background the following are useful:

E. Dowden, *Puritan and Anglican: Studies in English Literature*, 1900.
Caroline F. Richardson, *English Preachers and Preaching, 1640–1670: A Secular Study*, 1928.
C. E. Whiting, *Studies in English Puritanism from the Restoration to the Revolution, 1660–1688*, 1931.

NOTES

123, l. 45, *when I was a soldier:* The muster rolls of the Parliamentary garrison at Newport Pagnell show that he served from November, 1644, to June, 1647.

124, l. 48, *game at cat:* Tipcat, as it is usually called, is a game in which a small pointed piece of wood, known as a "cat" is tipped, or struck into the air, by a bat, and while it is in the air is batted by the same player.

125, l. 23, *Tom of Bedlam:* common designation for a madman.

127, l. 20, *Ranters' books:* The Ranters were a seventeenth-century religious sect who pushed so far the doctrine of justification by faith that they believed themselves emancipated from the obligations of moral law.

127, l. 23, *professors:* that is, persons who had made public profession of their religious faith. The term was a common one among the Puritans.

127, l. 32, *I Cor. 12:* In some places Bunyan's references are incomplete; the passage here indicated is I Cor. 12:8, 9.

DANIEL DEFOE

BIBLIOGRAPHY

There is no complete edition of Defoe's works; the following are the most accessible editions:
Oxford Edition, 20 vols., 1840, 1841.
G. A. Aitken, *Romances and Narratives*, 16 vols., 1895, 1896.
G. H. Maynadier edited a collection of the novels in 16 vols. in 1903.
Defoe's Novels and Miscellaneous Works appear in 7 vols. in the Bohn Library, 1888–93.
Editions of *Robinson Crusoe* are numerous.
Selected Writings of Daniel Defoe was published by Blackwell in 1927.
Novels and Selected Writings, Shakespeare Head Ed., 16 vols., 1928.
There is an excellent volume of *Selections* published by Nimmo of Edinburgh, 1870.
H. Morley, *Defoe's Earlier Life and Earlier Works*, 1889.
William Lee, *Life and Newly Discovered Writings of Daniel Defoe*, 3 vols., 1869.
There are several lives of Defoe, but none is entirely satisfactory; among them are those of George Chalmers, 1786; Walter Wilson, 3 vols., 1830; William Lee, in vol. 1 of above; W. Minto, in English Men of Letters Series, 1879; and T. Wright, 1894; new ed. revised, 1931.
Among recent critical works the following are important:
G. A. Aitken, Notes in *Contemporary Review*, Feb., 1890, and in the *Athenæum*, Apr. 30, 1889, and Aug. 31, 1890.
W. P. Trent, Four articles (chiefly bibliographical) in the New York *Nation*, 1907, 1908.
W. P. Trent, *Defoe: How to Know Him*, 1916.
See the same author's account in *CHEL*, vol. IX, chap. 1.
W. Nicholson, *The Historical Sources of Defoe's "Journal of the Plague Year,"* 1919.
P. Dottin, *Daniel Defoe et ses romans*, 1924. Pt. I translated by Louise Regan as *The Life and Surprising Adventures of Daniel Defoe*, 1929.
A. W. Secord, *Studies in the Narrative Method of Defoe*, 1924.
W. Gückel und E. Günther, *D. Defoes und J. Swifts Belesenheit und literarische Kritik*, 1925.
A. E. Levett in F. J. C. Hearnshaw, *The Social and Political Ideas of Some English Thinkers of the Augustan Age*, 1928.
Ernst G. Jacob, *Daniel Defoe, Essay on Projects, eine wirtschafts- und sozialgeschichtliche Studie*, 1929.
G. Roorda, *Realism in Daniel De Foe's Narratives of Adventure*, 1929.
Armin Blass, *Die Geschichtsauffassung Daniel Defoes*, 1931.
Paula van Beek, *Der psychologische Gehalt in den Romanen Defoes*, 1931.

NOTES

AN ESSAY UPON PROJECTS

133, l. 3, *Under this head of Academies:* Defoe has been considering some of the traditional arguments for the establishment in England of an Academy similar to the French. During the latter part of the seventeenth and the early part of the eighteenth centuries this project received a good deal of attention. In 1664 a committee, of which Dryden, Waller, and Evelyn were members, was appointed by the Royal Society to take steps "for improving the English tongue." Three years later Sprat in the *History of the Royal Society* discussed "A Proposal for Erecting an English Academy." In 1712 Swift in an open letter to Oxford published *A Proposal for Correcting, Improving, and Ascertaining the English Tongue.* The neglect of this proposal is significant of the whole history of the neo-classical movement in England: British inertia and deep-rooted individualism constantly opposed and eventually nullified all attempts to impose such literary and social discipline as were exerted abroad by the French Academy. See Matthew Arnold's essay, *The Literary Influence of Academies.*

133, l. 37, *Advice to the Ladies: Serious Proposal to Ladies* (1694) by Mary Astell.

134, l. 47, *felony without clergy:* that is, without benefit of clergy, a mediæval privilege by which the clergy, and afterwards all who could read, might escape the death penalty by appealing to the jurisdiction of an ecclesiastical court. At this time the privilege had been so widely extended that it had become the practice to make especially heinous crimes punishable without benefit of clergy. Defoe thus proposes that the law should be enacted in the strictest possible form.

A JOURNAL OF THE PLAGUE YEAR

137, l. 21, *the place where I lived:* The supposititious narrator is represented as a saddler, dealing with "the merchants trading to the English colonies in America." He was unmarried but had a house with a number of servants as well as a shop and warehouses. He lived "without Aldgate, about midway between Aldgate Church and Whitechapel Bars," in the East End of London.

137, l. 22, *Dr. Heath:* a physician, a friend of the narrator's, whom he frequently visited.

137, l. 24, *When any one... they:* Here and in many other places Defoe's style is loosely colloquial rather than literary.

138, l. 23, *the weekly bill:* Official bills or reports of mortality in London were issued weekly.

144, l. 9, *in case of the approach of a like visitation:* Here and elsewhere Defoe shows his journalistic purpose in relating his account of the plague of 1665 to contemporary apprehensions of another visitation. See introduction.

146, l. 7, *the mob:* This word, against the use of which Swift protested, was at this time coming into popular use; it is a contraction of *mobile* (neuter form of *mobilis*) *vulgus* and refers to the fickle and easily moved multitude. *Cf. Spectator*, Nos. 62 and 135.

146, l. 35, *there wants two days of two months in the account of time:* As has often been pointed out, the period from Aug. 8 to Oct. 10 comprises two days more than two months.

147, l. 22, *without the bars:* outside the limits of the City proper.

JOHN LOCKE

BIBLIOGRAPHY

Locke's *Works* have been published in numerous editions, of which that in 10 volumes, 1801, 1812, 1823 is most easily accessible.

Two Treatises of Government, together with Sir John Filmer's *Patriarcha* was edited by Henry Morley, 1884. It has also been published in Everyman's Library.

Among biographical works and critical works useful for the study of his contributions to political theory are the following:

Lord King, *Life and Letters of John Locke*, 1829.
H. R. Fox-Bourne, *Life of John Locke*, 1876.
T. Fowler, *Locke* in Eng. Men of Letters Series, 1880.
Sir F. Pollock, *Locke's Theory of the State*, in *Proceedings of the British Academy*, 1904.
Charles Bastide, *John Locke, ses théories politiques et leur influence en Angleterre*, 1907.
S. T. Lamprecht, *The Moral and Political Philosophy of John Locke*, 1918.
S. G. Hefelbower, *Relation of John Locke to English Deism*, 1919.
G. Tarozzi, *John Locke*, 1926.
Benjamin Rand, *The Correspondence of John Locke and Edward Clarke, with a Biographical Study*, 1927.

Among general reference works see the following:

Sir Leslie Stephen, *History of English Thought in the Eighteenth Century*, 2 vols., 1876.
H. J. Laski, *Political Thought in England from Locke to Bentham*, Home Univ. Library, 1920.
C. H. Driver in F. J. C. Hearnshaw, *The Social and Political Theories of Some English Thinkers of the Augustan Age, 1650–1750*, 1928.

NOTES

152, l. 46, *the late relation of Ceylon:* In *An Historical Relation of the Island Ceylon, in the East-Indies: together with an Account of the Detaining in Captivity the Author and Divers other Englishmen now Living there, and of the Author's Miraculous Escape. By Robert Knox, a Captive there near Twenty Years.* London, 1681. See especially Part II, Chap. III, "Of the King's Tyrannical Reign."

153, l. 28, *"No man in civil society can be exempted from the laws of it":* "Civil law, being the act of the whole body-politic, doth therefore overrule each several part of the same body." Hooker, *Ecclesiastical Polity*, Book I, section 10, note. Throughout this part of the treatise, Locke makes numerous references to Hooker.

154, l. 15, *the mighty Leviathan:* the commonwealth. After the publication of Hobbes's *Leviathan* (1651), this use of the word was not uncommon.

154, l. 41, *Josephus Acosta's word:* José de Acosta (1539?–1600), Spanish Jesuit, missionary to Peru, whose *Historia Natural y Moral de la Indias*, 1590, was widely read. It had been translated into English in 1601. Locke shows here characteristic prejudice against the Jesuits.

155, l. 14, *those who went away from Sparta, with Palantus, mentioned by Justin:* Early in the eighth century B.C. a group of Spartan emigrants led by Phalanthus founded a colony at Tarentum. Junianus Justinus, the Roman historian, tells the story in *Trogi Pompei Historiarum Philippicarum Epitoma*, III, 4.

157, l. 43, *amor sceleratus habendi* (Ovid, *Met.* I, 131): "Accursed greed of possession."

158, l. 22, *jure divino:* "By divine right." While this doctrine was not new in the seventeenth century, it had been much emphasized by English Churchmen at this time. See J. N. Figgis, *The Divine Right of Kings.*

160, l. 6, *in vacuis locis:* "In unoccupied places."

SIR GEORGE SAVILE, MARQUIS OF HALIFAX

BIBLIOGRAPHY

The standard edition of Halifax is by H. C. Foxcroft. See also Walter Raleigh, *Miscellanies*, 1912. Miss Foxcroft is also the author of *Life and Letters of Sir George Savile, First Marquis of Halifax*, 2 vols., 1898.

Herbert W. Paul, "The Great Tractarian," in *Men and Letters*, 3d ed., 1901.

A. W. Reed, "George Savile, Marquis of Halifax," in *The Social and Political Ideas of Some English Thinkers of the Augustan Age*, ed. by F. J. C. Hearnshaw, 1928.

NOTES

162, l. 20, *Quod principi placuit lex esto:* "Let what has pleased the emperor be the law."

164, l. 9, *two Czars of Muscovy:* Between 1682 and 1689 Peter the Great and his brother, Ivan, were joint rulers of Russia. When Halifax wrote these words, he could not foresee that within four years he would be the agent deputed to offer the crown of England to the joint sovereigns, William and Mary.

166, l. 34, *the Triennial Act:* The act requiring the meeting of a new Parliament at least once in three years was passed in 1641, but was disregarded, and repealed in 1664. Later (in 1694) it was re-enacted, but repealed by the Septennial Act of 1716.

SIR WILLIAM TEMPLE

BIBLIOGRAPHY

There are numerous editions of Temple's *Works*: the Edinburgh edition in 4 vols., 1754, was several times reprinted and is most frequently referred to.

J. E. Spingarn edited *Essays on Ancient and Modern Learning and on Poetry*, 1909.

G. C. Moore Smith edited *Early Essays and Romances of Sir William Temple. With the Life and Character of Sir William Temple by his sister Lady Giffard*, 1930.

H. Luden, *Sir William Temple. Biographie.* Kleine Aufsätze, meist historischen Inhalts, vol. II, 1808.

Charles Lamb, "The Genteel Style in Writing," *The Last Essays of Elia*, 1833.

T. P. Courtenay, *Memoirs of the Life, Works, and Correspondence of Sir William Temple*, 2 vols., 1836.

T. B. Macaulay, "Life and Writings of Sir William Temple," 1838. This essay was published as a review of the preceding work.

M. L. R. Beavan, *Sir William Temple*, 1908.

E. S. Lyttel, *Sir William Temple*, 1908.

Clara Marburg, *Sir William Temple; a Seventeenth Century "Libertin,"* 1932.

NOTES

167, l. 3, *... In such poor wretched weeds as these was poetry clothed:* Temple has been speaking of the "Gothic runes" of the Middle Ages, charms, ballads, romances, and miscellaneous rhymes. His attitude toward "the fairy way of writing," which the eighteenth century was to find attractive, is illustrated in the following words, "all the visionary tribe of fairies, elves, and goblins, of sprites and of bull-beggars that serve not only to fright children into whatever their nurses please, but sometimes, by lasting impressions, to disquiet the sleeps and the very lives of men and women till they grow to years of discretion; and that, God knows, is a period of time which some people arrive to but very late, and perhaps others never."

168, l. 30, *the true religion was not found to become fiction so well as false:* Boileau's attack upon the Christian epic in *L'Art poëtique*, III, 193 ff., is here reflected.

168, l. 43, *After these three... none of the moderns... worth recording:* The inclusion of Spenser among the greatest of modern epic poets and the omission of Milton may be alike surprising at first sight. That Temple, in spite of his dislike of allegory, should thus rate Spenser very high is a piece of evidence to show that this age had more appreciation of *The Fairy Queen* than has sometimes been supposed. The omission of Milton is probably to be explained by the odium attached to his political principles; then too Temple probably classed him with the writers of the Christian epic. It is worthy of note that English, as well as French, contemporaries are also omitted. Perhaps Temple's partisanship of the ancients may have led him to slight these recent writers whose works were being claimed as evidence of the superiority of the moderns.

169, l. 14, *Absentum qui rodit... caveto* (Horace, *Sat.* I, 4, 81–85): "Whoever criticizes an absent friend, whoever fails to defend him when another blames; whoever tries to win the loud guffaws of men, and a reputation as a wit; whoever can invent what he never saw, who cannot keep secret questionable things; he is a reprobate: beware of him, O Roman."

169, l. 46, *La Secchia Rapita:* Alessandro Tassoni published in 1622 this mock epic on "The Stolen Bucket."

169, ll. 47–49, *Scarron... Sir John Mince... Hudibras... and Cotton:* Paul Scarron published *L'Énéide Travestie* in 1648–53, which was paraphrased in English by John Cotton under the title, *Scarronides* in 1664. Sir John Mennes or Mince (1599–1671) is the supposed author of burlesque and satiric verses that appeared in *Wit's Recreation* and *Musarum Deliciæ*. For the work of Samuel Butler, author of *Hudibras*, see page 1.

169, l. 48, *humour, a word peculiar to our language:* This statement was often repeated during the eighteenth century. Critics were generally agreed that the excellence of English comedy lay in its use of the humours. See J. E. Spingarn, *Critical Essays of the Seventeenth Century*, Introduction, pp. lx ff.

171, l. 18, *Rosicrucian principles:* Rosicrucianism was a system of occult knowledge that created some stir in the seventeenth century.

171, l. 5, *Phalaris:* In *An Essay upon the Ancient and Modern Learning*, first published in 1690, Temple had praised the *Epistles* of Phalaris, the Sicilian tyrant, as having "more race, more spirit, more force of wit and genius than any others I have ever seen, either ancient or modern." In the controversy that followed between Richard Bentley and Robert Boyle the former definitely proved these epistles a forgery.

ISAAC BARROW

BIBLIOGRAPHY

The Works of Isaac Barrow were published by John Tillotson, with a Life of the Author by Abraham Hill, 1683–87.

The Theological Works, ed. by A. Napier, 9 vols., 1859.

Sermons on Evil-Speaking, ed. by Henry Morley in Cassell's National Library, No. 59, 1887.

Among general works on the English preachers of the Restoration see W. H. Hutton, "Divines of the Church of England, 1660–1700," *CHEL*, vol. VIII, chap. XII.

J. Hunt, *Religious Thought in England to the End of the Eighteenth Century*, 3 vols., 1870–73.

J. H. Overton, *Life in the English Church, 1660–1717*, 1885.

W. H. Hutton, *The English Church from the Accession of Charles I to the Death of Anne*, 1903.

Caroline F. Richardson, *English Preachers and Preaching, 1640–1670*, 1928.

W. F. Mitchell, *English Pulpit Oratory from Andrewes to Tillotson; a Study of its Literary Aspects*, 1932.

NOTES

174, l. 4, "*I exhort therefore... authority*": the text upon which this sermon was preached. Barrow divided his treatment into the two main heads of the duty of prayer for kings and the duty of thanksgiving for kings. Of the first division the first eight sections are omitted; the rest of the sermon is reprinted entire, except that the references for a large number of the Biblical quotations are in the original printed in the margins. Since these references are not necessary for the present purpose, they are not here reproduced either in the text or in the notes. Any one who desires may easily find the passages by the use of a Bible concordance.

174, l. 34, *As the good bishop, observing St. Austin's mother:* Saint Augustine (*Confessions*, bk. III, chap. 12) tells how a certain bishop returned this answer to St. Monica, when she had importuned him to attempt Augustine's conversion. The form, Austin, was formerly often used for Augustine.

174, l. 43, *Fieri non potest... pereat:* "It is impossible that a prince of those tears should perish."

174, l. 50, "*All things, whatsoever we shall ask...*": This passage is slightly adapted from St. Matt. 21:22, substituting *we* for *ye*. In several other places Barrow has made slight changes in his quotations, none of which seriously affect the sense.

175, l. 3, *how the prayer of Hannah did procure Samuel to her, as his name doth import:* See I. Sam. chap. 1. The name, Samuel, means "Asked of God."

175, l. 5, *Elias:* In the Old Testament the Heb. form of this name, *Elijah,* is used.

175, l. 7, *reduce:* "Bring back," from Lat. *reducere.*

175, l. 24, *re-edifying:* "Rebuilding," the Latin meaning.

175, l. 10, *the Preacher's doctrine:* The title of the Old Testament book from which the preceding quotation is taken is Ecclesiastes, or The Preacher.

175, l. 21, *stomach:* "Anger, resentment."

175, l. 51, *These were the misdemeanours of those in the late times:* The reference is to the recent Civil War raised by Parliament against Charles I. The word, *misdemeanours*, here means *misdeeds*, without suggestion of the legal distinction between misdemeanour and felony. Barrow, as the context indicates, regarded the actions of Cromwell and his associates as crimes of the deepest dye.

176, l. 19, *This is the only method St. Paul did prescribe, even when Nero...* : The High Church clergymen of this time in preaching the duty of non-resistance to kings were never weary of pointing out that the Roman Emperor who was on the throne when St. Paul urged upon the early Christians the duty of obedience to temporal rulers, was Nero. The word, *naughty*, had not yet acquired its modern sense of mild censure such as is applied to children; here it means *wicked.*

176, l. 48, *orators:* "Those who petition or pray." The Lat. *orare* means either *to speak* or *to pray.*

178, l. 5, *experiments:* "Experiences."

178, l. 7, *the throne of his Blessed Father:* Though the Church of England possessed no machinery for formal canonization, by common consent Charles I was honoured as St. Charles the Martyr; January 30 (the anniversary of his death) was celebrated as his day, and churches were dedicated in his name.

ROBERT SOUTH

BIBLIOGRAPHY

South's sermons have been several times reprinted; modern editions include one in 4 vols., 1843, and another in Library of Old English Divines, 5 vols., 1866–1871

NOTES

179, l. 10, ...*In fine:* The omitted portion of this sermon may be briefly summarized as follows. From a consideration of the majesty of God emphasized in the text, South declares "that premeditation of thought, and brevity of expression, are the great ingredients of that reverence that is required to a pious, acceptable, and devout prayer." He then shows that prayer is neither to give God information, to persuade him, to move his pity, or to weary him by importunity; but it is the fulfilling of the "condition upon which God has freely promised to convey his blessings to men." After elaborating these ideas and answering objections, he continues: "Now in all addresses, either to God or man, by speech, our reverence to them must consist of, and show itself in these two things: first, a careful regulation of our thoughts, that are to dictate and to govern our words, which is done by premeditation; and secondly, a due ordering of our words, that are to proceed from and to express our thoughts, which is done by pertinence and brevity of expression." Under the first head, premeditation, he discusses "1. The person whom we pray to; 2. The matter of our prayers; and 3. The order and disposition of them." The extract here reprinted begins near the end of section 2 of this last subdivision.

181, l. 29, *a Popish priest... counterfeiting himself a Protestant:* Accusations such as this were common in the seventeenth century, though details vary surprisingly in different accounts.

181, l. 51, *one of the greatest monsters:* This interesting character has been identified as a certain Major John Weyer. He is too obscure for inclusion in *DNB*.

184, l. 9, *But this I cannot dispatch now:* In a second sermon on the same text South pleads for a "pertinent brevity of expression," and shows that this quality is best found in the Anglican *Book of Common Prayer.*

JOHN TILLOTSON

BIBLIOGRAPHY

The standard edition of Tillotson's *Works*, to which is prefixed the *Life* by T. Birch, was published in three vols., folio, 1725, and republished in 10 vols., 1820. The only recent reprint is a volume of selections entitled *The Golden Book of Tillotson*, ed., with a sketch of his life, by James Moffatt, 1926.

NOTES

185, l. 5, *Thus saith the Lord...* : Tillotson discusses this text under two heads: "First, what we are not to glory in; Secondly, what it is that is matter of true glory." In treating the second of these heads he says, "I shall only make two observations or inferences from what hath been said, and then apply the whole discourse to the great occasion of this day; and they are these.

"First, that the wisest and surest reasonings in religion are grounded upon the unquestionable perfections of the divine nature.

"Secondly, that the nature of God is the true idea and pattern of perfection and happiness." It is with the second of these inferences that our selection begins.

186, l. 33, *cœlum non animum mutavit* (Horace, *Epist.* I, xi, 27, altered): "He has changed his sky, not his soul."

186, l. 17, *the great and glorious occasion of this day:* The immediate occasion was thanksgiving for the naval victory at La Hogue, May 19, 1692, in which the French fleet had been destroyed and the transports that had been prepared for the invasion of England had been burned. La Hogue has been called "the greatest naval victory won by the English between the defeat of the Armada and the battle of Trafalgar." Its immediate consequences were to give England command of the seas and to remove the threat of French invasion.

186, l. 33, *that horrid and most barbarous attempt... those great and manifold dangers:* An attempt had been made to murder King William in Flanders. He had recently returned from the Continent where the land operations had been unsuccessful. It will be noted that the archbishop makes only this distant allusion to William's defeat at Steenkirk the preceding July.

187, l. 55, *these two characters exemplified:* In the following portrayal of Louis XIV as the ungodly king and William III as the godly king, we have an example of the application of the seventeenth-century "character" to the sermon.

188, l. 28, *those who have so long pretended conscience against submission to the present government:* the Nonjurors.

189, l. 18, *believed him to have been slain at the Boyne:* On the eve of the Battle of the Boyne, William III had been grazed by a cannon ball; for a time it was supposed that he had been killed.

189, l. 31, *he is as much above being flattered:* In view of the presence of the king and queen when this sermon was delivered, this disclaimer of the worthy prelate was, of course, a refinement of flattery.

189, l. 13, *Two sovereign princes reigning together:* William and Mary were joint sovereigns.

THOMAS RYMER

BIBLIOGRAPHY

There is no modern edition of Rymer's critical works. Some extracts are included in Vol. II of J. E. Spingarn's *Critical Essays of the Seventeenth Century*.

Albert Hofherr, *Thomas Rymers dramatische Kritik*, 1908.

George B. Dutton, "The French Aristotelian Formalists and Thomas Rymer," *PMLA* (1914), 5:152-88.

NOTES

191, l. 48, *Sed non ut placidis... agni* (*Art of Poetry*, ll. 12, 13): Ben Jonson translates,

> "Yet not as therefore cruel things should cleave
> To gentle; not that we should serpents see
> With doves, or lambs with tigers coupled be."

191, l. 21, *Di non si accompagnare... noi* (*Ecatommiti*, III, 7): "Not to marry a man whom nature and heaven and manner of life separate from us."

191, l. 45, *And of the cannibals that each others eat:* As Spingarn has pointed out, Rymer's quotations from the play seem "in general to follow the Players' Quarto of 1687."

191, l. 55, *Aqua Tetrachymagogon: Cf. Tatler* No. 240, which refers to *tetrachymagogon* as a very hard word posted upon every corner in the streets by a quack doctor some twenty years before to excite popular curiosity and draw patients.

192, l. 11, *Intererit multum... Argis* (*Art of Poetry*, ll. 114 and 118): "It will make a great difference... whether a Colchian or an Assyrian, one reared in Argos or in Thebes."

192, l. 21, *latitude of Gotham...* : Gotham was an English village the people of which were proverbially foolish. *Cf.* the Mother Goose rhyme about the "Three wise men of Gotham."

192, l. 38, *Littora littoribus contraria* (Virgil, *Æneid*, IV, 628): "Shores hostile to shores." The quotation is from the curse of Dido against Æneas and his descendants, prophesying the hatred of Carthage and Rome.

192, l. 16, *Impiger, iracundus, inexorabilis, acer* (*Art of Poetry*, l. 121): "Energetic, passionate, ruthless, fierce." So Horace says that Achilles must be represented on the stage. Neo-classical criticism laid great stress on consistent portrayal of type characteristics.

192, l. 42, *alla soldatesca:* "Soldierlike."

192, l. 43, *Non sia egli... mano:* "He is not one to take vengeance by deceitful means, but sword in hand."

193, l. 24, *Step then amongst the scenes to observe the conduct in this tragedy...* : Here follows a detailed examination of the play in the same spirit as the preceding. Lack of space necessitates its omission until we come to the last scene of the play.

193, l. 31, *some machine for her deliverance:* some supernatural agency. The reference is to the use of "a god from a machine" in ancient tragedy — the introduction of a god upon the stage to overcome difficulties insuperable by human means.

193, l. 48, *Soles occidere et redire possunt* (Catullus, V, 4): "Suns may set and rise again."

193, l. 50, *The very soul and quintessence of Sir George Etherege:* contemporary dramatist and man-about-town, famous for his creation, Sir Fopling Flutter, the principal character in *The Man of Mode.* The meaning seems to be that Othello here shows himself not a rough soldier but a fop. No better illustration of Rymer's poetic insensibility can be found than his treatment of these beautiful lines. At the same time it must be remembered that his objection is to their dramatic propriety; he considers them out of place.

193, l. 8, *sub tam lentis maxillis* (Suetonius, *Tiberius*, 21): "Under such slow jaws," i.e., to be ground by jaws that crunch so slowly.

193, l. 22, *in parvis litibus... movere* (*Inst.* VI, 1, 36): "To produce tragedies about small matters of dispute."

193, l. 46, *lâcheté:* "Baseness, or contemptible thing."

193, l. 48, *Lardella... in The Rehearsal: The Rehearsal* (1671) by the Duke of Buckingham and various collaborators was a burlesque play ridiculing the contemporary heroic play and especially Dryden's part in it. In IV, 1, from the coffin of the supposedly dead Lardella is taken a paper in which she speaks in the character of a humble bee, promising her lover that she would hum and buzz before him. Rymer's frequent references to *The Rehearsal* seem to have irritated Dryden considerably.

194, l. 3, *Flamsteed:* John Flamsteed was astronomer-royal, 1675–1719.

194, l. 6, *Gresham College:* The Royal Society held its meetings here.

194, l. 29, *John an Oaks, John a Stiles:* fictitious names used in legal papers as we use John Doe and Richard Roe.

194, l. 35, *σπουδαιότερον και φιλοσορώτερον...* (*Poetics*, IX, 3): translated in the context.

195, l. 1, *hare:* harass.

195, l. 3, *tintamarre:* loud or unpleasant noise.

JEREMY COLLIER

BIBLIOGRAPHY

There is no modern reprint of *A Short View of the Immorality and Profaneness of the English Stage.* For books dealing with the Collier controversy, see the following:

A. Hofherr, *Thomas Rymers dramatische Kritik*, 1908.

J. Ballein, *Jeremy Colliers Angriff auf die englische Bühne*, 1910.

G. H. Nettleton, *English Drama of the Restoration and Eighteenth Century*, 1914.

E. Bernbaum, *The Drama of Sensibility: A Sketch of the History of English Sentimental Comedy and Domestic Tragedy*, 1915.

J. W. Krutch, *Comedy and Conscience after the Restoration*, 1924.

Bonamy Dobrée, *Restoration Comedy, 1660–1720*, 1924.

H. T. E. Perry, *The Comic Spirit in Restoration Drama: Studies in the Comedy of Etherege, Wycherley, Congreve, Vanbrugh, and Farquhar*, 1925.

See also Charles Lamb's essay, "On the Artificial Comedy of the Last Century," 1822, and T. B. Macaulay's review of Leigh Hunt's edition of *Comic Dramatists of the Restoration, Edinburgh Review*, July, 1841.

NOTES

197, ll. 13, 15, *Wildblood... Bellamy:* characters in Dryden's early comedy, *An Evening's Love; or, The Mock Astrologer.*

197, l. 16, *Lorenzo... calls his father "bawdy magistrate"*: Lorenzo is one of the principal characters in the comic part of Dryden's tragi-comedy, *The Spanish Friar*. See act 5, scene 2.

197, ll. 17, 18, *Horner... Harcourt:* characters in Wycherley's comedy, *The Country Wife.*

197, l. 19, *The Plain Dealer:* Wycherley's comedy.

197, ll. 23, 24, *Mellefont... Careless... Lady Plyant:* characters in Congreve's comedy, *The Double-Dealer.*

197, l. 27, *Don Sebastian:* Dryden's tragedy. The characters mentioned are important in the comic parts of this play.

197, l. 30, *Love for Love:* Congreve's comedy.

198, l. 5, *The Provoked Wife:* comedy by Sir John Vanbrugh, act 3, scene 1. In later versions, the first quoted sentence is omitted.

198, l. 19, *The Relapse:* comedy by Sir John Vanbrugh.

198, l. 29, *Morayma... runs away with Antonio:* in *Don Sebastian.*

198, l. 31, *Angelica:* in *Love for Love.*

198, l. 32, *Belinda:* in *The Provoked Wife.*

198, l. 36, *Orphan:* tragedy by Otway.

198, l. 36, *Double-Dealer:* comedy by Congreve.

198, l. 37, *Love Triumphant:* tragi-comedy by Dryden.

198, l. 43, *Philolaches, in Plautus: Mostellaria.*

198, l. 46, *Lysiteles:* in Plautus's *Trinummus.*

198, l. 52, *Chremes, in Terence: Eunuchus.*

198, l. 55, *Hecyra:* by Terence.

199, l. 3, *Plautus's Pinacium: Stichus.*

199, l. 10, "*Virtue is an ass...*": Act I, scene 1. In later versions of the play this sentence, together with other parts of the same soliloquy, is omitted.

199, l. 21, "*What will become of us*": This and the following quotations are from *The Mock Astrologer.*

199, l. 15, *Horace... seems to be of another opinion:* The references are to the *Art of Poetry.*

200, l. 3, *chorus was added...*: *Poetics*, chapter V.

200, l. 7, *Molière has now revived them:* i.e., the use of the chorus. The marginal note in the original edition shows that Collier had in mind *Psyché*, which is rather opera than comedy.

200, l. 22, *Mr. Dryden makes homewards:* In his Preface to *An Evening's Love; or, The Mock Astrologer*, he speaks of having "launched out farther than I intended in the beginning of this preface," and then adds, "'Tis time now to draw homeward; and to think rather of defending myself, than assaulting others."

200, l. 26, *Ben Jonson's Fox:* This play bears the title, *Volpone or The Fox.*

200, l. 28, *He declares the poet's end...*: See Dryden, *An Essay of Dramatic Poesy.*

200, l. 40, *Falstaff goes off in disappointment:* He is dismissed from favour in *II Hen. IV*, v, 5, and his death is reported in *Hen. V*, ii, 3.

200, l. 54, *Flowerdale, the prodigal:* a character in *The London Prodigal*, a play that was often attributed to Shakespeare. It was included in the Third Folio (1664) and the Fourth Folio (1685).

201, l. 9, *Heaven helping me...*: Act 5, scene 1, l. 437 with *of* inaccurately quoted for *as.*

201, l. 20, *he makes a wide difference between... tragedy and comedy:* The reference is again to Dryden's Preface to *An Evening's Love; or, The Mock Astrologer.*

201, l. 24, *Monsieur Rapin affirms: Réflexions sur la poëtique d'Aristote*, 1674.

JOHN POMFRET

BIBLIOGRAPHY

Poetical Works in R. Anderson, *British Poets*, vol. 6, 1792–94, and in A. Chalmers, *The Works of the British Poets*, vol. 8, 1810.

Life in Dr. Johnson's *The Lives of the English Poets.*

G. Baumann, *Leben und Dichtungen des Rev. John Pomfret*, 1931.

NOTES

203, l. 4, *spend:* The first four lines are the protasis to which the remainder of the poem serves as apodasis.

204, l. 86, *huffing:* bluster.

204, l. 94, *Cæsar:* the king.

204, l. 109, *Coy:* modest, retiring.

205, l. 151, *rate:* tax or fee.

BERNARD MANDEVILLE

BIBLIOGRAPHY

The Fable of the Bees: Or, Private Vices, Public Benefits by Bernard Mandeville. With a Commentary Critical, Historical, and Explanatory by F. B. Kaye, 2 vols., 1924.

Sir Leslie Stephen, *Essays on Freethinking and Plainspeaking*, 1873.

Sir Leslie Stephen, *History of English Thought in the Eighteenth Century*, 2 vols., 1876.

Robert Browning, *Parleyings with Certain People of Importance in their Day*, "With Bernard de Mandeville," 1887.

Paul Sakmann, *Bernard de Mandeville und die Bienenfabel-Controverse: Eine Episode in der Geschichte der englischen Aufklärung*, 1897.

NOTES

THE GRUMBLING HIVE

206, l. 7, *No bees had better government... less content:* It was a commonplace of the time to apply such terms to the English people. The next two couplets have a similar application.

207, l. 48, *without a cross:* a coin, so called because it was customary to use the cross in designs of various coins.

207, l. 62, *Dipp'd:* mortgaged.

207, l. 92, *cabbage:* cloth pilfered by tailors when cutting out garments.

209, l. 269, *Squire Catch:* The traditional name for a public executioner was Jack Ketch.

209, l. 275, *bums:* Bumbailiff was a contemptuous name for a bailiff.

209, l. 289, *journey-bees:* The curate who attended to the duties of an absentee clergyman was popularly nicknamed a "journeyman parson."

AN ENQUIRY INTO THE ORIGIN OF MORAL VIRTUE

212, l. 26, *Fortior est qui... Mœnia: Cf.* Proverbs, 16:32.

214, l. 26, *the incomparable Mr. Steele:* See, for example, *Tatler* No. 87.

214, l. 50, *Lorenzo Gratian:* Baltasar Gracián (1601–1658), Spanish Jesuit, whose works were published under the name of his brother, Lorenzo.

ANTHONY ASHLEY COOPER, EARL OF SHAFTESBURY

BIBLIOGRAPHY

The best edition of *Characteristics of Men, Manners, Opinions, Times* is that edited by J. M. Robertson, 2 vols., 1900.

For biography and criticism the following will be useful:

T. Fowler, *Shaftesbury and Hutcheson*, 1882.

B. Rand, *Life, Letters, and Philosophical Regimen of Shaftesbury*, 1900.

Sir Leslie Stephen, *History of English Thought in the Eighteenth Century*, 2 vols., 1876.

C. A. Moore, "Shaftesbury and the Ethical Poets in England," *PMLA*, 31:264–325, June, 1916.

E. Tiffany, "Shaftesbury as Stoic," *PMLA*, 38:642–84, Sept., 1923.

NOTES

SOLILOQUY, OR ADVICE TO AN AUTHOR

217, l. 20, *je ne sais quoi:* This expression, which is translated in the context, was characteristic of the school of taste which opposed the more mechanical application of the rules; it was applied to those nameless beauties which can neither be taught nor adequately explained by rules. Thus Pope says,

"Some beauties yet no precepts can declare,"

and recognizes that it is possible to "snatch a grace beyond the realm of art." *Essay on Crit.*, ll. 141 and 153. See J. E. Spingarn, *Critical Essays of the Seventeenth Century*, Introduction to vol. I.

217, l. 38, *virtuoso:* This word generally had an unfavourable connotation at this time, being applied to a mere empiric, or to a collector of curios. Shaftesbury uses it sometimes with a favourable connotation, in contrast to the pedant, who concerns himself so much with mechanical details that he loses the spirit of what he studies. In *Miscellaneous Reflections*, III, 1 (our second extract), he distinguishes between two types of virtuosos.

217, l. 45, *faciuntne intellegendo,... intellegant?* (Terence, *Andria*, Prol., l. 17): "Do they not bring it about by their understanding that they understand nothing?"

219, l. 42, *the same method and manner of soliloquy as above:* Note that the title of this selection is *Soliloquy, or Advice to an Author*. In pt. I, sec. 1, Shaftesbury explains his method of soliloquy, or self-discourse, in which he is both "pupil and preceptor."

220, l. 53, *the Nore:* a sandbank at the mouth of the Thames, below Gravesend.

220, l. 28, *Of antres vast...* : Shakespeare, *Othello*, I, 3, 140–46, with omissions.

MISCELLANEOUS REFLECTIONS

222, l. 52, *in favour of our author:* In *Miscellaneous Reflections* Shaftesbury announces as his purpose "to write on every subject and in every method as I fancy." Among other things he discusses the earlier essays which are also included in *Characteristics*.

222, l. 34, *these inferior virtuosos:* This paragraph is an excellent brief expression of the typical neoclassical attitude toward those whose interest in the unusual led them to disregard the typical and the universal.

223, l. 14, *Quid sumus,... gignimur* (Persius, *Sat.* III, 67): "What are we, and destined to live what life, pray, are we born?"

224, l. 21, *Quid verum... sum* (Horace, *Epist.* I, 1, 11): "What is true and also fitting is my concern and quest, and my thought all centres on this."

ANNE, COUNTESS OF WINCHILSEA

BIBLIOGRAPHY

Miscellany Poems, 1714.
The Poems of Anne, Countess of Winchilsea, ed. M. Reynolds, 1903.
Poems, selected and ed. J. M. Murry, 1928.
Sir Edmund Gosse in *Gossip in a Library*, 1891.
M. Reynolds in *The Treatment of Nature in English Poetry*, 1909.
E. Dowden in *Essays Modern and Elizabethan*, 1910.

NOTES

THE TREE

226, l. 14, *chaplets:* garlands.

226, l. 26, *Prevent:* anticipate, blowing the tree down before it is felled by the axe

TO THE NIGHTINGALE

227, l. 8, *unconfined:* With the thought, compare Keats's *Fancy*.

227, l. 13, *thorn:* a popular superstition.

227, l. 17, *thy:* the poet's.

227, l. 18, *refine:* This and the two lines following indicate an ideal of versification far in advance of Lady Winchilsea's time.

227, l. 23, *division:* a rapid melodic phrase sung on one breath to one syllable.

227, l. 32, *fluent vein:* an easy style in poetic composition.

A NOCTURNAL REVERIE

227, l. 1, *In such a night:* The entire poem, which is written in one sentence, is a fantasia upon this phrase from the opening lines of *The Merchant of Venice*, Act V.

227, l. 6, *hollowing:* hallooing.

227, l. 19, *Salisbury:* Lady Salisbury, wife of the Third Earl.

228, l. 46, *her own:* the soul's world, heaven. The line shows how remote Lady Winchelsea's religious belief was from the pantheism of the younger Wordsworth.

THE PETITION FOR AN ABSOLUTE RETREAT

228, l. 3, *retreat:* The rhyme with *fate* was sufficiently close in the pronunciation of the time.

228, l. 29, *truffle:* an edible fungus.

228, l. 29, *morillia:* morel, a kind of mushroom.

228, l. 31, *ortolan:* the garden bunting of Europe, a table delicacy.

228, l. 39, *cup:* skin of the grape.

228, l. 59, *monarch:* See I Kings, 7:1–12.

228, l. 84, *partially:* with the partiality of affection.

229, l. 115, *subterranean:* to shut off the sun's rays and see the stars by day.

229, l. 116, *engine:* a mechanical device, the telescope.

229, l. 120, *frame:* of mind.

FRAGMENT

229, l. 2, *Ardelia's:* Ardelia was the poet's pen-name.

229, l. 6, *dedicate:* Supply "made her" from l. 4.

229, l. 11, *placed:* The reference is to Anne's position at the court of James II and to the subsequent fall of that king.

229, l. 14, *wheel's:* the Wheel of Fortune.

229, l. 20, *in vain:* by themselves, alone.

229, l. 23, *monastic walls:* of Wye College, Kent, once a priory, near Lady Winchilsea's home.

229, l. 31, *ineffable recess:* This magical phrase and the lines following show the vagueness and ecstasy of mystical language and cannot be accurately glossed.

JOHN DYER

BIBLIOGRAPHY

A. Chalmers, *The Works of the British Poets*, vol. 13, 1810.
Poetical Works ed. with Life by G. Gilfillan, 1858.
Poems, ed. with Biographical Introduction by E. Thomas, 1903.
S. Johnson in *The Lives of the English Poets*.
E. Dowden in Ward's *The English Poets*.

GRONGAR HILL

231, l. 1, *Silent nymph:* the Muse of painting.

231, l. 2, *the purple ev'ning:* i.e., during the evening.

231, l. 3, *van:* brow.

231, l. 10, *Muse:* of poetry.

231, l. 13, *Grongar Hill:* in Carmarthenshire, near Aberglasney, where Dyer was born.

231, l. 23, *Towy's:* The Towy is a river flowing into Carmarthen Bay.

231, l. 66, *lawn:* grassy field.

231, l. 73, *creeps:* a transitive verb.

232, l. 113, *pearls:* The image is vaguely recollected from *Romeo and Juliet*, I, 5, 48.

232, l. 118, *streaks of meadows:* narrowed by perspective.

232, l. 132, *laid:* quieted, like waves.

THE COUNTRY WALK

232, l. 18, *Augusta:* London.

233, l. 116, *wildernesses:* parts of a garden allowed to grow wild.

AN EPISTLE TO A FRIEND IN TOWN

234, l. 8, *Virtue:* here, the sense of public duty.

THE TATLER

BIBLIOGRAPHY

The best edition of the *Tatler* is edited by G. A. Aitken, 4 vols., 1898, 1899.

Lives of Steele have been published by A. Dobson, 1888, and G. A. Aitken, 2 vols., 1889. See also references listed under the *Spectator.*

For an account of the predecessors of the *Tatler* see W. J. Graham, *Beginnings of English Literary Periodicals,* 1926, and for its successors see G. S. Marr, *Periodical Essayists of the Eighteenth Century,* 1925.

The most complete list of periodicals is to be found in *Tercentenary Handlist of English and Welsh Newspapers, 1620–1920,* 1920.

The rich but scattered collections of English periodicals in American libraries have been listed by R. S. Crane, and F. B. Kaye, in *Census of British Newspapers and Periodicals, 1620–1800,* 1927; and by W. Gregory, in *Union List of Serials,* 1927.

NOTES

NO. I

235, l. 1, *Motto:* The same motto was used until No. 41, when different quotations from Latin literature, suited to the theme for the day, were employed instead. Nos. 49 to 80 (with a few exceptions) revert to the first motto, which applied to the purpose of the *Tatler* as a whole rather than to the particular essay. Beginning with No. 81 varied mottoes were used, though a number of papers were left without mottoes.

236, l. 10, *White's Chocolate-house:* a fashionable resort known especially because of gambling for high stakes.

236, l. 11, *Will's Coffee-house:* Since the time of Dryden it had been the favourite meeting place of men of letters, though its literary reputation had been growing less. Addison, however, continued to frequent it until 1712, when he transferred his patronage to Button's.

236, l. 12, *Grecian:* Although chiefly a resort of lawyers, it had many patrons of other trades and professions who gathered there to discuss questions of learning and philosophy. Its name came from its original proprietor, a Greek.

236, l. 13, *St. James's Coffee-house:* a fashionable meeting place for Whigs on St. James's Street.

236, l. 23, *Kidney:* a waiter at St. James's.

236, l. 32, *the power of divination:* Mr. Bickerstaff had been represented by Swift as an astrologer. See note on Mr. Partridge below.

236, l. 29, *Love for Love:* a celebrated comedy by William Congreve, originally produced in 1695. Thomas Betterton, the celebrated tragic actor, who was now an old man, died the following year. The three players mentioned as acting on the occasion of this benefit performance were among the most famous of the period.

237, l. 27, *Mr. Thomas D'Urfey:* Though now comparatively forgotten, Tom D'Urfey (1653–1723) was well known as a dramatist and a song writer. He was a popular man-about-town and was also a friend of Addison's.

237, l. 36, *From... Apartment:* The letter from St. James's Coffee-house, which deals with reports from Holland about the progress of the war, is here omitted. The War of the Spanish Succession was then nearing its close, though the Treaty of Utrecht was not signed until 1713. Negotiations for peace were at this time in progress; but they were broken off, and the Battle of Malplaquet was fought on September 11 of the same year.

237, l. 40, *Mr. Partridge:* Swift's famous practical joke at the expense of John Partridge, a London almanac maker, was still fresh in the popular mind when the *Tatler* made its appearance. Under the pseudonym, Isaac Bickerstaff, Esq., Jonathan Swift had published *Predictions for the Year 1708,* in which he attacked the so-called astrological predictions of the popular almanacs and made *Merlinus Liberatus* of Partridge his special target. Instead of the vague and indefinite predictions then common, Bickerstaff, who professed to be a true astrologer, set down a definite forecast of the future, among other things predicting the death of Partridge on March 29. On March 30 he published a second pamphlet giving full details of the accomplishment of this prediction, which he said had come to pass within four hours of the time mentioned. In his almanac for 1709 Partridge protested loudly that he was still living, but Swift returned to the attack with *A Vindication of Isaac Bickerstaff, Esq.,* which asserted that Partridge could not be alive because the almanac which had recently appeared with his name contained such foolishness that it could have been written by no man alive. Accordingly he was urged to remain decently dead. In continuation of this joke, which had been taken up by the town wits, Steele made Isaac Bickerstaff his mouthpiece in the new magazine.

NO. 25

238, l. 24, *From... Apartment:* The article from St. James's Coffee-house is omitted here. It deals with reports from Vienna and the Hague about the progress of the war.

NO. 106

240, l. 3, *let me have a particular:* a phrase commonly used by auctioneers.

240, l. 6, *sonnets:* At this time the term, *sonnet,* was not restricted to the fixed form of lyric to which it is now exclusively applied. *Cf. Tatler,* No. 163.

240, l. 16, *in solitude:* Note the striking difference between this conception of solitude and that which was expressed by the romantic poets of the latter part of the century.

240, l. 35, *it might probably pass for a very good Pindaric:* Compare Addison's remarks on English Pindarics, *Spectator,* Nos. 58 and 160.

240, l. 19, *one of my late lucubrations: Tatler,* No. 104.

241, l. 35, *Company of Upholders: Upholders* here means *undertakers.*

241, l. 50, *Mr. Bickerstaff's dead warrant:* In *Tatler,* No. 96 Addison had supported the thesis that every worthless man is a dead man. Among other things he had said as follows: "In the number of the dead I comprehend all persons, of what title or dignity soever, who bestow most of their time in eating and drinking, to support that imaginary existence of theirs which they call life; or in dressing and adorning those shadows and apparitions which are looked upon by the vulgar as real men and women. In short, whoever resides in the world without having any business in it, and passes away an age without ever thinking on the errand for which he was sent hither, is to me a dead man to all intents and purposes; and I desire that he may be so reputed. The living are only those that are some way or other laudably employed in the improvement of their own minds, or for the advantage of others; and even among these, I shall only reckon into their lives that part of their time which has been spent in the manner above mentioned." At the end he returns to the old joke about John Partridge and prints a communication in which that worthy is made to assert that he is still living. *Cf.* No. 1.

NO. 163

241, l. 54, *little Gothic ornaments: Cf. Spectator,* No. 61.

242, l. 12, *sonnet:* See note to *Tatler,* No. 106.

NO. 165

243, l. 1, *that which is generally known by the name of a critic:* In this paragraph of generalizations and in the character of Sir Timothy Tittle which follows, Addison satirizes the small wits who set up as critics without either natural endowment or adequate knowledge. These are the fop-critics, the petty Hectors of the pit, the coffee-house oracles to whom prologues and epilogues, character-books, satires, and essays make frequent reference. At a time when all gentlemen were supposed to be amateur critics, it was inevitable that many should essay the part without much preparation. Such men were likely to fall back upon the French Aristotelian formalists for a few mechanical rules which they applied without taste or discrimination.

243, l. 26, *Rapin and Bossu:* René Rapin (1621–1687) was the author of numerous literary *Comparaisons* which were known both in French and in English translation, but he was most famous for *Réflexions sur la Poétique d'Aristote et sur les ouvrages des poètes anciens et modernes* (1674). René Le Bossu (1631–1680) was the best known authority of the time on epic poetry. His *Traité du poème épique* (1675) was widely read in England. Of the two, Le Bossu was the more formalistic; Rapin, like Boileau, laid a good deal of stress on those nameless graces that the rules are powerless to teach. Addison seems to have had respect for both these critics and to have been especially indebted to Le Bossu, whom he used particularly in his criticism of Milton.

244, l. 22, *that natural sense:* Here we have a reference to "good sense" as a saving antidote to critical formalism, a point of view much emphasized both by French and English critics of the time. See A. F. B. Clark, *Boileau and the French Classical Critics in England,* Chap. VI.

244, l. 51, *Dacier:* André Dacier (1651–1722) was a somewhat pedantic French critic, best known for his translation of Aristotle's *Poetics* and his remarks upon it.

NO. 181

245, l. 10, *resolved to be sorrowful:* Steele had a large vein of "sensibility" which at times suggests late eighteenth-century romantic sentimentality.

246, l. 34, *a hamper of wine:* This reference to an advertisement which appeared in the same number of the *Tatler* was at the same time a wine-merchant's "puff" and also, what is more important, a half humorous expedient to break off the sentimental reflections and provide a sharp contrast at the end.

NO. 196

246, l. 15, *patron's service:* With this essay on literary patronage compare Dr. Johnson's famous letter to Lord Chesterfield.

247, l. 4, *the upholder's goods: Upholder* here means a tradesman who deals in small wares. *Cf.* note to No. 106.

NO. 216

248, l. 31, *a virtuoso:* an empirical investigator; this word is almost always used by writers of this period in a depreciatory sense. On the common attitude toward the Royal Society and the satiric representation of the scientist, see C. S. Duncan, *The New Science and English Literature in the Classical Period* (Univ. of Chicago dissertation, 1913).

NO. 263

249, l. 37, *crimp and basset:* popular card games.

NO. 271

251, l. 36, *the purpose of it wholly lost by my being so long understood as the author:* While, of course, popular penetration of Steele's anonymity may have had something to do with the abandonment of the *Tatler* at this time, it is likely that his chief desire was to establish another magazine that would give greater freedom to develop the most valuable features of the journal.

251, l. 14, *The hand that has assisted me:* The reference is, of course, to Addison.

251, l. 38, *Major General Davenport, Brigadier Bisset, and my Lord Forbes:* Steele's attacks upon gamblers having resulted in threats by sharpers, on at least one occasion these gentlemen came to his assistance.

THE SPECTATOR

BIBLIOGRAPHY

A. Chalmers, *British Essayists* is a convenient collection of the more important eighteenth-century periodical essays.

Good editions of the *Spectator* are as follows: Henry Morley, 1889–91; G. A. Aitkin, 8 vols., 1898; G. G. Smith, 8 vols., 1897, 1898, and 4 vols., 1907.

For Addison see A. C. Guthkelch, *Miscellaneous Works of Joseph Addison*, 2 vols., 1914.

William Wheeler, *Concordance to the Spectator*, 1898.

Lives of Addison have been published by Lucy Aikin, 2 vols., 1843; W. J. Courthope, E.M.L., 1884; and Sir Leslie Stephen, in *DNB.*

A. Beljame, *Le public et les hommes de lettres en Angleterre au dix-huitième siècle, 1660–1774*, 1881, contains an important chapter on Addison.

Bonamy Dobrée, "The First Victorian," in *Essays in Biography*, 1925.

Well-known discussions, which, however, reveal more of their authors than they do of their subjects, are W. M. Thackeray, *The English Humorists of the Eighteenth Century;* William Hazlitt, *Lectures on the English Comic Writers;* and T. B. Macaulay, *Essay on Addison.*

Important material for the study not only of Addison and Steele but also of all the principal men of letters of the eighteenth century is to be found in Joseph Spence, *Anecdotes, Observations, and Characters*, 1820; and in John Nichols, *Literary Anecdotes of the Eighteenth Century*, 1782, and *Literary Illustrations of the Eighteenth Century*, 1817.

NOTES

NO. 2

254, l. 8, *Soho Square:* still a fashionable quarter in 1711, though, like Sir Roger himself, less fashionable than it had been some years before. The name, Soho, may be supposed to have appealed to Sir Roger since it recalls the hunters' cry when the dogs are called off from the hare.

255, l. 42, *Longinus:* Though the *Treatise on the Sublime* which bears his name had already been three times translated into English before the end of the seventeenth century, it was through the translation and the *Réflexions* of Boileau that this important work of ancient criticism chiefly came to be known in England. About this time there was unusual interest in Longinus; the Templar was therefore in the best literary mode of the day. Littleton and Coke are, of course, among the best known English authorities on law.

255, l. 13, *exactly at five:* The dinner hour about 1711 was usually three or four in the afternoon; the play began at six. These hours had been retarded since 1660 when the play had begun at three. Compare *Tatler*, No. 263, pp. 249–51.

NO. 35

257, l. 19, *Risu inepto:* The motto is in the original wrongly ascribed to Martial.

257, l. 3, *The deceased Mr. Shadwell:* Shadwell had prided himself on the humours in his plays. See note on Dryden's *Absalom and Achitophel*, l. 15.

257, l. 17, *as Cowley has done:* See Cowley's ode, *Of Wit*, especially the seventh stanza.

NO. 41

258, l. 48, *The Silent Woman:* In Ben Jonson's *Epicœne, or The Silent Woman*, V, 1, these two characters discuss the question.

NO. 50

260, l. 54, *the four Indian kings:* Swift in the *Journal to Stella*, April 28, 1711, the morning after the publication of this paper, speaks of "a noble hint" he had given Steele, "long ago for his Tatlers, about an Indian supposed to write his travels into England. I repent he ever had it. I intended to have written a book on that subject. I believe he has spent it all in one paper, and all the under hints there are mine too; but I never see him or Addison." In the *Tatler*, No. 171 (May 13, 1710), the four kings had already been introduced. During the preceding month four American Indian chiefs had been in London and had excited a good deal of popular interest.

261, l. 42, *little black spots:* Of course these are the patches that were then much in vogue; Addison again satirizes them in *Spectator*, No. 81.

NO. 58

262, l. 14, *Ut pictura poesis erit:* As Gregory Smith points out in his notes to the Everyman's Library *Spectator*, the quotation in the form given in the motto comes from Du Fresnoy's *De Arte Graphica* (1658); Horace's words in *Ars Poetica*, ll. 361 ff., do not mean that poetry and painting are alike in all respects, but that they have certain points of similarity. See *The New Laokoön*, by Irving Babbitt.

262, l. 30, *the censure which a famous critic bestows:* The reference is to Longinus's objections to Cæcilius's work *On the Sublime*.

263, l. 54, *Mr. Herbert's poems:* This particular kind of false wit is exemplified in but two poems in George Herbert's *The Temple* (*The Altar* and *Easter Wings*), but other kinds such as anagram and "echo" poems are also found there. *Cf.* Dryden, *Mac Flecknoe*, ll. 203–08.

263, l. 1, *Du Bartas:* The reference, as Gregory Smith points out, is to the Dedication in Joshua Sylvester's translation of Du Bartas.

263, l. 49, *Pindaric writers:* Compare Addison's further references in No. 160.

NO. 61

264, l. 1, *No. 61:* The second and third papers on wit are omitted. They discuss the verses of lipogrammatists or letter-droppers, rebuses, echo poems, anagrams, acrostics, *bouts-rimés*, and the use of doggerel rhymes.

264, l. 20, *a famous university:* The references to fens and marshes indicates that Cambridge is meant.

265, l. 11, *recover itself in some distant period of time:* Addison's prophecy was strikingly fulfilled in the romantic revival of the nineteenth century, notably in the work of Lamb and Hood.

265, ll. 4, 5, *Induitur... forma est:* It is not always noticed that Addison ends his essay on puns by playing on the words, *formosa* (beautiful) and *ipsa forma* (form or beauty itself).

NO. 62

267, l. 32, *Mr. Dryden's definition of wit:* Quoted from his *Apology for Heroic Poetry and Poetic Licence* prefixed to *The State of Innocence* (1677): "From that which has been said, it may be collected that the definition of wit (which has been so often attempted, and ever unsuccessfully by many poets) is only this: that it is a propriety of thoughts and words; or, in other terms, thoughts and words elegantly adapted to the subject."

267, l. 51, *Bouhours... the most penetrating of all the French critics:* The reference is to the fourth of Père Bouhours's dialogues which bears the title, *La Manière de bien penser dans les ouvrages d'esprit.* For Bouhours's influence on Addison see A. F. B. Clark, *Boileau and the French Classical Critics in England,* 1925, chap. V and pp. 266, 267 especially.

267, l. 49, *Gothic:* On the varying meanings and connotations of this word see *NED.* Here it refers to the rude taste which is unpurified by classical influences.

267, l. 49, *He quotes Monsieur Segrais:* from *Virgil and the Æneid,* Dryden's dedication of his translation of the *Æneid* (1697). Jean Regnauld de Segrais (1624–1701) prefixed to his translation of the *Æneid,* a dissertation of which Dryden has much to say in this work.

268, l. 10, *mob readers: Cf.* p. 146, l. 7, note.

NO. 63

268, l. 33, *pulvillios:* scent bags fashionable at the time.

NO. 70

271, l. 19, *Sir Philip Sidney:* Note that Sidney had praised the ballad because of its similarity to classical poetry and had objected to its crude style, while Addison in similar fashion compares *Chevy Chase* in this essay to Virgil's *Æneid.* But in the ballad revival of the late eighteenth and the nineteenth century it was the primitive qualities of the ballads that were appreciated.

271, l. 51, *time the poem... was written:* Addison had no idea of the distinction between oral and written poetry which was much emphasized later.

273, l. 6, *another opportunity: Spectator,* No. 74, published the following Friday, further elaborated the comparison between *Chevy Chase* and the *Æneid.*

NO. 102

273, l. 1, *No. 102:* In *Tatler,* No. 52, Steele had already treated the idea of this paper, and in *Tatler,* No. 239 Addison had touched upon it incidentally in the verses on Flavia's fan.

274, l. 50, *I teach young gentlemen:* In the advertisement to *Spectator,* No. 138 Steele develops this idea further, as follows: "The exercise of the snuff-box, according to the most fashionable airs and motions, in opposition to the exercise of the fan, will be taught with the best plain or perfumed snuff, at Charles Lillie's, perfumer, at the corner of Bauford-Buildings in the Strand, and attendance given for the benefit of the young merchants about the Exchange for two hours every day at noon, except Saturdays, at a toy-shop near Garraway's Coffee-house. There will be likewise taught the ceremony of the snuff-box, or rules for offering snuff to a stranger, a friend, or a mistress, according to the degrees of familiarity or distance; with an explanation of the careless, the scornful, the politic, and the surly pinch, and the gestures proper to each of them. N.B. The undertaker does not question but in a short time to have formed a body of regular snuff-boxes ready to meet and make head against all the regiment of fans which have been lately disciplined, and are now in motion."

NO. 119

275, l. 31, *conversation among men of mode: Cf.* Dryden's statements in the Prologue to the Second Part of *The Conquest of Granada,* p. 62, about the difference between the wit of conversation in this age and the last.

NO. 135

276, l. 2, *one of the greatest geniuses:* The reference is evidently to Swift, who had written *Tatler,* No. 230 on the same subject about a year before, and who published *A Proposal for Correcting... the English Language* the following year. *Cf. A Complete Collection... of Conversation,* pp. 440 ff.

276, l. 20, *single letter... does the office of a whole word:* In this matter as well as in the substitution of "s" for "eth" modern historical grammar has shown that the facts are not quite as here represented. M.E. *-es* or *-is* was shortened to *'s*; *his,* as in *John Smith his mark,* was the result of confusion with this termination. The third person singular present ending *-s* is not an abbreviation of the form *-eth,* but resulted from the substitution of the northern dialect ending in Standard English.

277, l. 2, *Sir Roger L'Estrange* (1616–1704): journalist and minor man of letters; under Charles II and James II, Surveyor of Printing Presses and Licencer of the Press.

277, l. 25, *academy:* For further references to the project of establishing an English academy see Swift's *Proposal* mentioned above.

NO. 157

277, l. 13, *indoles:* This Latin word means *inborn* or *native quality*. *Cf.* Addison's remarks on Genius in No. 160.

277, l. 48, *misfortune of the children:* In thus attacking abuses in contemporary education Steele was espousing the cause of another unpopular reform; compare his attitude toward duelling, gambling, etc. Steele takes up the same subject again in *Spectator*, No. 168.

279, l. 10, *of either robe:* that is, the law or the church.

279, l. 33, *Mr. Cæsar:* The context seems to demand Mr. Darcy.

NO. 160

279, l. 12, *natural geniuses:* In this paper Addison foreshadows the controversy about original genius that was to bulk large in the latter part of the eighteenth century and was to play an important part in the romantic movement. *Cf.* Young's *Conjectures on Original Composition.*

279, l. 51, *a large field of raillery:* Homer's comparison of Ajax to an ass belaboured by boys (*Iliad*, II, 558 ff.) and of Odysseus to a piece of flesh broiled on the coals (*Odyssey*, XX, 25 ff.) had given rise to much discussion among Renaissance critics, some of whom (Vida and Scaliger, for example) laid stress upon Virgil's superiority to Homer in the matter of decorum. The little wits to whom Addison here refers are probably contemporary beau-critics who repeat commonplaces of censure about authors whom they know slightly, if at all.

280, l. 8, *bienséance:* "Decorum or propriety."

280, l. 26, *Pindarics: Cf. Spectator*, No. 58.

280, ll. 34–36, *Incerta hæc... insanias* (*Eun.*, act I, sc. i, ll. 16–18): "You may as well pretend to be mad and in your senses at the same time as to think of reducing these uncertain things to any certainty by reason."

280, l. 39, *Camisars:* The Camisars (or Camisards), sometimes called "French prophets," were French Calvinists who had taken arms after the revocation of the Edict of Nantes. They were often ridiculed because of their eccentricity.

NO. 262

281, l. 24, *the late designed procession:* Since the time of the "Popish Plot" it had been customary to celebrate Nov. 17, Queen Elizabeth's Accession Day, by means of a burlesque procession in which the Pope, cardinals, Jesuits, and various allegorical figures were taken through the streets of London and then publicly burned. In 1711 the procession had been planned on a scale more elaborate than usual; but the government feared public disturbances and so prevented its taking place.

281, l. 43, *as tubs and barrels are to a whale:* Swift's *Tale of a Tub* had appeared in 1704.

NO. 409

284, l. 7, *I entertained the town: Spectator*, Nos. 58–63, four of which are included in the present collection.

284, l. 13, *I afterwards gave an instance: Spectator*, Nos. 70 and 74, the former of which is included in the present collection.

284, l. 18, *I have likewise examined:* Addison's series of papers on *Paradise Lost*, which ran in the *Spectator* on successive Saturdays from No. 266 to No. 369.

NO. 419

284, l. 46, *fairy way of writing:* This paper is the ninth of the series on "The Pleasures of the Imagination" promised in No. 409. *Cf.* Hurd's *Letters on Chivalry and Romance*, pp. 754 ff.

284, l. 12, *Sylvis deducti... versibus* (*A.P.*, 244):

> "A satyr that comes staring from the woods
> Must not at first speak like an orator."
>
> ROSCOMMON.

284, l. 16, *Mr. Bayes in The Rehearsal: The Rehearsal* (1671) by George Villiers, Duke of Buckingham, and others ridiculed the heroic play and introduced Dryden under the name, Bayes. See 5, 1, 113–115:

"BAYES. Plain? Why, did you ever hear any people in clouds speak plain? They must be all for flights of fancy, at its full range, without the least check or control upon it. When once you tie up spirits and people in clouds to speak plain, you spoil all."

THOMAS TICKELL

BIBLIOGRAPHY

Works in A. Chalmers, *The Works of the English Poets*, 1810.
Life, by Dr. Johnson, *The Lives of the English Poets.*
R. E. Tickell, *Thomas Tickell and the Eighteenth Century Poets*, 1931.

NOTES

286, l. 3, *Warwick:* Addison had married, three years before his death, the Countess-dowager of Warwick.

286, l. 12, *dead:* Addison's tomb is in the "Poets' Corner," Westminster Abbey.

286, l. 22, *Montagu:* Charles Montagu, Earl of Halfax, 1661–1715, friend and patron of Addison.

286, l. 27, *memorial:* remembrance.

286, l. 33, *alone:* The following lines were probably suggested by Addison's Essay, "A Walk Through Westminster Abbey."

287, l. 56, *hymns:* such as *The Spacious Firmament on High.*

287, l. 74, *Cato:* Addison's drama of that name.

287, l. 76, *grove:* probably at Holland House, Kensington, where Addison spent his last years and where he died.

287, l. 82, *die:* On his death-bed Addison called for the Earl of Warwick, that he might see "how a Christian can die."

287, l. 83, *hill:* the eminence above the Avon River on which Warwick Castle stands.

287, l. 102, *Craggs:* James Craggs the younger, 1686–1721, a friend of Pope, Gay, Tickell, and Addison, who had served with the last two in the Cabinet of 1717.

287, l. 106, *convey'd:* Dr. Johnson says that Addison, on his death-bed, dedicated his works to Craggs and "gave directions to Mr. Tickell for their publication."

287, l. 110, *lies:* James Craggs was also buried in the Abbey.

ISAAC WATTS

BIBLIOGRAPHY

Works, 6 vols., 1753.
Poems in A. Chalmers, *The Works of the English Poets*, 1810.
Thomas Gibbons, *Memoirs of the Rev. Isaac Watts, D.D.*, 1780.
Brief lives by Dr. Johnson and by Jeremy Belknap (1793).
W. M. Stone, *The Divine and Moral Songs of Isaac Watts*, 1918.

NOTES

THE DAY OF JUDGMENT

288, l. 34, *Dooming:* judging.

MAN FRAIL, AND GOD ETERNAL

289, l. 10, *frame:* shape.

WILLIAM LAW

BIBLIOGRAPHY

Works, 9 vols., 1756–76. Also ed. by G. B. Morgan, 1892–93.
A Serious Call has appeared in numerous editions; see especially those of J. H. Overton, 1898, and of C. Bigg, 1899. It is also included in Everyman's Library.

Among works of biography and criticism see the following:
Christopher Walton, *Notes and Materials for an Adequate Biography of... Law...*, 1854.
J. H Overton, *William Law, Nonjuror and Mystic*, 1881.
[G. Moreton], *Memorials of the Birthplace and Residence of... Law at King's Cliffe*, 1895.
Stephen Hobhouse, *William Law and Eighteenth Century Quakerism*, 1927.
Sir Leslie Stephen, *History of English Thought in the Eighteenth Century*, 2 vols., 1876.
C J. Abbey and J. H. Overton, *The English Church in the Eighteenth Century*, 2 vols., 1878.
W. R. Inge, *Studies in the English Mystics*, 1899.
Rufus M. Jones, *Studies in Mystical Religion*, 1909.
J. H. Overton, *The Nonjurors, their Lives, Principles and Writings*, 1902.
A volume of selections from Jacob Boehme is published in Everyman's Library under the title, *The Signature of All Things*.

NOTES

291, l. 18, *Julius:* One of the characteristic features of *A Serious Call* is the "characters" with which it is interspersed. These are an interesting development from seventeenth-century character-writing, and may be advantageously compared with the verse characters in Pope's *Moral Essays*.

294, l. 16, *a natural:* an idiot.

COLLEY CIBBER

BIBLIOGRAPHY

The best modern version of Cibber's *Apology* is edited with notes and supplement by R. W. Lowe, 2 vols., 1889.
Two recent works of biography and criticism are D. M. E. Habbema, *An Appreciation of Colley Cibber*, which includes a reprint of his play, *The Careless Husband*, 1928; and F. Dorothy Senior, *The Life and Times of Colley Cibber*, 1928.

NOTES

295, l. 4, *the master of our theatre:* Christopher Rich, manager of Drury Lane Theatre. Cibber's opinion of his character, which is writ large in the *Apology*, can readily be estimated from this extract.

296, l. 14, *The Funeral, or Grief à la Mode:* comedy by Richard Steele, first acted, 1701.

296, l. 20, *utile dulci* (Horace, *Art of Poetry*, 343): "The useful with the agreeable." These words, together with *prodesse, delectare* (*Ib.*, 333), which are translated in the context, are among the commonplaces of critical reference.

297, l. 10, *The Pilgrim:* Fletcher's play, revised by Vanbrugh under conditions explained in the context. This Epilogue is of the more significance since it is one of the very last things that Dryden wrote; he died on May 1, 1700.

298, l. 32, *View of the Stage, etc., about the year, 1697: A Short View of the Immorality and Profaneness of the English Stage* was published in 1698; see Introduction to Jeremy Collier, p. 196.

298, l. 1, *The authors of the Old Bachelor and of The Relapse:* William Congreve and Sir John Vanbrugh.

298, l. 21, *nolo prosequi:* "I am unwilling to prosecute," a legal expression (usually written *nolle* in the infinitive) indicating that the prosecutor wishes to proceed no further in the action. See Introduction to Jeremy Collier.

298, l. 44, *sic volo:* "Thus I will."

298, l. 52, *King Henry the Sixth, who is killed by Richard in the first act:* As indicated in the context, this play was not *Richard III* as Shakespeare wrote it, but Cibber's revision which begins with the scene of the king's murder from the Third Part of *Henry VI*. Cibber's version held the stage until comparatively recent times.

299, l. 18, *The patent granted... to Sir Richard Steele:* After the accession of George I, Steele was given the patent of the Theatre Royal of Drury Lane.

LADY MARY WORTLEY MONTAGU

BIBLIOGRAPHY

The standard edition, *Letters and Works of Lady Mary Wortley Montagu*, was ed. by her great-grandson, Lord Wharncliffe, in 3 vols., 1837. Moy Thomas published a revised edition in 2 vols. with additions and a Memoir, 1861; this edition was republished with slight additions in Bohn's Library, 2 vols.,

1886; Thomas's edition reappeared in 1887 and 1893. The Letters were also published in Everyman's Library, 1906.

Lewis Melville [pseud. for Lewis S. Benjamin], *Lady Mary Wortley Montagu: Her Life and Letters (1689–1762)*, n.d. A selection from the Letters with comment was published by A. R. Ropes under the title, *Lady Mary Wortley Montagu*, 1892.

For biography, in addition to the above, see George Paston [pseud. for Miss E. M. Symonds], *Lady Mary Wortley Montagu and her Times*, 1907.

Iris Barry, *Portrait of Lady Mary Wortley Montagu*, 1928, is an imaginative work "in almost every detail based on fact."

For background see Myra Reynolds, *The Learned Lady in England 1650–1760*, 1920.

NOTES

300, l. 8, *a journey not undertaken by any Christian for some hundred years:* In 1716 Lady Mary left England for Constantinople whither her husband was sent as English ambassador. They remained in Turkey from March, 1717, until July, 1718. Her letters written during her stay at Constantinople were published shortly after her death. These are famous for their vivid descriptions of little known places, but since they were evidently written for general reading, if not for publication, they have less of vivid personality than is to be found in her later correspondence.

300, l. 7, "*Caput a cervice... ripæ*":

"Then, when his head, from his fair shoulders torn,
Wash'd by the waters, was on Hebrus borne,
Ev'n then his trembling tongue invok'd his bride;
With his last voice, 'Eurydice,' he cried.
'Eurydice,' the rocks and river banks replied."

301, l. 5, "*As equal were our souls...*": Dryden, "An Ode to the Pious Memory of... Mrs. Anne Killigrew," l. 164, slightly altered, "As equal were their souls, so equal was their fate."

301, l. 31, *I read over your Homer:* Pope's translation of the *Iliad*, the first four books of which had appeared in 1715.

303, l. 35, *the Countess of Mar:* Lady Mary's younger sister, Frances, had married the Earl of Mar, who joined the Pretender in the rising of 1715. The fact that he was now in exile accounts for the writer's uncertainty about her sister's address.

304, l. 12, *ruelle:* bedchamber or alcove arranged as a private drawing-room.

305, l. 48, *soucoupes:* saucers or salvers.

307, l. 5, *Poloneze:* a Pole. Kamieniec is the Polish name of Kamenetz-Podolsk, which was an important fortress in the seventeenth and eighteenth centuries.

307, l. 41, *the Countess of Pomfret:* She had been one of the Ladies of the Bedchamber to Queen Caroline, at whose death the countess and her husband had gone abroad.

307, l. 52, "*Rien n'est beau... aimable*": "Nothing is beautiful but the true; the true only is lovely."

307, l. 7, *the gifts of Lilly or Partridge:* the power of foretelling the future, claimed by the popular almanac makers. Partridge was the man whom Swift had held up to ridicule a generation before.

308, l. 27, *the Countess of Bute:* Her daughter, Mary, who had been born in Turkey, had in spite of her mother's disapproval married a Scottish peer, Lord Bute, who later attained a high position in the state. During the last years of Lady Mary's life many of her letters were addressed to Lady Bute with whom she had become completely reconciled.

309, l. 15, *Randolph's poems:* Thomas Randolph (1605–1635), poet and dramatist, and friend of Ben Jonson. There were probably few people in the eighteenth century who had read his works.

309, l. 9, *Lady——... or Mrs.——*: Thomas points out in a note that the blanks are in the original manuscript letter.

309, l. 15, *Pope's unintelligible essays:* Personal prejudice against Pope was responsible for this surprising statement. At this time Lady Mary could not tolerate the work of Pope or of any of his friends.

MATTHEW PRIOR

BIBLIOGRAPHY

Miscellaneous Works, ed. A. Drift, 2 vols., 1740.

The Writings of Matthew Prior (prose and verse), ed. A. R. Waller, 2 vols., 1905–07.

Dialogues of the Dead, ed. A. R. Waller, 1907.

Poems on Several Occasions, 2 vols., 1718.

Poetical Works, ed. with memoirs and notes by T. Evans, 1779.

Poetical Works, with Memoir by J. Mitford, 2 vols., 1835, 1866.
Poetical Works, with Memoir by G. Gilfillan, 1858.
Poetical Works, with Memoir by R. B. Johnson, 2 vols., 1892.
Selected Poems, with introduction and notes by A. Dobson, 1889.
Shorter Poems, ed. Francis Bickley, 1923.
A. Dobson, in *Eighteenth Century Vignettes*, third series, 1896.
A. C. Swinburne, in *Miscellanies*, 1886.
W. M. Thackeray, in *English Humorists of the Eighteenth Century*, 1853.
L. G. W. Legg, *Matthew Prior*, 1921.

NOTES

TO A LADY

312, l. 31, *reed:* arrow or javelin.

A BETTER ANSWER (TO CLOE JEALOUS)

312, l. 20, *Thetis's:* Thetis, a sea-goddess.

AN EPITAPH

313, l. 48, *bottom:* a thread used to wind round loose papers and the like.
313, l. 53, *ringers:* of the church bells.

THOMAS PARNELL

BIBLIOGRAPHY

Poems on Several Occasions, ed. A. Pope, 1721.
Poetical Works, ed. with Memoir by G. A. Aitken, 1846, 1894.
Poetical Works (with Churchill and Tickell), 1854.
Poetical Works, ed. with Life by G. Gilfillan, 1855.
Poems, selected by L. Robinson, 1927.
O. Goldsmith, *Life of Dr. Parnell*, 1770.
S. Johnson, *The Lives of the English Poets*.

NOTES

TO MR. POPE

317, l. 19, *Egypt's princess:* Berenice, wife of Ptolemy III. She dedicated her hair to Venus for the safe return of her husband from a military expedition, and when it disappeared from the temple a court astrologer explained that it had been carried to the sky and had there become the constellation *Coma Berenices*. The Greek poet Callimachus (*ca.* 250 B.C.) celebrated the incident in a mock-heroic poem which exists only in a translation by Catullus, but which had some influence upon *The Rape of the Lock* (cf. V, 129 ff.).

317, l. 22, *for gods:* in the form or aspect of gods.

317, l. 23, *new machines:* In dedicating *The Rape of the Lock* to Miss Arabella Fermor, Pope wrote: "The machinery, madam, is a term invented by the critics to signify that part which the deities, angels or demons are made to act in a poem.... These machines I determined to raise on a very new and odd foundation, the Rosicrucian doctrine of spirits."

317, l. 24, *chymic fool:* The Rosicrucians used the technical terms of alchemy as a sort of secret language for the expression of their moral and religious ideas.

318, l. 27, *satyr:* The word "satire" was erroneously connected with "satyr" during the eighteenth century, both spelling and pronunciation helping the confusion.

318, l. 78, *unfertile ground:* Ireland.

A HYMN TO CONTENTMENT

319, l. 26, *trailing purple:* walking in the purple robes of a king.

319, l. 42, *Grace:* Peace personified.

319, l. 73, *speak their Maker:* reveal. The idea that Nature is a secondary revelation of the Creator was prominent in all Deistic thinking, and from it was drawn the corollary that the contemplation and study of Nature leads to knowledge of God.

A NIGHT-PIECE ON DEATH

319, l. 29, *osier:* twigs of willow.

320, l. 50, *visionary:* imagined.

320, l. 71, *stoles:* ecclesiastical vestments usually consisting of narrow strips worn over the shoulders and falling to the knees.

320, l. 72, *cypress:* a kind of crape.

320, l. 72, *mourning poles:* either the funeral staffs upon which the cross was carried in the funeral procession, or else the poles on which the hatchments of the deceased were borne.

320, l. 73, *weeds:* mourning garments.

320, l. 76, *'scutcheons:* coats of arms.

THE HERMIT

320, l. 10, *sprung:* caused.

320, l. 26, *scallop:* A scallop-shell was commonly worn by mediæval pilgrims both as an emblem and as a utensil.

320, l. 38, *deceived:* made it seem shorter.

321, l. 52, *flourish:* ostentation.

321, l. 103, *eager:* sour.

322, l. 152, *writhed:* in the transitive sense, twisted.

322, l. 161, *Perplexed:* crossed confusingly.

322, l. 163, *nice:* difficult.

322, l. 179, *gradual:* growing.

322, l. 183, *wist:* knew.

322, l. 199, *second:* indirect.

323, l. 220, *artists:* artisans.

323, l. 221, *coals of fire:* quoted from Romans, 12:20.

323, l. 230, *go:* die.

JOHN GAY

BIBLIOGRAPHY

Poems, 1720, 1727, 1752.
Works, 4 vols., 1770.
Poetical, Dramatic, and Miscellaneous Works, with Life by S. Johnson, 6 vols., 1793.
Poetical Works, ed. J. Underhill (Muses' Library), 2 vols., 1893.
Poetical Works, ed. G. Faber, 1926.
Trivia, ed. W. H. Williams, 1922.
W. Coxe, *Life of Gay*, 2nd ed., 1797.
W. Hazlitt in *Lectures on the English Poets.*
Lewis Melville [pseud. for Lewis S. Benjamin], *Life and Letters of John Gay, 1685–1732*, 1921.
Oscar Sherwin, *Mr. Gay; being a Picture of the Life and Times of the Author of the Beggar's Opera*, 1929.

NOTES

THE SHEPHERD'S WEEK, "TUESDAY"

326, l. 13, *misling:* misty.

326, l. 14, *nappy:* strong.

THE SHEPHERD'S WEEK, "FRIDAY"

326, l. 16, *sonnets:* used in the contemporary sense of songs or ballads.

326, l. 19, *Patient Grissel:* the phenomenally long-suffering wife in Chaucer's "Clerk of Oxford's Tale."

326, l. 19, *devise:* intend.

327, l. 55, *hatch:* a half-door or wicket.

327, l. 58, *pinners:* pinafores.

327, l. 60, *lily:* a tool used in stamping impressions upon butter.

327, l. 79, *every deal:* entirely.

327, l. 85, *butter-flowers:* buttercups.

327, l. 86, *hemlock:* the poisonous plant, not the tree.
327, l. 99, *wether's:* the old ram with a bell attached to its neck that led the flock.
328, l. 135, *Sprigg'd:* arranged in sprays or branches.
328, l. 151, *Gaffer:* grandfather.
328, l. 155, *standing:* stagnant.

TRIVIA

328, l. 4, *Billingsgate:* London fish-market, below London Bridge.
328, l. 7, *asses:* The milk of asses, which were driven through the streets like the goats of Italian cities, was at this time often prescribed for invalids. *Cf. Dunciad* II, 247.
328, l. 11, *drummers:* hired to serenade the newly-wed.
328, l. 14, *state of peace:* i.e., in married life. See *Spectator*, No. 364.
328, l. 16, *hawker:* street-vendor.
329, l. 29, *small-coal:* broken into small pieces.
329, l. 40, *The wall:* that part of the sidewalk nearest the wall, and so farthest from the muddy road.
329, l. 48, *mantling peruke:* full and flowing periwig.
329, l. 56, *kennel:* gutter of the street.
329, l. 61, *signs:* used to identify houses and other buildings, which were not numbered.
329, l. 67, *St. Giles's* (in the Fields): a parish in the northwest of Gay's London, once a separate village.
329, l. 69, *sev'n dials:* These have given their name to the modern district.
329, l. 84, *fob:* a pocket in the waistband.
329, l. 85, *stunted besom:* worn broom.
329, l. 86, *rid:* clear.
329, l. 86, *slabby:* sloppy.
329, l. 91, *billets:* chunks of wood.
329, l. 92, *post:* used to mark the edge of the pavement.
329, l. 94, *board:* of the pillory, used to punish perjurers.
330, l. 109, *Samian:* Pythagoras, born at Samos.
330, l. 115, *Watling Street:* dangerous because narrow.
330, l. 117, *rugged street:* Thames Street.
330, l. 118, *Fleet-ditch:* once a brook, but in Gay's time little better than an open sewer.
330, l. 124, *trainy oil:* tried from whale's blubber.
330, l. 126, *Cornavian:* from Cheshire.
330, l. 128, *chaplain:* supposed to leave the table of his host when dessert was served, together with all other persons of low social rank.
330, l. 129, *Pell Mell:* a fashionable street in western London, now Pall Mall, so-called from a game resembling croquet, of the same (French) name.
330, l. 133, *lets:* obstructions.
330, l. 149, *beaver:* a hat made of beaver's fur.
330, l. 156, *draper's:* a dealer in cloth, linen, etc.
330, l. 160, *Meuse:* The Mews, where originally the king's falcons were "mewed," later became the royal stables, on the site of Trafalgar Square.
330, l. 160, *thimble's cheats:* thimble rigging, a sleight-of-hand played with cups and a ball.

THE TWO MONKEYS

331, l. 5, *Don:* a Spaniard.
331, l. 6, *Monsieur's:* a Frenchman's.

THE HARE AND MANY FRIENDS

332, l. 2, *stint:* confine.

MATTHEW GREEN

BIBLIOGRAPHY

The Spleen, ed. R. Glover, 1737.
Third edition, with other pieces, 1738.
Fourth edition, ed. J. Aikin, 1796.
Poetical Works, ed. G. Gilfillan, 1858.

NOTES

334, l. 35, *chief:* a housekeeper.

334, l. 43, *plate:* silver.

334, l. 53, *Eurus:* the east wind.

334, l. 56, *quit-rents:* sums paid by freeholders of a manor in the place of other services.

335, l. 62, *embodied:* grouped together.

335, l. 68, *dark decrees:* an allusion to the ancient Roman custom of divination by interpreting the sounds of leaves in the wind.

335, l. 96, *sphincter:* a muscle encircling a natural opening or passage, and able to close it.

335, l. 100, *livery-smile:* donned as though it were a uniform worn as a token of service.

335, l. 108, *coming down:* returning from London to the country.

ALEXANDER POPE

BIBLIOGRAPHY

The standard edition of Pope's Works is edited by Whitwell Elwin and W. J. Courthope, 10 vols., 1871–89.

Poetical Works, edited by A. W. Ward, the Globe Edition, 1869.

The Complete Poetical Works, edited by H. W. Boynton, the Cambridge Edition, 1903.

The Essay on Man, edited by Mark Pattison, 1869.

Satires and Epistles, edited by Mark Pattison, 1872.

Selections, edited by George Sherburn, 1929.

The Dunciad Variorum, facsimile of the edition of 1729, edited by R. K. Root, 1929.

The best bibliography is that by R. H. Griffith in two parts, 1922, 1927.

Edwin Abbott, *A Concordance to the Works of Alexander Pope*, 1875.

For biography see the following:

Samuel Johnson, *The Lives of the English Poets*, 1779–81.

Joseph Spence, *Anecdotes, Observations, and Characters of Books and Men. Collected from the Conversations of Mr. Pope and other Eminent Men of his Time*, 1820.

R. Carruthers, *The Life of Alexander Pope, including Extracts from his Correspondence*, Second Edition, 1857.

Sir Leslie Stephen, *Alexander Pope*, E. M. of L. Series, 1880.

W. J. Courthope, *The Life of Alexander Pope*, 1889. Vol. 5 of the Elwin and Courthope edition of Pope's *Works*.

George Paston [pseud. for Miss E. M. Symonds], *Mr. Pope: his Life and Times*, 2 vols., 1909.

Edith Sitwell, *Alexander Pope*, 1930.

Among the large number of critical works the following will be useful:

Joseph Warton, *An Essay on the Genius and Writings of Pope*, vol. I, 1756; vol. II, 1782.

Albrecht Deetz, *Alexander Pope. Ein Beitrag zur Literaturgeschichte des achtzehnten Jahrhunderts, nebst Proben Pope'scher Dichtungen*, 1876.

A. Beljame, *Le public et les hommes de lettres en Angleterre (1660–1744)*, 1881.

James W. Tupper, "Pope's Imitations of Horace," *PMLA*, 15:181 ff., 1900.

Ludwig Lochner, *Popes literarische Beziehungen zu seinen Zeitgenossen*, 1910.

Paul Elmer More, *With the Wits*, 1918.

J. W. Mackail, *Pope*, The Leslie Stephen Lecture, 1919.

Lytton Strachey, *Pope*, The Leslie Stephen Lecture, 1925.

C. W. Broadribb, *Pope: his Friendships and his Poetry*. National Home-Reading Union Pamphlets, Literature Series, No. 9, 1925.

George Sherburn, "The Fortunes and Misfortunes of *Three Hours after Marriage*," *MP*, 24:91–109; 1926. (Discusses the early attacks on Pope.)

Ralph Straus, *The Unspeakable Curll*, 1927.

Austin Warren, *Alexander Pope as Critic and Humanist*, 1929.

E. Audra, *L'Influence française dans l'œuvre de Pope*, 1931.

NOTES

AN ESSAY ON CRITICISM

338, l. 34, *Mævius:* an ancient poet who attacked Virgil. He is here referred to as a classic example of the bad poet and critic.

338, l. 68, *First follow Nature:* As has often been pointed out, Pope uses the word *nature* with a variety of meanings. This confusion of uses is due partly to his unmethodical mind and partly to the common practice of the age. In general *nature* meant the best and most universal aspects of human nature as dependent upon a regular and ordered world. Professor A. O. Lovejoy defines it as "the universal and immutable in thought, feeling, and taste." "Nature as Æsthetic Norm," *MLN*, XLII (1927), 447. For a discussion of *nature*, as well as *wit, sense*, and *taste*, see Austin Warren, *Alexander Pope as Critic and Humanist*, pp. 26 ff.

338, ll. 88, 89, *Those rules of old... Nature methodiz'd:* Pope here presents the idea, common in eighteenth-century criticism, that the rules were merely certain aspects of universal Nature reduced to a code for practical application. On the relation of the Rules, Nature, the Models, and Reason, see the Introduction to Edward Young, p. 492.

338, l. 112, *Some on the leaves of ancient authors prey:* the Italian verbal critics and their followers, mere grammarians and scholiasts, whom Pope later attacked in *The Dunciad*.

338, l. 115, *dull receipts how poems may be made:* The Aristotelian formalists, members of the "school of preceptism" are here ridiculed. Pope, as we have seen above, respected the rules, but he believed that rules could be overdone when they were substituted for the true poetic inspiration. See "A Receipt to Make an Epic Poem," p. 379.

339, l. 129, *Mantuan Muse:* Virgil, whose full name was Publius Vergilius Maro (l. 130), was born in Mantua.

339, l. 138, *the Stagirite:* Aristotle, so-called from his birthplace, Stagira in Macedonia.

340, II, l. 16, *the Pierian spring:* Pieria in Thessaly, the birthplace of the Muses; here was the fountain of Hippocrene.

340, II, l. 67, *La Mancha's knight:* Don Quixote de la Mancha. The episode that Pope mentions is in the second part of *Don Quixote*.

341, II, l. 128, *Fungoso in the play:* Jonson's *Every Man out of his Humour*.

341, II, ll. 144–47, *These equal syllables... in one dull line:* Here and in the famous passage, ll. 154–73, Pope aptly illustrates the qualities of verse that he discusses.

341, II, ll. 172, 173, *Not so when swift Camilla... along the main:* See Dryden's translation of Virgil's *Æneid*, VII: 1094–1113.

341, II, l. 174, *Timotheus' varied lays:* See Dryden's *Alexander's Feast*.

342, II, l. 191, *For fools admire: Admire* is here used with the sense of "wonder at," suggesting the Horatian *nil admirari*.

342, II, l. 244, *Scotists and Thomists:* followers of Thomas Aquinas and Duns Scotus, and members of rival parties of Mediæval Schoolmen whose philosophy had fallen into disrepute after the Renaissance.

342, II, l. 245, *Duck Lane:* a lane in London formerly occupied by second-hand book dealers.

342, II, l. 259, *parsons, critics, beaux:* The reference is to Jeremy Collier (see Introduction and notes to *A Short View*, pp. 196 ff.) and to the Duke of Buckingham and his associates in the authorship of *The Rehearsal*, a farce which ridiculed Dryden under the name of Mr. Bayes.

342, II, l. 263, *Blackmores and new Milbournes:* See notes to Dryden's Preface to *Fables*.

342, II, l. 265, *Zoilus:* a Greek critic who attacked Homer.

343, II, l. 345, *the dregs of bold Socinus:* Unitarianism infecting Latitudinarian divines. See the following lines.

344, III, ll. 26–28, *But Appius... in old tapestry:* John Dennis, author of the unsuccessful tragedy, *Appius and Virginia*, a critic whose furious quarrel with Pope began as a result of this satirical reference. Pope said that Dennis took the previous mention of his name in II, 70, as a compliment.

344, III, l. 58, *Durfey's Tales:* Thomas D'Urfey, or Durfey (1653–1723), a poet of a low order, whose songs and verse *Tales* had been popular with country squires and tavern frequenters.

344, III, l. 60, *Garth did not write his own Dispensary:* a common but unfounded report. Sir Samuel Garth, physician and poet, published in 1699 a mock-heroic poem, *The Dispensary*, which ridicules the apothecaries who opposed the establishment of a dispensary for the treatment of the poor.

344, III, l. 64, *Paul's churchyard:* St. Paul's churchyard had been, previous to the London fire, the resort of booksellers. The neighbourhood is still used by the book trade.

345, III, l. 89, *the Mæonian star:* Homer, who was born, according to one tradition, in the province of Mæonia in Asia Minor.

345, III, l. 106, *Dionysius:* Dionysius of Halicarnassus, Greek rhetorician and critic of the first century B.C.

345, III, l. 108, *gay Petronius:* Petronius, called "Arbiter Elegantiæ," companion of Nero; and probable author of the *Satiricon*.

345, III, l. 110, *grave Quintilian's copious work: Institutiones Oratoriæ*, a well-known work on oratory.

345, III, l. 138, *Leo's golden days:* The papacy of Leo X, from 1513 to 1521, was one of the flowering times of the Italian Renaissance.

345, III, l. 148, *Cremona:* the birthplace of Bishop Vida, famous Latin poet and author of the *Art of Poetry*, a verse treatise on epic poetry.

345, III, l. 170, *Walsh:* William Walsh (1663–1708) is now remembered less for his poems than for his friendship with Pope, which is here celebrated.

THE RAPE OF THE LOCK

346, I, l. 1, *What dire offence...*: the conventional statement of the epic theme.

346, I, l. 3, *Caryll:* John Caryll, a member of an old Roman Catholic family in Sussex, and a common friend of Pope and of Lord Petre (the Baron of the poem) and of Arabella Fermor (Belinda). He had suggested that Pope write about the theft of the lock of hair.

347, I, l. 44, *the box... the ring:* the box, at the theatre or opera; the ring, in Hyde Park.

349, II, l. 132, *rivell'd:* shrivelled.

350, III, l. 3, *a structure of majestic frame:* Hampden Court Palace, one of the royal residences near London.

350, III, l. 27, *ombre:* a fashionable card game of the period, played by three people. The nomenclature shows its Spanish origin: the Matadores were the three principal trumps, first Spadillio, or the ace of spades, second, Manillio, or the deuce of clubs when as here the trumps were black, third Basto, or the ace of clubs; Pam was the knave of clubs (in the game of loo, l. 62, it was the highest card); Codille was the term applied to gaining or losing the tricks necessary to win the game. See Charles Lamb's essay, "Mrs. Battle's Opinions on Whist." Pope presented the game in terms of an heroic battle, following the model of Vida's *The Game of Chess*.

351, III, l. 107, *shining altars of japan:* small japanned tables.

351, III, l. 123, *Changed to a bird:* "Ovid, *Metam.* VIII." Pope's note.

351, III, l. 147, *forfex:* pair of scissors.

351, III, l. 165, *Atalantis: The New Atalantis*, by Mrs. Manley, was a work then popular in which contemporary scandal was presented in thinly disguised form.

352, IV, l. 16, *Cave of Spleen:* In the classical epic there is usually a descent into hell; Spleen (*cf.* Introduction to Green, p. 334) is the appropriate genius of the lower world in a mock epic of society.

352, IV, l. 24, *Megrim:* Here probably personifies sick-headache. The word (like "the vapours" in l. 59) was also used to signify what we call "the blues."

352, IV, l. 56, *A branch of healing spleenwort in his hand:* Suggests Virgil's golden bough, *Æneid*, VI.

352, IV, l. 69, *Like citron-waters matrons' cheeks inflame:* Distilled spirits made from citron rind; they were often drunk by women, sometimes with disastrous results to the complexion.

353, IV, l. 118, *wits take lodgings in the sound of Bow:* The church of St. Mary le Bow in the heart of London has a famous peal of bells. "Within the sound of Bow bells" meant the City, where of course courtiers and wits did not lodge.

353, IV, l. 121 ff., *Sir Plume:* His conduct and especially his unmeaning speech full of fop-diction was resented by Sir George Brown, who was understood to be the original of Sir Plume. Thalestris (l. 87) was Mrs. Morley, his sister.

354, V, ll. 5, 6, *Not half... vain:* Æneas, commanded by Jupiter to leave Carthage, could not be restrained by Dido or her sister, Anna. *Æneid*, IV.

354, V, l. 53, *Triumphant Umbriel... sate to view the fight:* "Minerva, in like manner, during the battle of Ulysses with the suitors, perched on a beam of the roof to behold it." Pope's note.

355, V, l. 125, *So Rome's great founder:* an allusion to the tradition that Romulus was carried up to the skies later appearing to Proculus, who alone saw him return thither.

355, V, l. 129, *Berenice's locks:* Berenice (accented on third syllable) wife of Ptolemy III of Egypt. See note on Thomas Parnell's *To Mr. Pope*, l. 19.

355, V, l. 133, *the Mall:* at this time a fashionable promenade in St. James's Park, London.

355, V, l. 136, *Rosamonda's lake:* formerly in St. James's Park, known as a rendezvous for lovers. *Cf.* Waller, *On St. James's Park*, pp. 22 ff.

355, V, l. 137, *Partridge:* John Partridge, the astrologer upon whom Swift had played the famous joke in 1708. Galileo invented the telescope, here referred to as his eyes.

AN ESSAY ON MAN

356, l. 1, *St. John:* Henry St. John, Viscount Bolingbroke.

356, l. 15, *candid:* favourable in judgment.

356, l. 42, *satellites:* Pronounced in four syllables as in Latin.

358, l. 156, *a Borgia or a Catiline:* Cesare Borgia, one of the famous members of the brilliant and wicked Italian Renaissance family to which he belonged. Catiline is remembered, because of Cicero's orations, as another monster of wickedness.

358, l. 160, *young Ammon:* Alexander the Great, who was called the son of Jupiter Ammon.

EPISTLE TO DR. ARBUTHNOT

360, l. 1, *good John:* John Searl, Pope's old servant.

360, l. 8, *thro' my grot they glide:* Pope's famous grotto was an underground passage beneath the London road that separated his garden from his house on the Thames at Twickenham. With the help of his friends he succeeded in decorating what was originally merely a necessary tunnel.

360, l. 13, *the Mint:* a place of refuge for insolvent debtors. Since no one could be arrested for debt on Sunday, impecunious poets could then come abroad.

360, l. 21, *Twit'nam:* a playful shortening of Twickenham, affected by Pope and his friends. The name is now pronounced Twickenham or "Twick'num," and seems to have been generally so pronounced in the eighteenth century.

360, l. 23, *Arthur:* Arthur Moore, a prominent politician of Queen Anne's time; his son, James, who took the name, Moore-Smythe, was a small poet whom Pope often ridiculed. *Cf.* l. 98, below.

361, l. 40, *"Keep your piece nine years"*: Horace's famous advice. *A. P.*, 388.

361, l. 44, *Obliged by hunger, and request of friends:* The sting of this line lies in the contrast between the real and the commonly affected reasons for immediate publication.

361, l. 49, *Pitholeon:* "The name taken from a foolish poet of Rhodes, who pretended much to Greek." Pope's note. Leonard Welsted, a poetaster who had translated Longinus, is probably here referred to. See note to l. 299 below.

361, l. 53, *Curll:* Edmund Curll was a bookseller against whom Pope had many grievances. The *Journal* in the following line was the *London Journal* which supported Sir Robert Walpole. Though Pope abstained from direct participation in politics, his sympathies were with the Tories among whom most of his friends were numbered.

361, l. 62, *Lintot:* Bernard Lintot, Pope's usual publisher.

361, l. 85, *Codrus:* a minor Roman poet satirized by Juvenal; hence a poetaster.

361, l. 98, *His butchers, Henley:* John Henley, a popular preacher and lecturer, whose auditors were largely recruited from butchers and other city tradesmen and artisans.

361, l. 99, *Bavius:* a Roman poet who had attacked both Virgil and Horace; hence a jealous poetaster.

361, l. 100, *Still to one bishop, Philips seems a wit:* Ambrose Philips, "Namby Pamby," member of Addison's circle and author of *Pastorals*, was one of Pope's favourite antipathies. Bishop (afterwards Archbishop) Boulter was Philips's friend and patron.

361, l. 101, *Sappho:* The reference is probably to Lady Mary Wortley Montagu; see also l. 369 below.

362, ll. 135–37, *Granville... Walsh... Garth:* George Granville (afterwards Lord Lansdown), Walsh (see note to *An Essay on Criticism*, III, l. 170), and Dr. Garth, were friends who encouraged Pope's earliest poetry.

362, l. 139, *Talbot, Somers, Sheffield:* great lords who also encouraged Pope's early poetry.

362, l. 140, *mitred Rochester:* Francis Atterbury, Bishop of Rochester.

362, l. 146, *Burnets, Oldmixons, and Cookes:* Gilbert Burnet, Bishop of Salisbury (author of *History of my own Times*), John Oldmixon (poet, pamphleteer, and partisan historian), and Thomas Cooke (translator and journalist) are here classified together as violent party writers, though Pope in a note admits that Burnet was in most respects superior to the other two.

362, l. 148, *pure description held the place of sense:* Pope's mature comment on his own early *Pastorals*.

362, l. 149, *Like gentle Fanny's:* The reference is to John, Lord Hervey, friend of Lady Mary Wortley Montagu. Pope gives a bitterly satiric "character" of him under the name, "Sporus," below. Here he merely suggests that his own poems, *The Rape of the Lock* ("a painted mistress") and *Windsor Forest* ("a purling stream") were flowery like Hervey's work.

362, l. 151, *Gildon draw his venal quill:* Charles Gildon, a critic who had attacked Pope. The poet believed that Addison had hired him to do so.

362, l. 153, *Dennis:* See note to *An Essay on Criticism*, III, ll. 26–28. The quarrel between Pope and Dennis had become furious in the mean time.

362, l. 164, *slashing Bentley... piddling Tibbalds:* Richard Bentley, the scholar and critic with whom Temple and Swift had quarrelled about the *Letters* of Phalaris. On his ed. of Milton see *Imit. of Hor.*, 1, Ep., Bk. II, ll. 103–04. Lewis Theobald (Pope often wrote his name Tibbald as pronounced) was the first hero of *The Dunciad*. *Cf.* Introd. to *Satires*, p. 359.

362, ll. 179, 180, *The bard... half a crown:* Ambrose Philips (see l. 100 above) was the author of *Persian Tales* as well as *Pastorals*.

362, l. 190, *nine such poets made a Tate:* Nahum Tate, author of *Absalom and Achitophel*, Part II, and with Nicholas Brady, of a metrical version of the Psalms. Tate was Poet Laureate from 1690 to 1715.

362, ll. 193–214, *Peace to all such... if Atticus were he:* This "character" of Addison has been the subject of interminable discussion, but there is no dispute about its satiric power. Pope and Addison had been friends but had drifted apart because of incompatability of temper; Addison was reserved while Pope was impulsive, but both were jealous. Even more important than these personal differences were the political. Addison was a Whig leader, and Pope, though not active in politics, was drawn by his sympathies, and even more by his friendships, toward the Tories; in this age of partisan rancour there was a deep gulf fixed between the parties.

The power of the satire lies in the sober sadness with which it exposes the faults of one whom its author in the main appreciates and admires. For the most part the delineation of Addison is just; it tells the truth though it does not tell the whole truth. The value of the "character," however, no more depends on its personal application than Browning's *The Lost Leader* depends on its accurate portrayal of Wordsworth. "Atticus" is a perennial type: a great man who is coldly selfish, distrustful, and grudging of recognition to others. The language is simple but exquisitely chosen, and the whole is charged with suppressed emotion that expresses itself in the rhythm of the lines. Cato in Addison's play of that name is shown surrounded by the "little senate" of Utica, while Addison had an admiring group of authors about him (Ambrose Philips, Thomas Tickell, Eustace Budgell, and others.) Atticus was a gifted Roman of high character, a friend of Cicero's. The name had previously been applied to Addison.

363, ll. 230 ff., *Bufo:* Lord Halifax may be meant here, though the reference is to any noble and powerful patron of letters.

363, l. 260, *Queensb'ry:* The Duchess of Queensbury had been John Gay's friend and patron.

363, l. 280, *Sir Will or Bubo:* Sir William Yonge, a Whig politician and minor author, who had taken a prominent part in the prosecution of Bishop Atterbury for his Jacobite activities; and George Bubb Doddington, afterwards Lord Melcombe, remembered as a diarist and a friend of Frederick, Prince of Wales.

363, ll. 299 ff., *Who to the dean...:* Pope had been accused of satirizing in his *Epistle on Taste*, afterwards incorporated in *Moral Essays*, Ep. IV (see ll. 99 ff.), the decorations and furniture of the Duke of Chandos's house at Canons, in spite of the fact that he had enjoyed the latter's hospitality there. Pope denied the charge and in *Moral Essays*, Epistle I, ll. 54 ff. he had praised Chandos. *Welsted's lie*, l. 375 below, refers to this charge.

364, l. 305, *Sporus:* a favourite of Nero's. For the application see note to l. 149 above.

364, l. 319, *at the ear of Eve...:* See Milton, *Par. Lost*, IV, 799 ff.

364, l. 363, *Japhet in a jail:* Japhet Crooke, alias Sir Peter Stranger, punished for forgery, 1731.

364, l. 365, *Knight of the post... or of the shire:* A knight of the post was a professional bondsman, who waited near a sheriff's court; a knight of the shire was a gentleman who represented his county in Parliament.

364, ll. 370, 371, *Dennis... friend to his distress:* In 1733 Pope contributed a Prologue to a play given for the benefit of his enemy, Dennis, who was then old and blind.

364, ll. 378, 379, *Let Budgell... except his will:* Eustace Budgell, a follower of Addison's, contributor to the *Spectator*, later attacked Pope in a weekly pamphlet called the *Bee*. Budgell was accused of forging a will, fell into distress, and committed suicide in 1737.

364, l. 380, *the two Curlls of town and court:* For Edmund Curll (of town) see note to l. 53 above; the second Curll (a gentlemen of the court who, like the disreputable bookseller, had libelled Pope) was Lord Hervey.

364, l. 391, *And better got than Bestia's:* L. Calpurnius Bestia, a Roman proconsul who was bribed into making a peace with Jugurtha unfavourable to Roman interests. The Duke of Marlborough is here meant.

365, l. 397, *Nor dar'd an oath:* Pope never took the oaths of allegiance to the king.

THE FIRST SATIRE OF THE SECOND BOOK OF HORACE

365, *Mr. Fortescue:* The speakers in Horace are G. Trebatius Testa, a famous lawyer, and the poet, who comes to ask his legal advice about satiric writing. The Hon. W. Fortescue, his "counsel learned in the law," was Pope's intimate friend. For the original see H. R. Fairclough, *Horace, Satires, Epistles, and Ars Poetica* (Loeb Library), pp. 126–33, where the Latin and an English prose translation appear on pages facing each other.

365, l. 3, *wise Peter:* Peter Walter, an attorney praised in *Mor. Essays*, Ep. III, ll. 123 ff.

365, l. 4, *Chartres: Francis Chartres*, an infamous scoundrel; see *Mor. Essays*, Ep. III, l. 20.

365, l. 18, *probatum est:* "It has been proved."

365, l. 19, *Celsus:* probably refers to any physician.

365, l. 23, *Sir Richard:* Sir Richard Blackmore; *cf.* notes to Dryden's *Fables*.

365, l. 30, *Carolina:* Caroline of Brandenburg-Anspach, the Queen of George II.

365, l. 31, *Amelia's liquid name:* Princess Amelia, second daughter of George II.

365, l. 42, *Timon... Balaam:* Timon, whose magnificent villa is satirized in *Moral Essays*, Ep. IV, ll. 99 ff. (see note on *Ep. to Arbuth.*, ll. 299 ff.), and Sir Balaam whose progress to the devil is portrayed in *Moral Essays*, Ep. III, ll. 341 ff., are examples of the poet's use of imaginary names to indicate types.

365, l. 44, *Bond is but one, but Harpax is a score:* See *Moral Essays*, Ep. III, ll. 91 and 100.

365, l. 46, *Scarsdale... Darty:* Lord Scarsdale and Charles Dartineuf were famous epicures.

365, l. 47, *Ridotta:* a name suggested by *ridotto*, the Italian word for an assembly.

365, l. 49, *F——... his brother:* Probably refers to Henry Fox, Lord Holland; "his brother," who loves Hockley-in-the-Hole, a well-known bear-garden in London, would then be Stephen Fox, afterwards Lord Ilchester.

365, l. 52, *downright Shippen:* William Shippen, an outspoken Jacobite.

366, ll. 65, 66, *Papist or Protestant... an honest mean:* On Pope's religious opinions see his letter to the Bishop of Rochester on page 380. Erasmus, like Pope, though adhering to the Roman Catholic Church, was very tolerant of those who did not do so.

366, l. 75, *Peace... not Fleury's more:* Cardinal Fleury, Prime Minister of France, 1726–43, was at this time pacific in his policy.

366, l. 81, *poison dread from Delia's rage:* refers to a current rumour that Mary Howard, Countess of Deloraine, had poisoned a certain Miss Mackenzie through jealousy.

366, l. 82, *Page:* Sir Francis Page, a "hanging judge."

366, l. 83, *furious Sappho:* generally believed to be Pope's ungentlemanly reply to some of Lady Mary Wortley Montagu's equally vicious personal attacks.

366, l. 100, *Lee or Budgell:* Nathaniel Lee (1657–1692), tragic poet, was for a time confined in Bedlam, and Budgell (*cf. Ep. to Dr. Arbuthnot*, ll. 378, 379) was in the Fleet prison. Both were insane.

366, l. 103, *Shylock and his wife:* the Wortley Montagus.

366, l. 104, *testers:* sixpences.

366, ll. 129–32, *he, whose lightning... conquer'd Spain:* The Earl of Peterborough, who in 1705, 1706, had achieved surprising conquests in Spain, was a close friend of Pope's. *Quincunx* is a term used to denote an arrangement of five trees in gardening.

366, ll. 147, 148, *quart.... Eliz.*: the usual legal designation of statutes by the year of the sovereign's reign.

366, ll. 150–53, *Libels... Sir Robert would approve:* Sir Robert Walpole, the prime minister. Horace makes a similar turn using the double sense of *malum* as *libellous* and *of bad quality*; his verses were *good verses* such as the emperor would approve.

THE FIRST EPISTLE OF THE SECOND BOOK OF HORACE

367, *To Augustus:* Whereas Horace addressed the Emperor Augustus, a real patron of letters, Pope addressed George Augustus II, King of England, who cared little for them. George II was at this time, 1737, unpopular because of his treatment of the Prince of Wales, and because of his preference for the interests of Hanover over those of Great Britain. The poet's praises of the king are thus ironic, and his discussion of English literature, though itself to be taken literally, is given point by the king's neglect.

367, ll. 1–3, *While you... abroad defend:* ironic reference to the king's unpopular pacific policy, which had opened the ocean by leaving the Spaniards in control.

367, l. 38, *beastly Skelton:* one of the chief English poets at the end of the fifteenth and the beginning of the sixteenth century. Though Skelton's language is often indecorous, Pope's epithet is too severe.

367, l. 40, *Christ's Kirk o' the Green:* a sixteenth-century Scottish poem, attributed to King James V.

367, l. 41, *Ben:* Ben Jonson, one of whose literary resorts was the Devil Tavern.

367, l. 66, *Stowe:* John Stowe, Elizabethan writer of chronicle history.

368, l. 88, *eldest Heywood:* John Heywood, early English dramatist, author of interludes.

368, l. 91, *Gammer Gurton: Gammer Gurton's Needle*, an early English comedy.

368, l. 92, *The Careless Husband:* one of Cibber's most popular comedies.

368, l. 98, *Sidney's verse... Roman feet:* Sir Philip Sidney was one of the Elizabethan poets who experimented with English poetry in classical metres.

368, ll. 122, 123, *Betterton's grave action... well-mouth'd Booth:* Thomas Betterton (1635–1710), one of the greatest of Shakespearean actors and an early friend of Pope's; Barton Booth (1681–1733) was famous for his articulation on the stage.

368, l. 132, *Merlin's prophecy:* Various prophecies attributed to Merlin were in circulation at this time.

368, l. 144, *Newmarket's glory:* horse racing.

368, ll. 149–50, *Lely... the melting soul:* Sir Peter Lely (1618–1680) painted many of the beauties of the court of Charles II.

368, ll. 153, 154, *On each enervate string... a eunuch's throat:* the introduction of opera into England.

369, l. 182, *Ward tried... his drop:* Joshua Ward, a well-known quack doctor of the time.

369, l. 183, *Radcliffe's doctors:* Holders of the Radcliffe fellowships in medicine spent at least half their time in foreign study and travel.

369, l. 186, *Should Ripley venture:* Thomas Ripley, an architect who, though of poor beginnings, was patronized by Sir Robert Walpole and made Comptroller of his Majesty's Board of Works.

369, l. 230, *Hopkins and Sternhold:* Their metrical version of the Psalms (1562) remained in popular use throughout the eighteenth century in spite of its crudity.

370, l. 289, *Van:* Sir John Vanbrugh, architect and dramatist.

370, l. 290, *Astræa:* Aphra Behn, well-known woman dramatist of the Restoration period; her comedies are like those of most of her contemporaries, neither "looser" nor more moral.

370, l. 293, *poor Pinkey eat with vast applause:* William Pinktheman, well-known low comedian of the time. One of his popular stage tricks was the eating of a cold chicken.

370, l. 309, *black-joke:* an indecent song sometimes sung at the conclusion of a theatrical performance.

370, l. 318, *The Champion:* The Champion of England is a figure in the coronation of English kings. In 1727, when George II was crowned, a spectacle representing the coronation of Henry VIII and Anne Boleyn ran for forty nights. To garb the Champion as realistically as possible, the armour of one of the kings of England was borrowed from the Tower of London.

370, l. 320, *Democritus:* Greek philosopher of the fourth century B.C. known as "the laughing philosopher."

370, l. 328, *Orcas' stormy steep:* a promontory at the extreme northern extremity of Scotland.

370, l. 331, *Quin's high plume, or Oldfield's petticoat:* Quin was a famous tragic actor of this time; "Nance" Oldfield had been the most popular comic actress of the preceding generation.

370, l. 337, *Cato's long wig... and lacquer'd chair:* used in the production of Addison's *Cato.*

370, ll. 354, 355, *How shall we fill... half unfurnish'd yet?*: Merlin's Cave, a grotto in the royal gardens at Richmond. Pope in a note says ironically that Queen Caroline had there "a small but choice collection of books."

371, ll. 380, 381, *Charles to late times... Bernini's care:* Giovanni Lorenzo Bernini (1598–1680), an Italian sculptor, made a bust of Charles I.

371, ll. 382, 383, *And great Nassau to Kneller's hand...* : Sir Godfrey Kneller, a German painter, did the well-known equestrian portrait of William III of England.

371, l. 387, *Blackmore... Quarles:* Sir Richard Blackmore (see note to Dryden's Preface to the *Fables*) was knighted by "the hero William" (Pope had no love for William III) in recognition chiefly of his services as court physician. Francis Quarles (1592–1644), a Royalist, whose poetry was full of "metaphysical conceits."

371, l. 395, *your repose, to sing:* This phrase and the verb *bought* in l. 397 are among the most stinging pieces of satire on George II in the whole poem.

371, l. 405 ff., *And I'm not us'd to panegyric strains:* The conclusion, though following Horace at no great distance, carries new and daring satiric implications in the light of the ironic praise of the king that has preceded.

371, l. 417, *Eusden, Philips, Settle:* all mentioned as bad poets who have flattered kings. Laurence Eusden (1688–1730) had been Poet Laureate; Ambrose Philips was Pope's frequent butt; Elkanah Settle (1648–1724) had been satirized by Dryden.

371, l. 419, *Bedlam and Soho:* Wardour Street, or "Old Soho," as well as the neighbourhood of Bedlam, contained second-hand book shops.

EPILOGUE TO THE SATIRES

371, l. 1, *Fr.*: This dialogue is between the *Poet* and his *Friend.*

371, l. 8, *Tories call'd him Whig...* : See *First Sat. of the Second Book of Hor.*, l. 68. For l. 10 below see *ibid.*, l. 40.

371, ll. 12, 13, *Bubo... Sir Billy:* See note to *Ep. to Dr. Arbuth.*, l. 280.

371, l. 14, *H–ggins:* Huggins, "Formerly jailor of the Fleet Prison, enriched himself by many exactions, for which he was tried and expelled," Pope's note.

371, ll. 17, 18, *And own the Spaniard...* : A reference to the famous story of Jenkins's ear, cut off by a Spanish captain from an English captain who was told that he could carry it to the King of England. This insult led to war between England and Spain in 1739.

372, l. 24, *Patriots:* Those in opposition to the Court and Sir Robert Walpole were at this time called "Patriots." Pope, though in sympathy with this group, suggests that some of those who were so called were undeserving of the name.

372, l. 34, *what he thinks mankind:* Walpole is still remembered for his maxim, "Every man has his price."

372, ll. 39, 40, *A joke on Jekyl...*: "Sir Joseph Jekyl, Master of the Rolls, a true Whig in his principles, and a man of the utmost probity. He sometimes voted against the court, which drew upon him the laugh here described of *One* [i.e., Sir Robert Walpole] who bestowed it equally upon religion and honesty." Pope's note.

372, l. 47, *Lyttleton:* "George Lyttleton, secretary to the Prince of Wales, distinguished both for his writings and speeches in the spirit of liberty." Pope's note.

372, l. 51, *Sejanus, Wolsey... honest Fleury:* Sejanus was the minister of the Roman Emperor Tiberius; Cardinal Wolsey, of Henry VIII; for Fleury see the *First Sat. of the Second Bk. of Horace*, l. 75.

372, l. 66, *Osborne's wit:* T. Pitt edited the London *Journal*, a government newspaper, as "F. Osborne."

372, l. 68, *Y—ng:* Sir William Yonge; for him and Bubo see *Ep. to Arbuth.*, l. 280, note.

372, ll. 71, 72, *H—vy's, F—'s... The S—te's:* Lord Hervey's, Henry Fox's and the Senate's. The first had written on the death of Queen Caroline (1737), and the second had presented an address in the House of Commons on the same occasion.

372, l. 75, *Middleton and Bland:* The epitaph with its poor Latin style is worthy of Conyers Middleton, author of the *Life of Cicero*, and Dr. Bland, of Eton.

372, l. 82, *All parts perform'd, and all her children blest:* The story had been circulated that the queen had died without receiving the Sacrament or being reconciled to the Prince of Wales.

372, l. 92, *Immortal S—k and grave De—re:* The Earl of Selkirk had held a court position under three kings. Lord Delaware was a court favourite.

373, l. 112, *Who starves a sister, or forswears a debt:* current gossip about Lady Mary Wortley Montagu.

373, l. 119, *Ward draw contracts:* John Ward, a member of Parliament, was expelled from the House and convicted of forgery.

373, l. 120, *Japhet:* See *Ep. to Arbuth.*, l. 363, note.

373, ll. 123, 124, *If Blount... Passeran:* Charles Blount, a Deist writer, had committed suicide in 1693; Passeran was the author of *A Philosophical Discourse on Death*, in which he defended suicide.

373, l. 130, *hurls the thunder of the laws on gin:* Gin, which was cheap at this time, had done so much harm among the poorer classes that its use was restrained by an Act of Parliament in 1736.

373, ll. 131, 132, *Let modest Foster... preaching well:* a dissenting minister, known for his eloquence and his defence of Christianity against the Deist, Tindal. A metropolitan is an archbishop.

373, l. 134, *Llandaff:* "A poor bishopric in Wales, as poorly supplied." Pope's note. The Quaker's wife was Mrs. Drummond, who made a sensation with her preaching.

373, ll. 135, 136, *Let humble Allen... fame:* Ralph Allen of Prior Park, close friend of Pope and later a patron of Fielding, who drew his idealized portrait as Squire Allworthy in *Tom Jones*.

373, l. 150, *pale Virtue carted:* "Modern readers may require to be reminded that in Pope's days carting, or exhibiting from a cart, was a punishment of prostitutes and procuresses." Croker's note.

THE DUNCIAD

373, l. 2, *The Smithfield Muses:* Smithfield was the scene of the famous Bartholomew Fair, where low farces and extravagant entertainments were performed before vulgar throngs. Pope means that this type of theatrical entertainment had been brought to the best London theatres by Colley Cibber and his associates. This opening imitates in mock-heroic form the conventional epic opening.

373, l. 6, *Still Dunce the second reigns like Dunce the first:* The new Emperor of Dullness has succeeded to Dryden's mock-hero in *Mac Flecknoe*; yet it must not be forgotten that George II had succeeded George I in 1727, the year before the first edition of this poem was published. *Cf.* p. 60, l. 48.

374, ll. 19–26, *O thou! whatever title...*: These references will be clear after reading the selections from Swift in this volume.

374, l. 30, *Monroe:* physician to Bedlam Hospital.

374, ll. 31, 32, *Where o'er the gates... brothers stand:* Caius Gabriel Cibber, father of Colley Cibber, was the sculptor of the two figures of lunatics over the gates of Bedlam Hospital.

374, l. 40, *Curll's chaste press, and Lintot's rubric post:* For Curll and Lintot see *Ep. to Arbuth.*, notes to ll. 53 and 62. Curll had been fined for publishing obscene books; Lintot, Pope tells us in a note, "usually adorned his shop with titles in red letters."

374, l. 41, *Tyburn's elegiac lines:* Last confessions of criminals executed at Tyburn and lurid accounts of their crimes and deaths were frequently published.

374, l. 57, *Till genial Jacob, or a warm third day:* Jacob Tonson, a well-known bookseller who published both for Dryden and Pope. The receipts of the third night's performance usually went to the dramatist.

374, l. 63, *clenches:* puns. See *Spectator*, Nos. 58–63, on the types of false wit referred to below.

374, l. 85, *'Twas on the day when* **, *rich and grave:* Earlier editions gave the name *Thorold.* Sir George Thorold was Lord Mayor of London in 1720. The formal procession on Lord Mayor's Day was made both by land and by water. Cimon, the Athenian general, obtained victories by land and by water, on the same day.

374, l. 90, *Settle's numbers:* Elkanah Settle, Dryden's old enemy, had been "City Poet" and so had written panegyrics on the Lord Mayors.

375, l. 98, *Heywood's days:* See *The First Epist. of the Second Book of Horace*, l. 88.

375, l. 103, *old Prynne in restless Daniel:* William Prynne was in 1633 fined and put in the pillory for publishing *Histriomastix*, an attack on the stage in which there were reflections on Queen Henrietta. Daniel Defoe was pilloried in 1703 for publishing *The Shortest Way with the Dissenters*.

375, l. 108, *Bayes's monster-breeding breast:* Cibber was Poet-Laureate.

375, l. 126, *sooterkins:* false-births.

375, ll. 131, 132, *poor Fletcher's half-eat scenes... crucified Molière:* Cibber in his comedies drew upon and adapted both Fletcher and Molière.

375, l. 133, *hapless Shakespeare, yet of Tibbald sore:* Lewis Theobald had published *Shakespeare Restored* in 1715. See Introduction to the *Satires*.

375, l. 134, *Wish'd he had blotted for himself before:* Ben Jonson wrote in *Timber:* "I remember the players often mentioned it as an honour to Shakespeare that in his writing (whatsoever he penned) he never blotted out a line. My answer hath been, 'Would he had blotted a thousand.'"

375, l. 141, *Ogilby the great:* John Ogilby (1600–1676), minor poet and printer. *Cf.* p. 44, l. 102, and note.

375, l. 142, *Newcastle:* Margaret, Duchess of Newcastle (1624?–1674) and her husband wrote numerous volumes which were often magnificently bound.

375, l. 146, *Banks, and Broome:* John Banks, a late seventeenth-century tragic poet. Pope in a note says that Broome was "a serving man of Ben Jonson who once picked up a comedy from his betters." The more obvious reference is to William Broome, one of Pope's assistants in translating the *Odyssey*, with whom he had quarrelled but was again reconciled when *The Dunciad* was published in its revised form.

375, l. 149, *Caxton... Wynkyn:* William Caxton (1422–1491) first English printer, Wynkyn de Worde, his successor.

375, l. 153, *De Lyra:* "Nich. de Lyra, or Harpsfield, a very voluminous commentator, whose works in five vast folios were printed in 1472." Pope's note. A note in the Elwin-Courthope ed. explains that Nicholas Harpsfield was a sixteenth-century theological controversialist and ecclesiastical historian of England.

375, l. 154, *Philemon:* Philemon Holland (1552–1636), an industrious translator.

375, ll. 167, 168, *E'er since Sir Fopling's periwig... butt and bays:* Cibber had played Sir Fopling Flutter in a very large wig. The butt (of wine) and the bays were traditionally associated with the laureateship.

376, l. 200, *the Bible, once my better guide:* Cibber had originally been intended for the Church.

376, l. 203, *at White's amidst the doctors sit:* For *White's* see Introduction and Notes to the *Tatler*; *doctors* was a slang expression for false dice.

376, l. 208, *Ridpath... Mist:* "George Ridpath, author of a Tory paper called the *Flying-Post*; Nathaniel Mist, of a famous Tory Journal." Pope's note.

376, l. 216, *Ralph:* James Ralph, an American, who went to England with Benjamin Franklin and became a successful party writer.

376, l. 222, *This mess... Hockley Hole and White's:* See note to *First Sat. of the Sec. Book of Horace*, l. 49. The next couplet explains the meaning: a mixture of the vulgar and the aristocratic.

376, ll. 225–230, *Oh, born in sin... walk the streets:* The meaning is that Cibber's plays, which he speaks of in his *Apology* as his children, were most fortunate when they failed, since then they rose to the skies purified by flames, instead of remaining like their successful sisters to exhibit themselves in town.

376, ll. 231, 232, *Ye shall not beg... vagrant thro' the land:* See note to *Epilogue* I, 75. "It was a practice so to give the Daily Gazetteer and ministerial pamphlets (in which this B was a writer), and send them post-free to all the towns in this kingdom." Pope's note.

376, l. 233, *sail with Ward to ape-and-monkey climes:* Ned Ward, comic poet and author of *The London Spy*, whose works, Pope asserts, were sold in the colonies.

376, l. 234, *mundungus:* bad-smelling tobacco.

376, ll. 238–40, *Tate... Shadwell's:* Both had held the laureateship.

376, ll. 250–53, *The Cid... Perolla... Cæsar... King John... The Nonjuror:* all plays of Cibber's.

376, l. 258, *Thule:* An unfinished poem by Ambrose Philips.

376, l. 270, *quidnuncs:* gossips, from the Latin phrase *quid nunc?*, what now?

377, l. 281, *less reading than makes felons scape:* Very little learning was required to secure "benefit of clergy." *Cf.* p. 134, l. 47, note.

377, l. 286, *Ozell:* John Ozell, translator of French plays.

377, l. 290, *a heideggre:* "A strange bird from Switzerland, and not (as some have supposed) the name of an eminent person who was a man of parts." Pope's note. The veiled allusion here is to the German, John James Heydegger, who was an operatic manager in England.

377, l. 293, *Eusden thirsts no more for sack or praise:* Lawrence Eusden (1688–1730) had been Poet-Laureate.

377, l. 296, *Withers, Ward, and Gildon:* All three were wretched; the eighteenth century considered them all very bad poets, though Withers (or Wither) now has a higher reputation than the other two. See note to Dryden's *Es. of Dram. Poesy*, p. 66, l. 16.

377, ll. 297, 298, *high-born Howard...fool of quality:* Hon. Edward Howard and Lord Hervey.

377, ll. 305 ff., *And thou! his aid-de-camp, lead on...: Cf.* Addison's essays on True and False Wit, *Spectator*, Nos. 58–63.

377, l. 324, *pious Needham:* Mrs. Needham, whose portrait appears in the first scene of Hogarth's "Harlot's Progress," was a well-known procuress.

377, l. 325, *Back to the Devil:* The Laureate's odes were rehearsed at the Devil Tavern in Fleet Street before they were presented at court.

377, ll. 327–30, *So when Jove's block... King Log:* The quotation is from the story of the frogs who desired a king in Ogilby's *Æsop's Fables.*

THE GUARDIAN

378, l. 25, *Baiana nostri villa... lætatur (Epigrams,* III, 58, ll. 1–5): "The Baian villa of our friend, Faustinus, O Bassus, does not occupy ungrateful stretches of wide field laid out in idle myrtle-beds, with the plane trees unwedded to the vines, and with the close-cropped box tree, but it revels in rusticity which is genuine and artless."

378, l. 7, *Virgil's account: Georgics,* IV, 116–48.

378, l. 9, *Homer's... in the seventh Odyssey:* ll. 78–132.

378, l. 11, *Sir William Temple has remarked: Upon the Gardens of Epicurus.*

378, l. 20, *the trees, which were standards:* That is, they were not dwarfed by grafting or distorted in any way from their natural growth.

379, ll. 9–15, *Hinc et nexilibus... vallos:* "Next one sees gardens of intertwined branches, twisted hedgewalls, battlements extending all about and broad towers rising, fashioned from branches; one sees even the myrtle bent out of shape into sterns and also bronze prows, and in the box trees one sees the undulating sea and ship rigging of rosemary; in another part the tents leafing out from their camps, and shields and darts made of the citron tree."

379, l. 27, *giants, like those of Guildhall:* two wooden figures known as Gog and Magog.

379, l. 30, *the Champion flourishing on horseback:* See note to *The First Epistle of the Second Book of Horace,* l. 318.

379, l. 20, "*Thy wife shall be as the fruitful vine...*": Psalm 128:3, with a slight omission.

A RECEIPT TO MAKE AN EPIC POEM

379, l. 54, *fable:* plot or story.

379, l. 56, *Geoffrey of Monmouth or Don Belianis of Greece:* the first, a twelfth-century Latin chronicler who wrote about King Arthur, and the second, a fifteenth-century Spanish Romance of Chivalry.

380, l. 20, *the moral and allegory:* Bossu and other critics had laid great emphasis upon these aspects of the epic and had taught that they were central in the poetic practice of Homer and Virgil.

380, l. 4, *Nec deus intersit... Inciderit* — ll. 191–92:

> "Nor in the unravelling be a god displayed,
> Save where the knot disdains all humbler aid."
> Howes's translation.

380, l. 13, *quantum sufficit:* "As much as is necessary."

380, l. 28, *the Theory of the Conflagration:* a sarcastic reference to the work of Thomas Burnet, whose *Theory of the Earth* was published in 1684.

380, l. 30, *succedaneum:* substitute.

LETTERS

380, l. 40, *The Bishop of Rochester:* Francis Atterbury.

381, l. 1, *Genetrix est mihi:* Pope's mother survived for many years, dying in 1733 at the age of ninety-three.

381, l. 3, *Necqueam lacrymas perferre parentis* (Virgil, *Æneid*, IX, 289): "I could not bear a mother's tears."

381, l. 10, *Ignaram hujus quodcunque... linquam?* (*Ibid.*, IX, 287, adapted): "Shall I leave her now without knowledge of this danger, whatever it may be?"

381, l. 32, *all that had been written... in the reign of King James the Second:* During the last years of Charles II, when the succession of his brother was being much discussed, and during the short reign of James II, 1685–88, there was a perfect flood of theological controversy published in England.

381, l. 21, *I am not a Papist... I am a Catholic:* As the context shows, he means that he accepted the spiritual authority of the Roman Pontiff, but denied the temporal. The word, *Papist,* which is now used opprobriously only, was in the eighteenth century the common term in England for a Roman Catholic. Its use indicated the claim of the Church of England to be primitive and Catholic. This letter clearly shows Alexander Pope's liberal and tolerant religious views. Because he was not much concerned with theology, and because he was unwilling to hurt his mother's feelings, he was content to remain in the Church of his birth and early training, though by so doing he subjected himself to legal and social disabilities.

381, l. 37, *sermo ad clerum* not *ad populum:* "Speaking to the clergy" not "to the people."

381, l. 47, *the Travels of one Gulliver: Gulliver's Travels* when first published purported to be the work of Captain Lemuel Gulliver; it did not bear the name of Swift. Pope and Gay were well acquainted with the facts of its authorship, though they here pretend ignorance. At this time while there was some danger that the book might be the occasion of legal prosecution, it was injudicious to admit the facts in a letter that might be opened by the postal authorities *en route.* At the same time an affectation of ignorance was a humorous device that was doubtless congenial to the authors and to the recipient of this letter.

382, l. 18, *Your friend, my Lord Harcourt:* See note to Swift's *Journal to Stella*, p. 394, l. 39.

382, l. 21, *The Duchess Dowager of Marlborough:* Sarah Jennings, the widow of the first Duke of Marlborough. She was not a friend of Pope or of Swift.

382, l. 53, *nemine contradicente:* "Without contradiction."

382, l. 11, *cum hirundine prima:* "With the first swallow."

382, l. 15, *style Gregorian:* the New Style calendar. For some time before 1752, when the calendar change was made in England, both the Old Style and the New Style of reckoning were common.

382, l. 26, *the thing that is not... Houyhnhnm... Yahoo:* For these terms see the Fourth Voyage of *Gulliver's Travels* in this volume.

382, l. 43, *Mrs. Martha Blount:* Martha Blount (Mrs. is the eighteenth-century prefix used for unmarried as well as married women) was an intimate friend of Pope's and the woman whom, in happier circumstances, he might have married.

383, l. 1, *Mrs. Howard:* Henrietta Howard, Countess of Suffolk, mistress of George II. She had a villa at Marble Hill, Twickenham, near Pope's house. The death of her friend, John Gay, Dec. 4, 1732, is referred to here.

383, l. 19, *Mr. Bethel:* Hugh Bethel, a Yorkshire gentleman who was a friend both of Pope and of the Blount family.

VISCOUNT BOLINGBROKE

BIBLIOGRAPHY

Bolingbroke's *Works* were collected and published by David Mallet in 5 vols., 1754, and republished in various forms during the following century.

Letters and Correspondence, Public and Private of Henry St. John, Viscount Bolingbroke, during the Time he was Secretary of State to Queen Anne, ed. by Gilbert Clarke, 2 vols., 1798.

Lettres historiques, politiques et particulières de H. St. John, Vic. Bolingbroke, depuis 1710 jusqu'à 1736, 3 vols., 1808.

G. W. Cooke, *Memoirs of Bolingbroke*, 2 vols., 1835.

T. Macknight, *The Life of Henry St. John, Viscount Bolingbroke*, 1863.

M. Brosch, *Lord Bolingbroke und die Whigs und Tories seiner Zeit*, 1883.

R. Harrop, *Bolingbroke*, 1884.

J. C. Collins, *Bolingbroke, a Historical Study*, 1886.

A. Hassall, *The Life of Viscount Bolingbroke*, 1889.

W. Sichel, *Bolingbroke and his Times*, 2 vols., 1901–02.

Sir Leslie Stephen, *History of English Thought in the Eighteenth Century*, 2 vols., 1876.

F. J. C. Hearnshaw, ed., *The Social and Political Ideas of Some English Thinkers of the Augustan Age, 1650–1750*, 1928.

NOTES

384, l. 2, *The Right Honourable Lord Bathurst:* Allen Bathurst, First Earl Bathurst, was a friend of Pope, Swift, Prior, and other Tory wits.

385, l. 14, "*Toute opinion... vie*": "Every opinion is strong enough for some one to hold at the risk of his life."

386, l. 28, *as the second Scipio took in his dream:* The dream of Scipio is related in the sixth book of Cicero's *De Republica*.

387, l. 33, *Deo immortale,... prodere* (Cicero, *De Senectute*, 25, slightly altered): "To the immortal God, who has wished me not only to receive these things from past generations but to hand them down to future generations."

387, l. 10, *all his nerves and sinews as well braced as Jacob Hall:* Jacob Hall the rope-dancer, said to have been a lover of Barbara Villiers, Countess of Castlemain, mistress of Charles II. See Pepys's *Diary*, April 7, 1668.

387, l. 51, *Manent ingenia senibus... industria* (Cicero, *De Senectute,* 22): "Natural abilities remain with old men, only if love of study and industrious application continue."

388, l. 12, *Solve senescentem mature sanus equum* (Horace, *Epistles*, 1, 1, 8): "Be wise in time and loose the aging horse."

388, l. 13, *the demon of Socrates:* genius or supernatural voice, not an evil spirit.

388, l. 5, *Stagirite:* Aristotle, so-called from his birthplace, Stagira, a town in Macedonia.

389, l. 24, "*literæ nihil sanantes*": "Letters not at all curative."

389, l. 42, *The Tartar believes... that the soul of Foe inhabits in his Dairo:* The reference is probably to an account of the religion of the Tartars in some book of oriental travel, not identified.

389, l. 44, *the hypostatic union:* the union of the divine and human natures in the person of Christ. This passage is a good example of Bolingbroke's rationalistic scepticism; he does not explicitly assert belief or disbelief in the articles of the creed, but he links Christian teaching with Tartar superstition.

390, l. 9, *the disputes that have arisen between the followers of Omar and Ali:* the Sunnis, and the Shi'ites, Moslem sects, which quarrelled originally over the question whether the Caliphate is an elective or a hereditary office, and later came to differ about many other matters.

391, l. 8, "*Dulce est desipere*" (Horace, *Carm.*, 4, 12, 28): "It is pleasant to be foolish." The concluding words, "*in loco*" ("at the right time"), are omitted, probably because of the familiarity of the quotation.

391, l. 9, "*Vive la bagatelle!*": "Hurrah for trifles!"

391, l. 30, *In his studiis... extinguitur* (Cicero, *De Senec.*, 38): "Living in the midst of these studies and tasks one does not realize when old age steals upon him: thus gradually and imperceptibly life passes into old age, not suddenly ended, but extinguished with the passing of much time."

391, l. 13, *Vivendi recte... amnis* (Horace, *Ep.*, 1, 2, 32): "Who postpones the season of living aright, [is like] the peasant [who] waits until the river ceases flowing."

391, l. 21, *the fleetest courser of Newmarket:* Newmarket in Cambridgeshire has been since the seventeenth century famous for its horse-races.

JONATHAN SWIFT

BIBLIOGRAPHY

There is no satisfactory edition of Swift's complete works. Indeed, the Swift canon is far from being established; while there is no doubt about the attribution of the major works, a large number of doubtful and supposititious writings have at various times been published as his. The fact that few of Swift's genuine works were published under his own name has increased the difficulty.

Among collected editions that of Sir Walter Scott, 19 vols., Edinburgh, 1814 and 1824, is important.

The most accessible edition of Swift's prose is that edited by Temple Scott in 12 vols., 1897–1908.

The Poems of Jonathan Swift, edited by W. E. Browning, 2 vols., 1910, is supplementary to this edition.

Sir Henry Craik's *Swift: Selections from his Works*, 2 vols., 1892–93, is valuable for its introductions and notes, though the text has been heavily cut by expurgation and other omission.

Editions of particular works have been very numerous. The best of these is *A Tale of a Tub*, etc., by A. C. Guthkelch and D. Nichol Smith, 1920.

Gulliver's Travels has appeared hundreds of times (usually in expurgated form). Émile Pons has an excellent edition with French Introduction and English Notes, 1927. Harold Williams has presented the text of the first ed. with Introduction, Bibliography and Notes, 1926.

The Correspondence of Jonathan Swift, D.D., has been well edited by F. Elrington Ball in 6 vols., 1910–14.

W. D. Taylor has edited a well-chosen volume, *Select Letters of Jonathan Swift, D.D.*, in Bohn's Popular Library, 1926.

Among biographical and critical works the following are important:

Sir Walter Scott, *Memoirs of Jonathan Swift*, in the first vol. of his edition of the *Works*, 1814.

John Forster, *Life of Jonathan Swift*, 1875; vol. 1 only, 1667–1711. (Most complete so far as it goes.)

Sir Henry Craik, *Life of Jonathan Swift*, 2 vols., 1882. (On the whole the best complete biography.)

Sir Leslie Stephen, *Jonathan Swift*, 1882, Eng. Men of Letters Series.

J. C. Collins, *Jonathan Swift, A Biographical and Critical Study*, 1893.

Henriette Cordelet, *Swift*, 1907.

Émile Pons, *Swift: les années de jeunesse et le "Conte du tonneau,"* 1925. (A work of first-rate importance.)

Carl Van Doren, *Swift*, 1930. (Sound on the whole but adds nothing to our knowledge of the man.)

Dr. Johnson's *Swift* in *The Lives of the Poets* is one of the least satisfactory treatments in the work of a critic who is never negligible.

W. M. Thackeray's discussion in *English Humorists of the Eighteenth Century*, 1853, is responsible for much current misunderstanding of Swift.

C. H. Firth, "Political Significance of 'Gulliver's Travels,'" *Proceedings of the British Academy*, vol. ix, 1919, is one of the best brief discussions of its subject.

W. A. Eddy, *"Gulliver's Travels": A Critical Study*, Princeton Univ. dissertation, 1923.

W. Gückel and E. Günther, *D. Defoes und J. Swifts Belesenheit und literarische Kritik*, 1925.

J. O. Wedel, "The Philosophical Background of 'Gulliver's Travels,'" *Studies in Philology*, Oct., 1926.

F. Elrington Ball, *Swift's Verse*, 1929.

Hans Glaser, *Jonathan Swifts Kritik an der englischen Irland-politik*, 1932.

Harold Williams, *Dean Swift's Library*, 1932.

NOTES

JOURNAL TO STELLA

394, l. 6, *Presto:* a punning reference to the Italian form of his own name, Swift.

394, l. 8, *MD:* My dears; the letters were addressed to Stella and Rebecca Dingley. While it is obvious that they were written primarily for the former, it is equally obvious that the latter was not forgotten. See Mrs. Meynell's essay, "Mrs. Dingley."

394, l. 15, *My shin mends:* On March 13 Swift, while walking in the Strand, had stumbled over a tub of sand left in the street, and severely hurt his shin.

394, l. 16, *Ned Southwell's:* Ned Southwell, clerk of the council, son of Sir Robert Southwell, former secretary to the Lord Lieutenant of Ireland, and a patron of Swift's.

394, l. 24, *Stella:* The name, Stella, does not occur in those letters of which we have the original MSS.; Swift probably did not use it until some time later. It was substituted by Deane Swift (a second cousin of Dr. Swift's, and the first editor of Letters 1–40 of *The Journal*) for ppt., which seems to stand for Poppet or Poor Pretty Thing. In spite of this fact, the collection has come to be universally known as the *Journal to Stella*.

394, l. 26, *This illness of Mr. Harley:* On March 8, Robert Harley, Chancellor of the Exchequer, had been stabbed at a meeting of the council by a half-mad Frenchman named Guiscard. Harley was at this time recovering from his wounds. Guiscard had been severely handled by those present, and had died on March 17. Harley is better known by his title, Earl of Oxford, which was conferred upon him shortly after this time.

394, l. 33, *Biddy Floyd:* A reigning beauty and a friend of Swift's; she had the smallpox. One is glad to read on April 7 that Swift called on her and reported that she was " very red, but I believe won't be much marked."

394, l. 36, *a merry new year:* According to the old calendar, the year began on March 25, which is also the feast of the Annunciation, commonly known in England as Lady Day.

394, l. 39, *my Lord-Keeper:* Sir Simon Harcourt, Lord Keeper of the Great Seal.

394, l. 41, *Mr. Secretary St. John:* Henry St. John, Secretary of State and one of the most important members of the ruling Ministry. He is better known by his title, Viscount Bolingbroke, which was conferred on him in 1712. See Introduction, p. 384.

394, l. 43, *Mrs. de Caudres':* Mrs. Johnson (Stella) and Mrs. Dingley had recently taken lodgings at her house, near St. Mary's Church, in Dublin.

394, l. 21, *the caprice of Radcliffe:* Dr. Radcliffe, the famous physician.

394, l. 26, *Laracor:* Swift held at this time the living of Laracor in Ireland.

394, l. 36, *my neighbour Vanhomrigh:* Mrs. Vanhomrigh, widow of Bartholomew Vanhomrigh, a wealthy Dutch merchant, and mother of Hester Vanhomrigh, of whom Swift wrote in *Cadenus and Vanessa*. It is significant that, though the *Journal* makes frequent references to Mrs. Vanhomrigh, Hester is referred to on only three occasions, and then without quoting her name.

394, l. 38, *Dr. Freind:* a well-known physician, who was also an author.

394, l. 46, *Patrick:* Swift's Irish servant, whose drunkenness and consequent quarrelsomeness caused his master frequent annoyance. *Cf.* the reference on March 30. Swift dismissed Patrick, though not until about a year later.

394, l. 55, *Walls's hand:* Archdeacon Walls, rector of Castle Knock in Ireland.

395, l. 12, *exchequer trangum:* trangam, a toy or trifle.

395, l. 14, *Ben Tooke's:* the bookseller who had published *A Tale of a Tub;* he sometimes transacted financial business for Swift.

395, l. 16, *Vedeau:* Several references in the *Journal* mention a certain Vedeau, who had been a shopkeeper but had turned soldier. See below, April 4 and 5.

395, l. 27, *the Lord Treasurer:* The reference here is to Godolphin, the Lord Treasurer in the recent Whig cabinet.

395, l. 38, *your dean's:* Dr. Sterne, who was then Dean of St. Patrick's Cathedral, Dublin. On his appointment as Bishop of Dromore in 1713, Swift succeeded him.

395, l. 40, *Charles Barnard's library:* On March 19 Swift had expressed his intention of inspecting the books of Charles Bernard [*sic*], a bookseller whose stock was to be sold at auction.

395, l. 1, *the grease ran down upon the paper:* "It caused a violent daub on the paper, which still continues much discoloured in the original." (Note in original edition.)

395, l. 21, *Sir Thomas Mansel:* Obviously these words were written in the evening, though Swift forgot to indicate the fact.

395, l. 24, *Teaguelander:* Irishman.

396, l. 10, *that ugly grease:* the spot referred to two days before, which had soaked through the paper.

396, l. 44, *Mrs. Barton:* Widow of Colonel Barton, and niece of Sir Isaac Newton; she was a famous beauty.

396, l. 29, *Mrs. Masham's brother:* Mrs. Abigail Masham was the queen's favourite at this period of her reign. Her brother, Col. John Hill, was made a brigadier general about this time.

396, l. 32, *my old friend, Rollinson:* William Rollinson, a retired wine merchant, whose home was in Oxfordshire; he was a friend of Pope's.

397, l. 11, *Mr. Dopping:* Samuel Dopping was an Irish friend of Stella's.

397, l. 17, *Stoyte and Catherine:* Alderman Stoyte, afterwards Lord Mayor of Dublin; Catherine was his sister.

397, l. 46, *Parvisol:* Swift's steward and tithe agent at Laracor.

397, l. 1, *Mrs. Edgworth:* a friend by whom Swift had sent a box to Ireland.

397, l. 4, *Leigh stays till Sterne:* Jemmy Leigh, an Irish landlord who lodged in London with Enoch Sterne, Collector of Wicklow, and Clerk to the Irish House of Commons.

397, l. 16, *what I did with Mr. Harley:* Harley had sent Swift a bank note for fifty pounds, which the latter had indignantly returned, since he did not wish to be considered a hired writer. On March 7 he had told Stella of the matter and had written, "Did I not do right?"

397, l. 53, *this way:* "The writing gives example of the right and the wrong mode of sloping the letters." (Note in original edition.)

398, l. 7, *this Clements:* As the context indicates, Clements was an acquaintance who had been recommended to Swift's good graces. On Feb. 12, 1712, he wrote in the *Journal*, "I find Clements, whom I recommended to Ld. Anglesey [*sic*] last year, at Walls's desire, or rather the Bishop of Cl's, is mightily in Lord Anglesea's favr."

GULLIVER'S TRAVELS

400, l. 8, *what country it was:* The map of Houyhnhnms' Land in early editions of *Gulliver's Travels* shows it as an island south of Australia and west of Tasmania. In each of the voyages Swift placed his imaginary land in identifiable relation to parts of the world that were known, but not accurately known, to Englishmen of his own day.

402, l. 13, *Houyhnhnm:* usually pronounced " whinnim," suggesting the "whinny," of a horse. The other native words quoted in this voyage are similarly imitative in sound.

403, l. 54, *a fetlock full of oats:* A man would say, *a handful.*

403, l. 7, *any sensitive being:* any being with the usual physical senses.

404, l. 54, *at a great loss for salt:* Swift is in error in his statement that no animal but man is fond of salt; many animals, including horses, are fond of it.

409, l. 51, *whether flesh be bread... whether the juice... be blood or wine:* an obvious reference to the Consecrated Elements in the Eucharist.

409, l. 53, *whether whistling be a vice or a virtue:* refers to the controversies about church music.

409, l. 54, *to kiss a post, or throw it into the fire:* suggests the disputes about relics.

409, l. 55, *what is the best colour for a coat:* Quarrels about ecclesiastical vestments are here indicated. In *A Tale of a Tub* Swift had made similar references to matters of religious belief and ceremonial.

421, l. 24, *indocible:* incapable of being taught.

427, l. 24, *Mr. Herman Moll:* He had made the maps for a collection of voyages published in 1705 by John Harris, and he had also engraved the plates for Grierson's atlas, Dublin, 1720. These remarks about the correction of well-known maps are, of course, a part of Swift's attempt to give a realistic tone to his imaginary voyages.

427, l. 32, *admiration:* wonder.

428, l. 13, *my three years' residence:* Since Gulliver was set ashore on May 9, 1711, and departed Feb. 15, 1715, his residence was of nearly four years' duration, — three years, nine months, and six days.

429, l. 53, *stone-horses:* stallions.

430, l. 7, *other* ...: Chapter XII, which is omitted, is really a conclusion to the whole book rather than a part of the Fourth Voyage.

ON THE DEATH OF MRS. JOHNSON

430, l. 28, *as soon as I am left alone:* Swift was entertaining friends at one of the regular Sunday evening dinners at the Deanery, when the news of Stella's death was brought to him.

430, l. 52, *another lady:* Rebecca Dingley; see note to p. 394, l. 8.

430, l. 2, *a person on whom she had some dependence:* Sir William Temple, who left her a small legacy.

430, l. 28, —— *in the year 170–*: Swift seems to have left blanks which he intended to fill later with the details that he could not at that moment recollect. Esther Johnson came to Ireland early in 1701.

431, l. 20, *several of her sayings:* Swift left a brief paper entitled *Bons Mots of Stella*, which gives several examples of her sharp wit; but they are scarcely brilliant enough to warrant the description here given.

433, l. 7, *to offend in the least word against modesty:* This passage is one that must be taken into account in considering the problem of Swift's indecency. That he considered verbal coarseness an effective weapon against hateful things is obvious; it is also obvious that this explanation does not account for all the indecencies of his correspondence and his writings intended for publication. There can be no doubt that he is here expressing a sincere admiration of Stella's attitude on the subject.

ON THE DEATH OF DR. SWIFT

435, l. 59, *St. John:* See the *Journal to Stella*, p. 394, l. 41, note.

435, l. 59, *Pultney:* William Pultney (1684–1764; after 1742, Earl of Bath). He and St. John were attacking Walpole in the *Craftsman* about this time.

435, l. 83, *That old vertigo in his head:* Vertigo is here accented on the second syllable. In *Anecdotes of the Family of Swift*, he says of himself, writing in the third person, "For he happened before twenty years old, by a surfeit of fruit, to contract a giddiness and coldness of stomach that almost brought him to his grave; and this disorder pursued him with intermissions of two or three years to the end of his life." This giddiness or vertigo has often been regarded as a symptom of the disease which was to cloud the last years of his life, but the two probably had no connection.

435, l. 108, *well remembers Charles the Second:* Swift was about 18 years old at the death of Charles II in 1685.

436, l. 156, *'Tis all bequeath'd to public uses:* Swift left the bulk of his little fortune to found St. Patrick's Hospital for Lunatics and Incurables. *Cf.* the closing lines.

436, l. 162, *No worthy friend, no poor relation:* Swift's will, which was dated 1740, nine years after the writing of this poem, did leave small bequests to a few individuals, though the bulk of his property went to "public uses," as indicated above.

436, l. 168, *To curse the Dean, or bless the Drapier:* He assumes that his old political enemies will continue to attack his memory, but that his services to Ireland in *The Drapier's Letters* will be remembered by some with thankfulness.

436, l. 179, *Kind Lady Suffolk:* Mrs. Howard, afterwards Countess of Suffolk, had at one time professed friendship for Swift. See note on *Mrs. Howard*, Pope's letter to Martha Blount, Dec., 1732, p. 383, l. 1, note.

436, l. 184, *the medals were forgot:* Queen Caroline, while Princess of Wales, had promised to give Swift a present, which he never received.

436, l. 189, *Chartres:* Colonel Francis Chartres, a rake of unsavoury reputation, whom Pope satirized. He died in 1731, the same year this poem was written.

436, l. 189, *Sir Robert's:* Sir Robert Walpole, the prime minister, was Swift's political enemy.

436, l. 194, *my good friend Will:* See note on Pultney above. He had formerly been Walpole's friend but later became his bitter enemy.

436, l. 197, *Curll:* Edmund Curl, or Curll, an unscrupulous bookseller, who had published three volumes of work attributed to Swift, though without his consent. It was his practice to publish lives, letters, and remains of well-known men who died, from ministers of state to highwaymen.

436, l. 200, *Tibbalds, Moore, and Cibber:* Lewis Theobald, James Moore, and Colley Cibber; all had been satirized by Pope in *The Dunciad.* The last-named was at this time Poet-Laureate.

436, l. 230, *I'll venture for the vole:* in quadrille, a play in which the dealer takes all the tricks or suffers a heavy loss. *Cf.* the bid of a "grand slam" in bridge.

437, l. 253, *Lintot:* Bernard Lintot, a famous bookseller. *Cf.* p. 361, l. 62.

437, l. 258, *Duck Lane:* a London lane in which obscure booksellers sold unfashionable or out-of-date publications.

437, l. 272, *Stephen Duck:* the "Thresher Poet," who had been patronized by the queen.

437, l. 278, *Mr. Henley's last oration:* a clergyman who had left the Established Church and had set up what he called an "Oratory" where he gave fantastic lectures on religious and other topics. *Cf.* note to p. 361, l. 98.

437, l. 281, *Woolston's tracts:* Thomas Woolston (1670–1733), freethinker, whose *Discourses on the Miracles of our Saviour*, 1727–29, were making a ensation. W. E. Browning (*Poems of Jonathan Swift*, I, 256, n. 3) thinks that Swift confused him with William Wollaston (1660–1724), whose *Religion of Nature Delineated*, 1724, had an even wider sale.

438, l. 378, *Two kingdoms... Had set a price upon his head:* In 1713 the English government had offered a reward of £300 for the apprehension of the author of Swift's anonymous pamphlet, *The Public Spirit f the Whigs*, and in 1724 the Irish government had offered a similar reward when the fourth of *The Drapier's Letters* was published. While "six hundred pound" had thus been offered, the first of these rewards was offered by Swift's friends in the ministry, and the second was probably not taken very seriously.

438, l. 404, *Too soon that precious life was ended:* The death of Queen Anne, August 1, 1714, came just at the moment when Bolingbroke was reorganizing the government. Had it come a few weeks later, the Whigs might not have been able to seize the power as they did and so crush the hopes of Swift and his friends.

438, l. 444, *A wicked monster on the bench:* William Whitshed, Lord Chief Justice of Ireland, who was an enemy of Swift's and did everything in his power to persecute him. Sir William Scroggs, who was Lord Chief Justice of England under Charles II, was known for his subservience to the court. Sir Robert Tresilian was an infamous "hanging judge" in the reign of Richard II, whose perversions of justice led to his own execution in 1388.

439, l. 498, *Biennial:* The words in square brackets are conjectural fillings of the blanks left in the original edition. The reading here given is that of W. E. Browning in Bohn's Standard Library. Other editors supply the blanks differently. *Biennial squires* refers to members of the Irish Parliament, which met once in two years.

439, l. 501, ——: Henry Craik interprets *rob.*

439, l. 502, *rapparees:* Originally this name was given to those Irish irregular soldiers who had been accustomed to rob the Protestants during the recent wars; later it was applied to common highwaymen.

439, l. 545, *Methinks you may forgive his ashes:* With these words ends the speech of the impartial critic who discusses the character of Dr. Swift before the "club assembled at the Rose." Apparently his speech is broken from time to time by the words of another man who acts as a sort of *advocatus diaboli.* The use of quotation marks in the text as here given is conjecturally emended in order to bring out this important element of structure, which is obscured by the pointing of the ordinary editions.

A COMPLETE COLLECTION OF GENTEEL AND INGENIOUS CONVERSATION

441, l. 40, *Mr. Creech's admirable translation:* Swift is here writing in the person of a typical beau, who is so much afraid of being thought pedantic that he affects complete ignorance of Latin. Compare the later reference to Lily, who had taught words "in a language wholly useless."

441, l. 14, *Simon Wagstaff, Esq.:* The name suggests one of the many variations upon Bickerstaff which had appeared in the *Tatler.* It will be remembered that Swift had himself introduced Isaac Bickerstaff as the author of *Predictions for the Year 1708*, in which he had ridiculed Partridge, and that Steele had shortly after adopted the name for use in his journal.

442, l. 10, *proverbs and those polite speeches:* The irony of this statement becomes apparent when one notices the large number of proverbs that are used in the dialogues.

442, l. 8, *the whole exercise of the fan: Cf.* the *Spectator*, No. 102.

442, l. 32, *Isaac the dancing-master:* a well-known French dancing-master. Steele refers to him in the *Tatler*, No. 34.

443, l. 6, *cant words:* In the *Tatler* No. 230, Swift gives a letter which embodies some of "the late refinements crept into our language," and in *A Proposal for Correcting, Improving, and Ascertaining the English*

Tongue he comments upon the probability that the language of his own day would soon become so antiquated as to be unintelligible.

443, l. 13, *Colonel James Graham:* "I dined with the Secretary as usual, and old Colonel Graham that lived at Bagshot Heath, and they said it was Colonel Graham's house." The *Journal to Stella*, June 3, 1711.

443, l. 23, *the late D. of R—— and E. of E——*: Temple Scott regards these names as probably fictitious.

443, l. 41, *abbreviating or reducing words:* This practice, which is illustrated later in this Introduction, was especially obnoxious to Swift; he attacked it repeatedly.

444, l. 22, *the great Bishop Burnet:* Gilbert Burnet, Bishop of Salisbury, was one of Swift's favourite antipathies.

444, l. 22, *selling of bargains:* See note to Dryden's *Mac Flecknoe*, p. 45, l. 181.

444, l. 23, *free-thinking:* Swift's lifelong fight against Deism and other forms of free-thinking found expression in numerous works.

445, l. 15, *the converted rumpers:* members of the "Rump" Parliament, after "Pride's Purge," 1648.

445, l. 50, *applied in some manner by an appendix:* The context seems to demand *supplied.*

446, l. 5, *the clergy,... polite assemblies:* Swift never failed by word or deed to protest against the contemporary low estimate of the clergy.

446, l. 37, *an ancient poet:* Temple Scott believes that this couplet was written by Swift himself.

447, l. 11, *Lilly:* William Lily's *Latin Grammar* was long a standard school textbook.

447, l. 32, *e'n't:* ain't.

447, l. 53, *name the particular speakers:* Though there is some elementary characterization in these dialogues, the point of the satire is in the conventional sallies and retorts, which fit one character about as well as another.

449, l. 36, *push-pin:* a child's game in which pins are pushed over each other.

450, l. 39, ***the bishop has set his foot in it:*** See *NED*, *Bishop*, n.[1], 5, where the following passage from Tindale is quoted: "If the porage be burned to, or the meat ouer rosted, we say the bishop hath put his foote in the potte or the bishop hath played the cooke, because the bishops burn who they lust, and whoever displeaseth them."

450, l. 33, *the devil was beating his wife:* That is, he is laughing and she is crying. For variants on this proverbial expression see G. L. Apperson, *English Proverbial Phrases*, 1919.

451, l. 50, *Lob's pound:* a difficulty. This is another proverbial expression.

451, l. 24, *I never take snuff, but when I'm angry:* "Snuff," archaically, means resentment expressed by sniffing; offence. *Cf.* the expression, "To take it in snuff."

JOHN ARBUTHNOT

BIBLIOGRAPHY

George A. Aitken, *The Life and Works of John Arbuthnot*, 1892, is the best biographical treatment and also the best modern reprint of Arbuthnot's work, complete except for a few scientific writings.

The History of John Bull is included in Edward Arber's *English Garner*, vol. 6, 1883, and in Cassell's National Library, ed. by Henry Morley, 1889.

Memoirs of the Extraordinary Life, Works, and Discoveries of Martinus Scriblerus is included in the Elwin and Courthope edition of *The Works of Alexander Pope*, vol. v.

H. Teerink, *The History of John Bull for the First Time Faithfully Reissued from the Original Pamphlets, 1712, together with an Investigation into its Composition, Publication, and Authorship*, 1925.

For the political situation, see J. W. Greene, *History of the English People*, book VIII, chap. III.

The most recent work on the subject is George Macaulay Trevelyan, *England under Queen Anne*, vol. I, *Blenheim*, 1930, vol. II, *Ramillies and the Union with Scotland*, 1932.

NOTES

453, l. 8, *the late Lord Strutt:* Charles II of Spain died in 1700 without issue.

453, l. 8, *the parson and a cunning attorney:* Cardinal Portocarero and the Marshal of Harcourt, the French envoy at Madrid, were the chief supporters of the French interest in Spain.

453, l. 10, *his cousin, Philip Baboon:* Philip Bourbon, Duke of Anjou, had a claim to the Spanish throne through his grandmother, Maria Theresa, wife of Louis XIV. By the terms of the first Partition Treaty, 1698, the greater part of the Spanish dominions had been settled on the Electoral Prince, Joseph, who claimed the succession through his grandmother, Margaret, sister of Charles II and wife of the Emperor Leopold I. After the death of Joseph in 1699, Louis XIV, by the second Partition Treaty had renounced the rights of his grandson, the Duke of Anjou, in favour of the Archduke Charles of Austria; but when the former was named as heir by the will of Charles II, he disregarded this treaty, thus bringing on the War of the Spanish Succession.

453, l. 11, *his cousin Esquire South:* the Archduke Charles of Austria.

454, l. 10, *John Bull, the clothier:* England.

454, l. 11, *Nic. Frog, the linen-draper:* Holland.

454, l. 29, *Lewis Baboon:* Louis XIV of France.

454, l. 40, *Charles Mather:* a well-known English toyman.

455, l. 4, *coming to Mrs. Bull's ears:* John Bull's wife represents the English government: the ministry or the Parliament.

455, l. 26, *their lawsuit:* the War of the Spanish Succession, waged by England and Holland against France and Spain to prevent the union of these two kingdoms, through the heir to the throne of the former becoming the king of the latter. See previous notes. Disturbance of the European balance of power and danger to Dutch security and English trade were among the causes of this war.

455, l. 34, *lying Ned, the chimney-sweeper of Savoy:* the Duke of Savoy.

455, l. 35, *Tom, the Portugal dustman:* the King of Portugal. Savoy and Portugal joined the allies against France and Spain.

455, l. 37, *Humphry Hocus, the attorney:* the Duke of Marlborough, general-in-chief of the allied armies. His character is sketched in the last paragraph of this chapter, emphasis being laid upon his love of money and upon his relations to his wife, to whom the epithet, "mild-spirited," is of course applied ironically.

456, l. 32, *Doily stuffs:* cheap material, named after Doily, a dealer who introduced it.

456, l. 14, *Blackwell Hall:* a woollen market in London. The name was sometimes written Bakewell Hall.

456, l. 51, *Hocus had dealings with John's wife:* It was a common charge that Marlborough had bribed some members of Parliament.

457, l. 15, *Hocus's country-house:* Blenheim House was built for the Duke of Marlborough by the British nation in recognition of his military success.

457, l. 19, *The parson of the parish:* Dr. Henry Sacheverell in November, 1709, preached a sermon on the divine right of kings and the sin of popular resistance to their authority. Parliament considered this an attack on the Revolution of 1688, and impeached Sacheverell. His trial resulted in a nominal sentence that was interpreted as a practical acquittal. This case made a great popular sensation, and contributed largely to the defeat of the Whigs the following year.

458, l. 10, *Polemia, Discordia, and Usuria:* war, faction, and usury.

458, l. 13, *John Bull's Second Wife:* The new Tory government was generally unfavourable to the war. Parliament investigated mismanagement and misappropriation of funds expended for war supplies.

459, l. 27, *Daniel Burgess:* a dissenting preacher, whose meeting house had been wrecked by the mob in the riots at the time of the Sacheverell trial.

459, l. 35, *Sir Roger Bold:* Robert Harley, who succeeded Godolphin as Treasurer. See note to Swift's *Journal to Stella*, p. 394, l. 26.

459, l. 53, *Mrs. Bull should sell her linen and wearing-clothes:* the end of the first part of *The History of John Bull,* except for a short chapter XIII, not afterwards reprinted in the complete edition.

JAMES THOMSON

BIBLIOGRAPHY

Poetical Works, with Memoir and Critical Appendices by D. C. Tovey, 1897.
Complete Poetical Works, ed. J. L. Robertson, 1908.
Leon Morel, *James Thomson, sa vie et ses œuvres*, 1895.
William Bayne, *James Thomson* (Famous Scots Series), 1898.
G. C. Macaulay, *James Thomson* (English Men of Letters Series), 1907.
Herbert E. Cory, "Spenser, Thomson and Romanticism," *PMLA*, 26:51–91 (1911).
Erna Anwader, *Pseudoklassizistisches und Romantisches in Thomsons "Seasons,"* 1930.

NOTES

WINTER

460, l. 6, *horrors:* a weaker word than it now is.

461, l. 17, *essay:* The first edition (1726) of *Winter*, which was the first of the Seasons to be published, had been dedicated to Sir Spencer Compton, who in 1730 became the Earl of Wilmington.

461, l. 43, *year:* i.e., in late December.

461, l. 65, *root:* the turnip, recently introduced as winter feed by Jethro Tull and Lord Townshend, with great benefit to agriculture.

462, l. 139, *downs:* open highlands.

462, l. 144, *cormorant:* sea raven.

462, l. 146, *hern:* the heron, which neither shrieks nor soars.

462, l. 150, *Eat:* eaten.

462, l. 174, *round:* This picture of storm at sea is based upon *Æneid*, I, 81–124.

463, l. 189, *dome:* house, from Latin *domus*.

463, l. 194, *devoted:* doomed.

463, l. 208, *aside:* The present passage was suggested by Milton's *Il Penseroso*, 76–120.

463, l. 244, *store:* of grain, from which the farmer is fanning the chaff.

463, l. 267, *at will:* as much as they wish.

464, l. 311, *vain:* With this passage compare Gray's *Elegy*, 21–24, and note, p. 519.

464, l. 322, *proud:* an early example of the sentimental view that the wealthy and cultivated classes are wicked and hard-hearted, and that the poor and ignorant — at any rate, when they live in the country — are always virtuous. Compare Gray's *Elegy*, and Burns's *The Cotter's Saturday Night*.

464, l. 358, *work:* This faith in the social sense — "a determination to be pleased with the happiness of others, and to be uneasy at their misery" — may be traced to Shaftesbury, and to Francis Hutcheson, whose *Essay on the Conduct of the Passions*, 1728, had deep influence upon the "sentimentalists" of the century.

464, l. 359, *band:* a group appointed in 1729 to report upon the prisons of England. The shocking conditions found by them were not improved fifty years later when John Howard published his investigations or, indeed, until 1814.

465, l. 390, *horrid:* bristling.

465, l. 406, *stands:* according to mediæval superstition.

465, l. 415, *Grisons:* people of the easternmost Swiss canton.

465, l. 424, *Now...:* another passage suggested by *Il Penseroso*.

465, l. 437, *volume:* Plutarch's *Lives*.

465, l. 446, *Solon:* Athenian lawgiver (638–559 B.C.).

466, l. 453, *Lycurgus:* legendary Spartan lawgiver (*ca.* 800 B.C.).

466, l. 457, *chief:* Leonidas, king of Sparta, died at Thermopylæ, 480 B.C.

466, l. 459, *Aristides:* Athenian statesman and soldier, died 468 B.C.

466, l. 464, *fame:* that of Themistocles, whom Aristides assisted in the campaign of Salamis.

466, l. 466, *Cimon:* Athenian statesman, to whom Aristides gave command of the fleet.

466, l. 474, *Timoleon:* liberator of Sicily from Carthage (411–337 B.C.). For the good of Corinth he allowed his brother to be put to death.

466, l. 476, *pair:* Epaminondas and Pelopidas, generals in the war against Sparta.

466, l. 481, *Phocion:* Athenian statesman (402–318 B.C.).

466, l. 488, *Agis:* King of Sparta, strangled by his people in 241 B.C.

466, l. 491, *Aratus:* a Greek statesman (271–213 B.C.), supporter of the Achæan League.

466, l. 494, *Philopœmen:* commander of cavalry in the Achæan League.

466, l. 503, *Numa:* legendary king of Rome.

466, l. 504, *Servius:* sixth king of Rome.

466, l. 507, *father:* Marcus Junius Brutus, founder of Roman civil law.

466, l. 510, *Camillus:* a patrician first exiled and then recalled.

466, l. 511, *Fabricius:* a consul, died 275 B.C.

466, l. 512, *Cincinnatus:* an early Roman hero twice called from his farm to the dictatorship.

466, l. 513, *victim:* Regulus, slain at Carthage on his return from Rome on parole.

466, l. 517, *Scipio:* surnamed "Africanus," conqueror of Hannibal.

466, l. 521, *Tully:* Marcus Tullius Cicero.

466, l. 523, *Cato:* Roman farmer and statesman, opponent of Hellenism and author of *De Re Rustica*.

466, l. 524, *Brutus:* Marcus Brutus (78–42 B.C.), hero of Shakespeare's *Julius Cæsar*.

466, l. 532, *Mantuan swain:* Virgil.

467, l. 555, *Hammond:* James Hammond (1716–1742), author of *Love Elegies*.

467, l. 587, *good:* The optimism of this passage, together with the expectation that order, harmony, and unity will be discovered in the natural world, is derived chiefly from the writings of Shaftesbury.

467, l. 603, *life: Cf.* Gray's *Elegy*, ll. 75, 76.

467, l. 617, *Meantime...:* The outline of the following forty lines was suggested by the night scenes in Milton's *L'Allegro*, ll. 100 ff.

467, l. 630, *city:* It is observable that Milton, the alleged Puritan, takes only pleasure in his thought of metropolitan delights — *L'Allegro*, ll. 117 ff. — and that Thomson, although by no means a strict moralist, describes the city as a scene of riot, vice, and ruin, sharpening the contrast between it and rural virtue by every means in his power.

468, l. 647, *Monimia:* heroine of Otway's *The Orphan*, 1690.

468, l. 648, *Belvidera:* heroine of Otway's *Venice Preserved*, 1682.

468, l. 653, *strain:* in what is now called "sentimental comedy."

468, l. 655, *Bevil:* a character in Sir Richard Steele's *The Conscious Lovers*, 1722.

468, l. 664, *Chesterfield:* Philip Dormer Stanhope, fourth Earl of Chesterfield, 1694–1773, Ambassador to Holland, Lord Lieutenant of Ireland, and Secretary of State. The present passage, quite inorganic and in almost the worst vein of literary sycophancy, is rendered less painful to read by the recollection of Dr. Johnson's Letter to Lord Chesterfield. See pp. 647, 648.

468, l. 710, *luculent:* lucid.

468, l. 714, *stores...:* a passage based upon the atomic theory of Lucretius, and especially upon *De Rerum Natura*, vi, 527 ff.

469, l. 740, *cope:* vault.

469, l. 768, *Batavia:* Holland.

469, l. 782, *gelid:* frozen.

469, l. 804, *vast:* wilderness.

469, l. 813, *Sables:* The fur of the sable is in fact not black but brown. Thomson is deceived by the use of the word in heraldry.

469, l. 814, *freaked:* spotted.

469, l. 820, *toils:* traps.

469, l. 824, *bray:* make a loud outcry.

470, l. 827, *half-absorbed:* half-wallowed up or covered by snow.

470, l. 835, *Boötes:* "The ploughman," a constellation near the Great Dipper or Charles's Wain.

470, l. 836, *Caurus:* the west northwest wind.

470, l. 845, *gives...:* The pure "primitivism" of this passage, suggesting Rousseau and Chateaubriand, had been anticipated many times, as in Henry Brooke's *Universal Beauty*, 1735, and even in Pope's *Essay on Man*, I, 99 ff.

470, l. 875, *Niëmi's:* a lake in Lapland.

470, l. 886, *woe...:* This idyllic picture, based upon an account of Lapland in P. de Maupertuis's *Sur la figure de la terre*, 1738, is highly fanciful, for the Lapps have been enslaved in turn by the Norse, the Swedes, and the Russians.

470, l. 887, *Tornea's lake:* in northern Sweden.

470, l. 888, *Hecla:* a volcanic mountain in Iceland.

470, l. 893, *sky:* i.e., of another hemisphere.

470, l. 901, *globe...:* a passage suggested by Virgil's hall of Æolus, *Æneid*, I, 52 ff.

470, l. 902, *eastward:* really southward from the pole, but toward the Orient.

470, l. 912, *pole:* imagined pictorially.

471, l. 925, *Briton's:* Sir Hugh Willoughby, who perished in 1554 on the coast of Lapland while searching for a northeastern passage to Cathay.

471, l. 930, *Arzina:* the Kola Peninsula.

471, l. 937, *Oby:* a river of Siberia emptying into the Arctic Ocean.

471, l. 955, *Peter:* Peter the Great (1672–1725), emperor of Russia.

471, l. 971, *skill:* Peter's tour of western Europe, including England, was made in 1697.

471, l. 976, *roar:* referring to Peter's naval expedition down the River Don against the Turkish fortress of Azov on the inland sea of that name.

471, l. 980, *Alexander of the north:* Charles XII of Sweden (1682–1718).

471, l. 981, *sons:* successors in the Caliphate of Othman (574–656).

472, l. 1007, *sea: Cf. Paradise Lost*, I, 207, 208.

A HYMN

473, l. 1, *These:* the seasons of the year, described in the foregoing portions of the book for which the present poem was written as an epilogue.

473, l. 21, *round:* circle of the year.

473, l. 22, *train:* succession.

TO THE MEMORY OF SIR ISAAC NEWTON

474, Title, *Newton:* Newton died on the twentieth of March, 1727, and the present poem appeared in folio three months later.

474, l. 2, *his:* in the sense that he had understood them.

474, l. 2, *Muse:* poet.

474, l. 5, *light:* the stars with reference to the "music of the spheres."

474, l. 17, *bound:* by the law of gravitation.

474, l. 18, *unequal:* too difficult.

474, l. 25, *names:* in the speculations about nature, largely resting upon authority in the ages before the application of scientific method.

475, l. 45, *tracts:* orbits.

475, l. 51, *main:* the sea, whose tides are affected by the moon.

475, l. 88, *pleasing:* perhaps in the sense that the older cosmology seemed to give more importance to the earth and to man. After Newton's discoveries "the scenery became too wide for the drama."

475, l. 100, *his:* its.

475, l. 118, *new*... : With this glowing passage compare Keats's *Lamia,* II, 231–38.

476, l. 131, *way:* a reference to Newton's *The Chronology of Ancient Kingdoms,* first published in English in 1728, but before that in French.

476, l. 143, *whole:* Newton was in fact deeply religious, and he wrote extensively upon theological topics.

476, l. 157, *Conduitt:* John Conduitt, who was Newton's deputy as Warden of the Mint and who promised, but never wrote, a life of the scientist. He had married Newton's favourite niece.

476, l. 165, *privilege:* immortality.

476, l. 209, *kings:* Newton was buried in Westminster Abbey.

THE CASTLE OF INDOLENCE

477, Prefatory stanza, l. 1, *hight:* called.

477, l. 3, *emmet:* ant.

477, l. 3, *moil:* labour.

477, l. 4, *sentence:* laid upon Adam.

477, l. 8, *bale:* evil.

477, l. 10, *dale*... : *Cf. The Faerie Queene,* I, 1, stanza 34.

477, l. 18, *wight:* creature.

477, l. 18, *ne:* nor.

477, l. 21, *kest:* cast.

477, l. 25, *sheen:* shining.

477, l. 27, *still:* continually.

477, l. 31, *vacant:* idle.

477, l. 35, *coil:* disturbance, noise.

477, l. 35, *keep:* maintain.

477, l. 36, *yblent:* The *y* is the old sign of the past participle.

477, l. 40, *Idless:* Idleness.

477, l. 46, *drowsyhed:* The suffix is equivalent to *-ness.*

478, l. 55, *landskip:* the common form of the word at this time, and more correct than landscape. After this word supply *was.*

478, l. 66, *breathe:* rest.

478, l. 70, *Ymolten:* melted.

478, l. 86, *emove:* move, suggested by *emotion.*

478, l. 96, *Interest:* self-interest, private profit.

478, l. 97, *Astræa:* the "star maid," last goddess to leave earth when the iron age succeeded to the golden.

478, l. 103, *sweep:* an allusion to the myth of Sisyphus.

478, l. 110, *stounds:* pangs of pain.

478, l. 111, *louting:* bowing.

479, l. 126, *Sybarite:* citizen of ancient Sybaris, in Southern Italy, famous for its wealth and luxury.

479, l. 152, *Scipio:* See p. 466, l. 517, note. His retirement, at the height of his great fame, to his small native village is frequently cited in the literature of solitude.

479, l. 152, *Cumæan:* Campanian.

479, l. 159, *fry:* trout.

479, l. 172, *trembling:* from Milton's *Lycidas,* l. 77.

479, l. 180, *stream:* suggested by the entry of Milton's fallen angels into Pandemonium.

479, l. 181, *smooth:* in almost the slang sense of today.

479, l. 184, *han:* have.

479, l. 187, *perdie:* a mild oath, from *par Dieu.*

479, l. 195, *giant-crew:* the Titans.

480, l. 205, *losel's:* of a loose or idle fellow.
480, l. 218, *to weet:* to wit.
480, l. 233, *fain:* gladly.
480, l. 240, *nepenthe:* a care and pain-dispelling drug. *Cf. Faerie Queene,* IV, 3, 43–45.
480, l. 241, *Dan:* Master, a shortened form of *Dominus.*
480, l. 241, *sings: Odyssey,* iv, 228.
480, l. 245, *trump:* sound of trumpet.
480, l. 246, *will:* This is the motto and only rule of the Abbey of Theleme, described in Rabelais's *Gargantua,* chapter 57.
480, l. 255, *eftsoons:* soon after.
480, l. 261, *was:* commonly used with the second person by good writers of the time.
480, l. 268, *wain:* literally, a wagon, but here the chariot of the sun.
481, l. 278, *place:* Thomson's confession of his own indolence, *cf.* ll. 604 ff.
481, l. 281, *imp:* child.
481, l. 288, *age:* an outline of Thomson's literary plans, most of which he fulfilled in *Liberty* and in his dramas.
481, l. 306, *played . . . :* A comparison of this stanza with Keats's *Eve of Saint Agnes,* stanzas 29–31, will reveal — when due allowance is made for the fact that Keats was a first-rate, and Thomson a second-rate poet — some of the fundamental differences between the neo-classical and the romantic manner.
481, l. 312, *desire: Cf.* l. 246, and note.
481, l. 326, *Depeinten:* depicted.
481, l. 327, *land:* Genesis 11:31.
481, l. 334, *pencil:* artist's paint-brush.
482, l. 341, *Lorrain:* Claude Lorraine, 1600–82.
482, l. 342, *Rosa:* Salvator Rosa, 1615–73.
482, l. 342, *Poussin:* Nicolas Poussin, 1594–1665. The three great painters of landscape admirably characterized in these few words were extremely influential in England at just this time, doing much to shape English taste in the "picturesque" and strongly affecting the work of landscape poets such as Thomson.
482, l. 352, *before:* scarcely true. The æolian harp — so named after Æolus, god of the winds — was first described by Athanasius Kircher in his *Musurgia Universalis,* 1650. It became familiar in England, however, in Thomson's time, and it grew into favour with the growth of the romantic movement for the reason suggested in l. 369. Thomson wrote *An Ode on Æolus's Harp.*
482, l. 383, *mell:* mingle.
482, l. 393, *Titian's:* Venetian painter, 1477–1576, supreme as a colourist.
482, l. 404, *heaven:* The Mohammedan paradise is enlivened by nymphs or *houris* of the sort here described.
483, l. 409, *for:* as to.
483, l. 409, *fiends:* of nightmare.
483, l. 432, *abide:* await.
483, l. 450, *pot:* of ale.
483, l. 463, *Thespian:* from Thespis, a Greek poet, supposed inventor of tragedy.
483, l. 474, *rout:* crowd.
484, l. 479, *cabals:* political cliques or factions.
484, l. 479, *juntos:* same as *cabals.*
484, l. 483, *Lucifer:* the morning star.
484, l. 504, *moe:* more.
484, l. 506, *man:* probably the poet, William Collins, whose indolence entitled him to admission. Thomson knew Collins only during the last year of his life, but it was at this time that he was working on the present poem.
484, l. 509, *soote:* sweetly.
484, l. 511, *stark:* entirely.
484, l. 513, *boon:* generous.
484, l. 514, *incontinent:* immediately.
484, l. 517, *broom:* a yellow-flowered shrub.
484, l. 534, *One:* the poet and physician, John Armstrong, 1709–1779, author of a famous didactic poem, *The Art of Preserving Health.*
484, l. 538, *wroke:* wreaked.
484, l. 541, *wretch:* Henry Welby, an eccentric solitary.
485, l. 551, *youth:* John Forbes, son of Duncan Forbes of Culloden, Lord President of the Scottish Court of Sessions.

485, l. 577, *guest:* George Lyttelton, 1709–1773, statesman and man of letters; Thomson's patron.

485, l. 581, *lad:* led.

485, l. 594, *Hagley Park:* Lyttelton's estate in Worcestershire, adjoining William Shenstone's Leasowes.

485, l. 595, *whilom ligged:* formerly lay.

485, l. 595, *the Esopus of the age:* James Quin, 1693–1766, an actor second only to Garrick in popularity, here called Esopus because, like that Roman tragedian, he had killed a man in personal combat. Quin won Thomson's friendship by giving the poet a hundred pounds when he was in jail for debt.

485, l. 604, *dwelt . . .*: This description of Thomson himself was written by Lyttelton.

485, l. 614, *mote:* might.

485, l. 615, *oily man of God:* the Rev. Patrick Murdoch, tutor to John Forbes, and first biographer of Thomson. He was so old and close a friend that the poet could take liberties with him, as he does here and in his verse epistle, *To the Incomparable Soporific Doctor*.

485, l. 619, *tight:* neat.

485, l. 620, *mew:* cage or enclosure.

486, l. 638, *knot:* knit.

486, l. 648, *vapoury god:* the "vapours," a fashionable complaint akin to the "spleen" but even more imaginary — boredom and *ennui*.

486, l. 658, *change:* The following stanzas were written by Dr. John Armstrong.

486, l. 663, *eath:* easy.

486, l. 675, *frantic:* insane.

486, l. 679, *spittles:* hospitals.

486, l. 689, *Tertian:* fever and ague returning every other day.

MARK AKENSIDE

BIBLIOGRAPHY

Poetical Works, with *Life*, by A. Dyce, 1835.
Poetical Works, ed. by R. A. Willmott, 1855.
Poetical Works, with *Life*, by G. Gilfillan, 1857.
C. Buck: *On the Life, Writings, and Genius of Akenside*, 1832.
E. Dowden, article in Ward's *English Poets*, vol. 3.
S. Johnson, in *The Lives of the English Poets.*

NOTES

THE PLEASURES OF IMAGINATION

488, l. 66, *forms eternal:* The thought behind this passage is derived from Plato.

THE REMONSTRANCE OF SHAKESPEARE

490, l. 23, *shameful bands:* Apparently refers to the Reformation, which of course Shakespeare did not see.

491, l. 98, *vaunting race:* the French.

EDWARD YOUNG

BIBLIOGRAPHY

Works, 6 vols., 1757–78; new ed., 1774–78; revised with *Life* by J. Doran, 2 vols., 1854.
Poetical Works, with *Life* by J. Mitford, 2 vols., Aldine Poets, 1834, 1858, 1871.
Poems, with *Memoir* by W. M. Rossetti, 1871.
The Complaint, or Night Thoughts on Life, Death, and Immortality has appeared in many editions.
Conjectures on Original Composition, edited by Edith J. Morley, 1918.
H. C. Shelley, *Life and Letters of Edward Young*, 1914.
Among critical works the following are important:

G. Eliot, "Worldliness and Otherworldliness: the Poet Young," in *Essays*, 1884.
J. Texte, *Rousseau et la cosmopolitisme littéraire*, 1895; English translation by J. W. Matthews, 1899.
W. Thomas, *Le poète Edward Young*, 1901.
J. L. Kind, *Edward Young in Germany*, 1906.

M. W. Steinke, *Edward Young's "Conjectures on Original Composition" in England and Germany*, 1917.

Harry H. Clark, "The Romanticism of Edward Young," *Transactions of Wis. Acad. of Sciences, Arts, and Letters*, XXIV, 1–45, Nov., 1929.

Marjorie Bowen, "Edward Young," in *Transactions of the Royal Society of Literature*, n.s., vol. VIII, 1928.

NOTES

NIGHT THOUGHTS

493, l. 15, *The day too short for my distress:* The death of Young's wife in 1741, together with other domestic losses, was in part responsible for the gloomy cast of his reflections in this poem.

496, l. 321, *Lorenzo:* an infidel, probably an imaginary figure, to whom are addressed the poet's arguments in support of belief in immortality.

497, l. 344, *Philander:* perhaps the poet's son-in-law, who had died in 1740. Such identification is of no great importance for the comprehension of the poem, however, since Philander stands for any dear friend who has departed.

497, l. 406, *vails:* gratuity.

498, l. 449, *Mæonides:* Homer.

498, l. 451, *his... own:* Pope's.

CONJECTURES ON ORIGINAL COMPOSITION

498, Title, *The Author of Sir Charles Grandison:* Samuel Richardson (1689–1761), the famous novelist; he was a friend of Young's.

498, l. 17, *subjects more important, and more suitable to my season of life:* The reference is to the account of Addison's death (omitted here) with which the letter ends. The introduction of "monumental marbles," "a churchyard walk of mournful yews," and "sepulchral lamps" shows Young's characteristic preoccupation with such subjects as he treats in *Night Thoughts.*

498, l. 19, *original composition... seen nothing hitherto written on it: Cf.* introductory remarks on Young and the fuller treatment of the subject in the Introduction to Edith J. Morley's ed. of the *Conjectures.*

499, l. 9, *the first Brutus:* Lucius Junius Brutus took a prominent part in the expulsion of the Tarquins from Rome, became one of the first two consuls and sentenced to death his own sons, who had conspired to restore the Tarquins.

499, l. 5, *In uxoris infirmitate... confugio* (*Epis.* 8, 19, 1, considerably changed): "Distracted by the ill-health of my wife and by the dangerous illness or the death of my friends, I flee for succour to my studies, the most potent assuagers of my grief."

499, l. 25, *tædium vitæ:* "Weariness of life."

499, l. 36, *imitations:* The classical theory of imitation on its higher levels involved not mechanical copying but rather work inspired by, and done in the spirit of the original. Young generally ignores this finer imitation and uses the word to indicate "a sort of duplicates of what we had, possibly much better, before," though later he refers to it when he advises imitating, "not the composition but the man," or when he speaks of "a sort of noble contagion from a general familiarity with their writings." *Cf.* Reynolds's *Sixth Discourse*, pp. 682 ff.

499, l. 54, *Armida's wand:* Armida, the enchantress who opposed the Crusaders in Tasso's *Jerusalem Delivered.*

500, l. 13, *Meo sum pauper in ære* (*Epis.* 2, 2, 12): "I am poor but live on my own means."

500, l. 43, *old Omar lighted up but a small bonfire:* The story is that Omar, the second of the Mohammedan caliphs (reigned 634–644), on taking Alexandria burned the world-famous Alexandrian Library, which was so large that its contents supplied fuel for six months to the furnaces that heated the public baths. This story is open to much doubt. In any event it was not Omar, but his general 'Amr, who captured the city.

501, l. 13, *you must either imitate Homer or depart from nature: Cf.* Pope, *An Essay on Criticism*, ll. 130–35. The neo-classical teaching was that since Homer had exactly imitated nature, one could learn of nature from Homer. See Introduction to Young.

502, l. 10, *Stat contra... es* (I, LV, 12): "Your page confronts you and says that you are a thief."

502, l. 50, *Nemo unquam vir... divino* (Cicero, *De Natura Deorum*, II, 167, inaccurately quoted): "No one was ever a great man without some divine inspiration."

502, l. 17, *Jura negat... arrogat* (Horace, *A. P.*, 122): "He denies that laws were intended to apply to him and claims everything as his own."

502, l. 34, *Pecuniam negligere... lucrum* (*Adelphæ*, 216, altered): "Sometimes to despise riches is the greatest gain."

502, l. 47, *Vossius:* Gerhard Johann Vossius (1577–1649), Dutch classical scholar.

503, l. 2, *Sacer nobis inest Deus:* "God dwells within us."

503, l. 34, *Neve minor... Fabula* (*A. P.*, 189, 190): "To five acts lengthened be the piece, not more." Howes.

503, l. 21, *vigor igneus... cœlestis origo:* "Ardent force," "Heavenly origin."

504, l. 54, *dii minorum gentium:* "Lesser gods."

505, l. 1, *Ostia septem... valles* (*Met.* II, 255, 6): "Seven dusty mouths are empty, seven valleys without a stream."

505, l. 12, *Joseph's brethren:* See Genesis, chap. 42, *et seq.*

505, l. 15, *the widow's cruse:* See II Kings, 4:1–7.

505, l. 21, *Collectas fugat... reducit* (*Æn.*, I, 143): "Drives away the gathered clouds and brings back the sun."

506, l. 40, *Nil tam prope, proculque nobis* (I, LXXXVI, 10): "No one so near and yet so far from us."

507, l. 18, *Cynthius aurem Vellit* — (*Ecl.* 6, 4): "Apollo twitches at my ear." I.e., gives warning.

507, l. 15, *Phœben alieno... suo* (III, 9, 10): "He had decreed that the moon should be filled with a fire not her own, but that the sun should be filled with his own fire."

508, l. 55, *Parrhasius for Zeuxis:* Parrhasius of Ephesis, Greek painter, here said to have been the predecessor of Zeuxis in the same way that Æschylus preceded Sophocles in tragedy.

509, l. 15, *Natos sine semine flores* (*Met.* I, 108): "Flowers produced without seed."

509, l. 41, *Why condemned Maro...:* It is said that Virgil desired the *Æneid* to be burned after his death because it had not been completely revised.

510, l. 1, *...minima contentos nocte Britannos* (not Virgil, but Juvenal. *Sat.*, II, 161): "Britons satisfied with the shortest night."

510, l. 25, *A friend of mine has obeyed that injunction:* As the next paragraph indicates, this friend is Richardson himself, to whom the letter is addressed. The meaning is that Richardson had used the novel, which in its earlier forms had had a bad influence, to teach moral lessons.

ROBERT BLAIR

BIBLIOGRAPHY

Poetical Works, ed. R. Anderson, *The Works of the British Poets*, vol. 8, 1795.
The Works of the English Poets, ed. A. Chalmers, vol. 15, 1810.
Poetical Works, ed. G. Gilfillan, 1854.
The Grave, Illust. by Schiavonetti from designs by William Blake, 1808, 1813, 1903.
The Grave, ed. F. W. Farrar, 1860.
H. G. Graham, in *Scottish Men of Letters in the Eighteenth Century*, 1901.
Carl Müller, *Robert Blairs "Grave" und die Grabes- und Nachtdichtung*, 1909.

NOTES

THE GRAVE

513, l. 31, *There lie:* i.e., within the church edifice.

513, l. 35, *Rook'd:* crouched low.

513, l. 45, *pile:* church.

513, l. 47, *rift:* split.

513, l. 54, *gossipping:* christening.

513, l. 85, *Invidious:* envious.

513, l. 99, *errors:* wanderings.

513, l. 113, *smirking:* smiling.

514, l. 116, *Complexionally:* by natural disposition.

514, l. 125, *youth:* Alexander the Great.

514, l. 450, *'Tis long... majority: Cf.* Sir Thomas Browne in *Urn-Burial*: "The number of the dead long exceedeth all that shall live."

514, l. 462, *clubs:* contributes to the common stock.

515, l. 498, *balance:* possibly "balance of power," or perhaps the law, with reference to the symbolic figure of Justice.

515, l. 513, *lawn-robed:* The sleeves of the bishop's rochet are of lawn.

515, l. 536, *downright:* blunt in speech and manner.

THOMAS GRAY

BIBLIOGRAPHY

Works, ed. E. Gosse, 4 vols., 1884, revised edition, 1902–06.
Letters, ed. D. Tovey, 1900–12.
Selections from the Poetry and Prose, ed. W. L. Phelps, 3 vols., 1894.
Essays and Criticisms, ed. with Introd. by C. S. Northup, 1911.
E. Gosse, *Life of Gray*, English Men of Letters Series, 1882.
D. Tovey, *Gray and His Friends*, 1890.
A. S. Cook, *A Concordance to the English Poems of Thomas Gray*, 1908.
W. H. Hudson, *Gray and his Poetry*, 1911.
C. S. Northup, *A Bibliography of Thomas Gray*, 1917.
Amy L. Reed, *The Background of Gray's Elegy; a Study in the Taste for Melancholy Poetry, 1700–1751*, 1924.

NOTES

ODE ON A DISTANT PROSPECT OF ETON COLLEGE

517, l. 3, *Science:* knowledge.

517, l. 4, *Henry's:* Eton was founded in 1440 by Henry VI, who was noted for his piety.

517, l. 6, *Windsor's:* the royal palace of Windsor Castle, across the Thames from Eton.

517, l. 28, *succeed:* to the schoolboys of Gray's generation.

517, l. 29, *circle's:* poetic diction for "hoop." Dr. Johnson remarks in his Life of Gray: "His supplication to Father Thames, to tell him who drives the hoop or tosses the ball, is useless and puerile. Father Thames has no better means of knowing than himself."

517, l. 32, *labours:* studying aloud.

517, l. 33, *hours:* of recitation.

517, l. 34, *sweeten:* by contrast.

517, l. 36, *reign:* realm, the school grounds.

517, l. 81, *beneath:* later.

517, l. 83, *family:* of diseases.

518, l. 89, *hand: Cf.* Gray's *Elegy*, ll. 51, 52.

ODE ON THE SPRING

518, l. 1, *Hours:* The epithet "rosy-bosomed" is taken from Milton's *Comus*, l. 986. The Hours were regarded as companions of Venus who ushered in the seasons.

518, l. 3, *long-expecting:* long-expected.

518, l. 4, *purple:* highly coloured.

518, l. 5, *warbler:* the nightingale.

ELEGY WRITTEN IN A COUNTRY CHURCHYARD

519, l. 16, *rude:* unlettered, simple-minded.

519, l. 24, *share:* The ultimate source of this scene may be Lucretius, *De Rerum Natura*, III, 894–96, imitated by Horace in *Epode* II, 39 ff. Eighteenth-century poets were very fond of it. See, for example, in this book, Thomson's *Winter*, 311–21, and Collins's *Popular Superstitions of the Highlands*, 121–37.

519, l. 33, *heraldry:* noble lineage.

519, l. 35, *Awaits:* The hour of death *lies in wait for* beauty, wealth, power, and noble birth.

519, l. 38, *trophies:* memorials.

519, l. 39, *fretted:* decorated.

519, l. 41, *storied urn:* a funeral urn with an inscription.

519, l. 41, *animated:* lifelike.

519, l. 43, *provoke:* call forth.

519, l. 51, *rage:* enthusiasm.

519, l. 52, *genial:* life-giving.

519, ll. 53–56, *Full many... air:* more than thirty "sources and analogues" of this famous stanza have been discovered by Gray's many editors, but all of them — like Pope's *Rape of the Lock*, IV, 157, 158 — mention either the flower or the gem alone. The true source of the stanza, bringing the flower and the gem metaphors together with just the purpose Gray has in mind, is to be found in the eleventh Canzone of the Venetian poet, Celio Magno (1536–1602):

Ma (qual in parte ignota
Ben ricca gemma altrui cela il suo pregio,

O fior, ch'alta virtù ha in se riposta)
Visse in sen di castità nascosta,
In sua virtute e'n Dio contento visse.
Lunge dal visco mondan, che l'alma intrica

"But (as in some unknown place a truly rich gem hides its worth from those around, or a flower that has excellence deeply concealed within itself) lived hidden in the heart of virtue, content in his own excellence and in God, far from worldly snare that entangles the soul."

519, l. 57, *Hampden:* John, 1595–1643, antagonist of Charles I at the outbreak of the Civil War

519, l. 60, *blood:* The unfavourable attitude toward Cromwell is characteristic of the time. In an earlier version of the poem the names Cato, Tully, and Cæsar stood in the places of the present English names.

520, l. 72, *incense:* of poetic flattery. After this line Gray originally wrote the following four stanzas with which he intended that the poem should end:

The thoughtless world to majesty may bow,
  Exalt the brave, and idolize success;
But more to innocence their safety owe
  Than pow'r or genius e'er conspired to bless.

And thou, who, mindful of th' unhonoured dead,
  Dost in these notes their artless tale relate,
By night and lonely contemplation led
  To wander in the gloomy walks of Fate:
Hark! how the sacred calm, that breathes around,
  Bids ev'ry fierce tumultuous passion cease;
In still small accents whisp'ring from the ground
  A grateful earnest of eternal peace.

No more, with reason and thyself at strife,
  Give anxious cares and endless wishes room;
But through the cool sequestered vale of life
  Pursue the silent tenor of thy doom.

520, l. 78, *still:* always.

520, l. 82, *elegy:* a versified eulogium of an illustrious person, just deceased (such as Tickell's lines *On the Death of Mr. Addison*) highly popular both in England and America for a century before 1750.

520, l. 93, *thee:* Usually interpreted as referring to Gray himself, but this interpretation, when applied to l. 94, forces a choice between two awkward corollaries: that "these lines" are the misspelled epitaphs of the churchyard and were written by Gray, or that Gray refers to the *Elegy* itself as an "artless tale." A further difficulty is that this forces one to read all that follows, including the rather fulsome Epitaph, as Gray's description of himself — a real difficulty because Gray was shy, modest, and a gentleman. The best solution seems to be that this stanza, bad in many ways, is a bungling attempt to join two poems, one of which was to have ended with the last of the four rejected stanzas in a modest reference to the poet himself, and the other of which was a poem of mourning for Gray's dearest friend, Richard West, who died just before the *Elegy* was begun. Gray's motive for concealing the reference to West may have been that he alone had been entrusted with the terrible secret of the young man's sorrow and broken-hearted death: that West's mother had poisoned his father in order that she might marry another man. (For a full discussion of these problems, see "A Youth to Fortune and to Fame Unknown" by Odell Shepard, in *Modern Philology*, vol. xx, 1923, pp. 347–73.)

520, l. 116, *thorn:* hawthorn tree. Here follows, in one manuscript, the stanza:

There scattered oft, the earliest of the year,
  By hands unseen are shower of violets found;
The redbreast loves to build and warble there,
  And little footsteps lightly print the ground.

520, l. 119, *Science: Cf.* p. 517, l. 3, note. The line means that although of low birth he was able to secure education.

HYMN TO ADVERSITY

520, l. 7, *purple:* in the ancient sense, a sort of crimson worn by emperors.

520, l. 8, *pangs unfelt before:* a phrase from *Paradise Lost*, II, 703.

520, l. 13, *lore:* teaching or discipline.

520, l. 16, *woe:* The thought of this line is taken from *Æneid*, I, 630.

521, l. 20, *good:* suggested by John Oldham's *Satire against Virtue*, l. 119.

521, l. 21, *Light:* swiftly.

521, l. 28, *leaden: Cf. Il Penseroso*, l. 44. The entire mood and manner of this stanza, together with the device of surrounding the central figure with a "philosophic train" of congenial abstractions, is derived from Milton's poem.

521, l. 36, *band:* the Furies.

521, l. 37, *impious:* in the older sense, undutiful to parents. The Furies pursued Orestes, who slew his mother.

521, l. 47, *Exact:* an adjective.

THE PROGRESS OF POESY

521, l. 1, *lyre:* of Pindar, chief master of the strict Greek ode here imitated, who himself called his verse "Æolian" — i.e., soft, melting, musical.

521, l. 3, *Helicon:* a mountain range in Bœotia, home of the Muses.

521, l. 9, *reign:* realm.

522, l. 15, *shell:* the lyre, first made of a tortoise shell.

522, l. 21, *king:* the eagle of Jove.

522, l. 27, *Idalia's:* a town, sacred to Venus, in Cyprus.

522, l. 38, *sublime:* held high.

522, l. 46, *fond:* foolish.

522, l. 47, *Jove:* suggested by Milton's line, "And justify the ways of God to men," *Paradise Lost*, I, 26.

522, l. 53, *Hyperion's:* the sun.

522, l. 54, *beyond the solar road:* a translation of *Æneid*, VI, 796, *extra anni solisque vias.* In this stanza Gray has in mind, as he says, the influence of poetry among uncivilized peoples, as shown by "the Erse, Norwegian, and Welsh fragments, the Lapland and American songs."

522, l. 60, *repeat:* tell the story or the names of.

522, l. 64, *pursue:* plural after the first part of a compound subject.

522, l. 66, *steep:* Mount Parnassus, haunt of the Muses, at the foot of which was the Delphic oracle of Apollo.

522, l. 68, *Ilissus:* a river near Athens.

522, l. 69, *Mæander:* a winding river in Asia Minor.

522, l. 84, *darling:* Shakespeare, called the child of Nature because his genius was considered far greater than his art.

522, l. 95, *he:* Milton, whom Gray considers not "second" or inferior to Shakespeare.

522, l. 96, *the seraph wings of Ecstasy: Cf. Paradise Lost*, VI, 771, "He on the wings of cherubs rode sublime."

522, l. 98, *flaming . . . time:* imitated from Lucretius's famous phrase, *flammantia mœnia mundi*, *De Rerum Natura*, I, 73.

523, l. 105, *Two coursers:* perhaps intended to recall Dryden's mastery of the heroic couplet.

523, l. 106, *pace:* Gray says that these two lines were "meant to express the stately march and sounding energy of Dryden's rhymes." The "Necks in thunder cloth'd" was suggested by Job, 39:19.

523, l. 112, *spirit:* Thomas Gray.

523, l. 115, *Theban eagle:* Pindar.

523, l. 123, *great:* The idea of this half-line, probably Stoic in origin, is illustrated by Gray's *Ode on the Spring*, ll. 19, 20, and by several passages in the *Elegy*.

THE BARD

523, Fifth l. of note, *death:* Gray's note. The last survivor of the bards is speaking. The date of Edward's invasion of Wales was 1282.

523, l. 2, *Confusion:* destruction.

523, l. 8, *Cambria's:* Latin name for Wales.

523, l. 13, *Glo'ster:* Earl of Gloucester and Hertford, Edward's son-in-law. Like Edmond de Mortimer, mentioned below, he held lands on the borders of Wales.

523, l. 16, *Conway's:* a picturesque stream in North Wales.

523, l. 20, *air:* Gray says that he took this image from a picture by Raphael of "the Supreme Being in the vision of Ezekiel."

523, l. 28, *Hoel's:* Howel ab Owain Gwynedd, a royal poet of the twelfth century.

523, l. 28, *lay:* the poem, by Davydd Benvras about Llewelyn ab Iorwerth, greatest of Welsh kings.

523, l. 33, *Modred:* a name apparently taken at random from the Arthurian legends. As Gray does not use Welsh spelling, it is not easy to make sure what poets he referred to by the names "Cadwallo" and "Urien."

523, l. 34, *Plinlimmon:* a mountain in Wales.
523, l. 35, *shore:* opposite Anglesea.
524, l. 56, *king:* Edward II, murdered in Berkeley Castle.
524, l. 57, *She-wolf of France:* Isabel of France, the queen of Edward II.
524, l. 60, *him:* Edward III.
524, l. 67, *warrior:* Edward the Black Prince, who died before his father.
524, l. 71, *Fair...:* These lines, says Gray, are intended to suggest the "magnificence of Richard the Second's reign," and to foreshadow its ruin.
524, l. 82, *guest:* Gray explains, in a note, that "Richard the Second... starved to death."
524, l. 85, *havoc:* the Wars of the Roses.
524, l. 87, *towers:* the Tower of London.
524, l. 89, *consort's:* Margaret of Anjou, wife of Henry VI.
524, l. 89, *father's:* Henry V.
524, l. 90, *usurper's:* Henry VI, considered almost a saint.
524, l. 92, *foe:* the red rose of Lancaster, foe to the white rose of York.
524, l. 93, *boar:* emblem of Richard III, who "wallowed" in the infant-gore of the two young princes.
524, l. 99, *heart:* Gray says that this refers to Queen Eleanor, at whose loss Edward I was overwhelmed with grief.
524, l. 101, *stay:* From this point the bard speaks for himself alone.
524, l. 109, *Arthur:* regarded by the Welsh as still living and as future king of Britain.
524, l. 110, *kings:* of the House of Tudor, which was of Welsh origin.
524, l. 115, *form:* Queen Elizabeth.
524, l. 120, *strains:* Elizabethan poetry.
524, l. 121, *Taliessin:* a half-legendary Welsh bard of the sixth century.
524, l. 127, *drest:* in Spenser's *Faerie Queene.*
525, l. 128, *measures:* of Shakespeare's tragedies.
525, l. 131, *voice:* Milton.
525, l. 133, *warblings:* of the poets following Milton.
525, l. 135, *man:* Edward I.

THE FATAL SISTERS

525, l. 32, *king:* Sictryg.
525, l. 37, *They:* the Norse.
525, l. 40, *plain:* of the region near Dublin.
526, l. 41, *earl:* Sigurd.
526, l. 44, *king:* Brian.
526, l. 56, *king:* Sictryg.

ODE ON THE PLEASURE ARISING FROM VICISSITUDE

526, Title, *vicissitude:* change. This poem, left unfinished by Gray, is here printed as it was found in his pocket-book for 1754.
526, l. 3, *vermeil:* vermillion.
526, l. 37, *Still:* always.

LETTERS

527, l. 2, *Peterhouse:* the college of that name at Cambridge University.
527, l. 9, *came:* to Cambridge.
527, l. 11, *companions:* Greek and Latin authors.
527, l. 41, *rest:* Isaiah XIII, 21; XXXII, 14; XXXIV, 14.
527, l. 45, *habitation:* at Christ Church College, Oxford.
527, l. 49, *hyp:* hypochondria.
527, l. 15, *Richard West:* This fragmentary letter, probably written in 1742, is given here in the original spelling and punctuation.
527, l. 26, *files:* probably an error for "flies."
527, l. 31, *Mad. de Sévigné:* Madame de Sévigné, most famous of French letter-writers, 1626–1696.
527, l. 34: Οὐδέποτε γυνή: "Never, woman!"
527, l. 40, *Bussy Rabutin:* a French soldier, courtier, and writer of memoirs, 1618–1693.
527, l. 44, *Bruyère:* Jean de la Bruyère, 1645–1696, author of a famous book of "characters."
527, l. 47, *Malebranche:* a French philosopher, 1638–1715.
527, l. 48, *Gronovius:* German classical scholar, 1611–1671.
527, l. 53, *Ray, the Naturalist:* John Ray, 1628–1705, father of English natural history.

528, l. 1, '*Me vero... Accipiant!*': "As for me, may the dear Muses take me to themselves." *Georgics*, II, 475–77.

528, l. 4, *H. More:* an English philosopher, 1614–1687, foremost of the "Cambridge Platonists."

528, l. 8, *Cheyne:* George Cheyne, 1671–1743, an English physician.

528, l. 27, *cough:* West had just sent Gray a Latin poem on this topic.

528, l. 42, *Dunciad:* the fourth book, which appeared in 1742.

528, l. 46, *Joseph Andrews:* the novel by Fielding, published in 1742.

528, l. 12, *Marivaux:* French novelist and dramatist, 1688–1763.

528, l. 12, *Crébillon:* French novelist, 1707–1777.

528, l. 15, *harangues:* a reference to Gray's drama *Agrippina*, never completed, which he had sent to West for criticism.

528, l. 55, *Rowes:* Nicholas Rowe, 1674–1718, a poet and dramatist.

529, l. 4, *But I,...:* Shakespeare's *Richard III*, I, 1, 14–21.

529, l. 19, *expression:* in his own drama.

529, l. 32, *una litura:* "One erasure."

529, l. 41, *ἐν ἀμαθίᾳ ... καταβιῶναι:* "In ignorance and without art to waste one's life."

529, l. 9, *Dodsley:* Robert Dodsley, 1703–1764, poet, anthologist, and publisher.

529, l. 26, *let it alone:* The *Elegy* was published by Dodsley, without Gray's name, five days after this letter was written.

529, l. 27, *Richard Hurd:* Bishop Hurd, author of *Letters on Chivalry and Romance*: see p. 753.

529, l. 32, *right and title to:* copies of *The Bard* and *The Progress of Poesy*, just published.

529, l. 54, *Mason's:* William Mason, 1724–1797, a second-rate poet and Gray's first biographer.

WILLIAM COLLINS

BIBLIOGRAPHY

Poems: ed. W. C. Bronson, 1898.
Poems, ed. by E. Blunden, 1929.
A. C. Swinburne, *Miscellanies*, 1886.
E. Montegut, *Heures de lecture d'un critique*, 1891.
H. W. Garrod, *Collins*, 1928.

NOTES

ODE TO SIMPLICITY

532, l. 9, *gauds:* ornaments.

532, l. 9, *pall:* a long cloak.

532, l. 10, *decent:* decorous.

532, l. 14, *Hybla's:* a district in Sicily famous for honey.

532, l. 16, *her:* the nightingale, praised by Electra in Sophocles's tragedy of that name.

532, l. 18, *poet's ear:* the phrase is taken from Milton's sonnet, *When the Assault was Intended to the City*.

532, l. 19, *Cephisus:* a river in Attica.

532, l. 21, *retreat:* Athens.

532, l. 32, *theme:* that of physical courage.

532, l. 33, *band:* of poets.

532, l. 35, *throne:* of Augustus, patron of poets.

532, l. 37, *bow'r:* the private apartment of a castle, which would have a poetry different from that of the hall, or great public room.

532, l. 39, *her:* Rome's, or Italy's.

532, l. 42, *scene:* the typical British attitude of the time toward Italian poetry and drama, caused in part by the presence in England of the Italian opera. See Collins's poem, *On Our Late Taste in Music*.

532, l. 49, *these:* taste and genius.

ODE TO EVENING

532, l. 1, *If aught of oaten stop:* if any music from a shepherd's flute. The conclusion following "If" is not reached until line 15.

533, l. 7, *brede:* embroidery.

533, l. 9, *Now:* supply "while."

533, l. 21, *folding-star:* at the rising of which shepherds fold their sheep.

533, l. 28, *car:* triumphal chariot.

533, l. 29, *vot'ress: Cf.* l. 2. Evening is imagined throughout as somewhat like a nun.
533, l. 32, *gleam:* a reflection, apparently, from the lake.
533, l. 41, *wont:* is accustomed to do.

ODE TO FEAR

533, l. 18, *allied:* to the phantoms.
533, l. 22, *brood:* called by Sophocles the "unescapable hounds" of Fate.
533, l. 30, *bard:* Æschylus, the Greek tragic poet, 525–456 B.C., who fought at Marathon.
534, l. 33, *reach'd:* took.
534, l. 34, *he:* Sophocles, 495–406 B.C.
534, l. 35, *Hybla's:* See note to p. 532, l. 14. The allusion is to the sweetness of Sophocles, except in the *Œdipus Coloneus.*
534, l. 37, *grove:* scene of *Œdipus Coloneus.*
534, l. 38, *veil:* of a thunderstorm.
534, l. 38, *queen:* Jocasta.
534, l. 43, *line:* of Sophocles's tragedy.
534, l. 45, *scene:* stage.
534, l. 59, *eve:* Hallowe'en.
534, l. 70, *cypress:* crown of the tragic poet.
534, l. 71, *thee:* suggested by Milton's *L'Allegro* and *Il Penseroso.*

ODE ON THE POETICAL CHARACTER

534, l. 1, *As:* to be connected with *thus* in l. 17.
534, l. 2, *bard:* Spenser.
534, l. 4, *Queen:* Elizabeth.
534, l. 6, *wear: Cf. The Faerie Queene,* IV, 5, 16–19.
534, l. 19, *cest:* girdle.
534, l. 22, *gaze:* supply *upon.*
534, l. 29, *enthusiast:* i.e., Fancy.
534, l. 29, *woo'd:* implored.
534, l. 39, *youth:* the sun.
534, l. 46, *whose:* i.e., by whose eyes.
534, l. 46, *tarsel's:* the male falcon's.
535, l. 54, *work:* the girdle.
535, l. 55, *cliff:* Each detail of the following description is intended to suggest some phase of Milton's poetry.
535, l. 57, *jealous:* hard to climb.
535, l. 63, *oak:* see *Il Penseroso,* l. 60.
535, l. 66, *spher'd:* placed in one of the concentric spheres in which, according to Ptolemy, the heavenly bodies move.
535, l. 67, *trump:* trumpet, called "ancient" to suggest that none but he had blown it since ancient times.
535, l. 69, *myrtle:* sacred to Venus. The most popular of Waller's poetry was erotic.
535, l. 72, *alone: Cf.* l. 5.

THE PASSIONS

535, Title, *Passions:* the emotions.
535, l. 3, *shell:* lyre.
535, l. 26, *sounds:* in apposition with "measures."
535, l. 36, *theme:* that of love.
535, l. 43, *denouncing:* announcing.
536, l. 75, *sisters:* wood-nymphs.
536, l. 75, *queen:* Diana.
536, l. 81, *viny:* suggesting that Joy is identified with Bacchus, as Cheerfulness is with Diana.
536, l. 86, *vale:* in Thessaly.
536, l. 108, *sister's:* poetry's.
536, l. 110, *reed:* flute.
536, l. 114, *world of sound:* the pipe organ, which St. Cecilia was supposed to have invented.
536, l. 115, *endeavours:* in the elaborate Italian opera which was at the height of fashion in London when this poem was written. Collins expressed the same attitude in his most vigorous poem, *On Our Late Taste in Music.*
536, l. 118, *relate:* One of Collins's last poems was an *Ode on the Music of the Greek Theatre,* now lost.

ODE WRITTEN IN THE BEGINNING OF THE YEAR 1746

536, Subtitle, *1746:* This almost perfect poem, which has the strong simplicity of a Greek epitaph, was probably written to commemorate the English soldiers who fell at Fontenoy in May, 1745, at Preston Pans in September of that year, and at Falkirk in January, 1746. In all these battles the British were defeated.

A SONG FROM SHAKESPEARE'S "CYMBELINE"

536, Sub-title, *Guiderus:* spelled Guiderius in Shakespeare.

536, Sub-title, *dead: Cf. Cymbeline,* IV, 2.

AN ODE ON THE POPULAR SUPERSTITIONS OF THE HIGHLANDS OF SCOTLAND

537, l. 1, *H——:* John Home, Scotch dramatist, 1722–1808, who came to London in 1749 with a tragedy which was refused by Garrick. Seven years later his *Douglas* — a tragedy based upon the old ballad of *Child Maurice* and not entirely unlike the poetry Collins is here describing — won a great success.

537, l. 5, *youth:* John Barrow, a friend who lived near Collins in Sussex.

537, l. 13, *soil:* Home was in fact returning not to the Highlands but to the parish near Edinburgh of which he had recently been made vicar in succession to Robert Blair, author of *The Grave.*

537, l. 18, *Doric:* simple, rural.

537, l. 21, *birken:* birch.

537, l. 23, *tribes:* the "Brownies" or "dark ones" — Celtic fairies. *Cf. L'Allegro,* 105.

537, l. 26, *herd:* herdsman.

537, l. 37, *run:* in the Hebrides.

537, l. 40, *possest:* spell-bound.

537, l. 41, *bards:* old poets who used the runic alphabet — later suggestive of magic and mystery.

537, l. 42, *vest:* garb.

537, l. 44, *hind:* peasant.

537, l. 45, *dirge:* the coronach.

538, l. 48, *shiel:* hut.

538, l. 52, *prove:* test.

538, l. 56, *Uist's:* an island near Skye.

538, l. 57, *sight:* "second sight." See the article *s.v.* in *Encycl. Brit.* by Andrew Lang. Gray uses a supposed example in *The Fatal Sisters* and exemplifies it in *The Bard.* Collins found many alleged instances in his chief source of information, Martin's *Description of the Western Islands,* 1716.

538, l. 59, *strath:* river valley.

538, l. 68, *heartless:* dismayed.

538, l. 73, *Charles:* Charles I of England.

538, l. 77, *slain:* a reference to the Jacobite insurrection of 1715.

538, l. 81, *Culloden:* In the first two of the battles here named the Scottish supporters of the Stuarts were successful against England. In the last, fought in April, 1746, they were defeated.

538, l. 83, *William:* of Orange, afterwards William III of England.

538, l. 85, *thou:* William, Duke of Cumberland, hero of Culloden.

538, l. 91, *Will:* the will-o'-the-wisp.

539, l. 121, *wait:* For the sources of this passage see the note on l. 24 of Gray's *Elegy.*

539, l. 126, *Her:* his wife's.

539, l. 126, *travell'd:* probably for *travailed,* worn by labour.

539, l. 136, *osier'd:* overgrown with willows.

539, l. 137, *kelpie's:* water-sprite's.

539, l. 137, *more:* The preceding lines are based upon Ovid's *Metamorphoses,* XI, 654 ff.

539, l. 139, *tribes:* of gannets or solan geese.

539, l. 142, *pile:* a burial place on the island of Benbecula described by Martin Martin.

539, l. 147, *kings:* of Norway, Scotland, and Ireland, supposed to be buried on the Island of Iona.

539, l. 155, *race:* the inhabitants — seldom over one hundred in number — of St. Kilda, a precipitous island of the Outer Hebrides.

539, l. 162, *but:* only.

539, l. 164, *sainted:* regarded as holy because medicinal.

539, l. 166, *solan:* the solan goose or gannet.

539, l. 169, *tasteful:* appetizing.

539, l. 172, *false:* The thought is that these themes have not yet been accepted by poets and critics or that they are mere superstitions: *cf.* ll. 189, 190 below.

539, l. 173, *gentle:* cultivated, as a gentleman's, in classic literature.

539, l. 178, *sisters:* the Weird Sisters of *Macbeth.*

539, ll. 182, 183, *shadowy kings... passed:* see *Macbeth,* IV, 1.

540, l. 198, *Fairfax:* Edward Fairfax produced in 1600 a good English translation of Tasso's *Gerusalemma Liberata.* The passages mentioned are in Canto xiii, stanzas 41–46.

540, l. 204, *num'rous:* musical, well versified.

540, l. 207, *friths:* arms of the sea at the mouths of rivers.

540, l. 215, *shade:* alluding to the visit paid in 1618 by Ben Jonson to the poet, William Drummond, at Hawthornden.

540, l. 216, *dale:* The valley of the Tiviot, in Roxburghshire, is the scene of many Scottish ballads.

540, l. 217, *And mourn... laid:* The Yarrow, a picturesque stream near Edinburgh, has long been famous in poetry. By "Willy" is probably meant William, Knight of Liddesdale, known as the "Flower of Chivalry," murdered near Yarrow in 1353 by the first Earl of Douglas. See William Hamilton's poem *The Braes of Yarrow.*

540, l. 219, *youth: Cf.* l. 5.

THOMAS WARTON, THE ELDER

BIBLIOGRAPHY

The Three Wartons, A Choice of Their Verse, ed. by Eric Partridge, 1927.

"*Poems on Several Occasions*" *Reproduced from the Edition of 1748.* Facsimile Text Society, 1930.

NOTES

RETIREMENT: AN ODE

542, l. 36, *St. James's:* the palace of that name in London, during most of the eighteenth century the royal residence and center of the court; now the residence of the Prince of Wales.

AN ODE WRITTEN IN A GROTTO

542, l. 1, *retreat:* The natural cavern called Mother Ludlam's (not Ludlow's) Cave is in Moor Park, Surrey, the country home of Sir William Temple, where Swift lived as Temple's secretary and first met Stella.

542, l. 4, *Sirius:* the chief star in the constellation Canis Major, and so often called the dog star. It rises with the sun during the hottest part of the summer, and therefore the ancients thought that it helped to cause the heat of the "dog days."

542, l. 9, *circling wood:* a grove of ancient limes, still standing, near the cave.

542, l. 10, *flood:* a small stream called the Wey.

542, l. 18, *witch:* the legend of the "white witch," Mother Ludlam, was occasioned, probably, by the strange and wild appearance of the cavern, which contains a bubbling spring.

542, l. 23, *Lud:* The story of the visit paid by Lud, king of the West Saxons, to Mother Ludlam's cave is told by John Aubrey in his *Perambulation of Surrey.*

542, l. 35, *trepan:* more properly, *trapan,* to ensnare.

AN INVOCATION TO A WATER-NYMPH

542, l. 8, *blasting sprite:* an evil spirit causing disease.

THOMAS WARTON, THE YOUNGER

BIBLIOGRAPHY

Poetical Works, 2 vols., ed. with *Memoir* by R. Mant, 1802.

The Three Wartons, A Choice of Their Verse, ed. by Eric Partridge, 1927.

J. Dennis, in *Studies in Literature,* 1876.

W. P. Ker, *Thomas Warton,* 1911.

Maurice Denby, *Die Brüder Warton und die romantische Bewegung,* 1913.

C. Rinaker, *Thomas Warton,* 1916.

NOTES

THE PLEASURES OF MELANCHOLY

543, The title, *Melancholy:* Warton uses this word in a sense, somewhat different from ours, which may be deduced from a study of Shakespeare's Jaques, Burton's *Anatomy of Melancholy,* John Fletcher's song, *Melancholy,* and *Il Penseroso.* Its central meaning is solitary meditation.

543, l. 13, *wild uproar:* The thought and the image are derived from Lucretius, *De Rerum Natura*, II, 1 ff.
543, l. 19, *seats:* country houses or castles.
543, l. 26, *Tempe:* a beautiful valley in Thessaly, the type of all charming natural landscape.
543, l. 28, *ruin'd abbey's:* Thomas Warton's interest in mediæval architecture was second only to his interest in literature.
543, l. 31, *light:* This line is taken almost *verbatim* from Milton's *Comus*, l. 340.
543, l. 32, *sullen:* sad, or solemn.
544, l. 41, *horror:* awe.
544, ll. 46, 47, *airy voices... walls:* taken from Pope's *Eloisa to Abelard*, l. 306.
544, l. 63, *Spenser saw: The Faerie Queene*, III, 11, 12.
544, l. 66, *Milton knew: Paradise Lost*, VI, 110.
544, l. 86, *unweeting:* unknowing or unsuspecting.
544, l. 87, *blear:* blinding. The phrase is quoted from Milton's *Comus*, l. 155.
544, l. 88, *charmèd cup:* See Milton's *Comus*, l. 51.
544, l. 92, *elegance:* finished excellence founded upon good taste.
544, l. 93, *quicker:* livelier.
544, l. 99, *tapers of the dead:* See Pope's *Eloisa to Abelard*, ll. 261, 262.
544, l. 107, *dædal:* ingeniously contrived, complex, or many-coloured.
544, l. 121, *devise:* plan.
545, l. 154, *Attic:* classical, as contrasted with Spenser.
545, l. 159, *wasteful:* probably, full of wastes or wildernesses.
545, l. 159, *lurid:* mingling light with gloom.
545, l. 160, *fair:* heroine of *The Rape of the Lock*.
545, l. 171, *assuasive:* soothing. Warton takes the word from Pope's *Ode for Music on St. Cecilia's Day*, l. 26.
545, l. 185, *illuded:* deceived by illusion.
545, l. 195, *taste:* This description of the solitude of the lover is in accord with a tradition which goes back at least to Petrarch.
545, l. 196, *taper'd:* lighted by tapers.
545, l. 215, *Monimia:* heroine of Otway's *The Orphan*, 1680.
546, l. 220, *Jaffier:* hero of Otway's *Venice Preserved*, 1682.
546, l. 232, *ken:* prospect.
546, l. 247, *Hymettus':* a mountain in Attica, famous for its honey.
546, l. 249, *Plato's:* whose school or Academy was in a grove.
546, l. 256, *sage-inspiring:* see Plato's *Phædrus*.
546, l. 261, *Persepolis:* an ancient city of Persia destroyed by Alexander.
546, l. 265, *Parian:* made of marble from the Ægean island of Paros. The ruins of Persepolis are indeed of marble, but of a local and dark-hued variety.
546, l. 266, *Horrid:* bristling.
546, l. 271, *Spires:* rises like a spire.
546, l. 277, *moles:* artificial mounds.
546, l. 285, *Euphrosyne:* one of the Three Graces who presided over social pleasures. See opening lines of Milton's *L'Allegro*.
546, l. 303, *Cirrha's:* one of the two peaks of Parnassus, sacred to Apollo.
547, l. 308, *Mona's:* the island of Anglesea, chief abode of the Druids.
547, l. 315, *Menai:* the strait of that name which separates Anglesea from Carnarvon in Wales.

ON THE APPROACH OF SUMMER

547, l. 14, *train:* a group of allegorical personages, loosely related to the figure chiefly invoked, such as Milton employs in *L'Allegro* and *Il Penseroso*. The use of these "trains" in the verse of the eighteenth century is one of the marks of Miltonic influence, and indeed it seems likely that much of the stiff and frigid personification in that verse is ultimately traceable to them.
547, l. 15, *Eurus:* the east wind.
547, l. 19, *Auster:* the south wind.
547, l. 20, *watchet:* pale blue.
547, l. 43, *embrown'd:* darkened.
547, l. 45, *amaranthine:* made of unfading flowers.
547, l. 67, *Zephyr:* the west wind.
547, l. 75, *confess'd:* revealed or identified.
548, l. 92, *Cherwell's:* a small tributary of the Thames, flowing through Oxford.

548, l. 99, *wattled cotes:* shelters — or in this case perhaps pens — made of wicker-work.

548, l. 106, *besprent:* besprinkled.

548, l. 112, *bosom'd:* half-hidden by trees. Derived from *L'Allegro*, l. 76.

548, l. 114, *deep-embattled:* standing in serried ranks.

548, l. 114, *ears of corn:* the spikes or heads of barley, oats, wheat, not of Indian corn.

548, l. 116, *chaffer-swarms:* swarms of cockchafer, a kind of beetle.

548, l. 123, *dight:* adorned.

548, l. 142, *To... mead:* This line is taken *verbatim* from *L'Allegro*, l. 90.

548, l. 151, *shrill-tinkling:* because of the bells hung from the necks of the horses.

548, l. 183, *Clio:* the Muse of history.

548, l. 185, *Sylvan:* the god of forest glades.

548, l. 186, *Lycæum's:* apparently a reference to the mountain Lycæus, in Arcadia, which Warton confuses with the gymnasium at Athens, where Aristotle taught, called the Lyceum.

549, l. 191, *hedger:* a labourer who trims hedges.

549, l. 208, *Genius:* spirit.

549, l. 210, *imps:* children.

549, l. 211, *Pierian:* referring to the mountains of that name, in Thessaly, which were a favourite haunt of Apollo.

549, l. 212, *Ilissus':* a small stream near Athens on the bank of which Plato set the scene of one of his *Dialogues*. There seems to be no better reason for calling it "laureate" than for referring to its "shore."

549, l. 227, *scene:* Supply *which.*

549, l. 240, *umbrage:* shadow.

549, l. 243, *Hardyknute:* the hero of a so-called ballad of the same name probably written in part by Lady Wardlaw, first published in 1719, and reprinted by Bishop Percy in his *Reliques*. As this poem is fragmentary, it is evident that Warton refers to it in order to provide a parallel with the passage in *Il Penseroso* where Milton thinks of calling up "him that left half-told the story of Cambuscan bold."

549, l. 251, *spelt:* told.

549, l. 257, *Let not... climb:* Compare *Il Penseroso*, l. 155.

549, l. 268, *grange:* isolated farm-house.

549, l. 278, *reed:* a symbol of pastoral song or verse.

549, l. 285, *pedant cloisters:* of Oxford.

549, l. 286, *votive:* due in fulfillment of a vow.

549, l. 287, *use:* habitually stay.

550, l. 300, *Tusculane:* referring to Cicero's rural retreat at Tusculum.

550, l. 323, *Brutus':* the legendary founder of Britain, here called "lawless" for the reason that he had caused the death of his parents.

550, l. 324, *Bonduca:* usually called Boadicea, and correctly called Boudicca, a queen in Britain of the time of Nero who revolted against the Romans.

TO THE RIVER LODON

550, *The title:* The River Lodon is a small tributary of the Thames, rising in Hampshire, not far from Basingstoke, Warton's birthplace.

VERSES ON SIR JOSHUA REYNOLDS'S PAINTED WINDOW

551, l. 28, *Vitruvian:* referring to Marcus Vitruvius Pollio, a Roman architect of the Augustan age whose treatise on architecture was followed by all the builders of the classic revival.

551, l. 29, *genius:* peculiar nature.

551, l. 55, *stole:* a long robe.

551, l. 89, *round:* circle.

551, l. 92, *Picture's:* the art of painting, personified.

551, l. 93, *crystal plain:* glass.

JOSEPH WARTON

BIBLIOGRAPHY

The Three Wartons, A Choice of Their Verse, ed. E. Partridge, 1927.

J. Dennis, in *Studies in English Literature*, 1876.

H. A. Beers, in *A History of English Romanticism in the Eighteenth Century*, 1899.

Maurice Denby, *Die Brüder Warton und die romantische Bewegung*, 1913.

NOTES

THE ENTHUSIAST

552, l. 6, *Parterres:* flower-beds elaborately arranged.

552, l. 8, *Stowe:* a great private estate in Buckinghamshire, considered the masterpiece of the landscape gardener, William Kent.

553, l. 22, *Numa:* a legendary king and law-giver of Rome. The story of his meetings with the nymph Egeria is told by Livy and Plutarch.

553, l. 26, *Versailles:* In the magnificent gardens designed by Le Notre for Louis XIV the chief attractions are the fountains and waterworks, for the supply of which water was brought from a distance at enormous cost in money and human lives.

553, l. 31, *Anio:* an Italian rive famous for the cascades in which it falls at Tivoli.

553, l. 47, *Kent:* William Kent, 1685–1748, called by Horace Walpole "the father of modern gardening." His effort, often carried to ludicrous extremes, was to imitate nature.

553, l. 75, *horrid:* bristling.

553, l. 77, *ægis:* a storm cloud round a thunderbolt, on the breastplate of Zeus.

553, l. 81, *Evander's:* See *Æneid*, VIII, 167 ff.

553, l. 86, *Lydian airs:* music of a relaxing influence. *Cf.* Milton's *L'Allegro*, l. 136.

553, l. 87, *Happy:* The following dream picture of the Golden Age, as fervid and as false as Rousseau's, is an extraordinary early example of the "primitivism" which was to become a main ingredient of romanticism.

554, l. 108, *bard:* Lucretius, *De Rerum Natura*, V, 925–1010.

554, l. 122, *pine:* pain.

554, l. 151, *close:* enclosure.

554, l. 169, *Shakespeare's:* Warton's opinion that Shakespeare, though "incorrect" was superior to Addison in "original genius" had, of course, highly important implications for literary criticism. Thomas Gray, imitating the present passage in *The Progress of Poesy*, l. 84, suggests a similar view by calling Shakespeare "Nature's darling," and even Milton may have had the same thought in calling him "Fancy's child." The comparison would have been made not with Addison, whose "lays" were of slight importance, but with Pope, if Pope had not been still living when the poem was composed.

554, l. 180, *walk:* The passages following were obviously suggested by *Il Penseroso*.

555, l. 229, *She spoke:* The next three lines are almost literally translated from *Æneid*, I, 401–404.

555, l. 233, *western climes:* The following confused dream of the American Arcadia is vaguely related to the close of Virgil's second *Georgic*. Joseph Warton was much interested in the "forest primeval," and he even wrote a soliloquy of a dying Indian based upon the Old Norse Death-Song of Ragnar Lodbrok. His sigh for the American wilderness was to be echoed scores of times in the later literature of romanticism.

555, l. 235, *Iberian:* Spanish.

555, l. 247, *Thetis:* queen of the under-sea.

WILLIAM SHENSTONE

BIBLIOGRAPHY

Works in Verse and Prose, 2 vols., 1764–69.
Poetical Works, ed. G. Gilfillan, with *Life*, 1854.
Essays on Men and Manners, 1868.
Essays on Men and Manners, ed. H. Ellis, 1927.
R. Graves, *Recollections of Some Particulars in the Life of the Late William Shenstone*, 1788.
R. Graves, *Columella, or the Distressed Anchoret*, 2 vols., 1779.
D. Otto, *William Shenstones "Schoolmistress" und das Aufkommen des Kleinepos*, 1908.
A. I. Hazeltine, *A Study of William Shenstone and his Critics*, 1918.
E. M. Purkis, *William Shenstone, Poet and Landscape Gardener*, 1931.

NOTES

THE SCHOOLMISTRESS

559, Motto, *Auditæ voces,... primo: Æneid*, VI, 426, 427:

"Voices are heard and loud wailing —
Spirits of infants that cry at the very sill of the portal."

Virgil is describing the entrance to hell.

559, l. 18, *shent:* blamed.

559, l. 20, *dome:* house.

559, l. 21, *Whilom:* formerly.
559, l. 23, *mickle:* great.
559, l. 29, *phantom:* scarecrow.
559, l. 30, *wanton:* joyous.
559, l. 35, *Ne:* nor.
560, l. 41, *perdie:* indeed; a weakened form of *par Dieu.*
560, l. 45, *wheel:* spinning-wheel.
560, l. 56, *faces:* representations of the winds as found on the margins of old maps. Shenstone has in mind the description of Æolus ruling the winds given in *Æneid*, I, 50 ff.
560, l. 65, *kirtle:* outer petticoat.
560, l. 72, *wight on ground:* creature on earth.
560, l. 73, 74, *ne... Ne:* neither, nor.
560, l. 75, *Goody:* goodwife.
560, l. 75, *gossip:* godmother.
560, l. 75, *n'aunt:* made by misdivision of *mine aunt, thine aunt. Cf. nuncle.*
560, l. 76, *additions:* titles of dignity.
560, l. 78, *as mought behove:* becomingly.
560, l. 95, *gray renown:* long-standing reputation.
560, l. 97, *baum:* balm.
561, l. 114, *wassel:* festive.
561, l. 117, *thane:* a member of one of the higher social classes.
561, l. 119, *Sternhold:* Thomas (1500–1549), with John Hopkins, the writer of a metrical version of the Psalms, long standard in England and used in Massachusetts until superseded by the *Bay Psalm Book.*
561, l. 119, *mete:* paraphrase metrically.
561, l. 123, *king:* The reference is to the Babylonian Captivity, and to Psalm 137.
561, l. 129, *elfins':* children's. The word is used as a noun by Spenser, though not in this sense.
561, l. 131, *tortious:* wrongful.
561, l. 133, *nould:* would not.
561, l. 134, *lawny:* white, like well-bleached cambric or "lawn."
561, l. 135, *forfend:* forbid.
561, l. 135, *thilk:* those.
561, l. 136, *stem:* the Stone of Scone, made into a chair in which British monarchs are crowned. The stone, but not the chair, was brought from Scotland.
561, l. 139, *liefest:* dearest.
561, l. 165, *bard:* Spenser. The river Mulla flowed near his home, Kilcolman Castle, in Ireland.
561, l. 169, *brogues:* trousers.
561, l. 171, *ermilin:* ermine.
562, l. 191, *device:* description.
562, l. 207, *y-rare:* the "y," an old sign of the past participle, is incorrectly used here, but correctly in the following stanza.
562, l. 211, *fourm:* form, a long seat.
562, l. 213, *snubs:* sobs.
562, l. 227, *caitiff:* originally, captive. From this sense the word developed in two directions, so as to suggest both villainy and misfortune.
562, l. 242, *Vernon's:* Edward Vernon, 1684–1757, an English admiral.
562, l. 243, *pimps:* panders.
562, l. 251, *weeting:* knowing.
563, l. 254, *build:* And perhaps this boy who, disapproving the plan of it, lays low the house of cards built by that other.
563, l. 255, *Dennis:* John Dennis, 1657–1734, an English literary critic notorious for his severity. Satirized in Pope's *Dunciad.*
563, l. 257, *Aonian field:* Helicon, in Bœotia, the home of the Muses.
563, l. 265, *han:* plural of *have.*
563, l. 279, *kesar:* Cæsar.
563, l. 299, *posies:* bunches.
563, l. 304, *cakes:* "invented" at Shrewsbury in Shropshire or "Salopia," and called by the name of the town.

A PASTORAL BALLAD

564, l. 32, *fond to resign:* so foolish as to leave.

ODE TO MEMORY

564, l. 14, *Isis:* the River Thames above Oxford.
564, l. 16, *Cherwell's:* a small tributary entering the Thames at Oxford.
564, l. 18, *Lycon:* probably the poet Richard Jago, 1715–1781, Shenstone's lifelong friend.

AN HUMORIST

566, l. 34, *discovery:* revelation.
566, l. 16, *complexion:* disposition.
566, l. 26, *seat:* country estate.
567, l. 8, *ingenuous:* ingenious.
567, l. 13, *want:* lack, as above.
567, l. 17, *contemplating:* meditating.
567, l. 33, *earwig:* an insect.
567, l. 33, *nectarine:* a kind of peach.

DETACHED THOUGHTS

567, l. 46, *compromise:* lessen or nullify.
567, l. 23, *stickle:* take sides in a dispute.
567, l. 30, *standish:* inkstand.
567, l. 33, "*Midst many faithless...*": misquoted from *Paradise Lost*, V, 894.
567, l. 37, *non est tanti:* "It is no great matter."
567, l. 51, *conceit:* far-fetched analogy.
568, l. 5, *nightgown:* dressing-gown.

WILLIAM WHITEHEAD

BIBLIOGRAPHY

Plays and Poems. Collected by the author, 1774.
Complete Poems, with Memoir, ed. by W. Mason, 1788.
Poems, in Chalmers, *Works of the English Poets*, vol. 17.
Plays, in Bell's *British Theatre*, vols. 3, 7, 20.

CHARLES CHURCHILL

BIBLIOGRAPHY

Poetical Works. With memoirs by J. L. Hannay, 2 vols., 1892.
P. Fitzgerald, *The Life and Times of John Wilkes*, 2 vols., 1888.
F. Putschi, *Charles Churchill, sein Leben und seine Werke*, 1909.
W. J. Courthope, *History of English Poetry*, 1925, vol. V, chap. 8.
R. W. Postgate, *That Devil Wilkes*, 1929.

NOTES

THE AUTHOR

572, l. 20, *Sleep over books:* Churchill himself, though entered at St. John's College, Cambridge, left very soon and never took a degree.

573, l. 111, *bill of privilege:* a claim to exemption based upon high birth, or upon membership in Parliament.

574, l. 189, *Sandwich:* John Montague, fourth Earl of Sandwich, a corrupt and hated politician, at one time the associate and later a powerful enemy of Churchill's friend, John Wilkes.

574, l. 216, *Smollett... Johnson:* Dr. Johnson was a pensioner of the crown, and Smollett may have received some payments from the king while editing *The Briton* for Lord Bute.

CHRISTOPHER SMART

BIBLIOGRAPHY

Poems, in *The Works of the English Poets*, ed. A. Chalmers, 1810, vol. **XVI.**
A Song to David, with other Poems, ed. E. Blunden, 1924.
A Song to David, facsimile of first ed., 1926.

E. Gosse, "Smart's Poems," in *Gossip in a Library*, 1891.
John Middleton Murry, "A Note on the Madness of Christopher Smart," in *Discoveries: Essays in Literary Criticism*, 1924.

NOTES

A SONG TO DAVID

576, l. 13, *charge:* duty.
576, l. 26, *horn: Cf.* I Samuel, XVI, 1–13.
576, l. 36, *war: Cf.* I Samuel, XVII, 40.
576, l. 38, *plann'd: Cf.* I Chronicles, XXVIII.
577, l. 43, *vein:* David's ancestry was traced, through Boaz and Ruth, to the ancient nobility of Judah.
577, l. 44, *grain:* intrinsically or innately.
577, l. 47, *cave: Cf.* I Samuel, XXIV.
577, l. 48, *dart: Cf.* II Samuel, XVI, 5–14.
577, l. 69, *Kidron:* a brook flowing from the region of Bethlehem into the Salt Sea.
577, l. 77, *bear: Cf.* I Samuel, XVII, 34, 35.
577, l. 84, *attend, Cf.* II Samuel, XVI, 1–4.
577, l. 88, *ephod:* the coloured vestment of a Hebrew priest.
577, l. 91, *fall: Cf.* II Samuel, XI and XII.
577, l. 96, *child:* Solomon.
577, l. 101, *Michal:* daughter of Saul, and David's first wife.
577, l. 102, *Abishag: Cf.* I Kings, I, 1–4.
577, l. 103, *sung:* The following nine stanzas all depend upon this verb.
577, l. 111, *citterns:* lutes.
577, l. 119, *his:* God's.
577, l. 127, *virtuous:* having medicinal "virtue."
577, l. 128, *Gem:* bud.
578, l. 143, *shoals:* schools.
578, l. 148, *coney:* in England, the rabbit; in Biblical usage, the rock-badger.
578, l. 152, *device:* skill.
578, l. 162, *Saul: Cf.* I Samuel, XVI, 23.
578, l. 171, *stood: Cf.* I Samuel, XVIII, 20.

578, l. 175, *seven: Cf.* Proverbs, IX, 1: "Wisdom hath builded her house; she hath hewn out her seven pillars," and I Samuel, II, 8: "For the pillars of the earth are Jehovah's, and he hath set the world upon them." The difficulties of the seven stanzas that follow cannot be fully elucidated, but it is clear that each pillar symbolizes the work of God in a single day of the Creation as narrated in Genesis. The chief problem concerns the names of the pillars. Alpha and Omega have an obvious significance, and Smart may have confused Sigma with the character Stigma, the Greek sign for six. It seems possible that the other four names were chosen for some fanciful appropriateness in the shape of the Greek capital letter to the works of the day concerned. The entire passage, however, is saturated with Masonic symbolism. The seven pillars are themselves a Masonic emblem. Alpha and Gamma, taken together, suggest the Compasses and Square; Eta may stand for Jacob's Ladder, Theta for the Eye, and Iota for the Plumb-line. Obviously, the Creator is imagined as the architect or mason of the universe. The passage is organic in a poem addressed to David, who planned the Temple at Jerusalem — with which the Masonic Order was supposed, in Smart's time, to have begun.

578, l. 199, *Supreme:* It stands "next," perhaps, in the sense that it is the initial letter of θεός, God.
578, l. 200, *sign:* constellation.
578, l. 202, *one:* the sun.

578, l. 222, *draught:* by separating cosmos from chaos. The shape of the capital letter Omega may have some significance here.

578, l. 225, *degree:* either in the Masonic or the academic sense.
578, l. 228, *bee: Cf.* Judges, XIV, 18.
579, l. 244, *fool:* St. Matthew, V, 22.
579, l. 249, *wilk:* whelk, a shell-fish.
579, l. 256, *wilt:* St. Matthew XXVI, 39.
579, l. 267, *bull: Cf.* Deuteronomy, XXII, 10.
579, l. 270, *wool: Cf.* Deuteronomy, XXII, 11.
579, l. 286, *Grutch:* grudge.
579, l. 310, *checks:* checkers.
579, l. 313, *prime:* ripeness.

579, l. 315, *gems:* buds, as in l. 128.

579, l. 316, *Ivis:* "the humming-bird" (Smart's note).

579, l. 318, *bell-flowers:* either daffodils or campanulas.

579, l. 323, *nature:* a clear example of the tendency to see nature chiefly in terms of art.

580, l. 327, *feed:* supply *upon.*

580, l. 328, *embark:* "There is a large quadruped that preys upon fish, and provides himself with a piece of timber for that purpose, with which he is very handy." (Smart's note.)

580, l. 329, *ark:* the nest of the halcyon or kingfisher, which was supposed to build on the waves and to charm them into quiet.

580, l. 331, *fig: Cf.* Micah, IV, 4.

580, l. 339, *spirits:* of the seasons.

580, l. 340, *coasting:* moving along the coast.

580, l. 341, *silverlings:* tarpons.

580, l. 341, *crusions:* crucians, fish of the carp family.

580, l. 356, *thyine:* precious or sweet. Taken from Revelations, XVIII, 12.

580, l. 374, *thorn:* the hawthorn, called "holy" because associated with Christ and with St. Joseph of Arimathea.

580, l. 384, *translation:* to heaven.

580, l. 386, *bullfinch:* a European bird that can be taught to whistle a tune.

580, l. 392, *philosopher:* a student of "natural philosophy" who strives to interpret God's revelation in Nature.

580, l. 394, *ring:* of Saturn.

580, l. 397, *strings:* of the Æolian harp.

580, l. 400, *voice:* of God.

580, l. 404, *bezoar:* a concretion found in the intestines of ruminating animals, once much used in magic and medicine — but not in making incense.

580, l. 405, *fur:* The fatty substance of the civet cat, from which perfumery is made, is found, not in the fur, but in a pouch.

580, l. 408, *galbanum:* a Persian gum used in perfumery.

580, l. 410, *crown:* the tuft of stiff leaves on the pineapple — called *ananas* in tropical America.

581, l. 426, *Church:* This stanza is a paraphrase of Psalm LXXXIV, 3.

581, l. 445, *speed:* These two stanzas on the strength and speed of animals, birds, and fish rest chiefly upon Job, XXXIX.

581, l. 446, *glede:* hawk.

581, l. 450, *xiphias:* the sword-fish, or *xiphias gladius. Cf. The Faerie Queene,* II, 12, 24.

581, l. 452, *mole:* a mound of earth or stone.

581, l. 454, *gier-eagle:* vulture.

581, l. 462, *wide:* a paraphrase of St. Matthew, VII, 7.

581, l. 467, *meditated:* left wild by design, with reference to the "wilderness" of the "English garden."

581, l. 478, *conceit:* understanding.

581, l. 480, *dust: Cf.* II Samuel, XII, 16.

581, l. 481, *mite: Cf.* St. Mark, XII, 43.

581, l. 483, *churl: Cf.* I Samuel, XXV, 2–19.

581, l. 485, *alba's: Cf.* Revelations, II, 17.

581, l. 492, *sod: Cf.* Leviticus, XXIII, 40.

581, l. 494, *heart: Cf.* Acts, XIII, 22.

581, l. 508, *den: Cf.* Daniel, VI, 13–22.

DAVID HUME

BIBLIOGRAPHY

The standard edition of Hume's *Essays* was edited by T. H. Green and T. H. Grose in 2 vols., 1875.

A Treatise of Human Nature, ed. by L. A. Selby-Bigge, 1896.

Dialogues Concerning Natural Religion, ed. by B. McEwen, 1907.

Political Discourses, ed. by W. B. Robertson, 1908.

C. W. Hendel, *Hume Selections,* Mod. Students' Lib., Philos. Series, 1928.

J. Y. T. Greig, *Letters of David Hume,* 1932.

A complete list of the books that discuss Hume would be very large. In addition to the standard works on philosophy, the following biographical and critical works will be useful:

J. H. Burton, *Life and Correspondence of David Hume*, 1846.
F. Jodl, *Leben und Philosophie Humes*, 1872.
T. H. Huxley, *Hume*, E. M. of L., 1879.
G. B. Hill, *Letters of David Hume to W. Strahan*, 1888.
A. Thomsen, *David Hume. Sein Leben und seine Philosophie*, 1912.
W. Knight, *Hume*, 1914.
A. Meinong, *Hume-Studien*, I, 1877; II, 1882.
G. Lechartier, *David Hume, moraliste et sociologue*, 1900.
O. Quast, *Der Begriff der Belief bei Hume*, 1903.
A. E. Taylor, *David Hume and the Miraculous*, 1927.
A. Leroy, *La critique et la religion chez David Hume*, 1929.
J. Y. T. Greig, *David Hume*, 1931.
Sir Leslie Stephen, *History of English Thought in the Eighteenth Century*, 2 vols., 1876.
H. J. Laski, *Political Thought in England from Locke to Bentham*, Home Univ. Library, 1920.
E. G. Braham, *The Life of David Hume*, 1931.
B. M. Laing, *David Hume*, 1932.

NOTES

583, l. 9, *Fénelon:* See note on William Godwin, p. 846, l. 4.

584, l. 26, *Ogilby:* See note on Dryden's *Mac Flecknoe*, p. 44, l. 102.

584, l. 26, *Bunyan:* Hume here reflects an estimate of Bunyan common in the eighteenth century when *The Pilgrim's Progress* and Bunyan's other works were considered important merely as popular theological treatises.

587, l. 15, *The most vulgar ballads are not entirely destitute of harmony or nature:* Interest in the popular ballads had increased since the time of Addison, but it had not yet mounted very high by 1757, when this essay was first published; Percy's *Reliques of Ancient English Poetry* appeared in 1765.

590, l. 9, *Clitia of Machiavel: Clizia* is a comedy by Niccolò Machiavelli, 1469–1527, author of *Il Principe*.

591, l. 38, *Of all speculative errors, those which regard religion:* This paragraph and the two following are typical of Hume's guarded, yet unmistakable, gibes at religion.

591, l. 20, *Polyeucte and Athalie:* Hume here refers to Corneille's *Polyeucte*, 1642, and Racine's *Athalie*, 1691. Joad and Josabet are characters in the latter. The quotation is from V, 3, 1–8.

PHILIP DORMER STANHOPE, EARL OF CHESTERFIELD

BIBLIOGRAPHY

Miscellaneous Works of the late Philip Dormer Stanhope, Earl of Chesterfield, with Memoirs of his Life, 2 vols., 1777.

Chesterfield's *Letters to his Son, Philip Stanhope* was edited by C. Strachey with notes by A. Calthrop, 2 vols., 1901.

A convenient edition, which also includes selections from his other correspondence and an introduction by R. K. Root, appeared in Everyman's Library, 1929.

The most recent edition is *The Letters of Philip Dormer Stanhope, Fourth Earl of Chesterfield*, ed. by Bonamy Dobrée, 6 vols., 1932.

There are numerous volumes of selections; among the most recent is that by Phyllis Jones, in the World's Classics, 1929.

Letters to his Godson and Successor was first ed. by the Earl of Carnarvon, 1890.

Characters, ed. by Charles Whibley, 1927, and *Poetical Works*, 1927, are, except for slight additions in the latter, reprints from *Miscellaneous Works*.

For biography and criticism see the following:

W. Ernst, *Memoirs of the Life of the Fourth Earl of Chesterfield; with Numerous Letters now First Published*, 1893.
W. H. Craig, *Life of Chesterfield*, 1907.
Roger Coxon, *Chesterfield and his Critics*, 1925.
Temple Scott, *Lord Chesterfield and his Letters to his Sons*, 1929.

See also the Introduction to Strachey's edition of the *Letters*, above, and the essays by Churton Collins in *Essays and Studies* and by Paul Elmer More in the Fifth Series of *Shelburne Essays*.

NOTES

593, l. 22, *an Elzevir classic:* one of the small, beautifully printed volumes of the classics published by the Elzevirs, a family of seventeenth-century Dutch printers. They are such works as a connoisseur would be proud to own.

594, l. 2, *Leonidas and Curtius:* Leonidas was the King of Sparta who perished at Thermopylæ when Xerxes invaded Greece in 480 B.C. Marcus Curtius was a hero of Roman legend, who is said to have leaped into a deep gulf, which opened in the forum in 362 B.C. and remained until by his sacrifice it was closed. These two men are cited as examples of sacrificial fidelity to the state.

594, l. 16, *geese in the Capitol:* It is said that the cackling of geese, sacred to Juno, saved the Roman Capitol when it was besieged by the Gauls in 390 B.C.

594, l. 19, *Vittorio Siri:* Italian historian (1608–85), patronized by Cardinal Mazarin in France.

594, l. 33, *Mr. Grevenkop:* a Danish gentleman, who seems to have been in the earl's service.

595, l. 22, *Les Réflexions Morales de Monsieur de la Rochefoucauld:* François, Duc de la Rochefoucauld (1613–80), whose most important work, *Réflexions ou sentences et maximes morales* is here referred to. The perfection of form and the cynicism in these maxims are alike famous.

595, l. 23, *Les Caractères de la Bruyère:* Jean de la Bruyère, French character-writer, in 1688 first published *Les caractères de Thêophraste, traduits du Grec, avec les caractères ou les mœurs de ce siècle.* He continued to add further characters to this work until his death in 1696.

595, l. 51, *On trouve dans le malheur... pas:* See Swift's poem "On the Death of Dr. Swift," p. 434, where this maxim is quoted in a slightly different form.

597, l. 14, *the line:* the equator.

597, l. 30, *My dear Friend:* Early in 1750, when Philip was about eighteen, his father changed the style of salutation, thus indicating that the boy had become a man.

597, l. 11, *Sardanapalus:* according to tradition the last King of Assyria, most corrupt and effeminate of his line. He is said to have burned himself in his palace with his wives and treasures, when he could no longer defend Ninevah against the rebels, 880 B.C.

597, l. 14, *Alcibiades:* brilliant, unprincipled Athenian (c. 450–404 B.C.), admirer of Socrates; he was famous as a military leader.

597, l. 45, *ruelles:* "Ladies' chambers, or drawing-rooms."

598, l. 6, *Mais c'est là leur affaire:* "But that is their concern."

598, l. 12, *improve in your German:* German was little studied by Englishmen at this time. Since the boy was destined for a diplomatic career, his father was particularly interested in his acquiring familiarity with as many languages as possible.

598, l. 34, *ogni fatica è vana:* "All labour is useless."

HORACE WALPOLE

BIBLIOGRAPHY

The Works of Horatio Walpole, Earl of Orford, edited by Mary Berry, 5 vols., 1798; 4 additional vols. appeared between 1818 and 1825.

The *Letters* have been several times published: *Private Correspondence of Horace Walpole*, 4 vols., 1829; *Letters*, ed. by John Wright, 6 vols., 1840; *Letters*, ed. by Peter Cunningham, 9 vols., 1857–59; *Letters*, ed. by Mrs. Paget Toynbee, 16 vols., 1903, the standard edition which includes many letters not included in the earlier editions. *Supplement to the Letters of Horace Walpole*, ed. by Mrs. Paget Toynbee, 1919, makes still further additions. Various selections from the *Letters* have been published: among others *The Best Letters of Horace Walpole*, ed. by Anna B. McMahan, in Laurel-Crowned Letters series, 1890; *Horace Walpole and his World: Select Passages from his Letters*, ed. by L. B. Seeley, 1895; *Horace Walpole's Letters*, ed. by William Hadley, 1926; *A Selection of the Letters of Horace Walpole from the Oxford Edition*, 2 vols., ed. by W. S. Lewis, 1926.

For biography and criticism see the following:

Austin Dobson, *Horace Walpole, a Memoir*, 1890, 1910, revised by P. Toynbee, 1927.

M. A. Havens, *Horace Walpole and the Strawberry Hill Press*, 1901.

Alice D. Greenwood, *Horace Walpole's World*, 1913.

Paul Yvon, *La vie d'un dilettante, Horace Walpole*, 1924.

Dorothy M. Stuart, *Horace Walpole*, E.M.L., 1927.

Anna De Koven, *Horace Walpole and Madame du Deffand. An Eighteenth Century Friendship*, 1929.

Stephen Gwynne, *The Life of Horace Walpole*, 1932.

NOTES

600, l. 1, *The Hon. Henry Seymour Conway:* Walpole's cousin, brother of the Marquis of Hertford. He was born in 1719, entered the army in 1741, rose to be commander-in-chief in 1782, and died in 1795. He was a frequent correspondent of Walpole with whom he maintained a lifelong friendship.

600, l. 8, *Mrs. Chenevix's shop:* Walpole had recently leased from Mrs. Chenevix, a fashionable toy dealer, the cottage here described, at Twickenham, near London. The following year he bought the property, which he called Strawberry Hill, where he erected his famous villa in the Gothic manner.

600, l. 11, *A small Euphrates...*: Pope, *Epistle to Addison*, ll. 25, 26, with alteration of "eagles" to "finches."

600, l. 46, *the Marquis of Rockingham:* Conway had sat in Parliament from 1741 to 1747. It was said that he owed his seat to the influence of the Marquis of Rockingham.

600, l. 3, *your campaign:* At this time Conway was in Flanders with the British army.

600, l. 48, *George Montagu:* an old schoolfellow at Eton with whom Walpole maintained a friendship for many years.

601, l. 54, *the honeymoon of a new reign:* George III had just ascended the throne.

601, l. 11, "*No petticoat government...*": The new king had been under the domination of his mother, the Princess Dowager of Wales. John Stuart, Earl of Bute, is probably the Scotchman referred to; he was a friend and adviser of the king's mother, and was popularly suspected of being her lover. (He was the husband of Lady Mary Wortley Montagu's daughter.) Lord George Sackville was a friend of the Earl of Bute. Shortly before this time he had been found guilty by a court-martial of disobedience of orders at the Battle of Minden (1759), but was received at court by George III nevertheless.

601, l. 16, *Lady Susan Stuart:* daughter of the Earl of Galloway, appointed Lady-in-Waiting to the Princess Augusta.

601, l. 17, *Sir Harry Erskine:* He had been dismissed from the army because of parliamentary opposition while he was a member of Parliament from Ayre; subsequently he was restored and became a lieutenant general. He was a favourite of Lord Bute.

601, l. 31, *the Duke of Newcastle:* Thomas Pelham Holles, Duke of Newcastle, Prime Minister, and Chancellor of Cambridge University at this time. The Chancellors of Cambridge and Oxford are honourary officials; the Vice Chancellors are the actual heads of these universities.

601, l. 32, *Médecin malgré lui:* the chief character (the physician in spite of himself) in Molière's comedy of the same name. He is represented as an ignorant pretender to learning.

601, l. 34, *my Lord Westmoreland:* The Earl of Westmoreland was Chancellor of Oxford.

601, l. 42, *the burying:* The funeral here described is that of George II.

602, l. 15, *I had been in dread of being coupled with some boy:* Walpole is described as being slender and somewhat boyish in appearance.

602, l. 33, *a dark brown adonis:* a kind of wig.

602, l. 12, *the King of Prussia... Marshal Daun:* On November third, Frederick the Great of Prussia had defeated Marshal Daun, the Austrian commander, at the Battle of Torgau. At this time England and Prussia were fighting the Seven Years' War against a European coalition headed by France.

602, l. 18, *Leicester Fields:* the old name for Leicester Square in London. Leicester House, which was on this square, had been the residence of Prince George before his accession to the throne.

602, l. 23, *John Chute* (1701–1766): an English gentleman with whom Walpole had become acquainted at Florence in 1740. He was a frequent guest at Strawberry Hill and remained on intimate terms with Walpole during the latter part of his life.

602, l. 43, *haut-pas:* a raised platform.

602, l. 45, *two of my eagles:* suggesting one of the antiquarian treasures at Strawberry Hill, a marble eagle found at Rome in 1742 and purchased for Horace Walpole.

602, l. 55, *a soupçon:* a suspicion, the merest trifle.

603, l. 24, *The Rev. William Mason* (1724–1797): poet and dramatist, friend of Gray, and his biographer. It is to Mason's *Life of Gray* that this letter refers.

603, l. 4, *non est tanti:* "It is not worth so much."

603, l. 15, *the censure on David:* See Gray's letter to James Beattie, July 2, 1770: "I have always thought Hume a pernicious writer, and believe he has done as much mischief here as he has in his own country." For the whole passage see D. C. Tovey, *The Letters of Thomas Gray*, III, 289.

603, l. 18, *an imbelle javelin sine ictu:* "A harmless javelin without force."

603, l. 41, *a Strulbrug:* Walpole's spelling of Struldbrug, one of the useless immortals described by Swift in the Third Voyage of Gulliver.

603, l. 52, *the Macphersons and Dalrymples:* James Macpherson, the reputed translator of Ossian. It is, however to his historical writings (published 1775) that Walpole here refers. Sir John Dalrymple (1726–1810), had begun to publish in 1771 *Memoirs of Great Britain and Ireland from the Dissolution of the*

Last Parliament of Charles II until the Sea Battle of La Hogue. Horace Walpole disliked both these authors and more than once ridiculed them.

604, l. 42, *Foote:* Samuel Foote (1720–77), actor, dramatist, and wit.

604, l. 45, *Dr. Murray:* William Murray, the Earl of Mansfield, Chief Justice of the King's Bench; he was the uncle of the English Ambassador at Paris, David Murray, Viscount Stormont.

604, l. 4, *Sir Horace Mann:* While travelling in Italy Walpole met Sir Horace Mann, the English Ambassador at Florence, and began a friendship with him which found expression in a correspondence continued vigorously for more than forty years, though the two did not meet again.

605, l. 8, *Mrs. Montagu:* Mrs. Robinson Montagu (1720–1800), the famous "blue-stocking," had published in 1769 her *Essay on the Writings and Genius of Shakespeare,* in which she had defended Shakespeare against the criticisms of Voltaire.

605, l. 10, "*Je crois, madame... d'entendre*": "I suppose, madam, that you are somewhat displeased at what you have just heard."

605, l. 13, "*Moi, monsieur!... Monsieur Voltaire*": "Not at all, sir! I am not a friend of Monsieur Voltaire's."

SAMUEL JOHNSON

BIBLIOGRAPHY

The most accessible complete editions are those by Arthur Murphy, 12 vols., 1792, 1796, 1801, etc., and by A. Chalmers, 12 vols., 1806, etc., and the Oxford Edition, 1825, 9 vols. plus 2 supplementary vols.

The Lives of the English Poets has been fully edited by G. B. Hill, 3 vols., 1905. The same editor has also done *Johnsonian Miscellanies*, 2 vols., 1897, and *The Letters of Samuel Johnson*, 2 vols., 1892.

London: A Poem, and The Vanity of Human Wishes, with an Introductory Essay by T. S. Eliot, 1930.

S. C. Roberts has a volume of *Selected Letters*, 1927.

Among recent editions of journals and letters are the following:

The French Journals of Mrs. Thrale and Doctor Johnson, edited by Moses Tyson and Harry Guppy, 1932.

Johnson and Queeney: Letters from Dr. Johnson to Queeney Thrale, from the Bowood Papers, ed. by the Marquis of Lansdowne, 1932.

Some Unpublished Letters to and from Dr. Johnson, ed. by J. D. Wright, 1932.

An excellent volume of *Selections from the Works of Samuel Johnson* was edited by C. G. Osgood in 1909.

Boswell's *Life* is the great biography of Johnson. See Boswell bibliography. Sir Leslie Stephen wrote a good short biography for the English Men of Letters Series, 1878.

G. B. Hill, *Dr. Johnson: His Friends and his Critics*, 1878, and *Footsteps of Dr. Johnson*, 1890, are important contributions by the foremost editor of Johnson.

John Bailey, *Dr. Johnson and his Circle*, is small but useful.

Among recent works of criticism the following a e important:

Sir Walter Raleigh, *Six Essays on Johnson*, 1910.

P. E. More, *With the Wits*, Shelburne Essays, Tenth Series, 1919.

P. H. Houston, *Dr. Johnson, a Study in Eighteenth Century Humanism*, 1923.

J. E. Brown, *The Critical Opinions of Dr. Johnson*, 1926.

R. Lynd, *Dr. Johnson and Company*, 1927.

C. Hollis, *Dr. Johnson*, 1928.

R. B. Adam, *The R. B. Adam Library Relating to Dr. Samuel Johnson and his Era*, 3 vols., 1929.

D. Nichol Smith, R. W. Chapman, and L. F. Powell, *Johnson and Boswell Revised by Themselves and Others*. Three Essays, 1928.

Harry Salpeter, *Dr. Johnson and Mr. Boswell*, 1929.

Aleyn L. Reade, *Johnsonian Gleanings*, Parts I–V, 1909–30.

S. Christiani, *Samuel Johnson als Kritiker im Lichte von Pseudo-Klassizismus und Romantik*, 1931.

F. M. Smith, *Some Friends of Doctor Johnson*, 1931.

A. S. Turberville, *Johnson's England*, 2 vols., 1933.

Mildred C. Struble, *A Johnson Handbook*, 1933.

NOTES

THE VANITY OF HUMAN WISHES

607, l. 49, *Democritus:* Greek philosopher of the fourth century B.C., commonly known as "the laughing philosopher."

608, l. 97, *septennial ale:* ale that was furnished by candidates for Parliament. In 1716 the term had been lengthened from three to seven years. Osgood, *Selections from the Works of Samuel Johnson* calls attention to Hogarth's *Election*, Plate I, which shows an election dinner at a country inn.

608, l. 99, *Wolsey:* Cardinal Wolsey (1475?–1530), the great minister of Henry VIII. *Cf.* Shakespeare's *Henry VIII*, 2:4 and 3:2.

608, l. 129, *What gave great Villiers to th' assassin's knife:* George Villiers, Duke of Buckingham (1592–1628), minister of Charles I, killed by a fanatic.

608, l. 130, *Harley's closing life:* Robert Harley, Earl of Oxford, minister of Queen Anne. See Swift's *Journal to Stella*, p. 394, l. 26, note.

608, l. 131, *What murder'd Wentworth, and what exil'd Hyde:* Thomas Wentworth, Earl of Strafford (1593–1641), minister of Charles I, attainted by Parliament and executed shortly before the outbreak of the Civil War. Edward Hyde, Earl of Clarendon (1609–1674), minister of Charles II. See the Introduction to his work in this volume, p. 114.

608, l. 139, *Bodley's dome:* the Bodleian Library at Oxford. *Dome* is here used in the sense of the Lat. *domus: house, building.*

608, l. 140, *And Bacon's mansion trembles o'er his head:* According to tradition Roger Bacon (1214–94) had his cell in a tower on the bridge over the Thames at Oxford. It was said that if any man greater than Bacon should pass under this tower, it would fall on his head. *Mansion* is here used in the sense of *abode. Cf.* Lat. *mansio* and Fr. *maison.*

608, l. 160, *the patron: Cf.* Boswell, p. 648.

608, l. 164, *Here Lydiat's life, and Galileo's end:* Thomas Lydiat (1572–1646), a learned mathematician who suffered for his loyalty to Charles I and died in misery. Galileo Galilei (1564–1642), commonly known by his first name, famous Italian astronomer, who was persecuted by the Inquisition and died in blindness.

608, l. 168, *Rebellion's vengeful talons seize on Laud:* William Laud (1573–1645), Archbishop of Canterbury under Charles I, impeached by the Long Parliament and beheaded. While Johnson's High Church sympathies are reflected in this passage, it should be remembered that the revulsion of feeling against the Roundheads, which set in at the Restoration, continued throughout the eighteenth century. *Cf.* Gray's *Elegy*, l. 60. Not until the nineteenth century did the reaction against this opinion begin to produce the opposite prejudice.

609, l. 179, *the rapid Greek:* Alexander the Great.

609, l. 182, *the Danube or the Rhine:* The Battle of Blenheim, 1704, was fought near the Danub ; Marlborough had previously conducted brilliant campaigns along the Rhine.

609, l. 192, *Swedish Charles:* Charles XII of Sweden (1682–1718), after brilliant successes against Danes, Poles, Saxons, and Russians, was defeated at the Battle of Pultowa in 1709, took refuge in Turkey for several years, and finally fell at Frederikshald in Norway. L. 220 refers to the unsettled question whether he was shot by an enemy or a traitor. Charles XII is here substituted for Hannibal in Juvenal.

609, l. 227, *Great Xerxes:* The example of Xerxes' pride and his defeat by the Greeks is taken from Juvenal.

609, l. 241, *The bold Bavarian:* Charles Albert, Elector of Bavaria, who had contended with Maria Theresa, Queen of Hungary in the War of the Austrian Succession for the crown of the Holy Roman Empire. This queen is the "fair Austria" of l. 245. The war involved Prussia, France, Spain, Saxony, and Poland on one side and Hungary, England, and Holland on the other. It had been brought to a close by the Treaty of Aix-la-Chapelle in 1748, shortly before the publication of this poem.

610, l. 313, *Lydia's monarch:* The following lines refer to the well-known story of Crœsus, King of Lydia (560–546 B.C.), who was warned by Solon not to consider himself happy until the end of his life.

610, l. 317, *From Marlb'rough's eyes:* The Duke of Marlborough (1650–1722), the great English commander under Queen Anne, suffered two paralytic strokes several years before his death, but his condition in his last years was probably not so bad as Johnson here suggests.

610, l. 318, *And Swift expires a driv'ller and a show:* Swift had died in 1745, less than four years before this poem was published. During his last years he had sunk into a lethargic insanity.

610, l. 321, *Yet Vane could tell what ills from beauty sprung:* Anne Vane, mistress of Frederick, Prince of Wales, the son of George II. She had died at Bath, deserted.

610, l. 322, *And Sedley curs'd the form that pleas'd a king:* Catherine Sedley, Countess of Dorchester, mistress of James, Duke of York, before he ascended the throne as James II in 1685. She was the daughter of Sir Charles Sedley, the poet and wit.

RAMBLER, NO. 161

611, l. 5, *Tully sought... the tomb of Archimedes:* Cicero tells (*Tusc. Disp.*, V, 23) how, when he was quæstor, he found the grave of Archimedes at Syracuse, forgotten among the bushes, identifying it by the sphere and cylinder that had been set up over it.

IDLER, NO. 60

613, l. 44, *profession has one recommendation:* Of course this statement is an intentional paradox. The common opinion of the eighteenth century was that critics, especially bad ones, worked much harm and triumphed only with others' pain.

614, l. 5, *Otway... making a conspirator his hero:* in his tragedy, *Venice Preserved.*

614, l. 11, *Southerne:* Thomas Southerne (1660–1746). Of his ten plays *The Fatal Marriage* and *Oroonoko* are best known.

614, l. 35, *Phædra and Hippolitus:* a tragedy by Edmund Smith (1672–1710). Johnson in *The Lives of the Poets* wrote that it pleased the readers rather than the spectators, and, though it was the work of a vigorous and elegant mind, it showed "little acquaintance with the course of life."

615, l. 15, *the bell was rung twice in Barbarossa: Barbarossa* is a tragedy by the Reverend John Brown (1715–1766); it was produced by Garrick in 1754. Johnson objected to the use of a bell in the play because it was not true to Mahometan custom.

615, l. 17, *the author of Cleone:* Robert Dodsley (1703–1764), the well-known bookseller, was also a poet and dramatist. *Cleone* was produced by Garrick in 1758.

615, l. 27, "*the sound an echo to the sense*": Pope, *An Essay on Criticism,* l. 365. In his *Life of Pope* Johnson says, "This notion of representative metre and the desire of discovering frequent adaptations of the sound to the sense have produced, in my opinion, many wild conceits and imaginary beauties."

615, l. 33, *And pulpit...*: Samuel Butler, *Hudibras,* 1, 1, 11, 12.

615, l. 38, *Honour is like the glassy bubble: Ibid.,* 2, 2, 385–88, inaccurately quoted. The reference is not to a soap bubble but to a "Prince Rupert's drop," a tear-shaped bit of hollow glass which explodes when the lower end is broken.

IDLER, NO. 61

615, l. 24, *an academy of criticism:* In the Preface to his *Dictionary* and in his *Life of Roscommon* (*The Lives of the Poets*) Johnson opposed the project of founding an English academy.

615, l. 46, "*the great vulgar and the small*": Cowley, *Imit. of Horace, Ode* 3, 1.

616, l. 1, *the monkish barbarity of rhyme:* Johnson's love of rhyme is well known; *cf.* p. 662, first col., ll. 29–40.

616, l. 32, *the ground Burns frore...*: a misquotation of Milton, *Par. Lost,* 2, 595.

616, l. 36, *So thick a drop...*: *Ibid.,* 3, 25.

PREFACE TO SHAKESPEARE

617, l. 14, *Pythagorean scale of numbers:* To Pythagoras (sixth century B.C.) and to his followers were attributed many important discoveries about the properties of numbers, including the doctrine of the arithmetical, geometrical, and harmonical proportions, and the "Pythagorean triangle."

618, l. 51, *a character is too often an individual:* The romantic critics later praised Shakespeare for exactly the opposite quality. Johnson saw in his characters, above all, "the grandeur of generality," the representation of the type in the individual.

619, l. 1, *Dennis:* See John Dennis, *On the Genius and Writings of Shakespeare,* 1711; see note to p. 563, l. 255. For Rymer see Introduction, p. 190.

619, l. 2, *Voltaire:* See *Du Théâtre anglais par Jérôme Carré,* 1764. For a discussion of Voltaire's criticism of Shakespeare see J. J. Jusserand, *Shakespeare en France,* and T. R. Lounsbury, *Shakespeare and Voltaire.*

619, l. 28, *comic and tragic scenes:* Johnson had in 1751 given expression to somewhat less pronounced views on this subject in the *Rambler,* No. 156.

620, l. 48, *The players... in their edition:* The first folio of Shakespeare, published in 1623 by John Heminge and Henry Condell, two members of Shakespeare's company, had divided the plays into the three classes of which Johnson speaks.

621, l. 26, *candour:* "Freedom from malice, favourable disposition, kindliness." Obsolete in this sense. *NED.*

622, l. 18, *Hector quoting Aristotle: Troilus and Cressida,* II, 2, 166.

622, l. 19, *the loves of Theseus and Hippolyta: A Midsummer-Night's Dream.*

624, l. 35, *The humour of Petruchio:* in Shakespeare's *The Taming of the Shrew.*

624, l. 38, *the soliloquy of Cato:* Addison's *Cato,* V, 1, contains the famous soliloquy which begins

"It must be so. Plato, thou reason'st well! —"

625, l. 17, *Non usque... tolli* (Lucan, *Pharsalia,* III, 138): "The long day has not so far confused high things with low that if the laws were to be saved by the voice of Metellus, they would not choose rather to be destroyed by Cæsar."

625, l. 2, *Æneas withdrew from the defence of Troy:* Virgil, *Æneid*, II, 604 ff.

625, l. 10, *Every man's performances:* Compare Johnson's remarks on the same subject in his *Life of Dryden*, and Pope's in *An Essay on Criticism*, ll. 118–23. Such recognition of the importance of knowing an author's historical background is a very different thing from the historical criticism which was later developed under romantic auspices: Johnson lays the emphasis on the universal, unchanging aspects of literature; romantic critics lay it on the temporal and changing.

625, l. 34, *The philology of Italy: Philology* is here used in its etymological sense of "love of letters," a sense that includes literary as well as linguistic studies.

626, l. 5, *The Death of Arthur:* Malory's *Le Morte Darthur*.

626, l. 11, *Palmerin and Guy of Warwick:* Palmerin is the hero (or the father of the hero) of several sixteenth-century Spanish chivalric romances of which *Palmerin of England* is the most important. Guy of Warwick is the hero of one of the most popular early English metrical romances. These works were no longer admired by discriminating readers in the eighteenth century; their readers were now found only among children, or adults of the lower classes, who had access to them in crude chapbook versions.

626, l. 28, *As You Like It... from Chaucer's Gamelyn: The Coke's Tale of Gamelyn*, once falsely ascribed to Chaucer, was the basis of Thomas Lodge's novel, *Rosalynde, Euphues' Golden Legacie* (1590), which was the immediate source of Shakespeare's comedy.

626, l. 31, *the tale of Hamlet in plain English prose:* For *The Historie of Hamblet*, an English prose rendering from Belleforest's *Histoires Tragiques*, see H. H. Furness, *Hamlet*, in the Variorum ed.

627, l. 28, "*Go before, I'll follow*": Zachary Grey in *Notes on Shakespeare* (1754) had attempted to find a source for Gloucester's words, *Richard III*, I, 1, 144,

"Go you before, and I will follow you,"

in Terence, *Andria*, I, 1, 144.

627, l. 31, "*I cried to sleep again*": *The Tempest*, III, 2, 152,

"I cried to dream again."

627, l. 54, *Rowe*: Nicholas Rowe, *Some Account of the Life &c. of Mr. William Shakespear*, 1709. He was also the author of several dramas, the best known of which is *Jane Shore.* Johnson refers to this dramatic work later.

628, l. 3, *Boyle... high birth:* Robert Boyle, 1627–1691, famous as a scientist and one of the founders of the Royal Society, was a son of the Earl of Cork.

628, l. 20, "*as dew-drops from a lion's mane*": Shakespeare, *Troilus and Cressida*, III, 3, 224, 225:

"And, like a dew-drop from the lion's mane,
Be shook to air."

629, l. 15, "*He seems," says Dennis:* John Dennis, *On the Genius and Writings of Shakespeare*, 1711.

629, l. 29, *Gorboduc:* the well-known tragedy by Thomas Sackville and Thomas Norton, produced about 1562.

629, l. 31, *Hieronymo:* better known as *The Spanish Tragedy*, by Thomas Kyd, produced about 1585–88.

629, l. 7, *book of some modern critic:* John Upton, *Critical Observations on Shakespeare*, 1746.

629, l. 46, "*declined into the vale of years*": *Othello*, III, 3, 265, 266.

LIFE OF DRYDEN

631, l. 1, *The praise lavished by Longinus: On the Sublime*, chap. 16.

632, l. 14, *Trapp:* the Reverend Joseph Trapp, first Professor of Poetry at Oxford, 1708–18. His lectures were delivered in Latin. The following extract is from *Prælectiones Poeticæ* (1722), p. 386.

632, l. 16, "*Novimus judicium... occupatur*": "We know the judgment of Dryden on a certain poem of Chaucer — truly a beautiful poem it is, and most worthy of praise — that doubtless it is not only genuinely epic but also that it equals even the *Iliad* and the *Æneid* too; nay rather it surpasses them. But at the same time we know that the judgments of that most distinguished man are neither always very accurate nor worked out according to the most exacting standard of criticism: in his judgment the best is usually that which he has before him and that with which he is now occupied." Trapp misquotes a passage in Dryden's *Preface to the Fables*: "I prefer in our countryman far above all his other stories the noble poem of *Palamon and Arcite*, which is of the epic kind, and perhaps not much inferior to the *Ilias* or the *Æneis*."

632, l. 28, *Spence, in his remarks on Pope's Odyssey:* the Reverend Joseph Spence, *Essay on Mr. Pope's Odyssey*, 1726/27.

632, l. 49, *Sewel:* George Sewell (d. 1726) in his Preface to Ovid's *Metamorphoses*.

632, l. 55, *Quæ superimposito... colosso* (*Sylv.*, I, 1, 1): "What heavy mass doubled by the huge form placed upon it...?"

632, l. 4, *condemned him to straw:* Adjudged him insane; see above. Dryden in *A Parallel of Poetry and Painting* wrote: "Virgil, if he could have seen the first verses of the *Sylvæ* would have thought Statius mad, in his fustian description of the statue on the brazen horse."

632, l. 9, *Gorboduc:* See note on the *Preface to Shakespeare*, p. 629, l. 29.

632, l. 10, *Chapman's versification:* In the Preface to *Annus Mirabilis* Dryden wrote: "And besides this, they [the French] write in Alexandrines, or verses of six feet; such as, amongst us, is the old translation of Homer by Chapman." George Chapman (1559–1634) used verses of fourteen syllables in his translation.

632, l. 17, *the tuition of Busby:* Richard Busby was headmaster of Westminster School, 1638–95. He is said to have "educated more youths that were afterwards eminent in Church and State than any master of his time." Wood, *Ath. Oxon.*, IV, 418.

633, l. 32, *His conversation...*: *Threnodia Augustalis*, 337–45.

634, l. 43, *Feltham:* Owen Feltham (1609?–1668?), said to have been the only man in his day who had the courage to attempt putting Ben Jonson in his place. He was the author of *Resolves: Divine, Moral, and Political.*

634, l. 46, *Sandys:* George Sandys (1578–1644), translator of Ovid's *Metamorphoses.*

634, l. 50, *Holyday:* Barten Holyday (1593–1661), translator of Juvenal and Persius.

634, l. 16, "*Translation therefore," says Dryden:* Preface to the *Translation of Ovid's Epistles.*

634, l. 36, *Sir Edward Sherburne* (1618–1702): poet and translator of Seneca and Horace.

635, l. 11, *What had been...*: *Don Sebastian*, IV, 3.

635, l. 30, *forced conceits:* The following passage from the *Life of Cowley* will explain not only Johnson's point of view here but also the attitude of the neo-classical poets and critics toward one important aspect of mid-seventeenth-century poetry: "About the beginning of the seventeenth century appeared a race of writers that may be termed the metaphysical poets... If wit be well described by Pope as being 'that which has been often thought, but was never before so well expressed,' they certainly never attained, nor ever sought it; for they endeavoured to be singular in their thoughts, and were careless of their diction. But Pope's account of wit is undoubtedly erroneous: he depresses it below its natural dignity, and reduces it from strength of thought to happiness of language.

"If by a more noble and more adequate conception that be considered as wit which is at once natural and new, that which, though not obvious, is, upon its first production, acknowledged to be just; if it be that which he that never found it wonders how he missed; to wit of this kind the metaphysical poets have seldom risen. Their thoughts are often new, but seldom natural; they are not obvious, but neither are they just; and the reader, far from wondering that he missed them, wonders more frequently by what perverseness of industry they were ever found.

"But wit, abstracted from its effects upon the hearer, may be more rigorously and philosophically considered as a kind of *discordia concors*; a combination of dissimilar images, or discovery of occult resemblances in things apparently unlike. Of wit, thus defined, they have more than enough. The most heterogeneous ideas are yoked by violence together; nature and art are ransacked for illustrations, comparisons, and allusions; their learning instructs, and their subtlety surprises; but the reader commonly thinks his improvement dearly bought, and, though he sometimes admires, is seldom pleased."

635, l. 30, *his verses on the Restoration: Astræa Redux, A Poem on the Happy Restoration and Return of his Sacred Majesty, Charles the Second* (1660).

635, l. 42, *Monk's dexterity:* General Monk, who by declaring for a free Parliament in March, 1660, took the step which led to the Restoration.

636, l. 43, *second part, written by Tate:* See notes on *Absalom and Achitophel*, p. 44, l. 15.

638, l. 39, *the Religio Medici of Browne:* Sir Thomas Browne (1605–1682), physician, antiquarian, speculative philosopher, and master of rich and majestic English prose.

638, l. 24, *Nicene Fathers:* the fathers of the Christian Church, theological writers about the time of the Council of Nicæa, 325.

638, l. 27, *The City Mouse and Country Mouse:* In 1687 Matthew Prior and Charles Montague, afterwards Earl of Halifax, collaborated in writing *The Hind and the Panther Transversed to the Story of the Country and the City Mouse*, a parody which uses machinery suggested by *The Rehearsal.*

639, l. 36, *the poem On the Birth of the Prince of Wales:* published under the title, *Britannia Rediviva.*

640, l. 31, *the old poem of Boiardo... new-dressed by Domenichi and Berni:* Count Matteo Maria Boiardo (1434–94) wrote *Orlando Furioso*, which later Italian poets made the subject of completions, remodellings, and imitations. Among these are the *rifacimenti* of Lodovico Domenichi (1515–64) and of Francesco Berni (about 1498–1535).

640, l. 52, *one of the Beroalds:* Philip Beroald the elder, about 1495.

640, l. 8, *The Ode for St. Cecilia's Day: Alexander's Feast; or, The Power of Music; an Ode in Honour of*

St. Cecilia's Day, not to be confused with *A Song for St. Cecilia's Day, 1687*, to which Johnson has previously referred. As G. B. Hill has pointed out in his edition of *The Lives of the English Poets*, I, 456, *n.* 3, this ode was not "the last effort of Dryden's poetry," for he wrote several other poems between 1697 and his death in 1700.

641, l. 1, *Love various minds...* : *Tyrannic Love*, II, 3.

641, l. 22, *Otway:* Thomas Otway (1651?–1685) is generally considered one of the best, if not the best, of the tragic poets of his day.

641, l. 21, *Move swiftly, sun...* : *Conquest of Granada*, Pt. II, V, 2.

641, l. 24, *Amariel flies...* : *Tyrannic Love*, IV, 1.

641, l. 30, *Then we upon our orb's last verge...* : *Annus Mirabilis*, stanza 164.

641, l. 38, *'Tis so like sense...* : Cowley in *Ode to Mr. Hobbes*, had written,

"'Tis so like truth, 'twill serve our turn as well."

641, l. 44, *I am as free...* : *Conquest of Granada*, Pt. I, I, 1.

641, l. 47, *'Tis but because the living...* : *Tyrannic Love*, V, 1.

641, l. 51, *There with a forest...* : *Ibid.*, I, 1.

642, l. 1, *I beg no pity...* : *Don Sebastian*, I, 1.

642, l. 14, *No, there is a necessity...* : *Conquest of Granada*, Pt. I, IV, 2.

642, l. 26, *What precious drops...* : *Ibid.*, Pt. II, III, 1.

642, l. 30, *Resign your castle...* : *Ibid.*, Pt. II, III, 3. This passage and the preceding are not quoted quite accurately, though the textual variations do not affect the purpose of their quotation.

642, l. 36, "*Delilahs of the theatre*": Dryden wrote in the Dedication of *The Spanish Friar*, 1681: "I remember some verses of my own Maximin and Almanzor which cry vengeance upon me for their extravagance,... All I can say for those passages, which are, I hope, not many, is that I knew they were bad enough to please, even when I writ them; but I repent of them amongst my sins; and if any of their fellows intrude by chance into my present writings, I draw a stroke over all those Delilahs of the theatre; and am resolved I will settle myself no reputation by the applause of fools." The reference is, of course, to the Philistine woman who tempted Samson to his fall.

642, l. 52, "*tack to the larboard*": translation of Virgil's *Æneid*, III, 525. Johnson's objection here and in the following quotations is to the use of technical terms, which the neo-classical poets generally rejected because they are opposed to the grandeur of generality.

642, l. 54, "*virtue spooming before the wind*": *The Hind and the Panther*, III, 96.

642, l. 1, *They Nature's King...* : *Ibid.*, I, 57.

642, l. 10, *A hollow crystal pyramid...* : *Annus Mirabilis*, stanza 281.

642, l. 17, *When rattling bones...* : *Ode to Mrs. Anne Killigrew*, ll. 184, 185.

643, l. 17, *Waller was smooth...* : *Imitations of Horace*, Epistle II, 1, 267 ff.

643, l. 1, *Relentless Time, destroying power...* : Thomas Parnell (1679–1717) in *An Imitation of some French Verses.*

643, l. 6, *Drayton's Polyolbion:* by Michael Drayton (1563–1631), a topographical description of England.

643, l. 14, *The triplet and Alexandrine:* The lines which Swift wrote in ridicule of these metrical variations of the heroic couplet conclude *A Description of a City Shower*:

"Sweepings from butcher's stalls, dung, guts and blood,
Drown'd puppies, stinking sprats, all drench'd in mud,
Dead cats and turnip-tops come tumbling down the flood."

643, l. 39, *the braces of the margins:* In printing of this period it was customary to mark triplets by printing in the margin the curved lines known as braces.

644, l. 1, *Fenton:* Elijah Fenton (1683–1730) is most frequently remembered as one of Pope's assistants in translating the *Odyssey*. Johnson wrote a short account of him in *The Lives of the English Poets*.

644, l. 9, *Together o'er the Alps:* Pope, *Epistle to Mr. Jervas*, ll. 25, 26.

644, l. 14, *Laugh all the powers...* : *Palamon and Arcite*, III, 671.

644, l. 3, *And with paternal thunder...* : *The Hind and the Panther*, II, 535.

644, l. 16, *Though Davies has reasoned in rhyme:* Sir John Davies (1569–1626) in *Nosce Teipsum*, which deals with human knowledge and the immortality of the soul.

644, l. 23, *lateritiam... reliquit:* Suetonius, *Aug.*, chap. 29.

JAMES BOSWELL

BIBLIOGRAPHY

The standard edition of Boswell's *Johnson* is by G. B. Hill, 6 vols., 1887.
For Boswell biography and criticism see the following:
Percy Fitzgerald, *Life of James Boswell*, 2 vols., 1891.

W. K. Leask, *James Boswell*, in "Famous Scots Series," 1897.
George Mallory, *Boswell the Biographer*, 1912.
C. B. Tinker, *Young Boswell*, 1922.
F. A. Pottle, *The Literary Career of James Boswell, Esq.*, 1929.
The most important recent Boswell publication is *Private Papers of James Boswell from Malahide Castle in the Collection of Lt.-Colonel Ralph Heyward Isham*, 18 vols. Ed. by Geoffrey Scott; later vols. ed. by F. A. Pottle, 1928–34.
See also F. A. and M. S. Pottle, *The Private Papers of James Boswell from Malahide Castle... a Catalogue*, 1931.
C. E. Vulliamy, *James Boswell*, 1932.
The two famous essays by T. B. Macaulay (1831) and by Thomas Carlyle (1832) are now of more importance for the understanding of their authors than of their subject.

NOTES

646, l. 7, *the "Plan" of his Dictionary:* In 1747, when he was beginning work on his *Dictionary*, Johnson had written a plan or prospectus, which he had addressed to Philip Dormer Stanhope, Earl of Chesterfield, the famous statesman and wit. See Introduction, p. 592.

646, l. 19, *Colley Cibber:* Pope's old enemy, the hero of *The Dunciad*, who was Poet-Laureate from 1730 until his death in 1757.

646, l. 24, *George Lord Lyttelton* (1709–1773): poet and statesman, as well as the patron of several men of letters, including James Thomson and Henry Fielding. See in *An Eighteenth-Century Gentleman and Other Essays* by S. C. Roberts, the title essay.

646, l. 14, *the World:* a periodical in the *Spectator* tradition, which ran from the beginning of 1753 to the end of 1756. It had several other contributors of rank besides Lord Chesterfield.

647, l. 18, *Mr. Dilly's:* the elder brother of Edward and Charles Dilly, the booksellers frequently mentioned by Boswell.

647, l. 22, *Mr. Baretti:* Joseph Baretti, an Italian friend of Johnson's, who came to England about 1753 and lived there most of the time until his death in 1789. Johnson wrote the Dedication for his *Italian and English Dictionary.*

647, l. 24, *Mr. Langton:* Bennet Langton, Esq., a gentleman of Lincolnshire, who had while still a youth admired the *Rambler* and sought Johnson's acquaintance. He became a fast friend of the philosopher, and was one of the original members of the Club.

647, l. 47, *le vainqueur... la terre:* "The conqueror of the conqueror of the earth." *Cf.* the first line of Scudéry's *Alaric* (1654), cited by Boileau, *Art Poëtique*, III, 272, as an example of pretentious opening: *Je chante le vainqueur des vainqueurs de la terre.*

648, l. 14, *The shepherd in Virgil: Eclogue* VIII, 43 ff.

648, l. 24, *till I am solitary:* His wife had died in 1752, while he was at work on the *Dictionary.*

648, l. 44, *Dr. Adams:* the Master of Pembroke College, Oxford, whose acquaintance with Johnson had begun when the latter was a student.

648, l. 45, *Dr. Warburton:* the Reverend William Warburton (1698–1779), friend of Pope, editor of Shakespeare. He became Bishop of Gloucester in 1759.

648, l. 5, *Imitations of Juvenal: The Vanity of Human Wishes*, ll. 159, 160.

648, l. 26, *Mr. Robert Dodsley:* bookseller and publisher. He was one of the publishers of Johnson's *Dictionary.*

649, l. 30, *Mr. Derrick, the poet:* Samuel Derrick (1721–1769), a minor man of letters, at this time "King" or Master of Ceremonies at the Pump-Room of Bath.

649, l. 41, *Mr. Thomas Sheridan:* father of the dramatist, Richard Brinsley Sheridan. See the later reference to his activities at Bath where he delivered lectures on oratory.

650, l. 25, *Mr. Alexander Wedderburne:* Lord Loughborough, a friend of Johnson's, who had been of service in helping to secure his pension.

650, l. 5, *Nam vos mutastis:* "For you have changed, Ovid, *Met.*, I, 2.

651, l. 33, *Garrick:* David Garrick (1717–1779), the famous actor and dramatist, Johnson's former pupil and his life-long friend. At this time he was manager of the Drury Lane Theatre. As Boswell explains in a note, Johnson did not here voice his real conviction, since on all other occasions when the subject came up, the doctor praised Garrick's liberality.

651, l. 35, *Miss Williams:* Anna Williams, daughter of a Welsh physician, whom Boswell described as "of more than ordinary talents and literature," had come to London in the hope of being cured of cataracts and was hospitably received by Mrs. Johnson. Afterwards she became totally blind, and Johnson, who had great respect for her, lodged her "during the rest of her life at all times when he had a house." She had a small income.

652, l. 24, *The Elements of Criticism:* by Henry Home, Lord Kames (1696–1782), Scottish judge, and writer upon philosophical and other subjects.

652, l. 36, *tædium vitæ:* "Weariness of life."

652, l. 18, *Messieurs Thornton, Wilkes, Churchill, and Lloyd:* This list of wits with whom Boswell was acquainted is representative of his wide and undiscriminating association with people of contemporary reputation. Bonnell Thornton (1724–1768), the author of the burlesque quoted by Dr. Johnson on the first of July following, was a minor poet. Charles Churchill (1731–1764), was a disreputable clergyman, who had become famous two years before by his satire on the stage, *The Rosciad*. *Cf.* Introduction, p. 571. Johnson disapproved even more vigorously of John Wilkes (1727–1797), the witty, profligate politician. In spite of the fact that Johnson and Wilkes were opposites in character and in political views, Boswell managed to bring them together at a famous dinner in 1776. Robert Lloyd (1733–1764), poet and friend of Churchill's.

652, l. 23, *Dr. Blair:* the Reverend Hugh Blair (1718–1800), Scottish divine and man of letters, famous for his *Lectures on Rhetoric and Belles Lettres* and his *Sermons*.

652, l. 33, *Mr. James Macpherson:* Twelve years later, Dr. Johnson wrote him the following letter which is scarcely less famous than the one to Chesterfield.

"Mr. James Macpherson.

"I received your foolish and impudent letter. Any violence offered me I shall do my best to repel; and what I cannot do for myself, the law shall do for me. I hope I shall never be deterred from detecting what I think a cheat by the menaces of a ruffian.

"What would you have me retract? I thought your book an imposture; I think it an imposture still. For this opinion I have given my reasons to the public, which I here dare you to refute. Your rage I defy. Your abilities, since your Homer, are not so formidable; and what I hear of your morals inclines me to pay regard not to what you shall say, but to what you shall prove. You may print this if you will. Sam. Johnson."

653, l. 25, *My poor friend Smart:* See the Introduction to Smart, p. 575.

653, l. 23, *Grotius:* Hugo Grotius (1583–1645), famous Dutch writer on law and religion.

653, l. 23, *Dr. Pearson:* John Pearson (1613–1686), Bishop of Chester, widely known for his theological writings. His *Exposition of the Creed* is still a classic.

653, l. 23, *Dr. Clarke:* the Reverend Samuel Clarke (1675–1719), theological and philosophical writer, friend and supporter of Newton.

654, l. 2, *Johnson ride upon three horses:* an Irishman who had been exhibiting feats of horsemanship in London.

655, l. 11, *Whitehead:* William Whitehead (1715–1785) had succeeded Cibber as Poet-Laureate in 1757; he was a minor poet and dramatist who is now remembered less for his own work than for the ridicule he excited. See p. 569.

655, l. 21, *Gray:* These ideas are developed at greater length in Johnson's treatment of Gray in *The Lives of the Poets*. The ode quoted is *The Bard*.

656, l. 22, *Mallet's tragedy of Elvira:* David Mallet, or Malloch (1705–1765), minor poet and dramatist; he is now remembered chiefly for his ballad, *William and Margaret*. "Rule Britannia" first appeared in the masque, *Alfred*, in which he collaborated with his friend Thomson; but the famous song is generally attributed to the latter.

656, l. 38, *paternal estate:* His father, Alexander Boswell, was the Laird of Auchinleck (pronounced äfflĕck) in Ayrshire.

657, l. 27, *Mrs. Piozzi:* Hester Lynch Thrale, Johnson's intimate friend during the lifetime of her husband, afterwards married Gabriel Piozzi, an Italian musician. This marriage, which broke her friendship with Johnson, took place in 1784, the year of the latter's death. She published *Anecdotes of Dr. Johnson*, the "small volume" here referred to. As later references indicate, Boswell considered it inaccurate.

657, l. 9, *Dr. Oliver Goldsmith:* Boswell did not like Goldsmith; in the following account the facts are more trustworthy than the interpretations.

657, l. 16, *Mr. Malone:* Edmond Malone (1741–1812), well known as a Shakespearean critic and editor. He was a member of the Club, and was of much assistance to Boswell in preparing *The Life of Johnson*.

657, l. 50, *Nihil quod ... ornavit:* "He touched nothing he did not adorn." Slightly altered from a line of the epitaph which Johnson wrote for Goldsmith's cenotaph in Westminster Abbey.

658, l. 11, *un étourdi:* "A rattle-brain."

658, l. 25, *Fantoccini:* marionettes: puppet-show.

658, l. 39, *Dean of Durham:* "I am willing to hope that there may have been some mistake as to this anecdote, though I had it from a dignitary of the church. Dr. Isaac Goldsmith, his near relation, was Dean of Cloyne, in 1747." (Boswell's note.) His honesty as a literary historian impelled Boswell to add this note though not to expunge the passage in which he had made what seems to be a baseless charge against Goldsmith.

658, l. 4, *Sir John Hawkins:* a member of the Club who had written a life of Johnson, which Boswell criticized severely. Among the latter's strictures on this volume the following sentences from the account of the year 1778 are typical. Johnson had been talking with Boswell and Mrs. Thrale about the effects of carelessness upon truth. He concluded: "Some men relate what they think as what they know; some men of confused memories and habitual inaccuracy ascribe to one man what belongs to another; and some talk on, without thought or care. A few men are sufficient to broach falsehoods, which are afterwards innocently diffused by successive relaters." Boswell adds the comment: "Had he [Johnson] lived to read what Sir John Hawkins and Mrs. Piozzi have related concerning himself, how much would he have found his observation illustrated."

658, l. 45, *Mr. Levet:* Robert Levet, whom Boswell describes as "an obscure practicer in physic amongst the lower people," had been a friend of Johnson's since 1746 and stood high in his opinion. "Mr. Levet had an apartment in his house, or his chambers, and waited upon him every morning, through the whole course of his late and tedious breakfast. He was of a strange, grotesque appearance, stiff and formal in his manner, and seldom said a word while any company was present."

659, l. 29, *Connoisseur:* a weekly periodical in the *Spectator* tradition, which ran from 1754 to 1756. Thornton was one of the editors.

660, l. 23, *Sir John Fielding's:* half-brother of Henry Fielding the novelist, and his successor as justice of the peace.

661, l. 3, *Bayle's Dictionary: Dictionnaire historique et critique* of Pierre Bayle (1697).

662, l. 31, *Dr. Adam Smith* (1723–1790): the distinguished Scottish economist and author of *Inquiry into the Nature and Causes of the Wealth of Nations*, 1776. He became a member of the Club.

662, l. 47, *Canada is taken:* In 1759 Quebec had been captured by the English army under General Wolfe; and the following year, with the fall of Montreal, the whole of Canada had been conquered.

662, l. 49, *King James's health:* the "Old Pretender," son of James II, who claimed the English crown as James III. Many staunch Tories, like Squire Western, cursed the "Hanover rats," and drank to the "King over the water," rather from tradition than from any real desire to overturn the ruling dynasty in England. See Johnson's reference below to the Battle of Culloden, 1746, in which Prince Charles, "Bonnie Prince Charlie," known to his enemies as "the Young Pretender," was defeated and the Stuart hopes were finally crushed.

663, l. 28, *Mr. Walmsley:* Gilbert Walmsley, Registrar of the Ecclesiastical Court at Lichfield, of whom Johnson said: "He was a Whig, with all the virulence and malevolence of his party; yet difference of opinion did not keep us apart." He died in 1751.

664, l. 11, *Ita feri ut se sentiat emori:* "So strike that he may feel himself dying." Suetonius (*Cal.* xxx) says that the Emperor Caligula's desire to put men to death by numerous slight wounds made this cruel order famous.

664, l. 45, *tall Sir Thomas Robinson:* So called to distinguish him from Sir Thomas Robinson, Lord Grantham; he was a close friend of Lord Chesterfield.

664, l. 15, *"jargonnant un François barbare"*: "Using a rude French jargon."

665, l. 23, *Mr. David Hume's style:* See Introduction to Hume in this volume, p. 582. Johnson disliked him because of his religious scepticism.

665, l. 34, *Rousseau's treatise: Discours sur l'origine et les fondements de l'inégalité parmi les hommes,* 1754. Johnson suspected the democratic ideas of the French political philosophers.

666, l. 8, *Sir William Petty* (1623–1687): political economist, one of the founders of the Royal Society, and a Commissioner of the Navy, in which last position he was an associate of Pepys.

666, l. 25, *cæteris paribus:* "Other things being equal."

667, l. 14, *Academy della Crusca:* founded at Florence in 1582.

667, l. 3, *plenum... vacuum:* "A space entirely filled with matter," and "one entirely empty of matter."

668, l. 37, *Dr. Joseph Warton:* The first volume of this work had appeared in 1756; the second was not published until 1782, long after this conversation but previous to the writing of Boswell's *Life of Johnson.* He became a member of the Club. See Introduction to Joseph Warton in this volume, p. 552.

669, l. 50, *Tale of a Tub:* See *The Journal of a Tour to the Hebrides* (3d edition), p. 32, for another statement of this opinion. However, in *The Lives of the Poets* he says of this book: "That Swift was its author, though it be universally believed, was never owned by himself nor very well proved by any evidence; but no other claimant can be produced, and he did not deny it when Archbishop Sharpe and the Duchess of Somerset, by showing it to the Queen, debarred him from a bishopric." Swift's authorship of *A Tale of a Tub* is well established.

670, l. 12, *Foote:* Samuel Foote (1720–1777), prolific dramatist and popular comic actor. *Cf.* p. 604.

670, l. 6, *Sir Isaac Newton:* This assertion, which Johnson undoubtedly believed, seems to be without foundation.

672, l. 5, *Buchanan:* George Buchanan (1506–1582), Scottish poet, scholar, and historian. Johnson, whose own learning was similar to that of the Renaissance humanists, admired Buchanan for that use of Latin which has prevented his works from being widely read in our day.

672, l. 9, *Johnston:* Arthur Johnston (1587–1641), Scottish poet whose Latin verses had been famous.

672, l. 17, *Formosam resonare... silvas* (Virgil, *Eclogue* I, 5): "You teach the woods to re-echo with the name of fair Amaryllis."

673, l. 5, *restore the Convocation:* From early times there had been a convocation or assembly of clergy from the ecclesiastic provinces of Canterbury and York, during the meeting of Parliament. Between 1717 and 1861 the licence from the Crown, necessary for the legal transaction of business, was withheld.

674, l. 6, *Pomponius Mela De Situ Orbis:* Pomponius Mela (c. A.D. 40), Roman geographer.

674, l. 24, *Mr. Blacklock's poetry:* the Reverend Thomas Blacklock (1721–1791), a poet, who had lost his sight as the result of smallpox when he was six months old.

674, l. 30, *That foolish fellow, Spence:* The Reverend Joseph Spence (1699–1768), the author of the *Anecdotes* (pub'd posthumously in 1820), had published in 1754 *An Account of the Life, Character, and Poems of Mr. Blacklock.*

674, l. 18, *Jean Bull philosophe:* "John Bull philosopher," i.e., the typical Englishman trying to justify his hearty appetite.

675, l. 6, "*Gordon's palates*": After his tour to the Hebrides in 1773, Johnson was entertained in Edinburgh by Alexander Gordon and by Mr. Maclaurin. Both these gentlemen attained distinction at the Scottish bar.

675, l. 29, *Bishop Berkeley's ingenious sophistry:* This well-known example of the "common sense" treatment of metaphysical subtlety does not, as Johnson doubtless knew, prove the existence of matter; the experiment merely demonstrates the feeling of solidity — something which Berkeley did not deny. It is a good example of Johnson's methods in controversy: vigorous, picturesque, effective for the purpose, illuminating the question, but not finally answering it.

675, l. 39, *Père Bouffier:* Claude Buffier (1661–1737), a French Jesuit philosopher. His chief work, *Traité des vérités premières*, 1724, is here referred to.

675, l. 40, *Reid and of Beattie:* Thomas Reid (1710–1796) and James Beattie (1735–1803) were two important Scottish philosophers; the former was one of the chief opponents of Berkeley's idealistic philosophy; the latter is better remembered for his poem, *The Minstrel*, 1771–1774, than for his reply to Hume. *Cf.* Introduction, p. 776.

675, l. 47, *one of the most luminous minds of the present age:* Edmund Burke. The quoted lines at the top of p. 676 are from Goldsmith's poem, *Retaliation*, ll. 31, 32.

FRANCES BURNEY

BIBLIOGRAPHY

Diary and Letters of Madame D'Arblay, 1778–1840, edited by her niece, Charlotte Barrett, 7 vols., 1842–46; with preface and notes by Austin Dobson, 6 vols., 1904, 1905.

Early Diary of Frances Burney, 1768–1778, with a Selection from her Correspondence and from the Journals of Susan and Charlotte Burney, edited by A. R. Ellis, 2 vols., 1889; and reprinted in Bohn's Library.

L. B. Seeley, *Fanny Burney and her Friends. Select Passages from her Diary and Other Writings*, 1890.

Her best novels, *Evelina* and *Cecilia*, have been frequently reprinted.

For biography and criticism the following volumes will be useful:

Austin Dobson, *Fanny Burney*, E. M. of L., 1903.

Constance Hill, *The House in St. Martin's Street, being Chronicles of the Burney Family*, 1907.

Constance Hill, *Fanny Burney at the Court of Queen Charlotte*, 1912.

R. Brimley Johnson, *Fanny Burney and the Burneys*, 1926.

Muriel Masefield, *The Story of Fanny Burney*, 1927.

See also T. B. Macaulay's *Essay on Madame D'Arblay*, 1843.

NOTES

677, l. 4, *Susan:* Fanny's sister.

677, l. 5, *Mrs. Thrale:* Hester Lynch Thrale, the wife of a wealthy brewer. The Thrales were intimate friends of Dr. Johnson, who in his later years spent a great deal of time at their house in Streatham, near London. See p. 657, l. 27, note.

677, l. 6, *Madame Riccoboni:* contemporary French novelist, whose work was popular at this time.

678, l. 27, *Mr. Crisp:* better known as "Daddy" Crisp, an elderly friend of the Burney family, who was lodging at this time in Chessington Hall, a country house near Kingston, Surrey. He was a great favourite with the children.

678, l. 53, *Mrs. Williams:* Anna Williams, the blind dependent of Dr. Johnson, whom he sheltered in his home for many years. She seems to have been highly respected by the doctor and his friends. The epithet "exceeding pretty" obviously applies to "poetess" in a literary sense. See note on Boswell, p. 651, l. 35.

679, l. 55, *Lowndes:* Thomas Lowndes, the publisher of *Evelina*; he paid £20 for the manuscript and afterwards voluntarily added £10 more.

680, l. 11, *Mr. Smith ... the fine gentleman manqué:* "The Holborn beau," the would-be fine gentleman, was one of the humorous characters in *Evelina* that Dr. Johnson particularly admired. On a later occasion he said, "Harry Fielding never drew so good a character! such a fine varnish of low politeness! such a struggle to appear a gentleman! Madam, there is no character better drawn anywhere — in any book or by any author." *Diary*, Aug. 23, 1778.

680, l. 28, *Mr. Seward:* William Seward, a well-known dilettante, a friend of the Thrales's. Fanny had met him the year before.

680, l. 40, *Bonduca:* George Colman's adaptation of Beaumont and Fletcher's tragedy. Austin Dobson says in his note, *Diary and Letters*, I, 57, that Garrick's contribution was a Prologue.

681, l. 2, *Wilkes:* John Wilkes, the well-known radical politician. About two years before this time Dr. Johnson had been inveigled by Boswell into dining in Wilkes's company and had apparently enjoyed the meeting. See note on "Junius," p. 800, l. 38.

681, l. 22, *Sir John Hawkins:* one of the original members of Johnson's Club, though he withdrew later. He was one of Dr. Johnson's executors, and the author of a biography. *Cf.* note to p. 658, l. 4. Austin Dobson suggests that Johnson refers to the Ivy Lane Club, which continued its meetings between 1749 and 1756; the Literary Club, commonly called Johnson's, was not founded until 1764.

681, l. 10, *Madame Duval:* the grandmother of Evelina. She was a woman of low birth and vulgar manners; after the death of Evelina's grandfather she married M. Duval.

681, l. 29, *agreeability: NED* points out that Chaucer had used *agreablete*, adapted from OF. *agréableté.* This word had been obsolete in Eng. for 400 years, until it was freshly formed from *agreeable* as here indicated. After this passage *NED* gives no further examples until the nineteenth century, when it quotes uses by Lady Lytton and by Thackeray. It is curious that the corresponding French word had been long obsolete until it was reformed by Sainte-Beuve in the nineteenth century as *agréabilité.*

SIR JOSHUA REYNOLDS

BIBLIOGRAPHY

The most accessible edition of the *Works* is that edited by H. W. Beechy, 2 vols., 1835 (Bohn, 1852).

Editions of the *Discourses* are numerous; among them the following are to be noted: J. Burnet, 1842; Edmund Gosse, 1884; Roger Fry, 1905; and Austin Dobson, 1907. There is a convenient edition in Everyman's Library.

Letters of Sir Joshua Reynolds, collected and ed. by F. W. Hilles, 1929.

For biography see the following:

Sir Walter Armstrong, *Sir Joshua Reynolds*, 1900.

Lord Ronald Gower, *Sir Joshua Reynolds*, 1902.

M. Osborn, *Joshua Reynolds*, in Künstler-Monographien, 1908.

NOTES

687, l. 42, *Guido was thus meanly copied by Elisabetta Sirani, and Simone Cantarini:* Guido Reni (1575–1642), the celebrated Bolognese painter had among his pupils Simone Cantarini and Giovanni Andrea Sirani, who in turn taught his daughter Elisabetta. Because the references in the text are sufficiently clear for the present purpose, no further notes are included on the painters mentioned.

689, l. 35, *Gothic essays:* crude or barbaric attempts. This is the customary eighteenth-century use of these words.

689, l. 44, *the luxuriant style of Paul Veronese:* Though Reynolds was himself much influenced by the Venetian painters, he condemned their colouring as ornamental, and contrasted with it the ideal beauty of form in the work of Michael Angelo. In so doing he was consistently following neo-classical critical principles. Du Fresnoy in *De Arte Graphica*, 1668, had declared that invention is the first part of painting, design the second, and colouring the third. Dryden in *A Parallel of Poetry and Painting*, 1695, prefixed to his translation of Du Fresnoy's poem says, "Expression, and all that belongs to words, is that in a poem which colouring is in a picture."

OLIVER GOLDSMITH

BIBLIOGRAPHY

J. F. Waller, *The Works of Oliver Goldsmith*, 1864, 1865.
David Masson, *The Miscellaneous Works of Oliver Goldsmith*, Globe Edition, 1869; reprinted 1925.
J. W. M. Gibbs, *The Works of Oliver Goldsmith*, Bohn's Standard Library, 5 vols., 1885, 1886.
A. Dobson, *Complete Poetical Works*, 1906.
A. Dobson and G. P. Baker, *Plays of Goldsmith*, Belles Lettres Series, 1903.
Padraic Colum, *Essays, Poems, Letters and Plays of Oliver Goldsmith*, 1928.
J. Earnshaw, *Selections from Oliver Goldsmith*, 1929.
Among the many editions of separate works the following will be useful:
A. Dobson, *The Bee*, 1903.
A. Dobson, *The Citizen of the World*, 1891.
H. J. Smith, *The Citizen of the World*, 1926.
R. S. Crane, *New Essays by Oliver Goldsmith*, 1927.
Katherine C. Balderstone, *The Collected Letters of Oliver Goldsmith*, 1928.
C. E. Doble, *The Vicar of Wakefield*, 1909.
For biography and criticism see the following:
Sir James Prior, *Life of Oliver Goldsmith*, 2 vols., 1837.
Washington Irving, *Life of Oliver Goldsmith*, 2 vols., 1844; revised ed., 1849.
J. Forster, *Life and Adventures of Oliver Goldsmith, A Biography*, 2d ed., 2 vols., 1854; final ed., 1877.
W. Black, *Goldsmith*, E. M. of L. Series, 1878.
A. Dobson, *Life of Goldsmith*, Great Writers Series, 1888; revised ed., 1899.
R. A. King, *Oliver Goldsmith*, 1910.
F. F. Moore, *Goldsmith*, 1910.
Temple Scott, *Oliver Goldsmith, Bibliographically and Biographically Considered;* Introduction by A. E. Newton, 1928.
K. C. Balderstone, *A Census of the Manuscripts of Oliver Goldsmith*, 1927.
Iolo A. Williams, *Seven Eighteenth Century Bibliographies*, 1924. (Armstrong, Akenside, Churchill, Collins, Goldsmith, Shenstone, Sheridan.)
A. Dobson, *Eighteenth Century Vignettes*, 1892.
A. L. Sells, *Les Sources françaises de Goldsmith*, 1924.
James H. Pitman, *Goldsmith's "Animated Nature": A Study of Goldsmith*, in *Yale Studies in Eng.*, LXVI, 1924.
H. J. Smith, *Oliver Goldsmith's "The Citizen of the World": A Study*, in *Yale Studies in Eng.*, LXXI, 1926.
A. Bosker, *Literary Criticism in the Age of Johnson*, 1930.

NOTES

AN INQUIRY INTO THE PRESENT STATE OF LEARNING

693, l. 1, *An Inquiry into the Present State of Polite Learning in Europe, Chapter X:* The text here given is that of the revised edition of 1774; this chapter is made up of chapter VI and chapter XI of the original edition.

693, l. 6, *Of all misfortunes ... is the most severe:* This sentence is the key to Goldsmith's attack on criticism. He opposes the formalism of the school of rules — the same thing that most of the greater critics of this period condemned — and sets against it "judging from feeling," which means not the romantic spontaneity but rather the school of taste.

694, l. 19, *The ingenious Mr. Hogarth:* William Hogarth (1697–1764), the famous realistic painter, a friend of Goldsmith's.

695, l. 4, *The Celtic ... Edda of Iceland:* Goldsmith's knowledge of the history of language was obviously inadequate even for a day when the subject had been comparatively little studied. There were, however, scholars in England who could have put him right on the language of the Eddas.

695, l. 8, *Olaus Wormius:* Ole Worm (1588–1654), Danish antiquary, author of *Monumenta Danica*.

695, l. 10, *Pontoppidan, Bishop of Bergen:* Erik Pontoppidan (1698–1764), Danish scholar.

695, l. 6, *humour acts a contrary part:* Goldsmith's concept of *humour* is here the orthodox classical one, eccentricity.

695, l. 50, *Civem, mehercule! ... possit:* Paraphrased in the following line and a half.

THE BEE, NO. 2

696, l. 23, *No. 2:* Each number of the *Bee* contained several essays. This contribution was afterwards republished by Goldsmith, slightly altered, as Essay XV.

696, l. 14, *trollopees:* loose gowns at this time worn by women.

697, l. 3, *Quanto si mostra... bella* (*La Gerusalemme Liberata,* XVI, 14, 4.): "The less it is shown, the more beautiful it is."

697, l. 40, *those odious muffs:* Muffs were carried by men — especially the dandies — during much of the eighteenth century.

697, l. 49, *the White Conduit House:* a resort at Islington, near London, somewhat after the style of Vauxhall.

THE BEE, NO. 5

699, l. 14, *Colley Cibber:* Goldsmith probably introduced Cibber into this eminent company for the sake of the jest about the black eye: that is, his abuse of Pope which led the latter to make him the hero of *The Dunciad* in later editions of the poem. Cibber was a leading exponent of sentimental comedy, which Goldsmith opposed.

699, l. 50, *The next... a most whimsical figure indeed:* Dr. John Hill was an industrious minor writer of the time, who had published among other things a periodical called the *Inspector,* 1751–53. He had written books on botany and was noted for his dress.

699, l. 41, *The person who after him appeared:* Arthur Murphy (1727–1805), man of letters and popular dramatist. The tragedy referred to is *The Orphan of China,* produced in April, 1759.

700, l. 12, *a very grave personage:* Dr. Johnson, whose close friendship for Goldsmith is said to have resulted from this essay.

700, l. 43, *another,... something more modern:* David Hume. See Introduction, p. 582.

700, l. 13, *a person... inclined to the Stagecoach of Riches:* Tobias George Smollett (1721–1771), physician, author of *Roderick Random, Peregrine Pickle,* and other famous novels, and also of a *History of England,* the first four volumes of which had been published in 1757. Shortly after the publication of this essay, Goldsmith, who seems not to have been personally acquainted with Smollett before, was engaged by the latter to write for his new *British Magazine.*

700, l. 30, *Segrais:* J. R. de Segrais was the pseudonym of Mme. de La Fayette (1634–93), author of *La Princesse de Clèves.*

700, l. 37, *I found them grumbling at each other:* Smollett had attacked Hume; Johnson's opinion of Scotchmen is well known — Smollett and Hume were both Scots.

701, l. 8 (*To be continued*): Goldsmith published no continuation of this *Reverie*; the *Bee* ran to only eight numbers.

THE CITIZEN OF THE WORLD, LETTER IV

702, l. 5, *the great man's gentleman:* The term, "gentleman's gentleman" was often applied to a valet.

LETTER XXX

702, l. 26, *repeated our visit to the club of authors:* Letter XXIX is "A Description of a Club of Authors."

703, l. 32, *The royal game... the royal martyr drew:* For the game of goose and the twelve rules, see notes to *The Deserted Village,* p. 723, l. 232.

703, l. 34, *listing:* selvage, border.

703, l. 14, *ex ungue Herculem:* "One may know Hercules by his finger nail."

703, l. 54, *my Lord Squash, the Creolian:* i.e., the Creole.

704, l. 50, *door of a sponging-house:* a house kept by a bailiff where persons under arrest for debt were sometimes temporarily lodged.

LETTER LI

705, l. 22, *my old friend and companion:* The Man in Black is a benevolent eccentric who attempts to conceal his goodness of heart beneath a pretence of hardness and cynicism. He is referred to throughout the whole series; Letter XXVI gives his character, and Letter XXVII tells his history.

705, l. 50, *strokes — and dashes:* The reference seems to be to Sterne's *Tristram Shandy,* the first two volumes of which appeared in 1760. See Letter LIII on "The Absurd Taste for Obscene and Pert Novels. Such as 'Tristram Shandy' Ridiculed."

705, l. 55, *seventy-two ha-ha's:* James Towneley's farce, *High Life Below Stairs,* 1759, is probably referred to.

706, l. 47, *Suppose... a volume of Chinese Letters:* In the sentences which follow, Goldsmith replies to critics who had censured him because the character of his Chinese philosopher was too carefully — or not carefully enough — preserved in his comments upon English affairs.

LETTER LIV

706, l. 44, *Letter LIV:* This sketch was republished by Goldsmith with slight alterations as Essay X, under the title, "Beau Tibbs, a Character."

LETTER LV

708, l. 22, *Letter LV:* Republished as Essay XI.

709, l. 54, *in the manner of Grisoni:* Giuseppe Grisoni, eighteenth-century Italian painter of the Florentine School.

LETTER LXXXIX

709, l. 47, *The Folly...*: Compare the *Tatler*, No. 216.

710, l. 32, *Sesostris:* a legendary King of Egypt, who was said to have been a world conqueror.

711, l. 28, *Magog, Meshech, and Tubal:* three of the sons of Japheth, the son of Noah. See Genesis 10:2.

LETTER XC

711, l. 45, *the spleen:* The word was commonly used in the eighteenth century to cover a variety of meanings from ill humour or lowness of spirits to hypochondria or melancholia. See Pope's description of the Cave of Spleen, *The Rape of the Lock*, Canto IV and Matthew Green's *The Spleen*, p. 334.

712, l. 11, *ambusheer:* correct placing of the lips and tongue in playing a wind-instrument, usually spelled *embouchure*.

712, l. 23, *deathwatches:* Certain small beetles sometimes make a peculiar ticking sound that is superstitiously regarded as a warning of approaching death.

LETTER XCIII

713, l. 8, *All seem convinced... probability of success:* Goldsmith himself made use of the popular opinion that he here ridicules, when in 1764 he published *An History of England in a Series of Letters from a Nobleman to his Son*. The success of this work was, at least in part, due to its popular attribution to the Earl of Chesterfield or to Lord Lyttelton.

LETTER CXI

713, l. 24, *Methodists:* Compare Walpole's letter to John Chute, Oct. 10, 1766, and the Introduction to Wesley's *Journal*, p. 741.

713, l. 27, *to hire a conventicle:* The meaning here is a building in which dissenters from the English Church held their meetings. *Conventicle* usually means such a meeting. Of course at this time the Methodists had not yet separated from the Established Church.

713, l. 41, *white gowns and black mantles:* The Puritans generally objected to the use of the surplice in church services and often substituted the black Geneva gown.

714, l. 37, *Zoroaster,... Brahmins:* He was the religious leader of the Parsees, not of the Brahmins.

714, l. 54, *Ridicule... the most powerful enemy of enthusiasm:* Compare Shaftesbury's *Characteristics*, p. 222.

THE TRAVELLER

715, l. 8, *thee:* the poet's brother, the Reverend Henry Goldsmith, to whom this poem was dedicated.

716, l. 69, *the line:* the equator.

718, l. 190, *the struggling savage:* The wild beast is here meant.

718, l. 253, *gestic lore:* knowledge of bodily motion (*cf.* gesticulate); here refers to dancing.

719, l. 286, *rampire's artificial pride:* the dikes of Holland.

720, l. 420, *To stop too fearful...*: "And here it is proper to settle with authentic precision what has long floated in public report as to Johnson's being himself the author of a considerable part of that poem [*The Traveller*]. Much, no doubt, both of the sentiments and the expression were derived from conversation with him; and it was certainly submitted to his friendly revision: but in the year 1783 he at my request marked with a pencil the lines which he had furnished, which are only line 420th and the concluding ten lines except the last couplet but one.... He added, 'These are all of which I can be sure.'" Boswell, *The Life of Johnson*, under the year 1766.

720, l. 436, *Luke's iron crown:* "Goldsmith in the couplet which he inserted [see note above], mentions Luke as a person well known.... The truth is that Goldsmith himself was in a mistake. In the *Respublica Hungarica* there is an account of a desperate rebellion in the year 1514, headed by two brothers of the name of Zeck, George and Luke. When it was quelled, George, not Luke, was punished by his head being encircled with a red hot iron crown." Boswell, *The Life of Johnson*, under the year, 1766. Boswell is not entirely accurate, himself. George (Gyorgy) Dozsa was the man's name; he was a Szeckler, one of a Magyar people of eastern Transylvania.

720, l. 436, *Damiens' bed of steel:* In 1757 Robert François Damiens attempted to assassinate Louis XV of France. The unfortunate man was subjected to the most excruciating tortures before he was put to death.

THE DESERTED VILLAGE

723, l. 232, *The twelve good rules:* These rules of conduct, commonly ascribed to Charles I, were often hung up in inns.

723, l. 232, *the royal game of goose:* a game not unlike parchesi.

724, l. 316, *artist:* artisan.

726, ll. 427–30, *That trade's proud empire... and the sky:* Dr. Johnson told Boswell that he had supplied only the last four lines to *The Deserted Village.*

EDWARD GIBBON

BIBLIOGRAPHY

The standard edition of *The Decline and Fall of the Roman Empire* is edited by J. Bury, 7 vols., 1896–1900; new ed., 1909–13.

Gibbon's *Autobiography* has appeared in numerous editions with different titles:

The Life of Edward Gibbon, Esq., with Selections from his Correspondence, and Illustrations, by H. H. Milman, 1839.

Autobiographies of Edward Gibbon, ed. by John Murray, 1896.

Memoirs of the Life and Writings of Edward Gibbon, ed., with introduction and notes, by O. F. Emerson, Athenæum Press Series, 1898.

The Memoirs of the Life of Edward Gibbon, with Various Observations and Excursions by Himself, ed. by G. B. Hill, 1900. (Excellent notes and appendixes.)

The Autobiography of Edward Gibbon, ed. by Oliphant Smeaton, Everyman's Library, n.d.

The Private Letters of Edward Gibbon (1753–1794) were edited by R. E. Prothero, 2 vols., 1896.

Gibbon's Journal to Jan. 28, 1763 has been ed. by D. M. Low, 1929.

For biography and criticism see:

J. C. Morison, *Gibbon*, E. M. of L., 1878.

Algernon Cecil, *Six Oxford Thinkers*, 1909.

J. M. Robertson, *Gibbon*, 1925.

Lytton Strachey, *Portraits in Miniature*, 1930.

Gibbon's work as a historian has been frequently discussed, notably by the following:

Eduard Fueter, *Geschichte der neueren Historiographie*, 1911.

J. B. Black, *The Art of History*, 1926.

NOTES

THE HISTORY OF THE DECLINE AND FALL OF THE ROMAN EMPIRE

727, l. 7, *Constantinople and the Greek fire... the conquerors of Spain:* Chapters L, LI, and LII tell the story of the rise of Mohametanism and the earlier conquests of the Arabs. In 668–75 and again in 716–18 the Arabs had besieged Constantinople but had been repulsed, chiefly by the use of Greek fire, a compound of naphtha and certain other secret ingredients, which struck terror into the hearts of the besiegers. Shortly before the events narrated in this extract, 721–32, Spain had been overrun by the Moslems.

728, l. 41, *The memory of these devastations... romances of chivalry... Italian Muse:* the Charlemagne romances and their later treatment in the poems of Pulci, Boiardo, and Ariosto.

729, l. 8, *Neustria and Austrasia:* dominions respectively of the Western and the Eastern Franks.

730, l. 26, *His merits were forgotten:* Here and elsewhere Gibbon shows his characteristic animus against the Church.

MEMOIRS

730, l. 29, *a gentleman-commoner:* a student paying higher fees than the "commoners" and enjoying certain special privileges.

731, l. 10, *the Hookers, the Chillingworths, and the Lockes:* Richard Hooker (1554?–1600), a distinguished Anglican theologian, author of *Ecclesiastical Polity.* For William Chillingworth (1602–1644) see below; for John Locke see Introduction to the selections from his work, p. 150.

731, l. 28, *the intolerant zeal which Warburton had ascribed to the genius of the place:* William Warburton (1698–1779), Bishop of Gloucester, is most frequently remembered for his defence of Pope's *Essay on Man,* which brought him the poet's friendship and literary executorship, and for his edition of Shakespeare. The reference here is to Warburton's controversy with Robert Lowth (1710–87), later Bishop of Oxford and still later Bishop of London. After this sentence, Gibbon, in the fragment of autobiography known as Memoir B, adds, "It may indeed be observed that the atmosphere of Oxford did not agree with Mr. Locke's constitution, and that the philosopher justly despised the academical bigots who expelled his person and despised his principles."

732, l. 20, *budge doctors: Cf.* Milton's *Comus,* ll. 708, 709,

> Oh, foolishness of men! that lend their ears
> To these budge doctors of the Stoic fur.

"Budge" is a kind of lambskin formerly used on academic gowns; as an adjective it had come to mean "scholastic," and afterwards "austerely stiff."

732, l. 52, *the three faculties:* theology, law, and medicine.

732, l. 9, *Dr. Adam Smith* (1723–1790): philosopher and political economist, author of *Inquiry into the Nature and Causes of the Wealth of Nations.* The quotation above is from book V, chap. 1.

733, l. 29, *the monks of Magdalen:* the fellows of the college, so called by Gibbon because they showed qualities popularly ascribed by Protestants to Roman Catholic monks.

733, l. 37, *the common room:* in an English college a room set apart for the use of the fellows, where they retire after dinner. The gentlemen-commoners were also admitted.

733, l. 11, *Wenman and Dashwood ... Cicero and Chrysostom:* The reference is to the parliamentary election of 1754 in which Lord Wenman and Sir James Dashwood, who were supported by the fellows of Magdalen, were defeated. Gibbon means that politics occupied their interest to the exclusion of the classics and church history.

733, l. 20, *ascribi quietis ordinibus ... deorum* (Hor., *Odes,* III, 3, 35): "To be admitted to the peaceful ranks of the gods."

733, l. 38, *Burmann or Bernoulli:* Pieter Burmann (1668–1741), a well-known Dutch classical scholar, professor in the universities of Utrecht and Leyden. As a matter of fact, Burmann taught oratory, history, and politics as well as Greek. Several members of the family of Bernoulli, or Bernouilli, attained distinction as mathematicians; the reference here is probably to Daniel Bernoulli, who was a professor at Basel, 1733–1785.

734, l. 15, *Pococke and Hyde:* Edward Pococke (1604–1691) was a celebrated oriental scholar. Thomas Hyde (1636–1703) was Pococke's successor as Laud Professor of Arabic at Oxford.

JAMES HERVEY

BIBLIOGRAPHY

There is no recent reprint of Hervey's works, but eighteenth-century versions are easily accessible. Most writers on the literature of the period make brief reference to Hervey. See Sir Leslie Stephen, *History of English Thought in the Eighteenth Century,* 2 vols., 1876.

A. L. Reed, *The Background of Gray's Elegy,* 1924.

J. W. Draper, *The Funeral Elegy and the Rise of English Romanticism,* 1929.

NOTES

738, l. 8, *How often has the schoolboy: Cf.* Robert Blair, *The Grave,* ll. 56 ff.

738, l. 37, *"I'll meet thee there":* Hervey's note illustrates the deadly seriousness of his literary allusions. "The story of Brutus and his evil genius is well known. Nor must it be denied that the precise words of the spectre to the hero were, 'I'll meet thee at Philippi.' But as this would not answer my purpose, I was obliged to make an alteration in the circumstance of place." See Shakespeare's *Julius Cæsar,* IV, 3, 284, where the phrasing is slightly different from that quoted in the note.

738, l. 15, *the book of Job:* chap. IV, especially verses 12–19. In an elaborate note Hervey explains this passage not as a vision but as the appearance of a spirit to Eliphaz.

738, l. 49, *It spoke, and this was the purport of its words:* "I have given this solemn picture a modern dress, rather for the sake of variety and illustration than from any apprehension of improving the admirable original. Such an attempt, I am sensible, would be more absurdly vain than to lacquer gold or paint the diamond. The description in Eliphaz's own language is awful and affecting to the last degree, a night-piece dressed in all the circumstances of the deepest horror. I question whether Shakespeare himself, though so peculiarly happy for his great command of terrifying images, has anything superior or comparable to this. The judges of fine composition see the masterly strokes, and I believe the most ordinary reader feels them chilling his blood and awakening emotions of dread in his mind." Hervey's note.

740, l. 14, *The hatchment suspended on the wall:* a display of the arms of the deceased, used in mourning.

JOHN WESLEY

BIBLIOGRAPHY

Works, 32 vols., 1771–74; 11th ed., 15 vols., 1856–62.
The standard edition of the *Journal* is by N. Curnock, 8 vols., 1909–16.
J. Whitehead, *Life of John Wesley*, 2 vols., 1791–93.
T. Coke and H. Moore, *Life of John Wesley*, 2 vols., 1792; new ed., 2 vols., 1824, 1825.
R. Southey, *Life of Wesley*, 2 vols., 1820.
L. Tyerman, *The Life and Times of Wesley*, 3 vols., 1870, 1871.
Julia Wedgwood, *John Wesley*, 1870.
C. T. Winchester, *Life of Wesley*, 1906.
A. Léger, *La jeunesse de Wesley*, 1910.
A. Léger, *John Wesley's Last Love*, 1910.
W. H. Hutton, *John Wesley*, 1927.
John Simon, *John Wesley, the Master Builder*, *1757–72*, 1927.
Henry Bett, *Studies in Literature*, 1929. "Evangelical Religion and Literature," and "Wesley's Journal."
Arnold Lunn, *John Wesley*, 1929.
J. D. Wade, *John Wesley*, 1930.
Sir Leslie Stephen, *History of English Thought in the Eighteenth Century*, 2 vols., 1876.
C. J. Abbey and J. H. Overton, *The English Church in the Eighteenth Century*, 2 vols., 1878; new ed., 1887
J. H. Overton, *The English Church from the Accession of George I to the End of the Eighteenth Century*, 1906

NOTES

742, l. 10, *these horrid mountains:* Wesley was certainly not, in Charles Lamb's phrase, "romance-bit about nature"; mountains were to him chiefly an obstacle to travel.

742, l. 48, *quid mea refert?:* "What is it to me?"

743, l. 43, *the Foundery:* A large building near Moorfields, London, formerly used by the government as a cannon-foundery, had been taken over by the Methodists very early as a city meeting-house.

744, l. 47, *The rage of Arctos...:* Prior, *Solomon*, I, 266.

744, l. 42, *enthusiasts: NED, Enthusiast*, 2, B, "one who erroneously believes himself to be the recipient of special divine communications; in wider sense, one who holds extravagant and visionary religious opinions, or is characterized by ill-regulated fervour of religious emotion."

747, l. 14, *Essay on Music: An Essay on Musical Expression*, 1752, by Charles Avison.

747, l. 51, *the expulsion... at Oxford:* On March 11 of this same year six students who were Calvinistic Methodists had been expelled from the university for "attending conventicles."

747, l. 54, *summum jus:* "The utmost rigour of the law."

CHARLES WESLEY

BIBLIOGRAPHY

Poetical Works of John and Charles Wesley, 13 vols., 1868.
Methodist Hymn Book Illustrated by J. Telford, 1906.
L. Tyerman, *Life and Times of Samuel Wesley, M.A.*, 1866.

RICHARD HURD

BIBLIOGRAPHY

Hurd's *Complete Works* were published in 8 vols. in 1811. The best modern reprint of *Letters on Chivalry and Romance* was edited by Edith J. Morley in 1911.

The Correspondence of Richard Hurd and William Mason and Letters of Richard Hurd to Thomas Gray, with Introduction and Notes by E. H. Pearce; ed. with Additional Notes by Leonard Whibley, 1932.

Memoirs of the Life and Writings of the Right Rev. Richard Hurd was published by F. Kilvert, 1860.

For criticism see the following works:

W. L. Phelps, *The Beginnings of the English Romantic Movement*, 1893.

Paul Hamelius, *Die Kritik in der englischen Literatur des 17 und 18 Jahrhunderts*, 1897.

H. A. Beers, *A History of English Romanticism in the Eighteenth Century*, 1898.

A. Bosker, *Literary Criticism in the Age of Johnson*, 1930.

NOTES

754, l. 7, *Gerusalemme Liberata: Jerusalem Delivered*, Torquato Tasso's epic of the First Crusade, 1581.

754, l. 9, *heroic and Gothic manners:* the manners and customs of the ancient Greeks, as shown in the Homeric poems; and those of the Middle Ages, as shown in *Jerusalem Delivered* and in the mediæval romances.

754, l. 39, "*— omnes illacrymabiles... sacro*" (Horace, *Odes*, IV, 9, 26–28): "All are encompassed by enduring night, unwept and unknown, because they lack an inspired poet."

755, l. 1, *the Canidia of Horace:* a sorceress often mentioned by him.

755, l. 3, *Virgil's myrtles... Tasso's enchanted forest: Cf. Æneid*, III, 19 ff., and *Jer. Del.*, canto 13.

755, l. 11, *His ego sæpe lupum... messes* (*Eclogues*, VIII, 97–99): "Through these I have often seen Mœris become a wolf and hide himself in the forests, often call spirits from the depths of graves, and charm away sown grain to other fields."

755, l. 19, *fascination:* enchantment.

755, l. 21, *Non isthic obliquo... Limat...* (Horace, *Epistles*, I, 14, 37): "No one there takes away from my good things with the evil eye." The context clearly shows that Hurd supposed *obliquo oculo* to carry this meaning.

755, l. 33, *... I have bedimm'd...*: *The Tempest*, V, 1, 41–49.

755, l. 42, *animas imis excire sepulchris:* See quotation from Virgil's *Eclogues*, above.

755, l. 2, *... nor stay'd the terror there...*: IV, 421–24.

755, l. 8, *Thus pass'd the night...*: IV, 426–30.

755, l. 27, "*The ancients have not much of this poetry...*": *Spectator*, No. 419, on "The Fairy Way of Writing." See p. 284.

756, l. 41, *his growing fanaticism:* Puritanical zeal.

756, l. 45, *the immortal satire of Cervantes: Don Quixote.*

756, l. 6, *Towered cities please us then...*: lines 117–24.

756, l. 23, *Or call up him that left half-told...*: lines 109–20. Milton here refers to Chaucer's *Squire's Tale*, which was never finished by the author.

758, l. 28, *Kent and Nature:* William Kent (1685–1748), the most famous landscape gardener of his time, was a leader in the movement for a return to nature by substituting natural foliage and serpentine paths for the clipped hedges and the straight lines of the formal gardens, which had previously been popular.

758, l. 37, *In lieto aspetto... scopre:* Wiffen translates as follows,

These windings passed, the garden-gates unfold,
And the fair Eden meets their glad survey, —
Still waters, moving crystals, sands of gold,
Herbs, thousand flowers, rare shrubs, and mosses grey;
Sunshiny hillocks, shady vales; woods gay,
And grottos gloomy, in one view combined,
Presented were; and what increased their play
Of pleasure at the prospect, was, to find
Nowhere the happy Art that had the whole designed.

JAMES MACPHERSON

BIBLIOGRAPHY

Works of Ossian, ed. by W. Sharp, Edinburgh, 1896.
B. Saunders, *The Life and Letters of James Macpherson*, 1894.
A. Nutt, *Ossian and the Ossianic Literature*, 1899.
J. S. Smart, *James Macpherson: An Episode in Literature*, 1905.
Keith N. Macdonald, *In Defence of Ossian, Being a Summary of the Evidence in Favour of the Authenticity of the Poems*, 1906.
Carl Meyer, *Die Landschaft Ossians*, 1906.
A. Tedeschi, *Ossian "l'Homère du Nord" en France*, 1911.
George F. Black, *Macpherson's Ossian and the Ossianic Controversy: A Contribution towards a Bibliography*, 1926.

NOTES

761, l. 27, *Toscar:* The speaker, throughout, is supposed to be Ossian, or Oisin, the legendary Irish blind bard of the third century.

762, l. 15, *Ossian:* the son of Fingal.

762, l. 27, *blood:* an example of the "second sight" of which Collins had made much in his *Ode on the Superstitions of the Highlands.*

764, l. 29, *foe:* "A man who tells his name to an enemy" was of old an ignominious term for a coward. — Macpherson's note.

THOMAS CHATTERTON

BIBLIOGRAPHY

Poetical Works, 2 vols., ed. with Essay on the Rowley Poems, by W. W. Skeat, 1871.
Complete Poetical Works, 2 vols., ed. with Life by H. D. Roberts, 1906.
The Rowley Poems, ed. with Introd., by M. E. Hare, 1911.
D. Wilson, *Thomas Chatterton*, 1869.
D. Masson, *Chatterton*, 1899.
C. E. Russell, *Thomas Chatterton, the Marvellous Boy*, 1908.
J. H. Ingram, *The True Chatterton*, 1910.
Esther P. Ellinger, *Thomas Chatterton, the Marvelous Boy, to which is Added The Exhibition, a Persona. Satire*, 1930.
E. H. W. Meyerstein, *A Life of Thomas Chatterton*, 1930.

NOTES

BRISTOWE TRAGEDIE

767, Subtitle, *Bawdin:* probably Sir Baldwin Fulford, a Lancastrian executed at Bristol in 1461.
767, l. 2, *Han:* has.
767, l. 9, *quod:* quoth.
767, l. 13, *nappy:* strong.
767, l. 45, *Canynge:* mayor of Bristol, patron of the imaginary poet Thomas Rowley.
768, l. 58, *rewyn'd:* ruined.
768, l. 66, *meede:* reward.
768, l. 73, *reines:* loins or kidneys.
768, l. 75, *Christ's vycarr:* the Pope.
768, l. 78, *faste:* fasten.
768, l. 104, *flowe:* a line borrowed from Dryden's *Alexander's Feast*, l. 88.
769, l. 141, *Henrie:* Henry VI, 1421–71, a pious feeble king deposed by Edward IV.
769, l. 141, *forfende:* defend. The true sense is *forbid.*
769, l. 183, *sonnes:* Edward IV and Richard III were sons of Richard, Duke of York.
769, l. 187, *choppe:* exchange.
769, l. 190, *hynde:* peasant.
770, l. 263, *enshone:* showed.

770, l. 269, *Freers:* friars.
770, l. 271, *weedes:* garments.
770, l. 272, *plyghte:* condition.
770, l. 276, *bataunt:* an adjective meaning *eager*, mistaken for the name of an instrument.
771, l. 335, *Gloucester:* afterward Richard III.

ÆLLA, A TRAGYCAL ENTERLUDE, *FIRST* MYNSTRELLES SONGE

771, l. 1, *boddynge:* budding.
771, l. 2, *mees:* meadows.
771, l. 2, *sprenged:* sprinkled.
772, l. 3, *dyghte:* adorned.
772, l. 4, *nesh:* delicate.
772, l. 5, *straughte:* stretched.
772, l. 8, *The roddie... eyne:* The ruddy sky shines to the eyes.
772, l. 9, *alestake:* the sign of a tavern. Chatterton misunderstands its position.
772, l. 16, *kynde:* womankind.
772, l. 19, *blake:* bare.
772, l. 20, *guylteynge:* gilding.
772, l. 23, *woddie:* willow.
772, l. 24, *levynne-fyres:* lightning.
772, l. 24, *lemes:* gleams.
772, l. 25, *even:* evening.
772, l. 26, *fructyle:* fertile.
772, l. 30, *steyncèd:* stained.
772, l. 31, *kynde:* sex.
772, l. 32, *chafe:* hot.
772, l. 33, *Dheere:* there.
772, l. 34, *Yatte:* that.
772, l. 35, *botte:* but.
772, l. 39, *an ynutyle membere:* a useless member, Adam's rib.
772, l. 43, *pheeres:* mates.
772, l. 45, *efte:* often.
772, l. 45, *cheres:* cherishes.
772, l. 46, *Tochelod:* may perhaps mean "joined."
772, l. 46, *heie:* they.
772, l. 47, *swythyn:* at once.
772, l. 48, *bante:* banned, cursed.
772, l. 48, *hie:* highly.

SECOND MYNSTRELLES SONGE

772, l. 1, *synge... roundelaie:* join in my song.
772, l. 3, *hallie daie:* holiday.
772, l. 4, *reynynge:* running.
772, l. 7, *wyllowe:* emblem of mourning.
772, l. 8, *cryne:* hair.
772, l. 9, *rode:* neck.
772, l. 9, *snowe:* perhaps as seen on mountain tops.
772, l. 10, *Rodde:* ruddy.
772, l. 11, *Cale:* cold.
772, l. 14, *tree:* In this stanza particularly, Chatterton follows Ophelia's song in *Hamlet*, IV, 5.
773, l. 15, *Swote:* sweet.
773, l. 17, *taboure:* a small drum.
773, l. 17, *stote:* stout.
773, l. 31, *yanne:* than.
773, l. 38, *hallie:* holy.
773, l. 39, *celness:* coldness.
773, l. 43, *dente:* plant.
773, l. 44, *gre:* grow.
773, l. 45, *Ouphante:* elfin.

773, l. 57, *reytes:* water-flags.
773, l. 58, *leathalle:* deadly.
773, l. 60, *Thos:* thus.

AN EXCELENTE BALADE OF CHARITIE

773, Title, *Charitie:* the last of the "Rowley poems," written in London.
773, Sub-title, *1464:* "Thomas Rowley, the author, was born at Norton Malreward, in Somersetshire, educated at the convent of St. Kenna, at Keynesham, and died at Westbury, in Gloucestershire." — Chatterton's note.
773, l. 1, *Virgynè:* the Virgin, a sign of the zodiac which the sun enters in August.
773, l. 1, *gan:* did.
773, l. 4, *mole:* soft.
773, l. 5, *The peede chelandri:* the pied or variegated goldfinch.
773, l. 7, *aumere:* mantle.
773, l. 13, *Hiltring... face:* hiding at once the sun's festive face.
773, l. 15, *holme:* an oak.
773, l. 16, *covent:* convent. "It would have been *charitable* if the author had not pointed at personal characters in this 'Ballad of Charity.' The abbot of St. Godwin's at the time of writing this was Ralph de Bellomont, a great stickler for the Lancastrian family. Rowley was a Yorkist." — Chatterton's note.
773, l. 17, *moneynge:* moaning.
773, l. 18, *ungentle in his weede:* not dressed like a gentleman.
773, l. 19, *bretful:* brimful.
773, l. 20, *almer:* beggar of alms.
773, l. 23, *forwynd:* sapless.
773, l. 24, *church-glebe-house:* the grave.
773, l. 25, *kiste:* coffin.
773, l. 25, *dortoure:* dormitory.
773, l. 30, *forswat:* hot.
773, l. 30, *smethe:* steam.
773, l. 30, *drenche:* drink.
774, l. 31, *ghastness:* terror.
774, l. 33, *flott:* fly.
774, l. 35, *smothe:* steam.
774, l. 35, *lowings:* flashes.
774, l. 36, *clymmynge:* noisy.
774, l. 37, *Cheves:* moves.
774, l. 37, *embollen:* swollen, strengthened.
774, l. 39, *gallard:* frightened.
774, l. 40, *swanges:* sways.
774, l. 45, *chapournette:* small hat.
774, l. 45, *drented:* drenched.
774, l. 46, *pencte:* painted.
774, l. 47, *bederoll:* "He told his beads backwards: a figurative expression to signify cursing." — Chatterton's note.
774, l. 49, *mist:* poor.
774, l. 50, *cope:* cloak.
774, l. 52, *autremete:* defined by Chatterton as "a loose white robe worn by priests."
774, l. 53, *his shoone... binne:* His pointed shoes might have been a lord's.
774, l. 54, *coste:* expense.
774, l. 55, *trammels:* shackles, used to make a horse amble.
774, l. 63, *crouche:* crosse.
774, l. 66, *faitour:* vagabond.
774, l. 67, *rynge:* door-knocker.
774, l. 69, *shettynge:* shooting.
774, l. 74, *jape:* a short surplice.
774, l. 75, *A limitoure... seene:* He was seen to be a limiter — i.e., a friar licenced to beg.
774, l. 81, *groate:* a coin worth four pence.
774, l. 82, *mister:* poor.
774, l. 82, *halline:* joy.
774, l. 83, *eathe:* ease.
774, l. 84, *nete:* naught.

774, l. 85, *unhailie:* unhappy.
774, l. 86, *Scathe:* scarce.
774, l. 86, *rentrolle:* account of income.
774, l. 87, *semecope:* under-cloak.
774, l. 89, *aborde:* took up.
774, l. 90, *gloure:* glory.
774, l. 91, *mittee:* mighty.
774, l. 91, *will:* the will to do the good they can.

JAMES BEATTIE

BIBLIOGRAPHY

Poetical Works, ed. with Memoir by A. Dyce, 1831, 1866.
Poetical Works, ed. with Life by G. Gilfillan, Edinburgh, 1854.
A. Bowyer, *An Account of the Life of James Beattie*, 1804.
W. Forbes, *An Account of the Life and Writings of James Beattie*, 1807.
M. Forbes, *Beattie and His Friends*, 1904.

NOTES

776, l. 9, *unknown:* With the ideas — chiefly "sentimental" — implicit in this stanza compare Gray's *Elegy*, 45–60.
776, l. 15, *obstreperous:* turbulent.
776, l. 27, *sung:* This description tallies closely with that in *An Essay on the Ancient Minstrels of England* prefixed to Percy's *Reliques*, 1765.
777, l. 91, *Gothic:* mediæval.
777, l. 95, *the north countrie:* Scotland.
777, l. 123, *roam'd: Cf.* Gray's *Elegy*, 73–76.
777, l. 136, *vulgar:* common, ordinary.
777, l. 138, *gaud:* gaily coloured trinket.
778, l. 153, *team:* the horses of Apollo's chariot, the sun.
778, l. 175, *smoky:* misty.
778, l. 183, *sublime:* on high.
778, l. 195, *soul:* Here and in the following lines Gray's *Ode on the Pleasure Arising from Vicissitude*, p. 526, is followed.
779, l. 279, *expire: Cf.* Gray's *Ode on a Distant Prospect of Eton College.*
780, l. 299, *valves:* doors of a gate.
780, l. 322, *spill:* ruin, overcome.
781, l. 357, *Pyrrho's:* a Greek philosopher, 360–270 B.C., whose system leads to complete agnosticism. Perhaps a covert reference to Hume.
781, l. 357, *Epicurus':* a Greek philosopher, 342–270 B.C., whose teaching of an exalted doctrine of pleasure has been grossly misunderstood and degraded.
781, l. 394, *trade: Cf. Macbeth*, IV, 1.
782, l. 466, *nice:* delicate, refined.
783, l. 523, *Lapponian's . . . land:* Lapland.
783, l. 534, *Montagu:* Elizabeth Robinson Montagu, 1720–1800, leader of London society and a famous woman of letters. *Cf.* p. 605.

THOMAS RUSSELL

BIBLIOGRAPHY

The Poems of Cuthbert Shaw and Thomas Russell, ed. by Eric Partridge, 1925.

NOTES

785, l. 3, *Pœan's son:* Philoctetes, a hero of the Trojan War who was left alone on Lemnos for nine years. The story is told by Sophocles in a tragedy named after the hero. His father was not the god Pæan but King Pœas of Mt. Œta, at the head of the Sea of Eubœa.

GILBERT WHITE

BIBLIOGRAPHY

The Natural History and Antiquities of Selborne has been frequently reprinted. One of the most accessible editions is that of Frank Buckland, 1880. Editions of *The Natural History* alone are more numerous, many of them having been done by naturalists with illustrations and supplementary notes; see those of John Burroughs, 1895; L. C. Miall and W. W. Fowler, 1901; Grant Allen, 1902; Richard Kearton, 1902, 1924. There are also reprints in Everyman's Library and in the World's Classics series. For biography see R. Holt-White, *The Life and Letters of Gilbert White of Selborne*, 1901, and Walter Johnson, *Gilbert White, Pioneer, Poet, and Stylist*, 1928.

NOTES

786, l. 1, *As to swallows... being found in a torpid state during the winter:* At this time it was commonly believed that swallows hibernated, usually in the mud of pools or streams. White is much interested in this theory and frequently discusses it. Though, on the whole, he is inclined to favour it because he finds swallows hovering about muddy places late in the autumn and early in the spring, because he notices that fine weather sometimes brings them suddenly and cold weather causes them to disappear, and because he has evidence that bats, insects, and turtles do actually so hibernate, he keeps an open mind about the matter and refuses to confound speculation with proof. More recent investigators have abandoned this theory entirely.

787, l. 5, *Brighthelmstone, in Sussex:* now Brighton.

787, l. 39, *your Zoölogy:* Thomas Pennant published a number of works on natural history; his *British Zoölogy* appeared in 1768, the year after the date of this letter.

787, l. 50, *Ray's Philos. Letters:* John Ray (1627–1705), Fellow of Trinity College, Cambridge, and prominent as a naturalist. Ray's *Philosophical Letters* were collected and published by the Rev William Derham in 1718.

787, l. 54, *Mr. Stillingfleet:* Benjamin Stillingfleet (1702–71), poet and naturalist, best known for his botanical works. He was the grandson of the famous Edward Stillingfleet, Bishop of Worcester from 1689 to 1699.

787, l. 19, *Linnæus:* Carl von Linné (1707–78), Swedish botanist, famous for his scientific classifications.

788, l. 7, *the Plestor:* "In the centre of the village, and near the church, is a square piece of ground surrounded by houses, and vulgarly called the Plestor." White, Let. II. The name is understood to be a corruption of Pleystow, playing-place.

788, l. 37, *The late vicar...*: adapted from Swift, *Baucis and Philemon*, l. 178.

788, l. 44, *Religione... annos:* Virg., *Æneid*, II, 715.

788, l. 49, *Forte puer... vocantem:* "The youth being separated by chance from his faithful attendants, calls aloud, 'Is there any one here?' and echo answers, 'Here.' He is amazed; he casts his eyes on every side and calls with a loud voice, 'Come!' whereupon echo calls the youth who calls."

789, l. 21, *Tityre, tu patulæ recubans* — (Virgil, *Ecl.* I, 1): The passage of which these are the opening words is thus translated by Dryden:

"Beneath the shade which beechen boughs diffuse
You, Tityrus, entertain your sylvan Muse."

789, l. 33, *Monstrum horrendum, informe, ingens* — (Virgil, *Æn.*, III, 658): Dryden translates as follows:

"A monster grim, tremendous, vast, and high."

789, l. 48, ... *aut ubi concava pulsu... imago* (Virgil, *Georg.*, IV, 47–50): The passage of which these words are the conclusion is thus translated by Dryden:

"Nor place them where too deep a water flows,
Or where the yew, their poisonous neighbour, grows;
Nor near the steaming stench of muddy ground,
Nor hollow rocks that render back the sound,
And double images of voice rebound."

790, l. 6, *Anathoth:* The Heb. name means "answers."

790, l. 50, *quæ nec reticere... Echo:* Ovid, *Met.*, 3, ll. 357, 358.

790, l. 1, *Quæ bene quom videas... musam:* In Creech's translation as follows:

"This shows thee why, whilst men, through caves and groves
Call their lost friends, or mourn unhappy loves,
The pitying rocks, the groaning caves return
Their sad complaints again, and seem to mourn:
This all observe, and I myself have known
Both rocks and hills return six words for one;
The dancing words from hill to hill rebound,
They all receive, and all restore the sound:
The vulgar and the neighbours think, and tell,
That there the Nymphs, and Fauns, and Satyrs dwell:
And that their wanton sport, their loud delight,
Breaks through the quiet silence of the night:
Their music's softest airs fill all the plains,
And mighty Pan delights the list'ning swains:
The goat-faced Pan, whose flocks securely feed;
With long-hung lip he blows his oaten reed:
The horned, the half-beast god, when brisk and gay,
With pine-leaves crowned, provokes the swains to play."

790, l. 25, *the vizier of the Spectator:* No. 512.

790, l. 50, *vox humana:* "Human voice," the name of an organ stop for producing tones resembling those of the human voice.

791, l. 42, *the crested cock...*: Milton, *Par. Lost*, VII, 443, 4.

792, l. 13, *The old Sussex tortoise...*: This famous tortoise, who bore the name Timothy, had been brought, according to White's account, from America and had been the property of his aunt in Sussex. A letter has been preserved, written in Timothy's name to Miss Mulso, afterwards Mrs. Chapone, whom White unsuccessfully wooed.

792, l. 11, *Much too wise...*: *Imits. of Horace*, Second Epistle of Second Book, l. 191.

792, l. 12, *not to fall down a haha:* a sunken fence or wall, used to enclose a park or garden without interfering with the view.

793, l. 53, *ne plus ultra:* "No more beyond," the uttermost point capable of attainment.

"JUNIUS"

BIBLIOGRAPHY

A complete bibliography of the *Junius Letters* and of the controversy about their authorship would run to great length. In 1890–92 J. Edmunds compiled a list of 49 editions of the *Letters* and 289 books and articles about their author, and considerable new material has appeared since that time.

The most accessible edition is that edited by John Wade, 2 vols., 1850, which contains, in addition to the *Junius Letters* proper, their author's private correspondence with H. S. Woodfall, the editor of the *Public Advertiser*, and with John Wilkes, as well as many other letters which appeared over different signatures but which have been ascribed to "Junius." In the second volume is a long essay in support of the "Franciscan" theory.

C. W. Everett reprinted the *Letters of Junius* in 1927 with an Introduction which attributes them to Lord Shelburne.

The following list contains a few of the more important books on the controversy:

J. Taylor, *A Discovery of the Author of the Letters of Junius*, 1813.

J. Taylor, *The Identity of Junius with a Distinguished Living Character Established*, 1816. (Sir Philip Francis.)

I. Newhall, *Letters on Junius... showing that the Author of that Celebrated Work was Lord Temple*, 1831.

J. Jaques, *The History of Junius and his Works*, 1843.

C. Chabot, *The Handwriting of Junius Professionally Investigated*, 1871.

A. Hayward, *The Handwriting of Junius*, 1874.

F. Brockhaus, *Die Briefe des Junius*, 1876.

H. R. Francis, *Junius Revealed, by his Surviving Grandson*, 1894.

B. Francis and E. Keary, eds., *The Francis Letters. By Sir Philip Francis and Other Members of the Family*, 2 vols., 1901.

James Smith, *Junius Unveiled*, 1909.

Frank Monaghan, "A New Document on the Identity of *Junius*," *Journ. of Mod. History*, 4:68–71, 1932.

Helen B. Bates, "Some Notes on Thomas Mante (Alias 'Junius')," *Journ. of Mod. History*, 4:232–34, 1932.

NOTES

795, l. 2, *His Grace the Duke of Bedford:* John Russell, fourth Duke of Bedford (1710–1771). He had taken an important part in the negotiations leading to the Peace of Paris in 1763 by which the war against France, Spain, and Portugal had been brought to an end. This treaty of peace had met with popular disfavour in England, and in consequence the Duke of Bedford had become unpopular. In 1766 he had entered the cabinet of which the Duke of Grafton was the head.

796, l. 37, *a domestic misfortune:* The duke's only son had recently been killed by a fall from his horse while hunting. This son was the father of Francis Russell, fifth Duke of Bedford. See Burke's *Letter to a Noble Lord*, pp. 817 ff.

796, l. 50, *the favourite of his sovereign:* John Stuart, third Earl of Bute (1713–92). See note to Walpole, p. 601, p. 11. Bute was hated as a royal favourite and as a Scot, as well as for his part in the unpopular treaty of peace in 1763, which ended the Seven Years' War.

797, l. 18, *the purchase and sale of a borough:* "In an answer in chancery, in a suit against him to recover a large sum of money paid him by a person whom he had undertaken to return to Parliament from one of his grace's boroughs. He was compelled to repay the money." Junius's note.

797, l. 52, *the recorded stripes:* "Mr. Heston Humphrey, a country attorney, horsewhipped the duke with equal justice, severity, and perseverance, on the course at Lichfield. Rigby and Lord Trentham were also cudgelled in a most exemplary manner." Junius's note.

797, l. 3, *any of his Majesty's kingdoms, except France:* Between 1340 and 1802 the English sovereigns included among their official titles King of France. The sting in this sentence is the reference to the popular belief that the Duke of Bedford and others had received French bribes at the time of their negotiation of the unpopular treaty of peace in 1763. See next paragraph.

797, l. 24, *Belleisle... the Havanna:* English conquests surrendered by the treaty of 1763. The French were also at the same time admitted to a share in the Newfoundland fisheries. Though the English government did not get the best possible terms by this treaty, it did thereby add greatly to the extent of the British possessions over seas.

798, l. 6, *you would not permit him to preserve the honour of a gentleman:* "The ministry having endeavoured to exclude the dowager out of the regency bill, the Earl of Bute determined to dismiss them. Upon this the Duke of Bedford demanded an audience of the king, reproached him in plain terms with his duplicity, baseness, falsehood, treachery, and hypocrisy — repeatedly gave him the lie, and left him in convulsions." Junius's note.

798, l. 8, *Mr. Mackenzie's history:* The reference is probably to the dismissal of James Stuart Mackenzie, brother of Lord Bute, from the office of Privy Seal of Scotland in 1765. In spite of the king's promise that Mackenzie should have this sinecure office for life, Pitt forced the dismissal and also exacted from the king a promise never again to have a private interview with Bute.

798, l. 40, *Woburn... Plymouth... Exeter:* Woburn, Bedfordshire, was the duke's family seat. The duke held large possessions in Devonshire, of which county he was lord-lieutenant. In July, 1769, he had been stoned by a mob while in Devonshire.

799, l. 1, *As well might Verres have returned to Sicily:* Gaius Verres, Roman governor of Sicily (B.C. 74–71) was charged with oppression and extortion and prosecuted by Cicero in a famous trial.

799, l. 34, *To the Printer of the "Public Advertiser"*: This address to the king caused very great public excitement. Though 1750 additional copies of the *Public Advertiser* were published on this occasion, the whole edition was exhausted within a few hours after publication. It was for printing this letter that the editor was brought to trial.

799, l. 28, *the pernicious lessons you received in your youth:* The reference here is to the dominance of George III while he was Prince of Wales by his mother and her favourite, the Earl of Bute.

800, l. 34, *When you affectedly renounced the name of Englishman:* George III in his speech to Parliament on his accession had said, "Born and educated in this country, I glory in the name of Briton." His initial popularity was largely owing to the fact here stated, since both George I and George II had been born in Germany. The use of the word "Briton" instead of "Englishman" had become frequent after the legislative union of England and Scotland in 1707, but it was often objected to as truckling to the prejudices of the Scotch. The reference of this paragraph, and especially of the last sentence, is to the influence of the Scottish Lord Bute upon George III during his minority.

800, l. 38, *A man, not very honourably distinguished:* In the next few paragraphs particularly, and to some extent throughout this whole letter, "Junius" makes frequent references to John Wilkes (1727–97), a brilliant demagogue who is conspicuous in the history of the time. In spite of personal profligacy, Wilkes succeeded by reason of his wit, his personal charm, and his political shrewdness in attaining great popularity. He had entered the House of Commons in 1755 but had been disappointed of political preferment by Lord Bute. He then turned to journalism in order to attack the government. In 1762 he began publication of the *North Briton*, the editor of which is ironically represented as a Scotchman who exults in the influence of his countrymen in the government of Great Britain. This appeal to English national prejudice was very successful for a time and provoked the government to reprisals. The opportunity came with No. 45, which charged the king with falsehood in his speech from the throne on the Treaty of Peace of 1763. Wilkes was arrested but claimed immunity as a member of Parliament and succeeded in obtaining damages for illegal imprisonment. Then the House expelled him as the author of a seditious libel. In 1768 Wilkes was re-elected to Parliament but was ordered arrested as an outlaw because of his libels. Riots followed in London, where he became a hero with the mob. Once more he was expelled from the House, but was re-elected as often as he was excluded. When this letter was written, Wilkes was in prison. "Junius," though not a partisan of Wilkes, supported the latter's claim to his seat in Parliament.

802, l. 10, *They complained of an act of the legislature:* The Stamp Act, 1765, and the tax on tea and various other imports, 1767, were stirring up the American colonies at this time.

803, l. 33, *that part of our history when the unhappy Charles:* In 1646 Charles I, after his armies had been defeated in England, threw himself on the protection of the Scottish army, his own countrymen, since the Stuarts had been Kings of Scotland before they were Kings of England. He was afterwards handed over to his rebellious subjects in England.

803, l. 7, *the uses to which one part of the army has been too frequently applied:* On May 10, 1768, several battalions of foot-guards had dispersed a great crowd that had gathered opposite the King's Bench Prison where Wilkes was at this time imprisoned. During the rioting fourteen civilians were killed and more were wounded.

804, l. 32, *the Long Parliament:* the Parliament that met for the first time in November, 1640, and that afterwards conducted the rebellion against Charles I.

EDMUND BURKE

BIBLIOGRAPHY

Burke's *Works* have been several times published. Among the more accessible editions are the following:

Works, 9 vols., 1839; revised ed., 12 vols., 1865–67, and 1894.
Works and Correspondence, 8 vols., 1852.
Works, 8 vols., Bohn Ed., 1854, 1855.
Complete Works, 6 vols., ed. by H. H. Willis and F. W. Raffety, World's Classics, 1906–08.
Select Works, 3 vols., ed. by E. J. Payne, 1874–78 and 1892–98.
Correspondence between 1744 and 1797, ed. by Earl Fitzwilliam and Sir R. Bourke, 4 vols., 1844.
There are many editions of the speech, *On Conciliation with America*. *American Speeches and Letters* were edited for Everyman's Library by H. Law in 1908.
Reflections on the Revolution in France has been edited by F. G. Selby, 1890; G. Sampson, 1905; A. J. Grieve for Everyman's Library, 1910.

Biographical and critical works are numerous:

R. Bisset, *The Life of Edmund Burke*, 1798; 3 vols., 1800.
Sir James Prior, *Memoir of the Life and Character of the Rt. Hon. E. Burke*, 1824, 1878.
G. Croly, *A Memoir of the Political Life of the Rt. Hon. E. Burke*, 1840.
T. McKnight, *History of the Life and Times of Edmund Burke*, 3 vols., 1858–60.
J. Morley, *Edmund Burke. A Historical Study*, 1867, 1893.
J. Morley, *Burke*, E. M. of L., 1879, 1888.
T. D. Pillans, *Edmund Burke, Apostle of Justice and Liberty*, 1905.
J. MacCunn, *The Political Philosophy of Burke*, 1913.
F. Meusel, *Edmund Burke und die französische Revolution*, 1913.
Bertram Newman, *Edmund Burke*, 1927.
J. Rowley, *Wordsworth and Other Essays*, 1927.
Alfred Cobban, *Edmund Burke and the Revolt against the Eighteenth Century*, 1929.
Arthur A. Baumann, *Burke: the Founder of Conservatism. A Study*, 1929.
R. H. Murray, *Edmund Burke. A Biography*, 1931.
E. Dowden, *The French Revolution and English Literature*, 1897, presents the political background of Burke's *Reflections*.

NOTES

REFLECTIONS ON THE REVOLUTION IN FRANCE

807, l. 1, *Reflections on the Revolution in France:* As Burke explained in a preliminary note, these *Reflections* grew out of a letter to a young Frenchman, P. M. Dupont, who had written to ask his opinion on the events of 1789. Burke's reply grew under his hand so that it was not published until 1790.

807, l. 8, *they look abroad:* the English supporters of the French Revolution, especially the members of the Revolution Society, who had listened with approbation to a sermon by the Reverend Richard Price, a non-conformist minister, in which the actions of the French revolutionists had been praised. It had been the annual custom of this society to celebrate November 4, the anniversary of the landing of William of Orange, and the outbreak of the Revolution of 1688. At this time Dr. Price had asserted in his sermon (which had been published under the title, *A Discourse on the Love of our Country*) that the French Revolution, which had begun with the destruction of the Bastille on July 14, 1789, was in conformity with the principles of the English Revolution, a century earlier. Burke absolutely denied this statement and pointed out that the English Revolution had been in support of the constitution, endangered by the illegal practices of James II, while the French aimed to subvert the foundations of state, church, and society.

807, l. 41, *Illa se jactet... regnet* (Virgil, *Æneid*, I, 140, 141): "In that hall let Æolus vaunt himself and rule in the closed prison-house of the winds."

807, l. 44, *a Levanter:* a strong easterly wind in the Mediterranean.

809, l. 3, *Liceat perire poetis* (Horace, *A. P.*, 466): "Poets should be permitted to perish as they please."

809, l. 5, *Ardentem frigidus Ætnam insiluit* (*Ib.*, 465, 466): "In cold blood he leaped into fiery Etna." The reference is to Empedocles, who is said to have perished by jumping into the crater of Mount Etna, in Sicily. One of his slippers was reported to have been cast forth afterwards, by an eruption.

809, l. 35, *cum perimit sævos... tyrannos* (Juvenal, VII, 151): "When the sing-song class destroys the cruel tyrants." The reference is to school boys reciting in a sing-song fashion.

810, l. 13, *the Old Jewry:* the London street on which stood the meeting-house in which Dr. Price had preached the sermon to which Burke makes frequent mention.

810, l. 37, "*Lord, now lettest thou...*" (St. Luke, II, 29, 30): The opening words of the Song of Simeon, commonly called *Nunc dimittis* (so referred to by Burke later) from the opening words of the Latin version. It is used in Evening Prayer in the Church of England.

811, l. 5, *the Rev. Hugh Peters:* an Independent preacher, once prominent in Salem, Massachusetts, who supported Cromwell in the Civil War and was put to death on the Restoration in 1660 for having abetted the killing of Charles I. It must be remembered that English public opinion in the eighteenth century almost unanimously condemned the execution of King Charles. Burke's implication is that Price's sentiments are not those of the patriots of 1688 but those of the regicides of 1649.

811, l. 48, *a foreign republic:* i.e., Paris, the newly formed government of which was vested in sixty departments ruled by the revolutionary clubs.

812, l. 20, *Catiline... Cethegus:* leaders of a Roman rebellion which Cicero put down. They were denounced by Cicero in his *Orations against Catiline* as monsters of wickedness.

812, l. 51, *explode:* the Latin sense of driving from the stage by noisily expressed disapprobation: opposite of *applaud*.

812, l. 5, *nec color imperii... senatus* (Lucan, *Pharsalia*, ix, 207): Translated by the words which immediately precede.

812, l. 28, *un beau jour:* "A beautiful day." Oct. 6, 1789, to the events of which day Burke refers at length a little later.

812, l. 31, "*that the vessel of the state*": a translation of Mirabeau's words.

813, l. 25, *our ordinary of Newgate:* the prison chaplain.

813, l. 35, *lèse nation:* "Treason against the nation," a phrase modelled after *lèse majesté*, "treason against the king."

813, l. 45, "*the balm of hurt minds*": Shakespeare, *Macbeth*, II, 2, 30.

814, l. 42, *the projected fifth monarchy:* A small party of fanatics during the English civil wars tried to establish by force the "fifth monarchy" or reign of Christ in the world. See Daniel, II, esp. v. 44. The implication is that the French revolutionists were more radical even than Cromwell, who had put down the Fifth Monarchy Men. *Cf.* Pepys's *Diary*, pp. 101 ff.

814, l. 4, *is to be seen hereafter:* Burke's prediction came true about three years later when the French king and queen were guillotined.

816, l. 25, *Non satis est pulchra... sunto* (Hor., *A. P.*, 99): "It is not enough that poems be beautiful in form; they must have charm."

816, 33, *cast into the mire: Cf.* St. Matt., VII, 6.

A LETTER TO A NOBLE LORD

817, Title, *A Letter from the Right Hon. Edmund Burke to a Noble Lord:* In 1794, after the conclusion of the Hastings trial, Burke retired from Parliament. The government had intended to reward his long services to the public by elevating him to the peerage. However, in August of the same year, his only son, Richard, died. Because a hereditary peerage would have been an empty honour to a childless old man, Pitt gave him instead a pension of £1200 a year from the Civil List, supplemented by £2500 from the Crown funds. Since Burke was in financial distress, these grants were particularly welcome in themselves as well as in recognition of his public services. The opposition, however, attacked them on the grounds that they had been made without the consent of Parliament, and in defiance of the need for economic reform. The Duke of Bedford and the Earl of Lauderdale were particularly loud in their protests. To the former, Burke addressed in 1796 this reply.

817, l. 39, *the Duke of Orleans:* The cousin of Louis XVI, who renounced his title and assumed the name of Philip Égalité; he became a member of the Constituent Assembly and concurred in the execution of the king. He was himself guillotined in 1793.

817, l. 40, *Citizen Brissot:* Girondist leader, executed when the moderate revolutionary party fell from power in 1793. By associating the names of the Duke of Bedford and the Earl of Lauderdale with those of the Duke of Orleans and Brissot, Burke implies that these British peers were animated by opposition to the English constitution similar to that which actuated the apostate Bourbon and the other revolutionary leaders in France. Here and elsewhere he suggests that they might suffer the same fate if they were successful in their revolutionary propaganda.

817, l. 54, *the Priestleys and the Paines:* Dr. Joseph Priestley (1733–1804), English clergyman and chemist. Because of his revolutionary sympathies he had migrated to America in 1794. For Thomas Paine see the Introduction to the selections from *The Rights of Man*, p. 837. He had fled to France and become a member of the Convention.

817, l. 7, *Lord Grenville:* He had defended Burke's pension when it was attacked in the House of Lords.

817, l. 30, *like old John Zisca's:* John Zisca (1360?–1424), the Bohemian Hussite, who is said to have desired that after his death his skin should be make into drumheads.

817, l. 41, *Lord Verulam:* better known as Lord Bacon.

818, l. 10, *unplumb the dead:* That is, remove from their lead coffins.

818, l. 31, *the heaviest of all calamities:* the death of his son, in whom all his hopes had been centred.

818, l. 7, *Corresponding Society:* The London Corresponding Society was a radical organization formed in 1792 by Thomas Hardy. It rapidly grew in numbers and importance until checked by the rising tide of anti-French feeling excited by the Reign of Terror.

818, l. 52, *The Dukes and Earls of Brentford:* The allusion is to the two Kings of Brentford, twin characters in *The Rehearsal* (1671), a satiric play by the Duke of Buckingham and others. These two kings always appear together in the play and act alike. Brentford is a suburb of London.

819, l. 15, *quantum meruit:* "How much did he deserve?" a legal phrase used in connection with suits about professional services.

819, l. 52, *"from its horrid hair..."*: Milton, *Par. Lost*, II, 710.

819, l. 53, *"with fear of change...:"* *Ib.*, I, 598.

820, l. 36, *a sort of national convention:* At the time of the Anti-Popery riots of 1780, tumultuous crowds threatened Parliament. Burke compares them to the French National Convention.

820, l. 47, *Lord North:* Prime Minister, 1770–1782.

820, l. 5, *Ipse diem... unda* (Virgil, *Æneid*, III, 201, 202): "Palinurus himself says that he does not distinguish day from night in the sky or remember his way in the midst of the waves."

822, l. 43, *Hamlet says:* Shakespeare, *Hamlet*, III, 4, 48.

823, l. 10, *St. Stephen's chapel:* The House of Commons, so called because it met in a hall originally built as a chapel dedicated to St. Stephen.

824, l. 6, *Nitor in adversum* (Ovid, *Metamorphoses*, II, 72): "I struggle."

825, l. 25, *sans-culottes:* "Fellows without breeches." The extreme republicans who abandoned the aristocratic short breeches of the old régime for the new pantaloons.

825, l. 33, *Mr. Thelwall's lecture:* John Thelwall was a political agitator of the time.

825, l. 39, *Senatus consultum:* "A decree of the senate."

825, l. 40, *Cludere ludum impudentiæ jussit* (Tacitus, *De Oratoribus*, 35): "He gave orders to close the school of shamelessness."

826, l. 20, *"the stuff of which his dreams are made"*: *Cf.* Shakespeare, *The Tempest*, IV, 1, 156, 157:

"We are such stuff
As dreams are made on,"

826, l. 30, *"he lies floating many a rood"*: Milton, *Par. Lost*, I, 196.

826, l. 28, *the Garters, and Norroys... and Rouge Dragons:* officers of the Herald's College in England.

826, l. 49, *Guillim, Edmondson, and Collins:* writers on heraldry and the English peerage.

830, l. 47, *Dum domus Æneæ... habebit* (Virgil, *Æneid*, IX, 448, 449): "While the race of Æneus shall dwell on the immovable rock of the Capitol, and the Roman Father shall maintain the sovereignty."

830, l. 32, *Ça ira:* "That shall go on," a song popular among the French revolutionists, so called from its refrain.

831, l. 40, *douce humanité:* "Sweet humanity" or "human kindness."

831, l. 2, *mauvais plaisant:* "Mischievous wag."

832, l. 23, "*the compunctious visitings of nature*": *Macbeth,* I, 5, 46.

832, l. 16, *Harrington's seven different forms of republics:* James Harrington (1611–77), radical political theorist, published in 1646, *Oceana,* in which there is both political allegory and speculation.

832, l. 22, *Abbé Sieyès:* a French churchman who supported the Revolution.

832, l. 31, *boue de Paris:* "Paris mud."

833, l. 17, *Woburn Abbey:* The country home of the Duke of Bedford, originally a monastery; it had been granted to the head of the Russell family after the dissolution.

833, l. 20, *Covent Garden:* a square in London, originally the property of a convent (the name is a corruption of *convent garden*) about which the Dukes of Bedford have large holdings of real estate, which came into their possession in the sixteenth century. Inigo Jones, the famous architect, designed a number of the buildings. The neighbourhood was much frequented by prostitutes; see further references below.

833, l. 26, *per antiphrasin:* "Through expression by opposites." *Cimento* in Italian means "experiment." Such revolutionary chemists as Morveau and Hassenfratz will not "cement" stones together as the result of their experiment but will do exactly the opposite.

833, l. 5, *Condorcet's:* The Marquis de Condorcet, famous philosopher and mathematician, was a member of the Girondist, or moderate, French revolutionary group.

833, l. 22, *Marquis of Tavistock:* one of the titles of the Duke of Bedford.

833, l. 35, *Legendre:* famous contemporary French geometrician.

833, l. 54, *Pleas'd to the last...*: Pope, *Essay on Man,* ll. 83, 84.

834, l. 12, *Lord Keppel* (1725–1786): Vice admiral of the British navy; he was defeated in battle with the French in 1778, was tried for neglect of duty and acquitted. Later he was made First Lord of the Admiralty and a viscount.

836, l. 7, *Grotius:* Hugo Grotius (1583–1645), well-known Dutch writer on international law.

836, l. 17, *the house of Nassau:* the family of William III of England. When Burke wrote, the Prince of Orange had been expelled from Holland by the French, and the Austrian Netherlands (now Belgium) had also been overrun.

THOMAS PAINE

BIBLIOGRAPHY

The most available edition of Paine's works is *The Writings of Thomas Paine,* ed. by M. D. Conway, 4 vols., 1894–96.

W. M. Van der Weyde, *The Life and Works of Thomas Paine,* 10 vols., 1925.

The Rights of Man is included in Everyman's Library.

Selections from the Works of Thomas Paine, with Introduction by A. W. Peach, 1928.

Most of the lives of Paine are partisan documents; the early ones were written by his enemies, and the later ones (that of Conway especially), by enthusiastic admirers.

"Francis Oldys" [George Chalmers], *The Life of Thomas Pain* [*sic*], 1791.

James Cheetham, *Life of Thomas Paine,* 1809.

M. D. Conway, *The Life of Thomas Paine,* 2 vols., 1892.

F. J. Gould, *Thomas Paine,* 1925.

M. A. Best, *Thomas Paine, Prophet and Martyr of Democracy,* 1927.

Among critical works the following are important:

J. M. Robertson, *Thomas Paine. An Investigation,* 1888.

Kingsley Martin, *Thomas Paine,* Fabian Society Tract, No. 217, 1925.

See also Sir Leslie Stephen, *History of English Thought in the Eighteenth Century,* 2 vols., 1876.

Harry Hayden Clark, "Thomas Paine's Relation to Voltaire and Rousseau," *Rev. Anglo-américaine,* 9:305–18 and 393–405, 1932.

Harry Hayden Clark, "Toward a Reinterpretation of Thomas Paine," *Am. Lit.,* 5:133–45, 1933.

Harry Hayden Clark, "An Historical Interpretation of Thomas Paine's Religion," *Univ. of Calif. Chron.,* 35:56–87, 1933.

Harry Hayden Clark, "Thomas Paine's Theories of Rhetoric," *Transactions of the Wis. Acad. of Sciences, Arts, and Letters,* 28:307–39, 1933.

NOTES

839, l. 50, *"Othello's occupation's gone!"*: Shakespeare, *Othello,* III, 3, 357.

839, l, 9, *Among the few who fell...*: written at the close of the year 1790, before the Reign of Terror.

839, l. 13, *that long, cold-blooded, unabated revenge... the affair of 1745:* After the suppression of the Stuart rising in Scotland led by "Bonny Prince Charlie" (or the "Young Pretender" as he was called by his enemies), the Duke of Cumberland, second son of George II, executed a terrible vengeance on the rebellious Highlanders.

839, l. 25, *a madman, like the person called Lord G[eorge] G[ordon]*: After the passage in 1778 of a law which relieved Roman Catholics from some of the religious and civil disabilities from which they had suffered in England since the Reformation, and especially since the Revolution of 1688, there was an outbreak of religious prejudice that culminated in the "No Popery" riots of 1780. In June of that year, Lord George Gordon, President of the Protestant Association, headed a great mob, which protested against all indulgence to Roman Catholics. For nearly four days London was in the hands of the mob which opened the prisons and did enormous damage to property. Gordon was afterward acquitted of high treason but was imprisoned for libel until his death in 1793. Recollection of the Gordon Riots was a strong factor at this time in marshalling popular sentiment against the French Revolution; consequently Paine tried to minimize their importance.

840, l. 10, *As Mr. Burke has passed over... the enemies of the Revolution...* : Paine here gives an extended account of the outbreak of the French Revolution, which is omitted as less important than the following part of this extract.

WILLIAM GODWIN

BIBLIOGRAPHY

An Inquiry Concerning Political Justice has not appeared in full since the fourth edition of 1842. An abridged edition was edited by R. A. Preston, 2 vols., 1926.

Among biographical and critical works the following will be found useful:

C. K. Paul, *William Godwin: His Friends and Contemporaries*, 2 vols., 1876.
E. Dowden, "Theorists of Revolution," in *The French Revolution and English Literature*, 1897.
H. Saitzeff, *William Godwin und die Anfänge des Anarchismus im XVIII Jahrhundert*, 1907.
P. Ramus, *William Godwin der Theoretiker des kommunistischen Anarchismus*, 1907.
R. Gourg, *William Godwin: sa vie, ses œuvres principales*, 1908.
H. N. Brailsford, *Shelley, Godwin, and their Circle*, Home University Library, 1913.
Henri Roussin, *William Godwin*, 1913.
F. K. Brown, *The Life of William Godwin*, 1926.

NOTES

846, l. 4, *the illustrious Archbishop of Cambrai:* François de Salagnac de La Mothe-Fénelon (1651–1715), Archbishop of Cambrai, commonly known by his last name, Fénelon, was the author of *Télémaque* (1699), a romance which deals with the education of Telemachus, the son of Ulysses. Fénelon had been intrusted with the education of the Duke of Burgundy and other princes of the blood royal. This work, together with the *Fables* and the *Dialogues of the Dead*, was written for his royal pupils. The benevolence of Fénelon appealed especially to Godwin.

850, l. 21, *Clément, Ravaillac, Damiens, and Gerard:* famous for their assassination or their attempted assassination of kings. The first killed Henry III of France; the second killed Henry IV of France; the third tried to kill Louis XV, and the fourth killed William of Orange (William the Silent).

850, l. 27, *the fires of Smithfield:* Smithfield in London was formerly outside the city walls. During the reign of Queen Mary many Protestants were burned here.

850, l. 28, *the daggers of Saint Bartholomew:* the massacre of St. Bartholomew, August 24, 1572, when thousands of Huguenots were killed in France.

850, l. 29, *Gunpowder Treason:* the famous Gunpowder Plot to blow up the Parliament House on November 5, 1605, and kill James I and the whole English Parliament. Guy Fawkes Day, as it is commonly called, was celebrated on November 5 every year as a time of Protestant rejoicing and anti-Catholic demonstration.

850, l. 3, *Servetus:* Michael Servetus was burned in 1553 by Protestants because he denied the Trinity. John Calvin, the leader of the Calvinists, was largely instrumental in his condemnation.

854, l. 45, "*at a time when neither the people of France...*": Quoted inexactly from the opening paragraph of Thomas Paine's *The Rights of Man*.

GEORGE CRABBE

BIBLIOGRAPHY

Poetical Works, with his Letters and Journals and his Life by his Son, 8 vols., 1834. The same in 1 vol., 1901.
Poems, ed. A. W. Ward, 3 vols. 1905–07.
Poetical Works, ed. A. J. and R. M. Carlyle, 1914.

Biography and criticism:
F. Jeffrey in the *Edinburgh Review:* April, 1808; April, 1810; November, 1812; July, 1819.
G. Saintsbury: *Essays in English Literature, 1780–1860*, 1890.
L. Stephen: *Hours in a Library*, 1892, vol. II.
P. E. More: *Shelburne Essays*, First Series, 1906.
G. E. Woodberry: *Makers of Literature*, 1901.
A. Ainger: *Crabbe*, in English Men of Letters Series, 1903.
C. K. Shorter: *Immortal Memories*, 1907.
R. Huchon: *George Crabbe and His Times*, trans. Frederick Clarke, 1907.
F. J. F. Jackson: *Social Life in England*, 1916.
L. J. Wylie: *Social Studies in English Literature*, Boston, 1916.
J. Patton: *The English Village*, 1919.

NOTES

THE VILLAGE

857, l. 2, *swains:* It is characteristic of the several ways in which Crabbe mingled conservatism with his innovations that he retained this name for the rural labourer, which had grown hackneyed in the poetic diction of the previous century, even while doing his utmost to change the word's connotation.

857, l. 12, *Corydons:* a conventional name for lovers in pastoral poetry.

857, l. 15, *Mincio's banks:* The reference is to the banks of the Mincius in Italy, not far from Mantua, where Virgil was born and where he lived during the reign of the Emperor Augustus. Tityrus, who stands for the poet himself, is one of the two speakers in Virgil's first Eclogue.

857, l. 27, *honest Duck:* Stephen Duck, 1705–1756, a rural poet of considerable powers whose account of country life — especially in his poem *The Thresher's Labour* — lost nothing in enthusiasm because he knew the facts.

857, l. 49, *frowning coast:* the coast of Suffolk near the village of Aldeburgh where Crabbe was born.

858, l. 69, *thistles:* The list of "rank weeds" that follows may remind one that Crabbe was an amateur botanist.

858, l. 89, *lawless merchant:* smuggler.

858, l. 114, *septennial bribe:* given by candidates for Parliament. See Johnson's *The Vanity of Human Wishes*, l. 97, and note.

858, l. 122, *fled:* to London.

860, l. 282, *potent quack:* The anger in which this portrait is drawn may be due to the fact that Crabbe had himself worked for a time as physician in his native village.

860, l. 303, *passing rich*... : Quoted from Goldsmith's *The Deserted Village*, l. 142.

861, l. 326, *Churchwarden:* His duties included the collection of tithes, as those of the overseer did the collection of rents.

861, l. 327, *farmer:* in England usually one who leases or rents the land he works from a landed proprietor. He may be a person of some local importance.

PETER GRIMES

862, l. 115, *hatchway:* an opening in the deck of a ship or boat giving access to the decks below or to the hold.

863, l. 155, *hall:* The trial would be conducted by the local justice of the peace in the "hall" or main room of his private house.

863, l. 181, *neap:* lowest.

863, l. 208, *reach:* a straight course between two bends of a river.

WILLIAM COWPER

BIBLIOGRAPHY

Works, 15 vols., with Life, by R. Southey, 1836, 1837.
Poems, ed. by H. S. Mitford, 1906.
Letters, sel. and ed. by E. V. Lucas, 1908, 1911.
Letters, sel. and ed. by W. Hadley, 1925.
G. Smith, *Cowper* (English Men of Letters Series), 1880.
T. Wright, *The Life of William Cowper*, 1921.
Hugh I'Anson Fausset, *William Cowper*, 1928.
D. Cecil, *The Stricken Deer*, 1929.

NOTES

RETIREMENT

867, Motto, ... *studiis... oti:* "Flourishing in the pursuits of inglorious ease."

867, l. 1, *Hackney'd:* worn out.

869, l. 227, *creature:* instead of the Creator.

870, l. 234, *Strait'ning:* restricting.

870, l. 279, *Heberden:* a famous English physician, 1710–1801.

870, l. 283, *comes:* The following picture of a person "melancholy-mad" is obviously drawn from Cowper's own experience.

871, l. 421, *balks:* strips of unploughed land between cultivated fields in "open-field" farming.

872, l. 467, *cross:* mount.

872, l. 490, *milestone:* measuring from the centre of London.

872, l. 516, *Tunbridge Wells:* a fashionable resort in the south of England.

873, l. 521, *caravans:* large covered wagons.

873, l. 521, *hoys:* small sloop-rigged vessels.

873, l. 559, *rents:* the raising of ready money upon an heir's "expectations."

873, l. 571, *Cobham's groves:* the estate of Viscount Cobham at Stowe, described by Pope, *Moral Essays*, Epistle IV, ll. 70–75.

873, l. 572, *describes:* in his *Windsor Forest.*

873, l. 598, *Granby:* John Manners, Marquis of Granby, 1721–1770, English hero of the Seven Years' War.

874, l. 687, *his:* Voltaire built a church at Ferney in 1760, with the inscription, *Deo erexit Voltaire.*

875, l. 739, *Frenchman:* La Bruyère, echoing J. B. Balzac.

875, l. 767, *king:* David. *Cf.* I Samuel, 19–25.

875, l. 804, *Ouse:* a small stream flowing through Olney, in Buckinghamshire.

YARDLEY OAK

876, l. 5, *excoriate:* barkless. This word and "deform" are past participles, the *-ed* being omitted in imitation of Milton.

876, l. 10, *Druids:* of course not in any strict sense to be regarded as "forefathers" of the English.

877, l. 12, *act:* the death of Christ.

877, l. 34, *instinct:* filled, charged.

877, l. 35, *twins:* Castor and Pollux, born from an egg.

877, l. 41, *Dodona:* the oracle which spoke through rustling oak leaves, interpreted by priests.

877, l. 53, *champaign:* field.

877, l. 85, *tone:* health.

877, l. 96, *admiral:* flag-ship. *Cf. Paradise Lost,* I, 292–94.

877, l. 96, *tortuous arms:* twisted boughs.

878, l. 103, *honours:* political office bought with money gained from the sale of timber.

878, l. 110, *Embowell'd:* the same as *disembowelled.*

878, l. 116, *sincere:* whole, of one piece.

878, l. 144, *Thou:* The passage extending from here through l. 166 was crossed through in the manuscript and so was not printed by the poet Hayley in his first edition of the poem. It was first printed in 1900. The passage within quotation marks is taken from Cowper's translation of the *Iliad*, VI, ll. 175–79.

878, l. 145, *bourn:* limit or goal.

878, l. 152, *Jacob:* See Gen., 47:7–9.

878, l. 154, *prediluvian:* before the flood.

878, l. 155, *theirs:* the word "years" or "days" is to be understood.

878, l. 162, *Mæonian:* Homer.

878, l. 171, *articulation:* speech.

THE TASK

879, l. 10, *inn:* from which the rural mail was redistributed.

879, l. 27, *Snore:* referring to the inaction of the British troops in the war with the American Colonies. Cowper began *The Task* in the summer of 1783. When he wrote this line he may not have heard of the treaty of peace between England and America, signed at Paris in September of that year.

879, l. 28, *India:* Cowper is probably thinking of the First Mahratta War, which ended in 1782.

879, l. 49, *placemen:* office-holders.

879, l. 50, *folio:* the newspaper.

880, l. 78, *wilderness:* i.e., of advertisements.

880, l. 85, *Ethereal journeys:* The first ascents in a balloon were made in 1783.

880, l. 86, *Katterfelto:* a quack-doctor who, in 1782, advertised in the newspapers under the heading, "Wonders! Wonders! Wonders!"

880, l. 107, *expatiates:* roams. Cowper is thinking here less of newspapers than of the narratives of sea voyages such as those of Cook and Anson, which he read eagerly.

881, l. 190, *Sabine bard:* Horace, in *Satires*, II, ii, 65.

881, l. 195, *tragic:* because secured by the deaths of animals.

881, l. 221, *mast:* in later editions, *mace.* A cue.

881, l. 227, *back-string:* a leading-string, by which a child is supported while learning to walk.

882, l. 313, *lands:* ploughed fields.

883, l. 437, *Plash'd:* with interwoven branches.

884, l. 460, *ebriety:* drunkenness.

884, l. 473, *Indian fume:* tobacco smoke.

884, l. 504, *excise:* an inland tax, in this case upon liquor.

884, l. 516, *poetic prose:* in his *Arcadia.*

885, l. 533, *tramontane:* barbarous, eccentric, or naïve.

885, l. 540, *lappets:* flaps or pendants on a head-dress.

885, l. 579, *fatal:* determined by fate. The belief in steady and inevitable deterioration here expressed was common in the ancient world and Middle Ages, but in Cowper's time was giving way before the modern theory of progress.

885, l. 596, *magisterial sword:* symbol of his office as magistrate or justice of the peace.

885, l. 603, *ghostly:* spiritually.

886, l. 681, *factories:* These lines were written at the beginning of the "Industrial Revolution."

886, l. 728, *Chertsey's:* a village on the Thames, scene of Cowley's retirement.

887, l. 738, *obtains:* is true.

887, l. 748, *villas:* the exodus from London to the suburbs began in Cowper's time.

887, l. 765, *Frenchman's darling:* mignonette.

ON THE RECEIPT OF MY MOTHER'S PICTURE

888, l. 53, *pastoral house:* the parsonage at Great Berkhamstead.

888, l. 67, *humour:* caprice, whim.

889, l. 97, "*Where... roar*": misquoted from Garth's *The Dispensary*, canto 3, l. 226.

889, l. 99, *side:* Cowper's father died in 1756.

889, l. 108, *birth:* On his mother's side Cowper was in fact a descendant of Henry VII.

TO MARY

889, l. 1, *twentieth year:* since the attack of insanity which had prevented Cowper's marriage to Mrs. Unwin.

889, l. 21, *indistinct expressions:* caused by paralysis.

890, l. 41, *Such:* This stanza, taken from the original manuscript, was not published until 1900.

THE CASTAWAY

890, l. 3, *destin'd:* doomed.

890, l. 7, *chief:* George, Lord Anson, 1697–1762.

LETTERS

891, l. 1, *William Unwin:* only son of Mrs. Mary Unwin.

891, l. 12, *biographies: The Lives of the Poets*, just beginning to appear.

892, l. 28, *four quires:* twenty-four sheets of writing paper make a quire. This was the manuscript of *The Task.*

892, l. 32, *points:* punctuation.

892, l. 53, *compliment: The Winter Evening*, 427, 428.

892, l. 3, *Mr. Throckmorton: The Task*, I, 262.

892, l. 4, *Mr. Smith:* the anonymous benefactor of the poor at Olney.

893, l. 1, *John Newton:* an evangelical clergyman of whom Cowper stood usually in awe. In a recent letter he had criticized the manuscript of *The Task* adversely — as Cowper thought, because his advice had not been previously asked about it.

893, l. 25, *volume:* that of 1782.
893, l. 49, *Olio:* miscellany.
893, l. 16, "*The Time-piece*": the title of the second book of *The Task.*
893, l. 49, *Lady Hesketh:* Cowper's cousin Harriet, whom he had not seen for twenty years.
894, l. 37, *another:* His *Homer* was not published until 1791.
894, l. 43, *proposals:* advance advertisements of a book published by subscription.
895, l. 41, *Troy:* at work upon his translation of Homer.
896, l. 16, *fifty-four:* from London stone.
896, l. 37, *Newport:* five miles from Olney.

ROBERT BURNS

BIBLIOGRAPHY

Among the more accessible of the numerous editions are the following:

The Works of Robert Burns, ed. by W. Scott Douglas, 6 vols., 1877–79.
The Complete Writings of Robert Burns, with an Essay by W. E. Henley, Introduction by John Buchan; the Letters ed. by F. H. Allen, 10 vols., 1926, 1927.
The Poetical Works of Robert Burns, ed. with a Memoir by G. A. Aitken, 3 vols, 1893.
The Poems of Robert Burns, ed. by Andrew Lang and W. A. Craigie, 1896.
The Complete Poetical Works of Robert Burns, ed. by J. L. Robertson, 3 vols., 1896.
The Poetry of Robert Burns, ed. by W. E. Henley and T. F. Henderson, 4 vols., 1896, 1897. Condensed in Cambridge Ed., 1897.
Complete Poetical Works of Robert Burns, with an Appreciation by Lord Rosebery, 1902.
Poetical Works of Robert Burns, ed with Life and Notes by William Wallace, 1902.
The Poetical Works of Robert Burns, ed. with Biographical Introduction by Charles Annandale, 4 vols., 1913.
Robert Burns: Poems, Epistles, Songs, Epigrams, and Epitaphs, ed. by Charles S. Dougall, 1927.
The Letters of Robert Burns, ed. by J. DeLancy Ferguson, 2 vols., 1931.

Biography and Criticism:

J. Cuthbertson, *Complete Glossary to the Poetry and Prose of Robert Burns*, 1886.
J. Stuart Blackie, *Life of Robert Burns* (Great Writers Series), 1888.
A. Angellier, *Robert Burns: la vie et les œuvres*, 2 vols., 1893.
James C. Higgins, *Life of Robert Burns*, 1893.
W. A. Craigie, *A Primer of Burns*, 1896.
H. Molenaar, *Robert Burns' Beziehungen zur Litteratur*, 1899.
J. B. Reid, *A Complete Word and Phrase Concordance to the Poems and Songs of Robert Burns*, 1899.
T. F. Henderson, *Robert Burns* (Oxford Biographies), 1904.
William A. Neilson, *Robert Burns: How to Know Him*, 1917.
Duncan McNaught, *The Truth about Burns*, 1921.
Dudley Wright, *Robert Burns and Freemasonry*, 1921.
James L. Hughes, *The Real Robert Burns*, 1922.
Andrew Dakers, *Robert Burns, his Life and Genius*, 1923.
Jessie P. Findlay, *Footprints of Robert Burns*, 1923.
John Drinkwater, *Robert Burns: A Play*, 1925.
Sir James Crichton-Browne, *Burns from a New Point of View*, 1926.
Henry A. Kellow, *Burns and his Poetry*, 1927.
James D. Law, *A New and True Account of Robert Burns*, 1927.
Dudley Wright, *Robert Burns and his Masonic Circle*, 1929.
Catherine Carswell, *The Life of Robert Burns*, 1930.
A. Jamieson, *Burns and Religion*, 1931.
John D. Ross, *A Burns Handbook*, 1931.
A. A. Thomson, *The Burns We Love*, with a Foreword by G. K. Chesterton, 1931.
Franklin B. Snyder, *The Life of Robert Burns*, 1932.

NOTES

THE COTTER'S SATURDAY NIGHT

899, l. 1, *friend:* Robert Aiken, a lawyer of Ayr, one of Burns's earliest admirers.
899, l. 10, *sugh:* sough, the sound of the wind.
899, l. 12, *pleugh:* plough.

900, l. 21, *stacher:* stagger.
900, l. 22, *flichterin:* fluttering, as fledglings in the nest.
900, l. 23, *ingle:* hearth.
900, l. 26, *kiaugh:* anxiety.
900, l. 28, *Belyve:* soon.
900, l. 30, *tentie:* watchful.
900, l. 30, *rin:* run.
900, l. 35, *deposite:* Accent the first syllable.
900, l. 38, *spiers:* asks.
900, l. 40, *uncos:* uncommon things.
900, l. 48, *eydent:* diligent.
900, l. 49, *jauk:* dally.
900, l. 62, *hafflins:* half.
900, l. 64, *ben:* into the parlour.
900, l. 67, *cracks:* chats.
900, l. 69, *blate:* bashful.
900, l. 69, *laithfu':* sheepish.
900, l. 72, *lave:* rest.
901, l. 92, *parritch:* oatmeal porridge.
901, l. 93, *hawkie:* cow.
901, l. 94, *hallan:* partition wall.
901, l. 96, *weel-hained kebbuck:* well-saved cheese.
901, l. 96, *fell:* pungent.
901, l. 99, *towmond:* twelve-month.
901, l. 99, *sin' lint... bell:* since flax was in blossom.
901, l. 105, *lyart haffets:* gray locks.
901, l. 107, *wales:* chooses.
901, l. 113, *beets:* kindles.
901, l. 138, "*springs exulting...*": adapted from Pope's *Windsor Forest*, ll. 111, 112.
902, l. 166, "*An honest man...*": Pope's *Essay on Man*, l. 248.

THE HOLY FAIR

902, l. 4, *caller:* cool.
902, l. 5, *Muirs:* moors.
902, l. 7, *hirplin:* limping.
903, l. 12, *hizzies:* wenches.
903, l. 13, *skelpin:* hurrying.
903, l. 15, *lyart:* gray.
903, l. 22, *slaes:* sloes, the plum-like fruit of the blackthorn.
903, l. 34, *feck:* the bulk, or greater part.
903, l. 36, *screed:* rip or tear.
903, l. 42, *daffin:* larking.
903, l. 43, *Gin:* if.
903, l. 43, *runkled:* wrinkled.
903, l. 47, *sark:* shirt.
903, l. 50, *crowdie-time:* breakfast-time; literally, porridge-time.
903, l. 55, *gash:* wise.
903, l. 55, *graith:* gear.
903, l. 56, *hoddin:* trotting.
903, l. 59, *thrang:* crowded.
903, l. 61, *whang:* slice.
903, l. 62, *farls:* oat-cakes.
903, l. 63, *crump:* crisp.
903, l. 66, *glow'r:* stare.
903, l. 66, *black bonnet:* the elder taking the church collection.
903, l. 70, *dails:* planks.
903, l. 71, *bleth'rin:* talking nonsense.
903, l. 77, *tittlin jades:* whispering girls.
903, l. 79, *wabster:* weaver.
903, l. 84, *fyl'd:* dirtied.

903, l. 86, *swatch:* sample — of the "elect."
903, l. 91, *blest:* the line is quoted *verbatim* from the Scottish metrical version of Psalm 146.
903, l. 98, *loof:* the palm of the hand.
903, l. 102, *Moodie:* Alexander Moodie, 1722–1799, a local minister of great severity.
903, l. 102, *speels:* climbs.
903, l. 104, *Hornie:* Satan.
904, l. 122, *Smith:* George Smith, a moderate minister of the "New Light" party whom Burns approved of.
904, l. 138, *Peebles:* William Peebles, 1752–1826, a versifying divine, one of Burns's inveterate enemies.
904, l. 138, *water-fit:* river's mouth.
904, l. 141, *mim:* primly.
904, l. 143, *Cowgate:* a street in Mauchline.
904, l. 145, *Miller:* Alexander Miller, died 1804. His career in the ministry was ruined by the present passage.
904, l. 145, *niest:* next.
904, l. 146, *raibles:* gabbles.
904, l. 149, *birkie:* conceited fellow.
904, l. 150, *hums:* talks humbug.
904, l. 152, *hafflins-wise:* partly.
904, l. 154, *butt an' ben:* front and back.
904, l. 154, *change-house:* tavern.
904, l. 155, *yill-caup:* ale-cup.
904, l. 156, *bakes an' gills:* biscuits and whiskey.
904, l. 163, *Leeze me on:* dear to me is.
904, l. 165, *lear:* learning.
904, l. 166, *pangs:* crams.
904, l. 167, *penny-wheep:* small beer.
904, l. 170, *kittle:* tickle, incite.
904, l. 176, *leuk:* look.
904, l. 178, *neuk:* the ingle by the fire.
904, l. 184, *Russell:* John Russell, 1740–1817, a severe and hated schoolmaster and Calvinistic minister.
904, l. 191, *lowin:* flaming.
904, l. 193, *whun-stane:* whinstone.
904, l. 203, *cogs:* wooden cups.
904, l. 207, *dawds:* lumps.
905, l. 208, *gausie:* buxom.
905, l. 208, *gash:* complacent.
905, l. 210, *kebbuck:* cheese.
905, l. 217, *Waesucks:* alas.
905, l. 220, *melvie:* dust with meal.
905, l. 226, *tow:* rope.
905, l. 227, *jow:* "a verb which includes both the swinging motion and pealing sound of a large bell." Burns's note.
905, l. 228, *dow:* can.
905, l. 230, *slaps:* fence-openings.
905, l. 230, *blink:* moment.
905, l. 234, *crack:* chat.
905, l. 242, *houghmagandie:* fornication.

ADDRESS TO THE DEIL

905, l. 5, *Spairges... cootie:* splashes about the brimstone dish.
905, l. 11, *skelp:* strike.
905, l. 15, *lowin heugh's:* flaming pit is.
905, l. 18, *blate, nor scaur:* bashful nor timid.
905, l. 22, *Tirlin the kirks:* unroofing the churches.
906, l. 32, *douce:* sober.
906, l. 33, *yont the dyke:* beyond the wall.
906, l. 35, *boortrees:* elders.
906, l. 40, *lough:* lake.
906, l. 41, *rash-buss:* clump of rushes.

906, l. 42, *sugh:* sound of the wind.
906, l. 43, *nieve:* fist.
906, l. 45, *stoor:* hoarse.
906, l. 54, *howkit:* dug up.
906, l. 56, *kirn:* churn.
906, l. 59, *dawtit ... bill:* the favourite twelve-pint cow is as dry as the bull.
906, l. 62, *croose:* self-assured.
906, l. 64, *cantraip:* magic.
906, l. 66, *bit:* critical moment.
906, l. 67, *thowes:* thaws.
906, l. 73, *spunkies:* will-o'-the-wisps.
906, l. 91, *snick-drawing:* cheating.
906, l. 93, *brogue:* trick.
906, l. 95, *shog:* shake.
906, l. 98, *reekit ... gizz:* smoking clothes and singed wig.
906, l. 101, *sklented:* turned.
906, l. 107, *scaul:* scold — i.e., Job's wife.
906, l. 108, *ava:* of all.
906, l. 110, *fechtin:* fighting.
906, l. 113, *ding:* beat.
906, l. 113, *Lallan:* Lowland.
906, l. 117, *linkin:* tripping.
906, l. 119, *jinkin:* dodging.
906, l. 123, *aiblins:* perhaps.
906, l. 124, *stake:* gambler's chance.

TO A MOUSE

907, l. 1, *sleekit:* sleek.
907, l. 4, *bickering brattle:* scampering haste.
907, l. 6, *pattle:* plough-staff.
907, l. 13, *whyles:* at times.
907, l. 15, *A daimen icker in a thrave:* an occasional ear in twenty-four sheaves.
907, l. 17, *lave:* rest.
907, l. 20, *silly:* weak, useless.
907, l. 21, *big:* build.
907, l. 22, *foggage:* coarse grass.
907, l. 24, *snell:* biting.
907, l. 34, *But:* without.
907, l. 34, *hald:* property.
907, l. 35, *thole:* endure.
907, l. 36, *cranreuch:* hoarfrost.
907, l. 37, *no thy lane:* not alone.
907, l. 40, *Gang aft agley:* go oft astray.

TO A MOUNTAIN DAISY

907, l. 3, *stoure:* dust.
907, l. 6, *gem:* bud.
907, l. 20, *maun:* must.
907, l. 21, *bield:* shelter.
907, l. 23, *histie:* bare.
908, l. 39, *card:* compass-card.

GREEN GROW THE RASHES, O

908, l. 1, *rashes:* rushes.
908, l. 9, *war'ly:* worldly.
908, l. 13, *cannie:* happy.
908, l. 16, *tapsalteerie:* topsy-turvy.
908, l. 17, *douce:* sedate, sober.

THE RANTIN DOG, THE DADDIE O'T

908, l. 1, *babie-clouts:* baby-clothes.
908, l. 2, *tent:* heed, care for.
908, l. 4, *rantin:* roistering.
908, l. 5, *faut:* fault.
908, l. 6, *maut:* ale for the midwife.
908, l. 7, *ca't:* call it.
908, l. 9, *creepie-chair:* stool of repentance in church.
908, l. 13, *crack:* chat.
908, l. 13, *my lane:* alone.
908, l. 14, *fidgin fain:* tingle with pleasure.

WHISTLE O'ER THE LAVE O'T

908, l. 3, *spier:* ask.
908, l. 4, *lave o't:* rest of it.

EPISTLE TO JAMES SMITH

909, l. 1, *pawkie:* artful.
909, l. 2, *rief:* thieving.
909, l. 3, *warlock-breef:* wizard's control.
909, l. 5, *prief:* proof.
909, l. 14, *scrimpit:* saved.
909, l. 20, *barmie:* yeasty.
909, l. 21, *yerkit... sublime:* jerked aloft.
909, l. 27, *clash:* gossip.
909, l. 29, *fash:* trouble about.
909, l. 37, *my notions... sklent:* my mind has taken a turn.
909, l. 40, *Hoolie:* slowly.
909, l. 41, *red:* advise.
909, l. 41, *tent:* heed.
909, l. 52, *thrang:* busily.
909, l. 53, *howes:* dells.
909, l. 74, *speel'd:* climbed.
909, l. 75, *Eild:* old age.
910, l. 77, *hostin:* coughing.
910, l. 77, *hirplin:* hobbling.
910, l. 100, *But:* without.
910, l. 126, *rowth:* plenty.
910, l. 131, *yill:* ale.
910, l. 131, *cairds:* tinkers.
910, l. 132, *sconner:* sicken.
910, l. 141, *water-brose:* oatmeal porridge.
910, l. 141, *muslin-kail:* broth of water, barley, and greens.
910, l. 146, *lug:* ear.
910, l. 147, *jouk:* crouch.
910, l. 151, *douce:* soberly respectable.
910, l. 164, *Nae ferly:* no wonder.
910, l. 165, *ram-stam:* headstrong.
910, l. 172, *quat:* quit.

WILLIE BREW'D A PECK O' MAUT

911, l. 1, *fou:* full, drunk.
911, l. 2, *drappie:* small drop.
911, l. 4, *barley-bree:* barley-brew: i.e., ale or whiskey.
911, l. 7, *lee-lang:* live-long.
911, l. 12, *mae:* more.
911, l. 14, *lift:* sky.
911, l. 15, *wyle:* entice.
911, l. 18, *loun:* rascal.

TAM O' SHANTER

911, l. 1, *chapman billies:* pedlars.
911, l. 2, *drouthy:* thirsty.
911, l. 4, *tak the gate:* go home.
911, l. 5, *nappy:* strong ale.
911, l. 7, *Scots miles:* longer than the English.
911, l. 8, *slaps:* gates.
911, l. 19, *skellum:* good-for-nothing.
911, l. 20, *blellum:* babbler.
911, l. 23, *melder:* grinding of grain.
911, l. 25, *ev'ry... on:* every time a horse was shod.
911, l. 31, *warlocks:* wizards.
911, l. 31, *mirk:* dark.
911, l. 33, *gars me greet:* makes me weep.
912, l. 40, *reaming swats:* foaming new ale.
912, l. 41, *Souter:* cobbler.
912, l. 81, *skelpit:* hurried.
912, l. 81, *dub:* puddle.
912, l. 83, *Whiles:* now.
912, l. 84, *sonnet:* song.
912, l. 86, *bogles:* goblins.
912, l. 88, *ghaists:* ghosts.
912, l. 90, *smoored:* smothered.
912, l. 91, *birks:* birches.
912, l. 91, *meikle:* great.
912, l. 93, *whins:* stones.
912, l. 103, *bore:* hole.
912, l 107, *tippeny:* two-penny ale.
912, l. 108, *usquebae:* whiskey.
912, l. 110, *boddle:* farthing.
912, l. 116, *brent:* brand.
912, l. 119, *winnock-bunker:* window-seat.
912, l. 121, *towsie tyke:* shaggy dog.
912, l. 123, *gart them skirl:* made them squeal.
912, l. 124, *dirl:* ring.
912, l. 127, *cantraip:* magic.
913, l. 147, *cleekit:* clutched.
913, l. 148, *Till... reekit:* till every hag sweated and steamed.
913, l. 149, *coost... wark:* threw off her clothes for the work.
913, l. 150, *And linket... sark:* tripped the dance in her shirt.
913, l. 151, *queans:* young women.
913, l. 153, *creeshie flannen:* greasy flannel.
913, l. 154, *seventeen hunder linen:* woven in a reed of 1700 divisions.
913, l. 155, *Thir breeks:* these breeches.
913, l. 157, *hurdies:* haunches.
913, l. 160, *Rigwoodie... foal:* ancient hags that would wean a foal, with disgust.
913, l. 161, *crummock:* crutch.
913, l. 164, *wawlie:* well-built.
913, l. 165, *core:* corps.
913, l. 166, *kend:* known.
913, l. 169, *bear:* barley.
913, l. 171, *cutty sark:* short shirt.
913, l. 171, *harn:* coarse cloth.
913, l. 174, *vauntie:* proud of it.
913, l. 176, *coft:* bought.
913, l. 177, *pund Scots:* the Scottish pound was worth one-twelfth of the English; thus the shirt cost less than one dollar.
913, l. 186, *hotched:* hitched.
913, l. 188, *tint:* lost.
913, l. 193, *fyke:* fury.
913, l. 194, *herds:* shepherds.

913, l. 194, *byke:* hive.
913, l. 195, *pussie's:* the hare's.
913, l. 201, *fairin:* reward.
913, l. 210, *fient:* devil.
913, l. 213, *ettle:* intention.
913, l. 217, *claught:* seized.

COMIN THRO' THE RYE

913, l. 3, *draigl't:* bedraggled.
913, l. 9, *Gin:* if.

OF A' THE AIRTS

914, l. 1, *airts:* directions.
914, l. 5, *row:* roll.
914, l. 8, *Jean:* Jean Armour, whom Burns finally married.
914, l. 14, *shaw:* woodland.

I HAE A WIFE O' MY AIN

914, l. 12, *dunts:* blows.

JOHN ANDERSON, MY JO

914, l. 1, *jo:* darling.
914, l. 4, *brent:* upright, with hair.
914, l. 5, *beld:* bald.
914, l. 7, *pow:* head.
914, l. 11, *cantie:* happy.

FOR A' THAT

915, l. 8, *gowd:* gold.
915, l. 10, *hoddin:* homespun.
915, l. 17, *birkie:* conceited fellow.
915, l. 20, *cuif:* blockhead.
915, l. 28, *fa':* claim.
915, l. 36, *gree:* prize.

AULD LANG SYNE

915, Title, *Auld Lang Syne:* Old long since, a common phrase in the Scottish dialect of Burns's time.
915, l. 9, *ye'll . . . pint-stowp:* You will drink and pay for your pint-cup. The Scottish ale-pint was equal to three English pints.
915, l. 14, *pou'd the gowans:* plucked the wild daisies.
915, l. 15, *fit:* foot.
915, l. 17, *paidled in the burn:* paddled in the brook.
915, l. 19, *braid:* broad.
915, l. 21, *fiere:* comrade.
915, l. 23, *guid-willie:* hearty, expressing good will.
915, l. 23, *waught:* a deep draught.

DUNCAN GRAY

916, l. 5, *coost:* tossed.
916, l. 6, *skeigh:* shy.
916, l. 7, *Gart:* made.
916, l. 7, *abeigh:* aside.
916, l. 9, *fleeched:* teased.
916, l. 11, *Ailsa craig:* a great rock off the coast of Ayrshire.
916, l. 14, *Grat:* wept.
916, l. 15, *lowpin o'er a linn:* leaping down a waterfall.
916, l. 19, *bide:* endure.
916, l. 38, *smoored:* smothered.
916, l. 39, *crouse and canty:* contented and happy.

HIGHLAND MARY

916, Title, *Mary:* probably Mary Campbell, who died in 1786, shortly after her betrothal to Burns.
916, l. 1, *braes:* hillsides.
916, l. 2, *Montgomery:* the house of Burns's friend Gavin Hamilton, in Mauchline, where Mary Campbell served as a dairy-maid.
916, l. 4, *drumlie:* muddy.
916, l. 9, *birk:* birch.

THE JOLLY BEGGARS

917, l. 1, *lyart:* faded.
917, l. 1, *yird:* earth.
917, l. 2, *bauckie-bird:* bat.
917, l. 4, *skyte:* dash.
917, l. 6, *cranreuch:* hoarfrost.
917, l. 7, *core:* corps, group.
917, l. 8, *randie, gangrel bodies:* lawless vagabonds.
917, l. 9, *Poosie-Nansie's:* a tavern at Mauchline.
917, l. 9, *splore:* spree.
917, l. 10, *drink... duddies:* sell their extra clothes for drink.
917, l. 14, *girdle:* griddle.
917, l. 18, *doxy:* wench.
917, l. 21, *tozie:* tipsy.
917, l. 22, *skelpin:* smacking.
917, l. 24, *aumous dish:* alms basin.
917, l. 26, *cadger's whup:* hawker's whip.
917, l. 35, *Abrám:* at Quebec, in 1759.
917, l. 37, *Moro:* at Santiago de Cuba, 1762.
917, l. 38, *batt'ries:* at Gibraltar, 1782.
917, l. 40, *Eliott:* defender of Gibraltar.
917, l. 44, *callet:* trull.
918, l. 51, *kebars:* rafters.
918, l. 53, *rattons:* rats.
918, l. 54, *benmost bore:* farthest hole.
918, l. 55, *neuk:* corner.
918, l. 56, *skirl'd:* screamed.
918, l. 57, *chuck:* darling.
918, l. 74, *spontoon:* infantry officer's pike.
918, l. 85, *Merry-Andrew:* a clown.
918, l. 86, *tinkler-hizzie:* tinker-wench.
918, l. 90, *stoiter'd:* staggered.
918, l. 105, *stirk:* bullock.
918, l. 108, *daffin:* play.
918, l. 112, *Premier:* Pitt.
919, l. 119, *chiel:* fellow.
919, l. 121, *raucle carlin:* sturdy old woman.
919, l. 122, *cleek the sterlin:* snatch the money.
919, l. 124, *doukèd:* ducked.
919, l. 126, *weary... woodie:* bad luck to the gallows.
919, l. 130, *Lalland:* Lowland.
919, l. 137, *philibeg:* kilt.
919, l. 138, *claymore:* sword.
919, l. 139, *trepan:* insnare.
919, l. 155, *can:* of ale.
919, l. 162, *trystes:* cattle-markets.
919, l. 162, *driddle:* toddle.
919, l. 163, *gawsie:* buxom.
919, l. 165, *hol'd... riddle:* pierced his heart like a sieve.
919, l. 172, *giga:* Italian for "jig."
919, l. 173, *ryke:* reach.
919, l. 173, *dight:* wipe.
919, l. 176, *lave:* rest.

919, l. 181, *kirns:* harvest-homes.
920, l. 185, *pyke:* pick.
920, l. 190, *kittle ... thairms:* tickle hair on catgut.
920, l. 197, *caird:* tinker.
920, l. 202, *speet him ... pliver:* spit him like a plover.
920, l. 206, *hunkers:* haunches.
920, l. 211, *snirtle:* snicker.
920, l. 220, *clout:* patch.
920, l. 224, *budget:* tool-bag.
920, l. 225, *stowp:* ale mug.
920, l. 226, *Kilbaigie:* a kind of whiskey.
920, l. 228, *craigie:* throat.
920, l. 238, *hurchin:* urchin.
920, l. 239, *shavie:* trick.
920, l. 241, *cavie:* coop.
920, l. 242, *Homer's craft:* ballad-singing.
920, l. 243, *spavie;* spavin.
920, l. 244, *hirpl'd:* hobbled.
920, l. 244, *lap like daft:* leaped like mad.
920, l. 245, *sho:'d:* offered.
920, l. 246, *boot:* gratis.
920, l. 258, *glowrin byke:* staring crowd.
921, l. 264, *stank:* pool.
921, l. 265, *burn:* brook.
921, l. 266, *there:* in his mug of ale.
921, l. 271, *thraw:* thwart.
921, l. 275, *law:* decide.
921, l. 283, *till't:* to it.
921, l. 287, *toom'd their pocks:* emptied their pockets.
921, l. 288, *coor their fuds:* cover their tails.
921, l. 289, *lowin:* burning.
921, l. 292, *wale:* choose.

MARY MORISON

922, l. 5, *bide the stoure:* endure the strife.
922, l. 13, *braw:* handsome.

YE FLOWERY BANKS

922, l. 1, *Doon:* a little river of Ayrshire.
922, l. 19, *staw:* stole.

WILLIAM BLAKE

BIBLIOGRAPHY

Works, Poetic, Symbolic, and Critical, 3 vols., ed. with Memoir and Interpretation by E. J. Ellis and W. B. Yeats, 1893.
Poetical Works, ed. by J. Sampson, 1905, 1913, 1925.
Poetry and Prose, ed. by G. Keynes, 1927.
The Writings of William Blake, 3 vols., ed. by G. Keynes, 1925.
A. Gilchrist, *Life of William Blake,* 2 vols., 1863 and 1906.
A. C. Swinburne, *William Blake, a Critical Essay,* 1868 and 1906.
G. K. Chesterton, *Blake,* 1910.
S. F. Damon, *William Blake: His Philosophy and Symbols,* 1924.
Helen C. White, "The Mysticism of William Blake," *Univ. of Wisconsin Studies in Language and Literature,* No. 23, 1924.
D. Figgis, *The Paintings of William Blake,* illustrated, 1925.
O. Burdett, *William Blake,* 1926.
Mona Wilson, *The Life of William Blake,* 1927. New edition, 1932.
Denis Saurat, *Blake and Modern Thought,* 1929.

Thomas Wright, *The Life of William Blake*, 1929.
Thomas Wright, *Key to Blake, Blake for Babes. A Popular Illustrated Introduction to the Works of William Blake*, 1932.

NOTES

THE MARRIAGE OF HEAVEN AND HELL

927, Title, *Hell:* The title, as well as many ideas of the poem, was suggested by Swedenborg's *Heaven and Hell*, in which the two are strongly contrasted. Blake's deeper thought is that each needs the other as its complement.

927, l. 1, *Rintrah:* the spirit of the present day.

927, l. 37, *advent:* Swedenborg had said that a new spiritual era began in 1757, the year of his mystical illumination. Blake, born in that year, accepted the prophecy, as meaning that he was to correct and complete Swedenborg's teaching. The present poem was written when he was thirty-three.

927, l. 36, *it:* unwilling energy.

933, Subtitle, *Liberty:* For the comprehension of the following passage the date, 1790, must be remembered. In the following year Blake wrote his poem, *The French Revolution.*

933, l. 9, *rocks:* a passage intended to suggest the fall of the angels in *Paradise Lost.*

933, l. 17, *commands:* The King of France, likened to Satan just above, is here likened to Jehovah, over whom Satan, the active principle, triumphs.

THE TIGER

933, l. 12, *feet:* the splendid anacoluthon of this line was due to accident. Having first written

> What dread hand and what dread feet
> Could fetch it from the furnace deep,

Blake changed l. 13 to its present form without seeing that this required a change in l. 12. In a later version, however, he wrote

> What dread hand forged thy dread feet?

AUGURIES OF INNOCENCE

934, Title, *Auguries of Innocence:* The text here given is that prepared by Rossetti.

INDEX OF FIRST LINES OF POETRY

INDEX OF AUTHORS AND TITLES